YVES KLEIN

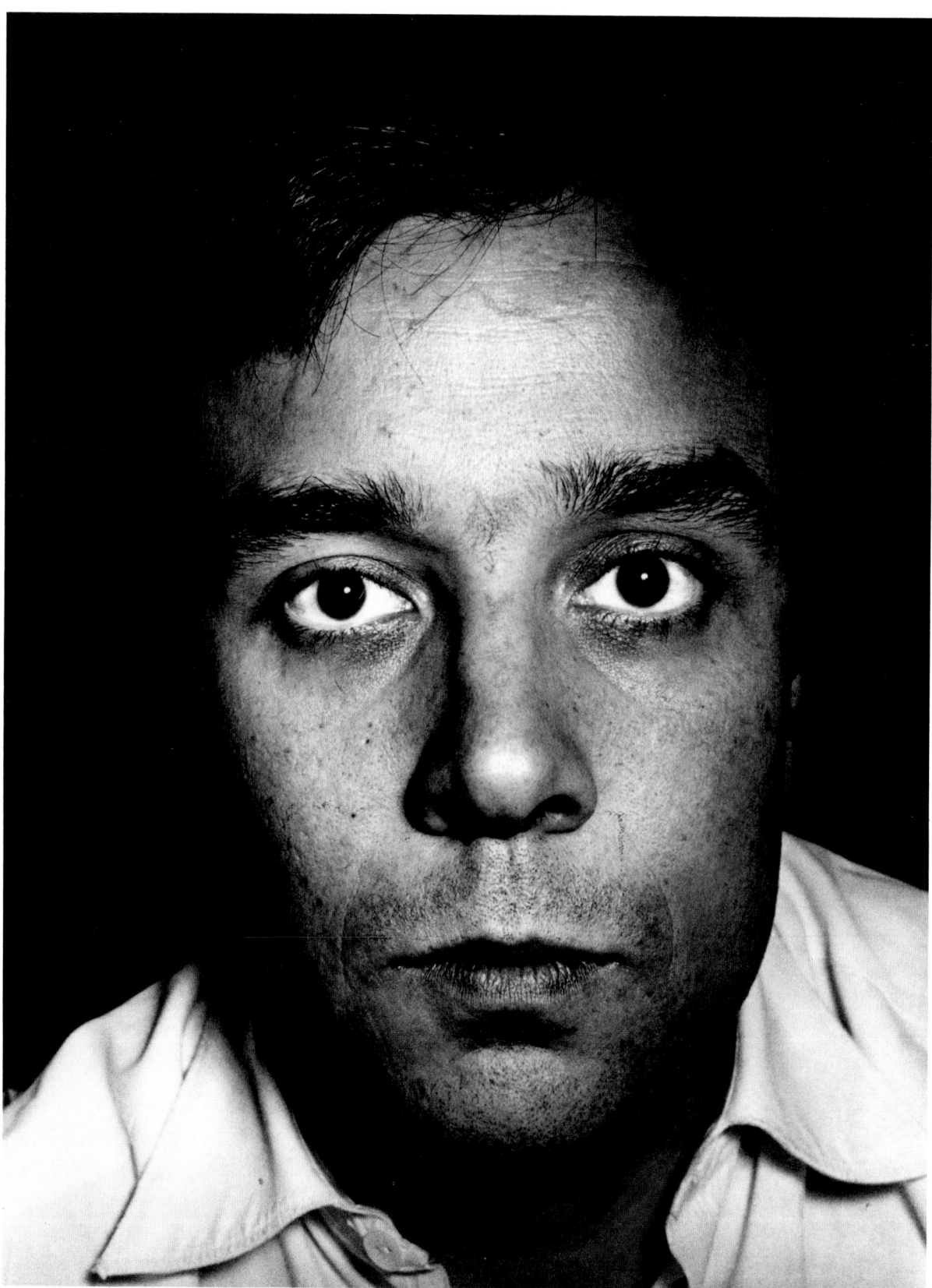

YVES KLEIN

1928-1962

A RETROSPECTIVE

Institute for the Arts, Rice University, Houston

in association with

The Arts Publisher, Inc., New York

Exhibition Dates

Rice Museum, Houston: February 5–May 2, 1982

Museum of Contemporary Art, Chicago: June 18–August 29, 1982

The Solomon R. Guggenheim Museum, New York: November 18, 1982–January 9, 1983

Musée National d'Art Moderne, Centre Georges Pompidou, Paris: February 17–May 1983

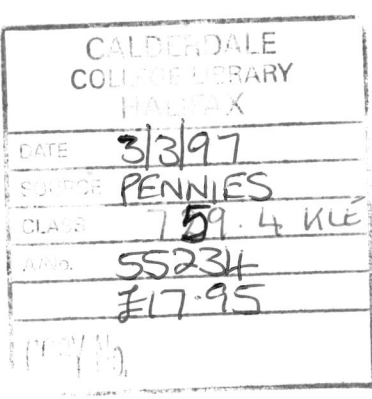
Library of Congress Catalogue Card Number: 81-86085
ISBN: 0-914412-27-2
Printed and bound in the United States of America.

Cover: cat. no. 62
Frontispiece: Yves Klein, March 17, 1961

This Yves Klein retrospective exhibition is placed under the high patronage
of Monsieur Jack LANG, the Minister of Culture of France;
of Monsieur Bernard VERNIER-PALLIEZ, Ambassador of France to the United States of America;
and of Monsieur Didier QUENTIN, Consul General of France in Houston.

The exhibition officially opens in the presence of
the Minister of Culture of France and Madame Jack LANG;
Madame Georges POMPIDOU, Honorary Chairman of the Georges Pompidou Art and Culture Foundation;
Monsieur Paul GUIMARD, Chargé de Mission with the Secretariat General of the Presidency of the French
      Republic;
Monsieur André LARQUIE, Chargé de Mission with the French Ministry of Culture;
Monsieur Christian DUPAVILLON, Technical Counselor with the French Ministry of Culture;
Monsieur Jean-Claude GROSHENS, President of the Centre Georges Pompidou;
Monsieur André-Jean LIBOUREL, Cultural Counselor of the French Embassy to the United States;
Monsieur Didier QUENTIN, Consul General of France in Houston; and
Monsieur Dominique BOZO, Director of the Musée National d'Art Moderne, Centre Georges Pompidou.

The exhibition has been organized and the catalogue published by the Institute for the Arts, Rice University,
Houston, with generous grants from the National Endowment for the Arts, Washington, D.C.; the Cultural
Arts Council of Houston; Banque Française du Commerce Exterieur, New York; Banque Nationale de Paris
(Houston, Chicago, New York); Michel David-Weill, New York; the Fribourg Foundation, Inc., New York; the
Menil Foundation, Houston; Schlumberger Horizons, Inc., New York; and Henry J.N. Taub, Houston.

The Georges Pompidou Art and Culture Foundation, New York, has acted as general sponsor.

Lenders to the Exhibition

Stephen S. Alpert, Wayland, Massachusetts
Yves Arman, New York
Mr. and Mrs. Jacob Baal-Teshuva, New York
Gerard Bonnier, Stockholm
Mr. and Mrs. Andrew P. Fuller, New York
Walter Hopps, Pasadena, California
Sidney Janis Gallery, New York
Ed and Nancy Kienholz, Hope, Idaho
Rotraut Klein-Moquay, Paris
Jan Eric von Löwenadler, New York
D. & J. de Menil Collection, Houston
Mizne-Blumenthal Collection, Monte Carlo, Monaco
Karl-Heinrich Müller, Düsseldorf
Robert Rauschenberg, New York
Marie Raymond, Paris
Fredirick Roos, Stockholm
Mr. and Mrs. P. M. Schlumberger, Houston
Richard Stankiewicz, Huntington, Massachusetts
Henry J. N. Taub, Houston
Mr. and Mrs. Burton Tremaine, Meriden, Connecticut
Anonymous lenders

Stedelijk Museum, Amsterdam
Albright-Knox Art Gallery, Buffalo, New York
Van Abbemuseum, Eindhoven, The Netherlands
Dartmouth College Museum & Galleries, Hanover, New Hampshire
Menil Foundation Collection, Houston
Louisiana Museum of Modern Art, Humlebaek, Denmark
The Solomon R. Guggenheim Museum, New York
The Museum of Modern Art, New York
Musée National d'Art Moderne, Centre Georges Pompidou, Paris
Moderna Museet, Stockholm

Contents

About Yves Klein

Yves Klein's short career as an artist, marked by high-voltage showmanship, irritated many and left most bewildered. Only a few sensitive people perceived that the oldest dreams of humanity had suddenly found a new poetical expression.

Using natural elements — pure pigments, gold leaf, female bodies, fire and water — Klein created works of stunning beauty. His monochrome paintings shine today with a magic glow, his body imprints have the mysterious fascination of ancient and forgotten signs, and his legend, which he helped fashion, is itself a work of art.

Considering the short duration of his active career — seven or eight years — the number of works Klein left behind is amazing. Most arresting is the decoration of the entrance hall of the theater of Gelsenkirchen, Germany. Its vast panels of undulating gesso and the myriads of sponges, ultramarine blue all over, have a monumental nobility. This may well be the greatest work of art to be found in a public building of the fifties and sixties.

Always treading the fine line separating the sublime from the absurd, Klein pushed his ideas to their utmost extreme with a fierce determination. Conceptual art was still in its infancy when he clearly formulated the notion of immaterial works, exhibiting the Void and selling zones of empty space previously impregnated with his own sensibility. This was in 1958.

Besides such tangible and intangible works, Klein left a mass of "philosophical" writings and plans for extraordinary projects which were to be carried out in collaboration with architects and other artists — Ruhnau, Kricke, Tinguely....Some, like the fire fountains emerging from water basins or spouting through cascades, were feasible. Others were totally impossible, like an "architecture of the air" in which roofs and walls would be made of laminated air currents blown at great pressure and thus be capable of stopping rain and intruders. In this technological Eden people would live in perfect climatization and bliss. This was to be the age of levitation!

About the Exhibition

Commemorative exhibitions took place after Yves Klein's death in June 1962. A small one opened in Tokyo that same year. Three years later Amsterdam's Stedelijk Museum presented a large exhibition. In 1967, Kynaston McShine organized an important retrospective at the Jewish Museum in New York. Thanks to François Mathey, always two steps ahead, France recognized Klein at the Musée des Arts Décoratifs in 1969. Denmark's Louisiana Museum, in 1968, and Yugoslavia's Museum of Contemporary Arts in Belgrade, in 1971, also paid homage to Klein. Three years later a well-documented show opened in London at the Tate Gallery. Finally, in 1976, a prestigious exhibition of Yves Klein's major works was held at the Nationalgalerie of Berlin.

Then silence settled over the golden tomb Yves Klein had built and on which he had laid a blue sponge wreath and a spray of pink artificial roses. The void he had conjured engulfed him; the music and the dance were elsewhere.

With the approach of the twentieth anniversary of Yves Klein's death, a rediscovery and a reevaluation of his work were appropriate; and a tribute had to be paid by France to a French artist who could measure up to the artists of the New York School. These thoughts were in the mind of Pontus Hulten, then Director of the Musée National d'Art Moderne at the Centre Georges Pompidou, when I mentioned to him my wish for an Yves Klein retrospective. An exhibition was decided upon, and we agreed that it would travel to three or four cities in the United States and end triumphantly in Paris, within easy reach of Germany, Italy, and the northern countries, where Klein's work had first been acknowledged.

Plans were made and carried out jointly between the Centre Georges Pompidou and the Rice Museum in Houston. Jean-Yves Mock, *commissaire* for the Paris exhibition, has been a generous co-worker and indispensable coordinator. Dominique Bozo, who succeeded Pontus Hulten as Director of the Musée National d'Art Moderne, Alfred Pacquement, in charge of exhibitions, and Germain Viatte, Curator of Paintings, gave their full support to the project.

Thomas Messer and John Neff enthusiastically welcomed the proposal to share this retrospective exhibition with the Solomon R. Guggenheim Museum, New York, and with the Museum of Contemporary Art, Chicago.

Rotraut Klein-Moquay and Daniel Moquay played a major part in the preparation of the exhibition. They made available all the Klein material they had, and assisted in the organization in every possible way. Rotraut's recollections and her intimate knowledge of Yves Klein were of prime importance. My most heartfelt gratitude goes to both of them.

My very sincere thanks also go to Marie Raymond, Klein's mother, and to Rose Gasperini, his aunt, who generously opened their archives and searched among their souvenirs. Bernadette Allain, who was Klein's companion in the 1950s, consented to break a silence of twenty years. Her acute memory and her insight into Klein's personality made her contribution particularly valuable, and I wish to express to her my warm appreciation.

As acknowledged herein, this catalogue owes a great deal to Klein's closest friends, Claude Pascal and Arman, who consented to be repeatedly interviewed. I thank them especially, as well as Jean Tinguely, a comrade in arms and devoted friend to Klein. My gratitude goes also to Pierre Restany, who helped me to see the true dimension of Klein's work, and to Karl Flinker, who from the start provided indispensable information and assistance.

With the help of Véronique Legrand and Agnès Angliviel de La Beaumelle, the Klein archives deposited by Rotraut Klein-Moquay at the Centre Georges Pompidou were thoroughly explored by Virginie de Caumont, who also made a major contribution by conducting many interviews. The work of Bénédicte Pesle and Marian McEvilley during the research is also gratefully acknowledged.

The following people cannot be forgotten:

Dr. Paul Wember, Iris Clert, Guido Le Noci, and the late Dr. Alfred Schmela, who shared with me their deep and personal involvement in Yves Klein's life and work.

Yves Arman, who generously made available his knowledge and the legacy he received from Yves Klein, his godfather.

Alexander Iolas, Tarica, Jan Runnqvist, and Liliana Dematteis, who provided both information and assistance.

Dr. Reinhold Lange, who kindly opened the theater in Gelsenkirchen for me.

Dr. Gerhard Storck of the Kaiser Wilhelm Museum in Krefeld, who arranged a special viewing of the museum's Klein works.

Dr. Evelyn Weiss of the Museum Ludwig in Cologne, and Dr. Sabine Kimpel of the Städtisches Museum, Mönchengladbach.

Harry Shunk, who was Klein's personal photographer, and who contributed important data to the project.

William Zamprelli, whose advice on the logistics of the exhibition was indispensable.

People interviewed have been listed elsewhere in this catalogue. In addition I wish to thank Ichiro Abe of the Tokyo Kodokan Judo Institute, Kazuo Anazawa, Shinichi Segi, Yuki Tatsura, Yoshiaki Tono, and Takachiyo Uemura, who were interviewed by letter; Jean de Galzain of the Rosicrucian Society, who was interviewed by Thomas McEvilley in Oceanside, California; and Larry Rivers, who shared his remembrances with me in New York.

Without the understanding and cooperation of numerous collectors, museum directors, and curators, this large and complex exhibition could not have taken place. I am especially grateful to all those who have lent their precious Yves Kleins to this retrospective. In addition to the collectors, I would particularly like to acknowledge the assistance of Robert T. Buck, Dr. E.L.L. de Wilde, Knud Jensen, Margaret J. Moody, Jane Nitterauer, Nina Ohman, Cora Rosevear, William Rubin, Margriet Suren, Louise Averill Svendsen, and Germain Viatte.

The authors of the catalogue essays are Pierre Restany, Thomas McEvilley, and Nan Rosenthal. Pierre Restany, well-known French art critic, is the author of innumerable articles in major art publications, including *Art International, Art Magazine, XXe Siècle, Connaissance des arts, L'Oeil,* and *Coloquiu de Artes* (Lisbon). A regular contributor to *Domus,* he has written monographs on Chryssa, Cesar, Niki de Saint-Phalle, and others, and is the author of *Yves Klein le monochrome* and *Le Nouveau Réalisme.*

Thomas McEvilley, a classicist and poet whose interests include mythology, comparative philosophy, and the history of film, teaches at Rice University and is a recent contributor to *Artforum* and *Images and Issues.*

Nan Rosenthal is an associate professor of art history at the University of California, Santa Cruz. Her doctoral dissertation, "The Blue World of Yves Klein" (Harvard, 1976), has been invaluable to all those researching this exhibition and catalogue.

Though considerable help came from Paris, the bulk of the work for the exhibition and the catalogue was carried out in Houston. My immediate collaborators — Harris Rosenstein, Administrator of the Institute for the Arts, Rice University; Heidi Rentería, Associate Curator; Walter Hopps, Director of the Menil Collection; and Thomas McEvilley — have done most of the work. They are the true artisans of the catalogue and deserve more than gratitude. So does Elsian Cozens, who has been an indefatigable and indispensable assistant.

Others who have made major contributions are Mary Ellen Sheridan, the catalogue's designer; Molly Kelly, copy editor; Linny Goldstein, registrar; Joe Dugan and Bear Parham, technicians; Jesse Lopez, production manager; Carol Mancusi-Ungaro, conservator; and Paula Webb, publicist.

Dominique de Menil

Yves Klein: Arrogance and Angelism

Two exhibitions opening within a month of each other — Yves Klein in Houston, Jackson Pollock in Paris — illustrate the desire, here and there, to share and confront two cultures which have continuously nourished one another and stimulated creativity. This preamble is not intended to raise the question of the respective importance of these two artists, but rather to point out the efforts being made on both sides of the Atlantic to promote exchange and dialogue. In this context, Dominique de Menil, who originated the Yves Klein exhibition, has contributed to the movement of ideas, following the tradition of the great initiator, Alfred Barr, founding director of the Museum of Modern Art. Through this exhibition she has once more shown the intercultural fabric, inextricably complex, of America and France. For this initiative may she find here the expression of our gratitude.

Why Yves Klein? In the United States, he is one of the most famous postwar European artists, yet his work is relatively little known. In this century, when each artist must invent his own means of creation, there are few whose *oeuvre* is as concentrated and yet as multifaceted as Klein's. And few artists can claim as many inventions as he in his lightning-brief trajectory.

There was an arrogance in Klein's attitude toward art — arrogance or insolence that challenged art, that went beyond art (as he said himself). He used this insolence, this fire burning within him, to minimize and reinvent art, all the while knowing, through some essential intuition, that his time was short.

From the start Klein gave himself a vocabulary — color, monochrome, imprints, and anthropomorphic casts — and he resorted to elements — water, air, and fire — to which he added action. This strategic reversal of values and statements fooled his critics, who called him the gravedigger of art — and he was, but in a positive way: he became the sower, dispensing his experiences. His influence is visible today in the varied manifestations of his ideas throughout France and beyond. So many developments which seem to have another formal origin in fact come from an experience of Yves Klein.

In this attitude of arrogance there was also angelism, inasmuch as the spirit of the leap into the void involves generosity and foresight. Here Klein was typically a product of postwar Europe, a Europe feeling itself at the extreme limit of nothingness and feeling the urge, new and fresh, to reinvent everything. This is what gave the stricken old continent the aspect of a testing laboratory where the need for diverse, multiple, and rapid experiences is expressed. On the other hand, in America, works less ambitiously speculative but more concrete, more self-assured, were being developed.

Yves Klein is probably the most perfect expression of a Europe that wants everything, particularly the freedom to think about everything and to rethink, starting from ground zero. This experience of the absolute, this attitude à la Rimbaud, appears destructive. With Klein, however, it implies a renaissance, since his angel-leap into the void is synonymous with the role of the artist who has the power and the mission to act upon the elements, to transmute nature.

There is arrogance in the monochrome, but only apparently. If we project ourselves into the blue of the sky, a sky untroubled by the flight of birds, then little by little the angel in us leaps into the depth, the depth Klein saluted in Gaston Bachelard's words: "First there is *nothing*, then there is a *deep* nothing; then there is a blue *depth*."

That's all. That's immense.

Dominique Bozo

Yves Klein: An Appreciation

The life and work of every artist raise certain questions: what the artist tried to achieve, what he succeeded in doing, where he failed. Eventually, if the work is great, the questions are answered, for those who know how to "read" it, by the work itself. In a sublimated and positive way, the work reveals the man who is no more, whereas the factual traces of his life are only shadows, an absence, and even stains.

The concentrated power of Yves Klein's work lies in the shortness of his life and its concise dramatization of an artistic development. Take-off, trajectory, stop. In that *oeuvre* we can see a prophecy that is now working itself out, step by step.

Each moment of Klein's life bears the stigmata of an enlarged, almost collective self-awareness. Both in Europe and in America, his quest became that of the generation succeeding him — a quest of the spirit, inquiring, concentrating, advancing, directed towards the sacred, the absolute.

His life and his work reconcile destiny and daily life, the incidental and the imagination, the ordinary and the heroic. His work and his life restore, nourish the spirit. The reality of inspiration rejoins the body of the universe, no longer trivial, offering us a luminous, ethereal vision.

In Klein's work, the elements — earth, air, fire, and water — are grasped, captured at their source. Their metamorphosis gives form to a unique *oeuvre* that goes beyond the usual norms of the foreseeable and the aesthetic. Klein's life and work, his visionary search, are a kind of testing of the law which posits a reciprocal balance between the mundane and the divine, between man and nature.

To some, Klein's *oeuvre* may seem fragmentary; and so, perhaps, it is. But it is like the rediscovered fragments of an essential artifact or text, at one and the same time a blueprint and the indications of a search. Klein takes his place in the perspective of a semantic reconciliation of appearance and reality, essence and personality, that is all the more important for breaching the historical materialism of the twentieth century and pointing toward a new spirituality that lies still ahead.

Few anniversaries, like this twentieth commemoration of Yves Klein's death, also celebrate an eternal continuation.

Jean-Yves Mock

Who Is Yves Klein?

Pierre Restany

The flashing brilliance of Yves Klein's Achillean destiny so fascinates his contemporaries that, twenty years after he passed away in Paris in 1962, at the age of thirty-four, he is a figure of legend. A few years of intense activity enabled him to build an *oeuvre* rigorously logical in the complexity of its internal dimensions, and whose prophetic influence on the course of aesthetic research is of vast importance.

I. Not many people knew Yves Klein...

I owe it to myself to state that few people *really* knew Yves Klein in the sense that they were party to the whole development of his career. Not many were close enough to him to get beyond the surface, the appearances. On the other hand, for his close friends the encounter was overwhelming, decisive. When failure to understand him was at its height, or when controversy about his work was widespread, there was always, among the artists of his generation, a minority, alive, disturbed, directly touched by and sensitive to his message. No one of his presentations, however great the scandal it caused, failed to evoke a response. A monochrome exhibition in Milan or Düsseldorf was enough to galvanize the local milieu, bring out revelations, and give direction to movements that were still erratic and unsure of themselves. Examples abound, from the Zero Group in Düsseldorf to the Milanese painter Manzoni. On the Côte d'Azur, where he grew up and where he spent time regularly, Klein started a School of Nice, and his friends Arman and Martial Raysse, its leaders, rightly claim to have been influenced by him. His meeting in Paris with Tinguely and later with Raymond Hains, which had a decisive bearing on the spiritual development of both these men, was of great importance in the artistic climate of the late fifties; my own thinking about this triple association — Klein, Tinguely, Hains — led me to found the Nouveaux Réalistes group in 1960.

II. All that does not belong to us is of the order of God

A mystical vitalist, Yves Klein was a realist in his vision of the immediate future. He was a master of judo, and, although born into a family of painters, as a painter was completely self-taught. He ordered his work around a fundamental intuition: that a new world calls for a new man. The mutations that affect the human species primarily concern the realm of sensibility, emotion, and perception. In the Third Mil-

lennium, a time of unbounded energy and the reign of the new sensibilities, the creative person will find no technical obstacle in his way. Artistic realization will no longer be a problem. In the "technological Eden," history will stop, the eternal present will have arrived. Art will be the language of pure, synthetic, sovereign emotion, the language of direct communication among perceptive individuals, the language of the eternal present.

Man must begin now to experiment with these modes of cosmic perception, to see and feel things on the scale of the new age. Yves Klein devoted himself to the search for this absolute dimension of expression. In 1959 he laid the foundations of a "school of sensibility" open to all those who wanted to learn the new language of art: he had the faith of the great visionaries and their power to communicate. The source of his faith was his love of life, which is the proper object of art. *Life which does not belong to us* is the supreme concept and the fundamental reality, the manifestation of cosmic energy. Pictorial sensibility is identical with the perception of this immaterial and therefore divine reality: *all that does not belong to us is of the Order of God.* Life is the absolute.

Yves Klein lived by the rhythm of his truth and of the material proofs he left us of that truth. Each new realization corresponds to a forward step in the demonstration: properly speaking it is not an experiment, a tryout, but a phenomenon of cognition, a localized, partial manifestation of a clarity which can only be fully appreciated by those whose sensibilities are tuned to the future. We are, it seems to me, in the presence of an intuitive thought that reveals itself continuously to itself and allows no fissure.

III. A whole destiny in color

It is through pure color that Yves Klein materialized his sensory intuitions and activated a mechanism of extra-lucid perception, a totally affective psychosensory language that cannot be tested or verified by rational processes.

Like destiny, color is a reality in itself: it fixes the image of the world through the creator's consciousness of it. At the same time color, by its direct action on people's sensibility, is the essential element in affective communication among them. Color shocks us or irritates us, charms or fascinates us, moves us to reverie or meditation. It is the sensory vehicle of the cosmic energies freely diffused in space, and it conditions us — or, to use Klein's terminology, it *im-*

pregnates us. It impregnates us the way happiness and the sense of fate impregnate us.

The idea of universal impregnation by color came forcibly to him in Nice in 1946, when he was only eighteen, and was the starting point of his monochrome work. The "monochrome propositions" — panels uniformly covered by a layer of color with a base of pure industrial paint — were never intended by their author to be decorative "pictures." Their function was entirely different: they were meant to gather the diffused energy that acts on our senses and to fix it, by means of color, in a certain space. In order to dispel any confusion in the mind of the public, Klein, after having used several tones without preference for any one of them, in late 1956 fixed on a particular variety of ultramarine blue. To him this one color represented revelation; it was the plastic base of unformulable intuitions, the vehicle of the grand emotions. It was also the captured image of the firmament and of the infinity of worlds: it recalled the *immaterial* dimension of the universe.

IV. All color is in blue, all blue in the Void, all the Void in Fire

The Blue Period, officially inaugurated in January 1957 by an exhibition at the Galleria Apollinaire in Milan, had within it the seeds of further development. To Klein, in his pursuit of the absolute, the Blue appeared as an approach to imminent reality, which is infinite; this immaterial energy is self-sufficient. The question was how to become conscious of it and how to hold onto that consciousness. Hence the famous exhibition of the Void in 1958, when on the night of the opening 2,000 people came to view the bare walls of the Galerie Iris Clert in Paris. In late 1959 came the zones of immaterial pictorial sensibility, which were "relinquished" to purchasers in exchange for a weight of fine gold.

What next, after going from the Blue to the Void? Klein answered the call of a Promethean vocation, which also corresponded to a return to universalistic humanism in the cosmogonic tradition of the Rosicrucians. In the trilogy of the colors of fire — blue, pink, and gold — the artist rediscovered the alchemical expression of the universal synthesis. He went back to monochrome and to blue, but also to pink, which he fixed in a carmine tone, and to gold, for which he used gold leaf. His cosmic vision aimed still higher; soon he was integrating every manifestation of the elemental forces into his creative activity. He used "living brushes" in his Anthropome-

tries, which are prints on paper made by nude models coated with blue paint. He enlisted the inclemency of the weather, painting the rain blue by going out in a storm and grinding pure pigment into a strong emulsion as the rain fell into it. The raindrops thus "impregnated" at shoulder height fell on a canvas laid flat on the ground and printed their colored images on it — the "Cosmogonies" of rain.

V. Air, ether, space, and its theater

In the course of a long stretch of work on monumental decoration for the theater in Gelsenkirchen (1957–59), done in close collaboration with the superintendent, Werner Ruhnau, Klein became familiar with the problems of architecture and constructed his own theories: he built on air in the air with air. His plans for the climatization of space with layers of atmosphere created by compressed-air blowers and his projects for a return to a technological Eden are related to the old dream of universal levitation — paradisiacal harmony by autosublimation into the ether. Here the Promethean dimension reflected the spiritual climate of the artist. Klein acted as a prophet, but in the service of the Order of God. His vitalist attitude and surrender to pantheistic effusion suggest his anticipation of a syncretistic harmonizing of occult Rosicrucian mysticism and the dogmatic legitimacy of faith. The prophet of the new age behaves as a gallant Knight of Saint Sebastian; the alchemist of energy is also a good Christian. It was in conformity with the Order of God that Klein would work out the rites of impregnation of the Nouveaux Réalistes at the time the group was established.

In the same effusive spirit he carried out one of the most meaningful acts of his entire career — the appropriation of a day of the world. From midnight to midnight of Sunday, November 27, 1960, the planet Earth became the Theater of the Void. The appropriation was accomplished by making use of the printed page: as his submission to the third Festival d'Art d'Avant-garde, held at the Palais des Expositions at the Porte de Versailles, Paris, Klein published his *Dimanche: The Newspaper of a Single Day* in the exact format of the *Journal du Dimanche* (the Sunday edition of the daily *France-Soir*). This document, of which several thousand copies were printed, brought together all his ideas on the Theater of the Void, the reversal of the actor-spectator and stage-auditorium relationships, and so forth.

On page 1 a photomontage titled "A Man in Space," with a caption reading, "The painter of space launches himself into the void," shows Klein setting off in gliding flight from the roof of a suburban building. This leap into space symbolized syncretistic harmony and access to the ether, the ethereal region of the physical world.

Unlike the sculptor Takis, who was the first to send a man — a living sculpture — into space by means of a magnetic launcher, Klein did not treat the space adventure ironically; on the contrary, it fascinated and thrilled him. Paralleling the flights of Russian and American astronauts, he executed "Planetary Reliefs" — advance topographical surveys of Mars and Venus and of the earth as seen from the moon — thus laying the foundation for a cosmogony on the scale of our solar system. Gagarin, the Russian cosmonaut, confirmed Klein's thought: from far out in space the earth is blue.

As a final stage in this system of symbols representing universal impregnation he tamed fire, using it to make both sculptures (jets of incandescent gas under pressure, in Krefeld in 1961) and paintings (by turning industrial coke-gas torches on sheets of Swedish cardboard treated with asbestos). And his ultimate human message, undertaken in the last months of his life, took the form of a fantastic series of portrait reliefs based on life-size plaster molds made directly from the body. The only one he was able to finish (in March 1962) was the portrait of Arman, blue on a gold background.

VI. Harmony of heart and head

Considered in its chronological sequence, Klein's evolution is significant. He embodied a total urge — the urge to give whatever he created the fundamental norms of a cosmogony. For him it was not enough to foresee the world of the future; he sought to fix its image for us through a new language, a new method by which to perceive the energies of the cosmos. And that is how he exerts a powerful attraction, an undeniable fascination upon us as we stand on the threshold of a new world and are forced to create a completely new understanding and psychology. Today we need above all to learn to see and to feel. Klein illustrates the coming of a different sensibility on the scale of the planetary world of tomorrow. While he marks out our present limitations, he opens the way to the greatest hopes. He recharges our feelings and sharpens our perceptions: with Klein and through the medium of his message, we have the impression of no longer being the passive toys of events, and we seem to feel things differently, seeing better and big-

ger, conjugating life in the future tense.

Settled at the heart of his language and entirely one with it, Yves Klein was a man of faith who lived by his own sense of the divine, and a man of the future responsible to the highest degree for his vision. Vital energy, the source of every mutation, is the Order of God. How else to take hold of it than by the synthesis of syntheses, the intuition of the senses, the Void? Hence the monochrome painter's fascination with all the formulas of esoteric Christianity, with Rosicrucian occultism, knighthood (he was a Knight of the Order of Saint Sebastian), the rules of Masonry, and the myth of the Man-Christ. For help against the temptations of pride he prayed to Saint Rita, patron saint of hopeless causes and his last resort when, face to face with the ineffable Void, he experienced a holy fear of the Order of God. For Yves Klein there were no problems, there were only answers. His sudden death is one of them: it seems like a limit imposed upon his vitalistic lack of limits — a call to order. Yves Klein, the man of faith, took on the monochrome adventure in perfect harmony of head and heart.

VII. The more I think about Klein the man

The more I think about Klein the man, the more I appreciate the specific dimension of his faith. It was natural, as natural as breathing: it was a form of sensibility, a quality of life — his sensibility and his life. He was "chosen," but the pride of election was immediately tempered by the Order of God. Klein believed that he was the holder of a fundamental truth, but believed that he held it on loan, so to speak, and not outright. He had only a leasehold on the energy that he sold in zones of sensibility, and he would not keep the whole price for himself. He appropriated the anthropometric measure of the human body through the blue of sensibility rather than the red of blood, which inevitably would soil the print. Everything happened as if he were voluntarily exposing himself to all the temptations of Prometheus, taking them on as a trial, a test revealing the Order of God. The Order of God appears as the most ineffable of limits — all that does not belong to us. In his prophetic role Klein had no thought of challenging that Order; his intention was to bring to fullness the resources of his humanity, making maximum use of them on the way to knowing. Ideal knowledge is the eternal present; we will attain it only at the end of a mutation which is to happen suddenly and soon. That is the significance of the return to the state of nature in a technological Eden and of its two corollaries, the architecture of air and the disappearance of individual intimacy — i.e., the sublimation of the ego and the power of levitation. Yves Klein was the great artist of the environment, but his intention was to work on the *ethereal* nature of the world. His action upon physical nature was only a preamble, the prefiguration of a future that will be an eternal present. "The transcending of the problematical in art" fitted into the logic of his faith. The transitional period will be the time when all technical problems of artistic process will be overcome.

By making his own the affective fullness of his faith, Yves Klein became the archetype of the artist of our time. Instinctively he lived with the kind of sensibility that gives priority to the gesture, the action, by which an idea takes flesh. He placed himself at the crossroads of all active and creative spiritualities. Obviously he was "in on" a secret, because the Order of God is ineffable; but he did not want to make this secret the privilege of a caste. The rhythm of planetary transition will proliferate perceptive individuals; it was in order to speed this process that he laid the foundation of a theoretical and practical teaching in the form of a "school of sensibility." The Man-Christ is the conscious instrument of a transitory mutation. No audacity is forbidden as long as the goal is to "feel higher and see bigger."

When I say that Yves Klein's sudden death was an answer, I am not only alluding to his "transcending of the problems"; I am thinking of the coherence and cohesion of his system-message. The essential has been taken care of, the rest lies in the domain of proof — a race against the clock, against the material time of change. A prolongation of his physical existence would have added nothing.

VIII. Yves Klein continues to be an immensely present idea

Yves Klein as an idea is still very much of our day, present in absence, in monochromy, and in the immaterial. The idea corresponds to a double profile, comprising both thought and practice, of the sensibility of a period — our period, which is also Yves Klein's. Not by chance does Klein dominate the most forward-moving sectors of the visual arts. He gives body to a generalized poetic dynamism which has a dozen or more facets today, among them the monochromy of minimal painting, body art with its corporeal transfer of the ego, the various systems by which reality is perceived through cultural anthropology,

the statements of conceptual art, investigation of the environment through the elements (fire sculptures, nature prints), problems connected with the dematerialization of the art work/art object, the Void, the air, antigravitation, space at every level, planetary climatization, futuristic architecture and urbanism, and so on.

Yves Klein is a contemporary of Newman the kabbalist, of the Reinhardt of black painting, of the almost monochrome Kelly; the inspirer of artists like Manzoni and Piene; the catalyzer of Fontana's spatialism; the spiritual father of all the Rymans in the world. He is the prophet who brings out the basics and reveals the operative concepts that have shaped the cultural landscape of our time — the body as medium, space as structural laboratory, nature and the elements as prime matter.

Lastly, our mystical vitalist inaugurated in thought and feeling this syncopated period we live in, made up of conflicting alternatives of hope and fear, joy and anxiety — the end of a century and of a millennium, a time of anticipation of the new millennium to come. As the great fear before the year 1000 was the plague, before the year 2000 it is the atom: the paranoia is the same. Given the body's limitations and the mind's deficiencies, it is well that sensibility has taken over for the sovereign emotions.

IX. Well then, who is Yves Klein?

Lawrence Weiner writes like Klein, and Klein talks like Malevich; Yona Friedman thinks like Klein, and Klein sees the way Sant'Elia does; Vito Acconci sleeps like Klein, and Klein dreams like Bachelard. Klein has no fear of anything except God, and no one knows how he prays when he is afraid. No one, that is, save Saint Rita of Cascia, the only one who could tell us whether Klein's sacred fear is that of Saint John of the Cross or of Gilles de Rais or of Antoni Gaudí. And does it matter anyway?

(translated by W.G. Ryan)

Yves Klein: Conquistador of the Void

Thomas McEvilley

Yves Klein died prematurely. He is almost a heroic figure to the postwar art world of Europe. Legends and controversy still surround the artist and his extraordinary career....His life was a symbolic poetic act.

Kynaston McShine[1]

Unlike most artists, Yves Klein was not inferior to his works. We consider them as the highlights of an exceptional adventure and to a large extent they bear witness to this adventure. But of many other stages only memories remain. For Yves Klein took as much trouble with what was to disappear as with what was to endure. That's why it's not proper only to show his paintings, his weldings, his prints, his fires, his golds; one must also try to recount that part of his work whose traces exist only in memory.

Pierre Descargues[2]

His influence has been exerted not so much through his paintings as through the character of his activities generally.

Michael Compton[3]

He was like one who, in a state of sudden intoxication, fills life with meaning to the point of overflowing.

Giuliano Martano[4]

It is not easy to follow him into his innermost spaces....He had his own ideas, his own drunkenness.

Paul Wember[5]

He didn't paint to paint, but to reveal his truth....To grasp it, one has to...enter into his game.

Pierre Restany[6]

Part One

1

*The painter only has to paint one masterpiece,
himself, constantly.*

Yves Klein

Yves Klein was a myth-making artist. He declared that his *manner of existence* would be the foremost artistic event of our time; and his strategy for realizing this goal involved the propagation of an explicit personal myth, left behind as the trace, or ashes, of his life. So brilliantly was this myth presented, with such daring, charm, and (usually) good humor, that it caught fire at once in the public imagination; yet its real shape, its sources, its purposes, and its relationship to his everyday life have not yet been made clear.

Klein was a craftsman of myth, working directly with it as an artist with his material. With both deliberation and flair, he acted out the fulfillment of an ancient prophecy by incorporating its symbols into his life as a series of ideographic Moments or Kratophanies; these he proffered to the public like Stations or Labors of a sacrificial monotheater, to mark the stages of his progress along a path of transcendence. When he showed himself, he was often in costume, acting out one current or another of his overflowing mythic energy. At one such Moment he was the apotheosized Yves the Monochrome, at others the Proprietor of Color, the Champion of Color, the Conquistador of the Void. By such apparitions he hoped to install himself in the realm of the archetypes, all traces of personal origin concealed.

Klein's writings supported these visual Moments by evoking related literary codes. Sometimes the sorcerer's:

I have manipulated the forces of the void...[7]

Sometimes the messiah's:

My original goal [was]...to restore the lost Eden.[8]

Sometimes the mystic's:

I, without the "I," became one with life itself. All my gestures, movements, activities, creations, were this life, original or essential in itself.[9]

But Klein's myth was not primarily a literary product; it was rooted in what he felt were the deficiencies of his life. For as Roland Barthes pointed out, no myth is innocent; each tries to force reality into a certain shape, for certain motives. And to conceal its motivation "myth has the task...of making contingency appear eternal."[10] Just so, the contingent Yves Marie Klein was gradually submerged beneath the eternalized Yves the Monochrome.

Still, despite the compelling obviousness of its motivation, such a myth is not altogether produced, as an object, by the decision of a subject. It has a momentum of its own, like a game which "draws the players into its own realm and fills them with its spirit. The player experiences the game as an overpowering reality."[11] And just so, again, the historical Yves Marie Klein experienced the mythical Yves the Monochrome with the overpowering reality of a game which he could not stop playing until it stopped playing him. The myth and the man, reciprocally, created one another.

It is not easy to enter into the processes of this extraordinary adventure. The appearance of eternality must be reduced back to contingency. And the lost Eden of the myth's original horizon must be reconstituted from within.

2

The solemn geography of human limits...

Paul Eluard

The village of Cagnes-sur-Mer in the south of France fills, in the early summer, with the odor of the mimosa groves, the cries of children released from school, and the arrivals of summer visitors from the cities. For generations artists have gathered there, drawn by the Mediterranean light, the beauty of the seashore and the countryside. Renoir painted there, Modigliani, Braque, Soutine, and others. It was to figure prominently in Yves Klein's life.

Yves' grandfather, a businessman from Hanover, was established in Java as a planter toward the end of the nineteenth century. There Fred Klein, Yves' father, was born of a Dutchwoman whose grandmother was Javanese. Educated in Europe, Fred Klein became, in his early twenties, a painter in a pointillist neo-impressionist mode — delicate landscapes with gamboling horses, Monet-like surfaces of water. In 1925, at age twenty-seven, he bought an old ruin on a hillside just behind Cagnes and spent his summers there, restoring it as a studio.

Yves' mother, Marie Raymond, was from a middle-class family in Nice (her grandfather a buyer of flowers for perfume makers, her father a pharma-

---

Footnote numbers which appear in bolder type throughout the text (e.g. 12) indicate important additional information beyond the citation of a source document.

cist). Rose Raymond, Marie's sister, married a medical doctor who often vacationed in nearby Cagnes. When Marie was fifteen she accompanied her sister and brother-in-law when he was called to Cagnes to tend to an ailing artist. It was her first exposure to the artistic milieu, and at once she recognized her metier. Back in Nice she bought a box of paints and began to work. In the following summers she returned to Cagnes on her own. In July 1926, at age eighteen, she met Fred Klein in Cagnes at an outdoor party where a guitarist was playing. That October they were married in Nice, and she returned to Paris with him.

Soon — perhaps sooner than penniless young artists would have hoped — she was pregnant. The child was due in April 1928, but there was no money to pay a hospital and a doctor. Fred and Marie drove to Nice and awaited the event in Marie's sister's house, where Marie's brother-in-law, the doctor, could preside. Here, in the bosom of his mother's family, Yves Klein entered the world on April 28, 1928, when the sun was in Taurus and Gemini was on the eastern horizon.[12] A handsome baby with unusual eyes — the Javanese strain left an exotic touch — he was hugged to the breasts of grandmother, childless aunt, and mother.

Having no money to set up a household in Paris, the Kleins retired to the villa at nearby Cagnes, where Yves spent his first months in a paradisal ambience of sunlight, flowers, and relaxed country living. His father painted; his mother took a correspondence course to become a drawing teacher and worked sometimes in the decorative arts center in nearby Nice. But in Cagnes, Fred Klein could not make the contacts which would be necessary to start selling his work. "A charming man, but absolutely in the clouds"[13] (words which might later have been spoken of his son), he successfully resisted wage slavery all his life. As years passed, they would sell the furniture in the villa in Cagnes to buy food, parting even with the Japanese cloisonné vases cherished by Marie (which her sister bought), and finally with the villa itself. Their financial situation never visibly improved.

Before Yves was one year old Fred traveled to cities in the north, seeking contacts in the art world, and arranged a show in Amsterdam for 1930. Marie soon joined him, reluctantly leaving the child with her sister in Nice, where, at least, there was money to feed and house him. This was the first dislocation in a childhood which was to become increasingly confused and fragmented, with many comings and goings, many changes of residence, role model, and attitude.

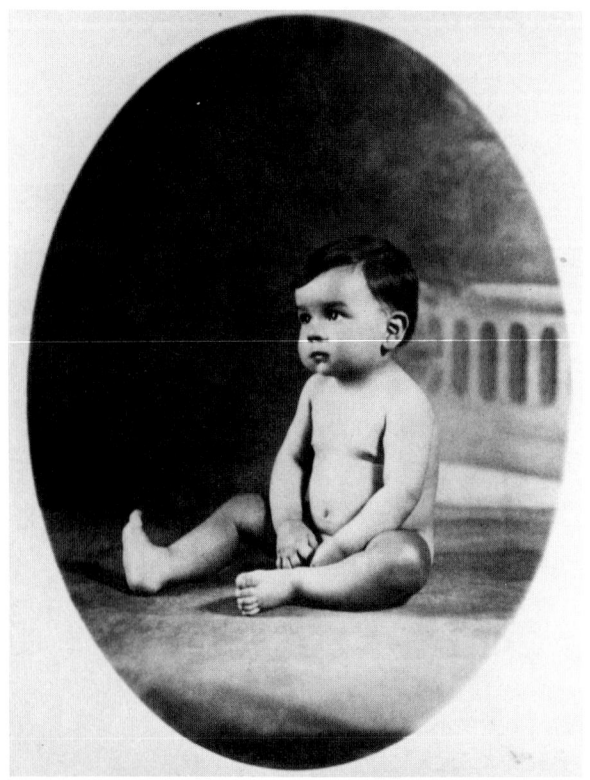

Yves Klein, age one

Rose Raymond, childless and now divorced, was living in her mother's house again. She took Yves into her care with something more than willingness, more than affection. As she walked him in the pram, held him, doted on him, fussed over him, he became in a sense as much her son as Marie's. The infant had in effect two mothers, between whom a certain competition existed for his affections and the right to guide his development; the situation was as confusing to him as to the only child of divorced parents shuttling back and forth between their homes. As the years passed, and the parents came and went (to Cagnes for the summer, back to Paris at summer's end), young Yves was subjected to contradictory role conditioning. It was Aunt Rose who "had her feet on the ground," who had money and knew its value, who cared for schooling and hard work. "It was she to whom he would return each time he had some need for the rest of his life, because with her he could find himself on solid ground again."[14]

Yves' grandmother and aunt were devotees of the Italian Saint Rita of Cascia, whose miracle cult had many adherents in the south of France. Their attachment to Saint Rita provided the background for

Yves' ritualism and religious ambitions, his obsession with magic and miracle. As a child he was ritually presented to a statue of the saint and consecrated to her care forever. (Ominously, perhaps: Saint Rita was known as the patroness of lost causes.) Years later, when Yves felt he needed heavenly intervention, he would ask his aunt to pray to Saint Rita for him. When he got what he wanted, he would say, "Saint Rita got it for me." Four times he himself would make pilgrimages to Cascia to leave gifts for the saint and make requests of her. This imprint of rustic piety never left him.

When Yves was two years old his mother "languished" from desire for him, and Aunt Rose ("in despair" at losing him) took him to her in Paris. For two years he came and went between Paris and Nice. Then at age four he was settled in Aunt Rose's house more solidly, to stay for almost six years. During most of the summers he was with his parents in Cagnes; for the rest of the year he lived in Nice and attended a Catholic school. He was living, really, in two worlds, and the contradictions between them became ingrained in his personality. For the rest of his life he would swing between the poles of the creative, free-roaming parents and the pious, respectable aunt, emulating both, but never making them one. Like the parents, he would avoid conventional employment, acquire debts, devote himself to art, learn to disappear. Like the aunt, he would practice religion, dress like a business person, and consecrate himself to a kind of respectability. It was his parents' world, where his imagination and sense of freedom and adventure grew almost pathologically intense, which attracted him most; yet each September this world would reject him, sending him back to the solidity and careful supervision of his aunt. As his two "mothers" competed for his affections, he learned to control them both and get what he wanted; the temper tantrum became a part of his arsenal for surviving. At once spoiled and rejected, he felt both in control of the world and outside of it. It was his parents whom he would finally emulate, finding a way into the Paris art world where he was to surpass them both quickly; but it was his aunt who would be called on, at the height of his adventure, to intercede with Saint Rita and to accompany him to the saint's shrine to give thanks for his attainments.

3

When I was young, I opened my arms to purity. This was only a beating of wings in the sky of my eternity.

Paul Eluard

"He was a sort of holy child," says his friend Arman: a person of special power and charisma from the beginning. "He had the power to convince people by his charm," says his mother. "He was always surrounded by a group of children who looked to him for leadership." In the summers in Cagnes they would come to the house in the morning, saying, "What will we do today, Yves?" He would organize treasure hunts and games of knights in armor. (The age of chivalry continued to fascinate him throughout his life. "Tintin seeking the Holy Grail," François Mathey would call him years later.)[15] He would go for long walks in the woods and come back, his arms filled with flowers. "The great freedom he enjoyed," his mother says, "certainly developed his sense of adventure, and his imagination." But already he was a fighter *(un bagarreur)*, with a sense of military victory. At age ten, he would demand a written surrender from a beaten foe: "I lay down my arms. Signed, Antoine."

In the summer of 1937 there was an artists' festival in Cagnes for which Yves' parents decorated a pavilion with themes of air, earth, water, and fire (a structure he would later repeat in his own works). Someone organized a "racecourse of cockroaches," which he would also repeat, more than once, in Paris and Germany in his twenties. His admiration for his parents, his resentment of the time they spent away from him, and his desire to emulate their freedom and creativity were enduring parts of his character.

When his parents returned to Paris in September, he would return to Nice and attend the Catholic school. There things did not go so well. His thoughts were already far removed from ordinary things, and he fought with the priests and the other boys. The freedom of his summers undermined the discipline of his winters; he became a rebel. His attendance at the Catholic school ended with the year of his private first communion, May 27, 1937. The following year he attended a private (tutorial) school, and began to do better. Each evening he would sit with Aunt Rose while she patiently checked his homework. His education seemed about to get back on track—when his mother called for him in Paris again.

In Paris at age ten, he became a confirmed *bagarreur* and was asked to leave one school after another. In the summer of 1939 his family returned to Cagnes and was caught there by the war. For four years he lived with his parents in Cagnes, and though the "freedom he enjoyed" there set fire to his imagination, his discipline, in effect his formal education, was over for good.

Many artists left Paris for the south at this time, and many of them passed through the Klein-Raymond home. Yves was introduced to the Paris art world in exile. Hans Hartung and others were frequent visitors; Nicolas de Staël lived nearby.

Away from Aunt Rose's supervision, Yves ceased caring about school altogether, and spent more and more of his time at hero's games, or imitating the activities of the grown-ups. He wore a military cap which his mother had given him, and was known throughout the village as "the Captain." He and de Staël's son once took paintings from the artist's dustbin, grasped them by the stretcher braces, and used them as shields in knightly battles. He began to write little poems which gave a sense already of the literary power he would later attain. Painting itself, however, did not interest him. He was, in fact, "fed up with it," even "against it," because it had separated him from his parents for so long.[16] Instead he spent hours at the piano, learning to play basic jazz motifs by ear, and read comic books. His favorites were Tintin, who even as a boy achieved knightly adventures, and Mandrake the Magician, who wore a black tie and cape, read minds, and was a master of illusion.

In the summer of 1940, while France still drifted in the *drôle de guerre*, Yves organized a children's theater in the basement of the Maison Musée in Cagnes. While the village youths built benches of planks and stones and brought electricity into the room, he conceived and directed, making up sketches and rehearsing the other children in them. On the day before the performance he distributed invitations throughout the village, in the cafés and the streets. "Already he was able to organize everything and get his audience," his mother says. Many artists in the village attended; the Renoir family came from nearby; even the famous Valentine Tessier, who likewise was waiting out the war in Cagnes, appeared. The little Captain had won a choice audience indeed!

But the Captain was soon pubescent, and he became fiercely independent, beyond anyone's control. In the summer of 1942 his parents financed a trip to St. Dalmas, in the Alps, by renting out the villa, and left Yves behind in Nice. He sorely resented it. In the following summer, at age fourteen, he took off alone on his bicycle to see St. Dalmas for himself, and was gone for days. "I knew then," his mother says, "that he had gone his own way for good." He was terribly stubborn ("the freedom he enjoyed...")

and would not take no for an answer. (Years later his friends would say, "He admitted no obstacle, tolerated no one who resisted him.")

But life in Cagnes was becoming difficult. Even food was scarce in the south of France. In the summer of 1943 the family moved back to occupied Paris, and Yves learned war, the black market, and the streets. Everything was difficult now. Fred Klein had to sell the villa in Cagnes, and Marie's parents sold a lot in Nice, dividing the money between Rose and herself. Mere survival was a problem. Debts accumulated.

Still Paris was fairly stable, and galleries began to open again in 1943. Fred Klein worked desperately to get a show and make some money. Occasionally he sold a painting, but the earnings came to little. Yves, in love with jazz, would play the piano with friends who came over on Sundays bearing trumpets, flutes, drums.

In June 1944, Yves went with a Boy Scout group on a camping trip to Normandy. They returned to Paris one day before the landing of a million and a half American and British troops. Fearing for his safety, his parents sent him to stay with friends in the village of Milhars (Tarn). He remained there for about three months, while they lived through the liberation of Paris—blockades in the streets, gunfire at their doorstep, Leclerc's tanks tearing down the barricades; by August 26 the Germans were gone from Paris, and soon Yves was summoned back. Sixteen years old, he returned eager to join the Resistance, carrying a hand grenade hidden in a loaf of bread. His mother kept it under the tiles of the kitchen floor until the war was over, then turned it in to the army.

The war had aroused his taste for adventure, and in the following year his troubles in school increased. More and more often he failed to attend, and no one could force him. He took to frequenting nightclubs and daydreamed of being a jazz musician and playing in the Claude Luther band (with which he was occasionally allowed to sit in on piano for an easy number). In 1946, his mother recalls, he presented himself for the baccalaureate exams and failed them. It was a disappointment which he felt increasingly as the years passed, and which he tried to compensate for by various mythic inventions. Even more serious was a consequence of this failure. Eager to set out on travels and adventures of his own, Yves had planned for two years to enter the Merchant Marine Academy. Now his failure at the baccalaureate rendered him ineligible for the entrance exam. It was a second major disappointment, which he later tried to rectify through invention. The common story that he attended the Merchant Marine Academy was created by Yves himself, who was ashamed, in later years, of his lack of formal education. Translating his early life into myth, he claimed imaginatively some credentials which cannot be seen by daylight. At the moment, the disappointment was softened by the opportunity to travel in the company of his parents.

As soon as the war ended, the art world came to life again. In 1946 Marie Raymond, who had begun painting abstracts during the war, began exhibiting at the young Galerie Denise René; Fred Klein was invited to show at the Anglo-French Art Centre in London. In July, Marie and Fred went to London, but had difficulty obtaining a visa for Yves. A month or so later the visa was cleared, and Yves joined them. For several weeks they stayed with friends who had a handicapped son. Yves befriended the boy and showed the graciousness and kindness which throughout his life would coexist paradoxically with his arrogance and egocentricity.

Back in France after a taste of travel and freedom, Yves found himself, at age eighteen, living in his aunt's house in Nice again. She had remarried (becoming Mme. Taramasco) and was running a Phillips appliance store and doing well. Yves was already at a kind of dead end in the world. His education had been aborted by familial instability, poverty, and the war. He could not enter the Merchant Marine or any school of higher education. His personality was already too brilliant, too strong and assertive, for conventional limits. And though physically an adult, he was still wrapped up in the dreams of his childhood, still reading Tintin and Mandrake the Magician.

Hoping to groom him for a career in commerce, his aunt set up a bookshop for him to run in one room of her appliance store. Yves was "very competent," she says. But inwardly he dreaded becoming the next generation's Phillips dealer. He played the piano desultorily and began to tell his friends that he had been a member of the Claude Luther band. (He had never perceived a clear boundary between his imagination and the world of plain facts, and never would.) In the evenings he strolled on the promenade by the sea and went to dances; he was an excellent jitterbugger and was popular with the girls. Occasionally the bandleader would let him sit in on piano. Life was pleasant enough, but dull; he yearned for the more exciting world of his parents and openly resented the fact that they had sent him away from it. The restlessness which would become so famous in later years ("He was the most restless man I have ever known," says Tinguely) began to show.

Outside of his fantasy life (where he was Mandrake and Tintin and Perceval and Claude Luther and

a famous artist all rolled into one), nothing that he had experienced was really his own. It was his parents' world, from which he was repeatedly sent away, or his aunt's world, which tempted him with a suffocating security. The confusion of his childhood was maturing into a kind of desperation. The paradox of being simultaneously neglected and spoiled was a difficult one; the neglect left a residue of anger, the pampering a false sense of omnipotence. He wanted a world of his own, a reality which would assuage his inner anger and reflect his inner sense of omnipotence. He wanted to go "beyond" everything he had seen.

4

I am a child of the Earth and the starry Sky,
But the Sky alone is where I belong.

Orphic inscription,
circa 300 B.C.

In 1947 something moved Yves to join the judo school at the police headquarters in Nice, where courses were offered to the public. At once he met Claude Pascal, and two weeks later Armand Fernandez (later simply Arman). These were the most important friends of his life. With them in the next few years he underwent a "mystic crisis" (as Claude Pascal calls it) which introduced him to his personal myth and established, once and for all, the governing symbols of his life—the symbols of "spiritual space."

Yves was quick and strong, though not large, and the combat on the judo mats aroused his energies fully for the first time. Judo, he would say later, was his first experience of "spiritual space," that "sensorium of god," as Henry More called it, which was to preside over the end of his adventure as much as its beginning. The straining of muscles, the flying through the air, the landing unhurt—these released him from the limitations of "plain facts," and made him feel free and powerful.

He was to seek the unobstructed freedom of empty space for the rest of his life—to evoke it in his art of emptiness, to activate it with his immaterial works, to mark its flight and fall in his Imprints, to consummate his sex-and-death relationship with it in his Leap—even to sell it, though the proceeds went into the river of time, not his own pockets. Space, transparent and shining, whole and without blemish, which contains Everything but is Nothing—this was his embarkation and his terminal, the prelude of the sermon he preached with his life and its peroration.

But judo by itself was not enough for Yves and

his friends. They wanted hardships and adventures, explorations in the nighttime world of magic and lunar vision. They were ready for a teacher; and when the student is ready, says the occult tradition, the teacher will appear.

"One day [late in 1947 or early in 1948]," says Claude Pascal, "Yves arrived saying, 'Look, I have found it!' He showed me the *Cosmogonie* of the Rosicrucians. We tried reading it and found that without a master it could not be understood. We asked everyone, 'Do you know anybody who understands the *Cosmogonie* of the Rosy Cross?' After about two months, as we were leaving a judo class, Yves said, 'I have found someone.' We went to a house at about eleven o'clock at night, which in Nice at that time was very late, and knocked on the door. When it opened, we saw a very old man in a white shirt, who said, 'What can I do for you?' Yves showed him the *Cosmogonie* and he said at once, 'Ah! Come in, my children.' " This was Louis Cadeaux, a man in his seventies who operated inconspicuously as an astrologer, occultist, and proselytizer for the Rosicrucian Society. Through some inscrutable dispensation, he acted as the artificer of Yves' Icarus-like adventure in fiery space.

For almost a year the three youths visited Cadeaux's apartment twice a week. He gave them lessons in casting horoscopes and meditating, lectures on Rosicrucian doctrines, on the rising of the world of forms out of formless unity—and on the taming of the ego that is necessary to return to that unity.

Yves underwent a dramatic change. This at last was schooling which aroused not only his interest, but his passionate dedication. In June 1948 he and Claude joined the Rosicrucian Society (Arman did not) and began to work the biweekly lessons that were sent from Oceanside, California. With surprise and pleasure Aunt Rose saw him working studiously at this "homework" (as she calls it) every evening.

The central source used by Cadeaux, and by the Rosicrucian Society in general,[17] was Max Heindel's *La Cosmogonie des Rose-Croix*. In this book Yves found his myth. The shock of recognition made a believer of him, and for years he read the *Cosmogonie* daily with what can only be described as religious faith. As late as 1952, says his mother, "he would read this book for hours every day. He would read it for entire nights. You could see the light in his window from the street. At two or three in the morning he would still be reading. He was deeply penetrated by Rosicrucianism." In fact, Yves was still, as far as books went, an intellectual child. His mind had rejected what was taught in school and remained empty, even

innocent; and it was through this emptiness or innocence that the doctrines of the Rosy Cross penetrated to his very depths. He was never to forget them.

Yves did not read many books, but those he did read (or read parts of) influenced him deeply, Heindel's *Cosmogonie* above all. Yves' own writings, which he began to publish while still a Rosicrucian, show an increasing cleverness at balancing several cultural codes, or finding interfaces between them, so that he could retreat, when pursued on the basis of one interpretation, into another. The first of these, and the most basic to the very end, was the Rosicrucian code as set forth in the *Cosmogonie*. The structure of Heindel's thought became basic to Yves', and other codes, when he learned them, were fitted to it. Heindel's dogmatic certainty recompensed Yves' lack of higher education. Rosicrucianism was, in effect, his *baccalauréat* and his university.[18]

"The Spirit penetrates all things, even the most solid bodies," says the *Tractatus Micreris*, an alchemical text. Max Heindel's Rosicrucianism is a psychological alchemy which aspires to set spirit free from solid bodies and restore it to the Eden of unity—to render it one with the seamless transparency of Space before the first "Fiat" was uttered. This dream, of a self-transcending fecundity which can be attained by ascending the Great Chain of Being, arose before European occultism in the Platonic schools, before them in Orphism, and before Orphism it was shadowed forth in Egyptian afterlife myth and shamanic rite. It has captured many spiritual adventurers, and now it captured Yves.

What Yves learned from Heindel was that he "had a rendezvous with the end of an age."[19] We are now, Heindel says, approaching the end of the Age of Matter, when Spirit lies captive in solid bodies, and the beginning of the age of open Space, when Spirit will exist free of form, at one with the boundlessness of Space. The law of gravity is about to be rescinded. Soon solid bodies will levitate, and personalities will be able to slip out of matter at will and travel, in an immaterial or "etheric" form, through invisible realms, traversing great distances in the wink of an eye. This airy body will be equipped with an immaterial sensibility empowered to read the "Memory of Nature," which is inscribed on empty space, and, by manipulating its circuits, to exercise a godlike power over the world of form.

Here was a path which led "beyond" the limits of things, a magic which would dissolve the boundaries which separated Yves Klein from Tintin and Mandrake and the Knights of the Grail. Here was a way to make (or believe) one's fantasies real. Yves' face brightened as he read this, and his inner world became both excited and still. He was a child of the imagination, after all. (As late as 1960, Tinguely says, "he would tell us stories of knights and the Holy Grail.")

Yves was one of those who do not feel at home in the world of facts ("His passion," says Tinguely, "always went beyond, beyond the plain state of things"; "He had a great, an amazing, power to live an imaginary life," says Bernadette Allain), one of those for whom life in a body seems, by reason of its limitations, an insult and a punishment. He had lived in many homes, but none was his. Now Heindel's words seemed like a message from his true home, summoning him back at last. That he should be a citizen of infinity, should have a limitless home with no barriers, no inside and outside, no owner and no stranger, seemed right and natural. It was what he had always felt without realizing it. ("For Yves," says Tinguely, "megalomania was just a natural state, not something added on.") At the time, being reminded that his true home was in infinite space and that the central purpose of his life was to find his way back to it was enough. It was later, when forced deep into myth by the "plain facts" of life, that he assigned himself the messianic role which Heindel calls the "highest initiate," who will be the first to attain immaterial sensibility, and who will pass it on to others, ushering in the new age. Night after night Yves sat by the reading lamp until the early morning hours, recognizing, and then recognizing more strongly, his own hidden face, in that infinity where the omnipotence of the spoiled child may expand to fill the universe and the anger of rejection dissolve into invisibility.

Yves' Rosicrucianism was no passing fancy. "It gave him his foundation," says his mother; and one's foundation does not change. He read Heindel daily and worked the Rosicrucian lessons faithfully (far more faithfully than he had ever done schoolwork) for four or five full years, the duration of an ordinary college education. Even after that, Heindel's idea system remained his "foundation." A friend of almost ten years later describes him then as still "passionate" about the Rosy Cross.[20] At that time, when he returned to Paris after his wanderings and began publicly promoting his myth, he would say that he was "an initiate," that he had "undergone an initiation," and would mysteriously say no more. This was a reference to his year of working with Cadeaux and his all-night sessions with the *Cosmogonie*, after which the world seemed entirely different to him. His art works, his writings, and the series of symbolic *personae* he

adopted were all attempts, more or less serious, to embody this myth in his life. As his "beautiful megalomania" (as Tinguely calls it) grew, he would even try (or pretend to try) to enforce it on the history of his time. How much of the latter activity was dandyism, how much Dadaism, how much religious faith, and how much personal pathology, no one precisely knows. Yves became a master of the poetic act, and clouds of interpretations surround him. These range from Harold Rosenberg's "able to make a good show out of nothing" to Pierre Restany's "the latest prophet of Europe."

5

From the sky moved the charms of my dreams
And came to eclipse the banner of the real.

Max Jacob

On the practice mats as in a kind of theater Yves acted out the role of spiritual warrior which was to become central to his self-image. This "holy child," remember, was a *bagarreur*, deeply drawn toward power and domination. The attraction of judo was not simply that it gave one power, but that it made power beautiful and harmless; it made it a game, a dance, an art. He gained the black belt in the school at Nice and would in time write a book on judo and operate judo schools in Paris and Madrid. Judo and Rosicrucianism were for ten years the center of his life. His sense of manhood, his sense of "being at home in the world," came to be based on generating, through judo, the ability to dominate others and, through Rosicrucianism, the self-restraint not to do so.

Claude Pascal, who was a couple of years older, had a room of his own, and Arman, who was already involved in art, had made a studio in his parents' basement. A room in the basement was prepared as a "cave" or "temple," with one wall painted blue (for Heindel's new age and the sky) and imprinted with their hands. Gathering every day in one of these places, or on the roof of the apartment house where Arman's parents lived (Aunt Rose's house was "too bourgeois"), they would practice judo, study Zen, and cultivate the ability to sit properly for meditation. At this time Yves revealed again the stubbornness which, at age fourteen, had sent him off to explore the Alps on his own. He learned to endure physical pain until he could sit in the difficult full-lotus position for up to three hours without moving his legs. The three would concentrate their minds on "holy places" in India and

Japan and practice the tantric-style visualization exercises prescribed by Heindel. (Yves' long practice of visualizations was the basis, in later years, of his "art of the immaterial.")

Also on Heindel's instructions, they became vegetarians (for about five years) and abstained from alcohol, cigarettes, and sex, feeling a certain guilt when, on the summery streets and beaches of Nice, an erotic urge would overtake them. And they fasted ("very seriously," says Arman) for one day each week, one week each month, and one month each year.

On the roof of the apartment house, during the long summer fast of 1948, they would meditate without pausing for two or three days at a time, lying in *shavasana* and walking in the Zen fashion. High on fasting and concentration (in the pre-psychedelic age), they talked of leaping from the roof and flying into the full moon overhead. Yves especially was lost in the dream of flying. The Rosicrucian texts said quite simply that it could be done by anyone with proper training. The Catholic church recognized flight as an activity of saints. Sorcerers, shamans, monks, yogis, and alchemists could all, their traditions claimed, fly without wings. There seemed no reason why Yves himself could not fly; his intense personal feeling of its rightness was like a guarantee. His lack of grounding in history and science made it easy for him, as for a child, to believe his fantasies.

As the months passed and the ascetic life seemed to dissolve their old limits, they adopted new names, like knights at the commencement of their official adventures. Armand Fernandez (thinking of Van Gogh) became Arman; Yves Klein (getting back at his parents?) became Yves; Claude Pascal (lover of paradox) became Pascal Claude.

Lying on the beach one afternoon, their adventure—and so the whole world—still unspoiled, they divided the universe among themselves (as Zeus, Poseidon, and Hades had done at the beginning of *their* careers). Arman, procreator and protector, maker of fullnesses, took charge of the animal realm. Claude, gentle and slow of memory, gathered to himself the safety of all plants. And Yves, harder, more abstract, and less at home in the world than the others, defined his realm, the mineral, as the blue emptiness of the distant sky.[21] Ascending mentally into the empyrean, he signed his new name on the *other* side of the sky— the side with no birds, no planes, no clouds, only pure and irreducible Space. It was the signature of an omnipotent creator: "The blue sky is my first art work," he said.[22]

This ambiguous act (or fantasy) of his twentieth year, with its resonances of Plato's *Phaedrus* and

shamanic myth, became the central symbol of his life. He had come from beyond the sky, and he was going to return there. A kingdom as vast as the cosmos, spreading unimaginably far beyond the boundaries of his body-and-ego, of his personal history, of his parents' home and his aunt's, of Nice, and France, and all the closed-in spaces of ordinary life, awaited him—it was the destruction of the world, the matrix of the immaterial, the destination of the Leap into the Void.

"The daydream," wrote Gaston Bachelard (an author who would later influence Yves greatly), "transports the dreamer outside the immediate world into a world that bears the mark of infinity."[23] But for Yves it was more than a daydream; it gripped him too strongly to be that. The belief that he might one day ascend to his aerial kingdom, expand through all space and become one with it, never really left him. In 1959, giving a talk at Tinguely's exhibition in Düsseldorf, he declared (secretly referring to Heindel's prophecy),

> We will all become aerial men, we will know the force of upward attraction, toward the void and the totality at one and the same time; when the forces of terrestrial attraction have been dominated in this way we will literally levitate to total physical and spiritual liberty.[24]

And in 1960, when Russian cosmonauts were threatening to encroach on his dominion, he set them straight:

> Today anyone who paints space must actually go into space to paint, but he must go there without any faking, and neither in an airplane, a parachute, nor a rocket; he must go there by his own means, by an autonomous individual force: in a word, he must be capable of levitating.[25]

And again:

> I would like to present myself on the stage of a theater hanging in space several meters from the floor without any gimmick or hoax, hanging for five or ten minutes at least without any commentary at all.[26]

"The sky," as Eliade says, " 'symbolizes' transcendence, power and changelessness simply by being there....The whole nature of the sky is an inexhaustible hierophany."[27] This hierophany transformed Yves' sense of the meaning of life; he had been given a purpose: he had been shown the sacred space toward which his current flowed.

It is a fundamental (and common) error to disregard the mystical and miraculous tone of Yves' writings as an empty posture or a display of Dada. It is an error which his own behavior sometimes seemed to confirm, but it is still an error—because, as Arman says, "he was a very special and complex character," and as Tinguely adds, "he was very contradictory inside." His systematic mixing of codes, designed, as we will see, to protect his inner world from the dangerous intrusion of uncontrolled facts, was confusing. He used forms related to Dada to express ideas which were absolutely counter to it. He caricatured himself, yet resented ridicule.

"Yves knew how to joke," says Tinguely; "he would roll on the ground laughing—but at the same time he was taking himself very seriously."

And Claude Pascal: "He was not a Dada. He was a mystic. He laughed all the time and joked, so people didn't take him seriously—but Yves was *always* dead serious."

And Arman: "A mystic, yes. He was shy, and his showing off was to hide shyness. He was *always* a mystic."

And Rotraut Klein: "He was absolutely a mystical man. He was like Jesus."

6

Follow my tracks,
You can come,
My best friends,
The road is open
The sky is clear.

Jules Supervielle

Yves' desire to travel, to claim for himself the free-roaming life of Fred Klein and Marie Raymond, had not ended with his failure to enter the Merchant Marine Academy. In the summer of 1948 he hitch-hiked through Italy, staying at convents to save money. Costumed in a shirt imprinted with his hands and feet, he visited museums and monuments. Rosicrucianism had done what school had utterly failed to do: it had aroused his interest in the past. He began to regret more deeply his lack of academic grounding; he dreamed of being a traveling writer, sending back to France his impressions of the world, and began to study languages.

The army could offer travel, if less than the Merchant Marine, and in November 1948 Yves entered military service. He was sent to French-occupied Germany, where he stayed for eleven months, training in artillery. There he imitated what he had seen of his parents' life, making a racecourse of cockroaches to amuse his fellows, and visiting museums and galleries during his furloughs. The Rosicrucian lessons still came from Oceanside and still were faithfully worked and returned.

Meanwhile he dreamed of a more radical adventure, fit for knights in armor. Two roads beck-oned, one to Oceanside to live with the sages of the Rosicrucian Society, the other to Japan to pursue the "spiritual space" of judo. Japan was the more attractive, for it offered scope for an adventure worthy of Tintin himself: the Grail knights would go first to Ire-land (which seemed to the three French youths a land of horsemen and horsemanship), learn to ride, and then, mounted on good steeds, crusade across Europe and Asia, climaxing the great adventure by sailing from Korea to Japan and entering a judo academy. Yves returned to Nice on furlough and discussed it with Claude and Arman.

Arman, who was already busy with art work and had just met his wife-to-be (and who no longer read Tintin!), begged off the lengthy adventure. But late in 1949, when Yves was discharged from the army, he and Claude crossed the Channel to London to learn English before proceeding to Ireland and their private *fiana*.

In London for about four months, Yves and Claude shared a room near Earl's Court, attended judo classes and Rosicrucian meetings, and took English lessons three times a week from James Shorrocks. They continued the mystical life, conscientiously working the Rosicrucian lessons and maintaining the Hein-delian discipline. Claude worked at a tuxedo rental firm, and Yves, calling on contacts of his parents, worked in the shop of the framer who had prepared his father's exhibition in 1946.[28] Yves' parents sent some money when they could, and Aunt Rose was often called upon.

In London in 1950 Yves' "vocation" as a painter began to force itself into his awareness. He was still, and would remain for several years, "fed up with painting" as Claude Pascal puts it, even hostile to it. His desire to differentiate himself from his parents, to create his own world rather than tamely enter theirs, led him to judo, to an assertion of warlike individuality quite distinct from their artistic receptiveness. But an inner discord was involved here. Yves' talents as an artist were enormous, and his rejection of art did violence to his inner nature at the same time that it freed him outwardly from his past. While moving judo and Rosicrucianism into the foreground as the coor-dinates of his personal identity, he began to catch hold, in the background, of the threads of his own artistic direction.

By his own later account, Yves began painting monochromes in 1946; but there is no witness who confirms this. In 1948, however, not long after signing the sky, his first art work, he attached a round blue disc to the notebook in which he did his Rosicrucian work. When Arman inquired about the disc, he was told, "This is what the paintings of the future will look like." Now, working at the frame shop in London, Yves found himself attracted to the powdered pigments, which for him were always the "pure" colors. One day, Claude recalls, Yves disappeared into the bathroom for a long time and emerged carrying monochromes done in various pastels on small squares of cardboard. "I have found what I want to do," he announced to Pascal Claude. And so attuned was Claude that he credited the news at once, replying only, "Of course!"

Such was the beginning of Yves' extraordinary career—hands smudged with color, eyes glowing, "a man infested with dreams,...overtaken by the divine infection."[29] Carefully he placed the paintings on the table and bed and, fastidious, washed the color from his hands. Soon he tacked the cardboards to the wall and invited Shorrocks and two or three other friends to see them.

But Yves' return to the occupation of his parents was not to be so easy or so quick; the London monochromes are merely the first stage of a difficult change of direction which represents, in effect, the end of Yves' prolonged adolescence and his adoption of an adult vocation which truly satisfied his inner needs. For him the monochrome was from the beginning an expression of Rosicrucian thought (Arman associates it directly with the influence of Cadeaux's teachings), but on another level it was an attack on the whole world of painting as then known—an attack on the figurative painting of his father and the abstract painting of his mother. It made both seem unnecessary and by implication mocked them. "Everyone who saw these monochromes," says Claude, "died laughing; and Yves and I laughed too." Yves still "detested" all paintings except for the monochromes; but he was gradually becoming, as Claude Pascal says, "an involuntary painter."

In Yves' later mythic record of his early life this event is recorded as his first exhibition of monochromes—described sometimes as a public and sometimes as a private showing. Earlier than Rauschenberg's 1951 exhibition of white paintings, it became, in Yves' mind, an event of art historical weight and importance. To an immaterialist, to one who scorned the "plain dull skin of a man,"[30] who wrote that it is only when "transported by the Imagination" that "we attain to the immaterial space of Life itself,"[31] the "factual" record is a contemptible thing,

not equal to describing Truth. However slight the event in worldly terms, it grew, in Yves' mythic theater, to its proper size—not merely a young artist's first tentative experimentation, but an announcement, like the prophecy of John the Baptist, of a turning point in human history: the first public signal of the dawning of Heindel's Age of Space. This "exhibition," Yves was to declare in 1957, marked the beginning of the "Age of Bypassing the Problematics of Art." The monochrome painting had no problematics because it represented, not a selection of objects from the All, but the All Itself. *"Solvite corpora et coagulate spiritum."*[32] In the monochrome all bodies are dissolved into the pristine ground where spirit coagulates into chromatic fullness. The Age of Form ends, and human evolution begins its ascending Return to Space. Thus the event in the London boardinghouse bathroom overflowed Yves' mental space, passed through the channel of his private myth, and began its appropriation of the universe: the future of human evolution became a ramification of his private thoughts.

7

Flee as far as possible from murderous Conceits,
Cruel Wit and impure Laughter,
Which make the eyes of the blue sky weep.

Paul Verlaine

In April 1950, Yves and Claude were ready to push on to Ireland. Emulating wandering monks, they left their goods (except for the *Cosmogonie*) with English friends and set out hitchhiking, with only three pounds, a loaf of bread, and a bag of sugar between them. ("We were afraid of nothing in those days," says Claude.) In Ireland they simply wandered into the countryside, found their way to the horse-breeding area, and inquired until they found work. For three months they lived on a horse farm, cleaning stables in return for riding lessons. (Yves would later describe himself as "an experienced trainer of horses.")

But the equestrian life was not smooth. They received few lessons in return for much shoveling, and in time tensions set in between them. Yves kept a journal, written in his left hand, largely in English;[33] in his determination to make up for years of neglected studies, he was memorizing ten English words a day, practicing English composition, and learning to write ambidextrously. The journal shows a sensitive and decent youth who was remarkably aware of his own shortcomings and seriously trying to soften the corners of his one-day-to-be-famous ego. The glimpse it offers

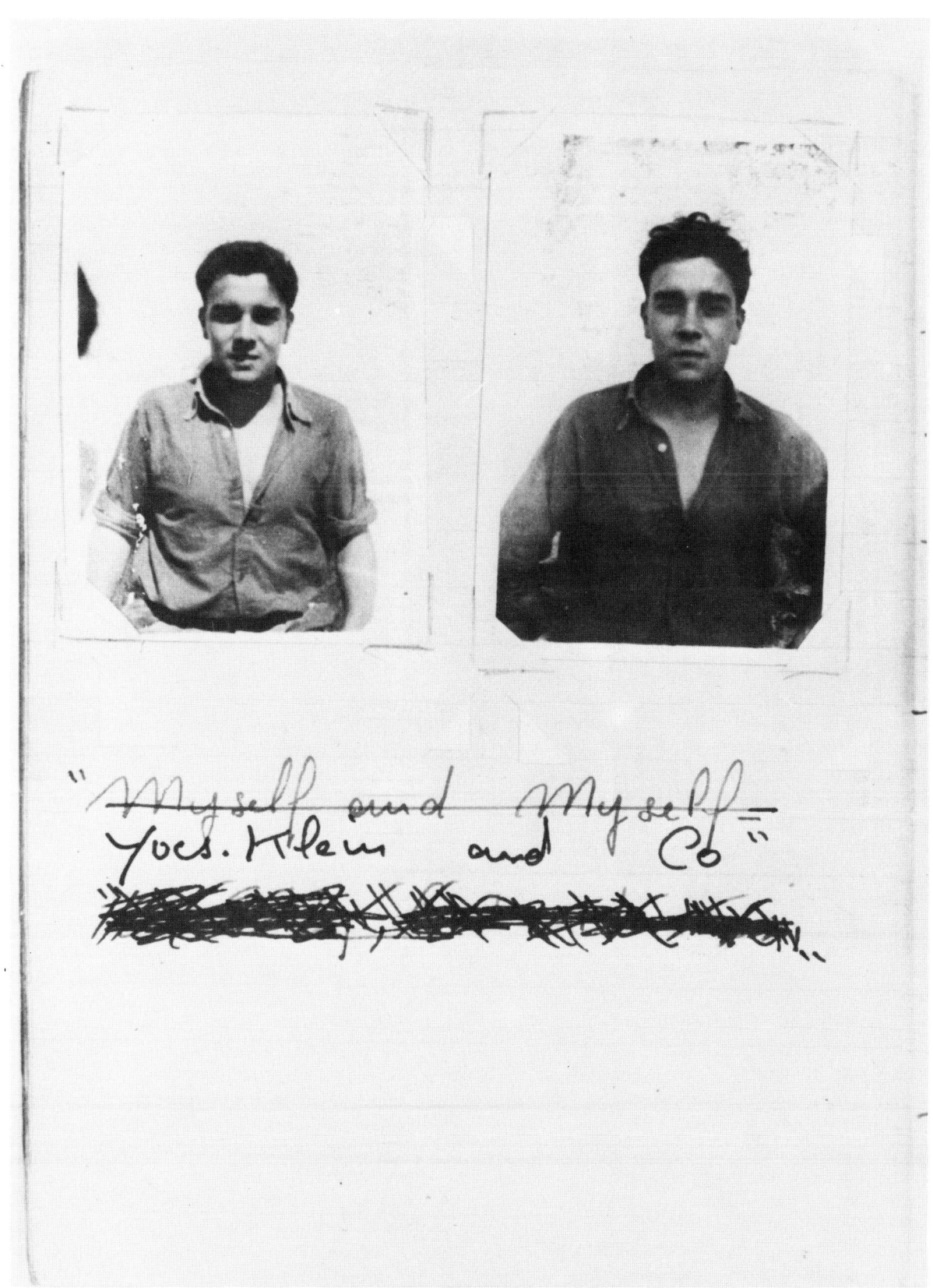

Frontispiece of Yves Klein's Irish journal, 1950

of his character should be carefully considered by all who would understand clearly the record of his later life.

Weds. the 11th of July and Thursday the 12th of July.

Last night after the ride, or more exactly after the practise in the ring, I felt happy and in Peace with myself, and suddenly when we were dining the idea comes to me that I had not told Claude about the money I was going to receive from my parent, and also that I had to get it in New Bridge as quick as possible. . . . So I broke the usual silence, telling Claude all about; and asking him for his advice how to ask the permission to Allan [the farm manager]!!! First he said that it was no need that he comes and second—well, a bad interpretation of dry answer from me made him furious and angry!

Now, that book here, will be never read by somebody else without my permission—I will be very strict—so I can speak clearly about ourselves and our two difficults caracters—then Claude these last days was in the very same bad period which I was a month ago—I have watched him for a fortnight quite intensely—my purpose was not to be happy looking at an unhappiness, but just to try to find how and why, you are catch so strongly by this "Discord Spirit" without any apparent reason at all.

Yves' effort to study the Discord Spirit in himself went to the roots of his psyche; it may be that he never solved the matter, and that his failure to do so cost him his life.

Claude after that prelude cloudy—start a deep complaining speech about our comportement one to each other. I was listening, recognizing myself in the same bad state of mind in which I was a month ago—"It's something to become mad, he said, we must do something for it;" I said the very same words in this dayry in the pages of about one month ago. But it was nice and I was happy to heard that because I could understand him so well. I know many people would laught at something like that—but just to give an idea of the strength of that Spirit—when you look at your friend just without any purpose and then when suddenly you see him ugly, bad, dirty fellow, etc. . . . at the point then when you want to speak to him you are so upset that the words stay in your throat, no

there is no laughing matter. . . .

. . . Now I just know that 'to be in peace with oneself is to be [in] peace with everybody else' that means when I you do in everything, every gesture, what the little voice of conscience tell you to do inside, everything goes well.

And I realize now that if we beat all that we will be *free* really in this world!!!

Making up their dispute, the young men went to a local party, and Yves remarked in his diary:

Very funny this world. . . . I was not shave and I looked very wild among these fraiche and white skins girls! They do not mind at all.

In fact, Yves was discovering, during these years, that sexuality was not to be easy for him. His impatience and overexcitable nature brought with them a proclivity to premature ejaculation which encouraged the Heindelian practice of sublimation. It was a heavy burden for a young man who was attractive to girls and disposed to their company. It did not help in his struggles against the Discord Spirit, which were always intense—sometimes unbearably so—and seem never to have gotten easier.

When the Discord Spirit comes it is a strange feeling, this is exactly a fact, that this spirit appear suddenly as quick as a flash—I have no idea at all how and from where he comes, I just know that it is very hard to take it away. When it comes I make me cold and absolutely without any emotion in order to analyse all the facts and reasons who might have bring this spirit. . . . All the day I was again angry, not against Claude and not against somebody else, but just against everything—the reason was silly, again a question of no control of myself. . . . I should be able to ignore an unsmart and ugly gesture like that now! No, I can't, I fall in the snare every time and the anger live in me for as long as it want.

Still, he learned much, in those months, of gentleness and nonviolence toward life situations in general:

Friday the 13th of July—

. . . An amazing ride on Pat tonight, has again proved to me that softness and softness again is the only way in everything! Remember!

If only he could have remembered!

Saturday the 14th of July

. . . I don't want to say anymore about him [Allan], because I know too well now what it cost to judge our fellow creatures and never one's self.

Throughout this period the Rosicrucian lessons arrived with their worksheets to be sent back to Oceanside. After the day's work, Yves and Claude ate their vegetarian meal (sometimes in monastic silence) and worked at the Rosicrucian studies into the night. Yves read the Bible along with the theosophic interpretations of Max Heindel, and was often moved to longing for a gentler, freer, less ego-serving frame of mind:

Sunday the 15th of July—

...How to do all my possible for everybody? how to help everybody as much as I can? Just following the little voice...I know that it is the only way now, but in spite of that I still turn my head and I still look aside Knowing perfectly well where is the Good—I look at the Bad or not especially the Bad but I should say that I still make calculs and follow my cunning instinct, which is very clumsy. Oh God, if I could only forget for a little while the World Wisdom, the Civilization Wisdom and go in the natural love-way perhaps I would be able afterwards to carry on, looking a foolish at the everybody's eyes but happy inside myself knowing that I am doing my Best Sincerely—

My left hand start to write better now—

But alongside his pious desire to "do all my possible for everybody" he was also developing his wicked satanic mask, partly in imitation of the farm manager, Allan, whose personal style he had earlier loathed:

Friday the 11th

...I have perfectly understood today the laught of Allan—when he chuckle sometimes as a devil—I know now what that means exactly and I start to take a plaisure to do it either!

With the characteristic ambivalence of spiritual seekers raised in dualistic traditions, he fancied himself both potential devil and potential saint:

"To challenge the evil" that should be my motto—I don't think I can really have hatred against anybody now but still too many voices hum in my innermost—If only my jaw could remember me each time swallow a mouthful, that I am eating the Christ's body! I am still not rife [ripe?] at all!—too young!

(His ten English words for Friday, August 11, included "motto = devise, to challenge = défier, mal = evil, to hum = murmurer, jaw = mâchoir, mouthful = bouchée, rife = mur.")

Yves' desire that his jaw would "remember" him "each time swallow a mouthful" reveals a spiritual program related to the "self-remembering" of Gurdjieff, the "Attention!" of Zen, and the "mindfulness" practices of southern Buddhism.

The 5th of August 1950[34]

Many persons are like I am, when relaxing my mind and my body I start to dream about...I don't know...just about the first picture who come into my mind—then my eyes look completely mad and lost in the space—if someone speak to me when I feel like that it may get the impression so unpleasant of a person who does not listen at all and pay any attention at what it is said!

This state is the result of a simple lasyness, I realize that now, as well as we have some difficulties to keep our back straight as well we have difficulties to pay constantly attention at everything around....that question goes very far and I can't really [think] about it tonight properly—but I feel that it might be a big question—I have to think about—because I am afraid it is a little negative to be like that—So now I have to keep a back straight a permanent vision of everything!

Clearly Yves had not yet begun to doubt Heindel's assurances that the human being is perfectible through his own effort, which no external force (such as childhood experiences) can countervail. Throughout these years Heindel presided over his life with minutely detailed instructions: what to eat, how much, and how often; how to breathe; even how to dream. The accumulated force of these disciplines, Heindel promised, maintained for at least seven years, would not only tame the "cunning" ego, but would actually "transfigure" the physical body, atom by atom, into a nobler creature, able to float at its ease through silken space and decipher at a glance the rebus of nature.

This laborious "transfiguration" was the organizing purpose of Yves' life for nearly ten years and, goaded by Heindel, he invested much effort and expectation in it. Many of his later works are (among other things) attempts to translate this purpose into symbols and, in effect, escape from it. But during the period of the Irish journal the promise was still newly made, too fresh and sweet to be doubted; as late as 1954 Yves wrote:

Transfiguration
To be transfigured is to think at each instant of the very essence of the purity of sanctity, and the breathing does the rest—that is, it spreads through the body a new life which

enters into every separate atom and remakes each infinitesimal particle of the ordinary body into a body transfigured.

What is necessary then is to breathe with joy an atmosphere and a climate intensely spiritual, which creates in the ego the power to purify the physical body and the astral body and the body of desire.

Every instant
every act
every word
every perception
of my five senses
must be for me
steeped in joy
a joy perhaps
artificial and
a little too self-conscious
at first, but
which will be little by little
a continual
illumination
to drink to eat
to breathe only
joy
It is necessary to breathe the divine everywhere.[35]

These themes of his journal at age twenty-two—the struggle with the Discord Spirit, the acceptance of the satanic laughing mask, the belief that transfiguration would come in the not-too-distant future—all remained prominent in Yves' life until the end. Later, after he had assumed his mythic role in public, when his "omnipotence" was challenged (or, worse, mocked) he reacted with violent anger; but when his claims on the cosmos were not in question, he was profoundly gentle. The ambivalence between the worldly life, in which he was forced to defend his appropriated zones of reality, and the life of the "innermost," where no claim was at issue, is expressed most poignantly in a brief entry toward the end of the stay in Ireland:

It is better to have no friends and so no enemies!
I am afraid it is World-Wisdom
And I don't want World-Wisdom
Do I?

8

And then he mounted upon his horse, and rode into many strange and wild countries, and through many waters and valleys.

Sir Thomas Malory, *Morte d'Arthur*

One day while working in the stable, Yves entered a deep daydream. In his mind's eye he had mounted on horseback, cantered across Europe and Asia, passed through the gateway of a judo school, and donned a kimono, when, roused from his daydream, he saw Claude grimacing unhappily at him over his manure shovel.

He forced a departure, returning to London by himself at the end of August; Claude joined him there about a month later. By the end of the year they were back in Nice. But the long ride could not get started. Arman had other involvements, and just as Claude was applying for a passport, he discovered he had tuberculosis. Almost two years passed before the pilgrimage got under way, but Yves didn't sit still. ("He was too impatient," says Tinguely. "There was such anguish in him, such longing for paradise, that he could not wait for anything.")

On February 3, 1951, he left for Madrid alone, to study Spanish. There he joined a judo club, and when the instructor got sick was asked to replace him. This was Yves' first employment as a judo teacher, which was to be his source of livelihood for much of the rest of his life. He became very friendly with the director of the school, Fernando Franco de Sarabia, whose father was a publisher.

Meanwhile, his subterranean vocation as an artist continued to thrust itself upward toward awareness. He wrote in his diary (February 18, 1951) an idea, neither an actual plan nor a mere daydream, of exhibiting monochrome paintings with unspecified musical accompaniment.[36] Very probably this was a reference to the idea of one-note or one-chord music (later the *Monotone Symphony*), which, according to Claude Pascal, Yves had "discovered" in London not long after "discovering" the monochrome, and which he specifically regarded as the musical correlate of the one-color painting.

Yves, the international traveler, now reversed roles on his parents, inviting them to visit him in Madrid. The money was difficult to find, but in June, at last, Fred, Marie, Aunt Rose, and Yves' maternal grandmother (the instigator of the family's devotion to Saint Rita) traveled to Madrid and spent ten days or so touring Spain. At the end of June he returned with them, on a steamer by way of the Balearic Islands. But first Arman, who needed a job, was summoned by Yves to Madrid, and took over for a while Yves' "professorship" of judo.

Throughout his travels Yves wrote to both his parents and his aunt, often to ask for money, sometimes just to keep in touch. His closeness to his mother's family, and above all to his Aunt Rose, never ceased. His letters are almost childishly affectionate. When his mother shared the Kandinsky Prize in 1949, he wrote from England: "Hurray for Mama! Both abstract *and* famous!! Bravo!!" To Aunt Rose, from London: "A thousand thanks for the candied fruits! With thousands of big kisses and a great big hug!"[37] In fact, he was finding it difficult to break away from his mother's family and strike out on a path of his own. His adolescence was unnaturally prolonged both by the excessive care of his aunt and by his own refusal to follow his increasingly frequent impulses toward a career in art.

From January 1951 until the end of summer 1952, Yves lived in Paris in a rented room a hundred yards or so from his parents. Away from Claude and Arman, he felt himself an outsider and began to worry about finding a place in the world. Because Paris frightened him, he sought anchorage in Rosicrucianism, which he studied through the night: Rosicrucianism, like judo, was his own, not something given to him by his parents or his aunt. Twenty-three years old now, he was ready for the second time to try to enter the adult world.

His mother's reputation was then very high, and she held a weekly open house ("Marie Raymond's Monday") through which much of the Parisian art world passed. Yves attended regularly. ("He loved those gatherings," says his mother. "He loved the ambience of artists.") His sense of the art historical moment could not have been more finely tuned than by alert attendance at these salons. It was here that he grasped his second code, that of twentieth-century avant-gardism; later, in his writings, he would conflate it, with deliberate ambiguity, with the Rosicrucian code.

Among the avant-garde activities which Yves now witnessed at first hand were those of the Lettrists, who professed to continue the tradition of Dada and surrealism through concrete poetry, glossolaliac performances, and multimedia projects. He met young artists such as Raymond Hains who were about his age and already had careers under way. "I am a little afraid," he wrote to Aunt Rose, "to be so hesitant before life, to be still and always in so much doubt. . . . I still dream of Japan."[38] Still hoping to remedy his lack of education, he attended the School of Oriental Languages informally, studying Japanese. ("I have no

diploma," he wrote with a touch of desperation in a letter never mailed. "But I have been studying Japanese furiously for months.")[39] The great question was whether or not to seek entrance into his parents' world, hitching his carriage to their train. But the little Captain was too independent for that. He remained fixed in the desire to make his own way, in a profession as close to a Knight of the Grail as he could find—as a judo master!

In the summer of 1952 he arranged contacts in Japan through his parents' circle, asked his aunt to pay his steamship fare ("Of course I said yes"), and set out alone, not on horseback, but on the *Marseillaise*, through the Suez Canal, cruising the warm seas around India, by Singapore and Hong Kong, arriving in Yokohama on September 23, 1952.[40] He was met by Takachiyo Uemura, an art critic acquainted with his parents, and stayed briefly in Uemura's house. "My dear aunt," he wrote, "See! I'm in Japan at last!" Soon he moved on to Tokyo and on October 9, 1952, enrolled in the Kodokan Judo Institute, the most prestigious judo center in the world.

9

"Sirs," said the youth, "you would do well to be still, for I will not be stopped for anything or for any man in the world."

Chrétien de Troyes, *Perceval*

Yves stayed in Japan for fifteen months. Rose Raymond sent money regularly, and in addition Yves tutored two French children and taught French to Japanese and American students. Investigating the art world, he arranged three shows of his parents' works. At the same time he pursued his experiments in monochromy, making small cardboard monochromes, as he had done in England, and inviting Japanese friends to his (characteristically empty) apartment to see them. As in England, he received no encouragement from their reaction.[41]

Still thinking of a career as a traveling journalist, Yves wrote an article on Japan which he sent to his mother, asking her to try to place it in a magazine, and promising more ("I have written a lot") if they were wanted.[42] The article is very interesting by way of contrast both with the Irish journal and with the mythic essays he would begin to publish in 1958. When Yves wrote of his own feelings, as in the Irish journal, he was often charming, in a rather touchingly innocent way. When he wrote his self-glorifying essays of the late fifties, he had found a voice (partly from Bachelard) of power and poetic beauty. But in writing on a subject outside of himself, such as Japanese culture, he is a deadly bore. There is none of the passion, none of the flashes of exalted mood or imagery, none of the taut phrases, of his essays on himself. Wisely, Marie refrained from forwarding the essay to any editor; its voice is that of a schoolboy trying to sound grown up.

Above all, Yves practiced judo, flying through "spiritual space" for hours a day at the Kodokan Institute. With characteristic grandiosity he was fiercely determined that upon his return he would be the foremost *judoka* in Europe. The plan had two parts. First was the publication of a book which would clarify through photographs the set of *judokata*, or slow movements, which are the basis of the training. (With relentless determination Yves would practice each of these movements for a thousand repetitions at a time.) No European book really made the positions clear. With borrowed camera equipment and a cameraman, he managed to have a film made from which the stills for such a book could be derived. But the second part of his plan was of the essence. In Europe there were many *judokas* with the third degree, or *dan*, of the black belt. But of the fourth *dan* there were very few. Yves was determined to return to France with the fourth *dan* black belt from the prestigious Tokyo Kodokan, win the European judo championship, and take over the French Federation of Judo.

Laying down his French belts, which were not recognized in Japan, he started over again from the beginning and worked at the almost pathologically high energy level which would come to characterize his activities more and more as the years passed. His judo master, Tashiro, wrote to Aunt Rose that "he has practiced judo so intensely since his arrival in Japan that his friends have sometimes been worried about his health."[43] In fact, Tashiro's concern for Yves' health was justified. Following the examples of Japanese sumo wrestlers and *judokas*, Yves began taking various stimulants to prepare himself for judo performances. These included calcium injections and amphetamines, which were legally obtainable at that time in both Japan and France. The regular use of legally obtained amphetamine products continued until the end of his life and may have contributed to the apparent change—toward greater intensity and grandiosity—which his personality underwent in Japan, and to the inability to sleep for which he was famous among his friends in later years.[44] His letters to his family from Japan show a growing strain and an increasing rigidity of ambition.

On Christmas day, 1952, he wrote to his grandfather about his grandmother's death (which had occurred the previous July): "Her photo is constantly on my table in my bedroom. I look at it as often as possible. . . . I am absolutely certain that she protects and helps us without us being aware of it. . . . She will fence off from me all possible dangers and for that I thank her often." His grandmother, who had first entrusted him to the care of Saint Rita, seemed now to share in that saint's activity.

In January he wrote to Aunt Rose, asking for money to relieve him of the need to give French lessons so he could "work judo from morning till night. . . . I think of nothing else right now." Receiving it, he replied, "You are truly a Fantastic Tantine!" Hoping to hit it rich on his own, he entered a business arrangement for importing kimonos from Indonesia to Marseilles, and was gypped. Again Aunt Rose came to the rescue. Yves replied, "Thank you, thank you a thousand times as always. . . . You have again saved me from catastrophe, with those brigands. I have the most formidable Tantine in the world."

But the strain of his effort, and the difficulty he was encountering at succeeding in anything, were showing. "It is hard here," he wrote to Aunt Rose, "and I constantly remember how sweet life is in Nice, well taken care of by Tantine. But I absolutely must work at this damn judo and return to France a Grand Master and Champion. It is my future!" ("I have no diploma!")

After a year he requested the fourth *dan* belt (his "future") and was told that he qualified only for the second. He wrote to Aunt Rose in a frenzy:

I am fed up with this country. I am a nervous wreck and desire only one thing, to return to France as soon as possible. But I desire above all to obtain what I came for; it is absolutely necessary that I get the 4th dan from the Kodokan. Without that I could not return, I would have lost everything, because today in France if I wish to be someone in Judo I must have the 4th dan, the third, which is offered me [!] is insufficient, there are too many third dans in France at present (about sixty), but there are only five fourth dans, and you see I will not be the very foremost even if I extract the fourth dan from them. . . . I am regarded as the best foreign student and all the professors think I deserve the fourth dan, and even the fifth. But alas they are against foreigners and have decided not to give promotion to a foreigner without his having won at least ten times or their being tempted by money. But this last way does not please me.

I have been too sincere in judo up till now; I do not want any trafficking in money to buy my rank. But there is a way, that is to impress them, to make them understand that on my return I am going to be a very powerful figure in France, and that it will be to their advantage to keep me on their side by doing me this special favor, of giving me the 4th dan before I leave. To this end I have asked the Spanish Federation of Judo [through his friend Franco de Sarabia] to recognize me as their technical director; they have very kindly done that for me and at present the Kodokan is aware that I will be the master of Judo for all of Spain....I have explained further to the Kodokan that I am going to establish in Paris the largest and best Judo club in the city and perhaps in Europe....and that I will devote it exclusively to the Judo of the Kodokan (BLUFF) if I get the 4th dan.

Aunt Rose's complicity in the "bluff" was requested. She was to write to Tashiro and inform him, "clearly and discreetly," that if and only if Yves received the fourth *dan*,

I will have at my disposition three or four million francs for the establishment of my Judo club in Paris....This letter must be genteel and familial but unhesitating in its request for the 4th dan, and about the three or four million francs....If I lose this, I do not think that I will ever get over it....Write quickly, tantine, but construct your letter well....I am in a hurry to see you again; embrace Grandpa for me, and for you hundreds of thousands of big kisses, BRAVO TANTINE!

On November 18, Tantine did as she was asked: "My heart is filled with hope that I have the honor of addressing the master of the prestigious Kodokan Judo Institute, famed throughout the entire world, so that he might deign to honor with his attention the situation of one of his students, my nephew Yves Klein."

Yves, it turned out, had read the psychology of the Kodokan well. On December 7 Tashiro replied to Aunt Rose in a letter that is a masterpiece of doublespeak. "Yves," he wrote, "has become a second Dan in a very short time: his progress is truly impressive." But the shortness of time is precisely the problem: "Myself, I began to practice Judo at the age of fourteen and after three difficult exercises a day for eight years finally became third Dan." Having established the necessity for rejection, he slips out of it with amazing ease: "I understand well your affectionate

concern and that of Yves' parents. But, to speak frankly, the situation being as above described, it is impossible to give him the fourth or fifth Dan in so short a time, that is to say, before the end of this year." Before the end of *this* year—the date of writing being December 7! Eleven days later, on December 18, the Kodokan issued Yves' diploma—fourth *dan* black belt.[45] A diploma at last! On February 9, 1954, on the *Marseillaise* at Hong Kong, en route to France, Yves wrote to Aunt Rose, "And so I am fourth Dan, which is the highest in judo in France, it is truly marvelous....I hope that I will be at the very top in Judo....You are, without exaggeration, the only Tantine of your class in the world!"

Behind the record of this successful "bluff" several tendencies lie: a determination to be *first* in whatever he did ("in Paris, or perhaps in all of Europe"); a refusal to recognize boundaries between fact and fantasy when the fantasy was intense and personal ("I think if I don't get this I will never get over it"); a desperate dependence on childish appeals ("a thousand big kisses for Tantine"); and, perhaps most important, a tendency to "set himself up" for disappointment by nurturing unrealistic expectations ("I hope that I will be at the very top in judo"). Combined with his unwillingness to admit any obstacle, this latter trait, in years to come, would join forces with the Discord Spirit.

In fact, Yves seems to have undergone an important change in Japan. In Ireland he had not been thinking of power and primacy, but of "softness and softness again." ("Remember!") But now he was impatient to make up for lost time, to overtake those of his generation who had entered careers more easily and quickly—in short, to assume at last the destiny of a hero. Early in 1953 he stopped communicating with Oceanside, and six months later his membership in the Rosicrucians lapsed. There were still darknesses inside him where the Discord Spirit waited. But his mastery on the judo mats deceived him. He was a champion already. He could now demand a deeper response from the world. He was no longer a mere seeker, but One Who Has Attained.

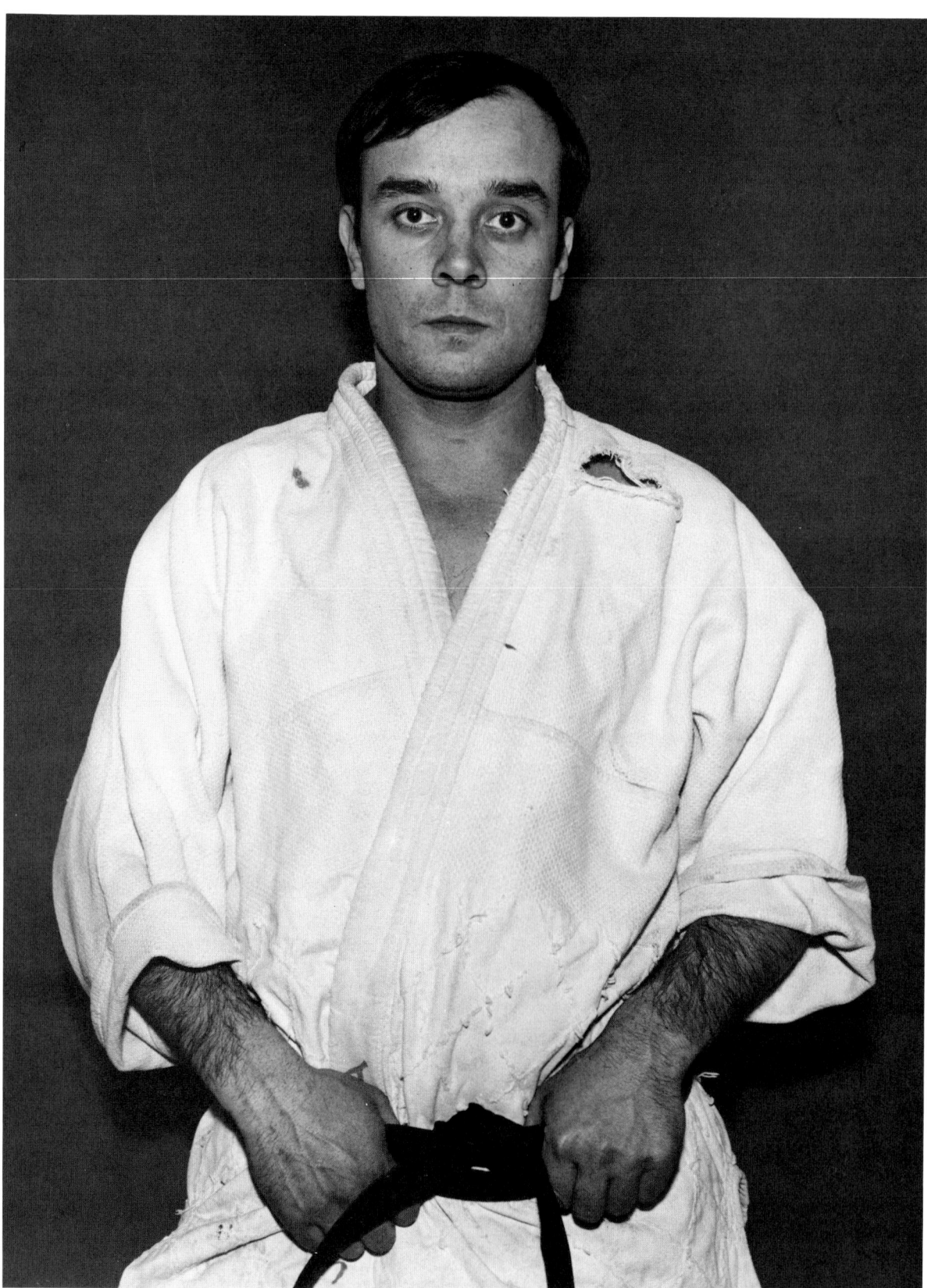

Yves Klein, fourth dan black belt in judo, 1960

10

*Patience, patience,
Patience in the blue sky.*

Paul Valéry

Early in 1954 Yves returned to France, and at once Franco de Sarabia invited him to Madrid to teach. But Yves had greater things in his sights: the European championship beckoned. He traveled to judo clubs in France and Italy, giving talks and demonstrations. The advertisements—written, it seems, by himself—are almost sinister in the intensity of the demands they make upon the world:

There are in the world heroes of adventure whom the public at large does not know. Yves KLEIN is one of these. . . .

It is not every day that one has the chance to meet and even to watch at work one of the great masters of judo. . . .[46]

Unfortunately, this approach was not the right one. The situation was more delicate than Yves had thought, and his reading of French psychology less precise than of Japanese. Judo was a big business in France already, and the French Federation of Judo, which had no master trained in Japan, was teaching it commercially as a sport. Yves, who had been disappointed by the lack of mysticism in the Tokyo Kodokan, was deeply offended by the commercialism of French judo. Rashly he took on the establishment, talking against the Federation in the clubs. *He* represented the lineage of the Tokyo Kodokan. *He* had the highest rank in Europe. And he believed that *he,* not the Federation, should be the guiding power of French judo.

Predictably, the Federation did not like him. Yves may indeed have been, as he claimed, "the most advanced judo expert in France," but the Federation, claiming that his Japanese belts were not recognized in France, nevertheless demanded that he take a new examination.[47] He refused, in self-righteous anger, and was prohibited from participating in the European championships and even from joining the Federation. Privately it was said that he was a grabber, a troublemaker—he advertised himself too much.

Suddenly the goal for which he had worked with such determination, which was the basis of his differentiation as a self, and on which all his expectations were placed (*"It is my future!"*), had disappeared from sight. His *Fundamentals of Judo* was published by Bernard Grasset in Paris in November; but despite the book, he saw that he could not be a real judo master—with the prestige which, in his eyes, the position entailed—in France. The most he could hope for was to run a private club. His first and, he thought, best option for a career of his own was over before it had begun. Filled with bitterness, and preferring to endure his humiliation away from French eyes, he made plans to move to Madrid—"out of sheer disappointment," says Arman.

As usual in a time of need, he called on Aunt Rose. "I need a car," he said, "to organize my kingdom of judo in Spain." "I went to Paris," she says, "and bought him a little four-CV Renault, with which he was enchanted." ("My dear Tantine…the car is absolutely Sensational!…and thank you for the card of Saint Rita, in which I truly believe.") Soon thereafter, promising her (or himself) that this was "your last surge of spoiling me," he left for Spain. There he poured the energy of his frustration into teaching, and made a powerful showing.

Clearly, Yves did return from Japan a more impressive figure than before. "Judo gave him strength and life," his mother says. And Bernadette Allain, who practiced judo with him in Paris in the following year, says: "His true métier was as a *judoka.* On the judo mats he was serene, strong, and inwardly at peace. He had learned in Japan the true judo, which was nonexistent in the French schools—judo as an intensive discipline and ascesis, which confers on the body itself a knowledge that has never passed through the intellectual mind." Yves had that "other" knowledge, that infraverbal, pre- or postintellectual knowledge; his body and countenance, as long as he remained a true *judoka,* radiated strength and self-confidence. He developed the Spanish Federation of Judo from a mere name into an ongoing institution and obtained accreditation from the Kodokan to leave a lineage of black belts, the first in Spain.

But this did not supply what he had wanted, or needed: preeminence of some sort in Paris itself, in his parents' milieu. During the months in Spain he planned a second attempt at the conquest of Paris, this time on another flank. He would develop his second career option, the one for which his attendance at his mother's Monday salons had prepared him. The dead end of his career in judo pointed him toward art. ("He did not so much come to painting," Edouard Adam says, "as come back to it.")

There was, however, a problem. He was now twenty-six years old and had honestly acquired a profession already. To return to Paris as a beginner, as, in effect, a child, so far behind Hains and Villeglé and others of his own age who, unobstructed by a parental example to rebel against, had started in art a decade before, was too humiliating.

It is beyond doubt that Yves had at least conceived the idea of the monochrome painting as early as February 1951, when he mentioned it in his journal. Almost certainly the first primitive examples had been made as early as 1949, as Claude Pascal recalls—perhaps as early as 1948, as Arman says. The physical record is gone—at some point Yves destroyed the earliest works—and the documentary record has been deliberately tampered with. The latter date is perhaps the most plausible, since Yves, who claimed to have painted monochromes in 1946, seems to have commonly backdated his "discoveries" by about two years. In any case, he decided to date his career as a painter of monochromes from 1951, and, in company with Claude Pascal, who now joined him in Madrid, set out to produce evidence to support the claim.

He was in fact still engaged in the making of little monochromes of pastel on cardboard, as he had done in England and Japan. It had become his practice to put such objects on the walls of his environments, a kind of Rosicrucian icon beside the pictures of his grandmother and Saint Rita. Now, in Madrid, he hung monochromes in the hall where he taught judo. Judo, Rosicrucianism, and the monochrome, three approaches to "spiritual space," were all "his"—they did not bear the taint of parental example. Now the monochrome began to come to the foreground and offer itself as his ticket of admission to the adult world.

With money supplied by Rose Raymond, Yves and Claude prepared, in Franco de Sarabia's father's print shop, a book of reproductions of monochromes. In a gesture with distinct Dada overtones, they published two versions, one entitled *Yves Peintures*, the other *Haguenault Peintures* (after a brand of gingerbread, Yves was later to say). Inside both was a preface of blank lines, divided into paragraphs and signed with the name of power, Pascal Claude,[48] and ten color plates of monochromes in green, yellow, blue, pink, red, and orange—each dated (1951–54), some with city names and dimensions indicated, and each signed, at the lower right, "Yves."

Clearly these reproductions were meant to imply a group of larger originals made in various cities between 1951 and 1954. Back in Paris Yves would use the book to establish the "fact" that he had already been for some years a practicing painter, and that his work was already mature enough to warrant publication. Yet each of these claims is highly questionable. There is no evidence that Yves had yet made monochromes as large as the reproductions imply. In fact, these plates have been identified not as photographic reproductions but as pieces of inked paper tipped onto the page;[49] if this identification is correct, then there is no guarantee that the implied originals ever existed.

Yves' deception here (if indeed it was a deception) is of great interest in revealing his style as trickster; for every feature of the little book can respond to either of two interpretations. For example, the attributions ("London, 1950," "Paris, 1951," "Tokyo, 1952") seem to have been secretly justified by Yves not as details of manufacture but as titles. Aldo Passoni relates a story, probably originated by Yves in reference to this pamphlet, that Yves had organized in Madrid "an exhibition of ten monochrome paintings, each one dedicated to a different city."[50] Thus "Tokyo, 1952" may be read as meaning "This is my impression of Tokyo in 1952." The "exhibition" seems to have been no more than the hanging of small monochromes in the judo hall.

In any case, Yves had prepared himself, by the end of his period of exile, to make his second "entrance into Paris" with a revised strategy. The decision was of crucial importance. Judo, the passion of his youth, was thrust to the background; into the foreground stepped the alchemical artist, keeping his "rendezvous with the end of an age."

Part Two

11

"This is Tintin speaking. I've just put on my space-suit and am now standing in the air-lock. They're just going to reduce the pressure to a vacuum in here ..."

Hergé, *The Adventures of Tintin: Explorers on the Moon*

In December 1954, Aunt Rose visited Yves in Madrid. He returned with her to France, moved into his mother's Paris apartment (she was now living separately from her husband), and began to experiment with materials and methods for more mature monochrome paintings. Rose and Marie sold a lot they jointly owned in Nice and used the proceeds to help set up the Judo Club of Montmartre on the Boulevard de Clichy, in a studio formerly used by Léger where, between his judo classes, Yves began, says Arman, "to paint like mad." From this base he began at last to drift away from his mother's family and acquire a new circle of associates.

At this point Yves' horizon expanded, and his remarkable and variegated talents began to flower. He underwent, in the next two years, a transition from boy-in-family to artist-in-world, and he must be seen increasingly as a public rather than a private figure. But the child remained unusually prominent in him until the end; in fact it gained strength. In ferocious compensation for his late start in the art world, Yves asserted his grandiosity with increasing insistence. In effect, he transited from a "kingdom of judo in Spain" to claiming (with a certain sense of dynastic right?) a kingdom of art in Paris. Now, and increasingly in the following years, he drew on the ability demonstrated at age twelve in the children's theater at Cagnes to mobilize other people for his own purposes.

One important friend and adviser was Robert Godet, a colorful figure on the edge of the Paris art world. An occultist and Gurdjieffian who was interested in Eastern religions, avant-garde art, utopian prophecy, and the martial arts, he and Yves were kindred spirits. A pilot and, like Yves, a worshiper of the "inexhaustible hierophany" of the sky, Godet lived in a fairly sumptuous style which was rumored to be based on gun-running activities. For years he was at Yves' side in La Coupole, the famous Left Bank café, urging him always to "go beyond" the present state of his work. They were close until Godet's death in 1960, rumored to have occurred while Godet was piloting a load of guns to Tibet in his own plane, after the Chinese invasion.

Godet in turn introduced Yves to Bernadette Allain, a precocious young architect who for years lived with Yves and helped him with the techniques and materials of his work. Yves introduced her to judo and she guided his experiments to find a binder which would fix powdered pigments without "murdering their color," as Yves and Bernadette said. She found him, in 1955, still "passionately devoted to Rosicrucianism," in which the "world of pure color" represents the higher metaphysical realm (the realm of the "astral" body) which it is the goal of the initiate's labors to attain. She also, she recalls, was "passionately interested in pure color" at this time, and together they spoke of the mysticism of color, of "going beyond the limits, beyond the gamut of sensations," of finding out "what would happen if one's personal intensity increased beyond known frontiers." They were convinced that there was a "certain hypersensitivity" which would permit one actually "to enter into the world of color" and exist as color. It was "a physical matter, a question of vibrations, wavelengths, and resonances." (Bernadette identified herself with ultramarine blue, the color with which she was "exactly in resonance.") Finding, after much experiment, the necessary ingredients, they made the first exhibited monochromes together, in Yves' mother's kitchen, painting with rollers on vellum mounted on wooden panels.

It is important to dwell upon Bernadette Allain's insistence that she and Yves regarded "entering into the world of color" as "a physical matter, a question of vibrations, wavelengths, and resonances." For this is pure Rosicrucianism, of the same stuff as Heindel's insistence that one can literally learn to fly. Yet the phraseology, divorced from its Rosicrucian sources and viewed in terms of Parisian culture of the fifties, sounds like phenomenology, as Bachelard or Gadamer, for example, will speak of entering into the world of a work of art. This example of a phrase which relates simultaneously to two existing codes, hanging ambiguously on the interface between them, foreshadows many such careful formulations in Yves' writings. Phenomenology, at first picked out of the Paris air, later buttressed by a superficial reading of Bachelard, was the third of the three codes which Yves was to weave together in his rich literary statements of 1957 and after.

In these writings Rosicrucianism provides the basic structures of thought to which the other codes are fitted to create the multidirectional ambiguity which, as in the Madrid pamphlet, was Yves' artful way of mediating between his desires and the world of facts. Whether this constitutes a belief or a habit is perhaps not a proper question. But if one judges by

Yves' writings and by the persistence of certain ideas (such as flight or levitation) in his life, then the Rosicrucian code would seem to be a belief system, a structure to which his inner self-definition was inextricably bound.

Although Yves stopped working the Rosicrucian lessons in early 1953, he continued to read in Heindel's book until at least 1956, by which time he had it virtually memorized. Upon returning from Madrid to Paris, he spoke openly of his Rosicrucianism within the art world and was mocked for it. He did not make that mistake again. Henceforth, phenomenology mediated his Rosicrucianism to the outside world, and Neo-Dada provided an escape route from explanations and demands for consistency. "Yves' culture," as Pierre Restany says, "was very personalized and had many gaps in it. But in a sense it was the very gaps which made his remarkable personality."

During the period of the first monochromes, Yves was also teaching in the judo club of Montmartre, where Bernadette Allain demonstrated the *judokatas* with him. Yves' personal charisma attracted many of the neighborhood hoodlums and delinquents; they made up perhaps half his students. He sympathized with their rebelliousness, their violence, their resistance to formal education; they were better potential warriors than the bourgeois students. He in turn influenced them deeply. As Allain says, "When the neighborhood tough is thrown to the mat time and time again without exception, in three months this eighteen-year-old boy will be transformed, because he has come into contact with a *force*." He taught them the ethic of the Kodokan, the fraternity of the *judokas*, the quietness of the judo master who when he walks on the street looks like anyone else. "Already," says Bernadette, "he had an insane need to be admired," but in the hero cult of this "pure judo period" he had not yet begun to caricature himself. He was peaceful and dignified. He was, in her eyes at least, at his best.

Yves' "insane need to be admired" never abated. The shock of his near "failure" at judo had alarmed him. He began to feel, perhaps as a kind of compensation, an inner conviction of his own importance which grew more rigid and fanatical as time passed. Always a devotional personality drawn to the supernatural, he began to regard his life, through its secret connection with Rosicrucian prophecy, as sacred history. He assimilated himself to Jesus Christ, telling Bernadette that he would die at age thirty-three. ("In fact," she says, "he died every time he didn't get what he wanted.... Yves Klein, mental age: ten." She laughs.)

When he wanted to rush into the art world at once, confident of his success, she tried to pull him back. ("I knew how they buy, how they manipulate, how they sell.") His head was still filled with Tintin and knights in armor. He was "too naïve, too infantile—and too fascinating. He had a certain...power." Competing for attention in the avant-garde, he was in danger of throwing away whatever degree of inner peace he had gained in judo. It was the first of the disputes which were to bring their relationship to an end.

Nevertheless, impatient, as always, for paradise, Yves submitted an orange monochrome to the Salon des Réalités Nouvelles in 1955. When he refused to add an element of drawing, the painting was rejected (though the judges disliked barring the son of Marie Raymond, who had participated in the exhibition for several years). Rejection only increased Yves' energy level. ("He would not tolerate anyone who resisted him," says Bernadette.) He arranged a show of monochromes at the Club des Solitaires in October 1955. The exhibition went almost unnoticed except by the young critic Pierre Restany, whose work was to be linked with Yves' for their mutual benefit. As the years passed, Restany would write Yves' catalogues and, on at least one occasion, arrange for his shows. "Restany," says a mutual friend, "wanted to *become* Yves."[51] "I owe him very much," says Restany. "I owe to him both the structure of my thought and the conduct of my life, my style of life." Yves in turn found in Restany the educated voice which he himself lacked but deeply desired. When words were required, he interposed Restany between himself and the world, while secretly searching (through Voltaire, Hugo, Flaubert, Proust) for a writing style of his own.

Equally important was Yves' meeting with Jean Tinguely (who had been standing by the judges' table when Yves' orange monochrome was rejected). Tinguely was beyond convention and as the years passed would greet Yves' increasingly flamboyant mythic gestures with delight. The little Captain, with his childlike beliefs and laughing intensity, made life into a poem overflowing with good humor, and that was a magic beyond questioning.

In the next years several young artists from Nice (the "School of Nice," actually formed in 1961) — would arrive in Paris: Arman, Martial Raysse, César. They all had a certain intensity, or "anguish," as Tinguely calls it. "It was astonishing," he says, "to see such anguish coming from the Côte d'Azur. But Yves Klein was absolutely the champion in every category of anguish. He was the most anguished man

I have ever met. He had too much positive force in a climate of materialism which was impossible for him to bear."

The little group which would become the New Realists was forming. Yves' glowing eyes and inexhaustible childish energy propelled him toward its center. ("He was," says Tinguely, "a superb companion," as well as the "champion of anguish.") With supreme — indeed, exaggerated — self-confidence, he promised the others that he would quickly become famous and then sponsor their careers.

In 1956, after an introduction by his mother, he exhibited monochromes of various colors at the Galerie Colette Allendy; the preface to the catalogue was written at his request by Pierre Restany.[52] Restany suggested that Yves was carrying to its conclusion the adventure begun by Malevich (a comparison which would disturb Yves more and more as the years passed), denounced *l'art informel*, and characterized the monochromes as icons of "asthenic silence" and "pure contemplation." But there is an interesting contrast between Restany's "pure contemplation" and Tinguely's description of Yves' state of mind as he made the paintings: "He had no contemplation, no calm, no inner balance. While he painted the monochromes he was going crazy with anxiety about whether the three materials he was using would mix properly." The discrepancy between Yves' high-voltage personal style and the ideal of "pure contemplation" would become more pronounced as time passed.

But the show did not satisfy Yves. The effect of several colors was too decorative to express the profound sensibility of pure color. In the following year he would use only one color, ultramarine blue (later International Klein Blue) — Bernadette's color, and the color of his first art work, the blue sky of Nice.[53]

Prowling the galleries in search of a dealer, Yves appeared one day at Iris Clert's, a blue monochrome under his arm. At first, like the judges of the salon, she denied that it was a painting. But after hanging it (at Yves' insistence) for several days, she realized that it had "a certain power," a certain "positive force," like its maker. It was the force of "spiritual space," of the "upward attraction" toward limitless blue freedom in the sky. It was the force that would draw Yves more and more strongly back toward his infinite home.

12

I am obsessed! The Blue! The Blue! The Blue! The Blue!

Stéphane Mallarmé

At the time, Iris Clert was not yet a dealer to whom serious artists were offering their work. But she was ambitious and excitable and wanted to be part of the avant-garde. For this she needed a group of "anguished" young artists, and Yves was offering her one. The arrangement was advantageous to both. In the next few years she exhibited the works of Yves, Tinguely, Arman, and others who would become the New Realists, at times (e.g., the exhibition *Le Vide*, 1958) performing curatorial heroics. Fired up by the youthful exuberance of her new associates, she encouraged their tendency toward radical innovation, as opposed to a slower deepening and maturing of vision, to the point of psychological strain. Yves in particular underwent pronounced personality changes as the game of avant-gardism became an overpowering reality. He grew increasingly hungry and manipulative ("No one could refuse anything to Yves," Iris Clert says). He became, she remembers, "a kind of Nietzsche of painting"; the "hypertrophy of his ego" became overwhelming; he was *"un gros bébé," "un grand naïf,"* and, above all, *"un dictateur."* Their ruptures as time passed were passionate and nearly hysterical.

In collaboration with Robert Godet, Jean Tinguely, Pierre Restany, and Iris Clert, Yves began the process feared by Bernadette Allain, the process of becoming a caricature of himself; he began to make his personal myth public by stages, along with his work. At once he found that the technique brought him worldly success, and he pushed on with it regardless of what it was doing to his inner world. The presentation of a mythic persona which at times he seems to have literally believed, but which, in self-defense, he buffered with the fashionable codes of the day, became increasingly a game which had its own momentum, which pushed on toward its conclusion with a ruthless dynamism, a game from which the player himself could not simply escape by an act of choice.

But concealing his Rosicrucian "foundation" concealed the inner coherence of his *oeuvre* also and opened him to constant misinterpretation as a mere showman or opportunist. This blindness to his inner seriousness frustrated Yves deeply, and as in his rash decision to challenge the Judo Federation, he responded with more and more assertive claims. And as his claims became more extreme, Yves found himself increasingly caught up in them.

Perhaps the first of the symbolic Stations or Labors were motivated primarily by an opportunistic desire for publicity. But as his self-image came to depend more and more on the status of his claims, his commitment to the myth became less playful, his identification with it more complete and more dangerous. As Yves' identification with his symbolic personae grew, his mood became increasingly doomed, heroic, and tragical.

Those who watched him undergo this process evaluated it differently. Tinguely, for example, romanticizes it and regards Yves' self-crucifixion (through self-caricature) as beautiful poetry. His mother chooses to regard it as unavoidable, a "destiny that had tracked him from the day he was born." Bernadette Allain, on the other hand, regards it as a growing pathology, brought on by overexcitement and loss of inner balance, and intensified by the encouragement of those whose careers would profit from his drama of self-immolation.

In 1957 Yves began to act out his mythic function as Messenger of the incoming age. The Blue Epoch was inaugurated by an exhibition of identical blue monochromes at Guido Le Noci's Galleria Apollinaire in Milan. Yves' artfully interpenetrating code system was now solidly in place on several levels. The title of the exhibition, *l'Epoca Blu*, makes ironic reference, in art historical terms, to Picasso's famous Blue Period; but in Rosicrucian terms it indicates the age in which matter will be dissolved and humanity will return to the bodiless Eden of space-as-pure-spirit, which Heindel symbolized by blue. The blue monochromes themselves represent the melting of forms into prime matter beyond internal differentiations, while in terms of art history they are a sharp (and timely) rejection of *l'art informel*; phenomenologically they deny the subject-object dichotomy by forcing the "observer" to participate in the creation of their meaning. The fact that the paintings were hung about eight inches in front of the wall is also a conflation of codes; in Rosicrucian terms it indicates the end of the age of gravity and the beginning of the age of levitation (Yves began at this time to speak "obsessively" about levitation); in art historical terms it relates to the project of "proclaiming ... the activity of painting in real space ... [and revealing] the picture as an object within that space." [54] As Yves was to write in "The Monochrome Adventure," [55] he wanted the painting to "invade the space of the observer," both by controverting habitual modes of perceiving a painting, and by signifying the Rosicrucian doctrine of the onrushing invasion of all matter by spirit.

The fact that the paintings were more or less identical is again an expression of the triple code: in Rosicrucian terms it refers to the underlying sameness of the absolute or ground of being beneath all individual beings; in art historical terms it is anti-illusionistic, "insisting upon the material 'thinghood' of the components"; [56] phenomenologically regarded, it is a strategy to break up the viewer's complacency of perceptual habit.

It must be stressed that these paintings could very well have been exhibited without the implied claim that they ushered in not only a new age of art but a new phase of human evolution. But Yves' grandiosity required the myth. Art in and by itself, without exalted spiritual implications and claims, was never enough for him. He was later to say to Claude Parent that "the monochromes are me": they were his calling card as Messenger from the Blue Void, the heraldic emblem of his ethereal kingship in the sky.

In purely art historical terms they were as timely at that moment in Europe as the more or less contemporary works of Newman and Reinhardt, or Rauschenberg's white paintings, were in America. But it was not only the perfection of the gesture at that moment that put the blue monochromes in the art history books; the brilliant presence of these paintings cannot be denied. Each of them preserves still its maker's magnetic gaze and high-voltage surface. Quite without any myth they exerted an immediate influence on serious artists. In Milan, Fontana bought an International Klein Blue monochrome and subsequently moved his own work further into monochromy. Piero Manzoni was converted by the IKBs from a figurative style to his "achromes." In the following years he made repeated trips to Paris to knock on Yves' door and hang around Iris Clert's gallery. His *oeuvre* became a strange parody, or deliberate inversion, of Yves'.

Later that year the blue monochromes were exhibited at Iris Clert's. In conjunction with the exhibition, Yves showed at Colette Allendy's an astonishingly varied group of works which presaged not only much of his own later career, but in a sense the next ten or twenty years of Western art. There the first blue sponge sculpture appeared, alluding to the Rosicrucian doctrine of the permeation of matter by Spirit and foreshadowing the development of new media in the sixties; blue painted screens gestured both toward Japanese influence and toward the sculptural transformation of the painting; upstairs, a room was left empty as an exhibition of "the surfaces and volumes of pure pictorial sensibility"; and on the evening of the opening, Yves performed a "One-Minute Fire Painting," made up of four rows of four signal flares each, mounted on a square plywood support. As the exhibition of blue monochromes at Iris Clert's was the announcement of the beginning of Yves' career as self-appointed art messiah or Messenger of the New Age, the show at Colette Allendy's laid claim to the whole range of art as his domain.

Still later in 1957, groups of monochromes in various colors were exhibited in Düsseldorf and London. Though London and Paris remained unconvinced, the effect in Düsseldorf was as positive as in Milan. Young German artists (Heinz Mack, Otto Piene, and others) were electrified by directions implicit in Yves' work and, after meeting him, by his "man of destiny" style. The groups N in Milan and Zero in Düsseldorf purveyed his influence and, when they came to know it, his myth.

Ten years or so earlier, Yves Marie Klein had rejected his personal origin and history, becoming simply "Yves," and like an Orphic devotee had chosen a mythic origin and cast his true home beyond the sky. Now, launching the Blue Epoch in which all humanity, catalyzed by him, was to recall and regain the Sky-nature, he called himself "Yves the Monochrome." It was in part a knightly title for his adventures in the infinity of color-space-spirit. But in part it was a claim, perhaps ill advised, to a seamless wholeness like that of his paintings, to an inner space uniformly and serenely blue, where no darknesses or entanglements of lines might conceal the Discord Spirit.[57]

13

*Shall we admit that in the blue void
is limitless pleasure?*

Lu Kuei-meng

Yves' essays combining prophecy, theory of art, and claims of occult attainments began to be written in 1954 (the year of exile and wounded pride) and began to be published in 1958. The most accomplished of these — "Truth Becomes Reality," "Due to the Fact That," "The Monochrome Adventure" — reveal a poetic talent and have a certain interest as pure literature.

The earliest of them, "The War: A Little Personal Mythology of the Monochrome" (parts of which were written as early as 1954), presented a mythic interpretation of the monochrome exhibitions.[58] The Rosicrucian opposition between Space (unity) and

Form (multiplicity) was translated into art historical terms as the Battle between Color and Line. As human evolution, according to Heindel, is on the verge of a return from Form (separateness, limitation) to Space (wholeness, infinity), so the artist, Yves wrote, should reject Line (division, entanglement, neurosis) in favor of Color (unity, openness, enlightenment). Whereas Line divides and fragments space, Color fills it completely and becomes one with it:

It is color which bathes in cosmic sensibility. The line does not have the ability to impregnate, as color does.
The line cuts space.... Color impregnates it.
Line rushes through infinity; color just "is" in infinity.

Color, as Heindel taught, is Spirit when it has coagulated enough to become visible in space, but not enough to fracture into forms:

Before the colored surface, one finds oneself directly before the matter of the soul.[59]

The dichotomy between Delacroix (color) and Ingres (line) was the paradigm of this battle. Yves had discovered Delacroix's *Journals* in 1956 and it remained his bedside book for the rest of his life, the record not only of a comrade in arms but of a spiritual brother. He was drawn by the romantic mysticism of this painter who wrote, "In some people the inner spark scarcely exists. I find it dominant in me. Without it I should die — but it will consume me."[60] This Werther-like spirit, Yves wrote, "sought the total expression of himself in and by color,"[61] and was in a sense the first prophet of the return to Space. But it was above all Delacroix's insistence on the "indefinable" factor that aligned him, Yves thought, with the alchemical approach to art.

Alchemical texts speak of a real, although invisible and ineffable, substance which distinguishes the "gold of the philosophers" from "common gold," the "fire of the philosophers" from "common fire," and so forth. Control of this substance, symbolized by the Philosopher's Stone, was the goal of the Work; by isolating it in his own person, the alchemist gains the power to inject it into other entities at will. Guided by Heindel, Yves had been seeking this power for years:

The gold of the ancient alchemists can be extracted from anything. The difficult part is uncovering the gift of the Philosopher's Stone, which exists in each of us.[62]

Now, inspired by Delacroix's "indefinable," he transposed the alchemical doctrine into artistic terms; a true painting contains an invisible, indefinable "substance" which transmutes it into an eternal absolute:

> Painting is alchemical, and beyond time. It represents nothing.[63]

An immaterial substance, which Yves called "pure pictorial sensibility," is injected into the art work by the alchemist/artist who has isolated and purified this sensibility in himself; it can be experienced in the painting, after any number of years, by a viewer whose own sensibility is sufficiently developed. Art, then, is not a sensory but an extrasensory experience. Of two visually identical paintings, one possessing this substance is art, and the other, lacking it, is not. A sensitive viewer can distinguish at once.

The theory was based on Heindel, but Yves heard resonances of it in Delacroix, who said, "It is not a painting if it doesn't point beyond the finite; the value of a painting is the indefinable factor."[64] Yves read Delacroix's "indefinable" as equivalent to his own "pure sensibility," and both of them as equivalent to Heindel's "Spirit." The indefinable, said Delacroix, is "what the soul [of the artist] has added to the lines and colors to reach out to the soul [of the viewer]."[65] Similarly, Van Gogh (whom also Yves enlisted on his side in the Battle, because he "foresaw the monochrome") wrote to his brother Theo that "paintings have their own life which comes entirely from the soul of the painter."[66] Heindel, the ultimate authority, also had said that a true work of art has a soul like a living creature. The artist, then, is truly godlike. Said Yves:

> *He puts a soul in his creation.*

A synopsis of art history emerges which consists of Yves and his "precursors," to wit, Giotto, Rembrandt, Delacroix, and Van Gogh, all of whom had managed to "put a soul" in their creations.

Such claims are, of course, grandiose. As Bachelard put it, "Alchemical gold is a reification of a strange need for royalty, superiority and domination which animates the...solitary alchemist."[67] This "strange need" may reach back, through the "timelessness of the unconscious," to the child in the cradle, bawling his claim to omnipotence.

Yves' alchemical theory of art might be discredited on the ground that, since (it seems) he "could not hold a pencil,"[68] he was forced to argue for a nonvisual criterion of value. After all, if Yves claimed — as he did — that he had isolated the Philosopher's Stone in himself, that his inner world was open and clear, and that he had injected "pure sensibility" into his works, who could deny it? Yves would simply retort that his critic's sensibility was not sufficiently developed. The theory of the immaterial essence, in other words, could be a charlatan's disguise. But it is

not so easy to dismiss either Yves' work or his theory.

Iris Clert relates that in the year after showing Yves' "monoblues" she exhibited "monoblacks" by another painter which aroused no response at all: they lacked the magnetic gaze of "pure sensibility."[69] Indeed, many have discovered that, face to face, these paintings have "an unmitigated, pure, but very sensuous beauty."[70] An IKB monochrome viewed out of context on the other side of the world still breathes the fierceness of Yves' ego and his fiery drive toward transcendence. Such vibrations seem, quite as he said, to cling round his work, or emanate from it, invisibly.

Finally, it must be noted that Yves' art is hard to define — thus hard to criticize. ("Am I a painter?" he asks in "The Monochrome Adventure"; "oh all right then, I'm a painter.") He was not in fact devoted to any single medium, but to the general aim of giving a body, a voice, and a soul to the absolute — of making it a living mythic presence in our time. This was a composite project, for which Yves intended to employ the arts and sciences in general. At the time of his death he had already employed painting, sculpture, event art, photographs, music, and literature, and had clear plans for works in theater, ballet, and film (not to mention the various scientific, political, and economic projects conceived in the name of the Void).

14

The eyes in the countenance of the young barbarian were bright and smiling. Though no one who saw him thought him other than mad, all found him handsome and noble.

Chrétien de Troyes, *Perceval*

At the Colette Allendy exhibition of 1956, Yves met a friend of his father who was involved with heraldry and an order of "archers," the Knights of Saint Sebastian, which traces its origins to the time of Charlemagne. He invited Yves to join, and Yves was delighted: here was a Round Table still active in his own day!

Yves was accepted on a Friday, rented a cape and sword on Saturday ("He loved costumes," says Arman; "He loved disguises," says Claude Pascal), passed the night in a vigil with the other inductees, and on Sunday, in the presence of his parents, at the touch of a bishop's hand he was made a knight, at last!

A cartoon panel, Station, or Labor, of the Myth: Yves, Knight of Saint Sebastian, stands trim, compact, straight, in the plumed hat and black cape with

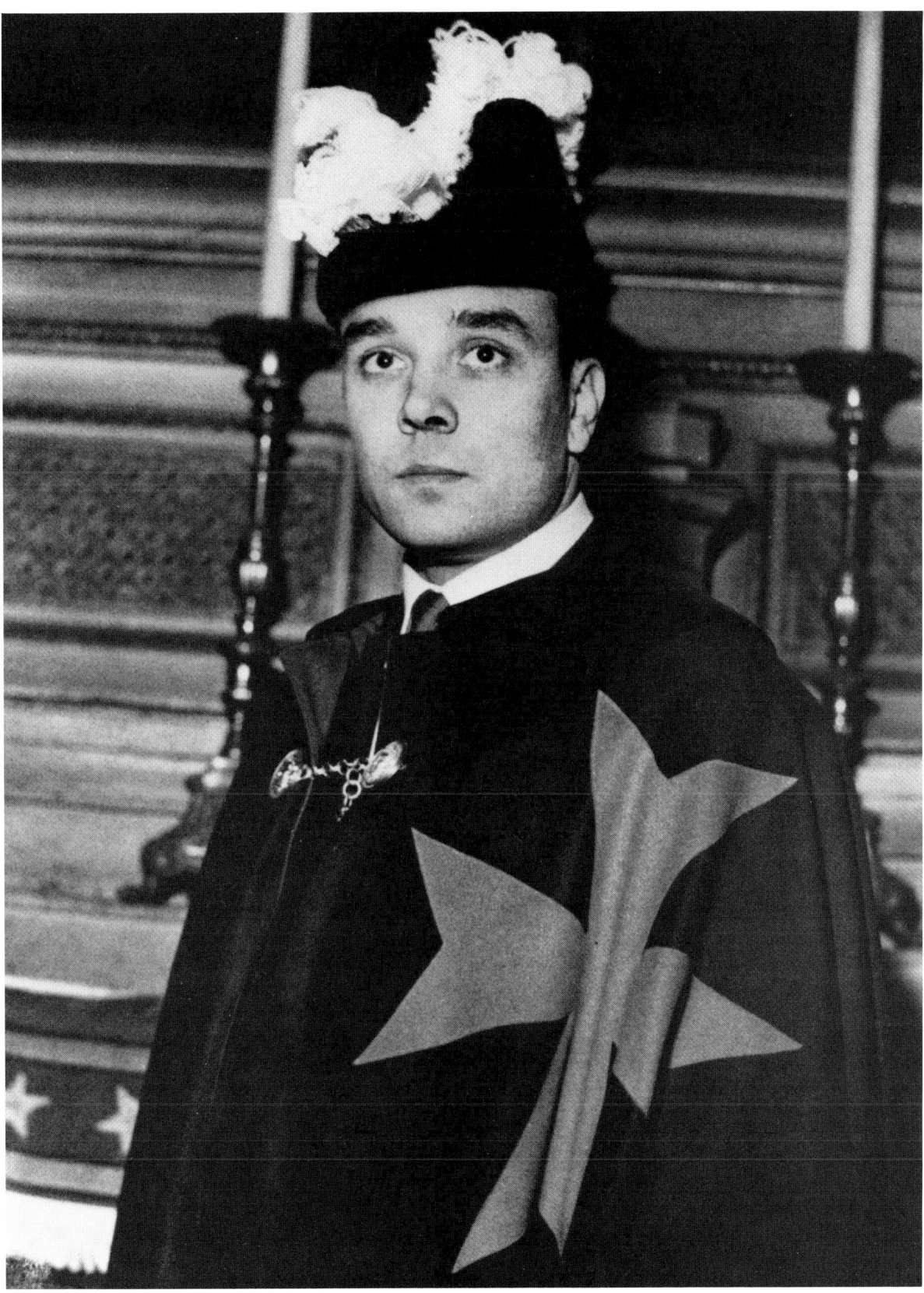

Yves Klein in the regalia of the Knights of Saint Sebastian

Crusader's cross, a veiled challenge in the famous Javanese eyes as he stares into Space, poised for combat. He holds in his right hand a blue monochrome painting which his left hand points to as the symbol of the kingdom he serves. "Having been made a knight of the Order of Saint Sebastian," he proclaims in a hero's ringing voice, "I espouse the cause of Pure Color, which has been invaded and occupied guilefully by the cowardly line and its manifestation, drawing in art. I will defend color, and I will deliver it, and I will lead it to final triumph."[71]

(In the following year he asked his aunt for a new costume to wear each Saint Sebastian's day. She sent a red velvet waistcoat with "Italian trousers." The Champion of Color, ever a child to his aunt, replied: "What a formidable red velvet! Really this time I have been re-spoiled and super-spoiled by my tantine! It is getting terrible, everyone tells me that I am spoiled rotten.")

15

"Moon rocket calling Earth...This is Tintin here. I am no longer subject to ordinary gravitational pull..."

Explorers on the Moon

Jean Tinguely: "Yves was very earthy. He loved to eat well. He loved the good things of the earth. But at the same time he was transported toward the opposite—the ethereal, the immaterial, the void. He was very contradictory inside. I think that at a certain age this contradiction began to take over his personality. He would spend an entire evening trying to convince someone that the earth was flat and square. It was hard, at that time, with satellites orbiting the earth, to prove to people that the earth was flat and square. But he managed to do it. He would spend insane amounts of energy to convince some fellow — it didn't matter who — someone he had met by accident in La Coupole. He would even search for victims to persuade. And they believed him. He had such fire, such force, in conversation, he marshaled so many proofs of an unrecognizable metaphysical character, that the idiots would leave feeling sure he was right.

"This was not a man who was interested in material things. He was profoundly nonmaterialistic. For him money meant a good meal, and he always shared what he had with a friend, as a sign of respect. Once Eva and I did not have a cent. Yves said, 'I have twenty thousand francs. I'm giving you ten thousand.' It was like Saint Martin's cloak.

"He had an aerial walk that created a happy mood around him. He would go out walking in May still wearing his winter coat (I don't think he even noticed). He would stride into La Coupole, the Saint Sebastian cape flying around him, his eyes shining, with the new Tintin book under his arm. He shocked the intellectuals.

"He read comic books and talked about knights and the Holy Grail. Those marvelous things that exist in the world of a child still worked for him."

16

"Greetings, spirit of the air, greetings, spirit that penetratest from heaven to earth and from earth to the uttermost abyss, greetings, spirit that penetratest into me and shakest me."

Great Magical Papyrus of Paris

Sitting around La Coupole, Tinguely, Iris Clert, Robert Godet, and others encouraged Yves to "go beyond" the monochrome. In a sense, he already had, for he had already declared his belief in the immaterial essence of the art work, which of course implies the irrelevance of color quite as much as of line. Clearly the unbroken field of color was not the ultimate symbol for Prime Matter before it has separated into forms. In 1958, aware of these problems and encouraged by his friends, Yves redefined his kingdom. No longer bound to any ordinary human experience — such as the visual experience of the blue of the sky — it was now the actual emptiness which had been hinted by the blue, the immaterial itself. He and Iris began to prepare for the classic exhibition *Le Vide*.

(Just prior to the opening of *Le Vide*, at the beginning of April 1958, Yves rooted the event in the basal level of his religious personality—the nourishing and protecting female deities of his mother's family— by flying secretly to Cascia and visiting Saint Rita at her own shrine for the first time. There he prayed to her for an ability to penetrate Rosicrucian magic without losing his soul. As he explained later to his Aunt Rose, "I said to myself, 'I think this exhibition of the Void is rather dangerous....It is necessary to go to Saint Rita....'")

Station or Labor: it is April 1958. Yves is alone in the Iris Clert gallery. Moving quickly, carefully, and silently, on feet accustomed to "spiritual space," he carries the furniture to storage, sweeps the floor, and slowly, through two long days, paints the interior walls white. Concentrating his mind as in the old

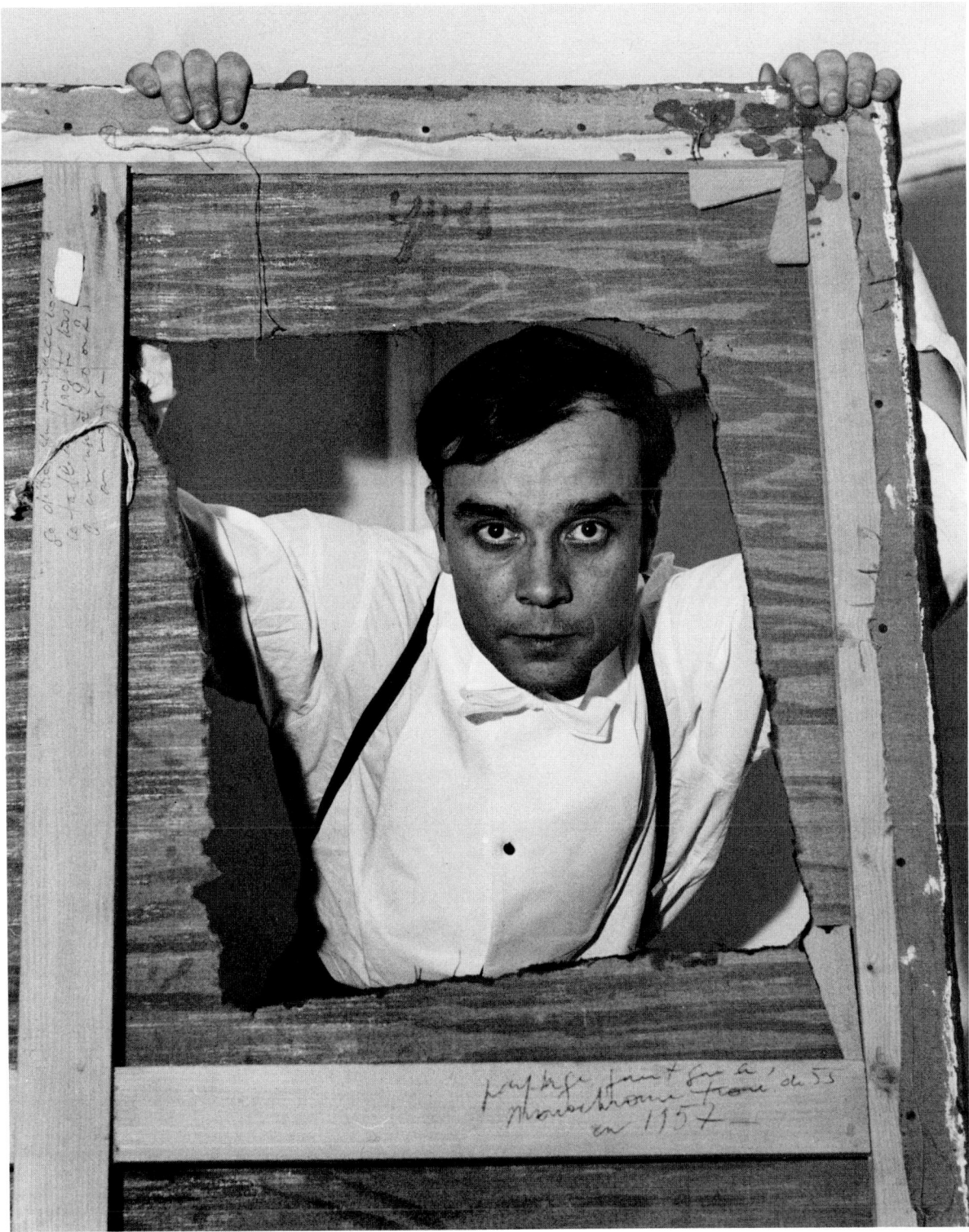

Yves Klein, 1961

days of meditation on the terrace in Nice, he gains access to the first immaterial realm and begins to manipulate its forces. Projecting images onto its Prime Matter, he draws them up from potentiality and stabilizes them in the space of the room. It is his thirtieth birthday, an occasion traditionally associated with the commencement of spiritual ministries.

As evening falls, crowds of thousands gather in the narrow street—the Void itself is about to open its secrets to them. Guards of the Republic flank the doors to the *sanctum sanctorum*. Glasses of blue liquid are passed out like a communion drink ("The blood of the body of sensibility is blue").[72] The door opens and Yves-the-Sorcerer appears in formal dress. He guides small groups into the Void while striving "to create a magnetic current and enthrall or enchant the guests."[73] Many laugh and leave at once. Some stay silent for an hour or more. One man "trembled and couldn't hold back his tears."[74] Camus himself enters and writes in the guest book, "With the void, full powers." (Casual flattery? Or did he *feel* a power in that room?) Yves' judo students try to keep order. The fire trucks come, and then the police. As the crowd disperses, many people who went inside emerge strangely excited or moved. They walk away "impregnated" with the new sensibility of the incoming age. At midnight, at La Coupole, Yves proclaims that four millennia of civilization have been culminated; a new age of human sensibility has arrived. He quotes Socrates and Cicero, denounces Einstein and Roosevelt, and announces that henceforth "leprous France" will be governed by Blue, concluding with a magician's prayer to reify his words: "May this be said and done." (And remember: "Yves was *always* dead serious.") Still, inside, despite the protection of Saint Rita and his grandmother, he feels a little frightened at what he has done; he feels, somehow, that he has contacted his own death that night.[75]

For a week all those who drank the blue "cocktail" urinate blue: the blood of pure sensibility issuing from their bodies.

Other Void or Immaterial works followed, as Yves pursued the project of eliminating the visible art object altogether. The artist of the future, he wrote (following Heindel), will only leave his vibration in a space, to be picked up later by the immaterial antennae of others walking there.[76] In the following years he demonstrated the art of his invisible kingdom, opening the door to the age of immateriality.

Station: it is 1959. Yves is asked to participate in a group show *(Vision in Motion—Motion in Vision)* in Antwerp. At the opening, he stands for a while in the place allotted for his piece, recites a passage from

Bachelard on the color blue, then returns to Paris. An empty space in the gallery is his work—a vibration left hanging in the air, a bodiless magnetism with his ego patterns in its waves. In Paris, he works on plans to sell invisible paintings and to give a public demonstration of flying.

17

In the bright crystal of your eyes
Show the havoc of fire, show its inspired works
And the paradise of its ashes.

Paul Eluard

Yves understood that his writings were as essential to the program of mythic theater as were his art works and events. Yet his Heindelian belief system was an anachronism, with its wholehearted commitment to the priority of unchanging essence. It could have no place in the Paris of Sartre, Barthes, Lévi-Strauss, and Robbe-Grillet (whose 1958 essay "Nature, Humanism, Tragedy" simply pulverizes the "spiritual" approach to art). Yet it was a part of Yves' genius—indeed, his method—to be archaic while seeming ultramodern. He found his strongest link to modern thought in the works of Gaston Bachelard.

Bachelard was superficially much like Heindel; he too wrote about alchemy and the four elements, about spiritual space and the soul's voyages in it. Yet his modernism was guaranteed by none other than Sartre, who praised him for several pages in *Being and Nothingness*.[77] Yves read (or read parts of) Bachelard's books on the four elements and space, deriving from them a thin overlay of phenomenology with which to soften his Heindelian literalism.[78]

"We can classify poets," said Bachelard, "by asking them to answer the question: 'Tell me what your infinite is…: is it the infinite of the sea or sky, is it the infinite of the earth's depths or of the pyre?'"[79] Yves, the child who had no home on earth but, he suspected, a whole kingdom in the sky, seems nevertheless to have regarded himself not as an air but a fire type: it is fire which burns away limits, which produces change, which converts solid matter to spirit-like ash on the wind. "The alchemist," of course, "is a 'master of fire.' It is with fire that he controls the passage of matter from one state to another."[80] "In comparison with the intensity of fire," said Bachelard, "how slack, inert, static and aimless seem the other intensities that we perceive. They are not embodiments of growth. They do not fulfill their promise. They do not become active in a flame and a light which symbolizes transcendence."[81] "I hold that in the heart of the void, as in the heart of man, fires are burning,"[82] wrote Yves, echoing the ancient image of the universal soul as a central fire whose scattered sparks are individual souls. "Fire is dialectical in all its properties," said Bachelard; "...it only has to flame up to contradict itself."[83] To Yves this became a desperate moral imperative:

> One must be like untamed fire....One must
> know...how to contradict oneself.[84]

For the same fire which burns through into the void is, says Bachelard, the fundamental symbol of sexuality. (Consider the ithyphallic angle of the flame-thrower in the photographs of Yves making fire paintings, consider the interplay of sex and death in those works.) "My paintings are only the ashes of my art," said Yves;[85] "He was always speaking of ashes," says Tinguely. "Whatever he did, he would say, 'It's the ashes that interest me.'" There is danger in this preoccupation. As Bachelard said, "In the last analysis, all the complexes attached to fire are painful complexes."[86]

"Repression," wrote Bachelard, "is a normal activity, a useful activity, a joyous activity," when it is performed in the service of an "absolute sublimation."[87] "Sublimation" of course is an alchemical as well as a psychoanalytic term, denoting the ascension phase of the Great Work ("It rises from the earth to the sky and again descends into the earth," says the *Emerald Tablet*). Yves' dreamed flight to the other side of the sky was an analogue of alchemical sublimation; but his life partook of psychoanalytic repression and sublimation as well. His Rosicrucian belief that sexual energies must be stored up for the great burst of the Transfiguration never completely left him. It was perhaps sustained by his ongoing problem in sexual performance. "Eroticism, for him, was something transformed," says Tinguely. "It had nothing of the pornographic in it." And Arman recalls: "Sublimation was a key word in his vocabulary."

Indeed Yves borrowed Bachelard's term "absolute sublimation" to describe his own inner alchemy:

> I seek the effective liberation of the per-
> sonality in all its aspects in the individual,
> by the exasperation of the Me practiced to
> the point of an absolute, purifying
> sublimation.[88]

We can recognize still the archaic and painful ascesis of Heindel, only superficially tamed by the stylish Bachelardian terminology. Art remained for Yves a ritual of self-sacrifice and self-liberation, the cannibalistic communion rite of a dying god:

> The painter, like Christ, says the mass while
> painting and gives his body and soul as
> nourishment for other people; he realizes a
> little the miracle of the Last Supper in every
> painting.[89]

In fact, Yves had a growing problem with Heindel, to which Bachelard seemed to offer a solution. As the years passed and Yves found himself still not "*free* really in this world" (as he had written with boyish enthusiasm in the Irish journal), he came to doubt more and more the radical Transfiguration which was promised in the *Cosmogonie* and in which he had invested a decade's faith and effort. But Bachelard dissolved all such goals into symbols; magic he called imagination; ascension and transfiguration he called the glories of reverie, not of the physical body. All value, in fact, he shifted from the objective to the subjective pole of the intentional vector: it is the inner disposition that matters, not the outer act.

Yves pricked up his ears at this. Here was a door through which he might escape the devouring sky. But what if Heindel was right — Heindel through whom a thousand sages spoke? What did Bachelard know of the lonely truth of the hermit and yogi? In his writings Yves plays sleight-of-hand with these two, now making the absurdly literalist claims which made him seem to many an impostor, and again retreating from literalism into Bachelard's "imagination." In the end, however, there was no contest, for only one truly promised omnipotence and transcendence.

The same problem besets the "invitation to a voyage." Every poet, said Bachelard, proffers to the reader an "invitation to voyage" into his imagination, into "the land of the infinite," "the realm where the imagination...is free and alone,...[and] the reality of unreality asserts itself."[90] Yves' career as an artist is a long and often-reformulated invitation to voyage into his kingdom of infinite space beyond the sky.

> Now I want to go beyond art, beyond sensi-
> bility, beyond life; I want to go into the void.[91]

Clearly this is a dangerous desire, this sublimation of oneself right out of the world. But on the very danger of it hung its amazing heroism, and on its literal truth depended its glory. Yves was not ready to abandon ontology for epistemology, to give up heaven for dreams of heaven, to consider Heindel merely one of Bachelard's "poets." Perhaps if he had lived longer....But he was still devastatingly innocent. He was still burning too brightly to touch. He still wanted to live with untamed fire.

So the question, as Bachelard put it, was whether "to seize fire or to give oneself to fire, to annihilate or to be annihilated, to follow the Prometheus complex or the Empedocles complex."[92] Surely Yves (the Conquistador of the Void!) thought he was acting out the Prometheus complex; as events would show, however, he was an Empedocles walking toward the mouth of the volcano.

18

A true dream unfolds ...
The wind, only the wind, takes me where I please.

André Frenaud

Yves had begun to meet the artists of the Zero Group in 1955, and his exhibition of monochromes in Düsseldorf in May 1957 brought him more centrally to their attention at a propitious moment. On the day of the opening, the city of Gelsenkirchen announced a competition for the commission to decorate its new opera house. Norbert Kricke, a young German sculptor, invited Yves to join a group of artists taking part in the competition. Yves accepted eagerly and was introduced to the architect, Werner Ruhnau, who became fascinated by him. Over the following months, Pierre Restany says, "Yves gradually, imperceptibly, took over Kricke's place as the leader of the group." Following the directions of his shows at Iris Clert's and Colette Allendy's, he proposed for the foyer of the opera house a set of monumental paintings and sponge reliefs in ultramarine blue.

Characteristically he mobilized his forces (primarily female) in pursuit of the commission. Bernadette Allain was set to work on the maquettes, and Aunt Rose was asked to intercede on high. "How I prayed to Saint Rita," she recalls. Several months later Yves phoned her, saying not, "I won it," but, "Tantine! Saint Rita won it!" Soon, however, the Gelsenkirchen commission was to bring about a shift in his relationship with the female deities.

In the summer of 1958, not long after the exhibition of the Void, Yves traveled to Nice and in Arman's house met a beautiful eighteen-year-old German girl, Rotraut Uecker (sister of the Zero Group artist Gunther Uecker, and herself a painter), who was babysitting young Yves, Arman's son and Yves' namesake. They locked archetypes at once, and he began to expose to her that side of himself which felt profound and tragical and secretly doomed. (Yves' "technique" with girls, says Marcel Boulois, was to appeal

to their motherly, protective impulses.) He was offering Rotraut, in effect, a front-row seat in his mythic theater. The first emblem of his identity he extended to her was the myth of his imminent dematerialization in the Void. "He was leaving Nice soon," says Rotraut, "and he said, 'I don't know if I will see you again. I have made an exhibition that has led me onto a very dangerous path. And I think that I may have to die for it.'" His eyes had a darkened, almost tearful look; the prophetic intensity of his voice frightened her.

He was in fact about to leave for the Gelsenkirchen project, which had him traveling a good deal. In September he went with Aunt Rose to Cascia for his second, and her first, visit to the saint's own shrine, to thank her for winning the commission for her favorite. He left among the *ex voto* objects a blue monochrome, once again involving the patroness of his art in Rosicrucian mysticism. The monochrome represented both thanks for success so far attained and a promise of greater things to come. In October he was back in Gelsenkirchen and found himself in need of an assistant and a translator. He phoned Rotraut and asked her to join him. She came at once.

Soon he was at work on the huge sponge reliefs which, according to Tinguely, "were his death." He soaked the sponges in polyester resins to harden them before applying the color, working without a mask, and at high intensity, for twelve hours a day. "At that time," says Tinguely, "no one was aware of the dangers of synthetic resins."

Back in Paris in June, Yves showed the *Bas-Reliefs in a Forest of Sponges* at Iris Clert's — sponge reliefs like those for Gelsenkirchen but smaller, and blue sponges mounted like the foliage of trees on metal stems. Like the blue monochromes and the immaterial pieces, this exhibition seems to have roots in Heindel, in whose writings the saturation of sponges is a standard image for the permeation of all matter by Spirit — and blue the color most closely connected with Spirit. The mounting of the sponges on slender stalks again suggests Heindel's description of saturated sponges floating in empty space, and, like the mounting of the blue monochromes away from the wall, was a sign of Yves' ambition to make truly levitating art, sculptures which would float in the air, freed from any base.

Shortly after the opening of the *Forest* Yves traveled for a third time to Cascia, leaving four tiny ingots of gold for Saint Rita. In an accompanying prayer he dedicated the forthcoming Gelsenkirchen paintings to God the Father and the sponge reliefs to Saint Rita herself, praying fervently "that the impossible may arrive and establish its kingdom *quickly.*" [93]

In December 1959, Yves attended the impressive Gelsenkirchen opening with his mother and aunt. "The president of the German Republic was there," says Aunt Rose. "How proud I was!" Yves seemed really to be achieving the ambition (to be at "the very top") of which he had written to her on the voyage back from Japan.

Yet his success, ominously, did not bring much financial reward. Rotraut, who returned to Paris to live with him, recalls that their first dinner together after Gelsenkirchen was on credit at La Coupole. The experience would become familiar in the years that followed.

Yves' conjunction with Rotraut, both charmed and tumultuous, lasted until the end of his life. Rotraut's sweetness of temper and childlike openness to the imagination mingled happily with the same qualities in him, though his infantile and tyrannical angers drove her at times toward estrangement. "He was a child," she says, "who was both very happy and very sad at the same time."

Rotraut became both presiding goddess and chief spectator of his monotheater — the spectator who watched both from backstage and from front row center. Further, she is present in his works in the most direct way: many of the classic imprints are of her body — her tissue, texture, heartbeat, in the "trace of the immediate" in the paint.

More Stations of the Myth: alone at home with Rotraut Yves puts on a vampire cape, makes paper fangs, marks her throat with red ink. She removes the cross from her neck, and he pretends to drink from her throat. "Don't worry," he says, "I just took a little. I'm the vampire who will die by self-starving."

Arman hailed this "very special and complex character" in free verse:

Master of the Blue Sky
Monogold vampire
O! Great master of the school of Nice—
Let the school of New York be over
and all the American renunciations. [94]

Spurred on by accelerating success, Yves made his gestures of appropriation more extensive and fantastic. On May 29, 1958, he wrote to President Eisenhower announcing the termination of the French national government by the Blue Revolution. Receiving no answer, he sent the same message to Premier Khrushchev, again receiving no answer.

To the astonished architect Werner Ruhnau, he proposed plans for altering the earth's climate and building cities of compressed-air currents which would neither break up the visual unity of space nor obstruct the flight patterns and telepathic communications of the levitating, mind-reading humans of the Blue Age. The power of Yves' personality is demonstrated by the fact that he often convinced people that he might actually be able to do such things. Ruhnau carried out experiments with him at a factory near Hamburg and soon concluded that the air roof was impossible. Yves, however, was by no means convinced.

Station: fighting his inner war, he fills pages of his notebook with the word "humility, humility, humility…."

19

The alchemist is a dreamer who wishes, who enjoys wishing, who magnifies himself in his "wishing big."

Gaston Bachelard

After the success of *Le Vide* in 1958, Yves did in fact bring Arman and Tinguely and others to Iris Clert to launch their careers. Still eager to "do all my possible for everybody," he delighted in advancing his friends. He encouraged their work in the directions that seemed natural to them, introduced them to dealers in Paris, Milan, Düsseldorf, lent them the aura of his burgeoning fame, praised their works to critics, became a kind of beneficent patriarch to his own contemporaries. But the "Proprietor of Color" had to come first in all things—that was his condition. As Restany says, "I would see that from time to time a new carriage would be added to Yves' train." There was no question about who was the locomotive. As he helped his friends, he also created a school of "followers" around (and behind) himself.

Soon, problems arose. In collaborating with Tinguely for their joint show, *Vitesse pure et stabilité monochrome* (1958), he referred to their work as "mine." But Tinguely, a bit of a samurai himself, did not want to be owned. Yves wrote at torturous length, explaining that for one who has gone beyond ego, the word "mine" is quite different in intentionality. In the egoless Age of Space, all art belongs to all artists. One must resist "the temptation to materialize pure spirit," and the consequent fall into passion. "The Sabbath Queen, Iris," was invoked to write an affidavit, specifying the "domain" of each of the collaborators, much as Yves, Claude, and Arman had once divided up the world. "The air, the atmosphere," Iris declared, "are the domain of Klein, while the magnetism, that is the earth … is the domain of Tinguely."

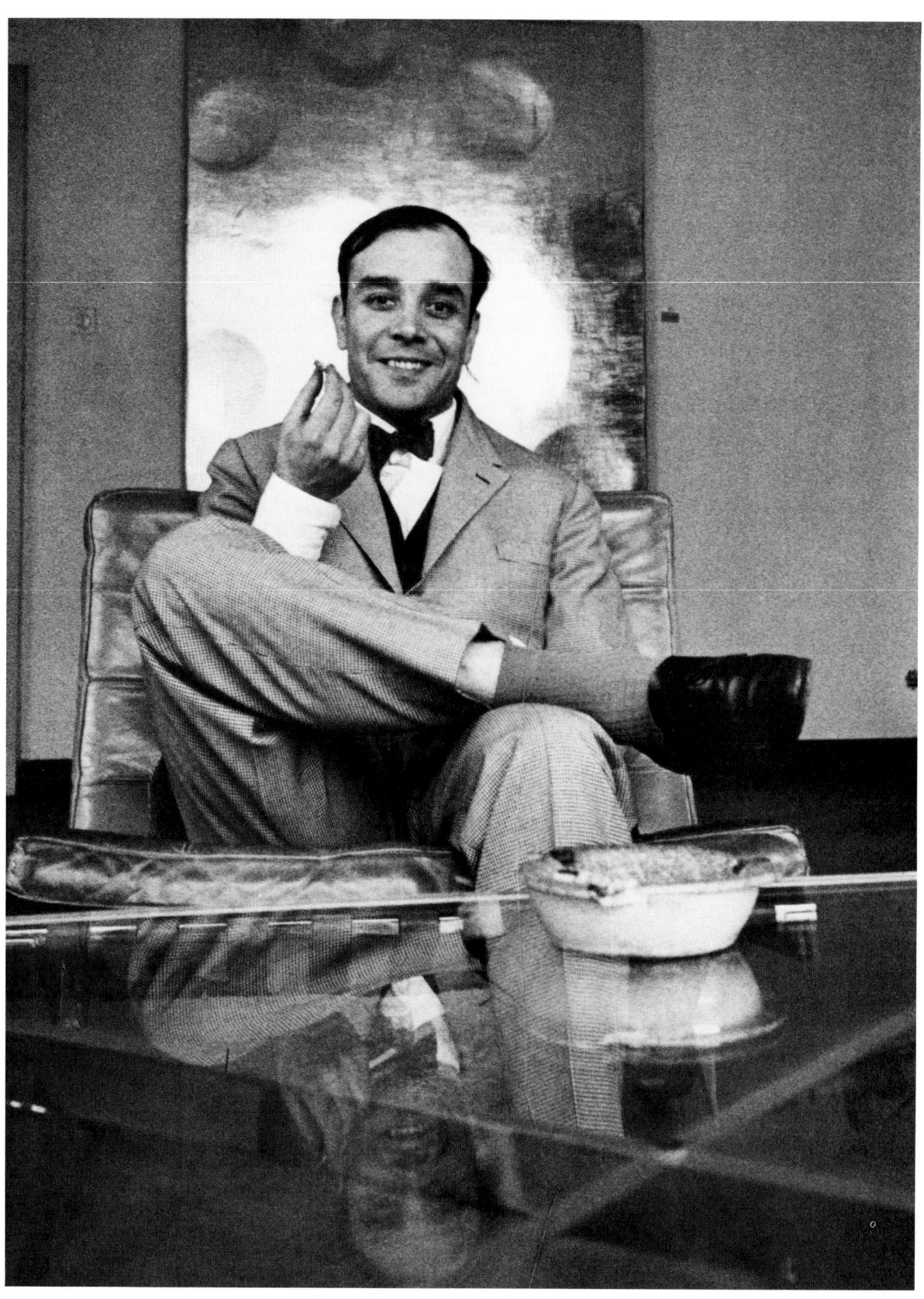

Yves Klein, circa 1961

This controversy with a close friend was of serious moment to Yves. He was depressed by the clash of egos. Contemplating his dematerialization in the Void, he wrote wearily of life:

Is it then a game, that it is necessary to live in the skin of a plain dull human? and in society as a pure spirit which has put on a costume and plays on the stage of a theater one role as well as another?

He even offered, in the context of his deep friendship for Tinguely, a prophetic Station of the Myth, forecasting more publicly now his own death, which he saw draw nearer in his incursions into the Void:

The immaterial blue color presented in April '58 at Iris' had rendered me ... inhuman. It had excluded me from the society of the world of tangible reality. I was outside of society, living in space, and unable to return to the earth. Jean Tinguely saw me in space and signaled to me by speed to show me the path of volumetric return to the ephemerality of material life. This is what I call my "salvation" by Tinguely.[95]

This pattern of disturbing ego clashes followed by tense reconciliations became a constant feature of Yves' last years; he quarreled over priority, at one time or another, with virtually all his friends. Still, he remained a "superb companion" much of the time, eager for collaboration with his friends.

In October 1960, after Iris Clert had exhibited the work of Yves, Arman, Tinguely, and others, Pierre Restany forged them into an official group, the New Realists. The manifesto was drawn up and signed in Yves' apartment. Yves exerted a strong influence (stronger even than over the others) over Restany, who soon came to see him as the central figure in the group, and whose book, *Yves Klein le monochrome*,[96] is the main external support for Yves' myth of himself as prophet and superman.

For in 1959, buoyed by the onrushing success of his adventure in the world of Blueness, Yves had taken an irrevocable step into the horizon of pure myth. Pol Bury, in Belgium, published a collection of Yves' writings[97] which required a wholehearted commitment to live up to, or which were, in plain fact, impossible to live up to. There for all to see were the announcements of the new age and his role in it, his plans to replace Keynesian economics, his prophecies of immediate evolution into the age of levitation, telepathy, and immateriality. It was a severe case of developmental forcing. His "beautiful megalomania" and "delusions of grandeur"[98] (the fantasied omnipotence of the little Captain: "I lay

down my arms. Signed: Antoine") were now in the public domain. There was no longer much possibility of escaping from the myth and becoming a "plain dull human" among the others. In Germany and Italy his myth was received with good humor. But Paris did not make peace with him until 1965 — three years after his death. Many were fascinated or amused by his provocation of the public mind; others considered him a braggart and awaited his downfall with pleasure.

He began to live with a sense that "the public" was daring him to carry the myth all the way. If he backed down from it, he would be considered a "phony." And the myth began at some point to reveal a negative side. At first he had thought only of the scenes of the hero's victories; later the sacrificial ending came to the foreground. He was writing a beautiful poem with his life — but the poem had a tragic ending. Sooner or later he would have to face it.

Increasingly as the fifties rolled on Yves felt the strain of his uncompromising self-advertment. When Rotraut awakened at night she would find him already awake (or not yet asleep), writing or meditating to calm himself. In 1959 he tried to raise money for a full-page advertisement in *Paris-Match* declaring, in ultramarine blue, "The greatest painter in the world, Yves Klein, is a Frenchman." "His great naïveté and his exacerbated ambition," wrote Iris Clert, "frightened me. They made him fragile. The least setback shattered him."[99] He projected now a sculpture magnetically suspended in the air, now an IKB Stations of the Cross (fourteen blue monochromes in an all-white chapel). As his territory became more complex, boundary disputes arose. He quarreled over priority constantly.

This in itself was not unusual. It was one of the dangers that Bernadette Allain had tried to warn him about. "The whole artistic milieu," she says, "*forced* people to do something new every time. If someone else had done it before, then your work was worth nothing. In other words, the work itself had no value; it was only a publicity device. One had to do something *new*, to say something *new*, rather than deepening one's work and reflecting on its quality. One fabricates a legend about oneself for publicity, and before long the legend takes possession of the man and the man is forced to behave in conformity with the legend, to do what publicity requires. And it is from this that he died."

"He had none of the qualities you would expect of someone who made monochromes," says Tinguely, "— a kind of quietude, a capacity to contemplate himself, a kind of balance. He made monochromes as an iconoclast, an anti-painter. He was fighting his mother, he was fighting his father...."

Since the "mystic crisis" with Claude and Arman in 1948, Yves' inner world had expanded for about ten years, then had begun to contract and harden around certain contradictions. The serious and likable youth of the Irish journal, conscientiously and quietly striving for inner growth, had hardened into the apotheosized "Yves the Monochrome," whose inner world was now, supposedly, all of one texture. Yet that inner oneness was belied by his ambitions, his jealousies, and, above all, his "celebrated temper tantrums."[100] For the Discord Spirit was still with him, ambushing him with increasing frequency. "He had a violent temper but almost always controlled it," says Rotraut. "He would turn white in the face, and then blue. You would think he was going to explode." And Claude Pascal, his oldest friend: "His biggest problem — and I think in fact he died of it — was those terrible angers that seized him; his face would go completely, *completely* white. And sometimes for nothing. It was something that came out from inside him and he could not resist it. And I think that's what destroyed him."

The myth of the clear blue sky was proving hard to live up to. In fact, it was a trap. He had drawn for himself a role of prophet and perfect master and struggled desperately to fulfill it. "The Void belongs to me," he insisted — and it was a hard claim to live up to. He wrote:

I am in a spiritual state which grows from day to day; my only problem is to keep it pure and authentic and not allow it to be contaminated by the psychological domain.[101]

The "psychological domain" is the bound thrashings of ego, with its "cunning" and its *"calculs"*; the "spiritual state," the unlimited freedom which (according to Heindel) underlies it. This "only problem" which Yves mentions so lightly was in fact a terrifying inner battle:

My fundamental nature is at war with the psychological multiplicity of my personality.[102]

For Yves, the true artist had to be a kind of saint or yogi who has purified his essence beyond all contamination. He sought to unify his character, life, and art by rooting them all in the stratum of pure Spirit. This inner unity is, as the alchemists said, the Great Art:

The fact that I exist as a painter will be the most formidable pictorial work of our

time.[103]

But what would one be, or would one be anything at all, after attaining the psychological monostate? Yves ruminates along Zen lines, not knowing:

The author of a play lives his spectacle, his creation, he is his public and his triumph or disaster. And gradually even the author is not there anymore, and still the play goes on.[104]

20

I saw the tremendous sky, the beautiful look of people deprived of everything.

Paul Eluard

In August 1959, while vacationing in Greece, Iris Clert received a note from her assistant in Paris: "M. Klein came to take all his works. He told me that if a customer wished to buy one, I should say that his paintings are invisible, because immaterial, in the space of the gallery, and that if he wanted to buy one, it would suffice to write me a check. He was clear that the check should be quite visible. I think that M. Klein has gone mad."[105] Yves, his career now under way, was abandoning Iris for the more established dealer Jean Larcade.

But such was the charm of Yves the Monochrome that the first customer to whom the gallery attendant actually said these words[106] replied that he did indeed want to buy an invisible painting, asking only for a receipt signed by Yves. Yves showed his seriousness by rejecting the chance to make a Duchampian gesture. The transfer of immaterial realities had profound implications, and Yves understood them. In a few months he had devised the "Ritual for the Relinquishing of Immaterial Zones of Pictorial Sensibility, 1957 – 59" (note the two-year backdating), including a sharp reprimand to the customer for wanting something visible to indicate possession:

Every possible buyer of an immaterial zone of pictorial sensibility must realize that the fact that he accepts a receipt for the price which he has paid takes away all authentic immaterial value from the work, although it is in his possession.

In order that the fundamental immaterial value of the zone belong to him and become a part of his life, he must solemnly burn his receipt.[107]

(There it is again, the fire which burns through into

the Void—as Taoist priests would send a message to Hell by burning it, as Paracelsus says the soul must be raised to the highest vibration by burning.) An immaterial zone, after all, is more or less a *soul*. Only gold can buy it (since "spirits are commixed with gold, and by it fixed"), and nature must receive its due (since "transmutation is the work of Nature, only aided by the Art").[108]

> Yves Klein must, in the presence of... witnesses, throw half of the gold received into the ocean, a river, or some other place in nature where this gold cannot be retrieved by anyone.[109]

Station: November 18, 1959, the bank of the Seine. Yves, in bow tie and overcoat, smiling and energetic, even businesslike, sells a ticket to the other side of the sky, a zone of pregnant emptiness, for gold which flows away upon the river. The event is recorded in photographs. ("Was this," asks Iris Clert, "the birth of conceptual art?")[110]

21

> *The fire in the clouds*
> *The fire in the birds*
> *The fire in the cellars...*
> *All empties and refills*
> *In the rhythm of the infinite*
>
> Paul Eluard

The swarm of works and ideas which Yves produced without pause after becoming, in 1955, "an involuntary painter" was not simply the result of trying "to go farther each time, because it was necessary to be avant-garde," as Bernadette Allain suggests. While that compulsion did of course enter into it, Yves' *oeuvre* displays an underlying wholeness of program. At the foundation was Heindel's Rosicrucianism. But it is questionable whether after a certain age Yves should be called a Rosicrucian. There is something to Arman's statement that "he was not a Rosicrucian, he was not anything; he just used whatever was useful to him." As Bernadette Allain says, Yves had "a certain flair or intuitive knowledge of what he could use, in regard to people, books, materials. He nourished himself on things, which he made into food and then intuitively transformed....When by chance he found a text he could use, even a paragraph he could make into food, or on which he could lean, then he became an enthusiast."

But the point that must be made clear is that Yves did not "use" just anything; he exercised a refined and intelligent choice. First of all he was nourished by Heindel, and his artistic program was to translate Heindel's Rosicrucianism into visual terms, as a kind of sympathetic magic to induce the dawning of a new age in which Yves himself might feel more at home. But in artistically articulating Heindel, in giving Heindel poetic rather than dogmatic force, Yves was secondarily nourished by Gaston Bachelard. He found in Bachelard many passages which he could use as food because they seemed to parallel Heindel. By overlaying Bachelard on Heindel, Yves could more clearly see Heindel in artistic terms.

Yves' first public acknowledgment of the influence of Bachelard occurred in April 1959, at his immaterial exhibition in the Hessenhuis in Antwerp, where he read a passage of *L'Air et les songes* — from the chapter entitled "Le Ciel bleu":

> First there is *nothing*, then there is a *deep* nothing; then there is a blue *depth*.[111]

In December of that year, at the Gelsenkirchen opening attended by his "two mothers," a text purportedly by Yves but in fact consisting of passages from the same chapter of Bachelard was read for Yves in German. The lack of acknowledgment was not unusual. Only once in his extensive writings does Yves mention Max Heindel. His desire to give the appearance of excelling at all things (great athlete, artist, lover, and man of intellect) became especially fierce in areas in which he did not in fact excel. ("He had such desire," says Edouard Adam, "to be what he was not — it ate him away.")

In June of the same year, in his lecture at the Sorbonne, Yves was careful to assign a date for his first reading of Bachelard: April 1958.[112] The date, which is called into question by the very fact that he published it, may yet reveal more than he intended. April 1958 was the month of the opening of *Le Vide* at Iris Clert's. Clearly for Yves that exhibition had Rosicrucian associations. But in addition, the transition from blue-as-absolute to immaterial is specifically mentioned by Bachelard in the chapter from which Yves quoted repeatedly in the following year. After discussing "*l'azur*," Bachelard notes:

> The mark of a true aerial [or ethereal] nature is found, among us, in another direction [i.e., other than blueness]. It is based, in effect, on the dynamic of dematerialization. The substantial imagination of air is only truly active in a dynamic of dematerialization.
>
> It is in surveying the degrees of dematerialization of celestial blue that we can see the ethereal revery in action, ...the *fusion* of

the dreaming being in a universe as little differentiated as possible, in a universe blue and sweet, infinite and without form, *with the least possible structure*. [113]

Yves later, in fact, referred to *Le Vide* as an exhibition of "an immaterial blue color." It is possible that he had read in Bachelard earlier than April 1958, and the transition from blue to immaterial may reflect in part the convergence of Bachelard and Heindel, both of whom felt that blue was the last veil over the face of the Void. Yves' conception of the Battle between Line and Color may also reflect the influence of Bachelard's claim that "the feeling of the blue sky appears as an expansiveness without line."[114]

In general, Yves' "method" was to respond to convergences between Heindel, Bachelard, and his immediate environment. His attempt at an "architecture of the air" is a clear example. Heindel specifically calls for the dematerialization of the human environment (through a union of science, art, and religion) for the incoming age of the "etheric" body. This remaking of the environment is one of the duties of the highest initiate, who must lead the way. This is the "mythic" or "prophetic" basis of the architecture of the air (Yves' works *all* had a mythic or prophetic basis), made explicit in the levitation Imprint called *L'Architecture de l'air* (ANT 102). Yet Yves seems not to have turned his attention directly to this part of the Rosicrucian system until he was stimulated by an apparent parallel in Bachelard. *The Poetics of Space* (of which Yves owned six copies when he died) was published in 1958, the year in which Yves first mentioned the architecture of the air; in the second chapter (section 6) he found the following lines:

"My house...is diaphanous, but it is not made of glass. It is more of the nature of vapor. Its walls contract and expand as I desire."

An immense cosmic house is a potential of every dream of houses. Winds radiate from its center....A house that is as dynamic as this allows the poet to inhabit the universe. Or, to put it differently, the universe comes to inhabit his house.[115]

...houses that integrate the wind, aspire to the lightness of air...

...wind house, abode that a breath effaced...

Bachelard then set the hook in Yves by noting that such houses would "be rejected by a positive, realistic mind." To Yves — the man who would spend an entire evening trying to convince a listener that the earth was flat and square — this was a challenge;

he proposed a universe opposite to that of "the positive, realistic mind," a universe based on inspired irrationality.

Yet Iris Clert says that Bernadette Allain gave Yves the first vague suggestion of the architecture of the air, and Bernadette Allain confirms this, saying, "I was the precursor of the architecture of the air." In fact, Werner Ruhnau makes a similar claim for himself. But it should be pointed out that such assertions show an incomplete understanding of Yves' method— understandably, since his method was so ambiguous and secretive. From the "prophetic" point of view, it is Heindel who was the precursor, and Bernadette Allain or Werner Ruhnau, or someone, merely acted as the trigger to set Yves' energy loose on that aspect of Heindel's prophecy. The fact that, as Bernadette Allain says, "he was the least intellectual person I have ever known" should not obscure the more important fact that he was influenced by certain books to an extraordinary degree (primarily the *Cosmogonie*, secondarily the works of Bachelard). His ideas seem to have arisen not simply from his environment, but from the interplay between events (or remarks) in his environment and the patterns of thought imprinted in him by these books.

In fact, many of the claims on Yves' work seem to arise from an incomplete understanding of his method. Bernadette Allain, for example, feels that she suggested to Yves the priority of blue among colors; Iris Clert, on the contrary, feels that it was *she* who made this suggestion. But ultimately it seems that Heindel, for whom blue was the color of Spirit, was the crux of Yves' decision — though others, by their suggestions, may unwittingly have pointed him toward this element of Heindel's system. The same confusion can be seen in Takis' belief that Yves borrowed from him the idea of gravity-free or aerostatic sculpture.[116]

Such claims cannot be rejected as without basis, but they are only a part of the story. Clearly Yves *was* a "grabber." But he grabbed only what he felt already belonged to him due to his privileged relationship to Rosicrucian prophecy. The deeply imbibed Rosicrucian structures, overlaid with Bachelardian "poetics," formed a net held out to his environment; when something caught in the net, he used it, but he used *only* what caught. When an idea (like the blue monochrome, the sponge sculpture, the aerostatic sculpture, or the architecture of the air) obviously fit into his system, he seems to have felt that it belonged to him by right. Though another person might articulate the idea first, that person still did not have real priority, because Yves' system, containing the idea latently, had been there still earlier. (Such is the irrationality of a prophet.) For Yves, who had picked art theory and phenomenology "out of the air," it was clear that, as Georges Poulet wrote, "ideas belong to no one. They pass from mind to mind as coins pass from hand to hand."[117] In a sense, of course, the "origin" of the ideas is irrelevant. It was Yves who molded the varied elements into a distinctive and consistent body of work, each part of which bears his personal touch.

Yves spoke openly about his "system" and the "prophetic" basis of his art to few people — in fact, only to those of whose sympathy he was certain. In the late fifties, for example, he stopped talking to Arman about Rosicrucianism, because Arman would no longer take it seriously (*or* the pilgrimages to Cascia!). To Robert Godet he told it, and, more briefly, to Tinguely. ("He is a messenger," Tinguely wrote, "of the future age.")[118] Unaware of his "system," and seeing his apparently random forays into various media, one might easily regard him as an opportunist and a Dada. It was precisely this opinion, widely held by people around him, that caused him such pain and frustration. ("The word Dada was used as an insult," says Tinguely, who heard it as much as Yves.)

After 1958 he tried to establish himself as a Bachelardian. But while Yves understood Heindel well enough, he did not really understand Bachelard's phenomenological side, which he misinterpreted in terms of Heindel. This was made painfully clear to him by Bachelard himself when Yves visited him in 1961. Yves began to explain that Bachelard was a kind of crypto-Rosicrucian, and Bachelard threw him out at once. The saintly elder thought Yves was "a crazy man," Arman recalls.

There was also a persistent problem in Yves' understanding of Heindel. The plans for altering and reclimatizing the environment were based ultimately on the *Cosmogonie*, in which Yves had read at age eighteen about the coming age of Space, levitation, and telepathy. But a crucial point which Yves did not understand (or accept) is that Heindel did not predict the dawning of that age until several more centuries had passed. Yves, like an ancient priest performing rites to reconstitute the universe at the New Year, was trying to force it to happen *now*. ("May the impossible arrive and establish its kingdom *quickly!*")

22

All my desires are born of my dreams. To what fantastic creatures have I entrusted myself, in what dolorous and ravishing world has my imagination enclosed me?

Paul Eluard

When Bernadette Allain passed out of Yves' circle of intimates, he needed a new "hand" to make his drawings and engineer his maquettes. It was at this juncture that he met the architect Claude Parent.

"What interested me about Yves," says Parent, "was a kind of generosity, and a power of positive scandal....The liberty with which he lived radiated out of him; everyone felt it, in his actions, his character, his way of being with people. He was extremely spontaneous....He was an extraordinary comrade and always full of ideas....Whatever you did with him was an adventure.

"It was very difficult at first, in drawing for Yves, to find out what he wanted. Then suddenly I realized that the more romantic it was, the more dynamically the sky was drawn, the more he liked it. It was a type of drawing that was completely out of style at the time.

"I didn't make him pay for my work. It was a matter between friends. Then one day he wanted to give me something. He said, 'What would you like, from my works?' I said, 'A sponge relief.' He replied, 'No. Those are not really me. You should have a monochrome. That is me.'"

In June 1959, Iris Clert arranged lectures at the Sorbonne for Yves and Ruhnau, on "The Evolution of Art toward the Immaterial." For Yves, who still read Tintin and Mandrake the Magician (*"I have no diploma"*), it was a special triumph, a kind of confirmation (as if, now, any more were needed) of his special role as Highest Initiate, as favorite of Saint Rita, as lost cause of all lost causes. Tinguely and Claude Parent both were present at the Amphithéâtre Turgot, where Yves outlined his plans for a World Center of Sensibility, talked of reforming the world economic system, and spoke of making an art work which would consist of reclimatizing all of France — later the world. ("The alchemist is a dreamer...who magnifies himself by 'wishing big.'")

"Lectures at the Sorbonne," says Claude Parent, "were usually very cold and intellectual — a monstrous bore, but irreproachable. But Yves emanated charm. He absolutely seduced the audience. Everyone saw it. It was a genteel seduction of the entire audience."

The newspapers covered the event as grand Dada. The only people who took it very seriously were some members of the activist left, who interpreted Yves' plans not as a Dada gesture, nor as the fantasies of a solitary alchemist, but as the beginning of a Fascist movement. His visits to Japan and Spain, his interest in the martial arts, and his evident desire to launch movements contributed to this impression.

But Yves was of course not political in any ordinary sense of the word — the repeal of the law of gravity was his program! Matters of practical policy never entered his head, any more than they would a child's. He organized movements in Paris as once ("the little Captain") he had organized children's games in Cagnes-sur-Mer. As Tinguely says, "He was neither left nor right. He was nothing at all. He was above all that. He was a true poet, who was living a trance of total dream."

23

"Ha! ha! ha! You see, Captain! On the moon gravity is actually six times less than on the Earth!"

Tintin, in *Explorers on the Moon*

Stations/Labors/Cartoons: 1960 — Yves pushes on through the spectrum of nature, pursuing his symbolic alchemy to its conclusion.

He exhibits the first Monogold, symbolic of the completion of the Great Work, at the Musée des Arts Décoratifs, in the show *Antagonismes*.

He appears in blue formal dress before a seated audience in the Galerie Internationale d'Art Contemporain and gestures to the orchestra; the musicians begin to play the *Monotone Symphony*. He gestures again. Three naked girls appear, smear their bodies with blue paint, and press themselves against sheets of paper under his guidance.

Writing about this event, Yves stresses his separateness, his voyeurism if you will, as he controls but does not touch:

I could continue to maintain a precise distance from my creation and still dominate its execution. In this way I stayed clean. I no longer dirtied myself with color, not even the tips of my fingers.

(Now even color is profane before the sanctity of the immaterial!)

The work finished itself there in front of me with the complete collaboration of the model. And I could salute its birth into the tangible

world in a fitting manner, in evening dress.[119]

He extends the magico-artistic function of "supporting birth into the tangible world," seeking the birth of nature revealed in the "trace of the immediate," where realms meet, by allowing the elements to state their projects directly upon the material: he straps a canvas to the roof of his car and drives from Paris to Nice and back. As citizen of infinity, he inspects the processes of the finite:

I bound outside and down to the river. Among the rushes and reeds I dust color over everything I see there, and the wind making the long stems bow, sets them with delicacy and precision against the canvas I present to trembling nature; I obtain a mark of plant life.... It begins to rain; a fine spring shower. I hold out my canvas to the rain and it is done! I have the mark of the rain, of the stirring of the atmosphere.[120]

Unfortunately, the Imprints involved him in increasing tension and strained some of his closest relationships. The first performance had been at Godet's apartment in 1958 (the result an all-blue canvas, not a silhouette). But it was unclear who had originated the idea. Iris Clert felt that Yves had borrowed it from her, Arman that it had been borrowed from him. Yves replied that at age eighteen, in first "projecting my mark outside myself," he had imprinted his hands and feet upon his clothing.[121]

Still the outside world increased its invasions of his domain, and he sprang to the defense, at times hysterically. According to Iris Clert, he sued the film director Claude Chabrol for the film *Les Godelureaux*, in which Chabrol portrayed an artist making body prints as an example of the degeneracy of art. Yves' lawyer compared him to Giotto for the profundity of his blue — and lost the case. Hearing that Iris Clert had imprints by another artist in her gallery, he called the police on her and threatened to sue.

His domain had grown too large to defend effectively. His closest friends wrangled with him over priority. He was in constant need of money and wrote Aunt Rose frequent appeals, which she usually responded to. When money arrived he would spend it in one night with a crowd of friends in Montparnasse. When it did not, he would tear up the offending letter and pound his fists into the wall, as he might have done when he was three. In fact, he was growing increasingly rebellious toward the female deities. When in Nice, he stayed not at his aunt's home, but at Arman's.

Meanwhile, his relationship with Rotraut was destabilized by his abrupt changes in mood and role,

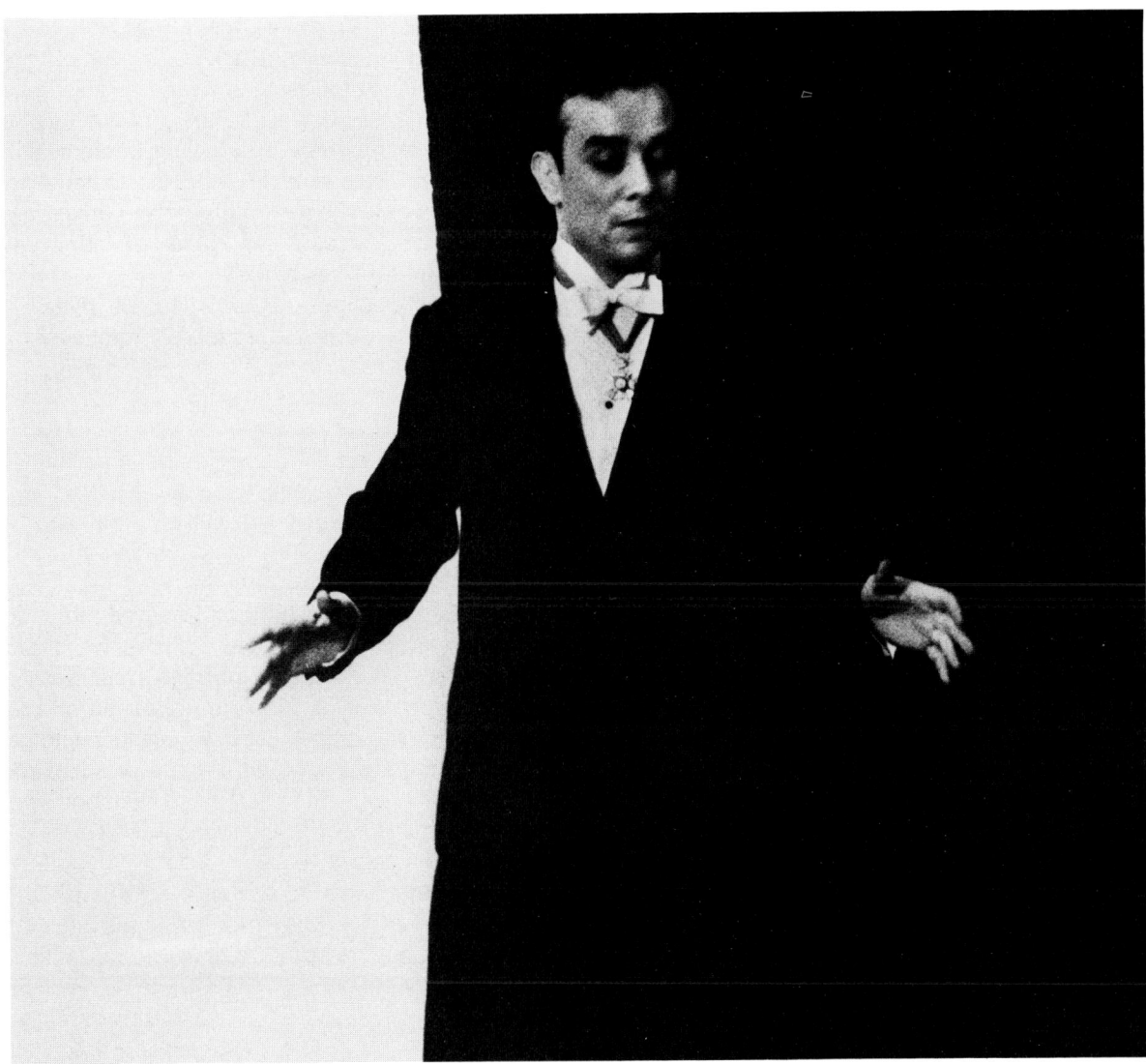

Yves Klein directing the making of Imprints, 1960

which she had difficulty following: when he was authoritarian, she was submissive, sent to her room like a child if Iris came round on business; when he was the libertine, she was the procuress, helping him find girls in the bars; when he was the voyeur, she was the performer, dancing erotically at parties. More than once she left him, and returned.

The problem of debt was aggravated when Yves stopped giving judo lessons in 1959, and so were all the other problems. "It was when he abandoned judo," says Bernadette Allain, "that he lost the ability to adjust himself inside, to keep the physical balance necessary to live as intensely as he did. He did not even seem physically solid anymore." A German *judoka* of lesser rank threw him three times easily in what was to have been a collaboration.[122] His friends began to experience him as paranoid and hyper-motivated. "He was so restless that he could not even sleep," says Tinguely. "He was the most restless man I have ever known. At night he had to write to avoid being torn apart by despair. He wrote, and he invented other methods to avoid sinking into a nightmare." "He lived," says Iris Clert, "as if his days were numbered."[123]

It was at this time, in this situation, that Yves decided to put his myth "at the very *top*" — to make his Leap into the Void. ("That whole world of young artists who gravitated around him — little by little I developed a real aversion to them, because they were killing the man. That's what it came to, obliging him to go farther each time because it was necessary to be avant-garde, it was necessary to go 'beyond' the others. One was forced, you might say, to throw oneself into the void," says Bernadette Allain.)

24

That absurd leap of body and soul, that cannonball that strikes its target in the act of exploding, yes, that, surely, is the life of a man!

René Char

The dream of flight was very old with Yves. It had dominated his spiritual ambitions at least since his liberating first reading of Heindel under Cadeaux's guidance in 1948. The sky as transcendence meant both fulfillment and escape to one who was basically discontented with the things of this world. He had flown in imagination to the far side of the sky from the beach in Nice, and, while meditating on Arman's rooftop, had visualized intensely, for hours, the act of rising and flying through the moon.

Like the monochrome painting, which seems to have entered his consciousness at the same time and with related associations, magical flight remained a constant which went with him everywhere. This was more than an icon, more than an image to define oneself; it was a belief. As Rotraut says: "He was sure he could fly. He used to tell me that at one time monks knew how to levitate, and that he would get there too. It was an obsession. Like a little child he really was convinced that he could do it. He even talked about a machine in which to train people to fly."

This of course was a central part of Yves' role as Highest Initiate and Messenger of the Age of Levitation. Within the terms of that myth, it was not only his destiny, but even his duty, to be the first to demonstrate flight and to teach others to fly until everyone could do it. From 1957 on, the myth seemed really to be unfolding, and the dream of flying once again seemed near. He talked about it obsessively, not only to Rotraut but to everyone.

It is also true that flying and dematerialization— the alternate climaxes of his myth — were both associated in his mind with death, and that the act of flying away to the sky seemed a form of magical sacrifice. A common element in the myth of the Messenger or Savior is that his own sacrificial death is necessary to cement the new age in place. As Yves' state of mind grew increasingly tragic and doomed, he spoke more often both of flying and of death, usually together.

"He would talk about his death," says Claude Parent: "It was passionately interesting to him....What was it he used to say? He would tell me that he would leap, that he would make a famous leap...."

And Tinguely: "He always talked about two things: he talked about levitation, and he talked about just vanishing."

Station: it is autumn, 1960. The King of the Sky pulls back the curtain for another act of his Mono-drama. Yves, in a business suit and necktie, gives a demonstration of flying. He stands on a second-story ledge and gazes down at the street, then up at the sky, his home. When the photographers are ready, he tenses his judo-trained muscles and dives out and up in splendid freedom. Gazing intently above (glowing eyes) without thought of the hard street below, he hangs for a moment at the top of his leap (cameras clicking), then rises gracefully over the roofs of Paris, is lost among clouds for a while, and vanishes into his true home, beyond the sky.

This magnificent photograph is a numinous object around which rumors and controversy have clus-

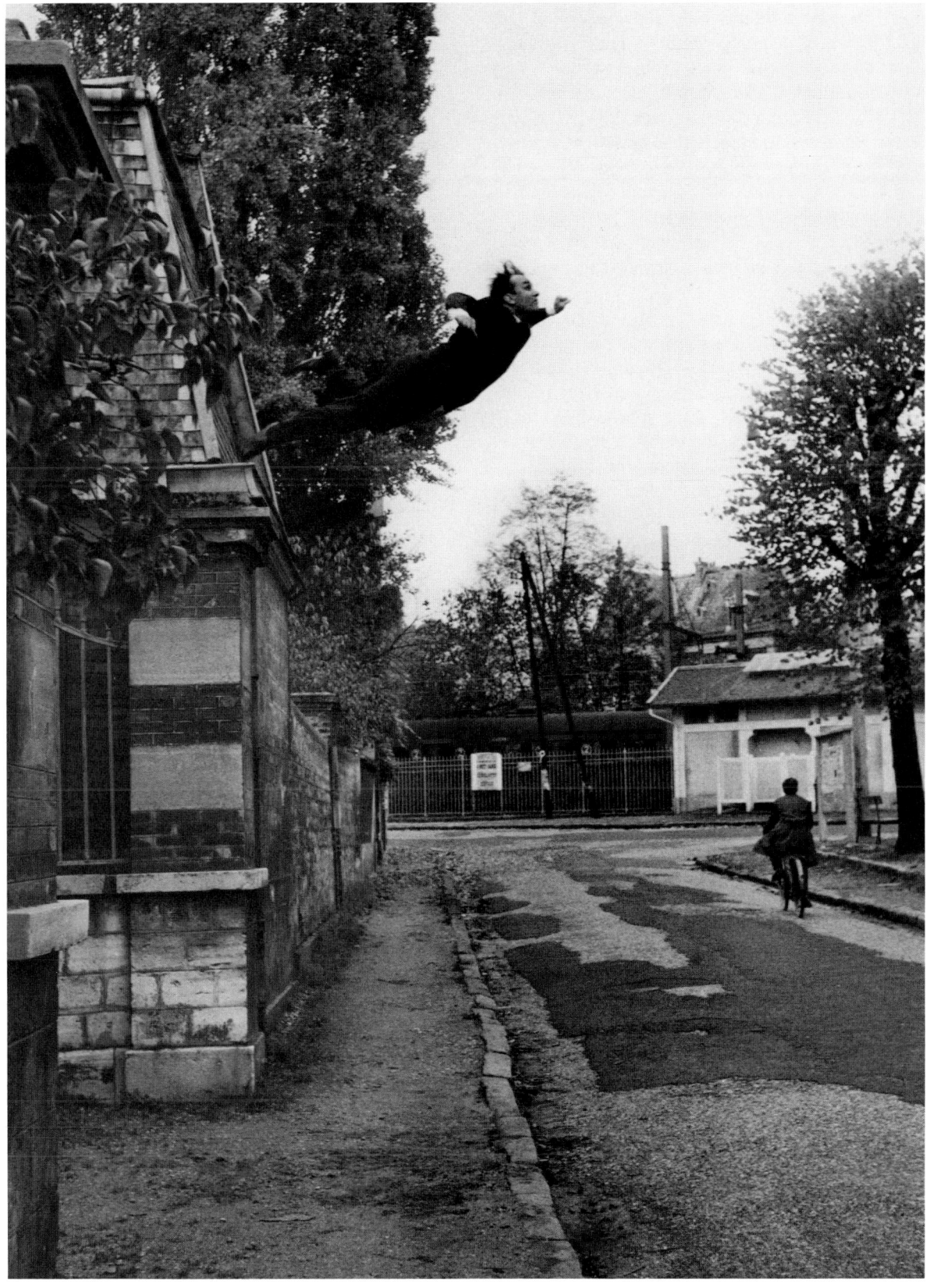

"The Painter of Space Hurls Himself into the Void!" 1960

tered as around the miracles claimed for a candidate for sainthood who is suspected of fraud. It has been pointed out that Yves himself, in the first publication of the photograph (in *Dimanche*, November 27, 1960), raised the question of whether the leap was made "with or without a net," and that the subsequent publication history, controlled by Yves, may have been designed to increase ambiguity on this point.[124] Specifically, the bicyclist in the lower right-hand corner of the photograph in *Dimanche* (the ploughman who did not see Icarus fall from the sky— a motif which Breughel had adapted from Ovid) is omitted in a later publication. Today various people, including the photographers, claim to know the inside story, then proceed to give wildly conflicting accounts. Even more striking, Yves' own reports were as conflicting as those of the eyewitnesses. To Arman, who was not an eyewitness, "he said, right out, no problem, that it was a montage.... But then he insisted that he *could* do it anyway." And Claude Parent: "He swore to me that he levitated. He would not let me alone about it." So skillfully disguised are the plain facts of the event, so effectively has the image been cleansed of historical origin, that protective clouds still cling around it. One thing is certain about the photograph in *Dimanche*: magnification of a print made directly from the negative shows with absolute clarity a montage line running from right to left along the ledge beneath Yves' feet and in a zig-zag path through the foliage behind that ledge.

But this photograph by no means tells the whole story. As we will see, the question of the net was not in fact *first* raised by Yves; the question preceded the photographed event and had been forced upon him by circumstances, so that he could not avoid it. First of all, a minimum of three leaps, witnessed by different people and made under different circumstances, must be sorted out from one another. It is probable that no single individual except Yves himself was aware of the series as a whole.

Pierre Restany provides a date and framework for the first leap. "With Yves," he says, "many things happened as a result of fixation, of a sort of intense insistence.... One day he told me he was going to do something 'very important.' He said, 'I'm going to give a practical demonstration of levitation,'" Restany was asked to come to Yves' apartment on the rue Campagne Première, to go with him to the leap site, and to witness the "demonstration." Unfortunately, detained by other business, Restany arrived at Yves' apartment late, just as Yves was returning from the event. "When I got there," Restany says, "Yves was tremendously excited; he was in a kind of mystical

ecstasy. He truly seemed to have just accomplished some prodigious physical feat. He said to me, 'You have just missed one of the most important events of your life.' He was limping slightly from a twisted ankle. I tell you, if I hadn't gone there and seen the state he was in, I would always have believed that it was a photomontage."

Two crucial points must be made. First, Restany's appointment book for 1960 indicates that this "practical demonstration of levitation" took place on January 12; but a bill for work done for Yves by the photographers Harry Shunk and John Kender shows two dates for a *saut* (leap): October 19 and 25, 1960.[125] The Shunk-Kender dates pinpoint the leap publicized in *Dimanche*; the event referred to by Restany took place ten months earlier. They were separate events. Secondly, Restany's recollection that Yves was limping from a twisted ankle agrees precisely with the recollection of Bernadette Allain, and with no one else's; it is highly probable that the leap missed by Restany was the same which she attended.

Bernadette Allain, who has not previously made a public statement on the question, asserts that she was present at a leap, and that it occurred at Colette Allendy's house on the rue de l'Assomption. She describes it as follows: "For a *judoka* who knew how to fall it was not extraordinary.... It would be expected of someone at his level of training to know how to recover and fall. He did it as a challenge or act of defiance, to prove that he was capable of leaping into the void — that is, not leaping out of a window, but leaping *toward the sky*. He wanted this known.... He had nothing underneath him but the pavement—nothing! There was no faking.... I was not amazed because I had seen him do far more extraordinary things on the judo mats.... He knew that he could do it, too. It was only the public who were amazed.... But as soon as he became a celebrity, everyone in the world claimed to have been there and told stories and more stories."

Subsequent events were directly influenced by the fact that Restany had not managed to attend this leap. When they met afterward at the apartment, Yves said, "I am terribly disappointed that you were not there, because *you are my witness*." It is easy to appreciate Yves' dilemma and the courses of action which it led to. He had in fact leapt without a net, and wished to publish the fact; but his official witness, who would be widely believed in the art world, could not guarantee the fact.

It is worth asking why Yves went ahead with the leap on January 12 when he saw that his official witness was not present. First, Yves had repeatedly told his judo companion Marcel Boulois that he was frightened of the leap. On January 12 the stage was set, his nerve was up, and rather than try to prepare himself again on another day, he went ahead with the event. Second, there is the strange poetic-symbolic connection between Yves' obsession with flight-and-death and that of his friend Robert Godet. Pierre Restany's appointment book for January 12, the day of the leap, indicates that later in the afternoon he and Yves went together to Godet's apartment (Yves was limping along the way). The occasion was special. "This," says Restany, "was the day of Godet's departure on that journey from which he would never return." Godet's fiery plunge out of the sky in the Himalayas, which Yves was to consider as a foreshadowing of his own death, was itself shadowed forth by Yves' fanatical leap from Colette Allendy's wall. To Yves himself such synchronicity might have suggested a mythic force.

For some time after January 12 Yves boasted of his leap, and found that no one believed him. The second and third leaps must be seen not as separate events in their own right but as attempts to generate credibility for the unwitnessed first leap. These attempts were not, however, successful. "When he talked about the leap," says Arman, "everyone said it was impossible. They laughed at him. There was a stairway at the Rive Droite Gallery, and Yves wanted to prove that he could leap from some height. He jumped from the stairway and hurt his shoulder badly. It was hurt for two or three months. He had to have it bandaged and everything." Both Jean Larcade and Rotraut recall this leap being made not from a staircase but over a table. In any case, it did nothing to help Yves' credibility.

It was at this point, brooding on the series of events while his shoulder mended, that Yves decided to falsify the event, over a net, in front of photographers. (Why risk a broken leg or dislocated shoulder again, when in fact the feat itself was already accomplished?) This leap was not to be the important, the magical event, as the first one was, but a mere complement or completion of that earlier event, providing the documentation which the real leap, through unhappy chance, had lacked. Therefore it became necessary to obscure the time and place of the photographed leap so that the fiction could be grafted onto the reality of the earlier event.

Shunk and Kender were engaged to record the leap on October 19 and to create the illusion by photomontage. A new leap site was chosen, in Fontenay-aux-Roses, both because Colette Allendy had died in the meantime (on February 22) and because there was a judo club across the street from the new site; Yves knew all the *judokas* in Paris and could count on them to help. Kender recalls that a dozen or so of the *judokas* were enlisted as catchers.[126] Extant photographs show these catchers in place. When Yves leapt, they caught him in a tarpaulin. The leap was made repeatedly to get the facial expression just right. The *judokas* and the tarpaulin were photomontaged out.

Rotraut (not Bernadette Allain) was present at this event and recalls it as follows: "Do you really want to know the truth?...It's idiotic to hide it. He really leapt, [but] first he went to the judo club to get the *judokas*, and they held a sort of tarpaulin....He leapt three, four, maybe five times....[Then] he was getting ready to leap without anything underneath him. It was terrible. I became completely unnerved. At one moment I was furious....I thought, *He's going to kill himself*. He was extremely fascinated by that."

Dissuaded by Rotraut, he did not make that final leap which, if successful, would have established his credibility before acceptable witnesses. Instead, knowing that such a leap had in fact been made ten months earlier, he swore Rotraut, Shunk, and Kender to secrecy about the presence of the net, and proceeded to publish the photograph with no date or specification of site. (The second Shunk-Kender date — October 25 — may represent darkroom work, perhaps the inclusion of the street view with the bicyclist.)

Finally, of course, the history of the icon is not the most important point: it is a time-canceling image, an image of escape from the bonds of history and conditionality, and its message does not hang upon the details of its manufacture. The intensity of the image itself, and the richness of its meaning, are its validation. At one level it is an unbearably poignant image of impatient longing for paradise, a desperate attempt to make paradise disclose itself *now*, before it is too late. If the Messenger of the New Age has already appeared, has already trumpeted forth from the rooftops his symbolic announcement, can the age itself be far behind?

Viewed not as magic but as art, the Leap is perhaps the most startling and arresting formulation of Yves' "invitation to a voyage." It is a classic icon of the urge to transcendence and of its dire consequences for body and ego.

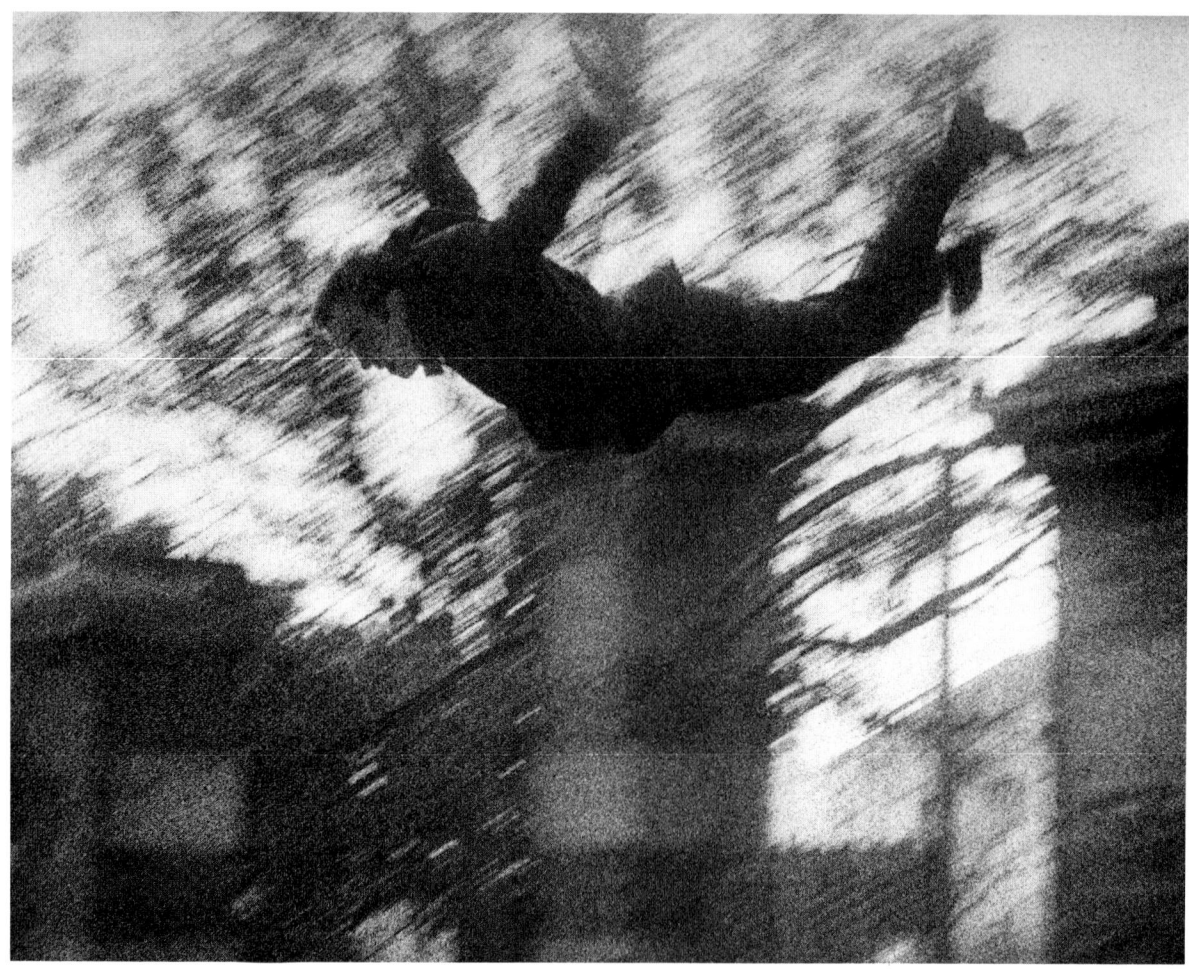

Yves Klein, 1960

25

This king flies away from you, ye mortals.
He is not of the earth, he is of the sky.
This king flies as a cloud to the sky.
He goes to the sky! He goes to the sky!
On the wind! On the wind!

Egyptian pyramid texts

"Space takes on quite a different aspect in the countless myths, tales, and legends concerning human or superhuman beings who fly away into Heaven and travel freely between Earth and Heaven, whether they do so with the aid of birds' feathers or by any other means. It is not the speed with which they fly, nor the dramatic intensity of the aerial voyage that characterises this complex of myth and folk-lore; it is the fact that weight is abolished, that an ontological mutation has occurred in the human being himself....The motif is of universal distribution, and is integral to a whole group of myths concerned both with the celestial origin of the first human beings and with the paradisiac situation during the primordial *illud tempus....*

"Now, if we consider the 'flight' and all the related symbolisms as a whole, their significance is at once apparent: they all express a break with the universe of everyday experience; and a dual purposiveness is evident in this rupture: both transcendence and, at the same time, freedom are to be obtained through the 'flight.'...The creation, repeated to infinity, of these countless imaginary universes in which space is transcended and weight is abolished, speaks volumes about the true nature of the human being. The longing to break the ties that hold him in bondage to the earth is not a result of cosmic pressures or of economic insecurity — it is constitutive of man, in that he is a being who enjoys a mode of existence unique in the world. Such a desire to free himself from his limitations, which he feels to be a kind of degradation, and to regain spontaneity and freedom—the desire expressed, in the example here discussed, by symbols of the 'flight' — must be ranked among the specific marks of man.

"The breaking of the plane effected by the 'flight' signifies... an act of transcending, ... [a] longing to go beyond and 'above' the human condition, to transmute it by an excess of 'spiritualisation.' For one can only interpret all the myths, rites, and legends to which we have been referring by a longing to see the human body behaving like a 'spirit,' to transmute the corporeal modality of man into a spiritual modality."

Mircea Eliade[127]

26

I breathe the elusive smoke I shall become
And to my incandescent soul the sky
Sings alteration in the restless shores.

Paul Valéry

Yves' career was a long process of appropriating the entire universe — element by element, stratum by stratum — into his myth, of symbolically enforcing his concept of essence on all being. In one sense this activity is metaphysics ("Isn't the metaphysician," asks Bachelard, "the alchemist with ideas too big to be realized?"),[128] but in another sense it is cosmic theater — the imaginary installation of oneself as "director" of the universal drama.

Yves was, of course, as Tinguely says, "a superdramatic case," and in one sense it was the everpresent theatrical implications which unified his *oeuvre.* Insofar as he was acting out the myth of the hero's quest for transcendence, his whole life was theater. His various immaterial events *(Le Vide,* the Relinquishments) and the performances of Anthropometries were a kind of theater. In fact, most of his art objects (the sponge works, IKB sculptures, Cosmogonies, Imprints) announce the processes of their making, thus positing a time axis and implying a form of theater. Georges Mathieu had made the theatrical implications of action painting explicit in 1956, when he painted a large canvas before an audience in the Théâtre Sarah Bernhardt. That event may have influenced Yves, who seems deliberately to have gone beyond it in the performances of Anthropometries (the first of which, ironically, was attended by Mathieu).

But Yves always had other sources than the contemporary art world. As he knew, Japanese painters traditionally painted before audiences works "which must be executed...without hesitation" in order to embody "that indefinable something" without which "the painting...must be considered a failure."[129] Yves echoed this Zen tradition in his term "indefinable" and when he wrote:

When everything goes well, when I am in form, my best paintings are executed very quickly, without hesitation, directly, and I am pleased with them.[130]

In 1960 Yves' thoughts turned directly to the theater, and his gestures of appropriation reached to the very limits of the universe, in what may be his most brilliant work: *Dimanche, the Newspaper of a Single Day.* This four-page imitation newspaper — Yves' contribution to the Festival d'Art d'Avant-garde

—reproduced the format of a Parisian daily and was distributed to newsstands one Sunday morning (creating amusing theater over many a breakfast table). The text is an astonishing tour de force, Yves Klein pursued by Yves Klein through a maze of imaginary theaters and disguises, simultaneously asserting and exposing the myth of his own omnipotence. If indeed he wrote these pieces on sleepless nights, to avoid "being torn apart by despair" or "sinking into a nightmare," then one must again be struck with admiration by his alchemical ability to transmute inner tension into creative force.

Yves begins, in the dateline, as God himself: "Yves Klein presents Sunday, November 27, 1960." (*Fiat lux!*) Beneath it: "The Blue Revolution Continues." "THEATER OF THE VOID," declares the headline, beside it the numinous photograph—Yves' upward gaze, his flying hair—"The Painter of Space Hurls Himself into the Void." The lead story proclaims an ultimate, godlike omnipotence — the appropriation of all space and all beings within it:

> The theater which I propose is not only the
> city of Paris, but is also the countryside, the
> desert, the mountain, even the sky, in fact,
> the whole universe. Why not?

For one day every person in the world was cast by Yves Klein as actor-spectator upon his universal stage. It was "an historic day for the theater," which for the first time expanded to include all "being itself." This universal theater is a piece of conceptual art which, by declaring our everyday actions to be dramatic performances, distances us from them, as in Shklovsky's definition of art as "a defamiliarization, a making strange ... a renewal of perception."[131]

Within this macrocosmic theater various microcosmic theaters are nested, some carrying to the limit the gestures of Meyerhold, Brecht, and Dada (for example, handcuffing the members of the audience to their seats), others approaching the Void through metaphysical reductionism and the reification of absences. A "Monotheater" is proposed with "no actors, no audience, no decor, no scene," expressing the unity and mystery of what is happening everywhere all the time. For a fee, an empty seat with your name on it would sit forever beside other empty seats facing an empty stage in a hall whose doors are closed and locked:

> This constant *arepresentation*, in this hall
> which no one enters after the installation,
> must have some moments more intense than
> others, indicated to the subscribers at the
> beginning by a program....At these particu-
> lar moments...the theater must be brilliantly

illuminated so that the light can be seen from outside.

> The director of such a theater should
> seek,...in long journeys made for this pur-
> pose only, actors who will...constantly re-
> new the troupe....The new actor so chosen
> will have nothing to do except know that he
> is an actor...and be aware of the "moments
> of hyperintensity" indicated to the subscrib-
> ers in the program. After an engagement, the
> actor will be charged with his new solemn
> responsibility of being an actor and will dis-
> appear into the crowd, into society, to be-
> come finally a serious visitor in the gigantic
> museum of the past.

There is a nest of theaters and metatheaters here, interlocking in circular infinities. And at the center, as at the periphery enclosing them, is the theater of Yves' personal myth as self-appointed representative of the Void. On the front page, Yves flies off into space; beneath him a reproduction of one of his own monochromes is captioned "Space Itself" (i.e., he Leaps into his own painting!). Inside, he explains the significance of his upward flight for others:

> To tell the truth, all this is only one step in the
> long expedition to really capture the void,
> which will happen after my final dis-
> appearance....This capture of the void will
> be realized by those who have understood
> this idea, or rather this principle, and who
> will live it as a pure ecstatic activity in a
> manner at last altogether natural.

This of course, is sheer messianism: not "my death," but "my final disappearance"! (Cf. Zalmoxis, Mithra, Quetzalcoatl, Christ.) He is the Redeemer, who, when he ascends to the sky, will open the way to others after him.

But this is only one glance into the kaleidoscope. In the next, the "final disappearance" is recast as an anima fantasy shot through with romantic longing; and here we encounter what must be considered Yves' most explicit "invitation to a voyage":

> When I think of you
> The same dream always comes back
> We are walking hand in hand
> On the wild path of our holidays
> When little by little
> Everything seems to disappear around us
> The trees, the flowers, the sea
> On one side of the path,
> Suddenly there is no longer anything at all
> We are at the end of the world
> And then...do we turn back?

No...I know that you say no
Come with me into the void!
If you return someday
You who dream also
Of this marvelous void
Of this absolute love
I know that together
Without saying a word
We will leap
Into the reality of that void
Which awaits our love
As I wait for you each day:
Come with me into the void!

There is a cry of loneliness in that song which echoes the fantasies found by Jung in the works of "solitary alchemists." A psychiatrist once remarked that Yves' ideas were remarkably similar to a delusion system. Yet unlike the truly deluded individual, Yves was able to bracket his private reality as myth, art, and theater. Within these privileged arenas, like a monk in a monastery, he was able to live out his myth as "pure" action which did not refer outside the brackets at all.

Still, the separate reality which the mythophile carries around with him, though it may not threaten society, does threaten to engulf his own ordinary humanity and leave him only the shadowy life of a monument, artifact, or symbol. On the last page of Yves' newspaper there is a strange little essay, "The Statue," which shows that he did at times find his myth burdensome and ossifying, that he sometimes wished to escape from its brackets and, like Odysseus in Plato's *Laws*, lay down the hero's burden and become a plain citizen of the world again:

> When I will finally become like a statue by the practice of exasperating my ego (*l'exaspération de mon moi*), which will have led me to this ultimate rigidity....Then, then alone, I will be able to set this statue in its place and go off by myself into the crowd, to go and see the world at last. No one will notice, because they will all be looking at the statue, and I will be able to walk away, free at last.[132]

27

Good luck, I cried, and I saw a sea of flames and smoke in the sky.

Arthur Rimbaud

The last years of Yves' life were enormously productive. His energy was at its peak, and his use of time, while studiedly casual, was fiendishly efficient. Wember's catalogue lists 1,077 pieces made between 1956 and 1962.[133] One does not produce such a body of work by mere publicity-seeking. It may or may not be the case that Yves used work to avoid some inner nightmare; but it is certainly the case that he worked hard and constantly. ("It was as relentless as an army mobilizing," Arman says, "when he decided to do something.")

Early in 1961 Yves received the ultimate mark of success for a young artist, a major retrospective of his works, at the Museum Haus Lange in Krefeld. It was at a time when his program of artistic alchemy, the art of fire, earth, air, water, prime matter, and gold, was nearing completion. The series of Monogolds (1959–61) symbolically completed nature's Great Work of perfecting matter. ("Gold is the sun; to make gold is to be god," says an alchemical text). The great triptych *Monoblue, Monopink, Monogold* (1960) crowned, with its Rosicrucian associations, the mysticism of color and brought it to an end. The theme of the unity of the absolute beginning and the absolute end was rendered into Egyptian form in the three obelisks, blue, rose, and gold, of the following year. This path leads no further, except to dissolve again what it has begun.[134]

It is this dissolution, this evanishment of forms through the inner combustion of the overheated spirit, which is shadowed forth in the Fire pieces of 1961. The theme of man as a perfected part of nature, at home in any of the elements, has appeared in the architecture of the air as a symbol of freedom and ascension; now, in the architecture of fire at Krefeld, it took on the more aggressive overtones of destruction.

Station: Yves becomes Prometheus in a vested suit and tie, taming fire into fountains, walls, paintings. At Krefeld in January he exhibits the Fire Walls and Fire Fountains of a city beyond the need for nourishment. Back in Paris, at the Centre d'Essais du Gaz de France, he makes the first Fire-Color paintings, burning composition board with a huge flamethrower, adding color selectively.

The Fire pieces (mostly 1961-62), while beautiful in themselves and an appropriate climax to the

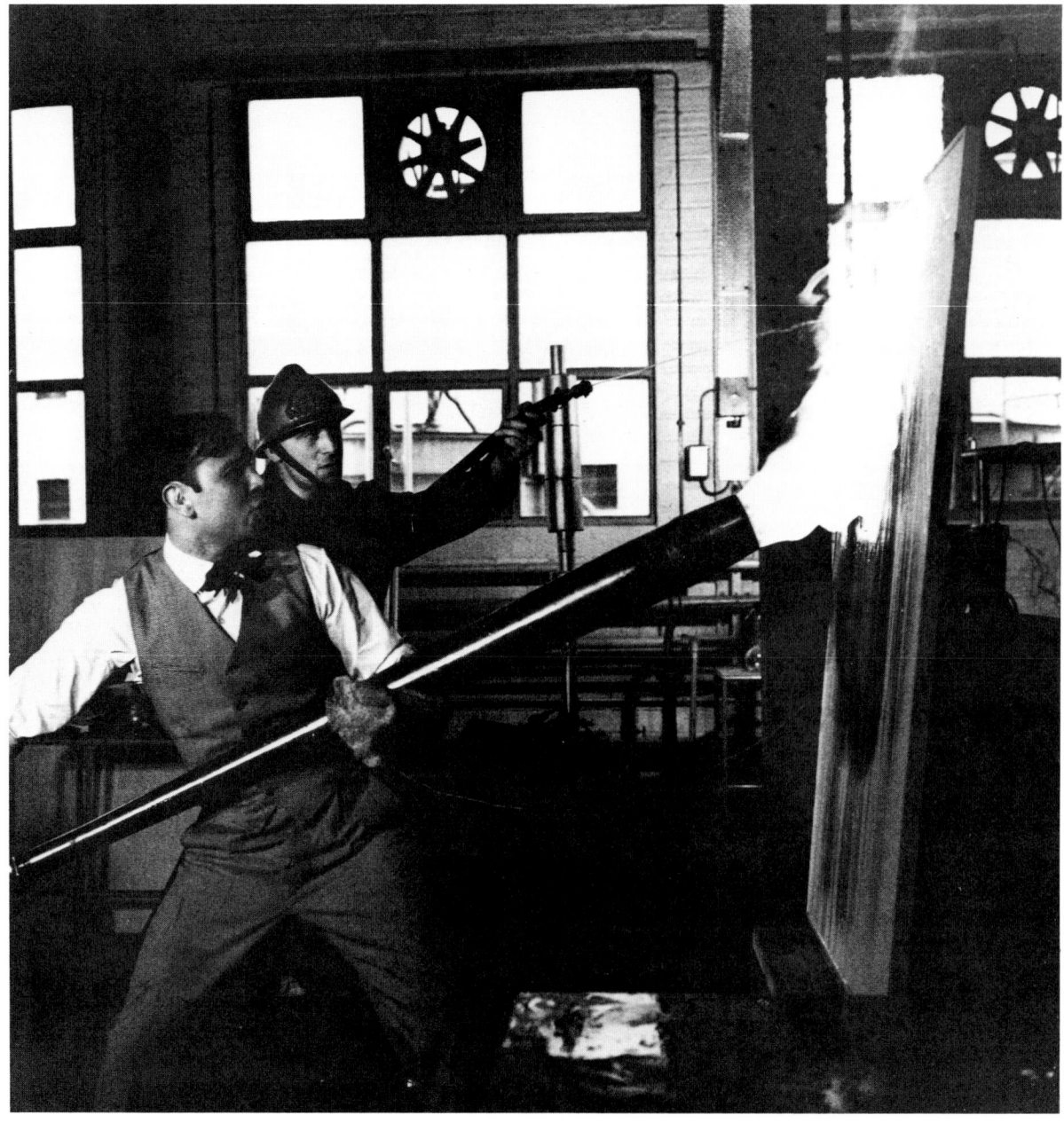

Yves Klein making Fire Paintings at the Centre d'Essais du Gaz de France, Paris, 1961

"...to seize fire or to give oneself to fire, to annihilate or to be annihilated, to follow the Prometheus complex or the Empedocles complex."

Gaston Bachelard

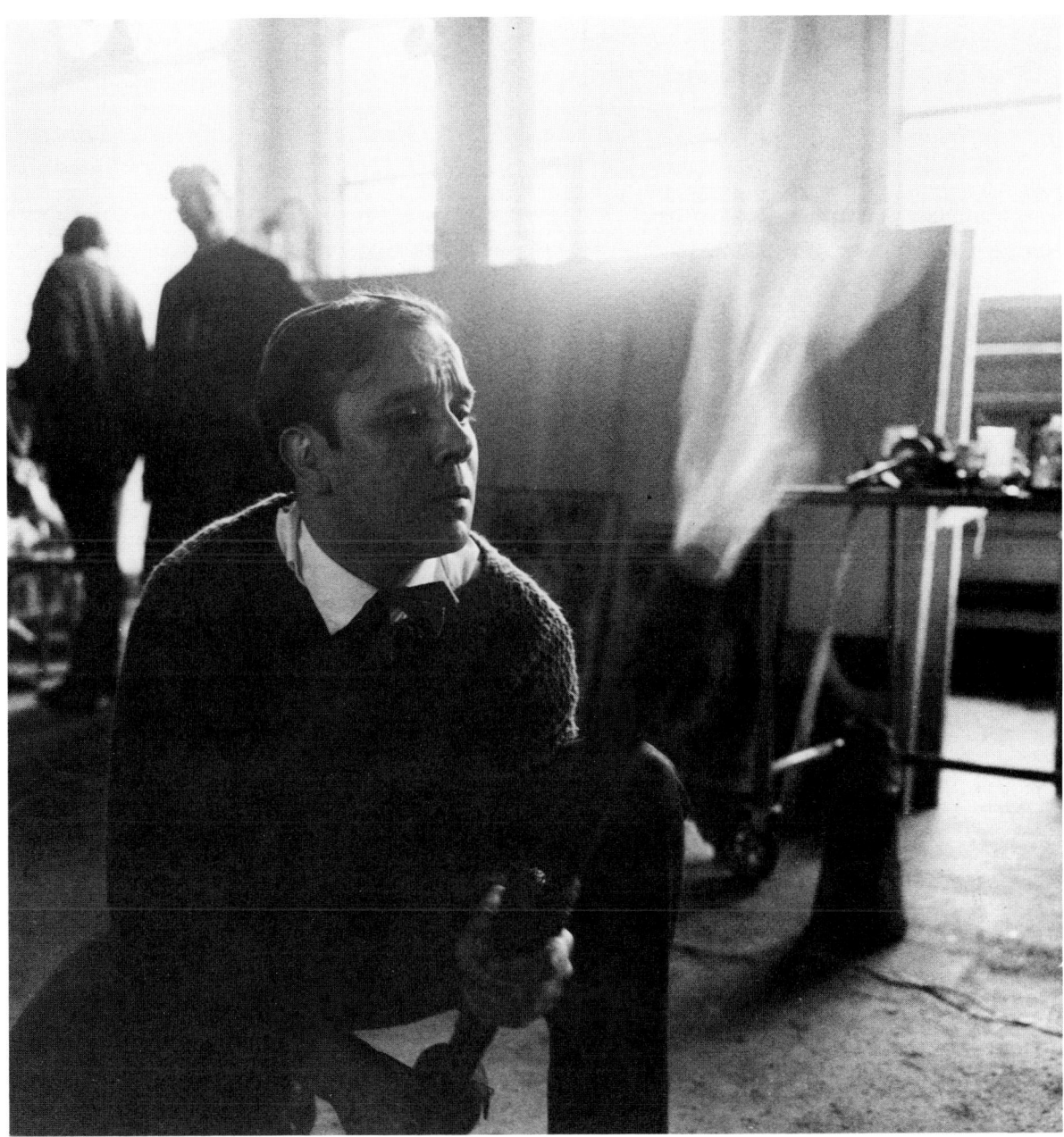

alchemical period, nonetheless radiate sinister overtones in terms of Yves' myth. "The last phase of the Opus," says the alchemical tradition, "during which the alchemist contemplates the appearance of fiery Light, is the most dangerous."[135] There is more than the "trace of the immediate" in these works: a sex-and-death thrill, a Promethean aggression, an Empedoclean walk to the very edge of the smoky crater. The Fire Paintings with added color have something of Nietzsche's "voluptuousness of hell." The famous photograph of the *Fire Wall* at Krefeld is a deathlike Station of the Myth: Yves' body is consumed by the fifty flames while his head floats in ghostly isolation above them. The *Fire Fountain*, innately awesome, scorches us with Heraclitean law: "All things are exchanged for fire, and fire for all things."

In November 1960, Yves and Rotraut traveled to Cascia (for his fourth and last time), to thank Saint Rita for the success of this "lost cause." Yves left an *ex-voto* object (pure pigments and gold from the sales of "zones of immateriality") accompanied by a long prayer ending "may all my enemies become my friends, and if that is impossible, may all their attacks on me be in vain—make me, and all my works, totally invulnerable!"[136]

28

"Moon rocket to earth....The air's becoming unbreathable,...the last cylinder from the spacesuits has been used up....The others are already unconscious....I wonder if we can possibly get back alive."

Tintin, in *Explorers on the Moon*

Tinguely: "It was his personality which prevented him from being taken seriously. He was too alive. An artist cannot be so charming, so powerfully persuasive; an artist can't articulate ideas that well. It was almost inconceivable that an artist could be like Yves Klein. It was a handicap to him, his extraordinary charm, his graciousness, his comradely side. He was too fine—not *low* enough. You have to be *low* to be an artist—drunk or sick or have ten children. But he was just simply superb! And that, that is dangerous."

Bernadette Allain: "After the judo period he needed a crowd around him—friends, girls—it was his relaxation. You might say he was indifferent to most of them, and in a sense treated them badly. But, from another point of view, he *did* accept them; he

did let them embark on his adventure with him. They were like his attendants or servants; they waited on him, men and women alike, as if he were a pampered child, an only son whose parents, whose whole family adored him."

Tinguely: "His studio was painted white, but really he wanted to line it entirely with mirrors — floor, ceiling, and walls. So he would see only himself. If he had had the money he would surely have done it. It was not one of those projects you think of vaguely for the future—if he had had a little money he would have done it at once. He had great hopes of being able to do it someday."

Yves Klein: "Saint Rita of Cascia, saint of impossible and desperate causes, thank you for all the powerful, decisive, and marvelous help you have given me to the present day—thank you infinitely."

Fred Klein: "We were one hundred percent companions. He was a real friend. But later, he became a little lost from view."

29

No longer any doubt, they're tugging me from below, loading me with ballast, I'm going down, the weight in me, again the weight, again the ground at my feet, what am I doing on the earth again?

Henri Michaux

Early in 1961, Leo Castelli, in New York, announced an exhibition, *Yves Klein the Monochrome*, to open on April 11. It was an invitation (at last!) to extend his domain over the ocean to America —from which, said Heindel, the new humanity of the Age of Space would arise. Yves and Rotraut flew to New York and lived for two months at the Chelsea Hotel.

On April 12, the day after the Castelli opening, Yuri Gagarin made the first manned space flight and reported (to Yves' delight) that from space the earth looked blue! Yves felt confirmed in his conviction that the Blue Age, the age of return to Space, would dawn in his own time. Still, a rocket is not levitation, and science alone (Heindel was explicit on this point) could not fulfill the ancient prophecies. Yves remained true to Heindel, though he could easily have slipped away from him through a relaxed interpretation. Yuri Gagarin was not the Messenger; his flight was a sign—but it was not the event itself. Yves wrote:

It is not with rockets, Sputniks, and missiles

that modern man will achieve the conquest of space....It is by means of the powerful yet pacific force of his sensitivity that man will inhabit space.[137]

Yet despite the more or less propitious omen, the show at Castelli's did not go well. The New York critics ridiculed it. "Have you ever been all blue?" asked the *Herald Tribune*. "I've got the Yves Klein blues," lamented the *New York Times*. *Art News* called him "the latest sugar-Dada to jet in from the Parisian common market," "the George M. Koan of French Neo-Dada," and "a Dali—junior grade." In fact, the show was misconceived, an anachronism; featuring the blue monochromes, as in 1957, it gave little hint of the range and depth that Yves' work had achieved by 1961.

The New York artists' reactions were mixed, as Yves for two months tried to annex them to his kingdom (hadn't the School of New York, after all, been replaced by the School of Nice?). Some (Larry Rivers, Barnett Newman, Marcel Duchamp) welcomed him; others were put off. He met Rothko, who turned away without a word. Reinhardt was pleasant but noncommittal. To all those working in monochrome styles Yves said they could be barons of the monochrome—but he was the king. In much the same spirit he regarded Rothko as a precursor of his own work. This kind of talk did not go over. Most New York artists pointedly boycotted the show. Nothing sold.

It was a disaster, and Yves felt the strain. Here he was not the "only son, adored by all the family." When mocked publicly as a failure, he underwent a rare break ("When the Discord Spirit come, I make me absolutely cold and without any emotion...") and hospitalized his tormentor with judo blows. He smoked constantly and at times drank too much.

Outwardly there was still the challenging smile and the laughter of a "superb companion." But privately, with increasing frequency he told Rotraut, "I feel so old and so lonely," and other remarks not particularly healthy for a very young man. As he felt the myth's sacrificial ending tightening around him, death entered his thoughts more and more.

He was thirty-three years old.

He wrote:

Only very recently I have become a sort of undertaker....Some of my latest works have been tombs and coffins.[138]

In June, Yves and Rotraut flew to Los Angeles for a show at the Dwan Gallery and quickly found they were in a different and friendlier atmosphere. A group of Los Angeles artists asked him if he had really jumped as on the front page of *Dimanche*, and when he said yes—they simply believed him! Partly it was because Tinguely had prepared the way for him the year before, becoming great friends with Ed Kienholz and others, but partly it was a cultural stance which naturally approved many of the things New York naturally condemned. In the looser, warmer, less intimidating West Coast atmosphere, Yves and Rotraut became vacationers, visiting the Hearst castle, the bullfights in Tijuana, and Disneyland, which (like all children) they greatly enjoyed, bringing home two souvenir booklets.

Still a strange and deadly vibration hung over Yves, who was painfully stung by his failure in New York. He and an associate of the gallery went shark-shooting with 30/30 rifles in the Pacific, watching the blood-maddened sharks devour each other in the water around the boat. Later Yves talked of the experience in a fascinated but loathing way.

One day he and Rotraut went driving with Ed Kienholz and Walter Hopps in a Land Rover, navigating by compass on the Mojave Desert. Yves insisted that he wanted to go to Death Valley to make a Fire Fountain there. He kept asking if they were in Death Valley yet, and even when repeatedly assured that they were not going that far seemed convinced that they were indeed in Death Valley; he was amused and fascinated by the theme of death.

"One afternoon," says the Los Angeles painter Ed Moses, "I took him up to my place in the hills to see my work. I had been told that he would be a supersophisticated operator. But instead he was charming, open, friendly. He looked right at everything, very simple and curious....

"Afterward, he had to get back to the gallery fast. So I gave him a Death Ride down the canyon—a real Death Ride. But that guy didn't flinch a muscle—he was ice cold. Just joked, as we tore around the curves, about how he had been making coffins or something...the undertaker artist...." ("Tantine! The car is absolutely sensational!") He rode through the woods on the back of Ed Kienholz's motorcycle, and was once provided a helicopter by the Dwan Gallery, delighting to descend from the sky—and return to it.

30

I am going to unveil all the mysteries: religious mysteries, or natural mysteries, death, birth, the future, the past, cosmogony, nothingness. I am a master of phantasmagoria.

Arthur Rimbaud

Back in Paris, inspired in part by Gagarin's flight, Yves began the series of Planetary Reliefs. But he was losing interest in the usual materials of art and wanted to work with the raw fabric of life, eliciting its hidden forces and expressions.

I shall give up the use of color, I think. I shall work with the perspiration of the models, mixed with dust, and even, perhaps, with their own blood.[139]

The idea was occultly powerful. Heindel had written,

The blood is...the vehicle of the subconscious memory, and in touch with the Memory of Nature, situated in the highest division of the Etheric Region.[140]

Having read in a book on sorcery that menstrual blood was the most powerful, Yves hired a Montmartre prostitute at the right time of the month, to make Anthropometries of her own lunar blood. The girl panicked midway—when the blood had been applied to her, but not to the canvas yet—and became hysterical. Pierre Restany was called over to calm her down.

Undaunted, Yves revised his strategy. A second attempt was made with Rotraut—using beef blood this time—and ten blood imprints of her body were made. Then terrible news came. A young Japanese artist, inspired in part by Yves' Leap and his Anthropometries (especially, perhaps, the "Hiroshima" imprint, ANT 79), was reported to have leapt from a high building onto a canvas in the street, killing himself and willing the canvas to the Tokyo Museum of Modern Art, which, according to the story, rejected it.

Yves was deeply shaken. He feared that the blood imprints had occultly brought about this tragedy. After all, blood is "in touch with the Memory of Nature," the central switchboard of the universe, whose circuits were infinite and inscrutable. The blood imprints were "diabolical." Or were they cryptic notices, from the central switchboard, of how closely death was approaching him? Was the event in Japan, in a sense, an invitation? To take the weight of the omen from Rotraut onto himself, Yves signed each of the canvases with a single thumbprint of his own blood, then called Restany over at midnight to witness the burning of the series.

31

I am the lover
I have wings
I will teach you to fly.

Max Jacob

On January 21, 1962, Yves and Rotraut were married in the church of Saint-Nicolas des Champs, Paris, to the accompaniment of the *Monotone-Silence Symphony*. Yves, lover of ritual and disguise, wore the plumed hat and crusader's cape of a Knight of Saint Sebastian and was attended by a retinue of knights. The wedding was an extraordinary event, a ceremonial pageant, like the ritual mating which preceded the sacrifice in ancient fertility religions.

Rotraut was pregnant with their son, Yves.

There was partying into the night. Old friends who had fallen away returned and were reconciled.

Soon thereafter, the Discord Spirit laid its final marks upon him.

32

He moves toward a place of quietude and peace where he can finally stop being wind. But his nightmare has already lasted a long time.

Henri Michaux

As soon as the New Realists had been officially formed, in his apartment in October 1960, Yves had attempted to appropriate the movement into his work, to make his work the matrix in which the others' hopes for immortality would reside. In November he had gathered the members in his apartment again for a collective imprint on the theme of the Void.

Now, in 1962, when his own drama was drawing toward its close, he moved even more emphatically to incorporate the others into his approaching transfiguration. The perishable Collective Imprint would be eternalized in a Collective Portrait Relief. Plaster casts of the New Realists would be made, converted into bronze, then painted in Yves' heraldic colors (the colors of the Void), and, rendered timeless like the statues of Egyptian pharaohs, exhibited together. But the composition of the group was clearly hierarchical. The other New Realists were to be painted in International Klein Blue and exhibited against a gold ground; Yves himself, in the center, would be gold, against a blue ground—supernatural,

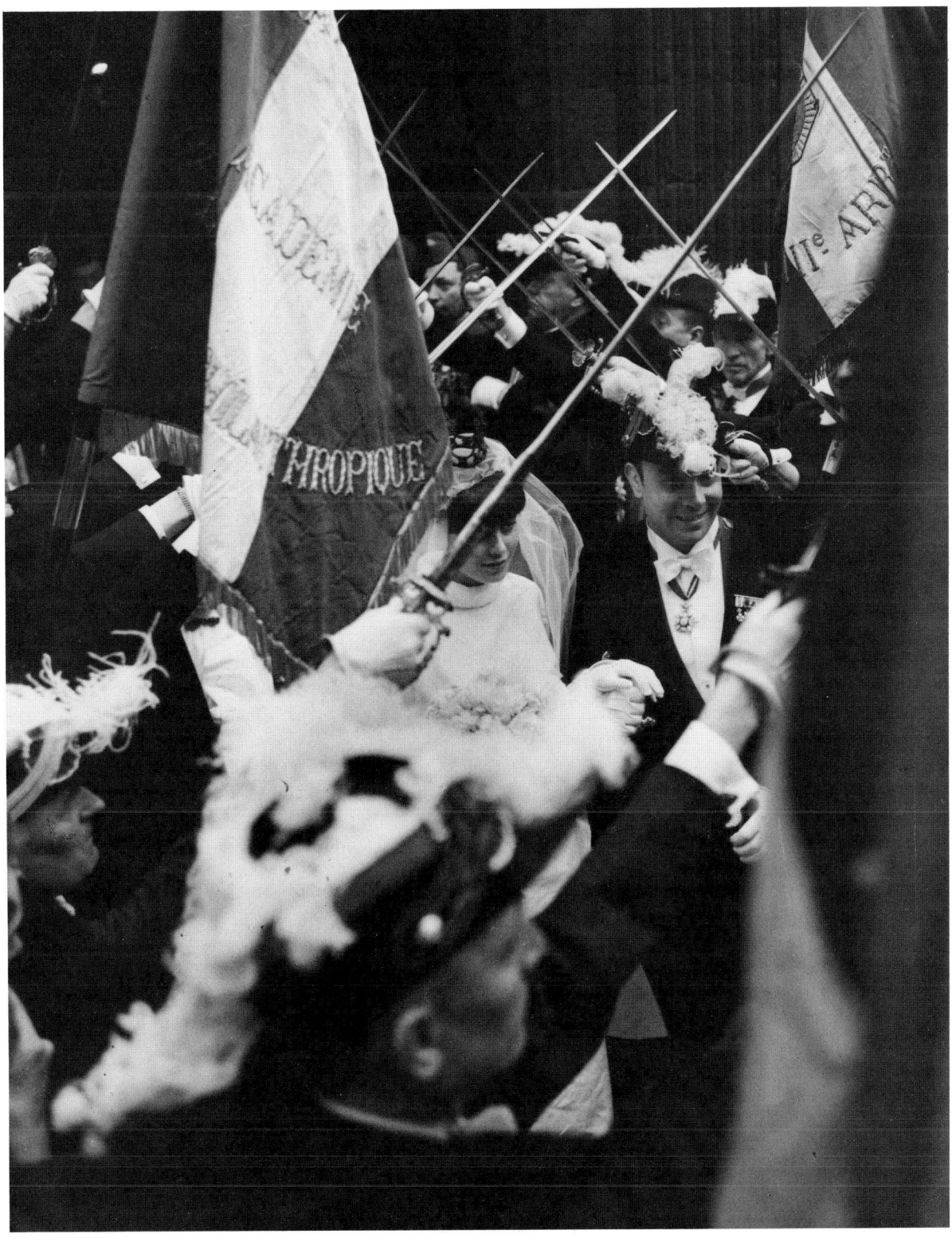

The wedding of Rotraut Uecker and Yves Klein, January 21, 1962

otherworldly, in this world but not of it, a ghostly king among his *chevaliers*. This project was terminated by the very transfiguration which it heralded. Only the cast of Arman was finished; those of Martial Raysse and Claude Pascal remain unpainted plaster. The others were never cast.[141]

Station: in the company of Jean-Pierre Mirouze (who had helped Yves at Gelsenkirchen, and with whom Yves planned to make films), and his oldest friends, Arman and Claude Pascal, the Monogold Vampire makes his will: as Proprietor of the Void, he leaves all immaterial space to the others, as well as the right to make monochromes of International Klein Blue and sign them with his name. Sacramentally, he perpetuates his nature in his disciples.

Station: The Citizen of Infinity is photographed lying as if dead beneath the gold-leafed "Tomb of Space," safely returned to his home in the absolute.

33

They made you pay for the bread
The sky earth water sleep
And the misery
Of your life.

Paul Eluard

In 1961, George Marci, an associate of Yves' dealer, Jean Larcade, arranged for an Italian director to make a film of Yves and his work—a film which would present performances of Anthropometries in a serious light, repairing the damage done by Chabrol in *Les Godelureaux*. The film was directed by Gualtiero Jacopetti, but Yves was filmed by Paolo Cavara, a cameraman with whom he felt a certain bond of trust. He was paid three thousand francs to cover expenses, and in July 1961 performed Anthropometries (ANT SU 8.1 and 8.2) to the accompaniment of the *Monotone Symphony*, a re-creation of the famous performance of March 1960, which had been parodied by Chabrol. For weeks Yves talked about the film, which he was convinced would put his reputation "at the very top." In fact, his critical sense of the situation was askew.

Back in Italy, unknown to Yves, the footage was mutilated. A brief sequence (only five minutes) was taken out of context, giving it a comical air. The *Monotone Symphony* was removed from the soundtrack and replaced by an insipid American popular song. The passage was edited into the film *Mondo Cane*, a vulgar collection of oddities ridiculed by a contemptuous voice-over narration.

Much more negative than Chabrol's film, *Mondo Cane* would also be distributed much more widely.

The film was to preview at Cannes in May 1962. Rotraut, then about six months pregnant, did not attend. Yves flew to Cannes on May 11 or 12 and there met George Marci, with whom, on the evening of the twelfth, he rode to the screening in a taxi. (The legend that he drove down in a blue Rolls Royce and blue tuxedo is not founded on fact, though Yves himself seems to have begun it.) Yves' honest expectation was to witness a film about twenty minutes long, entirely about himself.

So there was Yves, caught at last—crushed in the collision between his private myth and the outside world. Sitting in the darkened theater among people he had expected to impress, he watched himself, a Mandrake the Magician cartoon, absurdly overplaying with gestures of eye and hand which the camera made into comedy. It is difficult for one who admires Yves' career to watch this sequence; his self-importance, his apparent lack of ironic distance, make one almost wish to turn away. (How must it have made *him* feel?) And he was not even the centerpiece of this freak show, but just another trivial absurdity among sequences of people eating insects and drinking turtles' blood.

No better trap was ever devised for a hunted animal! Yves with his uncompromising *imago*, Yves who always had to be first at everything, Yves who would tolerate no resistance, the Master of the Blue Sky, the Proprietor of Color, the Conquistador of the Void! If there was one thing—and there was—which he absolutely could not deal with, it was to be ridiculed. ("His biggest problem—and I think in fact he died of it—was those terrible angers.... It was something that came out from inside of him, and he could not resist it.") ("Softness and softness again... Remember!")

After the showing Yves was "furious and nervous," says George Marci, as he struggled to repress his anger. ("His face would go completely, *completely* white...") Even before the screening he had complained repeatedly that he did not feel well—unusual for Yves, who had once defined art as health. He retired alone to his hotel room to pass a sleepless night fighting his personal nightmares as the Discord Spirit went berserk in his mind. The next morning, when George Marci was to meet him at his hotel, he had disappeared, flying back to Paris alone.

For several days Yves struggled with the Discord Spirit. The sense that his destiny was threatened by ridicule made him increasingly brittle. Unfortunately he had to make a public appearance almost at once, before the Discord Spirit had been exorcised.

Three days after the screening of *Mondo Cane*, Yves was to take part in a public discussion on the relationship of art and industry at the Musée des Arts Décoratifs. Eugène Claudius-Petit, who was presiding, could not have known how delicate Yves' mental and physical condition was.

Not long before, François Mathey of the Musée des Arts Décoratifs had arranged a meeting for Yves, Restany, and Tinguely with an industrialist involved in compressed-air products, to discuss the practical possibilities of the architecture of the air. The businessman had treated them "like fools," remembers Restany—especially Yves, who was the spokesman.

Now, in the debate on art and industry, the memory of this event took Yves in its grip, and he launched a furious diatribe on the stupidity of businessmen. Turning on Restany and Tinguely, who were also members of the discussion panel, he shouted, "You did nothing, you said nothing, you did not come to my aid at all." Claudius-Petit, perceiving him as a child in a tantrum, silenced him peremptorily. "Yves went white as a sheet," says François Mathey. For a Knight of the Grail, with his "strange need of royalty," to be dismissed in midsentence in the midst of his own court was an unbearable humiliation.

After the debate Yves walked with Restany and Rotraut to the opening of the show *Donner à voir* at the Galerie Creuze, where Restany had arranged a New Realist room, including the Portrait Relief of Arman. Yves was silent, strained, and pale. He may already have been in an infarction. At one point he said that he had to sit down, and stopped for a cognac. At the gallery an unfamiliar pain gradually suffused his chest and shoulders; by the end of the opening it was intolerable. He could not walk properly. He was taken to a doctor. There was no ambiguity: his heart was "breaking." Even for one who had tried to eternalize himself, time had become impossible to ignore.[142]

Two days later, sitting "very quietly" on the floor of his almost-empty apartment, he told Claude Pascal that he had nearly died. His eyes had a new expression, solemn, sober, no longer playing a game.

His doctor laid down strict conditions for the continuance of his life—conditions which the Conquistador of the Void could hardly accept. One night as Jean Laffont, manager of La Coupole and long a close friend, walked him to the door after dinner, Yves' frustration burst out. "Everything is going wrong," Yves said. "The doctor says that I've got to

stay home. I'm hardly allowed to move. When I was in Japan I started taking stimulants. It helped me in judo, but look where I am now. You know me. For me to stay lying down is out of the question. It's just impossible."

34

Had I not once a lovely youth, heroic, fabulous, to be written on sheets of gold, good luck and to spare!

Arthur Rimbaud

The end was appropriately mythic, and marked by omens. Death seemed to draw nearer to him, and he seemed to know it. On May 13 Franz Kline died, and Joan Miró, thinking that it was Yves, sent Rotraut a letter of condolence. Yves carried the letter in his pocket, showing it to friends for amusement. On June 2 he wrote to Miró: "Just a little note to show you that I am really alive."

Yet at the same time he seemed to feel that Miró had been prophetically, if not factually, correct: that his time was in fact up. On May 26 he wrote to Larry Rivers, saying, "I have had a heart attack just ten days ago, and I am going to have another one." Death seemed easier to accept than an invalid's life. "It's funny," says Rotraut, "that he had finished everything, just like someone who is getting ready to go on a trip—or to die. He answered all his letters and made sure there was money for me, fixed the name of his son in advance, and designated a godparent [Arman]. Everything was ready." He did not seem frightened or despondent. Death, after all, had always been associated with his deepest and fondest dream, that of flying away from the world, or dematerializing out of it. "He always thought of death as the immaterial," says Rotraut. "It was an obsession with him."

Still, his intention wavered. He believed that his career was at some crucial turning point, but at times was not certain what it was. Was this to be the final performance, death, or merely another turning point along the way? Late in May he broke off with the dealer Larcade, as once he had abruptly left Iris Clert, and on June 4, two days before his death, he dropped by Karl Flinker's gallery unannounced, asking to talk. They made a dinner appointment for June 7.

The next day Yves met Edouard Adam and complained, as he had to others, about the effect of stimulants on his health and the severity of his doctor's advice: "He wants me to relax my efforts; he wants me to paint miniatures, I who wish only to paint space! It is impossible!"

In fact he was deeply depressed by the breakdown of his health and the impossible instructions of his doctor. That night, as he sat in La Coupole with Rotraut, "he had the same dark sad eyes that I had seen when he was about to go to Gelsenkirchen and was telling me that he was going to die [because of *Le Vide*]. He had the same eyes, almost filled with tears. 'Yves,' I said, 'it's strange; you have the same look you had that day'; and then the tears did come out. When we left, I had the sensation that he was being threatened every moment; as we walked back to the apartment I kept turning around as if someone were about to attack him with a knife."

And indeed someone or something seemed to be on Yves' trail that night. "About three or four o'clock in the morning," Rotraut recalls, "there was a knock at the door. Yves said, 'That's strange. Go see who it is.' And it was a German architect or something, no one we knew, who wanted to meet Yves. I didn't let him in." The anonymous predawn summons reverberated like an omen in the nearly empty apartment.

The next morning another unaccustomed visitor arrived. Yves' doctor had phoned Fred Klein to inform him of the gravity of Yves' condition, and Fred made a rare visit to his son's apartment to communicate his concern. He advised Yves to leave at once for a vacation in the south of France. But Yves, of course, had appointments to keep. When his father left he went to lunch with Jean Larcade, and it seemed that a reconciliation between them was approaching. Both excited and confused by his dilemma, Yves ate heavily and drank wine, then said that he had to go home and rest for several hours, as his doctor had advised. At home, finding the elevator broken, he climbed the stairs.

Yet still he did not rest immediately, but fretted for a while over the question of how, considering the state of his health, his career could continue. Rather than make "miniatures," as he contemptuously said, he would concentrate on immaterial works, to relieve himself of the physical labor which his doctor warned him he would not survive. For a moment the idea pleased him, as it rid him at last of the need for a separate studio, which had always been financially out of reach and a source of great frustration. He stood looking at a red monochrome hanging on the wall. "From now on the whole world will be my studio," he said in his last claim to omnipotence, his last appropriation of the universe into his art, "and I will make only immaterial works."

But meanwhile, if he was not allowed to work,

he could at least, as his father had suggested, go on a vacation. A friend came by, and Yves asked him to drive his car to Nice while he and Rotraut took a plane, since the doctor had said that driving was too strenuous for him. But even as the arrangement was being made, there was another call to the doctor, who said that he absolutely must not go on a vacation or indeed go anywhere. He was only to "rest." The Conquistador of the Void was to sit like a tame bird and make no further efforts to fly.

When he and Rotraut were alone, he seemed at last ready to "rest." "He was sitting on the bed and now he stretched out. He was lying stretched out on the bed and I blew a kiss to him and said, 'I love you,' as I often did. He said, 'Don't say that; never say that,' which he had never said before....Then in a moment he said, 'Call the doctor; I feel strange.' " When she left the room to phone, the "strange" feeling spread quickly through his entire being. His heart opened up, the "absolute love" of the Void at last rushing in, while something of him, some gold vibration or fiery paradox, rushed out ("free at last!"), to fly weightlessly, in an instant, beyond the sky.

When she returned, his body lay still in a smear of vomit on the bed. It was about six o'clock in the evening, five weeks after Yves' thirty-fourth birthday. Arman, Protector of Animals, arrived minutes later and helped tend to the body.

("When I was told that he had died," says Tinguely, "I was very suspicious. I thought it was one of those extraordinary things he used to put over on us. Because he had always talked about two things: he talked about levitation, and he talked about just vanishing.")

35

Thy mother the sky reaches forth her arms to thee.
Now thou art one with thy mother the sky.

Egyptian hymn at the pharaoh's death

Station: In the newspaper *Dimanche*, Yves foresees his death as brought on by the utter loneliness and isolation of being not an ordinary person but a myth. On a certain day, at a certain hour, every citizen of France goes indoors. Streets, countryside, public squares are absolutely empty. But Yves alone is taken up violently by his fellow men and thrust, against his will, out of doors. Totally alone, unseen by human eyes, he begins to cease to exist as he walks through the empty streets. Soon he has disappeared altogether — and the citizens of France,

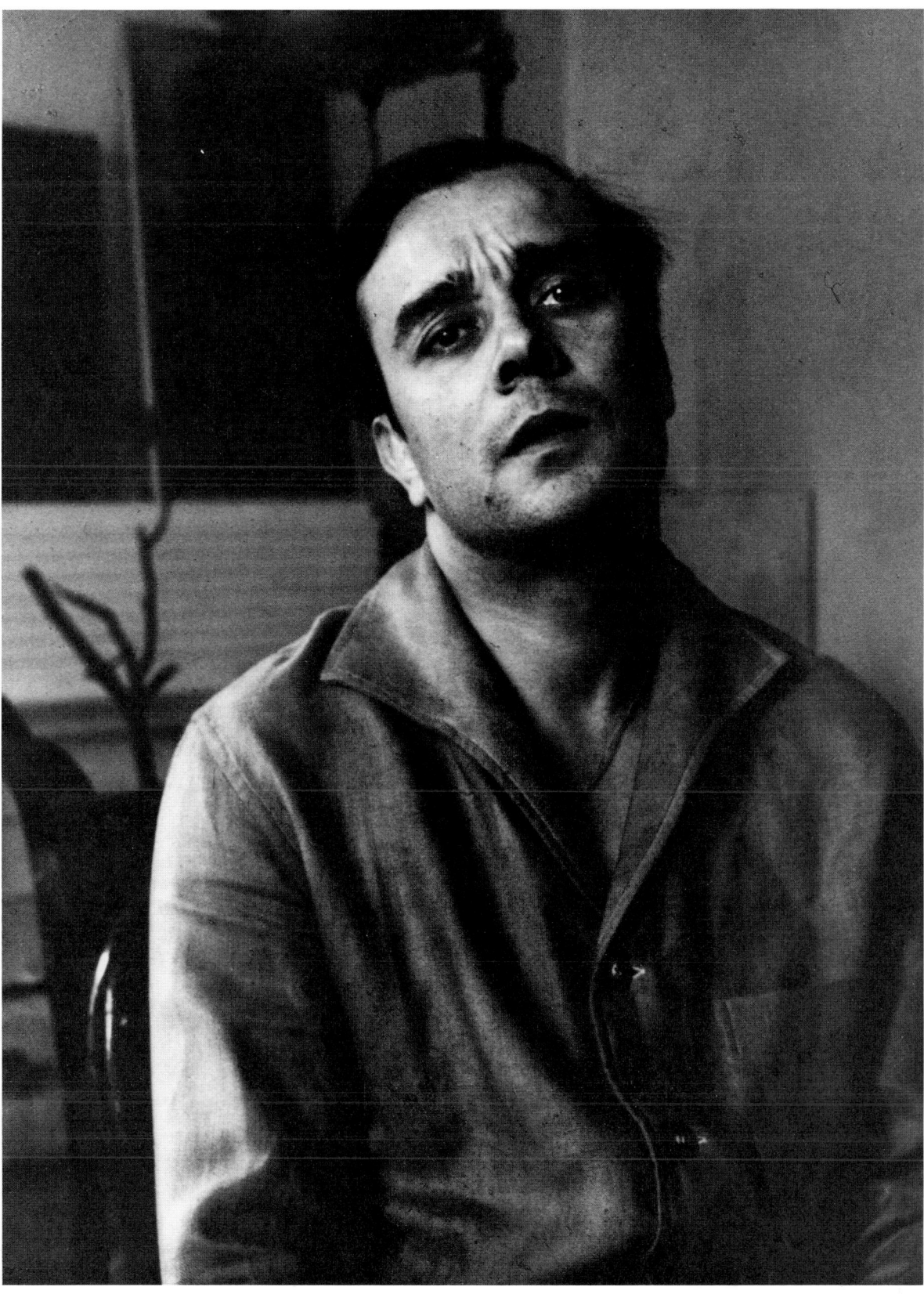

Yves Klein shortly before his death, 1962

opening their doors, resume life again.

His constantly shifting approach to the Void, marked by the Stations or Labors, ended in this desolate separation from mankind: Yves the little Captain, walking from the forest, his arms filled with mimosa blossoms; Yves flying from the summer terrace through the moon; Yves signing his name on the far side of the sky; Yves in crusader's costume, the Champion of Color, ready to free us all from the entanglements of line; Yves, his magnetic eyes glowing, shaping pure space in the empty gallery; Yves selling zones of the Void (were they *really* his to sell?), pursuing the Great Work through the four elements toward Prime Matter, leashing destructive fire (how long would it stay tame?); Yves delighting to be the warlock-master of naked young women who groveled in slime at his feet; Yves leaping into the Void, grinning with vampire teeth, lying in the Tomb of Space; Yves fading into thin air as he walks alone through deserted streets, fading…fading…finally, gone.

("From now on I will make *only* immaterial works!")

These gestures still rustle with life in our minds. It is their very smallness which writes them in letters of gold. Compacted into real moments of an individual life, the most fundamental questions gazed out in all honesty. Universals forced their way through his small density and opened spaces in it, zeros of meaning, question marks.

For Yves, art, like spiritual ascesis, meant an attempt to eradicate the self in favor of a higher principle which perhaps could be induced to flow through the gutted channel. It was a path to the blue deep from which all gods and angels arose or descended or were temporarily and apparitionally constituted like clouds. His works were pointers toward the "innermost," icons of the abyss within oneself and each thing, whereby one might plummet through to infinity.

Obviously his works contributed greatly toward giving direction to the art of the sixties and after — monochrome painting, environmental sculpture, nonstatic art, conceptual art, minimal art, new media, mixed media — but it is the radical purity of his endeavor, granting all its problems and imperfections, that is most impressive. He gave both a body and a voice to absolutist art, and as if that were not enough, he gave it a myth too. His attempts to absorb universal meaning into his public image through symbolic acts must be seen as heroic if, like much heroism, fatal.

Edward Lucie-Smith, among critics, seems to have fairly appraised his career:

> I do believe that Klein was perfectly sincere and serious in what he did, and I do believe, in addition, that what he did was pointful rather than pointless. Klein also wanted to cleanse the temple; he wanted to rob art of the materialism (which he equated with materiality) which seemed to him to corrupt it, to weight it down…. Heroes are commonly thought of as men whose actions make some kind of statement, stress a moral value. By this definition, Klein was certainly a hero of sorts.

And these lines of Mallarmé (whose blank page gobbled Yves up) may stand as his epitaph:

> Gilt by the chaste dawn of the Infinite,
>   I admire myself, see me as angel! I die, I adore
> —may the glass be art, may it be mysticity—
> to be reborn, with my dreams a crown for me,
> in the anterior sky where beauty flowers.
>   But, alas, Here-below is master, his intimacy
> sickens me sometimes in this certain shelter,
> and the dirty vomit of Stupidity
> makes me hold my nose before the azure.
>   Are there ways, O self who know asperity,
> to break the crystal outraged by this monster
> and to escape, on these wings without feathers,
> —at the risk of falling throughout eternity?[143]

36

*Let us contemplate undazed
the extent of my innocence.*

Arthur Rimbaud

Language is never innocent.

Roland Barthes

"The function of writing," says Roland Barthes, "is to maintain a clear conscience."[144] The author's "self" is validated by the imposition upon it, as a kind of mask, of a literary sign to which the writer entrusts his claims of identity. It is an attempt to create oneself anew through a style of words.

Yves Klein was unusually open or direct (or naïve) in the act of entrusting himself, for definition, to a literary sign. For various reasons less naïve and more cunning, he defused his primary sign—that of the occult initiate—by interpenetrating it with the sign of the ironist, which in turn he defused by leading it back into the first, as the laugh of the master who is above it all.

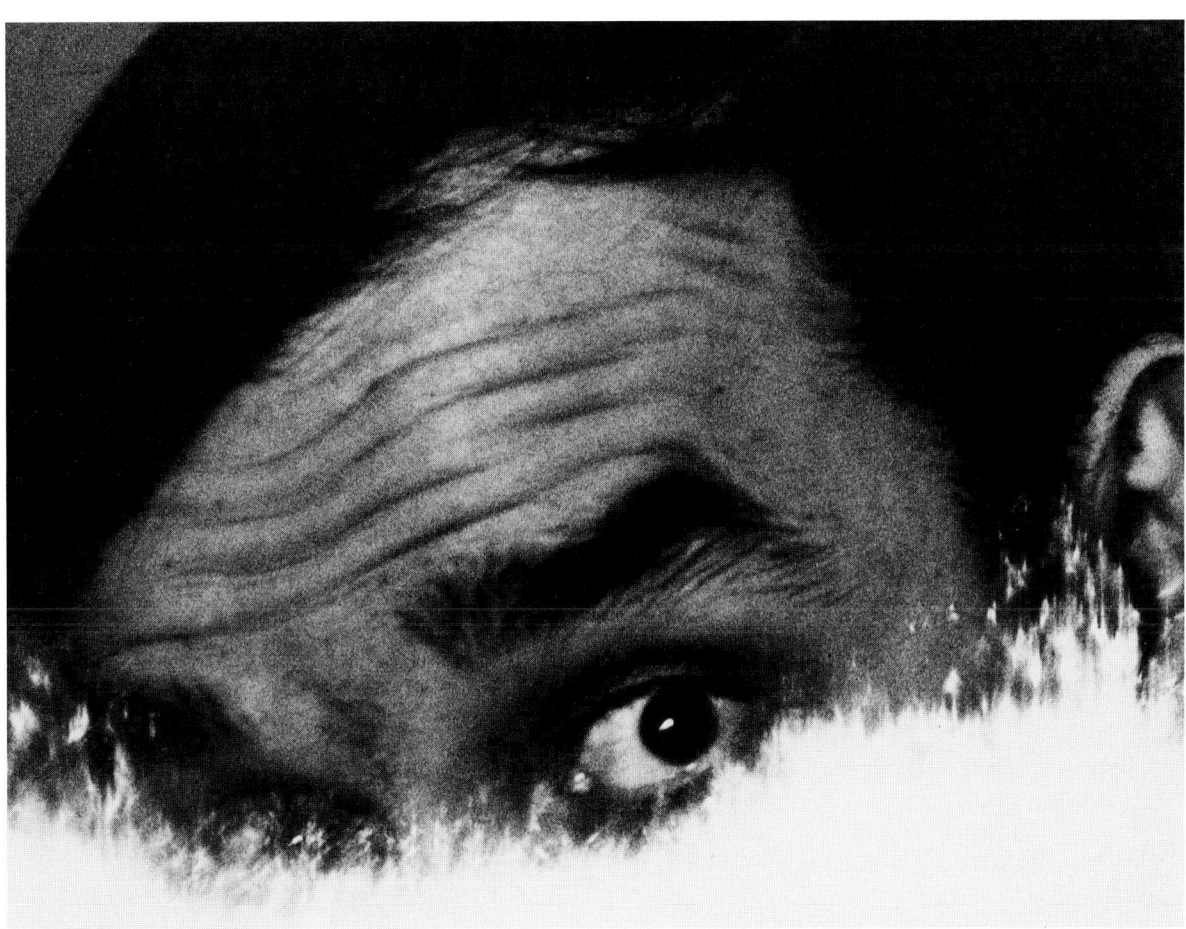

This system of reciprocally confirming and canceling signs, designed to give space in which to operate as an unashamed self, seems to have provided little real freedom. There are various views about what Yves would have done if he had lived longer. Restany suggested that he would have pursued the immaterial architecture and related technological prophecies; Arman, that he would have gone into politics; Rotraut, the theater; to George Marci he declared his intention to "paint" with a movie camera. Perhaps his unrelentingly contradictory and creative character would have produced some hitherto undefined occupation involving these activities and more. But in any case it seems certain that he would have had to escape from his myth somehow, to "live it down," to dissociate himself from the literary sign system which, designed as a solution, became a cul-de-sac. The belief that an artist can fashion himself in a form of human perfection as he can fashion an inanimate art material seems ill-founded. He is already fashioned. The marks of early experience cannot be gessoed over. Under pressure of frustration the rigorous requirements of the claim of personal perfection drift into the zone of *sprezzatura*.[145]

Various reductionist models—mostly involving overcompensation for deficiencies of early experience—are available for Yves' motivation in undertaking his mythic project. On top of this is a certain false expectation arising from the tradition of grace—of Saul's instant and permanent transformation into Paul—which implies that peak experiences are permanent. Yves had the misfortune not merely to regard his own early peak experiences as signs of permanent transformation, but even to advertise them as such.

But, questions of personal motivation aside, one must acknowledge his accomplishment. There is no doubt that he created a myth—a variant, an instantiation, of a basic mythic structure—and that his myth must be regarded as an art work. The famous photographs—the Champion of Color, the Leap into the Void—present to us a mythological character ritually garbed in the vestments of art as he performs his mythological Labors. The work overall is finished, subtle, humorous, daring, and powerful.

Disraeli aptly described dandies as "princes of a fantasy world,"[146] and the peculiarly French combination of romanticism, mysticism, and dandyism offers a tradition for Yves. Balzac, Barbey d'Aurevilly, Baudelaire, and Sartre cumulatively described dandyism as a type of transcendental spirituality;[147] Barbey in particular identified the dandy as the fore-

most of artists, *because his life is his art*. Indeed, insofar as the dandy creates himself, he reflects the activity of an absolute; he abrogates time and causality and transcends their conditions. Dandyism at all levels involves "perpetual contradiction and ambiguity" as one of its constants.[148]

Yves' love of costumes and public posturing, his fastidiousness, his pretense of complete self-control, his constant advertisement of himself as an art work or a perfect being, his desire to incorporate into his character the most enormous contradictions, are all traits related to the transcendental dandyism of which Barbey, Baudelaire, and Sartre wrote. But Yves expanded this tradition into even more difficult realms and claims by his incorporation of the Japanese posturing of the samurai (to avoid the association of dandyism with homosexuality?), by his marriage and procreation (both rigorously excluded from pure dandyism), and above all by the incorporation of a full-scale hero myth which he feigned to act out and pretended to want others to take seriously. The difficulty of this multifaceted undertaking, combined with the production of a major body of external art works, can hardly be overestimated.

Schelling, spokesman for the romantic transcendentalist aesthetic, defined art as "the resolution of an infinite contradiction in a finite product."[149] Yves, whose view of art was similar, attempted to make *himself* the finite object within which infinite forces strain to annihilate one another, to bring them directly into his own body and mind in an attempt at perfection which resembles religious self-sacrifice.

The minor adjustments of the outer record which were necessary to fulfill this program are trivial. They are a small price for the remarkable image which he offered up, as a free gift, with such simplicity and curiosity. The maintenance of so elaborate and excessive a pose was a kind of ravaging ascesis. There is some merit to the view, enunciated occasionally, that for Yves early death was a solution.

In Yves' body of work as a whole, the myth may be viewed either as one artifact among many, underscoring the astonishing diversity of materials and genres he worked in, or as a matrix within which the other works exist and by which they are given a supererogatory thematic coherence. More than a single mythologem is involved. Restany has compared Yves to both Prometheus and Achilles.[150] The latter exemplum is the less accurate (except for the famous childishness of the perpetually eighteen-year-old hero); the former is of limited relevance.

The essential structure of Yves' myth is magical flight, or ascension, or, in its mentalist (Platonic) version, magical vision, seeing into the realm of Forms. In terms of art, the artist becomes a hierophant, opening the vision of Reality to all; as Schelling said, "When a great painting comes into being, it is as though the invisible curtain that separates the real from the ideal world is raised."[151] Whether by flight, by vision, or by expansion into oneness with space, the hero of such a myth establishes in his own person a symbolic link between above and below, suggesting a fructifying exchange of sacred power.

Yves' myth, energized by the antitheses material/immaterial, earth/sky, line/color, and by the mediating structures of magical flight and dematerialization, is as ancient as the "Bird-Man" of Lascaux. It refracts into many aspects hinted at by Yves' rich and contradictory nature, which contains microcosmically the strata of human history. A shamanic level is intimated by the concrete imagery of flying to the sky, and by the interest in taboo materials such as blood; the Neolithic spirituality of the Dying God is disclosed in Yves' sacramental theory of painting; in his love of royalty and flight, the Bronze Age king who returns to the far sky, as in Egyptian afterlife myth the pharaoh presides over the court of Re— Osiris among the circumpolar stars. But Yves' myth is most closely paralleled in the Orphic structure of descent from the sky and hope to reascend there through ascetic and magical means. In Persian messianism and Christianity, the being from beyond the sky descends in order to lead others after him in his reascent. This motif is echoed in the alchemical pattern of sublimation and precipitation, and is clearly stated by Yves in *Dimanche*.

In terms of literary genre-criticism Yves' myth has various associations, not least the inevitable resonance with Aristotle's definition of the tragic flaw. "The great majority of tragic heroes," says Northrop Frye, "do possess hybris, a proud, passionate, obsessed or soaring mind which brings about a morally intelligible downfall....The tragic hero usually belongs...to the *alazon* group, an imposter in the sense that he is self-deceived, or made dizzy by hybris."[152]

When Yves' life-myth is regarded as a series of symbolic tableaux, it shows affinities to the medieval procession or pageant and the related miracle and passion plays. When viewed from the hostile point of view of those who awaited his downfall, he swaggers like the *miles gloriosus*.

It is remarkable that the literary genres to which Yves' life bears the least resemblance are the most realistic ones, the novel and the history. His quick and sensitive mind picked up and resonated to every motif in the zone of the quest and the ascent, while attempting to edit out all that was soiled with history and origins.

To quote Tinguely once more: "It was a dream he was living. And he lived it altogether truly. He was a true poet."

Notes

1. In *Yves Klein,* catalogue of exhibition at the Jewish Museum, New York City, 1967, pp. 4, 7 (hereafter "Jewish Museum cat.").

2. Ibid., p. 16.

3. In *Yves Klein,* catalogue of exhibition at the Tate Gallery, London, 1974, p. 8.

4. Giuliano Martano, *Yves Klein, Il Mistero Ostentato* (Turin: Martano Editore, 1970), p. 154.

5. Paul Wember, *Yves Klein* (Cologne: Verlag DuMont Schauberg, 1969), p. 45.

6. Jewish Museum cat., p. 11.

7. "Due to the Fact That," in *Yves Klein,* catalogue of exhibition at the Alexandre Iolas Gallery, New York, 1962. Translated by Klein in collaboration with Neil Levine and John Archambault in spring, 1961.

8. Ibid.

9. "Truth Becomes Reality" (printed elsewhere in this catalogue).

10. Roland Barthes, *Mythologies* (New York: Hill and Wang, 1972), p. 142.

11. Hans-Georg Gadamer, *Wahrheit und Methode: Grundzüge einer philosophischen Hermeneutik* (Tübingen: J. C. B. Mohr, 1960), p. 104.

12. In the late forties Klein became interested in astrology and cast some horoscopes. This in itself makes his own horoscope relevant, and it was interpreted for researcher Virginie de Caumont on March 16, 1981, by one M. Berthon. The most salient feature he noticed was precisely the "temperamental duality" between the sun sign, Taurus, and the ascendant sign, Gemini, which he describes as "very contradictory signs." "Taurus is a patient worker,...[but] Gemini always wants to give the impression of playing, of irony, of being at ease....I think there was a kind of humor in his lifestyle but this humor was not free: it leaned on...the Taurean universe, which is...slow, patient, industrious.... He had two personalities....[In addition] a triplicity of fire gives much exuberance, vitality, and self-confidence; and alongside it ... there is Saturn squared with Mars in opposition to the ascendant; this is a cyclo-thymic or manic-depressive situation, with periods of low energy, depression, inhibition. At one moment one is dealing with a strong man, sure of himself,...at other moments a depressed man, who is restless,...in anguish, who believes that the world is lost, that he is dying, and so forth.... The emotional relationships of his life were far from simple.... At the amorous level I think he must have had many problems.... In order to love intensely he needs anguish, drama, a kind of little cinema....He was able to live intensely because he was a Taurus and as such was inside the role; but at the same time he was able, as a Gemini, to disengage himself from the role and change the game. He was a double man....He is capable of speaking with ease, and at the same time is profoundly introverted."

13. References to interviews will be made by the name of the interviewee, in this case Bernadette Allain. Interviews have been conducted by me, by Dominique de Menil, by Benedicte Pesle, and by Virginie de Caumont, as follows: Bernadette Allain, May 22, 1980, Paris. Rotraut Klein-Moquay, June 30, 1977, Paris; May 25, 1979, Houston; March 26, 1981, Paris. Claude Pascal, July 3, 1977, March 26 and May 4, 1981, Paris. Arman, December 29, 1977, New York; May 27, 1979, Houston; January 15, 1981, Paris. Rose Raymond Taramasco Gasperini, June 30, 1980, April 16 and 29, 1981, Nice. Marie Raymond, June 10, 1980, and April 17, 1981,

Paris. Fred Klein (by telephone), December 12, 1980, Paris. Pierre Restany, June 28 and December 26, 1980, April 30, 1981, Paris. François Mathey, April 3, 1980, Paris. Jean Tinguely, June 17, 1980, Paris. Claude Parent, July 1, 1980, Paris. Edouard Adam, February 24, 1981, Paris. Karl Flinker, March 7, 1981, Paris. Ed Moses, February 26, 1981, Los Angeles. Iris Clert, March 10, 1981, Paris. Jean Larcade, March 26, 1981, Paris. Tarica, March 20, 1981, Paris. Marcel Boulois, May 2, 1981, Paris. Jean Laffont, May 6, 1981, Paris. George Marci (by telephone), June 14, 1981. Walter Hopps, October 13, 1981, Houston.

14. Bernadette Allain.

15. In *Yves Klein,* catalogue of exhibition at the Palais des Beaux-Arts, Brussels, 1966.

16. Claude Pascal.

17. The Rosicrucian Society of Oceanside, California, should be distinguished from the Rosicrucian Order (or AMORC); it became a separate organization at about the turn of the century.

18. The essay "Yves Klein and Rosicrucianism," printed elsewhere in this catalogue, documents this influence in detail. Only broad outlines will be mentioned here.

19. St-John Perse, *Winds,* trans. Hugh Chisholm (New York: Bollingen, 1953), p. 210.

20. Bernadette Allain.

21. The division into animal, vegetable, and mineral realms came from Heindel. Arman recalls that they patterned the event after the story in Homer (*Iliad* V. 185 ff.).

22. Arman.

23. *The Poetics of Space,* trans. Maria Jolas (Boston: Beacon, 1969), p. 183.

24. "Discourse on the Occasion of Tinguely's Exhibition in Düsseldorf, January 1959" (printed elsewhere in this catalogue).

25. *Dimanche, the Newspaper of a Single Day,* p. 1, Klein's tour de force imitation newspaper that he submitted to the Paris Festival d'Art d'Avant-garde, 1960 (photographically reproduced elsewhere in this catalogue).

26. "Du vertige au prestige" (printed elsewhere in this catalogue).

27. *Myths, Rites, and Symbols: A Mircea Eliade Reader,* 2 vols., ed. W. C. Beane and W. G. Doty (New York: Harper and Row, 1975), II:354.

28. Robert Savage, on Old Brompton Road.

29. St-John Perse, *Winds,* p. 190.

30. MS V 2288: "Compte rendu de l'exposition en collaboration avec Jean Tinguely chez Iris Clert," Klein archive, Documentation Arts Plastiques, Musée National d'Art Moderne, Centre National d'Art et de Culture Georges Pompidou, Paris (hereafter "Klein archive").

31. "Discourse on the Occasion of Tinguely's Exhibition."

32. "Dissolve the body and coagulate the spirit," Nicolas Valois, alchemist. Cited in Stanislas K. De Rola, *Alchemy, the Secret Art* (New York: Bounty, 1973), p. 17.

33. Klein archive.

34. This is the only entry which specifies the year of writing, and it is not consistent with the day-date correlations on all the entries: July 14, for example, was a Friday in 1950, a Saturday in 1951. In other words, either Klein specified the wrong year in the entry of August 5, or the wrong (by one digit) date of the month in *all* the entries. The latter assumption is almost certainly correct, as an abundance of external evidence shows. The same error occurs in a letter Klein wrote on July 11 but is corrected in his letter of July 21 (see n. 37 below).

35. Klein archive. My translation.

36. Ibid.

37. Klein's relatives generously provided many personal letters from him for photocopying. Copies of all letters cited in this essay are in the author's archive.

38. April 20, 1952.

39. Rough draft of letter, November 1951, Klein archive.

40. The exact departure date is not known, but seems to have been either August 22 or 23.

41. Mr. Shinichi Segi of Tokyo (interviewed by Jean-Yves Mock of the Centre Georges Pompidou in August 1980), met Klein at the exhibition of his parents' works at the Bridgestone Gallery, Tokyo, and attended the private showing of monochromes at Klein's apartment. He notes that Klein employed only primary colors in these pieces, a practice which he would later return to.

42. A photocopy of the Japanese article, provided by Marie Raymond, is now in the author's archive.

43. Letter to Rose Raymond Gasperini, December 7, 1953.

44. Klein was later to complain (to Marcel Boulois, Jean Laffont, Edouard Adam, and others) that these stimulants had weakened his heart. Edouard Adam recalls Klein taking amphetamines "in connection with judo performances" after his return from Japan. Marcel Boulois agrees, adding that "all students took Benzedrine in those days." Rose Raymond recalls that Klein frequently took Maxiton, an amphetamine product. Rotraut Klein-Moquay recalls that "Yves had some capsules which he always took when he was tired or starting to work. He would say that they were a mixture of calcium and something. I don't know who gave him these capsules; he always had them." It would be ill-advised to ignore the influence which this practice may have had on his lifestyle. Claude Pascal, in speaking of the years in which he knew Klein most intimately (1948–52), recalls that Klein slept a good deal—usually eight, sometimes nine or ten hours a night. But those who knew him after his return from Japan declare unanimously that he slept very little. George Marci says: "That boy never slept. I would leave him, to go home to bed, at eleven at night, and when I met him the next morning at eight or nine he would tell me all the things he had done in the meantime." Tinguely agrees, saying that Klein complained often that he was tormented by lack of sleep. Rotraut Klein-Moquay recalls that usually when she awakened in the night Klein would already be awake and out of bed.

45. The Kodokan Institute states that "he was confirmed 4th dan as of December 12[?], 1953." Letter to author, October 27, 1980, from Ichiro Abe, International Division, Kodokan Judo Institute, Tokyo.

46. Klein archive.

47. Actually Klein's competence in comparison with the members of the Federation cannot be evaluated precisely. Arman and Bernadette Allain feel that for a year or two after returning from Japan he was probably the best in France. But Marcel Boulois, a judo teacher himself, says: "Yves was a mediocre *judoka*. There were members of the Federation who, although they were only first *dan*, were five times better than he was."

48. The preface of blank, paragraphed lines was, says Claude Pascal, Klein's idea, and Klein later explained it in terms of heraldry: "You know that horizontal lines in heraldry mean 'blue.'...At the time I did not know that, and the coincidence is curious" (MS I 2174, Klein archive: fragments of an interview of Klein by Pierre Restany).

49. Nan Rosenthal [Piene] was, as far as I know, the first to focus critical attention on this pamphlet and to recognize it as not precisely a fraud but a trick. See "The Blue World of Yves Klein," Ph.D. dissertation, Harvard University, 1976, pp. 81–87. This study pursues, often with interesting results, an analysis of Klein's deliberate ambiguity similar to that of Ronald Hunt in "Yves Klein," *Artforum* (January 1967), pp. 33–37.

50. In *Yves Klein, Paintings, Reliefs, Sculptures* (Belgrade: Museum of Contemporary Arts, 1971), translated from Serbo-Croatian by Goran Milutinovic for the Institute for the Arts, Rice University, Houston, Texas.

51. Edouard Adam.

52. "La Minute de vérité"; the exhibition, which ran from February 21 to March 7, was titled *Yves: Propositions monochromes.*

53. Klein patented his distinctive blue in May 1960, as International Klein Blue. It has sometimes been described as cobalt; visually it is somewhere between ultramarine and cobalt, but closer to the former. The Klein archive contains a typescript of the formula, as follows: "Médium fixatif de l'IKB./ 1 kilo 200 Rhodopas (c'est un produit pâteux) M A (Rhône poulenc) (Chlorure de Vinyle)/ 2 kilo 200 Alcool Ethylique. 95% Industriel. Dénaturé/ 0 kilo 600 Acetate d' Ethyle./ [total:] 4 kilo 000/ Mélanger à froid/ en agitant énergiquement/ ne jamais chauffer à feu nu. Danger." Then, in Klein's handwriting: "700 kg Outremer Blue Pur/ ref 1311."

54. So Sheldon Nodelman speaks of Stella's paintings, in *Marden, Novros, Rothko: Painting in the Age of Actuality* (Seattle: University of Washington Press for the Institute for the Arts, Rice University, 1978), p. 13.

55. "The Monochrome Adventure" is a group of Klein's writings which he collected for publication as a book; his death aborted the project. The typescript is in the Klein archive. Selections from the text are printed elsewhere in this catalogue.

56. *Marden, Novros, Rothko*, p. 65

57. Klein also asserted "the glaring obviousness of my paternity of the monochrome in the twentieth century." In fact, it was not all that obvious. Miro's blue monochrome of 1925 may be regarded as an exception. But around 1950 a number of artists had seen that twentieth-century painting was headed toward the monochrome as one of its ultimate expressions. In 1951 Rauschenberg exhibited white monochromes; in 1953 Reinhardt confined himself to a monochrome style. Others were quick to follow.

58. The complete text of "The War" was published in *Dimanche* in 1960; selections from this essay are printed elsewhere in this catalogue.

59. Ibid.

60. *The Journal of Eugène Delacroix*, trans. Walter Pach (New York: Crown, 1948), entry for October 5, 1882.

61. "The War."

62. "The Monochrome Adventure."

63. Ibid.

64. Quoted by Klein in "The War."

65. Ibid.

66. Letter 459; quoted by Klein in "The War."

67. *The Poetics of Reverie*, trans. Daniel Russell (Boston: Beacon, 1969), pp. 72–73.

68. Iris Clert, François Mathey, etc.

69. *Iris-Time (L'Artventure)* (Paris: Editions Denoël, 1978), pp. 146–47.

70. *Donald Judd, Complete Writings, 1959–1975* (New York: New York University Press, 1978), p. 68.

71. Klein added this text to the photograph in his scrapbook; it may be compared to a speech balloon in a cartoon panel.

72. "Preparation and Presentation of the Exhibition of 28 April 1958" (printed elsewhere in this catalogue).

73. *Iris-Time*, p. 155. The record is strangely confused on the question of how many visitors entered at a time; Klein says ten, Iris Clert three, Claude Pascal five.

74. Ibid., p. 156.

75. *Le Dépassement de la problématique de l'art* (La Louvière: Editions de Montbliart, 1959); Rotraut Klein-Moquay.

76. The idea appears repeatedly in Klein's writings, for example in the essay "Preparation and Presentation of the Exhibition of 28 April 1958."

77. *Being and Nothingness*, trans. Hazel E. Barnes (New York: Philosophical Library, 1956), pp. 600–603.

78. The Klein archive contains the following books by Bachelard: *L'Eau et les rêves* (Paris: José Corti, 1942); *La Terre et les rêveries de la volonté* (Paris: José Corti, 1948); *La Terre et les rêveries du repos* (Paris: José Corti, 1948); *La Philosophie du non* (Paris: Presses Universitaires de France, 1949); *La Dialectique de la durée* (Paris: Presses Universitaires de France, 1950); *La Formation de l'esprit scientifique* (Paris: Librairie Philosophique J. Vrin, 1957); and *La Poétique de l'espace* (Paris: Presses Universitaires de France, 1958). The Klein archive contained, in July 1977, six copies of the last-named work. Although the archive contained no copy of *La Psychanalyse du feu* (Paris: Gallimard, 1949), or of *L'Air et les songes* (Paris: José Corti, 1943), it is certain from other evidence that Klein read them.

79. *On Poetic Imagination and Reverie*, trans. C. Gaudin (New York: Library of Liberal Arts, 1971), p. 23.

80. *Myths, Rites, and Symbols: A Mircea Eliade Reader*, I:195.

81. *The Psychoanalysis of Fire*, trans. Alan C. M. Ross (Boston: Beacon, 1964), p. 111.

82. "Due to the Fact That."

83. *Psychoanalysis of Fire*, p. 111.

84. "Truth Becomes Reality."

85. *Dépassement.*

86. *Psychoanalysis of Fire*, p. 112.

87. Ibid., pp. 100–101; see also *Poetics of Space*, p. xxv, and *Poetics of Reverie*, p. 58.

88. "Du vertige au prestige."

89. "The War."

90. *On Poetic Imagination and Reverie*, p. 23.

91. "Les Vrais Créateurs," Klein archive.

92. *Psychoanalysis of Fire*, p. 112. Prometheus stole fire from heaven; Empedocles leapt into the mouth of the active volcano Mount Aetna.

93. Klein archive.

94. Ibid.

95. See MSS V 2288 and C 2310, Klein archive: "Compte rendu de l'exposition en collaboration avec Jean Tinguely chez Iris Clert," and Iris Clert's statement, "A la suite d'une série de terribles malentendus." In 1967 Tinguely described Klein as "a beautiful megalomaniac,...the best friend and best provocateur I have ever encountered" (Martano, *Mistero*, p. 110).

96. Paris: Librairie Hachette, 1974.

97. *Dépassement.*

98. Jean Tinguely.

99. *Iris-Time*, p. 175.

100. Ibid.

101. "The Void belongs to me": letter to a M. Yamazaki, February 15, 1960, typescript in Klein archive; "The Monochrome Adventure."

102. "The Monochrome Adventure."

103. Ibid.

104. Ibid.

105. *Iris-Time*, p. 185.

106. Peppino Palazzoli, director of the Galleria Apollinaire in Milan, where the Blue Epoch had been inaugurated in 1957.

107. Klein archive.

108. Geber, *The Sum of Perfection*, cited in E. J. Holmyard, *Alchemy* (Baltimore: Penguin, 1957), pp. 134, 140.

109. See "Ritual for the Relinquishment of the Immaterial Pictorial Sensibility Zones," quoted in full in Nan Rosenthal's essay in this catalogue.

110. *Iris-Time*, p. 192.

111. *L'Air et les songes*, p. 194.

112. Klein's Sorbonne lecture was made into two long-playing records titled *Conférences à la Sorbonne, 3 juin 1959* (Paris: RPM, n.d.).

113. *L'Air et les songes*, p. 188.

114. Ibid., p. 191.

115. Compare Klein's wording in *Dépassement*, p. 19: "the real life in which a man no longer thinks he is the center of the universe, but the universe is the center of man." Whereas the substance of Klein's writings is primarily from Heindel, his style contains many artful echoes of Bachelard.

116. It is worth noting that the idea is actually very ancient; it had occurred in the context of the Greco-Egyptian mystery religions which lie at some remove in the background of Rosicrucianism. Pliny the Elder wrote (XXXIV.xlii [148]):

    The architect Timochares had begun to use lodestone [magnetic oxide of iron] for constructing the vaulting in the Temple of Arsinoë at Alexandria, so that the iron statue contained in it might have the appearance of being suspended in mid-air; but the project was interrupted by his own death and that of King Ptolemaus, who had ordered the work to be done in honor of his sister.

    Klein and Takis also planned to use magnets.

117. "Criticism and the Experience of Interiority," in *The Structuralist Controversy*, ed. Richard Macksey and Eugenio Donato (Baltimore: Johns Hopkins University Press, 1972), p. 59.

118. *Inner and Outer Space*, catalogue of exhibition at the Moderna Museet, Stockholm, 1966.

119. "Truth Becomes Reality."

120. Ibid. The "Cosmogonies" are another case of convergence of Heindel and Bachelard. The basis in Heindel is discussed in the essay "Yves Klein and Rosicrucianism." In Bachelard (*Poetics of Space*, p. 15) Klein read of "the images of the four material elements, the four principles of the intuitive cosmogonies."

121. Shinichi Segi (interviewed in Tokyo by Jean-Yves Mock in August 1980) recalls an interesting conversation with Klein in Japan in 1953. They were talking about the Japanese tradition of inking a fish and applying it to paper to obtain an imprint of the scale pattern. The word for this process, when transliterated into the Latin alphabet, is *gyotaku*; Klein, as a Frenchman, pronounced it *jyotaku*, and Segi replied that that pronunciation changed the meaning: it was now a woman,

not a fish, who was being inked and printed.

122. The story is told by Werner Spies, who attributes it to Norbert Kricke as eyewitness.

123. *Iris-Time*, p. 175.

124. See Nan Rosenthal's essay elsewhere in this catalogue.

125. Klein archive.

126. As interviewed by Nan Rosenthal in New York City in 1975; see "The Blue World of Yves Klein," pp. 256–57.

127. Mircea Eliade, *Myths, Dreams, and Mysteries* (New York: Harper, 1967), pp. 104–107.

128. *Poetics of Reverie*, p. 79.

129. See Henry T. Bowie, *On the Laws of Japanese Painting* (New York: Dover, n.d.), pp. 15, 79, 82–83.

130. "The Monochrome Adventure." Also, the influence of the Japanese *gassaku*, "an impromptu picture in which several artists will in turn participate" (*On the Laws of Japanese Painting*, p. 13), may be seen in the collective imprint of New Realists (ANT SU 11) and the "blind poem" made collectively, on a long scroll, by Klein, Arman, Claude Pascal, and Restany (ANT SU 15), in which the mixture of poetry and visual image is also in the Sino-Japanese tradition. In fact, all the Imprints and some Cosmogonies show Japanese influence. See "Yves Klein and Rosicrucianism."

131. Frederick Jameson, *The Prison House of Language* (Princeton: Princeton University Press, 1972), pp. 50–51.

132. This passage suggests that Klein had read some alchemical literature other than the Rosicrucian texts. Jung has found many passages where "the statue evidently denotes the end-product of the process, the lapis Philosophorum or its equivalent." In the Book of Komarios, for example:

> The body clothed itself in the light of divinity, and darkness departed from it, and all were united in love, body, soul, and spirit, and all became one…
> and the house was sealed and the statue was erected, filled with light and divinity.

See C. G. Jung, *Mysterium Conjunctionis*, 2d ed. (Princeton, N.J.: Princeton University Press, 1970), pp. 391 ff.

133. Wember, *Yves Klein.*

134. The status of this triptych is, however, not altogether unambiguous. The evidence is that the three paintings were made separately by Klein, bought separately by the same buyer, and formed into a triptych either by the original buyer or by the present owner, the Louisiana Museum. It is not known whether Klein's agreement was ever obtained. The amalgamation of the three works into a triptych is not without justification, however. After the show of varicolored monochromes at Colette Allendy's in 1956 Klein denounced the practice of establishing a polychromatic interplay between his monochromes of different colors. In 1960, however, at the show *Yves Klein le monochrome* at Jean Larcade's Galerie Rive Droite, Klein returned to the practice of hanging monochromes of different colors in relation with one another, and specifically monochromes of blue, rose, and gold. These three colors were of special sacredness in Heindel's Rosicrucianism, where they represent the body of God. In his transference of Rosicrucian magic to his worship of Saint Rita, Klein came to associate these three colors with her. The ex-voto piece which he dedicated to her in November 1961 was a triptych of pure pigments in gold, blue, and pink. If the the Louisiana Museum triptych is to be criticized, it is for the arrangement of the colors in order of the natural spectrum (red, yellow, blue). The evidence suggests that Klein would have put blue in the center.

135. M. Caron and S. Hutin, *The Alchemists* (New York: Grove, 1961), p. 147.

136. This piece is described in detail by Pierre Restany elsewhere in this catalogue.

137. "Truth Becomes Reality."

138. "Due to the Fact That."

139. "Truth Becomes Reality."

140. *The Rosicrucian Cosmo-conception* (Oceanside, California, 1937), p. 397.

141. The plaster cast of Arman had been painted blue and mounted on a gold ground before Klein's death. The bronze casting of Arman was made from the plaster after Klein's death. It is worth mentioning that the genitals of the three casts are identical, having been cast from a classical statue.

142. The legend that *Mondo Cane* "killed" Klein is very strong in the oral tradition. George Marci, however, denies emphatically that Klein had a heart attack at Cannes, and Klein himself seems to agree, since various references in his letters and conversations indicate that he thought his first heart attack took place at the opening at the Galerie Creuze.

In fact, neither George Marci's nor Klein's opinion can be taken as medical authority. A heart attack (understood as the moment when a major part of the heart tissue dies) may either precede or follow, by several days or even weeks, the pain which is its outer sign; it may be accompanied at onset only by the sort of mild discomfort of which Klein complained at Cannes, or by no immediate discomfort at all. All that can be said about the date of Klein's first heart attack is that is seems to have occurred somewhere in the period including both the Cannes screening and the opening at the Galerie Creuze.

In considering the actual "cause" of the heart attacks, whether prolonged use of stimulants, inhalation of synthetic resins, or his "celebrated temper tantrums," it is well to remember that Klein seems to fit rather closely what medical doctors call the "cardiac profile" or "cardiac personality."

143. "Les Fenêtres," trans. C. F. MacIntyre, in *Stéphane Mallarmé, Selected Poems* (Berkeley: University of California Press, 1965), p. 11.

144. *Writing Degree Zero*, trans. Annette Lavers and Colin Smith (New York: Hill and Wang, 1968), p. 25.

145. On *sprezzatura,* the self-eternalizing posturing of the Renaissance aristocrats, Castiglione cautioned, "Nor must one be more careful of anything than of concealing it, because if it is discovered, this robs a man of all credit." Baldesar Castiglione, *The Book of the Courtier*, trans. Charles S. Singleton (New York: Doubleday, 1959), p. 43.

146. Ellen Moers, *The Dandy: Brummell to Beerbohm* (New York: Viking, 1960), p. 101.

147. Ibid., passim.

148. Maud Sacquard de Belleroche, *Du dandy au playboy* (Paris: Editions Mondiales, 1964), p. 55.

149. Friedrich Wilhelm Joseph von Schelling, *System of Transcendental Idealism*, VI.3, in Albert Hofstadter and Richard Kuhns, eds., *Philosophies of Art and Beauty* (Chicago: University of Chicago Press, 1964), p. 372.

150. In *Yves Klein,* catalogue of exhibition at the Palais des Beaux-Arts, Brussels, 1966. And see Restany's 1981 essay elsewhere in this catalogue, which shows that the myth still lives.

151. *System of Transcendental Idealism*, VI.3, in *Philosophies of Art and Beauty*, p. 373.

152. *The Anatomy of Criticism* (Princeton: Princeton University Press, 1957), pp. 210, 216.

Assisted Levitation: The Art of Yves Klein

Nan Rosenthal

Untitled blue monochrome (IKB 193), 1957; 78 × 55.5 (30¾ × 21⅞); private collection

1

If you become like a mirror
Those who look at you
See themselves in you
You are then invisible!

Yves Klein, diary entry
for March 15, 1952[1]

Yves Klein's public career as an artist lasted from 1954 to 1962, years of pivotal importance in the history of postwar art. From the evidence of his series of monochrome panels, his assembled reliefs, his body prints and fire paintings, his performed events, his frequent use of photographs, and his enormous body of published and unpublished texts, it can be argued that he is easily the most interesting European artist of his generation, the generation to emerge after Abstract Expressionism or its approximate counterpart in Europe, *art informel.*

Klein is also one of few Europeans of the second generation of postwar artists who have continued to interest the American audience. This is partly because of the quality of his work. It is equally because of the radical issues his work has raised: as Frank Stella said about Klein fifteen years ago, "What's not radical about the idea of selling air?"[2]

Klein interests historians partly on account of his origins in the School of Paris, the center for modernism in visual art prior to New York. If we are to understand the art of the postwar second generation, we need to examine and understand its premises beyond the borders of the School of New York. Klein's work was invented and developed independently of American art of the same period. It thus constitutes an excellent litmus by which to test the presence of certain acids — certain general characteristics — of the art of his generation, the generation of Jasper Johns, Robert Rauschenberg, Andy Warhol, Donald Judd, Ellsworth Kelly, and Allan Kaprow, each of whom was born within a few years of Klein's birth in 1928.

Klein has often been understood as a central figure in the revival of interest, on the one hand, in the example of Malevich or, on the other, in the example of Duchamp — revivals, or reinflections, which characterize much art of the postwar second generation. It is more to the point that Klein's work consistently embodies a *range* of meaning that could be said to incorporate simultaneously certain characteristics of the work of both of these artists. This could be described as a range which shuttles between the profoundly idealistic and the cynical or misanthropic, or it could be described as a range from the utopian to the conspicuously fraudulent (conspicuous in the sense that tricks are not concealed but instead are left for the observer to notice). Klein's work repeatedly puts forward the *question* of whether it is the creation of a mystic concerned with transcendence, silence, and purity or whether it is the production of a dystopian armed with humor. This question, that is, the exploration of various inflections of the relationship between the ideal and the actual, is a major theme of Klein's work.

Corresponding to the oscillation between seeming contradictions put forward by Klein's objects and prose, there is also in his imaginative self-mythologizing a heroic image of the artist and a debunking of that heroic image, present simultaneously. In this respect Klein's work questions half a millennium of Western tradition: the tradition which originated in the Renaissance and which flourished even as it was being tested in the course of the nineteenth century that "art presents a superior, more perfect world than the one we inhabit, . . . [that] the artist is like a god inspired by a vision of a higher order."[3]

A version of this idealist view of art and the artist continued to thrive in the France in which Klein grew up. It functioned in the context of the intellectual fashion for existentialism. It was part of the system of belief among intellectuals in Paris during and just after World War II that an existentialist artist, facing a blank canvas or chunk of unshaped clay, was a person whose decisions were supremely worth making, a person who continually risked being untrue to his heroic selfhood. While Klein was attracted to the idealist tradition that artists possess special powers of sensitivity and that the painter of even modern life is a "spiritual citizen of the universe" and a "prince,"[4] nevertheless, in Klein's work and working methods, which he publicized flamboyantly, he regularly mocked the idealist tradition, particularly as it was enacted by existential decision-making in the studios of Montparnasse. In doing so, he expressed grave doubts about the viability, in the postwar world, of the myth of the superiority of the artist.

Klein wrote extensively. There are four particularly useful long collections of his writing which he made public in the course of his short career. One of these is a printed anthology of manifestos, narrative descriptions of events, speeches proclaimed at openings, and autobiographical notes, published in 1959 as *Le Dépassement de la problématique de l'art (Going Beyond the Problematical in Art).*[5] Another printed collection of texts and photographs on the subjects of visual art, theater, and film appeared in late 1960 in the form of a four-page fake edition of the Paris newspaper, *Dimanche*.[6] *Dimanche* includes "La Guerre" ("The War"), Klein's imaginary history of art from the Paleolithic to Impressionism, and the first publication by Klein of his extraordinary photographic self-portrait, captioned "Le Peintre de l'espace se jette dans le vide!" ("The Painter of Space Throws Himself into the Void!"). A third long text by Klein is the manuscript and tape-recording of a seventy-minute speech, "L'Evolution de l'art vers l'immatériel" ("The Evolution of Art toward the Immaterial"), which he delivered at the Sorbonne in June 1959.[7] There is also a typewritten manuscript of 145 pages, "L'Aventure monochrome" ("The Monochrome Adventure"), which contains extremely various writings by Klein (and other acknowledged and occasionally unacknowledged authors).[8] These range from a poem Klein wrote in 1939 at the age of eleven, to brief excerpts from certain of his diaries, to letters to and from public officials about Klein's events, to theoretical statements about art, often cast in anecdotal form. Klein began to circulate this manuscript to artists, museum curators, and critics during 1959 and 1960, in the hope of getting it published in several languages.

These writings and other documents — Klein's extensive correspondence; diaries kept sporadically between 1948 and 1957; frequently modified *curricula vitae;* scrapbooks containing photographs, press releases, memorabilia, and reviews pertaining to his exhibitions; diagrams and ballpoint pen sketches; film footage reenacting exhibitions and events — and Klein's library are obviously valuable tools for reconstructing the facts of his work and the ways in which he presented it.[9] Together with the testimony of many witnesses to Klein's activities, Klein's writings and the large body of other documents he left make it possible to perform a kind of archaeology and to distinguish the historical Klein from the mythological Klein, a creation begun by the artist himself. Thus they enable us to undertake a critical interpretation of the work and the myth and to begin to relate that interpretation to the larger culture from which Klein's art sprang and to which it was addressed: the art historical culture (Klein's parents are painters, and through them he was familiar with the immediate issues of vanguard art in postwar Paris) and the social culture (like Alain Robbe-Grillet and Jean-Luc Godard, Klein was an adolescent during World War II and as a young adult read newspapers offering rhetorical falsehoods and half-truths about the Cold War and the disintegration of the French colonial empire).

In the essay which follows I shall briefly discuss the immediate Parisian context from which Klein's art emerged and biographical details necessary to comprehend the content of some of his objects and events. I shall then examine the range from utopianism to misanthropy in compelling examples of his work: the resonant blue monochrome panels and the supplementary objects of art he created to suggest various meanings for these paintings; his presentation of "voids" or the "immaterial" — his selling air — as a work of art; and a category of his work which approaches visual representation in such a way as to illustrate a subject and show, simultaneously, its literal traces, for example, his works made with the imprint of a nude model's paint-covered body.

When I began to conduct archival research on Klein some years ago, an awareness of his psychological characteristics proved helpful to me in reconstructing certain facts about the chronology of his work and the ways in which he produced it. However, I believe that the task of offering a critical interpretation of Klein's art should not depend on such an awareness. One should distinguish between the psychology of the man and the meanings of the work he produced. This is especially important in the case of an artist who might be seen in the Duchampian tradition as having made a work of art out of his own life.

A further note on method: when I write about Klein's art I mean not only his extant objects but also his events, his public speeches, and the texts and photographs which he published or planned to publish before he died of a heart attack at the age of thirty-four. While these events and texts are often extrinsic to the material objects Klein left, they are as intrinsic to his art as Duchamp's *Green Box* notes are to the *Large Glass*. Indeed, Klein's seemingly outrageous tip, "My paintings are the ashes of my art," happens to be a helpful one.[10]

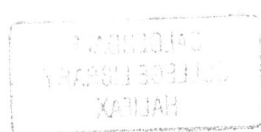

2

I loathe artists who empty themselves into their painting, as is quite often the case today. Morbidism [sic], rather than thinking of the beautiful, the good, the true in their painting: they express, they ejaculate, they spit out every horrible, rotten, and infectious complexity in their painting as if relieving themselves and putting the burden on others, "the readers of their works," of all their sorry failures.

I execute my paintings very quickly, in very little time.

Yves Klein,
"The Monochrome Adventure"[11]

Because both of his parents were painters, Klein was unusually knowledgeable about modern art and the Parisian art world, which became part of the subject matter of his work. Although not an intellectual, he possessed a tremendous intuitive intelligence and a quick, absorptive mind. The circumstance that he was an undisciplined student who failed to obtain a baccalaureate within the French school system made him particularly alert to information he obtained from other sources, for example, inside dope acquired from his parents' world and the people he met through it.

In the years immediately following World War II, Klein's mother, Marie Raymond, was an active member of vanguard art circles in Paris, and through her and her regular Monday evening gatherings of artists and critics Klein became intimate with this milieu. By the real beginning of Klein's own career as an artist in 1954, he was well aware of the nuances of contemporary artistic issues discussed by his mother's *lundistes*.

Unlike Marie Raymond, Klein's Dutch father, Fred Klein, never became an avant-garde artist. After moving from Holland to Paris, in the course of the 1920s he developed a skilled, if unoriginal, representational style that reflects the influence of Monet, pointillist neo-Impressionism, Redon, and Dufy. The typical subjects of his oils, watercolors, and pastels are gardens in bloom, Mediterranean beach scenes, and circus figures. He has sold modestly yet steadily over the years, often through little-known galleries in Holland. In the late 1940s and early 1950s, Fred Klein began increasingly to use pastel as a principal medium. It is probable that this, as well as his continuing interest in highly keyed color, partly stimulated Yves Klein's attempts in the middle 1950s to invent a kind of paint that might suspend pigment in a pure powdery form, unadulterated by a binder that would diminish the intensity of dry specks of color.[12]

Advanced painting in Paris in the decade just after World War II encompassed a variety of complex features. Although Picasso and Matisse remained towering heroes in the hierarchy, they were, in terms of daily vanguard currents, almost *hors concours* in the opinion of many artists of the following generation, artists born, like Klein's parents, between the turn of the century and about 1920. Both Picasso and Matisse stood for a refusal to paint abstractly. This perhaps had the effect of making almost any abstract art in the context of the *école de Paris* look more radical than it actually was.

Immediately after the war, geometric abstraction, with its roots for the French most obviously in Mondrian, in the prewar Paris groups Cercle et Carré and Abstraction-Création, and in middle and late Kandinsky, whose post-Expressionist painting the French discovered chiefly after the war, was the movement that carried the banner for abstract painting. In 1945 there were important exhibitions of *art concret* and Kandinsky at the Galerie René Drouin. In spring 1949 Michel Seuphor organized a large historical show at Galerie Maeght, *Les Premiers Maîtres de l'art abstrait*, which emphasized the Constructivist origins of abstract painting and resulted in a book that became a standard reference on both sides of the Atlantic. The annual Salon des Réalités Nouvelles, begun in 1946, was devoted exclusively to abstract art and, in its first years, also favored geometric abstraction, as did André Bloc's monthly magazine, *Art d'aujourd'hui*, begun in 1949. The Galerie Denise René, also devoted to geometric abstraction, opened in 1945.

A different current, which produced some of the finest new art during the first postwar years of the *école de Paris*, is exemplified by the painting of Jean Dubuffet and Jean Fautrier, who were championed by prominent literary figures such as Jean Paulhan, Francis Ponge, and André Malraux. It seemed to these writers that the radically distorted crudeness of the painters' human imagery bore witness to the tragedy of the war and the absurdity of the human condition. One characteristic of their painting was a high-relief or textured surface that came to be called *matièrisme*. This stylistic label was applied to many other artists as well, whether their work was figurative or abstract; these included Nicolas de Staël and André Lanskoy, who were both friends of Klein's parents.[13]

It is significant that a number of Surrealist painters and poets, including André Breton, having been dispersed by the war, returned to Paris and continued to work, exhibit, and publish. The lessons of Dada had been evident during the war in the Midi in the work of Picabia, an almost legendary figure in Cannes, and in the years right after the war Picabia's work —

including many examples from his period as a Dadaist between 1915 and 1925 — was frequently exhibited in Paris.

The stylistic development which emerged almost simultaneously with and partly in reaction to the clean orthodoxy of geometric abstraction, and the style for which this period is best known, was so-called gestural abstraction. This was practiced in various ways by painters such as Wols (Wolfgang Schulze) and Hans Hartung, both prewar German émigrés to France, the Canadian Jean-Paul Riopelle, the former Surrealist poet Camille Bryen, Pierre Soulages, and Georges Mathieu. Mathieu used the term *abstraction lyrique* to describe their style.[14] Some of the roots of this freely painted nonfigurative art lay in the psychic automatism promulgated earlier by Surrealist theory.

Mathieu was extremely active in writing as a proselytizer of lyrical abstraction and as an organizer of several key exhibitions, such as *H.W.P.S.M.T.B.* at the Galerie Colette Allendy in 1948.[15] For the catalogue of this exhibition Mathieu wrote a statement which reflects the existentialist ethics of the moment:

Liberty is the void.

To accord man a total metaphysical enfranchisement would be to frustrate him of the last pretexts that justify his presence. If he has not yet done anything to merit his liberation, he has hardly lost such esteem that anyone should be so cruel as to set him free.

It seems that it is only recently that our civilization has become conscious of this state of affairs, the tragedy of which is illustrated in the contemporaneity and necessity of the notion of choice. The debate is open, ambiguity has replaced exiguity....

Poetry, music, painting are in fact shaking off the last servitudes: word, tonality, figuration.

Since the reassuring asperities to which the secretions of men clung have disappeared, two means of transcendence remain open to them: the one, illusory, which coagulates the sensibilities in a cosmic universality; the other, which exacerbates them and exalts them by revalorizing all the possibilities in the watertightness of individual consciousness.[16]

Mathieu was sensitive at least as early as 1948 to the significance of new American abstract painting, which probably encouraged him to widen greatly the size of his calligraphic oils. Mathieu was also a showman: on May 28, 1956, on the stage of the Théâtre Sarah Bernhardt, before an audience of two thousand, he painted a twelve-meter-long canvas in twenty minutes. He continued such demonstrations of the spontaneous recording of "creative moments" in a number of European cities in subsequent years.[17] Yves Klein knew Mathieu personally, and it is clear that Mathieu's public existential performances, his intellectual pamphleteering, and perhaps even his lavish style of living became for Klein, who was seven years his junior, an example to challenge.[18]

Along with completely abstract painters who emphasized gesture, there were a number of artists, such as Roger Bissière, Jean Bazaine, Alfred Manessier, Maurice Estève, and Marie Hélène Viera da Silva, who worked in styles that appeared to be abstract but were often residually figurative and which employed Cubist-derived space and composition. The critic Michel Ragon called this *paysagisme abstrait* and abstract naturalism, terms which serve to describe the painting of Klein's mother, Marie Raymond, at this time. She had been mostly self-taught as an artist. Around 1938 she began to paint more or less abstractly; her imagery emerged from Picasso's curvilinear late Cubism of the 1930s. Her brightly colored oils and gouaches of the 1940s and 1950s are balanced compositionally and have a shallow Cubist space and linear arabesques which make slight symbolic reference to aspects of nature in imaginary landscapes or skyscapes. Occasionally the formal vocabulary of de Staël is visible in her work.

Raymond was friendly with both painters of abstract naturalism and artists associated with geometric abstraction. She showed regularly at the Salon des Réalités Nouvelles and in small group exhibitions at the galleries of Denise René and Colette Allendy. In 1949 she won the Prix Kandinsky; she continued to be sufficiently highly regarded to earn a half-column entry in an index of mid-1950s Paris taste, Seuphor's *Dictionary of Abstract Painting*. One of Marie Raymond's supporters was the older critic Charles Estienne, who initially after the war had championed geometric abstraction. Later Estienne turned on this style as a formularized academicism, and in 1954 he began to use the term *tachisme* for gestural abstraction.

Georges Mathieu's friend, the critic and occasional sculptor Michel Tapié, was, like Mathieu, receptive to the new American painting, particularly to the work of Jackson Pollock. In his book of 1952, *Un Art autre*, where the term of the title and the term *art informel* were launched, Tapié attacked the tradition of *la belle peinture*, claiming that "since Nietzsche and Dada art appears as the most inhumane of adventures.... Notions of Beauty, Form, Space, Aesthetics [no longer apply]."[19] He was writing in support both of the raw art of Dubuffet and of what he called the "paroxism" of gestural abstraction. In view of the way American art criticism of the 1960s has often appeared to claim almost exclusively for America serious appreciation during the 1950s of the work of Duchamp, it is worth noting that Tapié, in this essay of 1952, stressed the significance for postwar art of Duchamp and Picabia. Other French critics were beginning to reexamine the work of Duchamp for its irony and emphasis on the cerebral, for example, Alain Jouffroy, in a long interview with Duchamp in November 1954 published in the Paris cultural tabloid *Arts*.[20]

It is difficult to pin down with precision the extent of Klein's detailed knowledge of Dada and Surrealism prior to the start of his own career. Klein knew Duchamp's French biographer, Robert Lebel; this does not establish that Klein had a great deal of particularized information about the work of Duchamp, whom Klein did not meet until his one trip to New York in spring 1961.[21] Klein's friend from Nice, the artist Arman, recalls that Klein lent him the catalogue *Le Surréalisme en 1947*, with its cover by Duchamp bearing a foam-rubber breast over the request "Please Touch," a year or so after this large exhibition at the Galerie Maeght.[22]

Klein may have been unusually well informed about Dada through his minor connections to the Lettrist movement during the winter he spent in Paris in 1951-52. The Lettrists, led first by the Rumanian poet Isidore Isou and later by the French poet Maurice Lemaître, were an aggressively vanguardist group who theorized ceaselessly and hailed Dada and Surrealism as direct ancestors.[23] As Lemaître wrote later, referring to the years immediately after the war:

> In those dark days for French culture, when the obscurantist waste products of the "poetry of the resistance" and of its chief [Louis] Aragon were tarnishing the golden course of French lyricism, the Lettrists were almost the only ones [Lemaître adds in a note, "with the great Surrealists, such as Breton..."] to uphold the idea that Dada was a necessary moment for art. They passionately supported the correct position that Tzara and Breton were by no means "surpassed" or made "old-fashioned" by the Zhdanovist error of neoclassical patriotism.[24]

The Lettrists were committed to a form of concrete poetry that emphasized nonsense words and pictographs. They stressed the legitimacy of working simultaneously in many media: film, theater, music, and painting as well as poetry. Klein was acquainted with the movement and with Isou through his friend François Dufrêne, who was then a Lettrist poet. The Lettrists wrote social theory which substituted youth for the proletariat as the desirable agent of revolution, and early in the 1950s they published a periodical broadsheet, *Soulèvement de la jeunesse*, for which Klein in June 1952 wrote an article condemning the staidness of the older generation and calling for a utopian society based on "enthusiasm."[25]

3

Fortunately I have my entire life ahead of me and I don't wish at all to become bogged down at this point in . . . a "Stable Situation." . . . I am going to ask you something again, this time very precise: can you quickly (in order to have a choice if possible) write or contact a person likely to issue you a work permit — that is, for this certificate, the person guarantees to be able to employ me at it doesn't matter what work, supposedly capable of supporting me, this only to make me, in the opinion of the English authorities, sufficiently qualified so that they leave me alone and let me live in England for at least one year.

Yves Klein, letter from Nice to his parents
in Paris, October 31, 1949[26]

While as a child Klein sometimes spent winters in Nice at the home of his mother's sister, during the final years of World War II he lived in Paris with his parents in their small apartment south of the Luxembourg Gardens. Immediately after the war, in the course of the decade of the *école de Paris* I have just described, Klein was in and out of Paris frequently, and on at least two occasions he traveled with his parents to their exhibitions in England and Holland. He also hitchhiked through Italy, touring monuments of ancient and Renaissance art and several resorts fashionable then, such as Capri.[27]

In 1947, in Nice, he began to study judo in classes at the police academy, where he became close to Arman and another young man his age, Claude Pascal, who later aspired to be a poet. The following year Klein and Pascal together became correspondence students of a Rosicrucian sect headquartered near San Diego.[28] In late 1949, after Klein had completed his military service in the French sector of West Germany, he and Pascal went for about ten months to London and Ireland, where they rapidly learned English and continued to study judo and Rosicrucian lessons.[29] Through his father Klein got a job in London for several months at the shop of Robert Savage, a framemaker of excellent reputation. Savage has said that Klein at twenty-one in London "did no painting. I had the impression he was rejecting art because of his interest in judo."[30] He remembers Klein as a cheerful, friendly, bright young person, neither knowledgeable about technique, nor very practical with his hands, nor particularly interested in increasing his manual dexterity at the shop. Klein's duties there consisted primarily of applying several coats of gesso to wood frames and rubbing each coat absolutely smooth with glass paper. This was in preparation for work done by others in a more skilled department: the application of red grounds followed by the actual gilding of the frames. Klein also learned to apply linen to flat wooden frames with size, so that the grain of the wood would not show through the finish. This is similar to the technique Klein used from late 1955 forward to prepare the wood or composition board supports of his monochrome panels. Apart from what Klein may have learned at home, the months at Savage's shop constituted his chief training in handling art materials prior to the beginning of his own career as a painter.[31]

Klein's friend Pascal maintains that during their months in London Klein made several small nonfigurative pastels of one color. According to Pascal, Klein hung these on a wall of their flat in a rooming house near Earl's Court and invited a few friends, such as their English teacher, James Shorrocks, to see them.[32] Shorrocks does not recall the medium of these little drawings but reports that they were greeted by general laughter, which Klein encouraged.[33] This was the exhibition which Klein claimed later, in many speeches and documents, had been his first one-man show.[34]

There is no mention of these one-color pastels or of any monochromes either in Pascal's extensive diary of the London-Ireland trip, which records such details as works of art they saw at the National Gallery, or in Klein's two journals of their stay in Ireland. These journals make it very clear that he had not yet decided upon a career.

In April 1950 Klein and Pascal departed London for a horse farm near Dublin, where for six months they earned room and board as kitchen helpers and stableboys. They wished to learn to ride to carry out a fantasy: to travel to Japan on horseback in order to study judo at the source. Their wish was somewhat frustrated by the reluctance of their employer to teach them about horsemanship. In Klein's journal, which he was by then keeping in English, he commented,

revealingly for his future attitude towards artistic activities, "We know, now just enough to stay [a] few minutes on a horse back and that will probably be enough for the *idea* 'to travel on horseback to Japan!' " [Italics and quotation marks Klein's.][35]

In early 1951 Klein went (without Pascal, who was recuperating from tuberculosis) to Madrid. The earliest documentary evidence of his intention to make two-dimensional works of one color is in one of his diaries of his stay there between February and June 1951.[36] These journals reflect enlightened tourism and concern about how he will earn his living while studying Castilian and how he will pursue judo in the Spanish capital. Two short entries over this five-month period appear relevant. On February 22 Klein noted, in ungrammatical but swiftly acquired Spanish, that on the previous evening, as he and a South American friend were leaving the Café Gijón (a well-known writers' hangout),

> while walking I suddenly began to think about the paintings in a single color. As that seemed to interest him I talked to him about the exhibit I would like to present with appropriate music. Also to him everything seemed interesting and he will ask about an exhibition room and [word illegible] musicians also (Be Bop!).[37]

And on February 25 Klein recorded that the same friend

> has insisted so much that I have begun to paint but warning him that my painting (if it can be called painting) will not please him. In fact he was disappointed and to repair the disastrous impression which was made, I went out and painted rapidly a little watercolor of Toledo according to a card: this, more realistic, he liked.[38]

Klein's long journal and loose manuscript pages that date from his winter in Paris in 1951-52 make no reference whatsoever to monochrome painting and reveal that he was still completely undecided — unhappily so — about a career. Among this substantial body of introspective material, which is preponderantly about the Rosicrucians, judo, his war of nerves with a concierge, his lack of discipline (particularly in respect to a Japanese language class he was auditing), his opinion of works by the Lettrists, as well as primitive plans for a utopian society, located on a Mediterranean island and governed by a "little king" who inspires his subjects to economic prosperity, there are two pages, undated but in penmanship that resembles dated diaries of 1952, that appear to anticipate Klein's later career as a believer in the affective properties of color and, specifically, the primaries. The passage makes no connection between color and visual art, nor does it refer to Klein's making art. Rather, it is a sketch for an imaginary public opinion poll in which Klein asks what is represented by the colors blue, red, and yellow, which is the most powerful, which the weakest, what is the normal psychological effect of each, and whether the sight of one of these colors in "the pure state" awakens in the respondent some sentiment.[39]

Klein's longed-for trip to Japan was brought about with the help of acquaintances of Marie Raymond, among them the Japanese art critic Takachiyo Uemura. In Tokyo from the fall of 1952 to the end of 1953, Klein lived mostly "European style" and studied judo almost daily at the *dojos* of the police academy and the Kodokan Judo Institute, the more or less official international arbiter of ranks in the sport. He lived on remittances from his Niçoise aunt, by giving French lessons, and through the sale of his parents' paintings at an exhibition in November 1953 at the Bridgestone Gallery in Tokyo.[40] The Kodokan finally awarded Klein the grade of fourth *dan*, black belt, then considered exceptionally high for a non-Japanese. The letter of award and other documents make clear that Klein's enthusiasm and manipulations rather than his skill earned the designation.[41] While in Tokyo, with a cameraman he met through Uemura, Klein made a short film about judo.

Letters Klein wrote from Asia to his family and his Japan journal and photo albums make no reference to his painting. In the case of his albums — a rich record of his travels containing photographs of shipboard stops throughout Southeast Asia, his judo companions, his Japanese and Western friends in Tokyo, sites he visited in Kyoto, and installation shots of the exhibition of his parents' art which he had arranged with the help of Uemura — the absence of any verbal or visual trace of Klein's own art seems telling. His journal records his reluctance to accept suggestions that he earn his living in Tokyo as a fashion or advertising illustrator; he preferred a job that expected no "genius" from him and that allowed him to concentrate on judo. Uemura, who saw Klein often in Tokyo, has written that Klein seemed to show no interest in becoming an artist at that time, that he saw no exhibition there of works of art by Klein, and that Klein did not seek the company of artists during his stay.[42] The view that Klein was not making art in Japan is supported by one of his close friends from the period, Malcolm Gregory. An English *judoka* whom Klein knew from London, Gregory was in Japan, also studying judo at the Kodokan, throughout Klein's stay

there.[43] Gregory was well aware of Klein's parents' art and attended the Fred Klein–Marie Raymond exhibition at the Bridgestone Gallery. Klein often claimed later, in letters, *vitae*, catalogues, and, by implication, in speeches, that he had had a one-man show in Tokyo in 1952 or 1953; sometimes he tempered the claim by calling this a "private monochrome manifestation."[44] It seems unlikely, if even a private show of his work had taken place, that both the art critic Uemura and Klein's friend Gregory would have been absent from it and completely unaware of its occurrence.

When Klein returned from Tokyo to Paris in 1954, he found that despite his Kodokan rank of fourth *dan*, black belt, he was not embraced as a star by the Fédération Française de Judo. Although he then wrote a book, *Les Fondements du judo*, which was published by Grasset late in 1954, and although during 1954 he taught judo on and off for at least six months in Madrid before settling permanently in Paris, a career in the sport, which he had seriously contemplated, was apparently no longer a possibility for him. This point marks the real beginning of his career as an artist, that is, as an individual who thought of himself as an artist and made works of art which were intended to go out into the world.

4

One does not become a painter, one discovers suddenly that that is what one is!

Yves Klein,
"The Monochrome Adventure"[45]

Klein initiated his public career as an artist in late 1954 with *Yves Peintures (Yves Paintings)*, a booklet of carefully captioned reproductions of monochrome paintings that there is no evidence he had previously painted. He made *Yves Peintures* in Madrid, at a printshop run by one of his judo companions there. This remarkable little book of purported reproductions boldly forecast three central characteristics of Klein's subsequent work: first, his mockery, through advertisements for himself, of the idealist tradition of the superiority of the artist; second, his habit of adumbrating meanings for his utterly imageless monochromes with a set of works *supplementary* to the paintings themselves; and third, his presentation of a range of alternative meanings such that no one meaning may be settled upon as exclusively correct.

The booklet *Yves Peintures* measures approxi-

pp. 138–39

mately 9½ by 7½ inches and is made of thick, heavily textured white paper. Printed on the cover in black ink are the words "Yves/ Peintures/ 10 Planches/ Préface de Pascal Claude." The preface consists of three pages. Except for the word "Préface" at the top of the first page and the inverted name of his friend, "Pascal Claude," at the bottom of the third, these pages are bare of typography. Instead of lines of type there are horizontal black lines, indented to indicate paragraphs and broken to indicate sentences. Except for the removal of one black line on the third page, presumably to make room for the writer's name, the "paragraphs" and the "sentences" of black lines are identical on each page.

The preface is followed by the plate pages, ten sheets of the same textured white paper used for the cover and preface. On each of these plate pages, different sizes of rectangular one-color papers, probably commercially inked and purchased, have been pasted, one to a page. Below each tip-in a caption is printed on the backing paper. The first pasted paper, captioned "Yves" to the left and "à Londres, 1950 (195 × 97)" to the right, is robin's-egg blue and measures exactly 195 by 97 millimeters. This is followed by a rust-brown paper captioned "Yves/ à Madrid, 1951 (130x81)"; a purple paper captioned "Yves/ à Nice, 1951 (195 × 97)"; a green paper captioned "Yves/ à Paris, 1951 (130 × 81)"; a nasturtium paper captioned "Yves/ à Tokio, 1952 (195 × 97)"; a yellow paper captioned "Yves/ à Tokio, 1953 (100 × 65)"; an ultramarine paper captioned "Yves/ à Paris, 1954 (195 × 97)," and so on. In each case the measurements in the caption, which conventionally in reproductions of European paintings would stand for centimeters, conform in millimeters to the size of the pasted papers.

Yves Peintures concludes with a colophon page which reads:

> This illustrated edition of ten color plates was printed on the presses of the master printer Fernando Franco de Sarabia at Jaen 1, Madrid, on November 18, 1954. One hundred and fifty copies were printed, numbered 1 to 150. Copy No. _____. All rights reserved for all countries. Copyright by the author.[46]

There is also another edition of this book, nearly identical except that it is titled *Haguenault Peintures,* and the name Haguenault is substituted for Yves in the captions to the plates. These captions, printed in a type style slightly different from that used for *Yves Peintures,* have an additional category of information common to labels for reproductions of paintings, one which reports on the ownership of the

works. For example, there are captions which read "Haguenault — Tokyo, 1952 (130 × 81) Private Collection" and "Haguenault — Paris, 1951 (162 × 97) Collection Raymond Hains."[47]

> Last Wednesday night we went to a café frequented by abstracts...some abstracts were there. They are easily recognizable because they create an abstract-picture atmosphere, and one sees their pictures in their eyes. Maybe I have illusions but I have the impression of seeing all that. In any case we sat down with them....then people began to talk about the book *Yves Peintures.* Later as they kept insisting I produce it, I went to fetch it from the car and threw it on the table. From the very first pages the eyes of the abstracts changed. Their eyes lit up and in the depths beautiful and pure uniform colors seemed to appear.[48]

In early 1955 Klein settled in Paris for good. As his text above and other documents indicate, within weeks of completing *Yves Peintures* in Madrid he troubled to show the little book to recognized — at any rate, recognizable — artists in the cafés of Montparnasse.

What is the meaning of the book? First of all, it appears to present the idea of making paintings that consist of a single, evenly applied color. The title of the book and the information in the captions underneath the plates imply that the plates are supposed to be reproductions of unique paintings. This is an implication Klein often spelled out, for example in correspondence and in the biographical notes printed at the end of his pamphlet of 1959, *Le Dépassement de la problématique de l'art,* in which the book of 1954 is referred to as "a selection of reproductions of his works."[49] In a letter to a Paris art critic which Klein drafted several times in the summer of 1955, he used the book (along with references to shows in foreign cities, private collections in which his work figured, and so forth) to suggest his identity as a promising painter. He wrote to the critic that "a small book of reproductions of my work was published in Madrid in June 1954 [sic]. Out of print for the moment but I think the publisher has some personal copies at his disposal"; Klein next provided the critic with the Madrid printer's address. In an early draft of this letter, Klein has inked quotation marks around the words "of reproductions"; in later drafts these quotation marks are gone.[50]

If we inquire why Klein used commercially inked papers instead of a photomechanical method to reproduce his paintings, several answers suggest them-

selves. It is difficult to reproduce monochrome paintings effectively, and this is one possible way to deal
with the problem. It became evident fairly soon after
the publication of his book that Klein liked the appearance of dry pigment and disliked oil paint, so we
may imagine that he selected the somewhat matte
finish of the cut papers in preference to the glossiness
of most printed color plates. No doubt it was much
cheaper for the young artist to paste in colored papers by hand than to order *clichés* and have them
printed. There was also the example, of which Klein
cannot have been ignorant, of Matisse's *papiers
découpés* in highly saturated colors.[51]

Still another reason why Klein may have used
pasted papers instead of a photomechanical method
of reproduction is that the paintings he wished to reproduce did not really exist. As my earlier discussion
of Klein's activities between 1950 and 1953 suggests, this was almost certainly the case. If we are
supposed to take the dimensions given in the captions in the conventional sense, as indications of
centimeters, then we must assume that every one of
these sizable paintings is lost, for none in these sizes
appears in Paul Wember's *catalogue raisonné* of
Klein's work,[52] and none in these sizes appeared during Klein's lifetime in exhibitions about which we have
information, for example, his large retrospective at the
Museum Haus Lange in Krefeld in early 1961.[53] If we
are supposed, instead, to take the dimensions in the
captions as indications of millimeters, we still find no
works of corresponding size in either the *catalogue
raisonné* or lists of works in exhibitions before Klein's
death. Furthermore, we have been misled — by a
deviation from standard practice for which the very
correctness of the colophon page hardly prepares us.
A historian examining *Yves Peintures* today has to
conclude that the book presents evidence of an idea,
not evidence of previously made paintings. Thus it
suggests Klein's concern to establish, with dates and
places that are autobiographically accurate as well
as glamorizing (travel was not easy for Europeans in
the early 1950s), that he had the idea of painting
monochromes at least five years before he made a
point of showing the book to artists in Paris cafés in
January 1955. The conception appears to have
counted at this point as much as or more than the
execution of actual paintings. But these conclusions — that the book presents highly exaggerated or
false information about previous work, that this indicates Klein's desire to build a career retroactively,
and that being first with an idea was important to
Klein — are the evaluations of a historian. The issue
remains whether critical analysis of the book *Yves*

Peintures and its fraternal twin *Haguenault Peintures* leads us elsewhere.

In a number of respects the books do not present
themselves in such unequivocal terms that it can be
assumed that everyone will know what they are and
how to interpret them. The title page, the colophon
page, and, to a degree, the pages with the plates set
up certain conventional expectations: that *Yves
Peintures* is a limited-edition book of reproductions
of serious, if radically unusual, paintings, apparently
intended to present pure color. However, the pages
with the plates present standard data for books of this
kind in a slightly disturbing fashion. The captions have
too much and too little information. First, an art book
reproducing the work of only one artist does not repeat the artist's name under every color plate; in the
case of a little book called *Yves/Paintings* surely the
title of the book itself should suffice. Second, we expect from legends under reproductions in art books
the titles of works, not information in caption form
about where the artist was when he made the work —
that is, autobiography — presented as a sort of title.
Third, the dimensions of height and width in each
caption are dimensions which convention, in the absence of the abbreviation "cm" or the word "centimeters," decrees, in the case of paintings, to *mean*
centimeters, but Klein's dimensions turn out to describe not what is purportedly being miniaturized by
reproduction but exactly what is *there*, the height and
width in millimeters of the colored papers.

These may seem to be relatively minor oddities
and they may — mistakenly, I believe — be written
off as evidence of Klein's youthful inexperience when
he made the book or as an example of what we know,
in retrospect, of his fondness for self-promotion.
However, we cannot ignore that these minor oddities
have been introduced by a major one, the astonishing preface of three pages of black lines, these "first
pages" at which, Klein wrote, "the eyes of the abstracts changed." One can well imagine that they did.
The reader is challenged not only to accept one-color
plates as reproductions of paintings but, in place of
the laudatory *belles lettres* of Jean Paulhan on Dubuffet or Jean-Paul Sartre on Giacometti, a wordless
essay as prose. What do these black lines of 1954
mean? That the reader may write his own preface, that
is, conduct his own hermeneutics, upon them? That
the paintings which follow are meaningful beyond
words and too significant to be cheapened by the
specificities of art criticism? Or that if you take blank
lines seriously, you are a fool, and the whole book
is a satire on collections of plates by well-known artists? We are given enough cues to distinguish such

alternatives as these, but not enough information to decide firmly among them. A range of meanings is forced upon us. This may be one explanation of why Klein attributed authorship of the paintings to two different people, Yves and Haguenault. That is, the books may be read in at least two ways, as the creation of an artist concerned with silence and pure color or as the production of a satirist.[54]

The meaning of the book *Yves Peintures* shifts in other ways as well. On the one hand, the book did serve in Paris in early 1955 and afterward to suggest that Yves Klein's biography as an artist dates back at least to 1950, and further that his reputation in 1954 as the artist Yves was important enough for a publisher to reproduce his work. That is, he introduced his career to Paris not only as preexisting but as already validated. On the other hand, in addition to what I have pointed out — that deviations from convention within the object *Yves Peintures* lead us to suspicions about what it appears to be — there is the context of its presentation by Klein, which does likewise. Most painters of Klein's generation launched their careers by showing paintings, not by showing reproductions. The very act of presenting, as his first public work, a book of reproductions of paintings no one has seen is peculiar enough to be conspicuous; it calls attention to the possibility that the paintings don't exist and that what you see is what is there: an *original* that presents itself as if it were a set of reproductions.

It might be said that part of the subject matter of this original is that vanguard artists of this place and period sometimes backdated their work. With *Yves Peintures* Klein does just that and, at the same time, by pointing us to the possibility of his having done so, he mocks the not uncommon art world practice. To believe that he has merely tried to fool us is on a par with accepting at face value such statements of his as "In any case I do not consider myself an artist of the avant-garde. I wish to make clear quite the contrary, that I think and believe myself to be a classic, perhaps even one of the rare classics of the century!"[55] This is printed in boldface type in Klein's 1959 pamphlet, *Le Dépassement de la problématique de l'art*, a few pages after his detailed (and hilarious) description of the infamous evening on which he presented an empty art gallery as a work of art. When Klein exaggerates vanguard practices to the point of mockery, he forces us to question the canon of the idealist tradition that equates creativity and originality.

Looking back, it is not surprising that in 1954, just three years after the much-discussed publication in France of André Malraux's *Voices of Silence*,[56] a young Frenchman whose writings show concern with the sweep of art history from cave paintings to Sung landscape and Van Gogh would make an original work of art, *Yves Peintures*, which turns out to be *about* works of art which go unseen except in reproduction. Despite the criticism it immediately received, Malraux's construction of a Museum without Walls, built of vast numbers of reproductions, endowed reproductions and in particular color plates with a certain revitalized status as cultural artifacts. Malraux in passing laments about his imaginary museum that, as works of art of different media, different size, and different periods become color plates in a book, the works of art lose their status as objects.[57] In other words, as Walter Benjamin had pointed out fifteen years earlier in "The Work of Art in the Age of Mechanical Reproduction," they lose the "aura" of originals;[58] and, Malraux mentions, works of art taken out of context also lose their originally intended functions. However, Malraux leaves the impression that, in his view, these losses of aura and function are compensated for by what man discovers, when many reproductions are juxtaposed, about the history of art's "great styles," and thus, according to Malraux, by what Man discovers about his Fate.[59] There is the proposal that by tracking his destiny through the history of artistic styles, man may recover the humanism he mislaid in the wars and aborted revolutions of the twentieth century.

When Klein began his career he was working, whether consciously or not, in the context of Malraux's *Voices of Silence* and myriad reactions to it.[60] These reactions considered in a general way some of the issues which Benjamin had raised years before (with very different conclusions) and which Malraux's book popularized. As Benjamin put it in his essay, mechanical reproduction depreciates the quality of the presence of the actual work of art; it jeopardizes the authority of the object. Duchamp made a related point in 1919 when he drew a moustache and goatee on a small reproduction of the Mona Lisa and captioned it *L.H.O.O.Q.* On the eve of World War II, with his portable museum, the *Box in a Valise*, Duchamp showed something different: that reproductions in miniature may become highly effective carriers of ideas. Benjamin had also pointed this out: "Technical reproduction can put the copy of the original into situations which would be out of reach for the original itself, . . . [enabling] the original to meet the beholder halfway." This, he wrote, "reactivates the object reproduced."[61]

With *Yves Peintures* Klein demonstrated his

sensitivity to such issues and further, that he wished to have it both ways. The book is, on the one hand, an original work, albeit one that is supposed to exist in an edition of 150. If we follow Klein's clues that it is not simply a publisher's *livre de luxe* but an original, then it takes on an "aura" of its own; at least, according to Klein, the book made artists' eyes light up and "pure uniform colors" seem to appear in them. Here his little text functions as a supplement to the original, by describing to us how to react to it. On the other hand, the captioned colored papers of the book, which purport to be reproductions, refer *outside* the book to hypothetical original paintings. The captioned colored papers are themselves supplements which create the fiction of the central idea: the idea that a rectangular field of nothing but pure uniform color may constitute a painting. Klein's pretense that the colored papers are reproductions keeps alive the ideal quality of the hypothetical originals, and, not incidentally for his later work, it keeps the hypothetical original paintings in a state of immateriality. *Yves Peintures* considered as a supplement to original paintings also suggests that the originals are not strong enough (yet?) to stand by themselves — or they would not need a supplement. They require explanation. The idea of painting pure monochromes is "explained" as a valid form of art by a little book — a subordinate object — which proposes that the idea must be valid because it was worth reproducing. Such supplements to a central idea are abundant in Klein's work.

5

The paucity of possibilities for perspective in painting, "trompe l'oeil" as it is so aptly called, are the lot of the impotent who feel they are unsuccessful sculptors. The true painter lives only in his color and its brew, applying it to the whole of his canvas as if reweaving it anew with all the knowledge of the surface tension which ought to be innate.

Yves Klein,
"The Monochrome Adventure"[62]

While *Yves Peintures* is compendious and reliable as an introduction to Klein's ideas and *modus operandi* — most noticeably the little book demonstrates the possibility that art may consist of communicating information about art — it is hardly an object so appealing in visual terms as to establish the career of a painter. It may be useful at this point to leap forward five years to examine some of Klein's most sensuous and visually compelling works: a series of dark ultramarine monochrome panels which date chiefly from 1960 and 1961 and which measure approximately 2 meters by 1½ meters. There are at least sixteen ultramarine monochromes in variations of this size, a size Klein referred to as "2m × 1,50." They are about 6½ by slightly under 5 feet; thus they are a little taller than most of us and somewhat slimmer than the width of our outstretched arms.

p. 148

Like much of Klein's work, these paintings call attention to surface. That is, they concern the place where illusion and reality, or the deep space of painting and the real world, quite literally coalesce. They appear to the viewer to have deep space for several reasons. We bring to paintings, even to paintings as flat and apparently imageless as these, our previous experience that paintings *are* windows into an ideal world. If we bring to these paintings our experience of the river below and the clouds above the buildings in the *View of Delft*, whose author Klein hugely admired, or our experience of any other great painting, which in a world of museums without walls is not always easy but is also an experience we cannot dismiss once we have had it, then we quite simply expect paintings to have depth. We inject depth into them because the convention is there. Another reason these paintings have depth also has to do with association and memory, but of nature, not art. That is the obvious fact that the sea and the sky, which are the deepest things and the things most like infinity in our daily experience of nature, are blue. It is difficult to look at an expanse of blue paint without making an association, however fleeting, with the sea and the sky. Another reason that these paintings have depth has to do with Klein's artistry — the particularly resonant blue he chose. Klein's ultramarine is not only opulent, it is dark — darker than the ultramarine in a number of monochromes by Ellsworth Kelly, and darker than the blue in so many of the *papiers découpés* of late Matisse.[63] The darkness lends the paintings depth.

Works in the series of this size also have depth because they happen to look more like conventional paintings than many monochromes Klein made. They are neither mural size nor easily portable *tableaux objets*, and the sides of the panels, which as usual Klein painted, are shallow relative to the height and width of the pictures.

At the same time these paintings have depth, they are among the flattest paintings ever painted: they have no internal composition, and there are no marks upon their surfaces which distinguish figure from ground. Instead, they have texture — a dry, grainy surface which is very lush, which makes pigment evident, and which appeals to our haptic sense. This is partly the result of Klein's paint formula, which he patented in 1960 as International Klein Blue, and which I will discuss below. The viewer wants to touch these paintings, a little like the way one wants to touch velvet or stroke skin or let sand run through one's fingers. This, along with the undeniably objectlike qualities of these works — their four slightly rounded corners, their painted sides, the fact that the thin canvases are glued around wood or composition-board panels — brings them into our actual space in a very direct way.

At their best, Klein's blue monochromes manage to carry an illusion of pure, undisturbed depth forward into the real space of the real world. This is as much, in a way, as anyone can ask of a painting. The illusion that infinity has been made present to our ordinary lives does not, in my experience of these paintings, sustain itself for very long, probably not as long as the "minute of truth" Klein often said he wanted, and not as long as in the case of the *View of Delft*, whose mysterious play with sky and water, illusion and surface, defies explanation or maintains wonderment for a longer time. So we are left standing in a gallery of "2m × 1,50" International Klein Blue monochromes wondering about something else: about what are we doing looking at these blue panels. That is, we are left in doubt about whether we are crazy to be there, and we are left with the hope that we can return to look at them another time and again have, for a second, the experience of infinity made present in reality.

To approach the meaning of these works we should backtrack to observe how Klein developed their visual properties and how he determined to present such works to an audience. He first attempted to show a painting publicly in Paris in mid-1955 at a salon.

p. 140 top

This work was a horizontal orange monochrome, slightly larger than three by seven feet; the fairly matte orange paint (probably an early version of Klein's formula) has been applied evenly over a white ground covering the surface of thin composition board. It differs from monochromes Klein made soon after this in a number of respects. It has a title, *Expression du monde de la couleur Mine Orange (Expression of the World of the Color Orange Mineral)*; it is signed on the front, quite prominently, in a calligraphic monogram of the letters *Y* and *K* with a date, "mai 55"; it has sharply right-angled corners; and contemporary photographs suggest that Klein put a narrow strip frame around the painting. When Klein submitted this work to the salon for abstract art, the Salon des Réalités Nouvelles, in July 1955, the rad-

ical character, in the context, of an abstract painting with no composition within its perimeters was immediately given an official seal: in a burlesque of the history of modern French art, the painting was refused. Klein went to considerable trouble to tell part of the story a few years later in "The Monochrome Adventure."

In the presence of monochrome paintings the Boeotians say to me again and again, "But what does that represent?" I could answer and moreover I have already done so, that it represents quite simply blue in itself, or red in itself, or indeed that it is the landscape of the world of the color yellow for example, which is not imprecise, but what matters most in my opinion is the fact that in painting a single color for itself this way I escape the phenomenon of "spectacle" which conventional ordinary classic easel painting is.

You could say to me "okay," no more lines or drawing, but why not two colors? On this subject I think it might be amusing to relate how I was refused at the Salon des Réalités Nouvelles in 1955, this doesn't lack relish and relates well to the point here.

In 1955, then, I register at the appointed time after having made it clear to the Secretariat that I am not at all figurative, and I show some photos (about these I'm told that it will perhaps be difficult to print a good plate for the catalogue). They accept my application and register me. A few months later I receive notice to bring my entry for hanging at the Palais des Beaux-Arts de la Ville de Paris.

There, in the presence of my canvas, various members of the Committee hesitate an instant but agree quite rapidly, with a kind of "Yes, of course," that it can go. They then give me a receipt in exchange and they store my picture, which I had titled *Expression du monde de la couleur Mine Orange*. And what's more, it was quite orange. (That was not yet the period when I was claiming that orange was blue and vice versa.)

I go home enthusiastic at the idea of being hung for the first time in a Grand Salon, but this illusion does not last long, alas! The next afternoon I receive a very dry letter giving me notice of the refusal to show me and asking me to come as quickly as possible to take away my canvas: "Lack of space to store rejected entries." Such is the brutal tone of the letter.

Stupefied, I reply by *pneumatique* (there were only two days left before the opening) to protest, to point out that I am in perfect accord with their regulations, that they never refuse nonfigurative painters, and that I do not understand their attitude. In a few words I assure them of my sincere and serious intention in presenting my entry to their salon, fearing perhaps that they had believed it a provocative joke in bad taste on my part, counter to the spirit of the Salon, which was always very avant-garde and often scoffed at by the press because of that.

My mother, who is well acquainted with all the members of the Salon committee, her colleagues, then receives an extraordinary phone call from one of these notables, whose name I can of course not mention here, and the conversation amounts to this: "You understand, it is really not enough all the same, well then, if Yves would agree at least to add a little line, or a dot, or even simply a spot of another color. We might be able to hang it, but a single plain color, no, no, really that is not enough, it's impossible!"

As I refuse categorically to add anything whatsoever, I receive a second letter the next morning, this time very polite and courteous, but still very firm. I will only mention the last paragraph, absolutely incredible in its totalitarian spirit: "We will be happy, another year, if, considering matters as I have stated them to you, you decide to show with us, providing that, having seen our salon, you can envisage the possibility of reconciling your efforts with ours."

In short, complete dictatorship, in a salon which prided itself on being completely open to all the most advanced endeavors, ideas, and investigations.[64]

Why did Klein make such a lengthy parable (typically, one involving the response of others to his work) out of this incident? Clearly, by doing so he declared his break from official representatives of abstract painting of his mother's generation, and further, he attempted to demonstrate with his story that he was more advanced and more open-minded than the artists of that generation, the "abstracts" to whom he had shown *Yves Peintures* some months earlier. Klein continued to enact this break from both geometric abstraction and gestural abstraction on numerous subsequent occasions, and the style in which he did so is fairly consistent. Instead of naming names — erasing a de Kooning — Klein characteristically questioned the sincerity of decisions made by painters of *art informel* by dramatizing with his behavior the possibility that art is a fraud. His text is an instance of this.

At the outset of this passage Klein widened the audience we might expect him to be addressing to include a constituency beyond the art world, the Boeotians, which we might translate as the Philistines, or, more literally, as ignorant dunces or thickheads. By means of their voice, he introduced a question about the emperor's new clothes, that is, a question which was not commonly raised among the cognoscenti about abstract painting in the middle of the 1950s: "What does that represent?" While Klein attributes the nagging query to thick-heads, it is he as author who has brought the issue "what does this mean?" into the discussion and who thereby attaches the question immediately and directly to his monochromes. Moreover, he tells us that his story is "amusing" and "doesn't lack relish," a tone that hardly matches what follows, his "stupefied" indignation and hurt at the "totalitarian spirit" he encountered. In the course of assuring the Salon (and the reader) of his "sincere and serious intentions . . ., fearing perhaps that [the Salon committee] believed it a provocative joke in bad taste" on his part, Klein himself raised the alternative possibility that he was insincere and that perhaps his monochromes were a joke. Unless he wished to give the reader the opportunity at least to consider this alternative, there is no reason to propose it, particularly in a text assembled several years after the actual event, at a time when Klein was becoming recognized. In addition, rather than soberly describe the rejected painting, he bantered about it himself: "And what's more, it was quite orange. (That was not yet the period when I was claiming that orange was blue and vice versa)." There was no "period" when Klein "claimed" this; indeed, there exist only three or four other orange monochromes. What is this light tone and seemingly preposterous claim doing in the midst of this story in any case? Such bantering hints to the reader not to take everything Klein says at face value. No doubt the parenthetical remark also signals Klein's attraction to the complementaries, that is, to the phenomenon that, by staring at an orange monochrome, one may produce blue before one's eyes in the immaterial form Klein came to favor.

In a sense Klein's orange monochrome *was* represented at the 1955 Salon in immaterial form. For despite the length of his tale, Klein failed to tell all of it: that, by prearrangement, he and several friends attended the opening of the salon and (like a troupe of Walter Arensbergs going to the Independents show and asking to see the *Fountain* by R. Mutt) inquired at intervals where Klein's painting (which was at home in his studio) was hanging.[65]

6

After having passed through several periods, my experiments led me to paint uniform monochrome pictures. My canvases are each layered with one or more coats of a single even color after a certain preparation of the support and by multiple technical processes. No drawing, no variation of hue is visible; there is only the plain, UNIFORM color. Thus, the dominant overruns the whole picture.

I seek in this way to individualize color, because I have come to believe that there is a living world of each color and I express these worlds. My pictures represent an idea of absolute unity in perfect serenity; an abstract idea represented in an abstract manner, which has made me place myself on the side of the abstract painters. I quickly point out that the abstracts themselves do not understand it this way and reproach me among other things for refusing to provoke color relations.

I think that the color yellow, for example, is quite sufficient in itself to create an atmosphere and a climate "beyond the thinkable"; besides, the nuances of yellow are infinite, which makes it possible to interpret it in many ways....

Yves Klein, portion of text
posted at his first Paris
exhibition, *Yves Peintures*,
Club des Solitaires, October 1955[66]

p. 140; cat.
nos. 4–8

In the course of 1955 and 1956 Klein painted monochromes in all the colors of the spectrum and black, in sizes ranging from the seven-foot-wide Salon submission to a vertical yellow panel of 8½ by 6½ inches. The medium of most of these works was Klein's own plastic paint, applied with rollers directly to thin white cloth which had been mounted on wood or fiberboard. The immediate example of *matière* painters such as Dubuffet and Fautrier had made the surface of a painting once again an important focus, and it is likely that the complex mixture of materials (for example, asphalt, plaster, cement, sand, tar) which these artists sometimes used, either instead of or in combination with oil paint, encouraged Klein to experiment with materials.

According to Edouard Adam, the retailer of chemicals and art supplies whose Montparnasse store Klein patronized, Klein was seeking to show pigment itself in as direct and matte a form as possible, and he also wished to work very quickly.[67] Oil hardly permits this, and acrylic colors were not yet stocked in French stores. Like most paints, the synthetic medium which Adam developed for Klein consisted of pigment, binder, and thinner. The novel ingredient for the period was the transparent binder, a polymerized vinyl acetate made by Rhône Poulenc under the name Rhodopas M 60 A; it was an industrial product, a component of varnishes used by manufacturers of maps and books. This binder was not water soluble; the solvents used with it in Klein's paint were alcohol and ethyl acetate. Klein purchased the ingredients from Adam in substantial quantities and mixed them in his studio.[68] The paint dried quickly and left a hard surface.

The monochromes of the period between mid-1955 and middle or late 1956 vary greatly in facture. Some have a low, sandpaperlike surface, some are flat, others in their swirls and pockets of texture resemble icing spread roughly on a homemade cake. A few others are cracking severely today. The variations make clear that Klein was at this point experimenting with the proportions of the ingredients in his paint formula and with housepainters' rollers of different nap.[69] In nearly all cases he attached four sides to his wood or composition-board supports so as to construct what are actually shallow boxes, open at the back. Some of these are as deep as 3⅛ inches. He filed the four front corners of these boxes so that they are rounded, and he painted the sidebars in the same way he painted the front of the panels. In some cases the panels have wood brackets fixed to the back so that the pictures may be hung not against but a few inches in front of the wall, and at his second Paris exhibition, at the Galerie Colette Allendy in late February and early March 1956, some of the dozen or so monochromes in the show were installed in this way.[70] Still another characteristic that contributes to the objectlike quality of some of these rectangular chunks of color is the fact that a few are in proportions of height to width unusual for painting at the time. One, for example, is square, and several others are extremely elongated.

Klein's texts about the monochromes written at the time of his 1955 and 1956 shows in Paris have a neo-Symbolist flavor that disappears in his later writing. But even at this point, when we think that a statement of his is about to hint at what he may intend a certain color to suggest, it turns out that the nuances of the color "are infinite, which furnishes the possibility of interpreting it in many ways."[71] This statement is absolutely characteristic of Klein in that it refuses to settle on a single meaning and encourages the viewer to engage in interpretation. Writing later about the 1956 show, Klein omitted to describe the actual paintings but instead described his work by describing the reactions of spectators to it, reactions he claims to have observed when he scheduled an evening discussion about his monochromes at the gallery:

> On this occasion I immediately noticed an important thing: in the presence of a wall on which canvases of different colors were hung, the public reconstituted the elements into a decorative polychromy. Prisoners of their habitual way of looking, the members of the public, although a select group, didn't place themselves in the presence of the "COLOR" of a single picture. This is what provoked my Blue Period.[72]

Here Klein has coached the reader of his text how not to look at his work, and he has done so tactfully, the implication being that the reader is somehow wiser than members of the art world who erroneously read a wall of Klein monochromes as a kind of Mondrian or single, compositionally relational painting.

7

> At the Galleria Apollinaire in Milan [I had] an exhibition devoted to what I dared to call my Blue Period. (I had in fact already dedicated myself for more than a year to the pursuit of the most perfect expression of "Blue.")
>
> This show consisted of some ten dark blue ultramarine pictures, all rigorously alike in tone, value, proportions, and dimensions. The rather impassioned controversies created by this demonstration proved to me the value of the phenomenon and the genuine degree of the confusion [bouleversement] which it created in men of good will who cared very little about passively supporting the sclerosis of recognized concepts and established rules....
>
> I am happy, despite all my errors and naïvetés and the utopias in which I live, to find myself investigating so contemporary a problem.
>
> All of these blue propositions, all alike in appearance, were recognized by the public as quite different from one another. The amateur passed from one to another as he liked and penetrated in a state of instantaneous contemplation, into the worlds of the blue.
>
> However, each blue world of each picture, although of the same blue and treated in the same manner, revealed itself to be of an entirely different essence and atmosphere; none resembled another, no more than pictorial moments or poetic moments resemble each other. Although all were of the same nature, superior and subtle (registering the immaterial).

> The most sensational observation was that of the "buyers." Each selected out of the...pictures that one that was his, and each paid the asking price. The prices were all different of course. This fact proves, for one thing, that the pictorial quality of each picture was perceptible through something other than the material physical appearance, and for another, that those who made selections were obviously cognizant of that state of things that I call "Pictorial Sensibility."...
>
> So I am in search of the real value of the picture, that is, suppose two paintings rigorously identical in all visible and legible effects, such as lines, colors, drawing, forms, format, density of surface, and technique in general, but the one is painted by a "painter" and the other by a skilled "technician," an "artisan," albeit both officially recognized as "painters" by the public. This invisible real value means that one of these two objects is a "picture" and the other isn't. (Vermeer, van Meegeren.)

Yves Klein,
"The Monochrome Adventure"[73]

Klein's Blue Period began with preparations for *L'Epoca Blu,* his show of eleven virtually identical blue monochromes in the very small Galleria Apollinaire in Milan in January 1957. It reached a kind of apogee in May of the same year in Paris, where, in the tiny Saint-Germain-des-Prés gallery of Iris Clert, Klein repeated the Milan show and, halfway across the city, at Colette Allendy's on the edge of the Bois de Boulogne, he had a concurrent exhibition of objects which instructed the viewer about sundry ways in which the mysterious monochromes might be read.

Each of the virtually identical ultramarine monochromes in the Milan and Paris shows of 1957 *p. 90* measured approximately 30¾ by 22 inches (about 78 by 56 centimeters), and each had a matte, allover, slightly rippled surface, "lightly and regularly wrinkled like the plaster in our apartments," a Milanese critic observed.[74] This texture extended around the sides of the unframed panels. The paintings were hung *fig. 26* on brackets in such a way that they projected in front of the wall, perhaps as much as eight inches. Klein wrote some months after these exhibitions that he had "succeeded in abolishing the space which exists in front of the picture in the sense that the presence of the picture invades this space and the public itself."[75]

These shows and this statement were remarkable as responses to European *art informel* painting. However energetically applied, the personalized strokes of its practitioners tended either to remain well bordered by the grounds on which they were painted or to meet some and echo other of their perimeters in asymmetrical balance. By contrast, Klein's roll-ered finish not only banished composition, it appeared—at least at first glance—impersonal, a quality intensified by the presentation of a series of paintings which looked just like one another and which apparently were easily repeatable. The rich chroma of the panels, their lightly textured surfaces, and their frameless painted sides suggest that these are paintings which extend frontally and laterally beyond the boundaries of traditional pictorial space. Klein's unusual installation of the monochromes some inches in front of the wall, in the setting of very small galleries, emphasized the nature of the panels (and it might be recalled that they *are* panels) as solids in the ambient space of the observer. These monochromes raise the question of whether we should call them paintings at all or whether we should resort to a term coined later, chiefly for three-dimensional art, by an admirer of Klein's work, Donald Judd: "specific objects."[76] If we do we are left with an interesting fact about these 30¾-by-22-inch monochromes: their proportions of 5 to 3.5. These proportions are like those of many prestretched canvases on sale in ordinary art supply stores. Thus on the undoubtedly startling occasion of presenting as one exhibition eleven imageless pictures which appeared identical, Klein did not show rectangles in any of the unusual sizes he had tried out the previous year but employed a format which served to reassure his viewers that the curious blunt boards they encountered looked, in at least one respect, a great deal like what the viewers used to know as paintings.

Between 1957 and his death in 1962 Klein continued to use proportions of height to width of about 5 to 4 for a number of different series of blue monochromes whose dimensions and facture, within a particular series, are almost alike; on occasion he used these 5-to-4 proportions for other works whose status as "paintings" was questionable.[77] He also continued from time to time to create monochromes in sizes which would neither overwhelm nor be diminished by the given situation for which they were initially intended. For example, when planning for his 1961 retrospective, held in the ample but not vast environment of the Museum Haus Lange in Krefeld, a building designed in the 1920s as a private house by Mies van der Rohe, Klein made a number of blue panels in the "2m × 1,50" size.[78]

Klein continued on occasion to install his monochromes so that they projected or appeared to project in front of the wall. An extreme example of this occurred when he became part of a team of artists commissioned in late 1957 to make art on a large scale for the new city theater of Gelsenkirchen, Germany. This commission eventually enabled Klein to make

six huge works: four ten-meter-long blue sponge reliefs — two for the long rear wall of the glass-facaded main foyer and two for the lower-level cloakroom — and two blue monochrome paintings, approximately 7 by 20 meters, for the side walls of the main foyer.[79] These paintings are actually reliefs, made of gypsum inlaid with wire and sprayed with a variant of Klein's paint formula. They are between about 10 and 20 centimeters thick, with a very obvious dry surface texture, indented in mainly vertical waves in the painting on the left of the foyer and in horizontal ripples in the painting at the right. Even these, Klein's largest material works, conformed to his ideas about hanging, for they are not precisely murals. Rather, they are installed on structural members of the building, which jut forward considerably from nonbearing side walls attached to them. These side walls extend above the paintings but not below them. Indeed, the bottom edges of the paintings, with their curved corners, overlap the bottoms of the side walls by several inches. This is no doubt why these works were enlarged from the six-meter height envisioned on an early plan to the seven-meter height that was executed. Because the paintings are fixed to the protruding vertical structural members and overlap the side walls, they appear, despite their enormity, to hover in front of the walls.

p. 161

In the cases I have just discussed Klein has tried by means of the physical characteristics of his monochromes and their installation to collapse the distance between the world of the imagination — that is, the world of pictorial space — and our so-called real world. It is typical of the style of his visual art to attempt such a bridge between the virtual and the actual with means that are sensuous, literal, and explicit. However, it is characteristic of the meaning of his work to resist being limited to any single, direct, unambiguous interpretation.

One response to the 1957 Milan exhibition he received was this: if you have seen one ultramarine monochrome by Yves of a certain size and facture, you have perhaps seen them all. Indeed, a sympathetic review of the show, which Klein read, described this reaction.[80] Klein himself of course provoked this by the act, almost surely unprecedented at the time, of presenting as one exhibition a series of separate imageless paintings which appeared identical in every way. If Klein had been concerned only about color and environment — about forcefully presenting a single stunning hue so as to "invade" the viewer's real space — he might have shown dark ultramarine paintings of several distinctly different yet compatible sizes, and he did do this on certain later occasions. He could surely have availed himself of a straightforward, unprovocative convention for distinguishing among works in series: he could have given his monochromes descriptive titles or simply titles which distinguished one blue panel from another by a label of numbers. It is striking that, although Klein often gave individual titles to works in other media, in the case of his serial monochromes he did not.[81] The point was to leave the discernment of differences up to the viewer — in a context which obviously questioned whether such discernment was possible and whether such discernment made any difference.

That Klein's shows at the Galleria Apollinaire and Galerie Iris Clert in 1957 raised sly questions about the unique worth of individual paintings may be understood as another of Klein's attempts to challenge the aesthetics of *art informel* painting. At least these exhibitions are an attack on the ideology of *art informel* as promoted by outspoken critics such as Tapié, whose writing Klein knew. Both Tapié's insistence that works of *art informel* are made by "paroxysms" of expression and Mathieu's demonstrations on stage of such paroxysms were mocked by an exhibition of eleven paintings which appeared identical and showed no trace of line and very little trace, at first examination, of the artist's hand. As challenges to the aesthetics of gestural abstraction, Klein's Milan and Paris shows of 1957 may be compared to Robert Rauschenberg's nearly identical collages of the same year, *Factum I* and *Factum II*. By repeating drips and smears associated with Abstract Expressionist style in virtually the same manner on both of these "things made," Rauschenberg raised questions about the advice of the critic Harold Rosenberg in his 1952 essay, "The American Action Painters," that the spectator "must become a connoisseur of the gradations among the automatic, the spontaneous, the evoked."[82]

The phenomenon of Duchamp's ready-mades is in certain respects the apposite antecedent of Klein's Milan show. The ready-mades were selected from mass-produced objects and, if lost, could be repeated. There is a sense in which the sight of a gallery hung with eleven virtually identical pictures raises more immediately than a ready-made the issue of the irrelevance of the uniqueness of a material object of art.

Characteristically, Klein on a number of public occasions re-created his 1957 shows of identical blue monochromes in the medium of language, supplementing the central fact of the paintings with a range of different perspectives on them. He did this in a talk at the Institute of Contemporary Art in London in June 1957;[83] in an essay for the Düsseldorf artists' journal, *ZERO*, published in April 1958; in a speech of early 1959 delivered to city officials of Gelsenkirchen, in connection with the mural commission; in his lecture at the Sorbonne in June 1959; and in his continually expanding book, "The Monochrome Adventure," which is the source of the passage I quoted at the beginning of this discussion of the Blue Period. I wish to note in passing that, while each of these descriptions by Klein draws upon the language I have quoted, Klein edited this language fairly drastically according to the audience he was addressing, with the result that he emphasizes different qualities of the Blue Period shows at different times. It is a text which may serve to evoke the ineffable or serve to bait collectors, and in some versions, such as the one I have quoted, it appears to do both at once, leaving the reader with the question of whether the speaker is a mystic or the perpetrator of a put-on.

Klein's first verbal supplement to the Milan show was on the announcement of the exhibition. While the individual paintings were left untitled both to ensure the impact of their sameness and to leave it to the spectators to perceive their differences, the show as a whole did have a title: the outrageously comic label *L'Epoca Blu*, or *Blue Period*.[84] There is no hint in Klein's papers that we are actually to compare the sentimentalizing turquoise of 1901–1904 Picasso to Klein's ultramarine (or that Klein seriously comprehended a certain trend toward single-toned painting from Whistler forward), nor, obviously, was Klein old enough in 1957 or well known enough to have earned classification of his work into art historical periods. That he chose to present himself in this fashion was no doubt partly a publicity stunt, one which, like the book *Yves Peintures*, implied, retroactively, a considerable career. But what the label Blue Period chiefly did was to jest about yet exploit the conventions of the art world, in this instance conventions as commonplace as reproductions of the Mona Lisa. By using these conventions, Klein framed his frameless panels and again raised the possibility that they may be a joke.

In the text itself Klein clinched the joke of the Blue Period label by expressing a certain humility about it ("what I dared to call..."). He went on to suggest how controversial the Milan show was and to state, disingenuously, that its value lay in the confusion it created. After describing how rigorously alike the works were, Klein made a point that his prose could accomplish more effectively than his paintings: he asserted that the observers recognized each of these works of the same hue, dimensions, and so forth, to be different, "of an entirely different essence and atmosphere...none resembled another." As the reader begins to be convinced that Klein is talking about spirit, not matter ("something other than the material physical appearance...'Pictorial Sensibility'"), Klein shuttles swiftly back to the material world with the statement that "the prices were all different of course." Of course? It is hardly surprising that when Klein repeated this sentence at his Sorbonne lecture in 1959, his audience laughed.

The historical fact is that the idea of charging different prices for paintings of the same hue and size occurred to Klein not before but either in the course of or after the Milan exhibition. In contrast to Klein's tale, a reliable review of the show notes that the prices of the blue monochromes were extremely modest, about $56 *per painting*.[85]

Also, in contrast to the implication in Klein's text that all the paintings were sold, which has the effect of advertising their attractiveness and demonstrating that quite a number of people agreed that they had value, in fact there were only three or four buyers, among them the Milanese painter, sculptor, and designer of environments, Lucio Fontana.[86]

There is evidence that Klein did develop the idea of different prices for apparently identical works within a month of the Milan show; in the February 15, 1957, *Le Monde* a critic mentioned that Klein "a little while ago offered rigorously monochrome canvases of the same format at different prices."[87] In a review in the Stockholm newspaper, the *Tidningen*, on October 30, 1957, which discussed Klein's double Blue Period shows in Paris of the previous May, Pontus Hulten noted that Klein was "even able to sell at the same exhibition paintings of the same color and same size at different prices."[88] Whether Klein or Iris Clert actually did this on the occasion of Klein's May 1957 exhibitions remains unclear and hardly matters. That Klein conveyed the *idea* of doing so to critics is significant, because it points to the fact that he was concerned about making an issue, rather than merely a living, out of the monetary value of works of art considerably before he began to try to sell his "voids" in 1958 and his "Immaterial Pictorial Sensibilities" in 1959, and before he first exhibited a Monogold, or panel covered with gold leaf, in Paris in February 1960.

The fact that it was not until after the Milan exhibition that Klein said that different sums were charged for virtually identical paintings is an example of the way Klein, through the medium of prose and conversation, applied meanings to his objects after

he had received some response to them.

A close examination of some of the works in the several series of blue monochromes of course shows that there are differences among the paintings. For example, the panels in the "2m × 1,50" series of 1960 and 1961 often vary in dimensions by several inches, and the surfaces of these large pictures may differ slightly also. For example, if one compares IKB 68 to IKB 69 (the numbers are posthumous), one notices that Klein has mixed some tiny pebbles into the lower left-hand area of the surface of the former, so that the panels are clearly not quite identical. In addition to writing about the paintings' being different, and in addition to building differences into the almost identical works for the small but perhaps significant part of his audience who might look very closely, Klein pointed to the varying factures of successive series by making two assemblages out of used lambskin paint rollers of noticeably different nap.

p. 164

Minute differences among the monochromes in a series of the same format and nearly identical texture are necessary to maintain the tension in these works, when they were hung together as Klein wished, between their immediate impact as works that are alike and the interest in individual surfaces that arises from the perception of small variations: the differences would not be so telling if they did not occur in the context of overall sameness. Klein's paintings are not simple copies of one another or of some single original nor, obviously, is each unique, and this formal tension, visible when one experiences a room of blue monochromes, gives the works part of their vitality.

The formal tension just described has its counterpart in the effect of the works as statements about the nature of art. In this context, Klein's paintings are perhaps close to what Walter Benjamin has termed the "manual reproduction, which was usually branded as a forgery."[89] The usefulness of Benjamin's term is that it discriminates a gray area between originals ("High Art") and mechanical reproductions: the gray area of the handmade copy, which hovers ambiguously between forgery and a new view of an old subject. It is not clear which of these an assembly of Klein's monochromes is intended to be, and it is this that generates both the possibility that they are a gigantic joke and the possibility that they are authentic art.

The issue of forgery also arises in Klein's text about the Blue Period paintings. He wrote that he was in search of their "real value," and that their real value was "invisible." He enlarged on this claim, an unusual one to make for visual art, by writing that the "public" cannot distinguish between a "painter" and an "artisan" or see the difference between a Vermeer and a van Meegeren. Simply by mentioning the subject of the famous craftsman of fakes, who was a kind of folk hero during the late 1940s, Klein raised the question of how the public is to distinguish authentic art from art which has been authenticated by experts, in this case the scholarly representatives of the Dutch art world who bought van Meegerens for Dutch museums believing that they were Vermeers.[90] The question proposes that the public cannot determine authentic from fake art through appreciation of an artist's craftsmanship or by traditional methods of connoisseurship. The real value of art, Klein wrote, is invisible; it lies beyond what one can see.

By implication Klein's question about authentic versus authenticated art also challenged certain conventions of the vanguard world in which Klein had grown up and in which he worked: that it was forbidden to doubt the sincerity of the hundreds and hundreds of abstract painters whose works filled the annual independent salons, and that it was perhaps bad form to demur about their talents.

In addition, by bringing up the subject of van Meegeren Klein once more employed the technique he used when he raised the possibility that his submission of the orange monochrome to the Salon des Réalités Nouvelles was a "provocative joke in bad taste" on his part. That is, his mention of the forger has the effect of pointing to the possibility that there may have been an element of fraud in his own stance.

There are, then, at least three tones of voice for the same set of words about the problem of discerning the "real value" of painting: the tone of a critic, who laments the situation that art historians have questionable motives for making attributions and that abstract painters may be perpetrating frauds; the tone of an impostor, who suggests that he may share in the activity he is criticizing; and the tone of a real artist, who by breaking the artists' taboo and allowing the imputation, even about himself, that some artists may be hypocrites shows how sincere *he* is. We have no way of establishing unequivocally which tone of voice dominates.

Earlier I said that on the occasion of his two concurrent exhibitions in Paris in May 1957, Klein instructed observers not only with words but also with sundry objects and activities about ways in which the eleven Blue Period panels on view at Iris Clert's might be understood. The publicity and invitations to both shows, and in particular the contents of the show at Colette Allendy's, constituted a set of interpretations or deformations of the monochromes. These deformations stress various single or multiple aspects of the paintings which the paintings themselves may not make entirely obvious. With the Allendy show Klein "illustrated" his own pictures with other works of art. In this sense the show was a microcosm of his subsequent work: the parade of little books and long texts, of acts of theater, of photographs, and of illusionistic objects with which Klein expressed doubt about the capacity of abstract painting to signify unaided.

The show at Iris Clert's opened Friday evening, May 10, 1957, four days before a second opening at Colette Allendy's. An audience from slightly beyond the art world was summoned to the first opening by grape clusters of blue balloons — according to Klein, 1,001 of them — which were paraded from the gallery itself in the rue des Beaux-Arts to the Place Saint-Germain-des-Prés, where the bunches were let loose in the church courtyard. The sidewalk outside the gallery was painted blue.[91] With this festive advertisement from the street to the sky, Klein reaffirmed his ability to get himself into the newspapers and demonstrated for the first time in public, in the literal manner typical of his style, his attraction to the ephemeral and the unfettered. He later claimed that the blue balloons were his first "aerostatic sculpture," sculpture which, he wrote, would solve the "problem of the base."[92]

fig. 29

Publicity about the double shows advertised "paintings" at Clert's and "pure pigments" at Allendy's, and for the first time in a public document described Klein as "Yves le monochrome," that is, as Yves the monochrome, not Yves the monochromist. The intimate connection that Klein wove between himself and his objects probably begins with the autobiographical legends ("à Londres, 1950"; "à Tokio, 1952") under the pasted papers in the booklet of 1954, *Yves Peintures*, and it could be said to culminate in his decision in 1960 to patent his synthetic paint as International Klein Blue and henceforth to name his serial paintings after the paint — for short, IKBs. It is a paradox characteristic of Klein that while his artist's *patte* appears impersonal, he personalized his paint and, as I will show, anthropomorphized many of his paintings.

The postcards which announced the double exhibitions suggest another attempt by Klein to attract an audience beyond the art world. The postage on these cards consisted of Klein's own blue stamps: ultramarine stamp-size paper rectangles with perforated edges. Klein continued to use these "stamps" to mail announcements within France at least as long as he exhibited with Iris Clert (through 1959), and he was sufficiently concerned to establish whether announcements bearing fake stamps such as these ac-

figs. 28, 44

tually went through the mail that he repeatedly addressed invitations to himself and saved envelopes returned to the sender because the addressee had moved. According to Iris Clert, these mailings were arranged by paying the normal required postage at the post office while simultaneously tipping the postal clerk to cancel the postcards or envelopes over or near Klein's stamps.[93] It was an effort by Klein to widen the dragnet for his art — in this instance to include and co-opt the government. Each postmark was an official validation, a stamp of approval on top of Klein's stamp of blue, and each postman who carried one of these postcards had briefly to become the deliverer of Klein's blue, as the addressees had to become on some level receivers of it.

Klein's stamps were also a spurious self-decoration: like stamps issued by the French government in reproduction of well-known paintings or in commemoration of nationally significant cultural figures, Klein's stamps proposed that his ultramarine paintings were important. However, like the pasted papers in Klein's 1954 booklet, the stamps are best understood as original monochromes which belong to an extremely large series. Each stamp measures 2½ by 2 centimeters, like the proportions of so many of Klein's serial panels, a proportion of height to width of 5 to 4.

If we consider the various works in proportions of about 5 to 4, including the monochrome panels in the series I described earlier and still other works which remain to be discussed, then we become conscious not only of their relationship, in terms of literal size, to the spaces for which they were intended, but also of their relationship to one another. Regarded this way, Klein's sense of scale, like his ideas about the surface of a painting, seems to be concerned with the place where the physicality of his objects meets what we might consider to be his projections about their metaphysics. That is, if we were to line up the proportionally similar blue monochromes, from the postage stamp to the "2m × 1,50" size (an order which is not one of chronological appearance), it could be suggested that Klein, as he made works which deeply respected specific environments, was at the same time making works which advanced the idea that their literal size could be expanded to any situation which called for it. By drawing attention to the way his objects might be scaled down or scaled up, Klein suggested the possibility that their size might be reduced to nothing or expanded infinitely.

Among the most blunt, seemingly simple, and didactic works in the Allendy show was a set of eight small, hollow, box-like objects, which Klein in his

scrapbook termed *reliefs bleus*. These have been p. 144 posthumously classified as sculpture, and the four examples extant appear in Wember's catalogue as Sculptures 1, 3, 4, and 5. At Allendy's the eight reliefs were cantilevered from the wall in two vertical rows of four each, spaced at approximately even intervals from one another. Each of these objects is 7⅝ inches deep by 4¾ by 3¾ inches (19.5 by 12 by 9.5 centimeters), that is, each projects forward 7⅝ inches from the wall and has a front face that is 4¾ inches high and 3¾ inches wide. The seams where any two planes meet have been slightly rounded, and so have the corners of the front faces. S 1, 3, 4, and 5 have been substantially restored, so it is difficult to discuss with any authority the nature of their surfaces as Klein made them in 1957. Today they appear porous but not yielding.

Judging from the relationship of the objects to a door in Allendy's gallery which is visible in a photograph of the original installation — a photo Klein pasted into his scrapbook — the blue reliefs appear to have been hung at a height that began somewhat above eye level and continued down to about chest level or perhaps slightly lower. While today we can easily appreciate that an artist who carefully continued the texture of the front of his paintings around to their sides did not intend these sides to be encased by frames, it is less immediately apparent that the artist who installed his paintings several inches in front of the wall in fact originally hung his blue reliefs directly against it. An awareness of Klein's original installation is important if we understand the works in the Allendy show as signposts in object form to qualities of the monochromes simultaneously on view at Iris Clert's.

The blue reliefs refer to the monochrome panels in many ways. The most immediately noticeable characteristic of the reliefs is that their longest dimension is perpendicular to the wall, a condition that is most unusual even for high relief. They protrude forward into the real space of the observer in a direct fashion, which may have put early observers of Klein's paintings on notice about the way the paintings at the Iris Clert show were hung forward from the wall, also in our real space. It is also obvious that, hung together closely as they were, the reliefs are a group of works in a series — or perhaps even one work. This collocation in unity points to the ambiguity of the show at Clert's — to the way that the ten or eleven monochromes there were identical yet different. Because the reliefs exist clearly in three dimensions, the rounding, where two planes meet and where three corners come together, is particularly manifest. This perhaps indicated the less noticeable rounding of the corners of the panel paintings, a fact about the paintings which, as noted, encourages us to view them as a kind of object. Indeed, the boxlike morphology of these *reliefs bleus* encourages us to look at the paintings as boxes instead of as paintings. The most interesting correspondence between these reliefs and the monochrome panels at Clert's is that, if we stand in a traditional posture in relation to the works (that is, if we face them frontally), the facades of the boxes are in Klein's favored proportions: the ratio of height to width, 12 to 9.5 centimeters, works out to a proportion of 5 to 3.9. This anchors the relationship of these works to the paintings at Iris Clert's, to the stamps on the invitations to both shows, and to the subsequent series of paintings in very similar proportions. Therefore these reliefs suggest that Klein's paintings, which have obvious surfaces and a blatant existence in our real space, also have depth: these objects, which Klein called reliefs, have deepness as their most dominant dimension. The illusion of deep space in the paintings is "illustrated" by the fact of this depth.

The show at Colette Allendy's was the first occasion on which Klein exhibited works made of sponge, a curious and elegant found material which proved to be a telling metaphor for his desire to involve his audience in his blue world and which he employed brilliantly to exaggerate certain formal questions raised by the serial monochromes. Between 1957 and 1961 Klein made several hundred of what he called "sponge sculptures" and nearly fifty of what he called "sponge reliefs."

One quality of the monochrome paintings which he reiterated with this large number of sponge works was the ambiguity he wrote about: the issue of whether the panels were all alike or all different. Klein did this both by grouping many different sponges on one sponge relief and by showing, on several occasions, many sponge sculptures grouped together, for example, in a June 1959 show at Iris Clert's which he *fig. 45* called *Bas-reliefs in a Forest of Sponges*. While each tree in this forest was unique in appearance, each was also similar to its neighbor in being made of the same arresting phylum *(poriphera)* of *objet trouvé* and, in most cases, in being blue. Klein varied the types of sponges he used, generally employing soft ones of the kind used for bathing or cleaning, which he hardened with a binder before painting, but occasionally using the kind of spiny, calcified sponge known as white coral. As unique objects, the sponge sculptures partake of the aura which surrounds an original. However, as part of a series that Klein demonstrated was very large and that was obviously easily

expandable, these objects might be available to many people. Indeed, a note at the end of the catalogue of Klein's retrospective exhibition in Krefeld offered a blue Yves Klein sponge to visitors who purchased a catalogue.[94] Most artists, when requested by a museum director to make a work in an edition available for sale by the museum, would make a numbered edition of identical fine prints. It is typical of Klein that in such a situation he chose to offer objects in a series whose members were in fact each visibly different.

Klein was perhaps stimulated to use sponges as a material by the example of Dubuffet's soft, uncolored sponge figures of 1954, such as *The Maestro* or *The Duke*. Some of Klein's sponge sculptures are remarkably anthropomorphic. They are commonly, although not always, vertical; many are mounted on bases of metal or stone with a stem of wire or metal pipe. Several which have entered museum collections were given titles identifying them as "portraits" of Klein's audience, for example, the works of 1960 such as *Lecteur IKB (IKB Reader)*, SE   *p. 167* 171, or Krefeld's *Le Veilleur IKB (IKB Watcher)*, SE 174. In a paragraph from "Notes on some works shown at Colette Allendy's," a two-page text Klein wrote some months after the 1957 exhibition, he made vividly clear what he wished such objects to depict:

> In working on my pictures in my studio, I sometimes used sponges. They became blue very quickly, obviously! One day I noticed the beauty of the blue in the sponge; at once this working tool became raw material for me. It is that extraordinary faculty of the sponge to become impregnated with whatever may be fluid that seduced me. Thanks to the sponges — raw living matter — I was going to be able to make portraits of the observers [*lecteurs*] of my monochromes, who, after having seen, after having voyaged in the blue of my pictures, return totally impregnated in sensibility, as are the sponges.[95]

Klein's sponge reliefs can be described as monochrome panels to which many rather flat, roundish sponges painted the color of the ground have been fixed. A number of them, for example RE 10, 1960 —   *cat. no. 45* *L'Accord bleu (Blue Harmony)* — and RE 20, 1960,   *p. 156* are in the approximately "2m × 1,50" size used for the particularly impressive series of monochrome paintings. At his Krefeld retrospective Klein installed sponge reliefs of this size in rooms together with paintings from the series of the same size, as if they were interchangeable. The fact that the sponges literally project forward from their grounds —and in   *p. 157 top;* some cases project laterally beyond the perimeters of   *p. 158* their rectangular grounds so as to suggest a strangely organic version of what was soon after termed a "shaped canvas" — once again points to the way the monochrome panels themselves come forward from pictorial space to inhabit the viewer's actual space.

The sponge reliefs were also an inventive way for Klein to reintroduce composition into wall-hung objects without abandoning monochromy and without recourse to "relational" painting. The distribution of sponges on these panels constitutes a composition which appears neither asymmetrically balanced, in the tradition of much Western painting, nor aggressively, mindlessly scattered. Rather, the placement of the sponges appears random yet calmly controlled, and it surely drew upon Klein's memory of the Zen gardens he had visited in Kyoto. The arrangement at the Ryoan temple garden there, of five groups of stones within an architecturally bounded rectangle of raked gravel, presents an order that looks at once mentally conceived and natural, as if the stones had grown in place. That the sponge reliefs were made of materials we associate with nature reinforces the parallel between them and the gardens of Kyoto, and again it introduces the puzzle of a dichotomy into Klein's work.

Among the most inventive supplements to the monochromes on view at Iris Clert's that Klein installed in the show of "pure pigments" at Colette Allendy's was just that: a low tray, placed on the floor, containing dry ultramarine pigment in powder form.[96] At his Krefeld retrospective Klein reconstructed this, showing a tray of blue pigment, 47½ by 39⅓ inches (120 by 100 centimeters), and a second tray of rose pigment, 36¼ by 28¾ inches (92 by 73 centimeters).[97] Not surprisingly, these dimensions are in Klein's favored proportions of height to width, and the rose tray was the same size as Klein's most extensive series of monochrome panels of virtually identical format.

p. 145

In his 1957 newspaper article Pontus Hulten noted about the Blue Period shows that a small rake lay in the tray of blue and that one could, if one wished, use this to create patterns on the surface.[98] No doubt the idea of the rake also sprang from Klein's knowledge of Japanese gardens of gravel or sand raked carefully into patterns. The rake in the pigment engages the actual participation of the observer in the work in a direct and conspicuous fashion: decisions about where imagery or configuration of any kind might go are left to the player in the sandbox, and such decisions may be quickly reversed. Like the *Métamatics* of Klein's friend, Jean Tinguely, whose do-it-yourself machines invite the observer to create

his own abstract paintings, Klein's rake gently mocked *art informel*. The position of the tray on the floor perhaps made oblique reference also to American Abstract Expressionist painting — or rather to documents of its making: Hans Namuth's early 1950s photographs of Jackson Pollock pouring paint from above onto unstretched canvas on the floor. These icons of information about artistic process were well known to European artists of Klein's generation, and it is unlikely that an artist as aware as Klein of issues relating to vanguardism was unaware of their general content. However, the important point here is that in Klein's typically literal style, the rake in the pigment put the observer, not the artist, in the purported "arena" of picture-making, and thereby called attention to the hermeneutical quality of the blank monochromes — to the fact that these panels derive most of their meaning from the interpretation we choose to bring to them. To put it another way, one of their central meanings is to raise the question, What does this mean? The rake in the tray pushes the question to, Observer, what will you make this mean?

Klein's paragraph about the tray of blue in his notes on the Allendy show indicates his interest in something as minute in size as an individual particle of pigment and his awareness that he was changing the axis of the pictorial rectangle from vertical to horizontal in a way that would alter the viewer's relationship to the work. As Klein described it,

> pure pigment shown on the floor became a picture on the ground and no longer on the wall [*cimaise*], the fixative medium then being the most immaterial possible, that is, the force of gravity itself. This didn't alter the grains of pigment individually, as happens inevitably with oil, glue, and even with my particular fixative medium. The only drawback of this: man naturally holds himself upright and looks toward the horizon.[99]

In terms of the "drawback" of altering the viewer's relationship to a work in a literal way, Klein's "pure pigment" and his comment upon it remind us of Duchamp's ready-made of 1917, *Trébuchet*, the coat rack he nailed to the floor of his studio. And they anticipate certain later works by Klein, for example, *La Tombe — ci-gît l'espace (The Tomb — Here Lies Space)*. Klein installed this 50-by-40-inch gold panel of 1960 not on the wall but on blocks as a kind of low table, roughly parallel to the floor but at a distinct tilt, and he had himself photographed with his eyes closed lying under the "tomb," thus making a direct connection between the panel and his body.

p. 214

Because Klein's trays are peculiarly insistent

about entering our physical space and because at the same time these works are resolutely abstract (they have no image that can be read — unless we make one — yet if they are in an art exhibition, they must *mean* something), they address both the actual world and the world of the imagination in a way that teases and frustrates our attempts to achieve a clear image of the relationship between these two worlds. As we have seen, this situation recurs repeatedly in Klein's work and suggests that exploration of various inflections of the relationship between the ideal and the actual is one of the major themes of the work as a whole. His work shows that he recognized the distinction an audience often makes between something called "art" or aesthetic experience and the variously muddled, whether trivial or impelling, aspects of experience that we do not immediately associate with art. (It is classical, and perhaps classically confusing, to call these things "life," but perhaps "ordinary experience" will do.) One of the remarkable things about Klein's work is the way in which it continually confronts us with the distinction itself — questioning it, exploring it, pinpointing its inadequacies, yet recognizing something essential to it, and passing on, perhaps, his own uncertainties about it to us. It is this concern that I term thematic.

Klein made it clear that he wished to rain blue on the milieu of the Allendy exhibition by installing a kind of sculpture, the *Pluie bleue (Blue Rain)* to hang near or over the tray of pigment. He reconstructed the *Blue Rain* for the Krefeld retrospective and added a *Red Rain* there. These works each consisted of several slender painted wooden dowels, slightly longer than two meters, hung from nylon filament at slightly different heights so that, according to witnesses, they did not quite reach the tops of the blue and red trays.

Another work introduced in the Allendy show with which, it appears, Klein intended to instruct his viewers to enter his blue world was the *Paravent*, IKB 62 in Wember's catalogue, a five-part folding screen of canvas stretched on hinged wooden frames, 59 inches high by 137¾ inches in total length (1½ by 3½ meters). Klein wrote about the screen that it "enabled envelopment in blue. One could arrange [it] in a semicircle in such a way as to be able to place oneself as observer of the work at the center of the diameter."[100]

Like much of Klein's later work, one of the more startling objects in the exhibition was both aggressive in its approach to viewers, and ephemeral. This was the *Feux de Bengale — Tableau de feu bleu d'une minute (Bengal Flares — One-Minute Blue*

p. 168

Fire Painting), as Klein called the work in his writings about the Allendy show. He was making reference by this informal title to Pierre Restany's short critical explication of monochrome paintings, "La Minute de vérité" ("The Minute of Truth"), which had appeared on the invitations to Klein's first show at Allendy's the year before. The *Tableau de feu* (M 41 in Wember's catalogue) was a plywood panel, 44 by 29½ inches (112 by 75 centimeters). Klein had rendered it blue in what was for him a painterly fashion, possibly with a brush, and fitted it with sixteen Bengal lights, a kind of cylindrical signal flare that gives off a fairly sustained, vivid, blue illumination. Klein set these, in four evenly spaced rows of four, so they protruded forward and skyward from the panel at an angle of about thirty degrees. He mounted the panel on an ordinary studio easel, presumably to reinforce, as did his paint strokes, the notion that this object was a painting, and to remind his observers that it was a painting still in the process of being made. He placed this in the garden of Colette Allendy's house and, after having himself photographed beside it, at the opening ignited the lights. Today the panel, minus the Bengal lights, is slightly charred and uninteresting visually, except as a document of the first material ashes of Klein's art. As an object in this form, however, it still possesses a certain meaning about the relationship between a work and its audience: it serves to suggest that to have witnessed its making would have been a more intense experience than to observe its charred remains.

fig. 31

cat. no. 11

In Klein's first written comments about the *Tableau de feu*, he said that the effect of the burning "gave to the observers, after the picture consumed itself, the sensation of expanding in recollection, in the visual memory."[101] In a later description he enlarged on the effects of the work:

> I was at once able to envisage the immense possibilities of the Ultra Living element. If all that changes slowly is explained by life, all that changes quickly is explained by fire.... The visible duration: one minute. The observer, visually illuminated, carried away his vision in recollection — but not in the past — because the affective impression, the sensual image of the tablet of fire, became more and more present and increased in the visual memory. You might as well say that the duration of a minute plus the sensation of the immobile speed of fire suppressed the phenomenology of time.[102]

It is clear from Klein's text that he had read some of Gaston Bachelard's *Psychoanalysis of Fire*, for the following words appear in the midst of the first paragraph of the first chapter of this essay: "If all that changes slowly may be explained by life, all that changes quickly is explained by fire. Fire is the ultra-living element."[103] Klein's absorption of Bachelard's prose extends to the phrase about suppressing "the phenomenology of time," which reflects Bachelard's book of 1936, *The Dialectic of Duration*. Klein owned this book and appears to have read at least up to part three of the second chapter, after which the pages are uncut. Bachelard argues against what he describes as a Bergsonian notion of time, that is, that we experience time psychologically in a continuous thread; and he writes in favor of the thesis that "duration is metaphysically complex and that the decisive centers of time are its discontinuities." There is, Bachelard writes,

> beyond lived time, thought time. This thought time is more aerial, more free, more easily broken off and recaptured....It is in this time that a fact becomes a factor.[104]

The notion of time Bachelard presents in this book has to do in part with moments of poetic intensity such as we may imagine Klein sought with the *Tableau de feu,* and Bachelard's evocative language explains or, at any rate, puts forth the idea that such moments are recoverable in memory. Bachelard's statement early in the book that "the problem of the recall of memories may be illuminated...by paying more attention to the instant in which the memories are really fixed"[105] is one we may link directly to Klein's description of the blue fire painting of a minute, which, Klein wrote, will expand in the recollection of the viewer, after he has been "visually illuminated" by the Bengal lights.

It seems obvious that Bachelard's prose style in his lighter works, of which Klein owned seven volumes, appealed to Klein on account of its sensuousness, and an extensive argument can be made about Klein's assimilation of certain Bachelardian imagery and language into his art during and after 1958.[106] Nevertheless, it would be a mistake to take either Bachelard's appeal for Klein or Klein's original statement about the *Tableau de feu* at face value as concerns the notion that poetic moments are necessarily recoverable and expandable in memory.

First of all, Klein's insertion of Bachelard's words into his own and onto his object is a good example of the way Klein attached interpretation and reinterpretation to his objects *after* they had appeared in the world. The irony of this in this instance is that Bachelard's term "ultra-living" has been applied to a work that is in reality quite dead visually, a fact Klein

knew and a fact we know, whether or not we are sorry we were not present at the minute of creation. By adding to the charred blue panel something extrinsic to it — both his own words and lines from the first paragraph of an eloquent essay all about fire, which by implication carries Bachelard's entire short book into the meaning of the panel — Klein demonstrated his doubts precisely about whether a "painting of one minute" can last in memory. If it can, it is perhaps not necessary to describe it, nor to attach to it, after this memory was supposedly made, the poetics of someone else. In other words, in order for the fact of this particular painting to become a factor for more than a minute, it had to be reconstructed in language, which Klein made clear by doing so.

To conclude this discussion of the *Tableau de feu,* Klein's statement — which also grew from this work — that his paintings were the ashes of his art should be considered in the range of its implications: from what it evokes about immateriality and spirit to what such a statement may mean to the lover of visual art (that is, to someone who prefers Vermeer to ashes), and in terms of the fact that the statement teases us swiftly into thinking about Klein.

Finally, it should be noted that the *Tableau de feu,* like so many objects in the Allendy show, was the initial experiment in a series of works — in this case works relating to fire. These were mostly developed from late 1960 onward, and they include Klein's Fire Fountain and Fire Wall at the Krefeld museum during his retrospective, his fire drawings and fire paintings, and his projects for an architecture of air, fire, and water, elements which were to provide the walls for his utopian communities.

Klein's *Cris bleus* ("blue cries") — human cries which he tape-recorded as a soundtrack to accompany film footage about the Paris Blue Period shows — constituted yet another supplement to the shows themselves, and like many of Klein's texts, the cries appear to coach the witness about appropriate behavior in the presence of Klein's works: sustained, active participation. It could be said that Klein used the cries to validate the worth of his art, for they were shouts in its favor by representatives of the art world. However, at the same time, and in the same spirit in which he toyed with collectors about prices, he used them to make fun of a well-known older critic, Charles Estienne. Klein's deadpan description of having asked Estienne to sing for the Blue Period monochromes is particularly amusing if we keep in mind that the critic was a partisan of *tachisme* and Klein's mother's work, and was famous among other reasons for an interview with Matisse published in 1909. Klein wrote about the "blue cries of Charles Estienne":

I made a little 16mm color film on my Blue Period shows in 1957. I needed a commentary, preferably spoken by an art critic. Therefore I asked Charles Estienne to agree to utter some blue cries for the roughly twenty minutes the short film lasted. The blue cries — the longest and most volumetric possible of them — were inspired by my canvases in my rue Campagne-Première studio.

That was very successful, and I must say that the film will retain the prestigious commentary that Charles had the courage at this period to back up with his profound conviction.

These cries are fairly long, continuous, and uttered with vigor (he had asked me for two weeks to train before letting himself be recorded). To give only an approximate idea of these cries: they are somewhat like the cries which sailors utter at regular intervals to avoid collisions when the mist is thick.[107]

Klein's use of conspicuous charlatanry showed itself in connection with the cries when he played tape recordings of them at his Sorbonne lecture in 1959. The context was a discussion of the Japanese habit of presenting honorific awards to nonprofessionals in a given field, a subject he raised to justify his own entry into the field of music with his *Monotone Symphony,* a one-chord composition of adjustable duration, and with his *Cris.* He told the Sorbonne audience:

Several years ago I created a monotone symphony of which this is an extract. [About seven seconds of what sounds like unbroken bowing of a stringed instrument at F-sharp below C below middle C.]

Now, a cry from François Dufrêne, a monotone cry. [About fifteen seconds of a high, piercing, continuous cry.]

Now, a cry — listen! — a cry from Charles Estienne. [About ten seconds of a low, steady "ohhhhhhh."]

And now, a very beautiful cry from Antonin Artaud. [About twelve seconds of an anguished, scratchy, unsteady shriek.][108]

During the playing of the tape-recorded cries, the Sorbonne audience laughed hard, for these sounds of adult male voices uttering commitment to Klein's work are funny to listen to. In the case of the "very beautiful cry" attributed to Artaud, the sounds were quite evidently faked as commentary on Klein's work,

for the playwright and theoretician of theater had died in 1948 — a fact which no doubt occurred to some of Klein's listeners. One effect of this conspicuous charlatanry was to broaden the constituency for Klein's work: skeptics could at least laugh when they heard the cries, and in that way be drawn in to react to Klein's world.

The literal-mindedness Klein demonstrated with the tape-recorded cries relates to the issue of the presence of his painting in the real space of the observer. With the cries Klein again tried to collapse the distance that is conventionally said to exist between the world of the imagination and our so-called real world, by getting grown men to make noises that purportedly express aesthetic experience.

I said earlier that by "illustrating" aspects of the monochromes at Iris Clert's with sundry didactic objects at Colette Allendy's, Klein expressed doubt about the capacity of abstract art to signify unaided. Later he expressed a related anxiety: that the public for art might not bother to stop and notice the significant qualities of the monochromes. He did this in a brief article, "Les Cinq Salles," published on November 27, 1960, in his fake newspaper, *Dimanche.*[109] Here Klein amplified the example of the eleven Blue Period panels installed together and expanded on an earlier formulation in "The Monochrome Adventure," that his "pictures create ambiences." He opens "Les Cinq Salles" by writing that "the bond between spirit and matter is energy." He proceeds to describe a kind of ideal (and theatrical) situation for showing his monochromes, so that, according to his text, they will convey a "moment of extraordinary and extra-dimensional illumination." In sum, he proposes a "demonstration in five rooms crossed by spectators dragging balls and chains on their feet." This was to consist first of a room of nine blue monochromes, all the same color (IKB) and format; next, an empty room, immaculately white (IKI — International Klein Immaterial); third, a room of nine Monogolds, the same format as the blues; fourth, a dark, almost black empty room of International Klein Nothingness *(néant);* and fifth, a room of nine Monopinks, the same format as the blues and golds.

Klein appears to have written this text detailing an environmental installation of his work in the late summer or early fall of 1960, during the same months that he began to work on designs for the installation of his retrospective at Krefeld, which opened in mid-January 1961. A draft of one of his first letters to the director of the museum in Krefeld, Paul Wember, shows that Klein was hoping (although it did not quite work out that way) to have a room which showed the Blue Period — five or seven 200×150 cm pictures, and with that some pictorial sponge sculptures, some sponge reliefs, a big blue monochrome screen, some pure pigments.... [110]

In other words he wanted to reproduce an entirely blue environment with paintings of a certain size, and his later notations about the installation, worked out with floor plans of the Mies building that he had requested from the museum director, specified that the paintings be hung forward from the wall. [111] The retrospective turned out to display many more — in fact, most — aspects of Klein's work. As an exhibition finally hung in an attractive public museum on the scale of a private house, it seems to have showed off particularly well Klein's personal modification of the primaries into ultramarine, gold, and deep pink. It is significant that Klein at first planned to repeat his Blue Period as an important part of the show, and that he thought of the installation as something he wished firmly to control.

Klein did not, in late 1960 when he was planning the Krefeld show, possess nine blue, nine gold, and nine pink monochromes of the same format — the ideal installation he proposed in "Les Cinq Salles" (although in one of his plans for the museum show he colored one large room blue, one yellow, and one red). Nor did he ever make as many as nine pink or gold monochromes of the "200×150" size. What is most curious about the text "Les Cinq Salles" is the way it reveals that, by the time of its appearance in 1960, the reasonably gentle — if sometimes hilarious — seduction, provocation, teasing, and cajoling of his audiences which characterized his Blue Period in 1957 had hardened into something with a distinctly misanthropic undertone. In order to experience "extraordinary illumination," the observers, Klein wrote, would traverse the five rooms dragging balls and chains on their feet. This discomfort and humiliation may be understood as Klein's method of forcing art lovers to slow down their progress to involve themselves deeply in the experience of the rooms. This would be one art exhibition which, despite its apparent directness and simplicity, would be impossible to run through quickly. Klein would literally control the hasty, superficial habits of visitors to galleries. Weighty balls and chains might also be understood as the inverse of the freedom and immateriality which the paintings in some respects suggest: thus, paradoxically, the wearers of the weights might come to know the paintings more richly because of the contrast between what they saw and their physical condition. However, read in the context of

other texts in *Dimanche* (in one, for example, Klein proposed that theater-goers be gagged and chained to their seats to experience "pure sensibility"), [112] the necessity for the bondage of balls and chains suggests what it may cost to arrive at a moment of transcendence. The means to this end are uneasy, even totalitarian; a certain ruthlessness in the course of the search for purity of vision had by 1960 come to interest Klein.

In summary, we have seen Klein write about the importance of the space in front of his paintings, about making portraits of his observers as sponges impregnated with blue, about his pictures creating an ambience in the real space of the observers; and we have noted the particularly objectlike nature of the Blue Period paintings and their saturated and sometimes relieflike surfaces. There is also the condition, referred to briefly earlier, that the pure monochromy of Klein's paintings pushes forward in a peculiarly intense fashion the question raised by all nonobjective painting: "What does this mean?" This question is an aggressive part of the content of Klein's monochromes, and the spectator himself must supply at least some of the answer. In addition to the extreme pressures toward vanguardism which flourished in the art world Klein inhabited and about which he was often witty, the fact that the question "What does this mean?" was an inherent part of Klein's objects partly explains his passion to establish his originality in regard to the monochromes, for the less novel they are, the less demanding the question becomes. While it is quite possible to conjecture with good sense and plausible evidence about Klein's "iconography," it is a central characteristic of his work to avoid settling on any specific meaning for, say, the color blue. For him to close in on a specific meaning might exclude a potential member of the audience who, by inventing his own meaning, engages with the work itself.

The show at Colette Allendy's was a remarkable storehouse of the possibilities contained in the mysterious monochromes hanging at Iris Clert's. Works such as the tray of pigment demand that we participate and address the issue of our bodies and the issue of the surface of a painting; the sponges are portraits of our heads and refer to nature and series; the cantilevered boxes protrude into our space yet illustrate depth. The summonses to both exhibitions — the balloons released skyward, which forecast Klein's interest in immateriality, and the blue stamps, which were validated and delivered by government officials — also injected meaning into the monochromes. These works exaggerate certain qualities of the monochromes but do not specify which qualities are to be taken most seriously: surface or depth, anthropomorphization or immateriality.

Because the Allendy show interacted with the monochromes in this way, it is an example of what I have called a supplement. The show was a kind of microcosm of Klein's subsequent work, not only because it contained the beginnings of kinds of objects he was later to develop more fully, such as fire paintings, but because of its complex, supplementary relationship to the blank blue pictures. Like the book *Yves Peintures*, the Allendy show is both a collection of independent originals and a set of subordinate objects that refer to (and in this case help to explain, or·gloss) something beyond them, although, as was not the case with *Yves Peintures*, the referent, the blue monochromes, actually existed. What is interesting is the way they demonstrate the complexity of these seemingly simple paintings — or perhaps create it.

As Jacques Derrida uses the term, a supplement is something that is double, paradoxical and contradictory in its nature and basic structure.[113] It is by definition something extra added to a preexisting whole, and therefore excluded from the whole and dependent on it. It is "only a supplement" to the completed work. At the same time, however, a supplement supplies something *lacking* from the wholeness of the original work and reveals it as incomplete, precisely because it needs to be supplemented, needs to have its deficiencies made up.

In ordinary life the paradoxical structure of the supplement generally remains buried. We are used to supplements, such as footnotes or appendices, and we do not feel the need to question them. But Klein's practice tends to evoke this structure and to make it conspicuous. It does so because of the extraordinarily strong claims to wholeness, unity, originality, and independence that the traditional ideology of artistic creation makes for works of art. Klein's exalted language of "pure sensibility" and the like does nothing to reduce these claims. But at the same time, there is the blankness of the monochromes themselves, a blankness which proclaims a striking absence of clues to their meaning. The paintings are thus at once wholes and holes, as it were; they simultaneously make claims to independence and depend on explanation. Klein, by supplying the explanations, the supplements, *calls attention* to the original lack in the act of making it up. From one point of view the supplements in the Allendy show stress the priority and fertility of the monochromes by showing how much can be made out of them, how much they supposedly contain. Simultaneously and in the same gesture, however, the

supplements *refer* us to the monochromes; they continually carry us back to them in their original and persistent blankness. By doing so the supplements make us more aware of their own independent originality — they are less blank than what they seem to be based on. They thus raise the question of whether the complexity really is or ever was in the monochromes, whether it is not created by the supplements and arbitrarily applied back to the "originals." A decision cannot be made between these alternatives; they establish the range of possibilities for the meaning of the monochromes, a range within which we are forced to shuttle back and forth.

This analysis helps to define the kind of meaning Klein's art has, the meaning of a process. One effect of continually producing supplements is to keep the objects to which they are supplements *unfinished*, to keep them alive and in dialogue with the interpreting audience. Without this dimension the objects are relatively lifeless and tend to get taken over by the conventional expectations of the art world or the general public, which, by closing down the ambiguity of the objects and forcing determinate meanings upon them, kill them. It is in this sense that Klein's paintings, as mere objects, are "the ashes of [his] art."

That Klein continued, in the Allendy show and later, to apply meanings to his objects after he had made them and after he had received responses to them further suggests something about his notion of value and his notion of what a "work" was. For Klein the value of a picture was something it took on in the continuing process of interpretation. This value inevitably shifts, depending on differences of audiences and time, and Klein's own interest seems to have been in the process itself, in valuing rather than in mere value. For him art was something living, something that continued to work and continued to produce effects in the world. His art is not objects — "works" in the conventional sense — but "workings" or processes. If there is an obvious sense in which a central theme of Klein's work is the relation of made material objects to some form of spirit or transcendence, his remark that "the bond between spirit and matter is energy" provides a clue to his handling of the theme. His concern was with the ambiguous energies expressed in interpretation and reinterpretation, in valuing and testing values, and of investigating the act of valuing itself ("I am in search of the real value of the picture." "The prices were all different of course").

8

Klein's best-known exhibition, one which increased the infamy he had acquired in the popular press on account of his 1957 monochrome shows (in addition to the Milan and Paris exhibitions, he had also had one-man shows of monochromes in Düsseldorf and London that year), took place on the evening of his thirtieth birthday, April 28, 1958. On this occasion and for the next two weeks, Klein presented at Iris Clert's a white-walled empty art gallery as a work of art. *Le Vide (The Void)*, as Klein came to call it, involved many issues. Certainly it may be understood as a limiting instance of Klein's presentation of ambience or environment — the space around his monochromes — and as an attempt to showcase, literally, the spiritual. However, as Klein's written account of the opening makes vividly clear, the Void was not empty; it was so packed with people that the police came to disperse the crowds on several streets. But in its hypothetical emptiness and in its insurance of the presence of interpreters, this work tested to the limit whether it was still possible for an artist to stimulate sentiment. Klein was not at all sure that it was, and this event was one of the experiments he made to find out.

fig. 34 That the opening was, in a way, a big birthday party, complete with engraved invitations, was not a fact Klein announced in so many words, and previous critics of Klein's work have not discussed it. Yet surely causing so many Parisians to celebrate with him was part of the humor of the evening, and this was another occasion on which Klein arranged an intimate connection between his person and his work.

The 1958 exhibition was not the first example of Klein's voids; in a sense such absences had been part of his approach to his work from the beginning. There was the book *Yves Peintures*, which presented the idea of monochrome paintings while hinting by means of its peculiarities that the paintings had no material form; and there was the appearance of Klein's friends at the Salon in 1955, requesting to see a picture by Klein that he and they knew was not in the exhibition. The first time Klein seems to have identified an empty room in a gallery as a container of what he then called "invisible pictorial sensibility" was at the 1957 Blue Period show at Allendy's. This is not surprising in view of the richness of that exhibition in terms of ideas, and it suggests yet another way to think about the blue monochrome panels. There is evidence that in the course of the Allendy show Klein decided, simply by saying so, that an empty room on the second floor of Colette Allendy's house, a room that was

not always regularly used as part of the gallery space, was to be part of the show also. There is a photograph in Klein's scrapbook of Iris Clert, Pierre Restany, and Klein's friend, the artist Raymond Hains, standing in this room, and on the top of the gray cardboard photo mount Klein has written, "In the room on the second floor at Colette Allendy's where surfaces and blocks of invisible pictorial sensibility were shown."[114] According to Hains, Klein was aware that this particular room had been the consulting room, before his death, of Dr. René Allendy, a noted Parisian psychiatrist who had treated and been a friend for many years of Antonin Artaud. Hains believes that Klein understood the "presence" of Artaud to be in the room.[115] That Klein perhaps thought of the room this way is plausible, not only because Klein later put "blue cries" into Artaud's mouth and wrote about him in an article on theater in *Dimanche*, but also because Klein would, I believe, have admired Artaud instinctively for the way that, as Susan Sontag has pointed out, Artaud's "violent discontinuity of discourse" and "excruciating carnality" in accounting for his mental life are, finally, extreme examples of purity of moral purpose.[116]

fig. 33

The famous void at Iris Clert's in 1958, which Klein described as part of his "Pneumatic Period," was not a work easily rendered lifeless by the conventional expectations of the art world, but it did of course rely on those expectations to achieve some of its effects. So that the empty room would continue to have effects and remain in dialogue with an interpreting audience, Klein provided a supplement — a remarkable narrative account of the Pneumatic Period which he caused to be published the year after the event itself in his pamphlet *Le Dépassement de la problématique de l'art*.[117] His use of the historical present tense through most of this account vivifies it and causes it to waver between something that is supposed to have taken place in the past and something that is being made present now. It might be suggested that whether or not the events of April 28, 1958, did happen as Klein described them, they are happening in the speaking in the text. In other words, this text is a supplement which *creates* many of the complexities of the event itself. Because the text is so characteristic of Klein's style and so closely reflects central thematic concerns of his art, and because an immaterial picture cannot be hung in a posthumous retrospective or be reproduced visually (though Klein attempted the latter), I shall ask the reader to turn to the English translation of the essay, printed elsewhere in this catalogue, to read Klein's entire high-spirited account of showing and selling air.

fig. 35

Reading Klein's account of the empty gallery that he seriously or jokingly — at any rate, enthusiastically — termed "the interior of the century," one is confronted with the range from put-down to put-on to make-perfect within which his art usually operates. The contradictions in the text are such that it is impossible to pronounce it either essentially dystopian or essentially utopian. Rather, it oscillates between these poles, and this is the point.

There are first of all the obvious senses in which the show and the text may be apprehended on the one hand, while not the interior of the century, as one of the most explicit hoaxes of twentieth-century art, and on the other, as a demonstration that "sensibility" (spirit, aesthetic quality) ought not to be for sale. Reversal: the artist, who people like to believe is above such things, sells it. Next reversal: he sets a price cheap enough actually to lure buyers, a price so cheap that you wonder just what you are buying. Can "sensibility" really be had for three dollars? If not, how much should it cost? Next reversal: since what you have bought is air — presumably, as the crowded April evening in the tiny gallery progressed, hot air — you can't resell it; unlike Duchamp's *Paris Air*, "immaterial pictorial sensibility" is not contained by a pharmacist's ampoule and is most likely a poor investment. Next reversal: while you can't resell it, you can surely dine out on having bought it, and there is the hint that this is one of the main things buyers of art do with their purchases anyway.[118] Klein wants us to think about this and shows his awareness of the issue by making the event appear to be the place to be that night. While patently designed to attract a crowd, the event also purports to be exclusive; it is only those who did not receive invitations who were supposed to pay, the text tells us. The invitations project another ambiguity: this show of immateriality requires engraved cards worthy of an embassy ball. Yet as Klein's text also makes clear, as he anticipated, the event once under way is so appealing to so many that its exclusivity cannot be maintained even by hired guards.

The presence of the private guards returns us again to the dystopian pole. We tend to take for granted that the Mona Lisa hangs under bulletproof glass and that Picasso stored his work during World War II in the vaults of the Bank of France. Does an exhibition of pure spirit also need to be controlled by bodyguards? Is it fair to present white walls which invite such acts of interpretation as drawing upon them ("I expect some acts of vandalism"), and then to order your guards to seize the young draftsman and "eject him forcibly!"? It is Klein's text which poses such questions about the human cost of maintaining purity.

The presence of members of the Garde Républicaine, the arrival of the firemen and the police ("three wagons full"), and the partial cooperation of the Electricité de France are a different matter. As in the case of the canceled stamps, Klein has co-opted the government into participating in his work, and he has shown that his work can generate effects in not only the art world but also the real world. His text leaves mysterious just how he arranged for the presence of members of the Garde Républicaine, whose customary duties are to attend the president and cabinet ministers of France; in fact it was accomplished because a cabinet minister acquaintance of Restany was, in theory, expected at the opening.[119] In his text Klein uses the "official" presence of the Garde to bring up one of his favorite subjects, authenticity, and one of his favorite questions, How are we to determine real from fake? The twist in the case of the members of the Garde is that, in the context, they *look* fake (art students, Klein's text says, take them for movie extras in rented costumes) but *are* real.

Klein's text also omits to mention the effect, on the members of the Garde and on other visitors, of drinking the mixture of gin, Cointreau, and methylene blue prepared for Klein by La Coupole. As Jean Tinguely wrote happily to Pontus Hulten just after the opening, "Tomorrow they'll all pee blue!!!"[120] He was referring to the fact, which Klein had clearly told him in advance, that methylene blue is a biologist's stain which, taken internally, dyes the urine. In a second enthusiastic communication to Hulten, Tinguely wrote that the effects would last a week or ten days, "approximately the run of the show."[121] This aspect of the exhibition suggests the lengths to which Klein would go to get into people's systems. Of course it degrades people to impregnate them with blue in this way, and it runs counter to notions of purity, sensibility, or immateriality. What humor there is is mostly at the expense of the audience, but the myth of the artist is also called into question by this physical parody of transmitting a special vision.

One special vision Klein debunked with *Le Vide* was the popular notion of the agonized, existential vision of artists of *art informel*. That during the second half of the 1950s Georges Mathieu painted works of *art informel* on stage and before audiences in museums and galleries provided an obvious and immediate example sanctioning Klein's use of "theater" — an event such as the evening of the Void — as a mode of communication. However, Mathieu was making a public spectacle out of self-expression; he was staging existential acts as if to turn

Hans Namuth's film of Pollock painting in his studio into live theater. This is precisely what Klein was not doing. His text tells us that he wished "by the act of painting the walls white not only to purify the premises [to paint out previous artists] but especially through this action and this gesture" to make the gallery his studio. His words were no doubt deliberately chosen: "action" and "gesture" are of course what his blank white walls did not reveal, and he was careful in his text to let us know that the particular aspect of the Void he handled "all alone" in private was the painting of the gallery. According to Klein's account the "actions" performed at the Void evening were largely those of the crowd and the cops, not the artist. His favorite adjective throughout his text is "laconic," which sets a tone remote from that of the "paroxysms" or romantic frenzies acted out by Mathieu.

Klein re-created "immaterial pictorial sensibility" on a number of occasions. The first was in April 1959 in the loftlike vaulted spaces of the Hessenhuis, a seventeenth-century warehouse in Antwerp, which was being used for one of the earliest shows of European art of Klein's generation to repudiate gestural abstraction in favor of painting based on serial structure, undivided fields of color, or the excitation of real motion or light-reflecting surfaces. As his text tells us, for this group show Klein rejected any "gesture" related to painting — such as sweeping the walls with a dry brush; instead, at the opening he pronounced a phrase about blue from Bachelard's *L'Air et les songes* in the spot reserved for his work and made the "immaterial" slightly visible by smoking a cigarette. Klein claimed he sent three "immaterials" to the show, for which the price, instead of money, was a kilo of gold per work. Klein's decision to ask for gold, followed up in ceremonies and paintings I will discuss below, had a number of effects: it called attention to the issue of valuing works of art; it lent a certain quality of precious ritual to the idea of the immaterials; and through the very materiality of gold weights it suggested, by contrast, the otherworldliness of the immaterials. Also, whether the effect was deliberate or not, to ask for gold instead of cash at a time when the French franc was in crisis and undergoing repeated devaluation gave an impression of worldly good sense. As usual with Klein the virtual is countered by the actual, and we are left to consider their relationship.

Klein next ritualized the selling of "zones" of the immaterial with rules:

fig. 43

Ritual for the Relinquishment of the Immaterial Pictorial Sensibility Zones

The immaterial pictorial sensibility zones of Yves KLEIN the Monochrome are relinquished against a certain weight of fine gold. Seven series of these pictorial immaterial zones, all numbered, exist already. For each zone relinquished a receipt is given. This receipt indicates the exact weight of pure gold which is the material value correspondent to the immaterial acquired.

The zones are transferable by their owner. (See rules on each receipt.)

Every possible buyer of an immaterial pictorial sensibility zone must realize that the fact that he accepts a receipt for the price which he has paid takes away all authentic immaterial value from the work, although it is in his possession.

In order that the fundamental immaterial value of the zone belong to him and become a part of him, he must solemnly burn his receipt, after his first and last name, his address, and the date of the purchase have been written on the stub of the receipt book.

In case the buyer wishes this act of integration of the work of art with himself to take place, Yves Klein must, in the presence of an Art Museum Director, or an Art Gallery Expert, or an Art Critic, plus two witnesses, throw half of the gold received into the ocean, into a river, or in some place in nature where this gold cannot be retrieved by any one.

From this moment on, the immaterial pictorial sensibility zone belongs to the buyer absolutely and intrinsically.

Zones having been relinquished in this way are not transferable by their owners.

Y.K.

P.S. It is important to point out that, beyond the rites of relinquishment above, there exist, disengaged from all rules and convention, relinquishment-transfers of the void and of immaterials in the most absolute anonymity.[122]

Klein had meticulous checkbooks printed to use at the ceremonies for relinquishing the zones, and on several occasions between 1959 and 1962 he sold some of these immaterials: to his old friend, Claude Pascal, for example; to the Italian novelist who had

p. 206

favorably reviewed his 1957 show in Milan, Dino Buzzati; and to Dorothy and Michael Blankfort, a Los Angeles couple whom he had met on the occasion of his show at the Dwan Gallery in June 1961. For various reasons each of these buyers had a friendly stake in Klein and his work.[123] For Klein the sales meant that he could publish such statements as "Incredible as it may seem, I have actually sold a number of these immaterial pictorial states" and be speaking the truth.[124] Some of the ceremonies were held on the Right Bank of the Seine using the cathedral of Notre Dame as a backdrop, and in 1962 photographers hired by Klein were present to record each scene of the narrative.

pp. 208–209

While sales of the zones were hardly a major profit-making venture for Klein — the Blankforts recall that the gold ingots they purchased cost about $250 — it is worth noting that Klein's rules allowed him to keep half of the gold but that the purchasers had to burn their receipts. Unlike Dr. Tzanck, the dentist whom Duchamp paid with a check drawn on Teeth's Loan and Trust, Klein's buyers could not resell the artist's currency later at a profit. The art world was of course drawn into the "ritual" as well, for each immaterial was signed — on the receipts to be burned and on the receipt stubs which Klein kept — by an expert with official or quasi-official status, such as François Mathey, curator of the Musée des Arts Décoratifs in Paris.

Klein reified the conception of the immaterials by making monochromes which are by no means spare in their materials, the Monogolds. There are about forty-five of these gold-leaf panels; most date from 1960 and 1961, and many are in Klein's favored proportions of about 5 to 4. Three are approximately 2 by 1½ meters. The visual facts are that the works fall into three fairly straightforward categories. There are gold monochromes made out of small rectangles (somewhat like Klein's panes of stamps), for example MG 6. Such works are made out of series of sheets of gold leaf just as it comes, like Klein's pigment, from the supplier. These paintings

p. 155

made out of what might be described as smaller paintings — rectangles made out of smaller rectangles — form very obvious grids.

The second type of Monogold asserts itself as relief. Works such as these consist of fluttery pieces of gold leaf fixed to a panel previously covered with burnished gold leaf. The fluttery pieces of gold on the surface move according to the slightest current of air, including the natural breathing of an observer. That is, they not only exist in an obvious fashion in our optical and physical space, they respond delicately

and instantly to changes in the space they are in and we are in. During Klein's lifetime these fluttery pieces of gold leaf on the surface sometimes got lost, got stolen, vanished into the ordinary world, or simply disappeared. That he intended these fragile leaves to be lost seems clear. Klein of course also demonstrated the phenomenon of losing gold, literally throwing it away, in the relinquishment ceremonies.

The third kind of Monogold — the ones that appear to depict moonscapes because of shallow, oval depressions carved into the gesso ground — are concave reliefs, usually highly burnished as well. An obvious quality of these shiny concave reliefs, for example MG 16, which is 199 by 153 centimeters and which Klein titled *Résonance*, is their reflectivity. This is not simply a matter of projecting a certain energy into the viewer's space. These works also mirror the viewer: as the viewer observes one of these objects, the object — in the case of MG 16, partly on account of the panel's human scale — appears to be observing the viewer. Some of the immediacy and directness of these works has to do with their lavishness; they tend to be the works by Klein which are noticed first and sell the most quickly. Works made of gold have to do with selling in a way that continues to seduce and mock viewers.

p. 153

That these Monogold panels offer an immediately sensuous promise of a rich golden world, perhaps related to Klein's utopian ideas, and at the same time reflect the real world — by fluttering in response to it or by mirroring it — is consistent with the range of meaning, the hope and the doubt, the illusion and disillusionment that run through Klein's work as a whole.

9

I want to show man in nature by the traces and marks he leaves there in spite of himself, which are always of a marvelous grandeur, artificial, ephemeral, yet forever indestructible.

Yves Klein,
"The Trace of the Immediate"[125]

While Klein's reputation appears to be based on works which are conspicuously vacant of imagery — the monochromes, the voids — he supplemented these works so as to adumbrate a range of meaning for them, either with other objects or with series of photographs and texts whose narrative structure is patent. Indeed, Klein seems often to be straining to seduce his observers — his "readers" as he sometimes called them — not only with sensuous materials such as rich ultramarine pigment and gold leaf, but with his urgent address to our appetite for narrative: in short, with stories.

Many of the works of visual art which Klein made or caused to be made between 1960 and his death in June 1962 are not at all abstract. On the contrary, many are what we customarily term naturalistic or figurative, and they bring to the surface, literally and metaphorically, the issue of how things are made to stand for other things. Among these works are Klein's *pp. 172–81* body prints or Anthropometries, paintings on paper made either by the press of a nude model's paint-smeared body or by spraying paint around a model's body, which served as a kind of template. Klein termed the models employed to make these works *pinceaux vivants,* living brushes.[126] There is a variant of the body *pp. 182–84* prints which Klein called Shroud Anthropometries, and the grounds of these Veronica's veil-like works are silk or unstretched canvas. There are also the Fires, *pp. 186–90* works on coated cardboard made by the marks of a large gas jet and water or by flames emitting from *fig. 61* Klein's *Fire Wall,* which was a grid of Bunsen burners installed outdoors at the Krefeld retrospective. The Fire *p. 191* Colors, also on coated paper, are a variant of these; they were made by the marks of flame and the flow of paint, usually in Klein's ultramarine and deep pink, the scorched grounds constituting a variation of the third primary, yellow (or in Klein's system, gold). Also *p. 151; cat.* in this category are Klein's Cosmogonies, works on *no. 51* paper made with paint and, at some stage, the presence of an element of nature: for example, as Klein's titles and texts tell us, a spring rain, or the wind, or reeds and beach grass used, like the nude models, as brushes and negative stencils.[127] In addition there *p. 171* are the Portrait Reliefs Klein was working on just before he died: life casts of the nude bodies, above the knees, of his friends Arman, Claude Pascal, and the artist Martial Raysse.[128]

During the three years before his death Klein also tremendously increased the number of occasions on which he commissioned posed or semi-posed photographs, most of them taken by two Paris-based Hungarians, Harry Shunk and John Kender, or by a Düsseldorf photographer, Charles Wilp. For example, the *fotoromanzi* of sales of Immaterial Pictorial Sensibility date from this period. There are photo-*pp. 198–201* graphs recording a ceremonial evening at which models made Anthropometries in front of an audience, and photographs of Klein wielding a huge gas *pp. 70–71,* jet to make his Fire pictures. There are also photo-*188;* graphs of Klein at home in sundry didactic stances next *figs. 67–68* to his works, of Klein lying underneath *La Tombe*

— *ci-gît l'espace,* of Klein gazing at an IKB-dipped globe of the world which is hovering magically in *p. 205* the air above its stand, of Klein pointing a camera at the observer, and of Klein soaring in the air, appearing to fly.

If we consider Klein's approach to visual representation, the remarkable common denominator of all of these categories of works — the Anthropometries, Cosmogonies, Fires, Portrait Reliefs, and the many photographs — is that they appear both to illustrate a subject and to show its literal traces. In the language of semiotics, these works are (or at any rate, at first glance seem to be) simultaneously iconic and indexical.[129]

For example, many of the Anthropometries clearly look like groups of female bodies and at the same time show the imprints of breasts, midriffs, bellies, sometimes pubic hair, and thighs. To take another example, the Fire Colors tend both to depict — on account of their colors and morphology — large, leaping tongues of flame, and to give evidence, with molten bubbles, soot, and scorched crusts of paint, of being the by-products of an actual conflagration. As a number of writers on photography have noted, photographs are both images and physical traces; they register light waves reflected from the objects they represent. Sontag has pointed out that the way in which photographs are a material vestige of their subjects, as most paintings are not, lends something magical to photographs. Proposing the hypothetical alternatives of possessing a portrait in oil of Shakespeare by the meticulous delineator Holbein the Younger or a faded, barely legible photograph of the Bard, she suggests that most Bardolators would choose the photograph over the Holbein because to possess the photograph "would be like having a nail from the True Cross."[130] Her simile is particularly apt as directed to Klein's trace works, because it at once suggests the powerfully convincing quality of photographs, the literal-mindedness of believers in relics, and our present-day suspicions about the source and veracity of such objects as the Shroud of Turin.

It seems clear that Klein wished for a number of reasons to exploit the special credibility which trace images possess. Perhaps the least interesting reason is that images made this way did not require Klein to draw in order to create an icon. While he often sketched the outlines of an idea energetically with a ballpoint pen, sustaining illusion with the shading of a pencil was a skill that he neither possessed nor as an adult was concerned to acquire. In Klein's lexicon, color meant good and line meant evil. Line equals evil because it specifies and thus it sets limits, it bounds, it binds; as Klein put it in several texts, lines are like the bars of a prison.[131] Color, on the other hand, for Klein meant incommensurate space — space in which to liberate oneself from cares, and space in which to conduct continual reinterpretation. As we see in certain works such as *Europe-Afrique*, 1961, Klein used color as though it could be an explicit and overtly political tool for ending wars, because if you paint a single color over a relief map of Western Europe and North Africa, you thereby eliminate the boundaries between the countries with a unifying bath of blue. You have thus eliminated from view the differences between France and Algeria, and you have literally painted over the differences that used to exist between France and Germany. Here is an instance where Klein's utopianism overrides realities which cannot be ignored: that World War II cannot unhappen and that the *pieds noirs* and brown-skinned Algerians were still killing each other when Klein took a found object — a relief map — and made the work. Although a relief map, unlike tracks in the snow or an electrocardiogram, is not exactly an indexical object, it shares with such trace images the capacity to invoke belief in its reliability as record: it is scientific reportage, a miniaturized account of the contours of the earth. By employing a relief map, Klein was able both to provide a credible icon and make a monochrome at the same time.

p. 163

In his essay "The War" Klein complained about line that "drawing is writing in a painting. One draws a tree, but that would come to the same as painting a color and writing at the side: tree." This statement suggests that for Klein mere iconicity (the drawing) and mere symbol (the word) are insufficiently convincing. Something which is only a representation of a thing puts you off from that thing's actuality and thus, for Klein, from its capacity to continue to produce effects. Klein's trace works — the body prints, the vegetable prints, the fire paintings, and so on — allude conspicuously to the process of their making, so that you must take that into consideration when you look at them and so that you will not be tempted to regard them only as aesthetic objects, as "mere" works of art ("My paintings are the ashes of my art").

In the case of most categories of Klein's trace works, he created supplements to the objects. These supplements usually call further attention to the processes by which the objects were made, and in the course of doing so provide a range of connotations for the objects which the objects alone lack or only hint at. These supplements are in the form of other objects, captions, longer texts, events, photographs of events, and the contexts in which some of these

photographs were published. For example, when in 1961 Klein decided to follow up the imprints of rosettes of soot he had made from the burners of his *Fire Wall* at Krefeld with more fire pictures, he did not stay in his studio and work out compositional strategies with clumps of candles. Instead he employed an extravagant method hardly necessary to achieve the trace images themselves: he arranged to spend two days at the Centre d'Essais du Gaz de France plant near Paris being photographed and filmed using a giant flamethrower to scorch paper. This was in the presence of firemen and two of Klein's nude models, who, for some of the pictures made at the Gaz de France, pressed their previously water-drenched bodies on the coated paper grounds before Klein used the flamethrower.[132] *Fire 24* is one result of this process, which sometimes left a ghostly silhouette of the models as well as marks of flame. The photographs, in this case commissioned by Klein from Pierre Joly and Vera Cardot, connote a good deal more than the registration of process signified by the works on paper in isolation. We learn from the presence of a fireman spraying water on the same paper ground that Klein is branding with flame, that this is collaborative work, and that it is perhaps dangerous as well; the fireman is protected by his firesuit and helmet, while Klein, in white shirt, tie, and vest, wears asbestos mitts. The presence of the nude models together with the suggestive position in which Klein is holding the long flamethrower in several of the photographs intimates that the artist has fire in his loins. The Centre d'Essais du Gaz de France is a research center owned by the government; the presence of nude "living brushes" in its laboratories indicates that once again Klein has not only co-opted officialdom but ridiculed it.

p. 186

p. 70; figs. 67–68

cat. no. 70

Shortly after Klein conceived the idea of painting with body prints he arranged an evening event, *Anthropometries of the Blue Period,* for an invited audience of about a hundred people, collectors and some artists and critics. At this performance he showed the process by which many of the body paintings were made.[133] Held on March 9, 1960, at the Galerie Internationale d'Art Contemporain — a posh Right Bank establishment associated with Georges Mathieu, who edited a magazine backed by the gallery, and with other artists of *art informel* — Klein's event was fairly brief. Sheets of blank white paper had previously been placed on a wall at one end of the main room of the spacious gallery prior to the performance. In front of the white paper were pedestals of different heights for the "living brushes" to mount. Sheets of white paper had also been spread on the floor of the spectacle area. The audience stood or sat on gilt chairs at the other

pp. 198–201

end of the gallery, facing the action. To one side there was a string chamber group which during the event played a version of Klein's one-chord *Monotone Symphony.* Klein wore tuxedo and white tie and gave directions, partly by gesture, to his models, three nude young women with attractive bodies. The models entered carrying small pails of ultramarine paint which they spread on their torsos and thighs before pressing their skin against the sheets of white paper. In one instance, a model pulled another along a sheet of paper on the floor to make a kind of body print which Klein later called a "dragging."

To photograph this event Klein commissioned the team of Shunk and Kender and Charles Wilp. The photographs they took are sufficiently compelling that their content, particularly when considered together with several texts Klein quickly published about the making of the body prints, tends to spill over by implication onto other body prints, that is, Anthropometries Klein made subsequently, in the privacy and concentration of his studio. The photographers were present at a rehearsal of the event and helped Klein set up the gallery on the evening the event took place.[134] Their function — to register the humorous yet erotic ceremonial effect of the immediacy of the models' actions — was planned by Klein in advance, as was the event itself.

pp. 174–75

I pointed out earlier that Namuth's portraits of Pollock painting were well known to European artists of Klein's generation.[135] In an essay which seeks to distinguish between Pollock's paintings and the way that the myth of Pollock partly established by Namuth's photographs has inflected our understanding of these paintings, Barbara Rose described these photographs as pictures of "a tormented, agonized man, torn by self-doubt, the victim of an inner *Sturm-und-Drang* nakedly revealed in his contorted face, ... the romantic Genius, possessed by demonic *terribilità,*" and so on.[136] One of the chief purveyors of information about Pollock in Klein's Paris was, as I have also pointed out, Georges Mathieu. The version of Pollock he was propounding in the 1950s was close to that suggested by Harold Rosenberg's essay "The American Action Painters," to which Mathieu sometimes referred in his own writings. In an essay published in 1958 Mathieu set the following criteria for the execution of "up-to-date non-figurative painting": "1. First and foremost, speed in execution. 2. Absence of premeditation, either in form or movement. 3. The necessity for a sublimated state of concentration."[137] Mathieu enacted this program in his public performances of painting huge canvases very quickly.

At least one of the meanings of Klein's event (to which, not incidentally, Mathieu had been invited and which he attended) was that the purported heroic selfhood and existential risk-taking of such artists of *art informel* as Mathieu is being made fun of when it is not the artist but naked girls who do the painting and take the risks. Klein's event questioned the idealist tradition that the artist is a person who conveys an inspired vision, just as the worth of Mathieu's hypothetically unpremeditated public risk-taking was cast into doubt by an event which was rehearsed and proceeded calmly.

That Mathieu understood Klein's event as something of an attack is suggested by the fact that the gallery, whose operations he influenced, did not show Klein again. Klein himself made a number of statements concerning the relationship of the Anthropometries to action painting. In one written within a year of the event he said:

> These living brushes are under the constant direction of my commands, such as "a little to the right; over to the left now; to the right again, etc." ... Many art critics claimed that via this method of painting I was in fact merely reenacting the technique of what has been called "action painting." I would like to make it clear that this endeavor is opposed to "action painting" in that I am actually completely detached from the physical work during its creation.
>
> Just to cite one example fostered by the misrepresentation of anthropometry by my coverage in the international press — a group of Japanese painters eagerly applied this method in their own very different manner. These painters in fact transformed themselves into living brushes. By drowning themselves in color and then rolling on their canvases, they became ultra-action-painters! Personally I would never attempt to smear paint over my own body and become a living brush; on the contrary, I would rather put on my tuxedo and wear white gloves. I would not even think of dirtying my hands with paint. Detached and distant, the work of art must complete itself before my eyes and under my command. Thus, as soon as the work is realized, I stand there, present at the ceremony, spotless, calm, relaxed, worthy of it, and ready to receive it as it is born into the tangible world.[138]

He managed with these disingenuous words to exaggerate a popular view of action painting to the point of absurdity while dissociating himself from it.

The event on March 9, 1960, and the paintings and photographs linked to it had other implications as well, and as in so much of Klein's work, these range from the utopian to the misanthropic. Klein's attempt to separate his work from *art informel* by making fun of some of the latter's techniques is utopian in this sense: it is an attempt to rid the world of the torment, agony, and gloom with which *art informel* was often popularly associated. It is worth recalling that Klein wrote that he detested "artists who empty themselves into their painting... [and] spit out every horrible, rotten, and infectious complexity" as if to burden others with "all their sorry failures."

Klein also appears to have been suggesting that a little society, namely the models, had formed to help the master artist execute creations performed under his direction. This is collaborative work, he tells us, and his texts do not fail to amuse us in their claims about the devotion of the models, who, while Klein never says so in print, were of course paid by him.[139] "At first," he wrote, "they thought me crazy; afterwards they could no longer keep themselves away from coming to pose for me or rather from coming to work with me."[140]

p. 181   Several of the Anthropometries, including *Architecture de l'air*, actually illustrate Klein's Utopia in perspectival diminution with vanishing orthogonals. It is a palm-treed place where people live nude, are sheltered by Klein's architecture of air and fire, and have the capacity to fly. Directly on the surface of this large painting Klein wrote a text which describes how his plans for the climatization of the surface of the earth will bring about a return to the "Eden of legend." To achieve this there will have to be a disappearance of all familial and personal intimacy, he wrote. It is worth noting that to achieve even this image of the edenic, or indeed, to achieve most of the Anthropometries, misanthropic or, more precisely, misogynist means were employed. For it is difficult to ignore completely the acute discomfort the models suffered in covering their bodies and sometimes their hair with blue paint, in the service of an artist who said he would not dream of being a "living brush" himself. Klein hinted at their discomfort by noting in passing in a text that after "these fantastic sessions," once the paintings were finished, "my model took a bath."[141] My aim here is not to accuse Klein of antifeminist practices but rather to suggest that his work was structured in such a way as to bring out the tensions between collaboration and exploitation, between the ideal and what it may cost to achieve it.

The issue of what Klein's method of painting did

to the women willing to assist it is inflated by presenting the process to an audience who sat and watched it. The audience, on the one hand rendered glamorous by being in the presence of beautiful girls at a chic cultural event, has on the other hand been turned into voyeurs: both the sexual kind, who get a kick out of watching naked women make fools of themselves in public, and the art world kind, who desire to watch the artist at the moment of creation. As performance, Klein's event, like the glittering scene at Andy Warhol's Factory in the mid-1960s, raised questions about what it means to make an artist into a celebrity. While Klein did not get his hands dirty, his dramatization of stardom forces us to question whether our association, since the sixteenth century, of artistic creation with divine creation is still believable.

Klein made nearly two hundred Anthropometries and Shroud Anthropometries, and they vary greatly in appearance. If we examine them as material artifacts, what they share, in addition to (in most cases) the signature of blue paint, is that the process of their making has left marks which are literally at human scale. As in the case of Rauschenberg's *Female Figure (Blueprint)*, ca. 1949 (a monoprint made by exposing to light blueprint paper on which a nude woman was lying), with Klein's body prints the observer is confronted not only by bodies which are the approximate size of his own but by a process which insists that an actual body was there. The mere illusion of bodies that we find in most figurative art is, for Klein, not sufficient. This is emphasized by the heterogeneity of these works. For if we examine them as pictorial objects whose formal characteristics are to be analyzed in terms of composition, figure-ground relationships, spatial illusion, paint handling, and so on, we find that Klein has undermined the usefulness of this sort of analysis by presenting an inventory of referents to different styles, as if to say that to aestheticize these works is to remove not only art but art history from life.

For example, in the case of ANT 104 and several   p. 180
like it, the marks of the models' body parts are barely recognizable as such and appear to have been employed to render a pastiche of a painterly *art informel* work. ANT 82 has a series of torsos and thighs   p. 172
which are rigidly frontal and regularly distributed across the surface in such a way as to invoke a Justinianic mosaic. ANT 96, *People Begin to Fly*,   p. 179
has negative traces of the models' bodies in sundry postures of motion, facing forward and in profile; the figures overlap at baroque angles of flight and are cut off by the perimeter of the paper ground like

so many dancers by Degas. In still others, the clear imprint of separate body parts, the postures of the models, and the blueness of the traces force comparison to Matisse's cut papers of *Blue Nudes* of the early 1950s.

A close reading of a number of the body prints also leads us to have doubts about whether the immediacy of the trace process — vivified by the scale of the figures and demonstrated by Klein's supplements in the form of performance, photographs, and texts — is all that was involved in the making of these *p. 183* works. With ANT SU 20, *Vampire*, a work which was made in Klein's studio and which registers the body of his wife, Rotraut, it appears that great care was taken to create an illusion of facial features with a kind of shading to render depth at the cheekbones. The areas of paint indicating the breasts are circular, and we are left wondering just how this effect was achieved: by applying paint to a breast in circles before the imprint was made, by using a breast as a brush in motion, or, perhaps, by using a brush? ANT 102, *Architecture de l'air*, with its grid of receding orthogonals, palm trees, and figures in diminution, is clearly the product of premeditation and careful execution. It turns out that it, too, manages to constitute the product of traces: the negative silhouettes of palm trees derive from a tracing of a photograph of the beach at Martinique;[142] the silhouettes of the diminished figures were made by spraying around dolls.[143] These works and certain other of the body prints, which we might term "assisted" traces, both recall the real flesh involved in their making and remind us that artists continue to fool the eye.

I have discussed how Klein began his public career as a painter with a booklet of carefully captioned reproductions of paintings which he seems never to have painted — that is, with an original work of art, the book, which calls attention to the probability that it is not what it purports to be, a set of reproductions. The most stunning instance in Klein's art of such conspicuous fraudulence — fraudulence designed to show — and the most remarkable use by the artist of the medium of a captioned, mechanically repro-*p. 204* duced image are the famous self-portraits of Klein flying, which were crafted by the photographers Shunk and Kender. Like the book *Yves Peintures*, the self-portraits are structured to call attention to the likelihood that what they denote at first glance is a fiction.

Klein had the self-portraits made in October 1960, for publication on the front page of his fake *p. 192* edition of the newspaper *Dimanche*.[144] The four-page paper, rich with texts by Klein, appeared on November 27, 1960, as his contribution to a festival

of avant-garde art, music, poetry, film, theater, and stage design then taking place in Paris. Unwilling as usual to settle for only the art world as an audience, Klein immediately sent eight copies of the paper to the Ministry of Information, with a brief business letter noting that in doing so he was acting "in compliance with the law."[145]

In addition, on the day that *Dimanche* was published, Klein hung it alongside real newspapers on sale at kiosks in Paris and then had the kiosks photographed. In some of these photographs of the kiosks, *fig. 59* both Klein's *Dimanche* and the real *Dimanche* are simultaneously visible. This juxtaposition of real and fake is one of several clues provided by Klein to what citizens innocent of his art may well have assumed about a news photo of a man flying unaided by mechanical means: that there was a trick involved.

If we know something about the history of iconography and something about the brighter side of Klein's art and ideology, the photographic image of him soaring upward into the air from a fifteen-foot-high wall may be read at one level as a compelling icon of transcendence. It depicts what millennia of ancient Western art and Christian art have also depicted: the human image in ascension. However, the artist has shown himself — not a Winged Victory, nor a member of the Holy Trinity, nor Superman — doing the ascending, a vision that reminds us that it is artists, not gods, who often people modern myths. If we examine Klein's icons of transcendence closely, we find that at the same time that Klein appears to be dramatizing his own myth, he is once again raising questions about our belief in the divine capacities of artists.

Klein headlined the brilliant illusion of himself soaring "A Man in Space!"; under the newspaper photograph a second headline announces, "The painter of space throws himself into the void!" This is followed by an extended caption below the photograph, in which a bylineless reporter (the author is of course Klein) tells a little feature story about the visual image and quotes the artist. The extended caption reads:

> The Monochrome, who is also a fourth *dan* black belt judo champion, regularly practices dynamic levitation! (with or without a net, at the risk of his life).

> He means to be in shape to go into space soon to join his favorite work: an aerostatic sculpture composed of 1,001 blue balloons which, in 1957, escaped from his exhibition into the sky over Saint-Germain-des-Prés, never to return.

To liberate sculpture from the base has been his preoccupation for a long time. "Today the painter of space ought actually to go into space to paint, but he ought to go there without tricks or fraud, not any longer by plane, parachute, or rocket: he must go there by himself, by means of individual, autonomous force, in a word, he ought be capable of levitating."

Yves: "I am the painter of space. I am not an abstract painter but on the contrary a figurative one, and a realist. Let's be reasonable, to paint space I owe it to myself to go there, into space itself."

In the essay "The Photographic Message," published in Paris a few months after Klein published his newspaper self-portrait, Roland Barthes observed about texts which accompany press photographs that they constitute an important historical reversal of the accustomed relationship between text and image: "The image no longer *illustrates* the words; it is now the words which, structurally, are parasitic on the image. . . . Formerly, the image illustrated the text (made it clearer); today, the text loads the image, burdening it with a culture, a moral, an imagination."[146] Barthes goes on to explain ways in which the text adds such "signifieds of connotation" to the fundamental denotation given by the photographic image, writing that sometimes "the text produces (invents) an entirely new signified which is retroactively projected into the image, so much so as to appear denoted there."[147]

Barthes' observation applies to the way that texts connote images in Klein's work as a whole. In the case of Klein's press photograph of himself flying, the message connoted by the text in the extended caption forces us to question our habit of placing particularly firm trust in a photograph which reports on an instant of motion, whether it be the so-called photo finish of a horserace or the scientific inquiry of a Muybridge. For the first paragraph of Klein's text tells us that the pictured judo champion-artist who practices dynamic levitation "at the risk of his life" does so "with or without a net." This introduces to our reading of the astonishing photograph the serious possibility that to achieve this image — which either successfully defied gravity or ended on the street in a splat — there was, in fact, a net. Indeed, at no point in the short text does Klein state that he has done just what the image pictures; repeatedly he writes that he "must" be or "ought" to be capable of doing so, "without tricks or fraud." The text is Klein's second clue to the fact that to create the image, there was a trick involved.

The self-portrait published in *Dimanche* is, of course, a photomontage, executed for Klein by Shunk and Kender, who took the shots involved and skillfully printed this montage and one closely related to it. The mental leap, the selection of the site, and the act of arranging for publication of the images were Klein's.

It has emerged since Klein's death that like many movies, these photomontages were made at a time when streets are supposed to be empty, a quiet Sunday morning, in this case one in October 1960.[148] They were made by putting a Rolliflex camera with six-by-six-centimeter film on a tripod facing down a street in the Paris suburb of Fontenay-aux-Roses and shooting the street scene from exactly the same position at least three times: once with the little man on the bicycle in the middle ground in the picture, an appearance that was probably accidental; once without the man on the bicycle; and once with Klein diving upward off the wall while about a dozen of his judo companions, from a judo school across the street, stood underneath with a tarpaulin to catch him as he sprang from the wall. Shunk was using the Rolliflex. According to Kender, who was using a 35-millimeter Leica with a telephoto lens to take shots that show Klein plunging down, not ascending — shots Klein did not publish — Klein had to jump several times for the elegant and slightly devilish pose, which we now see, to be achieved, and he hurt himself slightly. Splicing of the upper and lower portions of the montages was accomplished in the darkroom.[149]

Within six weeks of publishing the flying self-portrait in *Dimanche*, Klein published it again in the catalogue of his retrospective exhibition at Krefeld, *Yves Klein: Monochrome und Feuer*, which appeared on January 14, 1961. But in this second publication, while the upper part of the picture, with the image of Klein making his leap, is absolutely identical to the image in *Dimanche*, the little man on the bicycle has been removed — and so have any doubts about whether or not the photograph is a photomontage. This switch in photographs is Klein's third clue to the facts that artists still fool the eye and that perhaps what one could read in French newspapers in 1960 might not be entirely trustworthy.

For Klein's immediate audience, to be in possession of both his *Dimanche* and his Krefeld catalogue was not unusual; in other words, the opportunity to doubt the "objective truth" of one or the other photo through comparing the two was provided by the artist himself. Klein provided his audience another opportunity to discern his illusionism in July 1961, six months after the Krefeld catalogue ap-

p. 204 rt.

peared, when he published the self-portrait yet again in the Düsseldorf artists' journal *ZERO;* this time the little man on the bicycle was back in the picture.[150] Düsseldorf and Krefeld are about twenty-five miles apart, and their audience for art was then the same audience.

Klein's correspondence establishes that these switchbacks in publication were no accident. For example, he wrote twice to the museum director in Krefeld, in late November and early December 1960, urging him to substitute the second "photo...of me in the void" for the first one (with the bicyclist), which Klein had sent for the catalogue originally, because, Klein wrote, the second (without the bicyclist) was "cleaner" [*plus nette*].[151] Even if the opportunity to compare the two versions was unavailable, the other photographic material Klein provided for the catalogue and the layout of this material set up ambiguities which suggest to the reader the alternatives of believing and disbelieving in the image of Klein risking his life to leap into the Void. Next to the leap photomontage in the Krefeld catalogue is a documentary photo of Klein engaged in judo; like the press-photo context of the leap in *Dimanche,* this reminder of Klein's acrobatic skill lends a certain veracity to the possibility that he could have made the leap without serious injury. But this is undercut by two other photos on the same page which instantly denote sleight-of-hand in the darkroom: one of Klein gazing at his blue globe hovering in the air above its base, another of Klein holding flame in his bare right hand.

There seems little question that in creating a persuasive image of himself soaring or flying or levitating or reaching heavenwards or liberating himself from the base (the real world), Klein was drawing upon what Barthes has called "stock metaphors" or a "'historical grammar' of iconographic connotation."[152] In Klein's case this grammar hints at secret oriental knowledge of levitation, or adolescent Christian mysticism, or athletic prowess that rivals and humanizes an astronaut's, or artistic talent that surpasses Malevich's desire — which Klein knew well — to make art reach the other side of the sky.[153]

In the "Introductory" to *Studies in Iconology,* Erwin Panofsky uses for one of his main arguments two different examples of paintings in which something is suspended in space in violation of the laws of gravity, as Klein is in his photographic self-portraits.[154] The works to which Panofsky refers are from two different historical periods, and part of his point is that the way these images were read and understood at the time of their making depended, in effect, on the systems of belief of the eras which produced

them. The system of belief dominant among intellectuals in Klein's Paris included the panoply of connotation which was installed between the two book covers of Malraux's Museum without Walls. But the system of belief was dominated, as I have said, by existentialism. So whatever Klein may have wished his leap from the wall to accrue from history and autobiography, it read to his intelligent contemporary audience as a metaphor of existential risk — this in part because his extravagant image implied real physical risk, an artist willing to die or break bones and endure pain for his art. By setting us up to catch him in the act of faking existential risk, Klein raised doubts about whether existential acts work. I think it seemed to Klein that the existential acts being undertaken in many studios of Montparnasse did not work and were not above suspicion: they did not stop wars, and their performers did not buy newspapers in which more than the political party allegiance of the publisher could be reliably depended upon.

Klein knew as well as the rest of us that in the modern Western world, men do not levitate unassisted except in the imagination. It is precisely in order to make his leaps of imagination, and not of physical flight, credible that Klein permits the curtain — what he often called the temple veil of the studio — to be pulled back, to let us in on his makebelieve. By revealing to us that he arranged for the camera to deceive, Klein suggests to us that the moral of this story is that he does not, and therefore that his vision of a brighter world is trustworthy — that it contains the potential of being achieved or, at any rate, that we ought to try to achieve it.

The issue is a complex one. As we have seen, a pattern of fraudulence designed to show runs through Klein's work: the booklet *Yves Peintures,* which reproduced nonexistent paintings; the exhibition of virtually identical Blue Period monochromes for which the prices were all different, of course; the gallery exhibition of nothing at all; the icons of flight that are really darkroom manipulations; "action paintings" purportedly made by models, not the artist. In each case (and in many others not discussed here), Klein's utopian vision — the exaltation of pure, undisturbed, intense color, the value of spirit over matter, the ability to fly unfettered, pictures of an Eden in which the entire community is capable of ascendance — is proposed and then undercut in a version of the Brechtian method, whereby the creator forces us to stop and stand outside of what we have just seen and to reflect upon it. This has its counterpart in Klein's self-mythologizing: like Norman Mailer's advertisements for himself, the persona Klein created and the antics he indulged in — that is, his willingness to make a fool (or little dictator) of himself in public by, say, pretending to have the ability to fly, or proposing to change the world through the Blue Revolution — are what might be called real existential acts. Through them he constructed a myth which, during the time when he was working, was possibly more believable than the myth of the previous generation, repeated so often in Klein's Paris that it lost its force and at times seemed little more than bad faith. By revealing his tricks, Klein shows that he is honest.

That Klein's objects often seem to call into question not only ordinary notions (including vanguard ones) of what constitutes "good" art, but even the notion that what he did was art at all, is a part of his achievement. I believe that while he was attracted to the Saint-Simonian concept of the artist as priest, Klein was also acutely aware that, in the modern world, the priest is often difficult to distinguish from the charlatan. The man who offers what Klein claimed to offer — the possibility of universal peace and spiritual fulfillment in this world — has become a suspicious character, much as the idealist tradition — that artistic creativity is close to divine creativity — has come increasingly in the course of late modernism to be questioned. Klein accepted these implications, and the extent to which he mocked those who would believe that art is magic born of demi-gods by dramatizing the possibility that art is a fraud, is a measure of how compelling the brighter vision was for him. Like the many two-faced images of his persona which he made, his work presents us not with a double bind but with the sensation that we live with choices.

Marginal references are made throughout this essay to material printed elsewhere in this catalogue; "cat. no." refers to entries in the Catalogue Listing, and "fig. no." to illustrations in the Chronology.

Notes

1. Reentered in "The Monochrome Adventure," also known as "Mon Livre," p. 50. In this essay I am quoting from the particular typewritten manuscript of this partly published 145-page anthology which has notations in Klein's hand and which was loaned to me in 1973 by Dr. Paul Wember, Krefeld. Dr. Wember consulted this typescript heavily in late 1960 when he worked with Klein to prepare the catalogue of Klein's retrospective at the Museum Haus Lange, Krefeld, January 14–February 26, 1961. Thus a firm *terminus ad quem* for the document is late 1960; internal evidence makes clear that much of it was written earlier. Several slightly varying versions of the manuscript are in the Klein archive, Documentations Arts Plastiques, Musée National d'Art Moderne, Centre National d'Art et de Culture Georges Pompidou, Paris. Extracts, edited in a manner which tends to distort Klein's text, were published in English in *Yves Klein,* the catalogue of the exhibition at the Jewish Museum, New York, 1967. Selections from the text are printed elsewhere in this catalogue.

   Translations throughout are mine unless noted. I would like to thank Sylvia Huot and Richard Miller for their generous assistance with Klein's French. His prose is erratic in style and occasionally ungrammatical; I aimed for fidelity to the original and tried to avoid editing for smoothness.

   The present version of this essay owes a huge debt to the criticisms of H. Marshall Leicester, Jr. I wish to thank him and James S. Ackerman, Harry Berger, Jr., Neil Levine, Sheldon Nodelman, and Laura A. Slatkin for their suggestions, and the Research Committee of the Faculty of the University of California, Santa Cruz, the University Art Museum, Berkeley, and the Department of Fine Arts, Harvard University, for partial support of my study.

2. "Questions to Stella and Judd," interview by Bruce Glaser, ed. Lucy R. Lippard, in *Minimal Art: A Critical Anthology,* ed. Gregory Battcock (New York: E. P. Dutton & Co., 1968), p. 164. This interview was taped in February 1964.

3. James S. Ackerman, "On Judging Art without Absolutes," *Critical Inquiry* 5 (Spring 1979): 444.

4. Charles Baudelaire, "The Painter of Modern Life," *The Painter of Modern Life and Other Essays,* trans. and ed. Jonathan Mayne (London: Phaidon Press, 1964), pp. 7, 9.

5. *Le Dépassement de la problématique de l'art* (La Louvière, Belgium: Editions de Montbliart, 1959).

6. *Dimanche, the Newspaper of a Single Day,* prepared as part of the Paris Festival d'Art d'Avant-garde and published on November 27, 1960 (photographically reproduced elsewhere in this catalogue).

7. "L'Evolution de l'art vers l'immatériel," lecture delivered at the Sorbonne on June 3, 1959, in connection with an exhibition at the Galerie Iris Clert of maquettes by Klein and other artists commissioned to make art for the city theater of Gelsenkirchen, Germany. Klein's Sorbonne lecture was tape-recorded and made posthumously into two long-playing phonograph records, *Conférence à la Sorbonne, 3 juin 1959* (Paris: RPM, n.d.).

8. See n. 1.

9. Most of Klein's papers have been deposited by Rotraut Uecker Klein-Moquay, the artist's widow, in the Documentations Arts Plastiques, Musée National d'Art Moderne, Centre National d'Art et de Culture Georges Pompidou, Paris, where they constitute the Klein archive. For a detailed discussion of this archive and other unpublished sources on the artist, see Nan Rosenthal [Piene], "The Blue World of Yves Klein," Ph.D. dissertation, Harvard University, 1976. Virtually all the primary documents I cite in this essay are in my files in the form of photocopies or photographs which Rotraut Klein-Moquay and Marie Raymond kindly permitted me to make in 1973–74.

10. *Dépassement,* p. 3.

11. Pp. 27–28.

12. Fred Klein, interview with author, May 15, 1974, Paris; Sadi de Gorter, [Fred] *Klein* (Libourne: Editions Arts Graphiques d'Aquitaine, 1972).

13. Marie Raymond, interview with author, May 18, 1974, Paris; Fred Klein, interview with author, May 15, 1974.

14. See Georges Mathieu, "L'Abstraction lyrique" and "Esquisse d'une embryologie des signes," *Au-delà du Tachisme* (Paris: René Julliard, 1963), pp. 13–154, 164–71.

15. The initials stand for the surnames of the participating artists: Hartung, Wols, Picabia, Stahly, Mathieu, Tapié, and Bryen.

16. *H.W.P.S.M.T.B.* (Paris: Imprimerie d'Astorg, 1948), unpaginated.

17. François Mathey, *Georges Mathieu* (Paris: Hachette-Fabbri, 1969), pp. 10–24, 43–47.

18. E.g., in a letter of February 14, 1957, from Klein in Paris to his parents (probably in the Low Countries), Klein described his first visit, the previous evening, to Mathieu's distinctly unbohemian establishment: "He has a mansion three stories high in Passy and he received us with champagne. It has huge rooms and paintings which are six meters long" (Klein archive).

19. *Un Art autre: ou il s'agit de nouveaux dévidages du réel* (Paris: Gabriel-Giraud & Fils, 1952), p. 3.

20. Alain Jouffroy, "Marcel Duchamp: l'idée de jugement devrait disparaître...," *Arts* (Paris), November 24, 1954, p. 13. It is also worth noting the publications in Paris of Duchamp's almost complete writings, *Marchand du sel,* ed. Michel Sanouillet (Paris: Le Terrain Vague, 1958), and of his authorized biography, Robert Lebel, *Sur Marcel Duchamp* (Paris: Trianon Press, 1959).

21. Rotraut Klein-Moquay, interview with author, November 10–17, 1973, Ibiza, Mallorca.

22. Arman (Armand Fernandez), interview with author, May 25, 27, 1975, New York.

23. Regarding Klein's knowledge of the Lettrist movement, see the journal he kept in Paris and on his voyage to Asia, January 21 to mid-September, 1952, Klein archive. The pertinent entries are January 25, where he writes about having seen a good film by Isidore Isou, and March 12, where he writes, "Les Lettrists ne sont pas au point—Isou et Dufrène sont bien, le rest 0."

24. Maurice Lemaître, *Le Lettrisme devant dada et les nécrophages de dada!* (Paris: Centre de Créativité, 1967), p. 15.

25. "Des bases (fausses), principes, etc....et condamnation de l'évolution," *Soulèvement de la jeunesse* (Paris), June 1952, p. 3.

26. Letter in possession of Marie Raymond, Paris.

27. Letter, fourteen pages, from Yves Klein, Nice, to Marie Raymond and Fred Klein, probably in Paris, circa late August 1948, Klein archive, giving a detailed account of Klein's trip beginning August 3, 1948, from Nice through Italy.

28. See Thomas McEvilley, "Yves Klein and Rosicrucianism," elsewhere in this catalogue. For a different assessment of the impact of Max Heindel's and Joséphin Peladan's Rosicrucianism on Klein's art, see Rosenthal [Piene], "The Blue World of Yves Klein," pp. 34–40.

29. Claude Pascal, interview with author, April 11, 1974, Paris. See also Klein's two Irish journals, of April 30 to June 19, 1950, and June 22 to September 19, 1950, Klein archive, and Pascal's Nice/London journal of October 25, 1949, to October 29, 1950, in the possession of Arman, New York.

30. Interview with author, July 10, 1974, Sudbury, Suffolk.

31. In late 1959 Klein began to use gold leaf on his monochrome panels. The tale he fostered, that he had learned the craft of handling this delicate material while working for the frame-maker in London in 1950, is an exaggeration. According to Savage, when Klein returned to London in June 1957 for his exhibition of variously colored monochromes at the Gallery One, he visited his former employer and asked to be shown how to gild. That Klein was thinking in 1957 about using gold leaf seems very likely; the bronze monochrome M 23, 1957, was almost certainly in his Gallery One show.

32. Pascal, interview with author, April 11, 1974.

33. James Shorrocks, interview with author, July 11, 1974, London.

34. Among the examples of this claim in the Klein archive, see sundry *curricula vitae* made by Klein before his death; the exhibition chronology in *Yves Klein: Monochrome und Feuer*, preface by Paul Wember, catalogue of exhibition at the Museum Haus Lange, Krefeld, 1961 (hereafter cited as "Kre-feld cat."); and three drafts of a typewritten, hand-corrected letter of August 5, 1955, from Klein in Nice to the writer Jacques Tournier in Paris. In this letter about his "toiles...d'une seule couleur unie" Klein seeks to establish himself as a promising painter, and in what appears to be the first draft, he writes that he has had "Expositions Particulières à Londres en 1950, à Tokio en 1953, à Madrid en 1954." In the second draft the "Londres en 1950" is typed but crossed out, and in the apparently final draft, typed in the form of a normal French business letter, only "Expositions à Tokio en 1953, à Madrid en 1954" appears, as if Klein decided to reduce the extent of the previous career he was claiming for himself.

35. Irish journal, entry for May 21, 1950.

36. Entries in Klein's two Madrid diaries, both in the Klein archive, run from February 18 to June 26, 1951, and are mainly in Spanish.

37. Translated by Hannah Hanna.

38. Translated by Hannah Hanna and Gabriel Berns.

39. Loose manuscript page, recto and verso in handwriting and on graphed school notebook paper identical to that in the journal Klein kept in Paris and on his voyage to Asia, January 21 to mid-September, 1952, Klein archive. The relevant passage, with minor omissions, reads:

> Que représente pour vous la couleur: Bleu/Rouge/ Jaune/..../ Quelle est la plus puissante des trois/ ..../ Quelle est la plus faible/ Quelle est la plus agréable à regarder/..../ à votre avis la vue d'une de ces trois couleurs à l'état pur/ éveille-t-elle chez vous un sentiment quelconque/ Vos idées personnelles sur ces trois c./ (si ce n'est pas trop indiscret)/ les employez vous souvent/ pourriez-vous vous passer de ces/ trois couleurs/ quel rôle joue le Bleu/Rouge/Jaune/ en tant que couleur dans la Chimie/Physique/dans la Psych/ Quel est l'effet normal psychologique de/ chacun de ces [word illegible, probably "pures" or "trois"] couleurs sur l'homme/ et les animaux.

40. My account here and below of Klein's activities in Japan draws on Klein's Japan journal, on loose pages of circa 11-by-8½-inch graph paper, written mainly in late September and October 1952, Klein archive; Klein's Japan photo albums, thirty-six pages dating from September 23, 1952, to late November 1953, reproduced in Rosenthal [Piene], "The Blue World of Yves Klein," figs. 68–85; letters from Klein to his parents from Tokyo, November 5, 1952, and from Hong Kong, January 9, 1954, and from Tokyo to his aunt, Rose Raymond, November 8, 1952, and n.d., 1953, in the possession of Marie Raymond, Paris; Marie Raymond, interview with author, May 18, 1974; Yoshiaki Tono, Tokyo, letter to author, September 6, 1975; Takachiyo Uemura, Tokyo, letter to author, November 7, 1975.

41. Letter to Klein, Tokyo, from Risei Kano, president, Kodokan Judo Institute, Tokyo, December 19, 1953, Klein archive. See also letter from S. Tachiro, instructor at Kodokan Judo Institute, Tokyo, to Klein's aunt, Rose Raymond, Nice, December 7, 1953, Klein archive, in response to a letter of November 18, 1953, from her, explaining that it is impossible for the Institute to give the grade of fourth or fifth *dan* to someone such as Klein who had studied judo for, by Japanese standards, such a short time.

42. Uemura, letter to author, November 7, 1975.

43. Malcolm Gregory, interview with author, Los Angeles, September 20, 1975.

44. See n. 34. See also the carbon of a three-page letter from Klein, Paris, to Takachiyo Uemura, Tokyo, October 4, 1960, Klein archive.

45. P. 18.

46. The particular version of *Yves Peintures* I have described belongs to the Klein archive, Paris. This archive copy is missing the tenth plate page; according to Pierre Restany, in *Yves Klein le monochrome* (Paris: Librairie Hachette, 1974), p. 27, the color plate on this page was orange, captioned Paris, 1954. This is an example of the version I regard as having been carefully collated by Klein in late 1954; by contrast to some haphazardly assembled versions also in the Klein archive, which have been exhibited posthumously, it may be described as the correct *Yves Peintures*. It is extremely unlikely that the 150 booklets referred to on the colophon page of *Yves Peintures* were ever all assembled in the correct version I have described, or in any version. No version I have seen is actually numbered on the colophon page, and the Klein archive contains many loose, unmounted inked colored papers and uncollated parts of the booklet.

    A number of identically sized, unmounted, loose colored papers in the archive are printed "Yves" at the lower right in the same size of cursive type, to simulate a signature on a painting. Had Klein trimmed these "signed" colored papers to the varying sizes of the plates in the correct version, it would have produced the appearance of varying sizes of signature.

47. Hains, who, like François Dufrêne, later became a founding member of the Nouveaux Réalistes, knew Klein originally from Marie Raymond's Monday salon, perhaps as early as the late 1940s. Two years older than Klein, Hains during most of the 1950s was a photographer and filmmaker of fractured images of Paris street scenes and poster lettering. Knowledgeable about Dada and Surrealism, an admirer of Duchamp, and himself an inspired punster, Hains may have contributed substantially to Klein's general knowledge of Duchamp. Hains says that he did not own a monochrome by Klein in 1951 and that Klein took the pseudonym

Haguenault from the wrapper of a mass-produced brand of pastry, but Hains does not recall why (interview with author, July 17, 1974, Paris). There are plate pages from *Haguenault Peintures* in the Klein archive.

48. Posthumously typed Paris journal entry, January 13, 1955, Klein archive.

49. *Dépassement*, p. 28.

50. See Klein's letter to Jacques Tournier, August 5, 1955.

51. Klein was unquestionably aware of the chromatic opulence of Matisse's painting and in 1951 visited the Dominican chapel at Vence designed by Matisse. Matisse's *papiers découpés* were published and exhibited many times in Paris and Nice between 1945 and 1954. Even if Klein missed all of the museum and gallery exhibitions of the cut papers during this period, which despite his travels is highly unlikely, he certainly knew of the existence of these works. In 1953, following a brief interview with Matisse, Marie Raymond wrote an article about Matisse's figuration for an Amsterdam periodical, "Matisse contra de Abstracten," *Kroniek van Kunst en Kultur* 13 (December 1953): 227–29, in which the cut papers are discussed at length and reproduced. Klein kept close track of his parents' careers, and when he returned from sixteen months in Asia to their apartment in Paris in late January or early February 1954, his mother's article must have been one of the first pieces of art criticism he encountered. Soon after, Klein inquired in a letter to his Madrid friend, Franco de Sarabia, after pages of negotiating his contract to teach at Franco de Sarabia's judo school in Madrid, about whether his friend was still a printer. If so, Klein wrote, "that is also a major reason for me to go to Spain and publish some books with you" (draft of a letter in Spanish to "Fernando," n.d., from internal evidence early 1954, Klein archive).

Klein was very likely aware of Matisse's cut papers in terms of the novelty of the medium, and possibly thought about their relevance to the production of limited-edition books. In the case of Matisse's *Jazz*, published in 1947, a book that Klein because of his fondness for jazz was especially likely to have known about, Matisse made the original cut-outs for the pochoir illustrations with paper painted with printer's ink.

52. Paul Wember, *Yves Klein*, chronology, bibliography, and list of exhibitions compiled by Gisela Fiedler (Cologne: Verlag M. DuMont Schauberg, 1969).

53. Wember, "Austellungsverzeichnis," Krefeld cat.

54. There is a precedent for such satire on French luxury books: the *Album primo-avrilesque* (Paris: Librairie Ollendorf, 1897) by the humorous writer Alphonse Allais, who was lampooning Symbolism. The *Album* contains seven single-color engravings, one in black captioned "Combat de nègres dans une cave pendant la nuit," one in red captioned "Récolte de la tomate par des cardinaux apoplectiques au bord de la mer rouge," one in blue captioned "Stupeur de jeunes recrues apercevant pour la première fois ton azur, ô Méditerranée!" and so on. The book concludes with a "marche funèbre spécialement composée pour les funérailles d'un grand homme sourd," which is scored with two pages of empty staves. Despite the striking similarities between Allais' book and Klein's, Klein's friend Arman seriously doubts that Klein was aware of the *Album* when he produced *Yves Peintures* (Arman, interview with author, May 27, 1975).

55. *Dépassement*, p. 28.

56. Malraux's *The Voices of Silence*, trans. Stuart Gilbert (Garden City, New York: Doubleday, 1953), was first published in France as *Les Voix du silence* (Paris: Nouvelle Revue Fran-

çaise, 1951). The gist of the book had appeared earlier in Malraux's *Psychologie de l'art* (Geneva: Albert Skira, 1947); parts of the first volume of this work, "Le Musée imaginaire" (in the English-language edition "The Museum without Walls"), had been published before and immediately after the war in French art and literary journals.

57. Malraux, *Voices of Silence*, pp. 44, 46.

58. In *Illuminations*, ed. Hannah Arendt, trans. Harry Zohn (New York: Schocken Books, 1969), pp. 220–21.

59. Malraux, *Voices of Silence*, pp. 44, 46.

60. E.g., Georges Duthuit, "Malraux et son musée I," *Les Lettres nouvelles* 2 (March 1954): 334–57.

61. Benjamin, "The Work of Art in the Age of Mechanical Reproduction," pp. 220–21.

62. P. 38.

63. There is no evidence in Klein's papers that he was aware of the monochrome paintings and reliefs Kelly made in Paris as early as 1950.

64. Pp. 11–13. While in this text and other texts in the Klein archive Klein wrote that he had titled the refused orange monochrome *Expression du monde de la couleur Mine Orange*, he inscribed the back of the work with the title *Expression de l'univers de la couleur mine orange*.

65. Catherine Krahmer, *Der Fall Yves Klein: Zur Krise der Kunst* (Munich: R. Piper & Co. Verlag, 1974), p. 35.

66. Yves Klein, "Texte de présentation de l'exposition aux Editions Lacoste, Oct-Sept 1955" [sic], penned title in Klein's hand on a typescript identical to the text posted at his October 1955 Paris exhibition (Klein archive). This text is almost identical to Klein's description of his work in his letter to Tournier, August 5, 1955.

67. Edouard Adam, interview with author, May 16, 1974, Paris.

68. Ibid. See also the typescript formula in the Klein archive for International Klein Blue paint (IKB), and patent no. 63471, issued to Klein on May 19, 1960, for IKB, Ministère de l'Industrie, Paris. In Klein's patented formula, the binder Rhodopas MA is described as a vinyl chloride; however, according to Rhône-Poulenc, Rhodopas M is a solid form of polyvinyl acetate also sold in solution as M60A.

69. There has been one large traveling exhibition of Klein's early (mostly 1955–1957) monochromes, at the Kaiser Wilhelm Museum, Krefeld, *Frühe gelbe, schwarze, weisse, orange, grüne, Bilder von Yves Klein*, May 27–July 29, 1973, and at the Städtische Kunstsammlungen, Ludwigshafen, *Yves Klein*, March 20–April 28, 1974. I am grateful to Manfred Fath, then director of the municipal gallery in Ludwigshafen, for helping me examine these works closely.

70. Bernadette Allain, "Propositions monochromes du peintre Yves," *Couleurs* 15 (1956): 25.

71. See n. 66. For a discussion of the way that Klein's language in 1955 and 1956 echoes Symbolist literature and hints that colors may represent certain moods, see Rosenthal [Piene], "The Blue World of Yves Klein," pp. 106–11.

72. *Dépassement*, p. 3.

73. Pp. 20–22. Cf. Klein's almost identical descriptions of his 1957 Milan exhibition in "Meine Stellung im Kampf zwischen Linie und Farbe," *ZERO* (Düsseldorf), no. 1 (April 1958), pp. 8–9, and in the manuscript of a speech to city officials of Gelsenkirchen, early 1959, Klein archive. In these versions for German audiences, Klein edited out the paragraphs stating that the pictures did not resemble one another and that their "prices were all different of course."

74. Dino Buzzati, "Blu Blu Blu," *Corriere d'Informazione* (Milan),

January 10, 1957.

75. "The Monochrome Adventure," p. 47. Klein made an almost identical statement on May 28, 1957, in a radio interview in English with "Marjorie D." conducted for broadcast in the U.S. (see varying transcriptions of the broadcast in the Klein archive).

76. Donald Judd, "Specific Objects," *Arts Yearbook* 8 (1965), reprinted in *Complete Writings 1959–1975* (Halifax: Press of the Nova Scotia College of Art and Design, 1975), pp. 181–89. In his essay Judd uses Klein's work three times to exemplify characteristics of the term of the title.

77. E.g., there are twenty-four ultramarine monochrome panels dating from 1959 to 1961 that are about 36¼ by 28¾ inches (92 by 73 centimeters), a proportion of height to width of 5 to 3.9; nine dating from 1959 to 1962 that are about 23½ by 18¾ inches (60 by 48 centimeters), proportions of 5 to 4; and the series dating mainly from 1960 and 1961 that Klein called "2m × 1,50," most of which are in proportions of 5 to 3.8. There is also a 1959 series of blue monochromes on paper, destined to be included in a deluxe edition of *Dépassement*; these measure 8⅛ by 6⅝ inches (21 by 17 centimeters), proportions of 5 to 4.

78. See Krefeld cat.; draft of letter about Krefeld retrospective from Klein, Paris, to Wember, Krefeld, n.d. (from internal evidence early or mid-1960), Klein archive; and Klein's installation designs on architectural blueprint of 1961 Krefeld retrospective, Klein archive.

79. Norbert Kricke, interview with author, December 9, 1973, Düsseldorf; Werner Ruhnau, interview with author, December 10, 1973, Essen; Städtische Kunstaustellung Gelsenkirchen, *Bildende Kunst am Neubau des Theaters der Stadt Gelsenkirchen* (Gelsenkirchen, 1957).

80. Buzzati, "Blu Blu Blu."

81. The numeration in Wember's *catalogue raisonné* is posthumous.

82. In *The Tradition of the New* (New York: Grove Press, 1961), p. 29.

83. On June 26, 1957, two evenings after the opening of his first one-man show in London, *Monochrome Propositions of Yves Klein* at the Gallery One, Klein showed a short film about the Paris Blue Period shows and gave a talk about his work at the Institute of Contemporary Art; this event was advertised on the invitations to the Gallery One exhibition and on a press release about the show sent out by Victor Musgrave, director of the gallery. While no transcript of Klein's remarks at the I.C.A. exists, Klein wrote about the evening in "The Monochrome Adventure," p. 47. Characteristically, he describes audience reactions to his work which protest that it is a "gigantic joke" and complains that "some friends" (although he does not name them, he probably refers to Iris Clert and Pierre Restany, who were present) "defended me badly" that evening by describing him as "pure purity." According to the British artist Richard Hamilton, whose late wife wrote him a detailed account of the I.C.A. evening, Klein repeatedly provoked the I.C.A. audience to laughter (interview with author, March 4, 1974, London).

84. The January 1957 Galleria Apollinaire announcement was titled "Yves Klein: proposte monocrome epoca Blu" and contained a text by Pierre Restany, "L'Epoca blu, il secondo minuto della verità."

85. Buzzati, "Blu Blu Blu"; Krahmer, *Klein*, p. 35.

86. The subject of the possible mutual influences of the much older (b. 1899) Italian-Argentinian artist and Klein on one another is beyond the scope of this essay. The two met at Klein's 1957 Milan show and became friends soon after; their correspondence (in Spanish) is in the Klein archive. At some point Fontana gave Klein copies of his Manifesto Blanco of 1946. No doubt much could be written on the complex subject of Fontana's relationship to second-generation postwar European artists. This relationship might be compared to the subtleties of Barnett Newman's relationships—in terms of artistic influence and personal generosity of spirit—to younger artists working in New York during the 1960s.

It is clear from what I have written that I rarely assume Klein's claims about dates, precedence, and so forth to be necessarily true. However, I doubt strongly that Klein's Blue Period shows of 1957 were seriously influenced by Fontana's environmental installations of paintings away from the wall in the early 1950s. Peculiar as it may sound now, Fontana's work was not well known in Paris in the mid-1950s; he did not exhibit there until after 1957, and his name does not appear in Seuphor's *Dictionnaire de la peinture abstraite* (1958), although an artist as little known today as Klein's mother has an entry. Klein could have been well informed about *spazialismo* and northern Italian art, from mid-1955 forward, through Pierre Restany's connections with Milan, which were strong. But I doubt that Fontana had a serious influence on Klein because, first, when Klein did borrow from a source, he tended to leave some clues to the fact and his anxiety about it, and second, I know of no exhibition by Fontana of monochromes of only one color prior to Klein's Milan show of 1957. See Fontana's intelligent remarks on Klein and European artists of the second postwar generation in *Art et création* 1 (January-February 1968): 78.

87. Michel Conil-Lacoste, "Comparaisons," *Le Monde* (Paris), February 15, 1957, p. 8.

88. K. G. Pontus Hultén, "Pariskonst och Jiujitsu," *Stockholms-Tidningen*, October 30, 1957, trans. Marion Dansky.

89. Benjamin, "The Work of Art in the Age of Mechanical Reproduction," p. 220.

90. It seems likely that the sensational story of the investigation and trial of van Meegeren between 1945 and 1947 made a considerable impression on Klein, who was between seventeen and nineteen when the story unraveled. His Dutch father, who may well have known van Meegeren when the forger was part of the artistic community on the Côte d'Azur during most of the 1930s, was once again having one-man exhibitions in the Netherlands in the immediate postwar years. Klein accompanied his parents to Holland on the occasion of at least one of these exhibitions, probably in 1947.

It is worth remembering that van Meegeren himself called attention to his forgeries of Vermeer and de Hoogh, in part to clear himself of the charge—far more grave than fraud in the liberated Netherlands—that he had collaborated with the Germans by selling them a Dutch Baroque masterpiece. When it emerged that not only Goering but also a sizable group of professional experts, including the directors of important museums in the Netherlands, had been taken in, van Meegeren became a popular hero.

An adolescent might have drawn a number of lessons from the complex story. One may have been that while van Meegeren had behaved like a knave, professional art historians and noted dealers and collectors had behaved like fools. Another lesson may have been that the professionals had committed themselves to works of art for reasons that were not really related to quality. For example, in 1937 Abraham

Bredius certified the van Meegeren *Christ at Emmaus* as an authentic Vermeer, possibly because it suited his previous theories about the Baroque painter's lost early work on religious subjects and because it corroborated his own belief, decades before, in the unusual Edinburgh Vermeer, *Christ with Mary and Martha*. Hannema, the director of the Boymans Museum, which had acquired the *Christ at Emmaus*, testified at van Meegeren's trial regarding the decision of a committee of experts in 1943 to advise the Dutch government to purchase Vermeer's *Washing of Christ's Feet*, which also turned out to be a van Meegeren. Hannema said at the trial that "none of us liked it much but we were afraid it would go to Germany." When the court inquired, "But you also bought it for its artistic value?" Hannema answered, "Of course. After all, Vermeers are scarce." See P. B. Coreman, *Van Meegeren's Faked Vermeers and de Hooghs: A Scientific Examination* (London: Cassel, 1949), and John Godley, *The Master Art Forger: The Story of Han van Meegeren* (New York: Wilfred Funk, 1951).

91. Hultén, "Pariskonst och Jiujitsu."

92. See fig. 36, a 1958 sketch by Klein for his project to illuminate the obelisk of Luxor in the Place de la Concorde with blue light above the base, Klein archive.

93. Interview with author, May 16, 1974, Paris.

94. "Ein von Yves Klein blau gefärbter Schwamm wird dem Käufer des Kataloges, der die Austellung in Krefeld besucht, hinzugeben" (Krefeld cat.).

95. "Remarques sur quelques oeuvres exposées chez Colette Allendy," Klein archive. There are three slightly varying versions of this important text in the Klein archive; internal and other evidence suggests that two were written before spring 1958 and that the third was modified after that date. The first pre–spring 1958 version consists of three pages in Klein's hand; the second pre–spring 1958 MS, from which I am quoting, is a typed carbon, identifiable by the provisional archival notations of K. G. Pontus Hulten: AA 20 and AA 21.

96. Ibid.

97. Krefeld cat.

98. Hultén, "Pariskonst och Jiujitsu."

99. "Remarques sur quelques oeuvres exposées chez Colette Allendy" (see n. 95 above).

100. Ibid.

101. Ibid.

102. Ibid. I quote here from what I called in n. 95 a third version of this text, dating from after spring 1958. As discussed below, this version established Klein's reading of Gaston Bachelard, whose work, according to Klein's Sorbonne lecture in 1959, he did not encounter until 1958. While Klein often willfully misdates events, I tend to believe his Sorbonne assertion because of other changes in these years in his prose style— from neo-Symbolist to Bachelardian—and because the third version of the "Remarques" reflects issues raised for the first time by his joint exhibition with Jean Tinguely, *Vitesse pure et stabilité monochrome*, held at the Galerie Iris Clert in November 1958.

103. *The Psychoanalysis of Fire*, trans. Alan C. M. Ross (Boston: Beacon Press, 1964), p. 7.

104. *La Dialectique de la durée* (Paris: Presses Universitaires de France, 1950), p. 38. Klein's copy of this book is in the Klein archive.

105. Ibid., p. 17.

106. In addition to Bachelard's *Dialectique de la durée*, Klein's library in the Klein archive contains *L'Eau et les rêves* (Paris: José Corti, 1942); *La Formation de l'esprit scientifique* (Paris: Librairie Philosophique J. Vrin, 1957); *La Philosophie du non* (Paris: Presses Universitaires de France, 1949); *La Poétique de l'espace* (Paris: Presses Universitaires de France, 1958); *La Terre et les rêveries de la volonté* (Paris: José Corti, 1948); and *La Terre et les rêveries du repos* (Paris: José Corti, 1948).

107. "Les Cris bleus de Charles Estienne," typed page signed "Y.K. 57," Klein archive.

108. *Conférence à la Sorbonne*.

109. *Dimanche*, p. 3.

110. Draft of letter from Klein in Paris to Paul Wember in Krefeld, n.d. (from internal evidence early or mid-1960), Klein archive.

111. In the Klein archive there are two floor plans of the Museum Haus Lange, Krefeld, on which Klein wrote, sketched, and color-penciled detailed instructions for the installation of his January-February 1961 retrospective; at the top of one is the note "accrochage en projection hors de la cimaise."

112. "Sensibilité pure," *Dimanche*, p. 1.

113. *Of Grammatology*, trans. Gayatri Chakravorty Spivak (Baltimore: Johns Hopkins University Press, 1976), pp. 141–47.

114. Klein archive.

115. Interview with author, July 17, 1974.

116. "Approaching Artaud," *The New Yorker*, May 19, 1973, p. 42.

117. "Preparation and Presentation of the Exhibition of 28 April 1958" (printed elsewhere in this catalogue).

118. Klein demonstrated his acute sensitivity to this issue during his May 1957 radio interview for broadcast in the U.S. (see n. 75), to which he brought along a letter from Stanley Marcus, the Dallas merchant and art collector, to Iris Clert, for the radio interviewer to read aloud on the air. In the transcript of the broadcast the interviewer quotes Marcus as follows: "Dear Iris, My Yves Klein has proved to be one of the most sensational purchases I have ever made. It has brought great laughter and fun whenever I show it. I will be sending you lots of customers this summer...." In a second, edited version of the radio transcript, one which Klein apparently planned to publish, though he never did, the sentence about "laughter and fun" has been excised, as if Klein wished to control the extent to which a collector regarded his art as a laughing matter.

119. Iris Clert, interview with author, May 16, 1974.

120. K. G. Pontus Hultén, *Jean Tinguely: Méta* (Boston: New York Graphic Society, 1975), pp. 62–63.

121. Ibid.

122. Typewritten manuscript, n.d., Klein archive.

123. E.g. in the case of Michael Blankfort, a novelist with a modest and interesting collection of postwar art, Klein had on the occasion of Blankfort's daughter's marriage in Paris early in 1962 helped the Blankfort family cut red tape to obtain a marriage license. Michael Blankfort, interview with author, November 23, 1974, Los Angeles.

124. "Due to the Fact That," a text datelined "Hotel Chelsea, New York, 1961," in *Yves Klein*, catalogue of exhibition at the Alexander Iolas Gallery, 1962, p. 11. This posthumously published text, which Neil Levine and John Archambault translated from French to English in collaboration with Klein in spring 1961, is a version of "Le Vrai devient réalité" ("Truth Becomes Reality"), ZERO (Düsseldorf), no. 3 (July 1961), reprinted in a facsimile edition of the journal, *Zero*, ed. Otto Piene and Heinz Mack (Cambridge, Mass.: MIT Press, 1973), pp. 85–95. Printed elsewhere in this catalogue.

125. *Dimanche,* p. 4.

126. "Viens avec moi dans le vide," *Dimanche,* p. 2.

127. "Truth Becomes Reality," printed elsewhere in this catalogue.

128. It is often suggested that George Segal's plaster sculptures stimulated Klein to make the life-cast Portrait Reliefs. It is more likely that the relevant example for Klein, if there was one, was Marcel Duchamp's *Female Fig Leaf* of 1950. This galvanized plaster object, which appears to be a cast of female sexual organs, was reissued in an edition of ten bronzes in 1961 by the Galerie Rive Droite, Paris, Klein's gallery at the time. Klein obtained one of the reissued *Fig Leaves* from Jean Larcade, director of the gallery, for his own collection, promising Larcade a Shroud Anthropometry in exchange (letter of November 14, 1962, from Jean Larcade to Rotraut Klein, in her personal files).

129. Rosalind Krauss, in "Notes on the Index: Seventies Art in America, Part 2," *October* 3 (1977): 58–67, has discussed the semiological terminology of C. S. Pierce very interestingly in relation to the 1976 painting of Lucio Pozzi.

130. *On Photography* (New York: Farrar, Straus, and Giroux, 1977), p. 154.

131. See, e.g., "The War," *Dimanche.*

132. Rotraut Klein-Moquay, interview with author, March 18, 19, and 21, 1974, London, and May 18, 19, 1974, Paris.

133. There is no objective evidence in the Klein archive to substantiate the story, suggested by Klein in "Viens avec moi dans le vide," "Le Vrai devient réalité," and "Due to the Fact That" and perpetuated by Restany in *Yves Klein le monochrome,* p. 173, that Klein used "living brushes" years before 1960 to paint monochromes; he used a roller.

134. John Kender, interview with author, May 28, 1975, New York.

135. Otto Piene, an artist friend of Klein who like him was born in 1928, has told me that even an article which predates the Namuth photographs and their publication in art journals during the 1950s ("Jackson Pollock: Is He the Greatest Living Painter in the United States?" *Life,* August 8, 1949, pp. 42 ff.) excited the attention of European vanguard artists.

136. "Namuth's Photographs and the Pollock Myth," in Hans Namuth, *Pollock Painting,* ed. Barbara Rose (New York: Agrinde Publications, 1980), unpaginated.

137. "Phenomenology of the Art of Painting," in *From the Abstract to the Possible* (Zurich: Cercle d'Art Contemporain, 1958), p. 20.

138. "Due to the Fact That," pp. 8–9.

139. Arman, interview with author, May 25, 27, 1975.

140. "Viens avec moi dans le vide," *Dimanche,* p. 2.

141. Ibid.

142. The photograph, labeled "La Plage du Diamant, Martinique," by H. Roger-Viollet, and the ink tracing, labeled "femmes et hommes" in Klein's hand, are in the Klein archive.

143. Rotraut Klein-Moquay, interview with author, March 18, 19, and 21, 1974.

144. John Kender, interview with author, May 28, 1975. An unsigned bill, almost certainly from Kender and Shunk, to Klein for nearly 400 photographs and slides made between February 1960 and October 1961 gives two dates, October 19, 1960, and October 25, 1960, on which Klein is charged for photos of his "leap" (*saut*). These dates, a Tuesday and a Wednesday, are probably the days on which the photographers either printed the photos or delivered them to Klein; as I discuss below, according to Kender the images of Klein flying were shot on a Sunday.

145. Carbon of letter of November 25, 1960, from Klein to Mi-nistère de l'Information, Klein archive.

146. "The Photographic Message," *Image-Music-Text,* trans. Stephen Heath (New York: Hill and Wang, 1977), pp. 25–26. Originally published as "Le Message photographique," *Communications* (Paris) 1 (1961).

147. Ibid.

148. John Kender, interview with author, May 28, 1975.

149. Ibid.

150. *ZERO* (Düsseldorf), no. 3 (July 1961), unpaginated, reprinted in *Zero,* ed. Piene and Mack, p. 111.

151. Letter of November 28, 1960, from Klein, Paris, to Paul Wember, Krefeld, Klein archive.

152. "The Photographic Message," p. 22.

153. For a discussion of Malevich's influence on Klein and the details of Klein's knowledge of the work and writing of Malevich and the Polish Unists, see Rosenthal [Piene], "The Blue World of Yves Klein," pp. 238–42 and 292–93. In sum: Klein was not initially stimulated to make monochromes on account of the Russian's example; he became very interested in Malevich's painting and theory in 1957 and had an unusual opportunity, some of which he created for himself, to see the painting, and learned enough about the theory to comprehend that Malevich was a mystic about space and the moral meaning of art. Klein appears to have understood nuances of the challenge of Malevich with considerable critical intuition. The issue was serious enough for Klein to make fun of the Russian artist in an amusing cartoon of 1958, *fig. 46* in which he depicts Malevich (who died when Klein was seven) using Klein's monochromes as a kind of still-life subject. I.e., he sketches Malevich as a painter of geometric abstraction, and to make the point utterly clear (and in a way, to pay homage), while Malevich at least wears a smock and thus has the status "painter," in this cartoon Kandinsky appears as a mere mouse (or rat?) on the floor. There are several versions of this cartoon by Klein in the Klein archive. It was based on a Folon cartoon, published in a Paris newspaper, that was probably intended to make fun of Magritte's paintings of easels framing windows on the landscape. Klein, employing Bachelard's language in the caption of one of his Malevich cartoons, proposes that we go outside "the phenomenology of time" to see that he preceded Malevich chronologically in space and monochromy. This obvious impossibility constitutes another of Klein's comments on the staleness of vanguardism.

154. *Studies in Iconology: Humanistic Themes in the Art of the Renaissance* (New York: Harper and Row, 1972).

Plates

Several works not in the exhibition are illustrated in the
Plates section because of their relation to exhibited works.
These unexhibited works have no catalogue numbers. The
Catalogue Listing gives detailed information on works in
the exhibition.

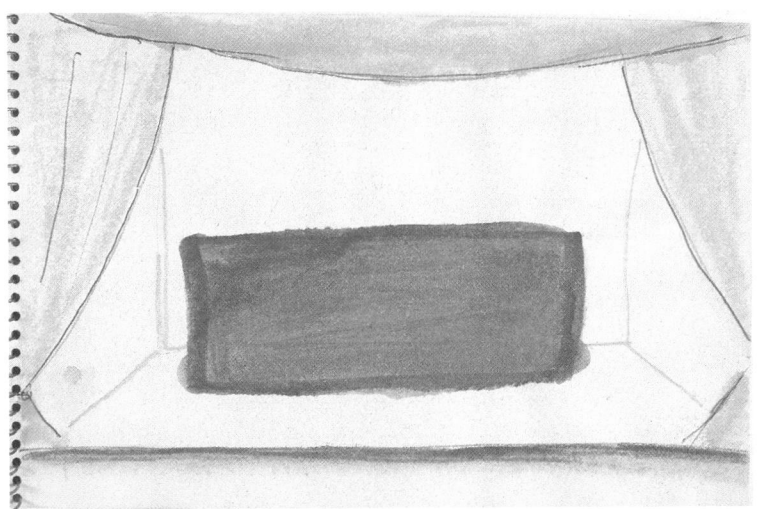

2. Untitled (red monochrome on stage), 1954

1. Untitled orange-red monochrome, [1950]

PREFACE

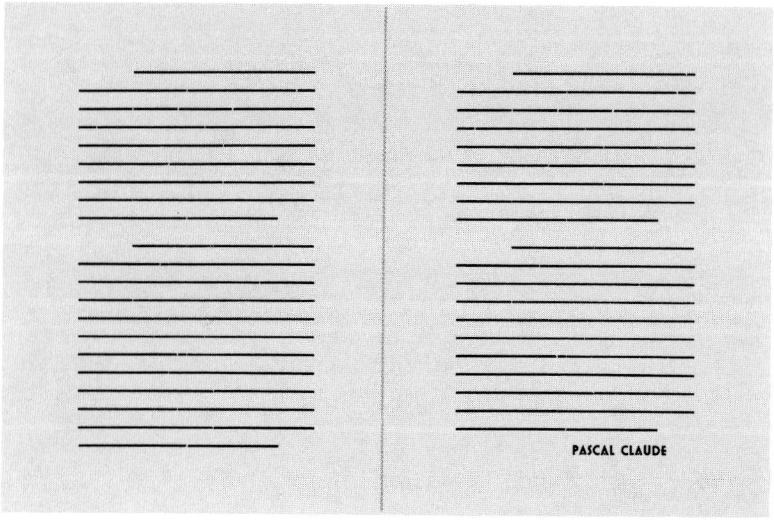

PASCAL CLAUDE

YVES   A LONDRES, 1950 (195 × 97)

YVES   A MADRID, 1951 (130 × 81)

YVES   A NICE, 1951 (195 × 97)

YVES   A PARIS; 1951 (130 × 81)

3. *Yves Peintures (Yves Paintings),* 1954

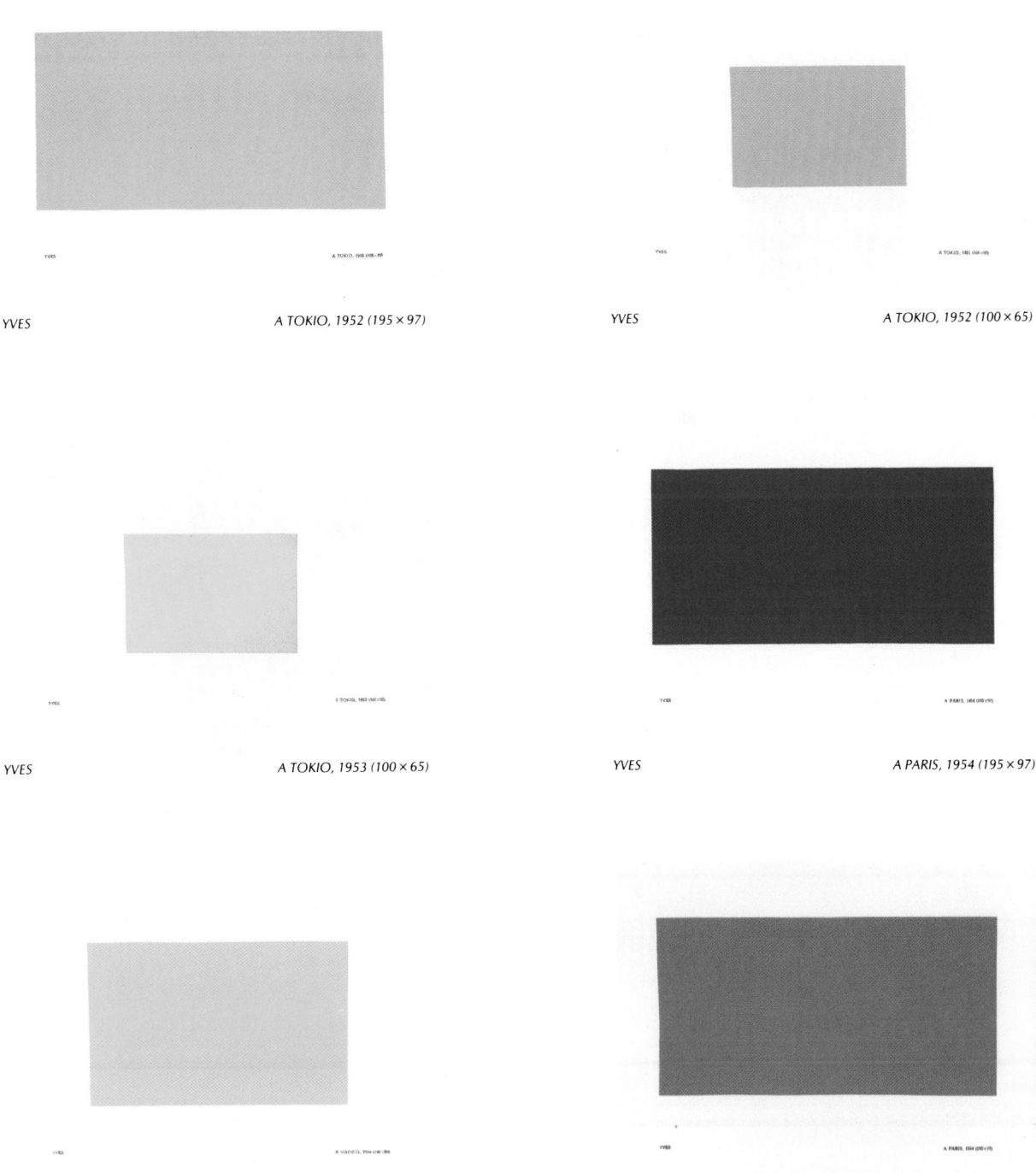

YVES   *A TOKIO, 1952 (195 × 97)*

YVES   *A TOKIO, 1952 (100 × 65)*

YVES   *A TOKIO, 1953 (100 × 65)*

YVES   *A PARIS, 1954 (195 × 97)*

YVES   *A MADRID, 1954 (146 × 89)*

YVES   *A PARIS, 1954 (195 × 97)*

5. *Expression de l'univers de la couleur mine orange (Expression of the Universe of the Color Orange Mineral),* orange monochrome, 1955

7. Untitled black monochrome, 1956

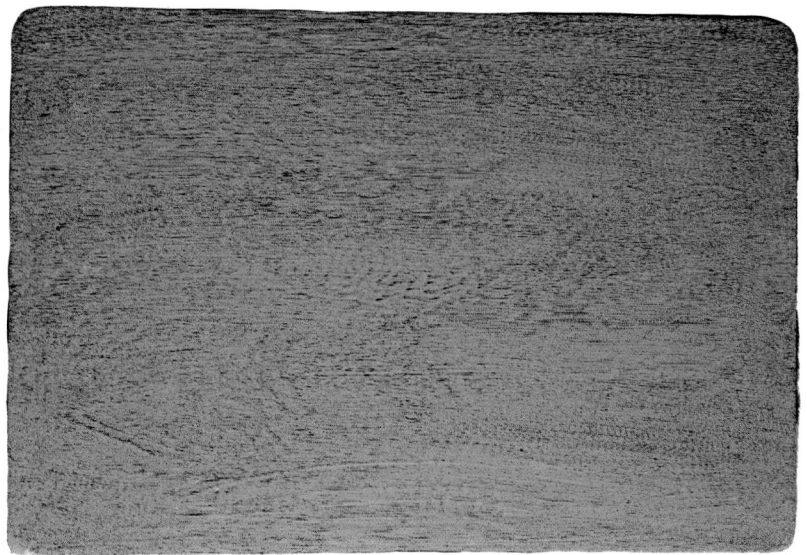

10.   Untitled green monochrome, 1957

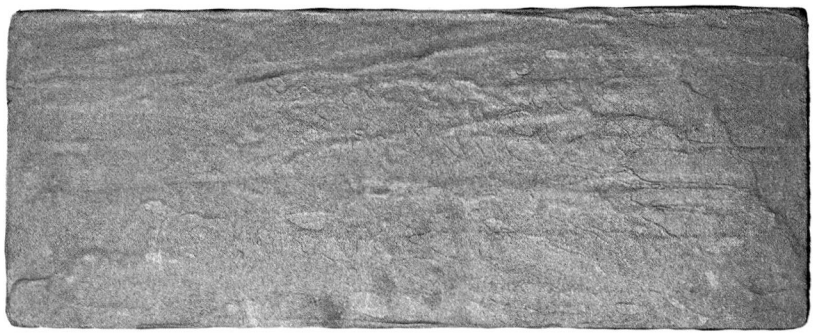

9.   Untitled bronze monochrome, 1957

13.   Untitled yellow monochrome, [1957]

12. Untitled white monochrome, 1957

14. Untitled red monochrome, 1959

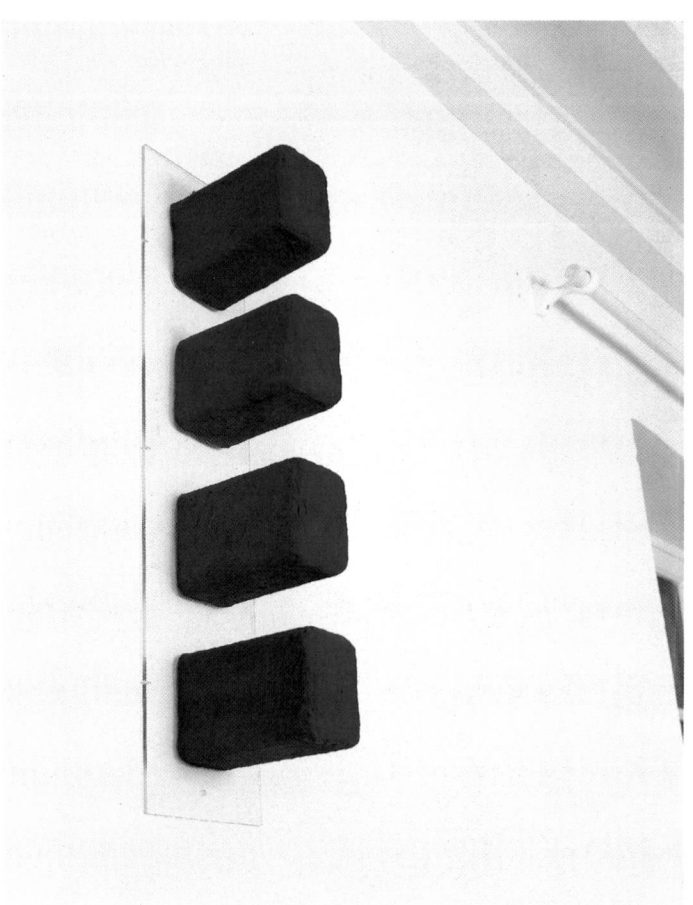

84.   *Relief bleu (Blue Relief)*, [1957]

85.   *Relief bleu (Blue Relief)*, 1957

86.   *Relief bleu (Blue Relief)*, 1957

87.   *Relief bleu (Blue Relief)*, [1957]

33. *Pigment pur bleu (Pure Blue Pigment)*, facsimile of 1957 and 1961 presentations of pure pigment

20.   Untitled blue monochrome, 1959

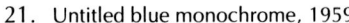

21. Untitled blue monochrome, 1959

26. Untitled blue monochrome, 1960

24. Untitled blue monochrome, 1960

31. Untitled blue monochrome, 1961

32. Untitled blue monochrome, 1962

35.   Untitled pink monochrome, [1962]

52. Untitled blue cosmogony (rain), [1961]

36.   Untitled monogold, undated

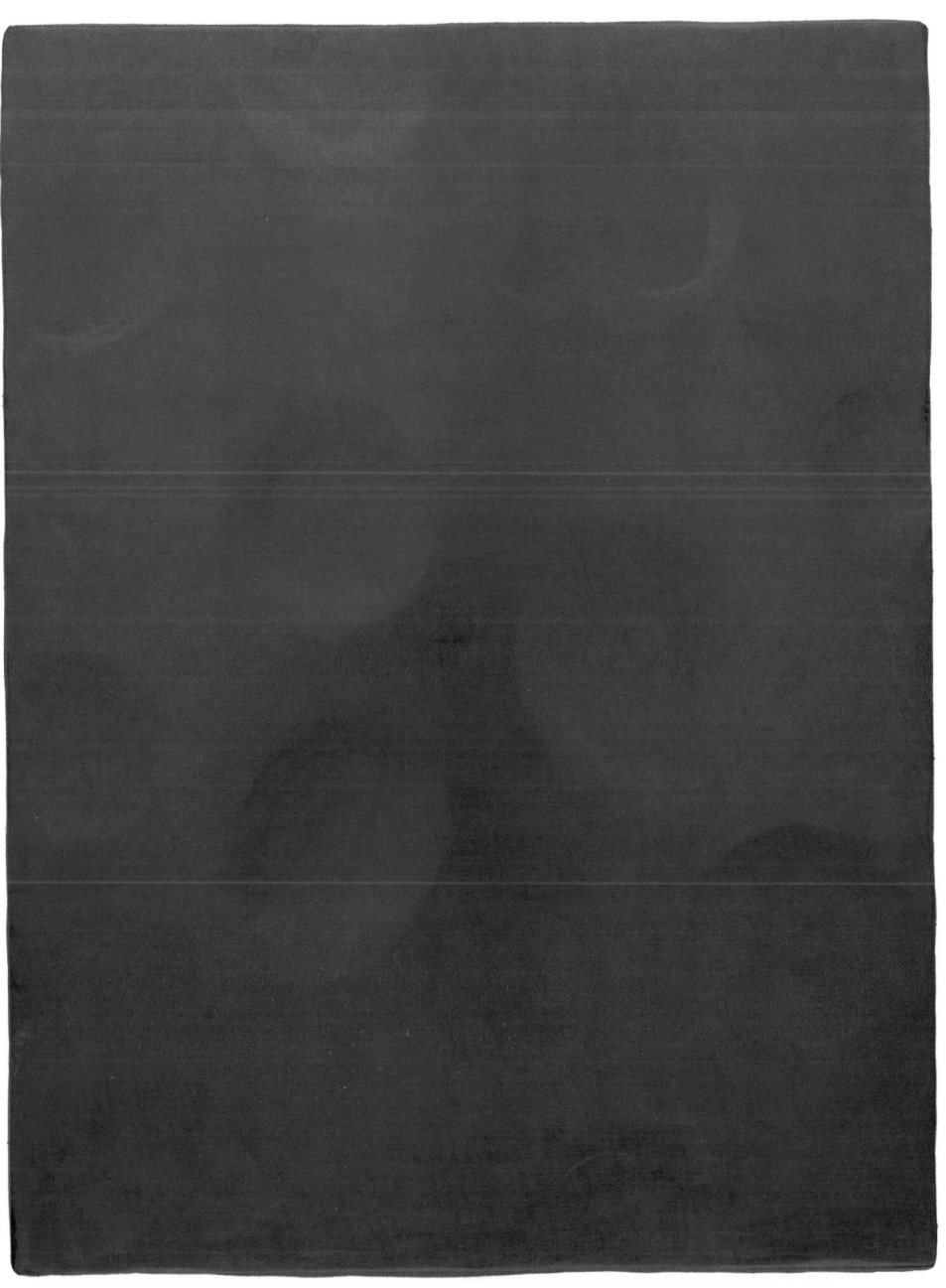

38. *Résonance (Resonance)*, 1960

40.   Untitled monogold, 1961

41. Untitled monogold, 1961

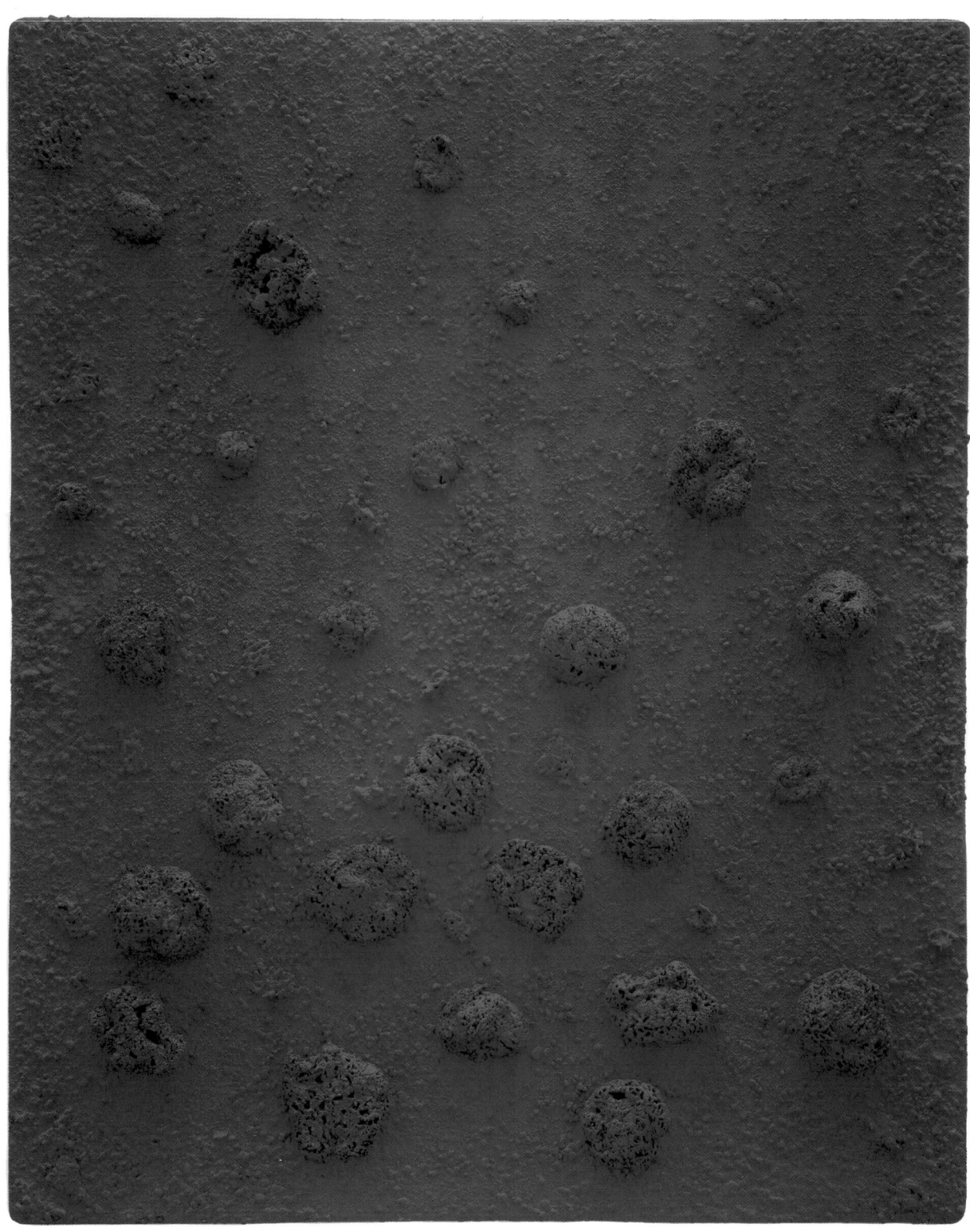

47. *Requiem*, 1960

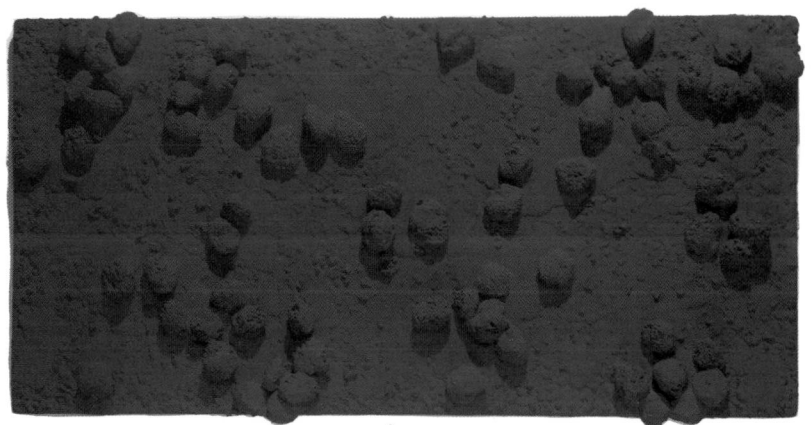

50. Untitled blue sponge relief, 1961

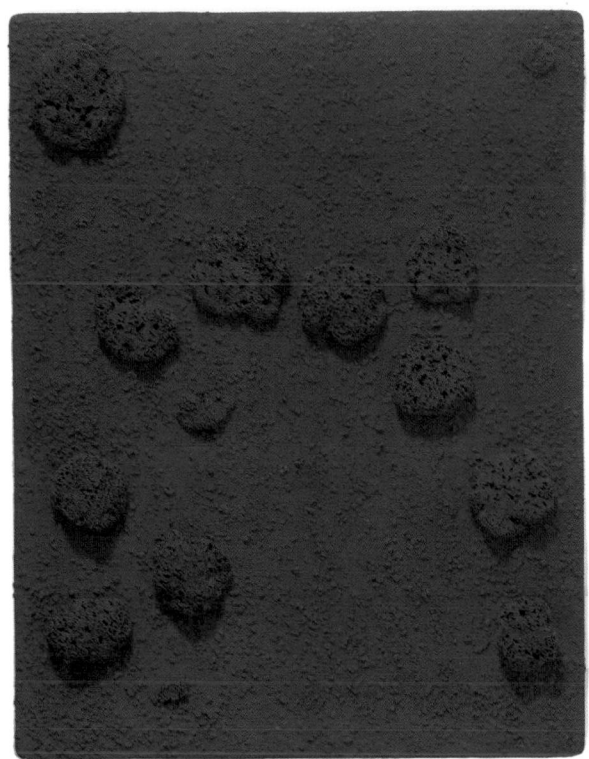

48. Untitled blue sponge relief, 1960

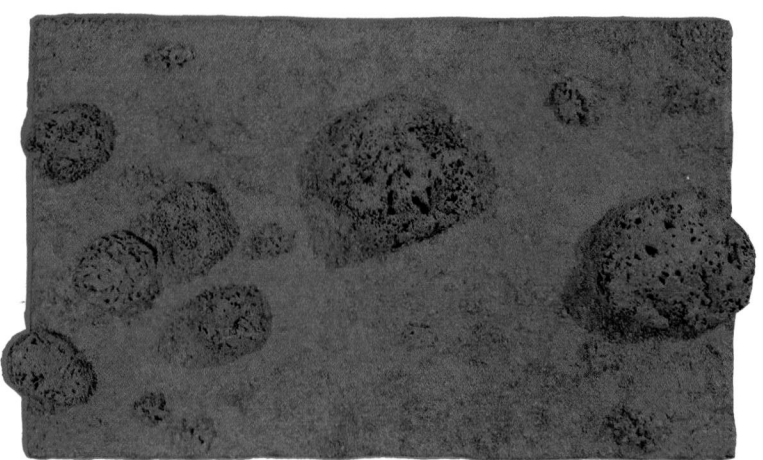

49. Untitled gold sponge relief, 1961

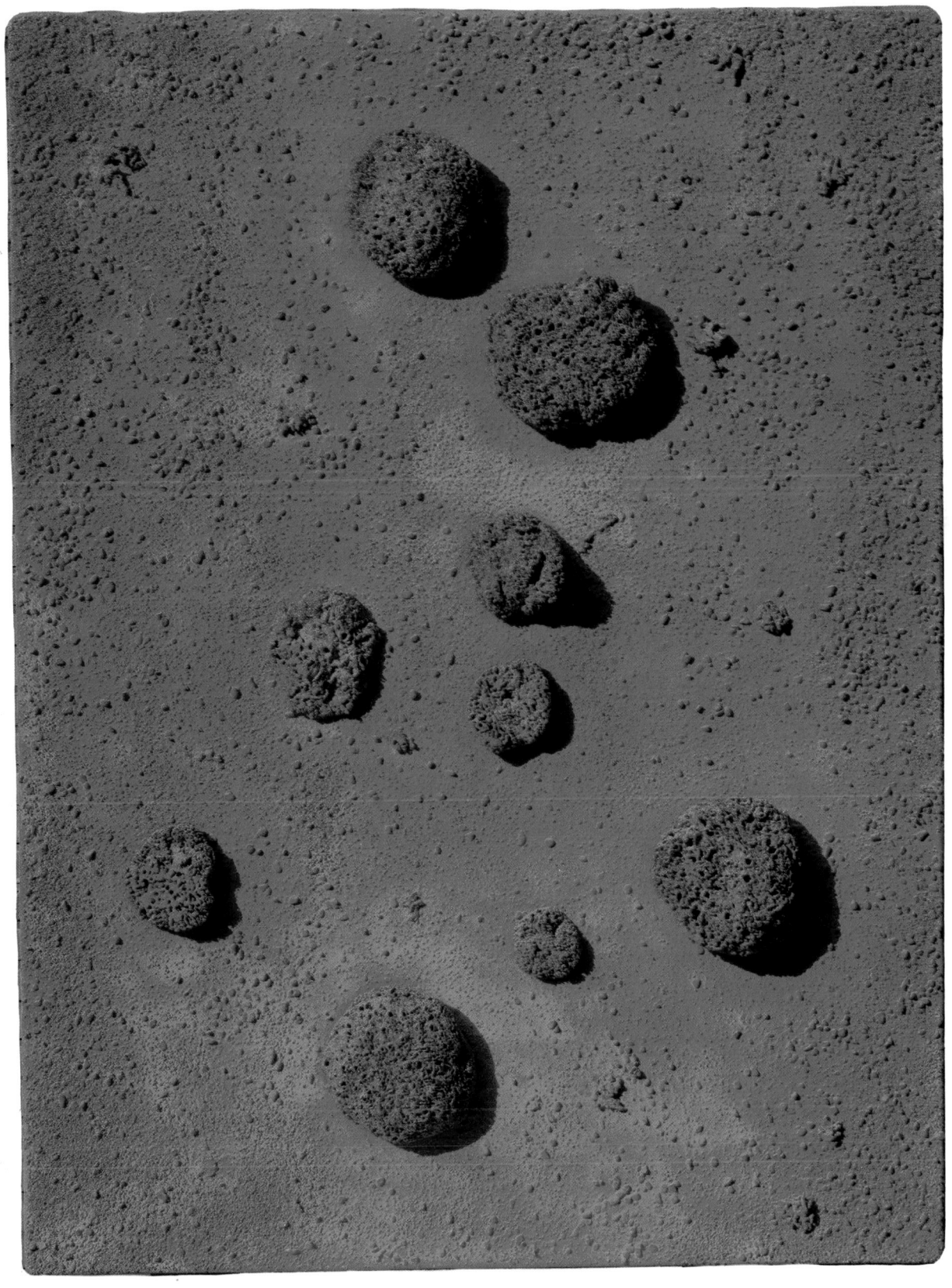

43. *Le Rose du bleu (The Rose of the Blue),* c. 1960

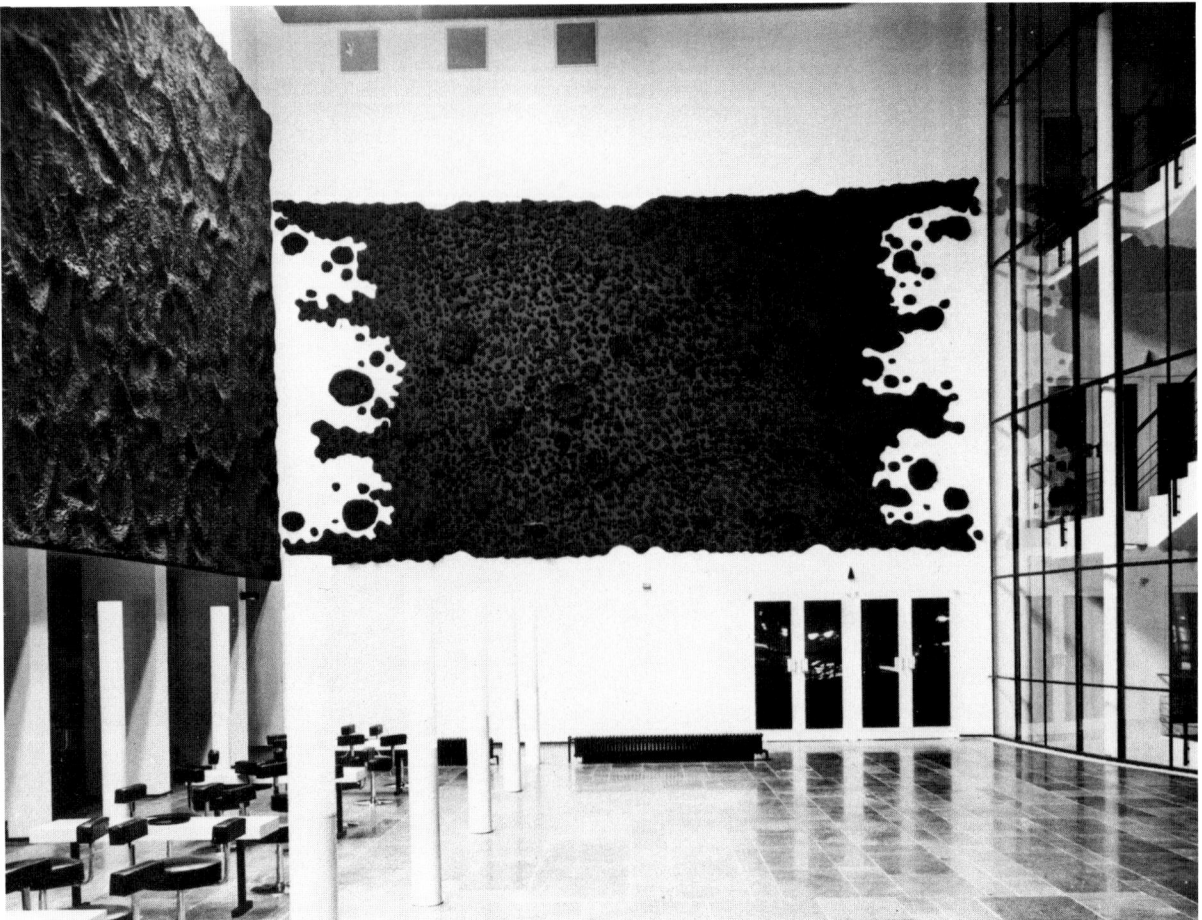

Klein's blue sponge reliefs and blue monochrome paintings in the Gelsenkirchen, Germany, city theater, 1957–59

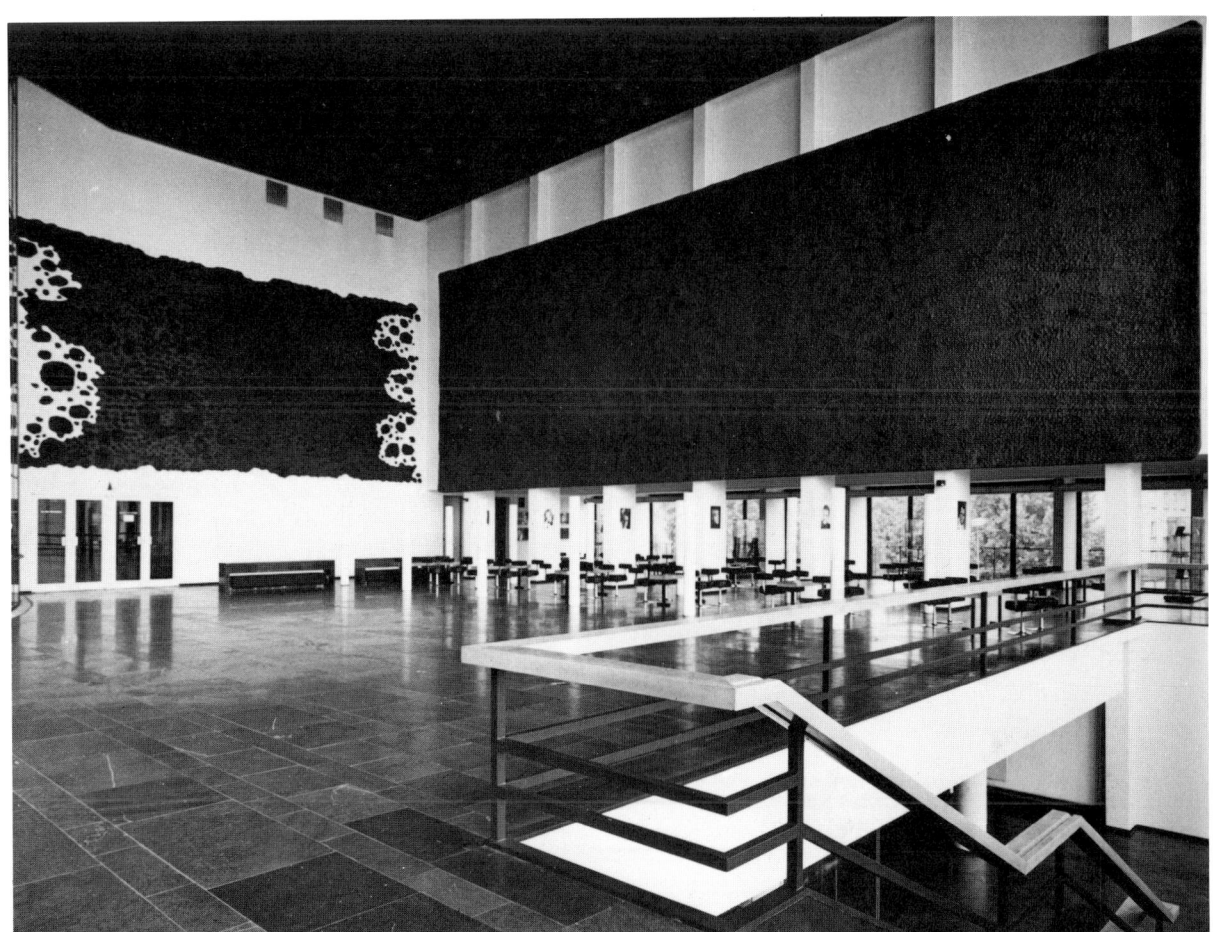

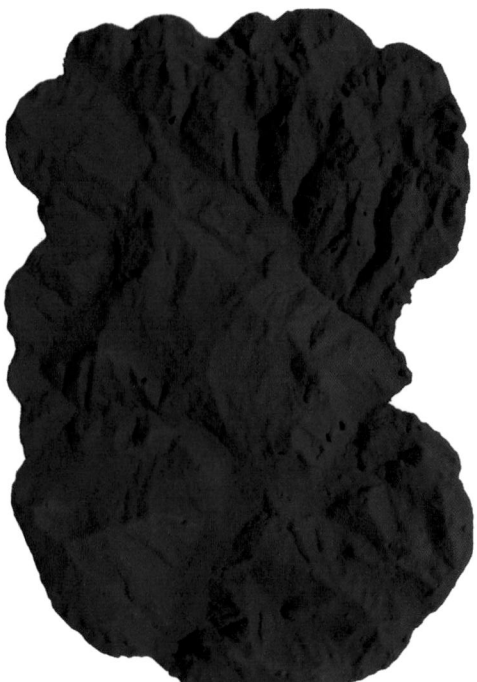

53. Untitled planetary relief, 1961

57. Untitled planetary relief, 1961

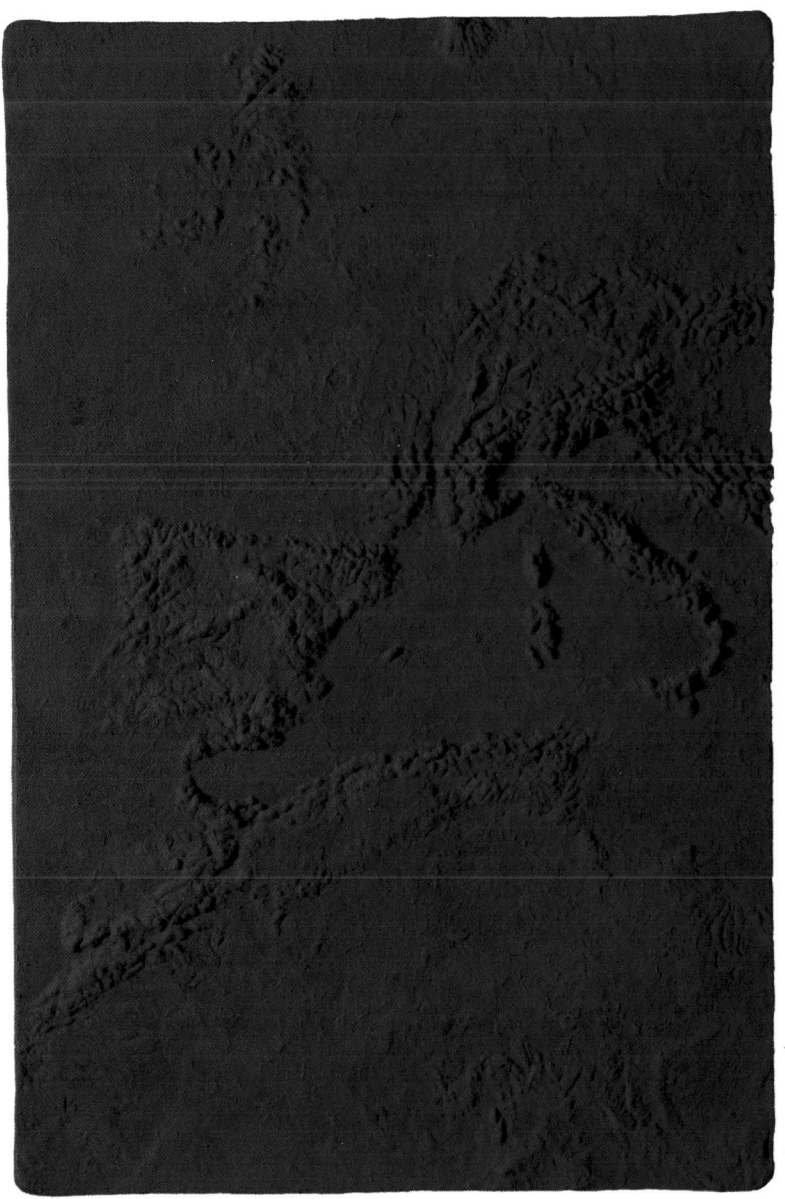

56. *Europe-Afrique (Europe-Africa)*, 1961

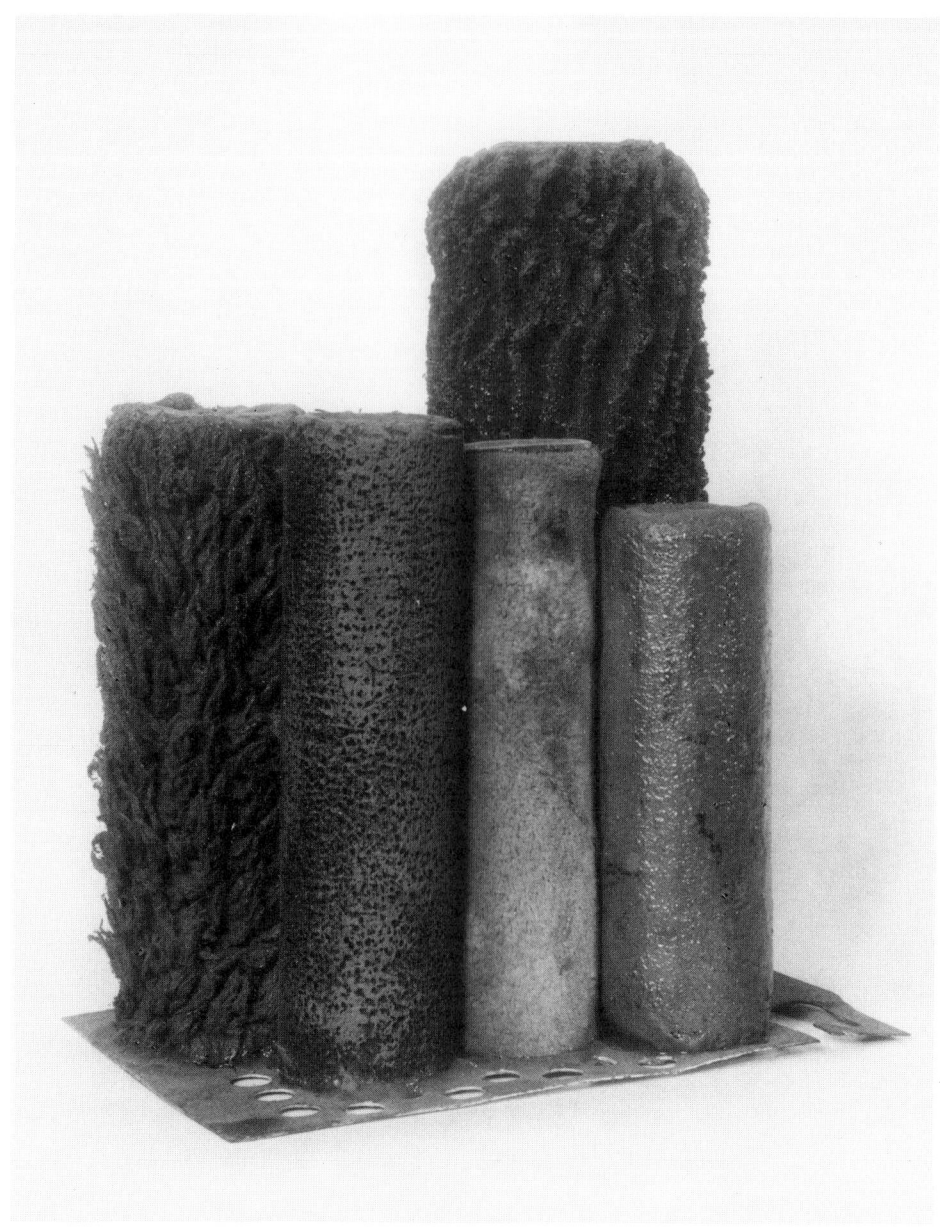

Untitled sculpture (S 7), 1956 (prototype), 1962 reconstruction shown; six rollers (blue, pink, orange, and white) on perforated metal plate; height 25.5 (10)

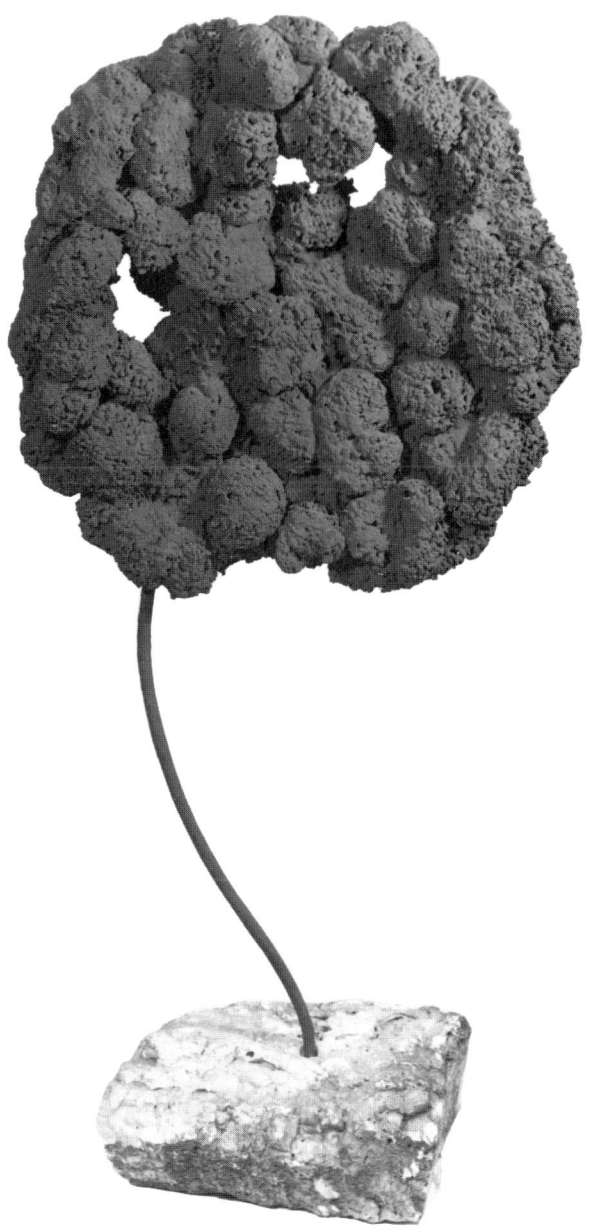

79.   Untitled blue sponge sculpture, [1959]

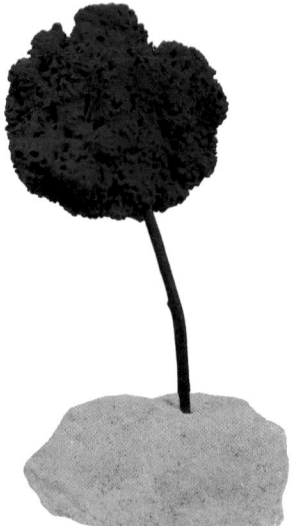

80.   Untitled blue sponge sculpture, 1959

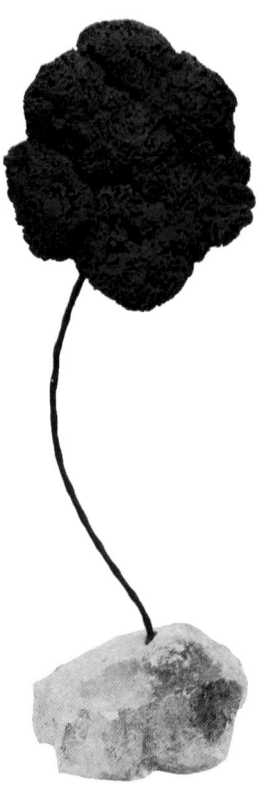

78.   Untitled blue sponge sculpture, [1959]

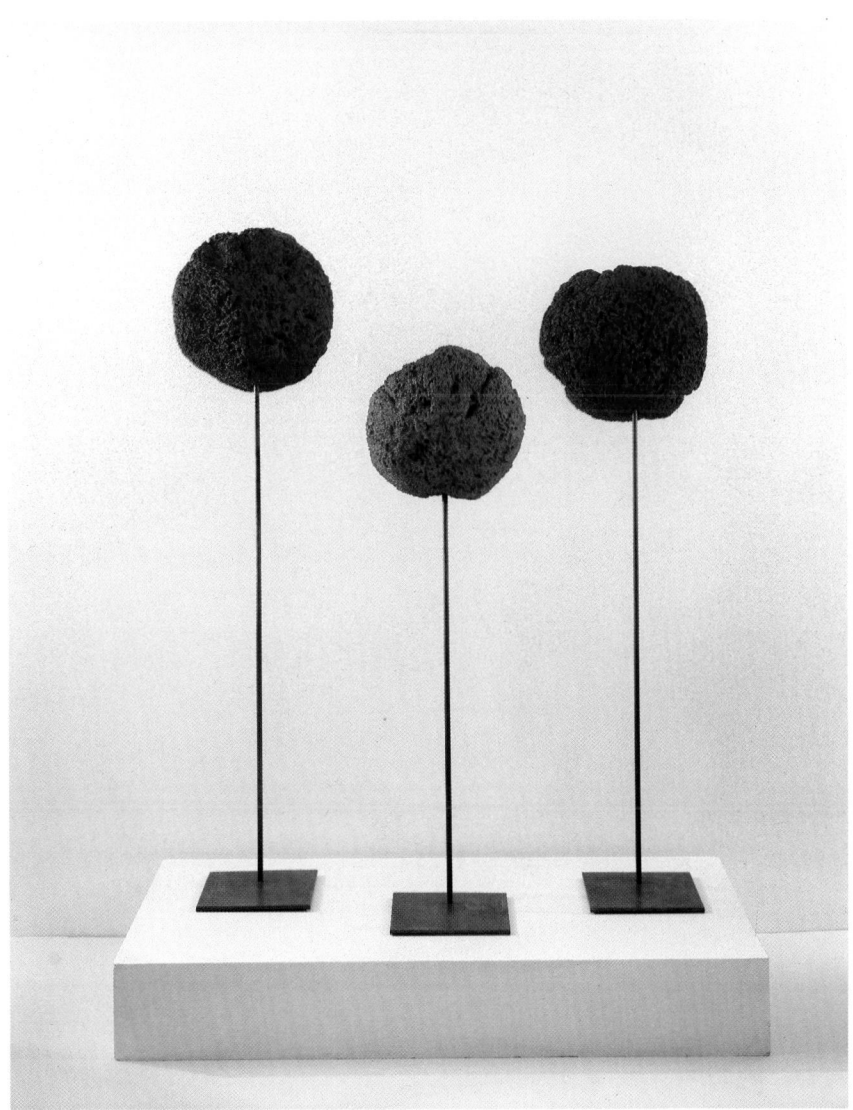

82. *Lecteur IKB (IKB Reader)*, 1960

83. *Lecteur IKB (Rose) (IKB Reader [Rose])*, 1960

81. *Lecteur IKB (IKB Reader)*, 1960

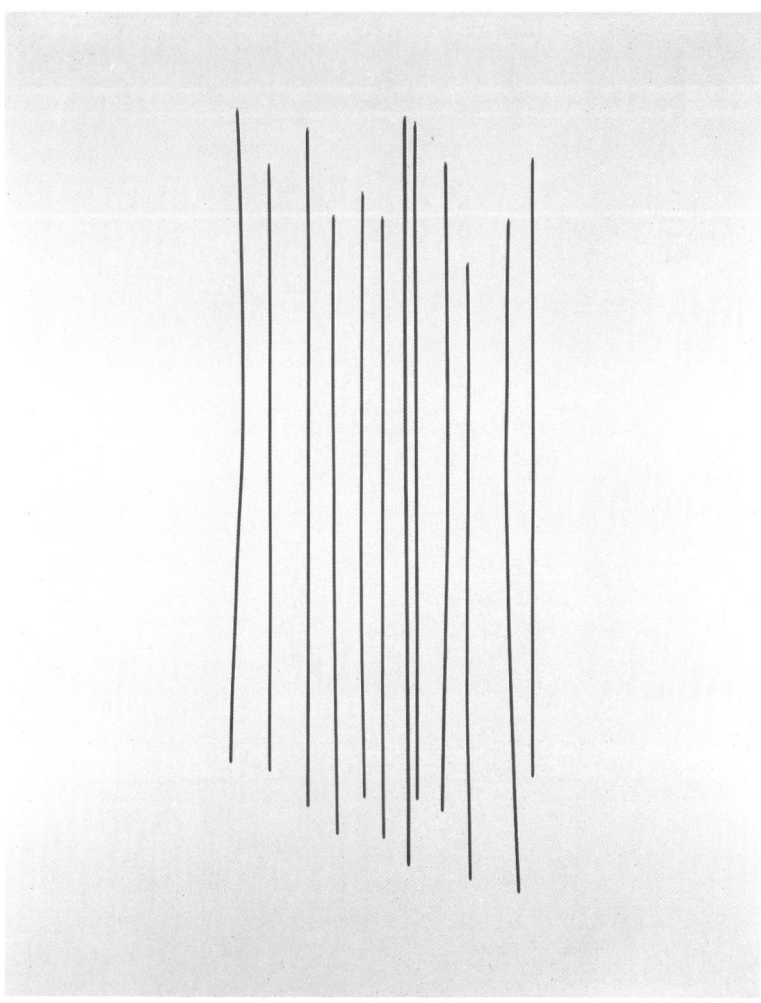

90. *Pluie bleue (Blue Rain)*, 1961

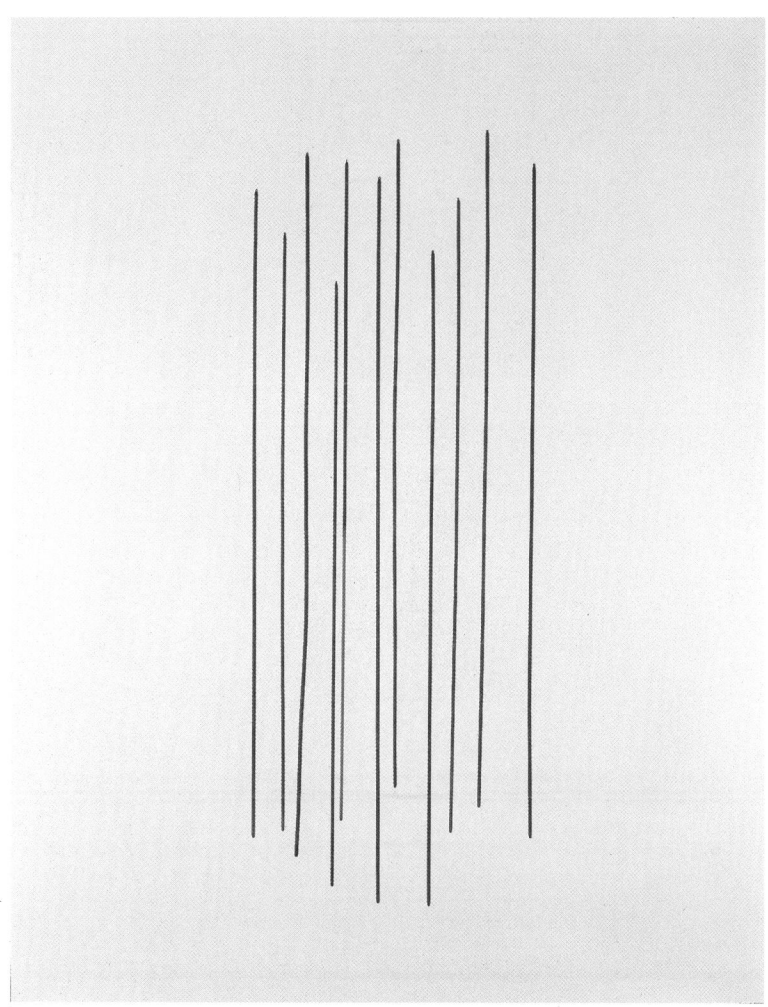

91. *Pluie rouge (Red Rain),* 1961

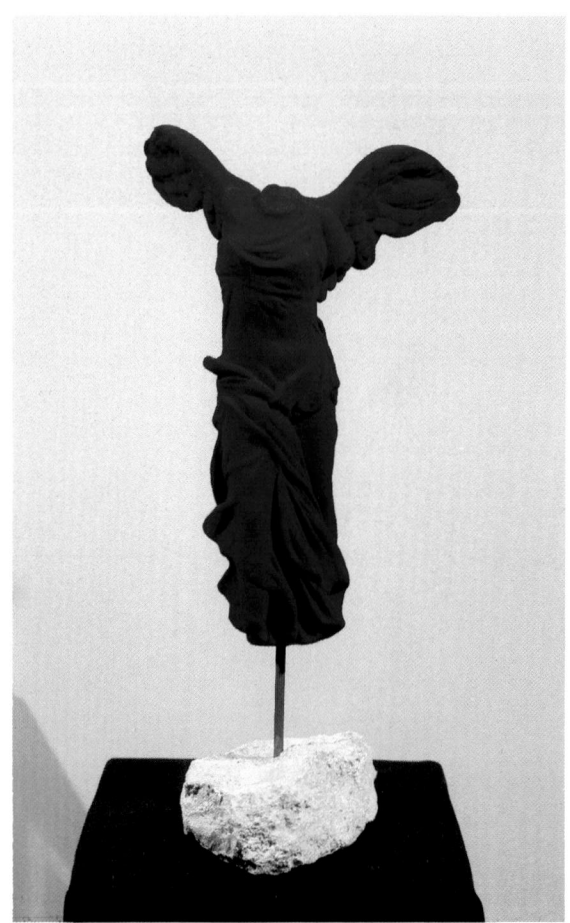

92. *Victoire de Samothrace (Victory of Samothrace)*, 1962
     (prototype), example of 1973 edition exhibited

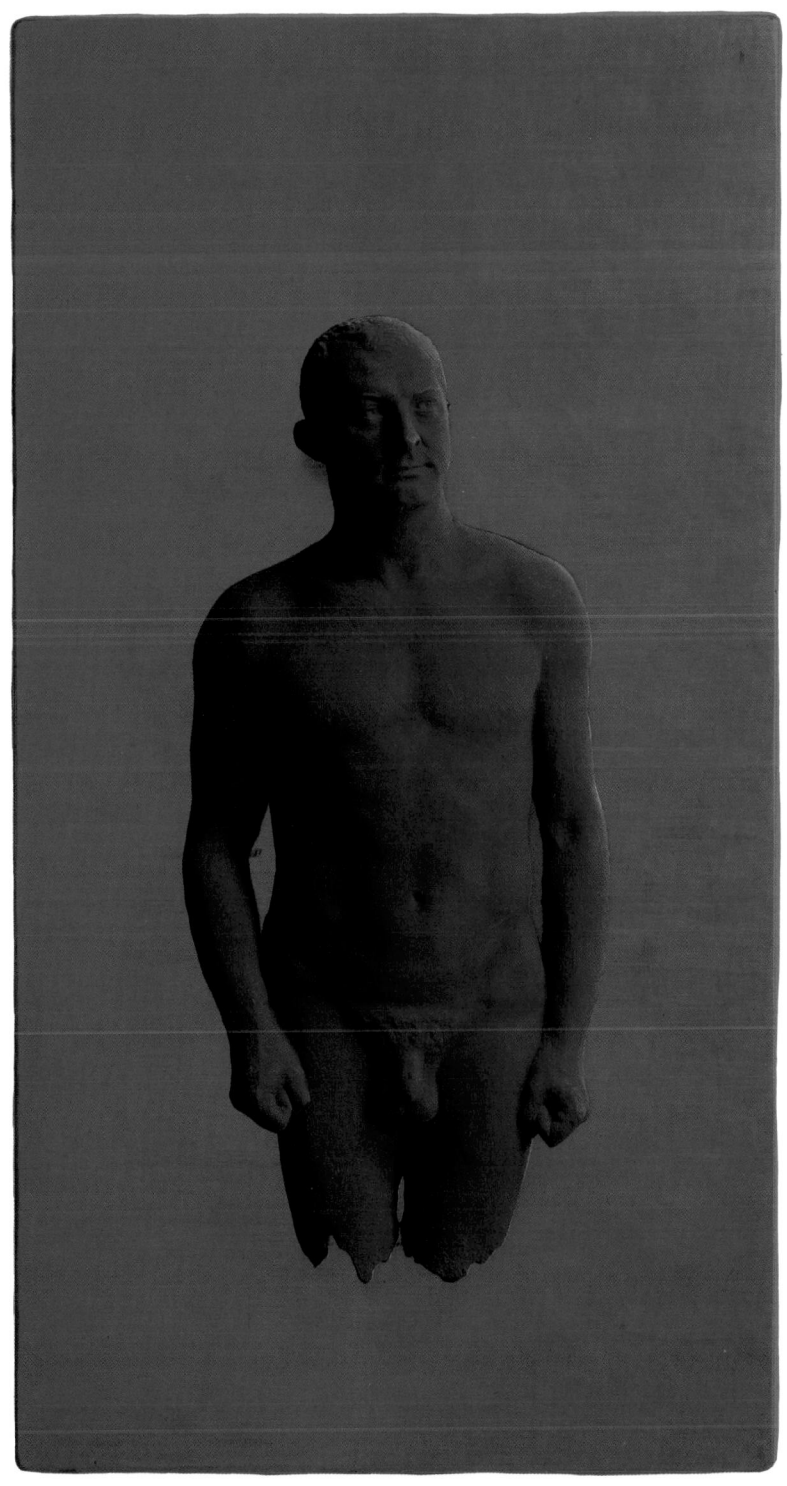

93. *Arman*, 1962 (prototype), example of undated edition exhibited

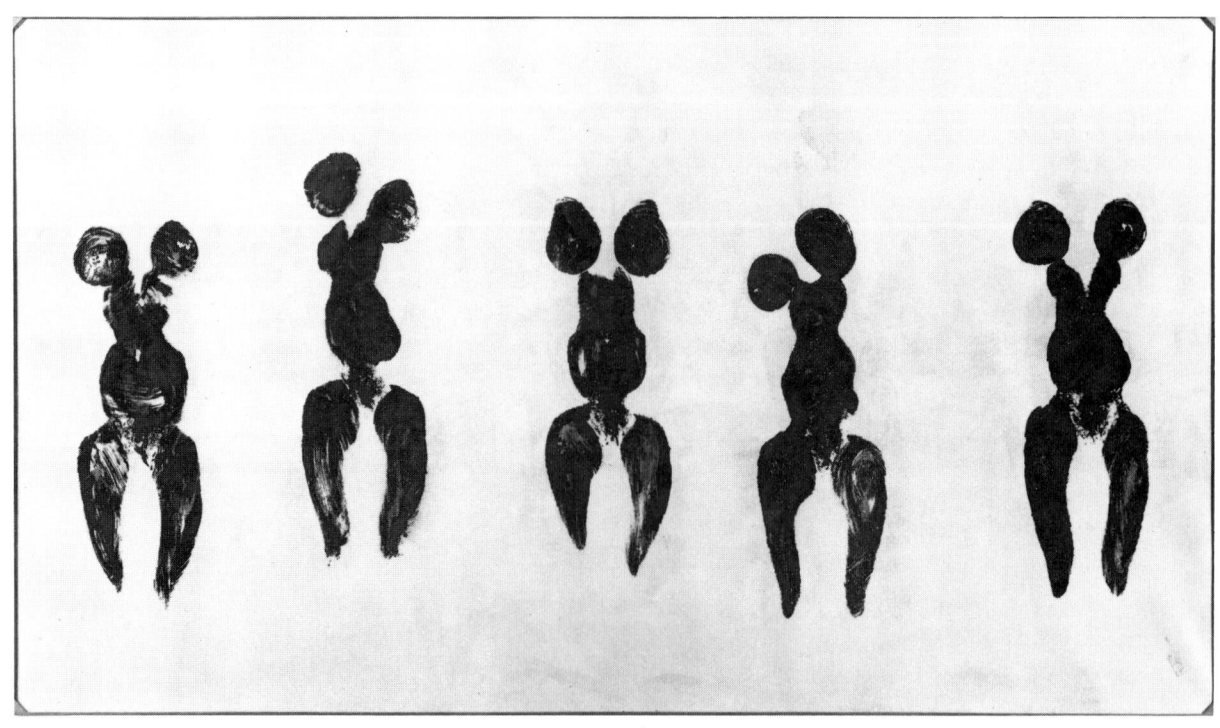

59. *Anthropométrie de l'époque bleue (Anthropometry of the Blue Period)*, 1960

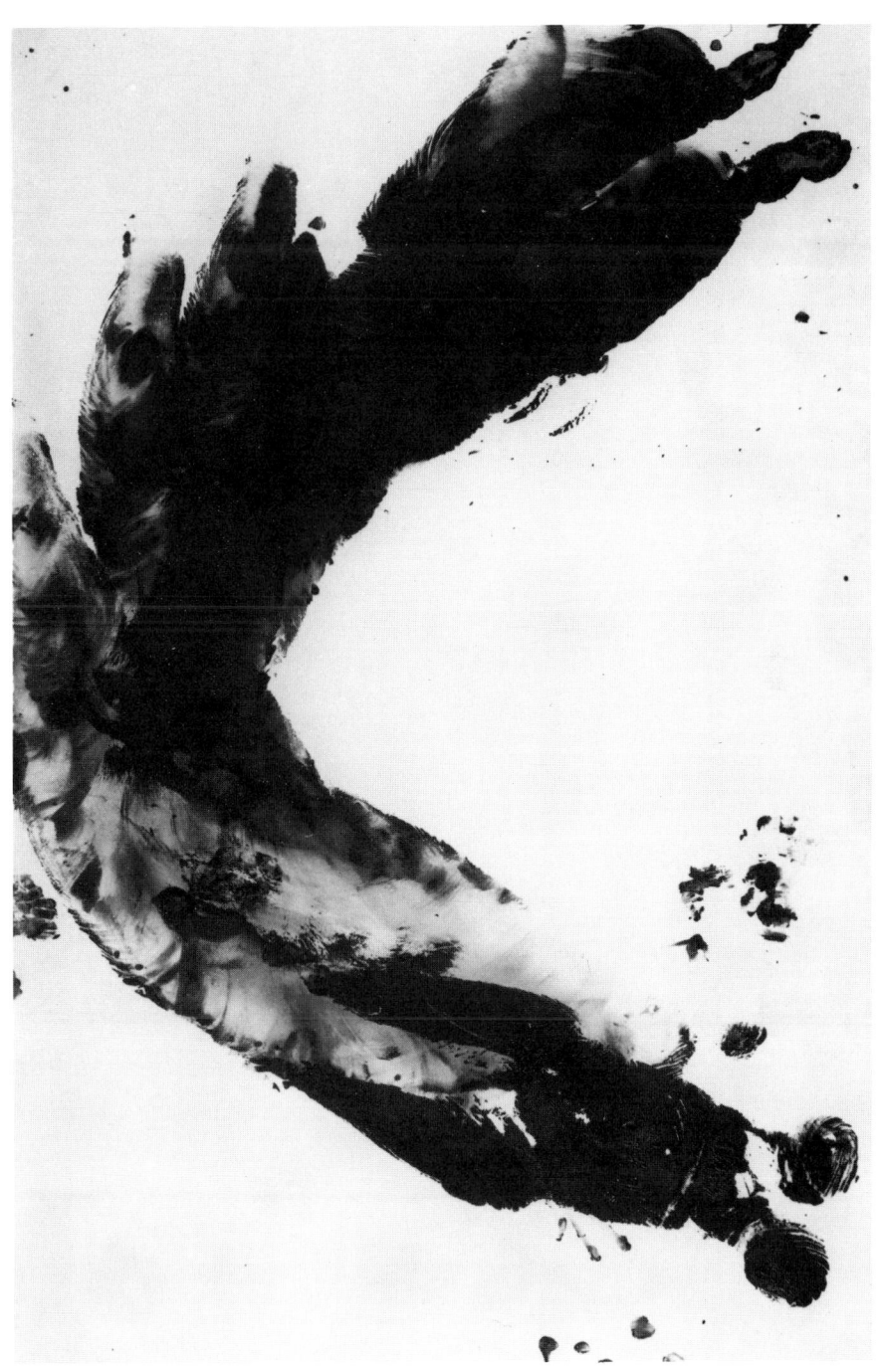

58. *Princesse Hélena,* 1960

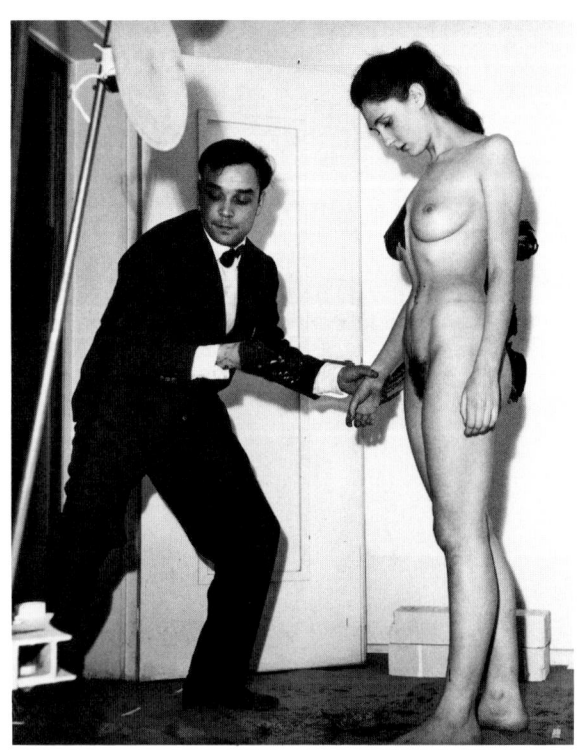

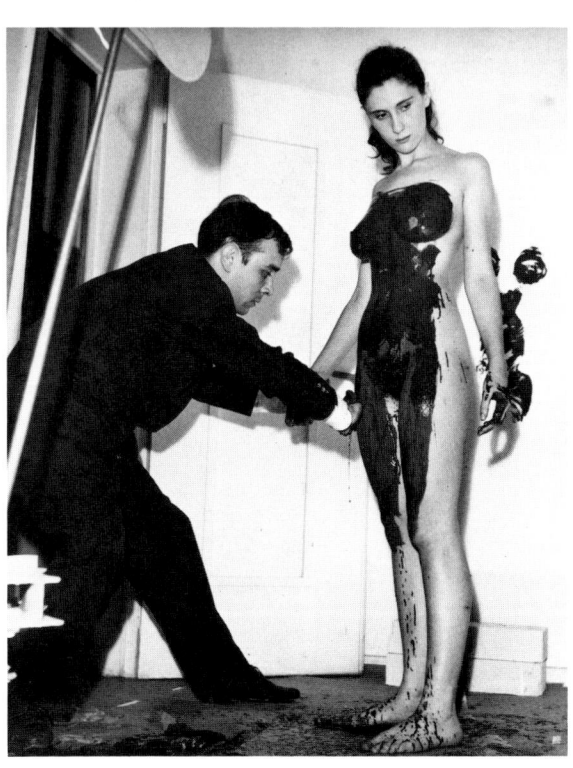

Klein making anthropometries with the model Michèle

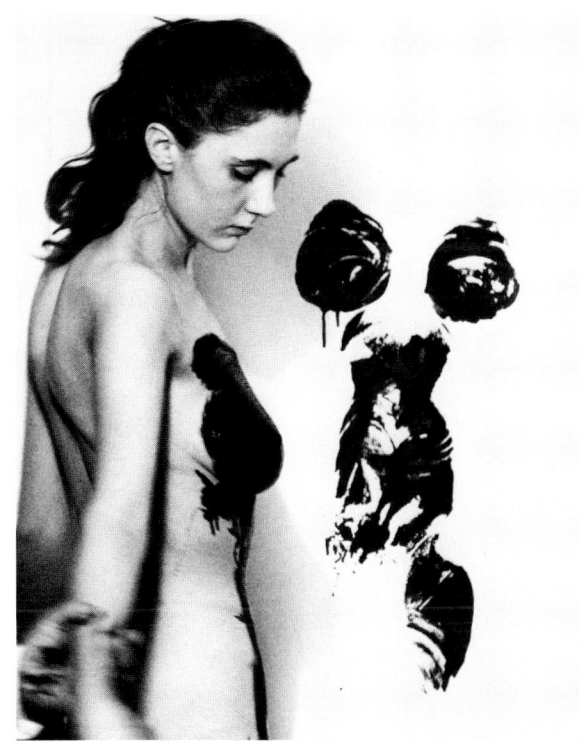

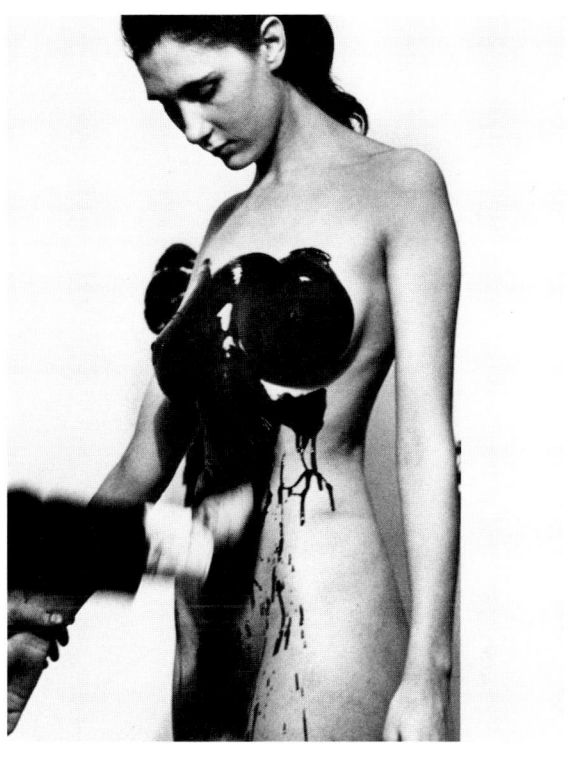

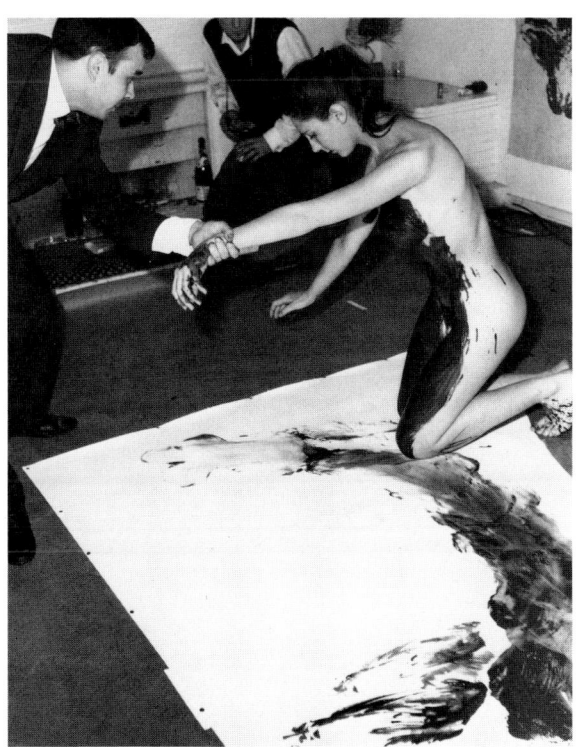

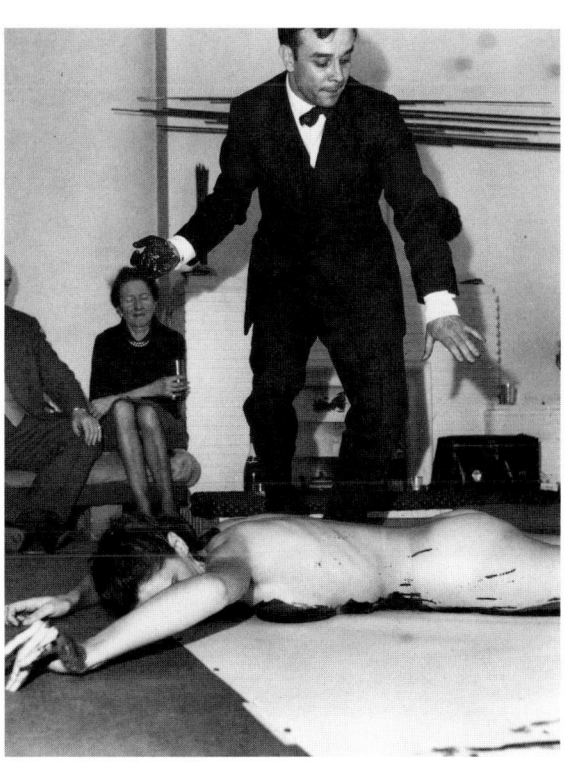

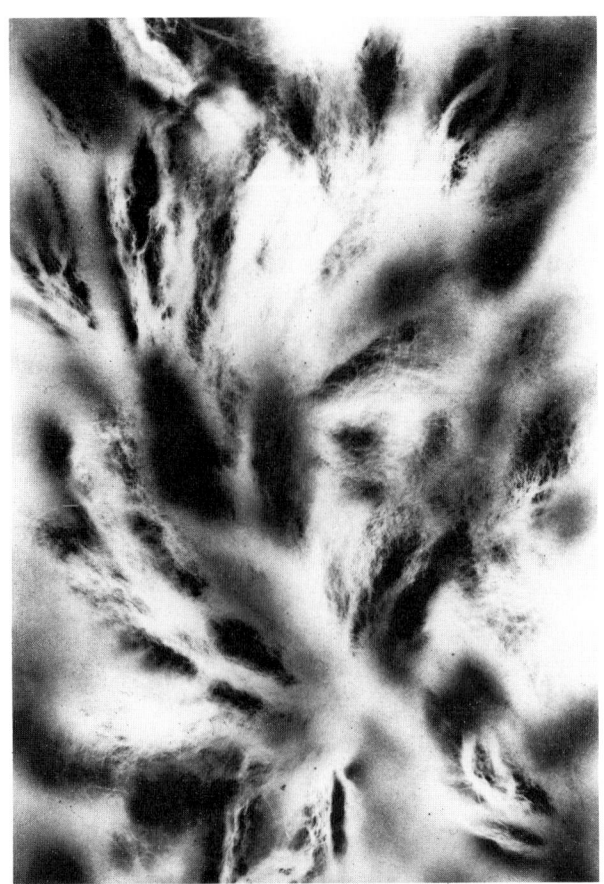

61. *Cheveux (Hair)*, [1961]

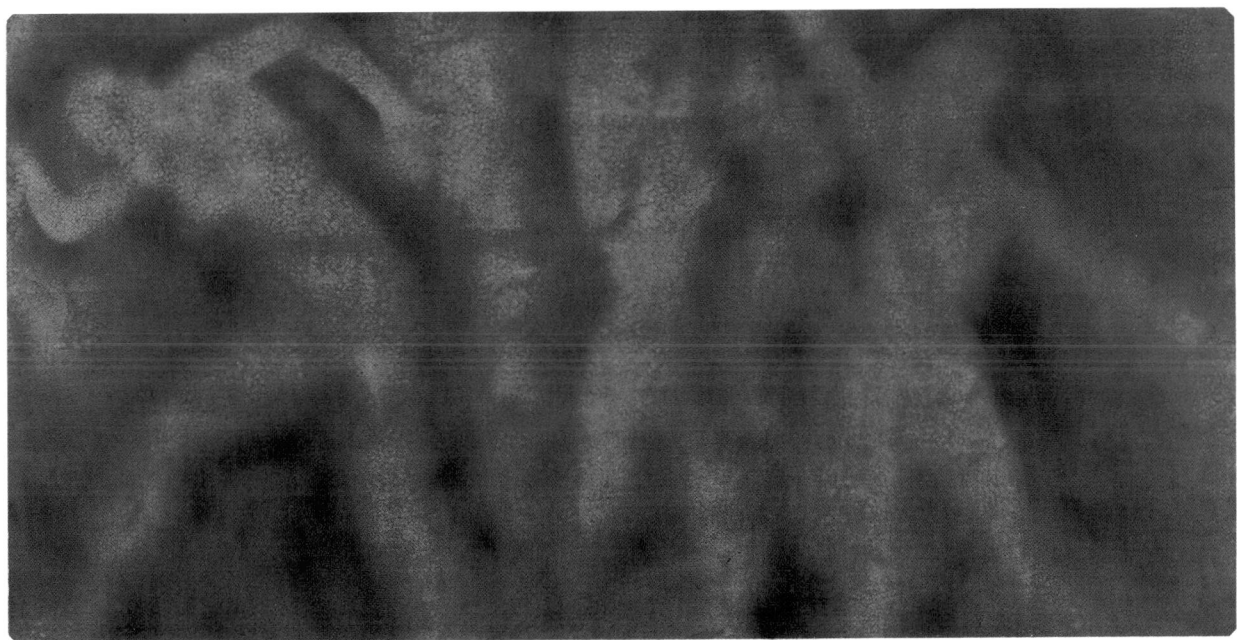

60. *Hiroshima*, c. 1961

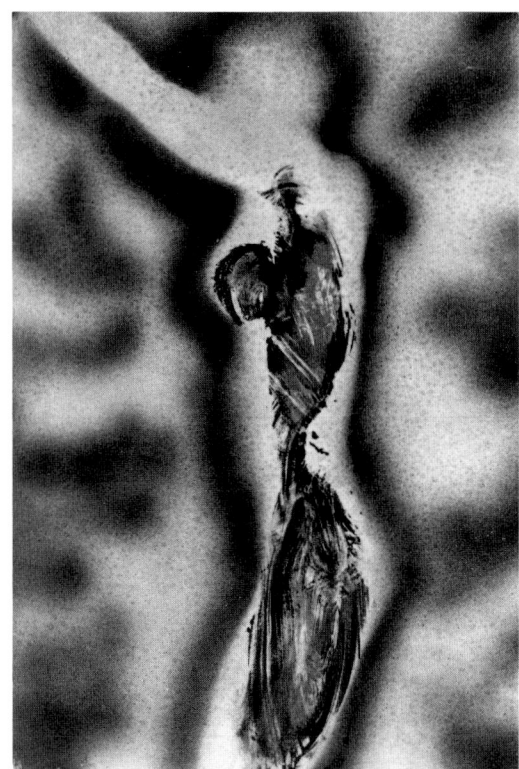

64.   Untitled anthropometry, [1962]

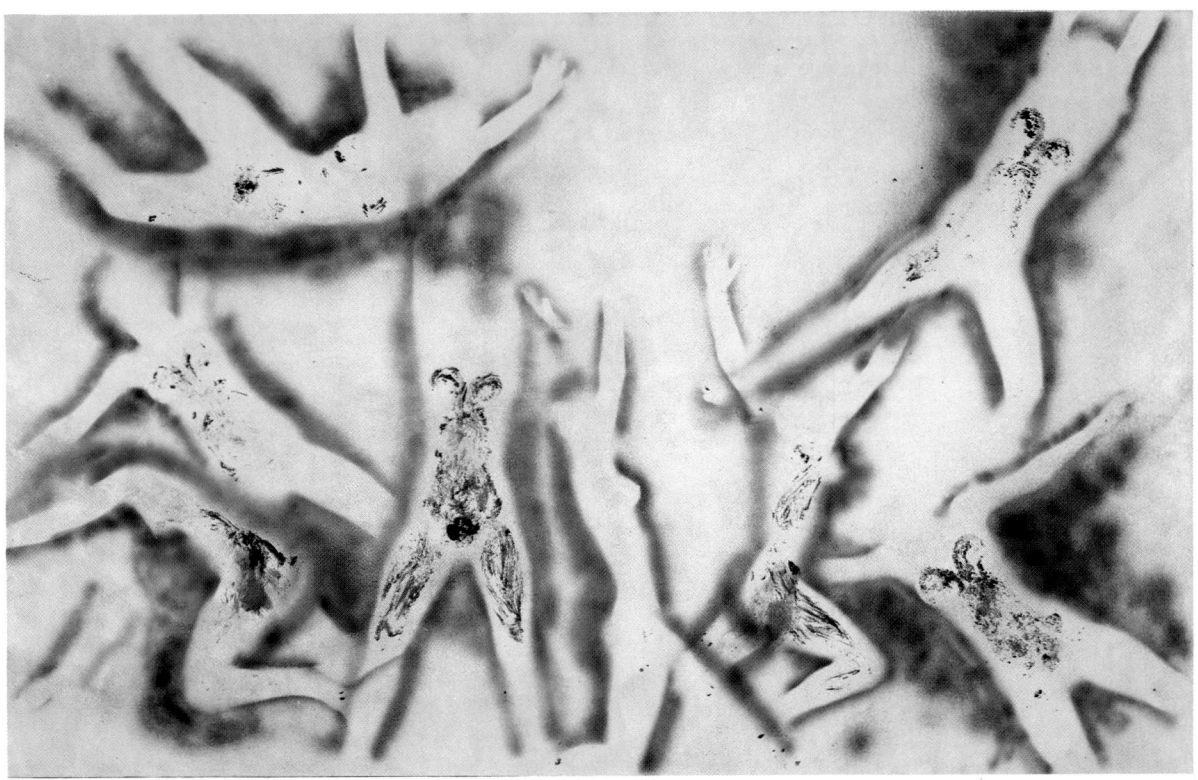

62. *People Begin to Fly,* [1961]

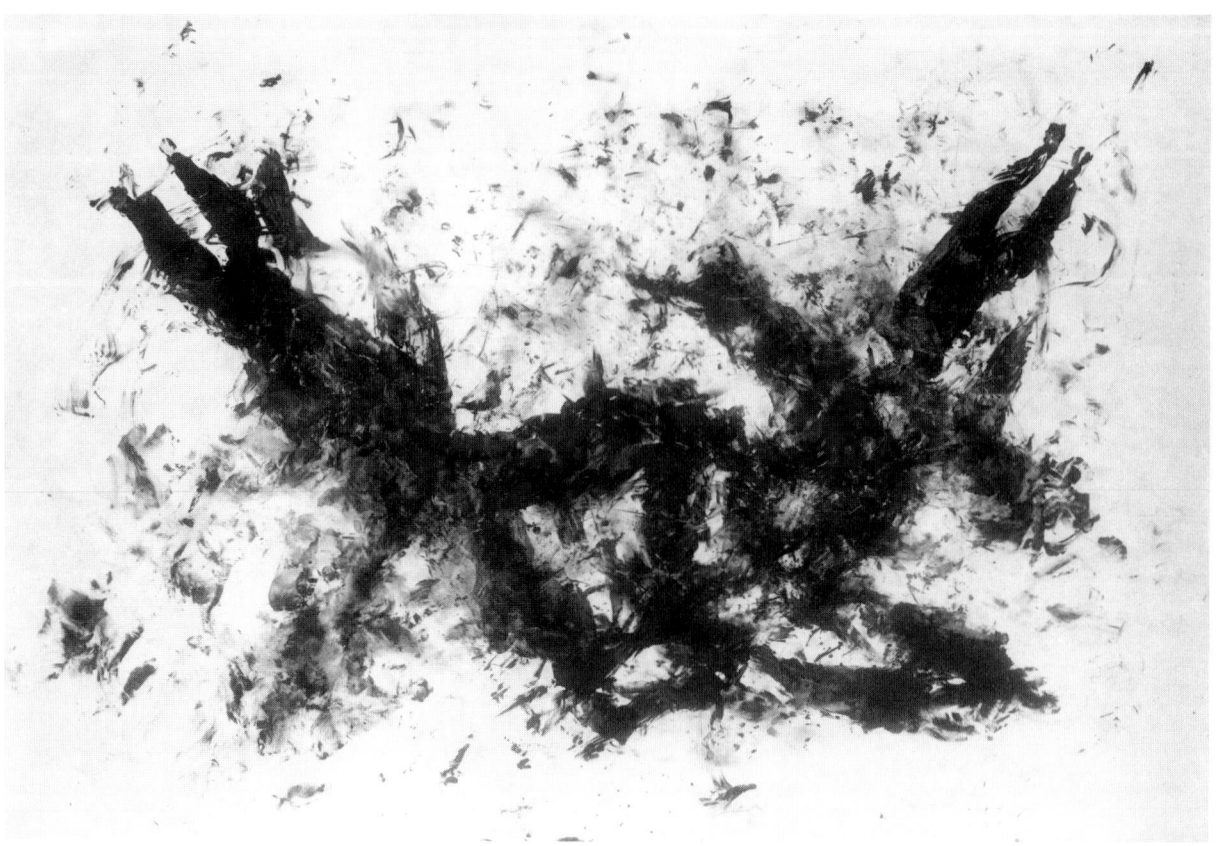

Untitled anthropometry (ANT 104), 1960; 278 × 410 (109½ × 161⅜); private collection

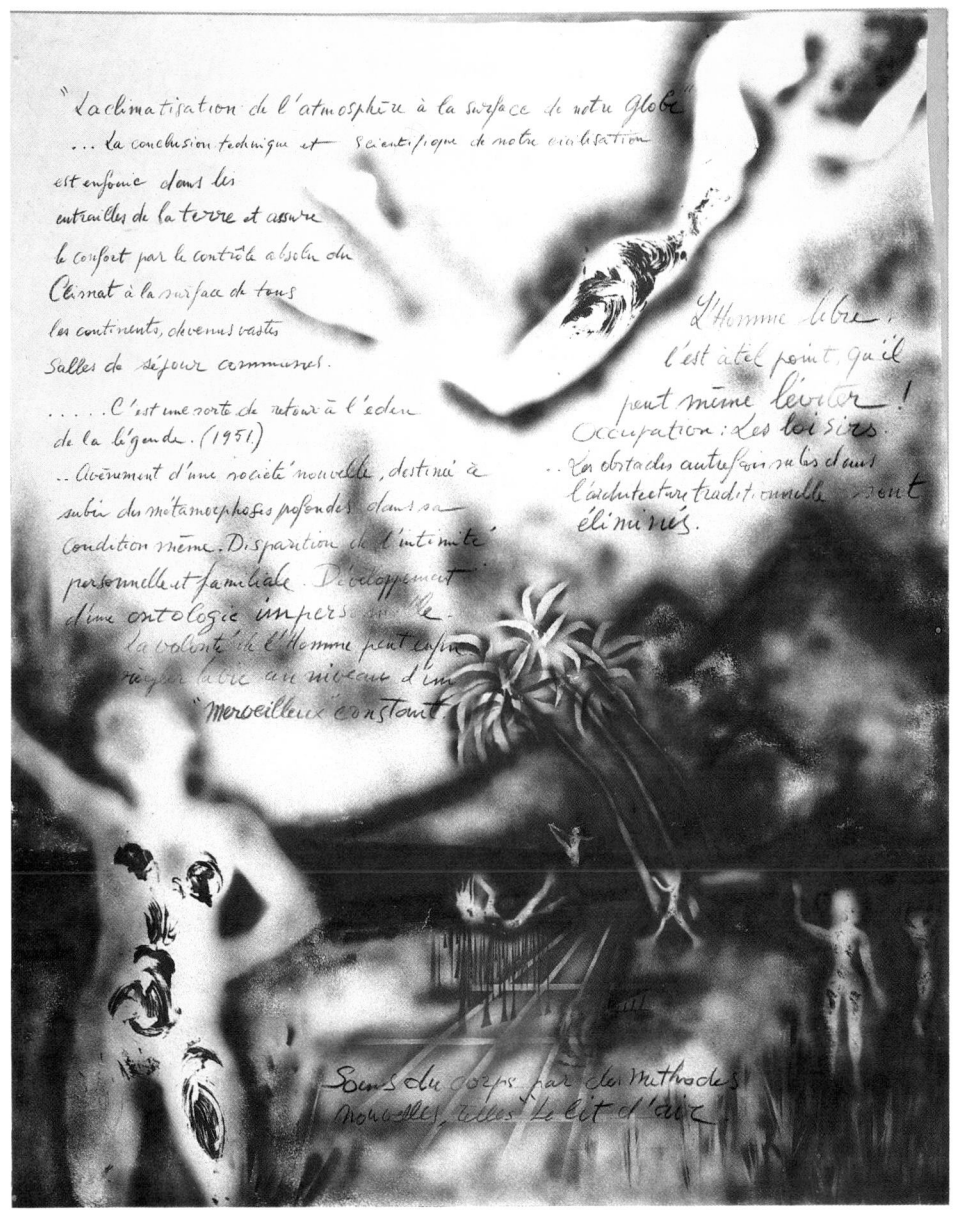

63. *Architecture de l'air (Architecture of the Air)*, [1961]

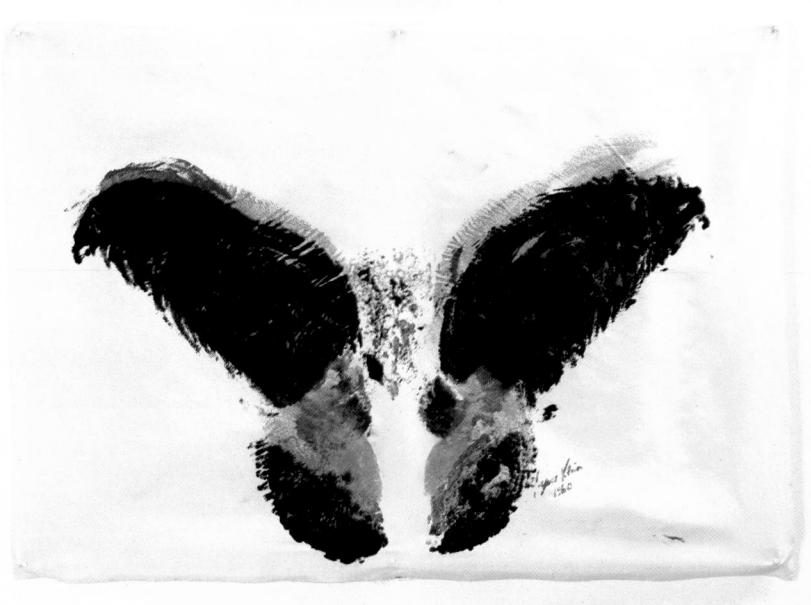

65.   Untitled shroud anthropometry, 1960

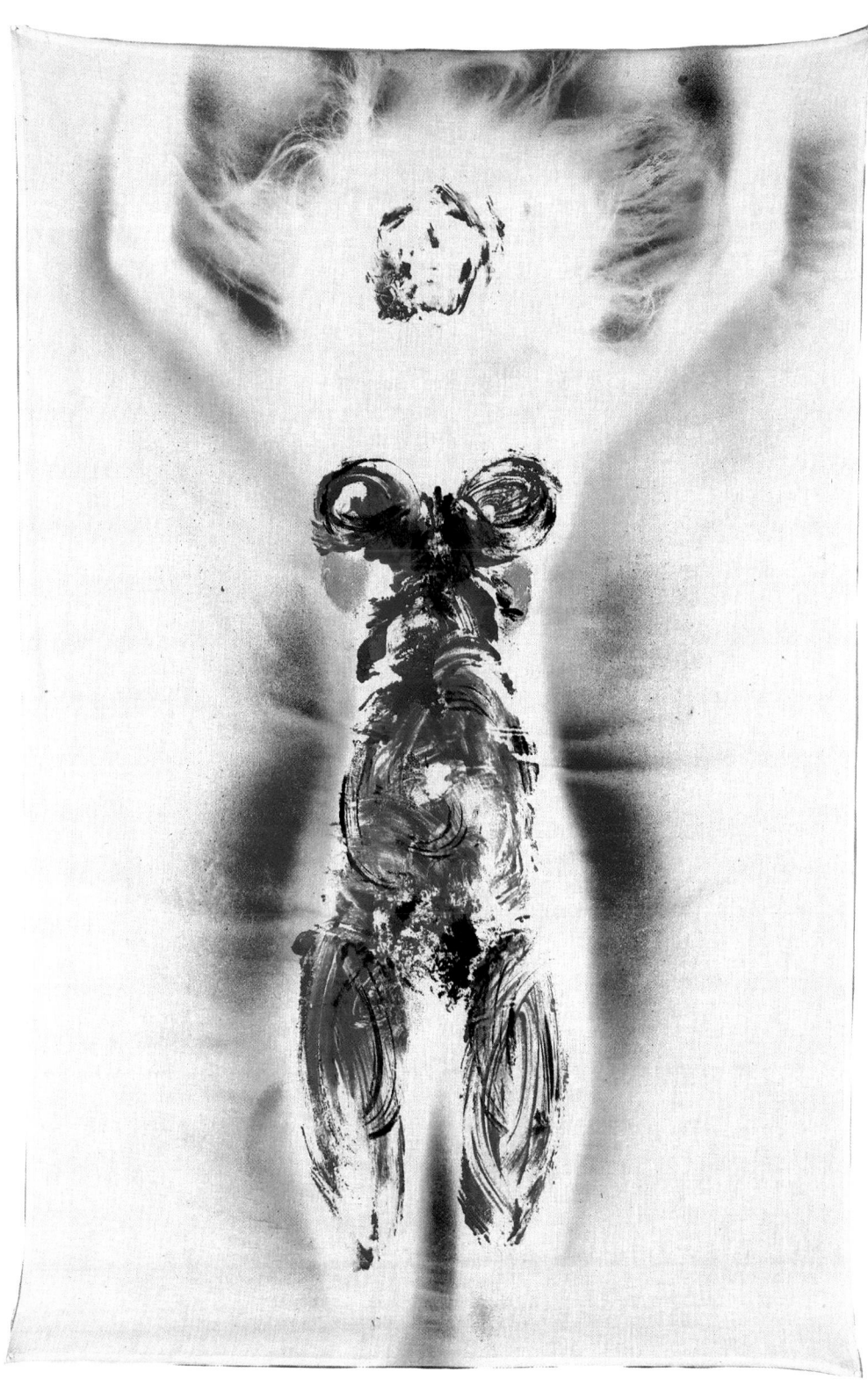

66. *Vampire*, c. 1960

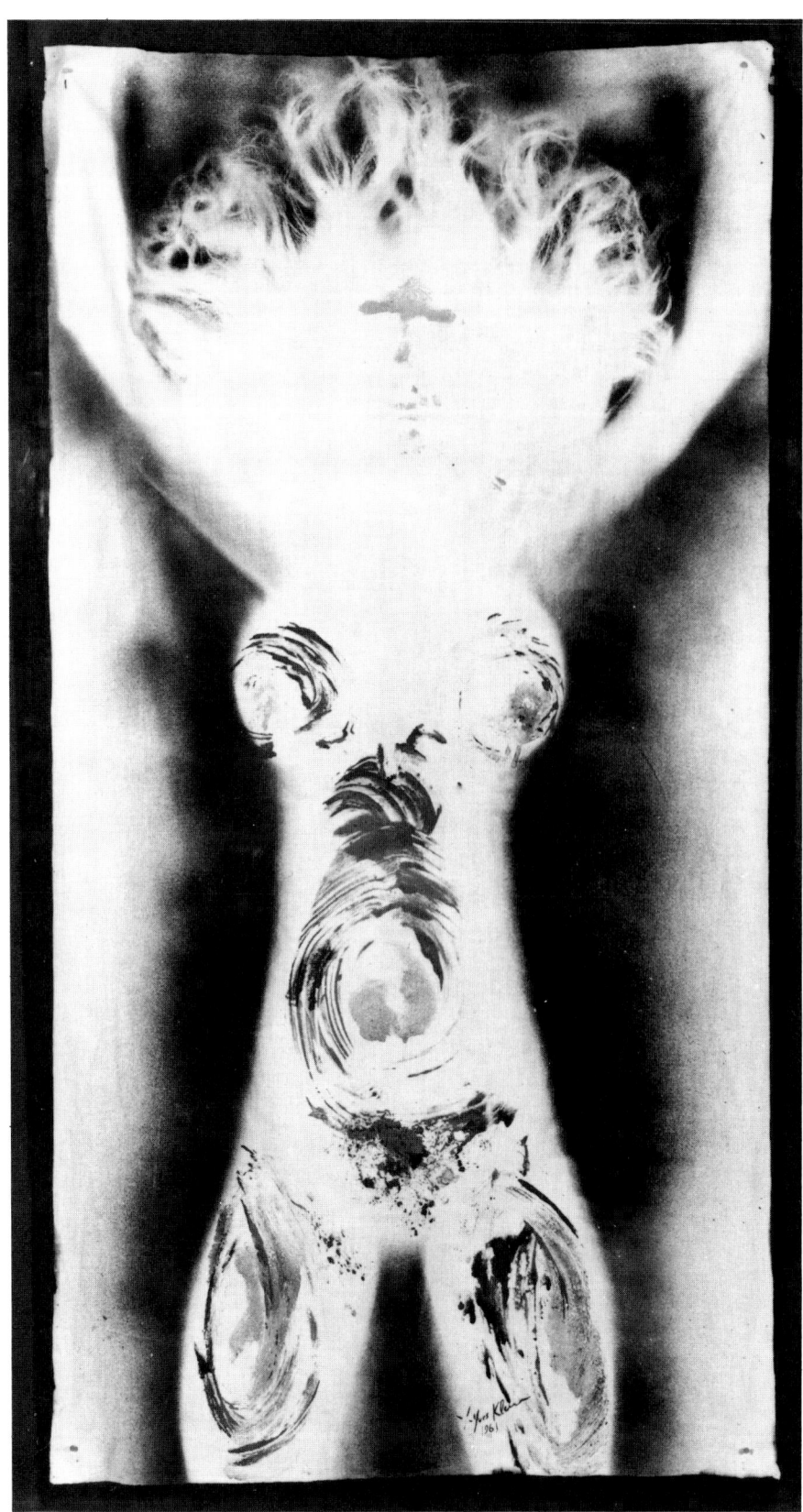

67. Untitled shroud anthropometry, 1961

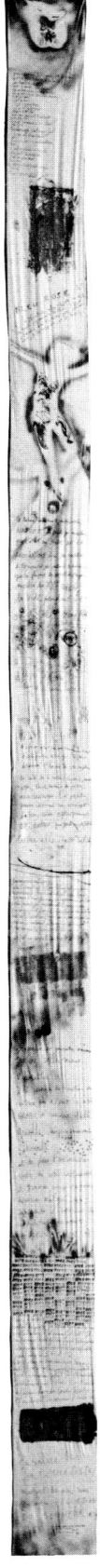

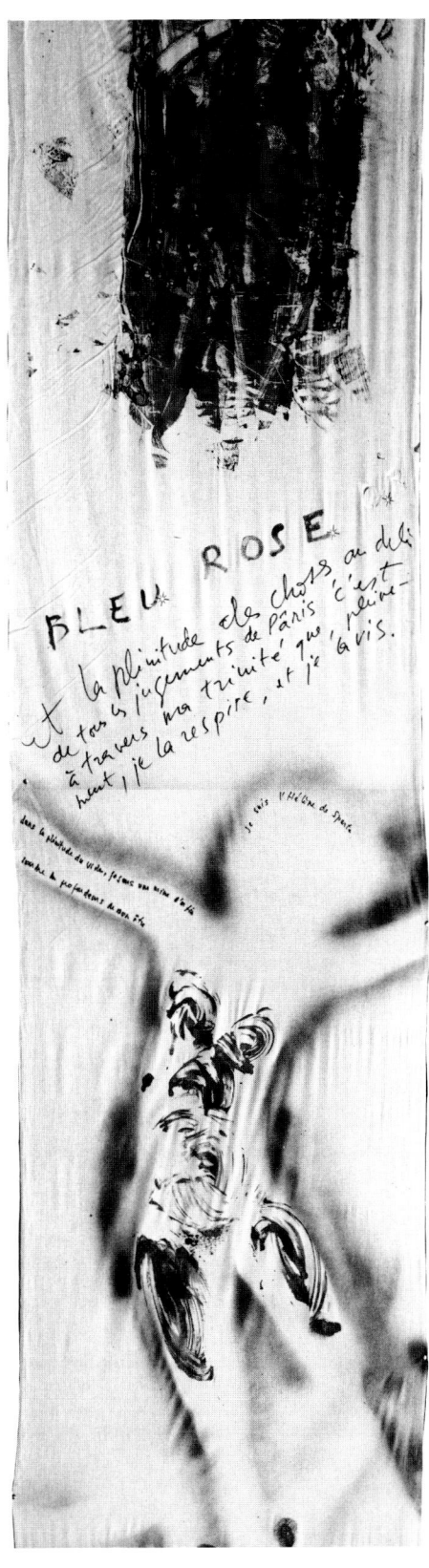

Store Poème (Scroll Poem) (ANT SU 15), March 1, 1962; by Yves Klein, Arman, Claude Pascal, and Pierre Restany; 1480 × 78 (582½ × 30¾); private collection; (detail at right)

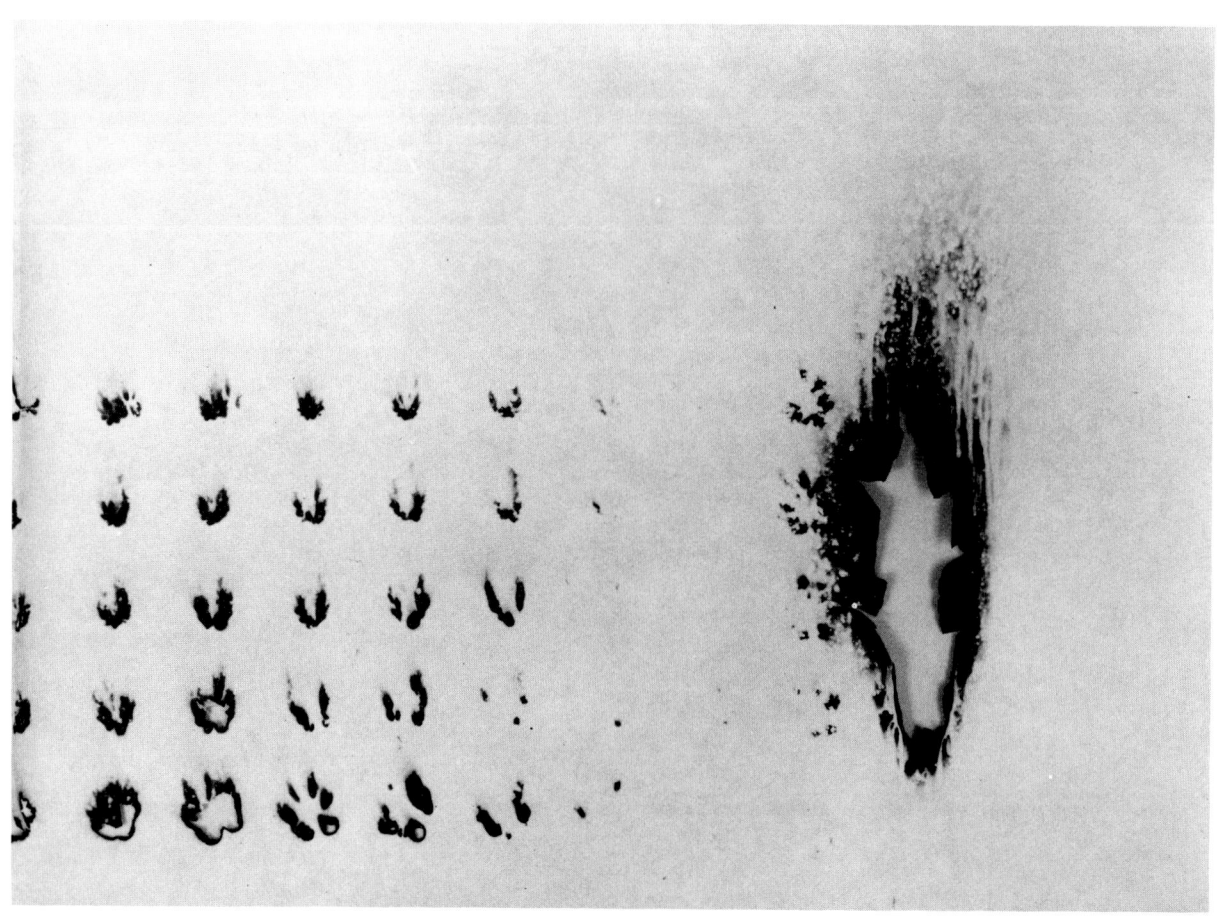

71.   Untitled fire painting, 1961

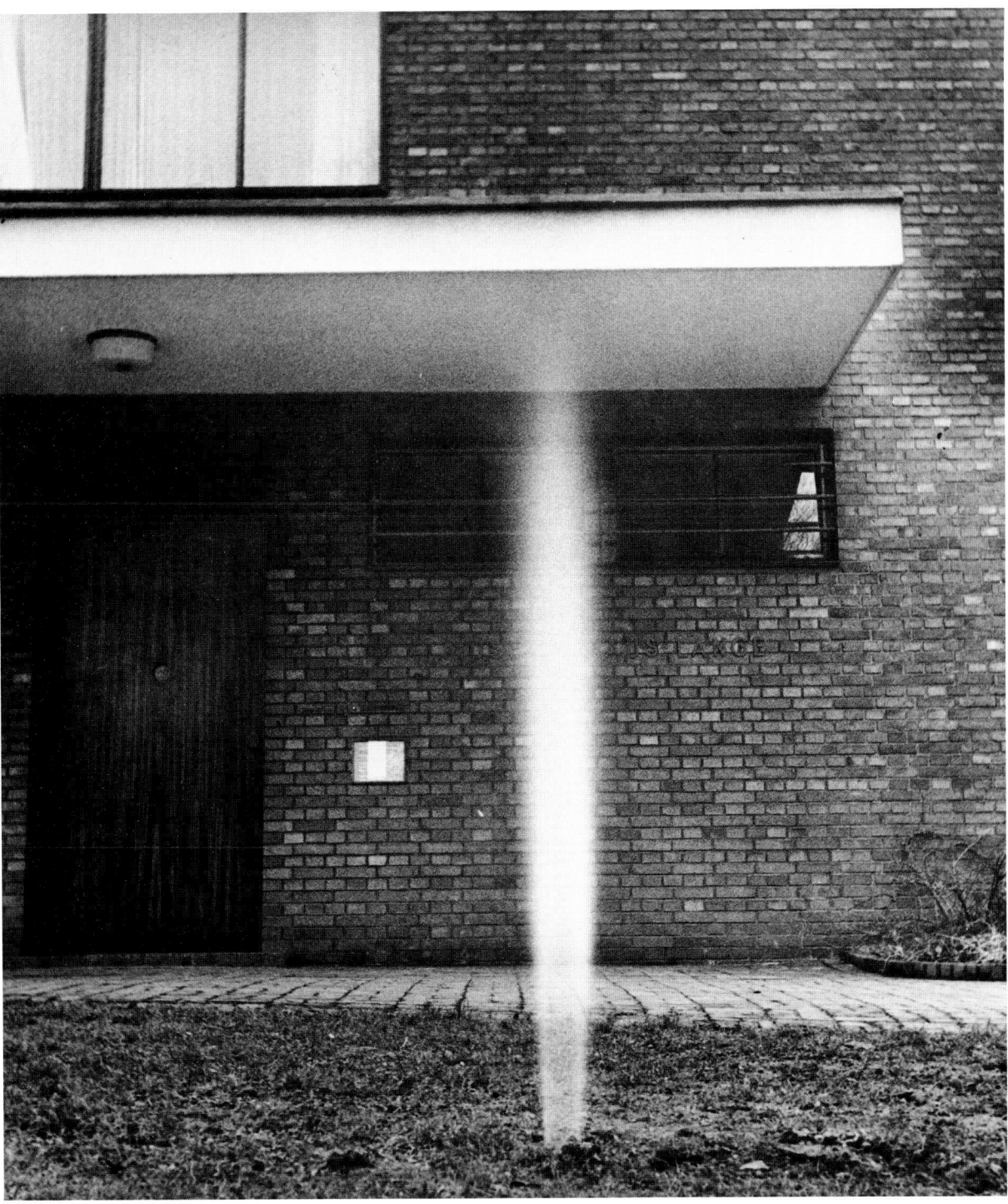

Klein's *Fire Fountain* at Krefeld, Germany, 1961

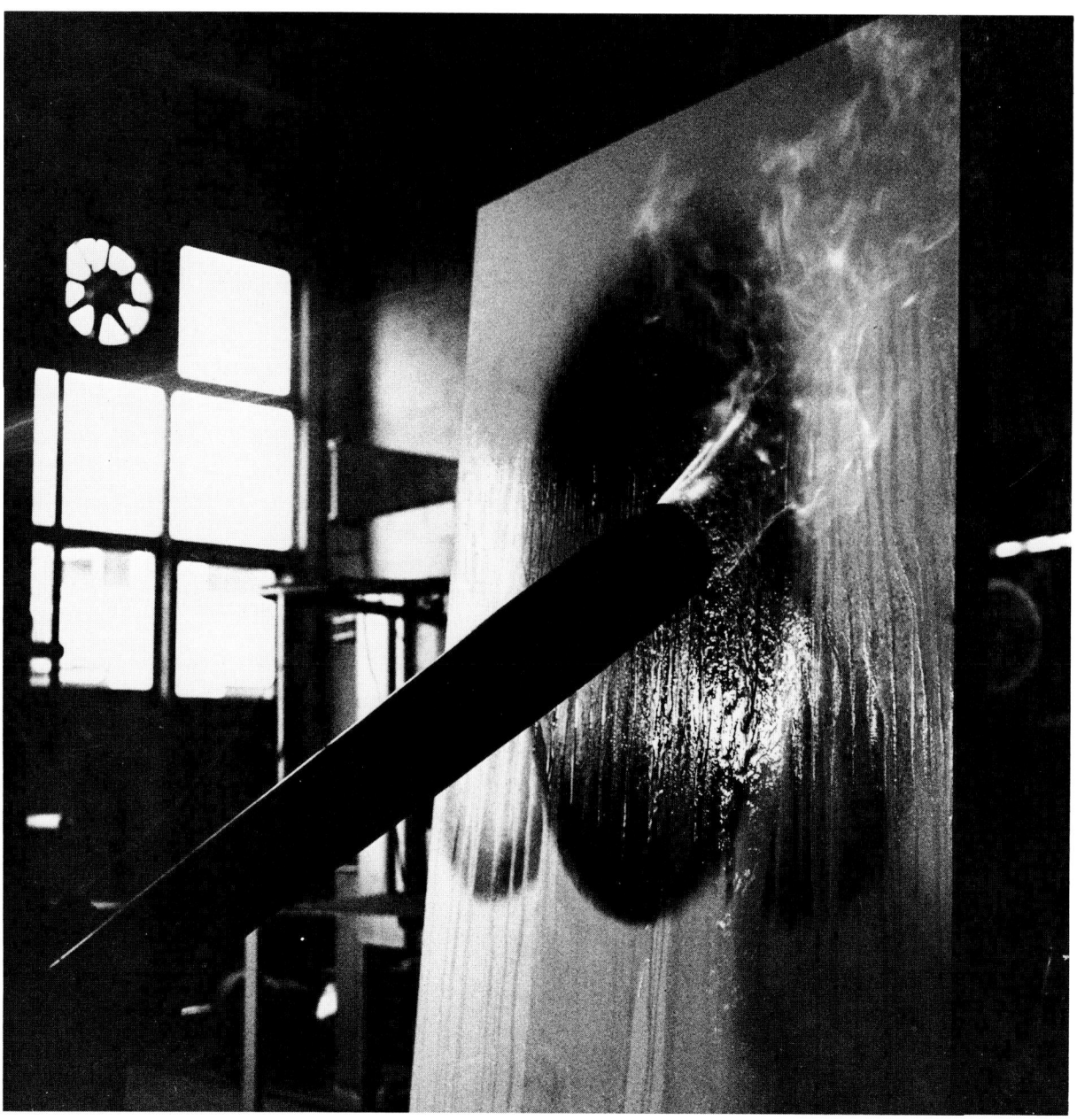

Klein making cat. no. 68

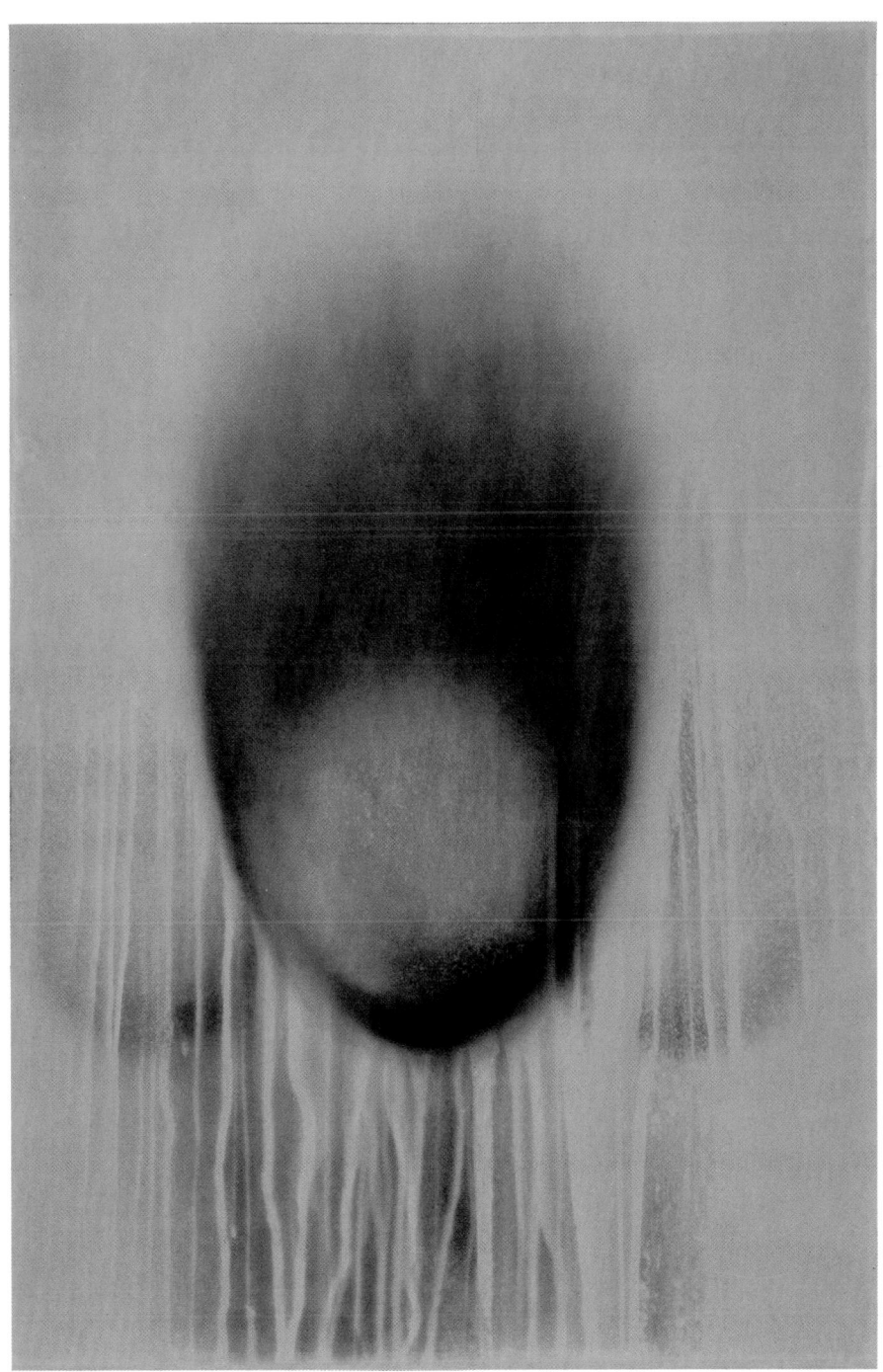

68.   Untitled fire painting, 1961

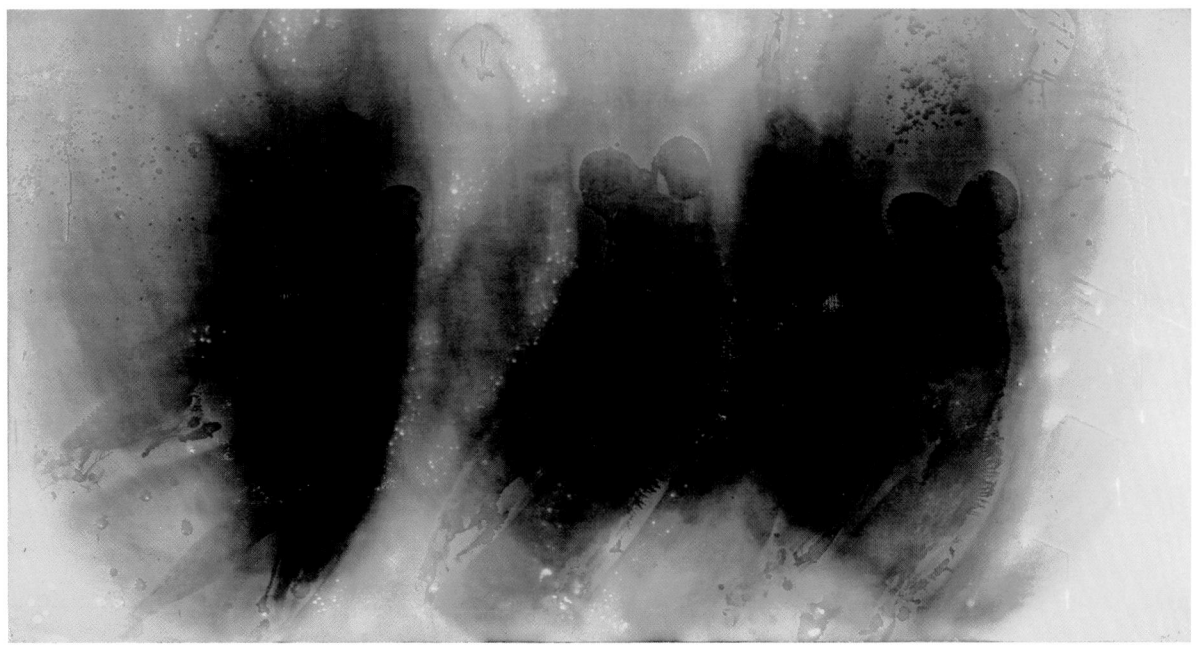

73.   Untitled fire painting, c. 1961

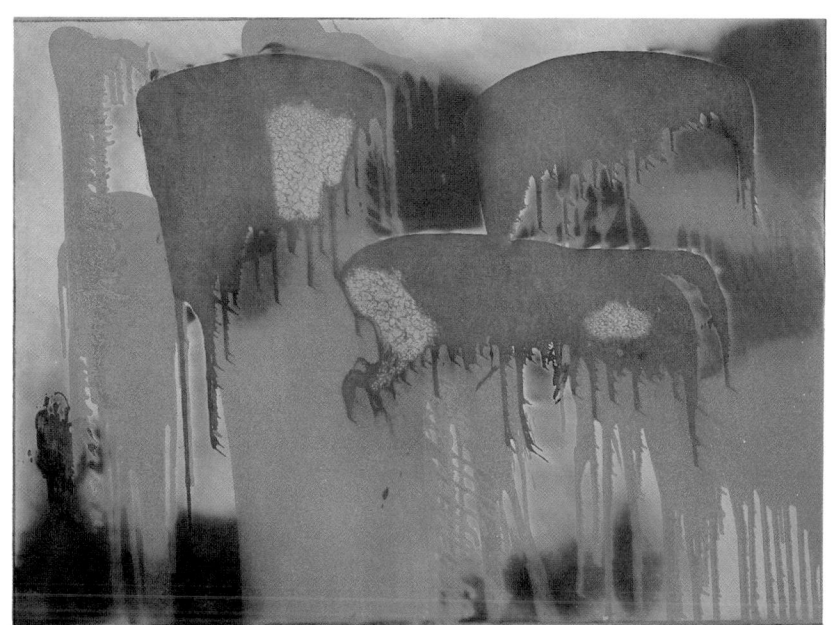

76. Untitled fire-color painting, c. 1962

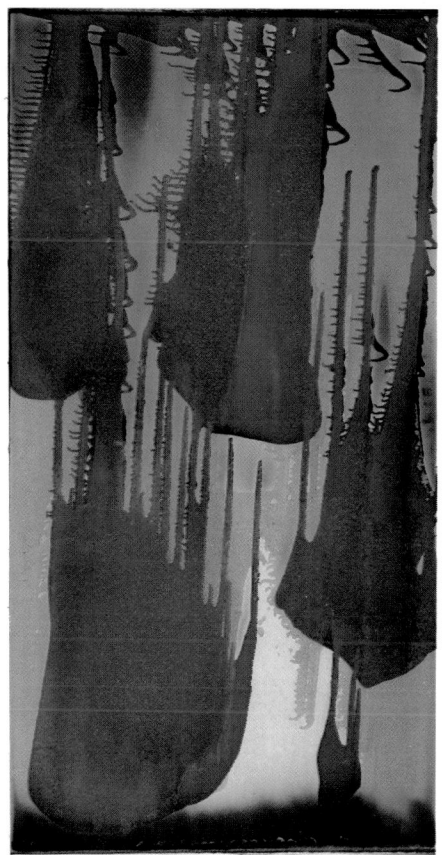

75. Untitled fire-color painting, c. 1962

YVES KLEIN PRÉSENTE :
LE DIMANCHE 27 NOVEMBRE
1960

NUMÉRO
UNIQUE

FESTIVAL D'ART
D'AVANT-GARDE
NOVEMBRE - DÉCEMBRE 1960

La Révolution
bleue
continue

SEANCE DE 0 HEURE A 24 HEURES

Dimanche
27 NOVEMBRE

Le journal
d'un
seul jour

0,35 NF (35 fr.)   Algérie : 0,30 NF (30 fr.) · Tunisie : 27 mill.
Maroc : 32 f m. · Italie : 50 lires · Espagne : 2 pes. 5

THEATRE DU VIDE

● SUITE EN PAGE 2

L'ESPACE, LUI-MÊME.

ACTUALITÉ

Yves KLEIN

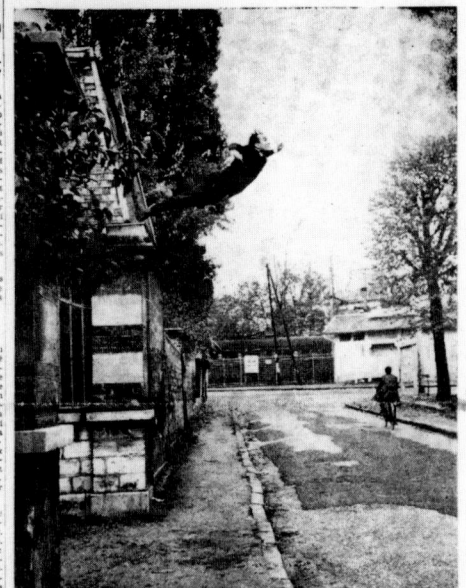

UN HOMME DANS L'ESPACE !

(Photo Shunk-Kender)

Le peintre de l'espace se jette dans le vide !

Yves

Sensibilité pure

● SUITE EN PAGE 2

105. *Dimanche, le journal d'un seul jour (Sunday, the Newspaper of a Single Day)*; November 27, 1960; page 1

Sensibilité pure (suite)

Quand tout est prêt, l'obscurité se fait dans la salle. Le rideau se lève lentement avec l'éclosion d'un pétillement continu, semblable à celui que fait l'eau gazeuse fraîchement débouchée, mais prodigieusement mineure. C'est une inondation sonore, monotone, s'imprégnant d'une manière volumétrique dans l'espace, perceptible par l'oreille sensible de chaque spectateur.

Sur la scène : une salle vide blanche, très blanche ; tous les anciens sont arrondis... Tout est vide, absolument vide avec le pétillement : dans je ne sais quelle sorte d'ouverture-boursiers isolonnés il faudrait couper l'acoustique.

Dans la salle de très belles filles nues où, à la rigueur, on y kini, sorte d'ouvreuses-hôtesses,

passent dans les rangs des spectateurs et leur distribuent ajustent leurs chaînes et leurs bâillons, leur disant l'heure et combien de temps je dois encore à supporter le spectacle (de très violence), ou bien encore mot uz en bikini, s'occupent des spectatrices).

La première demi-heure passée, le pétillement s'éteint peu à peu, se dissout complètement à quer autre disparues et se passe dans le silence absolu pour les spectateurs toujours face à la scène vide, blanche et brillamment éclairée.

Le rideau se baisse. La lumière revient dans la salle. Les groupes d'enchaîneurs reviennent délivrer de leurs chaînes et de leurs bâillons les spectateurs.

Capture du vide

Une ville entière, votre même une capitale, ou, encore mieux, un pays entier doit servir de scène et de décor.

L'État, lui-même, annonce la date de la représentation dans tout le territoire. Le jour dit, à l'heure dite, exactement, tout le monde rentre chez soi, s'enferme à double tour, et l'extérieur est vide de tout être humain pendant deux heures.

Dans les rues plus personne, plus personne du tout dans les bureaux administratifs et autres lieux publics ; plus personne dans les campagnes, tout est fermé tout le monde est chez soi et ne bouge plus.

Le territoire doit sembler aux yeux de l'Espace, pour deux heures, entièrement vide de sujets vivants !

Mais alors des compagnons-idées seront là autour de moi, chez moi, et me jetteront dehors, maigre moi, car j'aurai peur et il sera nécessaire que je sois là totalement expulsé dehors, dans le vide des rues et des campagnes, tout seul, face à la nature et à tout. À vrai dire, cela ne sera qu'un peu fait dans le chemin de la « capture du vide » réelle, où le vrai après ma disparition définitive, lors de l'une de ces relations nationales volontaires Cette « capture du vide » telle sera réalisée par moi qui sauront compris cette pensée ou plutôt ce principe et qui le vivront comme une action pure statique d'une manière toute naturelle enfin

Les voleurs d'idées

Quand l'urbanisme de l'air et encore, et surtout, après cette étape. Quand l'immatérialisation totale et définitive de l'architecture aura été accomplie, c'est-à-dire lorsque nous vivrons l'Éden perdu, de nouveau dans la nature véritable, non sans ditsface artificiel aucun, il est certain que notre conception actuelle de l'intimité, aura bien changé. Nous verrons en permanence tout ce qui, aujourd'hui est très secret et caché (avec les autres et les autres verront de même en nous, dans tous les moindres événements de notre vie quotidienne. Notre sensibilité sera alors développée d'une telle manière qu'il deviendra possible d'envisager même la possibilité de voir entre nous nos pensées les plus profondes ; ces pensées ne seront pas les plus intellectuellement « perçues », elles seront « saisies », et plutôt par imprégnation, toujours en « sensibilité » plus que par pénétration psychologique ; puisque la psychologie aura presque complètement disparu alors.

Cependant, si tous les hommes arrivent à conquérir cette possibilité de « rêver dans le rêve des

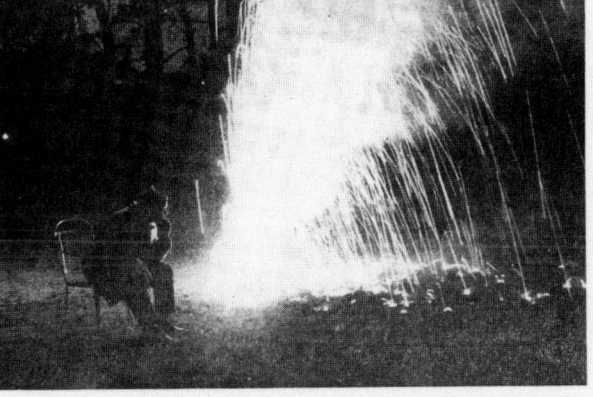

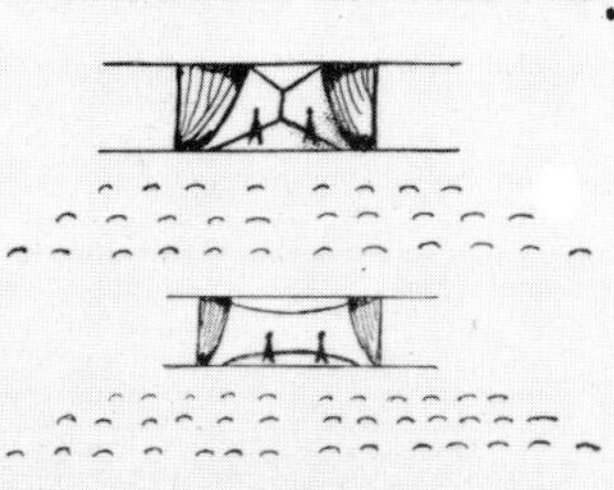

Les fontaines de feu, d'Yves. Pour un crépuscule de dimanche. *(Photo Verdi)*

pourtant pensé à cela le premier ! »

L'acteur de droite : « Quel merveilleux paysage ! »

L'acteur de gauche reçoit ces paroles comme un coup de poing à l'estomac et se tourne, convulsionné, vers le public, en montrant un visage défait... Dans le paysage de son côté, des nuages s'amassent et le vent redouble de violence. La voix, dans le vent, dit : « ...J'avais vu cela avant lui !... » « C'est lui. c'est le voleur d'idées ! » Et ainsi, d'idées en idées, et en constatations futiles en constatations futiles et universelles sans plus de valeur et sans propriété, l'acteur de gauche passe par tous les tourments absent tout le premier et d'entendre l'autre, l'acteur de droite, énoncer tout avant lui. La pièce

est presque un monologue puisque l'acteur de droite parle tout le temps, debout face aux écrans, tournant le dos aux spectateurs, ou considérant, de temps à autre, son seul au bord de plus en plus de désespoir à côté de lui, dans que série de mimes, qu'il exécute en faisant tantôt face aux spectateurs, tantôt face au décor-film.

Au lever du rideau, trente secondes se passent, montrant seule la scène vide violemment éclairée. Puis, avec l'action d'un ton continu l'éclairage baisse d'intensité, jusqu'au moment où un film est projeté au fond de la coulisse sur les écrans (ou tout l'écran panoramique)

À l'orchestre, sont assis assez loin l'un de l'autre, deux spectateurs, deux acteurs qui se lèveront soudain, s'apercevront et se font des gestes d'empressement d'aller se rencontrer sur la scène.

Ils se dirigent vers la scène à travers les rangs de spectateurs.

À présent, sur la scène, le film

L'acteur de droite reste toujours debout ; dans son secteur, le soleil brille et le paysage est toujours le même ; il est lumineux.

Dans la salle, une jeune fille se lève parmi les spectateurs de l'orchestre, et se dirige vers la scène.

L'acteur de gauche l'aperçoit le premier.

L'acteur de droite dit, cependant, encore le premier : « Comme elle est belle ! » La jeune fille sourit et le rejoint sur la scène ; en le regardant, ils se tournent autour, ils se prennent les mains...

Soudain la jeune fille voit l'épave vivante, à côté, par terre ; elle le secteur où tout est noir lamentable et désastreux.

Attiré, naturellement, par ce qui souffre, elle lâche brusquement les mains de l'acteur de droite et va, directement, se pencher sur l'épave de son secteur de douleur au sol en la dévorant des yeux. Elle le relève doucement.

Le bagage mental est dressé l'acteur de gauche a en tête l'image de sa compagne qui est venue à son secours instinctivement. Écœuré, ne laisse plus voir ses peines à l'autre. Le paysage merveilleux revient de son côté, il enlace la jeune fille.

Au même moment, l'obscurité brusque se fait dans le secteur de l'acteur de droite qui disparaît !

(Les dialogues sont en préparation)

quée jusqu'à une sorte de sublimation purificatrice absolue.

J'ai réellement déclaré, en janvier 1959, dans une communication en Allemagne, que, libéré du monde psychologique, l'artiste de demain créera et se recréera lui-même, capable de léviter dans une totale liberté physique !

Du vertige au prestige (1957-1959)

Depuis des années, je m'exerce à léviter et je connais bien les moyens d'y arriver effectivement (chutes judo).

Il y a d'une part le vampirisme légendaire et traditionnel pour la nuit avec l'immobilité physique absolue durant le jour. C'est une question de diastole et de systole, et d'autre part la libération effective de la personnalité dans tous ses aspect dans l'individu par l'exaspération du Moi, pratiquement

spiritualité. J'ai déjà procédé à des tentatives de réalisation d'œuvres de ce genre, telles les sculptures volantes aérostatiques de 1957, composées de mille et un ballons bleus, ou l'expérience de l'Obélisque de la place de la Concorde illuminé en bleu de nuit, le socle restant dans l'ombre et aussi les vapeurs de l'inauguration de l'époque bleue en 1957. C'est ce que j'appelle passer toujours le passage du vertige au prestige (libération de l'esclavage du socle en sculpture).

C'est ainsi qu'il me serait bien agréable bientôt de me présenter moi-même sur la scène d'un théâtre allongé dans l'espace à quelques mètres du sol, sans aucun truc ni supercherie, pendant quelque cinq à dix minutes au scénario dont l'atmosphère serait tel l'exutoire au spectacle...

« Viens avec moi dans le vide »

Je peins d'après modèle le plus souvent ni même avec la collaboration effective du modèle depuis quelques années déjà. En effet, depuis longtemps, je ne demande pourquoi les peintres figuratifs ou même abstraits quelque fois tel l'acteur par exemple, ressentent le besoin de peindre

d'après des nus. La raison de chercher une forme vivante humaine à dessiner et à copier s'est allongé dans l'espace à quoi bon mettre du sol, sans aucun truc ni supercherie, pendant quelque cinq à dix minutes au scénario dont l'atmosphère... Attention ! pas la sexualité ! Le modèle crée le climat sensuel à l'intérieur de l'atelier, comme éventuellement à l'extérieur, qui permet de stabiliser la matière picturale. C'est le gros bol sens à ne pas rompre quand l'artiste s'enferme dans les sphères de création d'art avec le centre de gravité des leurs charnelles dans le sens de la vraie foi chrétienne qui dit : « Je crois à l'incarnation du Verbe, je crois à la résurrection des corps » et il se trouve, au aussi, le Vrai sens du théâtre du Verbe : le Verbe, c'est la chair !

J'ai donc pris des modèles. J'ai essayé ; c'était très beau. La chair, la délicatesse de la peau vivante, sa couleur extraordinaire et si paradoxalement incolore à la fois me fascinaient.

Mes modèles riaient beaucoup de me voir exécuter d'après elles de splendides monochromes bleus sans unis ! Elles riaient, mais de plus en plus se sentaient attirées par le bleu.

Un jour j'ai compris que mes mains outils de travail pour manier la couleur ne suffisaient plus. C'était le modèle lui-même qu'il me fallait pour peindre la toile monochrome ; Non, ce n'était pas de la folie érotique !

C'était encore plus beau. J'ai jeté une grande toile blanche par terre, j'ai vidé au milieu vingt kilos de bleu et le modèle s'est littéralement rué dedans ; elle a peint le tableau en se roulant sur la surface de la toile dans tous les sens, avec son corps.

Je dirigeai l'opération debout, en tournant rapidement tout autour de cette fantastique surface au sol guidant tous les mouvements et déplacements du modèle. La fille, tellement grisée par l'action et par le bleu vu de si près et en contact avec sa chair finissait par ne plus m'entendre lui hurler : « Encore un peu plus à droite, là encore un revers roulant sur ce côté-là, c'est que n'est pas encore couvert dans cet angle contrôle, venez y appliquer votre sein droit. etc ».

Il n'y a jamais rien eu d'érotique, de pornographique ni de quoi que ce soit d'amoral dans ces séances fantastiques ; dès que le tableau était terminé, mon modèle grelottait un bain. Je ne les ai jamais touchées. d'ailleurs, c'est pour cela qu'elles avaient confiance et qu'elles aimaient à collaborer et aiment encore collaborer ainsi, de tout leur corps, à ma peinture. Et puis c'était la solution apportée au problème de la distance en peinture : mes pinceaux étaient vivants et télécommandés

Avec moi elles comprenaient, elles s'taient quelque chose, elles agissaient. Avant, avec les figuratifs qu'les dessinaient, elles se reconnaissaient aussi sur les peintures. Ensuite sont venus les abstraits et alors c'était inquiétant « psychologique mais... Elles ne comprenaient plus à quoi elles servaient en fait.

Avec moi, au début, elles m'ont cru fou ; après, elles ne pouvaient plus se passer de venir poser pour moi ou plutôt de venir travailler avec moi !

C'est ce que je veux représenter sur cette œuvre, comme fond musical, la chanson « Viens avec toi dans le vide », musique Hans Martin Malecki.

Quand je pense à toi !

Le même rêve revient toujours
Nous marchons enlacés
Dans le chemin sauvage de nos vacances

Et puis, peu à peu,
Tout semble disparaître autour de nous
Les arbres, les fleurs, la mer
Au bord du chemin,
Il n'y a plus rien non plus au monde
Nous sommes à notre bout du monde
Alors... Allons nous retourner ?
Non... Tu dis non je sais
Si tu reviens un jour
Toi qui rêves aussi
À ce vide merveilleux
À cet amour absolu
À ton que'ensemble,
Sans aucun mot à nous dire.
Nous nous jetterons
Dans la réalité de ce vide
Qui attend notre amour,
Comme moi je t'attends chaque jour :
Viens avec moi dans le vide !
1957.

Conclusion

Si mal, il y a : «...Je n'ai pas voulu ça ! »
Voir dans *Naturométrie* le développement pictural de cette proposition.

Ballet du feu

Dans un jardin : un immense écran hémisphérique de papier blanc ignifugé de manière que le feu d'une lampe à souder le perfore mais sans le faire s'enflammer.

Le public assis face à cette surface blanche unie voit soudain une flamme apparaître après avoir en une fraction de seconde foré un trou. La flamme disparaît — derrière l'écran de papier des hommes munis de lampes à souder dessinent ainsi par toute la surface de l'écran, par derrière, des vides au feu.

THÉÂTRE DU VIDE

● *Suite de la première page*

est en public, et son triomphe ou son désastre. Rapidement, l'auteur n'est même plus là lui-même, et pourtant tout continue.

...Vivre une constante manifestation, connaître la permanence d'être : être là, partout, ailleurs, dedans comme dehors, une sorte de sublime du désir, une matière imbibée, imprégnée dans « partout »... et tout continue, monothéâtre, hors du monde psychologique enfin... L'avenir du vide... c'est une salle de vide ! ce n'est plus de salle du tout !

★

Ce manifeste de 1954 m'a, depuis, inspiré des propositions médiatrices telles que celles qui vont suivre :

Créer une sorte de théâtre privé, à fréquenter (collectivement, par abonnement.

Les membres reçoivent chacun, en échange de leur cotisation, un siège à leur nom dans la salle de vide du théâtre où se donne la constante manifestation, avec accès sans autre spectateur, etc. Cette constante manifestation, dans cette salle où se pénètre plus de personne après son installation, doit avoir des moments plus intenses que d'autres ; signalés, aux abonnés par un programme qu'ils reçoivent par la poste ou... autrement ! À ces moments particuliers, le soir de

seulement (en passant leurs mains et leurs bras dans des manchons aux murs et tâter sans les voir) les sculptures tactiles hypersensibles qui sont de ravissants modèles vivants, au centre constitués hommes et femmes, exposés à la portée des spectateurs de l'autre côté des murs.

Ensuite après cotisation, les spectateurs sont plongés dans un sommeil artificiel de vingt-quatre heures, puis réveillés, massés, douchés, rhabillés et expulsés violemment dehors.

préférence, au petit matin, au lever du soleil, le théâtre doit être illuminé, brillamment, de manière que cela se voit bien de l'extérieur (la situation idéale d'un tel théâtre, pour l'instant, serait à Paris, celle du Marigny).

Encore une fois, je le répète, tout est fermé, personne ne peut entrer à l'intérieur, sauf le bureau de location à l'entrée ouvert pour que les retardataires et non abonnés puissent, au dernier moment, louer les quelques défections avant chaque manifestation. Le directeur d'un tel théâtre devra rechercher dans la ville, à la campagne ou au cours de longs voyages effectués à cet effet, les acteurs qui conviennent et ainsi constamment renouveler la troupe. Les acteurs seront choisis par lui dans la rue, partout ou ailleurs, et devront exiger aussitôt un contrat ferme, avec avance sur leurs honoraires.

Le nouvel acteur ainsi choisi travaura rien d'autre à faire qu'à savoir qu'il est un acteur et à passer pour toucher ses cachets après chaque séance où « au moment d'hyper intensité » indiqué dans le programme des abonnés. L'acteur s'entiura chargé de cette nouvelle et grave responsabilité d'être un acteur et disparaîtra dans la foule, dans le secrète pour devenir enfin un visiteur sérieux dans le spectacle monde de temps passé qu'est devenu le monde moderne d'aujourd'hui !

Projet pour un institut national théâtral

Les spectateurs sont reçus par un médecin psychiatre qui leur fait subir un examen général d'aptitude aux séances de l'Institut, puis ils passent tous dans une piscine où ils sont lavés et nettoyés à fond par de splendides et jeunes spécimens féminins de la race humaine.

Ils passent ensuite dans un sauna pendant vingt minutes puis, dans une chambre d'oxygénation où ils sont douchés à la lune pendant qu'ils peuvent admirer, par le sens du toucher

autres », comme on voie aujourd'hui d'huit des idées, des idées dites « dans l'air » à que certains osent tant plus rapidement que d'autres et que d'autres réalisent rapidement que certains. Il y aura toujours et le poète à qui au delà du rêve lui-même du contact avec le centre affectif de toute chose, avec le « je » et à l'état matière première cette douce. L'acteur de gauche arrive le premier sur la scène et rompt avec ravissement le paysage.

Cette pièce est une anticipation d'un tel état de choses, et c'est un paysage riant, des arbres, des collines, une rivière, le tout ensoleillé dans une atmosphère très Renoir, que perçoit du sa spiritualité l'acteur droit, il y aura toujours et le poète indéfinissable à l'horizon.

Ce son continu s'est transformé en une musique pastorale très douce. L'acteur de gauche arrive le premier sur la scène et rompt avec ravissement avec le paysage.

Le contrat

1er ACTE

Le rideau se lève, un la scène est un paysage riant, des arbres, des collines, une rivière, le tout ensoleillé dans une atmosphère très Renoir, que perçoit un peu en retrait, l'auteur. Discussion entre les trois personnages sur le théâtre d'Yves Klein et les autres possibilités théâtrales.

2e ACTE

Le rideau se lève sur une salle de théâtre avec l'orchestre, les balcons, etc., tous les sièges sont occupés par des acteurs c'est comble. La salle reconstituée sur scène est identique en tous points à celle dans laquelle se trouvent les vrais spectateurs au centre, entre les deux salles plusieurs auteurs se tiennent debout devant de petites tables et président, à tour de rôle, le débat.

Stupéfaction monochrome

Les spectateurs convoqués entrent dans une salle vide dont le sol est recouvert de riches tapis très épais en longue laine blanche et où leur sont distribuées des pilules bleues à consommer sur-le-champ.

Deux ou trois minutes plus tard, les personnages ayant consommé ces pilules tombent sous l'effet du stupéfiant : c'est-à-dire, une agréable torpeur dynamique

dans laquelle apparaît un espace lumineux intérieur comme extérieur bleu, celui-ci monochrome.

(Cependant, dans ce bleu, deux autres couleurs semblent bien distinctes et séparées les unes des autres : c'est l'or et le rose, mais tout est bleu uni I.K.B. en fin de compte.)

C'est la béatitude des paradis artificiels en bleu.

Tout le monde s'y prélasse.

Les cinq salles

Le lien entre l'esprit et la matière est l'énergie. Le mécanisme combiné de ces trois états donne notre monde tangible, prétendu réel m'a ébranlé. C'est ainsi que depuis si longtemps le théâtre est spectacle, et nous ne sortirons de ce désastre que lorsque nous prendrons la décision d'être indifférents vis-à-vis de l'énergie. C'est à ce moment-là que se fera l'illumination extraordinaire et extra-dimensionnelle et l'on sera alors dans l'esprit et la matière, en direct !

La manifestation en cinq salles parcourues par les spectateurs traînant des boulets aux pieds est une proposition dans ces esprits.

1. — Entrée par la salle des neuf tableaux monochromes bleus, tous du même format et du même bleu I.K.B.) (1).

2. — Passage dans la salle vide entièrement blanche immaculée (sol y compris) (I.K.I.) (2).

3. — Passage dans la salle des neufs Monogolds du même or fin 999.9 (I.K.G.) (3) et toujours tous du même format que les précédents bleus de la première salle.

4 — Passage dans la salle vide obscure presque noire (I.K.N.) (4).

5. — Passage dans la salle des neuf monochromes toujours du même format que les bleus et ors des salles précédentes (couleur exacte : I.K.P. (5) laque de garance rose...) (sortie).

La guerre

Petite mythologie personnelle de la monochromie, datant de 1954, adaptable en film ou en ballet

(Avertissement : J'ai tenu à laisser ce texte intact, tel qu'il a été écrit en 1954. Il est certain que si je le produisais plus tard, un peu naïf et n'emploierais plus sans doute les mêmes termes.)

Deux principaux personnages abstraits : la ligne et la couleur, qui se combinent, se multiplient, et s'interpénètrent par la suite. Pour tout décor un immense écran hémisphérique (écran destiné à recevoir une transparence la projection d'un film en couleur, ou de front).

Premier Tableau : Projection d'un blanc intense et immaculé sur l'écran pendant quatre secondes.

Deuxième Tableau : Passage progressif du blanc à l'or (couleur de l'or fin 999.9) quatre secondes fixes avec l'éclosion d'un son continu monoton (longueur d'onde de l'or).

Troisième Tableau : Passage progressif de l'or au rose (laque de garance, rose carminé). Passage progressif du son continu or au son continu rose. Quatre secondes fixes de rose sur l'écran ainsi que quatre secondes de monoton rose.

Quatrième Tableau : Passage progressif du rose au bleu (bleu I.K.B.) Passage progressif du son continu rose au son continu bleu. Quatre secondes bleu fixe sur l'écran accompagnées de quatre secondes de monoton bleu.

Cinquième Tableau : Sur l'image bleu uni apparaît soudain, gigantesque, une main (empreinte préhistorique de main, Castelio, Espagne, abbé Breuil). Un fort à-coup dramatique dans le son continu.

Commentaire : Profitant d'un besoin qu'éprouve le premier

scène invisibles, se relèvent lentement devant l'écran et commencent à danser les contours de la main gigantesque projetée sur l'écran. Lentement, la main s'anime sur l'écran. La main disparaît progressivement, trois doigts, puis deux seulement, dessinent dans la glaise découverte des traces linéaires. Apparaissent alors successivement les tracés sur doigts préhistoriques relevés par l'abbé Breuil à Ornos de la Pena et Alta Mira, Espagne.

Les danseurs, dans leurs mouvements, suivent les tracés digitaux sur l'écran.

Dans le même temps une musique concrète linéaire suit le tracé des doigts.

L'homme dans cette partie du ballet découvre toutes les formes de la nature, les formes du monde de la réalité tangible et manuelle sur laquelle viennent se s'ouvrir ses yeux. Il découvre les formes de la nature au même titre que celles d'un rocher, d'un lion, d'une plante, et il peut s'ajouter une danse légèrement suggestive, voire même érotique à la découverte mutuelle de l'émotion affective sensuelle entre l'homme et la femme.

Puis, c'est l'époque du meurtre (Abel et Caïn) le passage définitif du rêve à la réalité.

★

A PARTIR DE CE MOMENT C'EST AU CHORÉGRAPHE ÉVENTUEL A DÉCOUPER CE QUI VA SUIVRE EN TABLEAUX

Rapidement maîtrisée, la pure couleur, âme universelle dans laquelle baignait celle de l'homme et le paradis terrestre, est emprisonnée, compartimentée, cisaillée, réduite à l'esclavage. Sur l'écran, projection des traces cernés de rouge de Ornos de la Pena ou de Pech-Merle dans le Lot ; tracés australiens de la Tribu Worora, Port George, argumentés aussi de pieds.

La musique concrète continue en s'adaptant aux images projetées sur l'écran.

★

Dans le jour et le délire de sa victoire pure rude, la lutte sauvage l'homme et lui imprime son rythme abstrait à la fois intellectuel, matériel et émotionnel. Le réalisme va apparaître bientôt.

★

Le premier moment de stupéfaction passé, l'homme préhistorique réalise qu'il vient de perdre la vision.

Il se ressaisit en découvrant la forme dite figurative.

Réalisme et abstraction se combinent dans un horrible mélange machiavélique qui devient la vie humaine terrestre et c'est la mort vivable : « L'horrible cage » comme dira Van Gogh plusieurs milliers d'années plus tard. La couleur est asservie par la ligne qui devient l'écriture...

Sur l'écran, projection de cercis schématiques et chasseurs de

Nuestra Senore del Castillo, Aimaden, abbé Breuil. Hordes guerrières de Cueva del Val del Charco del Agua Amarga, Teruel. Musique concrète agrémentée de rythmes nègres.

Cette écriture d'une fausse réalité qui s'élabore, la réalité physique figurative, permet à la ligne de s'organiser presque définitivement déjà, en terrain conquis.

Son but : ouvrir les yeux de l'homme sur le monde extérieur de la matière qui l'entoure et lui permettre la marche vers le réalisme. Au loin, dans l'homme s'éloigne, sans pouvoir le quitter tout à fait cependant, sa vision intérieure colore perdue, à la place de laquelle se crée une sorte de vide atroce pour les uns, bouleversant ou merveilleusement romantique pour les autres et devient la vie intérieure, l'âme déchirée par l'actualité de la ligne.

La couleur souillée, humiliée, vaincue, va cependant préparer tout au long des siècles une revanche un soulèvement plus fort que tout. Sur l'écran, projection de figures courantes, de Bassosto. Afrique du Sud : Bisons de Lascaux avec larges taches de couleur rouge et vertes taches de couleur indépendantes du dessin. Dessins gravés abstraits sur objets néolithiques gravés, cerfs réduits à des signes, Andalousie du Sud cernés de rouge, l'abbé Breuil.

★

Enchantement musical sur la « Messe des pauvres » de Eric Satie

Ainsi l'histoire de la très longue guerre, de la ligne et de la couleur commence avec celle du monde, de l'homme et de la civilisation.

★

La couleur héroïque fait des signes à l'homme toutes les fois qu'il remet le destin de peindre (phénomène de tentative faite par le corps affectif pour sa libération dans l'espace) qui lui vient de très loin en lui, d'au-delà de son âme...

★

La couleur claime de l'œil à l'homme, enfermé dans les formes par le dessin. Des millénaires passeront avant que l'homme comprenne ces appels désespérés et se mette tout à coup fébrilement à l'action pour délivrer la couleur comme il le peut. Le paradis est perdu, l'enchevêtrement des lignes devient comme les barreaux d'une véritable prison qu'est d'ailleurs, de plus en plus, la vie psychologique humaine. Le drame de la nature inévitable à des mortels » où ils sont entraînés de par la coexistence orageuse de la ligne et de la couleur en guerre, provoque la naissance de l'art.

★

Cette lutte pour la création éternelle, et surtout immortelle, pour arriver à transmuter dans l'objet, dans la forme, dans le son, ou dans l'image, en la triangulant, cette âme universelle colore qui est la vie elle-même conquise, envahie, brimée par la ligne, puissance magique du mal

et des ténèbres, terrible, parce qu'elle tue.

De la situation des formes figuratives et de l'enchantement que l'homme ressent à savoir le dessin de la couleur qui lui laisse toujours une impression vague de remords lorsqu'il ne le fait pas, mais l'écriture. Sur l'écran, défilé de pièce maîtresses illustrant toujours les premiers symptômes de la naissance de l'écriture : véritable et unique mission valable de la ligne et du dessin. Hiéroglyphes. La couleur soulagée respire et redevient pure bien que toujours prudemment compartimentée dans l'Egypte ancienne. Chaque caste à ses couleurs (rituel des couleurs). Amérique : Civilisation aztèque, toltèque. maya.

En Chine, la couleur semble se libérer par un truchement, une ruse (plutôt encore, ici, le caractère rituel de la couleur auquel tente à se substituer le symbolisme graphique, l'idéographisme).

La couleur envahit dans les images les surfaces avec délicatesse et le dessin semble lui être soumis pour un temps ; mais ce n'est pas par des ruses que la couleur veut se libérer, elle le sent bien.

C'est dans le monochrome en effet, que la peinture chinoise a excellé, notamment à l'époque des « Song ». Parfois l'artiste ajoute aux teintes plates une pointillé à l'encre qui permet d'obtenir des jeux de lumière sur la soie, conservé au British Museum à Londres l'œuvre du peintre Koukai-tchi, IV° siècle. Ce n'est qu'au XIII° siècle que les tons violents, rouges et pourpres font leur apparition. Mais ce pendant la couleur reconnaît elle-même que ce clair-obscur cette peinture délicate d'atmosphère, ces nuages de ton et de demi-ton passant sans heurt de l'un à l'autre, bien que très peu striés par le dessin, ce n'est pas une vraie victoire ! Ce n'est qu'artistes et tout au plus compromis. La couleur ne veut pas d'une fausse libération. Elle veut une vraie victoire hors de tout malaise.

Bientôt grâce à de telles tentatives de coexistence, la ligne arrive à se faire aimer, on plaidit estimer, par la couleur même du concept forme « couleur, catégories logiques de la vision comme de l'entendement). Couleur et dessin s'adaptent l'un à l'autre et une v même, mais ils s'installe et pernd forme. Les civilisations devant les seulement apparente de paix qui règne entre les deux ennemis s'abonnent aux arts picturaux des grands mythes naissent), la couleur, comme la ligne, est plus ou moins mise en valeur selon les époques. Sur l'écran, observation sur les couleurs et lignes dans chacune de ces civilisations. Défile de pièces maîtresses montrant l'époque ou vécu la priorité de la ligne, tantôt celle de la couleur (déductions psychologiques). Ligne et couleur s'affrontent dans toutes les civilisations suivantes.

Mais c'est ce lien invisible, cette cible qui tient tout univers à travers le temps et qui est éternelle, qui devrait être perçu et transmué dans la création d'art. Les artistes véritables devraient être comme des prophètes de la paix, profonde et violente d'intensité, plus forte que la guerre destructrice. Aujourd'hui, la ligne me pourrait-elle jusque même dans ses retranchements les plus sûrs par cette nécessité de l'absolu à retrouver. L'évolution très rapide de ces dernières années dans la calligraphie japonaise en est la preuve, la ligne disparaît, se transforme plutôt en des formes dégagées de contours, ou presque, et remplissant toute la surface d'une matière presque uniforme.

La ligne jalouse de la couleur habitante authentique de l'espace vente de se libérer de sa condition de sourisse de l'espace le trait se dissout ci s'envahit la surface picturale. Couleur toute-puissante révélée à révéler au grand jour, l'évolution permet cette initiation qui ramènera tout dans l'ordre. Tous désirent, parfois, sans le savoir, le plus véritable : non pas ce mot plein de fausseté et malhonnête : « La Paix des Nations », mais cela bien ineffable dans la nature et dans l'homme d'avant l'intrusion de la ligne dans la couleur.

Aujourd'hui, le calligraphe japonais pourrait presque remplir de sa présence qualitative spatiale, d'une manière égale la

Observation et imagerie comparées sur l'écran

★

L'Inde, les Etrusques, le Japon, civilisation d'Asie Mineure, Moyen-Orient, Grèce, Rome. La religion qui défend souvent la représentation figurative dans l'art, la couleur chez les Nègres : b'en montrer le « rituel ».

★

Le monde pictural chrétien oriental et occidental.

★

Les enluminures irlandaises abstraites, le Moyen Age en Europe.

★

Les primitifs italiens, la Renaissance, pour atteindre jusqu'à nos jours, c'est-à-dire d'abord par les précurseurs de l'impressionnisme.

★

La couleur envahit dans les images les surfaces avec délicatesse et le dessin semble lui être soumis

Dernier sursaut et tentative de défense de la ligne dans l'opposition Ingres-Delacroix. « La couleur, disait Ingres, ajoute des ornements à la peinture ; il en tendait dessin, composition), mais elle n'en est que la dame d'atour... »

Mais Delacroix recopiait dans son journal des observations qui l'avaient frappé. « Les couleurs sont la musique des yeux... Certaines harmonies de couleurs produisent des sensations que la musique, elle-même, ne peut pas atteindre ».

Très important, le concept, lyrisme retrouvé

★

Opposition entre le pouvoir rituel essentiellement affectif de la couleur et le symbolisme rationalisant du graphisme.

★

L'histoire de l'art c'est l'âge de l'histoire des peuples. Les peuples heureux n'ont pas d'histoire : or, les peuples heureux sont ceux chez qui règne la paix, ce qui fait que pour qu'une histoire de l'art existe, comme une histoire des peuples, il faut tout simplement qu'il y ait de la guerre ! Il faut de la guerre et puis de la paix, et ensuite de la guerre à nouveau et de la paix encore — Dualité - Duel - Opposition - Opposition - Progression et évolution par comparaison et analogie.

C'est ce qu'on peut reprocher à l'art, sauf quelques exceptions, c'est, justement, de n'avoir été jusqu'à ce jour qu'une histoire de l'art, une sorte de constant témoignage de l'époque. Bien sûr, bien des génies ont vécu de même en véritables artistes : c'est-à-dire plus ou moins inconsciemment transportés par leur art bien au-delà, en marge de leur époque, parfois en avance de quelques siècles, souvent en arrière d'autant.

unie, une surface donnée, le résultat serait une dominante partout imprégnée de lui-même par son choix et sa qualité de créateur. Plus de barreaux psychologique linéaire. Devant la surface colore, on se trouve directement devant la matière d'âme.

Le dessin c'est de l'écriture dans un tableau. On dessine un arbre, mais ça reviendrait au même de peindre une couleur et d'écrire à côté : arbre. Dans le fond, le vrai peintre de l'avenir, ce sera un poète muet qui n'écrira rien mais qui racontera, sans articuler, en silence, un tableau immense et sans limite.

Chez les Egyptiens, la ligne sentant le danger de l'insurrection continuelle de la couleur vaincue et occupée par elle tente de remporter une victoire psychologique en imitant la nature, « toute sensibilité », de la couleur, elle amènera alors à la fausse illumination du plaisir, presque toujours sensuel, des sens et de l'œil en particulier. Les artistes seront alors des esthètes, abstraits ou réalistes ; en passant par toute la gamme de la figuration, la couleur agonise puis se ressaisit. Il y a des peu tes traités entre les deux adversaires avec l'avènement de telles ou telles civilisations. Souvent la couleur parvient à dominer sans pouvoir jamais toutefois se défaire complètement de la ligne.

Il apparaît toujours tout au long de l'histoire de l'art, qu'il est incompréhensible, invraisemblable et pourtant vrai que, pratiquement les artistes aient toujours choisi pour thème exactif ce qui est éphémère ou irréel.

Cependant, le pouvoir de l'image est tel que l'on voit, tour à tour, les civilisations entières affolées interdire tantôt la figuration, tantôt l'abstraction.

★

Parvenu au nadir du matérialisme au XX° siècle, le voile du temple de l'art se déchire enfin, l'imitation est pour tour le monde et chacun pourra apprécier et profondément comprendre l'art, autrefois réservé aux rares privilégiés. Dans les premiers chapitres de son traité, Léonard de Vinci s'évertue à démontrer la supériorité de la peinture sur la poésie, la musique et la sculpture.

La peinture et l'art sous toutes ses formes inquiétaient la nature. On reconnaît à l'image les possibilités d'exploration de l'inconscient. Des recherches conscientes ou inconscientes s'entreprennent pour retrouver quelque chose d'oublié, mais que tout le monde ressent.

La connaissance du réel fournit pas non sens est à la base des expériences de l'espace ; analogue sera la notion que s'en construit l'intelligence, Bergson l'a rappelé : « La prise physique, de même que celle des mots ou des notions claires, défaillie dès que l'on passe de ce qui se réunit par son intensité ou sa qualité seule. Il n'y a d'idée claire ou distincte que par analogie avec les séparations de l'espace. La sensibilité pure est confuse. Elle n'est que durée même, non communicabilité. »

« L'enfant s'est couché. La chambre est obscure. Il ferme les yeux. Il appuie deux doigts tendus un fourche sur ses paupières. Et il voit de grandes flammes. Il les voit et cependant elles sont là où sont les yeux, plus profondes même dans sa tête. Mais il n'y a plus ni dedans ni dehors plus d'objets, plus d'yeux. L'enfant voit, tout simplement de la couleur intense. Il die maintenant ses mains de ses yeux et c'est un merveilleux assemblage de losanges azolés, mobiles comme de l'eau, doux comme du velours qui serait liquide et répandrait la phosphorescence lumière comme des fleurs d'arbuste dans la nuit.

Mais cette étonnante lumière n'est ni du jour ni de la nuit. Elle est immuable et pourtant tremble doucement. Elle est là dans sa tête depuis toujours. Y ruisera-t-elle toujours ? Et la couleur est plus belle que toutes parce que plus vaste, somptueuse comme la couleur chargée des pensées du jardin, mais sans cette apparence d'étoffe ancienne moisie on ne sait où. L'enfant appelle sa mère et lui demande : « Qu'est-ce que c'est que tu vois quand on ferme les yeux ? » Mais sa mère ne comprend pas d'abord. Il explique et sa mère lui répond : « Il ne faut pas faire ça... tu deviendrais aveugle ! »

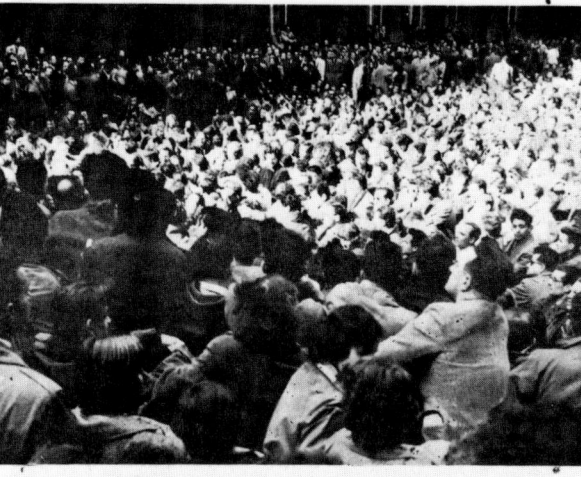

Les spectateurs assis sur la chaussée dans la rue sont contemplés par les acteurs sur les trottoirs !

● SUITE EN PAGE 4

---

(1) I.K.B. = International Klein Bleu

(2) I.K.I. = International Klein Immatériel (vide).

(3) I.K.G. = International Klein Gold.

(4) I.K.N. = International Klein Néant

(5) I.K.P. = International Klein Pink.

La guerre (suite)

Delacroix et le réalisme romantique : Le 20 février 1824, bien que décidé à calquer pour ainsi dire la nature, il écrira : « Hé ! réalisme maudit, voudrais-tu, par hasard, me produire une illusion telle que je me figure que j'assiste en réalité au spectacle que tu prétends m'offrir ? C'est la cruelle réalité des objets que je fuis quand je me réfugie dans les sphères des créations d'art, »

« Malheur au tableau qui ne montre rien au-delà du fini. Le mérite du tableau est l'indéfinissable : c'est justement ce qui échappe à la précision : qu'est-ce donc ? « C'est ce que l'âme a ajouté aux couleurs et aux lignes pour aller à l'âme : Delacroix cherchait l'expression totale de lui-même dans le spectre d'art.

[...]

★

★

★

Projet de ballet sur aspect de fugue et choral

(écrit en collaboration avec
Jean-Pierre MIROUSE.)

L'idée essentielle de ballet en trois mouvements est un aspect de fugue musicale, chorégraphique, chromatique. [...]

PROGRAMME DU FESTIVAL D'ART D'AVANT-GARDE
Paris, novembre-décembre 1960

Renseignements et location :
Durand, 4, place de la Madeleine — Salle Gaveau ; Pavillon Américain, Porte de Versailles ; Théâtre : Musée des Arts décoratifs ; Galerie des Quatre Saisons ; Studio Raznaigh ; Atelage française ; agences et S.V.P.

[...]

La marque de l'immédiat

En 1953, je propose à un producteur de cinéma à Tokio de tourner un petit film en couleurs sur un voyage visuel mystico-réaliste et très contemplatif mais aussi dynamique que possible. [...]

La statue

Lorsque je serai enfin devenu comme une statue par l'exagération de moi-même moi et m'aura amené à cette sclérose ultime. [...]

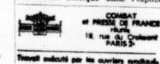

Le sommeil

Le rideau se lève sur une scène, où la trouve une chambre, un grand lit, dans un coin la mort. [...]

Renversement

Il serait peut-être intéressant de donner une fois une pièce de théâtre quelconque, à l'envers. [...]

Directeur-gérant : Yves KLEIN.

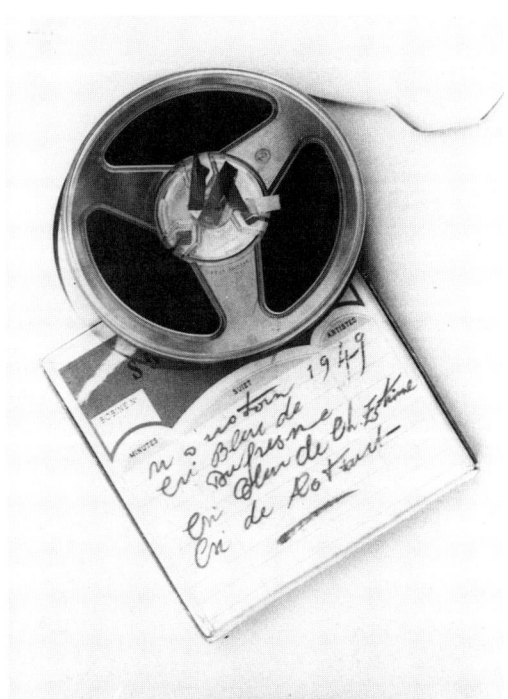

Tape recording of *Monotone Symphony* and *Blue Cries*
(see cat. nos. 94 and 96)

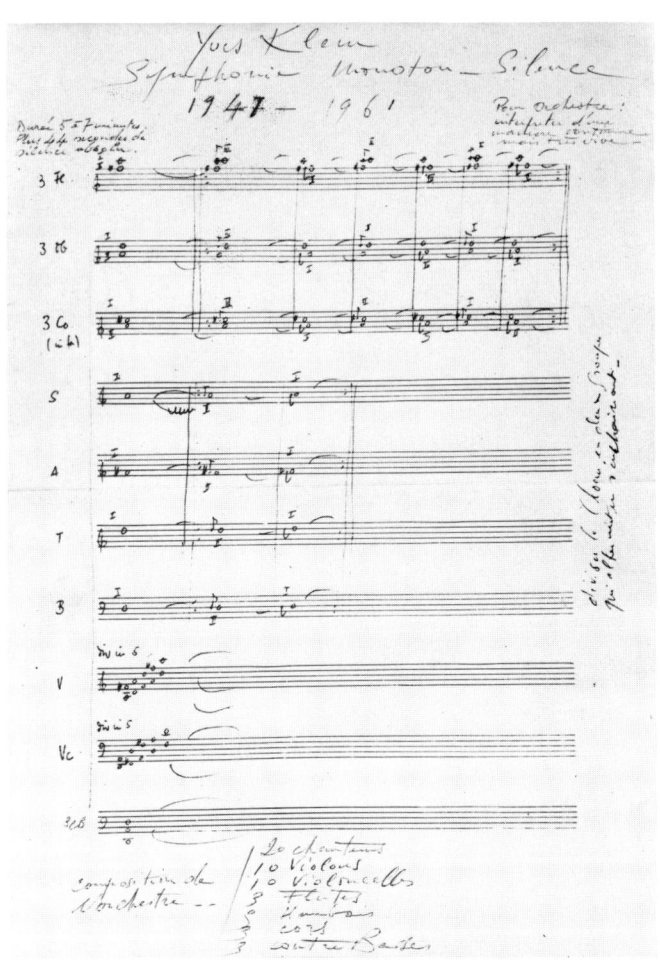

94.   Score for *Symphonie Monoton-Silence (Monotone-Silence Symphony)*, [1947], 1961

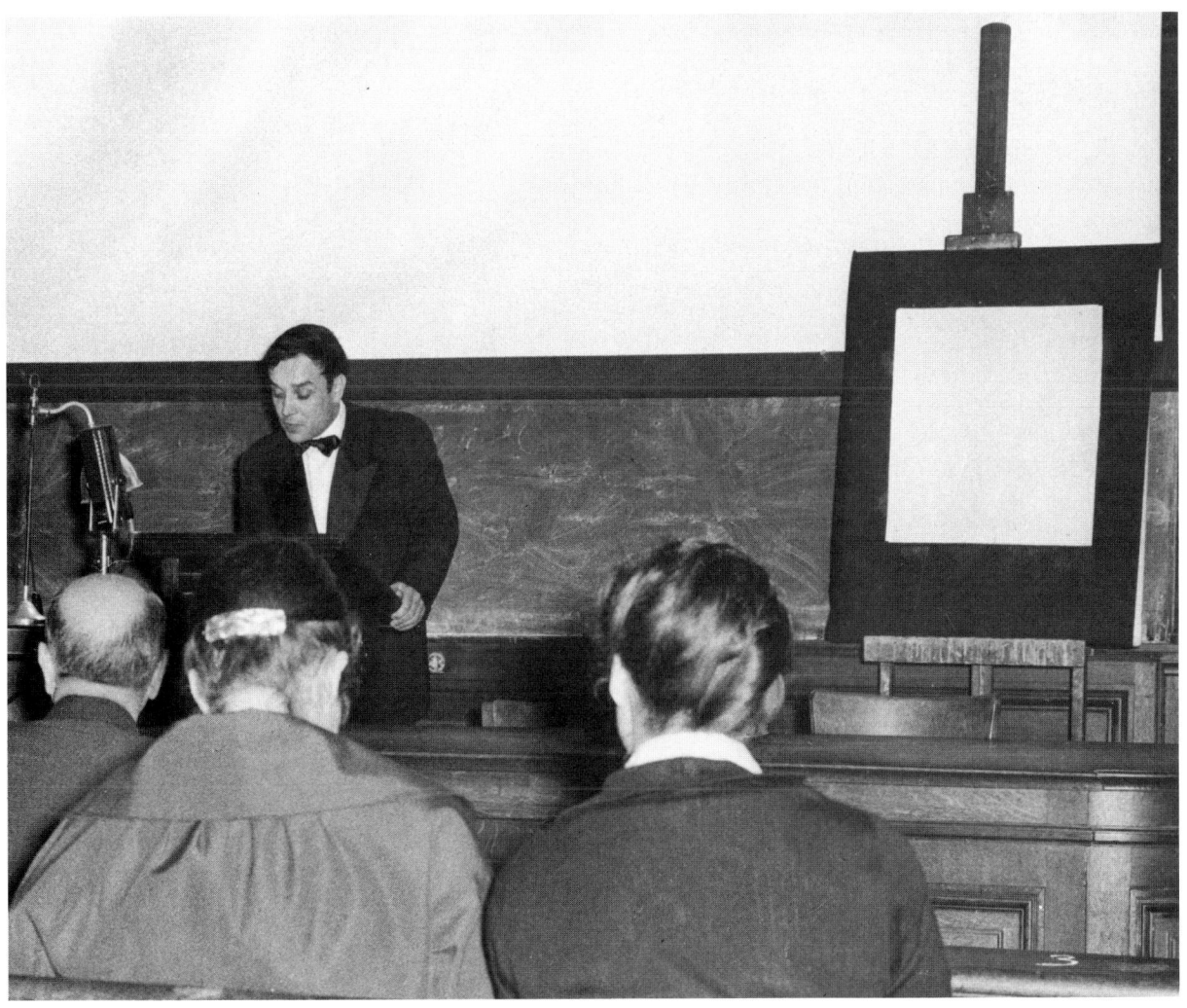

97. *L'Evolution de l'art vers l'immatériel (The Evolution of Art toward the Immaterial);* June 3, 1959; lecture by Yves Klein at the Sorbonne, Paris

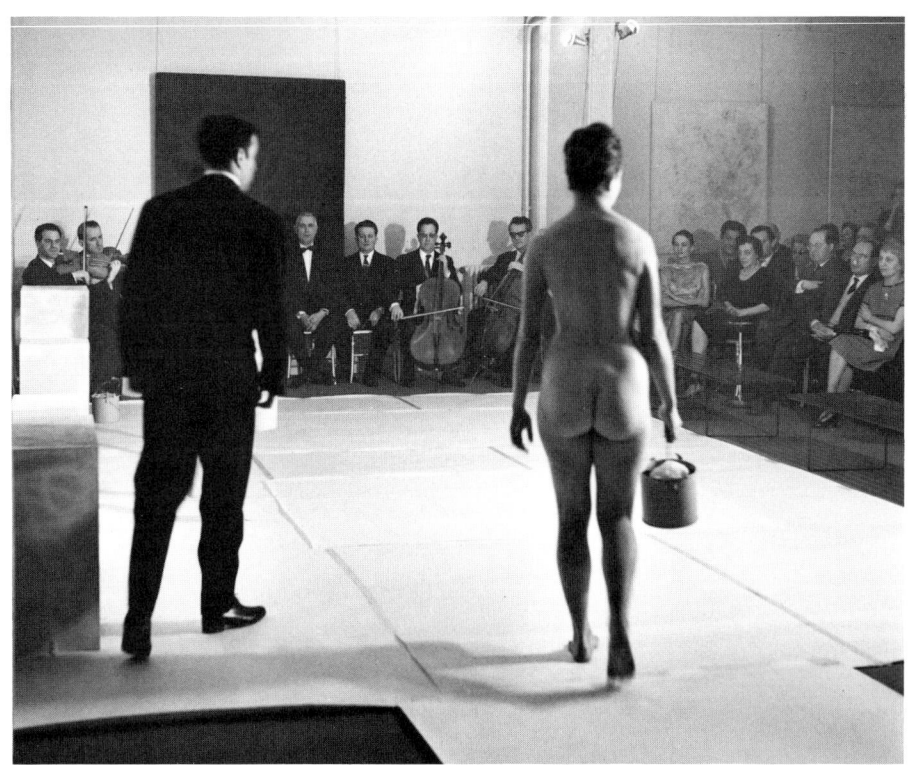

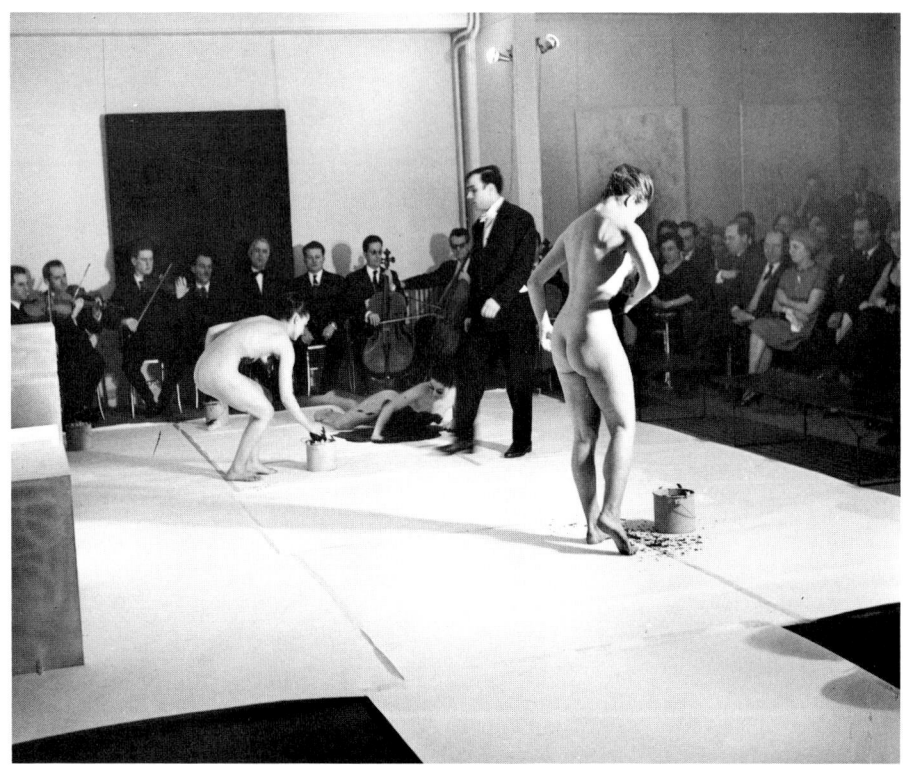

95. *Anthropométries de l'époque bleue (Anthropometries of the Blue Period)*, March 9, 1960; performance at Galerie Internationale d'Art Contemporain, Paris

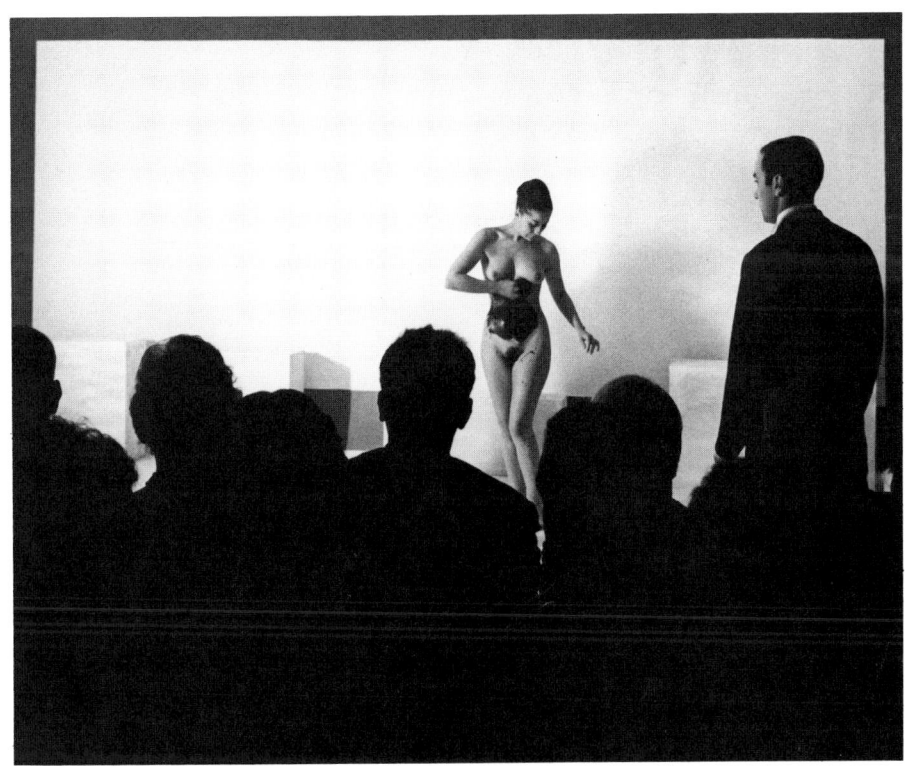

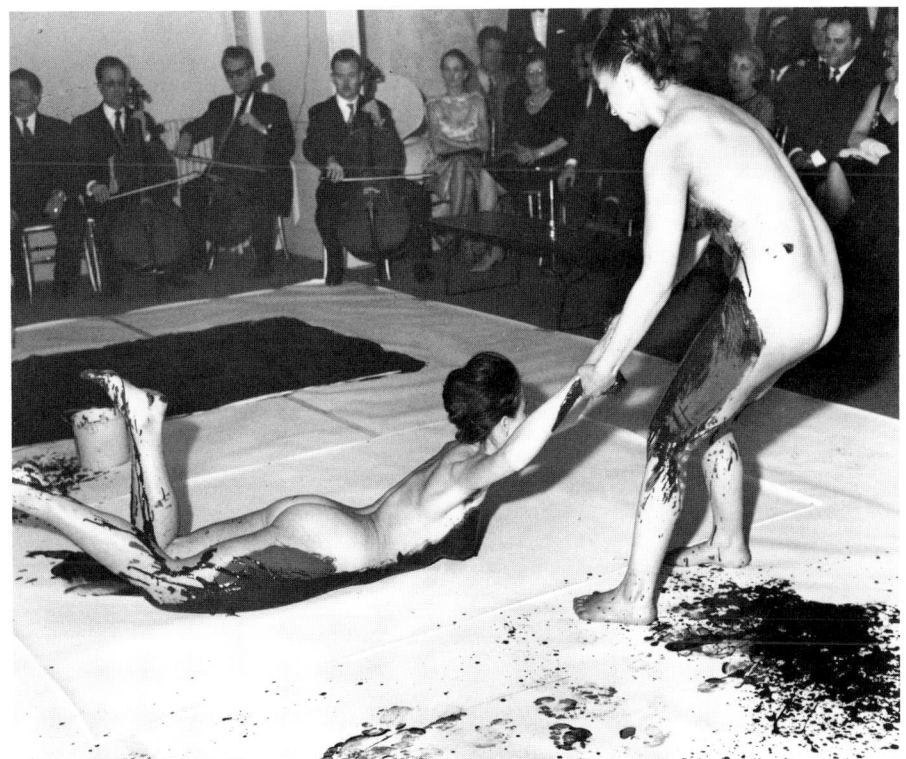

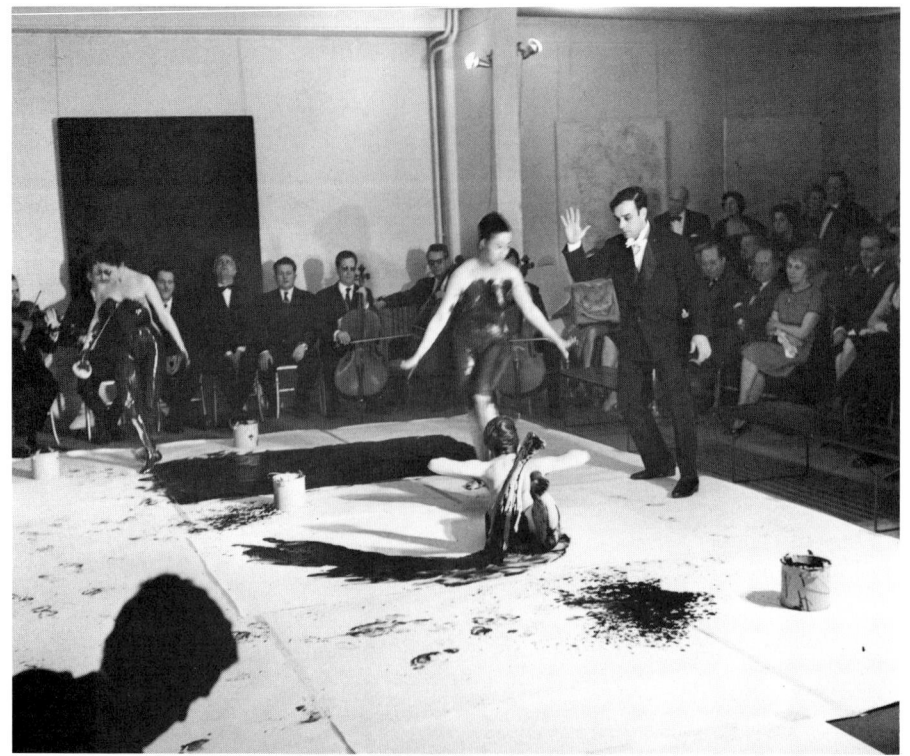

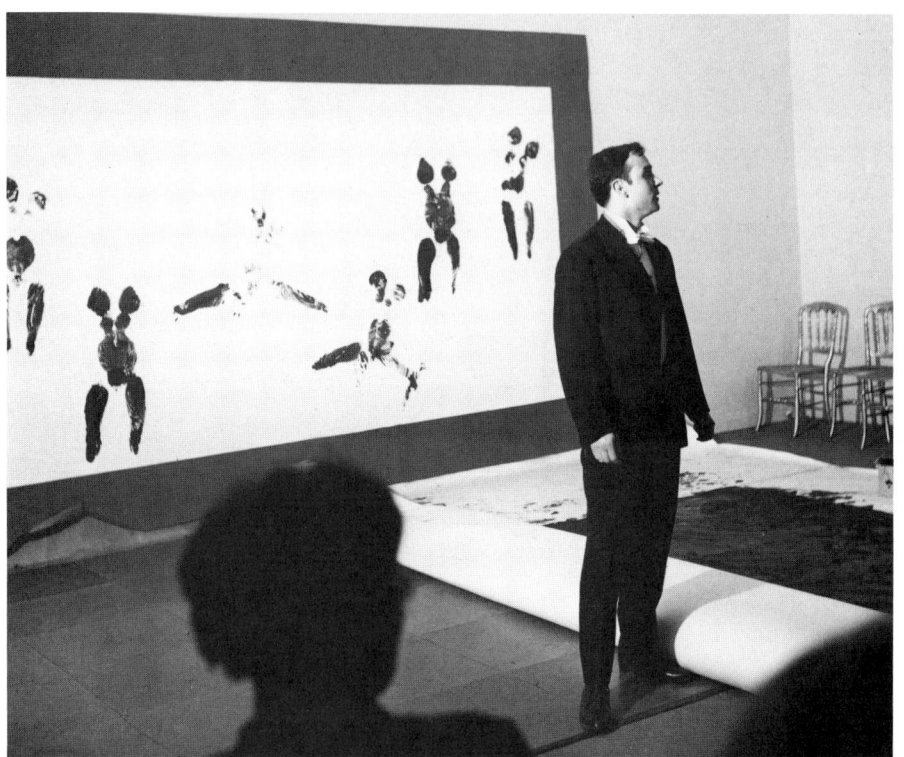

95.   *Anthropométries de l'époque bleue,* continued

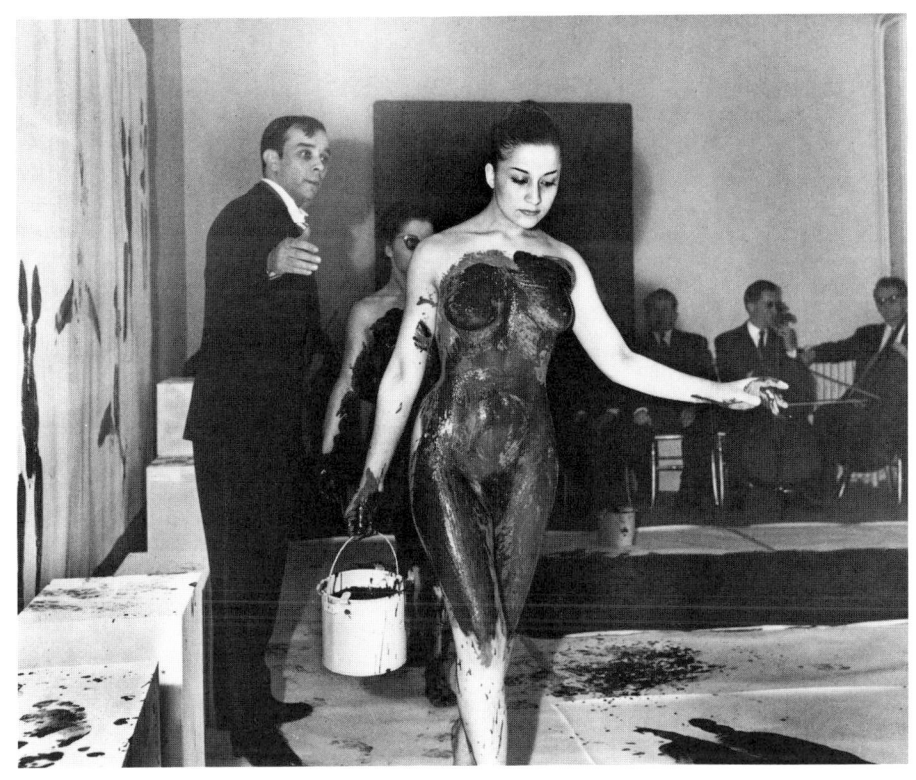

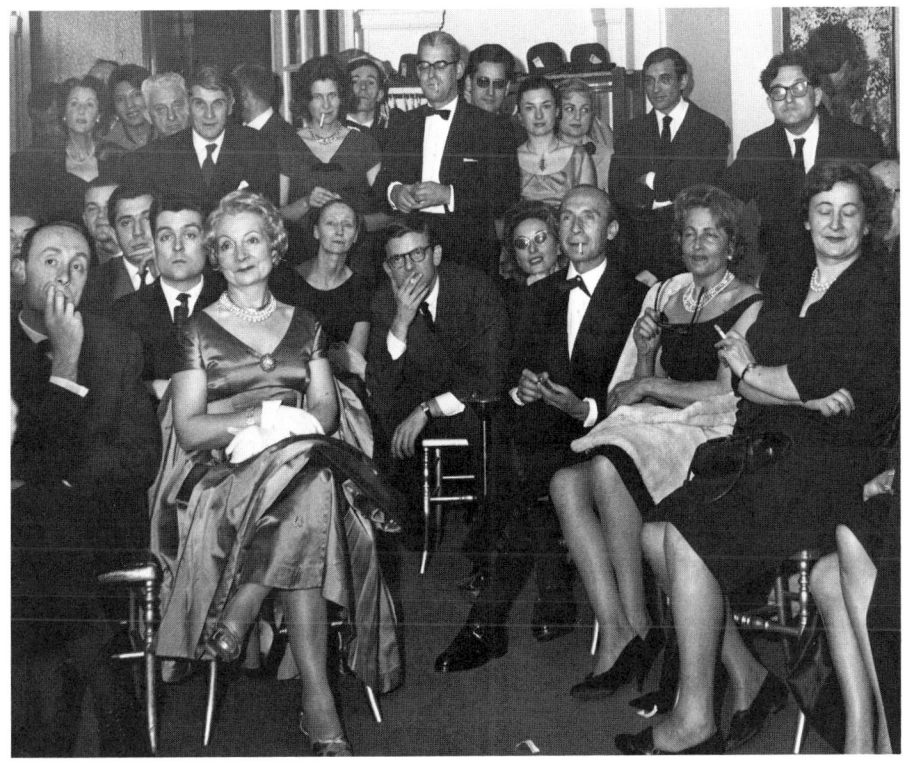

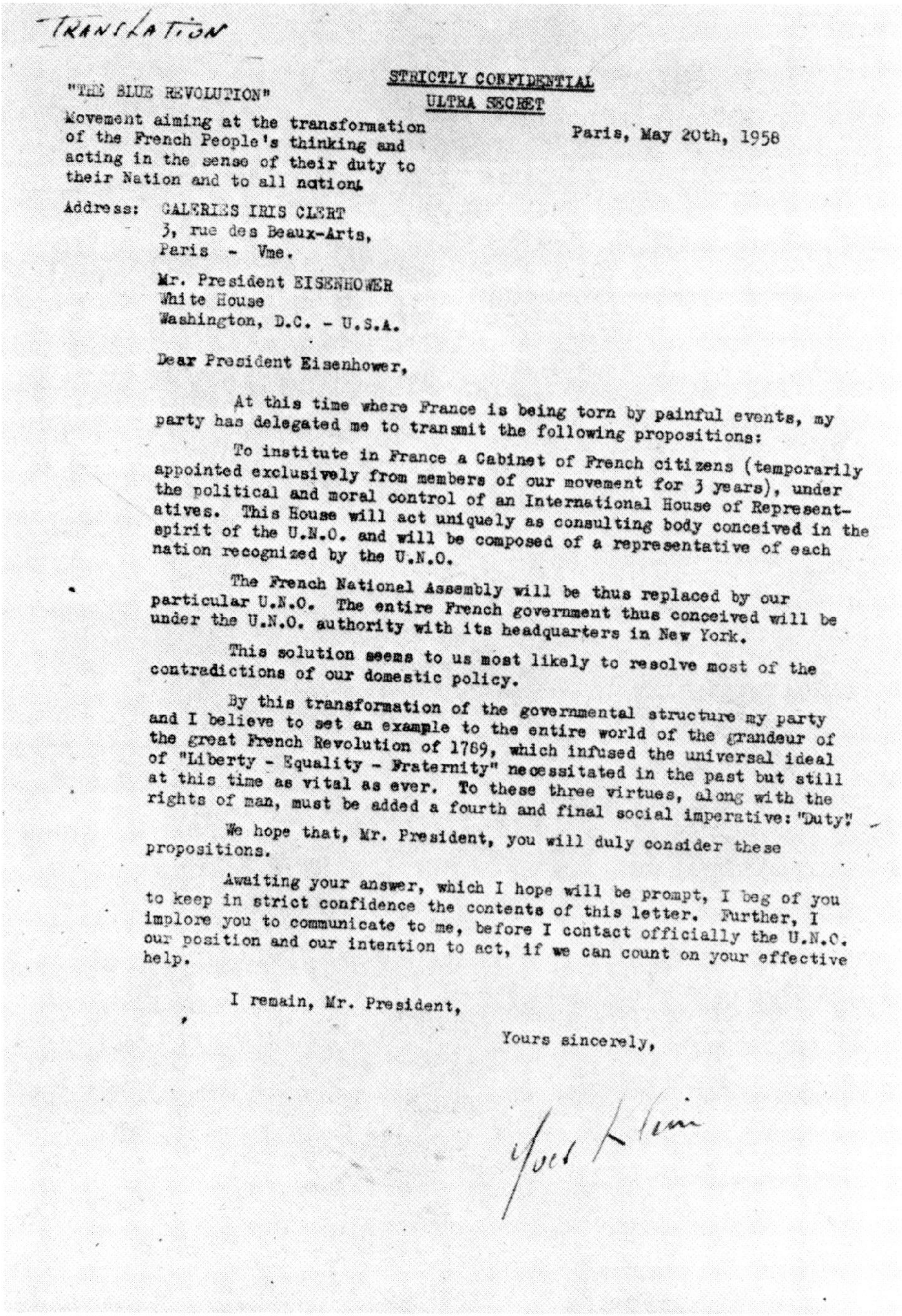

TRANSLATION

"THE BLUE REVOLUTION"

Movement aiming at the transformation
of the French People's thinking and
acting in the sense of their duty to
their Nation and to all nations.

<u>STRICTLY CONFIDENTIAL</u>
<u>ULTRA SECRET</u>

Paris, May 20th, 1958

Address: GALERIES IRIS CLERT
3, rue des Beaux-Arts,
Paris - Vme.

Mr. President EISENHOWER
White House
Washington, D.C. - U.S.A.

Dear President Eisenhower,

At this time where France is being torn by painful events, my party has delegated me to transmit the following propositions:

To institute in France a Cabinet of French citizens (temporarily appointed exclusively from members of our movement for 3 years), under the political and moral control of an International House of Representatives. This House will act uniquely as consulting body conceived in the spirit of the U.N.O. and will be composed of a representative of each nation recognized by the U.N.O.

The French National Assembly will be thus replaced by our particular U.N.O. The entire French government thus conceived will be under the U.N.O. authority with its headquarters in New York.

This solution seems to us most likely to resolve most of the contradictions of our domestic policy.

By this transformation of the governmental structure my party and I believe to set an example to the entire world of the grandeur of the great French Revolution of 1789, which infused the universal ideal of "Liberty - Equality - Fraternity" necessitated in the past but still at this time as vital as ever. To these three virtues, along with the rights of man, must be added a fourth and final social imperative: "Duty".

We hope that, Mr. President, you will duly consider these propositions.

Awaiting your answer, which I hope will be prompt, I beg of you to keep in strict confidence the contents of this letter. Further, I implore you to communicate to me, before I contact officially the U.N.O. our position and our intention to act, if we can count on your effective help.

I remain, Mr. President,

Yours sincerely,

Yves Klein

99. *The Blue Revolution*, 1958; letter from Yves Klein to President Eisenhower

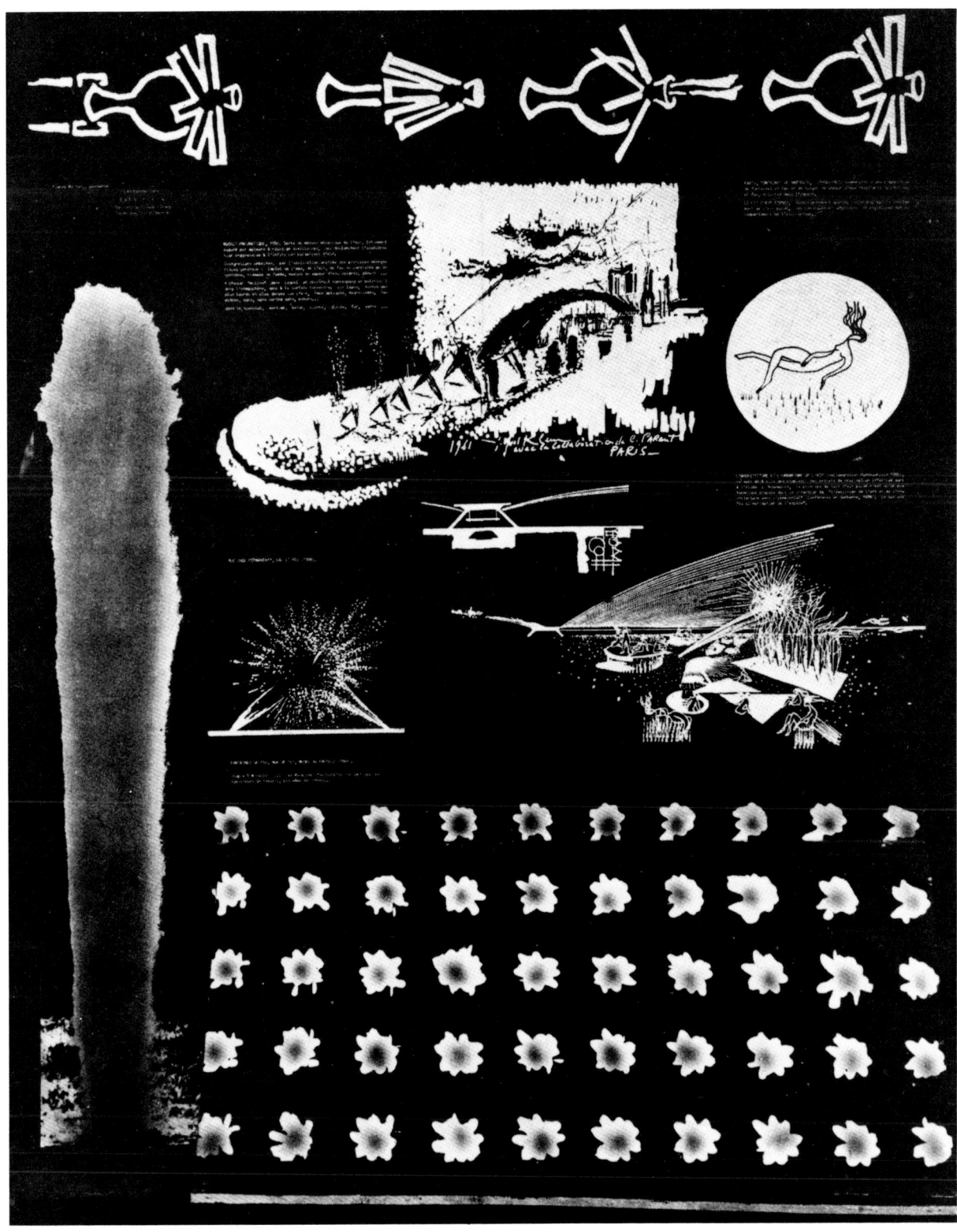

100. *L'Architecture de l'air (The Architecture of the Air)*, 1958–62; one of Klein's photomontage display panels, rendered with the aid of Claude Parent

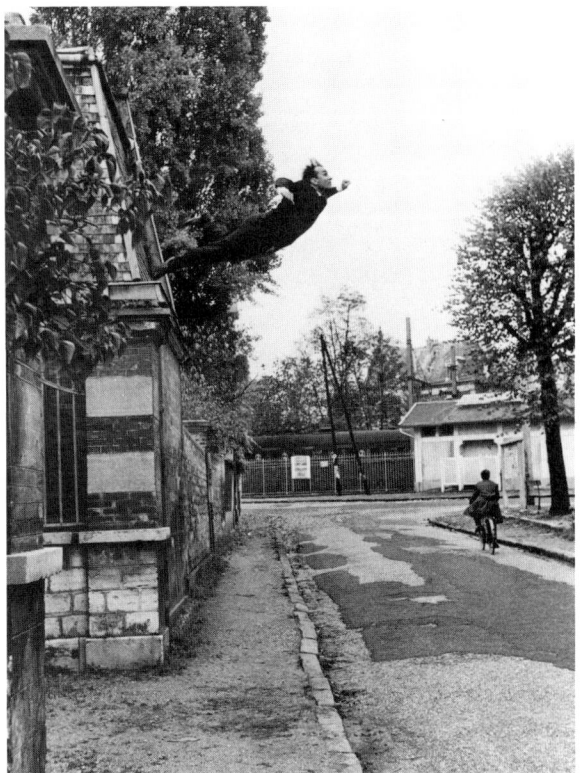 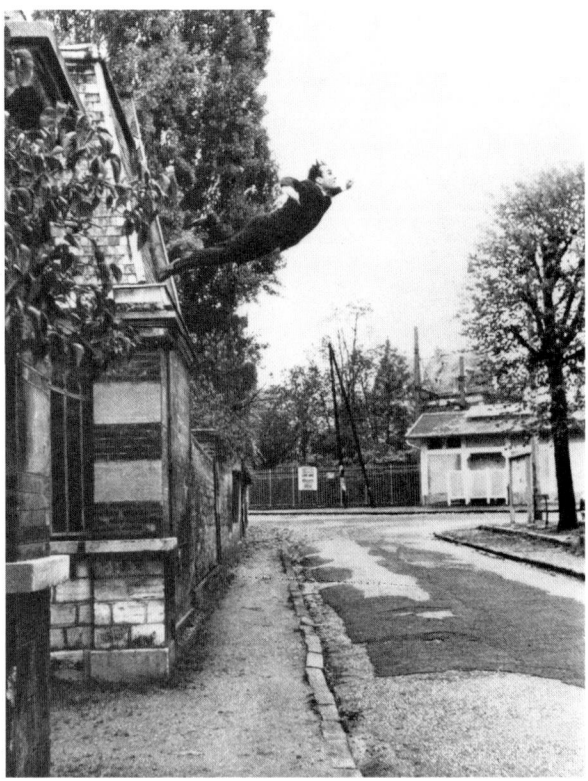

104. *The Leap into the Void*, 1960; at left, as published in *Dimanche*; at right, as published in Klein's Krefeld exhibition catalogue

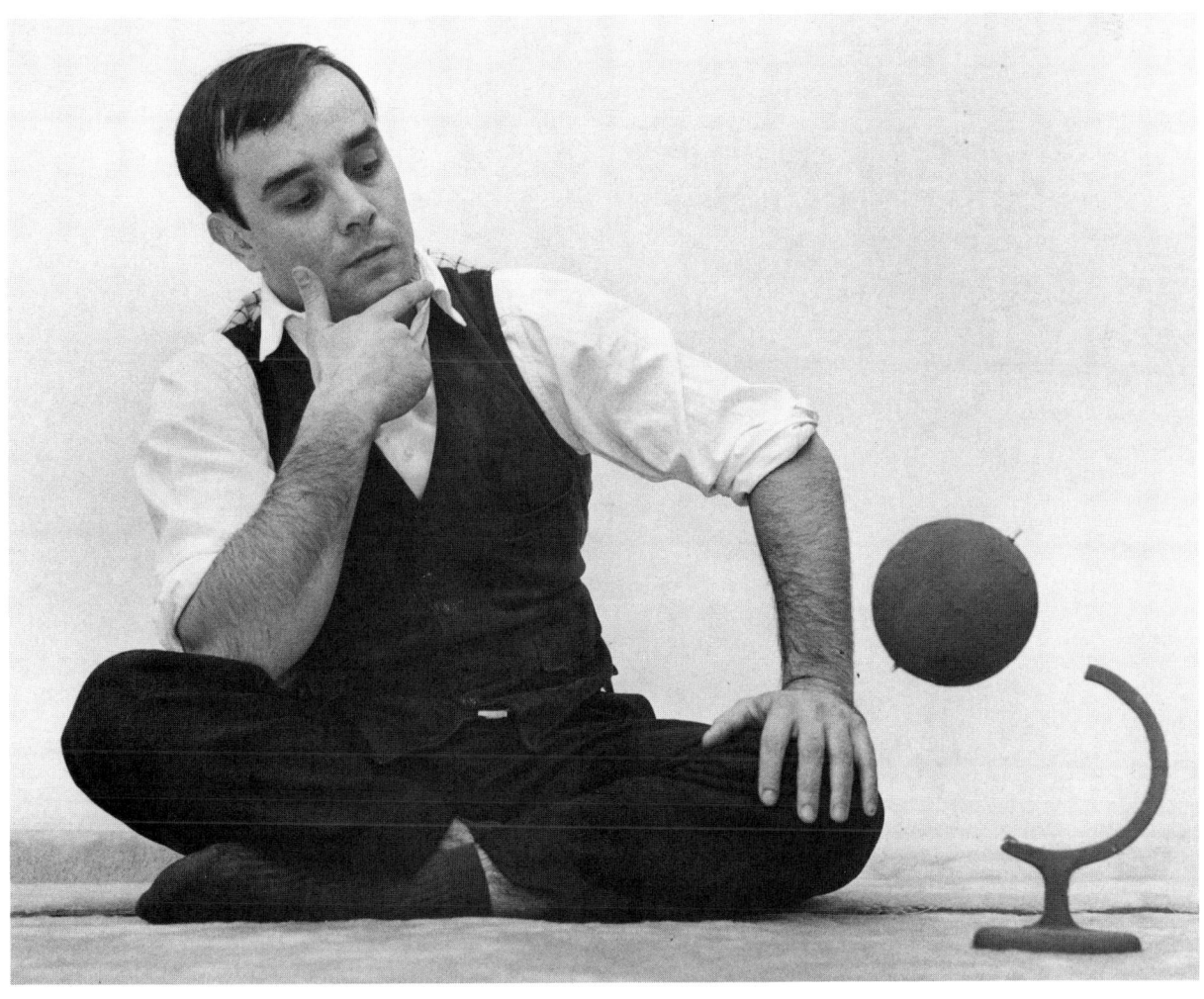

106. *Le Globe est bleu (The Globe Is Blue)*, c. 1961

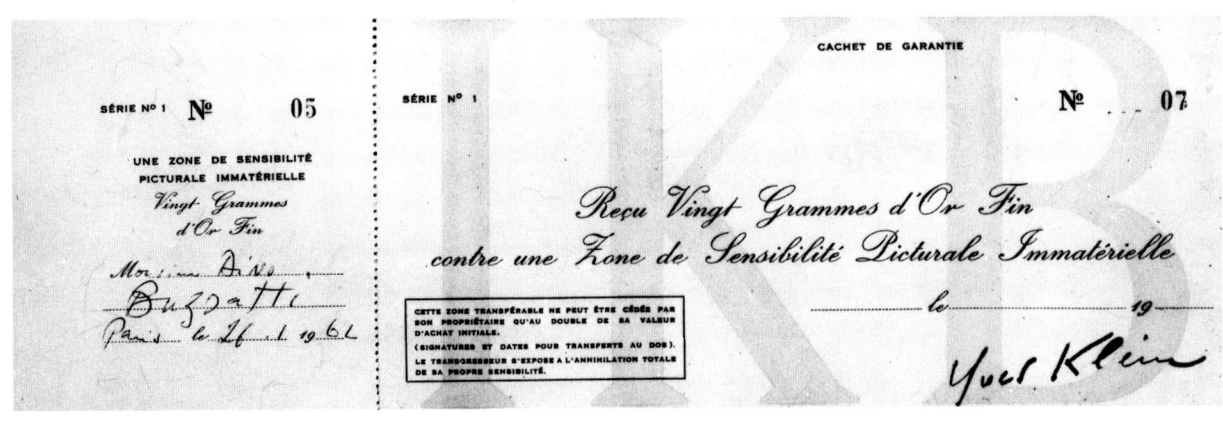

102. Receipt book for *Zones of Immaterial Pictorial Sensibility*, series 1, item 5

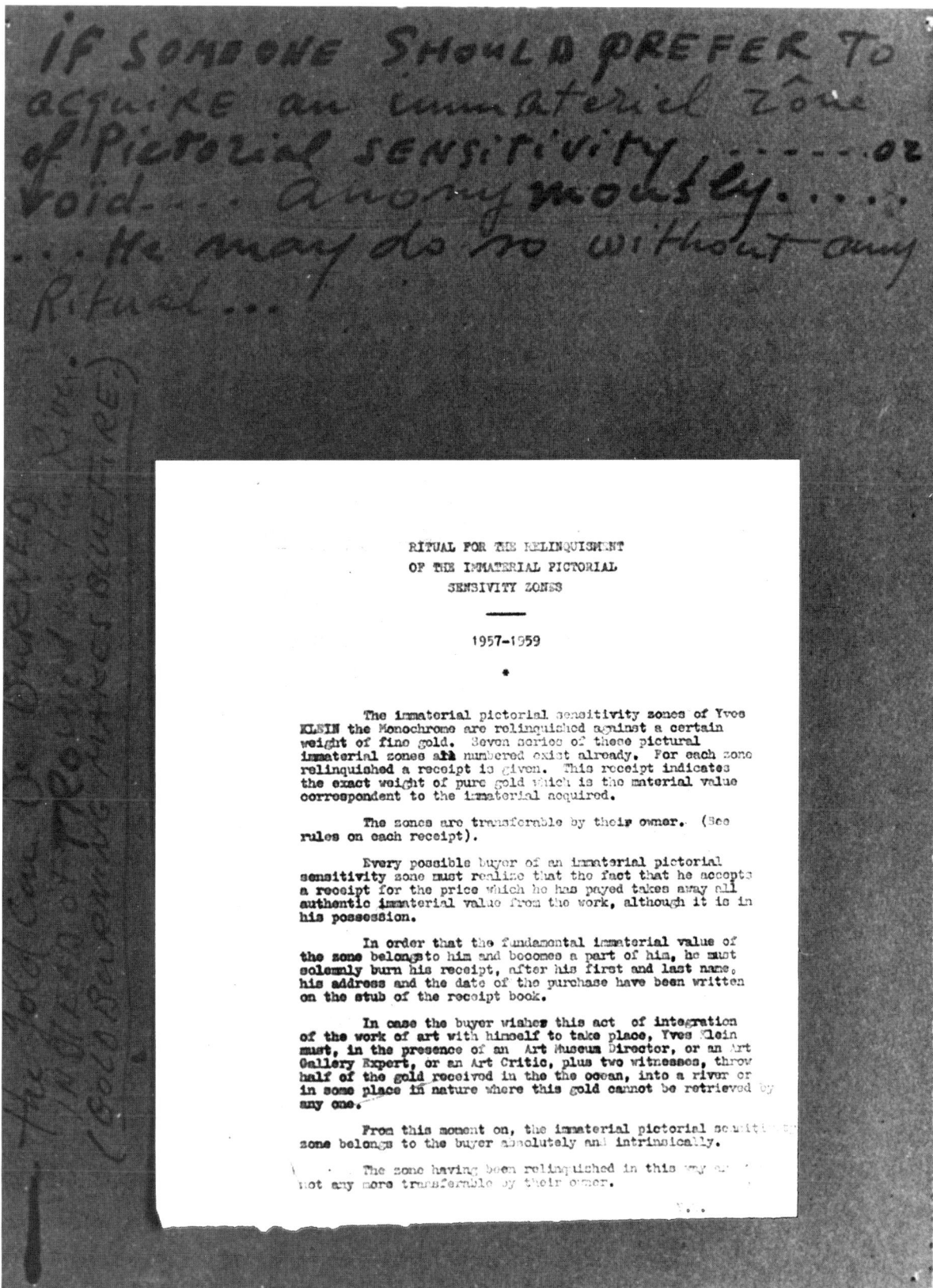

Klein's rules for ritual sales of *Zones of Immaterial Pictorial Sensibility*

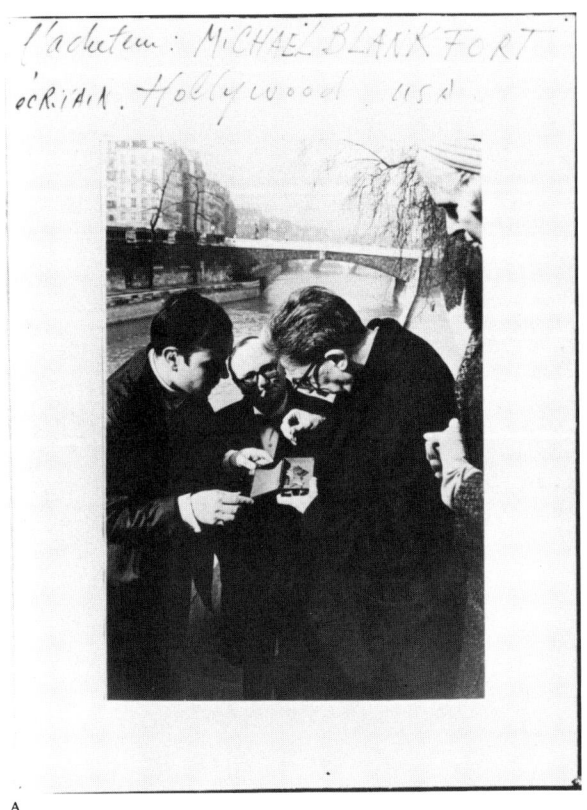

A

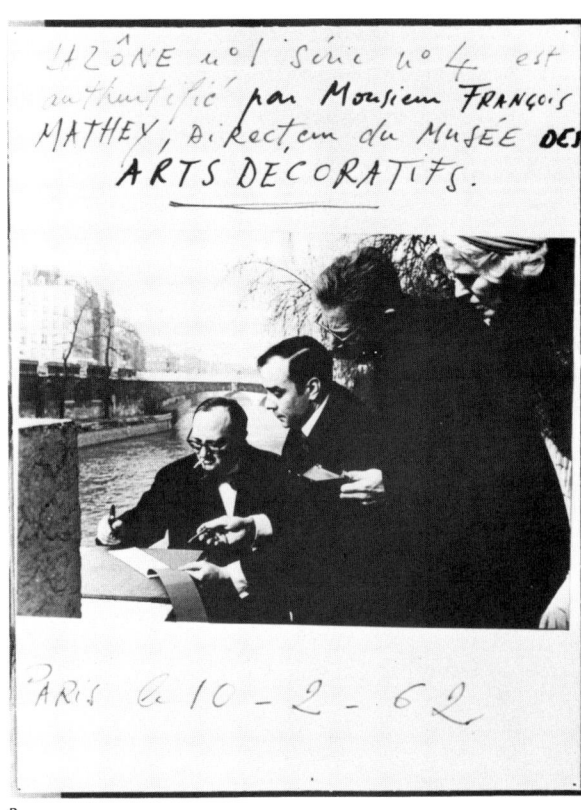

B

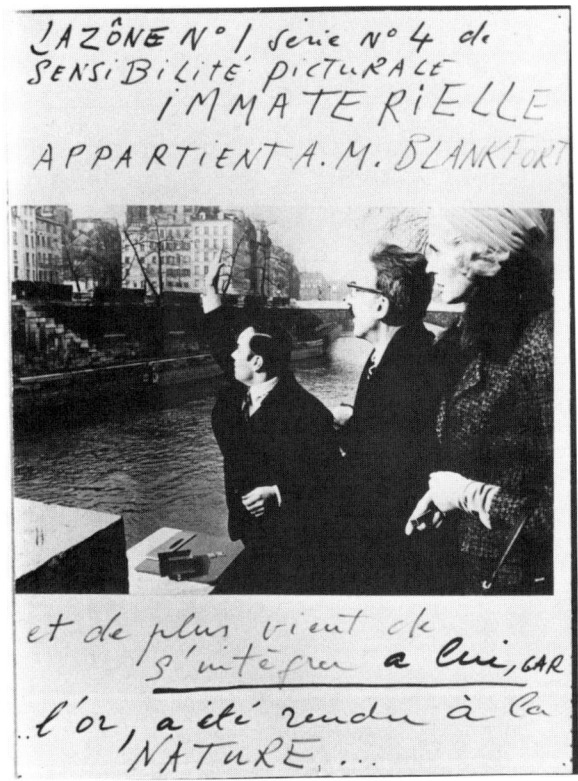

E

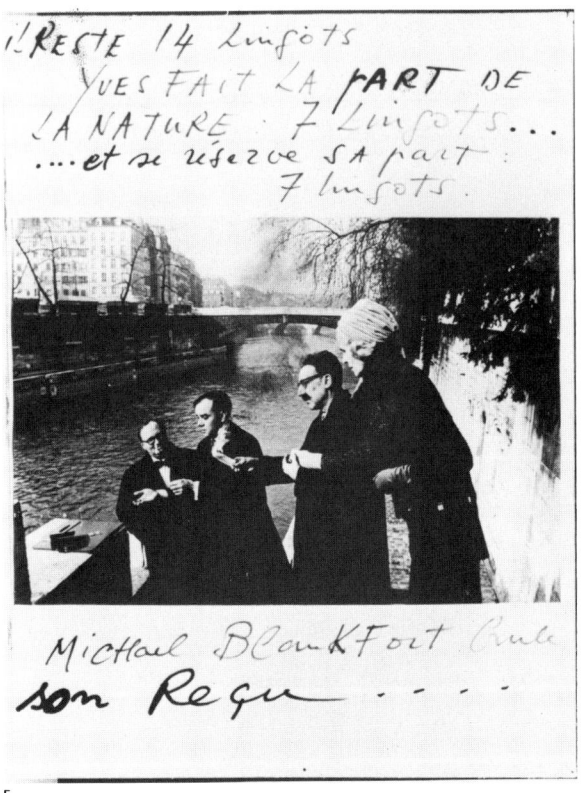

F

The ritual for a *Zone of Immaterial Pictorial Sensibility,* with Klein's notations (see cat. no. 101)

20 Grammes (soit deux lingots sont remis au Directeur du MUSÉE

commission pour le Musée qui a Authentifié l'œuvre immatérielle.)

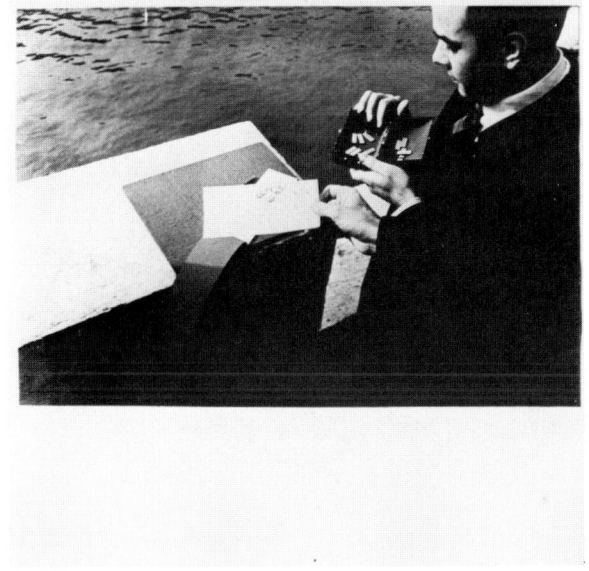

C

7 Lingots d'or Fin
soit
70 Grammes vont être jetés dans la Seine

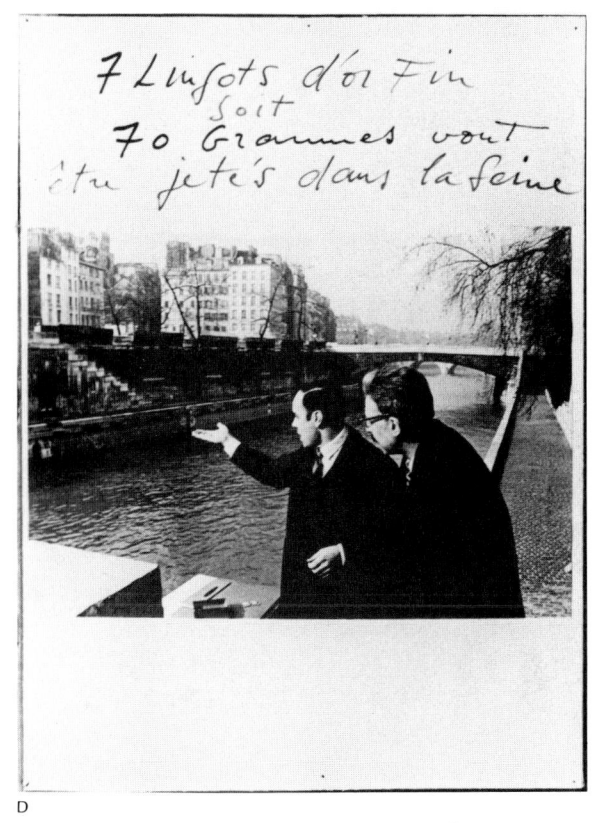

D

"DE LA MATIÈRE POUR DE L'IMMATÉRIEL."
"DE L'OR POUR LE VIDE"

TÉMOINS : Mr BLANKFORT, Mr
BORDEAUX. LEPECQ, Prés. "Henri SALON
COMPARAISONS", Mr VIRGINIA KONDRATIEF
de la DWAN GALLERY, LOS ANGELES,
Mr Jean LARCADE — Mr Jamin de Goldschmit
Mr PIERRE DESCARGUES.

G

VENTE-CESSION DE LA ZÔNE
N°1 de la SÉRIE N° 4.
160. Grammes d'or FIN (999,9)
contre SENSIBILITÉ PICTURALE IMMATÉRIELLE

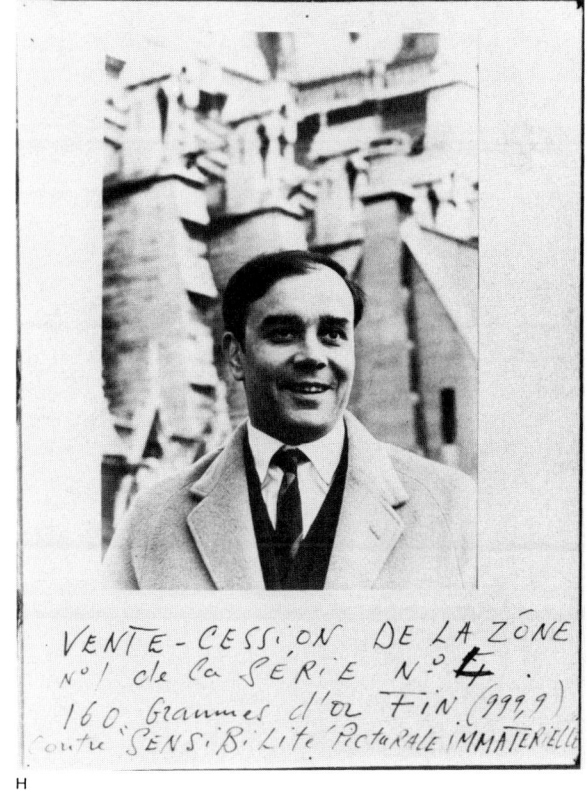

H

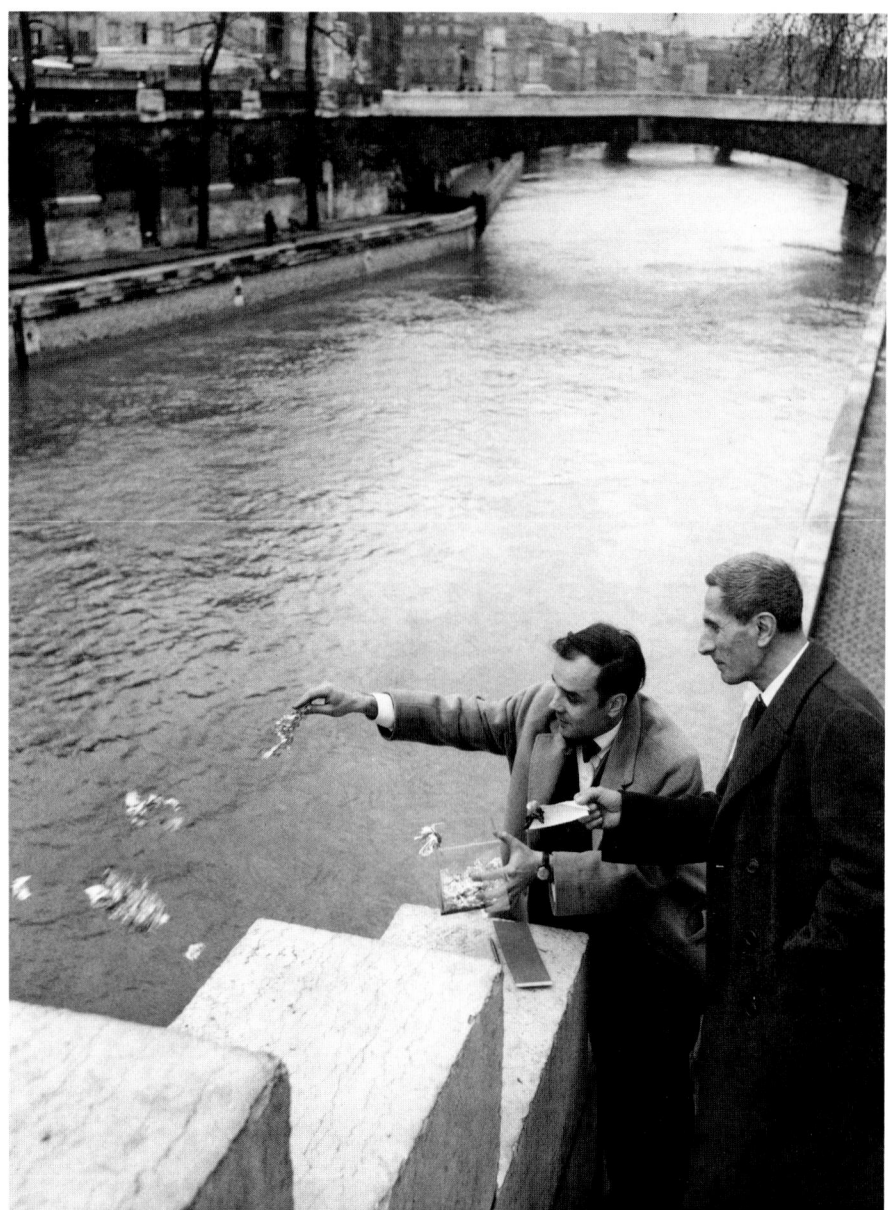

The ritual for a *Zone of Immaterial Pictorial Sensibility* (see cat. no. 102, item 5)

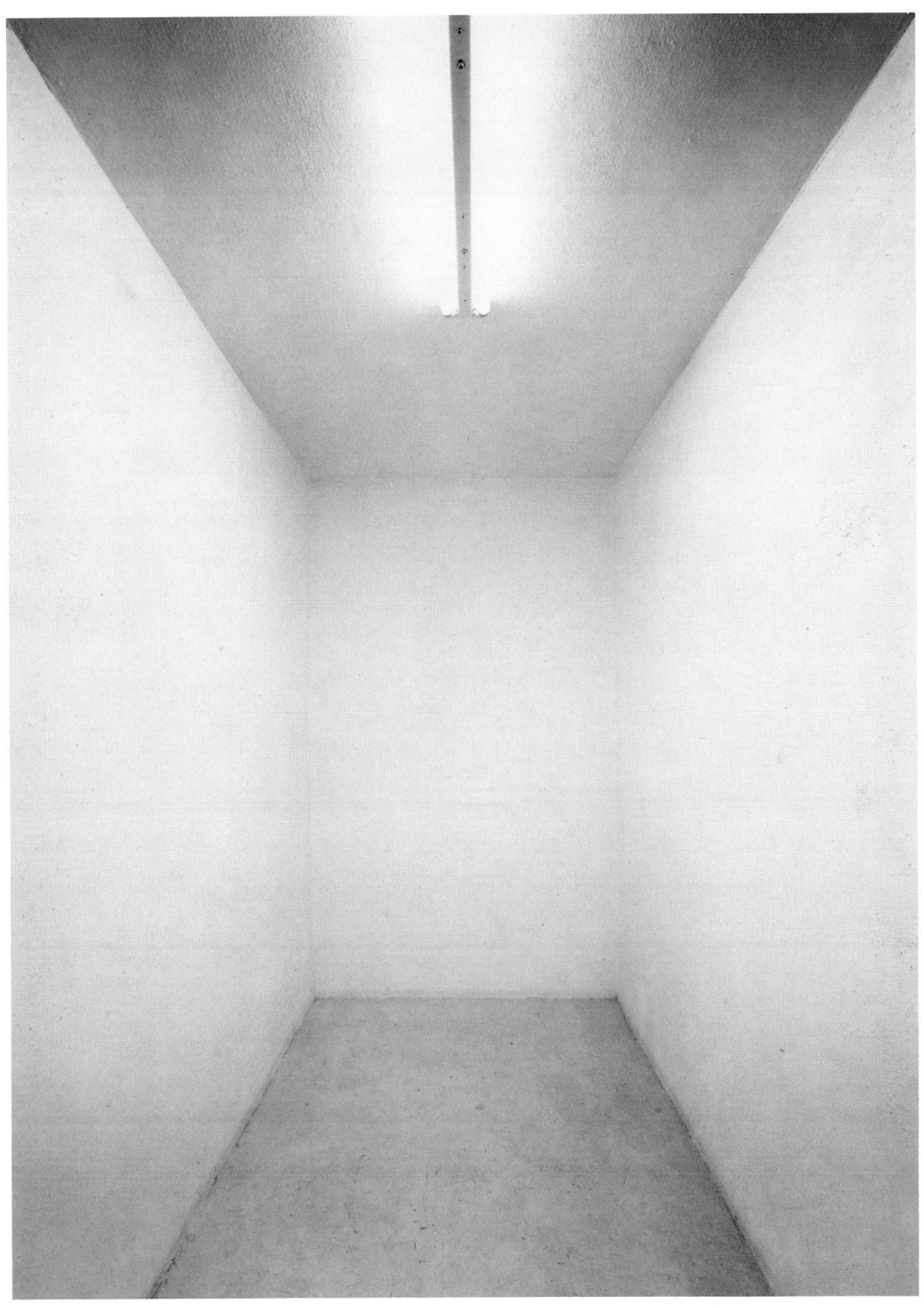

Klein's *Immaterial Room* at the Museum Haus Lange, Krefeld, Germany, 1961 (see cat. nos. 101 and 103)

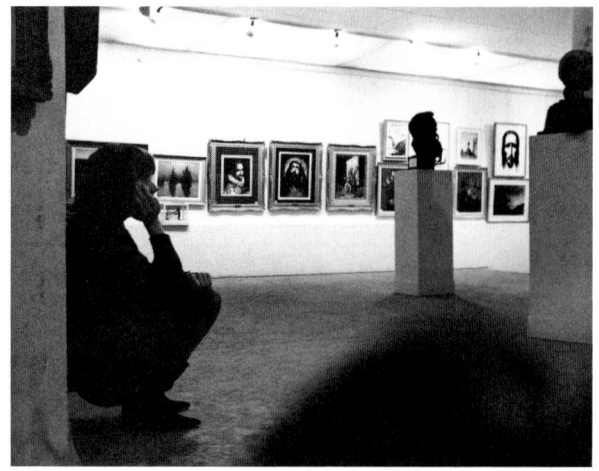

A

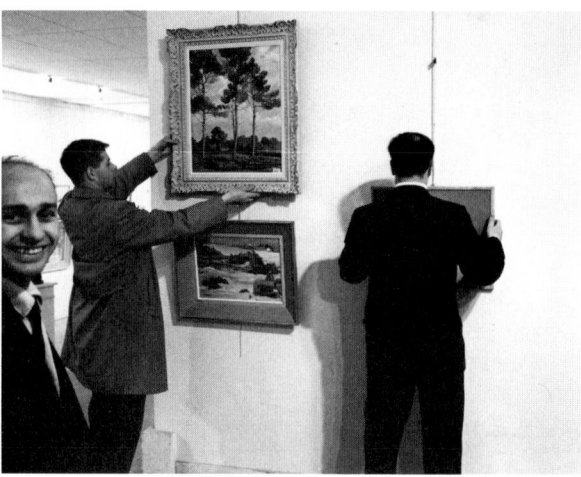

D

107. Removing Paintings from a Gallery to Make a Void, January 26, 1962; conceptual performance at the Musée d'Art Moderne de la Ville de Paris

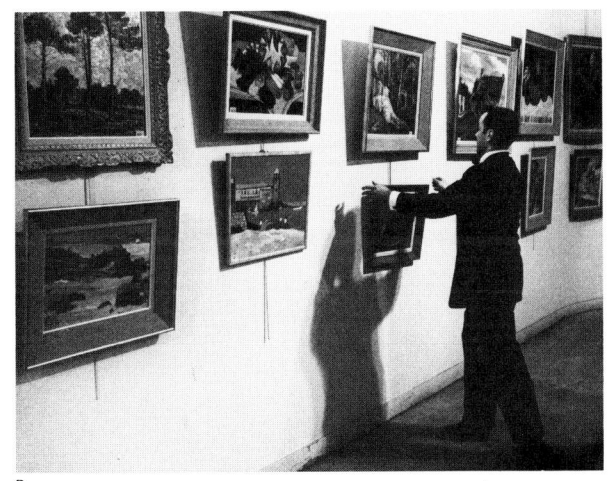

B

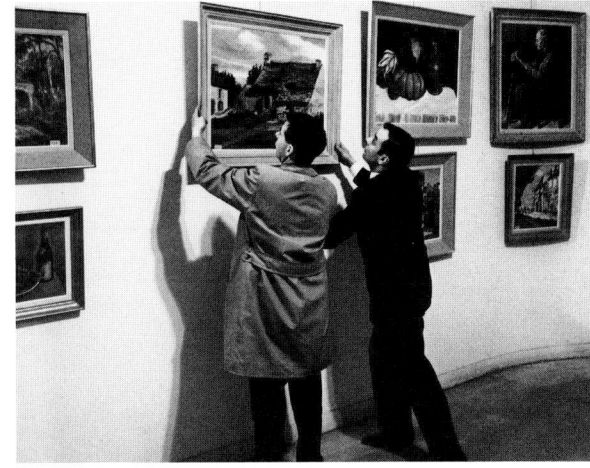

C

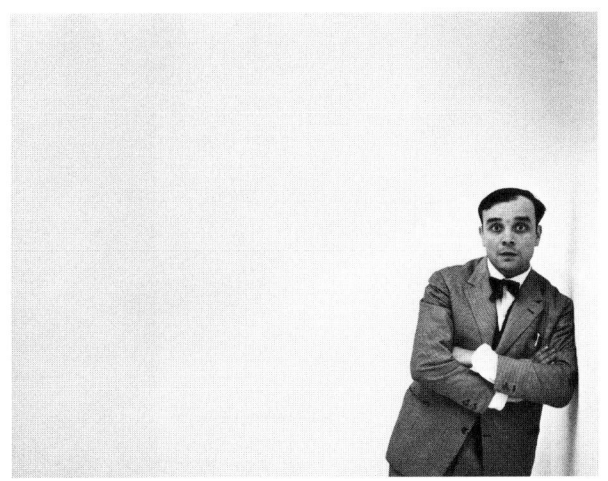

E

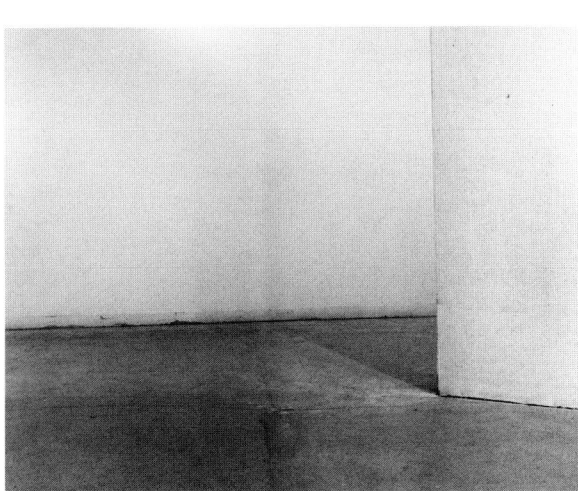

F

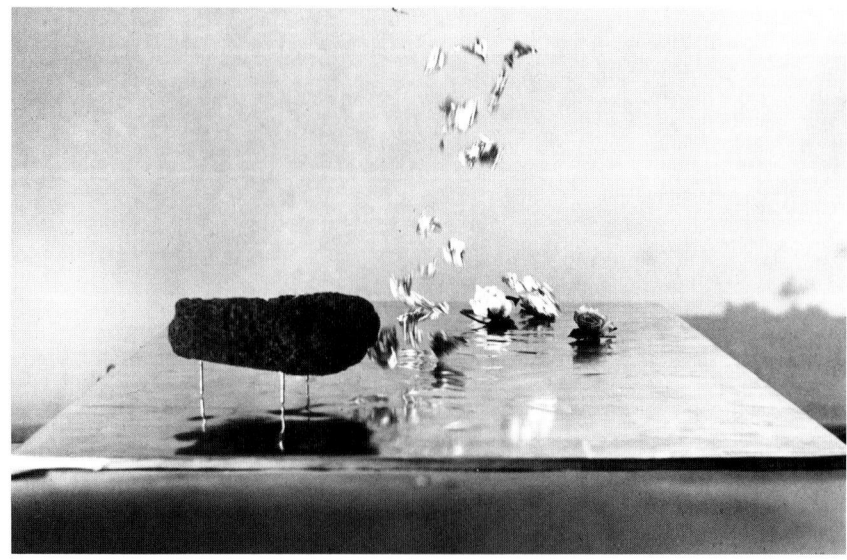

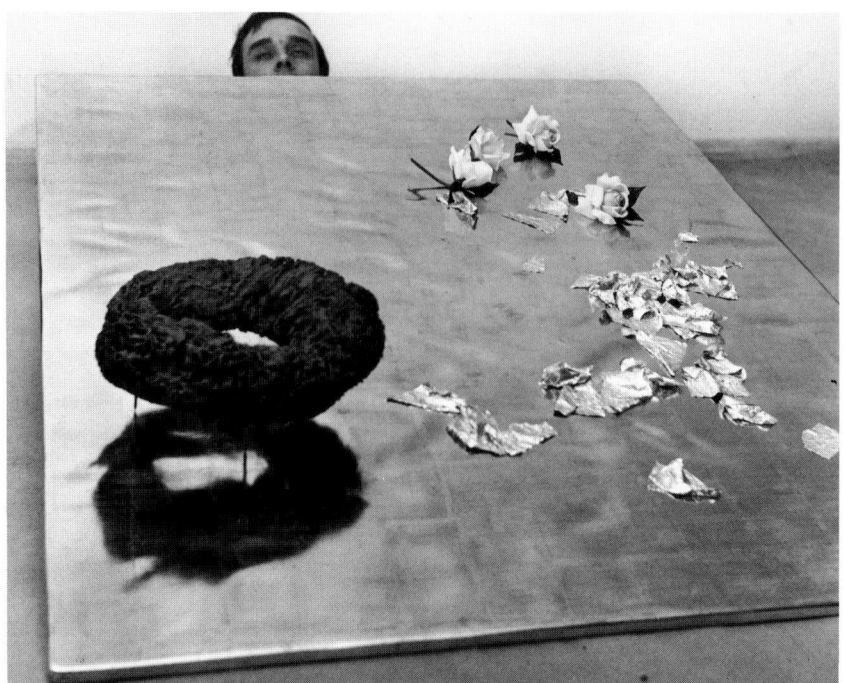

108.   Klein beneath *The Tomb—Here Lies Space*, March 30, 1962

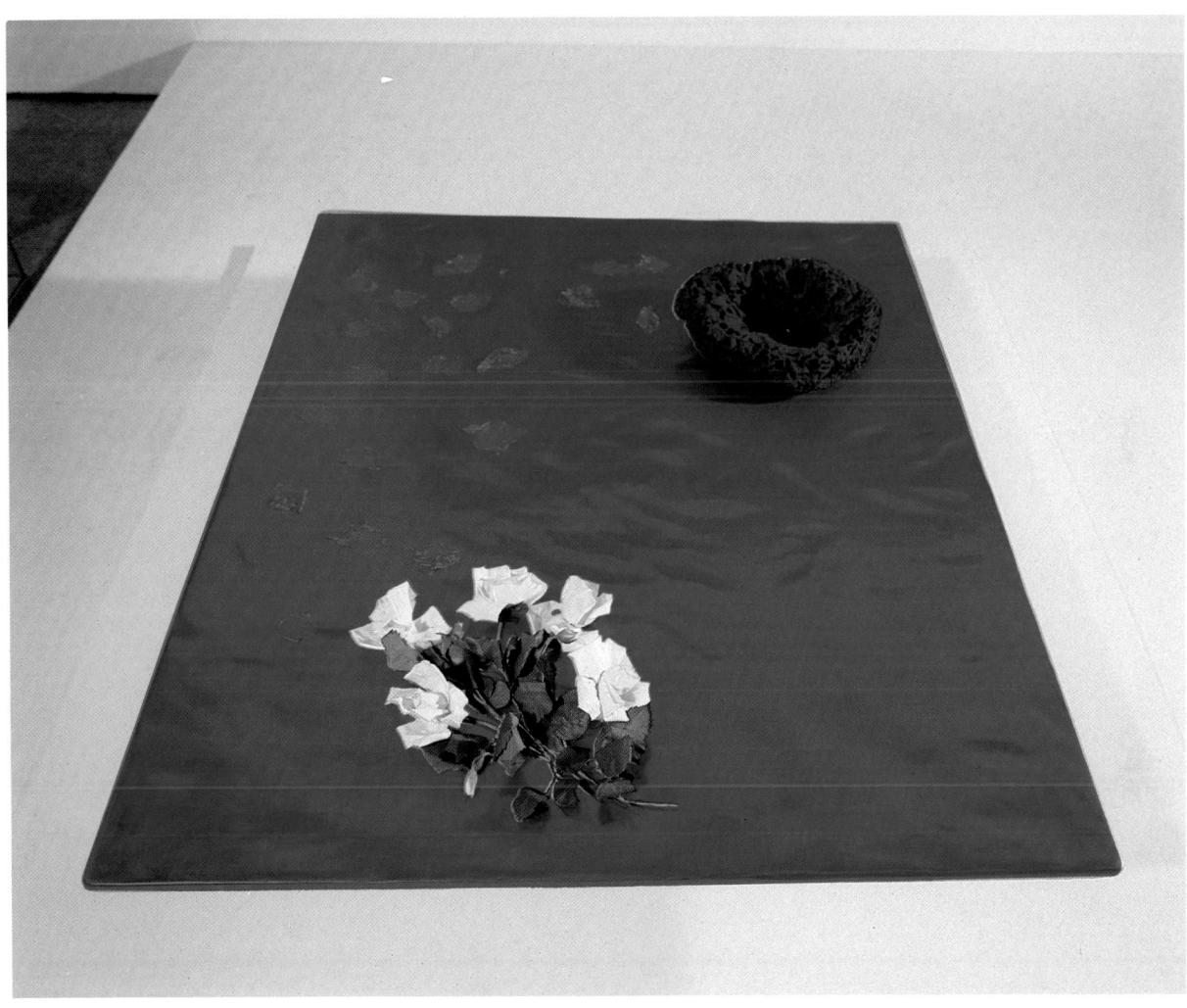

La Tombe—ci-gît l'espace (The Tomb—Here Lies Space), 1960; monogold with blue sponge-wreath and pink artificial roses; 125 × 100 (49¼ × 39⅜); collection Musée National d'Art Moderne, Centre Georges Pompidou

Selected Writings

Yves Klein

Selections from "The War: A Little Personal Mythology of the Monochrome"

[In the beginning] pure color, the universal soul in which the human soul was bathing in a state of earthly paradise, was mastered by the invasion of line, imprisoned, compartmentalized, cut apart, returned to slavery. In the joy and delirium of its guileful victory, line subjugated man and imprinted on him its abstract rhythm.

When the first moment of stupefaction had passed, prehistoric man realized that he had lost his vision. Seeking it, he came across the form called figurative. Realism and abstraction combined in a horrible, Machiavellian mixture which became earthly life—but is really a living death, the "horrible cage" of which Van Gogh spoke millennia later.

Having enslaved color, line proceeded to become writing. Writing elaborated a false reality, the physical, figurative reality, making it possible for line to organize itself definitively in the conquered terrain. The goal of line was to open man's eyes to the exterior world of matter which surrounds him and permits his approach to realism. Meanwhile, color vision retreated deep inside man, becoming more and more distant without being able to leave him altogether. Thus was created what some experience as an atrocious void, others as a stormy and romantic wonderment—the interior life, the life of the soul torn apart by the ascendancy of line.

Color—soiled, humiliated, defeated—prepared its revenge over long ages. Heroic, it made signs to man so that he felt the need to paint rising from far off in himself, from beyond his own soul; this was the first sign of the feeling-body's desire for liberation in space.

Color winked its eye at man, from the forms within which it had been enclosed by drawing. Millennia would pass before man understood these desperate appeals and turned himself feverishly to the task of setting free both color and himself.

Paradise had been lost. The entanglement of lines became the bars of a real prison which increasingly dominated human psychological life. The drama of the inevitable death of "mortals" when they had been carried away by the stormy coexistence of line and color in a state of war provoked the birth of art. Color and drawing adapted to each other, and a life took form and installed itself which, though livable, was basically deathly. Deceived by the illusion of peace between the two enemies, civilizations dedicated themselves to the pictorial arts. The great myths were born. Color, like line, rose or fell in value as the times changed.

The history of art is the soul of the history of nations. Happy nations have no history. But happy nations are those among whom peace reigns; and for a history of art to exist, as for a history of nations, it is quite simply necessary that there be war.

Yet it is the invisible bond, the glue which holds the universe together through time, and which is eternal, which should be perceived and transmitted in the creation of art. True artists should be prophets of a peace which is deep and violent in its intensity, and stronger than destructive war.

Today at last, line has bound itself by its own limitations to such a point that the absolute must be rediscovered. Line is disappearing at last. It is being transformed into shapes without contours, or nearly so, and is filling up the surface again in an almost uniform way. Jealous of color, which is the true inhabitant of space, line is trying to free itself from the condition of tourist in space. It is dissolving itself and invading the picture plane. Evolution calls for this initiation, which will put everything back in order again. It is not the false and dishonest "Peace of Nations," but that unspeakable peace which prevailed in both nature and man before the first intrusion of line into color.

No more linear psychological bars! Before the colored surface one finds oneself directly before the matter of the soul.

The true painter of the future will be a mute poet who will write nothing but will recount, without speech and in silence, an immense picture without limits.

It is incomprehensible, unreasonable, and nonetheless true, that throughout the long history of art, artists have almost always chosen as their most emotional themes things which are ephemeral and unreal.

The child is in bed. The room is dark. He closes his eyes and presses his fingers against his eyelids, and he sees great flames; he sees them, and they are there, where his eyes are, in fact deeper inside his head. And yet there is nothing there, no inside, no outside, no objects, no eyes. The child sees intense color in complete simplicity. He presses his hands on his eyes and there is a marvelous assemblage of linked lozenges, flowing like water, soft as velvet, which become liquid and pour out phosphorescent light like a flowering bush at night.

But this astonishing light is not of the day or of the night. It is unchanging, yet trembles sweetly. It is always there inside the head. And will it stay there always? The color is more beautiful than any colors on the earth, sumptuous like color charged with thoughts of the garden, without the appearance yet of old moldy matter. The child calls its mother and asks, "What is it that you see when your eyes are closed?" At first the mother doesn't understand; he explains; then she says: "Don't do that! You'll go blind."

The interior light is all color.

I have felt, before paintings that live and speak, a sensation of being imprisoned and looking through bars (which are the lines in the painting) at the real and free life of a world of color. I think this is what Van Gogh meant when he asked to be set free, by the alchemy of painting, from "I know not what horrible cage."

All this will be mocked by most people, who believe that the answer lies in balance, in achieving a balance between line and color. But balance is a *tour de force* which requires constant attention to maintain. It is a horrible and false solution which keeps people blind, because they are so occupied with their infinite precautions in weighing carefully the pros and cons of everything that they see nothing and pass to the wayside of life.

As soon as events become dark, there is an invasion of the picture plane by lines. The difficult periods of a civilization, or of the personal life of an artist, are immediately striated and darkened by lines appearing in their pictorial art. To return to balance then has no value. Life must be sought anew in its own element, its own species, its very self, its dominant. And the human dominant is color. All the immense evolution across the ages proves this, by leading up to the discovery of the mystery of color. It is an organic tendency, rising from the deepest strata of ourselves, that pushes us today toward the rediscovery of color, which is our life.

A painter is a man who, consciously or not, cuts apart and destroys his own soul, with or without sorrow, or even with joy, to transform the scraps of his soul, through the alchemy of painting, into physical, ephemeral matter for the picture.

The painter, like Christ, says the mass when he paints, and gives his own body and soul as nourishment to others. In a small way he realizes the mystery of the Last Supper in each painting.

Originally printed in Klein's *Dimanche, le journal d'un seul jour*, published November 27, 1960. Edited and translated by Thomas McEvilley.

Selections from "The Monochrome Adventure"

Through color, I experience a feeling of complete identification with space, I am truly free.

If a color is no longer pure, the drama may take on disquieting overtones.

For those who don't know what it is, total freedom is dangerous.

Certain people, confronted by my monochrome paintings, often ask "But what does it represent?" I might answer as I used to, that it quite simply represents blue in itself, or red, or even, for example, that it's the landscape of the world of the color yellow: that would be correct yet more important, to my mind, is that by painting one color for its own sake, I break with the "spectacle" of the ordinary, conventional, classic easel-painting.

I am in favor of more line, more design; why not, then, of two colors?

Well, because I refuse to provide a spectacle in my painting. I refuse to compare and put in play, so that some stronger element will emerge in contrast to other, weaker ones.

Even the most civilized representation is based on an idea of "combat" between different forces, and the onlooker assists at a death-scene in a painting, a drama, morbid by definition as it's a question of love and hate.

For me, the painting is an individual, I want to consider it as such and not judge, above all, not judge it!

As soon as there are two colors in a painting, combat begins; the permanent spectacle of this battle of two colors may give the onlooker a subtle psychological and emotional pleasure, that is nonetheless morbid from a purely human, philosophical point of view.

Of two people, I wish absolutely not to choose the better according to traditional and taught criteria, unless I am absolutely certain; or to reject one unless always keeping him by the other's side to conclusively prove that I've chosen the better!

I know that this reign of cruelty has existed and still does; for me it is living death, sweating morbidity, obscurantism and, above all, the ferocious condemnation of freedom.

Like the impressionists, of whom I regard myself as a continuator, especially like Delacroix, of whom I regard myself as the disciple, I have encounters with sympathetic things as they are, a real or imaginary landscape, an object, a person, or simply a new sensitivity I come across, an atmosphere.

From the mute conversation that follows between these states of things and myself, an impal-

pable affinity is born, "indefinable" as Delacroix said. It is this "indefinable," this ineffable poetic moment that I wish to fix on my canvas according to my mode of being (notice, I don't say expression) and thus make a painting. I paint, then, the pictorial moment born of an illumination by impregnation in life itself.

To experience spirit without explanation, without a vocabulary, and to represent this sensation. It is this that had led me to monochrome!

For me, art in painting is to produce, to create freedom in its raw state.

Color, in nature and man, is saturated with the cosmic sensitivity, a sensitivity without recesses, like humidity. For me, color is sensitivity "materialized."

It is saturated with the all just as everything is that's indefinable, formless, limitless sensitivity. It is, indeed, the abstract spacematter.

Line may be infinite, as wit is, but it lacks the ability to fill the immeasurable all, to impregnate itself with it, that color has.

"Wit is capable of many things, Sir," Delacroix wrote, "it is an adroit intelligent being, quick to profit from its neighbor's weakness, who knows how to lie low in the passions' storm, but worth is a strong fellow whom nothing can resist, who goes against wind and tide, and marches straight to his goal."

Taking this up, I would like to say: "Line is capable of many things, Sir, it is an adroit intelligent being, quick to profit from its neighbor's weakness, who knows how to lie low in the passions' storm. But color is a strong fellow whom nothing can resist, who goes against wind and tide, and marches straight to his goal."

For me, colors are living beings, highly developed individuals that become part of us, as of everything. Colors are the true inhabitants of space. Line merely travels through, crosses; it merely passes by. Every nuance, although of the same family as the base color, nonetheless has its own, autonomous life, a fact which makes it immediately clear that painting in one color is not limited; there are myriads of nuances of all colors, each with its particular worth.

The painting is merely the witness, the sensitive plate that has recorded what's happened. Color, in the chemical form in which all painters use it, is the best suited to be this medium of the event. My paintings represent poetic events or, rather, are immobile, silent, static witnesses of that essential movement and free life which, in the pictorial moment, is a flame of poetry!

What Pierre Restany has called my monochrome propositions (I've called them "paintings" outright) preserve the objective aspect of the traditional painting because in fact they are props to color.

Different-sized panels of wood or [Masonite] (size and chromatic value are not in general related), they are covered with a very thin, tight canvas. This canvas is to receive the color, after a scrupulous priming. A single color whose tone, once determined from the mixing of various pigments, will be uniform. I think one may fairly suppose, here, a sort of modern-day alchemy practiced by painters, born of the tension of experiencing each instant of pictorial matter, a bath in space vaster than infinity. At my second Paris exhibition at Colette Allendy, in 1956, I presented a selection of propositions of different colors and sizes. What I required of the public was that "moment of truth" mentioned by Pierre Restany in his preface to the exhibition, to free their mind from external contamination, and achieve that stage of contemplation in which color becomes pure, full sensitivity.

Unfortunately, as became evident from the manifestations that followed, in particular a debate sponsored by Colette Allendy, many spectators, victims of a conditioned way of seeing, insisted on a rapport between these different propositions (rapport of colors, values, dimensions, and architectural combinations): the elements, for them, of a reconstituted decorative polychrome. This led me to take the initiative and present, this time in Italy at the Galleria Apollinaire in Milan, an exhibition dedicated to what I ventured to call my Blue Period. (I had already spent more than a year, in fact, seeking the most perfect expression of "Blue").

This exhibition consisted of ten deep sea blue paintings, very similar in tone, value, proportion and size. The lively controversies that followed were proof of its worth and the real profundity of the surprise it caused intelligent people, unwilling to passively endure the sclerosis of accepted concepts and set rules.

These apparently exactly similar propositions in blue were recognized by the public to be quite diverse. The spectator went from one to the other, acquiescing in an instantaneous contemplation of blue worlds.

But each painting's blue world, although of the same blue and identical in execution, revealed an entirely other essence and atmosphere; none resembled each other, any more than do pictorial moments and poetic moments. Though all alike in nature, superior and subtle (the charting of the immaterial).

I decided now to penetrate further into this newly conquered terrain; the physical painting owes its existence to the sole fact of one's seeing it, even as one is obscurely aware of the essential presence of something else, more important in a very different way.

I thought, then, that the Blue Period's sequel would be the presentation to the public of pictorial sensitivity, the "poetic energy" of matter's impalpable liberty, unconcentrated and uncontracted.

It would be a truly informal painting, such as it is and should be! Thus, in my double exhibition in Paris, at Iris Clert and Colette Allendy in 1957, I presented, in one room of the [second] floor at Colette Allendy, a series of surfaces of pictorial sensitivity, invisible indeed to the naked eye, yet very present.

Painters are not, as is sometimes claimed, creators in the primary sense.

Paintings are living, autonomous presences; this fact is crucial because it proves that artistic creation is something subtler, much subtler than one thinks, even while being *real*. This reminds me, in its own way, of the Cathare movement of the Middle Ages.

Paintings create atmospheres, sensitive climates, phenomenal states and particular natures, perceptible yet not tangible.

To be exact, all objects and states of matter do also; but some less than others: paintings are nearer to perfection in their genre, shall we say.

The painter should resemble paintings which end by being examples, in a sense, because they create, they truly procreate art. They derive from that phenomenal substance which may be said to be that of pictorial sensitivity, of liberty in its raw state, of life, in fact, refined and made available to our higher perceptions, of the states of pure, abstract things.

This is why I often repeat, despite the deprecatory smiles of my colleagues, that it is valid to express "the best of oneself" only in that refining of space which constitutes the act of painting.

Paintings are examples, then, for the painters who produce them, who do not paint paintings because they no longer need to assure themselves in this way that they exist, that they, also, can create. Freed from such psychological pressures, they know and are paintings, quite simply yet also quite astonishingly.

At this stage of sensitivity (not to be confused with sentimentality) one may extract a painting, a "truth" from a work, which has remained in it long enough to refine its space, and thus immediately perceive that its absence, its presence having been very distinct, with the psychological effect of a support, allows one to safely expose oneself to the full void of pictorial sensitivity.

But having gotten used to its absence, one notices the new presence derived from and created by its physical sojourn; a kind of presence-presence, autonomous and different from all other phenomenal states in this work from which the painting is absent.

It's a question, really, of a creation of art, pure, true art. And no longer of suggestion, of picturesque this and that, crystallization of desires, or of a psychological state, etc. etc....

It was in 1947 that I had the "idea," the conscious vision of "monochrome." I should stress that it came to me intellectually; it was the result of passionate research.

At "Judo" (1947), a Rosicrucian cosmogony (a jazz interpretation of Max Heindel, Oceanside, California), I played the piano and dreamed of having a great orchestra, of composing, with music of a single tone, a "monochrome" symphony (not necessarily like jazz in spirit or rhythm), a single musical mass saturated with space, a melody melted into one note throughout. (By the way, I composed this symphony two years later in 1949. The "sound" was deprived of a beginning and end by an electronic process and thus came from space even while remaining in it, and reentered it in a return to silence; duration, twenty minutes). I also painted and drew during this period (1946-7) but not much: the fact that my mother and father were painters annoyed me and alienated me from painting. Thanks to them, however, I was aware of the most extremely avant-garde theories in painting. I was unconsciously trying, because of all this, to go even further.

It was in these circumstances that, I don't really know how, my research had led me to the gaudy painting, in gouache, of surfaces of monochrome spots in a sort of pointillism, but with only one color; then, thanks to youthful temerity and energy, I suppose, I decided to discard all this and cover the surface with one, uniform, scrupulously monochrome color.

I did not actually realize the value of my discovery until two years later in London, in 1949.

To earn my living, I worked illegally for about a year in the Old Brompton Road frame shop of Robert Savage, a friend of my father. It was there, assisting in the preparation of size, colors, varnish, of gilt bases, that I became familiar with the material, with han-

dling it "in bulk." In giving the frames coat after coat, in sandpapering them, in carefully eliminating the least spot or blemish, I arrived at a beautiful white distemper, pure, clean, and dry. This, after the second coat, was a very pale gray red or clear pink. It was necessary to repeatedly examine the surface from about two inches away (my eyesight was perfectly normal) to see if the desired consistency, effect of blurring, softness or roughness had been achieved.

And then, what gold! These leaves that literally fluttered in a breath of air, on the flat cushion which one held in one hand, with the other trapping them with a knife. Or with one's comb. The leaf that one delicately placed on the surface to be gilded, previously coated with a base and wet with gelatinous water. What matter! What better school in which to learn respect for pictorial matter! And then the polishing, like an agate....

I experienced the illumination of matter, its physicality and depth, that year at "SAVAGE." In my room at night, I did gouache monochromes on pieces of white cardboard, using, also, more and more pastels. I was very fond of pastel's tone. It seemed to me that, in this pastel-matter, each grain of pigment remained utterly free and itself without being killed by the fixative; I did very large paintings in this mode but, alas, either fixed with a vaporizer they lost their brightness of tone and became dull, or un-fixed they irretrievably decayed and gradually turned to dust: the color kept its beauty without the pictorial strength.

I disliked colors ground in oil. They seemed dead to me; what pleased me above all were pure pigments, in powder, such as I saw them in the windows of retail paint-sellers. They had brightness and extraordinary, autonomous lives of their own. This was essential color. Living tangible colormatter.

It was depressing to see such glowing powder, once mixed in distemper or whatever medium intended as a fixative, lose its value, tarnish, become dull. One might obtain effects of paste but after drying it wasn't the same; the effective color magic had vanished.

Each grain of pigment seemed to have been individually killed by the size or whatever ingredient intended to connect it with the others, as well as the base.

Irresistibly attracted to this new monochrome manner, I decided to undertake the technical research necessary to find a medium capable of fixing the pure pigment to the base, without altering it. The color value would thus be represented in a pictorial way. The possibility of leaving the grains of pigment entirely free, such as they are in powder, mixed perhaps yet separate, even while exactly similar, seemed to me inducement enough. "Art is total freedom, and life: as soon as it's confined by any manner, it suffers damage; freedom and life are diminished according to the degree of confinement."

To leave this pigment powder free, such as I'd seen it at the paint-sellers, even while presenting it as a painting, one would simply have had to spread it on dirt. Gravity would have held it to the earth without altering it. At the time, I didn't consider this solution acceptable to the plastic arts public, even at its most permissive. I had already done one "Snow Job"—this wasn't another! Also, I had committed myself to the classical pictorial form, i.e. I was doing monochrome paintings.

My technique was, and still is, although at a much more advanced stage of course, as follows: I decided to retain the classic, rectangular shape so as not to shock the onlooker who thus would see a color surface rather than a flat color form. My desire at that time was to present, with an effect of slight artificiality, an opening on the world of the color represented, an open window on one's freedom to saturate oneself, in an infinite, unlimited way, with the immeasurable state of color. I wanted to offer the public a possibility of the illumination of pictorial, essential colormatter, impregnated with which all physical things, stones, rocks, bottles, clouds, become pretext for the voyage of human sensitivity in the cosmic sensitivity, unlimited, of everything.

Before one of my color surfaces the ideal onlooker would become, only as regards his sensitivity of course, "extradimensional" to the point of being "all in all," saturated with the sensitivity of the universe.

Line will enable you to do anything, to cut through the most secret strata of the mysteries of your unconscious, but it will never reveal the life of sensitivity. Its one victory will be that of sensuality.

Line, in the last analysis, can only suggest; while color "is."

It is a self-sufficient presence which the artist can endow with a particular life, putting it to the use of human sensitivity.

The scenes of the life of Jesus described in the gospel are vividly present to us, almost physically so; more than a story, more than a representation, they are a presence. Not one color is mentioned, neither face nor landscape described: we are constantly face to face and alone with "states."

I want to create works which will be spirit and mind.

WATER AND FIRE

The sculptor Norbert Kricke, for some time past, has been studying how to create Art with the material "water." As he himself says, it was necessary to *become* water to actually realize the full range of fluidic possibilities, and thus evolve a new hydraulic conception of art. His "hydrodynamics" corresponding to my own "pneumatic" conception of art, we decided to collaborate and, as a beginning, to create water and fire fountains; as creators we divided and shared the provinces and kingdom of the elements as follows:

KRICKE: *water* and *light.*

YVES: *air* (plus wind: the anger of sensitivity) and *fire.*

With his water fountains, KRICKE represents the plastic element of coolness in warm countries (a psychological rather than actual effect; water in public places of warm countries brings little real coolness; it's mostly the suggestion of coolness that is produced).

Thanks to air, I can produce real coolness in my collaboration with him. In this way: I cause great cold gusts of treated air to strike the water on all sides and in one main direction, continually modelling it like a living, glittering matter, and creating a genuine freshness within the chosen area. The water and fire fountains represent for me, if we succeed in realizing them, the same type of phenomena as the biblical "cast-iron sea" project, botched as the Queen of Sheba looked on, that age not having been ready for such events as "the mixture of water and fire."

The fountains of light and fire will be even subtler, as those of air and water (gusts of wind against the cascade).

Today I can say: I have found joy again with my monochrome painting and...

TODAY

I want everything to be marvelous, in myself and everywhere, in all my gestures and acts and anything, I want always to create the constant state of happiness, of rediscovered total freedom and the profound, joyous gladness of living.

If I make *trompe-l'oeil* realistic paintings of banknotes, their various significations and symbols will interest me only in their exact statement to each level of understanding of their eventual spectator.

I am a painter: I will make something that will be painting in everybody's eyes, and also (why not?) full of wit. So much the worse for those who don't get it. As for myself, I wish to be happy; I don't even wish it, I am so already: as long as I live as an artist in the kingdom of art, of truth!

THE HUMAN ATTRIBUTE: "QUALITY"

I am for a sort of depersonalization in art.

The artist who creates should no longer do so for the sake of signing his work, but as an honest citizen of the immeasurable space of sensitivity should create always from his awareness that he exists in a state of profound illumination, as does all the universe, but which we neither see nor feel, closed in the psychological world of our inherited optics.

Through absolute art, i.e. the living illumination which I become by sealing myself in the worlds of works of art, by saturating myself with the eternal limitless sensitivity of space, I return to Eden, as I certainly feel; and this is why, in my art, I refuse more and more emphatically the illusion of personality, the transient psychology of the linear, the formal, the structural. I want to be a sane, strong, very normal man, to live in outward nature with all sensitivity, with all confidence, constantly experiencing the immense joy of being life itself, eternal life, to go out to my subject, as did all the figurative impressionist painters and those who loved a simple life full of honest, true poetry, with my easel, my colors and my canvas under my arm. Evidently the subject I'm travelling toward is space, pure spirit but then, this is the same as the country, or the marvelous beach which our true painters have loved before us; once there, I will create an immense, immaterial painting, of an incomparable stable, static quality and radiant with real movement; and, already being there, I will have no need of space-travel, unlike the wretched yet great Malevich, his ponderous, academic personality plunging dramatically into space with all the good will of a dazzled tourist:

"The sky's color having been conquered by the suprematist system," Malevich wrote, "it became white whose existence and essence *represent infinity*. I have conquered the pale depth of the colored sky, I have detached its color, put it in a creative sack, and tied the knot. Aviators of the future, fly! White, free and endless, *infinity is before you*."

Reprinted with permission from *Yves Klein*, catalogue of exhibition at the Jewish Museum, New York City, 1967, pp. 28-35. Edited by Marcelin Pleynet. Translated by Lane Dunlop. Copyright © 1967 the Jewish Museum. The original typescript of "The Monochrome Adventure" is in the Klein archive, Documentations Arts Plastiques, Musée National d'Art Moderne, Centre National d'Art et de Culture Georges Pompidou, Paris.

Preparation and Presentation of the Exhibition of 28 April 1958

Preparation and Presentation of the Exhibition
of 28 April 1958
at Iris Clert's
3, rue des Beaux-Arts, Paris
"The Specialization of Sensibility
from the Status of Raw Material into Stabilized
Pictorial Sensibility"
PNEUMATIC PERIOD
(Numerous details will be omitted, they
would be too numerous.)

The object of this endeavor: to create, establish, and present to the public a palpable pictorial state in the limits of a picture gallery. In other words, creation of an ambience, a genuine pictorial climate, and, therefore, an invisible one. This invisible pictorial state within the gallery space should be so present and endowed with autonomous life that it should literally be what has hitherto been regarded as the best overall definition of painting: "radiance."

Invisible and intangible, this immaterialization of the picture — if the creative operation on the vessels or sensitive bodies of the visitors to the exhibition succeeds — must work much more effectively than ordinary, material, usual, representative pictures. These latter, when they are obviously good pictures, are also imbued with this special pictorial essence, this affective presence — in a word, with sensibility; however, in them it is transmitted through the suggestion of the entire physical and psychological appearance of the picture: lines, contours, forms, composition, opposition of colors, etc.... [Ellipses are Klein's throughout.] In the present case there are no such intermediaries: one finds oneself being literally impregnated by the sensitive pictorial state, previously specialized and stabilized by the painter in the given space, and this is direct and immediate perception-assimilation, devoid of any other effect, trick, or deception.

To this end, then, we compose with Iris Clert the invitation card to the opening. The text is by Pierre Restany. This brilliantly laconic text is very clear and we decide, in view of the importance of this exhibition for the history of art, to have it engraved on informals in London script, for the sake of solemn ceremony and especially so that the blind can read it. (They are all that — blind! Nothing pejorative or aggressive intended.) The ink used will be blue, obviously, printed on white cards.

This method, which seems to smack of Symbolism, is really not that, since in fact everything happens in space. It provides a fitting foretaste of what the exhibition will be: in actuality a space of Blue sensibility in the frame of the whitened walls of the gallery. (This sensitive body contains Blue blood.) A decision is also made to send out the invitations in envelopes bearing the formidable blue stamp of the blue period of the previous year.

Iris Clert invites you to honor, with all your affective presence, the lucid and actual event of a certain reign of the sensitive. This demonstration of perceptive synthesis sanctions, in the works of Yves Klein, the pictorial quest for an ecstatic and immediately communicable emotion.
(Opening, 3, rue des Beaux-Arts, Monday, April 28, 9–12 P.M.)
Pierre Restany

Thirty-five hundred invitations are sent, 3,000 of them in Paris alone. We decide also to add a sort of free entry card, stipulating that without this special little card the price of admission will be 1,500 francs [approximately three dollars] per person.

Invitation for
TWO PERSONS
from April 28 to May 5
For any person not furnished with this card
the price of admission is 1,500 francs.

This ploy is necessary because, although the pictorial sensibility I am exhibiting is for sale either piecemeal or in a single block, visitors endowed with a vessel or body open to sensibility will be able, despite me — notwithstanding the fact that I will exert all my strength toward keeping the entire exhibition together — to steal from me by impregnation, whether consciously or not, some degree of its intensity. And that, that especially should be paid for. After all, 1,500 francs is not really very much.

(For publicity: two big posters on the Place Saint-Germain-des-Prés, for just five days before the exhibition, blue letters in relief on a white background. Text: Galerie IRIS CLERT, 3, rue des Beaux-Arts, YVES LE MONOCHROME, April 28–May 5. Then we announce the exhibition with a simple notice inserted in *Arts* and *Combat* for Paris and in *Arts* for America.)

Next, we decide on the scenic arrangement and the material presentation of the exhibition.

The Galerie Iris Clert is very small: 20 square meters; it has a show window and an entrance on the street. We will close the street entrance and make the public enter through the lobby of the building, where there is a small doorway opening into the back of the gallery. From the street it will be impossible to see anything but Blue, because I will paint the window glass with the Blue of the previous year's blue period. On and around the lobby door through which the public will enter, I will erect a monumental canopy covered with Blue fabric, still in the same tone of dark ultramarine.

On the evening of the opening, members of the Garde Républicain in full dress uniform will be stationed at each side of the entrance, under the canopy. (This is necessary for the official character I want the exhibition to have and also because the true Republican principle, were it applied, pleases me although I don't find much evidence of it at the present time.)

We will receive the public in the lobby, which measures about 32 square meters; there, a blue cocktail will be served (prepared by the bar of La Coupole in Montparnasse — gin, Cointreau, methylene blue).

Once in the lobby the visitors will see on the left wall a large blue hanging which will mask the narrow door to the gallery.

We also plan to have four private guards ready for any eventuality in dealing with 3,000 people. This is very urgent and necessary, particularly since I expect some acts of vandalism. The guards are to mingle with the throng and will be given strict orders to extend the greatest courtesy to the public, so long as it behaves decently and does not react in too untoward a manner.

Two of these (more or less) bodyguards will be stationed on the street at the entrance to the lobby, with members of the Garde Républicain, to check the invitations, and two others will be stationed at the lobby entrance to the gallery to ensure that the public enter the gallery in groups limited to ten at a time. As for me, I will stand inside requesting that people stay no more than two or three minutes at the most, in order to enable everyone to get in.

Scenic preparation of the gallery: in order to make the ambience special, to render its pictorial sensibility from the status of raw material to an individual, autonomous, stabilized pictorial climate, I must, on the one hand — to clear out the impregnations left by many preceding shows — whiten the gallery. By the act of painting the walls white, I wish not only to purify the premises but, especially through this action and this gesture, to make it momentarily my space for work and creation — in short, my studio.

If, conscious of my act and enraptured by the principle of the demonstration, I put sundry coats of color on the walls of the gallery with my usual technique, if I work, as if on a large picture, with the best of myself and with all the good will I can muster, employing pure white lithopone, blended in my special alcohol, acetone, and vinyl-resin binder (which does not alter the pure pigment when fixing it to the support), and spreading it on with a Ripolin paint [enamel house paint] roller, I believe I shall reach my goal.

By not playing the house painter, that is, by giving free rein to my facture, my gesture of painting, free and perhaps slightly influenced by my sensual nature, I think that the pictorial space I had stabilized at other times in front of and around my monochrome pictures will be, from that time, well established in the gallery space. My presence in action during the execution of this gallery space will create that radiant pictorial climate that usually reigns in the studio of any artist endowed with true power; a sentient density, abstract but real, will exist and live, in and of itself, within the given confines.

For that reason, nothing about the sight of the gallery should be shocking; it must not be too deliberately naked. Thus, no furniture; we will leave the showcase set into the back wall on the left, and I shall simply paint it white like everything else, except for the metal frame. I shall leave the poster show window facing onto the street and paint the wooden part white, always in the same manner, and cover the upper part with white fabric.

The glass of the show window and street entrance door, which will be closed off, will be painted white like the rest. Everything will be white in order to receive the pictorial climate of the sentient, immaterialized blue. I will paint neither the ceiling nor the floor; on the latter I will leave the new gray-black velvet-pile carpet in place; it's a new one Iris just put down a few days ago.

To make it absolutely clear that I am abandoning material, physical Blue, offal and dried blood, issue of the raw material of spatial sensibility, I hope to obtain from the Préfecture de la Seine and the Electricité de France authorization to illuminate the obelisk on the Place de la Concorde in Blue — in such a way that, by placing Blue filters on the already existing projectors, the obelisk is illuminated while its pedestal is left in shadow, thereby restoring the mystic splendor of high antiquity to this monument and, simultaneously, providing the solution to the problem that has always arisen with sculpture: the "base." Indeed, lit up this way, the obelisk will hover, immutable and static, in a monumental movement of affective imagination in space, dominating the Place de la Concorde over its prehistoric gas lamps in the night, like a huge exclamation point without the period under it!

So, visible and tangible Blue will be outside, out of doors, in the street, and indoors will be the immaterialization of Blue. Color-space which is not seen but within which one is impregnated. The authorization to illuminate the obelisk in Blue for the evening of our opening having been granted by the Préfecture, on Wednesday, May 23, at 11 P.M. [Klein clearly meant April 23], Iris Clert and I make an appointment to meet at the Place de la Concorde with the technicians of the Electricité de France. From afar, as we make our way there, we are already transported with enthusiasm for this extraordinary vision of such a rare and exceptional quality. The surfaces covered with hieroglyphs become pictorial matter of a profound and mysterious richness, unprecedented and overwhelming.

It is grandiose.

The trials are decisive in all respects.

On Saturday morning at eight o'clock, I set to work in the gallery. I have 48 hours in which to paint it entirely, all alone. The whole thing must be finished on Sunday in order to air it out properly before the opening. The draper installs the canopy Monday morning. On Monday afternoon at two o'clock I write my inauguration speech, for the movement of sensibility, that I shall deliver after the opening, at around 1 A.M. at La Coupole, among friends, over one last drink.

Everything is in readiness: around 8 P.M. I am in the gallery. Suddenly the telephone rings (during the exhibition, the phone will be placed outside in the lobby). It's the Préfecture de Police. A laconic voice informs me that the Préfecture has decided to cancel the illumination of the obelisk because the character of the demonstration is too personal and because of the publicity the radio and newspapers have given the gesture. I collapse...

I try to reach Iris, who has left to get ready for the opening, which is going to start at 9 P.M. I find her, she is in despair and dashes to the Préfecture, but it's too late, everyone has left, nothing can be done. The next day we learn that this brusque and unforeseen decision of the authorities is the result of base and insulting phone calls from jealous types slanderously protesting against this official favor to me.

At 8 P.M. I go to La Coupole to get the "blue cocktail" prepared especially for the exhibition.

At 8:45 I am in the gallery. Final preparations. At 9 P.M., arrival of the members of the Garde Républicain, in full dress uniform. I immediately offer them a Blue cocktail of honor before they take up their posts under the canopy at the entrance, standing at attention.

Almost simultaneously, arrival of the four private guards. I explain to each his duty; they are still rehearsing when the first visitors arrive...

9:30 P.M. The place is jammed, the lobby is packed, the gallery also. Outside, the growing crowd begins to have difficulty getting inside.

9:45. It's frantic. The crowd is so dense that no one can budge. I stay in the gallery itself. Every three minutes I shout at the top of my lungs to the people who are crowding together in the gallery more and more (the guards are no longer able to contain them or to control the entrances and exits): "Ladies and gentlemen, please be good enough to agree not to stay in the gallery too long so that other visitors who are waiting outside may enter in their turn."

9:45 P.M. Restany arrives, having been driven by Brüning from Düsseldorf to Paris, at the same time as Kricke, accompanied by his wife.

9:50. Inside the gallery, I suddenly notice a young man drawing on one of the walls. I rush over to him, stop him, and politely but very firmly ask him to leave. Accompanying him to the narrow exit door outside, at which the two guards are posted (the crowd inside the gallery falls silent, waiting to see what will happen), I shout to the guard outside, "Seize this man and eject him forcibly!" He is literally uprooted and disappears in the clutches of my guards.

10 P.M. The police (three wagons full) arrive in force by the rue de la Seine. The firemen in force also, with truck and ladder, arrive by the rue Bonaparte, but they can only turn in as far as the Galerie Claude Bernard in the rue des Beaux–Arts because of the mob.

10:10 P.M. Twenty-five hundred to 3,000 people are in the street; the police in the rue de la Seine and the firemen in the rue Bonaparte are trying to push back the crowd toward the quays of the Seine. When a police patrol appears at the entrance to demand an explanation (some people, furious at having paid 1,500 francs admission to see, in their eyes, nothing at all in the interior, went to complain), my bodyguards laconically and firmly tell them, "We have a privately hired guard here, we do not require your services." The police patrol cannot gain entry legally and retreats.

10:20. Arrival of the representative of the Order of Saint Sebastian in full regalia (bicorne and cape with red Maltese cross). Many painters happen to be in the room at the same moment. Camille Bryen exclaims, "In short, this is an exhibition of painters!"

On the whole the crowd enters the gallery in a rage and exits fully satisfied. The important newspapers will be obliged to state officially in writing that 40 percent of the visitors are positive, won over by the sentient pictorial state and overwhelmed by the intense climate that, awesome in its apparent void, reigns in the exhibition room.

10:30 P.M. The Gardes Républicains leave in disgust; for an hour students from the [Ecole des] Beaux-Arts have been tapping them familiarly on the shoulder and asking them where they rented their costumes and if they are movie extras!

10:50. The supply of blue cocktail having been consumed, there is a run to La Coupole to get more. Arrival of two pretty Japanese girls in extraordinary kimonos.

11 P.M. The mob, which was dispersed outside by the police and the firemen, returns in little exasperated groups. Inside everything is still swarming.

Half past midnight. We close and leave for La Coupole.

At La Coupole, a big table in the back for forty people.

1 A.M. Trembling with fatigue, I deliver my revolutionary speech. (See the following text [in *Le Dépassement de la problématique de l'art*]).

1:15. Iris conks out!

The next morning. Iris receives a peremptory summons to Garde Républicain headquarters. There she undergoes a two-hour interrogation and is charged with an attempt to demean the dignity of the Republic. Everything is rectified the next day when the commander-in-chief of the Garde himself comes to visit the scene (of the so-called, by slanderers, misdemeanor).

Planned for eight days, the exhibition has to be extended for an additional week. Every day, more than 200 visitors rush to the interior of the century.

The human experience is one of a vast and almost indescribable scope. Some cannot enter, as if prevented by an invisible wall. One of the visitors yells to me one day from the door, "I'll be back when this void is full..." I reply, "When it's full you won't be able to come in."

Frequently people remain inside for hours without saying a word, and some tremble or begin to cry.

I sold two immaterial pictures at this exhibition.

Believe me, no one who buys such pictures is robbed. I am the one who is always robbed because I accept the money. That's why at the group show at the Hessenhuis in Antwerp with BREER, BURY, MACK, MUNARI, UECKER, PIENE, ROT, SOTO, SPOERRI, and TINGUELY, I no longer even wanted to paint one or several walls nor make some sort of figurative gesture such as sweeping or brushing the walls even with a dry brush. NO, I merely made it a point to go to the premises, on the day of the opening, to tell everyone, in the space reserved for me:

"FIRST THERE IS NOTHING, THEN THERE IS A PROFOUND NOTHING, THEN THERE IS A BLUE PROFUNDITY." (G. Bachelard)

I no longer want people to buy that from me for money. For the three pictorial states exhibited, I asked for pure GOLD. A kilo of GOLD per work. There it is, nice and clear [*net et clair*] at last...for the moment, anyway; afterwards, which was not slow in coming, we shall see.

For, for me, there are no problems any longer. As I said at the beginning of this text [*Le Dépassement*], "I have gone beyond the problematical in art."

This text originally appeared as "Préparation et Présentation de l'Exposition du 28 Avril 1958" in Yves Klein's *Le Dépassement de la problématique de l'art* (La Louvière, Belgium: Editions de Montbliart, 1959), pp. 4–13. Translated by Nan Rosenthal.

Truth Becomes Reality

...Leave my mark on the world, I have done it! When I was a child.... Hands and feet thick with color, applied to the surface; suddenly, there I was, face to face with my own psyche. I had the proof of my five senses: I knew I could function. Then I lost my childhood...just as everyone else (no illusions on that score). And when I tried the same game as an adolescent, I quickly encountered Nothingness.

I did not like Nothingness, and this is how I came to know the void, the deep void, those depths of blue!

As an adolescent I wrote my name on the sky's back in a flight of fantasy—real or imaginary—stretched out one day on a beach at Nice.... I have hated birds ever since that day, I have hated them for trying to pierce great dark holes in my greatest and most beautiful work. Away with all birds!

Having arrived at the monochrome adventure, I no longer needed to force myself to function; I functioned naturally.

I was no longer myself. I, without the "I," became one with life itself. All my gestures, movements, activities, creations were this life, original or essential in itself. It was at this time that I used to say that "painting for me is more than a function of the eye. My works are but the ashes of my art." I monochromed my canvases with devotion. And out of this arose the all-powerful blue, to dominate now and for ever. Then I became uneasy. I brought models to the studio, not to work from, but simply to work in their company.

I was spending far too much time in the studio. I did not want to be so alone in the magic blue void that was developing.

Here the reader will smile, no doubt,...but remember, I was still free of the vertigo that all my predecessors had experienced when faced with the absolute void. A void which must be and is the essence of pictorial space....But how much longer would it last?

In the old days, the painter used to go to the subject, work out of doors, in the landscape; he had both feet on the ground. How healthy! Today easel painting, fully academized, imprisons the painter in his own studio, face to face with the terrifying mirror that is his own canvas. In order not to retreat by shutting myself inside the excessively spiritual regions of creative art, with the plain common sense that is so necessary in our bodily condition and that benefits from the presence of flesh in the studio atmosphere, I employed nude models.

The shape of the body, its curves, its colors between life and death, are not of interest to me. The affective atmosphere of the flesh itself is what I value.

The flesh...!!!

For all that, I took a look at the model now and then....

...I very quickly perceived that it was the block of the body, that is to say the trunk and part of the thighs, that fascinated me. The hands, the arms, the head, the legs were of no importance to me. Only the body is alive, all-powerful, nonthinking. The head, the arms, the hands are only intellectual articulations around the bulk of flesh that is the body.

The heart beats without thought on our part; the mind cannot stop it. Digestion works without our intervention, be it emotional or intellectual. We breathe without reflection.

True, the whole body is made of flesh, but the essential mass is the trunk and the thighs. It is there that we find the real universe, hidden by the universe of our limited perception.

For a long time, then, the presence of this flesh in the studio steadied me during the enlightenment brought on by the execution of my monochromes. It preserved in me the spirit of health, the health that lets us participate, carefree and yet responsible, in the order of the universe. Strong, tough, powerful, and yet fragile, like dreaming animals waking in the perceptual world, like things vegetable and mineral entranced in this world of ephemeral perception....

...This health that makes us "exist." The nature of life itself. All that we are. As I continued to paint in monochrome, I reached the state of disembodiment almost automatically. This made me realize that I really was an Occidental, a proper Christian, believing with reason in the "resurrection of the body and in the resurrection of the flesh." An entire phenomenology took shape. But it was a phenomenology without ideas, or rather without any of the recognized conventions.

What appeared was clearly divorced from form. It became immediate experience. The mark of the immediate, that was my need.

...The stages are not hard to understand. At first my models laughed to see themselves transposed in monochrome on my canvas. Then they became accustomed to it and loved the shades, which differed from one painting to another, even during the blue period, when it was always the same hue, the same pigment, the same technique. Then gradually, pursuing the adventure of the immaterial, my work ceased to be tangible. My studio was empty. Even the monochromes were gone. At this moment my models felt they had to help me. They rolled in the pigment and painted my monochromes with their bodies.

They became living brushes.

I had rejected the brush long before. It was too psychological. I painted with the roller, more anonymous, hoping to create a "distance" between me and my canvases, which should be at least intellectual and unvarying. Now, like a miracle, the brush returned, but this time alive. At my direction, the flesh itself applied the color to the surface, and with perfect exactness. I could continue to maintain a precise distance from my creation and still dominate its execution. In this way I stayed clean. I no longer dirtied myself with color, not even the tips of my fingers. The work finished itself there in front of me with the complete collaboration of the model. And I could salute its birth into the tangible world in a fitting manner, in evening dress. It was at this time that I noticed the "marks of the body" after each session. They disappeared again at once, since the whole effect had to be monochrome.

These marks, pagans in my religion of the absolute monochrome, hypnotized me at once, and I worked on them secretly, always with the complete collaboration of the models, in order to share the responsibility in the event of spiritual weakness.

My models and I practiced a scientifically exact and irreproachable remote control. Thus I was able to present "The Anthropometries of the Blue Period," first of all privately, at Robert Godet's in Paris in the spring of 1958, and then in a far more perfected form on the ninth of March, 1960, at the Galerie Nationale d'Art Contemporain.

...Hiroshima, the shadows of Hiroshima; in the desert of the atomic catastrophe they constituted evidence, terrible evidence beyond any doubt, but still evidence of hope for the permanence (though immaterial) of the flesh.

This demonstration was rather technical. My particular aim was by this means to tear down the temple veil of the studio. To keep nothing of my process hidden, and by so doing, perhaps to merit the "grace" to receive later new reasons for amazement through such new gimmicks of technique just as valuable as they had ever been, and just as unimportant. The results continue to astonish even me... "With or without technique, it is always a good thing to win" had been my motto in Japan, competing in the judo championships. They taught me in judo that one must achieve technical perfection in order to be able to ignore it; that one should be able to show one's technique to one's adversary, and although he knows everything, still win.

The shreds of the temple veil of the studio enable me even today to obtain excellent winding sheets. Everything is of use to me.

My old Monotone Symphony of 1949, played by the little classical orchestra under my direction at the show of March 9, 1960, was intended to create the "silence after": after all was finished, in each one of us present at the exhibition.

Silence...That is really my symphony, and not the sound of its execution. It is this marvelous silence that grants "good fortune" and sometimes even the possibility of true happiness. If it only lasts a second, that second is of infinite duration.

To conquer silence, to shatter it, to take its skin and wrap oneself in it, never again to suffer from spiritual cold. I feel like a vampire sucking the blood of universal space!

But to return to the facts: still there in the studio with my models, in 1956 I was reading the journal of Delacroix when I came across these lines: "I adore this little vegetable garden, the gentle sun shining over it fills me with a secret joy, such as one feels when the body is in perfect health. But how transitory all this is; I have found myself in this delicious state many times in the twenty days I have been here. It seems there should be a 'mark,' a special memory for each of these 'moments.'"

What an artist needs is the temperament of a reporter, a journalist, but in the wider sense of these words, one perhaps no longer understood today.

I understand the spiritual mark of these captured moments. I have caught it with my monochromes. I have the mark of the captured moments of the flesh in the imprints snatched from the bodies of my models....But the captured moments of Nature?

...I bound outside and down to the river. Among the rushes and reeds, I dust color over everything I see there, and the wind bending the slender stems sets them with delicacy and precision against the canvas I present to trembling nature; I obtain a mark of plant life.

It begins to rain; a fine spring shower. I hold out my canvas to the rain and it is done! I have the mark of the rain, of an atmospheric occurrence.

I have an idea also. For a long time I have wanted to temper the whole of nature, with the aid, perhaps, of solar reflectors or some other scientific technique not yet discovered. When the first steps have been made with the architecture of the air, which we are working on at the moment in collaboration with the architect Werner Ruhnau, they will permit us to live naked in immense regions that we will have regulated and transformed into a veritable paradise on earth. Then it will at last be only natural that the model should leave the studio with me. And that I, I should take prints of nature, and that the model should all at once be there, taking her place in nature and in this way marking the canvas where she feels it best, in the grass, among the reeds, by the water's side or under the waterfall, naked, either static or in motion, as a true subject of nature, fully integrated at last.

All aspects of the "subjects" of nature interest me. Men, animals, plants, minerals, atmospheric states. I am interested in all these for my naturometries.

I shall give up the use of color, I think. I shall work with the perspiration of the models, mixed with dust, and even, perhaps, with their own blood; with the sap of plants, the color of the earth, and so on...and time will turn the results I obtain into the blue monochrome I.K.B.

Fire is there too, and I must have its mark!

We are coming into an anthropophagous era, frightening in appearance only. It will be the practical realization on a universal scale of the famous words, "He who eats of my flesh and drinks of my blood will live in me and I in him." Spiritual words, certainly, but words that will be put into practice for a time before the arrival of the blue era of peace and glory. Practiced in perfect Edenesque liberty. A freedom won by man from the immaterial sensitivity of the universe.

No matter what one thinks, all this is very bad taste, and indeed, that is my intention. I howl it from the rooftops: "Kitsch, corn, bad taste," this is the new notion in art. And while we are about it, let's forget art altogether!

Great beauty is only a reality when it contains, intelligently mixed into it, "genuine bad taste," "irritating and intentional artificiality," with just a dash of dishonesty!

One must be like untamed fire. One must know how to be gentle and at the same time cruel, how to contradict oneself. Then and only then has one really joined the family of the principles of universal enlightenment.

...No, I am not literary. All my past exhibitions have been "events." With the first showing of "The Void" at Colette Allendy's in 1957, I liberated at one fell swoop the entire live theater from the age-old yoke of perspective!

By publishing the text for all artists, young or not, I wish to make it clear that I spent the last few years following the path of the monochrome, here, there, and everywhere, then that of immateriality and nothingness (though I might add that they are still far from being achieved), and that I have not made an abrupt about-face.

In fact, for some time I have been told repeatedly that the followers of the monochrome movement that I started in the contemporary international art world are baffled by my recent works....

...Well then—nothing could be more natural than the fact that I have reached this point, and I am sure that they will reach it too. At first they were baffled by my monochromes, which afterwards they took up with enthusiasm, each in his own way.

Today I feel—thinking of everything that has happened—like the worm in the Swiss cheese of the history of science, which eats its way forward, making holes. It creates an empty space around itself and moves on.... From time to time, it meets a hole, which it must circle around in order to move forward, in order to live, to have something to eat!

One day there is no more cheese, because it has eaten the whole thing; there is nothing but emptiness, an enormous emptiness. Then it hovers in space, free and happy, but only for a moment, because naturally it falls onto another cheese and continues to eat and create emptiness around itself. That reminds me of a poem I wrote when I was eleven, which my mother wisely saved for me. It says just what I have always wanted to say:

Silence
The soft scraping of a dead leaf
dragged by the wind,
A falling stone
There the small hole is dug
The silent space struggles.
Suddenly, steps, shadows,
A shepherd, his regiment of sheep around him
Their little bells ring so sweetly.
That's it! He has won!
The silence around him is...
...Behind him.

Paris 1939

It is not with rockets, Sputniks, and missiles that modern man will achieve the conquest of space. That is the dream of present-day scientists who live in a state of mind romantic and sentimental enough for the last century.

It is by means of the powerful yet pacific force of his sensitivity that man will inhabit space. It is by the impregnation of space with human sensitivity that the much coveted conquest of this space will be achieved. For human sensitivity is omnipotent in immaterial reality; it can even read in the memory of nature about the past, the present, and the future!

It is our effective supply of extradimensional power.

Proofs? Precedents?

...Dante, in the *Divine Comedy*, accurately describes the Southern Cross, a constellation invisible in the northern hemisphere, and which no traveler of his time could have told him about. Swift, in his *Voyage to Laputa*, gives the distances and the rotation periods of the two satellites of Mars, unknown at the time. When the American astronomer Asaph Hall discovered them in 1877 and saw that his calculations corresponded to those of Swift, seized by a sort of panic, he called them Phobos and Deimos, Fear and Terror.

May the authentic realism of today and tomorrow flourish. I want it to live with the best of myself, in total freedom of mind and body. The universal cannibalism that is approaching, the anthropophagous era through which we are soon to pass, is not by nature cruel or fierce, nor inhuman; quite the contrary—it will become the living expression or rather the assimilation of a biological synthesis. It will finally free us from the few tyrannical aspects of nature vis-à-vis...such as...*

*In the original publication, Klein had the last page of his article burned off—dematerialized by fire—at this point.

Originally printed in *ZERO* (Düsseldorf), no. 3 (July 1961); reprinted with permission from a facsimile edition of the journal with English translations, *Zero*, ed. Otto Piene and Heinz Mack (Cambridge, Mass.: MIT Press, 1973), pp. 91-95. Translated by Howard Beckman. Copyright © 1973 The Massachusetts Institute of Technology.

Discourse on the Occasion of Tinguely's Exhibition in Düsseldorf, January 1959

Ladies and Gentlemen,

This evening, on the occasion of Jean Tinguely's formidable exhibition (which I consider the fixative medium of the age), I wish to propose to those who wish to hear: COLLABORATION. Consider the etymology of the word.

To collaborate is to work in common on the same project. The project for which I propose collaboration is Art.

In Art—Art without problematics—is found the source of inexhaustible LIFE; through this source, if we are true artists, freed from the dreaming and pictorial imagination of the psychological domain (which is the counter-space, the space of the PAST), we may attain to eternal life, to Immortality. Immortality is conquered through a common effort—that is one of the natural laws of man's relationship to the universe.

To create, one must never turn back to consider his work, for that way lies stasis and death. The work must be like a volumetric wake; it must involve penetration, by impregnation of the sensibility, into the immaterial space of LIFE itself. In such collaboration, each of us must practice "pure imagination."

This imagination of which I am speaking does not involve perception, or a trace of perception, or a personal memory, or a habit of colors and forms. It involves nothing which can be perceived by the five senses or by the domain of sentiment or even by the purest, most fundamental emotion. All that is the imagination of artists who cannot collaborate. Because by wishing to save their personalities at any cost, they kill their spiritual selves and lose their Life. These artists who cannot collaborate work from the stomach, the plexus, the intestines. The artists who collaborate are those who work with the heart and the head.

These are artists who understand the RESPONSIBILITY of being a MAN in relation to the UNIVERSE.

Among artists, the imagination is a psychic power, a continual experience of opening, an experience of newness itself (after G. Bachelard).

For artists who are ready to collaborate, to IMAGINE is to absent oneself, to propel oneself toward a new kind of life. In their many surges in every direction and dimension of this constantly new life, they are paradoxically united and separated at the same time. For them, imagination is the "daring" of sensibility.

What is sensibility?

It is that which exists beyond our being, yet belongs always to us. Life itself does not belong to us; it is with sensibility, which does belong to us, that we can attain to Life. Sensibility is the money of the universe, of space, of great nature which permits us to attain LIFE at the state of prime matter. Imagination is the vehicle of sensibility. Transported by imagination, we attain Life, that very Life which is the absolute art.

In the wake of such volumetric displacements, the Absolute Art suddenly materializes itself, with a dizzying yet static velocity, and appears in the tangible world; it is this materialized form of Absolute Art which mortals, with a sense of vertigo, call GREAT ART.

This evening, I am proposing collaboration to artists who already know about it, and who perhaps already know that they should mock their possessive, egotistical, egocentric personalities by the aggravation of the Me in all their "portrayals" in the theater–like world (the tangible, physical, ephemeral world) where they know well how to exist by playing a part. I propose to them to continue to say "my work," each separately, when speaking to the living dead (who surround us in everyday life) of the communal work which was realized through collaboration. I propose that they continue joyously to say Me, I, My, Mine, not the hypocritical Us, Our—but only after solemnly signing the pact of COLLABORATION this evening.

Then perhaps one day I will find that one of the members of this pact has suddenly and spontaneously signed one of my paintings somewhere in the world without even speaking to me about it. And in the same way, I may sign something which pleases me from the works of the other members of the pact, without being in the least concerned to indicate that it is not in fact mine.

I push the point to this perhaps eccentric extreme to make it clear that the collaboration which I am proposing means playing your way out of the psychological world in order to make yourself really free.

I do not speak as a Utopian this evening in proposing this new form of collaboration and trying to get a new and perfect "BAUHAUS" underway in 1959; rather, I speak from experience. For more than a year now, I have collaborated successfully with the architect Werner Ruhnau; together we created the Architecture of the Air, and other projects are now in preparation. With the sculptor Norbert Kricke, I have collaborated to create works of water, wind, fire, and light, which have not yet been realized. Jean Tinguely and I, working together for the last six months, have mined a constantly new and wonderful thing, the commotion of "the fundamental static movement of the universe.''

In conclusion, in proposing Collaboration in art to artists of the heart and head, I am in fact proposing that they bypass art altogether and work individually on the return to real life, the life in which a man no longer feels that he is the center of the universe, but where the universe is the center of every man. We will then know a magical honor [*prestige*] where in the past we knew only vertigo [*vertige*].

In this way, we will become aerial men; we will know the force of upward attraction toward space, toward nothing and everything at the same time; the force of terrestrial attraction having been mastered, we will literally levitate in total physical and spiritual freedom.

Originally printed in Klein's *Le Dépassement de la problématique de l'art* (La Louvière, Belgium: Editions de Montbliart, 1959), pp. 19-22. Translated by Thomas McEvilley.

Du vertige au prestige, 1957–1959

For years I have been training for levitation, and I am intimately familiar with the best means of attaining it—the judo falls.

On one side is the traditional legendary vampirism at night, combined with absolute physical immobility during the day (a sort of systole and diastole); and on the other is the actual liberation of every aspect of the individual personality by the aggravation of the Me, practiced to the point of an absolute purifying sublimation.

I rcently declared, in a talk in Germany in January 1959, that, once liberated from the psychological world, the artist of tomorrow will create himself anew in every work, through his power to levitate in total physical and spiritual freedom. I have already made the first steps toward works of this type, such as the flying aerostatic sculptures of 1957, made of a thousand and one blue balloons; and the experience of the obelisk of the Place de la Concorde lighted blue at night, while the base remained in shadow; and also the fumes of the inauguration of the Blue Age in 1957. This transition to the age of flight is what I call the transition from *vertige* to *prestige* (in sculptural terms it is the liberation from enslavement to the base).

In the same way, I would like to present myself on the stage of a theater, hanging in space several meters from the floor without any trick or deception, for five or ten minutes at least, without any commentary.

Originally printed in Klein's *Dimanche, le journal d'un seul jour,* published November 27, 1960. Translated by Thomas McEvilley.

Selections from "The Thieves of Ideas"

In the period of the urbanism of air, and above all after that stage, in the period of the complete and definitive immaterialization of architecture—that is, when we will have returned to the lost Eden, in a nature which has been climatized anew, living naked, without any artificial impediment at all—then our understanding of friendship will be very different. We will see, all the time, those aspects of other people which are now hidden and secret, and they will see the same in us, in all the smallest details of daily life. At that time, our sensibilities will be so developed that we may be able to see each other's deepest thoughts—not by intellectually reading or perceiving them, but by "seizing" them, through impregnation in sensibility, rather than through psychological penetration; at that time, the psychological aspect of the personality will have disappeared almost completely.

Nevertheless, if all men arrive at the ability to "dream the dreams of others" (as today one steals ideas "from the air," some being quicker at this than others), it will always be "the poet" who, going beyond the dream itself, will know the illuminated trance of contact with the feeling-center of the universe, of contact with joy at the state of Prime Matter which, while both deep and high, is beyond dimensions and lies at the origin of life itself. . . .

Then there will be no more ideas. It will be the "silence" which generates everything inside everyone. . . .

Originally printed in Klein's *Dimanche, le journal d'un seul jour,* published November 27, 1960. Excerpted and translated by Thomas McEvilley.

Supplementary Documentation

tincte du sentiment qu'elle fait naître. Cette impression est neutre ; c'est une activité manifestée dans la deuxième Région du Monde du Désir, où des images sont formées par les forces de la perception sensorielle dans le corps vital de l'homme.

Dans la troisième Région, l'Attraction — la force qui assemble et construit — l'emporte déjà sur la Répulsion, dont l'action est de détruire. Si nous comprenons que la caractéristique principale de cette force de Répulsion est une tendance à s'affirmer, à repousser les autres forces pour avoir plus de champ d'action, nous comprendrons aussi qu'elle cède très facilement le pas à un désir pour de nouvelles choses. La substance de la troisième Région du Monde du Désir est donc principalement soumise à la force d'Attraction vers de nouveaux objets, mais dans un but égoïste : c'est la Région des Souhaits.

La Région des Désirs vils peut être comparée aux solides du Monde Physique ; la Région de l'Impressionnabilité, aux liquides. La nature changeante de la Région des Souhaits la rend comparable à la partie gazeuse du Monde Physique. Ces trois subdivisions fournissent la substance des formes qui contribuent à l'expérience, au développement de l'âme et à l'évolution, éliminant les éléments complètement destructeurs et retenant ceux qu'il est possible d'utiliser pour le progrès.

La quatrième Région du Monde du Désir est la « Région du Sentiment ». C'est de là qu'émane notre sentiment au sujet des formes précédemment mentionnées. Leur corrélation avec nous et leur effet sur nous dépendent de ce qu'elles nous inspirent. Il importe peu, pour le moment, que les idées ou objets présentés soient bons ou mauvais ; l'Intérêt ou l'Indifférence sont les seuls facteurs qui déterminent leur sort.

Si l'impression faite sur nous par un objet ou une idée éveille notre Intérêt, celui-ci a sur elle le même effet que le soleil et l'air sur les plantes. Elle va croître et fleurir dans notre vie. Si, au contraire, l'impression est reçue avec Indifférence, elle se flétrit comme une plante placée dans l'obscurité d'une cave.

De cette région centrale du Monde du Désir émane donc le stimulant qui pousse à agir ou, au contraire, à empêcher toute action (ce qui est aussi une action au point de vue de l'occultisme scientifique). En effet, dans l'état actuel de notre évolution, les sentiments jumeaux d'Intérêt et d'Indifférence sont la source même de l'action ; ils sont les ressorts qui meuvent le Monde. Plus tard, ils n'auront plus aucun poids. Le facteur décisif de l'action sera alors le Devoir.

L'Intérêt met en mouvement les forces d'Attraction et de Répulsion. L'Indifférence flétrit simplement l'idée ou l'objet contre lequel elle est dirigée, tout au moins en ce qui concerne nos rapports avec lui.

Si notre intérêt pour un objet ou une idée engendre la Répulsion, cela

nous fait naturellement écarter de notre vie toute relation avec l'objet ou l'idée qui a mis cette force en jeu ; mais il y a une grande différence entre l'action de la Répulsion et le simple sentiment d'Indifférence.

Un exemple fera peut-être comprendre plus aisément la manière d'agir des deux Sentiments et des deux Forces.

Trois hommes passent le long d'un chemin. Ils aperçoivent un chien malade, couvert d'ulcères et qui souffre apparemment d'une douleur et d'une soif intenses. Tout cela est évident pour les trois hommes ; les témoignages de leurs sens sous ce rapport sont identiques. Maintenant, laissons le Sentiment entrer en scène. Deux d'entre eux éprouvent de l' « Intérêt » pour l'animal, mais le troisième ne ressent que de l' « Indifférence ». Il poursuit donc son chemin, abandonnant le chien à son sort. Les autres restent ; tous les deux s'intéressent à la pauvre bête, mais chacun manifeste son sentiment d'une manière différente. L'intérêt de l'un est fait de sympathie, du désir d'aider ; il le pousse à s'occuper du malade, à soulager ses souffrances et à lui prodiguer des soins pour le guérir. Chez lui, le sentiment a éveillé la force d'Attraction. L'intérêt de l'autre homme est d'un ordre différent. Il ne voit qu'un spectacle répugnant qui le révolte ; il veut s'en débarrasser et débarrasser le Monde au plus vite. Il conseille donc de tuer l'animal sur-le-champ et de l'enterrer. Chez lui, le sentiment a éveillé la force destructive de Répulsion.

Quand l'Intérêt met en œuvre la Force d'Attraction et qu'il a pour objet des choses et des désirs vils, ceux-ci gagnent les Régions inférieures du Monde du Désir, où agit la force neutralisante de Répulsion, comme nous l'avons vu précédemment. De la lutte entre les forces jumelles d'Attraction et de Répulsion proviennent toute la douleur et toute la souffrance qu'entraînent les mauvaises actions ou les efforts mal dirigés, intentionnellement ou non.

Nous voyons ainsi l'importance capitale du Sentiment que nous éprouvons envers toute chose, car c'est de lui que dépend la nature de l'ambiance que nous nous créons. Si nous aimons le bien, nous veillerons comme des anges gardiens sur tout ce que nous rencontrons de bon autour de nous ; dans le cas contraire, nous peuplerons notre route des démons que nous aurons créés.

Les noms des trois Subdivisions Supérieures du Monde du Désir sont : la Région de la « Vie de l'Ame », la Région de la « Lumière de l'Ame » et la Région du « Pouvoir de l'Ame ». Elles sont le domaine de l'Art, de l'Altruisme, de la Philanthropie et de toutes les activités de la vie supérieure de l'âme. En comprenant que ces régions rayonnent dans les formes des trois subdivisions inférieures les qualités que leurs noms indiquent, nous aurons une idée exacte des activités supérieures et inférieures du Monde du Désir. Néanmoins, le Pouvoir de l'Ame peut temporairement être mis aussi bien au service du mal qu'à celui du bien ; mais,

Cosmogonie 3.

Yves Klein's copy of La Cosmogonie des Rose-croix, *by Max Heindel*

Yves Klein and Rosicrucianism

Advance information about ... an artist's concepts is necessary to the appreciation and understanding of contemporary art.

Joseph Kosuth[1]

The artist's own comments about what is said in one or another of his works may certainly be of interest.... But the language of art means the excess of meaning that is present in the work itself. The inexhaustibility that distinguishes the language of art from all translations into concepts rests on the excess of meaning.

Hans-Georg Gadamer[2]

The relation of language to painting is an infinite relation....Neither can be reduced to the other's terms: it is in vain that we say what we see; what we see never resides in what we say.

Michel Foucault[3]

In concluding his essay on the myth of Isis and Osiris, Plutarch denies that any of the dozen or so interpretations he has reviewed is true by itself and affirms that all of them together (despite their contradictions) constitute a kind of truth. His intuition that hermeneutics must remain sufficiently open to embrace not only complementary but even contradictory readings foreshadows both the multimodel approach generated by modern positivism *and* the phenomenological insistence that a myth (or an art work) transcends any single horizon of subjectivity.

Basic philological work on Yves Klein's extensive *oeuvre* has hardly begun. It may eventually result in an integrated layering of readings which, like Plutarch's stratified approach to myth, can be held to constitute a meaning. But initially philology must proceed by isolating partial models, which may ultimately be merged in a synthesis.

It is well known that Klein's work has a remarkable inner consistency or logic. What is not widely understood is that this consistency reflects the faithfulness with which he translated into visual and art historical terms an idea system whose native context was not art, namely, the Rosicrucianism of Max Heindel. Philological analysis of the relationship between Klein's writings and Heindel's is necessary groundwork from which a more synthetic approach to Klein's art may develop. The task is undertaken here without any claim that this model can exhaust the meaning of Klein's works. On the contrary, it is not so much an interpretation of his works which is offered here as a reconstruction of his sources and intentions, which are of interest in themselves.

Around the end of 1947 or the beginning of 1948, when Klein was nineteen, he obtained a copy of Max Heindel's *La Cosmogonie des Rose-croix*, the "manual" of the Rosicrucian Society of Oceanside, California.[4] At once he began practicing the Rosicrucian teachings intensively, in the company of his close friends Claude Pascal and Armand Fernandez (later Arman), under the guidance of an older Rosicrucian, Louis Cadeaux. In June 1948 Klein officially joined the Rosicrucians. For more than three years he received monthly lessons (written, like the *Cosmogonie*, by Max Heindel) and faithfully sent his worksheets to Oceanside for review. For another year and a half (until mid-1953) he received the lessons but did not send back his worksheets. In mid-1953 his official membership lapsed.[5] He continued to read in the *Cosmogonie* for several more years; until about 1958, it was the central book of his life.

Between 1955 and 1962 Klein produced both a variegated body of art works and an interesting body of writings on the theory of art, his own art especially.[6] Through these writings a kind of luminous pattern seems to shine without entirely revealing itself. Much of that pattern can be clarified by a study of Klein's usually unacknowledged allusions to Heindel's works, especially the *Cosmogonie*. I will first summarize Klein's theory of art, then Heindel's Rosicrucian system, and then will explicate the detailed correspondences between them.

The central theme of Klein's essays is a mystical conception of space, conceived as free energy, in contrast to form, or bound energy. Space is identified with alchemical Prime Matter, containing a universal "memory" of past, present, and future, and functioning as the source of the world of form. Psychologically, pure space equates with the free (enlightened) mind, form with the bound (neurotic) mind. In terms of painting, this fertile space is called "pure pictorial sensibility." The artist whose mind is free like space can crystallize this pictorial energy into any object by mental concentration; the higher sensibility which has been locked into the object by the artist can be regained from it by the viewer, who can, in fact, be awakened to cosmic consciousness by the experience.

The metaphysical dichotomy between space and form appears in painting as the Battle between Line and Color. Line divides and obstructs the pure space of cosmic sensibility, while color asserts the freedom and fullness of space and tends to make the artist one with it (to "return him to Eden"). In fact, pure color is not merely an analogue of this cosmic space/sensibility, it is an actual materialization of it—

especially blue, the color of sea and sky, the two most abstract and illimitable natural entities. The artist who has realized the sensibility of pure space will express himself in pure color; the artist who lacks this cosmic openness of mind will express himself through the neurotic entanglements of line and form.

But the artist can express the sensibility of space in other ways, too. The "trace of the immediate" shows prime matter just beginning to crystallize into bound space. Above all, the "art of the immaterial" is the truest expression of this sensibility and will be the typical mode of future art in the technological Eden of aerial men. The artist makes immaterial art by leaving the aura of his sensibility in an apparently empty space, from which it can be regained by the sensitive observer at any time. The artist may also "specialize" his sensibility into specific, but invisible, forms, which are also works of immaterial art, or he may project it over long distances.

In a not very distant future, Klein wrote, all men will evolve into this sensibility and will become more or less one with space, able to levitate their physical bodies or to operate immaterially, out of their bodies altogether. At that time human societies will be reconstituted, through a union of science, art, and religion, in an Edenic state; the surface of the earth will be reclimatized to accommodate the new immaterial mode of living and, consonant with his new identity with space, man will live in houses of compressed-air currents. We are nearly in that age now, Klein held, as is shown by his own prophetic works and by the flight of the Russian spacecraft Vostok 1 (during which Yuri Gagarin said that the earth, from outer space, looks blue).

This theory, and to a degree the works which express it, are based primarily on the Rosicrucian thought of Max Heindel, with a smattering of Buddhism and glances at Gaston Bachelard thrown in. The central idea of Heindel's *Rosicrucian Cosmo-conception* is the polarity, and ultimate synthesis, of Life and Form.[7] Life is pure spirit, equated with apparently empty space; Form, on the other hand, is bound spirit, and equates with physical matter. These conditions alternate through long states of human evolution. At the beginning is the stage of Life, in which there is no illusion of ego separation but awareness of Oneness-with-the-All. In ensuing periods, the principle of Form gradually gains dominance over Life, and the illusion of ego separation smothers awareness of Oneness-with-the-All. Finally, awareness of separate existence will somehow combine with awareness of Oneness-with-the-All, at the triumphant culmination of human evolution.

At present we are nearing the end of the age of Form, and in the next Epoch we will begin to open up again to awareness of Life. When this happens we will no longer be bound to the gross physical body, the ultimate product of the age of Form, but will gain control, successively, of a series of higher vehicles which are now obscured from our awareness by our bondage to Form. The first sign of this upward trend toward Life will be control of the Desire Body (the grossest of six "immaterial" vehicles); at that point we will gain the ability to levitate, to read the memory of nature, and to manipulate the order of things through mental activity alone. In each new age the dominant vehicle remakes the environment to suit itself — as at present the gross physical body has created for itself an environment of solid matter. In the next Epoch, when the Desire Body needs an environment less bound to Form and more open to Life, the environment will be remade by science, which will become an arm of religion and will turn human life back in the direction of empty space, where alone Life and freedom are to be found.

Klein's career was an expression of this belief system; he regarded himself as the instrument of evolution, presaging and hastening the dawn of the new age.

The leading ideas of both Heindel's and Klein's thought were Space and Evolution. For Heindel, Space is equated with all six invisible realms higher than the physical and is accessible only to the initiate who has performed certain inner transformative works. Space is not dead emptiness, but invisible fullness:

> In our present materialistic period we have unfortunately lost the idea of all that lies behind that word Space. We are so accustomed to speaking of "empty" space, of the "great void" of space, that we have entirely lost the grand and holy significance of the word, and are thus incapable of feeling the reverence that this idea of Space and Chaos should inspire in our breasts.
>
> To the Rosicrucians, as to any occult school, there is no such thing as empty or void space. To them, *space* is *Spirit* in its attenuated form; while matter is crystallized space or Spirit.[8]

Heindel's equation of Space with Ovidian chaos, or with the undifferentiated Prime Matter of the alchemists, is transposed by Klein into painterly terms in his definition of space as "unlimited pictorial sensibility." In a passage which Klein underlined in his copy of the *Cosmogonie*, Heindel wrote:

> Chaos is the seed-ground of the Cosmos. . . .

we shall no longer wonder how "something can come out of nothing," because Space is not synonymous with "nothing." It holds within itself the germs of all that exists during a physical manifestation.[9]

All of Klein's art relates in some way to this central concept of featureless etheric fullness. As he wrote:

The void has always been my essential preoccupation.[10]

In rejecting nothingness I found the void. The meaning of immaterial pictorial zones issued from the depths of the void.[11]

I seek above all...to create in my realization this transparency, this void immeasurable, in which lives the Spirit permanent and absolute, freed from all dimensions.[12]

The absolute void...is entirely naturally the true pictorial space.[13]

It is Evolution which is carrying us toward the void. According to Heindel, we have reached the farthest extension into matter, and the next stage calls for our reawakening to Pure Spirit and simultaneously our expansion beyond the physical realm into space:

During the remaining half of this Period and the entire three remaining Periods, man must expand his consciousness so as to include all of the six Worlds above this Physical World.[14]

[Man's] next step in progress will be towards an expansion in consciousness that will include the Etheric Region, then the Desire World, etc.[15]

This transition will be marked by both mental and physical changes in the human vehicle and the human culture which is its expression and its matrix. One of these changes which was already visible in Klein's time was the exploration of outer space. Says Heindel:

[Modern science] does not recognize the... fact insisted upon by occult science...that the whole atmosphere around us, the space between the worlds, is Spirit.[16]

The Etheric Region extends beyond the atmosphere of our dense earth....the Desire World extends further into interplanetary Space than either of the others.[17]

Thus travel into outer space is travel toward Pure Spirit and away from matter. Klein viewed the flight of Yuri Gagarin as confirmation that we are now on the verge of this great turning point in human history.

According to Heindel, humanity, in the next Epoch, will gain control of the Desire Body, and

thereafter movement will be through levitation; truly spiritualized human beings will be able to separate themselves from the gross body at will, and will no longer need physical spacecraft:

In the Physical World, matter is subject to gravity...In the Desire World, ...forms levitate as easily as they gravitate. Distance and time are also governing factors of existence in the Physical World, but are almost nonexistent in the Desire World.[18]

Klein underlined in his copy of the *Cosmogonie* mostly passages describing the Desire World, and wrote "Transfiguration" large in the margin next to the description of levitation. His own desire to levitate was an anticipation of this stage of evolution, as were his Leap into the Void, the "Anthropometry" entitled *People Begin to Fly*, and the Düsseldorf speech announcing that

we will all become aerial men, we will know the upward force of attraction toward space, toward nothing and everything at once: earthly gravity having been overcome, we will literally levitate in a total physical and spiritual freedom.[19]

In fact, it seems that Klein viewed his own career as one of the announcements or signs of the impending transformation of humanity, using terminology to describe it which clearly derives from Heindel's theory of Evolution. Heindel uses the term "Period" for a vast cosmic phase (we are now, for example, in the "Earth Period"), and the terms "Revolution" or "Epoch" for smaller phases within Periods. Klein's announcement in 1957 of the "Blue Revolution" ushering in the "Blue Epoch" referred not merely to the displacement of one artistic style or school by another, but to this imminent spiritualization of all mankind.

Heindel, like writers in various Eastern traditions, specifically associated the void of Pure Spirit with the color blue, saying, "Blue shows the highest type of spirituality," that is, the spirituality which has become one with Space/Spirit.[20] Klein followed him in associating the Void, or Pure Spirit, with the color blue.[21] The Blue Epoch, then, is to be nothing less than the Epoch of return to Space/Spirit. President Eisenhower was the first head of state who was honored with a notice of this Revolution, perhaps because of Heindel's statements:

From the people of the United States will descend the last of all the Races in this scheme of evolution.[22]

[From the United States] will the next "chosen people"...be chiefly derived.[23]

Similarly, the Blue Revolution's plans to alter the surface of the earth spring from Heindel's assertion that

> before a new Epoch is ushered in…there must be "a new heaven and a new earth"; the physical features of the Earth will be changed and its density decreased.[24]

Klein's "architecture of the air" is a means to decrease the density of the environment, and his reclimatization schemes connect with Heindel's statement that

> climate, *flora* and *fauna* are altered by man under the direction of higher beings.[25]

Heindel and the Rosicrucian tradition in general describe the next Epoch (the return to Space) as a return to Eden, a term which recurs continually in Klein's writings.[26] For the individual, the return to Eden means escape from the body, reimmersion in Space/Chaos, and consequent realization of Oneness-with-the-All. For the community, it means the union of technology, religion, and art to create a milieu in which the transition to the Desire Body will be hastened and facilitated. Klein's attempt to synthesize Rosicrucianism, technology, and art was a response to Heindel's insistence that in order to make the transition to the Desire World,

> *Religion, Science* and *Art* must re-unite in a higher expression of the *Good*, the *True* and the *Beautiful*.[27]

His deliberate attempts to fulfill Heindel's prophecies suggest that Klein believed, or hoped, that he might be the transition figure announced by Heindel:

> At the end of our present Epoch the highest initiate will appear publicly when a sufficient number of ordinary humanity desire and will voluntarily subject themselves to such a leader.…After that time races and nations will cease to exist. Humanity will form one spiritual fellowship.[28]

Klein's announcement to President Eisenhower of the end of the French national government certainly sounds as if he is taking this mantle on himself, as do his statements that Space itself acknowledges him as its "Conquistador" and makes him the "Proprietor of COLOR."[29]

As Conquistador of Space it is the initiate's duty to champion the advancement of others on the path of Evolution, and as the Proprietor of Pure Color it is in his power to do so. Klein's announcement of the Battle between Line and Color, and of himself (in Knight of Saint Sebastian costume) as the Champion of Color, shows him at the forward edge of Evolution,

championing the incoming age against the reactionary attraction of the old. The distinction is not only based on Heindel but was explicitly laid out by Heindel when he said:

> The Physical World is the world of Form.
> The Desire World…is particularly the world of *Color*.[30]

The physical world is tied to Form (in Klein's terms, line) because it is centered in Ego; the Desire World expresses itself as Pure Color because it is Spirit, which knows no internal divisions. As Klein wrote:

> Pure color [is] the universal soul in which the human soul bathes in the state of earthly paradise.…This universal color soul…is life itself.[31]

The art of Pure Color, then, is equivalent to immersion in uninterrupted Space and constitutes a return to the Eden of Life-without-Ego. Klein expresses this in perfectly Heindelian terms:

> By saturating myself with the eternal limitless sensitivity of space I return to Eden…and that is why, in my work, I refuse more and more emphatically the illusion of personality, the transient psychology of the linear, the formal, the structural. Evidently the subject I am traveling toward is space, pure Spirit.[32]

Line, which must express itself by dividing, separating, and making limits, entangles and imprisons the openness of color and thus destroys paradise:

> Paradise is lost [when] the entanglement of lines becomes the bars of a prison.[33]

Human history is the long drama of line invading color (Heindel's "Age of Form") and color struggling to free itself (for the "Age of Spirit"):

> Line, jealous of color, the true inhabitant of space, tries to free itself from the condition of tourist in space; it breaks itself up and invades the picture surface.…
>
> Color, humiliated, defeated, prepares its revenge over long years.[34]

The Edenic age of unity at the beginning of time was the age of color; it was followed by a long degeneration into multiplicity, as line invaded and broke up the picture surface. Color began to reassert itself with the works of Delacroix and Van Gogh, and now, in Klein's work, stands ready to regain the field and usher in a new age of unity. The goal of art (as of life) is to regain

> that ineffable peace in nature and man before the intrusion of line into color.[35]

In terms of Evolution, then, art based on Line and Form is regressive; it is a remnant of the Epoch of the gross body, which is now ending. Art based on pure color with no internal division is prophetic of the incoming age. Thus Klein's announcement of the Battle between Line and Color is the announcement, in artistic terms, of the end of one age of human evolution and the beginning of another. When he writes,

> the whole immense evolution across the ages aims at the discovery of the mystery of color,[36]

he is evidently referring to Heindel's doctrine of our long evolution toward the Desire World, the realm of color.

This same Heindelian dichotomy — between Space as free Spirit and Form as bound Spirit—is the basis of Klein's theory of the monochrome, which is perhaps the cornerstone of his writings. A key passage from "The Monochrome Adventure" (Klein's most ambitious essay) deserves to be quoted in full:

> Through color I experience a feeling of complete identification with space. I am truly free. If a color is no longer pure, the drama may take on disquieting overtones. . . . As soon as there are two colors in a painting combat begins; the permanent spectacle of this battle of two colors may give the onlooker a subtle psychological and emotional pleasure, that is nonetheless morbid from a purely human, philosophical point of view. . . . Lines, bars of a psychological prison, . . . are our chains, they are the concretization of our mortality, our sentimentality, our intellect, even our spiritual domain. They are our heredity, our education, our framework, our vices, our aspirations, our qualities, our wiles. In short, our whole psychological world, with all its subtlest recesses.
>
> Color on the other hand, both in nature and in man, is that which is most immersed in cosmic sensibility. That sensibility has no recesses but is like humidity in the air. For me, color is sensibility "materialized." . . . Color is free, it is instantly dissolved in space. . . . The line goes toward infinity, but color has its being right in infinity. Colors are the true inhabitants of space. The line only travels across space.

Clearly he is thinking of Heindel's "The Desire World . . . is particularly the world of Color" when he writes, "Color has its being right in infinity. . . . Colors are the true inhabitants of space." Underlying the passage is Heindel's distinction between Life/Spirit/Open Space/Color and Ego/Matter/Closed Space/Form. In many passages Klein makes this quite explicit by using the term "Life" (or "LIFE") in ways which cannot really be understood without knowing the Rosicrucian usage:

> Life itself does not belong to us; it is through sensibility that we can achieve it.[37]
>
> [Art work] should be like an open channel for penetration by impregnation in the sensibility of the immaterial space of LIFE itself.[38]
>
> I propose to artists that they pass by art itself and work individually to return to the real life in which a man no longer thinks he is the center of the universe, but the universe is the center of the man.[39]
>
> I love in myself everything that does not belong to me, that is, my life, and I detest everything that belongs to me: my education, my psychological and optical inheritance, . . . my vices, my defects, my qualities, my manias.[40]

But it is probable that there is more than Rosicrucian influence here. Klein read several books on Buddhism during his formative Rosicrucian period, both in France and in Japan, and although his sources in Buddhist literature cannot be specifically identified,[41] it seems that in the passages just quoted and others like them he was synthesizing Zen and Rosicrucianism and expressing the synthesis in art historical terms.

In Buddhist literature, the enlightened mind is often likened to empty space or the open sky with no internal divisions. As Milarepa, a Tibetan Buddhist sage, put it:

> A wise man knows how to practice
> The space-like meditation.
> In all he does by day
> He attaches himself to nothing.[42]

Klein's art is spacelike in its monochromy and immateriality; in its rejection of form it "attaches itself to nothing." He entitled himself "the Painter of Space,"[43] hostile to the birds and clouds which limit the openness of the sky by drawing lines across infinity,[44] and Buddhist authors also speak this way, for example Milarepa:

> [The awareness of voidness]
> is like the feeling of staring
> into a vast and empty sky...
> Thinking of the magnitude of the sky
> Meditate on the vastness with no center and
> no edge...
> It was fine when I contemplated the sky!
> But I felt uneasy when I thought of the
> clouds ...[45]

The art of the empty sky is the blue monochrome, portrait of Space and of the mind which is clear like Space.

According to Buddhist psychology, the origin of neurosis is a tendency to solidify energy so that it ceases to fill space completely and be one with it (as pure color does), and becomes a barrier (a line) dividing space into subject and object, ego and other. The arising of this first mental barrier is called "primary dualistic fixation," and it equates with the one line Klein refused to add to a monochrome in 1955 to get it into a show. Once this first barrier is in place, others are produced from it by a kind of mechanical momentum. Finally, space—the mind like the open sky, which formerly was open and free—becomes clogged and obstructed by unnecessary barriers which force one's energy to flow in certain channels. The overall pattern of these channels comprises the individual personality, the "education, ... inheritance, ... vices, ... defects, [and] qualities" which the painter of space rejects. The cure consists in erasing these barriers through meditation until the mental space is open again.[46]

And in painterly terms all this, as Klein saw, points toward the monochrome, toward erasing the cloudlike forms from the pure skylike ground. Buddhist authors at times even express this process in terms of eliminating figure from ground; the Zen image is wiping the dust from the mirror. The monochrome is an analogue of the experience of emptiness *(shunyata)*:

> Attention can be directed either to the concrete, limited forms or to the field in which these forms are situated. In the shunyata experience, the attention is on the field rather than on its contents.[47]

We may compare the words of a developmental psychologist on the ego-discovering and ego-transcending stages of life:

> It is necessary that the ego discover itself by a figure-ground relationship to this material universe, but it is also necessary to transcend this relationship.[48]

In a similar spirit Klein said that the monochrome is

> the only physical way of painting which permits attaining the spiritual absolute.[49]

Heindel's system points to the same conclusion for the painter: Life pervades Space and is negated by Form, which divides and obstructs Space. Hence the painter who heralds the end of the age of Form and Ego and the beginning of the age of Space and Life must, like the Buddhist meditator, erase internal barriers and restore Space to its wholeness. This means abolishing figure (which represents Form and Ego) from the ground (which represents Space and Life). The art of Form is evolutionarily outdated, just as is the physical eye which perceives it; art must now move directly toward the Void:

> For me painting is no longer a function of the eye; it is a function of the only thing which does not belong to us: our LIFE.[50]

> I am against line and all its consequences: contours, forms, compositions. All paintings of that type, whether figurative or abstract, seem to me to be windows of a prison of which the lines themselves are the bars. Far away, where color dominates, is freedom! The viewer of a painting with lines, forms, and composition remains the prisoner of his five senses.[51]

In the next age, when the immaterial Desire Body arises, we will not only be freed from our senses, but will live naturally in the realm "where color dominates," the Desire Realm. The artist of that new age will produce works that are one with the infinite, that is, with Life:

> Life, Life itself ... is the absolute art.[52]

But this new art cannot be made authentically without a corresponding inner erasure of barriers from the artist's mind, restoring it, like the ground of the painting, to the state before "primary dualistic fixation" set in.[53] The artist's "education, inheritance, vices," and so forth are affronts to the infinity of primal mind, as lines and figures are affronts to the infinite ground of the painting, which is the seed-bed of art as Chaos is the "seed-ground of the Cosmos," holding all things in a state of "pure pictorial sensibility."

When in 1957 Klein adopted the title "Yves the Monochrome," he was announcing, or claiming, that he had erased dualistic fixation from his own mind as he had erased figure from his paintings; that he had, in other words, entered the Desire World, the realm of color. Other artists, he believed, would follow if he beckoned on the way. At this evolutionary turning point the artist must realize his true kinship with Space and disentangle himself from the deathlike art of Ego and Form, which negates Life:

> [Artists who] wish to save their personality at any cost will kill their spiritual self and lose their LIFE.[54]

> [Monochromism is] a sort of modern-day alchemy, practiced by painters, born of the tension of experiencing ... a bath in space vaster than infinity.[55]

> The artist who creates should no longer

do so for the sake of signing his work, but, as an honest citizen of the immeasurable space of sensitivity, should create always from his awareness that he exists in a state of profound illumination, as does all the universe — but which we neither see nor feel, enclosed in the psychological world of our inherited optics.[56]

The true painter of the future will be a mute poet who will write nothing, but recount, without detail and in silence, an immense picture without limit.[57]

My monochrome paintings are landscapes of freedom.[58]

By painting Space, Klein was painting the All and acting out in his own person the condition of return to the All, to the mind like open sky. It is this awareness that comprises the "monochrome spirit," which Klein insisted was the essence of his painting and which he said was lacking in, for example, the white monochromes painted by Rauschenberg around 1950.[59]

After 1957 Klein made monochromes only of what he called "rose, gold, and blue," but mostly of blue (a near-ultramarine patented in 1960 as International Klein Blue—the name suggesting the new age which these paintings inaugurate, an age beyond distinctions of race or nation). Rose, gold, and blue are in effect red, yellow, and blue, the three primaries, and Heindel gives special importance to these colors, which, he says, "are God and make up the triune godhead," and which "correspond to the three aspects of God."[60] By working with these colors Klein was reconstituting Space in the likeness of God. But it was especially blue which for both Heindel and Klein represented the absolute, or Life. This symbolism was, in a sense, confirmed for Klein when Gaston Bachelard (in a tradition going back to Mallarmé's *azur*) identified blue with the absolute.[61] Blue for Klein is above all the color of dimensionless Space:

Blue has no dimensions. It is beyond dimensions while the other colors are not.[62]

The blood of the body of sensibility is Blue.[63]

I have consecrated myself to finding the most perfect expression of Blue.[64]
(Note the Heindelian capitalization.)

Thus when Klein painted various objects (from a miniature Nike of Samothrace to a globe of the world) with International Klein Blue, he was expressing the idea that Life or Spirit permeates ("impregnates") all things, even when they seem bound to the rack of Form. As Klein himself said in a passage which para-

phrases many Heindelian statements:

It was an impregnation which went beyond dimensions, which traversed everything, which impregnated itself into everything, in matter as well as in the atmosphere or in the void.[65]

This "impregnation" of matter by Spirit is perhaps best exemplified by the blue sponge works, which, like the blue monochromes, were first exhibited in 1957, the year of the Blue Revolution. The first sponge sculpture was exhibited at the multifaceted show at Colette Allendy's, in conjunction with the exhibition of blue monochromes at Iris Clert's. It was followed in later years by more sponge sculptures (sponges painted blue and mounted on blue pedestals) and the sponge reliefs (sponges painted blue and mounted in groups on blue-painted wood), of which those at Gelsenkirchen are the most impressive examples.

Art historically the sponge works relate both to the found object and to the development of new media. In Heindelian terms they, like the Nike painted in IKB, represent the permeation of all things with the Life of the "blue deep" of Space. Klein's own statements on the sponge works clearly direct us to this interpretation:

I had this experience in 1956 while painting my monochromes with sponges; after the sponges had dried, they were impregnated with blue. And I said to myself, that is beautiful in itself, and even more it is remarkable because it is the portrait of someone who saw how I was making my monochromes. It [the sponge] was there. It was a presence. It was impregnated with blue. It is the phenomenon of impregnation that is important.[66]

While working on my paintings in my studio, I sometimes would use sponges. They became blue very fast, of course. One day I saw the beauty of the blue in the sponge; this instrument of work had become prime matter.... [They were] portraits of viewers of my monochromes who, after having seen them, after having voyaged into the blue of my paintings, come back totally impregnated in sensibility, like the sponges.[67]

In fact, Klein's interpretation of these works seems to be directly based on passages in Heindel's *Cosmogonie*: the sponge is the *only* image Heindel uses (and he uses it repeatedly) to illustrate the permeation of the material realm by Spirit.

Let us take a spherical sponge to represent the dense earth.... Imagine that sand permeates every part of the sponge and also forms a layer outside the sponge. Let the sand represent the Etheric Region, which in a similar manner permeates the dense earth and extends beyond its atmosphere.[68]

We may regard the solar systems as separate sponges, swimming in a World of Divine Spirit.[69]

But the blue works were not the ultimate expressions of Space art. They remained the material signs of an immaterial essence. Klein was able to deny that Rauschenberg's monochromes were *really* monochromes on the grounds that the essence of any work of art is immaterial:

The pictorial quality of each painting [is] perceptible by something other than its material physical appearance.[70]

In fact, in order to be real, a painting *must* be invisible.[71] The physical painting is only a remnant of the passing age of the Physical World:

The physical painting has a right to exist only because people believe only in the physical, even while they feel obscurely the essential presence of the other thing.[72]

Of two paintings physically identical, one may be a real work of art, the other not.[73] What matters is the condition of the artist's mind. If he has developed higher sensibilities which relate to Life rather than to Ego, then Life will be present in his work at the etheric level and can be picked up by the etheric sensors of the viewer. Thus a specially trained sensibility is necessary to experience art; only special viewers, those "gifted with a body or vehicle of sensibility," will be able to carry away the immaterial essence of what they see.[74]

Klein definitely felt that his own works were rich in this higher-dimensional essence, so much so that a really receptive viewer, standing before one of the IKB monochromes, becomes, through receiving the immaterial essence of the painting, "extra-dimensional in sensibility, all in all, impregnated [like the sponges] with the sensibility of the universe."[75]

From this denial that the power of an art work resides in its physical form, it is a small step to the actual elimination of the physical object altogether. As Heindel had asserted,

Life may exist independently of Concrete Form; may have Forms not perceptible to our present limited senses, and amenable to none of the laws which apply to this present concrete state of matter.[76]

In 1958 Klein took this step, declaring that

the sensibility of color, still very material, must be reduced to an airier, more immaterial sensibility.[77]

The Blue Epoch's sequel would be the presentation to the public of pictorial sensitivity…unconcentrated and uncontracted.[78] The decision to eliminate the art object altogether became a program which dominated the remainder of his life. "Painting is a mode of existence," he wrote; "it is indecent and obscene to materialize."[79] The artist of the future will simply stabilize his sensibility in a certain space and leave it there to be picked up by the higher vehicles of his viewers.[80] This will be true immaterial art.

This theory, again, seems based on Heindel. In the coming Epoch, according to Heindel, man will reside primarily in the nonphysical Desire World, and art will necessarily be immaterial. In a sense the IKB monochromes are the last paintings of the gross physical Epoch; the immaterial works are the first works of the new or dawning Epoch, the first works not bound to a physical vehicle at all.

Klein devoted at least seven years to Rosicrucian work, and his art of the immaterial seems to constitute a claim to adepthood. According to Heindel, the first higher ability that is gained is the ability to read, from the etheric realm, the memory of nature, on which future art will be based. Klein definitely is expressing this view when he writes:

Human sensibility can be all-powerful on the immaterial level. His sensibility can read the memory of nature, past, present, future.[81]

Next comes mastery of the Desire Body, which is, says Heindel,

a vehicle of transcendent qualities, marvelously adaptable and so responsive to the slightest wish of the indwelling spirit that in our present limitations, it is beyond our utmost comprehension.[82]

With this vehicle the artist will create through mental concentration alone works of art which are much more splendid than any which the physical body can experience:

The painter [who attains to the Desire World]…soon learns that his thought blends and shapes these colors at will. His creations glow and scintillate with a life impossible of attainment to one who works with the dull pigments of Earth.[83]

In more distant future Epochs, the artist's power will grow even more awesome. In fact, Heindel provides us with a preview of art history for the next few

Epochs: in the dawning Epoch the artist will create, through concentration projected onto the Prime Matter, "forms which will *live* and grow like plants." In the next, "he can create living, growing and *feeling* things"; finally, "creatures that will live, grow, feel and *think*."[84]

Klein's first immaterial work, the room left empty in the Colette Allendy exhibition in 1957, went unnoticed by the visitors. The next year saw a more direct and ambitious foray into the immaterial in the classic exhibition *Le Vide*, in which the Galerie Iris Clert was emptied entirely of furnishings, painted white by the artist's own hand, and exhibited with various associated Blue Revolution motifs to thousands of avant-garde enthusiasts. The event was art historically apposite to an extraordinary degree and in a distinctly French tradition. Consider a philosopher's remarks on the many attempts to respond to Mallarmé's seminal avant-gardism:

> The production [by Mallarmé] of the blank sheet of paper as the poem on which he was engaged would find its parallel in the area of the fine arts not in the production of a blank canvas, but in something like the gesturing toward the content of an empty studio.[85]

But this is by no means all that Klein meant by the exhibition, which expressed his Rosicrucianism quite as much as his sense of the art historical moment—in fact, it is Klein's great brilliance to combine the two approaches so smoothly that either may seem a complete account of his intention. In this case Klein was exhibiting more than an empty space with transcendental implications. Something of his intention is hinted at in Albert Camus' famous comment in the guest book of the opening: "With the void, full powers." In Klein's own words he was "manipulating the powers of the void."

Starting in 1947 in Nice, in the company of Claude Pascal and Armand Fernandez,[86] and continuing until the end of his life,[87] Klein had practiced meditation on the lines set forth by Heindel, who instructs the aspirant to still his mind and visualize some object:

> At first the pictures which the aspirant builds will be but shadowy and poor likenesses, but in the end he can, by concentrating, conjure up an image more real and alive than things in the Physical World.
>
> When the aspirant has become able to form such pictures and has succeeded in holding his mind upon the picture thus created, he may try to drop the picture suddenly and, holding his mind steady without any

thought, wait to see what comes into the vacuum.

> For a long time nothing may appear and the aspirant must carefully guard against making visions for himself, but if he keeps on faithfully and patiently every morning, there will come a time when, the moment he has let the imaged picture drop, in a flash the surrounding Desire World will open up to his inner eye. At first it may be but a mere glimpse, but it is an earnest of what will later come at will.[88]

In time, one who has mastered this technique will not merely behold the Desire World, he will be able to "mold the ever-changing matter of the Desire World into innumerable and differing forms of more or less durability."[89] At this stage,

> the painter has endless delights in the ever-changing color combinations....He is, as it were, painting with living glowing materials and able to execute his designs with a facility which fills his soul with delight.[90]

Both Arman and Claude Pascal, who were still Klein's constant friends at the time of the exhibition *Le Vide*, testify that, prior to the opening, Klein spent forty-eight hours alone in the gallery practicing visualization exercises on the Heindel method, leaving the apparently empty gallery space filled with the "glowing and scintillating" forms of the Desire World molded by his concentration. He was not exhibiting merely the idea of emptiness or minimalness, but the actual presence of Prime Matter (Life) activated into a certain "more or less durable" configuration by his concentration. The full title of the exhibition, written by Klein, read,

> The specialization of sensibility from the state of prime matter to the state of stabilized pictorial sensibility.[91]

The Prime Matter, or Spirit, which was diffused through that room as through all space, was *specialized* by the artist into a certain form by concentration, then stabilized by him in that form long enough for the exhibition to take place.[92]

> As Klein himself said,
> It was in short a gallery of paintings, although it was empty; I presented the atmosphere of painting in a picture gallery and not only the walls, as many have believed.[93]

The visitors, whether they realized it or not, were walking among specialized forms of the "living glowing material" of the Desire World. Accordingly, something more than art education was going on in them. The extradimensional faculties of the viewers were being shaped invisibly by Klein's immaterial works; far from merely seeing an exhibition, the viewers were being hastened on the evolutionary path toward the new age. Klein later estimated that about 40 percent of the visitors had been successfully "impregnated" with the new level of sensibility.[94]

It seems that the artist took the occult level of this event quite seriously. Sometime later he confided to his wife-to-be that he had done something "very dangerous" that night, for which he feared he might have to die.[95] Again, the source of this anxiety may be found in Rosicrucian teachings. According to Heindel, in order to manipulate the invisible worlds, the "vital body" must be separated from the physical body and enter temporary union with bodies from the planes being visited:

> When a medium allows his or her vital body to be used by entities from the Desire World who wish to materialize, the vital body generally oozes from the left side....Then the vital forces cannot flow into the body as they do normally, [and] the medium becomes very exhausted....The danger of contracting disease is much greater.[96]

If the vital body separates from the physical body too long or too completely, death may result.

In 1959, Klein began selling "zones of immaterial pictorial sensibility" for a quantity of gold leaf (a different quantity for each series!), which would then be thrown into a river or other natural body of water while the buyer burned his receipt, thereby finalizing the "transfer." The ritual, like the adoption of the name "Yves the Monochrome," was an announcement of Klein's claim to mastery of the Void and hence to proprietorship of it. The alchemical associations of gold make it a proper coin for such transcendent wares, and by throwing it away the artist demonstrates that his art, like the sky, is "attached to nothing."

In the same year Klein "participated immaterially" in a group exhibition in Antwerp, standing briefly in his space in the Hessenhuis gallery and leaving it impregnated with his sensibility, indicated thereafter only by a sign which read,

> At first, nothing; then a deep nothingness; then a blue depth. (After G. Bachelard.)[97]

On the one hand this event might be called conceptual art, and as such it shows Klein's usual keen awareness of the art historical moment. On the other hand, it is a display of yogic, indeed almost godlike, prowess. The artist, through the technique of impregnating space with his sensibility, reproduces the basic creative method of the universe as described by Heindel:

> When God desires to create, He seeks out an appropriate place in space, which He fills with His aura, permeating every atom of the cosmic Root-substance of that particular portion of space with His Life.[98]

Well might Klein boast, "I have created paintings in immaterial states....I have manipulated the forces of the void."[99] It is not known what further immaterial works he was planning, but clearly the art of the immaterial had come to the forefront of his career. Minutes before his sudden death he expressed the intention of making, thenceforth, *only* immaterial works.[100]

Klein's monochrome paintings and art of the immaterial were the center of his career and mark its two stages. But they were accompanied by other works, perhaps secondary, which function as elaborations and underscorings of his Rosicrucian ideas. They will be discussed more briefly.

At some time after reading Heindel's *Cosmogonie* Klein conceived the famous *Monotone Symphony*: a group of singers and instrumentalists produce a single chord (basically a D-major triad in second inversion — D, F-sharp, A, with emphasis on the A),[101] for a specific number of minutes (varying from performance to performance), and then keep silent for a specified time.

Like the monochrome paintings, this work has a Rosicrucian meaning, based on Heindel's *Cosmogonie*. In fact, in this case alone do we have Klein's specific acknowledgment of Heindel's influence:

> At "Judo" (1947), a Rosicrucian cosmogony (a jazz interpretation of Max Heindel, Oceanside, California), I played the piano and dreamed of having a great orchestra, of composing, with music of a single tone, a "monochrome" symphony (not necessarily like jazz in spirit or rhythm), a single musical mass saturated with space, a melody melted into one note throughout.[102]

According to the *Cosmogonie*, sound is metaphysically prior to color; it resides at a higher level of the universe:

> The Physical World is the world of *Form*. The Desire World is particularly the world of *Color*; but the World of Thought...is the sphere of *Tone*.[103]

The World of Thought lies beyond the Desire World and is the second of the six higher realms through which Evolution will lead us. At this level sound and color are inextricably mixed, though sound is more primal. Heindel explains:

When a certain note is struck, a certain color appears simultaneously....Color and sound are both present, but the Tone is the originator of the color....it is this tone which builds all forms in the Physical World.[104]

Heindel gives specific attention to single prolonged tones and their effects:

If one note or chord after another be sounded upon a musical instrument...a tone will finally be reached which will cause the hearer to feel a distinct vibration in the back of the lower part of his head....That note is the "key-note" of the person whom it so affects. If it is struck slowly and soothingly it will build and rest the body, tone the nerves and restore health. If, on the other hand, it be sounded in a dominant way, loud and long enough, it will kill as surely as a bullet from a pistol.[105]

Sound, then, is metaphysically prior to bodies and wields creative or destructive power over them.

A potential highest initiate could hardly ignore this power, especially when Heindel advertised it so temptingly, saying:

None ranks so high as the musician....His is the highest mission, because as a mode of expression for soul life, music reigns supreme....music is different from and higher than all the other arts.[106]

The *Monotone Symphony* seems an attempt to wield the power of the "key-note" as a creative, alchemical instrument, actually strengthening the bodies of the listeners and building them for their transfiguration into higher vehicles. In fact, the keynote theory applies to entities larger than human, and may even enable the initiate to wield cosmic power and exert an effect on the entire earth:

The musician can hear certain tones in different parts of nature....These combined tones make a whole which is the key-note of the Earth — its "Tone."[107]

There is no mistaking where the title of Klein's "Cosmogonies" came from. Their substance also may be largely based on Heindel. Klein wished to show the direct mark (the "trace of the immediate") of the traditional four elements: water (the traces of rain on a prepared canvas), air (powdered pigment blown by the wind against a prepared canvas), fire (the "Fire Paintings"), and earth (the "Planetary Reliefs"). This program shows the influence of Heindel in several ways. First, the artist working with the four elements just at the point where they rise from or return into Prime Matter duplicates the process of

alchemy whereby, Heindel said, Spiritual Evolution is advanced.[108] Secondly, not only does the title "Cosmogonies" recall Heindel's title, but the works themselves epitomize Heindel's theory of Evolution, which holds that at the beginning of each great cosmic Period one of the four elements came into existence: in the Saturn Period there was only fire; in the Sun Period air was added; in the Moon Period, water; and in the Earth Period, earth.[109] Each element, in other words, symbolizes the inception of a new phase of Evolution up to and including our present Period. Thirdly, the invitation to the elements to express themselves directly and "randomly" on the empty surface relates to Heindel's description of how forces from the Void reach through into the Physical World. These forces penetrate into our world along apparently random lines of force, such as "the lines of force along which ice crystals form in water," which are in fact reflections of lines of force in the higher, invisible realms. Thus the rain "Cosmogonies," "Fire Paintings," air "Cosmogonies," and "Imprints" are crystallizations of energy patterns from higher worlds, beckoning on the path of Evolution. This intimate connection of realms Klein called "the immediate" and associated with the pole of Life:

My goal is to extract and obtain the trace of the immediate in natural objects.

This manifestation is always distinct from form, and it is the essence of the immediate, the trace of the immediate.[110]

This concern with "the immediate" relates also to Klein's Zen experience, and it is worth noting that the air-and-plant "Cosmogonies" (especially numbers 17–20 and 31)[111] look very much like Japanese grass paintings.

The "Fire Paintings" have, in addition to their place in the alchemical scheme, the special significance which Heindel attributes to gas, describing it as "not far removed from Chaos" and quoting Commenius, *"Ad huc spiritum incognitum Gas voco"* ("This unknown spirit I call Gas").[112] The fact that gas flame is blue seemed additionally significant to Klein, who denied that red and yellow were true colors of fire: fire, like all things close to the infinite, must first of all be Blue.

In addition to their functioning as the earth element in Klein's artistic alchemy, the "Planetary Reliefs" relate to Heindel's emphasis on the differentiation of the planets from the sun as signs of Evolutionary Periods[113] and to his doctrine of the Planetary Spirits (occult cosmic masters residing in the different planets and guiding the Evolution of our solar system),[114] as well as to the imminent prospect of actual interplanetary travel after Vostok I.

The "Anthropometries" have art historical, Zen, and Rosicrucian content. Art historically they relate to Paleolithic cave art (the hand prints), and it is probably not accidental that most of them are female imprints which look very much like ancient elementary goddesses. Many of them deal with the theme of levitation and thus with Rosicrucian evolutionary theory, especially ANT 96, *People Begin to Fly*, and ANT 102, *Architecture of the Air*, of which Klein specifically spoke as prophecies of the coming age of aerial men. In addition it seems very likely that they had Zen associations for Klein. He spent two years in Japan and specifically refers to the work of Hokusai, about whom there is a famous anecdote which is supposed to express something of the essence of Zen art. Hokusai was ordered to produce works on a certain day for the shogun's amusement:

> The day came and Hokusai, not in the least awed, entered the august presence carrying a basket. He stretched out a long roll of paper on the floor, drew a few dark-blue lines along it with a brush, then took a chicken from the basket. As those present watched with bated breath he coated the chicken's feet in vermillion ink of the kind used for seals, and turned it loose on the paper. The chicken ran away over the paper, leaving a trail of brilliant footprints as it went. Hokusai prostrated himself before the Shogun. "Autumn Maple Leaves Drifting on the Tatsuta River," he announced, and with one more obeisance withdrew.[115]

Hokusai's type of Zen art was called *ukiyo-e*, "floating-world prints,"[116] of which Klein's phrase "trace of the immediate" may be a slightly loose translation. In the description of Hokusai preparing the chicken's feet while the audience watched "with bated breath" one may dimly hear the source of those performances (such as the one in *Mondo Cane*) in which Klein prepared his girls and "let them loose" on the canvas in front of an attentive audience.

The architecture of the air never got beyond the drawing-board stage, but it is easy enough to see where it fits into Klein's scheme. It, like the "Anthropometry" *People Begin to Fly*, prophesies that "technological Eden" in which a whole society will be living in the condition of free space. As Klein conceived this age, "spaced-out" humans will not only live in invisible dwellings and travel by levitation, but also communicate through telepathy: they will have the ability "to dream reciprocally each

others' dreams" and to perceive the "thoughts which fly through the air."[117]

These "thoughts which fly through the air" are surely parts of Heindel's "memory of nature," which is everywhere moving around us at the etheric level, and which at the beginning of the new Epoch human beings will gain the ability to read. Once this ability develops, Heindel noted, it will be used for telepathic conversation and will make spoken language more or less obsolete as a mode of communication.

In 1960 Klein published a photograph in which he seems to make a swan dive from a second-floor ledge. From the art historical point of view the leap is an immediate prototype for happenings, conceptual art in which a documentary record replaces the art object, and body art. From a Rosicrucian point of view it represents the ascent from the Physical World into the Desire World and is yet another prophecy of the incoming age of levitation by its first artistic explicator. The headline, "A Man in Space," identifies the picture as in part a parody of the incipient Soviet and American space programs, stressing Heindel and Klein's belief that soon we will not need external vehicles to enter space:

> Today anyone who paints space must actually go into space to paint, but he must go there without any faking, and neither in an airplane, a parachute, nor a rocket: he must go there by his own means, by an autonomous, individual force: in a word, he must be capable of levitating.[118]

> Not missiles, rockets, or Sputniks will make man the "conquistador" of space.... He could not truly conquer space.... until he has realized the impregnation of space by its own sensibility.[119]

But the subtitle, "The Painter of Space Throws Himself into the Void," has another intention. At the second publication of the photograph, in the Krefeld catalogue of 1961, Klein captioned it "The Leap into the Void." The phrase "Leap into the Void," as Klein knew from his long sojourn in Japan and his study and practice of meditation, is a technical term in Zen meditation manuals, signifying the moment when, being very advanced in concentration, the meditator lets go the last vestiges of self and becomes free like open Space.[120] It is worth noting that Klein, always a Westerner, translated into an image of physical derring-do what in its native tradition was an inward mental event.

The foregoing analysis of the sources of Klein's thought has not mentioned Gaston Bachelard very prominently, and it is well to explain why. Past writers on Klein[121] seem to exaggerate his debt to Bachelard. Klein encountered Bachelard's writings first in April 1958,[122] a full ten years after Klein's thought had been shaped by the sage of Oceanside, California. Clearly he felt sympathy with Bachelard's assertions that "by changing space, by leaving the space of one's usual sensibilities, one enters into communication with a space that is physically innovating," and that "every new cosmos is open to us when we have freed ourselves from the tie of a former sensitivity."[123] But Bachelard did not provide the rigorous system of Klein's thought; that came from Heindel, while Bachelard, ten years later, provided welcome confirmation from a compatriot. In addition, Klein found Bachelard convenient as, in effect, a "cover" for his own Rosicrucianism. Bachelard's writings on the poetic imagination provide a kind of vague mood study or reverie on ideas very similar to Heindel's but not enunciated with Heindel's old-fashioned dogmatic precision; Klein found that when he presented himself as inspired by Bachelard he was taken more seriously than he was as a Heindelian disciple.[124] By that time Klein himself had come to see the label "Rosicrucian" as an embarrassing one to bear. He was happy to bring his ideas, based on Heindel though they were, into the wider cultural arena where Bachelard's writings (or at least his name) circulated. And, in case this sounds like an (at least nominal) apostasy, Heindel himself had advised:

> [An initiate] does not call himself a Rosicrucian; no true Brother does so publicly ....Not even the most intimate friends or relatives know of a man's connection with the order.[125]

In reading Klein's writings it is well to be aware that his apparent allusions to Bachelard are in fact often disguised allusions to Heindel. Bachelard, for example, uses the term "imagination" a great deal, and Heindel does not. Klein picked it up from Bachelard's works, but the meaning which he privately assigned to it is purely Heindelian. "Imagination" is in fact a synonym for "immaterial sensibility," which in turn signifies the mind which has become open like Space. As Klein wrote:

> This imagination of which I am speaking is not a perception, a trace of a perception, a memory, a familiar thing, a habit of colors and forms....It has nothing which can be perceived with the five senses, with the domain of sentimentality, or even of pure and fundamental emotion.[126]

In conclusion, there seems little doubt that Klein's brilliant theory of art and his multifaceted work involved the conscious and deliberate translation of the Rosicrucian system of Heindel into mid-twentieth-century art historical terms. Though other models may be useful also, it would be unwise for any interpreter to disregard this aspect of his career, which is unmistakably indicated by the biographical evidence, the testimony of his closest friends, and the documentary evidence in the Klein archive.

Although it seems both clear-cut and pervasive, Heindel's influence does not in the least detract from the originality of Klein's career — it makes it, in fact, more impressive. Many abstract artists have felt that their work was an expression of some traditional body of ideas, but none has arrived at so strong and solid a connection between the art historical context and the traditional ideas as has Klein. Malevich's "Ouspenskyism," Mondrian's Theosophy, Newman's Cabalism, Reinhardt's Zen are correspondences less clearly and fully articulated than Klein's Rosicrucianism. In short, Klein's career is a paradigmatic expression of the fact that abstract art may have both a philosophical content and a spiritual direction.

Thomas McEvilley

Notes

1. Joseph Kosuth, "Art after Philosophy," in Gregory Battcock, ed., *Idea Art: A Critical Anthology* (New York: Dutton, 1973), p. 168.

2. Hans-Georg Gadamer, *Philosophical Hermeneutics*, trans. and ed. David E. Linge (Berkeley: University of California Press, 1976), pp. 102–103.

3. Michel Foucault, *The Order of Things* (English translation of *Les Mots et les choses*) (New York: Random House, Vintage Books, 1973), p. 9.

4. Paris, 1947. Published in English as *The Rosicrucian Cosmo-conception* (Oceanside, California, 1937), from which all my citations are taken; the two editions are identical except for minor changes in format. Klein's own copy of the *Cosmogonie* (much annotated and dog-eared), as well as many of his Rosicrucian lessons and related journals, are gathered in the archive of the Musée National d'Art Moderne, Centre Georges Pompidou, Paris. My thanks to Rotraut Klein-Moquay for her permission to study these and other materials in the Klein archive.

   It should be noted that the Rosicrucian Society centered in Oceanside is to be distinguished from the Rosicrucian Order or AMORC, which is a separate organization with different literature. (The AMORC is the one which advertises in magazines.)

5. My thanks to Jean de Galzain, director of French students at the Rosicrucian headquarters in Oceanside, California, for kindly opening the Klein file for my inspection on August 6, 1979.

   Certain misapprehensions about the Rosicrucians and Klein's relationship with them have entered the record. In general, all authors have underestimated his devotion to this body of doctrine. In his journal for May 8th,1950, for example, Klein wrote, "Je n'ai plus qu'une chose à faire, la Cosmogonie et l'étude constante de la merveilleuse science que j'ai à ma disposition!" In 1952 he wrote that he was still devoting four hours a day to the study of this book.

   In addition there are various specific misapprehensions. Paul Wember, for example, underestimates the duration of Klein's Rosicrucian period (*Yves Klein* [Cologne: Verlag M. DuMont Schauberg, 1969], p. 45). Giuliano Martano confuses the Rosicrucian Society with the AMORC, and wrongly attributes the *Rosicrucian Manual*, an AMORC publication, to Max Heindel (*Yves Klein: Il Mistero Ostentato* [Turin: Martano Editore, 1970], p. 48, n. 14) (hereafter "*Mistero*"). Several authors treat the Rosicrucian Society as a continuation of the seventeenth-century Rosicrucian Brotherhood, with which in fact it has no known connection (e.g., *Mistero*, p. 41). The distinction is important, because Heindel, like Blavatsky and other nineteenth-century-type occultists, had received Indian and Tibetan input which seventeenth-century occultists lacked.

6. No definitive edition of the writings exists; the manuscripts are in the Klein archive. Several of Klein's essays are printed elsewhere in this catalogue. Where possible, I will cite the published selections of these works: in this catalogue; in the catalogue of the exhibition *Yves Klein*, at the Jewish Museum, New York, 1967 (hereafter "Jewish Museum cat."); the catalogue of the exhibition *Yves Klein* at the Union Centrale des Arts Décoratifs, Paris, 1969 (hereafter "Union Centrale cat."); *Le Dépassement de la problématique de l'art* (La Louvière, Belgium: Editions de Montbliart, 1959) (hereafter "*Dépassement*"); and *Mistero*. Translations from *Dépassement*, the Union Centrale cat., and *Mistero*

are my own.

7. Terms capitalized with surrounding quotation marks are generic titles of Klein's works ("Cosmogonies"); terms capitalized without quotation marks are those which Klein and Heindel capitalized as religious terms (Space, God, Life, etc.).

8. *Cosmo-conception*, p. 247.

9. Ibid., p. 252.

10. "Due to the Fact That," in *Yves Klein,* catalogue of exhibition at the Alexander Iolas Gallery, New York, 1962. Translated by Klein in collaboration with Neil Levine and John Archambault in spring, 1961.

11. Ibid.

12. "The Monochrome Adventure" (selections from the text are printed elsewhere in this catalogue).

13. "Due to the Fact That."

14. *Cosmo-conception*, p. 189.

15. Ibid., p. 190.

16. Ibid., p. 249.

17. Ibid., pp. 178–79.

18. Ibid., p. 29.

19. *Dépassement*, p. 22.

20. Max Heindel, *Occult Principles of Health and Healing*, 4th ed. (London: L. N. Fowler and Co., 1919), p. 163. Various Eastern traditions have the same doctrine, and they probably lie behind Heindel, as behind Blavatsky. See, e.g., Swami Muktananda, *Play of Consciousness* (San Francisco: Harper and Row, 1978), pp. 141, 146, 177–78, 184, etc., on "the eternal Blue of Consciousness," which "lives within all, pervades the entire universe, and sets it in motion."

21. *Dépassement*, p. 22: "Vide [=] Lumière bleue."

22. *Cosmo-conception*, p. 306.

23. Ibid., p. 315.

24. Ibid., p. 311.

25. Ibid., p. 125.

26. See, e.g., Francis Yates, *The Rosicrucian Enlightenment* (London: Routledge and Kegan Paul, 1972), pp. 48, 57, 97, 119, 129, 213. In Heindel, Eden was the "Lemurian Epoch" of the Earth Period (two Epochs ago), and the next Epoch will recapture the essential feature of the Edenic or Lemurian condition, access to the Desire World (see *Cosmo-conception*, pp. 275–82, 305). In Klein's writings, see the Union Centrale cat., p. 12; "Due to the Fact That"; "The Monochrome Adventure"; and "Le Théâtre du vide" in *Dimanche, the Newspaper of a Single Day*, an imitation newspaper that Klein published on November 27, 1960 (photographically reproduced elsewhere in this catalogue). See also Pierre Restany, *Yves Klein le monochrome* (Paris: Librairie Hachette, 1974), p. 24.

27. *Cosmo-conception*, p. 517.

28. Ibid., p. 305.

29. *Dépassement*, p. 2.

30. *Cosmo-conception*, p. 119.

31. "The War" (selections from this essay are printed elsewhere in this catalogue).

32. "Due to the Fact That."

33. "The War."

34. Ibid.

35. Ibid.

36. Ibid.

37. *Dépassement*, p. 19.

38. Ibid.

39. Ibid.

40. Preface to "The Monochrome Adventure," Klein archive.
41. They certainly included D. T. Suzuki's *Studies in Zen Buddhism* and Eugene Herrigel's *Zen and the Art of Archery*, but just as certainly there were others which are not known (interview with Arman, New York City, December 13, 1977).
42. G. C. C. Chang, ed., *The Hundred Thousand Songs of Milarepa* (New Hyde Park, New York: University Books, 1962), p. 102.
43. *Dimanche*, p. 1.
44. "Due to the Fact That."
45. Chang, ed., *Songs of Milarepa*, pp. 128, 146–47.
46. See, e.g., Chogyam Trungpa, "Space Therapy," *The Middle Way, the Journal of the Buddhist Society of London* 50.3 (November 1975): 107–11.
47. Herbert V. Guenther and Chogyam Trungpa, *The Dawn of Tantra* (Berkeley and London: Shambala, 1975), p. 27.
48. John Curtis Gowan, *Development of the Psychedelic Individual* (Buffalo: Creative Education Foundation, 1974), p. 55.
49. Jewish Museum cat., p. 22.
50. *Dépassement*, p. 1.
51. Ibid., p. 2.
52. Ibid., p. 20.
53. In fact, the earliest true monochromes are seventeenth-, eighteenth-, and nineteenth-century Tantric depictions of Pure Consciousness or the Unmanifest Absolute as an empty monochromatic ground. See, e.g., A. Mookerjee, *Tantra Asana* (New York: G. Wittenborn, 1971), pl. 97, and *Tantra Art* (New Delhi, New York, Paris: Kumar Gallery, 1966), pl. 95.
54. *Dépassement*, p. 19.
55. "The Monochrome Adventure."
56. Ibid.
57. "The War."
58. Union Centrale cat., p. 21.
59. Interview with Rotraut Klein-Moquay, June 30, 1977, Paris.
60. *Cosmo-conception*, p. 253. For other traditional interpretations of these colors see Wember, *Yves Klein*, pp. 21–24.
61. The chapter "Le Ciel bleu" in *L'Air et les songes* (Paris: José Corti, 1950).
62. "The Monochrome Adventure."
63. *Dépassement*, p. 5.
64. "The Monochrome Adventure."
65. MS I 2174, Klein archive: fragments of an interview of Klein by Pierre Restany.
66. Ibid.
67. Typescript carbon, Klein archive: "Remarques sur quelques oeuvres exposés chez Colette Allendy."
68. *Cosmo-conception*, p. 53.
69. Ibid., p. 55.
70. "The Monochrome Adventure."
71. *Dépassement*, p. 4.
72. "The Monochrome Adventure."
73. Ibid.
74. *Dépassement*, p. 6.
75. "The Monochrome Adventure." This essentially alchemical view of art, which makes both the producing and the beholding of art works into a kind of yoga, has a parallel in the tradition of Taoist painting, where it is understood that, if the artist's mind is established in the non-ego of *wu-wei* ("actionless action"), then the *ch'i*, or universal vital energy, flows through his brush and is crystallized onto the surface of the paper, from whence it may be regained by a viewer also in the state of *wu-wei*. Like Klein, the Taoist painters

worshipped space: "Space of any sort was regarded as filled with meaning since it was filled with Tao" (Mai-mai Sze, *Tao of Painting* [New York: Bollingen, 1956], p. 17). The Taoists' emphasis on the "unhewn block" is again similar to Klein's rejection of Form in favor of Prime Matter, as is the Taoist penchant for *i-hua* or "one-painting," "painting-the-oneness." (See Mai-mai Sze, *Tao of Painting*, p. 88 et passim, and Philip Rawson and Laszlo Legeza, *Tao* [New York: Crown Publishers, 1973], pp. 19–20.) It is quite possible that Klein encountered something of this view in the Zen painting tradition of Japan, but the evidence indicates that his own system had already been formed, by long study of Heindel, before his visit to Japan.
76. *Cosmo-conception*, pp. 248–49.
77. *Dépassement*, p. 24.
78. "The Monochrome Adventure." This statement, along with many writings on Klein, implies that *l'époque pneumatique*, the age of immaterial art, succeeded and replaced *l'époque bleue*; this seems not to be the case, however. The exhibition *Le Vide*, for which the term *époque pneumatique* was coined, involved many Blue Epoch motifs, and as late as 1960–62 Klein was making "Anthropometries of the Blue Epoch." It should be noted that Klein himself provided the term *époque bleue*, whereas Pierre Restany, who was not totally privy to Klein's Rosicrucianism, supplied the term *époque pneumatique*.
79. "The Monochrome Adventure."
80. Ibid.
81. "Due to the Fact That."
82. *Cosmo-conception*, p. 423.
83. Ibid., p. 118.
84. Ibid., p. 427.
85. Richard Wollheim, in *Minimal Art*, ed. Gregory Battcock (New York: Dutton, 1968), p. 392.
86. Interviews with Claude Pascal, July 3, 1977, Paris, and Arman, December 13, 1977, New York.
87. Interview with Rotraut Klein-Moquay, June 30, 1977, Paris.
88. *Cosmo-conception*, pp. 488–89.
89. Ibid., p. 41.
90. Ibid., pp. 118–19.
91. *Dépassement*, p. 4.
92. In fact, it seems possible that Klein had performed this "specialization" of the Prime Matter for each of his monochromes, too, as is suggested by his statement that of the visually identical blue monochromes exhibited in 1957 each "revealed an entirely different essence; ... none resembled another" ("The Monochrome Adventure"). This would seem to be the basis of Klein's idea of selling physically identical paintings for different prices.
93. MS I 2174, Klein archive: fragments of an interview of Klein by Pierre Restany.
94. Restany, *Yves Klein le monochrome*, p. 61.
95. Interview with Rotraut Klein-Moquay, June 30, 1977, Paris.
96. *Cosmo-conception*, pp. 62, 64.
97. *Dépassement*, p. 13.
98. *Cosmo-conception*, p. 186.
99. "Due to the Fact That."
100. Interview with Rotraut Klein-Moquay, June 30, 1977, Paris.
101. This has often been misreported; the Jewish Museum catalogue, for example, says, "Single C Major note is played for ten minutes" (p. 37; and cf. p. 24); need I point out that there is no such thing as a "single C Major note"? A glance at the music itself would show the D-major triad.

102. So the Jewish Museum catalogue translates this passage from "The Monochrome Adventure" (p. 32). But the typescript in the Klein archive reads:

> ... elle etait le résultat de toutes mes recherches passionées d'alors.
> Judo (1946), cosmogonie des roses-croix (1947) (interprétation Max Heindel, Océan-side, Californie), jazz, je jouais du piano et rêvais d'avoir un grand orchestre.

Note the punctuation: no quotation marks around "judo"; comma after the parenthesis; "jazz" outside the parenthesis. The syntax is confusing. Most likely the catalogue that begins the new paragraph is meant to explicate the phrase "toute mes recherches passioneés d'alors." I suggest: "it [the monochrome] was the result of all my passionate researches at that time, to wit, judo (which I was practicing in 1946), the *Cosmogonie des Rose-Croix* (which I was studying in 1947) (the interpretation [of everything] of Max Heindel of Ocean-side, California), and jazz; I used to play the piano and dream," etc. The disadvantage of this reading is that I have to insert a stop after "jazz." If the first translation is preferred, then the *Monotone Symphony* was originally to be entitled *Judo* and is identified as an interpretation of Heindel's *Cosmogonie*. If the second, then judo and Heindel's *Cosmogonie* are both asserted as sources for the monochrome idea, and the passage then modulates into the Heindel-and-jazz background of the *Monotone Symphony*.

103. *Cosmo-conception*, p. 119.

104. Ibid., p. 123.

105. Ibid., pp. 369–70.

106. Ibid., p. 127.

107. Ibid., p. 123.

108. Ibid., p. 438. It should be noted, however, that Klein showed virtually no interest in the earth element, which represented the age of bondage to matter and thus was in effect the enemy of his cause. In some passages he refers specifically to "the three elements, air, water, and fire"; occasionally, when four are implied, they seem to be air, water, fire, and light. See, e.g., "L'Eau et le feu" and "Avec les trois éléments classiques, feu, air, et eau," typescripts, Klein archive. The Planetary Reliefs, though they relate to the earth element, are redeemed by their reference to outer space.

109. Ibid., p. 234.

110. "Due to the Fact That."

111. Following the numeration of Paul Wember, *Yves Klein*.

112. *Cosmo-conception*, pp. 250–52.

113. Ibid., pp. 258 ff.

114. Ibid., p. 180.

115. Muneshige Narazaki, *Hokusai* (Tokyo: Kodansha International, 1968), p. 16.

116. See e.g., Henry P. Bowie, *On the Laws of Japanese Painting* (New York: Dover, n.d.), pp. 20–26.

117. Restany, *Yves Klein le monochrome*, pp. 146–47.

118. *Dimanche*, p. 1.

119. "Due to the Fact That."

120. See, e.g., Chang Chung-yuan, *Original Teachings of Ch'an Buddhism* (New York: Vintage, 1971), p. 43 et passim.

121. See, e.g., *Mistero*.

122. Both Klein's Sorbonne lecture (recorded on two long-playing records titled *Conférences à la Sorbonne, 3 juin 1959* [Paris: RPM, n.d.]) and a manuscript note in the Klein archive give this date.

123. *The Poetics of Space* (New York: Orion, 1964), p. 206.

124. Interview with Arman, May 27, 1979, Houston.

125. *Cosmo-conception*, pp. 250–51; see also pp. 400, 521, 528–29. It is interesting to note that Klein's one meeting with Bachelard was "a disaster " (Rotraut Klein-Moquay): Bachelard regarded him as "a crazy man" (Arman), and did not in the least accept him as a companion in the realm of ideas.

126. "Discourse on the Occasion of Tinguely's Exhibition in Düsseldorf, January 1959" (printed elsewhere in this catalogue).

Yves Klein: The Ex-Voto for Saint Rita of Cascia

Toward the end of February 1961, after the opening of his retrospective show at the Krefeld museum in Germany, Yves Klein took leave of Dr. Paul Wember, director of the museum, and set out for Italy, and the monastery of Saint Rita of Cascia in Umbria. The purpose of his journey was to deliver a votive offering, or ex-voto, honoring the saint; and without identifying himself, he left his offering with the sister portress at the door of the cloistered convent of the Augustinian nuns. These religious women follow the Rule of Saint Benedict. Those in the monastery of Saint Rita in Cascia have as their sole responsibility the upkeep of the saint's shrine.

The ex-voto that Klein gave to the convent in February 1961 consisted of a transparent plastic box about sixteen by twelve by two inches, divided into three compartments. The top compartment had three sections, each filled with a pigment — sequentially rose (monopink), ultramarine blue (International Klein Blue), and gold leaf (monogold). The entire length of the bottom compartment was occupied by three gold bars of different weights on a bed of blue pigment. The bars of fine gold represented the proceeds of sales of zones of immaterial pictorial sensibility. Yves Klein sold these zones of sensibility — pure space suffused with his presence — in exchange for gold: he gave the buyer a check representing the value of the gold received. If the buyer agreed to destroy the check, i.e., his title of ownership, by burning it immediately, all the gold was restored to the cosmos by being thrown into the Seine. In the opposite case only a part of the gold was so disposed of: the rest came to Klein for the time being, he having only a temporary and conditional title to it.

The first four sales of the immaterial took place in Paris. The new owners were, in chronological order, Peppino Palazzoli (November 18, 1959), Jacques Kugel (December 7, 1959), Paride Accetti (December 7, 1959), and Alain Lemée (December 8, 1959). In his ex-voto Yves Klein gave Saint Rita the gold left to him as a result of these first transactions, since three of the buyers had kept their checks and the fourth had not destroyed his until some time after the purchase.

The middle section of the plastic box was a wide slot containing a text by Klein, written on paper folded in pleats. The text is a hymn of thanksgiving to Saint Rita. After thanking her for past favors, Klein places himself under the saint's protection and invokes her aid to assure the success, beauty, and eternal survival of his work.

The sisters kept the anonymous ex-voto in the depository of offerings at the shrine. Following the 1979 earthquake, which shook the foundations of the monastery, it was necessary to do some remodeling. Rosario Scrimieri, the architect in charge, commissioned Armando Marocco, the painter, to execute a series of painted glass windows for the chapel. As his work progressed, the artist needed some gold leaf and asked the people at the monastery to provide it. The sisters brought him Klein's ex-voto. Marocco recognized it immediately, and when he went back to Milan, where he had lived for several years, he got in touch with me through Guido Le Noci (the "inspired" dealer in whose gallery I had opened the world premiere show of Klein's blue period, *L'Epoca Blu*, the first IKBs — on January 2, 1957). I met Marocco on May 19, 1980. We arranged for a meeting with the ecclesiastical authorities on June 18 at Cascia. This allowed me to talk with the Mother Superior of the convent for nearly an hour in the parlor, and to make photographs of the ex-voto and photocopies of the text — all with the consent of the hierarchy.

I knew about Yves Klein's devotion to Saint Rita (a devotion that was very popular in Nice, his native town); his aunt had taught him to practice it. He had told me about his earlier pilgrimages to Cascia. He had gone there twice before 1961 to pray to the saint of hopeless causes, and to beg her to help him in the important, critical moments of his career. Only two persons, Dr. Paul Wember and Rotraut Klein, knew of the existence of the recently rediscovered text, and they had both lost track of it. It seems that Dr. Wember had mailed what was presumably a copy of the manuscript, entrusted to him by Klein before he left for Cascia, to Rotraut, who had never received it. The text gives clear evidence of the depth and sincerity of the artist's faith; there is certainly no hint of fetishism. The invocation to Saint Rita and the plea for her intercession were the heart of Klein's prayer and the high point of his spiritual life within dogmatic ritual, as well as a reference to God the Father, to his Son Jesus Christ, to the Holy Spirit, and to the Virgin Mary.

Pierre Restany

(translated by W.G. Ryan)

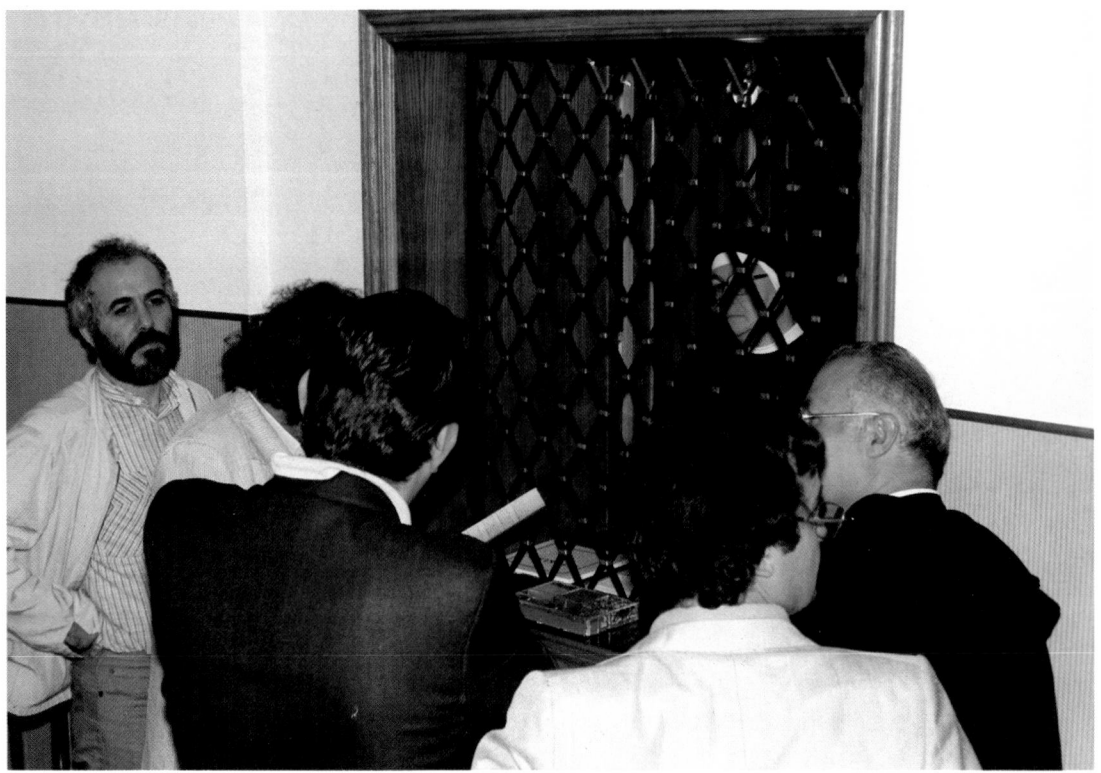

Pierre Restany at cloister window, shrine of Saint Rita of Cascia, Italy, June 18, 1980

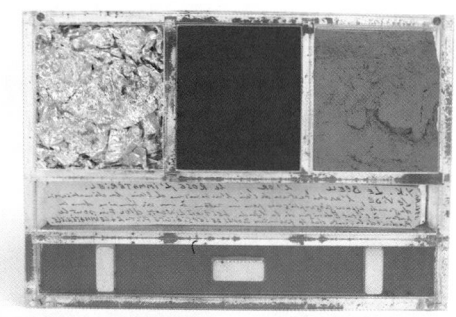 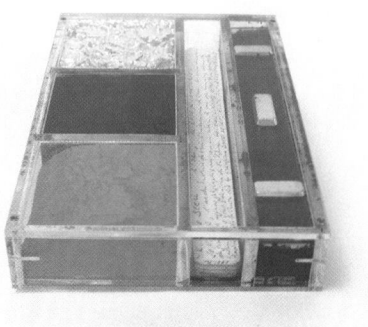

Yves Klein's ex-voto (two views)

1961, Feb.   Y.K.

—The BLUE, the GOLD, the PINK, THE IMMATERIAL. THE VOID, the architecture of the air, the urbanism of the air, the climatization of great geographic spaces for a return to a humane life in nature in the Edenic state of legend. The three bars of fine gold are the proceeds of the sale of the first 4 ZONES OF IMMATERIAL PICTORIAL SENSIBILITY.

—To God the Almighty Father in the name of the Son, Jesus Christ, in the name of the Holy Spirit and of the Blessed Virgin Mary.

By Saint Rita of Cascia under her guard and protection, with all my infinite gratitude. Thanks; Y.K.

—Saint Rita of Cascia, I ask thee to intercede with God the Almighty Father that he may always grant me in the name of the Son Jesus Christ and in the name of the Holy Spirit and of the Blessed Virgin Mary that I may live in my works and that they may become ever more beautiful; and may he grant also that I may discover always continually and regularly new things in art more beautiful every time even though alas I am not always worthy to be a tool to build and create Great Beauty. That everything that comes out of me be Beautiful. Amen. Y.K.

—Under the earthly guard of Saint Rita of Cascia: Pictorial Sensibility, the monochromes, the IKBs, the sponge sculptures, the immaterial, the static, positive, negative, and moving anthropometric imprints, the shrouds. The Fountains of Fire, of Water and Fire — the architecture of the air, the urbanism of the air, the climatization of geographic spaces thus transformed into constant Edens rediscovered on the surface of our globe — the Void.

—The theater of the Void — all the particular marginal variations in my oeuvre — the Cosmogonies — my Blue sky — all my theories in general —That my enemies may become my friends, and if that is impossible that all they may attempt against me may never result in anything that touches me, ever — make me, me and all my works, totally invulnerable. Amen.

—That all my works in Gelsenkirchen may always be Beautiful, more and more beautiful, and that they may be recognized as such more and more and as quickly as possible. That the Fountains of Fire and walls of Fire may be executed by me on the Operplatz in Gelsenkirchen without delay — That my exhibition at Krefeld may be the greatest success of the century and be recognized by all.

—Saint Rita of Cascia, saint of impossible and hopeless causes, thanks for the powerful, decisive, wonderful help thou hast given me until now — Thanks infinitely. Even if personally I am not worthy; grant me thy aid still and always in my art and always protect all I have created so that even in spite of myself it may always be of Great Beauty. Y.K.

Yves Klein's prayer to Saint Rita of Cascia, Italy, accompanying his ex–voto

A Technical Note on IKB

Yves Klein's synthesis of International Klein Blue (IKB) paint resulted from his desire to explore unencumbered color. Pure dry pigment, clear synthetic resin, and compatible solvents are the basic constituents of the paint. By skillfully manipulating the capabilities of the materials, the artist satisfied his aesthetic requirements without sacrificing artistic versatility.

In the mid-1950s Klein began to focus on pure color. Coincidentally, in 1954–55, he met Edouard Adam, a *droguiste* in Paris.[1] Although technically a purveyor of hardware, Adam also supplied various dry goods and chemicals, among them natural sponges and dry colored pigments. Klein came to Adam in search of materials he could not readily find in standard art supply shops. Adam in fact recalls the artist's joy at finding large quantities of dry pigments waiting to be sorted into specific drawers in the store. Klein purchased several colored pigments from Adam, but came to prefer an artificial ultramarine blue.[2] Though the artist had seen the pigment elsewhere, Adam was able to produce it more cheaply and in larger quantities than were commercially available.[3] Thus the artist was able to explore fully the rich blue pigment he so admired.

Klein sought to preserve "la matière colorée" in a medium that would bind colored particles to themselves and to the support yet not suppress their vibrancy as it dried.[4] Along with his contemporaries, he had experimented with variations of the traditional media available in the early 1950s—oil, glue, and other water-based binders. However, each appeared to smother and "kill" the individual grains of powder.[5] So the artist sought a newer matte medium capable of fixing pure pigment on the support without altering its appearance.

Klein's requisites were met by a synthetic resin also supplied by Edouard Adam.[6] The colorless medium, a polyvinyl acetate, was formulated by Rhône-Poulenc Industries and distributed under the name Rhodopas M.[7] To make the paint, pigment particles were blended with 95 percent pure ethyl alcohol and ethyl acetate in which solid pellets of Rhodopas M had been dissolved. The resin was also marketed as Rhodopas M60A, a stock 60 percent solution of Rhodopas M and ethyl alcohol. Stable in the presence of heat and light, this transparent material was an ideal carrier for the all-important colorant. It blended particularly well with the ultramarine blue pigment Klein purchased from Adam for his IKB paint.

By 1957 IKB had become the primary material Klein used to coat and color his work. Its formula included specific amounts of dry pigment, "Rhodopas MA," ethyl alcohol, and ethyl acetate. Indeed, by May 1960 Klein's affinity for his IKB paint prompted him to seek an official patent to protect the formula.[8] In his patent application, noting that he had used IKB from 1954 to 1958, he documented the major ingredients and specified proportions and methods of mixture. The only inconsistency in the patent is a description of "Rhodopas MA" as "chlorure de vinyl." Although Rhône-Poulenc produces a copolymer of vinyl chloride and vinyl acetate, its designation is Rhodopas AX, and it remains insoluble in ethyl alcohol and produces cloudy solutions with ethyl acetate.[9] Moreover, according to Rhône-Poulenc, "Rhodopas M" signifies the *M*edium-viscosity polyvinyl acetate, while "Rhodopas M60A" denotes the solution formed by the addition of *A*lcohol; the product identification and nomenclature within the company have remained relatively constant.[10] Therefore, one must conclude that Klein erred in designating "Rhodopas MA" as "chlorure de vinyl." Other details in the patent application are consistent with the use of polyvinyl acetate.

Although details of Klein's working methods remain unknown, the versatile IKB paint is readily adaptable to sundry applications. By varying the pigment concentration and the type of solvent, the mixture can be applied with brush, spray gun, or paint roller. Likewise, by manipulating the same variables, the paint could be suited to different substrates such as absorbent sponge or polyester resin. Finally, again by including more or less pigment and a faster- or slower-evaporating solvent, the material could appear chalky or fluid. Indeed, Yves Klein's mastery of his well-chosen medium enabled him to achieve his goal of enshrining pure color in a myriad of forms.

IKB became one the artist's trademarks. Pure pigment from a reliable supplier and quality synthetic resin in industrial solvents made such a paint possible. Yet, though quantifiable, this quintessence of unencumbered color owes its vitality and beauty to the magic of the artistic endeavor—a factor that can never be measured or duplicated.

Carol C. Mancusi-Ungaro
Conservator, Menil Collection

Notes

1. From the transcript of an interview with Edouard Adam by Nan Rosenthal, May 16, 1974, p. 1.
2. From the transcript of an interview with Edouard Adam by Virginie de Caumont, February 24, 1981, p. 2; regarding other colors that Klein may have used, Adam referred the interviewer to Jean-Paul Ledeur of Paris, a conservator familiar with Klein's work and recognized by Rotraut Klein-Moquay, the artist's widow.
3. Ibid., p. 4.
4. Extracts from Yves Klein's journal of 1957. Reprinted in *Yves Klein*, the catalogue of the exhibition at the Union Centrale des Arts Décoratifs, Paris, 1969, p. 27.
5. Ibid., p. 28.
6. From the transcript of an interview with Edouard Adam by Virginie de Caumont, February 24, 1981, p. 2.
7. Rhône-Poulenc Polymères, *Rhodopas: Documentation-Technique* (Courbevoie Cedex, October 1977), pp. 2-3; letter to author from Zora Pinney, Zora's Artists' Materials, Los Angeles, November 3, 1981.
8. Patent no. 63471, issued to Yves Klein on May 19, 1960, by L'Institut National de la Propriété Industrielle, Klein archive, Documentation Arts Plastiques, Musée National d'Art Moderne, Centre National d'Art et de Culture Georges Pompidou, Paris.
9. Rhône-Poulenc Polymères, *Rhodopas AX: Copolymères* (Courbevoie Cedex, September 1977), p. 5.
10. Author's telephone conversation with N. A. Sullo, Chemicals Division, Rhône-Poulenc Chemical Company, Monmouth Junction, New Jersey, December 11, 1981.

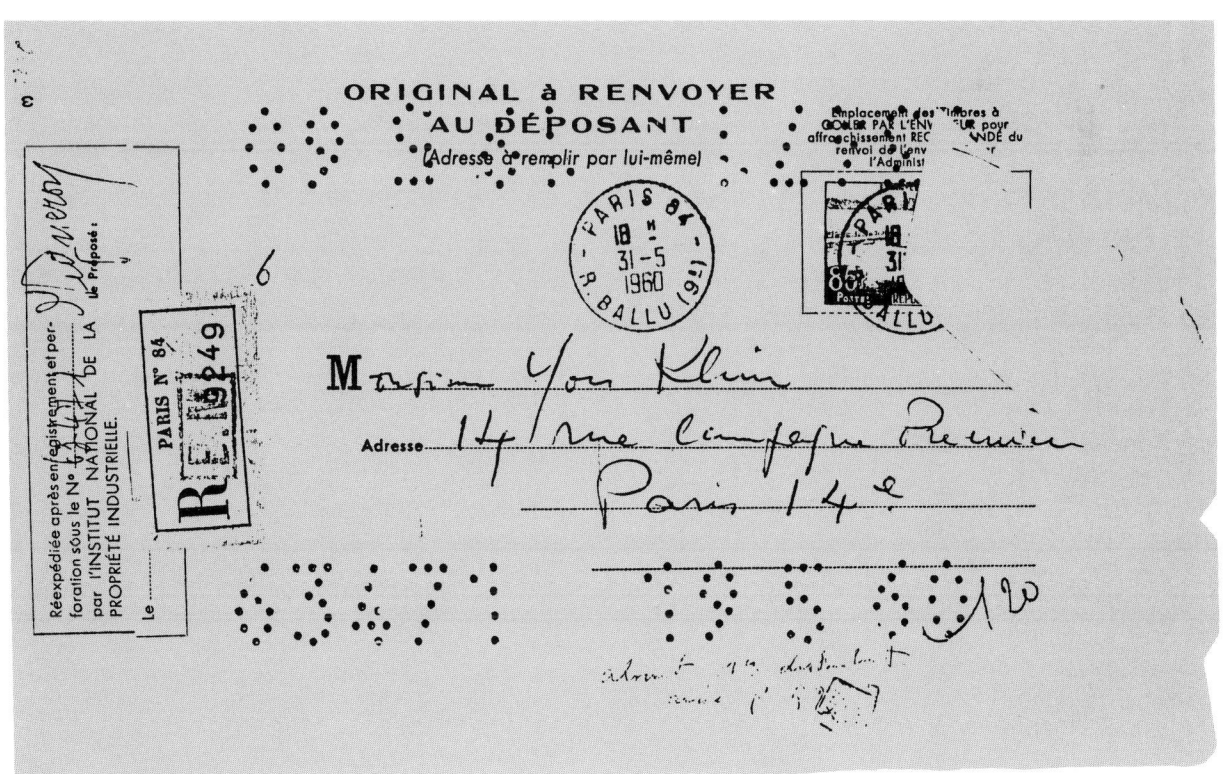

Klein's patent for International Klein Blue

Chronology

1928

April 28   Yves Marie Klein is born to Fred Klein and Marie Raymond, at 7:15 a.m., in the home of his maternal grandparents, rue Verdi, Nice, France. He is baptized in the Roman Catholic rite and dedicated to Saint Rita of Cascia. Fred Klein, born in 1898, is a painter whose works will be first exhibited in Holland in 1930. Marie Raymond, born in 1908, is a painting student who will begin to exhibit her works in Paris in 1945.

After several months his parents go to Paris, leaving him in the care of his maternal aunt, Rose Raymond (presently Rose Gasperini), in his grandparents' house.

Kasimir Malevich writes, "The painter is no longer bound to the canvas, but can transfer his composition to space."

1929

Remains in Nice.

Albert Einstein publishes the Universal Field Theory.

The American stock market crashes; worldwide depression deepens.

The Museum of Modern Art founded in New York City.

1930

Spring   Taken to Paris to live with his parents.

Autumn   Has a serious illness which endangers his life.

France begins building the Maginot Line.

Art Concret founded in Paris; includes Hélion and Van Doesburg.

Publication of *Civilization and Its Discontents*, by Sigmund Freud.

1931

Pierre Laval elected premier of France.

1932

Economic pressure forces the Klein family to return to the home of Marie's parents in Nice. After several months his parents return to Paris; he remains in Nice.

Franklin Roosevelt elected U.S. president.

Surrealism introduced to the U.S. through an exhibition organized by Julien Levy at his gallery in New York City (previewed in 1931 at the Wadsworth Atheneum, Hartford, under the title *Newer Super-Realism*).

1932–1939

Living in his grandparents' house, in his aunt's care, in Nice. His parents spend several summers with him in Cagnes-sur-Mer.

1933

Adolph Hitler appointed chancellor of Germany.

Wassily Kandinsky leaves Germany for France.

1934

Publication of *Art as Experience*, by John Dewey.

1935

Autumn   Enters the Ecole Masséna in Nice, where he remains until 1938; not generally successful in his schoolwork there.

Widespread government support of art begins in the U.S. as part of the New Deal economic recovery program.

Malevich dies in the U.S.S.R.

1936

Léon Blum elected premier of France.

Hitler and Mussolini proclaim the German-Italian Axis.

Exhibitions, *Fantastic Art, Dada, and Surrealism* and *Cubism and Abstract Art,* Museum of Modern Art, New York City.

1937

May 27   Makes his private first communion in Nice.

Summer   Artists' festival in Cagnes-sur-Mer; his parents participate.

Guernica bombed in the course of the Spanish Civil War.

1938

Autumn   Enrolled in private school on the rue Dante in Nice; his academic performance improves.

Early careers of such American artists as Barnett Newman, Jackson Pollock, Ad Reinhardt, Mark Rothko, and Clyfford Still under way.

1939

Returns to Paris early in the year to live with his parents.

May 25   Makes his public first communion at Notre-Dame-des-Champs, Paris.

Summer   In Cagnes-sur-Mer with his parents. Surprised by the declaration of war and unable to leave, they remain there until 1943.

Autumn   Enters school in Cagnes-sur-Mer.

France and Great Britain declare war on Germany.

Einstein takes a secret letter to President Roosevelt explaining the nature of atomic power and urging that the U.S. harness it before Germany does.

First arrivals of vanguard artists in New York City from war-torn Europe.

Founding of the Museum of Non-Objective Art (now the Solomon R. Guggenheim Museum), New York City.

1940

France falls to Germany. Marshal Pétain heads the French government.

Charles de Gaulle establishes a Free French government in exile.

Japan joins the German-Italian Axis.

Piet Mondrian leaves France for New York City to stay.

Kandinsky paints *Sky Blue* in Paris.

1941

Japan bombs Pearl Harbor. The U.S. enters World War II.

The Manhattan Project to build an atomic bomb begins in secret in the U.S.

Germany invades the U.S.S.R.

1942

World War II rages in Europe, Africa, and Asia.

Peggy Guggenheim opens a gallery, Art of This Century, in New York City, exhibiting European moderns and younger, advanced American artists.

Clyfford Still paints *Untitled (PH-613)*, revealing a vast, post-cubist space, in Oakland, California.

Marcel Duchamp arrives in New York City to stay.

1943

Returns to Paris with his parents; lives at 116 rue d'Assas. Plays the piano and generally neglects his schoolwork.

The French Resistance takes shape.

Roosevelt, Churchill, and Stalin meet in Teheran to discuss the future partition of Europe.

Publication of *Being and Nothingness*, by Jean-Paul Sartre.

Jackson Pollock paints *Guardians of the Secret* and has his first one-man exhibition at Art of This Century, New York City.

Clyfford Still retrospective, San Francisco Museum of Art, California.

1944

June   Goes on a Boy Scout camping trip to Normandy, returning to Paris just before the Allied landing. Is sent to the village of Milhars in the Tarn until late August.

Liberation of Paris by the Allies.

Jean Dubuffet has his first exhibition in Paris.

Deaths of Kandinsky in Paris and Mondrian in New York City.

1945

Autumn
:   Enters the Ecole du Génie Civil, 52 avenue des Wagrams, 75017 Paris, a private school that prepared students to take the Merchant Marine examination after the baccalaureate.

    Marie Raymond exhibits paintings in the Salon des Surindépendents, her first showing in Paris.

Surrender of Germany.

Death of Roosevelt.

The first atomic bomb is tested in New Mexico, then dropped on Hiroshima and Nagasaki. Japan surrenders.

De Gaulle elected president of the French provisional government.

Execution of Mussolini. Suicide of Hitler.

1946

Spring
:   Attempts the first baccalaureate exam and fails, thus becoming ineligible for the Merchant Marine Academy. Is never again formally enrolled in an academic institution.

    Marie Raymond participates in a group show at the Galerie Denise René, Paris; Fred Klein has a show at the Centre Anglo-Français, London.

Summer
:   Goes to London with his parents.

    Back in Paris, Marie Raymond begins her Monday night salons, which continue until 1954.

    Works in a bookstore, the Librairie des Champs-Elysées.

The United Nations founded.

Barnett Newman paints *The Beginning* and *Euclidian Abyss*.

Ad Reinhardt's first exhibition, Betty Parsons Gallery, New York City.

1947

August
:   Returns to Nice when his parents go to Holland for a show of Fred Klein's works. In Nice, begins painting scarves, some abstract, some figurative, a practice he continues off and on for several years.

September
:   Rose Raymond sets up a bookshop for him in her Philips appliance store, 39 rue de l'Hôtel des Postes, Nice. He works in the shop until October 1948.

    Enrolls in judo classes at police headquarters in Nice; there meets Claude Pascal and Armand Fernandez.

September 2	Becomes white belt in judo, that is, his formal instruction begins.
December 19	Becomes yellow belt in judo.
	Around the end of 1947 or the beginning of 1948, discovers Max Heindel's *La Cosmogonie des Rose-Croix*.

The U.S. program for European economic recovery (Marshall Plan) developed.

Manned supersonic flight achieved in California.

Publication of *Psychologie de l'art*, including "Le Musée imaginaire," by André Malraux.

Jean Dubuffet exhibits in New York City.

Jackson Pollock paints *Galaxy* and *Alchemy*.

Pollock, Rothko, and Still each has his first exhibition at Betty Parsons Gallery, New York City.

1948

January	Begins the systematic practice of Rosicrucianism with Claude Pascal and Armand Fernandez.
May	Klein, Claude Pascal, and Armand Fernandez meet Louis Cadeaux, who instructs them in Rosicrucianism and puts them in touch with the Rosicrucian Society of Oceanside, California.
May 4	Becomes orange belt in judo.
June 18	Klein and Pascal become members of the Rosicrucian Society.
	Attaches a small blue monochrome disc to his Rosicrucian notebook.
	The three friends divide the universe among themselves and alter their names: Yves Klein becomes Yves, Armand Fernandez becomes Arman, Claude Pascal becomes Pascal Claude. They become vegetarians and practice meditation daily, creating a "temple" in the cellar of Arman's parents' house; Klein paints one wall of the "temple" blue.
	Imprints hands, feet, and question marks on his shirt.
	Speaks (according to Arman's recollection in 1960) of "covering *judokas* with blue to obtain sharp, violent imprints."
September	Hitchhikes through Italy (Genoa, Portofino, Rapallo, Pisa, Rome, Capri, Ischia, Naples, Pompeii, Messina, Venice, Genoa, Nice).
September 24	Becomes green belt in judo.
November 16	Enters military service and is stationed in Germany, on the Lake of Constance.

Harry Truman elected U.S. president.

The Cold War intensifies. U.S.S.R.'s blockade of Berlin.

1949

October 27   Discharged from the army.

November   Goes to England with Claude Pascal; they live first on Hollywood Street, then at 69 Cromwell Road, SW7. Works at Robert Savage's frame shop on Old Brompton Road. Takes English lessons, attends Rosicrucian meetings and judo classes. Attempts to sell his parents' paintings at various galleries.

Conceives the idea of one-note or one-chord music as the visual corollary of one-color painting.

In late 1949 or early 1950, executes small rectangular monochromes of pastel on paper or cardboard; exhibits them privately to friends in his room.

The People's Republic proclaimed in China under Mao Tse-Tung.

The German Federal Republic established.

The U.S.S.R. tests its first atomic bomb. The U.S. test launches guided missiles.

Publication of *Essays in Zen Buddhism*, by D. T. Suzuki; it is translated into many languages.

Jackson Pollock paints *Number 10*; Mark Rothko paints *Violet, Black, Orange, Yellow on White and Red*; Clyfford Still paints *1949-C (PH-110)*.

Robert Rauschenberg creates *Female Figure (Blueprint)*.

Lucio Fontana creates *Black Environment* and his first perforated monochrome canvases.

1950

April   Klein and Claude Pascal hitchhike to Ireland and work at Jockey Hall, an equestrian club. Pascal mentions in his journal that Klein is drawing and painting.

April 4–26   Marie Raymond participates in a group show at Colette Allendy's gallery, Paris.

May   Tries with no success to sell his parents' paintings in Dublin galleries.

May 21   Writes a long reflection on painting in his journal.

July   Completes the Rosicrucian Society's intermediate course in philosophy.

August 25   Goes to London and resumes working in the frame shop. Claude Pascal arrives soon thereafter.

Autumn   Sends a postcard from London to Arman in Nice, one side monochrome pink, the other bearing a text by Claude Pascal: "The year 1951 will be pink Massacre."

Returns to Nice, stopping at Rosicrucian headquarters in Paris.

December 27   Completes the Rosicrucian Society's third course in philosophy.

December 31   Visits the Matisse chapel at Vence with his grandparents and aunt.

The Korean War begins.

Tachiste painting in Paris and Abstract Expressionism in New York and San Francisco at full tide.

Pollock paints *Autumn Rhythm* and *Lavender Mist*; Newman paints *The Name II* and *Vir Heroicus Sublimis*; Rothko paints *Green, Red on Orange*.

Newman's first one-man exhibition, Betty Parsons Gallery, New York City.

Sam Francis (one of a wave of younger American artists) settles in Paris and begins large "all-over" near-monochromatic paintings.

Nicolas de Staël's first one-man show in New York City.

Young Painters in New York and France organized by Leo Castelli at the Sidney Janis Gallery, New York City.

1951

January	Takes Spanish lessons.
February 4	Goes to Madrid, lives at 5 Calle de Puebla, and trains at two judo schools.
	Makes journal references to (1) "ideas capable of revolutionizing the world"; (2) presentation of monochrome paintings with appropriate musical accompaniment; (3) an allegory of colors. Conceives the idea of fountains of fire and water (according to his statement in 1958).
March	Begins to teach in two judo schools and makes a strong impression in both.
June	Travels in Spain with his parents, grandmother, and aunt, then returns to France with them.
August 30	Becomes brown belt in judo.
September	Tours Italy with his aunt, Rose Raymond.
Autumn	Lives in Paris near his parents, attending his mother's salons and auditing a course in Japanese at the Ecole des Langues Orientales. Writes a letter of inquiry to the Institut Franco-Japonais of Tokyo.

John Cage and Robert Rauschenberg make *Automobile Tire Print*, and Rauschenberg creates his series of *White Paintings*.

Barnett Newman paints *Cathedra*.

Ellsworth Kelly's first one-man show in Paris.

Publication of *Abstract Painting: Background and American Phase*, by Thomas Hess.

1952

February

Writes in his journal that he should spend four hours a day on Heindel's *Cosmogonie*.

July

His maternal grandmother (and godmother) dies in Nice.

August 22 or 23

Embarks for Japan at Marseilles, stopping at Crete, Suez, Djibouti, Colombo, Singapore, Saigon, and Hong Kong.

September 23

Arrives in Yokohama.

October

Engaged as a teacher at the Institut Franco-Japonais, Tokyo. Enrolls in the Kodokan Judo Institute, starting over again with the white belt and progressing quickly through brown.

Dwight D. Eisenhower elected U.S. president.

Ellsworth Kelly paints *Painting for a White Wall* and *Red, Yellow, Blue, and White*.

John Cage, with Rauschenberg, Merce Cunningham, David Tudor, and Charles Olsen, creates the first proto-happenings at Black Mountain College, North Carolina.

Jackson Pollock exhibition, Galerie Fachetti, Paris.

Georges Mathieu exhibition, Stable Gallery, New York City.

Harold Rosenberg's essay "The American Action Painters" published in *Art News*.

1953

January

Awarded the first *dan* black belt at the Kodokan Institute, Tokyo.

July

Second *dan*.

December

Obtains the diploma of fourth *dan*.

Invites a group of Japanese friends to his home to see small monochrome paintings in primary colors on paper or cardboard. Arranges shows of his parents' works at the Institut Franco-Japonais, the Bridgestone Gallery, and the Museum of Modern Art, Tokyo.

Death of Stalin.

End of the Korean War.

Publication in English of *The Voices of Silence*, including "Museum without Walls," by André Malraux.

Jean Tinguely begins making Meta-Machines in France.

Un Art autre (A Different Art) exhibition organized by Michel Tapié in France.

Clement Greenberg asserts the superiority of the new American painting over the French in a symposium titled "Is the French Avant-garde Overrated?"

Jasper Johns creates his first important abstract work, *Untitled*, a green painting.

1954

February	Arrives in Paris after a month's travel. The French Federation of Judo rejects his Kodokan diploma.
April	Signs a contract with Bernard Grasset, Paris, for publication of his book, *Les Fondements du Judo*, which appears in November.
May	Goes to Madrid, with Claude Pascal, as "technical director" of the Spanish Federation of Judo and is actively involved in teaching judo. Klein hangs monochrome paintings of unknown colors and sizes in the judo hall.
	Publishes the booklets *Yves Peintures* and *Haguenault Peintures*.
November	Rose Raymond visits him in Madrid, and he returns to France with her.
December	Attends the European judo championships in Brussels as a spectator.
	A drawing possibly of this period, signed "Gi 1954" and dedicated to Klein, is titled *Project for a Machine to Capture Pictorial Sensibility*; draftsman unknown (Klein archive, Centre Georges Pompidou, Paris).

The first hydrogen bomb exploded in a test in the South Pacific.

End of the French Indo-China War.

Beginning of the war in Algeria.

Ad Reinhardt exhibits yellow and blue near-monochrome paintings in New York City.

César and Jean Tinguely have their first exhibitions in Paris.

Death of Henri Matisse.

1955

January 11	Dines with his mother at Hans Hartung's house, where Sam Francis' work is described to him. Refers to the plates in *Yves Peintures* as "unicolor."
February	Begins teaching judo at the American Center, and continues to teach there until 1959.
Spring	Submits an orange painting to the Salon des Réalités Nouvelles; the painting is rejected on July 5.
	Meets Jean Tinguely.
	Meets Bernadette Allain, a young architect.
August 5	Uses the term "monochrome" in a letter and writes of it as "an idea of absolute unity in perfect serenity."

September	Opens a judo school at 104 boulevard de Clichy, Montmartre; in the judo hall he hangs several seven- or eight-meter-long monochromes in various colors, including blue, white, and pink, before which he sits to meditate.
October 15	First public exhibition, *Yves: Peintures*, Editions Lacoste—Club des Solitaires, 121 avenue de Villiers, 75017 Paris: shows monochromes of various colors.
October 24	Phones Pierre Restany, whom he has not met, and asks his help in arranging an exhibition at Colette Allendy's gallery. The next day Restany goes to Colette Allendy's and broaches the subject.
December 1	Meets Restany.

Meets Heinz Mack, who visits his studio in the foyer of the judo school.

Meets Iris Clert.

Death of Albert Einstein.

Jasper Johns paints *Green Target* and *Large White Flag*.

Robert Ryman makes his first white painting.

The Gutai Art Association, Osaka, presents art and performances by advanced Japanese artists. Kazuo Shiraga creates *Making a Work with His Own Body on a Slab of Wet Clay.*

Death of Nicolas de Staël.

1956

February 21–March 7	Exhibition, *Yves: Propositions monochromes*, Galerie Colette Allendy, 67 rue de l'Assomption, 75016 Paris; the catalogue's preface, "La Minute de Vérité," is written by Pierre Restany. At the gallery, meets Marcel Barillon de Murat, a Knight of Saint Sebastian, who invites him to join the order.
March 11	Dubbed a Knight of Saint Sebastian in the church of Saint-Nicolas-des-Champs.
Summer	Closes his judo school in Montmartre because of financial difficulties. The monochromes which had hung there are destroyed.
October 25	Appeals to the French Federation of Judo to recognize his Kodokan diploma.

Fidel Castro begins the revolution in Cuba.

Georges Mathieu creates "Paintings in Performance" before an audience at the Théâtre Sarah Bernhardt, Paris.

Sam Francis and Ellsworth Kelly have their first American exhibitions.

Arman's first one-man exhibition, Paris.

John Cage tours the U.S., lecturing.

Michel Tapié tours the U.S., lecturing on *art informel*.

Death of Jackson Pollock. Pollock retrospective, Museum of Modern Art, New York City.

1957

January 2–12	Exhibition, *Yves Klein: Proposte Monocrome, Epoca Blu*, Galleria Apollinaire, Milan. Eleven identical blue monochromes hang in one room, several monochromes of different colors in another. A red monochrome is bought by Count Panza de Biumo, a blue by Lucio Fontana.
May	Double exhibition: May 10–25, *Yves le monochrome*, Galerie Iris Clert; May 14–23, *Pigments purs*, Galerie Colette Allendy. At the Iris Clert opening, 1,001 blue balloons are released and the *Monotone Symphony* is played in a version recorded by Pierre Henry.
	Records the "Blue Cries" soundtrack for a short film he makes about his Paris Blue Period exhibitions.
May 31–June 23	Exhibition, *Yves: Propositions monochromes*, Galerie Schmela, Düsseldorf.
June 24–July 13	Exhibition, *Monochrome Propositions of Yves Klein*, Gallery One, London.
	Group shows: April, *Micro Salon d'avril*, Galerie Iris Clert, Paris; summer, *Ouverture sur le futur*, Galerie Kramer, Paris; August, *Internationaler Bericht der Gesellschaft der Freunde Junger Kunst*, Kunsthalle, Düsseldorf; October 12–30, *Arte Nucleare*, Milan.

The European Common Market created.

The U.S.S.R. launches the first earth satellites (Sputniks I and II).

Piero Manzoni creates his first "achromes."

Founding of the Zero Group, Cologne.

The Gutai Group presents *Art on Stage* in Osaka, including voices and sounds from an empty stage and an archery performance.

Imaginary Spaces exhibition organized by Pierre Restany, Paris.

1958

January	Commissioned to decorate the foyer of the new city theater in Gelsenkirchen, Germany.
Spring	Moves to 14 rue Campagne Première, Paris, where he lives till the end of his life.
April	Makes his first pilgrimage to the shrine of Saint Rita in Cascia, Italy, leaving a prayer that "the blue may be accepted everywhere." Writes Iris Clert from Assisi about "entirely blue monochrome panels" by Giotto, and declares Giotto his predecessor.
April 28	Opening of the exhibition *La Spécialisation de la sensibilité à l'état matière première en sensibilité picturale stabilisée* (*The Specialization of Sensibility from the State of Prime Matter to the State of Stabilized Pictorial Sensibility*)—also known as *Le Vide* (*The Void*)—at Iris Clert's gallery in Paris. Attempts to sell immaterial paintings in the gallery space. For his thirtieth birthday, his mother gives him Gaston Bachelard's *L'Air et les songes*.

May 20	Writes to President Eisenhower declaring the termination of the French national government by the Blue Revolution. A related letter from the same period, to the president of the International Conference on the Detection of Atomic Explosions, proposes that all future nuclear explosions be colored blue.
June 5	First "living brush" work, at Robert Godet's apartment on the Ile Saint-Louis (the term "Anthropometry" will be coined by Pierre Restany in 1960).
August	Meets Rotraut Uecker in Nice.
September	Goes to Cascia with his aunt, Rose Raymond, to leave a small blue monochrome for Saint Rita.
October	In Gelsenkirchen, meets with Werner Ruhnau; they carry out experiments which fail to produce an "air roof."
November 17	Opening of a joint exhibition with Tinguely, *Vitesse pure et stabilité monochrome* (*Pure Speed and Monochrome Stability*), at the Galerie Iris Clert. The exhibition includes blue discs turning at 300 kilometers per hour.
	Indicates in sketches and notes various projects never realized: (1) an "air roof" for a ruined German church; (2) the blue illumination of all paintings in the Salon des Réalités Nouvelles; (3) a blue monochrome Stations of the Cross for the chapel of Saint Martin, Pontoise; (4) a "pneumatic rocket"; (5) an exhibition of chemically prepared paintings on the theme "Evil and War Disappearing before John XXIII," some of which were to change color, others to disintegrate into powder within thirty minutes of being exposed to air.

Charles de Gaulle elected president of the Fifth French Republic.

Publication of *Zero 1* in Düsseldorf.

Rothko begins his Four Seasons project, a unified series of near-monochromatic murals.

1959

January	Speaks at the opening of Tinguely's exhibition at the Galerie Schmela in Düsseldorf.
March 17	Shows an immaterial piece at a group show, *Vision in Motion*, at the Hessenhuis, Antwerp; offers it for sale for one kilogram of gold.
Spring	Begins working with Claude Parent on drawings for the "architecture of the air."
	Draws up a proposal for aeromagnetic sculpture, asserting his priority in the idea over Takis.
June 3 and 5	Lectures at the Sorbonne on "The Evolution of Art toward the Immaterial" and "Architecture of the Air."
June 15–30	Exhibition, *Yves Klein: Bas-reliefs dans une forêt d'éponges*, Galerie Iris Clert, Paris.
July 7	Breaks with Iris Clert.
October 12	Writes to architect Philip Johnson requesting that he and Ruhnau be invited to the United States to lecture on the "architecture of the air."
November 18	First sale of a Zone of Immaterial Pictorial Sensibility, to Peppino Palazzoli. In December he sells three more zones.

December 15	Attends the opening of the city theater in Gelsenkirchen.

Stops teaching judo.

Publication of *Le Dépassement de la problématique de l'art*.

A film by Jean-Pierre Mirouze, *L'Ecole de Nice*, includes sequences of Klein.

Group shows: May 29, *Artistes et architectes de Gelsenkirchen*, Galerie Iris Clert, Paris; July 3, *Junge Maler der Gegenwart*, Künstlerhaus, Vienna; September 4, *Sélection pour le XI Premio Lissone*, Galleria l'Attico, Rome; October 2, *Première Biennale des Jeunes de Paris*; October 7, Leo Castelli Gallery, New York; November 8, *Kunstsammler am Rhein und Ruhr, Malerei 1900–1959*, Städtisches Museum, Leverkusen; *Dynamo I*, Galerie Renate Boukes, Wiesbaden.

Fidel Castro becomes premier of Cuba.

Publication of *Marcel Duchamp*, by Robert Lebel, in Paris and New York City: first comprehensive review of Duchamp's work.

The New American Painting, Alfred Barr's major exhibition including Newman, Pollock, Rothko, and Still, opens in Paris as part of its European tour.

Takis exhibits "telemagnetic" sculptures in Paris.

Manzoni exhibits *Air Bodies* (balloon works) and his canned excrement, each work offered for sale at the price of its weight in gold.

Allan Kaprow presents *Eighteen Happenings in Six Parts* in New York City.

Frank Stella paints his first series of black abstract paintings.

Robert Irwin paints his first near-monochrome "line paintings."

1960

January 12	Leaps from the ledge of Colette Allendy's house, 67 rue de l'Assomption, in the presence of Bernadette Allain.
March 9	Performance, *Yves Klein: Anthropométries de l'époque bleue*, Galerie Internationale d'Art Contemporain, Paris.
April 23	At La Coupole, founds ADAM, the Association pour le Dépassement de l'Art Moderne (Association for the Bypassing of Modern Art); the association has no further meetings.
May	Obtains a patent on a paint formula under the title International Klein Blue.
	With Restany, Mirouze, Pascal, and Arman, founds the International Klein Bureau, empowering the others to make IKB monochromes and sign them with his name.
Summer	Makes the first Cosmogonies.
October 11– November 13	Exhibition, *Yves Klein le monochrome*, Galerie Rive Droite, Paris.

Leap photographed at 3 rue Gentil Bernard, at the corner of Maréchal Gallieri in the suburb of Fontenay-aux-Roses, Paris.

October 27   Les Nouveaux Réalistes founded by Restany in Klein's apartment; signers of the group's first manifesto, written by Restany, are Arman, François Dufrêne, Raymond Hains, Martial Raysse, Daniel Spoerri, Jean Tinguely, and Jacques de la Villeglé. A quarrel that erupts at this first meeting leads to the verbal dissolution of the group, which however remains precariously intact for some time.

November 10   Makes a "Collective Anthropometry" of New Realists Arman, Hains, Restany, Tinguely, and himself.

November 27   *Dimanche, le journal d'un seul jour* goes on sale.

Considers undertaking two lawsuits: one against Iris Clert for selling "false anthropometries," the other against filmmaker Claude Chabrol for a fictional portrayal of the making of Anthropometries in the film *Les Godelureaux*.

Group shows: February, *Antagonismes*, Musée des Arts Décoratifs, Paris; March 18, *Monochrome Malerei*, Städtisches Museum, Leverkusen; April, *Les Nouveaux Réalistes*, Galleria Apollinaire, Milan; November 18, second Festival d'Art d'Avant-garde, Paris.

John F. Kennedy elected U.S. president.

Ad Reinhardt devotes the rest of his life to making 60-inch-square black paintings of almost imperceptibly trisected space. His black paintings are exhibited at the Galerie Iris Clert, Paris.

Jean Tinguely creates *Homage to New York* at the Museum of Modern Art and visits southern California.

Arman exhibits *Le Plein* (the gallery filled with garbage), Galerie Iris Clert, Paris.

A Zero Group exhibition in Düsseldorf includes inflated forms illuminated in the night sky by searchlights.

Edward Kienholz conceives "Concept Tableaux" (written propositions such as *The World*) in Los Angeles.

La Monte Young performs his *Butterfly Sonata* in Berkeley, California. The composition is silent: the composer sits at a piano, releases a butterfly from a jar, and leaves the stage when the butterfly has vanished from sight.

1961

January 14–
February 26   Exhibition, *Yves Klein: Monochrome und Feuer*, Museum Haus Lange, Krefeld, Germany.

April   Travels to New York with Rotraut Uecker and stays at the Chelsea Hotel.

April 11–29   Exhibition, *Yves Klein le monochrome*, Leo Castelli Gallery, New York City.

April 25   Accredited by the French Federation of Judo, long after he has stopped teaching judo.

Various journal entries attest to extreme financial difficulties.

May	Travels to Los Angeles with Rotraut Uecker.
May 17–June 10	In a group show, *A 40° au-dessus de Dada*, Galerie J, Paris, organized by Restany. In connection with this exhibition Restany writes a second manifesto, declaring the New Realists to be descendants of Dada; Klein writes from the United States objecting violently, and only Restany signs the manifesto. On October 8, Klein, Raysse, and Hains declare the New Realists dissolved because of the manifesto.
May 29–June 24	Exhibition, *Yves Klein le monochrome*, Dwan Gallery, Los Angeles.
June	Exhibition, *Yves Klein*, Galleria La Salita, Rome.
July 17–18	Back in Paris, performs, for cameraman Paolo Cavara, sequences of Anthropometries which will appear in Gualtiero Jacopetti's film *Mondo Cane* the following year.
July 18–19	Makes thirty Fire Paintings at the Centre d'Essais du Gaz de France, Paris. The presence of a naked woman for the Fire Anthropometries on the second day causes the center's director to withdraw permission for further sessions. (Klein had worked at the center several days earlier in the year.)
August 17	Writes to Philip Johnson objecting to Fire Fountains and Fire Paintings by others planned for the upcoming New York World's Fair. No known response.
Summer	Makes a film with Sacha Sosnowsky of imprints of Rotraut Uecker's body in sand.
November	Occupied with making Planetary Reliefs.
November 1	His contract with art dealer Jean Larcade goes into effect: Klein is to be paid 3,500 francs per month, in return for which Larcade can buy Klein's works at one-third normal price and receives a 20 percent commission on sales in Europe and 5 percent on architectural projects.
	Visits Cascia, accompanied by Rotraut Uecker, leaving an ex-voto with a long prayer. A few weeks later, makes his last visit to Cascia.
November 21	Exhibition, *Yves Klein le Monochrome: Il Nuovo Realismo del Colore*, Galleria Apollinaire, Milan.
	In collaboration with Claude Parent, plans fountains of fire and water, *Les Fontaines de Varsovie*, for the Palais de Chaillot, Paris (never realized).

First manned space flight: a U.S.S.R. satellite orbits the earth with Yuri Gagarin, and U.S. astronaut Alan Shepard mans a rocket into space. The earth is directly observed as a blue sphere in the black void of space.

Joseph Beuys begins teaching at the Düsseldorf Art Academy.

Manzoni exhibits *Line 1000 Meters Long*, in response to Klein's championing of color in the "Battle between Line and Color." Manzoni also signs and exhibits living human begins.

Robert Rauschenberg and Frank Stella have exhibitions in Paris.

Sixteen Americans exhibition at the Museum of Modern Art, New York City, includes works by Kelly, Johns, Rauschenberg, and Stella.

Publication of *Silence*, by John Cage.

Dan Flavin begins making monochrome art works, which include electric light fixtures.

Mark Rothko retrospective, Museum of Modern Art, New York City, followed by a European tour, including Paris.

1962

January or February	Begins casting Portrait Reliefs of the New Realists.
January 21	Marries Rotraut Uecker in the church of Saint-Nicolas-des-Champs, Paris. A party is held afterward in Larry Rivers' studio. Pierre Henry presents Klein with his second recorded version of the *Monotone-Silence Symphony.*
January 26	Sale of a Zone of Immaterial Pictorial Sensibility to Dino Buzzatti.
February 2	Sale of another zone to Michael Blankfort. (Edward Kienholz has bought a zone as well, but the ritual of transfer is completed only after Klein's death, by Rotraut Klein and Arman.)
March 1	Makes a collaborative "Scroll Poem" on a cloth scroll about fifteen feet long, with Claude Pascal, Arman, and Restany.
March 7	In the group show *Antagonismes 2: L'Objet,* Musée des Arts Décoratifs, Paris, contributing maquette drawings (by Claude Parent) for the "architecture of the air" and related projects, and the "Scroll Poem."
March 30	Photographed lying beneath *The Tomb—Here Lies Space.*
May 11 or 12	Flies to Cannes for the premiere of *Mondo Cane;* suffers shock and humiliation at the manner in which he is portrayed.
May 14	In Paris, breaks off with Jean Larcade by letter, complaining that his monthly salary has not been paid regularly.
May 15	Participates in a panel discussion at the Musée des Arts Décoratifs, at which he becomes agitated and angry. Afterward he goes to the opening of the exhibition *Donner à voir* at the Galerie Creuze, where he experiences severe chest pain later diagnosed as a heart attack.
June 6	Dies of heart failure in his apartment on the rue Campagne Première in the presence of Rotraut Klein.
July 23–31	Exhibition, *Rétrospective Yves Klein,* Tokyo Gallery, Tokyo.
August	Rotraut Klein gives birth to Yves Klein's son, Yves, in Paris.
November 5–24	Exhibition, *Yves Klein,* Alexander Iolas Gallery, New York City.

Georges Pompidou forms a government in France.

The U.S. military council established in South Vietnam.

Cuban missile crisis.

Pope John XXIII convenes the Second Vatican Council.

Tinguely stages *Study for the End of the World* in the Nevada desert.

Jasper Johns exhibition, Galerie Sonnabend, Paris.

An exhibition at the Janis Gallery, New York City, shows French New Realists and U.S. and English Pop artists together for the first time.

Ben Vautier puts himself on sale as a "living, moving sculpture" and "signs" Yves Klein's death as an art work.

1963

April	Exhibition, *Yves Klein et le langage du feu*, Kaiser Wilhelm Museum, Krefeld.
April 30–May 20	Exhibition, *Yves Klein le monochrome: Peintures de feu*, Galerie Tarica, Paris.
May	Exhibition, *Yves Klein*, Svensk-Franska Konstgalleriet, Stockholm.

John F. Kennedy assassinated. Lyndon B. Johnson becomes U.S. president.

Hans Haacke begins his water and wind sculptures.

Rauschenberg retrospective, Jewish Museum, New York City.

Death of Piero Manzoni.

Ben Vautier "signs" Manzoni's death as an art work.

1964

March–April	Exhibition, *Yves Klein, le monochrome: Empreintes*, Galerie Bonnier, Lausanne.
April 15–May 20	Exhibition, *Peintures de feu*, Galerie Schmela, Düsseldorf.

The U.S.'s Ranger III takes the first photographs of the dark side of the moon.

Rauschenberg wins the grand prize at the Venice Biennale.

Brice Marden begins making monochromatic paintings.

Dan Flavin exhibition of fluorescent light, Green Gallery, New York City.

Robert Mangold's first one-man exhibition, New York City.

Arman exhibition, Stedelijk Museum, Amsterdam.

1965

April 12	Exhibition, *Yves Klein*, Galerie Alexandre Iolas, Paris.
October 22–December 13	Exhibition, *Yves Klein, a Retrospective Exhibition*, Stedelijk Museum, Amsterdam.

De Gaulle reelected president of France.

Tinguely retrospective, Jewish Museum, New York City.

Joseph Beuys' *Twenty-four-Hour Piece*, Düsseldorf.

Stan Vanderbeek begins developing his *Movie Drome*, which relates to some of the projects Klein outlined in *Dimanche*.

Günter Brus and Rudolf Schwarzkogler begin their self-injury pieces in Vienna.

Exhibition, *Inner and Outer Space, an Exhibition Concerning Universal Art*, organized by Pontus Hulten, Moderna Museet, Stockholm, includes a major Yves Klein selection.

1966

March 3–April 3   Exhibition, *Yves Klein*, Palais des Beaux-Arts, Brussels.

Summer   Exhibition, *Yves Klein, peintures de feu*, Galerie Bonnier, Lausanne.

France leaves NATO.

Major public demonstrations in the U.S. against the Vietnam War.

Daniel Buren makes identical "paintings" of stretched red fabric in Paris for two years.

Major early earthworks by Richard Long, Robert Morris, and Robert Smithson, which relate to Klein's project of remodeling and reclimatizing the face of the earth.

Bruce Nauman and Vito Acconci begin body works in the U.S.

James Turrell makes his first Projection Pieces in southern California.

Ad Reinhardt retrospective, Jewish Museum, New York City.

Brice Marden one-man exhibition, New York City.

Death of André Breton.

1967

January 25–March 12   Exhibition, *Yves Klein*, Jewish Museum, New York City.

Exhibition, *Yves Klein*, Galerie Bischofberger, Zurich.

Israeli-Egyptian War in the Middle East.

Robert Ryman's first one-man exhibition, New York City; he creates the *Standard* series (thirteen all-white paintings on steel).

Daniel Buren and others hang paintings in an inaccessible room and distribute a leaflet describing them in detail.

Claes Oldenburg installs an "invisible sculpture" behind the Metropolitan Museum of Art, New York City, digging a grave-size hole and filling it up again.

Hans Haacke creates *Sky Line* (a balloon piece), Central Park, New York City.

Publication of "Art as Idea as Idea," by Joseph Kosuth.

Joseph Beuys founds the German Student Party, Düsseldorf.

Michael Heizer's first earthworks, Nevada.

Rockne Krebs creates his first laser light structures, Washington, D.C.

Zero Group dissolved.

Jackson Pollock retrospective, Museum of Modern Art, New York City.

Death of Ad Reinhardt.

1968

February 17–March 17	Exhibition, *Yves Klein—Louisiana*, Louisiana Museum, Humlebaek, Denmark.
April 2–May 12	Exhibition, *Yves Klein in Nürnberg*, Institut für Moderne Kunst, Kunsthalle, Nuremberg.
June	Exhibition, *Yves Klein*, National Gallery, Prague.
November 7–December 15	Exhibition, *Yves Klein*, Galerie Michel Couturier, Paris.

Assassinations of Martin Luther King and Robert Kennedy in the U.S.

Richard M. Nixon elected U.S. president.

Tet offensive in Vietnam.

The U.S.S.R. invades Czechoslovakia.

Worker and student demonstrations in France.

James Lee Byars sends a mile of gold thread into space on a series of helium balloons, New York City.

Robert Irwin and James Turrell begin perceptual phenomena research with Dr. Edward Wortz in southern California.

Death of Lucio Fontana.

Death of Marcel Duchamp.

1969

January 25–March 11	Exhibition, *Yves Klein, 1928–1962*, Musée des Arts Décoratifs, Paris.
June 30–August 15	Exhibition, *Yves Klein*, Galerie Lambert-Monet, Geneva.
November	Exhibition, *Le Monochrome*, Galleria Blu, Milan.
November–December	Exhibition, *Yves Klein*, Galleria d'Arte Martano, Turin.
	Exhibition, *Yves Klein*, Musée d'Art Moderne, Grenoble.

American astronaut Neil Armstrong becomes the first man on the moon.

First Concorde flight, Paris–New York.

De Gaulle resigns as president of France; Georges Pompidou elected as his successor.

Exhibition of Takis' *Magnetic Fields*, Guggenheim Museum, New York City.

Jean Tinguely's *Kamikaze Monument*, Kanagawa, Japan.

Christo's *Wrapped Coast: One Million Square Feet* performed on the South Australian coast; photodocumentation by Shunk-Kender.

Exhibition, *The Ghost of James Lee Byars* (an apparently empty room), Kunsthalle, Düsseldorf.

Exhibition, *Number 7*, organized by Lucy Lippard for the Paula Cooper Gallery, New York City: an apparently empty room contains a magnetic field by Robert Barry, air currents by Hans Haacke, existing shadows by Robert Huot, and other works.

Exhibition, *Invisible Painting and Sculpture*, organized by Tom Marioni for the Richmond Art Center, Richmond, California.

Joseph Beuys accepts full responsibility for any snowfall in Düsseldorf from February 15 through February 20.

James Turrell and Sam Francis make aerial pieces with planes and clouds over Pasadena, California.

Exhibition, *When Attitude Becomes Form*, including a major Yves Klein selection, organized by Harold Szeemann, Berne.

1970

January 26	Exhibition, *Yves Klein le monochrome*, Galleria dell'Obelisco, Rome.
November–December	Exhibition, *Klein–Manzoni*, Studio C Arte Moderna, Brescia.
December 2–31	Exhibition, *Yves Klein*, Galleria Civica d'Arte Moderna, Turin.

China launches its first space satellite.

Robert Barry's exhibition of a closed gallery, Los Angeles.

Deaths of Mark Rothko and Barnett Newman.

1971

February–March	Exhibition, *Yves Klein*, Museum of Modern Art, Belgrade.
June 9–July 25	Exhibition, *Yves Klein*, Kunstverein, Hanover.
August 4–29	Exhibition, *Yves Klein*, Kunsthalle, Berne.

Presidents Pompidou and Nixon meet in Paris.

Massive U.S. bombing in Cambodia and North Vietnam.

Tinguely retrospective at the Centre National d'Art Contemporain, Paris.

Barnett Newman retrospective, Museum of Modern Art, New York City.

Chris Burden's *Shoot*, F Space, Santa Ana, California: the artist is shot through the arm with a .22-caliber rifle bullet.

The Rothko Chapel inaugurated in Houston, with eight murals by Mark Rothko.

1972

December 16, 1972– February 17, 1973	Exhibition, *Marie Raymond—Yves Klein*, Château-Musée, Cagnes-sur-Mer.

President Nixon visits China, opening diplomatic and cultural relations.

Daniel Spoerri retrospective at the Centre National d'Art Contemporain, Paris.

Documenta V exhibition, Kassel, Germany, presents the largest international survey of advanced and controversial art forms since World War II.

1973

February 3–March 14	Exhibition, *Yves Klein*, Galerie Karl Flinker, Paris.
March 30–May 5	Exhibition, *Yves Klein*, Gimpel-Hanover Galerie, Zurich.
May 30–June 23	Exhibition, *Yves Klein*, Gimpel Fils, London.
May 27–July 29	Exhibition, *Frühe Gelbe, Schwarze, Weisse, Orange, Grüne: Bilder von Yves Klein*, Kaiser Wilhelm Museum, Krefeld.

U.S. troops withdraw from Vietnam.

Eric Orr creates *Zero-Mass Space* (the first of a series of dematerializing spaces), Pomona College, California.

Ellsworth Kelly retrospective, Museum of Modern Art, New York City.

Death of Robert Smithson.

1974

March 20–April 28   Exhibition, *Yves Klein*, Städtische Kunstsammlungen, Ludwigshafen, Germany.

March 20–May 15   Exhibition, *Yves Klein, 1928–1962*, Tate Gallery, London.

Death of Georges Pompidou.

Richard Nixon resigns as U.S. president.

The world oil shortage and increasing prices disrupt the international economy.

James Turrell begins the Roden Crater Project in Arizona.

Arman retrospective, La Jolla Museum of Contemporary Art, California.

1975

First international manned space flight: U.S. and U.S.S.R. satellites link up in earth orbit.

1976

June 4–July 12   Exhibition, *Yves Klein*, Nationalgalerie Berlin, Neue Berliner Kunstverein, and July 20–August 28, Städtische Kunsthalle, Düsseldorf.

October 19–
November 20   Exhibition, *Yves Klein, Feux*, Galerie Karl Flinker, Paris.

American scientists land a robot on Mars.

Inauguration of the Musée National d'Art Moderne, Centre Georges Pompidou, Paris.

Gerhardt Richter begins sets of identical *Gray Paintings*.

Robert Rauschenberg retrospective, Smithsonian Institution, Washington, D.C., followed by a U.S. tour.

1977

March 3–April 2   Exhibition, *Yves Klein*, Sidney Janis Gallery, New York City.

Launching of the first U.S. space shuttle.

Jasper Johns retrospective, Whitney Museum, New York City.

1978

The United Nations opens its conference on disarmament.

Mark Rothko retrospective, Guggenheim Museum, New York City.

1979

October 19–
November 17

Exhibition, *Yves Klein*, Fuji Television Gallery, Tokyo.

Eric Orr's *Space as Prime Matter, Gold as Prime Matter, Fire as Prime Matter* exhibited in Los Angeles.

Clyfford Still retrospective, Metropolitan Museum of Art, New York City.

1980

The price of gold reaches a record high on the international market.

1981

Westkunst exhibition, including a major Yves Klein selection, organized by Kasper Koenig, Cologne.

1982

Jackson Pollock retrospective, Centre Georges Pompidou, Paris.

This chronology was compiled by Thomas McEvilley with help from many sources. He was especially aided by Virginie de Caumont's detailed chronology of Klein's life, by the research of Nan Rosenthal, and by materials in the Klein archive, Centre Georges Pompidou.

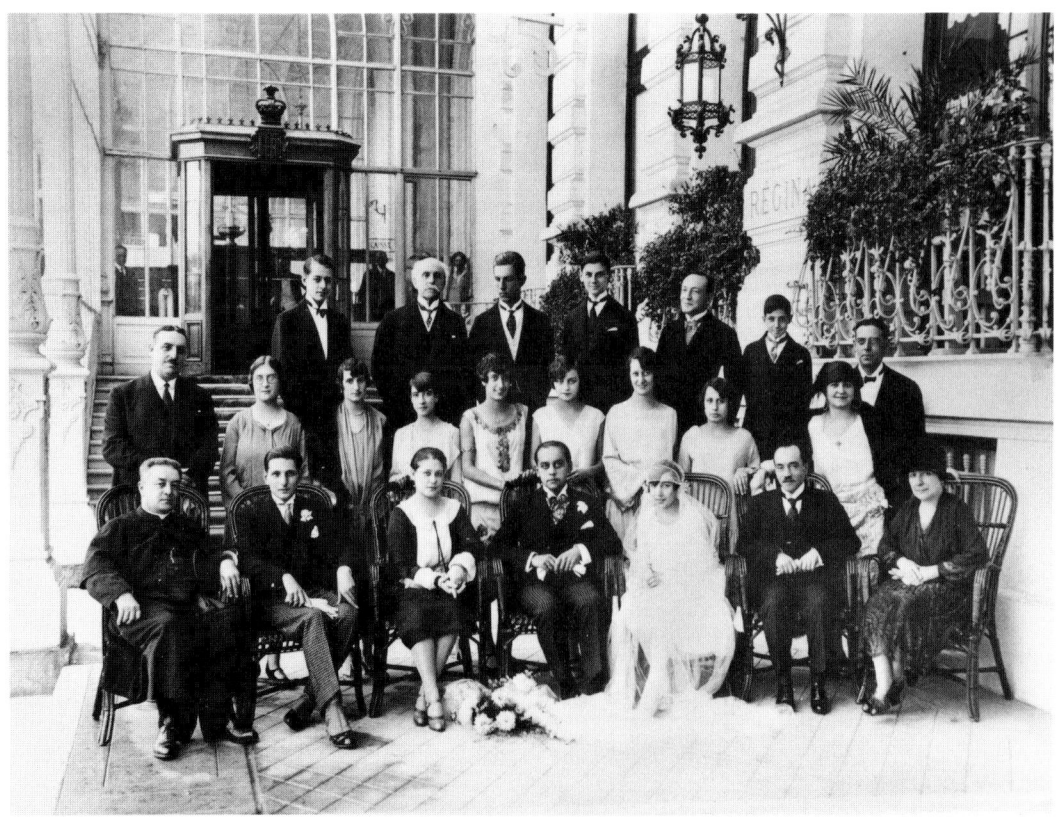

fig. 1. The wedding of Fred Klein and Marie Raymond, Nice, October 26, 1926

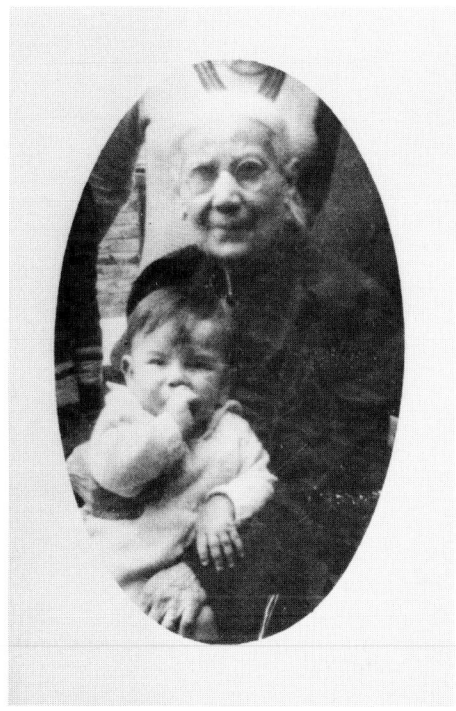

fig. 2. Yves Klein and his maternal grandmother, 1928

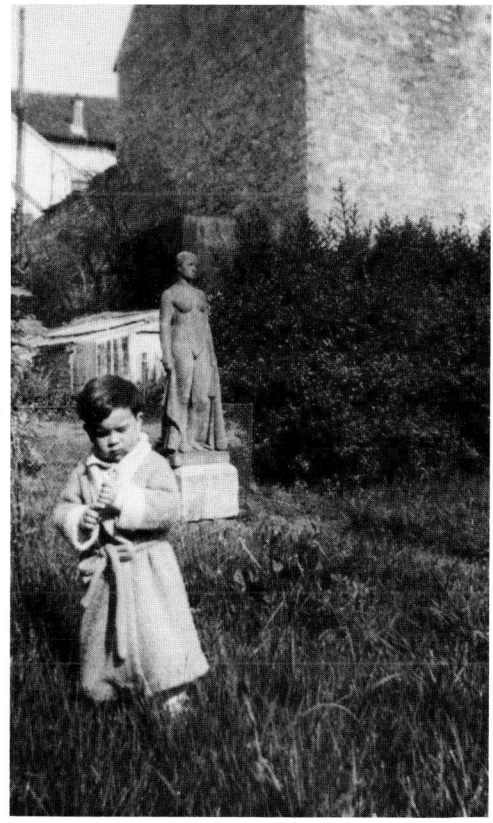

fig. 3. Yves Klein, c. 1931

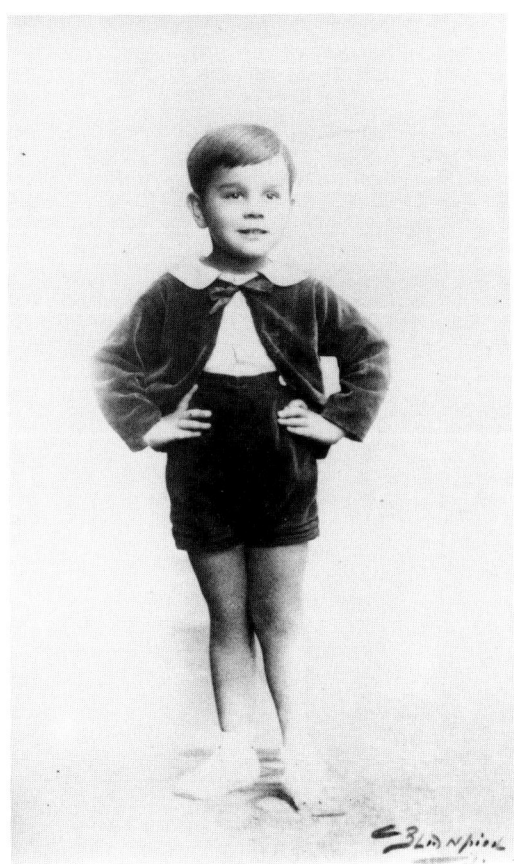

fig. 4. Yves Klein, 1933

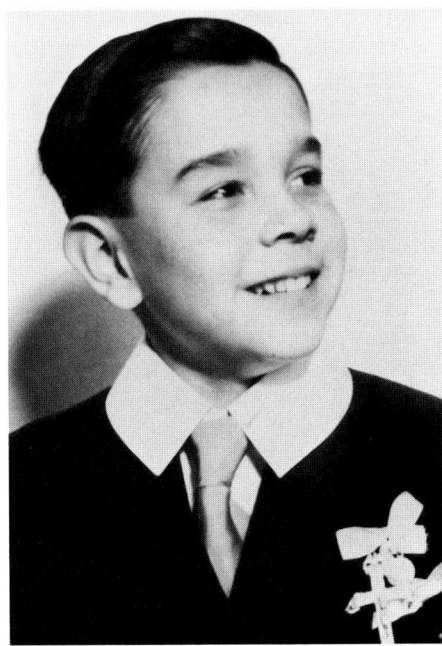

fig. 5. Yves Klein at the time of his first public communion, Paris, May 25, 1939

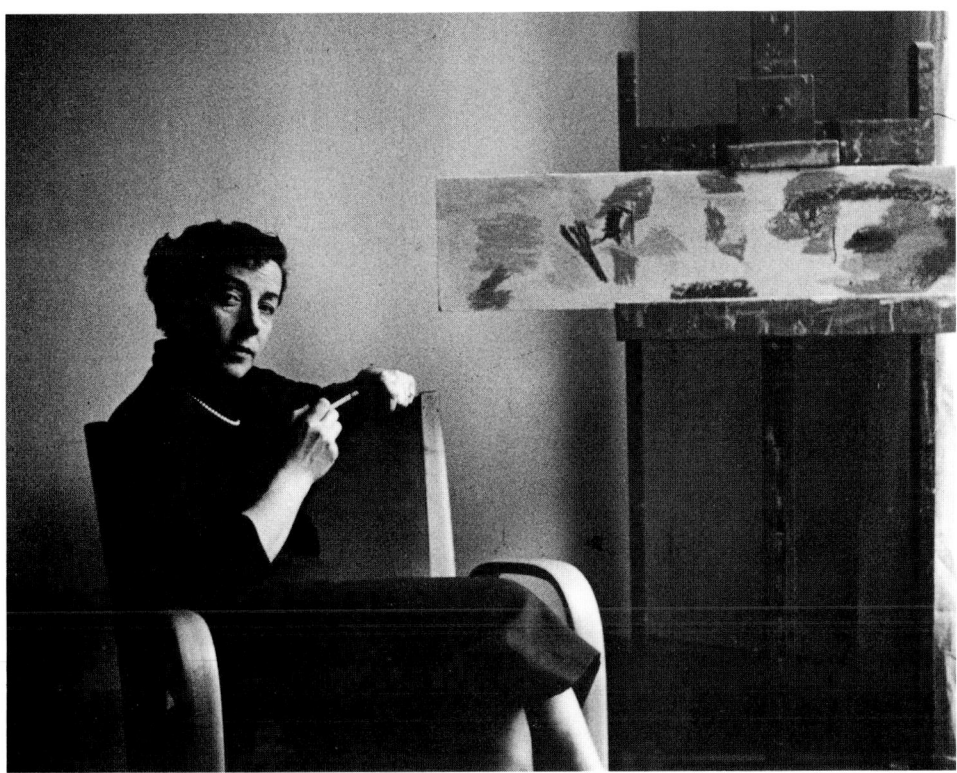

fig. 6. Marie Raymond and her work, c. 1958

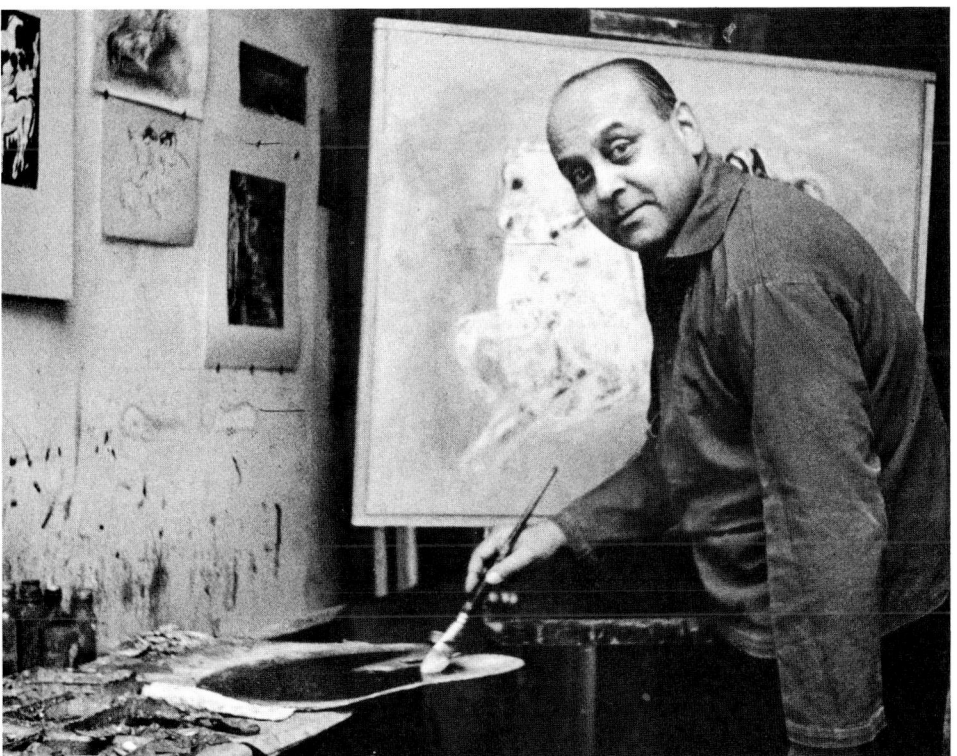

fig. 7. Fred Klein in his studio, c. 1958

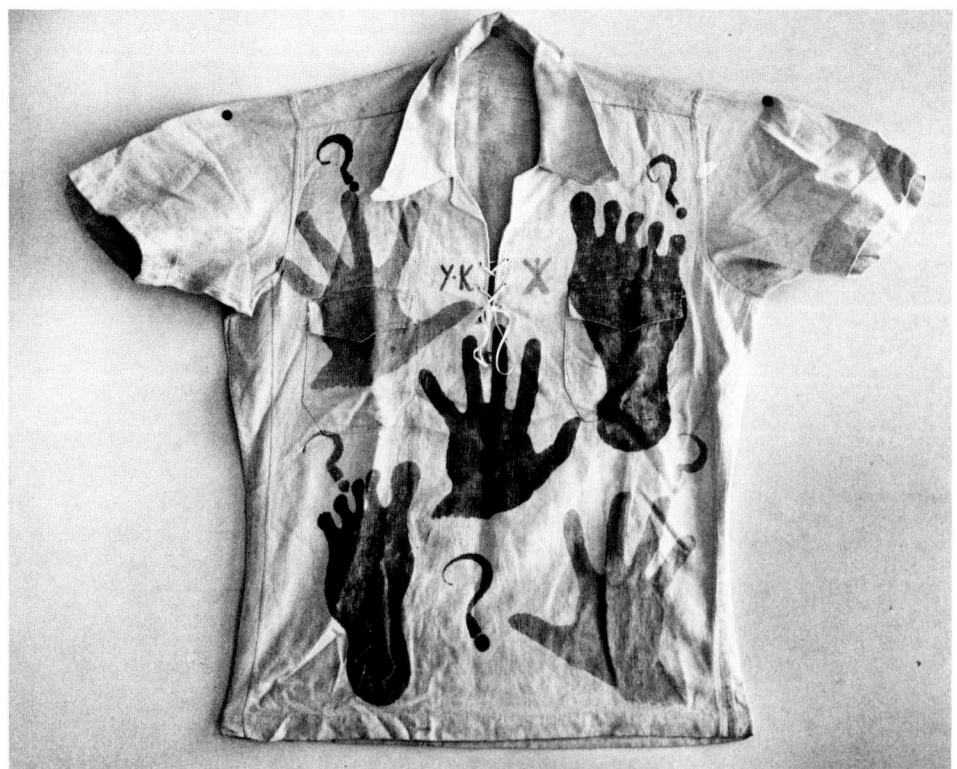

fig. 8. Yves Klein's handpainted shirt, 1948

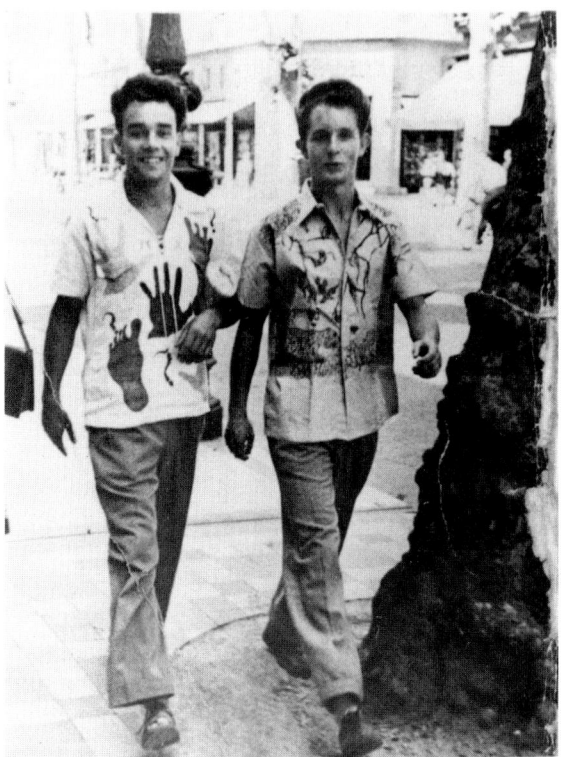

fig. 9. Yves Klein and Claude Pascal, Nice, 1951

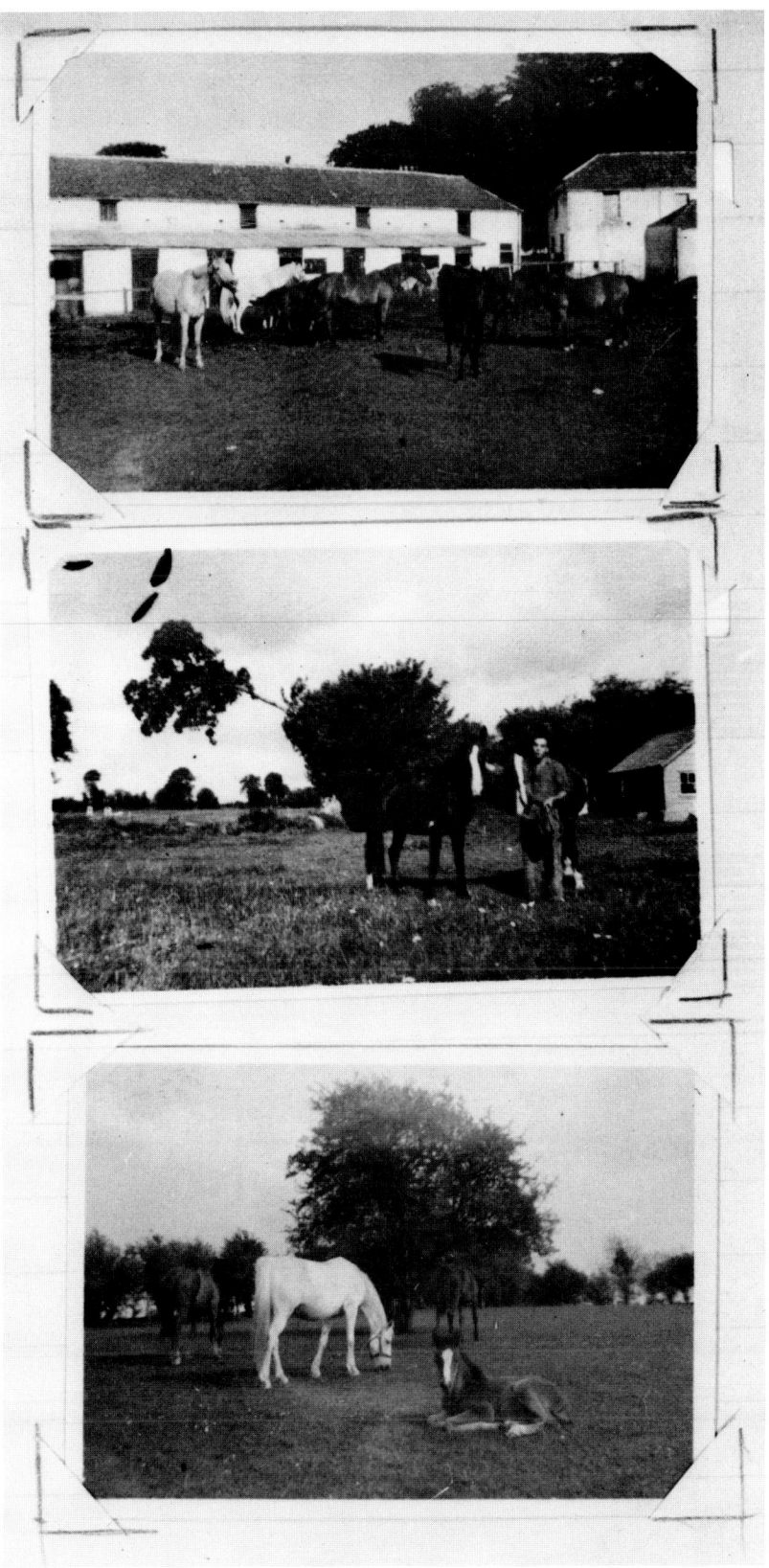

fig. 10. Yves Klein at Jockey Hall, Ireland, early 1950

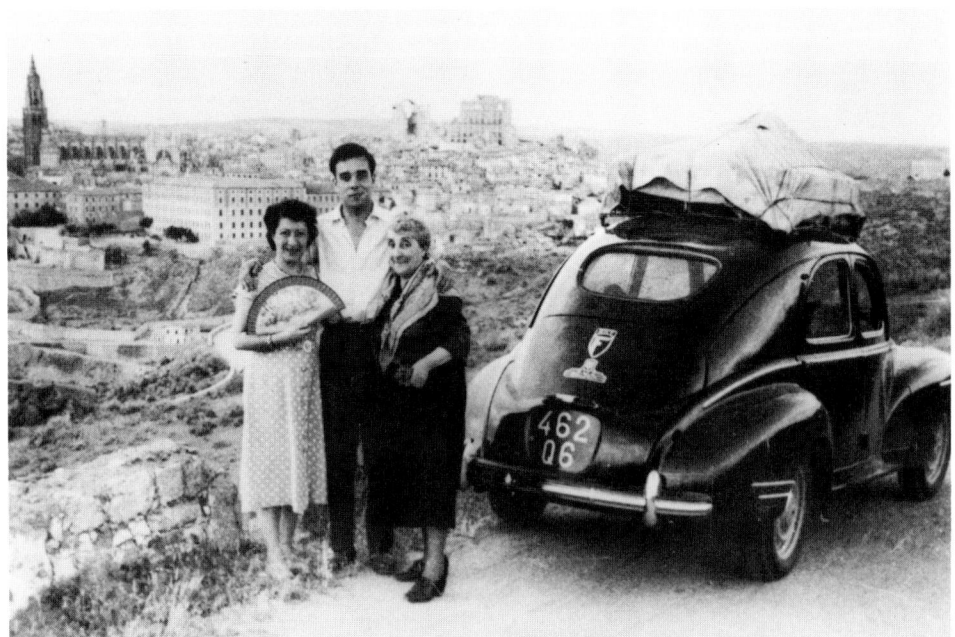

fig. 11. Rose Raymond, Yves Klein, and Grandmother Raymond, Toledo, Spain, June 1951

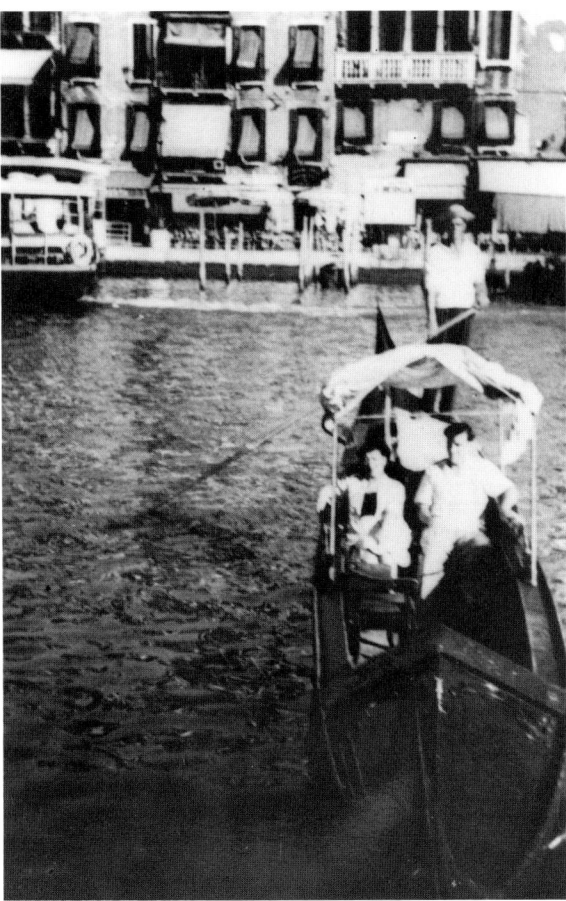

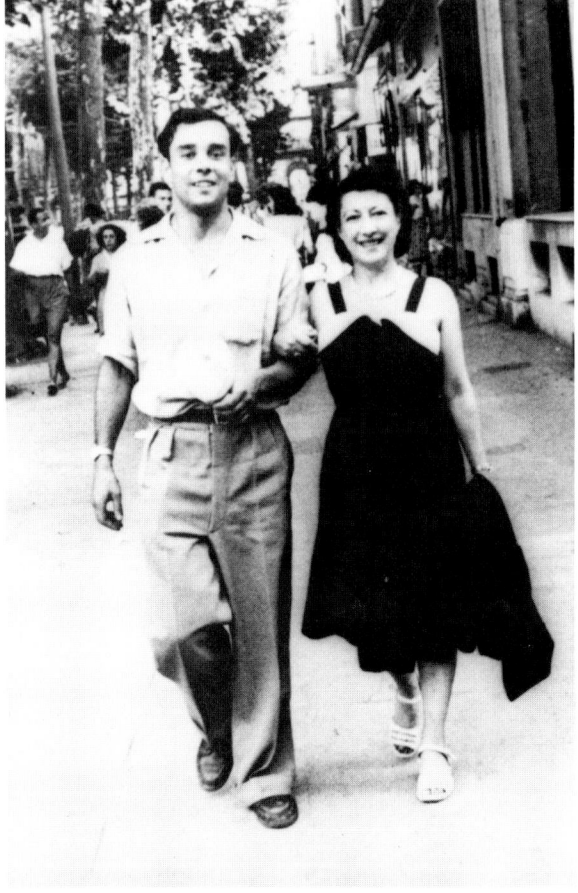

fig. 12. Rose Raymond and Yves Klein, Venice, September 1951   fig. 13. Yves Klein and Rose Raymond, Nice, 1952

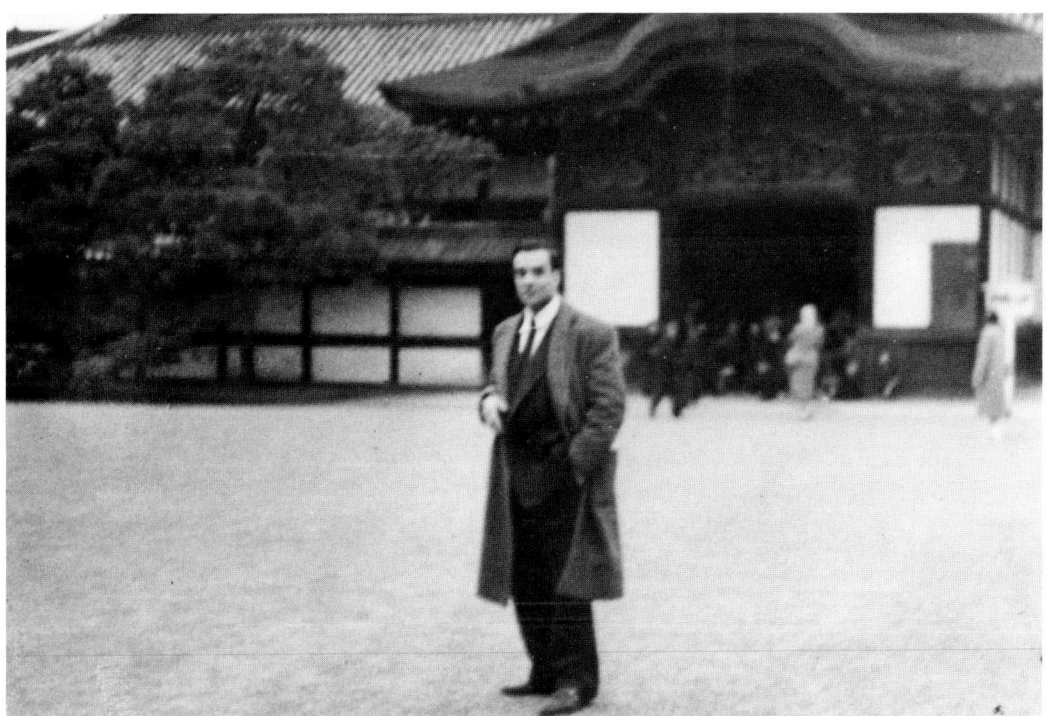

fig. 14. Yves Klein in Japan, c. 1952

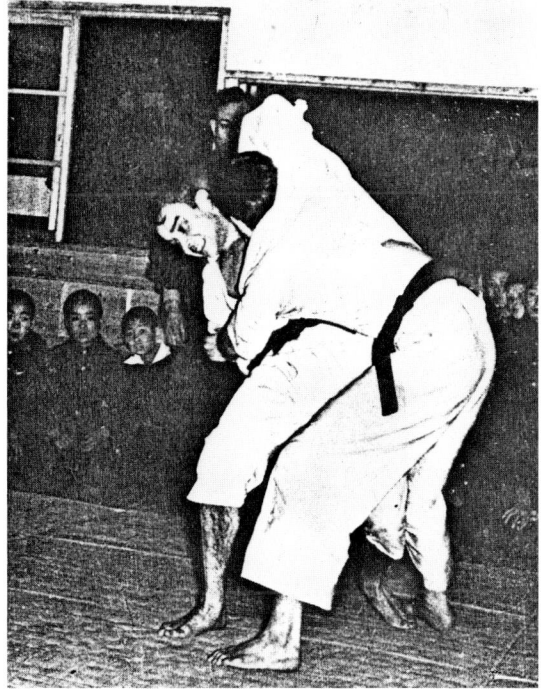

fig. 15. Yves Klein at the Kodokan Judo Institute, Tokyo, c. 1953

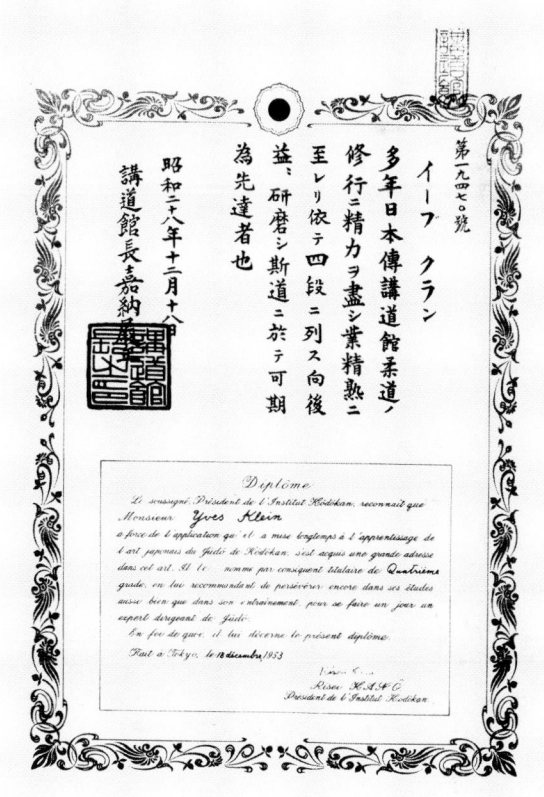

fig. 16. Yves Klein's diploma, fourth *dan* black belt, from Kodokan Judo Institute, Tokyo

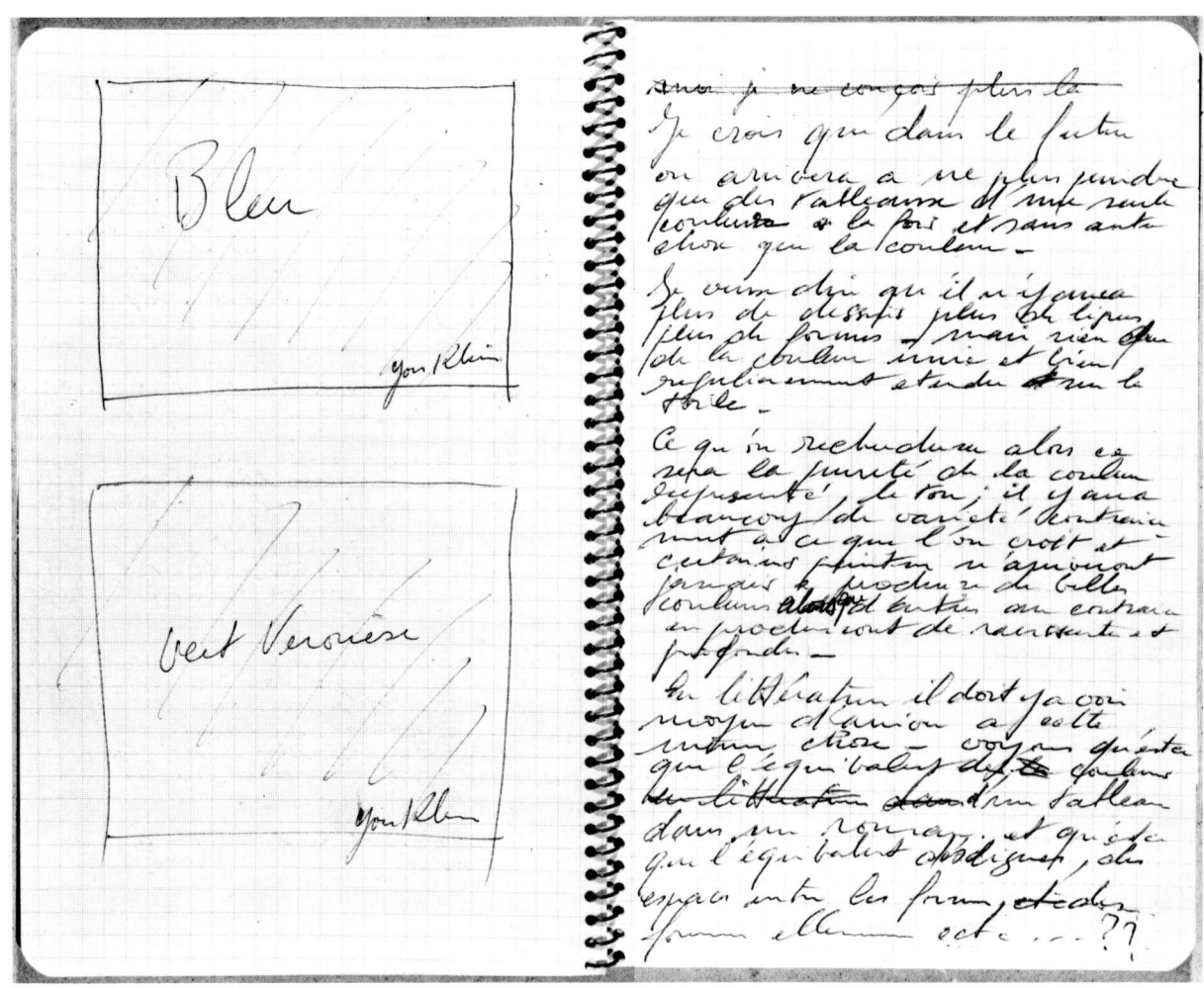

figs. 17-18.   Two pages from Yves Klein's Paris journal, December 27, 1954

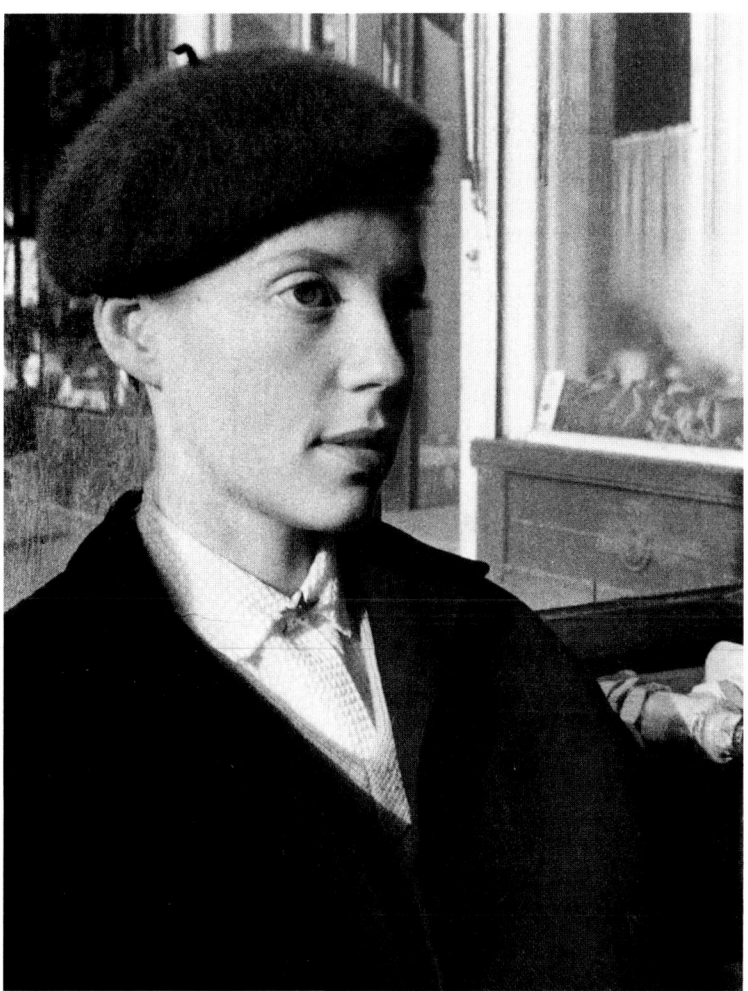

fig. 19. Bernadette Allain, c. 1956

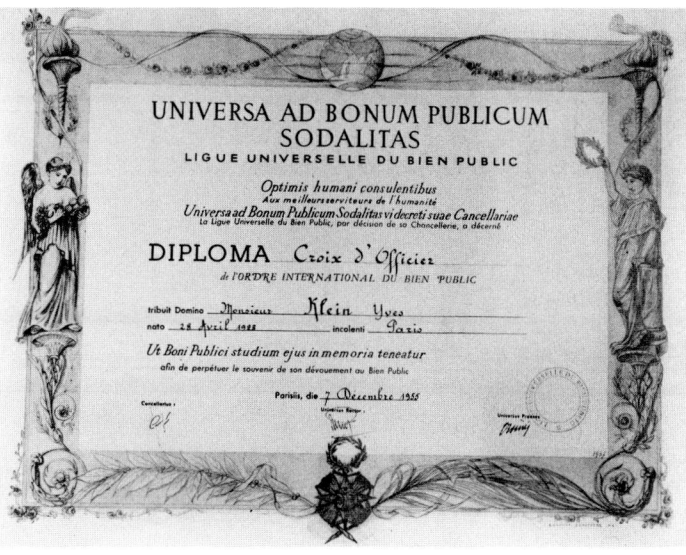

fig. 20. Yves Klein's diploma for "public good," December 7, 1955

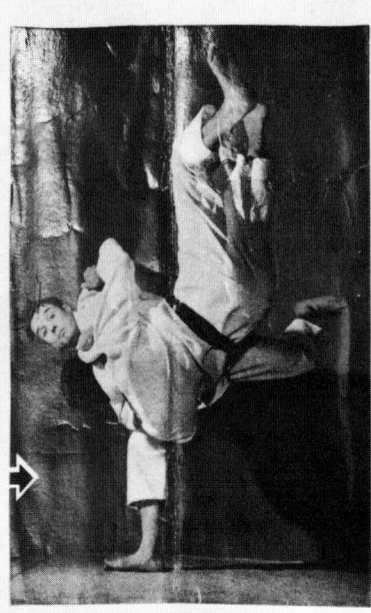

fig. 21. Advertising poster for Yves Klein's judo school, c. 1955

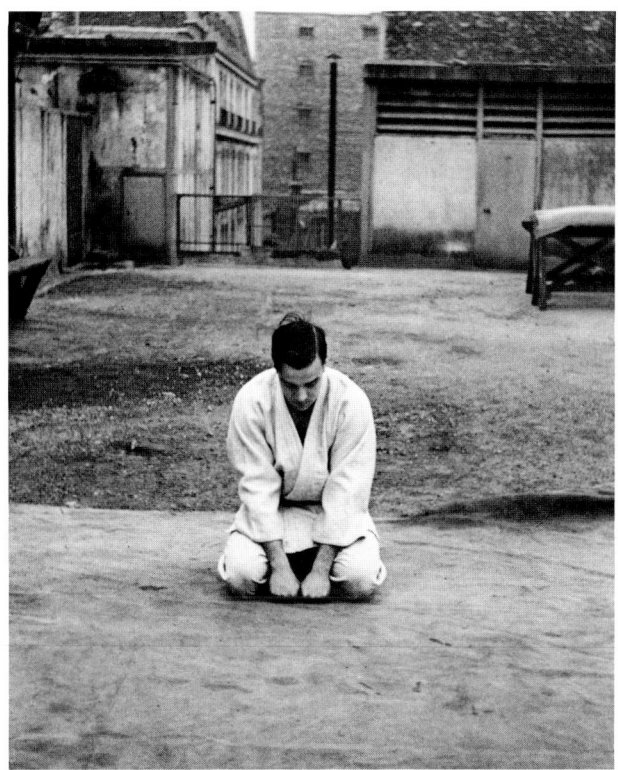

fig. 22.   Yves Klein in his judo uniform

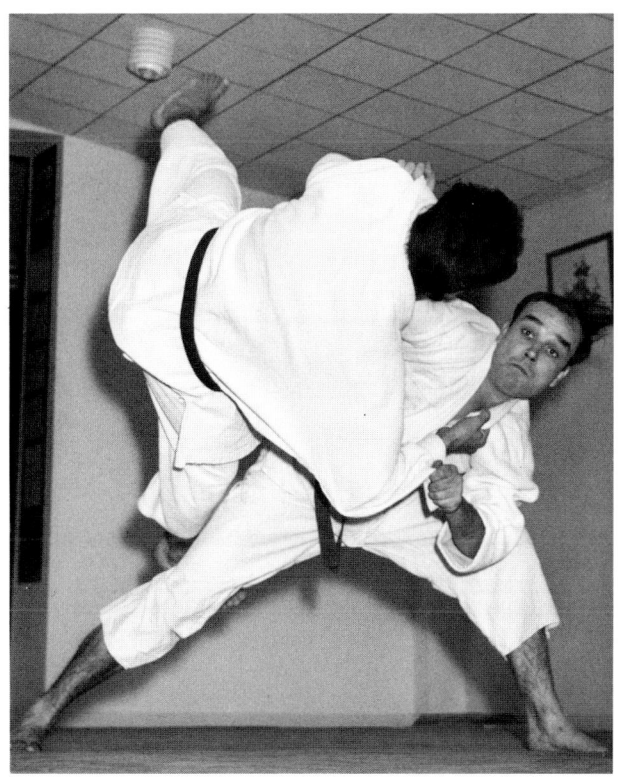

fig. 23.   Yves Klein practicing judo, Fontenay-aux-Roses, Paris, October 1960

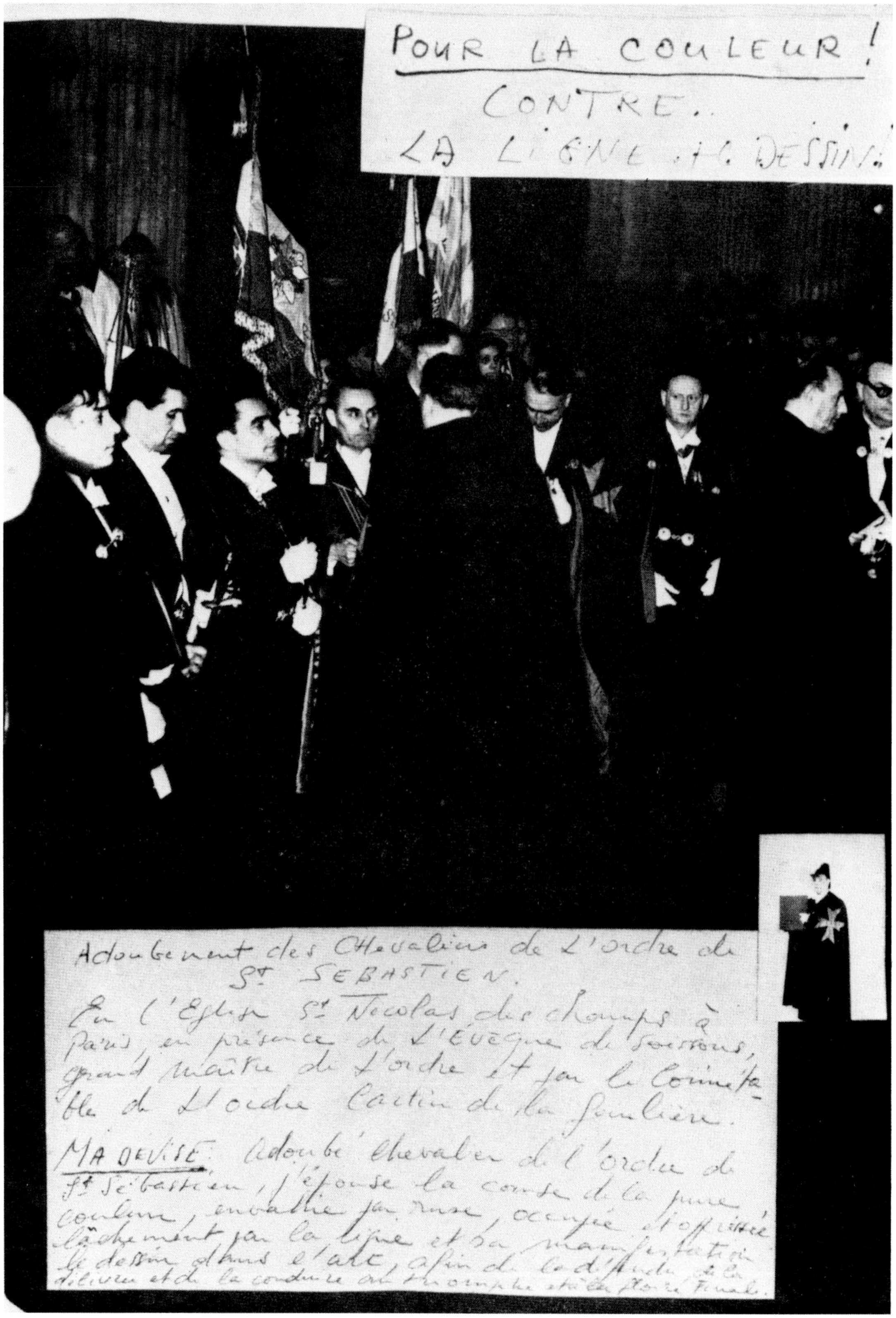

fig. 24. Page from Yves Klein's journal, 1956, declaring his initiation into the Order of Saint Sebastian to be the beginning of his crusade, as Champion of Color, against line

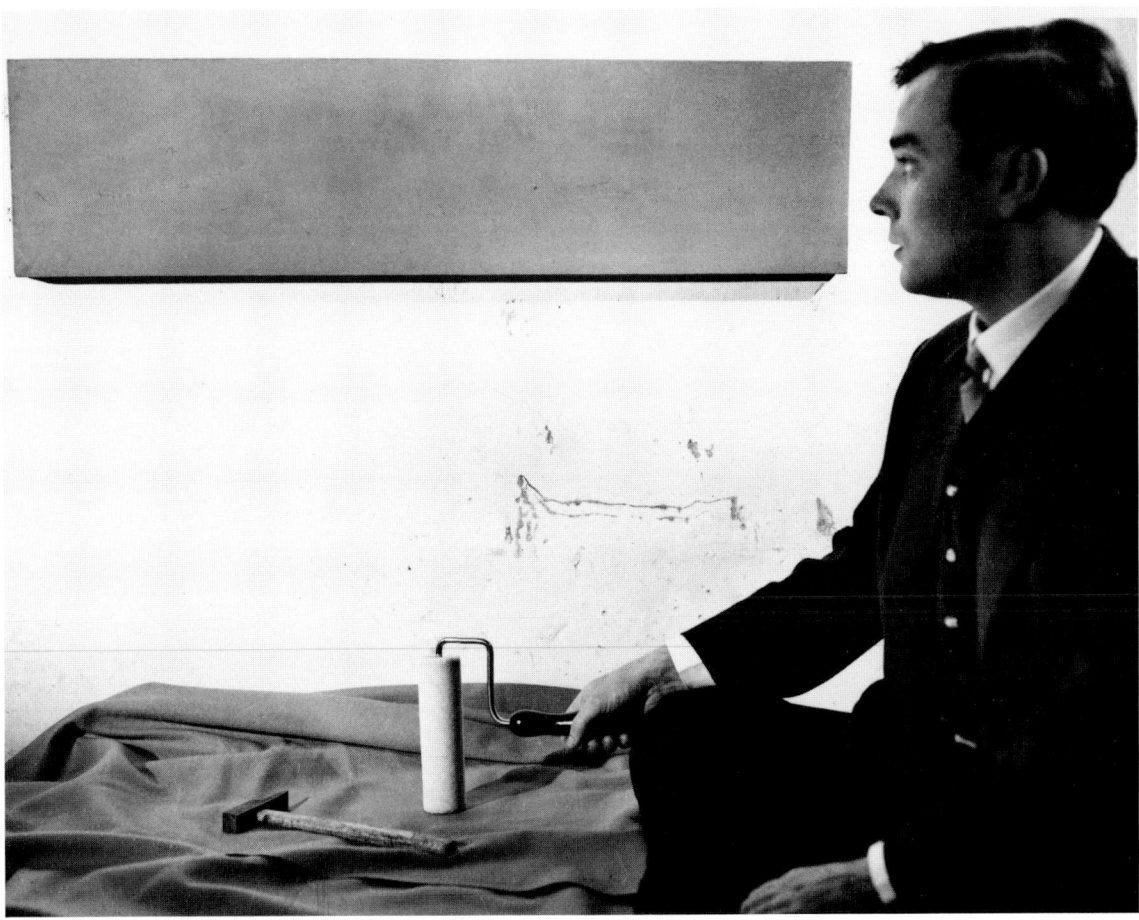

fig. 25. Yves Klein in his studio, c. 1956

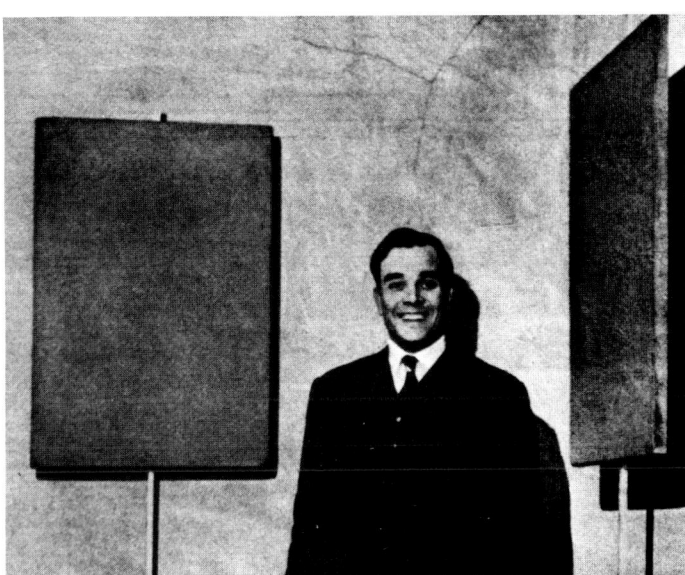

fig. 26. Yves Klein at the *Epoca Blu* exhibition, Galleria Apollinaire, Milan, January 1957

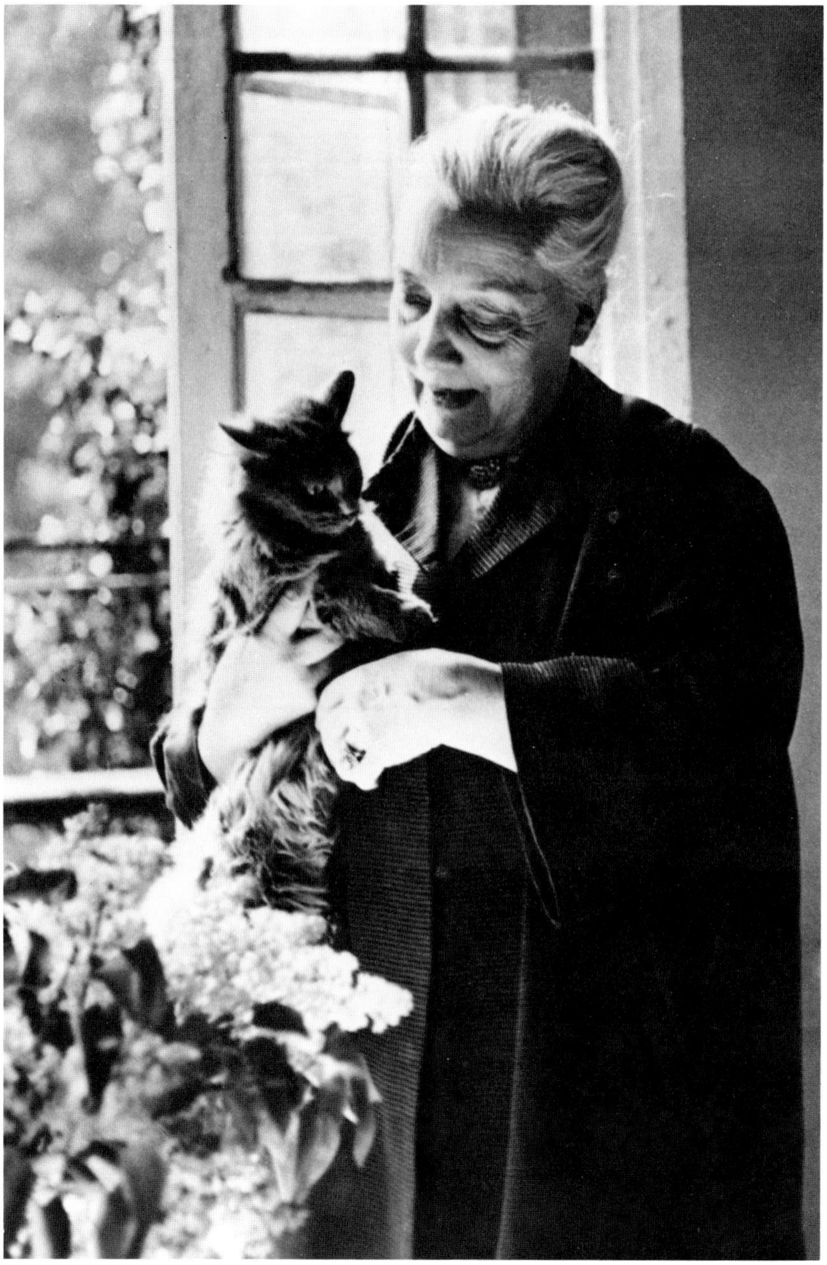

fig. 27. Colette Allendy

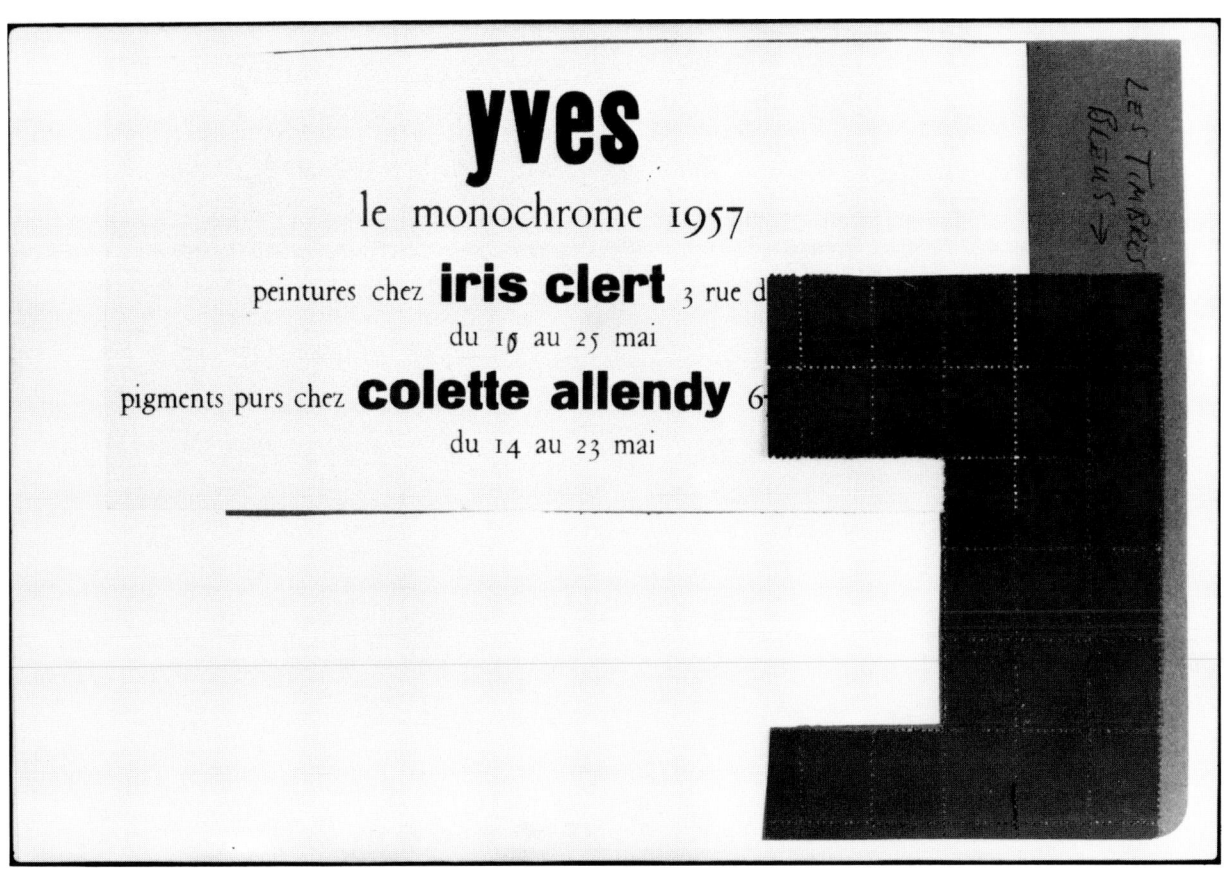

fig. 28. Exhibition announcement and IKB postage stamps, from Yves Klein's journal, 1957

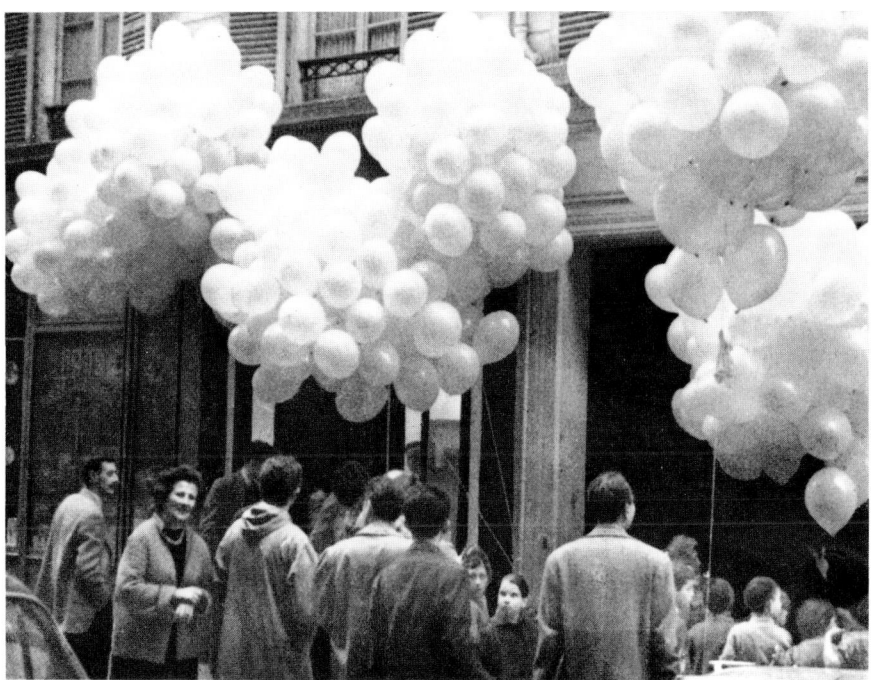

fig. 29. A thousand and one blue balloons are released at the Galerie Iris Clert opening, May 10, 1957

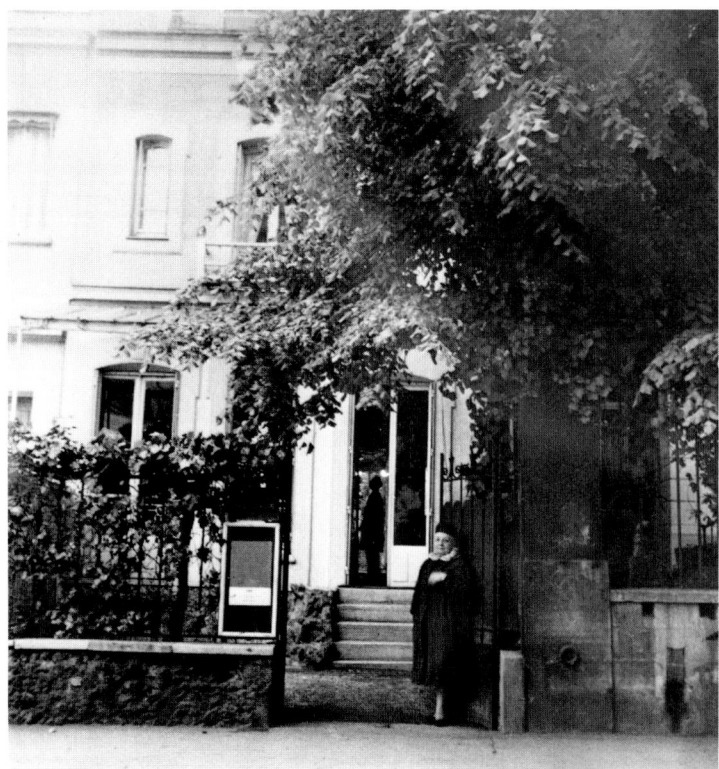

fig. 30. Colette Allendy in front of her house and gallery, 67 rue de l'Assomption, Paris, 1957

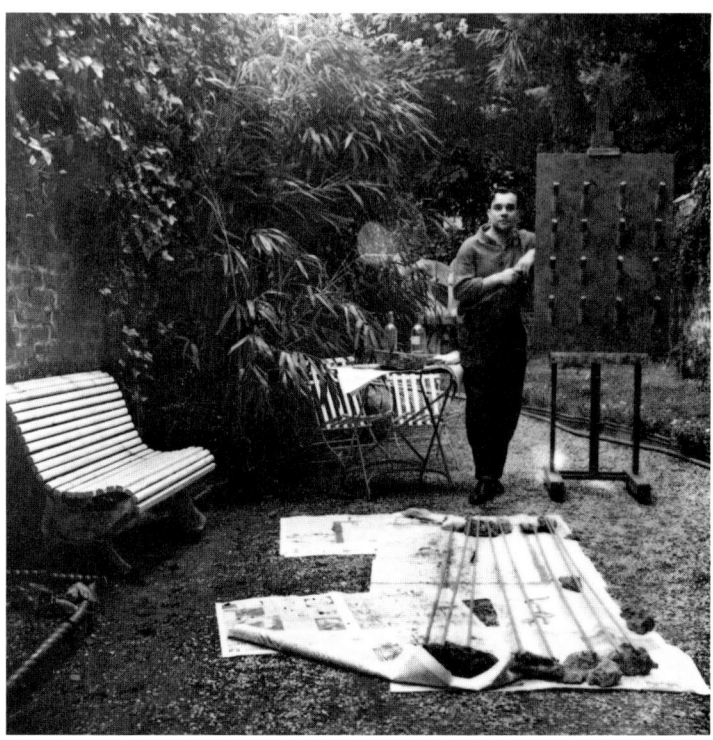

fig. 31. Yves Klein in Colette Allendy's garden with *Feux de Bengale—Tableau de feu bleu d'une minute* (cat. no. 11) and *Pluie bleue* (cat. no. 90), May 1957

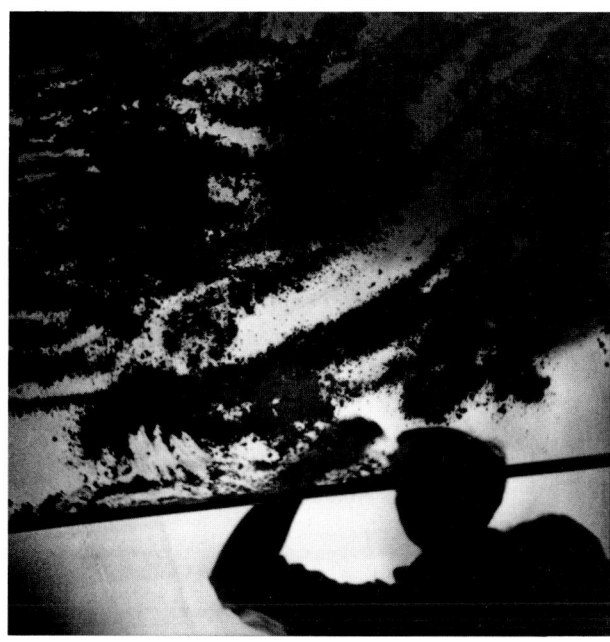

fig. 32. Yves Klein moving blue pigment on a plastic sheet (photographed from below), Galerie Colette
Allendy, Paris, May 1957

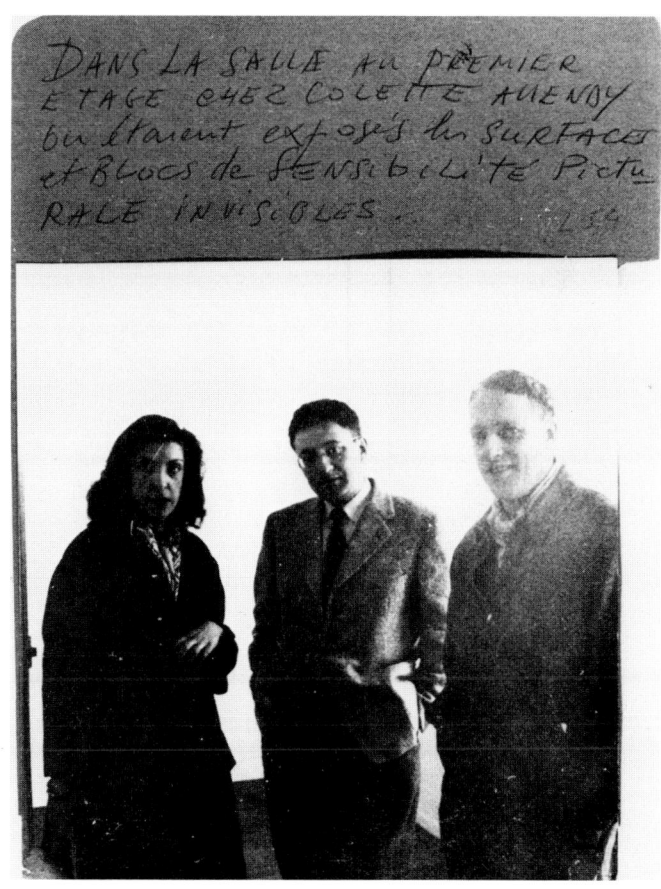

fig. 33. Iris Clert, Pierre Restany, and Raymond Hains in the second-floor Immaterial Room, Galerie
Colette Allendy, May 1957

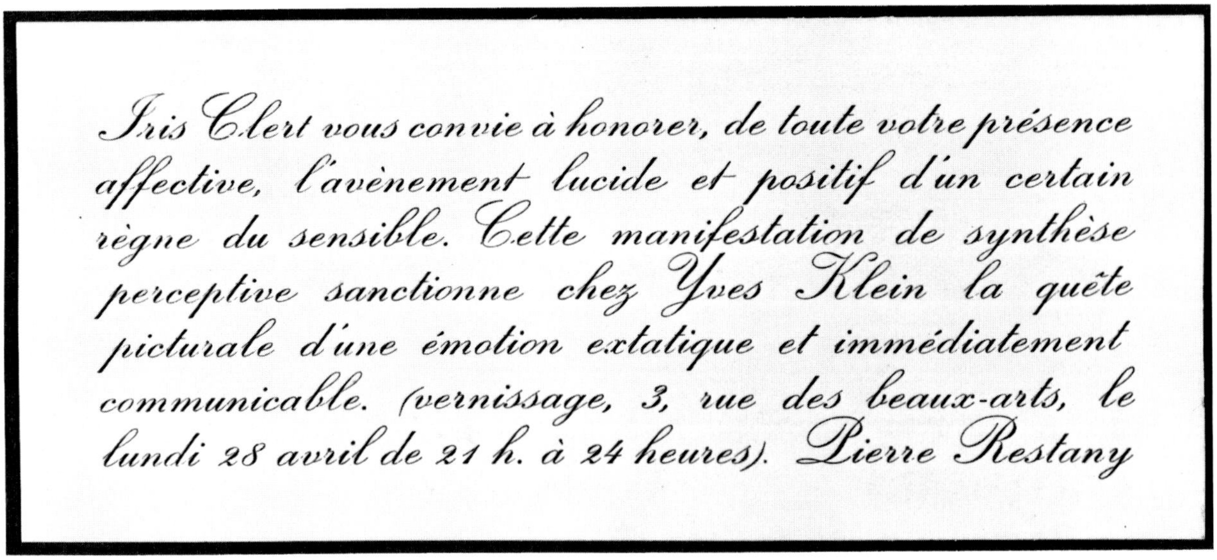

Iris Clert vous convie à honorer, de toute votre présence affective, l'avènement lucide et positif d'un certain règne du sensible. Cette manifestation de synthèse perceptive sanctionne chez Yves Klein la quête picturale d'une émotion extatique et immédiatement communicable. (vernissage, 3, rue des beaux-arts, le lundi 28 avril de 21 h. à 24 heures). Pierre Restany

fig. 34. Invitation to the exhibition *Le Vide*, Galerie Iris Clert, Paris, 1958

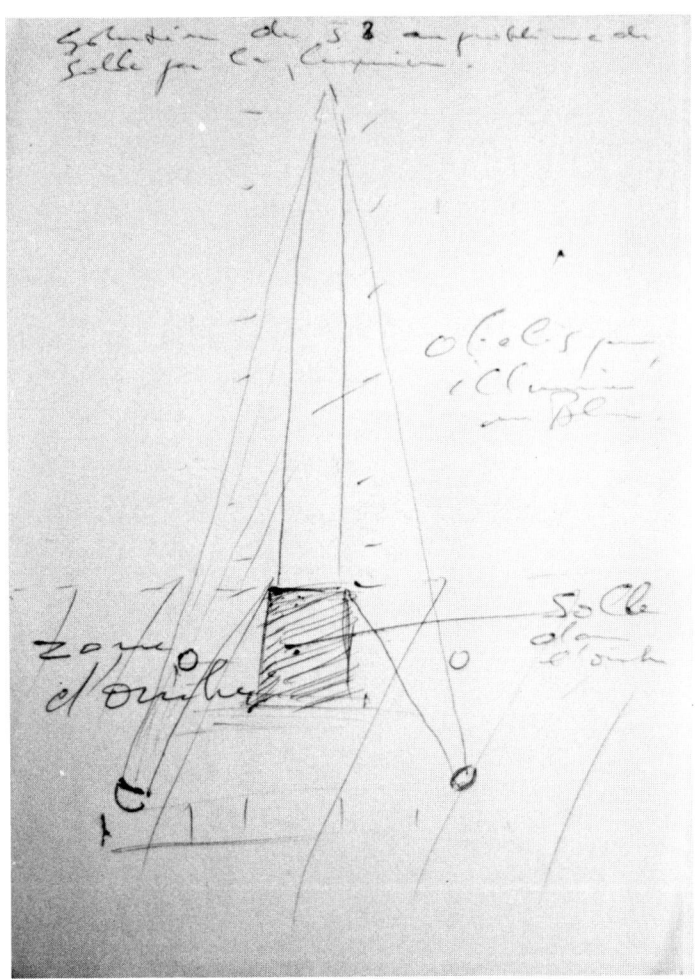

fig. 36. Yves Klein's drawing for the blue illumination of the obelisk in the Place de la Concorde, Paris, 1958

fig. 35. *Le Vide*: interior of the Galerie Iris Clert, April or May 1958

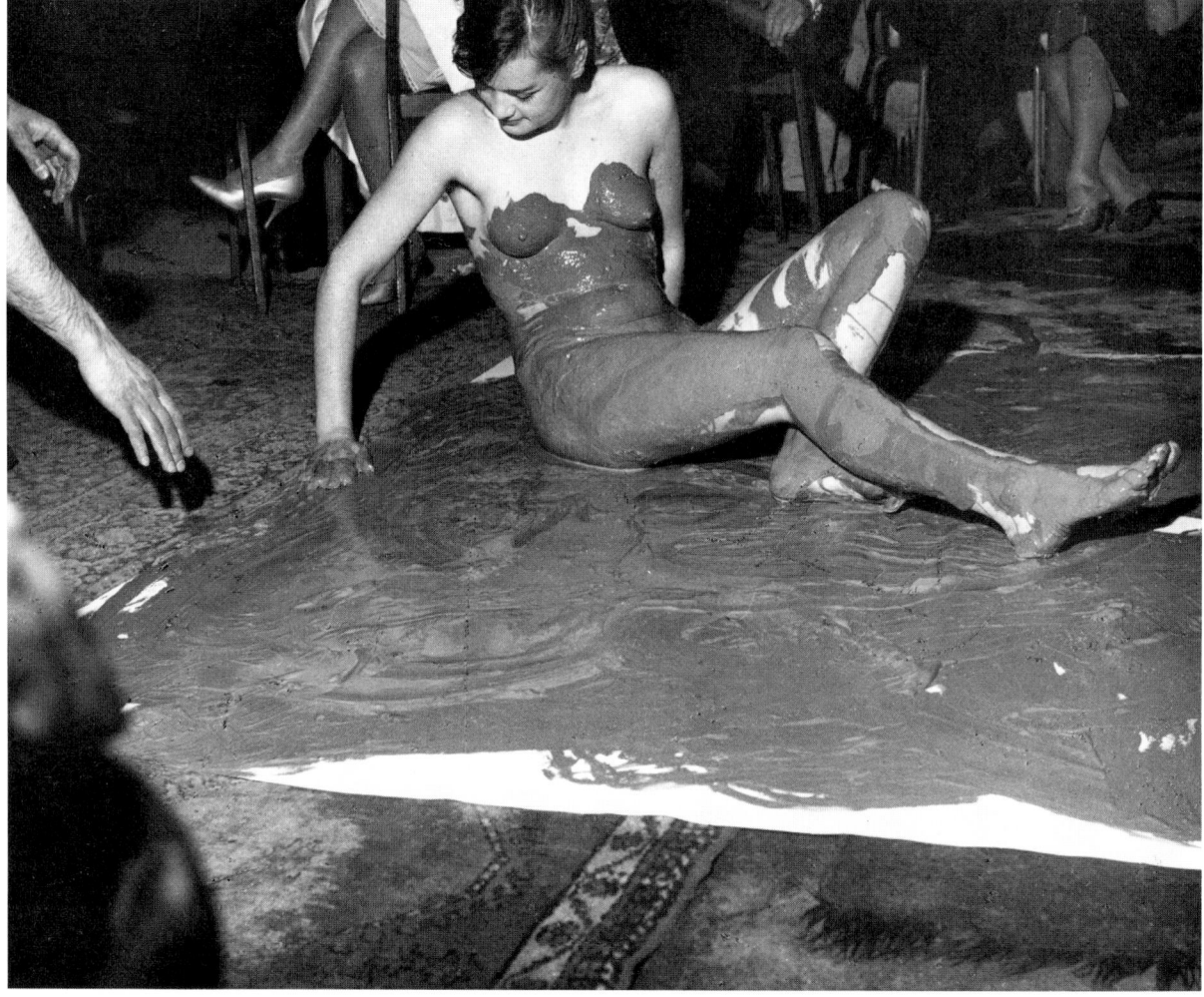

fig. 37.   The first "living brush," Robert Godet's apartment, Ile Saint-Louis, Paris, June 5, 1958

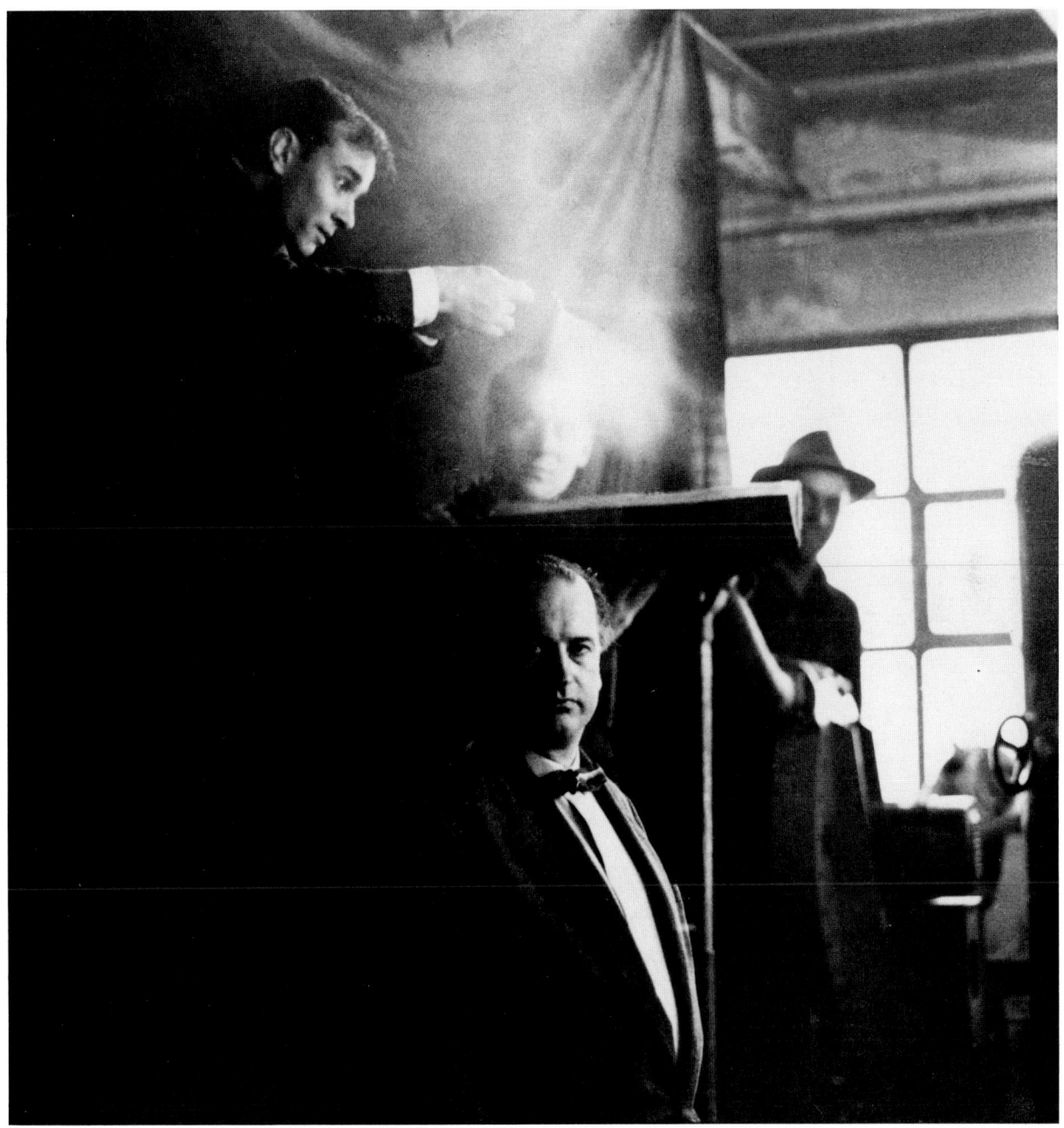

fig. 38. Yves Klein and Werner Ruhnau conducting experiments for an ''air roof,'' Kuppersbusch Factory, Germany, 1958

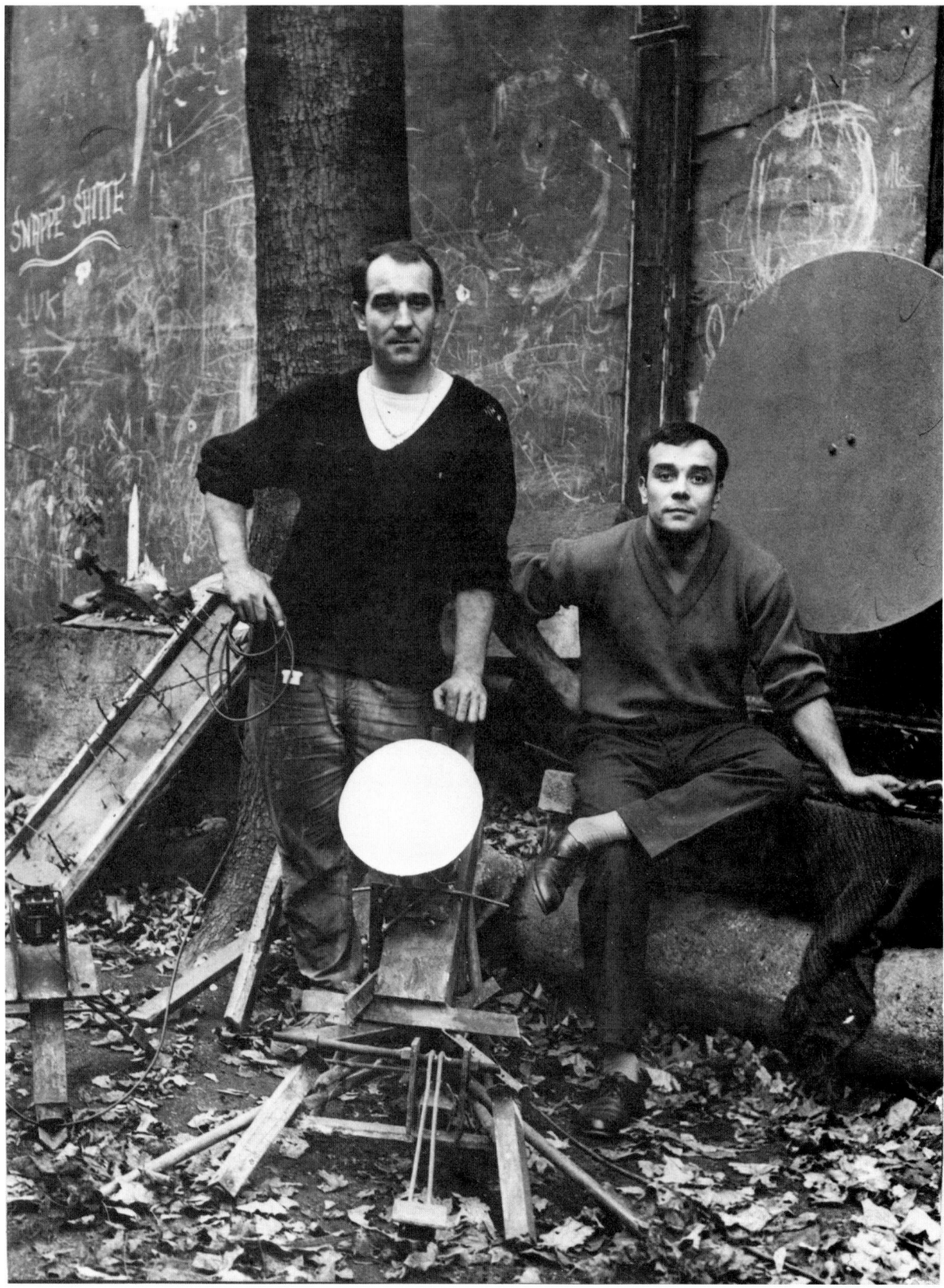

fig. 39.   Jean Tinguely and Yves Klein preparing for their joint exhibition, *Vitesse pure et stabilité monochrome*, 1958

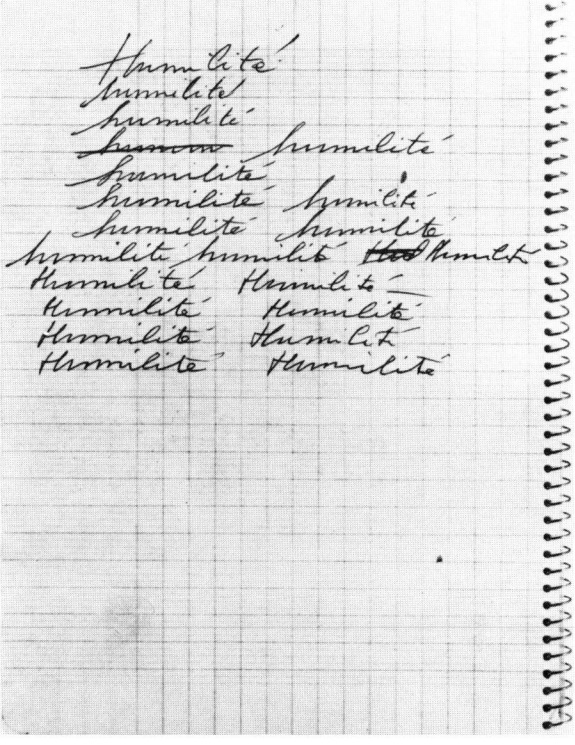

fig. 40. Page from Yves Klein's journal, 1958

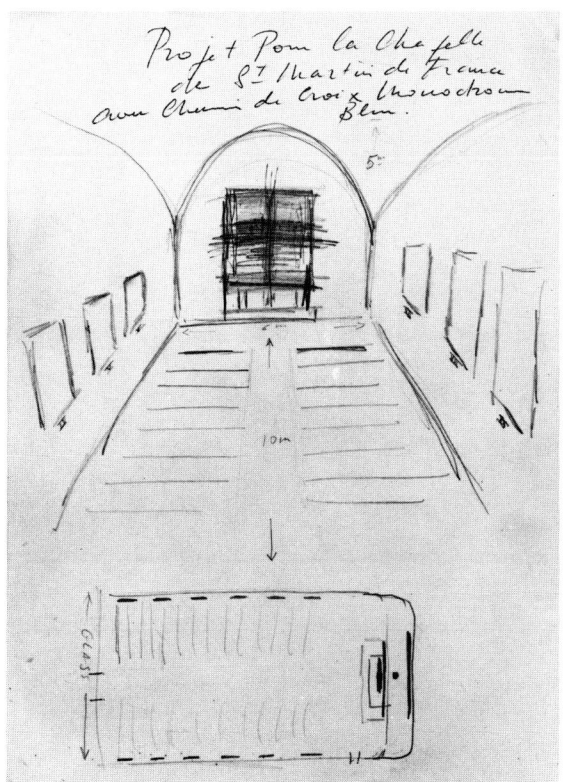

fig. 41. Yves Klein's drawing for Blue Stations of the Cross in the Chapel of Saint Martin, Pontoise, 1958

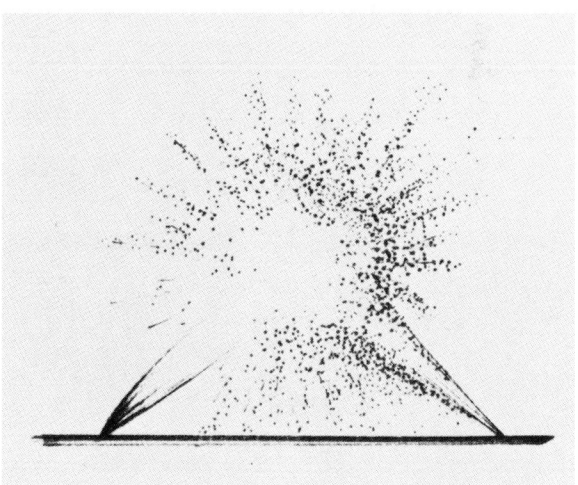

fig. 42. Drawing by Claude Parent or his assistant for Fountains of Fire and Water, c. 1958

fig. 43. Yves Klein preparing an immaterial work, Hessenhuis, Antwerp, March 17, 1959

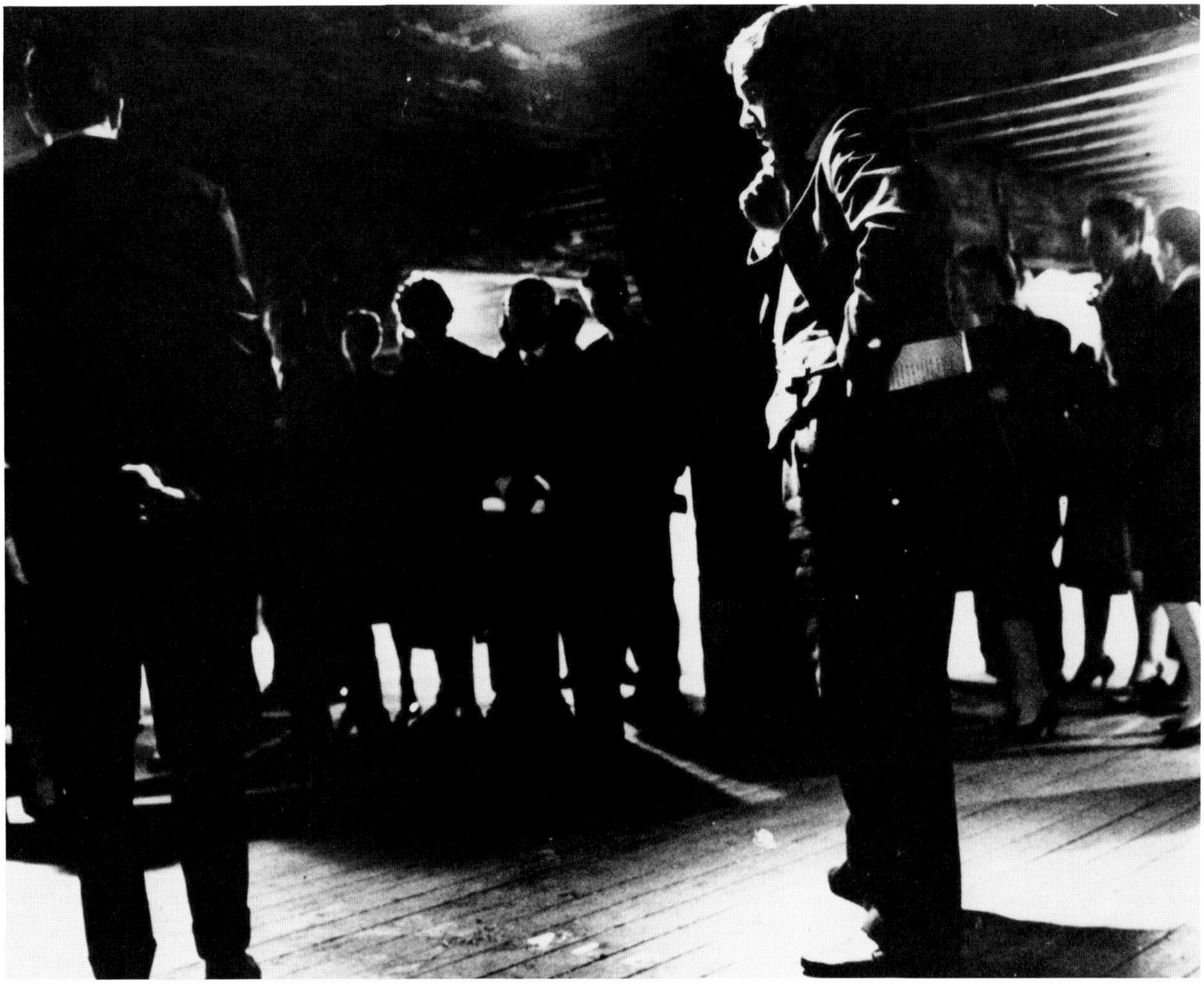

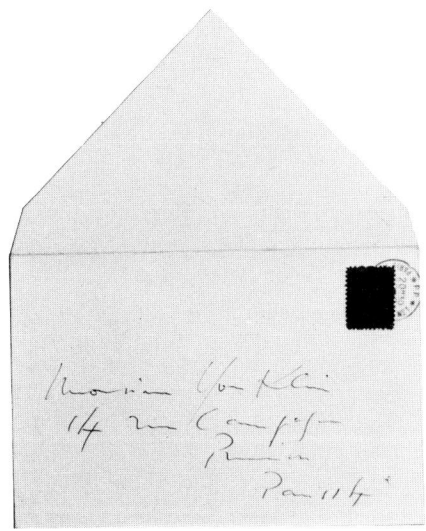

fig. 44. Envelope mailed by Yves Klein to himself with IKB postage stamp, 1959

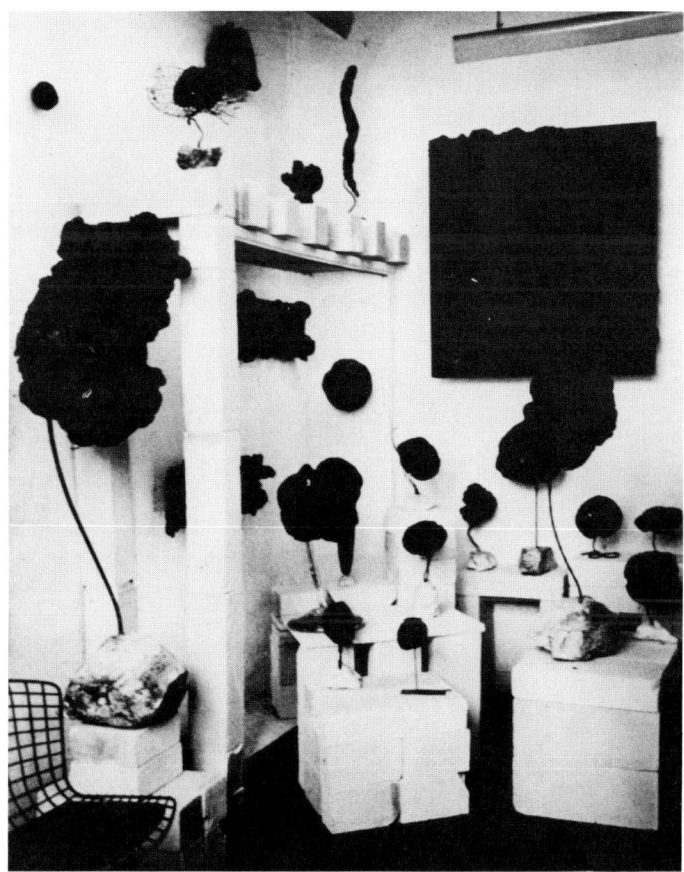

fig. 45. Installation view of the exhibition *Bas-reliefs dans une forêt d'éponges*, Galerie Iris Clert, June 1959

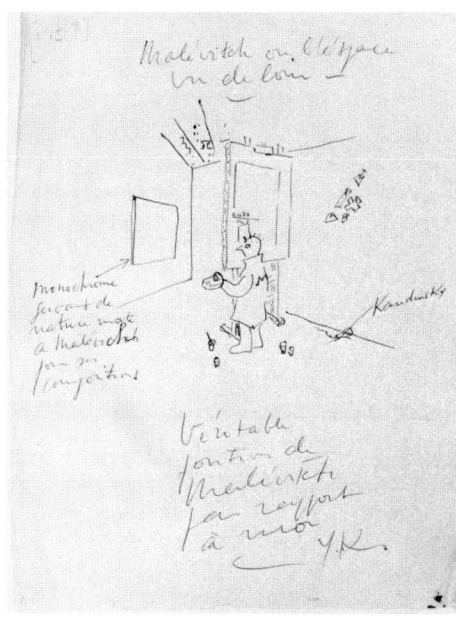

fig. 46. Yves Klein's cartoon "The True Position of Malevich in Relation to Me," showing Malevich imitating a Klein monochrome, c. 1959

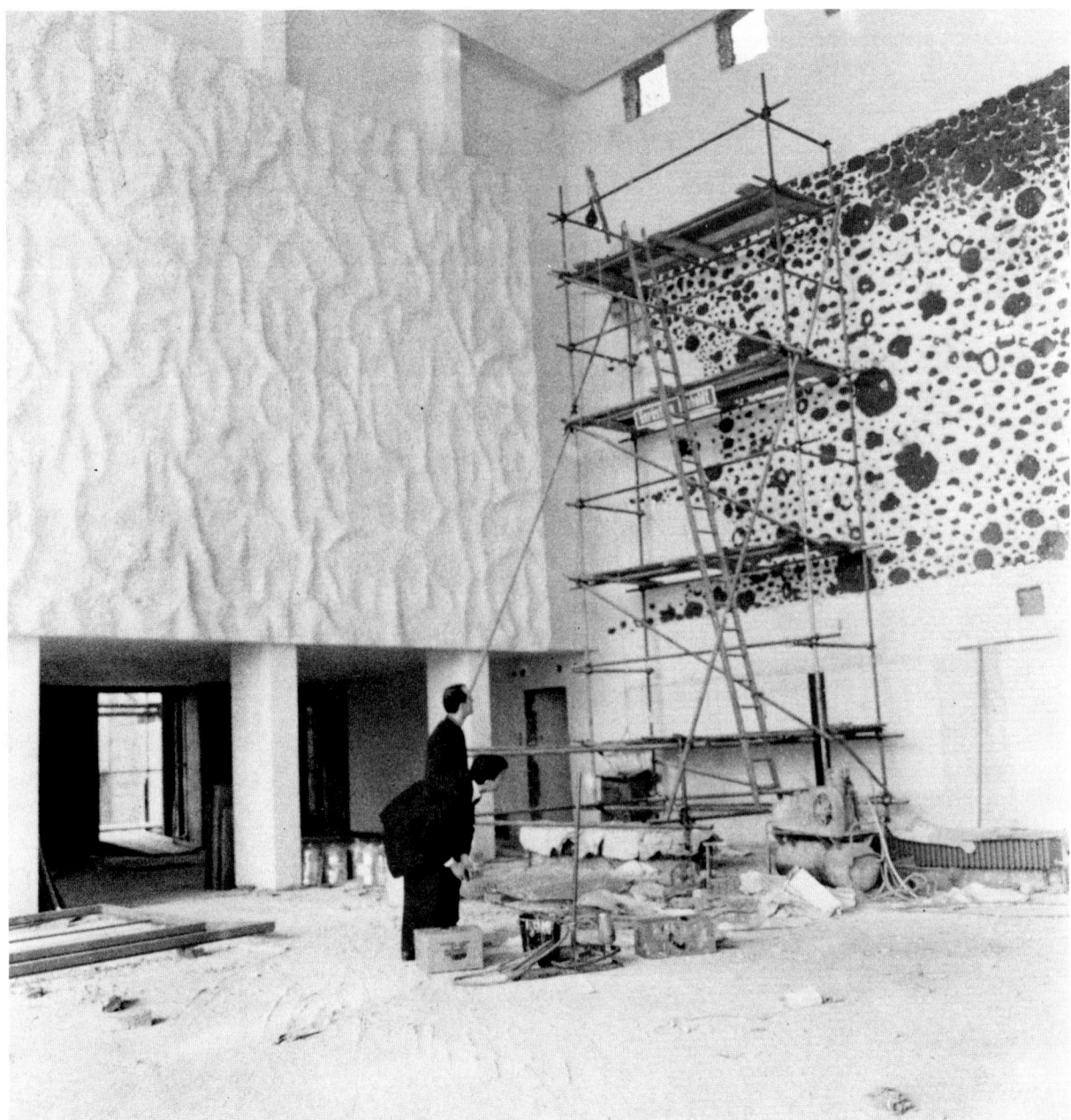

fig. 47. The Gelsenkirchen, Germany, city theater murals in progress, 1959

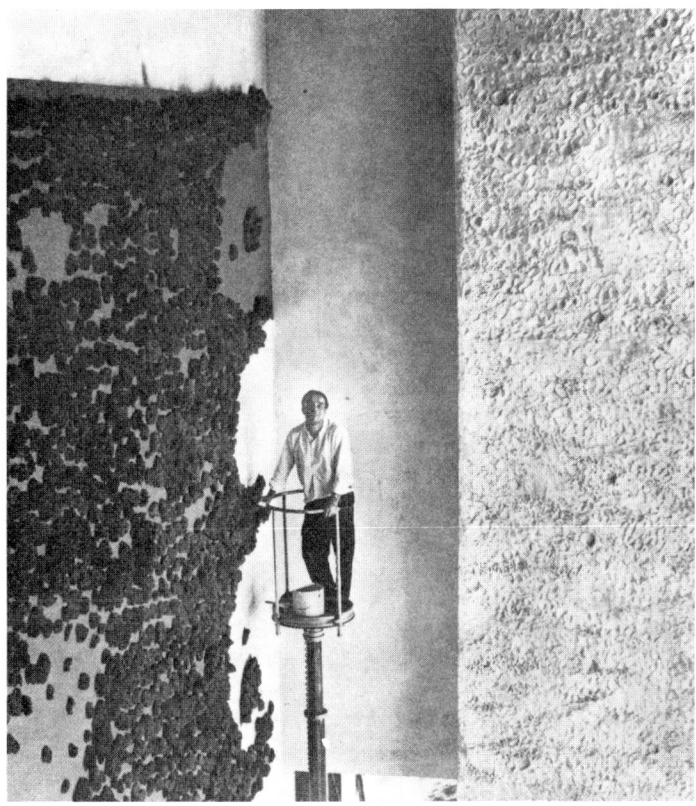

fig. 48. Yves Klein working on the Gelsenkirchen murals, 1959

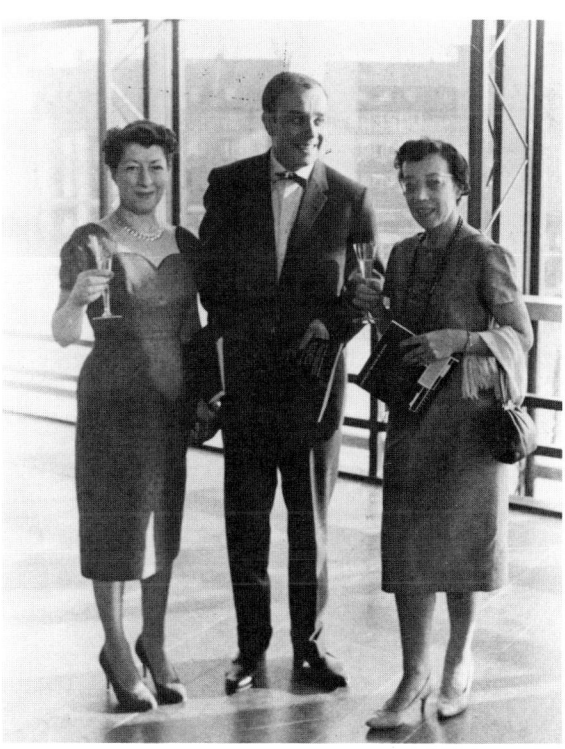

fig. 49. Rose Raymond, Yves Klein, and Marie Raymond at the opening of the Gelsenkirchen city theater, December 15, 1959

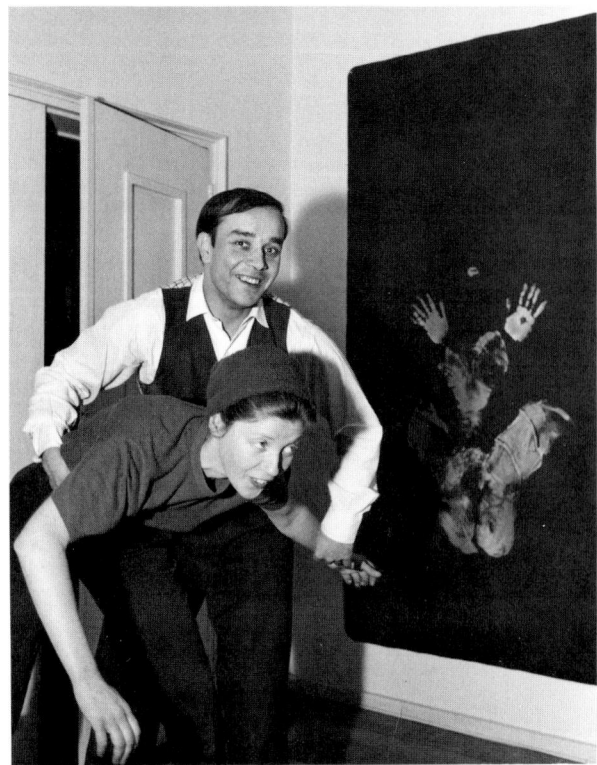

fig. 50. Yves Klein and Bernadette Allain, Paris, c. 1960

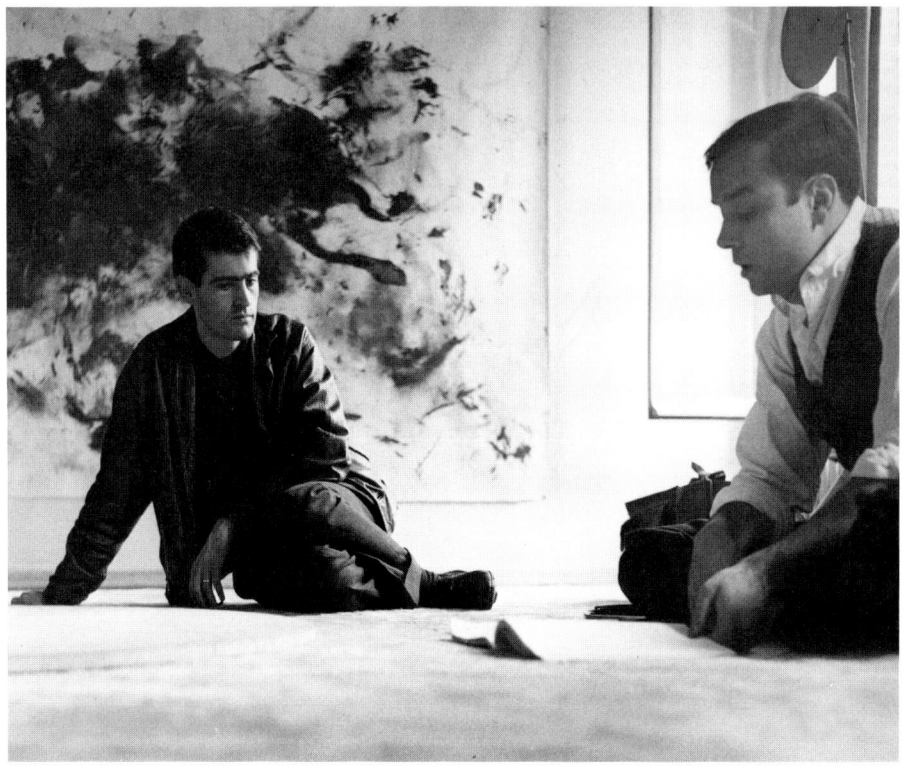

fig. 51. Martial Raysse and Yves Klein, Paris, c. 1960

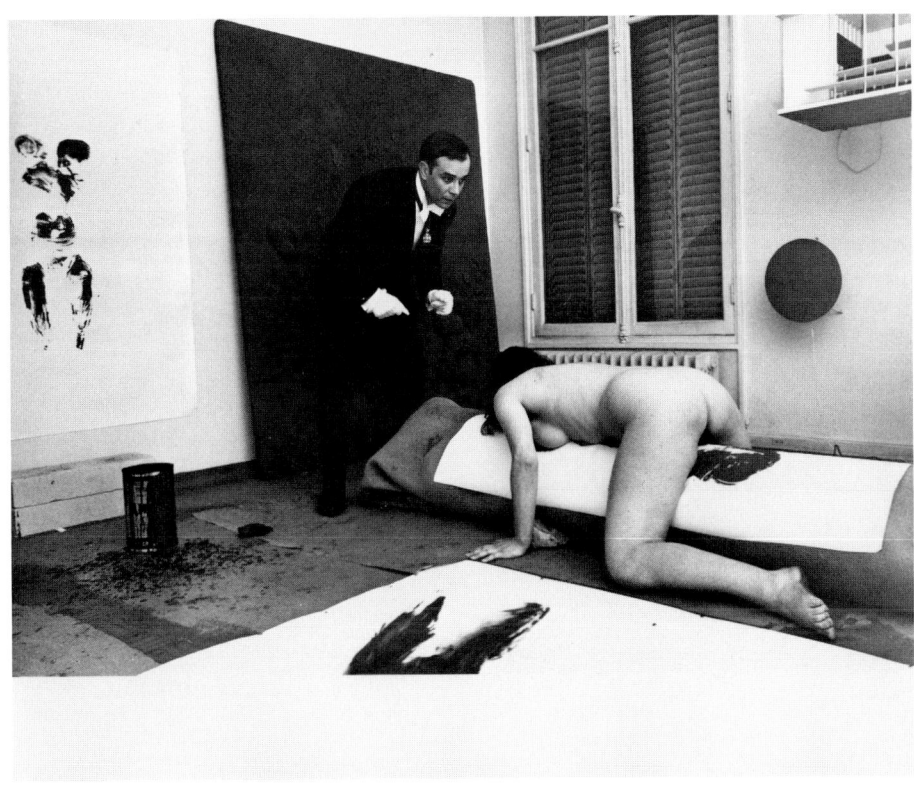

fig. 52. Yves Klein and a model making a Shroud Anthropometry, 14 rue Campagne Première, Paris, February 17, 1960

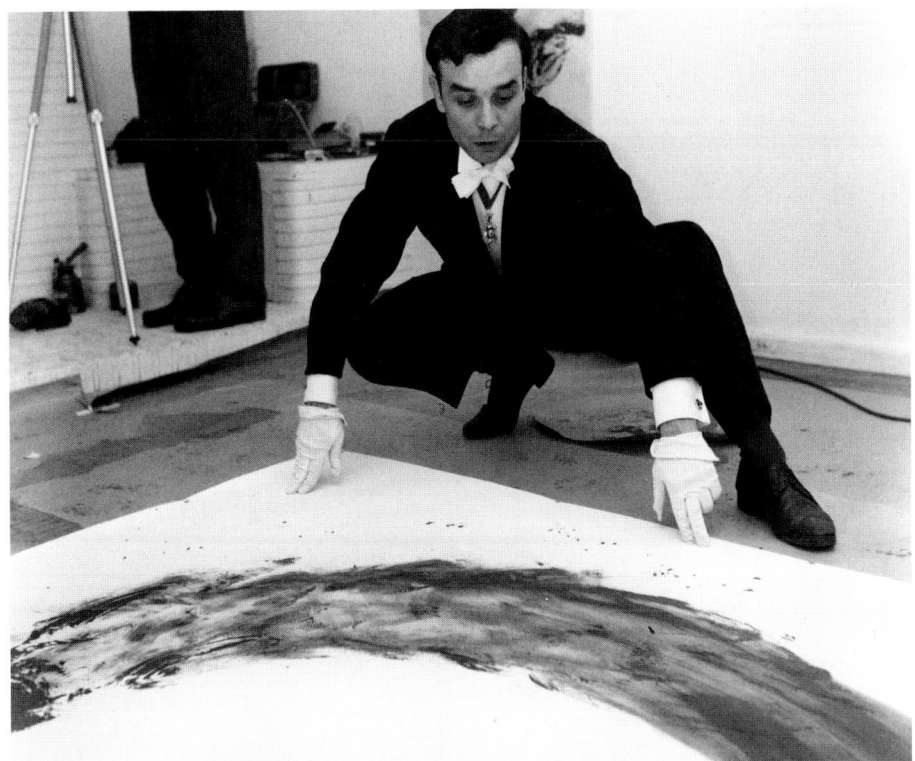

fig. 53. Yves Klein working on an Anthropometry, Paris, c. 1960

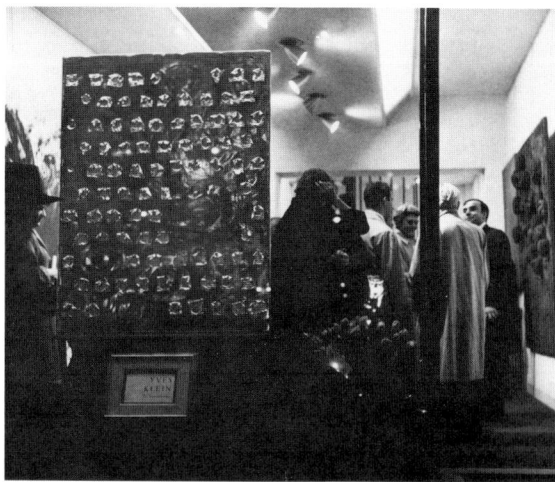

fig. 54. The opening of the exhibition *Yves Klein le monochrome* at the Galerie Rive Droite, Paris, October 11, 1960

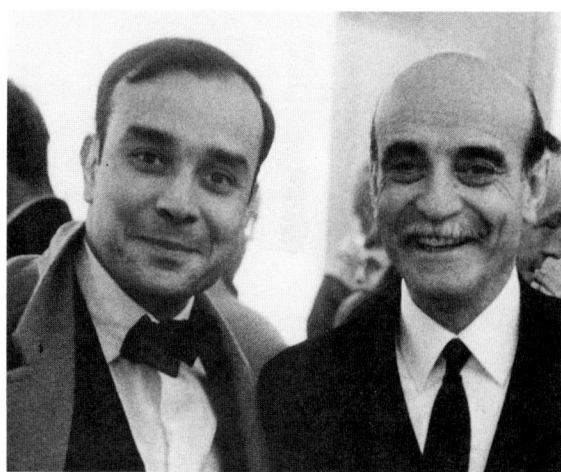

fig. 55. Yves Klein and Lucio Fontana at the Galerie Rive Droite, Paris, October 11, 1960

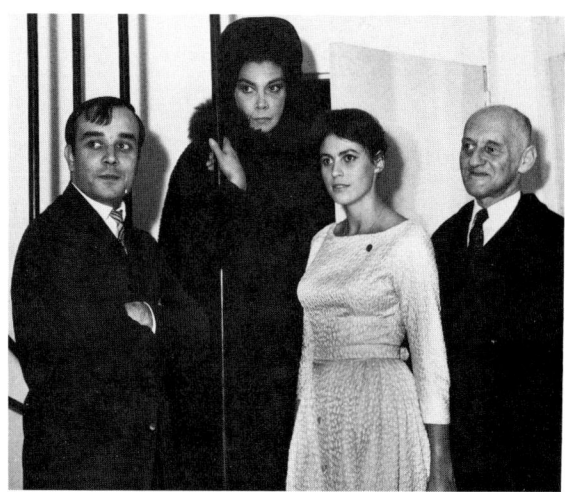

fig. 56. Yves Klein, Leonor Fini, Rotraut Uecker, and Victor Brauner at the Galerie Rive Droite, Paris, October 11, 1960

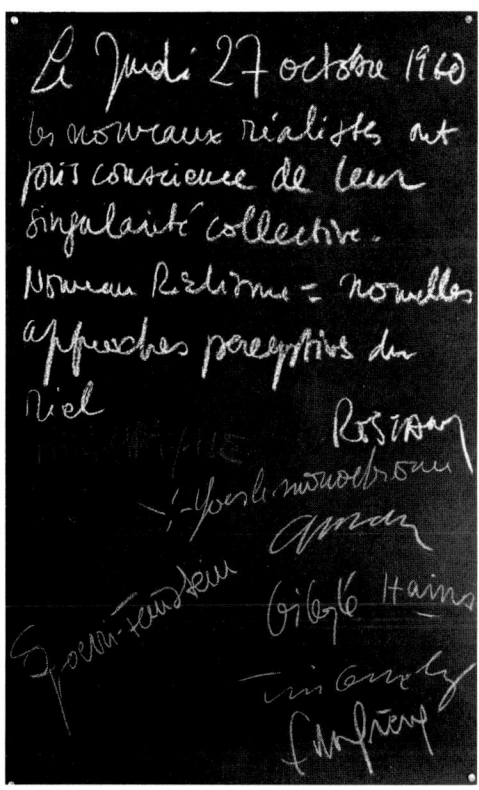

fig. 57. Signatures on the manifesto of the Nouveaux Réalistes, October 27, 1960

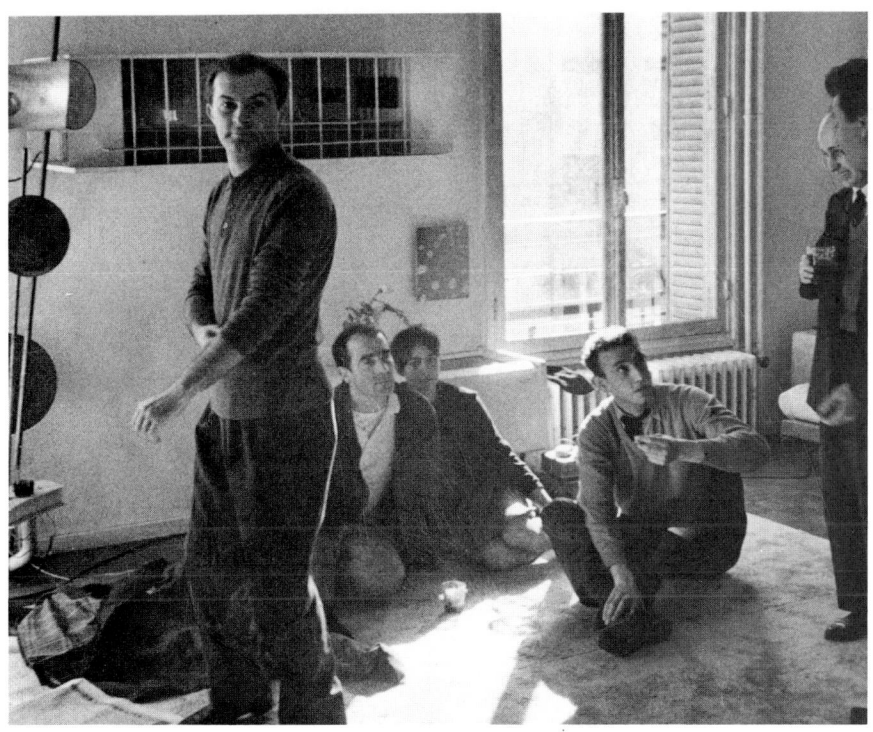

fig. 58. The founding of the Nouveaux Réalistes: Arman, Jean Tinguely, Rotraut Uecker, Daniel Spoerri, Jacques de la Villeglé, and Pierre Restany at 14 rue Campagne Première, Paris, October 27, 1960

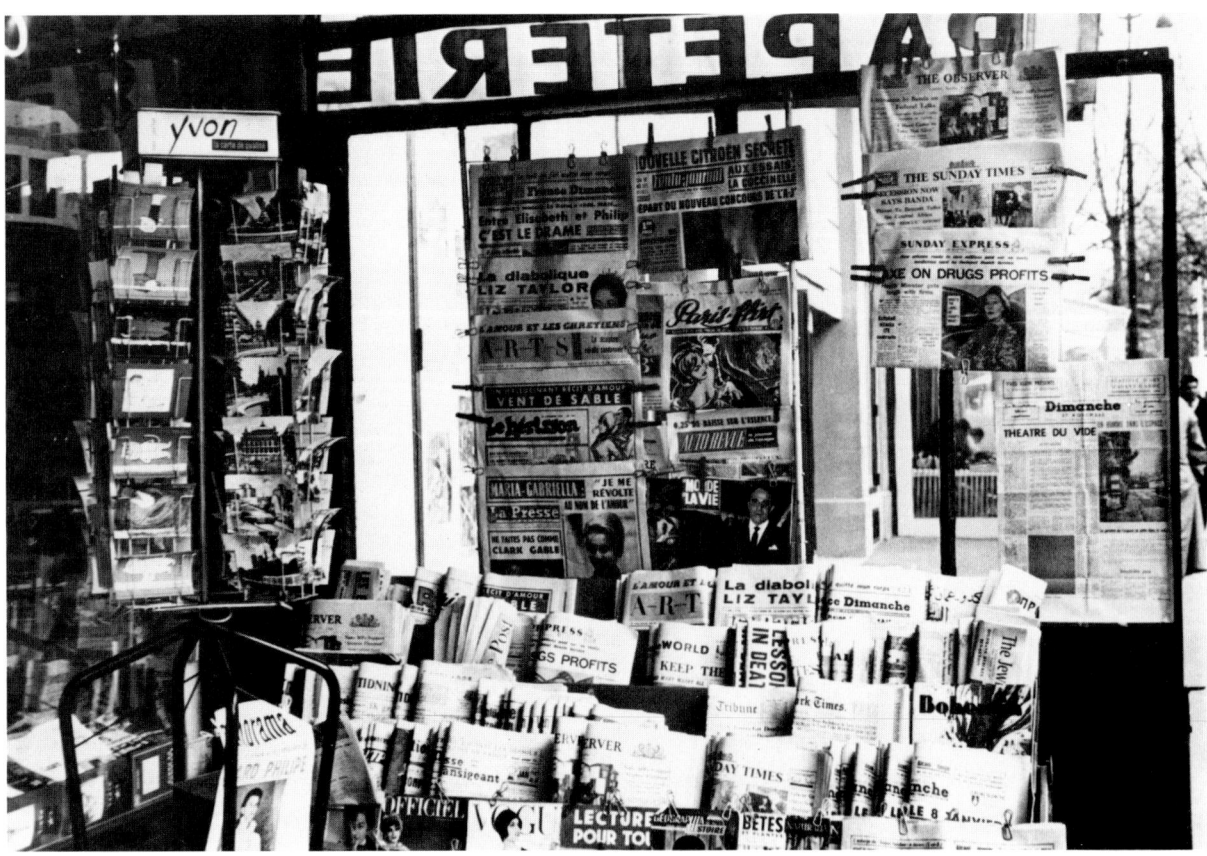

fig. 59. *Dimanche, le journal d'un seul jour* on sale at a Paris newsstand, November 27, 1960

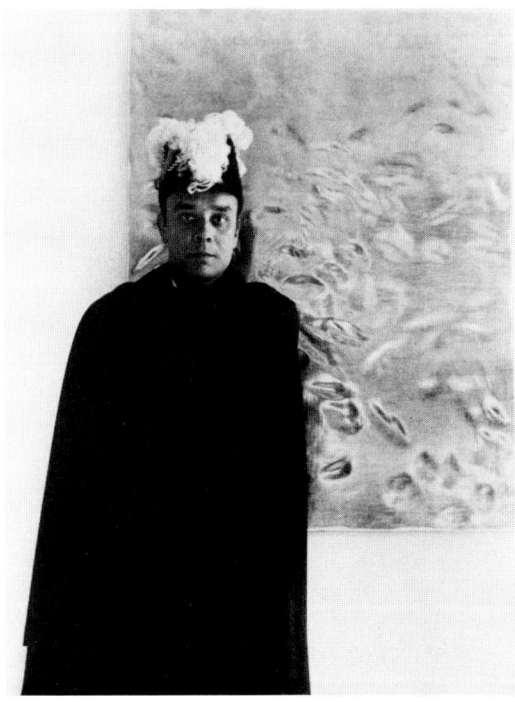

fig. 60. Yves Klein in the regalia of the Order of Saint Sebastian, Paris, 1960

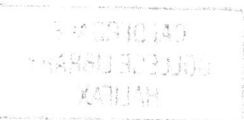

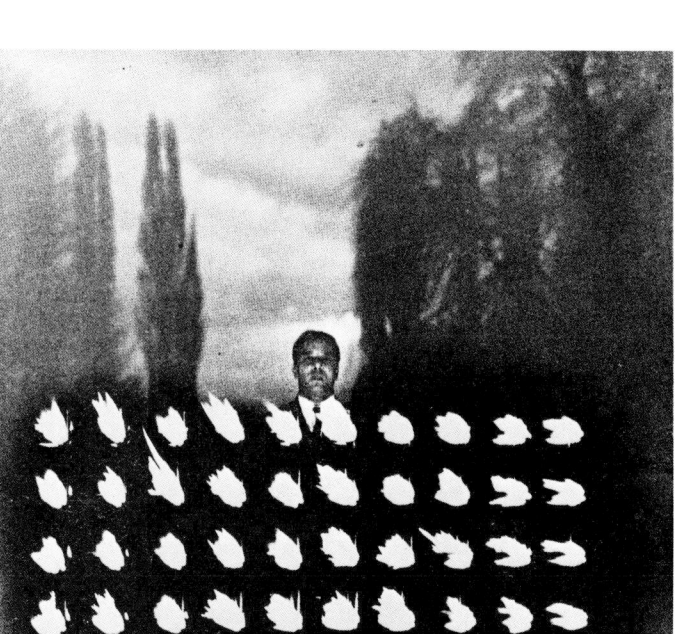

fig. 61. Yves Klein standing behind his Fire Wall, Museum Haus Lange, Krefeld, Germany, January 1961

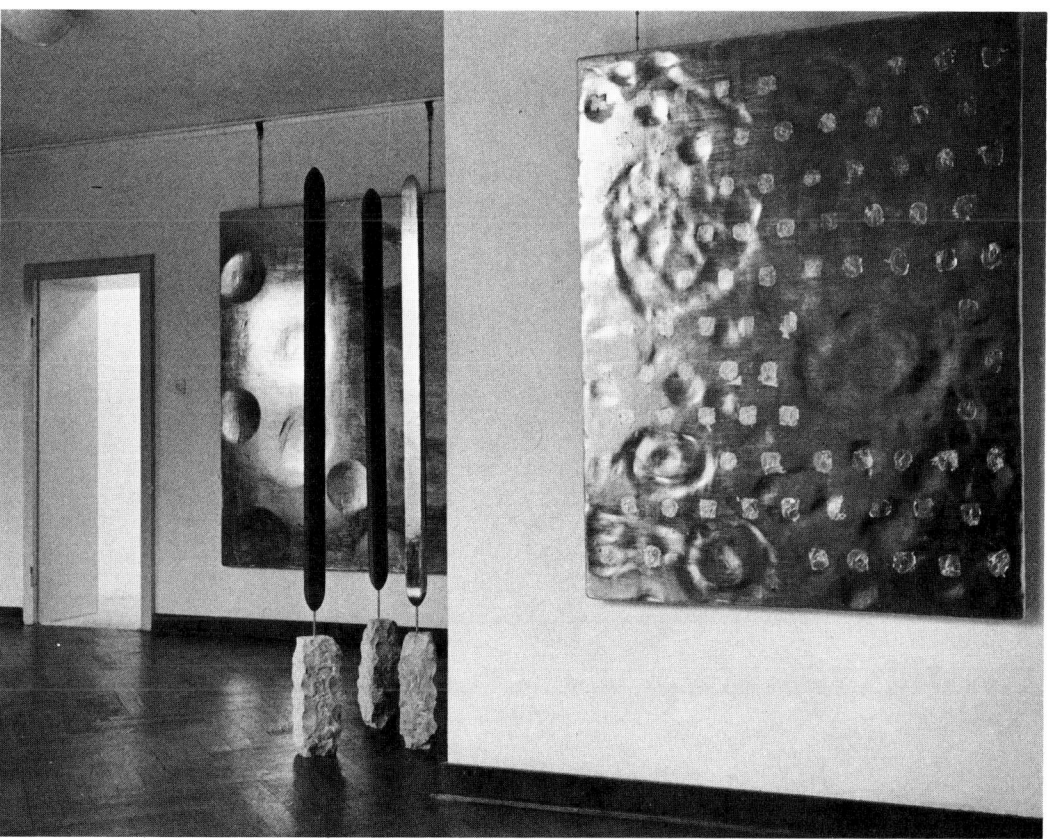

fig. 62. Installation view of the exhibition *Yves Klein, Monochrome und Feuer*, Museum Haus Lange, Krefeld, January 1961

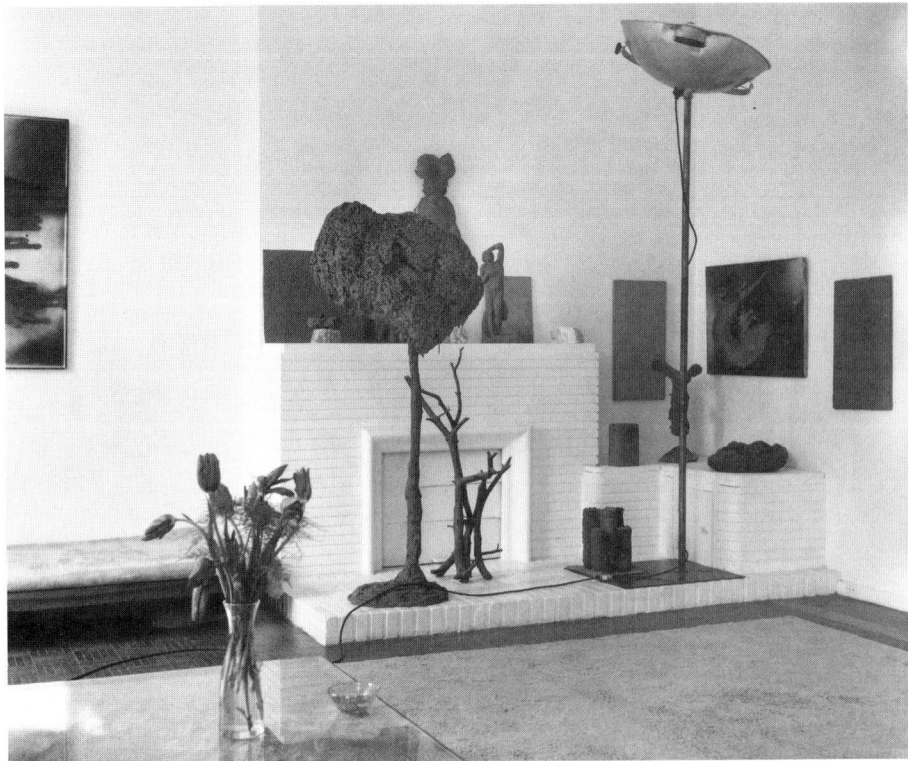

fig. 63. Interior, 14 rue Campagne Première, Paris, 1961

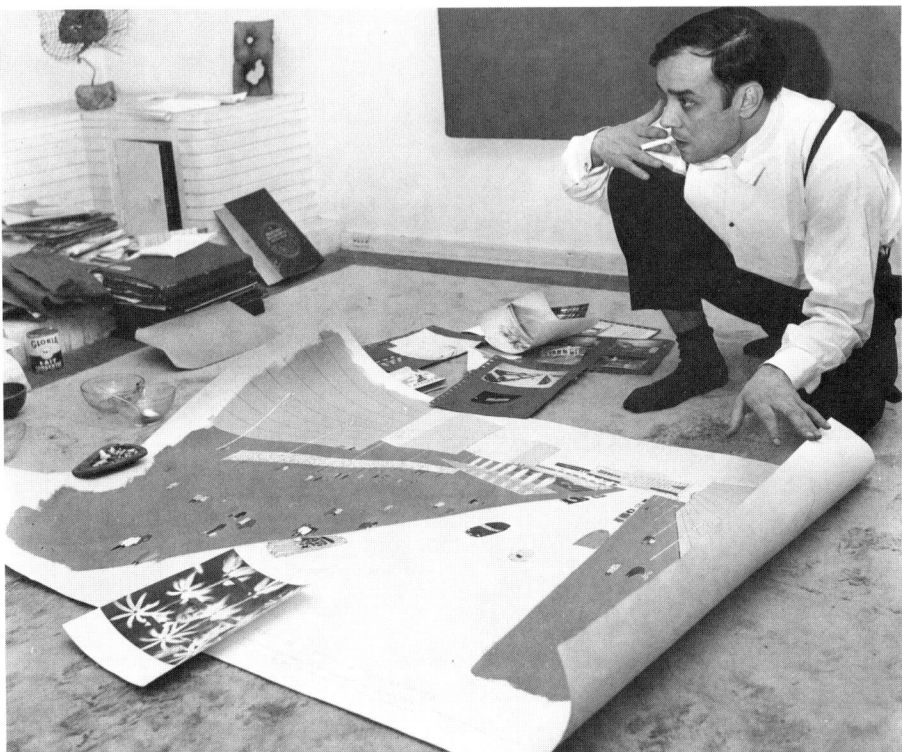

fig. 64. Yves Klein working with Claude Parent's renderings for fire and water walls and fountains, Paris, March 17, 1961

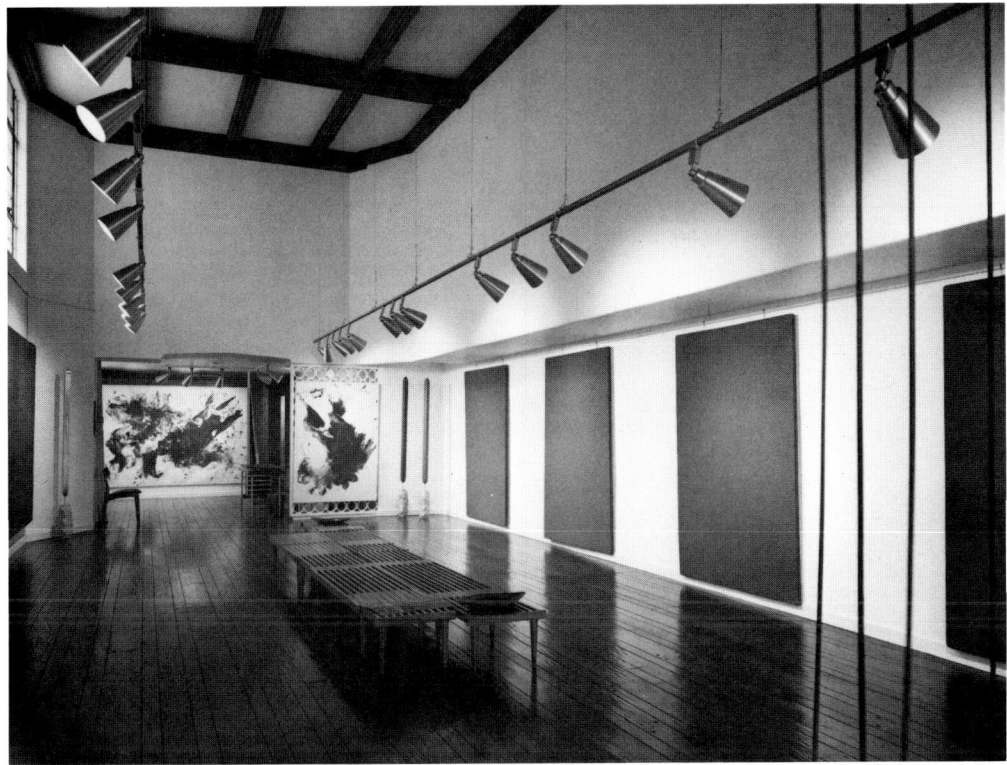

fig. 65. Installation view of the exhibition *Yves Klein le monochrome*, Dwan Gallery, Los Angeles, May–June 1961

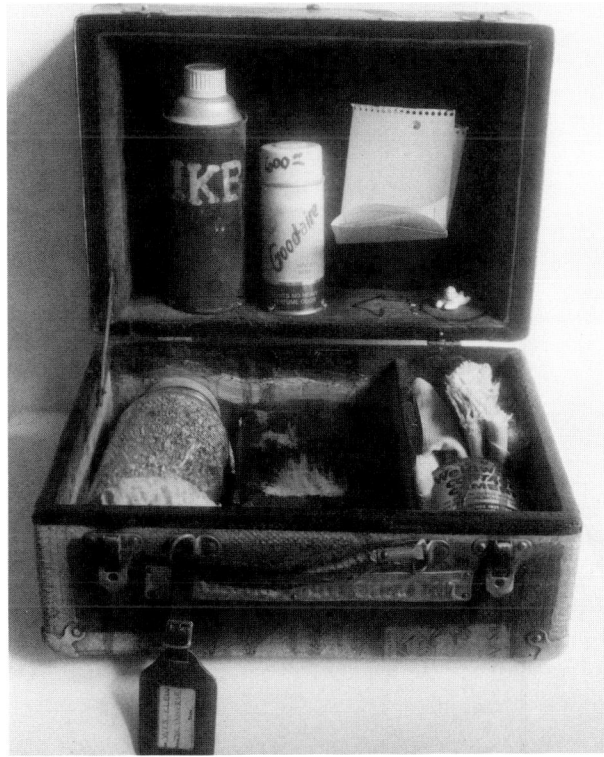

fig. 66. *Yves Klein, Address: The Universe*, gift to Klein from Ed Kienholz, c. 1961

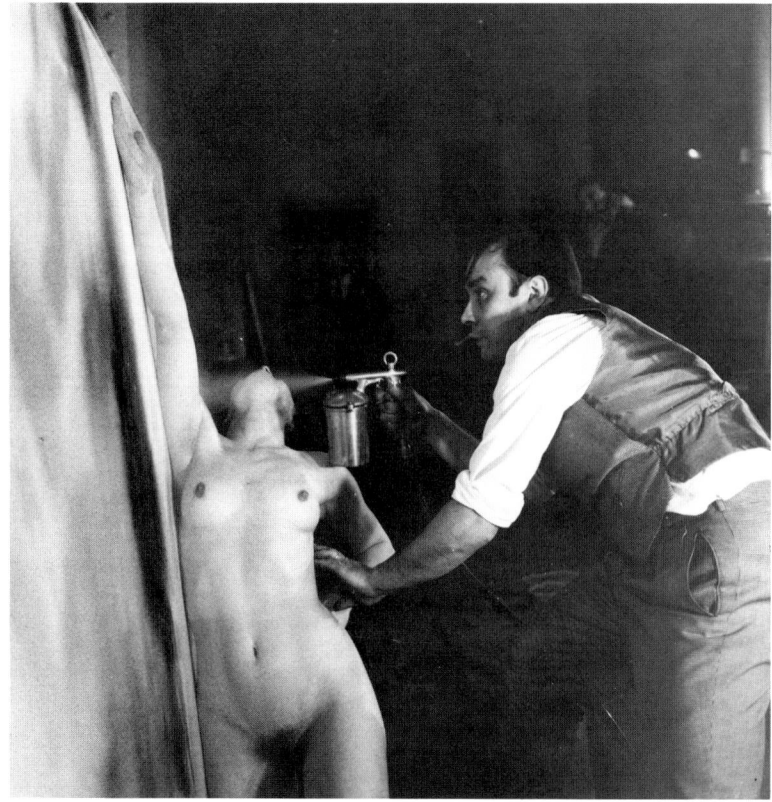

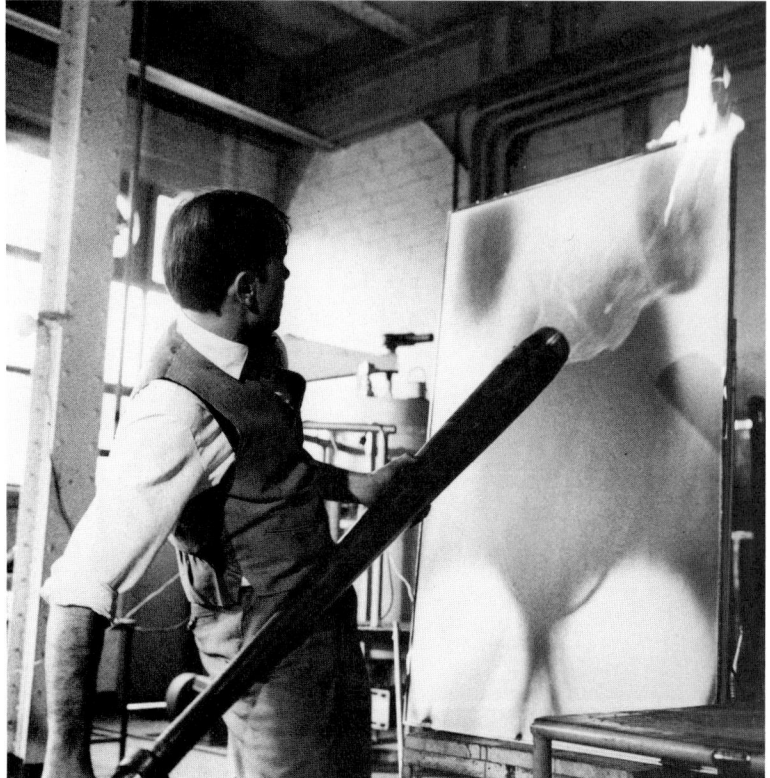

figs. 67-68.   Yves Klein making Fire Anthropometries, Centre d'Essais du Gaz de France, Paris, July 19, 1961

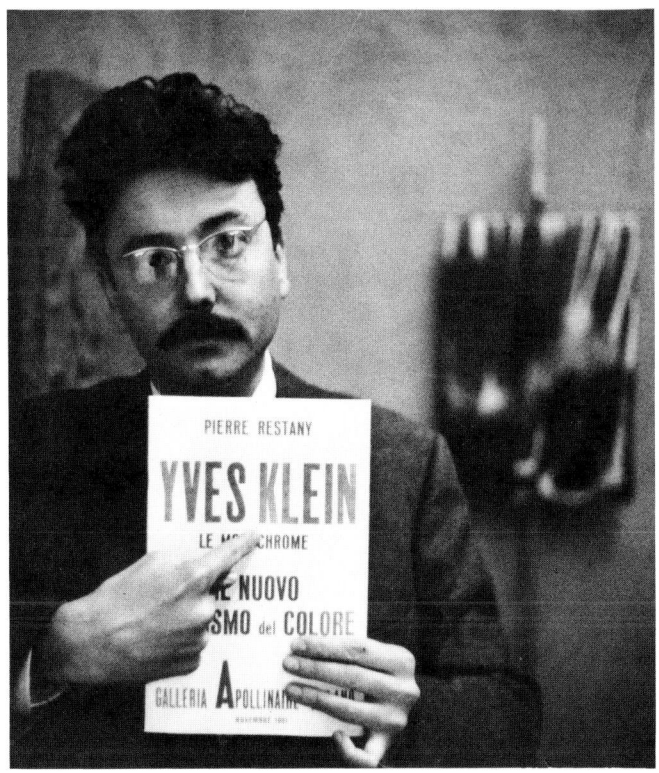

fig. 69. Pierre Restany, November 1961

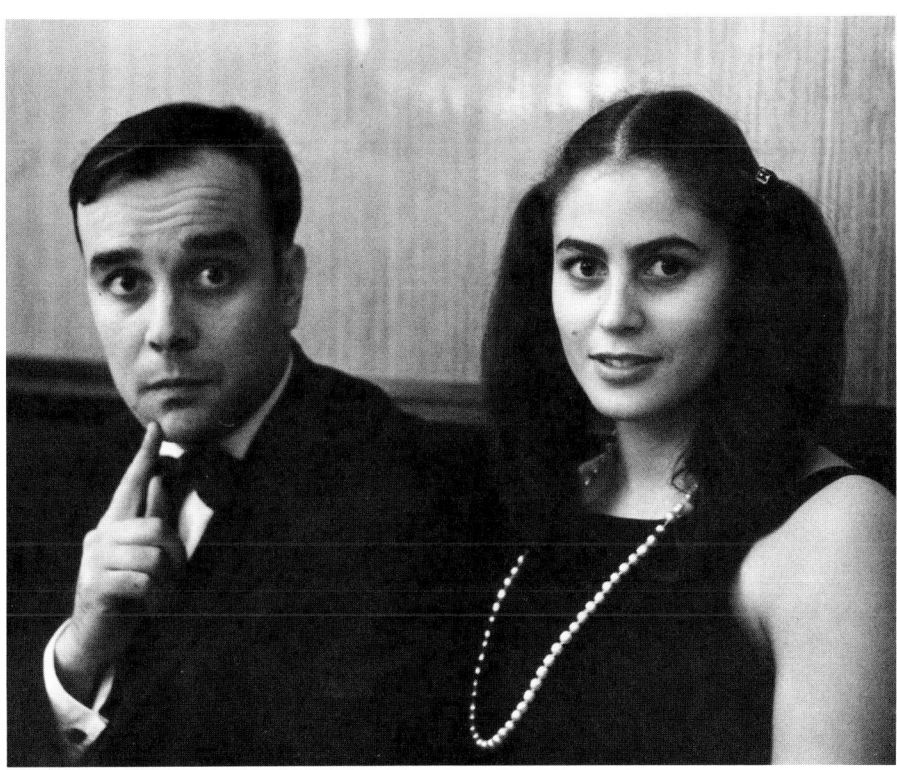

fig. 70. Yves Klein and Rotraut Uecker at La Coupole, Paris, November 9, 1961

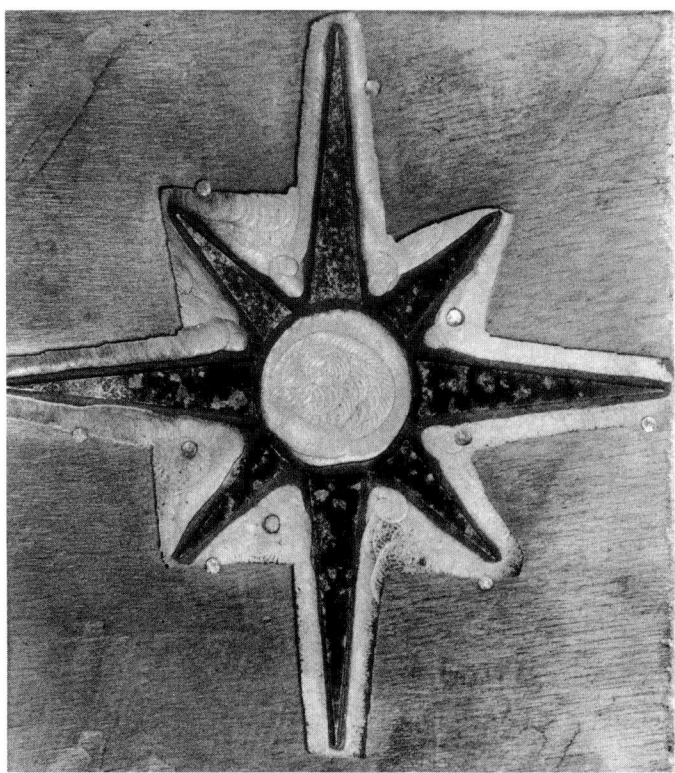

fig. 71. Yves Klein's star stamp, used on the back of some paintings

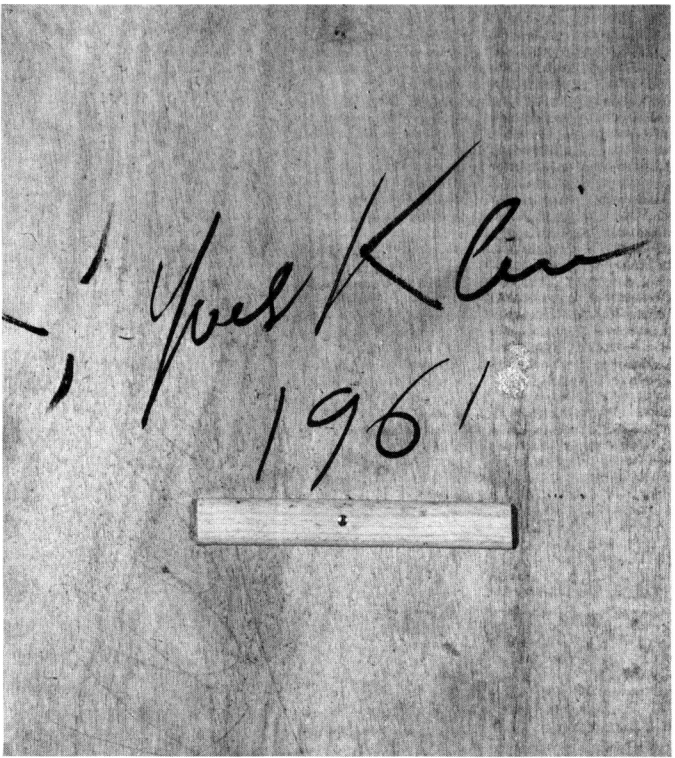

fig. 72. Signature on the back of a Klein painting

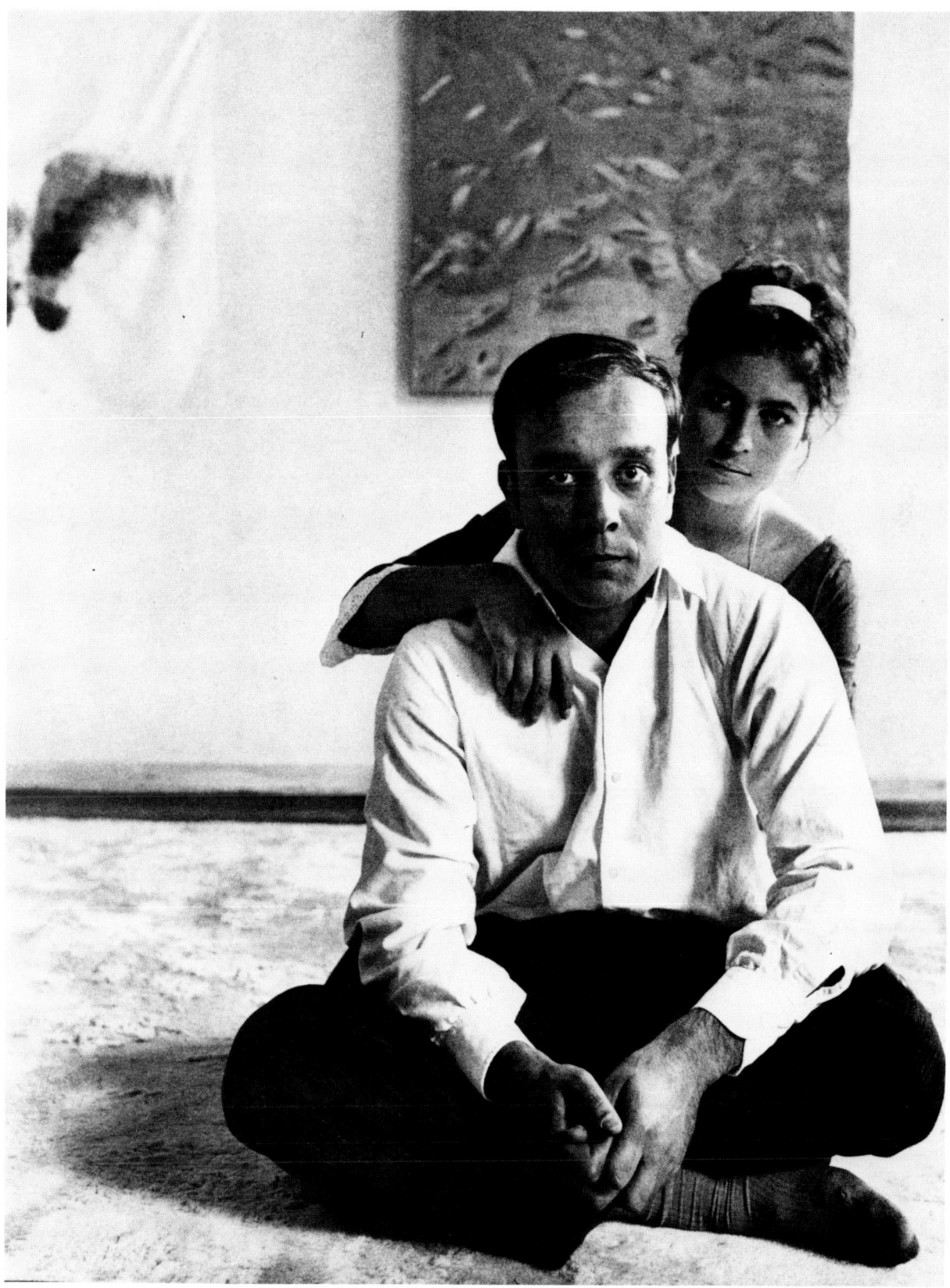

fig. 73. Yves Klein and Rotraut Uecker, Paris, 1961

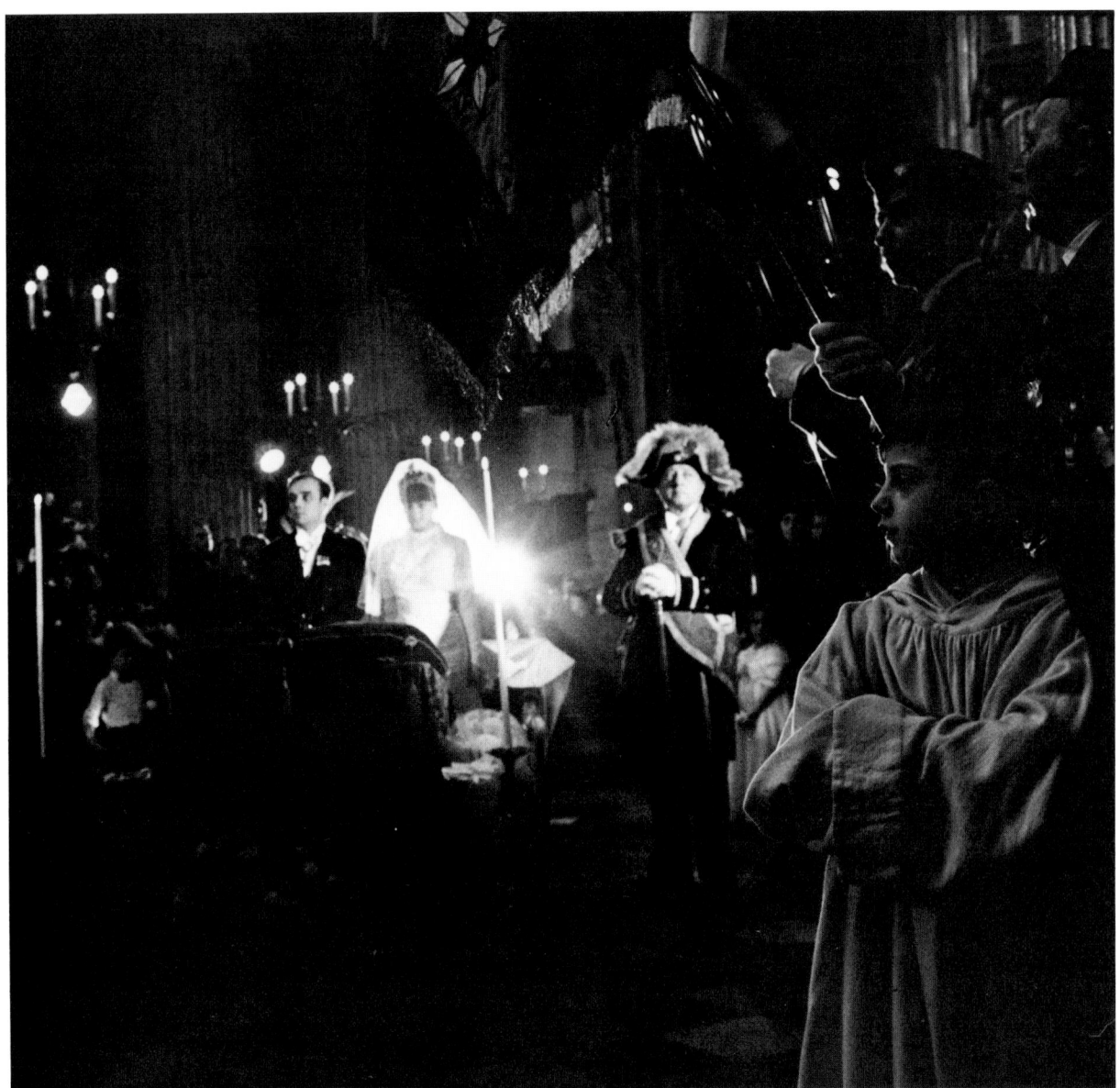

fig. 74. The wedding of Yves Klein and Rotraut Uecker, Church of Saint-Nicolas-des-Champs, Paris, January 21, 1962

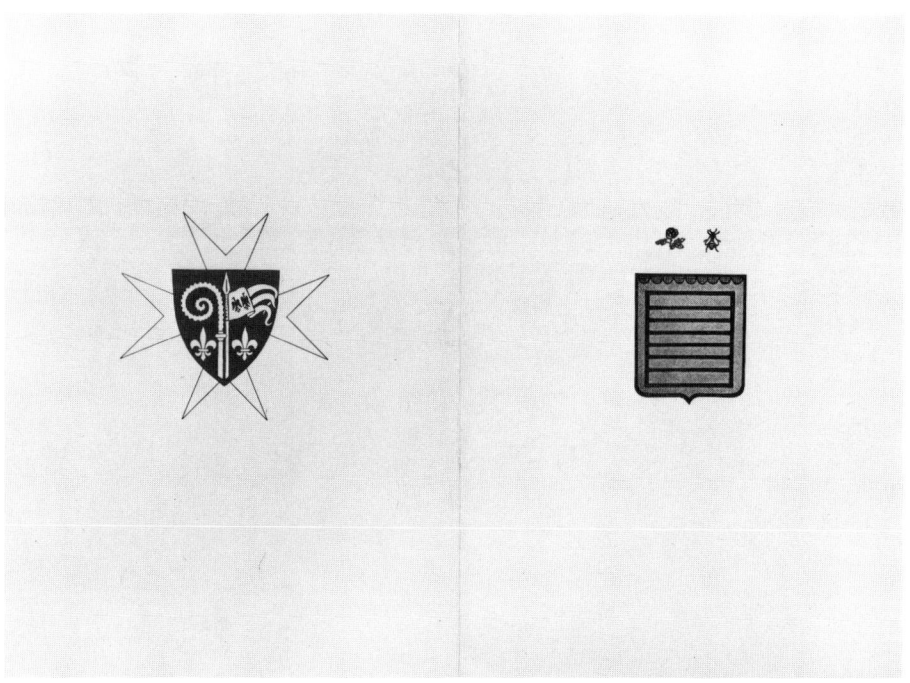

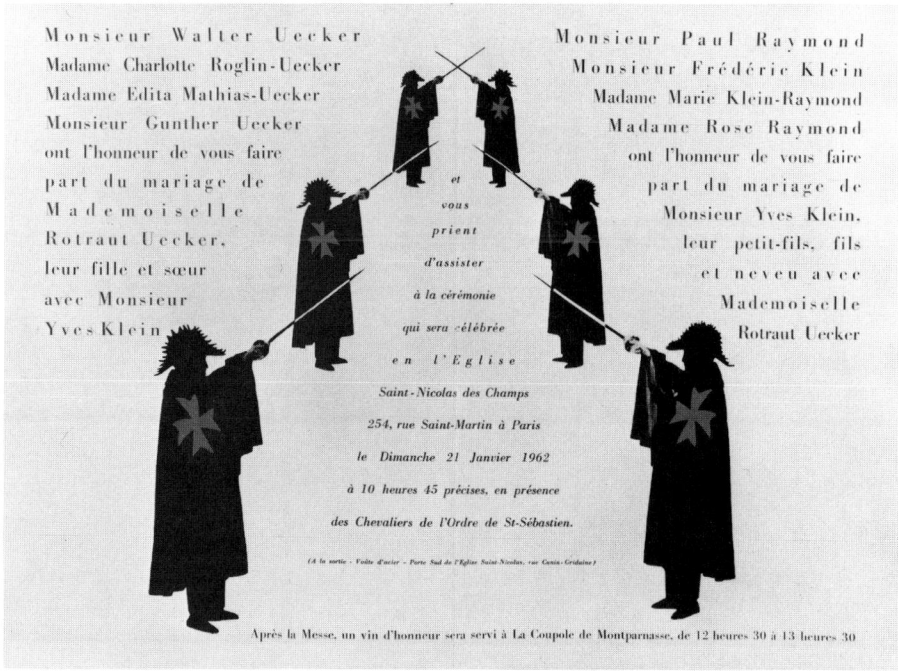

figs. 75-76.   Wedding invitation of Yves Klein and Rotraut Uecker

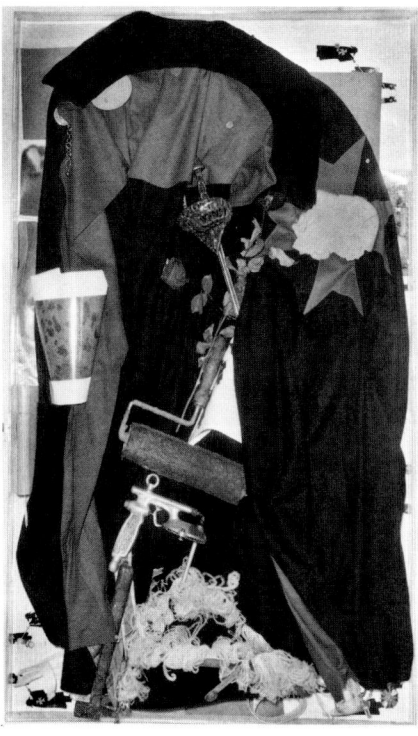

fig. 77.   Arman's *Portrait of Yves Klein*,
a wedding present, 1962

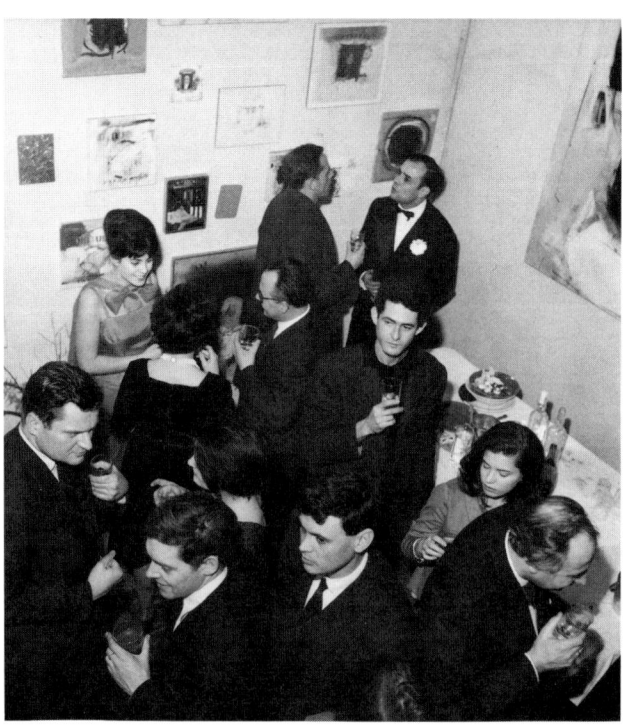

fig. 78.   Party at Larry Rivers' Paris studio after the wedding of Yves Klein and
Rotraut Uecker, January 21, 1962. Extreme left: John Ashbery; center:
James Metcalf; lower right: Norbert Kricke

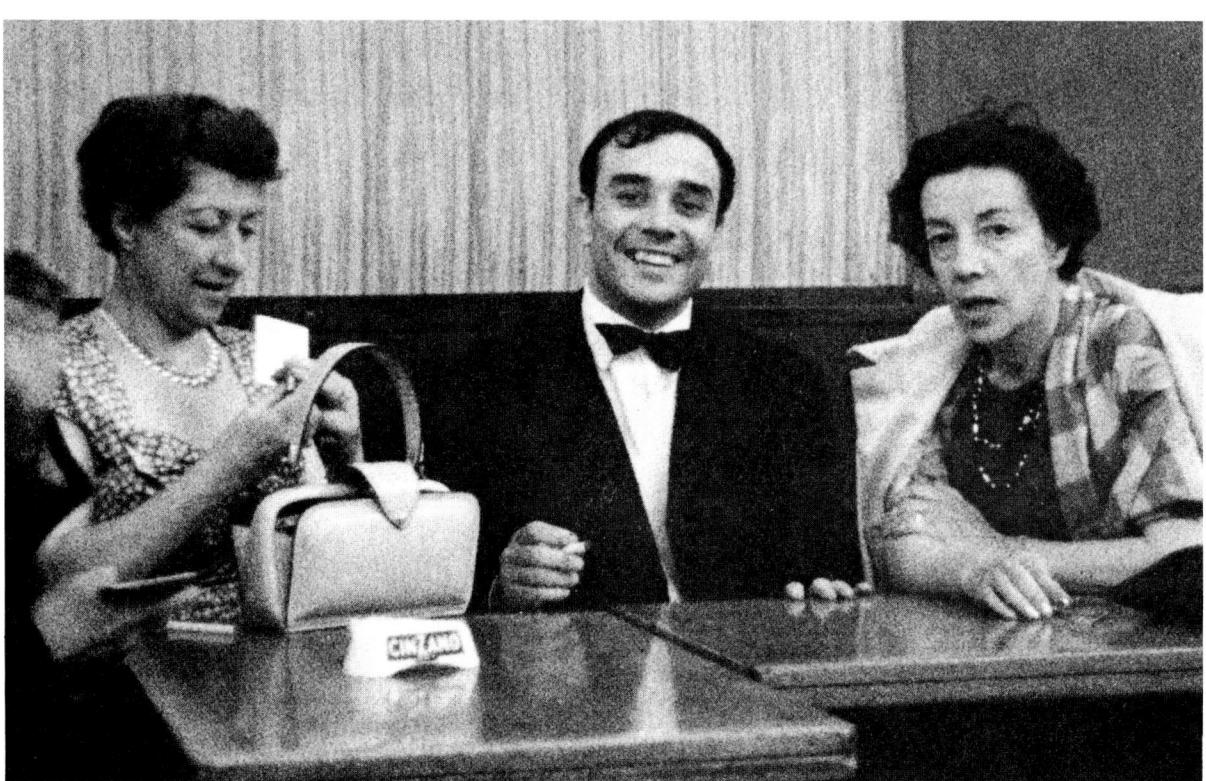

fig. 79.   Rose Raymond, Yves Klein, and Marie Raymond at La Coupole, Paris, c. 1962

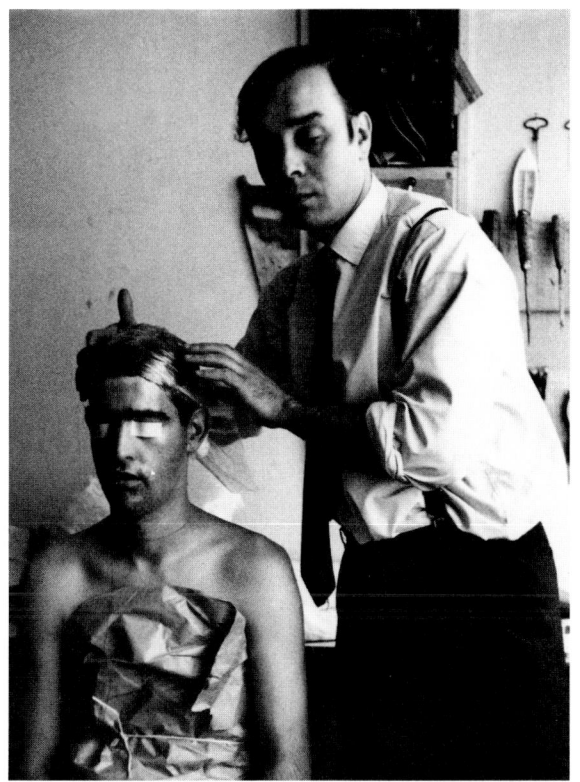
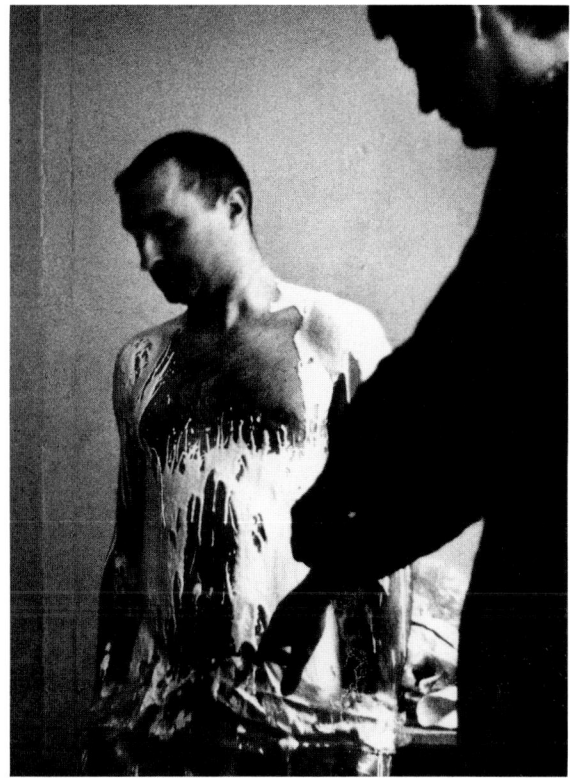
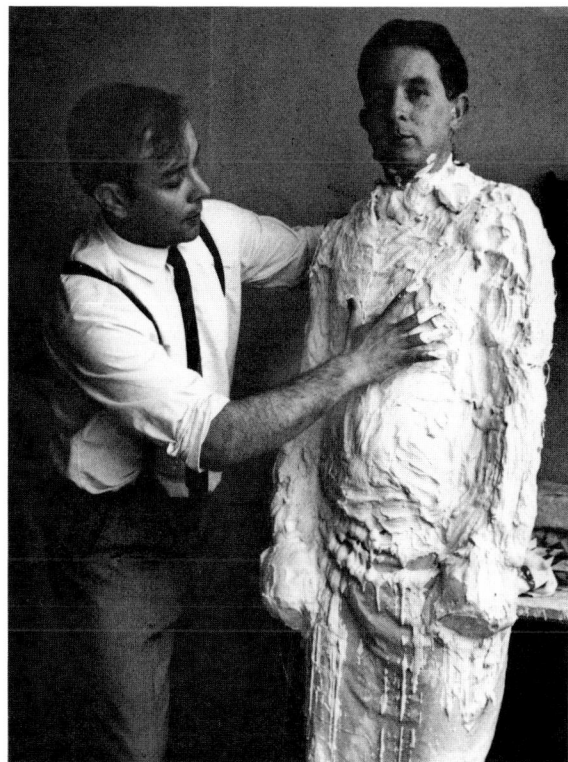
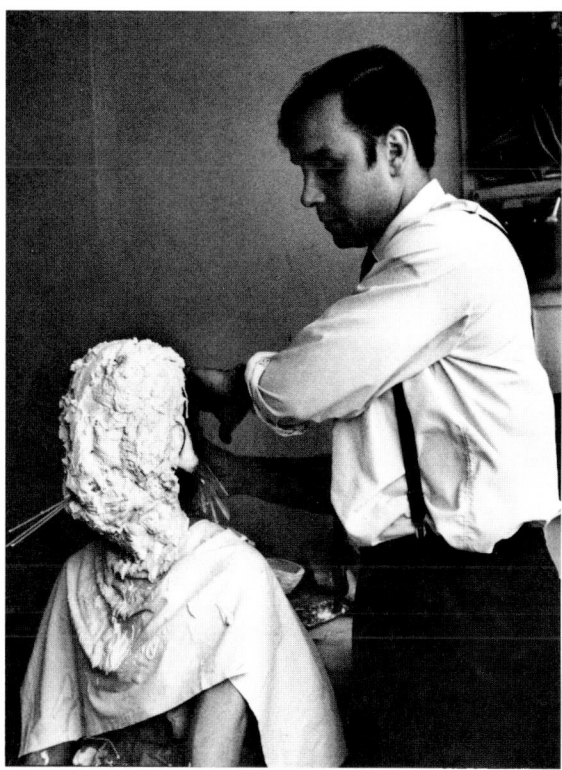

figs. 80-83.   Yves Klein preparing the Portrait Reliefs of (fig. 80) Martial Raysse, (fig. 81) Arman, (fig. 82) Claude Pascal, and (fig. 83) one of the preceding, February 1962

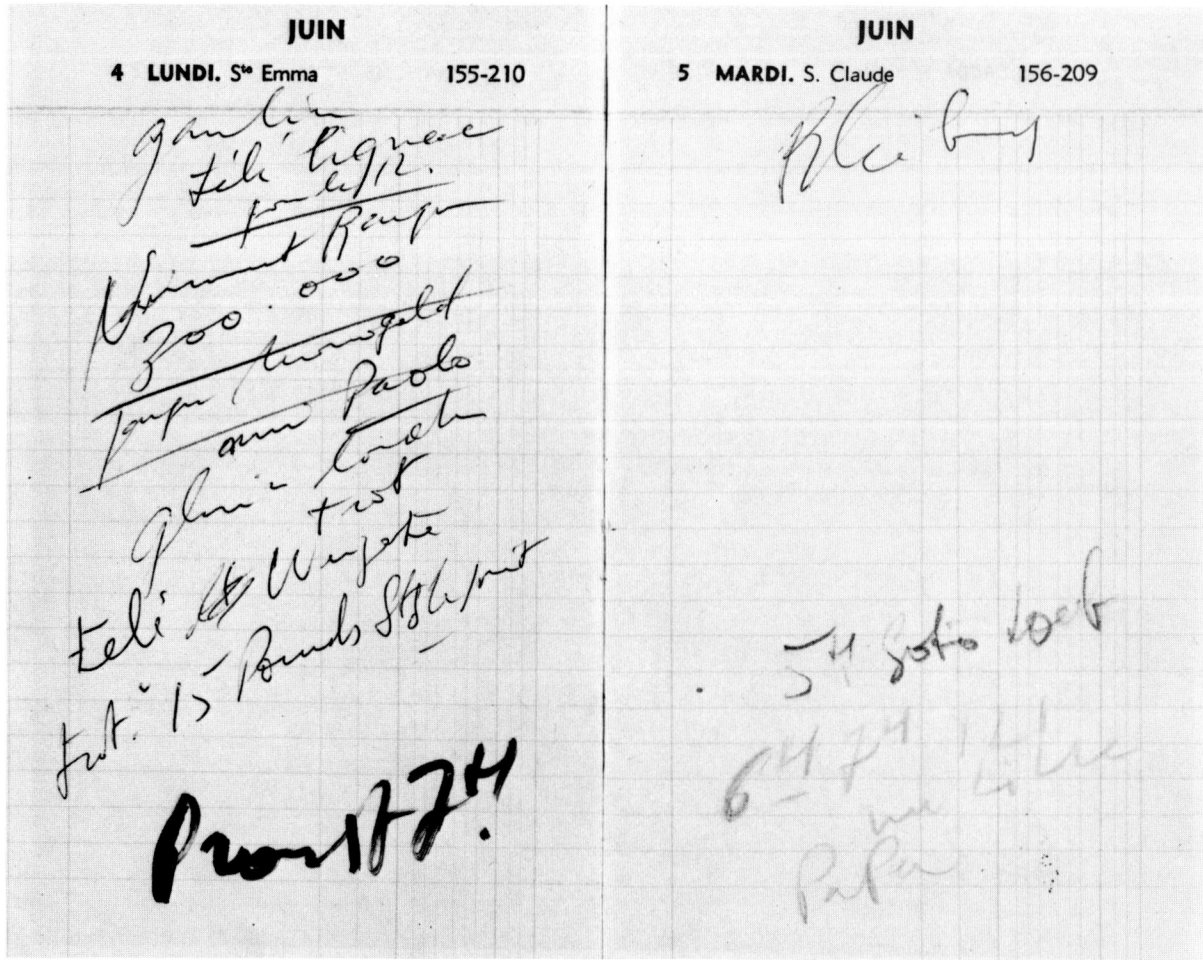

fig. 84. Yves Klein's appointment book for June 4 and 5, 1962 (he died June 6)

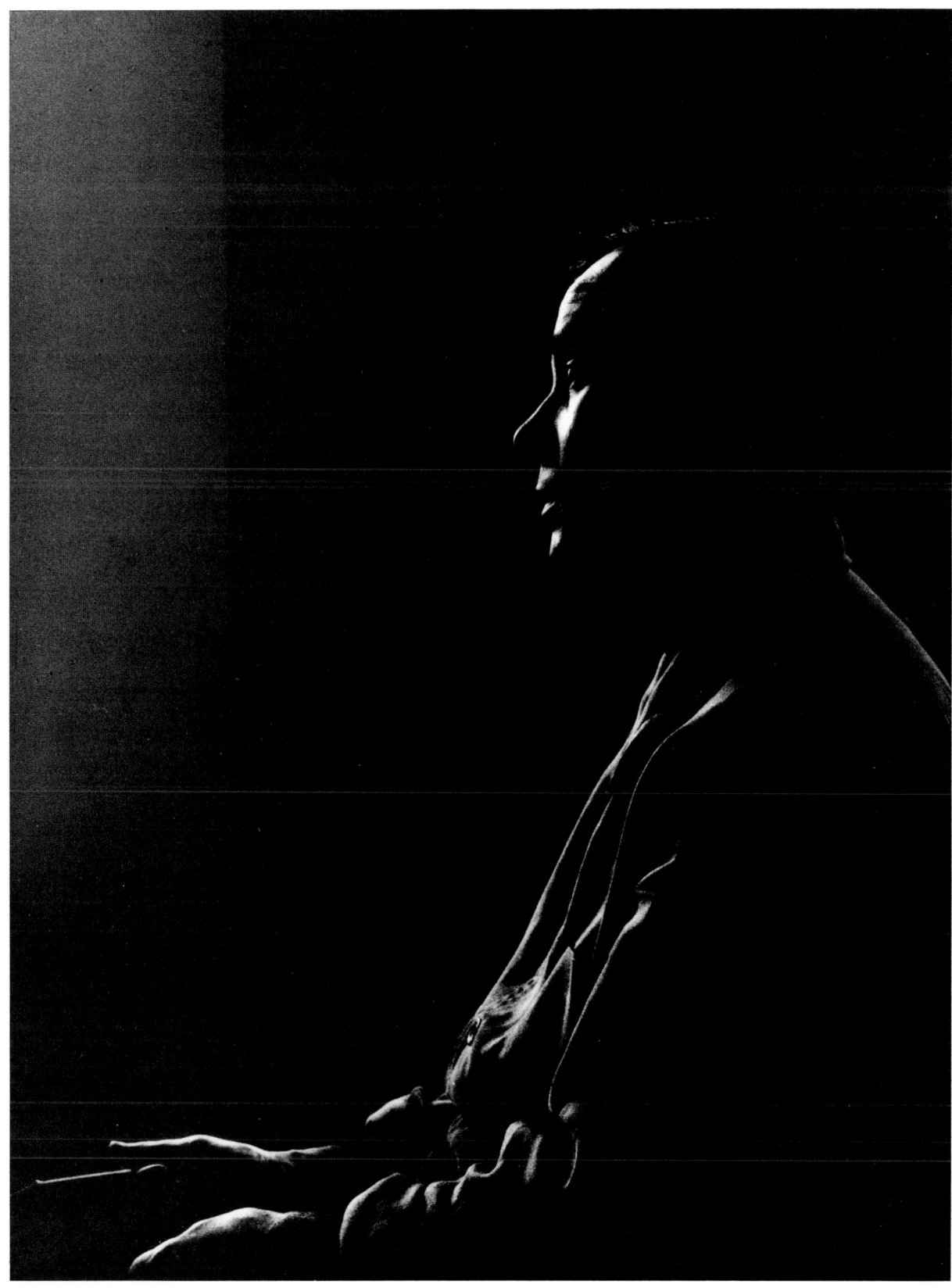

fig. 85. Yves Klein shortly before his death, May 1962

Bibliography

I. Published Writings by Yves Klein

1. "Des bases (fausses), principes, etc.... et condamnation de l'évolution." *Soulèvement de la jeunesse* (Paris), no. 1 (June 1952).

2. *Yves Peintures.* Preface by Pascal Claude [Claude Pascal]. Madrid: Fernando Franco de Sarabia, 1954.

3. *Haguenault Peintures.* Preface by Pascal Claude [Claude Pascal]. Madrid: Fernando Franco de Sarabia, 1954.

4. *Les Fondements du Judo.* Preface by Ichiro Abe. Paris: Editions Bernard Grasset, 1954.

5. "Propositions monochromes du peintre Yves." Interview with Bernadette Allain. *Couleurs* (Paris) 15 (1956): 25–27.

6. "Meine Stellung im Kampf zwischen Linie und Farbe." *ZERO* (Düsseldorf) 1 (April 1958); reprinted as "Ma Position dans le combat entre la ligne et la couleur," in Otto Piene and Heinz Mack, eds., *Zero.* Cambridge: MIT Press, 1973.

7. Reply to an inquiry made by *Arts* magazine. *Arts* (Paris), May 14, 1958.

8. *Le Dépassement de la problématique de l'art.* La Louvière, Belgium: Editions de Montbliart, 1959. Contains:
   "Le Dépassement de la problématique de l'art"
   "Préparation et présentation de l'exposition du 28 avril 1958"
   "Discours prononcé après le vernissage de l'époque pneumatique"
   "Esquisse du manifeste technique de la révolution bleue"
   "Esquisse et grandes lignes du système économique de la révolution bleue"
   "Discours prononcé à l'occasion de l'exposition Tinguely à Düsseldorf (janvier 1959)"
   "Exemple de collaboration realisée, evolution générale de l'art actuel vers l'immatérialisation" (with Werner Ruhnau)
   "Ma Systématique d'évolution"
   "Yves Klein (dit le monochrome)"
   "Histoire personnelle"
   "N.B."
   "Création d'un centre de la sensibilité"

9. *Dimanche, le journal d'un seul jour.* Paris: Festival d'Art d'Avant-garde, November 27, 1960. Printed by Combat et Presse de France. Contains:
   Page 1: "Le Théâtre du vide"
   "Actualité"
   "Un Homme dans l'espace"
   "Le Peintre de l'espace se jette dans le vide"
   "Sensibilité pure"
   Page 2: "Capture du vide"
   "Les Voleurs d'idées"
   "Du vertige au prestige (1957–1959)"
   "Viens avec moi dans le vide"
   "Projet pour un institut national théâtral"
   "Le Contrat"
   "Ballet du feu"
   Page 3: "Stupéfaction monochrome"
   "Les Cinq Salles"
   "La Guerre (petite mythologie personnelle de la monochromie datant de 1954, adaptable en film ou en ballet)"
   Page 4: "Projet de ballet sur aspect de fugue et choral"
   "La Statue"
   "La Marque de l'immédiat"
   "Le Sommeil"
   "Renversement"
   "Programme du Festival d'Art d'Avant-garde"

10. "My monochrome attempt has conducted me...." From the catalogue of the exhibition *Yves Klein le monochrome.* Leo Castelli Gallery, New York; April 11–29, 1961.

11. "Le Vrai devient réalité." *ZERO* 3 (July 1961).

12. "Nice 1947, l'époque de la rencontre...." *ZERO* 3 (July 1961).

13. In collaboration with Werner Ruhnau. "Projekt einer Luft-Architektur." *ZERO* 3 (July 1961).

14. "Yves Klein et le Globe terrestre Bleu!" From the catalogue of the exhibition *Yves Klein le monochrome, il nuovo realismo del colore.* Galleria Apollinaire, Milan; opening November 21, 1961.

15. "Climatisation de l'espace." From the catalogue of the exhibition *Antagonismes 2: L'Objet.* Musée des Arts Décoratifs, Pavillon de Marsan, Paris; opening March 7, 1962.

16. "La Climatisation de l'atmosphère." Ibid.

17. With Claude Pascal, Pierre Restany, and Armand Fernandez. "Store-poème." Ibid.

18. In collaboration with Neil Levine and John Archambault. "Due to the Fact That." From the catalogue of the exhibition *Yves Klein.* Alexander Iolas Gallery, New York; November 5–24, 1962.

19. "Le Réalisme authentique d'aujourd'hui." *KWY* (Paris) 11 (Spring 1963). A journal published by Lourdes Castro, Christo Javacheff, Jan Voss, and René Bertholo. This issue edited by Christo Javacheff.

20. "Pour satisfaire la sensualité...." From the catalogue of the exhibition *Peintures de feu.* Galerie Schmela, Düsseldorf; April 15–May 20, 1964.

21. "Après mon vide, le plein d'Arman." From the catalogue of the exhibition *Arman* (cat. no. 365). Stedelijk Museum, Amsterdam; September 22–November 2, 1964.

22. "Extraits de 'Journal' ('Rien n'est bleu...')." From the catalogue of the exhibition *Yves Klein.* Palais des Beaux-Arts, Brussels; March 3–April 3, 1966.

23. "Extraits d'une conversation avec P. Restany ('Moi, je suis jaloux...')." Ibid.

24. Extracts from "The Monochrome Adventure." Edited by Marcelin Pleynet. Translated by Lane Dunlop. From the catalogue of the exhibition *Yves Klein*. The Jewish Museum, New York; January 25–March 12, 1967.

25. Receipt for a Zone of Immaterial Pictorial Sensibility, December 8, 1959. Ibid.

26. Invitation card for Klein's marriage to Rotraut Uecker on January 21, 1962. Ibid.

27. "Symphonie—'Monoton Silence.' " Ibid.

28. "Quelques extraits de mon journal en 1957." *Art et création* (January–February 1968).

29. "L'Aventure monochrome." Ibid. The selection differs in several respects from the Jewish Museum text.

30. Receipt for a Zone of Immaterial Pictorial Sensibility, November 18, 1959, made out to Peppino Palazzoli (recto and verso). In the catalogue of the exhibition *Le Monochrome*. Galleria Blu, Milan; November 1969.

31. "Lorsque je serai...." From the catalogue of the exhibition *Yves Klein*. Galleria d'Arte Martano, Turin; November–December 1969.

32. "Humilité...." In Martano, Giuliano. *Yves Klein: Il Mistero Ostentato*. Turin: Martano Editore, 1970.

33. Cartoon, "Malévitch...." Ibid.

34. Postcard, "Ma chère Maman...Il n'y a que le grand art qui compte." Ibid.

35. "I Pennelli umani" ("Les Pinceaux vivants"). Ibid.

36. "Yves il monocromo naturometria" ("Yves le monochrome naturométries"). Ibid.

37. "Le Spugne" ("Les Éponges"). Ibid.

38. "Ma devise, pour la couleur! Contre la ligne et le dessin!" (motto written for the occasion of Klein's induction into the Order of Saint Sebastian). Ibid.

39. "Solution de 58 au problème de socle...." Ibid.

40. "Il Fuoco, ou l'avenir sans oublier le passé (1961)." Ibid.

41. *Dimanche, le journal d'un seul jour*. Ibid. A facsimile on glossy stock included in a pocket in the back cover.

42. "On est en train de créer quelquechose...." Translated into German by Manfred de la Motte. From the catalogue of the exhibition *Yves Klein*. Kunstverein, Hanover; June 19–July 25, 1971.

43. "Extrait d'une conférence en Sorbonne, 1959." From the catalogue of the exhibition *Yves Klein*. Galerie Karl Flinker, Paris; 1973.

44. *Yves Klein, 1928–1962: Selected Writings*. London: The Tate Gallery, 1974. Brief textual extracts and photographs of documents.

45. *Conférence à la Sorbonne, 3 juin 1959* (two long-playing phonograph records). Paris: RPM, n.d.

II. Archives of Yves Klein Papers and Documents

46. Archives Yves Klein, Documentation Arts Plastiques, Musée National d'Art Moderne, Centre National d'Art et de Culture Georges Pompidou, Paris.

47. The Yves Klein Archive of the Menil Foundation, Houston, Texas.

III. Exhibition Catalogues with Texts

48. *Yves Peintures*. Editions Lacoste, Paris; October 15, 1955. Text by Yves Klein.

49. *Yves: Propositions monochromes*. Galerie Colette Allendy, Paris; February 21–March 7, 1956. Text, "La Minute de Vérité," by Pierre Restany.

50. *Yves Klein: Proposte monocrome, epoca blu*. Galleria Apollinaire, Milan; January 2–12, 1957. Text, "L'Epoca blu, il secondo minuto della verità," by Pierre Restany.

51. *Monochrome Propositions of Yves Klein*. Gallery One, London; June 24–July 13, 1957. Text, "An Act of Truth," by Pierre Restany.

52. *Yves Klein le monochrome*. Galerie Rive Droite, Paris; October 11–November 13, 1960. Essay, "Monochromie et vitalisme," by Pierre Restany. Text by Werner Ruhnau.

53. *Yves Klein: Monochrome und Feuer*. Museum Haus Lange, Krefeld; January 14–February 26, 1961. Preface by Paul Wember.

54. *Yves Klein le monochrome*. Leo Castelli Gallery, New York; April 11–29, 1961. Statements by Yves Klein, Pierre Restany, and Paul Wember.

55. *Yves Klein le monochrome, il nuovo realismo del colore*. Galleria Apollinaire, Milan; opening November 21, 1961. Texts by Guido Le Noci and Yves Klein. Essay by Pierre Restany.

56. *Rétrospective Yves Klein*. Tokyo Gallery, Tokyo; July 23–31, 1962. Texts by Claude Pascal, Takachiyo Uemura, Yukiko Katsura, Yoshiaki Tono, and Shinichi Segi.

57. *Yves Klein*. Alexander Iolas Gallery, New York; November 5–24, 1962. Text, "Due to the Fact That," by Yves Klein in collaboration with Neil Levine and John Archambault.

58. *Yves Klein le monochrome, peintures de feu*. Galerie Tarica, Paris; April 30–May 20, 1963. Texts by André Verdet and Pierre Restany.

59. *Yves Klein*. Svensk-Franska Konstgalleriet, Stockholm; May 1963. Text by Yves Klein.

60. *Yves Klein le monochrome, empreintes*. Galerie Bonnier, Lausanne; March–April 1964. Texts by Pierre Restany and Ulf Linde.

61. *Peintures de feu*. Galerie Schmela, Düsseldorf; April 15–May 20, 1964. Texts by Otto Piene and Pierre Restany.

62. *Yves Klein*. Galerie Alexandre Iolas, Paris; opening April 12, 1965. Texts by Yves Klein and Pierre Restany.

63. *Yves Klein*. Stedelijk Museum, Amsterdam; October 22–December 13, 1965. Texts by Yves Klein, Ulf Linde, and Pierre Restany.

64. *Yves Klein*. In *Den inre och den yttre rymden en utställning rörande en universell konst (Inner and Outer Space, an Exhibition Concerning Universal Art)*. Moderna Museet, Stockholm; December 26, 1965–February 13, 1966. Texts by Ulf Linde, Pierre Restany, and Yves Klein.

65. *Yves Klein*. Palais des Beaux-Arts, Brussels; March 3–April 3, 1966. Texts by Yves Klein, Pierre Restany, and François Mathey.

66. *Yves Klein, peintures de feu*. Galerie Bonnier, Lausanne; summer 1966. Texts by Yves Klein and Pierre Restany.

67. *Yves Klein*. The Jewish Museum, New York; January 25–March 12, 1967. Texts by Kynaston McShine, Pierre Descargues, Pierre Restany, and Yves Klein.

68. *Trois Artistes de l'école de Nice: Arman, Yves Klein, Martial Raysse*. Musées de Nice, Galerie des Ponchettes; December 1967–February 1968. Texts by Jacques Médecin, Hervé de Fontmichel, Jacques Lepage, Alain Jouffroy, Pierre Restany, and Otto Hahn.

69. *Yves Klein — Louisiana*. Louisiana Museum, Humlebaek, Denmark; February 17–March 17, 1968. Texts by Pierre Descargues, Knud W. Jensen, Pierre Restany, and Yves Klein.

70. *Yves Klein in Nürnberg*. Institut für Moderne Kunst, Kunsthalle, Nuremberg; April 2–May 12, 1968. Texts by Dietrich Mahlow, Paul Wember, and Yves Klein.

71. *Yves Klein, 1928–1962*. Musée des Arts Décoratifs, Paris; January 25–March 11, 1969. Texts by Pierre Restany, Paul Wember, and Yves Klein.

72. *Le Monochrome*. Galleria Blu, Milan; November 1969. Texts by Pierre Restany and Dino Buzzati.

73. *Yves Klein*. Galleria d'Arte Martano, Turin; November–December 1969. Texts by Yves Klein, Pierre Restany, and Paul Wember.

74. *Yves Klein*. Galleria Civica d'Arte Moderna, Turin; December 2–31, 1970. Edited by Aldo Passoni. Texts by Yves Klein.

75. *Yves Klein*. Kunstverein, Hanover; June 9–July 25, 1971. Texts by Carlo Huber, Manfred de la Motte, Paul Wember, Werner Ruhnau, Yves Klein, Claude Pascal, and André Verdet.

76. *Yves Klein*. Kunsthalle, Berne; August 4–29, 1971. Texts by Carlo Huber, Manfred de la Motte, Paul Wember, Werner Ruhnau, Yves Klein, Claude Pascal, and André Verdet.

77. *Marie Raymond–Yves Klein*. Château-Musée de Cagnes-sur-Mer; December 16, 1972–February 17, 1973. Texts by Pierre Sauvaigo, Yves Klein, Pierre Restany, Michel Gaudet, and Charles Estienne.

78. *Yves Klein*. Galerie Karl Flinker, Paris; February 3–March 14, 1973. Text by Yves Klein.

79. *Yves Klein*. Gimpel-Hanover Galerie, Zurich; March 30–May 5, 1973. Text by Yves Klein.

80. *Yves Klein*. Gimpel Fils, London; May 30–June 23, 1973. Text by Yves Klein.

81. *Yves Klein*. Städtische Kunstsammlungen, Ludwigshafen; March 20–April 28, 1974. Texts by André Verdet, Manfred Fath, and Yves Klein.

82. *Yves Klein, 1928–1962, Selected Writings*. The Tate Gallery, London; March 20–May 15, 1974. Foreword by Norman Reid. Preface by Michael Compton. Introduction and annotated chronology by Jacques Caumont and Jennifer Gough-Cooper. Text by Yves Klein.

83. *Yves Klein*. Nationalgalerie and Neue Berliner Kunstverein, Berlin, June 4–July 12, 1976, and Städtische Kunsthalle, Düsseldorf, July 20–August 28, 1976. Foreword by Jürgen Harten, Lucie Schauer, and Dieter Honisch. Edited with commentary by Angela Schneider and Hannah Weitemeier. Text by Yves Klein.

84. *Yves Klein*. Fuji Television Gallery, Tokyo; October 19, 1979. Text in Japanese.

IV. Books about Yves Klein

85. Krahmer, Catherine. *Der Fall Yves Klein: Zur Krise der Kunst*. Munich: R. Piper and Co. Verlag, 1974.

86. Martano, Giuliano. *Yves Klein: Il Mistero Ostentato*. Turin: Martano Editore, 1970.

87. Restany, Pierre. *Yves Klein le monochrome*. Paris: Librairie Hachette, 1974.

88. ———. *Yves Klein*. Paris: Le Chêne, forthcoming.

89. ———. *Yves Klein et la mystique de Sainte Rita de Cascia*. Milan: Domus, 1981.

90. Rosenthal [Piene], Nan. "The Blue World of Yves Klein." Ph.D. dissertation, Harvard University, 1976.

91. Wember, Paul. *Yves Klein: Catalogue raisonné*. Monographie zur Zeitgenossischen Kunst, Institut für Moderne Kunst, Nuremberg. Cologne: Verlag M. DuMont Schauberg, 1969.

V. Selected Periodical Literature on Yves Klein

92. Allain, Bernadette. "Propositions monochromes du peintre Yves." *Couleurs* 15 (1956).

93. Alloway, Lawrence. "Spectrum of Monochrome." *Arts* 45 (December 1970).

94. *Art et création* 1 (January–February 1968).
    This issue was devoted to Klein. It contains:
    Cabanne, Pierre. "Le Rappel à l'ordre."
    Klein, Yves. "L'Aventure monochrome, extraits inédits."
    ——— . "Quelques extraits de mon journal en 1957."
    Parent, Claude. "Yves Klein et son architecture."
    ——— . "La 'Seconde Demeure' d'Yves Klein."
    Restany, Pierre. "Yves le monochrome."
    "L'Héritage impossible." Interview with Otto Hahn.

Statements by Sami Tarica, Raphael Soto, Jean Tinguely, Martial Raysse, Arman, Claude Pascal, and Lucio Fontana.

95. "Bluff mit Farbtafeln." *Neue Rheinzeitung* (Düsseldorf), June 3, 1957.

96. Buzzati, Dino. "Blu Blu Blu." *Corriere d'Informazione* (Milan), January 9–10, 1957.

97. "Ein neues Altstadt-Sensatiönchen." *Rheinische Post* (Düsseldorf), June 6, 1957.

98. Huelsenbeck, Richard. "Der Tod eines Malers." *Frankfurter Allgemeine*, July 27, 1962.

99. Hultén, K. G. Pontus. "Pariskonst och Jiujitsu." *Stockholms-Tidningen*, October 30, 1957.

100. Hunt, Ronald. "Yves Klein: Fragments from a Conversation with Rotraut Klein." *Icteric* (Newcastle-on-Tyne) 1 (January 1967).

101. _____. "Yves Klein." *Artforum* 5 (January 1967).

102. Janis, Sidney, and Jouffroy, Alain. Correspondence. *L'Oeil*, no. 155 (November 1967).

103. Jouffroy, Alain. "Le Grand Jeu de la Biennale." *L'Oeil*, no. 139–40 (July–August 1966).

104. _____. "L'Absolu d'Yves Klein." *XXᵉ Siècle* 41 (December 1973).

105. Judd, Donald. "Yves Klein." *Arts* 37 (January 1963). Review of Klein's show at Iolas Gallery.

106. Levine, Bernard. "The Kleins of D'Arvlay Street." *The Spectator*, July 5, 1957.

107. Lippard, Lucy R. "The Silent Art." *Art in America* 1 (January–February 1967).

108. Melville, Robert. "Exhibitions." *Architectural Review* 122 (September 1957).

109. Parent, Claude, with Jouffroy, Alain. "L'Utopie architecturale, condition de survie." *XXᵉ Siècle* 48 (June 1977).

110. Restany, Pierre. "Yves Klein, le jaillissement du futur." *Arts* Special Edition (June 23–July 6, 1955).

111. _____. "Die Beseelung des Objektes." *Das Kunstwerk* 15 (1961–62).

112. _____. "Le Nouveau Réalisme und was darunter zu verstehen ist." *Das Kunstwerk* 18 (January 1963).

113. _____. "New Realism." *Art in America* 51 (February 1963).

114. _____. "L'Avventura di Yves Klein." *Domus* 428 (July 1965).

115. Rivers, Larry. "Blues for Yves Klein." *Art News* 65 (February 1967).

116. Simon, Sidney. "Yves Klein." *Art International* 11 (October 1967).

117. Thwaites, John Anthony. "A Turning-Point: Notes on Norbert Kricke and Yves 'le monochrome.' " *Art International* 2 (September–October 1958).

118. _____. "Yves le monochrome...The Career of Yves Klein." *Art & Artists* 9 (July 1974).

119. "Voyage through the Void." *Time*, January 27, 1961.

120. Watt, Alexander. "Nouveaux Réalistes." *Art in America* 49 (1961).

121. Wember, Paul. "Yves Klein." *Art International* 5 (March 1961).

VI. Selected General Works Dealing with Yves Klein

122. Arnason, H.H. *History of Modern Art*. New York: Harry N. Abrams, 1977.

123. Becker, Jürgen, and Vostell, Wolf. *Happenings, Fluxus, Pop Art, Nouveau Réalisme*. Reinbek bei Hamburg: Rowohlt Paperback, 1965.

124. Brett, Guy. *Kinetic Art*. New York: Reinhold Book Corporation, 1968.

125. Burnham, Jack. *Beyond Modern Sculpture*. New York, 1968.

126. Celant, Germano, ed. *Conceptual Art, Arte Povera, Land Art*. Turin: Galleria Civica d'Arte Moderna, 1970.

127. Gottlieb, Carla. *Beyond Modern Art*. New York: E.P. Dutton, 1976.

128. Grohman, Will, ed. *Kunst unserer Zeit: Malerei und Plastik*. Cologne, 1966.

129. Henri, Adrian. *Total Art: Environments, Happenings, and Performance*. New York: Oxford University Press, 1974.

130. Janis, Harriet, and Blesh, Rudi. *Collage, Personalities, Concepts, Techniques*. Philadelphia and New York: The Chilton Company, 1962.

131. Kultermann, Udo. *Dynamische Architektur*. Munich, 1959.

132. _____. *Neue Dimensionen der Plastik*. Tübingen, 1967.

133. Lucie-Smith, Edward. *Late Modern: The Visual Arts since 1945*. New York: Praeger, 1969.

134. _____. *Art Now: From Abstract Expressionism to Superrealism*. New York: William Morrow, 1977.

135. Restany, Pierre. *Les Nouveaux Réalistes*. Paris: Planète, 1968.

136. Tono, Yoshiaki. *Passport No. 328309*. Tokyo, 1962.

137. Wember, Paul. *Malerei in unserem Jahrhundert*. Krefeld, 1963.

Catalogue Listing

In the listing below, the only titles given are those known to have been assigned by Yves Klein. The letters and numbers in parentheses before the works' dates refer to an inventory system which was made by Klein's widow, Rotraut Klein-Moquay, after his death, and which attempted to follow categories Klein himself used. These letters and numbers are unrelated to the works' dates of facture. They are furnished when known because they have become a customary means of identifying the pieces, which are often untitled. Frequently mistaken for titles (as in the Jewish Museum's 1967 Klein catalogue), these designations appear in the most complete cataloguing to date of Klein's work, Paul Wember's 1969 monograph.

Dates are given when they were noted on works by Klein or on the basis of existing definitive external information. Approximate dates are indicated by "c.," and undocumented dates are in brackets.

Dimensions are given first in centimeters, then in inches parenthetically, in the order of height, then width, then depth.

Only inscriptions on the works known or judged to be in Klein's hand are given. The end of an inscribed line is indicated by a diagonal slash (/). A symbol drawn with four short lines (less frequently, six or eight), in a configuration resembling a star or cross with an open center, is indicated by the words "star drawing." Klein used an inked stamp to put a similar mark — eight pointed rays around an open, circular center — on some works; this is indicated by the words "star stamp."

Works are listed by the categories below, by year within each category, and by inventory number within years:

> Paintings, Relief Paintings, and Related Works
> > Monochromes (M), International Klein Blue Monochromes (IKB), Monopinks (MP), Monogolds (MG), Sponge Reliefs (RE), Cosmogonies (COS), Planetary Reliefs (RP), Anthropometries (ANT), Shroud Anthropometries (ANT SU), Fire Paintings (F), Fire-Color Paintings (FC)
>
> Sculptures and Related Studies
> > Sponge Sculptures (SE), Sculptures (S), Portrait Relief (PR)
>
> Performance and Conceptual Works

Paintings, Relief Paintings, and Related Works

Monochromes

1. Untitled orange-red monochrome (M 7)   [1950]
    Paint (undetermined type) on paper on fabric
    25.7 × 20.6 (10⅛ × 8⅛)
    No inscription visible
    Lent anonymously

2. Untitled (red monochrome on stage)   1954
    Watercolor, pastel, ink, and pencil on paper, in an
        eighteen-page spiral-bound sketchbook
    13.5 × 21 (5⁵⁄₁₆ × 8¼)
    Inscrip.: *1954* (underlined twice), in pencil, on
        sketchbook cover; various inscriptions
        throughout sketchbook; *Scène avec un
        seul son/ continu—/ Un seul Rythme
        pour le ou la/ Danseur.—/ Une seule
        couleur au décor—*, in pencil, on facing
        page
    Lent anonymously

3. *Yves Peintures (Yves Paintings)*   1954
    Printed portfolio consisting of wraparound cover;
        title page; three pages titled "Preface," signed
        "Pascal Claude"; page indicating "Planches"
        ("Plates"); ten loose pages with captioned,
        tipped-in paper rectangles of various dimen-
        sions and colors; and colophon page stating that
        150 copies were printed at the press of Fer-
        nando Franco de Sarabia, Jaen 1, Madrid, No-
        vember 18, 1954
    24.4 × 19.7 (9⅝ × 7¾)
    Unsigned
    Lent by Marie Raymond

4. Untitled red monochrome (M 38)   1955
    Dry pigment in synthetic resin on fabric on board
    50 × 50 × 5 (19¹¹⁄₁₆ × 19¹¹⁄₁₆ × 2)
    Inscrip.: star drawing, *YK 55*, in pencil, on back of
        center support; star stamp on back
    Lent anonymously

5. *Expression de l'univers de la couleur mine
        orange (Expression of the Universe of the
        Color Orange Mineral)*, orange monochrome
        (M 60)   1955
    Dry pigment in synthetic resin on board
    95 × 226 (37⅜ × 89)
    Inscrip.: Calligraphic monogram of *Y* and *K*, and *.mai.
        55.*, in black paint, at lower right of front; *Yves
        K. mai 55./ "Expression de l'univers/ de la
        couleur mine orange,"* in black paint, at top
        center of back; *YVES*, in black paint, lower
        on back
    Lent anonymously

Note: In "The Monochrome Adventure" and other
texts in the Klein archive, Klein referred to this
painting as *Expression du monde de la
couleur Mine Orange.*

6. Untitled orange monochrome (M 6)   1956
Dry pigment in synthetic resin on fabric on board
37 × 57.5 (14⁹⁄₁₆ × 22⁵⁄₈)
Inscrip.: *Yves. 56,* in pencil, on fabric at bottom of back
Lent anonymously

7. Untitled black monochrome (M 22)   1956
Dry pigment in synthetic resin on fabric on board
24 × 41 × 2 (9⁷⁄₁₆ × 16⅛ × ¾)
Inscrip.: *Yves 56,* in pencil, on fabric over top sup-
port on back
Lent by Karl-Heinrich Müller

8. Untitled red monochrome (M 27)   1956
Flocking in undetermined binder on fabric on board
11.5 × 17.5 (4½ × 6⅞)
Inscrip.: star stamp, *Yves 56,* in black ink, on fabric
at top of back
Lent anonymously

9. Untitled bronze monochrome (M 23)   1957
Gold and bronze powdered paint over dry pig-
ment in synthetic resin on board
15.5 × 41 (6⅛ × 16⅛)
Inscrip.: *Fev 57,* in blue pencil, at top right of back
Lent anonymously

10. Untitled green monochrome (M 35)   1957
Dry pigment in synthetic resin on fabric on board
40 × 60 × 3.5 (15¾ × 23⅝ × 1⅜)
Inscrip.: star drawing, *Yves 57,* in black ink, on fabric
over bottom support on back
Lent anonymously

11. *Feux de Bengale — Tableau de feu bleu d'une
minute (Bengal Fires — One-Minute Blue
Fire Painting)* (M 41)   1957
Dry pigment in synthetic resin and charring
from fireworks on board
110 × 74.8 × 2.1 (43⁵⁄₁₆ × 29⁷⁄₁₆ × ⅞)
Unsigned
Lent anonymously
Note: Klein had fitted this painting with sixteen
Bengal lights fireworks, which he ignited
at the opening of his exhibition at the Galerie Colette Allendy, Paris, on May 14,
1957.

12. Untitled white monochrome (M 45)   1957
Oil over dry pigment in synthetic resin on fabric on
board
50 × 50 × 5.5 (19¹¹⁄₁₆ × 19¹¹⁄₁₆ × 2³⁄₁₆)

Inscrip.: star stamp, *Yves 57,* in blue crayon, on top
half of back; star stamp near bottom of right
side
Lent by Karl-Heinrich Müller

13. Untitled yellow monochrome (M 46)   [1957]
Dry pigment in synthetic resin on fabric on board
100 × 100 × 8.5 (39⅜ × 39⅜ × 3⁵⁄₁₆)
Unsigned
Lent anonymously

14. Untitled red monochrome (M 63)   1959
Dry pigment in synthetic resin on board
23.7 × 33 × .5 (9⅜ × 13 × ⅜)
Inscrip.: *To Mrs. A. Fuller/ avec ma profonde/ ad-
miration/* star drawing, *Yves Klein/ Juin
1959,* in black ink, on right half of back
Lent by Mr. and Mrs. Andrew P. Fuller

International Klein Blue Monochromes

15. Untitled blue monochrome (IKB 48)   1958
Dry pigment in synthetic resin on fabric on board
150.5 × 125 × 6 (59¼ × 49¼ × 2⅜)
Inscrip.: star drawing, *Yves 58* (sideways), in black
ink, near top of back center support; star
drawing, *Yves/ 58,* in black ink, at top right
of back
Lent by Moderna Museet, Stockholm

16. Untitled blue monochrome (IKB)   1959
Dry pigment in synthetic resin on paper
21.5 × 18 (8½ × 7⅛)
Inscrip.: *Yves,* in black ink, at bottom right of back
Lent by Menil Foundation Collection
Note: Cat. nos. 16, 17, 18, and 19 are four of sixty
original works done for a projected deluxe
edition of Klein's book *Le Dépassement
de la problématique de l'art.*

17. Untitled blue monochrome (IKB)   1959
Dry pigment in synthetic resin on paper
21.6 × 18.1 (8½ × 7⅛)
Inscrip.: *Yves 59,* in blue ink, at bottom right of back
Lent by D. & J. de Menil Collection

18. Untitled blue monochrome (IKB)   1959
Dry pigment in synthetic resin on paper
21.5 × 18 (8½ × 7⅛)
Inscrip.: *YVES,* in black ink, at bottom right of back
Lent anonymously

19. Untitled blue monochrome (IKB)   1959
Dry pigment in synthetic resin on paper
21.5 × 18 (8½ × 7⅛)
Inscrip.: *Yves 59,* in blue ink, at bottom right of back
Lent by Henry J. N. Taub

20. Untitled blue monochrome (IKB 63)   1959
    Dry pigment in synthetic resin on fabric on board
    92 × 73.5 × 3 (36¼ × 28¹⁵⁄₁₆ × 1³⁄₁₆)
    Inscrip.: star drawing, *Yves Klein 59,* in pencil, on
          fabric at top of back
    Lent by Van Abbemuseum, Eindhoven, The Neth-
          erlands

21. Untitled blue monochrome (IKB 82)   1959
    Dry pigment in synthetic resin on fabric on board
    92 × 73 × 2.5 (36¼ × 28¾ × 1)
    Inscrip.: star drawing, *Yves Klein/ 1959,* in dark ink,
          at center of fabric at bottom of back; star
          drawing, in dark ink, left of center on fab-
          ric at top of back
    Lent by Mr. and Mrs. Andrew P. Fuller

22. Untitled blue monochrome (IKB 172)   [1959]
    Dry pigment in synthetic resin on fabric on board
    74 × 27.5 × 2.5 (29⅛ × 10⅞ × 1)
    Inscrip.: star drawing, *Yves Klein/ Le Mono-
          chrome,* in red ink, on fabric at top back;
          star stamps at center back of top support,
          left of center back, and upper right of back
    Lent by Jan Eric von Löwenadler

23. Untitled blue monochrome (IKB 3)   1960
    Dry pigment in synthetic resin on fabric on board
    199 × 153 × 2.5 (78⅜ × 60¼ × 1)
    Inscrip.: star drawing, *Yves Klein/ le mono-
          chrome/ 1960,* in blue paint, on upper
          third of back
    Lent by Musée National d'Art Moderne, Centre
          Georges Pompidou

24. Untitled blue monochrome (IKB 42)   1960
    Dry pigment in synthetic resin on fabric on board
    199 × 153 × 2.5 (78⅜ × 60¼ × 1)
    Inscrip.: star drawing, *Yves Klein/ le mono-
          chrome/ 1960,* in blue paint, on top third
          of back; star stamp on fabric over top
          third of right support on back
    Lent by Menil Foundation Collection

25. Untitled blue monochrome (IKB 75)   1960
    Dry pigment in synthetic resin on fabric on board
    199 × 153 × 2.5 (78⅜ × 60¼ × 1)
    Inscrip.: star drawing, *Yves Klein/ le mono-
          chrome/ 1960,* in blue paint, on top third
          of back
    Lent by Louisiana Museum of Modern Art, Hum-
          lebaek, Denmark
    Note: Rice Museum exhibition only.

26. Untitled blue monochrome (IKB 83)   1960
    Dry pigment in synthetic resin on fabric on board
    92 × 73 × 2.5 (36¼ × 28¾ × 1)

    Inscrip.: star drawing, *Yves Klein/ le mono-
          chrome 1960,* in dark ink, on back of top
          support; star drawing, *I.K.B.,* in dark ink,
          on upper half of back
    Lent by Sidney Janis Gallery

27. Untitled blue monochrome (IKB 128)   1960
    Dry pigment in synthetic resin on fabric on board
    25 × 40 × 1.5 (9¹³⁄₁₆ × 15¾ × ⅝)
    Inscrip.: *Pour Antonio Saura/ avec l'amitié de/
          Yves Klein/ Paris 1–2–60,* in blue-black
          ink, on left half of back
    Lent by Sidney Janis Gallery

28. Untitled blue monochrome (IKB)   1961
    Dry pigment in synthetic resin on fabric on board
    195.1 × 140 × 2.5 (76⅞ × 55⅛ × 1)
    Inscrip.: star drawing, *Yves Klein/ le mono-
          chrome/ Paris 1961* and *California,* in
          black ink, on back
    Lent by The Museum of Modern Art, New York, The
          Sidney and Harriet Janis Collection, 1967

29. Untitled blue monochrome (IKB)   1961
    Dry pigment in synthetic resin on fabric on board
    73 × 54 × 2.5 (28¾ × 21¼ × 1)
    Inscrip.: star drawing/ *I.K.B./ Yves Klein/ 1961/* star
          stamp, in black paint, on top half of back;
          *Pour Alain Bedel/ avec toute l'amitié/ de
          Yves,* in black ink, on bottom half of back;
          star stamp at center back of right support
    Lent by D. & J. de Menil Collection

30. Untitled blue monochrome (IKB 68)   1961
    Dry pigment in synthetic resin on board
    195 × 140 × 3 (76¾ × 55⅛ × 1³⁄₁₆)
    Inscrip.: star drawing, *Yves Klein/ le mono-
          chrome/Paris 1961,* in black ink, at cen-
          ter of back
    Lent anonymously

31. Untitled blue monochrome (IKB 111)   1961
    Dry pigment in synthetic resin on fabric on board
    60 × 48 × 1 (23⅝ × 18⅞ × ⅜)
    Inscrip.: *Pour Bob R/ avec l'amitié/ de Yves K/ 1961,*
          in red ink, on back
    Lent by Robert Rauschenberg

32. Untitled blue monochrome (IKB)   1962
    Dry pigment in synthetic resin on fabric on board
    43 × 35 × 1 (16⅞ × 13¾ × ⅜)
    Inscrip.: star drawing, *Yves Klein/ 1962/ a wavy line/
          I.K.B.,* in black crayon, on back
    Lent by Walter Hopps

33. *Pigment pur bleu (Pure Blue Pigment)*
          facsimile of 1957 and 1961

presentations of pure pigment
Horizontal wooden tray containing dry, powdered
ultramarine blue pigment
Surface 120 × 100 (47¼ × 39⅜)
Note: Klein is known to have presented blue
powdered pigment on three occasions: at
the Galerie Colette Allendy, Paris, in 1957;
at the Museum Haus Lange, Krefeld, in
1961; and at the Dwan Gallery, Los Angeles, in 1961. The Krefeld exhibition also
included a tray of rose powdered pigment, *Pigment pur rose,* whose surface
measured 92 × 73 (36¼ × 28¾).

Monopinks

34. *Grand Monopink (Large Monopink)*
    (MP 16)   1960
    Dry pigment in synthetic resin on fabric on board
    199 × 153 × 3 (78⅜ × 60¼ × 1³⁄₁₆)
    Inscrip.: *Grand Monopink,* in red chalk, at top of
        back; star drawing, *Yves Klein/ le mono-
        chrome/ 1960,* in pink paint, on top third
        of back
    Lent by Louisiana Museum of Modern Art, Hum-
        lebaek, Denmark
    Note: Rice Museum exhibition only.

35. Untitled pink monochrome (MP 19)   [1962]
    Dry pigment in synthetic resin on fabric on board
    92 × 72.5 × 2.5 (36¼ × 28½ × 1)
    Inscrip.: star stamp, on lower right of back
    Lent anonymously

Monogolds

36. Untitled monogold (MG 7)   undated
    Gold leaf on primed board
    199.5 × 153 × 2 (78½ × 60¼ × ¾)
    Unsigned
    Lent anonymously

37. *Le Silence est d'or (Silence Is Golden)*
    (MG 10)   1960
    Gold leaf on primed board
    148.5 × 114 × 1.5 (58½ × 44⅞ × ⅝)
    Inscrip.: star drawing, *Yves Klein/ 1960,* in pencil,
        on upper back
    Lent anonymously

38. *Résonance (Resonance)* (MG 16)   1960
    Gold leaf on primed board
    199 × 153 × 2 (78⅜ × 60¼ × ¾)
    Inscrip.: star drawing, *Yves Klein/ le mono-
        chrome/ 1960,* in blue paint, on top half
        of back; *13* (circled) *"résonance"* and
        monogold, in pink crayon, on back

Lent by Stedelijk Museum, Amsterdam

39. Untitled monogold (MG 6)   1961
    Gold leaf on primed board
    60 × 48 × 2 (23⅝ × 18⅞ × ¾)
    Inscrip.: star drawing, *Yves Klein/ 1961,* in black
        paint, on back
    Lent anonymously

40. Untitled monogold (MG 21)   1961
    Gold leaf on primed board
    62.2 × 45.2 × 1.3 (24½ × 17¹³⁄₁₆ × ½)
    Inscrip.: star drawing, *Yves Klein/ le mono-
        chrome/ 1961,* in blue ink, at center top
        of back
    Lent by Sidney Janis Gallery

41. Untitled monogold (MG 24)   1961
    Gold leaf on painted board
    60 × 42 × 2 (23⅝ × 16½ × ¾)
    Inscrip.: star drawing, *Yves Klein/ 1961,* in black
        paint, on back
    Lent by Gerard Bonnier

42. Untitled monogold (MG 25)   1961
    Gold leaf on primed board
    53.5 × 50.4 × 2 (21 × 19⅞ × ¾)
    Inscrip.: *Pour Richard Stankiewicz/ avec l'amitié
        de/* star drawing, *Yves K/ New York 1961,*
        in dark ink, on back
    Lent by Richard Stankiewicz

Sponge Reliefs

43. *Le Rose du bleu (The Rose of the Blue)*
    (RE 22)   c. 1960
    Sponges, pebbles, and dry pink pigment in syn-
        thetic resin on board
    199 × 153 × c. 16 (78⅜ × 60¼ × c. 6¼)
    Inscrip.: *12* (circled) *le rose du Bleu,* in pink chalk,
        on upper back
    Lent anonymously

44. *Sol (The Note G),* blue (RE)   1960
    Sponges, pebbles, and dry pigment in syn-
        thetic resin on board
    71 × 153.5 × 12 (28 × 60½ × 4¾)
    Inscrip.: *1960/* star drawing, *Yves Klein/ le mono-
        chrome,* in blue paint, on back; *"Sol"*
        (sideways), in red crayon, on left of back
    Lent by Mizne-Blumenthal Collection

45. *L'Accord bleu (Blue Harmony)* (RE 10)   1960
    Sponges, pebbles, and dry pigment in synthetic
        resin on board
    198 × 164.5 × c. 13.5 (77¹⁵⁄₁₆ × 64¾ × c. 5⁵⁄₁₆)
    Inscrip.: *1960,* star drawing, *Yves Klein/ le mono-*

chrome, in blue paint, on back; *l'accord bleu,* in pink crayon, on back
Lent by Stedelijk Museum, Amsterdam

46. *Do, Do, Do (The Note C),* blue (RE 16)   1960
    Sponges, pebbles, and dry pigment in synthetic resin on board
    200 × 165 × 18 (78¾ × 65 × 7¹⁄₁₆)
    Inscrip.: star drawing, *Yves K/ le monochrome/ 1960,* in blue paint, on top half of back; *"Do, Do, Do"* (upside down), in red crayon, at bottom of back
    Lent anonymously

47. *Requiem,* blue (RE 20)   1960
    Sponges, pebbles, and dry pigment in synthetic resin on board
    198.6 × 164.8 × 14.8 (78⅜ × 64⅞ × 5⅞)
    Inscrip.: *1960,* star drawing, *Yves Klein/ le monochrome,* in blue paint, on top half of back; *4* (circled) *Requiem,* in pink chalk, on top quarter of back
    Lent by D. & J. de Menil Collection

48. Untitled blue sponge relief (RE 24)   1960
    Sponges, pebbles, and dry pigment in synthetic resin on board
    145 × 114 × 13 (57⅛ × 44⅞ × 5⅛)
    Inscrip.: *1960/* star drawing, *Yves Klein/ le monochrome,* in blue paint, on top quarter of back
    Lent by Dartmouth College Museum & Galleries, Gift of Mr. and Mrs. Joseph H. Hazen

49. Untitled gold sponge relief (RE 47)   1961
    Sponges, pebbles, gold paint, and gold leaf in synthetic resin on board
    45.5 × 80 × 7.5 (17¹⁵⁄₁₆ × 31½ × 3)
    Inscrip.: star drawing, *Yves Klein/ 61,* in pencil, on left center of back
    Lent anonymously

50. Untitled blue sponge relief (RE 27)   1961
    Sponges, pebbles, and dry pigment in synthetic resin on board
    60 × 122.5 × 7.5 (23⅝ × 48¼ × 3)
    Inscrip.: *Yves Klein/ 1961,* in blue paint, on back; star stamp on left back; star stamp on right back
    Lent by Sidney Janis Gallery

Cosmogonies

51. Untitled blue cosmogony (wind, Paris/Nice) (COS 10)   [1960]
    Dry pigment in undetermined fixative on paper on fabric on board

93 × 73 (36⅝ × 28¾)
No inscription visible
Lent anonymously

52. Untitled blue cosmogony (rain) (COS 12)   [1961]
    Dry pigment in undetermined fixative on paper on board
    105 × 76 (41⅜ × 29¹⁵⁄₁₆)
    No inscription visible
    Lent anonymously

Planetary Reliefs

53. Untitled planetary relief (RP 4)   1961
    Dry blue pigment in synthetic resin on polyester and fiberglass
    55 × 38 × 5.5 (21⅝ × 15 × 2³⁄₁₆)
    Inscrip.: star drawing, *YK/ 61,* in blue paint, on back
    Lent anonymously

54. Untitled planetary relief (RP 6)   [1961]
    Dry blue pigment in synthetic resin on polyester, fiberglass, vinyl, and wood
    40 × 56 × 5.5 (15¾ × 22¹⁄₁₆ × 2⅛)
    Unsigned
    Lent anonymously

55. Untitled planetary relief (RP 10)   [1961]
    Dry blue pigment in synthetic resin on bronze
    86 × 65.5 × 5 (33⅞ × 25¾ × 2)
    Inscrip.: *Yves Klein,* cast in bronze under paint, on lower left front
    Lent anonymously
    Note: This relief, which bears the foundry mark *Godard* on its lower right side, is a cast from an original destroyed by 1969.

56. *Europe-Afrique (Europe-Africa)* (RP 11)   1961
    Dry blue pigment in synthetic resin on gesso on board
    78 × 53 × 2 (30¾ × 20⅞ × ¾)
    Inscrip.: star drawing, *Yves Klein/ le monochrome/ 1961/ Relief Planétaire/ "Europe-Afrique,"* in charcoal, superimposed on *Yves Klein 1961,* in ink, on back
    Lent anonymously

57. Untitled planetary relief (RP 17)   1961
    Dry blue pigment in synthetic resin on gesso on board
    52 × 74 × 3.8 (20½ × 29⅛ × 1½)
    Inscrip.: *Relief/ Planétaire/ Yves Klein/ 1961,* in blue paint, on back
    Lent by Stephen S. Alpert

Anthropometries

58. *Princesse Hélena* (ANT)   1960
    Dry blue pigment in synthetic resin on paper on

board
198 × 128.2 (78 × 50½)
Inscrip.: *Yves Klein/ le monochrome 1960,* in dark
ink, on back; *Princesse Hélena,* in red
crayon, on back
Lent by The Museum of Modern Art, New York, Gift
of Mr. and Mrs. Arthur Wiesenberger, 1969

59. *Anthropométrie de l'époque bleue (Anthropometry of the Blue Period)* (ANT 82)   1960
Dry blue pigment in synthetic resin on paper on
fabric
155 × 281 (61 × 110⅝)
Previously documented inscriptions, obscured by
mounting
Lent anonymously

60. *Hiroshima* (ANT 79)   c. 1961
Dry blue pigment in synthetic resin on paper on
fabric
139.5 × 280.5 (54¹⁵⁄₁₆ × 110⁷⁄₁₆)
No inscription visible
Lent anonymously

61. *Cheveux (Hair)* (ANT 46)   [1961]
Dry blue pigment in synthetic resin on paper on
fabric
105.5 × 75.5 (41½ × 29¾)
No inscription visible
Lent anonymously

62. *People Begin to Fly* (ANT 96)   [1961]
Dry blue pigment in synthetic resin on paper on
fabric
246.4 × 397.6 (97 × 156½)
No inscription visible
Lent by D. & J. de Menil Collection

63. *Architecture de l'air (Architecture of the Air)*
(ANT 102)   [1961]
Dry blue pigment in synthetic resin and charcoal on
paper on fabric
261 × 213 (102¾ × 83⅞)
Extensive inscription in charcoal on front; no
inscription visible on back
Lent anonymously

64. Untitled anthropometry (ANT 134)   [1962]
Dry blue pigment in synthetic resin on paper on
fabric
108.6 × 76 (42¾ × 29⅞)
No inscription visible
Lent by Mr. and Mrs. P. M. Schlumberger

Shroud Anthropometries

65. Untitled shroud anthropometry (ANT SU 4) 1960

Dry blue, black, and pink pigment in synthetic resin
on unstretched fabric
65.5 × 94 (25¾ × 37)
Inscrip.: star drawing, *Yves Klein/ 1960,* in black ink,
on lower right of front
Lent anonymously

66. *Vampire* (ANT SU 20)   c. 1960
Dry blue, black, and pink pigment in synthetic
resin on unstretched fabric
142.5 × 94 (56⅛ × 37)
Unsigned
Lent anonymously

67. Untitled shroud anthropometry (ANT SU 2) 1961
Dry blue, black, and pink pigment in synthetic
resin on unstretched fabric with charred edges;
mounted with nails in light blue Plexiglas case
designed by Klein
Shroud 128 × 66 (50⅜ × 26); case 138.2 × 75.5 × 4.2
(54⅜ × 29¾ × 1⅝)
Inscrip.: star drawing, *Yves Klein/ 1961,* in black ink,
on figure's thigh at lower right of front
Lent by Moderna Museet, Stockholm

Fire Paintings

68. Untitled fire painting (F 2)   1961
Charred paper on board
146 × 97 (57½ × 38¼)
Unsigned
Lent anonymously

69. Untitled fire painting (F 20)   c. 1961
Charred paper on board in charred wood strip frame
74.5 × 55.5 (29⅜ × 21⅞)
Unsigned
Lent anonymously

70. Untitled fire painting (F 24)   c. 1961
Charred paper on board in charred wood strip frame
139 × 300 (54¾ × 118⅛)
Unsigned
Lent anonymously

71. Untitled fire painting (F 54)   1961
Charred paper on fabric
149 × 200 (58¹¹⁄₁₆ × 78¾)
Unsigned
Lent anonymously

72. Untitled fire painting (F 74)   c. 1961
Charred paper on fiberboard on board
139.5 × 102 (54⅞ × 40⅛)
Unsigned
Lent anonymously

73. Untitled fire painting (F 81)   c. 1961

Charred paper on fiberboard on board
130 × 250 (51³⁄₁₆ × 98⁷⁄₁₆)
Unsigned
Lent anonymously

Fire-Color Paintings

74. Untitled fire-color painting (FC 1)   c. 1962
    Dry blue and pink pigment in synthetic resin on
        paper, partially charred, on board; in charred
        wood strip frame with paint traces
    139 × 300 (54³⁄₄ × 118⅛)
    Unsigned
    Lent anonymously

75. Untitled fire-color painting (FC 3)   c. 1962
    Dry blue and pink pigment in synthetic resin on
        paper, partially charred, on board; in charred
        wood strip frame
    135 × 72 (53⅛ × 28³⁄₈)
    Unsigned
    Lent anonymously

76. Untitled fire-color painting (FC 27)   c. 1962
    Dry blue and pink pigment in synthetic resin on
        paper, partially charred, on board; in charred
        wood strip frame
    76 × 109 (29⁷⁄₈ × 43)
    Unsigned
    Lent anonymously

Sculptures and Related Studies

Sponge Sculptures

77. Untitled blue sponge sculpture (SE)   1959
    Dry pigment in synthetic resin on sponge and metal
        rod, with stone base
    c. 54 × 23 × 16 (21¼ × 11 × 6¼)
    Inscrip.: *Yves/ 59*, in blue paint, on lower side corner
        of stone
    Lent by Fredirick Roos

78. Untitled blue sponge sculpture (SE 160)   [1959]
    Dry pigment in synthetic resin on sponge and metal
        rod, with stone base
    99 × 33.7 × 27 (39 × 13¼ × 10⅝)
    Unsigned
    Lent by The Solomon R. Guggenheim Museum, New
        York, Gift of Mrs. Andrew P. Fuller, 1964

79. Untitled blue sponge sculpture (SE 168)   [1959]
    Dry pigment in synthetic resin on sponge and metal
        rod, with stone base
    114.9 × 57.2 × 31 (45¼ × 22½ × 12³⁄₁₆)
    Unsigned
    Lent by Mr. and Mrs. Burton Tremaine

80. Untitled blue sponge sculpture (SE 205)   1959
    Dry pigment in synthetic resin on sponge and metal
        rod, with stone base
    42 × 22 × 18 (16½ × 8⅝ × 7⅛)
    Inscrip.: *YVES/ 59*, in pencil, on bottom of stone
    Lent by Fredirick Roos

81. *Lecteur IKB (IKB Reader)*, blue (SE 171)   1960
    Dry pigment in synthetic resin on sponge, with brass
        base
    117 × 29.5 × 22 (46 × 11⅝ × 8⅝)
    Inscrip.: *"Lecteur/ IKB"/* star drawing, *Yves Klein/
        1960*, in black ink, on bottom of base
    Lent by Albright-Knox Art Gallery, Buffalo, New
        York, Gift of Seymour H. Knox, 1961

82. *Lecteur IKB (IKB Reader)*, blue (SE 172)   1960
    Dry pigment in synthetic resin on sponge, with brass
        base
    119 × 30.5 × 22 (46⁷⁄₈ × 17 × 8⅝)
    Inscrip.: *lecteur/ IKB/* star drawing, *Yves Klein/ 1960*,
        in black ink, on bottom of base
    Lent by Albright-Knox Art Gallery, Buffalo, New
        York, Gift of Seymour H. Knox, 1961

83. *Lecteur IKB (Rose) (IKB Reader [Rose])*
        (SE 198)   1960
    Dry pigment in synthetic resin on sponge, with brass
        base
    95.5 × 28 × 22.2 (37½ × 11 × 8³⁄₄)

Inscrip.: *"lecteur/ IKB"/ Yves Klein/ 1960/ Rose,* in black ink, on bottom of base
Lent by Albright-Knox Art Gallery, Buffalo, New York, Gift of Seymour H. Knox, 1961

Sculptures

84. *Relief bleu (Blue Relief)* (S 1) [1957]
Dry pigment in synthetic resin on cardboard, mounted with board on Plexiglas
12 × 19.5 × 19 (4¾ × 3¾ × 7¹¹⁄₁₆)
No inscription visible
Lent anonymously

85. *Relief bleu (Blue Relief)* (S 3) 1957
Dry pigment in synthetic resin on cardboard, mounted with board on Plexiglas
12 × 19.5 × 19 (4¾ × 3¾ × 7¹¹⁄₁₆)
Previously documented inscriptions, obscured by mounting
Lent anonymously

86. *Relief bleu (Blue Relief)* (S 4) 1957
Dry pigment in synthetic resin on cardboard, mounted with board on Plexiglas
12 × 19.5 × 19 (4¾ × 3¾ × 7¹¹⁄₁₆)
Previously documented inscriptions, obscured by mounting
Lent anonymously

87. *Relief bleu (Blue Relief)* (S 5) [1957]
Dry pigment in synthetic resin on cardboard, mounted with board on Plexiglas
12 × 19.5 × 19 (4¾ × 3¾ × 7¹¹⁄₁₆)
No inscription visible
Lent anonymously

88. Untitled sketchbook with drawings of various fire and water sculptures 1958
Eight-page spiral-bound sketchbook with drawings in charcoal, pencil, and colored pencil
54 × 37 (21¼ × 14½)
Inscrip.: various notations throughout
Lent anonymously

89. *Sculpture Tactile (Tactile Sculpture)* (S 22)
1960 (prototype), facsimile exhibited
Painted wood box and stand, mixed-media interior
141.5 × 50 × 50 (55¾ × 19¹¹⁄₁₆ × 19¹¹⁄₁₆)

90. *Pluie bleue (Blue Rain)* (S 36) 1961
Dry pigment in synthetic resin on twelve separate, hanging wood dowels
Diameter 1.1 (⁷⁄₁₆) each; length 200.9 to 208.9 (79¹⁄₁₆ to 82¼) each
Overall configuration varies with installation

Unsigned
Lent anonymously

91. *Pluie rouge (Red Rain)* (S 37) 1961
Dry pigment in synthetic resin on eleven separate, hanging wood dowels
Diameter 1.1 (⁷⁄₁₆) each; length 202 to 208.9 (79½ to 82¼) each
Overall configuration varies with installation
Unsigned
Lent anonymously

92. *Victoire de Samothrace (Victory of Samothrace)*
(S 9) 1962 (prototype),
example of 1973 edition exhibited
Dry blue pigment in synthetic resin on plaster reproduction of the Louvre's *Nike of Samothrace,* metal rod, and stone base
50.5 × 25.5 × 36 (19⅞ × 10 × 14⅛)
Inscrip.: *YK,* inscribed in plaster under paint, top surface of right wing
Lent by Mr. and Mrs. Jacob Baal-Teshuva
Note: A posthumous edition of 175 examples was made by the Galerie Karl Flinker, Paris, after a single original. Inscriptions, not in Klein's hand, on the exhibited piece are a fabricator's mark and *111/175,* in black paint, on bottom of base, and *111/175,* in black paint, on back of figure's drapery.

Portrait Relief

93. *Arman* (PR 1) 1962 (prototype),
example of undated edition exhibited
Dry blue pigment in synthetic resin on bronze, mounted on primed and gold-leafed board
175.5 × 94 × 26 (69⅞ × 37 × 10¼)
Unsigned
Lent by Musée National d'Art Moderne, Centre Georges Pompidou
Note: The piece exhibited is one of an edition of six made after Klein's death from a life plaster cast of the artist Arman. Inscribed in the bronze of the figure's left thigh is the foundry's mark, *2/6/ Susse Fonderie, Paris.*

Performance and Conceptual Works

Although the terms "performance art" and "conceptual art" came into general use after Yves Klein's death in 1962, they nonetheless describe activities which Klein believed to be a specific and important part of his art. He documented these performance and conceptual works in several ways, including photographs, sound recordings, typed or written manuscripts, and printed or graphic matter of his design. The entries below list works represented in this exhibition by specific photographs, documents, or graphic matter conceived by Klein. Entries have been grouped where conceptual relationships exist among them, thus altering chronological order in some cases.

94. Score for *Symphonie Monoton-Silence (Monotone-Silence Symphony)*   [1947], 1961
    Photostat of a sheet of hand-scored musical staff-paper, with handwritten notations
    41.7 × 29.5 (16⅜ × 11⅝)
    Signed, titled, dated, and variously annotated on front, in red and blue inks
    Lent anonymously
    Note: The exhibited score directs that a D-major triad be sounded by twenty voices and thirty-two instruments for five to seven minutes, followed by forty-four seconds of absolute silence.

    There is evidence that a musician, Pierre Henry, scored this work for Klein. The two basic forms for the piece — the *Monotone-Silence Symphony* and the *Monotone Symphony* — are orchestrated with various numbers of instruments and voices. There is at least one tape recording of a performance of this work.

95. *Anthropométries de l'époque bleue (Anthropometries of the Blue Period)*   March 9, 1960
    Performance before an audience at the Galerie Internationale d'Art Contemporain, Paris, where Klein directed three nude female models ("living brushes") in the making of Anthropometries, accompanied by string musicians playing a version of the *Monotone Symphony*
    Exhibited are photographs by Harry Shunk documenting this performance.
    Lent by Menil Foundation Collection

96. *Cris bleus (Blue Cries)*   1957
    Sound recording of human vocalizations which Klein stated were made by Charles Estienne, François Dufrêne, and Antonin Artaud
    A taped excerpt of *Blue Cries* (from cat. no. 97) is included in this exhibition.
    Lent by Menil Foundation Collection
    Note: Klein said that the *Blue Cries* were recorded as a soundtrack for a short 16mm film he made to document his 1957 Blue Period exhibitions. Klein played a brief selection of *Blue Cries* at a lecture at the Institute of Contemporary Art, London, June 24, 1957, and at his Sorbonne lecture (see cat. no. 97).

97. *L'Evolution de l'art vers l'immatériel (The Evolution of Art toward the Immaterial)*
                                    June 3, 1959
    Lecture by Yves Klein at the Sorbonne, Paris
    Exhibited is "Yves Klein: Conférence à la Sorbonne," an album of two twelve-inch LP phonograph records of Klein's lecture, published by RPM, Paris, in an edition of 500. Undated.
    Inscrip.: *IKB 1, IKB 2, IKB 3,* and *IKB 4,* incised by hand on each recording side, consecutively
    Lent by Menil Foundation Collection

98. IKB Postage   1958
    Hand-colored (International Klein Blue) postage stamps
    Stamps 2.5 × 2 (1 × ¾) each
    Exhibited is an envelope bearing an IKB postage stamp canceled May 25, 1959; the envelope is addressed to Mr. and Mrs. Fuller, Hotel Ritz, Place Vendôme, Paris 1ᵉʳ, and contains invitations.
    Lent by Mr. and Mrs. Andrew P. Fuller
    Note: Beginning with invitations to the openings of his two Paris exhibitions in May 1957, Klein was able to use his own IKB stamps as postage by paying the standard mailing costs at the post office.

99. *The Blue Revolution*   1958
    Exhibited is a photograph of a one-page, typed letter from Yves Klein to President Eisenhower, U.S.A., dated May 20, 1958, informing him of the termination of the French national government by Klein's "political party," the Blue Revolution.
    Lent by Menil Foundation Collection
    Note: Following his exhibition *Le Vide* at the Galerie Iris Clert in April 1958, Klein mailed a number of letters to government officials announcing the Blue Revolution and calling for or announcing a variety of actions.

100. *L'Architecture de l'air (The Architecture of the Air)*   1958–62
    A concept developed by Klein in 1958 and pursued

to the end of his life, involving the idea of using controlled air currents to form habitations literally in the air for human beings adapting to the "new age of levitation."

Exhibited are photographs of 1962 photomontage display panels.

Lent by Menil Foundation Collection

Note: This concept appears numerous times in Klein's work: in his writings, as an extensive inscription on a painting (cat. no. 63), through research and experiments with the German architect Werner Ruhnau, and on the large photomontage displays rendered with the aid of architect Claude Parent and exhibited at the Musée des Arts Décoratifs, Paris, in March 1962.

101. Receipt book for *Zones of Immaterial Pictorial Sensibility*, series 0   1959

Printed on paper, originally thirty-one unnumbered receipts, each for an unspecified amount of gold

8.6 × 29.8 (3⁷⁄₁₆ × 11¹¹⁄₁₆)

Unsigned; the first two receipts were used, and their stubs remain, made out to the Museum Haus Lange, Krefeld, on February 28, 1961, and to Ed Kienholz, Los Angeles, on June 14, 1961.

Lent by Yves Arman

Note: Klein had five receipt books printed, identified as being for *"Zones de Sensibilité Picturale Immatérielle."* Series 2 contains ten numbered receipts, each for forty grams of gold; series 3, which has been lost, probably contained ten numbered receipts, each for eighty grams; series 4 originally contained ten numbered receipts, each for 160 grams, of which the first was used and the stub made out to Michael Blankfort of Los Angeles, in Paris, February 2, 1962, *à midi* (at noon).

102. Receipt book for *Zones of Immaterial Pictorial Sensibility*, series 1   1959

Printed on paper, originally ten numbered receipts, each for twenty grams of gold

8.6 × 29.8 (3⁷⁄₁₆ × 11¹¹⁄₁₆)

Unsigned; the first seven receipts were used, and their stubs remain, made out as follows:

1. Peppino Palazzoli, Paris, November 18, 1959
2. Jacques Kugel, Paris, December 7, 1959
3. Paride Accetti, Paris, December 7, 1959
4. Alain Lemée, Paris, December 8, 1959
5. Dino Buzzati, Paris, January 26, 1962
6. Claude Pascal, Paris, February 4, 1962
7. Karl-Heinrich Müller, Goussonville, May 16, 1975 [sold after Klein's death]

Lent by Yves Arman

103. *Zone of Immaterial Pictorial Sensibility*
    June 14, 1961

Exists without dimension

Lent by Ed Kienholz

Note: Of the *Zones of Immaterial Pictorial Sensibility* that Klein created during his lifetime, three are referred to in this exhibition and catalogue. Cat. no. 103 is lent by the artist Ed Kienholz of Hope, Idaho, who during a visit to Houston on January 3, 1982, directed that his zone would be located with the exhibition at the Rice Museum and throughout the exhibition tour. The only other American to acquire a zone was the writer Michael Blankfort, whose zone is presumed to be with him at his and his wife Dorothy Blankfort's residence in Los Angeles. The one *Zone of Immaterial Pictorial Sensibility* acquired by an art institution within Klein's lifetime is represented by the *Immaterial Room* at the Museum Haus Lange, Krefeld.

104. *The Leap into the Void*   1960

A conceptual event principally embodied in a photograph by Harry Shunk of Klein leaping from the roof-ledge of a pavilion at 3, rue Gentil Bernard, in the Paris suburb of Fontenay-aux-Roses

Exhibited is an enlargement of Shunk's photograph.

Lent by Menil Foundation Collection

Note: During 1960, Klein literally made several leaps as a "practical demonstration of levitation." Some were witnessed, and some were performed for photographic documentation. One important leap took place outside Colette Allendy's house at 67, rue de l'Assomption, Paris, on January 12, 1960.

Two differing images of the Fontenay-aux-Roses leap were published during Klein's lifetime: one in *Dimanche*, November 27, 1960, captioned "A Man in Space: The Painter of Space Hurls Himself into the Void!"; the other in the catalogue for Klein's 1961 Krefeld exhibition (bibliography no. 53), captioned "The Leap into the Void, 1960." The first version includes a figure on a bicycle and a moving train; the second does not.

105. *Dimanche, le journal d'un seul jour (Sunday, the Newspaper of a Single Day)*
    November 27, 1960

Four-page illustrated newspaper, written and designed by Klein

55.7 × 38 (21^{15}/$_{16}$ × 14^{15}/$_{16}$)
Lent by Menil Foundation Collection
Note: This newspaper was printed in one edition
only, and copies were distributed at Paris
newsstands on its date of issue as Klein's
contribution to the Festival d'Art d'Avant-
garde, Paris.

Itself a conceptual-performance work,
Dimanche contains plans or descriptions
of other conceptual-performance works by
Klein, especially *Le Théâtre du vide (The
Theater of the Void)*. It stands as well as
an important collection of Klein's writings
(see bibliography no. 9).

106. *Le Globe est bleu (The Globe Is Blue)*   c. 1961
A concept embodied in a photograph by Harry Shunk
of Yves Klein gazing at an apparently levitating International Klein Blue globe of the
world, his untitled sculpture of c. 1957(RP 7)
Exhibited is a print of Shunk's photograph.
Lent by Menil Foundation Collection
Note: The first known publication of this photographic image appears in the 1961 Krefeld
exhibition catalogue (bibliography no. 53),
where it was captioned "The Liberation of
Sculpture from Its Base: The Blue Globe."

107. Removing Paintings from a Gallery to Make a Void
January 26, 1962
Conceptual performance at the Musée d'Art Mo-
derne de la Ville de Paris, documented in a
series of photographs by Harry Shunk
Exhibited are prints of Shunk's photographs.
Lent by Menil Foundation Collection
Note: Friends assisting Klein in this work in-
cluded Niki de Saint-Phalle, François Du-
frêne, and Jacques de la Villeglé.

108. Klein beneath *The Tomb — Here Lies Space*
March 30, 1962
A conceptual event embodied in a series of photo-
graphs by Harry Shunk
Exhibited are prints of two of Shunk's photographs.
Lent by Menil Foundation Collection
Note: One photograph shows Rotraut Klein in the
act of placing the IKB sponge wreath on *La
Tombe — ci-gît l'espace* of 1960 while,
from beneath the painting, Klein observes.
Loose gold leaf was scattered on the mono-
gold surface for this photograph. Another
view depicts Klein lying as if dead beneath
the work.

Photo Credits

Bureau Parisien, Paris: fig. 10. Centre Georges Pompidou, Paris: pp. 171, 172, 207–209. Geoffrey Clements, N.Y.: pp. 143 bot., 147, 149 top, 170, 189. D. James Dee, N.Y.: p. 166 top. Jacques Faujour, Paris: pp. 90, 137 top. Hickey-Robertson, Houston: cover, pp. 148, 149 bot., 156, 157 bot., 167–69, 179. Pierre Joly et Véra Cardot, Paris: pp. 70, 71, 188, figs. 67, 68. Sigwart Korn, Krefeld: p. 211. Christian Larrieu, Paris: pp. 141, 142, 150–52, 162 top, 181–83, 190, 191 bot., 215. Robert E. Mates, N.Y.: p. 166 bot. Moderna Museet, Stockholm, p. 184. Museum of Modern Art, N.Y.: p. 173. Photo Diska, Paris: fig. 27. Presseamt der Stadt Gelsenkirchen: p. 161. Martha Rocher, Paris: fig. 39. Paul Sarisson, Paris: fig. 29. I. Serisawa, Los Angeles: fig. 65. Harry Shunk, N.Y.: pp. 2, 38, 49, 54, 61,63, 66, 75, 79, 81, 140 bot., 143 top, 164, 174, 175, 180, 185, 186, 192–95, 197–201, 204, 205, 210, 212–14; figs. 6–8, 19–23, 25, 37, 50–58, 60, 62–64, 66, 69–83, 85. Stedelijk Museum, Amsterdam: p. 153. Van Abbemuseum, Eindhoven: p. 146. Sylvaine Vaucher, Geneva: p. 162 bot. Bernward Wember, Krefeld: p. 187. Charles Wilp, Düsseldorf: figs. 38, 47, 48. Janet Woodard, Houston: pp. 145, 177, 178, 238, 259; figs. 34, 42.

Colophon

Yves Klein (1928–1962): A Retrospective has been published in paperback and hardcover editions by the Institute for the Arts, Rice University, Houston, in association with The Arts Publisher, Inc., New York.

Design: Mary Ellen Sheridan, Houston
Offset color lithography and printing: W.M. Brown and Son, Inc., Richmond, Virginia
Typeface: Optima
Paper: Northwest Vintage Enamel text, Frankote Cover cover

Accommodation

These are not hotels, but historic properties in which accommodation can be arranged. The standard ranges from basic comfort to ultimate luxury.

See page 27

Civil Weddings

Places with a marriage licence where the ceremony itself can take place. Many will also be able to provide facilities for receptions.

See page 29

Corporate Hospitality

Properties which are able to accommodate corporate functions, wedding receptions and events. Individual entries will give greater detail.

See pages 30 - 32

Special Events

Special Events, historical re-enactments, gardening festivals, country and craft fairs, concerts and fireworks, car and steam rallies are now an established part of the summer season and throughout the year.

Don't miss our Movie Map on page 53

See pages 33 - 37

Websites

Many properties have their own website with more extensive information. If you want to make life easy, without having to type in each address, all you have to do is go to www.hudsons.co.uk and click on the direct link to any of these sites. Make your first stop

www.hudsons.co.uk

See page 38 - 45

Plant Sales

Many historic properties and gardens offer collections of rare and unusual plants not generally available.

See page 46 - 47

Open All Year

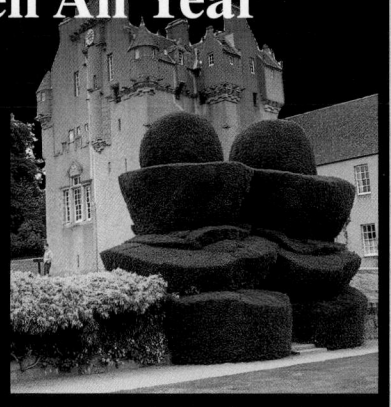

Properties and/or their grounds included in this list are open all or most of the year.

See pages 49 - 52

Access to Grant Aided Properties

English Heritage, as well as managing and opening properties in its care, has other equally important roles. It gives grants towards the cost of repairing outstanding buildings in private, National Trust and other ownerships. These grants are given subject to appropriate public access being given, details of which are incorporated in this section.

See pages 541

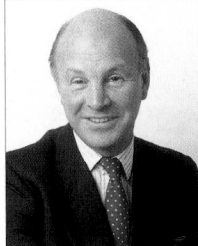

HUDSON'S

Gardens are the focus of much attention this year. They form the centrepiece of a worldwide campaign by the British Tourist Authority. The National Trust is also placing special emphasis on promoting the many gardens in their care.

A preoccupation with gardens and gardening, coupled with a climate favourable to a wide variety of plant species have produced in the British Isles some of the finest gardens in the world. They span many centuries in age and style. The process has not stopped. Private owners in particular continue to further enhance existing gardens and create new ones.

Garden visiting is a pastime for all seasons – providing you visit the right garden at the right time of year. In Spring, Summer and Autumn the choice is enormous.

Regular readers of *Hudson's* will also notice changes in region and county placements. In England we have listed properties within counties but otherwise, in co-ordination with The National Trust and English Heritage, have placed them in regions whose boundaries are aligned with the Regional Development Authorities. In Scotland, we have followed the boundaries of the Area Tourist Boards. Prefacing each section is a feature on a garden within the region.

Norman Hudson

Norman Hudson
Editor

Hudson's Historic Houses & Gardens

Editor .... Norman Hudson

Editorial/Production .... Edwina Brash

Administration .... Jennie Carwithen

Graphic Design .... KC Graphics

Page Layout & Maps .... Taurus Graphics

Scanning & Pre-press .... Spot-On Reprographics

Sales .... Fiona Rolt

Consultant/Maps .... Patrick Lane

Printed by .... E T Heron & Co Ltd

Distribution -
UK & Europe: .... Portfolio, tel: 020 8997 9000
USA:.......... The Globe Pequot Press, tel: 001 203 458 4505

Cover picture:
UK: Charlecote Park, Warwickshire.
© National Trust Photographic Library/Matthew Antrobus

USA: Newby Hall, Yorkshire
© R Compton

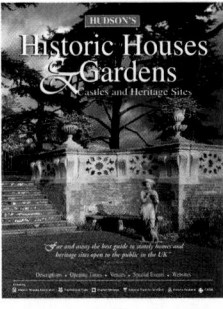

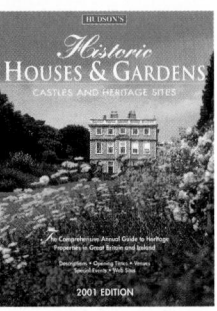

UK   USA

Published by:
Norman Hudson & Company,
High Wardington House, Upper Wardington,
Banbury, Oxfordshire OX17 1SP, UK
Tel: 01295 750750   Fax: 01295 750800
e-mail: enquiries@hudsons.co.uk
website: www.hudsons.co.uk

ISBN: 0-9531426-5-5

Co-published in the USA by:
The Globe Pequot Press,
246 Goose Lane, Guilford, Connecticut 06437, USA

**Library of Congress Cataloging-in-Publication
data is available.**
ISBN: 0-7627-0881-6

Foreword

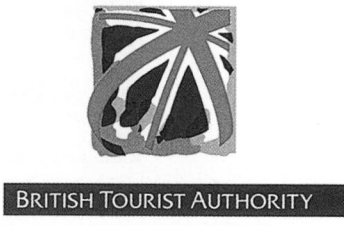

BRITISH TOURIST AUTHORITY

by David Quarmby

Chairman, British Tourist Authority

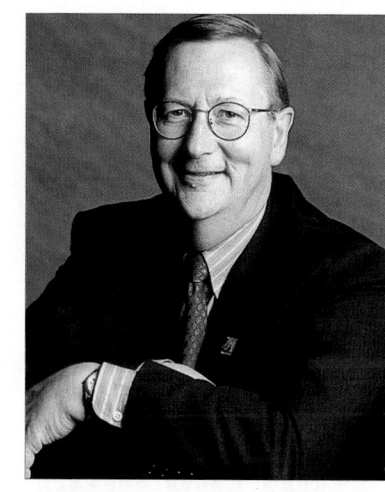

There is no question that our heritage and its history are at the heart of Britain's attraction to overseas visitors. Whether visiting historic houses, gardens and castles or seeing some of our wonderful museums, galleries and theatre, experiencing our heritage remains the number one reason for visiting our shores. *Hudson's* provides a definitive guide to the best that Britain has to offer.

Britain's history and tradition is our unique selling point – no other country rivals us in the quality and breadth of what we have to offer. As we in the British Tourist Authority plan our promotional programmes in 27 countries round the world, we recognise the vital importance of sustaining this interest whilst also promoting our rich contemporary culture.

'The garden' is one of the BTA's themes for the year 2001. In Britain we have the best and most interesting choice of gardens anywhere in the world. Many are featured in this splendid guide and will, I'm quite sure, provide a source of delight and inspiration to our visitors – whatever the time of year. I shall be among them myself!

David Quarmby

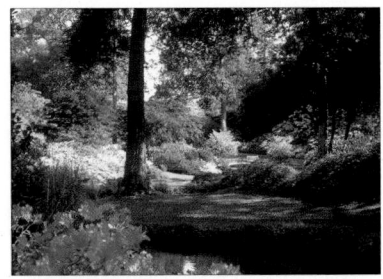
Exbury Gardens, Hampshire.

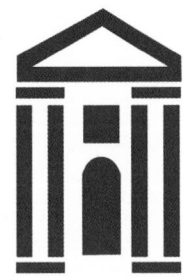

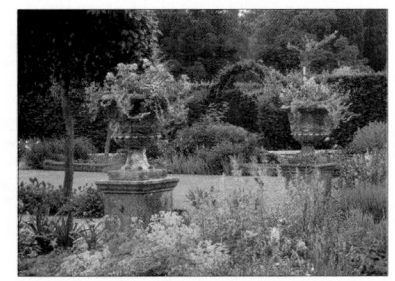
Cottesbrooke Hall Gardens, Northamptonshire.

"The HHA Friends scheme provides amazing value for the interested house and gardens visitor..."

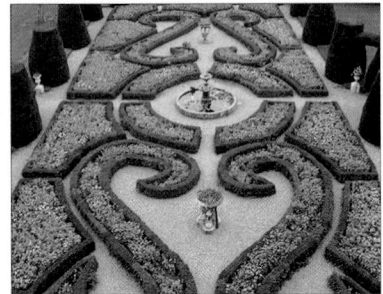
Bodrhyddan, Wales.

The HHA is a group of highly individualistic and diverse properties most of which are still lived-in family houses. They range from the great palaces to small manor houses.

Many HHA member properties are open to the public and offer free admission to Friends of the HHA.

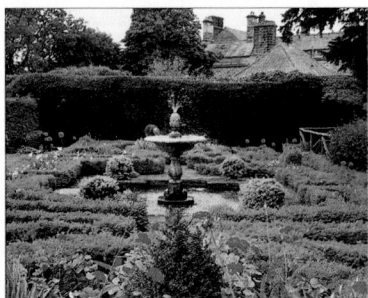
Dalemain, Cumbria.

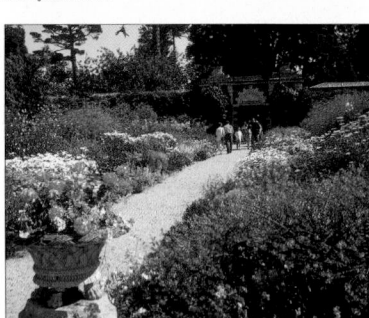
Somerleyton Hall, Suffolk.

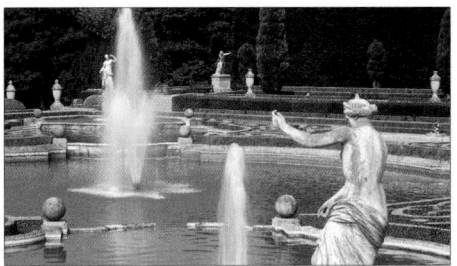
Blenheim Palace, Oxfordshire.

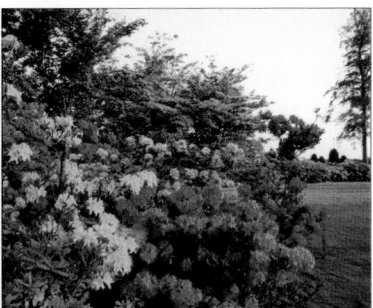
Borde Hill Garden, Sussex.

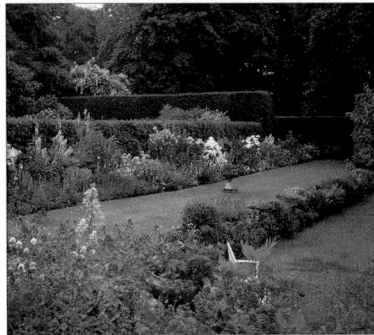
Coton Manor Garden, Northamptonshire.

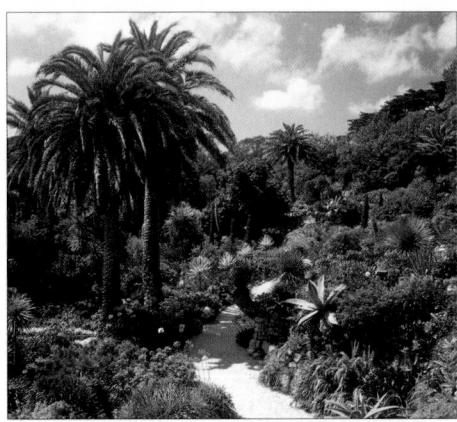
Tresco Abbey Gardens, Cornwall.

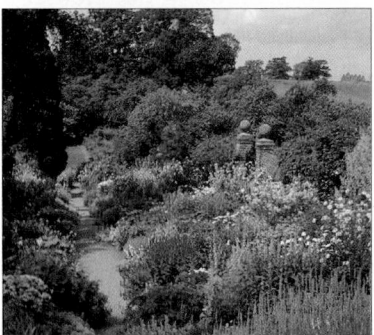
Benington Lordship Gardens, Hertfordshire.

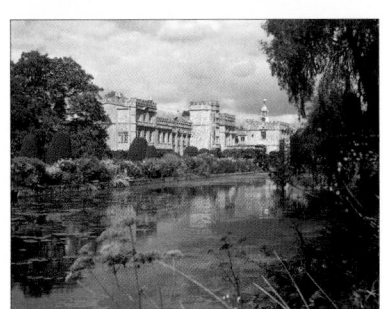
Forde Abbey, Dorset.

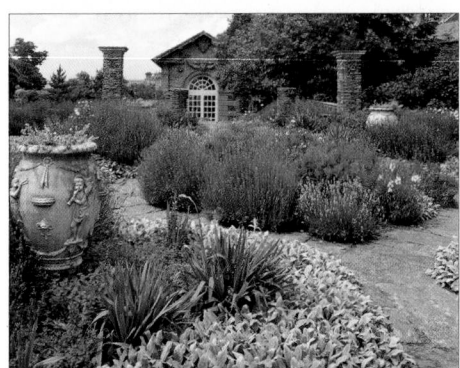
Hestercombe Gardens, Somerset.

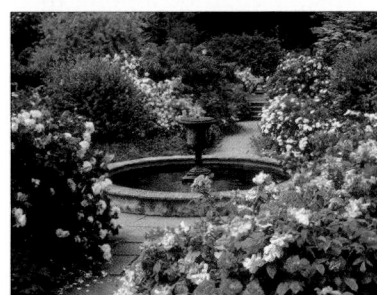
Newby Hall & Gardens, Yorkshire.

4

HISTORIC HOUSES ASSOCIATION

Become a Friend of the HHA and visit nearly 300 privately owned houses and gardens for FREE.

Other benefits:

- Receive the quarterly magazine of the HHA which gives news and features about the Association, its members and our heritage

- Take advantage of organised tours in the UK and overseas

- Join the specially arranged visits to houses, some of which are not usually open to the public

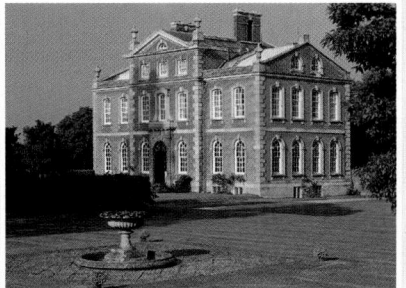

KINGSTON BAGPUIZE HOUSE, OXFORDSHIRE

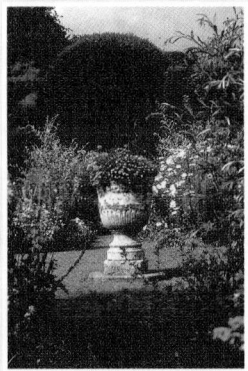

LEVENS HALL GARDENS, CUMBRIA

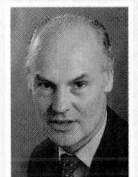

Richard Wilkin, Director General of the HHA, explains . . .

"It is not generally realised that two-thirds of Britain's built heritage remains in private ownership. There are more privately-owned houses, castles and gardens open to the public than are opened by the National Trust, English Heritage and their equivalents in Scotland and Wales put together.

Successive Governments have recognised the private owner as the most economic and effective guardian of this heritage. But the cost of maintaining these properties is colossal, and the task is daunting. The owners work enormously hard and take a pride in preserving and presenting this element of Britain's heritage.

The HHA helps them do this by:

- *representing their interests in Government*

- *providing an advisory service for houses – taxation, conservation, security, regulations, etc.*

- *running charities assisting disabled visitors, conserving works of art and helping promote educational facilities*

There is a fascinating diversity of properties to visit free with a Friends of the HHA card – from the great treasure houses such as Blenheim and Castle Howard through to small manor houses. What makes these places so special is their individuality and the fact that they are generally still lived in – often by the same family that has owned them through centuries of British history. As well as the stunning gardens which surround the houses, there are over 60 additional wonderful gardens to visit.

We have held the subscription rate again this year, so it remains outstanding value for money at £28.00 for an individual or £40.00 for two people at the same address. If you do wish to become a Friend of the HHA, and I very much hope you will, then you can join, using your credit/debit card by calling 01462 896688 or simply fill in the form below."

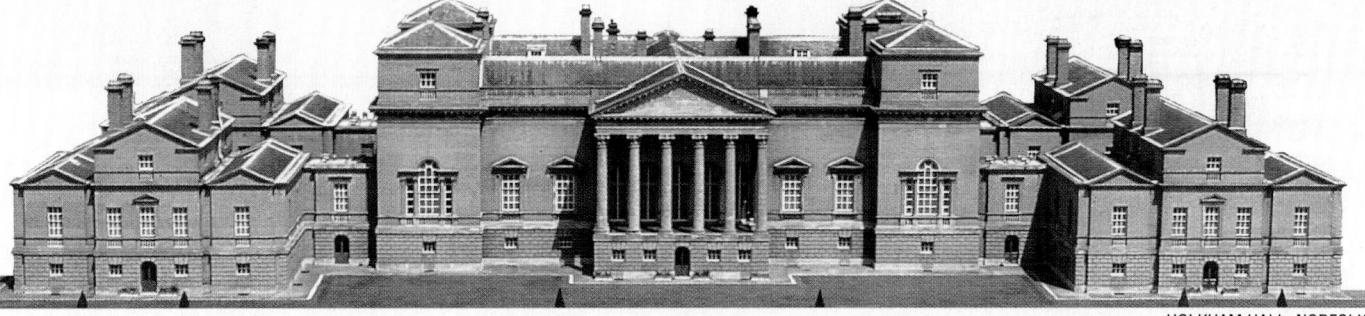

HOLKHAM HALL, NORFOLK

Membership: Single £28, Double £40, £10 additional Friend at same address. Members of NADFAS, CLA and NACF are offered special rates of £25 Individual and £37 Double (at same address).

FRIENDS APPLICATION FORM HHHG/01

PLEASE USE BLOCK CAPITALS *DELETE AS APPROPRIATE

MR/MRS/MS or MR & MRS* INITIALS _____

SURNAME _____

ADDRESS _____

_____

_____ POST CODE _____

ADDITIONAL FRIENDS AT SAME ADDRESS

_____

I/We* are members of NADFAS/NACF/CLA (please circle name of organisation to which you belong) our membership number is: ____

☐ I/We* enclose remittance of £____ payable to the Historic Houses Association.

☐ I/We* have completed the direct debit adjacent.

Please return to: Historic Houses Association, Friends Membership Department, Heritage House, PO Box 21, Baldock, Hertfordshire SG7 5SH. **Tel: (01462) 896688**

PHOTOCOPIES OF THIS FORM ARE ACCEPTABLE

INSTRUCTION TO YOUR BANK TO PAY DIRECT DEBITS

Please complete Parts 1 to 5 to instruct your Bank to make payments directly from your account. Then return the form to: Historic Houses Association, Membership Department, Heritage House, PO Box 21, Baldock, Herts, SG7 5SH.

1. Name and full postal address of your Bank

_____

_____

_____

Your Bank may decline to accept instructions to pay Direct Debits from some types of accounts.

2. Name of account holder _____

3. Account number ☐☐☐☐☐☐☐☐

4. Bank sort code ☐☐ ☐☐ ☐☐

Originator's identification number [9][3][0][5][8][7]

Originator's reference (office use only) ☐☐☐☐☐☐

IF COMPLETING THE DIRECT DEBIT FORM, YOU MUST ALSO COMPLETE THE APPLICATION FORM.

5. Your instructions to the Bank and signature.

- I instruct you to pay Direct Debits for my annual subscription from my account at the request of the Historic Houses Association.
- The amounts are variable and may be debited on various dates.
- I understand that the Historic Houses Association may change the amounts and dates only after giving me prior notice of not less than 21 days.
- Please cancel all previous Standing Order and Direct Debiting instructions in favour of the Historic Houses Association.
- I will inform the Bank in writing if I wish to cancel this instruction.
- I understand that if any Direct Debit is paid which breaks the terms of the instruction, the Bank will make a refund.

Signature(s) _____

_____

_____ Date _____

DIRECT Debit Completion of the form above ensures that your subscription will be paid automatically on the date that it is due. You may cancel the order at any time. The Association guarantees that it will only use this authority to deduct annually from your account an amount equal to the annual subscription then current for your class of membership.

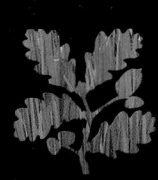

National Trust Gardens

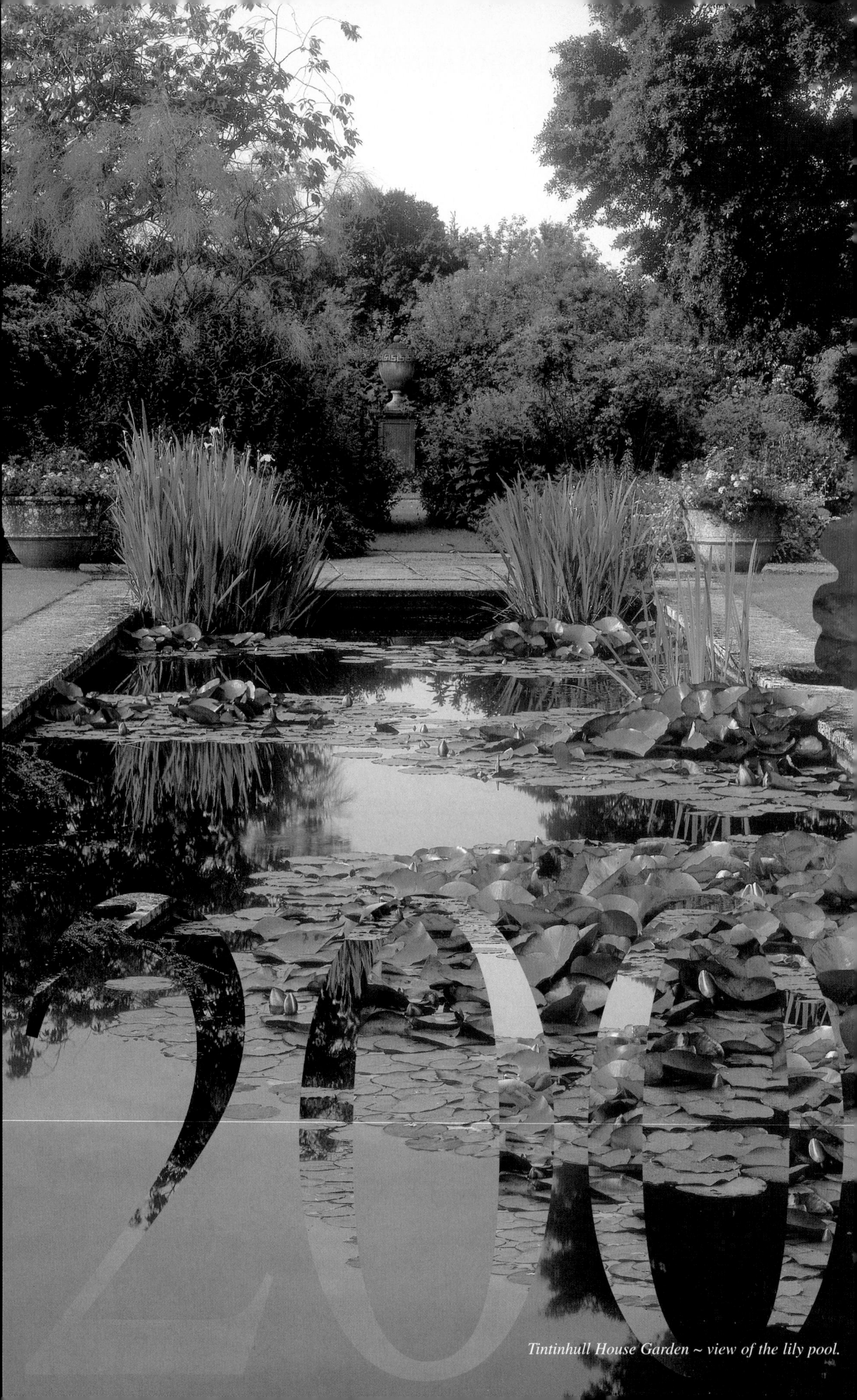

Tintinhull House Garden ~ view of the lily pool.

Rooted in history, growing forever

The National Trust looks after the largest and most important collection of historic gardens and cultivated plants in the world. Throughout 2001 the Trust will be celebrating its role as the world's leading garden conservation organisation, highlighting the work involved in caring for this living part of our cultural heritage and the need to consider the future of historic gardens at the beginning of a new millennium.

A major international gardens conference, a season of special nationwide garden events, an exhibition of contemporary art and craft inspired by historic gardens and a programme of lectures will focus on the Trust's collection of over 200 gardens and landscape parks.

National Trust 'Gardens Year 2001' has something to offer everyone who loves gardening and gardens from the horticultural professional to the millions who are passionate amatuer gardeners. It provides an opportunity for visitors to see what lies behind the Trust's garden gates, to share their own knowledge and passion for gardening and discover more about the Trust's collection of gardens, from those of internationally repute to less well-known garden treasures.

As part of Gardens Year celebrations, visitors can enjoy hundreds of different garden events taking place nationwide throughout the season. From Spring Plant Fairs to Paint the Garden and Tree Dressing days, the 2001 programme of activities explores the multifaceted nature of National Trust gardens, offering visitors the opportunity to discover more about their history, design and plant collections as well as the special gardening skills and behind the scenes work needed to maintain and care for historic gardens.

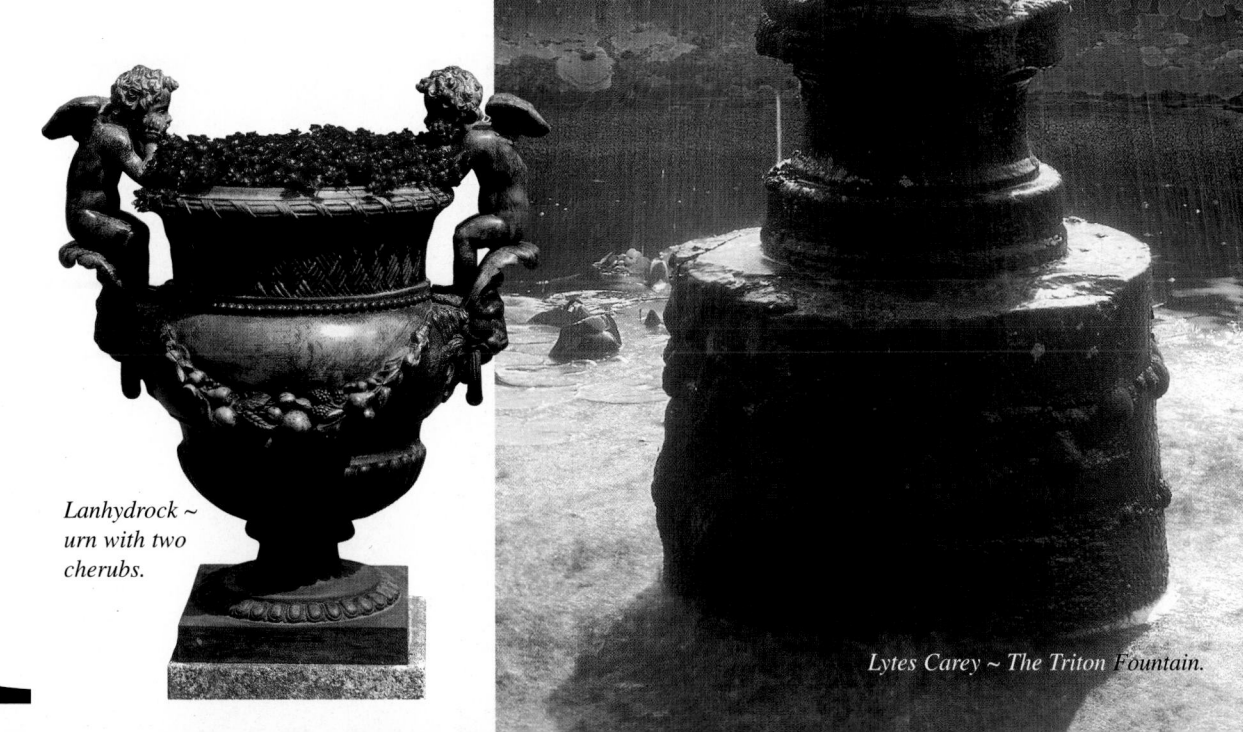

Lanhydrock ~ urn with two cherubs.

Lytes Carey ~ The Triton Fountain.

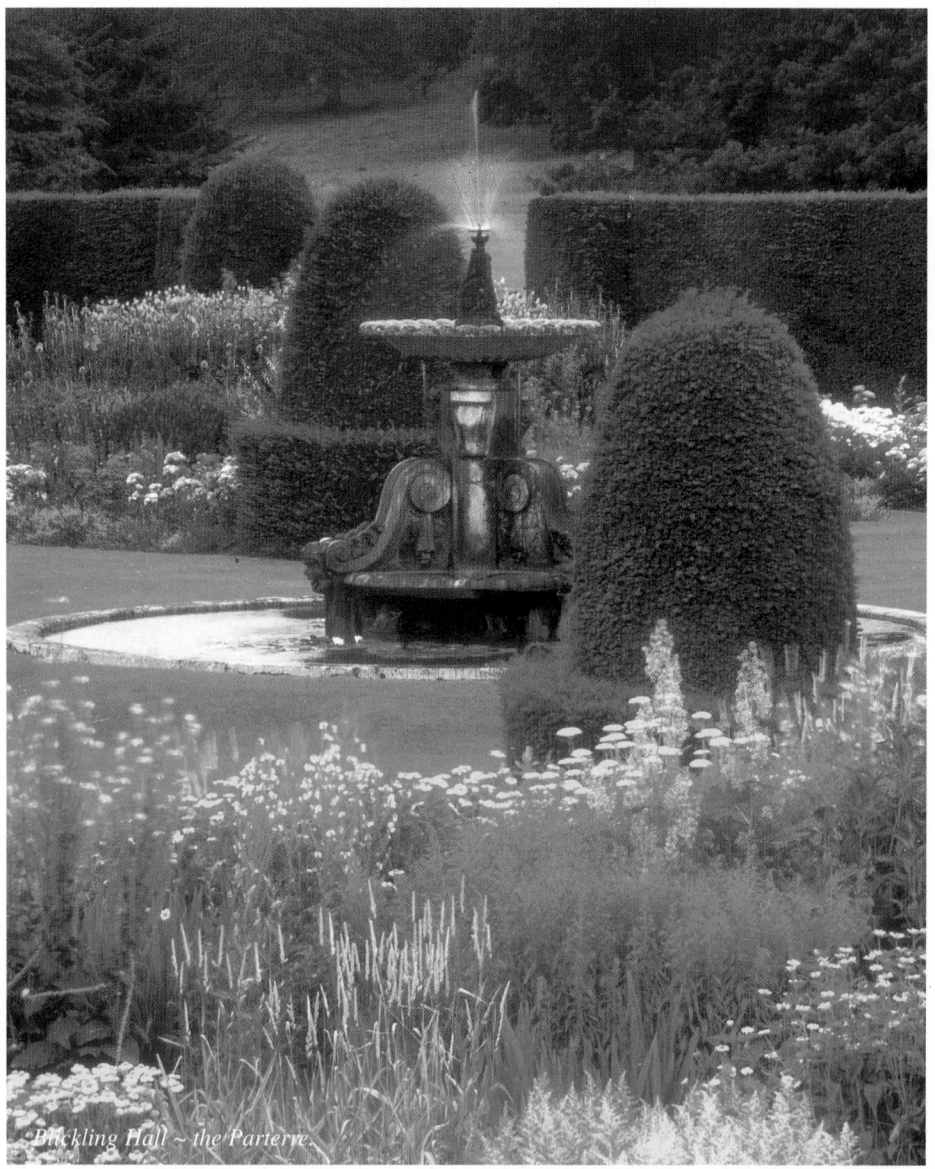

Blickling Hall ~ the Parterre.

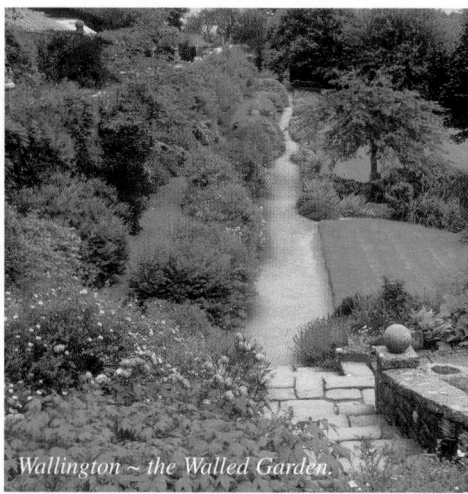

Wallington ~ the Walled Garden.

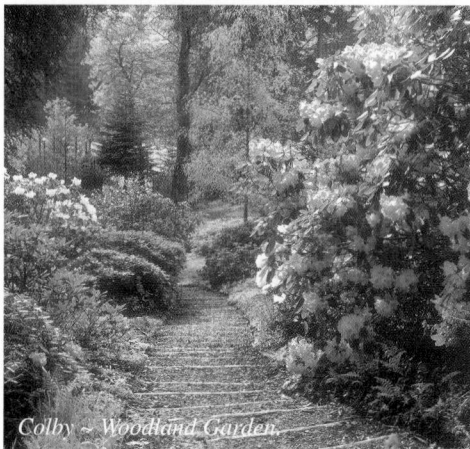

Colby ~ Woodland Garden.

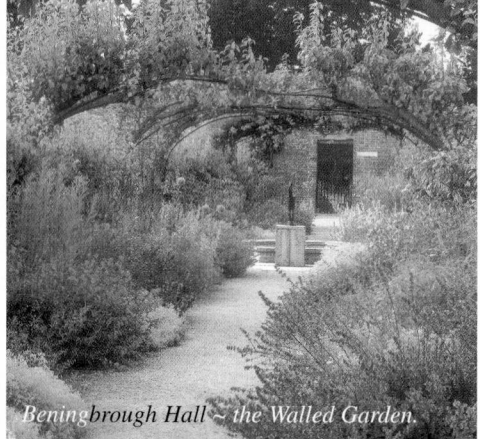

Beningbrough Hall ~ the Walled Garden.

The National Trust is also planning an exciting new exhibition of contemporary art and craft, inspired by and located within several Trust gardens. 'VISTA' aims to bring together some of the country's leading artists, commissioned by the Trust to create new work celebrating the legacy of craftmanship to be found within gardens in the charity's care.

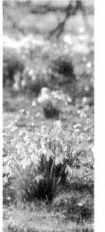
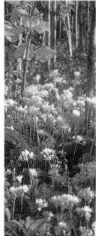
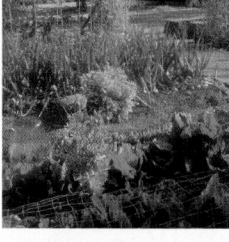

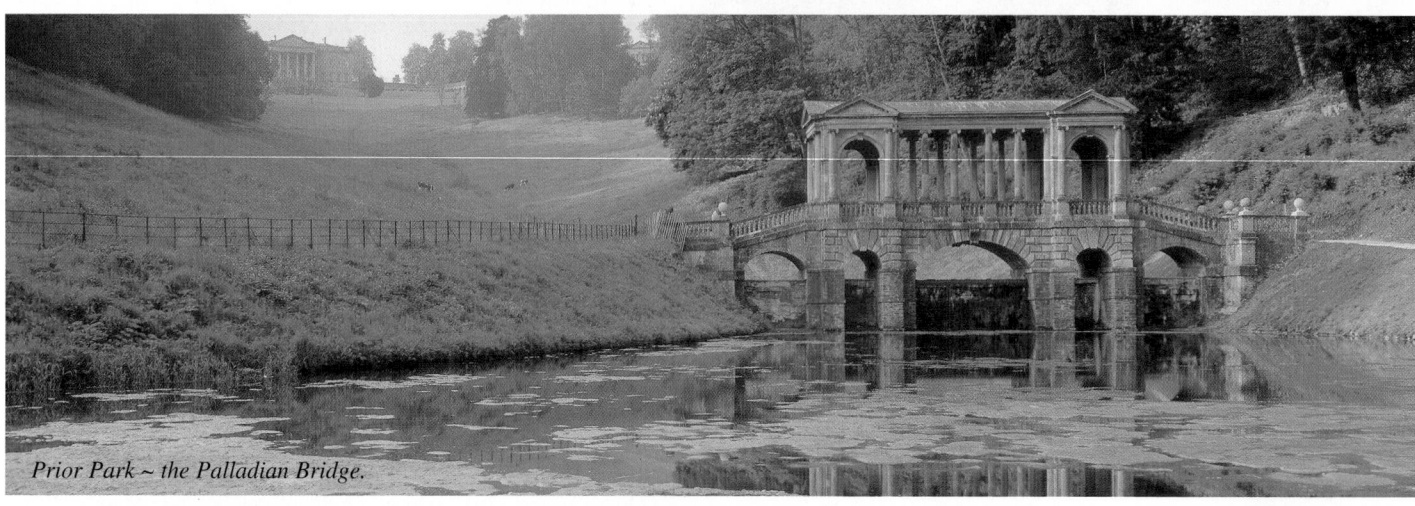

Prior Park ~ the Palladian Bridge.

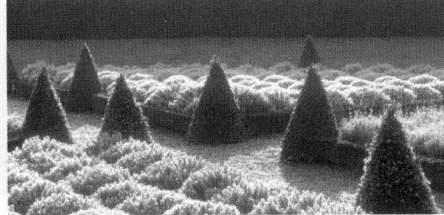

Ham House ~ the Knot Garden.

Some National Trust Garden Facts and Figures:

✻ **The National Trust looks after the largest and most important collection of historic gardens and cultivated plants in the world.**

✻ Over 200 gardens and landscape parks are open to the public throughout England, Wales and Northern Ireland.

✻ **Seven out of the top ten visited National Trust properties are those with gardens or landscape parks.**

✻ The National Trust employs over 450 skilled gardeners and hundreds more garden volunteers.

✻ National Trust gardens encompass over 400 years of history.

✻ **The National Trust is the world's leading conservation charity concerned for the long-term future of our garden heritage.**

Visitors can find more information about National Trust gardens and 'Gardens Year 2001' by telephoning: 020 8315 1111.

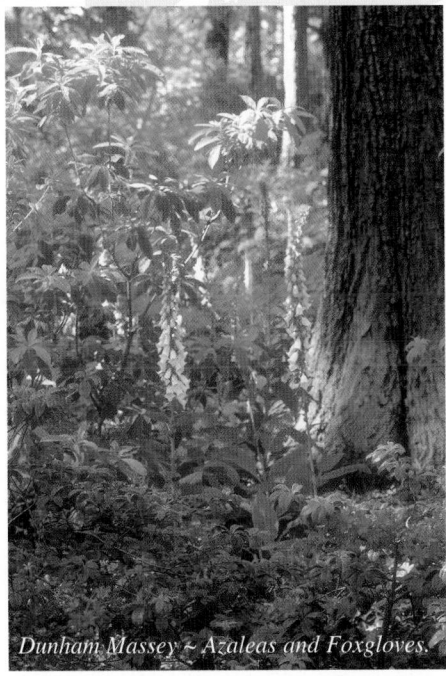

Dunham Massey ~ Azaleas and Foxgloves.

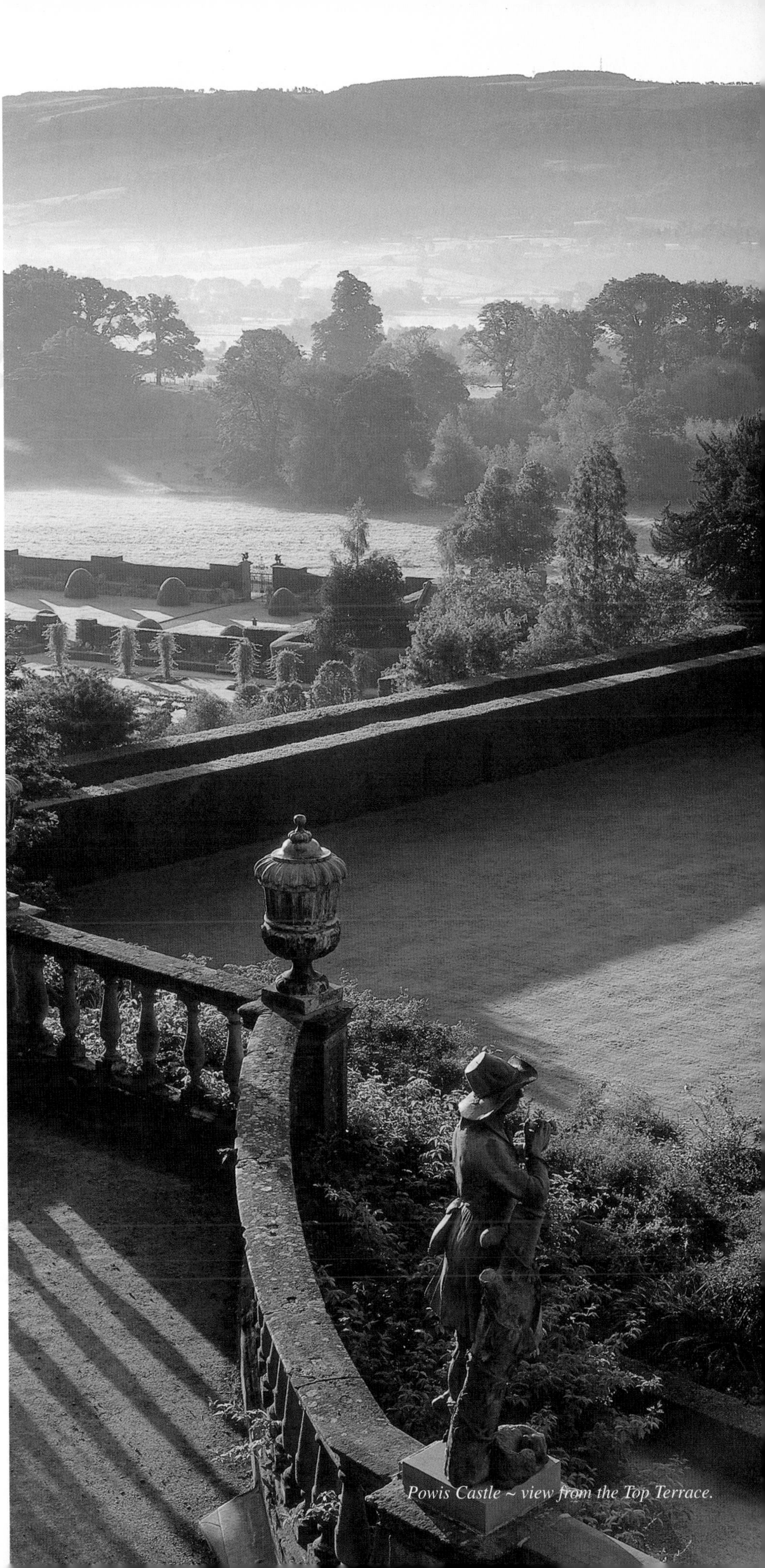

Powis Castle ~ view from the Top Terrace.

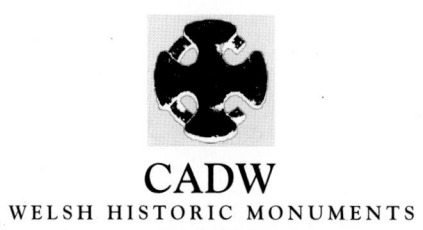

CADW

WELSH HISTORIC MONUMENTS

The National Assembly for Wales
Cathays Park
Cardiff CF10 3NQ
Telephone: 029 2050 0200   Fax: 029 2082 6375
E-mail: cadw@wales.gsi.gov.uk

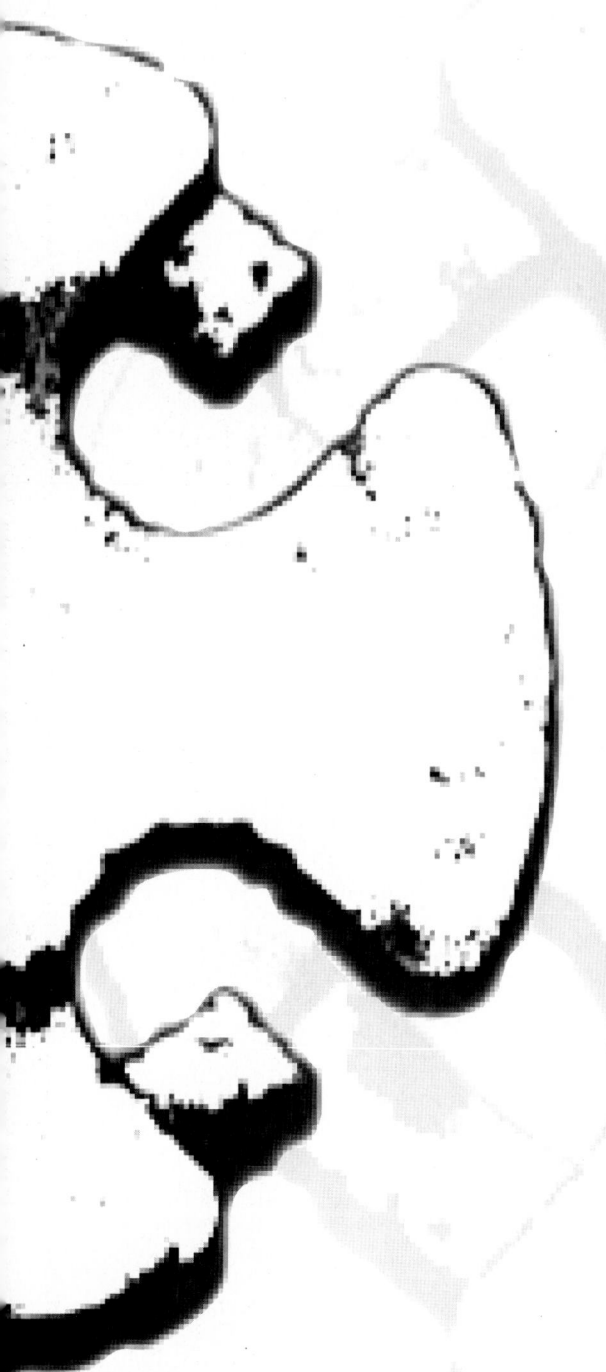

Cadw is the executive agency within the **National Assembly for Wales** that carries out the Assembly's statutory responsibilities to protect, conserve and promote an appreciation of the built heritage of Wales.

Cadw gives grant aid for the repair or restoration of outstanding historic buildings. Usually it is a condition of grant that the owner or occupier should allow some degree of public access to the property. Conditions of grant remain in force for ten years.

Details of properties grant aided by Cadw and to which the public currently enjoys a right of access can be found on Cadw's website: **www.cadw.wales.gov.uk**

Cadw's website contains a wide range of information, including details of buildings and monuments in its care and, where appropriate, related public access.

Cadw encourages you to visit these properties, as well as buildings and monuments in its care.

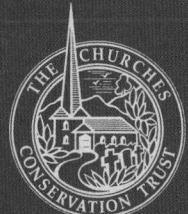

THE CHURCHES
CONSERVATION TRUST

Caring for historic churches throughout England

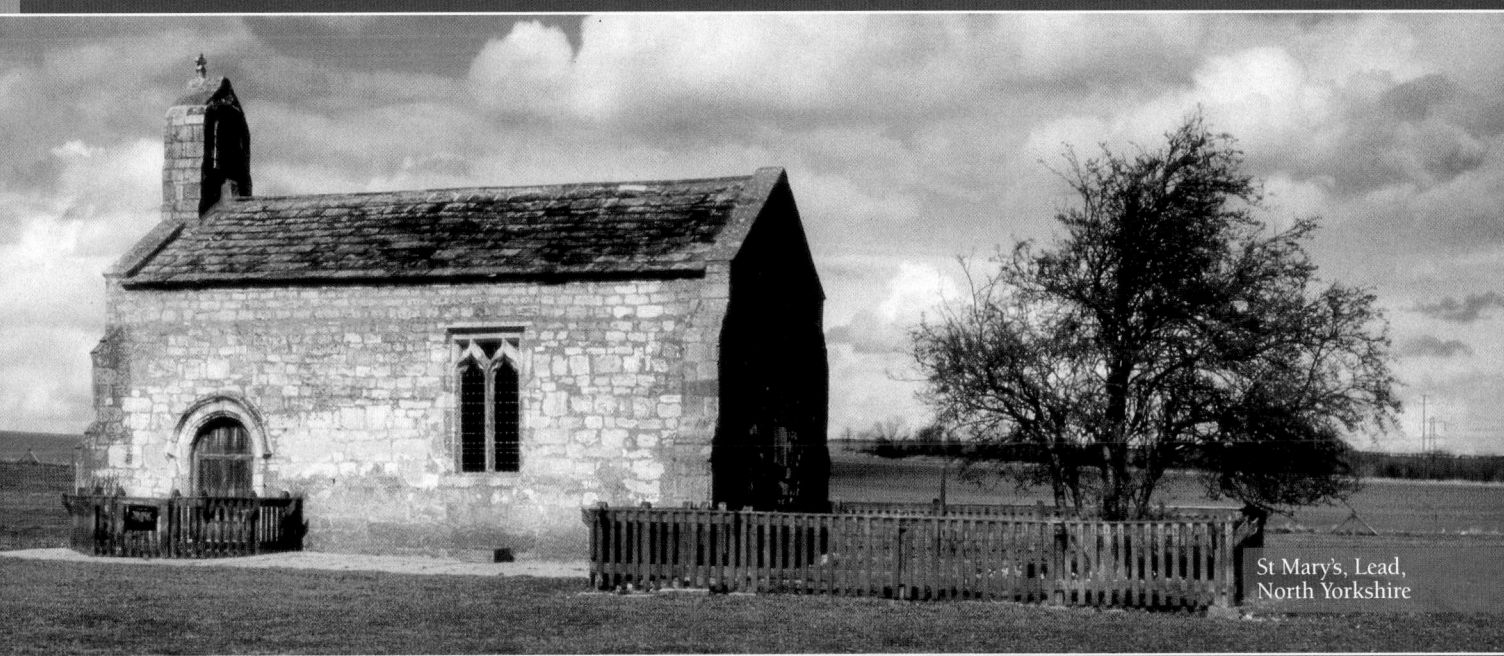

St Mary's, Lead,
North Yorkshire

St Mary's is just one of the 50 exceptional churches chosen by The Churches Conservation Trust to illustrate the gems it has in its care. *Your Starter for 50* churches all have something specially interesting or beautiful about them – and can be visited *free* throughout the year. Our map shows where they all are.

The job of The Churches Conservation Trust is to repair and preserve churches throughout England of outstanding architectural and historic interest when they are no longer needed for regular parish use. In many, you can see the results of conservation work we have undertaken to protect crumbling stone, or ancient stained glass or even mediaeval wall paintings.

We welcome visitors to all our churches; some are opened daily, others have more limited opening times and still others have nearby keyholders. Opening arrangements for the featured churches are included overleaf.

We have over 300 churches but why not begin your exploration by sampling the glories of our selected *Starter for 50*?

BRISTOL
Bristol, St John ▼

St John's is the sole survivor of four Bristol churches built on the city wall in the 12th century and its picturesque tower and spire surmount the old North Gate. Above an earlier 14th century vaulted crypt, the present Perpendicular church was founded by Walter Frampton (d 1388) whose tomb and fine effigy are in the north wall of the chancel. The small, but impressively tall interior has interesting and lovely fittings, mostly 17th century, and an air of mercantile splendour.

Bottom of Broad Street at intersection with Nelson Street, ST587732.
Open Tues-Fri 11-4.
or 07931 578 068.

CORNWALL
St Anthony-in-Roseland, St Anthony ▶

St Anthony's stands behind Place, looking across the creek to St Mawes, and is unusual in surviving in its 13th century form without later additions. Pevsner thought it 'the best example in the county of what a parish church was like in the 12th and 13th centuries.' The ingenious 1850 restoration was carried out by Revd C W Carlyon, an amateur architect, and a cousin of the Sprys of Place whose monuments are in the church. There is a fine Norman doorway which may have come from Plympton Priory nearby.

20m SW of St Austell off A3078 and opp. St Mawes, SW855320.
Open daily.

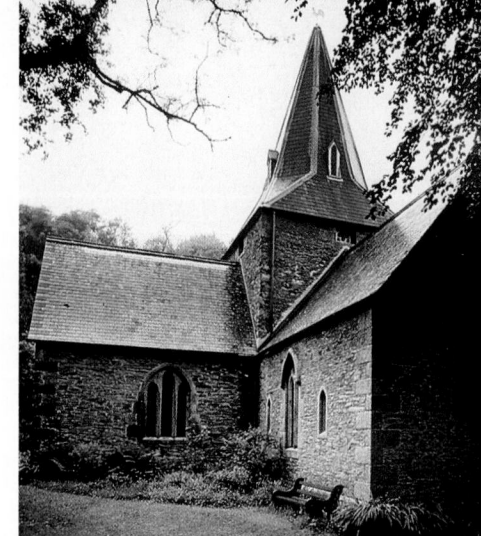

Boris Baggs

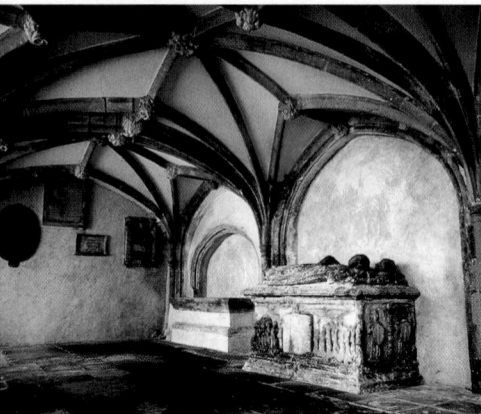

Boris Baggs

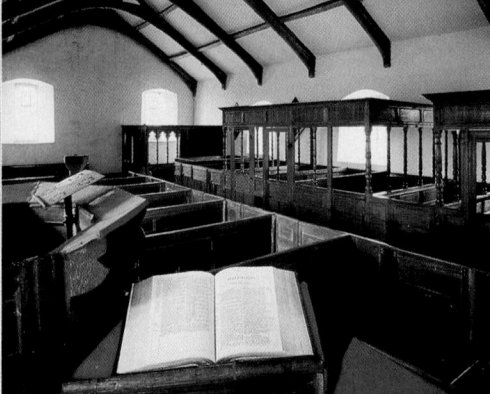

Boris Baggs

CUMBRIA
◀ Brougham, St Ninian

Known locally as Ninekirks, this lovely church is reached down a long track off the A66, and stands in fields above a bend in the River Eamont. In 1660 Lady Anne Clifford completely rebuilt the Norman church and it remains a fascinating example of what is known as Gothic Survival style, with furniture and fittings almost untouched. The simple whitewashed interior has clear glass in most windows and a stone-flagged floor. The family pews, complete with canopies, the box pews and benches, communion rails and screen, and the three-decker pulpit are all of late 17th century oak and of excellent quality.

3m E of Penrith off A66, NY559299. Open daily.

DORSET
▼ Winterborne Tomson, St Andrew

In a gentle farmyard setting, built of grey stone and flint with a bell-turret of board and tile, this small 11th century village church is a delight. It enchants on sight and is all one could hope for inside. Archbishop Wake of Canterbury presented the box pews, pulpit and other furnishings early in the 18th century and most are still there, under a barrel-roof whose arches continue over the apse. They are all of oak, bleached through the years to a magical silvery grey. The church was gently repaired in 1931 using money raised from the sale of Thomas Hardy manuscripts.

8m W of Wimborne Minster off A31, SY885974.
Open daily.

KENT
Sandwich, St Peter ▶

The tower and Flemish cupola of this great town centre church, as well as the gable of its south-eastern vestry, all show the influence of 16th and 17th century refugees from the Low Countries. But other parts of this church have stood for 900 years, so much of what we see was fashioned in the 1200s and 1300s. Mediaeval roofs, exquisite 14th century tombs under arches and a host of treasures, ancient and modern, may be enjoyed in this lofty, light and airy church, where we learn much about the history and life of the town and Cinque Port. St Peter's has a busy programme of events throughout the year.

In town centre, TR331580.
Usually open daily, or key available next door.

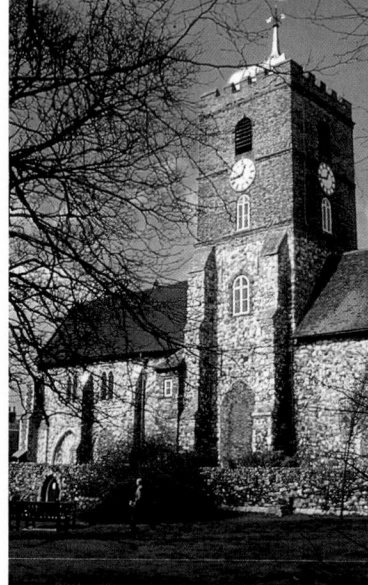

LINCOLNSHIRE
◀ Kingerby, St Peter

Set by fields in leafy countryside, this is a beautiful and unspoilt church. Its solid rustic tower may date from the 12th century or even earlier and the rest is mainly from the 13th and 14th. The nave roof timbers date from the 17th century. Three splendid 14th century monuments to the Disney family survive, two in the south aisle and one in the chancel. The church also had a north aisle, now long demolished. The church escaped Victorian restorers and the appealing simplicity of the interior remains.

5m NW of Market Rasen, TF057929.
Open daily.

Christopher Dalton

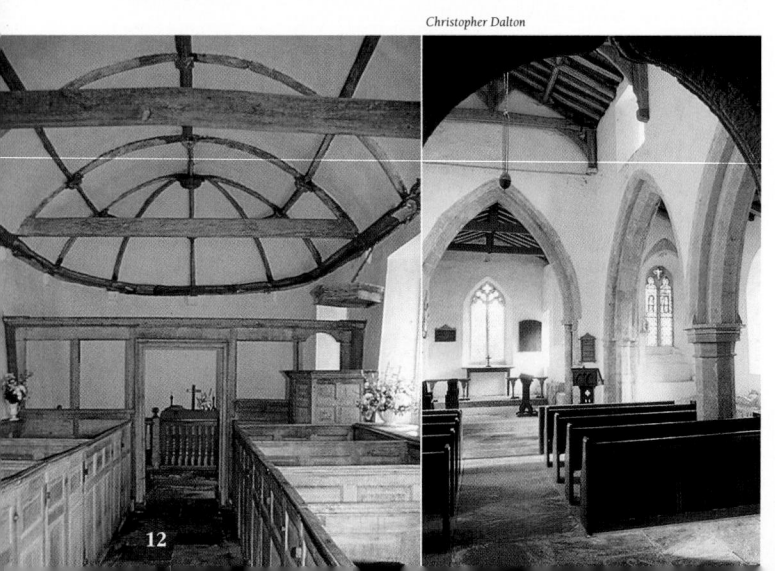

NORFOLK

Hales, St Margaret ▼

Known far and wide for its thatched roofs and round tower, Hales is Norfolk's best example of a 12th century Norman church essentially in its original form, with fascinating arcading around the apse, a magnificent north doorway of somewhat later date and a very good one to the south too. There are wall paintings including a St Christopher, the remains of a 15th century screen and a beautiful 15th century font. Despite its solitary position, remote from its village, it remains a place of pilgrimage for architectural students and church crawlers alike.

12m SE of Norwich and W of A146, TM384962.
Usually open daily April-Sept,
or keyholder nearby.

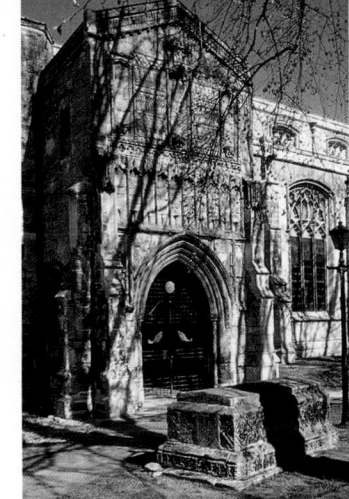
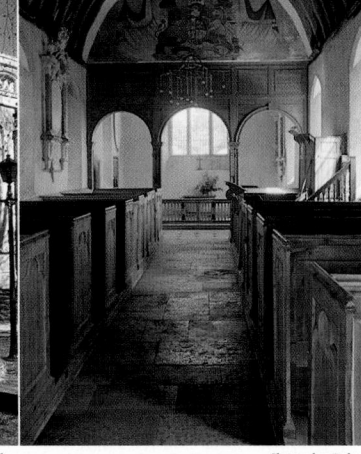

Christopher Dalton　　　*Christopher Dalton*

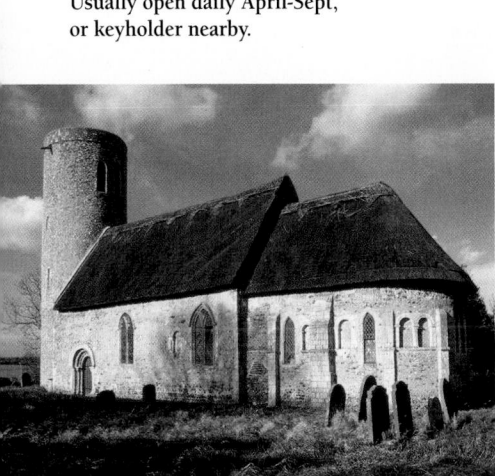

NORFOLK

King's Lynn, St Nicholas Chapel ▲

This striking building, splendidly light and spacious within, was built as a chapel of ease to St Margaret's. The fine tower is Early English, with a spire added by Sir George Gilbert Scott in 1869, but most of the church you see was finished in 1419. Its glories include a superb two-storied south porch, vaulted and richly ornamented, huge east and west windows and a very beautiful angel roof. There are fine fittings and interesting monuments, many commemorating Lynn merchants through the centuries.

St Anne's St, TF618205.
Key at True's Yard, call Andrew Lane
01553 770 479.

SUSSEX

▲ Warminghurst, The Holy Sepulchre

Up a narrow lane and on a walled bank with fine views to the south, Warminghurst church is one of the delights of Sussex. A simple mainly 13th century sandstone building, its 18th century interior is magical and unforgettable. A triple-arched screen, under a tympanum carrying a splendid Royal Arms robed in crimson drapery, separates nave from chancel; a complete set of box pews and a clerk's pew and pulpit fill the nave; there are hatchments and monuments from the 18th century and earlier; and the natural wood furnishings and uneven floor are all lit through clear glass.

10m N of Worthing off A24, TQ117169.
Keyholder nearby 01903 892 353.

WEST YORKSHIRE

Harewood, All Saints ▼

All Saints stands in the park of Harewood House and was built around 1410. Sir George Gilbert Scott's restoration in 1862–63 reordered the interior considerably to accord with the Victorians' idea of a mediaeval church. Inside, the building is severe and the lack of decorative carving contrasts strongly with its greatest treasures: the six superb alabaster tombs and pairs of effigies of the owners of Harewood and nearby Gawthorpe, dating from 1419 to 1510. These provide a unique display of costume, armour and funerary design during those years. There is good Victorian glass by Kempe and others.

6m N of Leeds off A61, SE314451
Open 10-6 April-October, 7 days a week. At other times call 0113 288 6331

Boris Baggs

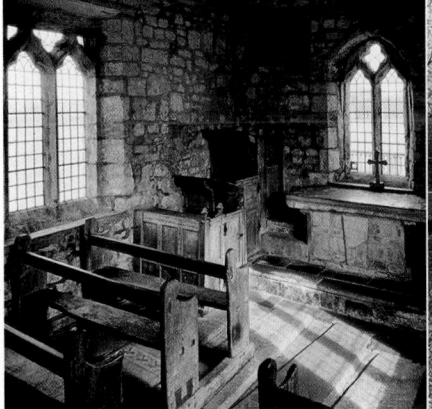

Christopher Dalton

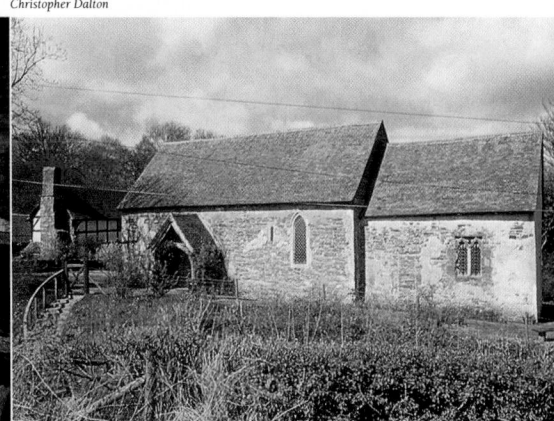

Boris Baggs

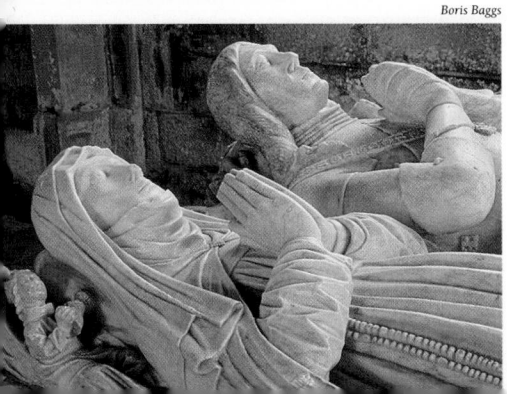

NORTH YORKSHIRE

Lead, St Mary ▲

Known as the Ramblers' Church this peaceful and well-visited place lies close to the battlefield of Towton where the wearisome Wars of the Roses ended. The field around is full of low earthworks, indicating the site of a manor house for which this was surely the chapel. It is tiny and rustic and the 14th century single cell building with a bell-cote is fitted with 18th century woodwork and earlier open benches. The floor includes mediaeval coffin lids and the font may be from an earlier church.

10m SE of Wetherby off B1217, SE464369.
Open daily.

WORCESTERSHIRE

Lower Sapey,
St Bartholomew Old Church ▲

This humble two cell building is a rare survival: a rustic Norman or late Saxon church, memorably set in beautiful and remote country next to a 17th century farmhouse and close to the site of a Saxon settlement. Some alterations were made in the 14th century, others in the 18th, but the importance and charm of this church is that little has changed from its early times. Years of neglect followed the building of a new church in the 1870s, but the efforts of local people and its vesting in the Trust in 1994 secured its future.

13m NW of Worcester off B4204, SO699602.
Open daily.

Your Starter for 50 churches in the care of The Churches Conservation Trust

All churches on the map are opened regularly or have keyholders nearby*. Further details may be obtained by ordering the leaflets below.

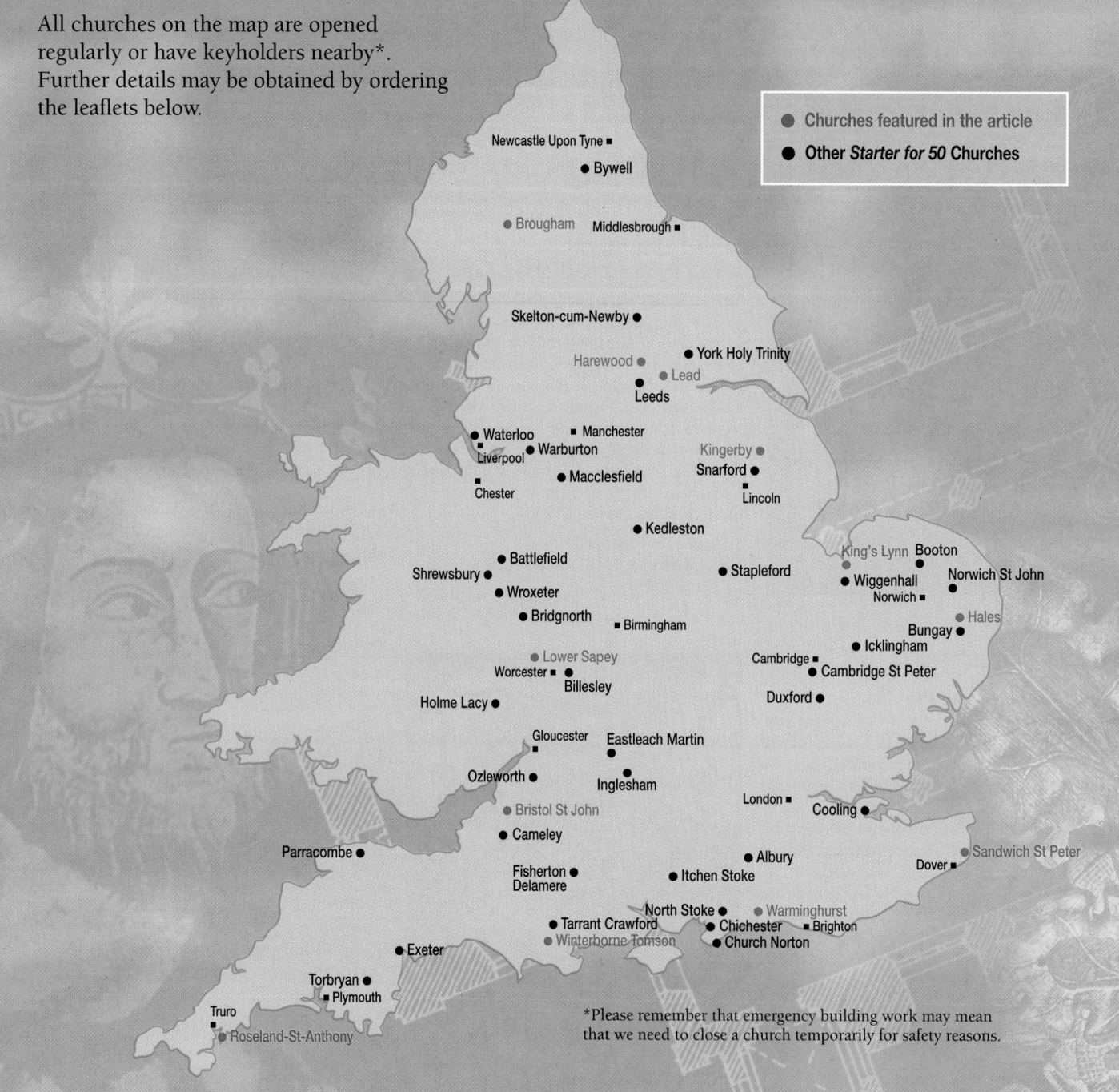

● Churches featured in the article
● Other *Starter for 50* Churches

Newcastle Upon Tyne ■
● Bywell
● Brougham   Middlesbrough ■

Skelton-cum-Newby ●
● York Holy Trinity
Harewood ●   ● Lead
Leeds ●

● Waterloo   ■ Manchester
Liverpool ■   Warburton ●   Kingerby ●
● Macclesfield   Snarford ●
Chester   Lincoln

● Kedleston

● Battlefield   King's Lynn ●   Booton
Shrewsbury ●   ● Stapleford   Wiggenhall ●   Norwich St John
● Wroxeter   Norwich ■
● Bridgnorth   ■ Birmingham   ● Hales
Bungay ●
Lower Sapey ●   ● Icklingham
Worcester ■   Cambridge ■
● Billesley   ● Cambridge St Peter
Holme Lacy ●   Duxford ●

Gloucester ■   ● Eastleach Martin
Ozleworth ●   London ■
Inglesham ●   ● Cooling
Bristol St John ●   ● Albury   Sandwich St Peter ●
● Cameley   Dover ■
Parracombe ●   Fisherton   ● Itchen Stoke
Delamere   North Stoke ●   Warminghurst ●
● Tarrant Crawford   ● Chichester   ● Brighton
Winterborne Tomson ●   ● Church Norton
● Exeter
Torbryan ●
Plymouth ■
Truro ■
● Roseland-St-Anthony

*Please remember that emergency building work may mean that we need to close a church temporarily for safety reasons.

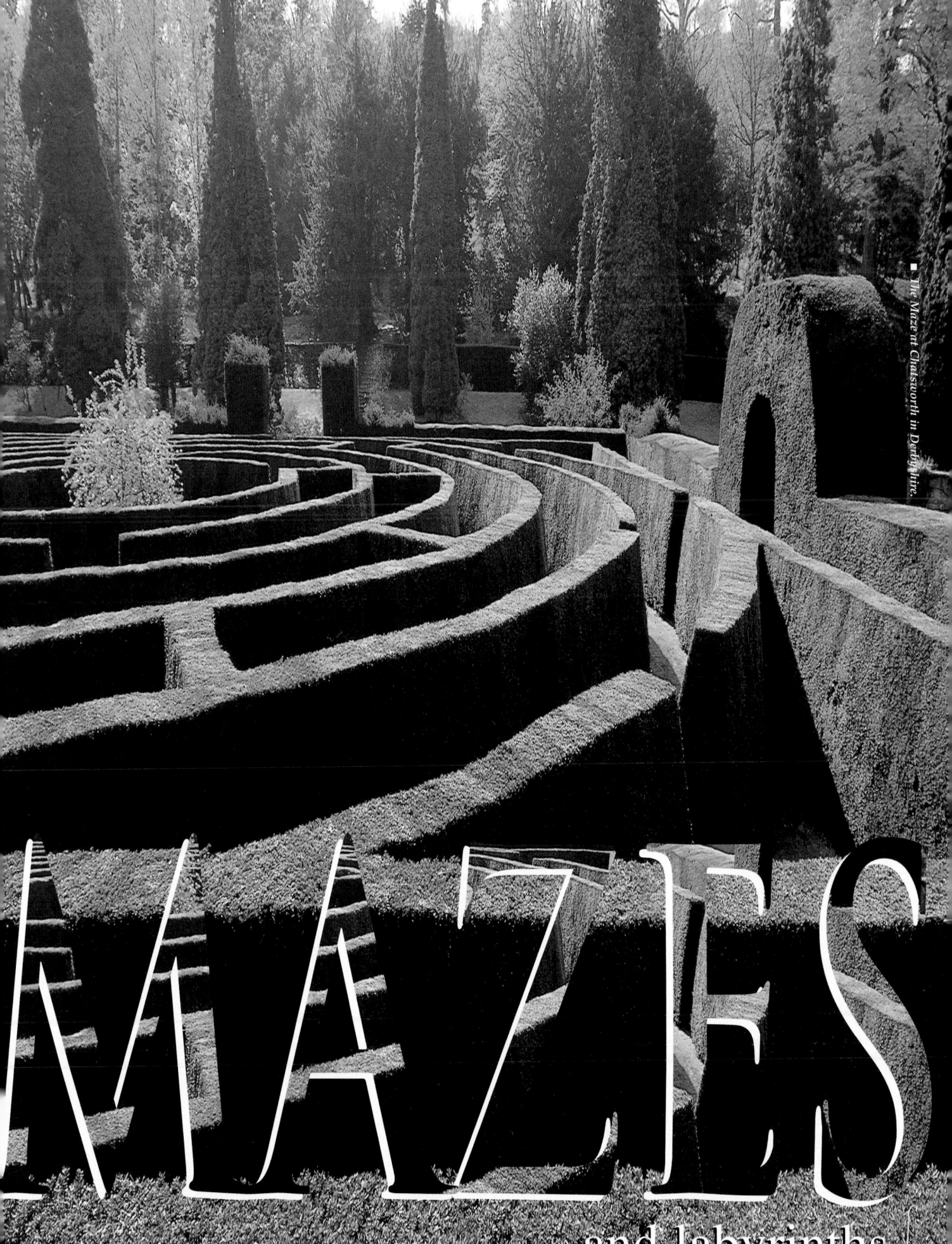

MAZES

and labyrinths

The maze is a device of great antiquity. The labyrinth symbol is found in many parts of the world. Although spread across different civilisations and cultures and during different periods of history, it is remarkable that an archetypal labyrinth design seems to have prevailed. Some of the earliest turf and stone labyrinths found in Scandinavia are thought to be 3,000 years old. How does a labyrinth differ from a maze? True labyrinths have a single, meandering pathway leading from the entrance to the centre and sometimes back out again. One pathway 'unicursal' was the only form used for thousands of years and it was only after the Middle Ages that 'multi-cursal' or puzzle mazes with dead ends, false paths and choices to confuse, became familiar.

We can readily understand the appeal and intrigue of a hedge puzzle maze but what was the purpose of a 'unicursal' labyrinth that does not hide the goal from view and is merely marked on the ground by stones or turf? Its origin remains a mystery. While as

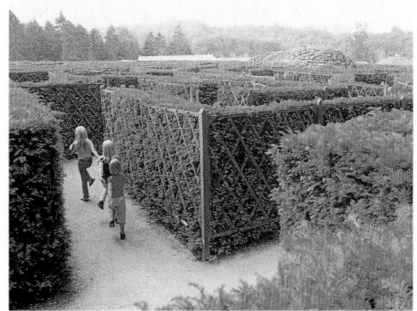

■ *The Maze at Leeds Castle, Kent.*

a symbol and concept often connected with the Minoan Temple at Knossos c1500 BC, and later popular with the Romans, there is evidence of labyrinths from much earlier time carved on rock faces in Africa and among remote jungle-dwelling tribes in Sumatra.

They had a religious significance also. Early Christians adopted the maze as they did other pagan symbols. In their symbolism the puzzle or labyrinth probably represented the

vicissitudes of life before the goal of Heaven could be obtained.

Mazes have been associated with British historic houses since Tudor times when they often had Royal connections. In the 19th century there was a resurgence of interest and there has been a remarkable revival since 1970. Britain has led the field and has the world's greatest concentration and variety of mazes and labyrinths. They take various forms: the traditional hedge maze, modern path and grass mazes, pavement mazes, colour mazes and mirror mazes. The Marquess of Bath at Longleat is a great enthusiast but by far the leading protagonist and most experience modern maze designer and builder is Adrian Fisher who has been responsible for many of the great diversity of contemporary British mazes, pioneering new forms of construction.

The best and simplest way to experience the compelling mystery is to walk or run through the various mazes and labyrinths open to the public.

■ *Aerial view of the Sun Maze and Lunar Labyrinth at Longleat in Wiltshire.*

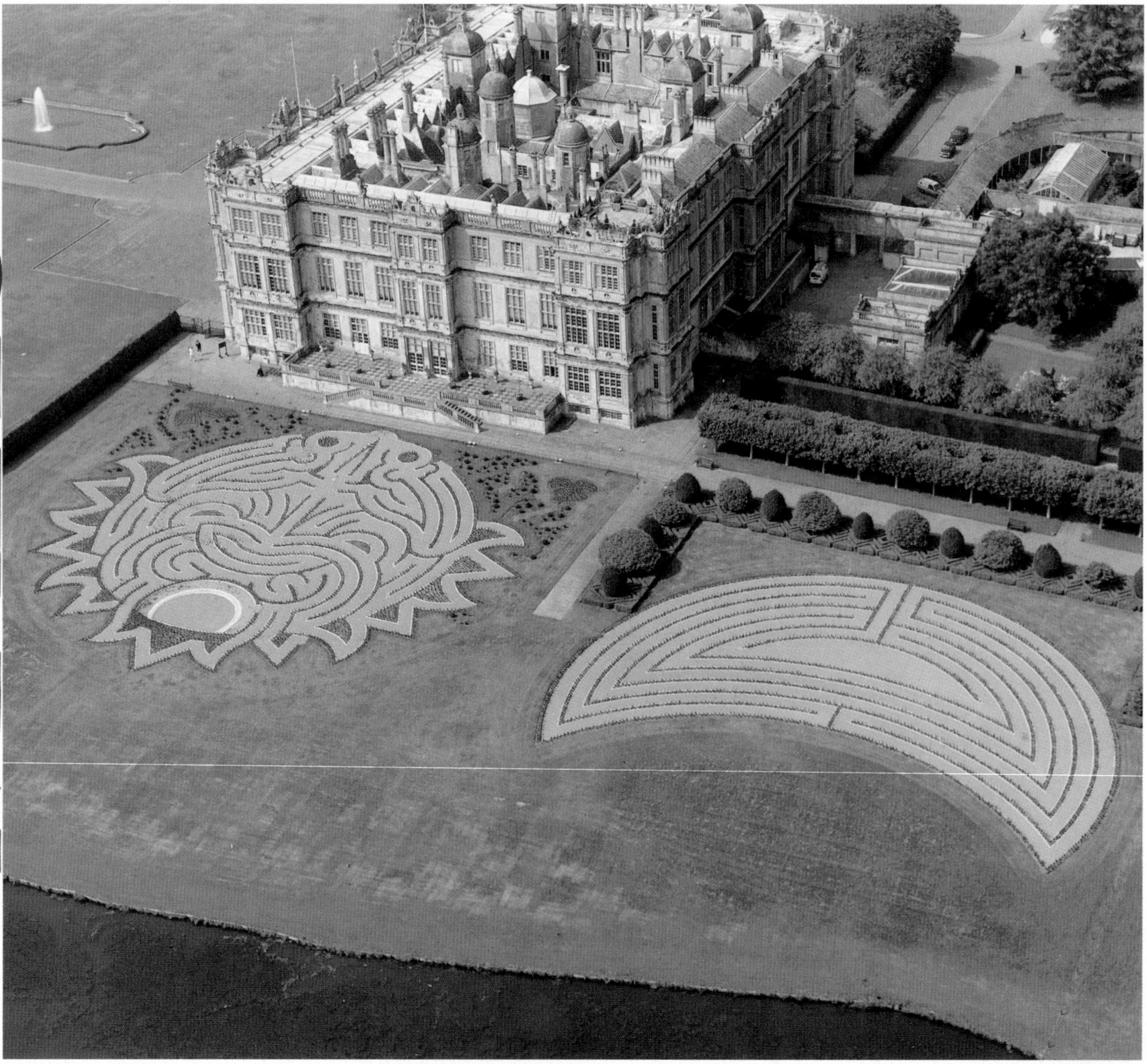

MAZES

LABYRINTHS

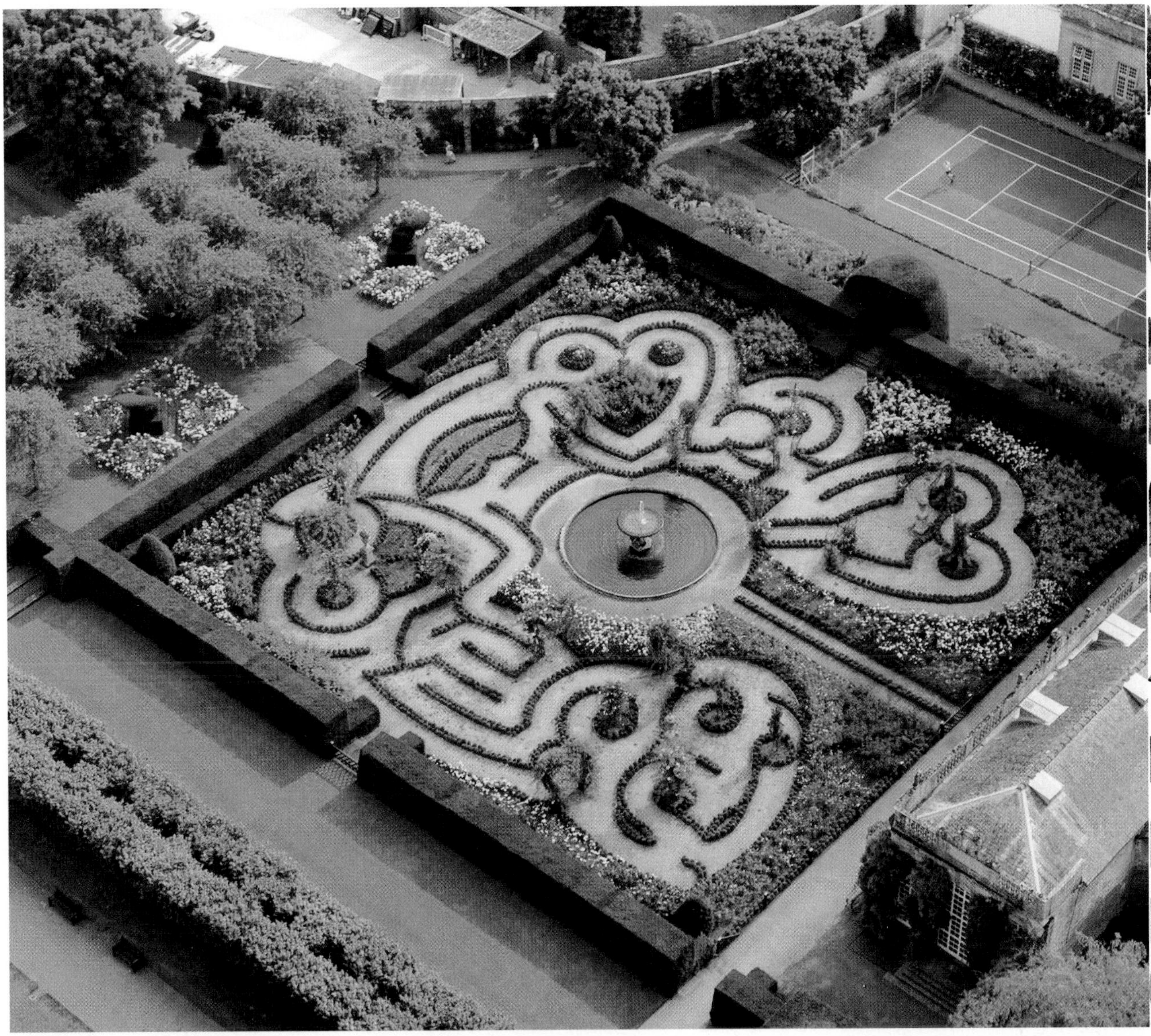

■ *The Love Labyrinth at Longleat, Wiltshire.*

■ *Enjoying the maze at Leeds Castle, Kent.*

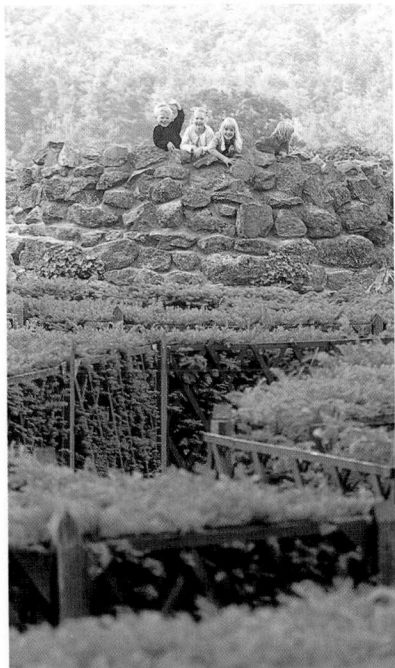

Mazes associated with historic houses and gardens which can be found in *Hudson's* are:

Buckinghamshire	Chenies Manor	turf and hedge
Cambridgeshire	Ely Cathedral	pavement
Cheshire	Tatton Park	hedge
Cornwall	Glendurgan	hedge
North Wales	Bodelwyddan	hedge
Derbyshire	Chatsworth	hedge
Herefordshire	Burford House	hedge
Hertfordshire	Hatfield House	low box
Kent	Hever Castle	hedge
Kent	Leeds Castle	hedge
Lancashire	Leighton Hall	turf
Lincolnshire	Doddington Hall	turf
London	Capel Manor	hedge
Highlands & Skye	Cawdor Castle	hedge
North Humberside	Burton Agnes Hall	hedge
Oxfordshire	Blenheim Palace	colour
Oxfordshire	Blenheim Palace	hedge
Oxfordshire	Greys Court	turf
Borders	Traquair House	hedge
Perthshire	Scone Palace	hedge
Suffolk	Kentwell Hall	courtyard
Suffolk	Somerleyton Hall	hedge
Surrey	Hampton Court Palace	hedge
Sussex	Parham Park	turf
Warwickshire	Ragley Hall	breezeblock
Wiltshire	Longleat	hedge

At Kentwell Hall, Suffolk, the maze is in the form of a brick-paved mosaic Tudor Rose. The owner, Patrick Phillips, takes the view that the concept of a 'goal' at the centre seems somewhat sterile as few mazes have a centre which is worth the effort when you get there, so the Kentwell maze has a start at the house and 'leads' eventually to the gardens. The maze is sited in the Courtyard, to pave that area in an interesting way, and to adapt the Tudor concept of a Knot Garden. Visitors have to 'submit' to the discipline of the maze which can be achieved merely by the path being clearly defined. Most obey the rules if they are interested. Where early mazes were largely two-dimensional, this differs by the introduction of junctions which notionally make it three-dimensional in that one path is deemed to pass 'over' or 'under' another.

The yew maze planted in 1906 by William Waldorf Astor at Hever Castle, Kent was a typical Victorian revival of a Renaissance tradition. It is situated at the edge of the Castle Courtyard, measuring 80' x 80' with almost a 1/4 mile of pathways inside. A very recent and exciting addition at Hever is the water maze, opened in 1997. This unique water maze with its 27m diameter pond and 4m high central folly and cascade is planted with a large collection of aquatic plants and ferns and complements the yew maze. Children and adults alike are challenged to avoid various water barriers and to reach the folly without getting wet. The stepping-stone path leads to water obstacles formed by jets of water, making the visitor divert to find an alternative way to the centre. Having reached the centre of the folly, visitors are greeted with a special water feature – a spiral staircase takes visitors to the top for an elevated view of the maze.

■ *The brick-paved mosaic Tudor Rose Maze at Kentwell Hall, Suffolk.*

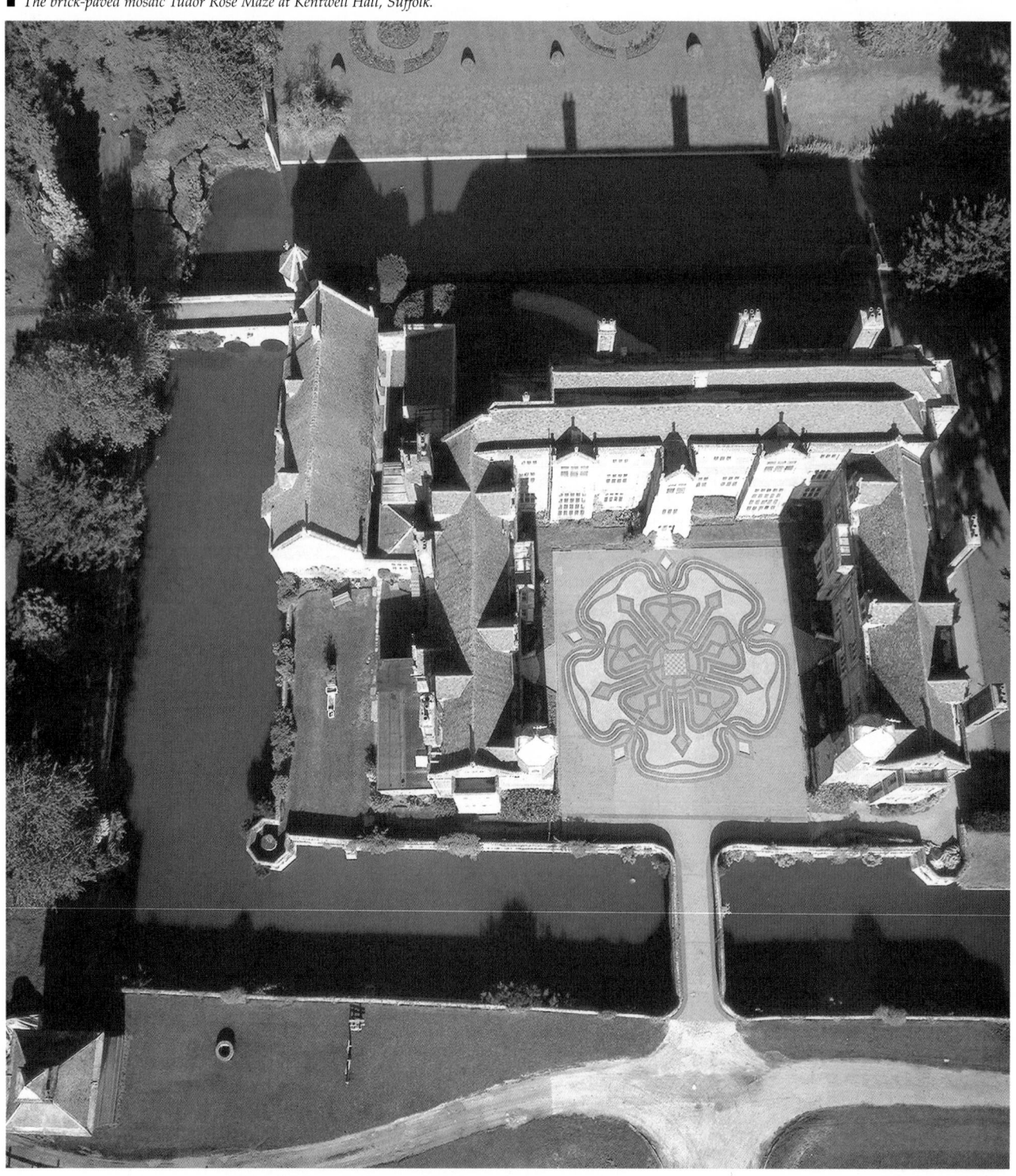

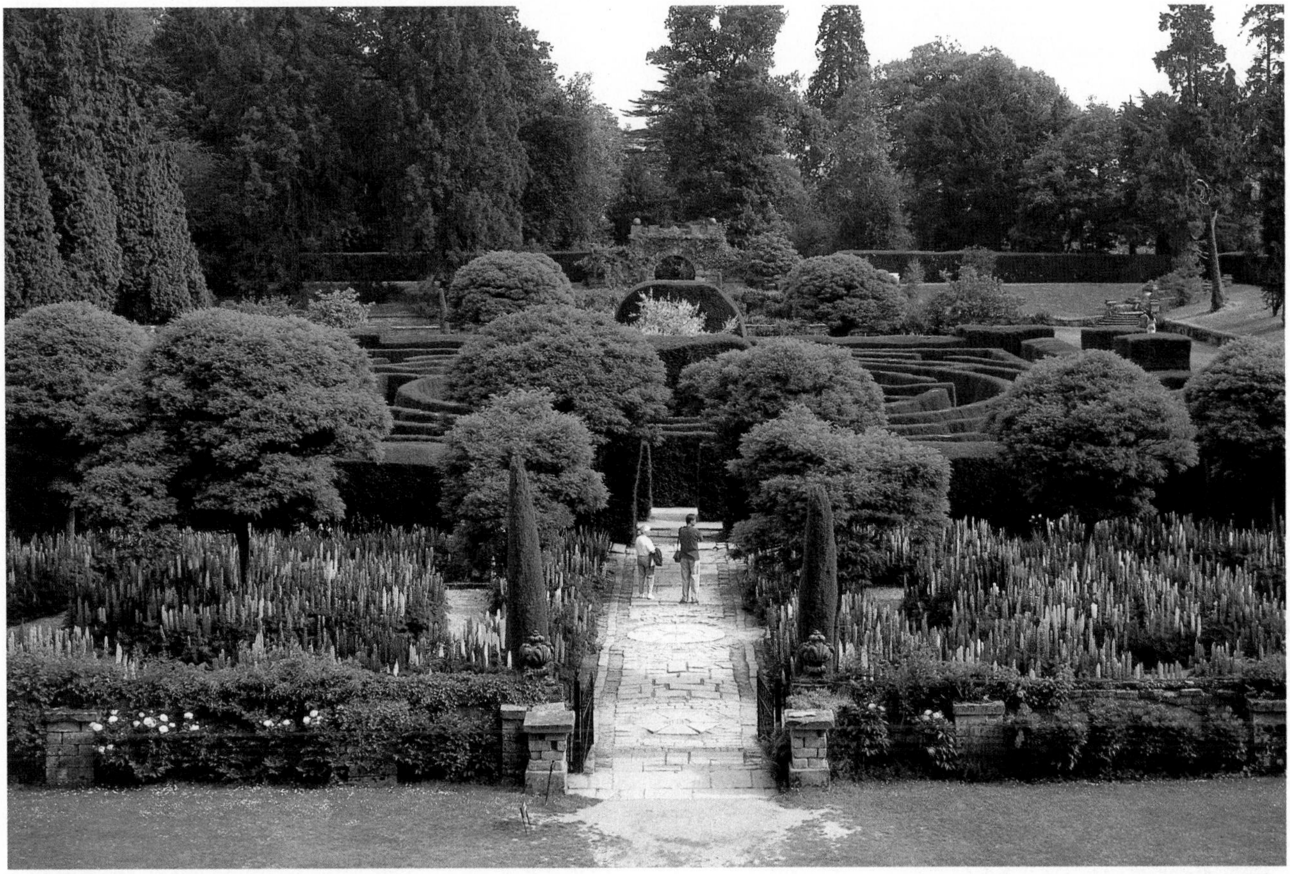

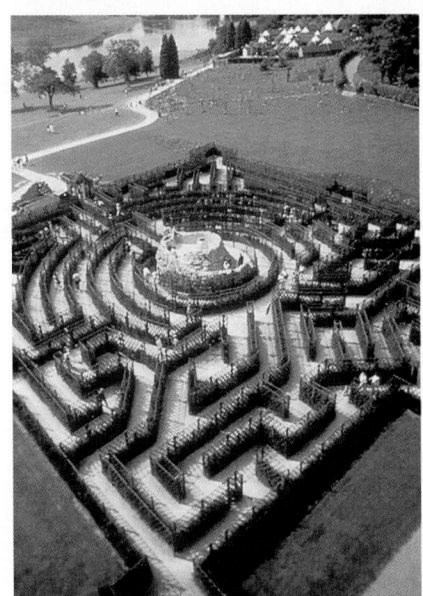

■ *The Maze at Chatsworth, Derbyshire.*

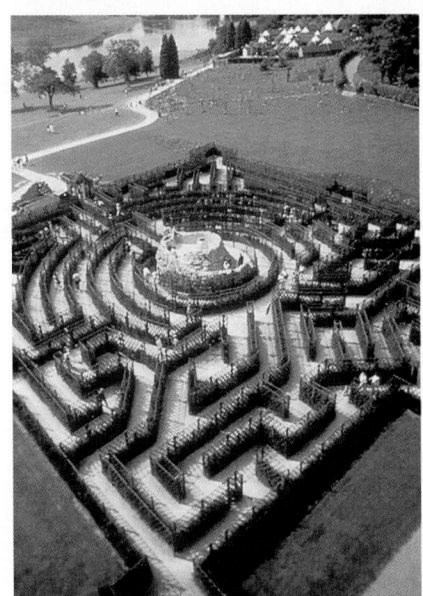

■ *Aerial view of the Maze at Leeds Castle.*

At Chatsworth, Derbyshire the garden which has been made within the foundation walls of the old conservatory has in part been created as a maze. Planted in 1962 with 1,209 yew trees, its setting is sensational. The North part of the garden is devoted to Autumn flowers, dahlias and Michaelmas daisies and the South end is all lupins. Peonies are planted round the outside of the foundation walls, the whole overlooked by towering Wellingtonias.

The hedge maze at Leeds Castle, Kent (designed by Adrian Fisher) was opened in 1998 by Princess Alexandra. It is a topiary castle with castellated yew hedges, an entrance bridge and a central tower. Inside it is challenging and teasing in several ways. From its central raised goal, the view from its stone parapet rewards the visitor with images of a Queen's crown and chalice, both laid out in the rows of the hedges. Looking down, visitors see splashing water and light 20' below them. Beneath the stone tower they discover the entrance to an underground grotto decorated with thousands of seashells, with statues in niches, and water cascading over a grotesque face. Still deeper, a 90' underground passage beneath the hedges of the maze leads through a dramatic vortex confronting visitors with a flooded cave, seat of the nymph of the grotto, before they ascend to the outside world. As Leeds Castle prepares to celebrate its Silver Jubilee as a charitable trust, they have developed the theme of mazes into a special event for May half-term. They will be holding a bonanza of 25 different mazes throughout the grounds on 26 May – 3 June 2001.

At Greys Court, Oxfordshire the Archbishop's maze is inspired by a dream of Dr Robert Runcie, formerly Archbishop of Canterbury. The turf maze abounds in Christian symbolism.

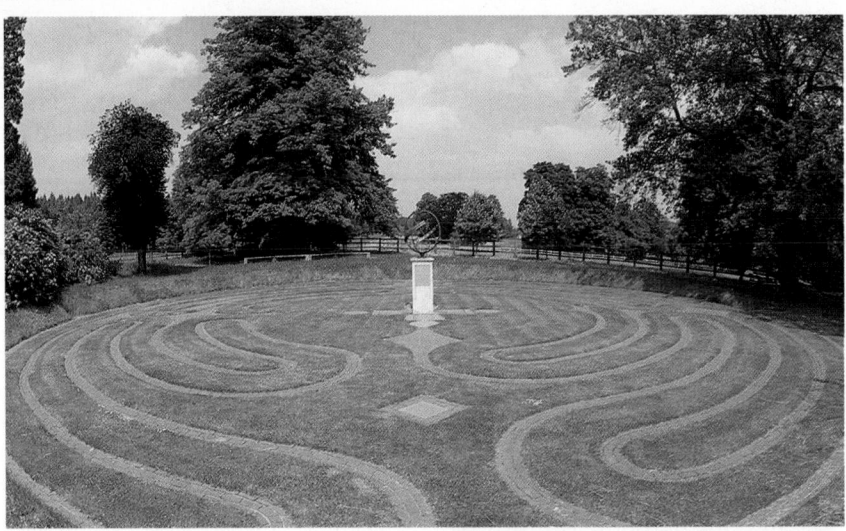

■ *The Archbishop's Maze, Greys Court, Oxfordshire.*

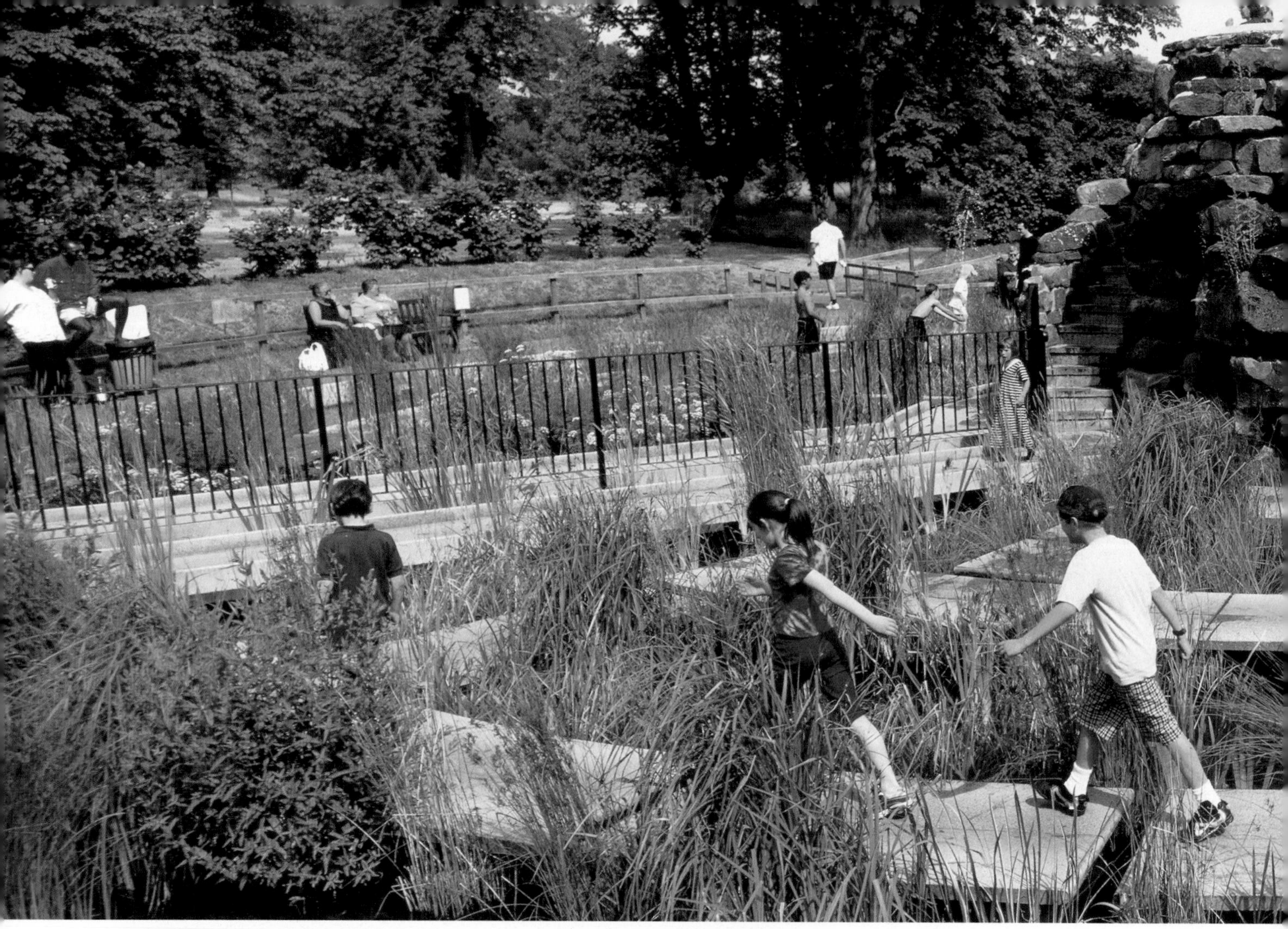

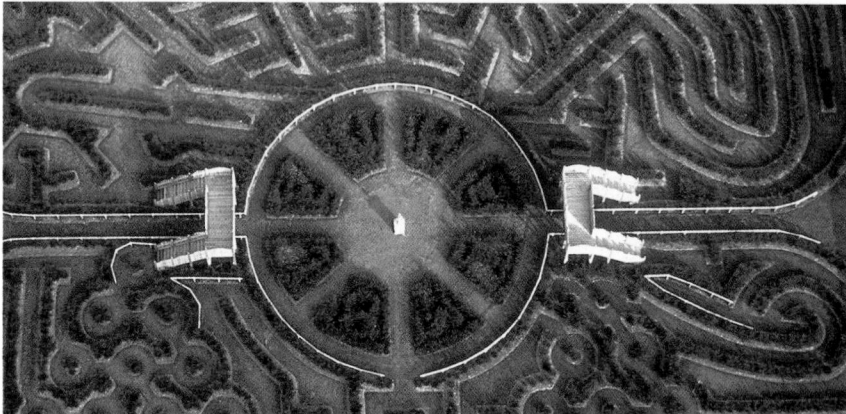

■ *The Maze at Blenheim Palace.*

■ *Below: The Hedge Maze at Longleat, Wiltshire.*

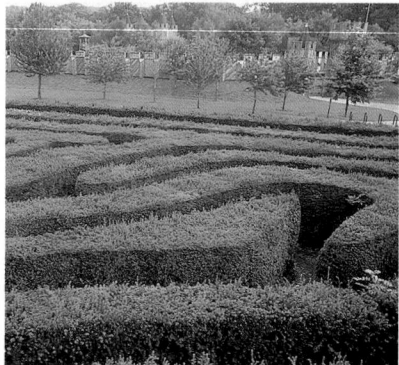

The inspiration for the Marlborough maze at Blenheim Palace, Oxfordshire came from stone sculptures depicting the Panoply of Victory carving by Grinling Gibbons from the roof of Blenheim Palace. Seen from above the lines of the yew hedges portray pyramids of cannonballs, a canon firing, and the air filled with banners, flags and the sound of trumpets. Two wooden bridges create a three-dimensional puzzle as well as giving tantalising views across parts of the world's largest symbolic hedge maze (designed by Adrian Fisher and Randoll Coat 1991).

The largest collection of mazes and labyrinths in Britain can be found at Longleat, Wiltshire. The 7th Marquess of Bath has an informed love of the ancient artefact. He has assigned a space for not one but two mazes immediately below his private apartments which look out on to a splendid vista of lawn, lake and rising parkland beyond. His challenge was to produce something which could measure up to the magnificence of its setting. His answer was to design a maze and join it to a labyrinth – perhaps a unique juxtaposition, each true to its definition and both highly symbolic in classical content and in their celestial shape. The two systems enable the visitor to savour their essential difference: the linear purity of the labyrinth with its unending unicursal corridor, and the dizzy gyrations of the maze with its multiple roots and wrong-turnings in the pursuit of an ultimate goal.

Longleat is now home to no less than five spectacular mazes. The latest maze, opened in 1998, is King Arthur's mirror maze. Visitors are invited to imagine they are knights who have set off from the Round Table to form a quest. On their journey they encounter mysterious sights, half-hidden faces, wild sounds, swirling fog and even seem to trigger off lightning and thunder. King Arthur's mirror maze, designed by Adrian Fisher, is a breakthrough in mirror maze design.

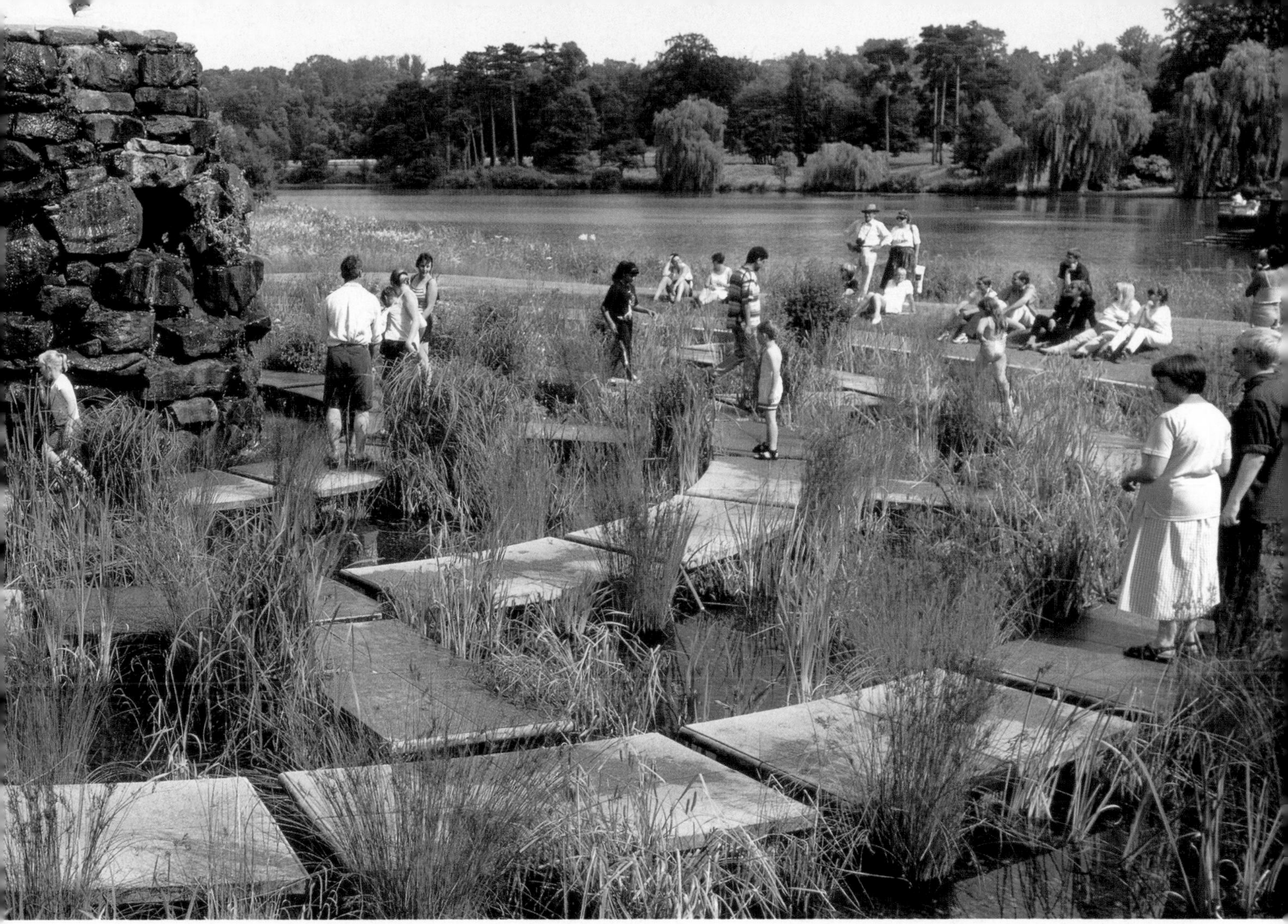

■ Above: The Water Maze at Hever Castle in Kent.

■ Below: The World's longest Hedge Maze at Longleat, Wiltshire.

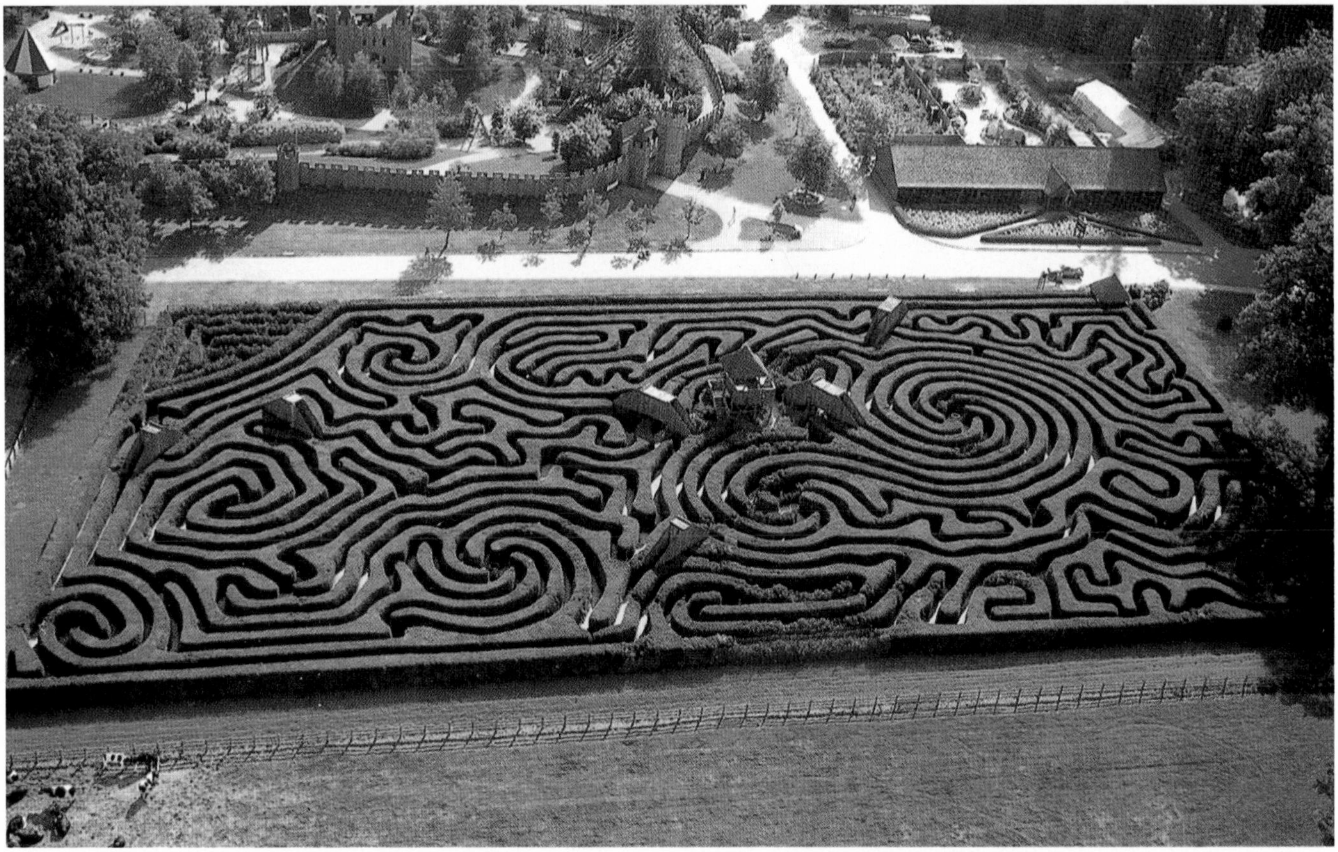

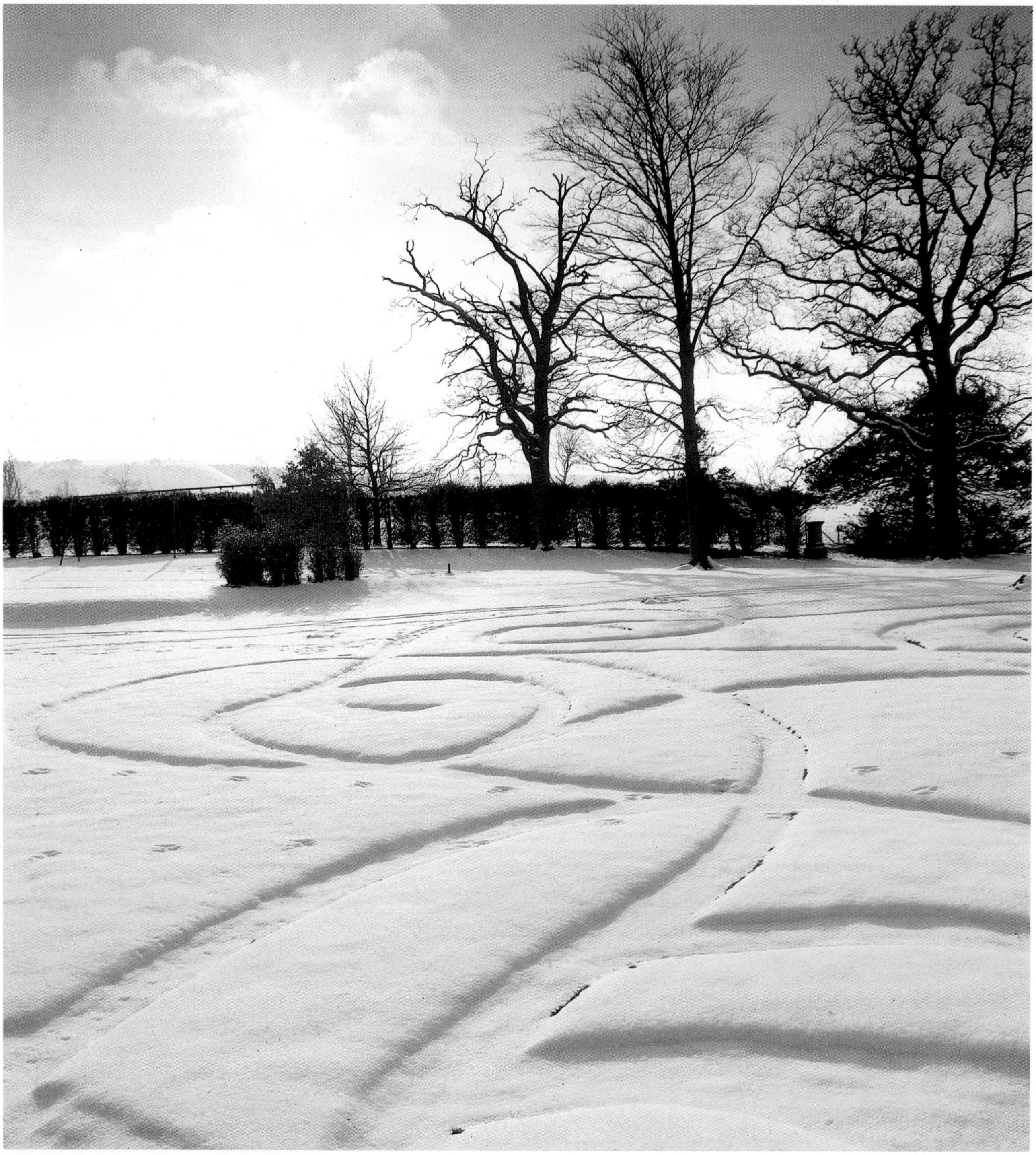

■ *Veronica's Maze at Parham in Sussex.*

Parham Park, Sussex is one of the loveliest Tudor houses in England, lying below the South Downs. The design for Veronica's maze was inspired by the embroidery over the 'Great Bed' in the principal bedroom of the house. This is an unusual one-way puzzle maze. The goal is the centre but once you start you have to keep going forward. When you reach forks in the path you choose which way to go. You cannot double-back when joined by other paths, nor make right-angled turns where paths cross over each other (designed by Adrian Fisher 1991).

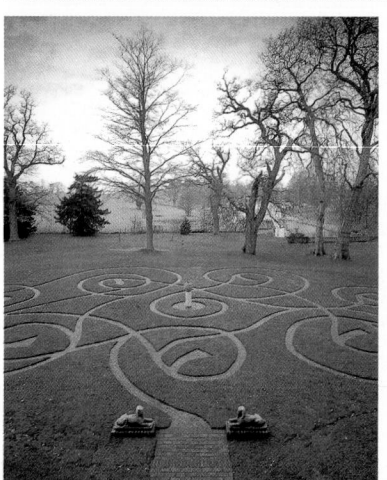

Further reading:

The Art of the Maze by Adrian Fisher and Georg Gerster, 1990
(available from Adrian Fisher Maze Design, Victoria Lodge, 5 Victoria Grove, Portsmouth, Hampshire PO5 1NE, tel: +44 (0) 2392 355500   website: www.mazemaker.com)

The British Maze Guide by Adrian Fisher and Jeff Saward (also available from Adrian Fisher)

Mazes - Adrian Fisher and Diana Kingham, Shire Publications, 1991 (revised 1997)

Secrets of the Maze - an interactive guide to the world's most amazing mazes by Adrian Fisher and Howard Loxton (Thames and Hudson)

HISTORIC CHAPELS TRUST

CHAIRMAN
Sir Hugh Rossi

29 Thurloe Street, London SW7 2LQ
Telephone: 020 7584 6072 Fax: 020 7225 0607

DIRECTOR
Dr Jennifer M Freeman

The Historic Chapels Trust has been established to take into ownership redundant chapels and other places of worship in England of outstanding architectural and historic interest. Our object is to secure for public benefit the preservation, repair and maintenance of our buildings including their contents, burial grounds and curtilages.

The trust now has twelve chapels in its care which can be visited on application to the keyholder:-

Biddlestone RC Chapel Northumberland	01665 574420
Coanwood Friends Meeting House Northumberland	01434 320256
Cote Baptist Chapel Oxfordshire	01993 850421
Farfield Friends Meeting House West Yorkshire	01756 710225
The Dissenters' Chapel Kensal Green Cemetery, London	020 7402 2749
Salem Chapel, East Budleigh Devon	01395 445236
St Benet's Chapel and Presbytery Netherton, Merseyside	0151 520 2600
St George's German Lutheran Church Tower Hamlets, London	020 8302 3437
Todmorden Unitarian Church West Yorkshire	01706 815648
Umbersland Baptist Church West Yorkshire	01564 783362
Wallasey Unitarian Church Merseyside	0151 639 5137
Walpole Old Chapel Suffolk	01986 798308

For further information please ring the Director at the office address.

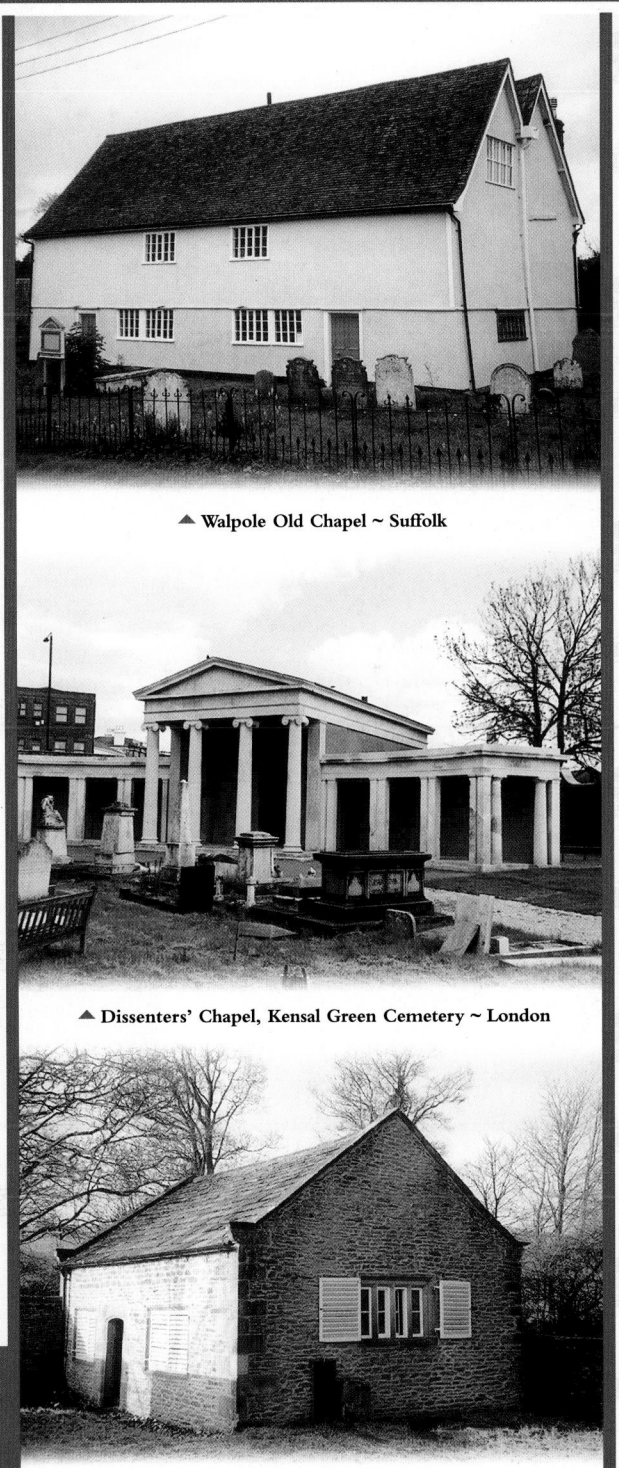

▲ Walpole Old Chapel ~ Suffolk

▲ Dissenters' Chapel, Kensal Green Cemetery ~ London

▲ Farfield Friends Meeting House ~ West Yorkshire

23

WORDSWORTH'S LAKE DISTRICT

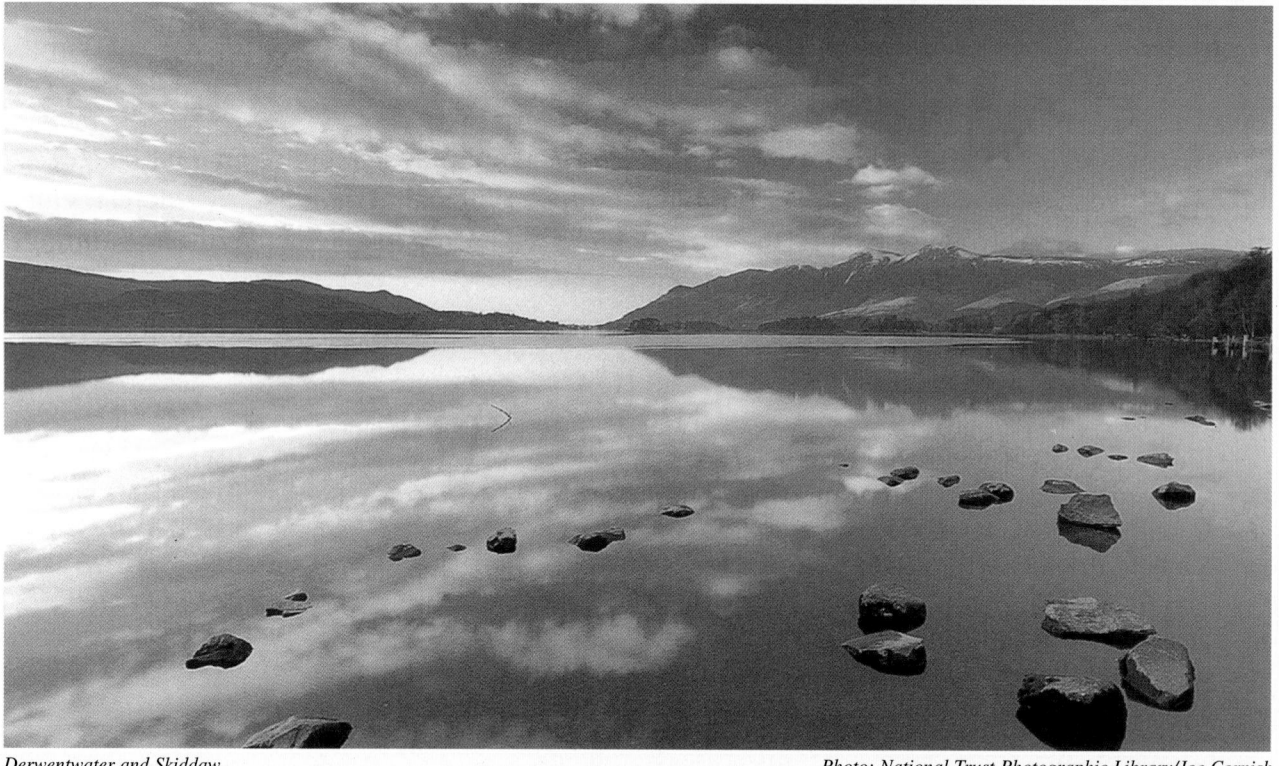

Derwentwater and Skiddaw

Photo: National Trust Photographic Library/Joe Cornish

"Here the rainbow comes - the cloud - And mists that spread the flying shroud..."

WORDSWORTH HOUSE
Cockermouth

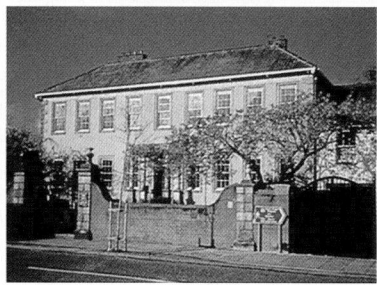

Birthplace of William Wordsworth in 1770

Open April to November, Monday to Friday and selected Saturdays in June, July and August. Restaurant. Shop. Events during season. Parking in town centre car parks. National Trust.

TEL: 01900 824805

DOVE COTTAGE
Grasmere

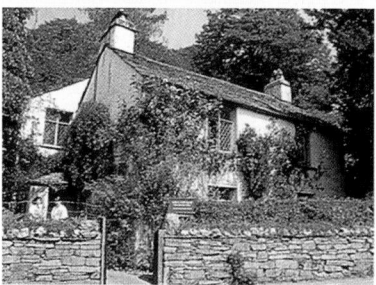

Dove Cottage & Wordsworth Museum, Grasmere

Open Daily 9.30 to 5.30pm. Closed 24th - 26th December

Parking next to Dove Cottage Tearoom & Restaurant immediately south of Grasmere village.

TEL: 015394 35544

RYDAL MOUNT & GARDENS
Near Ambleside

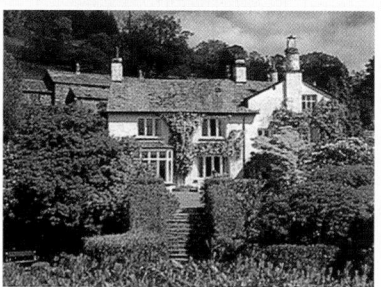

Rydal Mount Home of William Wordsworth from 1813 - 1850

Open:
Summer: Mar - Oct 9.30 - 5.00pm
Winter: Nov - Feb 10.00 - 4.00pm

(Closed Tuesdays in Winter)

FREE PARKING

TEL: 015394 33002

RECIPROCAL DISCOUNT OFFER - DETAILS FROM ANY OF THE ABOVE ATTRACTIONS

www.wordsworthlakes.co.uk

24

If you enjoy 'historic' Britain, you will love ...

Alastair Sawday's
Special
places to stay

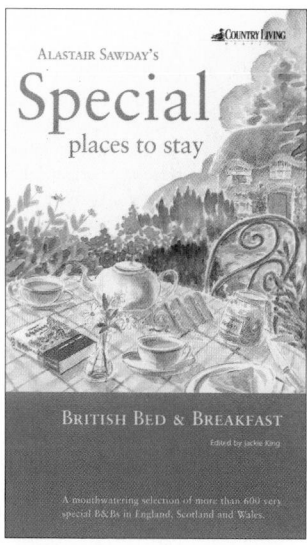

British Bed & Breakfast
£12.95

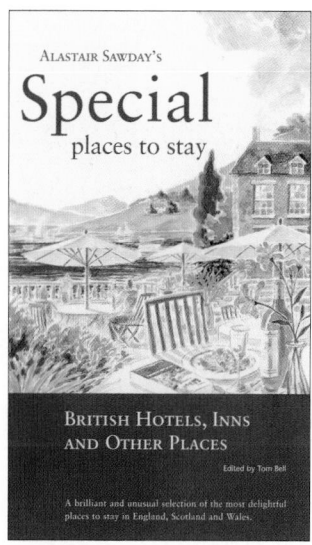

British Hotels & Inns
£10.95

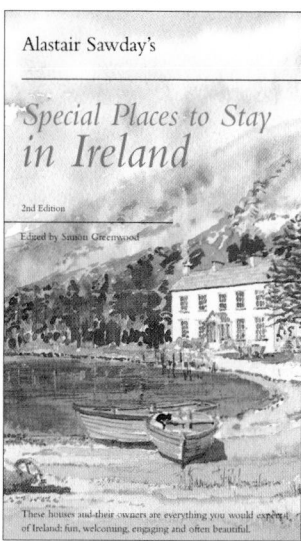

Special Places to Stay in Ireland £10.95

"Amid the myriad titles pedalled on the accommodation market, this eclectic series stands head and shoulders above the rest. Opinionated, lively and most important of all, totally independent"

The Bookseller

"Alastair Sawday's ideas about what makes a special place to stay are very similar to those of Country Living's... So it is with great pleasure that once again Country Living supports Special Places to Stay: British Bed & Breakfast... many are family-run enterprises and bring valuable income to country communities."

Susy Smith (Editor, Country Living magazine)

- **Discover** charming homes & hotels
- **Meet** owners who really ENJOY guests
- **Avoid** all things ugly, cold, functional & noisy
- **No** inflated prices - just terrific value for money

The Special Places series has:
- **Hand-picked** & inspected properties
- **Clear** symbols
- **Precise** directions & maps
- **Honest,** lively write-ups
- An **emphasis** on organic & home-grown food
- **Full** colour photos

Don't even <u>think</u> of exploring Britain and Ireland without these books!

To order a book - P&P free
Visit your local bookshop or order direct from the publisher *(credit cards accepted)* on: 01275 464891

Alastair Sawday Publishing
The Home Farm Barrow Gurney Bristol BS48 3RW Tel: +44 (0)1275 464891 Fax: +44 (0)1275 464887
e-mail: specialplaces@sawdays.co.uk web: www.sawdays.co.uk

The Landmark Trust

The Landmark Trust is a preservation charity which rescues and restores historic and architecturally important buildings at risk and lets them for holidays. There are 168 Landmarks where you can become, for a short time, the owner of such a building, including follies, forts, castles, gatehouses and towers. The Landmark Handbook illustrates every building with 184 pages of plans, location maps and black and white photographs. The price, including post and packing, is refundable against a booking.

Warden Abbey
Near Biggleswade, Bedfordshire

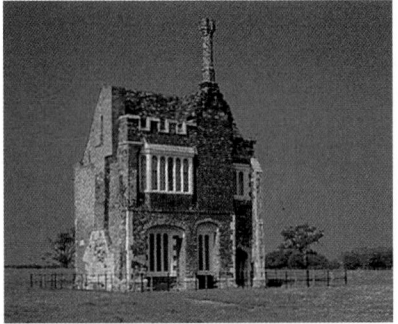

Landmarks are chosen for their historic interest or architectural importance, and also because many are in surroundings which give unexpected pleasure. Warden Abbey is a fragment of a great Cistercian Abbey and a Tudor House, set in fruitful countryside, once farmed by monks.

Lundy: Old Light
Lundy Island, Bristol Channel

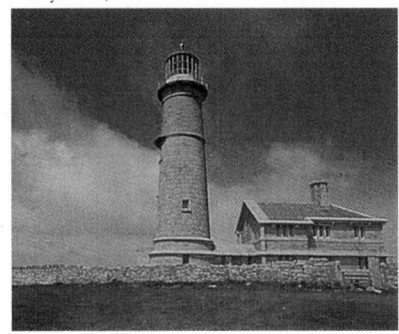

The beauty of the Landmark solution is not only that a building is saved and put to good use, but also that the restoration respects its original design. For a short time it is possible to live in surprising places. One of the light houses on Lundy Island, off the north coast of Devon, now provides unusual holiday accommodation.

Langley Gatehouse
Acton Burnell, Shropshire

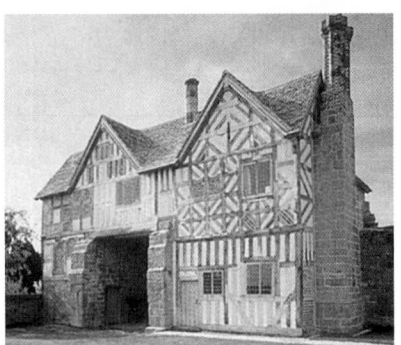

Landmarks often lie off the beaten track. Langley is no exception, set in a remote valley with a view to the Wrekin. In our restorations, we prefer to repair the old, and avoid renewal, to preserve the building's texture. When the building is timber framed, this can be like trying to patch a cobweb!

Saddell
Kintyre, Argyll

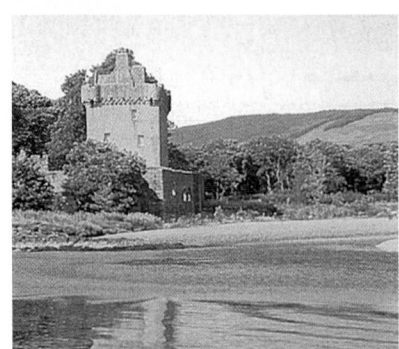

Some Landmarks, like this one, are connected with great families. Saddell Castle, a fine tower house with battlements, was in the hands of the Campbells for 400 years. Today the Castle cottages, and the long white strand of Saddell Bay are available for holidays.

Order Form
The Landmark Trust Handbook

The Handbook costs £9.50 including postage and packing when posted to an address in the UK, otherwise it costs £12.00 to Europe; £22.00 to the Americas*, Central Asia, Middle East and Africa; £26.00 to Australasia and Far East.
*Residents of USA and Canada can order a copy for US $25.00 from Landmark USA, 707 Kipling Road, Dummerston, Vermont 05301. Tel 802-254 6868.

Payment can be made by Mastercard/Visa/Switch/Delta, £sterling cheque drawn on a UK bank, or Eurocheque.

The cost of the Handbook is refundable against your first booking.

Once you have bought a Handbook, you will be put on our mailing list to receive up-to-date price and availability lists and bi-annual Newsletters.

Payment by credit or debit card can be made by telephoning our Booking Office on (01628) 825925 or by filling in this order form and sending it to:

The Landmark Trust, Shottesbrooke, Maidenhead, Berkshire SL6 3SW, England Charity number 243312

Telephone +44 (0) 1628 825925 Fax +44 (0) 1628 825417
www.landmarktrust.co.uk

Data Protection Act We promise that any information you give will be used for the purpose of the Landmark Trust only. We will write to you about our work and will occasionally include details of products developed by third parties in association with the Landmark Trust. Should you not wish to hear about such products please tick this box ☐

Credit card details   H
My Visa/Mastercard/Switch/Delta number is

Card expires   Switch issue No.

Please send me _____ copies @ _____ Total £ _____

Card holder's details:

Name _____

Address _____

_____ Postcode _____

Card holder's signature _____

Delivery details if different from above:

Name _____

Address _____

_____ Postcode _____

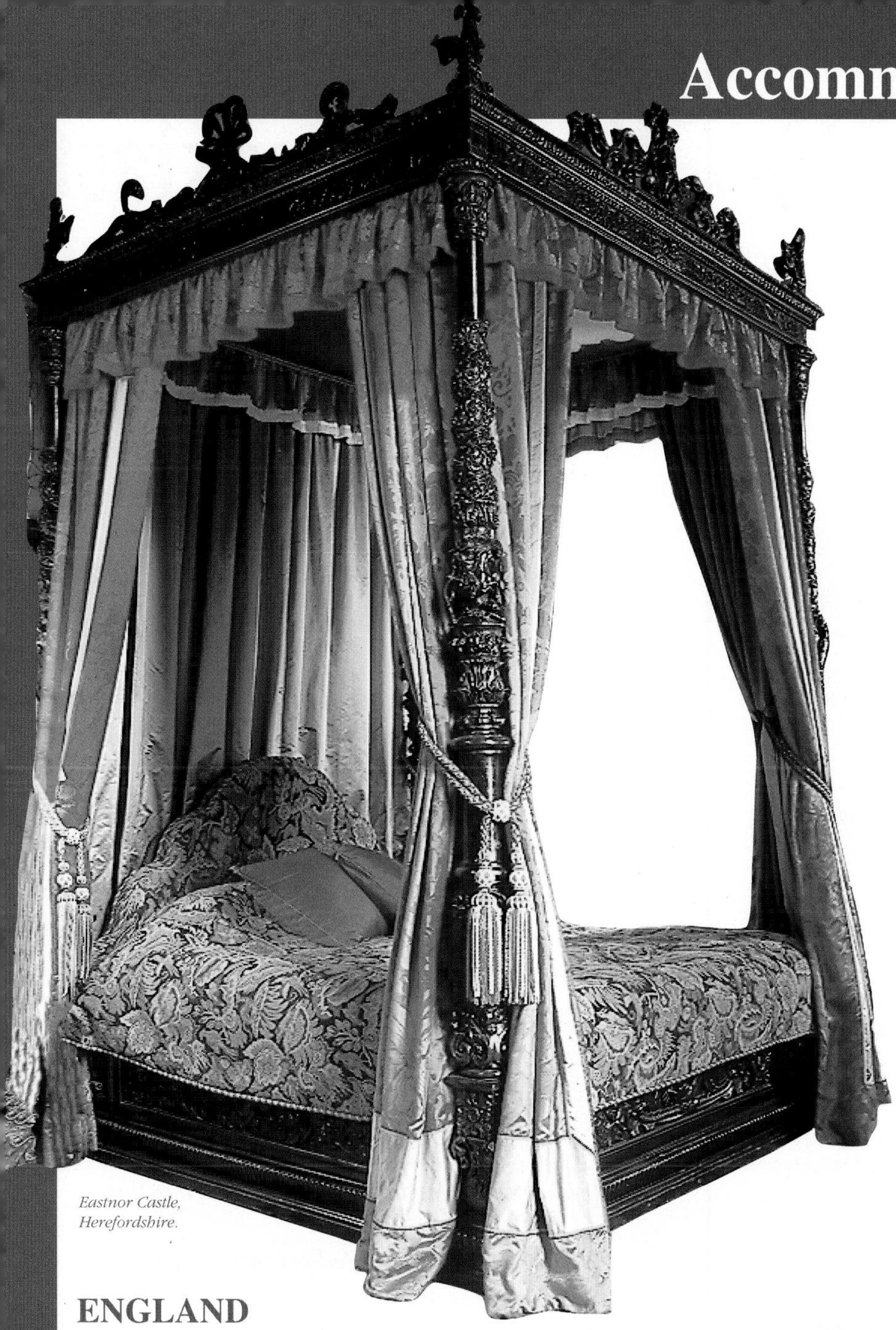

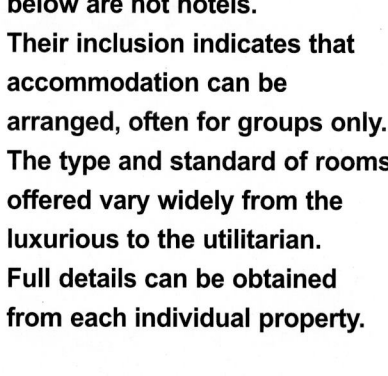
The historic properties listed below are not hotels. Their inclusion indicates that accommodation can be arranged, often for groups only. The type and standard of rooms offered vary widely from the luxurious to the utilitarian. Full details can be obtained from each individual property.

Eastnor Castle, Herefordshire.

This list is merely intended to draw attention to some properties which offer accommodation, it is only a guide.

HERITAGE VENUES

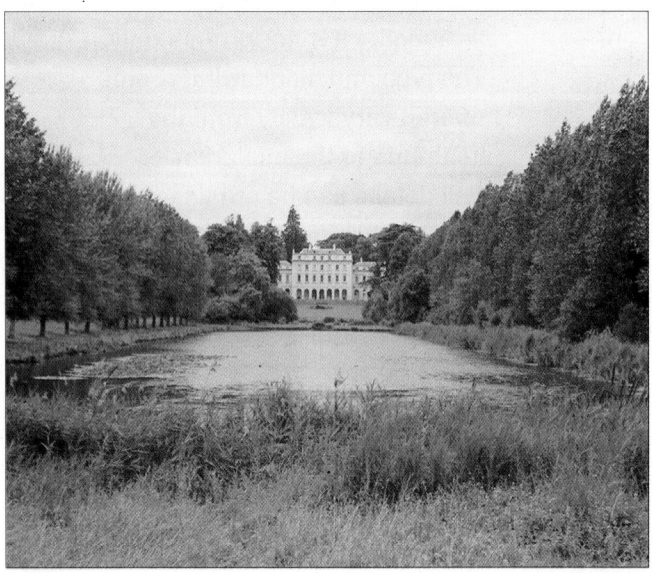

HERITAGE VENUES is the company that has access to some of the finest properties in the United Kingdom. All of them have intrinsic historical or architectural interest, most have beautiful gardens and parks but some have never been opened to the general public – they don't even appear in Hudson's!

For the finest properties Heritage Venues provides the most professional service, the best entertainment and delicious food and wine.

Heritage Venues is the sensible answer for the discerning corporate or private client who wants the top event or function, with the minimum of fuss in a unique setting.

Head Office
HERITAGE VENUES
Bagendon, Cirencester, Gloucestershire GL7 7DU
Tel/Fax: 01285 831417
e-mail: heritage.venues@virgin.net
www.heritagevenues.co.uk

Bed & Breakfast
for Garden Lovers

The original garden B&B guide founded in 1994

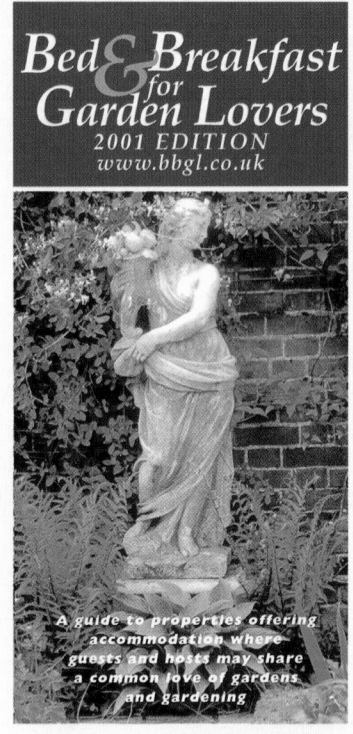

Quality accommodation in beautiful locations.

103 quietly situated private homes at various prices

Keen gardening hosts personally chosen for their kindness, courtesy and helpfulness and good local knowledge of horticultural matters

Useful tips to help plan garden visits

Excellent reputation for personal service built up over 7 years

TO OBTAIN BROCHURES:

From the UK: Send six loose first class stamps per copy required, with a 11 x 22cm sae

From abroad: Send four international reply-paid coupons per copy required, with a 11 x 22cm sae

To: BBGL/HD, Handywater Farm, Sibford Gower Banbury, Oxfordshire OX15 5AE

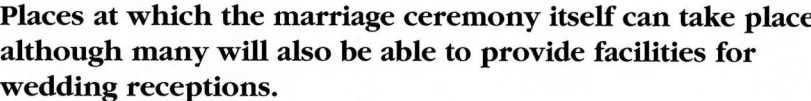

Places at which the marriage ceremony itself can take place although many will also be able to provide facilities for wedding receptions.

Full details about each property are available in the regional listings. There are numerous other properties included within Hudson's which do not have a Civil Wedding Licence but which can accommodate wedding receptions. The Marriage Act 1995, which has resulted in many more wedding venues in England, has not changed the situation in Scotland. In Scotland religious wedding ceremonies can take place anywhere subject to the Minister being prepared to perform them. Civil Weddings, however, are still confined to Registry Offices.

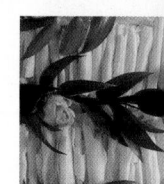

ENGLAND

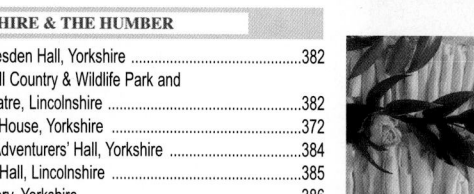
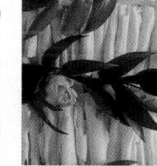
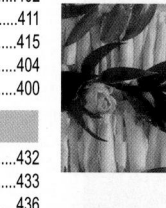
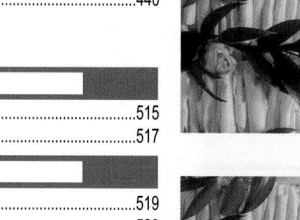
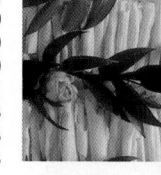
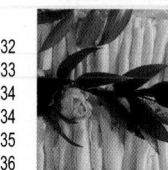
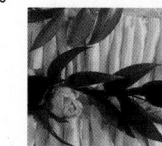

All Wedding Photographs
© Sarah Ward-Hendry
tel: 01295 811092 or 0385 901522
e-mail: ward-hendry@msn.com
website: www.ward-hendry.com

This list is merely intended to draw attention to properties which can host Civil Weddings, it is intended only as a guide.

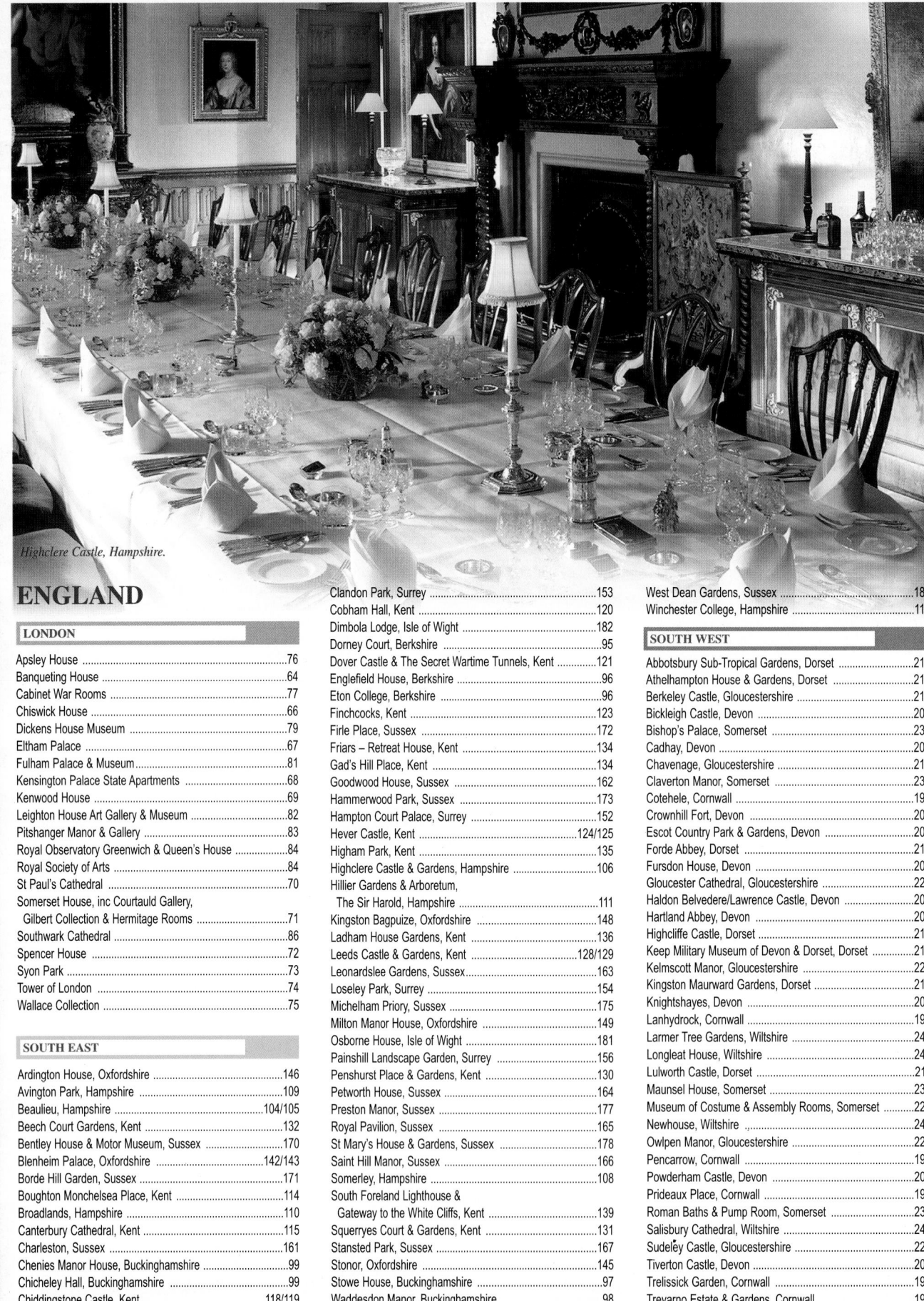

Highclere Castle, Hampshire.

ENGLAND

Properties which are able to accommodate corporate functions, wedding receptions and events.

Some properties specialise in corporate hospitality and are open only rarely, if ever, to day visitors. Others do both. See entry for details

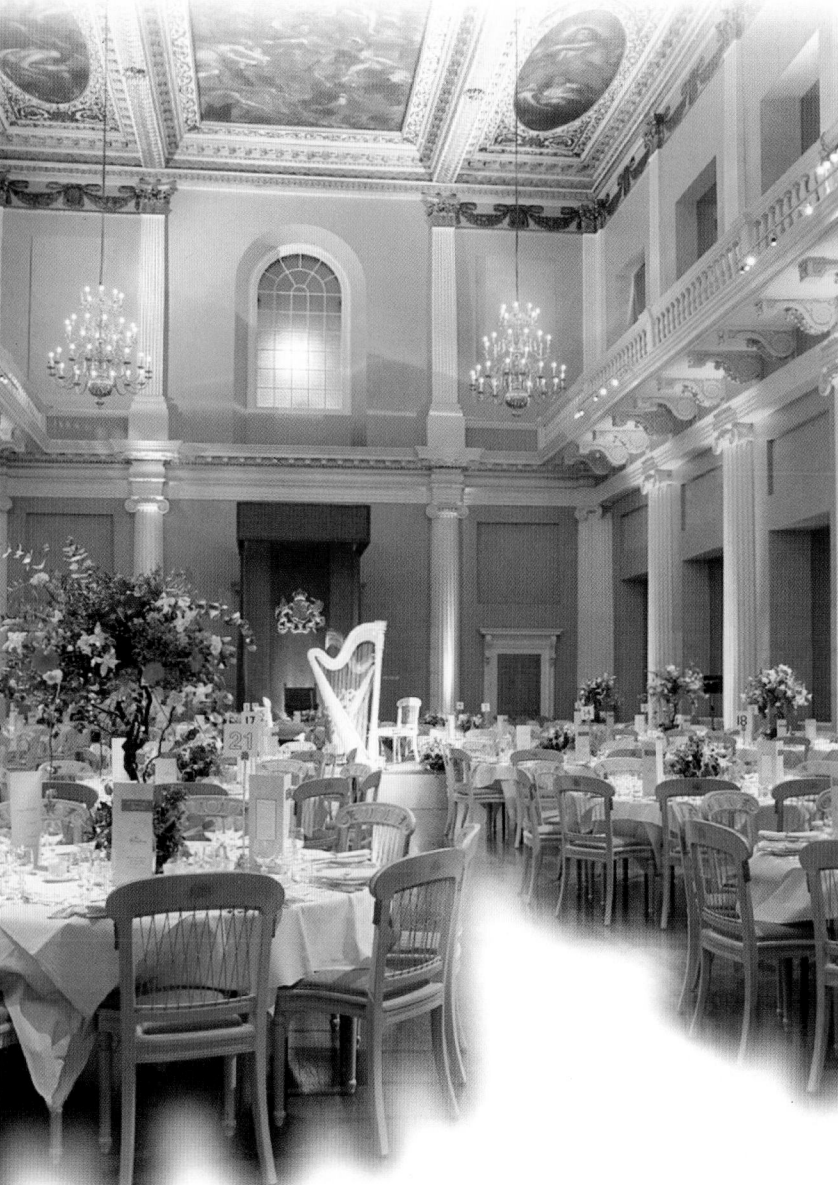

The Banqueting House, London.

This is not an exclusive list. It is intended to draw attention to some of these properties where functions or corporate hospitality is a major part of their business.

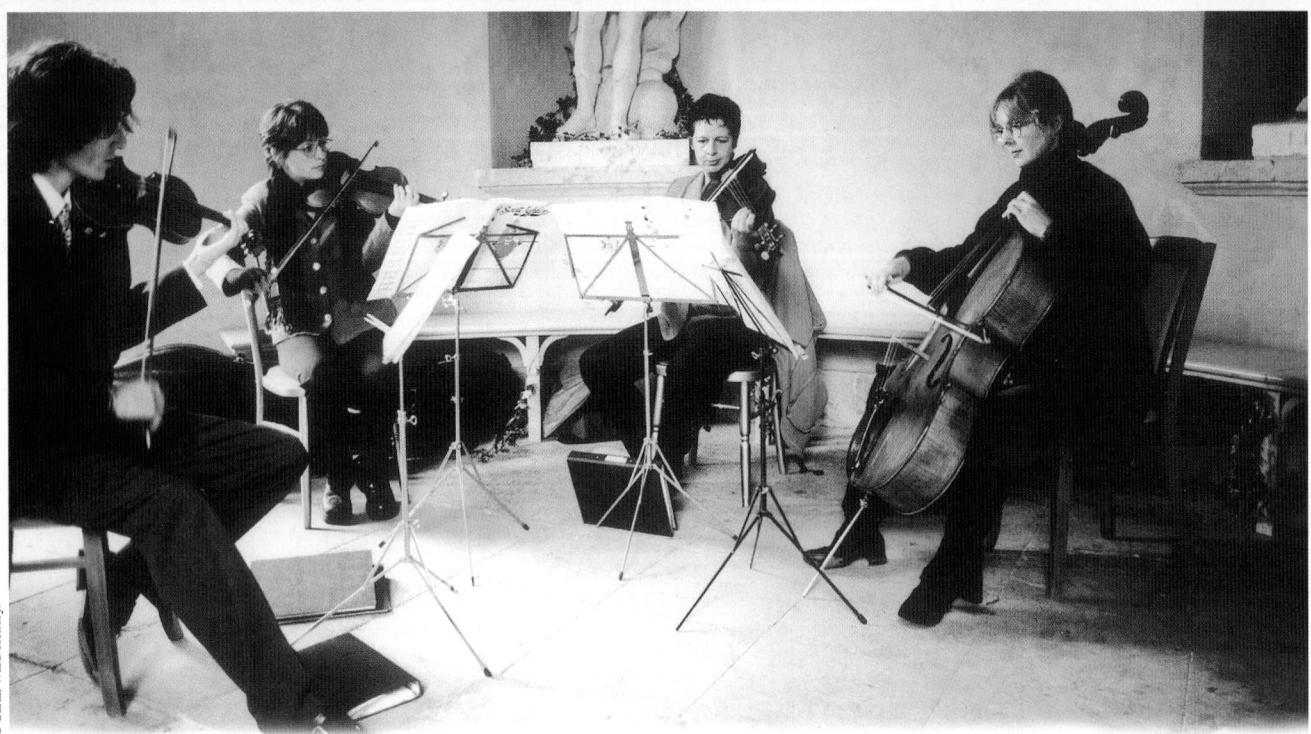

© Sarah Ward-Hendry.

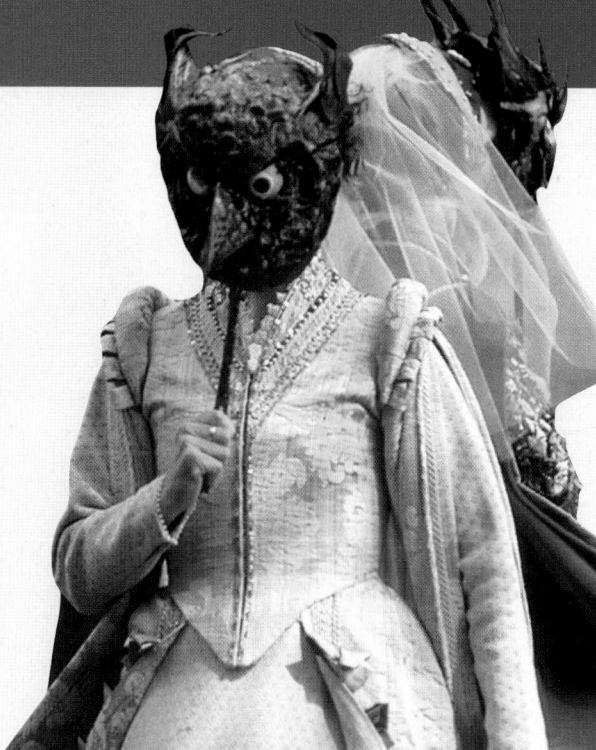

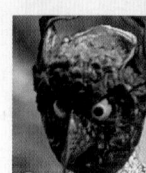
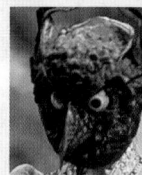
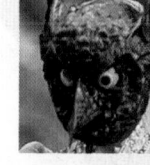
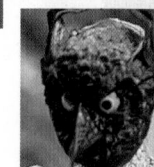
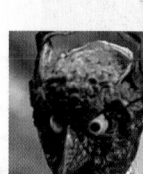
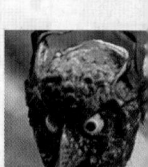
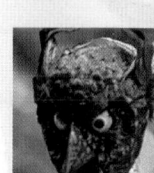
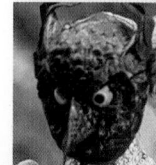

JANUARY

1
Leeds Castle, Kent
Treasure Trail.

1 – 6
Fairfax House, Yorkshire
Annual Exhibition on the 'Keeping of Christmas'.

1 – 31
Museum of Costume & Assembly Rooms, Somerset
'Fashion in the Fifties' traces the flowering of fashion talent in the glamorous decade following the War.

5
Harewood House, Yorkshire
Music at Harewood – Gallery Concert.

22 – 31
The Wallace Collection, London
"Thomas Sully and Queen Victoria" – marking the centenary of Queen Victoria's death, this exhibition will study Sully's portraits of the Queen and the objects associated with them.

FEBRUARY

1 – 28
Museum of Costume & Assembly Rooms, Somerset
'Fashion in the Fifties' traces the flowering of fashion talent in the glamorous decade following the War.

1 – 28
The Wallace Collection, London
"Thomas Sully and Queen Victoria" – marking the centenary of Queen Victoria's death, this exhibition will study Sully's portraits of the Queen and the objects associated with them.

3 – 4
Goodwood House, Sussex
Antiques Fair.

8 – 28
Abbot Hall Art Gallery, Cumbria
Andy Goldsworth – Photographic Works.

14
Baddesley Clinton, Warwickshire
Pruning Wall Climbers 'Wisteria', 10am.

19 – 23
Leeds Castle, Kent
Half Term Story-Telling.

23 – 25
Loseley Park, Surrey
Home Design Exhibition.

MARCH

1 – 18
Abbot Hall Art Gallery, Cumbria
Andy Goldsworth – Photographic Work.

1 – 31
Fairfax House, Yorkshire
Obsession – the collector and their collections.

1 – 31
Museum of Costume & Assembly Rooms, Somerset
'Fashion in the Fifties' traces the flowering of fashion talent in the glamorous decade following the War.

1 – 31
The Wallace Collection, London
"Thomas Sully and Queen Victoria" – marking the centenary of Queen Victoria's death, this exhibition will study Sully's portraits of the Queen and the objects associated with them.

2 – 4
Wilton House, Wiltshire
24th Annual Antiques Fair.

9 – 11
Hopetoun House, Edinburgh City, Coast & Countryside, Scotland
Antiques Fair.

10 – 11
Powderham Castle, Devon
Historic Devon Motor Rally.

12 – 18
Hever Castle, Kent
Spring Flower Week.

17 – 18
Ragley Hall, Warwickshire
Craft Fair.

22
Harewood House, Yorkshire
Music at Harewood – Gallery Concert.

23 – 25
Loseley Park, Surrey
Antique Fair.

25
Cobham Hall, Kent
National Garden Scheme.

25
Harewood House, Yorkshire
Mothers' Day.

26 – 29
Powderham Castle, Devon
Phillips Fine Art Sale.

27 – 31
Abbot Hall Art Gallery, Cumbria
Li Yuan-chia.

28
Holme Pierrepont Hall, Nottinghamshire
Old Photographs of Holme Pierrepont, coffee morning from 10 am - 1pm, fo raise funds for St Edmund's Church.

31
Leeds Castle, Kent
Gardeners' Weekend.

31
Nunnington Hall, Yorkshire
"Waltz of the Flowers" Art Exhibition by Angela McCall (normal opening times and prices apply).

APRIL

1
Leeds Castle, Kent
Gardeners' Weekend.

1 – 29
Nunnington Hall, Yorkshire
"Waltz of the Flowers" Art Exhibition by Angela McCall (normal opening times and prices apply).

1 – 29
The Wallace Collection, London
"Thomas Sully and Queen Victoria" – marking the centenary of Queen Victoria's death, this exhibition will study Sully's portraits of the Queen and the objects associated with them.

1 – 31
Abbot Hall Art Gallery, Cumbria
Li Yuan-chia.

1 – 30
Fairfax House, Yorkshire
Obsession – the collector and their collections.

1 – 30
Museum of Costume & Assembly Rooms, Somerset
'Fashion in the Fifties' traces the flowering of fashion talent in the glamorous decade following the War.

5 – 8
Ripley Castle, Yorkshire
Galloway Antiques Fair.

7 – 8
Capesthorne Hall, Cheshire
Rainbow Craft Fair.

7 – 12
Hopetoun House, Edinburgh City, Coast & Countryside, Scotland
Sotheby's Spring Sale.

8
Beaulieu, Hampshire
Boat Jumble.

10
Picton Castle, South Wales
RHS Lecture: Picton Castle Gardens in Early Spring.

13
Plas Newydd, North Wales
National Gardens Scheme Open Day.

13 – 16
Cobham Hall, Kent
Medway Craft Show.

13 – 16
Kentwell Hall, Suffolk
Re-creation: Easter.

13 – 16
Harewood House, Yorkshire
Easter Weekend.

13 – 16
Hever Castle, Kent
Easter Egg Trail and Brass Bands.

14 – 16
Leeds Castle, Kent
An Easter Celebration.

15
Plas Newydd, North Wales
Easter Eggstravaganza!

15
Lulworth Castle, Dorset
Easter Bunny Hunt.

15
Traquair, Borders, Scotland
Easter Egg Extravaganza.

15 – 16
Nunnington Hall, Yorkshire
Easter Egg Trail, 12.30-4.30pm (£1 per person, normal admission prices apply).

15 – 16
Rievaulx Terrace and Temples, Yorkshire
Easter Egg Trail, £1 per person (normal admission prices apply).

16
Ludlow Castle, Shropshire
Easter Egg Hunt.

20 – 22
Blair Castle, Perthshire, Scotland
Needlework & Lace Exhibition (contact: Lyndsey Dolliver on 01796 481207).

21 – 22
Goodwood House, Sussex
Home Design Interiors.

21 – 22
Shugborough, Staffordshire
Gamekeepers' Fair.

29
Wartnaby Gardens, Leicestershire
Plants for sale.

MAY

1 – 31
Abbot Hall Art Gallery, Cumbria
Li Yuan-chia.

1 – 31
Fairfax House, Yorkshire
Obsession – the collector and their collections.

1 – 31
Museum of Costume & Assembly Rooms, Somerset
'Fashion in the Fifties' traces the flowering of fashion talent in the glamorous decade following the War.

2 – 28
Nunnington Hall, Yorkshire
"Yorkshire Gems" Art Exhibition by G D Hemingway, a member of the British Watercolour Society (normal opening times and prices apply).

5 – 6
Kentwell Hall, Suffolk
Re-creation: May Day.

5 – 7
Hever Castle, Kent
May Day Music & Dance.

5 – 7
Leonardslee Gardens, Sussex
Bonsai Weekend.

6
Plas Newydd, North Wales
Spring Safari Family Fun Day.

6
Westbury Court Garden, Gloucestershire
Annual Plant Fair.

6 – 7
Catton Hall, Derbyshire
Classic Car Show.

6 – 7
Constable Burton Hall Gardens, Yorkshire
Tulip Festival.

6 – 7
Eastnor Castle, Herefordshire
Spring Country Crafts Fair.

8
Plas Newydd, North Wales
Walk with the Gardener, 2pm.

Special Events Index

9
Rievaulx Terrace and Temples, Yorkshire
History and Horticulture of Rievaulx Terrace –
explore this important 18th century landscape
garden, 2pm, £5 per person (normal admission
applies – booking essential 01439 798340).

10 – 13
Hatfield House & Gardens, Hertfordshire
Living Crafts.

12 – 13
Beaulieu, Hampshire
Spring Autojumble.

12 – 13
Chatsworth, Derbyshire
International Horse Trials.

12 – 13
Goodwood House, Sussex
Antiques Fair.

12 – 13
Leeds Castle, Kent
Festival of English Food & Wine.

12 – 13
Lulworth Castle, Dorset
Country Gardening & Food Fair.

12 – 31
Warwick Castle, Warwickshire
Mediaeval Festival.

13
Baddesley Clinton, Warwickshire
Wild Flower Identification Tour, 10am.

13
Hanbury Hall, Worcestershire
Annual Plant Fair.

13
Ludlow Castle, Shropshire
Vintage Vehicle Display.

13
Newby Hall & Gardens, Yorkshire
Spring Plant Fair.

13
Packwood House, Warwickshire
Annual Plant Fair.

13
Picton Castle, South Wales
National Gardens Scheme.

14
Plas Newydd, North Wales
Spring Plant Fair.

16
Rievaulx Terrace and Temples, Yorkshire
History and Horticulture of Rievaulx Terrace –
explore this important 18th century landscape
garden, 2pm, £5 per person (normal admission
applies – booking essential 01439 798340).

16
Westbury Court Garden, Gloucestershire
Meet the Gardener Evening Garden Tour.

17
Baddesley Clinton, Warwickshire
A Guided Tour of the Grounds, 10am.

19
Picton Castle, South Wales
Spring Plant Sale.

19
Ragley Hall, Warwickshire
Miniature Yacht Meet by the lake (free
admission for Season Ticket Holders).

19 – 20
Chatsworth, Derbyshire
Angling Fair.

19 – 20
Kentwell Hall, Suffolk
Re-creation: Land Girls.

19 – 20
Parham House & Gardens, Sussex
Needlework Event.

20
Harewood House, Yorkshire
Teddy Bears Picnic (inc National Kidney
Research Fund Sponsored Walk).

20
Wartnaby Gardens, Leicestershire
Plants for sale.

21 - 25
Chelsea Physic Garden, London
Chelsea Show Week, 12 noon - 5 pm with lunches.

24 – 28
Charleston, Sussex
Charleston Festival.

26
Blair Castle, Perthshire, Scotland
Atholl Highlanders' Parade (contact: Geoff Crerar
on 01796 481207).

26
Nunnington Hall, Yorkshire
"Create your own Wild Flower Garden" Workshop,
1.30-5pm, £20 including a Cream Tea (booking
essential).

26 – 27
Traquair, Borders, Scotland
Scottish Beer Festival.

26 – 28
Harewood House, Yorkshire
Live Crafts – May Bank Holiday Weekend.

26 – 28
Hever Castle, Kent
Merrie England Weekend.

26 – 28
Kentwell Hall, Suffolk
Re-creation: Whitsun.

26 – 28
Ludlow Castle, Shropshire
Festival of Crafts.

26 – 31
Leeds Castle, Kent
Amazing Mazes Week.

26 – 28
Shugborough, Staffordshire
Spring Craft Fair.

26 – 28
Skipton Castle, Yorkshire
Red Wyvern Society re-enactment of life in Skipton
Castle in the 15th century.

27
Blair Castle, Perthshire, Scotland
Atholl Gathering & Highland Games (contact: Mr J
Milliganr on 01796 481355).

27
Nunnington Hall, Yorkshire
Ryedale Centre Spring Fair, 12.30-5pm, £2
including NT Members (normal admission for
house – proceeds for conservation work).

27
Plas Newydd, North Wales
Dragon Day Treasure Trail Family Fun Day.

27
Powderham Castle, Devon
The Great Farm Shop Open Day.

27 – 28
Finchcocks, Kent
Spring Garden Fair & Flower Festival.

28
Eastnor Castle, Herefordshire
Steam Fair & Country Show with Fred Dibnah.

28
Mottisfont Abbey Garden, Hampshire
Spring Holiday Plant Fayre, 12 noon-6pm.

29
Picton Castle, South Wales
RHS Lecture: Rare Conifers at Picton Castle.

30
Nunnington Hall, Yorkshire
"Light and Shade" Art Exhibition by Jim Wright
(normal opening times and prices apply).

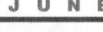

JUNE

1 – 2
Hopetoun House, Edinburgh City, Coast &
Countryside, Scotland
Hopetoun Carriage Driving Event.

1 – 3
Abbot Hall Art Gallery, Cumbria
Li Yuan-chia.

1 – 3
Holker Hall & Gardens, Cumbria
Holker Garden Festival.

1 – 3
Leeds Castle, Kent
Amazing Mazes Week.

1 – 3
Longleat, Wiltshire
Longleat Horse Trials.

1 – 3
Loseley Park, Surrey
Craft Fair.

1 – 30
Museum of Costume & Assembly Rooms,
Somerset
'Fashion in the Fifties' traces the flowering of
fashion talent in the glamorous decade
following the War.

1 – 30
Nunnington Hall, Yorkshire
"Light and Shade" Art Exhibition by Jim Wright
(normal opening times and prices apply).

1 – 31
Warwick Castle, Warwickshire
Mediaeval Festival.

2 – 3
Cawdor Castle, Highlands & Skye, Scotland
Special Gardens Weekend: guided tours of
gardens and Cawdor Big Wood.

3
Hopetoun House, Edinburgh City, Coast &
Countryside, Scotland
Dolls House & Miniatures Fair.

3
Sutton Park, Yorkshire
Specialist Plant Fair.

6
Plas Newydd, North Wales
Antiques Valuation Day with Sotheby's, 10am-3pm.

7 – 10
Bramham Park, Yorkshire
Bramham International Horse Trials & Yorkshire
Country Fair.

7 – 10
Ripley Castle, Yorkshire
Grand Summer Sale.

8 – 10
Newby Hall & Gardens, Yorkshire
Rainbow Craft Fair.

10
Burton Constable Hall, Yorkshire
Burton Constable Country Fair.

10
Harewood House, Yorkshire
Porsche Club – Yorkshire Region Annual
Concours.

10
Nunnington Hall, Yorkshire
Open Air Concert by local choral group
"Voicebox", 2pm (normal opening times and
prices apply).

12
Plas Newydd, North Wales
Walk with the Gardener, 2pm.

12 – 30
Abbot Hall Art Gallery, Cumbria
Paula Rego.

13
Hanbury Hall, Worcestershire
Concert.

13
Westbury Court Garden, Gloucestershire
Meet the Gardener Evening Garden Tour.

16
Nunnington Hall, Yorkshire
Oddsocks – Shakespeare, outdoor concert –
bring a picnic, £12.50, 7pm (tickets available
from Nunnington Hall 01439 748283 or
Fountains Abbey booking office 01765
609999).

16
Gilbert White's House & The Oates Museum,
Hampshire
Picnic to 'Jazz in June'.

16 – 17
Parham House & Gardens, Sussex
Steam Rally in Park.

16 - 17
Gilbert White's House & The Oates Museum,
Hampshire
Unusual Plants Fair.

17
Harewood House, Yorkshire
Vintage & Classic Car Rally.

17
Plas Newydd, North Wales
Fathers' Day Frolics.

17 – 30
Kentwell Hall, Suffolk
The Great Annual Re-creation (Sats & Suns only,
11am-5pm).

19
Picton Castle, South Wales
RHS Regional Lecture: Borders and Beyond
(Lecturer: Stephen Lacey).

21
Baddesley Clinton, Warwickshire
Evening Garden Tour, 6pm.

22 – 28
Hever Castle, Kent
Rose Week.

23 - 24
Arley Hall, Cheshire
Arley Garden Festival.

23 – 24
Hatfield House & Gardens, Hertfordshire
Festival of Gardening.

23 – 24
Leonardslee Gardens, Sussex
West Sussex Country Craft Fair.

23 – 30
Ludlow Castle, Shropshire
Ludlow Festival.

24
Longleat, Wiltshire
Radio Rally & Computer Fair.

24
Nunnington Hall, Yorkshire
Specialist Plant Fair, 11am-5pm (normal
admission).

24
Saint Hill Manor, Sussex
Open air production of Sheridan's "School for
Scandal" by "Rain or Shine Theatre", 4pm.

24
Wartnaby Gardens, Leicestershire
Plant Fair with 20 Nurserymen. Sketching Club
Exhibition.

☙ 25 – 28
Powderham Castle, Devon
Phillips Fine Art Sale.

☙ 27
Packwood House, Warwickshire
Evening Garden Tour, 7pm.

☙ 29 – 30
Powderham Castle, Devon
British Touring Shakespeare (open air).

☙ 30
Leeds Castle, Kent
Open Air Concert.

☙ 30
Shugborough, Staffordshire
Gardeners' Weekend.

J U L Y

☙ 1
Eastnor Castle, Herefordshire
Wood Festival.

☙ 1
Nunnington Hall, Yorkshire
"Light and Shade" Art Exhibition by Jim Wright
(normal opening times and prices apply).

☙ 1
Powderham Castle, Devon
British Touring Shakespeare (open air).

☙ 1
Ragley Hall, Warwickshire
Caspian Horse Society (free admission for
Season Ticket Holders).

☙ 1
Shugborough, Staffordshire
Gardeners' Weekend.

☙ 1 – 8
Kentwell Hall, Suffolk
The Great Annual Re-creation (Sats & Suns
only, and Fri 6 July, 11am-5pm).

☙ 1 – 8
Ludlow Castle, Shropshire
Ludlow Festival.

☙ 1 – 31
Abbot Hall Art Gallery, Cumbria
Paula Rego.

☙ 1 – 31
Museum of Costume & Assembly Rooms,
Somerset
'Fashion in the Fifties' traces the flowering of
fashion talent in the glamorous decade
following the War.

☙ 1 – 31
Warwick Castle, Warwickshire
Mediaeval Festival.

☙ 3
Plas Newydd, North Wales
Traditional Pole-lathe Turning, 11am-3pm.

☙ 3 – 29
Nunnington Hall, Yorkshire
"Nature on a Plate" Art Exhibition by Catherine
Bell (normal opening times and prices apply).

☙ 4
Leeds Castle, Kent
Children's Promenade Concert.

☙ 5
Blair Castle, Perthshire, Scotland
Charity Day in Aid of McMillan Cancer
Research (contact: Lyndsey Dolliver on 01796
481207).

☙ 6
Leighton Hall, Lancashire
Concert & Fireworks: 'Last Night of the Proms'.

☙ 6 – 8
Goodwood, Sussex
Goodwood Festival of Speed.

☙ 6 – 31
Blackwell – The Artistic House, Cumbria
Magdalene Odundo – Ceramic Vessels.

☙ 7
Nunnington Hall, Yorkshire
"Get Fruity with the Gardener" Workshop – how
to look after your fruit trees, 1.30-5pm, £20
including a Cream Tea (booking essential).

☙ 7
Leeds Castle, Kent
Open Air Concert.

☙ 7
Ragley Hall, Warwickshire
"Battle Proms Concert" outdoor concert.

☙ 7 – 8
Powderham Castle, Devon
Historic Vehicle Gathering.

☙ 7 – 8
Scone Palace, Perthshire/Fife, Scotland
Game Conservancy Scottish Fair.

☙ 8
Harewood House, Yorkshire
Jaguar Rally.

☙ 8
Plas Newydd, North Wales
Guided Archaeological Walk, 2pm.

☙ 8
Rievaulx Terrace and Temples, Yorkshire
Open Air Concert by local choral group
'Voicebox', 2-4pm (normal opening times and
prices apply).

☙ 10
Harewood House, Yorkshire
York Early Music Festival Concert.

☙ 10
Picton Castle, South Wales
RHS Lecture: Propagating Shrubs.

☙ 10
Plas Newydd, North Wales
An Evening Walk with the Gardener, 7pm.

☙ 12
Westbury Court Garden, Gloucestershire
Meet the Gardener Evening Garden Tour.

☙ 12 – 15
Ripley Castle, Yorkshire
Galloway Antiques Fair.

☙ 14
Nunnington Hall, Yorkshire
"Northanger Abbey" – outdoor concert – North
Country Theatre, £12.50, 7pm – bring a picnic.

☙ 14
Wilton House, Wiltshire
Classical Firework Proms Night.

☙ 14 – 15
Eastnor Castle, Herefordshire
Medieval Jousting & Hot Air Balloon Festival.

☙ 14 – 15
Leonardslee Gardens, Sussex
Model Boat Regatta.

☙ 14 – 15
Parham House & Gardens, Sussex
Garden Weekend.

☙ 15
Cobham Hall, Kent
National Garden Scheme.

☙ 15
Newby Hall & Gardens, Yorkshire
Historic Vehicle Rally.

☙ 15 - 31
Chelsea Physic Garden, London
Summer Exhibition: "Myth and Magic".

☙ 16 – 22
Blair Castle, Perthshire, Scotland
Contemporary Textile Art Exhibition by Northern
Fringes (tel: Lyndsey Dolliver on 01796 481207).

☙ 17
Plas Newydd, North Wales
Teddy Bear Family Fun Day.

☙ 19 – 22
Leeds Castle, Kent
A Festival of Summer Floral Art.

☙ 20 – 22
Loseley Park, Surrey
Garden Show.

☙ 21
Hever Castle, Kent
Jousting Tournament performed by 'The
Knights of Royal England'.

☙ 21
Longleat, Wiltshire
Longleat Balloon Festival & Nightfire.

☙ 21
Ragley Hall, Warwickshire
Outdoor Concert.

☙ 21 – 22
Dalemain, Cumbria
Dalemain Rainbow Craft Fair.

☙ 21 – 22
Holkham Hall, Norfolk
Holkham Country Fair.

☙ 22
Chenies Manor House, Hertfordshire
Plant and Garden Fair.

☙ 22
Hever Castle, Kent
Medieval Archery demonstrated by the
'Company of 1415'.

☙ 22
Leighton Hall, Lancashire
Classic Car Rally.

☙ 22
Longleat, Wiltshire
Longleat Balloon Festival.

☙ 22
Picton Castle, South Wales
National Gardens Scheme.

☙ 22
Plas Newydd, North Wales
Military Re-enactment – Napoleonic Alliance.

☙ 22
Westbury Court Garden, Gloucestershire
Pillowell Silver Band.

☙ 24
Plas Newydd, North Wales
All the Fun of the Annual Summer Fair!

☙ 26
Packwood House, Warwickshire
Evening Garden Tour, 7pm.

☙ 27
Rievaulx Terrace and Temples, Yorkshire
Bat Walk, 8.30pm, £2 per adult, £1 per child
including NT Members (booking essential).

☙ 28
Hever Castle, Kent
Jousting Tournament performed by 'The Knights
of Royal England'.

☙ 28
Ragley Hall, Warwickshire
Newfoundland Dog Trails (free admission for
Season Ticket Holders).

☙ 28 – 29
Lulworth Castle, Dorset
Lulworth Horse Trials & Country Fair.

☙ 28 – 30
Harewood House, Yorkshire
Leeds Championship Dog Show.

☙ 29
Hever Castle, Kent
Medieval Archery demonstrated by the
'Company of 1415'.

☙ 29
Plas Newydd, North Wales
Seaside Family Fun Day.

☙ 31
Goodwood House, Sussex
Race Week.

☙ 31
Nunnington Hall, Yorkshire
Art Exhibition by Stephanie Holmes (normal
opening times and prices will apply).

A U G U S T

☙ 1 – 4
Goodwood House, Sussex
Race Week.

☙ 1 – 8
Rievaulx Terrace and Temples, Yorkshire
History and Horticulture of Rievaulx Terrace –
explore this important 18th century landscape
garden, 2pm, £5 per person (normal admission
applies – booking essential 01439 798340).

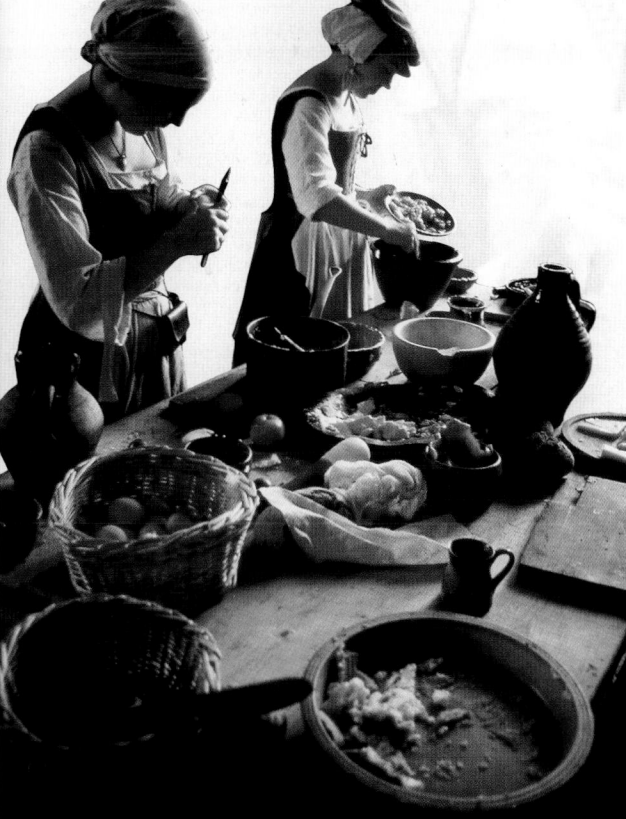

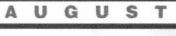

This list is merely intended to draw attention to properties who host Special Events, it is advisable to contact the property to confirm dates and times.

35

Special Events Index

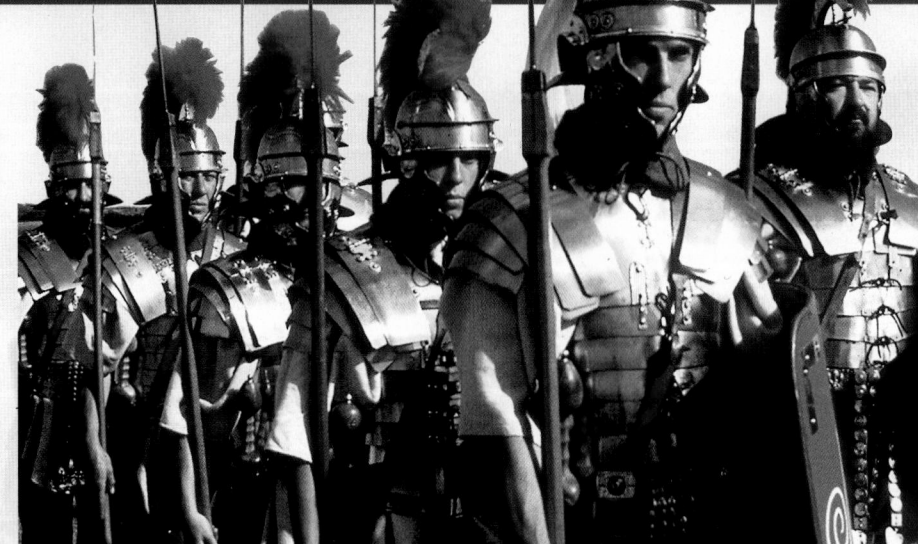

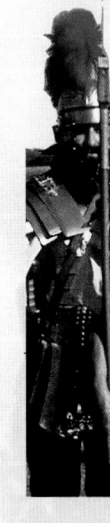

1 – 31
Abbot Hall Art Gallery, Cumbria
Paula Rego.

1 – 31
Blackwell – The Artistic House, Cumbria
Magdalene Odundo – Ceramic Vessels.

1 – 31
Chelsea Physic Garden, London
Summer Exhibition: "Myth and Magic".

1 – 31
Museum of Costume & Assembly Rooms,
Somerset
'Fashion in the Fifties' traces the flowering of
fashion talent in the glamorous decade following
the War.

1 – 31
Nunnington Hall, Yorkshire
Art Exhibition by Stephanie Holmes (normal
opening times and prices apply).

1 – 31
Warwick Castle, Warwickshire
Mediaeval Festival.

3
Nunnington Hall, Yorkshire
Bat Walk, 8.30pm, £2 per adult, £1 per child,
including NT Members (booking essential).

3
Powderham Castle, Devon
Bournemouth Symphony Orchester 'Last Night
of the Powederham Proms'.

3 – 4
Leighton Hall, Lancashire
Shakespeare in the Garden: 'Henry V'.

3 – 4
Scone Palace, Perthshire/Fife, Scotland
Perth Agricultural Show.

3 – 5
Hatfield House & Gardens, Hertfordshire
Art in Clay – Pottery & Ceramics Festival.

4
Powderham Castle, Devon
Open Air Rock Concert.

4
Ragley Hall, Warwickshire
"Fireworks & Laser Symphony"
outdoor concert.

4 – 5
Hever Castle, Kent
Jousting Tournament performed by 'The Knights
of Royal England'.

4 – 5
Kentwell Hall, Suffolk
Re-creation: World War II.

4 – 5
Traquair, Borders, Scotland
Traquair Fair.

5
Drummond Castle Gardens, Perthshire/Fife,
Scotland
Open Day – entertainments, teas, raffle.

5
Harewood House, Yorkshire
BMW Car Club 20th Annual Concours of the North.

5
Plas Newydd, North Wales
Clown Around with James the Juggler.

5
Shugborough, Staffordshire
Victorian Street Market.

8
Plas Newydd, North Wales
Evening Walk with the Gardener, 7pm.

11
Plas Newydd, North Wales
Worked Tapestry Pieces, 12 noon.

11 – 12
Hever Castle, Kent
Jousting Tournament performed by 'The Knights
of Royal England'.

12
Harewood House, Yorkshire
Rolls Royce Rally 21st Anniversary at
Harewood.

12
Loseley Park, Surrey
Outdoor Concert.

12
Plas Newydd, North Wales
Guided Archaeological Walk, 2pm.

13 – 17
Eastnor Castle, Herefordshire
Children's Fun Week.

16
Westbury Court Garden, Gloucestershire
Meet the Gardener Evening Garden Tour.

17 – 19
Parham House & Gardens, Sussex
Live Crafts in Park.

18
Chartwell, Kent
Opera Brava – an evening of Gilbert & Sullivan.

18
Nunnington Hall, Yorkshire
"The Art of Propagation" Workshop, 1.30-5pm,
£20 including a Cream Tea
(booking essential).

18
Plas Newydd, North Wales
Open Air Jazz Concert with Firework Finale, 7pm.

18 – 19
Bosworth Battlefield, Leicestershire & Rutland
Medieval Spectacular.

18 – 19
Hever Castle, Kent
Jousting Tournament performed by 'The Knights
of Royal England'.

18 – 19
Ragley Hall, Warwickshire
Warwickshire & West Midlands Game Fair
(Season Tickets do not apply this weekend).

18 – 19
Skipton Castle, Yorkshire
Feudal Archers: demonstration of arms, armour
and domestic life (1135 – 1216).

19
Chartwell, Kent
Opera Brava – "Tosca".

19
Harewood House, Yorkshire
Harewood Show.

19
Plas Newydd, North Wales
'Fleece to Garment.'

23
Baddesley Clinton, Warwickshire
A Guided Tour of the Grounds, 10am.

23 – 26
Blair Castle, Perthshire, Scotland
Bowmore Blair Castle International Horse Trials
& Country Fair (contact: The Horse Trials Office
on 01796 481543).

24 – 27
Kentwell Hall, Suffolk
Re-creation: High Summer.

24 – 27
Newby Hall & Gardens, Yorkshire
Rainbow Craft Fair.

25
Hever Castle, Kent
Jousting Tournament performed by 'The
Knights of Royal England'.

25
Rievaulx Terrace and Temples, Yorkshire
Peacocks & Dragons Workshop, starts at 12
noon, Art and Craft, £2 per person (normal
opening times and prices apply).

25 – 26
Plas Newydd, North Wales
Knights of Longshanks Combat Displays.

25 – 27
Harewood House, Yorkshire
Harewood Steam Rally.

25 – 27
Shugborough, Staffordshire
Summer Craft Fair.

26
Floors Castle, Borders, Scotland
Family Day with Massed Pipe Bands.

26 – 27
Eastnor Castle, Herefordshire
Berkeley Household: Living History in the 15th
century.

26 – 27
Finchcocks, Kent
Jane Austen Gala.

26 – 27
Hever Castle, Kent
Medieval Archery demonstrated by the
'Company of 1415'

28
Picton Castle, South Wales
RHS Lecture: Herbaceous Plants at Picton
Castle.

31
Ragley Hall, Warwickshire
"Last Night of the Ragley Proms" outdoor
concert.

30
Rievaulx Terrace and Temples, Yorkshire
Tribal Rhythms Workshop, starts at 12 noon,
Music and Dance, £2 per person (normal
opening times and prices apply).

SEPTEMBER

1
Hever Castle, Kent
Jousting Tournament performed by 'The
Knights of Royal England'.

1 – 2
Catton Hall, Derbyshire
National Carriage Driving Trials.

1 – 2
Chatsworth, Derbyshire
Country Fair.

1 – 2
Nunnington Hall, Yorkshire
Art Exhibition by Stephanie Holmes (normal
opening times and prices apply).

1 – 2
Parham House & Gardens, Sussex
Autumn Flowers at Parham House.

1 – 9
Chelsea Physic Garden, London
Summer Exhibition: "Myth and Magic".

1 – 9
Warwick Castle, Warwickshire
Mediaeval Festival.

1 – 23
Blackwell – The Artistic House, Cumbria
Magdalene Odundo – Ceramic Vessels.

1 – 30
Abbot Hall Art Gallery, Cumbria
Paula Rego.

1 – 30
Fairfax House, Yorkshire
Cutting Edge – the evolution of cutlery and
place settings.

1 – 30
Museum of Costume & Assembly Rooms,
Somerset
'Fashion in the Fifties' traces the flowering of
fashion talent in the glamorous decade
following the War.

2
Hever Castle, Kent
Medieval Archery demonstrated by the
'Company of 1415'

2
Plas Newydd, North Wales
Guided Fungus Foray Family Fun Day.

5 – 30
Nunnington Hall, Yorkshire
"Flower Power" Art Exhibition by Jeam Tilley
(normal opening times and prices apply).

7 – 9
Hatfield House & Gardens, Hertfordshire
Country Homes & Gardens Show.

7 – 9
Longleat, Wiltshire
Dog Agility Stakes.

7 – 9
Ludlow Castle, Shropshire
Food & Drink Fair.

8
Picton Castle, South Wales
Autumn Plant Sale.

▩ 8 – 9
Beaulieu, Hampshire
Autojumble.

▩ 8 – 9
Leeds Castle, Kent
Balloon & Vintage Car Weekend.

▩ 8 – 9
Leighton Hall, Lancashire
Rainbow Craft Fair.

▩ 8 – 9
Parham House & Gardens, Sussex
Country Show in Park.

▩ 8 – 9
Ragley Hall, Warwickshire
Garden Fair (Season Tickets holder free on
Saturday only).

▩ 9
Plas Newydd, North Wales
Guided Archaeological Walk, 2pm.

▩ 9
Shugborough, Staffordshire
Heavy Horse & Harvest.

▩ 11
Plas Newydd, North Wales
Walk with the Gardener, 2pm.

▩ 14 – 16
Goodwood House, Sussex
Motor Circuit Event.

▩ 14 – 16
Hever Castle, Kent
Patchwork & Quilting Exhibition.

▩ 14 – 16
Lulworth Castle, Dorset
International Floral Design Show & Competition.

▩ 15 - 16
Capesthorne Hall, Cheshire
Rainbow Craft Fair.

▩ 22 – 23
Kentwell Hall, Suffolk
Re-creation: Michaelmas.

▩ 22 – 23
Longleat, Wiltshire
Tipadel Hill Climb.

OCTOBER

▩ 1 – 7
Abbot Hall Art Gallery, Cumbria
Paula Rego.

▩ 1 – 31
Fairfax House, Yorkshire
Cutting Edge – the evolution of cutlery and
place settings.

▩ 1 – 31
Museum of Costume & Assembly Rooms,
Somerset
'Fashion in the Fifties' traces the flowering of
fashion talent in the glamorous decade
following the War.

▩ 3 – 31
Nunnington Hall, Yorkshire
"Aspects of Ryedale and the North York Moors"
Art Exhibition by Heather Watson (normal
opening times and prices apply).

▩ 4 – 31
Blackwell – The Artistic House, Cumbria
Kokten Korgei – Contemporary Crafts from
Japan.

▩ 6 – 7
Eastnor Castle, Herefordshire
Festival of Fine Food and Drink.

▩ 8 – 14
Hever Castle, Kent
Autumn Colour Week.

▩ 9
Plas Newydd, North Wales
Walk with the Gardener, 2pm.

▩ 10 – 14
Leeds Castle, Kent
Autumn Gold – A Celebration of Flowers &
Produce.

▩ 12 – 14
Finchcocks, Kent
Autumn Fair.

▩ 12 – 14
Hopetoun House, Edinburgh City, Coast &
Countryside, Scotland
Antiques Fair.

▩ 13
Leighton Hall,
Lancashire
Teddy Bear Fair.

▩ 13 – 14
Ragley Hall,
Warwickshire
Craft Fair.

▩ 13 – 14
**(Stop Press: this
event will now take
place on
27 – 28 Oct)**
Kentwell Hall, Suffolk
Re-creation:
World War II.

▩ 14
Leighton Hall,
Lancashire
Dolls House &
Miniaturist Fair.

▩ 16 – 31
Abbot Hall Art
Gallery, Cumbria
Hughie O'Donoghue
– Carborundum
Prints: Process
and Content.

▩ 17 – 21
Nunnington Hall,
Yorkshire
Apple Week –
display of apples
and appletising
recipes in the Tea
Room (normal
opening times and
prices apply).

▩ 19 – 21
Loseley Park, Surrey
Antique Fair.

▩ 20 – 21
Cobham Hall, Kent
Medway Craft Fair.

▩ 20 – 28
Rievaulx Terrace and Temples, Yorkshire
Sammy Squirrel's Survival Trail, £1 per Trail
(normal admission applies). Forage in the wood
for acorns to help you make it through the winter.

▩ 21
Plas Newydd, North Wales
Marvellous Shows of Magic.

▩ 21
Westbury Court Garden, Gloucestershire
Apple Day.

▩ 22 – 25
Powderham Castle, Devon
Phillips Fine Art Sale.

▩ 22 – 26
Leeds Castle, Kent
Half Term Halloween Event.

▩ 23
Plas Newydd, North Wales
Clowns & Kites Workshop.

▩ 27
Blair Castle, Perthshire, Scotland
Glenfiddich Piping Championships (contact:
Mrs L Maxwell on 01698 843843).

▩ 27 – 28
Kentwell Hall, Suffolk
Re-creation: World War II.

▩ 27 – 28
Stowe House, Buckinghamshire
Craft Fair.

▩ 28
Blair Castle, Perthshire, Scotland
Glenfiddich Fiddling Championships (contact:
Mrs L Maxwell on 01698 843843).

▩ 28
Plas Newydd, North Wales
Tricks & Treats.

▩ 30 – 31
Holme Pierrepont Hall, Nottinghamshire
Needlework: Ancient & Modern, open from 2 -
5.30pm, to raise funds for St Edmund's Church.

NOVEMBER

▩ 1
Holme Pierrepont Hall, Nottinghamshire
Needlework: Ancient & Modern, open from 2 -
5.30pm, to raise funds for St Edmund's Church.

▩ 1 – 4
Museum of Costume & Assembly Rooms,
Somerset
'Fashion in the Fifties' traces the flowering of
fashion talent in the glamorous decade
following the War.

▩ 1 – 4
Nunnington Hall, Yorkshire
"Aspects of Ryedale and the North York Moors"
Art Exhibition by Heather Watson (normal
opening times and prices apply)

▩ 1 – 20
Fairfax House, Yorkshire
Cutting Edge – the evolution of cutlery and
place settings.

▩ 1 – 30
Abbot Hall Art Gallery, Cumbria
Hughie O'Donoghue – Carborundum Prints:
Process and Content.

▩ 1 – 30
Blackwell – The Artistic House, Cumbria
Kokten Korgei – Contemporary Crafts from
Japan.

▩ 3
Leeds Castle, Kent
Grand Firework Spectacular.

▩ 3 – 4
Plas Newydd, North Wales
Autumn Book Fair.

▩ 10
Nunnington Hall, Yorkshire
"Putting the House to Bed", 10-12 noon, £5
adult, £2.50 child – coffee and biscuits
(booking essential).

▩ 10 – 11
Plas Newydd, North Wales
Patchwork Display & Workshop.

▩ 17
Plas Newydd, North Wales
Display of Worked Tapestry Pieces.

▩ 18
Plas Newydd, North Wales
Make a Seasonal Decorated Swag,
1.30-3.30pm (booking essential).

▩ 17 – 18
Goodwood House, Sussex
Goodwood Antiques Fair.

▩ 23 – 25
Hopetoun House, Edinburgh City, Coast &
Countryside, Scotland
Hopetoun's Present Event Shopping Fair.

▩ 24
Plas Newydd, North Wales
Sugarcraft Demonstration, 10am-12 noon,
1 - 3pm (booking essential).

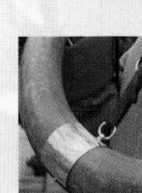

▩ 24 – 25
Ludlow Castle, Shropshire
Medieval Christmas Fayre.

▩ 24 – 25
Nunnington Hall, Yorkshire
Ryedale Craft Weekend, 10.30am-3.30pm,
£1.50, Tea Room and Shop open, House closed.

▩ 24 – 25
Ragley Hall, Warwickshire
Yuletide Craft Fair.

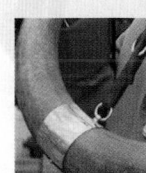

▩ 25
Gilbert White's House & Oates Museum, Hants
Annual Mulled Wine & Christmas Shopping
Day.

▩ 25
Plas Newydd, North Wales
Make a Foliage Welcome Ring, 1.30-3.30pm
(booking essential).

DECEMBER

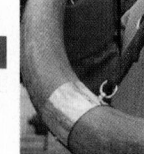

▩ 1
Plas Newydd, North Wales
National Tree Dressing Day.

▩ 1 – 21
Abbot Hall Art Gallery, Cumbria
Hughie O'Donoghue – Carborundum Prints:
Process and Content.

▩ 1 – 21
Blackwell – The Artistic House, Cumbria
Kokten Korgei – Contemporary Crafts from Japan.

▩ 1, 2, 8, 9, 15 & 16
Plas Newydd, North Wales
Father Christmas comes to Plas Newydd, 1-3pm.

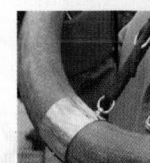

▩ 2
Plas Newydd, North Wales
Make a Gorgeous Garland, 1.30-3.30pm
(booking essential).

▩ 3 – 31
Fairfax House, Yorkshire
Annual Exhibition on the 'Keeping of Christmas'.

▩ 4 – 7
Shugborough, Staffordshire
Shuborough Victorian Christmas Evening.

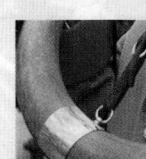

▩ 5
Baddesley Clinton, Warwickshire
Pruning Fruit & Nut Trees, 10am.

▩ 8
Nunnington Hall, Yorkshire
The Leeds Waites – Christmas Concert, 7pm –
Mulled Wine & Mince Pies, £10.

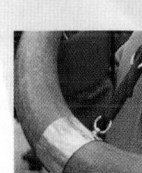

▩ 8
Plas Newydd, North Wales
Anglesey Farmhouse Chocolates, 1-4pm.

▩ 9
Plas Newydd, North Wales
Make a Christmas Arrangement, 1.30-3.30pm
(booking essential).

▩ 10
Plas Newydd, North Wales
Christmas Concert in the Music Room, 7.30pm.

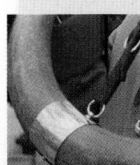

▩ 10 – 24
Leeds Castle, Kent
Christmas at the Castle.

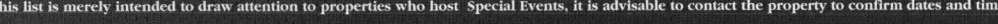

This list is merely intended to draw attention to properties who host Special Events, it is advisable to contact the property to confirm dates and times.

37

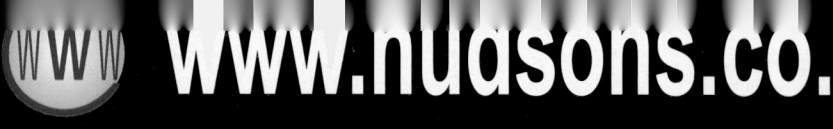

www.hudsons.co.uk –
your gateway to
heritage sites

Useful Web Addresses

Hudson's	www.hudsons.co.uk
Historic Houses Association	www.hha.org.uk
National Trust	www.nationaltrust.org.uk
English Heritage	www.english-heritage.org.uk
National Trust For Scotland	www.nts.org.uk
Historic Scotland	www.historic-scotland.gov.uk
CADW	www.cadw.wales.gov.uk
Dúchas	www.heritageireland.ie
Historic Royal Palaces	www.hrp.org.uk
The Royal Collection	www.the-royal-collection.org.uk
National Gardens Scheme	www.ngs.org.uk
British Tourist Authority	www.visitbritain.com
Wordsworth's Lake District	www.wordsworthlakes.co.uk
Heritage Venues	www.heritagevenues.co.uk

PLACES TO STAY

Landmark Trust	www.landmarktrust.co.uk
Alastair Sawday Publishing	www.sawdays.co.uk
Bed & Breakfast for Gardens Lovers	www.bbgl.co.uk

www.hudsons.co.uk

Make your life easier. Go to www.hudsons.co.uk and you can click on direct links to all the properties in this index. No need to type in each address. More are being added all

PROPERTY	COUNTY	WEB ADDRESS
1 Royal Crescent	Somerset	www.bath-preservation-trust.org.uk
Abbey Pumping Station	Leicestershire	www.leicestermuseums.ac.uk
Abbot Hall Art Gallery	Cumbria	www.abbothall.org.uk
Aberglasney Gardens	South Wales	www.aberglasney.org
Adlington Hall	Cheshire	www.adlingtonhall.com
Alnwick Castle	Northumberland	www.alnwickcastle.com
Althorp	Northamptonshire	www.althorp.com
Ancient House	Suffolk	www.landmarktrust.co.uk
Angus Folk Museum	Scotland	www.nts.org.uk/angus.html
Anne of Cleves House	Sussex	www.sussexpast.co.uk
Apsley House	London	www.vam.ac.uk/Infodome
Arbuthnott House	Scotland	www.arbuthnott.co.uk
Archaeological Resource Centre	Yorkshire	www.jorvik-viking-centre.co.uk/arc.html
Ardington House	Oxfordshire	www.ardingtonhouse.com
Arduaine Garden	Scotland	www.nts.org.uk/arduaine.html
Arley Hall	Cheshire	www.arleyestate.zuunet.co.uk
Armadale Castle Garden & Musuem of the Isles	Scotland	www.cland.demon.co.uk
Arniston House	Scotland	www.arniston-house.co.uk
Arundel Castle	Sussex	www.arundelcastle.org
Astley Hall	Lancashire	www.astleyhall.co.uk
Athelhampton House & Gardens	Dorset	www.athelhampton.co.uk
Auckland Castle	Co Durham	www.auckland-castle.co.uk
Avington Park	Hampshire	www.avingtonpark.co.uk
Bachelors' Club	Scotland	www.nts.org.uk/bachelor.html
Baddesley Clinton	Warwickshire	www.ntrustsevern.org.uk/baddesle.htm
Ballindalloch Castle	Scotland	www.ballindallochcastle.co.uk
Ballindoolin House & Garden	Ireland	www.ballindoolin.com
Ballywalter Park	Ireland	www.dunleath-estates.co.uk
Bamburgh Castle	Northumberland	www.bamburghcastle.com
Bannockburn Heritage Centre	Scotland	www.nts.org.uk/bannockburn.html
Banqueting House	London	www.hrp.org.uk/bh/indexbh.htm
Bantry House & Garden	Ireland	www.cork-guide.ie/bnry_hse.htm
Barnsley House	Gloucestershire	www.barnsleyhouse.com
J M Barrie's Birthplace	Scotland	www.nts.org.uk/barrie.html
Barry Mill	Scotland	www.nts.org.uk/barry.html
Beaulieu	Hampshire	www.beaulieu.co.uk
Beaumaris Castle	North Wales	www.cadw.wales.gov.uk
Belchamp Hall	Suffolk	www.belchamphall.com
Belmont	Kent	www.swale.gov.uk/sbctourism/sta/belmont.htm
Belvoir Castle	Leicestershire & Rutland	www.belvoircastle.com
Benington Lordship	Hertfordshire	www.beningtonlordship.co.uk
Berrington Hall	Herefordshire	www.ntrustsevern.org.uk/berringt.htm
Birmingham Botanical Gardens	West Midlands	www.bham-bot-gdns.demon.co.uk
Birr CastleDemesne	Ireland	www.birrcastle.com
Blackwell – The Artistic House	Cumbria	www.blackwell.org.uk
Blaenavon Ironworks	South Wales	www.cadw.wales.gov.uk
Blairquhan Castle	Scotland	www.blairquhan.co.uk
Blenheim Palace·	Oxfordshire	www.blenheimpalace.com
Bluecoat Arts Centre	Merseyside	www.bluecoatartscentre.com
Bodnant Garden	North Wales	www.sissons.demon.co.uk/bodnant.htm
Bolton Abbey	Yorkshire	www.boltonabbey.com
Bolton Castle	Yorkshire	www.boltoncastle.co.uk
Borde Hill Garden	Sussex	www.bordehill.co.uk
Bosworth Battlefield	Leicestershire & Rutland	www.leics.gov.uk
Boughton House	Northamptonshire	www.boughtonhouse.org.uk
Boughton Monchelsea	Kent	www.boughtonmonchelseaplace.co.uk
Bowood House	Wiltshire	www.bowood-estate.co.uk
Branklyn Garden	Scotland	www.nts.org.uk/branklyn.html

PROPERTY	COUNTY	WEB ADDRESS
Brodick Castle & Country Park	Scotland	www.nts.org.uk/brodick.html
Brodie Castle	Scotland	www.nts.org.uk/brodie.html
Broughton Castle	Oxfordshire	www.broughtoncastle.demon.co.uk
Broughton House & Garden	Scotland	www.nts.org.uk/broughton.html
Buckingham Palace	London	www.the-royal-collection.org.uk
Burghley House	Lincolnshire	www.burghley.co.uk
Burncoose Nurseries	Cornwall	www.burncoose.co.uk
Buscot Park	Oxfordshire	www.faringdon-coll.com
Cabinet War Rooms	London	www.iwm.org.uk
Cadhay	Devon	www.eastdevon.net/cadhay
Caerhays Castle	Cornwall	www.eclipse.co.uk/caerhays
Caerleon Roman Baths & Amphitheatre	South Wales	www.cadw.wales.gov.uk
Caerphilly Castle	South Wales	www.cadw.wales.gov.uk
Caernarfon Castle	North Wales	www.cadw.wales.gov.uk
Cambo Gardens	Scotland	www.camboestate.com
Canterbury Cathedral	Kent	www.canterbury-cathedral.org
Thomas Carlyle's Birthplace	Scotland	www.nts.org.uk/carlyles.html
Carreg Cennen Castle	South Wales	www.cadw.wales.gov.uk
Castell Coch	South Wales	www.cadw.wales.gov.uk
Castle Bromwich Hall Gardens	West Midlands	www.cbhgt.swinternet.co.uk
Castle Fraser & Garden	Scotland	www.nts.org.uk/fraser.html
Castle Howard	Yorkshire	www.castlehoward.co.uk
Cathedral Church of St Nicholas	Tyne & Wear	www.newcastle-ang-cathedral-stnicholas.org.uk
Catton Hall	Derbyshire	www.catton-hall.com
Cawdor Castle	Scotland	www.cawdorcastle.com
Charlecote Park	Warwickshire	www.ntrustsevern.org.uk/charleco.htm
Charleston	Sussex	www.charleston.org.uk
Chatsworth	Derbyshire	www.chatsworth-house.co.uk
Chavenage	Gloucestershire	www.chavenage.com
Chedworth Roman Villa	Gloucestershire	www.ntrustsevern.org.uk/chedwort.htm
Chepstow Castle	South Wales	www.cadw.wales.gov.uk
Chillingham Castle	Northumberland	www.chillingham-castle.com
Chillington Hall	Staffordshire	www.chillingtonhall.co.uk
Cilgerran Castle	South Wales	www.cadw.wales.gov.uk
Claverton Manor	Somerset	www.americanmuseum.org
Clifton Park Museum	Yorkshire	www.rma.org.uk
Cobham Hall	Kent	www.cobhamhall.com
Combermere Abbey	Shropshire	www.combermereabbey.co.uk
Conwy Castle	North Wales	www.cadw.wales.gov.uk
Corsham Court	Wiltshire	www.touristnetuk.com/S0/corsham/index.htm
Coton Manor Garden	Northamptonshire	www.cotonmanor.co.uk
Cottesbrooke Hall & Gardens	Northamptonshire	www.cottesbrookehall.co.uk
Coughton Court	Warwickshire	www.coughtoncourt.co.uk
Courtauld Gallery	London	www.courtauld.ac.uk
Coventry Cathedral	West Midlands	www.coventrycathedral.org
Cowper & Newton Museum	Buckinghamshire	www.mkheritage.co.uk/cnm
Cragside	Northumberland	www.ntnorth.demon.co.uk
Cranborne Manor Garden	Dorset	www.cranborne.co.uk
Crathes Castle & Garden	Scotland	www.nts.org.uk/crathes.html
Criccieth Castle	North Wales	www.cadw.wales.gov.uk
Croft Castle	Herefordshire	www.ntrustsevern.org.uk/croft.htm
Croome Park	Worcestershire	www.ntrustsevern.org.uk
Croxteth Hall & Country Park	Merseyside	www.croxteth.co.uk
Culloden	Scotland	www.nts.org.uk/culloden.html
Culross Palace	Scotland	www.nts.org.uk/culross.html
Culzean Castle & Country Park	Scotland	www.nts.org.uk/culzean.html
Cymer Abbey	North Wales	www.cadw.wales.gov.uk
Dalemain	Cumbria	www.dalemain.com
Dalmeny House	Scotland	www.dalmeny.co.uk

PROPERTY	COUNTY	WEB ADDRESS
Dapdune Wharf	Surrey	www.nationaltrust.org.uk/southern
Denbigh Castle	North Wales	www.cadw.wales.gov.uk
Dickens House Museusm	London	www.dickensmuseum.com
Dimbola Lodge	Isle of Wight	www.dimbola.co.uk
Docton Mill & Garden	Devon	www.doctonmill.co.uk
Doddington Hall	Lincolnshire	www.doddingtonhall.free-online.co.uk
Dolwyddelan Castle	North Wales	www.cadw.wales.gov.uk
Dorney Court	Berkshire	www.dorneycourt.co.uk
Dorset County Museum	Dorset	www.dorset.museum.clara.net
Dove Cottage & Wordsworth Museum	Cumbria	www.wordsworthlakes.co.uk
Drum Castle	Scotland	www.nts.org.uk/drum.html
Drumlanrig Castle	Scotland	www.drumlanrigcastle.org.uk
Duart Castle	Scotland	www.holidaymull.org/members/duart.html
Duncombe Park	Yorkshire	www.duncombepark.com
Duns Castle	Scotland	www.dunscastle.co.uk
Dunvegan Castle	Scotland	www.dunvegancastle.com
East Lambrook Manor Gardens	Somerset	www.margeryfish.com
Eastnor Castle	Herefordshire	www.eastnorcastle.com
Elgar Birthplace Museum	Worcestershire	www.elgar.org
Elsham Hall Country & Wildlife Park and Barn Theatre	Lincolnshire	www.brigg.com/elsham.htm
Englefield House	Berkshire	www.englefield-est.demon.co.uk
Essex Secret Bunker	Essex	www.essexsecretbunker.com
Escot Country Park & Gardens	Devon	www.escot-devon.co.uk
Exbury Gardens	Hampshire	www.exbury.co.uk
Eyam Hall	Derbyshire	www.eyamhall.co.uk
Fairfax House	Yorkshire	www.fairfaxhouse.co.uk
Falkland Palace	Scotland	www.nts.org.uk/falkland.html
Finchcocks	Kent	www.argonet.co.uk/finchcocks
Fishbourne Roman Palace	Sussex	www.sussexpast.co.uk
Ford Green Hall	Staffordshire	www.stoke.gov.uk/museums/fordgreen/
Forde Abbey	Dorset	www.fordeabbey.co.uk
Fountains Abbey	Yorkshire	www.fountainsabbey.org.uk
Freud Museum	London	www.freud.org.uk
Fursdon	Devon	www.fursdon.co.uk
Fyvie Castle	Scotland	www.nts.org.uk/fyvie.html
Gainsborough's House	Suffolk	www.gainsborough.org
Gardens of Easton Lodge	Essex	www.eastonlodge.co.uk
Gardens of the Rose	Hertfordshire	www.roses.co.uk/harkness/rnrs/gardens.htm
Gawsworth Hall	Cheshire	www.gawsworthhall.com
Georgian House	Scotland	www.nts.org.uk/georgian.html
Gilbert Collection	London	www.gilbert-collection.org.uk
Gladstone's Land	Scotland	www.nts.org.uk/gladstone.html
Glamis Castle	Scotland	www.great-houses-scotland.co.uk/glamis
Glastonbury Abbey	Somerset	www.glastonburyabbey.com
Glencoe	Scotland	www.nts.org.uk/glencoe.html
Glenfinnan Monument	Scotland	www.nts.org.uk/glenfinnan.html
Gloucester Cathedral	Gloucestershire	www.gloucestercathedral.uk.com
Goddards	Surrey	www.landmarktrust.co.uk
Goodwood House	Sussex	www.goodwood.co.uk
Great Comp	Kent	www.greatcomp.co.uk
Greenbank Garden	Scotland	www.nts.org.uk/greenbank.html
The Greyfriars	Worcestershire	www.ntrustsevern.org.uk/greyfria.htm
Greywalls	Scotland	www.greywalls.co.uk
Grimsthorpe Castle	Lincolnshire	www.grimsthorpe.co.uk
The Guildhall	Leicestershire	www.leicestermuseums.ac.uk
Guildhall Gallery	Hampshire	www.winchester.gov.uk/heritage/home.htm
Gwydir Castle	North Wales	www.gwydir-castle.co.uk
Haddo House	Scotland	www.nts.org.uk/haddo.html
Haddon Hall	Derbyshire	www.haddonhall.co.uk
Haddonstone Show Garden	Northamptonshire	www.haddonstone.co.uk

PROPERTY	COUNTY	WEB ADDRESS
Haldon Belvedere/ Lawrence Castle	Devon	www.haldonbelvedere.co.uk
Hall Place	Kent	www.bexley.gov.uk
Ham House	London	www.nationaltrust.org.uk/southern
Hammerwood Park	Sussex	www.name.is/hammerwood
Hampton Court	Herefordshire	www.hamptoncourt.org.uk
Hampton Court Palace	Surrey	www.hrp.org.uk/hcp/indexhcp.htm
Hanbury Hall	Worcestershire	www.ntrustsevern.org.uk/hanbury.htm
Harburn House	Scotland	www.harburnhouse.com
Harewood House	Yorkshire	www.harewood.org
Harlech Castle	North Wales	www.cadw.wales.gov.uk
Harmony Garden	Scotland	www.nts.org.uk/harmony.html
Hartland Abbey	Devon	www.hartlandabbey.com
Harvington Hall	Worcestershire	www.harvingtonhall.org.uk
Harwich Maritime & Lifeboat Museums	Essex	www.micrologic-ltd.co.uk/harwich/maritime.htm
Harwich Redoubt Fort	Essex	www.micrologic-ltd.co.uk/harwich/redoubt.htm
Hatchlands/Clandon Park	Surrey	www.nationaltrust.org.uk
Helmingham Hall Gardens	Suffolk	www.helmingham.com
Hengrave Hall Centre	Suffolk	www.hengravehallcentre.org.uk
Hergest Croft Gardens	Herefordshire	www.hergest.co.uk
Herstmonceux Castle Gardens	Sussex	www.seetb.org.uk/herstmonceux
Hestercombe Gardens	Somerset	www.hestercombegardens.com
Hever Castle	Kent	www.hevercastle.co.uk
Hidcote Manor Garden	Gloucestershire	www.ntrustsevern.org.uk/hidcote.htm
High Beeches Gardens	Sussex	www.highbeeches.com
Higham Park	Kent	www.higham-park.co.uk
Highclere Castle	Hampshire	www.highclerecastle.co.uk
Highcliffe Castle	Dorset	www.christchurch.gov.uk/highcliffecastle
Hill House	Scotland	www.nts.org.uk/hillhouse.html
Hill of Tarvit Mansionhouse	Scotland	www.nts.org.uk/hill.html
The Sir Harold Hillier Gardens & Arboretum	Hampshire	www.hillier.hants.gov.uk/
Holker Hall & Gardens	Cumbria	www.furness.co.uk/on-line/holker.htm
Holkham Hall	Norfolk	www.holkham.co.uk
Holme Pierrepont Hall	Nottinghamshire	www.holmepierreponthall.com
Holmwood House	Scotland	www.nts.org.uk/holmwood.html
Holst Birthplace Museum	Gloucestershire	www.holstmuseum.org.uk
Honeywood Heritage Centre	Surrey	www.sutton.gov.uk
Hopetoun House	Scotland	www.hopetounhouse.com
Houghton Lodge	Hampshire	www.hydroponicum.co.uk
House of Dun	Scotland	www.nts.org.uk/dun.html
House of the Binns	Scotland	www.nts.org.uk/binns.html
Hugh Miller's Cottage	Scotland	www.nts.org.uk/hugh.html
Hutchesons' Hall	Scotland	www.nts.org.uk/hutchesons.html
Hylands House	Essex	www.chelmsfordbc.gov.uk
Inverarary Castle	Scotland	www.inveraray-castle.com
Inveresk Lodge Garden	Scotland	www.nts.org.uk/inversk.html
Inverewe Garden	Scotland	www.nts.org.uk/inverewe.html
Iona Abbey & Nunnery	Scotland	www.historic-scotland.gov.uk
Irish Museum of Modern Art	Ireland	www.modernart.ie
Ironbridge Gorge Museums	Shropshire	www.ironbridge.org.uk
Judge's Lodging	South Wales	www.judgeslodging.org.uk
Keats House	London	www.keatshouse.org.uk
Kellie Castle & Garden	Scotland	www.nts.org.uk/kellie.html
Kelmscott Manor	Gloucestershire	www.kelmscottmanor.co.uk
Kensington Palace	London	www.hrp.org.uk/ken/indexken.htm
Kentwell Hall	Suffolk	www.kentwell.co.uk
Kidwelly Castle	South Wales	www.cadw.wales.gov.uk
King's College	Cambridge	www.kings.cam.ac.uk
Kinnersley Castle	Herefordshire	www.kinnersley.com/castle

Websites

PROPERTY	COUNTY	WEB ADDRESS
Knebworth House	Hertfordshire	www.knebworthhouse.com
Kylemore Abbey	Ireland	www.kylemoreabbey.com
Lamphey Bishop's Palace	South Wales	www.cadw.wales.gov.uk
Laugharne Castle	South Wales	www.cadw.wales.gov.uk
Layer Marney Tower	Essex	www.layermarneytower.co.uk
Leeds Castle	Kent	www.leeds-castle.co.uk
Leighton Hall	Lancashire	www.leightonhall.co.uk
Leighton House Art Gallery & Museum	London	www.rbkc.gov.uk/kcservices/libraries/leighton.htm
Leith Hall	Scotland	www.nts.org.uk/leith.htm
Lennoxlove House	Scotland	www.lennoxlove.org
Leonardslee Gardens	Sussex	www.leonardslee.com
Levens Hall	Cumbria	www.levenshall.co.uk
Lewes Castle & Barbican House Museum	Sussex	www.sussexpast.co.uk
Lichfield Cathedral	Staffordshire	www.lichfield-cathedral.org
Little Holland House	Surrey	www.sutton.gov.uk
David Livingstone Centre	Scotland	www.nts.org.uk
Lodge Park	Gloucestershire	www.ntrustsevern.org.uk
Lodge Park Walled Gardens & Steam Museum	Ireland	www.steam-museum.ie
Longleat House	Wiltshire	www.longleat.co.uk
Loseley Park	Surrey	www.loseley-park.com
Lost Gardens of Heligan	Cornwall	www.heligan.com
Lulworth Castle	Dorset	www.lulworth.com
Lydiard Park	Wiltshire	www.swindon.gov.uk/sbc.asp?s=CLMU
Macclesfield Museums	Cheshire	www.silk-macclesfield.org
Manderston	Scotland	www.manderston.co.uk
Mapledurham House & Watermill	Oxfordshire	www.mapledurham.co.uk
Mapperton	Dorset	www.mapperton.com
Marlipins Museum	Sussex	www.sussexpast.co.uk
Maunsel House	Somerset	www.sirbenslade.co.uk
Mawley Hall	Shropshire	www.mawley.com
Mellerstain House	Scotland	http://muses.calligrafix.co.uk/mellerstain
Merchant Adventurers' Hall	Yorkshire	www.theyorkcompany.sagenet.co.uk
Merriments Gardens	Sussex	www.merriments.co.uk
Michelham Priory	Sussex	www.sussexpast.co.uk
Milton's Cottage, John	Buckinghamshire	http:/home.clara.net/pbirger
Mount Stuart House & Gardens	Scotland	www.mountstuart.com
Muncaster Castle	Cumbria	www.muncastercastle.co.uk
Museum of Costume & Assembly Rooms	Somerset	www.museumofcostume.co.uk
Museum of Garden History	London	www.museumgardenhistory.org
Museum of Welsh Life	Wales	www.nmgw.ac.uk
New Lanark	Scotland	www.newlanark.org
Newby Hall	Yorkshire	www.newbyhall.co.uk
Normanby Hall	Yorkshire	www.northlincs.gov.uk
Norwood Park	Nottinghamshire	www.norwoodpark.org.uk
Nostell Priory	Yorkshire	www.nationaltrust.org.uk
Nymans Garden	Sussex	www.nationaltrust.org.uk/southern
Oakham Castle	Leicestershire & Rutland	www.rutnet.co.uk
Otley Hall	Suffolk	www.otleyhall.co.uk
Owlpen Manor	Gloucestershire	www.owlpen.com
Oxwich Castle	South Wales	www.cadw.wales.gov.uk
Packwood House	Warwickshire	www.ntrustsevern.org.uk/packwood.htm
Painshill Landscape Garden	Surrey	www.brainsys.com/cobham/painshill
Painswick Rococo Garden	Gloucestershire	www.rococogarden.co.uk
Palace of Holyroodhouse	Scotland	www.the-royal-collection.org.uk
Palace of Westminster	London	www.parliament.uk
Parham	Sussex	www.parhaminsussex.co.uk
Paxton House & Country Park	Scotland	www.paxtonhouse.com
Pencarrow	Cornwall	www.pencarrow.co.uk
Penhow Castle	South Wales	www.penhowcastle.com
Penshurst Place	Kent	www.penshurstplace.com

PROPERTY	COUNTY	WEB ADDRESS
Peto Garden at Iford Manor	Wiltshire	www.ifordmanor.co.uk
Petworth House	Sussex	www.nationaltrust.org.uk/southern
Picton Castle	South Wales	www.pictoncastle.co.uk
Pitmedden Garden	Scotland	www.nts.org.uk/pitmedden.html
Pitshanger Manor & Gallery	London	www.ealing.gov.uk/pitshanger
Plantation Garden	Norfolk	www.plantationgarden.co.uk
Plas Mawr	North Wales	www.cadw.wales.gov.uk
Polesden Lacey	Surrey	www.nationaltrust.org.uk/southern
Pollok House	Scotland	www.nts.org.uk/pollok.html
Portmeirion	North Wales	www.portmeirion.wales.com
Powderham Castle	Devon	www.powderham.co.uk
Powerscourt Estate	Ireland	www.powerscourt.ie
Prebendal Manor House	Northamptonshire	www.prebendal-manor.demon.co.uk
Preston Manor	Sussex	www.museums.brighton-hove.gov.uk
Preston Mill	Scotland	www.nts.org.uk/preston.html
The Priest House	Sussex	www.sussexpast.co.uk
Priorwood Garden & Dried Flower Shop	Scotland	www.nts.org.uk/priorwood.html
Provost Skene's House	Scotland	www.aagm.co.uk
Quaker Tapestry Exhibition Centre	Cumbria	www.quaker-tapestry.co.uk
Queen's Gallery	London	www.the-royal-collection.org.uk
RHS Garden Hyde Hall	Essex	www.rhs.org.uk
Raby Castle	Co Durham	www.rabycastle.com
Raglan Castle	South Wales	www.cadw.wales.gov.uk
Renishaw Hall	Derbyshire	www.sitwell.co.uk
Rhuddlan Castle	North Wales	www.cadw.wales.gov.uk
Ripley Castle	Yorkshire	www.ripleycastle.co.uk
Rochester Cathedral	Kent	www.rochester.anglican.org
Rockingham Castle	Northamptonshire	www.rockinghamcastle.com
Roman Baths & Pump Room	Somerset	www.romanbaths.co.uk
Rosslyn Chapel	Scotland	www.rosslynchapel.org.uk
Rousham House	Oxfordshire	www.information-britain.co.uk
Royal Mews	London	www.the-royal-collection.org.uk
Royal Observatory & Queen's House	London	www.rog.nmm.ac.uk
Royal Pavilion	Sussex	www.royalpavilion.brighton.co.uk
Royal Society of Arts	London	www.rsa.org.uk
Rug Chapel & Llangar Church	North Wales	www.cadw.wales.gov.uk
Rydal Mount	Cumbria	www.wordsworthlakes.co.uk
St Davids Bishop's Palace	South Wales	www.cadw.wales.gov.uk
St Edmundsbury Cathedral	Suffolk	www.stedmundsbury.anglican.org
St John's Gate	London	www.sja.org.uk/history
St Paul's Cathedral	London	www.stpauls.co.uk
Salisbury Cathedral	Wiltshire	www.salisburycathedral.org.uk
Sand	Devon	www.eastdevon.net/sand
Sandham MemorialChapel	Hampshire	www.nationaltrust.org.uk/southern
Sandon Hall	Staffordshire	www.sandonhall.co.uk
Sandringham	Norfolk	www.sandringhamestate.co.uk
Savill Garden	Berkshire	www.savillgarden.co.uk
Scampston Hall	Yorkshire	www.scampston.co.uk
Scone Palace	Scotland	www.scone-palace.co.uk
Shakespeare Houses	Warwickshire	www.shakespeare.org.uk
Sherborne Castle	Dorset	www.sherbornecastle.com
Sheffield Park Garden	Sussex	www.nationaltrust.org.uk/regionkentesussex
Shugborough	Staffordshire	www.staffordshire.gov.uk/shugboro/shugpark.htm
Sion Hill Hall	Yorkshire	www.sionhillhall.co.uk
Skipton Castle	Yorkshire	www.skiptoncastle.co.uk
Robert Smail's Printing Works	Scotland	www.nts.org.uk/robertsmail.html
Snowshill Manor	Gloucestershire	www.ntrustsevern.org.uk/snowshil.htm
Somerley	Hampshire	www.somerley.com
Somerleyton Hall	Suffolk	www.somerleyton.co.uk

PROPERTY	COUNTY	WEB ADDRESS
Somerset House	London	www.somerset-house.org.uk
Souter Johnnie's Cottage	Scotland	www.nts.org.uk
South Elmham Hall	Suffolk	www.southelmham.co.uk
Southwark Cathedral	London	www.dswark.org
Spencer House	London	www.spencerhouse.co.uk
Standen	Sussex	www.nationaltrust.org.uk/southern
Stansted Park	Sussex	www.stanstedpark.co.uk
Stoneleigh Abbey	Warwickshire	www.stoneleighabbey.org
Stonor	Oxfordshire	www.stonor.com
Stowe Gardens & Park	Buckinghamshire	www.nationaltrust.org.uk
Stowe House	Buckinghamshire	www.stowe.co.uk
Strata Florida Abbey	South Wales	www.cadw.wales.gov.uk
Sudeley Castle	Gloucestershire	www.stratford.co.uk/sudeley
Sulgrave Manor	Northamptonshire	www.stratford.co.uk/sulgrave
Sutton Park	Yorkshire	www.statelyhome.co.uk
Syon Park	London	www.syonpark.co.uk
Tate St Ives	Cornwall	www.tate.org.uk
Tatton Park	Cheshire	www.tatton.park.org.uk
Tenement House	Scotland	www.nts.org.uk/tenement.html
Thirlestane Castle	Scotland	www.thirlestanecastle.co.uk
Thorp Perrow Arboretum & The Falcons of Thorp Perrow	Yorkshire	www.thorpperrow.com
Threave Garden & Estate	Scotland	www.nts.org.uk/threave.html
Tintern Abbey	South Wales	www.cadw.wales.gov.uk
Tissington Hall	Derbyshire	www.tissington-hall.com
Titsey Place	Surrey	www.titsey.com
Torosay Castle & Gardens	Scotland	www.zynet.co.uk/mull/members/torosay.html
Tower of Hallbar	Scotland	www.vivat.org.uk
Tower of London	London	www.hrp.org.uk/tol/indextol.htm
Towneley Hall Art Gallery & Museums	Lancashire	www.burnley.gov.uk/towneley
Traquair	Scotland	www.traquair.co.uk
Trebah Garden	Cornwall	www.trebah-garden.co.uk
Treowen	South Wales	http://freespace.virginnet.co.uk/treowen.com
Tretower Court & Castle	South Wales	www.cadw.wales.gov.uk
Trewithen	Cornwall	www.trewithengardens.co.uk
Uppark	Sussex	www.nationaltrust.org.uk/southern
Upton House	Warwickshire	www.ntrustsevern.org.uk/upton.htm
Usk Castle	South Wales	www.castlewales.com/usk.html
Valle Crucis Abbey	North Wales	www.cadw.wales.gov.uk
The Vyne	Hampshire	www.nationaltrust.org.uk/southern
Waddesdon Manor	Buckinghamshire	www.waddesdon.org.uk
Wallace Collection	London	www.the-wallace-collection.org.uk
Waterperry Gardens	Oxfordshire	www.waterperrygardens.co.uk
Weaver's Cottage	Scotland	www.nts.org.uk/weaver.html
Weobley Castle	South Wales	www.cadw.wales.gov.uk
West Dean Gardens	Sussex	www.westdean.org.uk/gardens
Westbury Court Garden	Gloucestershire	www.ntrustsevern.org.uk/westbury.htm
Westminster Cathedral	London	www.westmintercathedral.org.uk
Weston Park	Shropshire	www.weston-park.com
White Castle	South Wales	www.cadw.wales.gov.uk
White Scar Cave	Yorkshire	www.wscave.co.uk
Whitehall	Surrey	www.sutton.gov.uk
Wilmington Priory	Sussex	www.landmarktrust.co.uk
Wilton House	Wiltshire	www.wiltonhouse.com
Wimpole Hall & Wimpole Home Farm	Cambridgeshire	www.wimpole.org
Winchester College	Hampshire	www.wincoll.ac.uk
Windsor Castle	Berkshire	www.the-royal-collection.org.uk
Winkworth Arboretum	Surrey	www.cornuswwweb.co.uk
Winton House	Scotland	www.wintonhouse.co.uk
Woburn Abbey	Bedfordshire	www.woburnabbey.co.uk
Wordsworth House	Cumbria	www.wordsworthlakes.co.uk

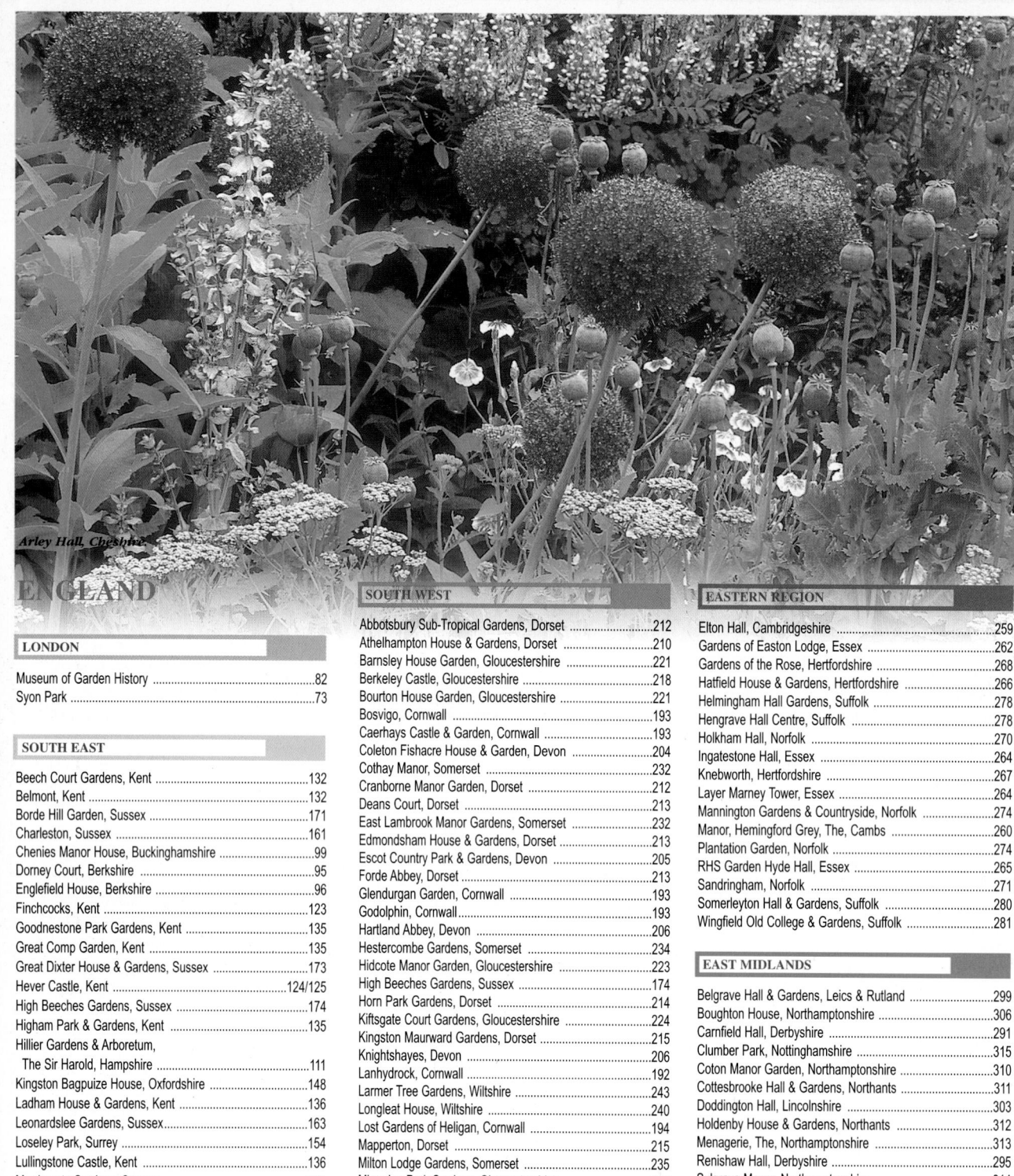

Arley Hall, Cheshire

ENGLAND

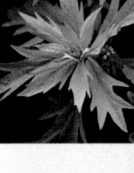
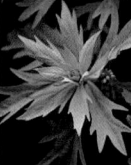
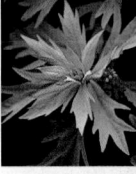
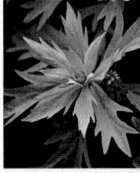
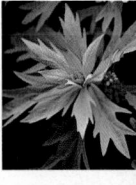
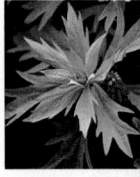
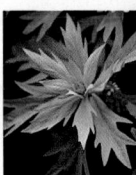
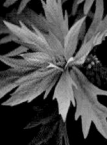

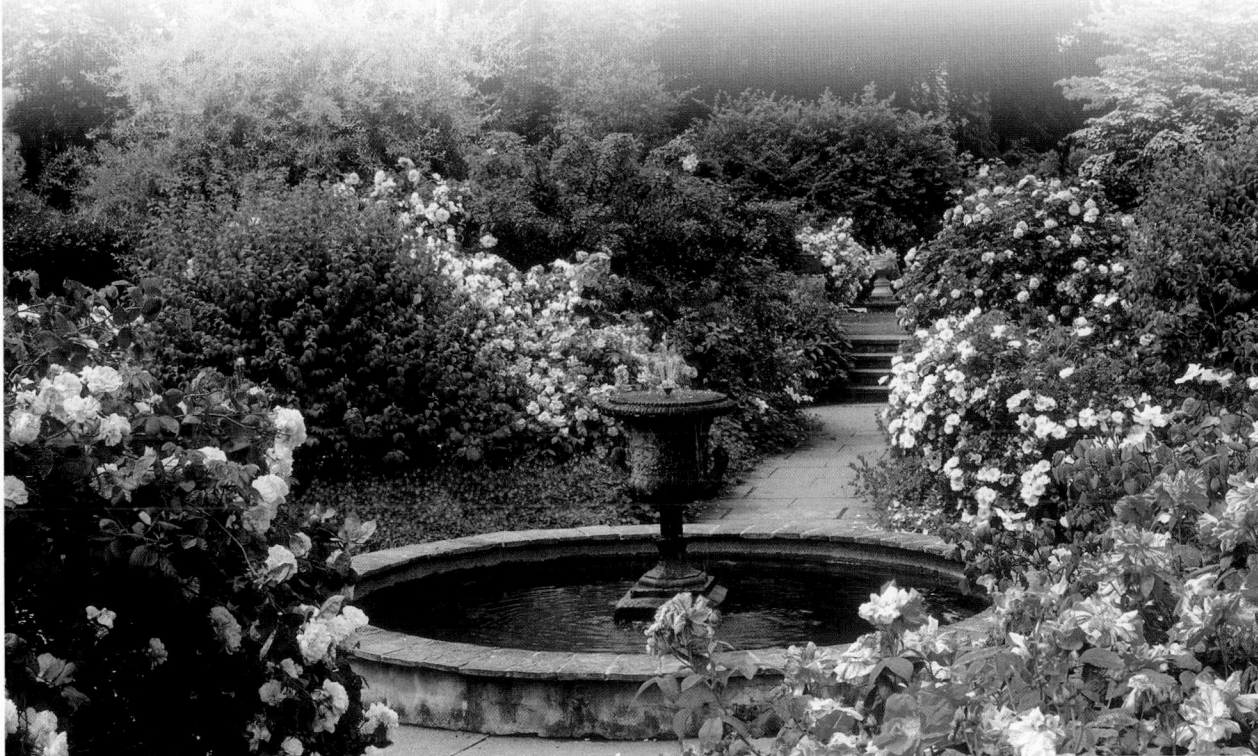

Newby Hall, Yorkshire.

This list is merely intended to draw attention to properties which have plant sales, it is intended only as a guide.

47

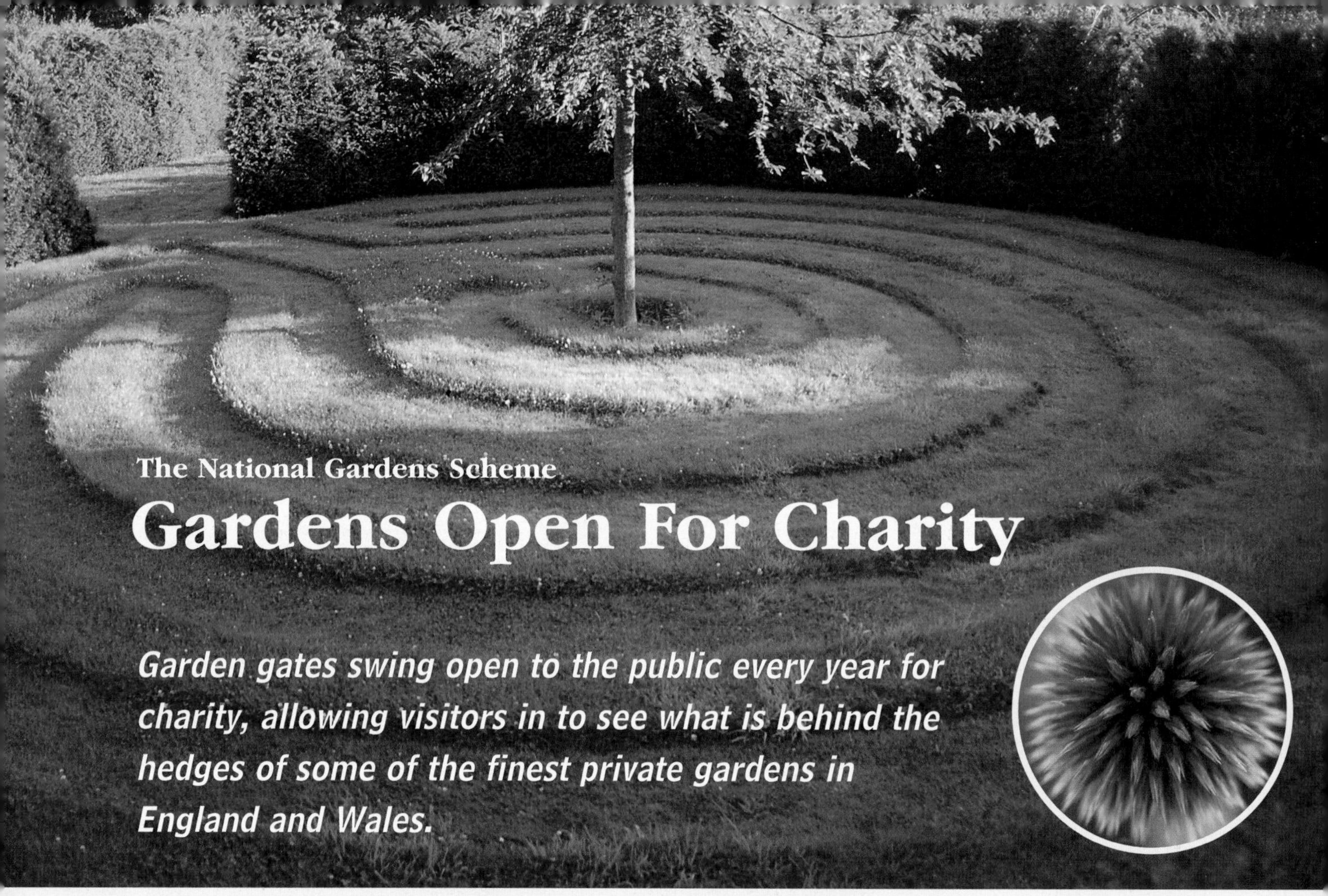

The National Gardens Scheme

Gardens Open For Charity

Garden gates swing open to the public every year for charity, allowing visitors in to see what is behind the hedges of some of the finest private gardens in England and Wales.

Innovative or classic, the NGS embraces them all, from intimate city courtyards and cottage plots to 18th Century landscapes. Find novel solutions to all kinds of garden problems and enjoy privileged insight into inventive planting schemes. Interesting and unusual plants are often available, along with expert tips from the people in the know.

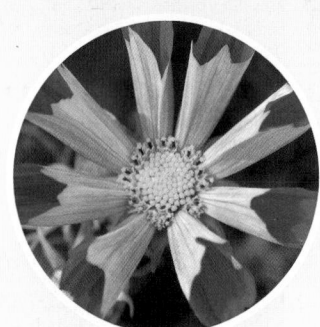

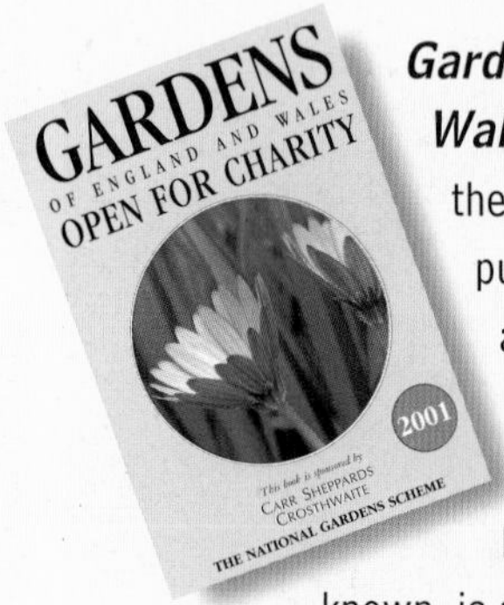

Gardens of England and Wales Open For Charity, the best-selling annual guide published by the NGS, lists all open days with short descriptions of the gardens. The 'Yellow Book', as it is familiarly known, is available at all major booksellers, and is also available on the NGS website.

Garden Finder, a search and mapping facility on the NGS website provides even more information about the gardens, often including photographs. Plan your itinerary using the latest opening information, including some garden openings exclusively announced on the NGS website **www.ngs.org.uk**

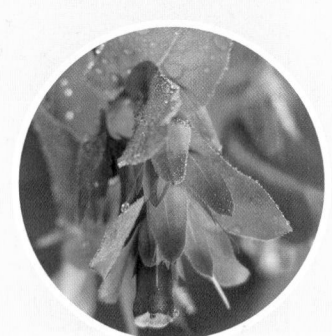

If you would like more information, or are interested in finding out about opening your own garden for the Scheme please contact:

Catherine Stepney, Public Relations Administrator
The National Gardens Scheme, Hatchlands Park, East Clandon, Surrey GU4 7RT

T 01483 211535   F 01483 211537   E ngs@ngs.org.uk

48

Properties included in this list are open to some extent for all or most of the year. See entry for details.

ENGLAND

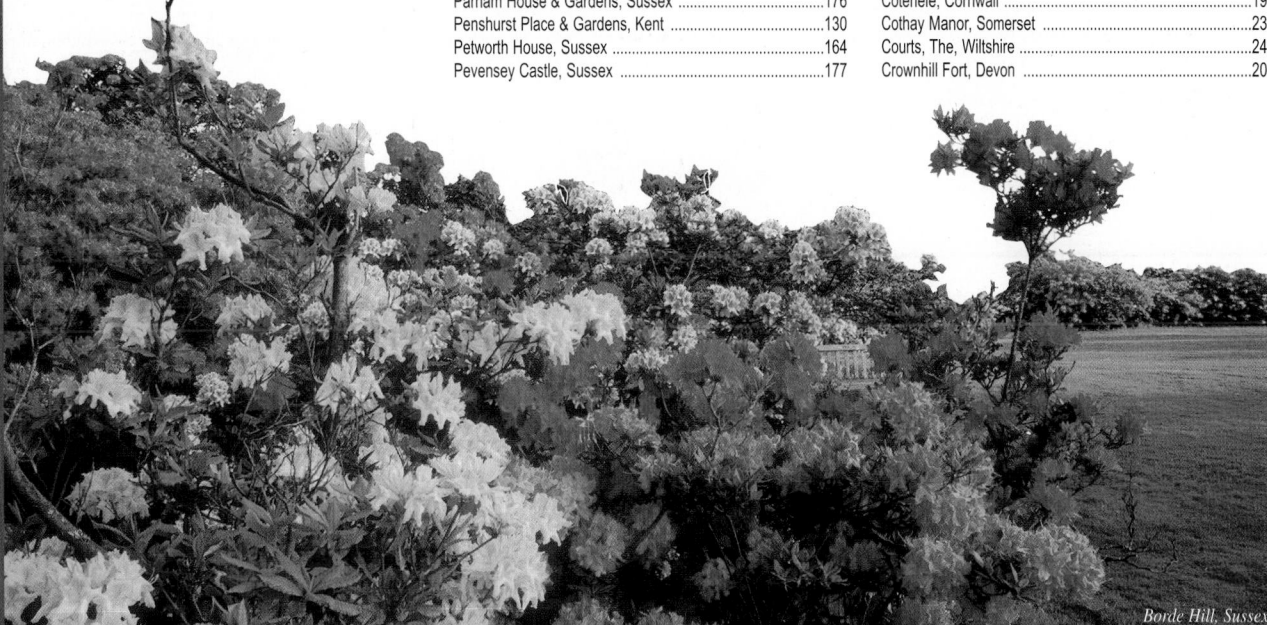

Borde Hill, Sussex.

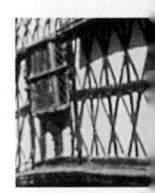
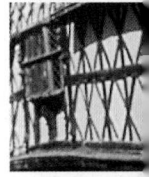
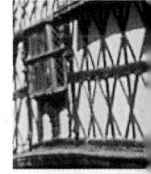
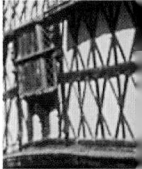
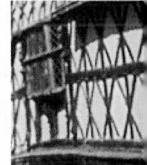
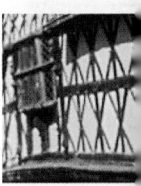
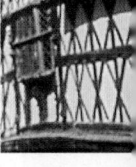
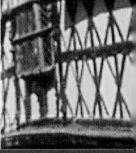

Linlithgow Palace. Historic Scotland.

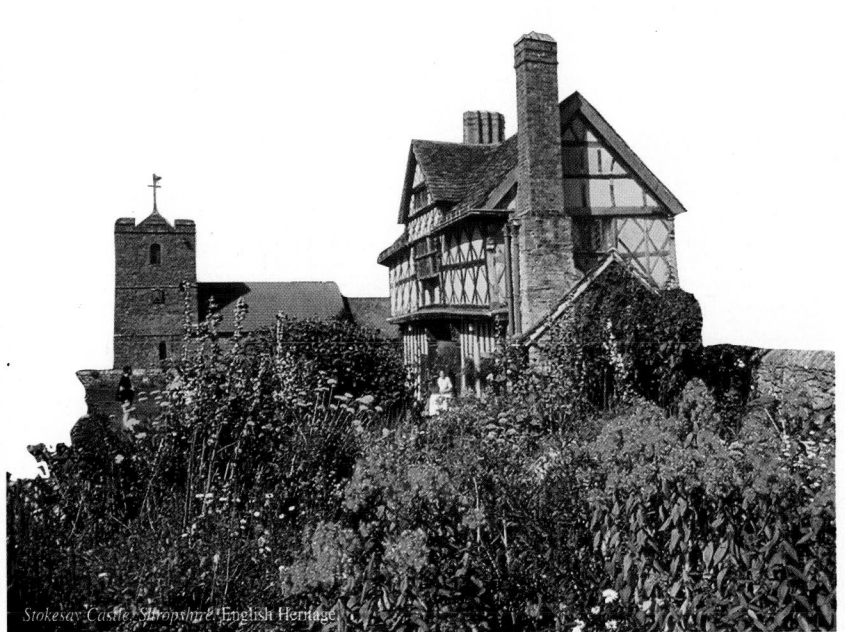

Stokesay Castle, Shropshire. English Heritage.

This list is merely intended to draw attention to properties which are open for most of the year, it is intended only as a guide.

5

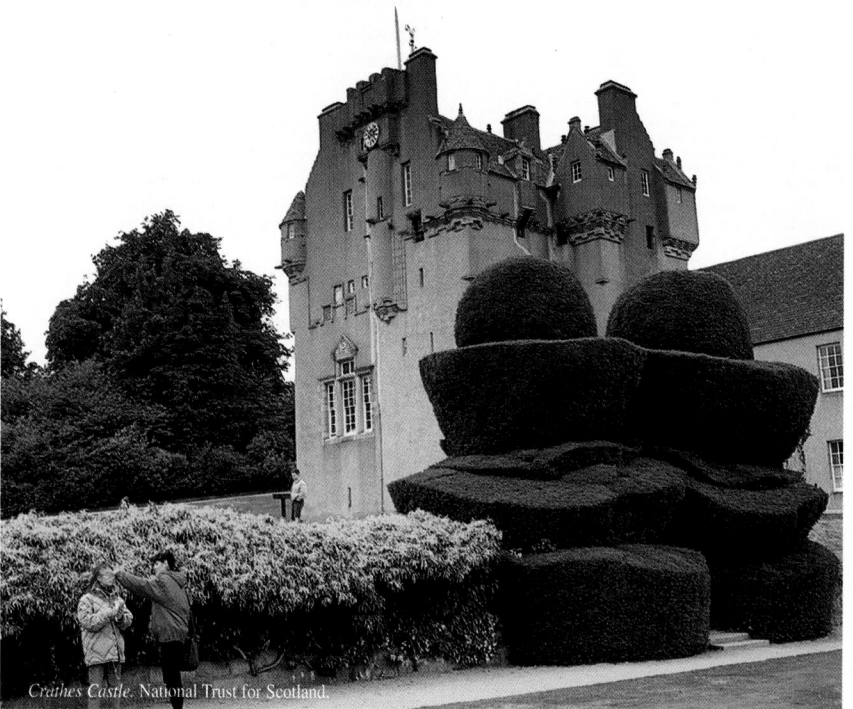

Crathes Castle. National Trust for Scotland.

WALES

IRELAND

SCOTLAND

MOVIES....

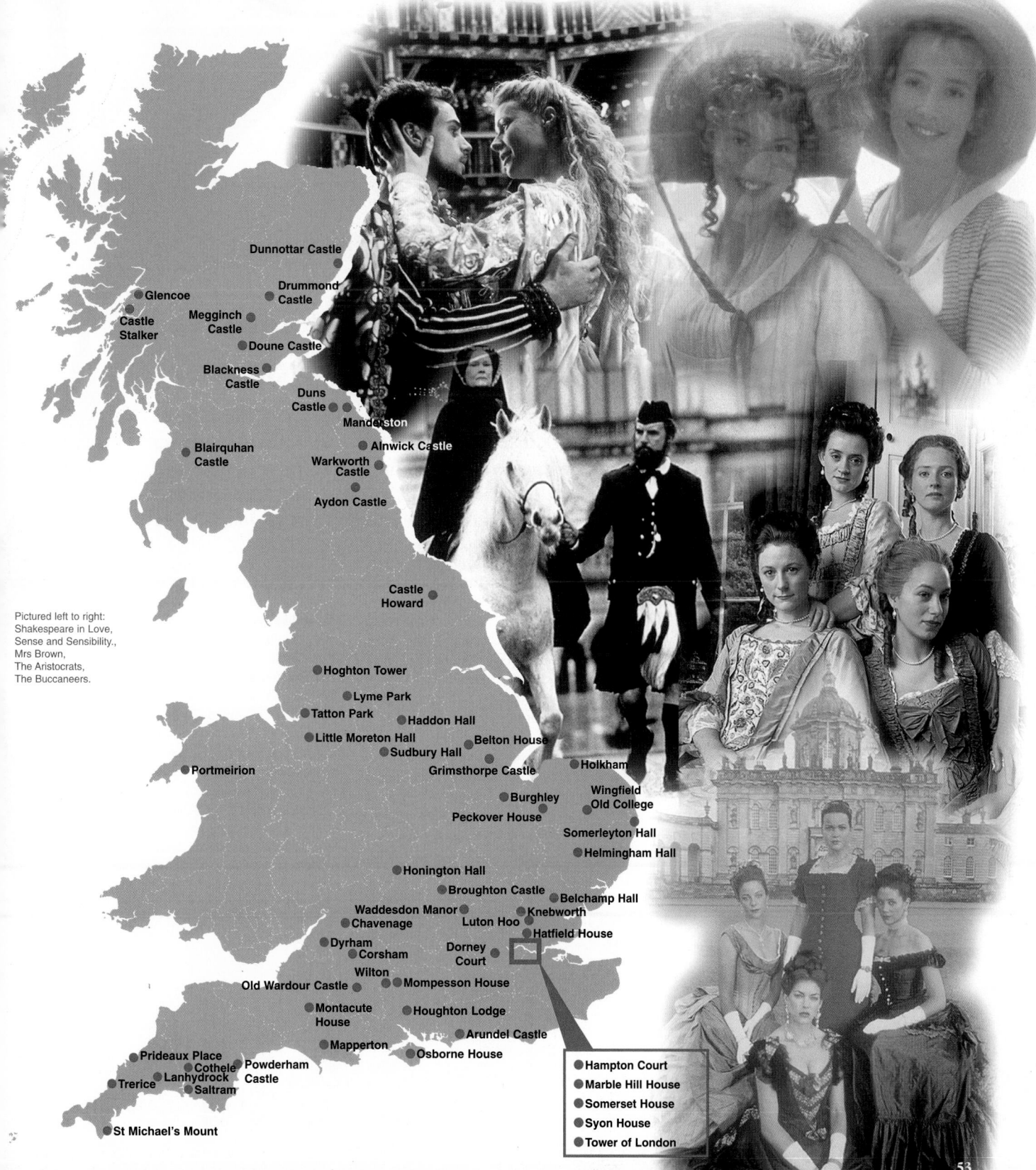

Pictured left to right:
Shakespeare in Love,
Sense and Sensibility.,
Mrs Brown,
The Aristocrats,
The Buccaneers.

Glencoe

Castle
Stalker

Megginch
Castle

Dunnottar Castle

Drummond
Castle

Doune Castle

Blackness
Castle

Duns
Castle

Manderston

Blairquhan
Castle

Alnwick Castle

Warkworth
Castle

Aydon Castle

Castle
Howard

Hoghton Tower

Lyme Park

Tatton Park

Haddon Hall

Little Moreton Hall

Belton House

Sudbury Hall

Portmeirion

Grimsthorpe Castle

Holkham

Burghley

Wingfield
Old College

Peckover House

Somerleyton Hall

Helmingham Hall

Honington Hall

Broughton Castle

Belchamp Hall

Waddesdon Manor

Knebworth

Chavenage

Luton Hoo

Hatfield House

Dyrham

Corsham

Dorney
Court

Wilton

Old Wardour Castle

Mompesson House

Montacute
House

Houghton Lodge

Mapperton

Arundel Castle

Osborne House

Prideaux Place

Cothele

Powderham
Castle

Trerice

Lanhydrock

Saltram

St Michael's Mount

- Hampton Court
- Marble Hill House
- Somerset House
- Syon House
- Tower of London

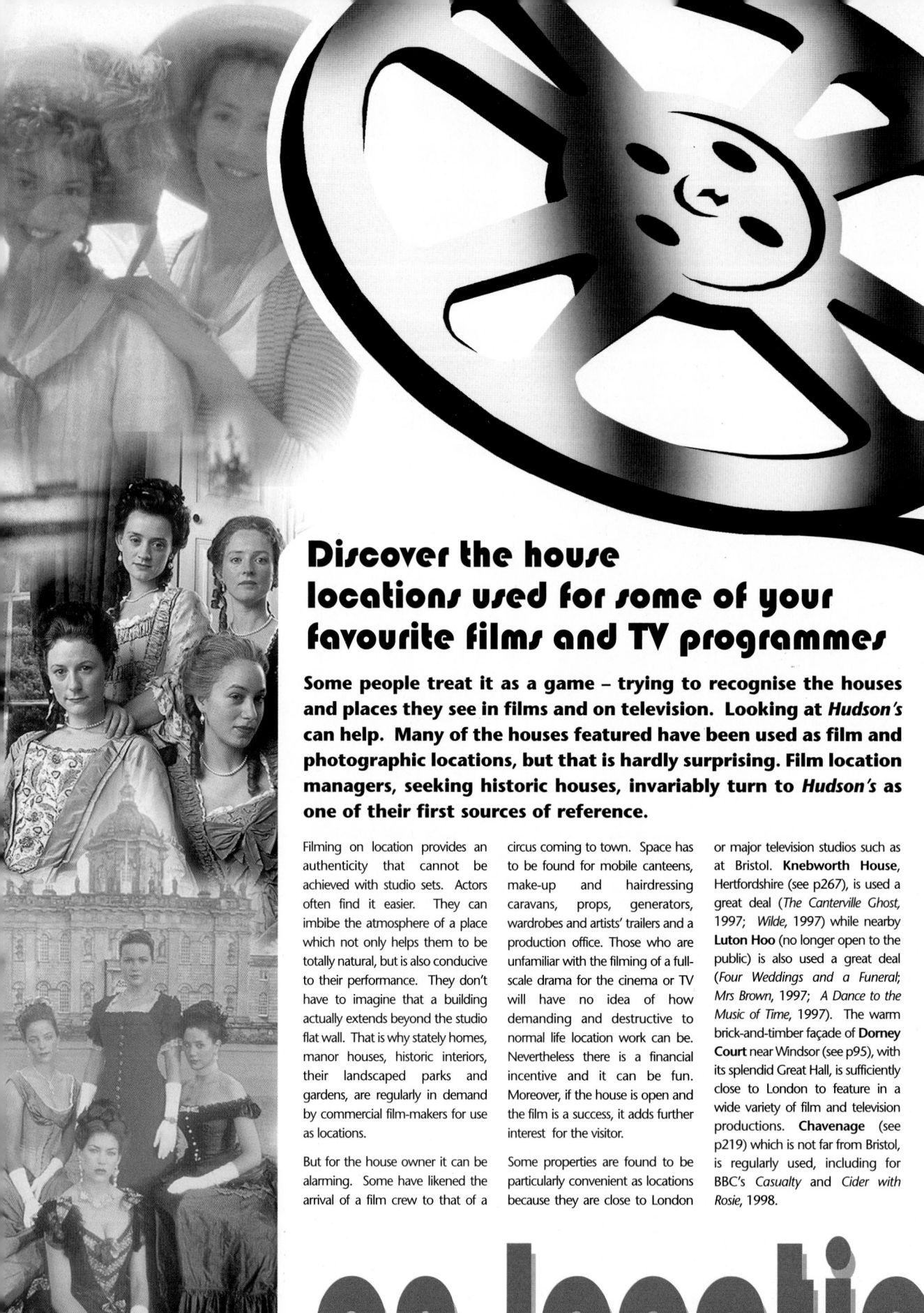

Discover the house locations used for some of your favourite films and TV programmes

Some people treat it as a game – trying to recognise the houses and places they see in films and on television. Looking at *Hudson's* can help. Many of the houses featured have been used as film and photographic locations, but that is hardly surprising. Film location managers, seeking historic houses, invariably turn to *Hudson's* as one of their first sources of reference.

Filming on location provides an authenticity that cannot be achieved with studio sets. Actors often find it easier. They can imbibe the atmosphere of a place which not only helps them to be totally natural, but is also conducive to their performance. They don't have to imagine that a building actually extends beyond the studio flat wall. That is why stately homes, manor houses, historic interiors, their landscaped parks and gardens, are regularly in demand by commercial film-makers for use as locations.

But for the house owner it can be alarming. Some have likened the arrival of a film crew to that of a circus coming to town. Space has to be found for mobile canteens, make-up and hairdressing caravans, props, generators, wardrobes and artists' trailers and a production office. Those who are unfamiliar with the filming of a full-scale drama for the cinema or TV will have no idea of how demanding and destructive to normal life location work can be. Nevertheless there is a financial incentive and it can be fun. Moreover, if the house is open and the film is a success, it adds further interest for the visitor.

Some properties are found to be particularly convenient as locations because they are close to London or major television studios such as at Bristol. **Knebworth House**, Hertfordshire (see p267), is used a great deal (*The Canterville Ghost*, 1997; *Wilde*, 1997) while nearby **Luton Hoo** (no longer open to the public) is also used a great deal (*Four Weddings and a Funeral*; *Mrs Brown*, 1997; *A Dance to the Music of Time*, 1997). The warm brick-and-timber façade of **Dorney Court** near Windsor (see p95), with its splendid Great Hall, is sufficiently close to London to feature in a wide variety of film and television productions. **Chavenage** (see p219) which is not far from Bristol, is regularly used, including for BBC's *Casualty* and *Cider with Rosie*, 1998.

...on location

ELIZABETH
1998 starring Cate Blanchett and Joseph Fiennes

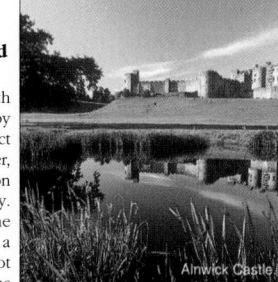
Alnwick Castle

The young Queen Elizabeth inherits a country wracked by internal religious conflict through the rule of her father, Henry VIII and the intervention of her Catholic half-sister, Mary. In a few short years she overcomes all odds to become a powerful monarch. Shot around the UK at locations which included **Alnwick Castle** (see p431) and Bamburgh beach, **Aydon Castle** (see p434) and **Warkworth Castle** in Northumberland (see p438); **Haddon Hall,** Derbyshire (see p289) and the **Tower of London** (see p74).

HAMLET
1990 starring Mel Gibson and Glenn Close

Impressive version of Shakespeare's dark tale of Hamlet's vengeance for the murder of his father with the setting of the menacing Castle Elsinore as much a character in the story as the rest of the cast. Shot on location in Scotland using the imposing medieval **Blackness Castle** in Falkirk (see p466) and **Dunnottar Castle** near Stonehaven, Grampian (see p491).

THE MADNESS OF KING GEORGE
1994 starring Nigel Hawthorne and Helen Mirren

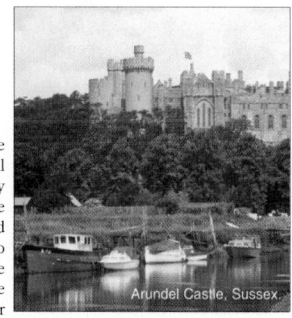
Arundel Castle, Sussex.

In the late 18th century the kindly King George is taken ill and his mental instability makes room for intrigue in the Court as his son and Parliament tussle to see who will take control. The Windsor Castle interiors were shot at **Wilton House** near Salisbury in Wiltshire (see p241) while also used were **Syon House** at Brentford (see p73), **Arundel Castle** in Sussex (see p159) and the impressive moated **Broughton Castle** near Banbury in Oxfordshire (see p144). Further scenes were shot in the Painted Hall of the Royal Naval College Greenwich and St Paul's Cathedral.

MRS BROWN (aka Her Majesty Mrs Brown),
1997 starring Judi Dench, Billy Connolly and Geoffrey Palmer

Much acclaimed and meticulously crafted drama about the extraordinary relationship between Queen Victoria, then the world's most powerful woman and John Brown, a simple but loyal Scottish Highlander. Filmed in **Osborne House**, Isle of Wight (see p181) (Victoria's elaborate holiday home), **Wilton House** near Salisbury (see p241) (doubling as Windsor Castle), **Duns Castle** west of Berwick-upon-Tweed in the Scottish Borders (see p452), and Lincoln's Inn Fields, London.

THE REMAINS OF THE DAY
1993 starring Anthony Hopkins and Emma Thompson

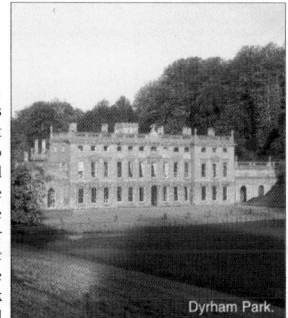
Dyrham Park.

Anthony Hopkins plays Mr Stephens the perfectionist butler at Darlington Hall, who watches over the ruling and serving classes during the 1930s and 40s but refuses to be emotionally drawn to events or even people. Four historic houses were used to create Darlington Hall. **Dyrham Park** near Bath (see p222) was used for exterior shots; **Corsham Court** near Chippenham (see p239) was used for the Library and Dining Room scenes; the Staircase Hall scenes were filmed at **Powderham Castle** near Exeter (see p201) and Badminton House, Gloucestershire (not open) was used for scenes of the servants' quarters.

ROB ROY
1995 starring Liam Neeson and Jessica Lange

Stirring adventure and fine retelling of the legend of the 18th century Scottish Highlander Rob Roy and his battles with the English. Shot around the west coast of Scotland and in Perthshire at **Megginch Castle** (see p481) and at **Drummond Castle** (see p479).

ROBIN HOOD PRINCE OF THIEVES
1991 starring Kevin Costner, Morgan Freeman and Alan Rickman

Shot almost everywhere except Sherwood Forest. Robin finds Marian at Hulme Priory, in the Park at **Alnwick Castle** in Northumberland (see p431); Locksley Castle is actually **Old Wardour Castle**, Wiltshire (see p245).

SENSE AND SENSIBILITY
1995 starring Emma Thompson, Kate Winslet and Alan Rickman

An Oscar winning adaptation of Jane Austen's classic novel about two sisters, one with good sense and the other with a wonderful excess of romantic sensibility. An elegant and witty film. Shot in part at **Montacute House**, Somerset (see p235); at **Saltram House** near Plymouth (see p208); at **Wilton** in Wiltshire (see p241) and at **Mompesson House** in Cathedral Close, Salisbury, Wiltshire (see p244).

SHAKESPEARE IN LOVE
1998 starring Gwyneth Paltrow, Joseph Fiennes, Judi Dench and Geoffrey Rush

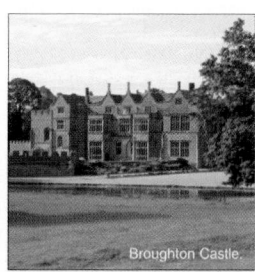
Broughton Castle.

Winner of 7 Oscars including Best Picture, this is a thoroughly enjoyable tale of a young Shakespeare (Fiennes) suffering from writer's block while setting out to write his new play, "Romeo and Ethel, the pirate's daughter". He falls for the beautiful Viola De Lesseps (Paltrow) who, in turn, disguises herself as a man to take part in his new play. Many sites were used including **Broughton Castle**, Oxfordshire (see p144) (stand-in for Viola's stately home); **Hatfield House**, Hertfordshire (see p266) doubled as Greenwich Palace, and the Great Hall at Middle Temple acted as the Banqueting Hall at Whitehall Palace (see p64). Other locations in London included **Marble Hill House** (see p82) and Spitalfields. The final scenes were shot at **Holkham** beach in Norfolk (see p270).

WILDE
1997 starring Stephen Fry and Jude Law

Impressive drama about the life of the playwright and *bon vivant* Oscar Wilde (wonderfully played by Fry), tracing his fame, family life and then fall from grace through his affair with Lord Alfred "Bosie" Douglas (Law). The film-makers made elegant use of locations which included Magdalen College, Oxford; Lulworth and Studland beaches and Swanage Pier in Dorset; **Houghton Lodge**, Hampshire (see p111); Luton Hoo near Luton; and **Somerset House** in London (see p71).

A MAN FOR ALL SEASONS
1966 starring Paul Schofield, Robert Shaw and Orson Welles

This Oscar winning adaptation of Robert Bolt's play about the politico-religious conflict between adulterous King Henry VIII and fervent Catholic Sir Thomas More, is an all-time classic. It was shot on location at **Hampton Court**, Surrey (see p152), the stunning 16th century Tudor Palace on the banks of the Thames.

MONTY PYTHON AND THE HOLY GRAIL
1975 starring John Cleese, Graham Chapman, Terry Jones, Terry Gilliam, Eric Idle and Michael Palin

This hilarious Python team send-up of Arthurian legend, the team of bungling knights encounter characters such as the Knights who say "Ni", flying cows, exploding rabbits, and a Knight who fights with all his limbs cut off. Though dealing with English legend, most of the film was shot in Scotland, including **Doune Castle** near Stirling (see p485), **Glencoe** (see p485) (where the knights must answer questions to cross the stunning 'Bridge of Death' at the Meeting of Three Waters) and **Castle Stalker** near Oban (see p484) (where the Grail is found).

TWELFTH NIGHT
1996 starring Nigel Hawthorne, Helena Bonham-Carter, Ben Kingsley, Imelda Staunton and Richard E Grant

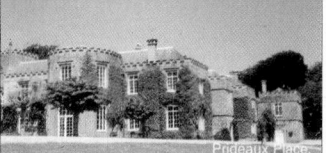
Prideaux Place.

Shot primarily in Cornwall including at **Prideaux Place**, Padstow (see p196); **Lanhydrock** (see p192) (Olivia's house, garden and estate), **Cotehele** (see p191) (quayside tavern and interior of Orsini's castle), **St Michael's Mount** (see p197) (Orsini's castle) and **Trerice** (see p199) (Olivia's estate – orchard). **Prideaux Place**, which was used extensively, was much altered for the film, but possibly the *piece de resistance* was one of the least expensive in terms of materials: an intricate ornamental grotto to form part of the Italian Garden contained thousands of shells coming from nearby beaches, local fishermen and Rick Stein's restaurant in Padstow.

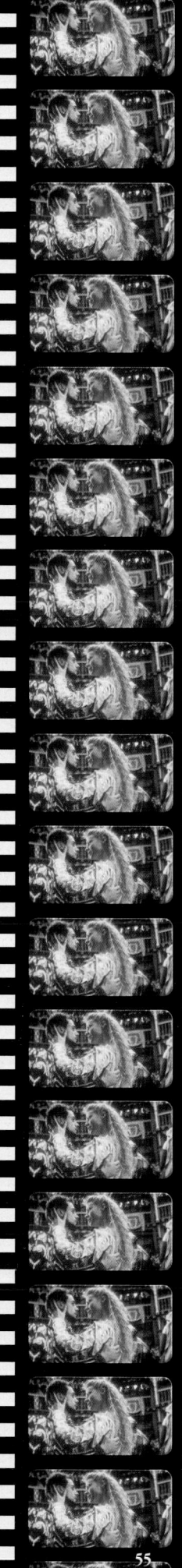

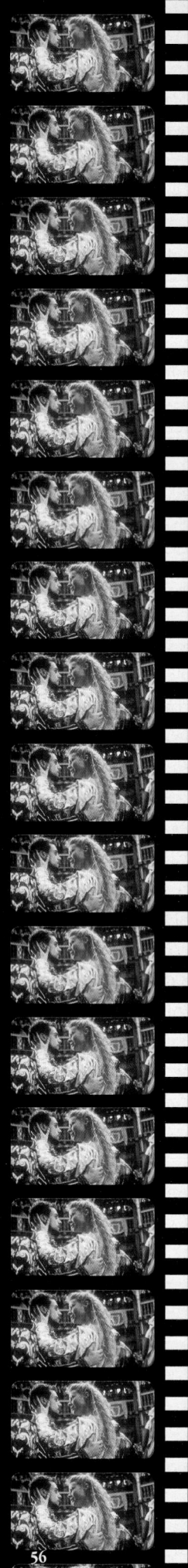

BRIDESHEAD REVISITED
1982 starring Jeremy Irons and Anthony Andrews
An epic ITV adaptation of Evelyn Waugh's novel has been a hit around the world, with a story of love, loyalty and passion amongst the upper classes during the inter-war years. **Castle Howard** near York (see p369) played the home of the Marchmain family but some interiors were also shot at **Tatton Park** in Cheshire (see p400).

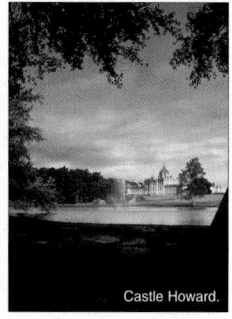
Castle Howard.

MIDDLEMARCH
1994 starring Juliet Aubrey, Patrick Malahide, Douglas Hodge and Rufus Sewell
This acclaimed and popular television version of George Eliot's classic novel tells of love and disillusionment against a backdrop of the 19th century Industrial Revolution. Filmed mainly in the historical Lincolnshire town of Stamford, using also nearby **Grimsthorpe Castle** (see p303) and **Burghley House** (see p301).

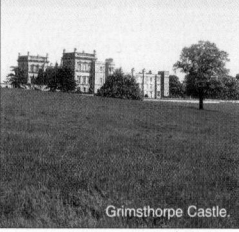
Grimsthorpe Castle.

PRIDE AND PREJUDICE
1995 starring Jennifer Ehle, Colin Firth and Alison Steadman
This very popular adaptation of Jane Austen's wonderful love story is about a young woman, Elizabeth Bennet (Ehle), her feminist views and her relationship with the dashing

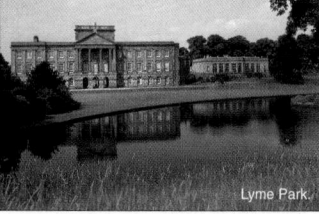
Lyme Park.

Mr Darcy (Firth). Shot at various locations including the National Trust village of Lacock in Wiltshire; the exteriors of Pemberley are **Lyme Park** in Cheshire (see p403); **Sudbury Hall**, Derbyshire (see p295); **Belton House** near Grantham (see p302); and the Cathedral Close in Salisbury.

THE PRISONER
1966-68 starring Patrick McGoohan
A cult series from the 60s. Patrick McGoohan, as a former secret service agent, is kidnapped and transplanted to a surreal village from which he constantly tries to escape. Filmed at the privately owned Mediterranean-style village of **Portmeirion** in North Wales (see p517). The village was the inspiration of architect Sir Clough Williams-Ellis who fell in love with the Italian fishing village of Portofino and was determined to recreate it in Britain.

AN IDEAL HUSBAND
1999 starring Rupert Everett and Cate Blanchett
Part of the exterior scenes featuring characters and horse riders used in this filmed version of Wilde's play, were filmed at **Waddesdon Manor**, Buckinghamshire (see p98) and were supposed to portray Rotten Row in Hyde Park.

MARTIN CHUZZLEWIT
1994
The BBC version of this Dickens novel starring Paul Schofield, John Mills and Peter Postlethwaite, used as locations **Honington Hall**, Warwickshire (see p352) and **Peckover House**, Cambridgeshire (see p260).

LOVEJOY
1980s
This popular television series about a roguish antiques dealer was shot primarily in East Anglia, where one of the principal locations was **Belchamp Hall**, Suffolk (see p277) as Lady Jane's house. Other house locations for this series were **Helmingham Hall** (see p278), **Wingfield Old College** (see p281) and **Somerleyton Hall** (see p280).

MOLL FLANDERS
1996 starring Alex Kingston, Daniel Craig and Diana Rigg
Wonderful adaptation of Daniel Defoe's widely-read novel with the story romping through the bedrooms and boudoirs of 18th century England. Filmed at **Hoghton Tower**, Preston (see p418); **Grimsthorpe Castle**, Lincolnshire (see p303) and **Little Moreton Hall**, Cheshire (see p403).

TOM JONES
1997
BBC1 television version of Fielding's novel. **Mapperton** in Dorset (see p215) and **Belton**, Lincolnshire (see p302).

CHARLES AND DIANA – UNHAPPY EVER AFTER
1994. A production for ABC starring Catherine Oxenburg
Shot primarily at **Manderston**, Berwickshire (see p450) where different aspects of the house could be portrayed variously as Buckingham Palace, Kensington Palace, Highgrove and Sandringham.

THE BUCCANEERS
1994.
The television adaptation of Edith Wharton's novel "The Buccaneers" included locations at **Castle Howard**, Yorkshire (see p369) and at **Houghton Lodge**, Hampshire (see p111).

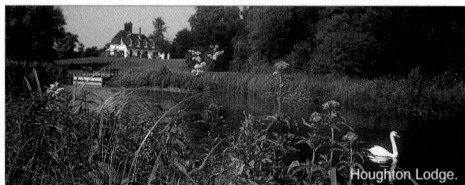
Houghton Lodge.

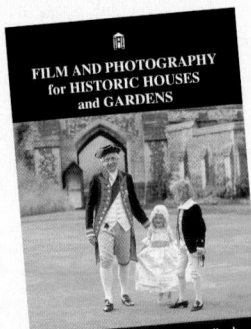
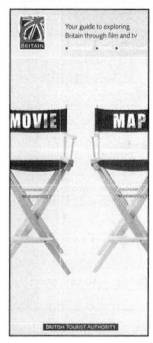

THE COUNTIES OF

ENGLAND

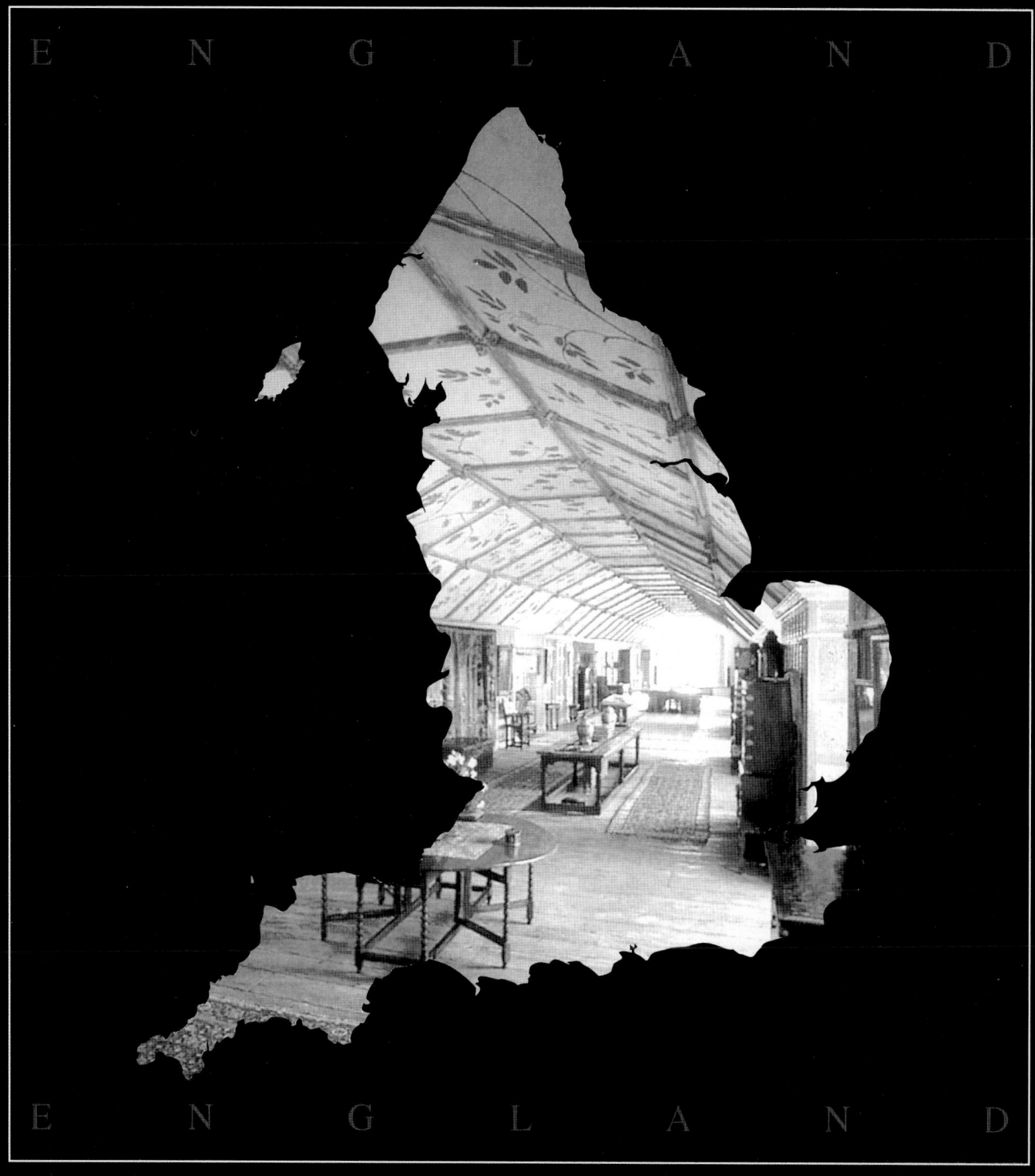

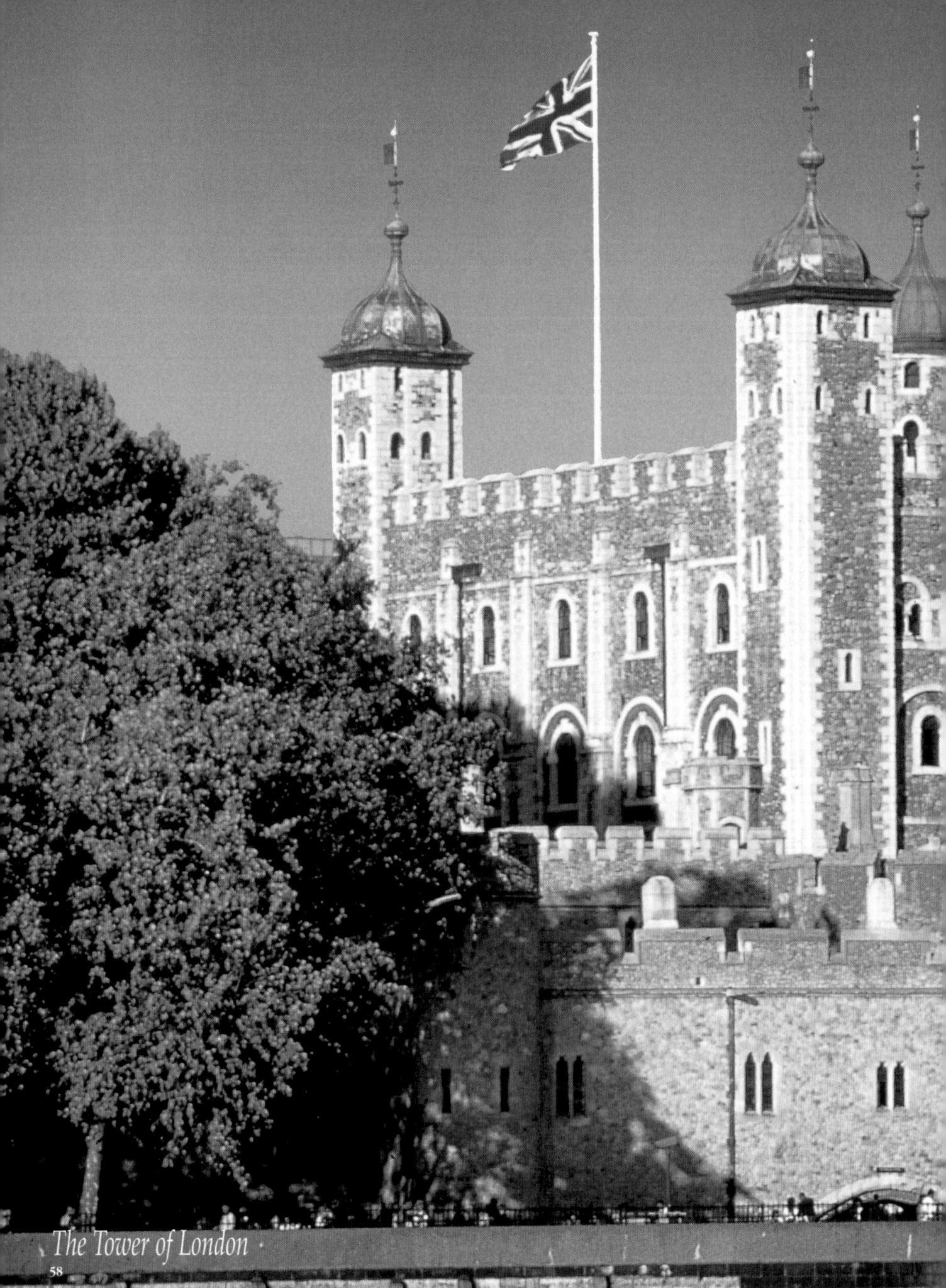

The Tower of London ·

London

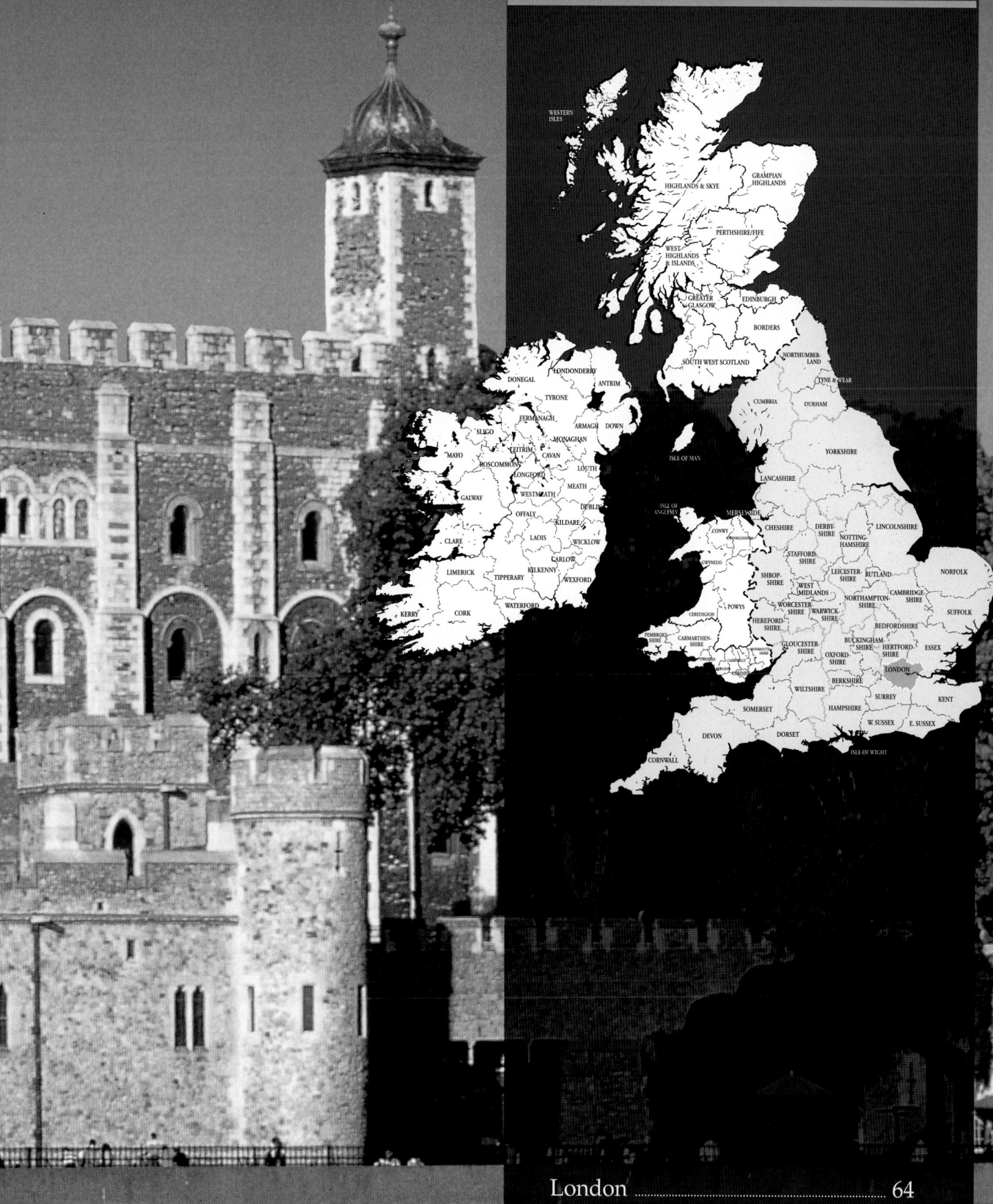

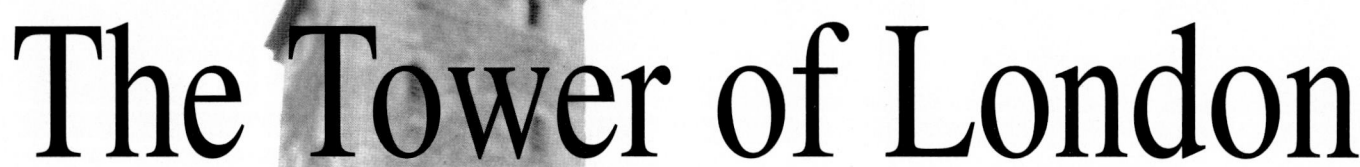

The Tower of London

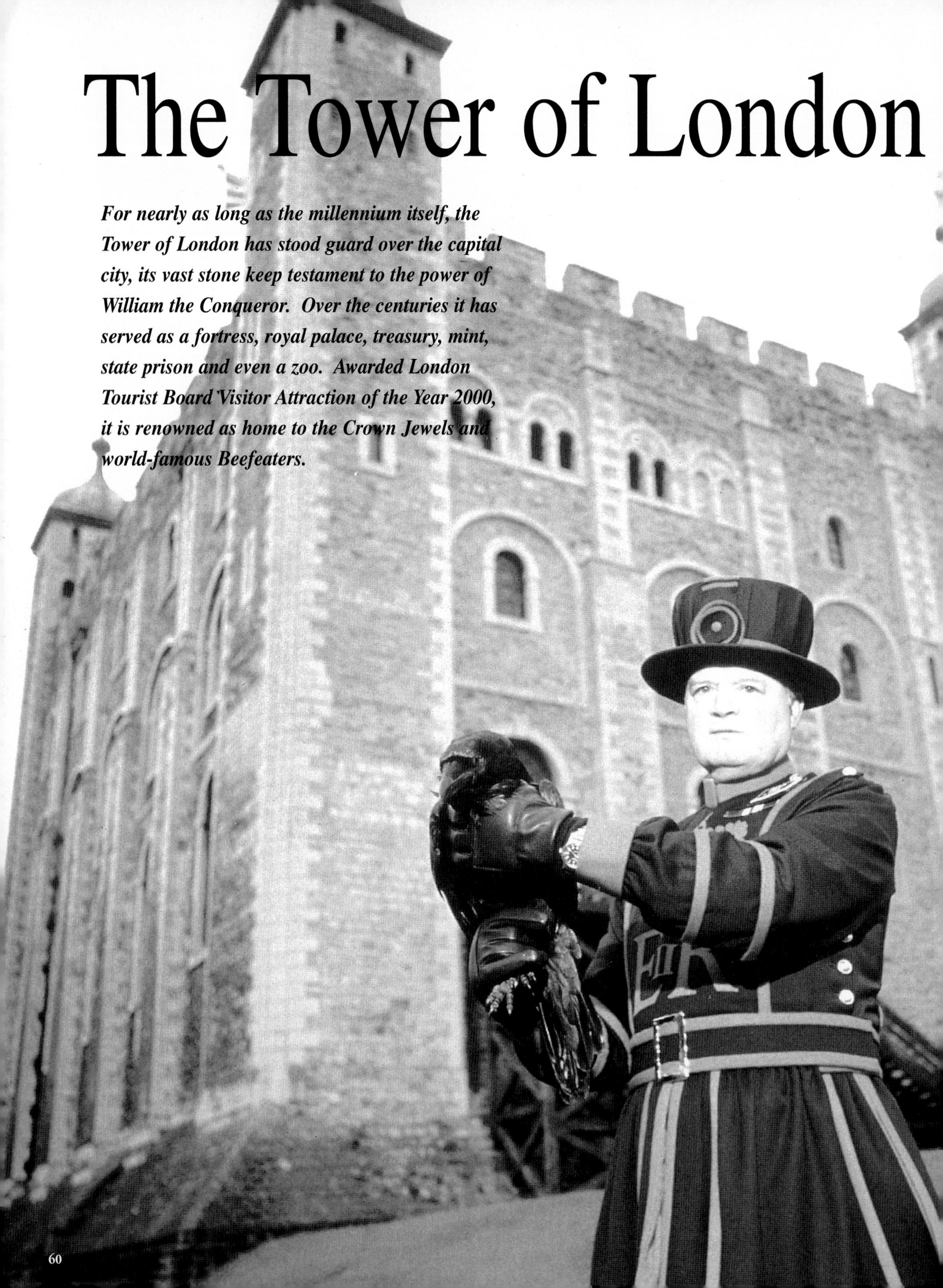

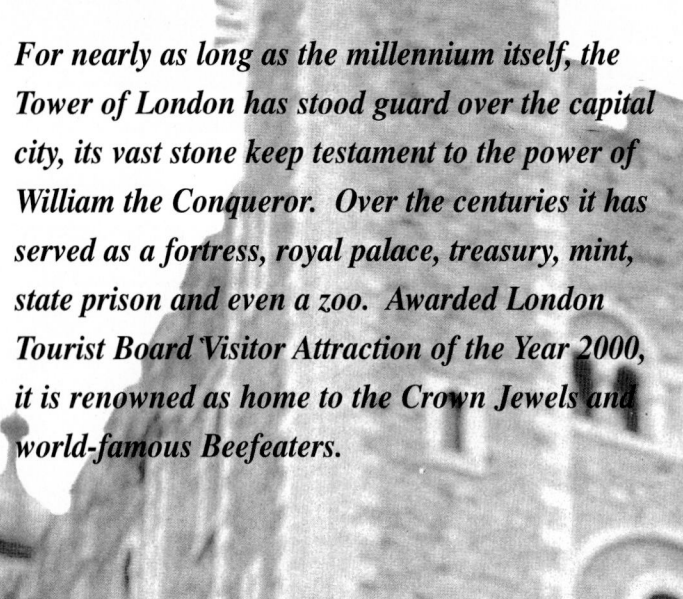

For nearly as long as the millennium itself, the Tower of London has stood guard over the capital city, its vast stone keep testament to the power of William the Conqueror. Over the centuries it has served as a fortress, royal palace, treasury, mint, state prison and even a zoo. Awarded London Tourist Board Visitor Attraction of the Year 2000, it is renowned as home to the Crown Jewels and world-famous Beefeaters.

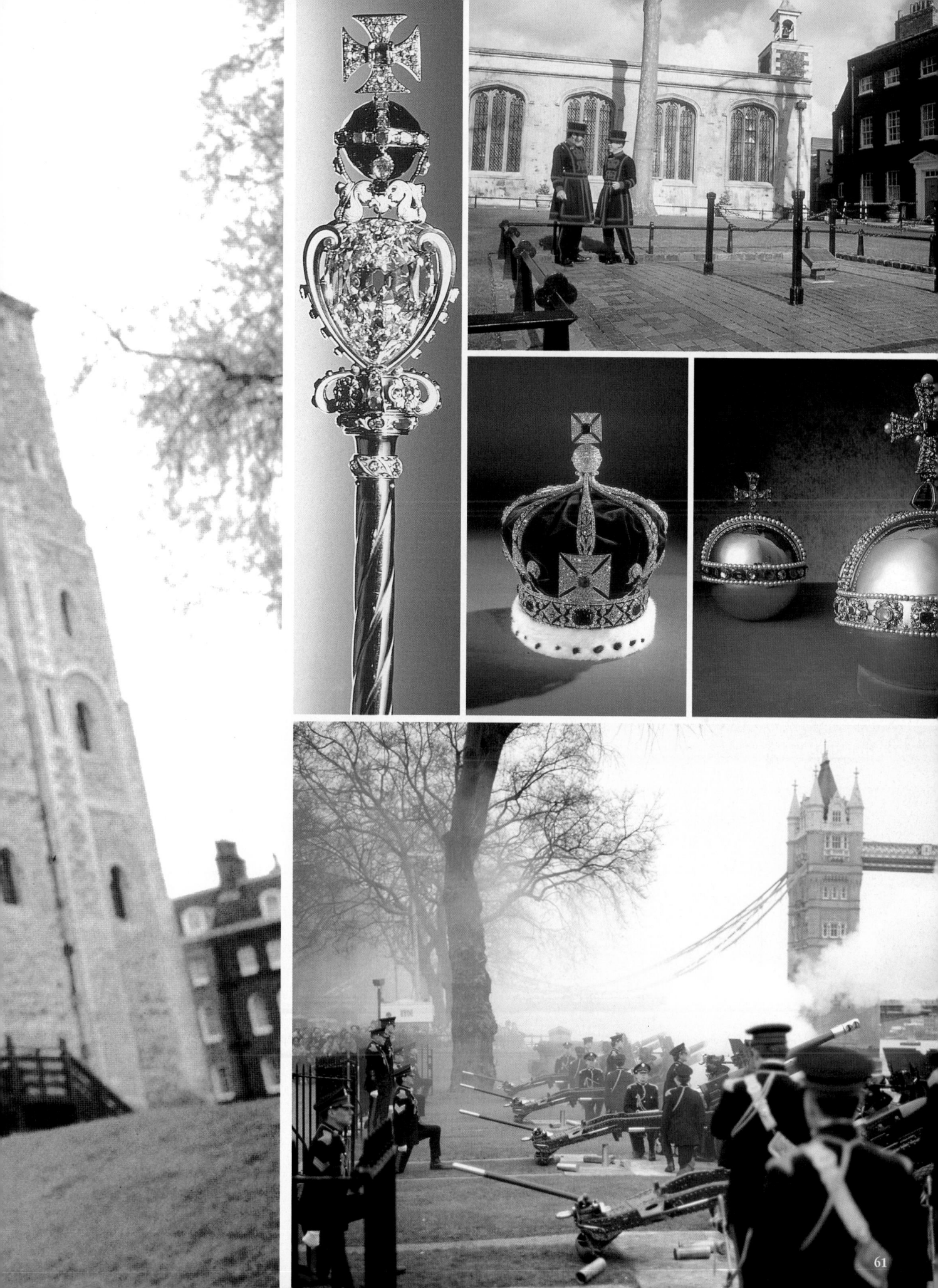

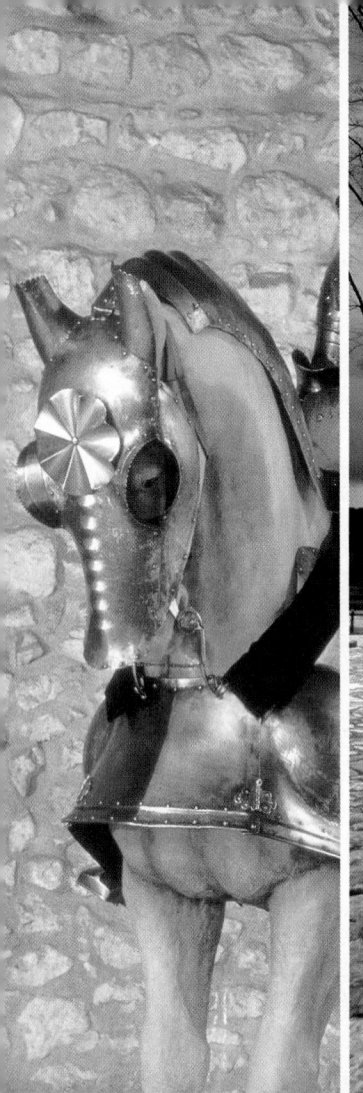

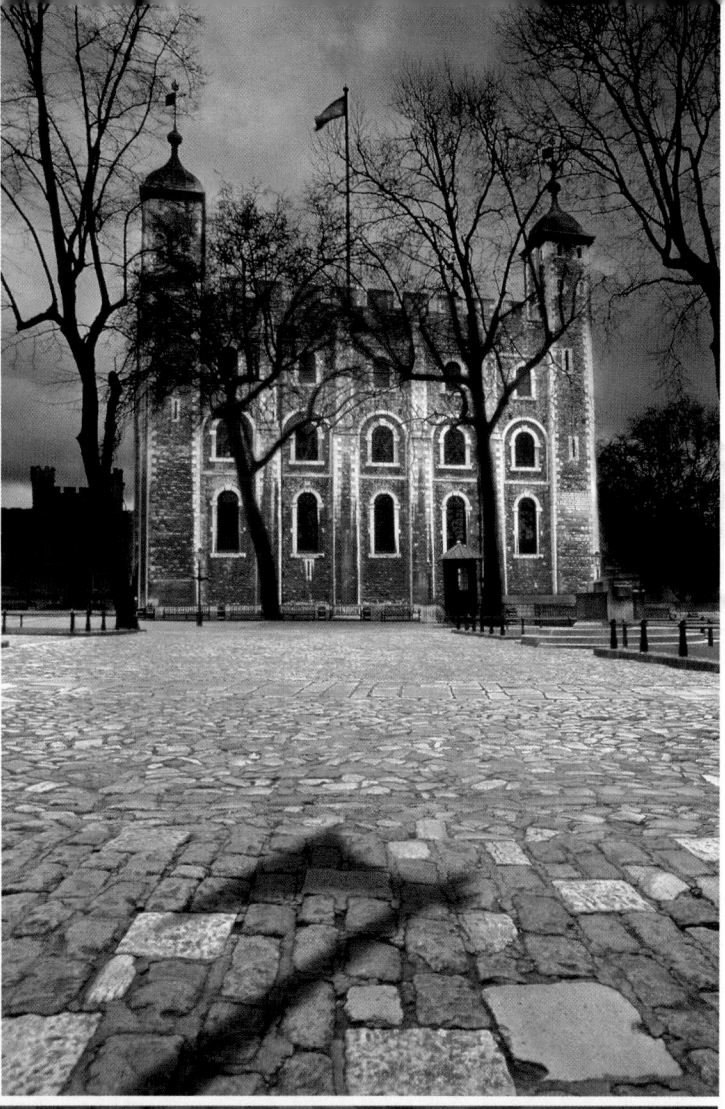

Since at least 1661, the Crown Jewels have been on display to the public and having moved from various locations in the Tower they now take pride of place in the new Jewel House, opened by Her Majesty the Queen in 1994. The items on show are priceless, representing far more than just precious stones and gold; they symbolise hundreds of years of the British Monarchy and the history that surrounds it.

No visit to the Tower is complete without taking a Yeoman Warder guided tour. Better known as Beefeaters, these former Warrant Officers regale visitors with tales of Kings, Queens, history and intrigue. What better way to discover 900 years of Britain's royal past in 60 minutes?

The great White Tower in the centre of the complex is the heart around which the rest of the fortress grew. Today it houses the Royal Armouries' displays of arms and armour, including two complete suits belonging to Henry VIII. Used throughout the Middle Ages by the sovereign and his court, it was the setting for some of the greatest events in British royal history.

Patrolling the Tower's lawns, the legendary ravens have played their role in Tower life since at least the reign of Charles II. It is said that should they ever leave, the White Tower will crumble and a great disaster befall England. Unwilling to take that chance, a complement of six of the huge black birds and one spare, are kept and tended by the Raven Master.

Home to some of Britain's most spectacular pomp and pageantry, the Tower hosts a series of special events throughout the year to bring history and tradition to life. Please telephone in advance for details.

For further details about *The Tower of London* see entry in London region.

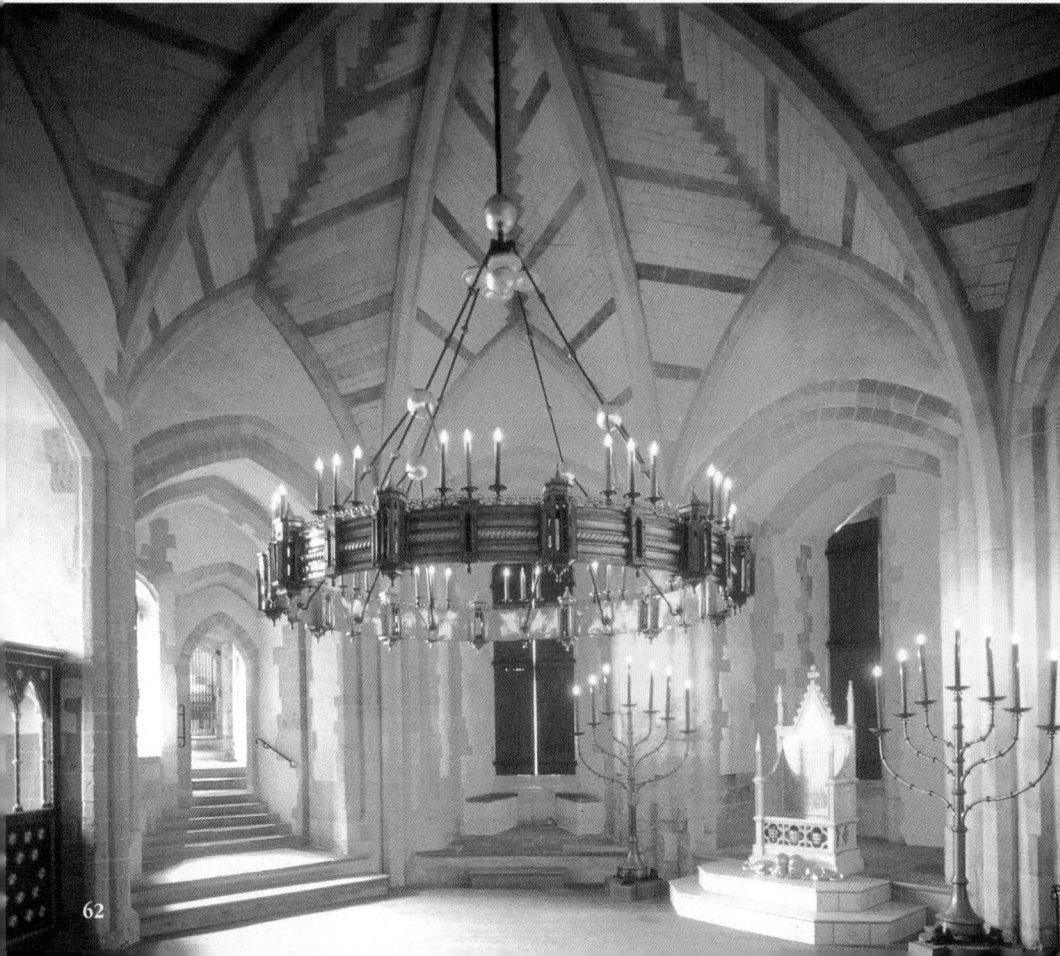

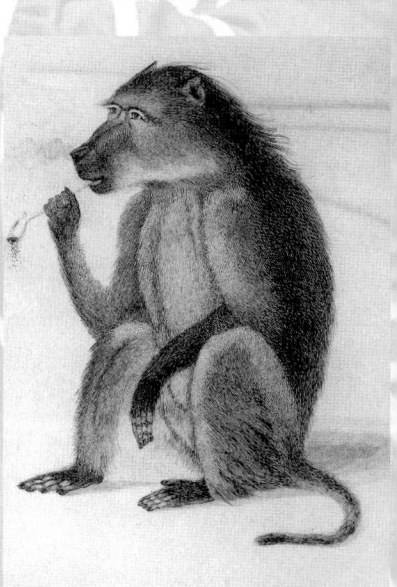

THE DOG-FACED BABOON.

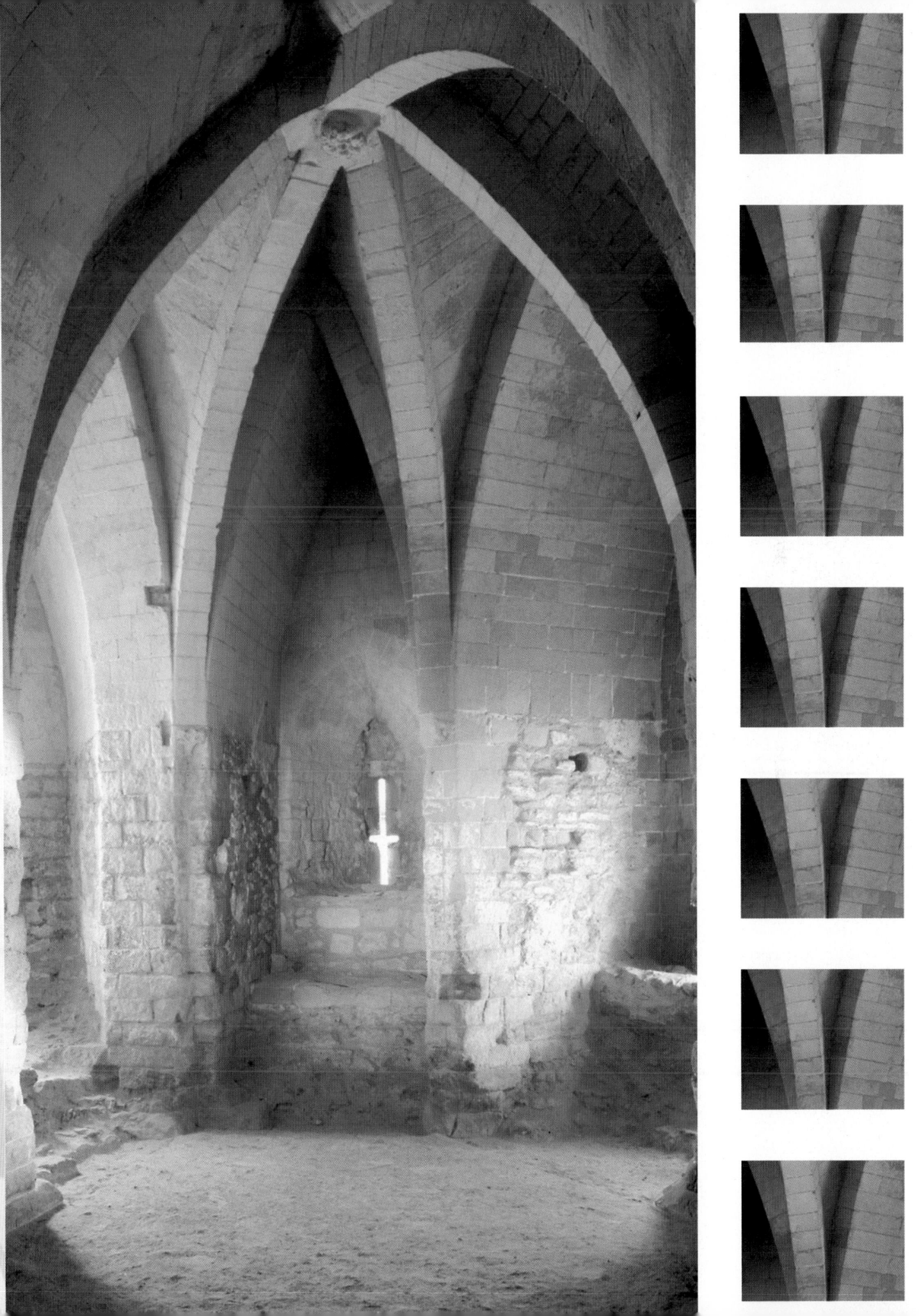

London England

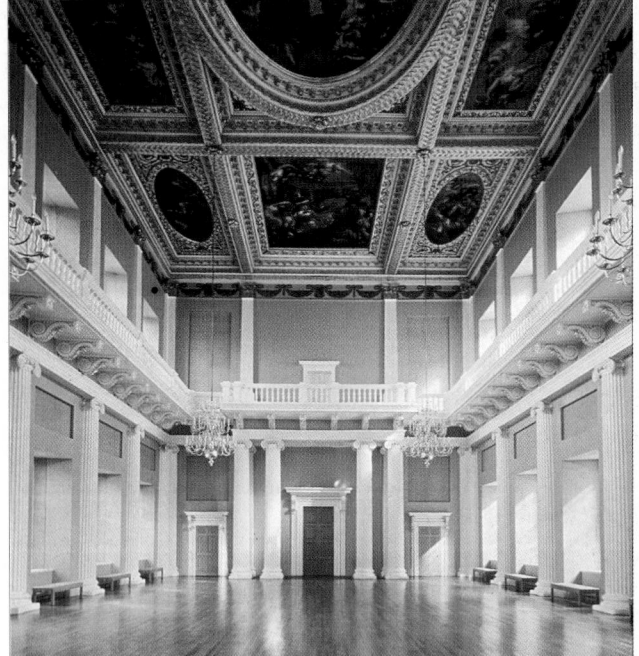

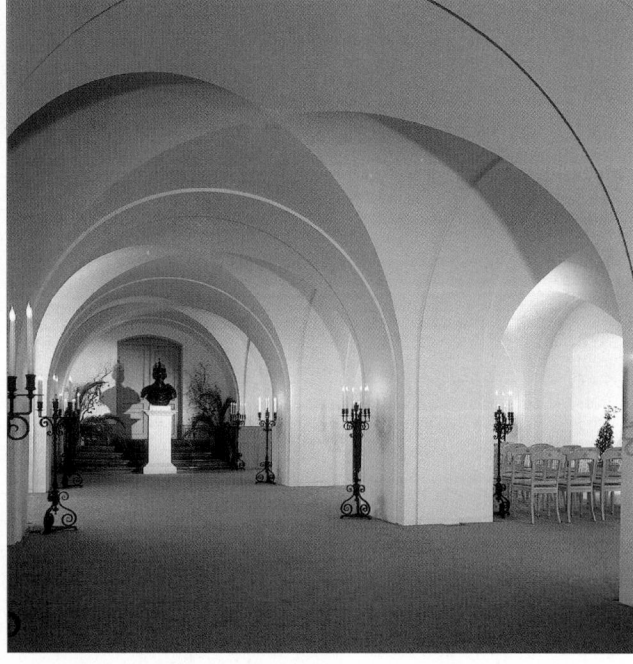

THE BANQUETING HOUSE
Whitehall

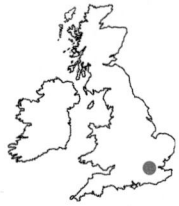

Owner:
Historic Royal Palaces

CONTACT

Irma Hay (day visitors)
Fiona Thompson
(functions)
The Banqueting House
Whitehall
London
SW1A 2ER

Tel: 020 7930 4179
or 020 7839 7569

Fax: 020 7930 8268

LOCATION

OS Ref. TQ302 801

Tube Stations:
Westminster,
Embankment
and Charing Cross.

Rail: Charing Cross.

The magnificent Banqueting House is all that survives of the great Palace of Whitehall which was destroyed by fire in 1698. It was completed in 1622, commissioned by King James I, and designed by Inigo Jones, the noted classical architect. In 1635 the main hall was further enhanced with the installation of 9 magnificent ceiling paintings by Sir Peter Paul Rubens, which survive to this day. The Banqueting House was also the site of the only royal execution in England's history, with the beheading of Charles I in 1649.

The Banqueting House is open to visitors, as well as playing host to many of society's most glittering occasions.

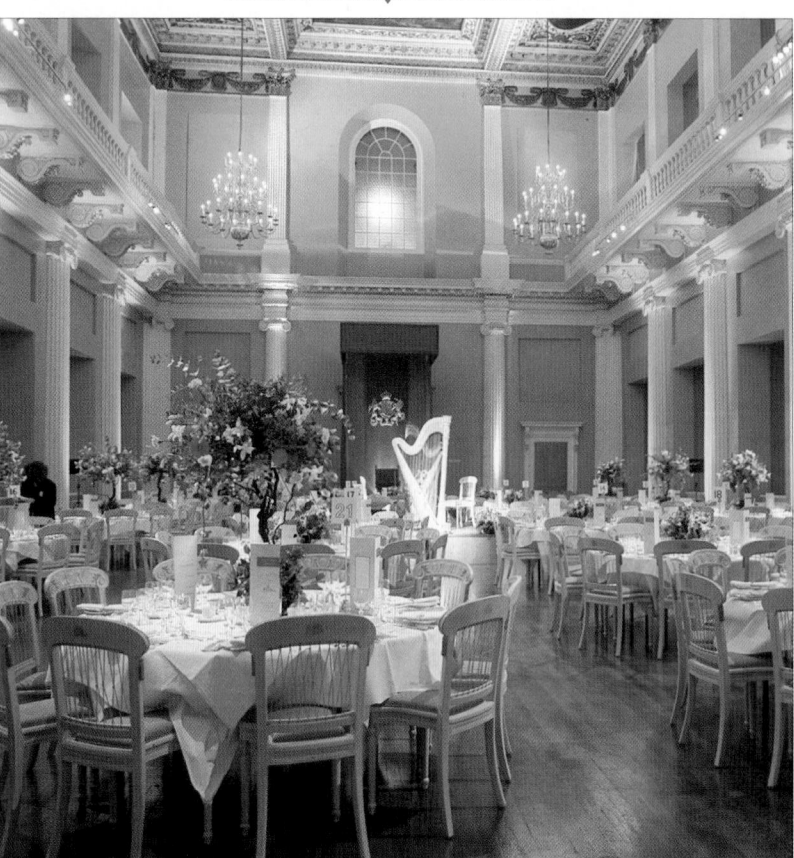

All year
Mon - Sat
10am - 5pm
Last admission 4.30pm.

Closed
24 December - 1 January,
Good Friday and other
public holidays.

NB. Liable to close at short
notice for Government
functions.

ADMISSION

Adult £3.90
Child (5-15yrs)..........£2.30
Student....................£3.10
OAP/Conc...............£3.10
Under 5s ....Free

Groups...please telephone:
020 7839 7569 for details.

 Concerts.
No photography in house.

Banquets.

Undercroft suitable.

Video and audio guide.

No parking.

Welcome.

CONFERENCE/FUNCTION		
ROOM	SIZE	MAX CAPACITY
Main Hall	110' x 55'	400
Undercroft	64' x 55'	350

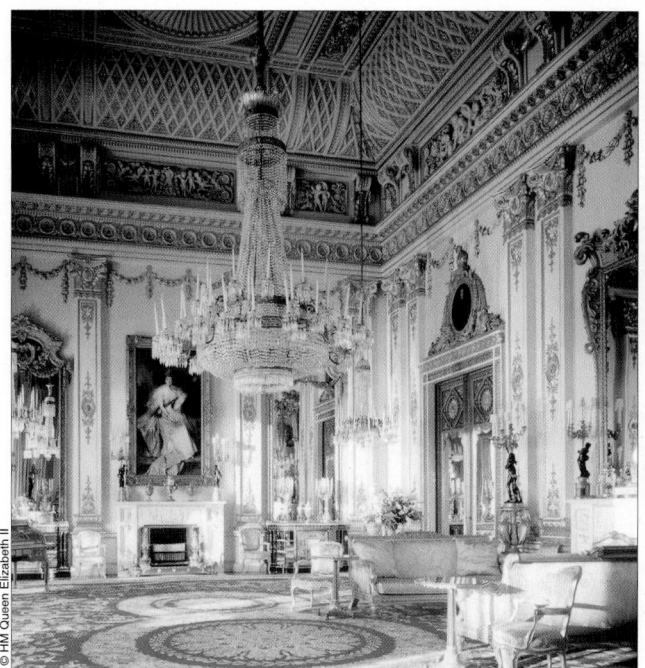

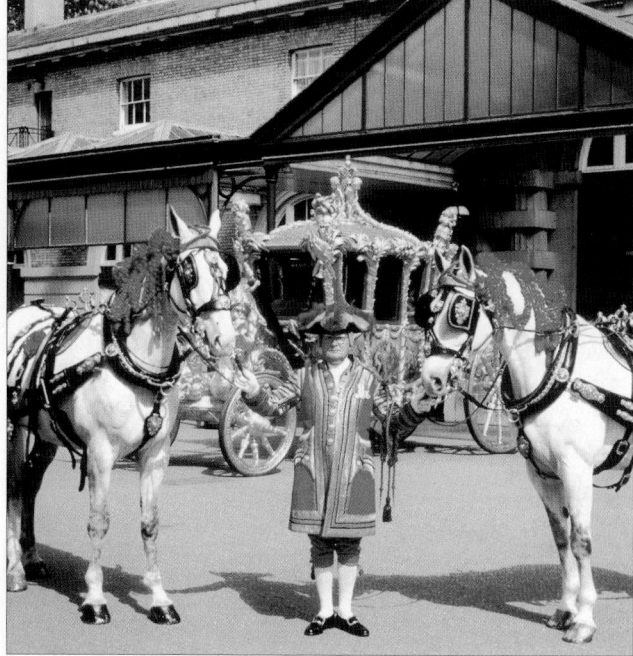

BUCKINGHAM PALACE
London

BUCKINGHAM PALACE, Windsor Castle and the Palace of Holyroodhouse are the Official residences of the Sovereign and are used by The Queen as both a home and office. The Queen's personal standard flies when Her Majesty is in residence. Furnished with works of art from the Royal Collection, these buildings are used extensively by The Queen for State ceremonies and Official entertaining. They are opened to the public as much as these commitments allow.

The Royal Mews is one of the finest working stables in existence. It provides a unique opportunity for visitors to see a working department of the Royal Household. The Monarch's magnificent Carriages and Coaches including the Gold State Coach are housed here, together with their horses and State liveries.

Owner:
HM The Queen

CONTACT

The Visitor Office
Buckingham Palace
London
SW1A 1AA

Tel: 020 7839 1377

Fax: 020 7930 9625

e-mail: information@
royalcollection.org.uk

LOCATION

OS Ref. TQ291 796

Nearest underground stations: Green Park, Victoria, St James's Park.

Rail: Victoria.

Air: Heathrow.

Sightseeing tours

A number of tour companies include a visit to the State Rooms in their sightseeing tours. Ask your concierge or hotel porter for details.

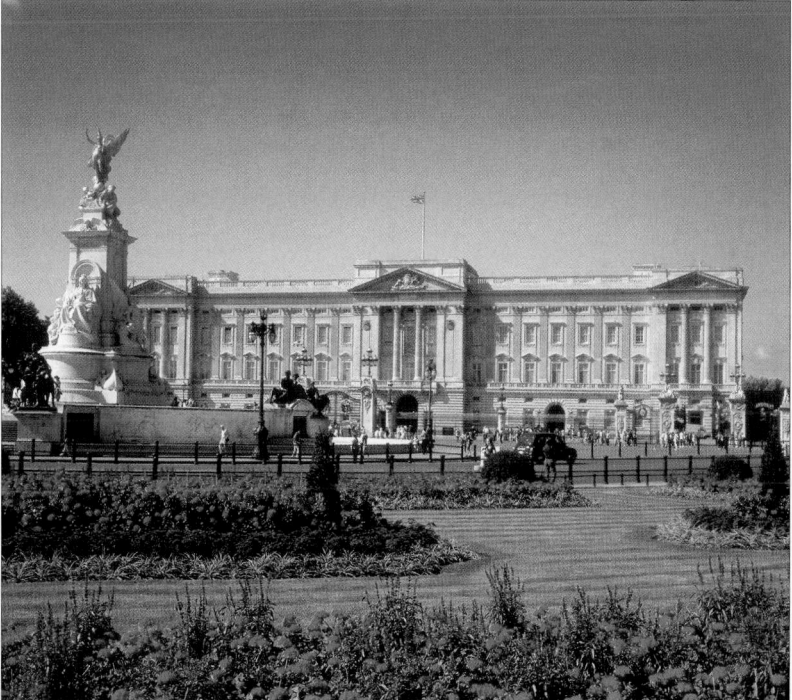

OPENING TIMES

Opening arrangements may change at short notice.

The State Rooms

6 August - 30 September*
Daily: 9.30am - 4.30pm.

Tickets available during Aug & Sept from the Ticket Office in Green Park.
To pre-book your tickets telephone the Visitor Office 020 7321 2233.

The Queen's Gallery

The Queen's Gallery is closed for refurbishment and will reopen in 2002, the year of The Queen's Golden Jubilee.

The Royal Mews

All year: Monday - Thursday
12 noon - 4pm
Last adm. 3.30pm.
Extra hours are added during the summer months.

* Further days may be added.

ADMISSION

The State Rooms

Adult	£11.00
Child (up to 17yrs)	£5.50
OAP	£9.00
Family (2+2)	£27.50

Groups (15+)	
Per person	£10.00

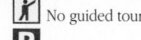 No photography inside.

 No guided tours.

Wheelchair users are required to pre-book for the summer opening. The Royal Mews is fully accessible.

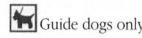 No parking. ■ Guide dogs only.

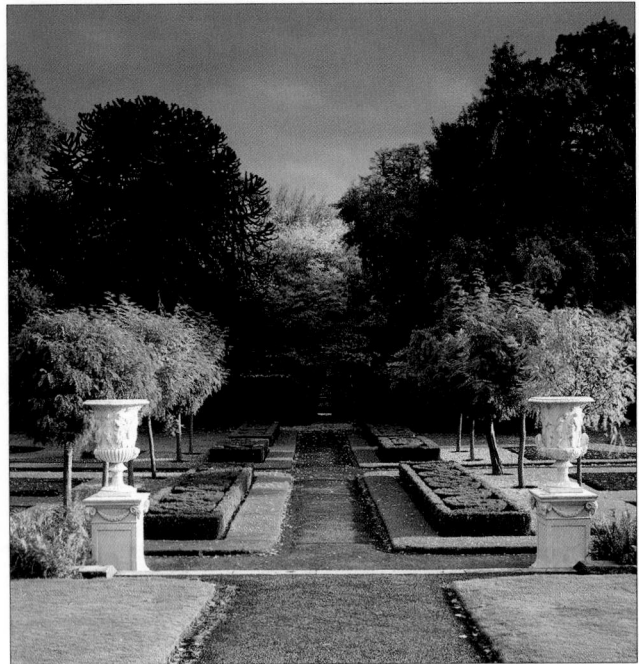

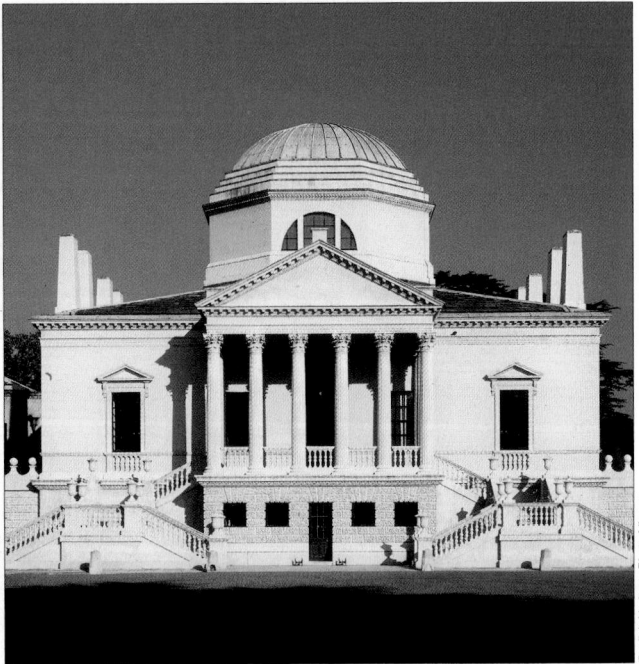

English Heritage Photo Library

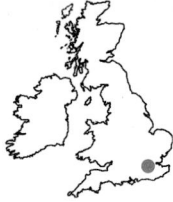

CHISWICK HOUSE
Chiswick

CHISWICK HOUSE is internationally renowned as one of the first and finest English Palladian villas. Lord Burlington, who built the villa from 1725 - 1729, was inspired by the architecture and gardens of ancient Rome and this house is his masterpiece. His aim was to create a fit setting to show his friends his fine collection of art and his library. The opulent interior features gilded decoration, velvet walls and painted ceilings. The important 18th century gardens surrounding Chiswick House have, at every turn, something to surprise and delight the visitor from the magnificent cedar trees to the beautiful Italianate gardens with their cascade, statues, temples, urns and obelisks.

English Heritage Hospitality

English Heritage Hospitality offers exclusive use of Chiswick House in the evenings for dinners, concerts, receptions and weddings.

Owner:
English Heritage

CONTACT

Visits:
House Manager
Chiswick House
Burlington Lane
London
W4 2RP

Tel: 020 8995 0508

English Heritage Hospitality:
The Hospitality Manager
Chiswick House
Burlington Lane
London
W4 2RP

Tel: 020 8742 1978

LOCATION

OS Ref: TQ210 775

Burlington Lane
London W4.

Rail: ¼m NE of Chiswick Station.

Bus: LT190, 290 (Hammersmith - Richmond).

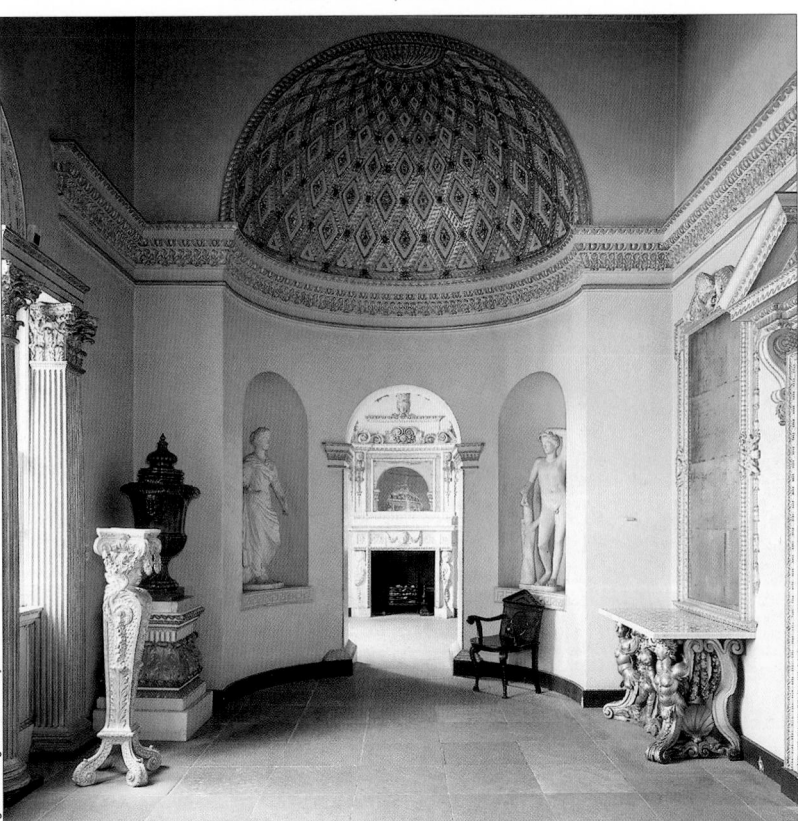

English Heritage Photo Library

CONFERENCE/FUNCTION	
ROOM	MAX CAPACITY
Domed Saloon	100 standing 48 dining
Red Velvet Room	24 dining
Green Velvet Room	24 dining
Whole House	150 standing 80 dining

OPENING TIMES

SUMMER
1 April - 30 September
Daily, 10am - 6pm.

AUTUMN
1 - 28 October
Daily, 10am - 5pm.
29 - 31 October:
Daily, 10am - 4.30pm.

WINTER
1 Nov - 31 March
Wed - Sun, 10am - 4pm.

Note: opening times may change in April 2001, please telephone for details before you visit.

ADMISSION

Adult £3.30
Child (5-15yrs) £1.70
Conc £2.50
Groups (11+)
.... 15% discount

Tour leader and coach driver have free entry. 1 extra place for every 20 additional people.

Filming, plays, photographic shoots.

Exclusive private & corporate hospitality.

Access to ground floor.

Personal guided tours must be booked in advance. Colour guide book £2.25.

Free audio tours in English, French & German.

Free if booked in advance. Tel: 020 7973 3485.

Guide dogs in grounds.

Civil Wedding Licence.

Telephone for details.

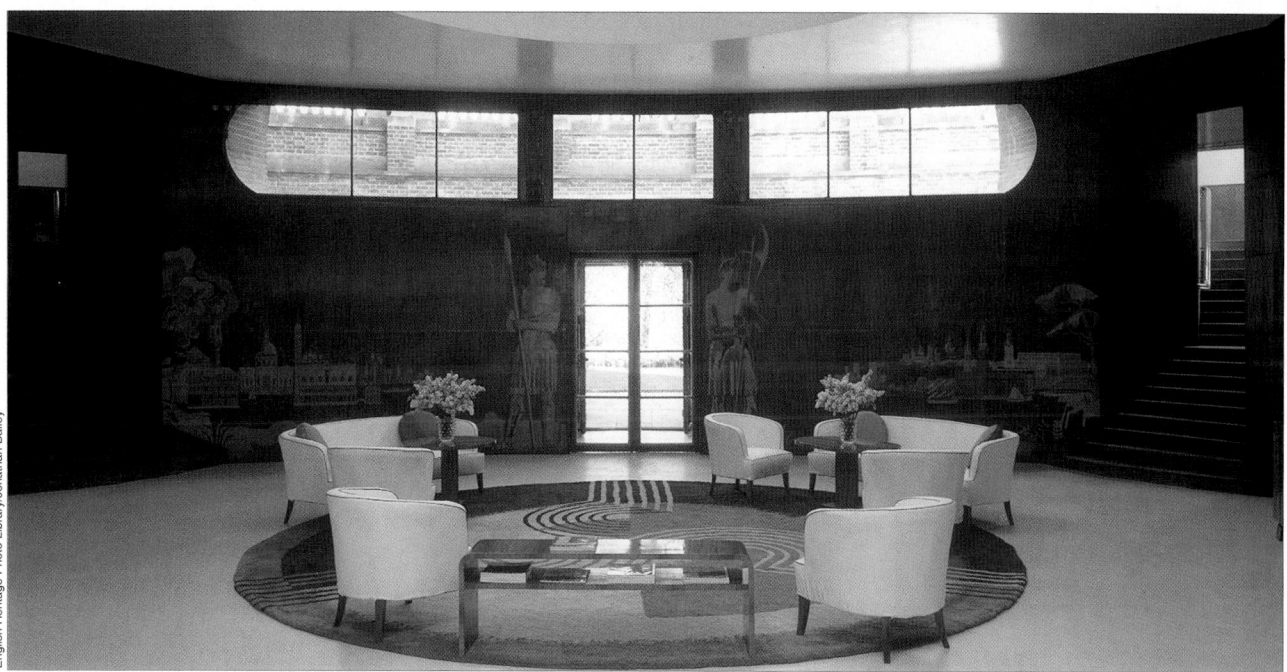

English Heritage Photo Library/Jonathan Bailey

ELTHAM PALACE
Eltham

The epitome of 1930s chic, Eltham Palace dramatically demonstrates the glamour and allure of the period.

Bathe in the light flooding from a spectacular glazed dome in the Entrance Hall as it highlights beautiful blackbeam veneer and figurative marquetry. It is a *tour de force* only rivalled by the adjacent Dining Room - where an Art Deco aluminium-leafed ceiling is a perfect complement to the bird's-eye maple walls. Step into Virginia's magnificent gold-leaf and onyx bathroom and throughout the house discover lacquered, 'ocean liner' style veneered walls and built-in furniture. A Chinese sliding screen is all

that separates chic '30s Art Deco from the medieval Great Hall. You will find concealed electric lighting, centralised vacuum cleaning and a loud-speaker system that allowed music to waft around the house. Authentic interiors have been recreated by the finest contemporary craftsmen. Their appearance was painstakingly researched from archive photographs, documents and interviews with friends and relatives of the Courtaulds.

Outside you will find a delightful mixture of formal and informal gardens including a rose garden, pergola and loggia, all nestled around the extensive remains of the medieval palace.

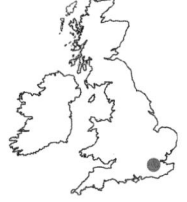

Owner: English Heritage

CONTACT

English Heritage Hospitality:
Hospitality Manager
Eltham Palace
Court Yard
Eltham
SE9 5QE

Tel: 020 8294 2577

Visits:
Property Secretary
Eltham Palace
Court Yard
Eltham
SE9 5QE

Tel: 020 8294 2548

LOCATION

OS Ref. TQ425 740

M25/J3, then A20 towards Eltham. The Palace is signposted from A20 and from Eltham High Street.

Rail: Eltham or Mottingham.

CONFERENCE/FUNCTION

ROOM	MAX CAPACITY
Great Hall	400 standing 200 dining
Entrance Hall	100 seated
Drawing Room	120 standing 80 theatre-style
Dining Room	50 dining

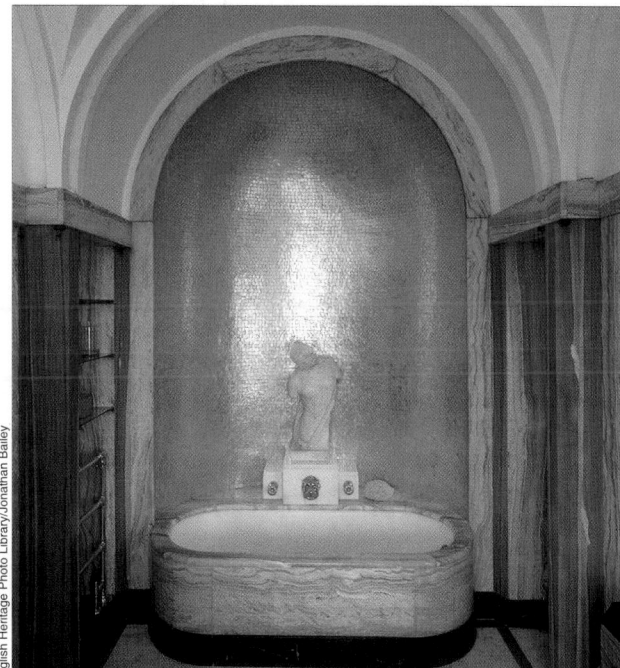

English Heritage Photo Library/Jonathan Bailey

OPENING TIMES

1 Apr - 30 September:
Wed - Fri & Sun
10am - 6pm.
1 - 31 October: Wed - Fri
& Sun, 10am - 5pm.
1 November - 31 March:
Wed - Fri & Sun,
10am - 4pm.
Open BH Mons
throughout the year.
Closed 24 - 26 December &
1 January 2001.
Groups visits must be
booked two weeks in
advance.

**English Heritage
Hospitality**
English Heritage Hospitality
offers exclusive use of the
Palace on Mons, Tues or
Sats for daytime
conferences, meetings and
weddings and in the
evenings for dinners,
concerts and receptions.

ADMISSION

House and Grounds
Adult £5.90
Child.......................£3.00
OAP........................£4.40

Grounds only
Adult £3.50
Child.......................£1.80
OAP........................£2.60

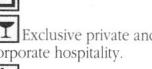 Filming, plays and photographic shoots.

 Exclusive private and corporate hospitality.

Free.

 Coaches must book.

London
England

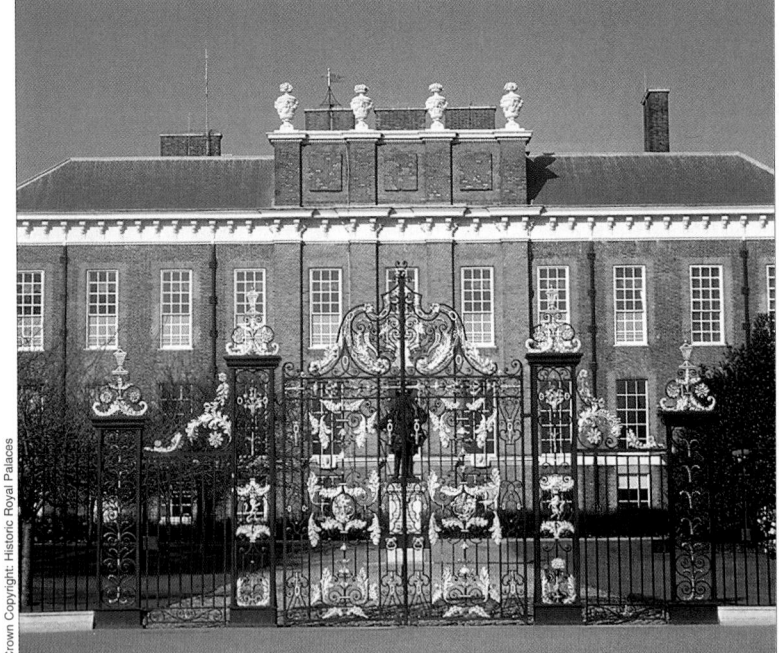

Crown Copyright: Historic Royal Palaces

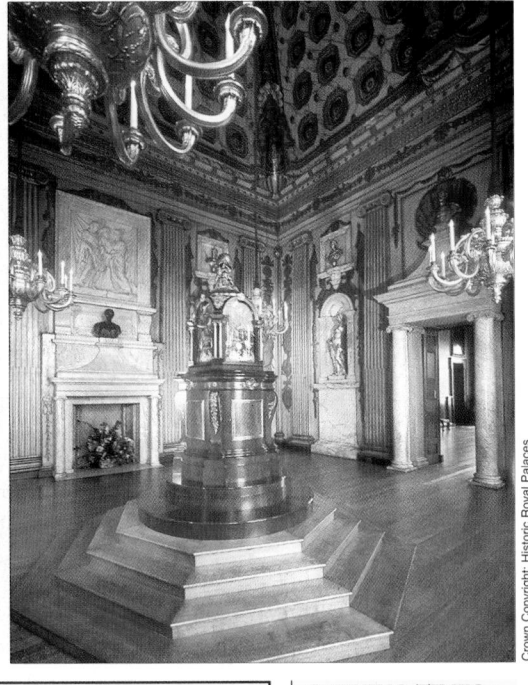

Crown Copyright: Historic Royal Palaces

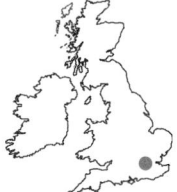

Managed by:
Historic Royal Palaces

CONTACT

Kensington Palace
State Apartments
London
W8 4PX

Tel: 020 7937 9561

LOCATION

OS Ref. TQ258 801

In Kensington Gardens.

Tube Station: Queensway
on Central Line,
High Street Kensington on
Circle & District Line.

KENSINGTON PALACE STATE APARTMENTS
Kensington

The history of Kensington Palace dates back to 1689 when the newly crowned William III and Mary II commissioned Sir Christopher Wren to convert the then Nottingham House into a Royal Palace. The Palace was again altered when George I had the artist William Kent paint the magnificent *trompe l'oeil* ceilings and staircases which can still be enjoyed at this most private of Palaces.

This beautiful historic building has seen such momentous events as the death of George II and the birth of Queen Victoria who began her long reign as Queen in 1837, with a meeting of her Privy Council in the Red Saloon.

Multi-language sound guides are available to lead visitors round the magnificent State Apartments. Highlights include the splendid Cupola Room, the most lavishly decorated state room in the Palace and where Queen Victoria was baptised, and the beautifully restored King's Gallery which is home to several Old Masters from the collection of HM the Queen.

Kensington Palace is also home to 'Dressing for Royalty' – a stunning presentation of Royal Court and Ceremonial Dress dating from the 18th century, which allows visitors to participate in the excitement of dressing for Court – from invitation to presentation. There is also a dazzling selection of 16 dresses owned and worn by HM Queen Elizabeth II.

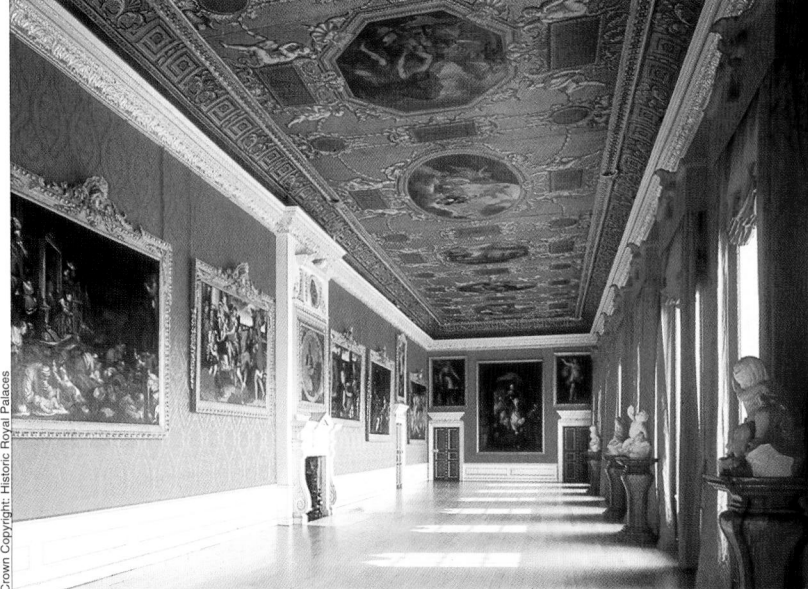

Crown Copyright: Historic Royal Palaces

No photography indoors.

The Orangery serves light refreshments.

Partially suitable.

Sound guides for Dress Collection and State Apartments.

P Nearby.

Welcome, please book.

In grounds, on leads. Guide dogs only in Palace.

FUNCTIONS		
ROOM	SIZE	MAX CAPACITY
Orangery	7.1 x 34m	250 receptions 150 dinners

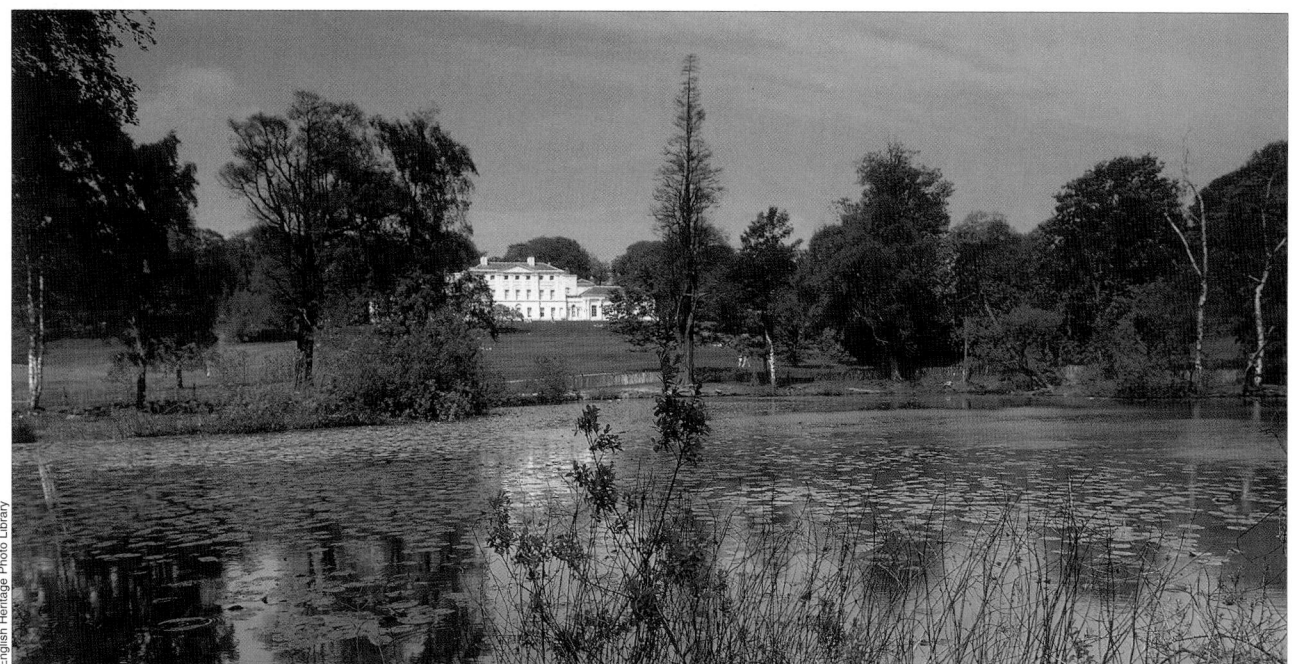

English Heritage Photo Library

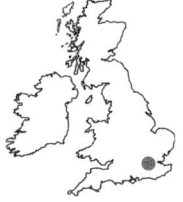

KENWOOD HOUSE
Hampstead

KENWOOD, one of the treasures of London, is an idyllic country retreat close to the popular villages of Hampstead and Highgate.

The house was remodelled in the 1760s by Robert Adam, the fashionable neo-classical architect. The breathtaking library or 'Great Room' is one of his finest achievements.

Kenwood is famous for the internationally important collection of paintings bequeathed to the nation by Edward Guinness, 1st Earl of Iveagh. Some of the world's finest artists are represented by works such as a Rembrandt *Self Portrait*, Vermeer's *The Guitar Player; Mary,*

Countess Howe by Gainsborough and paintings by Turner, Reynolds and many others.

As if the house and its contents were not riches enough, Kenwood stands in 112 acres of landscaped grounds on the edge of Hampstead Heath, commanding a fine prospect towards central London. The meadow walks and ornamental lake of the park, designed by Humphry Repton, contrast with the wilder Heath below. The open air concerts held in the summer at Kenwood have become part of London life, combining the charms of music with the serenity of the lakeside setting.

Owner:
English Heritage

CONTACT

Visits:
The House Manager
Kenwood House
Hampstead Lane
London
NW3 7JR

Tel: 020 8348 1286

English Heritage Hospitality:
The Hospitality Manager
Kenwood House
Hampstead Lane
London
NW3 7JR

Tel: 020 7973 3507

LOCATION

OS Ref. TQ271 874.

Hampstead Lane, NW3.

Bus: London Transport 210.

Rail: Hampstead Heath.

Underground: Archway or Golders Green Northern Line then bus 210.

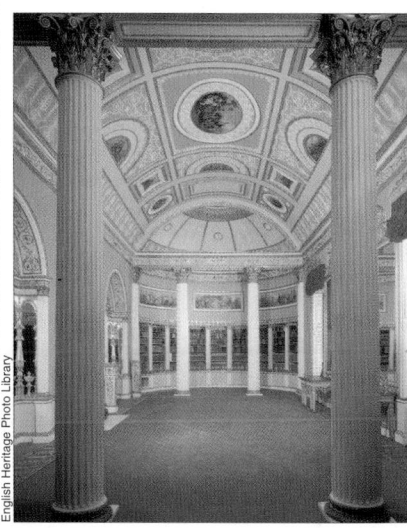

English Heritage Photo Library

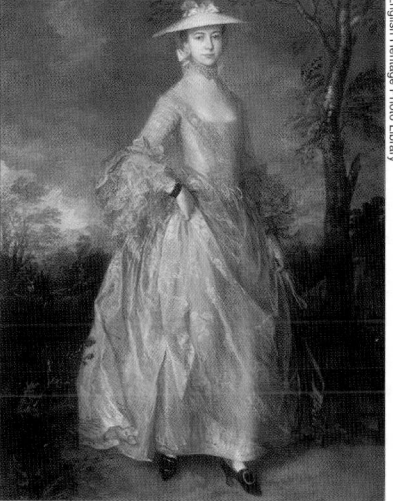

English Heritage Photo Library

OPENING TIMES

SUMMER
1 April - 30 September
Daily: 10am - 6pm.

1 - 31 October
Daily: 10am - 5pm.

WINTER
1 November - 31 March
Daily: 10am - 4pm.

Closed 24 & 25 December.

Open 1 January 2001.

English Heritage Hospitality offers exclusive use of Kenwood House in the evenings for dinners, concerts and receptions, and the lecture room for daytime events.

ADMISSION

House & Grounds:
Free. Donations welcome.

The 45 minute tour must be booked in advance. Please ask for details on tours available in different languages.

CONFERENCE/FUNCTION	
ROOM	MAX CAPACITY
Orangery	80 dining
Music Room	40 dining
Dining Room	50 dining
Lecture Room	80 theatre-style 300 dining
Whole House	150 dining

ℹ Concerts, exhibitions, filming. No photography in house.

Exclusive private and corporate hospitality.

Ground floor access.

Available in the Brew House.

Foreign language tours by prior arrangement.

Personal stereo tours.

West Lodge car park on Hampstead Lane. Parking for the disabled.

Free when booked in advance on 020 7973 3485.

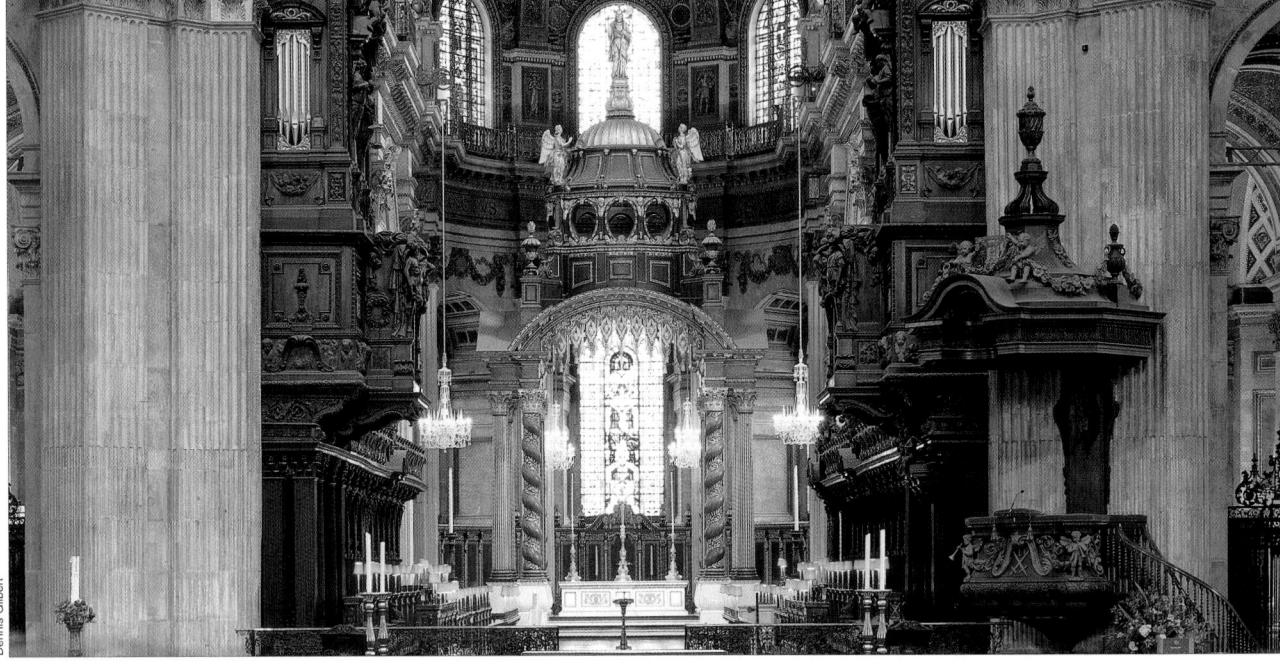

Dennis Gilbert

ST PAUL'S CATHEDRAL
London

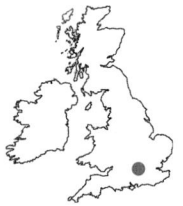

Owner: Dean & Chapter
of St Paul's Cathedral

CONTACT

Mark McVay
The Chapter House
St Paul's Churchyard
London
EC4M 8AD

Tel: 020 7246 8346
020 7246 8348

Fax: 020 7248 3104

e-mail: chapterhouse@
stpaulscathedral.org.uk

LOCATION

OS Ref. TQ321 812

Central London.
Nearest Underground:
St Paul's, Mansion House,
Blackfriars, Bank.

Rail: Blackfriars,
City Thameslink.

Air: London Airports.

A Cathedral dedicated to St Paul has stood at the heart of the City of London for 1400 years, a constant reminder of the spiritual life in this busy commercial centre.

The present St Paul's, the fourth to occupy the site, was built between 1675 - 1710. Sir Christopher Wren's masterpiece rose from the ashes of the previous Cathedral, which had been destroyed in the Great Fire of London.

Over the centuries, the Cathedral has been the setting for royal weddings, state funerals and thanksgivings. Admiral Nelson and the Duke of Wellington are buried here, Queen Victoria celebrated her gold and diamond jubilees and Charles, Prince of Wales married Lady Diana Spencer. Most recently, St Paul's hosted the thanksgiving service for the 100th birthday of HM Queen Elisabeth the Queen Mother.

Hundreds of memorials pay tribute to famous statesmen, soldiers, artists, doctors and writers and mark the valuable contributions to national life made by many ordinary men and women.

The soaring dome, one of the largest in the world, offers panoramic views across London from the exterior galleries. Inside, a whisper in the Whispering Gallery can be heard on the opposite side.

Far more than a beautiful landmark, St Paul's Cathedral is a living symbol of the city and nation it serves.

❖

Dennis Gilbert

🚫📷 ℹ️ No photography, video
or mobile phones.

🚫 Partially suitable.

☕🍴 Licensed.

🚶 No parking for cars, limited
for coaches.

🦮 Guide dogs only.

❄️

CONFERENCE/FUNCTION		
ROOM	SIZE	MAX CAPACITY
Conference Suite		100 (standing)

OPENING TIMES

Mon - Sat, 8.30am -
4.30pm, last admission
4pm.

Guided tours: daily,
11.30am, 1.30pm and 2pm.

Tours of the Triforium:
Mons & Thurs, 11.30am &
2.30pm.

Cathedral Shop & Café:
9am - 5.30pm,
Suns, 10.30am - 5pm.

Restaurant:
11am - 3.30pm.

Service Times
Mon - Sat
7.30am Mattins (Sat
8.30am)
8am Holy Communion
(said)
12.30pm Holy Communion
(said)
5pm Choral Evensong

Suns: 8am Holy
Communion (said)
10.15am Choral Mattins
& sermon
11.30am Choral Eucharist
& sermon
3.15pm Choral Evensong
& sermon
6pm Evening service

The Cathedral may be closed
to tourists on certain days of
the year. It is advisable to
phone or check our website
for up-to-date information.

ADMISSION

Adult £5.00
Child......................£2.50
Student....................£4.00
OAP........................£4.00

Groups (min 10)
Adult £4.50
Child......................£2.25
Student....................£3.75
OAP........................£3.75

(2000 prices)

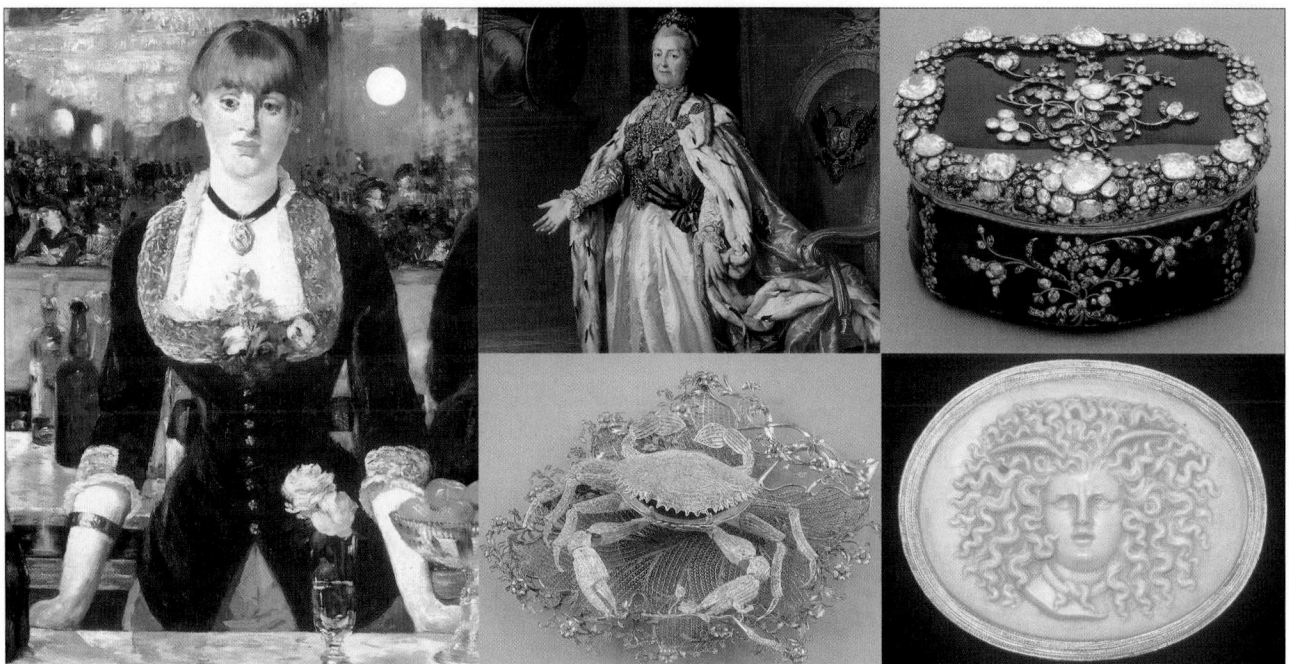

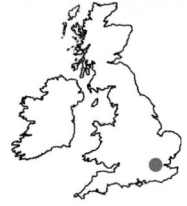

SOMERSET HOUSE
London
including Courtauld Gallery, Gilbert Collection and Hermitage Rooms

SOMERSET HOUSE, Sir William Chambers' 18th century architectural masterpiece, is open to the public for the first time. Situated between Covent Garden and the South Bank, it takes its place as one of Europe's great centres for art and culture, and the enjoyment of long-hidden classical interiors and architectural vistas.

The COURTAULD GALLERY has one of the greatest small collections of paintings in the world, including the finest Impressionist paintings in Britain.

The GILBERT COLLECTION is London's newest museum of the decorative arts. Given to the nation by Sir Arthur Gilbert, the magnificent collections of European silver, gold snuff boxes and Italian mosaics are pre-eminent in the world. Other displays include furniture, Russian Church art and portrait miniatures. The vaulted spaces of Somerset House provide an inspirational setting for these works of great historical and artistic importance.

The HERMITAGE ROOMS at Somerset House recreate, in miniature, the imperial splendour of the Winter Palace and its various wings, which now make up The State Hermitage Museum in St Petersburg. The inaugural exhibition 'Treasures of Catherine the Great' presents a dazzling mix of jewels, silver, antiquities and paintings.

CONTACT

Somerset House
Owner: Somerset House Trust
Strand, London
WC2R 1LA
Contact: Edward Schofield

Tel: 020 7845 4600
Fax: 020 7836 7613
e-mail: info@somerset-house.org.uk

Courtauld Gallery,
Courtauld Institute of Art
Tel: 020 7848 2526
e-mail: galleryinfo@courtauld.ac.uk

Gilbert Collection
Tel: 020 7420 9400
e-mail: info@gilbert-collection.org.uk

Hermitage Rooms
Tel: 020 7845 4630

LOCATION

OS Ref. TQ308 809

Entrances Victoria Embankment or Strand.
Rail: Underground: Temple or Covent Garden.
Air: London airports.

OPENING TIMES

Courtauld Gallery, Gilbert Collection & Hermitage Rooms
Mon - Sat except BHs, 10am - 6pm.
Suns & BHs, 12 noon - 6pm.
Last admission 5.15pm.

Closed 24 - 26 Dec & 1 Jan.

ADMISSION

Somerset House
Free except special exhibitions.

Courtauld Gallery & Gilbert Collection
Adult £4.00
Child (under 18) ......Free
Student (UK full)......Free
OAP.........................£3.00
Joint Ticket £7.00

Pre-booked Groups
Adult £3.00

Disabled & Helper.............
.............................£2.00pp

Courtauld Gallery
Mons, 10am - 2pm .....Free

Hermitage Rooms
Adult £6.00
Child (under 5) ....Free
Conc.........................£4.00
Pre-booked Groups
Adult £4.00

Advance booking advised for Hermitage Rooms: Ticketmaster 020 7413 3398

Peter Durant

Apply at desk for permission for photography/filming.	By arrangement.
Licensed.	Gilbert Collection and Hermitage Rooms.
	No parking.
	Guide dogs only.

FUNCTION/RECEPTION	
ROOM	MAX CAPACITY
Silver Gallery	350
Fine Rooms	250
Great Room	200
Fine & Gt Rm.	400
Seamen's Hall	200
Courtyard	2,700

London
England

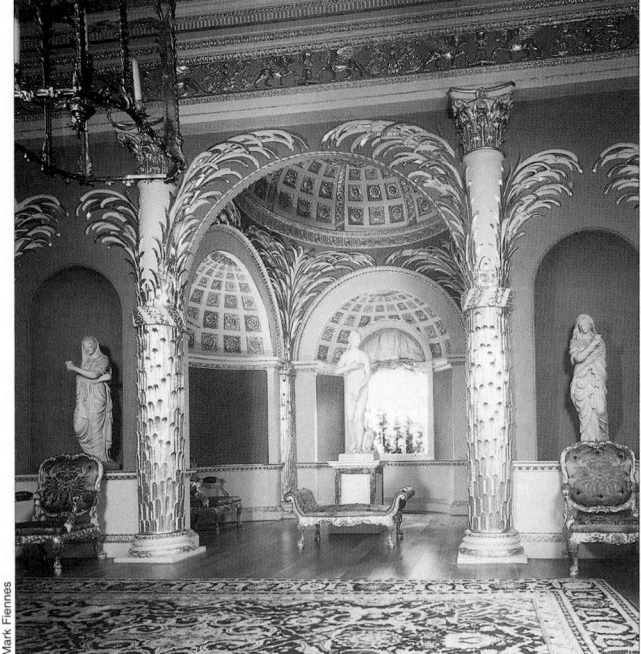

Mark Fiennes

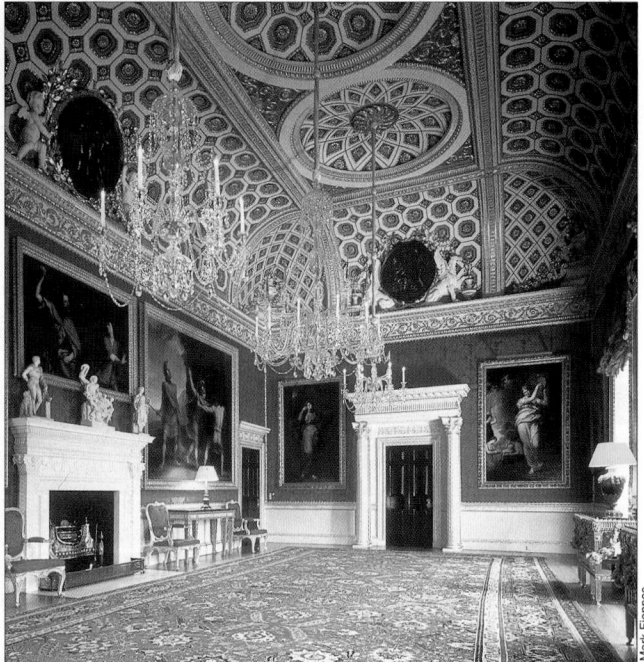

Mark Fiennes

SPENCER HOUSE
St James's Place

SPENCER HOUSE, built 1756 - 66 for the 1st Earl Spencer, an ancestor of Diana, Princess of Wales (1961-97), is London's finest surviving 18th century town house. The magnificent private palace has regained the full splendour of its late 18th century appearance, after a painstaking ten-year restoration programme.

Designed by John Vardy and James 'Athenian' Stuart, the nine state rooms are amongst the first neo-classical interiors in Europe. Vardy's Palm Room, with its spectacular screen of gilded palm trees and arched fronds, is a unique Palladian setpiece, while the elegant mural decorations of Stuart's Painted Room reflect the

18th century passion for classical Greece and Rome. Stuart's superb gilded furniture has been returned to its original location in the Painted Room by courtesy of the V&A and English Heritage. Visitors can also see a fine collection of 18th century paintings and furniture, specially assembled for the house, including five major Benjamin West paintings, graciously lent by Her Majesty The Queen.

The state rooms are open to the public for viewing on Sundays. They are also available on a limited number of occasions each year for private and corporate entertaining during the rest of the week.

❖

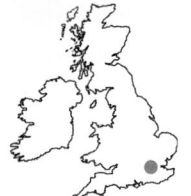

CONTACT

Jane Rick
Director
Spencer House
27 St James's Place
London
SW1A 1NR

Tel: 020 7514 1964

Fax: 020 7409 2952

Info Line: 020 7499 8620

LOCATION

OS Ref. TQ293 803

Central London:
off St James's Street,
overlooking Green Park.

Underground:
Green Park.

All images are copyright
of Spencer House Ltd
and may not be used
without the permission of
Spencer House Ltd.

CONFERENCE/FUNCTION		
ROOM	SIZE	MAX CAPACITY
Receptions		400
Lunches & Dinners		130
Board Meetings		40
Theatre Style meetings		100

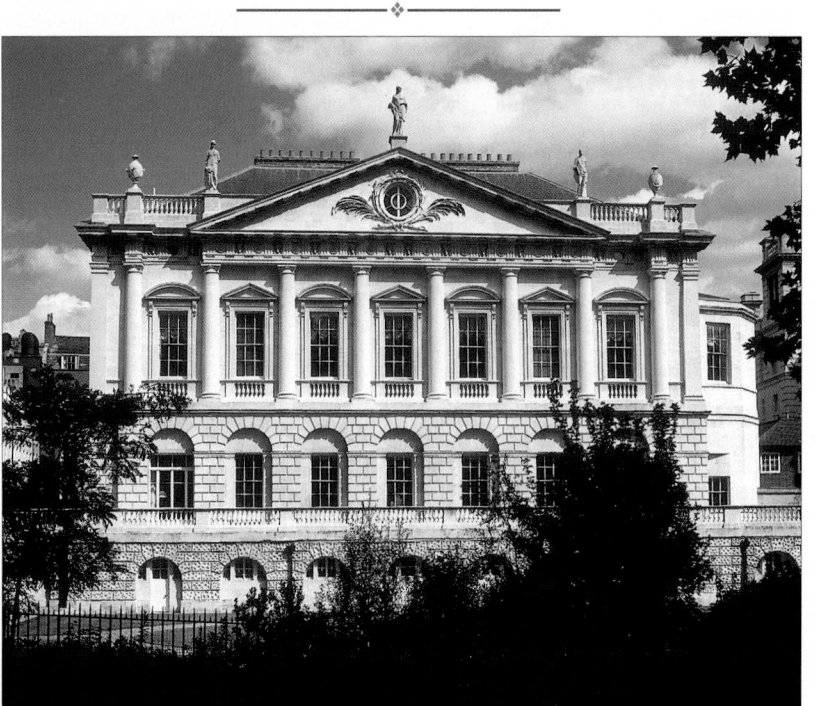

Mark Fiennes

OPENING TIMES

ALL YEAR

All year
(except January & August)
Suns, 10.30am - 5.30pm.

Last tour 4.45pm.

Tours begin approximately
every 20 mins and last
1hr 10 mins. Maximum
number on each tour is 20.

Mon mornings for
pre-booked groups only.

Open for corporate
hospitality except
during January & August.

ADMISSION

Adult £6.00
Conc.* £5.00

* Students, Friends of V&A,
Tate Gallery and Royal
Academy (all with cards),
children under 16
(no under 10s admitted).

Prices include guided tour.

ℹ️ No photography inside
House.

♿ Ramps and lifts. WC.

🚶 Obligatory.
Comprehensive colour guidebook £3.50.

🅿️ No parking facilities.
Coaches can drop off at door.

🛡️ **SPECIAL EVENTS**

• **SPECIFIC SUNDAYS:**
The authentically restored garden
of this 18th century London
palace will be open to the public
on specific Sundays during
Spring and Summer. For updated
information telephone 020 7499
8620 or see our website:
www.spencerhouse.co.uk

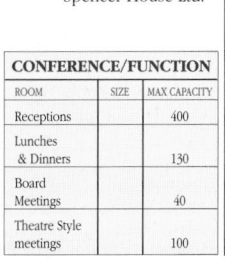

Mark Fiennes

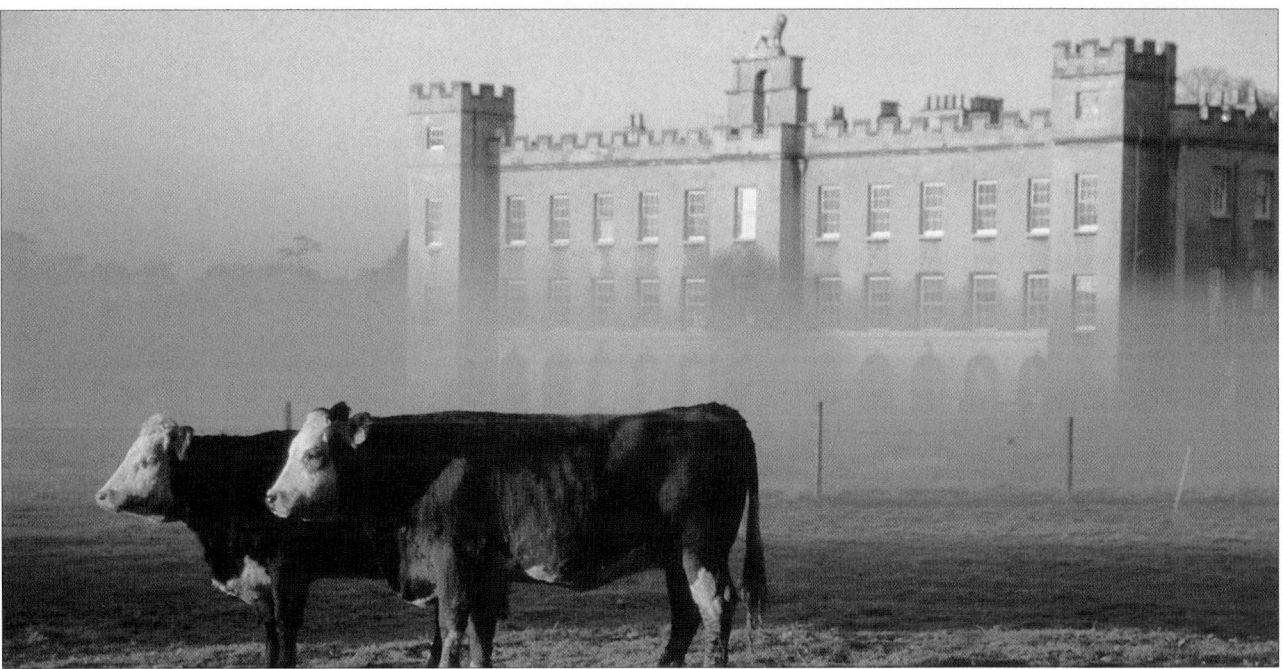

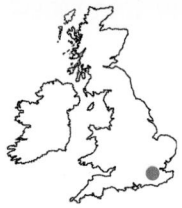

Owner: The Duke of Northumberland

CONTACT

Louise Page-Bailey
Syon House
Syon Park
Brentford
TW8 8JF

Tel: 020 8560 0881

Fax: 020 8568 0936

e-mail: louise@
syonpark.co.uk

LOCATION

OS Ref. TQ173 767

Between Brentford and
Twickenham, off the A4,
A310 in SW London.

Rail: Kew Bridge or
Gunnersbury
Underground then
Bus 237 or 267.

Air: Heathrow 8m.

CONFERENCE/FUNCTION		
ROOM	SIZE	MAX CAPACITY
Great Hall	50' x 30'	120
Great Conservatory	60' x 40'	150
Marquee		1000

SYON PARK
Brentford

Described by John Betjeman as 'the Grand Architectural Walk', Syon House and its 200 acre park is the London home of the Duke of Northumberland, whose family, the Percys, have lived here since the late 16th century.

Originally the site of a late medieval monastery, Syon Park has a fascinating history. The present house has Tudor origins but contains some of Robert Adam's finest interiors, which were commissioned by the 1st Duke in the 1760s.

Within the 'Capability' Brown landscaped park are 40 acres of gardens which contain the spectacular Great Conservatory designed by Charles Fowler in the 1820s. The House and Great Conservatory are available for corporate and private hire.

Syon House is an excellent venue for small meetings, lunches and dinners in the Duke's private dining room (max 22). The State Apartments make a sumptuous setting for dinners, concerts, receptions, launches and wedding ceremonies (max 120). Marquees can be erected on the lawn adjacent to the house for balls and corporate events. The Great Conservatory is available for summer parties, launches and wedding receptions.

❖

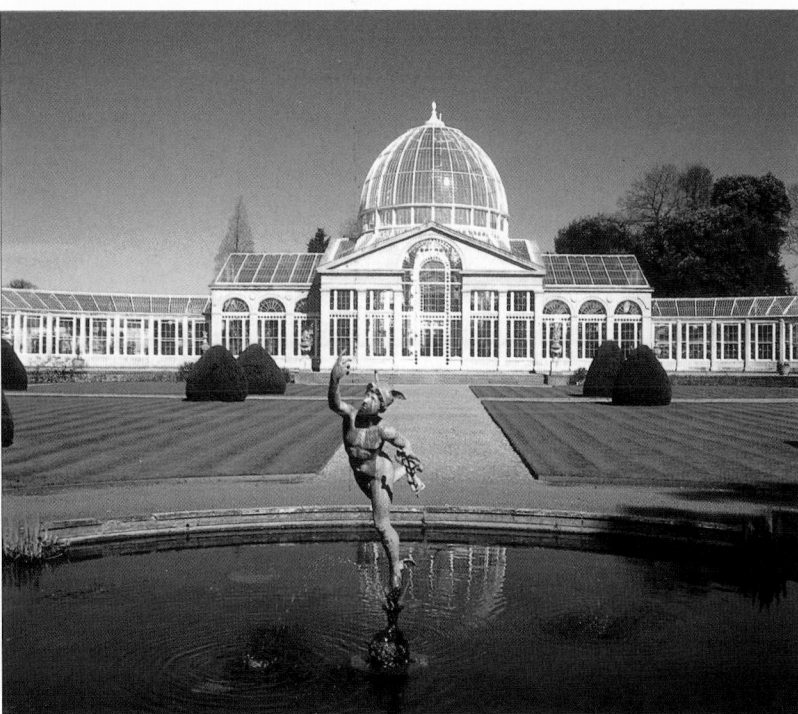

OPENING TIMES

House
14 March - 31 October only
Weds, Thurs, Suns & BHs
11am - 5pm
(open Good Fri &
Easter Sat).
Other times by
appointment for groups.

Gardens
Daily (except 25 & 26 Dec)
10am - 5.30pm or dusk if
earlier.

ADMISSION

House and Gardens
Adult £6.25
Child/Conc..............£5.25
Family (2+2) £15.00

Gardens only
Adult £3.00
Child/Conc..............£2.50
Family (2+2) £7.00

Groups (min 15, max 50)

House and Gardens
Adult £5.75
Child/Conc..............£4.75

Gardens only
Adult £3.00
Child/Conc..............£2.50

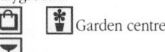 No photography in house. Indoor adventure playground.

Garden centre.

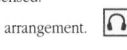 Partially suitable.

Licensed.

 By arrangement.

Guide dogs only.

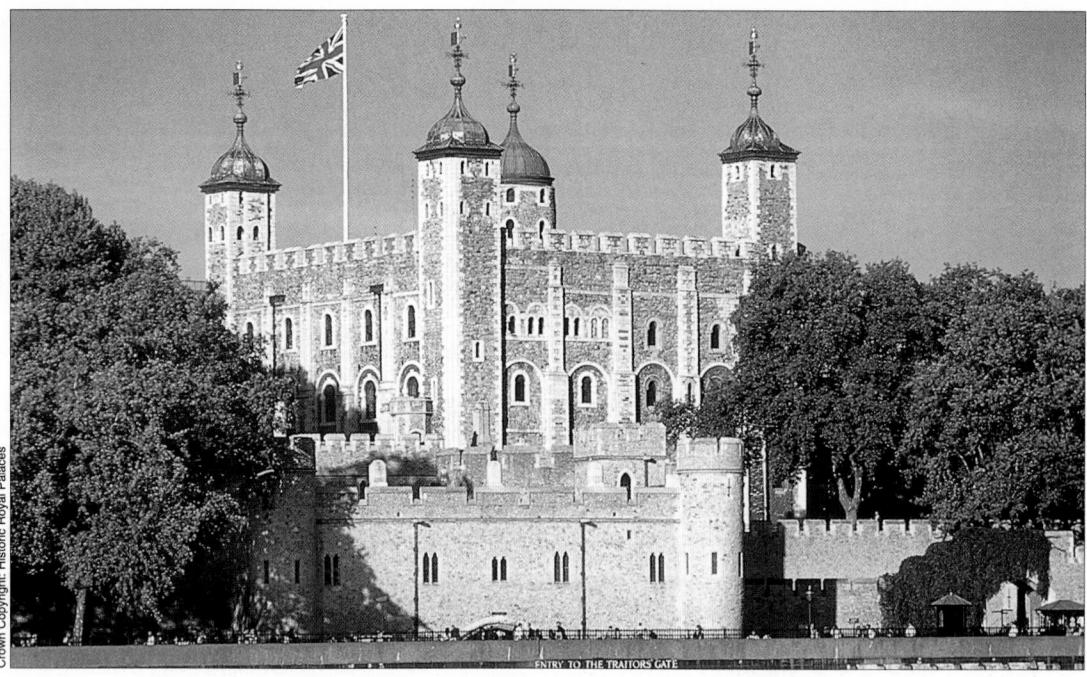

Crown Copyright: Historic Royal Palaces

ENTRY TO THE TRAITORS GATE

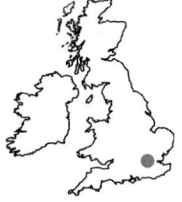

Managed by:
Historic Royal Palaces

CONTACT

The Tower of London
London
EC3N 4AB

Tel: 020 7709 0765

LOCATION

OS Ref. TQ336 806

Tube Station: Tower Hill
on Circle/District Line.
Monument on
Northern Line.

**Docklands Light
Railway:**
Tower Gateway Station.

Rail: Fenchurch Street
Station and
London Bridge Station.

Bus: 15, 25, 42,
78, 100, D1.

Riverboat: From Charing
Cross, Westminster or
Greenwich to Tower Pier.

THE TOWER OF LONDON
London

William the Conqueror began building the Tower of London in 1078 as a royal residence and to control the volatile City of London. Over the ensuing 900 years the Tower has served as a royal fortress, mint, armoury and more infamously as a prison and place of execution.

The Tower of London has been home to the Crown Jewels for the last 600 years and today visitors can see them in all their glory in the magnificent new Jewel House. They are still used by HM The Queen for ceremonies such as the State Opening of Parliament and the 'Crowns and Diamonds' exhibition details the jewels' history, alongside a pile of 2,314 diamonds lent by De Beers.

Visit the White Tower, the original Tower of London, which features new displays by the

Royal Armouries including the Block and Axe, Tudor arms and armour and the Instruments of Torture.

Once inside, the Yeoman Warder 'Beefeaters' give free guided tours providing an unrivalled insight into the darker secrets of over 900 years of royal history. Above the notorious Traitors' Gate, costumed guides evoke life at the court of King Edward I in the recently restored rooms of his Medieval Palace.

See the execution site where many famous prisoners such as two of Henry VIII's wives were put to death and visit the Chapel Royal where they are buried. Special events take place throughout the year, including events during every school holiday, with costumed interpreters.

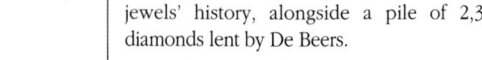

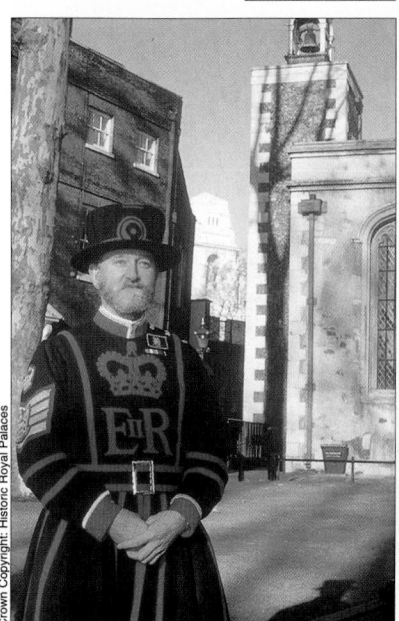

Crown Copyright: Historic Royal Palaces

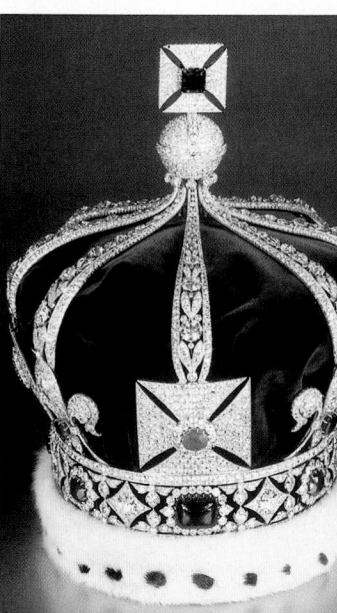

Crown Copyright: Historic Royal Palaces 2000

OPENING TIMES

SUMMER
1 March - 31 October
Daily
Mon - Sat: 9am - 5pm
(last admission)
Suns: 10am - 5pm.

WINTER
1 November - 28 February
Tues - Sat: 9am - 5pm
(last admission)
Mons & Suns: 10am - 4pm.

Closed 24 - 26 December
and 1 January.

Buildings close 30 minutes
after last admission.
Tower closes 1 hour after
last admission.

ADMISSION

Telephone Info Line for
admission prices:
020 7709 0765.

**Groups are advised to book,
telephone: 020 7488 5681.**

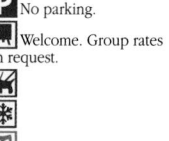 No photography
in Jewel House.

020 7488 5762.

Partially suitable. WC.

Available on the wharf.

Open from Feb 2001.

Obligatory. Yeoman
Warder tours are free and
leave front entrance every
1/2 hr.

No parking.

Welcome. Group rates
on request.

Telephone for details.

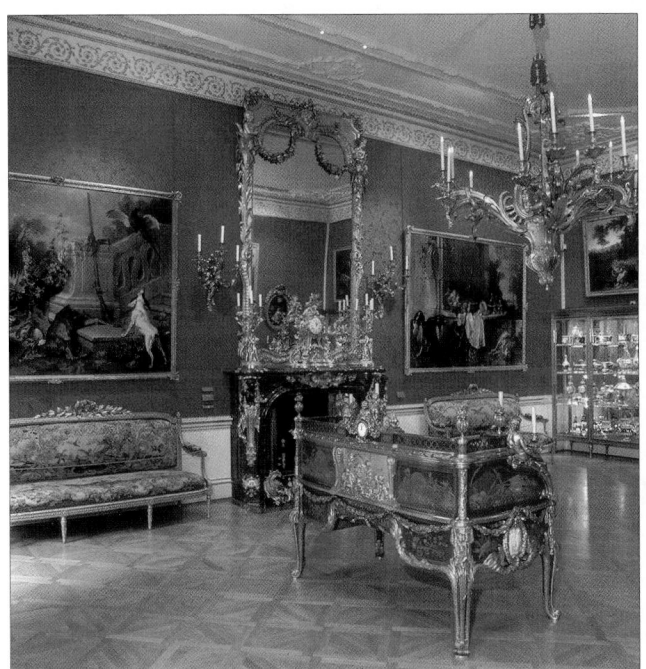
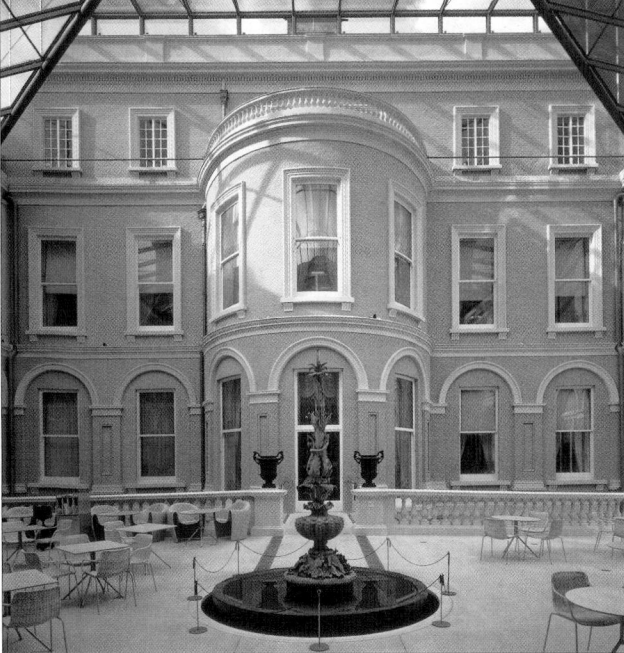

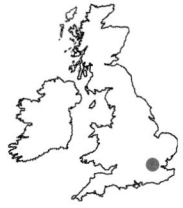

THE WALLACE COLLECTION
Manchester Square

Hertford House is home to the internationally renowned Wallace Collection, a national museum of fine and decorative arts principally from the 16th - 19th centuries. Originally built for the 4th Duke of Manchester between 1776 - 88, it was leased in 1797 by the 2nd Marquess of Hertford, so beginning 200 years of association between house and family. Today it still serves to display the family's treasures, which were accumulated over five generations, and then bequeathed to the nation by Sir Richard Wallace's widow in 1897.

The 5,470 works of art include some of the world's best-known paintings (among them Frans Hals's *The Laughing Cavalier*), over a thousand items of French 18th century furniture, sculpture and porcelain and the finest collection of princely arms and armour in this country. Masterpieces by Rubens, Rembrandt, Velázquez, Watteau and Boucher hang above furniture made for the kings and queens of France.

The rich interiors of the ground and first floors continue to evoke something of the domestic splendor and atmosphere of a grandiose 19th century home. This 19th century aesthetic is complemented by the internal courtyard and lower ground floor, which were redeveloped in 2000. Designed by award-winning Rick Mather, the elegant contemporary design extensively features glass, steel and oak, as illustrated by the Sculpture Garden that is crowned by a spectacular glass roof.

CONTACT

Press & Marketing Office
The Wallace Collection
Hertford House
Manchester Square
London
W1U 3BN

Tel: 020 7563 9500

Fax: 020 7224 2155

LOCATION

OS Ref. TQ283 813

Central London behind Selfridges department store.

Tube Station:
Bond Street.

CONFERENCE/FUNCTION		
ROOM	SIZE	MAX CAPACITY
Great Gallery	35.8x10.5m	120
Sculpture Garden	23.1x15.3m	100/250
State & Dining Rms		40
Galleries		300
Lecture Theatre		150
Meeting Rm		50

OPENING TIMES

ALL YEAR
Mon - Sat: 10am - 5pm
Sunday: 12 noon - 5pm

Closed
Good Friday, May Day, 24 - 26 & 31 December and 1 & 2 January.

ADMISSION

Free.

ℹ️ No photography in house.

🛍️ Full range of merchandise including catalogues, postcards, books & gifts.

🍸 Rooms are available for a range of events including formal dinners, receptions, seminars and conferences. Tel. Development Office 020 7563 9545.

♿ Ramp access is to the right of the main entrance. A parking space may be booked in advance. Lift to all floors. For full details tel. Access Co-ordinator 020 7563 9515.

☕ Café Bagatelle: morning coffee, lunch & afternoon tea.

🚶 Free lectures on the collection are given every day. Private tours can also be arranged. Please tel. Education Department on 020 7563 9551.

🎧

🅿️ Coaches may set down at Hertford House, parking is at Bayswater Road, W8. Meters in Manchester Square.

🖼️ A free programme of teaching sessions is available. Please tel. the Education Department on 020 7563 9551.

❄️ Open all year.

🛡️ Tel. for details.

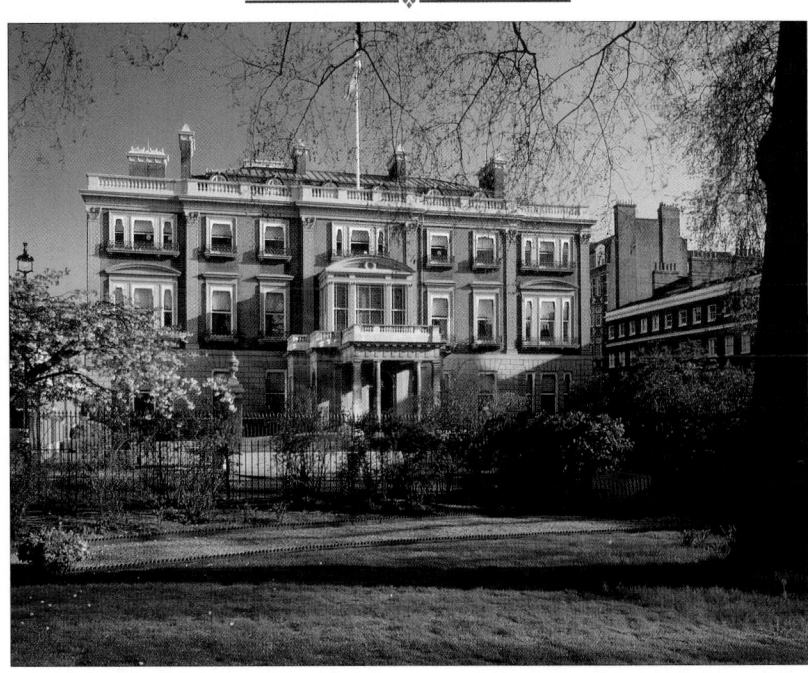

2 WILLOW ROAD

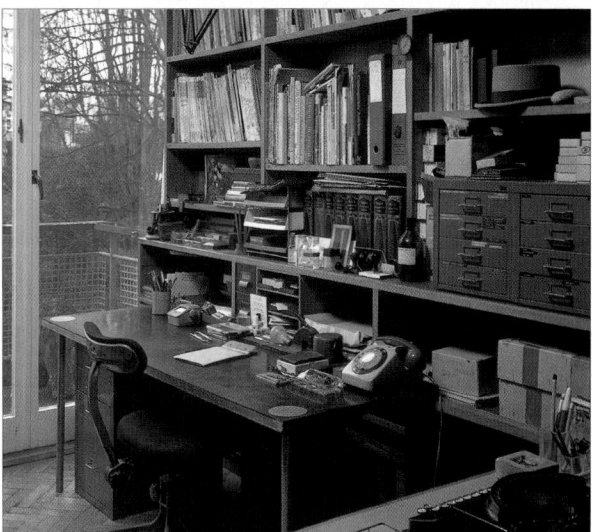

HAMPSTEAD, LONDON NW3 1TH

Owner: The National Trust *Contact:* The Custodian

Tel: 020 7435 6166 **e-mail:** twlgen@smtp.ntrust.org.uk

The former home of Erno Goldfinger, designed and built by him in 1939. A three-storey brick and concrete rectangle, it is one of Britain's most important examples of modernist architecture and is filled with furniture also designed by Goldfinger. The interesting art collection includes works by Henry Moore and Max Ernst.

Location: OS Ref. TQ270 858. Hampstead, London.

Opening Times: 4 - 24 Mar: Sats only, 12 - 5pm, free-flow with tours at 12.30 & 3.30pm; 30 Mar - 3 Nov: Thur - Sat, 12 - 5pm. Last admission 4pm. Guided tours every 45 mins.

Admission: Adult £4.30, Child £2.15. Joint ticket with Fenton House £6.30.

Small ground floor area accessible, filmed tour of whole house available.

Obligatory.

APSLEY HOUSE

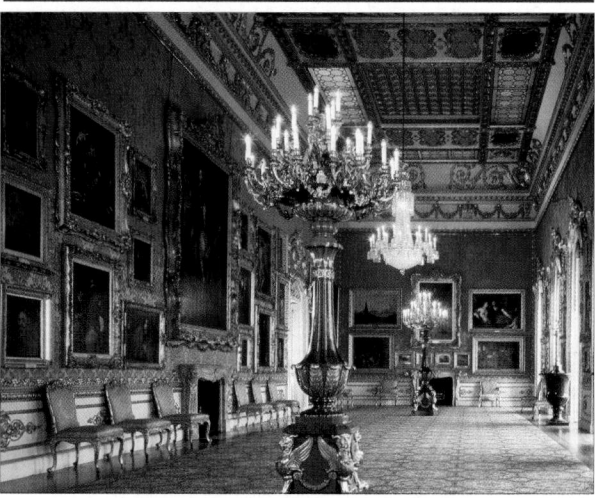

HYDE PARK CORNER, LONDON W1J 7NT

Owner: V & A Museum & Dept. for Culture, Media & Sport *Contact:* The Administrator

Tel: 020 7499 5676 / 495 8525 **Fax:** 020 7493 6576

Apsley House (No. 1, London) was originally designed by Robert Adam in 1771-8. In 1817 it was bought by the Duke of Wellington and enlarged. His London 'Palace' houses his magnificent collection: paintings by Velazquez, Goya, Rubens, Lawrence, Wilkie, Steen, de Hooch and other masters; sculpture, silver, porcelain, furniture, caricatures, medals and memorabilia.

Location: OS Ref. TQ284 799. N side of Hyde Park Corner. Nearest tube station: Hyde Park Corner exit 1 Piccadilly Line.

Opening Times: Tue - Sun, 11am - 5pm, last admission 4.30pm. Closed Mons, (except BHs), Good Fri, May Day BH, 24 - 26 Dec and New Year's Day.

Admission: Adult £4.50, Conc. £3 (both include Soundguide), Child (under 18yrs) Free. Pre-arranged groups (10+): £2.50. Over 60s Free.

No photography in house. Partially suitable. By arrangement. In Park Lane. Guide dogs only.

ALBERT MEMORIAL　　　　　　**Tel:** 020 7495 0916 (Booking Agency)

Princes Gate, Kensington Gore SW7

Contact: The Royal Parks Agency (management agency).

An elaborate memorial by George Gilbert Scott to commemorate the Prince Consort.

Location: OS Ref. TQ266 798. Victoria Station 1½ m, South Kensington Tube ½ m.

Opening Times: All visits by booked guided tours.

Admission: Adult £3, Child £2.50.

Sutton House.

THE BANQUETING HOUSE　　　**See page 64 for full page entry.**

BLEWCOAT SCHOOL　　　　　　**Tel:** 020 7222 2877

23 Caxton Street, Westminster, London SW1H 0PY

Owner: The National Trust　　　　　**Contact:** The Administrator

Built in 1709 at the expense of William Green, a local brewer, to provide an education for poor children. The building was used as a school until 1926, and is now the NT London Gift Shop and Information Centre.

Location: OS Ref. TQ295 794. Near the junction with Buckingham Gate.

Opening Times: All year: Mon - Fri, 10am - 5.30pm (Thurs 7pm). Also Sats 18 & 25 Nov & 2/9/16/23 Dec. Closed Bank Holidays.

BOSTON MANOR HOUSE　　　　**Tel:** 020 8560 5441

Boston Manor Road, Brentford TW8 9JX

Owner: Hounslow Cultural & Community Services　　**Contact:** Jerome Farrell

A fine Jacobean house built in 1623. The rooms that can be viewed include the State Drawing Room with a magnificent ceiling and fireplace designed in 1623.

Location: OS Ref. TQ168 784. 10 mins walk S of Boston Manor Station (Piccadilly Line) and 250yds N of Boston Manor Road junction with A4 - Great West Road, Brentford.

Opening Times: 1 Apr - 29 Oct: Sats, Suns & BHs, 2.30 - 5pm. Park open daily.

Admission: Free.

BRUCE CASTLE　　　　　　　　**Tel:** 020 8808 8772

Haringey Museum & Archive Service, Lordship Lane, London N17 8NU

Owner: London Borough of Haringey

A Tudor building. Sir Rowland Hill (inventor of the Penny Post) ran a progressive school at Bruce Castle from 1827.

Location: OS Ref. TQ335 906. Corner of Bruce Grove (A10) and Lordship Lane, 600yds NW of Bruce Grove Station.

Opening Times: All year: Wed - Sun & Summer BHs, 1 - 5pm. Organised groups by appointment.

Admission: Free.

BUCKINGHAM PALACE

See page 65 for full page entry.

BURGH HOUSE

Tel: 020 7431 0144 Buttery: 020 7431 2516 **Fax:** 020 7435 8817

New End Square, Hampstead, London NW3 1LT

Owner: London Borough of Camden   **Contact:** Ms Helen Wilton

A Grade I listed building of 1703 in the heart of old Hampstead with original panelled rooms, "barley sugar" staircase bannisters and a music room. Home of the Hampstead Museum, permanent and changing exhibitions. Prize-winning terraced garden. Regular programme of concerts, art exhibitions, and meetings. Receptions, seminars and conferences. Rooms for hire. Special facilities for schools visits. Wedding receptions.

Location: OS Ref. TQ266 859. New End Square, E of Hampstead underground station.

Opening Times: All year: Wed - Sun, 12 noon - 5pm. Sats by appointment only. BH Mons, 2 - 5pm. Closed Christmas fortnight, Good Fri & Easter Mon. Groups by arrangement. Buttery: Wed - Sun, 11am - 5.30pm. BHs, 1 - 5.00pm.

Admission: Free.

🖼 ♿ Ground floor & grounds suitable. WC. 🍽 Licensed buttery. 🅿 No parking. 🐕 Guide dogs only. 🔔 ❄

CABINET WAR ROOMS

See right for half page entry.

CAPEL MANOR GARDENS

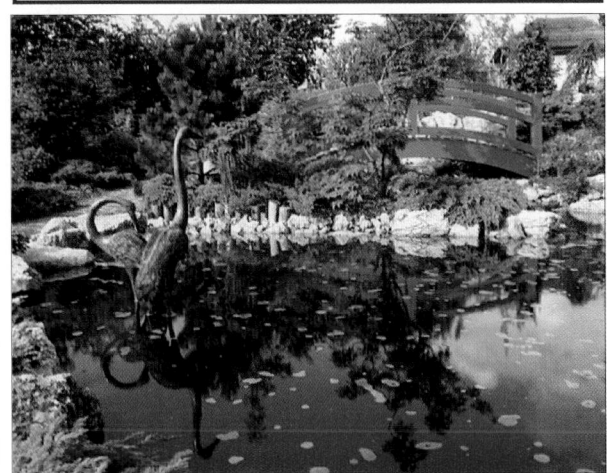

BULLSMOOR LANE, ENFIELD EN1 4RQ

Owner: Capel Manor Charitable Organisation   *Contact: Miss Julie Ryan*

Tel: 020 8366 4442 **Fax:** 01992 717544

These extensive, richly planted gardens are delightful throughout the year offering inspiration, information and relaxation. The gardens include various themes - historical, modern, walled, rock, water, sensory and disabled and an Italianate Maze, Japanese Garden and 'Gardening Which?' demonstration and model gardens. Capel Manor is a College of Horticulture and runs a training scheme for professional gardeners originally devised in conjunction with the Historic Houses Association.

Location: OS Ref. TQ344 997. Minutes from M25/J25. Tourist Board signs posted.

Opening Times: Daily in summer: 10am - 5.30pm. Last ticket 4.30pm. Check for winter times.

Admission: Adult £4, Conc. £3.50, Child £2, Family £10. Charges alter for special show weekends and winter months.

🖼 ♿ Grounds suitable. WC. 🍽 🐕 In grounds, on leads. ❄ 🛡 Tel. for details.

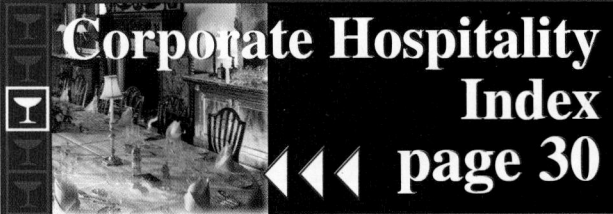
CABINET WAR ROOMS

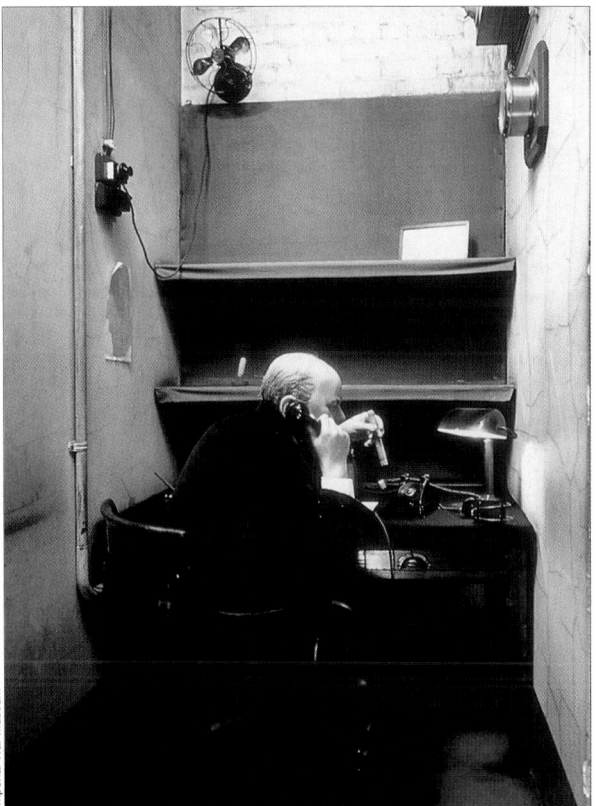

Imperial War Museum

CLIVE STEPS, KING CHARLES STREET, LONDON SW1A 2AQ

Director: Phil Reed   *Contact: Vanessa Rayner*

Tel: 020 7930 6961 **Fax:** 020 7839 5897 **e-mail:** cwr@iwm.org.uk

Visit the hidden world of Churchill's secret underground wartime headquarters and catch a glimpse of the spartan conditions in which he and his Cabinet worked and lived during the Blitz. A former storage basement, the bunker was hurriedly converted in 1939 to become the very nerve centre of the British war effort, operating around the clock, undisturbed by the heavy bombing raids above ground. Step back in time and view the original complex just as it was left at the end of six years of war, when the lights were finally extinguished. Free personal sound guides are provided for every visitor.

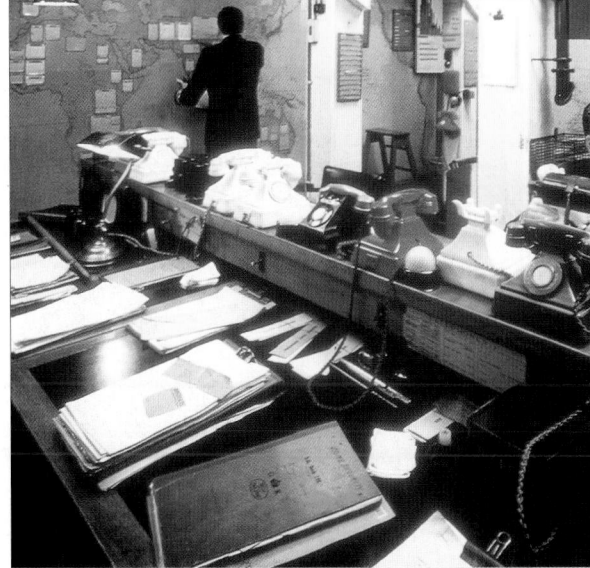

Location: OS Ref. TQ301 799. Buses: 3, 11, 12, 24, 53, 77a, 88, 159, 211. Westminster Underground.

Opening Times: All year: daily, 9.30am (1 Oct - 31 Mar: 10am) - 6pm. Last admission 5.15pm. Closed 24/25/26 Dec.

Admission: Adult £5, Child Free, Conc. £3.60. Booked groups (min 10): Adult £3.60, Child Free, Conc. £3.

🖼 🍴 ♿ 🚻 By arrangement. 🎧 🎬 🅿 None. ❄ 🅲

CARLYLE'S HOUSE

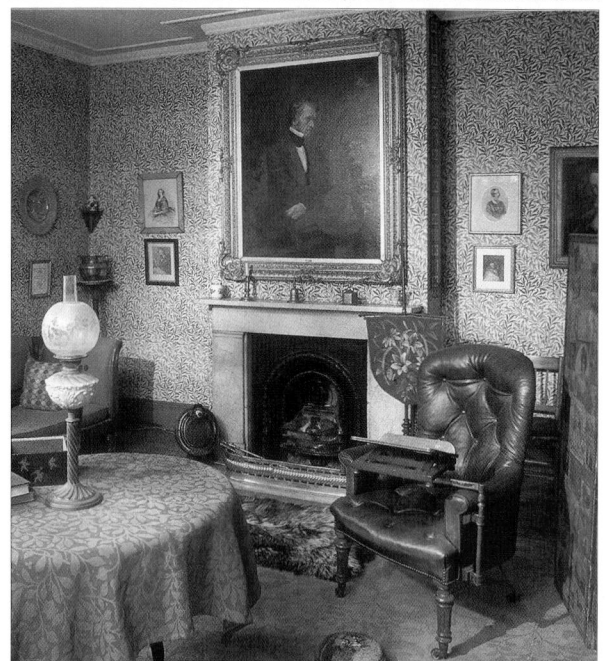

24 CHEYNE ROW, CHELSEA, LONDON SW3 5HL

Owner: The National Trust   *Contact: The Custodian*

Tel: 020 7352 7087 **Info Line:** 01494 755559

In a quiet and beautiful residential area of London, this Queen Anne house was the home of Thomas Carlyle, the 'Sage of Chelsea', for some 47 years until his death in 1881. The skilful Scottish home-making of his wife Jane is much in evidence: the Victorian period décor, the furniture, pictures, portraits and books are all still in place. As an historian, social writer, ethical thinker and powerful public speaker, Thomas is honoured in the house, while Jane's strong belief in his genius and her own brilliant wit and gift for writing are recognised in the many existing letters. Their academic and domestic lives can be experienced today in the evocative atmosphere of the house.

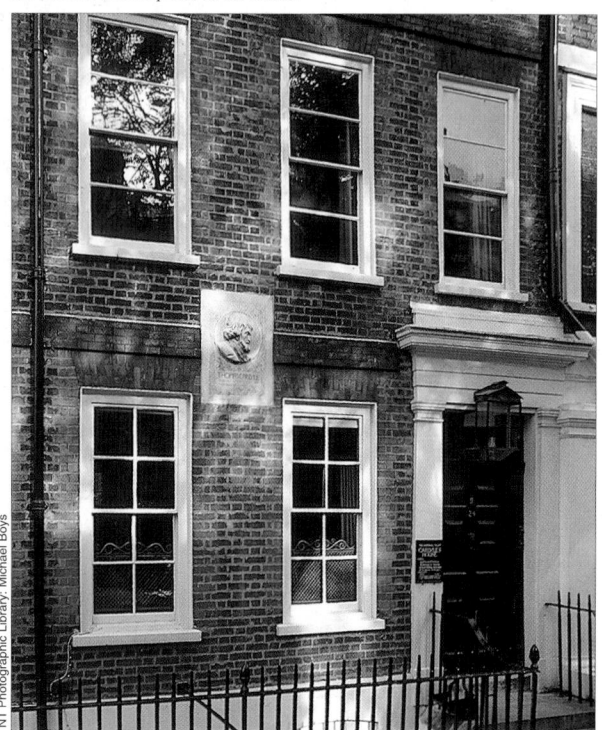

NT Photographic Library: Michael Boys

Location: OS Ref. TQ272 777. Off Cheyne Walk, between Battersea and Albert Bridges on Chelsea Embankment, or off the King's Road and Oakley Street.

Opening Times: 31 Mar - 4 Nov: Wed - Sun & BH Mons, 11am - 5pm. Last admission 4.30pm. Closed Good Fri.

Admission: Adult £3.50, Child £1.75.

By arrangement for groups.   Send SAE for details.

CHAPTER HOUSE, PYX CHAMBER & ABBEY MUSEUM

East Cloisters, Westminster Abbey, London SW1P 3PE   **Tel:** 020 7222 5897
Owner: English Heritage   **Contact:** Head Custodian

The Chapter House, built by the Royal masons in 1250 and faithfully restored in the 19th century, contains some of the finest examples of medieval English sculpture to be seen. The building is octagonal, with a central column, and still has its original floor of glazed tiles, which have been newly conserved. Its uses have varied and in the 14th century it was used as a meeting place for the Benedictine monks of the Abbey and as well as for Members of Parliament. The 11th century Pyx Chamber now houses the Abbey treasures, reflecting its use as the strongroom of the exchequer from the 14th to 19th centuries. The Abbey museum contains medieval Royal effigies.

Location: OS Ref. TQ301 795. Approach either through the Abbey or through Dean's Yard and the cloister.

Opening Times: 1 Apr - 30 Sept: daily, 9.30am - 5.30pm. 1 Oct - 31 Oct: daily 10am - 5pm. 1 Nov - 31 Mar: daily, 10am - 4pm. Liable to be closed at short notice on state occasions.

Admission: Adult £2.50, Child £1.30, Conc. £1.90.

Small charge.   Tel. for details.

CHELSEA PHYSIC GARDEN

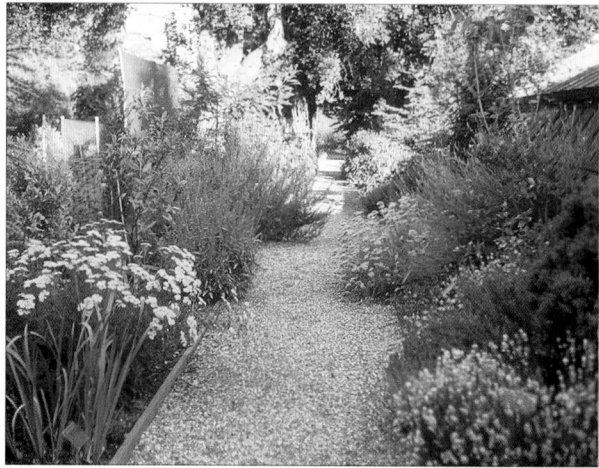

66 ROYAL HOSPITAL ROAD, LONDON SW3 4HS

Owner: Chelsea Physic Garden Company   *Contact: Sue Minter*

Tel: 020 7352 5646 **Fax:** 020 7376 3910

The second oldest botanic garden in Britain, founded in 1673. For many years these 4 acres of peace and quiet with many rare and unusual plants were known only to a few. Specialists in medicinal plants, tender species and the history of plant introductions.

Location: OS Ref. TQ277 778. Off Embankment, between Chelsea & Albert Bridges. Entrance - Swan Walk.

Opening Times: 1 Apr - 28 Oct: Weds, 12 noon - 5pm & Suns, 2 - 6pm. Snowdrop opening & winter festival: 4 & 11 Feb: 11am - 3pm.

Admission: Adult £4, Child £2, OAP £4, Conc. £2. Carers for disabled: Free.

SPECIAL EVENTS
MAY 21 - 25: Chelsea Show Week., 12 noon - 5pm with lunches.
JUL 15 - SEPT 9: Summer Exhibition: 'Myth and Magic'.

CHISWICK HOUSE   See page 66 for full page entry.

COLLEGE OF ARMS   **Tel:** 020 7248 2762   **Fax:** 020 7248 6448
Queen Victoria Street, London EC4V 4BT

Owner: Corp. of the Kings, Heralds & Pursuivants of Arms **Contact:** The Officer in Waiting
Mansion built in 1670s to house the English Officers of Arms and their records.

Location: OS Ref. TQ320 810. On N side of Queen Victoria Street, S of St Paul's Cathedral.

Opening Times: Earl Marshal's Court only; open all year (except BHs, State and special occasions) Mon - Fri, 10am - 4pm. Group visits (up to 10) by arrangement only. Record Room: open for tours (groups of up to 20) by special arrangement in advance with the Officer in Waiting.

Admission: Free (groups by negotiation).

COURTAULD GALLERY   See page 71 for full page entry.

THE DE MORGAN FOUNDATION

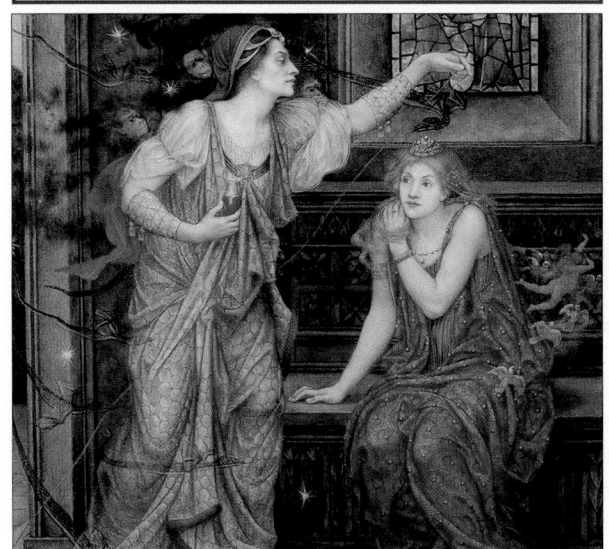

OLD BATTERSEA HOUSE, 30 VICARAGE CRESCENT, LONDON SW11 3LD

Contact: Susan Seagrave

Tel: 020 7371 8385

A substantial part of the De Morgan Foundation collection of ceramics by William De Morgan, and paintings by Evelyn De Morgan (née Pickering) are displayed on the ground floor of elegantly restored Old Battersea House - a Wren period building which is privately occupied.

Location: OS Ref. TQ267 767. Close to S shore of River Thames, $^1/_2$ m SW of S end of Battersea Bridge, via Battersea Church Road and Vicarage Crescent.

Opening Times: Weds by appointment.

Admission: Groups (4-15 persons) £2.50.

ℹ️ No photography in house.   ♿ Partially suitable.   🎟️ Obligatory.
🅿️ Cars limited, no coach parking.   ✖   ❄

THE DICKENS HOUSE MUSEUM

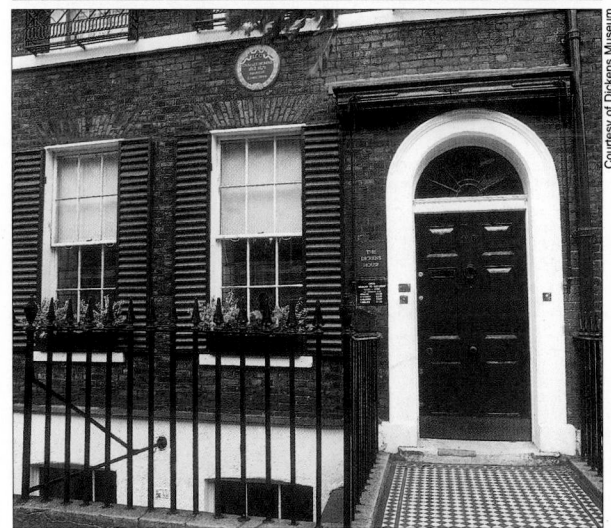

Courtesy of Dickens Museum

48 DOUGHTY STREET, LONDON WC1N 2LF

Owner: Dickens House Museum Trust   **Contact:** *Mr Andrew Xavier – Curator*

Tel: 020 7405 2127   **Fax:** 020 7831 5175   **e-mail:** dhmuseum@rmplc.co.uk

House occupied by Charles Dickens and his family from 1837 - 1839 where he produced *Pickwick Papers, Oliver Twist, Nicholas Nickleby* and *Barnaby Rudge*. Contains the most comprehensive Dickens library in the world as well as portraits, illustrations and rooms laid out exactly as they were in Dickens' time. The house is one of the few venues open over Christmas itself.

Location: OS Ref. TQ308 822. W of Grays Inn Road.

Opening Times: All year: Mon - Sat, 10am - 5pm (last admission 4.30pm).

Admission: Adult £4, Child £2, Conc. £3, Family £9. Booked groups (min 10): Adult £3, Child £2.

📷 🍽 🎟️ By arrangement. 🅿️ Limited. No coaches. 🚻
🐕 Guide dogs only. ❄ 🛏 Telephone for details. ♿

EASTBURY MANOR HOUSE 🌿   **Tel:** 020 8507 0119 **Fax:** 020 8507 0118

Barking IG11 9SN

Owner: The National Trust   **Contact:** The Administrator

Eastbury is a rare example of a medium-sized Elizabethan manor house. Leased to the Borough of Barking and Dagenham and used for a variety of arts and heritage activities.

Location: OS177, Ref. TQ457 838. In Eastbury Square, 10 mins walk S from Upney Station.

Opening Times: Mar - Dec: first Sat every month (except Aug), 10am - 4pm. Telephone for details.

Admission: Adult £1.80, Child 60p, Conc. £1, Family £4.20. Group visits by arrangement. Rates on application. Evening tours also available.

♿ Ground floor suitable.   📺 Visitor days.   🅿️ No parking.   🐕 Garden only.   🔔

ELTHAM PALACE ⌗   See page 67 for full page entry.

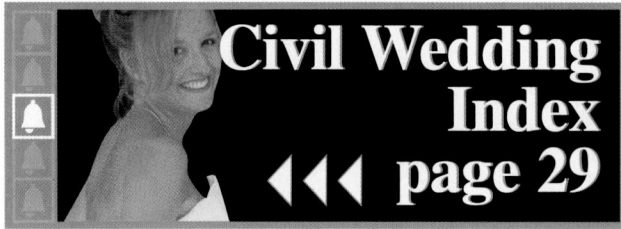

Civil Wedding Index ◀◀◀ page 29

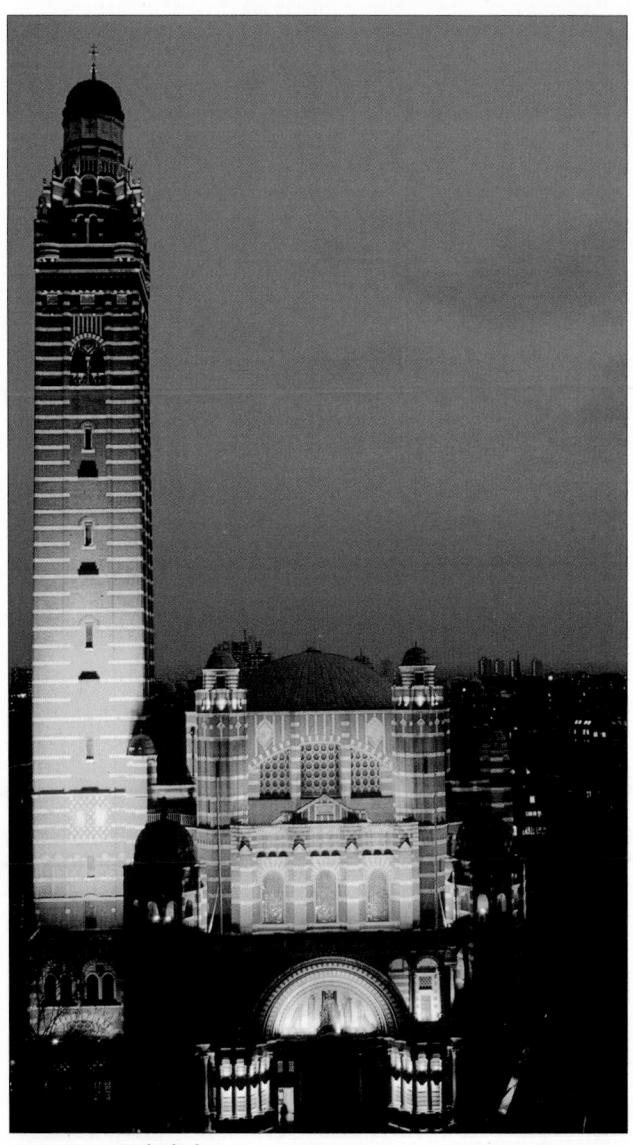

Westminster Cathedral.

London England

FENTON HOUSE

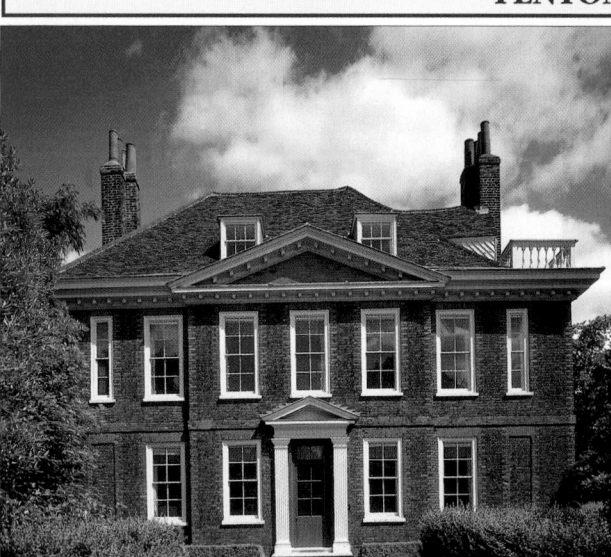

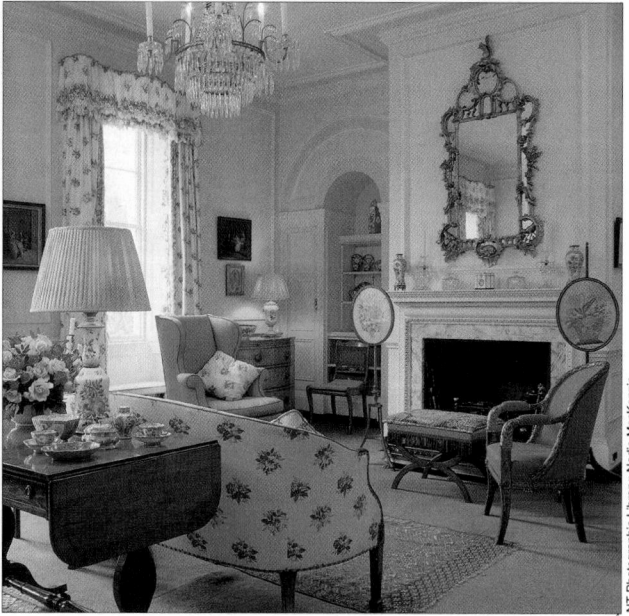

WINDMILL HILL, HAMPSTEAD, LONDON NW3 6RT

Owner: *The National Trust*   **Contact:** *The Custodian*

Tel: 020 7435 3471 **e-mail:** tfehse@smtp.ntrust.org.uk

A delightful late 17th century merchant's house, set among the winding streets of Old Hampstead. The charming interior contains an outstanding collection of Oriental and European porcelain, needlework and furniture. The Benton Fletcher Collection of beautiful early keyboard instruments is also housed at Fenton and the instruments are sometimes played by music scholars during opening hours. The walled garden has a formal lawn and walks, an orchard and vegetable garden and fine wrought-iron gates.

Location: OS Ref. TQ262 862. Visitors' entrance on W side of Hampstead Grove.

Hampstead underground station 300 yds.

Opening Times: 3 - 25 Mar: Sats & Suns, 2 - 5pm. 31 Mar - 4 Nov: daily except Mons & Tues (open BH Mons, closed Good Fri). Times: weekdays, 2 - 5pm. Weekends & BH Mons, 11am - 5pm. Groups at other times by appointment.

Admission: Adult £4.30, Child £2.15, Family £10.50. Joint ticket with 2 Willow Road, £6.30. No reduction for pre-booked groups. No picnics in grounds.

Ground floor accessible. No parking.

---

18 FOLEGATE STREET

Tel: 020 7247 4013

Spitalfields, East London E1 6BX

Owner: Spitalfields Historic Buildings Trust   **Contact:** Mick Pedroli

A time capsule furnished and decorated to tell the story of the Jarvis family, Huguenot silk weavers from 1725 - 1919.

Location: OS Ref. TQ335 820. ½ m NE of Liverpool St. Station. E of Bishopsgate (A10), just N of Spitalfields Market.

Opening Times: First Sunday each month, 2 - 5pm. First Mon following the first Sun by candlelight "Silent Night". Times vary with the light of the seasons and booking is required. Group visits can be arranged by appointment.

Admission: Non negotiable contribution £7.00 for the houses upkeep. "Silent Night" £10.

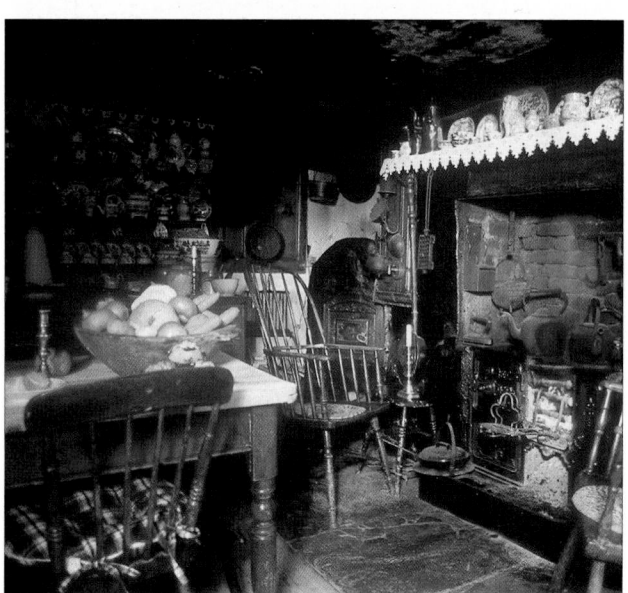

The Kitchen, 18 Folegate Street.

FREUD MUSEUM

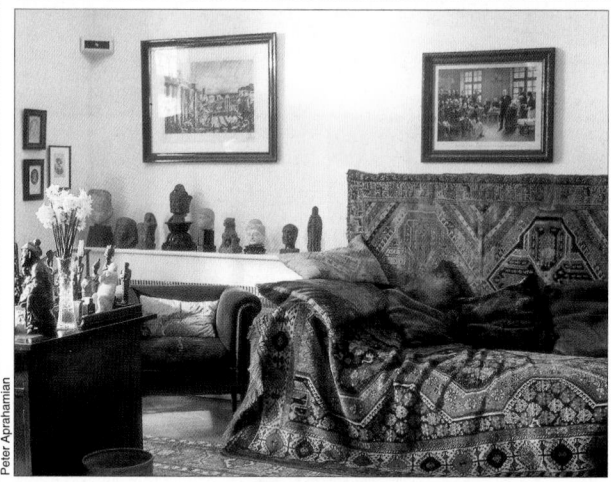

20 MARESFIELD GARDENS, LONDON NW3 5SX

Contact: *Ms E Davies*

Tel: 020 7435 2002 **Fax:** 020 7431 5452 **e-mail:** freud@gn.apc.org

The Freud Museum was the home of Sigmund Freud after he escaped the Nazi annexation of Austria. The house retains its domestic atmosphere and has the character of turn of the century Vienna. The centrepiece is Freud's study which has been preserved intact, containing his remarkable collection of antiquities: Egyptian, Greek, Roman, Oriental and his large library. The Freuds brought all their furniture and household effects to London; fine Biedermeier and 19th century Austrian painted furniture. The most famous item is Freud's psychoanalytic couch, where his patients reclined. Fine Oriental rugs cover the floor and tables. Videos are shown of the Freud family in Vienna, Paris and London.

Location: OS Ref. TQ265 850. Between Swiss Cottage and Hampstead.

Opening Times: Wed - Sun (inc) 12 noon - 5pm.

Admission: Adult £4, Child under 12 free, Conc. £2. Coach parties by appointment.

Ground floor suitable. Limited. Guide dogs only.

FULHAM PALACE & MUSEUM

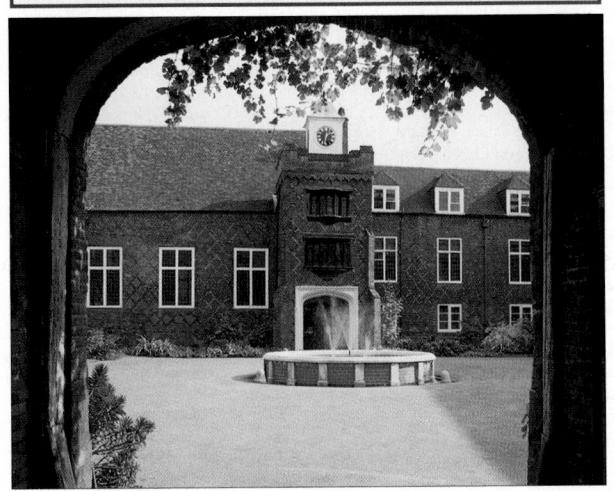

BISHOPS AVENUE, FULHAM, LONDON SW6 6EA

Owner: *London Borough of Hammersmith & Fulham & Fulham Palace Trust*

Tel: 020 7736 5821   **Museum:** 020 7736 3233

Former home of the Bishops of London (Tudor with Georgian additions and Victorian Chapel). The gardens, famous in the 17th century, now contain specimen trees and a knot garden of herbs. The museum tells the story of this nationally important site. Education service available. Rooms and grounds are available for private functions.

Location: OS Ref. TQ240 761.

Opening Times: Gardens: open daylight hours. Museum: Mar - Oct: Wed - Sun, 2 - 5pm. Nov - Feb: Thur - Sun, 1 - 4pm. Tours of principal rooms and gardens every 2nd Sun - contact Museum; selected other Suns contact Fulham Archaeological Rescue Group 020 7385 3723, £2. Private tours £5 each by arrangement with either organisation. Private tours with teas (50 max.).

Admission: Gardens: Free. Museum: Adult £1, Conc. 50p.

Private & wedding receptions.   Partially suitable.   Obligatory.
No parking.   Guide dogs only.

Reg. Charity No. 1020063

HAM HOUSE

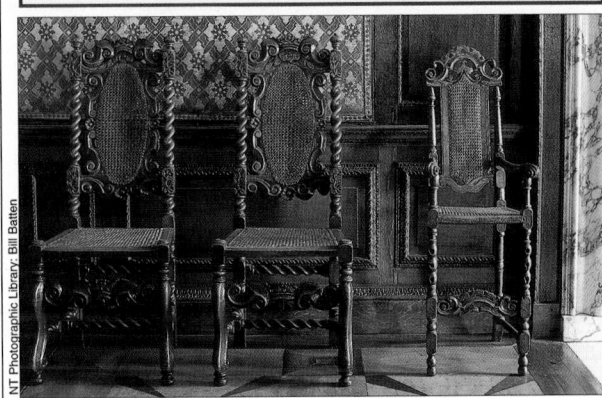

NT Photographic Library: Bill Batten

HAM, RICHMOND, SURREY TW10 7RS

Owner: *The National Trust*   ***Contact:*** *The Property Manager*

Tel: 020 8940 1950   **Fax:** 020 8332 6903   **e-mail:** shhgen@smtp.ntrust.org.uk

Ham House, on the banks of the River Thames, is perhaps the most remarkable Stuart house in the country. Apart from the fact that its architectural fabric has survived virtually unchanged since the 1670s, it still retains many of the furnishings from that period. Ham is presented today principally as the late 17th century Lauderdale residence with overlays of the 18th and 19th centuries. Visitors view the rooms in the sequence intended at the time, progressing through a hierarchy of apartments towards the Queen's Closet - the culmination of the sequence. The gardens are being restored using plans and images which were found in the house and were laid out in compartments, reflecting the ordered symmetry of the house and together they present the modern visitor with a complete picture of 17th century aristocratic life.

Location: OS Ref. TQ172 732. 1$\frac{1}{2}$ m from Richmond and 2m from Kingston. On the S bank of the River Thames, W of A307 at Petersham.

Opening times: 31 Mar - 1 Nov: daily except Thurs & Fris. House: 1 - 5pm, last adm. 4.30pm. Gardens: 11am - 6pm/dusk if earlier. Closed 25 - 26 Dec & 1 Jan.

Admission: House & Garden: Adult £6, Child £3, Family £15. Garden, Icehouse & Dairy: Adult £2, Child £1, Family £5. Pre-booked groups (min 15): Adult £5, Child £2.50.

Partially suitable. WC.   Guide dogs.

THE GEFFRYE MUSEUM

Tel: 020 7739 9893   **Fax:** 020 7729 5647

Kingsland Road, London E2 8EA

e-mail: info@geffrye-museum.org.uk

Owner: Independent Charitable Trust   **Contact:** Ms Nancy Loader

The Geffrye presents the changing styles of English domestic interiors through a series of period rooms from 1600 to present day.

Location: OS Ref. TQ335 833. 1m N of Liverpool St. Buses: 242, 149, 243, 67. Underground: Liverpool St. or Old St.

Opening Times: Museum: Tue - Sat, 10am - 5pm. Suns & BH Mons, 12 noon - 5pm. Closed Mons (except BHs) Good Fri, Christmas Eve, Christmas Day, Boxing Day & New Year's Day. Gardens: Apr - Oct.

Admission: Free.

GILBERT COLLECTION

See page 71 for full page entry.

GUNNERSBURY PARK MUSEUM

Tel: 020 8992 1612   **Fax:** 020 8752 0686

Gunnersbury Park, London W3 8LQ

e-mail: gp-museum@cip.org.uk

Owner: Hounslow and Ealing Councils   **Contact:** Vanda Foster

Built in 1802 and refurbished by Sydney Smirke for the Rothschild family.

Location: OS Ref. TQ190 792. Acton Town underground station. $\frac{1}{4}$ m N of the junction of A4, M4 North Circular.

Opening Times: Apr - Oct: daily: 1 - 5pm. (6pm weekends & BHs). Nov - Mar: daily: 1 - 4pm. Victorian kitchens summer weekends only. Closed Christmas Day and Boxing Day. Park: open dawn - dusk.

Admission: Free. Donations welcome.

HERMITAGE ROOMS

See page 71 for full page entry.

HOGARTH'S HOUSE

Tel: 020 8994 6757

Hogarth Lane, Great West Road, Chiswick, London W4 2QN

Owner: Hogarth House Foundation   **Contact:** Jerome Farrell

This late 17th century house was the country home of William Hogarth, the famous painter, engraver, satirist and social reformer between 1749 and his death in 1764.

Location: OS Ref. TQ213 778. 100 yds W of Hogarth roundabout on the Great West Road - junction of Burlington Lane. Car park in named spaces in Axis Business Centre behind house and Chiswick House grounds.

Opening Times: Apr - Oct: Tue - Fri, 1 - 5pm. Sats & Suns, 1 - 6pm. Nov - Mar: Tue - Fri, 1 - 4pm. Sats & Suns, 1 - 5pm. Closed Jan, Good Fri, 25 & 26 Dec. Closed Mons except BHs.

Admission: Free.

JEWEL TOWER

Tel: 020 7222 2219

Abingdon Street, Westminster, London SW1P 3JY

Owner: English Heritage   **Contact:** Head Custodian

Built c1365 to house the personal treasure of Edward III and one of two surviving parts of the Palace of Westminster.

Location: OS Ref. TQ302 794. Opposite S end of Houses of Parliament (Victoria Tower).

Opening Times: 1 Apr - 31 Mar: daily, 10am - 6pm (closes 5pm in Oct, & 4pm Nov - Mar).

Admission: Adult £1.60, Child 80p, Conc. £1.20.

DR JOHNSON'S HOUSE

Tel: 020 7353 3745

17 Gough Square, London EC4A 3DE

e-mail: curator@drjh.dircon.co.uk

Owner: The Trustees

Fine 18th century house, once home to Dr Samuel Johnson, the celebrated literary figure, famous for his English dictionary.

Location: OS Ref. TQ314 813. N of Fleet Street.

Opening Times: Oct - Apr: Mon - Sat, 11am - 5pm. May - Sept: Mon - Sat, 11am - 5.30pm.

Admission: Adult £4, Child £1 (under 10yrs Free), Conc. £3. Family Ticket £9.00. Groups: £3.

KEATS HOUSE

Tel: 020 7435 2062 **Fax:** 020 7431 9293
e-mail: keatshouse@corpoflondon.gov.uk

Keats Grove, Hampstead, London NW3 2RR

Owner: Corporation of London   **Contact:** C De' Freitas

Regency home of the poet John Keats (1795 - 1821).

Location: OS Ref. TQ272 856. Hampstead, NW3. Nearest Underground: Belsize Park & Hampstead.

Opening Times: Summer: May - end Oct: General opening: Tue - Sun & BHs, 12 noon - 5pm. Visits by appointment: Tues - Sat, 10am - 12 noon. Winter: Nov - Dec: General opening: Tues - Sun, 12 noon - 4pm. Visits by appointment, Tues - Sat, 10am - 12 noon. Due to ongoing building works from December 2001, please contact the house for opening times.

Admission: Adult £3, Under 16s Free, Conc. £1.50.

⬚ ♿ Ground floor & garden accessible 🅿 No parking. 🦮 Guide dogs only.
❄ Ⓦ

KENSINGTON PALACE STATE APARTMENTS

See page 68 for full page entry.

KENWOOD HOUSE ⌗

See page 69 for full page entry.

LEIGHTON HOUSE ART GALLERY & MUSEUM

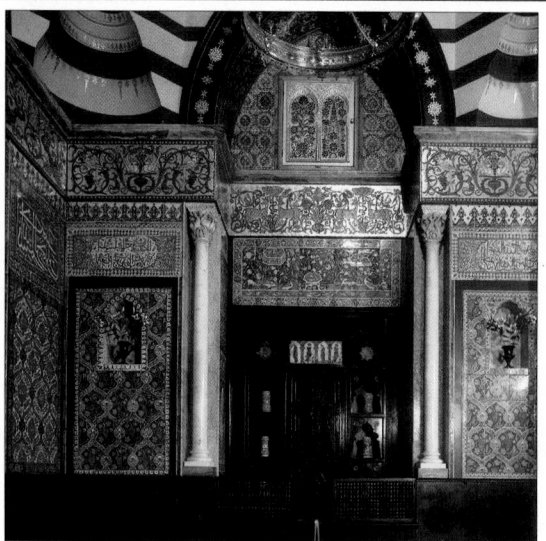

12 HOLLAND PARK ROAD, KENSINGTON, LONDON W14 8LZ
Owner: Royal Borough of Kensington & Chelsea Contact: Curator

Tel: 020 7602 3316 **Fax:** 020 7371 2467

Leighton House was the home of Frederic, Lord Leighton 1830 - 1896, painter and President of the Royal Academy, built between 1864 - 1879. It was a palace of art designed for entertaining and to provide a magnificent working space in the studio, with great north windows and a gilded apse. The Arab Hall is the centrepiece of the house, containing Leighton's collection of Persian tiles, a gilt mosaic frieze and a fountain. Victorian paintings by Leighton, Millais and Burne-Jones are on display.

Location: OS Ref. TQ247 793. N of High Street Kensington, off Melbury Rd, close to Commonwealth Institute.

Opening Times: Daily, except Tues. Spring & Summer BHs, 11am - 5.30pm.

Admission: Free. £3 per head for pre-booked tours.

⬚ 🍽 🎫 🎧 📷 ✂ ❄ 🛡 Please telephone for details. Ⓦ

LINDSEY HOUSE 🌿

Tel: 01494 528051

99 -100 Cheyne Walk, London SW10 0DQ

Owner: The National Trust   **Contact:** NT Regional Office

Part of Lindsey House was built in 1674 on the site of Sir Thomas More's garden, overlooking the River Thames. It has one of the finest 17th century exteriors in London.

Location: OS Ref. TQ268 775. On Cheyne Walk, W of Battersea Bridge near junction with Milman's Street on Chelsea Embankment.

Opening Times: By written appointment only. 17 May, 13 Jun, 12 Sept & 10 Oct: 2 - 4pm. Please write to (enc. SAE): The Secretary, 100 Cheyne Walk, London SW10 0DQ.

LINLEY SAMBOURNE HOUSE

Recorded Message: 020 7937 0663
Info: 020 7602 3316 **Fax:** 020 7371 2467

18 Stafford Terrace, London W8 7BH

Owner: The Royal Borough of Kensington & Chelsea   **Contact:** Assistant Curator

The home of Linley Sambourne (1844 - 1910) chief political cartoonist at Punch. A unique example of a late Victorian town house.

Location: OS Ref. TQ252 794. Bus: 9, 10, 27, 28, 31, 49, 52, 70 & C1. Tube: Kensington High Street. Parking on Sun in nearby streets.

Opening Times: Closed for conservation work, expected to re-open Autumn 2002.

MARBLE HILL HOUSE ⌗

Tel: 020 8892 5115

Richmond Road, Twickenham TW1 2NL

Owner: English Heritage   **Contact:** House Manager

This beautiful villa beside the Thames was built in 1724 - 29 for Henrietta Howard, mistress of George II. Here she entertained many of the poets and wits of the Augustan age including Alexander Pope and later Horace Walpole. The perfect proportions of the villa were inspired by the work of the 16th century Italian architect, Palladio. Today this beautifully presented house contains an important collection of paintings and furniture, including some pieces commissioned for the villa when it was built.

Location: OS Ref. TQ174 736. A305, 600yds E of Orleans House.

Opening Times: 1 Apr - 30 Sept: daily, 10am - 6pm. 1 Oct - 31 Oct: daily, 10am - 5pm. 1 Nov - 31 Mar, Wed - Sun, 10am - 4pm.

Admission: Adult £3.30, Child £1.70, Conc. £2.50.

⬚ ♿ Ground floor & grounds suitable. WC. 📷 ❄ 🛡 Tel. for details.

WILLIAM MORRIS GALLERY

Tel: 020 8527 3782 **Fax:** 020 8527 7070

Lloyd Park, Forest Road, Walthamstow, London E17 4PP

Owner: London Borough of Waltham Forest   **Contact:** Ms Nora Gillow

Location: OS Ref. SQ372 899. 15 mins walk from Walthamstow tube (Victoria line). 5 - 10 mins from M11/A406.

Opening Times: Tue - Sat and first Sun each month, 10am - 1pm and 2 - 5pm.

Admission: Free for all visitors but a charge is made for guided tours which must be booked in advance.

MUSEUM OF GARDEN HISTORY

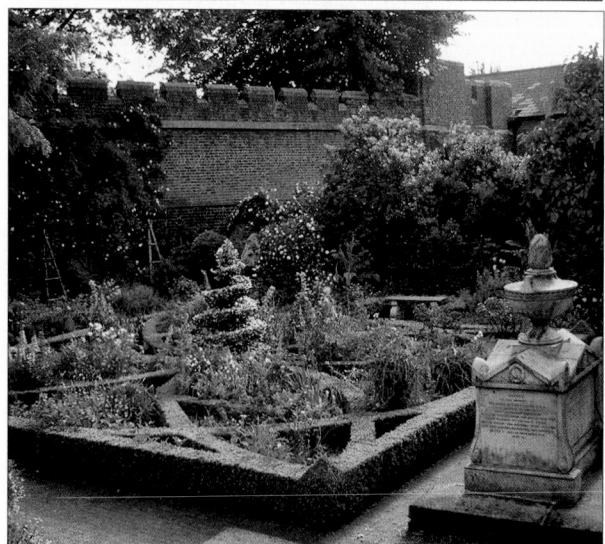

LAMBETH PALACE ROAD, LONDON SE1 7LB
Owner: The Tradescant Trust

Tel: 020 7401 8865 **Fax:** 020 7401 8869 **e-mail:** info@museumgardenhistory.org

Fascinating permanent exhibition of the history of gardens, collection of ancient tools and recreated 17th century garden displaying flowers and shrubs of the period – seeds of which may be purchased in the garden shop. Visit the tombs of the Tradescants and Captain Bligh of the Bounty. They have knowledgeable staff and lectures, concerts, courses and art exhibitions are held regularly. The Knot Garden, part of the churchyard, is shown above.

Location: OS Ref. TQ306 791. At Lambeth Parish Church, next to Lambeth Palace, at E end of Lambeth Bridge. Buses: 3, 77, 344, C10. Tube: Westminster or Waterloo.

Opening Times: 1st Sun in Feb - late Dec: Daily, 10.30am - 5pm.

Admission: Adult £2, Conc. £1.50

⬚ 🍽 ♿ Partially suitable. 🅿 No parking.

MYDDELTON HOUSE GARDENS

Tel: 01992 702200 **Fax:** 01992 702280

Bulls Cross, Enfield, Middlesex EN2 9HG

Owner: Lee Valley Regional Park Authority

Created by the famous plantsman E A Bowles.

Location: OS Ref. TQ342 992. ¹/₄ m W of A10 via Turkey St. ³/₄ m S M25/J25.

Opening Times: Mon - Fri (except Christmas), 10am - 4.30pm. Easter - Oct: Suns & BHs, 2 - 5pm.

Admission: Adult £1.90, Conc. £1.30.

THE OCTAGON, ORLEANS HOUSE GALLERY

Tel: 020 8892 0221

Fax: 020 8744 0501

Riverside, Twickenham, Middlesex TW1 3DJ

Owner: London Borough of Richmond-upon-Thames **Contact:** Rachel Tranter

Outstanding example of baroque architecture built by James Gibbs c1720. Adjacent wing now converted to an art gallery.

Location: OS Ref. TQ168 734. On N side of Riverside, 700yds E of Twickenham town centre, 400yds S of Richmond Road, A305 via Lebanon Park Road and 500yds W of Marble Hill House.

Opening Times: Tue - Sat, 1 - 5.30pm (Oct - Mar closes 4.30pm). Sun & BHs, 2 - 5.30pm. Closed Mons. Garden: open daily, 9am - sunset.

Admission: Free.

OSTERLEY PARK

See right for half page entry.

PALACE OF WESTMINSTER

Tel: 020 7219 3000 **Ticketmaster:** 0207344 9966

London SW1A 0AA

Recorded Info: 0207219 5532

Contact: Information Office

The first Palace of Westminster was erected on this site by Edward the Confessor in 1042 and the building was a royal residence until a devastating fire in 1512. After this, the palace became the two-chamber Parliament for government - the House of Lords (largely hereditary until the reforms of the present Government) and the elected House of Commons. Following a further fire in 1834, the palace was rebuilt by Sir Charles Barry and decorated by A W Pugin.

Location: OS Ref. TQ303 795. Central London, W bank of River Thames. 1km S of Trafalgar Square. Underground: Westminster.

Opening Times: Summer opening until 16 Sept: timed tours including both Houses of Parliament, can be booked through the Ticketmaster or website. Palace closed Suns, BHs and some mornings. **Strangers' Gallery**, **House of Commons**: open when the House is sitting: Mon - Wed, 2.30pm; Thurs, 11.30am and (occasionally) Fris, 9.30am (check recorded info line). UK residents can apply in advance to their MP for tickets but requests for specific days cannot be guaranteed. Otherwise join public queue outside St Stephen's Entrance, may take an hour or two before popular periods such as Prime Mininster's Questions (Wed, 3pm). Places usually available after 6pm. **Strangers' Gallery**, **House of Lords**: Open when House is sitting (see above), separate queue at St Stephen's Entrance. **The 'line of route' tour**: weekday group tours during recess. When the Houses are sitting, official tours, (1 hour), are restricted to before noon and Fri afternoons. Groups (max 16) must be sponsored by an MP. **Big Ben**: group tours (max 12): Mon - Fri, 10.30am, 11.30am & 2.30pm, must contact your MP for a booking. **Lord Chancellor's Apartments**: 2 tours per week (max 25): Tues & Thurs am. Fully booked until end 2001 (cancellation list: 020 7219 2184). **Westminster Hall**: Mon - Sat, (until 15 Sept), 9.30am - 5pm.

Admission: Ticketmaster admin charge £3.50. The 'line of route' tour: gratuity of £20 - £25 per group. Big Ben: Free.

PITSHANGER MANOR & GALLERY

Tel: 020 8567 1227 **Fax:** 020 8567 0595

Walpole Park, Mattock Lane, Ealing W5 5EQ

e-mail: pitshanger@ealing.gov.uk

Owner: London Borough of Ealing **Contact:** Neena Sohal

Set in Walpole Park, once owned by the architect Sir John Soane (1753 - 1837). He rebuilt most of the house to create a Regency villa. The later addition of a Victorian wing now houses a collection of Martinware pottery. Adjoining the Manor is Pitshanger Manor Gallery, the largest space for contemporary art in West London.

Location: OS Ref. TQ176 805. Ealing, London.

Opening Times: Tue - Sat, 10am - 5pm. Closed Suns & Mons. Also closed Christmas, Easter and New Year.

Admission: Free. Adult group tours (10+): £3.

  By arrangement. 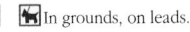 Limited. In grounds, on leads.

THE QUEEN'S GALLERY

Tel: 020 7839 1377

Buckingham Palace, London SW1A 1AA

Owner: HM The Queen **Contact:** The Visitor Office

Location: OS Ref. TQ290 795. Buckingham Palace.

Opening Times: The Queen's Gallery is closed for major remodelling and extension and will re-open in 2002, the year of The Queen's Golden Jubilee.

OSTERLEY PARK

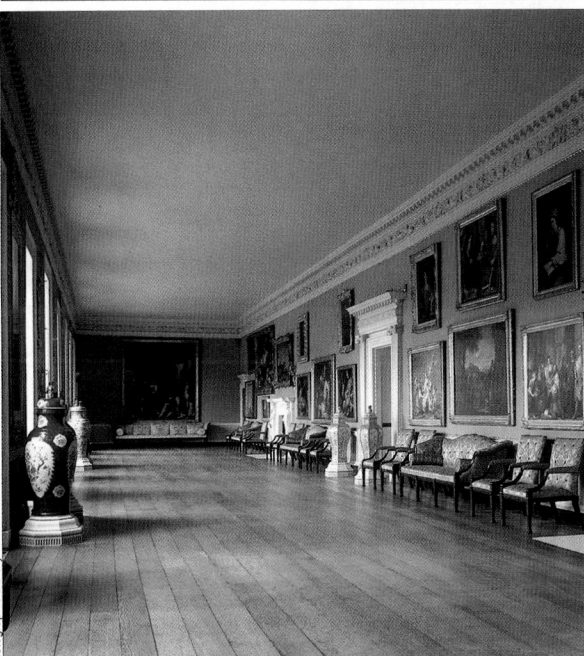

NT Photographic Library

ISLEWORTH TW7 4RB

Owner: The National Trust *Contact: The Property Manager*

Tel/Fax: 020 8568 7714

Osterley's four turrets look out across one of the last great landscaped parks in suburban London, its trees and lakes an unexpected haven of green. Originally built in 1575, the mansion was transformed in the 18th century into an elegant villa by architect Robert Adam. The classical interior, designed for entertaining on a grand scale, still impresses with its specially made tapestries, furniture and plasterwork.

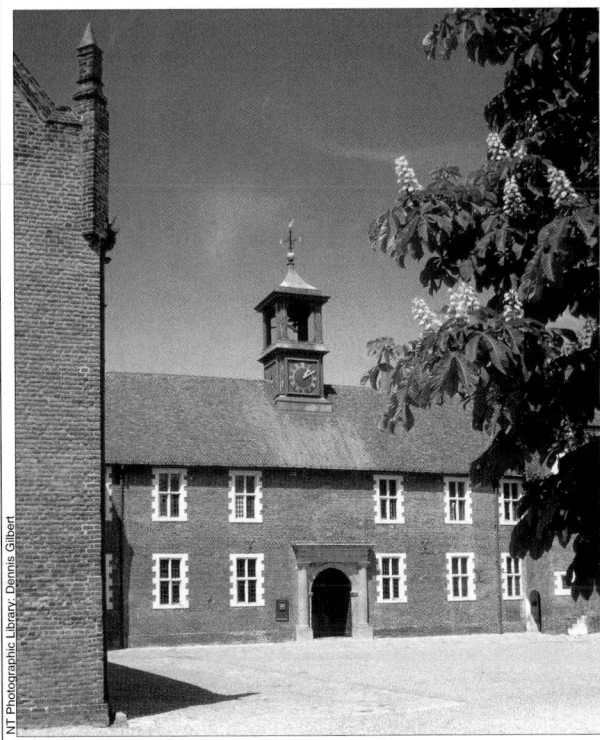

NT Photographic Library / Dennis Gilbert

Location: OS Ref. TQ146 780. Access via Thornbury Road on N side of A4.

Opening Times: House: 31 Mar - 4 Nov: daily except Mons & Tues, 1 - 4.30pm. Closed Good Fri, open BH Mons. Last admission: 4pm. Grand Stable: Sun afternoon in summer. Park & Pleasure Grounds: All year, 9am - 7.30pm or sunset if earlier. Park will be closed early during major events. Car park closed Good Fri, 25 & 26 Dec. Jersey Galleries: as house.

Admission: Adult £4.30, Child £2.15, Family £10.50. Group: Wed - Sat £3.50, pre-booking required. Car Park: £2.50.

  Suitable, phone for details. On leads in park.

London England

THE RANGER'S HOUSE   **Tel:** 020 8853 0035

Chesterfield Walk, Blackheath, London SE10 8QX

Owner: English Heritage   **Contact:** House Manager

A handsome, red-brick house which lies between two of London's great open spaces, Greenwich Park and Blackheath. The house was built for a successful seafarer, Admiral Francis Hosier around 1700 who sited the house within view of the Thames estuary. A later owner Lord Chesterfield, used to boast that the grand bow-windowed gallery commanded the three finest views in the world. Today Ranger's House is home to the Suffolk collection of paintings including elegant full-length Jacobean portraits. The first floor of the house contains an exhibition space. There is also an Architectural Study Collection, with features from 17th, 18th and 19th century dwellings. The first floor houses an exciting programme of contemporary exhibitions.

Location: OS Ref. TQ388 768. N of Shooters Hill Road.

Opening Times: 1 Apr - 30 Sept: daily, 10am - 6pm. 1 - 31 Oct: daily 10am - 5pm. 1 Nov - 31 Mar: Wed - Sun, 10am - 4pm. Ranger's House may close in winter 2000 for major refurbishment. Please call the house before you visit.

Admission: Adult £2.80, Child £1.40, Conc. £2.10.

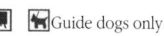 Limited, lift available. Guide dogs only. 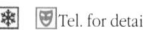 Tel. for details.

THE ROYAL MEWS   **Tel:** 020 7839 1377

Buckingham Palace, London SW1A 1AA

Owner: HM The Queen   **Contact:** The Visitor Officer

Location: OS Ref. TQ289 794. Entrance in Buckingham Palace Road, W of The Queen's Gallery.

Opening Times: Oct - Jul: Mon - Thur, 12 noon - 4pm. Aug & Sept: Mon - Thur, 10.30am - 4.30pm. Last admission 30mins before closing.

Admission: Adult £4.60, Child (under 17yrs) £2.60, OAP £3.60. Family ticket (2+2) £11.80.

ROYAL SOCIETY OF ARTS

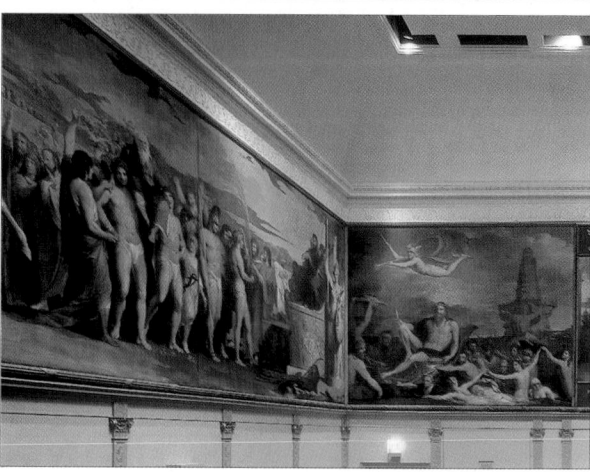

8 JOHN ADAM STREET, LONDON WC2N 6EZ

Owner: RSA Contact: Ms Nicki Kyle

Tel: 020 7839 5049   **Fax:** 020 7321 0271

e-mail: conference@rsa-uk.demon.co.uk

The house of the Royal Society of Arts was designed by Robert Adam specially for the Society in the early 1770s. One of the few remaining buildings from the original Adelphi development, its Georgian façade conceals many unexpected delights of both traditional and contemporary architecture. Designed as one of London's earliest debating chambers, the Great Room is one of the most spectacular theatres in the city. The Benjamin Franklin Room is spacious and elegant, featuring an antique chandelier and two Adam fireplaces. The Vaults were originally designed as river front warehouses. Now fully restored they offer a striking contrast to the splendour of the rooms above. All rooms may be hired for meetings, receptions and weddings.

Location: OS Ref. TQ305 806. Near to Charing Cross and Waterloo.

Opening Times: All year: 8am - 8pm. Closed last 2 weeks of Aug, 24 Dec & 2 Jan.

Admission: For room hire prices, contact the RSA Conference Officer.

  Licensed. By arrangement. None.

ROYAL OBSERVATORY GREENWICH & QUEEN'S HOUSE

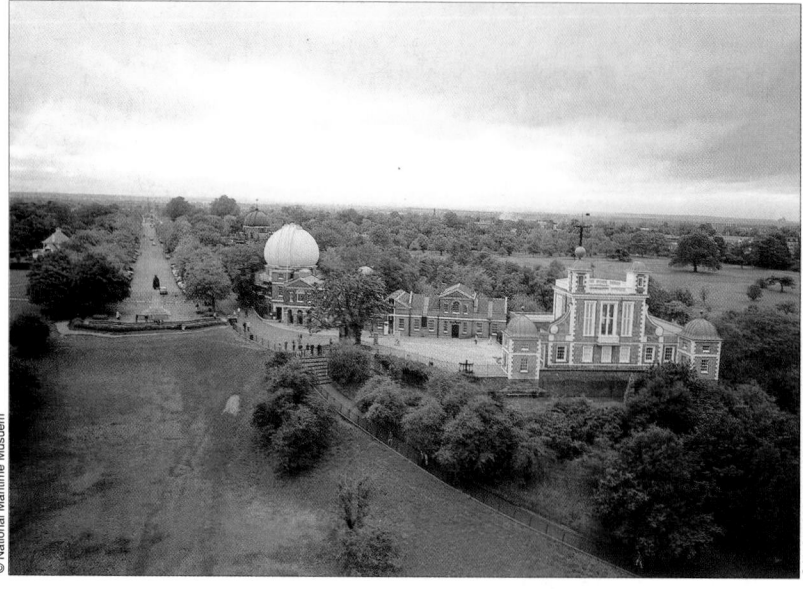 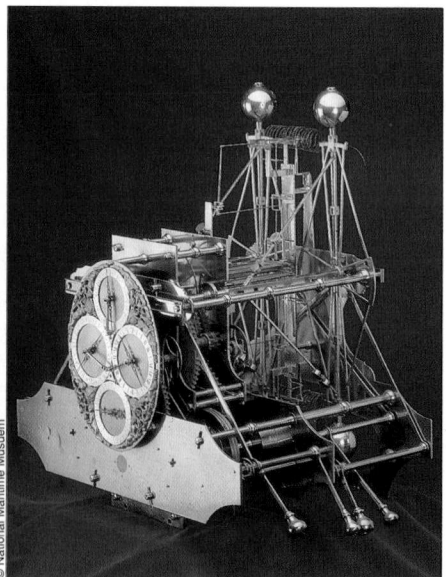

© National Maritime Museum

GREENWICH PARK, GREENWICH, LONDON SE10 9NF

Owner: National Maritime Museum Contact: Robin Scates

Tel: 020 8858 4422   **Fax:** 020 8312 6632

24-hour info: 020 8312 6565   **e-mail:** bookings@nmm.ac.uk

The Maritime Greenwich World Heritage Site encompasses Wren's imposing Royal Observatory (1675), the National Maritime Museum and the Queen's House (Inigo Jones c.1635). The Royal Observatory defines the Prime Meridian of the world – Longitude 0°. Visit the Astronomer Royal's apartments, see the 1833 time ball and admire Harrison's intricate marine timekeepers. The National Maritime Museum's 20 modern galleries chart Britain's history of seafaring and Empire ranging from Nelson's navy to recent environmental protection. The Queen's House (open from Easter 2001 onwards) contains a new exhibition of the rich history of Greenwich and also the magnificent portrait collection of the Museum.

Location: OS Ref. TQ388 773. On the South Bank of the Thames at Greenwich.

Opening Times: All year: daily, 10am - 5pm. Closed 24 - 26 Dec (Queen's House closed until Easter 2001).

Admission: Each site from £6 - £7.50, Child/Seniors (60+) Free. Disabled, student and unemployed 20% discount. Other concessions and group discounts available.

No indoor photography. Partially suitable. WC. Phone for details. Nearby. By arrangement. Coaches nearby.

ST GEORGE'S CATHEDRAL, SOUTHWARK

Tel: 020 7928 5256
Fax: 020 7787 8923

Westminster Bridge Road, London SE1 7HY
Contact: Canon James Cronin

Neo-Gothic rebuilt Pugin Cathedral bombed during the last war and rebuilt by Romily Craze in 1958.

Location: OS Ref. TQ315 794. Near Imperial War Museum. ^{1}/$_2$ m SE of Waterloo Stn.

Opening Times: 8am - 8pm, every day, except BHs.

Admission: Free.

ST JOHN'S GATE
THE MUSEUM OF THE ORDER OF ST JOHN

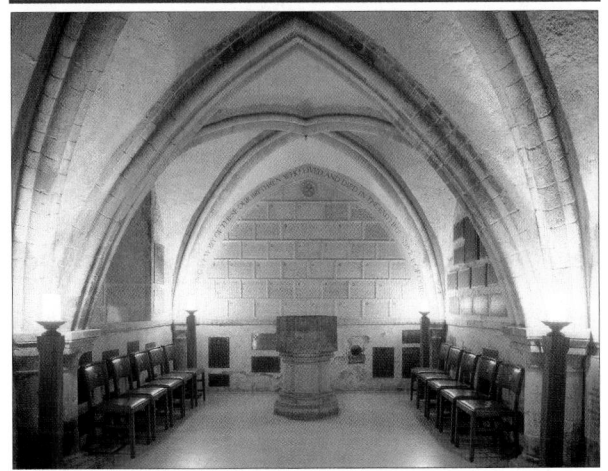

ST. JOHN'S GATE, LONDON EC1M 4DA
Owner: The Order of St. John   *Contact:* Pamela Willis

Tel: 020 7253 6644 **Fax:** 020 7336 0587

Discover the rich history of the Knights Hospitaller, a monastic order dedicated to serving the sick and defending the faith, dating back to the Crusades. The Museum is in a Tudor Gatehouse, once the entrance to their English Priory and visitors can also see the 16th century church with remarkable 12th century crypt. After the Dissolution, the Gate was Hogarth's home and Dr Johnson's workplace. In Victorian times, St John Ambulance was founded here and a new interactive gallery tells its story.

Location: OS Ref. TQ317 821. St. John's Lane, Clerkenwell. Nearest underground: Farringdon, Barbican.

Opening Times: Mon - Fri: 10am - 5pm. Sats: 10am - 4pm. Closed BHs & Sat of BH weekend. Tours: Tues, Fris & Sats at 11am & 2.30pm. Reference Library: Open by appointment.

Admission: Museum Free. Tours of the building: £4, OAP £3 (donation).

 Ground floor suitable. WC. Guide dogs only.

ST PAUL'S CATHEDRAL

See page 70 for full page entry.

SIR JOHN SOANE'S MUSEUM

Tel: 020 7405 2107 **Fax:** 020 7831 3957

13 Lincoln's Inn Fields, London WC2A 3BP

Owner: Trustees of Sir John Soane's Museum
Contact: Ms S Palmer

The celebrated architect Sir John Soane built this in 1812 as his own house. It now contains his collection of antiquities, sculpture and paintings.

Location: OS Ref. TQ308 816. E of Kingsway, S of High Holborn.

Opening Times: Tue - Sat, 10am - 5pm. 6 - 9pm, first Tue of the month. Closed BHs & 24 Dec.

Admission: Free. Groups must book.

SOMERSET HOUSE INCLUDING COURTAULD GALLERY,
GILBERT COLLECTION & HERMITAGE ROOMS

See page 71 for full page entry.

SOUTHSIDE HOUSE

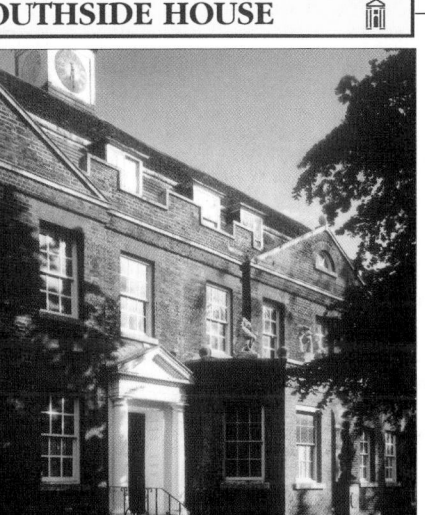

3 WOODHAYES ROAD, WIMBLEDON, LONDON SW19 4RJ
Owner: The Pennington-Mellor-Munthe Charity Trust   *Contact:* The Administrator

Tel: 020 8946 7643

Built by Robert Pennington in 1665, the family befriended or were related to many distinguished names - among others Ann Boleyn's descendents, Nelson, Hamilton, the 'Hell Fire Duke of Wharton' and Natalie, Queen of Serbia. Family portraits and possessions on show. Bedroom prepared for Prince of Wales in 1750. In 1907 the heiress, Hilda Pennington Mellor married Axel Munthe the Swedish doctor and philanthropist. After 1945 Hilda and her sons restored the house. Malcolm, who had lived extraordinary adventures during the war, determined to make a cultural art of the family inheritance. Guided tours give reality and excitement to the old family histories.

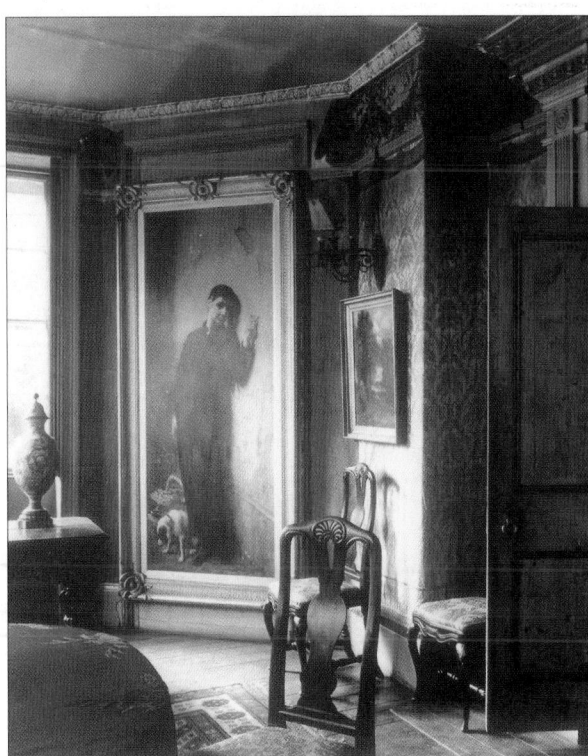

Location: OS Ref. TQ234 706. On S side of Wimbledon Common (B281), opposite Crooked Billet Inn.

Opening Times: 2 Jan - 24 Jun: Weds, Sats, Suns & BH Mons. Guided tours on the hour, 2 - 5pm (last tour 5pm). Also open for private parties by arrangement from 1 Dec - 24 Jun.

Admission: Adult £5, Child £3 (must be accompanied by an adult).

 Not suitable. Obligatory. Limited.

SOUTHWARK CATHEDRAL

Tel: 020 7367 6700 **Fax:** 020 7367 6725

Welcome Desk: 020 7367 6734 **e-mail:** cathedral@dswark.org.uk

Montague Close, Southwark, London SE1 9DA

Owner: Church of England   **Contact:** Welcome Desk

London's oldest gothic building and a place of worship for over 1,000 years, St Mary Overie Priory became St Saviour's Parish Church at the Dissolution. In 1905 it became an Anglican Cathedral. It has literary connections: Gower, Chaucer, Shakespeare and Dickens, and associations with Harvard, founder of the American university. Interesting links with the Royal family over the centuries.

Location: OS Ref. TQ327 803. South side of London Bridge, near Shakespeare's Globe and Tate Modern.

Opening Times: Daily: 8.30am - 6pm. Weekday services: 8am, 12.30pm and 5.30pm. Sat services, 9am and 4pm. Sun services: 9am, 11am and 3pm.

Admission: Recommended donation of £2.50 per person. Booked groups (min 15): Adult £2.50, Child £1, Conc. £2.

ℹ️ Indoor photography & video recording with permit. Exhibition centre (additional charge).
📷   🍴   ♿ Partially suitable. WCs. 💷   🍽 Licensed.   🎫 By arrangement. 🎧
🅿 No parking.   🚌   🐕 Guide dogs only.   ❄   ⓦ

SPENCER HOUSE

See page 72 for full page entry.

STRAWBERRY HILL

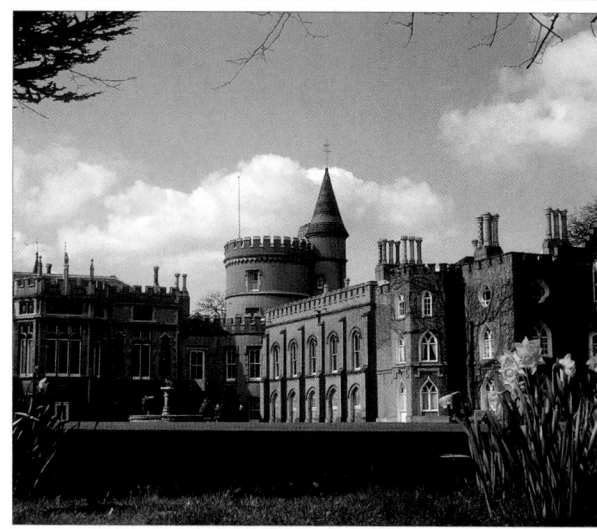

ST MARY'S, STRAWBERRY HILL, WALDEGRAVE ROAD, TWICKENHAM TW1 4SX

Contact: The Conference Office

Tel: 020 8240 4114/020 8240 4311/020 8240 4044

Horace Walpole converted a modest house at Strawberry Hill into his own version of a gothic fantasy. It is widely regarded as the first substantial building of the Gothic Revival and as such is internationally known and admired. A century later Lady Frances Waldegrave added a magnificent wing to Walpole's original structure. Lady Waldegrave's suite of rooms can be hired for weddings, corporate functions and conferences. Please telephone for details.

Location: OS Ref. TQ158 722. Off A310 between Twickenham & Teddington.

Opening Times: Easter - Oct: Suns. Please tel: 020 8240 4224 for opening times or to make an appointment 020 8240 4114.

Admission: Adult £5, OAP £4.25. Group bookings: £4.25.

ℹ️ Conferences.

SUTTON HOUSE

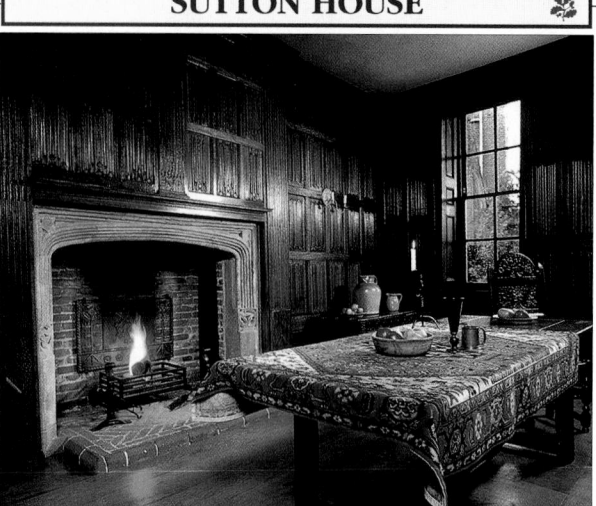

NT Photographic Library: Geoffrey Frosh

2 & 4 HOMERTON HIGH STREET, HACKNEY, LONDON E9 6JQ

Owner: The National Trust   *Contact:* The Property Manager

Tel: 020 8986 2264

A rare example of a Tudor red-brick house, built in 1535 by Sir Rafe Sadleir, Principal Secretary of State for Henry VIII, with 18th century alterations and later additions. Restoration revealed many 16th century details, even in rooms of later periods. Notable features include original linenfold panelling and 17th century wall paintings.

Location: OS Ref. TQ352 851. At the corner of Isabella Road and Homerton High St.

Opening Times: 7 Feb - 28 Nov & from 6 Feb 2002: Weds, Suns & BH Mons only, 11.30am - 5pm. Café Bar: All year: Wed - Sun & BH Mons, 11.30am - 5pm. Closed 21 Dec - 8 Jan 2002.

Admission: £2.10, Child 50p, Family £4.70. Group visits by prior arrangement.

📷   ♿ Ground floor only. WC. 💷   🅿 No parking.   🔔   🛡 Tel. for details.

SYON PARK

See page 73 for full page entry.

THE TOWER BRIDGE EXPERIENCE

Tel: 020 7378 1928 **Fax:** 020 7357 7935

Tower Bridge, London SE1 2UP

Owner: Corporation of London   **Contact:** Jo Skinner

One of London's most unusual and exciting exhibitions is situated inside Tower Bridge. Animatronic characters from the Bridge's past guide you through a series of audio-visual presentations.

Location: OS Ref. TQ337 804. Adjacent to Tower of London, nearest Tube: Tower Hill.

Opening Times: Nov - Mar: 9.30am - 6pm. Apr - Oct: 10am - 6.30pm (last entry 1¼ hrs before closing). Closed 24 - 25 Dec and 17 Jan 2001.

Admission: Adult £6.25, Child (5-15)/ Conc. £4.25, Family (2+2) £18.25 (subject to a small increase in Apr).

THE TOWER OF LONDON

See page 74 for full page entry.

THE WALLACE COLLECTION

See page 75 for full page entry.

Plant Sales Index ◀◀◀◀ page 47

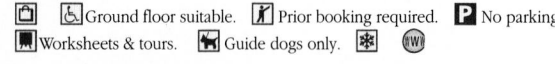

WESTMINSTER ABBEY

Tel: 020 7222 5152 **Fax:** 020 7233 2072

London SW1P 3PA   **e-mail:** press@westminster-abbey.org   **Contact:** Press Officer

Westminster Abbey is a living church that enshrines the History of the British nation.

Location: OS Ref. TQ301 795. Westminster.

Opening Times: Mon - Fri, 9am - 4.45pm (last admission 3.45pm), Sats, 9am - 2.45pm (last admission 1.45pm).

Admission: Adult £6, Child under 11yrs Free, Under 16yrs/Student/OAP £3, Family (2+2) £12 (prices from Feb 2001).

WESTMINSTER CATHEDRAL

Tel: 020 7798 9055 **Fax:** 020 7798 9090

Victoria, London SW1P 1QW

Owner: Diocese of Westminster   **Contact:** Rev Mgr George Stack

The Roman Catholic Cathedral of the Archbishop of Westminster. Spectacular building in the Byzantine style, designed by J F Bentley, opened in 1903, famous for its mosaics, marble and music. Westminster Cathedral celebrated the Centenary of its foundation in 1995.

Location: OS Ref. TQ293 791. On Victoria Street, between Victoria Station and Westminster Abbey.

Opening Times: All year: 7am - 7pm. Please telephone for times at Easter & Christmas.

Admission: Free. Lift charge: Adult £2. Child £1. Family (2+4) £5.

⬜   ♿ Ground floor suitable.   ✗ Prior booking required.   🅿 No parking.
📋 Worksheets & tours.   🐕 Guide dogs only.   ❋   ⓌⓌ

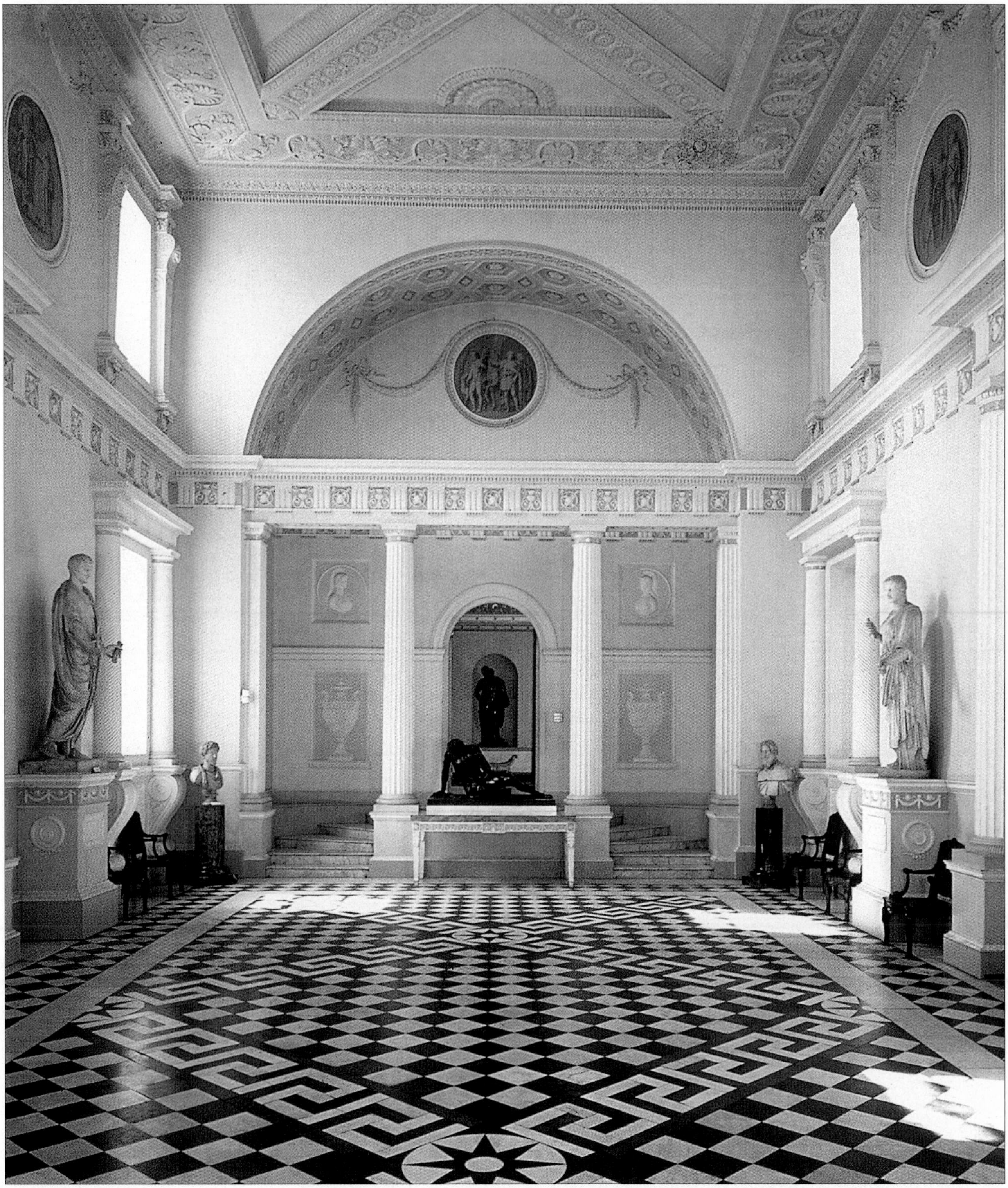

Syon Park, London.

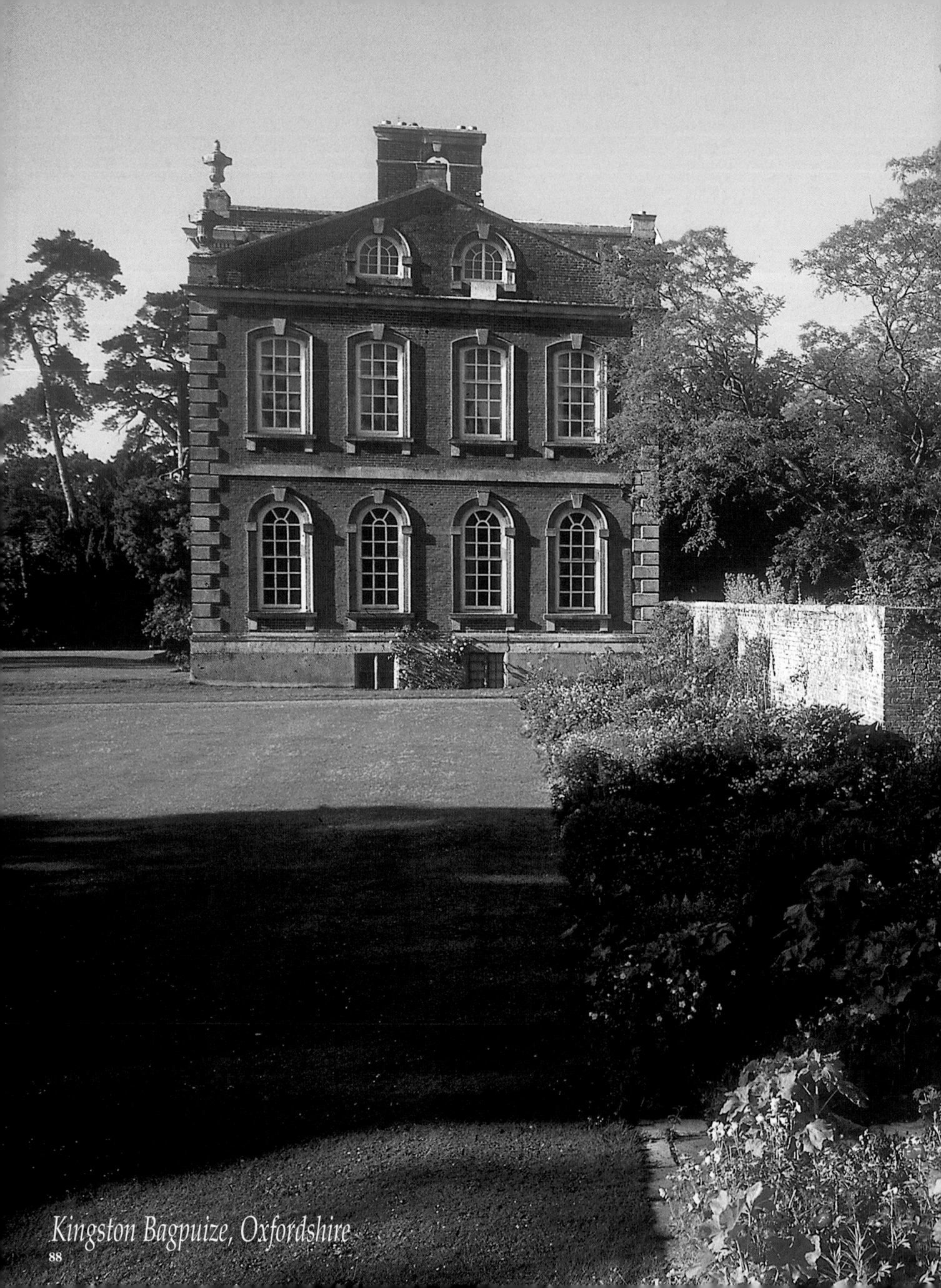

Kingston Bagpuize, Oxfordshire

88

South East

Kingston Bagpuize

Kingston Bagpuize, the beautiful Queen Anne manor house belonging to Mr and Mrs Francis Grant stands only nine miles from Oxford. In recent years, as well as being open to the public it has become an attractive and popular venue for special events, wedding receptions, filming and small conferences.

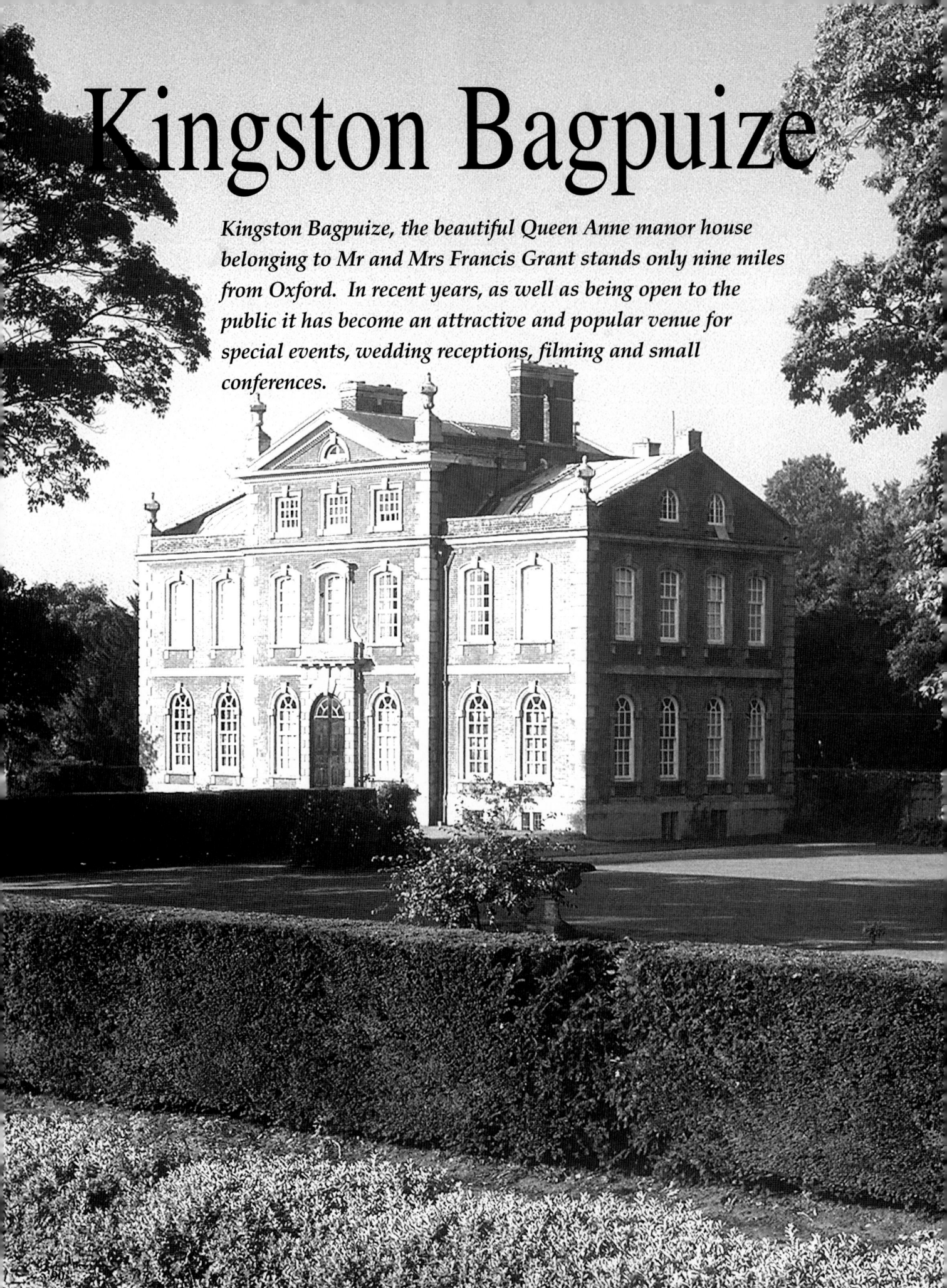

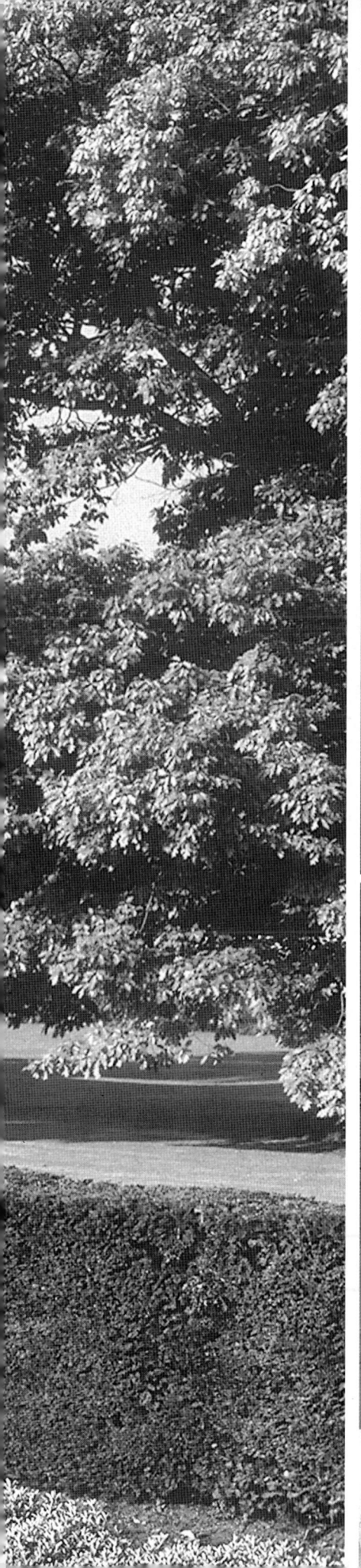

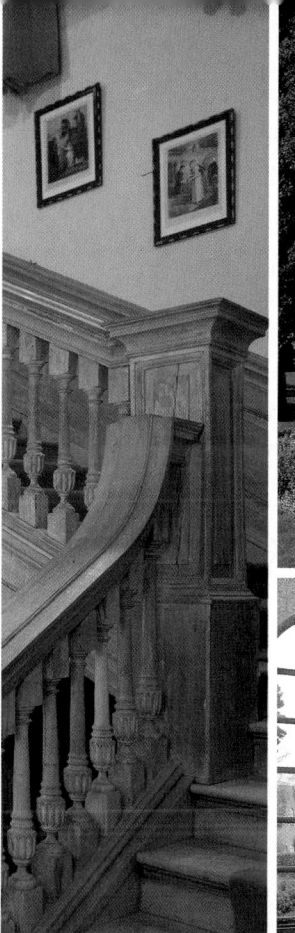

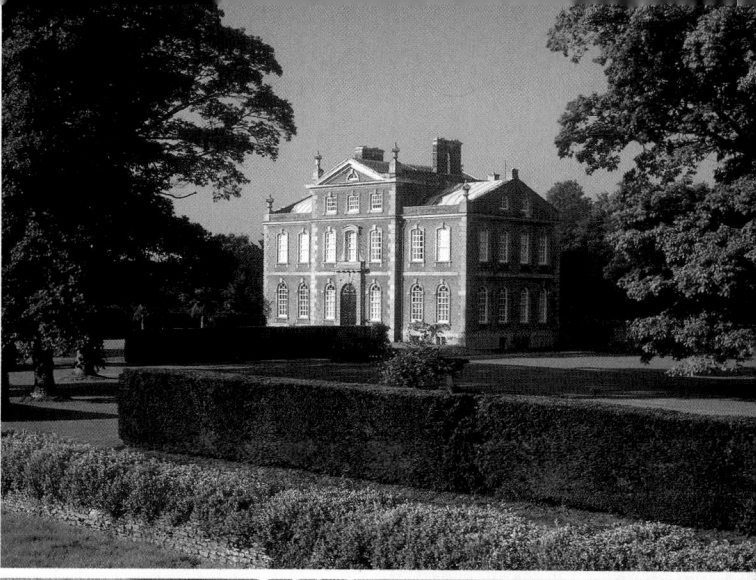

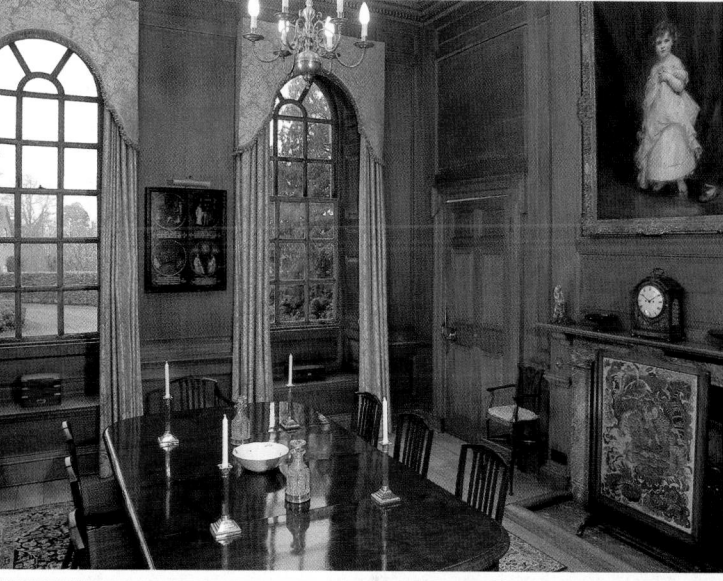

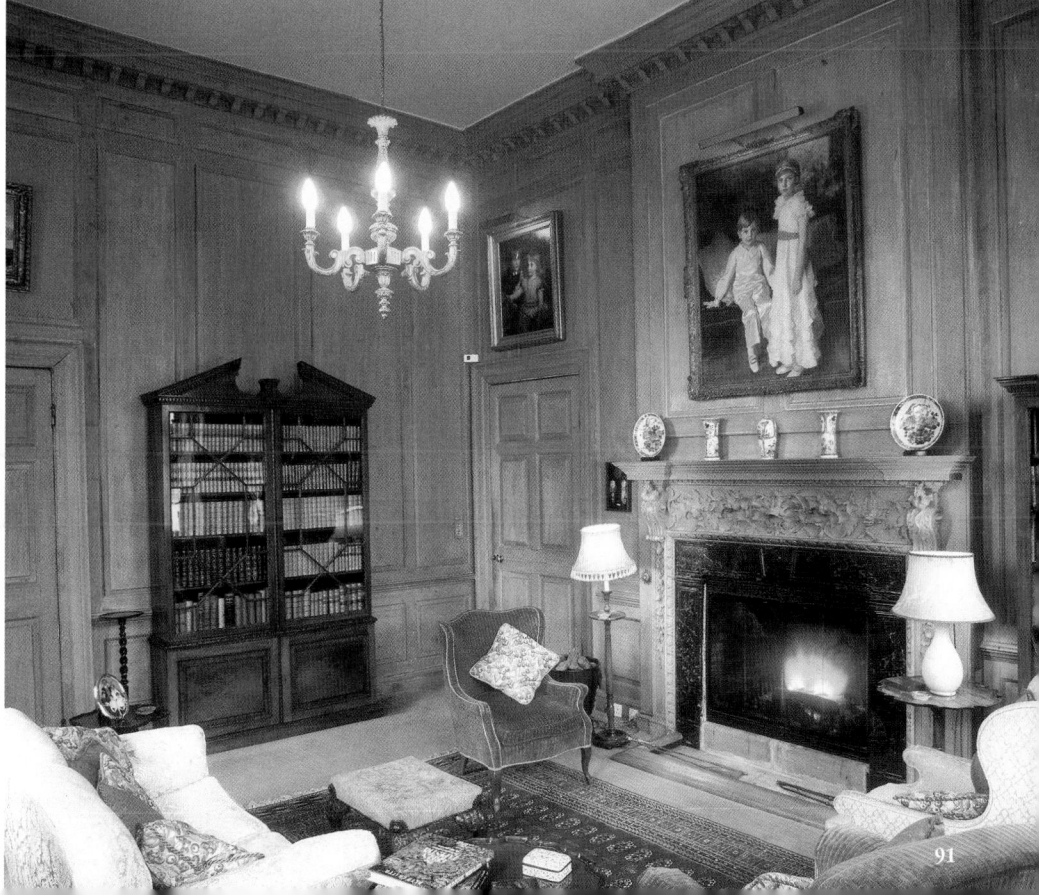

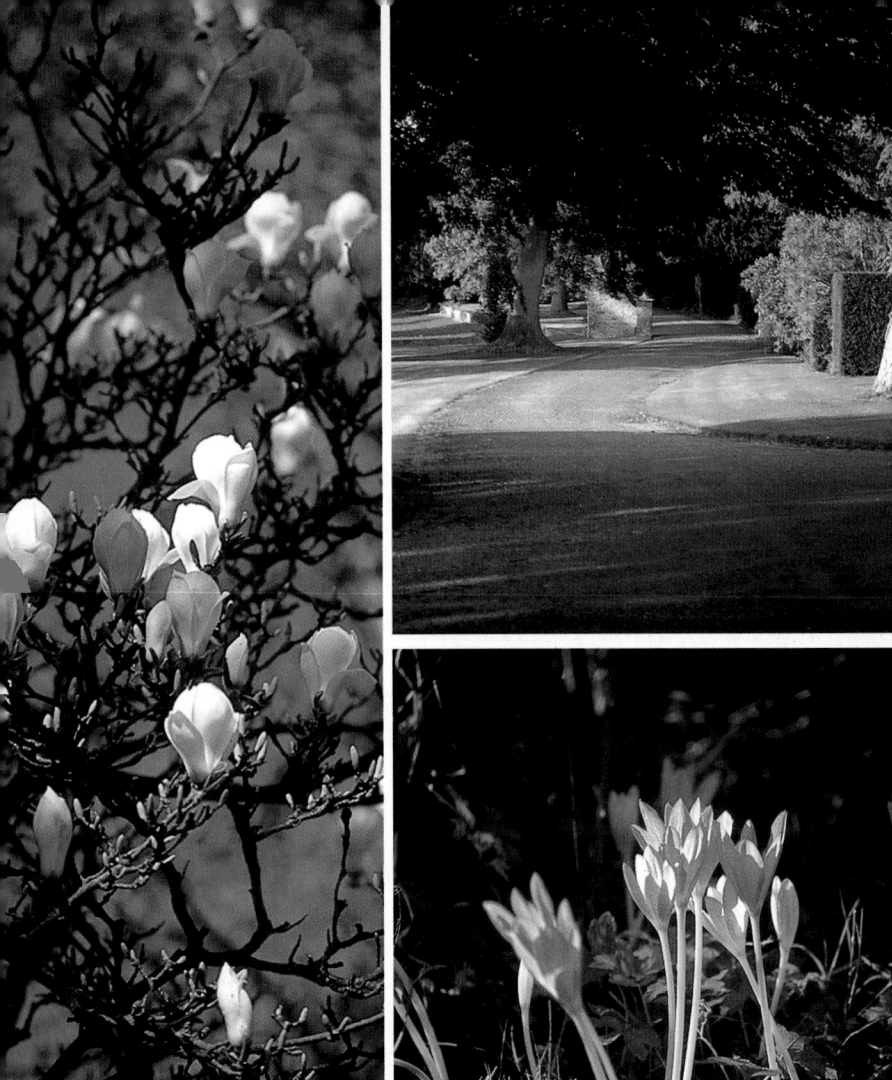

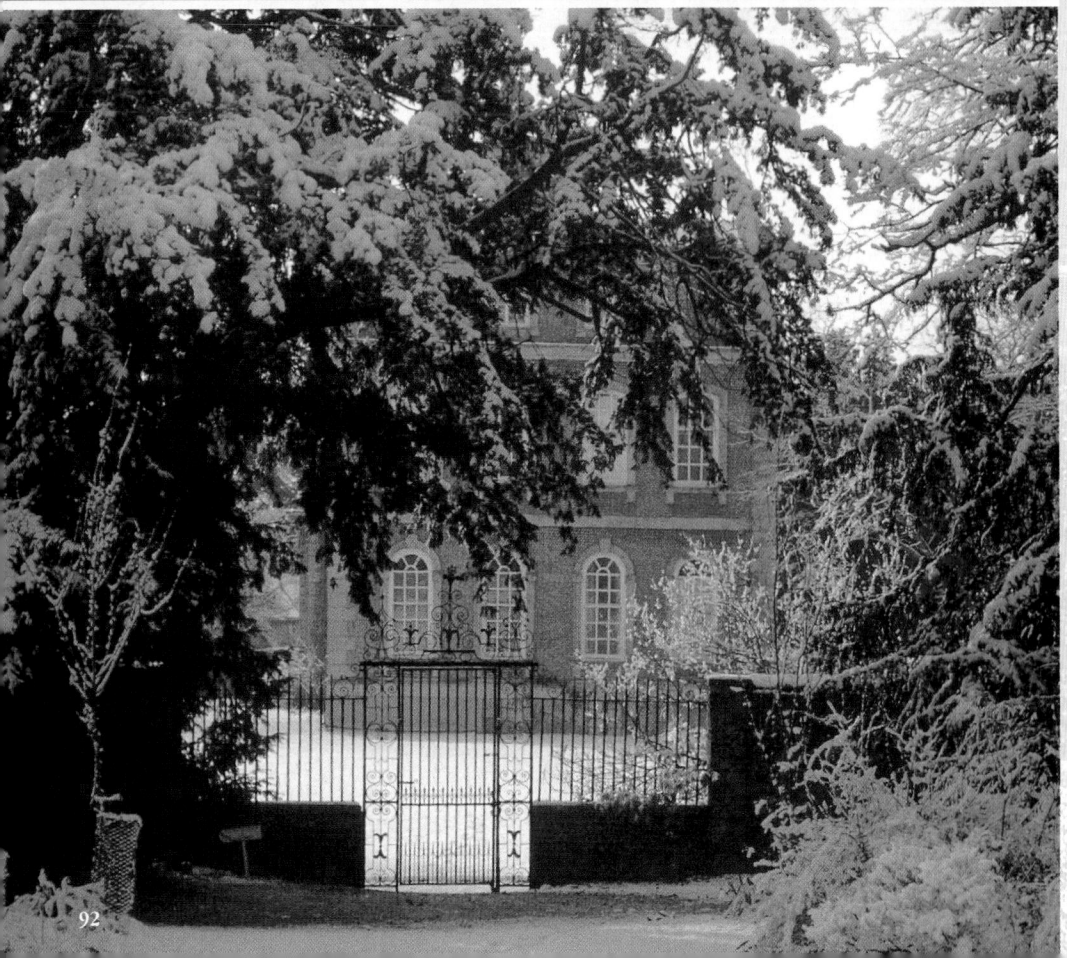

Set in mature parkland, the early origins of the house are unclear. A document of sale shows this present house to have been in existence since the 1660s, but it seems probable that it was substantially remodelled from the ground floor up in the 1720s. Townsend, a leading Oxford builder who worked under Nicholas Hawksmoor and others at Queen's College and elsewhere, may have been responsible for the alterations.

Despite the formal symmetry of the house, the interiors at Kingston Bagpuize feel immensely comfortable – the lightly coloured panelled main reception rooms creating a wonderful warm atmosphere. Dominating the Entrance Hall is the pine and oak cantilevered staircase and gallery. Thought to date from the 1720s, the staircase and gallery have no supporting columns, their weight being borne by the 3' thick walls.

Walking through the main reception rooms of the house, the visitor can see not only good Queen Anne and Georgian furniture but also in the Drawing Room beautiful French pieces from the 18th and 19th centuries. The house also has some fine paintings by Romney, Hoppner and Gainsborough.

In the Dining Room, over the fireplace, is a portrait of Marlie Raphael aged three, painted by Mrs Waller. Great Aunt of the current owner, it is to her that is owed much of the beauty of the formal and woodland gardens that surround the house today.

Marlie Raphael began adding to the existing formal gardens in the 1950s and, having removed the wartime Nissen huts from some areas of the estate, she planted the beech avenue and many specimen trees. Harold Hillier was one of the notable plantsmen who gave advice. The resulting collection contains many unusual species including *Albizia julibrissin, Ilex macrocarpa, Magnolia campbellii, Quercus pontica* and *Xanthoceras sorbifolium* as well as a wide variety of perennials and bulbs. These mature trees and shrubs today form a wonderful backdrop to the house.

The English, as a nation, have a passion for gardening. Gardens can be all things to all people and are never static. Francis and Virginia Grant, themselves keen and knowledgable gardeners, have over the last five years restored other areas of the garden and planted more specimen trees and shrubs to complement those already growing.

For further details about *Kingston Bagpuize* see entry in South East Region → Oxfordshire.

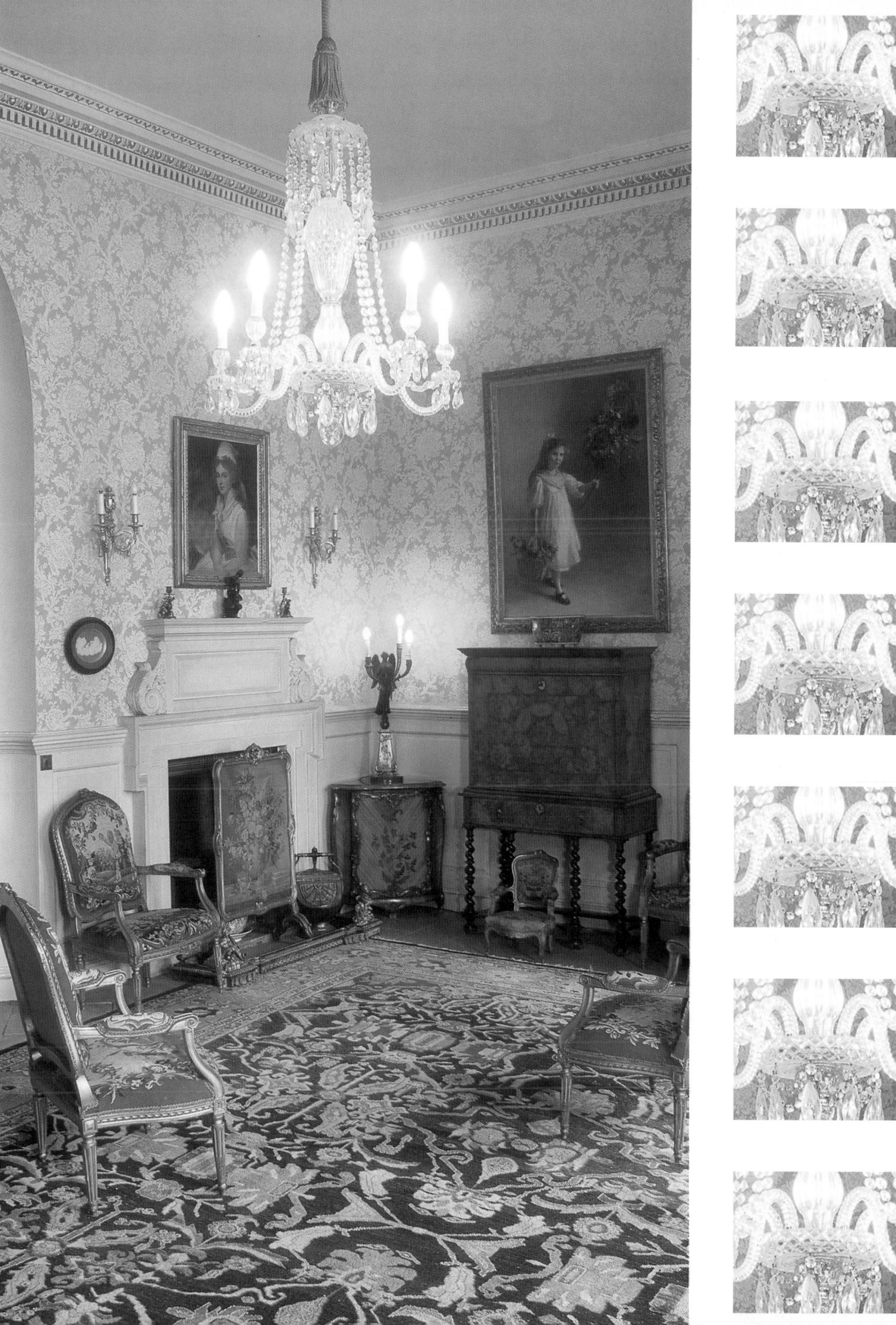

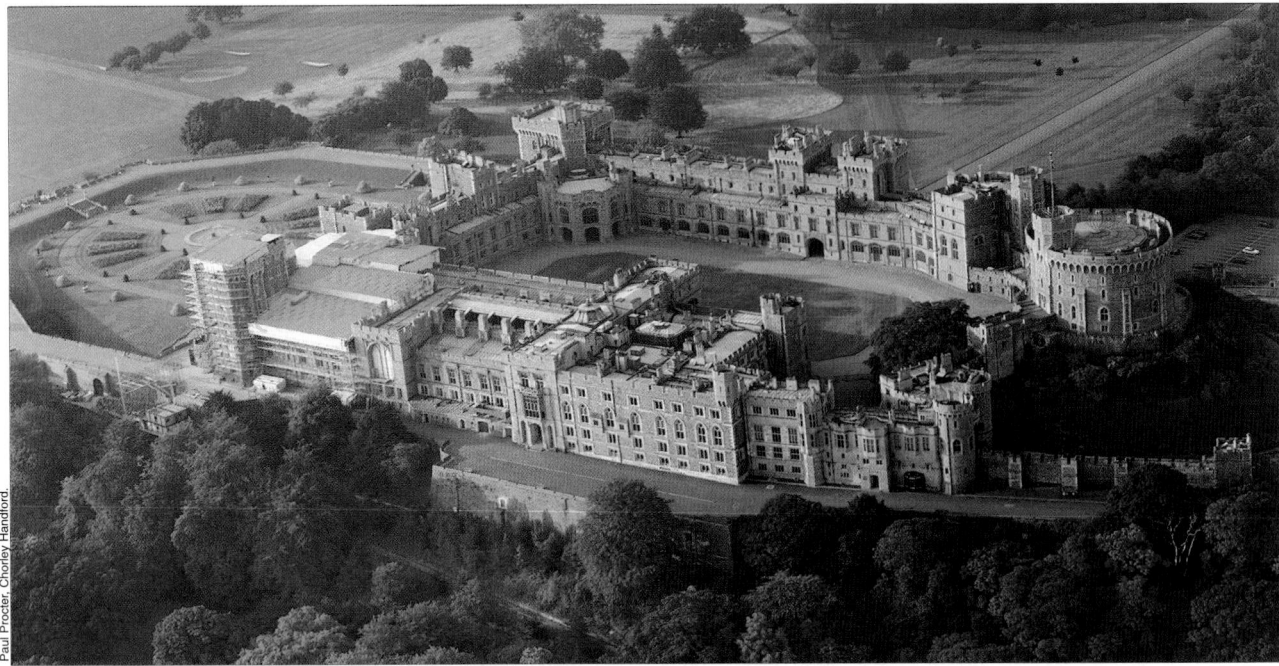

Paul Procter, Chorley Handford

WINDSOR CASTLE
Windsor

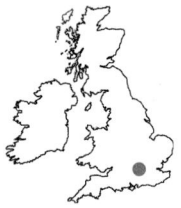

Owner: HM The Queen

CONTACT

The Visitor Office
Windsor Castle
Windsor
Berkshire
SL4 1NJ

Tel: 01753 869898
01753 831118

Fax: 01753 832290

e-mail: windsorcastle@
royalcollection.org.uk

WINDSOR CASTLE, Buckingham Palace, and the Palace of Holyroodhouse are the Official residences of the Sovereign and are used by The Queen as both a home and office. The Queen's personal standard flies when Her Majesty is in residence. Furnished with works of art from the Royal Collection, these buildings are used extensively by The Queen for State ceremonies and Official entertaining. They are opened to the public as much as these commitments will allow.

A significant proportion of Windsor Castle is opened to visitors on a regular basis including the Upper and Lower Wards, the North Terrace with its famous views towards Eton, Queen Mary's Dolls' House, the State Apartments including St. George's Hall and other newly restored rooms.

❖

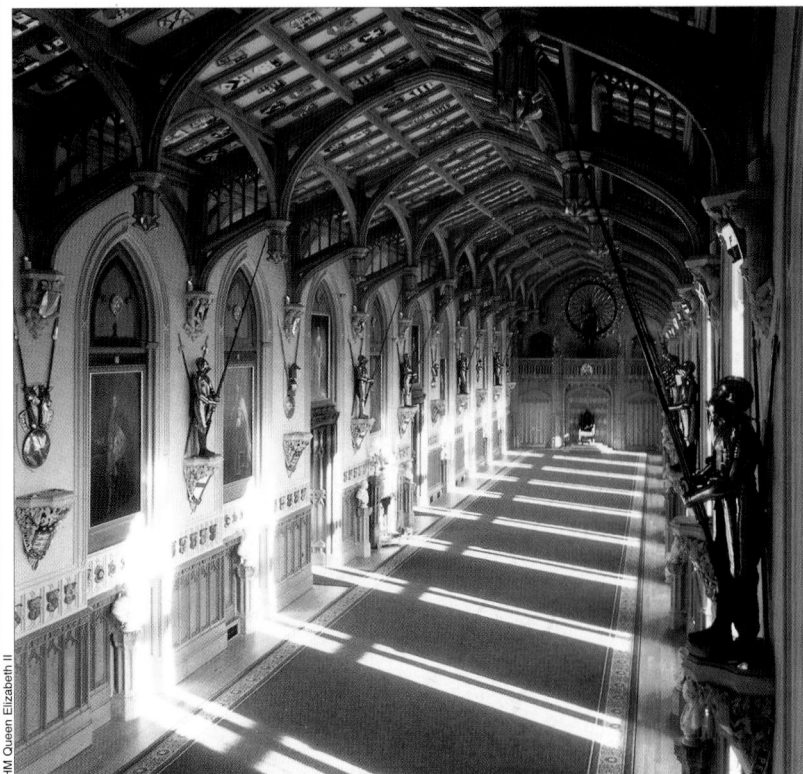

HM Queen Elizabeth II

LOCATION

OS Ref. SU969 770

M4/J6, M3/J3.
20m from central London.

Rail: Regular service from London Waterloo.

Air: London Airport (Heathrow) 15m.

Coach: Victoria Coach Station - regular service.

Sightseeing tours:
Tour companies operate a daily service with collection from many London Hotels. Ask your hotel concierge or porter for information.

OPENING TIMES

March - October:
Daily except 13 April
& 18 June
9.45am - 5.15pm
(last admission 4pm).

November - February:
Daily except 25/26 Dec
9.45am - 4.15pm
(last admission 3pm).

St George's Chapel is closed to visitors on Sundays as services are held throughout the day. Worshippers are welcome.

The State Rooms
are closed during
Royal and State visits.

**Opening arrangements
may change at
short notice.**

ADMISSION

Adult £11.00
Child (up to 17yrs)....£5.50
OAP.........................£9.00
Family (2+2) £27.50

Groups (15+)
Discounts available.

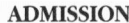

SPECIAL EVENTS

With the exception of Sundays, the Changing of the Guard takes place at 11am daily from April to the end of June and on alternate days at other times of the year.

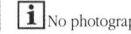 No photography.   **P** No parking.   Guide dogs only.

BASILDON PARK

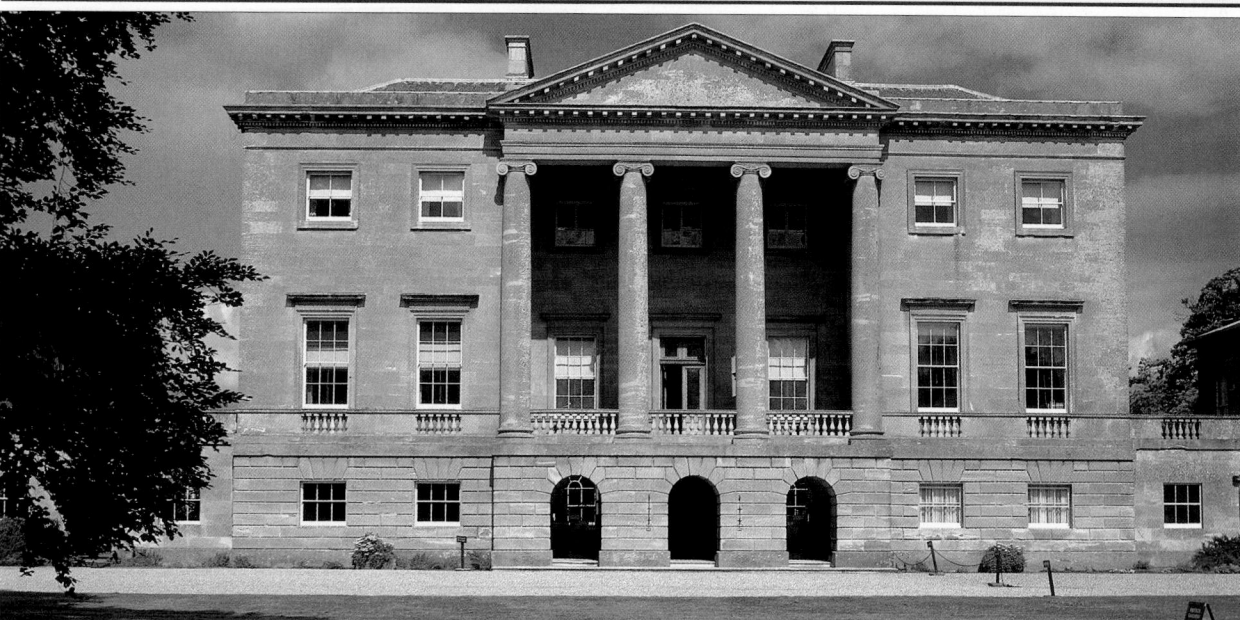

LOWER BASILDON, READING RG8 9NR

Owner: *The National Trust*   **Contact:** *The Property Manager*

Tel: 0118 984 3040 **Fax:** 0118 984 1267
e-mail: tbdgen@smtp.ntrust.org.uk

An elegant, classical house designed in the 18th century by Carr of York and set in rolling parkland in the Thames Valley. The house has rich interiors with fine plasterwork, pictures and furniture, and includes an unusual Octagon Room and a decorative Shell Room. Basildon Park has connections with the East through its builder and was the home of a wealthy industrialist in the 19th century. It was rescued from dereliction in the mid 20th century. Small flower garden, pleasure grounds and woodland walk.

Location: OS Ref. SU611 782. $2^1/_2$ m NW of Pangbourne on the west side of the A329, 7m from M4/J12.

Opening Times: House: 31 Mar - 4 Nov: daily except Mon & Tue (closed Good Fri, open BH Mons), 1 - 5.30. Park, Garden & Woodland Walk: as house 12 noon - 5.30pm. Property closes at 5pm on 17/18 Aug for concerts.

Admission: House, Park & Garden: Adult £4.30, Child £2.15, Family £10.50. Park & Garden only: Adult £1.80, Child 90p. Family £4.50. Groups of 15+ by appointment.

In grounds.   On leads, in grounds only.

DONNINGTON CASTLE

Tel: 02392 581059

Newbury, Berkshire

Owner: English Heritage   **Contact:** Area Manager

Built in the late 14th century, the twin towered gatehouse of this heroic castle survives amidst some impressive earthworks.

Location: OS Ref. SU463 691. 1m NW of Newbury off B4494.

Opening Times: Any reasonable time.

Admission: Free.

Patrick Lane.

Donnington Castle, Berkshire.

DORNEY COURT

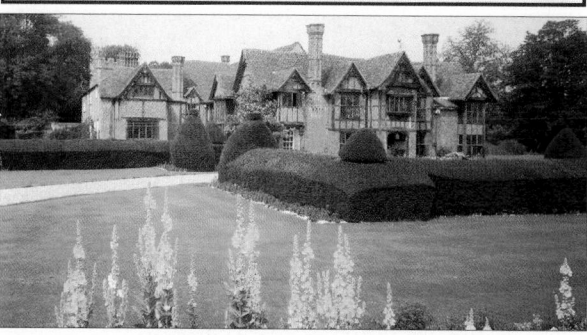

WINDSOR, BERKSHIRE SL4 6QP

Owner/Contact: *Mrs P P D Peregrine Palmer*

Tel: 01628 604638 **Fax:** 01628 665772 **e-mail:** palmer@dorneycourt.co.uk

Just a few miles from the heart of bustling Windsor lies "one of the finest Tudor Manor Houses in England", *Country Life*. Grade I listed with the added accolade of being of outstanding architectural and historical importance, the visitor can get a rare insight into the lifestyle of the squirearchy through 550 years, with the Palmer family, who still live there today, owning the house for 450 of these years. The house boasts a magnificent Great Hall, family portraits, oak and lacquer furniture, needlework and panelled rooms. A private tour on a 'non-open day' takes around $1^1/_2$ hours, but when open to the public this is reduced to around 40 mins. The adjacent 13th century Church of St James, with Norman font and Tudor tower can also be visited, as well as the adjoining Blooms of Bressingham Plant Centre in our walled garden where light lunches and full English cream teas are served in a tranquil setting throughout the day.

Location: OS Ref. SU926 791. 5 mins off M4/J7, 10mins from Windsor, 2m W of Eton.

Opening Times: May: BH Suns & Mons, 1.30 - 4.30pm. Aug: daily except Sats, 1.30 - 4.30pm. Last admission 4pm.

Admission: Adult £5, Child (10yrs +) £3. Groups: By arrangement throughout the year.

No photography in house. Film & photographic shoots. Pick your own: Jun - Aug.

Garden centre.   Garden centre suitable.

Guide dogs only.

ENGLEFIELD HOUSE

Tel: 01189 302221   **Fax:** 01189 303226

Englefield, Theale, Reading, Berkshire RG7 5EN   **e-mail:** benyon@netcomuk.co.uk

Owner: Sir William & Lady Benyon   **Contact:** Mrs Gloria Sleep

Seven acres of woodland and water garden. Stone balustrades and staircases descending to terraces, herbaceous and rose borders. All set in a deer park. Elizabethan house is open by appointment.

Location: OS Ref. SU622 720. 6m W of Reading on A340. Theale 1m.

Opening Times: Garden only: All year: Mons, 10am - 6pm. Apr - Oct: Mon - Thur incl. 10am - 6pm.

Admission: £2.

ⓘ No photography in house.   Partially suitable.WC.

By arrangement.   P Ample for cars, limited for coaches.

ETON COLLEGE

Tel: 01753 671177   **Fax:** 01753 671265

Windsor, Berkshire SL4 6DW   **e-mail:** visits@etoncollege.org.uk

Owner: Eton College   **Contact:** Rebecca Hunkin

Eton College, founded in 1440 by Henry VI, is one of the oldest and best known schools in the country. The original and subsequent historic buildings of the Foundation are a part of the heritage of the British Isles and visitors are invited to experience and share the beauty of the ancient precinct which includes the magnificent College Chapel, a masterpiece of the perpendicular style.

Location: OS Ref. SU967 779. Off M4/J5. Access from Windsor by footbridge only. Vehicle access from Slough 2m N.

Opening Times: Mar - early Oct: Times vary, best to check with the Visits Office.

Admission: Ordinary admissions and daily guided tours. Groups by appointment only. Rates vary according to type of tour.

Ground floor suitable. WC.   P Limited.   Guide dogs only.

ST GEORGE'S CHAPEL WINDSOR

Tel: 01753 868286

Fine example of perpendicular architecture. Open only in conjunction with Windsor Castle.

Location: OS Ref. SU968 770.

Opening Times: As Windsor Castle, but opening times subject to change at short notice.

Admission: Admission as part of Windsor Castle ticket.

SAVILL GARDEN

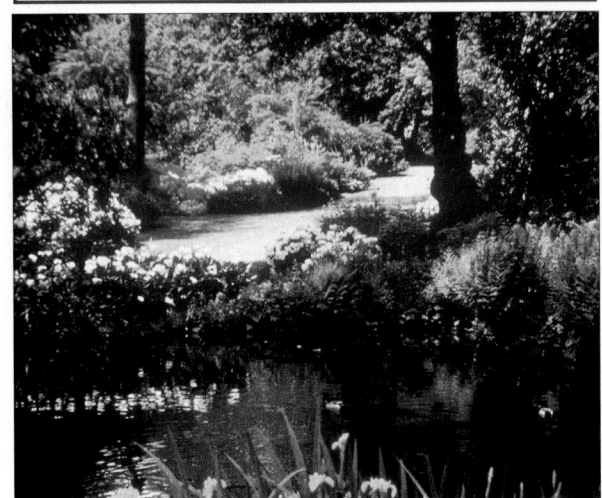

WINDSOR GREAT PARK, BERKSHIRE SL4 2HT

Owner: Crown Estate Commissioners   *Contact:* Jan Bartholomew

Tel: 01753 847518   **Fax:** 01753 847536   **e-mail:** savillgarden@crownestate.org.uk

World-renowned 35 acre woodland garden, providing a wealth of beauty and interest in all seasons. Spring is heralded by hosts of daffodils, masses of rhododendrons, azaleas, camellias, magnolias and much more. Roses, herbaceous borders and countless alpines are the great features of summer, and the leaf colours and fruits of autumn rival the other seasons with a great display.

Location: OS Ref. SU977 706. Wick Lane, Englefield Green. Clearly signposted from Ascot, Bagshot, Egham and Windsor. Nearest station: Egham.

Opening Times: Mar - Oct: 10am - 6pm. Nov - Feb: 10am - 4pm.

Admission: Apr - May: Adult £5, Child (6-16) £2, Conc. £4.50. Jun - Oct: Adult £4, Child (6-16) £1, Conc. £3.50. Nov - Mar: Adult £3, Child (6-16) £1, Conc. £2.50. Child under 6 Free. Prices subject to chnge from 1 Apr 2001.

Plant centre.   Grounds suitable. WC.   Licensed.

Guide dogs only.

TAPLOW COURT

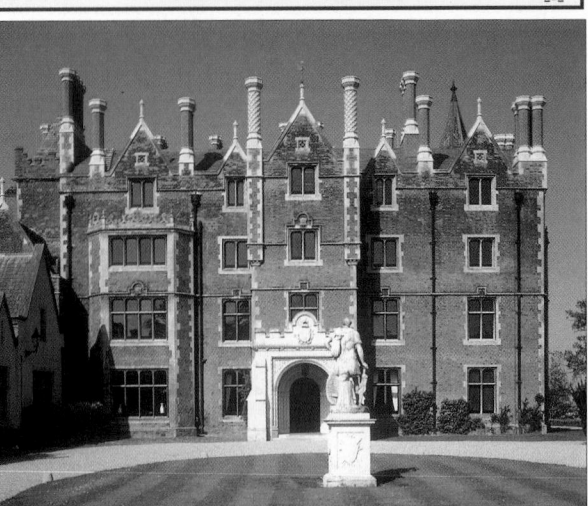

BERRY HILL, TAPLOW, Nr MAIDENHEAD, BERKS SL6 0ER

Owner: SGI-UK   *Contact:* Robert Samuels

Tel: 01628 591215   **Fax:** 01628 773055

Set high above the Thames, affording spectacular views. Remodelled mid-19th century by William Burn. Earlier neo-Norman Hall. 18th century home of Earls of Orkney and more recently of Lord and Lady Desborough who entertained 'The Souls' here. Tranquil gardens & grounds. Anglo-Saxon burial mound. Permanent and temporary exhibitions.

Location: OS Ref. SU907 822. M4/J7 off Bath Road towards Maidenhead. 6m off M40/J2.

Opening Times: House & Grounds: Easter Sun & Mon, Suns & BH Mons up to the end of Jul: 2 - 6pm.

Admission: No charge. Free parking.

P Guide dogs only.

WELFORD PARK

Tel: 01488 608203

Newbury, Berkshire RG20 8HU

Owner/Contact: Mr J Puxley

A Queen Anne house, with attractive gardens and grounds. Riverside walks.

Location: OS Ref. SU409 731. On Lambourn Valley Road. 6m NW of Newbury.

Opening Times: 28 May, 1 - 26 Jun, 27 Aug: 11am - 5pm.

Admission: House by prior arrangement. Adult £3.50, Child Free, Conc. £2. Grounds Free.

Grounds suitable.   On leads, in grounds.

WINDSOR CASTLE

See page 94 for full page entry.

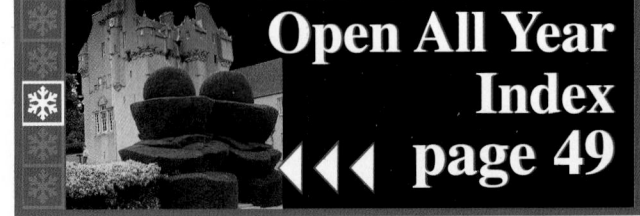

Open All Year
Index
◀◀◀ **page 49**

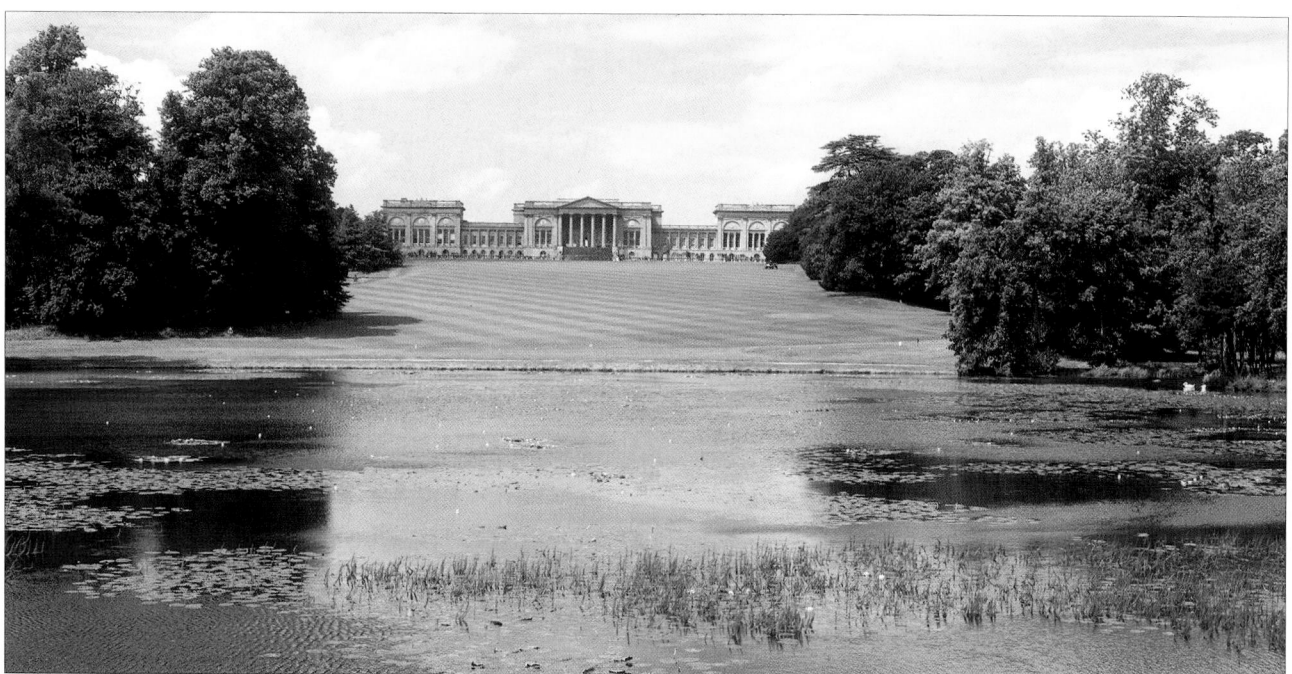

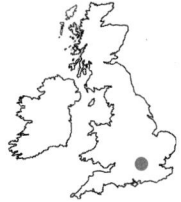

STOWE HOUSE
Buckingham

STOWE owes its pre-eminence to the vision and wealth of two owners. From 1715 to 1749 Viscount Cobham, one of Marlborough's Generals, continuously improved his estate, calling in the leading designers of the day to lay out the gardens, and commissioning several leading architects – Vanbrugh, Gibbs, Kent and Leoni – to decorate them with garden temples. From 1750 to 1779 Earl Temple, his nephew and successor continued to expand and embellish both Gardens and House. The House is now a major public school. Restoration of North Front and Colonnades will take place from August 2000 - October 2002.

Around the mansion is one of Britain's most magnificent landscape gardens now in the ownership of the National Trust. Covering 325 acres and containing no fewer than 6 lakes and 32 garden temples, it is of the greatest historic importance. During the 1730s William Kent laid out in the Elysian Fields at Stowe, one of the first 'natural' landscapes and initiated the style known as 'the English Garden'. 'Capability' Brown worked there for 10 years, not as a consultant but as head gardener, and in 1744 was married in the little church hidden between the trees.

❖

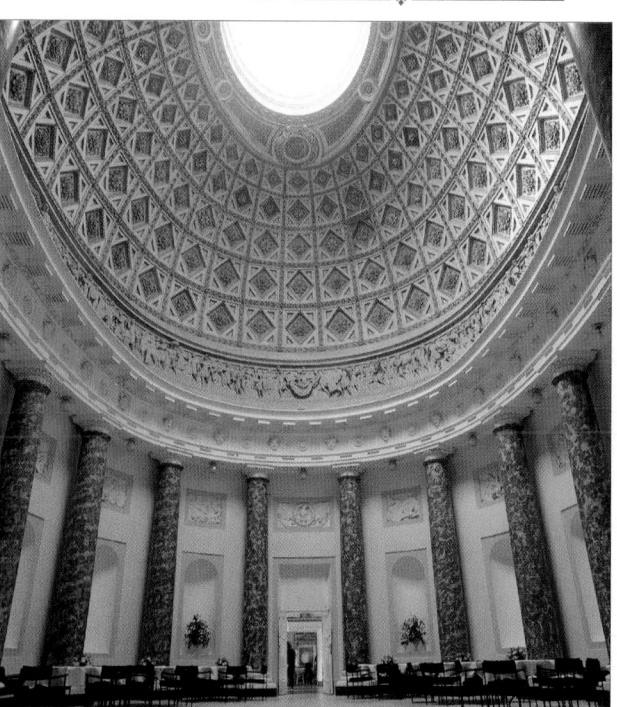

Owner: Stowe House Preservation Trust

CONTACT

The Commercial Director
Stowe School
Buckingham
MK18 5EH

Tel: 01280 818282
House only
or 01280 822850
Gardens

Fax: 01280 818186

e-mail: sses@stowe.co.uk

LOCATION

OS Ref. SP666 366

From London, M1 to Milton Keynes, 1½ hrs or Banbury 1¼ hrs, 3m NW of Buckingham.

Bus: from Buckingham 3m.
Rail: Milton Keynes 15m.
Air: Heathrow 50m.

CONFERENCE/FUNCTION

ROOM	SIZE	MAX CAPACITY
Roxburgh Hall	–	460
Music Room	–	120
Marble Hall	–	150
State Dining Rm	–	160
Garter Room	–	180
Memorial Theatre	–	120

i Indoor swimming pool, sports hall, tennis court, squash courts, parkland, cricket pitches and golf course. No photography in house.

Call for opening times.

Y International conferences, private functions, weddings, and prestige exhibitions. Catering on request.

Visitors may alight at entrance. Allocated parking areas. WC in garden area. 'Batricars' available.

Morning coffee, lunch and afternoon tea available by pre-arrangement only, for up to 100.

For parties of 30 at additional cost. Tour time: house and garden 2½ hrs, house only 45 mins.

P Ample.

In grounds on leads.

Civil Wedding Licence.

 Available. ❄

OPENING TIMES

SUMMER
House
24 Mar - 16 Apr:
Wed - Fri, 2 - 5pm,
Sats & Suns, 10am - 1pm.
8 Jul - 31 Aug:
Weds & Thurs, 2 - 5pm.
Fri - Sun, 10am - 1pm.
14 - 23 Dec: Fris & Sats,
10am - 1pm.

For other dates and for groups (by appointment: 17 Apr - 6 Jul & 3 Sept - 21 Oct), telephone Christine Shaw on 01280 818282.

NB: It may be necessary to close the house at times when it is being used for private functions. Please telephone first to check.

ADMISSION

Adult £3.00
Child (under 16yrs) ...£1.50

SPECIAL EVENTS

• Oct 27/28:
Craft Fair

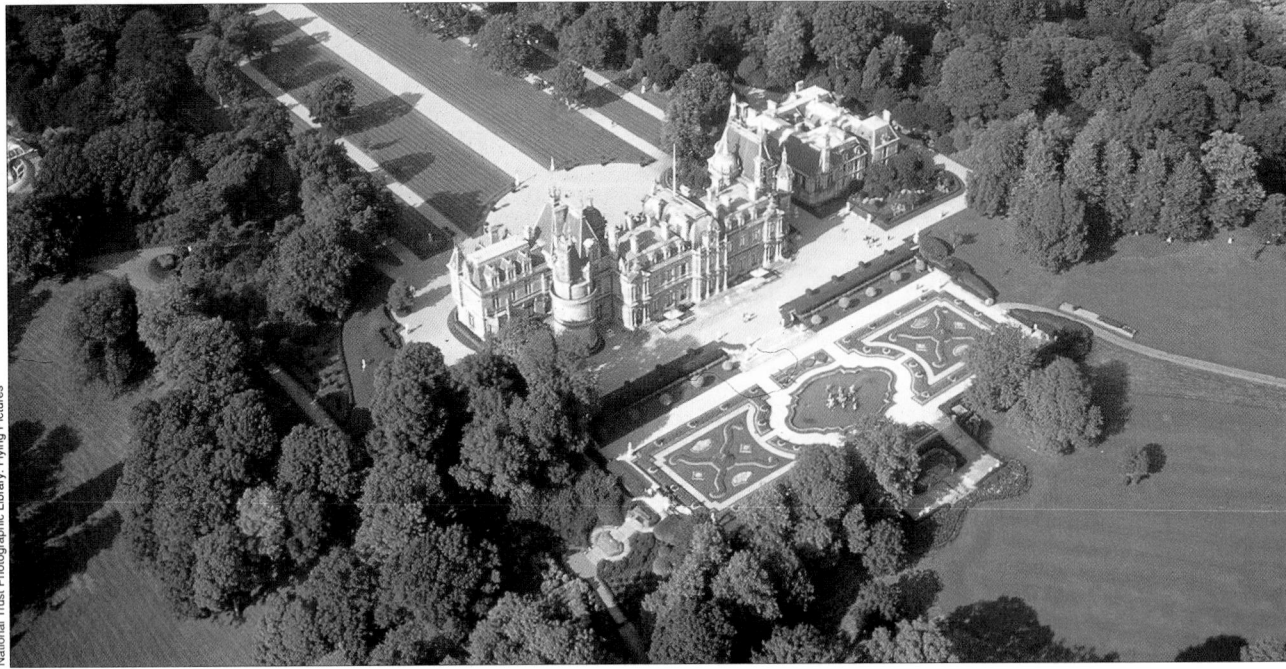

National Trust Photographic Library: Flying Pictures

WADDESDON MANOR
Nr Aylesbury

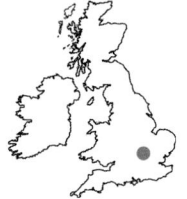

WADDESDON MANOR was built (1874-89) for Baron Ferdinand de Rothschild to entertain his guests and display his vast collection of art treasures. It has won many awards including the Silver Award for Best Overall Property and the Europa Nostra Garden Award 1999.

This French Renaissance-style château houses one of the finest collections of French 18th century decorative arts in the world: Savonnerie carpets, Sèvres porcelain, Beauvais tapestries and furniture, as well as important portraits by Gainsborough and Reynolds and works by Dutch and Flemish Masters of the 17th century.

Waddesdon has one of the finest Victorian gardens in Britain, renowned for its seasonal displays, colourful shrubs, mature trees and parterre. A children's garden has recently opened. Carpet bedding displays are newly created each year. In 2001 they will be created by the fashion designer, Oscar de la Renta. The rococo-style aviary houses a splendid collection of exotic birds, and thousands of bottles of vintage Rothschild wines are found in the wine cellars.

There is an award-winning gift shop, wine shop with a full selection of Rothschild wines and a licensed restaurant. Many events are organised throughout the year including special interest days, wine tastings and garden workshops.

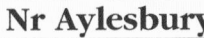

CONTACT

Waddesdon
Nr Aylesbury
Buckinghamshire
HP18 0JH

Tel: 01296 653211

Booking: 01296 653226

Fax: 01296 653208

e-mail: twmsep
@smtp.ntrust.org.uk

LOCATION

OS Ref. SP740 169

Between Aylesbury & Bicester, off A41.

Rail: Aylesbury 6m.

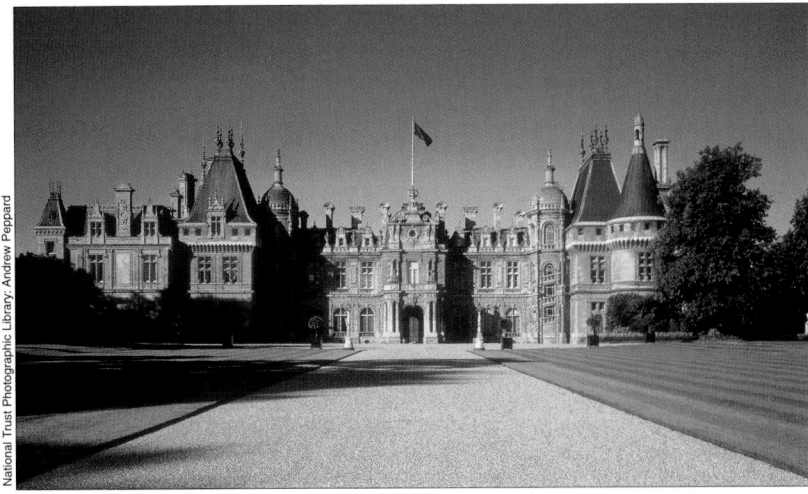

National Trust Photographic Library: Andrew Peppard

OPENING TIMES

House
(including wine cellars)
28 Mar - 4 Nov: Wed - Sun,
also BH Mons, 11am - 4pm.
Last recommended
admission 2.30pm.
Bachelors' Wing
Wed - Fri, 11am - 4pm
(space is limited and entry cannot therefore be guaranteed).

Grounds
(including garden, aviary, restaurant and shops)
28 Feb - 23 Dec: Wed - Sun & BH Mons, 10am - 5pm.

ADMISSION

House & Grounds
Adult £10.00
Child (5-16 yrs) £7.50
Groups (15+)
Adult £8.00
Child £6.00

Grounds only
Adult £3.00
Child (5-16 yrs) £1.50
1 Nov - 24 Dec.........Free
Groups (15+)
Adult £2.40
Child £1.20
Bachelors' Wing.........£1.00
NT members free. HHA Members free entry to grounds.
Timed tickets to the house can be purchased on site or reserved in advance by phoning 01296 653226 Mon - Fri, 10am - 4pm. Advance booking fee: £3 per transaction.
Children under 5yrs are not allowed in the house. Babies must be carried in a front-sling carrier.

SPECIAL EVENTS

Wine Tasting, Study Days, Garden Workshops and tours, Family Events, Floodlit Evenings: please telephone 01295 653226 for details.

No photography in house.		By arrangement.	
		Ample for coaches and cars.	
Conferences, corporate hospitality.		Guide dogs only.	
Suitable. WCs.		Civil Wedding Licence.	
Licensed.			

ASCOTT

Wing, Leighton Buzzard, Bucks LU7 0PS

Tel: 01296 688242 **Fax:** 01296 681904
e-mail: tacgen@smtp.ntrust.org.uk

Owner: The National Trust **Contact:** The Administrator

Originally a half-timbered Jacobean farmhouse, Ascott was bought in 1876 by the de Rothschild family and considerably transformed and enlarged. It now houses a quite exceptional collection of fine paintings, Oriental porcelain and English and French furniture. The extensive gardens are a mixture of the formal and natural, containing specimen trees and shrubs, as well as an herbaceous walk, lily pond, Dutch garden and remarkable topiary sundial.

Location: OS Ref. SP891 230. ¹/₂ m E of Wing, 2m SW of Leighton Buzzard, on A418.

Opening Times: House & Garden: 1 - 29 Apr & 7 Aug - 14 Sept: daily except Mons, 2 - 6pm, last admission 5pm. Garden only: 1 May - 1 Aug: every Wed & last Sun in each month, also 19 & 26 Sept, 2 - 6pm, last admission 5pm.

Admission: House & Garden: £5.60. Garden: £4. Child half price. No reduction for groups which must book.

Ground floor & grounds. 3 wheelchairs available. WCs. P 220 metres.

In car park only, on leads.

BLETCHLEY PARK

Tel: 01908 640404 **Fax:** 01908 274381
e-mail: majenkins@bletchleypark.org.uk

The Mansion, Wilton Avenue, Bletchley, Milton Keynes MK3 6EB

Owner: Bletchley Park Trust **Contact:** Merrill Jenkins

Centre of World War II Enigma code breaking operations.

Location: OS Ref. SP858 340. 200yds from Bletchley railway station. Just off the B4034 Bletchley to Buckingham road.

Opening Times: Every other weekend: 10.30am - 5pm, last admission 3.30pm. Last tour begins at 3pm.

Admission: Adult £5, Child & Conc. £4. Accompanied Child (under 8yrs) Free.

BOARSTALL DUCK DECOY

Tel: 01844 237488

Boarstall, Aylesbury, Buckinghamshire HP18 9UX

Owner: The National Trust **Contact:** The Administrator

A rare survival of a 17th century decoy in working order, set on a tree-fringed lake, with nature trail and exhibition hall.

Location: OS Ref. SP624 151. Midway between Bicester and Thame, 2m W of Brill.

Opening Times: 24 Mar - 26 Aug: Weds, 5 - 8pm, Sats, Suns & BH Mons, 10am - 5pm. Talk/demonstration: Sats, Suns & BH Mons if Warden available, tel. for details.

Admission: Adult £2.10, Family £5. Groups (6+) must book: £1.

Partially suitable. By arrangement. In car park only, on leads.

BOARSTALL TOWER

Boarstall, Aylesbury, Buckinghamshire HP18 90X

Owner: The National Trust **Contact:** The Tenant

The stone gatehouse of a fortified house long since demolished. It dates from the 14th century, and was altered in the 16th and 17th centuries, but retains its crossloops for bows. The gardens are surrounded by a moat on three sides.

Location: OS Ref. SP624 141. Midway between Bicester and Thame, 2m W of Brill.

Opening Times: 1 Apr - 31 Oct: Wed & BH Mons, 2 - 6pm. Also Sats by prior arrangement with tenant.

Admission: Adult £2.10, Child £1.05.

No WC. Ground floor & garden. In car park only.

BUCKINGHAM CHANTRY CHAPEL

Tel: 01280 823020

Market Hill, Buckingham, Buckinghamshire

Tel: 01494 528051

Owner: The National Trust **Contact:** Buckingham Heritage Trust

Rebuilt in 1475 and retaining a fine Norman doorway. The chapel was restored by Gilbert Scott in 1875, at which time it was used as a Latin or Grammar School.

Location: OS Ref. SP693 340. In narrow lane, NW of Market Hill.

Opening Times: Daily by written appointment with the Buckingham Heritage Trust, c/o Old Gaol Museum, Market Hill, Buckingham MK18 1JX.

Admission: Free.

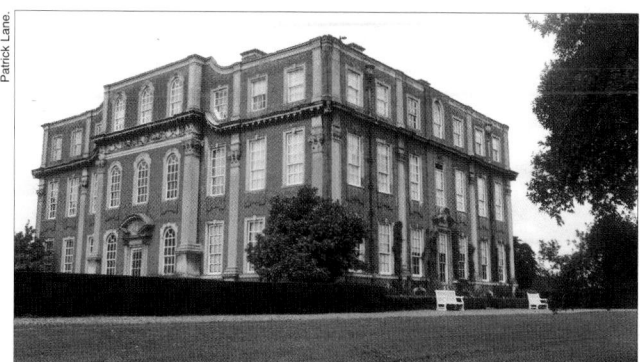

Chicheley Hall.

Patrick Lane.

CHENIES MANOR HOUSE

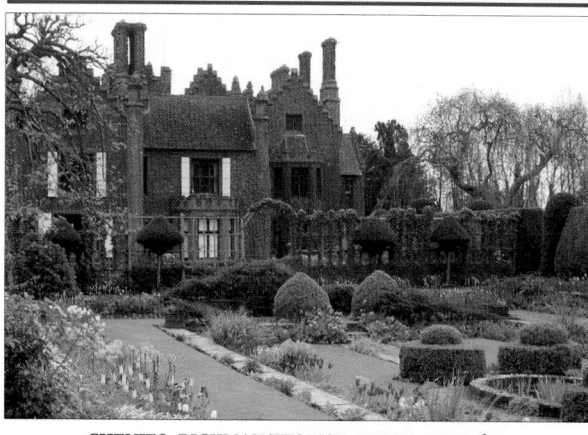

CHENIES, RICKMANSWORTH, HERTS WD3 6ER

Owner: *Lt Col & Mrs MacLeod Matthews* **Contact:** *Lt Col & Mrs MacLeod Matthews or Sue Brock*

Tel/Fax: 01494 762888

15th & 16th century Manor House with fortified tower. Original home of the Earls of Bedford, visited by Henry VIII and Elizabeth I. Home of the MacLeod Matthews family. Contains contemporary tapestries and furniture, hiding places, collection of antique dolls, medieval undercroft and well. Surrounded by beautiful gardens which have featured in many publications and on TV, a Tudor sunken garden, a white garden, herbaceous borders, a fountain court, a physic garden containing a very wide selection of medicinal and culinary herbs, a parterre and two mazes. The kitchen garden is in the Victorian style with unusual vegetables and fruit. Special exhibitions, flower drying and arrangements. Many specialist and rare plants in a charming setting.

Location: OS Ref. TQ016 984. N of A404 between Amersham & Rickmansworth. M25/J18, 3m.

Opening Times: 1 Apr - 28 Oct: Wed & Thur & BH Mons, 2 - 5pm. Last entry to house 4.15pm. Groups by arrangement at other times.

Admission: House & Garden: Adult £5, Child £3. Garden only: Adult £3, Child £1.

Unusual plants for sale. Grounds suitable. P Free nearby.

CHICHELEY HALL

Tel: 01234 391252 **Fax:** 01234 391388

Newport Pagnell, Buckinghamshire MK16 9JJ

Owner: The Hon Nicholas Beatty **Contact:** Mrs V Child

Fine 18th century house. Naval museum, English sea paintings and furniture. Suitable for residential conferences up to 15 delegates.

Location: OS Ref. SP906 458. 2m from Milton Keynes, 5 mins from M1/J14. 10m W of Bedford.

Opening Times: All year: By appointment only

Admission: Groups (20+): Adult £5. Groups under 20: Adult £6, Child £2.

Conferences. By arrangement. Not suitable. Obligatory.

CHILTERN OPEN AIR MUSEUM

Tel: 01494 871117 **Fax:** 01494 872774

Newland Park, Gorelands Lane, Chalfont St Giles, Buckinghamshire HB8 4AB

Owner: Chiltern Open Air Museum Ltd **Contact:** Dr J Moir

A museum of historic buildings showing their original uses including a blacksmith's forge, stables, barns etc.

Location: OS Ref. TQ011 938. At Newland Park 1¹/₂ m E of Chalfont St Giles, 4¹/₂ m from Amersham. 3m from M25/J17.

Opening Times: Sat 31 Mar - end of Oct: daily, 10am - 5pm.

Admission: Adult £5.50, Child under 5yrs Free, Child (5-16yrs) £3, Over 60s £4.50, Family £15. 10% discount for groups (10+).

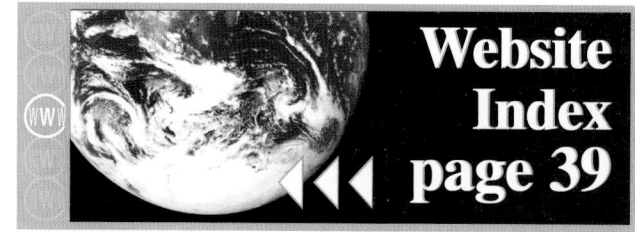

Website Index page 39

CLAYDON HOUSE

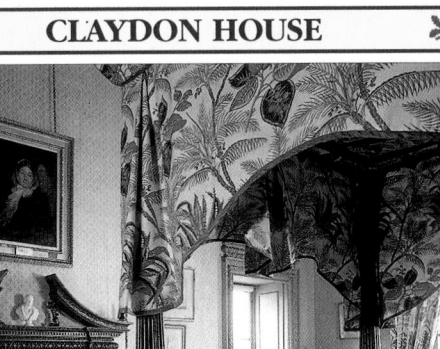

MIDDLE CLAYDON, Nr BUCKINGHAM MK18 2EY

Owner: *The National Trust*   **Contact:** *The Custodian*

Tel: 01296 730349 **Fax:** 01296 738511 **e-mail:** tcdgen@smtp.ntrust.org.uk

A fine 18th century house with some of the most perfect rococo decoration in England. A series of great rooms have wood carvings in Chinese and Gothic styles, and tall windows look out over parkland and a lake. The house has relics of the exploits of the Verney family in the English Civil War and also on show is the bedroom of Florence Nightingale, a relative of the Verneys and a regular visitor to this tranquil place.

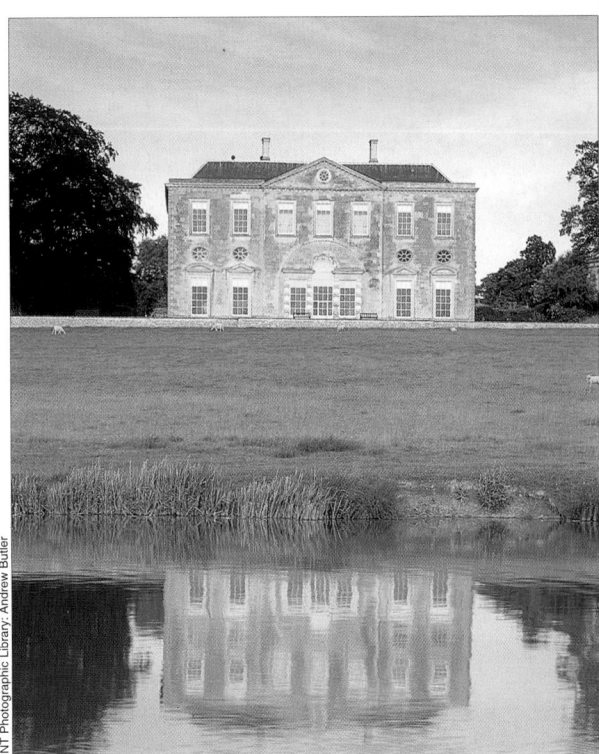

Location: OS Ref. SP720 253. In Middle Claydon, 13m NW of Aylesbury, signposted from A413, A421 and A41. 3¹/₂ m SW of Winslow.

Opening Times: 31 Mar - 4 Nov: daily except Thur & Fri, 1 - 5pm. House closes 1hr early on event days. Gardens, church & tearoom open at 12 noon.

Admission: Adult £4.30, Family £10.50. Groups 15+ (must book): Mon - Wed & Sat. £3.60. Garden only: £1.

♿ Ground floor & grounds. Braille guide. WC. 🐕 In park, on leads.
📞 Telephone for details.

CLIVEDEN

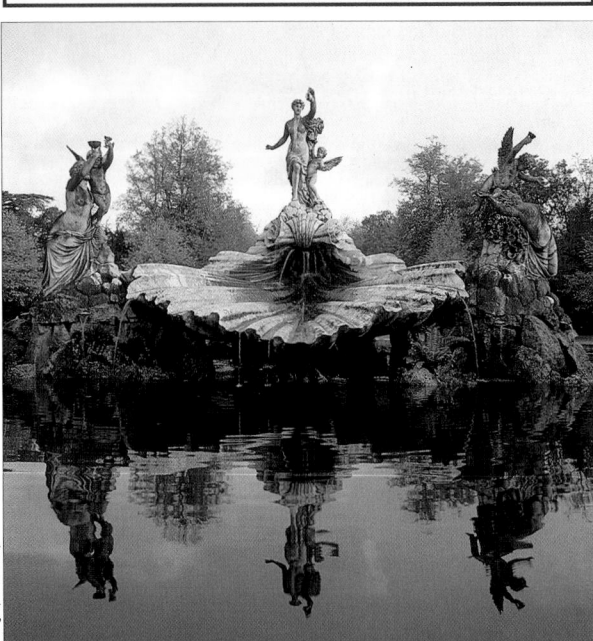

TAPLOW, MAIDENHEAD SL6 0JA

Owner: *The National Trust*   **Contact:** *Property Manager*

Tel: 01628 605069 **Fax:** 01628 669461

152 hectares of gardens and woodland. A water garden, 'secret' garden, herbaceous borders, topiary, a great formal parterre, and informal vistas provide endless variety. The garden statuary is one of the most important collections in the care of The National Trust and includes many Roman antiquities collected by 1st Viscount Astor. The Octagonal Temple (Chapel) with its rich mosaic interior is open on certain days, as are three of the principal rooms of the house (see below).

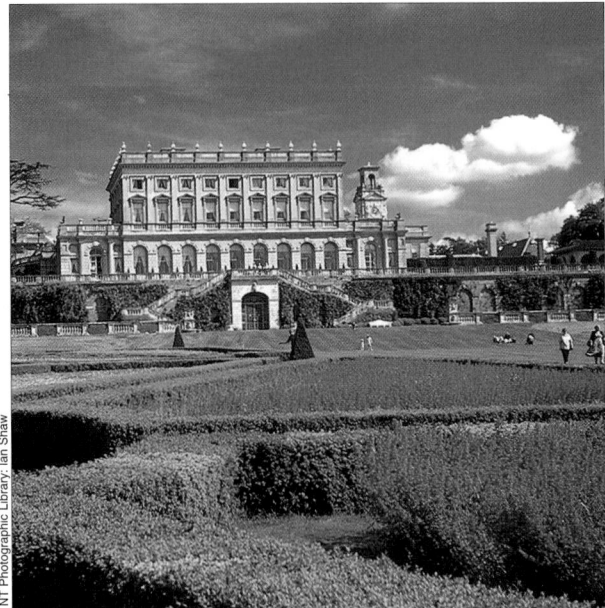

Location: OS Ref. SU915 851. 3m N of Maidenhead, M4/J7 onto A4 or M40/J4 onto A404 to Marlow and follow signs. From London by train take Thames Train service from Paddington to Burnham (taxi rank and office adjacent to station).

Opening Times: Estate & Garden: 14 Mar - 31 Dec, daily, 11am - 6pm (closes at 4pm from 1 Nov). House (3 rooms): Apr - Oct: Thurs & Sun, 3 - 6pm. Entry by times ticket from information kiosk. Otagonal Temple: as house. Woodlands car park: all year: daily, 11am - 5.30pm (closed at 4pm Nov - Mar).

Admission: Grounds: Adult £5, Child £2.50, Family £12.50. House: £1 extra, Child 50p. Groups (must book): Adult £4.50, Child £2.25. Woodlands car park: Adult £3, Child £1.50, Family £7.50. Note: Mooring charge on Cliveden Reach.

♿ Partially suitable. WC. 🍴 Licensed. 🐕 Specified woodlands only. ❄
📞 Telephone for details.

COWPER & NEWTON MUSEUM Tel: 01234 711516 e-mail: cnm@mkheritage.co.uk

Home of Olney's Heritage, Orchard Side, Market Place, Olney MK46 4AJ

Owner: Board of Trustees **Contact:** Mrs J McKillop

Once the home of 18th century poet and letter writer William Cowper and now containing furniture, paintings and belongings of both Cowper and his ex-slave trader friend, Rev John Newton (author of "Amazing Grace"). Attractions include re-creations of a Victorian country kitchen and wash-house, two peaceful gardens and Cowper's restored summerhouse. Costume gallery, important collections of dinosaur bones and bobbin lace, and local history displays.

Location: OS Ref. SP890 512. On A509, 6m N of Newport Pagnell, M1/J14.

Opening Times: 1 Mar - 23 Dec: Tue - Sat & BH Mons, 10am - 1pm & 2 - 5pm. Closed on Good Fri. Open on Sundays in June, July & August, 2 - 5pm.

Admission: Adult £3, Conc. £2, Child & Students (with card) £1.50, Family £7.50.

No photography. Gardens suitable. By arrangement. Guide dogs only.

DORNEYWOOD GARDEN Tel: 01494 528051 (NT Regional Office)

Dorneywood, Burnham, Buckinghamshire SL1 8PY

Owner: The National Trust **Contact:** The Secretary

The house was given to the National Trust as an official residence for either a Secretary of State or Minister of the Crown. Garden only open.

Location: OS Ref. SU938 848. SW of Burnham Beeches. 2m E of Cliveden.

Opening Times: By written appointment only - one week in advance – 27 June, 18 July & 4 August: 2 - 5pm. Write to The Secretary, Dorneywood Trust at above address.

Admission: £3.

FORD END WATERMILL Tel: 01582 600391

Station Road, Ivinghoe, Buckinghamshire **Contact:** David Lindsey

The Watermill, a listed building, was recorded in 1767 but is probably much older.

Location: OS Ref. SP941 166. 600 metres from Ivinghoe Church along B488 (Station Road) to Leighton Buzzard.

Opening Times: Please telephone for opening dates and milling times.

Admission: Adult £1, Child 30p. School Groups: 50p each adult and child.

JOHN MILTON'S COTTAGE Tel: 01494 872313 e-mail: pbirger@clara.net

21 Deanway, Chalfont St. Giles, Buckinghamshire HP8 4JH

Owner: Milton Cottage Trust **Contact:** Mr E A Dawson

Grade I listed 16th century cottage where John Milton lived and completed 'Paradise Lost' and started 'Paradise Regained'. Three ground floor museum rooms contain important 1st editions of John Milton's 17th century poetry and prose works. Amongst many unique items on display is the portrait of John Milton by Sir Godfrey Kneller. Well stocked, attractive cottage garden, listed by English Heritage.

Location: OS Ref. SU987 933. ½ m W of A413. 3m N of M40/J2. S side of street.

Opening Times: 1 Mar - 31 Oct: Tue - Sun, 10am - 1pm & 2 - 6pm. Closed Mons (open BH Mons). Coach parking by prior arrangement only.

Admission: Adult £2.50, under 15s £1, Groups (20+) £2.

  Ground floor suitable. Talk followed by free tour. P

NETHER WINCHENDON HOUSE Tel: 01844 290199

Aylesbury, Buckinghamshire HP18 ODY

Owner/Contact: Mr Robert Spencer Bernard

Medieval and Tudor manor house. There is a fine 16th century frieze, ceiling and original linenfold panelling. Altered in late 18th Century in the Strawberry Hill Gothick style. Fine furniture and family portraits. Continuous family occupation since mid-16th century. Home of the last British Governor of Massachussetts Bay, 1760. Interesting garden and specimen trees.

Location: OS Ref. SP734 121. 2m N of A418 equidistant between Thame & Aylesbury.

Opening Times: 1 - 28 May & 26/27 Aug: 2.30 - 5.30pm (last party at about 4.45pm).

Admission: Adult £4 (HHA members free), Child (under 12) & OAP £2 (not weekends or BHs). Groups: any time by written appointment, min charge £40.

By arrangement.

HUGHENDEN MANOR

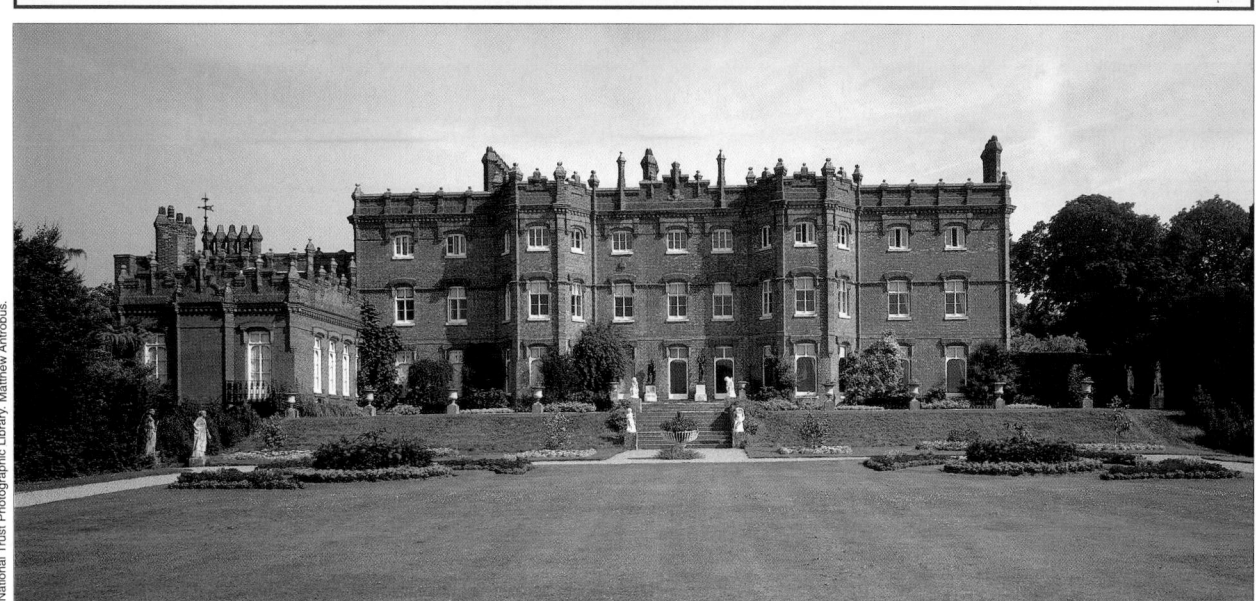

National Trust Photographic Library, Matthew Antrobus.

HIGH WYCOMBE HP14 4LA

Owner: *The National Trust* **Contact:** *The Property Manager*

Tel: 01494 755573

Home of Prime Minister Benjamin Disraeli from 1847 - 1881, Hughenden has a red brick, 'gothic' exterior. The interior is a comfortable Victorian home and still holds many of Disraeli's pictures, books and furniture, as well as other fascinating mementoes of the life of the great statesman and writer. The surrounding park and woodland have lovely walks, and the formal garden has been recreated in the spirit of Mary Anne Disraeli's colourful designs.

Location: OS165 Ref. SU866 955. 1½ m N of High Wycombe on the W side of the A4128.

Opening Times: House: 3 - 31 Mar: Sats & Suns. 1 Apr - 4 Nov: Wed - Sun & BH Mons, 1 - 5pm (last admission 4.30pm). Closed Good Fri. On BHs and busy days entry is by timed ticket. Gardens open same days as house, 12 noon - 5pm. Park & Woodland: All year.

Admission: House & Garden: Adult £4.30, Child £2.15, Family £10.50. Garden only: Adult £1.50, Child 75p. Park & Woodland Free. Groups must book, no groups on Sat, Sun or BH Mons.

Exhibition area. Limited. WC. In grounds, on leads. Guide dogs in house & formal gardens. Telephone for details.

South East England

PITSTONE WINDMILL

Ivinghoe, Buckinghamshire

Owner: The National Trust   **Contact:** The Administrator

One of the oldest post mills in Britain; in view from Ivinghoe Beacon.

Location: OS Ref. SP946 158. ¹/₂ m S of Ivinghoe, 3m NE of Tring. Just W of B488.

Opening Times: Jun - end Aug: Sun & BHs, 2.30 - 6pm.

Admission: Adult £1, Child 30p.

PRINCES RISBOROUGH MANOR HOUSE   Tel: 01494 528051

Princes Risborough, Aylesbury, Buckinghamshire HP17 9AW

Owner: The National Trust   **Contact:** The Owner

A 17th century red-brick house with Jacobean oak staircase.

Location: OS Ref. SP806 035. Opposite church, off market square.

Opening Times: House (hall, drawing room & staircase) and front garden by written appointment only with the owner. Apr - Oct: Weds, 2.30 - 4.30pm.

Admission: £1.20.

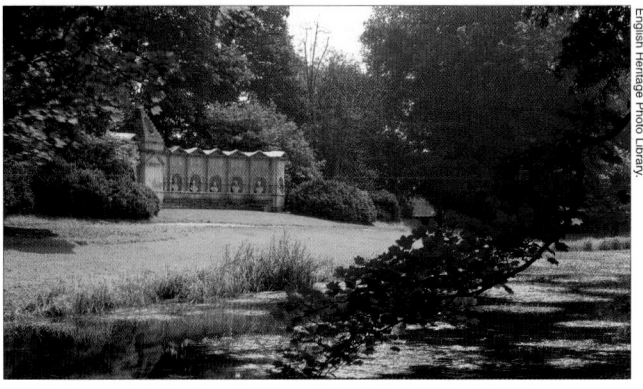

Stowe Gardens & Park.

English Heritage Photo Library

STOWE GARDENS & PARK

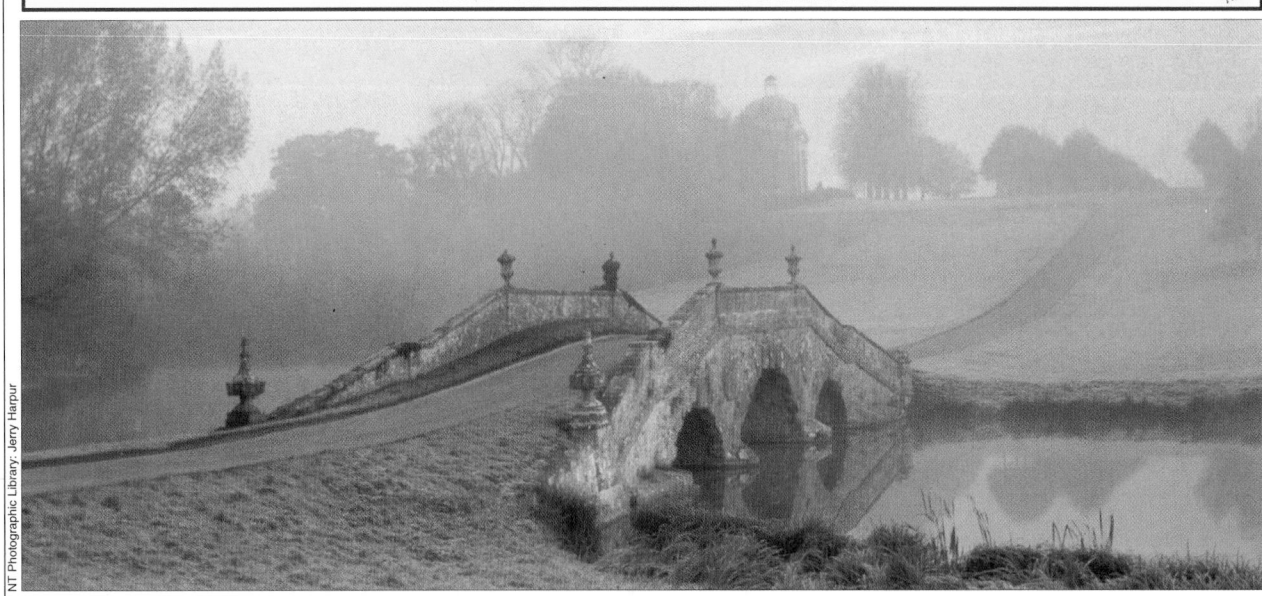

NT Photographic Library: Jerry Harpur

Nr BUCKINGHAM MK18 5EH

Owner: *The National Trust*   **Contact:** *The Property Manager*

Tel: 01280 822850 **Infoline:** 01494 755568   **Fax:** 01280 822437

One of the finest Georgian landscape gardens, made up of valleys and vistas, narrow lakes and rivers, with more than 30 temples and monuments designed by many of the leading architects of the 18th century. At the centre is Stowe House, occupied by Stowe School, and all around is Stowe Gardens & Park.

The creation of the Temple family, Stowe has been described as a 'work to wonder at' in its size, splendour and variety. Many of the garden buildings have now been conserved, and thousands of new trees and shrubs have been planted in recent years. Work continues on this as well as on the Mansion itself. What's new in 2001: Four newly restored monuments: the Fane of Pastoral Poetry and Lord Cobham's Monument in the garden, and the Conduit House and Wolfe's Obelisk in the Park.

Location: OS Ref. SP665 366. Off A422 Buckingham - Banbury Rd. 3m NW of Buckingham.

Opening Times: Gardens: 3 Mar - 28 Oct (closed 26 May) & 1 - 23 Dec: Wed - Sun (open BH Mons), 10am - 5.30pm, last admission 4pm. Dec: 10am - 4pm, last admission 3pm. Gardens may close in bad weather.

Admission: Gardens: £4.60. Family £11.50. House: Adult £2. Groups by arrangement.

Pre-booked self-drive powered chairs available. WC. Licensed. By arrangement. In grounds, on leads. Send SAE for details.

STOWE HOUSE   See page 97 for full page entry.

WADDESDON MANOR   See page 98 for full page entry.

WEST WYCOMBE PARK   Tel: 01494 513569

West Wycombe, High Wycombe, Buckinghamshire HP14 3AJ

Owner: The National Trust   **Contact:** The Head Guide

A perfectly preserved rococo landscape garden, created in the mid-18th century by Sir Francis Dashwood, founder of the Dilettanti Society and the Hellfire Club. The house is among the most theatrical and Italiante in England, its façades formed as classical temples. The interior has Palmyrene ceilings and decoration, with pictures, furniture and sculpture dating from the time of Sir Francis.

Location: OS Ref. SU828 947. At W end of West Wycombe S of the A40.

Opening Times: Grounds only: 1 Apr - end May: Suns, Weds & BHs, 2 - 6pm. House & Grounds: Jun, Jul & Aug: daily except Fris & Sats, 2 - 6pm. Weekday entry by timed tour. Last admission 5.15pm.

Admission: House & Grounds: Adult £4.60, Child £2.30, Family £11.50. Grounds only: £2.60. Note: The West Wycombe Caves and adjacent café are privately owned and NT members must pay admission fees. Groups by arrangement.

Grounds partly suitable. In car park only, on leads.

Special Events Index ◀◀◀ page 33

WINSLOW HALL
Tel: 01296 712323

Winslow, Buckinghamshire MK18 3HL

Owner/Contact: Sir Edward Tomkins

William and Mary house generally attributed to Wren. Virtually unchanged structurally and mostly original interiors. Attractive garden with unusual trees and shrubs.

Location: OS Ref. SP772 275. In the town of Winslow on N side of the A413.

Opening Times: By appointment.

Admission: Please contact for details.

WYCOMBE MUSEUM
Tel: 01494 421895 **Fax:** 01494 421897

e-mail: enquiries@wycombemuseum.demon.co.uk

Priory Avenue, High Wycombe, Buckinghamshire HP13 6PX

Owner: Wycombe District Council **Contact:** Vicki Wood (Museums Officer)

Set in historic Castle Hill House and surrounded by peaceful and attractive gardens, the Wycombe Museum explores the history of the Wycombe district.

Location: OS Ref. SU867 933. Signposted off the A404 High Wycombe/Amersham road. The Museum is about 5mins walk from the town centre and railway station.

Opening Times: Mon - Sat, 10am - 5pm. Open Suns, 2 - 5pm.

Admission: Free.

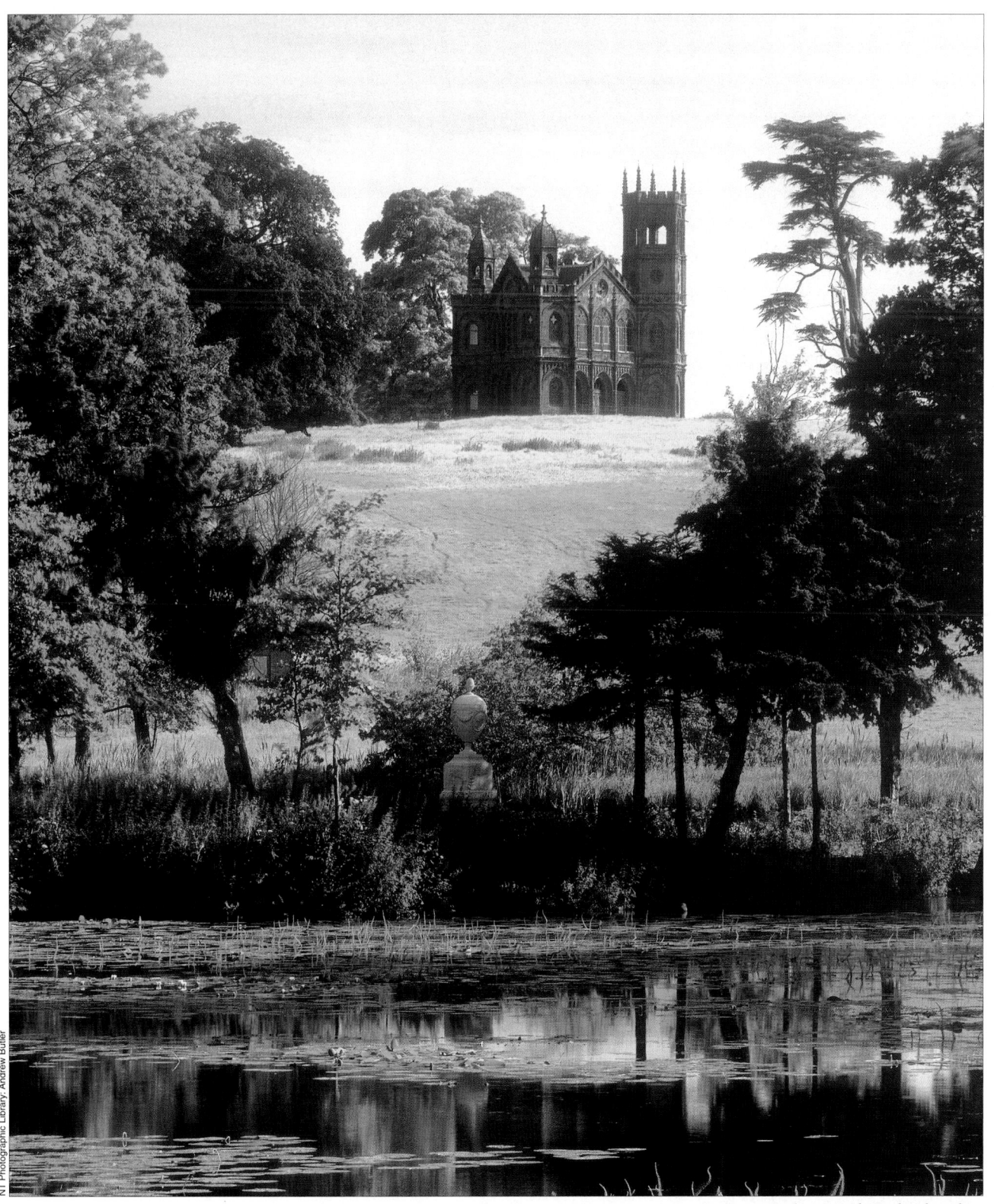

Stowe Gardens & Park, Buckinghamshire

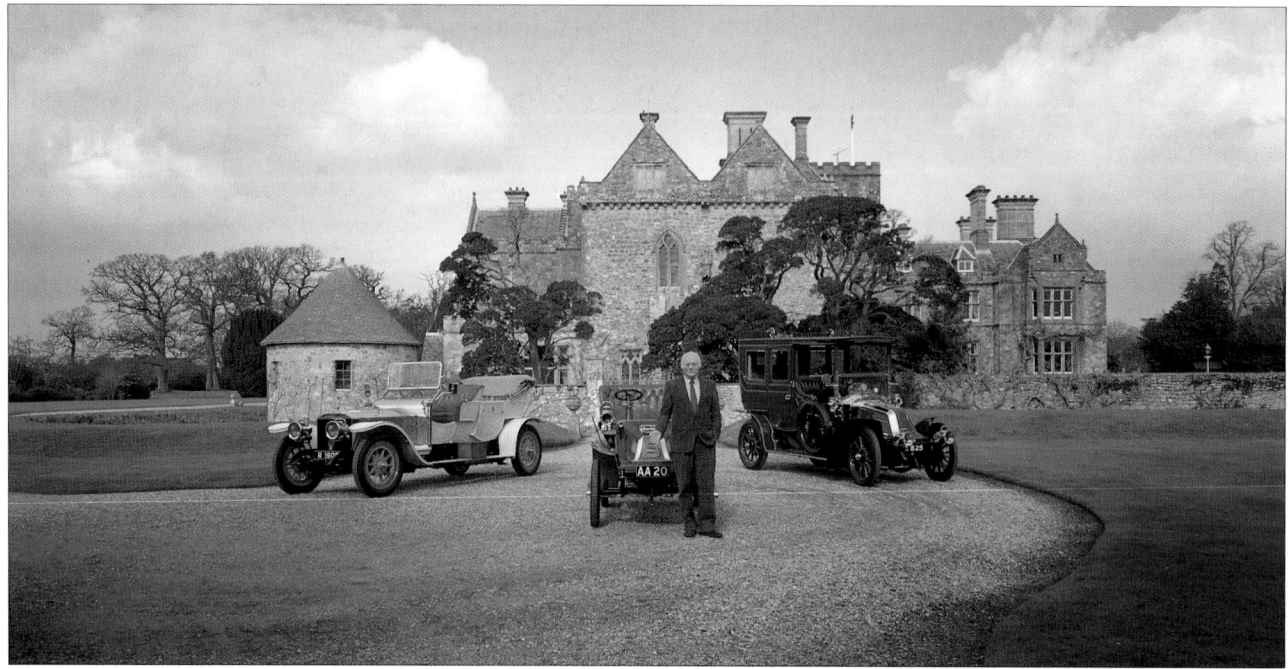

BEAULIEU
Beaulieu

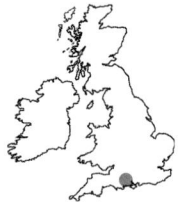

Owner: Lord Montagu

CONTACT

Conference Office
John Montagu Building
Beaulieu
Brockenhurst
Hampshire
SO42 7ZN

Tel: 01590 614604

Fax: 01590 612624

e-mail: conference@
beaulieu.co.uk

LOCATION

OS Ref. SU387 025

From London, M3,
M27 W to J2,
A326, B3054 follow
brown signs.

Bus: Bus stops
within complex.

Rail: Stations at
Brockenhurst and
Beaulieu Rd
both 7m away.

BEAULIEU is set in the heart of the New Forest and is a place that gives enormous pleasure to people with an interest in seeing history of all kinds.

Overlooking the Beaulieu River, Palace House has been the ancestral home of the Montagus since 1538. The House was once the Great Gatehouse of Beaulieu Abbey and its monastic origins are reflected in such features as the fan vaulted ceilings. Many treasures, which are reminders of travels all round the world by past generations of the Montagu family, can also be seen. Walks amongst the gardens and by the Beaulieu River can also be enjoyed.

Beaulieu Abbey was founded in 1204 and although most of the buildings have now been destroyed, much of the beauty and interest remains. The former Monks' Refectory is now the local Parish Church. The Domus, which houses an exhibition of monastic life, is home to beautiful wall hangings and 15th century beamed ceilings.

Beaulieu also houses the world famous National Motor Museum which traces the story of motoring from 1894 to the present day. 250 vehicles are on display including legendary world record breakers plus veteran, vintage and classic cars and motorcycles.

The modern Beaulieu is very much a family destination where there are various free and unlimited rides and drives on a transportation theme to be enjoyed by everyone, including a mile long monorail and replica 1912 London open-topped bus.

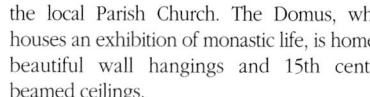

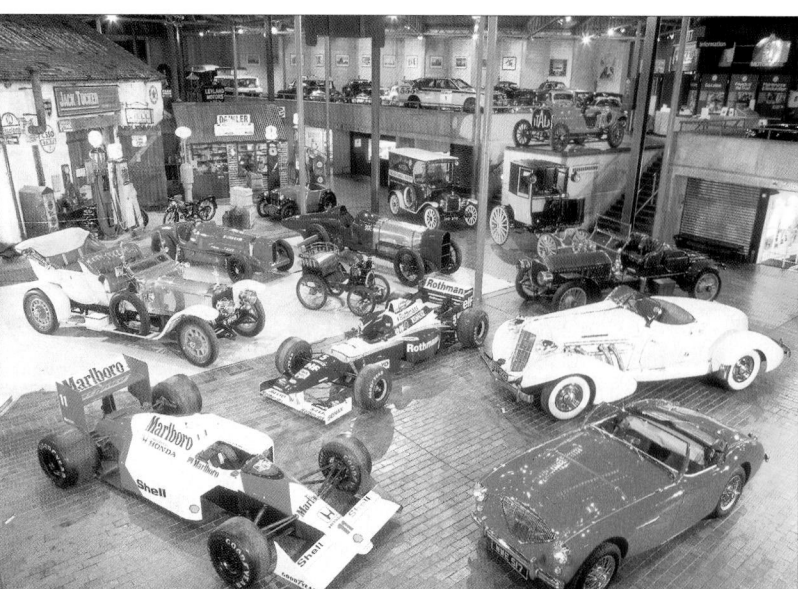

OPENING TIMES

SUMMER
May - September
Daily, 10am - 6pm.

WINTER
October - April
Daily, 10am - 5pm.

Closed Christmas Day.

ADMISSION

ALL YEAR

Individual rates upon application.

Groups (15+)
Rates upon application.

SPECIAL EVENTS

- **APR 8:**
  Boat Jumble.
- **MAY 12/13:**
  Spring Autojumble
- **SEPT 8/9:**
  Autojumble.

All enquiries should be made to our Special Events Booking Office where advance tickets can be purchased. The contact telephone is 01590 614645.

Other Event dates yet to be confirmed to include Motorcycle World, Palace House Prom, Fireworks Fair.

CONFERENCE/FUNCTION

ROOM	SIZE	MAX CAPACITY
Brabazon (x3)	40'x40'	120 (x3)
Domus	69'x27'	140
Theatre		200
Hartford Suite	39'x17'	50
Palace House		60
Motor Museum		300

BEAULIEU

Catering and Functions

Beaulieu also offers a comprehensive range of facilities for conferences, company days out, product launches, management training, corporate hospitality, promotions, film locations, exhibitions and outdoor events.

The National Motor Museum is a unique venue for drinks receptions and dinners or the perfect complement to a conference as a relaxing visit.

The charming 13th century Domus banqueting hall with its beautiful wooden beams, stone walls and magnificent wall hangings, is the perfect setting for dinners, buffets or themed evenings – 17th century Royal Feasts with period entertainment are a speciality.

Palace House, the ancestral home of Lord Montagu is an exclusive setting for smaller dinners, buffets and receptions. With a welcoming log fire in the winter and the coolness of the courtyard fountain in the summer, it offers a relaxing yet truly 'stately' atmosphere to ensure a memorable experience for your guests whatever the time of year

A purpose-built theatre, with tiered seating, can accommodate 220 people whilst additional meeting and syndicate rooms can accommodate from 5 to 200 delegates. With the nearby Beaulieu River offering waterborne activities and the Beaulieu Estate giving you the opportunity of indulging in a variety of country pursuits and outdoor management training, Beaulieu provides a unique venue for your conference and corporate hospitality needs.

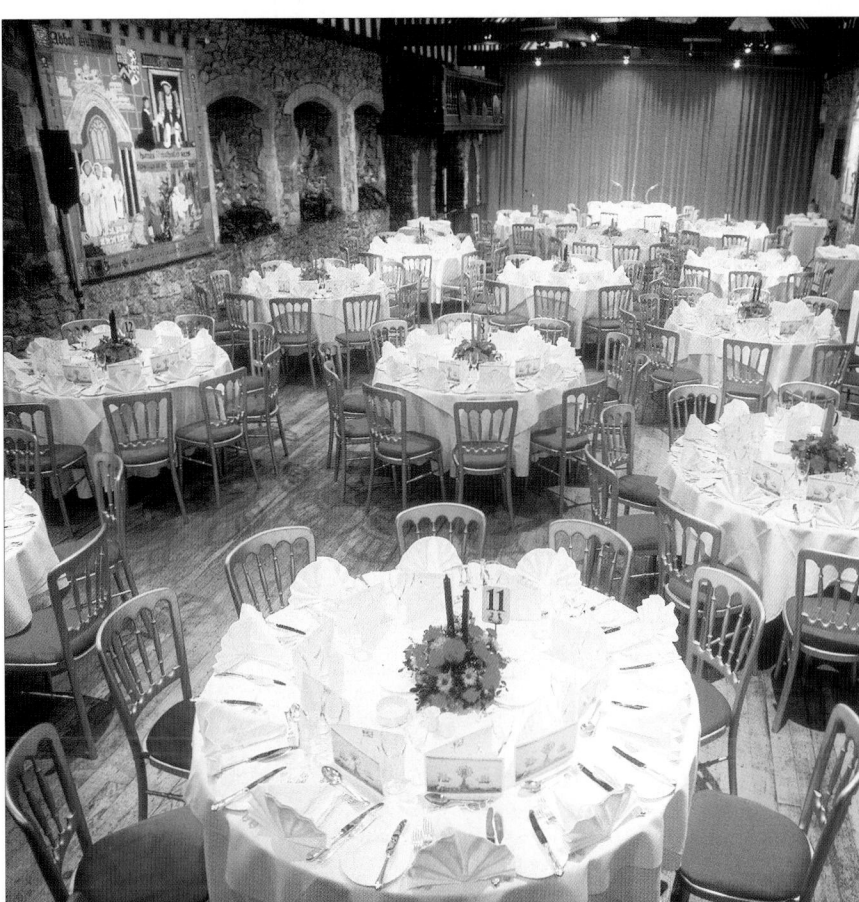

ℹ️ Allow 3 hrs or more for visits. Last adm. 40 mins before closing. Helicopter landing point. When visiting Beaulieu arrangements can be made to view the Estate's vineyards. Visits, which can be arranged between Apr - Oct, must be pre-booked at least one week in advance with Beaulieu Estate Office.

🛍️ Palace House Shop and Kitchen Shop plus Main Reception Shop.

🍷

♿ Disabled visitors may be dropped off outside Visitor Reception before parking. WC. Wheelchairs can be provided free of charge in Visitor Reception by prior booking.

🍴 The self-service Brabazon restaurant seats 300. Prices range to £7 for lunch. Groups can book in advance. Further details and menus from Catering Manager 01590 612345.

🚶 Attendants on duty. Guided tours by prior arrangement for groups.

🅿️ 1,500 cars and 30 coaches. During the season the busy period is from 11.30am to 1.30pm. Coach drivers should sign in at Information Desk. Free admission for coach drivers plus voucher which can be exchanged for food, drink and souvenirs.

📷 Professional staff available to assist in planning of visits. Services include introductory talks, films, guided tours, rôle play and extended projects. In general, educational services incur no additional charges and publications are sold at cost. Starter sets available free of charge to pre-booked parties. Information pack available from Education at Beaulieu, John Montagu Building, Beaulieu, Hants SO42 7ZN.

🐕 In grounds, on leads only.

❄️

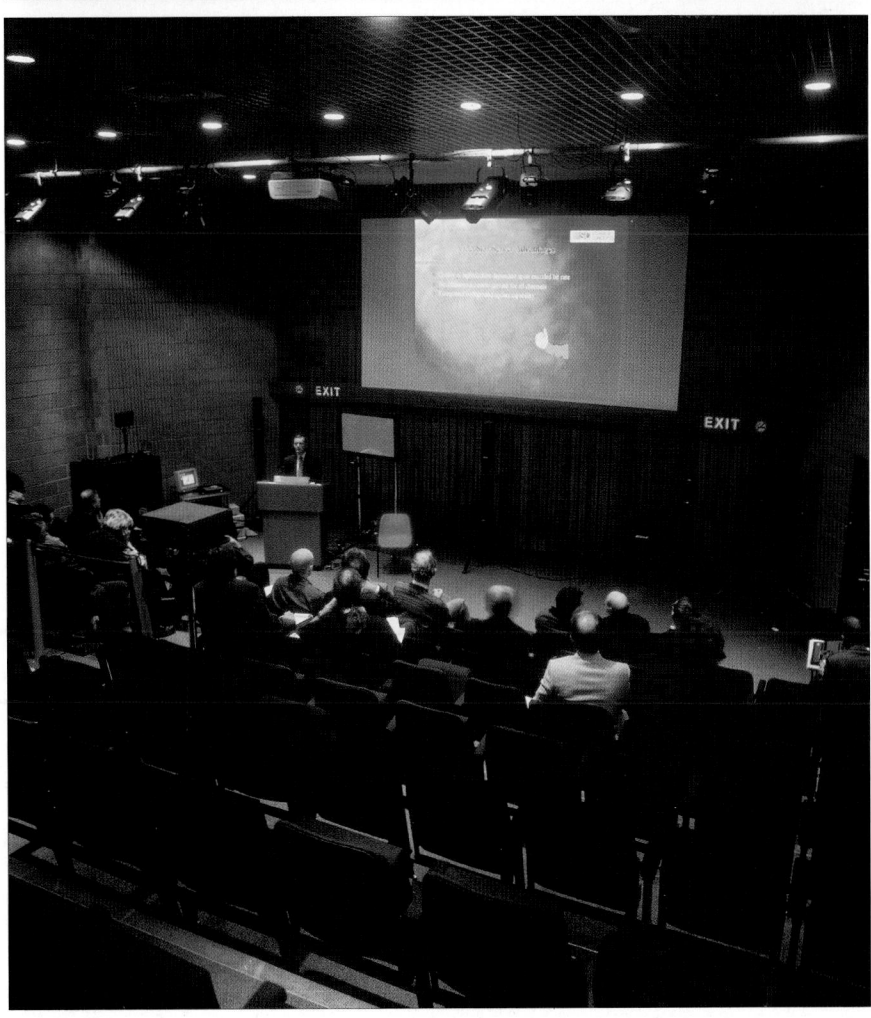

South East England

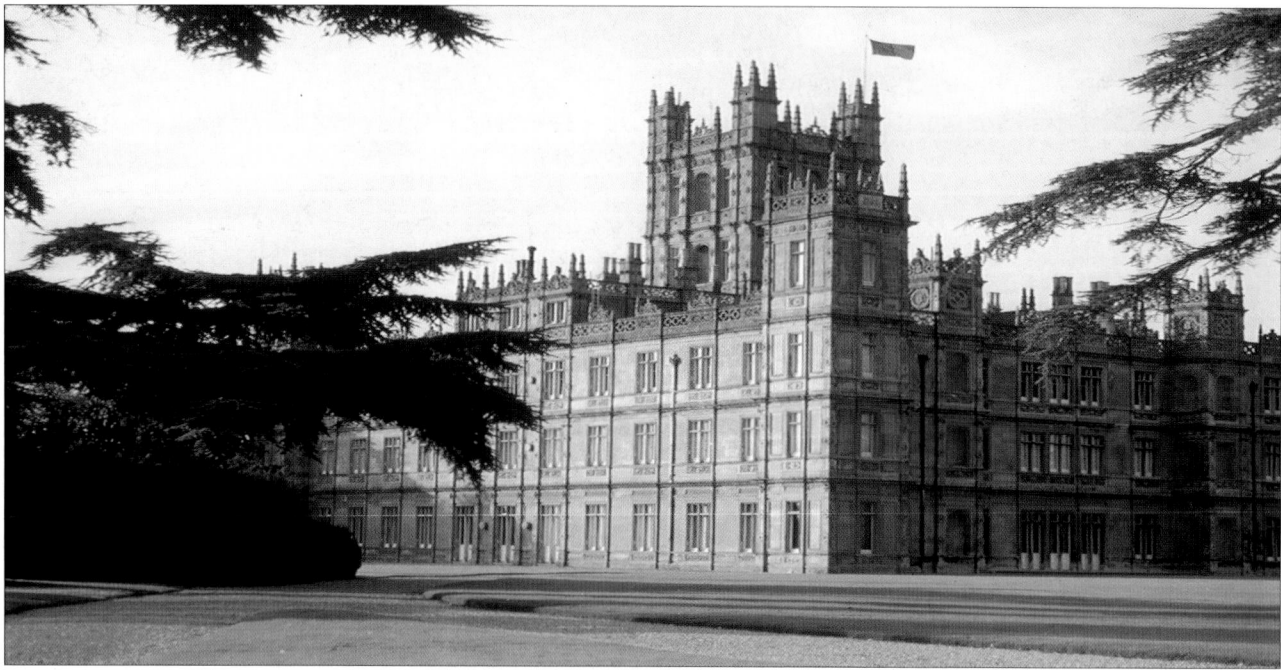

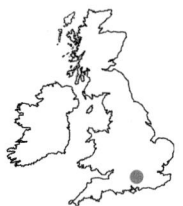

Owner:
The Earl of Carnarvon

CONTACT

Adrian Wiley
Highclere Castle
Newbury
Berkshire
RG20 9RN

Tel: 01635 253210

Fax: 01635 255315

e-mail: theoffice@
highclerecastle.co.uk

LOCATION

OS Ref. SU445 587

Approx 7m out
of Newbury on A34
towards Winchester.
From London: M4/J13,
A34 Bypass Newbury-
Winchester 20 mins.
M3/J5 approx 15m.

Air: Heathrow M4 45 mins.

Rail: Paddington -
Newbury 45 mins.

Taxi: 4¹/₂ m
01635 40829.

CONFERENCE/FUNCTION

ROOM	SIZE	MAX CAPACITY
Library	43' x 21'	120
Saloon	42' x 29'	150
Dining Rm	37' x 18'	70
Library, Saloon, Drawing Rm, Music Rm, Smoking Rm		400

HIGHCLERE CASTLE & GARDENS
Newbury

Designed by Charles Barry in the 1830s at the same time as he was building the Houses of Parliament, this soaring pinnacled mansion provided a perfect setting for the 3rd Earl of Carnarvon, one of the great hosts of Queen Victoria's reign. The extravagant interiors range from church Gothic through Moorish flamboyance and rococo revival to the solid masculinity in the long Library. Old master paintings mix with portraits by Van Dyck and 18th century painters. Napoleon's desk and chair rescued from St. Helena sits with other 18th and 19th century furniture.

The 5th Earl of Carnarvon discovered the Tomb of Tutankhamun with Howard Carter. The castle houses a unique exhibition of some of his discoveries which were only rediscovered in the castle in 1988. The current Earl is the Queen's Horseracing Manager. In 1993 to celebrate his 50th year as a leading owner and breeder 'The Lord Carnarvon Racing Exhibition' was opened to the public, and offers a fascinating insight into a racing history that dates back three generations.

GARDENS

The magnificent parkland with its massive cedars was designed by 'Capability' Brown. The walled gardens also date from an earlier house at Highclere but the dark yew walks are entirely Victorian in character. The glass Orangery and Fernery add an exotic flavour. The Secret Garden has a romance of its own with a beautiful curving lawn surrounded by densely planted herbaceous gardens. A place for poets and romantics.

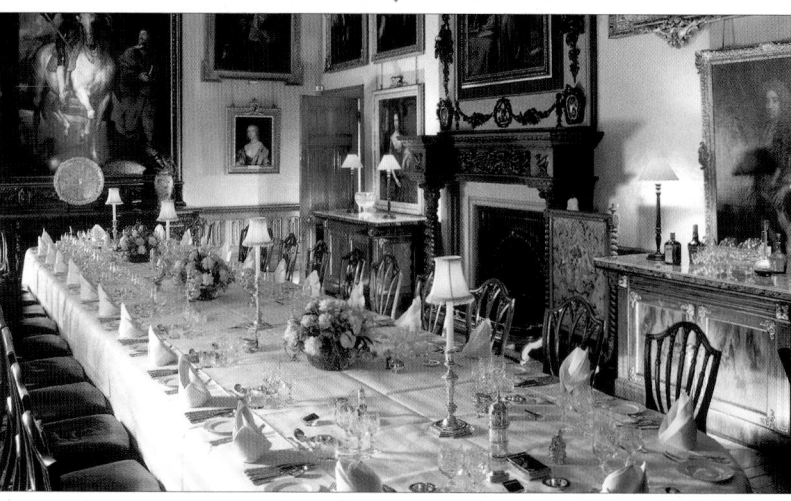

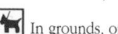 Conferences, exhibitions, filming, fairs, and concerts (cap. 8000). No photography in the house.

Receptions, dinners, corporate hospitality.

Visitors may alight at the entrance. WC.

Tearooms, licensed. Lunches for 20+ can be booked.

Ample.

Egyptian Exhibition: £3 per child. 1 adult free per every 10 children – includes playgroups, Brownie packs, Guides etc. Nature walks, beautiful old follies, Secret Garden.

In grounds, on leads.   Civil Wedding Licence.

OPENING TIMES

1 July - 30 August
Daily: 11am - 5pm.
Sats: 11am - 3.30pm. Last adm. 1 hour before closing.

The house is occasionally closed during this period - please call our information line.

Closed 21/22 July.

ADMISSION

Adult £6.50
Child (4-15yrs).........£3.00
Student/OAP...........£5.00
Wheelchair Pusher ..FOC

Grounds & Gardens only
Adult £3.00
Child (5-15yrs)........£1.50
Groups (20+)
Adult £5.00
Child (4-15yrs).......£3.00
Private guided tour by arrangement £10pp (min. £500 +VAT).

School Groups (to visit Egyptian Exhibition only)
Child £3.50
1 adult Free for every 10 children

VIP Season Ticket*
(2+3) £25.00
*Runs for one year from date of joining, Free admission for 2 adults & 3 children to the House, Exhibitions & Gardens: 1 Jul - 2 Sept & when special events are taking place. 10% off shop, tearooms, free admission to daytime events. Discounted rate for evening concerts, free admission to 'Shakespeare in the Park', £2 off Newbury Racecourse Members' Enclosure badges when pre-booked, Newbury Hilton - Fri, Sat, Sun evenings - dinner for two for the price of one from chef's hot or cold table, 10% off the price of lunch or dinner at Sharland's Restaurant, Newbury Manor Hotel.

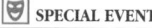 **SPECIAL EVENTS**

Please telephone
01635 253204 for details.

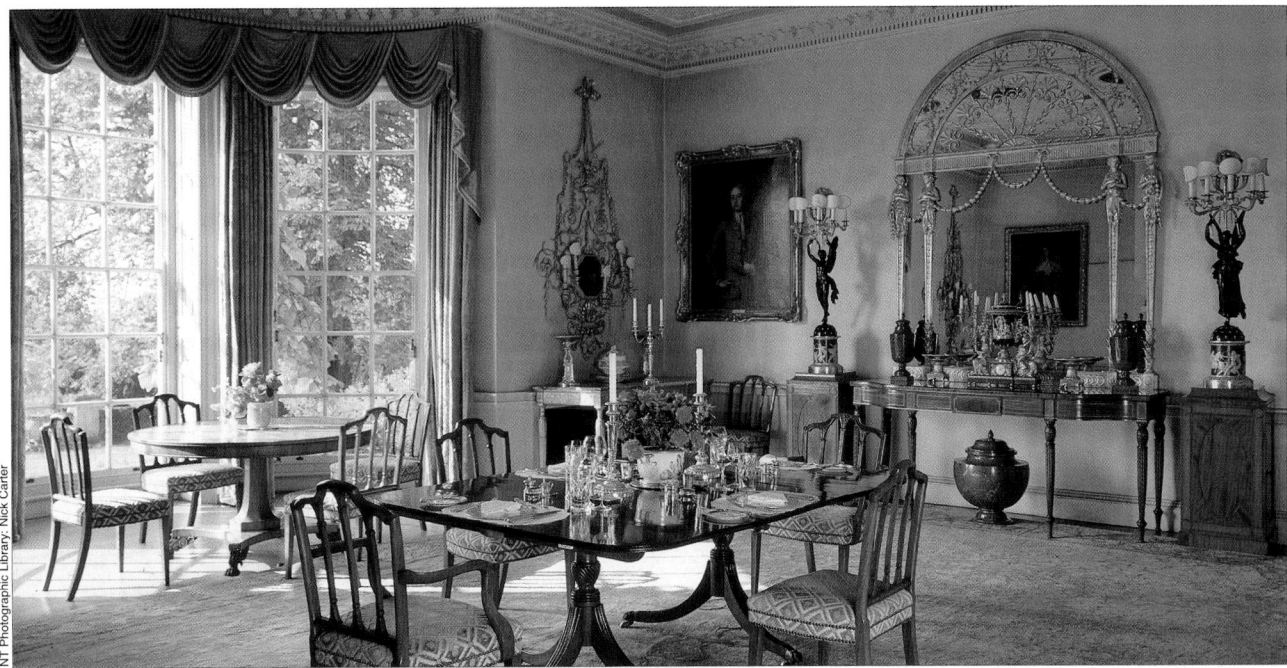

NT Photographic Library: Nick Carter

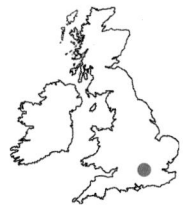

Owner: The National Trust

CONTACT

The Property Manager
Hinton Ampner Garden
Bramdean
Alresford
Hampshire
SO24 0LA

Tel: 01962 771305

Fax: 01962 793101

e-mail: shigen@
smtp.ntrust.org.uk

LOCATION

OS Ref. SU597 275

On A272, 1m W of
Bramdean village, 8m E of
Winchester.

HINTON AMPNER GARDEN
Bramdean

'I have learned during the past years what above all I want from a garden: this is tranquillity'. so said Ralph Dutton, 8th and last Lord Sherborne, of his garden at Hinton Ampner. He created one of the great gardens of the 20th century, a masterpiece of design based upon the bones of a Victorian garden, in which he united a formal layout with varied and informal planting in pastel shades. It is a garden of all year round interest with scented plants and magnificent vistas over the park and surrounding countryside.

The garden forms the link between the woodland and parkland planting, which he

began in 1930, and the house, which he remodelled into a small neo-Georgian manor house in 1936. He made further alterations when the house was reconstructed after a fire in 1960. Today it contains his very fine collection of English furniture, Italian paintings and hard-stones. Both his collection and every aspect of the decoration at Hinton Ampner reflects Ralph Dutton's sure eye and fine aesthetic judgement.

He placed the whole within the rolling Hampshire landscape that he loved and understood so well.

❖

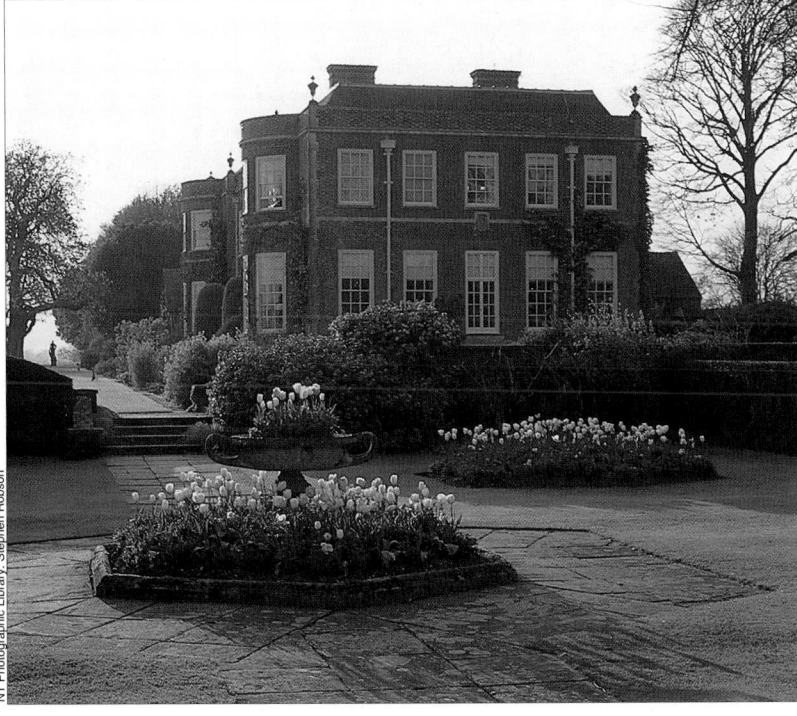

NT Photographic Library: Stephen Robson

OPENING TIMES

House
3 Apr - end Sept: Tues
& Weds,
also Sats & Suns in Aug,
1.30 - 5pm.

Garden
18 & 25 Mar,
1 Apr - end Sept:
Tues, Weds, Sats, Suns &
BH Mons, 1.30 - 5pm.

ADMISSION

House and Garden
Adult £5.00
Child (5-16)............£2.50

Garden only
Adult £4.00
Child (5-16)............£2.00

Children under 5yrs Free

Groups (min 15, max 60)
Adult £4.50
Child......................£2.25

NT Members free.

Limited for coaches.

South East England

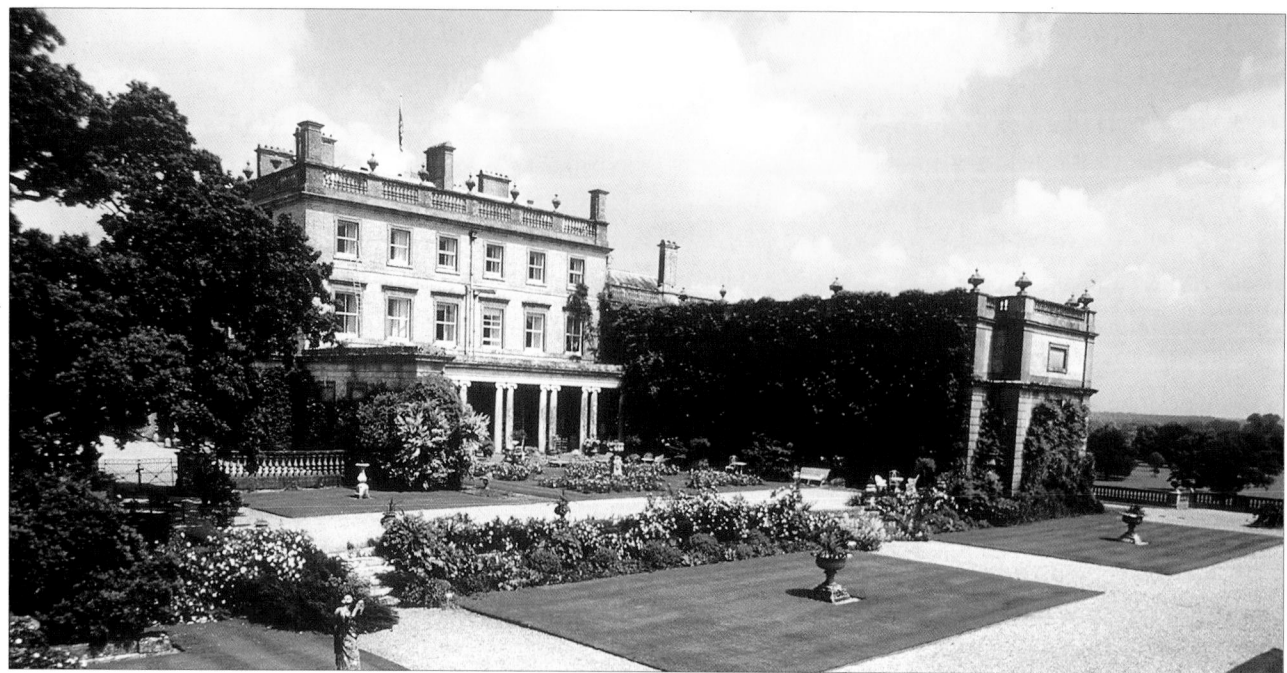

SOMERLEY
Ringwood

Sitting on the edge of the New Forest in the heart of Hampshire, Somerley, home of the 6th Earl of Normanton and his three children, is situated in 7,000 acres of meadows, woods and rolling parkland. Designed by Samuel Wyatt in the mid 1700s, the house became the property of the Normanton family in 1825 and has remained in the same family through the years. Housing a magnificent art and porcelain collection, the house itself, albeit impressively splendid, still retains the warmth and character of a family home.

Although never open to the public, Somerley is available for corporate events and its location, along with its seclusion and privacy, provide the perfect environment for conferences and meetings, product launches, lunches and dinners, activity and team building days (the estate boasts a hugely challenging off-road driving course) and film and photographic work.

Somerley only ever hosts one event at a time so exclusivity in an outstanding setting is always guaranteed. From groups as small as eight to perhaps a large dinner for 120, the style of attention and personal service go hand in hand with the splendour of the house and the estate itself.

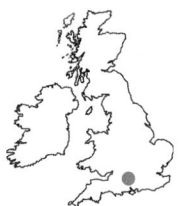

Owner:
The Earl of Normanton

CONTACT

Richard Horridge
Somerley
Ringwood
Hampshire
BH24 3PL

Tel: 01425 480819

Fax: 01425 478613

e-mail: info@somerley.com

LOCATION

OS Ref. SU134 080

Off the A31 to Bournemouth 2m. London 1³/4 hrs via M3, M27, A31. 2m NW of Ringwood.

Air: Bournemouth International Airport 5m.

Rail: Bournemouth Station 12m.

Taxi: A car can be arranged from the House if applicable.

CONFERENCE/FUNCTION		
ROOM	SIZE	MAX CAPACITY
Picture Gall.	80' x 30'	200
Drawing Rm	38' x 30'	50
Dining Rm	39' x 19'	50
East Library	26' x 21'	30

Privately booked functions only.

ADMISSION

Privately booked functions only.

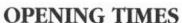

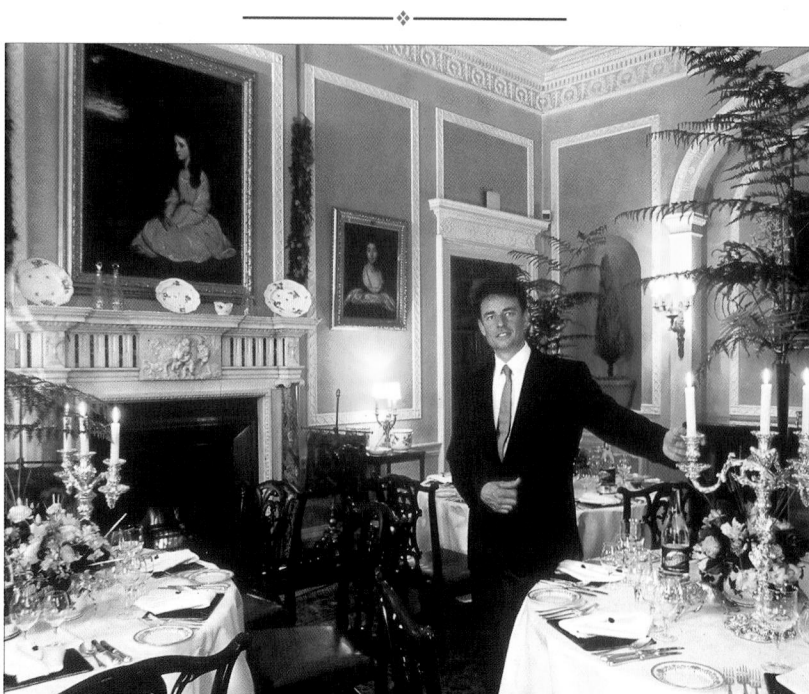

ℹ️ No individual visits, ideal for all corporate events, activity days and filmwork.

🍽️ Dining Room and picture gallery available for private parties.

🅿️ Unlimited.

🛏️ 4 twin & 4 double rooms.

JANE AUSTEN'S HOUSE

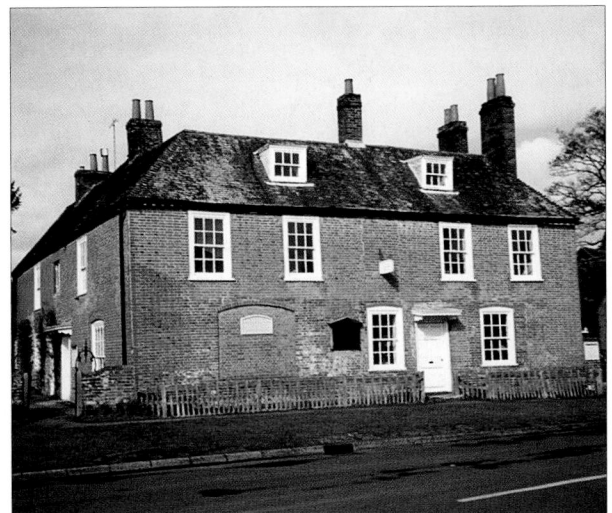

CHAWTON, ALTON, HAMPSHIRE GU34 1SD

Owner: *Jane Austen Memorial Trust*   **Contact:** *The Curator*

Tel/Fax: 01420 83262

17th century house where Jane Austen wrote or revised her six great novels. Contains many items associated with her and her family, documents and letters, first editions of the novels, pictures, portraits and furniture. Pleasant garden, suitable for picnics, bakehouse with brick oven and wash tub, houses Jane's donkey carriage.

Location: OS Ref. SU708 376. Just S of A31, 1m SW of Alton, signposted Chawton.

Opening times: 1 Mar - 1 Jan: daily, 11am - 4.30pm. Jan & Feb: Sats & Suns and half term in Feb (ring for dates). Closed 25 & 26 Dec.

Admission: Adult £3, Conc. £2.50. Groups (15+) £2.50, Child (8-18yrs) 50p.

Bookshop. Ground floor & grounds suitable. WC. Opposite house. Opposite house. Guide dogs only. ❄

BASING HOUSE

Tel: 01256 467294

Redbridge Lane, Basing, Basingstoke RG24 7HB

Owner: Hampshire County Council   **Contact:** Alan Turton

Ruins, covering 10 acres, of huge Tudor palace. Recent recreation of Tudor formal garden.

Location: OS Ref. SU665 526. 2m E from Basingstoke town centre. Signposted car parks are about 5 or 10 mins walk from entrance.

Opening Times: 1 Apr - 30 Sept: Wed - Sun & BHs, 2 - 6pm.

Admission: Adult £1.50, Child 70p.

BEAULIEU 🏛

See pages 104/105 for double page entry.

BISHOP'S WALTHAM PALACE ⛪

Tel: 01489 892460

Bishop's Waltham, Hampshire SO32 1DH

Owner: English Heritage   **Contact:** The Custodian

This medieval seat of the Bishops of Winchester once stood in an enormous park. There are still wooded grounds and the remains of the Great Hall and the three storey tower can still be seen. Dower House furnished as a 19th century farmhouse.

Location: OS Ref. SU552 173. In Bishop's Waltham, 5m NE from M27/J8.

Opening Times: 1 Apr - 30 Sept: daily, 10am - 6pm. 1 Oct - 31 Oct: 10am - 5pm.

Admission: Adult £2.10, Child £1.10, Conc. £1.60.

ℹ Exhibition. Grounds suitable. Grounds only, on leads. Tel. for details.

BOHUNT MANOR GARDENS

Tel: 01428 722208   **Fax:** 01428 727936

Liphook, Hampshire GU30 7DL

Owner/Contact: Lady Holman

Woodland gardens with lakeside walk, collection of ornamental waterfowl, herbaceous borders and unusual trees and shrubs.

Location: OS Ref. SU839 310. W side of B2070 at S end of village.

Opening Times: All year: daily, 10am - 6pm.

Admission: Adult £1.50, Child under 14 Free, Conc. £1. Group: 10% off.

AVINGTON PARK 🏛

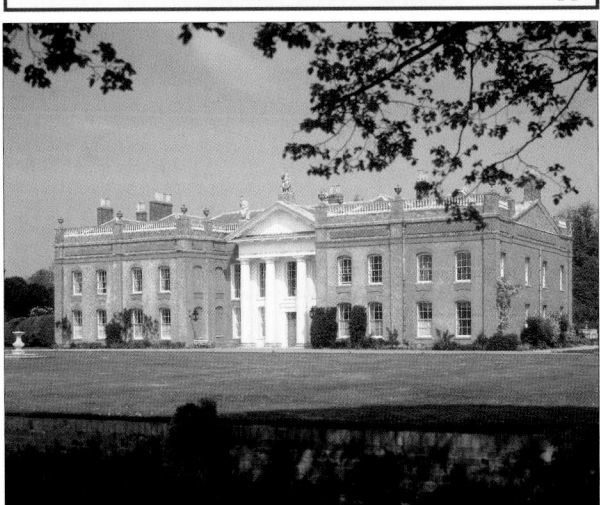

WINCHESTER, HAMPSHIRE SO21 1DB

Owner/Contact: *Mrs S L Bullen*

Tel: 01962 779260   **Fax:** 01962 779864   **e-mail:** sarah@avingtonpark.co.uk

Avington Park, where Charles II and George IV both stayed at various times, dates back to the 11th century. The house was enlarged in 1670 by the addition of two wings and a classical Portico surmounted by three statues. The State rooms are magnificently painted and lead onto the unique pair of conservatories flanking the South Lawn. The Georgian church, St. Mary's, is in the grounds.

Location: OS Ref. SU534 324. 4m NE of Winchester ½ m S of the B3047 in Itchen Abbas.

Opening Times: May - Sept: Suns & BH Mons, 2.30 - 5.30pm. Last tour 5pm. Other times by arrangement, coach parties welcome by appointment all year.

Admission: Adult £3.50, Child £2.

ℹ Conferences. Partially suitable. WC. Obligatory.   In grounds, on leads. Guide dogs only in house. 🔔 ❄ Ⓦ

BREAMORE HOUSE & MUSEUM 🏛

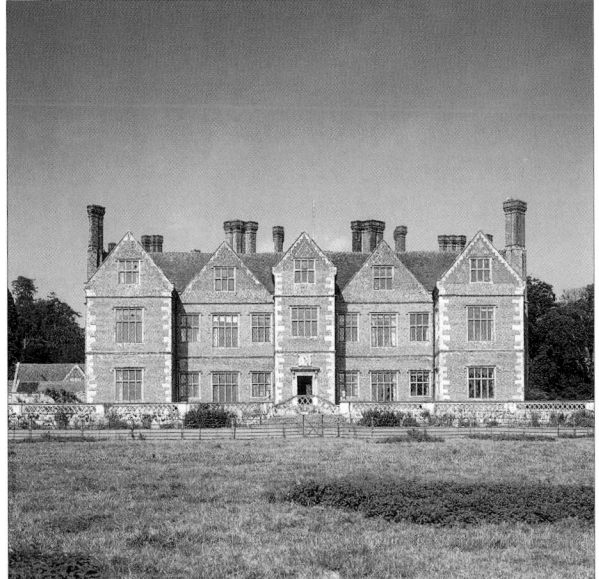

BREAMORE, FORDINGBRIDGE, HAMPSHIRE SP6 2DF

Owner/Contact: *Sir Edward Hulse Bt*

Tel: 01725 512233   **Fax:** 01725 512858   **e-mail:** breamore@estate.fsnet.co.uk

Elizabethan manor with fine collections of pictures and furniture. Countryside Museum takes visitors back to the time when a village was self-sufficient.

Location: OS Ref. SU152 191. W Off the A338, between Salisbury and Ringwood.

Opening Times: Apr: Easter Holiday, Tue, Wed & Sun. May, Jun, Jul & Sept: Tue, Wed, Thur, Sat & Sun & all hols. Aug: daily. House: 2 - 5.30pm. Countryside Museum: 1 - 5.30pm.

Admission: Combined ticket for house and museum: Adult £5, Child £3.50.

  Ground floor & grounds suitable. WC.

BROADLANDS

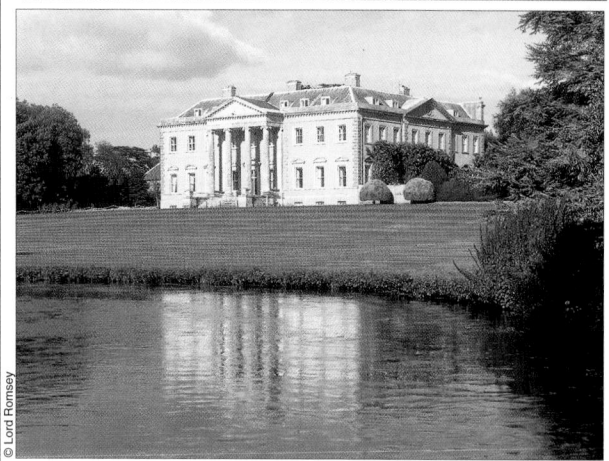

© Lord Romsey

ROMSEY, HAMPSHIRE SO51 9ZD

Owner: Lord & Lady Romsey   *Contact: Mrs S Armitage*

Tel: 01794 505010 **Event Enquiry Line:** 01794 505020

Famous as the home of the late Lord Mountbatten, and equally well known as the country residence of Lord Palmerston, the Great Victorian Prime Minister. Broadlands is an elegant Palladian mansion in a beautiful landscaped setting on the banks of the River Test. Visitors may view the House with its art treasures and mementoes of the famous, enjoy the superb views from the Riverside Lawns or relive Lord Mountbatten's life and times in the Mountbatten Exhibition and spectacular Mountbatten audio-visual presentation.

Location: OS Ref. SU355 204. On A31 at Romsey.

Opening Times: 11 Jun - 2 Sept: daily, 12 noon - 5.30pm. Last admission 4pm.

Admission: Adult £5.95, Child (12-16) £3.95, Conc. £4.95. Groups (10+): Adult £4.95, Child (12-16) £3.85, Conc. £4.65. All inclusive admission charges. Accompanied child under 12, Free.

🏛 🍴 ♿Ground floor & grounds suitable.WC. 📷 🅺Obligatory. 🐕Guide dogs only.

CALSHOT CASTLE ⊞   **Tel:** 023 8089 2023

Calshot, Fawley, Hampshire SO45 1BR

Owner: English Heritage   **Contact:** Hampshire County Council

Henry VIII built this coastal fort in an excellent position, commanding the sea passage to Southampton. The fort houses an exhibition and recreated pre-World War I barrack room.

Location: OS Ref. SU488 025. On spit 2m SE of Fawley off B3053.

Opening Times: 1 Apr - 30 Sept: daily, 10am - 6pm. 1 Oct - 31 Oct: 10am - 5pm.

Admission: Adult £2, Child £1.

ELING TIDE MILL   **Tel:** 023 8086 9575

The Toll Bridge, Eling, Totton, Southampton, Hampshire SO40 9HF

Contact: Mr David Blackwell-Eaton   **e-mail:** eling.tidemill@argonet.co.uk

Owner: Eling Tide Mill Trust Ltd & New Forest District Council

Location: OS Ref. SU365 126. 4m W of Southampton. 1/2 m S of the A35.

Opening Times: Wed - Sun and BH Mons, 10am - 4pm.

Admission: Adult £1.65, Child 90p, OAP £1.25, Family £4.60. Discounts for groups and joint entry with Totton and Eling Heritage Centre. (Prices will probably change 1 Jan 2001, phone to confirm details).

EXBURY GARDENS 🏛   **Tel:** 023 8089 1203 **Fax:** 023 8089 9940

Exbury, Southampton, Hampshire SO45 1AZ

Owner: Edmund de Rothschild Esq   **Contact:** Gardens Office

Extensive landscaped woodland gardens overlooking the Beaulieu River. World famous Rothschild plant collection (rhododendrons, azaleas etc.) as well as many rare and wonderful trees: Rock Garden, Cascades, Ponds, River Walk, Rose Garden, Water Garden, Heather Gardens, seasonal trails and themed walks. Ample seating throughout. Gardens spectacular in Spring and Autumn.

Location: OS Ref. SU425 005. 11m SE of Totton (A35) via A326 & B3054 & minor road.

Opening Times: 24 Feb - 25 Nov: daily, 10am - 5.30pm or dusk if earlier.

Admission: Please telephone for details.

🏛 ♿Grounds suitable. WC. 📷 🍴 🐕 In grounds, on leads. 🎫 Telephone for details. 🅦

FORT BROCKHURST ⊞   **Tel:** 023 9258 1059

Gunner's Way, Gosport, Hampshire PO12 4DS

Owner: English Heritage   **Contact:** The Head Custodian

This 19th century fort was built to protect Portsmouth, today its parade ground, moated keep and sergeants' mess are available to hire as an exciting setting for functions and events of all types. The fort is also open to visitors at weekends when tours will explain the exciting history of the site and the legend behind the ghostly activity in cell no. 3.

Location: OS196, Ref. SU596 020. Off A32, in Gunner's Way, Elson on N side of Gosport.

Opening Times: 1 Apr - 30 Sept: 10am - 6pm. 1 Oct - 31 Oct: 10am - 5pm. Weekends only.

Admission: Adult £2.10, Child £1.10, Conc. £1.60.

FURZEY GARDENS   **Tel:** 023 8081 2464 **Fax:** 023 8081 2297

Minstead, Lyndhurst, Hampshire SO43 7GL

Owner: Furzey Gardens Charitable Trust   **Contact:** Maureen Cole

Location: OS Ref. SU273 114. Minstead village 1/2 m N of M27/A31 junction off A337 to Lyndhurst.

Opening Times: Please contact property for details.

GREAT HALL & QUEEN ELEANOR'S GARDEN   **Tel:** 01962 846476
Fax: for bookings 01962 841326

Winchester Castle, Winchester, Hampshire SO23 8PJ

Owner: Hampshire County Council   **Contact:** Mrs Harris

The only surviving part of Henry III's medieval castle at Winchester, this 13th century hall was the centre of court and government life. The Round Table closely associated with the legend of King Arthur has hung here for over 700 years. Queen Eleanor's garden is a faithful representation of the medieval garden visited by Kings and Queens of England.

Location: OS Ref. SU477 295. Central Winchester. SE of Westgate archway.

Opening Times: All year: daily, 10am - 5pm (except weekends Nov - Feb, 10am - 4pm). Closed Christmas Day and Boxing Day.

Admission: Free .

🅺 By arrangement. ❄

GUILDHALL GALLERY   **Tel:** 01962 848289 (gallery) 01962 848269 (office)

The Broadway, Winchester SO23 9LJ   **Fax:** 01962 848299

e-mail: museums@winchester.gov.uk

Owner: Winchester City Council   **Contact:** Mr C Wardman Bradbury

A constantly changing programme of contemporary exhibitions including painting, sculpture, craft, photography and ceramics.

Location: OS Ref. SU485 293. Winchester - city centre. Situated above the Tourist Office in Winchester's 19th century Guildhall.

Opening Times: Apr - Oct: Mon - Sat, 10am - 5pm. Sun, 2 - 5pm. Nov - Mar: Tue - Sat, 10am - 4pm, Sun, 2 - 4pm.

Admission: Free.

♿ ❄ 🅦

HIGHCLERE CASTLE & GARDENS 🏛   See page 106 for full page entry.

HINTON AMPNER GARDEN 🌿   See page 107 for full page entry.

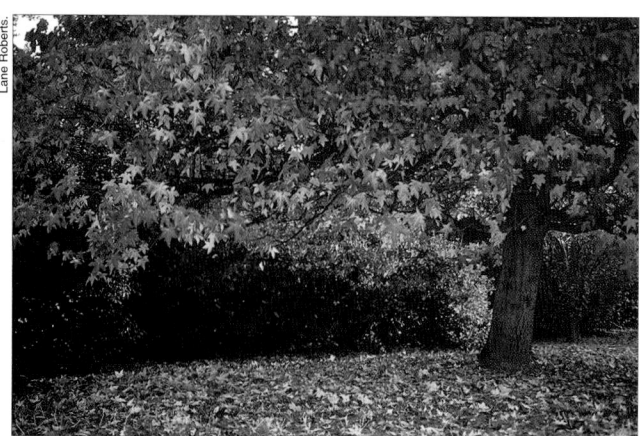

Lane Roberts.

The Sir Harold Hillier Gardens ~ Autumn colour in liquid amber.

THE SIR HAROLD HILLIER GARDENS & ARBORETUM

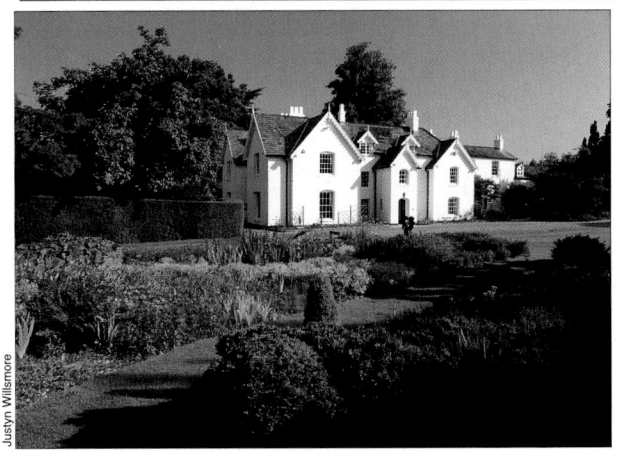

Justyn Willsmore

JERMYNS LANE, AMPFIELD, ROMSEY SO51 0QA
Managed by: Hampshire County Council
Contact: *Administration - Judith Drysdale   Marketing - Tim Brooks*

Tel: 01794 368787 **Fax:** 01794 368027

Set in the rolling Hampshire countryside between Winchester and the market town of Romsey, The Sir Harold Hillier Gardens & Arboretum comprises the greatest collection of hardy trees and shrubs in the world. Established in 1953, by the late Sir Harold Hillier, the 180-acre garden provides a stunning range of seasonal colour and interest and features 11 National Plant Collections, the Gurkha Memorial Gardens and the largest Winter Garden in Europe. A garden for all seasons.

Location: OS Ref. SU380 236. 3m NE of Romsey. Follow brown tourist signs from the town centre on A3090 (formerly A31) towards Winchester.

Opening times: Daily, 10.30am - 6pm or dusk if earlier. Closed Christmas BH.

Admission: Adult £4.25, Conc. £3.75, under 16s Free.

♿ Partially suitable. WC. ☕ Licensed. By arrangement. P Guide dogs only. ❄ Tel for details.

HOUGHTON LODGE

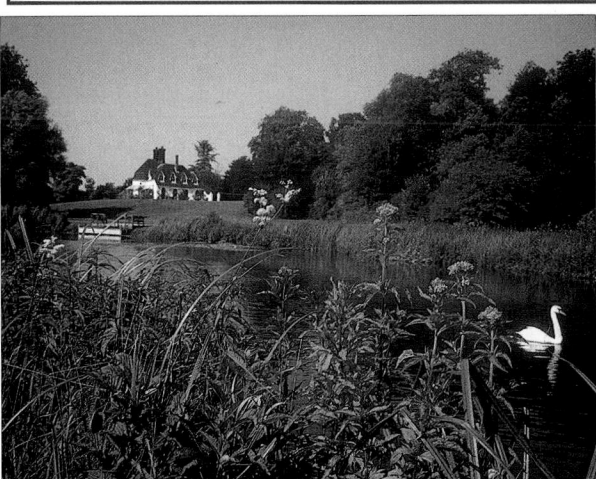

STOCKBRIDGE, HAMPSHIRE, SO20 6LQ
Owner/Contact: Captain M W Busk

Tel: 01264 810502/810912 **Fax:** 01264 810177
e-mail: info@hydroponicum.co.uk

Enjoy this haven of peace beside the tranquil beauty of the River Test. 5 acres of informal landscape (Grade II*) with fine trees surrounds an 18th century Cottage Ornée. Walled garden, ancient espaliers, greenhouses and herb garden. Formal topiary 'Peacock Garden'. Wild flowers; Children's puffing topiary dragon. Popular TV/film location. Indoor hydroponicum: learn how to garden without soil or toil and control greenhouse pests with natural predators.

Location: OS Ref. SU344 332. 1¹/₂ m S of Stockbridge (A30) on minor road to Houghton village.

Opening times: Garden: 1 Mar - 30 Sept: Sat, Sun & BHs, 10am - 5pm also Mon, Tue, Thur & Fri, 2 - 5pm. House: by arrangement.

Admission: Adult £5 (Child Free).

📷 ♿ ☕ Free tea or coffee. By arrangement. P In grounds, on leads.

HURST CASTLE
Tel: 01590 642344

Keyhaven, Lymington, Hampshire PO41 0PB
Owner: English Heritage   **Contact:** (Managed by) Hurst Castle Services

This was one of the most sophisticated fortresses built by Henry VIII, and later strengthened in the 19th and 20th centuries, to command the narrow entrance to the Solent. There is an exhibition in the Castle, and two huge 38-ton guns form the fort's armaments.

Location: OS196 Ref. SZ319 898. On Pebble Spit S of Keyhaven. Best approach by ferry from Keyhaven. 4m SW of Lymington.

Opening times: 1 Apr - 31 Oct: daily, 10am - 5.30pm. Café: open Apr - May weekends & Jun - Sept: daily.

Admission: Adult £2.50, Child £1.50, Conc. £2.

📷 ♿ Not suitable. ☕

MEDIEVAL MERCHANTS HOUSE
Tel: 023 8022 4854

58 French Street, Southampton, Hampshire SO1 0AT
Owner: English Heritage   **Contact:** The Custodian

The life of the prosperous merchant in the Middle Ages is vividly evoked in this recreated, faithfully restored 13th century townhouse.

Location: OS Ref. SU419 112. 58 French Street. ¹/₄ m S of Bargate off Castle Way. 150yds SE of Tudor House.

Opening Times: 1 Apr - 30 Sept: daily, 10am - 6pm. 1 - 31 Oct: daily, 10am - 5pm.

Admission: Adult £2.20, Child £1.10, Conc. £1.60.

MOTTISFONT ABBEY GARDEN, HOUSE & ESTATE

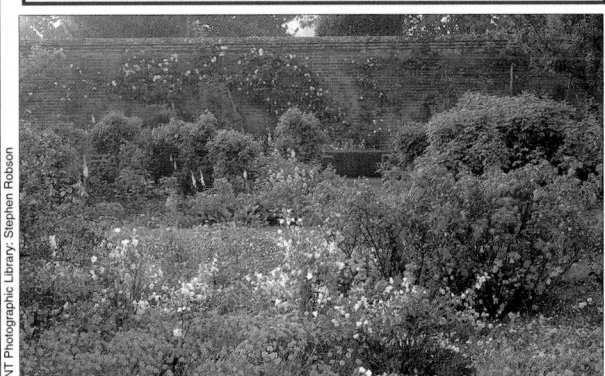

NT Photographic Library: Stephen Robson

MOTTISFONT, Nr ROMSEY, HAMPSHIRE SO51 0LP
Owner: The National Trust   Contact: The Property Manager

Tel: 01794 340757 **Fax:** 01794 341492 **Recorded Message:** 01794 341220

The Abbey and Garden form the central point of an 809 ha estate including most of the village of Mottisfont, farmland and woods. A tributary of the River Test flows through the garden forming a superb and tranquil setting for a 12th century Augustinian priory which, after the Dissolution, became a house. It contains the spring or "font" from which the place name is derived. The magnificent trees, walled gardens and the National Collection of Old-fashioned Roses combine to provide interest throughout the seasons. The Abbey contains a drawing room decorated by Rex Whistler and the cellarium of the old Priory. In 1996 the Trust acquired Derek Hill's 20th century picture collection.

Location: OS Ref. SU327 270. 4¹/₂ m NW of Romsey, 1m W of A3057.

Opening times: Garden, Grounds & House: 17 Mar - 4 Nov: Sat - Wed (open Good Fri), 11am - 6pm (or dusk if earlier). During peak rose season 9 - 24 Jun: (check recorded message for state of roses) open daily, 11am - 8.30pm. Last admission to grounds 1 hr before closing. House: 1 - 5pm. (Whistler Room & Cellarium: as garden). The Derek Hill picture collection: Sun, Mon & Tues, 1 - 5pm.

Admission: Adult £6, Child (5-18yrs) £3, Family £15. No reduction for groups. Coaches must book.

📷 ☕ Guide dogs only. 🔔 Tel. 01372 451596 for details.

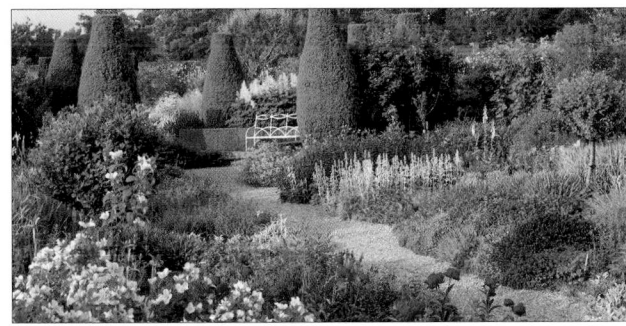

Mottisfont Abbey Garden, Hampshire.

NETLEY ABBEY

Tel: 023 9258 1059

Netley, Southampton, Hampshire

Owner: English Heritage   **Contact:** Area Manager

A peaceful and beautiful setting for the extensive ruins of this 13th century Cistercian abbey converted in Tudor times for use as a house.

Location: OS Ref. SU453 089. In Netley, 4m SE of Southampton, facing Southampton Water.

Opening Times: Any reasonable time.

Admission: Free.

OLD PORTSMOUTH CATHEDRAL

Tel: 023 9282 3300   **Fax:** 023 9229 5480

Portsmouth, Hampshire PO1 2HH   **Contact:** Rosemary Fairfax

Maritime Cathedral founded in 12th century and finally completed in 1991. A member of the ship's crew of Henry VIII's flagship *Mary Rose* is buried in Navy Aisle.

Location: OS Ref. SZ633 994. 1 1/2 m from end of M275. Follow signs to Historic Ship and Old Portsmouth.

Opening Times: 7.45am - 6pm all year. Sun service: 8am, 9.30am, 11am, 6pm. Weekday: 6pm (Choral on Tues and Fris in term time).

Admission: Donation appreciated.

PORTCHESTER CASTLE

Tel: 023 9237 8291   **Fax:** 023 9237 8291

Portsmouth, Hampshire PO16 9QW

Owner: English Heritage   **Contact:** The Custodian

The rallying point of Henry V's expedition to Agincourt and the ruined palace of King Richard II. This grand castle has a history going back nearly 2,000 years including the most complete Roman walls in Europe. Don't miss the interactive exhibition telling the story of the castle and see the newly conserved wallpaintings from the Viewing Gallery in the Keep.

Location: OS196, Ref. SU625 046. On S side of Portchester off A27, M27/J11.

Open: 1 Apr - 30 Sept: daily, 10am - 6pm. 1 - 31 Oct: 10am - 5pm. 1 Nov - 31 Mar: daily, 10am - 4pm. Closed 24 - 26 Dec & 1 Jan.

Admission: Adult £3, Child £1.50, Conc. £2.20. 15% discount for groups (11+). One extra place free for every additional 20.

ℹ Exhibition.   📷   ♿ Grounds & lower levels suitable.

🐕 In grounds, on leads.   ✳   🎫 Telephone for details.

SOMERLEY

See page 108 for full page entry.

STRATFIELD SAYE HOUSE

Tel: 01256 882882

Stratfield Saye, Basingstoke RG7 0AS

Owner: The Duke of Wellington   **Contact:** The Administrator

Family home of the Dukes of Wellington since 1817.

Location: OS Ref. SU700 615. Equidistant from Reading (M4/J11) & Basingstoke (M3/J6) 1 1/2 m W of the A33.

Opening times: Jun - Aug: Wed - Sun. Groups by arrangement – Mons & Tues in Jun, Jul & Aug. and Mon - Fri in Sept. Grounds & Exhibition: 11.30am - 5pm. House 12 noon - 3pm (last admission).

Admission: Adult £5.50, Child £2.50, OAP £5.

TITCHFIELD ABBEY

Tel: 01329 842133

Titchfield, Southampton, Hampshire

Owner: English Heritage   **Contact:** Mr K E Groves

Remains of a 13th century abbey overshadowed by the grand Tudor gatehouse. Reputedly some of Shakespeare's plays were performed here for the first time. Under local management of Titchfield Abbey Society.

Location: OS Ref. SU544 067. 1/2 m N of Titchfield off A27.

Opening Times: 1 Apr - 30 Sept: daily, 10am - 6pm. 1 - 31 Oct: daily, 10am - 5pm. 1 Nov - 31 Mar: daily, 10am - 4pm.

Admission: Free.

TUDOR HOUSE MUSEUM

Tel: 023 8063 5904   **Fax:** 023 8033 9601

Bugle Street, Southampton, Hampshire

Owner: Southampton City Council   **Contact:** Caroline Blott

Late 15th century half timbered house. Unique Tudor knot garden.

Location: OS Ref. SU418 113. Follow signs to Old Town and waterfront from M27/M3. 150yds NW of Merchants House.

Opening Times: From end of Oct 2000 - end of Mar 2001: Tues - Fri, 10am - 4pm. Sats, 10am - 12 noon. Suns, 1 - 4pm. Closed Mons. From end of Mar 2001 - end of Oct 2001: Tues - Fri, 10am - 5pm. Sats, 10am - 4pm. Suns, 2 - 5pm. Closed Mons. Closed for lunch 1 - 2pm.

Admission: Free.

SANDHAM MEMORIAL CHAPEL

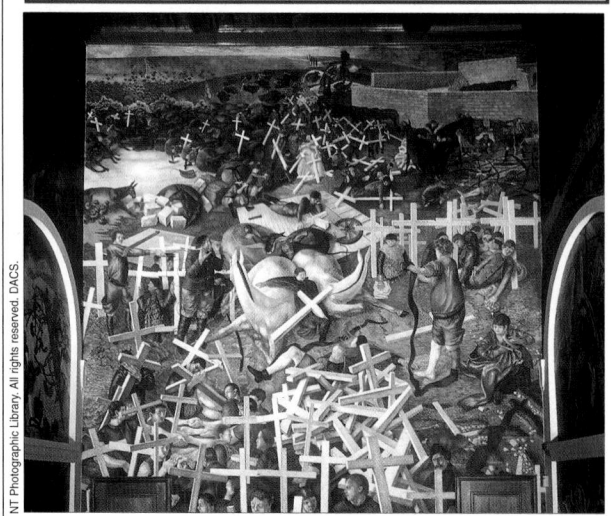

BURGHCLERE, Nr NEWBURY, HAMPSHIRE RG20 9JT

Owner: *The National Trust*   **Contact:** *Sarah Hook*

Tel/Fax: 01635 278394

Stanley Spencer's murals, which entirely cover the interior walls of this 1920s chapel, commemorate the First World War and constitute one of the greatest achievements of 20th century painting. The murals chronicle with minute accuracy the every day life of the soldier. Inspired by Giotto's Arena Chapel in Padua, this impressive project took Spencer five years to complete.

Location: OS Ref. SU463 608. 4m S of Newbury, 1/2 m E of A34, W end of Burghclere.

Opening times: Mar & Nov: Sats & Suns, Apr - end Oct: daily except Mons & Tues (open BH Mons): Dec - Feb 2002: by appointment only. Times: Mar & Nov: 11.30am - 4pm, Apr - end Oct: 11.30am - 5pm.

Admission: Adult £2.50, Child £1.25. Groups by prior arrangement, no reduction.

♿ Ramped steps.   🐕 In grounds, on leads.   ✳   🎫

Tall Chimneys at Houghton Lodge.

HUDSON'S

HAMPSHIRE

THE VYNE

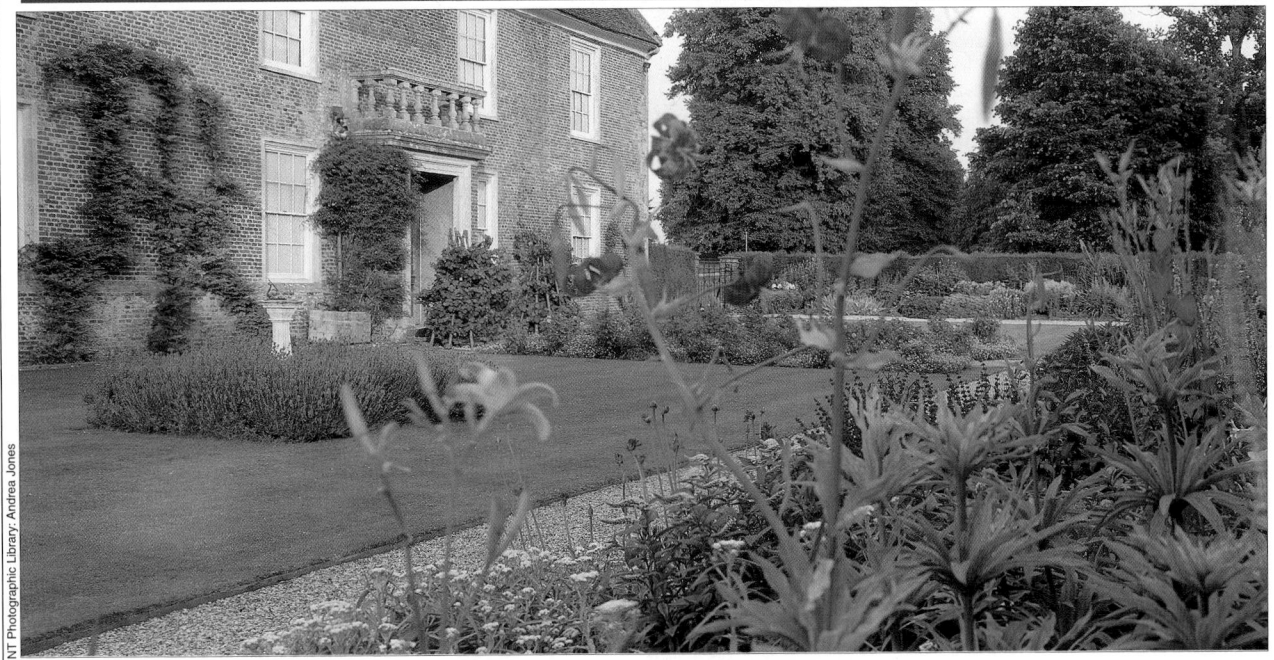

NT Photographic Library: Andrea Jones

SHERBORNE ST JOHN, BASINGSTOKE RG24 9HL

Owner: *The National Trust*   **Contact:** *The Property Manager*

Tel: 01256 881337 **Fax:** 01256 881720 **e-mail:** svygen@smtp.ntrust.org.uk

Built in the early 16th century for Lord Sandys, Henry VIII's Lord Chamberlain, the house acquired a classical portico in the mid-17th century (the first of its kind in England) and contains a fascinating Tudor chapel with Renaissance glass, a Palladian staircase and a wealth of old panelling and fine furniture. The attractive grounds feature herbaceous borders and a wild garden, with lawns, lakes and woodland walks.

Location: OS Ref. SU637 566. 4m N of Basingstoke between Bramley and Sherborne St John.

Opening times: House: 31 Mar - 4 Nov: daily except Thurs & Fris, 1 - 5pm (open Good Fri & BH Mons). Grounds: weekends in Feb & Mar, 11am - 4.30pm. 31 Mar - 4 Nov: daily except Thurs & Fris, 11am - 6pm (open Good Fri & BH Mons).

Admission: House & Grounds: Adult £5.50, Child £2.75, Family £13.75. Grounds only: Adult £3, Child £1.50. Groups: £4.50 (Mon - Wed only).

i No photography in house.   **P** Limited for coaches. By arrangement. Telephone for details.

GILBERT WHITE'S HOUSE & THE OATES MUSEUM

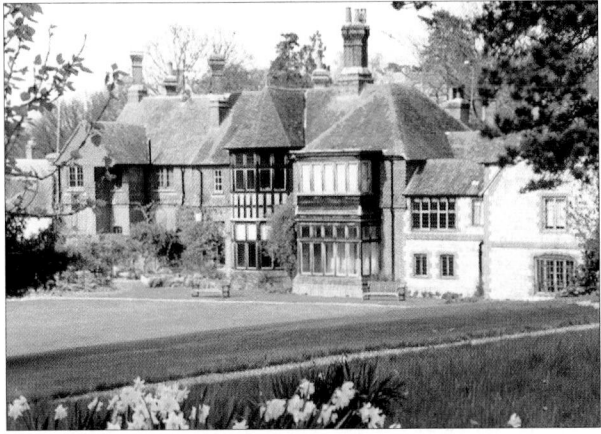

THE WAKES, HIGH STREET, SELBORNE, ALTON GU34 3JH

Owner: *Oates Memorial Trust*   **Contact:** *Mrs Anna Jackson*

Tel: 01420 511275

Charming 18th century house in heart of old Selborne, home of Rev Gilbert White, author of *The Natural History of Selborne*. Lovely garden with many plants of the 18th century. Museum devoted to Captain Oates of Antarctic fame. Tea parlour with 18th century fare.

Location: OS Ref. SU741 336. On W side of B3006, in village of Selborne 4m NW of the A3.

Opening Times: 1 Jan - 24 Dec: daily, 11am - 5pm. Evenings also for groups.

Admission: Adult £4, Child £1, OAP £3.50.

i No photography in house. Partially suitable. By arrangement. **P** Guide dogs only.

 SPECIAL EVENTS

JUN 16: Picnic to 'Jazz in June'   **JUN 16/17:** Unusual Plants Fair.
NOV 25: Annual Mulled Wine & Christmas shopping day.

WINCHESTER CATHEDRAL

Tel: 01962 857200 **Fax:** 01962 857201

Winchester, Hants SO23 9LS   **e-mail:** judy.george@winchester-cathedral.org.uk

The Cathedral was founded in 1079.   **Contact:** Mrs J George

Location: OS Ref. SU483 293. Winchester city centre.

Opening Times: 8.30am - 5pm. East end closes 5pm. Access may be restricted during services. Weekday services:7.40am, 8am, 5.30pm. Sun services: 8am, 10am, 11.15am, 3.30pm.

Admission: Recommended donations may increase: Adult £3, Child 50p, Conc. £2, Family £6, charges apply for Triforium gallery & Library - £1. Tower & Roof Tours £1.50. Group tours £3.50 should be booked through the Education centre. (Tel: 01962 857225 between 9am - 1pm).

WINCHESTER COLLEGE

Tel: 01962 621209 **Fax:** 01962 621215
e-mail: enterprise@bursary.wincoll.ac.uk

College Street, Winchester, Hampshire SO23 9NA

Owner: Winchester College   **Contact:** Marcus Van Hagen

Founded in 1382 with cobbled courtyards and vaulted ceilings to beautiful medieval stained glass windows.

Location: OS Ref. SU483 290. S of the Cathedral.

Opening Times: 1 Sept - 31 May: Mon - Sat, 11am, 12 noon, 2.15pm, 3.15pm. Sun, 2.15pm, 3.15pm. 1 Jun - 31 Aug: Mon - Sat, 10am, 11am, 12 noon, 2.15pm, 3.15pm. Sun, 2.15pm, 3.15pm. No tours Tues & Thurs afternoons all year.

Admission: Adult £1.50, Child/Conc. £1. Guided tours may be booked for groups (10+): Adult £2.50, Child/Conc. £2.

Ground floor & grounds suitable. Guide dogs only.

WOLVESEY CASTLE

Tel: 01962 854766

College Street, Wolvesey, Winchester, Hampshire SO23 8NB

Owner: English Heritage   **Contact:** The Custodian

The fortified palace of Wolvesey was the chief residence of the Bishops of Winchester and one of the greatest of all medieval buildings in England. Its extensive ruins still reflect the importance and immense wealth of the Bishops of Winchester, occupants of the richest seat in medieval England. Wolvesey was frequently visited by medieval and Tudor monarchs and was the scene of the wedding feast of Philip of Spain and Mary Tudor in 1554.

Location: OS Ref. SU484 291. 3/4 m SE of Winchester Cathedral, next to the Bishop's Palace; access from College Street.

Opening Times: 1 Apr - 30 Sept: 10am - 6pm. 1 - 31 Oct: 10am - 5pm.

Admission: Adult £1.90, Child £1, Conc. £1.40.

Grounds suitable. In grounds, on leads.

South East England

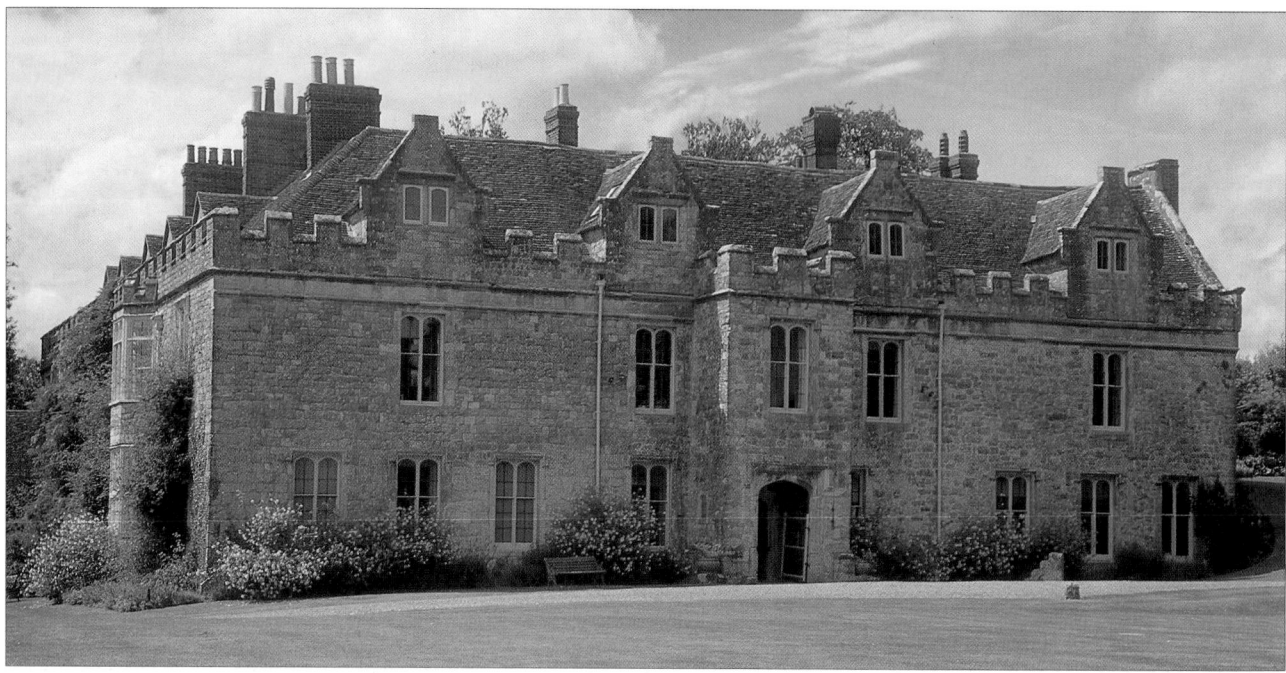

BOUGHTON MONCHELSEA PLACE
Nr Maidstone

BOUGHTON MONCHELSEA PLACE is a battlemented manor house dating from the 16th century, set in its own country estate just outside Maidstone, within easy reach of London and the channel ports. This Grade I listed building has always been privately owned and is still lived in as a family home.

From the lawns surrounding the property there are spectacular views over unspoilt Kent countryside, with the historic deer park in the foreground. These views are shared by the 20 acre activity site set back a little way from the house. A wicket gate leads from the grounds to the medieval church of St Peter, with its rose garden and ancient lych gate. At the rear of the house are to be found a pretty courtyard and walled gardens, together with an extensive range of Tudor barns and outbuildings. Inside the house, rooms vary in character from Tudor through to Georgian Gothic; worthy of note are the fine Jacobean staircase and sundry examples of heraldic stained glass. Furnishings and paintings are mainly Victorian, with a few earlier pieces; the atmosphere is friendly and welcoming throughout.

The premises are licensed for Civil marriage ceremonies, although wedding receptions may only be held on weekdays. In addition we welcome conferences, group visits, location work and all types of corporate, private and public functions, but please note times of availability. Use outside these hours is sometimes possible, subject to negotiation. All clients are guaranteed exclusive use of this prestigious venue.

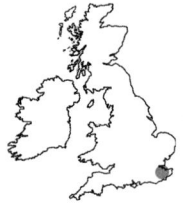

Owner:
Mr & Mrs D Kendrick

CONTACT

Mrs M Kendrick
Boughton Monchelsea Place
Boughton Monchelsea
Nr Maidstone
Kent
ME17 4BU

Tel: 01622 743120

Fax: 01622 741168

e-mail:
mk@boughtonmonchelsea
place.co.uk

LOCATION

OS Ref. TQ772 499

On B2163, 5$^{1}/_{2}$ m from M20/J8 or 4$^{1}/_{2}$ m from Maidstone via A229.

OPENING TIMES

By prior arrangement only.

House & Garden

Not open to individual visitors.

Private functions:
Mon - Fri, 9am - 8pm.

Group visits/ house tours:
(15-50 pax), Mon - Thur,
9am - 4pm.

Activity Site

365 days a year:
8am - 11.30pm.

ADMISSION

Gardens & Guided House Tour
   Adult £4.50

Gardens only
   Adult £2.75

Venue Hire
   Prices on application.

 By arrangement.

 By arrangement.

 By arrangement.

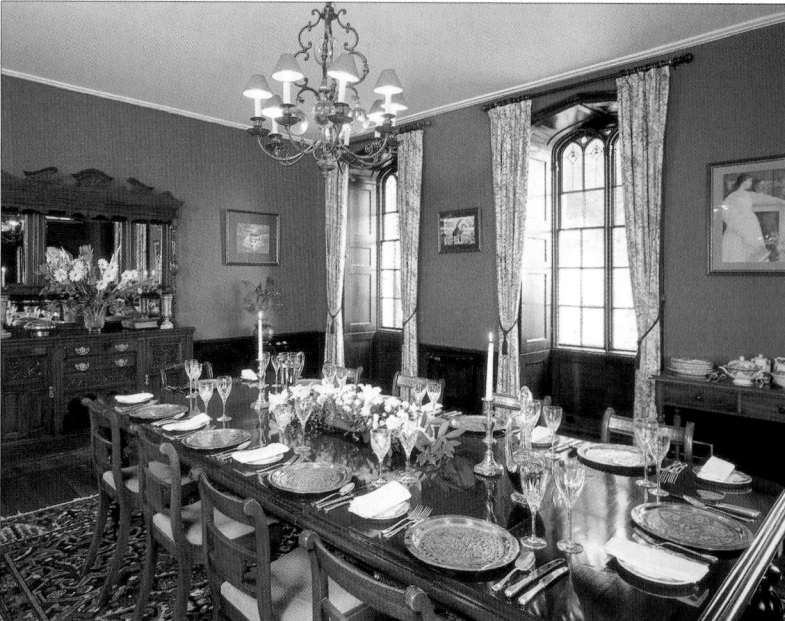

CONFERENCE/FUNCTION		
ROOM	SIZE	MAX CAPACITY
Entrance Hall	25' x 19'	50 Theatre
Dining Room	31' x 19'	50 Dining
Drawing Room	28' x 19'	40 Reception
Courtyard Room	37' x 13'	70 Theatre

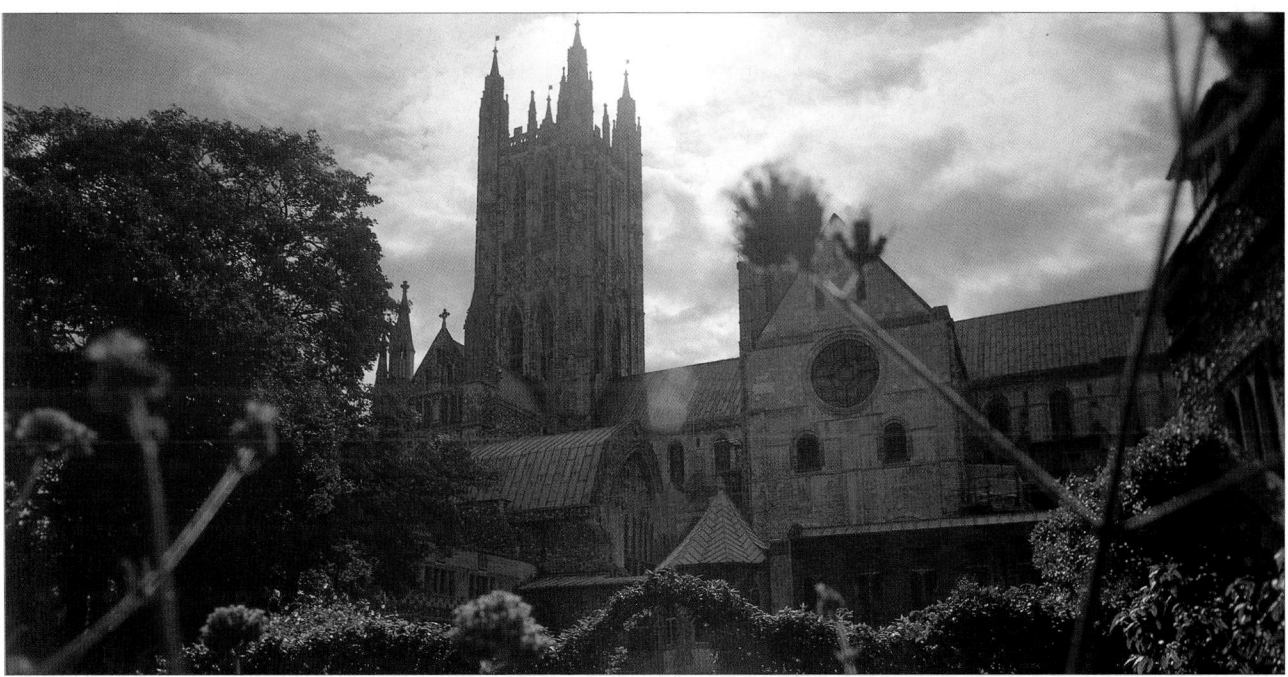

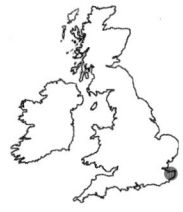

CANTERBURY CATHEDRAL
Canterbury

Canterbury Cathedral has a tradition of visitor welcome that reaches back to the days of medieval pilgrimages. A warm welcome is extended to all visitors and it is hoped that they will enjoy sharing the experience of one of the great holy places of Christendom.

St Augustine, sent by Pope Gregory the Great, arrived in 597 AD and became the first Archbishop, establishing his seat (or 'Cathedra') in Canterbury. In 1170 Archbishop Thomas Becket was murdered in the Cathedral and ever since, the Cathedral has attracted thousands of pilgrims.

The Cathedral is noteworthy for its medieval tombs of royal personages, such as King Henry IV and Edward the Black Prince, as well as numerous archbishops. To the later Middle Ages belong the great 14th century Nave and the famous central 'Bell Harry Tower'. The Quire dates back to the 12th century and the Crypt, the largest of its kind in the country, to the 11th century.

The Cathedral stands in spacious precincts amid the remains of the monastery – cloister, chapter house, and Norman water tower which have survived intact, from the Dissolution in the time of King Henry VIII to the present day.

Thomas Becket's shrine was destroyed by the Tudor King, but the site of that tomb is in the Trinity Chapel, near the High Altar. The saint is said to have worked miracles, and the Cathedral contains some rare stained glass depicting those events.

CONTACT

Visits Office
Canterbury Cathedral
The Precincts
Canterbury
CT1 2EH

Tel: 01227 762862

Fax: 01227 865222/865250

e-mail: visits@
canterbury-cathedral.org

LOCATION

OS Ref. TR151 579

Canterbury city centre.
M2/M20, then A2.

Bus: Victoria Station coach
– regular service.

Rail: London
Victoria/Dover Priory to
Canterbury East, London
Charing Cross to
Canterbury West.

Sightseeing Tours: Tour
operators operate a daily
service with collection from
most London hotels. Ask
your hotel concierge or
porter for information.

CONFERENCE/FUNCTION		
ROOM	SIZE	MAX CAPACITY
Clagett Auditorium	10.5 x 15m	250
'The Barn'	14 x 5m	92
Lecture Theatre (x2)	7 x 7m	60
Seminar rms	vary	12 - 50

OPENING TIMES

Summer
Mon - Sat, 9am - 7pm.

Winter
Mon - Sat, 9am - 5pm.

Crypt (all year):
10am - 7pm (5pm in winter)
Sundays (all year):
12.30 - 2.30pm,
4.30 - 5.30pm.

Restrictions during services
or special events.
Arrangements may vary
at short notice, always
check opening times
before visiting.

Main Services
Evensong:
Mon - Fri, 5.30pm
Sats & Suns, 3.15pm.

Eucharist:
Suns, 11am.

ADMISSION

Adult	£3.00
Conc.	£2.00
Pre-booked school groups	£1.50

(2000 prices)

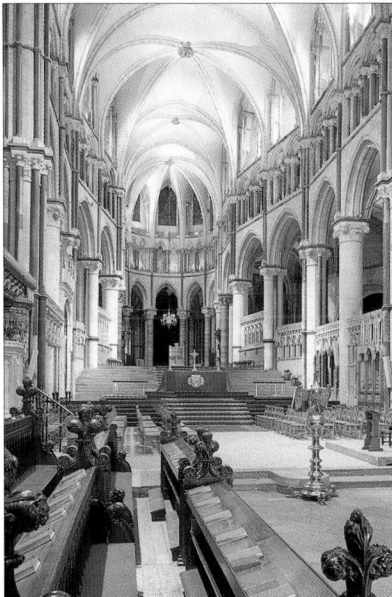

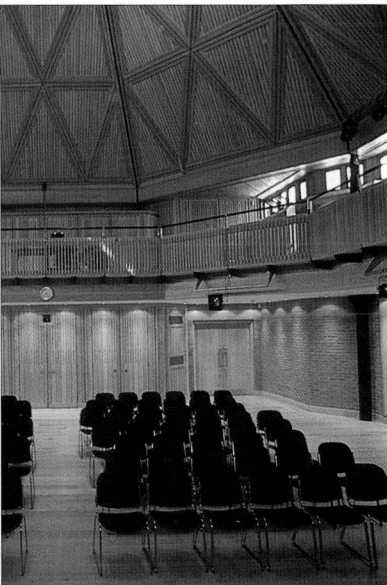

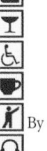

By arrangement.

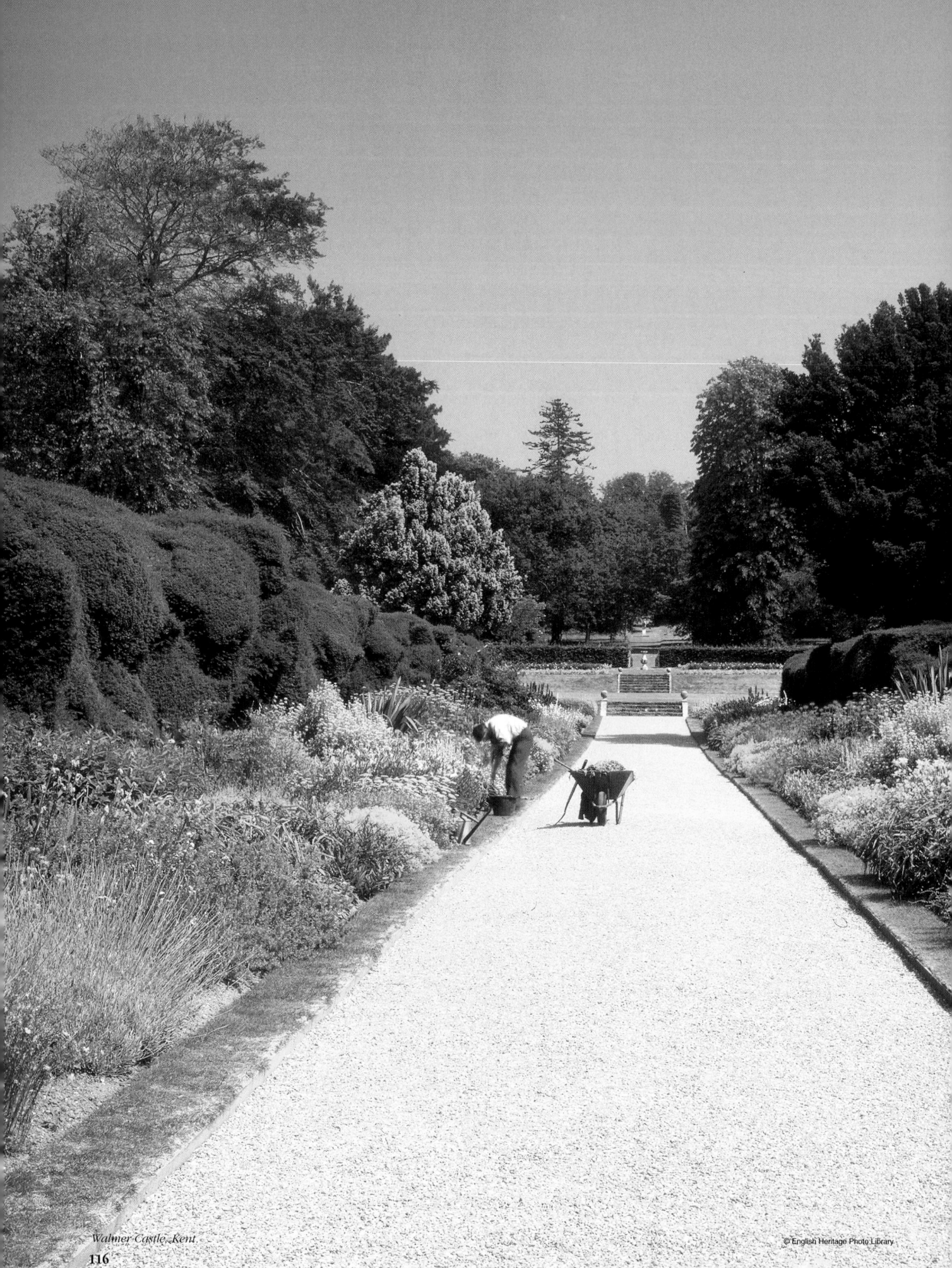

Walmer Castle, Kent.

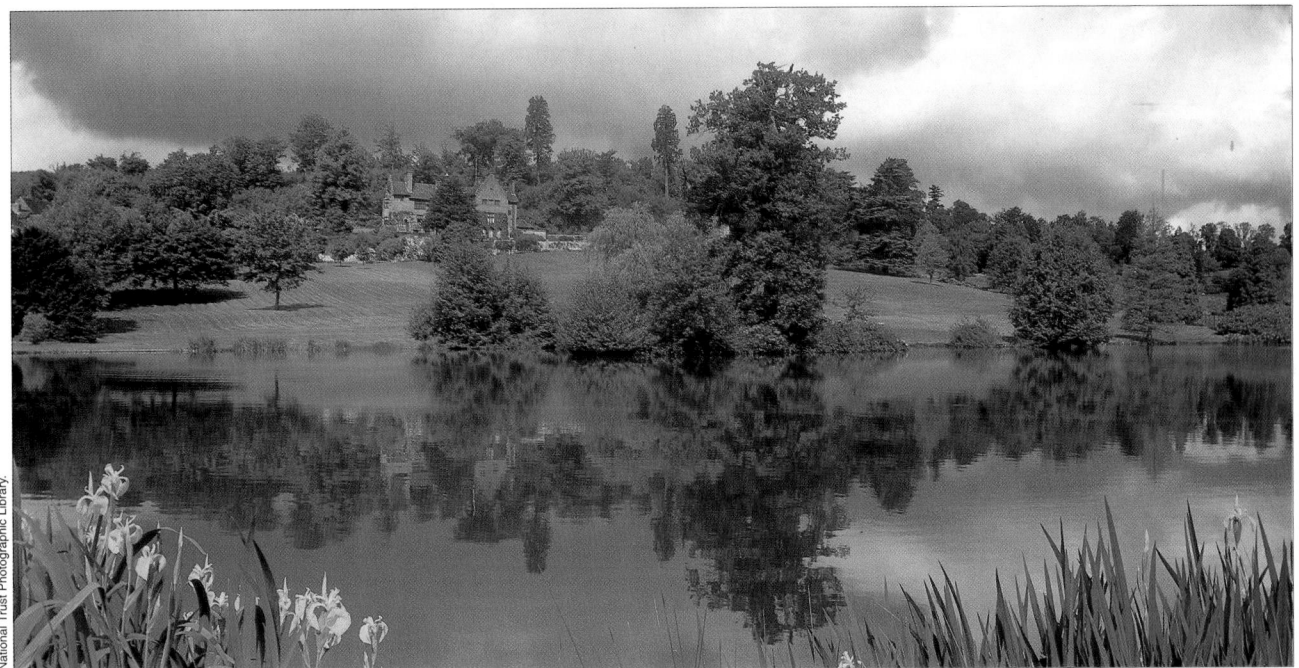

National Trust Photographic Library.

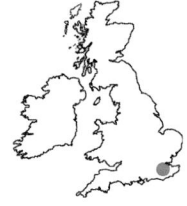

Owner: The National Trust

CONTACT

The Property Manager
Chartwell
Westerham
Kent
TN16 1PS

Tel: 01732 866368
01732 868381

Fax: 01732 868193

e-mail: kchxxx@
smtp.ntrust.org.uk

LOCATION

OS Ref. TQ455 515

2m S of Westerham,
forking left off B2026.

Bus: Chartwell Explorer
'green transport' bus link
with Sevenoaks &
Westerham. For more
information contact:
01732 866368

CHARTWELL
Westerham

The family home of Sir Winston Churchill from 1924 until the end of his life. He said of Chartwell, simply *'I love the place - a day away from Chartwell is a day wasted'*. With magnificent views over the Weald of Kent it is not difficult to see why.

The rooms are left as they were in Sir Winston & Lady Churchill's lifetime with daily papers, fresh flowers grown from the garden and his famous cigars. Photographs and books evoke his career and interests, as well as happy family life. Museum and exhibition rooms contain displays and sound recordings, superb collections of memorabilia from his political career, including uniforms and a 'siren-suit'.

The garden studio contains Sir Winston's easel and paintbox, as well as many of his paintings. Terraced and water gardens descend to the lake, the gardens also include a golden rose walk, planted by Sir Winston and Lady Churchill's children on the occasion of their golden wedding anniversary, and the Marlborough Pavilion decorated with frescoes depicting the battle of Blenheim. Visitors can see the garden walls that Churchill built with his own hands, the pond stocked with the golden orfe he loved.

The Mulberry Room and/or Cabinet Room at the restaurant can be booked for meetings, conferences, lunches and dinners. Please telephone for details.

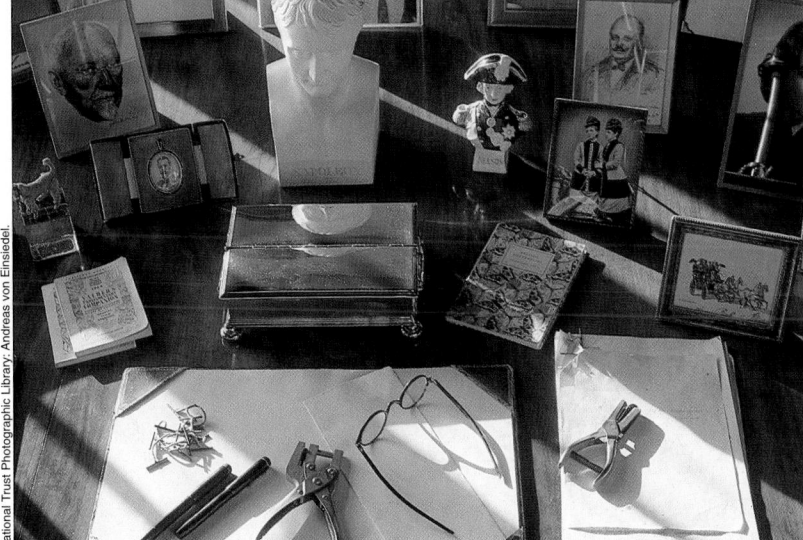

National Trust Photographic Library; Andreas von Einsiedel.

OPENING TIMES

31 March - 4 November
Wed - Sun & BH Mons
11am - 5pm.

July & August only
Tue - Sun & BH Mon
11am - 5pm.

Last admission 4.15pm.

ADMISSION

Adult £5.60
Child......................£2.80
Family £14.00

SPECIAL EVENTS

• **AUG 18**
Opera Brava presents 'An evening of Gilbert & Sullivan'.

• **AUG 19**
Opera Brava presents 'Tosca'.

Conference facilities. Partially suitable. WC. Please telephone before visit. Licensed. By arrangement. P In grounds, on leads.

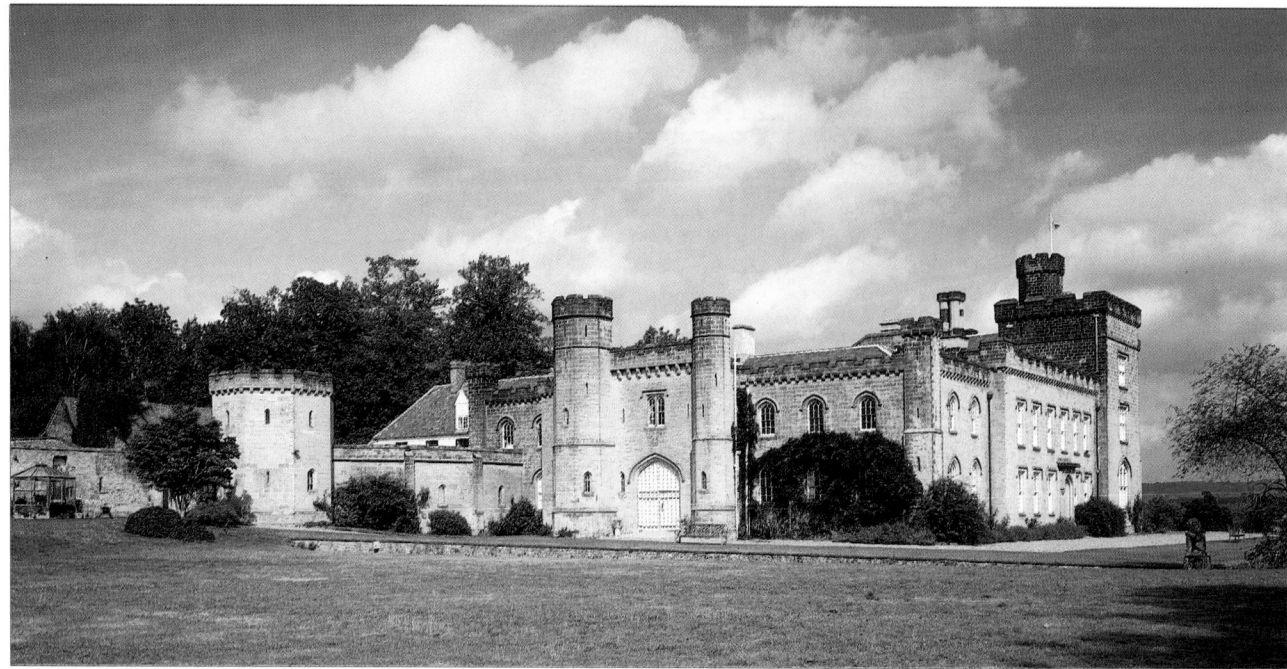

CHIDDINGSTONE CASTLE
Edenbridge

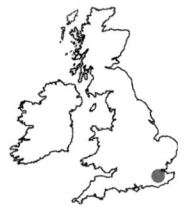

Owner: Denys Eyre Bower
Bequest Reg. Charity Trust

CONTACT

Mrs R Vernon
Chiddingstone Castle
Edenbridge
Kent
TN8 7AD

Tel: 01892 870347

LOCATION

OS Ref. TQ497 452

B2027, turn to
Chiddingstone at Bough
Beech, 1m further on
to crossroads, then
straight to castle.

10m from Tonbridge,
Tunbridge Wells and
Sevenoaks.
4m Edenbridge.
Accessible from A21
and M25/J5.
London 35m.

Bus: Enquiries: Tunbridge
Wells TIC 01892 515675.

Rail: Tonbridge,
Tunbridge Wells,
Edenbridge then taxi.
Penshurst then 2m walk.

Air: Gatwick 15m.

CHIDDINGSTONE CASTLE has never seen battle. Even the Civil War left it unscathed, though the village was Royalist amid Parliamentary territory. Tudor in origin, it was twice fundamentally altered by the Streatfeilds, whose family seat it was. But they never entirely erased its ancient foundation.

The final remodelling, c1805, was by William Atkinson, Master of the Picturesque, an effect, he commented, difficult to achieve intentionally, being generally due to accidents of time - in which Chiddingstone abounds. The romantic result aroused the contempt of the architectural establishment. It was saved from dereliction by the fierce championship of

Denys Bower, wayward connoisseur and collector, who in 1955 defied the trend and bought it as his home. When he died in 1977 he left it to the Nation, so that, as his Will said, 'future generations may enjoy it as I do now'.

It is now lovingly administered by a charitable trust, a fascinating place with contents to enthrall everyone. Superb Japanese lacquer and swords, Egyptian antiquities, Royal Stuart history, furnishings and pictures. The grounds, one of the listed gardens of Kent, are being developed as a haven for wildlife. An afternoon is all too short to explore this tranquil corner of a vanishing England.

Great Hall

OPENING TIMES

SUMMER
Easter Hol, Spring BH.

June - September
Wed - Fri & Sun
Weekdays: 2 - 5.30pm
Sun & BHs
11.30am - 5.30pm
Last admission 5pm.

WINTER
Open only for specially
booked groups (20+).

ADMISSION

Adult............................£4.00
  Child*......................£2.00

Groups** (pre-booked 20+)
  Adult.....................£3.50
  Child*....................£2.00

Fishing...........£8.00 per day
Onlooker....................£3.50
(1 onlooker per fisherman,
no children.)

* Child under 16yrs
  accompanied by adult.
  Under 5 yrs Free.

** Usual hours, other times by
  appointment. School groups
  only by appointment.

Chiddingstone may be
closed without notice for
Special Events.

CONFERENCE/FUNCTION		
ROOM	SIZE	MAX CAPACITY
Assembly Rm	14' x 35'	50
Seminar Rms	15' x 15'	
Stable Block	36' x 29'	

Conferences, receptions, concerts.
No photography in house, no smoking, no prams.

Available for special events. Wedding receptions

Partially suitable. WC.

Licensed. By arrangement.

By arrangement.

Ample hardcore parking. Coaches, please book.

Teachers' pack. Educational programme.

In grounds, on leads.

CHIDDINGSTONE CASTLE

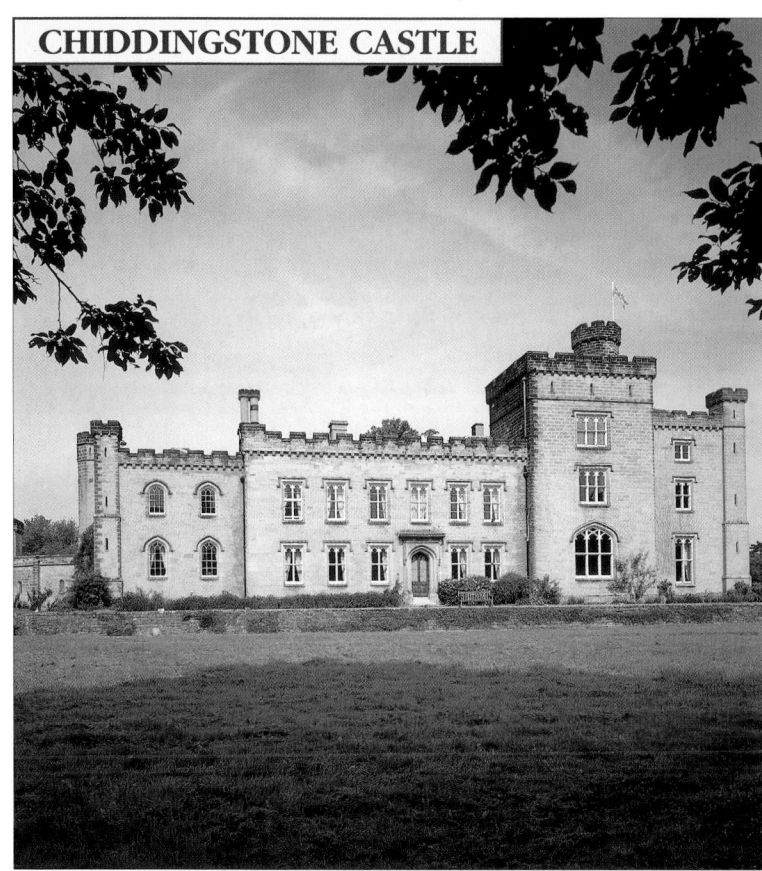

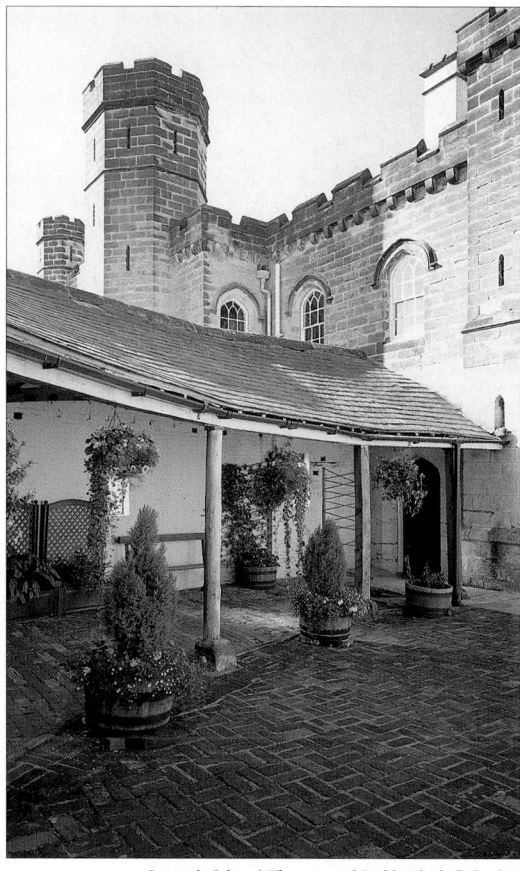

*Grounds (above), The restored Stable Block (below) &
The Assembly Room, Conference Centre (bottom right).*

SMALL CONFERENCES AND FUNCTIONS: the old domestic quarters, grouped around the courtyard, have been converted into a unique and elegant centre for various events. The self-contained Goodhugh Wing offers Assembly Room (capacity 50), three seminar rooms, and tea-kitchen. Meals can be provided in the refectory by our approved caterers. Additional lecture/meeting accommodation in the adjoining stable block, recently restored.

CIVIL MARRIAGES: The Great Hall is licensed by Kent County Council, and is specially attractive to those who desire the dignity of a church ceremony without the religious aspect. We offer all features of wedding celebrations, including reception of guests and refreshments.

EDUCATION: We welcome visits from schools who wish to use the collections in connection with classroom work. No anxiety for the teachers (admitted free). The children are safe here, can picnic and play in the grounds. We may have some exciting developments with adult education in the restored stable block. Please enquire.

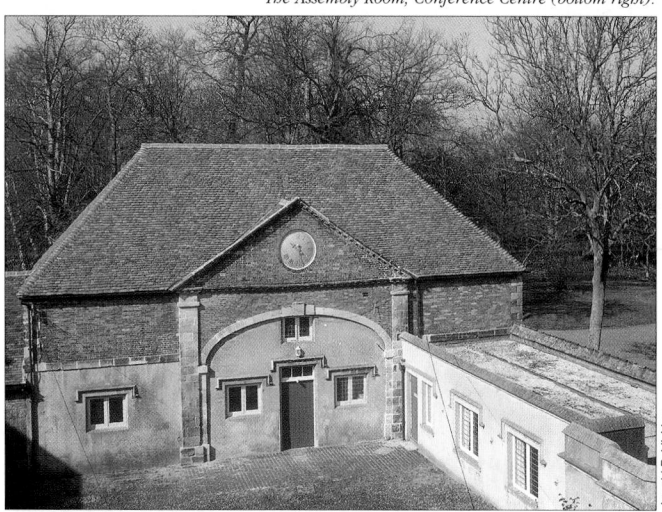

Jarrold Publishing.

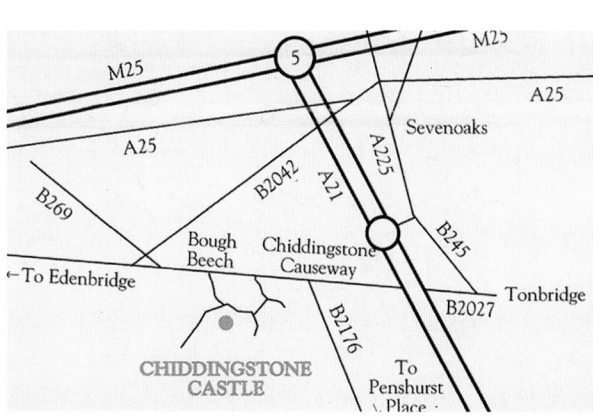

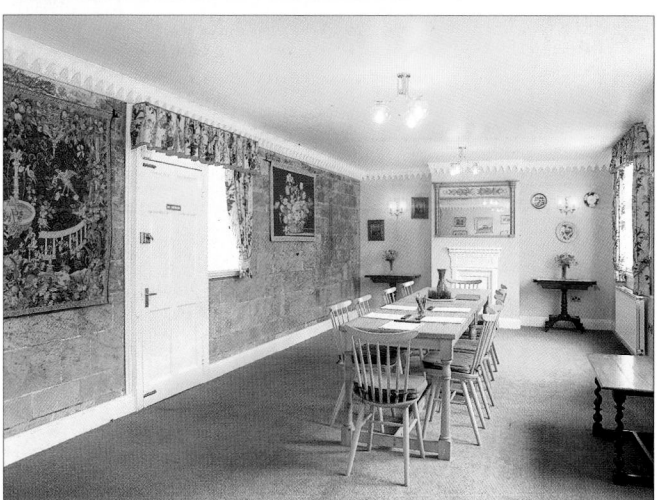

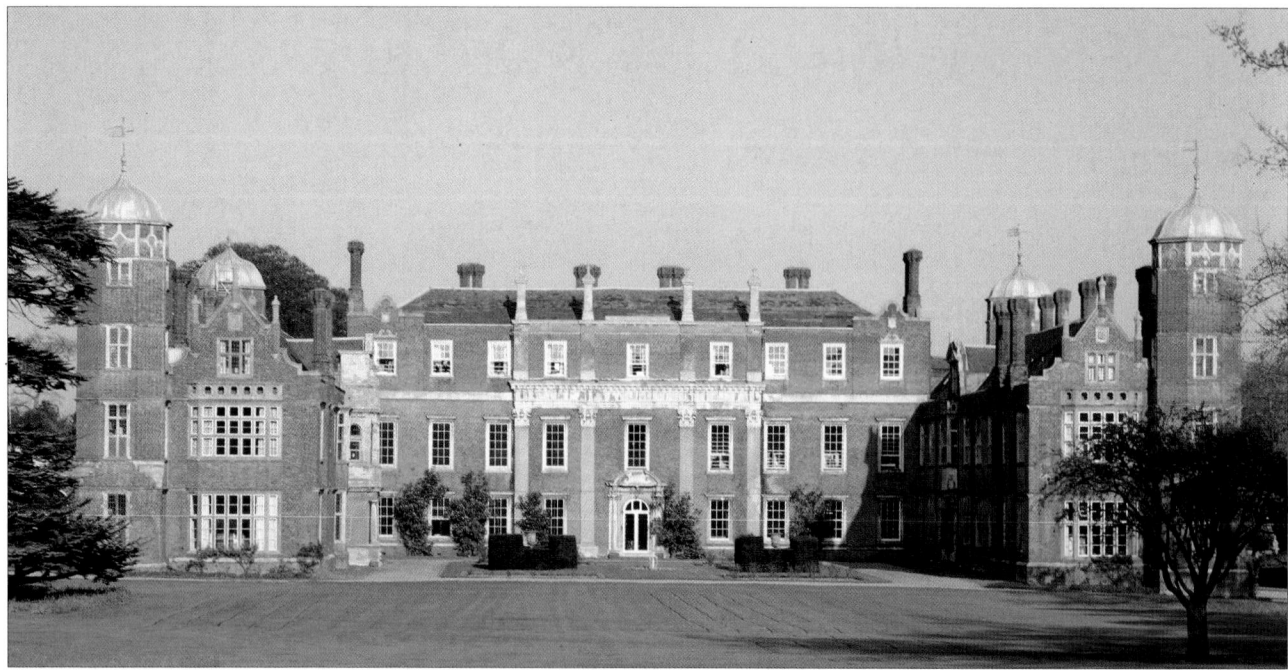

COBHAM HALL
Cobham

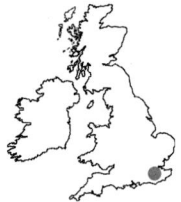

Owner: Cobham Hall Heritage Trust

CONTACT

Mr N Powell
Bursar
Cobham Hall, Cobham
Kent DA12 3BL

Tel: 01474 823371

Fax: 01474 825906
or 01474 825904

e-mail: cobhamhall@aol.com

LOCATION

OS Ref. TQ683 689

Situated adjacent to the A2/M2. ¹/₂ m S of A2 4m W of Strood. 8m E of M25/J2 between Gravesend & Rochester.

London 25m
Rochester 5m
Canterbury 30m

Rail: Meopham 3m
Gravesend 5m
Taxis at both stations.

Air: Gatwick 45 mins.
Heathrow 60 mins,
Stansted 50 mins.

CONFERENCE/FUNCTION		
ROOM	SIZE	MAX CAPACITY
Gilt Hall	41' x 34'	180
Wyatt Dining Rm	49' x 23'	135
Clifton Dining Rm	24' x 23'	75
Activities Centre	119' x 106'	300

'One of the largest, finest and most important houses in Kent', Cobham Hall is an outstandingly beautiful, red brick mansion in Elizabethan, Jacobean, Carolean and 18th century styles.

It yields much of interest to the student of art, architecture and history. The Elizabethan wings were begun in 1584 whilst the central section contains the Gilt Hall, wonderfully decorated by John Webb, Inigo Jones' most celebrated pupil, 1654. Further rooms were decorated by James Wyatt in the 18th century.

Cobham Hall, now a girls' school, has been visited by several of the English monarchs from Elizabeth I to Edward VIII, later Duke of Windsor. Charles Dickens used to walk through the grounds from his house in Higham to the Leather Bottle pub in Cobham Village. In 1883, the Hon Ivo Bligh, later the 8th Earl of Darnley, led the victorious English cricket team against Australia bringing home the 'Ashes' to Cobham.

GARDENS

The gardens, landscaped for the 4th Earl by Humphry Repton, are gradually being restored by the Cobham Hall Heritage Trust. Extensive tree planting and clearing have taken place since the hurricanes of the 1980s. The Gothic Dairy and some of the classical garden buildings are being renovated. The gardens are particularly delightful in Spring, when they are resplendent with daffodils and a myriad of rare bulbs.

❖

ℹ️ Conferences, business or social functions, 150 acres of parkland for sports, corporate events, open air concerts, sports centre, indoor swimming pool, art studios, music wing, tennis courts, helicopter landing area. Filming and photography. No smoking.

🍴 In-house catering team for private, corporate hospitality and wedding receptions. (cap. 200).

♿ House tour involves 2 staircases, ground floor access for w/chairs.

☕ Afternoon teas, other meals by arrangement.

🚶 Obligatory guided tours; tour time 1¹/₂ hrs. Garden tours arranged outside standard opening times.

🅿️ Ample. Pre-booked coach groups are welcome any time.

👥 Guide provided, Adult £3.50, Child / OAP £2.50.

🐕 In grounds, on leads.

🛏️ 18 single and 18 double with bathroom. 22 single and 22 double without bathroom. Dormitory. Groups only.

🔔

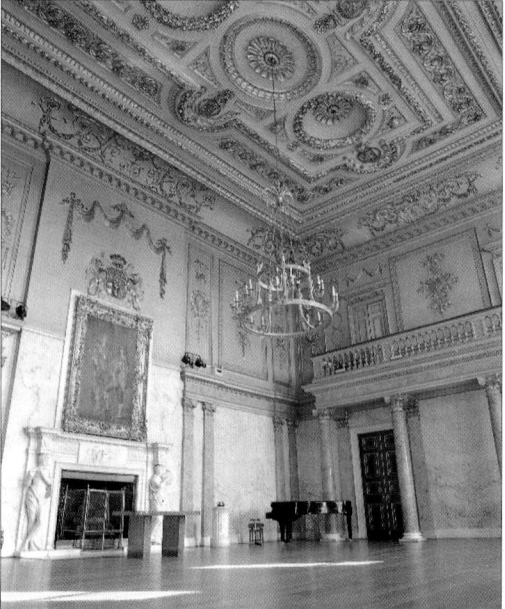

OPENING TIMES

SUMMER

March:
25, 28.

April:
1, 4, 8, 11, 13 - 16, 18.

July:
11, 15, 18, 22, 25, 29.

August:
1, 5, 8, 12, 15, 19, 22, 26, 27, 29.

October:
20, 21.

ADMISSION

Adult £3.50
Child (4-14yrs.) £2.75
OAP £2.75

Gardens & Parkland

Self-guided tour
and booklet £1.50

Historical/Conservation tour of Grounds (by arrangement)

Per person £3.50

SPECIAL EVENTS

• **MAR 25:**
National Gardens Scheme.

• **APR 13 - 16**
Medway Craft Show.

• **JUL 15:**
National Gardens Scheme.

• **OCT 20 - 21:**
Medway Craft Fair.

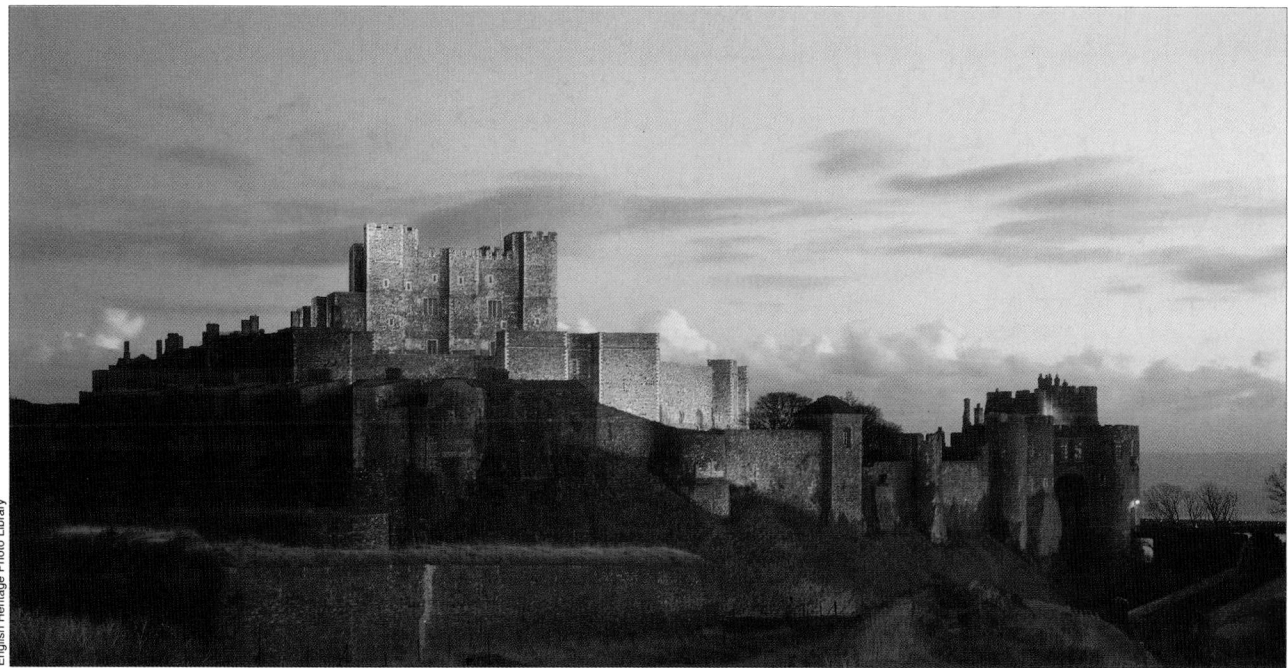

English Heritage Photo Library

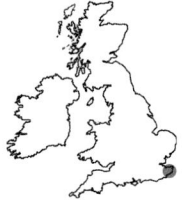

Owner: English Heritage

CONTACT

Mr K Scott
Dover Castle
Dover
Kent
CT16 1HU

Tel: 01304 211067

Info Line: 01304 201628

LOCATION

OS Ref. TR326 416

Easy access from A2 and M20. Well signed from Dover centre and east side of Dover. 2 hrs from central London.

Rail: London Charing Cross or Victoria 1^1/$_2$ hrs.

Bus: Freephone 0800 696996.

DOVER CASTLE & THE SECRET WARTIME TUNNELS
Dover

Journey deep into the White Cliffs of Dover and discover the top secret World War II tunnels. Through sight, sound and smells relive the wartime drama of the underground hospital as a wounded Battle of Britain pilot is taken to the operating theatre in a bid to save his life. Discover how life would have been during the planning days of the Dunkirk evacuation and Operation Dynamo as you are led around the network of tunnels and casements housing the communications centre.

Above ground you can explore the magnificent mediaeval keep and inner bailey of King Henry II. Visit the evocative Princess of Wales' Royal Regiment Museum. There is also the Roman Lighthouse and Anglo-Saxon church to see or take an audio tour of the intriguing 13th century underground fortifications and medieval battlements. Enjoy magnificent views of the White Cliffs from Admiralty lookout.

See the exciting 'Life Under Siege' exhibition, and discover, through a dramatic light and sound presentation, how it must have felt to be a garrison soldier defending Dover Castle against the French King in 1216. In the Keep, see a reconstruction of the Castle in preparation for a visit from Henry VIII and visit the hands-on exhibition explaining the travelling Tudor court. The land train will help you around this huge site.

Throughout the summer there are many fun events taking place, bringing the Castle alive through colourful enactments and living history.

❖

Two.

Functions catered for including themed evenings within the Keep. For private functions tel: 01304 205830.

Lift for access to tunnels. Courtyard and grounds, some very steep slopes.

2 restaurants, hot and cold food and drinks.

Tour of tunnels approx. every 20 mins, more at peak times when a 30 min. wait can occur.

Ample. Groups welcome, discounts available. Free entry for drivers. One extra place for each additional group of 20.

Free visits available for schools. Education centre. Pre-booking essential.

❄

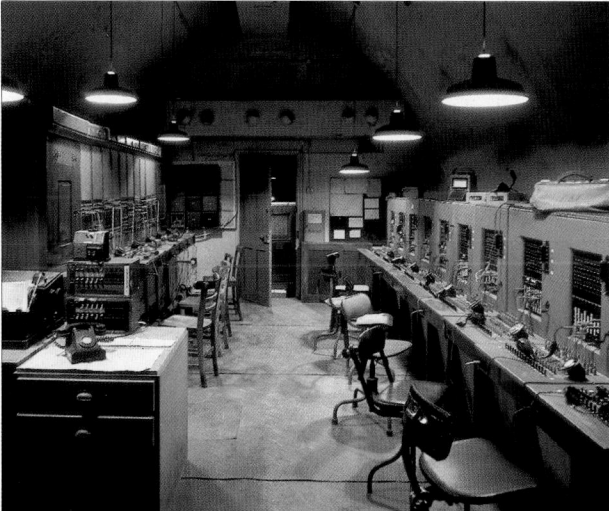

English Heritage Photo Library

OPENING TIMES

SUMMER
1 Apr - 30 Sept
Daily: 10am - 6pm.

1 - 31 Oct:
Daily: 10am - 5pm.

WINTER
1 November - 31 March
Daily: 10am - 4pm.

Closed 24 - 26 Dec & 1 Jan.

ADMISSION

Adult £7.00
Child......................£3.50
OAP......................£5.20
Family (2+3) £17.50

Groups
15% discount for groups (11+).

SPECIAL EVENTS

Please telephone for details.

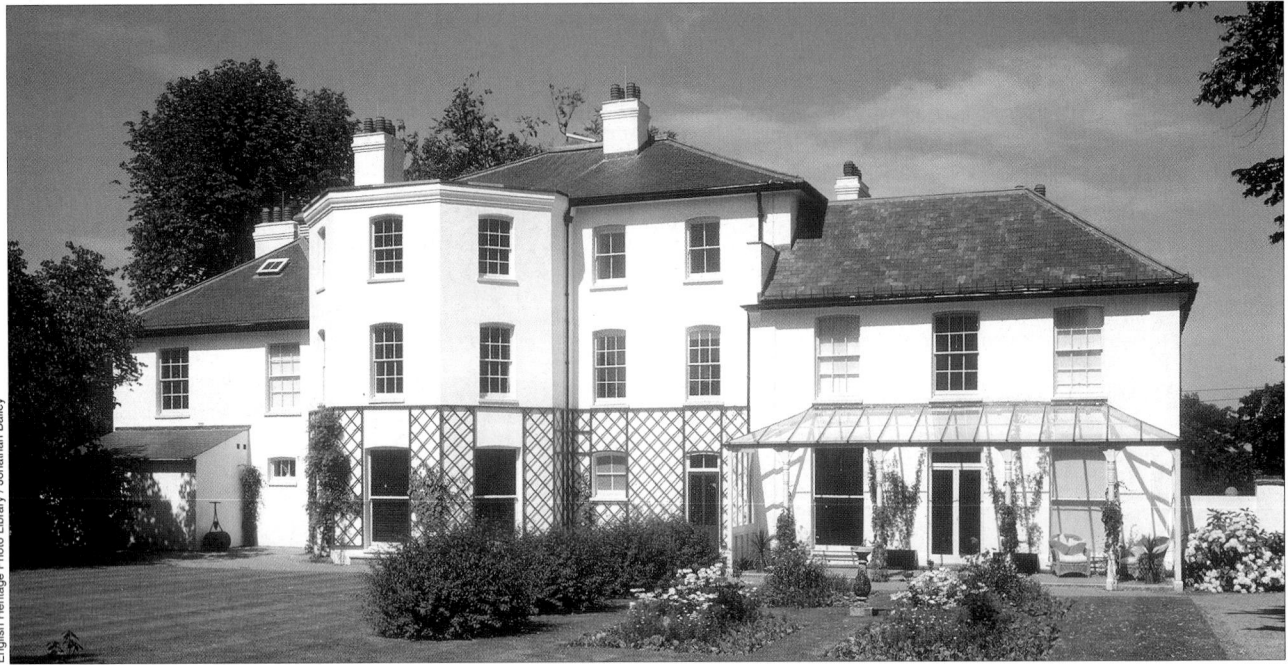

English Heritage Photo Library / Jonathan Bailey

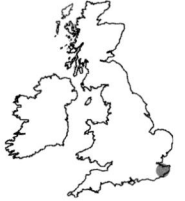

Owner: English Heritage

CONTACT

The House Manager
Down House
Luxted Road
Downe
Kent
BR6 7JT

Tel: 01689 859119

LOCATION

OS Ref, TQ431 611

In Luxted Road, Downe, off A21 near Biggin Hill.

Rail: From London Victoria or Charing Cross.

Bus: Orpington (& Bus R2) or Bromley South (& Bus 146). Buses R2 & 146 do not run on Sunday.

DOWN HOUSE
Downe

A visit to Down House is a fascinating journey of discovery for all the family. This was the family home of Charles Darwin for over 40 years and now you can explore it to the full.

See the actual armchair in which Darwin wrote 'On the Origin of Species', which shocked and then revolutionised the way we think about the origins of mankind. His study is much the same as it was in his lifetime and is filled with belongings that give you an intimate glimpse into both his studies and everyday life.

At Down House you will discover both sides of Darwin - the great thinker and the family man.

Explore the family rooms where the furnishings have been painstakingly restored. An audio tour narrated by Sir David Attenborough will bring the house to life and increase your understanding of Darwin's revolutionary theory. Upstairs you will find state-of-the-art interpretation of the scientific significance of the house - especially designed to inspire a younger audience.

Outside, take the Sandwalk which he paced daily in search of inspiration, then stroll in lovely gardens. Complete your day by sampling the delicious selection of home-made cakes in the tea room.

OPENING TIMES

10 Apr - 31 Oct:
Wed - Sun, 10am - 6pm.

1 Nov - 23 Dec:
Wed - Sun, 10am - 4pm.

7 Feb - 31 Mar:
Wed - Sun, 10am - 4pm.

Closed 24 Dec - 6 Feb 2001.

On BHs and throughout August visits to Down House must be booked in advance. It is not necessary to book if you travel by public transport.

ADMISSION

Timed ticketing: available on day or pre-booked on 01689 859119.

Adult £5.50
Child........................£2.80
Conc.......................£4.10

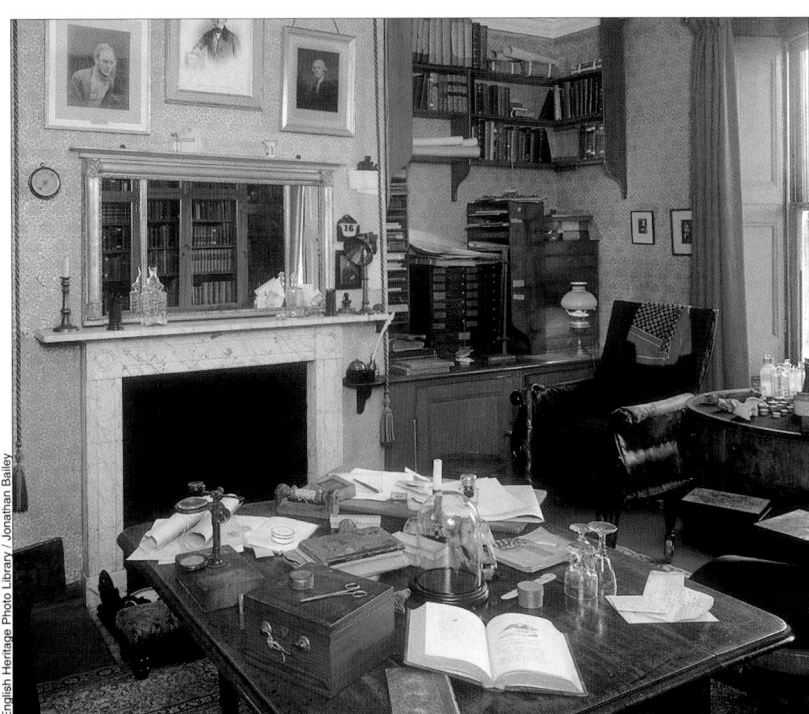

English Heritage Photo Library / Jonathan Bailey

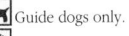

Inclusive.

Limited for coaches.

Guide dogs only.

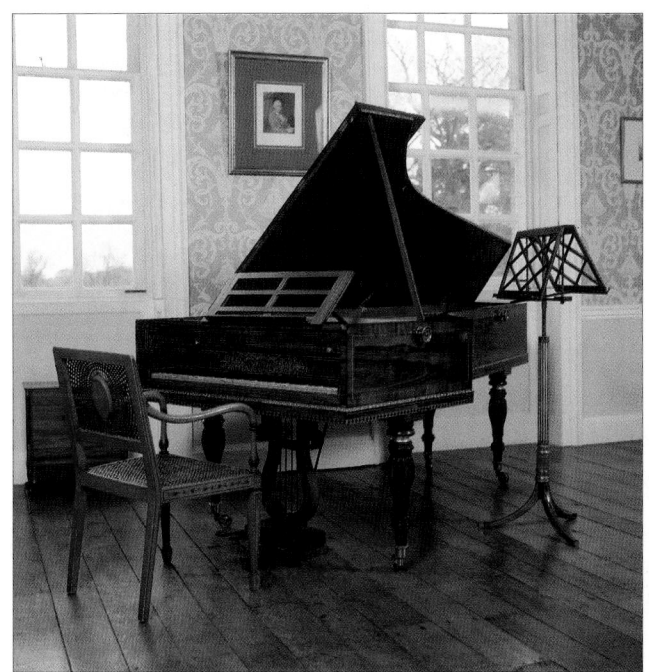

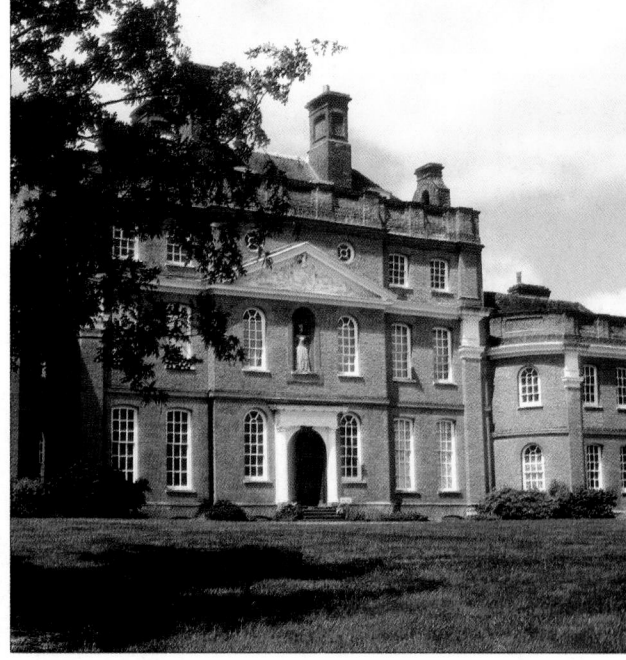

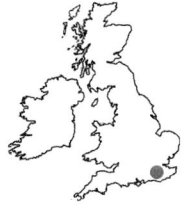

Owner:
Mr Richard Burnett

CONTACT

Mrs Katrina Burnett
Finchcocks
Goudhurst
Kent
TN17 1HH

Tel: 01580 211702

Fax: 01580 211007

e-mail: katrina@
finchcocks.co.uk

LOCATION

OS Ref. TQ700 365

1m S of A262, 2m W of
village of Goudhurst.
5m from Cranbrook, 10m
from Tunbridge Wells,
45m from London
(1¹/₂ hrs)

Rail: Marden 6m
(no taxi), Paddock
Wood 8m (taxi),
Tunbridge Wells
10m (taxi).

Air: Gatwick 1 hr.

FINCHCOCKS
Goudhurst

In 1970 Finchcocks was acquired by Richard Burnett, leading exponent of the early piano, and it now contains his magnificent collection of some eighty historical keyboard instruments: chamber organs, harpsichords, virginals, spinets and early pianos. About half of these are restored to full concert condition and are played whenever the house is open to the public. The house, with its high ceilings and oak panelling, provides the perfect setting for music performed on period instruments, and Finchcocks is now a music centre of international repute. Many musical events take place here.

There is also a fascinating collection of pictures and prints, mainly on musical themes, and there is a special exhibition on display on the theme of the 18th century pleasure gardens, such as Vauxhall and Ranelagh, which includes costumes and tableaux.

Finchcocks is a fine Georgian baroque manor noted for its outstanding brickwork, with a dramatic front elevation attributed to Thomas Archer. Named after the family who lived on the site in the 13th century, the present house was built in 1725 for barrister Edward Bathurst, kinsman to Earl Bathurst. Despite having changed hands many times, it has undergone remarkably little alteration and retains most of its original features. The beautiful grounds, with their extensive views over parkland and hop gardens, include the newly restored walled garden, which provides a dramatic setting for special events.

Music events, conferences, seminars, promotions, archery, ballooning, filming, television. Keyboard instruments and musical furniture for hire, marquees erected for large functions. No videos in house, photography by permission only.

Private and corporate entertaining, weddings. Full catering by arrangement. Fully licensed.

Limited. WC. Suitable for visually handicapped.

Licensed. Teas and light refreshments. Picnics permitted in grounds.

Musical tours / recitals on instruments whenever required. Tour time: 2¹/₂ - 4 hrs.

Ample. Pre-booked groups (25 - 100) welcome from Apr - Oct. Free meals for couriers and drivers.

Opportunity to play instruments. Can be linked to special projects and National Curriculum syllabus.

Music a speciality, and musicians can be provided.

OPENING TIMES

SUMMER

Easter Sun - end Sept
Sun & BH Mons, plus Wed
& Thur in August, 2 - 6pm.

Pre-booked groups and individuals welcome most days April to October mornings, afternoons and evenings and in some circumstances up to Christmas.

WINTER

Closed
January - mid-March
Available for private functions October, November & December.

ADMISSION

Open Days
House, Garden & Music
Adult £7.00
Child £4.00
Student...................£5.00

Garden Only
Adult £2.50
Child £0.50

Groups*
Adult £7.00
Child £4.00
Student...................£5.00

* Min. of 25 to open house.

SPECIAL EVENTS

- **MAY 27/28:**
  Spring Garden Fair & Flower Festival

- **AUG 26/27:**
  Jane Austen Gala

- **SEPT WEEKENDS:**
  Music Festival

- **OCT 12 - 14:**
  Autumn Fair

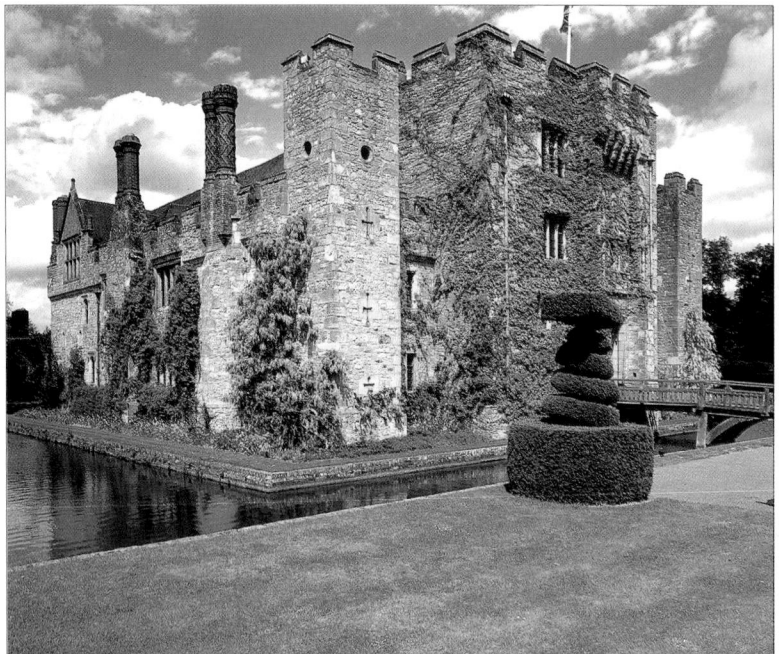

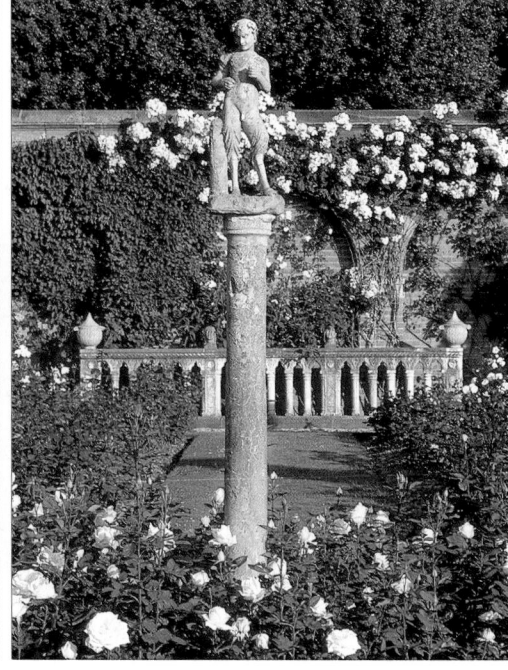

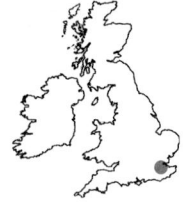

HEVER CASTLE
Edenbridge

HEVER CASTLE dates back to 1270, when the gatehouse, outer walls and the inner moat were first built. 200 years later the Bullen (or Boleyn) family added the comfortable Tudor manor house constructed within the walls. This was the childhood home of Anne Boleyn, Henry VIII's second wife and mother of Elizabeth I. There are many items relating to the Tudors, including two books of hours (prayer books) signed and inscribed by Anne Boleyn. The Castle was later given to Henry VIII's fourth wife, Anne of Cleves.

In 1903, the estate was bought by the American millionaire William Waldorf Astor, who became a British subject and the first Lord Astor of Hever. He invested an immense amount of time, money and imagination in restoring the castle and grounds. Master craftsmen were employed and the castle was filled with a magnificent collection of furniture, tapestries and other works of art. 'From Castles to Country Houses' the Miniature Model Houses exhibition, a collection of $1/12$ scale model houses, room views and gardens, depicts life in English Country Houses.

GARDENS

Between 1904-8 over 30 acres of formal gardens were laid out and planted, these have now matured into one of the most beautiful gardens in England. The unique Italian garden is a four acre walled garden containing a superb collection of statuary and sculpture. The award-winning gardens include the Rose garden and Tudor garden, a traditional yew maze and a 110 metre herbaceous border. A water maze has been added to the other water features in the gardens.

Owner:
Hever Castle Ltd

CONTACT

Anne-Marie
Critchley-Salmonson
Hever Castle
Hever, Edenbridge
Kent TN8 7NG

Infoline: 01732 865224
Fax: 01732 866796
e-mail: mail@HeverCastle.co.uk

LOCATION

OS Ref. TQ476 450

Exit M25/J5 & J6
M23/J10,
$1^1/2$ m S of B2027 at
Bough Beech,
3m SE of Edenbridge.

Rail: Hever Station
1m (no taxis),
Edenbridge Town
3m (taxis).

OPENING TIMES

SUMMER
1 March - 30 November
Daily:
Grounds: 11am - 6pm.
Castle: 12 noon - 6pm.
Last admission 5pm.

WINTER
March & November
Grounds: 11am - 4pm.

Castle: 12 noon - 4pm.

ADMISSION

Castle & Gardens
Adult £8.00
Child (5-16 yrs)........ £4.40
OAP £6.80
Family (2+2) £20.40
Please ring for group* prices.

Gardens only
Adult £6.30
Child (5-16 yrs)........ £4.20
OAP........................ £5.40
Family (2+2)...........£16.80
Please ring for group* prices.

*Min 15.

Pre-booked private guided tours are available before opening, during season.

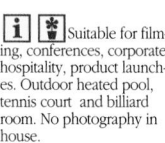

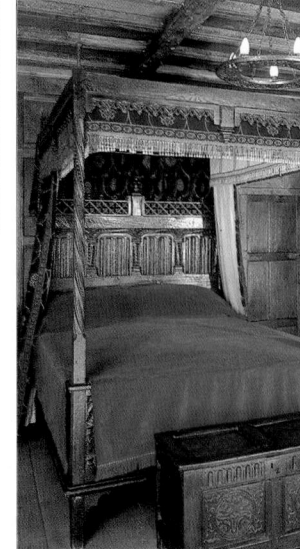

ⓘ ❀ Suitable for filming, conferences, corporate hospitality, product launches. Outdoor heated pool, tennis court and billiard room. No photography in house.

🛍 Gift, garden and book.

🍽 250 seat restaurant available for functions wedding receptions, etc.

♿ Access to gardens, ground floor only (no ramps into castle), restaurants, gift shop, book shop and water maze. Wheelchairs. WC.

🍴 Two licensed restaurants. Supper provided during open air theatre season. Pre-booked lunches and teas for groups.

🚶 Pre-booked tours in mornings. 1 Mar - 30 Nov. Tour time 1 hr. Tours in French, German, Dutch, Italian and Spanish (min 20). Garden tours in English only (min 15).

🅿 Free admission and refreshment voucher for driver and courier. Please book, group rates for 15+.

📖 Welcome (min 5). Guide provided for groups of 20. 1:10 ratio. Free preparatory visits for teachers during opening hours. Please book.

🐕 In grounds, on leads.

LOCATION

CONFERENCE/FUNCTION		
ROOM	SIZE	MAX CAPACITY
Dining Hall	35' x 20'	70
Breakfast Rm	22' x 15'	12
Sitting Rm	24' x 20'	20
Pavilion	96' x 40'	250
Moat Restaurant	25 'x 60'	75

HEVER CASTLE

Hever Castle Tudor Village was built in 1903 for William Waldorf Astor in the style of the Tudor period, to include every modern day comfort.

There are twenty individually designed rooms all with private bathroom, direct dial telephone, colour television, hair dryer, and tea and coffee making facilities. The billiard room, outdoor heated swimming pool, tennis court and croquet lawn are all available for guests to use. Hever Castle Estate includes Stables House, an imposing property with five bedrooms, overlooking the river Eden, providing additional accommodation.

The Tudor Village is a unique and unusual venue available only on an 'exclusive use' basis all year round for groups of 10 or more requiring the very highest standards of accommodation, dining and meeting facilities. There are three interconnecting reception rooms all available for private dining, receptions, product launches, private meetings or corporate hospitality.

The magnificent private dining rooms are able to seat up to 70 people for Tudor Banquets, lunches and dinners. Guests are able to enjoy a private guided tour of the Castle followed by a Tudor Banquet with Minstrels playing Tudor Music.

The Dining Hall, Sitting Room and Breakfast Room (which together form the Tudor Suite) provide formal meeting facilities for up to 30 people and 70 people 'theatre style'. Overhead projector, screen and flip charts can be provided and specialist audiovisual equipment hired. Additional arrangements can be made for laser clay pigeon shooting, archery, fishing, riding, golf and other pursuits on or near by the estate.

Hever Castle Tudor Village offers the following accommodation

- 4 single, 12 double, 4 twin bedded rooms in Tudor Village
- 4 twin, 1 double in Stables House

♜ SPECIAL EVENTS

- **MAR 12 - 18**
  Spring Flower Week
- **APR 13 - 16**
  Easter Weekend
- **MAY 5 - 7**
  May Day Music & Dance
- **MAY 26 - 28**
  Merrie England Weekend
- **JUN 22 - 28**
  Rose Week

- **JUL 21, 28, AUG 4, 5, 11, 12, 18, 19, 25, SEPT 1.**
  Jousting Tournaments
- **JUL 22, 29. AUG 26, 27. SEPT 2.**
  Medieval Archery
- **SEPT 14 - 16**
  Patchwork Quilting Exhibition
- **OCT 8 - 14**
  Autumn Colour Week

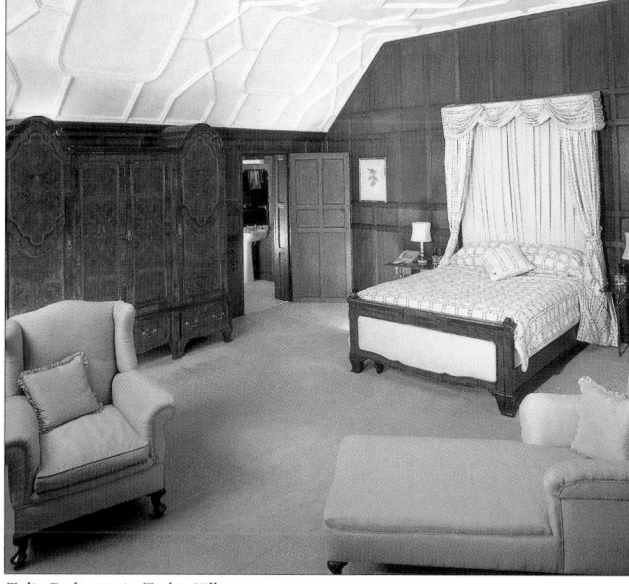

Tulip Bedroom in Tudor Village.

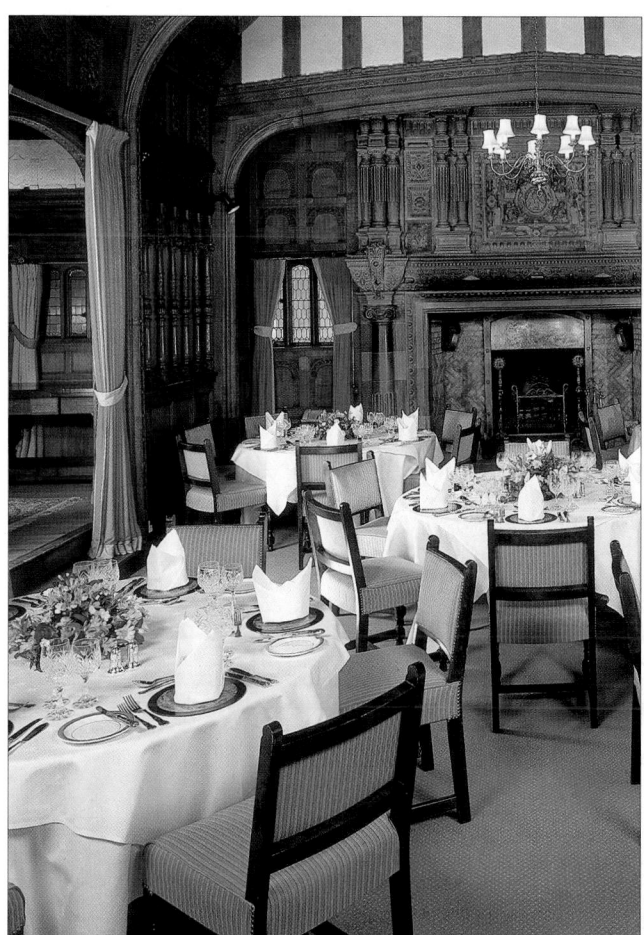

Tudor Suite Dining Room in Tudor Village.

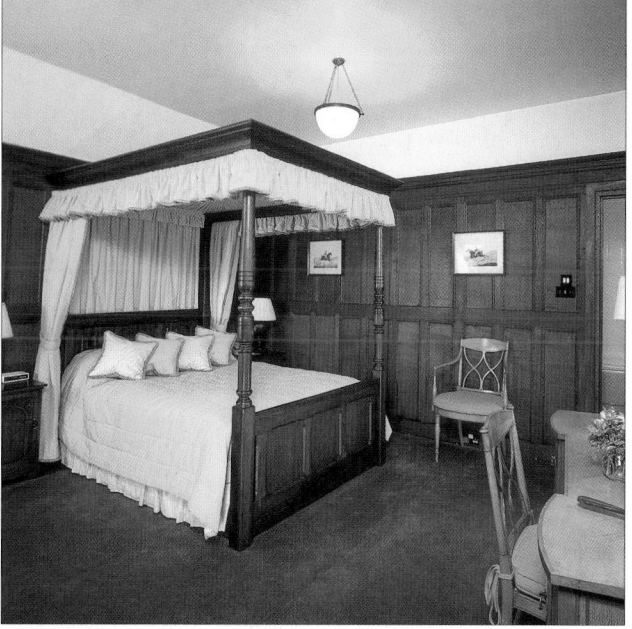

Panelled Bedroom.

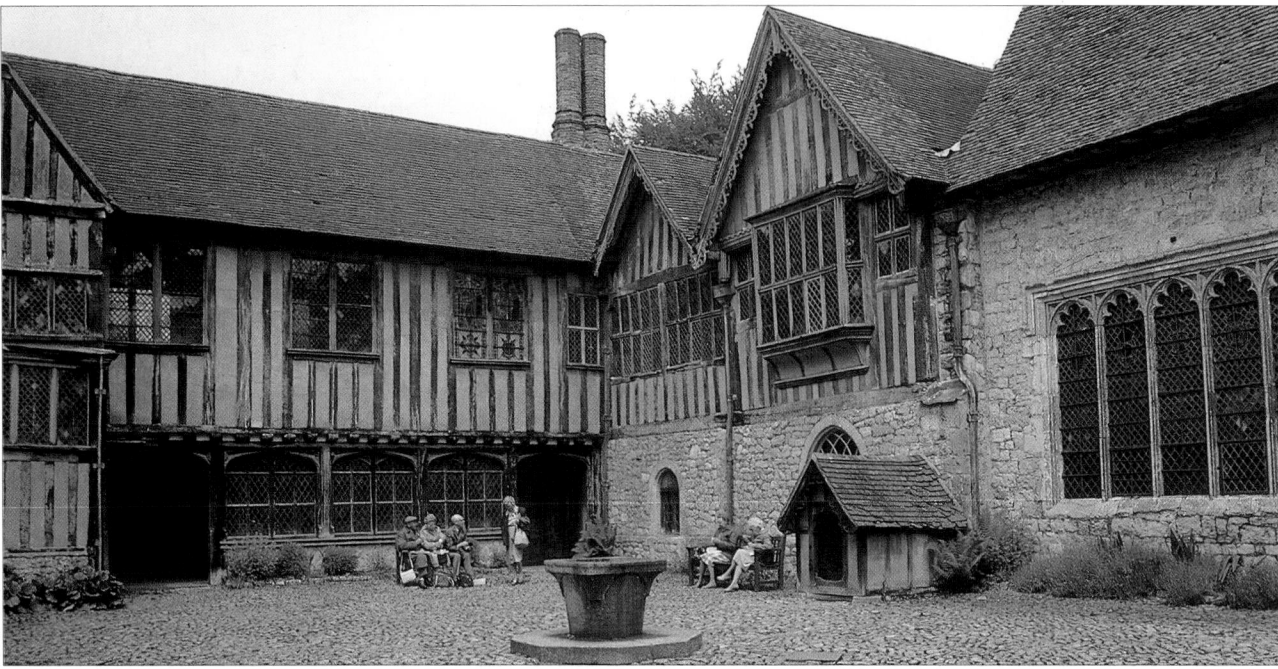

© National Trust.

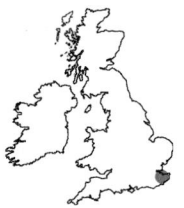

IGHTHAM MOTE
Sevenoaks

Beautiful moated manor house covering 650 years of history from medieval times to the 1960s. Extended visitor route now includes the newly refurbished North-West quarter with Tudor Chapel, Billiards Room and Drawing Room on view. Access in 2001 through the South West wing of the house for the first time ever. Ongoing conservation programme focusing on the Great Hall and Jacobean Staircase. Interpretation displays and special exhibition featuring Conservation in Action. Lovely gardens with lakes and woodland. Surrounding estate provides many country walks. Free introductory talks and garden tours.

Owner:
The National Trust

CONTACT

The Property Manager
Ightham Mote
Ivy Hatch
Sevenoaks
Kent
TN15 0NT

Tel: 01732 810378

Info: 01732 811145

Fax: 01732 811029

e-mail: kimxxx@
smtp.ntrust.org.uk

LOCATION

OS Ref. TQ584 535

6m E of Sevenoaks off
A25. 2$^{1}/_{2}$ m S of Ightham
off A227

OPENING TIMES

1 April - 4 November:
daily except Tues & Sats,
11am - 5.30pm.
Last admission 1 hr before
close.

ADMISSION

Adult £5.00
Child £2.50
Family £12.50

Groups (pre-booked)
Adult £4.25

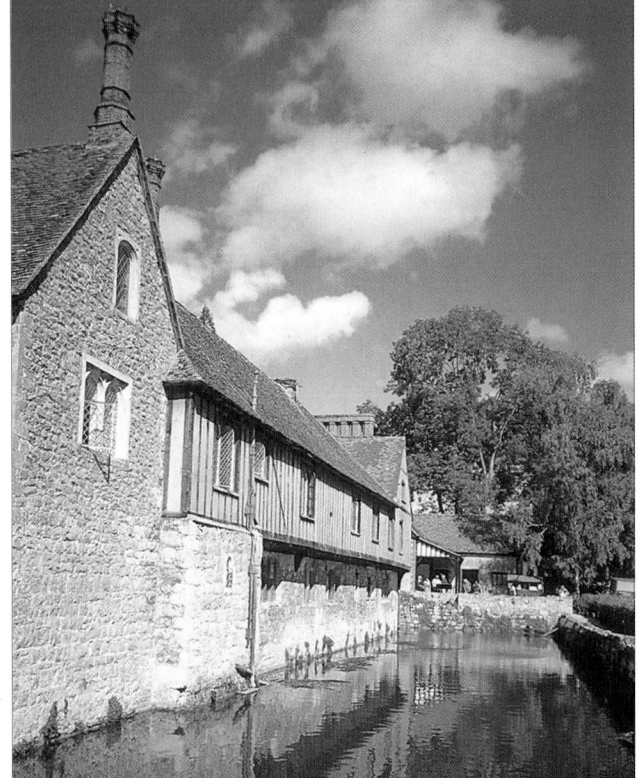

© National Trust.

Ground floor. WC.
Tea Pavilion.
On leads, Estate only.

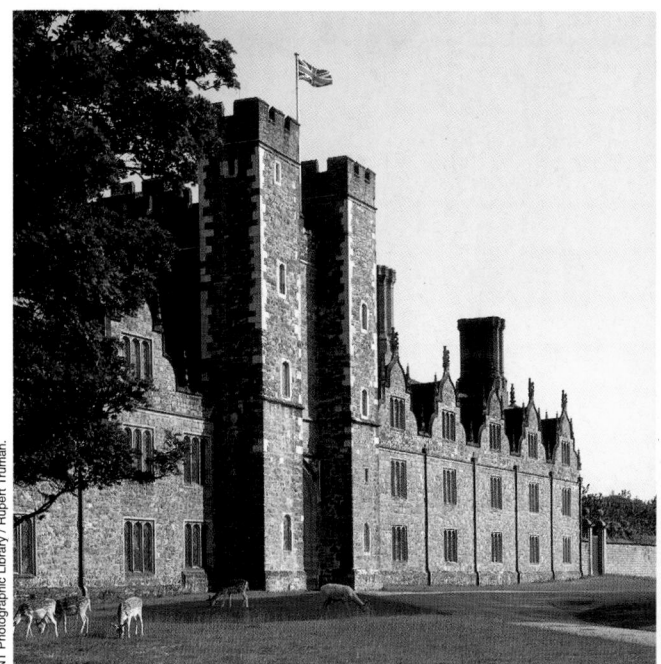

NT Photographic Library / Rupert Truman.

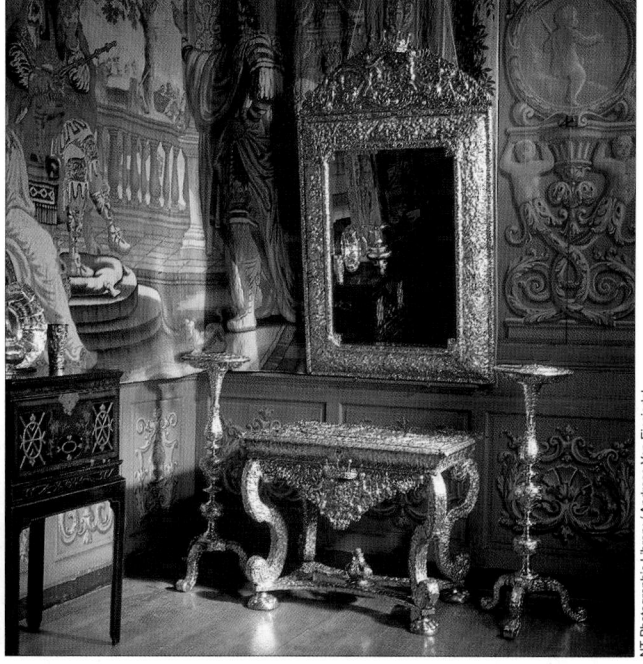

NT Photographic Library / Andreas Von Einsiedel.

KNOLE
Sevenoaks

Set in an extensive deer park owned by Lord Sackville, Knole is one of the great 'treasure houses' of England. It has been the home of the Sackville family since 1603, including four Dukes of Dorset, and houses an extensive collection of furnishings and paintings, many in the house since the 17th century.

The largest private house in England, Knole is a spectacular example of late medieval architecture overlaid with extensive Jacobean embellishments, including remarkable carving and plasterwork. The Sackville family crest of the leopard rampant recurs throughout.

An internationally renowned collection of Royal Stuart furnishings, including three state beds, celebrated silver furniture, and the prototype of the 'Knole' settee. Thirteen years were spent restoring the fabrics on the bed in the Kings' room.

The 6th Earl of Dorset played host to poets Pope and Dryden. Knole was the birthplace of the writer, Vita Sackville-West, and the setting for Virginia Woolf's novel *Orlando*.

Important collection of paintings, including works by Van Dyck, Lely, Kneller, Gainsborough, Hoppner, Wootton, and a room devoted to the works of Sir Joshua Reynolds, commissioned for the house by the 3rd Duke of Dorset, including portraits of Dr Johnson, David Garrick and Oliver Goldsmith.

The experience of visiting the house, which has been little altered since the 18th century, is like stepping back in time.

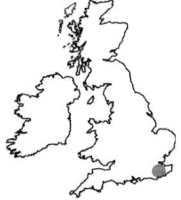

Owner:
The National Trust

CONTACT

Property Manager
Knole
Sevenoaks
Kent TN15 0RP

Tel: 01732 462100

Info: 01732 450608

Fax: 01732 465528

e-mail: kknxxx@
smtp.ntrust.org.uk

LOCATION

OS Ref. TQ532 543

25m SE of London. Just off A225 at S end of High Street, Sevenoaks.

Rail: 1/2 hr from London Charing Cross to Sevenoaks.

Bus: Chartwell Explorer 'green transport' bus link with Sevenoaks. Tel: 01732 462100

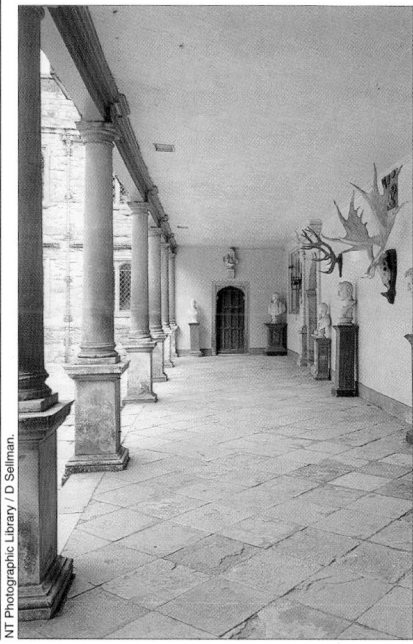

NT Photographic Library / D Sellman.

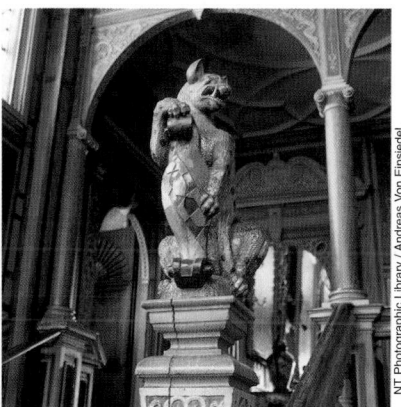

NT Photographic Library / Andreas Von Einsiedel.

🛍 ℹ Full range of NT goods and souvenirs of Knole.

♿ Wheelchair access to Green Court, Stone Court and Great Hall.

🍴 Brewhouse Restaurant serving morning coffee, lunch and teas. Also ice-creams and snacks in courtyard.

🚶 Guided tours for pre-booked groups: Thur mornings.

🅿 Ample.

▦ Welcome. Contact Education Officer.

OPENING TIMES

House

31 March - 4 November:
Wed - Sat, 12 noon - 4pm.

Last admission 3.30pm.

Sun, BH Mon & Good Fri
11am - 5pm.

Last admission 4pm.

Garden

May - September
1st Wed of month only
12 noon - 4pm.

Last admission 3pm.

Shop & Tearoom

1 April - 31 October:
11am - 4.30pm

ADMISSION

House & Garden

Adult	£5.00
Child	£2.50
Family	£12.50
Groups (pre-booked)	
Adult	£4.25
Parking	£2.50

Garden only £1.00

NT members Free.

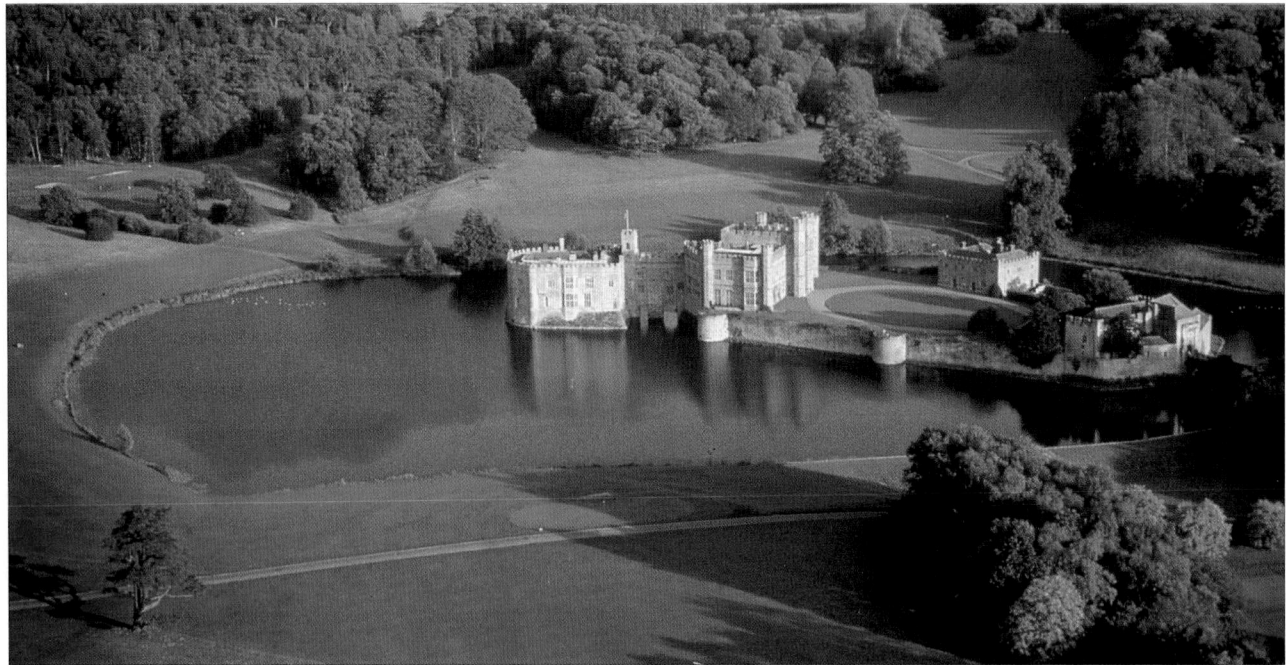

LEEDS CASTLE & GARDENS
Maidstone

This "loveliest castle in the world", surrounded by 500 acres of magnificent parkland and gardens and set in the middle of a natural lake, is one of the country's finest historic properties. Leeds is also proud to be one of the Treasure Houses of England.

The site of a Saxon royal manor, a Norman fortress and a royal palace to the Kings and Queens of England, the chequered history of Leeds Castle continues well into the 20th century. The last private owner, the Honourable Olive, Lady Baillie, purchased the Castle in 1926. Her inheritance helped to restore the Castle and, prior to her death, she established the Leeds Castle Foundation which now preserves the Castle for the nation, hosts important international conferences and supports the arts.

The Castle has a fine collection of paintings, tapestries and furnishings and is also home to a unique collection of antique dog collars. The Park and Grounds include the colourful and quintessentially English Culpeper Garden, the delightful Wood Garden, and the terraced Lady Baillie Garden with its views over the tranquil Great Water. An Aviary houses rare and endangered species from around the world and, next to the traditional Greenhouses can be found a Maze with its secret underground grotto.

A highly popular and successful programme of Special Events is arranged throughout the year, details of which can be found opposite.

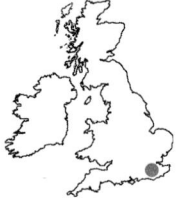

Owner:
Leeds Castle Foundation

CONTACT

Sandra Barrett
Leeds Castle
Maidstone
Kent
ME17 1PL

Tel: 01622 765400

Fax: 01622 735616

LOCATION

OS Ref. TQ835 533

From London to A20/M20/J8, 40m, 1 hr. 6m E of Maidstone, ¼ m S of A20.

Rail: BR Connex train and admission. London - Bearsted.

Coach: Nat Express/ Invictaway coach and admission from Victoria.

Air: Gatwick 45m. Heathrow 65m.

Channel Tunnel: 25m.

Channel ports: 38m.

CONFERENCE/FUNCTION		
ROOM	SIZE	MAX CAPACITY
Fairfax Hall	19.8 x 1m	200
Gate Tower	9.8 x 5.2m	50
Culpeper	7.65 x 7.34m	40
Terrace	8.9 x 15.4m	80

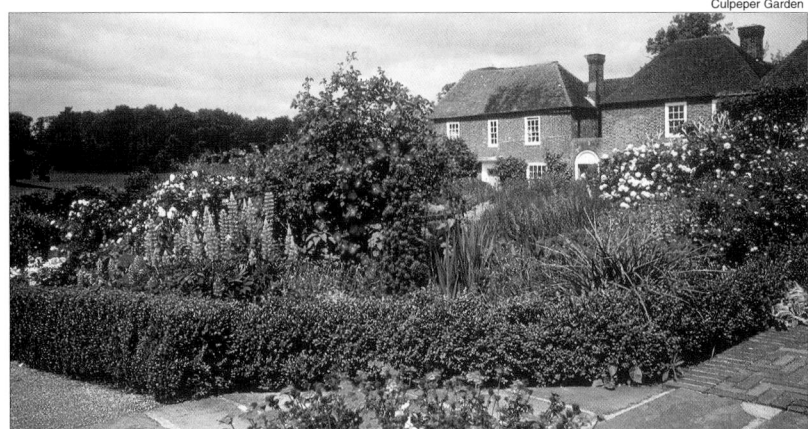
Culpeper Garden

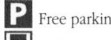 Residential conferences, exhibitions, sporting days, clay shooting, falconry, field archery, golf, croquet and heli-pad. Talks can be arranged for horticultural, viticultural, historical and cultural groups. No radios.

Corporate hospitality, large scale marquee events, wedding receptions, buffets and dinners.

Shuttle for elderly/disabled, wheelchairs, wheelchair lift, special rates. WC.

Two restaurants and a tearoom, group lunch menus. Refreshment kiosks.

Guides in rooms. French, Spanish, Dutch, German, Italian and Russian speaking guides.

Free parking.

Welcome, outside normal opening hours, private tours. Teacher's resource pack.

OPENING TIMES

OPEN ALL YEAR

SUMMER

1 March - 31 October
Daily:
10am - 5pm (last adm).

WINTER

1 November - 28 February
Daily:
10am - 3pm (last adm.).
(closed Christmas Day).

Also special private tours for pre-booked groups at any other time by appointment.

Castle & Grounds closed 30 Jun & 7 July prior to the Open Air Concerts.

ADMISSION

Rates from 1 March 2001.

Castle, Park & Gardens

Adult £10.00

Child (5 -15yrs).........£6.50

OAP/Student...........£8.50

Family (2+3)............£29.00

Disabled Visitors

Adult £5.50

Child (5 -15yrs).........£4.50

Groups (15+)

Adult £8.00

Child (5 -15yrs).........£6.00

OAP/Student...........£7.00

Park & Gardens

Adult £8.50

Child (5 -15yrs).........£5.20

OAP/Student...........£7.00

Family (2+3) £24.00

Disabled Visitors

Adult £4.50

Child (5 -15yrs).........£3.00

Groups (15+)

Adult £7.00

Child (5 -15yrs).........£5.00

OAP/Student...........£6.00

A guidebook is published in English, French, German, Dutch, Spanish, Italian and Japanese.

LEEDS CASTLE

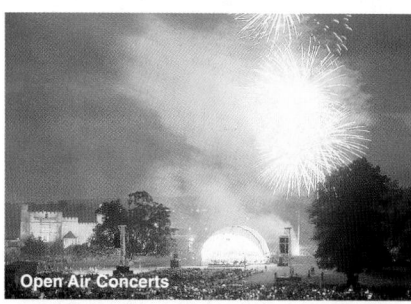
Open Air Concerts

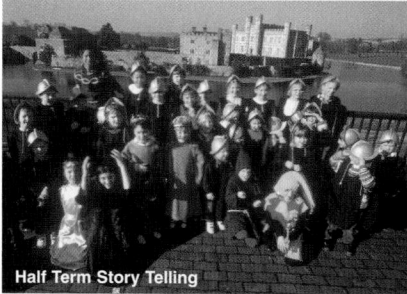
Half Term Story Telling

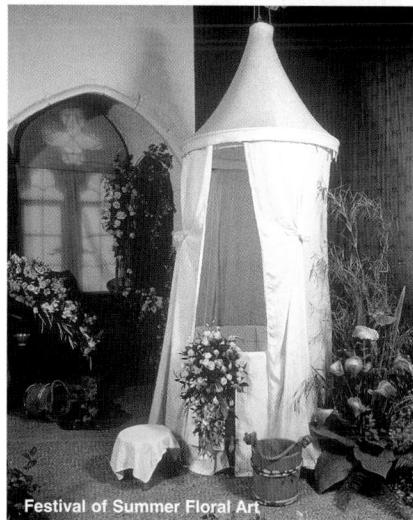
Festival of Summer Floral Art

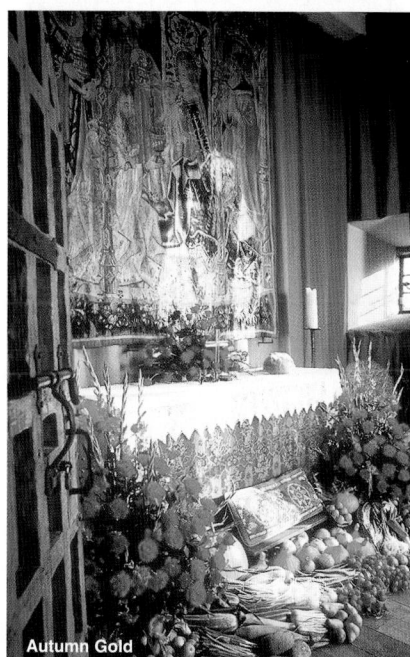
Autumn Gold

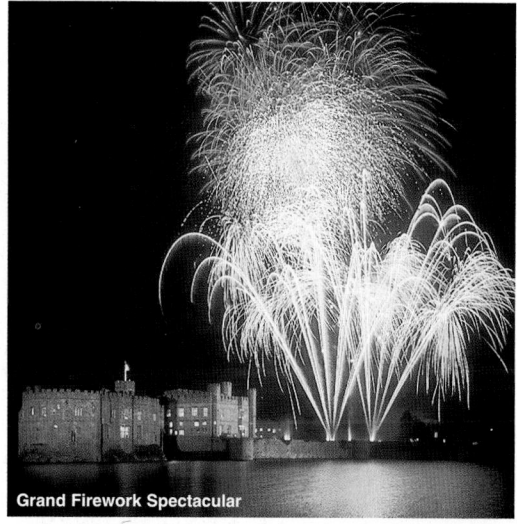
Grand Firework Spectacular

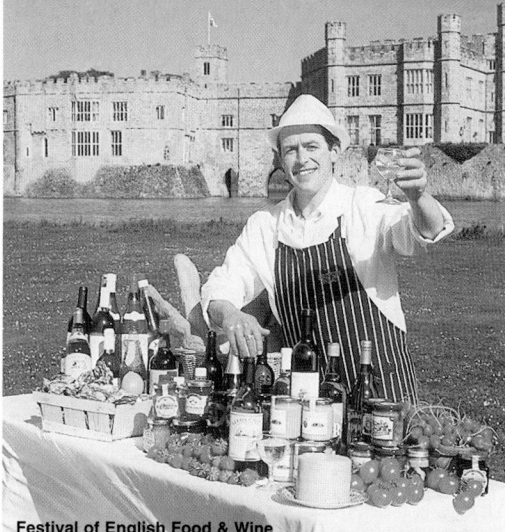
Festival of English Food & Wine

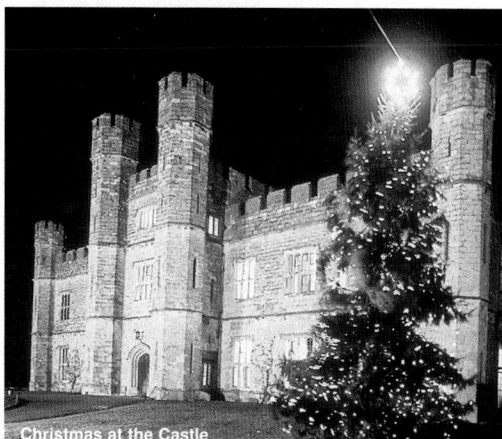
Christmas at the Castle

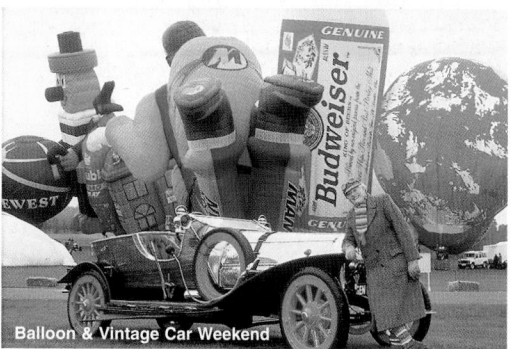
Balloon & Vintage Car Weekend

SPECIAL EVENTS

- **DEC 30/31 & JAN 1:**
  Treasure Trail
- **FEB 19 - 23:**
  Half Term Story-Telling
- **MAR 31 & APR 1:**
  Gardeners' Weekend
- **APR 14/15/16:**
  An Easter Celebration
- **MAY 12/13:**
  Festival of English Food & Wine
- **MAY 26 - JUN 3:**
  Amazing Mazes Week
- **JUN 30 & JUL 7:**
  Open Air Concerts
- **JUL 4:**
  Children's Promenade Concert
- **JUL 19 - 22:**
  A Festival of Summer Floral Art
- **SEPT 8/9:**
  Balloon & Vintage Car Weekend
- **OCT 10 - 14:**
  Autumn Gold - A Celebration of Flowers and Produce
- **OCT 22 - 26:**
  Half Term Halloween Event
- **NOV 3:**
  Grand Firework Spectacular
- **DEC 10 - 24:**
  Christmas at the Castle

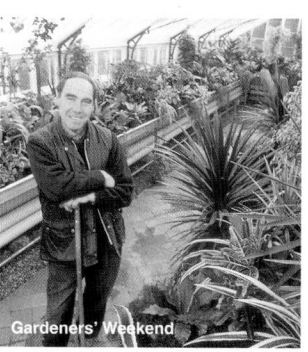
Gardeners' Weekend

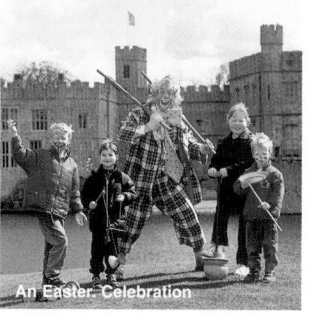
An Easter Celebration

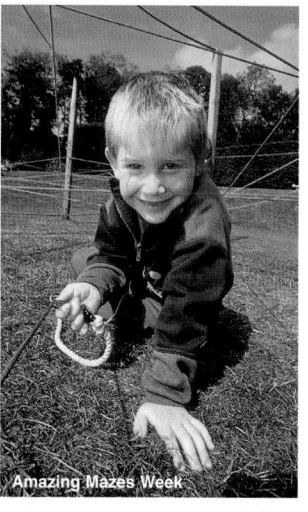
Amazing Mazes Week

South East
England

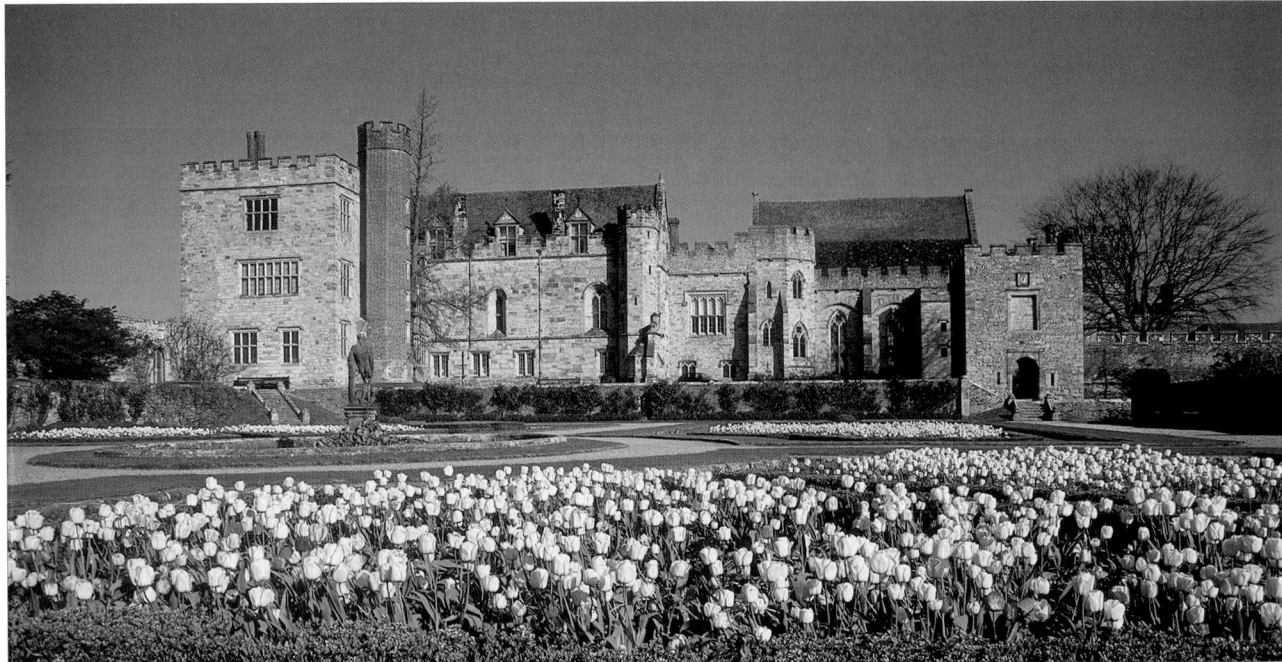

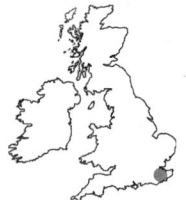

Owner:
Viscount De L'Isle

CONTACT

Bonnie Vernon
Penshurst Place
Penshurst
Nr Tonbridge
Kent
TN11 8DG

Tel: 01892 870307
Fax: 01892 870866

e-mail: enquiries
@penshurstplace.com

LOCATION

OS Ref. TQ527 438

From London M25/J5
then A21 to
Hildenborough, B2027 via
Leigh; from Tunbridge
Wells A26, B2176.

Visitors entrance at SE end
of village, S of the church.

Bus: Maidstone & District
231, 232, 233 from
Tunbridge Wells.

Rail: Charing Cross/
Waterloo - Hildenborough,
Tonbridge or Tunbridge
Wells; then taxi.

CONFERENCE/FUNCTION		
ROOM	SIZE	MAX CAPACITY
Sunderland Room	45' x 18'	100
Barons' Hall	64' x 39'	250
Buttery	20' x 23'	50

PENSHURST PLACE & GDNS
Nr Tonbridge

PENSHURST PLACE is one of England's greatest family-owned stately homes with a history going back six and a half centuries.

In some ways time has stood still at Penshurst; the great House is still very much a medieval building with improvements and additions made over the centuries but without any substantial rebuilding. Its highlight is undoubtedly the medieval Barons' Hall, built in 1341, with its impressive 60ft-high chestnut-beamed roof.

A marvellous mix of paintings, tapestries and furniture from the 15th, 16th and 17th centuries can be seen throughout the House, including the helm carried in the state funeral procession to St. Paul's Cathedral for the Elizabethan courtier and poet, Sir Philip Sidney, in 1587. This is now the family crest.

GARDENS

The Gardens, first laid out in the 14th century, have been developed over successive years by the Sidney family who first came to Penshurst in 1552. A twenty-year restoration and re-planting programme undertaken by the late Viscount De L'Isle has ensured that they retain their historic splendour. He is commemorated with a new Arboretum, planted in 1991. The gardens are divided by a mile of yew hedges into "rooms", each planted to give a succession of colour as the seasons change. There is also an Adventure Playground, Woodland Trail and Toy Museum for children and an exhibition "Celebrating Seven Centuries of Gardening at Penshurst Place".

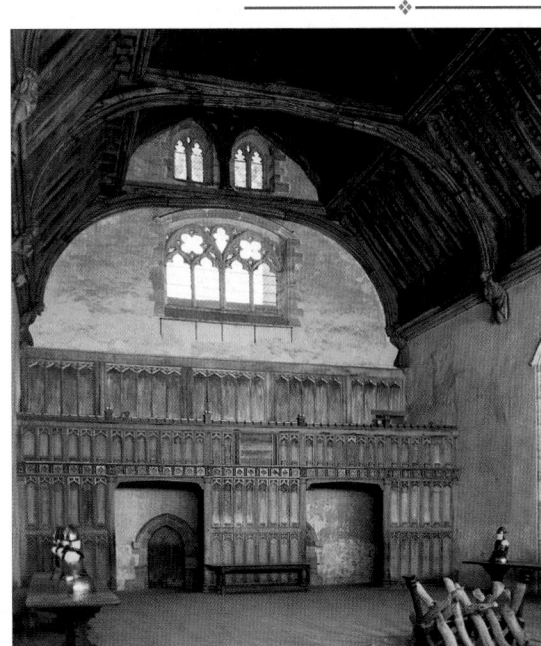

🛍 ❄ ℹ Product launches, garden parties, photography, filming, fashion shows, receptions, archery, clay pigeon shooting, falconry, parkland for hire, lectures on property, its contents and history. Conference facilities. Adventure playground & parkland & riverside walks. No photography in house.

🍽 Private banqueting, wedding receptions.

♿ Limited, disabled and elderly may alight at entrance. WC.

🍴 Licensed tearoom (waitress service can be booked by groups of 20+).

🚶 Mornings only by arrangement, lunch/dinner can be arranged. Out of season tours by appointment. Guided tours of the gardens.

🅿 Ample. Double decker buses to park from village.

🎒 All year by appointment, discount rates, education room and packs.

🐕 Guide dogs only

🔔

❄

OPENING TIMES

SUMMER
From 3 March
weekends only.

31 March - 31 October

House
Daily, 12 noon - 5.30pm.
Last entry 5pm.

Grounds
Daily, 10.30am - 6pm.

Shop & Plant Centre
10.30am - 6pm.

WINTER
Open to Groups by
appointment only
(see Guided Tours).

ADMISSION

House & Grounds
Adult £6.00
Child* £4.00
OAP..........................£5.50
Family (2+2) £16.00
Groups**
Adult £5.30
Child £3.20

Garden only
Adult £4.50
Child* £3.50
OAP..........................£4.00
Family (2+2) £13.00

Garden Season Ticket
................................£25.00

House Tours (pre-booked)
Adult..........................£6.00
Child £3.20

Garden Tours (pre-booked)
Adult £6.50
Child £4.00

House & Garden........£8.00

*   Aged 5-15yrs; under 5s Free.
** Min 20 people, afternoons only. Special rates for morning Guided Tours.

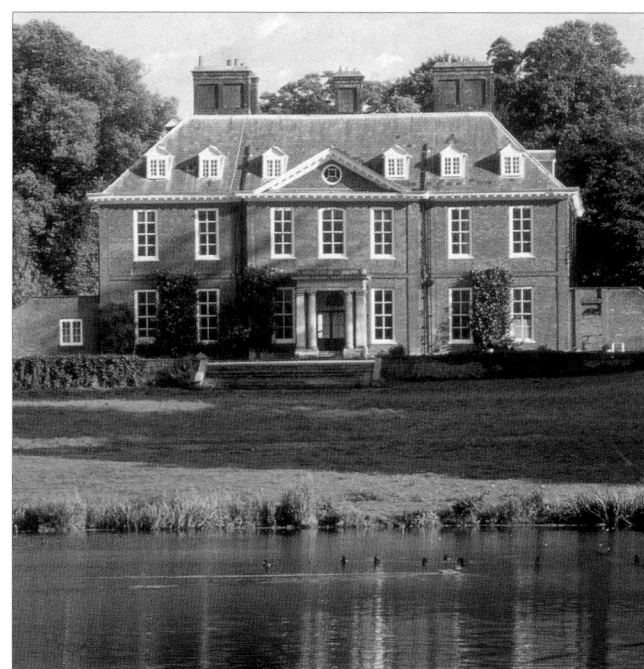

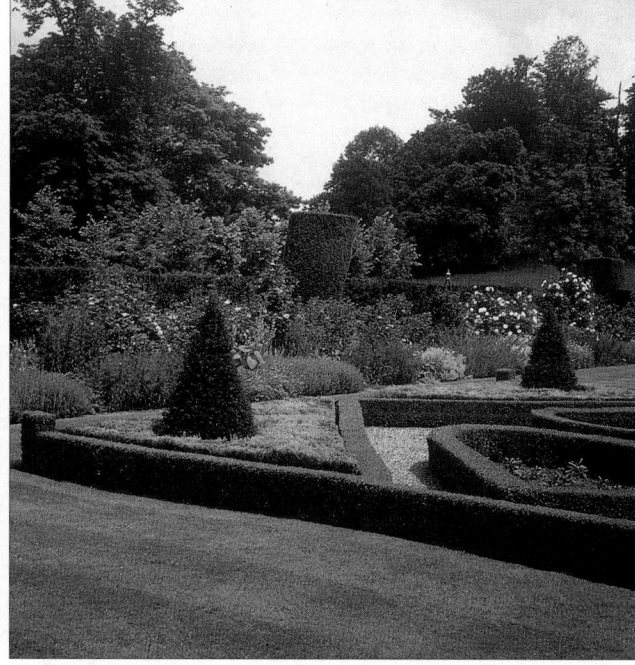

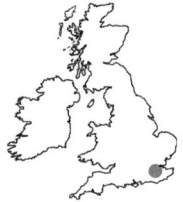

SQUERRYES COURT & GDNS
Westerham

SQUERRYES COURT is a beautiful 17th century manor house which has been the Warde family home since 1731. It is surrounded by 10 acres of attractive and historic gardens which include a lake, restored parterres and an 18th century dovecote. Squerryes is 22 miles from London and easily accessible from the M25. There are lovely views and peaceful surroundings. Visitors from far and wide come to enjoy the atmosphere of a house which is still lived in as a family home.

There is a fine collection of Old Master paintings from the Italian, 17th century Dutch and 18th century English schools, furniture, porcelain and tapestries all acquired or commissioned by the family in the 18th century. General Wolfe of Quebec was a friend of the family and there are items connected with him in the Wolfe Room.

GARDENS

These were laid out in the formal style but were re-landscaped in the mid 18th century. Some of the original features in the 1719 Badeslade print survive. The family have restored the formal garden using this print as a guide. The garden is lovely all year round with bulbs, wild flowers and woodland walks, azaleas, summer flowering herbaceous borders and roses.

Owner:
John St A Warde Esq

CONTACT

Mrs Vale or Mrs Warde
Squerryes Court
Westerham
Kent
TN16 1SJ

Tel: 01959 562345
or 01959 563118

Fax: 01959 565949

e-mail: squerryescourt
@pavilion.co.uk

LOCATION

OS Ref. TQ440 535

Off the M25/J6, 6m,
E along A25 $\frac{1}{2}$ m SW of
Westerham

London 1-1$\frac{1}{2}$ hrs.

Rail: Oxted Station 4m.
Sevenoaks 6m.

Air: Gatwick,
30 mins.

OPENING TIMES

SUMMER

1 April - 30 September
Wed, Sat, Sun & BH Mon.

Closed: Mon (except BH Mon), Tue, Thur & Fri.

Grounds: 12 noon - 5.30pm
House: 1.30 - 5.30pm
Last admission 5pm.

NB. Pre-booked groups welcome any day.

WINTER

October - 1 April
Closed.

ADMISSION

House & Garden
Adult £4.20
Child (under 14) £2.50
OAP........................£3.80
Groups (20+)
Adult £3.60
Child (under 14) £1.80
OAP........................£3.60

House only
Adult £4.20
Child (under 14) £2.50
OAP........................£3.80
Groups (20+)
Adult £3.60
Child (under 14) £1.80
OAP........................£3.60

Garden only
Adult £2.50
Child (under 14) £1.50
OAP........................£2.20
Groups (20+, booked)
Adult £2.20
Child (under 14) £1.10
OAP........................£2.20

CONFERENCE/FUNCTION		
ROOM	SIZE	MAX CAPACITY
Hall	32' x 32'	60
Old Library	20' x 25' 6"	40

Suitable for conferences, product launches, filming, photography, archery, clay pigeon shooting, garden parties. No photography in house.

Exclusive entertaining & wedding receptions (marquee).

Limited access in house and garden, please telephone before visiting. WC.

Home-made teas on open days. Groups must book for lunch or tea. Menus upon request.

For pre-booked groups (max 55), small additional charge. Owner will meet groups by prior arrangement. Tour time 1 hr.

Ample. Free teas for drivers and couriers.

Welcome, cost £1.50 per child, guide provided. Areas of interest: nature walk, ducks and geese.

On leads, in grounds.

THE ARCHBISHOPS' PALACE
Tel: 01622 663006 **Fax:** 01622 682451

Mill Street, Maidstone, Kent ME15 6YE
Owner: Maidstone Borough Council   **Contact:** Operations Manager
Recently refurbished 14th century Palace used as a resting place for Archbishops travelling from London to Canterbury.
Location: OS Ref. TQ760 555. On the banks of River Medway SW of the centre of Maidstone.
Opening Times: Daily: 10am - 4.30pm.
Admission: Entrance to 1st floor rooms is free.

BEDGEBURY NATIONAL PINETUM
Tel: 01580 211044   **Fax:** 01580 212423

Goudhurst, Cranbrook, Kent TN17 2SL   **e-mail:** bedgebury@forestry.gsi.gov.uk
Owner: Forestry Commission   **Contact:** Mr Colin Morgan
Location: OS Ref. TQ714 337 (gate on B2079). 7m E of Tunbridge Wells on A21, turn N on B2079 for 1m.
Opening Times: All year: daily, 10am - dusk or 7pm.
Admission: Adult £3, Child £1.50, OAP £2.50.

BEECH COURT GARDENS

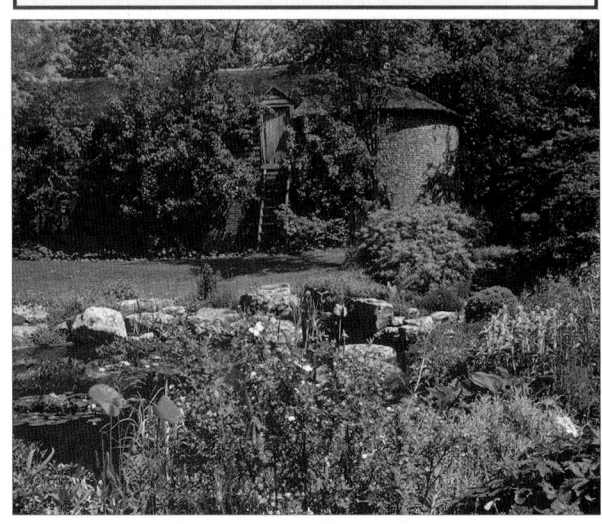

CANTERBURY ROAD, CHALLOCK, Nr ASHFORD, KENT TN25 4DJ
Owner: Mr V Harmsworth Contact: Mrs Miller-Thomas

Tel: 01233 740735 **Fax:** 01233 740842
Surrounding a medieval farm house the ten acre woodland garden has a fine collection of trees including many acers. Rhododendrons, azaleas, cascading roses, island beds and vivid blue hydrangeas with a finale of autumn colour makes this a true garden for all seasons. Tranquil atmosphere, bird song and surprising vistas.
Location: OS Ref. TQ999 501. Off A252 Charing side of Challock roundabout.
Opening Times: 31 Mar - 4 Nov: (Closed Good Fri) Mon - Thur, 10am - 5.30pm, Fri - Sun, 12 noon - 6pm.
Admission: Adult £3, Child £1, Conc. £2.50. Groups (12+): Adult £2.30, Child 50p, Conc. £2.

[i] Map available. [ ] [ ] [ ] [ ] [ ] [K] By arrangement. [P] Ample for cars, coaches limited. [ ] [ ] Guide dogs only.

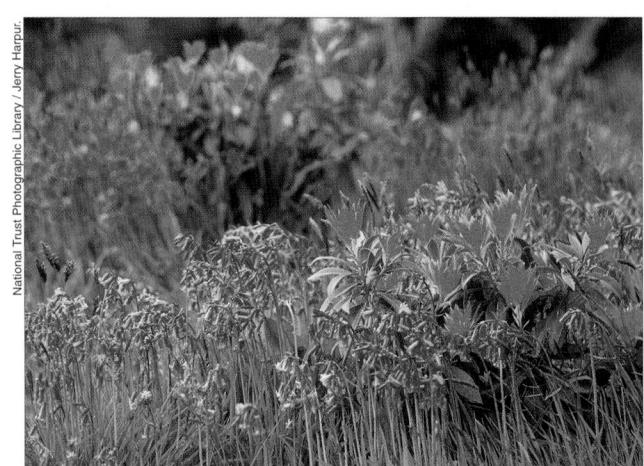

Emmetts Gardens, Kent.

BELMONT
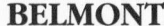

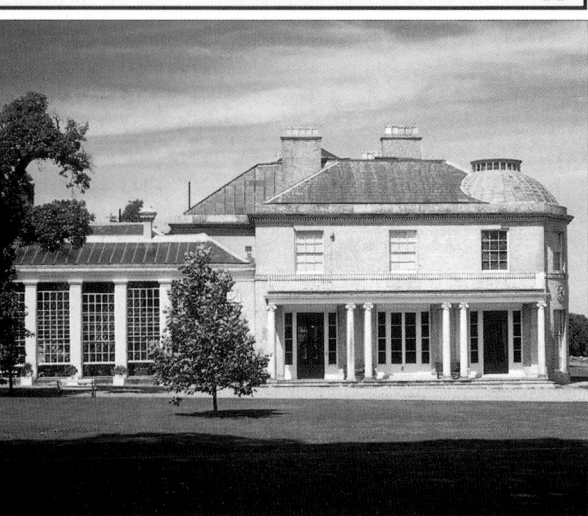

BELMONT PARK, THROWLEY, FAVERSHAM ME13 0HH
Owner: Harris (Belmont) Charity Contact: Lt Col F E Grant

Tel: 01795 890202 **Fax:** 01795 890042
Belmont is a charming late 18th century country mansion by Samuel Wyatt, set in delightful grounds. The seat of the Harris family since 1801 it is beautifully furnished and contains interesting items from India and Trinidad as well as the unique clock collection formed by the 5th Lord.
Location: OS Ref. TQ986 564. 4^1/$_2$ m SSW of Faversham, off A251.
Opening Times: 1 Apr - 30 Sept: Sats, Suns & BHs, 2 - 5pm. Last admission to house 4.30pm. Groups (20+) on other days by appointment.
Admission: House & Garden: Adult £5.25, Child £2.50, Conc. £4.75. Groups (20+): Adult £4.75, Child £2.50. Garden: Adult £2.75, Child £1. No discount for groups.

[i] No photography in house. [ ] [ ] [ ] Partially suitable. WC. [ ]
[K] Obligatory. [P] [ ] [ ]

BOUGHTON MONCHELSEA PLACE   See page 114 for full page entry.

CANTERBURY CATHEDRAL   See page 115 for full page entry.

CHARTWELL   See page 117 for full page entry.

CHIDDINGSTONE CASTLE [icon]   See pages 118/119 for double page entry.

COBHAM HALL   See page 120 for full page entry.

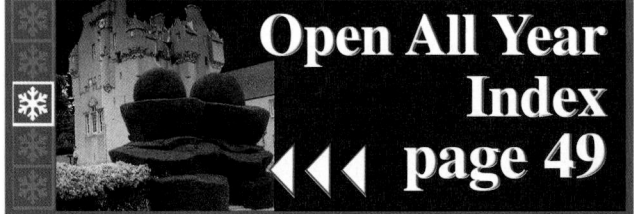
Open All Year
Index
◄◄◄ **page 49**

DEAL CASTLE

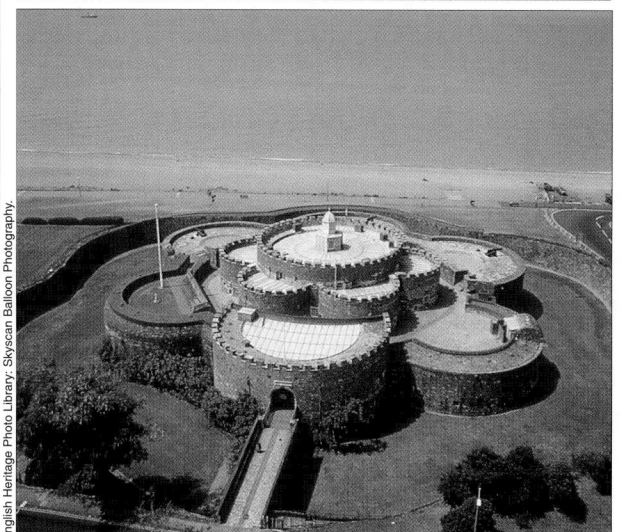

English Heritage Photo Library: Skyscan Balloon Photography.

VICTORIA ROAD, DEAL, KENT CT14 7BA

Owner: English Heritage **Contact:** *The Custodian*

Tel: 01304 372762

Crouching low and menacing, the huge, rounded bastions of this austere fort, built by Henry VIII, once carried 119 guns. A fascinating castle to explore, with long, dark passages, battlements and a huge basement. The interactive displays and exhibition give a fascinating insight into the Castle's history.

Location: OS Ref. TR378 521. SE of Deal town centre.

Opening Times: 1 Apr - 30 Sept: daily, 10am - 6pm. 1 - 31 Oct: 10am - 5pm. 1 Nov - 31 Mar: Wed - Sun only, 10am - 4pm. Closed 24 - 26 Dec & 1 Jan.

Admission: Adult £3.10, Child £1.60, Conc. £2.30.

Restricted. P Coach parking on main road.
Guide dogs only. Tel. for details.

DICKENS CENTRE - EASTGATE HOUSE

Tel: 01634 844176

High Street, Rochester, Medway ME1 1EW

Owner: Medway Council   **Contact:** Head Custodian

Much altered late 16th century brick house, now containing the Dickens Centre, with exhibits of his life and works, including his best known characters. At the rear is Dickens' prefabricated chalet, brought from Switzerland.

Location: OS Ref. TQ746 683. N side of Rochester High Street, close to the Eastern Road. 400yds SE of the Cathedral.

Opening Times: Daily, 10am - 4.45pm (last admission).

Admission: Adult £3.60, Child £2.50, Family £9.70 (2000 prices).

DODDINGTON PLACE GARDENS

Tel: 01795 886101

Doddington, Sittingbourne, Kent ME9 0BB

Owner: Mr & Mrs Richard Oldfield   **Contact:** Mrs Richard Oldfield

10 acres of landscaped gardens in an area of outstanding natural beauty.

Location: OS Ref. TQ944 575. 4m N from A20 at Lenham or 5m SW from A2 at Ospringe, W of Faversham. Signposted.

Opening Times: From Easter - Sept: Sun 2 - 6pm. Tues, Wed, Thurs & BHs 11am - 6pm. Groups at other times by appointment.

Admission: Adult £3, Child 50p. Groups: £2.50. Coaches by prior arrangement.

DOVER CASTLE & THE SECRET WARTIME TUNNELS

See page 121 for full page entry.

DOWN HOUSE

See page 122 for full page entry.

DYMCHURCH MARTELLO TOWER

Tel: 01304 211067

Dymchurch, Kent

Owner: English Heritage   **Contact:** Area Manager

Built as one of 74 such towers to counter the threat of invasion by Napoleon, Dymchurch is perhaps the best example in the country. Fully restored. You can climb to the roof which is dominated by an original 24-pounder gun complete with traversing carriage.

Location: OS189, Ref. TR102 294. In Dymchurch, access from High Street.

Opening Times: Please telephone 01304 211067 for details.

Admission: Adult £1, Child 50p, Conc. 80p.

EASTBRIDGE HOSPITAL OF ST THOMAS

Tel: 01227 471688

High Street, Canterbury, Kent CT1 2BD

Contact: Louise Fittall

Medieval pilgrims' hospital with 12th century undercroft, refectory and chapel.

Location: OS189, Ref. TR148 579. S side of Canterbury High Street.

Opening Times: Mon - Sat, 10am - 4.45pm.

Admission: Adult £1, Child 50p, Conc. 75p (1999 prices).

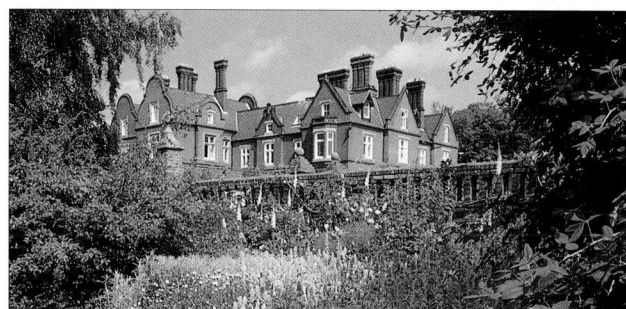

Doddington Place Gardens, Kent.

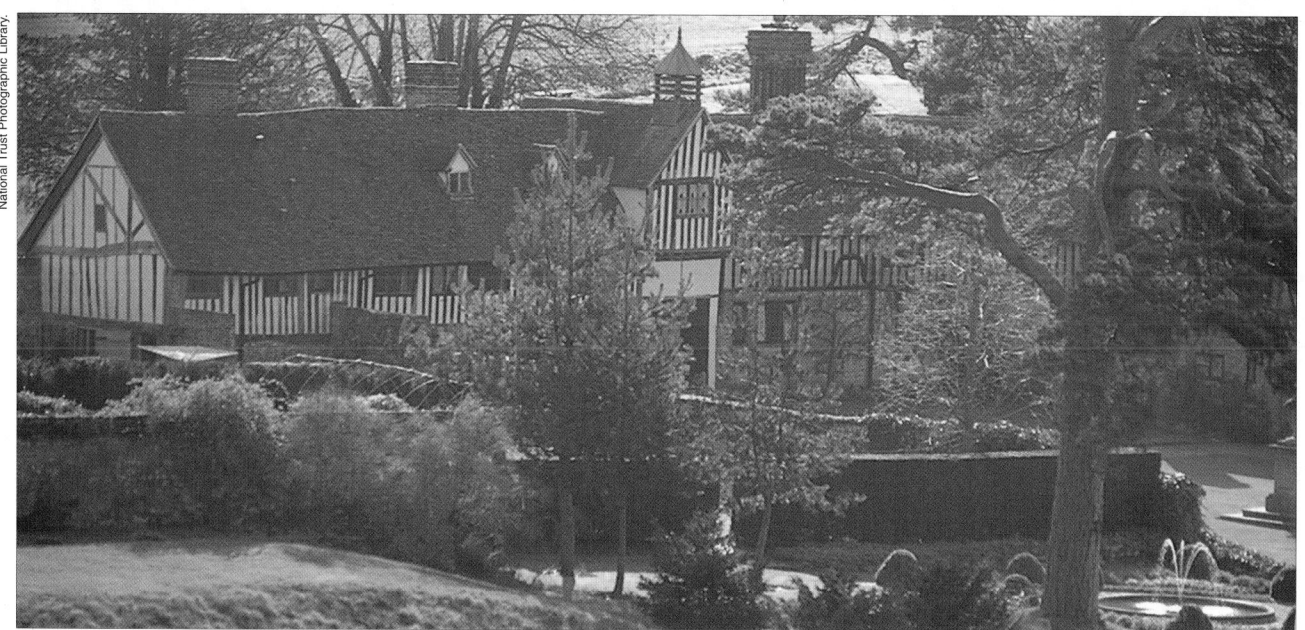

National Trust Photographic Library.

Ightham Mote, Kent.

EMMETTS GARDEN

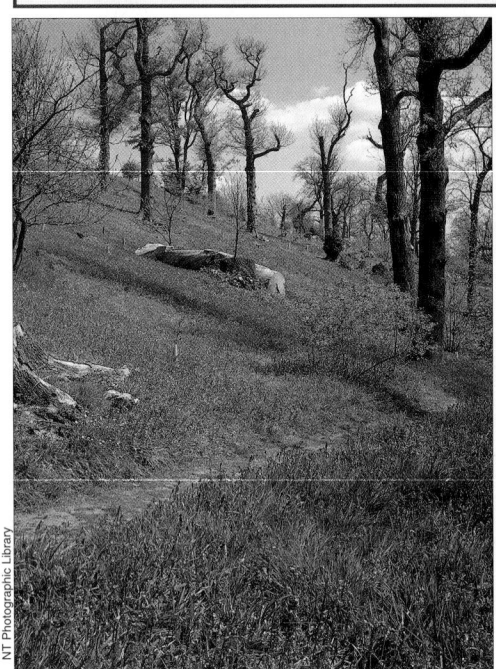
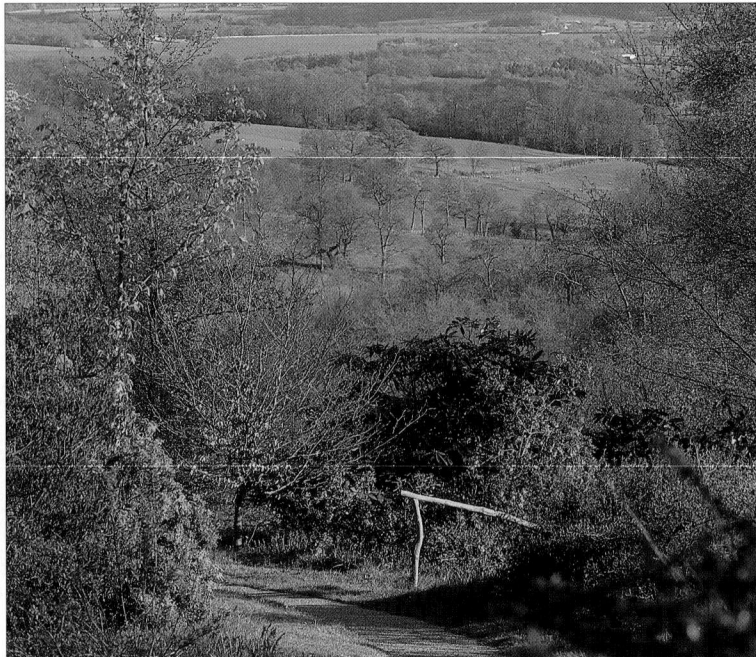

NT Photographic Library

IDE HILL, SEVENOAKS, KENT TN14 6AY

Owner: The National Trust **Contact:** *The Property Manager (Chartwell & Emmetts Garden, Mapleton Road, Westerham, Kent TN16 1PS)*

Tel: 01732 868381 (office)   **e-mail:** kchxxx@smtp.ntrust.org.uk
infoline: 01732 866368

Influenced by William Robinson, this charming and informal garden was laid out in the late 19th century, with many exotic and rare trees and shrubs from across the world. Wonderful views across the Weald of Kent – with the highest treetop in Kent. There are glorious shows of daffodils, carpets of bluebells, azaleas and rhododendrons, then acers and cornus in autumn, also a rose garden and rock garden.

Location: OS Ref. TQ477 524. 1¹/₂ m N of Ide Hill off B2042. M25/J5, then 4m.
Opening Times: 31 Mar - 3 Jun: Wed - Sun, Good Fri & BH Mons. 6 Jun - 4 Nov: Sats, Suns & Weds, 11am - 5.30pm. Last admission 1 hr before close.
Admission: Adult £3.40, Child £1.70, Family £8.50.

⬜   ♿ Steep in places. WC.   ▣   🐎 In grounds, on leads.   ♦ Tel: 01892 891001.

FINCHCOCKS   See page 123 for full page entry.

THE FRIARS - RETREAT HOUSE   **Tel:** 01622 717272 **Fax:** 01622 715575

Aylesford Priory, Aylesford, Kent ME20 7BX

Owner: Carmelite Friars   **Contact:** Margaret Larcombe

A peaceful, tranquil retreat house with 100 beds, set in 42 acres of lovingly tended grounds. Outstanding ceramic works of art by Adam Kossowski. Visitors are invited to picnic in the grounds, visit the tearooms situated in the restored 17th century Barn, which also houses the gift and bookshops. While you are there do call into the pottery and the upholsterers' workshops.

Location: OS Ref. TQ724 588. W end of Aylesford village. 3m NW of Maidstone.
Opening Times: Grounds open Summer & Winter, 24 hrs, 365 days.
Admission: No charge.

⬜   🍽   ♿ Partially suitable.   ▣   🎫 By arrangement.   🅿   🖼
🐎 Guide dogs only.   🔳   ❄

GAD'S HILL PLACE 🏛   **Tel:** 01474 822366 **Fax:** 01474 822977

Gad's Hill School, Higham, Rochester, Kent ME3 7PA

Owner: Gad's Hill School   **Contact:** Miss Anne Carter

This Grade I listed building dates from 1780. Charles Dickens lived here with his family from 1857 until his death in 1870, and wrote his last four novels here. Visitors can see his study, the newly restored conservatory, other rooms, the gardens and the grounds. Rooms can be hired for parties and weddings etc.

Location: OS Ref. TQ710 708. On A226, 3m from Rochester, 4m from Gravesend.
Opening Times: Apr - Oct: 1st Sun in month and BH Suns (inc Easter), 2 - 5pm. During Rochester Dickens Festivals (May/June & Dec), 11am - 4.30pm. At other times by appointment. Groups welcome.
Admission: Adult £2.50, Child £1.50, OAP £2.50, Student £1.50. Groups by arrangement.

⬜   🍽   ♿ Partially suitable.   ▣   🎫 Obligatory.   🐎 Guide dogs only.   🔔

GODINTON HOUSE & GARDENS

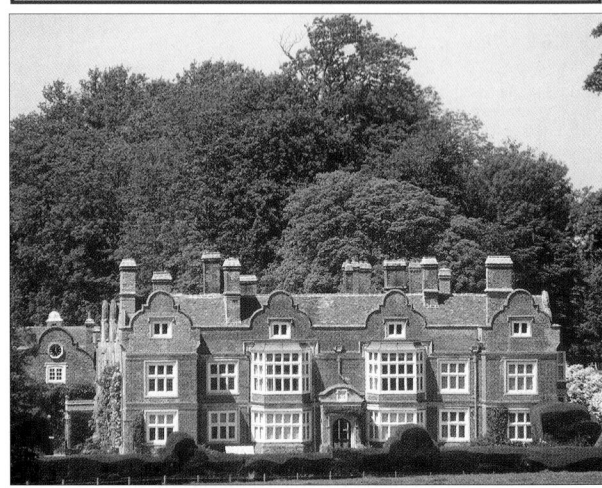

GODINTON PARK, ASHFORD, KENT TN23 3BP

Owner: Godinton House Preservation Trust **Contact:** *Mr D Bickle*

Tel: 01233 620773 **Fax:** 01233 632652 **e-mail:** ghpt@godinton.fsnet.co.uk

Jacobean House incorporating medieval hall, Tudor staircase and later additions, the carving, furniture, porcelain and contrasting decoration reflect its fascinating history. Topiary, terraces, ponds, herbaceous borders, new greenhouse, delphinium border, clematis collection, massed daffodils, wildflowers, fine trees, Italian, walled and formal gardens are surrounded by the famous yew hedge.

Location: OS Ref. TQ981 438. Godinton Lane, 2m NW of Ashford, off A20 (opposite Hare & Hounds public house).
Opening Times: Gardens: 17 Mar - 7 Oct: Thur - Mon, 2 - 5.30pm. House: 13 Apr - 7 Oct: Fris, Sats & Suns, 2 - 5.30pm. Last tour of house 4.30pm.
Admission: House & Gardens: Adult £5, Child £2. Garden only: Adult £2, Child £1.

ℹ No photography in house. Groups must book.   ♿ Partially suitable. WC.
▣ For booked groups.   🎫 Obligatory (house only).   🅿 Limited for coaches.
🖼   🐎 Guide dogs only.

GOODNESTONE PARK GARDENS

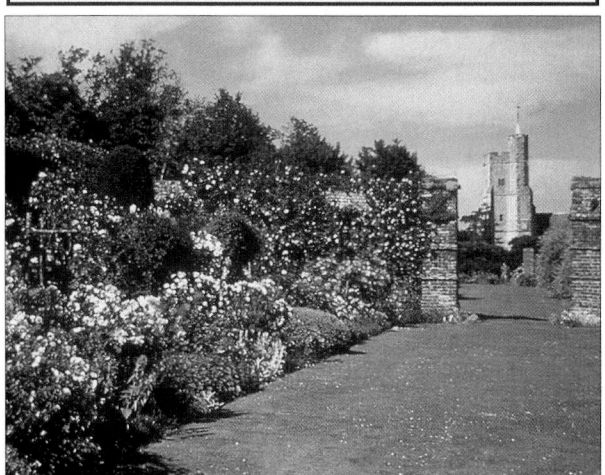

GOODNESTONE PARK, Nr WINGHAM, CANTERBURY, KENT CT3 1PL

Owner: The Lord & Lady FitzWalter   Contact: Lady FitzWalter

Tel/Fax: 01304 840107

The garden is approximately 14 acres, set in 18th century parkland. There are many fine trees, a woodland area and a large walled garden with a collection of old-fashioned roses, clematis and herbaceous plants. Jane Austen was a frequent visitor, her brother Edward having married a daughter of the house.

Location: OS Ref. TR254 544. 8m ESE of Canterbury, 1^1/$_2$ m E of B2046, at S end of village. The B2046 runs from the A2 to Wingham, the gardens are signposted from this road.

Opening Times: 26 Mar - 26 Oct: Suns, 12 noon - 6pm. Mons, Wed - Fri, 11am - 5pm. Closed Tues & Sats. House open by appointment, at any time, to groups of 20 at £1.80.

Admission: Adult £3, Child (under 12yrs) 30p, OAP £2.50, Student £1.50. Groups (20+): Adult £2.50. Wheelchair users £1, Guided groups (20+) £3.50. House by appointment £1.80.

GREAT COMP GARDEN

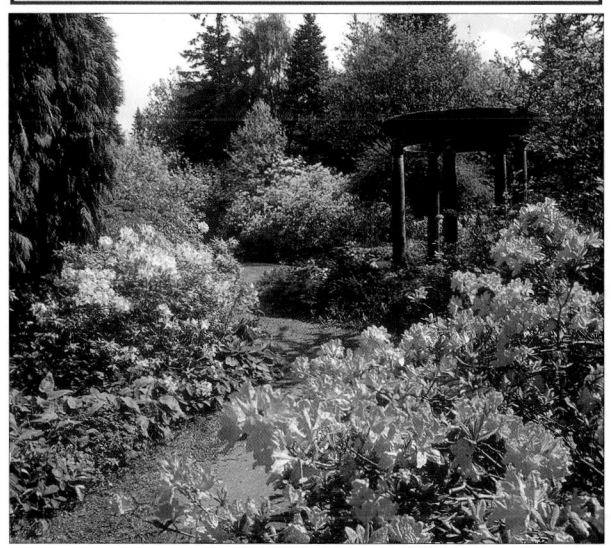

COMP LANE, PLATT, BOROUGH GREEN, KENT TN15 8QS

Owner: R Cameron Esq   Contact: Mr W Dyson

Tel: 01732 886154

One of the finest gardens in the country, comprising ruins, terraces, tranquil woodland walks and sweeping lawns with a breathtaking collection of trees, shrubs, heathers and perennials, many rarely seen elsewhere. The truly unique atmosphere of Great Comp is further complemented by its Festival of Chamber Music held in July/September.

Location: OS Ref. TQ635 567. 2m E of Borough Green, B2016 off A20. First right at Comp crossroads. ^{1}/$_2$ m on left.

Opening Times: 1 Apr - 31 Oct: daily, 11am - 6pm.

Admission: Adult £3.50, Child £1. Groups (20+) £3, Annual ticket: Adult £10, OAP £7.

Teas daily. Guide dogs only.

HALL PLACE
Tel: 01322 526574 **Fax:** 01322 522921

Bourne Road, Bexley, Kent DA5 1PQ

Owner: Bexley Council   **Contact:** Rosemary Evans

A fine Grade I listed country house built in 1540 for Sir John Champneis, a Lord Mayor of London. The house is set in beautiful formal gardens on the banks of the River Cray. Much of the house is open to the public, including the magnificent great hall.

Location: OS Ref. TQ502 743. Near the A2 less than 5m (London bound) from the M25/J2.

Opening Times: Mon - Sat, 10am - 5pm (4.15pm in winter), Sun & BHs, 2 - 6pm (BST only). Opening times may change from 2001, please phone to confirm times.

Admission: Free. Pre-arranged groups: £3.50.

House suitable, lift & WC. Licensed. By arrangement. Ample for cars, limited for coaches. Guide dogs only.

HEVER CASTLE   See pages 124/125 for double page entry.

HIGHAM PARK, HOUSE & GARDENS

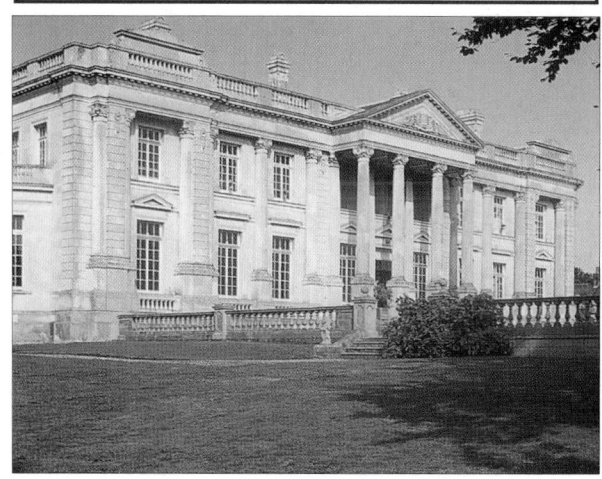

BRIDGE, CANTERBURY, KENT CT4 5BE

Owner/Contact: Patricia P Gibb

Tel/Fax: 01227 830830   **e-mail:** highampark@aol.com

Delight in Higham's (c1320) magnificently restored staterooms. Once home to Countess Margaret Zberanska (née Astor) and her son Louis, creator of the famous Chitty Chitty Bang Bang racing cars. Set on Barham Downs in 24 acres, surrounded by footpaths. Gardina d'Italiano. Trees, shrubs, roses, herbaceous. Kent's oldest acers, massed spring bulbs.

Location: OS Ref. TR183 541. On the A2 at Bridge between Canterbury and the channel ports.

Opening Times: Apr - end Sept: Garden: Suns, 11am - 6pm. Mon - Thur, 11am - 5pm. Closed Fris & Sats. House: Tours at 12.30pm, 2.30pm, 4pm (times may vary). Groups by arrangement at other times.

Admission: Garden: Adult £3, Child £1, OAP £2.50. Groups (20+): Adult £2.50. Guided groups (20+): £3.50. House Tours: £2.

Partially suitable. WC. Licensed. Light lunches. Obligatory. In grounds, on leads. Tel. for details.

HOLE PARK   **Tel:** 01580 241251 **Fax:** 01580 241882

Rolvenden, Cranbrook, Kent TN17 4JB

Owner/Contact: D G W Barham

A 15 acre garden with all year round interest, set in beautiful parkland with fine views.

Location: OS Ref. TQ830 325. 1m W of Rolvenden on B2086 Cranbrook road.

Opening Times: 8, 22, 29 Apr. 6, 20, 27 May. 17 June: HP Society Plant Fair. 14 & 21 Oct (Suns), for NGS. Also Weds, April, May, Jun & Oct. All 2 - 6pm. Groups and individuals by arrangement. Guided tours available for groups.

Admission: Adult £3, Child 50p.

IGHTHAM MOTE   See page 126 for full page entry.

KNOLE   See page 127 for full page entry.

LADHAM HOUSE GARDENS

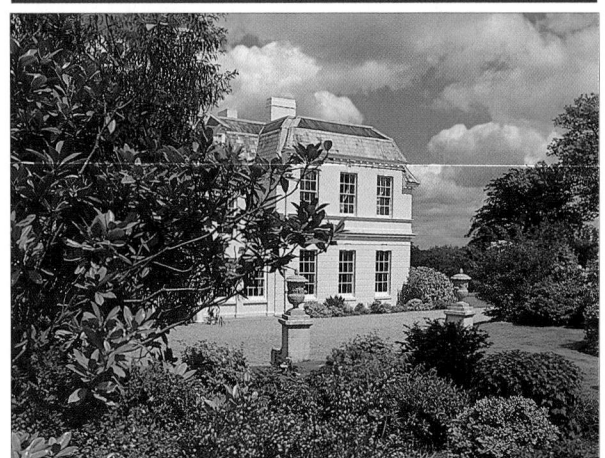

LADHAM LANE, GOUDHURST, KENT TN17 1DB

Owner: Mr & Mrs Alastair Jessel **Contact:** *Mrs Jessel*

Tel: 01580 212674/211203 **Fax:** 01580 212596

This Georgian house with additional French features has been in the family for over 120 years and the garden developed over that period. Mixed shrub borders with famous magnolias. Interesting bog garden replacing a leaking pond and arboretum replacing old kitchen garden. Rare trees and shrubs including cornus cousa, embothriums, American oaks, carpenteria californica and others. 10 acres of gardens set in magnificent Wealden countryside. Superb site for wedding receptions, ceremonies and private parties.

Location: OS Ref. TQ732 384. ³/4 NE of Goudhurst off A262. 5m NW of Cranbrook.

Opening Times: For NGS Sun 22 April, Sun 20 May, 2.30 - 5pm. All other times by prior arrangement.

Admission: Adult £3, Child 50p, OAP/Student £2.50. Groups (min 10, max 100): Adult £2.50, Child 50p, OAP/Student £2.

🐾 🎁 🍽 ♿Partially suitable. 🎿 By arrangement. 🏛
🅿 Limited for coaches. 🐕 🔔 ❄

LULLINGSTONE ROMAN VILLA ⊞

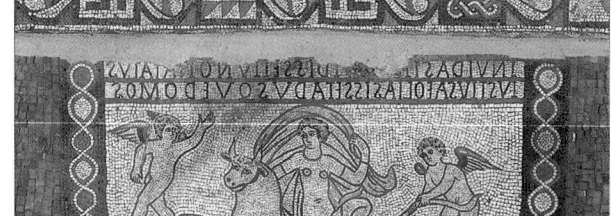

English Heritage Photo Library.

LULLINGSTONE LANE, EYNSFORD, KENT DA4 0JA

Owner: English Heritage **Contact:** *The Custodian*

Tel: 01322 863467

Recognised as one of the most exciting archaeological finds of the century, the villa has splendid mosaic floors and one of the earliest private Christian chapels. Take the free audio tour and discover how the middle-class owners lived, worked and entertained themselves.

Location: OS Ref. TQ529 651. ¹/2 m SW of Eynsford off A225, M25/J3. Follow A20 towards Brands Hatch. 600yds N of Castle.

Opening Times: 1 Apr - 30 Sept: daily, 10am - 6pm. 1 - 31 Oct: 10am - 5pm. 1 Nov - 31 Mar: 10am - 4pm. Closed 24 - 26 Dec & 1 Jan.

Admission: Adult £2.60, Child £1.30, Conc. £1.90.

📷 ♿ Ground floor & grounds suitable. WC. 🎧 ❄ 🛡Tel. for details.

LEEDS CASTLE   See pages 128/129 for double page entry.

LESNES ABBEY   **Tel:** 020 8303 9052

Abbey Road, Abbey Wood, London DA17 5DL

Owner: Bexley Council   **Contact:** TIC Manager

The Abbey was founded in 1178 by Richard de Lucy as penance for his involvement in events leading to the murder of Thomas à Becket. Today only the ruins remain.

Location: OS Ref. TQ479 788. In public park on S side of Abbey Road (B213), 500yds E of Abbey Wood Station, ³/4 m N of A206 Woolwich - Erith Road.

Opening Times: Any reasonable time.

Admission: Free.

LULLINGSTONE CASTLE 🏠   **Tel:** 01322 862114 **Fax:** 01322 862115

Lullingstone Castle, Eynsford, Kent DA4 0JA

Owner/Contact: Guy Hart Dyke Esq

Fine state rooms, family portraits and armour in beautiful grounds. The 15th century gatehouse was one of the first ever to be made with bricks.

Location: OS Ref. TQ530 644. 1m S Eynsford W side of A225. 600yds S of Roman Villa.

Opening Times: May - Aug: Sats, Suns & BHs, 2 - 6pm. Booked groups by arrangement.

Admission: Adult £4, Child £1.50, Conc. £3, Family £10. Groups (25+) 10% discount.

ℹNo interior photography. 📷 🐾 ♿ Partially suitable.
☕Teas at visitor centre, 1km. 🎿By arrangement. 🅿Limited. 🐕

MAISON DIEU ⊞   **Tel:** 01795 534542

Ospringe, Faversham, Kent

Owner: English Heritage   **Contact:** The Faversham Society

This forerunner of today's hospitals remains largely as it was in the 16th century with exposed beams and an overhanging upper storey.

Location: OS Ref. TR002 608. In Ospringe on A2, ¹/2 m W of Faversham.

Opening Times: 3 Apr - 31 Oct: Weekends & BHs, 2 - 5pm. Keykeeper in Winter.

Admission: Adult £1, Child/OAP 80p.

MILTON CHANTRY ⊞   **Tel:** 01474 321520

New Tavern Fort Gardens, Gravesend, Kent

Owner: English Heritage   **Contact:** Gravesend Borough Council

A small 14th century building which housed the chapel of the leper hospital and the chantry of the de Valence and Montechais families and later became a tavern and in 1780 part of a fort.

Location: OS Ref.TQ652 743. In New Tavern Fort Gardens ¹/4 m E of Gravesend off A226.

Opening Times: 1 Mar - 23 Dec: Wed - Sun & BH Mons, 10am - 4pm. Closed Jan & Feb.

Admission: Adult £1.50, Child 75p, Conc. 75p.

MOUNT EPHRAIM GARDENS 🏠   **Tel:** 01227 751496 **Fax:** 01227 750940

Hernhill, Faversham, Kent ME13 9TX

Owner: Mr & Mrs E S Dawes & Mrs M N Dawes   **Contact:** Mrs L Dawes

8 acres of superb gardens set in the heart of family run orchards.

Location: OS Ref.TR065 598. In Hernhill village, 1m from end of M2. Signed from A2 & A299.

Opening Times: Easter - end Sept: Mons, Weds, Thurs, Sats & Suns, 1 - 6pm. Groups at all times by arrangement. (Details apply to 2000 please confirm opening times).

Admission: Adult £3, Child £1. Groups: £2.50 (2000 prices).

OWL HOUSE GARDENS

Tel: 01892 890230 **Fax:** 01892 891222

Lamberhurst, Kent TN3 8LY   **Contact:** James & Angela Kelso

16.5 acres of romantic gardens surrounding a 16th century timber framed wool smuggler's cottage (not open to the public). Woodland walks with oaks, elm, birch and beech trees. Rhododendrons, azaleas and camellias surround sunken water gardens.

Location: OS Ref. TQ665 372. 8m SE of Tunbridge Wells; 1m from Lamberhurst off A21.

Opening Times: Gardens only: All year, daily, 11am - 6pm, except 25 Dec & 1 Jan.

Admission: Adult £4, Child £1. Coach parties welcome.

▢ ▦ ▧ ▣ Ⓟ Free. 🐕 On leads. ❄

PENSHURST PLACE & GARDENS

See page 130 for full page entry.

QUEBEC HOUSE 🎗

Tel: 01892 890651

Westerham, Kent TN16 1TD

Owner: The National Trust   **Contact:** Regional Office

General Wolfe spent his early years in this gabled, red-brick 17th century house. Four rooms containing portraits, prints and memorabilia relating to Wolfe's family and career are on view. In the Tudor stable block is an exhibition about the Battle of Quebec (1759) and the parts played by Wolfe and his adversary, the Marquis de Montcalm.

Location: OS Ref. TQ449 541. At E end of village, on N side of A25, facing junction with B2026, Edenbridge Road.

Opening Times: 3 Apr - 30 Oct: Suns & Tues, 2 - 6pm, last admission 5.30pm.

Admission: Adult £2.60, Child £1.30, Family (2+3) £6.50. Groups £2.20.

QUEX HOUSE & GARDEN & POWELL COTTON MUSEUM 🏛

Quex Park, Birchington, Kent CT7 0BH   **Tel:** 01843 842168

e-mail: powell-cotton-museum@virgin.net

Owner: Trustees of Powell Cotton Museum   **Contact:** John Harrison

Regency/Victorian country residence, walled gardens and Victorian explorers' museum.

Location: OS Ref. TR308 683. ½ m from Birchington Church via Park Lane.

Opening Times: Please contact Museum for details.

Admission: Summer: Adult £3.50, Child, OAP, Disabled & Carer £2.80, Student £2, Family (2+3) £11. Winter: Adult £2.50, Child, OAP, Disabled & Carer £1.80, Family (2+3) £7.50.

RECULVER TOWERS & ROMAN FORT ⊞

Tel: 01227 740676

Reculver, Herne Bay, Kent

Owner: English Heritage   **Contact:** Reculver Country Park

This 12th century landmark of twin towers has guided sailors into the Thames estuary for seven centuries. Walls of a Roman fort, which were erected nearly 2,000 years ago.

Location: OS Ref. TR228 694. At Reculver 3m E of Herne Bay by the seashore.

Opening Times: Any reasonable time. External viewing only.

Admission: Free.

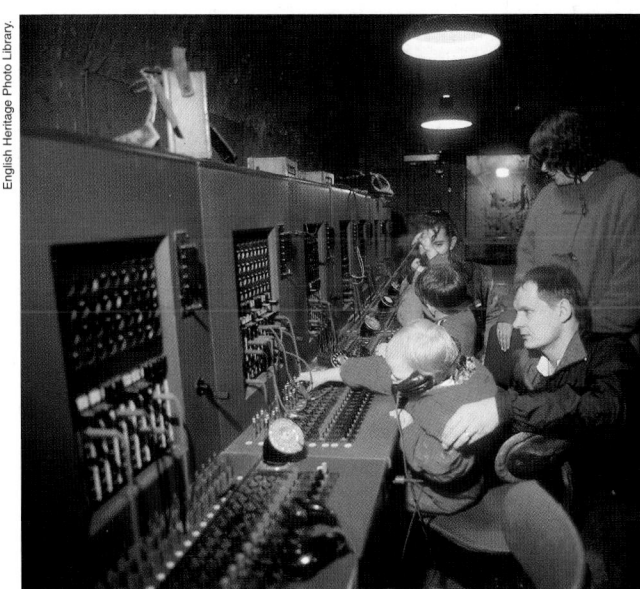

Dover Castle, Kent.

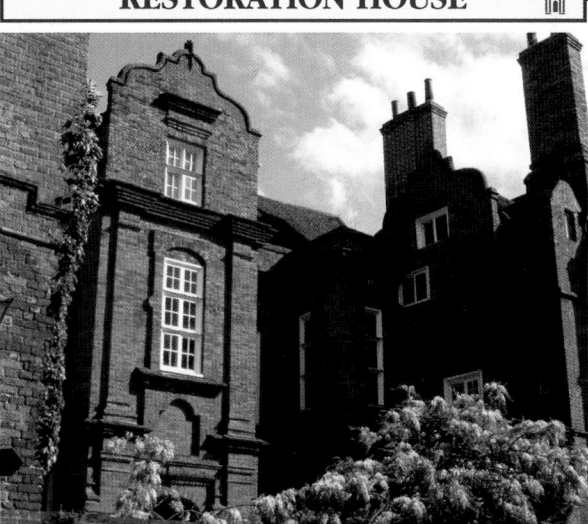

RESTORATION HOUSE 🏛

17 - 19 CROW LANE, ROCHESTER, KENT ME1 1RF

Owner: Messrs R Tucker & J Wilmot   *Contact:* Robert Tucker

Tel: 01634 848520 **Fax:** 01634 880058

Historic city mansion with unique old atmosphere. Links to Charles II, Pepys, Dickens (Miss Havisham's House). Beautiful interiors with early paintwork, fine furniture and pictures (including Kneller, Dahl, Reynolds, Gainsborough). Charming interlinked walled gardens of ingenious plan in classic English style. A private gem.

Location: OS Ref, TQ744 683. Historic centre of Rochester, off High Street, opposite the Vines Park.

Opening Times: 3 May - 28 Sept: Thurs & Fris, 10am - 5pm.

Admission: Adult £4.50 includes 24 page illustrated guidebook), Child £2. Booked groups (12+): Adult £4, Child £2.

ⓘ No stiletto heels. 🐕

RICHBOROUGH ROMAN FORT ⊞

Tel: 01304 612013

Richborough, Sandwich, Kent CT13 9JW

Owner: English Heritage   **Contact:** The Custodian

This fort and township date back to the Roman landing in AD43. The fortified walls and the massive foundations of a triumphal arch which stood 80 feet high still survive. The inclusive audio tour and the museum give an insight into life in Richborough's heyday as a busy township.

Location: OS Ref. TR324 602. 1½ m NW of Sandwich off A257.

Opening Times: 1 Apr - 30 Sept: daily, 10am - 6pm. 1 - 31 Oct: 10am - 5pm. 1 - 31 Nov: Wed - Sun only, 10am - 4pm. Weekends only in Dec, Jan & Feb, 10am - 4pm. 1 - 31 Mar: Wed - Sun, 10am - 4pm. Closed 24 - 26 Dec & 1 Jan.

Admission: Adult £2.70, Child £1.40, Conc. £2.

ⓘ Museum. ▢ ▧ Ground floor suitable. 🎧 Ⓟ 🐕 Guide dogs only. ❄ ▣ Tel. for details.

RIVERHILL HOUSE 🏛

Tel: 01732 458802/452557 **Fax:** 01732 458802

Sevenoaks, Kent TN15 0RR

Owner: The Rogers Family   **Contact:** Mrs Rogers

Small country house built in 1714, home of the Rogers family since 1840. Panelled rooms, portraits and interesting memorabilia. Historic hillside garden with extensive views, rare trees and shrubs. Sheltered terraces and rhododendrons and azaleas in a woodland setting. Bluebells.

Location: OS Ref. TQ541 522. 2m S of Sevenoaks on E side of A225.

Opening Times: Garden: Apr, May & Jun: Weds, Suns & BH weekends, 12 noon - 6pm. Coaches by arrangement. House: open only to pre-booked groups of adults (20+) on any day: Apr, May & Jun.

Admission: Adult £3, Child 50p. Pre-booked groups: £4.

ⓘ Conferences. ▢ ▧ Not suitable. ▣ 🚶 By arrangement. 🐕

ROCHESTER CASTLE ⊞

Tel: 01634 402276

The Lodge, Rochester-upon-Medway, Medway ME1 1SX

Owner: English Heritage   **Contact:** Head Custodian

(Managed by Medway Council)

Built in the 11th century. The keep is over 100 feet high and with walls 12 feet thick. At the top you will be able to enjoy fine views over the river and surrounding city of Rochester.

Location: OS Ref. TQ743 685. By Rochester Bridge (A2), M2/J1 & M25/J2.

Opening Times: 1 Apr - 30 Sept: daily, 10am - 6pm. 1 - 31 Oct: daily, 10am - 5pm. 1 Nov - 31 Mar: daily, 10am - 4pm. Closed 24 - 26 Dec & 1 Jan.

Admission: Please telephone for details.

ROCHESTER CATHEDRAL
Tel: 01634 401301 **Fax:** 01634 401410

c/o 70a High Street, Rochester, Kent ME1 1JY **Contact:** Mrs S Strong

Founded in 604AD, Rochester Cathedral has been a place of Christian worship for nearly 1,400 years. The present building is a blend of Norman and gothic architecture with a fine medieval crypt. In the cloister are the remains of the 12th century chapter house and priory. A focal point is the Doubleday statue.

Location: OS Ref. TQ742 686. Signposted from M20/J6 and on the A2/M2/J3. Best access from M2/J3.

Opening Times: All year: 8.30am - 5pm. Visiting may be restricted during services.

Admission: £2 donation. Groups: £2.50 guided. Groups must book on above number. Separate prices for schools.

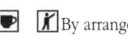

Photography permit £1. By arrangement.

ROMAN PAINTED HOUSE
Tel: 01304 203279

New Street, Dover, Kent CT17 9AJ

Owner: Dover Roman Painted House Trust **Contact:** Mr B Philip

Discovered in 1970. Built around 200AD as a hotel for official travellers. Impressive wall paintings, central heating systems and the Roman fort wall built through the house.

Location: OS Ref. TR318 414. Dover town centre. E of York St.

Opening Times: Apr - Sept: 10am - 5pm, except Mons.

Admission: Adult £2, Child/OAP 80p.

ROYDON HALL
Tel: 01622 812121 **Fax:** 01622 813959

Nr Tonbridge, Kent TN12 5NH **e-mail:** roydonhall@btinternet.com

Owner: Maharishi Foundation **Contact:** The Events Manager

Roydon Hall is a very fine Tudor manor house which was 'modified' by the Victorians.

Location: OS Ref. TQ664 518. M25 then M40 towards Paddock Wood. Follow signs for Paddock Wood into Seven Mile Lane. Sign for Roydon on right indicating turn to left on brow of hill about 4m down lane.

Opening Times: Available for film location work and corporate events. Bed and breakfast accommodation also.

ST AUGUSTINE'S ABBEY
Tel: 01227 767345

Longport, Canterbury, Kent CT1 1TF

Owner: English Heritage **Contact:** The Custodian

The Abbey, founded by St Augustine in 598, is a World Heritage Site. Take the free interactive audio tour which gives a fascinating insight into the Abbey's history and visit the museum displaying artifacts uncovered during archaeological excavations of the site.

Location: OS Ref. TR154 578. In Canterbury 1/2 m E of Cathedral Close.

Opening Times: 1 Apr - 30 Sept: daily, 10am - 6pm. 1 - 31 Oct: 10am - 5pm. 1 Nov - 31 Mar: daily, 10am - 4pm. Closed 24 - 26 Dec & 1 Jan.

Admission: Adult £2.60, Child £1.30, Conc. £1.90. 15% discount for groups (11+). One extra place for every additional 20.

Grounds suitable. WC. Free. Guide dogs only. Tel. for details.

ST JOHN'S COMMANDERY
Tel: 01304 211067

Densole, Swingfield, Kent

Owner: English Heritage **Contact:** The South East Regional Office

A medieval chapel built by the Knights Hospitallers. It has a moulded plaster ceiling and a remarkable timber roof and was converted into a farmhouse in the 16th century.

Location: OS Ref. TR232 440. 2m NE of Densole on minor road off A260.

Opening Times: Any reasonable time for exterior viewing. Internal viewing by appointment only.

Admission: Free.

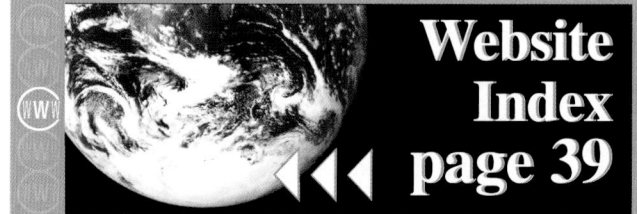

Website Index page 39

SCOTNEY CASTLE GARDEN

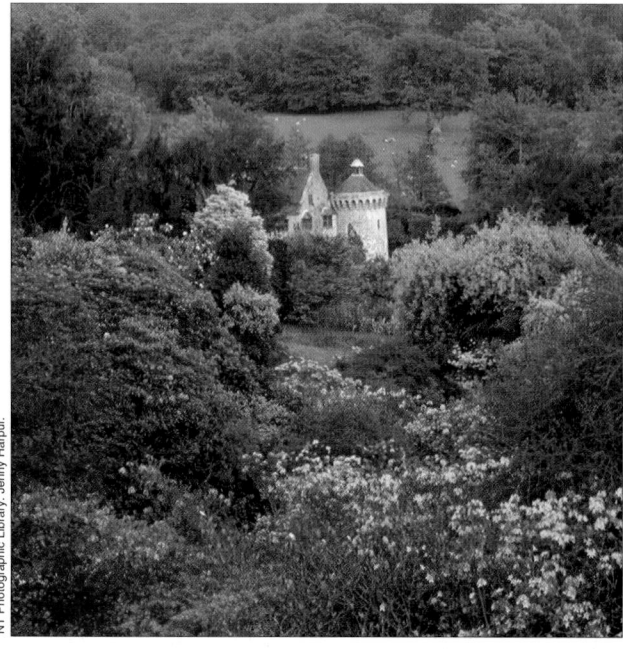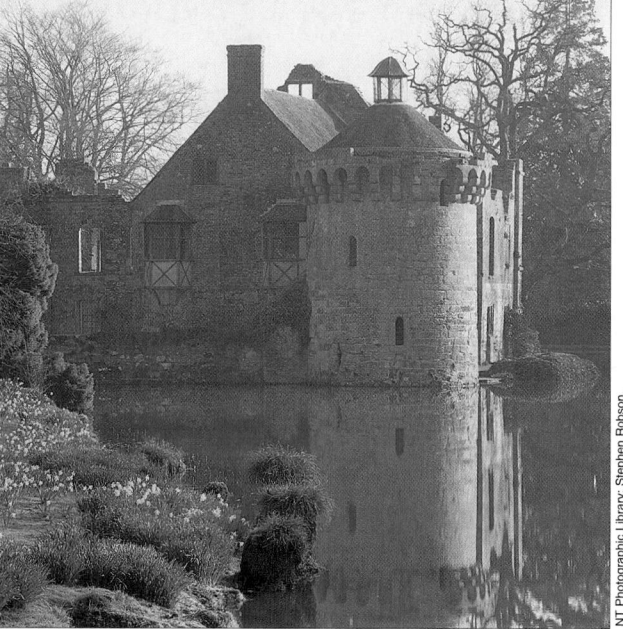

LAMBERHURST, TUNBRIDGE WELLS, KENT TN3 8JN

Owner: *The National Trust* **Contact:** *Administrative Assistant*

Tel: 01892 891081 **Fax:** 01892 890110 **e-mail:** kscxxx@smtp.ntrust.org.uk

One of England's most romantic gardens designed by Edward Hussey in the picturesque style. Dramatic vistas from the terrace of the new Scotney Castle, built in the 1830s, lead down to the ruins of a 14th century moated castle. Rhododendrons, kalmia, azaleas and wisteria flower in profusion. Roses and clematis scramble over the remains of the Old Castle, which is open for the summer. In autumn the garden's glowing colours merge with the surrounding woodlands where there are many country walks to be explored.

Location: OS Ref. TQ688 353. Signed off A21 1m S of Lamberhurst village.

Opening Times: 17 - 25 Mar: Sats & Suns, 12 noon - 4pm. 31 Mar - 4 Nov: Wed - Fri, 11am - 6pm, Sats & Suns, 2 - 6pm, BH Suns & Mons 12 noon - 6pm (closed Good Fri). Last adm. 1 hr before close. Car park: All year for estate walks.

Admission: Adult £4.40, Child £2.20, Family (2+3) £11. Pre-booked groups weekdays £3.80.

Grounds (but steep parts). Outside garden only, on leads.

SMALLHYTHE PLACE

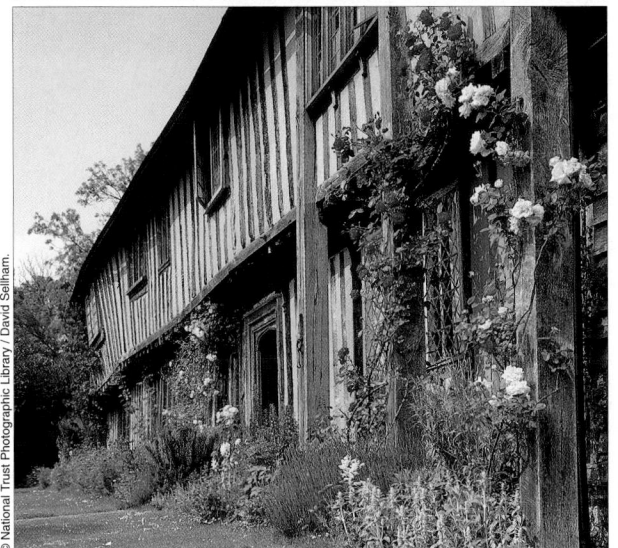

TENTERDEN, KENT TN30 7NG

Owner: The National Trust   Contact: The Custodian

Tel: 01580 762334 **Fax:** 01580 762334 **e-mail:** ksmxxx@smtp.ntrust.org.uk

This early 16th century half-timbered house was home to Shakespearean actress Ellen Terry from 1899 to 1928. The house contains many personal and theatrical mementoes including many of her lavish costumes. The charming cottage grounds include her rose garden and the Barn Theatre, which is open most days by courtesy of the Barn Theatre Society.

Location: OS Ref. TQ893 300. 2m S of Tenterden on E side of the Rye road B2082.

Opening Times: 31 Mar - 31 Oct: daily except Thurs & Fris (open Good Fri), 1.30 - 6pm or dusk if earlier. Groups (max. 25) Tues morning only.

Admission: Adult £3.20, Child £1.60, Family £8.

ℹ️ No photography in house. ♿ Not suitable. 🅿️ Limited. ✖️

SOUTH FORELAND LIGHTHOUSE & GATEWAY TO THE WHITE CLIFFS

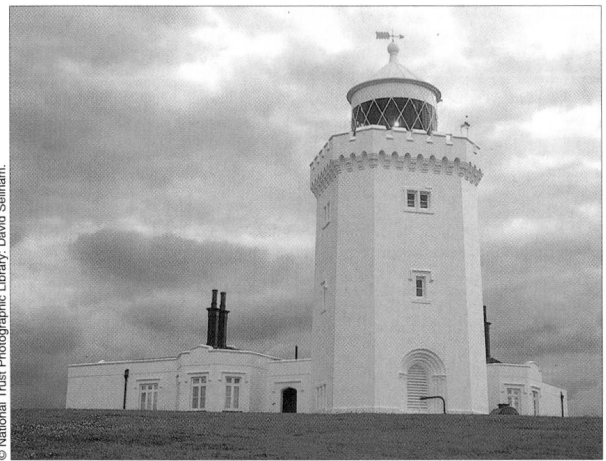

LANGDON CLIFFS, Nr DOVER, KENT CT16 1HJ

Owner: The National Trust   Contact: Countryside Manager

Tel: 01304 202756 **Fax:** 01304 205295 **e-mail:** kwcxxx@smtp.ntrust.org.uk

The Gateway to the White Cliffs is a visitor centre with spectacular views across the English Channel. It introduces the visitor to its coast and countryside through imaginative displays and interpretation. High up on the cliffs is South Foreland Lighthouse, used by Marconi for his first ship-to-shore radio experiments.

Location: OS138 Ref. TR336 422. Follow White Cliffs brown signs from roundabout 1m NE of Dover at junction of A2/A258.

Opening Times: Gateway: 1 Mar - 31 Oct: daily 10am - 5pm. 1 Nov - 28 Feb: daily 11am - 4pm. Lighthouse: 1 Mar - 31 Oct: daily except Tues & Weds, 11am - 5.30pm (last admission 5pm).

Admission: Adult £1.80, Child 90p. Car Park £1.50. Groups £1.50.

🛍️ Limited range. 🚻 ♿ Partially suitable. WC. 🎨 By arrangement.
🅿️ 🚌 🐕 In grounds, on leads. 🏠 Holiday cottage, 1dbl & 2 single. ✖️

SQUERRYES COURT & GARDENS 🏛️   See page 131 for full page entry.

STONEACRE 🌿   **Tel:** 01622 862871 **Fax:** 01622 862157

Otham, Maidstone, Kent ME15 8RS

Owner: The National Trust   **Contact:** The Tenant

A half-timbered mainly late 15th century yeoman's house, with great hall and crownpost, and restored cottage-style garden.

Location: OS Ref. TQ800 535. In narrow lane at N end of Otham village, 3m SE of Maidstone, 1m S of A20.

Opening Times: 4 Apr - 31 Oct: Weds & Sats, 2 - 6pm. Last admission 1hr before close.

Admission: Adult £2.60, Child £1.30, Family (2+3) £6.50. Groups £2.20.

TEMPLE MANOR 🏛️   **Tel:** 01634 827980

Strood, Rochester, Kent

Owner: English Heritage   **Contact:** Medway Council

The 13th century manor house of the Knights Templar which mainly provided accommodation for members of the order travelling between London and the Continent.

Location: OS Ref. TQ733 686. In Strood (Rochester) off A228.

Opening Times: 1 Apr - 30 Sept: weekends & BHs, 10am - 6pm.

Admission: Free.

THE THEATRE ROYAL, CHATHAM   **Tel:** 01634 306367

102 High Street, Chatham, Kent ME4 4BY

Owner: Chatham Theatre Royal Trust Ltd   **Contact:** The Administrator

Built in 1899, it is Kent's finest surviving Victorian Theatre.

Location: OS Ref. TQ755 679. In Chatham High Street.

Opening Times: Mon - Sat, 10am - 3pm. Guided tours most weekdays. Groups welcome by appointment.

Admission: Donation.

TONBRIDGE CASTLE   **Tel:** 01732 770929

Castle Street, Tonbridge, Kent TN9 1BG

Owner: Tonbridge & Malling Borough Council   **Contact:** The Administrator

Location: OS Ref. TQ588 466. 300 yds NW of the Medway Bridge at town centre.

Opening Times: All year: Mon - Sat, 9am - 4pm. Suns & BHs, 10.30am - 4pm.

Admission: Adult £3.60, Conc £1.80. Family £8.50. Admission includes audio tour.

UPNOR CASTLE 🏛️   **Tel:** 01634 718742

Upnor, Kent

Owner: English Heritage   **Contact:** Medway Council

Well-preserved 16th century gun fort built to protect Queen Elizabeth I's warships. However in 1667 it failed to prevent the Dutch Navy which stormed up the Medway destroying half the English fleet.

Location: OS Ref. TQ758 706. At Upnor, on unclassified road off A228. 2m NE of Strood.

Opening Times: 1 Apr - 30 Sept: daily, 10am - 6pm.

Admission: Please telephone for details.

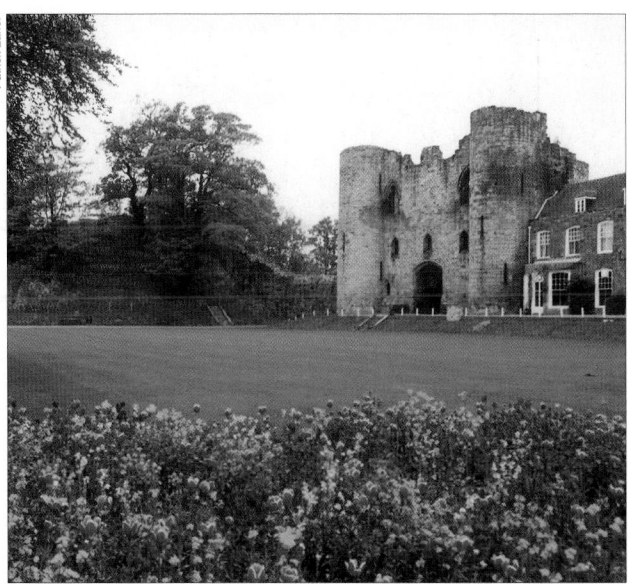

Tonbridge Castle, Kent.

WALMER CASTLE & GARDENS

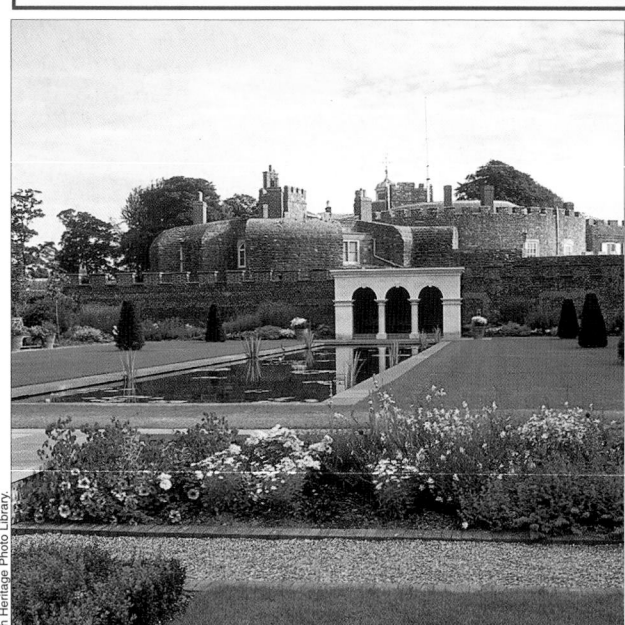
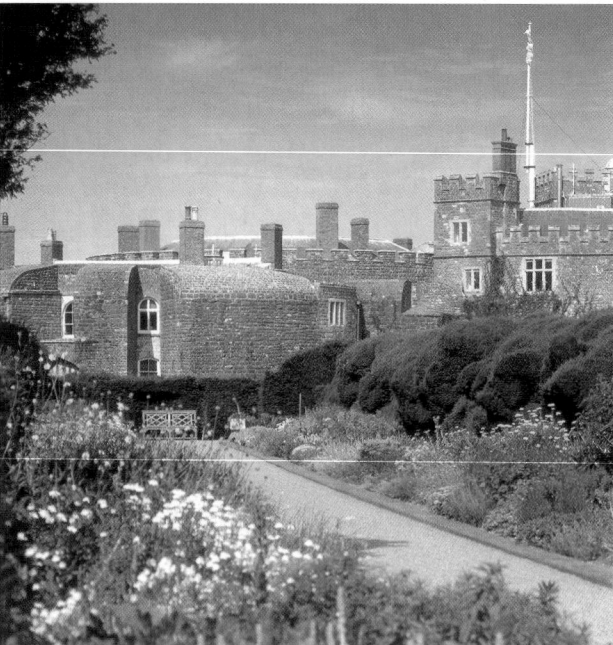

English Heritage Photo Library

WALMER, DEAL, KENT CT14 7LJ

Owner: *English Heritage*　　**Contact:** *The Custodian*

Tel: 01304 364288

A Tudor fort transformed into an elegant stately home. The residence of the Lords Warden of the Cinque Ports and still used by HM The Queen Mother today. Take the new free audio tour and see the Duke of Wellington's rooms and even his famous boots. Beautiful gardens including the Queen Mother's Garden, The Broadwalk with its famous yew tree hedge, Kitchen Garden and Moat Garden. Lunches and cream teas available in the delightful Lord Warden's tearooms.

Location: OS Ref. TR378 501. S of Walmer on A258, M20/J13 or M2 to Deal.

Opening Times: 1 Apr - 30 Sept: daily, 10am - 6pm. 1 - 31 Oct: daily, 10am - 5pm. 1 Nov - 31 Dec & 1 - 31 Mar: Wed - Sun only, 10am - 4pm. Jan & Feb: Sats & Suns, 10am - 4pm. Closed 24 - 26 Dec & 1 Jan and when Lord Warden is in residence.

Admission: Adult £4.80, Child £2.40, OAP/Student £3.60. 15% discount for groups (11+). One extra place for each additional 20. EH members free.

Grounds suitable.　Guide dogs only.　Tel. for details.

WILLESBOROUGH WINDMILL　　　　**Tel:** 01233 661866

Mill Lane, Willesborough, Ashford, Kent

125 year old restored smock mill.

Location: OS Ref. TR031 421. Off A292 close to M20/J10. At E end of Ashford.

Opening Times: Apr - Sept; Sats, Suns and BH Mons, 2 - 5pm or dusk if earlier.

Admission: Adult £1, Child/Conc. 50p. Groups 10% reduction by arrangement only.

YALDING ORGANIC GARDENS　　**Tel:** 01622 814650 **Fax:** 01622 814 650

Benover Road, Yalding, Maidstone, Kent ME18 6EX

Owner: HDRA - the organic organisation　　　**Contact:** David Holdsworth

Fourteen newly created gardens reflecting mankind's experience of gardening over the centuries.

Location: OS Ref. TQ698 492. 6m SW of Maidstone, 1/2 m S of village at Yalding on B2162.

Opening Times: Apr: w/ends only, 10am - 5pm. May - Sept: Wed - Sun, 10am - 5pm. Oct: w/ends only.

Admission: Adult £3 (no concessions), accompanied Child (up to 16yrs) Free. Groups (14+) £2.50 plus 50p for guided tour.

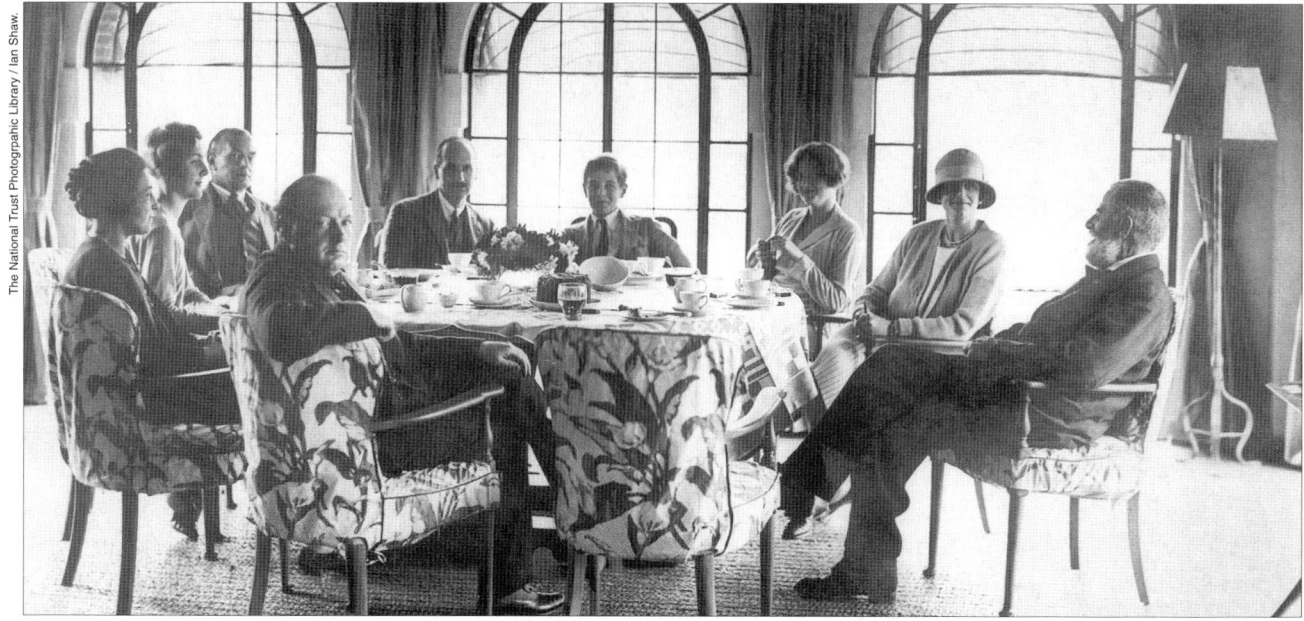

The National Trust Photogrpahic Library / Ian Shaw.

Sir Winston Churchill and others at Chartwell, Kent, of which he said " I love the place – a day away from Chartwell is a day wasted".

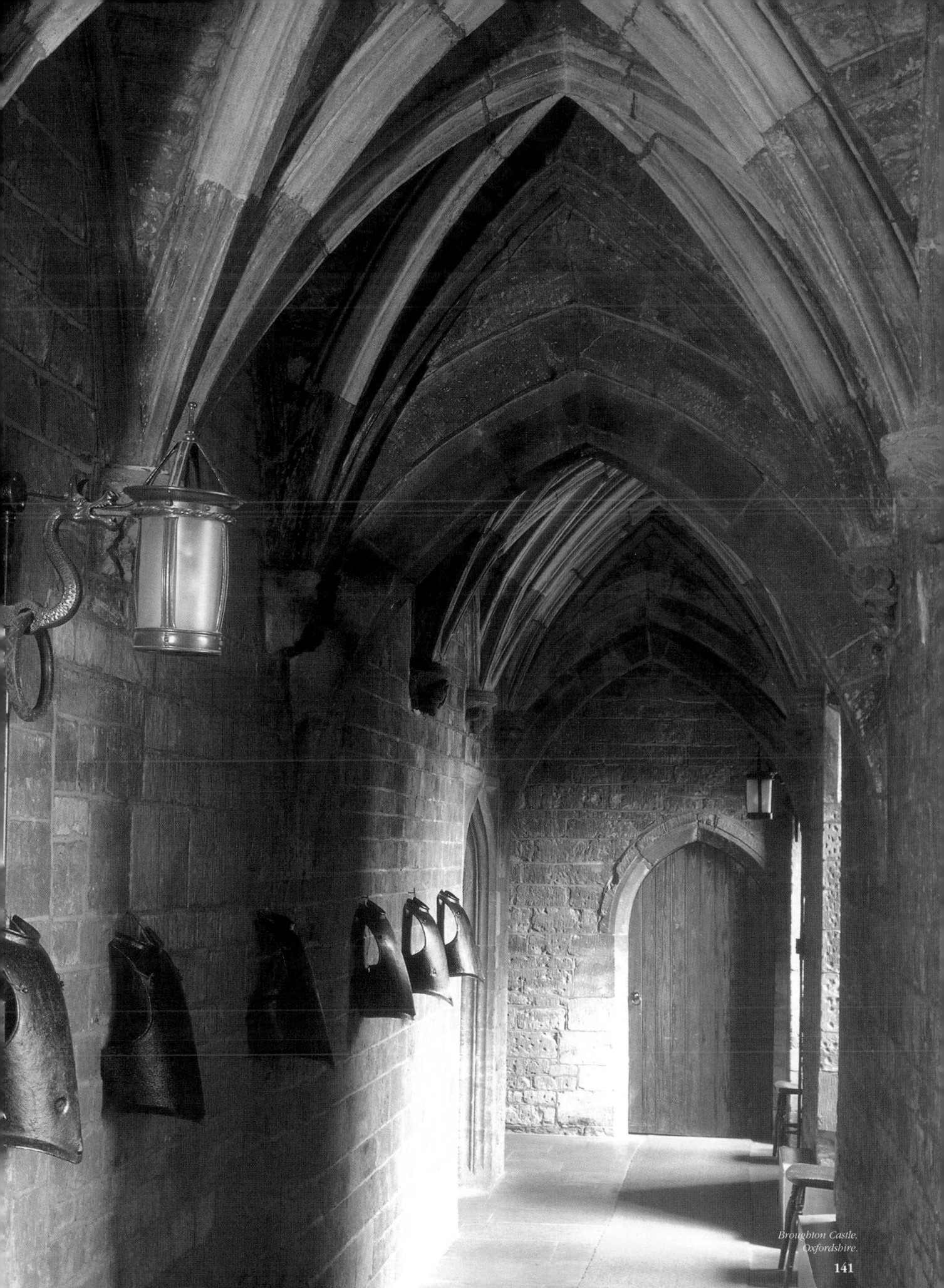

Broughton Castle,
Oxfordshire.

141

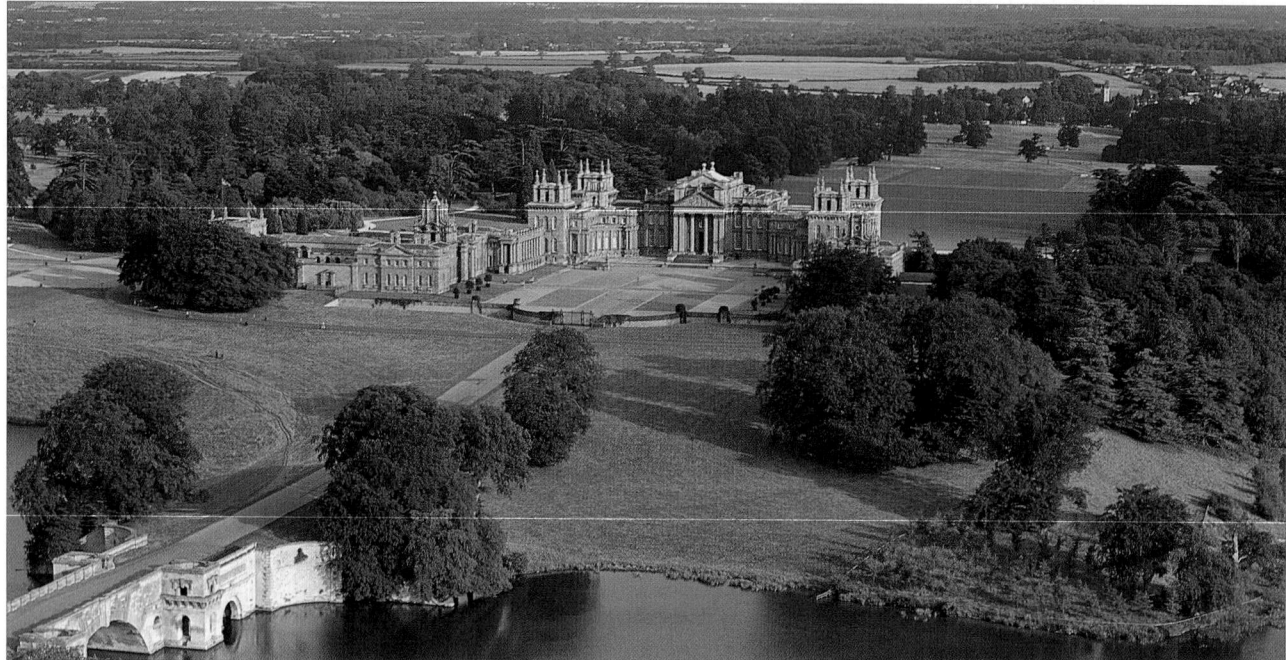

BLENHEIM PALACE
Woodstock

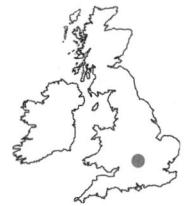

Owner:
The Duke of Marlborough

CONTACT

Nicholas Day
Blenheim Palace
Woodstock
OX20 1PX

Tel: 01993 811091

Fax: 01993 813527

e-mail: administration
@blenheimpalace.com

LOCATION

OS Ref. SP441 161

From London, M40, A44
(1½ hrs), 8m NW of
Oxford. London 63m
Birmingham 54.

Air: Heathrow 60m.
Birmingham 54m.

Coach: From London
(Victoria) to Oxford.

Rail: Oxford Station.

Bus: Oxford (Cornmarket)
- Woodstock.

CONFERENCE/FUNCTION

ROOM	SIZE	MAX CAPACITY
Orangery		200
Great Hall	70' x 40'	150
Saloon	50' x 30'	72
with Great Hall		450
with Great Hall & Library		750
Library	180' x 30'	300

BLENHEIM PALACE, home of the 11th Duke of Marlborough and birthplace of Sir Winston Churchill, was built between 1705-1722 for John Churchill, 1st Duke of Marlborough, in grateful recognition of his magnificent victory at the Battle of Blenheim in 1704. One of England's largest private houses, it was built in the baroque style by Sir John Vanbrugh and is considered his masterpiece. The land and £240,000 were given by Queen Anne and a grateful nation.

Blenheim's wonderful interior reveals striking contrasts – from the lofty Great Hall to gilded state rooms and the majestic Long Library. The superb collection includes fine paintings, furniture, bronzes and the famous Marlborough Victories tapestries. The five-room Churchill Exhibition includes his birth room.

GARDENS

The Palace grounds reflect the evolution of grand garden design. Of the original work by Queen Anne's gardener, Henry Wise, only the Walled Garden remains; but dominating all is the superb landscaping of 'Capability' Brown. Dating from 1764, his work includes the lake, park and gardens. Achille Duchêne, employed by the 9th Duke, subsequently recreated the Great Court and built the Italian Garden on the east and the Water Terraces on the west of the Palace. Recently the Pleasure Gardens complex has been developed. This includes the Marlborough Maze, Herb Garden, Adventure Playground, Butterfly House and Putting Greens.

❖

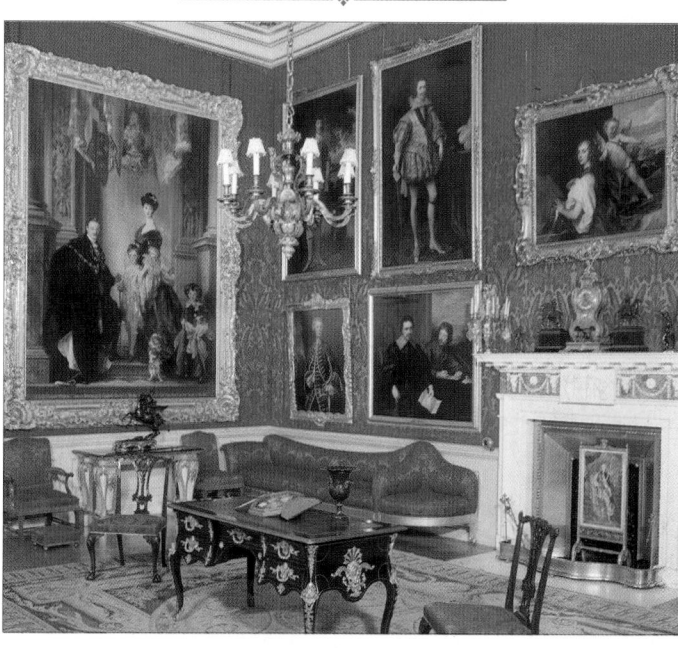

OPENING TIMES

SUMMER
Palace
Mid March - 31 October
Daily: 10.30am-5.30pm
Last admission 4.45pm.

WINTER
Park only
1 November - Mid March
The Duke of Marlborough reserves the right to close the Palace or Park or to amend admission prices without notice.

ADMISSION

(Prices: 12.3.01 - 31.10.01)
- Palace Tour and Churchill Exhibition
- Park
- Garden
- Butterfly House
- Herb & Lavender Garden
- Train
- Car or coach parking
- Maze & Adventure Play Area and rowing boat hire optional extras

    Adult £9.30
    Child (5 - 15 yrs.)......£4.80
    Child (16 & 17 yrs.)...£7.30
    OAP.........................£7.30
    Family £23.00
Groups
    Adult £7.50
    OAP/Student...........£6.50
    Child (5 - 15 yrs.)......£4.00
    Child (16 & 17 yrs.)...£6.50

- Blenheim Park, Butterfly House, Train, Parking, (Maze & Adventure Play Area and rowing boat hire optional extras).

    Coaches* £30.00
    Cars* £6.00
    Adult** £2.00
    Child** £1.00

- Private visits† £15.00

* Including occupants.
** Pedestrians.
† By appointment only.
  Min. charge of £375 (mornings and £525 (evenings).

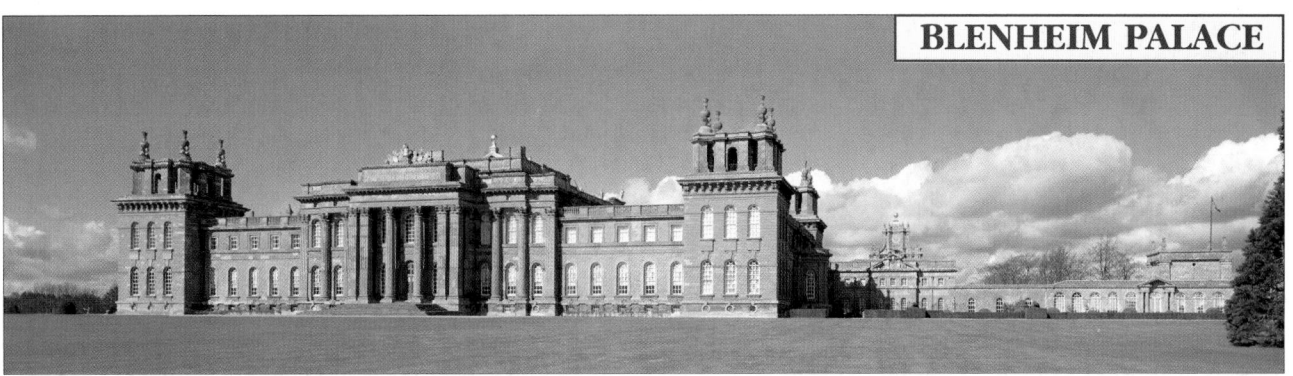

BLENHEIM PALACE

Five Shops. Filming, Equestrian Events, Craft Fairs. Will consider any proposals (contact Admin Office). Lake (Rowing Boats for hire), Golf Buggy rides, Train rides. Photography outside only.

Corporate hospitality, including dinners and receptions. The Orangery seats 200 for luncheon or dinner, throughout the year together with the Spencer Churchill Conference Room. For the Palace contact the Administrator, & for the Orangery contact Sodexho Prestige tel: 01993 813874/811274.

Visitors may alight at the Palace entrance then park in allocated area. WCs.

 2 Restaurants, 2 Cafeterias. Group capacity 150. Groups can book for afternoon tea, buffets and luncheon. Menus on request. Contact Sodexho Prestige for further info: 01993 813874/811274.

Included in the cost of entry. Private and language tours may be pre-booked.

Unlimited for cars and coaches. Advise Administrator's office for groups of over 100. Coaches/groups welcome, without pre-booking. Group organisers guide available by post.

Blenheim has held the Sandford Award for an outstanding contribution to Heritage Education since 1982. Operated by a very experienced headmaster, education groups may study virtually all subjects at all four stages of the National Curriculum as well as have general interest or leisure visits. Tourism Studies (all levels) available.

Dogs on leads in Park. Guide dogs for the blind & hearing dogs for the deaf only in house and garden.

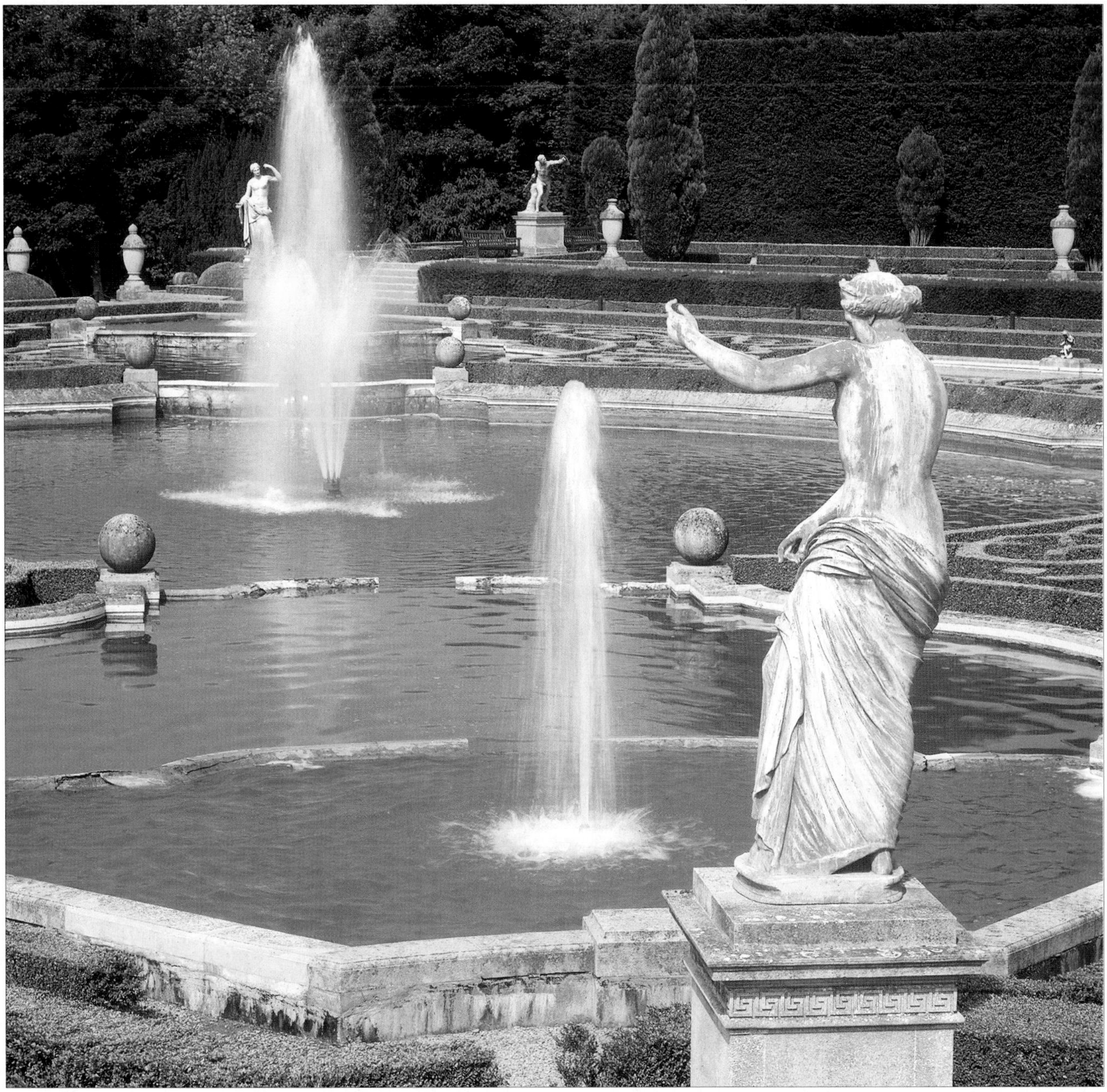

The Water Terrace

South East England

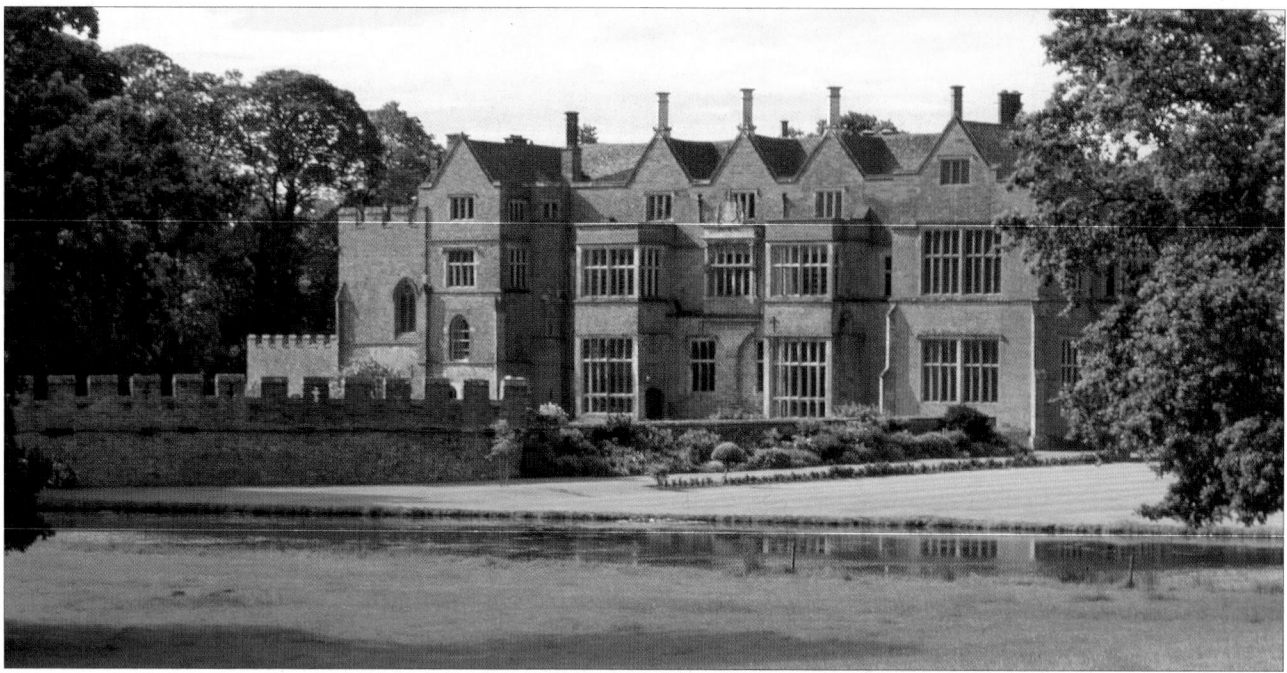

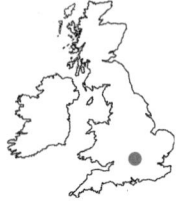

Owner:
Lord Saye & Sele

CONTACT

Mrs J Moorhouse
Broughton Castle
Banbury
OX15 5EB

Tel/Fax: 01295 276070

Tel/Fax: 01295 722547

e-mail: admin@broughton
castle.demon.co.uk

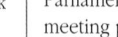

LOCATION

OS Ref. SP418 382

Broughton Castle is
2¹/₂m SW of Banbury Cross
on the B4035,
Shipston-on-Stour -
Banbury Road.
Easily accessible from
Stratford-on-Avon,
Warwick, Oxford, Burford
and the Cotswolds.
M40/J11.

Rail: From London/
Birmingham to Banbury.

BROUGHTON CASTLE
Banbury

BROUGHTON CASTLE is essentially a family home lived in by Lord and Lady Saye & Sele and their family.

The original medieval Manor House, of which much remains today, was built in about 1300 by Sir John de Broughton. It stands on an island site surrounded by a 3-acre moat. The Castle was greatly enlarged between 1550 and 1600, at which time it was embellished with magnificent plaster ceilings, splendid panelling and fine fireplaces.

In the 17th century William, 8th Lord Saye & Sele, played a leading role in national affairs. He opposed Charles I's efforts to rule without Parliament and Broughton became a secret meeting place for the King's opponents.

During the Civil War William raised a regiment and he and his four sons all fought at the nearby Battle of Edgehill. After the battle the Castle was besieged and captured.

Arms and armour for the Civil War and from other periods are displayed in the Great Hall. Visitors may also see the gatehouse, gardens and park together with the nearby 14th century Church of St Mary, in which there are many family tombs, memorials and hatchments.

GARDENS

The garden area consists of mixed herbaceous and shrub borders containing many old roses. In addition, there is a formal walled garden with beds of roses surrounded by box hedging and lined by more mixed borders.

❖

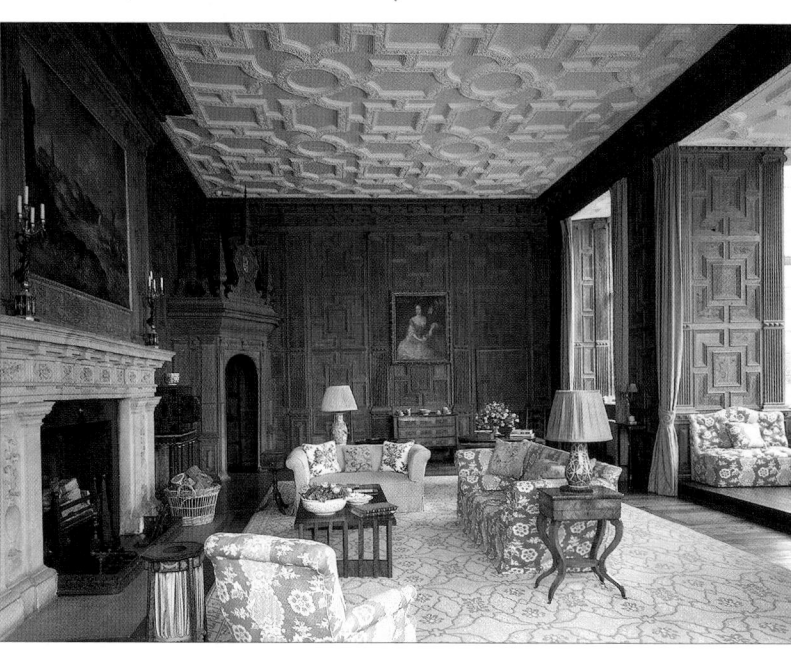

OPENING TIMES

SUMMER

20 May - 12 September
Weds & Suns
2 - 5pm.

Also Thurs in July and August and all Bank Holiday Suns and Bank Holiday Mons (including Easter) 2 - 5pm.

Groups welcome on any day and at any time throughout the year by appointment.

ADMISSION

Adult	£4.50
Child (5-15yrs)	£2.00
OAP/Student	£4.00
Groups*	
Adult	£4.00
Child (5-15yrs)	£1.75
Student	£3.00
OAP	£4.00

* Min payment: adults £80, children £50.

Filming, product launches, advertising features, corporate events in park. Photography permitted for personal use. Brief guidance notes available in French, Spanish, Dutch, Italian, Japanese, German, Polish, Greek & Russian.

Visitors allowed vehicle access to main entrance.

Tea/coffee for guided groups if pre-booked. Other meals by arrangement.

Available to pre-booked groups at no extra charge. Not available on open days.

P 300 yards from the castle.

Welcome.

No dogs inside House.

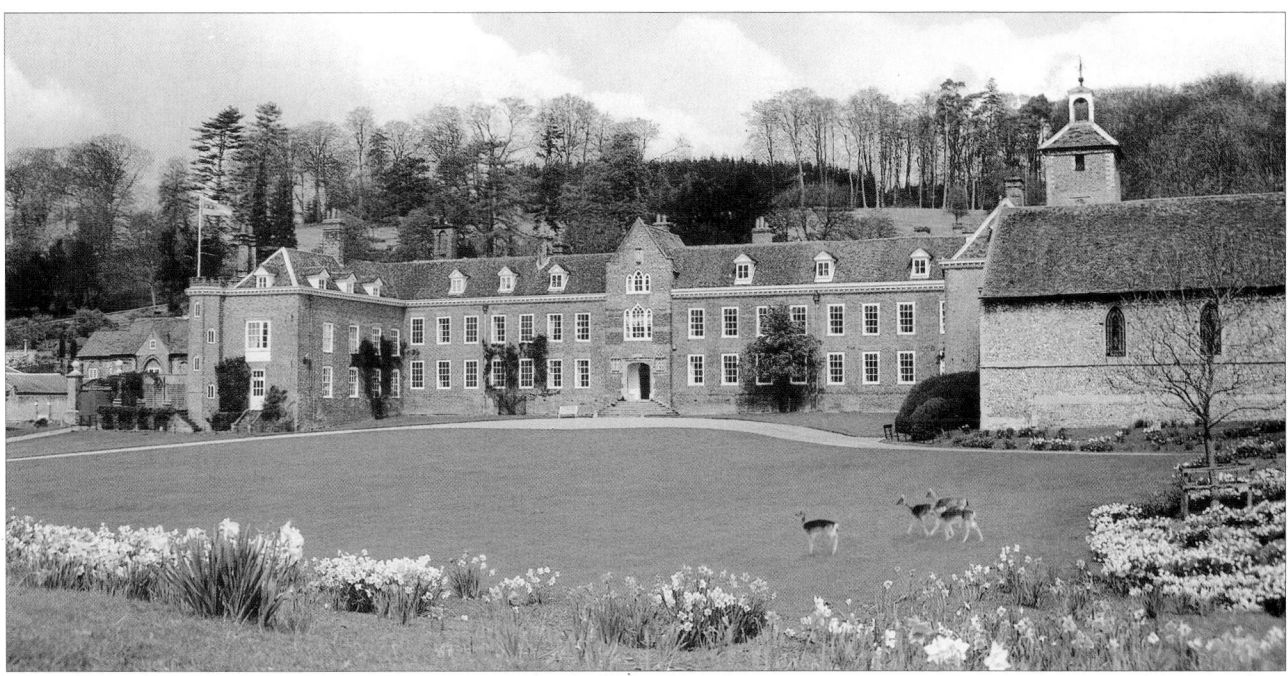

STONOR
Henley-on-Thames

STONOR, family home of Lord and Lady Camoys and the Stonor family for over 800 years, is set in a valley in the beautiful woods of the Chiltern Hills and surrounded by an extensive deer park.

The earliest part of the house dates from the 12th century, whilst most of the house was built in the 14th century. Early use of brick in Tudor times resulted in a more uniform façade concealing the earlier buildings, and changes to the windows and the roof in the 18th century reflect the Georgian appearance still apparent today.

Inside, the house shows strong Gothic decoration, also from the 18th century, and contains many items of rare furniture, sculptures, bronzes, tapestries, paintings and portraits of the family from Britain, Europe and America.

The Catholic Chapel used continuously through the Reformation is sited close by a pagan stone circle. In 1581 Stonor served as a sanctuary for St Edmund Campion, and an exhibition at the house features his life and work.

John Steane says of Stonor – *'If I had to suggest to a visitor who had only one day to sample the beauties of Oxfordshire I would suggest a visit to Stonor and a walk through its delectable park'.*

GARDENS

Extensive gardens enclosed at the rear of the house face south and have fine views over the park. The springtime display of daffodils is particularly outstanding. Fine irises and roses.

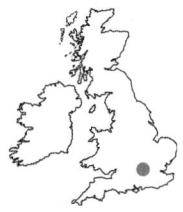

Owner:
Lord & Lady Camoys

CONTACT

Lisa Absalom
The Administrator
Stonor Park
Henley-on-Thames
Oxfordshire
RG9 6HF

Tel/Fax: 01491 638587

e-mail: lisa@
stonorpark.demon.co.uk

LOCATION

OS Ref. SU743 893

1 hr from London,
M4/J8/9. A4130 to
Henley-on-Thames.
On B480 NW of Henley.
A4130/B480 to Stonor.

Bus: 3m along the
Oxford - London route.

Rail: Henley-on-Thames
Station 5m.

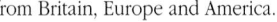

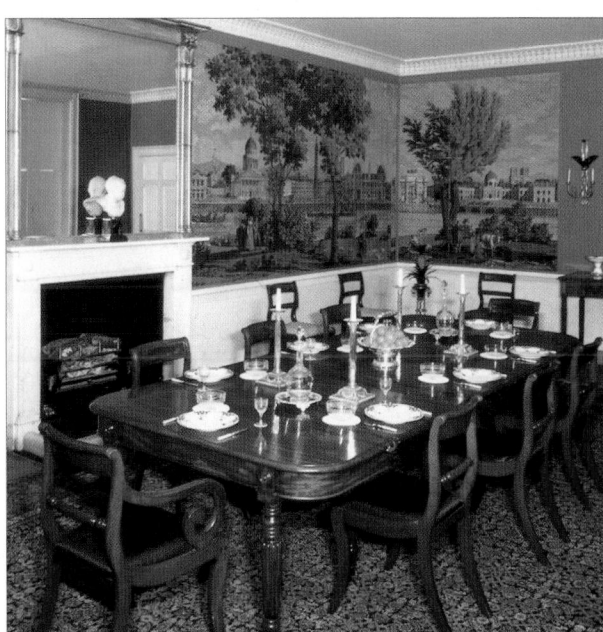

Filming, craft fairs, photo shoots, car displays, product promotion. Evening tours and buffet suppers by prior arrangement. Lectures can be given on the property, its contents and history. No smoking and no photography in house.

Visitors may alight at the entrance before parking. Ramp access to gardens, tearoom & shop. House not suitable.

Open as house. Lunches, teas & suppers by arrangement for groups (20+). Licensed.

Outside normal hours for 20 - 60 people per tour. Tour time: 1¼ hrs. Single payments for group bookings.

100 yds away.

In grounds, on leads.

Tel. for details.

OPENING TIMES

**Suns & Bank Holiday
Mons:** April - September,
2 - 5.30pm

Weds: July & August only:
2 - 5.30pm.

Private groups by
arrangement:
April - September,
Tue - Thur.

ADMISSION

House, Garden & Chapel
Adult £4.50
Child (under 14yrs).....Free
Groups* (12+) £4.00

Garden and Chapel
Adult £2.50

* Min. 12 persons by a single payment. Private guided tours £5pp, min. 20 persons and by a single payment.

School groups £2.50 per head, 1 teacher for every 10 children admitted free.

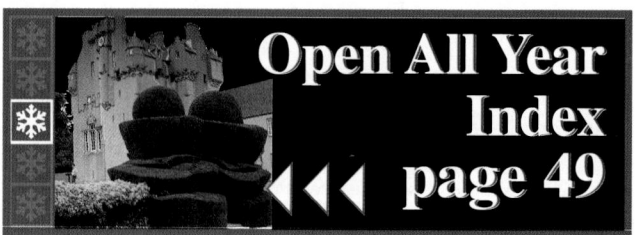

Open All Year
Index
◀◀◀ page 49

26A EAST ST HELEN STREET

Tel: 01865 242918

Abingdon, Oxfordshire

Owner: Oxford Preservation Trust   **Contact:** Ms Debbie Dance

One of best preserved examples of a 15th century dwelling in the area. Originally a Merchant's Hall House with later alterations, features include a remarkable domestic wall painting, an early oak ceiling, traceried windows and fireplaces. The remains of a 17th century boy's doublet found in the roof during restoration works is on display.

Location: OS Ref. SU497 969. 300 yards SSW of the market place and Town Hall.

Opening Times: By prior appointment.

Admission: Free.

ARDINGTON HOUSE

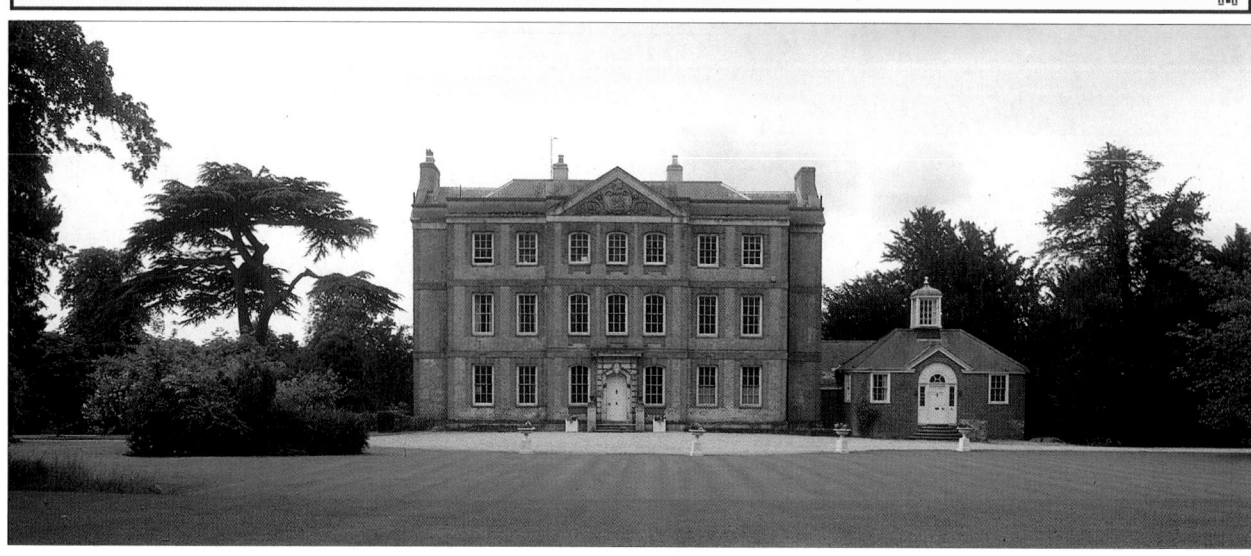

WANTAGE, OXFORDSHIRE OX12 8QA

Owner: The Baring Family   **Contact:** *Sharon Collerton*

Tel: 01235 821566   **Fax:** 01235 821151   **e-mail:** info@ardingtonhouse.com

Just a few miles south of Oxford stands the hauntingly beautiful, gracefully symmetric Ardington House. Surrounded by well-kept lawns, terraced gardens and peaceful paddocks this baroque house is still the private home of the Baring family. You'll find it in the village of Ardington in the lee of the Berkshire Downs close to the Ridgeway, the historic path that runs along the top of the Downs linking the Thames Valley to the Kennet. Its rooms to the south look across the garden and grazing horses to the river, well known to enthusiastic fly fisherman. To the front is an immaculately tended lawn, ideal for croquet and enjoyed by different generations of the Baring family as they grew up in this beautiful setting. Sir John Betjeman, one of the best loved poets of recent times, thought highly of this gracious home. But it doesn't end there because one of the greatest joys in this impressive home is the wood panelled dining room with its large oil painting of the father of the founder of this famous banking family.

The astonishing mixture of history, warmth and style you'll find at Ardington truly does place it in a class of its own.

Location: OS Ref. SU432 883. 12m S of Oxford, 12m N of Newbury, 2½ m E of Wantage.

Opening Times: 1 - 4, 7 - 11, 14 - 16, 18, 21 May; 1 - 3, 6 - 7, 9 - 10, 13 - 16 Aug & BH Mons, 2.30 - 4.30pm.

Admission: House & Gardens: Adult £3.50.

ℹ Conferences, product launches, films.   🍽   🍵 By arrangement. 🚶 By members of the family.   🅿   🐕 Guide dogs only.   🔔   Ⓦ

ASHDOWN HOUSE ✾

Tel: 01488 72584   **e-mail:** tadgen@smtp.ntrust.org.uk

Lambourn, Newbury RG16 7RE

Owner: The National Trust   **Contact:** Ashdown Estate Office

An extraordinary Dutch-style 17th century house, perched on the Berkshire Downs and famous for its association with Elizabeth of Bohemia (The Winter Queen), Charles I's sister, to whom the house was 'consecrated'. The interior has an impressive great staircase rising from hall to attic, and important paintings contemporary with the house. There are spectacular views from the roof over the formal parterre, lawns and surrounding countryside, as well as beautiful walks in neighbouring Ashdown Woods.

Location: OS Ref. SU282 820. 3½ m S of Lambourn, on W side of B4000.

Opening Times: Hall, Stairway, Roof & Garden: Apr - end Oct: Weds & Sats. Guided tours of house only at 2.15pm, 3.15pm & 4.15pm from front door. Woodland: All year: daily except Fris, dawn - dusk.

Admission: Adult £2.10, Woodland Free. No reduction for groups which must book in writing.

ℹ No WCs.   ♿ Garden suitable.   🚶 Obligatory.   🅿 250 metres from house. 🐕 Woodland only, on leads.   ❋   Ⓦ

BLENHEIM PALACE 🏛

See pages 142/143 for double page entry.

BROOK COTTAGE

Tel: 01295 670303 / 670590

Well Lane, Alkerton, Nr Banbury OX15 6NL

Owner/Contact: Mrs David Hodges

4 acre hillside garden. Roses, clematis, water gardens, colour co-ordinated borders, trees, shrubs.

Location: OS Ref. SP378 428. 6m NW of Banbury, ½ m SW of A422 Banbury to Stratford-upon-Avon road.

Opening Times: 16 Apr - 26 Oct: Mon - Fri, 9am - 6pm. Evenings, weekends and all group visits by appointment.

Admission: Adult £3, OAP £2, Child Free. In aid of National Gardens Scheme.

BROUGHTON CASTLE 🏛

See page 144 for full page entry.

BUSCOT OLD PARSONAGE ✾

Tel: 01793 762209

Buscot, Faringdon, Oxfordshire SN7 8DQ

e-mail: tbcjap@smtp.ntrust.org.uk

Owner: The National Trust   **Contact:** Coleshill Estate Office

An early 18th century house of Cotswold stone on the bank of the Thames with a small garden.

Location: OS Ref. SU231 973. 2m from Lechlade, 4m N of Faringdon on A417.

Opening Times: Apr - end Oct, Weds, 2 - 6pm by written appointment with tenant.

Admission: £1.20. Not suitable for groups.

BUSCOT PARK

Tel: 01367 240786 **Fax:** 01367 241794
e-mail: estbuscot@aol.com

Buscot, Faringdon, Oxfordshire SN7 8BU

Owner: The National Trust   **Contact:** Lord Faringdon

A late 18th century house with pleasure gardens, set within a park.

Location: OS Ref. SU239 973. Between Lechlade and Faringdon on A417.

Opening Times: House: 4 Apr - 28 Sept: Wed - Fri. Easter Sat & Sun, plus weekends of 28/29 Apr; 12/13, 26/27 May; 9/10, 23/24 Jun; 14/15, 28/29 Jul; 11/12, 25/26 Aug; 8/9, 22/23 Sept, last admission to house 5.30pm. Grounds: 2 Apr - 28 Sept: Mon - Fri (closed BH Mons) and same weekends as house, 2 - 6pm.

Admission: House & Grounds £4.40, Grounds only £3.30. Children half price. Groups must book in writing, or by fax or e-mail.

🚫 Not suitable. 📷 ♿

CHASTLETON HOUSE

Infoline/Fax: 01608 674355
e-mail: tchgen@smtp.ntrust.org.uk

Chastleton, Moreton-in-Marsh, Gloucestershire GL56 0SU

Owner: The National Trust   **Contact:** The Custodian

One of England's finest and most complete Jacobean houses, dating from 1612. It is filled with a mixture of rare and everyday objects and the atmosphere of four hundred years of continuous occupation by one family. The gardens have a Jacobean layout and the rules of modern croquet were codified here.

Location: OS Ref. SP248 291. 6m ENE of Stow-on-the-Wold. 1¹/₂ m NW of A436. Approach only from A436 between the A44 (W of Chipping Norton) and Stow.

Opening Times: 4 Apr - 29 Sept: Wed - Sat, 1 - 5pm, last admission 4pm. 3 Oct - 3 Nov: Wed - Sat, 1 - 4pm, last admission 3pm. Admission for all visitors (including NT members) by timed tickets booked in advance. Bookings can be made by telephone (01494 755585) on weekdays between 10am - 4pm.

Admission: Adult £5.20, Child £2.60. Family £13. Groups (11-25) by appointment.

🚫 Not suitable. 🅿 Coaches limited to 25 seat minibuses. 🐕 Guide dogs only.

CHRIST CHURCH CATHEDRAL

Tel: 01865 276154

The Sacristy, The Cathedral, Oxford OX1 1DP   **Contact:** Mr Jim Godfrey

12th century Norman Church, formerly an Augustinian monastery, given Cathedral status in 16th century by Henry VIII.

Location: OS Ref. SP515 059. Just S of city centre, off St Aldates. Entry via Meadow Gate visitors' entrance on S side of college.

Opening Times: Mon - Sat: 9am - 5pm. Suns: 1 - 5pm, closed Christmas Day. Services: weekdays 7.20am, 6pm. Suns: 8am, 10am, 11.15am & 6pm.

Admission: Adult £3, Child under 5 Free, Conc. £2, Family £6.

COGGES MANOR FARM MUSEUM

Tel: 01993 772602 **Fax:** 01993 703056

Church Lane, Witney, Oxfordshire OX8 6LA

Administered by: West Oxfordshire District Council   **Contact:** Carol Nightingale

The Manor House dates from the 13th century, rooms are furnished to show life at the end of the 19th century. Daily cooking on the Victorian range. On the first floor, samples of original wallpapers and finds from under the floorboards accompany the story of the history of the house. In one of the rooms, rare 17th century painted panelling survives. Farm buildings including two 18th century barns, stables and a thatched ox byre, display farm implements. Traditional breeds of farm animals, hand-milking demonstration each day. Seasonal produce from the walled kitchen garden sold in the museum shop.

Location: OS Ref. SP362 097. Just off A40 Oxford - Burford Road. Access by footbridge from centre of Witney, 600 yds. Vehicle access from S side of B4022 near E end of Witney.

Opening Times: Apr - end-Oct: Tue - Fri & BH Mons, 10.30am - 5.30pm; Sat & Sun, 12 - 5.30pm. Closed Good Fri. Early closing in Oct. Limited opening in Nov & Mar.

Admission: Adult £4, Child £2, Conc. £2.50 Family (2+2) £11.00

📷 ♿ Ground floor suitable. WCs. 📷 🅿 🐕 In grounds, on leads.

DEDDINGTON CASTLE ⌗

Tel: 023 9258 1059

Deddington, Oxfordshire

Owner: English Heritage   **Contact:** Area Manager

Extensive earthworks concealing the remains of a 12th century castle which was ruined as early as the 14th century.

Location: OS Ref. SP471 316. S of B4031 on E side of Deddington, 17m N of Oxford on A423. 5m S of Banbury.

Opening Times: Any reasonable time.

Admission: Free.

DITCHLEY PARK

Tel: 01608 677346

Enstone, Oxfordshire OX7 4ER

Owner: Ditchley Foundation   **Contact:** Brigadier Christopher Galloway

The most important house by James Gibbs with most distinguished interiors by Henry Flitcroft and William Kent.

Location: OS Ref. SP391 214. 2m NE from Charlbury. 13m NW of Oxford.

Opening Times: Visits only by prior arrangement with the Bursar.

Admission: £5 per person (minimum charge £40).

FAWLEY COURT

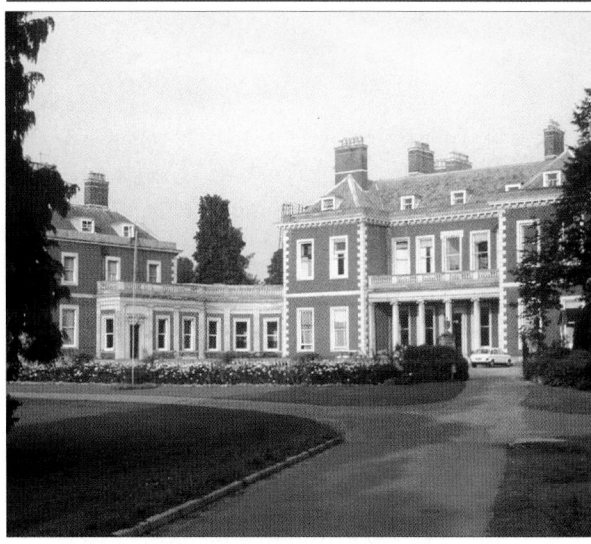

HISTORIC HOUSE & MUSEUM, HENLEY-ON-THAMES RG9 3AE

Owner: *Marian Fathers*   **Contact:** *The Secretary*

Tel: 01491 574917 **Fax:** 01491 411587

Designed by Christopher Wren, built in 1684 for Col W Freeman, decorated by Grinling Gibbons and by James Wyatt. The Museum consists of a library, various documents of the Polish Kings, a very well-preserved collection of historical sabres and many memorable military objects of the Polish army. Paintings, early books, numismatic collections, arms and armour.

Location: OS Ref. SU765 842. 1m N of Henley-on-Thames E to A4155 to Marlow.

Opening Times: May - Oct: Weds, Thurs & Suns, 2 - 5pm. Other dates by arrangement. Closed Whitsuntide and Nov - Apr inclusive.

Admission: House, Museum & Gardens: Adult £4, Child £1.50, Conc. £3. Groups (15+) £3.

📷 ♿ Ground floor & grounds suitable. WC. 📷 🐕 Guide dogs only.

GREAT COXWELL BARN

Tel: 01793 762209

Great Coxwell, Faringdon, Oxfordshire   **e-mail:** tbcjap@smtp.ntrust.org.uk

Owner: The National Trust   **Contact:** Coleshill Estate Office

A 13th century monastic barn, stone built with stone tiled roof, which has an interesting timber construction.

Location: OS Ref. SU269 940. 2m SW of Faringdon between A420 and B4019.

Opening Times: All year: daily at reasonable hours.

Admission: 50p.

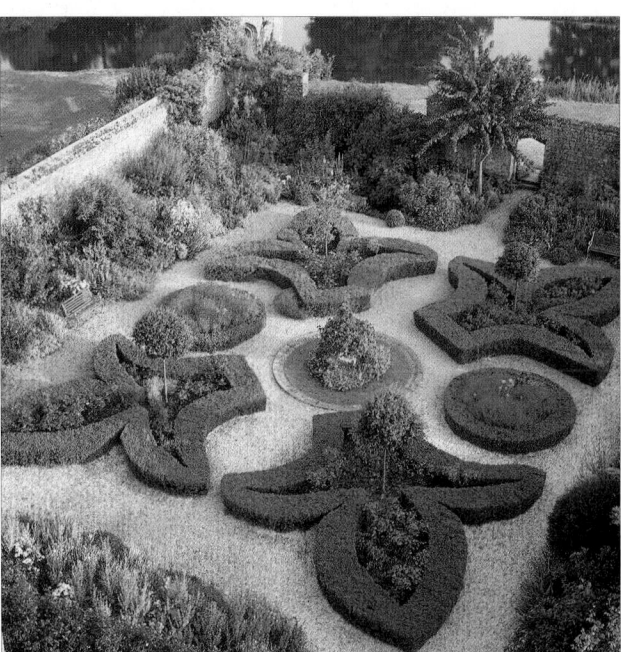

Broughton Castle, Oxfordshire.

South East
England

GREYS COURT

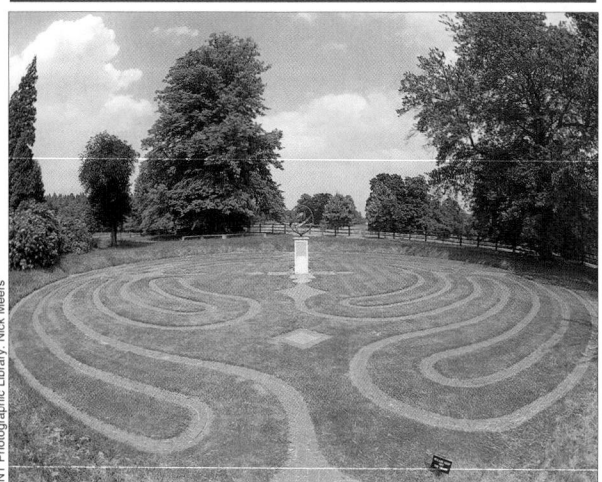

ROTHERFIELD GREYS, HENLEY-ON-THAMES, OXFORDSHIRE RG9 4PG

Owner: The National Trust   *Contact:* The Property Manager

Infoline: 01494 755564   **Tel:** 01491 628529

e-mail: tgrgen@smtp.ntrust.org.uk

Rebuilt in the 16th century and added to in the 17th, 18th and 19th centuries, the house is set amid the remains of the courtyard walls and towers of a 14th century fortified house. A Tudor donkey wheel, well-house and an ice house are still intact, and the garden contains Archbishop's Maze, inspired by Archbishop Runcie's enthronement speech in 1980.

Location: OS Ref. SU725 834. 3m W of Henley-on-Thames, E of B481.

Opening Times: 3 Apr - end Sept: House; Wed - Fri & BH Mons, 2 - 6pm (closed Good Fri) Garden: daily Tue - Sat & BH Mons 2 - 6pm (closed Good Fri) Last admission 5.30pm.

Admission: House & Garden: Adult £4.60, Child £2.30, Family £11.50. Garden only: £3.20, Family £8. Coach parties must book in advance.

Grounds partly suitable. WCs.   In car park only, on leads.

Contact Custodian.

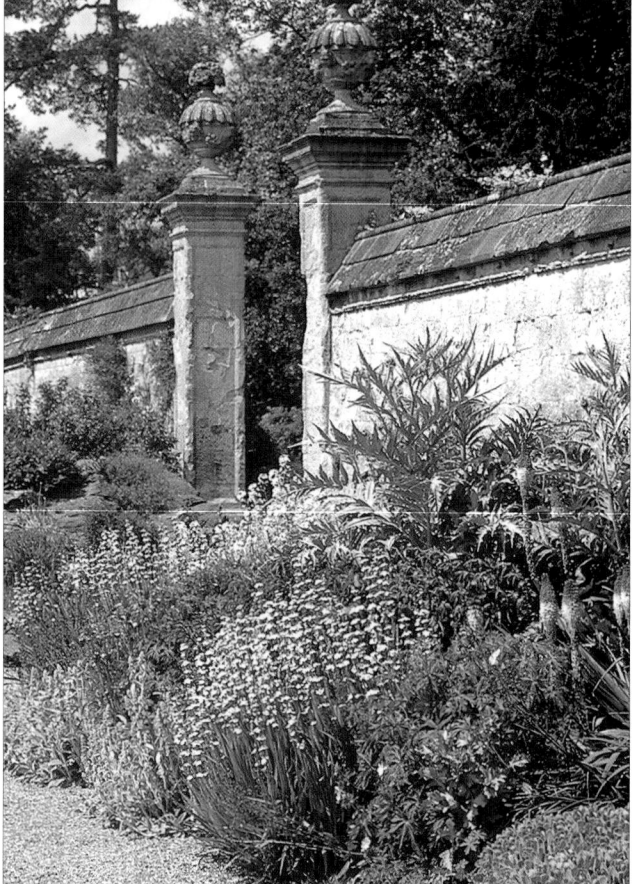

University of Oxford Botanic Garden.

KINGSTON BAGPUIZE HOUSE

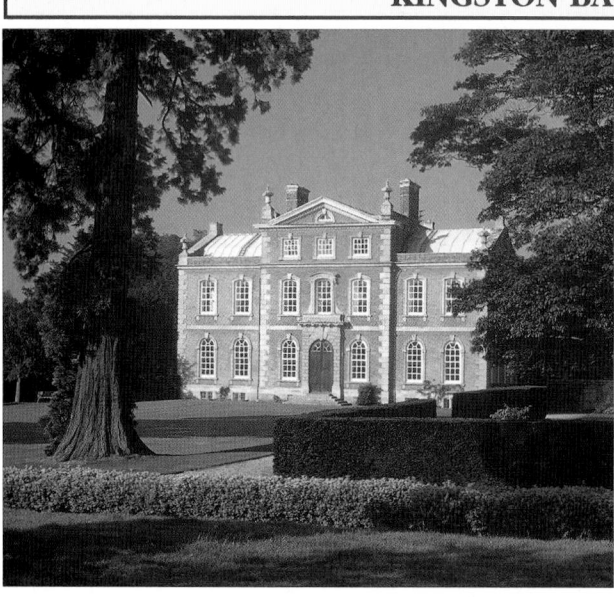

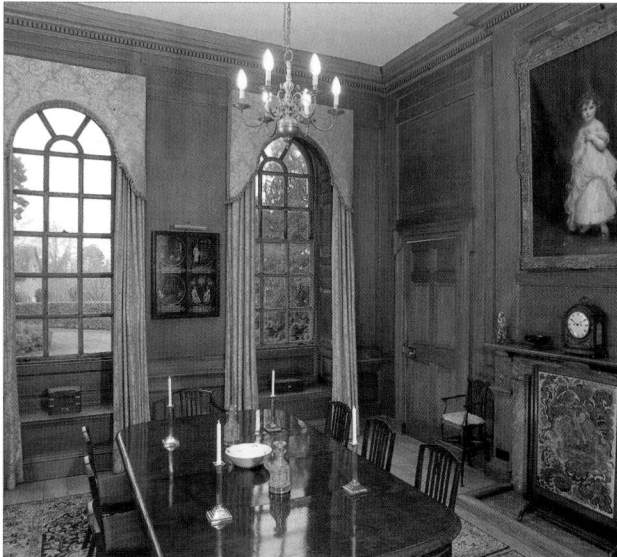

ABINGDON, OXFORDSHIRE OX13 5AX

Owner: Mr & Mrs Francis Grant   *Contact:* Mrs Francis Grant

Tel: 01865 820259 **Fax:** 01865 821659

A family home, this beautiful house originally built in the 1660s was remodelled in the early 1700s in red brick with stone facings. It has a cantilevered staircase and panelled rooms with some good furniture and pictures. Set in mature parkland, the gardens, including shrub border and woodland garden, contain a notable collection of trees, shrubs, perennials and bulbs planted for year round interest. A raised terrace walk leads to an 18th century panelled gazebo with views of the house and gardens, including a large herbaceous border and parkland. Available for special events, wedding receptions and filming. Facilities for small conferences.

Location: OS Ref. SU408 981. In Kingston Bagpuize village, off A415 Abingdon to Witney road S of A415/A420 intersection. Abingdon 5m, Oxford 9m.

Opening Times: Feb 18; Mar 4, 18; Apr 1, 14, 15, 16, 29; May 5, 6, 7, 26, 27, 28; Jun 10, 24; Jul 1, 21, 22; Aug 11, 12, 15, 25, 26, 27; Sept 8, 9, 12, 22, 23, 30; Oct 14; Nov 11. 2 - 5.30pm (tours of the house: 2.30 - 4.45pm). House: guided tours only. Last entry to garden 5pm.

Admission: House & Garden: Adult £3.50, Child £2.50, (children under 5yrs not admitted to house), OAP £3. Gardens: £1.50. (child under 5yrs Free). Groups (20-100) by appointment throughout the year, prices on request.

No photography.   Grounds suitable. WC.

Obligatory tours of house.

KINGSTONE LISLE PARK

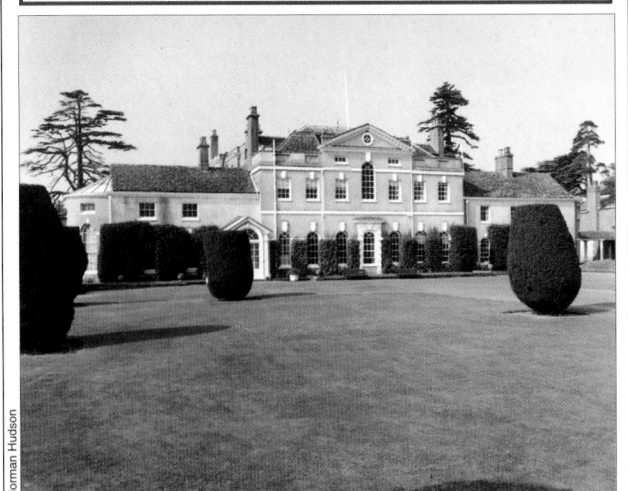

Norman Hudson

KINGSTONE LISLE PARK, WANTAGE, OXON OX12 9QG

Owner: *Mr James Lonsdale*   ***Contact:*** *The Secretary*

Tel: 01367 820599   **Fax:** 01367 820749

A sensational Palladian house, set in 140 acres of parkland. Superb views up to the Lambourn Downs. Three lakes beside the house complete this very attractive landscape. The hall, in the style of Sir John Soane, gives a strong impression of entering an Italian palazzo with beautiful ornate plaster ceilings, columns and figurines. In complete contrast the inner hall becomes the classical English country house, the most exciting feature being the Flying Staircase winding its way up, totally unsupported. A fine collection of art, furniture, clocks, glass and needlework, together with the architecture, evoke admiration for the craftsmanship that has existed in Britain over the centuries. 12 acres of gardens. Suitable for films, wedding receptions, functions and 'fun days'.

Location: OS Ref. SU326 876. M4/J14.

Opening Times: Coach parties only, strictly by appointment.

Admission: Telephone for details.

In grounds, on leads.

MAPLEDURHAM HOUSE & WATERMILL

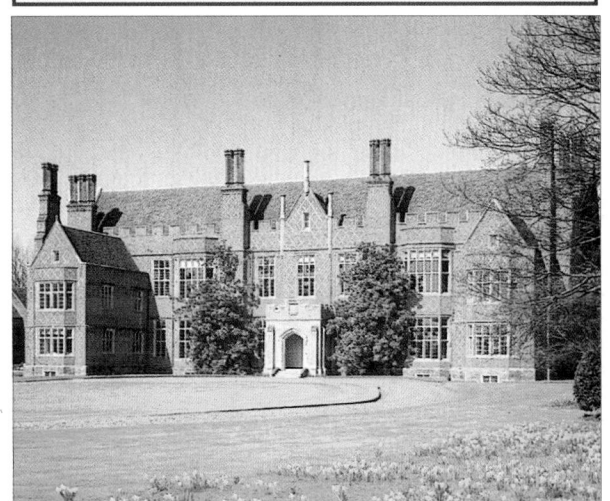

MAPLEDURHAM, READING RG4 7TR

Owner: *The Mapledurham Trust*   ***Contact:*** *Mrs Lola Andrews*

Tel: 01189 723350 **Fax:** 01189 724016 **e-mail:** mtrust1997@aol.com

Late 16th century Elizabethan home of the Blount family. Original plaster ceilings, great oak staircase, fine collection of paintings and a private chapel in Strawberry Hill Gothick added in 1797. Interesting literary connections with Alexander Pope, Galsworthy's *Forsyte Saga* and Kenneth Grahame's *Wind in the Willows*. 15th century watermill fully restored producing flour and bran which is sold in the giftshop.

Location: OS Ref. SU670 767. N of River Thames. 4m NW of Reading, 1½ m W of A4074.

Opening Times: Easter - Sept: Sats, Suns & BHs, 2 - 5.30. Last admission 5pm. Midweek parties by arrangement only (Tue - Thur).

Admission: Please call 01189 723350 for details.

Grounds suitable. WCs.   Guide dogs only.

11 holiday cottages available all year.

MILTON MANOR HOUSE

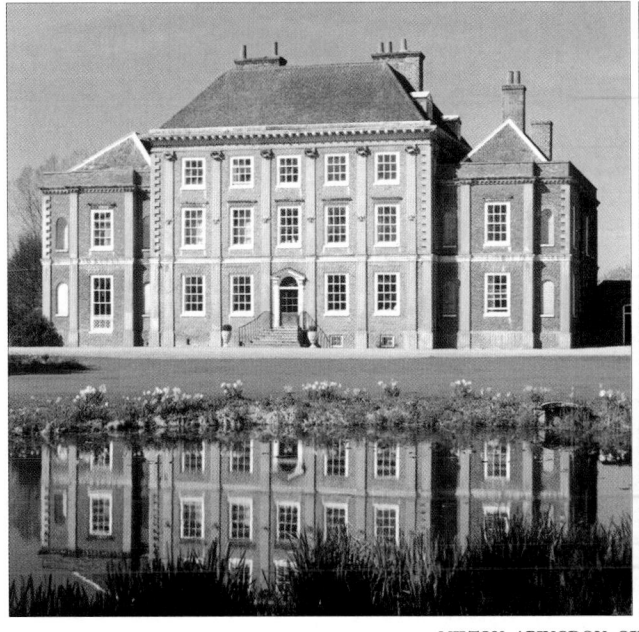

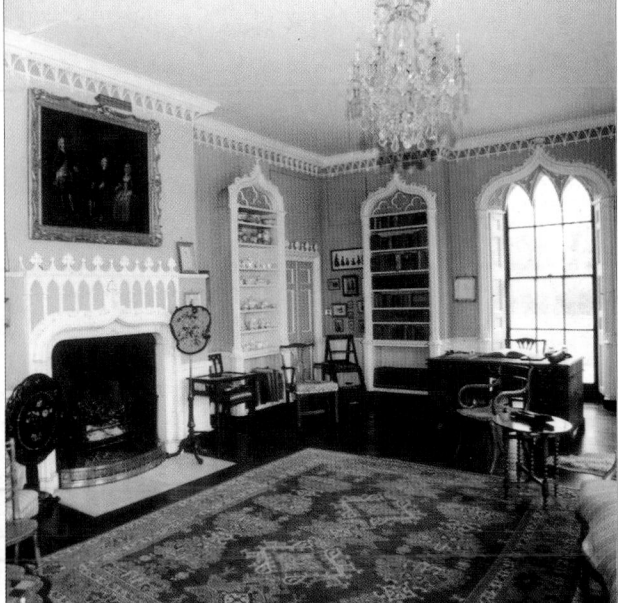

MILTON, ABINGDON, OXFORDSHIRE OX14 4EN

Owner: *Anthony Mockler-Barrett Esq*   ***Contact:*** *Gwendoline Marsh*

Tel: 01235 862321   **Fax:** 01235 831287

Dreamily beautiful mellow brick house, traditionally designed by Inigo Jones, with a celebrated Gothick library (pictured on right) and a startling Catholic chapel. Lived in by the family; pleasant, relaxed and informal atmosphere. Park with fine old trees, stables (pony rides usually available); swings, see-saw, small adventure playground. Walled garden, woodland walk, two lakes, variety of charming annuals and unusual ornaments. Plenty to see and enjoy for all ages.

Location: OS Ref. SU485 924. Just off A34, village and house signposted, 9m S of

Oxford, 15m N of Newbury. 3m from Abingdon and Didcot.

Opening Times: 1 - 15 May & 1 - 15 Aug: 2 - 5pm plus all BH weekends Easter - end Aug: Sat - Mon, 12 noon - 5pm. Guided tours of the house at 2pm, 3pm, 4pm.

Admission: House & Gardens: Adult £4, Child £2. House: Guided tours only. Grounds only: Adult £2.50, Child £1. Free parking. Groups by arrangement throughout the year. For group bookings only please write or phone 01235 831871.

Available.   Grounds suitable.   Guide dogs only.

MINSTER LOVELL HALL & DOVECOTE ⌗

Tel: 023 9258 1059

Witney, Oxfordshire

Owner: English Heritage   **Contact:** Area Manager

The ruins of Lord Lovell's 15th century manor house stand in a lovely setting on the banks of the River Windrush.

Location: OS Ref. SP324 114. Adjacent to Minster Lovell Church, ¹/₂ m NE of village. 3m W of Witney off A40.

Opening Times: Any reasonable time.

Admission: Free.

NUFFIELD PLACE

Tel: 01491 641224

Huntercombe, Henley-on-Thames, Oxfordshire RG9 5RY

Owner: Nuffield College   **Contact:** David Haenlein

The former home and gardens of Lord Nuffield founder of Morris Motors.

Location: OS Ref. SU679 879. Signposted off A4130 between Henley-on-Thames and Wallingford.

Opening Times: Apr - Sept: 2nd & 4th Suns in each month; 29 Apr, 13 & 27 May, 10 & 24 Jun, 8 & 22 Jul, 12 & 26 Aug, 9 & 23 Sept, 2 - 5pm.

Admission: Please contact for details.

PRIORY COTTAGES 🌿

Tel: 01793 762209   **e-mail:** tbcjap@smtp.ntrust.org.uk

1 Mill Street, Steventon, Abingdon, Oxfordshire OX13 6SP

Owner: The National Trust   **Contact:** Coleshill Estate Office

Former monastic buildings, converted into two houses. South Cottage contains the Great Hall of the original priory.

Location: OS Ref. SU466 914. 4m S of Abingdon, on B4017 off A34 at Abingdon West or Milton interchange on corner of The Causeway and Mill Street, entrance in Mill Street.

Opening Times: The Great Hall in South Cottage only: Apr - end Sept: Weds, 2 - 6pm by written appointment.

Admission: £1.

ROUSHAM HOUSE

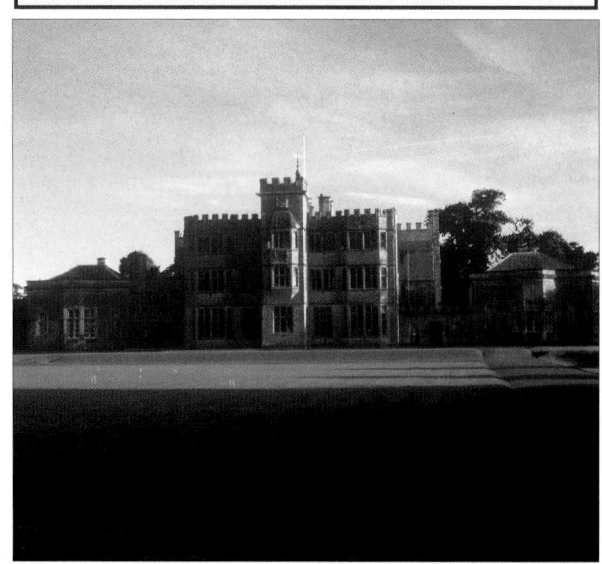

Nr STEEPLE ASTON, BICESTER, OXFORDSHIRE OX6 3QX

Owner/Contact: Charles Cottrell-Dormer Esq

Tel: 01869 347110/0860 360407

Rousham represents the first stage of English landscape design and remains almost as William Kent (1685 - 1748) left it. One of the few gardens of this date to have escaped alteration. Includes Venus' Vale, Townesend's Building, seven-arched Praeneste, the Temple of the Mill and a sham ruin known as the 'Eyecatcher'. The house was built in 1635 by Sir Robert Dormer.

Location: OS Ref. SP477 242. E of A4260, 12m N of Oxford, S of B4030, 7m W of Bicester.

Opening Times: House: Apr - Sept: Wed, Sun and BH Mon 2 - 4.30pm. Garden: All year: daily, 10am - 4.30pm.

Admission: House: £3. Garden: Adult £3. No children under 15yrs.

🚻 Partially suitable.   👤 Obligatory.   🅿

RYCOTE CHAPEL ⌗

Tel: 023 9258 1059

Rycote, Oxfordshire

Owner: English Heritage   **Contact:** Area Manager

A 15th century chapel with exquisitely carved and painted woodwork. It has many intriguing features, including two roofed pews and a musicians' gallery.

Location: OS165 Ref. SP667 046. 3m SW of Thame, off A329. 1¹/₂ m NE of M40/J7.

Opening Times: 1 Apr - 30 Sept: Fri - Sun & BHs, 2 - 6pm.

Admission: Adult £1.70, Child 90p, Conc. £1.30. 15% discount for groups (11+).

STANTON HARCOURT MANOR 🏛

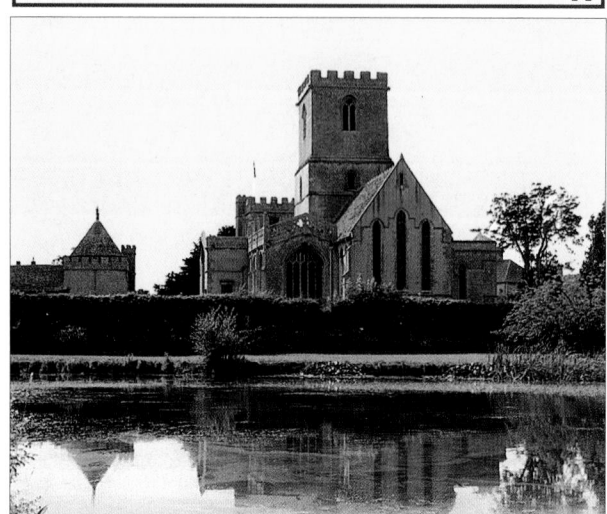

STANTON HARCOURT, Nr WITNEY, OXFORDSHIRE OX8 1RJ

Owner/Contact: The Hon Mrs Gascoigne

Tel: 01865 881928   **Answerphone / Fax:** 01865 880117

12 acres of garden with Great Fish Pond and Stew Ponds provide tranquil surroundings for the unique mediaeval buildings, Old Kitchen (Alexander) Pope's Tower and Domestic Chapel. The house, a fine example of a very early unfortified Manor House built to house the Harcourt family and its retainers, is still maintained as the family home.

Location: OS Ref. SP416 056. 9m W of Oxford, 5m SE of Witney off B4449 between Eynsham and Standlake.

Opening Times: 15, 16, 26, 29 Apr, 3, 6, 7, 17, 20, 24, 27, 28 May, 14, 17, 28 Jun, 1, 5, 8, 19, 22 Jul, 2, 5, 16, 19, 23, 26, 27 Aug, 6, 9, 20, 23 Sept: 2 - 6pm.

Admission: House & Garden: Adult £5, Child (under 12yrs)/OAP £3. Garden: Adult £3, Child (under 12yrs) /OAP £2. Group visits and access to the upper floors of Popes Tower by prior arrangement.

🚻 ☕ 🅿 Limited.   🐕 Guide dogs in grounds.

STONOR 🏛

See page 145 for full page entry.

SWALCLIFFE BARN

Tel: 01295 788278

Swalcliffe Village, Banbury, Oxfordshire   **Contact:** Jeffrey Demmar

15th century half cruck barn, houses agricultural and trade vehicles.

Location: OS Ref. SP378 378. 6m W of Banbury Cross on B4035.

Opening Times: Easter - end Oct: Suns & BHs, 2 - 5pm.

Admission: Free.

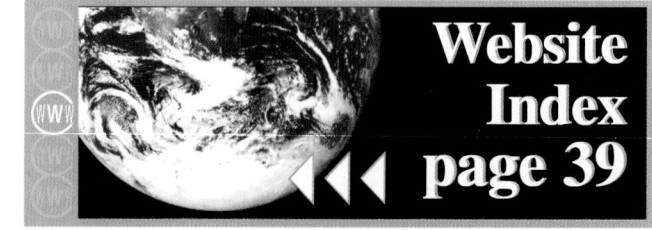

Website Index ◀◀◀ page 39

UNIVERSITY OF OXFORD BOTANIC GARDEN

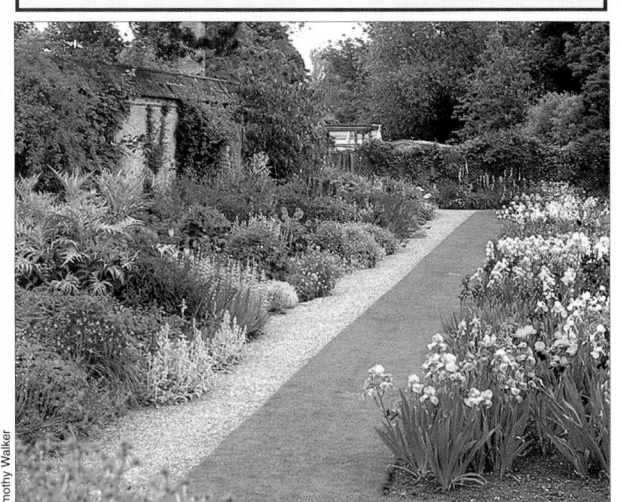

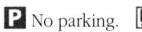

ROSE LANE, OXFORD OX1 4AZ

Owner: *University of Oxford*   **Contact:** *Timothy Walker*

Tel/Fax: 01865 286690 **e-mail:** postmaster@botanic-garden.ox.ac.uk

Founded in 1621; oldest botanic garden in Britain; 8,000 plants from all over the world; original walled garden; many trees over 200 years old; herbaceous borders, recently renovated rock and bog gardens; national collection of euphorbias, tropical glasshouses including a 100 year old cacti and waterlillies; a peaceful oasis in the city centre.

Location: OS Ref. SP520 061. E end of High Street, on the banks of the River Cherwell.

Opening Times: Apr - Sept: 9am - 5pm (glasshouses: 10am - 4.30pm). Oct - Mar: 9am - 4.30pm (glasshouses: 10am - 4pm). Closed 25 Dec & Good Fri. Last admission 4.15pm.

Admission: Adult £2, Child (under 12ys) Free.

ⓘ WCs for disabled only. ♿ 🅺 By arrangement. 🅿 No parking. 🔲 🐕 Guide dogs only. ❄

WATERPERRY GARDENS

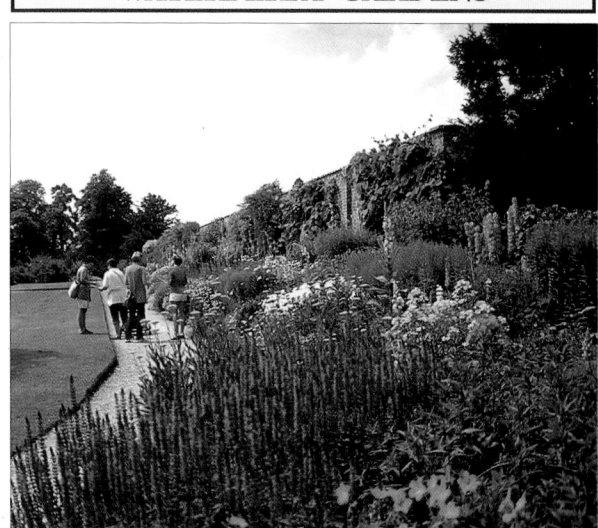

WATERPERRY, Nr WHEATLEY, OXFORDSHIRE OX33 1LB

Owner: *School of Economic Science*   **Contact:** *P Maxwell*

Tel: 01844 339226 **Fax:** 01844 339883

e-mail: office@waterperrygardens.f.s.net.co.uk

Here is the chance to enjoy the order of careful cultivation. See one of Britain's finest herbaceous borders which flowers continually from May to October. Rose garden; alpine gardens, formal garden, shrub borders, perennial borders and river walk.

Location: OS Ref. SP630 063. Oxford 9m, London 52m, Birmingham 42m. M40/J8. Well signposted locally.

Opening Times: Apr - Oct: 9am - 5.30pm. Nov - Mar: 9am - 5pm. Closed during Art in Action Festival.

Admission: Adult £3.40, Child £1.75, OAP £2.90. Groups (20+) £2.75, Child £1.50.

🗂 🚻 ♿ Partially suitable. 💻 🅺 By arrangement. 🅿 Limited for coaches. 🔲 🐕 In grounds, on leads. ❄ Ⓦ

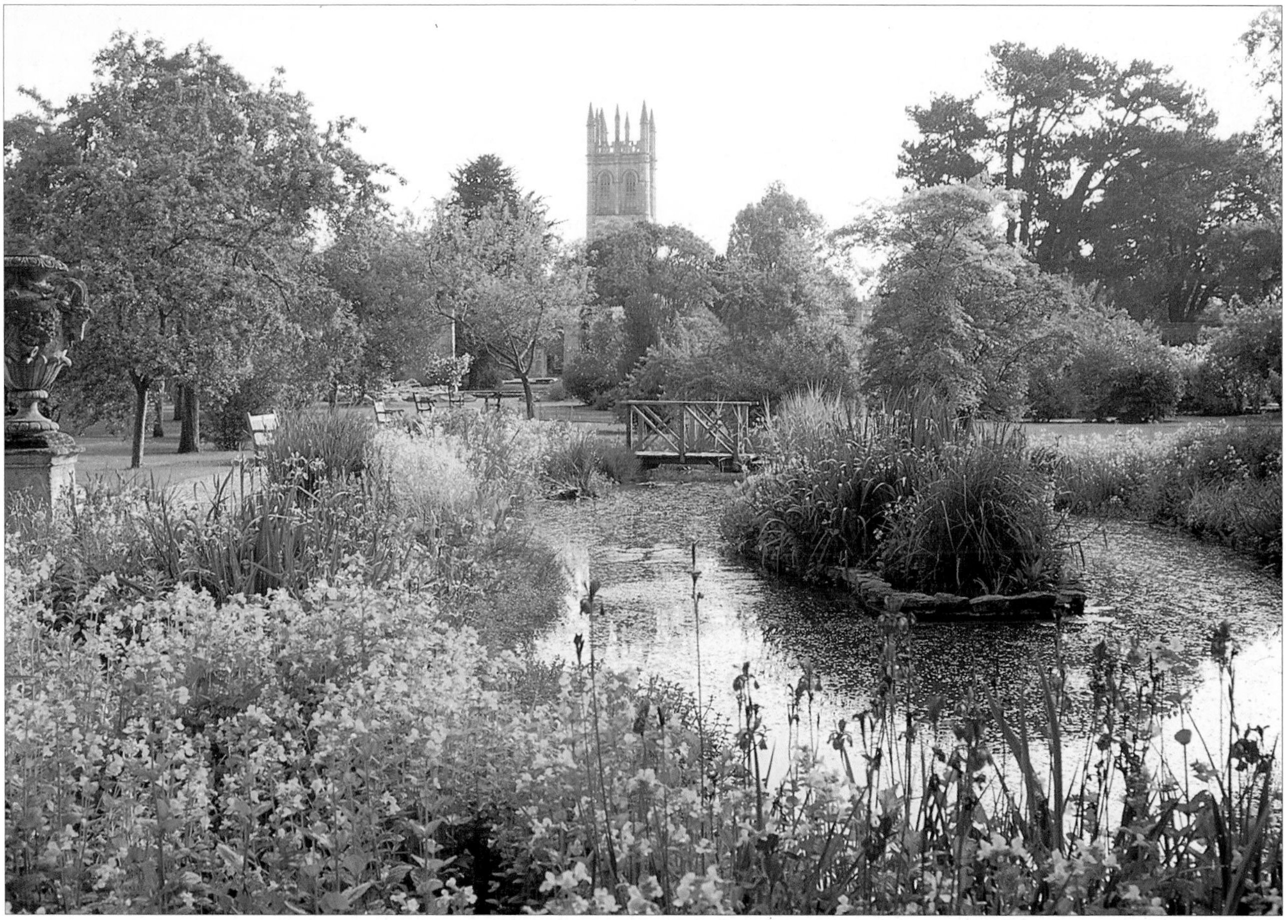

University of Oxford Botanic Garden.

South East England

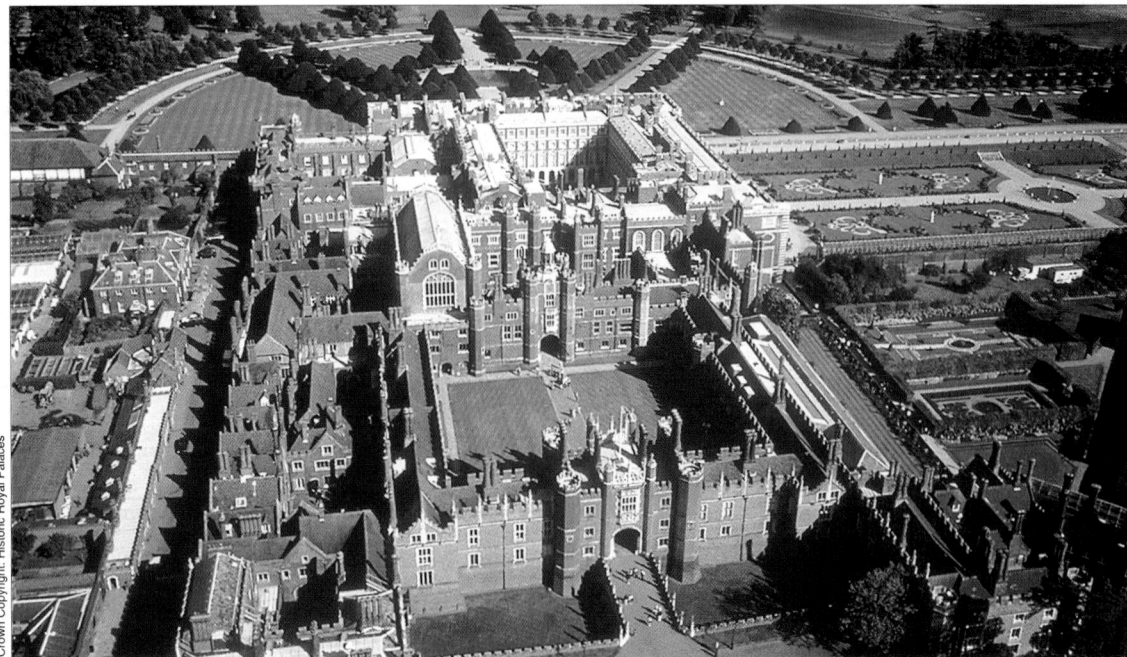

Crown Copyright: Historic Royal Palaces

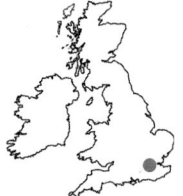

Managed by:

Historic Royal Palaces

CONTACT

Hampton Court Palace
Surrey
KT8 9AU

For all enquiries
please telephone:

Tel: 020 8781 9500

LOCATION

OS Ref. TQ155 686

From M25/J15 and A312,
or M25/J12 and A308, or
M25/J10 and A307.

Rail: From London
Waterloo direct to
Hampton Court (32 mins).

CONFERENCE/FUNCTION		
ROOM	SIZE	MAX CAPACITY
Great Hall	88'6" x 35'6"	280/400
Cartoon Gallery	22'6" x 116'	220/350
Gt Watching Chamber	66'6" x 25'	120
Painted Room	33'3" x 21'3"	60/100
Antc Room	22' x 21'6"	60/100
King's Award Chamber	60'3" x 36'4"	120/150
Public Dining Room	31'6" x 55'6"	80/150

HAMPTON COURT PALACE
Surrey

The magnificent Hampton Court Palace has been a favoured home to some of our most famous Kings and Queens from Henry VIII to George II. Today it serves to intrigue and amaze thousands of visitors a year.

Cardinal Wolsey created it; Henry VIII, Hampton Court's most famous occupant and first royal owner, spent £62,000 enlarging it (£18 million in today's terms); Charles I was imprisoned in it; William III and Mary II commissioned Sir Christopher Wren to rebuild it; and Queen Victoria opened its doors to the public. Today the beauty of Wren's building is combined with the finest Tudor architecture in Britain.

Costumed guides bring the Palace to life, with informative tours of the sumptuous interiors of the State Apartments, giving a unique insight into the daily lives of the Kings and their courtiers, and entertaining with tales of the etiquette and gossip of court life throughout the centuries.

The Chapel Royal is a stunning example of the Palace's rich interiors, while the Great Hall is still decorated with Henry VIII's priceless Flemish tapestries. Hampton Court is also home to important Renaissance paintings from the collection of HM The Queen.

The Tudor Kitchens are the most extensive surviving 16th century kitchens in Europe. They once cooked for over a thousand people a day, and are laid out as if a feast was being prepared, with a roaring log fire and boiling cauldrons.

Hampton Court Palace is set in sixty acres of beautiful riverside Tudor, baroque and Victorian gardens, which feature the world famous maze, and the Great Vine, the oldest and largest grapevine in the world, believed to have been planted in 1768 by 'Capability' Brown.

With its five hundred years of royal history, Hampton Court Palace is a living tapestry portraying the life and times of Henry VIII to George II. It is both visually and historically interesting, and a visit here has something for everyone.

❖

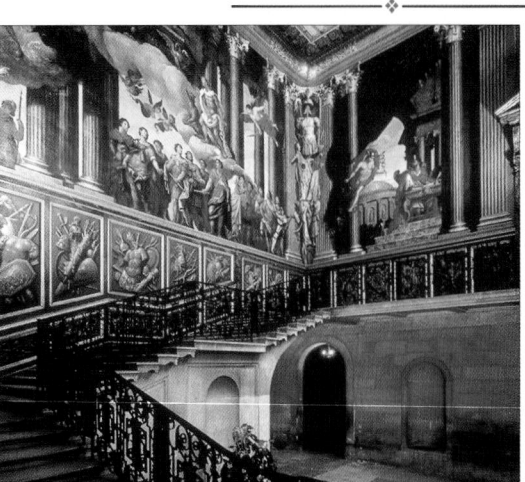

Crown Copyright: Historic Royal Palaces

  Information Centre.
No photography indoors.

Available by arrangement.

Motorised buggies available at main entrance. WCs.

Licensed.

Ample for cars, coach parking nearby.

Rates on request.

In grounds, on leads. Guide dogs only in Palace.

OPENING TIMES

SUMMER

Mid March - mid October
Tue - Sun:
9.30am - 6pm
Mon: 10.15am - 6pm.

WINTER

Mid October - mid March
Tue - Sun: 9.30am - 4.30pm
Mon: 10.15am - 4.30pm

Closed 24 - 26 December.

Last admission 45 mins before closing.

ADMISSION

Adult £10.50
Child (under 16yrs) ...£7.00
Child (under 5yrs) ......Free
OAP/Conc...............£8.00
Family (2+3) £31.40

SPECIAL EVENTS

For a full list of special events please telephone for details.

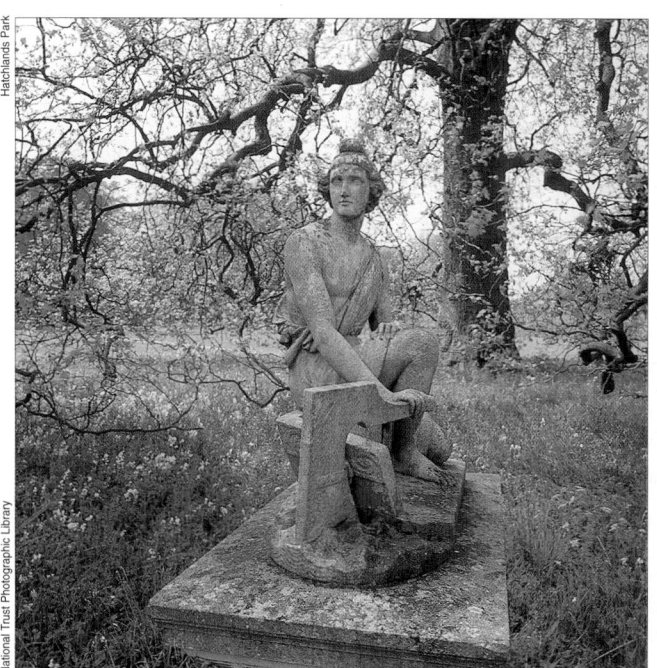

Hatchlands Park

National Trust Photographic Library

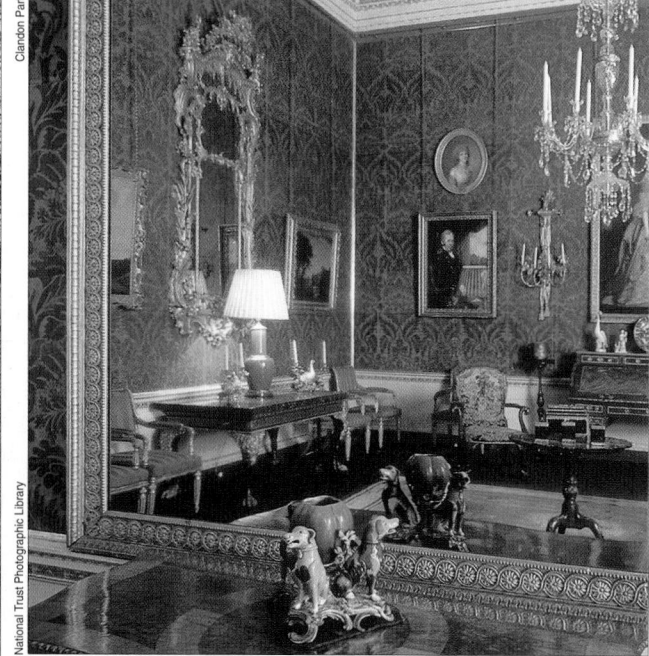

Clandon Park

National Trust Photographic Library

HATCHLANDS/CLANDON PARK
Guildford

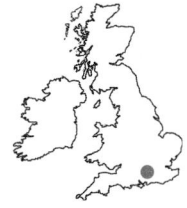

Owner: The National Trust

CONTACT

The Property Manager
Hatchlands Park/
Clandon Park
East Clandon
Guildford
Surrey
GU4 7RT

Tel: 01483 222482

Fax: 01483 223176

e-mail: shagen@
smtp.ntrust.org.uk

LOCATION

HATCHLANDS
OS Ref. TQ063 516

E of East Clandon
on the A246 Guildford -
Leatherhead road.

Rail: Clandon BR
2¹/₂ m,
Horsley 3m.

CLANDON
OS Ref. TQ042 512

At West Clandon on
the A247, 3m E of
Guildford.

Rail: Clandon BR 1m.

CONFERENCE/FUNCTION		
ROOM	SIZE	MAX CAPACITY
Marble Hall Clandon Pk	40' x 40'	160 seated 200 standing

HATCHLANDS PARK & CLANDON PARK were built during the 18th century and are set amidst beautiful grounds. They are two of England's most outstanding country houses and are only five minutes' drive apart.

Hatchlands Park was built in 1758 for Admiral Boscawen and is set in a beautiful Repton park offering a variety of park and woodland walks. Hatchlands contains splendid interiors by Robert Adam, decorated in appropriately nautical style. It houses the Cobbe Collection, the world's largest group of early keyboard instruments associated with famous composers, eg Purcell, J C Bach, Chopin, Mahler, Elgar and Marie Antoinette. There is also a small garden by Gertrude Jekyll

flowering from late May to early July.

Clandon Park is a grand Palladian mansion, built c1730 by the Venetian architect, Leoni and notable for its magnificent two-storey marble hall. The house is rightly acclaimed for its remarkable collection of 18th century porcelain, textiles and furniture, which includes the Ivo Forde Meissen collection of Italian comedy figures and a series of Mortlake tapestries. The attractive gardens feature a parterre, grotto, Dutch garden and a Maori house with a fascinating history. Clandon is also home to the Queen's Royal Surrey Regiment Museum. The excellent restaurant is renowned for its Sunday lunches - booking is advisable.

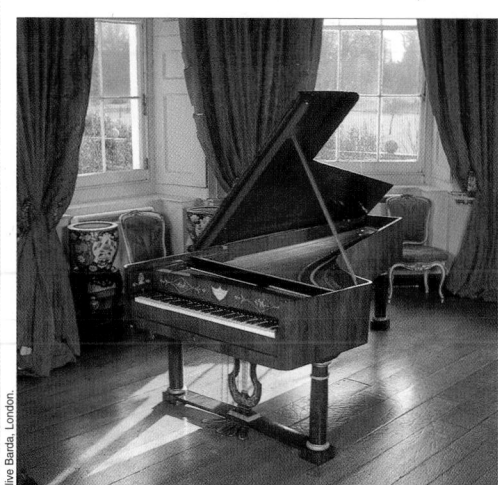

Clive Barda, London.

The Cobbe Collection of historic keyboard instruments can be seen at Hatchlands Park. Concerts and tours take place throughout the season. Both Beethoven and Schubert owned pianos made by Graf, the maker of the piano shown on the left, and many instruments in the collection were owned or played by great composers, including Chopin, Mahler and Elgar.

The Cobbe Collection Trust
Hatchlands Park, East Clandon
Guildford GU4 7RT
Tel: 01483 211474

Piano by Conrad Graf, Vienna, c.1820.

🏛 ℹ Clandon Park. Tel: 01483 222482. No photography.

🍴 For Clandon wedding receptions Tel: 01483 224912.

♿ Hatchlands suitable. Clandon partially suitable. WCs.

☕ Hatchlands: 01483 211120.

🍴 Licensed. Clandon: 01483 222502. H'lands: 01483 211120.

🚶 Clandon - by arrangement. Connoisseur Tours.

🎧 Hatchlands only.

🖼 Children's quizzes available.

🅿 Parking

🐕 Guide dogs only.

🔔 Clandon only.   🎭 01483 225804.

OPENING TIMES

HATCHLANDS
House
1 April - 31 October
Tue - Thur,
Suns & BH Mon,
Fris in August only.
2 - 5.30pm.

Park Walks
Daily (April - October)
11am - 6pm. Trail leaflets.

CLANDON
House
1 April - 4 November
Tue - Thur, Suns &
BH Mons, Good Fri
& Easter Sat
11am - 5pm.

Garden
As house: 9am - dusk.

Museum
1 April - 4 November
Tue - Thur & Suns,
BH Mons, Good Fri
& Easter Sat
12 noon - 5pm.

ADMISSION

Hatchlands
Adult £5.00
Park Walks £2.00
Child £2.50
Park Walks £1.00
Family £12.50
Groups (Tue - Thur only)
Adult £4.00

Clandon
Adult £5.00
Child £2.50
Family £12.50
Groups (Tue - Thur only)
Adult £4.00

Combined ticket
Hatchlands/Clandon .. £7.50
Family £18.00
Under 5s Free

South East England

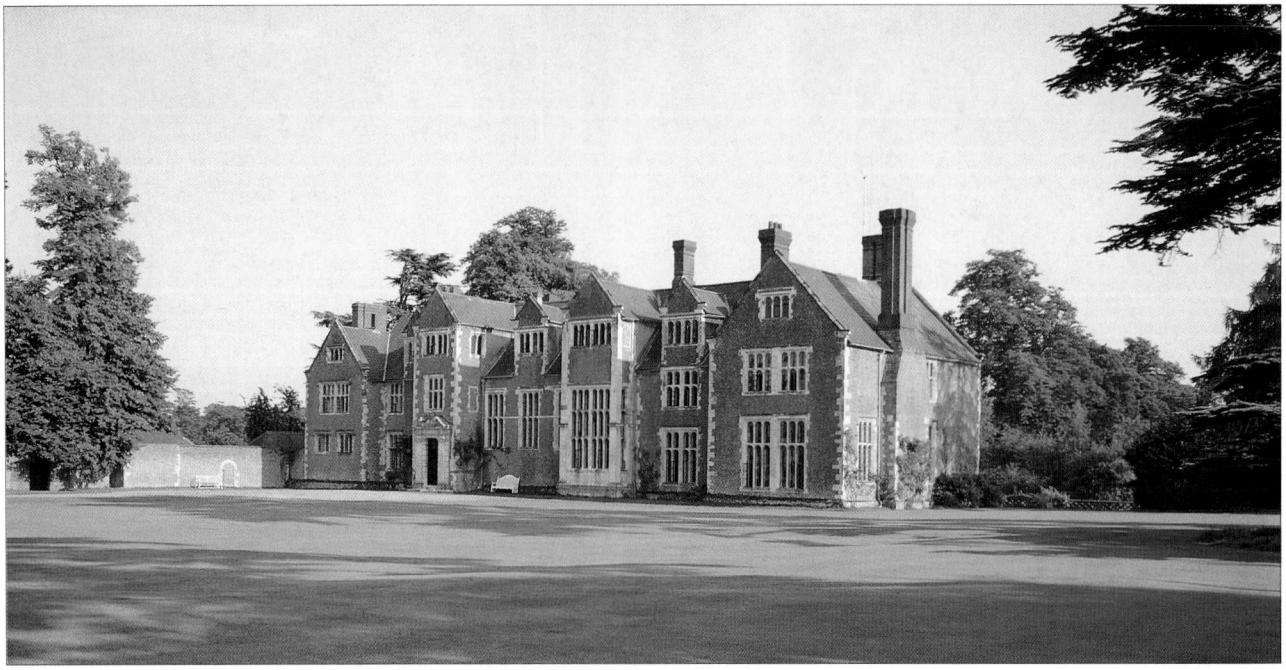

LOSELEY PARK
Guildford

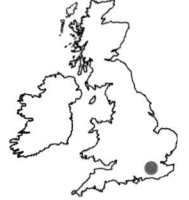

Owner:
Mr Michael
More-Molyneux

CONTACT

Michelle Wheeler
Loseley Park
Guildford
Surrey
GU3 1HS

Tel: 01483 304440

Fax: 01483 302036

e-mail: enquiries@
loseley-park.com

LOCATION

OS Ref. SU975 471

30m S of London, leave A3
S of Guildford on to B3000.
Signposted.

Bus: 1¼ m
from House.

Rail: Farncombe 1½m,
Guildford 2m,
Godalming 3m.

Air: Heathrow 30m,
Gatwick 30m.

CONFERENCE/FUNCTION

ROOM	SIZE	MAX CAPACITY
Tithe Barn	100' x 18'	200
Marquee	sites available	
Great Hall	70' x 40'	100
Drawing Rm	40' x 30'	50
Walled Gdn	Marquee	sites

LOSELEY PARK, built in 1562 by Sir William More, is a fine example of Elizabethan architecture, its mellow stone brought from the ruins of Waverley Abbey now over 850 years old. The house is set amid magnificent parkland grazed by the Loseley Jersey herd. Many visitors comment on the very friendly atmosphere of the house, it is a country house, the family home of descendants of the builder.

Furniture has been acquired by the family and includes an early 16th century Wrangelschrank beautifully inlaid with many different woods, a Queen Anne cabinet, Georgian armchairs and settee, a Hepplewhite four-poster bed and King George IV's coronation chair. The King's bedroom has Oudenarde tapestry and a carpet commemorating James I's visit.

The Christian pictures include the Henri Met de Bles triptych of the Nativity and modern mystical pictures of the living Christ, St Francis and St Bernadette. A Christian Cancer Help Centre meets twice monthly. Loseley House is available for dinners, functions and Civil weddings.

GARDEN
A magnificent Cedar of Lebanon presides over the front lawn. Parkland adjoins the lawn and a small lake adds to the beauty of Front Park. In the Walled Garden are mulberry trees, yew hedges, a grass terrace and a moat walk with herbaceous borders. Other features include an award-winning rose garden, a herb garden, flower garden, vegetable garden and idyllic fountain garden.

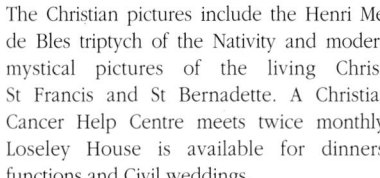 Chapel. New lakeside walk. Business launches & promotions. 10 - 12 acre field can be hired in addition to the lawns. Fashion shows, air displays, archery, garden parties, shows, rallies, filming, parkland, moat walk & terrace. Lectures can be arranged on the property, its contents, gardens & history. Loseley Christian Trust Exhibition, children's play area, picnic area, nature trail, home to Jersey herd since 1916; No unaccompanied children, no photography in house, no videos on estate. All group visits must be booked in advance.

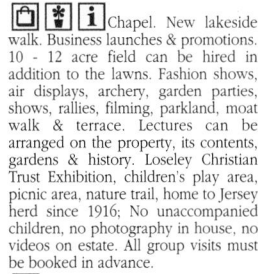

Special functions, banquets and conference catering. Additional marquees for hire. Wedding receptions.

May alight at entrance to property. Access to all areas except house first floor. WCs.

Courtyard Tea Room.

Obligatory. Tour time for house, 40 mins.

P 150 cars, 6 coaches. Summer overflow car park.

 Guide dogs only.

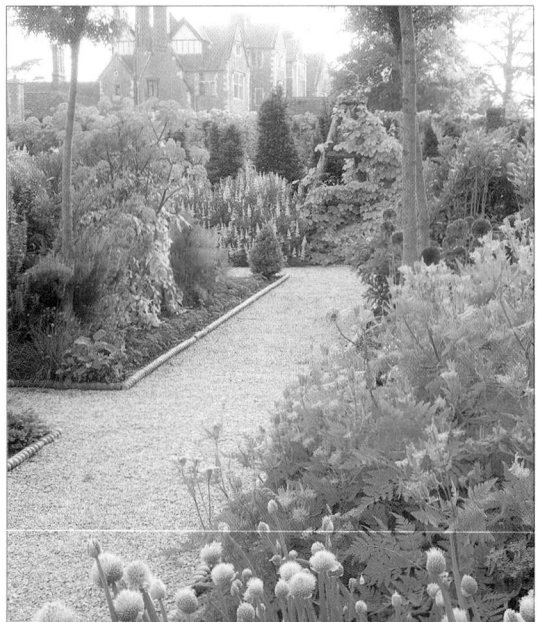

OPENING TIMES

SUMMER
Garden, Shop & Tea Room
May - September
Wed - Sun, 11am - 5pm.

House Tours
June - August
Wed - Sun, 1 - 5pm.

ALL YEAR
Tithe Barn, House and
Grounds available for
private/business functions,
Civil weddings and
receptions.

ADMISSION

House & Gardens
Adult £6.00
Child (3-16yrs)..........£3.00
Conc. £5.00
Child (under 3yrs) ......Free

Groups (15+)
Adult £4.50
Child (3-16yrs)..........£2.50
Conc. £3.50

SPECIAL EVENTS

• **FEB 23 - 25:**
Home Design Exhibition.

• **MAR 23 - 25:**
Antique Fair.

• **JUN 1 - 3:**
Craft Fair.

• **JUL 20 - 22:**
Garden Show.

• **AUG 12:**
Outdoor Concert.

• **OCT 19 - 21:**
Antique Fair.

CARSHALTON HOUSE

Tel: 020 8770 4781 **Fax:** 020 8770 4777

Pound Street, Carshalton, Surrey SM5 3PN

Owner: St Philomena's Catholic High School for Girls   **Contact:** Ms V Murphy

A Queen Anne mansion built c1707, now in use as a school, with grounds originally laid out by Charles Bridgeman.

Location: OS Ref. TQ275 644. On A232 just S of junction with B278.

Opening Times: Please telephone for details.

Admission: Adult £3, Child under 16/Full-time students £1.50.

CLANDON/HATCHLANDS PARK

See page 153 for full page entry.

CLAREMONT LANDSCAPE GARDEN

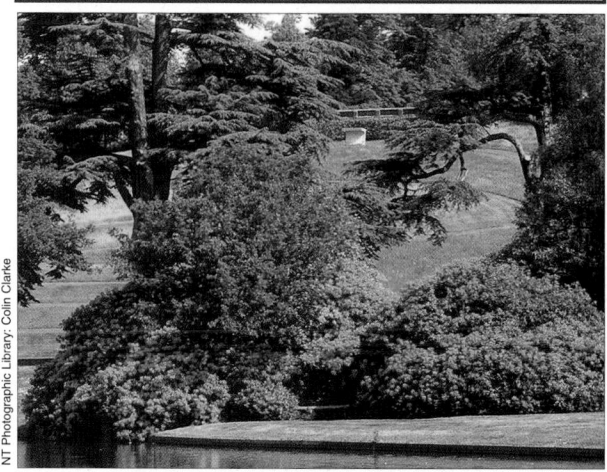

NT Photographic Library: Colin Clarke

PORTSMOUTH ROAD, ESHER, SURREY KT10 9JG

Owner: The National Trust **Contact:** *The Property Manager*

Tel: 01372 467806 **Fax:** 01372 464394 **e-mail:** sclgen@smtp.ntrust.org.uk

One of the earliest surviving English landscape gardens, restored to its former glory. Begun by Sir John Vanbrugh and Charles Bridgeman before 1720, the garden was extended and naturalised by William Kent. 'Capability' Brown also made improvements. Features include a lake, island with pavilion, grotto, turf amphitheatre, viewpoints and avenues.

Location: OS Ref. TQ128 632. On S edge of Esher, on E side of A307 (no access from Esher bypass).

Opening Times: Jan - end Mar, Nov - end Dec: daily except Mons: 10am - 5pm or sunset if earlier. Apr - end Oct: daily: Mon - Fri, 10am - 6pm, Sats, Suns & BHs, 10am - 7pm. NB: closed 10/11 Jul from 2pm, 12 - 15 Jul and all day 25 Dec & 1 Jan.

Admission: Adult £3.50, Child £1.75. Coach parties must book; no coach parties on Suns. Family (2+2) £8.75. Groups (15+), £3. 50p discount if using public transport.

📷 ♿ Limited suitability. WC. 🚻 🐕 No dogs (Apr - Oct).
🎧 Telephone for details.

CROYDON PALACE

Tel: 020 8688 2027

Old Palace Road, Croydon, Surrey CR0 1AX

Owner/Contact: The Whitgift Foundation

A residence of the Archbishops of Canterbury between the 12th and 18th centuries. 15th century Banqueting Hall (one of the outstanding great medieval halls of London); Norman Undercroft; 15th century Guard Room and Chapel; Tudor Long Gallery; Elizabeth I's bedroom. West wing contains some of the earliest medieval brickwork in England.

Location: OS Ref. TQ320 654. 200 yds S of Croydon parish church, 400 yds W of Croydon High St.

Opening Times: 17 - 21 Apr, 28 May - 1 Jun, 16 - 21 Jul and 23 - 28 Jul.

Admission: Adult £4, Child/OAP £3.

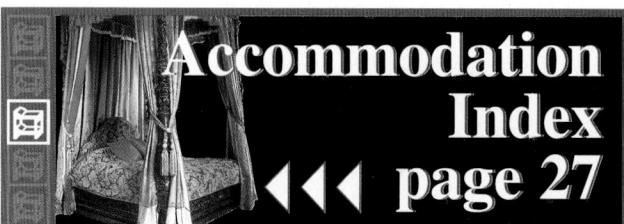

DAPDUNE WHARF

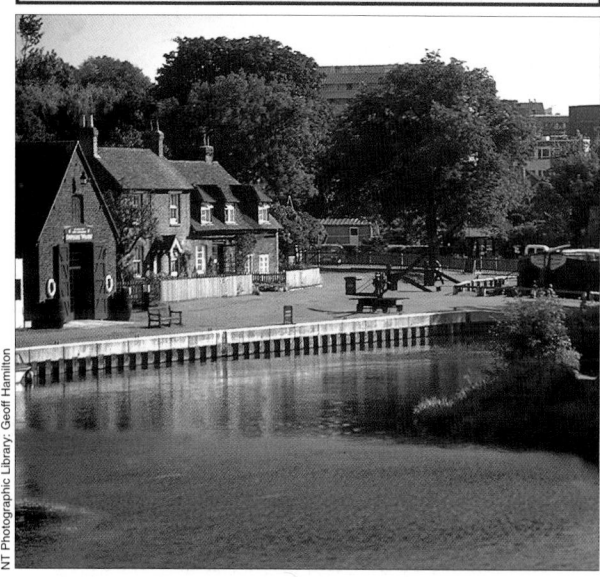

NT Photographic Library: Geoff Hamilton

RIVER WEY NAVIGATIONS, WHARF ROAD, GUILDFORD GU1 4RR

Owner: The National Trust **Contact:** *Andrea Selley*

Tel: 01483 561389 **Fax:** 01483 531667 **e-mail:** swybeb@smtp.ntrust.org.uk

Dapdune Wharf is the centrepiece of one of The National Trust's most unusual properties, the River Wey Navigations. Restored wharf buildings and a Wey barge can be seen. Interactive exhibits and displays tell the fascinating story of Surrey's secret waterway, one of the first British rivers to be made navigable.

Location: OS Ref. SU993 502. On Wharf Road to rear of Surrey County Cricket Ground, 1/2 m N of Guildford town centre off Woodbridge Road (A322).

Opening Times: 31 Mar - 4 Nov: Thurs, Sats, Suns & BHs, 11am - 5pm. River bus service 11am - 5pm

Admission: Adult £2.50, Child £1, Family £6. Groups (booked, min 15): Adult £2.

📷 ♿ 🚻 👣 By arrangement. 🎬 🅿 Limited. 🐕 In grounds, on leads.

FARNHAM CASTLE

Tel: 01252 721194 **Fax:** 01252 711283

Farnham, Surrey GU9 0AG   **e-mail:** info@cibfarnham.com

Owner/Contact: The Church Commissioners

Bishop's Palace built in Norman times by Henry of Blois, with Tudor and Jacobean additions.

Location: OS Ref. SU839 474. 1/2 m N of Farnham town centre on A287.

Opening Times: Please telephone for details.

Admission: Adult £2, Child, £1, Conc. £1.50 (2000 prices).

FARNHAM CASTLE KEEP

Tel: 01252 713393

Castle Hill, Farnham, Surrey GU6 0AG

Owner: English Heritage   **Contact:** The Head Custodian

Used as a fortified manor by the medieval Bishops of Winchester, this motte and bailey castle has been in continuous occupation since the 12th century. You can visit the large shell-keep enclosing a mound in which are massive foundations of a Norman tower.

Location: OS Ref. SU839 474. 1/2 m N of Farnham town centre on A287.

Opening Times: 1 Apr - 30 Sept: 10am - 6pm. 1 - 31 Oct, 10am - 5pm.

Admission: Adult £2.10, Child, £1.10, Conc. £1.60.

♿ Ground floor & grounds. 🎧 Free. 🐕 In grounds, on leads.

GODDARDS

Tel: 01628 825920 or 01628 825925 (bookings)

Abinger Common, Dorking, Surrey RH5 6TH

Owner: The Lutyens Trust, leased to The Landmark Trust   **Contact:** The Landmark Trust

Built by Sir Edwin Lutyens in 1898 - 1900 and enlarged by him in 1910. Garden by Gertrude Jekyll. Given to the Lutyens Trust in 1991 and now managed and maintained by the Landmark Trust, which let buildings for self-catering holidays. The whole house, apart from the library, is available for up to 12 people. Full details of Goddards and 170 other historic buildings available for holidays are featured in The Landmark Handbook (price £9.50 refundable against booking), from The Landmark Trust, Shottesbrooke, Maidenhead, Berkshire SL6 3SW.

Location: OS Ref. TQ120 450. 41/2 m SW of Dorking on the village green in Abinger Common. Signposted Abinger Common, Friday Street and Leith Hill from A25.

Opening Times: Strictly by appointment. Must be booked in advance, including parking, which is very limited. Visits booked for Weds afternoons from the Wed after Easter until the last Wed of Oct, between 2.30 - 5pm. Only those with pre-booked tickets will be admitted.

Admission: £3. Tickets available from Mrs Baker on 01306 730871, Mon - Fri, 9am & 6pm. Visitors will have access to part of the garden and house only.

HAMPTON COURT PALACE

See page 152 for full page entry.

HATCHLANDS/CLANDON PARK

See page 153 for full page entry.

HONEYWOOD HERITAGE CENTRE

Tel: 020 8770 4297 **Fax:** 020 8770 4777

e-mail: lbshoneywood@netscapeonline.co.uk

Honeywood Walk, Carshalton, Surrey SM5 3NX

Owner: London Borough of Sutton   **Contact:** The Curator

A 17th century listed building next to the picturesque Carshalton Ponds, containing displays on many aspects of the history of the London Borough of Sutton plus a changing programme of exhibitions and events on a wide range of subjects. Attractive garden at rear.

Location: OS Ref. TQ279 646. On A232 approximately 4m W of Croydon.

Opening Times: Wed - Fri, 10am - 5pm. Sat, Suns & BH Mons, 10am - 5.30pm. Tearooms open Tue - Sun, 10am - 5pm.

Admission: Adult £1.20, Child 50p, under 5 Free. Groups by arrangement.

Ground floor. WC.   Limited.   Guide dogs only.   Telephone for details.

KEW GARDENS

Tel: 020 8940 1171 **Fax:** 020 8332 5197

Kew, Richmond, Surrey TW9 3AB   **Contact:** Enquiry Unit

Kew's 300 acres offer many special attractions: including the 65ft high Palm House.

Location: OS Ref. TQ188 776. A307. Junction A307 and A205 (1m Chiswick roundabout M4).

Opening Times: 9.30am, daily except Christmas Day and New Year's Day. Closing time varies according to the season. Please telephone for further information.

Admission: Adult £5, Child £2.50, Conc. £3.50, Family £13. Groups 20% discount when pre-booked and paid. Prices subject to revision April 2001.

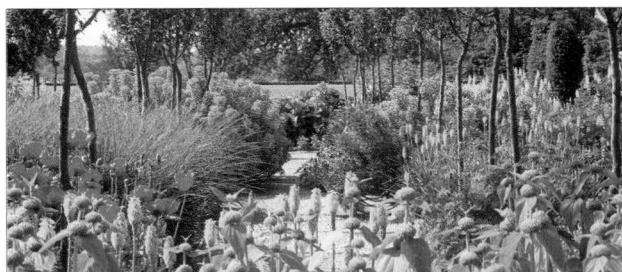

Loseley Park, Surrey.

LITTLE HOLLAND HOUSE

Tel: 020 8770 4781 **Fax:** 020 8770 4777

e-mail: valary.murphy@sutton.gov.uk

40 Beeches Avenue, Carshalton, Surrey SM5 3LW

Owner: London Borough of Sutton   **Contact:** Ms V Murphy

The home of Frank Dickinson (1874 - 1961) artist, designer and craftsman, who dreamt of a house that would follow the philosophy and theories of William Morris and John Ruskin. Dickinson designed, built and furnished the house himself from 1902 onwards. The Grade II* listed interior features handmade furniture, metal work, carvings and paintings produced by Dickinson in the Arts and Crafts style.

Location: OS Ref. TQ275 634. On B278 1m S of junction with A232.

Opening Times: First Sun of each month and BH Suns & Mons, 1.30 - 5.30pm.

Admission: Free. Groups by arrangement, £2 per person (includes talk and guided tour).

No photography in house.   Ground floor only.   By arrangement. No parking.   Guide dogs only.

LOSELEY PARK

See page 154 for full page entry.

OAKHURST COTTAGE

Tel: 01428 684090

Hambledon, Godalming, Surrey GU8 4HF

Owner: The National Trust   **Contact:** The Witley Centre

A small 16th century timber-framed cottage, painted by both Helen Allingham and Myles Birket Foster, containing furniture and artefacts reflecting two or more centuries of continuing occupation. There is a delightful cottage garden and a small barn containing agricultural implements.

Location: OS Ref. SU965 385. Hambledon, Surrey.

Opening Times: 31 Mar - 4 Nov: Weds, Thurs, Sats, Suns & BH Mons, 2 - 5pm. Strictly by appointment only.

Admission: Adult £2.50, Child £1.25 (including guided tour). No reduction for parties.

Not suitable.   Obligatory, by arrangement.   Limited.

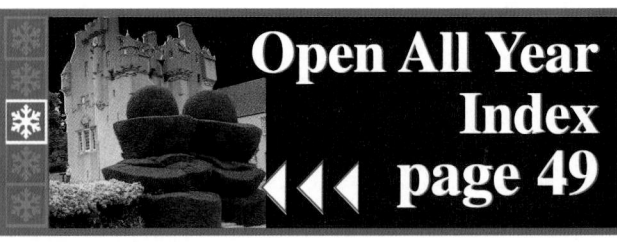

Open All Year

Index
◀◀◀ **page 49**

PAINSHILL LANDSCAPE GARDEN

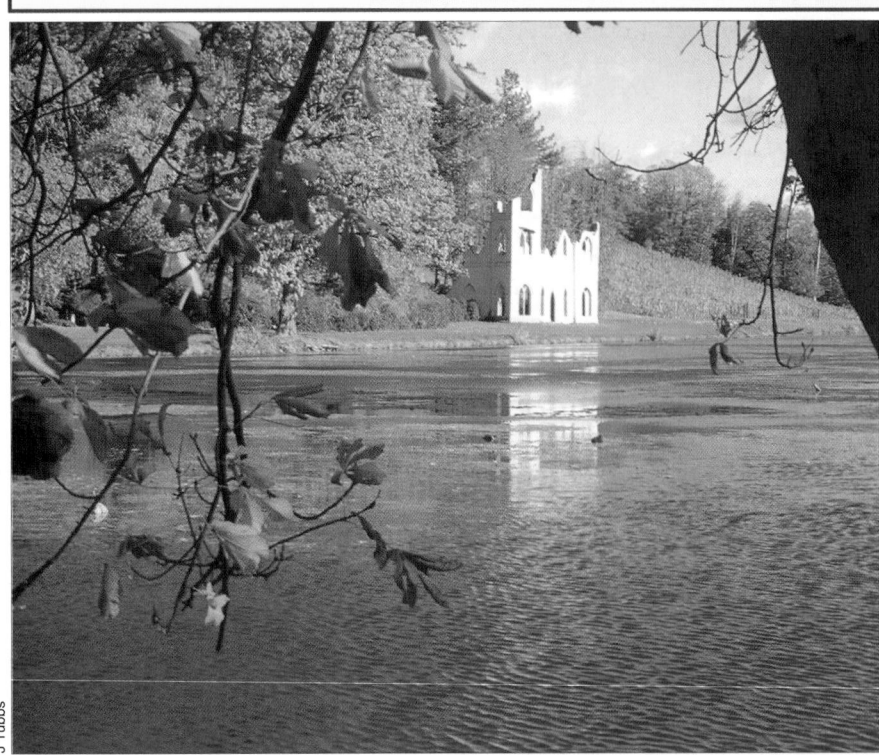

J Tubbs

PORTSMOUTH ROAD, COBHAM, SURREY KT11 1JE

Owner: Painshill Park Trust
Contact: Visitor Management

Tel: 01932 868113 **Fax:** 01932 868001

One of Europe's finest 18th century landscape gardens, contemporary with Stourhead and Stowe, created by the Hon Charles Hamilton between 1738 - 1773. Europa Nostra Medal winner for 'exemplary restoration'. Situated in 158 acres, visitors can take a circuit walk through a series of emerging scenes, each one more surprising than the last. A 14-acre lake fed by a massive waterwheel gives a breathtaking setting for a variety of spectacular features including a Gothic temple, ruined abbey, Turkish tent, crystal grotto, Chinese bridge, magnificent Cedars of Lebanon, replanted 18th century shrubberies and vineyard. Available for corporate and private hire, location filming, wedding receptions, etc.

Location: OS Ref. TQ099 605. M25/J10 to London. W of Cobham on A245. Entrance 200 yds E of A245/A307 roundabout.

Opening Times: Apr - Oct: Tue - Sun and BH Mons, 10.30am - 6pm (last admission 4.30pm). Gates close 6pm. Nov - Mar: daily except Mons & Fris (open BHs), 11am - 4pm or dusk if earlier (last admission 3pm). Closed Christmas and Boxing Day.

Admission: Adult £4.20, Child (5-16) £1.70, under 5 Free, Conc. £3.70. Groups (10+) £3.30.

Marquee site.   Guide dogs only.

POLESDEN LACEY

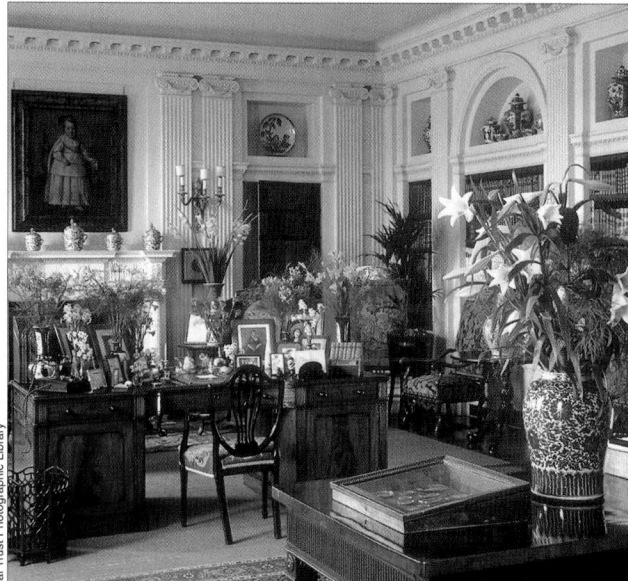

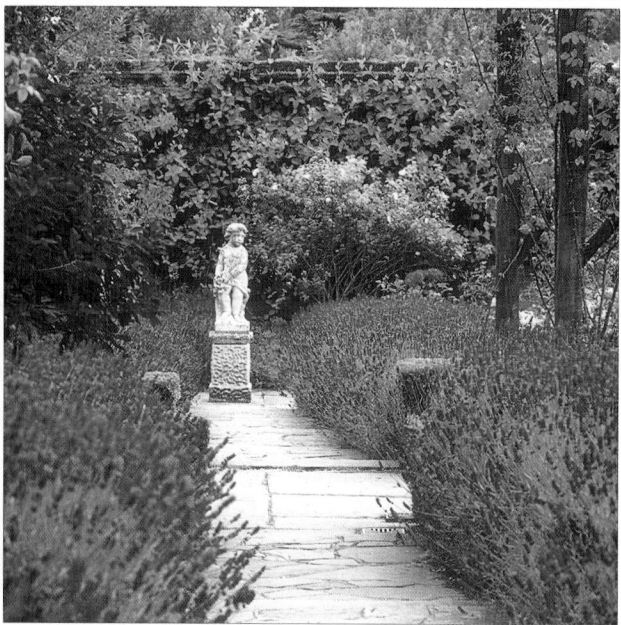

GREAT BOOKHAM, Nr DORKING, SURREY RH5 6BD

Owner: The National Trust   *Contact:* The Property Manager

Tel: 01372 452048   **Infoline:** 01372 458203
Fax: 01372 452023   **e-mail:** spljac@ smtp.ntrust.org.uk

Originally an elegant 1820s Regency villa in magnificent landscape setting. The house was remodelled after 1906 by the Hon Mrs Ronald Greville, a well-known Edwardian hostess. Her collection of fine paintings, furniture, porcelain and silver are still displayed in the reception rooms and galleries, which surround an inner courtyard. Extensive grounds, walled rose garden, lawns and landscaped walks. King George VI and Queen Elizabeth, The Queen Mother spent part of their honeymoon here.
Location: OS Ref. TQ136 522. 5m NW of Dorking, 2m S of Great Bookham, off A246.

Opening Times: House: 31 Mar - 4 Nov: Wed - Sun, 1 - 5pm also BH Mons starting with Easter, 11am - 5pm. Grounds: All year: daily, 11am - 6pm/dusk. Last admission to house ¹/₂ hr before closing.
Admission: Garden, grounds & landscape walks: Adult £4, Family £10. House: £3 extra. Family £7.50 extra. All year, booked groups £6 (house, garden & walks).

Licensed. Limited for coaches. In grounds on leads. Tel: 01372 452048 for info.

RHS GARDEN WISLEY

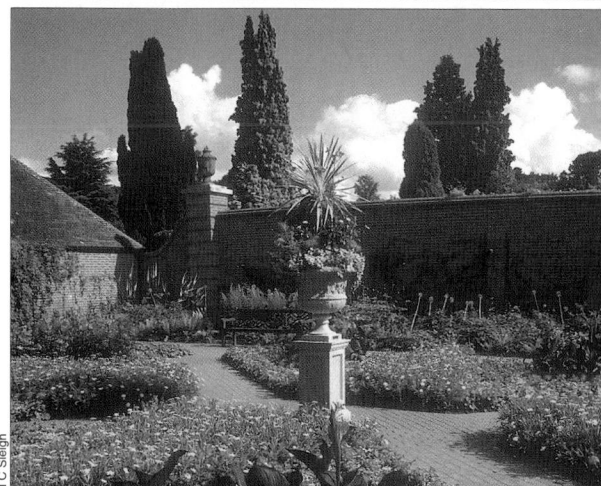

Nr WOKING, SURREY GU23 6QB

Owner/Contact: The Royal Horticultural Society

Tel: 01483 224234   **Fax:** 01483 211750

A world famous garden which extends to 240 acres and provides the chance to glean new ideas and inspiration. Highlights include the azaleas and rhododendrons in spring, the Glasshouses and the Model Gardens. The Giftshop and Plant Centre offer the world's finest collection of horticultural books and over 10,000 varieties of plants for sale.
Location: OS Ref. TQ066 583. NW side of A3 ¹/₂ m SW of M25/J10.

Opening Times: All year: Mon - Fri (except Christmas Day), 10am - sunset or 6pm during the summer; Sats, 9am - sunset or 6pm during summer. RHS members only on Suns.

Admission: Adult £5, Child (up to 6) Free, Child (6-16yrs) £2. Groups (10+) £4. Companion for disabled or blind visitors, Free.

Wheelchairs available tel: 01483 211113 & special map.
Guide dogs only.

RAMSTER GARDENS

Tel: 01428 654167   **Fax:** 01428 658345

Ramster, Chiddingfold, Surrey GU8 4SN
Owner/Contact: Mrs M Gunn
20 acres of woodland and shrub garden.
Location: OS Ref. SU950 333. 1¹/₂ m S of Chiddingfold on A283.
Opening Times: 14 Apr - 1 Jul: 11am - 5pm.
Admission: £3, Child Free.

SHALFORD MILL

Tel: 01483 561617

Shalford, Guildford, Surrey GU4 8BS
Owner: The National Trust
18th century watermill on the Tillingbourne, given in 1932 by 'Ferguson's Gang'.
Location: OS Ref. TQ000 476. 1¹/₂ m S of Guildford on A281, opposite Sea Horse Inn.
Opening Times: Daily, 10am - 5pm.
Admission: Free. No unaccompanied children.

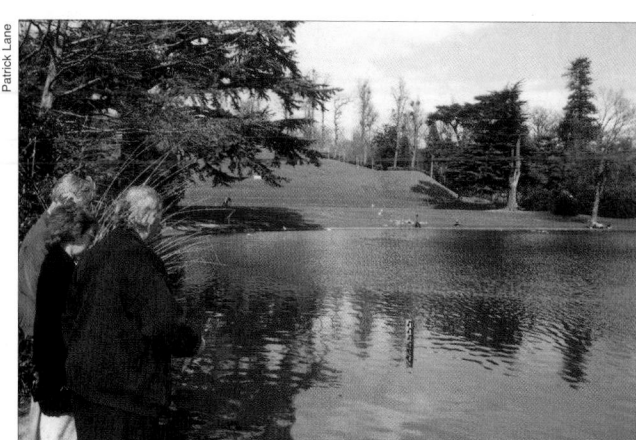

Claremont Landscape Garden, Surrey.

TITSEY PLACE

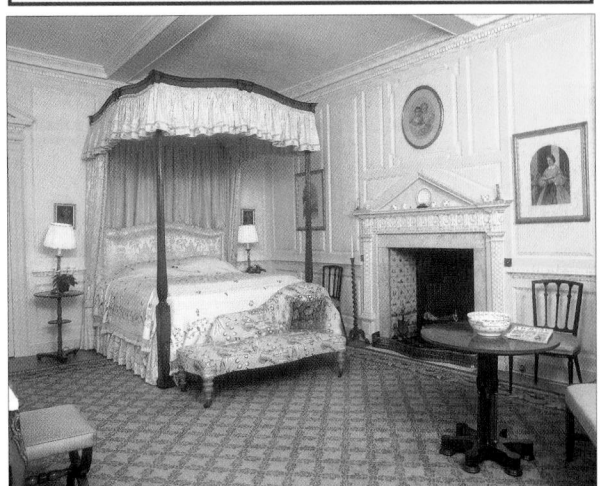

TITSEY, OXTED, SURREY RH8 0SD

Owner: *Trustees of the Titsey Foundation*   **Contact:** *Kate Moisson*

Tel: 01273 407056   **Fax:** 01273 478995
e-mail: kate.moisson@struttandparker.co.uk
Stunning mansion house. Situated outside Limpsfield. Extensive formal and informal gardens containing Victorian walled garden, lakes, fountains and rose gardens. Outstanding features of this house include important paintings and *objets d'art*. Home of the Gresham and Leveson Gower family since the 15th century. Infinite capacity in this magnificent garden, numbers unavoidably restricted on house tours.
Location: OS Ref. TQ406 553. A25 Oxted - Westerham, through Limpsfield and into Bluehouse Lane and Water Lane, follow blue signs.
Opening Times: 15 May - 30 Sept: Weds & Suns, 1 - 5pm including BH Mons. Garden only: Easter Mon.
Admission: Adult £4.50, Child £2. Groups (20+): Adult £5.50.

No photography in house. No barbecues.   Not suitable.
Obligatory.   Limited for coaches.

WHITEHALL

Tel: 020 8643 1236   **Fax:** 020 8770 4777
e-mail: curators@whitehallcheam.fsnet.co.uk

1 Malden Road, Cheam, Surrey SM3 8QD
Owner: London Borough of Sutton   **Contact:** The Curator
A Tudor timber-framed house, c1500 with later additions, in the heart of Cheam village conservation area. Twelve rooms open to view with displays on Nonsuch Palace, timber-framed buildings, Cheam pottery, Cheam school and William Gilpin. Changing exhibition programme and special event days throughout the year. Attractive rear garden features medieval well from c1400.
Location: OS Ref. TQ242 638. Approx. 2m S of A3 on A2043 just N of junction with A232.
Opening Times: 1 Oct - 31 Mar: Weds, Thurs, Suns, 2 - 5.30pm; Sats, 10am - 5.30pm. 1 Apr - 30 Sept: Tue - Fri, Sun, 2 - 5.30pm; Sats, 10am - 5.30pm; BH Mons, 2 - 5.30pm. Closed Christmas and New Year.
Admission: Adult £1.20, Child (under 16yrs) 50p, Child under 5yrs Free. Groups by arrangement.

 Ground floor only.   Guide dogs only. Tel. for details.

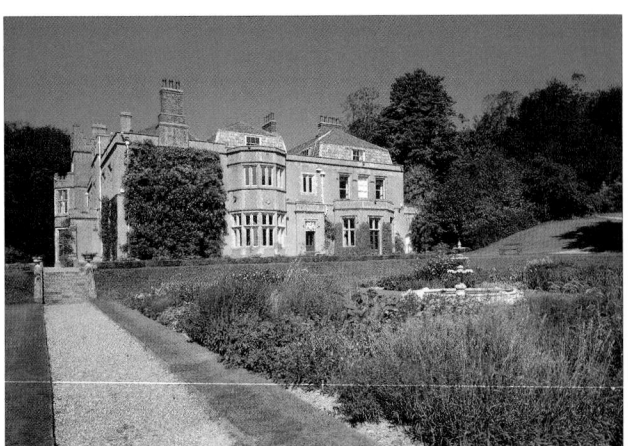

Titsey Place, Surrey.

WINKWORTH ARBORETUM

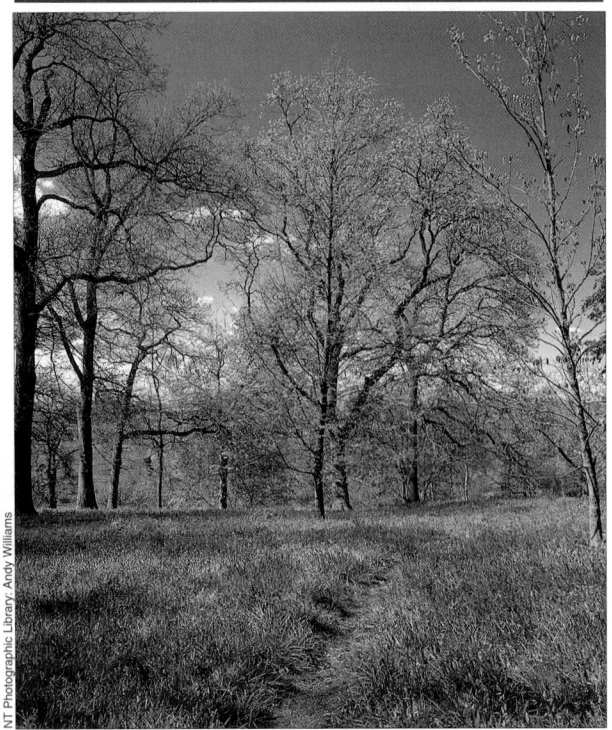

HASCOMBE ROAD, GODALMING, SURREY GU8 4AD

Owner: *The National Trust*   **Contact:** *The Head of Arboretum*

Tel: 01483 208477   **Fax:** 01483 208252   **e-mail:** swagen@smtp.ntrust.org.uk
Hillside woodland with two lakes, many rare trees and shrubs and fine views. The most impressive displays are in spring for bluebells and azaleas, autumn for colour and wildlife. Delightful 100 year old boathouse on Rowes Flashe lake. Seasonal opening.

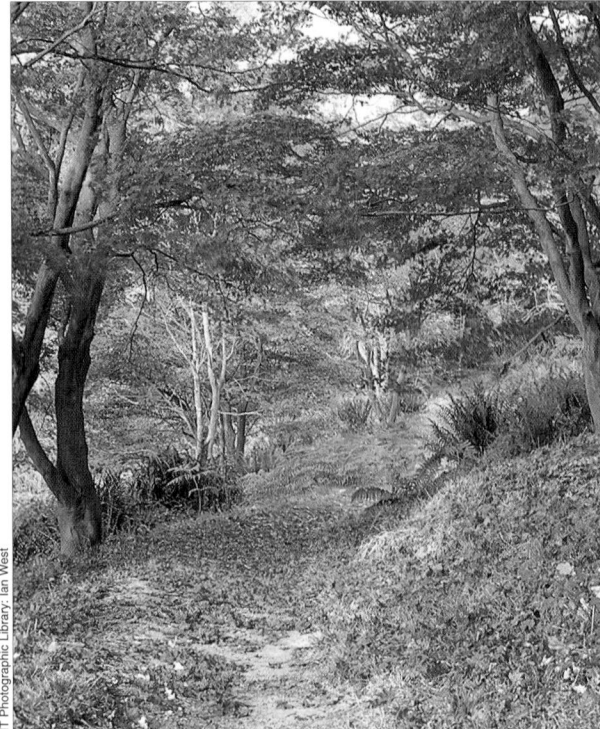

Location: OS Ref. SU990 412. Near Hascombe, 2m SE of Godalming on E side of B2130.
Opening times: All year: daily during daylight hours. May be closed due to high winds. Boathouse: 1 Apr - 31 Oct.
Admission: Adult £3.50, Child (5-16yrs) £1.75, Family (2+2) £8.75, additional family member £1.50. Discounts for 10 or more.

 Limited. WC.   In grounds, on leads.

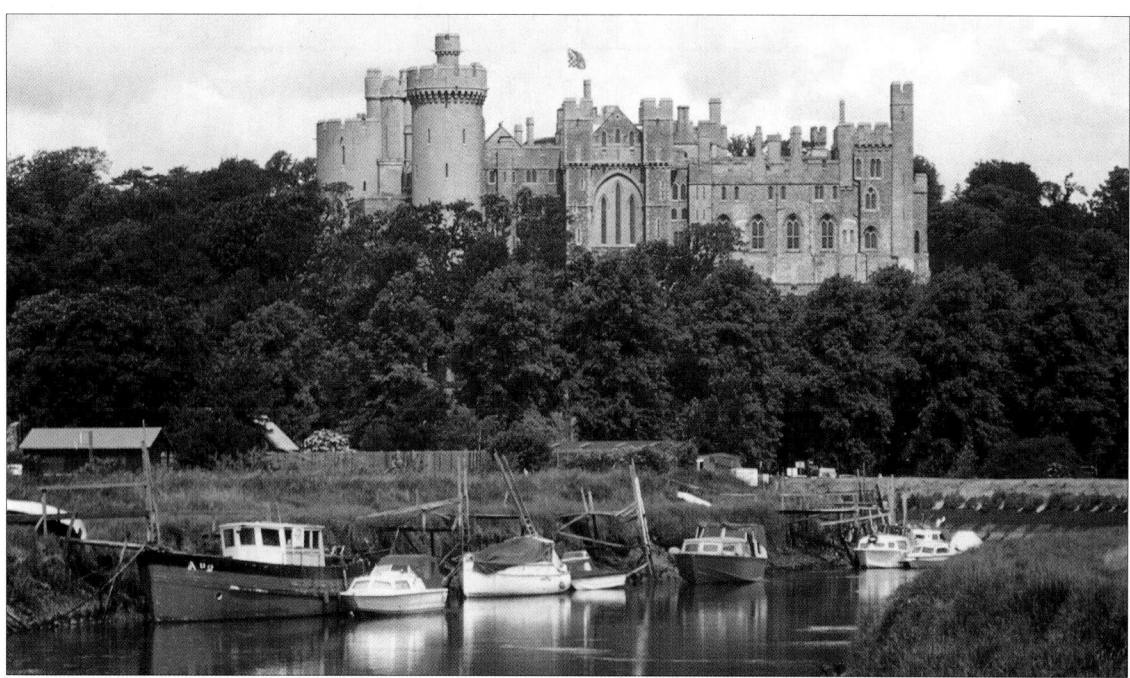

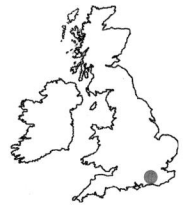

ARUNDEL CASTLE
Arundel

This great castle, home of the Dukes of Norfolk, dates from the Norman Conquest. Containing a very fine collection of furniture and paintings, Arundel Castle is still a family home, reflecting the changes of nearly a thousand years.

In 1643, during the Civil War, the original castle was very badly damaged and it was later restored by the 8th, 11th and 15th Dukes in the 18th and 19th centuries. Amongst its treasures are personal possessions of Mary Queen of Scots and a selection of historical, religious and heraldic items from the Duke of Norfolk's collection.

The Duke of Norfolk is the Premier Duke, the title having been conferred on Sir John Howard in 1483 by his friend King Richard III. The Dukedom also carries with it the hereditary office of Earl Marshal of England. Among the historically famous members of the Howard family are Lord Howard of Effingham who, with Drake, repelled the Spanish Armada; the Earl of Surrey, the Tudor poet and courtier and the 3rd Duke of Norfolk, uncle of Anne Boleyn and Catherine Howard, both of whom became wives of King Henry VIII.

❖

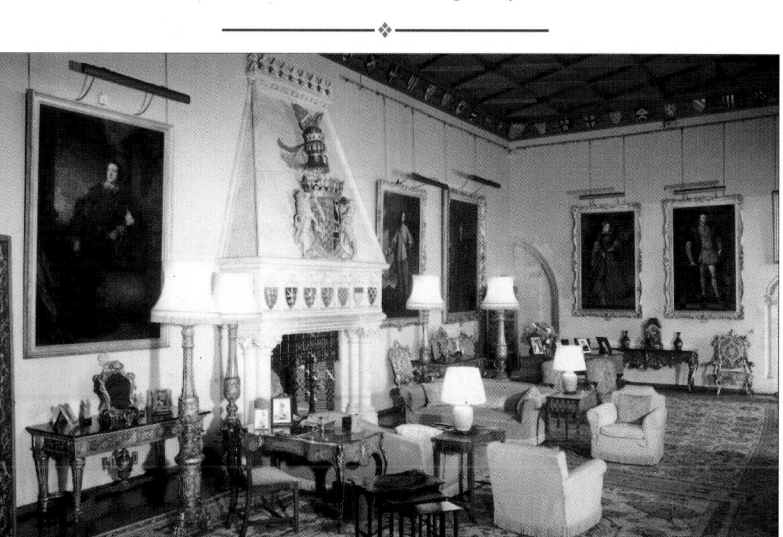

Owner:
Arundel Castle Trustees Ltd

CONTACT

The Comptroller
Arundel Castle
Arundel
West Sussex
BN18 9AB

Tel: 01903 883136
or 01903 882173

Fax: 01903 884581

e-mail: arundelcastle@
compuserve.com

LOCATION

OS Ref. TQ018 072

1m Arundel, N of A27
Brighton 40 mins,
Worthing 15 mins,
Chichester 15 mins.
From London A3 or A24,
1¹/₂ hrs.
M25 motorway, 30m.

Bus: Bus stop 100 yds.

Rail: Station ¹/₂ m.

Air: Gatwick 25m.

OPENING TIMES

SUMMER
1 April - 31 October
Daily (except Sats &
Good Fri)
12 noon - 5pm
Last admission 4pm.

WINTER
1 November - 31 March
Pre-booked groups only.

ADMISSION

SUMMER
Adult	£7.50
Child (5-15)	£5.00
OAP	£6.50
Family (2+2)	£21.00

Groups (20+)
Adult	£7.00
Child (5-15)	£4.50
OAP	£6.00

WINTER
Pre-booked parties
Mornings	£9.00
(Min Fee	£450.00)
Evenings, Sats &	
Suns	£10.00
(Min Fee	£500.00)

No unaccompanied children or photography inside the Castle.

Visitors may alight at the entrance, before parking in the allocated areas. WCs.

Restaurant seats 140. Special rates for booked groups. Self-service restaurant in Castle serves home-made food. Groups must book in advance for afternoon tea, lunch or dinner.

Pre-booked groups only, £9. Tour time 1¹/₂ hrs. Guide book translations in English, French and German.

Ample. Coaches can park opposite the Castle entrance.

Items of particular interest include a Norman Keep and Armoury. Special rates for schoolchildren (aged 5-15) and teachers.

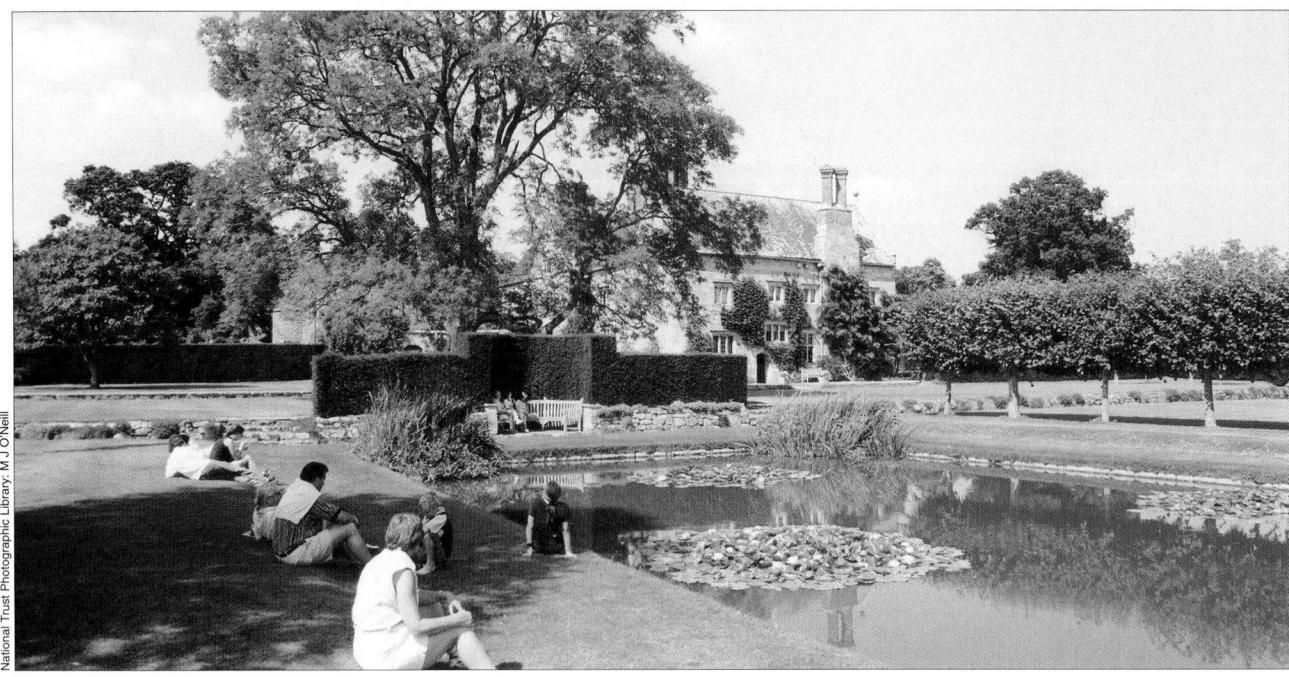

National Trust Photographic Library: M J O'Neill

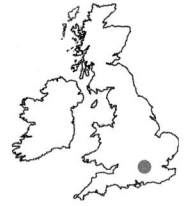

Owner: The National Trust

CONTACT

The Property Manager
Burwash
Etchingham
East Sussex
TN19 7DS

Tel: 01435 882302

Fax: 01435 882811

e-mail: kbaxxx@
smtp.ntrust.org.uk

LOCATION

OS Ref. TQ671 238

1/2 m S of Burwash off
A265.

Rail: Etchingham 3m, then
bus (twice daily).

Air: Gatwick 40m.

BATEMAN'S
Burwash

Built in 1634 and home to Rudyard Kipling for over 30 years, Bateman's lies in the richly wooded landscape of the Sussex Weald. Visit this Sussex sandstone manor house, built by a local ironmaster, where the famous writer lived from 1902 to 1936. See the rooms as they were in Kipling's day, including the study where the view inspired him to write some of his well-loved works including *Puck of Pook's Hill* and *Rewards and Fairies.* Find the mementoes of Kipling's time in India and illustrations from his famous *Jungle Book* tales of *Mowgli, Baloo* and *Shere Khan.*

Wander through the delightful Rose Garden with its pond and statues, with Mulberry and Herb gardens and discover the wild garden, through which flows the River Dudwell. Through the wild garden, you will find the Mill

where you can watch corn being ground on most Saturday afternoons and one of the world's first water-driven turbines installed by Kipling to generate electricity for the house. In the garage, see a 1928 Rolls Royce, one of several owned by Kipling who was a keen early motorist.

Savour the peace and tranquillity of this beautiful property which Kipling described as '*A good and peaceable place*' and of which he said '*we have loved it, ever since our first sight of it...*'.

There is a picnic glade next to the car park, or you can enjoy morning coffee, a delicious lunch or afternoon tea in the licensed tearoom where there is special emphasis on using local produce. The well-stocked gift shop offers the largest collection of Kipling books in the area.

OPENING TIMES

1 Apr - 1 Nov: Sat - Wed,
Good Fri & BH Mons,
11am - 5.30pm. Last
admission 4.30pm.

Wild Garden:
Open in March 2001.

ADMISSION

House and Garden

Adult	£5.00
Child	£2.50
Family (2+3)	£12.50
Groups	£4.25

SPECIAL EVENTS

• **AUG:**
Last Night of the Proms &
Sixties Concert.
Tel: 01892 891001 for details.

 Ground floor & grounds suitable. WC.

Licensed.

National Trust Photographic Library: Geoffrey Frosh

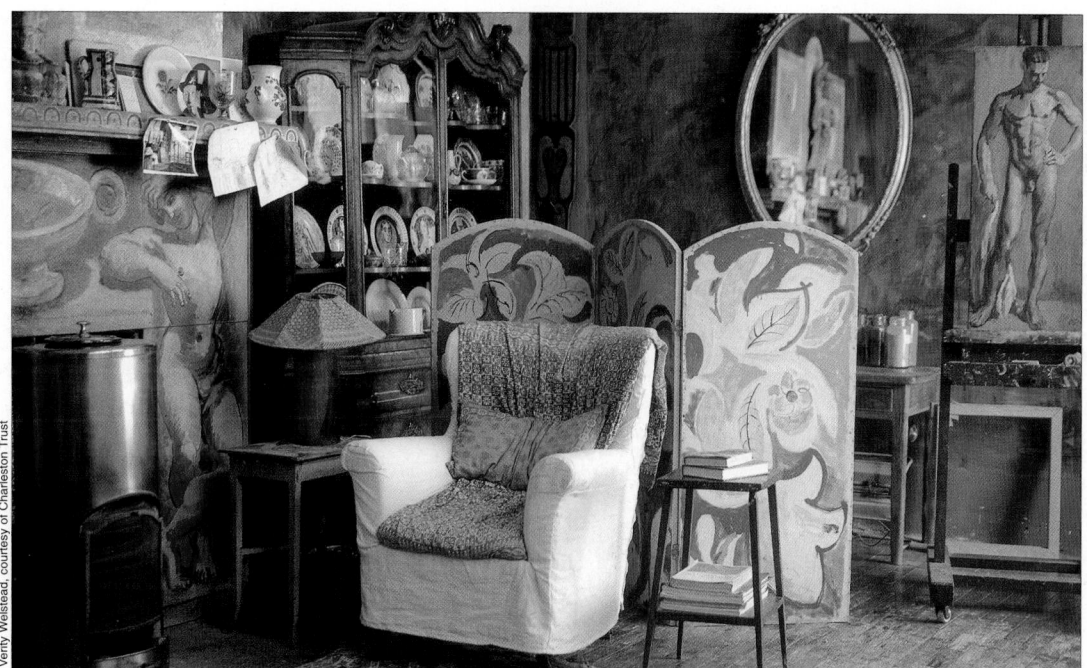

Verity Welstead, courtesy of Charleston Trust

CHARLESTON
Lewes

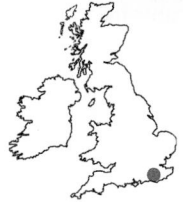

Owner:
The Charleston Trust

CONTACT

Emma Whelan
Charleston
Nr Firle
Lewes
East Sussex
BN8 6LL

Tel: 01323 811265
(Visitor information)
01323 811626 (Admin)

Fax: 01323 811628

e-mail: charles
@solutions-inc.co.uk

LOCATION

OS Ref. TQ490 069

6m E of Lewes on A27
between Firle & Selmeston.
The lane to Charleston
leads off the A27, 2m
beyond the Firle turning.

London 60m. Brighton 15m.
Monk's House, Rodmell
(Leonard and Virginia
Woolf's house) 11m.

Air: Gatwick 35m.

Rail: London (Victoria)
hourly to Lewes (65 mins).
Occasional train to Berwick.

Bus: Rider 125 Charleston
Rambler Suns & BHs
Route on A27.
Taxi: George & Graham,
Lewes 473692.

A mile or so from Firle village, near the end of a track leading to the foot of the Downs, lies Charleston. It was discovered in 1916 by Virginia and Leonard Woolf when Virginia's sister, the painter Vanessa Bell, was looking for a place in the country. Vanessa moved here with fellow artist Duncan Grant, the writer David Garnett, her two young sons and an assortment of animals. It was an unconventional and creative household which became the focal point for artists and intellectuals later to be known as the Bloomsbury set, among them Roger Fry, Lytton Strachey and Maynard Keynes.

Over the years the artists decorated the walls, furniture and ceramics with their own designs, influenced by Italian fresco painting and post-impressionist art. Creativity extended to the garden too. Mosaics were made in the piazza, sculpture was cleverly positioned to intrigue and subtle masses of colour were used in the planting.

After Duncan Grant's death in 1978, the Charleston Trust was formed to save and restore the house to its former glory. The task has been described as "one of the most difficult and imaginative feats of restoration current in Britain".

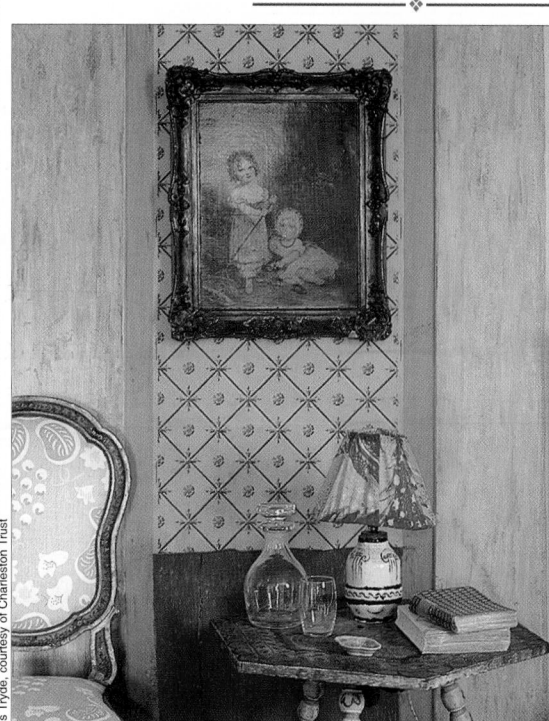

Pls Tryde, courtesy of Charleston Trust

Filming and photography contact Shaun Romain: 01323 811626. Small lecture room available by special arrangement. No filming, video or photography in house.

Visitors may alight at entrance. Wheelchair visitors by prior arrangement. Ground floor only suitable. WCs.

Wed - Sun, 2 - 5pm.

Obligatory.

50 spaces. Mini coaches and cars only. Mini coaches may use the lane to the property. It is essential to arrange group visits (up to 50) in advance and out of public hours. All group visits to the house are guided. Large coaches may set down at the start of the lane, 10 mins walk.

Student pack and a teacher's guide suitable for KS I & II.

Guide dogs only.

OPENING TIMES

1 April - 31 October
Wed - Sun: 2 - 5pm.

Extra Summer Opening
Times: July & August
Wed - Sat: 11.30am - 5pm.
Sun: 2 - 5pm.

November - December
Christmas shopping
Sat & Sun, 1 - 4pm.

Guided visits
Wed - Sat,
unguided on Suns.

House closed Mon & Tue
except BH Mons.

Connoisseur Fridays
April - June, September
and October, in-depth tour
of the house, including
Vanessa Bell's studio and
the kitchen.

ADMISSION

House & Garden

Adult	£5.50
Child (5+)/Conc*.	£4.00
Child (under 5)	Free
Disabled	£4.00

Groups (min 10)

Adult	£5.00
Child/Student	£4.00
OAP	£5.00

Connoisseur Fridays

Adult	£6.50

* OAPs, Students &
UB40 Wed & Thur
only throughout season.
Organised tours should
telephone for group rates.

SPECIAL EVENTS

• **MAY 24 - 28:**
Charleston Festival

For other events see
www. charleston.org.uk

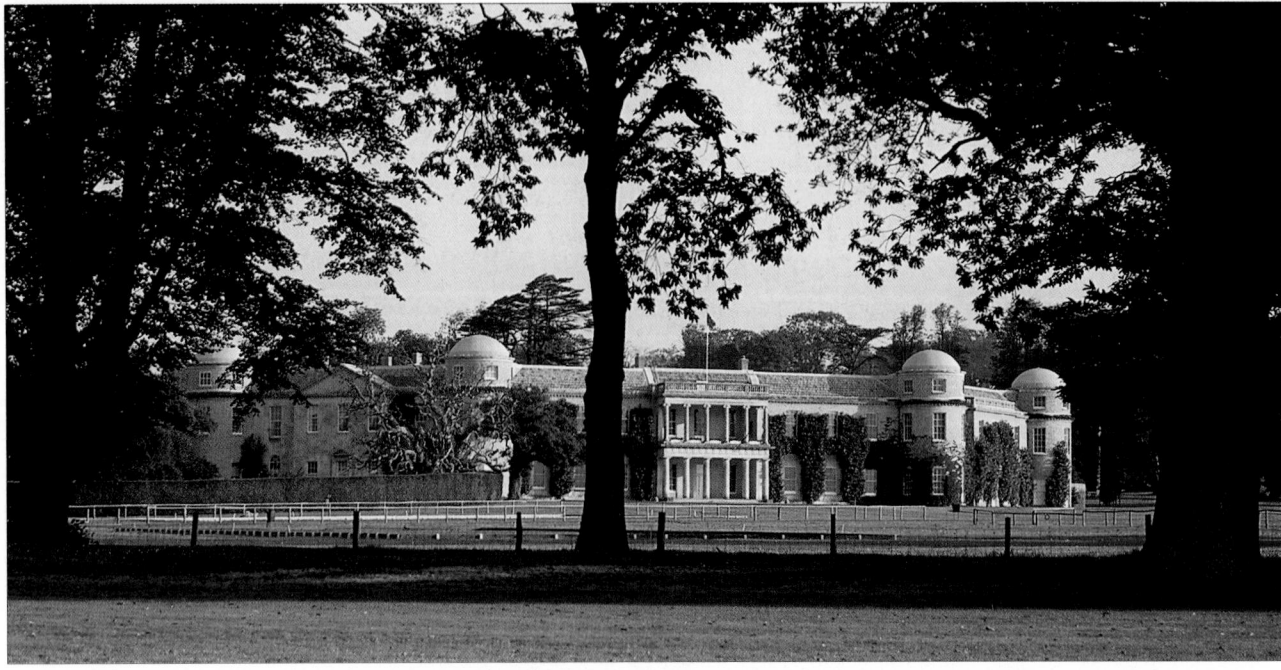

GOODWOOD HOUSE
Chichester

It is now 200 years since the 3rd Duke of Richmond embarked upon an ambitious scheme to turn his small country house into a magnificent ducal residence. In keeping with the fashion, the two new Regency wings were added to afford the best possible views of the picturesque parkland and beyond, to Chichester and the sea. Today, Goodwood encapsulates the flamboyance, innovation and style that have been the signature of the Richmond family ever since the time of the 1st Duke. The natural son of King Charles II and his beautiful French mistress, Louise de Keroualle, he was renowned for his love of life

and brilliance at entertaining – a tradition which continues to this day. The French interest was pursued by the 3rd Duke who, as British Ambassador to Paris, collected important French furniture which now sets off the newly restored Tapestry Drawing Room, and Sèvres porcelain, which can still be seen. Still owned and lived in by the Earl and Countess of March, Goodwood effortlessly exudes the glamour of a ducal seat and is not only a beautiful house to visit, but has also established a worldwide reputation for excellence as the location for corporate, private and incentive entertainment.

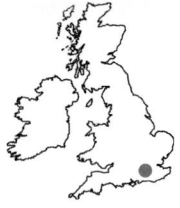

Owner:
The Earl of March

CONTACT

Kathryn Bellamy
Goodwood House
Goodwood
Chichester
West Sussex
PO18 0PX

Tel: 01243 755048

Fax: 01243 755005

Recorded info:
01243 755040

e-mail: enquiries
@goodwood.co.uk

LOCATION

OS Ref. SU888 088

4m NE of Chichester. A3 from London then A286 or A285. M27/A27 from Portsmouth or Brighton.

Rail: Chichester 4m
Arundel 9m.

Air: Heathrow 1¹/₂ hrs
Gatwick ³/₄ hr.

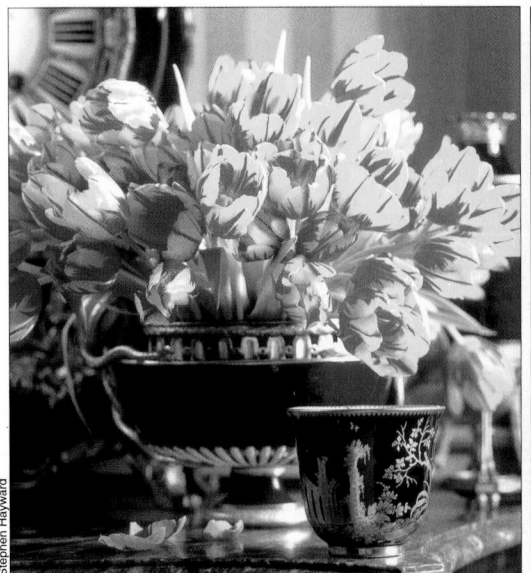

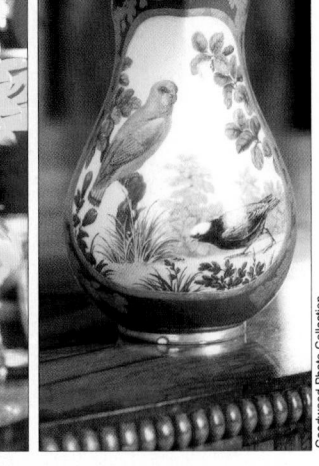

Stephen Hayward

Goodwood Photo Collection

  Conference facilities. No photography. Highly trained guides in every room. Shell House optional extra on Connoisseurs' Days only.

By appointment: open mornings & on Connoisseurs' Days.

Ample.

In grounds, on leads. Guide dogs only in house.

Suitable.

Civil Wedding Licence.

CONFERENCE/FUNCTION		
ROOM	SIZE	MAX CAPACITY
Ballroom	79' x 23'	200
11 other rooms also available		

OPENING TIMES

SUMMER

1 Apr - 1 Oct:
Most Suns & Mons.

5 Aug - 6 Sept:
Sun - Thur,
1 - 5pm.

Closed on Special Event Days (see list below): and occasional others including Sundays 6 & 27 May. To check please ring Recorded Information on 01243 755040.

Connoisseurs' Days
Group visits with special guided tours can be booked.

ADMISSION

House
Adult £6.50
Child* £3.00
Conc. £6.00

Groups (20 - 200)
Economy................£5.50
Connoisseur...........£8.50

*12 - 18 yrs, under 12 yrs free

⚅ SPECIAL EVENTS

• **FEB 3/4**
Antiques Fair.

• **APR 21/22**
Home Design Interiors.

• **MAY 12/13**
Antiques Fair.

• **JUL 31 - AUG 4**
Race Week.

• **MID SEPTEMBER**
Motor Circuit Revival Meeting.

• **NOV 17/18**
Antiques Fair.

Festival of Speed between mid-June & early July, please telephone to confirm the dates.

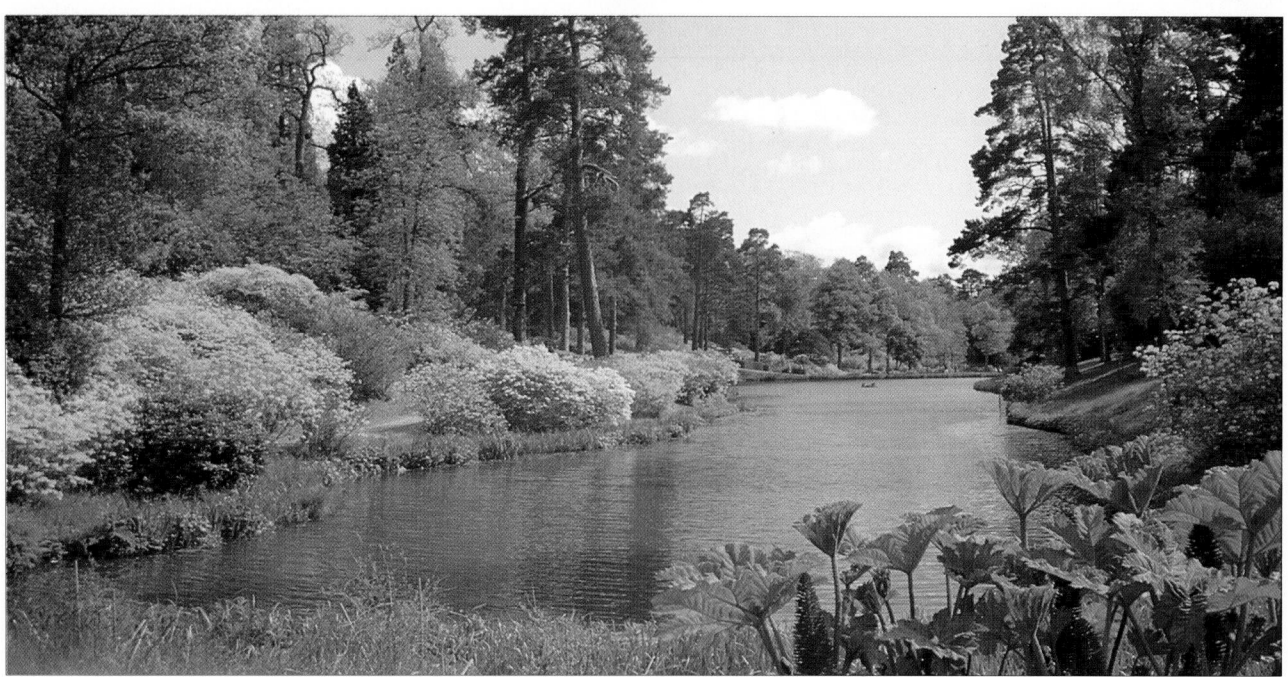

LEONARDSLEE GARDENS
Horsham

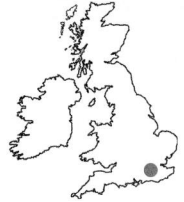

Owner:
R Loder Esq

CONTACT

R Loder Esq
Leonardslee Gardens
Lower Beeding
Horsham
West Sussex
RH13 6PP

Tel: 01403 891212

Fax: 01403 891305

LOCATION

OS Ref. TQ222 260

M23 to Handcross then
B2110 (signposted
Cowfold) for 4m.
From London:
1 hr 15 mins.

Rail: Horsham
Station 4$\frac{1}{2}$ m

Bus: No. 107 from
Horsham and Brighton

LEONARDSLEE GARDENS represent one of the largest and most spectacular woodland gardens in England with one of the finest collections of mature rhododendrons, azaleas, choice trees and shrubs to be seen anywhere. It is doubly fortunate in having one of the most magnificent settings, within easy reach of London, only a few miles from the M23. Laid out by Sir Edmund Loder since 1889, the gardens are still maintained by the Loder family today. The 240 acre (100 hectare) valley is world famous for its spring display of azaleas and rhododendrons around the 7 lakes, giving superb views and reflections.

The delightful Rock Garden, a photographer's paradise, is a kaleidoscope of colour in May. The superb exhibition of Bonsai in a walled courtyard shows the fascinating living art-form of Bonsai to perfection. The Alpine House has 400 different alpine plants growing in a natural rocky setting. Wallabies (used as mowing machines!) have lived wild in part of the garden for over 100 years, and deer (Sika, Fallow & Axis) may be seen in the parklands.

Many superb rhododendrons have been raised at Leonardslee. The most famous is *rhododendron loderi* raised by Sir Edmund Loder in 1901. The original plants can still be seen in the garden. In May the fragrance of their huge blooms pervades the air throughout the valley.

The Loder family collection of Victorian motorcars (1895 - 1900) provides a fascinating view of the different designs adopted on the first auto-mobile constructors.

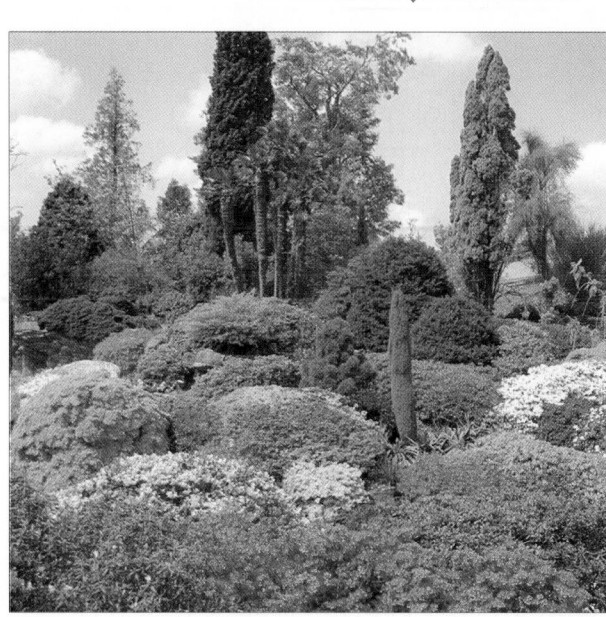

Photography - landscape and fashion, film location.

Restaurant available for private and corporate function in the evenings and out of season.

Not suitable.

Restaurant and café. Morning coffee, lunch and teas.

Ample. Refreshments free to coach drivers. Average length of visit 2 - 4 hours.

OPENING TIMES

SUMMER
1 April - 31 October
Daily 9.30am - 6pm

WINTER
1 November - 31 March
Closed to the general public.

Available for functions.

ADMISSION

April, June - October
Adult £5.00

May (Mon - Fri)
Adult £6.00

May (Sats, Suns & BH Mons)
Adult £7.00
Child (anytime) £3.00

Groups
April, June - October
Adult £4.00

May: (Mon - Fri) £5.00
Sat, Sun &
BH Mons: £6.00
Child (anytime) £2.50

SPECIAL EVENTS

• **MAY 5 - 7:**
Bonsai Weekend.

• **JUN 23 - 24:**
West Sussex Country Craft Fair.

• **JUL 14 - 15:**
Model Boat Regatta.

CONFERENCE/FUNCTION		
ROOM	SIZE	MAX CAPACITY
Clock Tower		100

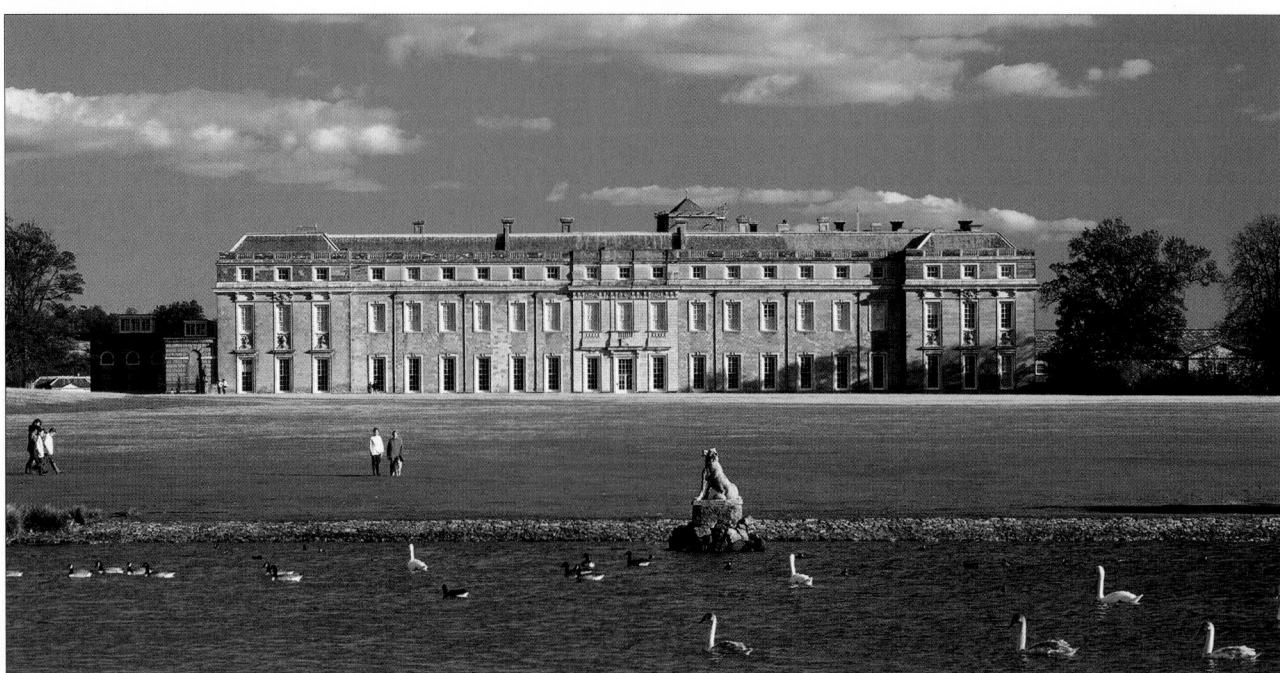

Oliver Benn

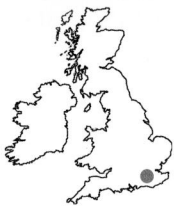

Owner:
The National Trust

CONTACT

The Administration Office
Petworth House
Petworth
West Sussex
GU28 0AE

Tel: 01798 342207

Info Line: 01798 343929

Fax: 01798 342963

e-mail: spegen@
smtp.ntrust.org.uk

LOCATION

OS Ref. SU976 218

In the centre of Petworth
town (approach roads
A272/A283/A285)
Car park signposted.

Rail: Pulborough
BR 5¼ m.

PETWORTH HOUSE
Petworth

PETWORTH HOUSE is one of the finest houses in the care of the National Trust and is home to an art collection that rivals many London galleries. Assembled by one family over 350 years, it includes works by Turner, Van Dyck, Titian, Claude, Gainsborough, Bosch, Reynolds and William Blake.

The state rooms contain sculpture, furniture and porcelain of the highest quality and are complemented by the opening of the old kitchens in the servants' block.

A continuing programme of repairs and restoration brings new interest for the visitor each year. Petworth House is also the home of Lord and Lady Egremont and extra family rooms are open on weekdays by kind permission (not Bank Holidays).

Petworth Park is a 700 acre park landscaped by 'Capability' Brown and is open to the public all year free of charge. Spring and autumn are particularly breathtaking and the summer sunsets over the lake are spectacular.

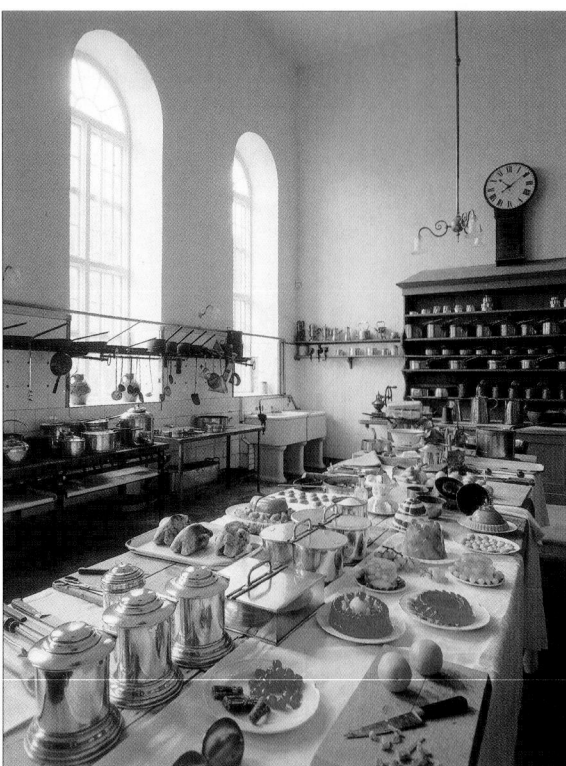

Andreas Von Einsiedel

Events throughout the year. Large musical concerts in the park. Baby feeding and changing facilities, highchairs. Pushchairs admitted in house but no prams, please. No photography in house.

Contact Retail & Catering Manager on 01798 344975.

Car park is 800 yards from house; there is a vehicle available to take less able visitors to house.

Licensed. 12-5pm.

By arrangement (Mon - Wed mornings) with the Administration Officer on variety of subjects, tailor-made to suit your group (additional charge).

800 yards from house. Coach parties alight at Church Lodge entrance, coaches then park in NT car park. Coaches <u>must</u> book in advance.

Welcome. Must pre-book. Teachers' pack available.

Guide dogs only in house. Dogs in park only.

Tel. for details.

OPENING TIMES

**House &
Servants' Quarters**
31 March - 4 November
Daily except Thurs & Fris
but open Good Fri and
every following Fri in
July & August. 1 - 5.30pm.
Last admission to house &
servants' quarters 5pm.
Extra rooms shown on
Mons, Tues & Weds,
not BH Mons.

**Pleasure Ground
and Car Park**
17/18 & 24/25 March
for spring bulbs, 12 noon -
4pm. Dates as house
12 noon - 6pm. BH Mons,
July & August, 11am - 6pm.

Park
All year: Daily, 8am - sunset.
Closed 29, 30 Jun & 1 Jul
for concerts.

**Servants Quarters,
Pleasure Grounds, Shop
& Restaurant:**
14 Nov - 22 Dec, Wed - Sat,
10.30am - 3.30pm. Thurs
only: guided tour of house
to see work in progess.

ADMISSION

**House, Servants'
Quarters &
Pleasure Ground**
Adult £6.00
Child* (5-17yrs) £3.00
Family (2+2) £15.00
Park Only .... Free
Groups (pre-booked 15+)
Adult £5.50

Pleasure Ground
Adult £1.50
Park ....Free
NT Members Free.

* Under 5yrs Free

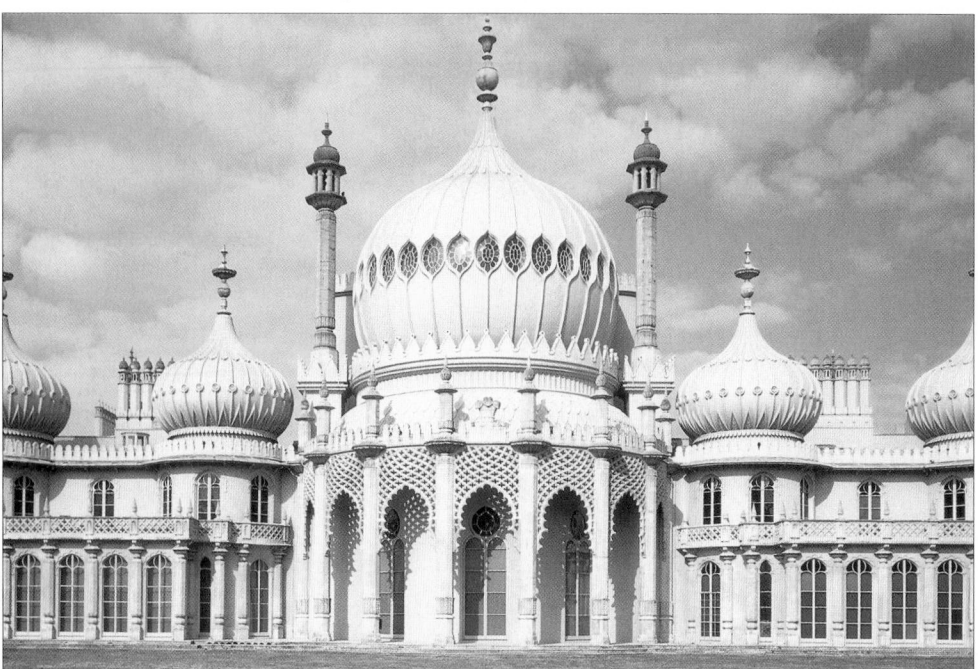

THE ROYAL PAVILION
Brighton

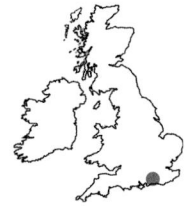

Owner:
Brighton & Hove Council

CONTACT

Visitor Services
The Royal Pavilion
Brighton
East Sussex
BN1 1EE

Tel: 01273 290900

Fax: 01273 292871

LOCATION

OS Ref. TQ313 043

The Royal Pavilion is in the
centre of Brighton easily
reached by road and rail.
From London M25, M23,
A23 - 1 hr 30 mins.

Rail: Victoria to Brighton
station 50 mins.
15 mins walk from
Brighton station.

Air: Gatwick 20 mins.

CONFERENCE/FUNCTION		
ROOM	SIZE	MAX CAPACITY
Banqueting Room		200
Great Kitchen		90
Music Rm		180
Queen Adelaide Suite		100
Small Adelaide		40
William IV		80

Universally acclaimed as one of the most
exotically beautiful buildings in the British
Isles, the Royal Pavilion is the former seaside
residence of King George IV.

Originally a simple farmhouse, in 1787 architect
Henry Holland created a neo-classical villa on
the site. It was later transformed into its current
Indian style by John Nash between 1815 and
1822. With interiors decorated in the Chinese
style and an astonishingly exotic exterior, this
Regency Palace is quite breathtaking.

Magnificent decorations and fantastic furnishings
have been re-created in the recent extensive
restoration programme. From the opulence
of the main state rooms to the charm of the
first floor bedroom suites, the Royal Pavilion
is filled with astonishing colours and superb
craftsmanship.

Witness the magnificence of the Music Room
with its domed ceiling of gilded scallop-shaped
shells and hand-knotted carpet, and promenade
through the Chinese bamboo grove of the
Long Gallery.

Lavish menus were created in the Great Kitchen,
with its cast iron palm trees and dazzling
collection of copperware, and then served in the
dramatic setting of the Banqueting Room, lit by a
huge crystal chandelier held by a silvered dragon.

Set in restored Regency gardens replanted to
John Nash's elegant 1820s design, the Royal
Pavilion is an unforgettable experience.

Visitors can discover more about life behind the
scenes at the Palace during the last 200 years with
a new specially commissioned interactive multimedia presentation. Public guided tours take
place daily at 11.30am and 2.30pm for a small
additional charge.

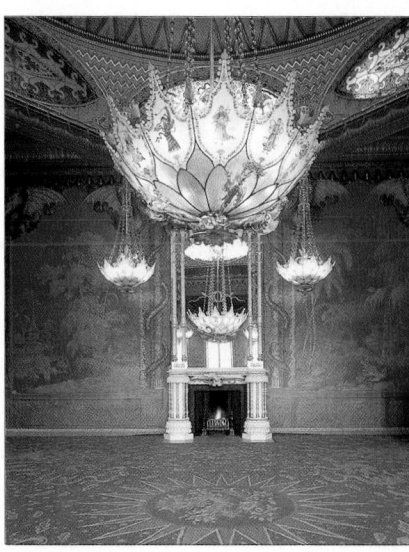

ℹ️ Location filming and photography, including feature
films, fashion shoots and corporate videos.

🎁 Gift shop with souvenirs unique to the Royal Pavilion.

🍽️ Spectacular rooms available for prestigious corporate
and private entertaining and wedding receptions.

♿ Access to ground floor. Free admission. Guided tours,
including tactile and signed tours, are free of charge to those
with disabilities but must be booked in advance with Visitor
Services Tel: 01273 292820/2.

☕ Tearooms with a balcony providing sweeping views
across the restored Regency gardens.

🚶 Tours in English, French and German by prior arrangement. General introduction and specialist tours provided.

🅿️ Close to NCP car parks, town centre voucher parking. Coach
drop-off point in Church Street, parking in Madeira Drive. Free
entry for coach drivers.

📚 Specialist tours relating to all levels of National
Curriculum, must be booked in advance with Visitor
Services. Special winter student rates. Slide lecture
presentations by arrangement.

💍 Civil Wedding Licence.

❄️

OPENING TIMES

SUMMER
June - September
Daily: 10am - 6pm
Last admission at 6pm.

WINTER
October - May
Daily: 10am - 5pm
Last admission at 5pm.

Closed 25/26 December.

ADMISSION

Adult	£4.90
Child	£3.00
Conc.	£3.55

Groups (20+)
Adult £4.10

Prices valid until 31.3.2001

SPECIAL EVENTS

- **SPRING & AUTUMN
  HALF TERM:**
  Children's Events.

- **OCT - MAR:**
  Winter programme of events –
  call for details.

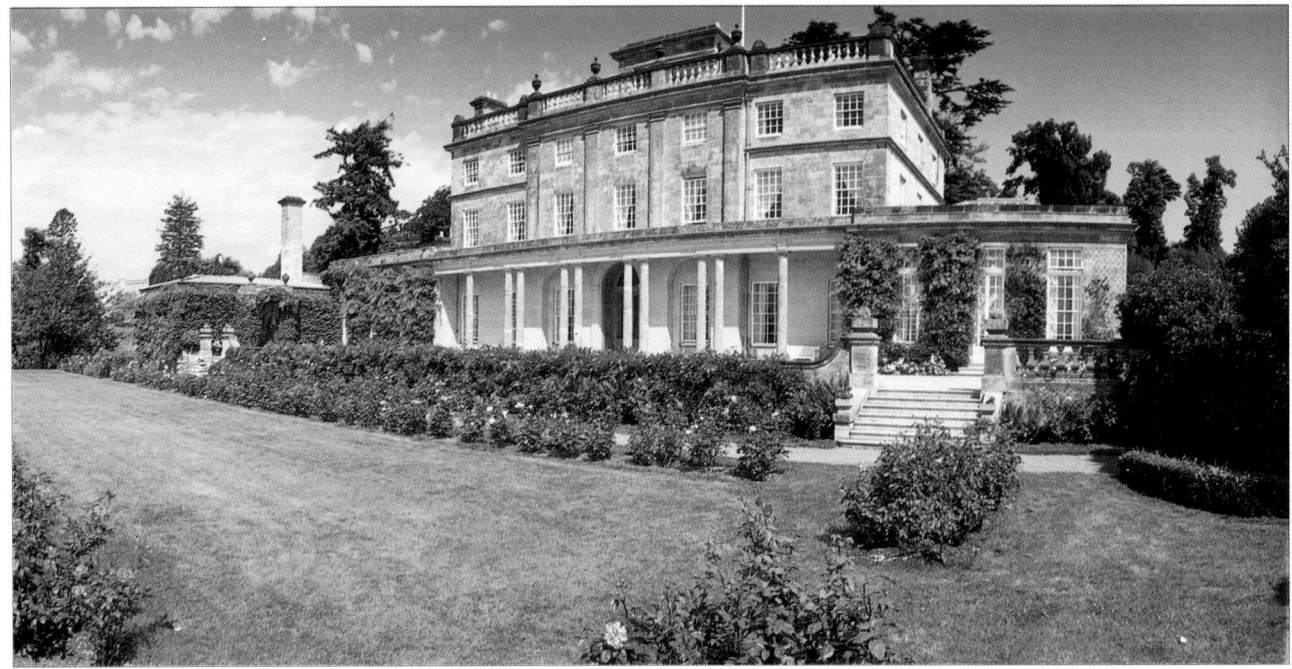

SAINT HILL MANOR
East Grinstead

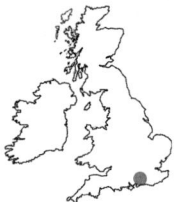

Owner: Church of Scientology

CONTACT

Mrs Liz Nyegaard
Saint Hill Manor
Saint Hill Road
East Grinstead
West Sussex
RH19 4JY

Tel: 01342 326711

Fax: 01342 317057

LOCATION

2m SW of East Grinstead. At Felbridge, turn off A22, down Imberhorne Lane and over crossroads into Saint Hill Road, 200yds on right.

Rail: East Grinstead station.

Air: 15 mins drive from Gatwick airport.

Built 1792 by Gibbs Crawfurd. One of the finest Sussex sandstone buildings in existence and situated near the breathtaking Ashdown Forest. Subsequent owners included Edgar March Crookshank and the Maharajah of Jaipur. In 1959, Saint Hill Manor's final owner, acclaimed author and humanitarian L Ron Hubbard, acquired the Manor, where he lived for many years with his family. As a result of the work carried out under Mr Hubbard's direction, the Manor has been restored to its original beauty, including the uncovering of fine oak wood panelling, marble fireplaces and plasterwork ceilings.

Other outstanding features of this lovely house include an impressive library of Mr Hubbard's works, elegant winter garden, and delightful Monkey Mural painted in 1945 by Winston Churchill's nephew John Spencer Churchill. This 100-foot mural depicts many famous personalities as monkeys, including Winston Churchill. Also open to the public are 59 acres of landscaped gardens, lake and woodlands. Ideal for corporate functions, wedding receptions and also available as a film location. Annual events include open-air theatre, arts festivals, classical and jazz concerts.

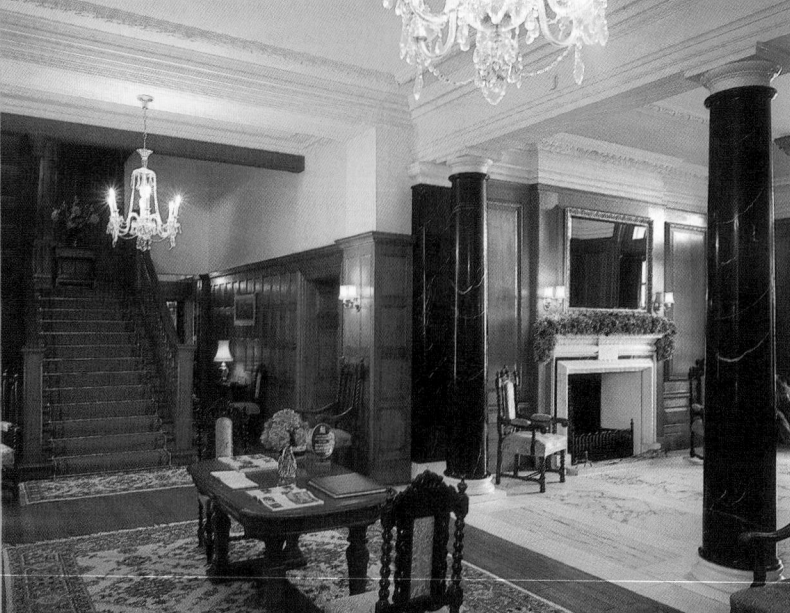

OPENING TIMES

All year: daily, 2 - 5pm, on the hour.
Groups welcome throughout the year.

ADMISSION

Free.

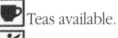
Ground floor suitable.
Teas available.
Obligatory.

SPECIAL EVENTS

• **JUN 24:**
Open air production of Sheridan's 'School for Scandal'

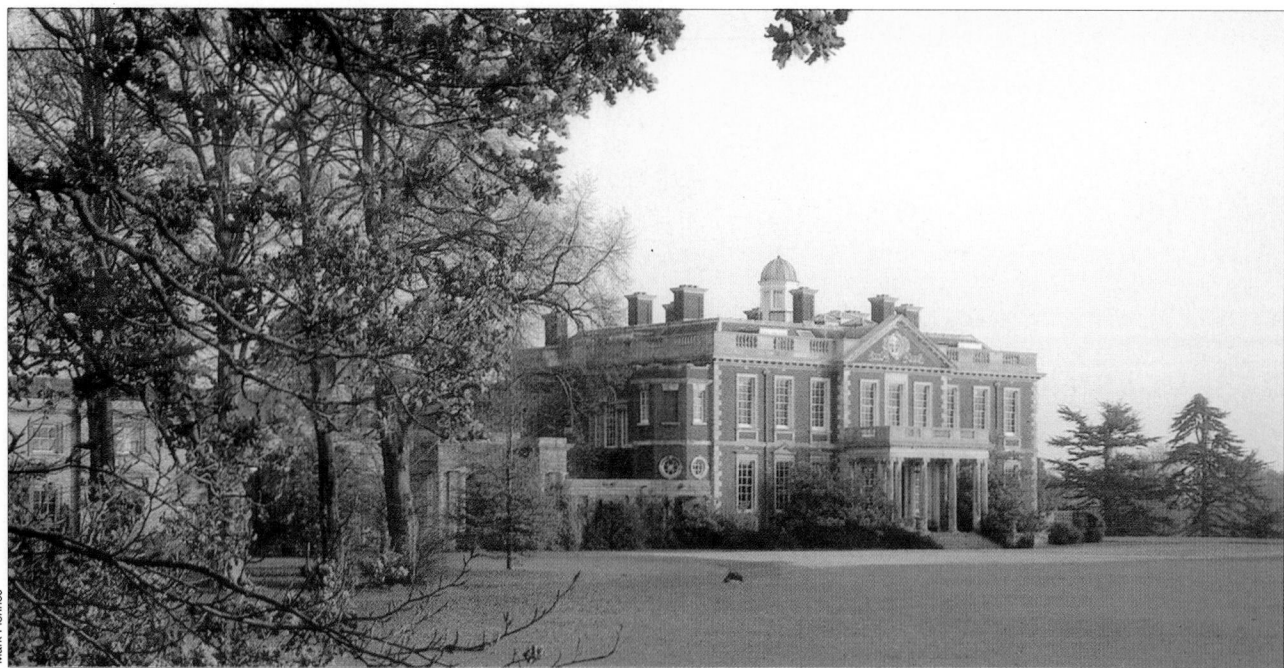

Mark Fiennes

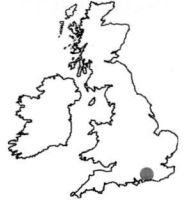

Owner: Trustees of Stansted Park Foundation

CONTACT

The House Manager
Stansted Park
Rowlands Castle
Hampshire
PO9 6DX

Tel: 023 9241 2265/
023 9241 3380

Fax: 023 9241 3773

e-mail: enquiries@
stanstedpark.co.uk

LOCATION

OS Ref. SU761 104

Follow brown heritage signs from A3 (Rowlands Castle) or A27 (Havant)

Rail: Rowlands Castle (London Waterloo 1¹/₂ hrs.

Air: Eastleigh, Southampton.

STANSTED PARK
Rowlands Castle

STANSTED is more than an elegant house. Set in 1750 acres of glorious park and woodland, rich in wildlife and famous for its tranquillity, it is a prime example of the Caroline revival. Not only is Stansted one of the South's most beautiful stately homes, it is also one of Sussex's best-kept secrets.

The contrast between the magnificent State Rooms and the purpose-built Servants' Quarters gives an insight into the social history of an English Country House in its heyday. The Bessborough family collection includes paintings of the famous Georgiana, Duchess of Devonshire and her sister Henrietta Frances, wife to the 3rd Earl and

mother of the equally famous Lady Caroline Lamb. The visionary stained glass windows in the exquisitely decorated Ancient Chapel inspired some of Keats' finest poetry.

The restored Dutch Garden, Circular Garden, Ivan Hicks' famous 'Garden in Mind' and the large, well-stocked Garden Centre within the unique Walled Gardens are a must for people who love plants.

Stansted's 12th century origins were related to hunting and hawking and Henry II visited often to enjoy the chase. The new Falconry revives this tradition and appeals to everyone, whatever their age.

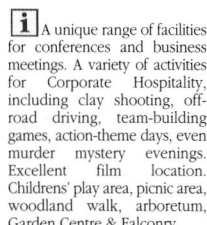
A unique range of facilities for conferences and business meetings. A variety of activities for Corporate Hospitality, including clay shooting, off-road driving, team-building games, action-theme days, even murder mystery evenings. Excellent film location. Childrens' play area, picnic area, woodland walk, arboretum, Garden Centre & Falconry.

Partially suitable. WC.

Licensed.

By arrangement.

In woods, on leads.

A wide variety of facilities to suit parties of all sizes. A complete package with both ceremony and reception is just one of the options offered. Every function is tailored to individual requirements and we guarantee a special day.

Please tel. for details.

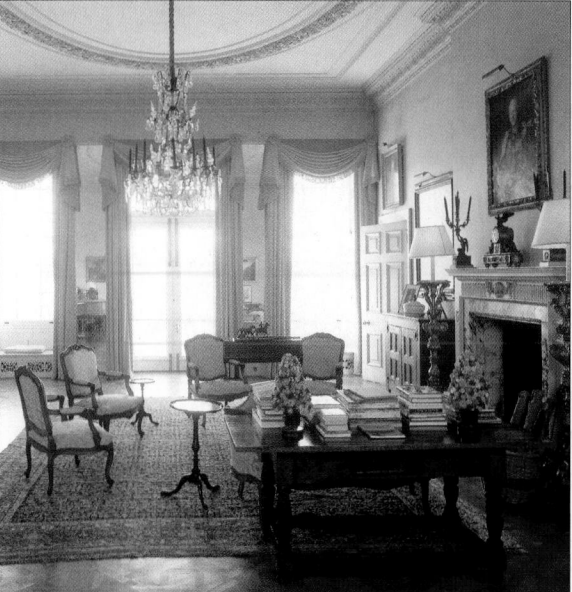

CONFERENCE/FUNCTION		
ROOM	SIZE	MAX CAPACITY
Mail Hall & Music Room		100 - 150

OPENING TIMES

House
1 April - 31 October:
Sun - Wed, 1 - 5pm.

Grounds, including Ivan Hicks' 'Garden in Mind' & Arboretum:
All year: daily, 1 - 5pm (closed Christmas & New Year BHs).

Falconry:
All year: daily except Thurs, 9am - 5pm. Flying times: 11am, 1pm & 3pm (weather permitting).

Garden Centre:
All year:
Mon - Sat, 9am - 5pm.
Suns, 10.30am - 4.30pm.

ADMISSION

House & Grounds
Adult £5.50
Child (5-17yrs)........£3.50
OAP/Student...........£2.70
Family (2+3) £14.50

Grounds
Adult £3.50
Child (5-17yrs)........£2.00
OAP/Student...........£3.00
Family (2+3) £9.00

Stansted Falconry
Adult £3.00
Child (5-17yrs)........£2.00
OAP/Student...........£2.50
Family (2+3) £8.00

Groups (30-50)
10% discount off the above prices.

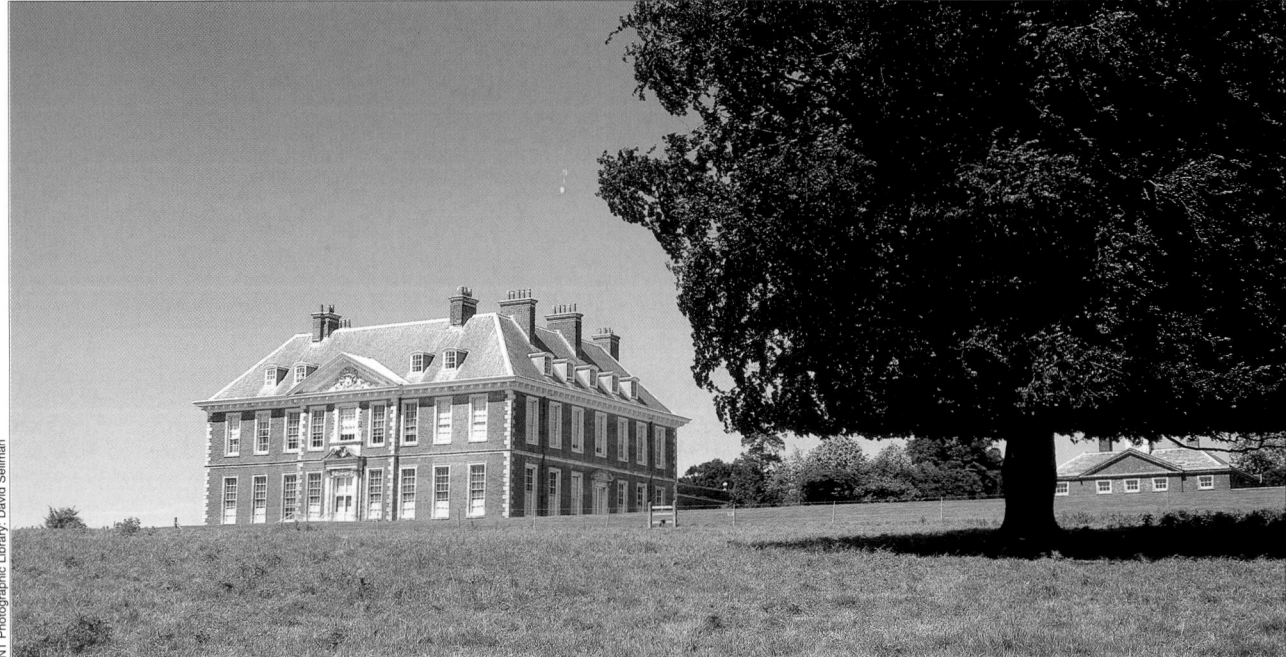

NT Photographic Library: David Sellman

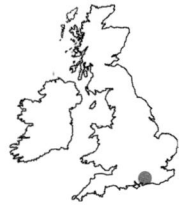

Owner: The National Trust

CONTACT

The Property Manager
Uppark
South Harting
Petersfield
GU31 5QR

Tel: 01730 825415

Info Line: 01730 825857

Fax: 01730 825873

e-mail: supgen@
smtp.ntrust.org.uk

LOCATION

OS Ref. 197 SU781 181

5m SE of Petersfield
on B2146, 1¹/₂ m S of
South Harting.

Bus: Stagecoach Sussex
Bus 54 (not Sun).

Rail: Petersfield 5¹/₂ m.

UPPARK
South Harting

A fine late 17th century house set high on the South Downs with magnificent sweeping views to the sea. An extensive, award-winning exhibition tells the dramatic story of the 1989 fire and restoration of the house and its collections.

The elegant Georgian interior houses a famous Grand Tour collection that includes paintings by Pompeo Batoni, Luca Giordano, and Joseph Vernet, with furniture and ceramics of superb quality. The famous 18th century dolls' house with original contents is one of the star items in the collection, and provides a rare insight into life in a great house 300 years ago.

The restaurant in the Georgian kitchen in the East Pavilion serves a Georgian themed menu using local produce. The West Pavilion houses the beautiful stables and the atmospheric and romantic Dairy. The complete servants' quarters in the basement are shown as they were in Victorian days when H G Wells' mother was housekeeper. From the basement visitors leave the house via the atmospheric subterranean passages.

The fine, peaceful, historic garden is now fully restored in the early 19th century 'Picturesque' style, with flowering shrubs and under-plantings of bulbs, perennials and herbaceous plants in a magical woodland and downland setting.

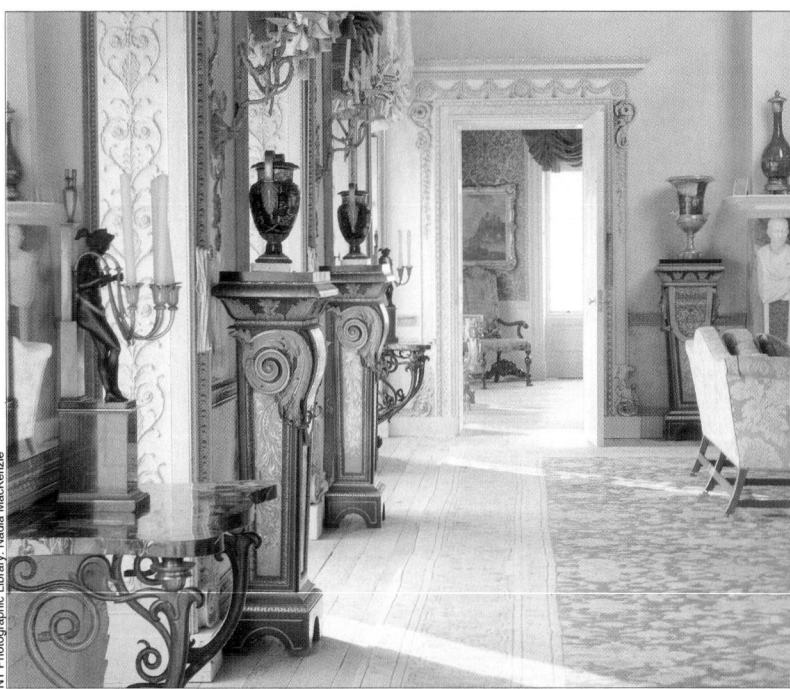

NT Photographic Library: Nadia MacKenzie

OPENING TIMES

1 April - 1 November:
Daily except Fris & Sats.

House: 1 - 5pm
(opens 12 noon on Suns
in Jul & Aug).

Last admission 4.15pm.

Print room open on 1st
Mon of each month.

Grounds, exhibition,
garden, shop & restaurant:
11.30am - 5pm.

ADMISSION

**House, Garden &
Exhibition**
Adult £5.50
Child......................£2.75
Family £13.75

Groups (min 15, week-
days only, must book)
Apr, May & Oct.......£4.50

Booked group guided
tours: mornings by
arrangement.

Special group catering
arrangements: please
telephone for details.

NT members Free.

ℹ️ Pushchairs on weekdays only. No photography, large bags or sharp heeled shoes in the house.

☕ Tel. for Xmas opening.

♿ Partially suitable. WC. Wheelchairs available.

☕ Licensed.

🅿️ Coaches must pre-book.

🐕 On leads, in Car Park (no shade) & woodland only.

🛡️ Please telephone for details.

CONFERENCE/FUNCTION		
ROOM	SIZE	MAX CAPACITY
Restaurant		50
Lower Servants Hall		50

ALFRISTON CLERGY HOUSE

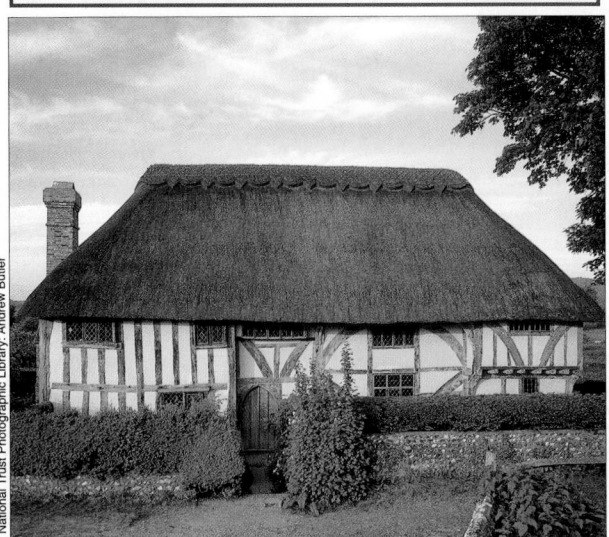

THE TYE, ALFRISTON, POLEGATE, EAST SUSSEX BN26 5TL

Owner: The National Trust   *Contact: The Property Manager*

Tel: 01323 870001   **Fax:** 01323 871318   **e-mail:** ksdxxx@smtp.ntrust.org.uk

Step back into the Middle Ages with a visit to this 14th century thatched Wealden 'Hall House'. Trace the history of this magnificent building - the first to be acquired by the National Trust in 1896. Discover why the chalk floor is soaked in sour milk, and visit the excellent shop with its local crafts. Explore the delightful cottage garden, filled with traditional cottage favourites and savour the idyllic setting beside Alfriston's famous parish church, with stunning views across the meandering River Cuckmere. An intriguing variety of shops, pubs and restaurants in Alfriston village make this a wonderful day out.

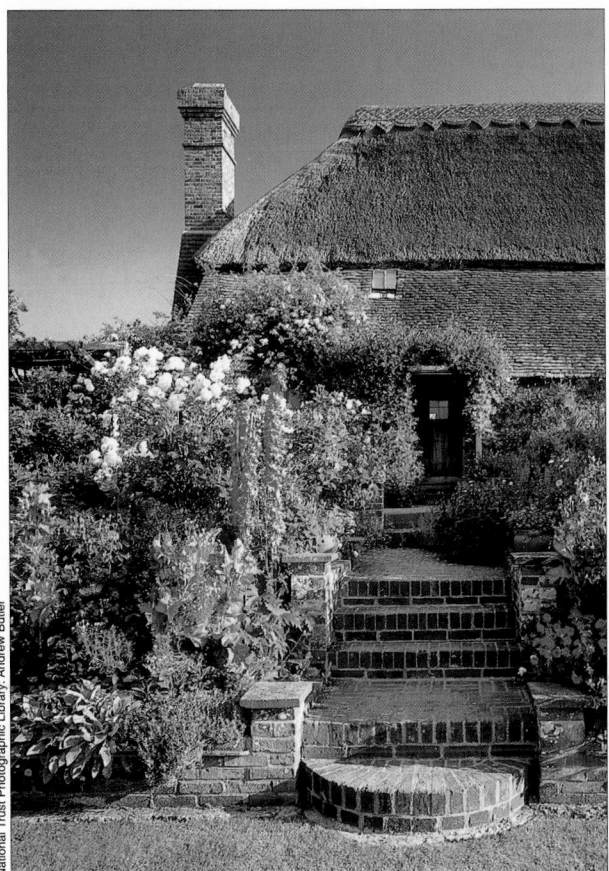

Location: OS Ref. TQ521 029. 4m NE of Seaford, just E of B2108.
Opening times: 3 - 25 Mar: Sats & Suns. 11am - 4pm. Last admission 3.30pm. 31 Mar - 4 Nov: daily except Tues & Fris, 10am - 5pm, last entry 4.30pm.
Admission: Adult £2.60, Child £1.30, Family (2+3) £6.50. Pre-booked groups £2.20 or £3.20 with guided tour.

⬛   ♿Not suitable.   🅿Parking in village car parks.

ANNE OF CLEVES HOUSE

Tel: 01273 474610   **Fax:** 01273 486990

52 Southover High Street, Lewes, Sussex BN7 1JA

Owner: Sussex Archaeological Society   **Contact:** Mr Stephen Watts

Anne of Cleves' house formed part of her divorce settlement from Henry VIII in 1541, although she never actually lived here. The 16th century timber-framed Wealden hall-house contains wide-ranging collections of Sussex interest. Furnished rooms give an impression of life in the 17th and 18th centuries. Artefacts from Lewes Priory, Sussex pottery and Wealden ironwork.

Location: OS198 Ref. TQ410 096. S of Lewes town centre, off A27/A275/A26.
Opening Times: 2 Jan - 17 Feb: Tues, Thurs & Sats, 10am - 5pm. 19 Feb - 4 Nov: Mon - Sat, 10am - 5pm; Sun, 12 noon - 5pm. 6 Nov - 23 Dec: Tue - Sat, 10am - 5pm; Sun, 12 noon - 5pm.
Admission: Adult £2.60, Child £1.30, Conc. £2.40, Family (2+2) £6.80 or (1+4) £5.20. Combined ticket with Lewes Castle is also available. Groups (15+): Adult £2.40, Child £1.10, Conc. £2.20.

⬛   ♿ Not suitable.   ⬛   🐕 Guide dogs only.   🔔   ❄   ⓘ

ARUNDEL CASTLE

See page 159 for full page entry.

ARUNDEL CATHEDRAL

Tel: 01903 882297   **Fax:** 01903 885335

Parsons Hill, Arundel, Sussex BN18 9AY   **e-mail:** aruncath1@aol.com

Contact: Rev A Whale

French Gothic Cathedral, church of the RC Diocese of Arundel and Brighton built by Henry, 15th Duke of Norfolk and opened 1873. Carpet of Flowers and Floral Festival held annually on the Feast of Corpus Christi (60 days after Easter) and day preceding.

Location: OS Ref. TQ015 072. Above junction of A27 and A284.
Opening Times: Summer: 9am - 6pm. Winter: 9am - dusk. Mass at 10am each day. Sun Masses: 8am, 9.30am & 11am, Vigil Sat evening: 6.30pm. Shop opened after services and on special occasions and otherwise at request.
Admission: Free.

1066 BATTLE OF HASTINGS BATTLEFIELD & ABBEY

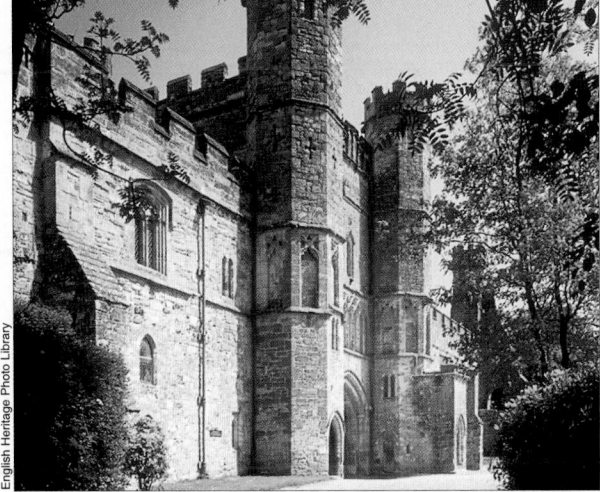

BATTLE, SUSSEX TN33 0AD

Owner: English Heritage   *Contact: The Custodian*

Tel: 01424 773792   **Fax:** 01424 775059

Visit the site of the 1066 Battle of Hastings. A free interactive audio tour will lead you around the battlefield and to the exact spot where Harold fell. Explore the magnificent Abbey ruins and see the fascinating exhibition in the gate house and '1066 Prelude to Battle' exhibition. Children's themed play area.

Location: OS Ref. TQ749 157. Top of Battle High Street. Turn off A2100 to Battle.
Opening Times: 1 Apr - 30 Sept: daily, 10am - 6pm. 1 - 31 Oct: 10am - 5pm. 1 Nov - 31 Mar: daily 10am - 4pm. Closed 24 - 26 Dec & 1 Jan.
Admission: Adult £4.30, Child £2.20, Conc. £3.20, Family £10.80. 15% discount for groups (11+). EH members Free.

⬛   ♿Ground floor & grounds.   🅿Free.   🐕In grounds, on leads.   ❄
🛡Tel. for details.

BATEMAN'S 🌿 See page 160 for full page entry.

BAYHAM OLD ABBEY ⎏ Tel/Fax: 01892 890381

Lamberhurst, Sussex

Owner: English Heritage **Contact:** The Custodian

These riverside ruins are of a house of 'White' Canons, founded c1208 and preserved in the 18th century, when its surroundings were landscaped to create its delightful setting.

Location: OS Ref. TQ651 366. 1³/₄ m W of Lamberhurst off B2169.

Opening Times: 1 Apr - 30 Sept: daily, 10am - 6pm. 1 - 31 Oct: 10am - 5pm. 1 Nov - 31 Mar: w/ends only 10am - 4pm. Closed 24 - 26 Dec & 1 Jan.

Admission: Adult £2.20, Child £1.10, Conc. £1.60.

📷 ♿ Grounds suitable. WC. 🐕 In grounds, on leads. ❄

BENTLEY HOUSE & MOTOR MUSEUM Tel: 01825 840573 Fax: 01825 841322

Halland, Lewes, East Sussex BN8 5AF **e-mail:** barrysutherland@pavilion.co.uk

Owner: East Sussex County Council **Contact:** Mr Barry Sutherland - Manager

Early 18th century farmhouse with a large reception room of Palladian proportions added on either end in the 1960s by the architect Raymond Erith, each lit by large Venetian windows. Furnished to form a grand 20th century evocation of a mid-Georgian house.

Location: OS Ref. TQ485 160. 7m NE from Lewes, signposted off A22, A26 & B2192.

Opening Times: Estate: 19 Mar - 31 Oct: daily, 10.30am - 4.30pm (last adm.). Nov, Feb - Mar: weekends only, 10.30am - 4pm (last adm.). House: 1 Apr - 31 Oct: daily 12 noon - 5pm. Estate closed Dec & Jan.

Admission: Adult £4.80 (£3.80 in winter), Child (4-15) £3, Conc. £3.80, Family (2+4) £13.50. Coach drivers free admission & refreshment ticket. 10% discount for groups of 11+. Special rates for the disabled. Call to verify prices (2000 rates).

📷 🍷 Wedding receptions. ♿ 📺 Licensed. 🎥 By arrangement. P 🐴 🐕 Guide dogs only. 🔔

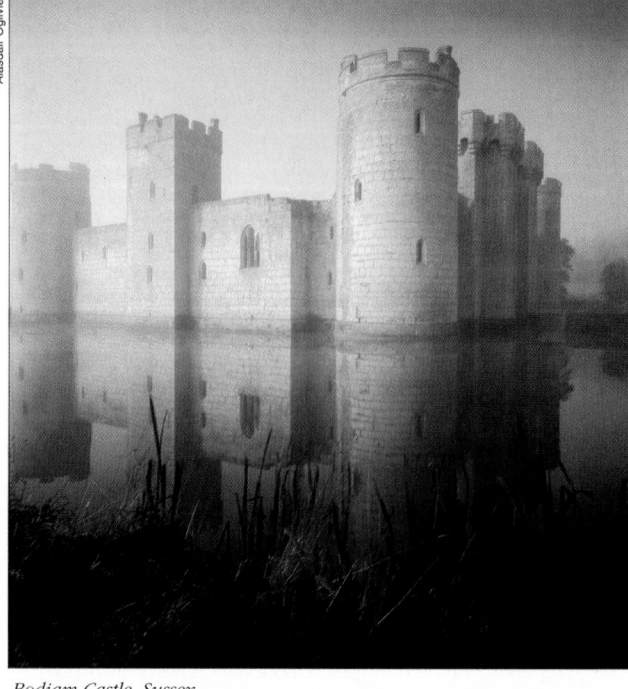

Bodiam Castle, Sussex.

BODIAM CASTLE 🌿

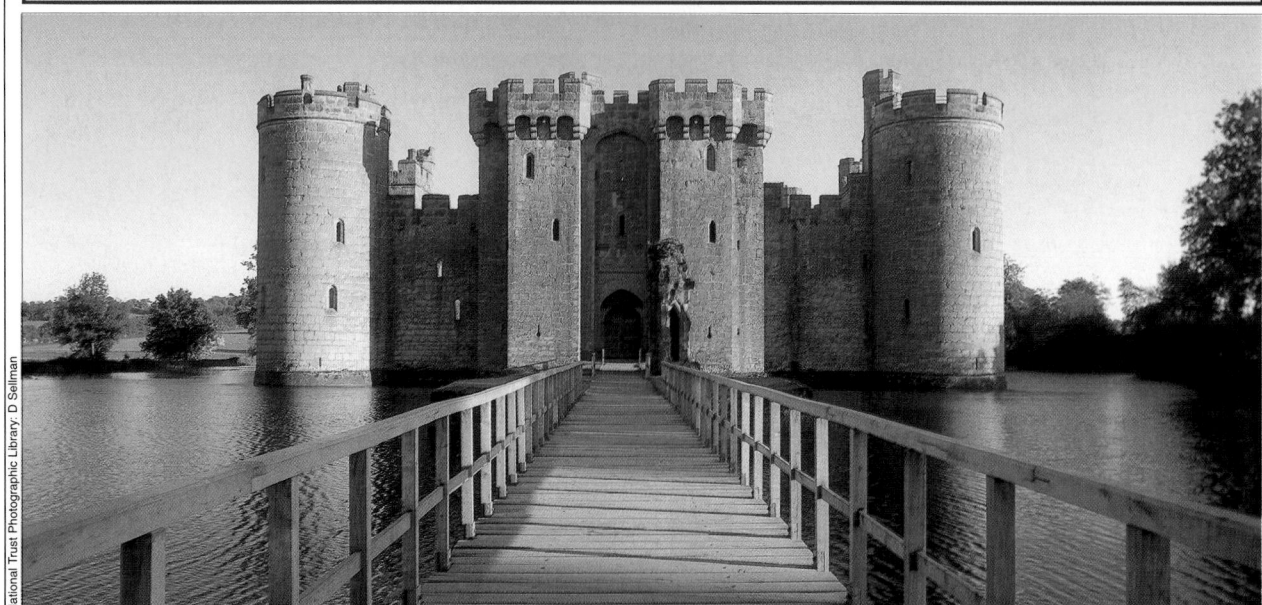

BODIAM, Nr ROBERTSBRIDGE, EAST SUSSEX TN32 5UA

Owner: The National Trust *Contact:* The Administrator

Tel: 01580 830436 **Fax:** 01580 830398 **e-mail:** kboxxx@smtp.ntrust.org.uk

Built in 1385 against a French invasion that never came and as a comfortable dwelling for a rich nobleman, Bodiam Castle is one of the finest examples of medieval architecture. The virtual completeness of its exterior makes it popular with adults, children and film crews alike. Inside, although a ruin, floors have been replaced in some of the towers and visitors can climb the spiral staircase to enjoy superb views from the battlements. Discover more of its intriguing past in the museum and video room, and wander in the romantic Castle grounds peacefully set on the banks of the River Rother.

Location: OS Ref. TQ782 256. 3m S of Hawkhurst, 2m E of A21 Hurst Green.

Opening Times: 6 Jan - 16 Feb: Sats & Suns, 11am - 4pm. 17 Feb - 31 Oct: daily, 10am - 6pm. 3 Nov - mid Feb 2002: Sats & Suns, 10am - 4pm. Last admission 1 hour before closing. Ring for information on Christmas Day and New Year holiday opening arrangements.

Admission: Adult £3.70, Child £1.85, Family ticket (2+3) £9.25. Groups £3.15. Car parking £1.50 per car.

ℹ Small museum. 📷 ♿ Ground floor & grounds suitable. 🍴 P 🐕 Teacher and student packs and education base. ❄

BORDE HILL GARDEN

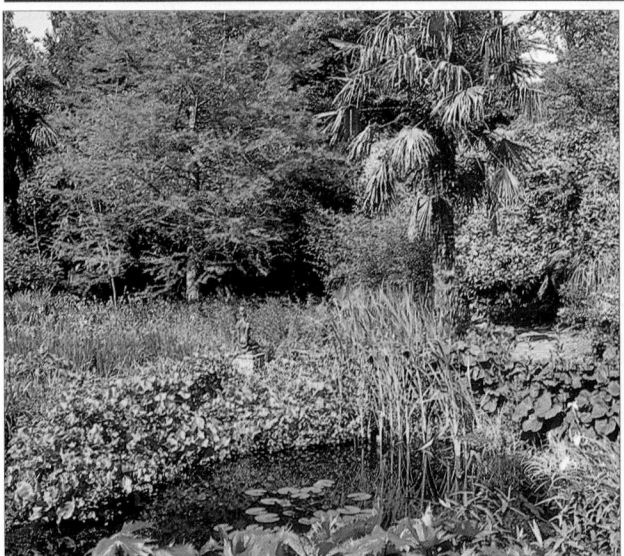
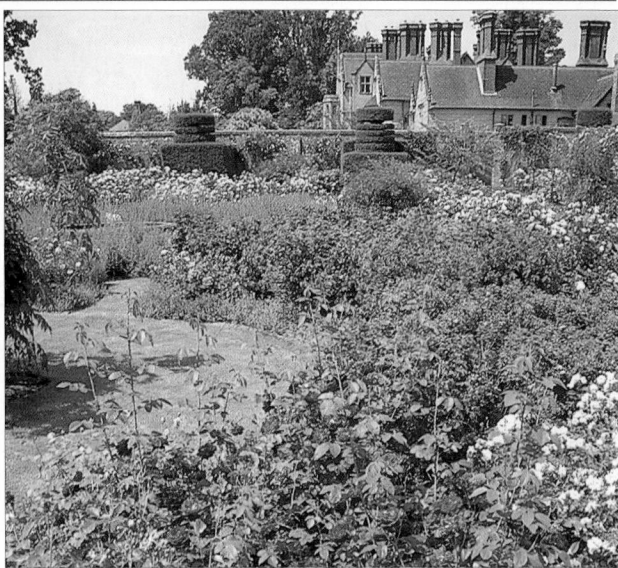

HAYWARDS HEATH, WEST SUSSEX RH16 1XP

Owner: *Mr & Mrs A P Stephenson Clarke*   **Contact:** *Sarah Brook*

Visitor Attraction of the Year 1999 SEETB

Tel: 01444 450326   **Fax:** 01444 440427   **e-mail:** info@bordehill.co.uk

Winner of two prestigious awards. A haven of peace and tranquillity can be found at Borde Hill Garden, created in the 1890s, where botanical interest as well as garden design and renaissance play equally important roles. 'Linked' gardens, each with their own unique style, offer a rich variety of seasonal colours. Marvel at the splendour of flowering bulbs in early spring and award-winning collections of camellias, rhododendrons and azaleas in May and June. In summer, the exuberant herbaceous borders and fragrant English roses give way to a vivid blaze of autumnal colour. Borde Hill House, dating from 1593, is open to groups by appointment.

Location: OS Ref. TQ324 265. 1^1/$_2$ m N of Haywards Heath on Balcombe Road, 3m from A23. 45mins from Victoria Station.

Opening Times: All year: daily (including Christmas Day), 10am - 6pm (dusk if earlier).

Admission: Adult £5, Child £2.50, OAP £4.50, Family (2+3) £13. Pre-booked groups (20+): £4.25.

Licensed. Licensed. By arrangement. P
In grounds, on leads. Tel. for details.

BOXGROVE PRIORY

Tel: 01424 775705

Boxgrove, Chichester, Sussex

Owner: English Heritage   **Contact:** Area Manager

Remains of the Guest House, Chapter House and Church of this 12th century priory, which was the cell of a French abbey until Richard II confirmed its independence in 1383.

Location: OS Ref. SU909 076. N of Boxgrove, 4m E of Chichester on minor road N of A27.

Opening Times: Any reasonable time.

Admission: Free.

BRAMBER CASTLE

Tel: 01424 775705

Bramber, Sussex

Owner: English Heritage   **Contact:** Area Manager

The remains of a Norman castle gatehouse, walls and earthworks in a splendid setting overlooking the Adur valley.

Location: OS Ref. TQ187 107. On W side of Bramber village NE of A283.

Opening Times: Any reasonable time.

Admission: Free.

BRICKWALL HOUSE & GARDENS

Tel: 01797 253388 **Fax:** 01797 252567

Northiam, Rye, Sussex TN31 6NL

Owner: Frewen Educational Trust   **Contact:** The Curator

Impressive timber-framed house. 17th century drawing room with magnificent plaster ceilings and good portraits including by Lely, Kneller and Vereist. Topiary, chess garden.

Location: OS Ref. TQ831 241. S side of Northiam village at junction of A28 and B2088.

Opening Times: By appointment only.

Admission: £3.

CAMBER CASTLE

Tel: 01797 223862

Camber, Nr Rye, East Sussex

Owner: English Heritage   **Contact:** Rye Harbour Nature Reserve

A fine example of one of many coastal fortresses built by Henry VIII to counter the threat of invasion during the 16th century. Monthly guided walks of Rye Nature Reserve including Camber Castle, telephone for details.

Location: OS189, Ref. TQ922 185. Across fields off A259, 1m S of Rye off harbour road.

Opening Times: 1 Jul - 30 Sept: Sat & Sun, 2 - 5pm.

Admission: Adult £2, Child £1, Conc. £1.50.

Not suitable. By arrangement. No parking. Guide dogs only.

CHARLESTON

See page 161 for full page entry.

CHICHESTER CATHEDRAL

Tel: 01243 782595 **Fax:** 01243 536190

Chichester, Sussex PO19 1PX   **Contact:** Mrs J Thom

In the heart of the city, this fine Cathedral has been a centre of Christian worship and community life for 900 years.

Location: OS Ref. SU860 047. West Street, Chichester.

Opening Times: Summer: 7.30am - 7pm, Winter: 7.30am - 5pm. Choral Evensong daily (except Weds) during term time.

Admission: Donation.

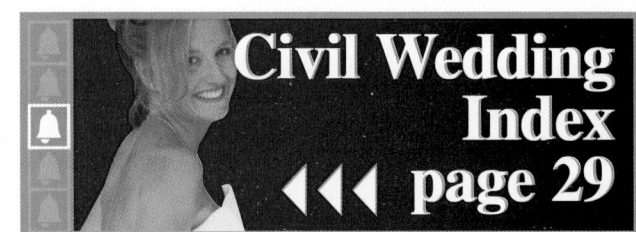

FIRLE PLACE

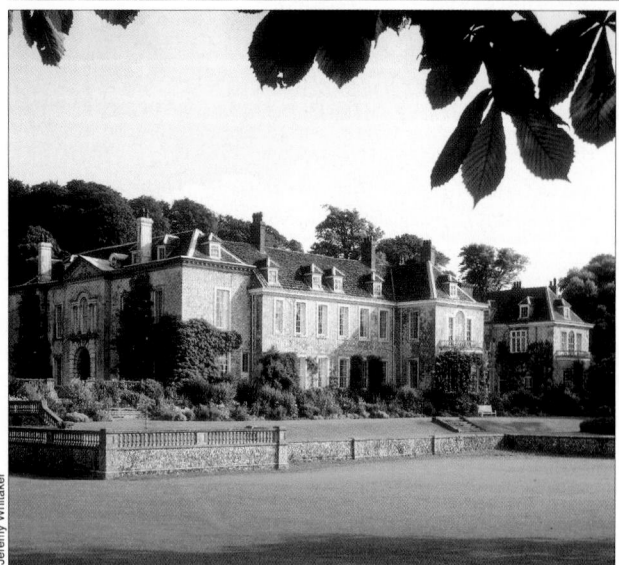

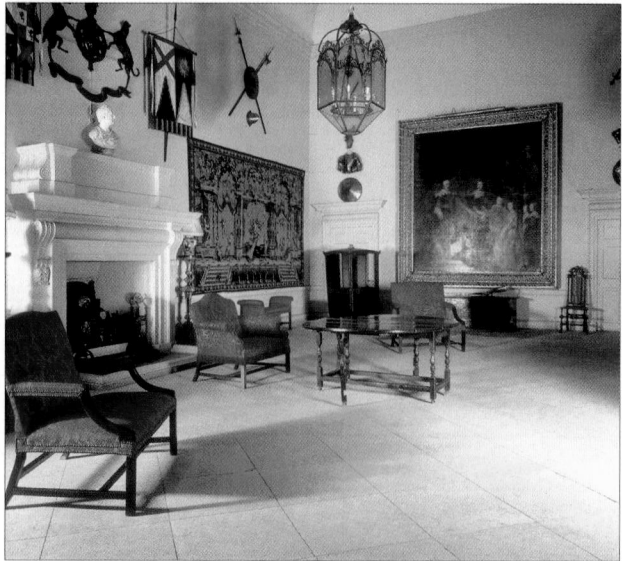

FIRLE, Nr LEWES, EAST SUSSEX BN8 6LP

Owner: The Rt Hon Viscount Gage

Tel: 01273 858307 (enquiries) **Info:** 01273 858335 **Events:** 01273 858567
Fax: 01273 858188 **Restaurant:** 01273 858307 **e-mail:** gage@firleplace.co.uk

Firle Place is the home of the Gage family, and has been for over 500 years. Set at the foot of the Sussex Downs within its own parkland, this unique house originally Tudor, was built of Caen stone, possibly from a monastery dissolved by Sir John Gage, friend of Henry VIII. Remodelled in the 18th century it is similar in appearance to that of a French chateau. The house contains a magnificent collection of Old Master paintings, fine English and European furniture and an impressive collection of Sèvres porcelain collected mainly by the 3rd Earl Cowper from Panshanger House, Hertfordshire.

Events: The Great Tudor Hall can, on occasion, be used for private dinners, with drinks on the Terrace or in the Billiard Room. A private tour of the house can be arranged. The paddock area is an ideal site for a marquee. The park can be used for larger events, using the house as a backdrop.

Location: OS Ref. TQ473 071. 4m S of Lewes on A27 Brighton/Eastbourne Road.

Opening Times: 15/16 Apr & 6/7 May. 23 May - 27 Sept: Wed - Thur, Suns & BHs, 2 - 4.30pm. Guided tours.

Admission: Adult £4.50, Child £2, Conc. £4 Connoisseurs' Day (last Thurs each month, Jun - Sept) £5.

i No photography in house. | | | Ground floor & restaurant suitable. Licensed. Tea Terrace. P | In grounds on leads.

FISHBOURNE ROMAN PALACE

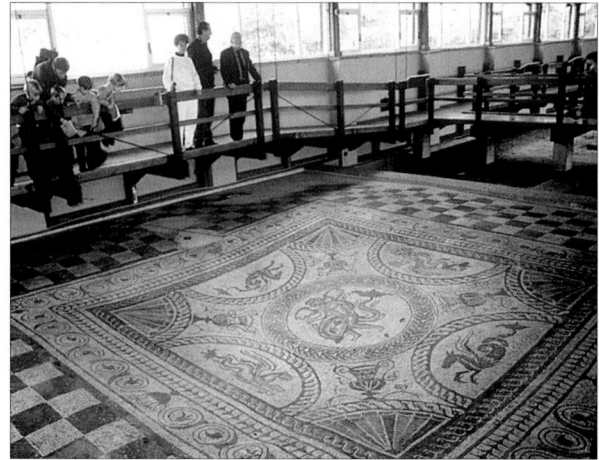

SALTHILL ROAD, FISHBOURNE, CHICHESTER, SUSSEX PO19 3QR

Owner: Sussex Archaeological Society   *Contact: David Rudkin*

Tel: 01243 785859   **Fax:** 01243 539266   **e-mail:** adminfish@sussexpast.co.uk

A Roman site built around AD75. A modern building houses part of the extensive remains including a large number of Britain's finest in-situ mosaics. The museum displays many objects discovered during excavations and an audio-visual programme tells Fishbourne's remarkable story. Roman gardens have been reconstructed and include a museum of Roman gardening.

Location: OS Ref. SU837 057. 1½ m W of Chichester in Fishbourne village off A27/A259.

Opening Times: 5 Feb - 14 Dec: daily. Feb, Nov - Dec: 10am - 4pm. Mar - Jul & Sept - Oct: 10am - 5pm. Aug: 10am - 6pm. 15 Dec - 4 Feb (excluding Christmas): Sats & Suns, 10am - 4pm.

Admission: Adult £4.50, Child £2.40, Conc. £3.90, Family (2+2): £11.70, Registered disabled £3.70. Groups (20+): Adult £3.90, Child £2.25, Conc. £3.70.

| | | | By arrangement. Guide dogs only.
Tel. for details.

GLYNDE PLACE

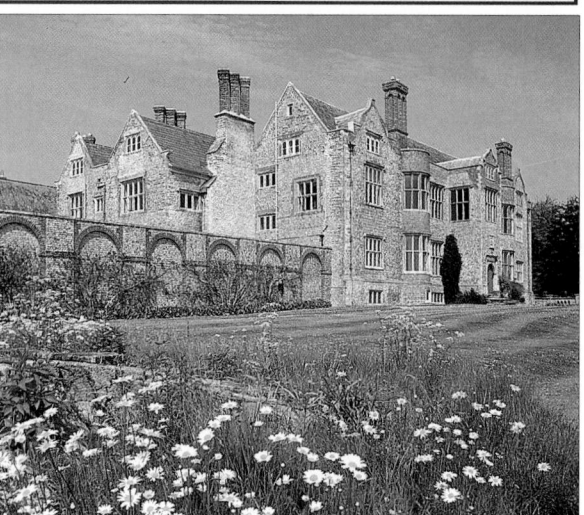

GLYNDE, LEWES, SUSSEX BN8 6SX

Owners: Viscount & Viscountess Hampden   *Contact: Viscount Hampden*

Tel: 01273 858224   **Fax:** 01273 858224

Glynde Place is a magnificent example of Elizabethan architecture commanding exceptionally fine views of the South Downs. Amongst the collections of 400 years of family living can be seen a fine collection of 17th and 18th century portraits of the Trevors and a room dedicated to Sir Henry Brand, Speaker of the House of Commons 1872 - 1884 and an exhibition of 'Harbert Morley and the Great Rebellion 1638 - 1660' the story of the part played by the owner of Glynde Place in the Civil War. Plus a collection of 18th century Italian masterpieces.

Location: OS Ref. TQ457 093. In Glynde village 4m SE of Lewes on A27.

Opening Times: House & Garden: Jun & Sept: Weds & Suns. Jul & Aug: Weds, Thus & Suns, 2 - 5pm. Last adm. 4.45pm.

Admission: Adult £5, Child £2.50.

| P Free.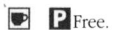

GOODWOOD HOUSE

See page 162 for full page entry.

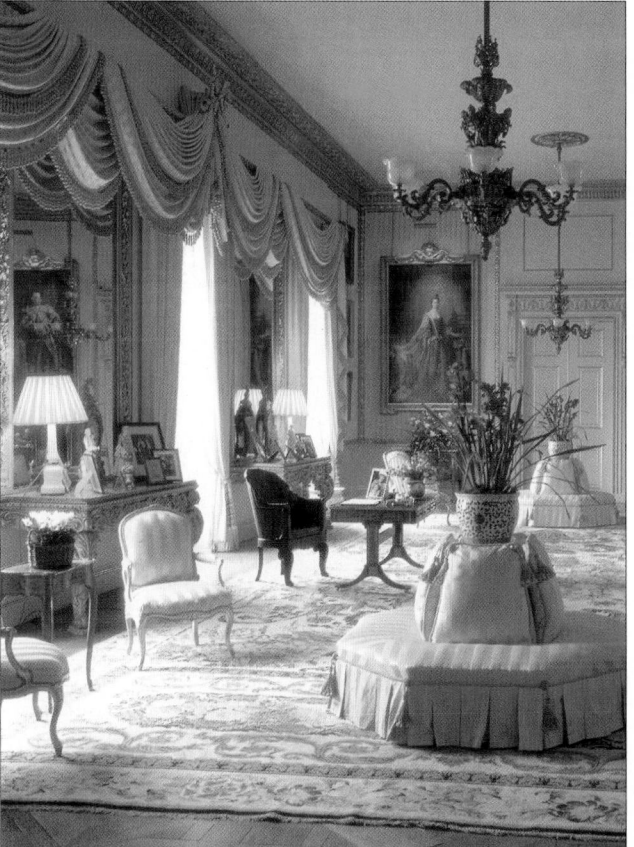

Goodwood House, Sussex.

GREAT DIXTER HOUSE & GARDENS

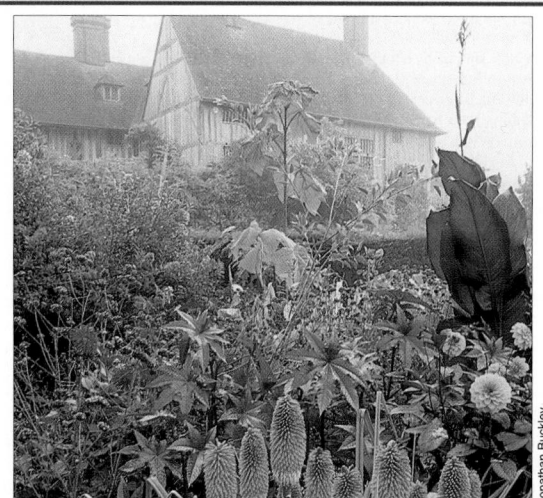

Jonathan Buckley

NORTHIAM, RYE, EAST SUSSEX TN31 6PH

Owner: Christopher Lloyd *Contact:* Elaine Francis, Business Manager

Tel: 01797 252878 **Fax:** 01797 252879 **e-mail:** greatdixter@compuserve.com

Great Dixter, birthplace and home of gardening writer Christopher Lloyd, was built c1450 and boasts one of the largest surviving timber-framed halls in the country. Lutyens was employed to restore both the house and gardens in 1910. The gardens are now the hallmark of Christopher Lloyd with an exciting combination of meadows, ponds, topiary and the famous Long Border and Exotic Garden.

Location: OS Ref. TQ817 251. Signposted off the A28 in Northiam.

Opening Times: 1 Apr - 28 Oct: Tue - Sun & BH Mons, 2 - 5.30pm (last admission 5pm). Gardens only open BH Suns & Mons, 11am - 5.30pm.

Admission: House & Garden: Adult £6, Child £1.50. Garden only: Adult £4.50, Child £1. Groups (25+) by appointment. House & garden: Adult £5, Child £1.50.

ⓘ No photography in House. 📷 🚻 🍴 Obligatory.
🅿 Limited for coaches. 🦮 Guide dogs only.

HAMMERWOOD PARK

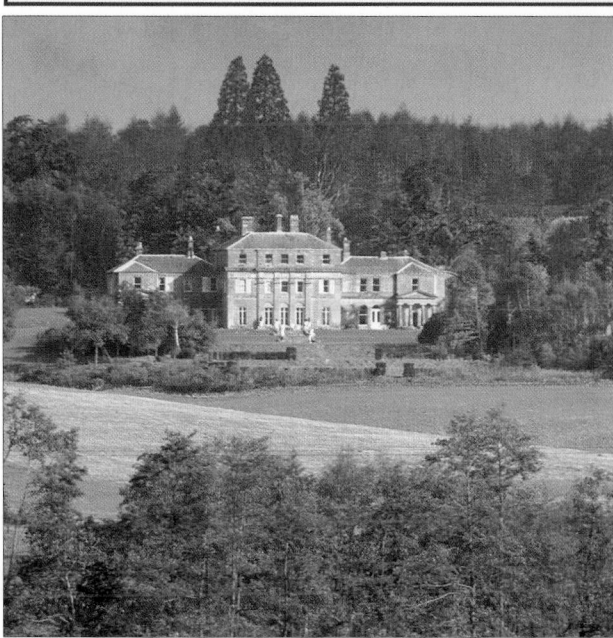 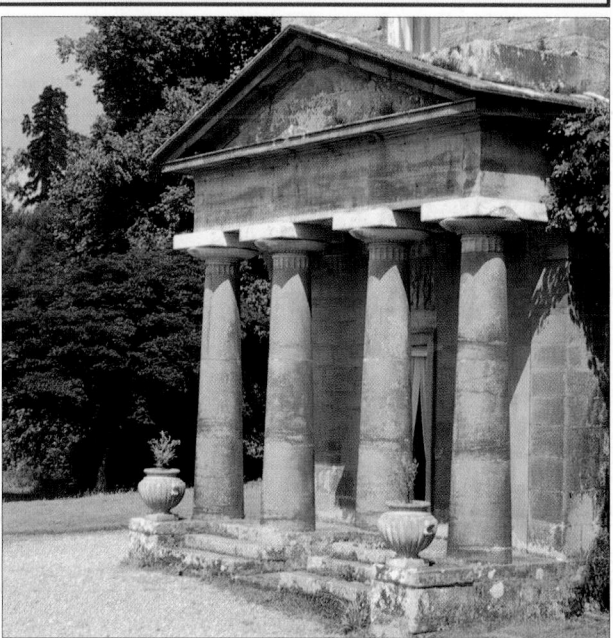

EAST GRINSTEAD, SUSSEX RH19 3QE

Owner/Contact: David Pinnegar

Tel: 01342 850594 **Fax:** 01342 850864 **e-mail:** latrobe@mistral.co.uk

Built in 1792 as an Apollo's hunting lodge by Benjamin Latrobe, architect of the Capitol and the White House, Washington DC. Owned by Led Zepplin in the 1970s, rescued from dereliction in 1982. Teas in the Organ Room; mural by French artists in the hall; and a derelict dining room still shocks the unwary. Guided tours (said by many to be the most interesting in Sussex) by the family.

Location: OS Ref. TQ442 390. 3¹/₂ m E of East Grinstead on A264 to Tunbridge Wells, 1m W of Holtye.

Opening Times: Easter Mon - end Sept: Wed, Sat & BH Mon, 2 - 5pm. Guided tour starts 2.05pm. Coaches strictly by appointment. Small groups any time throughout the year by appointment.

Admission: House & Park: Adult £5, Child £2. Private viewing by arrangement.

ⓘ Conferences. 🍴 🍽 🗝 Obligatory. 🔔
🐕 In grounds. 🛏 B&B. ✳ 🛡 Please tel for details. ⒸⓌ

South East England

HERSTMONCEUX CASTLE GARDENS   Tel: 01323 833816 Fax: 01323 834499

Hailsham, Sussex BN27 1RN   **e-mail:** c_cullip@isc.queensu.ac.uk

Owner: Queen's University, Canada   **Contact:** C Cullip

This breathtaking 15th century moated Castle is within 500 acres of parkland and gardens (including Elizabethan Garden) and is ideal for picnics and woodland walks. At Herstmonceux there is something for all the family. For information on our attractions or forthcoming events tel: 01323 834457.

Location: OS Ref. TQ646 104. 2m S of Herstmonceux village (A271) by minor road. 10m WNW of Bexhill.

Opening Times: 13 Apr - 28 Oct: daily, 10am - 6pm (last adm. 5pm) Closes 5pm from Oct.

Admission: Grounds and Gardens: Adults £4, Child under 5 Free, Conc. £3.
Castle Tour: Adult £2.50, Child £1 (under 5 Free). Group rates/bookings available.

ℹ️ Visitor Centre.   ♿ Suitable, limited for Castle Tour. 🍴 🎭 🅿️
🐕 On leads.   🔔 🛡️ Tel. for details. ♿

HIGH BEECHES GARDENS 🏛️

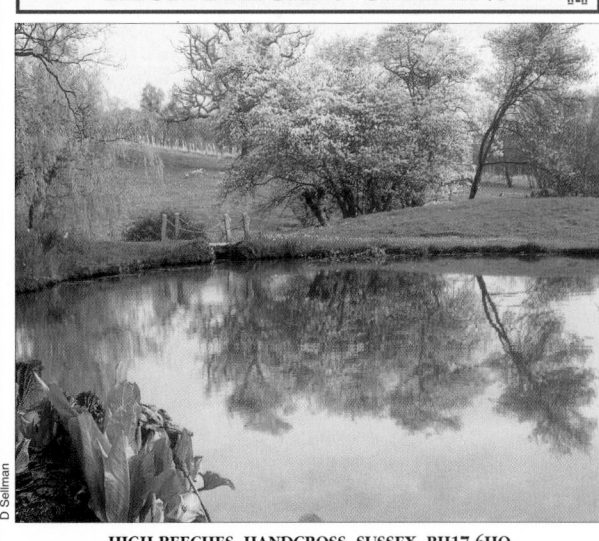

D Sellman

HIGH BEECHES, HANDCROSS, SUSSEX RH17 6HQ

Owner: *High Beeches Gardens Conservation Trust (Reg. Charity)* **Contact:** *Sarah Bray*

Tel: 01444 400589 **Fax:** 01444 401543 **e-mail:** office@highbeeches.com

Help preserve these 20 acres of magically beautiful, peaceful woodland and water gardens. Daffodils, bluebells, azaleas, naturalised gentians, autumn colours. Rippling streams, enchanting vistas. Four acres of natural wildflower meadows. Rare plants. Tree trail. Recommended by Christopher Lloyd. Picnic area. Gardens may be booked for photographic sessions.

Location: OS Ref. TQ275 308. S side of B2110. 1m NE of Handcross.

Opening Times: 17 Mar - 30 Jun & 1 Sept - 31 Oct: Thur - Tue, 1 - 5pm (last admission). Jul & Aug: Sun - Tue, 1 - 5pm. Coaches and guided tours by appointment only.

Admission: Adult £4, Child (under 14) Free. Season ticket (admits 2): £20. Groups (30+) anytime by appointment: £3.50pp. Guided tours for groups £5pp.

🎪 On Event Days. ♿ Not suitable. 🍴 🎭 By appointment. 🅿️ 🐕
🛡️ Tel. for details. ♿

HIGHDOWN GARDENS   Tel: 01903 501054

Littlehampton Road, Goring-by-Sea, Worthing, Sussex BN12 6PE

Owner: Worthing Borough Council   **Contact:** C Beardsley Esq

Unique gardens in disused chalk pit, begun in 1909.

Location: OS Ref. TQ098 040. 3m WNW of Worthing on N side of A259, just W of the Goring roundabout.

Opening Times: 1 Apr - 30 Sept: Mon - Fri, 10am - 6pm. W/ends & BHs, 10am - 6pm. 1 Oct - 30 Nov: Mon - Fri, 10am - 4.30pm. 1 Dec - 31 Jan: 10am - 4pm. 1 Feb - 31 Mar: Mon - Fri, 10am - 4.30pm.

Admission: Free.

LAMB HOUSE 🍂   Tel: 01892 890651 Fax: 01892 890110

West Street, Rye, Sussex TN31 7ES

Owner: The National Trust   **Contact:** Regional Office

The home of the writer Henry James from 1898 to 1916 where he wrote the best novels of his later period.

Location: OS Ref. TQ920 202. In West Street, facing W end of church.

Opening Times: 4 Apr - 31 Oct: Weds & Sats only, 2 - 6pm. Last admission 5.30pm.

Admission: Adult £2.60, Child £1.30, Family (2+3) £6.50. Group: £2.20.

LEONARDSLEE GARDENS   See page 163 for full page entry.

LEWES CASTLE & BARBICAN HOUSE MUSEUM

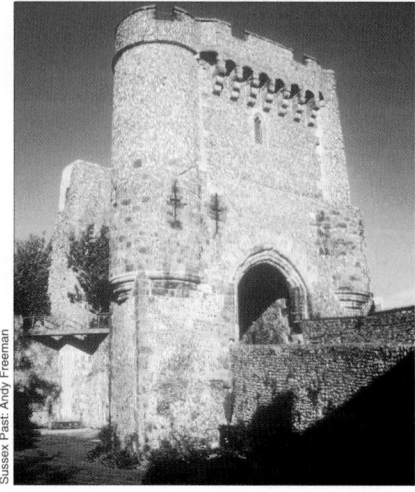

Sussex Past: Andy Freeman

169 HIGH STREET, LEWES, SUSSEX BN7 1YE

Owner: *Sussex Archaeological Society*   **Contact:** *Mrs Jill Allen*

Tel: 01273 486290 **Fax:** 01273 486990 **e-mail:** castle@sussexpast.co.uk

Lewes's imposing Norman castle offers magnificent views across the town and surrounding downland. Barbican House towered over by the Barbican Gate is home to the Museum of Sussex Archaeology; a superb scale model of Victorian Lewes provides the centrepiece of a 25 minute audio-visual presentation telling the story of the county town of Sussex.

Location: OS198 Ref. TQ412 101. Lewes town centre off A27/A26/A275.

Opening Times: Daily (except 8 Jan & 24 - 26 Dec). Mon - Sat: 10am - 5.30pm; Suns & BHs, 11am - 5.30pm. Castle closes at dusk in winter.

Admission: Adult £4, Child £2, Conc. £3.50 Family (2+2) £10.90 or (1+4) £8.00. Groups (15+): Adult £3.50, Child £1.60, Conc. £3. Combined ticket with Anne of Cleves House available.

📷 ♿ Not suitable. 🎭 By arrangement. 🔔 ❄️ 🛡️ Tel. for details. ♿

MARLIPINS MUSEUM   Tel: 01273 462994

High Street, Shoreham-by-Sea, Sussex BN43 5DA

Owner: Sussex Archaeological Society   **Contact:** Helen Poole

Shoreham's local and especially maritime history is explored at Marlipins, an important historic building of Norman origin.

Location: OS198 Ref. TQ214 051. Shoreham town centre on A259, W of Brighton.

Opening Times: Due to major rebuilding work Marlipins Museum's opening times during 2001 are uncertain. Please telephone 01273 487188 for details.

Admission: Adult £1.50, Child 75p (accompanied children, free), Conc. £1.

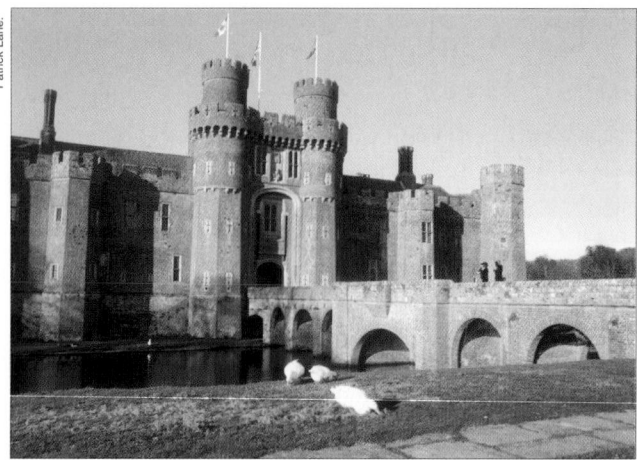

Patrick Lane.

Herstmonceux Castle Gardens, Sussex.

MERRIMENTS GARDENS

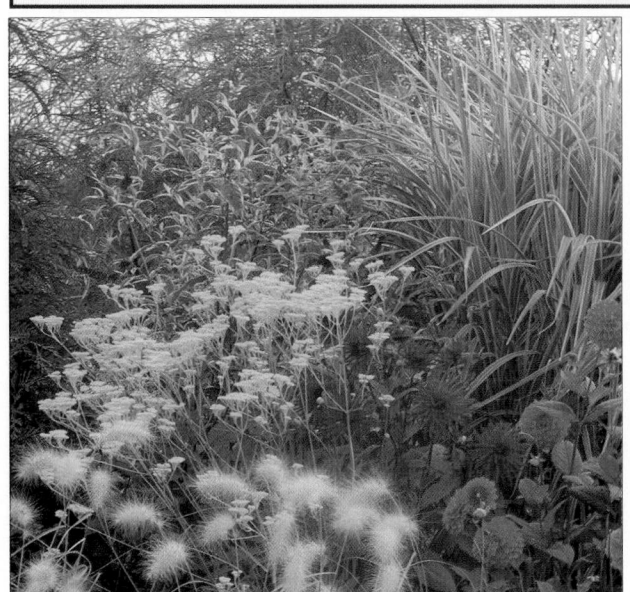
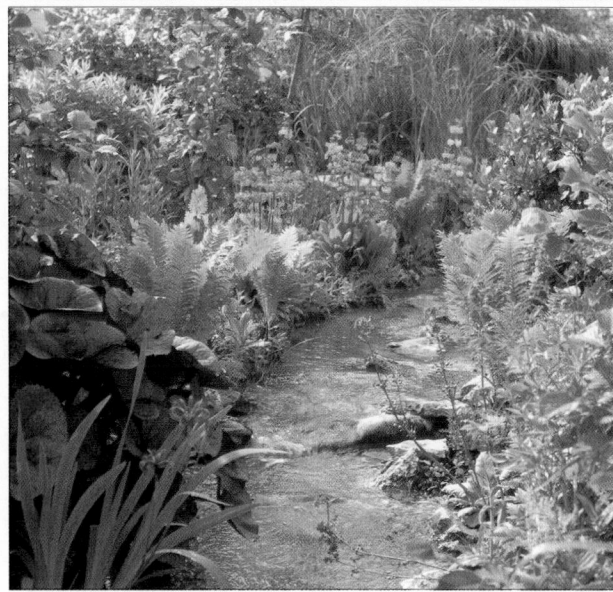

HAWKHURST ROAD, HURST GREEN, EAST SUSSEX TN19 7RA

Owner: *Family owned*　　　　**Contact:** *Mark Buchele*

Tel: 01580 860666　**Fax:** 01580 860324　**e-mail:** info@merriments.co.uk

'A unique experiment in colour composition'.

Set in 4 acres of gently sloping Weald farmland, a naturalistic garden which never fails to delight. Deep curved borders richly planted and colour themed. An abundance of rare plants will startle the visitor with sheer originality.

The garden is planted according to prevailing conditions and only using plants suited for naturalising and colonising their environment. This natural approach to gardening harks back to the days of William Robinson and is growing in popularity, especially in Northern Europe. Alternatively many borders are colour themed and planted in the great tradition of English gardening. These borders use a rich mix of trees, shrubs, perennials and grasses and give an arresting display from spring to autumn.

Location: OS198, Ref. TQ412 101. Signposted off A21 London - Hastings road, at Hurst Green.

Opening Times: Apr - Sept: Mon - Sat, 10am - 5pm, Suns, 10.30am - 5pm.

Admission: Adult £3.50, Child £2. Groups (5+) by arrangement.

🖼 🚻 ♿ Partially suitable. 🍴 Licensed. 🎨 By arrangement. 🅿
🐕 In grounds, on leads. 🆆

MICHELHAM PRIORY 🏛

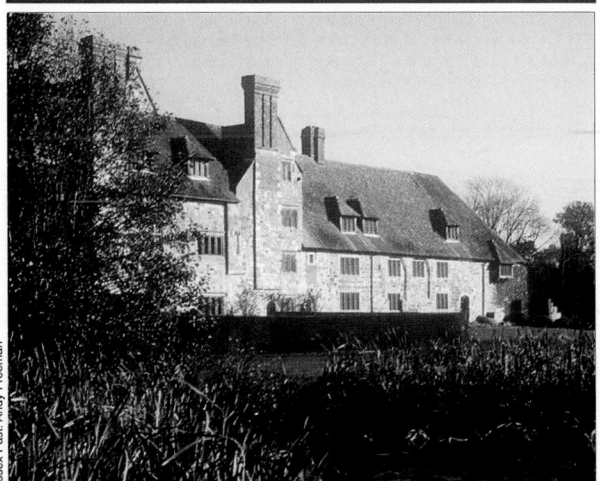

Sussex Past: Andy Freeman

UPPER DICKER, HAILSHAM, SUSSEX BN27 3QS

Owner: *Sussex Archaeological Society*　　**Contact:** *Mr Simon Turner*

Tel: 01323 844224　**Fax:** 01323 844030　**e-mail:** adminmich@sussexpast.co.uk

Set on a medieval moated island surrounded by superb gardens, the Priory was founded in 1229. The remains after the Dissolution were incorporated into a Tudor farm and country house that now contains a fascinating array of exhibits. Grounds include 14th century gatehouse, watermill, physic and cloister gardens and Elizabethan great barn.

Location: OS Ref. TQ557 093. 8m NW of Eastbourne off A22 / A27. 2m W of Hailsham.

Opening Times: 14 Mar - 28 Oct: Wed - Sun & BH Mons & daily in Aug. Mar & Oct: 10.30am - 4pm. Apr - Jul & Sept: 10.30am - 5pm. Aug: 10.30am - 5.30pm.

Admission: Adult £4.70, Child £2.30, Conc. £4, Family (2+2 or 1+4)) £11.50, Registered disabled & carer £2.35. Groups (15+): Adult/Conc. £3.80, Child £2.10.

🖼 🍴 ♿ 🍴 Licensed. 🎨 By arrangement. 🅿
🐕 Guide dogs only. 🔔 Tel. for details. 🆆

MONK'S HOUSE 🦋　　　**Tel:** 01892 890651　**Fax:** 01892 890110

Rodmell, Lewes　BN7 3HF

Owner: The National Trust　　　　**Contact:** Regional Office

A small weather-boarded house, the home of Leonard and Virgina Woolf until Leonard's death in 1969.

Location: OS Ref. TQ421 064. 4 m E of Lewes, off former A275 in Rodmell village, near church.

Opening Times: 4 Apr - 31 Oct: Weds & Sats, 2 - 5.30pm. Last admission 5pm.

Admission: Adult £2.60, Child £1.30, Family £6.50. Groups: Thurs only, 2 - 5.30pm, by arrangement with tenant.

MOORLANDS　　　　　　　　**Tel:** 01892 652474

Friar's Gate, Crowborough, East Sussex　TN6 1XF

Owner: Dr & Mrs Steven Smith　　　　**Contact:** Dr Steven Smith

Four acre garden set in a lush valley adjoining Ashdown Forest. Primulas, azaleas and rhododendrons flourish by streams and a small lake. New river walk with views over garden. Many unusual trees and shrubs. Good autumn colour. Featured in Meridien TV programme.

Location: OS Ref. TQ498 329. 2m NW of Crowborough. From B2188 at Friar's Gate, take left fork signposted 'Crowborough Narrow Road', entrance 100yds on left. From Crowborough crossroads take St John's Road to Friar's Gate.

Opening Times: 1 Apr - 1 Oct: Weds, 11am - 5pm. 20 May & 15 Jul: Suns, 2 - 6pm. Other times by appointment only.

Admission: Adult £2.50, Child Free.

🍴 ❄

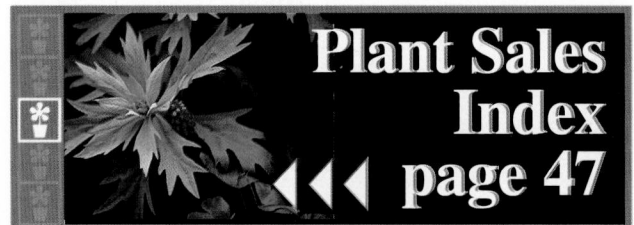

Plant Sales Index
◀◀◀ page 47

NYMANS GARDEN

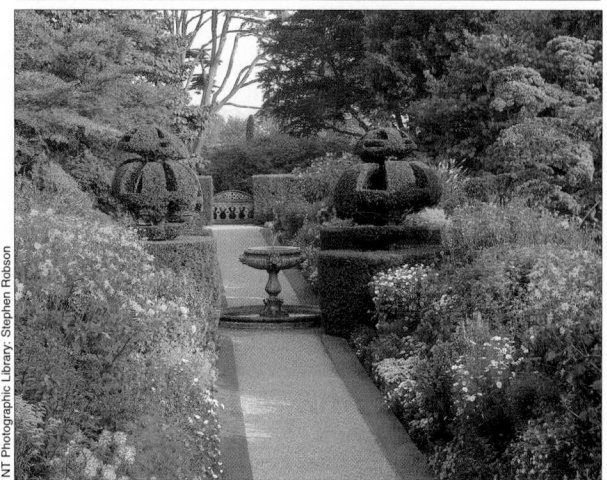

NT Photographic Library: Stephen Robson

HANDCROSS, HAYWARDS HEATH, SUSSEX RH17 6EB

Owners: *The National Trust* **Contact:** *The Property Manager*

Tel: 01444 400321/400777 **Fax:** 01444 400253 **e-mail:** snygen@smtp.ntrust.org.uk

One of the great gardens of the Sussex Weald, with rare and beautiful plants, shrubs and trees from all over the world. Wall garden, hidden sunken garden, pinetum, laurel walk and romantic ruins. Lady Rosse's library, drawing room and forecourt garden also open. Woodland walks and Wild Garden.

Location: OS Ref. TQ265 294. On B2114 at Handcross, 4^1/2 m S of Crawley, just off London - Brighton M23 / A23.

Opening Times: 1 Mar - 4 Nov: daily except Mon & Tue but open BHs, 11am - 6pm or sunset if earlier. House: 28 Mar - 4 Nov: same days as garden, closes at 4.30pm. Garden, tearoom & shop: Nov - Mar: Sats & Suns, 11am - 4pm. Closed 29 & 30 Dec 2001.

Admission: Adult £6, Child £3, Family £15. Pre-booked Groups £5. Joint group ticket which includes same day entry to Standen £9, available Wed - Fri only. Winter weekends: Adult £3, Child £1.50, Family £7.50. Booked groups: £2.50.

   Grounds suitable. WC. 🖪 🍴 Licensed. ❄ Ⓘ

PALLANT HOUSE GALLERY   **Tel:** 01243 774557 **Fax:** 01243 536038

9 North Pallant, Chichester, West Sussex PO19 1TJ

Owner: Pallant House Gallery Trust   **Contact:** Mr Andrew Churchill

Lovingly restored Queen Anne townhouse with historic rooms in Georgian style, fine antique furniture and formal garden. Highly important collection of Bow porcelain and displays of modern British art (Nicholson, Nash, Moore, Sutherland, Piper etc). Georgian style walled garden.

Location: OS Ref. SU861 047. City centre, SE of the Cross.

Opening Times: All year: Tue - Sat ,10am - 5pm. Suns & BHs 12.30 - 5pm. Last admission 4.45pm. Closed Mons.

Admission: Adult £4, OAP. £3, Student/Unemployed £2.50. West Sussex students and child under 16 Free.

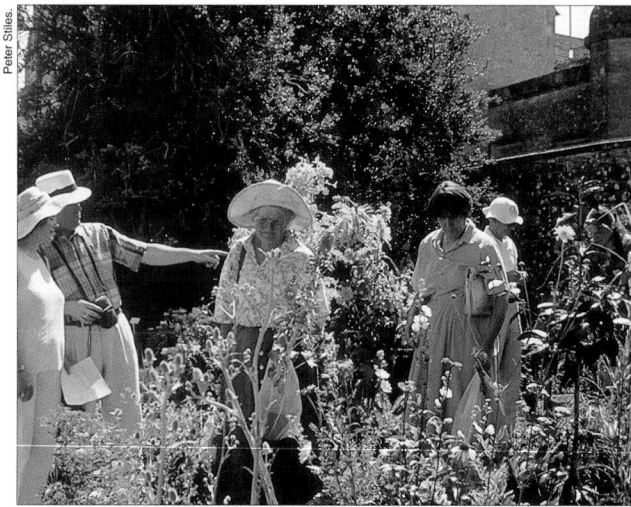

Peter Stiles.

Parham Park, Sussex.

PARHAM HOUSE & GARDENS 🏛

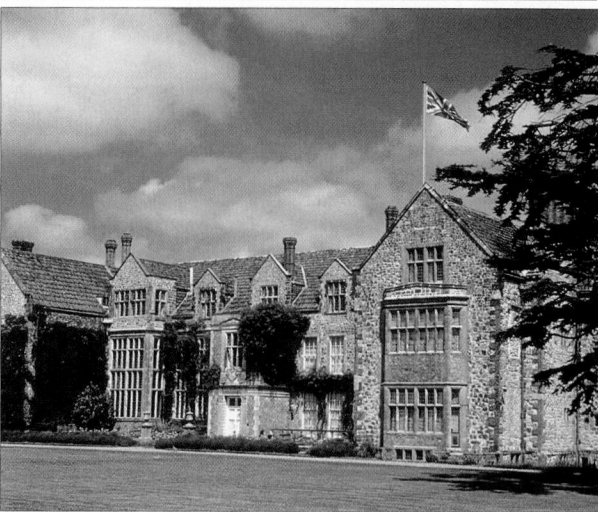

PARHAM PARK, Nr PULBOROUGH, WEST SUSSEX RH20 4HS

Owners: *Parham Park Trust* **Contact:** *Patricia Kennedy*

Tel: 01903 744888/742021 **Fax:** 01903 746557 **e-mail:** Parham@dial.pipex.com

Friendly staff give a warm welcome to this stunning Elizabethan house with award-winning gardens, set in the heart of a medieval deer park below the South Downs. The light, panelled rooms, from Great Hall to magnificent Long Gallery house an important collection of contemporary paintings, furniture, working clocks and needlework, all complemented by informal arrangements of flowers, freshly cut twice a week from the four acre walled garden. Light lunches and cream teas are served in the 15th century Big Kitchen (licensed), and souvenirs and gifts can be purchased from the shop, with plants and herbs on sale from the garden shop.

STITCHES IN TIME
A needlework weekend 19 - 20 May 2001
Official opening by Kaffe Fassett

Parham is home to perhaps the finest and most important collection of 17th century embroidery to be found anywhere in the United Kingdom. During this weekend there will be a display of 18th and 19th century Samplers never before seen by visitors to Parham, demonstrations of needleworking techniques, lectures and sales tables.

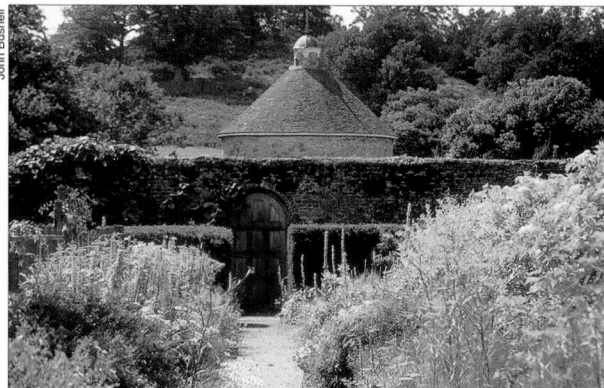

John Bushell

Location: OS Ref. TQ060 143. Midway between Pulborough & Storrington on A283.

Opening Times: 1 Apr - 31 Oct: Weds, Thurs, Suns & BH Mons. Also Sats 19 May, 14 Jul & 1 Sept (special events). Private groups by arrangement at other times. Picnic area, Big Kitchen, and Gardens, 12 noon - 6pm. House: 2 - 6pm. Last entry 5pm.

Admission(2000 prices): House & Gardens: Adult £5, OAP £4, Child £1, Family (2+2) £10. Unguided booked groups (20+) £4. Garden only: Adult/OAP £3, Child 50p.

ⓘ No photography in house. 🖻 🌲 👤 Partially suitable. 🖪 Licensed.
🧍 🎧 Ⓟ 🛏 🐕 In grounds, on leads. ❄ 🛡 Ⓘ

PASHLEY MANOR GARDENS

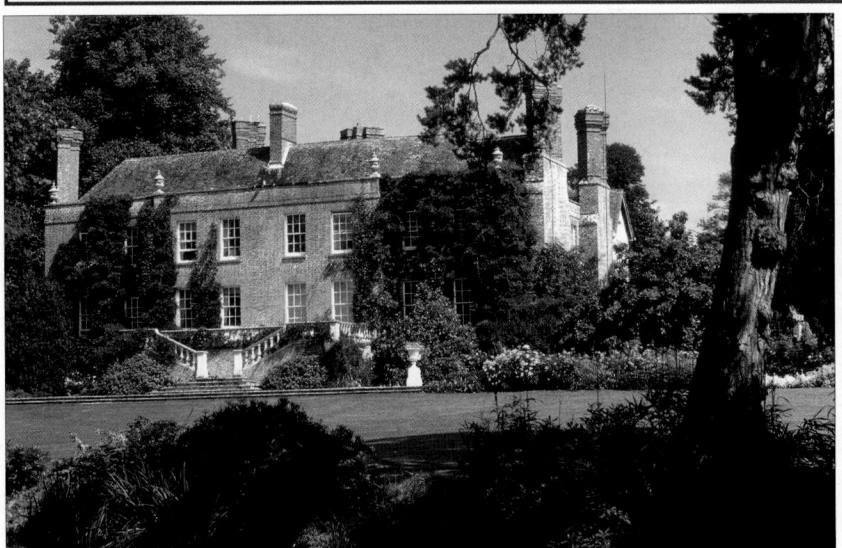

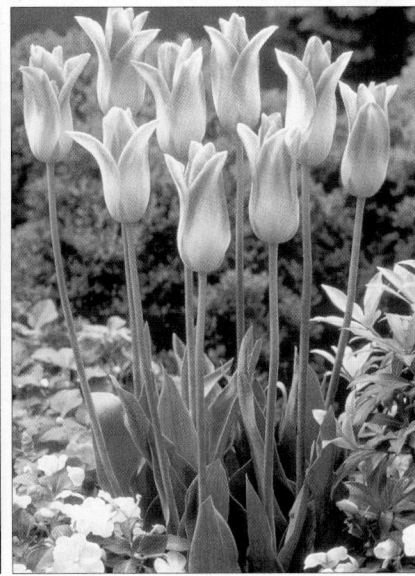

TICEHURST, WADHURST, EAST SUSSEX TN5 7HE

Owner: *James A Sellick*   ***Contact:*** *Caroline Foster*

Tel: 01580 200888 **Fax:** 01580 200102 **e-mail:** pashleymanor@email.msn.com

HHA/Christie's Garden of the Year 1999. The gardens offer a sumptuous blend of romantic landscaping, imaginative plantings and fine old trees, fountains, springs and large ponds. This is a quintessentially English garden of a very individual character with exceptional views to the surrounding valleyed fields. Many eras of English history are reflected here, typifying the tradition of the English Country House and its garden.

Pashley prides itself on its delicious food. Home-made soups, ploughman's lunches with pickles and patés, fresh salad from the garden (whenever possible), home-made scones and delicious cakes, filter coffee, specialist teas, fine wines - served at the Terrace Restaurant or in the Old Stables Tearoom. The gift shop caters for every taste… from postcards and local honey to traditional hand-painted ceramics and tapestry cushions. A wide selection of plants and shrubs, many of which grow at Pashley, are available for purchase.

Location: OS Ref. TQ 707 291. On B2099 between A21 and Ticehurst village.

Opening Times: 7 Apr - 29 Sept: Tues, Weds, Thurs, Sats and all BH Mons, 11am - 5pm. Garden only (restaurant & shop closed): 1 - 31 Oct: Mon - Fri, 11am - 4pm.

Admission: Adult £5, Child/OAP £4.50. Groups (min 20): £4.50. Coaches by appointment only.

🗖 ⚹ ⮾ Partially suitable. 🖵 Licensed. 🧍By arrangement. **P**
🐕 Guide dogs only.

PETWORTH HOUSE 🌿   **See page 164 for full page entry.**

PEVENSEY CASTLE ⬚   **Tel:** 01323 762604

Pevensey, Sussex BN24 5LE

Owner: English Heritage   **Contact:** The Custodian

Originally a 4th century Roman Fort, Pevensey was the place where William the Conqueror landed in 1066 and established his first stronghold. The Norman castle included the remains of an unusual keep within the massive walls. Free audio tour tells the story of the Castle's 2,000 year history.

Location: OS Ref. TQ645 048. In Pevensey off A259.

Opening Times: 1 Apr - 30 Sept: daily, 10am - 6pm. 1 - 31 Oct: 10am - 5pm. 1 Nov - 31 Mar: Wed - Sun only, 10am - 4pm. Closed 24 - 26 Dec & 1 Jan.

Admission: Adult £2.50, Child £1.30, Conc. £1.90. 15% discount for groups of 11+.

⮾ Grounds suitable. 🖵 🎧 Free. 🐕 In grounds, on leads. ✳ 🛡 Tel. for details.

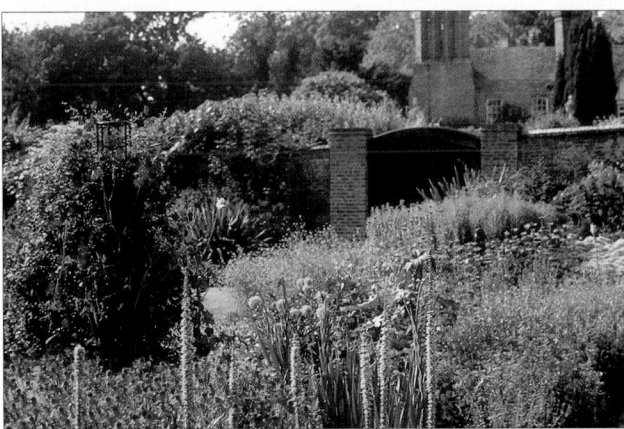

Pashley Manor Gardens, Sussex.

PRESTON MANOR

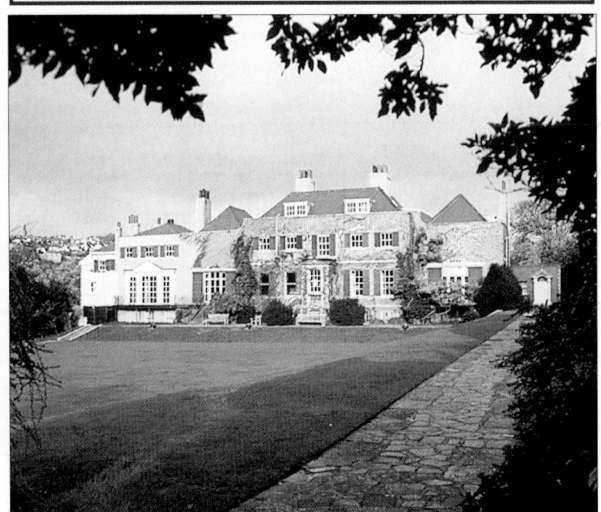

PRESTON DROVE, BRIGHTON, EAST SUSSEX BN1 6SD

Owner: *Brighton & Hove Council*   ***Contact:*** *David Beevers*

Tel: 01273 292770 **Fax:** 01273 292771

A delightful Manor House which powerfully evokes the atmosphere of an Edwardian gentry home both 'upstairs' and 'downstairs'. Explore more than twenty rooms over four floors – from the servants' quarters, kitchens and butler's pantry in the basement to the attic bedrooms and nursery on the top floor. Plus charming walled gardens, pets' cemetery and 13th century parish church.

Location: OS Ref. TQ303 064. 2m N of Brighton on the A23 London road.

Opening Times: All year: Tue - Sat 10am - 5pm, Suns 2 - 5pm, Mons 1 - 5pm (BHs 10am - 5pm). Closed Good Fri, 25/26 Dec.

Admission: Adult £3.20, Child £2, Conc. £2.70. Groups (20+) £2.70. Prices valid until 31 Mar 2001.

ℹ No photography. 🗖 Gift kiosk. 🍽 ⮾ Not suitable.
🧍By arrangement. ▦ **P** For coaches. 🚫 ✳ ⓦ

THE PRIEST HOUSE

Tel: 01342 810479

North Lane, West Hoathly, Sussex RH19 4PP

Owner: Sussex Archaeological Society   **Contact:** Antony Smith

Standing in the beautiful surroundings of a traditional cottage garden on the edge of Ashdown Forest, the Priest House is an early 15th century timber-framed hall-house. In Elizabethan times it was modernised into a substantial yeoman's dwelling. Its furnished rooms contain 17th and 18th century furniture, kitchen equipment, needlework and household items. Formal herb garden.

Location: OS187 Ref. TQ362 325. In triangle formed by Crawley, East Grinstead and Haywards Heath, 4m off A22, 6m off M23.

Opening Times: 1 Mar - 31 Oct: Mon - Sat, 11am - 5.30pm, Suns, 2 - 5.30pm.

Admission: Adults £2.50, Child £1.20, Conc. £2.30. Groups (15+): Adult £2.30, Child £1.10.

◻   �♻ Partially suitable.   🎦 By arrangement.   🅿 Limited.   ▥

🐾 Guide dogs only.   🌐

THE ROYAL PAVILION

See page 165 for full page entry.

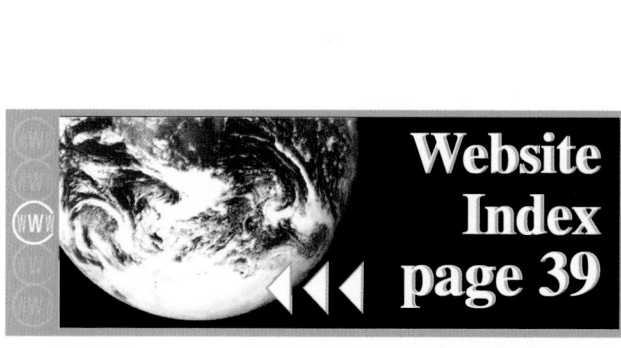

Website Index page 39 ◀◀◀

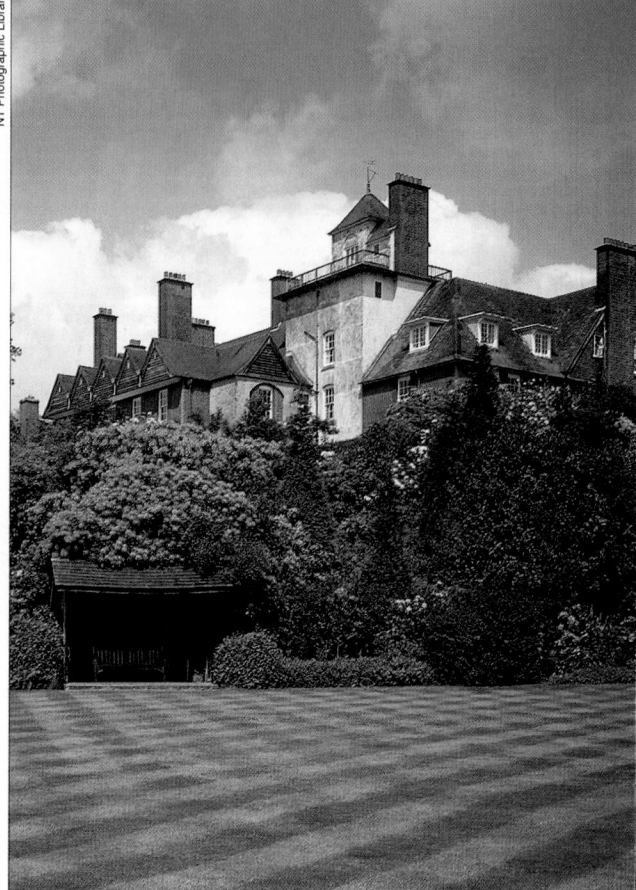

Standen, Sussex.

ST MARY'S HOUSE & GARDENS

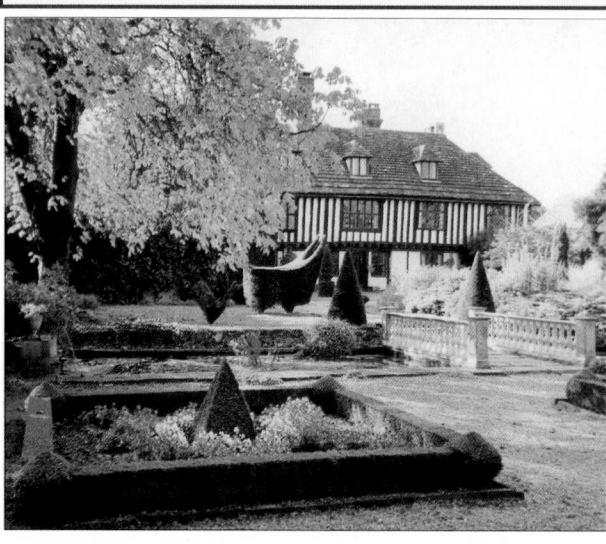

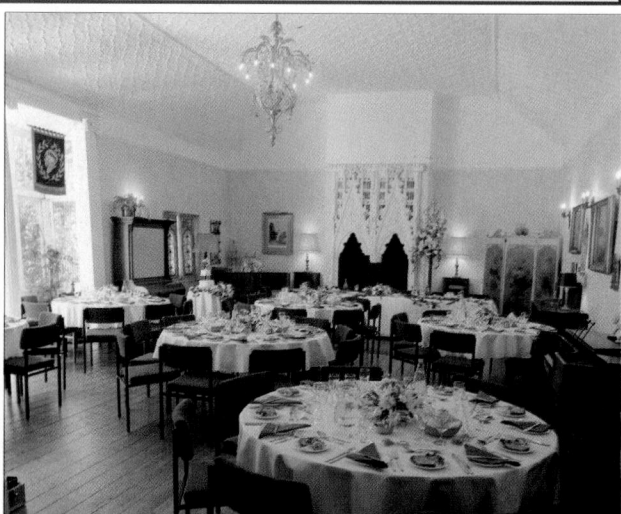

BRAMBER, WEST SUSSEX BN44 3WE

Owner/Contact: Mr Peter Thorogood

Tel/Fax: 01903 816205   **e-mail:** stmaryshouse@btinternet.com

This enchanting, medieval timber-framed house is situated in the downland village of Bramber. The fine panelled interiors of St Mary's, which include the famous 'King's Room' associated with the escape of Charles II in 1651, and the unique Elizabethan 'Painted Room' with its intriguing *trompe l'oeil* murals, give an air of tranquillity and timelessness. Informative guided tours tell of fact and legend from earlier Knights Templar foundations to the present day. Once the home of the real Algernon and Gwendolen, brilliantly portrayed in Oscar Wilde's comedy, *The Importance of Being Earnest*, St Mary's was more than likely the setting for the Sherlock Holmes story, *The Musgrave Ritual*, and has served as a location for a number of television series including the world-famous *Dr Who*. The formal gardens with amusing animal topiary include an exceptional example of the 'Living Fossil' tree, *Gingko biloba*, and a mysterious ivy-clad 'Monk's Walk'. In the 'Secret Garden' can still be seen the Victorian original fruit-wall, potting shed, circular orchard, and woodland walk.

St Mary's is a house of fascination and mystery. Many thousands of visitors have admired its picturesque charm and enjoyed its atmosphere of friendliness and welcome, qualities which make it a visit to remember.

Location: OS Ref. TQ189 105. Bramber village off A283. From London 56m via M23/A23 or A24. Bus from Shoreham to Steyning, alight St Mary's, Bramber.

Opening Times: Easter - Sept: Suns, Thurs & BH Mons, 2 - 6pm. Groups at other times by arrangement.

Admission: House & Garden: Adult £4, Child £2. Secret Garden: Adult £2, Child Free. Groups (25+) £3.80.

ℹ No photography in house.   ◻   🍴   ♻ Not suitable.   ▥

🎦 Obligatory. Groups (max 60). Visit time 2¹/₂hrs.   🅿 30 cars, 2 coaches.   ▥

  Tel. for details.

SHEFFIELD PARK GARDEN

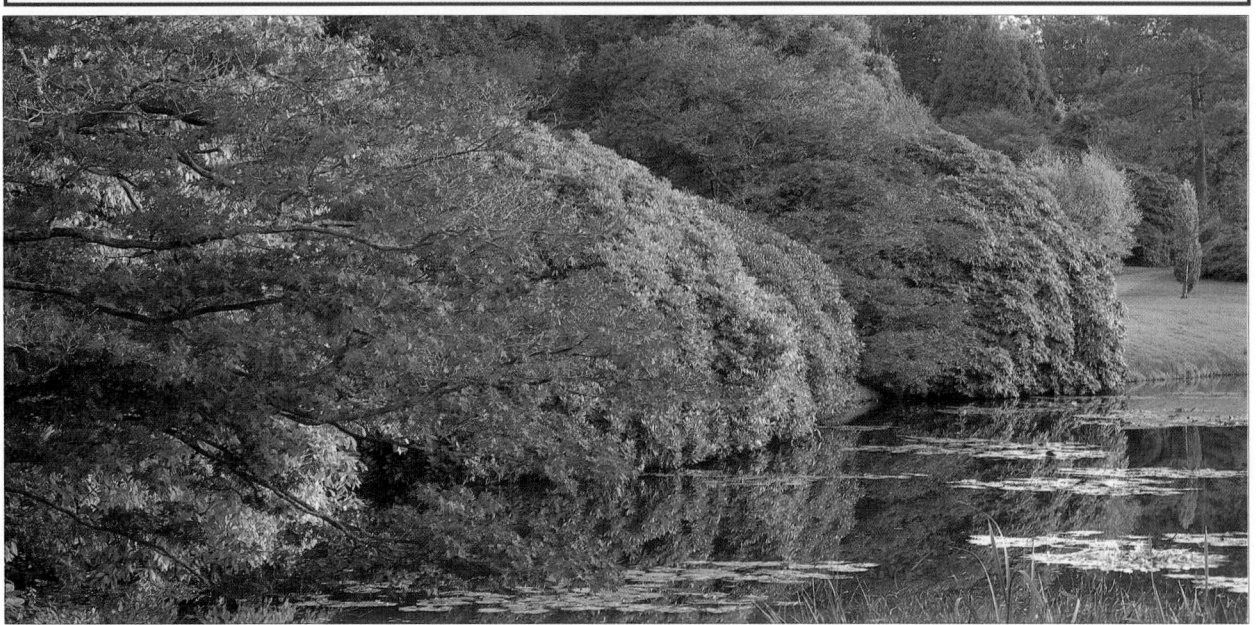

SHEFFIELD PARK, EAST SUSSEX TN22 3QX

Owner: The National Trust   *Contact:* The Property Manager

Tel: 01825 790231 **Fax:** 01825 791264 **e-mail:** kshxxx@smtp.ntrust.org.uk

A magnificent tranquil 120 acre landscape garden, with 4 lakes, laid out in the 18th century by 'Capability' Brown. A garden for all seasons. Daffodils, snowdrops and bluebells in spring, its rhododendrons, azaleas and spring garden are spectacular in early summer. Cool tree-lined paths and lake reflections make it perfect for a stroll in high summer and the garden is ablaze with colour from its rare trees and shrubs in autumn. The mists and frosts in wintertime create a mystical mood and give the garden a unique atmosphere.

Location: OS Ref. TQ415 240. Midway between East Grinstead and Lewes, 5m NW

of Uckfield on E side of A275.

Opening Times: Jan & Feb: Sats & Suns only, 10.30am - 4pm. Mar - end Oct: Tue - Sun, BH Mons & Good Fri, 10.30am - 6pm, last admission 5pm or sunset if earlier. Nov & Dec: Tue - Sun, 10.30am - 4pm.

Admission: Adult £4.60, Child £2.30, Family (2+3) £11.50. Pre-booked groups £4.00. Joint ticket available with Bluebell Railway.

 Grounds suitable. WC. Licensed (not NT). Guide dogs only.

STANDEN

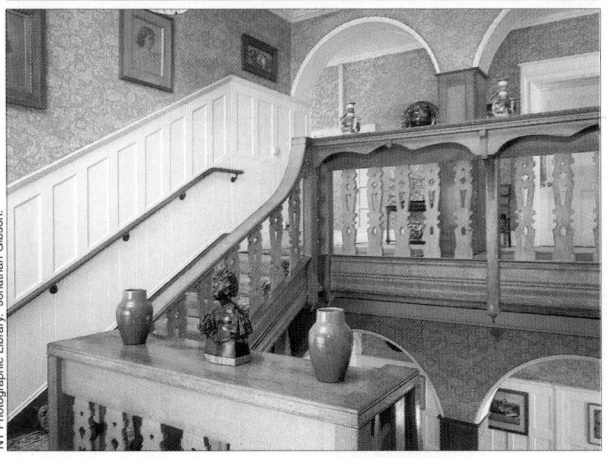

NT Photographic Library. Jonathan Gibson.

EAST GRINSTEAD, WEST SUSSEX RH19 4NE

Owner: The National Trust   *Contact:* The Property Manager

Tel: 01342 323029 **Fax:** 01342 316424 **e-mail:** sstpro@smtp.ntrust.org.uk

Dating from the 1890s and containing original Morris & Co furnishings and decorations, Standen survives today as a remarkable testimony to the ideals of the Arts and Crafts movement. The property was built as a family home by the influential architect Phillip Webb and retains a warm, welcoming atmosphere. Details of Webb's designs can be found everywhere from the fireplaces to the original electric light fittings.

Location: OS Ref. TQ389 356. 2m S of East Grinstead, signposted from B2110.

Opening Times: 28 Mar - 4 Nov: Wed - Sun & BH Mons. House: 12.30 - 4pm (last admission). Garden: As house, 11am - 6pm. Garden only: 9 Nov - 16 Dec: Fri - Sun, 11am - 3pm.

Admission: House & Garden: £5.50, Family £13.75. Garden only: £3. Joint ticket with same day entry to Nymans Garden £9, available Wed - Fri. Groups: £4.50, Wed - Fri only, if booked in advance.

 Partially suitable. WC. Licensed. By arrangement. In grounds on leads, not in garden.

SAINT HILL MANOR   See page 166 for full page entry.

STANSTED PARK   See page 167 for full page entry.

UPPARK   See page 168 for full page entry.

WAKEHURST PLACE   **Tel:** 01444 894066

Ardingly, Haywards Heath, Sussex RH17 6TN

Owner: The National Trust (managed by Royal Botanic Gdns) **Contact:** The Administrator

A superb collection of exotic trees, shrubs and other plants, many displayed in a geographic manner. Extensive water gardens, a winter garden, a rock walk and many other features. The Loder Valley Nature Reserve can be visited by prior arrangement.

Location: OS Ref. TQ339 314. 1½ m N of Ardingly, on B2028.

Opening Times: Daily (not 25 Dec & 1 Jan). Feb & Oct: 10am - 5pm. Mar: 10am - 6pm. Apr - end Sept: 10am - 7pm. Nov - end Jan 2000: 10am - 4pm. Mansion closed 1hr before gardens.

Admission: Adult £5, Child (5-16) £2.50, Conc. £3.50, Family (2+4) £13. Reductions for pre-paid booked groups. (Prices valid until 31 March 2001).

 Ground floor & grounds suitable. Tel. for details.

WEALD & DOWNLAND OPEN AIR MUSEUM   **Tel:** 01243 811363

Singleton, Chichester, Sussex PO18 0EU

40 original historic buildings. Interiors and gardens through the ages.

Location: OS Ref. SU876 127. 6m N of Chichester. SE side of A286. W of Singleton.

Opening Times: 1 Mar - 31 Oct: daily, 10.30am - 6pm. Nov - Feb: Weds & w/ends only. 10.30am - 4pm. 26 Dec - 3 Jan: 10.30am - 4pm.

Admission: Adult £7, Child/Student £4, OAP £6.50. Family (2+3) £17. Prices from 1 Mar 2001. Group rates on request.

WEST DEAN GARDENS

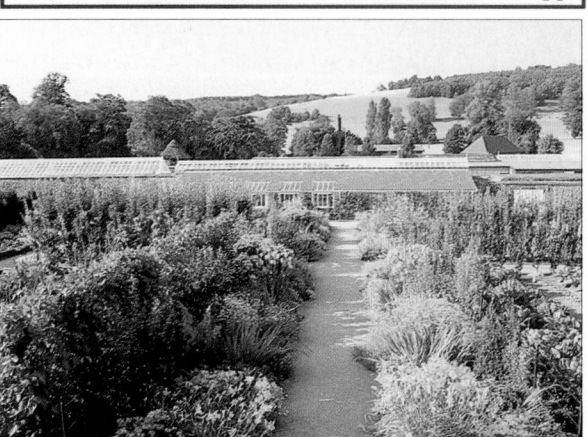

WEST DEAN, CHICHESTER, WEST SUSSEX PO18 0QZ

Owner: The Edward James Foundation　　　*Contact: Jim Buckland, Gardens Manager*

Tel: 01243 818210 **Fax:** 01243 811342 **e-mail:** westdean@pavilion.co.uk

Visiting the Gardens you are immersed in a classic 19th century designed landscape with its 2$\frac{1}{2}$ acre walled kitchen garden, 13 original glasshouses dating from the 1890s, 35 acres of ornamental grounds, 240 acre landscaped park and the 49 acre St Roche's arboretum, all linked by a scenic 2$\frac{1}{4}$ mile parkland walk. Features of the grounds are a lavishly planted 300ft long Edwardian pergola terminated by a flint and stone gazebo and sunken garden. The Visitor Centre (free entry) houses a licensed restaurant and an imaginative garden shop.

Location: OS Ref. SU863 128. SE side of A286 Midhurst Road, 6m N of Chichester.

Opening Times: 1 Mar - 31 October: daily. Mar, Apr & Oct: 11am - 5pm. May - Sept: 10.30am - 5pm.

Admission: Adult £4.50, Child £2, OAP £4. Groups (12+): Adult £4, Child £2.

No photography in house. Licensed. Limited for coaches. By arrangement. Guide dogs only. Telephone for details.

WILMINGTON PRIORY
Tel: 01628 825920 or 825925 (bookings)

Wilmington, Nr Eastbourne, East Sussex BN26 5SW

Owner: Leased to the Landmark Trust by Sussex Archaeological Society

Contact: The Landmark Trust

Founded by the Benedictines in the 11th century, the surviving, much altered buildings date largely from the 14th century. Managed and maintained by the Landmark Trust, which lets buildings for self-catering holidays. Full details of Wilmington Priory and 170 other historic buildings available for holidays are featured in The Landmark Handbook (price £9.50 refundable against booking), from The Landmark Trust, Shottesbrooke, Maidenhead, Berkshire, SL6 3SW.

Location: OS Ref. TQ543 042. 600yds S of A27. 6m NW of Eastbourne.

Opening Times: Grounds, Ruins, Porch & Crypt: on 30 days between Apr - Oct. Whole property including interiors on 8 of these days, 22 - 25 May & 7 - 10 Sept 2001. Telephone for details. Accommodation is available for up to 6 people for self-catering holidays.

Admission: Please contact Landmark Trust for details.

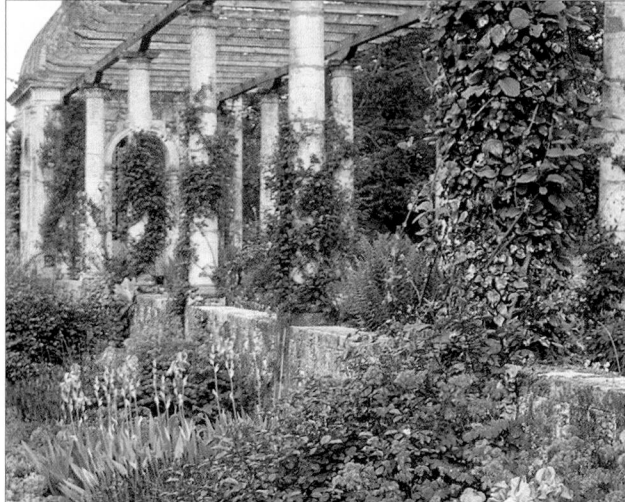

West Dean Gardens, Sussex.

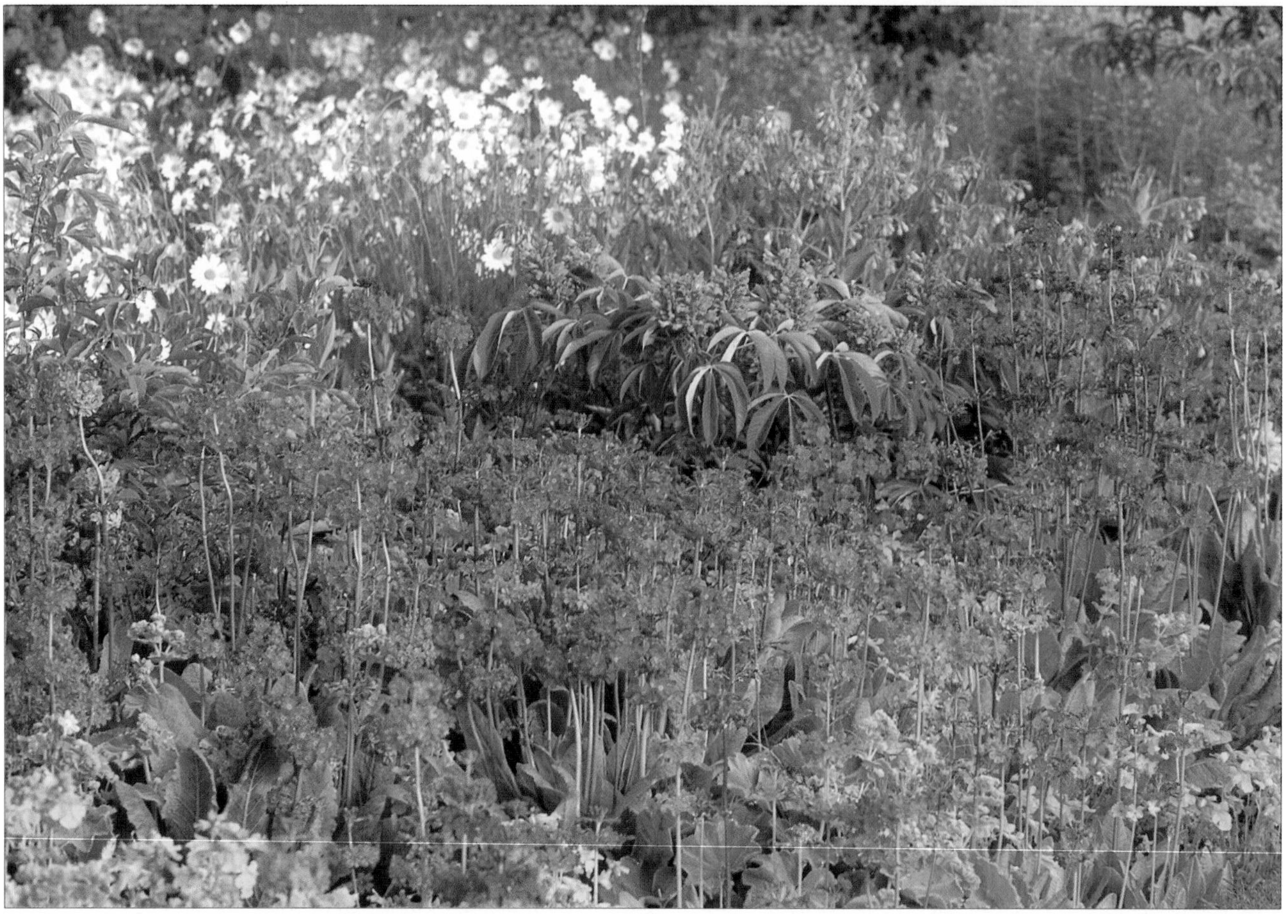

Merriments Garden, Sussex.

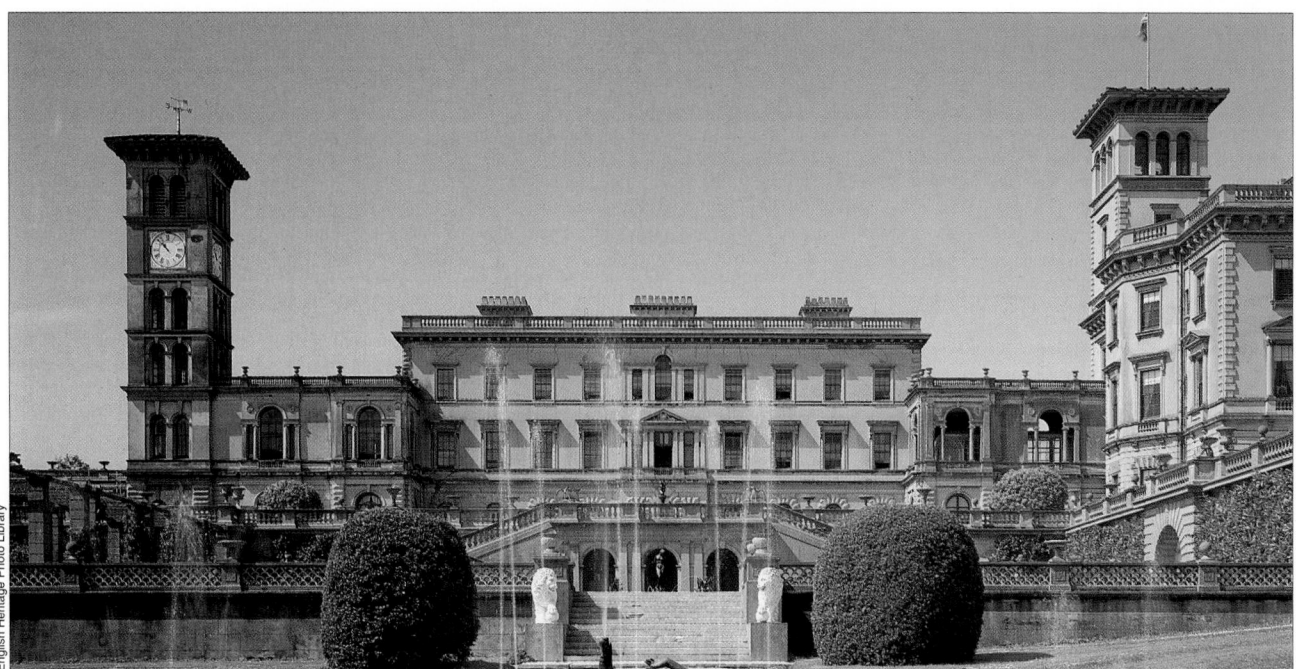

English Heritage Photo Library

OSBORNE HOUSE
East Cowes

OSBORNE HOUSE was the peaceful, rural retreat of Queen Victoria, Prince Albert and their family; they spent some of their happiest times here.

Many of the apartments have a very intimate association with the Queen who died here in 1901 and have been preserved almost unaltered ever since. The nursery bedroom remains just as it was in the 1870s when Queen Victoria's first grandchildren came to stay. Children were a constant feature of life at Osborne (Victoria and Albert had nine). Don't miss the Swiss Cottage, a charming chalet in the grounds built for the Royal children to play and entertain their parents in.

Enjoy the beautiful gardens with their stunning views over the Solent and the newly opened fruit and flower Victorian walled garden. In commemoration of the 100th anniversary of Queen Victoria's death the Durbar Wing has been refurbished. In addition, for 2001 only, the Queen's bedroom will be re-displayed to recreate the historic and atmospheric arrangement of the room after her death on 22 January 1901

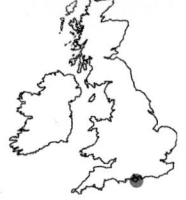

Owner: English Heritage

CONTACT

The House Administrator
Osborne House
Royal Apartments
East Cowes
Isle of Wight
PO32 6JY

Tel: 01983 200022

Fax: 01983 297281

LOCATION

OS Ref. SZ516 948

1m SE of East Cowes.

Ferry: Isle of Wight ferry terminals .

East Cowes 1$^{1}/_{2}$ m
Tel: 02380 334010.

Fishbourne 4m
Tel: 0870 58277441.

Suitable for filming, concerts, drama. No photography in the House. Children's play area.

Durbar Room available for functions.

Wheelchairs available, access to house via ramp, ground floor access only. WC.

Teas, coffees and light snacks. Waitress service in Swiss Cottage tearoom.

Ample. Coach drivers and tour leaders free, one extra place for every additional 20. Group rates.

Visits free, please book. Education room available.

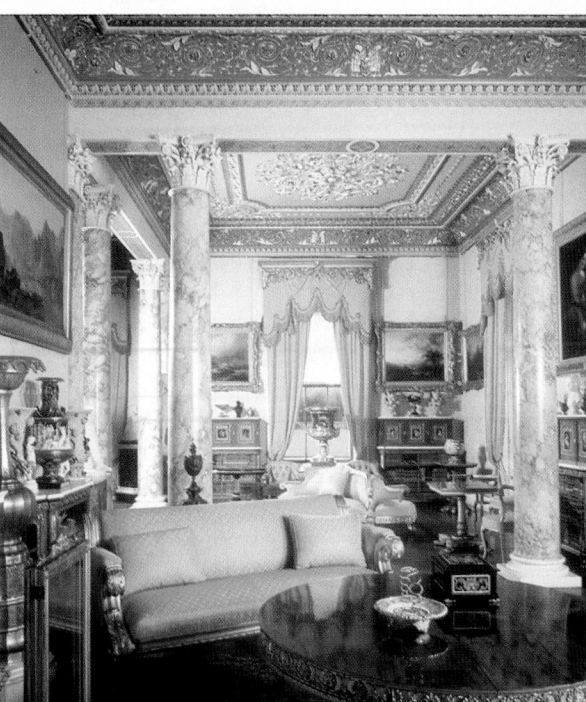

English Heritage Photo Library

OPENING TIMES

House

1 April - 30 September
Daily: 10am - 6pm.

1 - 31 Oct
Daily: 10am - 5pm
Last admission 4pm.

May close earlier on concert days, please telephone for details.

Winter Tours:

1 Nov - 9 Dec 2001
Daily: 10am - 2.30pm
Sun, Mon, Wed & Thur.
Guided tours only, booking essential - please telephone 01983 200022.

Closed 10 Dec - 2 Feb 2002.

ADMISSION

House & Grounds

Adult £7.20
Child* (5-15yrs) £3.60
Conc.......................£5.30
Family £18.00

Grounds only

Adult £3.80
Child* (5-15yrs) £1.90
Conc.......................£2.80

Winter & Spring Guided Tours

Adult £6.00
Child £3.30
Conc.......................£4.40

Plus normal 15% discount for groups.

* Under 5yrs Free.

APPULDURCOMBE HOUSE

Tel: 01983 852484

Wroxall, Shanklin, Isle of Wight

Owner: English Heritage   **Contact:** Mr & Mrs Owen

The bleached shell of a fine 18th century Baroque style house standing in grounds landscaped by 'Capability' Brown. New Falconry Centre.

Location: OS Ref. SZ543 800. ½m W of Wroxall off B3327.

Opening Times: 1 Mar - 31 Mar: Sat & Sun, 10am - 4pm. 1 Apr - 30 Sept, daily, 10am - 6pm (last entry 5pm). 1 Oct - 31 Oct, daily, 10am - 4pm. 1 Nov - 19 Dec, Sat & Sun, 10am - 4pm.

Admission: Adult £2, Child £1, Conc. £1.50.

    P Limited. In grounds, on leads. Tel. for details.

BARTON MANOR GARDENS

Tel: 01983 292835 **Fax:** 01983 293923

Wippingham, East Cowes, Isle of Wight PO32 6LB

Owner: Robert Stigwood   **Contact:** Julia Richards

Location: OS Ref. SZ519 944. Wippingham, East Cowes, Isle of Wight.

Opening Times: Four Sundays in the year, please telephone 01983 528989 for details. Hospice contact Julia Clifton.

Admission: Please telephone for details.

BEMBRIDGE WINDMILL

Tel: 01983 873945

Enquiries to: NT Office, Strawberry Lane, Mottistone, Isle of Wight PO30 4EA

Owner: The National Trust   **Contact:** The Custodian

Dating from around 1700, this is the only windmill to survive on the Island. Much of its original wooden machinery is still intact and there are spectacular views from the top.

Location: OS Ref. SZ639 874. ½m W of Bembridge off B3395.

Opening Times: 1 Apr - end Jun, Sept - 26 Oct: Sun - Fri, but open Easter Sat. Jul & Aug: daily, 10am - 5pm (last admission 4.30pm).

Admission: Adult £1.60, Child 80p. Special charge for guided tours.

    Not suitable. By arrangement.

CARISBROOKE CASTLE

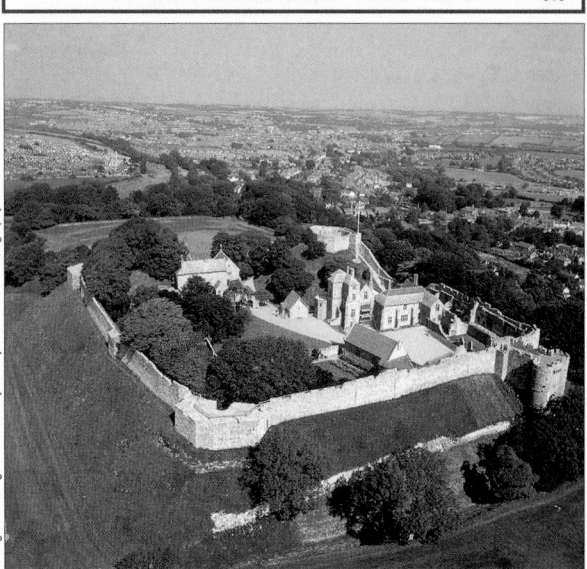

© English Heritage Photo Library © Skyscan Balloon Photography

NEWPORT, ISLE OF WIGHT PO30 1XY

Owner: English Heritage   *Contact:* The Custodian

Tel: 01983 522107 **Fax:** 01983 528632

The Island's Royal fortress and prison of King Charles I before his execution in London in 1648. See the famous Carisbrooke donkeys treading the wheel in the Well House or meet them in the donkey centre. Don't miss the castle story in the gatehouse, the museum in the great hall and the interactive coach house museum. Costumed guided tours available in summer.

Location: OS196 Ref. SZ486 877. Off the B3401, 1¼m SW of Newport.

Opening times: 1 Apr - 30 Sept: daily, 10am - 6pm. 1 - 31 Oct: 10am - 5pm. 1 Nov - 31 Mar: daily, 10am - 4pm. Closed 24 - 26 Dec & 1 Jan.

Admission: Adult £4.50, Child £2.30, Conc. £3.40, Family (2+3) £11.30. 15% discount for groups (11+), extra place for additional groups of 20.

    In grounds, on leads. Tel. for details.

DIMBOLA LODGE

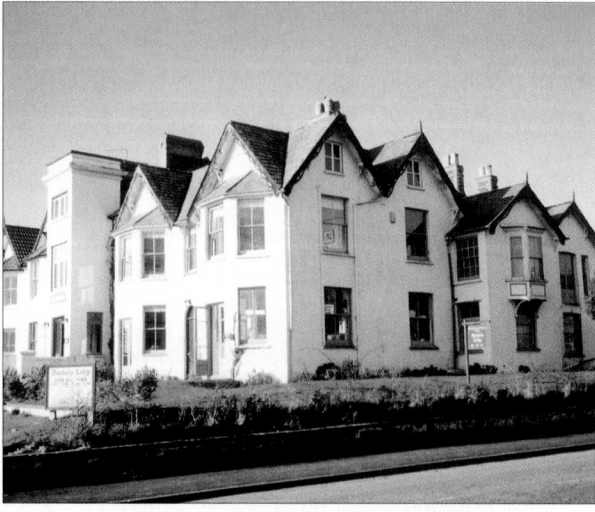

TERRACE LANE, FRESHWATER BAY PO40 9QE

Owner: Julia Margaret Cameron Trust   *Contact:* The Administrator

Tel: 01983 756814 **Fax:** 01983 755578
e-mail: administrator@dimbola.co.uk

Historic house, former home of internationally known 19th century photographer Julia Margaret Cameron, with museum and galleries. Permanent display of Cameron images. Contemporary revolving photographic exhibitions, lectures, photographic courses, and musical performances. Available for hire, book launches, etc.

Location: OS Ref. SZ348 858. From Lymington to Yarmouth and Portsmouth to Fishbourne, Wight Link Ferries. Then A3054 to Totland and then A3055. From Southampton, Red Funnel Ferries to Cowes then A3021 to A3054.

Opening Times: All year: Tue - Sun inclusive & BH Mons, 10am - 5pm. Closed for 5 days at Christmas.

Admission: Adult £3, Child (under 16yrs) Free. Groups (5 - 45) 10% discount.

i No photography in house. By arrangement.
P Limited.

MORTON MANOR

Tel: 01983 406168

Brading, Isle of Wight PO36 0EP

Owner/Contact: Mr J B Trzebski

Refurbished in the Georgian period. Magnificent gardens and vineyard.

Location: OS Ref. SZ603 863 (approx.). ¼m W of A3055 in Brading.

Opening Times: 8 Apr - end Oct: daily except Sats, 10am - 5.30pm.

Admission: Adult £4, Child £1.75, Conc. £3.50, Group £3. (Prices subject to review in 2001.)

MOTTISTONE MANOR GARDEN

Tel: 01983 741302

Mottistone, Isle of Wight

Owner: The National Trust   **Contact:** The Gardener

A haven of peace and tranquillity with colourful herbaceous borders and a backdrop of the sea making a perfect setting for the historic Manor House. An annual open air Jazz Concert is held in the grounds during July/August.

Location: OS Ref. SZ406 838. 2m W of Brightstone on B3399.

Opening Times: 25 Mar - 28 Oct: Suns, Weds & BH Mons, 2 - 5.30pm. House: Aug BH Mon only, 2 - 5.30pm.

Admission: Adult £2.50, Child £1.20.

  Not suitable. In grounds, on leads.

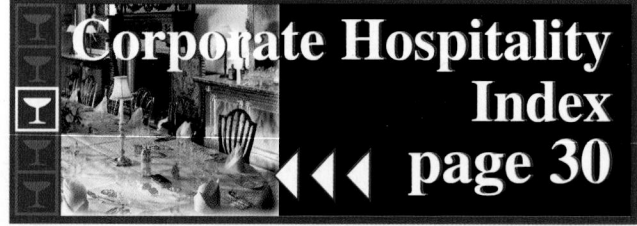

NEEDLES OLD BATTERY

Tel: 01983 754772

West High Down, Isle of Wight PO39 0JH

Owner: The National Trust   **Contact:** The Administrator

High above the sea, the Old Battery was built in the 1860s against the threat of French invasion.

Location: OS Ref. SZ300 848. Needles Headland W of Freshwater Bay & Alum Bay (B3322).

Opening Times: 1 Apr - 28 Jun, 2 Sept - 1 Nov: Sun - Thur (open Easter weekend) & Jul & Aug: daily, 10.30am - 5pm (last admission 4.30pm).

Admission: Adult £3, Child £1.50, Family £6. Special charge for guided tours.

⬚ Grounds suitable.   ⬚   ⬚ In grounds, on leads.

NUNWELL HOUSE & GARDENS

Tel: 01983 407240

Brading, Isle of Wight PO36 0JQ

Owner: Col & Mrs J A Aylmer   **Contact:** Mrs J A Aylmer

A lived in family home with fine furniture, attractive gardens and historic connections with Charles I.

Location: OS Ref. SZ595 874. 1m NW of Brading. 3m S of Ryde signed off A3055.

Opening Times: 27/28 May, then Mon - Wed, 2 Jul - 5 Sept: 1 - 5pm.

Admission: Adult £4, Pair of Adults £7.50 (inc guide book), OAP/Student £3, Child (up to 10yrs) £1. Garden only: Adult £2.50.

OLD TOWN HALL

Tel: 01983 531785

Newtown, Isle of Wight

Owner: The National Trust   **Contact:** The Custodian

A charming small 18th century building that was once the focal point of the 'rotten borough' of Newtown.

Location: OS Ref. SZ424 905. Between Newport and Yarmouth, 1m N of A3054.

Opening Times: 28 Mar - end Jun, Sept - 31 Oct: Mons, Weds & Suns (open Good Fri & Easter Sat) & Jul & Aug: daily except Fri & Sat, 2 - 5pm last admission 4.30pm.

Admission: Adult £1.50, Child 75p. Special charge for guided tours (written application).

⬚ Not suitable.   **P** Limited.   ⬚ Guide dogs only.

OSBORNE HOUSE

See page 181 for full page entry.

YARMOUTH CASTLE

Tel: 01983 760678

Quay Street, Yarmouth, Isle of Wight PO41 0PB

Owner: English Heritage   **Contact:** The Custodian

This last addition to Henry VIII's coastal defences was completed in 1547 and is, unusually for its kind, square with a fine example of an angle bastion. It was garrisoned well into the 19th century. It houses exhibitions of paintings of the Isle of Wight and photographs of old Yarmouth.

Location: OS Ref. SZ354 898. In Yarmouth adjacent to car ferry terminal.

Opening Times: 1 Apr - 30 Sept: daily, 10am - 6pm. 1 - 31 Oct: 10am - 5pm.

Admission: Adult £2.20, Child £1.10, Conc. £1.60.

⬚   ⬚ Ground floor suitable.   **P** No parking.   ⬚ In grounds, on leads.

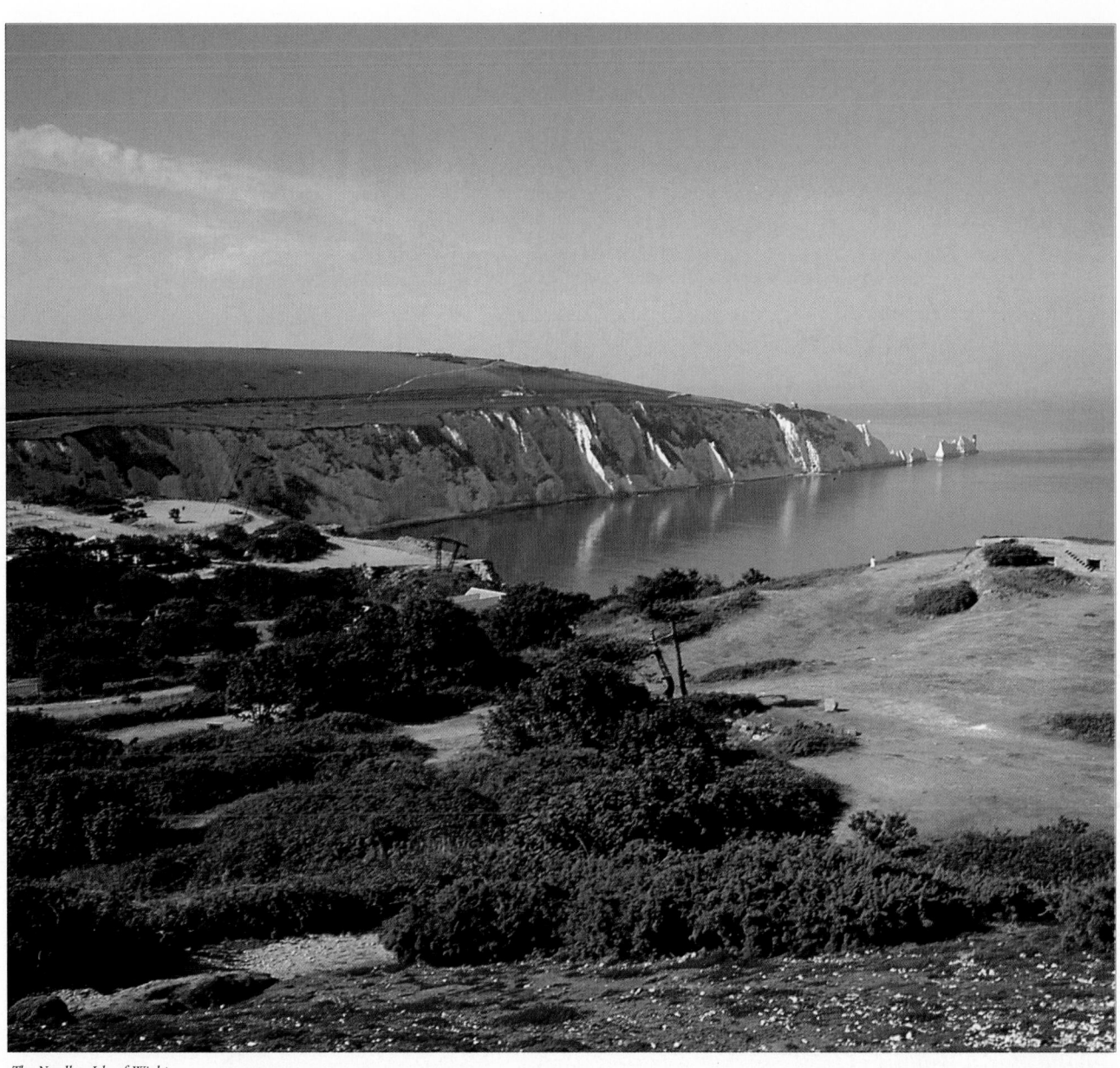

The Needles, Isle of Wight.

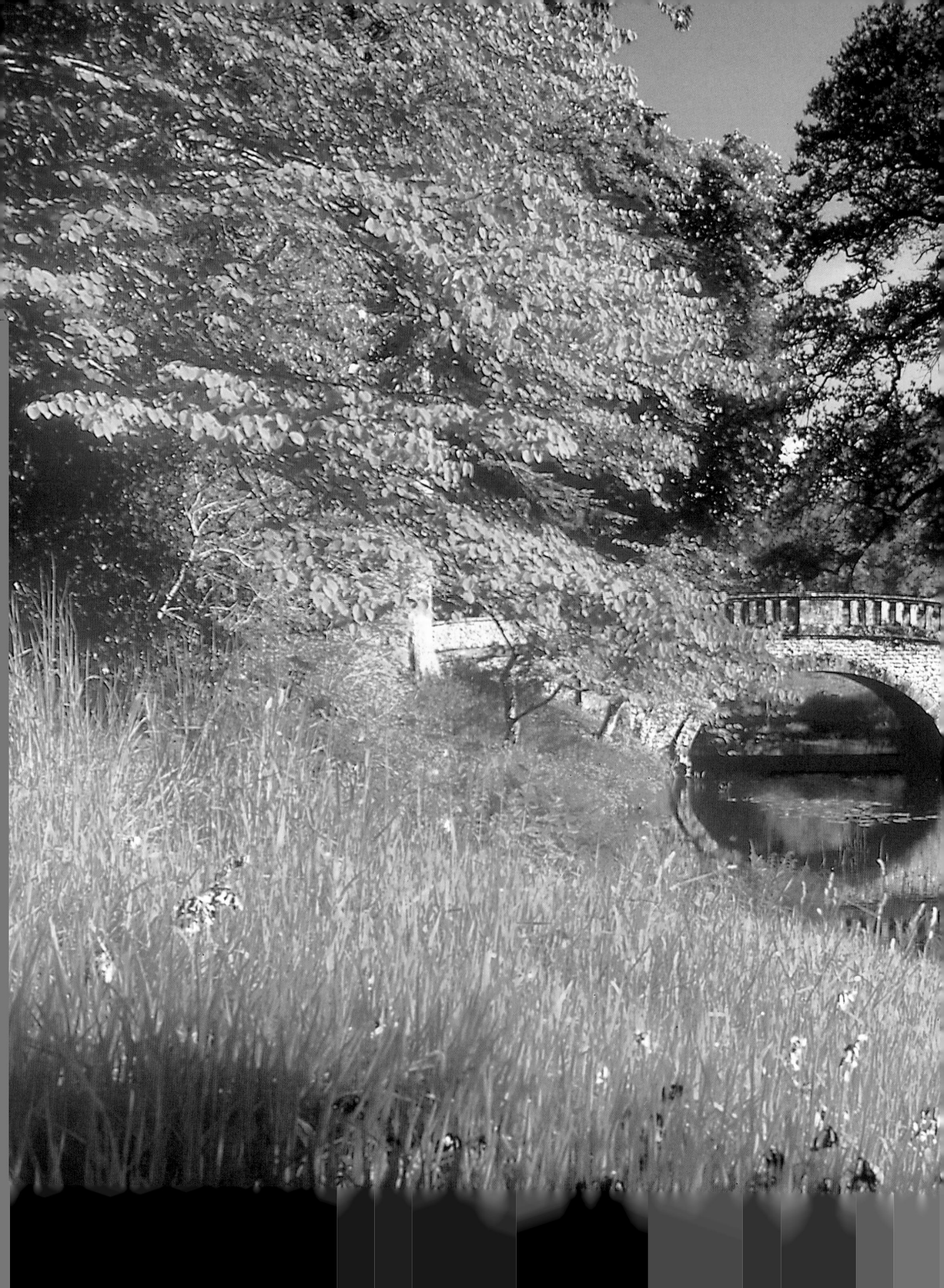

South West

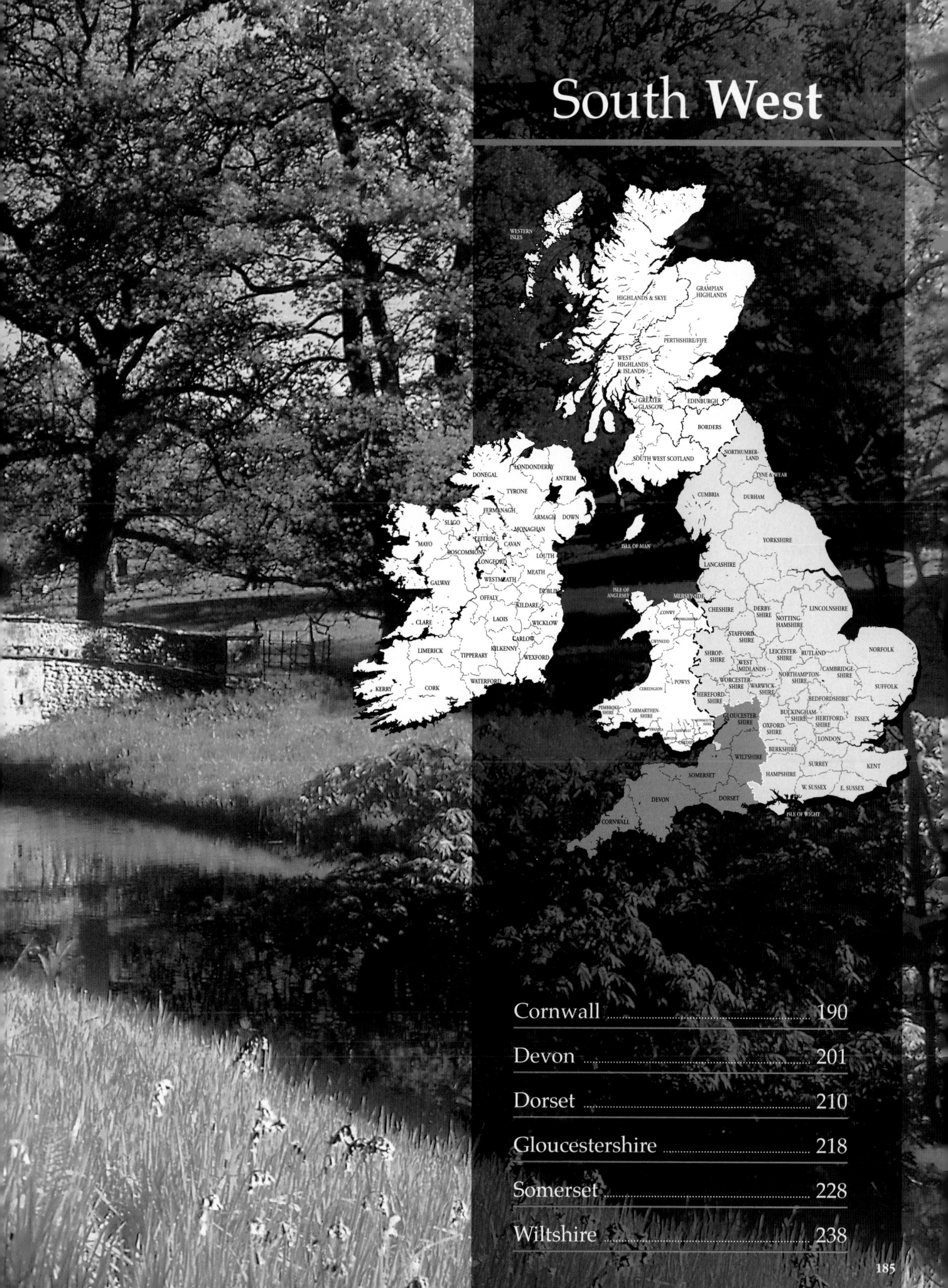

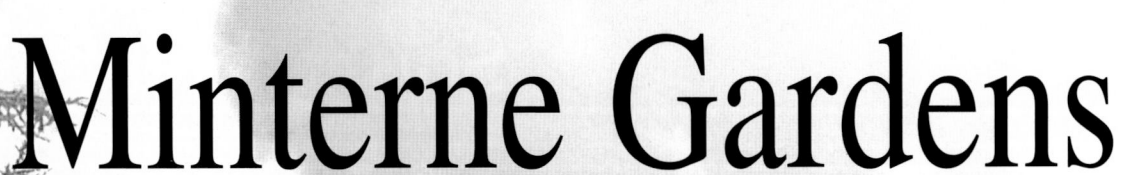

Minterne Gardens

*" If you want to visit a formal garden,
do not go to Minterne, but if you want to wander
peacefully through 20 wild woodland acres…
then you will be welcome"*

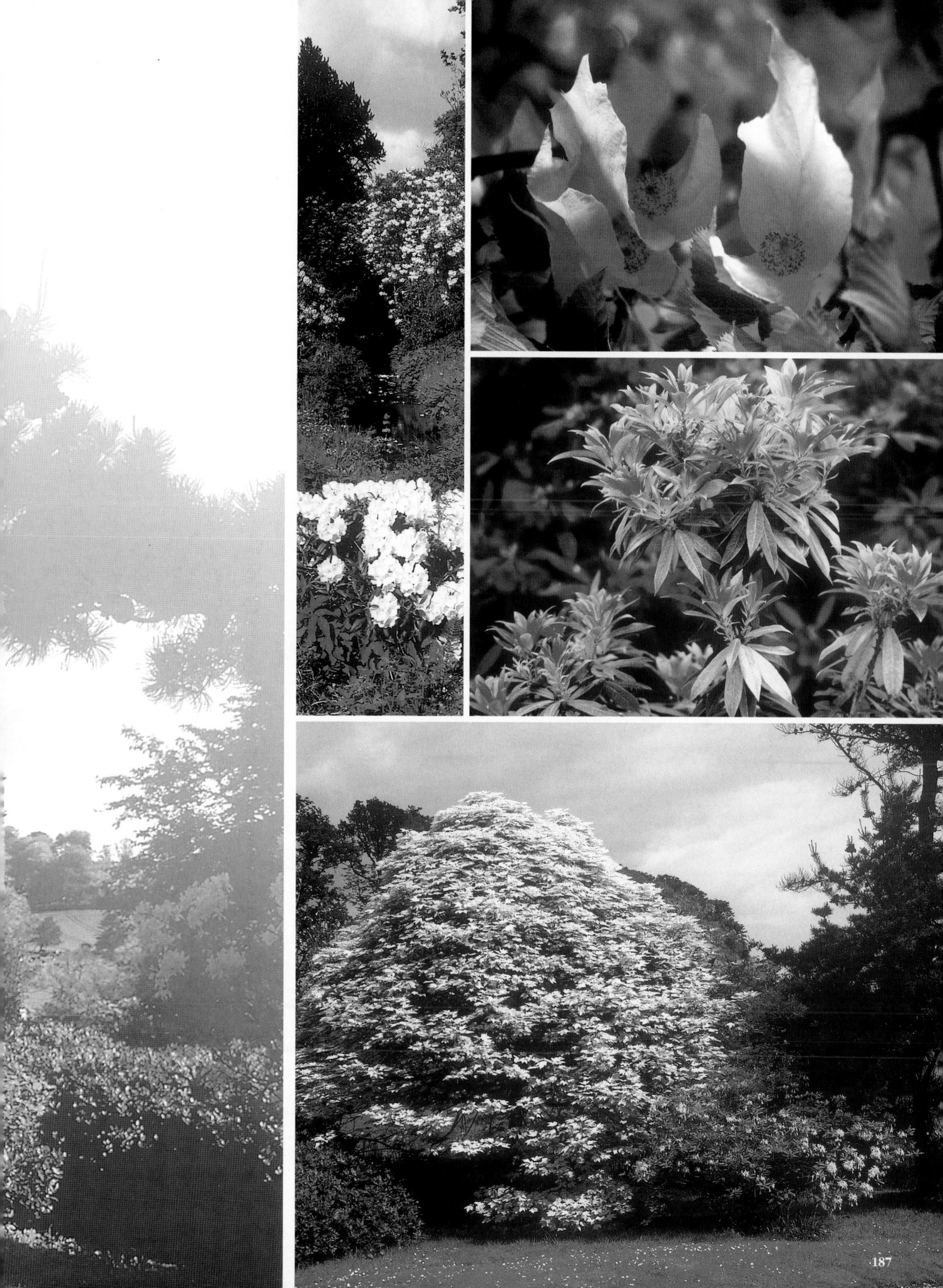

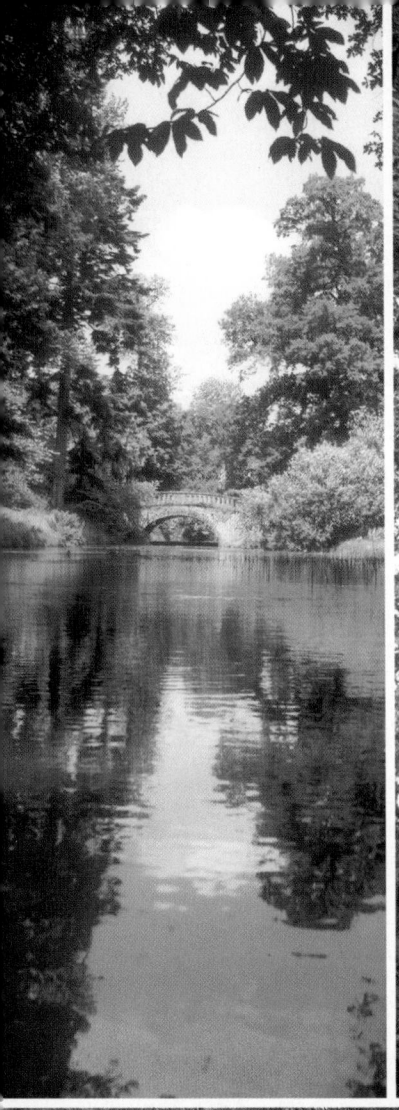

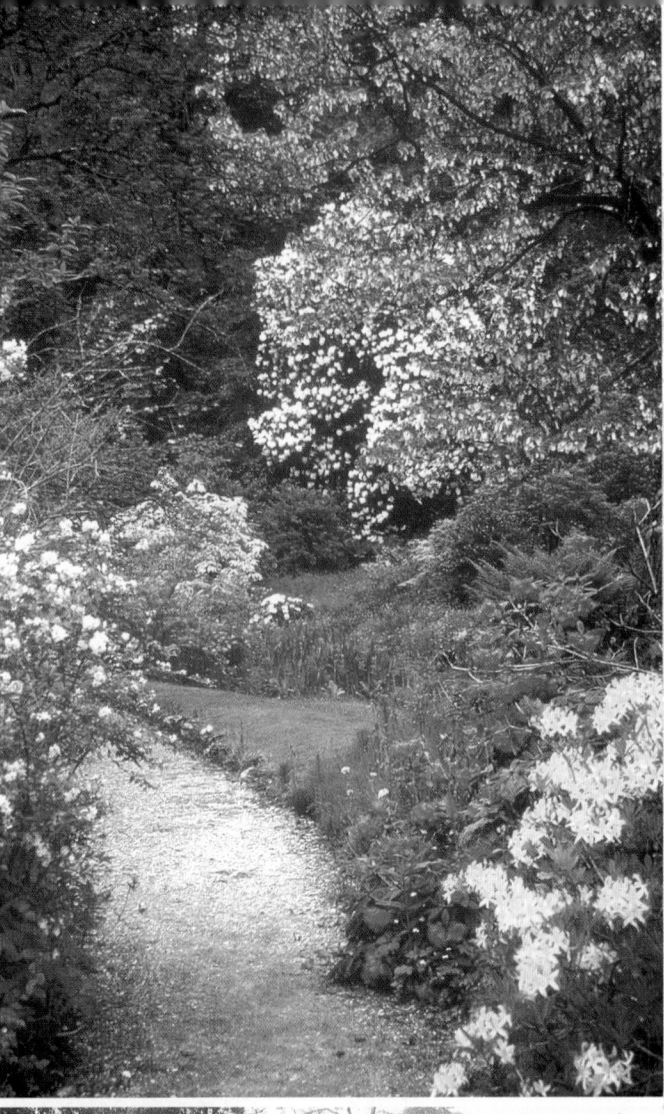

Once the home of the Churchill family, Minterne has been the property of the Digbys for the last 350 years. Admiral Robert Digby, on purchasing the estate in 1768, was to write, *"Visited my new estate, valley very bare, trees not thriving, house ill contrived and ill situated!"* – yet he obviously immediately saw the potential of this beautiful deep cut valley, as has every succeeding generation of the Digby family, all of whom are responsible for the interest found throughout the garden today.

The gardens are laid out in a horseshoe below Minterne House, with a chain of small lakes, streams and cascades. The house itself is not open to the general public but it is an integral part of the visit to the gardens. Built on the site of the original Churchill house, it is one of the great Edwardian houses of England. Designed by Leonard Stokes, a founder member of the Arts & Crafts movement and completed in 1906, built in soft apricot Ham Hill stone it shows an Elizabethan South Front and Gothic North Front.

The gardens are themselves composed of two quite different elements, an 18th century landscape, possibly influenced by 'Capability' Brown, and a 19th century woodland garden.

Admiral Robert Digby created the lakes, the cascades and Eleanor's bridge in 1785, together with the planting of the shelter belts of beech and pines along the tops of the hills and the park trees.

In the 1880s the family was to add rhododendrons from the Hooker expedition to the Himalayas and seedlings from the Wilson collection were brought back from China in 1903 and 1906.

Today, wandering along the paths and over the stepping stones and bridges, these two gardens seem to have meshed together imperceptibly, creating an atmosphere as rich as a Himalayan forest. At Minterne enjoy some of the most exciting varieties of azaleas, maples and magnolias, together with handkerchief trees, bamboos and swamp cypress – the result is a wonderfully lush and colourful visit.

The house, which contains magnificent Churchill tapestries and naval and other historical pictures, is open for special interest groups only, which may be arranged by prior appointment. Contact The Lord Digby on 01300 341370.

For further details about *Minterne Gardens* see entry in South West Region ➔ Dorset.

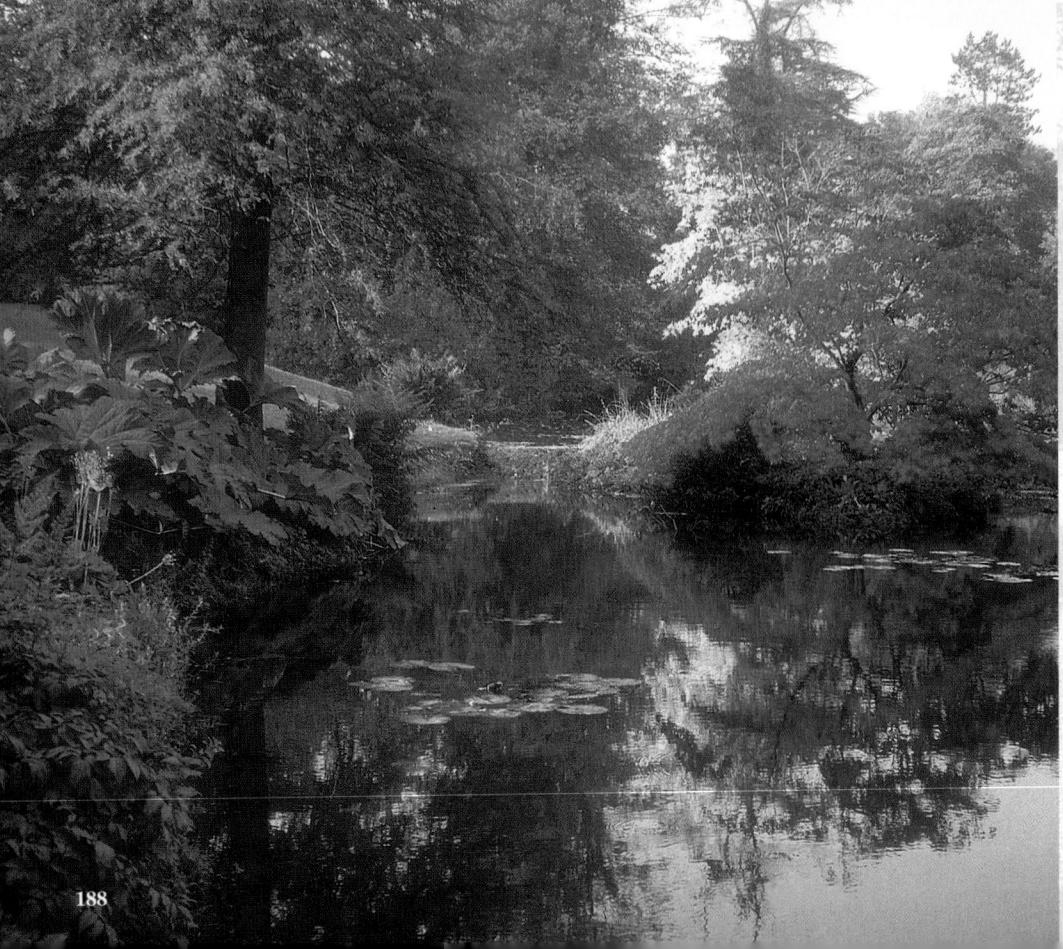

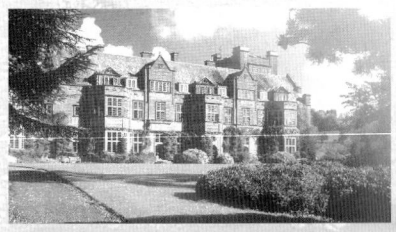

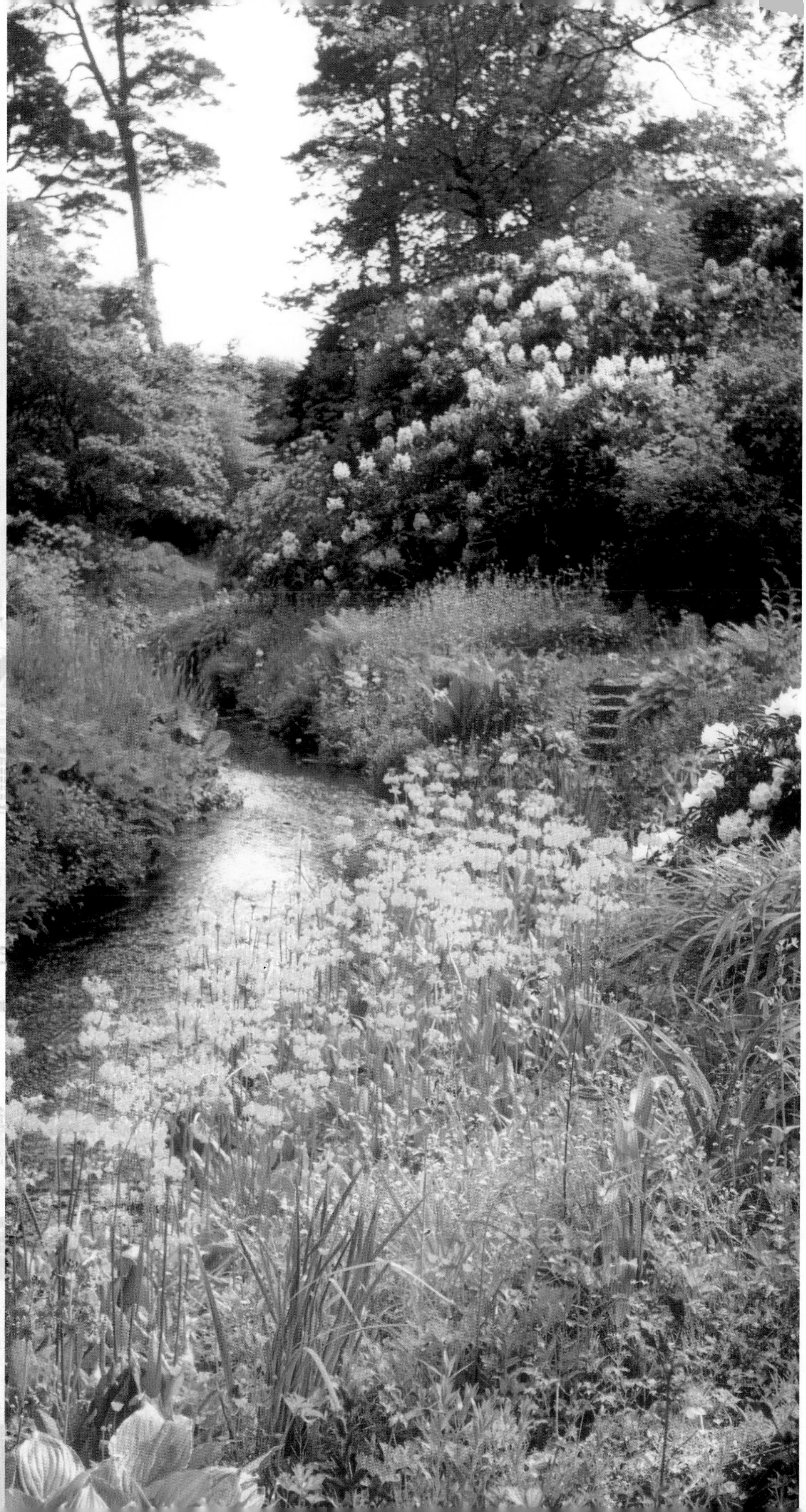

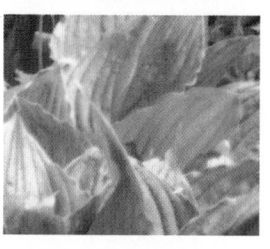

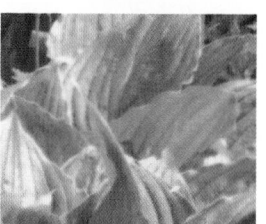

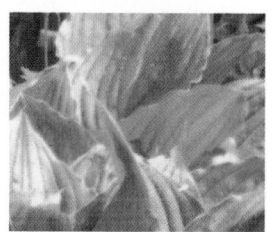

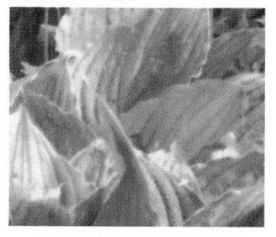

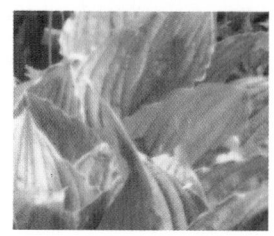

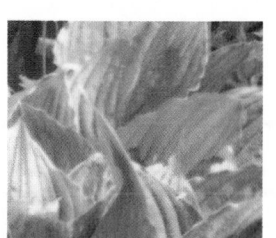

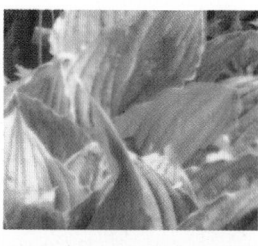

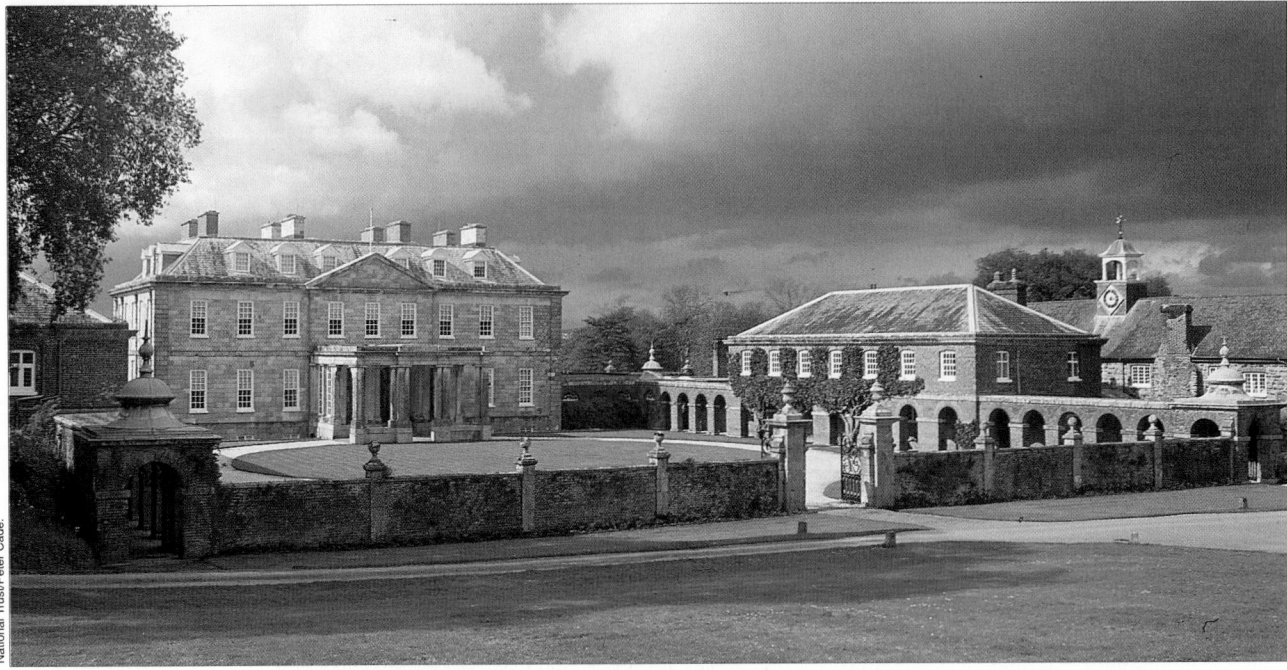

National Trust/Peter Cade.

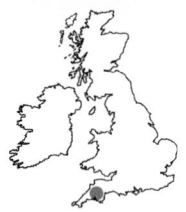

Antony House
Owner: The National Trust

Antony Woodland Garden Owner:
Carew Pole Garden Trust

CONTACT

Antony House
The Administrator
Antony House & Gdn
Torpoint
Cornwall
PL11 2QA

Tel: 01752 812191

Antony Woodland Garden
Mrs Valerie Anderson
Antony
Torpoint
Cornwall
PL11 2QA

Tel: 01752 812364

LOCATION

OS Ref. SX418 564

Antony House and Antony Woodland Garden
5m W of Plymouth via Torpoint car ferry,
2m NW of Torpoint.

ANTONY HOUSE & GDN. & ANTONY WOODLAND GDN.
Torpoint

ANTONY HOUSE AND GARDEN: A superb example of an early 18th century mansion. The main block is faced in lustrous silver-grey stone, flanked by mellow brick pavilions. The ancestral home of the Carew family for nearly 600 years, the house contains a wealth of paintings, tapestries, furniture and embroideries, many linking the great families of Cornwall – set in parkland and fine gardens (including the National Collection of day lilies), overlooking the Lynher river. An 18th century Bath House can be viewed by arrangement.

ANTONY WOODLAND GARDEN: The woodland garden was established in the late 18th century with the assistance of Humphrey Repton. It features numerous varieties of camellias, together with magnolias, rhododendrons, azaleas and other flowering shrubs, interspersed with many fine species of indigenous and exotic trees. A further 50 acres of natural woods bordering the tidal waters of the Lynher provide a number of delightful walks. The Woodland Garden is at its finest in the spring and autumn months.

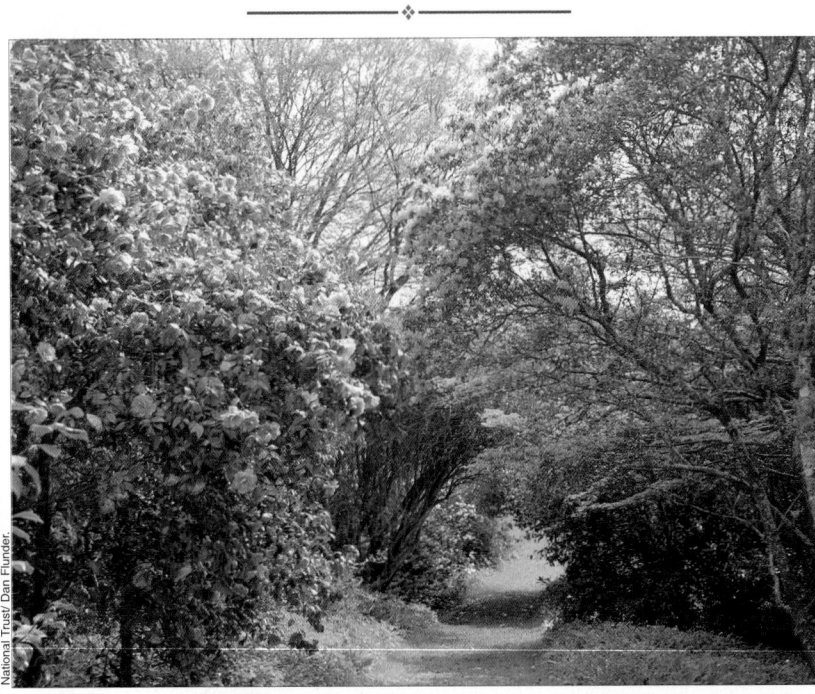

National Trust/Dan Flunder.

Braille guide.

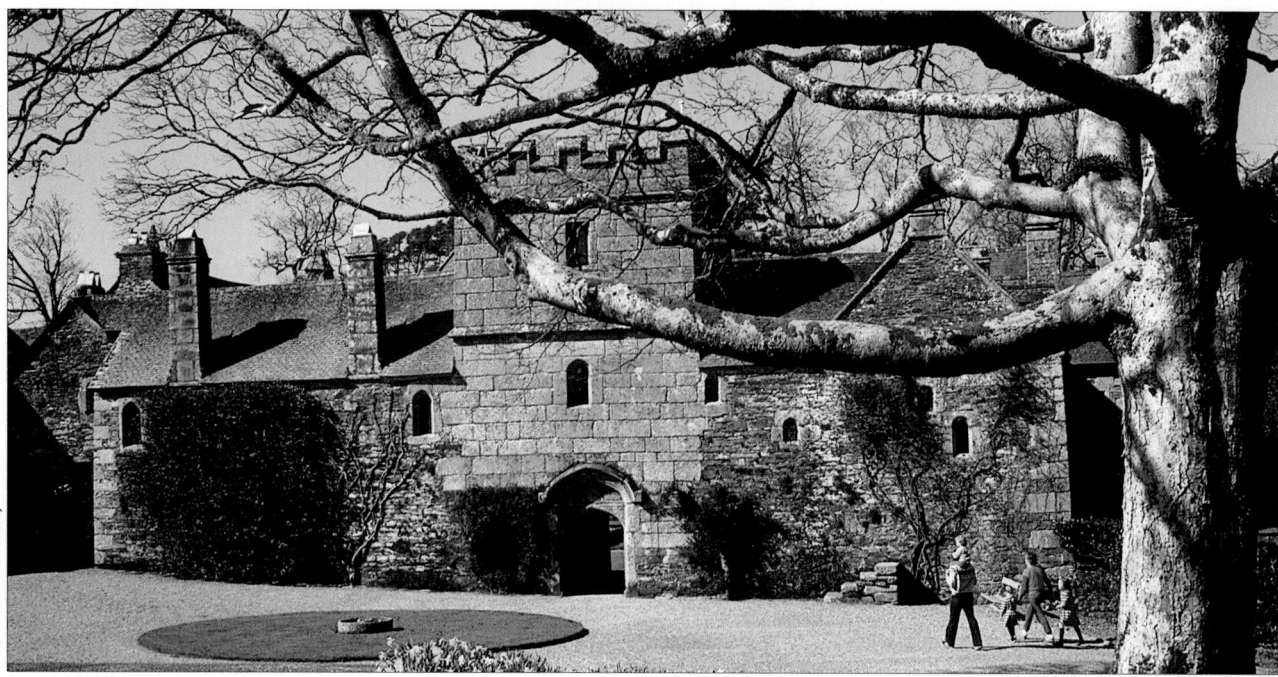

National Trust/Andrew Besley.

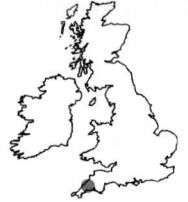

COTEHELE
Saltash

Owner: The National Trust

CONTACT

Lewis Eynon
Property Manager
Cotehele
St Dominick
Saltash
Cornwall
PL12 6TA

Tel: 01579·351346

Fax: 01579 351222

e-mail:
cctlce@smtp.ntrust.org.uk

LOCATION

OS Ref. SX422 685

1m SW of Calstock by foot.
8m S of Tavistock,
4m E of Callington,
15m from Plymouth via the
Tamar bridge at Saltash

Trains: Limited service
from Plymouth to Calstock
(1¼ m uphill)

Boats: Limited (tidal)
service from Plymouth to
Calstock Quay (Plymouth
Boat Cruises)
Tel: 01752 822797

River taxi: Privately run
from Calstock to Cotehele
Quay. Tel: 01579 351346

Buses: Western National
(seasonal variations)
Tel: 01752 222666

COTEHELE, owned by the Edgcumbe family for nearly 600 years, is a fascinating and enchanting estate set on the steep wooded slopes of the River Tamar. Exploring Cotehele's many and various charms provides a full day out for the family and leaves everyone longing to return.

The steep valley garden contains exotic and tender plants which thrive in the mild climate. Remnants of an earlier age include a mediaeval stewpond and domed dovecote, a 15th century chapel and 18th century tower with fine views over the surrounding countryside. A series of more formal gardens, terraces, an orchard and a daffodil meadow surround Cotehele House.

One of the least altered medieval houses in the country, Cotehele is built in local granite, slate and sandstone. Inside the ancient rooms, unlit by electricity, is a fine collection of textiles, tapestries, armour and early dark oak furniture. The chapel contains the oldest

working domestic clock in England, still in its original position.

A walk through the garden and along the river leads to the quay, a busy river port in Victorian times. The National Maritime Museum worked with the National Trust to set up a museum here which explains the vital role that the Tamar played in the local economy. As a living reminder, the restored Tamar sailing barge *Shamrock* (owned jointly by the Trust and the National Maritime Museum) is moored here.

A further walk through woodland along the Morden stream leads to the old estate corn mill which has been restored to working order.

This large estate with many footpaths offers a variety of woodland and countryside walks, opening up new views and hidden places. The Danescombe Valley, with its history of mining and milling, is of particular interest.

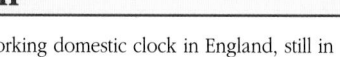

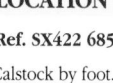

National Trust /Tymn Lintell.

ℹ️ No photography in house. *NPI National Heritage Award winners 1996 & 1999.*

🛍️ Cotehele Quay Gallery offers a wide range of local hand-made arts and crafts.

🍸 Available for up to 90 people.

♿ 2 wheelchairs at Reception. Hall & kitchen accessible. Ramps at house, restaurant and shop. Most of garden is very steep with loose gravel. Riverside walks are flatter (from Cotehele Quay) & Edgcumbe Arms is accessible. WCs near house and at Quay. Parking near house & mill by arrangement.

☕🍴 In Barn restaurant (can be booked) daily (except Fri), Apr - Oct. At the Quay, Edgcumbe Arms offers lighter meals daily, Apr - Oct (plus weekends in March). Both licensed.

🅿️ Near house and garden and at Cotehele Quay. No parking at Mill.

🚶 Groups (15+) must book with Property Manager and receive a coach route (limited to two per day). No groups Sun & BH weekends. Visitors to house limited to 80 at any one time. Please arrive early and be prepared to queue. Avoid dull days early and late in the season. Allow a full day to see estate.

🐕 Under control welcome only on woodland walks. ❄️

OPENING TIMES

House & Restaurant
31 Mar - 4 Nov: Daily
except Fris (but open
Good Fri), 11am - 5pm
(Oct & Nov:
11am - 4.30pm).

Mill
31 Mar - 30 June &
1 Sept - 4 Nov: Daily
except Fris (but open
Good Fri). Jul & Aug: Daily
Jul & Aug: 1 - 6pm
Mar, Jun & Sept: 1 - 5.30pm
Oct & Nov: 1 - 4.30pm.

Garden
All year: daily,
10.30am - dusk.

**Gallery & Tearoom
on Quay**
31 Mar - 4 Nov: Daily,
11am - 5pm.
Gallery: 12 noon - 5pm or
dusk. Nov & Dec:
Christmas openings,
telephone 01579 351494.

ADMISSION

House, Garden & Mill
Adult £6.20
Family Tickets.......£15.50

Pre-booked Groups
...............................£5.20

Garden & Mill only
Adult £3.40
Family £8.50

*Groups must book in
advance with the
Property Manager. No
groups Suns or BHs.

NT members free.
You may join here.

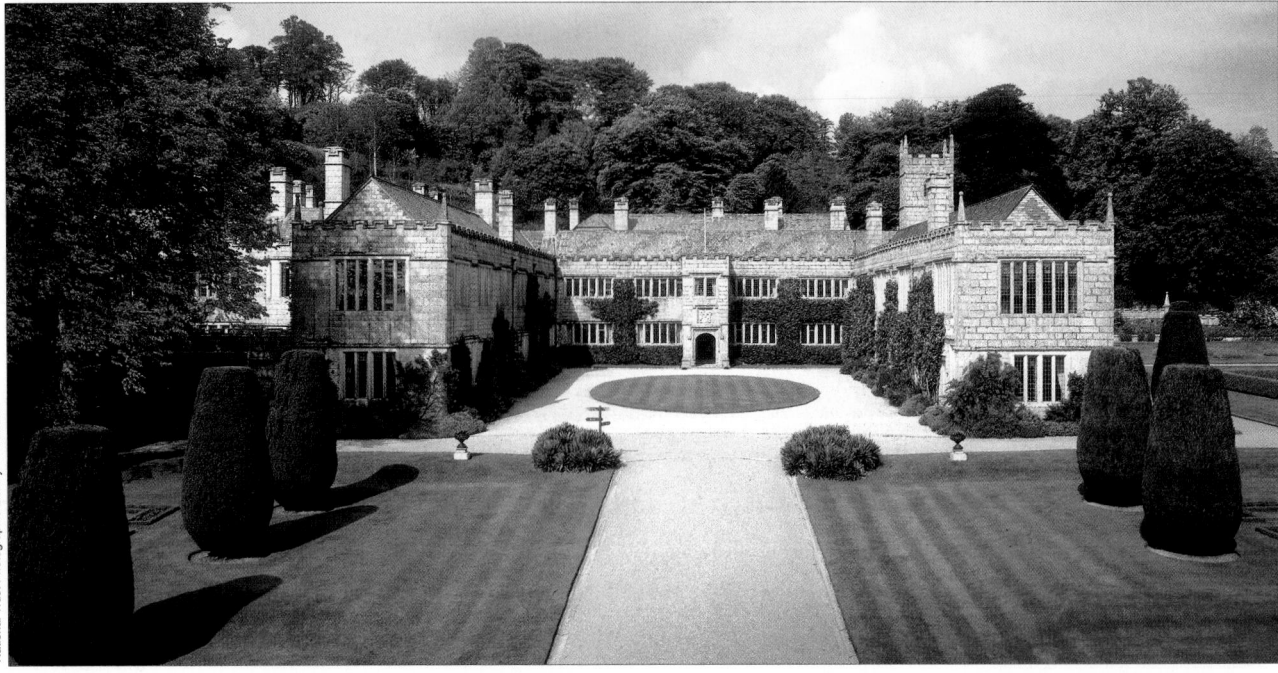

National Trust Photographic Library. R Truman.

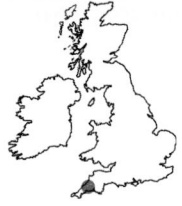

Owner: The National Trust

CONTACT

Property Manager
Lanhydrock
Bodmin
Cornwall
PL30 5AD

Tel: 01208 73320

Fax: 01208 74084

e-mail:
clhlan@smtp.ntrust.org.uk

LOCATION

OS Ref. SX085 636

2¹/₂ m SE of Bodmin,
follow signposts from
either A30, A38 or B3268.

LANHYDROCK
Bodmin

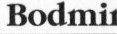

LANHYDROCK is the grandest and most welcoming house in Cornwall, set in a glorious landscape of gardens, parkland and woods overlooking the valley of the River Fowey.

The house dates back to the 17th century but much of it had to be rebuilt after a disastrous fire in 1881 destroyed all but the entrance porch and the north wing, which includes the magnificent Long Gallery with its extraordinary plaster ceiling depicting scenes from the Old Testament. A total of 49 rooms are on show today and together they reflect the entire spectrum of life in a rich and splendid Victorian household, from the many servants' bedrooms and the fascinating complex of kitchens, sculleries and larders to the nursery suite where the Agar-Robartes children lived, learned and played, and the grandeur of the dining room with its table laid and ready.

Surrounding the house on all sides are gardens ranging from formal Victorian parterres to the wooded higher garden where magnificent displays of magnolias, rhododendrons and camellias climb the hillside to merge with the oak and beech woods all around. A famous avenue of ancient beech and sycamore trees, the original entrance drive to the house, runs from the pinnacled 17th century gatehouse down towards the medieval bridge across the Fowey at Respryn.

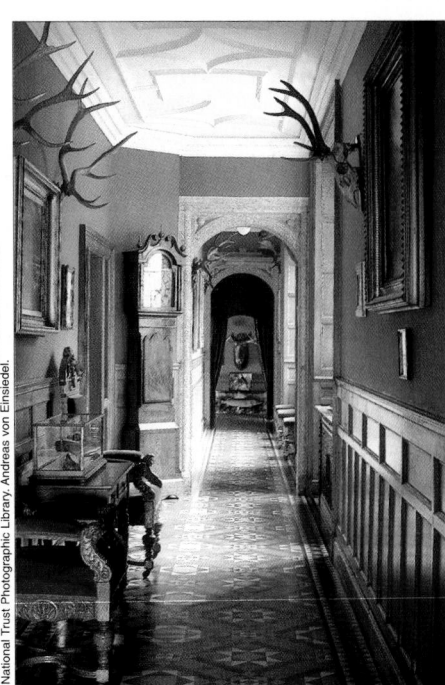

National Trust Photographic Library. Andreas von Einsiedel.

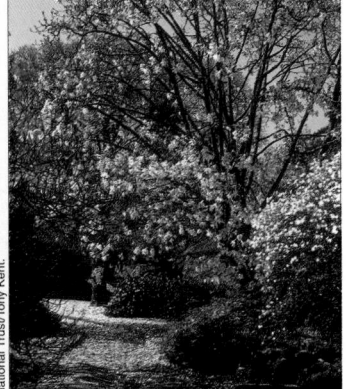

National Trust/Tony Kent.

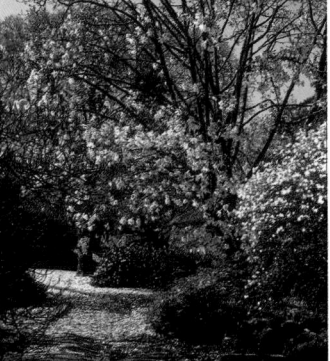

🖼 ✳ ℹ No photography in house.

🍽 By arrangement.

♿ Suitable. Braille guide. WC.

🍴🍽 Licensed restaurant

🐕 In park, on leads. Guide dogs only in house.

♿

🅿 Limited for coaches. ❄

OPENING TIMES

House:

31 Mar - 4 Nov:
Daily except Mons
(but open BH Mons)
31 Mar - 30 Sept:
11am - 5.30pm.
Oct - 4 Nov: 11am - 5pm.

Last admission ¹/₂ hr
before closing.

Garden:

All year: Daily.
17 Feb - 31 Mar
& Oct - 4 Nov:
10am - 5pm.
1 Apr - 30 Sept:
10am - 6pm.
5 Nov - mid-Feb: during
daylight hours.

Refreshments available
17 Feb - 4 Nov: Daily

ADMISSION

**House, Garden &
Grounds**

Adult £6.80
Family £17.00
Groups...................£5.80

**Garden & Grounds
only** £3.70

🎭 **SPECIAL EVENTS**

Please telephone for details.

ANTONY HOUSE & GARDEN
ANTONY WOODLAND GARDEN

See page 190 for full page entry.

BOSVIGO

Tel/Fax: 01872 275774

Bosvigo Lane, Truro, Cornwall TR1 3NH   **e-mail:** bosvigo.plants@virgin.net

Owner: Michael & Wendy Perry   **Contact:** Michael Perry

A series of small, densely planted 'rooms', each with its own colour theme, surround the Georgian house (not open). The mainly herbaceous plantings give non-stop colour from June to the end of September. The Hot Garden will 'blow your socks off' in August. Small specialist nursery attached.

Location: OS Ref. SW815 452. $^3/_4$ m W of Truro city centre. Turn off A390 down Dobbs Lane just W of Sainsbury foodstore.

Opening Times: Mar - end Sept: Thur - Sat, 11am - 6pm.

Admission: Adult £3, Child (5-15yrs) £1. No group concessions.

BURNCOOSE NURSERIES & GARDEN

Gwennap, Redruth, Cornwall TR16 6BJ   **Tel:** 01209 860316   **Fax:** 01209 860011

Owner/Contact: C H Williams   **e-mail:** burncoose@eclipse.co.uk

The Nurseries are set in the 30 acre woodland gardens of Burncoose.

Location: OS Ref. SW742 395. 2m SE of Redruth on main A393 Redruth to Falmouth road between the villages of Lanner and Ponsanooth.

Opening Times: Mon – Sat: 9am - 5pm, Suns, 11am - 5pm. Gardens and Tearooms open all year (except Christmas Day).

Admission: Nurseries: Free. Gardens: Adult/Conc. £2. Children Free. Group tours: £2.50 by arrangement.

CAERHAYS CASTLE & GARDEN

Tel: 01872 501310   **Fax:** 01872 501870

Caerhays, Gorran, St Austell, Cornwall PL26 6LY   **e-mail:** estateoffice@caerhays.co.uk

Owner: F J Williams Esq   **Contact:** Miss A B Mayes

One of the very few Nash built castles still left standing – situated within approximately 60 acres of informal woodland gardens created by J C Williams, who sponsored plant hunting expeditions to China at the turn of the century. Noted for its camellias, magnolias, rhododendrons and oaks. English Heritage listing - Grade I: Outstanding.

Location: OS Ref. SW972 415. S coast of Cornwall – between Mevagissey and Portloe. 9m SW of St Austell.

Opening Times: House: 19 Mar - 27 Apr: Mon - Fri (excluding BHs), 2 - 4pm, booking recommended. Gardens: 12 Mar - 18 May: Mon - Fri, 10am - 4pm. Charity openings (gardens only): 25 Mar, 15 Apr & 7 May: 10am - 4pm.

Admission: House: £3.50. Gardens: £3.50. House & Gardens: £6. Guided group tours by Head Gardener £4.50. These can be arranged outside normal opening times.

CHYSAUSTER ANCIENT VILLAGE

Tel: 07831 757934

Nr Newmill, Penzance, Cornwall TR20 8XA

Owner: English Heritage   **Contact:** The Custodian

On a windy hillside, overlooking the wild and spectacular coast, is this deserted Romano-Cornish village with a 'street' of eight well preserved houses, each comprising a number of rooms around an open court.

Location: OS203 Ref. SW473 350. 2$^1/_2$ m NW of Gulval off B3311.

Opening Times: 1 Apr - 31 Oct: daily, 10am - 6pm (5pm in Oct). Winter: closed.

Admission: Adult £1.70, Child 90p, Conc. £1.30. 15% discount for groups (11+).

P No coaches.   On leads.   Telephone for details.

CHYVERTON

Tel: 01872 540324   **Fax:** 01872 540648

Zelah, Truro, Cornwall TR4 9HD

Owner/Contact: Nigel Holman

The garden contains one of the finest collections of woody plants in private hands originating from all the temperate regions of the world, built up over the past 75 years by the Holman family. Exceptional magnolias. All growing in the setting of a Georgian landscape garden, creating 'The Magic Jungle of Chyverton' *(Tradescant - The Garden)*.

Location: OS Ref. SW797 512. A30, 20m W of Bodmin, 8m E of Redruth signed 1m W of Zelah.

Opening Times: 1 Mar - 30 Sept: by appointment.

Admission: Groups of 1-20 £4 and 21+ £3.50. Child under 16yrs Free.

Not suitable.   Lunch in House (II*) by arrangement (20 max).   Obligatory.   P Limited for coaches.   In grounds on leads.

COTEHELE

See page 191 for full page entry.

GLENDURGAN GARDEN

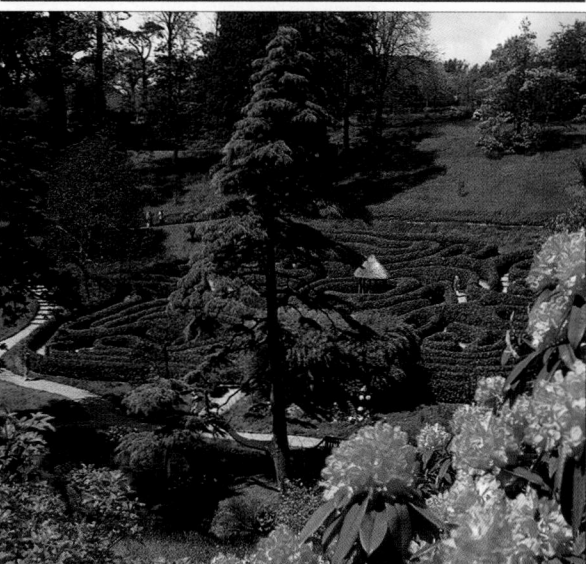

National Trust/David Hastilow

MAWNAN SMITH, FALMOUTH, CORNWALL TR11 5JZ

Owner: The National Trust   *Contact: Reception*

Tel: 01326 250906 (opening hours) or 01872 862090   **Fax:** 01872 865808

A valley garden of great beauty with fine trees, shrubs and water gardens. The laurel maze, recently restored, is an unusual and popular feature. The garden runs down to the tiny village of Durgan and its beach on the Helford River.

Location: OS Ref. SW772 277. 4m SW of Falmouth, $^1/_2$m SW of Mawnan Smith, on road to Helford Passage. 1m E of Trebah Garden.

Opening Times: 17 Feb - 3 Nov: Tue - Sat & BH Mons (closed Good Fri), 10.30am - 5.30pm. Last admission 4.30pm.

Admission: £3.60, Family £9. Pre-arranged groups: £3.

Braille guide.

GODOLPHIN

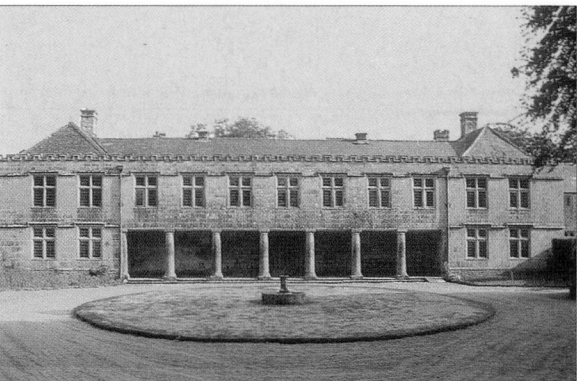

GODOLPHIN CROSS, HELSTON, CORNWALL TR13 9RE

Owner: Mrs L M P Schofield   *Contact: Mrs Joanne Schofield*

Tel/Fax: 01736 763194   **e-mail:** godo@euphony.net

A romantic Tudor and Stuart mansion, commenced in c1475. The development of the Godolphin family's courtly ambition and taste is beautifully expressed in the evolving architecture of the house. Exploitation of tin provided the wealth for this family of soldiers, entrepreneurs, poets and government officials. Birthplace of Queen Anne's Lord Treasurer. The large, compartmented Side Garden dates from the late 15th century also, though it grew out of an early 14th century Castle garden (still gardened). Good 16th and 17th century English Oak furniture. 1731 painting of the Godolphin Arabian by John Wotton and pictures by American impressionist Elmer Schofield. Godolphin is undergoing a programme of English Heritage funded repairs but works will cease from Easter to October 2001. Adjacent walks on the National Trust estate.

Location: OS Ref. SW602 318. Breage, Helston. On minor road from Breage to Townshend.

Opening Times: May - Jun: Thurs & Suns, 2 - 5pm. Jul, Aug & Sept: Thur & Fri & Suns, 2 - 5pm. Open BHs from Easter - end Sept: 2 - 5pm. Group bookings and tours by prior arrangement.

Admission: Adults £3, Child £1

Limited.   P Guide dogs only.

THE JAPANESE GARDEN & BONSAI NURSERY

Tel: 01637 860116

e-mail: rob@thebonsainursery.com   **Fax:** 01637 860887

St Mawgan, Nr Newquay, Cornwall TR8 4ET   **Owner/Contact:** Mr & Mrs Hore

Authentic Japanese Garden set in 1¹/₂ acres.

Location: OS Ref. SW873 660. Follow road signs from A3059 & B3276.

Opening Times: Summer: Daily 10am - 6pm. WInter: 10am - 5.30pm. Closed Christmas Day - New Year's Day.

Admission: Adult £2.50, Child £1. Groups (10+): £2.

KEN CARO

Tel: 01579 362446

Bicton, Liskeard PL14 5RF   **Owner/Contact:** Mr and Mrs K R Willcock

4 acre plantsman's garden.

Location: OS Ref. SX313 692. 5m NE of of Liskeard.

Opening Times: 15 Apr - 30 Aug, Sun - Thur, 2 - 6pm.

Admission: Adult £2.50, Child £1.

LANHYDROCK ✿

See page 192 for full page entry.

LAUNCESTON CASTLE ▢

Tel: 01566 772365

Castle Lodge, Launceston, Cornwall PL15 7DR

Owner: English Heritage   **Contact:** The Custodian

Set on the motte of the original Norman castle and commanding the town and surrounding countryside. The shell keep and tower survive of this medieval castle which controlled the main route into Cornwall. An exhibition shows the early history.

Location: OS201 Ref. SX330 846. In Launceston.

Opening Times: 1 Apr - 31 Oct: daily, 10am - 6pm (5pm in Oct). Winter: Fri - Sun, 10am - 4pm. Closed 24 - 26 Dec & 1 Jan.

Admission: Adult £1.90, Child 90p, Conc. £1.50. 15% discount for groups (11+).

📷   ♿ Grounds suitable.   📷   🅿 Limited.   🐕 In grounds, on leads.   🛡 Tel. for details.

MOUNT EDGCUMBE HOUSE & COUNTRY PARK

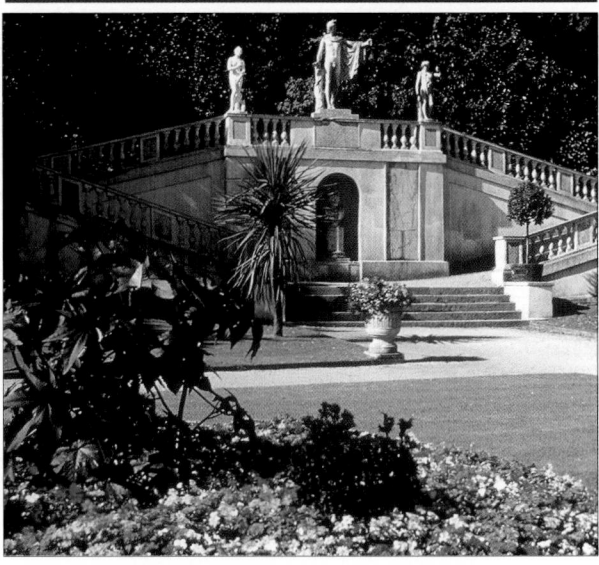

CREMYLL, TORPOINT, CORNWALL PL10 IHZ

Owner: *Cornwall County & Plymouth City Councils*   **Contact:** *Cynthia Gaskell Brown*

Tel: 01752 822236   **Fax:** 01752 822199

Tudor home of Earls of Mount Edgcumbe, set in historic 18th century gardens on the dramatic sea-girt Rame peninsula. Wild fallow deer, follies, forts; national camellia collection. One of the Great Gardens of Cornwall.

Location: OS Ref. SX452 527. 10m W of Plymouth via Torpoint.

Opening Times: House and Earls' Garden: 1 Apr - 30 Sept: Wed - Sun & BH Mons, 11am - 4.30pm. Country Park: All year, daily 8am - dusk.

Admission: Adult £4.50, Child (5-15) £2.25, Conc. £3.50, Family (2+2 or 1+3) £10, Season Ticket £7.50. Groups: £3.50. Park: Free.

📷   ♿   🍴 Licensed.   🅿   🐕 Grounds only.   ❄

THE LOST GARDENS OF HELIGAN

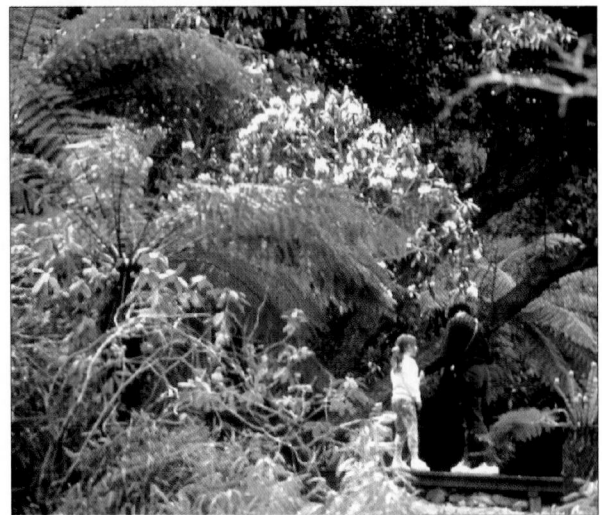

PENTEWAN, ST AUSTELL, CORNWALL PL26 6EN

Owner: *Mr T Smit*   **Contact:** *Mr C A Howlett*

Tel: 01726 845100   **Fax:** 01726 845101   **e-mail:** info@heligan.com

These award-winning Gardens are 80 acres of superb pleasure grounds together with a magnificent complex of four walled gardens and kitchen garden, all being restored to their former glory as a living museum of 19th century horticulture. An Italian Garden, Fern Ravine, Crystal Grotto, Summerhouses, Rides, Lawns and a 20 acre sub-tropical "Jungle Garden" are just some of the delights of this "Sleeping Beauty".

Location: OS Ref. SX000 465. 5m SW of St Austell. 2m NW of Mevagissey. Take the B3273 to Mevagissey – follow tourist signs.

Opening Times: Daily except 24 & 25 Dec: 10am - 6pm. Last adm. 4.30pm.

Admission: Adult: £5.50. Child (5-15) £2.50, OAP £5. Family £15. Groups: Adult £5, OAP £4.50. Children under 5 Free. Groups and tours by prior arrangement.

📷   🍴   ♿   📷   🅿   🐕 On leads only.   ❄

PENCARROW 🏛

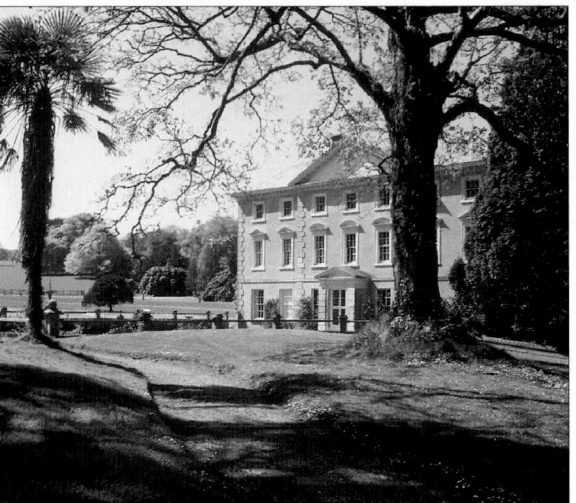

BODMIN, CORNWALL PL30 3AG

Owner: *Molesworth-St Aubyn family*   **Contact:** *The Administrator*

Tel/Fax: 01208 841369   **e-mail:** pencarrow@aol.com

Still owned and lived in by the family. Georgian house and listed gardens. Superb collection of pictures, furniture and porcelain. Marked walks through 50 acres of beautiful formal and woodland gardens, Victorian rockery, Italian garden, over 700 different varieties of rhododendrons, lake and ice house.

Location: OS Ref. SX040 711. Between Bodmin and Wadebridge. 4m NW of Bodmin off A389 & B3266 at Washaway.

Opening Times: 1 Apr - 14 Oct: Sun - Thur, 1.30 - 5pm. Spring BH through to Summer BH opens 11am.

Admission: House & Garden: Adult £5, Child £2.50. Garden only: Adult £2.50, Child Free. Groups (throughout year by arrangement): House & Garden: £4.

ℹ Craft centre, small childrens' play area, self-pick soft fruit.   ❄
🍴 By arrangement.   ♿   📷 Licensed.   🐕 Grounds only. 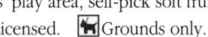

PENDENNIS CASTLE

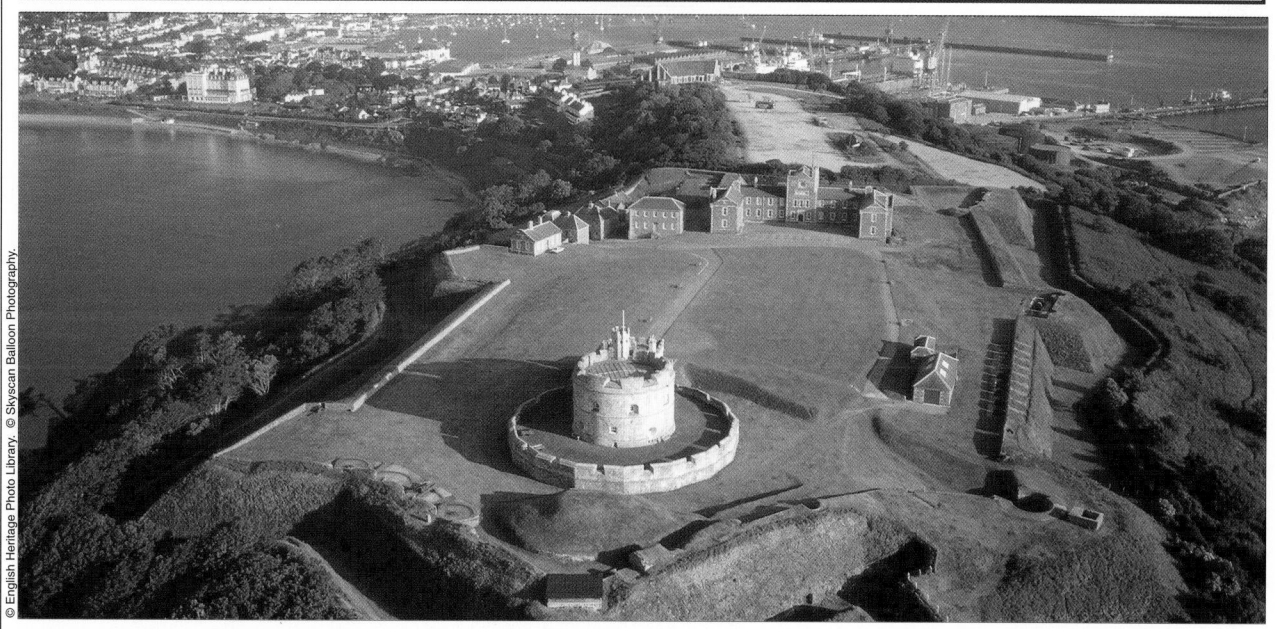

© English Heritage Photo Library. © Skyscan Balloon Photography.

FALMOUTH, CORNWALL TR11 4LP

Owner: *English Heritage*   **Contact:** *The Head Custodian*

Tel: 01326 316594

Pendennis and its neighbour, St Mawes Castle, face each other across the mouth of the estuary of the River Fal. Built by Henry VIII in 16th century as protection against threat of attack and invasion from France. Extended and adapted over the years to meet the changing threats to national security from the French and Spanish and continued right through to World War II. It withstood five months of siege during the Civil War before becoming the penultimate Royalist Garrison to surrender on the mainland. Pendennis today stands as a landmark, with fine sea views and excellent site facilities including exhibitions, a museum and guardhouse.

Location: OS204, Ref SW824 318. On Pendennis Head.

Opening Times: 1 Apr - 31 Oct: daily, 10am - 6pm or dusk if earlier. 1 Nov - 31 Mar: daily, 10am - 4pm. Closed 24 - 26 Dec.

Admission: Adult £3.80, Child £1.90, Conc. £2.90. 15% discount for groups of 11+.

⬚ ♿Partially suitable. ▣ ⬚By arrangement. 🅿Ample. ▮
🐾In grounds only. 🔔 ❄ ⬚Tel. for details.

PINE LODGE GARDENS

Tel/Fax: 01726 73500

Cuddra, St Austell, Cornwall PL25 3RQ   **Owner/Contact:** Mr & Mrs R H J Clemo

30 acre estate with a wide range of 5,500 plants.

Location: OS Ref. SX044 527. Signposted on A390.

Opening Times: April - September: Wed - Sun & Bank Holidays, 10am - 5pm.

Admission: Adult £3.50, Child half price.

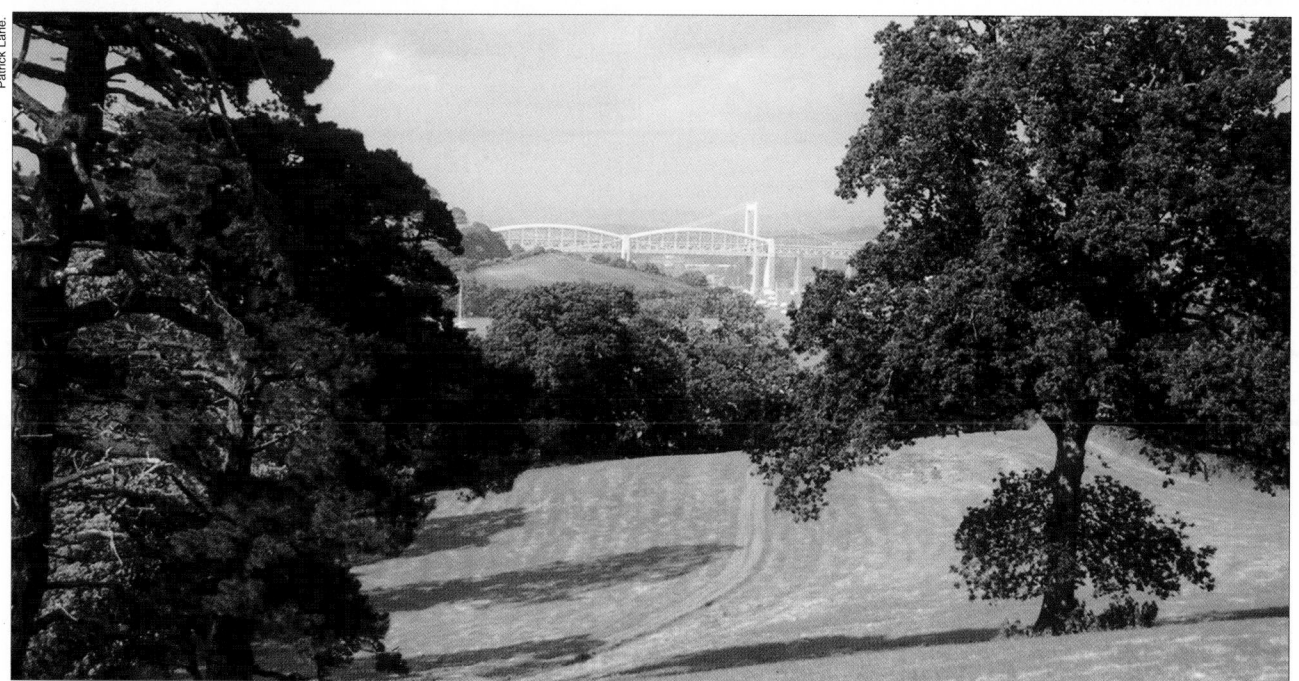

Patrick Lane.

Antony Woodland Garden, Cornwall.

PRIDEAUX PLACE

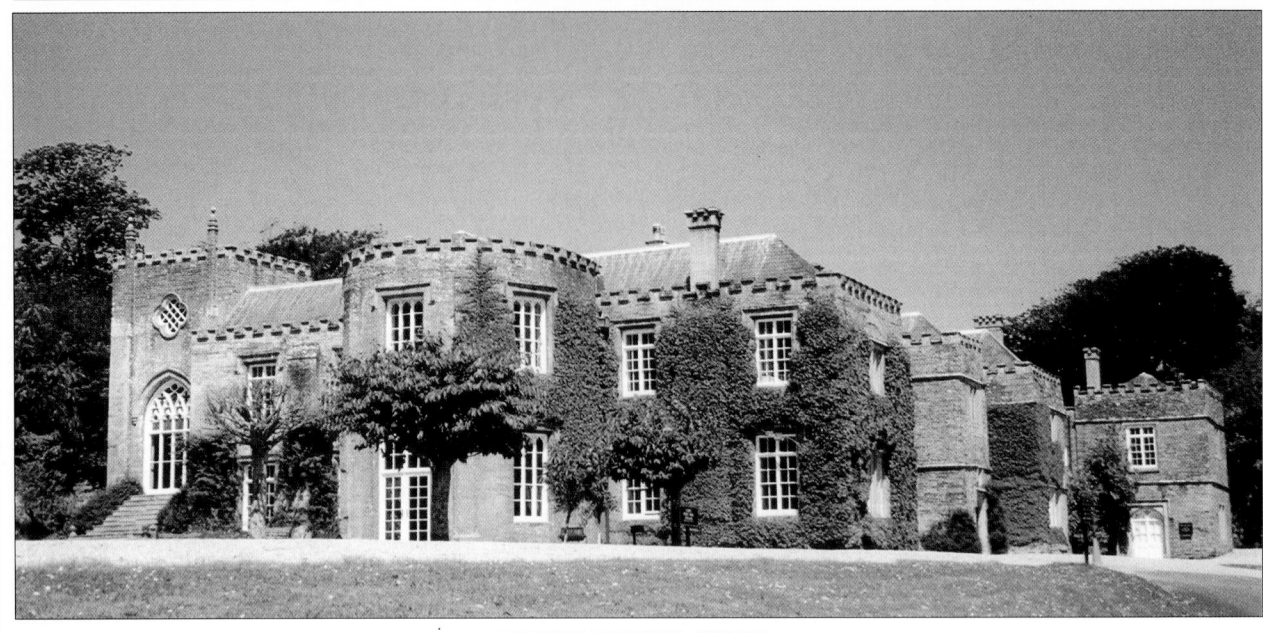

PADSTOW, CORNWALL PL28 8RP

Owner/Contact: Peter Prideaux-Brune Esq

Tel: 01841 532411   **Fax:** 01841 532945

Tucked away above the busy port of Padstow, the home of the Prideaux family for over 400 years, is surrounded by gardens and wooded grounds overlooking a deer park and the Camel estuary to the moors beyond. The house still retains its 'E' shape Elizabethan front and contains fine paintings and furniture as well as an exhibition reflecting its emergence as a major international film location. The impressive outbuildings have been restored in recent years and the 16th century plaster ceiling in the great chamber has been uncovered for the first time since 1760.

Location: OS Ref. SW913 756. 5m from A39 Newquay/Wadebridge link road. Signposted by Historic House signs.
Opening Times: Easter Sun 15 - 24 Apr & Sun 27 May - 4 Oct: Sun - Thur, 1.30 - 5pm. Open all year for groups 15+ by arrangement.
Admission: Adult £5, accompanied children £2. Grounds only: Adult £2 Child £1. Groups £4.

By arrangement.   Ground floor & grounds suitable.   By arrangement.   In grounds, on leads.

RESTORMEL CASTLE   **Tel:** 01208 872687

Lostwithiel, Cornwall PL22 0BD

Owner: English Heritage   **Contact:** The Custodian

Perched on a high mound, surrounded by a deep moat, the huge circular keep of this splendid Norman castle survives in remarkably good condition. It is still possible to make out the ruins of Restormel's Keep Gate, Great Hall and even the kitchens and private rooms.
Location: OS200 Ref. SX104 614. 1¹/₂ m N of Lostwithiel off A390.
Opening Times: 1 Apr - 31 Oct: daily, 10am - 6pm (5pm in Oct). Winter: closed.
Admission: Adult £1.80, Child 90p, Conc. £1.30. 15% discount for groups (11+).

Grounds suitable.   Limited for coaches.   In grounds, on leads.   Telephone for details.

ST CATHERINE'S CASTLE   **Tel:** 0117 9750700

Fowey, Cornwall

Owner: English Heritage   **Contact:** The South West Regional Office

A small fort built by Henry VIII to defend Fowey harbour, with fine views of the coastline and river estuary.
Location: OS200 Ref. SX118 508. ³/₄ m SW of Fowey along footpath off A3082.
Opening Times: Any reasonable time.
Admission: Free.

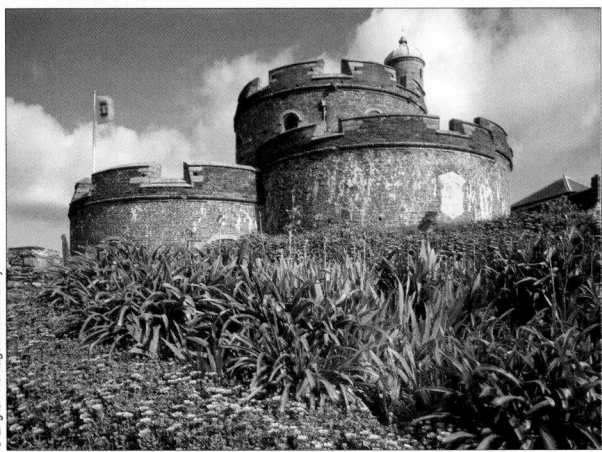

Patrick Lane.

Cornish Engines.

ST MAWES CASTLE

ST MAWES, CORNWALL TR2 3AA

Owner: English Heritage   *Contact:* The Head Custodian

Tel: 01326 270526

The pretty fishing village of St Mawes is home to this castle. On the opposite headland to Pendennis Castle, St Mawes shares the task of watching over the mouth of the River Fal as it has done since Henry VIII built it as a defence against the French. With three huge circular bastions shaped like clover leaves, St Mawes was designed to cover every possible angle of approach. It is the finest example of Tudor military architecture. The castle offers views of St Mawes' little boat-filled harbour, the passenger ferry tracking across the Fal, and the splendid coastline which featured in the *Poldark* TV series. Also the start of some delightful walks along the coastal path.
Location: OS204 Ref. SW842 328. W of St Mawes on A3078.
Opening Times: 1 Apr - 31 Oct: daily, 10am - 6pm (5pm in Oct). Winter: 1 Nov - 31 Mar: Wed - Sun, 10am - 4pm. Closed 1 - 2pm & 24 - 26 Dec & 1 Jan.
Admission: Adult £2.70, Child £1.40, Conc. £2.20. 15% discount for groups (11+).

Grounds suitable. WC.   Limited.   Guide dogs only.   Telephone for details.

© English Heritage Photo Library.

South West England

ST MICHAEL'S MOUNT

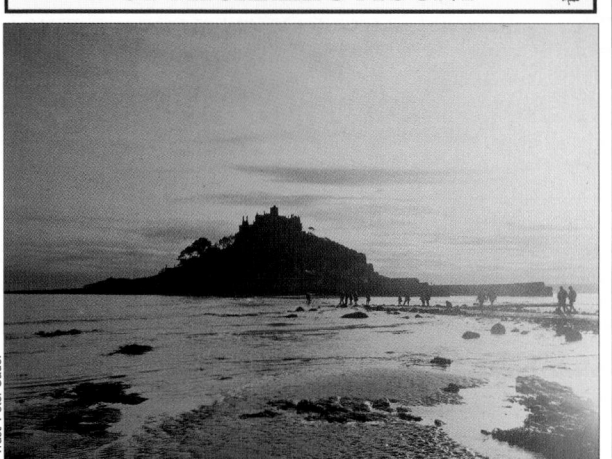

MARAZION, Nr PENZANCE, CORNWALL TR17 0EF

Owner: *The National Trust*   **Contact:** *The Manor Office*

Tel: 01736 710507 (710265 tide & ferry information) **Fax:** 01736 711544

This magical island is the jewel in Cornwall's crown. The great granite crag which rises from the waters of Mount's Bay is surmounted by an embattled medieval castle, home of the St Aubyn family for over 300 years. The Mount's flanks are softened by lush sub-tropical vegetation and on the water's edge there is a harbourside community which features shops and restaurants.

Location: OS Ref. SW515 300. At Marazion there is access on foot over causeway at low tide. In summer months there is a ferry at high tide. 4m E of Penzance.

Opening Times: 2 Apr - 2 Nov: Mon - Fri, 10.30am - 5.30pm. Last admission 4.45pm. 3 Nov - end Mar: guided tours as tide, weather and circumstances permit. Please telephone. Shops & restaurant: 2 Apr - 2 Nov: daily (restaurant closed Sats in Oct). The castle & grounds are open most weekends during the season. These are special charity days when National Trust members are asked to pay admission.

Admission: Adult £4.50, Family £12. Pre-arranged groups £4.10.

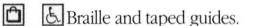 Braille and taped guides. Guide dogs only.

TINTAGEL CASTLE

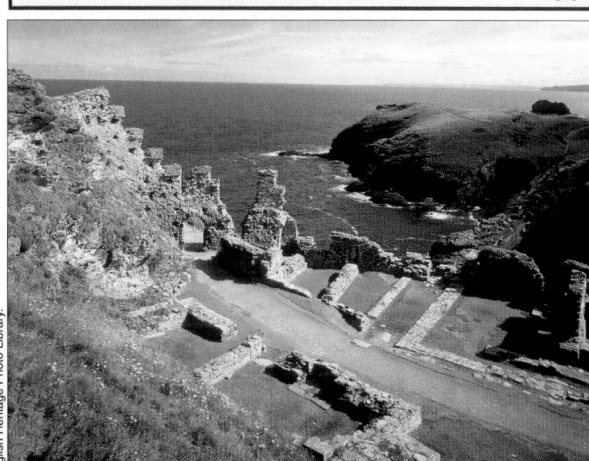

TINTAGEL, CORNWALL PL34 0HE

Owner: *English Heritage*   **Contact:** *The Head Custodian*

Tel: 01840 770328

The spectacular setting for the legendary castle of King Arthur is the wild and windswept Cornish coast. Clinging precariously to the edge of the cliff face are the extensive ruins of a medieval royal castle, built by Richard, Earl of Cornwall, younger brother of Henry III. Also used as a Cornish stronghold by subsequent Earls of Cornwall. Despite extensive excavations since the 1930s, Tintagel Castle remains one of the most spectacular and romantic spots in the entire British Isles. Destined to remain a place of mystery and romance, Tintagel will always jealously guard its marvellous secrets.

Location: OS200 Ref. SX048 891. On Tintagel Head, $^{1}/_{2}$ m along uneven track from Tintagel.

Opening Times: 1 Apr - 31 Oct: daily, 11am - 6pm (5pm in Oct). 1 Nov - 31 Mar: daily, 10am - 4pm. Closed 24 - 26 Dec & 1 Jan.

Admission: Adult £3, Child £1.50, Conc. £2.20. 15% discount for groups (11+).

[i] No vehicles. Telephone for details.

TATE ST IVES

Tel: 01736 796226 **Fax:** 01736 794480

Porthmeor Beach, St Ives, Cornwall TR26 1TG

Owner: Tate Gallery   **Contact:** Ina Cole

Changing displays from the Tate Gallery collection of British and modern art, focusing on the modern movement that St Ives is famous for. Also displays of new work by contemporary artists. Events programme, guided tours, gallery shop, rooftop café, with spectacular views over the beach. The Tate also manages the Barbara Hepworth Museum and Sculpture Garden in St Ives.

Location: OS Ref. SW515 407. Situated by Porthmeor Beach.

Opening Times: Tues - Sun, 10.30am - 5.30pm. Also open Mons in Jul/Aug & Bank Holidays.

Admission: Adult £3.95, Conc £2.50. Groups (10 - 30): Adult £2.50, Conc. £1.50.

 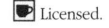 Licensed. 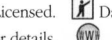 Daily. Nearby. 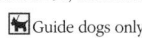 Guide dogs only. Telephone for details.

TINTAGEL OLD POST OFFICE

Tel: 01840 770024 or 01208 74281

Tintagel, Cornwall PL34 0DB

Owner: The National Trust   **Contact:** The Custodian

One of the most characterful buildings in Cornwall, and a house of great antiquity, this small 14th century manor is full of charm and interest.

Location: OS Ref. SX056 884. In the centre of Tintagel.

Opening Times: 31 Mar - 4 Nov: daily, 11am - 5.30pm (closes 4pm from Oct - 4 Nov).

Admission: Adult £2.30, Child £1.10. Family £5.70. Pre-arranged groups £1.80.

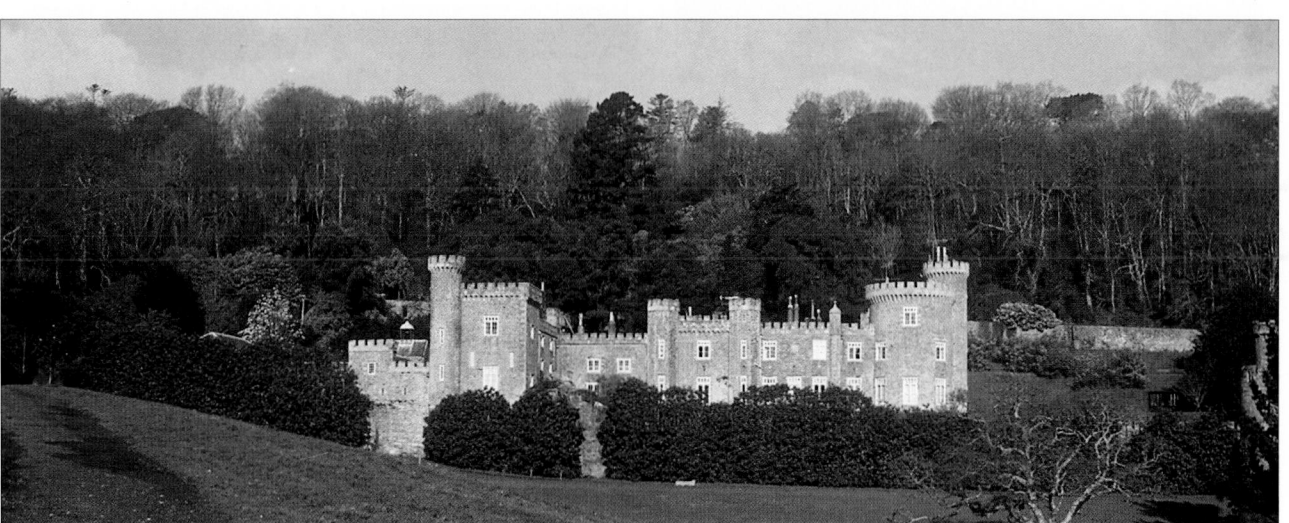

Caerhays Castle & Garden, Cornwall.

TREBAH GARDEN

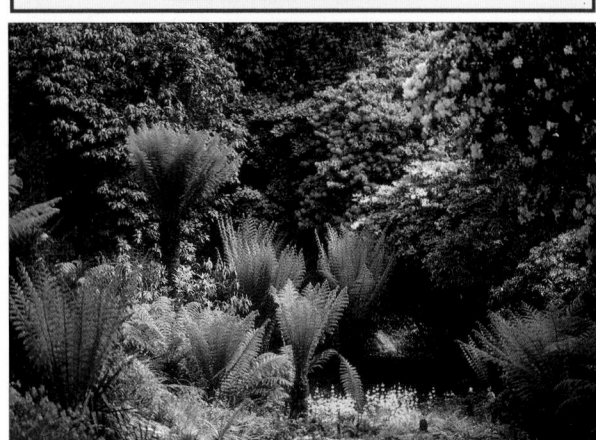

MAWNAN SMITH, Nr FALMOUTH, CORNWALL TR11 5JZ

Owner: Trebah Garden Trust   *Contact:* Vera Woodcroft

Tel: 01326 250448   **Fax:** 01326 250781   **e-mail:** mail@trebah-garden.co.uk

Steeply wooded 25 acre sub-tropical ravine garden falls 200 feet from 18th century house to private beach on Helford River. Stream cascading over waterfalls through ponds full of Koi Carp and exotic water plants winds through 2 acres of blue and white hydrangeas and spills out over beach. Huge Australian tree ferns and palms mingle with shrubs of ever-changing colours and scent beneath over-arching canopy of 100 year old rhododendrons and magnolias. A paradise for plantsmen, artists and families.

Location: OS Ref. SW768 275. 4m SW of Falmouth, 1m SW of Mawnan Smith. Follow brown and white tourism signs from Treliever Cross roundabout at A39/A394 junction through Mawnan Smith to Trebah.

Opening Times: All year: daily, 10.30am - 5pm (last admission).

Admission: Adult £3.75, Child (5-15yrs)/Disabled £2, OAP £3.50. Child under 5yrs Free, Groups (12 - 50): Adult £3.25, Child £1.75. RHS members have free entry all year, NT members have free entry 1 Nov - end Feb.

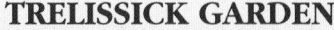
Partially suitable.   By arrangement.   In grounds, on leads.

TRELISSICK GARDEN

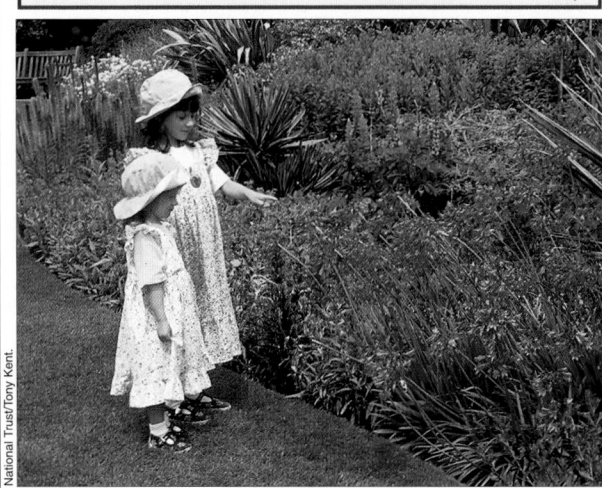

FEOCK, TRURO, CORNWALL TR3 6QL

Owner: The National Trust   *Contact:* The Property Manager

Tel: 01872 862090   **Fax:** 01872 865808

A garden and estate of rare tranquil beauty with glorious maritime views over Carrick Roads to Falmouth Harbour. The tender and exotic shrubs make this garden attractive in all seasons. Extensive park and woodland walks beside the river. There is an Art and Craft Gallery.

Location: OS Ref. SW837 396. 4m S of Truro by road, on both sides of B3289 above King Harry Ferry.

Opening Times: 17 Feb - 4 Nov: daily. Apr - Sept: Mon - Sat, 10.30am - 5.30pm, Suns, 12.30 - 5.30pm. Feb, Mar, Oct & Nov: Mon - Sat, 10.30am - 5pm, Suns, 12.30 - 5pm. Restaurant: as above but opens 12 noon on Suns. Shop, Art & Craft Gallery & Plant Sales: 17 Feb - 23 Dec: daily.

Admission: Adult £4.40, Family £11. Pre-arranged group £3.70. £1.50 car park fee (refundable on admission).

By arrangement.   By arrangement. In park on leads; only guide dogs in garden.

TRELOWARREN HOUSE & CHAPEL

Tel: 01326 221366

Mawgan-in-Meneage, Helston, Cornwall TR12 6AD

Owner: Sir Ferrers Vyvyan Bt   **Contact:** The Warden

Tudor and 17th century house. Chapel and main rooms of house are open to the public on a limited basis.

Location: OS Ref. SW721 238. 6m S of Helston, off B3293 to St Keverne.

Opening Times: Please telephone for details.

Admission: Please telephone for details.

TRENANCE HERITAGE COTTAGES

Tel/Fax: 01637 873922

Trenance Gardens, Newquay, Cornwall

Owner: Restormel Borough Council   **Contact:** Derek James Esq

The oldest cottages in Newquay now house an exhibition of life in the early 1900s, a traditional shop and photographic exhibition.

Location: OS Ref. SW815 612. In Newquay.

Opening Times: Mar - Oct: daily, 10am - 4pm. Closed on Sundays.

Admission: Adult £1, Child under 12yrs Free.

TRENGWAINTON GARDEN

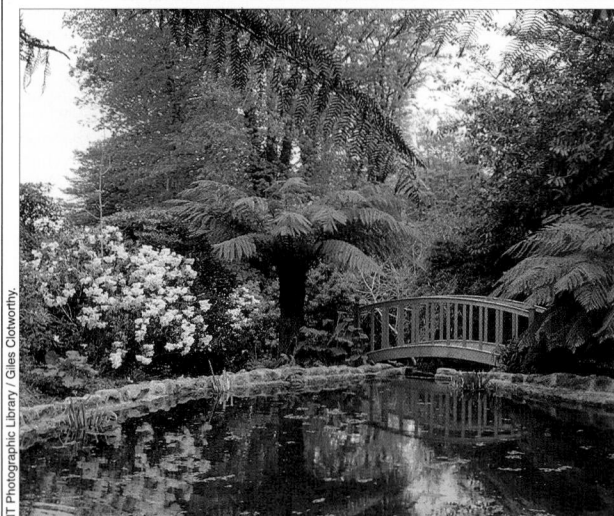

PENZANCE, CORNWALL TR20 8RZ

Owner: The National Trust   *Contact:* The Property Manager

Tel/Fax: 01736 362297

This large shrub garden, with many plants brought back from 1920s' plant-gathering expeditions, is a beautiful place throughout the year and a plantsman's delight. Splendid views over Mount's Bay can be gained from summer-houses at either end of the restored terrace. The walled gardens have many tender plants which cannot be grown in the open anywhere else in England and restoration of the kitchen gardens is underway. The new tea-house serves a full range of snacks and meals.

Location: OS Ref. SW445 315. 2m NW of Penzance, $^1/_2$ m W of Heamoor on Penzance - Morvah road (B3312), $^1/_2$ m off St. Just road (A3071).

Opening Times: 18 Feb - 4 Nov: Sun - Thur & Good Fri, 10am - 5.30pm. NB: Closes 5pm in Feb, Mar, Oct & Nov. Last admission $^1/_2$ hr before closing.

Admission: Adult £3.60. Family £9. Pre-booked groups: £2.90.

Partially suitable.   Tea-house.   On leads.

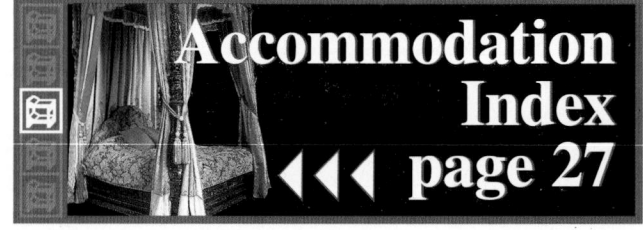
Accommodation Index ◀◀◀ page 27

South West England

TRERICE

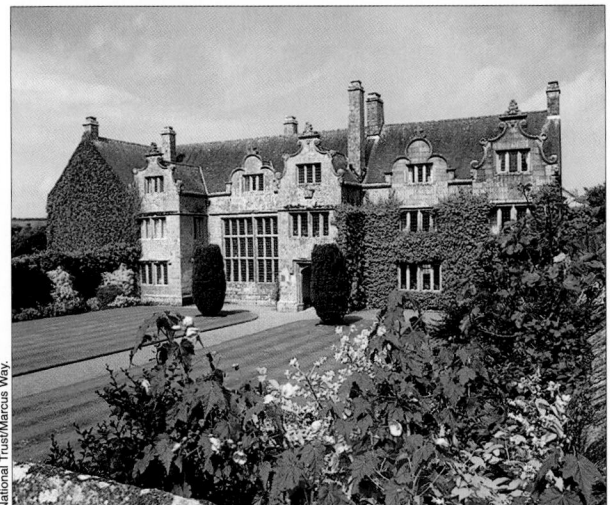

National Trust/Marcus Way.

NEWQUAY, CORNWALL TR8 4PG

Owner: The National Trust   *Contact:* The Property Manager

Tel: 01637 875404 **Fax:** 01637 879300

Trerice is an architectural gem and something of a rarity – a small Elizabethan manor house hidden away in a web of narrow lanes and still somehow caught in the spirit of its age. An old Arundell house, it contains much fine furniture, ceramics, glasses and a wonderful clock collection. A small barn museum traces the development of the lawn mower.

Location: OS Ref. SW841 585. 3m SE of Newquay via the A392 & A3058 (right at Kestle Mill).

Opening Times: 1 Apr - 16 Jul & 12 Sept - 4 Nov: daily except Tues & Sats. 17 Jul - 11 Sept: daily (except Sats), 11am - 5.30pm (closes 5pm in Oct & Nov).

Admission: £4.30, Family £10.75. Pre-arranged groups £3.60.

▢ ⚘ ♿ Braille & taped guides. WC. ▣ Licensed.
🐕 Guide dogs only.

TREVARNO ESTATE GARDENS & NATIONAL MUSEUM OF GARDENING

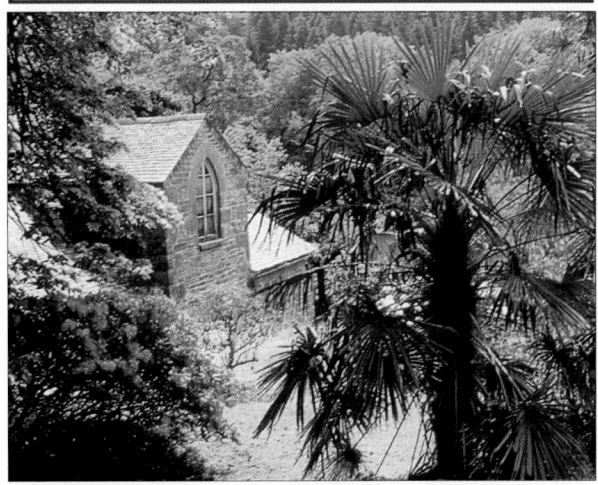

HELSTON, CORNWALL TR13 0RU

Contact: Kate Daughtery

Tel: 01326 574274 **Fax:** 01326 574282

An unforgettable gardening experience combining beautiful Victorian and Georgian gardens with the splendid fountain garden conservatory, unique range of craft workshops and the amazing National Museum of Gardening. Relax in the tranquil gardens and grounds, follow the progress of major restoration projects, visit the craft areas including handmade soap workshop and organic herbal workshop, explore Britain's largest and most comprehensive collection of antique tools, implements, memorabilia and ephemera creatively displayed to illustrate how gardens and gardening influence most peoples' lives.

Location: OS Ref. SW642 302. Leave Helston on Penzance road, signed from B3302 junction and N of Crowntown village.

Opening Times: All year, 10.30am - 5pm. Groups welcome by prior arrangement.

Admission: Adult £3.50, Child (5-14yrs) £1.25, Conc. £3.20.

▢ ♿ Partially suitable. ▣ Ⓟ ▤ 🐕 On leads. 🔔 ❄

TRESCO ABBEY GARDENS

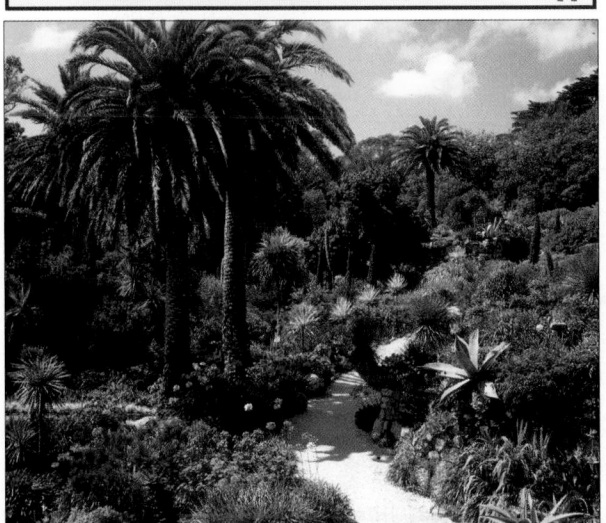

ISLES OF SCILLY, CORNWALL TR24 0QQ

Owner: Mr R A and Mrs L A Dorrien-Smith   *Contact:* Mr M.A Nelhams

Tel: 01720 424105 or **Tel/Fax:** 01720 422868 **e-mail:** mikenelhams@tresco.co.net

Tresco Abbey, built by Augustus Smith, has been the family home since 1834. The garden here flourishes on the small island. Nowhere else in the British Isles does such an exotic collection of plants grow in the open. Agaves, aloes, proteas and acacias from such places as Australia, South Africa, Mexico and the Mediterranean grow within the secure embrace of massive Holm Oak hedges. Valhalla Ships Figurehead Museum.

Location: OS Ref. SV895 143. Isles of Scilly. Isles of Scilly Steamship 0345 105555. BIH Helicopters 01736 363871. Details of day trips on application.

Opening Times: All year: 10am - 4pm.

Admission: Adult £6, (under 14yrs free). Weekly ticket £10. Guided group tours available.

▢ ♿ Grounds suitable. ▣ 🍴 🐕 In grounds, on leads. ❄

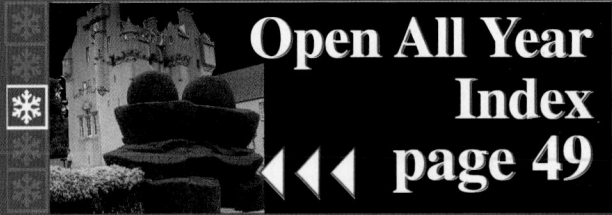

Open All Year
Index
◀◀◀ page 49

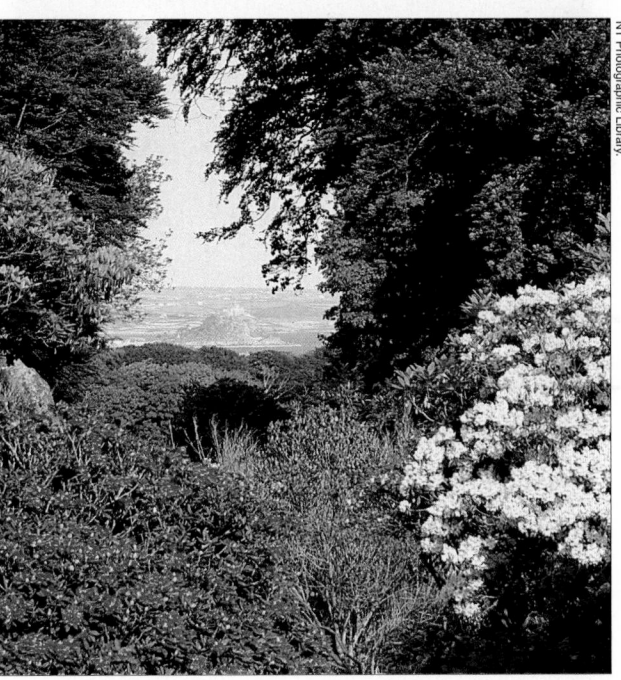

NT Photographic Library

Trengwainton Garden, Cornwall.

TREWITHEN

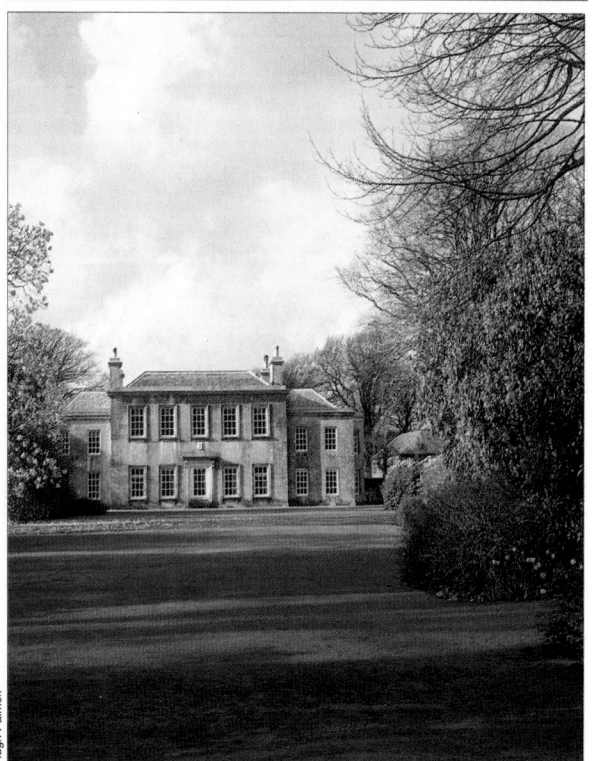

Hugh Palmer.

GRAMPOUND ROAD, TRURO, CORNWALL TR2 4DD

Owner: A M J Galsworthy *Contact: The Estate Office*

Tel: 01726 883647 **Fax:** 01726 882301
e-mail: gardens@trewithen-estate.demon.co.uk

Trewithen means 'house of the trees' and the name truly describes this fine early Georgian House in its splendid setting of wood and parkland. *Country Life* described the house as '*one of the outstanding West Country houses of the 18th century*'.

The gardens at Trewithen are outstanding and of international fame. Created since the beginning of the century by George Johnstone, they contain a wide and rare collection of flowering shrubs. Some of the magnolias and rhododendron species in the garden are known throughout the world. They are one of two attractions in this country awarded three stars by Michelin.

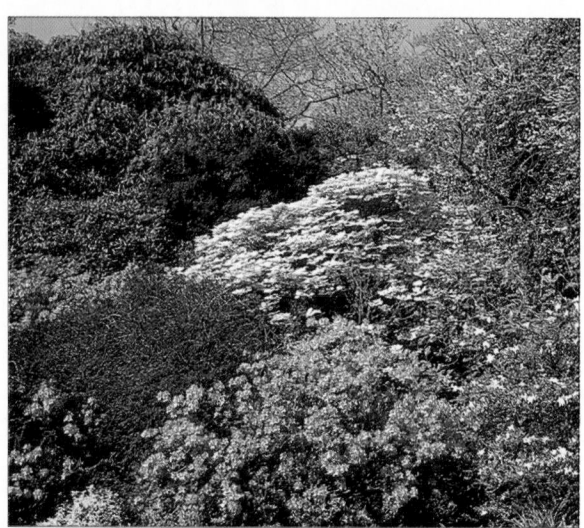

Location: OS Ref. SW914 476. S of A390 between Grampound and Probus villages. 7m WSW of St Austell.
Opening Times: Gardens: 1 Mar - 30 Sept: Mon - Sat, 10am - 4.30pm. Suns in Apr & May only. Walled Garden: Mons & Tues in June & 2/3 July only. House: Apr - Jul & Aug: BH Mons, Mons & Tues, 2 - 4pm.
Admission: Adult £3.75, Child £2. Pre booked groups (20+): Adult £3.50, Child £2. Combined gardens & house £6.

ℹ No photography in house. 🚻 ♿Partially suitable. WC.
🚶 By arrangement. 🅿 Limited for coaches. 🐕 In grounds, on leads.

TRURO CATHEDRAL

Tel: 01872 276782 **Fax:** 01872 277788

Truro, Cornwall TR1 2AF **Contact:** The Visitors Officer

It is a perfect example of a gothic Cathedral. The architect was J L Pearson. The Victorian stained glass is considered to be the finest in England.
Location: SW826 449. Truro city centre.
Opening Times: 7.30am - 6.30pm. Sun services: 8am, 9am, 10am and 6pm. Weekday services: 7.30am, 8am and 5.30pm.
Admission: Free.

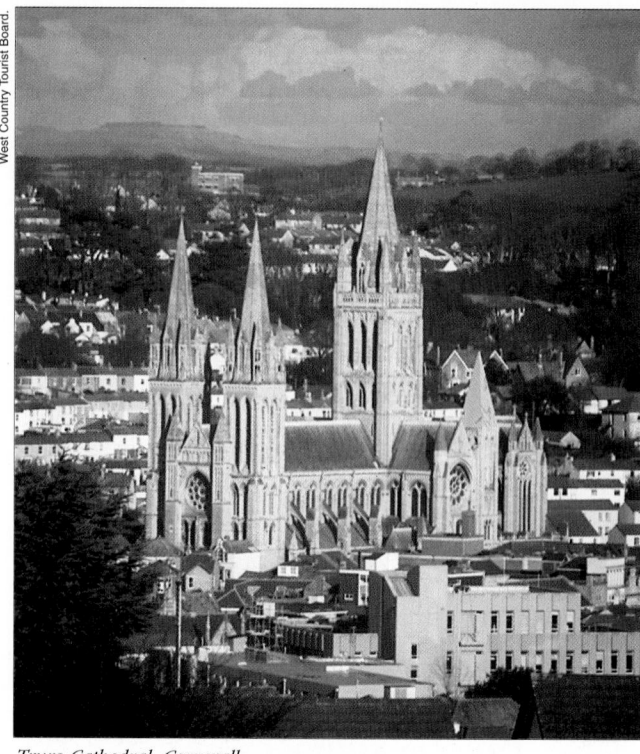

West Country Tourist Board.

Truro Cathedral, Cornwall.

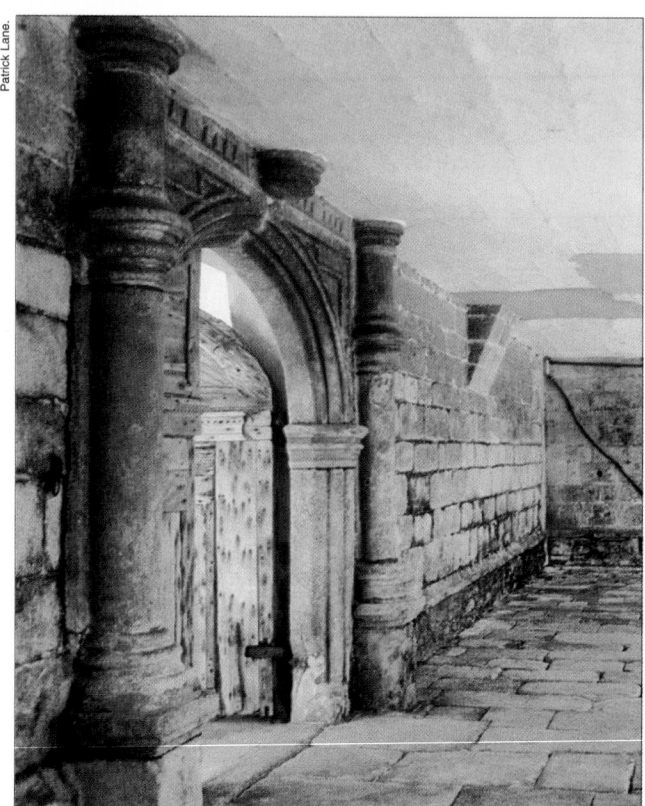

Patrick Lane.

Godolphin, Cornwall.

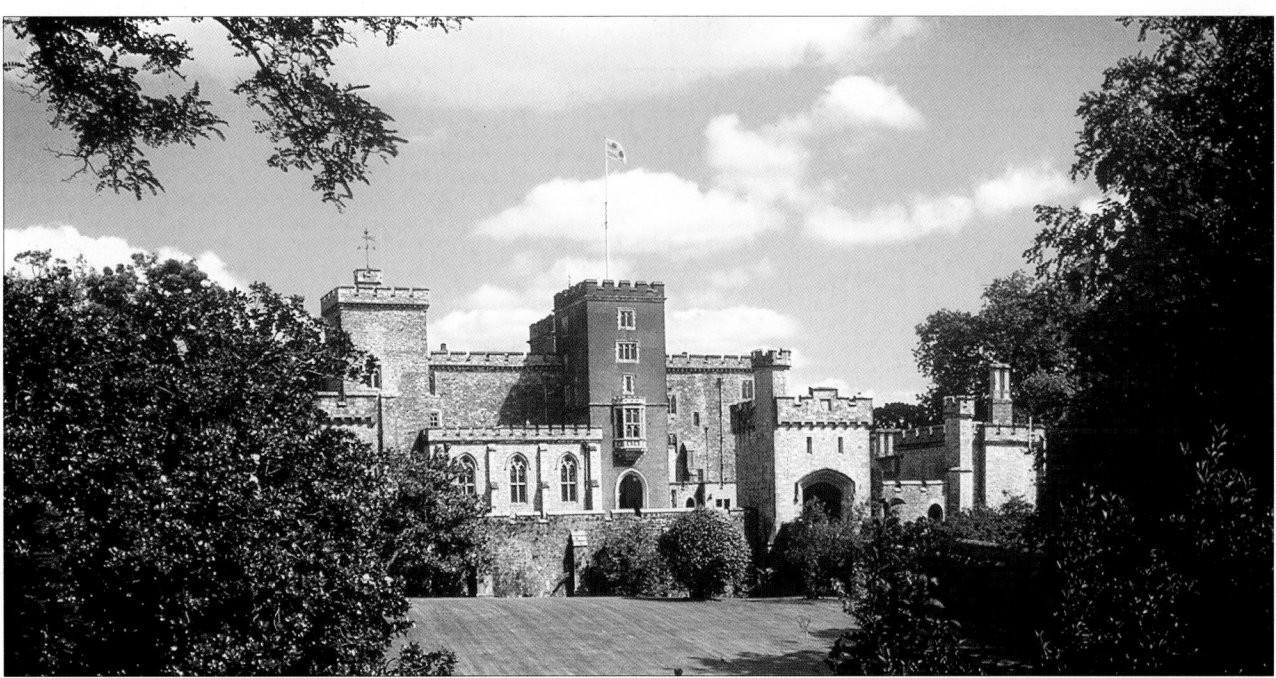

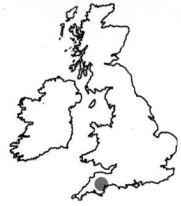

POWDERHAM CASTLE
Exeter

Historic family home of the Earl of Devon, Powderham Castle was built between 1390 and 1420 by Sir Philip Courtenay. The present Earl is his direct descendant. The Castle was extensively damaged during the Civil War and fell to the Parliamentary Forces after a protracted siege. When the family returned to the Castle seventy years later they embarked on a series of rebuilding and restoration which continued into the 19th century.

The Castle contains a large collection of portraits by many famous artists, including Cosway, Reynolds, Kneller and Hudson as well as some charming paintings by gifted members of the family. The 14ft high Stumbels Clock and the magnificent rosewood and brass inlaid bookcases by John Channon are particularly fine. One of the most spectacular rooms on view is the Music Room, designed for the 3rd Viscount by James Wyatt. It contains an exceptional Axminster carpet upon which sits recently commissioned carved gilt wood furniture.

GARDENS

2001 will see the opening of 'The Powderham Castle Steam Railway' taking visitors to the woodland gardens and smithy. The Castle is set within an ancient deer park beside the Exe Estuary and the Gardens and grounds are informally laid out. The fine Victorian Rose Garden is the home of Timothy, a 150 year old tortoise; The Children's Secret Garden houses a collection of pets and animals behind its walls to delight children and visitors of all ages; and the newly restored Woodland Garden is open in Spring and early Summer when at its best. Visit the new Farm Shop at Powderham Castle, open 364 days. Featuring high quality West Country food, a Plant Centre, Craft Shops and Restaurant, this free attraction adds another reason for visiting Powderham Castle. The Knights of Powderham joust daily (except Saturdays) in the grounds in the summer holidays at 3pm (separate admission applies).

Owner:
The Earl of Devon

CONTACT

Mr Tim Faulkner
The Estate Office
Powderham Castle
Kenton, Exeter
Devon
EX6 8JQ

Tel: 01626 890243

Fax: 01626 890729

e-mail:
castle@powderham.co.uk

LOCATION

OS Ref. SX965 832

6m SW of Exeter,
4m S M5/J30.
Access from A379 in
Kenton village.

Air: Exeter Airport 9m.

Rail: Starcross
Station 2m.

Bus: Devon General
No: 85, 85A, 85B to
Castle Gate.

CONFERENCE/FUNCTION		
ROOM	SIZE	MAX CAPACITY
Music Room	56' x 25'	170
Dining Room	42' x 22'	100
Ante Room	28' x 18'	25
Library 1	32' x 18'	85
Library 2	31"x18'	85

 Filming and car launches including 4WD vehicle rallies, open air concerts, etc. Grand piano in Music Room, 3800 acre estate, tennis court, cricket pitch, horse trials course. Deer park safari.

Conferences, dinners, corporate entertainment.

Limited facilities. Some ramps. WC.

Fully licensed restaurant and coach room access.

Fully inclusive. Tour time: 1 hr. Guide book available in French, Dutch & German.

Unlimited free parking. Commission and complimentary drinks / meals for drivers. Advance warning of group bookings preferred but not essential.

Welcome. Fascinating tour and useful insight into the life of one of England's Great Houses over the centuries. Victorian School Room and teacher pack.

In grounds, on leads.

Civil Wedding Licence.

South West England

A LA RONDE

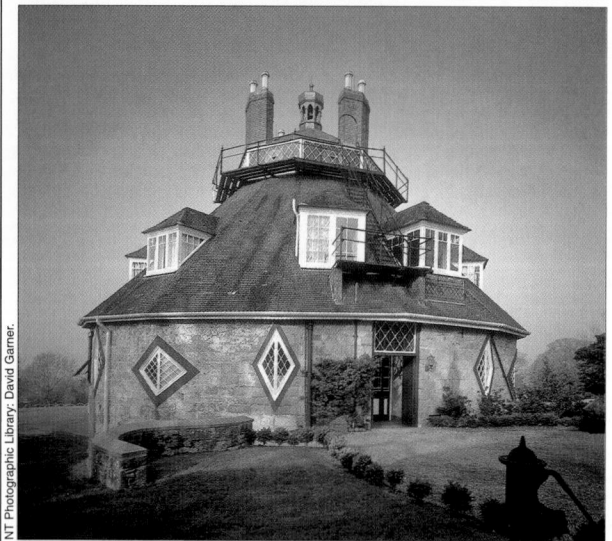

NT Photographic Library; David Garner.

SUMMER LANE, EXMOUTH, DEVON EX8 5BD

Owner: The National Trust   *Contact:* John Rolfe – Custodian

Tel: 01395 265514

A unique 16-sided house built on the instructions of two spinster cousins, Jane and Mary Parminter, on their return from a grand tour of Europe. Completed c1796, the house contains many 18th century contents and collections brought back by the Parminters. The fascinating interior decoration includes a feather frieze and shell-encrusted gallery which, due to its fragility, can only be viewed on closed circuit television.

Location: OS Ref. SY004 834. 2m N of Exmouth on A376.

Opening Times: 31 Mar - 4 Nov: daily except Fris & Sats, 11am - 5.30pm. Last admission 1/2 hr before closing.

Admission: Adult £3.30, Child £1.70. No reduction for groups.

ARLINGTON COURT

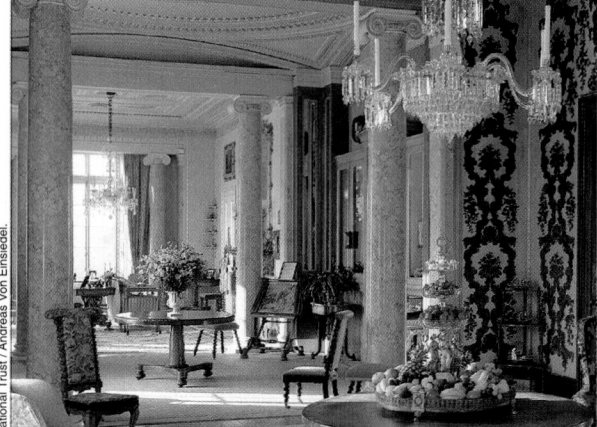

National Trust / Andreas Von Einsiedel.

Nr BARNSTAPLE, NORTH DEVON EX31 4LP

Owner: The National Trust   *Contact:* Susie Mercer - Property Manager

Tel: 01271 850296   **Fax:** 01271 850711

The house, built for the Chichesters in 1822 and still with much original furniture, is full of collections for every taste, including model ships, costume, pewter, shells and many other fascinating objects. Housed in the stables is the Trust's large collection of horse drawn carriages. Carriage rides through the 30 acres of peaceful informal gardens and past the formal terraced Victorian garden, start from the front of the house. Miles of walks through woods. Parks grazed by Shetland ponies and Jacob sheep.

Location: OS180 Ref. SS611 405. 7m NE of Barnstaple on A39.

Opening Times: 31 Mar - 4 Nov: daily except Tues, 11am - 5.30pm. Paths through park and woods open during daylight hours from Nov - Mar.

Admission: House & Garden: Adult £5.40, Child £2.70, Family £13.50. Booked groups (15+) £4.60, Child £2.30. Garden & Carriage Museum only: Adult £3.40, Child £1.70.

Ground floor & grounds suitable. WC.   Licensed.   P
Teachers' pack.   In grounds, on leads.

AVENUE COTTAGE GARDENS   **Tel/Fax:** 01803 732769

Ashprington, Totnes, Devon TQ9 7UT

Owner/Contact: R J Pitts Esq & R C H Soans Esq

A completely secluded and secret garden, yet one which has been in existence for over 200 years. For the last 10 years it has been undergoing restoration and recreation by the present owners. In this lovely valley site there is a large and fascinating collection of plants which is full of interest from spring until autumn.

Location: OS Ref. SX821 574. 3m SE of Totnes, from centre of village, up hill past church for 400 yds.

Opening Times: 1 Apr - 30 Sept, Tue - Sat, 11am - 5pm. Other times by appointment.

Admission: Adult £2, Child 25p. Entrance, guided tour & tea £3.50.

Wheelchairs in grounds.   By arrangement.   In grounds, on leads.

BAYARD'S COVE FORT   **Tel:** 01803 861234

Dartmouth, Devon

Owner: English Heritage   **Contact:** South Hams District Council

Set among the picturesque gabled houses of Dartmouth, on the waterfront at the end of the quay, this is a small artillery fort built 1509 - 10 to defend the harbour entrance.

Location: OS Ref. SX879 510. In Dartmouth, on riverfront 200 yds, S of South ferry.

Opening Times: Any reasonable time.

Admission: Free.

BERRY POMEROY CASTLE   **Tel:** 01803 866618

Totnes, Devon TQ9 6NJ

Owner: The Duke of Somerset   **Contact:** English Heritage

A romantic late medieval castle, dramatically sited half-way up a wooded hillside, looking out over a deep ravine and stream. It is unusual in combining the remains of a large castle with a flamboyant courtier's mansion. Reputed to be one of the most haunted castles in the country.

Location: OS202 Ref. SX839 623. 2 1/2 m E of Totnes off A385. Entrance gate 1/2 m NE of Berry Pomeroy village, then 1/2 m drive. Narrow approach, unsuitable for coaches.

Opening Times: 1 Apr - 31 Oct: daily, 10am - 6pm (5pm in Oct). Winter: closed.

Admission: Adult £2.20, Child £1.10, Conc £1.70. 15% discount for groups (11+).

Ground floor & grounds suitable.   Not EH.   P No access for coaches.
Telephone for details.

BICKLEIGH CASTLE

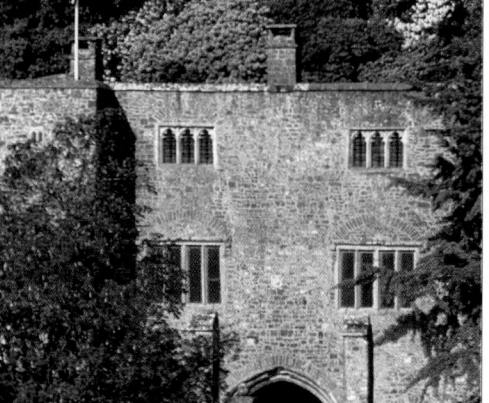

BICKLEIGH, Nr TIVERTON, DEVON EX16 8RP

Owner/Contact: M J Boxall Esq

Tel: 01884 855363

Royalist stronghold: 900 years of history and architecture. 11th century detached Chapel; 14th century Gatehouse – Armoury (Cromwellian), Guard Room – Tudor furniture and fine oil paintings, Great Hall – 52' long and 'Tudor' Bedroom, massive fourposter. 17th century Farmhouse: inglenook fireplaces, bread ovens, oak beams. The Spooky Tower, Great Hall and picturesque moated garden make Bickleigh a favoured venue for functions, particularly wedding receptions.

Location: OS Ref. SS936 068. Off the A396 Exeter-Tiverton road. Follow signs SW from Bickleigh Bridge 1m.

Opening Times: Easter Sun - Fri, then Weds, Suns & BHs until late May BH, then daily (except Sats) until 1st Sun in Oct, 2 - 5pm. Coaches & groups welcome at any time by appointment.

Admission: Adult £4, Child (5-15yrs) £2, Family £10.

Conferences.   Ground floor suitable.   Licensed.   Obligatory.

BICTON COLLEGE GARDEN & ARBORETUM   Tel: 01395 562400

East Budleigh, Budleigh Salterton, Devon EX9 7BY

Owner: Bicton College of Agriculture   **Contact:** Paul Champion
Grade I listed parkland, lake, monkey puzzle avenue, woodland garden.
Location: OS Ref. SY074 857. Off B3178 next door to Bicton Park, follow signs to plant centre.
Opening Times: Apr - Oct: daily 10am - 4.30pm. Nov - Mar: weekdays only 10am - 4.30pm.
Admission: Adult £2, Child (under 16yrs) Free.

BICTON PARK BOTANICAL GARDENS   Tel: 01395 568465   Fax: 01395 568374

Budleigh Salterton, Devon EX9 7DP

Owner: Mr & Mrs S E Lister   **Contact:** Mr Simon Lister
Over 60 acres of Parkland and Garden, Palm House and specialist greenhouses.
Location: OS Ref. SY074 856. 2m N of Budleigh Salterton on B3178.
Opening Times: Summer: 10am - 6pm. Winter: 10am - 5pm. Closed Christmas Day.
Admission: Adult £4.95, Child £2.95, Conc. £3.95.

BOWDEN HOUSE   Tel: 01803 863664

Totnes, Devon TQ9 7PW   **Owner/Contact:** Mrs Belinda Petersen

Elizabethan mansion with Queen Anne façade.
Location: OS Ref. SX800 600. Follow signs from Totnes. 1¹/₂ m S of Totnes, E of A381.
Opening Times: House: 2nd May BH - end Sept: Thur & Fri plus BH Suns. Museum opens 12 noon, Tours start at 2pm, or 1.30pm in high season, with ghost stories.
Admission: Adult £4.95, Child: (10-13yrs) £3.40, (6-9yrs) £2.20, (2-5yrs) £1. Tickets include Photo Museum and old film shows.

BRADLEY MANOR 🌱   Tel: 01626 354513

Newton Abbot, Devon TQ12 6BN

Owner: The National Trust   **Contact:** Mrs A H Woolner
A small medieval manor house set in woodland and meadows.
Location: OS Ref. SX848 709. On Totnes road A381. ³/₄ m SW of Newton Abbot.
Opening Times: Apr - end Sept: Weds & Thurs, 2 - 5 pm. Last admission 4.30pm.
Admission: £2.80, no reduction for groups.

BRANSCOMBE MANOR MILL, THE OLD BAKERY & FORGE 🌱

Tel: Manor Mill - 01392 881691   **Old Bakery** - 01297 680333   **Forge** - 01297 680481

Branscombe, Seaton, Devon EX12 3DB

Owner: The National Trust   **Contact:** NT Devon Regional Office
Manor Mill, still in working order and recently restored, is a water-powered mill which probably supplied the flour for the bakery, regular working demonstrations are held. The Old Bakery was, until 1987, the last traditional working bakery in Devon. The old baking equipment has been preserved in the baking room and the rest of the building is now a tearoom. Information display in the outbuildings. The Forge is open regularly and the blacksmith sells the ironwork he produces - please telephone to check opening times (01297 680481).
Location: OS Ref. SY198 887. In Branscombe ¹/₂ m S off A3052 by steep, narrow lane.
Opening Times: Manor Mill: 1 Apr - 4 Nov: Suns, 2 - 5pm; also Weds in Jul & Aug. The Old Bakery: Easter - Oct, daily, weekends in winter months, 11am - 5pm.
Admission: £1 Manor Mill only.

BUCKFAST ABBEY   Tel: 01364 645500   Fax: 01364 643891

Buckfastleigh, Devon TQ11 0EE

Owner: Buckfast Abbey Trust   **Contact:** The Warden
Medieval and modern Abbey.
Location: OS Ref. SX741 674. ¹/₂ m from A38 Plymouth - Exeter route.
Opening Times: Church & Grounds: All year: 5.30am - 7pm.
Admission: Free.

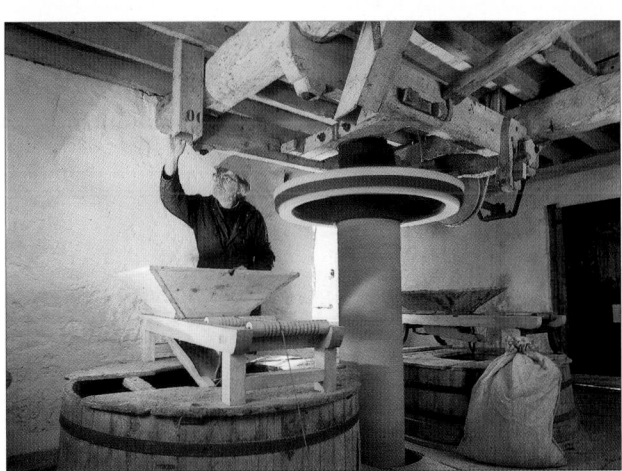

Branscombe Manor Mill, Devon.

BUCKLAND ABBEY 🌱

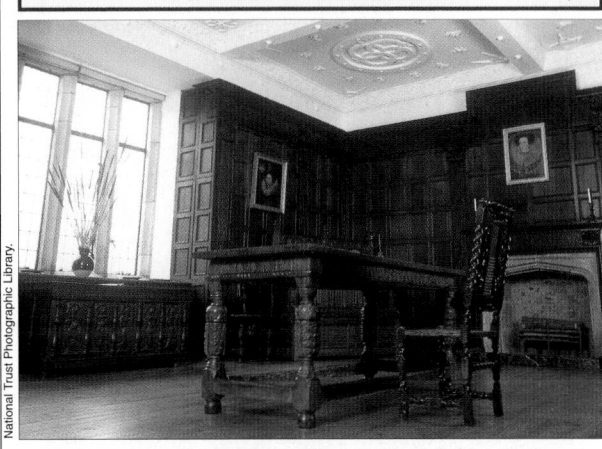

National Trust Photographic Library.

YELVERTON, DEVON PL20 6EY

Owner: The National Trust   *Contact:* Michael Coxson - Property Manager

Tel: 01822 853607   **Fax:** 01822 855448

The spirit of Sir Francis Drake is rekindled at his home with exhibitions of his courageous adventures and achievements throughout the world. One of the Trust's most interesting historical buildings and originally a 13th century monastery, the abbey was transformed into a family residence before Sir Francis bought it in 1581. Fascinating new decorated plaster ceiling in Tudor Drake Chamber. Outside there are monastic farm buildings, herb garden, craft workshops and country walks. Introductory video presentation. New Elizabethan garden under construction.
Location: OS201 Ref. SX487 667. 6m S of Tavistock; 11m N of Plymouth off A386.
Opening Times: 23 Mar - 4 Nov: daily except Thur, 10.30am - 5.30pm (last adm. 4.45pm). 5 Nov - 22 Mar 2002: Sat & Sun, 2 - 5pm, (last adm. 4.15pm). Closed 24 Dec - 15 Feb 2002. Other days for pre-booked groups.
Admission: Abbey & Grounds: Adult £4.60, Child £2.30, Family £11.50. Group: £3.80. Grounds only: Adult £2.40, Child £1.20. Winter: half price Abbey admission.

♿ Ground floor & grounds suitable. Wheelchair stairclimber may be available. WC. 🍴 🐕 Guide dogs only. ❄

CADHAY

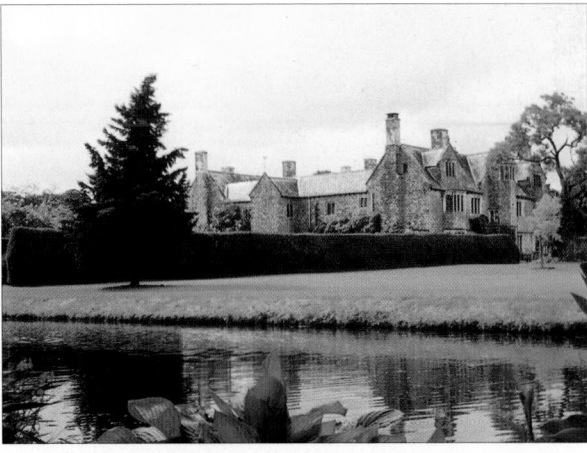

OTTERY ST MARY, DEVON EX11 1QT

Owner/Contact: Mr O N W William-Powlett

Tel/Fax: 01404 812432   **e-mail:** cadhay@eastdevon.net

Cadhay is approached by an avenue of lime-trees, and stands in a pleasant listed garden, with herbaceous borders and yew hedges, with excellent views over the original medieval fish ponds. The main part of the house was built about 1550 by John Haydon who had married the de Cadhay heiress. He retained the Great Hall of an earlier house, of which the fine timber roof (about 1420) can be seen. An Elizabethan Long Gallery was added by John's successor at the end of the 16th century, thereby forming a unique and lovely courtyard.
Location: OS Ref. SY090 962. 1m NW of Ottery St Mary. From W take A30 and exit at Pattersons Cross, follow signs for Fairmile and then Cadhay. From E, exit at the Iron Bridge and follow signs as above.
Opening Times: Jul & Aug: Tues, Weds & Thurs, also Suns & Mons in late Spring & Summer BHs, 2 - 5.30pm. Groups by appointment only.
Admission: Adult £4, Child £2.

♿ Ground floor & grounds suitable. 📷 Gardens available. 🐕 Guide dogs only. 🔔

CASTLE DROGO

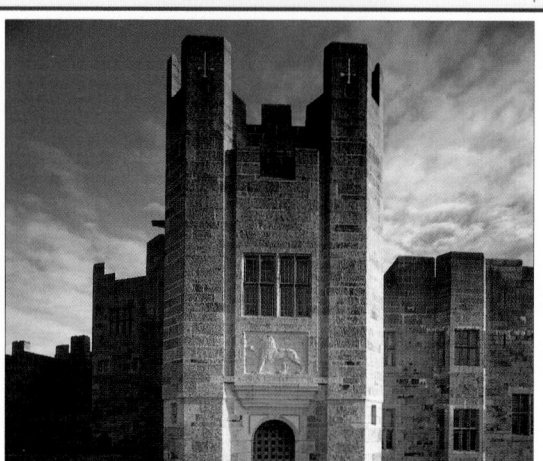

David Cripps.

DREWSTEIGNTON, EXETER EX6 6PB

Owner: The National Trust   *Contact: Peter Jennings, Property Manager*

Tel: 01647 433306 **Fax:** 01647 433186

Extraordinary granite and oak castle, designed by Sir Edwin Lutyens, which combines the comforts of the 20th century with the grandeur of a Baronial castle. Elegant dining and drawing rooms and fascinating kitchen and scullery. Terraced formal garden with colourful herbaceous borders and rose beds. Panoramic views over Dartmoor and delightful walks in the 300ft Teign Gorge.

Location: OS191 Ref. SX721 900. 5m S of A30 Exeter - Okehampton road.

Opening Times: Castle: 31 Mar - 4 Nov: daily except Fris (open Good Fri), 11am - 5.30pm (last admission 5pm). Sats & Suns in Mar: guided tours only (4 per day). Garden: All year: daily, 10.30am - dusk. Shop & tearoom open as Castle.

Admission: House & Garden: Adult £5.60, Child £2.80, Family £14. Group: £4.70. Garden only: Adult £2.80, Child £1.40.

⬚ ♿ Grounds floor & grounds suitable. WCs. 🍽 Licensed. 🧑 By arrangement. 🐕 Guide dogs only in certain areas. ❄

COLETON FISHACRE HOUSE & GDN

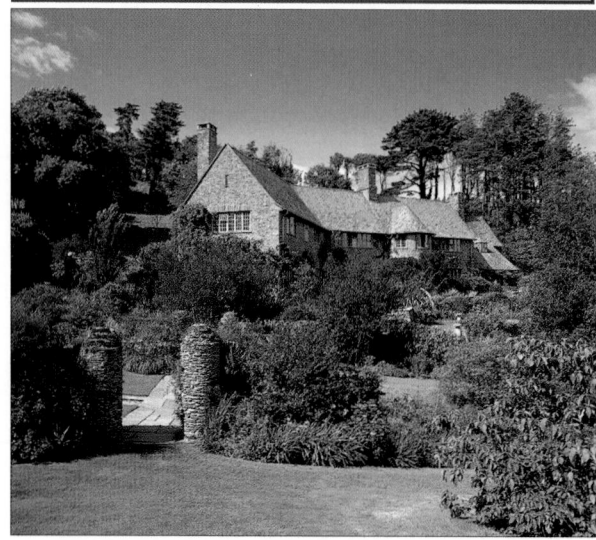

BROWNSTONE ROAD, KINGSWEAR, DARTMOUTH TQ6 0EQ

Owner: The National Trust   *Contact: David Mason, Property Manager*

Tel/Fax: 01803 752466 **e-mail:** dcfdmx@smtp.ntrust.org.uk

A 9 hectare property set in a stream-fed valley within the spectacular scenery of the South Devon coast. The Lutyenesque style house with art deco interior was built in the 1920s for Rupert and Lady Dorothy D'Oyly Carte who created the delightful garden, planted with a wide range of rare and exotic plants giving year round interest.

Location: OS202 Ref. SX910 508. 3m E of Kingswear, follow brown tourist signs.

Opening Times: Garden: Mar: Suns only, 11am - 5pm. House & Garden: 31 Mar - 4 Nov: Wed - Sun & BH Mons. House: 11am - 4.30pm, Garden: 10.30am - 5.30pm.

Admission: Adult £4.80, Child £2.40. Family £12. Booked groups (15+) £4.10. Garden only: Adult £3.80, Child £1.90, Booked groups (15+) £3.10.

ℹ No photography in house. ⬚ 🚻 ♿ Limited access to grounds. WC. 🍽 🅿 Limited. Coaches must book. 🐕 Guide dogs only in garden.

COMPTON CASTLE ✄

Tel: 01803 875740 (answerphone)

Marldon, Paignton TQ3 1TA

Owner: The National Trust   **Contact:** The Administrator

A fortified manor house with curtain wall, built at three periods: 1340, 1450 and 1520 by the Gilbert family.

Location: OS Ref. SX865 648. At Compton, 3m W of Torquay.

Opening Times: 2 Apr - 31 Oct: Mons, Weds & Thurs, 10am - 12.15pm & 2 - 5pm. The courtyard, restored great hall, solar, chapel, rose garden and old kitchen are shown. Last admission ½ hr before closing.

Admission: £2.90, pre-arranged groups £2.30.

CROWNHILL FORT

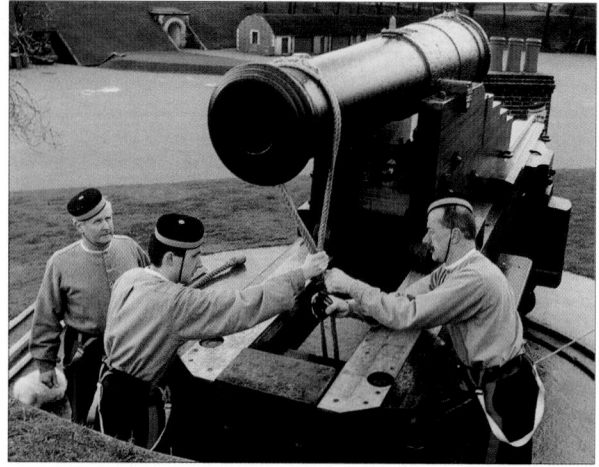

CROWNHILL FORT ROAD, PLYMOUTH, DEVON PL6 5BX

Owner: Landmark Trust   *Contact: James Breslin*

Tel: 01752 793754 **Fax:** 01752 770065 **e-mail:** ltcfort@aol.com

At Crownhill Fort you are free to explore the 16 acre site, honeycombed with tunnels, surrounded by massive ramparts, protected by a deep dry moat and guarded by many cannon. After a long restoration the Fort now stands proud as one of the largest and best preserved of Britain's great Victorian forts, and in particular boasts the Moncrieff Disappearing Gun, the only example in the world.

Location: OS Ref. SX487 593. 4m from Plymouth City Centre and less than 1m from A38, signposted from A386 Tavistock Road.

Opening Times: 8 Jan - 1 Apr: Groups by appointment only. 2 Apr - 28 Oct: daily, 10am - 5pm. Nov & Dec: Weekends, 10am - 5pm. Weekdays, groups by appointment only.

Admission: Adult £3.75, Child £2.25, OAP £3.50, Family (2+2) £10. Groups (15+) Adult £3.50, Child £2.

⬚ 🍽 ♿ Partially suitable. WC. 📷 🧑 By arrangement. 🅿 Ample for cars. Limited for coaches. 🍴 🐕 In grounds, on leads. ❄

DARTINGTON HALL GARDENS

Tel/Fax: 01803 862367

Dartington, Totnes, Devon TQ9 6EL   **e-mail:** graham@dartingtonhall.org.uk

Owner: Dartington Hall Trust   **Contact:** Mr G Gammin

28 acre gardens surrounds 14th century Hall.

Location: OS Ref. SX798 628. 30 mins from M5 at Exeter (off A38 at Buckfastleigh).

Opening Times: All year. Groups by appointment only. Guided tours by arrangement £4.

Admission: £2 donation welcome.

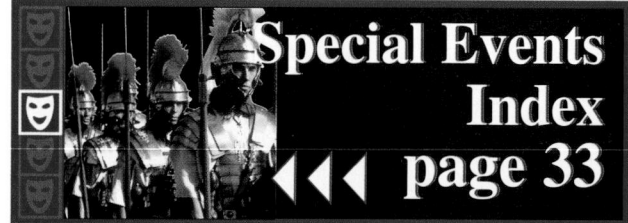

DARTMOUTH CASTLE

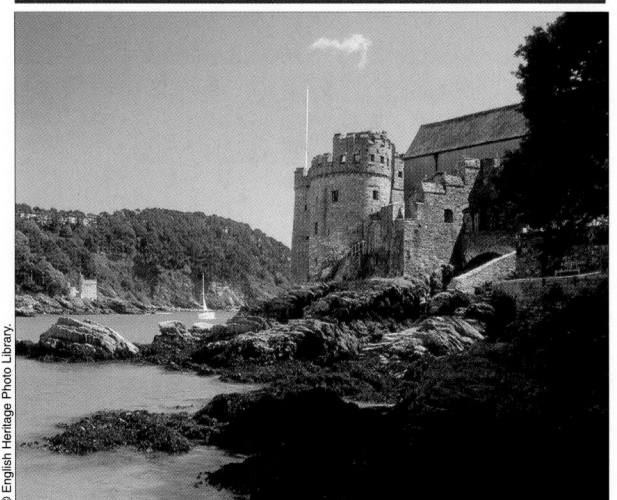

© English Heritage Photo Library

CASTLE ROAD, DARTMOUTH, DEVON TQ6 0JH

Owner: English Heritage   *Contact:* The Custodian

Tel: 01803 833588

This brilliantly positioned defensive castle juts out into the narrow entrance to the Dart estuary, with the sea lapping at its foot. When begun in 1480s it was one of the most advanced fortifications in England, and was the first castle designed specifically with artillery in mind. For nearly 500 years it kept its defences up-to-date in preparation for war. Today the castle is in a remarkably good state of repair, along with excellent exhibitions, the history of the castle comes to life. A picnic spot of exceptional beauty.

Location: OS202 Ref. SX887 503. 1m SE of Dartmouth off B3205, narrow approach road.

Opening Times: 1 Apr - 31 Oct: daily, 10am - 6pm (5pm in Oct). 1 Nov - 31 Mar: Wed - Sun, 10am - 4pm. Closed 24 - 26 Dec & 1 Jan.

Admission: Adult £3.20, Child £1.60, Conc. £2.50. 15% discount for groups (11+).

⬜ 🚻 Ground floor suitable. 💷 🅿 Limited. 🐕 ❄ 🖥 Tel. for details.

DOCTON MILL & GARDEN

Tel/Fax: 01237 441369

Spekes Valley, Hartland, Devon EX39 6EA   **e-mail:** john@doctonmill.freeserve.co.uk

Owner/Contact: John Borrett

Garden for all seasons in 8 acres of sheltered wooded valley, plus working mill.

Location: OS Ref. SS235 226. 3m Hartland Quay. 15m N of Bude. 3m W of A39, 3m S of Hartland.

Opening Times: Mar - Oct: 10am - 6pm. Coaches by appointment.

Admission: Adult £3.25, OAP £3.00, Child (under 14 yrs) £1.

🌐

THE ELIZABETHAN GARDENS

Tel: 01752 301010   **Fax:** 01752 312430

Plymouth Barbican Assoc. Ltd, New St, The Barbican, Plymouth

Owner: Plymouth Barbican Association Limited   **Contact:** Tony Golding Esq

Very small series of four enclosed gardens laid out in Elizabethan style in 1970.

Location: OS Ref. SX477 544. 3 mins walk from Dartington Glass (a landmark building) on the Barbican.

Opening Times: Mon - Sat, 9am - 5pm. Closed Christmas.

Admission: Free.

ESCOT COUNTRY PARK & GDNS

Tel: 01404 822188   **Fax:** 01404 822903

Escot, Ottery St Mary, Devon EX11 1LU   **e-mail:** escot@eclipse.co.uk

Owner/Contact: Mr J-M Kennaway

Otters, wild boar, birds of prey, 2 acre walled Victorian rose garden, 25 acres of shrubbery, rhododendrons and azaleas. 'Capability' Brown parkland, national award-winning pet & aquatic centre, wetlands and waterfowl park, Coach House Restaurant (all home cooking). The Kennaway family estate for over 200 years.

Location: OS Ref. SY080 977 (gate). 9m E of Exeter on A30 at Fairmile.

Opening Times: Easter - 31 Oct: Gardens, Aquatic Centre & Restaurant, daily, 10am - 6pm. 1 Nov - Easter: Gardens closed except by prior arrangement. Aquatic Centre & Restaurant: daily, 10am - 5pm except 25, 26 Dec & Mons in Jan, Feb & Mar.

Admission: Adult £3.50, Child £3, Child (under 4yrs) Free, OAP £3, Family (2+2) £12.

⬜ 🚻 🍴 🚻 Partially suitable. 💷 🍴 Licensed. 🐕 By arrangement. 📷 🅿
🐕 In grounds on leads. 🔔 ❄ 🖥 Tel. for details. 🌐

EXETER CATHEDRAL

Tel: 01392 255573   **Fax:** 01392 498769

Exeter, Devon EX1 1HS   **Contact:** Mrs Juliet Dymoke-Marr

Fine example of decorated gothic architecture. Longest unbroken stretch of gothic vaulting in the world.

Location: OS Ref. SX921 925. Central to the City - between High Street and Southernhay. Groups may be set down in South Street.

Opening Times: All year: Mon - Fri 7.30am - 6.30pm, Sats, 7.30am - 5pm, Suns, 8am - 7.30pm.

Admission: No formal charge – donation requested of £2.50 per person.

FURSDON HOUSE 🏛

Tel: 01392 860860   **Fax:** 01392 860126

Cadbury, Thorverton, Exeter, Devon EX5 5JS   **e-mail:** enquiries@fursdon.co.uk

Owner: E D Fursdon Esq   **Contact:** Mrs C Fursdon

The home of the Fursdon family is in beautiful hilly countryside above the Exe valley. The architecture reflects changes made throughout the centuries. Family memorabilia is displayed including scrap books, fine examples of 18th century costume and textiles and a letter from King Charles I during the Civil War.

Location: OS Ref. SS922 046. 1¹/₂m S of A3072 between Tiverton & Crediton, 9m N of Exeter. 2m N of Thorverton by narrow lane.

Opening Times: BHs Easter - August. Jun, Jul & Aug, Wed & Thurs. Gardens & Tearoom: 2 - 5pm. Guided house tours at 2.30pm & 3.30pm.

Admission: Adult £4, Child (11-16yrs) £2, (under 10yrs Free). Groups (20+) £3.50. Gardens only: £2.

ℹ️ Conferences. 🍴 🚻 Partially suitable. 💷 🐕 Compulsory. 🅿 🐕
🛏 Self-catering. 🌐

THE GARDEN HOUSE

Tel: 01822 854769   **Fax:** 01822 855358

Buckland Monachorum, Yelverton, Devon PL20 7LQ

Owner: Fortescue Garden Trust   **Contact:** Stuart Fraser

An 8 acre garden of interest throughout the year including a romantic terraced, walled garden around the ruins of a 16th century vicarage.

Location: OS Ref. SX490 682. Signposted W off A386 near Yelverton, 10m N of Plymouth.

Opening Times: 1 Mar - 31 Oct: daily, 10.30am - 5pm. Last admission 4.30pm.

Admission: Adult £4, Child £1, OAP £3.50, pre-booked groups (15+) £3 (if deposit paid).

HALDON BELVEDERE/LAWRENCE CASTLE

Tel/Fax: 01392 833668

e-mail: turner@haldonbelvedere.co.uk

Higher Ashton, Nr Dunchideock, Exeter, Devon EX6 7QY

Owner: Devon Historic Building Trust   **Contact:** Ian Turner

18th century Grade II* listed triangular tower with circular turrets on each corner. Built in memory of Major General Stringer Lawrence, founder of the Indian Army. Recently restored to illustrate the magnificence of its fine plasterwork, gothic windows, mahogany flooring and marble fireplaces. Breathtaking views of the surrounding Devon countryside.

Location: OS Ref. SX875 861. 7m SW of Exeter. Exit A38 at Exeter racecourse for 2¹/₂m.

Opening Times: Mar - Oct: Suns & BHs, 2 - 5pm.

Admission: Adult £1.50, Child 75p. No discount for groups (20-50).

🍴 🚻 Not suitable. 🐕 By arrangement. 🅿 Limited. 🖥
🐕 In grounds, on leads. 📷 🔔 🌐

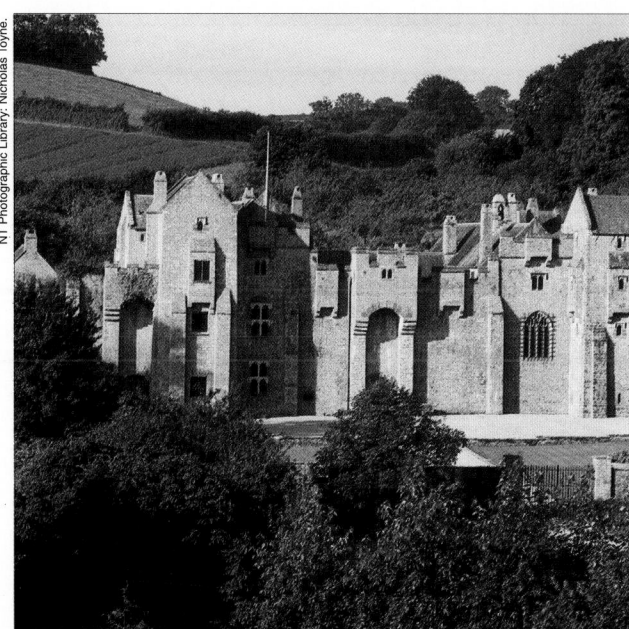

NT Photographic Library: Nicholas Toyne.

Compton Castle, Devon.

HARTLAND ABBEY

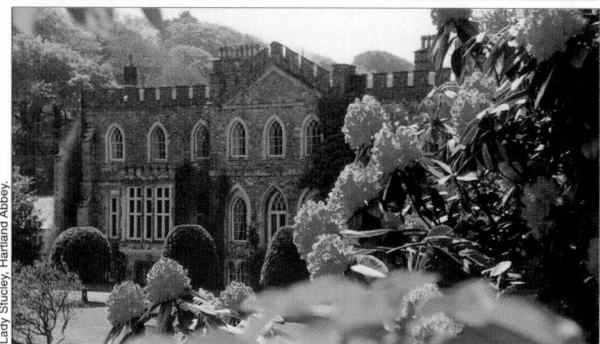

Lady Stucley, Hartland Abbey.

HARTLAND, BIDEFORD, DEVON EX39 6DT

Owner: Sir Hugh Stucley Bt   **Contact:** The Administrator

Tel: 01237 441264/441234   **Fax:** 01237 441264/01884 861134

Founded as an Augustinian Monastery in 1157 in a beautiful valley only 1 mile's walk from a spectacular Atlantic Cove, the Abbey was given by Henry VIII in 1539 to the Sergeant of his Wine Cellar, whose descendants live here today. Remodelled in the 18th & 19th century, it contains spectacular architecture and murals. Important paintings, furniture, porcelain collected over generations. Documents from 1160. Victorian and Edwardian photographs. Museum. Dairy. Recently discovered Victorian fernery and paths by Jekyll. Extensive woodland gardens of camellias, rhododendrons etc. Bog Garden. 18th century Walled gardens of vegetables, summer borders, tender and rare plants including echium pininana. Peacocks, donkeys and Welsh Mountain sheep in the park. NPI Heritage Award winner 1998.

Location: OS Ref. SS240 249. 15m W of Bideford, 15m N of Bude off A39 between Hartland and Hartland Quay.

Opening Times: 1 Apr - end Sept: Wed, Thur, Sun & BHs, plus Tues in Jul & Aug, 2 - 5.30pm. Gardens: 1 Apr - end Oct: daily except Sats, 2 - 5.30pm.

Admission: House, Gardens & Grounds: Adult £5, Child (9-15yrs) £1.50, OAP £4.50. Groups (20+): Adult £4, Child £1.50. Gardens & Grounds: Adult £3, Child 50p. Groups: £2.75.

Wedding receptions.   Partially suitable. WC.
By arrangement.   P   In grounds, on leads.

HEMERDON HOUSE   Tel: w/days 01752 841410 w/ends 01752 337350

Sparkwell, Plympton, Plymouth, Devon PL7 5BZ   **Fax:** 01752 331477

Owner: J H G Woollcombe Esq   **Contact:** Paul Williams & Partners

Late 18th century family house, rich in local history.

Location: OS Ref. SX564 575. 3m E of Plympton off A38.

Opening Times: 1 May - 30 Sept: for only 30 days including May & Aug BHs, 2 - 5.30pm. Last admission 5pm. Please contact the Administrator for opening dates.

Admission: £3.

Ground floor suitable.   Obligatory.   P

HEMYOCK CASTLE   Tel: 01823 680745

Hemyock, Cullompton, Devon EX15 3RJ

Owner/Contact: Mrs Sheppard

Former medieval moated castle, displays show site's history as fortified manor house, castle and farm. Medieval, Civil war and Victorian tableaux, archaeological finds, cider press and cow parlour.

Location: OS Ref. ST135 134. M5/J26, Wellington then 5m S over the Blackdown Hills.

Opening Times: BH Mons 2 - 5pm. Other times by appointment. Groups and private parties welcome.

Admission: Adult £1, Child 50p. Group rates available.

HOUND TOR DESERTED MEDIEVAL VILLAGE   Tel: 01626 832093

Ashburton Road, Manaton, Dartmoor, Devon

Owner: English Heritage   **Contact:** Dartmoor National Park Authority

The remains of the dwellings.

Location: OS191 Ref. SX746 788. 1¹/₂ m S of Manaton off Ashburton road. 6m N of Ashburton.

Opening Times: Any reasonable time.

Admission: Free.

KILLERTON HOUSE & GARDEN

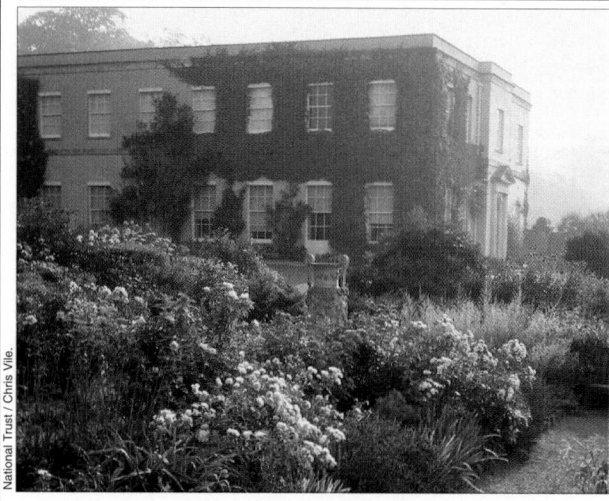

National Trust / Chris Vile.

BROADCLYST, EXETER EX5 3LE

Owner: The National Trust   **Contact:** Denise Melhuish - Property Manager

Tel: 01392 881345

The spectacular hillside garden is beautiful throughout the year with spring flowering bulbs and shrubs, colourful herbaceous borders and fine trees. The garden is surrounded by parkland and woods offering lovely walks. The house is furnished as a family home and includes a costume collection dating from the 18th century in a series of period rooms and a Victorian laundry.

Location: OS Ref. SS977 001. Off Exeter – Cullompton Rd (B3181). M5 N'bound J30, M5 S'bound J28.

Opening Times: House: 10 - 31 Mar & 1 Oct - 4 Nov, daily except Mons & Tues. 1 Apr - 31 Jul & Sept, daily except Tues. Aug: daily, 11am - 5.30pm (5pm during Oct) last entry ¹/₂ hr before closing.

Admission: House & Garden: Adult £5.20, Child £2.60, Family £13, Group £4.30. Garden only: Adult £3.70, Child £1.80. Reduced Nov - Feb.

      Guide dogs only in house.

KNIGHTSHAYES

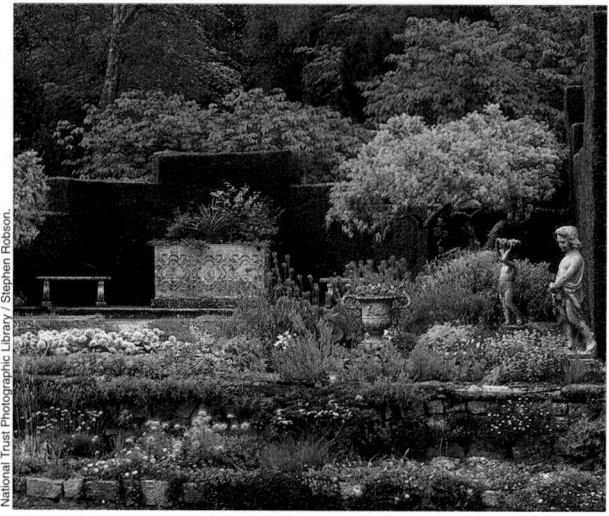

National Trust Photographic Library / Stephen Robson.

BOLHAM, TIVERTON, DEVON EX16 7RQ

Owner: The National Trust   **Contact:** Penny Woollams - Property Manager

Tel: 01884 254665   **Fax:** 01884 243050

The striking Victorian gothic house is a rare survival of the work of William Burges with ornate patterns in many rooms. One of the finest gardens in Devon, mainly woodland and shrubs with something of interest throughout the seasons. Drifts of spring bulbs, summer flowering shrubs, pool garden and amusing animal topiary.

Location: OS Ref. SS960 151. 2m N of Tiverton (A396) at Bolham.

Opening Times: House: 24 Mar - 4 Nov: daily except Fris (but open Good Fri), 11am - 5.30pm (Oct: 11.30am - 4.30pm. Closed Thurs/Fris). Nov/Dec: Suns, 2 - 4pm, pre-booked groups only. Gardens: 27 Mar - 31 Oct: daily, 11am - 5.30pm.

Admission: House & Garden: Adult £5.40, Child £2.70, Family £13.50. Group £4.70. Garden only: Adult £3.80, Child £1.90.

      Ground floor & grounds suitable. WC.
  Guide dogs in park.

LYDFORD CASTLES & SAXON TOWN

Tel: 01822 820320

Lydford, Okehampton, Devon

Owner: English Heritage   **Contact:** The National Trust

Standing above the lovely gorge of the River Lyd, this 12th century tower was notorious as a prison. The earthworks of the original Norman fort are to the south. A Saxon town once stood nearby and its layout is still discernible.

Location: OS191 Castle Ref. SX510 848, Fort Ref. SX509 847. In Lydford off A386 8m SW of Okehampton.

Opening Times: Any reasonable time.

Admission: Free.

MARKERS COTTAGE

Tel: 01392 461546

Broadclyst, Exeter, Devon EX5 3HR

Owner: The National Trust   **Contact:** The Custodian

Medieval cob house containing a cross-passage screen decorated with a painting of St Andrew and his attributes.

Location: OS Ref. SX985 973. $^1/_4$ E of B3181 in village of Broadclyst.

Opening Times: 1 Apr - 30 Oct: Sun - Tue, 2 - 5pm.

Admission: £1.

MARWOOD HILL

Tel: 01271 342528

Barnstaple, Devon EX31 4EB

Owner/Contact: Dr J A Smart

20 acre garden with 3 small lakes. Extensive collection of camellias, bog garden. National collection of astilbes.

Location: OS Ref. SS545 375. 4m N of Barnstaple. $^1/_2$ m W of B3230. Signs off A361 Barnstaple - Braunton road.

Opening Times: Dawn to dusk throughout the year.

Admission: Adult £3, Child (under 12yrs) Free.

MORWELLHAM QUAY

Tel: 01822 832766 **Fax:** 01822 833808

Morwellham, Tavistock, Devon PL19 8JL

Owner: The Morwellham & Tamar Valley Trust   **Contact:** Anne Emerson

Award-winning visitor centre at historic river port. Train ride into old mine workings. Shire horses and stables, staff in costume, costumes to try on. Museums, workshops, cottages, woodland walks in beautiful Tamar Valley. Average visit length 5 - 6 hours.

Location: OS Ref. SX446 697. Off A390 about 15 mins drive from Tavistock, Devon. 5m SW of Tavistock. 3m S of A390 at Gulworthy.

Opening Times: Summer: daily, 10am - 5.30pm, last adm. 3.30pm. Winter: daily, 10am - 4.30pm, last adm. 2.30pm.

Admission: Adult £8.80, Child £6. Family (2+2) £27. Group rate please apply for details. Usual concessions.

Licensed. In grounds, on leads.

OKEHAMPTON CASTLE

Tel: 01837 52844

Okehampton, Devon EX20 1JB

Owner: English Heritage   **Contact:** The Custodian

The ruins of the largest castle in Devon stand above a river surrounded by splendid woodland. There is still plenty to see, including the Norman motte and the jagged remains of the Keep. There is a picnic area and lovely woodland walks.

Location: OS191 Ref. SX584 942. 1m SW of Okehampton town centre off A30 bypass.

Opening Times: 1 Apr - 31 Oct: daily, 10am - 6pm (5pm in Oct). Winter: Closed.

Admission: Adult £2.50, Child £1.30, Conc. £1.80. 15% discount for groups (11+).

Grounds suitable. WC. In grounds, on leads. Tel. for details.

OLDWAY MANSION

Tel: 01803 201201 **Fax:** 01803 292866

Paignton, Devon

e-mail: webmaster@torbay.gov.org

Owner: Torbay Council   **Contact:** Peter Carpenter

Built by sewing machine entrepreneur I M Singer in the 1870s. Popular Civil wedding venue.

Location: OS Ref. SX888 615. Off W side of A3022.

Opening Times: Easter - Oct: Suns, 2 - 5pm. Visitors should note that not all rooms will always be open, access depends on other activities.

Admission: Free.

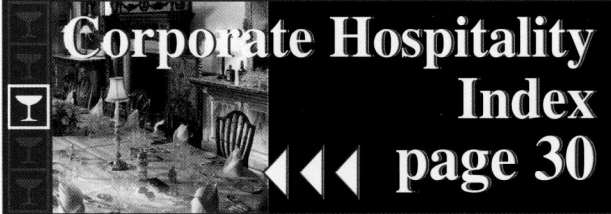

Corporate Hospitality Index page 30 ◀◀◀

OVERBECKS MUSEUM & GDN

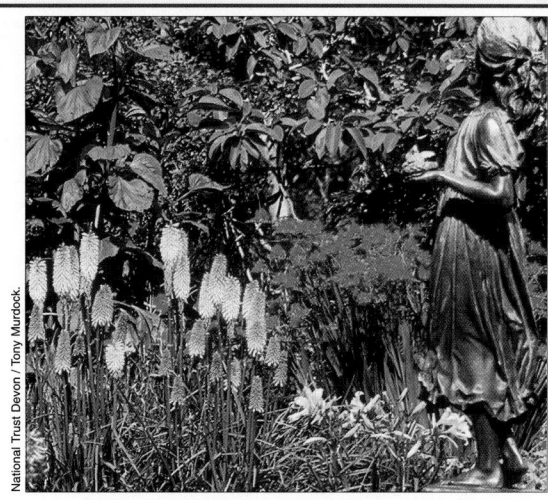

National Trust Devon / Tony Murdock.

SHARPITOR, SALCOMBE, SOUTH DEVON TQ8 8LW

Owner: The National Trust   **Contact:** Roy Chandler - Property Manager

Tel: 01548 842893

A sub-tropical garden with rare and tender plants thriving in the mild climate and spectacular views over the Salcombe Estuary. In the Edwardian house are curios such as a polyphon and rejuvenating machine and displays on the maritime history and wildlife of the area. There is also a secret room for children, with dolls, tin soldiers, other toys and a ghost hunt.

Location: OS202 Ref. SX728 374. $1^1/_2$ m SW of Salcombe. Signposted from Salcombe (single track lanes).

Opening Times: Museum: 1 Apr - 31 July, Sept: Sun - Fri (open Easter Sat), 11am - 5.30pm. August, daily, 11am - 5.30pm. October, Sun - Thur, 11am - 5pm. Garden: All year: daily, 10am - 8pm.

Admission: House & Garden: Adult £4.10, Child £2. Garden only: Adult £2.90, Child £1.40.

No photography in house. Partially suitable. By arrangement. Limited.

POWDERHAM CASTLE

See page 201 for full page entry.

PUSLINCH

Tel: 01752 880555 **Fax:** 01752 880909

Yealmpton, Plymouth, Devon PL8 2NN

Owner/Contact: Sebastian Fenwick

A perfect example of a medium sized early Georgian house in the Queen Anne tradition with fine contempary interiors. Built in 1720 by the Yonge family and still in their ownership.

Location: OS Ref. SX570 509. 1m SW of Yealmpton on Newton Ferrers Road.

Opening Times: Groups only (8-60). All year except Christmas & Boxing Day by prior written appointment only.

Admission: Adult £5.

No photography. Obligatory.

RHS GARDEN ROSEMOOR

Tel: 01805 624067 **Fax:** 01805 624717

Great Torrington, Devon   **Owner/Contact:** The Royal Horticultural Society

40 acres of gardens.

Location: OS Ref. SS500 183. 1m S of Great Torrington on A3124.

Opening Times: Apr - Sept: 10am - 6pm. Oct - Mar: 10am - 5pm.

Admission: Adult £4.50, Child (6 - 16yrs) £1, Child (under 6yrs) Free. Groups (10+) £3.50. Companion for disabled visitor Free.

ROYAL CITADEL

Tel: 01752 775841

Plymouth Hoe, Plymouth, Devon

Owner: English Heritage   **Contact:** Blue Badge Guides

A large, dramatic 17th century fortress, with walls up to 70 feet high, built to defend the coastline from the Dutch and still in use today.

Location: OS201 Ref. SX480 538. At E end of Plymouth Hoe. SE of city centre.

Opening Times: By guided tour only ($1^1/_2$ hrs) at 2.30pm. 1 May - 30 Sept. Tickets at Plymouth Dome below Smeaton's Tower on the Hoe and TIC in Plymouth.

Admission: Adult £3, Child £2, OAP £2.50.

SALTRAM HOUSE

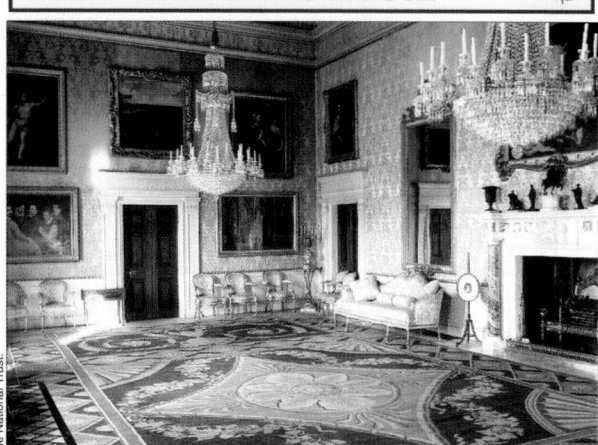

The National Trust.

PLYMPTON, PLYMOUTH, DEVON PL7 1UH

Owner: The National Trust   *Contact:* Kevan Timms - Property Manager

Tel: 01752 336546   **Fax:** 01752 336474

A magnificent George II mansion set in beautiful gardens and surrounded by landscaped park overlooking the Plym estuary. Visitors can see the original contents including important work by Robert Adam, Chippendale, Wedgwood and Sir Joshua Reynolds. You can explore the garden follies including Fanny's Bower and the Castle, follow the tree trail in the garden and enjoy fascinating walks beside the river, through the parkland and in the woods. Saltram starred as Norland Park in the award winning film *Sense & Sensibility.*

Location: OS Ref. SX520 557. 3¹/₂ m E of Plymouth city centre. ³/₄ m S of A38.

Opening Times: House & Great Kitchen: 1 Apr - 4 Nov: Sun - Thur & Good Fri, 12 noon - 5pm (from 1 Oct: 12 noon - 4pm). Art Gallery: open as house but from 10.30am. Garden: Feb & Mar: Sats & Suns only, 11am - 4pm; from 1 Apr - 4 Nov as house but from 10.30am - 5.30pm.

Admission: House & Garden: Adult £6, Child £3, Family £15. Groups £5.20. Garden only: Adult £3, Child £1.50.

ℹ️ Conferences.   📷   ♿ WC. Braille guide. Audio-visual tape.

🍴 Licensed.   🐕 In grounds, on leads. Guide dogs in house.

SAND

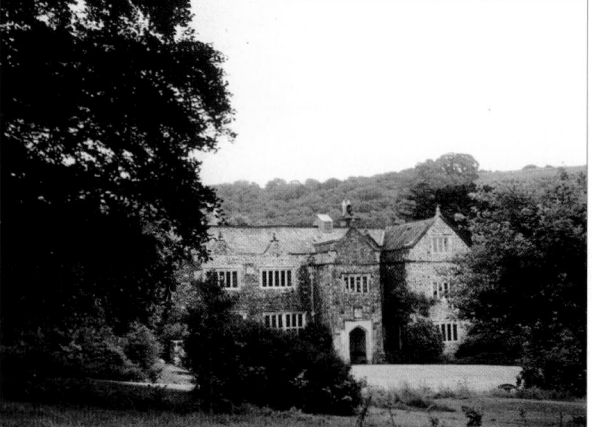

SIDBURY, SIDMOUTH EX10 0QN

Owner/Contact: Lt Col P Huyshe

Tel: 01395 597230

Lived-in manor house owned by the Huyshe family since 1560 rebuilt 1592-4 lying in unspoilt valley. Mixed 4-acre garden with something for everyone. Screens passage, panelling, family documents and heraldry. Also Sand Lodge, roof structure of late 15th century hall house.

Location: OS Ref. SY146 925. ¹/₄ m off A375, ¹/₂ m N of Sidbury. Well signed.

Opening Times: House: 15/16 Apr; 6/7/27/28 May; 10/11 Jun; 1/2/15/16/29/30 Jul; 12/13/26/27 Aug. Garden only: Apr - end Sept: Sun - Tue. 2 - 6pm, last admission to house and garden 5pm.

Admission: House & Garden: Adult £4, Child/Student £1. Garden only: Adult £2.50, accompanied Child (under 16) Free.

ℹ️ No photography in house.   ♿ Partially suitable.   📷 🎥 Obligatory.
🅿️ Limited for coaches.   🐕 In grounds, on leads.   📧 Tel. for details.

SHOBROOKE PARK

Tel: 01363 775153   **Fax:** 01363 775153

Crediton, Devon EX17 1DG

e-mail: admin@shobrookepark.com

Owner: Dr J R Shelley   **Contact:** Clare Shelley

A classical English 180-acre park. The lime avenue dates from about 1800 and the cascade of four lakes was completed in the 1840s. Millennium amphitheatre built in the year 2000. The southern third of the Park is open to the public under the Countryside Commission Access Scheme. The 15 acre garden, created c1845 with Portland stone terraces, roses and rhododendrons is being restored.

Location: OS Ref. SS848 010. 1m E of Crediton. Access to park by kissing gate at SW end of park, just S of A3072. Garden access on A3072.

Opening Times: South Park: All daylight hours. Gardens: Sats, 19 May, 9 & 23 Jun, 2 - 5pm.

Admission: Park: No charge. Gardens: NGS £2, accompanied children under 14 Free.

♿ Limited, wheelchairs in garden only.   🐕 Guide dogs only in garden.   ❄️

SHUTE BARTON

Tel: 01297 34692

Shute, Axminster, Devon EX13 7PT

Owner: The National Trust

One of the most important surviving non-fortified manor houses of the Middle Ages.

Location: OS Ref. SY253 974. 3m SW of Axminster, 2m N of Colyton, 1m S of A35.

Opening Times: 4 Apr - 31 Oct: Weds & Sats, 2 - 5.30pm. Last admission 5pm.

Admission: £1.80, No group reductions.

TAPELEY PARK

Tel 01271 342558   **Fax** 01271 342371

Watersdown Challenge

Instow, Bideford, Devon EX39 4NT

Owner: Tapeley Park Trust

Much altered Queen Anne building with extensive gardens and park.

Location: OS Ref. SS478 291. Between Bideford and Barnstaple near Instow. Follow brown tourist signs from the A39 onto B3233.

Opening Times: Good Fri - end Oct: daily except Sats, 10am - 5pm.

Admission: Adult £3.50, Child £2, OAP £3. House only open to pre-booked groups, extra £2 admission.

TIVERTON CASTLE

Tel: 01884 253200/255200   **Fax:** 01884 254200

Tiverton, Devon EX16 6RP

e-mail: tiverton.castle@ukf.net

Owner: Mr and Mrs A K Gordon   **Contact:** Mrs A Gordon

After nearly 900 years few buildings evoke such an immediate feeling of history as Tiverton Castle. Many ages of architecture can be seen, from medieval to modern. With continuing conservation there is always something new and interesting to see. Old walls, new gardens. Civil War Armoury – try some on.

Location: OS Ref. SS954 130. Just N of Tiverton town centre.

Opening Times: Easter - end of Jun, Sept: Sun, Thur, BH Mon, Jul & Aug, Sun - Thur, 2.30 - 5.30pm. Open to groups (12+) by prior arrangement at any time.

Admission: Adult £3.50, Child (7-16yrs) £2, Child under 7 Free. Groups (12+): Adult £4, Child £2.

📷   🌱 Plant centre.   ♿   🅿️ Ample for cars, limited for coaches.   🎥
🐕 In grounds, on leads.   🔔 📖 ❄️

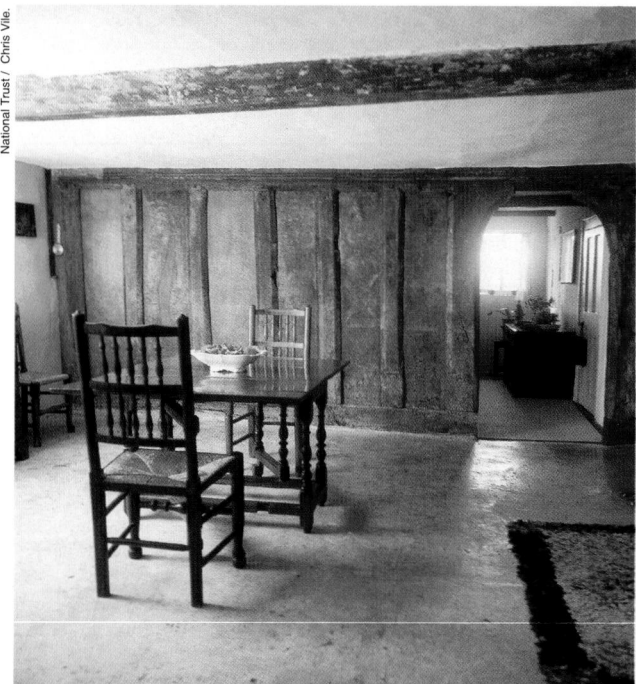

National Trust / Chris Vile.

Markers Cottage, Devon.

TORRE ABBEY

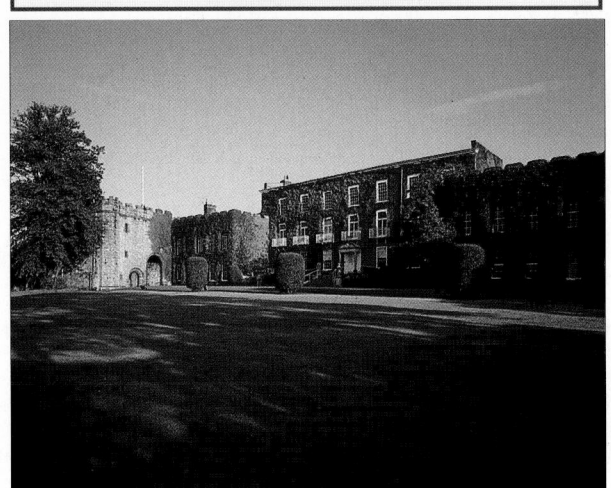

THE KINGS DRIVE, TORQUAY, DEVON TQ2 5JE

Owner: Torbay Council   *Contact:* L Retallick

Tel: 01803 293593 **Fax:** 01803 215948 **e-mail:** torre-abbey@torbay.gov.uk
Torre Abbey was founded as a monastery in 1196. Later adapted as a country house and in 1741-3 remodelled by the Cary family. Bought by the Council in 1930 for an art gallery. Visitors can see monastic remains, historic rooms, family chapel, mementoes of Agatha Christie, Victorian paintings including Holman Hunt & Burne-Jones & Torquay terracotta. Torre Abbey overlooks the sea and is surrounded by parkland and gardens. Teas served in Victorian Kitchen.
Location: OS Ref. SX907 638. On Torquay sea front. Between station and town centre.
Opening Times: Apr - 1 Nov: daily, 9.30am - 6pm, last adm. 5pm. Free access to members of the National Art Collections Fund.
Admission: Adult £3, Child £1.50, Conc. £2.50, Family £7.25. Groups (pre-booked, 10+): Adult £2.25, Child £1.30.
Conferences.   Not suitable.   By arrangement.
Schools' programme, apply for details.   Guide dogs only.

TOTNES CASTLE   **Tel:** 01803 864406

Castle Street, Totnes, Devon TQ9 5NU
Owner: English Heritage   **Contact:** The Custodian
By the North Gate of the hill town of Totnes you will find a superb motte and bailey castle, with splendid views across the roof tops and down to the River Dart. It is a symbol of lordly feudal life and a fine example of Norman fortification.
Location: OS202 Ref. SX800 605. In Totnes, on hill overlooking the town. Access in Castle St off W end of High St.
Opening Times: 1 Apr - 31 Oct: daily 10am - 6pm (5pm in Oct). 1 Nov - 31 Mar: Wed - Sun, 10am - 4 pm. Closed: 24 - 26 Dec & 1 Jan.
Admission: Adult £1.60, Child 80p, Conc. £1.20. 15% discount for groups (11+).
Not suitable.   In grounds, on leads.   Tel. for details.

UGBROOKE PARK   **Tel:** 01626 852179

Chudleigh, Devon TQ13 0AD
Owner: Captain The Lord Clifford of Chudleigh   **Contact:** Mrs Martin
Location: OS Ref. SX875 000. ³/₄ m NW of A380, 1m SE of Chudleigh.
Opening Times: Please contact for details.
Admission: Adult £4.80, Child (5-16yrs) £2. Groups (20+) £4.50 (2000/01 prices).

YARDE MEDIEVAL FARMHOUSE   **Tel:** 01548 842367

Malborough, Kingsbridge, Devon TQ7 3BY
Owner/Contact: John R Ayre Esq
Location: OS Ref. SX718 400. 5m S of Kingsbridge ¹/₄ m N of A381. ¹/₂ m E of Malborough. 1¹/₂ m W of Salcombe. Coaches only by appointment.
Opening Times: Easter - 30 Sept: Suns only, 2 - 5pm.
Admission: Adult £2.50, Child 50p, (under 5yrs Free). Groups by appointment only.

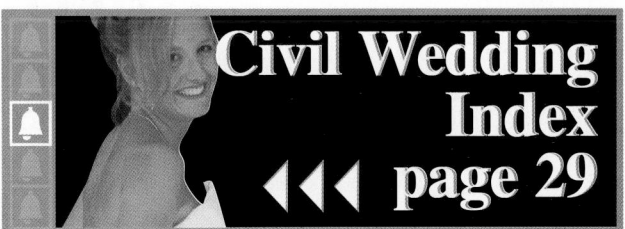
Fursdon House, Devon.

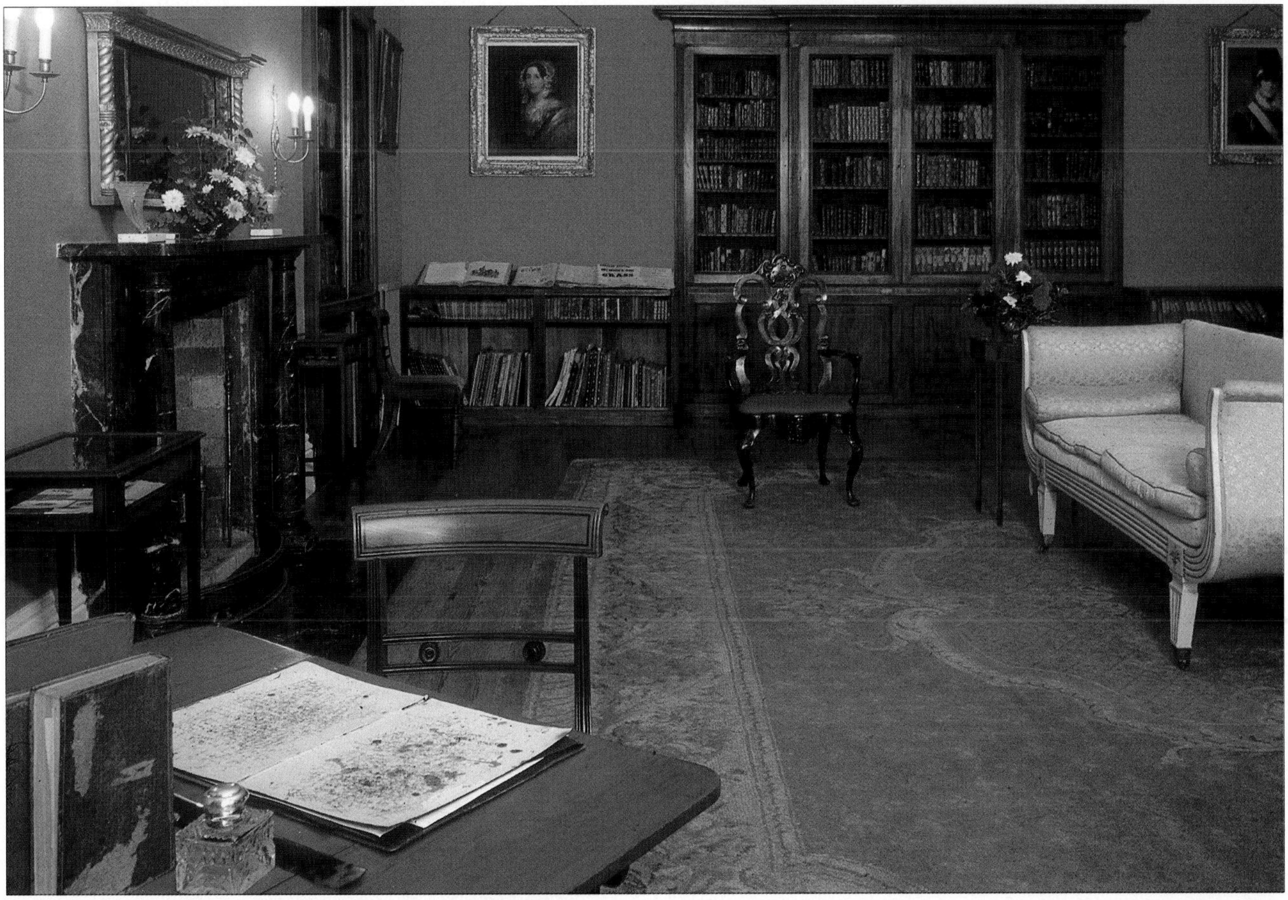

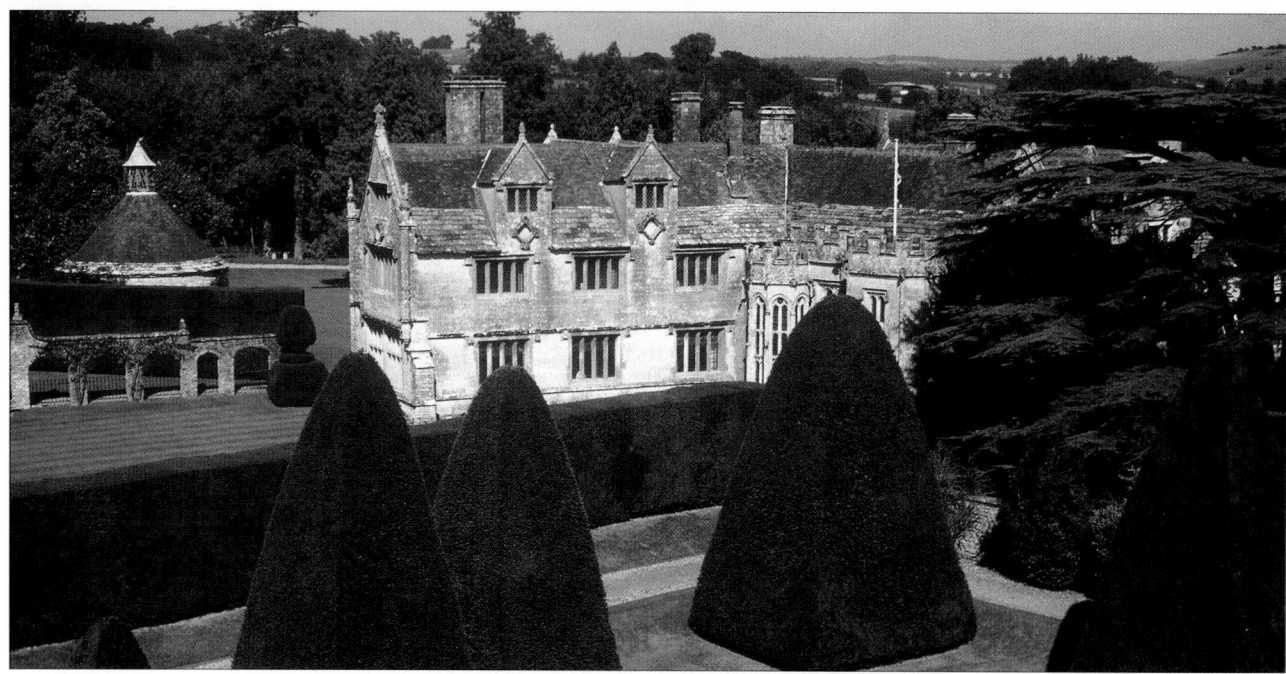

ATHELHAMPTON HOUSE & GARDENS
Dorchester

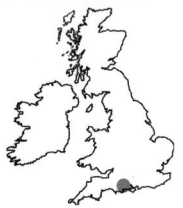

Owner:
Patrick Cooke Esq

CONTACT

Owen Davies
Athelhampton House
Dorchester
DT2 7LG

Tel: 01305 848363

Fax: 01305 848135

e-mail: pcooke@
athelhampton.co.uk

LOCATION

OS Ref. SY771 942

Off A35 (T) at Puddletown
Northbrook junction, 5m E
of Dorchester.

Rail: Dorchester.

CONFERENCE/FUNCTION

ROOM	SIZE	MAX CAPACITY
Coach House		
Long Hall	11 x 9m	80
Conservatory	16 x 11m	130
Main House		
Great Hall	12 x 8m	70
Great Chamber	10 x 6m	40
All four rooms are licensed for Civil wedding ceremonies.		

Athelhampton is one of the finest 15th century manor houses and is surrounded by one of the great architectural gardens of England. The Great Hall was built by Sir William Martyn in 1485. The West wing is Elizabethan in period and contains the Great Chamber, Library and Wine Cellar. On the East side of the house are the Green Parlour, Dining Room and three bedrooms opening off the Landing. Athelhampton houses a fine collection of English furniture starting in the Jacobean period leading on to late Victorian. There is also a collection relating to A W Pugin and The Palace of Westminster.

The glorious Grade I gardens, dating from 1891, contain the world-famous topiary pyramids, fountains and the River Piddle. Collections of tulips, magnolias, roses, clematis and lilies can be seen in season. Located in the gardens are a number of small buildings each with their own unique history. The two garden pavilions were used as water towers for the original fountain system. The Toll house was a collection point for the Wimborne turnpike trust between 1842 and 1878 and has now been restored along with its garden. The dovecote is one of the earliest in Dorset and with a capacity for 1200 birds would have supported a large household.

The Coach House contains all the facilities required for the comfort of daily visitors with private rooms available for visiting groups. The House and Gardens can be opened by appointment for evening visits and dinners. Saturdays are reserved exclusively for wedding ceremonies and receptions.

OPENING TIMES

March - October:
Daily (closed Saturdays).

Open Saturdays at Easter &
August BH weekends.

November - February:
Sundays only,
10.30am - 5pm/dusk.

Coach House Restaurant open
as house & gardens. Carvery on
Suns. Please book.

All facilities at Athelhampton are
available for private hire outside
our normal opening hours.
We specialise in weddings on
Saturdays and dinners on any
evening. Please contact
Owen Davies, Manager.

ADMISSION

House and Gardens
Adult £5.50
Child ....Free
Student....................£3.50
Disabled.................£3.50
OAP.......................£5.20

Groups (12+)
Adult £4.20

Gardens only
Adult £3.95
Child ....Free

By arrangement.
Partially suitable. WC.
Licensed.
Licensed.
By arrangement.

Guide dogs only.

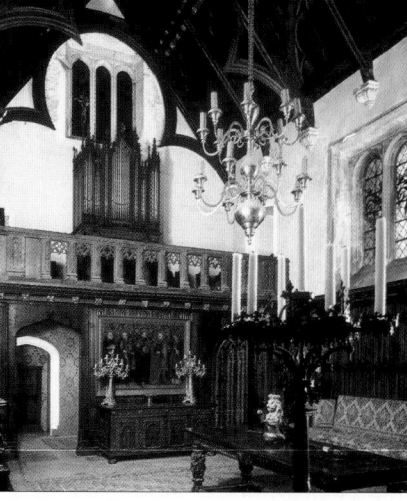
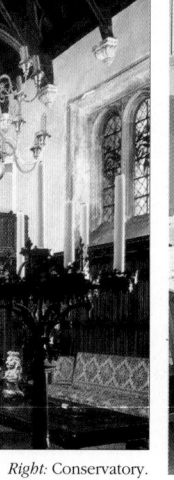
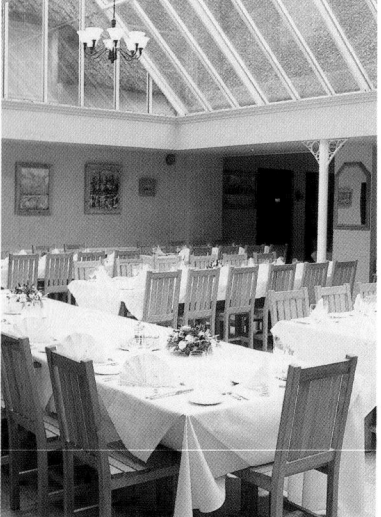

Above: Great Hall. *Right:* Conservatory.

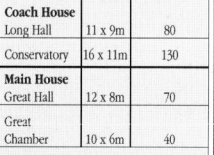

South West England

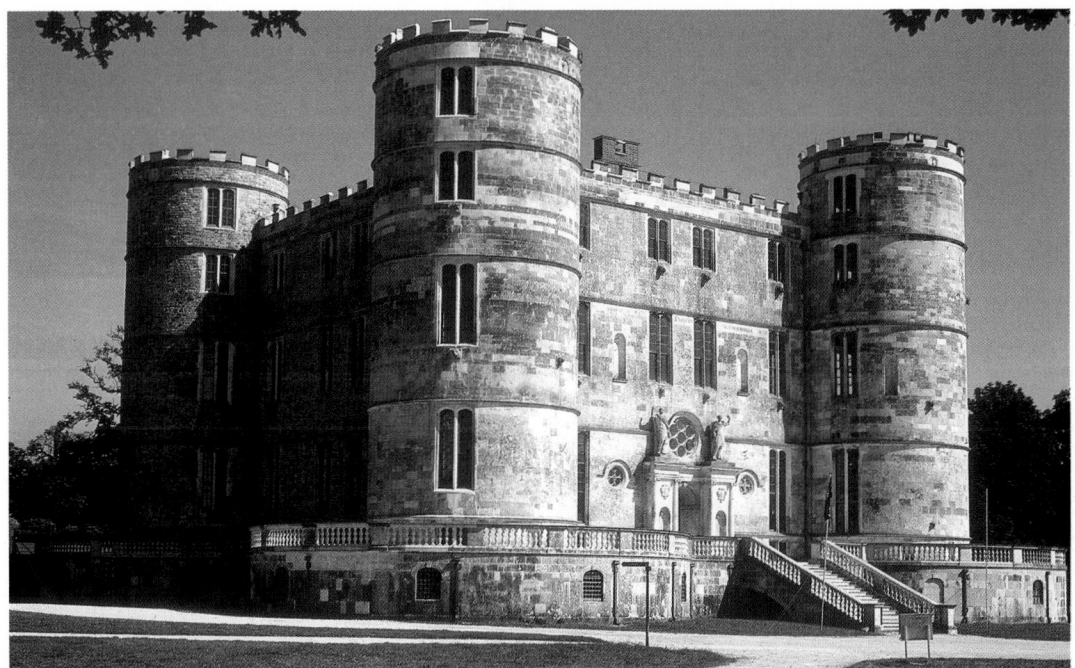

LULWORTH CASTLE
Dorset

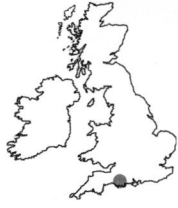

Owner: The Weld Estate

CONTACT

East Lulworth
Wareham
Dorset
BH20 5QS

Tel: 01929 400352

Fax: 01929 400563

LOCATION

OS194 Ref. SY853 822

In E Lulworth off B3070,
3m NE of Lulworth Cove.

A 17th century hunting lodge restored by English Heritage after the fire of 1929. Features include a gallery devoted to the Weld family, owners of the Castle and Estate since 1641. The kitchen and wine cellar have been furnished and the history of the building is brought to life through a video presentation. The Chapel of St Mary in the Castle grounds is reputed to be one of the finest pieces of architecture in Dorset. It is the first free standing Roman Catholic church to be built in England since the Reformation and contains an exhibition of 18th and 19th century vestments, church and recusant silver. A short walk from the Castle and Chapel is the Animal Farm, Play Area and Woodland Walk. The stables have been converted to house the licensed café serving morning coffee, light lunches and traditional cream teas. The Courtyard Shop offers a wide range of unusual gift items. Coach and car parking and access to the shop and café is free.

Lulworth Castle House

Modern house of the Weld family containing the Blundell collection of pictures and 18th century sculptures as well as portraits and furniture from Lulworth Castle. Walled garden and grounds.

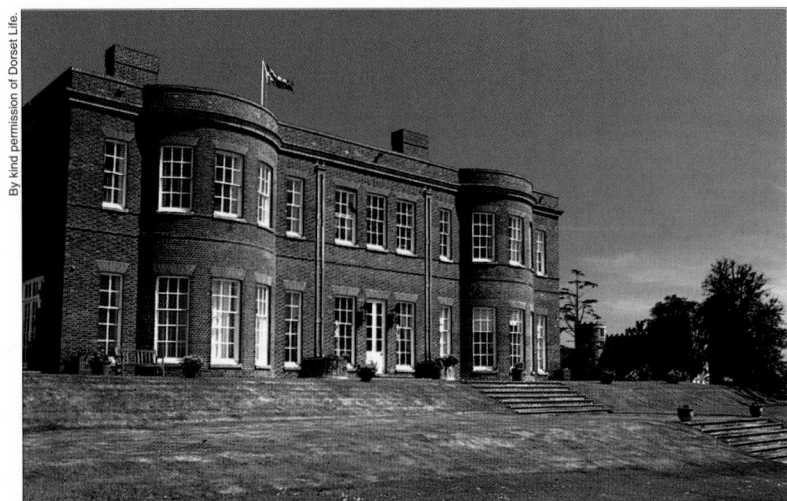

Lulworth Castle House

By kind permission of Dorset Life.

Corporate hospitality, conferences, receptions etc.

Partially suitable. WC.

Licensed.

By arrangement.

In grounds, on leads.

5 holiday cottages, tel: 01929 400100 (Mrs Weld).

OPENING TIMES

Lulworth Castle

30 Oct - 26 Mar 2001:
10am - 4pm or dusk if earlier.
27 Mar - 26 Oct 2001:
10.30am - 6pm. 28 Oct -
24 Mar 2002: 10.30am - 4pm
or dusk if earlier.
Sun - Fri, plus Easter Sat.
Closed Sats and 24/25 Dec.
Lulworth Leisure reserve the
right to close the Castle
without notice.

Lulworth Castle House

30 May - 26 Sept: Weds,
2 - 5pm. Groups: Mon - Fri
by appointment only.

ADMISSION

Lulworth Castle

Adult	£5.50
Child (5-16)	£3.00
Conc	£4.50
Family (2+3)	£14.00

Groups (10-200)

Adult	£4.95
Child (5-16)	£2.70
Conc	£4.05

Lulworth Castle House

Adult	£4.00
Child (5-16)	£1.50
OAP	£3.50
Family (2+3)	£10.00

Joint Ticket with Lulworth
Castle

Adult	£7.50
Child (5-16)	£3.50
OAP	£6.00
Family	£16.00

Children under 5yrs Free.

SPECIAL EVENTS

• **APR 15/16**
Easter Bunny Hunt.

• **MAY 12/13**
Country Gardening & Food Fair.

• **JUL 28/29**
Lulworth Horse Trials
& Country Fair.

• **SEPT 14 - 16**
International Floral Design
Show & Competition.

ABBOTSBURY SUB-TROPICAL GARDENS

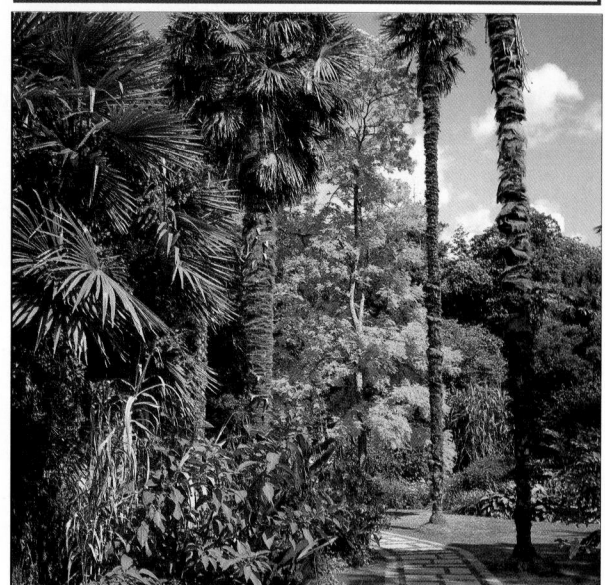

ABBOTSBURY, WEYMOUTH, DORSET DT3 4JT

Owner: *The Hon Mrs Townshend DL*   **Contact:** *Shop Manager*

Tel: 01305 871387

Over 20 acres of exotic and rare plants. Established in 1765. Superb colonial-style Teahouse. Extensively stocked plant centre. Quality gift shop.

Location: OS Ref. SY564 851. On B3157. Off the A35 between Weymouth & Bridport.

Opening Times: Mar - Nov, daily 10am - 6pm. Winter, daily 10am - 4pm. Last admission 1 hr before closing.

Admission: Adult £4.70, Child £3.20, OAP £4.50.

🖼 ❄ 🍽 ♿Partially suitable. 🍴 Licensed. 🍴 🍴By arrangement. 🅿Free. 🛏 🐕In grounds, on leads. ❄

ATHELHAMPTON HOUSE & GDNS   See page 210 for full page entry.

BROWNSEA ISLAND   **Tel:** 01202 707744   **Fax:** 01202 701635

Poole Harbour, Dorset BH13 7EE

Owner: National Trust   **Contact:** The Property Manager

A wonderfully atmospheric island of heath and woodland. Privately owned until aquired by the Trust in 1962 and now a haven for a rich variety of wildlife, including red squirrels and many species of bird. Part of the island is leased as a nature reserve to the Dorset Wildlife Trust. There are many fine walks and spectacular views of Poole Harbour. Note: Boats run from Poole Quay, Bournemouth and Sandbanks. Visitors may land from own boats at Pottery Pier at West end of island, accessible at all stages of the tide. Please note that the island's paths are uneven in places.

Location: OS Ref. SZ032 878. In Poole Harbour. Boats run from Poole Quay, Bournemouth and Sandbanks. Visitors may land on the beach with a dinghy.

Opening Times: 31 Mar - 7 Oct: daily, 10am - 5pm. Jul & Aug: 10am - 6pm.

Admission: Landing fee £3.50, Child £1.50, Family (2+3) £8.50 (1+3) £5. Groups £3.20, Child £1.20 by written appointment with the Property Manager.

🖼 ♿Partially suitable. 🍴 🍴 🛏 ♿Tel. for details.

CHETTLE HOUSE   **Tel:** 01258 830209   **Fax:** 01258 830380

Chettle, Blandford Forum, Dorset DT11 8DB

Owner/Contact: Patrick Bourke Esq

A fine Queen Anne manor house designed by Thomas Archer and a fine example of English baroque architecture. The house features a basement with the typical north-south passage set just off centre with barrel-vaulted ceilings and a magnificent stone staircase. The house is set in 5 acres of peaceful gardens and there is a new rose garden.

Location: OS Ref. ST952 132. 6m NE of Blandford NW of A354.

Opening Times: Easter Sun - end Sept: Suns only. Groups: by appointment any day.

Admission: Adult £2.50, Child Free (under 16yrs).

♿Grounds suitable. 🍴 🍴

CHRISTCHURCH CASTLE & NORMAN HOUSE   **Tel:** 0117 9750700

Christchurch, Dorset

Owner: English Heritage   **Contact:** The South West Office

Early 12th century Norman keep and Constable's house, built c1160.

Location: OS195. Ref. SZ160 927. In Christchurch, near the Priory.

Opening Times: Any reasonable time.

Admission: Free.

CLOUDS HILL 🌿   **Tel:** 01929 405616

Wareham, Dorset BH20 7NQ

Owner: The National Trust   **Contact:** The Custodian

A tiny isolated brick and tile cottage, bought in 1925 by T E Lawrence (Lawrence of Arabia) as a retreat. The austere rooms inside are much as he left them and reflect his complex personality and close links with the Middle East.

Location: OS Ref. SY824 909. 9m E of Dorchester, 1½ m E of Waddock crossroads B3390.

Opening Times: 1 Apr - 28 Oct: daily except, Mons, Tues, & Sats (open BH Mons), 12 noon - 5pm or dusk if earlier, (no electric light). Groups wishing to visit at other times must telephone in advance.

Admission: £2.60, no reduction for children or groups.

ℹNo WC. ♿Braille guide. 🅿No coaches.

CORFE CASTLE 🌿

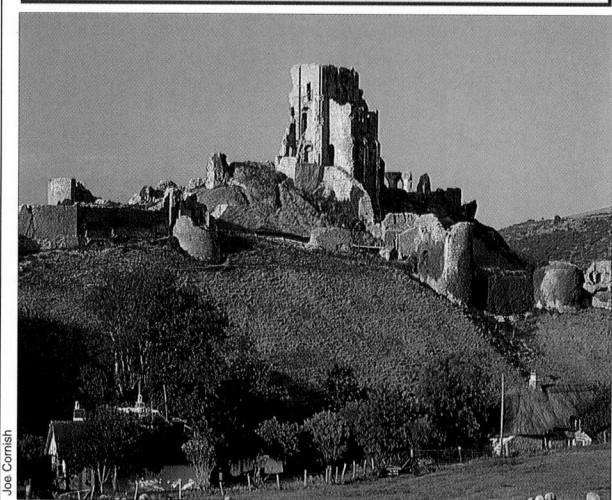

Joe Cornish

WAREHAM, DORSET BH20 5EZ

Owner: *The National Trust*   **Contact:** *The Property Manager*

Tel: 01929 481294

One of Britain's most majestic ruins, the Castle controlled the gateway through the Purbeck Hills and had been an important stronghold since the time of William the Conqueror. Defended during the Civil War by the redoubtable Lady Bankes, the Castle fell to treachery from within and was heavily slighted afterwards by the Parliamentarians. Many fine Norman and early English features remain. Visitor Centre at Castle View.

Location: OS Ref. SY959 824. On A351 Wareham - Swanage Rd. NW of the village.

Opening Times: All year: daily. Mar: 10am - 5pm; Apr - Oct: 10am - 6pm; Nov - Feb 2002: 10am - 4pm, last admission ½ hr before closing. Closed 25/26 Dec & 2 days end Jan, tel for details.

Admission: Adult £4.20, Child £2.10, Family (2+3) £10.50/ (1+3) £6. Groups: Adult £3.60, Child £1.80.

🖼 ♿Limited. WC. 🍴 🛏 🐕On leads. ❄

CRANBORNE MANOR GARDEN   **Tel:** 01725 517248   **Fax:** 01725 517862

Cranborne, Wimborne, Dorset BH21 5PP

Owner: The Viscount & Viscountess Cranborne   **Contact:** The Manor Garden Centre

The beautiful and historic gardens of yew hedges, walled, herb, mount and wild gardens originate from the 17th century – originally laid out by Mounten Jennings with John Tradescant supplying many of the original plants. Spring time is particularly good with displays of spring bulbs and crab apple orchard in the wild garden.

Location: OS Ref. SU054 133. On B3078 N of Bournemouth (18m), S of Salisbury (16m).

Opening Times: Mar - Sept: Weds, 9am - 5pm. Occasional weekends, phone for details. Entrance, parking and tearoom via the Garden Centre.

Admission: Adult £3, Child 50p, OAP £2.50.

🖼 🌿Garden centre. ♿Partially suitable. 🍴 🍴By arrangement. 🅿 🍴 🌍

DEANS COURT
Tel: 01202 886116

Wimborne, Dorset BH21 1EE

Owner: Sir Michael & Lady Hanham   **Contact:** Wimborne Tourist Information Centre
13 peaceful acres a few minutes walk south of the Minster. Specimen trees, lawns, borders, herb garden, kitchen garden with long serpentine wall and rose garden. Chemical-free produce usually for sale, also interesting herbaceous plants. Wholefood teas in garden or in Housekeeper's room (down steps).

Location: OS Ref. SZ010 997. 2 mins walk S from centre of Wimborne Minster.

Opening Times: 15 Apr, 6 & 27 May, 10 & 24 Jun, 22 Jul, 4/5 Aug: 2 - 6pm. 16 Apr, 7 & 28 May: 10am - 6pm. Organic Gardening Weekends: 26 Aug, 16 Sept: 2 - 6pm. 27 Aug: 10am - 6pm.

Admission: Adult £2, Child (5-15yrs) 50p, OAP £1.50. Groups by arrangement. Exhibition: Adult £3.50, Child (5-16yrs)/Student £1.50, Child (under 5yrs) Free, OAP £3. Family £6 (2+2).

Garden produce sales.   P   Guide dogs only.

EDMONDSHAM HOUSE & GARDENS
Tel: 01725 517207

Cranborne, Wimborne, Dorset BH21 5RE

Owner/Contact: Mrs Julia E Smith

Charming blend of Tudor and Georgian architecture with interesting contents. Organic walled garden, dower house garden, 6 acre garden with unusual trees and spring bulbs. 12th century church nearby.

Location: OS Ref. SU062 116. Off B3081 between Cranborne and Verwood, NW from Ringwood 9m, Wimborne 9m.

Opening Times: House & Gardens: All BH Mons & Weds in Apr & Oct 2 - 5pm. Gardens: Apr - Oct, Suns & Weds 2 - 5pm.

Admission: House & Garden: Adult £3, Child £1 (under 5yrs Free). Garden only: Adult £1.50, Child 50p. Groups by arrangement, teas for groups.

Available if booked, max 50 persons.   Obligatory.   Car park only.   (max 50).

FIDDLEFORD MANOR
Tel: 0117 9750700

Sturminster Newton, Dorset

Owner: English Heritage   **Contact:** The South West Regional Office

Part of a medieval manor house, with a remarkable interior. The splendid roof structures in the hall and upper living room are the best in Dorset.

Location: OS194 ST801 136. 1m E of Sturminster Newton off A357.

Opening Times: 1 Apr - 30 Sept: daily, 10am - 6pm. 1 Nov - 31 Mar: daily 10am - 4pm. Closed 24 - 26 Dec & 1 Jan.

Admission: Free.

DORSET COUNTY MUSEUM

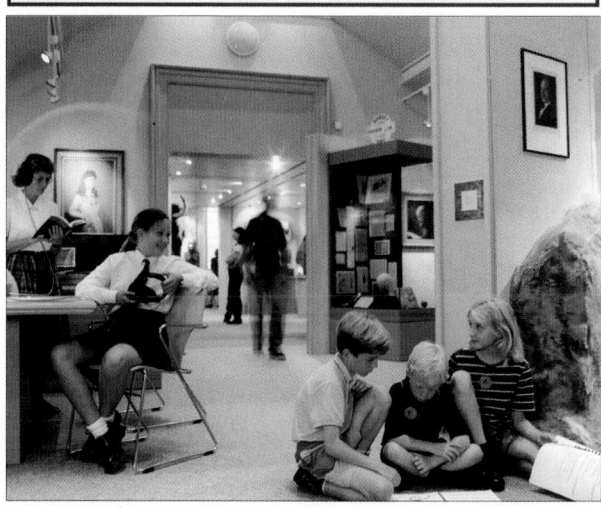

HIGH WEST STREET, DORCHESTER, DORSET DT1 1XA

Owner: The Dorset Natural History & Archaeological Society   *Contact:* Richard De Peyer

Tel: 01305 262735   **Fax:** 01305 257180

Sixteen exhibition rooms in a distinguished high Victorian museum building. New 'Dorset Writer's Gallery' includes a reconstruction of Thomas Hardy's study, displays on William Barnes, author of *Lyndon Lea* and many others. Evocative Victorian Hall paved with Roman mosaics; award-winning Archaeology Gallery, Geology, Natural History and local history displays; fine temporary exhibitions gallery. Interpret Britain commendation 1997. Best Social History Museum Award 1998.

Location: OS Ref. SY688 906. In the centre of Dorchester.

Opening Times: 1 Nov - 30 Apr: Mon - Sat, 10am - 5pm. May - Oct: daily, 10am - 5pm.

Admission: Adult £3.30, Child £1.60, Conc. £2.20, Family £8.20. Groups (15+): Adult £2.75.

Partially suitable.   P None - set down bay for coaches.   Guide dogs only.

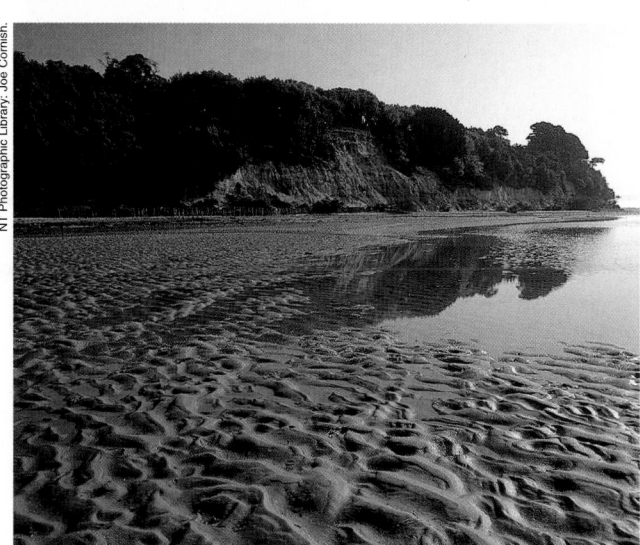

Brownsea Island, Dorset.

FORDE ABBEY

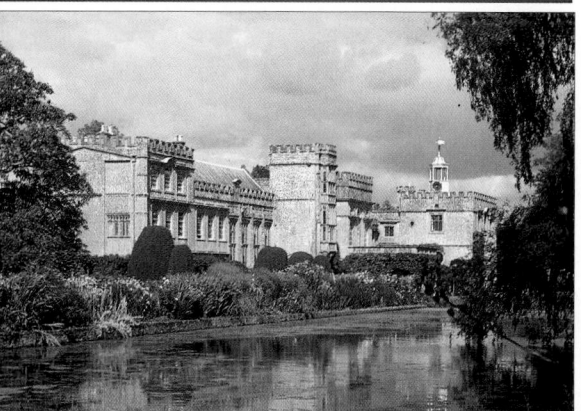

Nr CHARD, SOMERSET TA20 4LU

Owner/Contact: Mark Roper Esq

Tel: 01460 221290

One of the top ten gardens in England. 30 acres of timeless elegance, old walls, colourful borders, wide lawns, ponds, cascades, statuary, a walled working kitchen garden and huge mature trees surround a unique former Cistercian monastery that has been a private home since 1649. The medieval abbey was founded in 1140 and survives externally almost as the monks left it in 1539. Home to the Roper family and the world famous Mortlake tapestries and a host of outstanding pictures and furniture.

Location: OS Ref. ST358 041. Just off the B3167 4m S of Chard.

Opening Times: House: Apr - Oct, Suns, Tues - Thurs & BHs, 1 - 4.30pm. Gardens: All year: daily, 10am - 4.30pm.

Admission: House & Gardens: Adult £5.40, Child Free, OAP £5, Groups (20+) £4.50. Gardens: Adult £4.20, Child Free, OAP £3.95, Groups (20+) £3.75.

i Conferences. No photography in house.   Wedding receptions.
Ground floor & gardens suitable. WC. Wheelchair available, please telephone.
Licensed.   By arrangement.   P   In grounds, on leads.

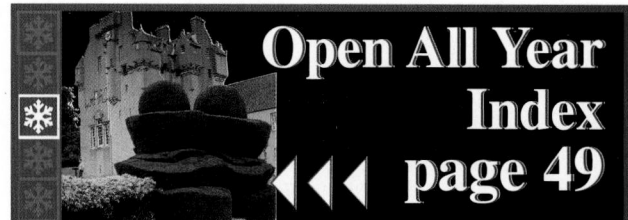

Open All Year
Index
◄◄◄ page 49

HARDY'S COTTAGE

Tel: 01305 262366

Higher Bockhampton, Dorchester, Dorset DT2 8QJ

Owner/Contact: The National Trust

A small thatched cottage where the novelist and poet Thomas Hardy was born in 1840, and from where he would walk to school every day in Dorchester, six miles away. It was built by his great-grandfather and is little altered since. The interior has been furnished by the Trust (see also Max Gate).

Location: OS Ref. SY728 925. 3m NE of Dorchester, ¹/₂ m S of A35. 10 mins walk through the woods from car park.

Opening Times: 1 Apr - 4 Nov: daily except Fris & Sats (open Good Fri), 11am - 5pm or dusk if earlier.

Admission: £2.60. No reduction for children or groups. School groups and coaches by arrangement only.

No WC. Garden suitable. No coach parking.

HIGHCLIFFE CASTLE

See below for half page entry.

HIGHER MELCOMBE

Tel: 01258 880251

Melcombe Bingham, Dorchester, Dorset DT2 7PB

Owner: Mr M C Woodhouse   **Contact:** Lt Col J M Woodhouse

Consists of the surviving wing of a 16th century house with its attached domestic chapel. A fine plaster ceiling and linenfold panelling. Conducted tours by owner.

Location: OS Ref. ST749 024. 1km W of Melcombe Bingham.

Opening Times: May - Sept by appointment.

Admission: Adult £2 (takings go to charity).

Not suitable. By written appointment only. Limited. Guide dogs only.

HORN PARK GARDENS

Tel: 01308 862212

Beaminster, Dorset DT8 3HB

Owner/Contact: John Kirkpatrick Esq

Large, beautiful garden; unique position, magnificent view to sea. Plantsman's Garden, unusual trees, shrubs and plants, in rock, water garden, terraces and herbaceous borders. Woodland Garden, Bluebell Woods. Wild Flower Meadow, with over 160 species, including orchids. Plants for sale. In "Twelve Beautiful Gardens" calendar for 1998 and "Twelve Gardens to Remember" for 1999.

Location: OS Ref. ST468 030. 1m NW of Beaminster, just S of the tunnel on the A3066.

Opening Times: 1 Apr - 31 Oct: Sun - Thur, 2 - 6pm.

Admission: Adult £3.50. Child (under 16yrs) Free. Groups £3.50.

 By arrangement. Dogs on leads.

THE KEEP MILITARY MUSEUM OF DEVON & DORSET   Tel: 01305 264066

Bridport Rd, Dorchester, Dorset DT1 1RN   **Fax:** 01305 250373

Owner: Ministry of Defence (Museums Trustees)   **Contact:** The Curator

There are four floors to explore in this Grade II listed building. Uniforms, medals and weapons reside alongside touch pad technology. Feel the experience of how it really was in the re-created world war bunker. Climb to the roof to view the county town and Hardy country. Lift available.

Location: OS Ref. SY687 906. In Dorchester at the top of High West Street.

Opening Times: All year: Mon - Sat 9.30am - 5pm (last admission 4.15pm). Suns during Jul & Aug, 10am - 4pm.

Admission: Adult £3, Conc. £2. Groups (10-100): Adult £2, Conc. £1.

No flash photography. By arrangement. Limited. Guide dogs only. Tel. for details.

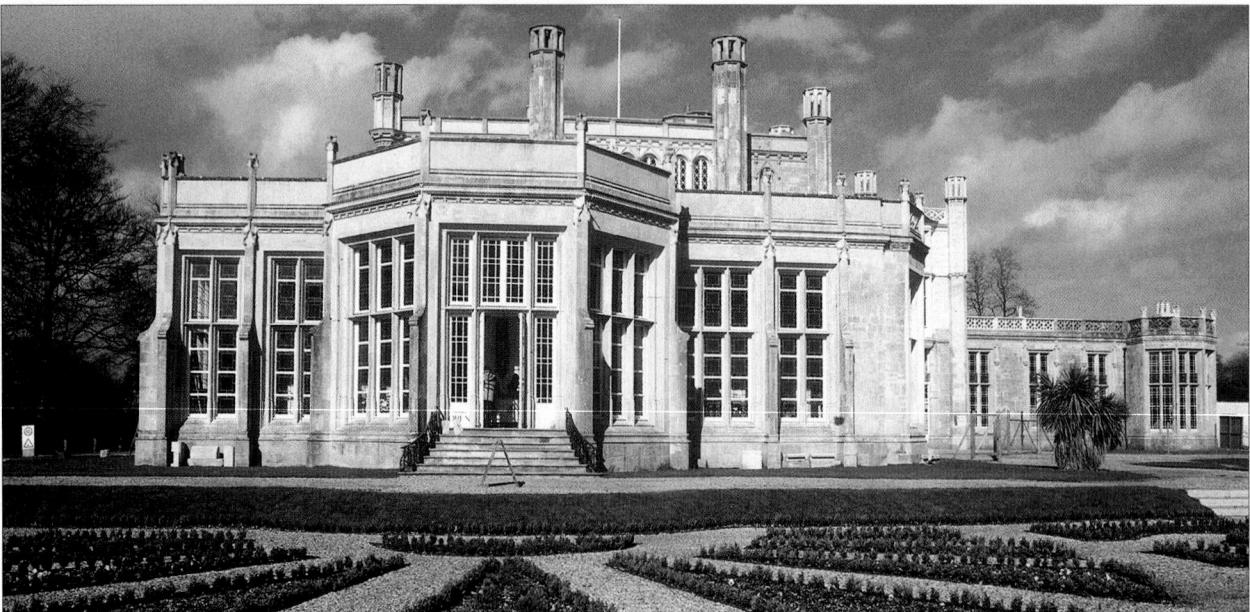

HIGHCLIFFE CASTLE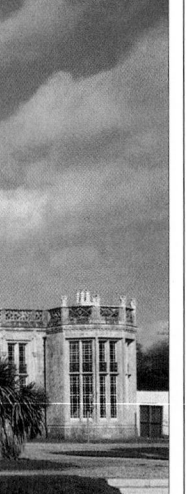

ROTHSAY DRIVE, HIGHCLIFFE-ON-SEA, CHRISTCHURCH BH23 4LE

Owner: Christchurch Borough Council   *Contact:* Mike Allen, Manager

Tel: 01425 278807 or 01202 495131 **Fax:** 01425 280423

e-mail: m.allen@christchurch.gov.uk

Built in 1830 in the Romantic and Picturesque style of architecture for Lord Stuart de Rothesay using his unique collection of French medieval stonework and stained glass. Recently repaired externally, it remains mostly unrepaired inside. Five rooms house a visitor centre, exhibitions, events and gift shop. Coastal grounds, village trail and nearby St Mark's church.

Location: OS Ref. SZ200 930. Off the A337 Lymington Road, between Christchurch and Highcliffe-on-Sea.

Opening Times: May - Oct (check exact dates): daily, 1 - 5pm. Grounds: All year.

Admission: Adult £1.50, Child Free. Group guided tour (min 12): Adult £2.50, Child £1. Grounds: Free.

 Partially suitable. WC. 10am - 5pm. By arrangement. Limited. Parking charge. By arrangement. In grounds, on leads.

KINGSTON LACY

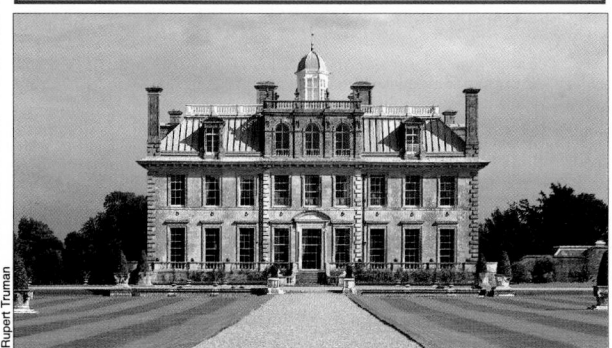

Rupert Truman

WIMBORNE MINSTER, DORSET BH21 4EA

Owner: The National Trust   *Contact:* The Property Manager

Tel: 01202 883402   **Infoline:** 01202 880413   **Fax:** 01202 882402

A 17th century house, designed by Sir Roger Pratt for Sir Ralph Bankes to replace his ruined family seat at Corfe Castle. Altered by Sir Charles Barry in the 19th century, the house contains the outstanding collection of paintings and other works of art accumulated by William Bankes. It is famous for its dramatic Spanish room, with walls hung in magnificent gilded leather. The house and garden are set in a wooded park with attractive waymarked walks and a find herd of Red Devon cattle. The surrounding estate is crossed by many paths (leaflet available from shop) and dominated by the Iron Age hill fort of Badbury Rings. The botanically rich rings are managed by grazing and dogs are not permitted. Point-to-Point races are held 24 Feb, 24 Mar & 14 Apr and on these days a charge is made for car-parking.

Location: OS Ref. ST978 013. On B3082 - Blandford / Wimborne road, 1$\frac{1}{2}$ m NW of Wimborne.

Opening Times: House: 31 Mar - 4 Nov: daily except Mons & Tues (open BH Mons, closed Good Fri), 12 noon - 5.30pm (last admission 4.30pm). Garden & Park: 3 Feb - 25 Mar: Sats & Suns only, 11am - 4pm. 31 Mar - 4 Nov: daily, 11am - 6pm; 9 Nov - 23 Dec: Fri - Sun, 11am - 4pm. Special Snowdrop Days early 2002, telephone infoline.

Admission: Adult £6.50, Child £3, Family £17. Park & garden only: Adult £3, Child £1.50. Pre-booked groups (15+): £5.

▢   ♿Garden only. Braille guide. WC.   🍴   ✗By arrangement.   P   ▥
🐾In park only.   ▨ Telephone for details.

KINGSTON MAURWARD GARDENS

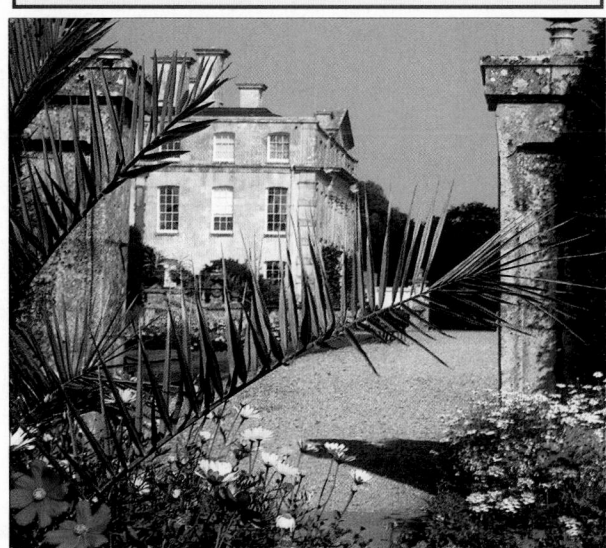

DORCHESTER, DORSET DT2 8PY

Contact: Mike Hancock

Tel: 01305 215003   **Fax:** 01305 215001   **e-mail:** administration@kmc.ac.uk

Classical Georgian mansion set in 35 acres of 18th century gardens including 5 acre lake. Restored Edwardian gardens with dividing hedges, stone balustrading features. Walled demonstration garden, National collections of Penstemons and Salvias. Animal park, Nature and Tree Trails. Visitors' Centre and restaurant.

Location: OS Ref. SY713 911. 1m E of Dorchester. Roundabout off A35 by-pass.

Opening Times: 6 Jan - 23 Dec: daily, 10am - 5.30pm or dusk if earlier.

Admission: Adult £3.75, Child £2 (under 3yrs Free). Groups (10+): Adult £3.25. Guided tours (by arrangement) (12+):£3.75.

ℹ️Conferences.   ▢   ♿   🍷Wedding receptions.   🍴   ✗By arrangement.
P   ▥   🐾 Guide dogs only.   ▨

KNOLL GARDENS & NURSERY   **Tel:** 01202 873931 **Fax:** 01202 870842

Stapehill Road, Hampreston, Wimborne BH21 7ND

Owner: J & J Flude & N R Lucas   **Contact:** Mr John Flude

Award-winning 6 acre gardens, with 6000+ named plants from the world over.

Location: OS Ref. SU059 001. Between Wimborne & Ferndown. Exit A31 Canford Bottom roundabout, B3073 Hampreston. Signposted 1$\frac{1}{2}$ m.

Opening Times: Mar: Wed - Sun, 10am - 4.30pm. Apr - Sept: daily 10am - 5pm. Oct & Nov: Wed - Sun, 10am - 4.30pm. Closed Dec - Feb inclusive.

Admission: Adult £4, Child (5-15yrs) £2, OAP £3.50, Student £3. Groups: Adult £3, Child £1.75, Student £2.50. Family (2+2) £9.75.

LULWORTH CASTLE ⛢ 🏛   **See page 211 for full page entry.**

MAPPERTON 🏛

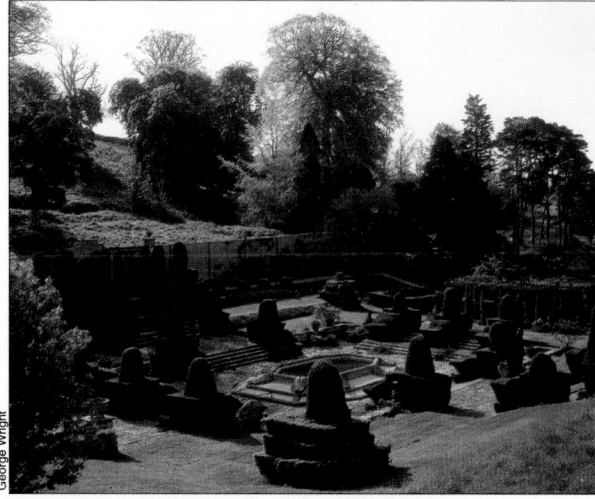

George Wright

BEAMINSTER, DORSET DT8 3NR

Owner/Contact: The Earl & Countess of Sandwich

Tel: 01308 862645   **Fax:** 01308 863348   **e-mail:** office@mapperton.com

Jacobean 1660s manor with Tudor features and classical north front. Italianate upper garden with orangery, topiary and formal borders descending to fish ponds and shrub gardens. All Saints Church forms south wing opening to courtyard and stables. Area of outstanding natural beauty with fine views of Dorset hills and woodlands. House and Gardens featured in *Restoration, Emma* and *Tom Jones.*

Location: OS Ref. SY503 997. 1m S of B3163, 2m NE of B3066, 2m SE Beaminster, 5m NE Bridport.

Opening Times: Gardens: 1 Mar - 31 Oct: daily, 2 - 6pm. House: Open only to groups by appointment (times as for gardens, but not Sat or Sun).

Admission: Gardens: £3.50. House (tour) £3.50. Child (under 18yrs) £1.50, under 5 Free.

▢   ⛲   ♿Partially suitable.   ▦   ✗By arrangement.   ▥
P Limited for coaches.   🐾Guide dogs only.   Ⓦ

MAX GATE   **Tel:** 01305 262538   **Fax:** 01305 250978

Alington Avenue, Dorchester, Dorset DT1 2AA   **e-mail:** max.gate@btinternet.com

Owner: The National Trust   **Contact:** The Tenant

Poet and novelist Thomas Hardy designed and lived in the house from 1885 until his death in 1928. The house is leased to tenants and contains several pieces of Hardy's furniture.

Location: OS Ref. SY704 897. 1m E of Dorchester just N of the A352 to Wareham. From Dorchester follow A352 signs to the roundabout named Max Gate (at Jct. of A35 Dorchester bypass). Turn left and left again into cul-de-sac outside Max Gate.

Opening Times: 1 Apr - 30 Sept: Mons, Weds & Suns, 2 - 5pm. Only dining and drawing rooms open.

Admission: Adult £2.30, Child £1.20.

♿Limited access to ground floor for wheelchairs.   P Limited.   🐾

MILTON ABBEY CHURCH   **Tel:** 01258 880489

Milton Abbas, Blandford, Dorset DT11 0BZ

Owner: Diocese of Salisbury   **Contact:** Chris Fookes

Abbey church dating from 14th century.

Location: OS117 ST798 024. 3$\frac{1}{2}$ m N of A354. Between Dorchester/Blandford Road.

Opening Times: Abbey Church: daily 10am - 6pm. Groups by arrangement please.

Admission: By donation except Easter & mid-Jul - end Aug. Adult £1.75, Child Free.

MINTERNE GARDENS   **Tel:** 01300 341370   **Fax:** 01300 341747

Minterne Magna, Nr Dorchester, Dorset DT2 7AU

Owner/Contact: The Lord Digby

If you want to visit a formal garden, do not go to Minterne, but if you want to wander peacefully through 20 wild woodland acres, where magnolias, rhododendrons, eucryphias, hydrangeas, water plants and water lilies, provide a new vista at each turn and where ducks enhance the small lakes and cascades, then you will be welcome at Minterne, the home of the Churchill and Digby families for 350 years. The house which contains magnificent Churchill tapestries and naval and other historical pictures is open for Special Interest groups only which may be arranged by prior appointment.

Location: OS Ref. ST660 042. On A352 Dorchester/Sherborne Road, 2m N of Cerne Abbas.

Opening Times: 1 Mar - 10 Nov: daily, 10am - 7pm.

Admission: Adult £3, accompanied children Free.

Not suitable.   In grounds on leads.

PORTLAND CASTLE   **Tel:** 01305 820539

Castletown, Portland, Weymouth, Dorset DT5 1AZ

Owner: English Heritage   **Contact:** The Custodian

Discover one of Henry VIII's finest coastal fortresses. Perfectly preserved in a waterfront location overlooking Portland harbour, it is a marvellous place to visit for all the family whatever the weather. You can try on armour, explore the Tudor kitchen and gun platform, see ghostly sculptured figures from the past, enjoy the superb battlement views or picnic on the lawn in front of the newly re-opened Captain's House. An excellent new audio tour, included in the admission charge, brings the castle's history and characters to life.

Location: OS194 Ref. SY684 743. Overlooking Portland harbour.

Opening Times: 1 Apr - 31 Oct: daily, 10am - 6pm (5pm in Oct). Winter 2000 closed. From Nov 2001 - Mar 2002: Fri - Sun, 10am - 4pm. Closed 24/26 Dec & 1 Jan.

Admission: Adult £3, Child £1.50, Conc. £2.20. 15% discount for groups (11+).

  Ground floor suitable. WCs.   P   Tel. for details.

PURSE CAUNDLE MANOR   **Tel:** 01963 250400

Purse Caundle, Sherborne, Dorset DT9 5DY

Owner/Contact: Michael de Pelet Esq

15th & 16th century manor house. Great Hall with minstrels gallery. Upstairs great chamber with barrel ceiling and oriel window. Family home.

Location: OS Ref. ST695 177. 4m E of Sherborne, just S of the A30.

Opening Times: 1 May - 30 Sept: Thurs by appointment, 2 - 5pm.

Admission: Adult £2.50, Child Free. Groups by appointment.

For groups.

ST CATHERINE'S CHAPEL   **Tel:** 0117 9750700

Abbotsbury, Dorset

Owner: English Heritage   **Contact:** The South West Regional Office

A small stone chapel, set on a hilltop, with an unusual roof and small turret used as a lighthouse.

Location: OS194 Ref. SY572 848. 1/2 m S of Abbotsbury by pedestrian track to the hilltop.

Opening Times: Any reasonable time.

Admission: Free at any reasonable daylight hour.

SANDFORD ORCAS MANOR HOUSE   **Tel:** 01963 220206

Sandford Orcas, Sherborne, Dorset DT9 4SB

Owner/Contact: Sir Mervyn Medlycott Bt

Tudor manor house with gatehouse, fine panelling, furniture, pictures. Terraced gardens with topiary and herb garden. Personal conducted tour by owner.

Location: OS Ref. ST623 210. 2 1/2 m N of Sherborne, Dorset 4m S of A303 at Sparkford. Entrance next to church.

Opening Times: Easter Mon, 10am - 6pm. May - Sept: Suns, 2 - 6pm, Mons, 10am - 6pm.

Admission: Adult £3, Child £1.50. Groups (10+): Adult £2.50, Child £1.

Not suitable.   Obligatory.   In grounds, on leads.

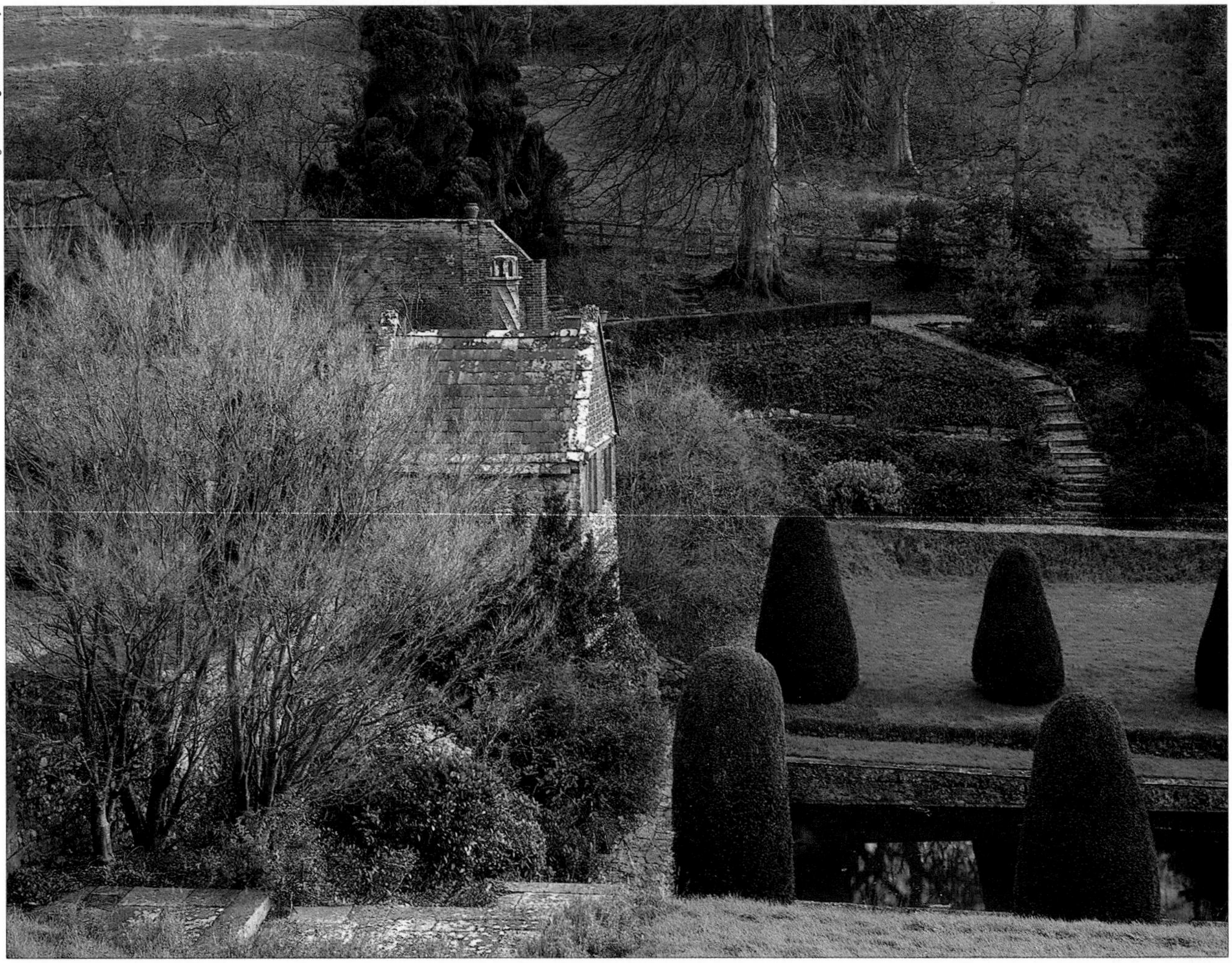

Mapperton, Dorset.

SHERBORNE CASTLE

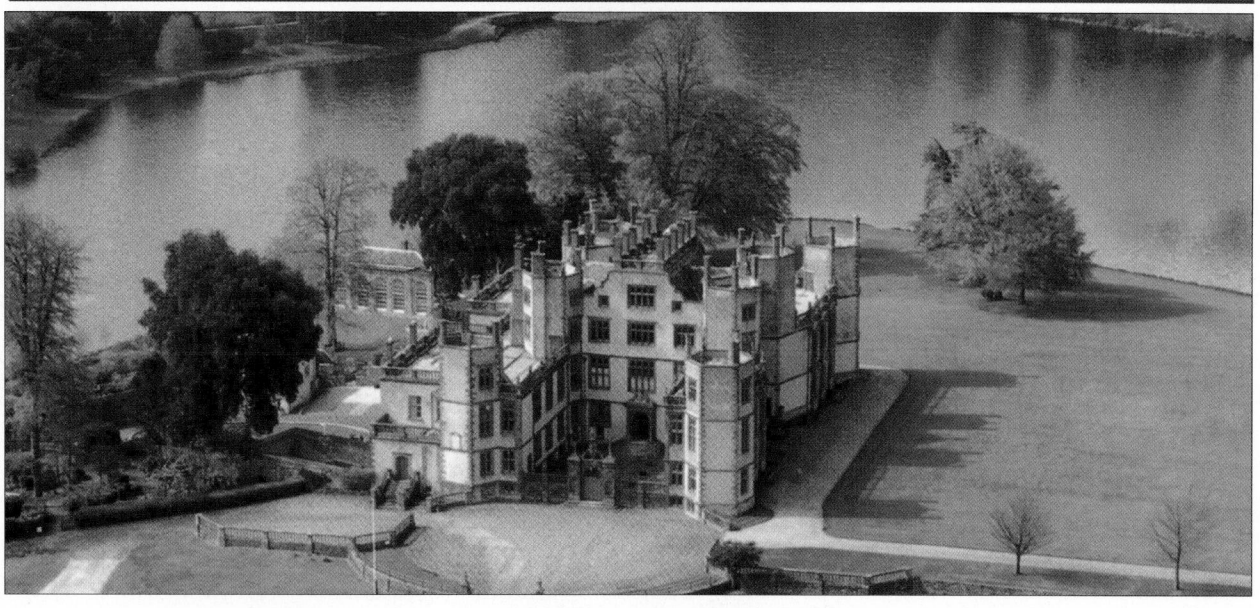

SHERBORNE, DORSET DT9 5NR

Owner: Mr & Mrs John Wingfield Digby *Contact:* Castle & Events Manager

Tel: 01935 813182 **Fax:** 01935 816727 **e-mail:** enquiries@sherbornecastle.com
Built by Sir Walter Raleigh in 1594, Sherborne Castle has been the home of the Digby family since 1617. Prince William of Orange was entertained here in 1688, and George III visited in 1789. Splendid collections of art, furniture and porcelain are on view in the Castle. Lancelot 'Capability' Brown created the lake in 1753 and gave Sherborne the very latest in landscape gardening.
Location: OS Ref. ST649 164. $^3/_4$ m SE of Sherborne town centre. Follow brown signs from A30 or A352. $^1/_2$ m S of the Old Castle.
Opening Times: 1 Apr - 31 Oct: Castle: Tues, Thurs, Suns & BH Mons, 12.30 - 4.30pm, Sats, 2.30 - 4.30pm (last admission). Gardens: daily except Weds, 10am -

5pm (last admission). Tearoom & Shop: daily (except Weds), 12.30 - 5pm (last admission). Groups (15+) by arrangement during normal opening hours and on other days if possible.
Admission: Castle & Gardens: Adult £5.50, Child (5-16yrs) £2.75, OAP £5, Family (2+2) £13.75. Groups (15+): Adult £4.75, Child (5-16) £2.30. Private Views: Adult £8.50, Child £4.25 (min charge for 15 people). Gardens only: Adult £2.75, Child (5-16) £1.30. Children under 5 Free, no concessions or group rates.

 Partially suitable. By arrangement.
In grounds, on leads. Telephone for details.

SHERBORNE OLD CASTLE

Tel: 01935 812730

Castleton, Sherborne, Dorset DT9 3SA
Owner: English Heritage **Contact:** The Custodian
The ruins of this early 12th century Castle are a testament to the 16 days it took Cromwell to capture it during the Civil War, after which it was abandoned. A gatehouse, some graceful arcading and decorative windows survive.
Location: OS183 Ref ST647 167. $^1/_2$ m E of Sherborne off B3145. $^1/_2$ m N of the 1594 Castle.
Opening Times: 1 Apr - 31 Oct: daily, 10am - 6pm (5pm in Oct). 1 Nov - 31 Mar: Wed - Sun, 10am - 4pm. Closed 24 - 26 Dec & 1 Jan.
Admission: Adult £1.80, Child 90p, Conc. £1.30. 15% discount for groups of 11+.

Grounds suitable. Limited for cars. No coach parking.

SMEDMORE HOUSE

Tel/Fax: 01929 480702

Smedmore, Kimmeridge, Wareham BH20 5BG
Owner: Dr Philip Mansel **Contact:** Mr B Belsten
The home of the Mansel family for nearly 400 years nestles at the foot of the Purbeck hills looking across Kimmeridge Bay to Portland Bill.
Location: OS Ref. SY924 787. 15m SW of Poole.
Opening Times: 13 May & 9 Sept: 2 - 5pm.
Admission: Adult £3.50, under 16s Free.

WHITE MILL

Tel: 01258 858051

Sturminster Marshall, Nr Wimborne, Dorset
Owner: The National Trust **Contact:** The Custodian
Rebuilt in 1776 on a site marked as a mill in the Domesday Book, this corn mill was extensively repaired in 1994 and still retains its original elm and applewood machinery (now too fragile to be operative). Peaceful setting with nearby riverside picnic area.
Location: OS Ref. ST958 007. On River Stour $^1/_2$ m NE of Sturminster Marshall from the B3082 Blandford to Wareham Rd, take road to SW signposted Sturminster Marshall. Mill is 1m on right. Car park nearby.
Opening Times: 31 Mar - 28 Oct: Weekends & BH Mons, 12 noon - 5pm.
Admission: Adult £2.50, Child £1.25.

Ground floor suitable. Large print guide. Obligatory.

WOLFETON HOUSE

Tel: 01305 263500 **Fax:** 01305 265090

Nr Dorchester, Dorset DT2 9QN **e-mail:** kthimbleby@wolfeton.freeserve.co.uk
Owner: Capt N T L L Thimbleby **Contact:** The Steward
A fine mediaeval and Elizabethan manor house lying in the water-meadows near the confluence of the rivers Cerne and Frome. It was much embellished around 1580 and has splendid plaster ceilings, fireplaces and panelling of that date. To be seen are the Great Hall, Stairs and Chamber, Parlour, Dining Room, Chapel and Cyder House. The mediaeval Gatehouse has two unmatched and older towers. There are good pictures and furniture.
Location: OS Ref. SY678 921. 1$^1/_2$ m from Dorchester on the A37 towards Yeovil. Indicated by Historic House signs.
Opening Times: 15 Jul - 15 Sept: Mons, Weds & Thurs. 2 - 6pm. Groups by appointment throughout the year.
Admission: Adult £4, Child £2.

By arrangement. Ground floor suitable. By arrangement.
By arrangement.

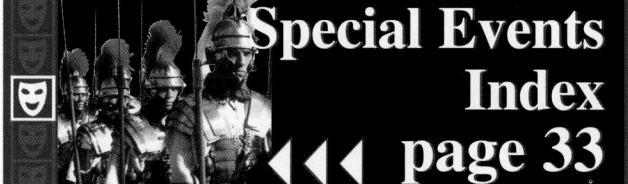

Special Events Index ◄◄◄ page 33

South West England

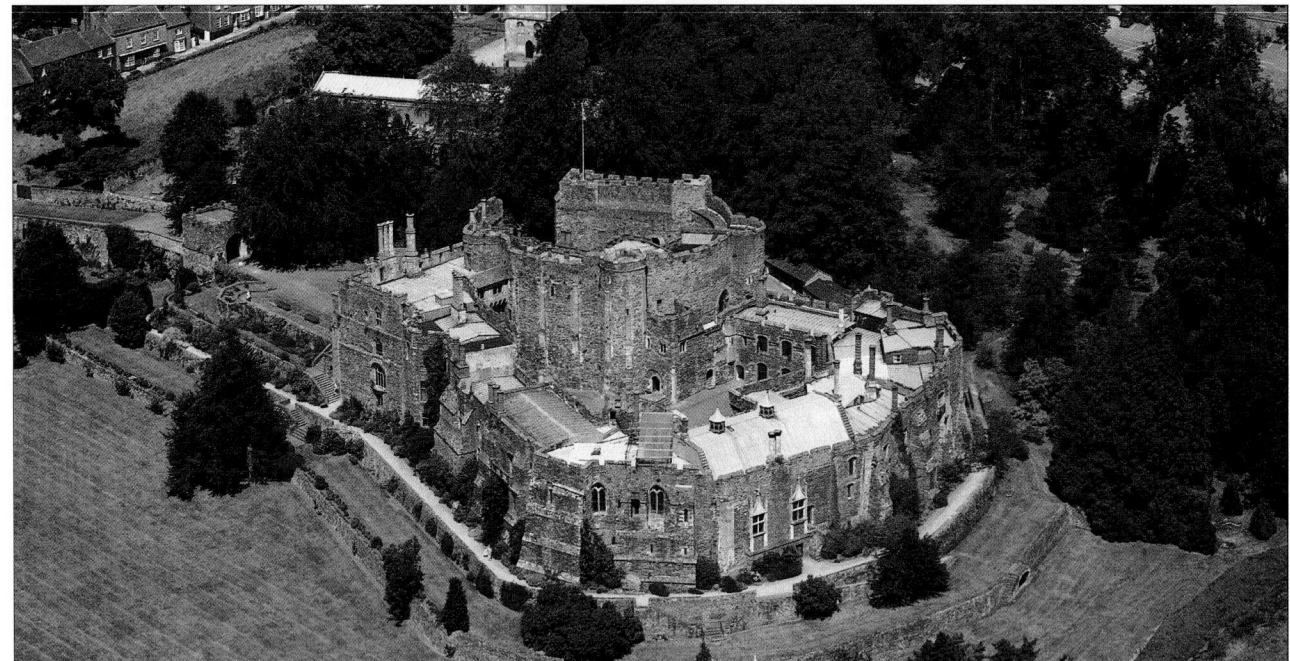

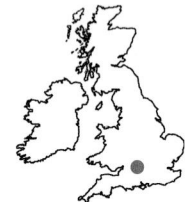

Owner: Mr R J G Berkeley

CONTACT

The Custodian
Berkeley Castle
Gloucestershire
GL13 9BQ

Tel: 01453 810332

LOCATION

OS Ref. ST685 990

SE side of Berkeley village.
Midway between
Bristol & Gloucester,
2m W off the A38.

From motorway
M5/J14 (5m) or
J13 (9m).

Bus: No 308 from
Bristol & Gloucester.

BERKELEY CASTLE
Berkeley

Not many can boast of having their private house celebrated by Shakespeare nor of having held it in the possession of their family for nearly 850 years, nor having a King of England murdered within its walls, nor of having welcomed at their table the local vicar and Castle Chaplain, John Trevisa (1342-1402), reputed as one of the earliest translators of the Bible, nor of having a breach battered by Oliver Cromwell, which to this day it is forbidden by law to repair even if it was wished to do so. But such is the story of Berkeley.

This beautiful and historic Castle, begun in 1117, still remains the home of the famous family who gave their name to numerous locations all over the world, notably Berkeley Square in London, Berkeley Hundred in Virginia and Berkeley University in California. Scene of the brutal murder of Edward II in 1327 (visitors can see his cell and nearby the dungeon) and besieged by Cromwell's troops in 1645, the Castle is steeped in history but twenty-four generations of Berkeleys have gradually transformed a Norman fortress into the lovely home it is today.

The State Apartments contain magnificent collections of furniture, rare paintings by primarily English and Dutch masters, and tapestries. Part of the world-famous Berkeley silver is on display in the Dining Room. Many other rooms are equally interesting including the Great Hall upon which site the Barons of the West Country met in 1215 before going to Runnymede to force King John to put his seal to the Magna Carta.

The Castle is surrounded by lovely terraced Elizabethan Gardens with a lily pond, Elizabeth I's bowling green, and sweeping lawns.

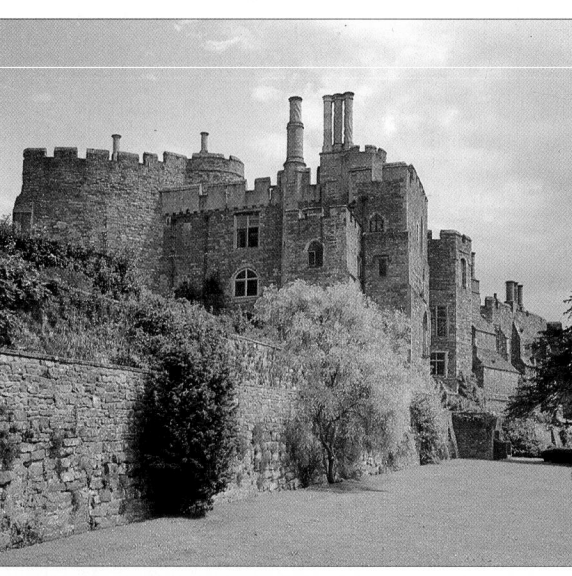

Fashion shows and filming. Butterfly farm. No photography inside the Castle.

Wedding receptions and corporate entertainment.

Visitors may alight in the Outer Bailey.

Licensed. Serving lunches and home-made teas.

Free. Max. 120 people. Tour time: One hour. Evening groups by arrangement. Group visits must be booked.

Cars 150 yds from Castle and up to 15 coaches 250 yds away.

Welcome. General and social history and architecture.

OPENING TIMES

April & May
Tue - Sun, 2 - 5pm.

June & September
Tue - Sat, 11am - 5pm,
Suns, 2 - 5pm.

July & August
Mon - Sat, 11am - 5pm
Suns, 2 - 5pm

October
Suns only, 2 - 5pm

BH Mons, 11am - 5pm

NB. Groups must book.

ADMISSION

Castle and Garden
Adult £5.50
Child £3.00
OAP......................£4.50
Family (2+2) £15.00

Groups (25+ pre-booked)
Adult £5.00
Child £2.70
OAP £4.20

Gardens only
Adult £2.00
Child £1.00

Butterfly Farm
Adult £2.00
Child/OAP £1.00
Family (2+2) £5.00
School Groups 80p

CONFERENCE/FUNCTION

ROOM	SIZE	MAX CAPACITY
Great Hall		200
Long Drawing Rm		100

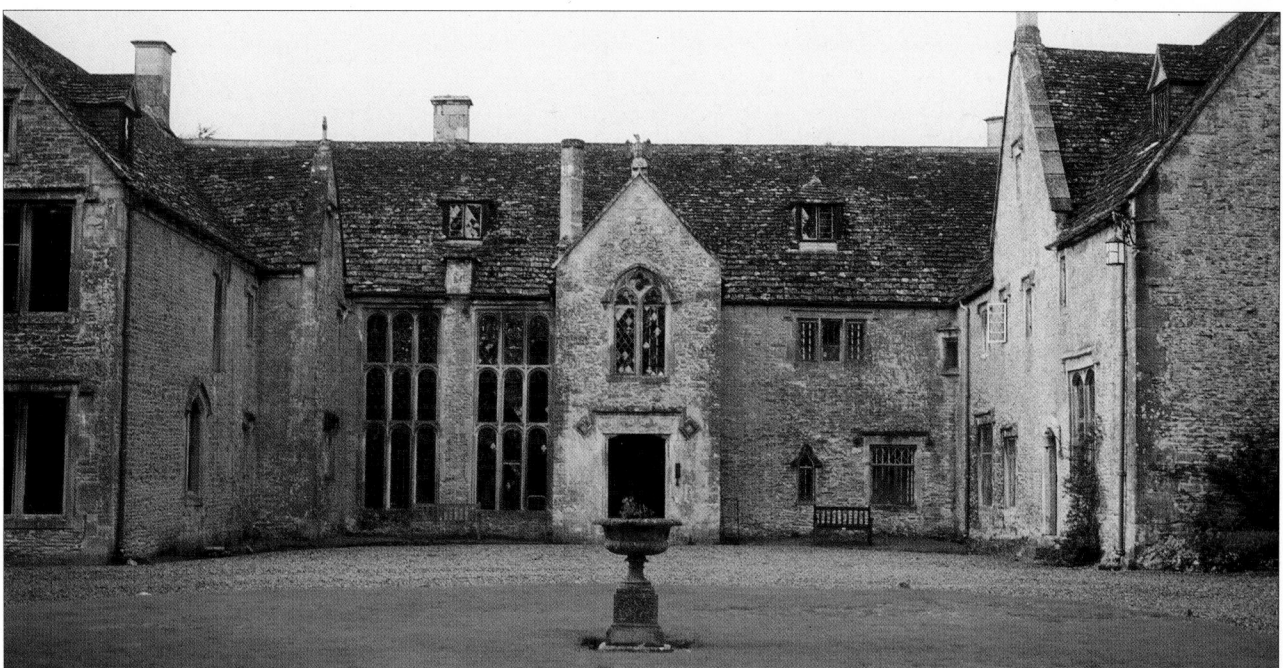

CHAVENAGE
Tetbury

CHAVENAGE is a wonderful Elizabethan house of mellow grey Cotswold stone and tiles which contains much of interest for the discerning visitor.

The approach aspect of Chavenage is virtually as it was left by Edward Stephens in 1576. Only two families have owned Chavenage; the present owners since 1891 and the Stephens family before them. A Colonel Nathaniel Stephens, MP for Gloucestershire during the Civil War was cursed for supporting Cromwell, giving rise to legends of weird happenings at Chavenage since that time.

Inside Chavenage there are many interesting rooms housing tapestries, fine furniture, pictures and many relics of the Cromwellian period. Of particular note are the Main Hall, where a contemporary screen forms a minstrels' gallery and two tapestry rooms where it is said Cromwell was lodged.

Recently Chavenage has been used as a location for TV and film productions including a Hercule Poirot story *The Mysterious Affair at Styles*, many episodes of the sequel to *Are you Being Served* now called *Grace & Favour*, a *Gotcha* for *The Noel Edmonds' House Party*, episodes of *The House of Elliot* and *Casualty* and in 1997/98 *Berkeley Square* and *Cider with Rosie*.

Chavenage is especially suitable for those wishing an intimate, personal tour, usually conducted by the owner, or for groups wanting a change from large establishments. Meals for pre-arranged groups have proved hugely popular. It also provides a charming venue for small conferences and functions.

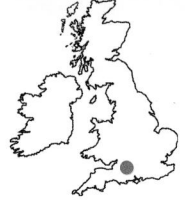

Owner:
Mr David Lowsley-Williams

CONTACT

D Lowsley-Williams
Chavenage
Tetbury
Gloucestershire
GL8 8XP

Tel: 01666 502329

Fax: 01453 836778

e-mail: caroline@chavenage.com

LOCATION

OS Ref. ST872 952

Less than 20m from M4/J16/17 or 18. 1³/₄ m NW of Tetbury between the B4104 & A4135. Signed from Tetbury. Less than 15m from M5/J13 or 14. Signed from A46 (Stroud -Bath road)

Rail: Kemble Station 7m.

Taxi: Pride Taxis: 01666 502555

Air: Bristol 35m. Birmingham 70m. Grass airstrip on farm.

CONFERENCE/FUNCTION		
ROOM	SIZE	MAX CAPACITY
Ballroom	70' x 30'	120
Oak Room	25 'x 20'	30

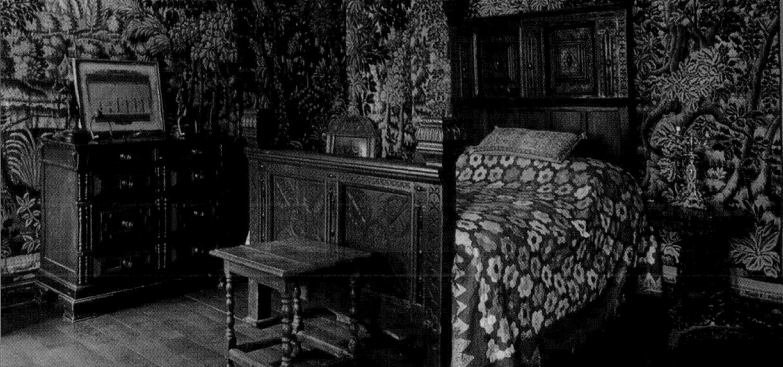

ℹ️ Clay pigeon shooting, archery, cross-bows, pistol shooting, ATV driving, small fashion shows, concerts, plays, seminars, filming, product launching, photography. No casual photography in house.

🍸 Corporate entertaining. In-house catering for drinks parties, dinners, wedding receptions. Telephone for details.

♿ Partially suitable. WC.

☕ Lunches, teas, dinners and picnics by arrangement.

👤 By owner. Large groups given a talk prior to viewing. Couriers and group leaders should arrange tour format prior to visit.

🅿️ Up to 100 cars and 2 - 3 coaches. Coaches only by appointment; stop at gates for parking instructions.

Chairs can be arranged for lecturing. Tour of working farm, modern dairy and corn facilities can be arranged.

🐕 In grounds on leads. Guide dogs only in house. ❄️

South West England

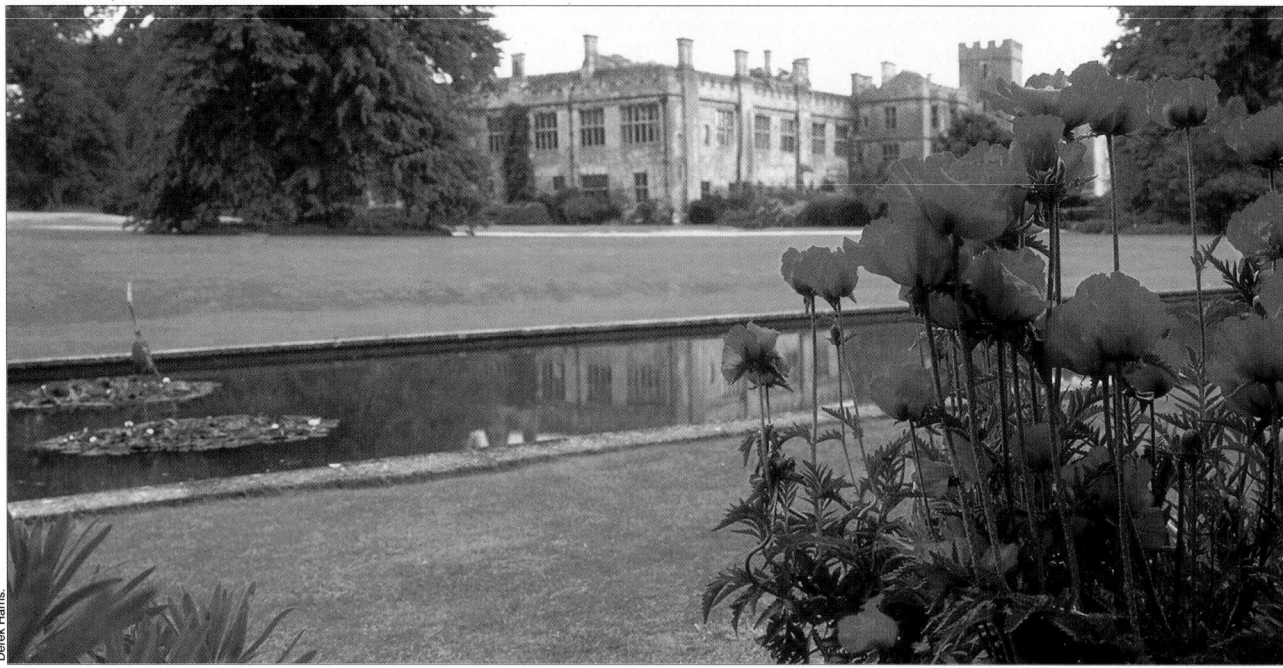

Derek Harris.

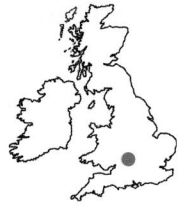

Owner: Lady Ashcombe

CONTACT

The Secretary
Sudeley Castle
Winchcombe
Nr Cheltenham
Gloucestershire
GL54 5JD

Tel: 01242 602308

Fax: 01242 602959

e-mail: marketing@
sudeley.org.uk

LOCATION

OS Ref. SP032 277

8m NE of Cheltenham,
at Winchcombe off B4632.

From Bristol or
Birmingham M5/J9.
Take A46 then B4077
towards Stow-on-the-Wold.

Bus: Castleways to
Winchcombe.

Rail: Cheltenham
Station 8m.

Air: Birmingham or
Bristol 45m.

CONFERENCE/FUNCTION		
ROOM	SIZE	MAX CAPACITY
Chandos Hall		80
North Hall		40
Library		80
Banquet Hall & Pavilion		150

SUDELEY CASTLE
Winchcombe

SUDELEY CASTLE, home of Lord and Lady Ashcombe, is one of England's great historic houses with royal connections stretching back 1000 years. Once the property of King Ethelred the Unready, Sudeley was later the magnificent palace of Queen Katherine Parr, Henry VIII's sixth wife, who is buried in St Mary's church, in the grounds. Henry VIII, Anne Boleyn, Lady Jane Grey and Elizabeth I all visited Sudeley. King Charles I stayed here and his nephew, Prince Rupert established it as his headquarters during the Civil War.

During the 19th century a programme of reconstruction, under the aegis of Sir Giles Gilbert Scott, restored Sudeley for its new owners, the Dent brothers. The interiors were largely furnished with pieces bought by the Dents at the famous Strawberry Hill sale, when the contents of Horace Walpole's house were sold.

Surrounding the Castle are the enchanting and award-winning gardens that have gained international recognition. Famous for its topiary and fine collection of old roses, the Queen's Garden is sited on the original Tudor parterre. The visitor must also see the Knot Garden, the Heritage Seed Library Garden and the recently replanted Secret Garden.

The Castle contains some interesting pieces of Civil War memorabilia, as well as pictures by Turner, Van Dyck and Rubens. The Emma Dent exhibition illustrates, at a personal level, the values and interests of the Victorian age. A licensed restaurant, gift shop and plant centre, specialising in old-fashioned roses, complete a perfect day.

Photography and filming, concerts, corporate events and conferences. Product launches, garden parties, craft fairs and activity days. Sudeley reserves the right to close part or all of the castle, gardens and grounds and to amend information as necessary.

Private dining, banquets, and medieval dinners.

Not suitable.

Licensed restaurant and tearooms. Groups should book.

Special interest tours can be arranged.

1,000 cars. Meal vouchers, free access for coach drivers.

14 holiday cottages for 2 - 5 occupants.

SUMMER
Gardens, Exhibition Centre, Shop & Plant Centre
3 March - 28 October
Daily: 10.30am - 5.30pm.

Castle Apartments & Church
31 March - 28 October
Daily: 11am - 5pm.

Restaurant
31 March - 28 October
Daily: 10.30am - 5pm.

WINTER
Groups (30+)
by appointment.

ADMISSION

Castle & Gardens
Adult £6.20
Child (5-15 yrs.)........£3.20
Conc.......................£5.20
Family (2+2) £17.00

Groups (min. 20)
Adult £5.20
Child (5-15 yrs.)........£3.20
Conc.......................£4.20

Gardens & Exhibitions
Adult £4.70
Child (5-15 yrs.)........£2.50
OAP.........................£3.70

Audio tour...............£2.00

Adventure Playground only (5-15 yrs.) £1.00

SPECIAL EVENTS

Please telephone for details.

ASHLEWORTH TITHE BARN

Tel: 01684 855300

Ashleworth, Gloucestershire

Owner: The National Trust   **Contact:** NT Regional Office

A c15th tithe barn with two projecting porch bays and fine roof timbers with queenposts.

Location: OS Ref. SO818 252. 6m NW of Gloucester, $1^{1}/_{4}$ m E of Hartpury A417.

Opening Times: 1 Apr - 31 Oct: daily, 9am - 6pm or sunset if earlier. Closed Good Fri (may be closed during part of 2001 for major repairs, please contact for details).

Admission: 60p.

BARNSLEY HOUSE GARDEN

Tel: 01285 740561 **Fax:** 01285 740628

Barnsley House, Cirencester GL7 5EE

Owner: Mr & Mrs Charles Verey   **Contact:** Charles Verey

Mature $4^{1}/_{2}$ acre garden designed by Rosemary Verey. Bulbs, mixed borders, autumn colours, knot of herb garden, laburnum walk (late May, early June). Decorative vegetable garden, garden furniture by Charles Verey. Fountain and statues by Simon Verity. Two 18th century summer houses. Winner of the HHA/Christie's Garden of the Year award, 1988.

Location: OS Ref. SP076 049. In Barnsley village, 4m NE of Cirencester on B4425.

Opening Times: 1 Feb - mid Dec: Mons, Wed - Sat, 10am - 5.30pm.

Admission: Adult £3.75, Child under 16 Free, OAP £3. No charge for group tour leader.

Partially suitable. By arrangement. Ample for cars. Limited for coaches.

BATSFORD ARBORETUM

Tel: 01386 701441 **Fax:** 01386 701829

Moreton-in-Marsh, Gloucestershire GL56 9QB

Owner: The Batsford Foundation   **Contact:** Admissions Centre

50 acres of arboretum.

Location: OS Ref. SP183 324. $1^{1}/_{2}$ m NW of Moreton-in-Marsh, off A44 to Broadway.

Opening Times: Jan, Feb & Dec: weekends only. Mar - Nov: daily.

Admission: Adult £4, Child Free, OAP £3.

BERKELEY CASTLE

See page 218 for full page entry.

BLACKFRIARS

Tel: 0117 9750700

Ladybellegate Street, Gloucester

Owner: English Heritage   **Contact:** The South West Regional Office

A small Dominican priory church converted into a rich merchant's house at the Dissolution. Most of the original 13th century church remains, including a rare scissor-braced roof.

Location: OS Ref. SO830 186. In Ladybellegate St, Gloucester, off Southgate Street and Blackfriars Walk.

Opening Times: Please contact the South West Regional Office.

Admission: Free.

BOURTON HOUSE GARDEN

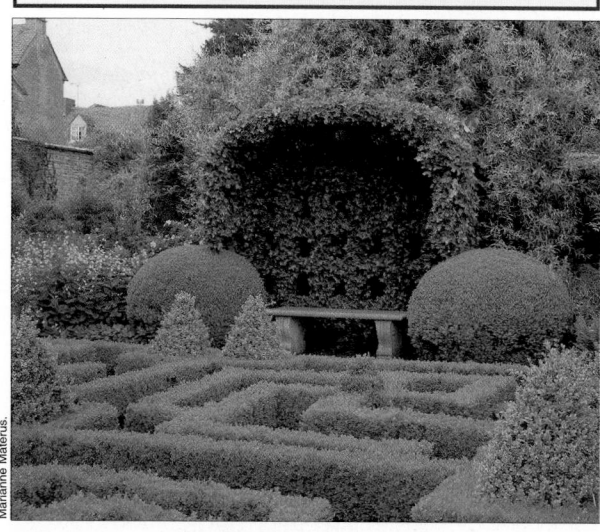

Marianne Majerus.

BOURTON-ON-THE-HILL GL56 9AE

Owner/Contact: Mr & Mrs Richard Paice

Tel: 01386 700121 **Fax:** 01386 701081

Exciting 3 acre garden surrounding a delightful 18th century Cotswold manor house and 16th century tithe barn. Featuring flamboyant borders, imaginative topiary, a unique shade house, a profusion of herbaceous and exotic plants and, not least, a myriad of magically planted pots. The mood is friendly and welcoming, the atmosphere tranquil yet inspiring. The garden... "positively fizzes with ideas".

Location: OS Ref. SP180 324. $1^{3}/_{4}$ m W of Moreton-in-Marsh on A44.

Opening Times: 24 May - 26 Oct: Thurs & Fris, 10am - 5pm. 27 - 28 May & 26 - 27 Aug: 10am - 5pm.

Admission: Adult £3.50, Child Free.

Partially suitable. By arrangement. Ample for cars. Limited for coaches.

CHAVENAGE

See page 219 for full page entry.

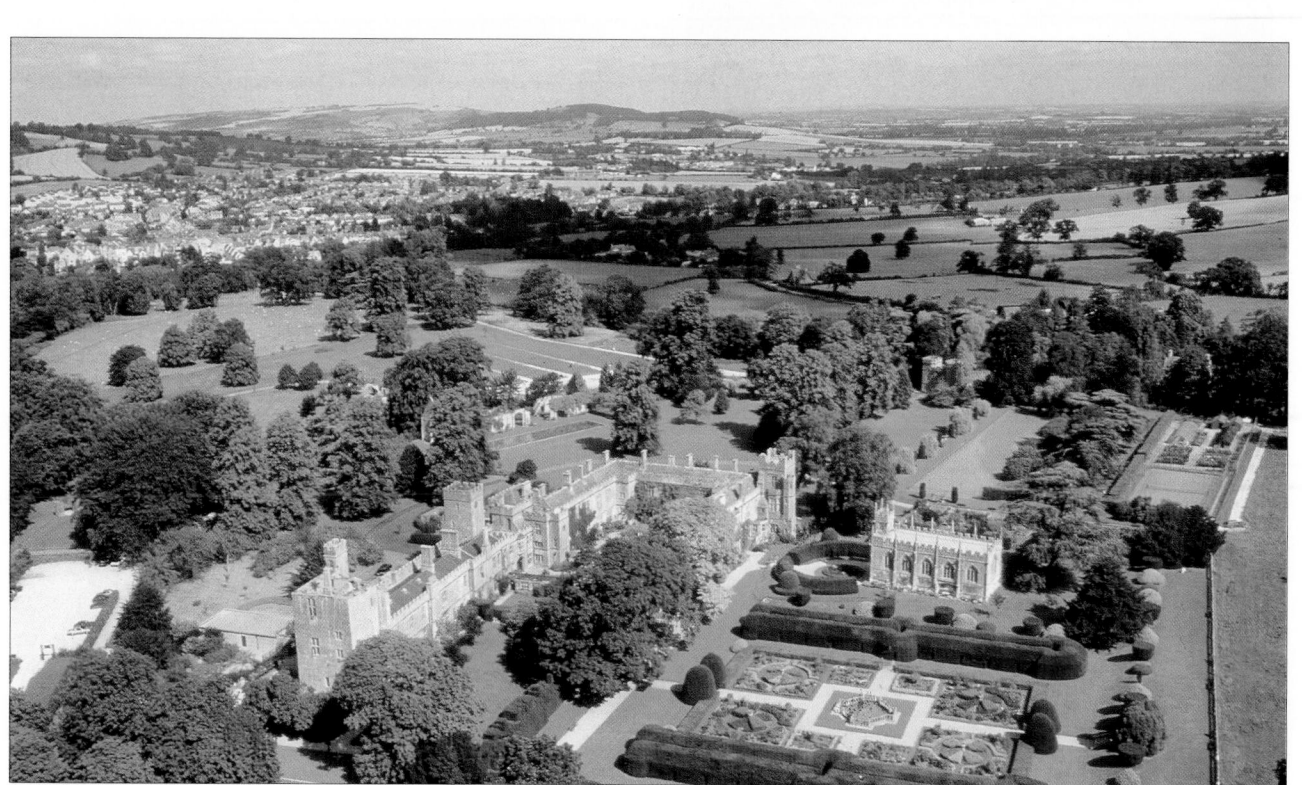

Sudeley Castle, Gloucestershire.

CHEDWORTH ROMAN VILLA

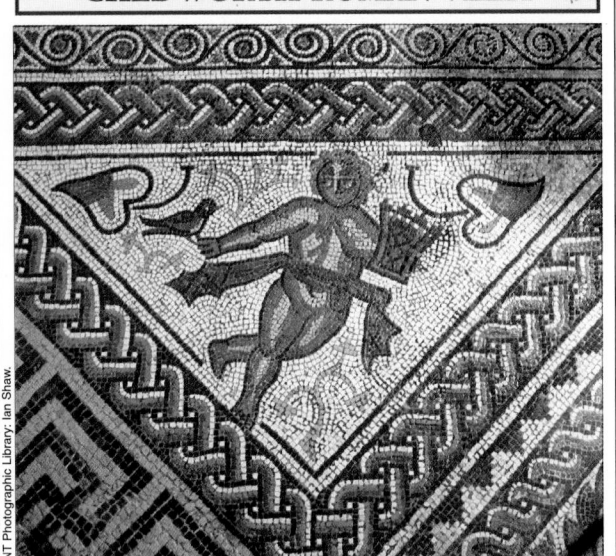

NT Photographic Library/ Ian Shaw.

YANWORTH, CHELTENHAM, GLOS GL54 3LJ

Owner: *The National Trust*   **Contact:** *The Property Manager*

Tel: 01242 890256 **Fax:** 01242 890544 **e-mail:** chedworth@smtp.ntrust.org.uk
The remains of a Romano-British villa, excavated 1864. Set in beautiful wooded combe. Includes fine 4th century mosaics, two bath houses, spring with temple. A museum houses the smaller finds.

Location: OS163 Ref. SP053 135. 3m NW of Fossebridge on Cirencester - Northleach road A429. Coaches must avoid Withington.

Opening Times: 27 Feb - 30 Mar: 11am - 4pm. 31 Mar - 28 Oct: 10am - 5pm; 30 Oct - 18 Nov: 11am - 4pm; daily except Mons (open BH Mons)

Admission: Adult £3.70, Child £1.85, Family £9.30. (Increased charge on special event days, including NT members).

⬜ ♿Grounds limited. WC. 🎨By arrangement. 🅿Limited. ✖
♨Tel. for details. · (WC)

DYRHAM PARK

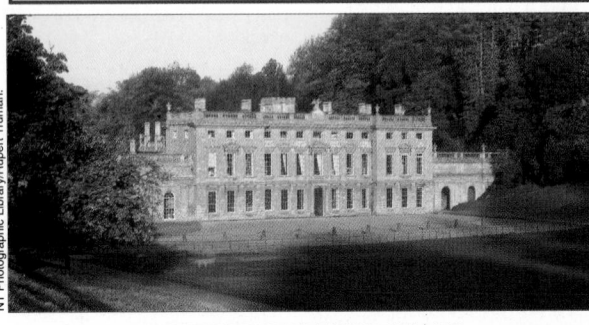

NT Photographic Library/Rupert Truman.

Nr CHIPPENHAM, WILTSHIRE SN14 8ER

Owner: *The National Trust*   **Contact:** *The Property Manager*

Tel/Fax: 0117 9372501
Crowned with a balustrade and with fine views over its ancient deer park, Dyrham was built between 1691 and 1702 for William Blathwayt, William III's Secretary at War and Secretary of State. The rooms have changed little since they were furnished by Blathwayt and their contents are recorded in his housekeeper's inventory. There are many fine textiles and paintings, as well as items of blue-and-white Delftware, reflecting the contemporary taste for Dutch fashions. Restored Victorian domestic rooms open (and for extended period, see below), including kitchen bells passage, bakehouse, larders, tenants' hall and Delft-tiled dairy. Car park has been relocated to the East Lodge and a free bus now takes visitors to and from the house, thereby restored to its original, car-free, setting. CD-ROM available for purchase.

Location: OS Ref. ST743 757. 8m N of Bath, 12m E of Bristol. Approached from Bath - Stroud road (A46), 2m S of Tormarton interchange with M4/J18.

Opening Times: House: 31 Mar - 4 Nov: Fri - Tue, 12 noon - 5.30pm, last admission 4.45pm. Garden: as house, 11am - 5.30pm or dusk if earlier. Park: daily (closed 25 Dec), 12 noon - 5.30pm or dusk if earlier (opens 11am if garden open). Winter opening for domestic rooms: 10 Nov - 16 Dec: Sats & Suns, 12 noon - 4pm. Note: property closed 6 - 9 Jul.

Admission: Adult £7.80, Child £3.90, Family £19. Grounds only: Adult £3, Child £1.50, Family £7. Park only (on days when house & garden closed): Adult £1.90, Child 90p. Winter: Park & Domestic Rooms: Adult £4, Child £2. Group rate weekdays only: contact the Property Manager.

⬜ 🍴Licensed. 🎧 ✖ ♨Tel. for details.

FRAMPTON COURT

Tel: 01452 740267 **Fax:** 01452 740698

Frampton-on-Severn, Gloucestershire GL2 7EU

Owner/Contact: Mrs Peter Clifford

Listed Grade I, by Vanburgh. 1732. Stately family home of the Cliffords who have lived at Frampton since granted land by William the Conqueror, 1066. Fine collection of original period furniture, tapestries, needlework and porcelain. Panelled throughout. The famous botanical paintings of *The Frampton Flora* are all on show. Fine views over parkland to extensive lake. A famous gothic orangery stands in the garden reflected in a Dutch ornamental canal.

Location: OS Ref. SO750 078. In Frampton, 1/4 m SW of B4071, 3m NW of M5/J13.

Opening Times: By arrangement.

Admission: House & Garden: £4.50.

ℹNo photography in house. ♿Not suitable. 🍴 🎨Obligatory.
🅿Limited for coaches. 🐕In grounds on leads. 🛏Ensuite. Tel for details. ✖

FRAMPTON MANOR

Fax: 01452 740698

Frampton-on-Severn, Gloucestershire GL2 7EU

Owner: Mr & Mrs P R H Clifford   **Contact:** Mrs P R H Clifford

Medieval/Elizabethan timber-framed manor house with walled garden. Reputed 12th century birthplace of 'Fair Rosamund' Clifford, mistress of King Henry II. Wool barn c1500 and c1800 granary with dovecote.

Location: OS Ref. SO748 080. 3m M5/J13.

Opening Times: House & Garden: open throughout the year by written appointment. Garden: 1 May - 17 Jul: Mons, 2 - 5pm.

Admission: House & Garden: £3.50. Garden only: £2.

✖

GLOUCESTER CATHEDRAL

Tel: 01452 528095 **Fax:** 01452 300469

Chapter Office, College Green, Gloucester GL1 2LR

Contact: Mrs L Henderson

Daily worship and rich musical tradition continue in this abbey church founded 1300 years ago. It has a Norman nave with massive cylindrical pillars, a magnificent east window with medieval glass and glorious fan-vaulted cloisters. You can also find the tombs of King Edward II and Robert of Normandy.

Location: OS Ref. SO832 188. Off Westgate Street in central Gloucester.

Opening Times: Daily, 8am until after Evensong. Groups must book via the Chapter Office.

Admission: £2.50 donation requested.

⬜ 🍴 ♿Partially suitable. WC. 🍴Licensed. 🎨By arrangement. 🏨
🅿None. 🐕In grounds, on leads. (WC)

HAILES ABBEY

Tel: 01242 602398

Nr Winchcombe, Cheltenham, Gloucestershire GL54 5PB

Owner: English Heritage & The National Trust   **Contact:** The Custodian

Seventeen cloister arches and extensive excavated remains in lovely surroundings of an abbey founded by Richard, Earl of Cornwall, in 1246. There is a small museum and covered display area.

Location: OS150, Ref. SP050 300. 2m NE of Winchcombe off B4632. 1/2m SE of B4632.

Opening Times: 1 Apr - 31 Oct: daily, 10am - 6pm (5pm in Oct). 1 Nov - 31 Mar: Sat - Sun, 10am - 4pm. Closed 24 - 26 Dec & 1 Jan.

Admission: Adult £2.60, Child £1.30, Conc. £2.

⬜ ♿Partially suitable. WC. 🍴 🐕In grounds, on leads. ✖ ♨Tel. for details.

HARDWICKE COURT

Tel: 01452 720212 **Fax:** 01452 724465

Gloucester GL2 4RS   **Owner/Contact:** C G M Lloyd Baker Esq

Early 19th century small country house designed by Robert Smirke.

Location: OS150, Ref. SO787 118. 6m S of Gloucester on A38.

Opening Times: Easter - end Sept: Mons, 2 - 4pm.

Admission: Please contact property for details.

Frampton Court, Gloucestershire.

HIDCOTE MANOR GARDEN

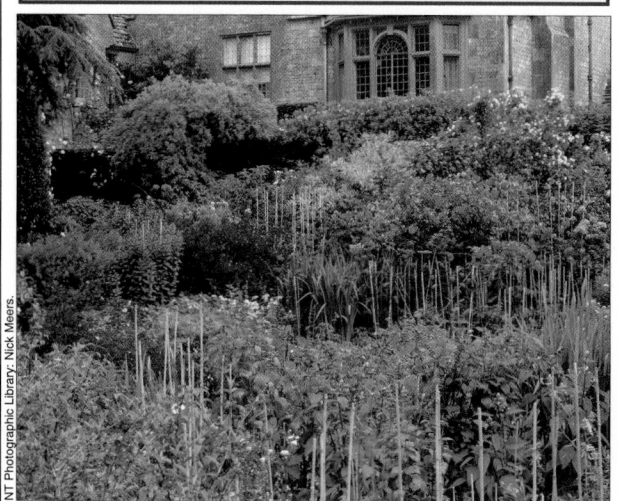

NT Photographic Library: Nick Meers.

CHIPPING CAMPDEN, GLOUCESTERSHIRE GL55 6LR

Owner: The National Trust   *Contact:* The Property Manager

Tel: 01386 438333 **Fax:** 01386 438817 **e-mail:** hidcote_manor@smtp.ntrust.org.uk

One of the most delightful gardens in England, created this century by the great horticulturist Major Lawrence Johnston; a series of small gardens within the whole, separated by walls and hedges of different species; famous for rare shrubs, trees, herbaceous borders, 'old' roses and interesting plant species.

Location: OS151 Ref. SP176 429. 4m NE of Chipping Campden, 1m E of B4632 off B4081. At Mickleton 1/4 m E of Kiftsgate Court.

Opening Times: 31 Mar - end May & Aug - 4 Nov: daily except Tues & Fris (open Good Fri). Jun & Jul: daily except Fris. Times: Apr - end Sept: 10.30am - 6.30pm; Oct: 10.30am - 5.30pm. Last admission 1 hour before closing or dusk if earlier.

Admission: Adult £5.70, Child £2.85, Family £14.

📷 ⚲ ♿Grounds, but limited. WC. 🍽Licensed. ✂
🛡Send SAE for details. Ⓦ

HOLST BIRTHPLACE MUSEUM

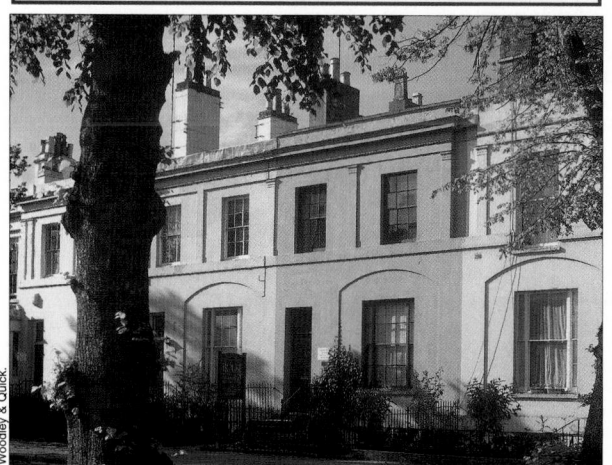

Woodley & Quick.

4 CLARENCE ROAD, PITTVILLE, CHELTENHAM GL52 2AY

Owner: Holst Birthplace Trust   *Contact:* Dr Joanna Archibald

Tel: 01242 524846 **e-mail:** holstmuseum@btconnect.com

Birthplace of Gustav Holst (1874 - 1934), composer of *The Planets*, containing his piano and personal memorabilia. (Holst's music is played.) The museum is also a fine period house showing the 'upstairs – downstairs' way of life in Regency and Victorian times, including a working kitchen, elegant drawing room and charming nursery.

Location: OS163 Ref. SO955 237. 5mins walk from town centre, opposite Pittville Gates.

Opening Times: All year: Tue - Sat, 10am - 4pm. Closed BHs. Guided tours for groups welcome by appointment.

Admission: Adult £2.50, Child/Conc. £1.25. Groups pay same prices unless having a guided tour (6-20): Adult £3.50, Conc. £2. Special rate for school groups: £75p.

ℹ Photography by prior permission only.   📷 ♿Not suitable.
✗ By arrangement.   ▣ P No parking.   🐕Guide dogs only. ✳
🛡 Tel. for details. Ⓦ

HORTON COURT ✿   **Tel:** 01249 730141

Horton, Nr Chipping Sodbury B17 6QR
Owner: The National Trust   **Contact:** Lacock Estate Office

A Cotswold manor house with 12th century Norman hall and early Renaissance features. Of particular interest is the late perpendicular ambulatory, detached from the house. Norman hall and ambulatory only shown.

Location: OS Ref. NT766 849. 3m NE of Chipping Sodbury, 3/4 m N of Horton, 1m W of A46.

Opening Times: 4 Apr - 31 Oct: Weds & Sats, 2 - 6pm or dusk if earlier.

Admission: Adult £2, Child £1.

KELMSCOTT MANOR 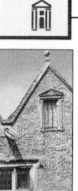

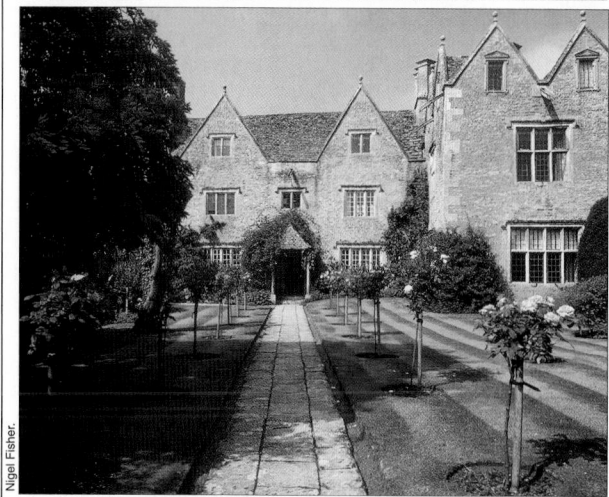

Nigel Fisher.

KELMSCOTT, Nr LECHLADE, GLOUCESTERSHIRE GL7 3HJ

Owner: Society of Antiquaries   *Contact:* Helen Webb

Tel: 01367 252486 **Fax:** 01367 253754 **e-mail:** admin@kelmscottmanor.co.uk

The home of William Morris, poet, craftsman and socialist from 1871 until his death in 1896. The house contains a collection of the possessions and works of Morris and his associates including furniture, textiles, carpets and ceramics. An exhibition of 'William Morris at Kelmscott' is being held in one of the barns during normal opening times.

Location: OS Ref. SU252 988. At SE end of the village, 2m due E of Lechlade, off the Lechlade - Faringdon Road.

Opening Times: Apr - Sept: Weds, 11am - 5pm. 3rd Sat in Apr, May, Jun & Sept, also 1st & 3rd Sat in July & Aug, 2 - 5pm. Private visits for groups on Thurs & Fris. Please note house only closed on Weds, 1 - 2pm.

Admission: Adult £7, Child/Student £3.50.

📷 ⚲ ♿ Grounds suitable. WCs. ▣ Licensed. ✗ By arrangement.
P Limited for coaches. ✂ Ⓦ

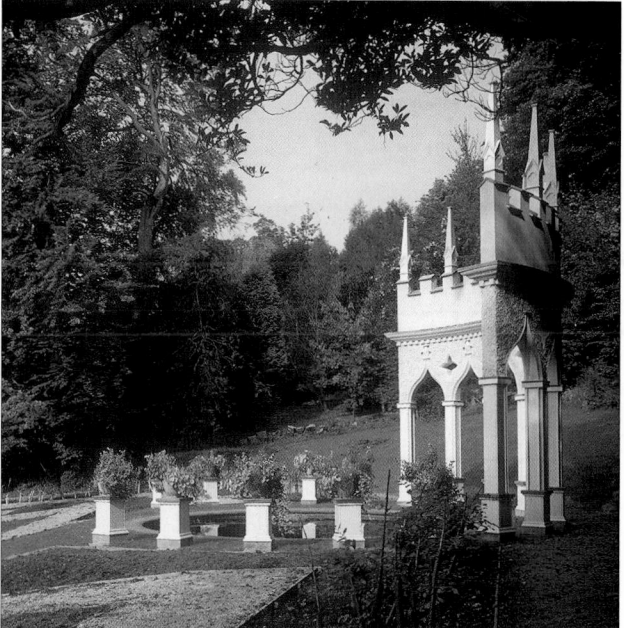

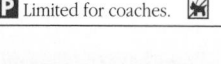

English Heritage Photo Library

Painswick Rococo Garden, Gloucestershire.

KIFTSGATE COURT GARDENS

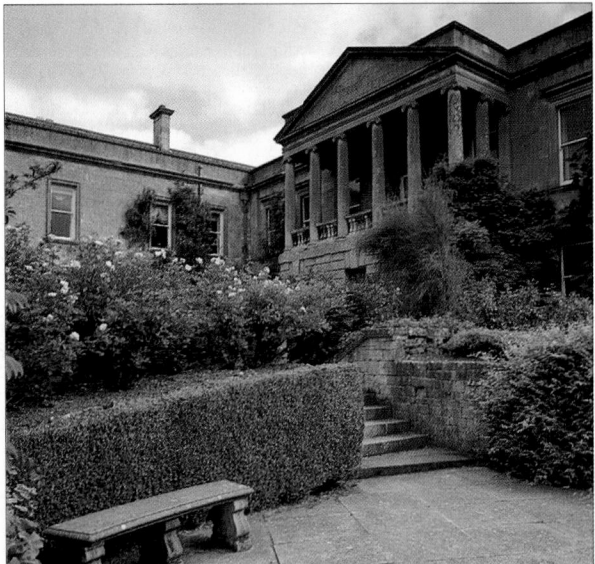

CHIPPING CAMPDEN, GLOUCESTERSHIRE GL55 6LW

Owner: Mr and Mrs J G Chambers **Contact:** Mr J G Chambers

Tel/Fax: 01386 438777

Magnificently situated garden on the edge of the Cotswold escarpment with views towards the Malvern Hills. Many unusual shrubs and plants including tree peonies, abutilons, specie and old-fashioned roses.

Location: OS Ref. SP173 430. 4m NE of Chipping Campden. 1/4 m W of Hidcote Garden.

Opening Times: Apr, May, Aug, Sept: Weds, Thurs & Suns, 2 - 6pm. Jun & Jul: Weds, Thurs, Sats & Suns, 12 noon - 6pm. BH Mons, 2 - 6pm. Coaches by appointment.

Admission: Adult: £4, Child £1.

LODGE PARK

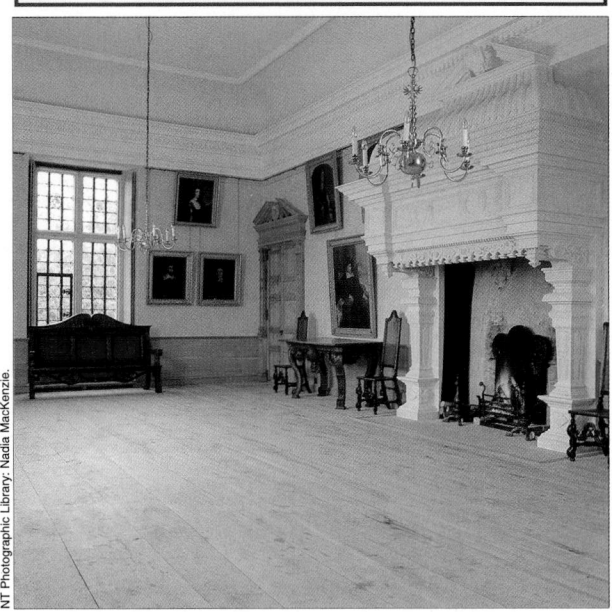

ALDSWORTH, Nr CHELTENHAM, GLOUCESTERSHIRE GL54 3PP

Owner: The National Trust **Contact:** The Property Manager

Tel: 01451 844130 **Fax:** 01451 844794 **e-mail:** lodgepark@smtp.ntrust.org.uk

Situated on the picturesque Sherborne Estate in the Cotswolds, Lodge Park was created in 1634 by John 'Crump' Dutton. Inspired by his passion for gambling and banqueting, it is a unique survival of a Grandstand, Deer Course and Park.

Location: OS163 Ref. SP146 123. 3m E of Northleach, approach only from A40.

Opening Times: 1 Mar - 4 Nov: Fri - Mon, 11am - 4pm. Slide talks at regular intervals.

Admission: Adult £4, Child £2, Family £10.

LITTLEDEAN HALL   Tel: 01594 824 213

Littledean, Gloucestershire GL14 3NR

Owner/Contact: Mrs S Anthony

'*Reputedly England's oldest inhabited house*', Guinness Book of Records. Site of Roman temple.

Location: OS Ref. SO673 131. 2m E of Cinderford, 500 yds S of A4151.

Opening Times: 1 Apr - 31 Oct: daily, 11am - 5pm.

Admission: Adult £3.50, Child £1.50, OAP £2.50. Groups £2.25 (by appointment).

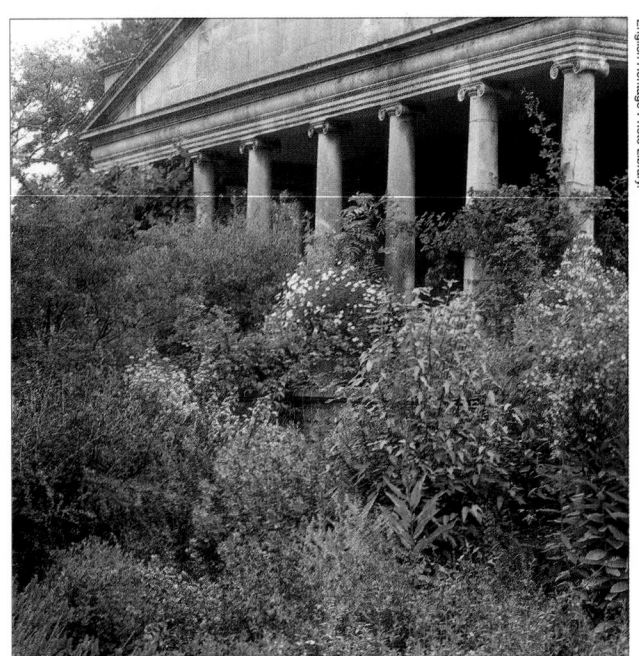

Kiftsgate Court Gardens, Gloucestershire.

LYDNEY PARK GARDENS & ROMAN TEMPLE SITE Tel/Fax: 01594 842027

Lydney, Gloucestershire GL15 6BU

Owner: The Viscount Bledisloe   **Contact:** Mrs Sylvia Jones

Eight acres of extensive valley gardens with trees and lakes. Roman temple site and museum.

Location: OS Ref. SO620 022. On A48 between Lydney and Aylburton.

Opening Times: 26 Mar - 3 Jun: Suns, Weds & BH Mons. Easter week & 27 May - 1 Jun: daily.

Admission: Adult £3 (Wed £2), Child 50p. Groups of (25+) by arrangement.

MISARDEN PARK GARDENS   Tel: 01285 821303 Fax: 01285 821530

Stroud, Gloucestershire GL6 7JA

Owner/Contact: Major M T N H Wills

Noted in the spring for its bulbs and flowering trees and in mid-summer for the large double herbaceous borders. Fine topiary throughout and a new parterre of hebes, aliums and lavender within the rose garden. Outstanding position, standing high overlooking the 'Golden Valley'.

Location: OS Ref. SO940 089. 6m NW Cirencester. Follow signs westward from A417 from Gloucester or Cirencester or B4070 from Stroud.

Opening Times: 3 Apr - 27 Sept: Tue - Thur, 10am - 5pm.

Admission: Adult £3 (guided tours extra), Child Free. 10% reduction for pre-arranged groups (20+).

Nurseries: daily except Mons. Grounds suitable. Guide dogs only.

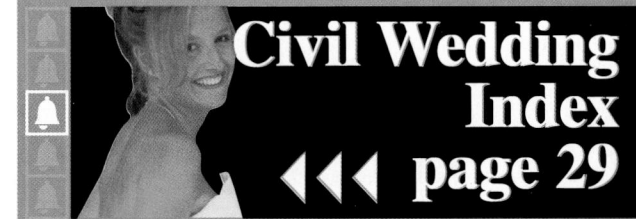

OWLPEN MANOR

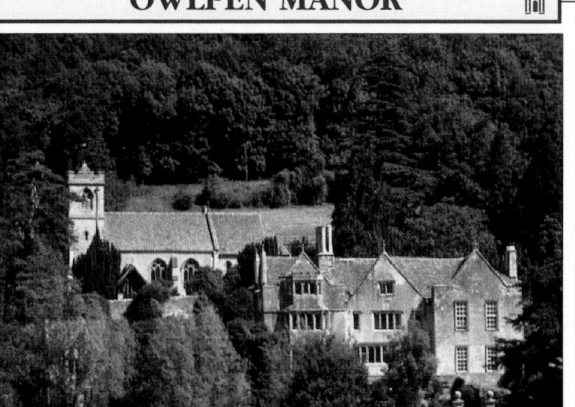

Nr ULEY, GLOUCESTERSHIRE GL11 5BZ

Owner: Mr & Mrs Nicholas Mander   *Contact:* Julia Webb

Tel: 01453 860261   **Fax:** 01453 860819   **Restaurant:** 01453 860816
e-mail: sales@owlpen.com

Romantic Tudor manor house, 1450-1616, with Cotswold Arts & Crafts associations. Remote wooded valley setting, with 16th and 17th century formal terraced gardens and magnificent yews. Contains unique painted cloth wall hangings, family and Arts & Crafts collections. Mill (1726), Court House (1620); licensed restaurant in medieval Cyder House. Victorian church. "*Owlpen - ah, what a dream is there!*" - Vita Sackville-West.

Location: OS Ref. ST801 984. 3m E of Dursley, 1m E of Uley, off B4066, by Old Crown pub.

Opening Times: Apr - Sept: daily, Tue - Sun & BH Mons, 2 - 5pm. Restaurant 12 noon - 5pm.

Admission: Adult £4.75, Child (5-14yrs) £2, Family (2+4) £13. Gardens and Grounds: Adult £3.25, Child £1. Group rates available.

🍴   ♿Not suitable.   🍽Licensed.   🅿   🏠Holiday cottages, sleep 2 - 9.   🔵

PAINSWICK ROCOCO GARDENS

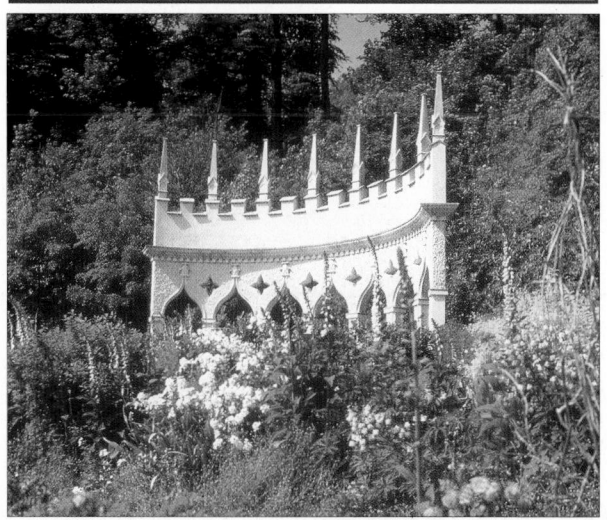

PAINSWICK, GLOUCESTERSHIRE GL6 6TH

Owner: Painswick Rococo Garden Trust   *Contact:* P R Moir

Tel: 01452 813204   **Fax:** 01452 814888   **e-mail:** paulmoir@rococogarden.co.uk

Unique 18th century garden restoration situated in a hidden 6 acre Cotswold combe. Charming contemporary buildings are juxtaposed with winding woodland walks and formal vistas. Famous for its early spring show of snowdrops. Newly planted maze.

Location: OS Ref. SO864 106. ½ m NW of village of Painswick on B4073.

Opening Times: Jan - Apr, Oct & Nov: Wed - Sun, 11am - 5pm. May - Sept: daily, 11am - 5pm.

Admission: Adult £3.30, Child £1.75, OAP £3. Family (2+2) £8.75. Free introductory talk.

📷   🍴   ♿Partially suitable. WC.   🍷Licensed.   🍽   🅿   🔲
🐕In grounds, on leads.   ❄   📞Tel. for details.   🔵

THE PRIORY GARDENS   **Tel/Fax:** 01386 725258

The Priory, Kemerton, Nr Tewkesbury GL20 7JN
Owner/Contact: The Hon Mrs Healing

This 4 acre garden was replanned and planted by the present owner and her husband in 1965, though tree planting had been thoughtfully planned since they came to the garden in 1939, and some 70 new specimen trees were planted. On the south facing slopes of Bredon Hill, the garden has matured and features long herbaceous borders planted in colour groups, at their best from mid-July through September and includes a stream garden, sunken garden and sweeping lawns down to a part reserved for wild flowers. There is a well-stocked kitchen garden.

Location: OS Ref. SO950 378. In Kemerton. 5m NE of Tewkesbury via B4080 at Bredon.

Opening Times: Jul - Sept: Thurs & selected Suns, 2 - 6pm. Groups (25+): by appointment, Jun - Sept.

Admission: Adult: Jun: £2.50, Jul - Sept: £2. Groups (min 20): £2.50 on non-open days.

🍴   ♿ Partially suitable. WC.   🚶By arrangement.   🅿Limited for coaches.
🐕In grounds on leads.

RODMARTON MANOR

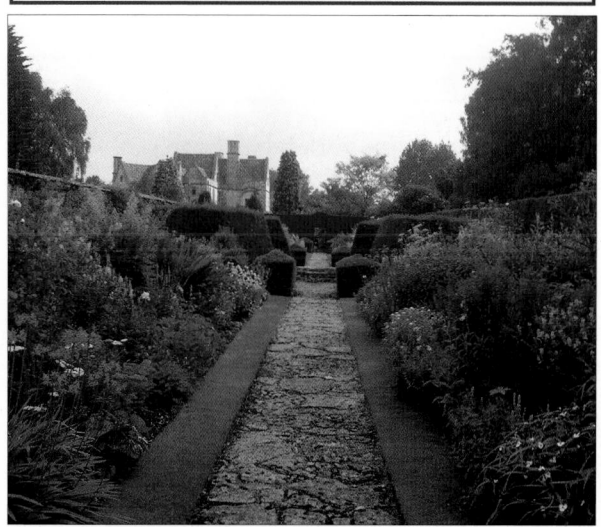

CIRENCESTER, GLOUCESTERSHIRE GL7 6PF

Owner: Mr & Mrs Simon Biddulph   *Contact:* Simon Biddulph

Tel: 01285 841253   **Fax:** 01285 841298

One of the last great country houses to be built in the traditional way and containing beautiful furniture, ironwork, china and needlework specially made for the house. The large garden complements the house and contains many areas of great beauty and character including the magnificent herbaceous borders, topiary, roses, rockery and kitchen garden.

Location: OS Ref. ST943 977. Off A433 between Cirencester & Tetbury.

Opening Times: House & Garden: 9 May - 29 Aug: Weds, Sats & BH Mons, 2 - 5pm. Groups please book. Guided house tours (20+) can be booked at other times by appointment. Guided tours of garden can also be booked.

Admission: House & Garden: £6, Child (under 14yrs) £3. Min. group charge £120. Garden only: £3, accompanied children Free.

🚶 By arrangement.

ST MARY'S CHURCH   **Tel:** 0117 9750700

Kempley, Gloucestershire
Owner: English Heritage   **Contact:** The South West Regional Office

A delightful Norman church with superb wall paintings from the 12th - 14th centuries which were only discovered beneath whitewash in 1871.

Location: OS149 SO670 313. On minor road. 1½ m SE of Much Marcle, A449.

Opening Times: 1 Apr - 30 Sept: 10am - 6pm, 1 Oct - 31 Mar: 10am - 4pm.

Admission: Free.

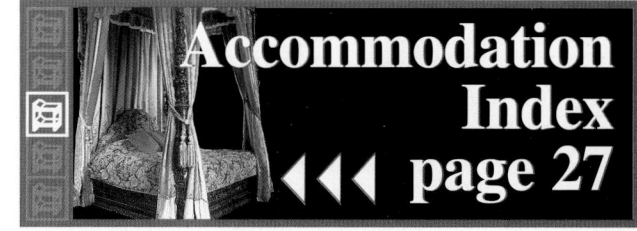

Accommodation Index ◀◀◀ page 27

SEZINCOTE

Moreton-in-Marsh, Gloucestershire GL56 9AW

Owner: Mr and Mrs D Peake　　　　　　**Contact:** Mrs D Peake

Exotic oriental water garden by Repton and Daniell. Large semi-circular orangery. House by S P Cockerell in Indian style was the inspiration for Brighton Pavilion.

Location: OS Ref. SP183 324. 2$\frac{1}{2}$ m SW of Moreton-in-Marsh. Turn W along A44 to Broadway and left into gateway just before Bourton-on-the-Hill (opposite the gate to Batsford Park), then 1m drive.

Opening Times: Garden: Thurs, Fris & BH Mons, 2 - 6pm (dusk if earlier) throughout the year except Dec. House: May, Jun, Jul & Sept, Thurs & Fris, 2.30 - 6pm. Groups by written appointment.

Admission: House & Garden £5 (no children in house). Garden: Adult £3.50, Child £1 (under 5yrs Free).

Not suitable.　Guide dogs only.

STANWAY WATER GARDEN

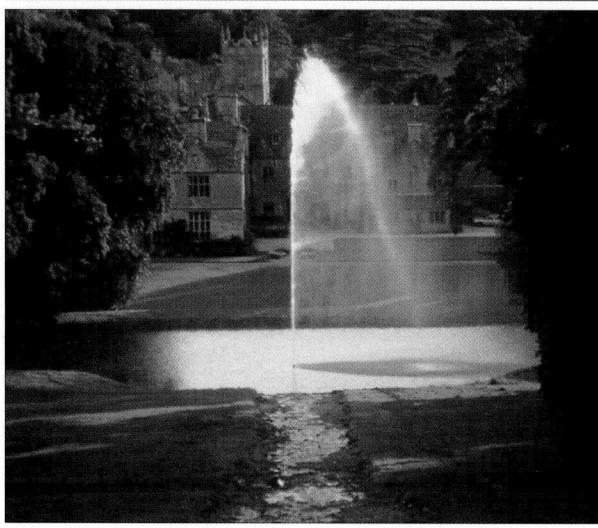

STANWAY, CHELTENHAM, GLOS GL54 5PQ

Owner: Lord Neidpath　Contact: Lorna Poulton

Tel: 01386 584469　**Fax:** 01386 584688

"*As perfect and pretty a Cotswold manor house as anyone is likely to see*" (Fodor's '*Great Britain '98* guidebook), Stanway's peaceful Jacobethan architecture and the beauty of its surrounding villages and parkland are now complemented by its magnificent, newly restored baroque water garden, with pyramid, cascade, upper pond, waterfall, grand canal and 70 ft high fountain.

Location: OS Ref. SP061 323. N of Winchcombe, just off B4077.

Opening Times: Gardens: Aug & Sept: Tues & Thurs, 2 - 5pm. Private tours by arrangement at other times.

Admission: Adult £3, Child £1, OAP £2.50.

Film & photographic location.　By arrangement.　P
In grounds on leads.

SNOWSHILL MANOR

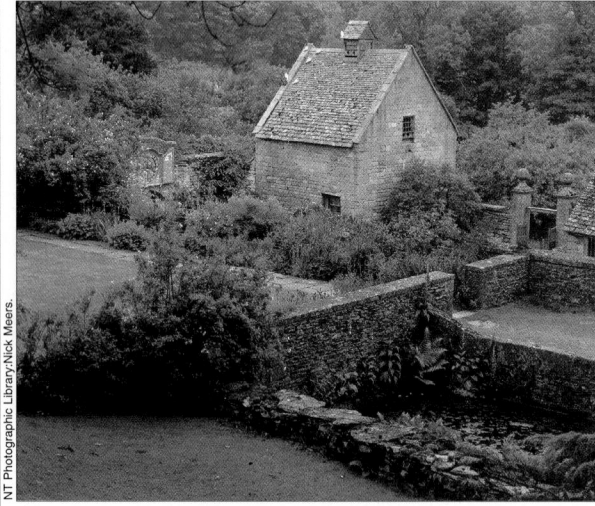

SNOWSHILL, Nr BROADWAY WR12 7JU

Owner: The National Trust　Contact: The Property Manager

Tel/Fax: 01386 852410　**e-mail:** snowshill@smtp.ntrust.org.uk

A Tudor house with a c1700 façade, 21 rooms containing Charles Paget Wade's collection of craftsmanship, including musical instruments, clocks, toys, bicycles, weavers' and spinners' tools, Japanese armour, small formal garden and Charles Wade's cottage. The Manor is a 10 minute walk (500 yds) along an undulating countryside path.

Location: OS150 Ref. SP096 339. 3m SW of Broadway, turning off the A44, by Broadway Green.

Opening Times: 31 Mar - 4 Nov: daily except Mons & Tues, 12 noon - 5pm (open BH Mons) & Mons in Jul & Aug. Last entry to Manor 4.30pm, last entry to the property 5pm. Timed tickets issued for Manor. Grounds: as house, 11am - 5.30pm.

Admission: Adult £6, Child £3, Family £15. Grounds, shop & restaurant £3.

SUDELEY CASTLE

See page 220 for full page entry.

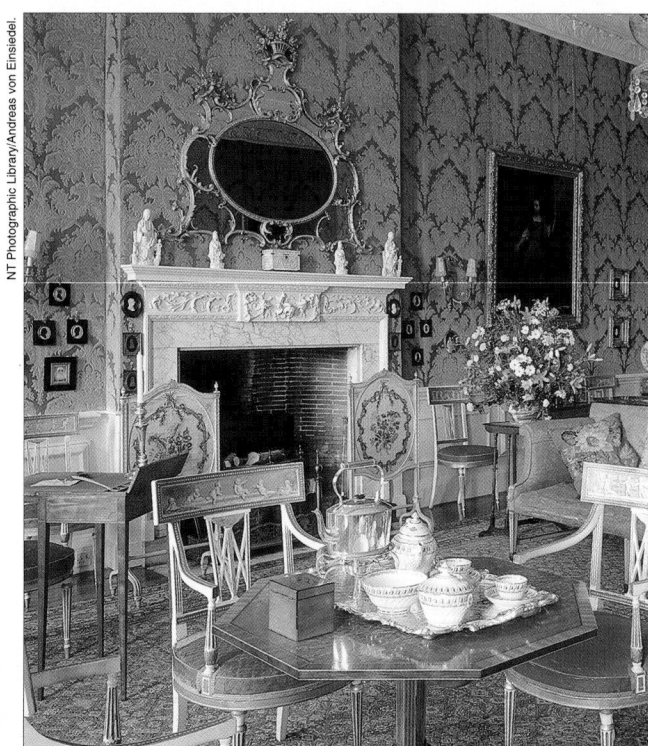

Dyrham Park, Gloucestershire.

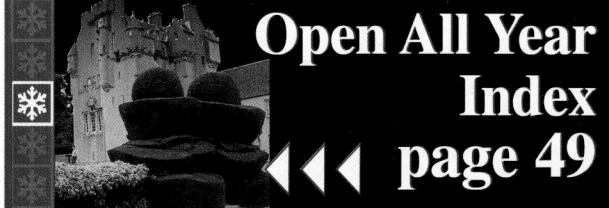

Open All Year
Index
◄◄◄ page 49

WESTBURY COURT GARDEN

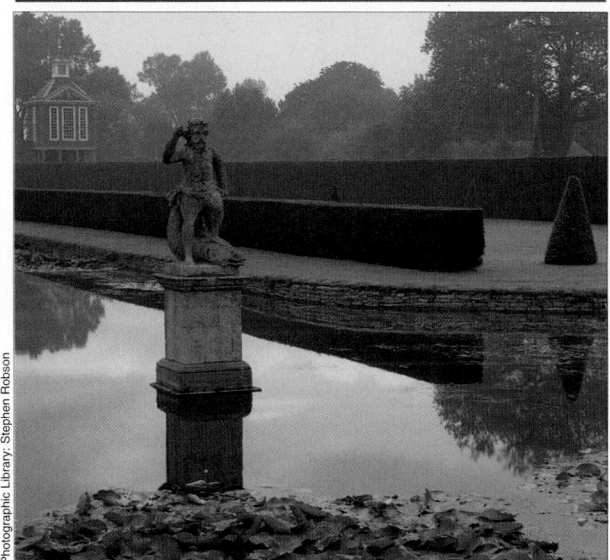

NT Photographic Library: Stephen Robson

WESTBURY-ON-SEVERN, GLOUCESTERSHIRE GL14 1PD

Owner: *The National Trust*   ***Contact:*** *The Head Gardener*

Tel: 01452 760461   **e-mail:** westbury@smtp.ntrust.org.uk

A formal water garden with canals and yew hedges, laid out between 1696 and 1705; the earliest of its kind remaining in England. Restored in 1971 and planted with species dating from pre-1700 including apple, pear and plum trees.

Location: OS162 SO718 138. 9m SW of Gloucester on A48.

Opening Times: 1 Mar - 30 Jun: Wed - Sun, Good Fri & BH Mons, 10am - 6pm. 1 Jul - 31 Aug: daily, 10am - 6pm. 1 Sept - 28 Oct: Wed - Sun, 10am - 6pm.

Admission: Adult £2.90, Child £1.45.

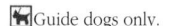Access to most parts of the garden. WC. Guide dogs only. ❄ Ⓦ

WESTONBIRT ARBORETUM
     Tel: 01666 880220   **Fax:** 01666 880559

Tetbury, Gloucestershire GL8 8QS

Owner: The Forestry Commission   **Contact:** Mr A Russell

600 acres arboretum begun in 1829, now with 18,000 catalogued trees.

Location: OS Ref. ST856 896. 3m S of Tetbury on the A433.

Opening Times: 365 days a year, 10am - 8pm (or dusk if earlier).

Admission: Adult £4.50, Child £1, OAP £3.50.

WHITTINGTON COURT 🏛
     Tel: 01242 820556   **Fax:** 01242 820218

Whittington, Cheltenham, Gloucestershire GL54 4HF

Owner: Mr & Mrs Jack Stringer   **Contact:** Mrs J Stringer

Elizabethan manor house. Family possessions.

Location: OS Ref. SP014 206. 4m E of Cheltenham on N side of A40.

Opening Times: 14 - 29 Apr & 11 - 27 Aug inclusive: 2 - 5pm.

Admission: Adult £3, Child £1, OAP £2.50.

WOODCHESTER PARK MANSION
     Tel: 01453 750455   **Fax:** 01453 750457

Stroud, Gloucestershire GL5 1AP

Owner: Woodchester Mansion Trust   **Contact:** Matthew Haynes

Hidden in a wooded valley near Stroud is one of the most intriguing houses in the country. Woodchester Mansion was started in 1856 but abandoned incomplete in 1870. It offers a unique insight into traditional building techniques. The Trust's repair programme includes courses in stone masonry and building conservation.

Location: OS Ref. SO795 015 (gateway on B4066). 5m S of Stroud on B4066. NW of the village of Nympsfield, then 1m path E from gate.

Opening Times: Weekends throughout the summer. Please telephone for details.

Admission: Adult £4, Child (under 12yrs) £2, Student £2. Groups (min 10 people or £50): Adult £5.

⬜ ♿Not suitable. ▯ 🕴 🅿 🐕Guide dogs only in Mansion.

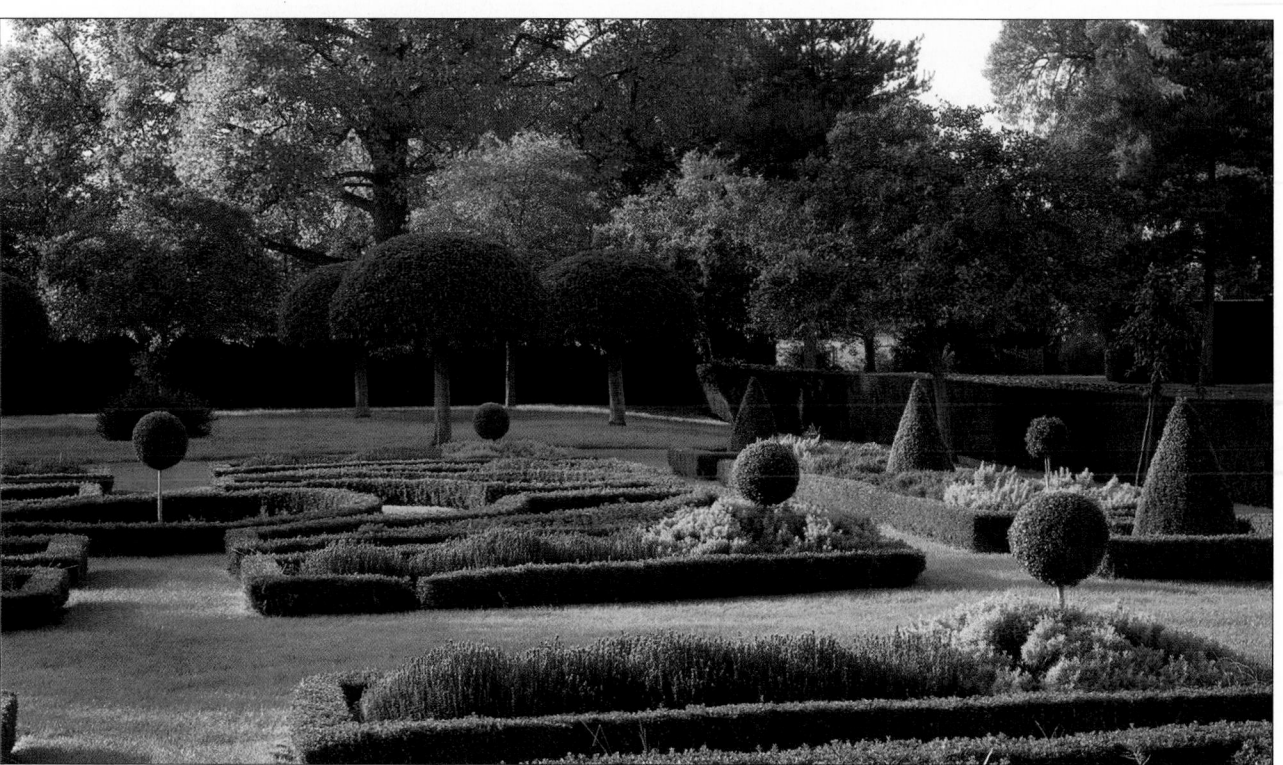

Westbury Court Garden, Gloucestershire.

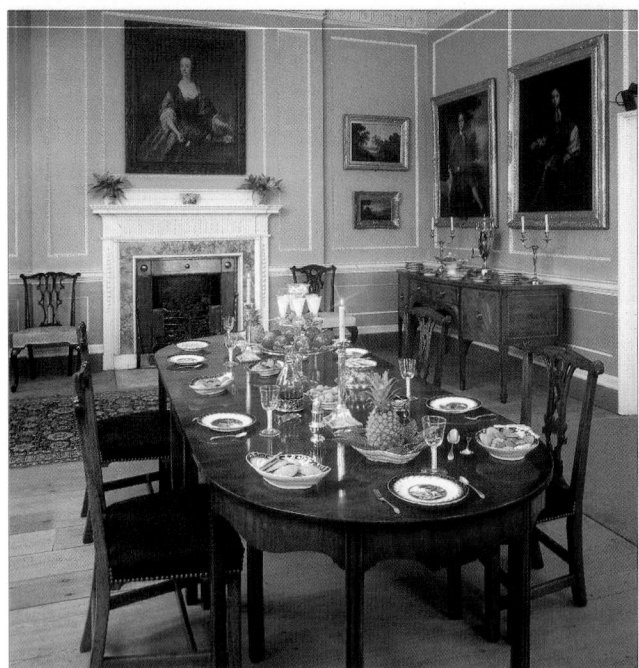
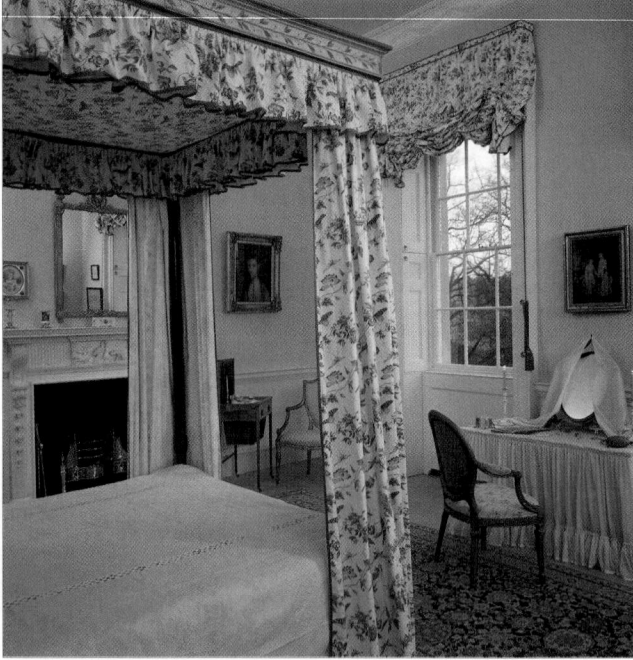

NO. 1 ROYAL CRESCENT
Bath

NUMBER 1 was the first house to be built in the Royal Crescent, John Wood the Younger's fine example of Palladian architecture. The Crescent was begun in 1767 and completed by 1774.

The House was given to the Bath Preservation Trust in 1968 and both the exterior and interior have been accurately restored. Visitors can see a grand town-house of the late 18th century with authentic furniture, paintings and carpets.

On the ground floor are the Study and Dining Room and on the first floor a Lady's Bedroom and Drawing Room. A series of maps of Bath are on the second floor landing. In the Basement is a Kitchen and a Museum Shop.

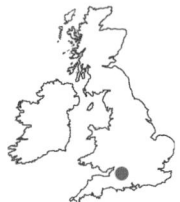

Owner:
Bath Preservation Trust

CONTACT

Mrs Ann Hollas
Administrator
1 Royal Crescent
Bath
BA1 2LR

Tel: 01225 428126

Fax: 01225 481850

OPENING TIMES

SUMMER

Mid February - End October
Daily except Mons
10.30am - 5pm
Closed Good Fri.
Open BHs and
Bath Festival Mon.

WINTER

November
Daily except Mons
10.30am - 4pm.

Last admission 30 mins before closing.

Special tours outside normal opening hours by arrangement with the administrator.

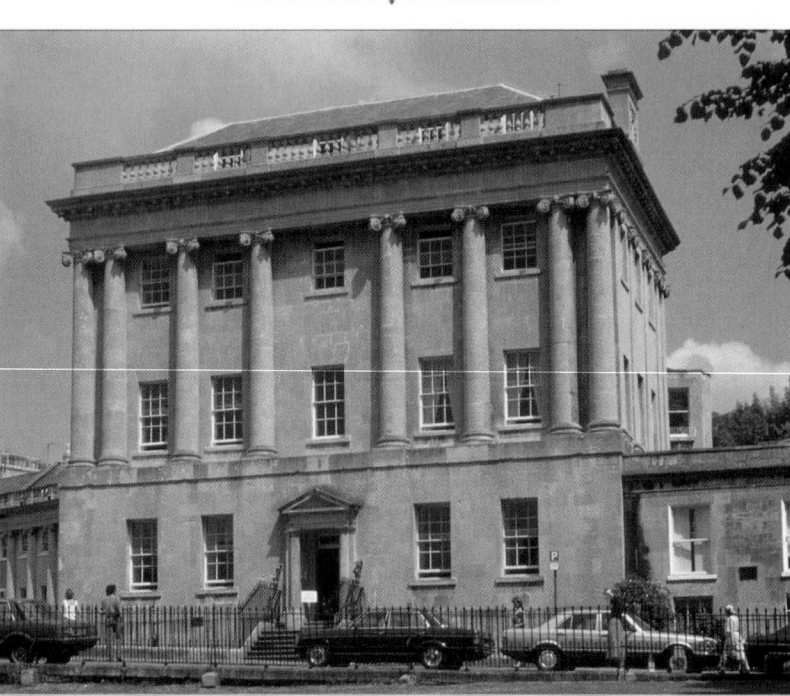

LOCATION

OS Ref. ST746 653

M4/J18,
then the A46 to Bath
2¹/₂ hrs from London
¹/₄ m NW of city centre.

Rail: Bath Spa
Railway Station
(1hr, 20 mins
from London).

Taxi: Streamline.

ADMISSION

ALL YEAR

Adult	£4.00
Child*	£3.50
Student	£3.50
OAP	£3.50
Family	£10.00

Groups

Adult	£2.50
School*	£2.50
Student	£2.50

* Aged 5 - 16yrs.

   Not suitable.   No restaurant or tearoom, but many facilities in Bath.

Guides in every room. Tours in French and Italian on request. Tour time 45 mins. Guide sheets available in French, German, Spanish, Italian, Japanese, Chinese, Danish, Dutch, Russian and Portuguese translations on request.

P Be aware of restrictions in The Royal Crescent and parking regulations in the centre of Bath.

The cost per child is £2.50. School group rates on request. Guides can be provided.

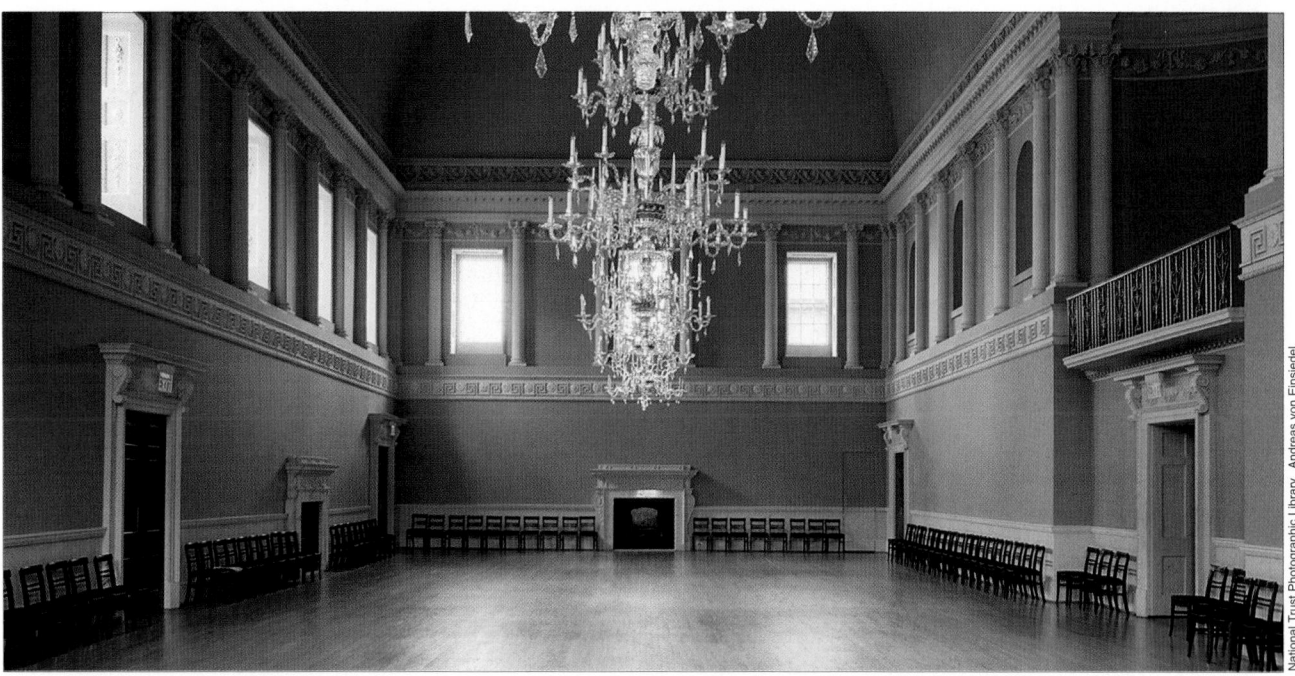

National Trust Photographic Library. Andreas von Einsiedel.

MUSEUM OF COSTUME & ASSEMBLY ROOMS
Bath

THE ASSEMBLY ROOMS in Bath are open to the public daily (free of charge) and are also popular for dinners, dances, concerts, conferences and civil weddings.

Originally known as the Upper Rooms, they were designed by John Wood the Younger and opened in 1771. The magnificent interior consists of a splendid Ball Room, Tea Room and Card Room, connected by two fine octagonal rooms. This plan was perfect for 'assemblies', evening entertainments popular in the 18th century, which included dancing, music, card-playing and tea drinking. They are now owned by The National Trust and managed by Bath & North East Somerset Council, which runs a full conference service.

The building also houses one of the largest and most comprehensive collections of fashionable dress in the country, the Museum of Costume. Its extensive displays cover the history of fashion from the late 16th century to the present day. Hand-held audioguides allow visitors to learn about the fashions on display while the lighting is kept to levels suitable for fragile garments. The 'Dress of the Year' collection traces significant moments in modern fashion history from 1963. 'Fashion in the Fifties', the special exhibition until 4 November 2001, traces the flowering of fashion talent in the glamorous decade following the war. For the serious student of fashion, the reference library and study facilities of the nearby Fashion Research Centre are available by appointment.

The museum shop sells publications and gifts associated with the history of costume and is open daily to all visitors.

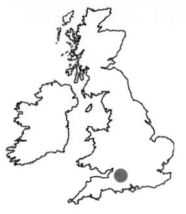

Owner: The National Trust

CONTACT

For Room Hire:
Mr Tom Deller
Room Hire Manager
Stall Street
Bath
BA1 1LZ

Tel: 01225 477734
Fax: 01225 477476
e-mail: tom_deller@
bathnes.gov.uk

Museum Enquiries:
Tel: 01225 477785
Fax: 01225 477743

LOCATION

OS Ref. ST750 648

Near centre of Bath,
10m from M4/J18.

Rail: Great Western from London Paddington (regular service) 1 hour 17mins duration.

Air: Bristol airport 40 mins.

CONFERENCE/FUNCTION		
ROOM	SIZE	MAX CAPACITY
Ballroom	103' x 40'	450
Octagon	47' x 47'	200
Tea Room	58' x 40'	250
Card Room	59' x 18'	70

OPENING TIMES

ALL YEAR
10am - 5pm

Closed 25 & 26 December

Last admission 30 mins before closing.

ADMISSION

Assembly Rooms:.....Free
Museum of Costume:
Adult £4.00
Child* £2.90
OAP.........................£3.60
Groups (20+)
Adult £3.80
Child* (summer) £2.30
Child* (winter)........£1.90

Combined ticket with Roman Baths
Adult £8.90
Child* £5.30
OAP.........................£8.00
Family (2+4) £23.50
Groups (20+)
Adult £6.80
Child* (summer) £4.00
Child* (winter)........£3.20

* Age 6 - 18yrs.
Child under 6yrs Free

(2000 prices)

- Conference facilities.
- Extensive book & gift shop.
- Corporate hospitality. Function facilities.
- Suitable. WC.
- Hourly. Individual guided tours by arrangement.
- English, French, German, Italian, Japanese, Spanish.
- Nearby car park.
- Teachers' pack.
- Guide dogs only.
- Civil Weddings/Receptions.

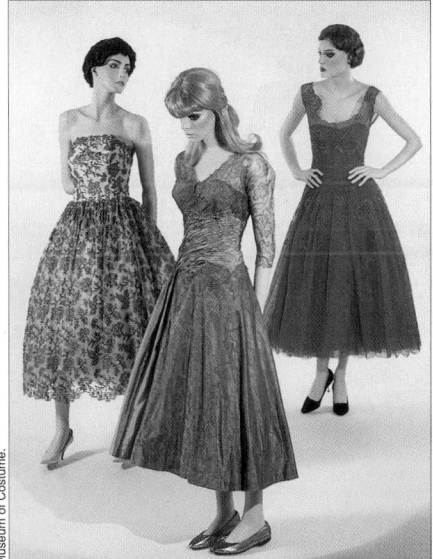

Museum of Costume.

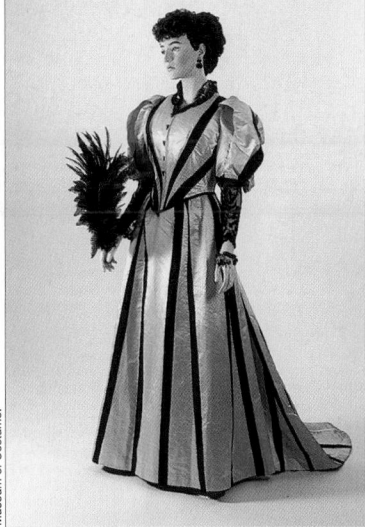

Museum of Costume.

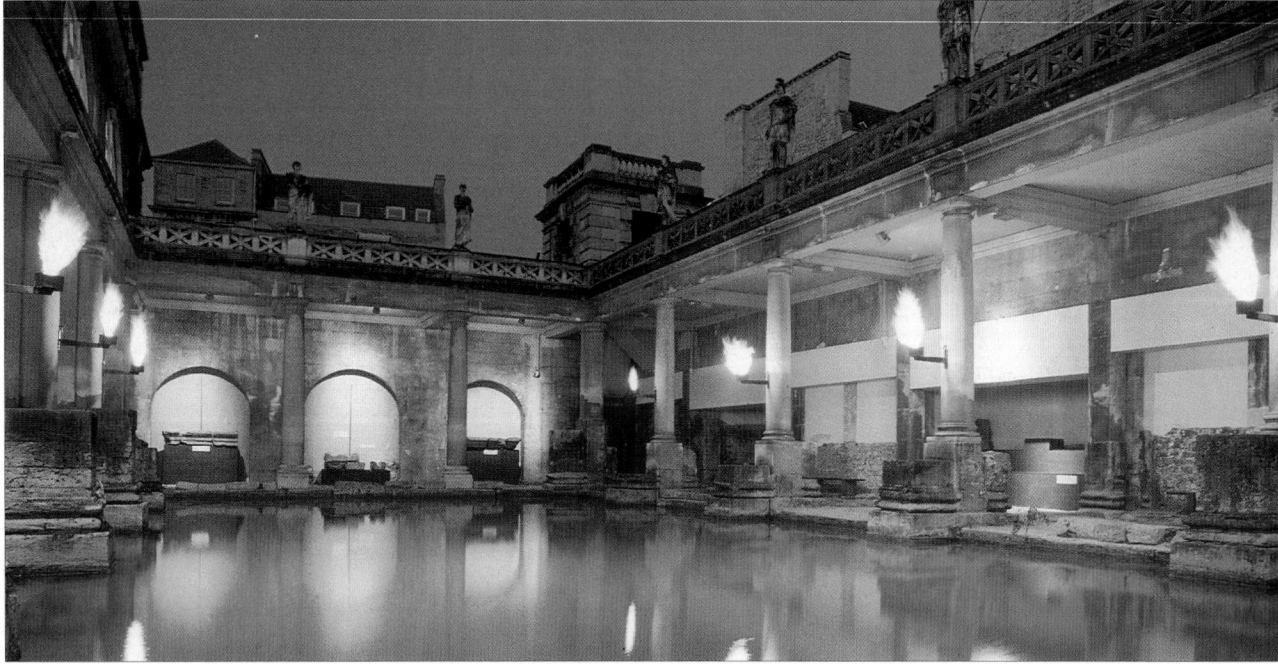

B & NES Council: Simon Mc Bride.

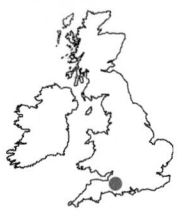

THE ROMAN BATHS & PUMP ROOM
Bath

The first stop for any visitor to Bath is the Roman Baths surrounding the hot springs where the city began and which are still its heart. Here you'll see one of the country's finest ancient monuments – the great Roman temple and bathing complex built almost 2000 years ago. Discover the everyday life of the Roman spa and see ancient treasures from the Temple of Sulis Minerva. A host of new interpretive methods bring these spectacular buildings vividly to life and help visitors to understand the extensive remains.

The Grand Pump Room, overlooking the Spring, is the social heart of Bath. The elegant interior of 1795 is something every visitor to Bath should see. You can enjoy a glass of spa water drawn from the fountain, perhaps as an appetiser to a traditional Pump Room tea, morning coffee or lunch. The Pump Room Trio and resident pianists provide live music daily. The Roman Baths shop sells publications and gifts related to the site.

In the evening, the Pump Room is available for banquets, dances and concerts. Nothing could be more magical than a meal on the terrace which overlooks the Great Bath, or a pre-dinner drinks reception by torchlight around the Great Bath itself.

❖

Owner:
Bath & North East
Somerset Council

CONTACT

For Room Hire:
Mr Tom Deller
Room Hire Manager
Stall Street
Bath BA1 1LZ
Tel: 01225 477734
Fax: 01225 477476
e-mail:
tom_deller@bathnes.gov.uk

For visits to Roman Baths:
Tel: 01225 477785
Fax: 01225 477743

LOCATION

OS Ref. ST750 648

Centre of Bath,
10m from M4/J18

Rail: Great Western from
London Paddington,
half hourly service,
1 hr 17 mins duration.
Good connection
to other UK cities.

CONFERENCE/FUNCTION		
ROOM	SIZE	MAX CAPACITY
Great Roman Bath		400 summer 200 winter
Pump Rm.	57' x 41'	180
Terrace overlooking Great Bath	83' x 11'	70
Concert Rm	56' x 44'	100
Smoking Rm & Drawing Rm	28' x 16'	40

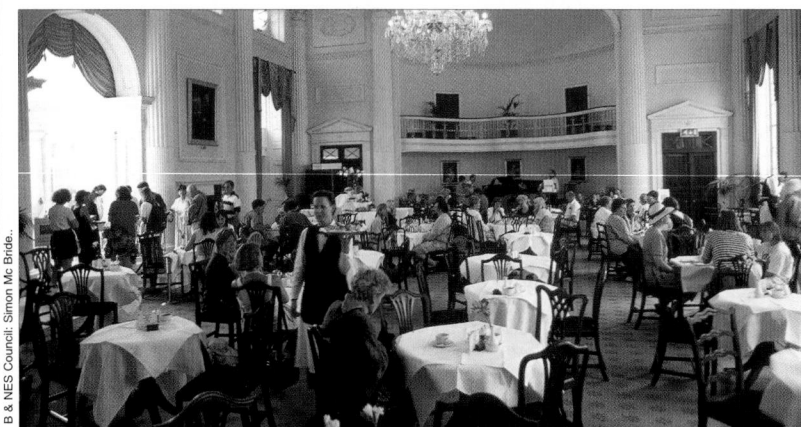

B & NES Council: Simon Mc Bride.

🛍 Extensive gift shop. ℹ Award-winning guide book in English, French and German. The Historic Buildings of Bath include the Assembly Rooms, Guildhall, and Victoria Art Gallery.

🍽 Comprehensive service for private and corporate entertainment. The Assembly Rooms, Guildhall, Victoria Art Gallery and Pump Room are all available for private hire, contact the Pump Room.

♿ Free access to terrace. Restricted access to the Museum, special visits for disabled groups by appointment. People with special needs welcome, teaching sessions available.

☕ Pump Room coffees, lunches and teas, no reservation needed. Music by Pump Room Trio or pianist.

🚶 Hourly. Private tours by appointment.

🗣 English, French, German, Italian, Japanese, Spanish.

📖 Teaching sessions available. Pre-booking necessary.

🔔 Civil Weddings in two private rooms with photographs around the Great Bath.

❄

OPENING TIMES

January - February:
9.30am - 5.30pm.
March - June: 9am - 6pm.
July - August: 9am - 10pm.
September - October:
9am - 6pm.
November - December:
9.30am - 5.30pm.
Last admission 1 hour
before closing.

Closed 25 & 26 December.

The Pump Room Trio plays
10am - 12 noon Mon - Sat
and 3 - 5pm Sunday.
During the summer it also
plays from 3 - 5pm, Mon -
Sat. Resident pianists play
at lunch-time.

ADMISSION

(2000 prices)

Adult £6.90
Child* £4.00
Family (2+4) £17.50
OAP.........................£6.00

Groups (20+)
Adult £5.30
Child* (summer)....£2.90
Child* (winter).......£2.50

**Combined ticket with
Museum of Costume,
Bath**

Adult £8.90
Child* £5.30
OAP.........................£8.00
Family (2 + 4).........£23.50

Groups (20+)
Adult £6.80
Child* (summer)....£4.00
Child* (winter).......£3.20

* 6 - 18 yrs.

NO. 1 ROYAL CRESCENT

See page 228 for full page entry.

BARRINGTON COURT

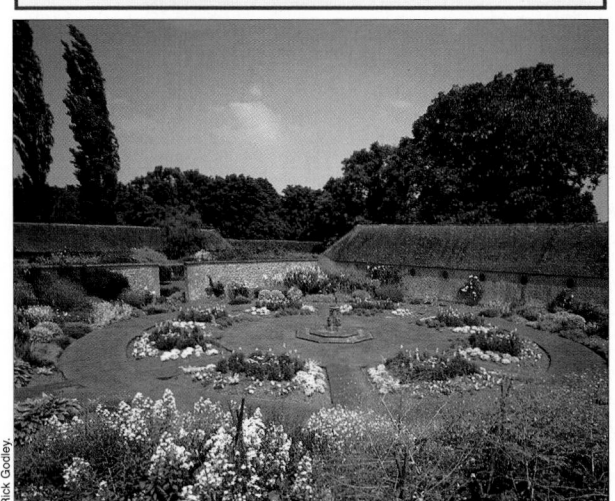

Rick Godley

BARRINGTON, ILMINSTER, SOMERSET TA19 0NQ

Owner: The National Trust   *Contact:* Visitor Reception Manager

Tel: 01460 241938

A beautiful garden influenced by Gertrude Jekyll and laid out in a series of walled rooms, including the white garden, the rose and iris garden and the lily garden. The working kitchen garden has apple, pear and plum trees trained along high stone walls. The Tudor Manor house was restored in the 1920s by the Lyle family. It is let to Stuart Interiors as showrooms with antique furniture for sale and is also open to NT visitors.

Location: OS Ref. ST395 181. In Barrington village, 5m NE of Ilminster, on B3168.

Opening Times: Mar & Oct - 4 Nov Thur - Sun: 11am - 4.30pm. 1 Apr - 30 Jun & Sept: daily except Fri, 11am - 5.30pm. Jul & Aug: daily (Fri: garden only), 11am - 5.30pm. Coach parties by appointment only.

Admission: Adult £5, Child £2.50, Family £12.50. Groups: Adult £4.50, Child £2.25.

⬜ ♿Grounds suitable. WC. 💷Licensed.

CLAVERTON MANOR

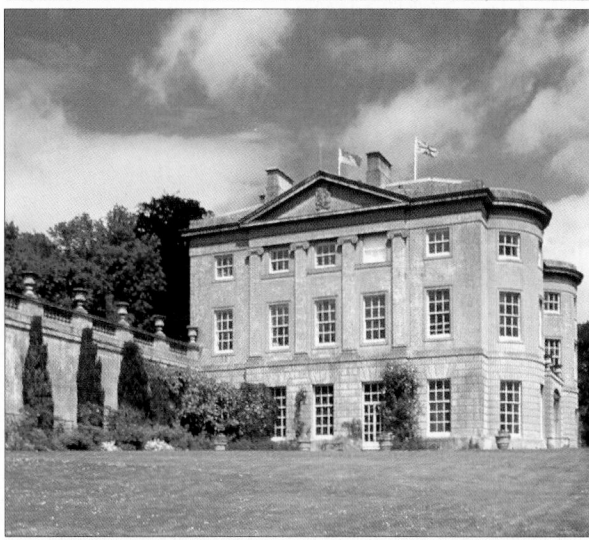

THE AMERICAN MUSEUM, BATH, SOMERSET BA2 7BD

Owner: The Trustees of the American Museum in Britain   *Contact:* Miss S Carter

Tel: 01225 460503   **Fax:** 01225 480726   **e-mail:** amibbath@aol.com

The American Museum is housed in a Georgian mansion set in extensive grounds which include a replica of George Washington's garden and arboretum of North American trees and shrubs. The museum shows, in a series of period rooms, life from early New England Colonies to New Orleans on the eve of the Civil War. 2001 Exhibition: The Textile Tradition Then and Now.

Location: OS Ref. ST784 640. 2m SE of Bath. Well-signed from city centre.

Opening Times: 24 Mar - 4 Nov: Tue - Sun. Grounds: 1 - 6pm. Museum: 2 - 5pm (closed Mons). Christmas openings: 24 Nov - 16 Dec, 1 - 4pm.

Admission: Adult £5.50, Child £3, Conc. £5. Group concessions available.

⬜ ☕ ♿Ground floor suitable. WC. 💷 🏛
🐕In grounds, on leads. ❄ ♨ Tel for details. 🆔

BECKFORD'S TOWER

Tel: 01225 422212 **Fax:** 01225 481850

Lansdown Road, Bath BA1 9BH

Owner: Bath Preservation Trust   **Contact:** The Administrator

Built in 1827 for eccentric William Beckford. The tower is a striking feature of the Bath skyline.

Location: OS Ref. ST735 676. Lansdown Road, 2m NNW of city centre.

Opening Times: Easter weekend - end of October: Sats, Suns & BH Mons, 10.30am - 5pm.

Admission: Adult £2.50, Child/OAP £2, Family £6. BPT & NACF members: Free. Groups by arrangement – Tel: 01225 460705.

THE BISHOP'S PALACE 🏛

Tel/Fax: 01749 678691

Wells, Somerset BA5 2PD

Owner: Church Commissioners   **Contact:** Mrs K J Scarisbrick

Fortified and moated medieval palace which is today the private residence of the Bishop of Bath and Wells. Extensive grounds and arboretum. Available for functions.

Location: OS Ref. ST552 457. 20m S of Bristol and Bath on A39.

Opening Times: 1 Apr - 31 Oct: Tue - Fri & BHs & daily in Aug, 10.30am - 6pm. Suns: 2 - 6pm.

Admission: Adult £3, Child (12 - 18) £1, OAP £2, Conc. £1.50. Groups (10+) £2. Guided tour £30 plus £2 per person.

☕Corporate hospitality. Wedding receptions. ♿Partially suitable. 💷 🍴
🎭By arrangement. 🐕In grounds on leads.

THE BUILDING OF BATH MUSEUM

Tel: 01225 333895 **Tel:** 01225 445473

The Countess of Huntingdon's Chapel, The Vineyards, The Paragon, Bath BA1 5NA

Owner: Bath Preservation Trust   **Contact:** The Administrator

Discover the essence of life in Georgian Bath.

Location: OS Ref. ST751 655. 5 mins walk from city centre. Bath M4/J18.

Opening Times: 15 Feb - 30 Nov: Tue - Sun and BH Mons, 10.30am - 5pm.

Admission: Adult £3.50, Child £1.50, Conc. £2.50. Groups: Adult £2.50. Child £1.50.

CLEEVE ABBEY 🏛

Tel: 01984 640377

Washford, Nr Watchet, Somerset TA23 0PS

Owner: English Heritage   **Contact:** The Custodian

There are few monastic sites where you will see such a complete set of cloister buildings, including the refectory with its magnificent timber roof. Built in the 13th century, this Cistercian abbey was saved from destruction at the Dissolution by being turned into a house and then a farm.

Location: OS181 Ref. ST047 407. In Washford, 1/4 m S of A39.

Opening Times: 1 Apr - 31 Oct: daily 10am - 6pm (5pm in Oct). 1 Nov - 31 Mar: daily 10am - 4pm (closed lunch 1 - 2pm). Closed 24 - 26 Dec & 1 Jan.

Admission: Adult £2.60, Child £1.30, Conc. £2. 15% discount for groups (11+).

⬜ ♿Partially suitable. 💷 🅿 🐕In grounds, on leads. ❄ ♨ Tel. for details.

CLEVEDON COURT 🌺

Tel: 01275 872257

Tickenham Road, Clevedon, North Somerset BS21 6QU

Owner: The National Trust   **Contact:** The Administrator

Home of the Elton family since 1709, this 14th century manor house, once partly fortified, has a 12th century tower and 13th century hall. Collection of Nailsea glass and Eltonware. Beautiful terraced garden.

Location: OS Ref. ST423 716. 1 1/2 m E of Clevedon, on B3130, signposted from M5/J20.

Opening Times: 1 Apr - 30 Sept: Weds, Thurs, Suns & BH Mons, 2 - 5pm.

Admission: Adult £4.50, Child £2. Groups & coaches by arrangement.

♿Ground floor suitable. 💷 🅿Limited. 🐕

COLERIDGE COTTAGE 🌺

Tel: 01278 732662

35 Lime Street, Nether Stowey, Bridgwater, Somerset TA5 1NQ

Owner: The National Trust   **Contact:** The Custodian

The home of Samuel Taylor Coleridge for three years from 1797, with mementoes of the poet on display. It was here that he wrote *The Rime of the Ancient Mariner*, part of *Christabel* and *Frost at Midnight*.

Location: OS Ref. ST191 399. At W end of Nether Stowey, on S side of A39, 8m W of Bridgwater.

Opening Times: 1 Apr - 30 Sept: Tue - Thur & Suns, 2 - 5pm.

Admission: Adult £3, Child £1.50, no reduction for groups, which must book.

🐕 ❄

COMBE SYDENHAM COUNTRY PARK

Tel: 01984 656284

Monksilver, Taunton, Somerset TA4 4JG

Owner: Theed Estates   **Contact:** Mr A Hudson

Built in 1580 on the site of a monastic settlement. Deer Park and woodland walks.

Location: OS Ref. ST075 366. Monksilver

Opening Times: Guided tours Mons, Weds, Thurs. Please telephone for details.

Admission: £3 per vehicle. Adult £5, Child £2.50 for guided tours. (2000 prices.)

COTHAY MANOR

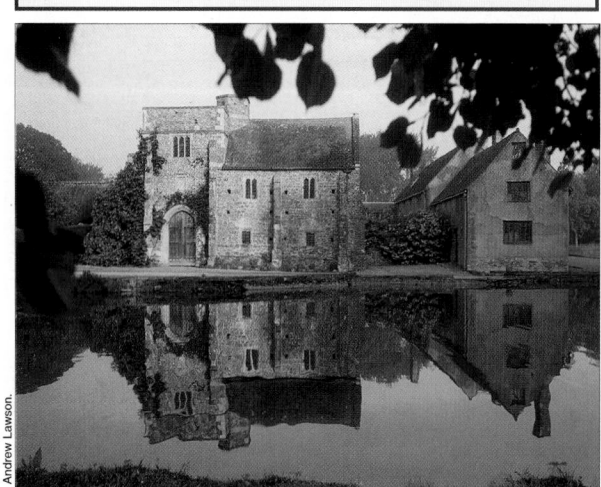

Andrew Lawson.

GREENHAM, WELLINGTON, SOMERSET TA21 0JR

Owner/Contact: Mr & Mrs Alastair Robb

Tel: 01823 672283 **Fax:** 01823 672345

It has been said that Cothay Manor is the finest example of a small classic, medieval manor house in England. The manor has remained virtually untouched since it was built in 1480. The gardens, laid out in the 1920s have been completely re-designed and replanted within the original framework of yew hedges. A white garden, scarlet and purple garden, herbaceous borders and bog garden are but a few of the delights to be found in this magical place.

Location: OS Ref. ST721 214. From M5 W J/27, take A38 dir Wellington. 3^1/$_2$ m left to Greenham. From N take A38 dir. Exeter. 3^1/$_2$ m right to Greenham (1^1/$_2$ m). On LH corner at bottom of hill turn right. Cothay 1^1/$_2$ m, always keeping left.

Opening Times: May - Sept: Weds, Thurs, Suns & BHs, 2 - 6pm.

Admission: Garden: Adult £3.50, Child (under 12yrs) Free. House: Groups (20+): by arrangement throughout the year, £4.50.

No photography in house. By arrangement.

CROWE HALL

Tel: 01225 310322

Widcombe Hill, Bath, Somerset BA2 6AR

Owner/Contact: John Barratt Esq

Ten acres of romantic hillside gardens. Victorian grotto, classical Bath villa with good 18th century furniture and paintings.

Location: OS Ref. ST760 640. In Bath, 1m SE of city centre.

Opening Times: Gardens only open 18 Mar, 22 Apr, 13 May, 10 Jun, 15 Jul: 2 - 6pm. House and Gardens by appointment.

Admission: House & Gardens: Adult £4. Gardens only: Adult £2, Child £1.

DUNSTER CASTLE

Tel: 01643 821314 **Fax:** 01643 823000

Dunster, Nr Minehead, Somerset TA24 6SL

Owner: The National Trust   **Contact:** The Property Manager

From Norman motte-and-bailey to Jacobean mansion and Victorian eccentricity there is something for everyone. 600 years of Luttrell family residence has groomed and moulded the property from coastal fortress to a secluded country seat. The house and medieval ruins are magically framed with sub-tropical plants including the famous Dunster Lemon.

Location: OS Ref. SS992 436. In Dunster, 3m SE of Minehead.

Opening Times: Contact property for details.

Admission: Contact property for details.

Guide dogs only.

DUNSTER WORKING WATERMILL

Tel: 01643 821759

Mill Lane, Dunster, Minehead, Somerset TA24 6SW

Owner: The National Trust   **Contact:** The Tenant

Built on the site of a mill mentioned in the Domesday Survey of 1086, the present mill dates from the 18th century and was restored to working order in 1979. Note: the mill is a private business and all visitors, including NT members are asked to pay the admission charge.

Location: OS Ref. SS991 434. On River Avill, beneath Castle Tor, approach via Mill Lane or Castle gardens on foot.

Opening Times: 1 Apr - 31 Oct: daily, 10.30am - 5pm.

Admission: £2.20. Family tickets available. Group rates by prior arrangement.

Ground floor suitable. P

EAST LAMBROOK MANOR GARDENS   **Tel:** 01460 240328   **Fax:** 01460 242344

South Petherton, Somerset TA13 5HL   **e-mail:** ELambrook@aol.com

Owner: Mr & Mrs Robert Williams   **Contact:** Mark Stainer - Head Gardener

Grade I listed cottage-style garden, developed by the famous Margery Fish, containing many rare and unusual plants saved from extinction.

Location: OS177 Ref. ST431 189. 2m N of S Petherton off A303 (signed).

Opening Times: Gardens only: All year: daily, 10am - 5pm. For winter opening hours please telephone first.

Admission: Groups by prior arrangement.

Art gallery. NCCPG National Geranium collection. Not suitable. By arrangement. P Limited for coaches.

ENGLISHCOMBE TITHE BARN

Tel: 01225 425073

Rectory Farmhouse, Englishcombe, Bath BA2 9DU   **e-mail:** tithebarn@ntlworld.com

Owner/Contact: Mrs Jennie Walker

An early 14th century cruck-framed Tithe Barn built by Bath Abbey.

Location: OS172 Ref. ST716 628. Adjacent to Englishcombe Village Church. 1m SW of Bath.

Opening Times: 15 - 20 Apr, 6 - 11 May, 27 May - 1 June, 25 - 29 June & 26 - 30 August, 3 - 6pm.

Admission: Free.

FARLEIGH HUNGERFORD CASTLE

Tel: 01225 754026

Farleigh Hungerford, Bath, Somerset BA3 6RS

Owner: English Heritage   **Contact:** The Custodian

Extensive ruins of 14th century castle with a splendid chapel containing wall paintings, stained glass and the fine tomb of Sir Thomas Hungerford, builder of the castle.

Location: OS173 Ref. ST801 577. In Farleigh Hungerford 3^1/$_2$ m W of Trowbridge on A366.

Opening Times: Apr - Oct: daily 10am - 6pm (5pm in Oct). Nov - Mar: Wed - Sun, 10am - 4pm (closed for lunch 1 - 2 pm). Closed 24 - 26 Dec & 1 Jan.

Admission: Adult £2.30, Child £1.20, Conc. £1.70. 15% discount for groups of 11+.

Grounds suitable. P Guide dogs only. Tel. for details.

GANTS MILL

Tel: 01749 812393

Bruton, Somerset BA10 0DB

Owner/Contact: Brian and Alison Shingler

4-storey working watermill with beautiful colour-themed designer garden.

Location: OS Ref. ST674 342. Off A359 ^{1}/$_2$ m SW of Bruton.

Opening Times: Mill: Easter - end of May, Thur & BH Mons. Mill & Garden: June - end Sept, Thurs, Suns & BH Mons, 2 - 5pm.

Admission: Adult £3.50, Child £1. Groups by arrangement.

GATCOMBE COURT

Tel: 01275 393141 **Fax:** 01275 394274

Flax Bourton, Somerset BS48 3QT

Owner: Mr & Mrs Charles Clarke   **Contact:** Mr Charles Clarke

A Somerset manor house, dating from early 13th century, which has evolved over the centuries since. It is on the site of a large Roman village, traces of which are apparent.

Location: OS Ref. ST525 698. 5m W of Bristol, N of the A370, between the villages of Long Ashton and Flax Bourton.

Opening Times: By written appointment only.

Not suitable. By arrangement. P

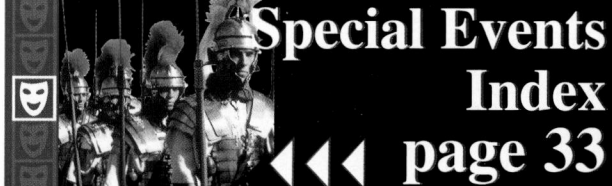

GAULDEN MANOR

Tel: 01984 667213

Tolland, Lydeard St Lawrence, Nr Taunton, Somerset TA4 3PN

Owner/Contact: James Le Gendre Starkie

Small historic manor of great charm. A real lived-in family home, guided tours by owner. Past seat of the Turberville family, immortalised by Thomas Hardy. Magnificent early plasterwork, fine furniture, many examples of embroidery by owner's wife. Interesting gardens include herb garden, old fashioned roses, bog garden and secret garden beyond monks fish pond.

Location: OS Ref. ST111 314. 9m NW of Taunton off A358 and B3224.

Opening Times: Garden: 3 Jun - 27 Aug. Thurs, Suns & BH Mons, 2 - 5pm. House & Garden: groups (15+): Jun, Jul & Aug: by written appointment at any time.

Admission: House & Garden: Adult £4.20, Child £1. Garden only: Adult £3, Child £1.

 Ground floor & grounds suitable. Obligatory. P

THE GEORGIAN HOUSE

Tel: 0117 921 1262

7 Great George Street, Bristol, Somerset BS1 5RR

Owner: City of Bristol Museums & Art Gallery

Contact: Karin Walton

Location: OS172 ST582 730. Bristol.

Opening Times: 1 Apr - 31 Oct: Sat - Wed, 10am - 5pm. 1 Nov - 31 Mar: closed.

Admission: Free.

THE WILLIAM HERSCHEL MUSEUM

Tel: 01225 311342 **Fax:** 01225 446865

19 New King Street, Bath, Somerset BA1 2BL

Owner: The Herschel House Trust

Contact: The Curator

The astronomer and musician William Herschel lived here with his sister Caroline during the latter part of the 18th century. 'Star Vault' opening 2001.

Location: OS Ref. ST750 648. Bath, Somerset.

Opening Times: Mar - Oct: daily, 2 - 5pm. Weekends throughout the winter, 2 - 5pm.

Admission: Adult £2.50, Child £1. Organised educational events: £2.50. Free entry to Herschel Society members and Museums Association members.

GLASTONBURY TRIBUNAL

Tel: 01458 832954

Glastonbury High Street, Glastonbury, Somerset

Owner: English Heritage

Contact: The TIC Manager

A well preserved medieval town house, reputedly once used as the courthouse of Glastonbury Abbey. Now houses Glastonbury Tourist Information Centre.

Location: OS182 Ref. ST499 390. In Glastonbury High Street.

Opening Times: Apr - Sept: Sun - Thur 10am - 5pm (Fri & Sat to 5.30pm). Oct - Apr: Sun - Thur, 10am - 4pm (Fri & Sat, 4.30pm). Closed 25 - 26 Dec & 1 Jan.

Admission: TIC Free. Display areas: Adult £2, Child £1.

GLASTONBURY ABBEY

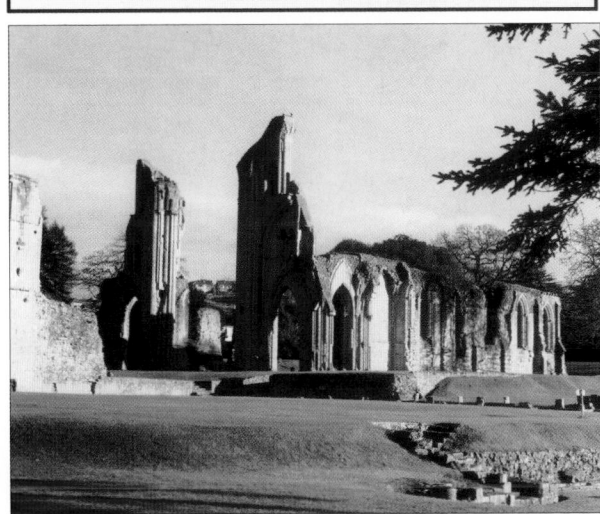

ABBEY GATEHOUSE, MAGDALENE STREET, GLASTONBURY BA6 9EL

Owner: Glastonbury Abbey Estate **Contact:** *F C Thyer - Deputy Custodian*

Tel/Fax: 01458 832267 **e-mail:** glastonbury.abbey@dial.pipex.com

Magnificent Abbey ruins steeped in history and legend, situated in 36 acres of glorious Somerset parkland. Traditionally the first Christian sanctuary in Britain and legendary burial place of King Arthur. Award-winning museum with model of pre-Reformation Abbey and 16th century Othery Cope. See the Holy Thorn Tree. Picnics welcomed

Location: OS Ref. ST499 388. 50 yds from the Market Cross, in the centre of Glastonbury. M5/J23, then A39.

Opening Times: Daily (except Christmas Day), 9.30am - 6pm or dusk if earlier. Jun, Jul & Aug: opens 9am. Dec, Jan & Feb: opens 10am.

Admission: Adult £3, Child £1, Conc. £2.50. Groups (booked, 10+): Adult £2.50.

  Summer only. By arrangement. P

In grounds, on leads. Tel. for details.

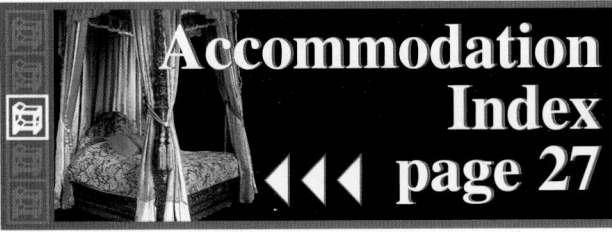

Accommodation Index ◀◀◀ page 27

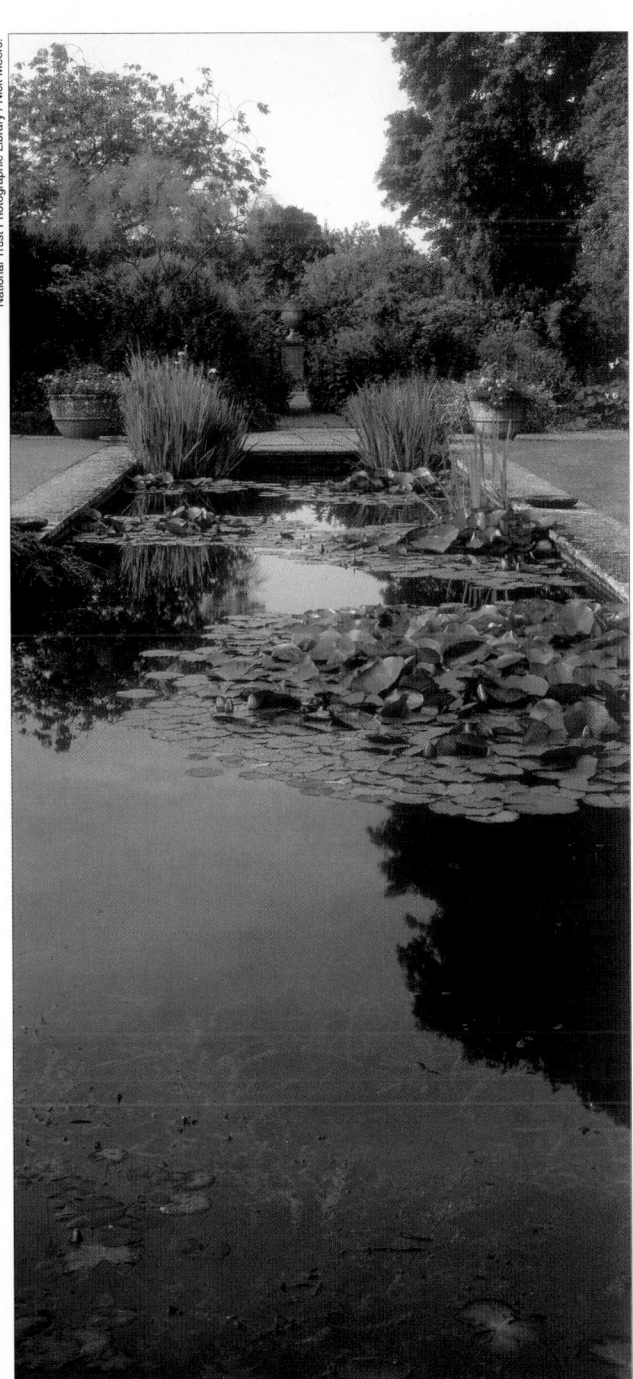

Tintinhull Garden, Somerset.

National Trust Photographic Library / Nick Meers.

HESTERCOMBE GARDENS

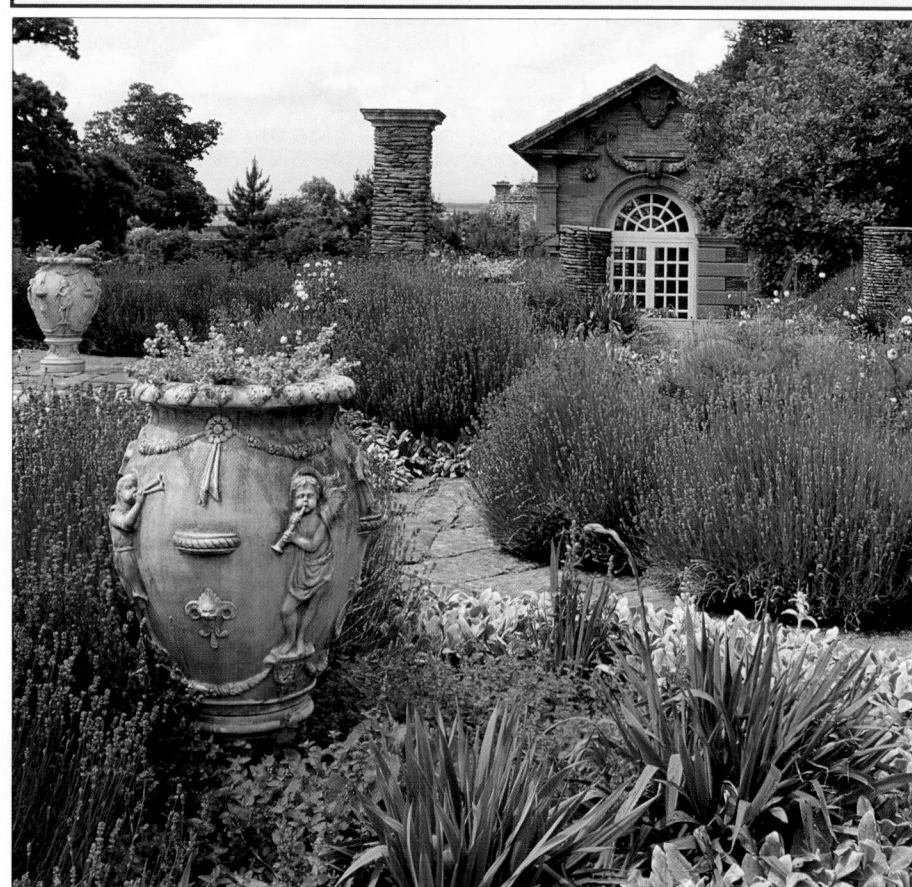

CHEDDON FITZPAINE, TAUNTON, SOMERSET TA2 8LG

Owner: *Somerset County Council & Hestercombe Gardens Project*

Contact: *Mr P White*

Tel: 01823 413923   **Fax:** 01823 413747

Hestercombe's 50 acres of gardens are listed Grade I on the English Heritage Register of Parks and Gardens and encompass over three centuries of garden history.

The formal gardens, designed by Sir Edwin Lutyens and planted by Gertrude Jekyll, were completed in 1906. With terraces, pools and an orangery, they are the supreme example of their famous partnership. These gardens are now reunited with Hestercombe's secret Landscape Garden, which opened in the Spring of 1997 for the first time in 125 years. Created by Coplestone Warre Bampfylde in the 1750s, these Georgian pleasure grounds comprise 40 acres of lakes, temples and delightful woodland walks. Our tearoom, shop and plant sales area are open daily from 10am to 5pm.

Location: OS Ref. ST241 287. 4m NE from Taunton, 1m NW of Cheddon Fitzpaine.

Opening Times: All year: daily, 10am - 6pm (last admission 5pm). Groups & coach parties by arrangement.

Admission: Adult £4. Child (5-15yrs) £1, Child under 5 Free, Conc. £3.80. Guided tour: £6.50 (min. charge £100).

▢ ▢ ▭ Partially suitable. WC.
▢ Licensed. ▯ Licensed.
▯ By arrangement.
▯ Limited for coaches.
▯ On short leads. ❄ (IW)

KENTSFORD

Tel: 01984 631307

Washford, Watchet, Somerset TA23 0JD

Owner: Wyndham Estate   **Contact:** Mr R Dibble

Location: OS Ref. ST058 426.

Opening Times: House open only by written appointment with Mr R Dibble. Gardens: 6 Mar - 27 Aug: Tues & BHs.

Admission: House: £2, Gardens: Free.

▭ Gardens only. ▯ Limited. ▯ In grounds, on leads. ❄

KING JOHN'S HUNTING LODGE

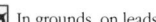

Tel: 01934 732012

The Square, Axbridge, Somerset BS26 2AP

Owner/Contact: The National Trust

An early Tudor merchant's house, extensively restored in 1971. Note: the property is run as a local history museum by Sedgemoor District Council in co-operation with Somerset County Museum's Service and Axbridge Archaeological & Local History Society.

Location: OS Ref. ST431 545. In the Square, on corner of High Street, off A371.

Opening Times: Easter - end Sept: daily, 2 - 5pm.

Admission: Free. School groups by arrangement.

▭ Ground floor suitable. ▯

LOWER SEVERALLS

Tel: 01460 73234   **Fax:** 01460 76105

Crewkerne, Somerset TA18 7NX

Owner: Mr & Mrs Howard Pring   **Contact:** Mary Cooper

2½ acre garden, developed over the last 25 years including herb garden, mixed borders and island beds with innovative features, ie a giant living dogwood basket and a wadi.

Location: OS Ref. ST457 112. 1½ m NE of Crewkerne, between A30 & A356.

Opening Times: 2 Mar - 20 Oct: daily (except Thurs), 10am - 5pm (Suns, 2 - 5pm in May/June only).

Admission: Adult £2, Child (under 16yrs) Free.

LYTES CARY MANOR

Tel: 01985 843600

Nr Charlton Mackrell, Somerset TA11 7HU

Owner: The National Trust   **Contact:** The Regional Office

A charming manor house with a 14th century chapel and Tudor Great Hall, much added to in the 16th century. Once the home of Henry Lyte, translator of Niewe Herball (1578). Attractive hedged garden.

Location: OS Ref. ST534 265. 1m N of Ilchester bypass A303, signposted from roundabout at junction of A303. A37 take A372.

Opening Times: 2 Apr - 31 Oct: Mons, Weds & Sats, 2 - 6pm or dusk if earlier. Also Fris in Jun, Jul & Aug: 2 - 6pm. Last admission 5.30pm.

Admission: £4.50, Child £2.

▭ Grounds suitable. ▯ Limited. ▯

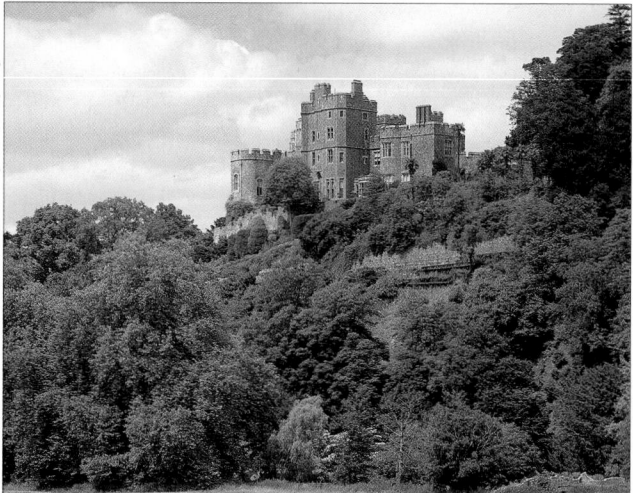

Dunster Castle, Somerset.

MAUNSEL HOUSE

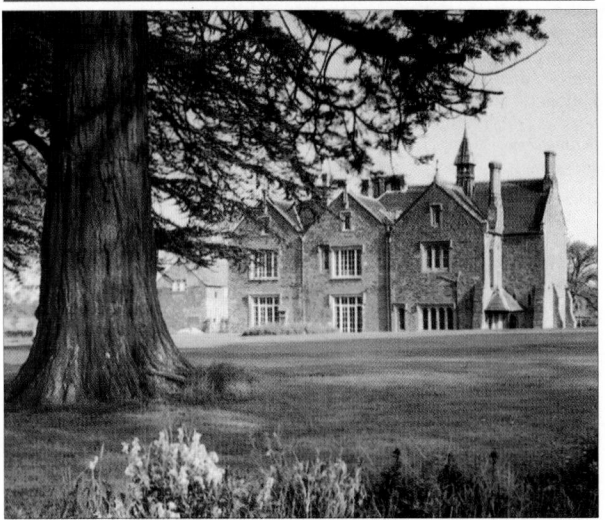

NORTH NEWTON, Nr BRIDGWATER, SOMERSET TA7 0BU

Owner: Sir Benjamin Slade *Contact: Olivia Boyle*

Tel: 0207 352 1132 **Fax:** 0207 352 5697

This imposing 13th century manor house offers the ideal location for wedding receptions, corporate events, private and garden parties, filming and family celebrations. The ancestral seat of the Slade family and home of the 7th baronet Sir Benjamin Slade; the house can boast such visitors as Geoffrey Chaucer, who wrote part of the *Canterbury Tales* whilst staying there. The beautiful grounds and spacious rooms provide both privacy and a unique atmosphere for any special event.

Location: OS Ref. ST302 303. Bridgwater 4m, Bristol 20m, Taunton 7m, M5/J24, turn left North Petherton. 2¹/₂ m SE of A38 at North Petherton.

Opening Times: Coach parties and groups welcome by appointment. Caravan rally field available.

⊤ Functions. ♿ Partially suitable. 🐕 In grounds, on leads. 🏳

MONTACUTE HOUSE

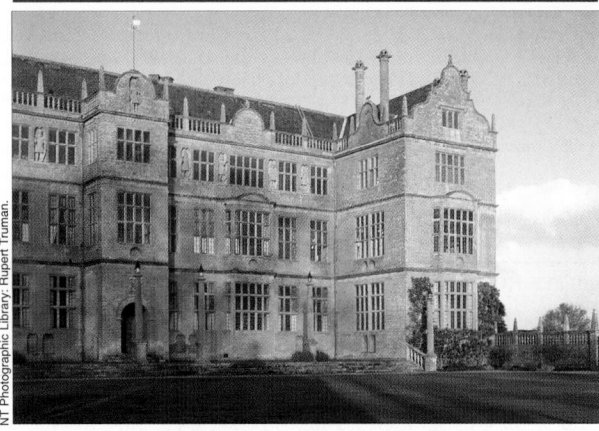

NT Photographic Library: Rupert Truman.

MONTACUTE, SOMERSET TA15 6XP

Owner: The National Trust *Contact: The Property Manager*

Tel/Fax: 01935 823289

A magnificent Elizabethan house, with an H-shaped ground plan and many Renaissance features, including contemporary plasterwork, chimneypieces and heraldic glass. The house contains fine 17th and 18th century furniture, an exhibition of samplers dating from the 17th century and Elizabethan and Jacobean portraits from the National Portrait Gallery displayed in the Long Gallery and adjoining rooms. The formal garden includes mixed borders and old roses, also a landscaped park. Montacute featured in the award-winning film *Sense & Sensibility*.

Location: OS Ref. ST499 172. In Montacute village, 4m W of Yeovil, on S side of A3088, 3m E of A303.

Opening Times: House: 31 Mar - 4 Nov: daily except Tues, 12 noon - 5.30pm. Garden & Park: 31 Mar - 4 Nov: daily except Tues, 11am - 5.30pm or dusk if earlier. 7 Nov - Mar 2002 daily except Mons & Tues, 11.30am - 4pm.

Admission: House, Park & Garden: Adult £6, Child £3, Family £15. Groups (15+) (must book): Adult £5.50, Child £2.80. Garden & Park only (31 Mar - 4 Nov): Adult £3.30, Child £1.50. 7 Nov - Mar 2002: Adult £2, Child £1.

📷 ♿ Grounds suitable. WC. ⊤ Licensed. 🅿 🐕 In park only.
🏛 ❄

MILTON LODGE GARDENS 🏛   **Tel:** 01749 672168

Wells, Somerset BA5 3AQ

Owner/Contact: D Tudway Quilter Esq

"The great glory of the gardens of Milton Lodge is their position high up on the slopes of the Mendip Hills to the north of Wells … with broad panoramas of Wells Cathedral and the Vale of Avalon", (Lanning Roper). Charming, mature, Grade II listed terraced garden dating from 1909. Replanned 1962 with mixed shrubs, herbaceous plants, old fashioned roses and ground cover; numerous climbers; old established yew hedges. Fine trees in garden and in 7-acre arboretum.

Location: OS Ref. ST549 470. ¹/₂ m N of Wells from A39. N up Old Bristol Road. Free car park first gate on left.

Opening Times: Garden & Arboretum: Easter - end Oct: Tues, Weds, Suns & BHs, 2 - 5pm Parties & coaches by prior arrangement.

Admission: Adult £2.50, Child (under 14yrs) Free. Open certain Suns in aid of National Gardens Scheme.

📷 🍴 ♿ Not suitable. 🛒 🅿 🐕

MUCHELNEY ABBEY 🏛   **Tel:** 01458 250664

Muchelney, Langport, Somerset TA10 0DQ

Owner: English Heritage   **Contact:** The Custodian

Well-preserved ruins of the cloisters, with windows carved in golden stone, and abbot's lodging of the Benedictine abbey, which survived by being used as a farmhouse after the Dissolution.

Location: OS193 Ref. ST428 248. In Muchelney 2m S of Langport.

Opening Times: 1 Apr - 31 Oct: daily 10am - 6pm (5pm in Oct). Winter: closed.

Admission: Adult £1.90, Child £1, Conc. £1.50. 15% discount for groups (11+).

📷 ♿ Ground floor & grounds suitable. 🛒 🅿 🐕 🎫 Tel. for details.

MUSEUM OF COSTUME & ASSEMBLY ROOMS

See page 229 for full page entry.

NUNNEY CASTLE 🏛   **Tel:** 0117 9750700

Nunney, Somerset

Owner: English Heritage   **Contact:** The South West Regional Office

A small 14th century moated castle with a distinctly French style. Its unusual design consists of a central block with large towers at the angles.

Location: OS183 Ref. ST737 457. In Nunney 3¹/₂ m SW of Frome, 1m N of the A361.

Opening Times: Any reasonable time.

Admission: Free.

Montacute House, Somerset.

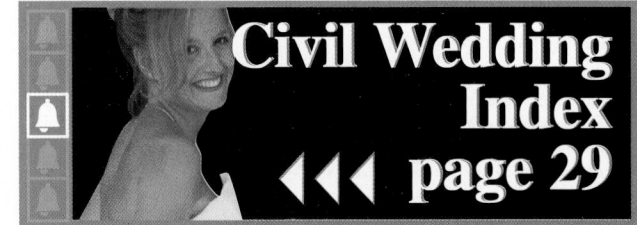

Civil Wedding Index ◄◄◄ page 29

South West England

ORCHARD WYNDHAM

Tel: 01984 632309 **Fax:** 01984 633526

Williton, Taunton, Somerset TA4 4HH

Owner: Wyndham Estate   **Contact:** Wyndham Estate Office

English manor house. Family home for 700 years encapsulating continuous building and alteration from the 14th to the 20th century. Limited showing space within the house. To avoid disappointment book places on tour by telephone or fax. Access only suitable for cars.

Location: OS Ref. ST072 400. 1m from A39 at Williton.

Opening Times: Aug: Thurs & Fris, 2 - 5pm; BH, 11am - 5pm. Guided tours only. Last tour at 4pm.

Admission: Adult £5, Child (under 12) £1.

⚑ Obligatory & pre-booked.   🅿 Limited. No coach parking.   🐕 In grounds, on leads.

PRIEST'S HOUSE

Tel: 01458 252621

Muchelney, Langport, Somerset TA10 0DQ

Owner: The National Trust   **Contact:** The Administrator

A late medieval hall house with large gothic windows, originally the residence of priests serving the parish church across the road. Lived-in and recently repaired.

Location: OS Ref. ST429 250. 1m S of Langport.

Opening Times: 1 Apr - 30 Sept: Suns & Mons, 2.30 - 5.30pm, last admission 5.15pm.

Admission: £2, no reduction for groups or children.

🐕

PRIOR PARK LANDSCAPE GARDEN

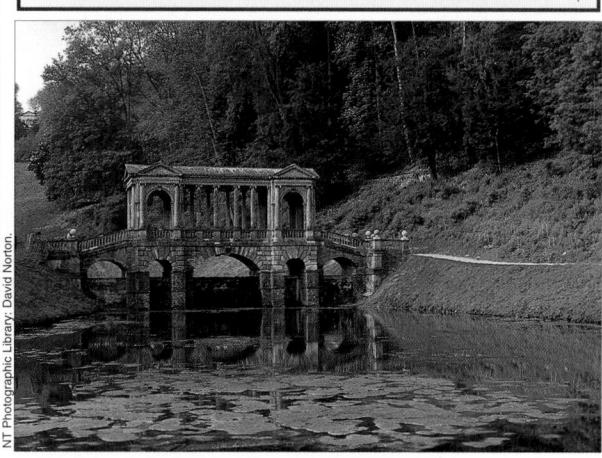

NT Photographic Library: David Norton.

RALPH ALLEN DRIVE, BATH BA2 5AH

Owner: The National Trust   *Contact:* Gardener-in-Charge

Tel: 01225 833422

Beautiful and intimate 18th century landscape garden created by Bath entrepreneur Ralph Allen (1693 - 1764) with advice from the poet Alexander Pope and Lancelot 'Capability' Brown. Sweeping valley with magnificent views of the City of Bath Palladian bridge and lakes. Restoration of the garden continues. All visitors must use public transport as there is no car park. For further details 01225 833422 or 24 hour information line 09001 335242 (60p per minute). Prior Park College, a co-educational school, operates from the mansion (not NT).

Location: OS Ref. ST760 632. Frequent bus service from City Centre. Badgerline 2 & 4.

Opening Times: Feb - Nov & 1 - 28 Feb 2002: daily except Tues. Dec & Jan 2002: Fri - Sun (closed 25/26 Dec & 1 Jan 2002). Times: Feb - Good Fri 12 noon - 5.30pm or dusk if earlier. Easter Sat - 11 Sept: 11am - 5.30pm. Oct - Feb 12 noon - 5.30pm or dusk if earlier.

Admission: Adult £4, Child £2. All visitors who produce a valid bus or train ticket will receive £1 off admission. NT members will receive a £1 voucher.

♿ Grounds suitable. WC.   🅿 No parking.   🐕 ❄

THE ROMAN BATHS & PUMP ROOM

See page 230 for full page entry.

STEMBRIDGE TOWER MILL

Tel: 01458 250818

High Ham, Somerset TA10 9DJ

Owner: The National Trust   **Contact:** The Administrator

The last thatched windmill in England, dating from 1822 and in use until 1910.

Location: OS Ref. ST432 305. 2m N of Langport, ¹/₂ m E of High Ham.

Opening Times: 1 Apr - 30 Sept: Suns, Mons & Weds, 2 - 5pm.

Admission: Adult £2, Child £1. Special arrangements may be made for coach/school groups.

🅿 Limited.   🐕

STOKE-SUB-HAMDON PRIORY

Tel: 01985 843600

North Street, Stoke-sub-Hamdon Somerset TA4 6QP

Owner/Contact: The National Trust

A complex of buildings, begun in the 14th century for the priests of the chantry chapel of St Nicholas, which is now destroyed.

Location: OS Ref. ST473 174. ¹/₂ m S of A303. 2m W of Montacute between Yeovil and Ilminster.

Opening Times: 31 Mar - 4 Nov: daily, 10am - 6pm or dusk if earlier. Only Great Hall open.

Admission: Free.

ℹ No WC.   🅿 Limited.   🐕

TINTINHULL GARDEN

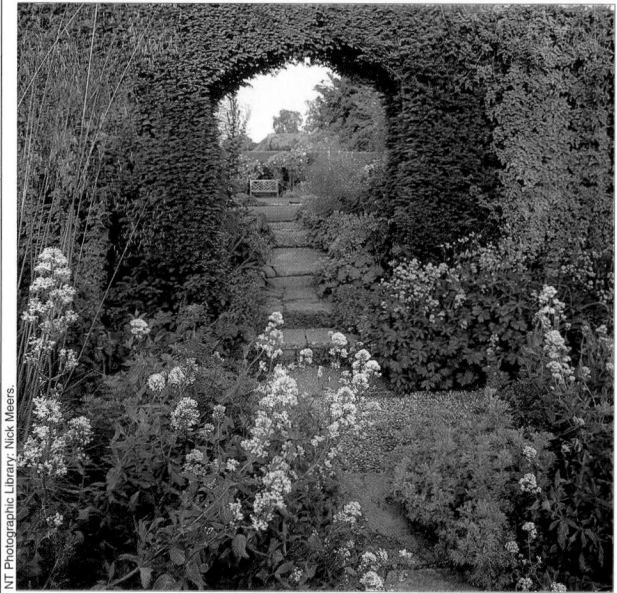

NT Photographic Library: Nick Meers.

FARM STREET, TINTINHULL, SOMERSET BA22 9PZ

Owner: The National Trust   *Contact:* The Head Gardener

Tel: 01935 822545

A delightful formal garden, created in the 20th century around a 17th century manor house. Small pools, varied borders and secluded lawns are neatly enclosed within walls and clipped hedges and there is also an attractive kitchen garden.

Location: OS Ref. ST503 198. 5m NW of Yeovil, ¹/₂ m S of A303, on E outskirts of Tintinhull.

Opening Times: 1 Apr - 30 Sept: Wed - Sun, 12 noon - 6pm (open BH Mons).

Admission: Adult £3.80, Child £1.80. No reduction for groups.

♿ Grounds suitable.   🅿 Limited.

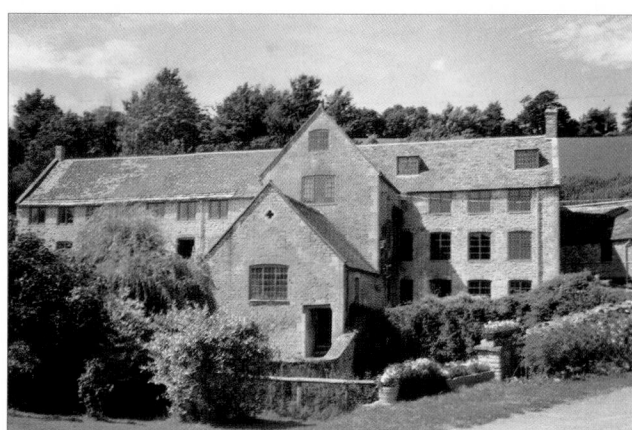

Gants Mill, Somerset.

TREASURER'S HOUSE ✿

Tel: 01935 825801

Martock, Somerset TA12 6JL

Owner/Contact: The National Trust

A small medieval house, recently refurbished by The Trust. The two-storey hall was completed in 1293 and the solar block is even earlier. There is also a kitchen, added later, and an interesting wall painting.

Location: OS Ref. ST462 191. 1m NW of A303 between Ilminster and Ilchester.

Opening Times: 1 Apr - 30 Sept: Sun - Tue, 2 - 5pm. Only medieval hall, wall paintings and kitchen are shown.

Admission: Adult £2 (no reduction for children). Groups by prior appointment.

🅿 Limited for cars. None for coaches & trailer caravans.

WELLS CATHEDRAL

Tel: 01749 674483 **Fax:** 01749 677360

Cathedral Green, Wells, Somerset BA5 2UE

Owner: The Chapter of Wells **Contact:** Mr John Roberts

Fine medieval Cathedral. The West front with its splendid array of statuary, the Quire with colourful embroideries and stained glass, Chapter House and astronomical clock should not be missed.

Location: OS Ref. ST552 458. In Wells, 20m S from both Bath & Bristol.

Opening Times: Daily: 7.15am - 8.30pm (summer), or 7.15am - 6pm (winter).

Admission: No entry charge. Donations welcomed. Photo permit £1.

WESTBURY COLLEGE GATEHOUSE ✿

Tel: 01985 843600

College Road, Westbury-on-Trym, Bristol

Owner: The National Trust **Contact:** Rev G M Collins

The 15th century gatehouse of the College of Priests (founded in the 13th century) of which John Wyclif was a prebend.

Location: OS Ref. ST572 775. 3m N of the centre of Bristol. Just E of main street.

Opening Times: Access by key only, to be collected by prior written or telephone appointment (0117 962 1536). Rev. G M Collins, The Vicarage, 44 Eastfield Road, Westbury-on-Trym, Bristol BS9 4AG.

Admission: Adult £1.10, Child 50p.

🅿 Limited. ✖ ❄

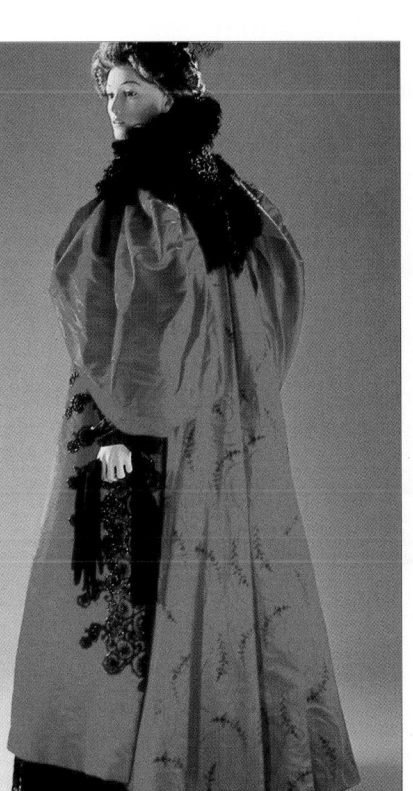
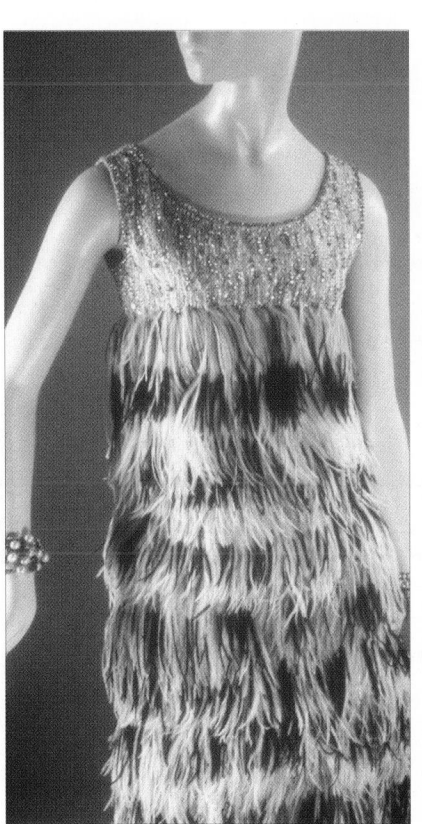
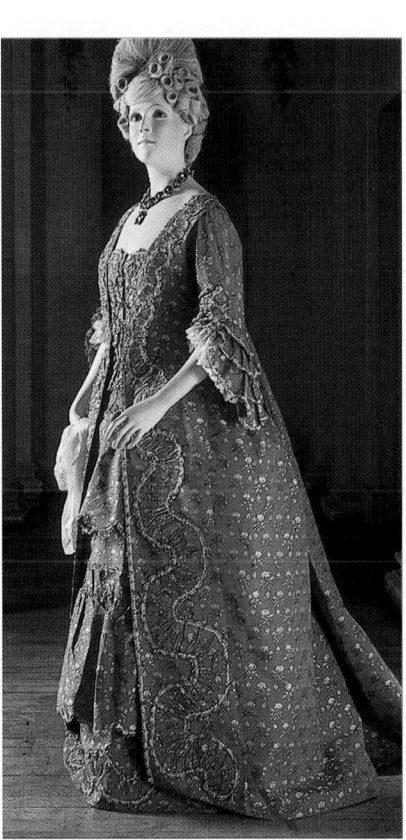

Costumes from the Museum of Costume and Assembly Rooms, Bath.

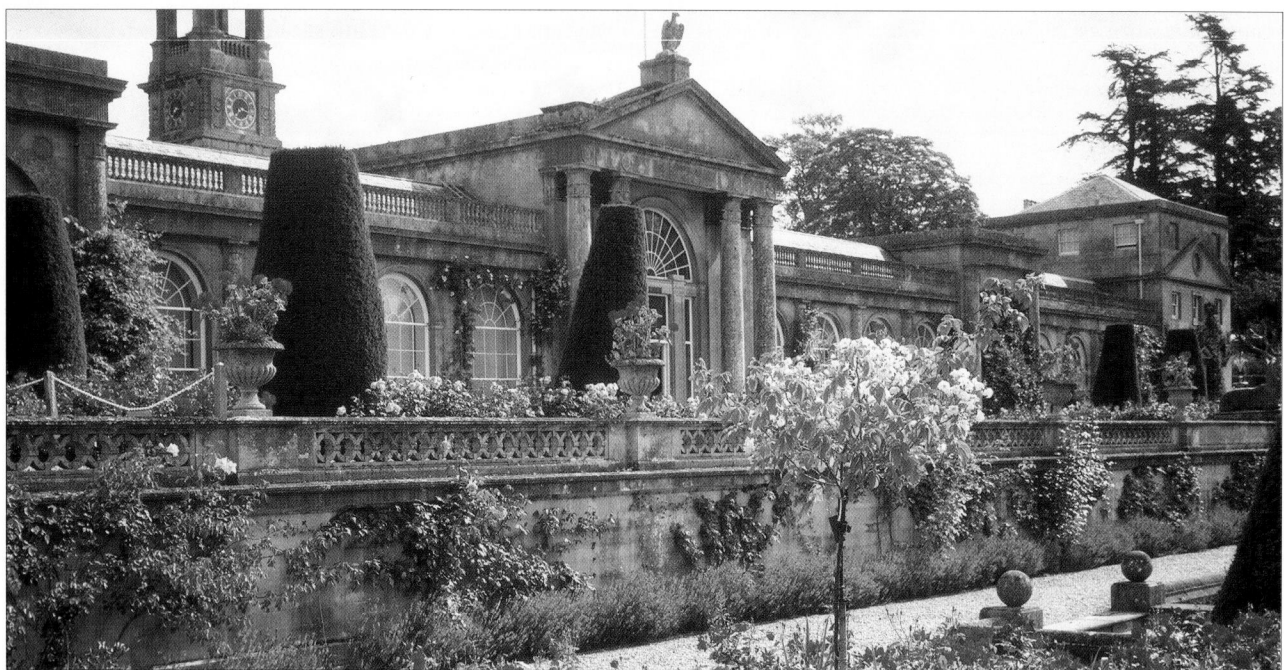

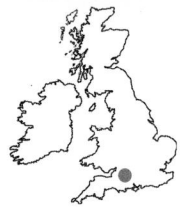

Owner:
The Marquis of Lansdowne

CONTACT

The Administrator
Bowood House and
Gardens
Calne
Wiltshire
SN11 0LZ

Tel: 01249 812102

Fax: 01249 821757

e-mail: houseandgardens@
bowood-estate.co.uk

LOCATION

OS Ref. ST974 700

From London M4/J17,
off the A4 between
Chippenham and Calne.
Swindon 17m,
Bristol 26m,
Bath 16m.

Bus: to the gate,
$1^1/2$ m through
park to House.

Rail: Chippenham
Station 5m.

Taxi: AA Taxis,
Chippenham 657777.

BOWOOD HOUSE & GARDENS
Calne

BOWOOD is the family home of the Marquis and Marchioness of Lansdowne. Begun c1720 for the Bridgeman family, the house was purchased by the 2nd Earl of Shelburne in 1754 and completed soon afterwards. Part of the house was demolished in 1955, leaving a perfectly proportioned Georgian home, over half of which is open to visitors. Robert Adam's magnificent Diocletian wing contains a splendid library, the laboratory where Joseph Priestley discovered oxygen gas in 1774, the orangery, now a picture gallery, the Chapel and a sculpture gallery in which some of the famous Lansdowne Marbles are displayed.

Among the family treasures shown in the numerous exhibition rooms are Georgian costumes, including Lord Byron's Albanian dress; Victoriana; Indiana (the 5th Marquess was Viceroy 1888-94); and superb collections of watercolours, miniatures and jewellery.

The House is set in one of the most beautiful parks in England. Over 2,000 acres of gardens and grounds were landscaped by 'Capability' Brown between 1762 and 1768, and are embellished with a Doric temple, a cascade, a pinetum and an arboretum. The Rhododendron Gardens are open for six weeks from late April to early June. All the walks have seats.

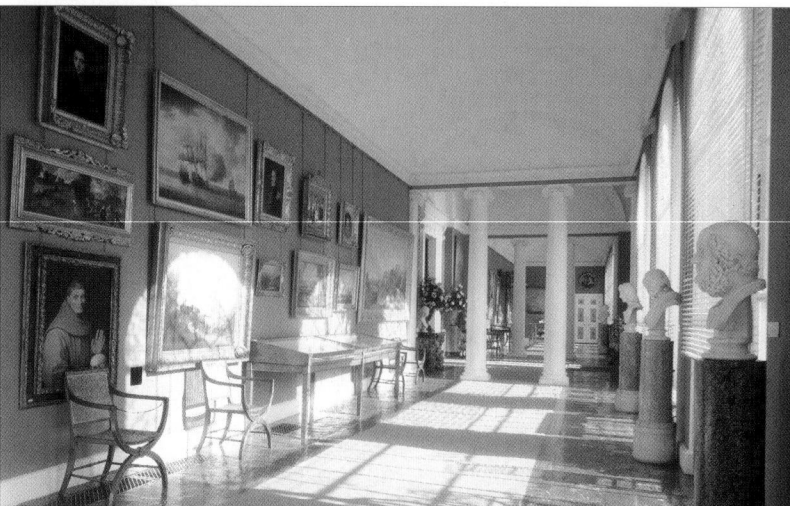

OPENING TIMES

House & Garden
1 Apr - 28 Oct:
Daily
11am - 6pm or
dusk if earlier.

Rhododendron Walks
Late April to early June
(depending on flowering
season) for 6 weeks
11am - 6pm.

ADMISSION

House and Garden
Adult £5.90
Child (5-15yrs)..........£3.70
OAP........................£4.90
Groups (20+)
Adult £4.95
Child (5-15yrs)..........£3.20
OAP........................£4.20
(children under 5yrs Free)

Rhododendron Walks
Adult £3.25
Child (0-15yrs) ....Free
OAP........................£3.25

The charge for
Rhododendron Walks is
£2.25 if combined on same
day with a visit to Bowood
House & Gardens.

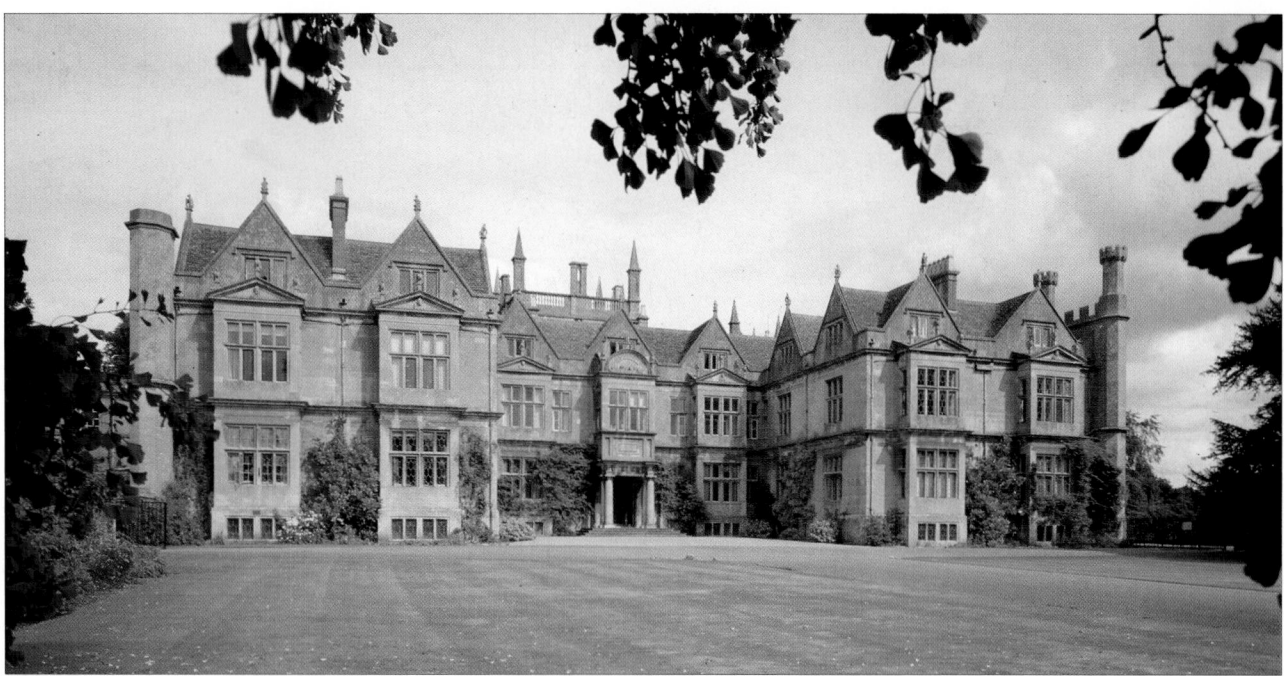

CORSHAM COURT
Corsham

CORSHAM COURT is an Elizabethan house of 1582 and was bought by Paul Methuen in the mid-18th century, to house a collection of 16th and 17th century Italian and Flemish master paintings and statuary. In the middle of the 19th century, the house was enlarged to receive a second collection, purchased in Florence, principally of fashionable Italian masters and stone-inlaid furniture.

Paul Methuen (1723-95) was a great-grandson of Paul Methuen of Bradford-on-Avon and cousin of John Methuen, ambassador and negotiator of the Methuen Treaty of 1703 with Portugal which permitted export of British woollens to Portugal and allowed a preferential 33$^1/_3$ percent duty discount on Portuguese wines, bringing about a major change in British drinking habits.

The architects involved in the alterations to the house and park were Lancelot 'Capability' Brown in the 1760s, John Nash in 1800 and Thomas Bellamy in 1845-9. Brown set the style by retaining the Elizabethan Stables and Riding School, but rebuilding the Gateway, retaining the gabled Elizabethan stone front and doubling the gabled wings at either end and inside, by designing the East Wing as Stateroom Picture Galleries. Nash's work has now largely disappeared, but Bellamy's stands fast, notably in the Hall and Staircase.

The State Rooms, including the Music Room and Dining Room, provide the setting for the outstanding collection of over 150 paintings, statuary, bronzes and furniture. The collection includes work by such names as Chippendale, the Adam brothers, Van Dyck, Reni, Rosa, Rubens, Lippi, Reynolds, Romney and a pianoforte by Clementi.

GARDENS
'Capability' Brown planned to include a lake, avenues and specimen trees such as the Oriental Plane now with a 200-yard perimeter. The gardens, designed not only by Brown but also by Repton, contain a ha-ha, herbaceous borders, secluded gardens, lawns, a rose garden, a lily pool, a stone bath house and the Bradford Porch.

Owner:
J Methuen-Campbell Esq

CONTACT
Corsham Court
Corsham
Wiltshire
SN13 0BZ

Tel/Fax: 01249 701610

LOCATION
OS Ref. ST874 706

Corsham Court is signposted from the A4, approx. 4m W of Chippenham. From Edinburgh, A1, M62, M6, M5, M4, 8 hrs. From London, M4, 2$^1/_4$ hrs. From Chester, M6, M5, M4, 4 hrs.

Motorway: M4/J17 9m.

Rail: Chippenham Station 6m.

Taxi: 01249 715959.

SUMMER
20 March - 30 September
Daily except Mons but including BH Mons
2 - 5.30pm
Last admission 5pm.

WINTER
1 October - 19 March
Weekends only
2 - 4.30pm
Last admission 4pm.

Closed December.

NB: Open throughout the year by appointment only for groups of 15+.

ADMISSION
House & Garden
Adult £5.00
Child (5-15yrs).......£2.50
OAP.......................£4.50
Groups (includes guided tour - 1 hr)
Adult £4.50

Garden only
Adult £2.00
Child (5-15yrs).......£1.00
OAP.......................£1.50
Groups
Per person £4.50

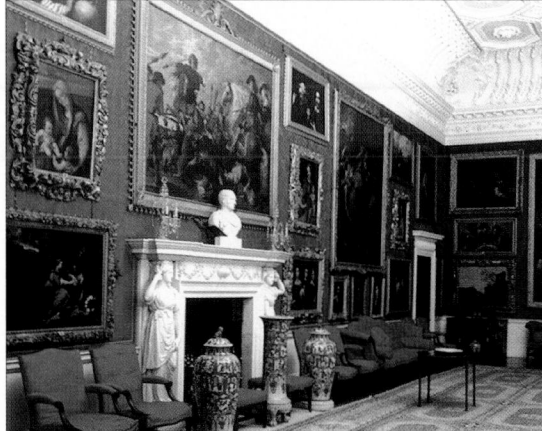

Souvenir desk. No umbrellas, no photography.

Visitors may alight at the entrance to the property, before parking in the allocated areas.

Tearooms nearby. Tel: Corsham 01249 713260.

For up to 55. If requested the owner may meet the group. Tour time 1$^1/_2$ hrs.

400 cars, 120 yards from the house. Coaches may park at the door to the house. Coach parties must book in advance.

Available: rate negotiable. A guide will be provided.

Must be kept on leads in the garden.

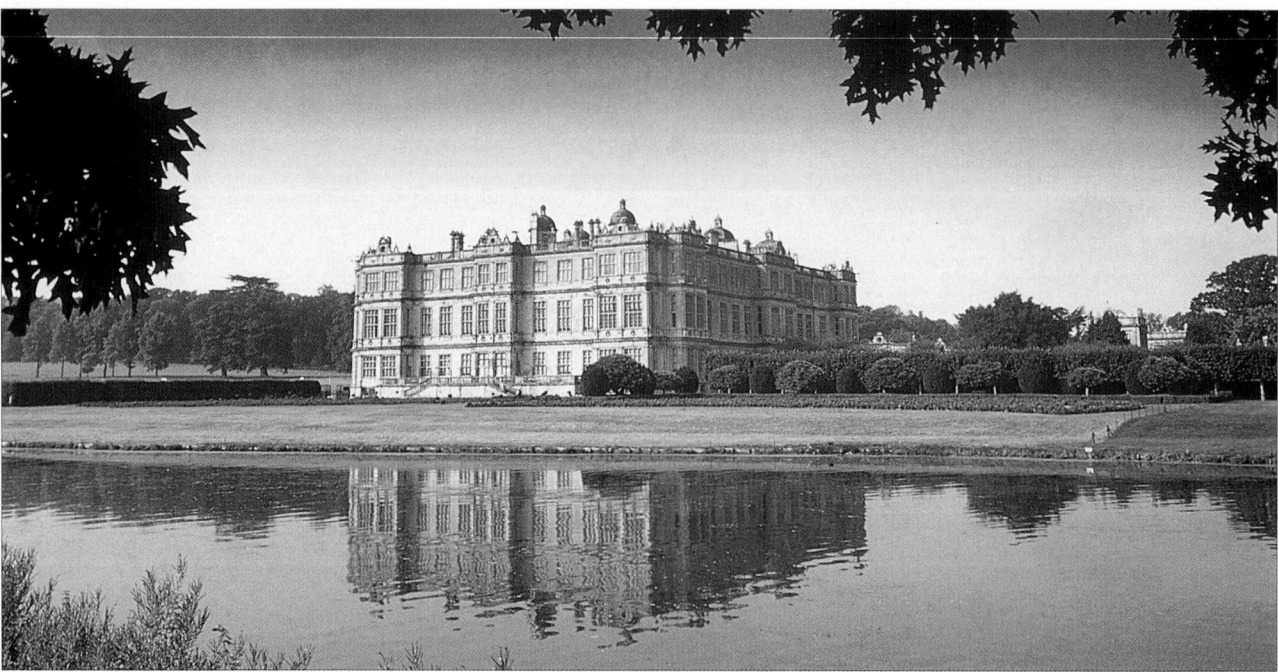

LONGLEAT
Warminster

Longleat hit the headlines in 2000 enjoying national recognition as one of the top tourist attractions in the UK. The prestigious 'Which? Guide to Tourist Attractions' voted Longleat one of the 'Best Animal Attractions' in the UK whilst early July saw Longleat voted as the 'Visitor Attraction of the Year' in the Southern Tourist Board's England for Excellence Awards. Special mentions were made in both reports on the excellent value for money Passport Ticket which offers entrance to all 12 of the Longleat attractions.

Set within 900 acres of 'Capability' Brown designed parkland the magnificent Elizabethan property, Longleat House, is widely regarded as the best example of Elizabethan architecture in Britain and one of the most beautiful stately homes open to the public. Built by Sir John Thynne and substantially completed by 1580, Longleat House has been the home of the same family ever since. Many treasures are included within; paintings by Tintoretto and Wootton, exquisite Flemish tapestries, fine French furniture and elaborate ceilings by John Dibblee Crace incorporating paintings from the 'School of Titian'. The Murals in the family apartments in the West Wing were painted by Alexander Thynn, the present Marquess, and are fascinating and remarkable additions to the collections.

Apart from the ancestral home, Longleat is also renowned for its Safari Park, the first of its kind outside Africa. Here, visitors have a remarkable opportunity to see hundreds of animals in a natural woodland and parkland setting. Amongst the most magnificent sights are the famous pride of lions, a white tiger, wolves, rhesus monkeys, elephants and giraffe..

Don't miss the other attractions which make Longleat a fun day out for all the family… get lost in the 'World's Longest Hedge Maze', let off steam in the Adventure Castle, travel on the Longleat Railway, get close to the creatures in Pets Corner and marvel at the sealions on the Safari Boats… your day at Longleat will never be long enough!

Rooms in Longleat House can be hired for conferences, gala dinners and product launches. Extensive parkland for car launches, ride n' drives, company fun days, marquee based events, concerts, balloon festivals, equestrian events, caravan rallies & fishing. Film location.

Licensed.

Cellar Café (capacity 80). Groups must book. From 3 course meals to cream teas, sandwiches & snacks. Traditional Wiltshire Fare. Not open all year.

Groups (max 20, 15 in murals). Booking essential.

Ample.

Welcome with 1 teacher free entry per 8 children. GNVQ talks and packs available on request. Booking essential. Education sheets.

In grounds, on leads.

Orangery.

PASSPORT TICKETS - includes all the following attractions:
Safari Park, Longleat House, Safari Boats, World's Longest Hedge Maze, King Arthur's Mirror Maze, Pets' Corner & Parrot Show, Adventure Castle, Longleat Railway, VirtuaScope Motion Ride, Butterfly Garden, Postman Pat Village, Dr Who Exhibition, Grounds & Gardens.

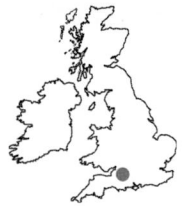

Owner:
The Marquess of Bath

CONTACT

The Estate Office
Longleat
Warminster
Wiltshire
BA12 7NW

Tel: 01985 844400

Fax: 01985 844885

e-mail: marketing@ longleat.co.uk

LOCATION

OS Ref. ST809 430

Just off the A36 between Bath & Salisbury.(A362 Warminster - Frome). Just 2hrs from London following M3, A303, A36, A362 or M4/J18/A46-A36.

Rail: Mainline Paddington to Westbury (12m) or Warminster station on Bristol-Salisbury line. Lion-Link bus from Warminster station to Longleat (tel. for details).

Air: Bristol airport 30m.

Taxi: Starline Taxis 01985 212215.

CONFERENCE/FUNCTION		
ROOM	SIZE	MAX CAPACITY
Banqueting Suite	2 x (10m x 7m)	40
Great Hall	8m x 13m	150

OPENING TIMES

SUMMER

24 March - 4 November
House: Easter - Sept: 10am - 5.30pm. Rest of year, guided tours at set times between 11am - 4pm

Safari Park: 10am - 4pm (10am - 5pm on weekends, BHs & in school holidays).

Other attractions: 11am - 5.30pm.

WINTER

House & grounds only: 1 January - 23 March Limited openings please telephone for details.

5 November - 31 December Guided tours at set times between 11am - 4pm (closed Christmas Day).

ADMISSION

House & Grounds
Adult £9.00
Child (4 -14yrs).........£6.00
OAP........................£6.00

Passport Ticket
(see left under photo)
Adult £14.00
Child (4 -14yrs).......£11.00
OAP......................£11.00
Groups (50+)
Adult £9.30
Child (4 -16yrs).........£7.30
OAP........................£7.30

Special discounted rates for groups of 12 - 49 & 50+.

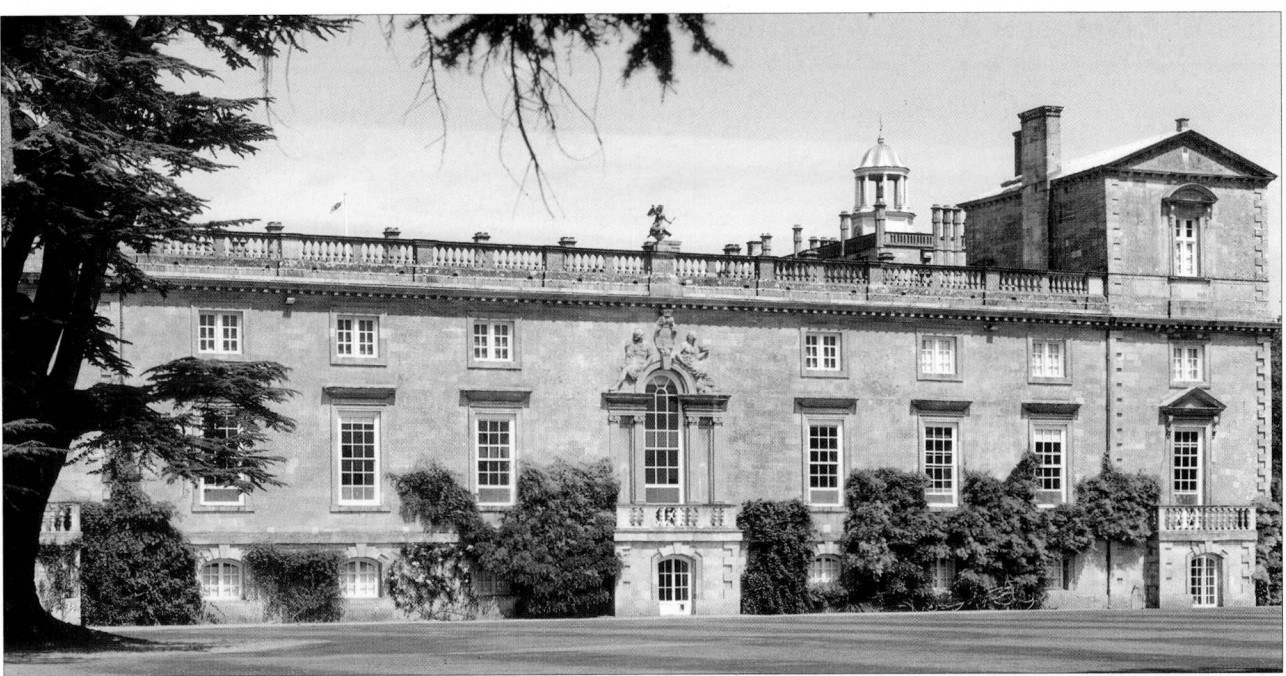

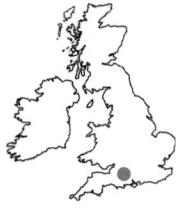

Owner:
The Earl of Pembroke

CONTACT

Sally Salmon
The Estate Office
Wilton House
Wilton
Salisbury
SP2 0BJ

Tel: 01722 746720

Fax: 01722 744447

e-mail:
tourism@wiltonhouse.com

LOCATION

OS Ref. SU099 311

3m W of Salisbury
on the A30.

Rail: Salisbury
Station 3m.

Bus: Every 10 mins from
Salisbury, Mon - Sat.

Taxi: Sarum Taxi
01722 334477.

WILTON HOUSE
Nr Salisbury

The 17th Earl of Pembroke and his family live in Wilton House which has been their ancestral home for 450 years. In 1544 Henry VIII gave the Abbey and lands of Wilton to Sir William Herbert who had married Anne Parr, sister of Katherine, sixth wife of King Henry.

The Clock Tower, in the centre of the east front, is reminiscent of this part of the Tudor building which survived a fire in 1647. Inigo Jones and John Webb were responsible for the rebuilding of the house in the Palladian style, whilst further alterations were made by James Wyatt from 1801.

The chief architectural features are the magnificent 17th century state apartments (including the famous Single and Double Cube rooms) and the 19th century cloisters.

The house contains one of the finest art collections in Europe, with over 230 original paintings on display, including works by Van Dyck, Rubens, Joshua Reynolds and Brueghel. Also on show are Greek and Italian statuary, a lock of Queen Elizabeth I's hair, Napoleon's despatch case, and Florence Nightingale's sash.

The visitor centre houses a dynamic introductory film (narrated by Anna Massey), the reconstructed Tudor kitchen and the Estate's Victorian laundry. The house is set in magnificent landscaped parkland, bordered by the River Nadder which is the setting for the majestic Palladian Bridge. The current Earl of Pembroke is a keen gardener who has created four new gardens since succeeding to the title in 1969 including the North Forecourt Garden, Old English Rose Garden, Water and Cloister Gardens.

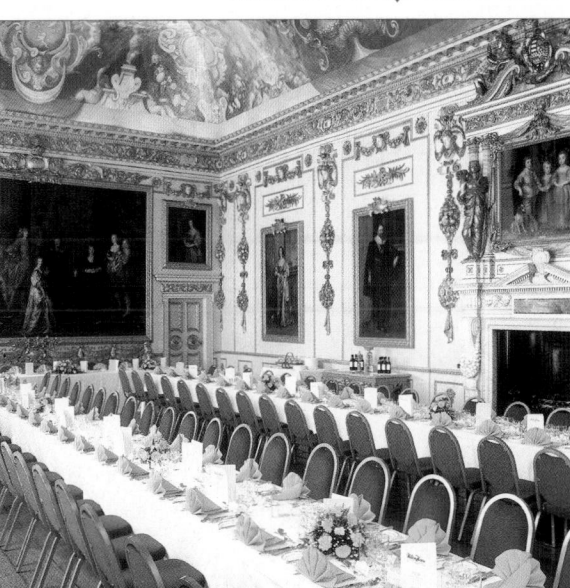

Film location, fashion shows, product launches, equestrian events, garden parties, antiques fairs, concerts, vehicle rallies. No photography in house. French, German, Spanish, Italian, Japanese and Dutch information.

Exclusive banquets.

Excellent access. Visitors may alight at the entrance. WCs.

Licensed. Self-service restaurant open 10.30am - 5pm. Groups must book. Hot lunches 12 noon - 2pm.

By arrangement.

200 cars and 12 coaches. Free coach parking. Group rates (min 15), meal vouchers, drivers' lounge.

Teachers' handbook for National Curriculum. EFL students welcome. Free preparatory visit for group leaders.

Guide dogs only.

OPENING TIMES

SUMMER
4 April - 28 October
Daily: 10.30am - 5.30pm

Last admission 4.30pm.

WINTER
Closed, except for private parties by prior arrangement.

ADMISSION

SUMMER
House, Grounds & Exhibition

Adult	£7.25
Child*	£4.50
OAP/Student	£6.25
Family (2+2)	£20.00

Groups (15+)

Adult	£5.50
Child	£4.00

Grounds only

Adult	£3.75
Child	£2.75

Season Tickets

Family	£43.00
Individual	£22.00

WINTER
Prices on application.

* 5 - 15 yrs - under 5s Free.

SPECIAL EVENTS

- **MAR 2 - 4:**
  24th Annual Antiques Fair.
- **JUL 14:**
  Classical Firework Proms Night.

CONFERENCE/FUNCTION

ROOM	SIZE	MAX CAPACITY
Double cube	60' x 30'	150
Exhibition Centre	50' x 40'	140
Film Theatre	34" x 20"	67

ALEXANDER KEILLER MUSEUM 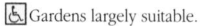   **Tel:** 01672 539250

Avebury, Nr Marlborough, Wiltshire SN8 1RF

Owner: The National Trust   **Contact:** The Custodian

The investigation of Avebury Stone Circles was largely the work of Alexander Keiller in the 1930s. He put together one of the most important prehistoric archaeological collections in Britain which can be seen at the Alexander Keiller Museum.

Location: OS Ref. SU100 699. In Avebury 6m W of Marlborough.

Opening Times: 1 Apr - 31 Oct: daily, 10am - 6pm/dusk if earlier. 1 Nov - 31 Mar 2002: daily, 10am - 4pm. Closed 24 - 26 Dec & 1 Jan.

Admission: Adult £2, Child £1. English Heritage members Free (tel. 01672 539250).

AVEBURY MANOR & GARDEN 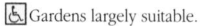   **Tel:** 01672 539250

Avebury, Nr Marlborough, Wiltshire SN8 1RF

Owner: The National Trust   **Contact:** The Custodian

A much altered house of monastic origin, the present buildings date from the early 16th century, with notable Queen Anne alterations and Edwardian renovation by Col Jenner. The topiary and flower gardens contain medieval walls, ancient box and numerous 'rooms'. Note: Manor house is occupied by tenants who open parts of it to visitors. Timed tickets may be in operation at busy times.

Location: OS Ref. SU101 701. 6m W of Marlborough, 1m N of the A4 on A4361 and B4003.

Opening Times: House: 1 Apr - 31 Oct: Tue - Wed, Suns & BH Mons, 2 - 5.30pm. Garden: 1 Apr - 31 Oct: daily except Mons & Thurs (open BH Mons), 11am - 5.30pm.

Admission: House & Garden: Adult £3.50, Child £1.70. Groups: Adult £3.20, Child £1.50. Garden only: Adult £2.50, Child £1.20. Groups: Adult £2.20, Child £1.

Gardens largely suitable.   No dogs in house. Guide dogs only in garden.

AVEBURY STONE CIRCLE 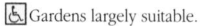   **Tel:** 01672 539250

Avebury, Nr Marlborough, Wiltshire SN8 1RF

Owner: The National Trust   **Contact:** The Property Manager

One of the most important Megalithic monuments in Europe, this $28\frac{1}{2}$ acre site with stone circles enclosed by a ditch and external bank, is approached by an avenue of stones. The site includes the Alexander Keiller Museum and is managed and owned by the National Trust.

Location: OS Ref. SU102 699. 6m W of Marlborough, 1m N of the A4 on A4361 and B4003.

Opening Times: Stone Circle: daily.

BOWOOD HOUSE   **See page 238 for full page entry.**

BRADFORD-ON-AVON TITHE BARN   **Tel:** 0117 975 0700

Bradford-on-Avon, Wiltshire

Owner: English Heritage   **Contact:** South West Regional Office

A magnificent medieval stone-built barn with a slate roof and wooden beamed interior.

Location: OS173 Ref. ST824 604. ¼ m S of town centre, off B3109.

Opening Times: Daily, 10.30am - 4pm. Closed 25 Dec.

Admission: Free.

BROADLEAS GARDENS   **Tel:** 01380 722035

Devizes, Wiltshire SN10 5JQ

Owner: Broadleas Gardens Charitable Trust   **Contact:** Lady Anne Cowdray

10 acres full of interest, notably The Dell, where the sheltered site allows plantings of magnolias, camellias, rhododendrons and azaleas.

Location: OS Ref. SU001 601. Signposted SW from town centre at S end of housing estate, (coaches must use this entrance) or 1m S of Devizes on W side of A360.

Opening Times: Apr - Oct: Sun, Weds & Thurs, 2 - 6pm or by arrangement for groups.

Admission: Adult £3, Child (under 12yrs) £1, Groups (10+) £2.50.

CORSHAM COURT   **See page 239 for full page entry.**

Open All Year
Index ◀◀◀ page 49

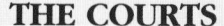

THE COURTS

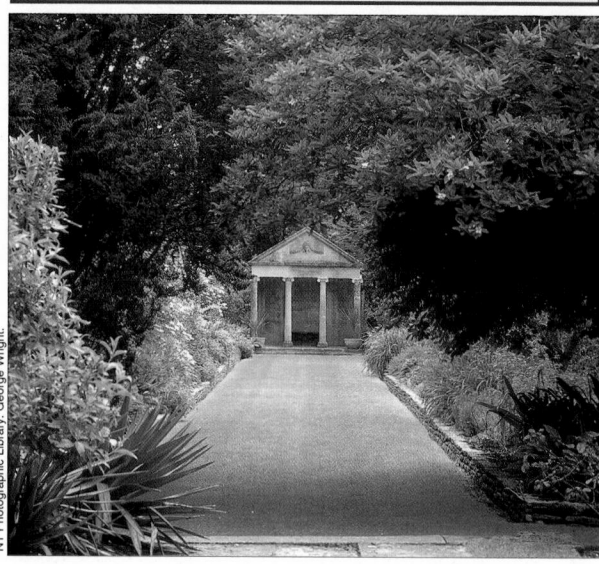

HOLT, TROWBRIDGE, WILTSHIRE BA14 6RR

Owner: *The National Trust*   **Contact:** *Head Gardener*

Tel: 01225 782340

One of Wiltshire's best-kept secrets, the English garden style at its best, full of charm and variety. There are many interesting plants and an imaginative use of colour surrounding water features, topiary and herbaceous borders. Complemented by an arboretum with natural planting of spring bulbs.

Location: OS Ref. ST861 618. 3m SW of Melksham, 3m N of Trowbridge, $2\frac{1}{2}$ m E of Bradford-on-Avon, on S side of B3107.

Opening Times: 1 Apr - 14 Oct: daily except Sats, 1 - 5.30pm. Out of season by appointment only.

Admission: Adult £3.50, Child £1.50. Groups by arrangement with Head Gardener.

No WC.   Limited.

GREAT CHALFIELD MANOR   **Tel:** 01225 782239   **Fax:** 01225 783379

Melksham, Wiltshire SN12 8NJ

Owner: The National Trust   **Contact:** The Tenant

A charming manor house enhanced by a moat and gatehouse and with beautiful oriel windows and a great hall. Completed in 1480, the manor and gardens were restored earlier last century (c1905 - 1911) by Major R Fuller, whose family live here and manage the property. The garden, designed by Alfred Parson, to compliment the Manor, has been replanted.

Location: OS Ref. ST860 633. 3m SW of Melksham via Broughton Gifford Common.

Opening Times: 3 Apr - 1 Nov: Tue - Thur, guided tours only at 12.15, 2.15, 3, 3.45 & 4.30pm. The tours take 45 mins and numbers are limited to 25. Visitors arriving during a tour can visit the adjoining parish church and garden first. Note: Group visits are welcome on Fris & Sats (not BHs) by written arrangement with Mrs Robert Floyd. Organisers of coach parties should allow 2 hours because of limits on numbers in the house.

Admission: £3.80, no reductions for children and groups.

Grounds suitable.   Obligatory.   Limited.

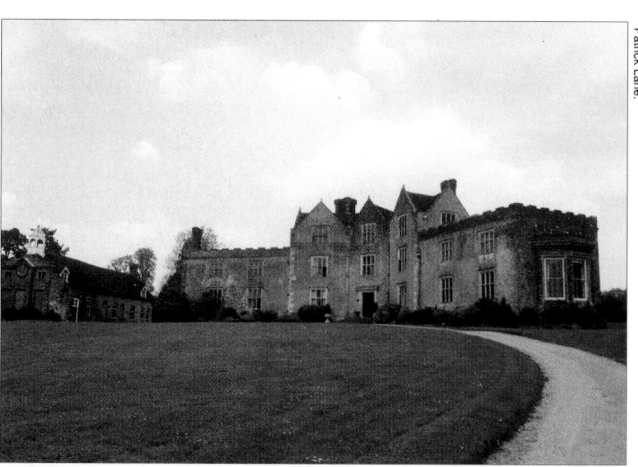

Newhouse, Wiltshire

HAMPTWORTH LODGE

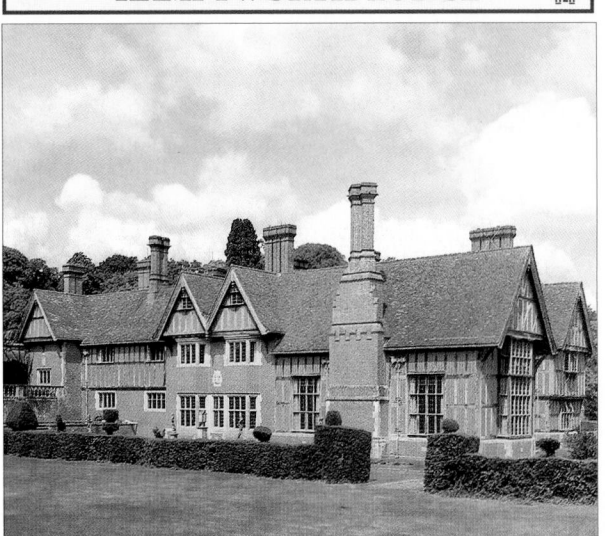

HAMPTWORTH, LANDFORD, SALISBURY, WILTSHIRE SP5 2EA

Owner/Contact: Mr N J M Anderson

Tel: 01794 390215 **Fax:** 01794 390644

Rebuilt Jacobean manor house standing in woodlands on the edge of the New Forest. Grade II* family house with period furniture including clocks. The Great Hall has an unusual roof construction. There is a collection of prentice pieces and the Moffatt collection of contemporary copies. Garden also open.

Location: OS Ref. SU227 195. 10m SE of Salisbury on road linking Downton on Salisbury/ Bournemouth Road (A338) to Landford on A36, Salisbury - Southampton.

Opening Times: 30 Mar - 30 Apr: 2.15 - 5pm except Suns. Coaches, by appointment only, 1 Apr - 30 Oct except Suns.

Admission: £3.50, Child (under 11yrs) Free. Groups by arrangement.

♿ Ground floor & grounds suitable.

THE KING'S HOUSE   **Tel:** 01722 332151 **Fax:** 01722 325611

SALISBURY & SOUTH WILTSHIRE MUSEUM
e-mail: museum@salisburymuseum.freeserve.co.uk
65 The Close, Salisbury, Wiltshire SP1 2EN
Owner: Occupied by Salisbury & South Wiltshire Museum Trust   **Contact:** P R Saunders
Location: OS Ref. SU141 295. In Salisbury Cathedral Close, W side, facing cathedral.
Opening Times: All year: Mon - Sat: 10am - 5pm. Suns in Jul & Aug: 2 - 5pm.
Admission: Adult £3, Child 75p, Conc. £2, Groups £2.

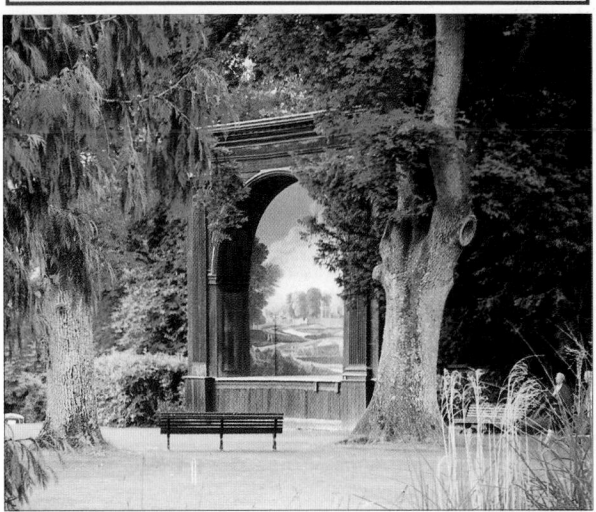

Salisbury Cathedral, Wiltshire

LACOCK ABBEY, FOX TALBOT MUSEUM & VILLAGE

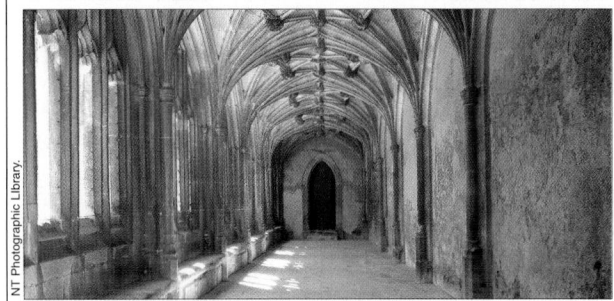

NT Photographic Library.

LACOCK, CHIPPENHAM, WILTSHIRE SN15 2LG

Owner: The National Trust   *Contact: The Property Manager*

Tel: 01249 730227/730459   *Watercolour Challenge*

Founded in 1232 and converted into a country house c1540, the fine medieval cloisters, sacristy , chapter house and monastic rooms of the abbey have survived largely intact. The handsome 16th century stable courtyard has half-timbered gables, a clockhouse, brewery and bakehouse. The Victorian woodland garden boast a fine display of spring flowers, magnificent trees, an 18th century summer house, Victorian rose garden and ha-ha. The Museum of Photography commemorates the achievements of a former resident of the abbey, William Fox Talbot (1800-77), inventor of the modern photographic negative and whose descendants gave the abbey and village to the Trust in 1944. The village, which dates from the 13th century and has many limewashed half-timbered and stone houses, featured in the TV and film production of *Pride & Prejudice*, *Moll Flanders* and *Emma*.

Location: OS Ref. ST919 684. In the village of Lacock, 3m N of Melksham, 3m S of Chippenham just E of A350.

Opening Times: Museum, Cloisters & Garden: 3 Mar - 4 Nov: daily, 11am - 5.30pm (closed Good Fri). Abbey: 31 Mar - 4 Nov: daily except Tues & Good Fri, 1 - 5.30pm. Museum: open weekends in winter, closed 22 & 23 Dec - 30 Dec. Tel for details.

Admission: Abbey, Museum, Cloisters and Garden: Adult £6, Child £3.30, Family £16.30. Groups: Adult £5.50, Child £2.80. Garden, Cloisters & Museum only: Adult £3.80, Child £2.30, Family £10.90. Abbey & Garden only: Adult £4.80, Child £2.70, Family £12.30.

▢ ♿ ☕ ✗ ❄ ▢ Tel. for details.

LARMER TREE GARDENS

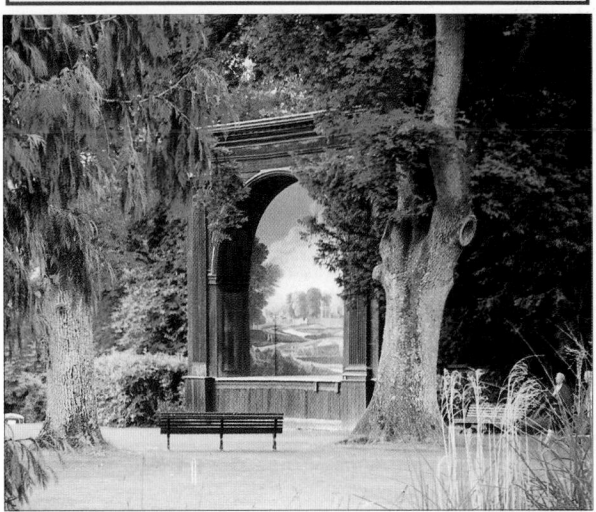

RUSHMORE ESTATE, TOLLARD ROYAL, SALISBURY, WILTSHIRE SP5 5PT

Owner: Mr William Gronow Davis (Pitt-Rivers Trustees)   *Contact: Tracey Hartles*

Tel: 01725 516228 **Fax:** 01725 516449

Historical gardens of General Pitt Rivers, set high on the Cranborne Chase. One of the most unusual gardens in England containing an extraordinary collection of Colonial and Oriental buildings, a Roman Temple and Open air Theatre. Created in 1880, the gardens are recognised as one of national importance and hold a unique place in history. Regular concerts, festivals, exhibitions and meetings. Licensed wedding venue available for hire all year.

Location: OS Ref. ST943 169. Tollard Royal.

Opening Times: Easter Sun - end Oct. Closed Sats.

Admission: Adult £3.50, Child £1.50, OAP/Student £3. Booked groups (15+): Adult £3.25, Child £1.35, OAP/Student £2.75.

▢ ♨ ⊤ ▢ Licensed. Closed Mons & Tues. ⚘ By arrangement. Ⓟ
▮ ⚘ Guide dogs only. 🔔 ▢ Tel. for details.

LITTLE CLARENDON

Tel: 01985 843600

Dinton, Salisbury, Wiltshire SP3 5OZ

Owner: The National Trust   **Contact:** The Regional Office

A Tudor house, but greatly altered in the 17th century. The principal rooms on the ground floor are open to visitors. There is also a 20th century Catholic chapel.

Location: OS Ref. SU015 316. 1/4 m E of Dinton Church. 9m W of Salisbury.

Opening Times: 31 Mar - 29 Oct:, Sats, 10am - 1pm, Mons, 1 - 5pm.

Admission: £2, no reductions.

ℹ️ No WC, no pushchairs or prams, no coaches. ♿ Unsuitable. 🅿️ At Dinton Post Office.

LONG HALL GARDENS

Tel: 01985 850424

Stockton, Warminster, Wiltshire BA12 0SE

Owner/Contact: N H Yeatman-Biggs Esq

4 acres of gardens. Long Hall Nursery is adjacent.

Location: OS Ref. ST982 381. Stockton 7m SE of Warminster, off A36, W of A303 Wylye interchange.

Opening Times: The gardens will be closed during 2001 except to groups by appointment, Mar - Aug.

Admission: Please contact for details.

LONGLEAT 🏛️

See page 240 for full page entry.

LYDIARD PARK

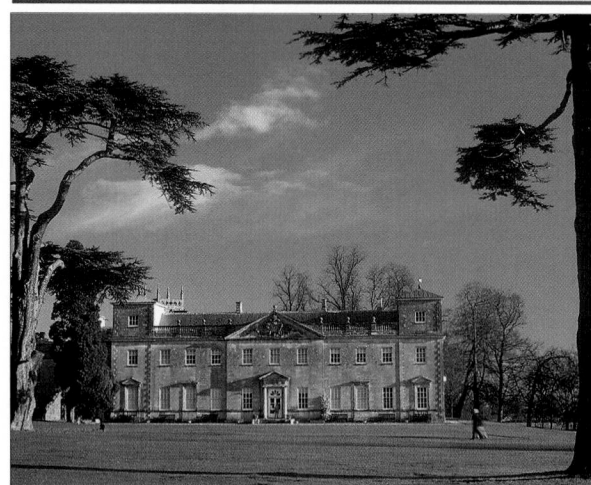

LYDIARD TREGOZE, SWINDON, WILTSHIRE SN5 9PA

Owner: Swindon Borough Council   *Contact: The Keeper*

Tel: 01793 770401 **Fax:** 01793 877909

Lydiard Park, ancestral home of the Bolingbrokes, is Swindon's treasure. Set in rolling lawns and woodland this beautifully restored Georgian mansion contains the family's furnishings and portraits, exceptional plasterwork, rare 17th century window and room devoted to 18th century society artist Lady Diana Spencer. Exceptional monuments such as the 'Golden Cavalier' in adjacent church.

Location: OS Ref. SU104 848. 4m W of Swindon, 1 1/2 m N of M4/J16.

Opening Times: House: Mon - Fri, 10am - 1pm, 2 - 5pm, Sat & school summer holidays, 10am - 5pm, Sun, 2 - 5pm. Nov - Feb: early closing at 4pm. Grounds: all day, closing at dusk. Victorian Christmas decorations throughout December.

Admission: Adult £1.20, Child 60p (reviewed April 2000). Groups by appointment.

ℹ️ No photography in house. 📷 ♿ ☕ 🎦 By arrangement. 🎧 🅿️ Limited for coaches. 🖼️ 🐕 In grounds on leads. ❄️ 🛡️ Tel. for details. 🌐

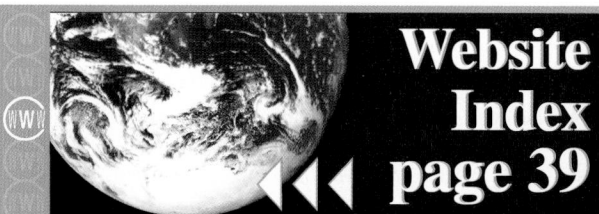

Website Index page 39

MOMPESSON HOUSE 🌿

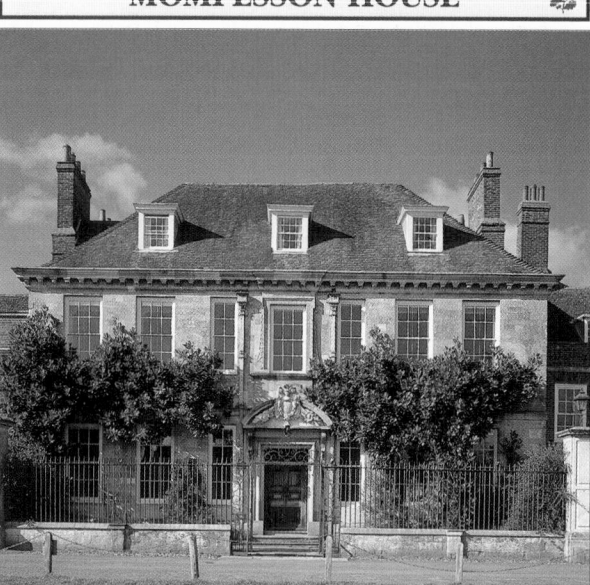

NT Photographic Library

THE CLOSE, SALISBURY, WILTSHIRE SP1 2EL

Owner: The National Trust   *Contact: The Property Manager*

Tel: 01722 335659

Fine Queen Anne town house containing high quality 18th century furniture, ceramics and textiles. Also the renowned Turnbull Collection of 18th century drinking glasses. Tranquil walled garden with many perfumed plants. Garden tea room serves home-made cakes. Featured in *Sense and Sensibility*.

Location: OS Ref. SU142 295. On N side of Choristers' Green in Cathedral Close, near High Street Gate.

Opening Times: 31 Mar - 4 Nov: Sat - Wed, 12 noon - 5.30pm.

Admission: Adult £3.90, Child £1.95. Groups: £3.40. Garden only: 80p.

📷 ♿ Ground floor & grounds suitable. WC. ☕ 🎦

NEWHOUSE 🏛️

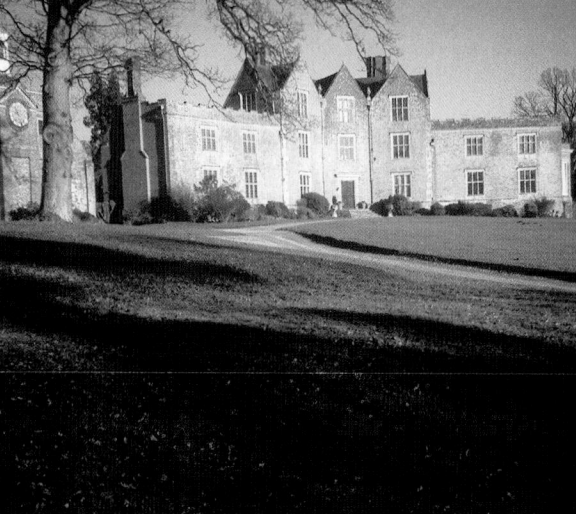

REDLYNCH, SALISBURY, WILTSHIRE SP5 2NX

Owner: George & June Jeffreys   *Contact: Mrs Jeffreys*

Tel: 01725 510055 **Fax:** 01725 510284

A brick, Jacobean 'Trinity' House, c1609, with two Georgian wings and a basically Georgian interior. Home of the Eyre family since 1633. Contents include costume, textiles and the Hare picture.

Location: OS184 Ref. SU218 214. 9m S of Salisbury between A36 & A338.

Opening Times: 2 Apr - 11 May: Mon - Fri, 2 - 5.30pm.

Admission: Adult £3.50, Child £2.50, Conc. £3.50. Groups (15+): Adult £3, Child £2.50, Conc. £3.

ℹ️ No photography in house, except at weddings. 🍴 ♿ Not suitable. 🎦 By arrangement. 🅿️ Limited for coaches. 🐕 Guide dogs only. 🔔

NORRINGTON MANOR

Tel: 01722 780367 **Fax:** 01722 780667

Alvediston, Salisbury, Wiltshire SP5 5LL

Owner/Contact: T Sykes

Built in 1377 it has been altered and added to in every century since, with the exception of the 18th century. Only the hall and the 'undercroft' remain of the original. It is currently a family home and the Sykes are only the third family to own it.

Location: OS Ref. ST966 237. Signposted to N of Berwick St John and Alvediston road (half way between the two villages)

Opening Times: By appointment in writing.

Admission: A donation to the local churches is asked for.

Not suitable. By arrangement. Limited for cars, none for coaches.

OLD SARUM

Tel: 01722 335398

Castle Road, Salisbury, Wiltshire SP1 3SD

Owner: English Heritage **Contact:** The Head Custodian

Built around 500BC by the iron age peoples, Old Sarum is the former site of the first cathedral and ancient city of Salisbury. A prehistoric hillfort in origin, Old Sarum was occupied by the Romans, the Saxons, and eventually the Normans who made it into one of their major strongholds, with a motte-and-bailey castle built at its centre. Old Sarum eventually grew into one of the most dramatic settlements in medieval England as castle, cathedral, bishop's palace and thriving township. When the new city we know as Salisbury was founded in the early 13th century the settlement faded away. With fine views of the surrounding countryside, Old Sarum is an excellent picnic spot.

Location: OS184 Ref. SU138 327. 2m N of Salisbury off A345.

Opening Times: 1 Apr - 31 Oct: daily, 10am - 6pm (5pm in Oct). 1 Nov - 31 Mar: daily 10am - 4pm. Closed 24 - 26 Dec & 1 Jan.

Admission: Adult £2, Child £1, Conc. £1.50. 15% discount for groups (11+).

  Grounds suitable. 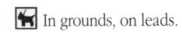 In grounds, on leads. 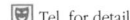 Tel. for details.

OLD WARDOUR CASTLE

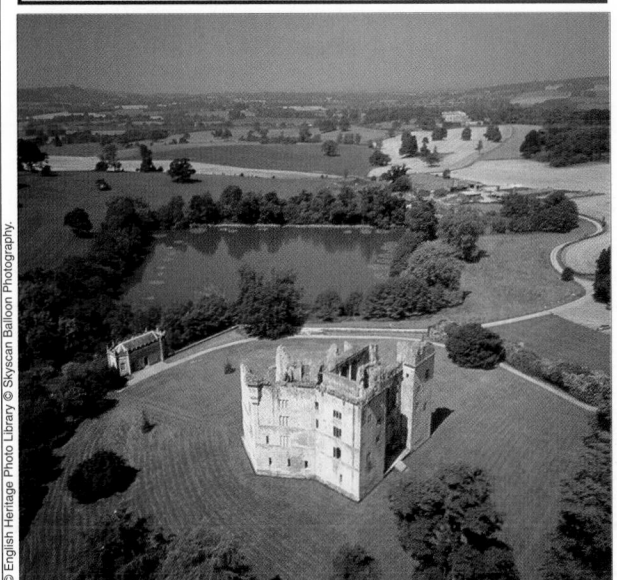

Nr TISBURY, WILTSHIRE SP3 6RR

Owner: English Heritage *Contact:* The Custodian

Tel: 01747 870487

In a picture-book setting, the unusual hexagonal ruins of this 14th century castle stand on the edge of a beautiful lake, surrounded by landscaped grounds which include an elaborate rockwork grotto.

Location: OS184 Ref. ST939 263. Off A30 2m SW of Tisbury.

Open: 1 Apr - 31 Oct: daily, 10am - 6pm (5pm in Oct). 1 Nov - 31 Mar: Wed - Sun, 10am - 4pm. Closed for lunch 1 - 2pm. Closed 24 - 26 Dec & 1 Jan.

Admission: Adult £2.50, Child £1.30, Conc. £1.90. 15% discount for groups (11+).

Grounds suitable. In grounds, on leads. Tel. for details.

THE PETO GARDEN AT IFORD MANOR

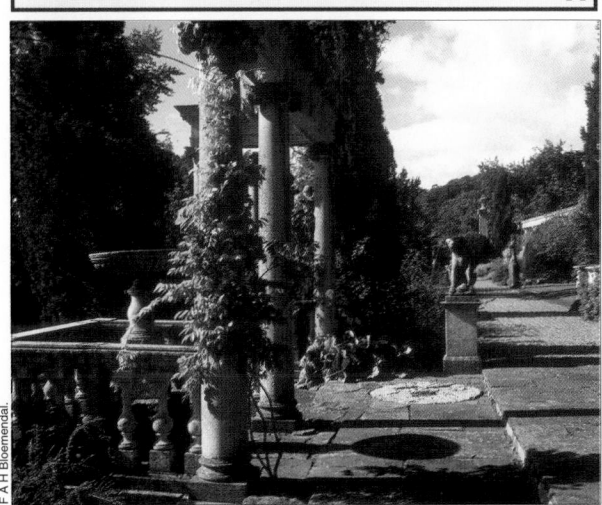

F A H Bloemendal.

BRADFORD-ON-AVON, WILTSHIRE BA14 2BA

Owner/Contact: Mrs E A J Cartwright-Hignett

Tel: 01225 863146 **Fax:** 01225 862364

This unique Grade I Italian-style garden is set on a romantic hillside beside the River Frome. Designed by the Edwardian architect Harold A Peto, who lived at Iford Manor from 1899 - 1933, the garden has terraces, a colonnade, cloister, casita, statuary, evergreen planting and magnificent rural views. Renowned for its tranquillity and peace, the Peto Garden won the 1998 HHA/Christie's Garden of the Year Award.

Location: OS Ref. ST800 589. 7m SE of Bath via A36, signposted Iford. 2m SW of Bradford-on-Avon via Westwood.

Opening Times: Apr & Oct: Suns only & Easter Mon, 2 - 5pm. May - Sept: Tue - Thur, Sats, Suns & BH Mons, 2 - 5pm. Coaches by appointment at other times. Children under 10yrs not admitted at weekends.

Admission: Adult £3, Child (10-16yrs)/OAP £2.50. Picnic area by River Frome.

Teas (May-Aug: Sats & Suns, 2 - 5pm). Coaches by appointment.

PHILIPPS HOUSE & DINTON PARK

Tel: 01985 843600

Dinton, Salisbury, Wiltshire SP3 5HJ

Owner: The National Trust **Contact:** The Regional Office

A neo-Grecian house by Jeffry Wyattville, completed in 1820. Principal rooms on ground floor are open and possess fine Regency furniture. Lovely walks in surrounding parkland.

Location: OS Ref. SU004 319. 9m W of Salisbury, N side of B3089, 1/2 m W of Little Clarendon. Car park off St Mary's Road next to church.

Opening Times: House: 31 Mar - 29 Oct: Mons, 1 - 5pm, Sats, 10am - 1pm. Park: All year: daily (may be closed for one day in Aug for music event).

Admission: House £3. Dinton Park Free.

No WC. House suitable, Park limited.

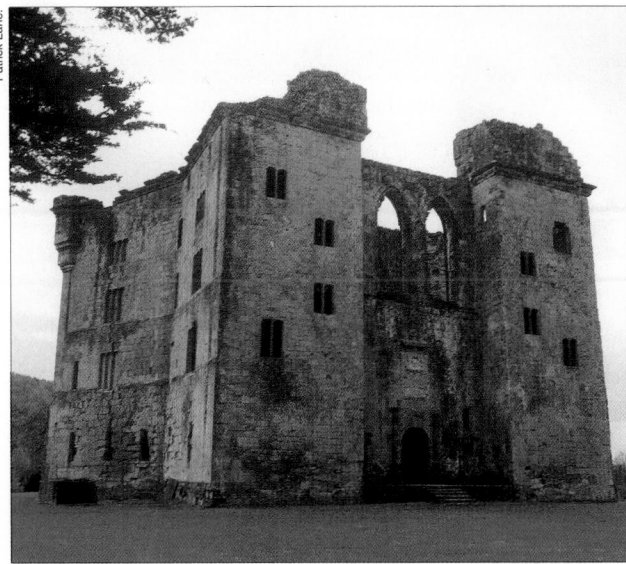

Patrick Lane.

Old Wardour Castle, Wiltshire

SALISBURY CATHEDRAL

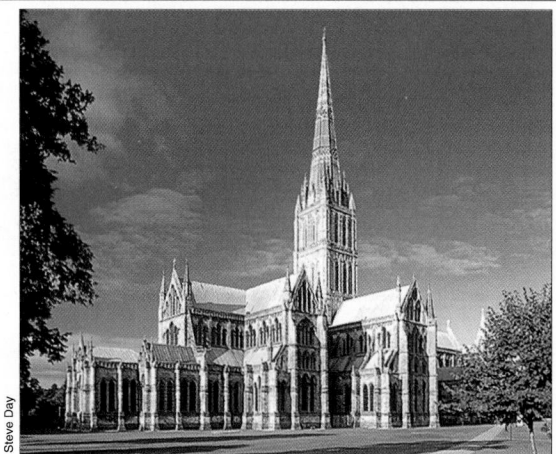

Steve Day

33 THE CLOSE, SALISBURY SP1 2EJ

Owner: The Dean & Chapter   *Contact:* Visitor Services

Tel: 01722 555120 **Fax:** 01722 555116 **e-mail:** visitors@salcath.co.uk

Salisbury Cathedral is a building of world importance. Set within the elegant splendour of the Cathedral Close it is probably the finest medieval building in Britain. Built in one phase from about 1220 to 1258 Britain's highest spire (123m/404ft) was added a generation later. Also, the best preserved Magna Carta, Europe's oldest working clock and a unique 13th century frieze of bible stories in the octagonal Chapter House. Boy and girl choristers sing daily services which follow a tradition of worship that goes back over 750 years. Join a tower tour climbing 332 steps to the base of the spire, and marvel at the medieval craftsmanship and the magnificent views.

Location: OS Ref. SU143 295. S of City. M3, A303, A30 from London or A36.

Open: All year: Every Sunday 7.15am - 6.15pm. Sept - May: Daily, 7.15am - 6.15pm. June - August: Daily, 7.15am - 8.15pm.

Admission: Donation: Adult £3.50, Child £2, Conc. £2.50, Family (2+2) £8.

🖼 ▼ ♿ Licensed. ¶¶ ⚹ By arrangement. 🅿 In city centre. ⬛
🐾 In grounds, on leads. ❊ ▽ Tel. for details. (RWB)

STONEHENGE

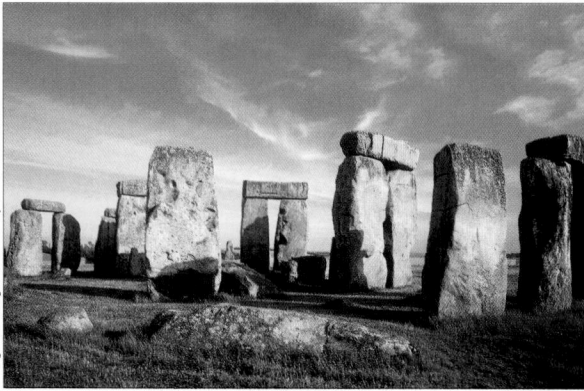

© English Heritage Photo Library.

AMESBURY, WILTSHIRE SP4 7DE

Owner: English Heritage

Tel: 01980 624715 (Information Line)

The mystical and awe-inspiring stone circle at Stonehenge is one of the most famous prehistoric monuments in the world, designated by UNESCO as a World Heritage Site. Stonehenge's orientation on the rising and setting sun has always been one of its most remarkable features. Whether this was simply because the builders came from a sun-worshipping culture, or because – as some scholars have believed – the circle and its banks were part of a huge astronomical calendar, remains a mystery. Visitors to Stonehenge can discover the history and legends which surround this unique stone circle, which began over 5,000 years ago, with a complimentary three part audio tour available in 9 languages (subject to availability).

Location: OS Ref. SU123 422. 2m W of Amesbury on junction of A303 and A344/A360.

Opening Times: 16 - 23 Oct: 9.30am - 5pm, 24 Oct - 15 Mar: 9.30am - 4pm, 16 Mar - 31 May & 1 Sept - 15 Oct: 9.30am - 6pm. 1 Jun - 31 Aug: 9am - 7pm. Closed 24 - 26 Dec & 1 Jan. Last adm. is ¹/₂ hr before advertised closing times and the site will be closed promptly 20mins after the advertised closing times.

Admission: Adult £4.20, Child £2.20, Conc. £3.20. Family (2+3) £10.60. Groups (11+) 10% discount.

❊ ▽ Tel. for details.

STOURHEAD

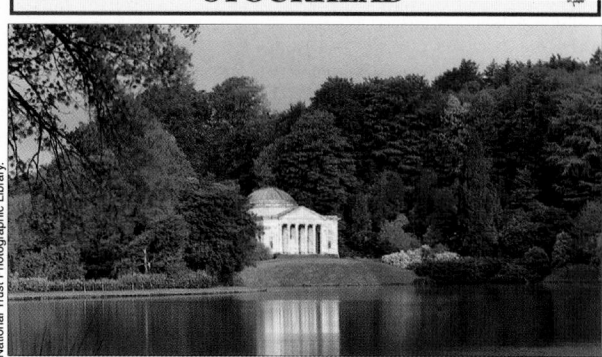

National Trust Photographic Library.

THE ESTATE OFFICE, STOURTON, Nr WARMINSTER BA12 6QD

Owner: The National Trust   *Contact:* The Property Manager

Tel: 01747 841152 **Fax:** 01747 841152 (office hours only)

An outstanding example of the English landscape style of garden. Designed by Henry Hoare II and laid out between 1741 and 1780. Classical temples, including the Pantheon and Temple of Apollo, are set around the central lake at the end of a series of vistas, which change as the visitor moves around the paths and through the magnificent mature woodland with its extensive collection of exotic trees. The house, begun in 1721 by Colen Campbell, contains furniture by the younger Chippendale and fine paintings. King Alfred's Tower, an intriguing red-brick folly built in 1772 by Henry Flitcroft, is almost 50m high and gives breathtaking views over the estate.

Location: OS183 Ref. ST778 341. At Stourton off the B3092, 3m N of A303 (Mere).

Opening Times: Garden: All year, daily, 9am - 7pm or sunset if earlier. House: 31 Mar - 4 Nov: daily (except Thur & Fri), 12 noon - 5.30pm or dusk. King Alfred's Tower: 31 Mar - 4 Nov: daily except Mon (open BH Mons). Times: Tue - Fri, 2 - 5.30pm; Sats, Suns & BH Mons: 11.30am - 5.30pm or dusk.

Admission: House & Garden: Adult £8.50, Child £4, Family £20. Booked groups (15+) by appointment: £8. House or Garden: Mar - Oct: Adult £4.80, Child £2.60, Family £12, Booked groups: £4.30. Garden only: Nov - end Feb: Adult £3.70, Child £1.80, Family £9. Booked groups: £3.50. King Alfred's Tower: Adult £1.60, Child 80p, Family £4.

ℹ Exhibition in Reception Building. 🖼 ♿ Wheelchair accessible. 🅿 ⬛
🐾 ❊ ▽ Tel. for details.

STOURTON HOUSE FLOWER GARDEN   **Tel:** 01747 840417

Zeals, Warminster, Wiltshire BA12 6QF

Owner/Contact: Mrs E Bullivant

Four acres of peaceful, romantic garden where grass paths lead through unique daffodils, spring flowers, camellias, azaleas, delphiniums, hydrangeas and hedged borders. Homemade refreshments.

Location: OS Ref. ST780 340. 2m NW of Mere next to Stourhead car park, A303. Follow blue signs.

Opening Times: Apr - end Nov: Weds, Thurs, Suns, and BH Mons, 11am - 6pm. Plants & dried flowers for sale during the winter on weekdays.

Admission: Please contact property for details. Group guided tours by appointment.

WESTWOOD MANOR 🌳   **Tel:** 01225 863374

Bradford-on-Avon, Wiltshire BA15 2AF

Owner: The National Trust   **Contact:** The Tenant

A 15th century stone manor house, altered in the early 17th century, with late gothic and Jacobean windows and fine plasterwork. There is a modern topiary garden. Note: Westwood Manor is administered for The National Trust by the tenant.

Location: OS Ref. ST813 589. 1¹/₂m SW of Bradford-on-Avon, in Westwood village, beside the church.

Opening Times: 1 Apr - 30 Sept: Suns, Tues & Weds, 2 - 5pm.

Admission: £3.80. No reduction for groups or children.

ℹ No WC. ♿ Not suitable. 🅿 Limited. 🐾

WILTON HOUSE 🏛   See page 241 for full page entry.

Eastern Region

Helmingham Hall

Helmingham 'both grand and lovable' – Sir Nikolaus Pevsner

The approach to Helmingham Hall is one of the loveliest in England.
The drive winds across an ancient, oak studded, 400 acre deer park
where large herds of red and fallow deer still graze.

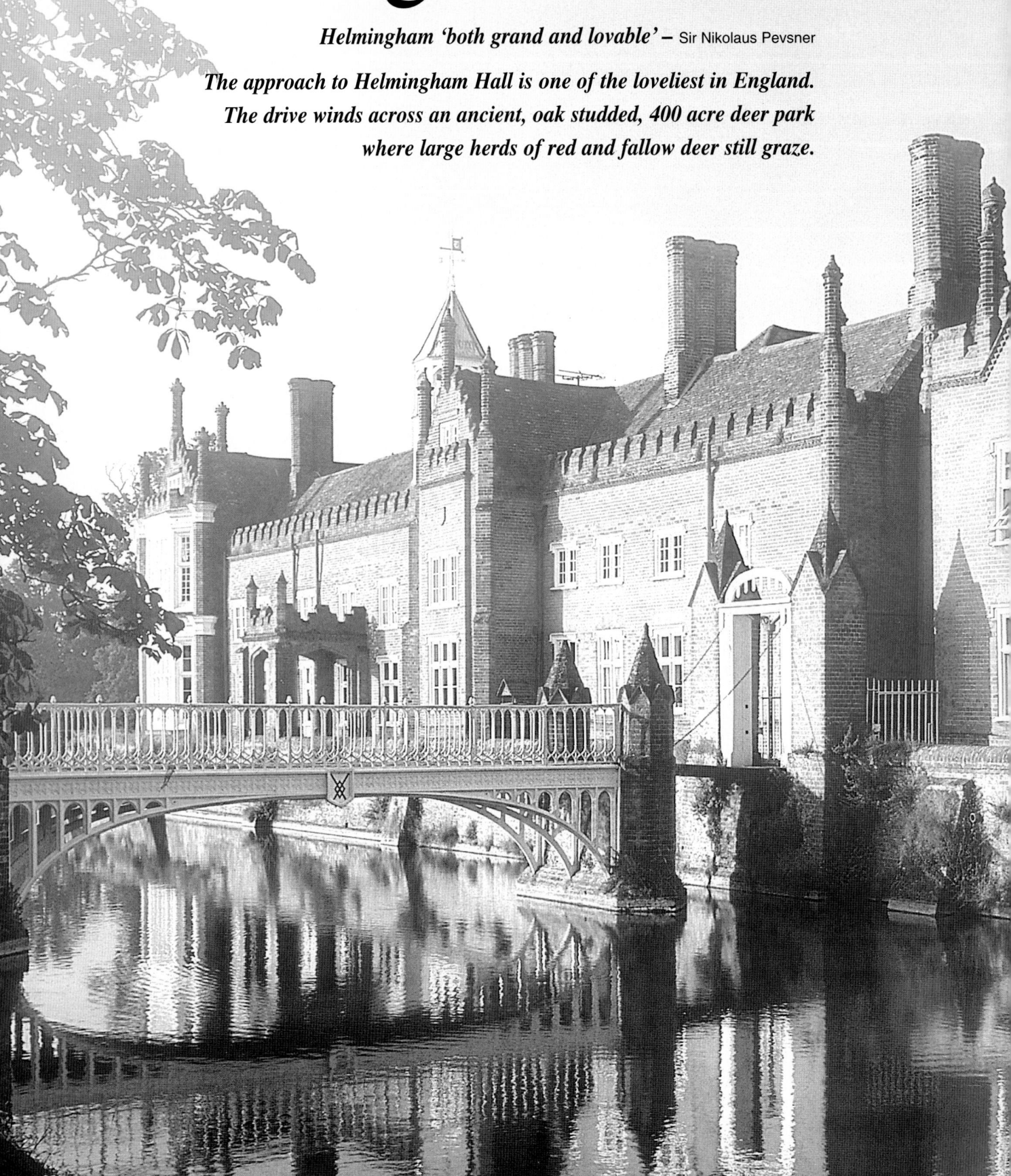

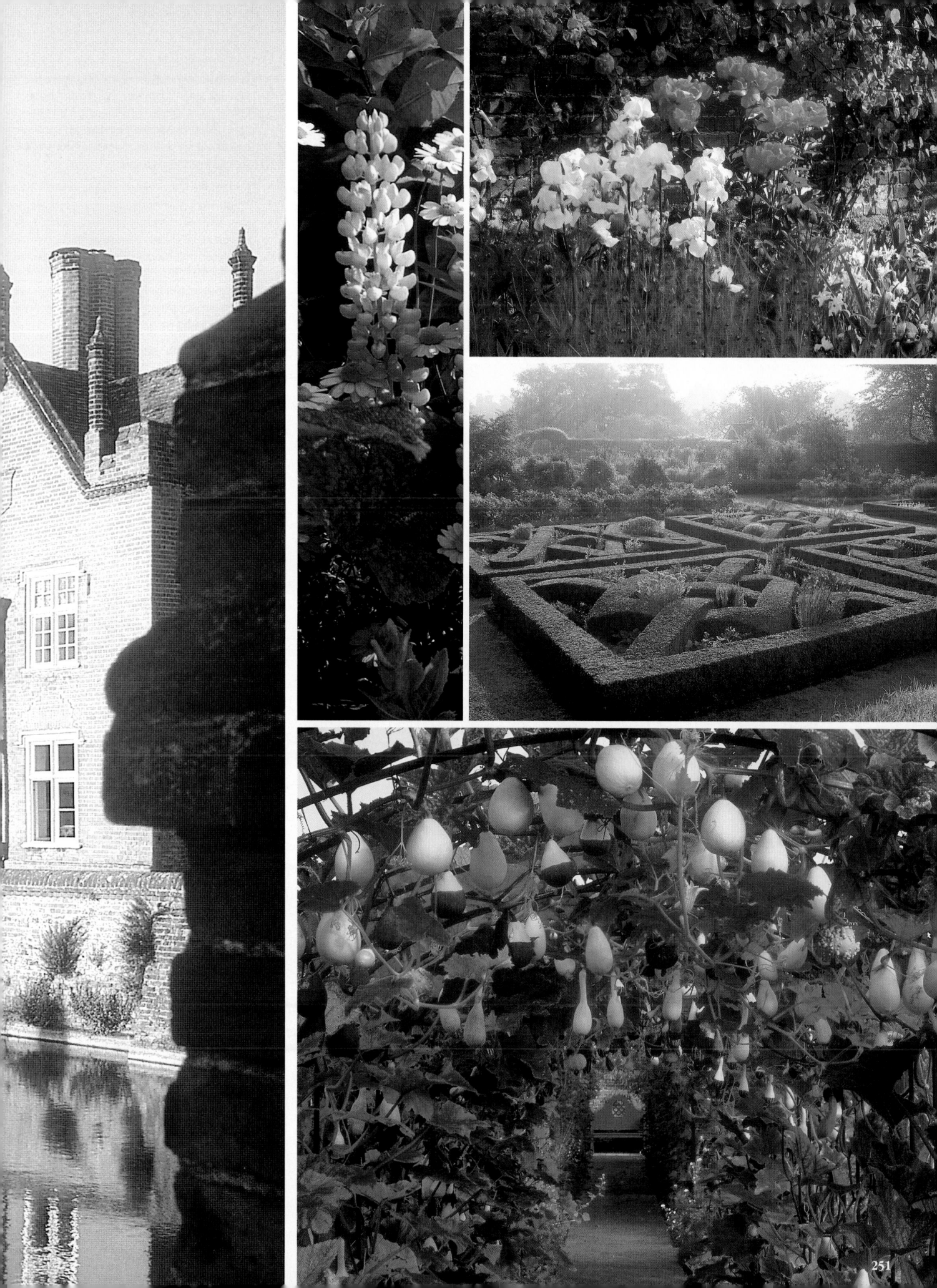

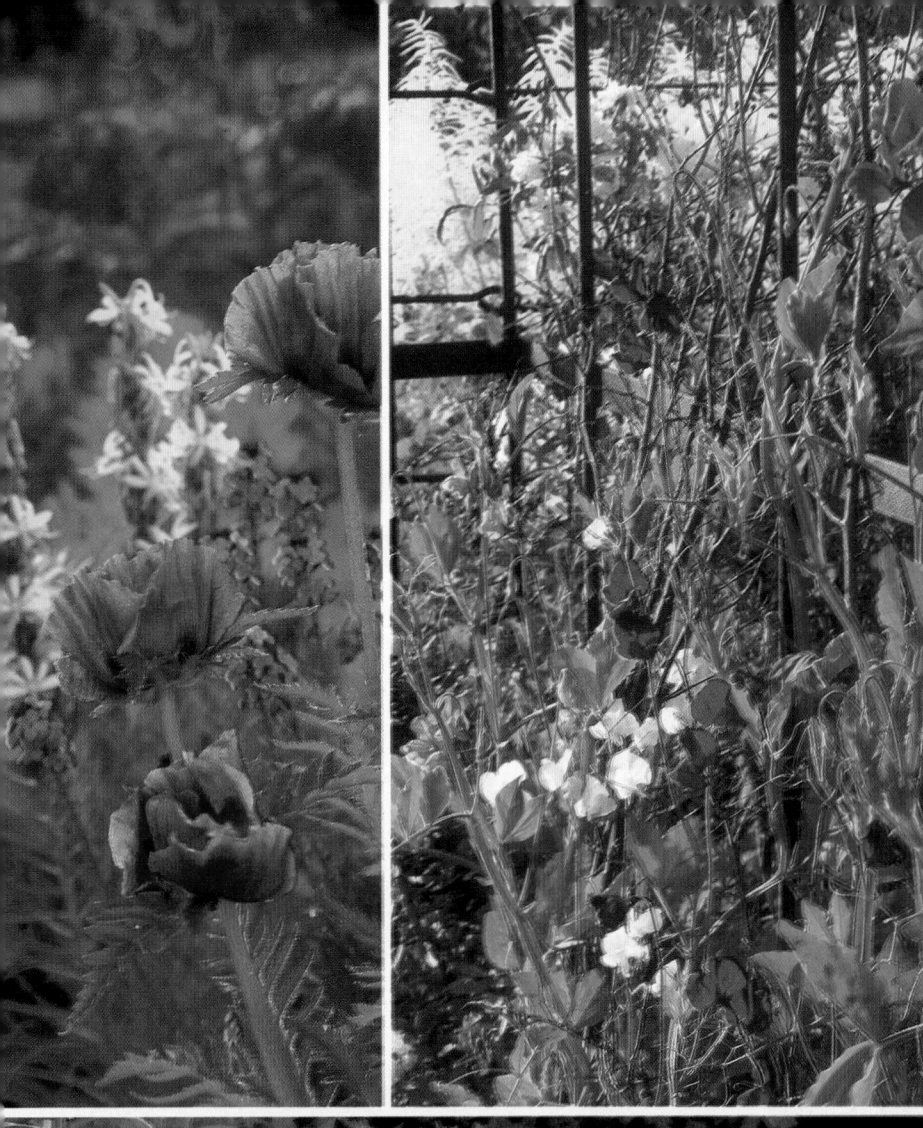

Helmingham Hall and the Tollemache family have been together for nearly 500 years, but it was not until 1510 that the present redbrick house was built. Although subsequent generations have added to and altered the house and its garden over the centuries, both retain a strong Elizabethan character.

Helmingham's romantic moat, with two drawbridges that are pulled up every night as they have been since 1510, fine barley twist chimneys, gables and decorative finials, provide the visitor with a wonderful timeless and secure atmosphere. It is, though, mainly due to the present Lord and Lady Tollemache that we owe the exquisitely planted gardens which clothe this early Tudor house.

Moated, like the house, the main part of the garden is reached by crossing a bridge, but between this and the elegant gates of the original walled kitchen garden is lawn patterned with a parterre of box-edged beds. Redesigned in 1978, the permanent planting of box hedging is infilled with *santolina incana*. Beyond the parterre and surrounding it on three sides is a rose garden planted in 1965 by Dinah, Lady Tollemache, mother of the present Lord Tollemache. The rose garden billows with an immense collection of hybrid musk roses edged with Hidcote lavender and underplanted with London Pride.

The cruciform herbaceous borders are the highlight of the walled kitchen garden. After finding old plans for this garden, in 1986 the garden was again divided into eight sections. The visitor can now wander through cross-paths planted with runner beans, sweet peas and gourds. Behind the garden's deep borders are walls covered in a rich combination of climbing roses, interplanted with clematis, hoheria and everlasting pea, to span the flowering times of the roses.

Two bridges lead out of the walled garden: an ancient one that takes visitors to the Apple Walk and a new bridge leading into the wild flower garden and orchard. This area of the garden, with cut paths making a walkway through long grass filled with cowslips, ox-eye daisies and orchids, provides a soft gentle contrast to the highly cultivated, more formal areas of Helmingham.

In 1982 Lord and Lady Tollemache decided to create a new garden historically sympathetic to the house – the result, a herb and knot garden stands on the far side of the house. These beautiful box-edged knot patterns are filled with herbs and flowers which were introduced to Britain before 1750 and, as with every other area of the gardens at Helmingham, they are an example of the perfectionist's eye. Beyond a wall of *rosa mundi* lie beds of old roses set against a tall yew hedge where a statue of Flora serenely surveys the scene.

The parks and gardens at Helmingham Hall are truly a gem, and richly deserve the Grade I status awarded by English Heritage. ⊹

For further details about *Helmingham Hall Gardens* see entry in Eastern Region ➜ Suffolk.

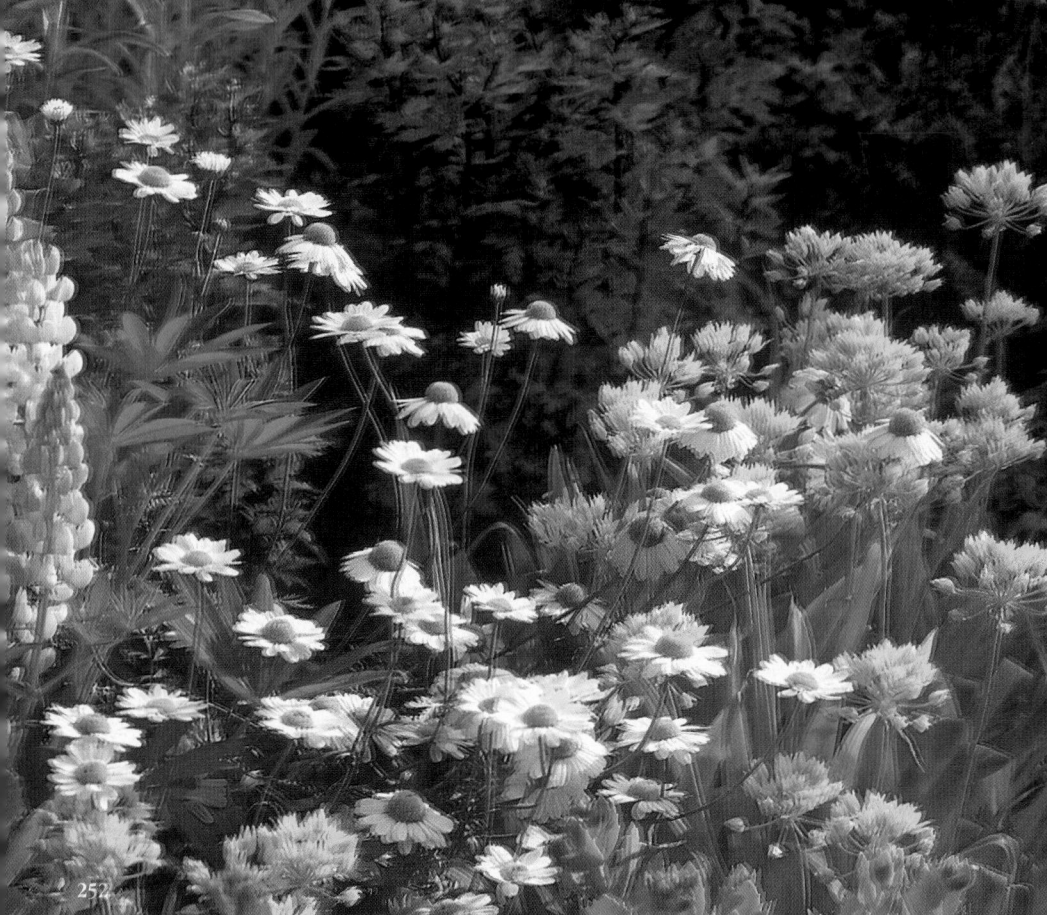

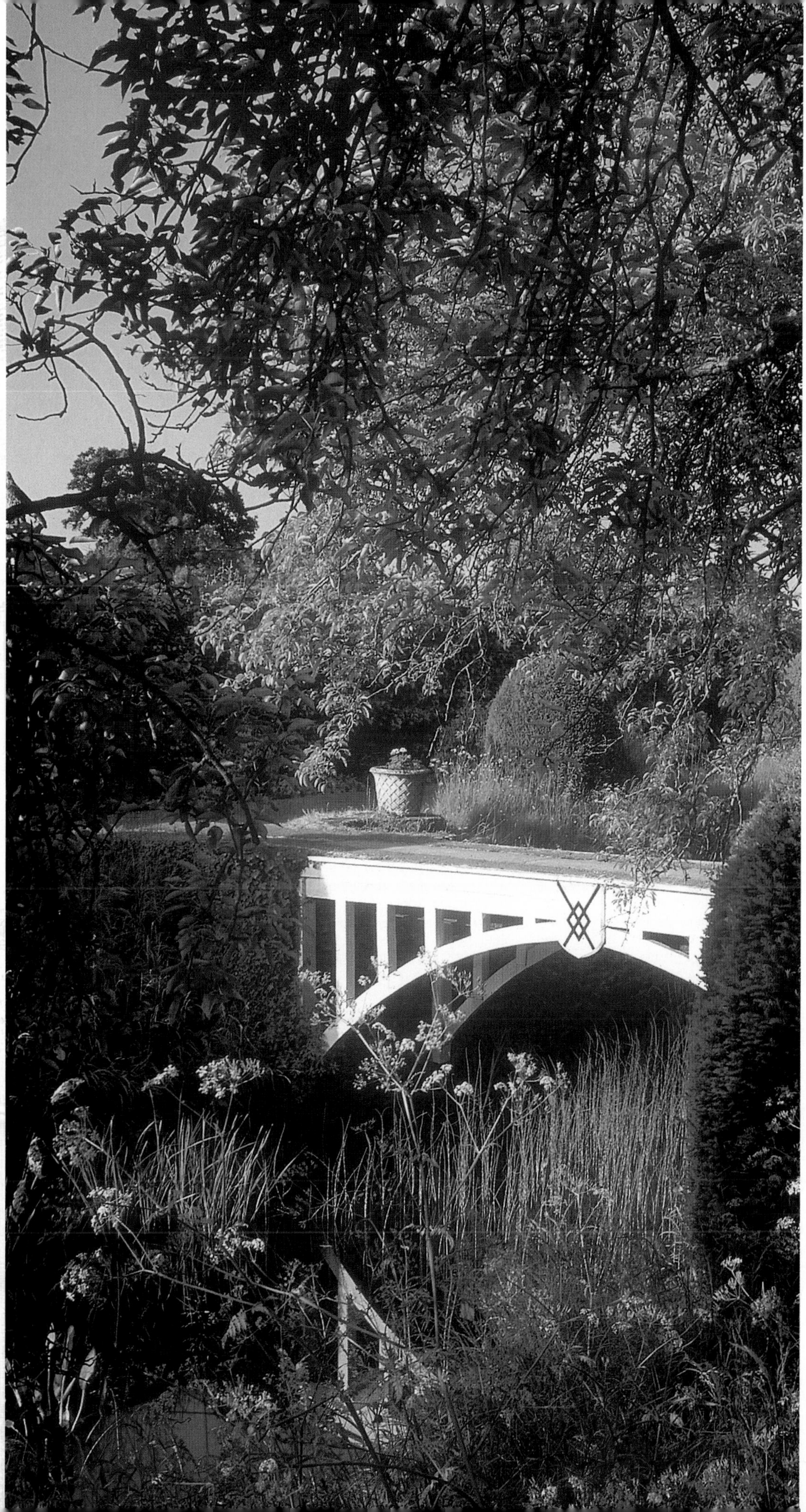

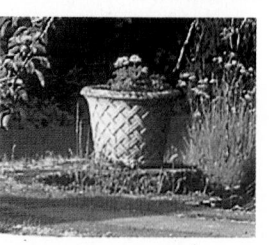

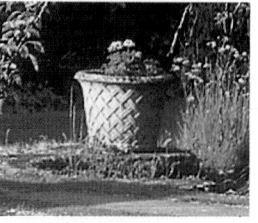

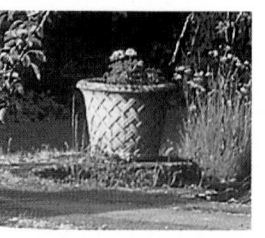

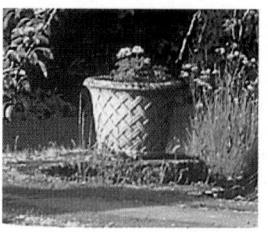

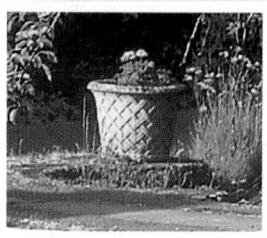

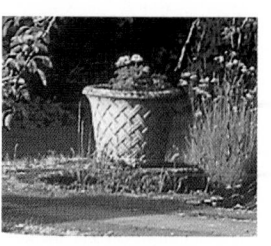

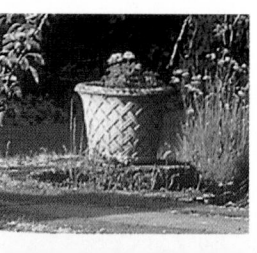

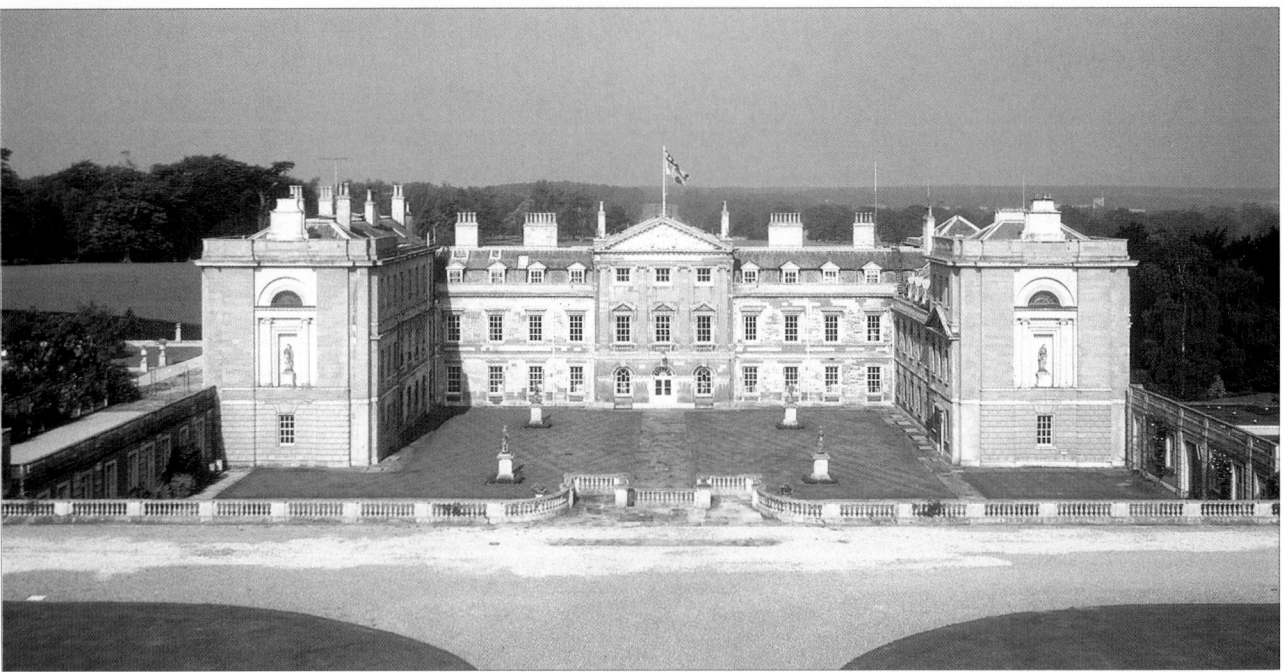

WOBURN ABBEY
Woburn

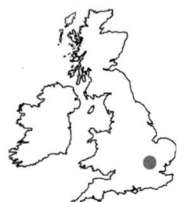

Owner: Trustees of Bedford Estates

CONTACT

William Lash
Woburn Abbey
Woburn
Bedfordshire
MK17 9WA

Tel: 01525 290666

Fax: 01525 290271

e-mail: enquiries@ woburnabbey.co.uk

LOCATION

OS Ref. SP965 325

On A4012, midway between M1/J13, 3m, J14, 6m and the A5 (turn off at Hockliffe). London approx. 1hr by road (43m).

Rail: London Euston to Leighton Buzzard, Bletchley/Milton Keynes. Kings Cross Thameslink to Flitwick.

Air: Luton 14m. Heathrow 39m.

CONFERENCE/FUNCTION		
ROOM	SIZE	MAX CAPACITY
Sculpture Gallery	130' x 25'	400 220 (sit-down)
Lantern Rm	24' x 21'	100

Set in a beautiful 3,000 acre deer park, Woburn Abbey has been the home of the Dukes of Bedford for nearly 400 years. It is now lived in by the present Duke's heir, the Marquess of Tavistock and his family. One of the most important private art collections in the world can be seen here, including paintings by Van Dyck, Cuyp, Gainsborough, Reynolds and Velazquez. In the Venetian Room there are 21 views of Venice by Canaletto. The collection also features French and English 18th century furniture and silver. The tour of the Abbey covers three floors, including vaults, where the fabulous Sèvres dinner service presented to the 4th Duke by Louis XV of France is on display.

The deer park has nine species of deer, roaming freely. One of these, the Père David, descended from the Imperial Herd of China, was saved from extinction at Woburn and is now the largest breeding herd of this species in the world. In 1985 22 Père David were given by the Family to the People's Republic of China and these are now successfully re-established in their natural habitat and number several hundred.

We carry out catering ourselves with banqueting, conferences, receptions and company days out our specialities in the beautiful setting of the Sculpture Gallery, overlooking the Private Gardens. It is also a popular choice for wedding receptions and we hold a Civil Wedding Licence.

There are extensive picnic areas. Events are held in the Park throughout the summer including the Woburn Garden Show, Craft Fair and the annual fly-in of the de Havilland Moth Club. The 40-shop Antique Centre is probably the most unusual such centre outside London.

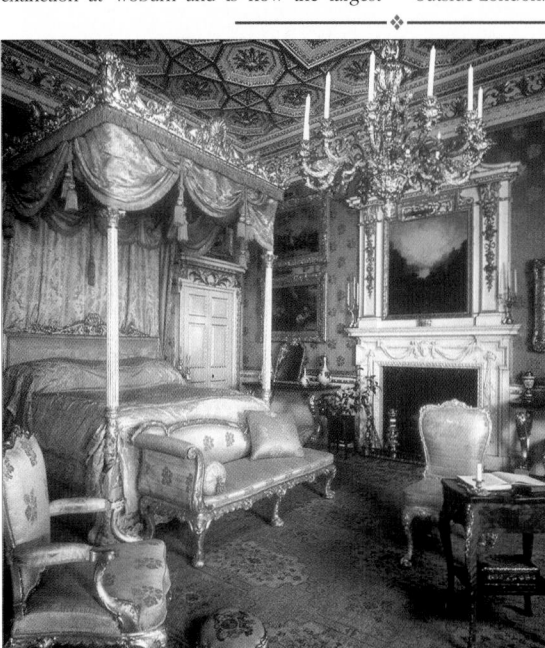

Suitable for fashion shows, product launches, filming & company 'days out'. Use of parkland and garden. No photography in House.

Two shops.

Conferences, exhibitions, banqueting, luncheons, dinners in the Sculpture Gallery, Lantern & Long Harness rooms.

Wheelchairs in the Abbey by prior arrangement (max. 8 per group).

Licensed. Group bookings in Sculpture Gallery. Flying Duchess Pavilion Coffee Shop.

By arrangement, max 15. Tours in French, German & Dutch at an additional charge of £10.00 per guide. Audio tape tour available – £1pp. Lectures on the property, its contents, gardens and history can be arranged.

P Ample. Free.

Welcome. Special programme on request. Cost: £2.50pp (group rate).

In park on leads, and guide dogs in house.

Civil Wedding Licence.

OPENING TIMES

1 January - 25 March
Abbey: weekends only 11am - 4pm*
Deer Park: Daily 10.30am - 3.45pm

26 March - 30 September
Abbey:
Mon - Sat: 11am - 4pm*
Sun & BHs: 11am - 5pm
Deer Park:
Mon - Sat: 10am - 4.30pm
Sun & BHs: 10am - 4.45pm

1 Oct - 28 Oct
Abbey: weekends only 11am - 5pm*
Deer Park: 10.30am - 4.45pm

Abbey closed: 29 Oct - end Dec

Antiques Centre:
All year, daily (except 24 - 26, 31 Dec 2000 & 1 Jan, 24 - 26 Dec 2001).

*last entry time

ADMISSION

Woburn Abbey
(Prices incl. Private Apts)
Adult £7.50
Child (12 - 16yrs) £2.50
OAP £6.50
Group rates & family tickets available.

Antiques Centre ..... Free

Grounds & Deer Park only
Car £5.00
Motorcycle £2.00
Coaches .... Free
Other...................... £0.50
Visitors from Safari Park .... Free

Reduced rates apply when Private Apartments are in use by the family.

SPECIAL EVENTS
Please telephone for details.

BROMHAM WATERMILL & ART GALLERY
Tel: 01234 824330

Bromham, Bedfordshire MK43 8LP

Owner: Bedfordshire County Council   **Contact:** Sally Wileman

Working water mill on River Ouse. Flour milling.

Location: OS Ref. TL010 506. Location beside the River Ouse bridge on N side of the former A428, 2$^{1}/_{2}$ m W of Bedford.

Opening Times: Wed - Sat, 12 noon - 4pm. Suns. 10.30am - 5pm. Last entry 30 mins before closing.

Admission: Please telephone for admission prices.

BUSHMEAD PRIORY
Tel: 01234 376614

Colmworth, Bedford, Bedfordshire MK44 2LD   **Regional Office:** 01223 582700

Owner: English Heritage   **Contact:** The Custodian

A rare survival of the medieval refectory of an Augustinian priory, with its original timber-framed roof almost intact and containing interesting wall paintings and stained glass.

Location: OS Ref. TL115 607. On unclassified road near Colmworth; off B660, 2m S of Bolnhurst. 5m W of St. Neots (A1).

Opening Times: Jul - Aug weekends & BHs only: 10am - 6pm. Closed 1 - 2pm.

Admission: Adult £2, Child £1, Conc. £1.50.

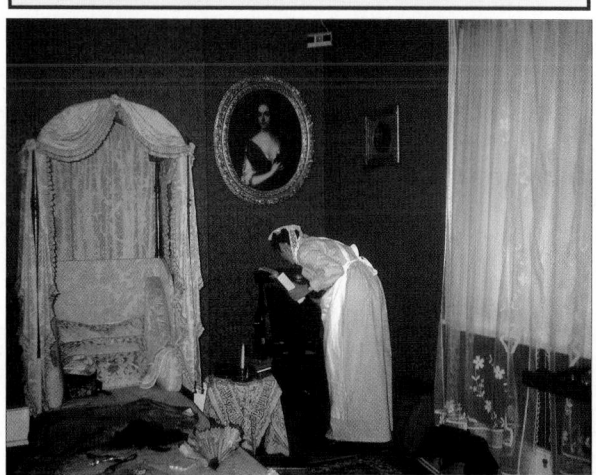

CECIL HIGGINS ART GALLERY

CASTLE CLOSE, CASTLE LANE, BEDFORD MK40 3RP

Owner: Bedford Borough Council & Trustees of Gallery   *Contact: The Gallery*

Tel: 01234 211222 **Fax:** 01234 327149 **e-mail:** chag@bedford.gov.uk

An unusual combination of recreated Victorian Mansion (originally the home of the Higgins family, wealthy Bedford brewers) and adjoining modern gallery housing internationally renowned collection of watercolours, prints and drawings, ceramics and glass. Room settings include many items from the Handley-Read Collection and furniture by Victorian architect William Burges. Situated in pleasant gardens near the river embankment.

Location: OS Ref. TL052 497. Centre of Bedford, just off The Embankment. E of High St.

Opening Times: Tue - Sat, 11am - 5pm (last admission 4.45pm). Sun & BH Mons, 2 - 5pm. Closed Mons, Good Fri & 25/26 Dec.

Admission: Adults £2, Conc. Free (includes visit to Bedford Museum).

ℹ Photography in house by arrangement. 📷 🍽 By arrangement.
♿ House & garden suitable. WC. 🖥 By arrangement. 🚶 By arrangement.
🅿 No parking. 🎧 🦮 Guide dogs only. ❄ ▣ Telephone for details.

HOUGHTON HOUSE
Tel: 01223 582700

Ampthill, Bedford, Bedfordshire

Owner: English Heritage   **Contact:** The East of England Regional Office

Reputedly the inspiration for "House Beautiful" in Bunyan's "Pilgrim's Progress", the remains of this early 17th century mansion still convey elements which justify the description, including work attributed to Inigo Jones.

Location: OS Ref. TL039 394. 1m NE of Ampthill off A421, 8m S of Bedford, then by footpath to NE.

Opening Times: Any reasonable time.

Admission: Free.

LUTON MUSEUM & ART GALLERY
Tel: 01582 546739

Wardown Park, Luton, Bedfordshire

Owner: Luton Borough Council   **Contact:** Lynette Burgess

Lively and varied collections housed in an impressive Victorian Mansion set in Wardown Park.

Location: OS Ref. TL089 230. 1$^{1}/_{4}$ m N of town centre between New and Old Bedford Rd.

Opening Times: Tue - Sat, 10am - 5pm, Suns, 1 - 5pm. Closed 25/26 Dec & New Year's Day.

Admission: Free.

MOOT HALL
Tel: 01234 266889

Elstow Green, Church View, Elstow, Bedford

Owner: Bedfordshire County Council

Timber framed market hall.

Location: OS Ref. TL048 475. 1m from Bedford, signposted from A6.

Opening Times: Apr - Oct: Tue, Wed, Thur, Sat, Sun & BHs: 2 - 5pm.

Admission: Adult £1, Conc. 50p.

STOCKWOOD PERIOD GARDENS
Tel: 01582 546739

Farley Hill, Luton, Bedfordshire

Owner: Luton Borough Council   **Contact:** Lynette Burgess

Includes Knot, Medieval, Victorian and Italian gardens.

Location: OS Ref. TL085 200. 1$^{1}/_{4}$ m SW of Luton town centre by Farley Road B4546.

Opening Times: Apr - Oct: Tue - Sun & BHs, 10am - 5pm. Nov - Mar: Sat - Sun, 10am - 4pm.

Admission: Free.

SWISS GARDEN
Tel: 01767 627666 **Fax:** 01767 627443

Old Warden Park, Bedfordshire

Operated By: Bedfordshire County Council

Laid out in the early 1800s and steeped in the indulgent romanticism of the time, Swiss Garden combines all the elements of high fashion: formal walks and vistas, classical proportions, tiny thatched buildings, woodland glades and, hidden away, a fairytale grotto with a brilliant glazed fernery, magnificent trees and a network of ponds and bridges. Shuttleworth Mansion, home of the family that owned Swiss Garden, is open on a number of days during the year. Cream teas are served during the summer on the lawn beside the house.

Location: OS Ref. TL150 447. 1$^{1}/_{2}$ m W of Biggleswade A1 roundabout, signposted from A1 and A600. Approached from Shuttleworth Mansion, Old Warden Park.

Opening Times: Mar - Sept: Sun & BHs, 10am - 6pm. Weekdays & Sat: 1 - 6pm. Jan, Feb & Oct: Suns & New Year's Day, 11am - 3pm. Last admission $^{3}/_{4}$ hr before closing. Groups at any time on request.

Admission: Adult £3, Conc. £2, Family £8. Season ticket available. Special rates for groups and guided tours.

♿ 🍽 Catering. ☕ Cream teas during summer. 🦮 ❄

WOBURN ABBEY
See page 254 for full page entry.

DE GREY MAUSOLEUM
Tel: 01525 860094 (Key-keeper)

Flitton, Bedford, Bedfordshire

Owner: English Heritage   **Contact:** Mrs Stimson

A remarkable treasure-house of sculpted tombs and monuments from the 16th to 19th centuries dedicated to the de Grey family of nearby Wrest Park.

Location: OS Ref. TL059 359. Attached to the church on unclassified road 1$^{1}/_{2}$ m W of A6 at Silsoe.

Opening Times: Weekends only. Key: Mrs Stimson, 3 Highfield Rd, Flitton.

Admission: Free.

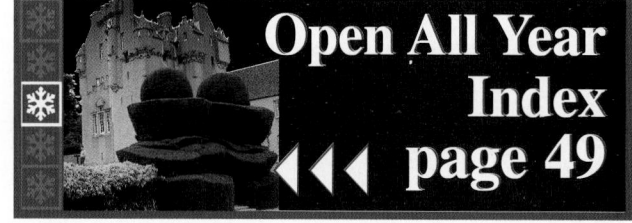

Open All Year
Index
◀◀◀ page 49

WREST PARK GARDENS

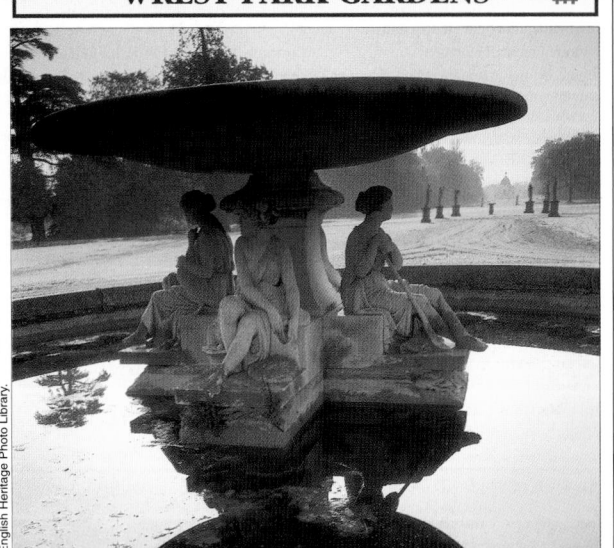

English Heritage Photo Library.

SILSOE, LUTON, BEDFORDSHIRE MK45 4HS
Owner: English Heritage   *Contact:* The Custodian

Tel: 01525 860152

Over 90 acres of wonderful gardens originally laid out in the early 18th century, including the Great Garden. During the 18th and 19th centuries the formal parterre was introduced together with marble fountains, the Bath House and the vast Orangery, built by the Earl de Grey. The gardens form a delightful backdrop to the house, built in the style of an 18th century French chateau.

Location: OS153, Ref. TL093 356. ¾ m E of Silsoe off A6, 10m S of Bedford.

Opening Times: 1 Apr - 31 Oct: Weekends and BHs only, 10am - 6pm (5pm in Oct). Last admission 1hr before closing time.

Admission: Adult £3.50, Child £1.75, Conc. £2.65. 15% discount for groups (11+). Family Ticket £8.75.

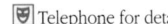 Telephone for details.

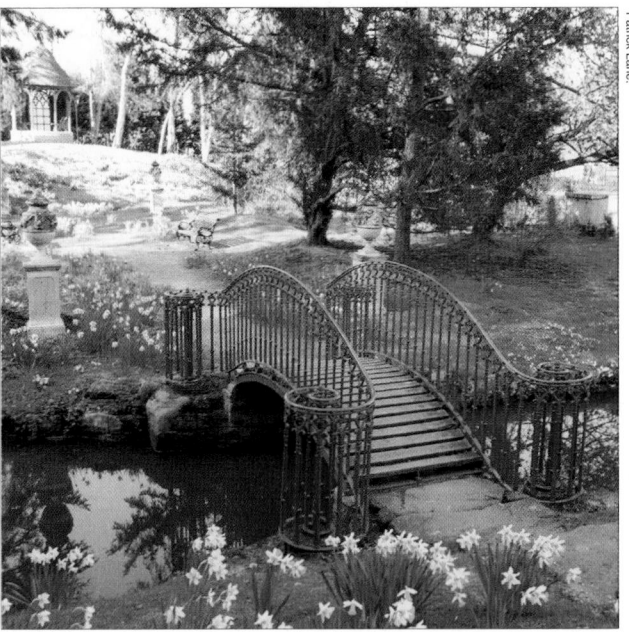

Patrick Lane.

Swiss Garden, Bedfordshire.

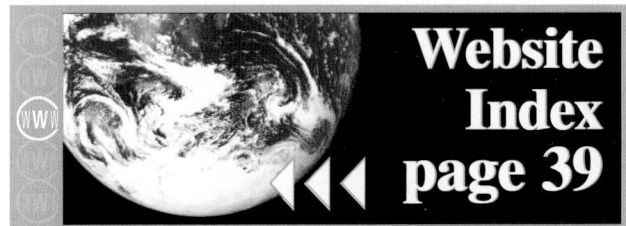

Website Index page 39

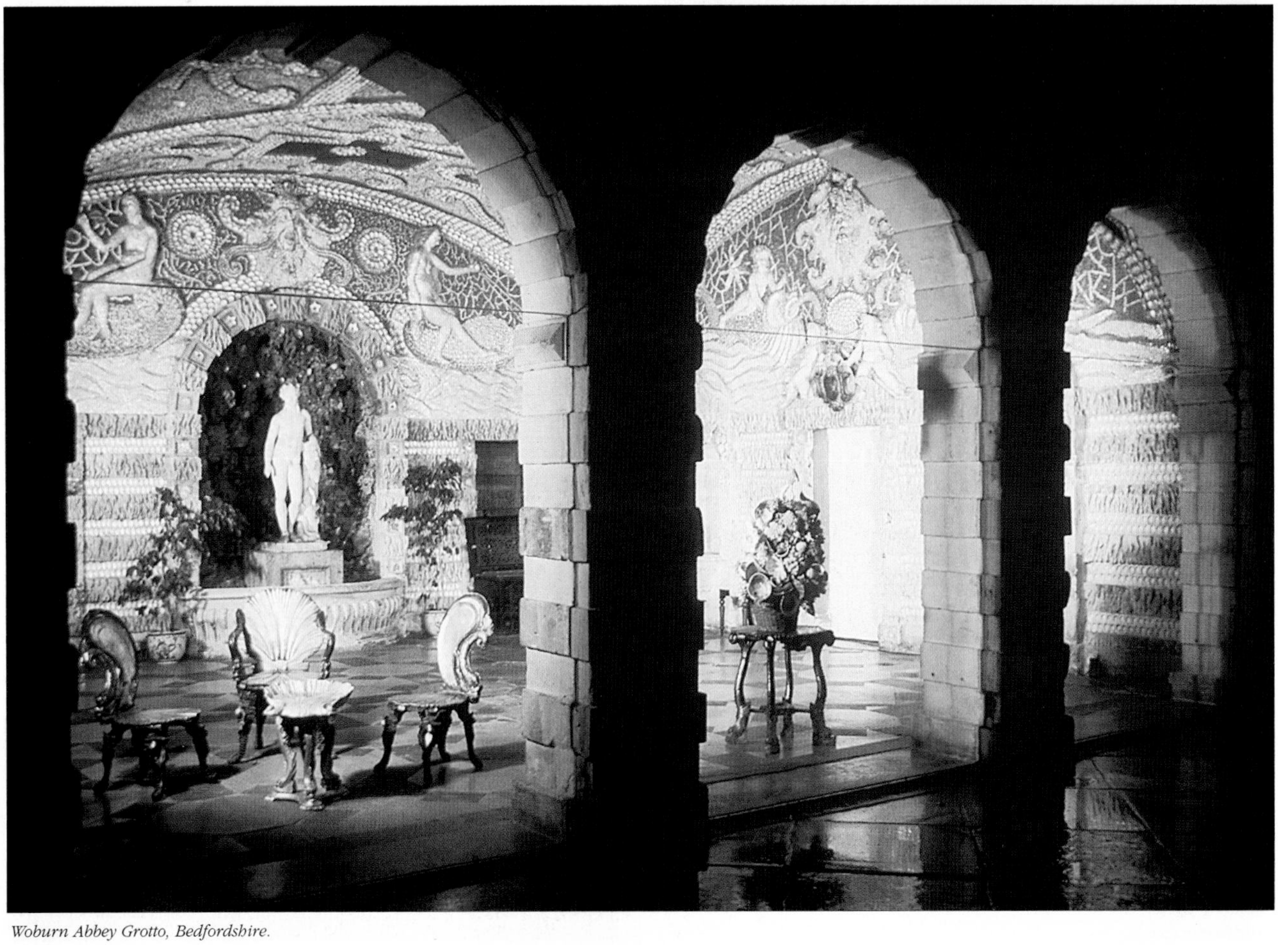

Website Index page 39

Woburn Abbey Grotto, Bedfordshire.

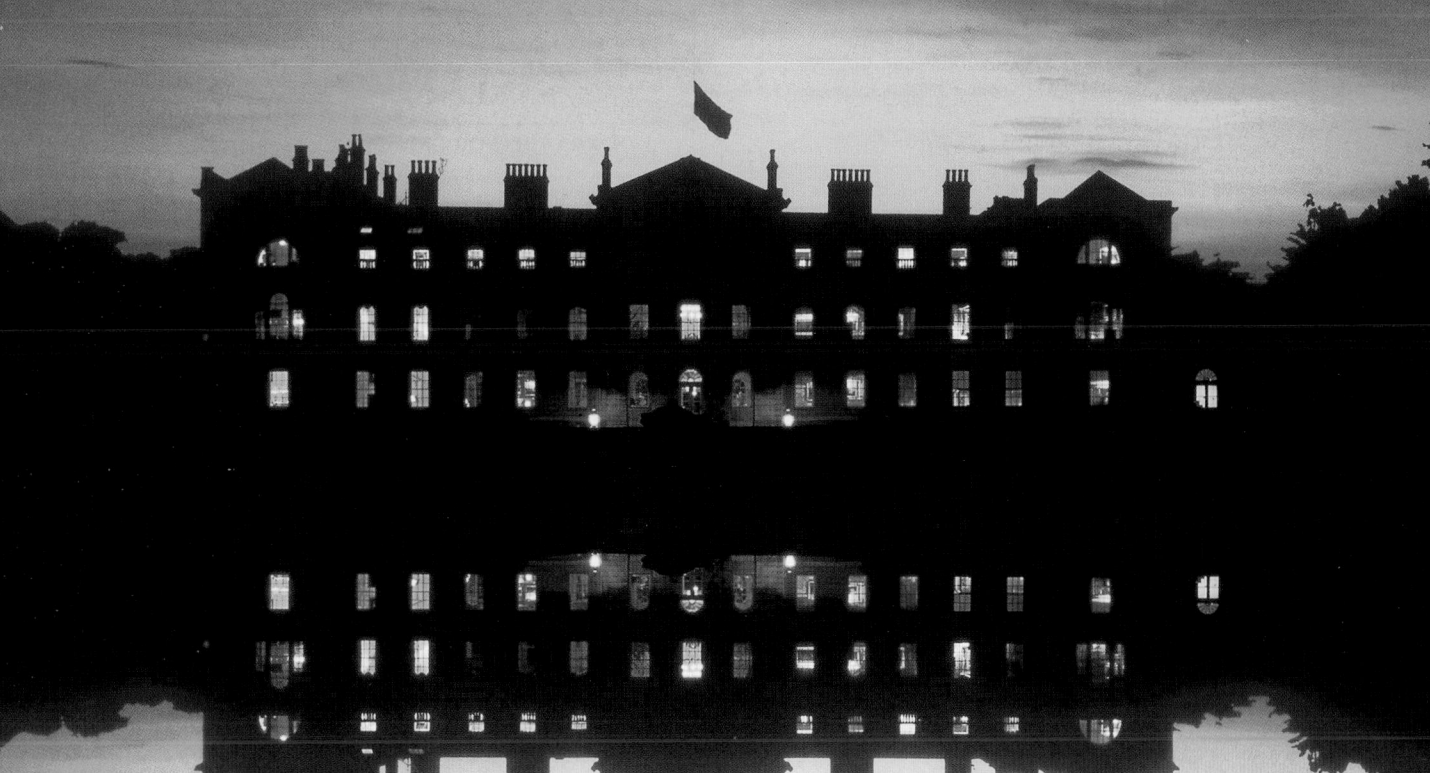

Woburn Abbey, Bedfordshire.

257

ANGLESEY ABBEY

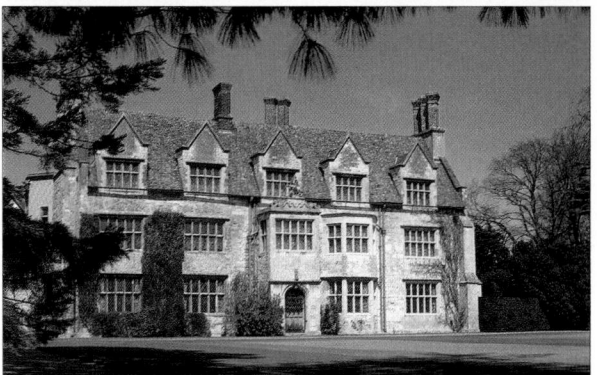

LODE, CAMBRIDGE, CAMBRIDGESHIRE CB5 9EJ

Owner: The National Trust   Contact: The Property Manager

Tel/Fax: 01223 811200

Dating from 1600, the house, built on the site of an Augustinian priory, contains the famous Fairhaven collection of paintings and furniture. Surrounded by an outstanding 100 acre garden and arboretum, with a wonderful display of hyacinths in spring and magnificent herbaceous borders and a dahlia garden in summer. A watermill in full working order is demonstrated on the first Saturday in each month.

Location: OS Ref 154. TL533 622. In Lode village, 6m NE of Cambridge on B1102, signs from A14.

Opening Times: House: 28 Mar - 21 Oct: Wed - Sun & BH Mons, 1 - 5pm (Noon opening for pre-booked groups). Garden: 28 Mar - 1 Jul: Wed - Sun; 2 Jul - 9 Sept: daily; 12 Sept - 21 Oct: Wed - Sun, 10.30am - 5.30pm. Winter Season: 24 Oct - 23 Dec:, 2 Jan - 24 Feb 2002: Wed - Sun, 10.30am - 4.30pm. Mar 2002 until 5.30pm. Lode Mill: As garden except 1 - 4.30pm. Winter season: Sats & Suns only, 11am - 4pm. Last admission to house & Mill 4.30pm (Mar - Oct). Timed entry to house on Suns & BH Mons. Closed Good Fri. Winter season part of gardens only.

Admission: House & garden: £6.25, Family discounts. Groups: £5. Garden & Mill only: £3.85 (groups £3.25). Group visit information pack (no groups Suns & BH Mons).

Partially suitable. Licensed. In park, on leads. Tel. for details.

CAMBRIDGE UNIVERSITY BOTANIC GARDEN

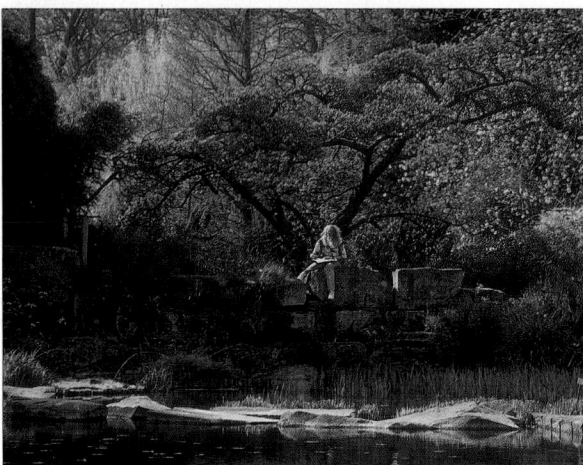

Bateman Street, Cambridge CB2 1JF

Owner: University of Cambridge   Contact: Mrs B Stacey, Administrative Secretary

Tel: 01223 336265 **Fax:** 01223 336278 **e-mail:** gardens@hermes.cam.ac.uk

40 acres of outstanding gardens with lake and glasshouses, near the centre of Cambridge, incorporating nine National collections, including Geranium and Fritillaria. Café and shop in the Gilmour building.

Location: OS Ref. TL453 573. 1m S of Cambridge city centre, off A1309 (Trumpington Rd).

Opening Times: Daily (except Christmas Day & Boxing Day), 10am - 6pm (Summer), 10am - 5pm (Spring & Autumn) 10am - 4pm (Winter). Glasshouses: daily, 10am - 3.45pm. Tours by arrangement.

Admission: Admission charged weekdays Mar - Oct inclusive, plus weekends & BHs all year.

Grounds suitable. WCs. Street/Pay & Display. Guide dogs only.

OLIVER CROMWELL'S HOUSE   **Tel:** 01353 662062 **Fax:** 01353 668518

29 St Mary's Street, Ely, Cambridgeshire CB7 4HF   **e-mail:** elytic@compuserve.com
Owner: East Cambridgeshire District Council   **Contact:** Mrs A Smith
The former home of the Lord Protector.
Location: OS Ref. TL538 803. N of Cambridge, ¼ m W of Ely Cathedral.
Opening Times: 1 Oct - 31 Mar, Mon - Sat, 10am - 5pm, Suns, 12 noon - 4pm. 1 Apr -30 Sept: daily, 10am - 5.30pm.
Admission: Adult £2.70, Conc. £2.20, Family £7. Joint Ticket (including Cathedral, Ely Museum and the Stained Glass Museum): Adult £8, Conc. £6. Group prices on application. (2000 prices - please confirm before visit).

DENNY ABBEY & THE FARMLAND MUSEUM

Ely Road, Chittering, Waterbeach, Cambridgeshire CB5 9TQ   **Tel:** 01223 860489
Owner: English Heritage/Managed by the Farmland Museum Trust   **Contact:** The Custodian
What at first appears to be an attractive stone-built farmhouse is actually the remains of a 12th century Benedictine abbey which, at different times, also housed the Knights Templar and Franciscan nuns. Founded by the Countess of Pembroke.
Location: OS Ref. TL495 684. 6m N of Cambridge on the E side of the A10.
Opening Times: 1 Apr - 31 Oct: 12 noon - 5pm..
Admission: Adult £3.50, Child £1.30, Conc. £2.50, Family £8.30.

DOCWRA'S MANOR GARDEN   **Tel:** 01763 261473 **Fax:** 01763 260677

Shepreth, Royston, Hertfordshire SG8 6PS
Owner: Mrs Faith Raven   **Contact:** Peter Rocket
Extensive garden around building dating from the 18th century.
Location: OS Ref. TL393 479. In Shepreth via A10 from Royston.
Opening Times: All year: Weds & Fris, 10am - 4pm & 1st Sun in month from Apr - Oct: 2 - 5pm.
Admission: £3.

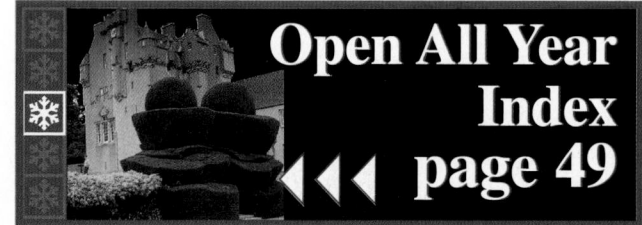Open All Year Index ◀◀◀ page 49

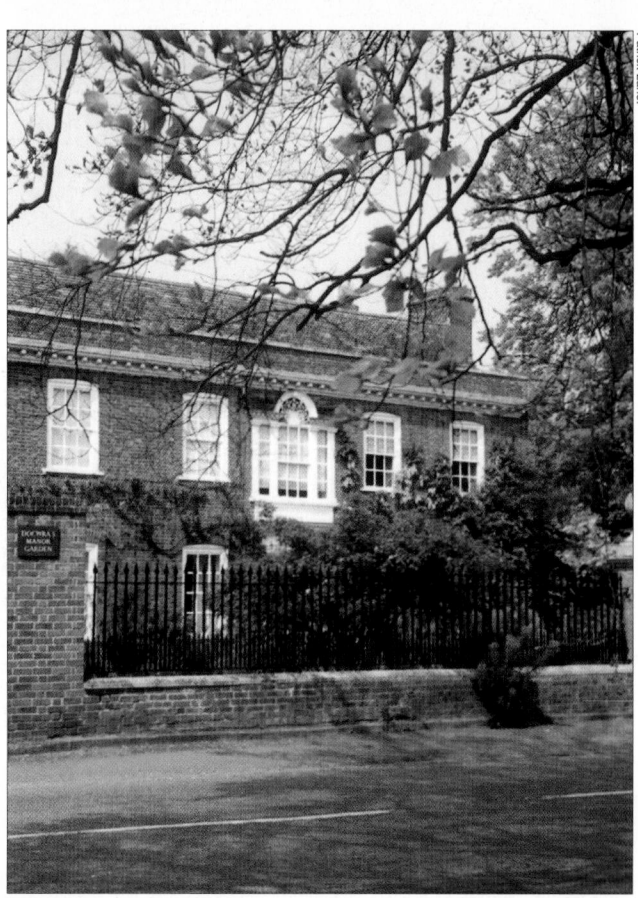
Docwra's Manor, Cambridgeshire.

ELTON HALL

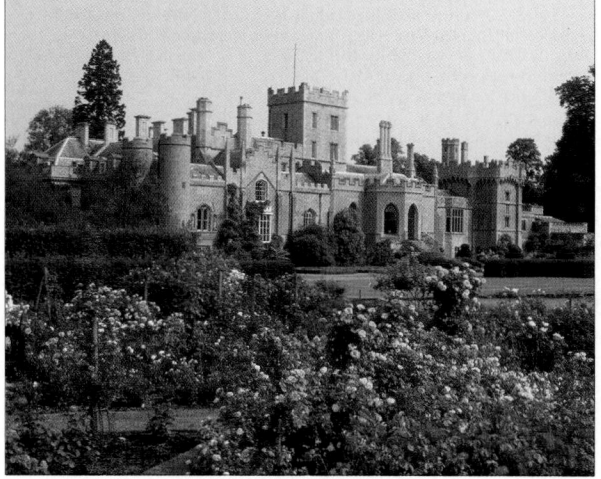

Nr PETERBOROUGH PE8 6SH

Owner: Mr & Mrs W Proby   *Contact:* The Administrator

Tel: 01832 280468 **Fax:** 01832 280584 **e-mail:** office@eltonhall.com

Elton Hall, the home of the Proby family for over 350 years is a fascinating mixture of styles. Every room contains treasures, magnificent furniture and fine paintings from the early 15th century. The library is one of the finest in private hands and includes Henry VIII's prayer book. The beautiful gardens have been carefully restored, with the addition of a new gothic Orangery to celebrate the Millennium.

Location: OS Ref. TL091 930. Close to A1 in the village of Elton, off A605 Peterborough - Oundle road.

Opening Times: 27/28 May. Jun: Weds. Jul & Aug: Wed, Thur & Sun. Plus Aug BH Mon. 2 - 5pm. Private groups by arrangement on weekdays Apr - Sept.

Admission: Hall & Gardens: Adult £5, Child (accompanied) Free. Gardens only: Adult £2.50, Child (accompanied) Free.

No photography in house. Hall not suitable. Obligatory. Guide dogs in gardens only. Tel. for details.

ISLAND HALL

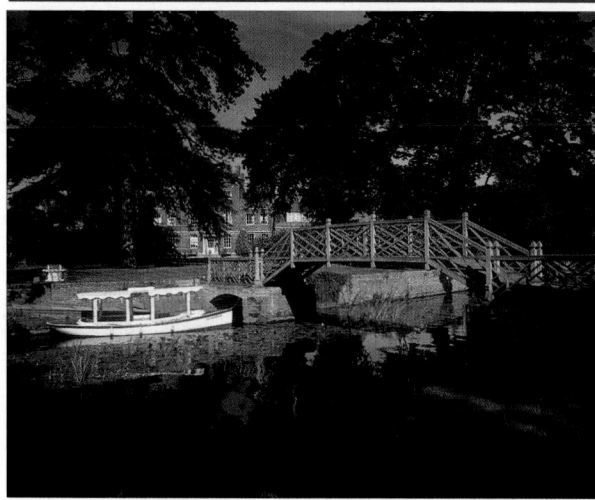

GODMANCHESTER, CAMBRIDGESHIRE PE29 2BA

Owner: Mr Christopher & Lady Linda Vane Percy   *Contact:* Mr C Vane Percy

Tel: 020 7491 3724 **Fax:** 020 7355 4006

An important mid 18th century mansion of great charm, owned and restored by an award-winning interior designer. This family home has lovely Georgian rooms, with fine period detail, and interesting possessions relating to the owners' ancestors since their first occupation of the house in 1800. A tranquil riverside setting with formal gardens and ornamental island forming part of the grounds in an area of Best Landscape. Octavia Hillwrote *"This is the loveliest, dearest old house, I never was in such a one before."*

Location: OS Ref. TL244 706. Centre of Godmanchester, Post Street next to car park. 1m S of Huntingdon, 15m NW of Cambridge A14.

Opening Times: Groups only, by arrangement: May - Jul & Sept.

Admission: (30+) Adult £3.50, (15-30 persons) Adult £4. Under 15 persons, min charge £60 per group (sorry but no children under 13).

Not suitable. Home made teas.

KIMBOLTON CASTLE   **Tel:** 01480 860505 **Fax:** 01480 861763

Kimbolton, Huntingdon, Cambridgeshire PE28 0EA

Owner: Governors of Kimbolton School   **Contact:** Mr J Mcleod

A late Stuart house, an adaptation of a 13th century fortified manor house, with evidence of Tudor modifications. The seat of the Earls and Dukes of Manchester 1615 - 1950, now a school. Katharine of Aragon died in the Queen's Room - the setting for a scene in Shakespeare's *Henry VIII*. A minor example of the work of Vanbrugh and Hawksmoor; Gatehouse by Robert Adam; the Pellegrini mural paintings on the Staircase, in the Chapel and in the Boudoir are the best examples in England of this gifted Venetian decorator.

Location: OS Ref. TL101 676. 7m NW of St Neots on B645.

Opening Times: 15/16 Apr, 27/28 May, 29 Jul & 5, 12, 19, 26/27 Aug: 2 - 6pm.

Admission: Adult £2.50, Child/Conc. £1.50. Groups by arrangement.

Not suitable. By arrangement. On leads in grounds.

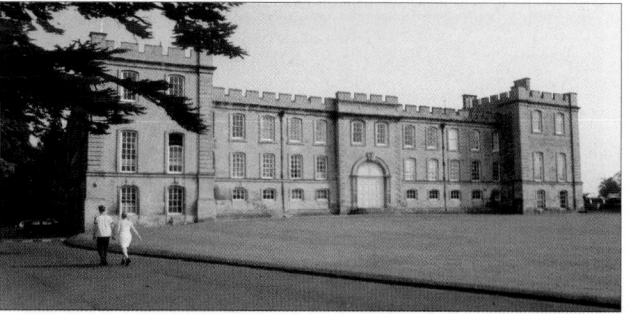

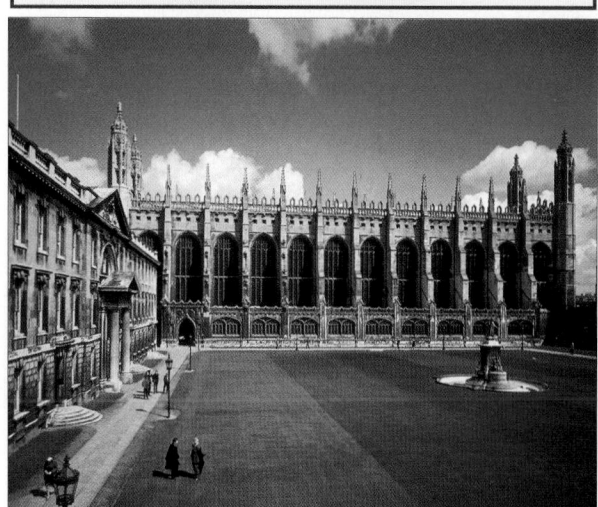

Patrick Lane.

Kimbolton Castle, Cambridgeshire.

KING'S COLLEGE

KING'S PARADE, CAMBRIDGE CB2 1ST

Owner: Provost and Fellows   *Contact:* Mr D Buxton

Tel/Fax: 01223 331212   **e-mail:** chapel.shop@kings.cam.ac.uk

Visitors are welcome, but remember that this is a working college. Please respect the privacy of those who work, live and study here. The Chapel is often used for services, recordings, broadcasts, etc, and ideally visitors should check before arriving. Recorded message for services, concerts and visiting times: 01223 331155.

Location: OS Ref. TL447 584.

Opening Times: Out of term: Mon - Sat, 9.30am - 4.30pm. Sun, 10am - 5pm. In term: Mon - Fri: 9.30am - 3.30pm. Sat: 9.30am - 3.15pm. Sun: 1.15 - 2.15pm, 5 - 5.30pm.

Admission: Adult £3.50, Child (12-17yrs)/Student (ID required) £2.50, OAP £3.50. Child (under 12 & accompanied) Free.

No photography inside Chapel. Conferences. By arrangement. By arrangement. No parking. Guide dogs only.

LONGTHORPE TOWER   **Tel:** 01733 268482

Thorpe Rd, Longthorpe, Cambridgeshire PE1 1HA

Owner: English Heritage   **Contact:** The Custodian

The finest example of 14th century domestic wall paintings in northern Europe showing a variety of secular and sacred objects. The tower, with the Great Chamber that contains the paintings, is part of a fortified manor house. Special exhibitions are held on the upper floor.

Location: OS Ref. TL163 983. 2m W of Peterborough just off A47.

Opening Times: 1 Apr - 31 Oct: weekends & BHs only: 12 noon - 5pm.

Admission: Adult £1.60, Child 80p, Conc. £1.20.

THE MANOR, HEMINGFORD GREY

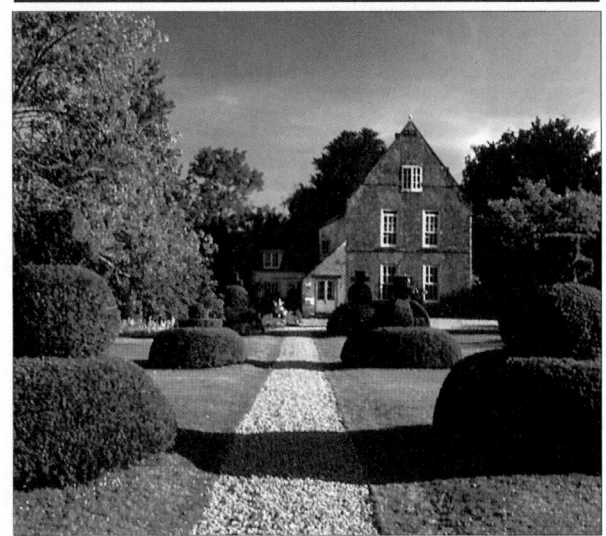

HUNTINGDON, CAMBRIDGESHIRE PE28 9BN

Owner: Mrs D S Boston   *Contact: Diana Boston*

Tel: 01480 463134 **Fax:** 01480 465026

Built about 1130 and made famous as 'Green Knowe' by the author Lucy Boston. Her patchworks are also shown. Four acre garden with topiary and old roses.

Location: OS Ref. TL290 706. Off A14, 3m SE of Huntingdon. 12m NW of Cambridge. Access is by a small gate on the riverside footpath.

Opening Times: House: All year (except Aug), by appointment only to individuals or groups. Aug: open access. Guided tours at 10am, 12 noon, 2pm & 4pm. Small house so tour size is limited. Advisable to book to avoid disappointment. Garden: All year, daily, 10am - 6pm (4pm in winter).

Admission: Adult £4, Child £1.50, OAP £3.50. Garden only: Adult £1, Child 50p.

ℹ️ No photography in house. ◻ ✲ ▣ Locally, by arrangement.
🏃 Obligatory. ▦ P Disabled only. 🐕 In garden, on leads. ✱

PECKOVER HOUSE & GARDEN 🌿

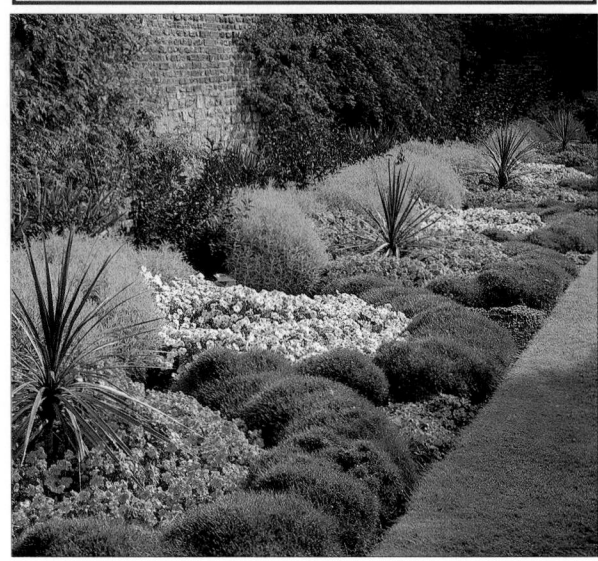

NORTH BRINK, WISBECH, CAMBRIDGESHIRE PE13 1JR

Owner: The National Trust   *Contact: The Property Manager*

Tel/Fax: 01945 583463 **e-mail:** aprigx@smtp.ntrust.org.uk

A town house, built c1722 and renowned for its very fine plaster and wood rococo decoration. The outstanding Victorian garden includes an orangery, summer-houses, roses, herbaceous borders, fernery, croquet lawn and reed barn.

Location: OS Ref. TF458 097. On N bank of River Nene, in Wisbech B1441.

Opening Times: House: 31 Mar - 30 Sept: Weds, Sats, Suns & BH Mons, 12.30 - 5.30pm. 3 Oct - 4 Nov: 12.30 - 4pm. Garden: 31 Mar - 4 Nov: Sat - Thur, 12.30 - 5.30pm. Groups welcome when house open and at other times by appointment.

Admission: Adult £3.80. Garden only: £2.50. Groups: £3.

🍽 ♿ Partially suitable. ▣ 🏃 By arrangement. P Signposted. 🚫
🔔 📻 Tel. for details.

PETERBOROUGH CATHEDRAL   **Tel:** 01733 343342 **Fax:** 01733 552465

Peterborough, Cambridgeshire PE1 1XS   **Contact:** Visitors' Officer

One of the finest Norman buildings in Europe, with a magnificent early English West Front. The 13th century painted Nave ceiling is the largest in the world. Admire the exquisite fan vaulting. You may also visit the tomb of Katharine of Aragon, the first wife of Henry VIII, and see the former burial place of Mary, Queen of Scots. Tourist Information Centre is also in the Cathedral precincts.

Location: OS Ref. TL194 986. 4m E of A1, in City Centre.

Opening Times: All year: daily, 8.30am - 5.15pm. Sats, 8.30am - 5.45pm. Suns, 12 noon - 5.45pm.

Admission: Donations are requested.

ℹ️ Visitors' Centre. ◻ ♿ 🍽 Mon - Sat. 🏃 By arrangement. P No parking. ▦
🐕 Guide dogs only. ✱

RAMSEY ABBEY GATEHOUSE 🌿   **Tel:** 01263 733471 (Regional office)

Abbey School, Ramsey, Cambridgeshire PE17 1DH

Owner: The National Trust   **Contact:** The Curator (in writing)

Remains of a 15th century gatehouse of the Benedictine Abbey.

Location: OS Ref. TL291 851. At SE edge of Ramsey at point where Chatteris road leaves B1096, 10m SE of Peterborough.

Opening Times: 1 Apr - end Oct: daily, 10am - 5pm, other times by written application to curator.

Admission: Donation.

P Limited. 🐕 Guide dogs only.

1/10/02

WIMPOLE HALL & HOME FARM 🌿

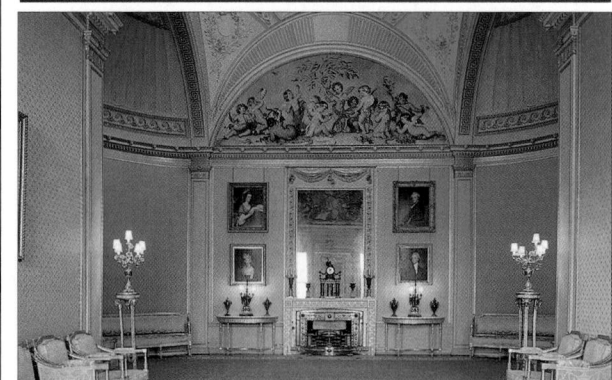

ARRINGTON, ROYSTON, CAMBRIDGESHIRE SG8 0BW

Owner: The National Trust   *Contact: The Property Manager*

Tel: 01223 207257 **Fax:** 01223 207838 **e-mail:** aweusr@smtp.ntrust.org.uk

Wimpole is a magnificent country house built in 18th century style with a colourful history of owners. The Hall is set in recently restored formal gardens including parterres and a rose garden. Home Farm is a working farm and is the largest rare breeds centre in East Anglia.

Location: OS154 Ref. TL336 510. 8m SW of Cambridge (A603), 6m N of Royston (A1198).

Opening Times: Hall: 17 Mar - 30 Jul & 2 Sept - 4 Nov: daily except Mons & Fris open Good Fri & BH Mons. Aug: Tue - Sun & BH Mons; 11, 18 & 25 Nov: Suns only. 1 - 5pm. BH Mons: 11am - 5pm. Closes 4pm after 28 Oct. Garden: As Farm. Park: dawn - dusk (closed 5pm on concert nights). Farm: 17 Mar - 2 Jul, 1 Sept - 4 Nov: daily except Mons & Fris (open Good Fri & BH Mons); Jul & Aug: Tue - Sun (open BH Mons), 10.30am - 5pm. Nov - Mar 2002: Sats & Suns (open Feb half-term week), 11am - 4pm.

Admission: Hall: Adult £5.90, Child £2.70. Joint ticket with Home Farm: Adult £8.50, Child £4.20, Family £21. Garden: £2.50. Group rates (not on Suns or BH Mons). Farm: Adult £4.70, Child (over 3yrs) £2.70. Discounts for NT members (not Suns or BH Mons).

◻ ♿ Partially suitable. ▣ 🍽 Licensed. 🏃 By arrangement.
P Limited. ▦ 🐕 In park only, on leads. 📻 Tel. for details.

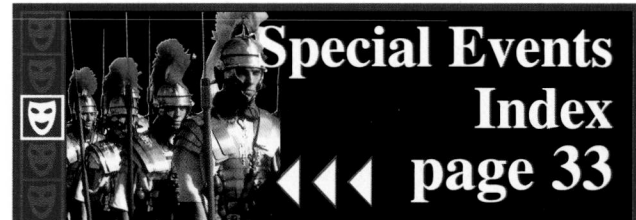

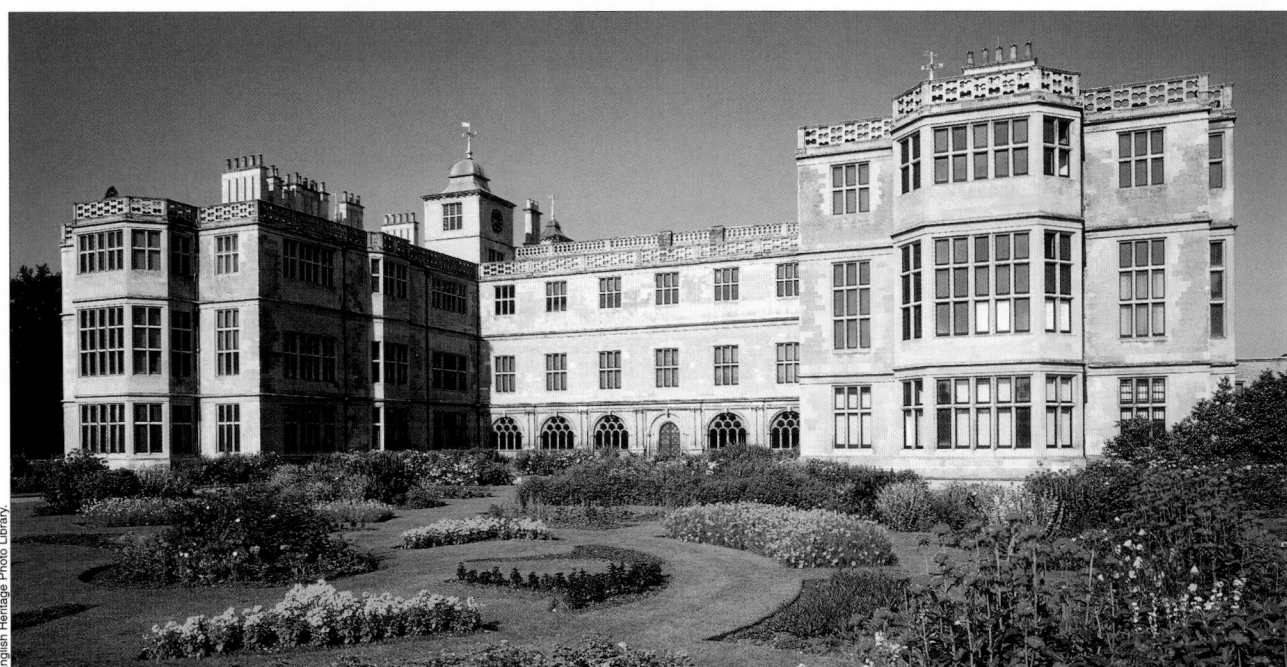

English Heritage Photo Library.

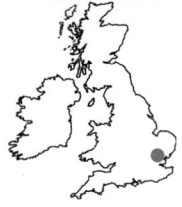

Owner:
English Heritage

CONTACT

The General Manager
Audley End House
Audley End
Saffron Walden
Essex
CB11 4JF

Tel: 01799 522842

Fax: 01799 521276

LOCATION

OS Ref. TL525 382

1m W of Saffron Walden
on B1383,
M11/J8 & 9 northbound
only & J10.

Rail: Audley End 1¼m.

AUDLEY END HOUSE & GDNS
Saffron Walden

AUDLEY END was a palace in all but name. Built by Thomas Howard, Earl of Suffolk, to entertain King James I. The King may have had his suspicions, for he never stayed there; in 1618 Howard was imprisoned and fined for embezzlement.

Charles II bought the property in 1668 for £50,000, but within a generation the house was gradually demolished, and by the 1750s it was about the size you see today. There are still over 30 rooms to see, each with period furnishings.

The house and its gardens, including a 19th century parterre and rose garden, are surrounded by an 18th century landscaped park laid out by 'Capability' Brown.

Visitors can now also visit the working organic walled garden and purchase produce from its shop. Extending to nearly 10 acres the garden includes a 170ft long, five-bay vine house, built in 1802.

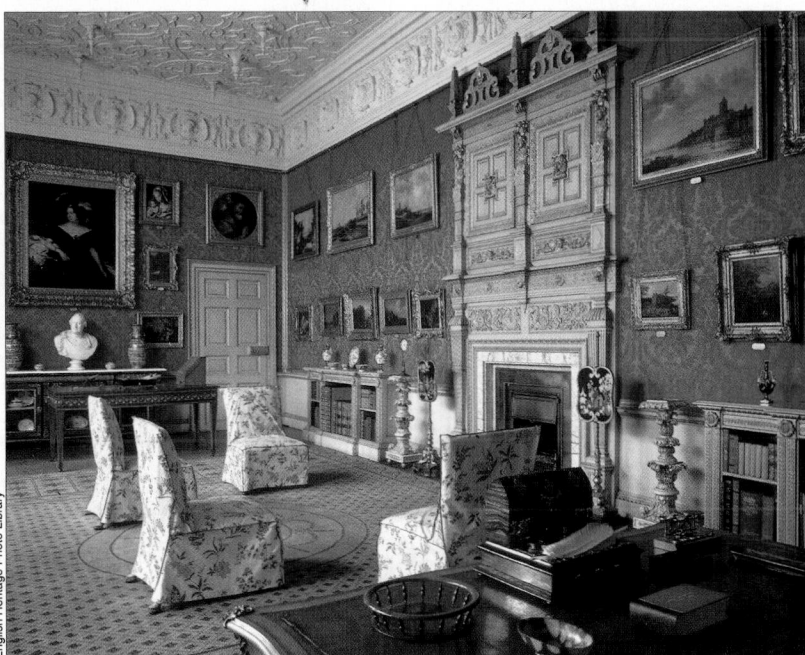

English Heritage Photo Library

🛈 Open air concerts and other events.

♿ Ground floor and grounds suitable.

🍴 Restaurant (max 50).

🚶 By arrangement for groups.

🅿 Coaches to book in advance, £5 per coach. Free entry for coach drivers and tour guides. One additional place for every extra 20 people.

School visits free if booked in advance. Contact the Administrator or tel. 01223 582700 for bookings.

🐕 On leads only.

OPENING TIMES

House
1 April - 30 September
Wed - Sun and BHs
1 - 6pm.
Last admission 5pm.

Grounds
1 April - 30 September
Wed - Sun and BHs
11am - 6pm.
Last admission 5pm.

House & Grounds
1 - 31 October
Wed - Sun
10am - 3pm
(site closes at 4pm).

House by pre-booked guided tour:
1 April - 30 Sept:
Wed - Fri,
10am - 12 noon (extra charge).

ADMISSION

House & Grounds
Adult £6.75
Child (5 - 15yrs) * £3.40
Conc........................£5.10
Family (2+3)...........£16.90

Grounds only
Adult £4.00
Child (5 - 15yrs) * £2.00
Concessions............£3.00
Family (2+3)...........£10.00

* Under 5yrs Free.

Groups (11+)
15% discount.

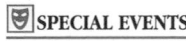 **SPECIAL EVENTS**
Please telephone for details of special events.

AUDLEY END HOUSE & GARDENS
See page 261 for full page entry.

BOURNE MILL
Tel: 01206 572422

Colchester, Essex CO2 8RT

Owner: The National Trust   **Contact:** The Custodian

Originally a fishing lodge built in 1591. It was later converted into a mill with a 4 acre mill pond. Much of the machinery, including the waterwheel, is intact.

Location: OS Ref. TM006 238. 1m S of Colchester centre, in Bourne Road, off the Mersea Road B1025.

Opening Times: BH Suns & Mons only; also Suns & Tues in Jun, Jul & Aug, 2 - 5.30pm.

Admission: Adult £2. No reduction for groups.

Guide dogs only.

CHELMSFORD CATHEDRAL
Tel: 01245 294480

New Street, Chelmsford, Essex CM1 1AT   **Contact:** Mrs Bobby Harrington

15th century building became a Cathedral in 1914. Extended in 1920s, major refurbishment in 1980s with contemporary works of distinction and splendid new organs in 1994 and 1996.

Location: OS Ref. TL708 070. In Chelmsford.

Opening Times: Daily: 8am - 5.30pm. Sun services: 8am, 9.30am, 11.15am and 6pm. Weekday services: 8.15am and 5.15pm. Tours by prior arrangement.

Admission: No charge but donation invited.

COLCHESTER CASTLE MUSEUM
Tel: 01206 282931/2   **Fax:** 01206 282925

14 Ryegate Road, Colchester, Essex CO1 1YG

Owner: Colchester Borough Council   **Contact:** Museum Resource Centre

The largest Norman Castle Keep in Europe with fine archaeological collections on show.

Location: OS Ref. TL999 253. In Colchester town centre, off A12.

Opening Times: All year: Mon - Sat, 10am - 5pm, also Suns, 11am - 5pm.

Admission: Adult £3.80, Child/Conc. £2.50, Saver ticket £10.20. Booked groups (20+) £3.30. Prices will increase from 1 April 2001.

ESSEX SECRET BUNKER
Tel: 01206 392271   **Fax:** 01206 393847
e-mail: info@essexsecretbunker.com

Crown Building, Shrubland Road, Mistley, Manningtree, Essex CO11 1HS

Owner: The Bunker Preservation Trust   **Contact:** The Curator

The huge concrete bunker half above and half below ground, gives a chilling insight into how 'Essex' stood ready for nuclear attack throughout the 40 years of the 'Cold War'. Cinemas, sound effects and historically accurate displays help you to explore the maze of passageways and rooms. Suitable for all the family.

Location: OS Ref.TM120 315. In Mistley near Manningtree on the B1352. Follow brown tourist signs from A120.

Opening Times: 1 Mar - 31 Oct: daily, 10.30am - 5pm (Aug 6pm). 1 Nov - 28 Feb: Sats & Suns, 10.30am - 4.30pm. Closed 20 Dec - 5 Jan.

Admission: Adult £4.95, Child £3.75, OAP £4.45, Student £2.50, Family £15.75. Groups (10-50): Adult £3.95, Child £2.75, OAP £3.45. Special evening tours throughout the year by appointment for groups: (10+) £6. Further discounts for groups of 30+.

Photography & video welcomed. Partially suitable. WC. By arrangement. Guide dogs only.

FEERINGBURY MANOR
Tel: 01376 561946

Coggeshall Road, Feering, Colchester, Essex CO5 9RB

Owner/Contact: Mrs Giles Coode-Adams

Location: OS Ref. TL864 215. 1½ m N of A12 at Feering, by B1024.

Opening Times: From 1st Tuesday in April to last Friday in July, Thurs & Fris only, 8am - 4pm.

Admission: £2 in aid of National Gardens Scheme.

COPPED HALL

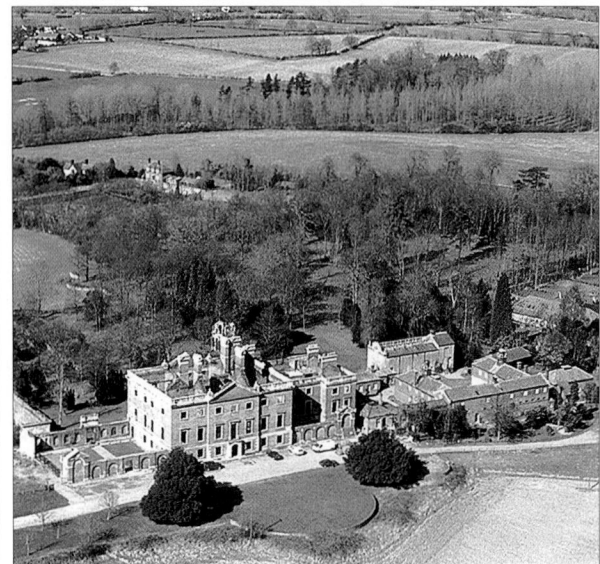

CROWN HILL, EPPING, ESSEX CM16 5HH

Owner: Copped Hall Trust **Contact:** *Alan Cox*

Tel: 020 7267 1679   **Fax:** 020 7482 0557

Burnt-out 18th century Palladian mansion situated on ridge overlooking excellent landscaped park. Built adjacent to site of 16th century mansion where *'A Midsummer's Night Dream'* was first performed. Former elaborate gardens gradually being rescued from abandonment. Victorian ancillary building including stables and small racquets court. Very large early 18th century walled garden.

Location: OS Ref. TL433 016. 4m SW of Epping, N of M25.

Opening Times: By appointment only.

Admission: Pre-arranged groups (20+) only: Adult £3, Child £1.

Partially suitable. Obligatory. In grounds on leads.

GARDENS OF EASTON LODGE

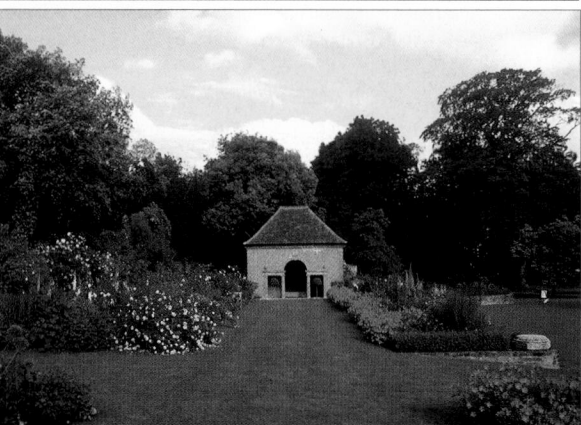

WARWICK HOUSE, EASTON LODGE, LITTLE EASTON, GT DUNMOW CM6 2BB

Owner/Contact: Mr Brian Creasey

Tel/Fax: 01371 876979   **e-mail:** enquiries@eastonlodge.co.uk

Beautiful gardens set in 25 acres. Horticultural associations from the 16th century to date. Visit the Italian gardens, currently undergoing restoration, designed by Harold Peto for 'Daisy' Countess of Warwick (Edward VII's mistress). In the dovecote, study the history of the house, garden and owners over 400 years. A peaceful and atmospheric haven! Millennium Project: Living yew and box sundial and Shakespeare border.

Location: OS Ref. TL593 240. 4m NW of Great Dunmow, off the B184 Dunmow to Thaxted road.

Opening Times: Feb/Mar (snowdrops): daily. Easter - 31 Oct: Fri - Sun & BHs, 12 noon - 6pm or dusk if earlier. Groups at other times by appointment.

Admission: Adult £3.80, Child (3-12yrs) £1.50, Conc. £3.50. Group (20+): £3.50. Schools (20+) £1.50 per child, 1 teacher free per 10 children.

Exhibition & Study Centre in Dovecote. Partially suitable. WC. Picnics. By arrangement. Limited for coaches. In grounds on leads.

GRANGE BARN, COGGESHALL

Tel: 01376 562226

Coggeshall, Colchester, Essex CO6 1RE

Owner: The National Trust   **Contact:** The Custodian

The oldest surviving timber framed barn in Europe, dating from around 1140, and originally part of a Cistercian Monastery. It was restored in the 1980s by the Coggeshall Grange Barn Trust, Braintree District Council and Essex County Council. Features a small collection of farm carts and wagons.

Location: OS Ref. TL848 223. Signposted off A120 Coggeshall bypass. West side of the road southwards to Kelvedon.

Opening Times: 1 Apr - 14 Oct: Tues, Thurs, Suns & BH Mons, 2 - 5pm.

Admission: £1.60. Joint ticket with Paycocke's £3.

Coaches must book. Guide dogs only.

HARWICH MARITIME & LIFEBOAT MUSEUMS

Tel: 01255 503429

Harwich Green, Harwich, Essex

Owner: The Harwich Society   **Contact:** Mr Sheard

One housed in a disused lighthouse and the other in the nearby disused Victorian Lifeboat House, complete with full size lifeboat.

Location: OS Ref. TM262 822. On Harwich Green.

Opening Times: 1 May - 31 Aug: daily, 10am - 1pm & 2 - 5pm. Groups by appointment at any time.

Admission: Adult 50p, Child Free (no unaccompanied children).

HARWICH REDOUBT FORT

Tel: 01255 503429

Main Road, Harwich, Essex

Owner: The Harwich Society   **Contact:** Mr Sheard

180ft diameter circular fort built in 1808 to defend the port against Napoleonic invasion. Being restored by Harwich Society and part is a museum. Eleven guns on battlements.

Location: OS Ref. TM262 322. Rear of 29 Main Road.

Opening Times: 1 May - 31 Aug: daily, 10am - 5pm. Sept - Apr: Suns only. Groups by appointment at any time.

Admission: Adult £1, Child Free (no unaccompanied children).

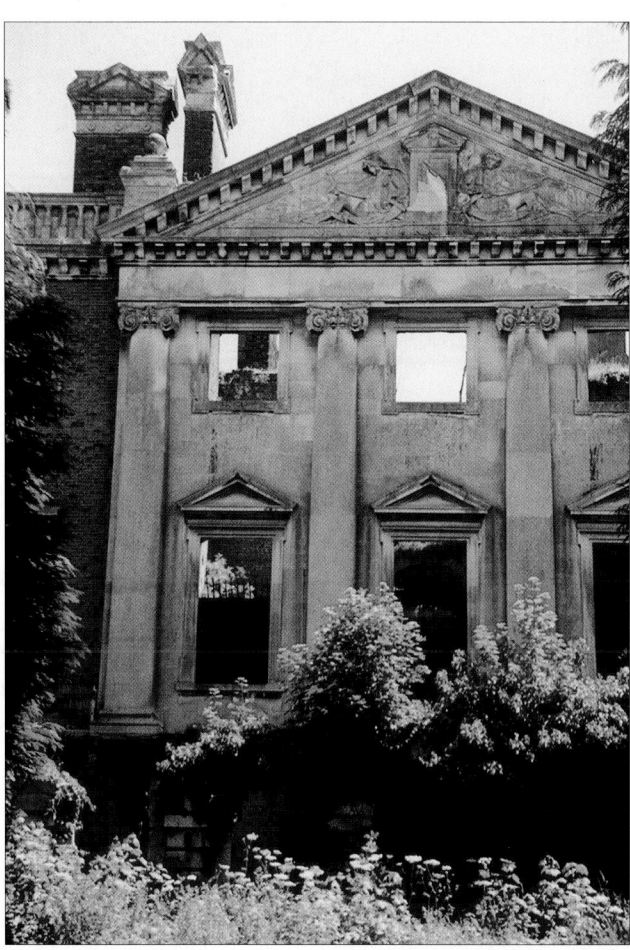

Copped Hall, Essex.

HEDINGHAM CASTLE

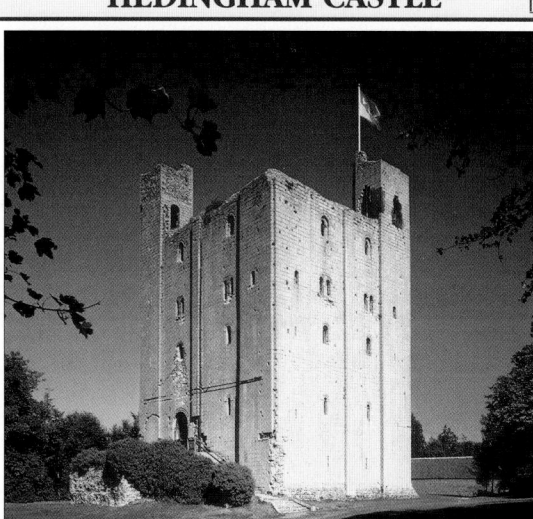

CASTLE HEDINGHAM, Nr HALSTEAD, ESSEX CO9 3DJ

Owner: The Hon Thomas Lindsay   Contact: Mrs Diana Donoghue

Tel: 01787 460261 **Fax:** 01787 461473 **e-mail:** hedinghamcastle@aspects.net

Splendid Norman keep built in 1140 by the famous de Veres, Earls of Oxford. Visited by Kings Henry VII and VIII and Queen Elizabeth I and besieged by King John. Magnificent banqueting hall with minstrel's gallery and finest Norman arch in England. Beautiful grounds, peaceful woodland and lakeside walks. Beside medieval village with fine Norman church.

Location: OS Ref. TL787 358. On B1058, 1m off A1017 between Cambridge and Colchester.

Opening Times: Week before Easter - 31 Oct: daily, 10am - 5pm.

Admission: Adult £4, Child £3, Conc. £3.50. Groups (20+): £3.50.

Partially suitable. By arrangement. In grounds, on leads. Tel. for details.

HYLANDS HOUSE

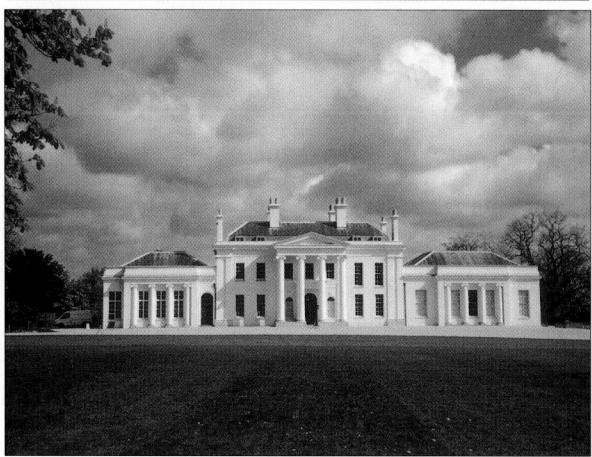

HYLANDS PARK, LONDON ROAD, CHELMSFORD CM2 8WQ

Owner: Chelmsford Borough Council   Contact: Ceri Lowen

Tel: 01245 606812 **Fax:** 01245 606970

This beautiful villa, with its neo-classical exterior is surrounded by over 500 acres of parkland, including formal gardens. The house re-opened at Easter 1999 after a period of restoration work. The Library, Drawing Room and Saloon have been restored to their appearance in the early Victorian period. The Entrance Hall was restored to its Georgian origins in the 1995 restoration. It is possible to view the Banqueting Room and Victorian staircase, as yet unrestored. There is an exhibition detailing the restoration work and the history of the house.

Location: OS Ref. TL681 054. 2m SW of Chelmsford. Signposted on A1016 near Chelmsford.

Opening Times: All year: Suns, Mons & BHs, 11am - 6pm, except Christmas Day.

Admission: Adults £3, Child (12-16 yrs) £2, (under 12yrs) Free, Conc. £2. Groups: £3pp or £75 (whichever greater).

No photography in house. Sun only. By arrangement. Limited for coaches. In grounds. Guide dogs only in house. Please tel. for details.

INGATESTONE HALL

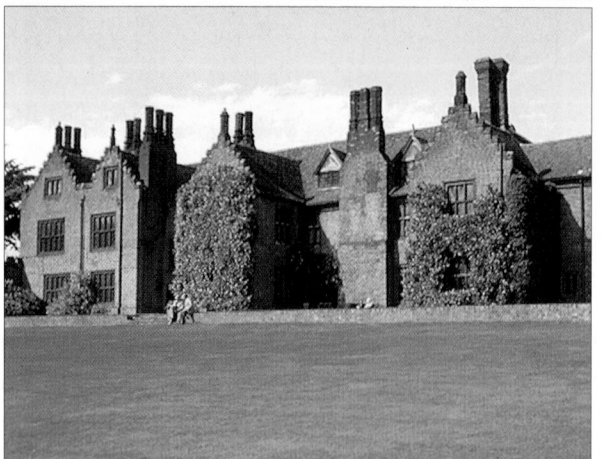

HALL LANE, INGATESTONE, ESSEX CM4 9NR

Owner: The Lord Petre   *Contact:* The Administrator

Tel: 01277 353010 **Fax:** 01245 248979

16th century mansion, set in 11 acres of grounds (formal garden and wild walk), built by Sir William Petre, Secretary of State to four Tudor monarchs, which has remained in the hands of his family ever since. The two Priests' hiding places can be seen, as well as the furniture, portraits and family memorabilia accumulated over the centuries.

Location: OS Ref. TQ653 986. Off A12 between Brentwood & Chelmsford. Take Station Lane at London end of Ingatestone High Street, cross level-crossing and continue for 1/2 m to SE.

Opening Times: 14 Apr - 30 Sept: Sats, Suns & BH Mons, plus 11 Jul - 7 Sept: Wed - Fri, 1 - 6pm.

Admission: Adult £3.50, Conc. £3, Child £2, Under 5yrs Free. 50p per head discount for groups (20+). Family Ticket (admits 5, up to 3 adults) £10.50.

ⓘ No photography in house. Ⓣ Ⓒ Ⓖ Grounds suitable. WC. Ⓦ By arrangement. Ⓟ Ⓜ Guide dogs only.

LAYER MARNEY TOWER

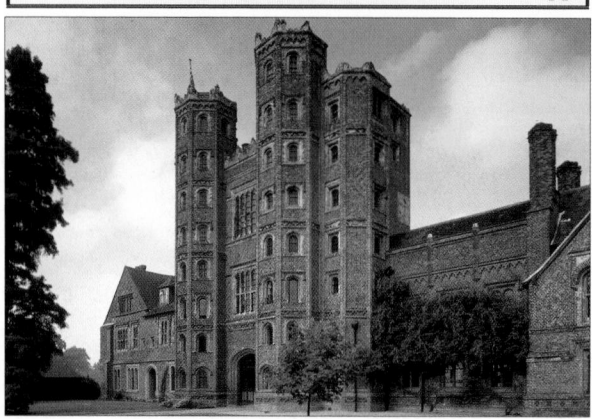

Nr COLCHESTER, ESSEX CO5 9US

Owner/Contact: Mr Nicholas Charrington

Tel/Fax: 01206 330784

Built in the reign of Henry VIII, the tallest Tudor gatehouse in Great Britain. Lord Henry Marney clearly intended to rival Wolsey's building at Hampton Court, but he died before his masterpiece was finished. His son John died two years later, in 1525, and building work stopped. Layer Marney Tower has some of the finest terracotta work in the country, most probably executed by Flemish craftsmen trained by Italian masters. The terracotta is used on the battlements, windows, and most lavishly of all, on the tombs of Henry and John Marney. Visitors may climb the Tower, passing through the History Room, and enjoy the marvellous views of the Essex countryside. There are fine outbuildings, including the Long Gallery with its magnificent oak roof and the medieval barn which now houses some of the Home Farm's collection of Rare Breed farm animals. Function room available for receptions, etc.

Location: OS Ref. TL929 175. 5m SW of Colchester, signed off B1022.

Opening Times: 1 Apr - 7 Oct: Sun - Fri, 12 noon - 5pm. Group visits and guided tours throughout the year by arrangement.

Admission: Adult £3.50, Child £2, Family £10. Groups (15+): Adult £3.25, Child £1.75. Guided tours (pre-booked) £4.75, min. charge £120. Schools by arrangement.

Ⓒ Ⓣ Ⓣ Ⓖ Partially suitable. WC. Ⓦ Ⓟ Ⓜ Ⓚ By arrangement. Ⓜ
Ⓜ In grounds, on leads. Ⓑ 1 dble, 2 single. Ⓐ ❄ Ⓦ Tel. for details. Ⓦ

LOWER DAIRY HOUSE GARDEN   **Tel:** 01206 262220

Water Lane, Nayland, Colchester, Essex CO6 4JS

Owner/Contact: Mr & Mrs D J Burnett

Plantsman's garden, approx 1 1/2 acres.

Location: OS Ref. TL966 330. 7m N of Colchester off A134. 1m SW of Nayland on E side of road to Little Horkesley.

Opening Times: Contact property for details. Groups by appointment only.

Admission: £2.

MISTLEY TOWERS ⧓   **Tel:** 01206 393884

Colchester, Essex

Owner: English Heritage   **Contact:** The Keykeeper (Mistley Quay Workshops)

The remains of one of only two churches designed by the great architect Robert Adam. Built in 1776. It was unusual in having towers at both the east and west ends.

Location: OS Ref. TM116 320. On B1352, 1 1/2 m E of A137 at Lawford, 9m E of Colchester.

Opening Times: Telephone for opening times.

Admission: Key available from Mistley Quay workshops - 01206 393884.

SIR ALFRED MUNNINGS ART MUSEUM

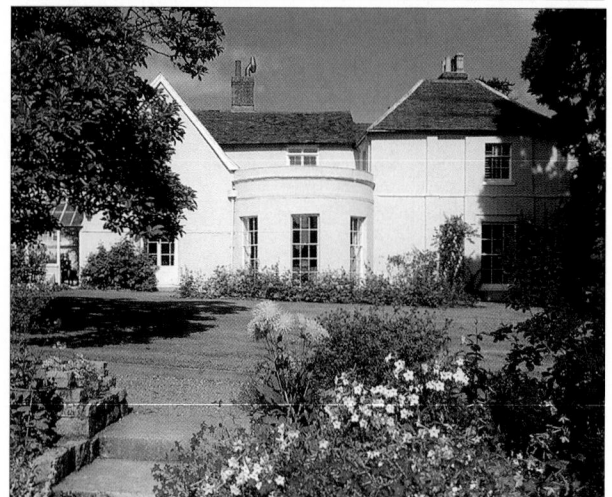

CASTLE HOUSE, DEDHAM, ESSEX CO7 6AZ

Owner: Castle House Trust   *Contact:* Mrs C Woodage

Tel/Fax: 01206 322127

The home, studios and grounds where Sir Alfred Munnings, KCVO, 1878 – 1959 (PRA 1944 – 1949) lived and painted for 40 years. Castle House, part Tudor part Georgian, restored and with original Munnings' furniture, exhibits over 200 Munnings' works representing his life's work, is augmented by private loans each season. Annual Special Exhibition.

Location: OS Ref. TM060 328. 3/4 m from Dedham centre. 8m from Colchester, 12m from Ipswich.

Opening Times: Easter Sun - first Sun in Oct: Weds, Suns & BH Mons, 2 - 5pm. Additionally Thurs & Sats in Aug, 2 - 5pm.

Admission: Adult £3, Child 50p, Conc. £2. Groups (25+): min. price £75, larger groups per admission prices.

ⓘ No photography in house. Ⓒ Ⓖ Partially suitable.
Ⓟ Ample for cars. Limited for coaches. Ⓜ In grounds, on leads.

PAYCOCKE'S ❀   **Tel:** 01376 561305

West Street, Coggeshall, Colchester, Essex CO6 1NS

Owner: The National Trust   **Contact:** The Tenant

A merchant's house, dating from about 1500, with unusually rich panelling and wood carving. A display of lace, for which Coggeshall was famous, is on show. Delightful cottage garden leading down to small river.

Location: OS Ref. TL848 225. Signposted off A120.

Opening Times: 1 Apr - 14 Oct: Tues, Thurs, Suns & BH Mons, 2 - 5.30pm, last adm: 5pm.

Admission: £2.20, groups (10+) by prior arrangement, no reduction for groups. Joint ticket with Coggeshall Grange Barn £3.

Ⓖ Access to ground floor and garden. Ⓟ NT's at the Coggeshall Grange Barn.

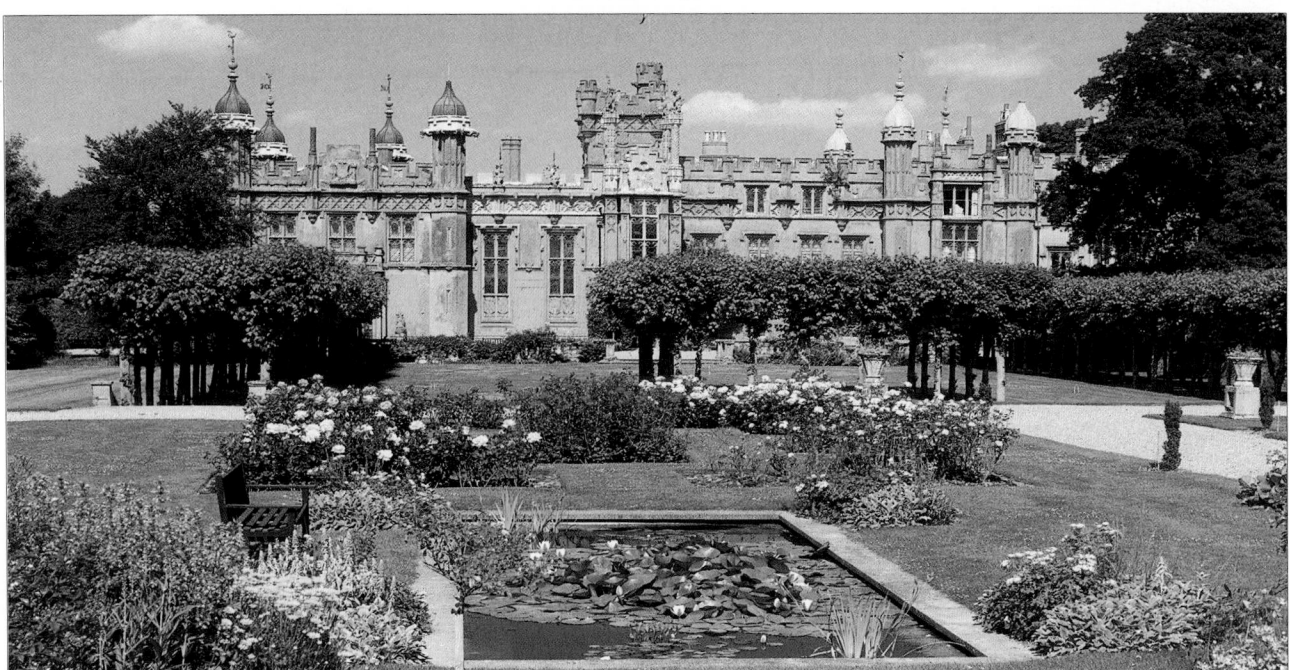

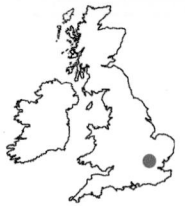

Owner: The Hon Henry
Lytton Cobbold

CONTACT

The Estate Office
Knebworth House
Knebworth
Hertfordshire
SG3 6PY

Tel: 01438 812661

Fax: 01438 811908

e-mail: info@
knebworthhouse.com

LOCATION

OS Ref. TL230 208

Direct access off the A1(M)
J7 (Stevenage South A602).
28m N of London. 15m N
of M25 J23.

Rail: Stevenage Station 2m
(from Kings Cross).

Air: Luton Airport 15m
Landing facilities.

Taxi: 01438 811122.

CONFERENCE/FUNCTION		
ROOM	SIZE	MAX CAPACITY
Banqueting Hall	26 'x 41'	80
Dining Parlour	21' x 38'	50
Library	32' x 21'	40
Manor Barn	70' x 25'	250
Lodge Barn	75' x 30'	150

KNEBWORTH
Nr Stevenage

Home of the Lytton family since 1490, and still a lived-in family house. Transformed in early Victorian times by Edward Bulwer-Lytton, the author, poet, dramatist and statesman, into the unique high gothic fantasy house of today, complete with turrets, griffins and gargoyles.

Historically home to Constance Lytton, the Suffragette, and her father, Robert Lytton, the Viceroy of India who proclaimed Queen Victoria Empress of India at the Great Delhi Durbar of 1877. Visited by Queen Elizabeth I, Charles Dickens and Sir Winston Churchill.

The interior contains various styles including the magnificent Jacobean Banqueting Hall, a unique example of the 17th century change in fashion from traditional English to Italian

Palladian. The high gothic State Drawing Room by John Crace contrasts with the Regency elegance of Mrs Bulwer-Lytton's bedroom and the 20th century designs of Sir Edwin Lutyens in the Entrance Hall, Dining Parlour and Library.

25 acres of beautiful gardens, simplified by Lutyens, including pollarded lime avenues, formal rose garden, maze and Gertrude Jekyll herb garden. 250 acres of gracious parkland, with herds of red and sika deer, includes children's giant adventure playground and miniature railway. World famous for its huge open-air rock concerts, and used as a film location for *Batman*, *The Shooting Party*, *Wilde*, *Jane Eyre* and *The Canterville Ghost*, amongst others.

The Jacobean Banqueting Hall.

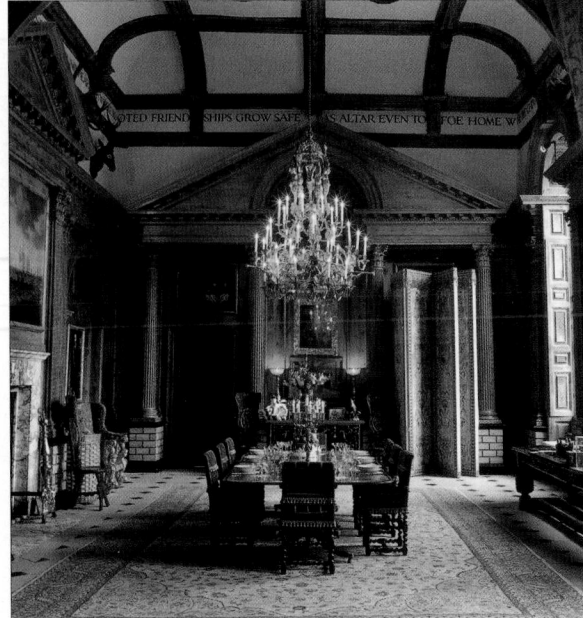

Suitable for fashion shows, air displays, archery, shooting, equestrian events, cricket pitch, garden parties, shows, rallies, filming, helicopter landing. No pushchairs, photography, smoking or drinking in House.

Indian Raj Evenings and Elizabethan Banquets with jousting. Full catering service.

Visitors may alight at entrance. Ground floor accessible to wheelchairs.

Licensed tearoom. Special rates for advance bookings, menus on request.

Unlimited parking. Group visits must be booked in advance with Estate Office.

Daily at 30 min intervals or at booked times including evenings. Tour time 1hr. Shorter tours by arrangement. Room Wardens on duty on busy weekends. 'Gothick Visions' tour.

National Curriculum based worksheets & children's guide.

Guide dogs only in House. In Park, on leads.

OPENING TIMES

**Park, Gardens,
Fort Knebworth
Adventure Playground
& Miniature Railway**
7 - 22 Apr; 26 May - 3 Jun;
7 Jul - 4 Sept: daily.

28 Apr - 20 May; 9 Jun -
1 Jul; 8 - 30 Sept:
weekends & BHs.

**Park, Gardens,
Playground & Railway**
11am - 5.30pm.

House & Exhibition:
12 noon - 5pm (last adm.
4.30pm)

Closed at other times, but
pre-booked groups (20+)
welcome all year (subject to
special events).

ADMISSION

**House, Gardens,
Park, Playground
& Railway**

Adult £7.00
Child*/OAP £6.50
Family (2+2) £23.50
Groups (20+)
Adult £6.00
Child*/OAP £5.50
(subject to special events)

**Gardens, Park,
Playground & Railway**

All persons..............£5.50
Family (2+2) £19.00
Groups (20+)
All persons..............£4.75
(subject to special events)

* Age 4 - 16yrs. Under 4s Free.
Season Tickets available.

ASHRIDGE

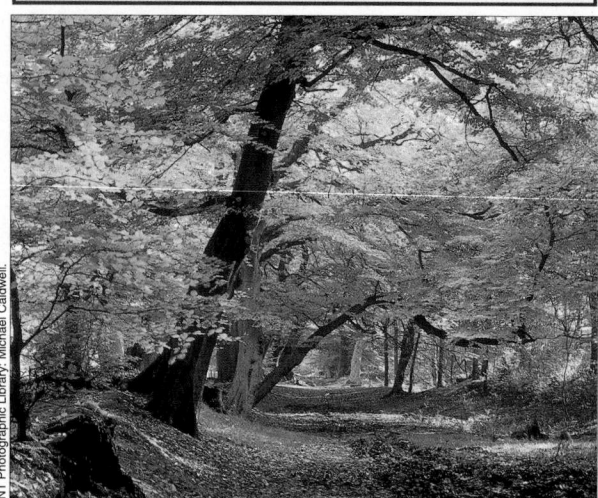

NT Photographic Library: Michael Caldwell.

RINGSHALL, BERKHAMSTED, HERTFORDSHIRE HP4 1LT

Owner: The National Trust   Contact: The Property Manager

Tel: 01442 851227 **Fax:** 01442 842062 **e-mail:** tasgsc@smtp.ntrust.org.uk

The Ashridge Estate comprises over 1800ha of woodlands, commons and downland. At the northerly end of the Estate the Ivinghoe Hills are an outstanding area of chalk downland which supports a rich variety of plants and insects. The Ivinghoe Beacon itself offers splendid views. This area may be reached from a car park at Steps Hill. The rest of Ashridge is an almost level plateau with many fine walks through woods and open commons.

Location: OS Ref. SP970 131. Between Northchurch & Ringshall, just off B4506.

Opening Times: Visitor Centre, Shop & Tearoom: Apr - Oct: daily except Fris (open Good Fri). Mon - Thur, 2 - 5pm, Sats, Suns, BHs, 12 noon - 5pm. Monument: Sats & Suns, 12 noon - 5pm, Mon - Thur, by arrangement. Please telephone for details on winter openings.

Admission: Monument: £1, Child 50p.

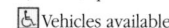 Visitor Centre.   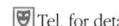 Vehicles available. 🛍 ❄ ⛨ Tel. for details.

BERKHAMSTED CASTLE ⛫

Tel: 01442 871737

Berkhamsted, St Albans, Hertfordshire

Owner: English Heritage   **Contact:** Mr Stevens - The Key Keeper

The extensive remains of a large 11th century motte and bailey castle which held a strategic position on the road to London.

Location: OS165 Ref. SP996 083. Adjacent to Berkhamsted rail station.

Opening Times: All year: daily, 10am - 4pm.

Admission: Free.

CATHEDRAL & ABBEY CHURCH OF ST ALBAN

St Albans, Hertfordshire AL1 1BY   **Tel:** 01727 860780 **Fax:** 01727 850944

e-mail: mail@stalbanscathedral.org.uk   **Contact:** Deputy Administrator

Abbey church of Benedictine Monastery founded 793AD commemorating Britain's first martyr.

Location: OS Ref. TL145 071. Centre of St Albans.

Opening Times: All year: 9am - 5.45pm. Tel for details of services, concerts and special events Mon - Sat, 11am - 4pm.

Admission: Free of charge. (AV show, Adult £1.50, Child £1).

CROMER WINDMILL

Tel: 01279 843301

Ardeley, Stevenage, Hertfordshire SG2 7QA

Owner: Hertfordshire Building Preservation Trust   **Contact:** Cristina Harrison

17th century Post Windmill restored to working order.

Location: OS165, Ref. TL305 286. 4m NE of Stevenage on B1037. 1m SW of Cottered.

Opening Times: Mid-May - mid-Sept: Sun, 2nd & 4th Sat & BHs, 2.30 - 5pm.

Admission: Adult £1.50, Child 25p. Groups by arrangement.

FORGE MUSEUM & VICTORIAN COTTAGE GARDEN Tel/Fax: 01279 843301

High Street, Much Hadham, Hertfordshire SG10 6BS

Owner: The Hertfordshire Building Preservation Trust   **Contact:** The Curator

The garden reflects plants that would have been grown in 19th century, also houses an unusual 19th century bee shelter.

Location: OS Ref. TL428 195. Village centre.

Opening Times: Fri, Sat, Sun & BHs, 11am - 5pm (dusk in winter).

Admission: Adult £1, Child/Conc. 50p.

BENINGTON LORDSHIP GARDENS 🏛

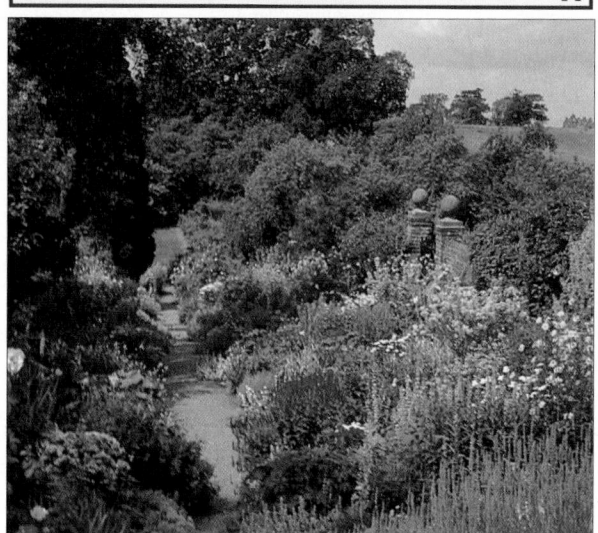

STEVENAGE, HERTFORDSHIRE SG2 7BS

Owner: Mr C H A Bott   Contact: Mr or Mrs C H A Bott

Tel: 01438 869668 **Fax:** 01438 869622 **e-mail:** rhbott@beningtonlordship.co.uk

A hilltop garden which appeals to everyone with its intimate atmosphere, ruins, Queen Anne Manor, herbaceous borders, old roses, lakes, vegetable garden, nursery and verandah teas. For films, fashion shoots etc. the gardens and estate offer excellent facilities. Mediaeval barns, cottages and other unique countryside features.

Location: OS Ref. TL296 236. In village of Benington next to the church. 4m E of Stevenage.

Opening times: Gardens only: Apr - Aug, Wed & BH Mons, 12 noon - 5pm, Sun 2 - 5pm. Sept: Weds only. Groups any time by arrangement.

Admission: Adult £3, Child Free.

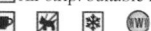 Air-strip. Suitable for filming & fashion shoots. ♿ Unsuitable.

🍴 ❀ ❄ 🅦

THE GARDENS OF THE ROSE

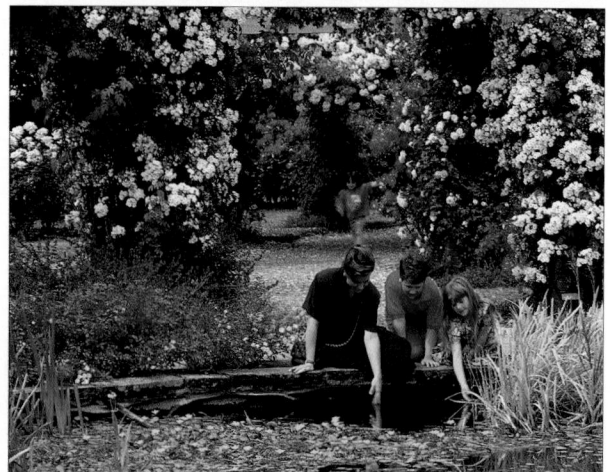

CHISWELL GREEN, ST ALBANS, HERTFORDSHIRE AL2 3NR

Owner: The Royal National Rose Society   Contact: Lt Col K J Grapes

Tel: 01727 850461 **Fax:** 01727 850360 **e-mail:** mail@rnrs.org.uk

The Royal National Rose Society Gardens provide a wonderful display of one of the best and most important collections of roses in the world. There are some 30,000 roses in 1800 different varieties. The Society has introduced many companion plants which harmonise well with roses including over 100 varieties of clematis. The garden, named for the Society's Patron Her Majesty The Queen Mother, contains a fascinating collection of old garden roses. Various cultivation trials show just how easy roses are to grow and new varieties can be seen in the International Trial Ground. There are excellent facilities for films and fashion photography.

Location: OS Ref. TL124 045. 2m S of St Albans, M1/J6, M25/J21A. 1/2 m W of B4630.

Opening times: 2 Jun - 30 Sept: Mon - Sat, 9am - 5pm, Sun & Aug BHs: 10am - 6pm.

Admission: Adult £4, Child (5-15) £1.50, OAP £3.50. Pre-arranged groups (min 20, max 100): Adult £3.50.

   ♿ 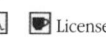 Licensed. 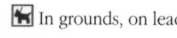 In grounds, on leads.

GORHAMBURY

Tel: 01727 854051 **Fax:** 01727 843675

St Albans, Hertfordshire AL3 6AH

Owner: The Earl Of Verulam **Contact:** The Administrator

Late 18th century house by Sir Robert Taylor. Family portraits from 15th - 20th centuries.

Location: OS Ref. TL114 078. 2m W of St Albans. Accessible via private drive from A4147 at St Albans.

Opening Times: May - Sept: Thur, 2 - 5pm.

Admission: House & Gardens: Adult £6, Child £3, OAP £4. Guided tour only. Groups by arrangement: Thursdays £5, other days £6.

HATFIELD HOUSE

See page 266 for full page entry.

HERTFORD MUSEUM

Tel: 01992 582686 **Fax:** 01992 534797

18 Bull Plain, Hertford

Owner: Hertford Museums Trust **Contact:** Andrea George

Local museum in 17th century house, altered by 18th century façade, with recreated Jacobean knot garden.

Location: OS Ref. TL326 126. Town centre.

Opening Times: Tue - Sat, 10am - 5pm.

Admission: Free.

HITCHIN BRITISH SCHOOLS

Tel/Fax: 01462 420144

e-mail: brsch@britishschools.freeserve.co.uk

41 - 42 Queen Street, Hitchin, Hertfordshire SG4 9TS

Owner: Hitchin British Schools Trust **Contact:** Mrs Judy Lee

Unique complex of school buildings dating from 1837 to 1905. Incorporates 1837 Lancasterian Schoolroom, believed to be the only surviving example, a now rare 1853 galleried classroom (both Grade II*), Girls and Infants School from 1857 as well as two Edwardian classrooms. Related displays and small museum.

Location: OS Ref. TL186 289. Hitchin town centre.

Opening Times: Feb - Nov: Tue, 10am - 4pm. Apr - Oct: Sun, 2.30 - 5pm. Feb - Nov: School visits, Wed & Thur, 9.45am - 12.45pm.

Admission: Adult £2, Child £1. Education programme with teaching session £2.75 plus VAT per child.

  Partially suitable. WC. 📷 🕴Obligatory. 🅿 🚋 🐕 Guide dogs only. ❄

KNEBWORTH

See page 267 for full page entry.

OLD GORHAMBURY HOUSE

Tel: 01223 582700 (Regional Office)

St Albans, Hertfordshire

Owner: English Heritage **Contact:** The East of England Regional Office

The remains of this Elizabethan mansion, particularly the porch of the Great Hall, illustrate the impact of the Renaissance on English architecture.

Location: OS166, Ref. TL110 077. 1/4 m W of Gorhambury House and accessible only through private drive from A4147 at St Albans (2m). Call 01727 843675 for more information.

Opening Times: Any reasonable time.

Admission: Free.

ST PAULS WALDEN BURY

Tel/Fax: 01438 871218/871229

Hitchin, Hertfordshire SG4 8BP

Owner: S Bowes Lyon **Contact:** S or C Bowes Lyon

A formal landscape garden, laid out in 1730, covering 40 acres. The childhood home of Queen Elizabeth, The Queen Mother.

Location: OS Ref. TL186 216. 5m S of Hitchin on B651.

Opening Times: By appointment.

Admission: Adult £2.50, Child 50p. Other times £5. (2000 prices.)

SCOTT'S GROTTO

Tel: 01920 464131

Ware, Hertfordshire

Owner: East Hertfordshire District Council **Contact:** J Watson

One of the finest grottos in England built in the 1760s by Quaker Poet John Scott.

Location: OS Ref. TL355 137. In Scotts Rd, S of the A119 Hertford Road.

Opening Times: 1 Apr - 30 Sept: Sat & BH Mon, 2 - 4.30pm. Also by appointment.

Admission: Suggested donation of £1 for adults. Children Free. Please bring a torch.

THE WALTER ROTHSCHILD ZOOLOGICAL MUSEUM

Tel: 020 7942 6171

Akeman Street, Tring, Hertfordshire HP23 6AP **Fax:** 020 7942 6150

Owner: The Natural History Museum **Contact:** Anne Chapman

The museum was opened to the public by Lord Rothschild in 1892. It houses his private natural history collection. More than 4,000 species of animal in a unique Victorian setting.

Location: OS Ref. SP924 111. S end of Akeman Street, 1/4 m S of High Street.

Opening Times: Mon - Sat, 10am - 5pm, Suns, 2 - 5pm.

Admission: Adult £3.50, Child (0-16yrs) Free, Conc. £2, Over 60s Free, School groups Free.

SHAW'S CORNER

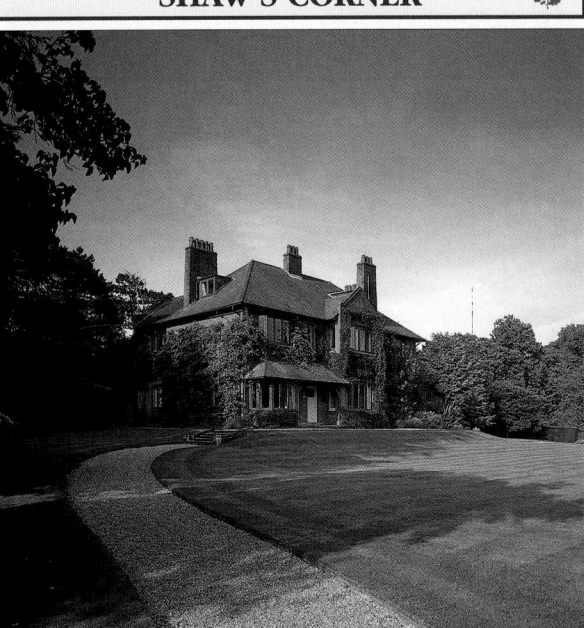

NT Photographic Library/Matthew Antrobus.

AYOT ST LAWRENCE, WELWYN, HERTFORDSHIRE AL6 9BX

Owner: *The National Trust* **Contact:** *The Custodian*

Tel/Fax: 01438 820307 **email:** tscgen@smtp.ntrust.org.uk

The fascinating home of playwright George Bernard Shaw until his death in 1950. The modest Edwardian villa contains many literary and personal relics, and the interior is still set out as it was in Shaw's lifetime. The garden, with its richly planted borders and views over the Hertfordshire countryside, contains the revolving summerhouse where Shaw retreated to write.

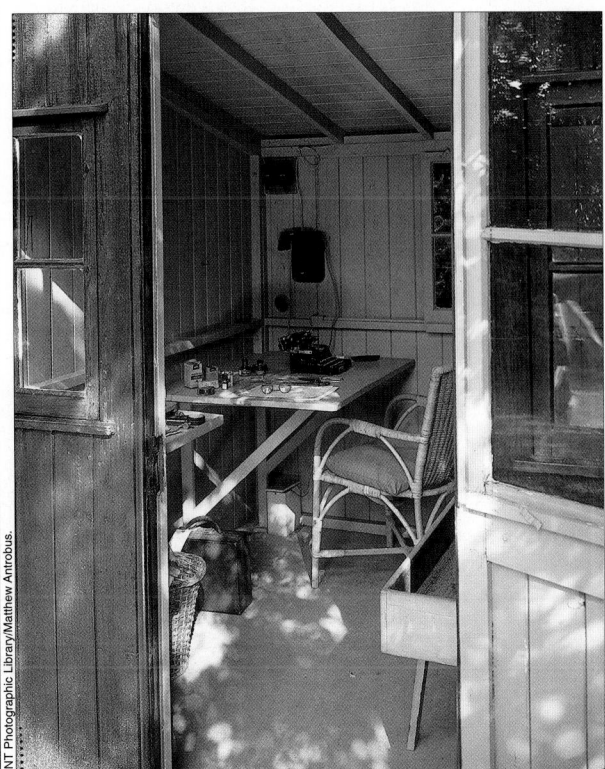

NT Photographic Library/Matthew Antrobus.

Location: OS Ref. TL194 167. At SW end of village, 2m NE of Wheathampstead, approximately 2m N from B653. A1(M)/J4, M1/J10.

Opening times: 31 Mar - 4 Nov: Wed - Sun & BH Mons, 1 - 5pm (closed Good Fri). Parties by written appointment, Mar - Nov. Last admission 4.30pm. On busy days admission by timed ticket. On event days closes at 3.30pm. No large hand luggage inside property.

Admission: Adult £3.50, Family £8.75.

🦽 House & garden but some steps. 🅿 Car park only. 🎫 Tel. for details.

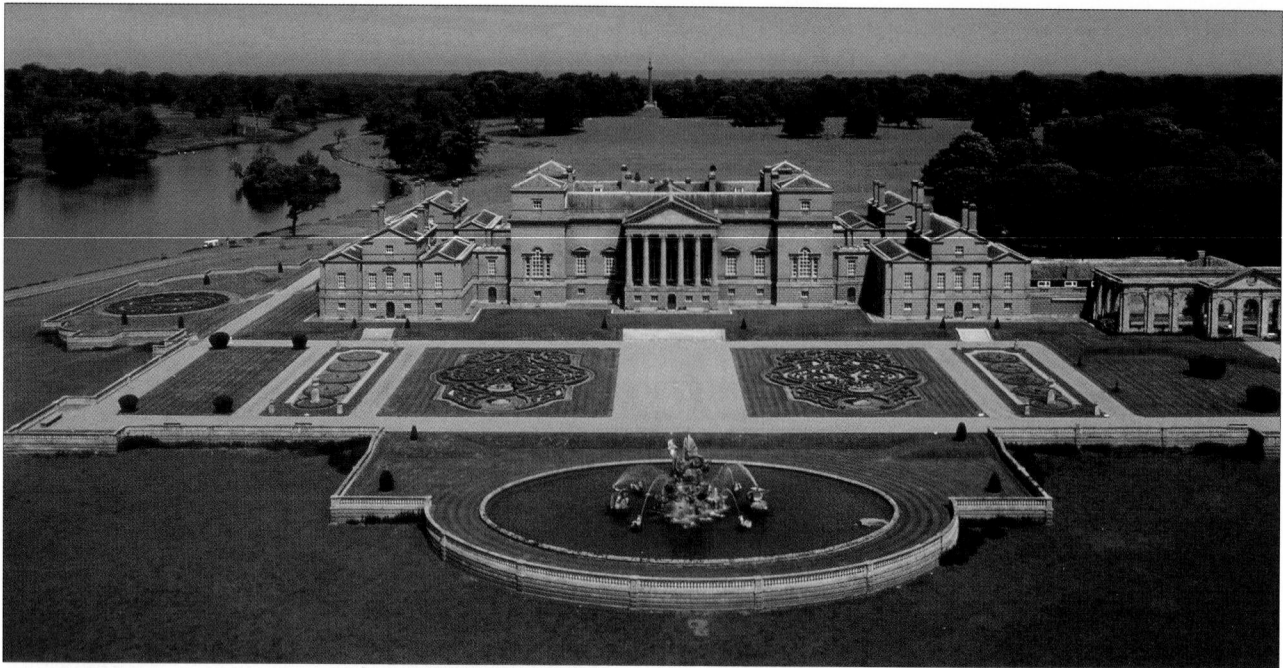

HOLKHAM HALL
Wells-next-the-Sea

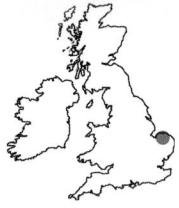

Owner:
The Earl of Leicester

CONTACT

The Administrator
Holkham Hall
Estate Office
Wells-next-the-Sea
Norfolk
NR23 1AB

Tel: 01328 710227

Fax: 01328 711707

e-mail: m.monk@
holkham.co.uk

LOCATION

OS Ref. TF885 428

From London 120m
Norwich 35m
King's Lynn 30m.

Rail: Norwich Station 35m
King's Lynn Station 30m.

Air: Norwich Airport 32m.

HOLKHAM HALL has been the home of the Coke family and the Earls of Leicester for almost 250 years. Built between 1734 and 1764 by Thomas Coke, 1st Earl of Leicester and based on a design by William Kent, this fine example of 18th century Palladian style mansion reflects Thomas Coke's natural appreciation of classical art developed during the Grand Tour. It is constructed mainly of local yellow brick with a magnificent Entrance Hall of English alabaster.

The State Rooms occupy the first floor and contain Greek and Roman statuary, paintings by Rubens, Van Dyck, Claude, Poussin and Gainsborough and original furniture.

On leaving the House visitors pass Holkham Pottery and its adjacent shop, both under the supervision of the Countess of Leicester. Fine examples of local craftsmanship are for sale including the famous Holkham Florist Ware.

Beyond are the 19th century stables now housing the Holkham Bygones Collection; some 4,000 items range from working steam engines, vintage cars and tractors to craft tools and kitchenware. A History of Farming exhibition is in the former Porter's Lodge.

The House is set in a 3,000-acre park with 600 head of fallow deer. On the lake, 1 mile long, are many species of wildfowl. Two walks encircle either the lake or agricultural buildings.

Holkham Nursery Gardens occupy the 18th century walled Kitchen Garden and a large range of stock is on sale to the public.

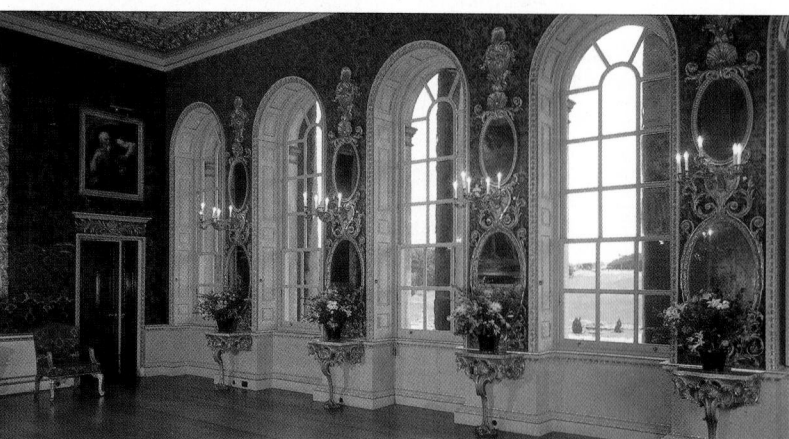

OPENING TIMES

SUMMER
27 May - 30 September
Sun - Thur (inclusive)
1 - 5pm.
Easter, May, Spring &
Summer BHs: Suns & Mons
11.30am - 5pm.
Last admission 4.45pm.
Restaurant, shop and
Holkham Nursery Gardens
from 10am.
21 & 22 July: Hall &
Museum closed for
Holkham Country Fair.

WINTER
October - May
By appointment for groups.

ADMISSION

SUMMER
Hall
　Adult £5.00
　Child (5-15yrs) £2.50
Bygones
　Adult £5.00
　Child (5-15yrs) £2.50
Combined Ticket
　Adult £8.00
　Child (5-15yrs) £4.00
GROUPS (min. 20)
Hall
　Adult £4.50
　Child (5-15yrs) £2.25
Bygones
　Adult £4.50
　Child (5-15yrs) £2.25
Combined Ticket
　Adult £7.20
　Child (5-15yrs) £3.60
Private guided tours by arrangement. Rates on application.

WINTER
By arrangement.
Visitors may walk in the Park without charge every day of the year.

SPECIAL EVENTS

• JUL 21/22
　Holkham Country Fair.

Grounds for shows, rallies and filming. No smoking or flash photography in the Hall.

Visitors may alight at entrance, stairs in Hall. WC.

Menus for pre-booked groups on request.

Guides are posted in each room. Audio tour £2, other times guided tours by arrangement.

Unlimited for cars, 20+ coaches. Parking, admission, refreshments free to coach drivers, coach drivers' rest room.

Welcome. Areas of interest: Bygones Collection, History of Farming, two nature walks, deer park, lake and wildfowl.

No dogs in Hall, on leads in grounds.

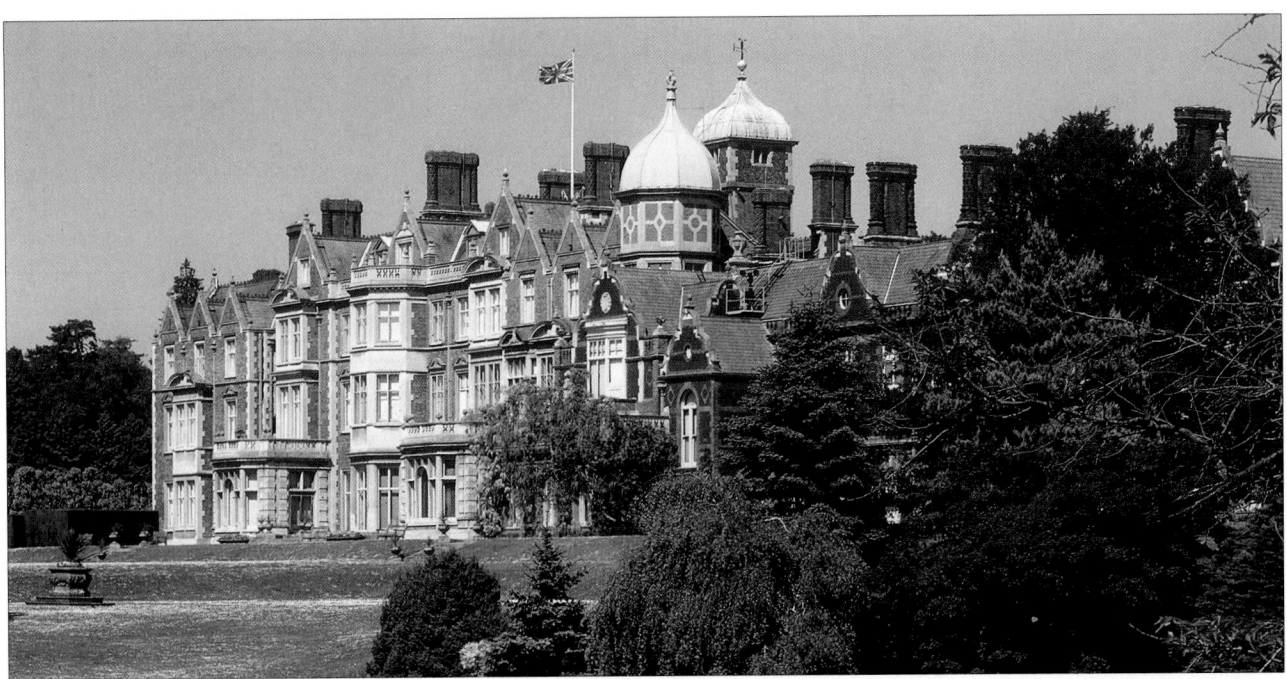

SANDRINGHAM
Norfolk

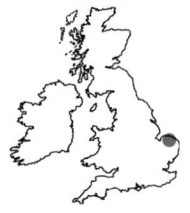

Owner: H M The Queen

CONTACT

Mrs Gill Pattinson
The Estate Office
Sandringham
Norfolk
PE35 6EN

Tel: 01553 772675

Fax: 01485 541571

LOCATION

OS Ref. TF695 287

8m NE of King's Lynn on B1440 off A148.

Rail: King's Lynn.

Air: Norwich.

SANDRINGHAM is the charming country retreat of Her Majesty The Queen, hidden in the heart of 60 acres of beautiful wooded grounds. Still maintained in the style of Edward and Alexandra, Prince and Princess of Wales (later King Edward VII and Queen Alexandra), all the main ground floor rooms used by The Royal Family, full of their treasured ornaments, portraits and furniture, are open to the public. A display of paintings will be on show in the ballroom.

More family possessions are displayed in the Museum housed in the old stable and coach houses including vehicles ranging in date from the first car owned by a British monarch, a 1900 Daimler, to a half-scale Aston Martin used by Princes William and Harry. A new display tells the mysterious tale of the Sandringham Company who fought and died at Gallipolli in 1915, recently made into a TV film 'All the King's Men'.

In the Gardens informal glades, dells, lakes and lawns are surrounded by magnificent trees and bordered by colourful shrubs and flowers. A free Land Train from within the entrance will carry passengers less able to walk through the grounds to the House and back.

OPENING TIMES

House, Museum & Gardens

14 April - 17 July
1 August - 28 October
Daily, 11am - 4.45pm.

ADMISSION

House, Museum and Gardens

Adult	£6.00
Child (5-15yrs)	£3.50
Conc.	£4.50

Groups (20+)
10% discount for payment one month in advance.

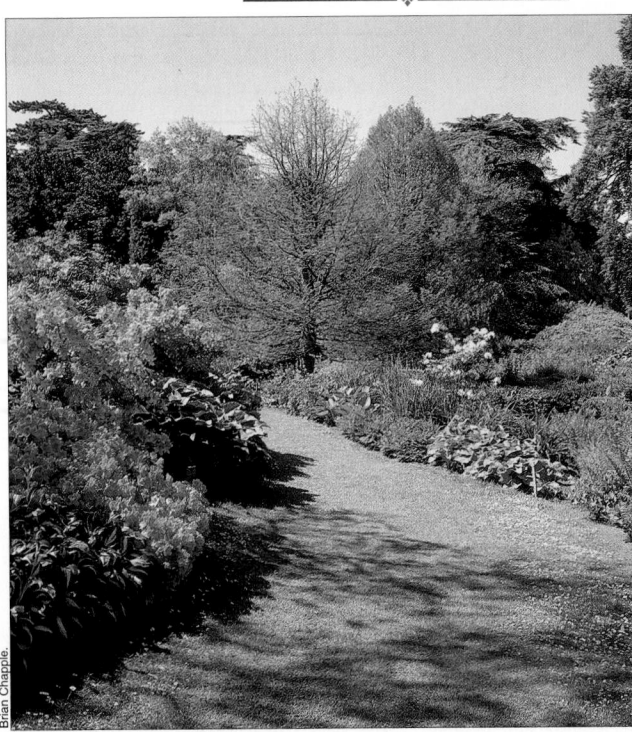

Brian Chapple.

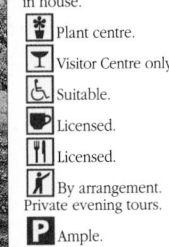

No photography in house.

Plant centre.

Visitor Centre only.

Suitable.

Licensed.

Licensed.

By arrangement. Private evening tours.

Ample.

Guide dogs only.

CONFERENCE/FUNCTION		
ROOM	SIZE	MAX CAPACITY
Restaurant		200
Tearoom		60

BERNEY ARMS WINDMILL ⬜

Tel: 01493 700605

c/o 8 Manor Road, Southtown, Gt Yarmouth NR31 0QA

Owner: English Heritage   **Contact:** The Custodian

A wonderfully situated marsh mill, one of the best and largest remaining in Norfolk, with seven floors, making it a landmark for miles around. It was in use until 1951.

Location: OS134 Ref. TG465 051. 3^1/$_2$m NE of Reedham on N bank of River Yare, 5m from Gt. Yarmouth. Accessible by boat or by footpath, from Halvergate (3^1/$_2$ m).

Opening Times: 1 Apr - 31 Oct: daily, 9am - 5pm (closed 1 - 2pm).

Admission: Adult £1.60, Child 80p, Conc. £1.20.

BINHAM PRIORY ⬜

Tel: 01223 582700 (Regional Office)

Binham-on-Wells, Norfolk

Owner: English Heritage   **Contact:** The East of England Regional Office

Extensive remains of a Benedictine priory, of which the original nave of the church is still in use as the parish church.

Location: OS132 Ref. TF982 399. ^{1}/$_4$ m NW of village of Binham-on-Wells, on road off B1388.

Opening Times: Any reasonable time.

Admission: Free.

BIRCHAM WINDMILL

Tel: 01485 578393

Snettisham Road, Great Bircham, Norfolk PE31 6SJ

Owner/Contact: Miss E Wagg/Mr S Chalmers

One of the last remaining complete windmills.

Location: OS Ref. TF760 326. ^{1}/$_2$ m W of Bircham. N of the road to Snettisham.

Opening Times: Please contact for details.

Admission: Adult £2.50, Child £1, Retired £2.25. (2000 prices).

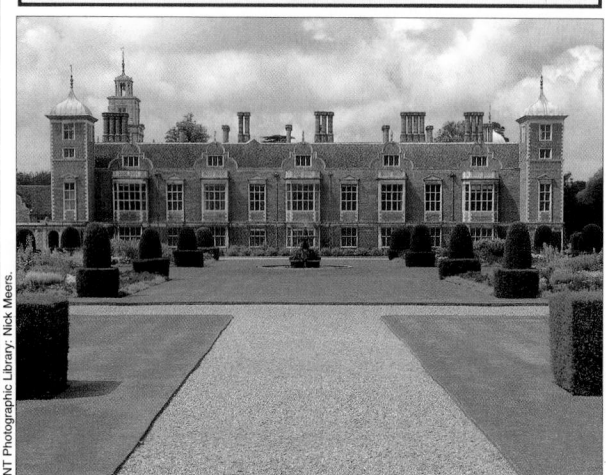

BLICKLING HALL 🌿

BLICKLING, NORWICH, NORFOLK NR11 6NF

Owner: The National Trust   *Contact:* The Property Manager

Tel: 01263 738030 **Fax:** 01263 731660

Built in the early 17th century and one of England's great Jacobean houses. Blickling is famed for its spectacular long gallery, superb library and fine collections of furniture, pictures and tapestries.

Location: OS133 Ref. TG178 286. 1^1/$_2$m NW of Aylsham on B1354. Signposted off A140 Norwich (15m) to Cromer.

Opening Times: House: 7 Apr - 28 Oct: Wed - Sun (open BH Mons), Apr - Sept: 1 - 4.30pm (last admission, house closes at 5pm). Oct: 1 - 3.30pm (last admission, house closes at 4pm). Garden: As house, also Tues in Aug. 1 Nov - 23 Dec: Thur - Sun. 5 Jan - end Mar 2002: Sats & Suns, 7 Apr - 28 Oct: 10.15am - 5.15pm. Nov - Mar 2002: 11am - 4pm. Park & Woods: daily, dawn - dusk.

Admission: Hall & Gardens: £6.70. Garden only: £3.80. Family & groups discounts. Groups must book.

Open as garden.   Partially suitable.   Licensed. By arrangement.   P   In park, on leads.   Tel for details.

NT Photographic Library: Nick Meers

BURGH CASTLE ⬜

Tel: 01223 582700 (Regional Office)

Breydon Water, Great Yarmouth, Norfolk

Owner: English Heritage   **Contact:** The East of England Regional Office

Impressive walls, with projecting bastions, of a Roman fort built in the late 3rd century as one of a chain to defend the coast against Saxon raiders.

Location: OS134 Ref. TG475 046. At far W end of Breydon Water, on unclassified road 3m W of Great Yarmouth. SW of the church.

Opening Times: Any reasonable time.

Admission: Free.

CASTLE ACRE PRIORY ⬜

Tel: 01760 755394

Stocks Green, Castle Acre, King's Lynn, Norfolk PE32 2XD

Owner: English Heritage   **Contact:** The Custodian

The great west front of the 12th century church of this Cluniac priory still rises to its full height and is elaborately decorated. Other substantial remains include the splendid prior's lodgings and chapel and the delightful modern herb garden should not be missed.

Location: OS Ref. TF814 148. ^{1}/$_4$ m W of village of Castle Acre, 5m N of Swaffham.

Opening Times: 1 Apr - 31 Oct: daily, 10am - 6pm (5pm in Oct). 1 Nov - 31 Mar: Wed - Sun, 10am - 4pm. Closed 24 - 26 Dec & 1 Jan.

Admission: Adult £3.50, Child £1.80, Conc. £2.60, Family £8.80.

📷   ♿ Ground floor & grounds.   **P**   ❄   Tel. for details.

CASTLE RISING CASTLE

Tel: 01553 631330 **Fax:** 01553 631724

Castle Rising, King's Lynn, Norfolk PE31 6AH

Owner: Greville Howard   **Contact:** The Custodian

Possibly the finest mid-12th century Keep left in England: it was built as a grand and elaborate palace. It was home to Queen Isabella, grandmother of the Black Prince. Still in surprisingly good condition, the Keep is surrounded by massive ramparts up to 120 feet high. Picnic area adjacent to tearoom.

Opening Times: 1 Apr - 31 Oct: daily, 10am - 6pm, (5pm in Oct). 1 Nov - 31 Mar: Wed - Sun, 10am - 4pm. Closed 24 - 26 Dec & 1 Jan.

Admission: Adult £3.25, Child £1.50, Conc. £2.50. 15% discount for groups (11+). Prices include VAT.

ℹ Picnic area.   ♿ Grounds suitable. WC.   ❄

DRAGON HALL

Tel: 01603 663922

115 - 123 King Street, Norwich, Norfolk NR1 1QE

Owner: Norfolk & Norwich Heritage Trust Ltd   **Contact:** Mr Neil Sigsworth

Magnificent medieval merchants' hall described as "one of the most exciting 15th century buildings in England". A wealth of outstanding features include living hall, screens passage, vaulted undercroft, superb timber-framed Great Hall, crown-post roof and intricately carved and painted dragon. Built by Robert Toppes, a wealthy and influential merchant. Dragon Hall is a unique legacy of medieval life, craftsmanship and trade.

Location: OS Ref. TG235 084. SE of Norwich city centre.

Opening Times: Apr - Oct: Mon - Sat, 10am - 4pm. Nov - Mar: Mon - Fri, 10am - 4pm. Closed 23 Dec - 2 Jan & BHs.

Admission: Adult £2, Child 50p, Conc. £1.50.

📷   ♿ House suitable.   Obligatory.   Guide dogs only.   ❄

FAIRHAVEN WOODLAND & WATER GARDEN

Tel: 01603 270449

2 The Woodlands, Wymers Lane, South Walsham NR13 6EA

Owner: The Fairhaven Garden Trust   **Contact:** George Debbage, Manager

180 acre woodland & water garden with private broad in the beautiful Norfolk Broads.

Location: OS Ref. TG368 134. 9m NE of Norwich just N of the B1140 at South Walsham.

Opening Times: Daily (except 25 Dec), 10am - 5pm, also May - Aug: Wed & Thurs evenings until 9pm.

Admission: Adult £3, Child £1 (under 5yrs Free), OAP £2.70. Group reductions.

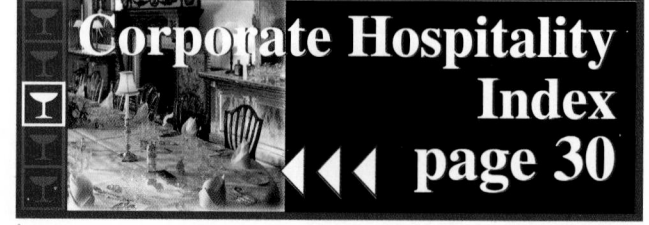

FELBRIGG HALL

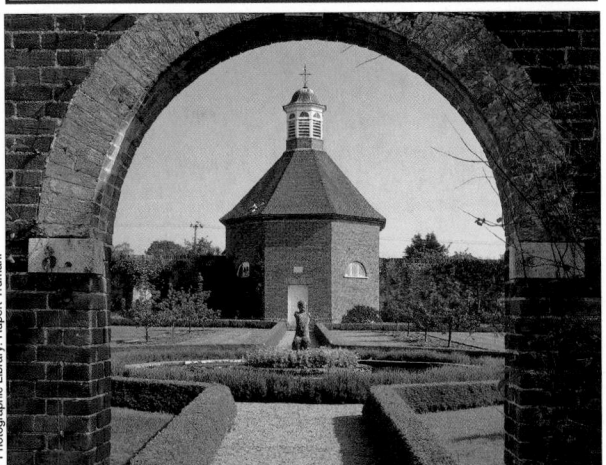

NT Photographic Library: Rupert Truman.

FELBRIGG, NORWICH, NORFOLK NR11 8PR

Owner: *The National Trust*   ***Contact:*** *The Property Manager*

Tel: 01263 837444 **Fax:** 01263 837032

One of the finest 17th century houses in East Anglia, the hall contains its original 18th century furniture and Grand Tour paintings, as well as an outstanding library. The walled garden has been restored and features a dovecote and small orchard.

Location: OS133 Ref. TG193 394. Nr Felbrigg village, 2m SW of Cromer, entrance off B1436, signposted from A148 and A140.

Opening Times: House: 31 Mar - 4 Nov: daily except Thurs & Fris, 1 - 5pm; BH Suns & Mons, 11am - 5pm. House will close at 4pm on and after 29 Oct. Garden: As house, 11am - 5.30pm.

Admission: House & Garden: Adult £5.80, Child £2.90, Family £14.50. Garden only: £2.20. Groups: (except BHs), £4.80. Groups please book with SAE to the Property Manager.

Tel: 01263 837040. 01263 838237. Licensed. Licensed. Partially suitable. By arrangement. In park, on leads. Park. Tel. 01263 838297 for details.

GRIME'S GRAVES

Tel: 01842 810656

Lynford, Thetford, Norfolk IP26 5DE

Owner: English Heritage   **Contact:** The Custodian

These remarkable Neolithic flint mines, unique in England, comprise over 300 pits and shafts. The visitor can descend some 30 feet by ladder into one excavated shaft, and look along the radiating galleries, from where the flint used for making axes and knives was extracted. Special flint-knapping days are advertised throughout the year.

Location: OS144 Ref. TL818 898. 7m NW of Thetford off A134.

Opening Times: 1 Apr - 31 Oct, daily, 10am - 6pm, (5pm in Oct). 1 Nov - 31 Mar: Wed - Sun, 10am - 4pm (closed 1 - 2pm) Closed 24 - 26 Dec & 1 Jan. Last visit to pit 20 mins before close. NB: Visits to pit for children under 5yrs at the discretion of the custodian.

Admission: Adult £2.10, Child £1.10, Conc. £1.60.

P Tel. for details.

HOLKHAM HALL

See page 270 for full page entry.

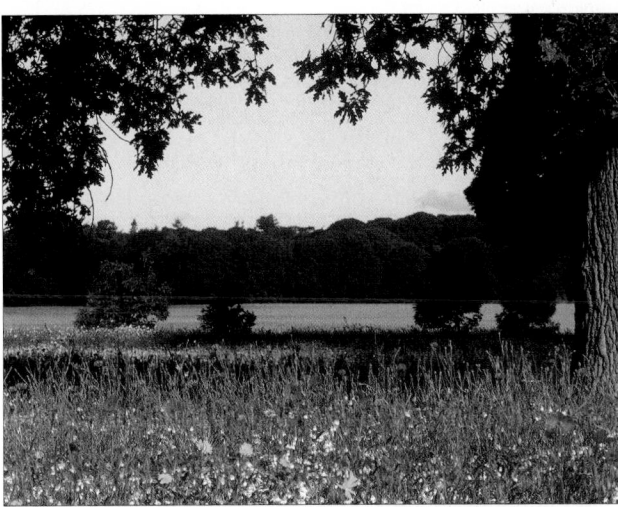

Wild Flowers at Houghton Hall, Norfolk.

HOUGHTON HALL

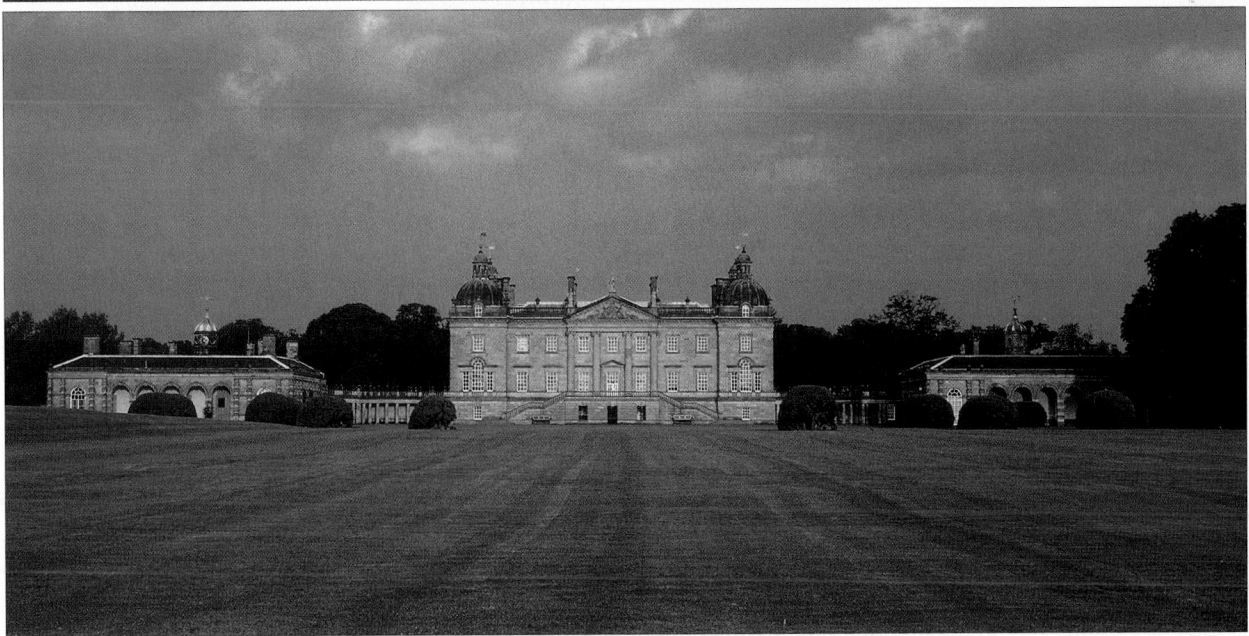

HOUGHTON, KING'S LYNN, NORFOLK PE31 6UE

Owner: *The Marquess of Cholmondeley*   ***Contact:*** *Susan Cleaver*

Tel: 01485 528569 **Fax:** 01485 528167 **e-mail:** enquiries@houghtonhall.com

Houghton Hall was built in the 18th century by Sir Robert Walpole. Original designs were by Colen Campbell and revised by Thomas Ripley with interior decoration by William Kent. It is regarded as one of the finest examples of Palladian architecture in England. Houghton was later inherited by the 1st Marquess of Cholmondeley through his grandmother, Sir Robert's daughter. Situated in beautiful parkland, the house contains magnificent furniture, pictures and china. A private collection of 20,000 model soldiers and militaria. 5-acre walled garden.

Location: OS Ref. TF792 287. 13m E of King's Lynn, 10m W of Fakenham 1¹/₂ m N of A148.

Opening Times: 15 Apr - 30 Sept: Suns, Thurs & BH Mons, 1 - 5.30pm. House: 2 - 5.30pm. Last admission 5pm.

Admission: Adult £6, Child (5-16) £3, Groups (20+): Adult £5.50, Child £2.50. Excluding house: Adult £3.50, Child £2, Groups (20+) Adult £3, Child £1.50.

HOVETON HALL GARDENS

Tel: 01603 782798 **Fax:** 01603 784564

Wroxham, Norwich, Norfolk NR12 8RJ

Owner: Mr & Mrs Andrew Buxton　　　　　　**Contact:** Mrs Buxton

10 acres of rhododendrons, azaleas, woodland and lakeside walks, walled herbaceous and vegetable gardens. Traditional tearooms and plant sales. The Hall (which is not open to the public) was built 1809 - 1812. Designs attributed to Humphry Repton.
Location: OS Ref. TG314 202. 8m N of Norwich. 1½ m NNE of Wroxham on A1151. Follow brown tourist signs.
Opening Times: Easter Sun - mid-Sept: Weds, Fris, Suns & BH Mons, 11am - 5.30pm. Also open Thurs in May.
Admission: Adult £3.50, Child £1, Wheelchairs users £2, Family £20, Season ticket £9.50. Groups: £3 (if booked in advance).

LETHERINGSETT WATERMILL

Tel: 01263 713153 **e-mail:** watermill@ic24.net

Riverside Road, Letheringsett, Holt, Norfolk NR25 7YD

Owner/Contact: M D Thurlow

Water-powered mill producing wholewheat flour from locally grown wheat. Built in 1802.
Location: OS Ref. TG062 387. Riverside Road, Letheringsett, Holt, Norfolk.
Opening Times: Whitsun - Oct: Mon - Fri, 10am - 5pm, Sat 9am - 1pm. Working demonstration, every afternoon, 2 - 4.30pm. Viewing may take place at any other time. Oct - Whitsun: Mon - Fri, 9am - 4pm. Sat, 9am - 1pm. Working demonstration, Tue - Fri, 1.30 3.30pm. BH Suns & Mons, 2 - 5pm.
Admission: Adult £2, Child £1.50. When demonstrating: Adult £3, Child £2, OAP £2.50, Family (2+2) £9.

MANNINGTON GARDENS & COUNTRYSIDE

Tel: 01263 584175

Mannington Hall, Norwich NR11 7BB　　　　**Fax:** 01263 761214

Owner: The Lord & Lady Walpole　　　　　　**Contact:** Lady Walpole

Gardens with lake, moat and woodland. Outstanding rose collection, heritage rose gardens.
Location: OS Ref. TG144 320. Signposted from Saxthorpe crossroads on the Norwich - Holt road B1149. 1½ m W of Wolterton Hall.
Opening Times: Gardens: May - Sept: Suns 12 - 5pm. Jun - Aug: Wed - Fri, 11am - 5pm. Walks: daily from 9am. Medieval Hall open by appointment.
Admission: Adult £3, Child (under 16yrs) Free, Conc. £2.50. Groups by arrangement.

ℹ No photography. 📷 🚻 ⛴ ♿ Grounds suitable. WCs. 🍴 Licensed.
🎫 By arrangement. 🅿 🛏 🐕 Guide dogs only.

THE MANOR HOUSE

Great Cressingham, Thetford, Norfolk IP25 6NJ

Owner/Contact: Mrs L R Chapman

Small Tudor manor house famous for its terracotta façade.
Location: OS Ref. TF852 020. 6m S of Swaffham. 1½ m E of A1065.
Opening Times: By written appointment only.
Admission: Prices on application.

NORWICH CASTLE MUSEUM

Tel: 01603 493625 **Fax:** 01603 493623

Norwich, Norfolk NR1 3JU　　　**e-mail:** museums@norfolk.gov.uk

Norman Castle Keep, housing displays of art, archaeology and natural history.
Location: OS Ref. TG233 085. City centre.
Opening Times: Norwich Castle Museum is closed until Spring 2001 due to extensive refurbishment of the historic Norman Keep and redisplay of the Museum's galleries.

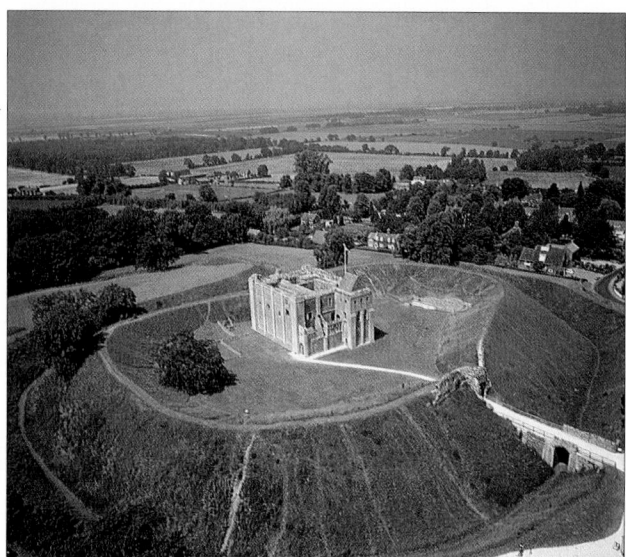

Castle Rising Castle, King's Lynn, Norfolk.

OXBURGH HALL, GDNS & ESTATE

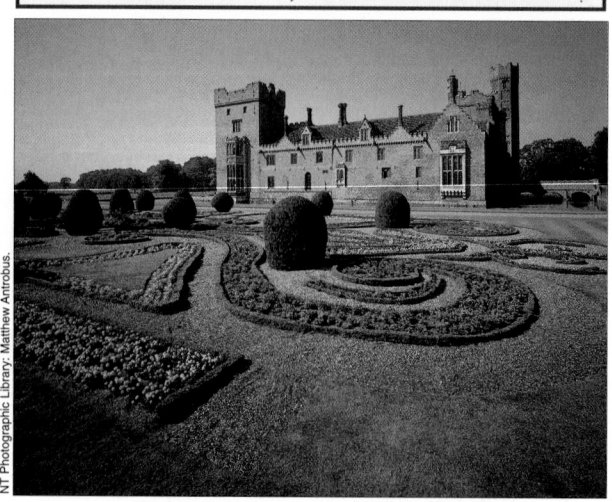

NT Photographic Library: Matthew Antrobus.

OXBOROUGH, KING'S LYNN, NORFOLK PE33 9PS

Owner: The National Trust　　*Contact:* The Property Manager

Tel: 01366 328258 **Fax:** 01366 328066

A moated manor house built in 1482 by the Bedingfeld family, who still live here. The rooms show the development from medieval austerity to Victorian comfort and include an outstanding display of embroidery done by Mary Queen of Scots. The attractive gardens include a French parterre, kitchen garden and orchard.
Location: OS143 Ref. TF742 012. At Oxborough, 7m SW of Swaffham on S side of Stoke Ferry road.
Opening Times: 31 Mar - 4 Nov: Sat - Wed, 1 - 5pm, BH Mons, 11am - 5pm. Last admission 4.30pm. Garden: 3 - 25 Mar: Sats & Suns, 11am - 4pm. 31 Mar - 4 Nov: Sat - Wed, also daily in Aug: 11am - 5.30pm.
Admission: Adult £5.30, Family discounts. Garden & Estate only: Adult £2.60. Groups: £4.20. Groups must book with SAE to the Property Manager.

📷 🍴 Licensed. ♿ Partially suitable. 🎫 By arrangement. 🛏 🅿
🐕 In grounds, on leads. ✉ Send SAE for details.

PLANTATION GARDEN

Tel: 01603 621868 **Fax:** 0870 1692343

4 Earlham Road, Norwich　　**e-mail:** chair@plantationgarden.co.uk

Owner: Plantation Garden Preservation Trust　　　　**Contact:** Chairperson
(Reg. Charity No. 801095)

The Plantation Garden is a Grade II English Heritage registered garden established 143 years ago in an abondoned chalk quarry some 600 yards from the city centre. It comprises nearly 3 acres in all, and includes a huge gothic fountain, flower beds, lawns, Italianate terrace, 'medieval' terrace wall, woodland walkways and rustic bridge.
Location: OS Ref. TG223 085. Leave inner ring road on B1108 Earlham Road, on left immediatly after St John's Roman Catholic Cathedral (entry shared with Beeches hotel driveway).
Opening Times: Apr - mid-October: daily, 9am - 6pm and other times 10am - 4pm.
Admission: Normally £1.50 (honesty box if garden unattended). Child Free.

📷 On Suns, pm only. 🚻 ⛴ ♿ Partially suitable. 🍴 On Suns, pm only.
🎫 By arrangement. 🅿 300 metres. 🛏 By arrangement. 📷 ❄
✉ Tel. for details. 🆆

RAVENINGHAM HALL GARDENS

Tel: 01508 548480 **Fax:** 01508 548958

Raveningham, Norwich, Norfolk NR14 6NS　　**e-mail:** raveningham@freenet.co.uk

Owner: Sir Nicholas Bacon Bt　　　　　　**Contact:** Mrs J Woodard

Gardens laid out approximately 100 years ago around a red brick Georgian house which is not open to the public.
Location: OS Ref. TM399 965. Between Beccles and Loddon off B1136/B1140.
Opening Times: 1 Apr - 30 Sept: Suns, Weds & BH Mons, 2 - 5.30pm.
Admission: Adult £2.50, Child (under 16yrs) Free, OAP £2. Groups by prior arrangement.

ROW 111 HOUSE, OLD MERCHANT'S HOUSE,
& GREYFRIARS' CLOISTERS

South Quay, Great Yarmouth, Norfolk NR30 2RQ　　**Tel:** 01493 857900

Owner: English Heritage　　　　　　**Contact:** The Custodian

Two 17th century Row Houses, rows 111 and 113, a type of building unique to Great Yarmouth, containing original fixtures and displays of local architectural fittings and early wall paintings.
Location: OS134 Ref. TG525 072. In Great Yarmouth, make for South Quay, by riverside and dock, ½ m inland from beach. Follow signs to dock and south quay.
Opening Times: 1 Apr - 31 Oct: daily, 10am - 5pm. Closed 1 - 2pm. Guided tours depart from Row 111 house at 10, 11am, 12 noon, 2, 3 & 4pm.
Admission: Adult £2.40. Child £1.20, Conc. £1.80. 15% discount for groups of 11+.

ST GEORGE'S GUILDHALL

Tel: 01553 765565

27-29 Kings Street, Kings Lynn, Norfolk PE30 1HA

Owner: The National Trust   **Contact:** The Administrator

The largest surviving English medieval guildhall, with adjoining medieval warehouse, now in use as an Arts Centre.

Location: OS132 Ref. TF616 202. On W side of King Street close to the Tuesday Market Place.

Opening Times: All year: Mon - Fri (closed Good Fri, BHs & 24 Dec - 1st Mon in Jan), 10am - 2pm. Times may vary in Jul & Aug. The Guildhall is not usually open on days when there are performances in the theatre, tel. box office 01553 764864 for details.

Admission: Free.

📷   ♿ Access to galleries.   🖼 🍴 Licensed.   ❄

SANDRINGHAM

See page 271 for full page entry.

WALSINGHAM ABBEY GROUNDS & SHIREHALL MUSEUM

Little Walsingham, Norfolk NR22 6BP   **Tel:** 01328 820259 **Fax:** 01328 820098

Owner: Walsingham Estate Company   **Contact:** The Agent

Set in Walsingham, a picturesque medieval village, the grounds contain the remains of an Augustinian Priory founded in 1153.

Location: OS Ref. TF934 367. B1105 N from Fakenham - 5m.

Opening Times: Please contact for details.

Admission: Please telephone for details.

WOLTERTON PARK

Tel: 01263 584175 **Fax:** 01263 761214

Norwich, Norfolk NR11 7BB

Owner: The Lord and Lady Walpole   **Contact:** The Lady Walpole

18th century Hall. Historic park with lake.

Location: OS Ref. TG164 317. Situated near Erpingham village, signposted from Norwich - Cromer Rd A140.

Opening Times: Park: daily from 9am. Hall: Fridays Spring - Autumn, 2 - 5pm and by appointment.

Admission: £2 car park fee only. Groups by application. Hall tours: See local press, from £4 groups, £5 individuals.

🚃   ♿ Partially suitable. WC.   🚶 Obligatory for Hall.   🅿   ▥
🐕 In grounds, on leads.   ❄

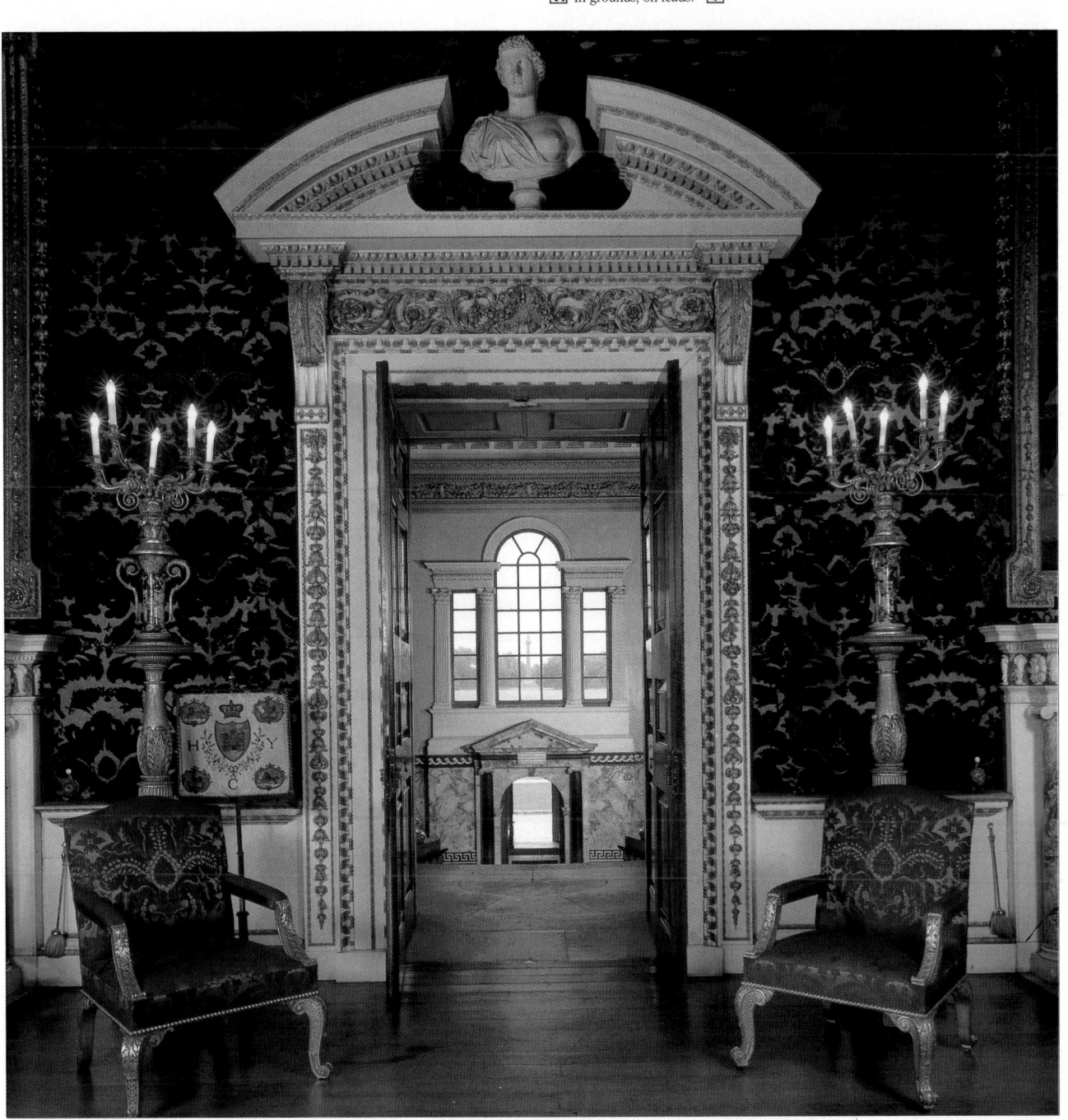

Holkham Hall, Norfolk.

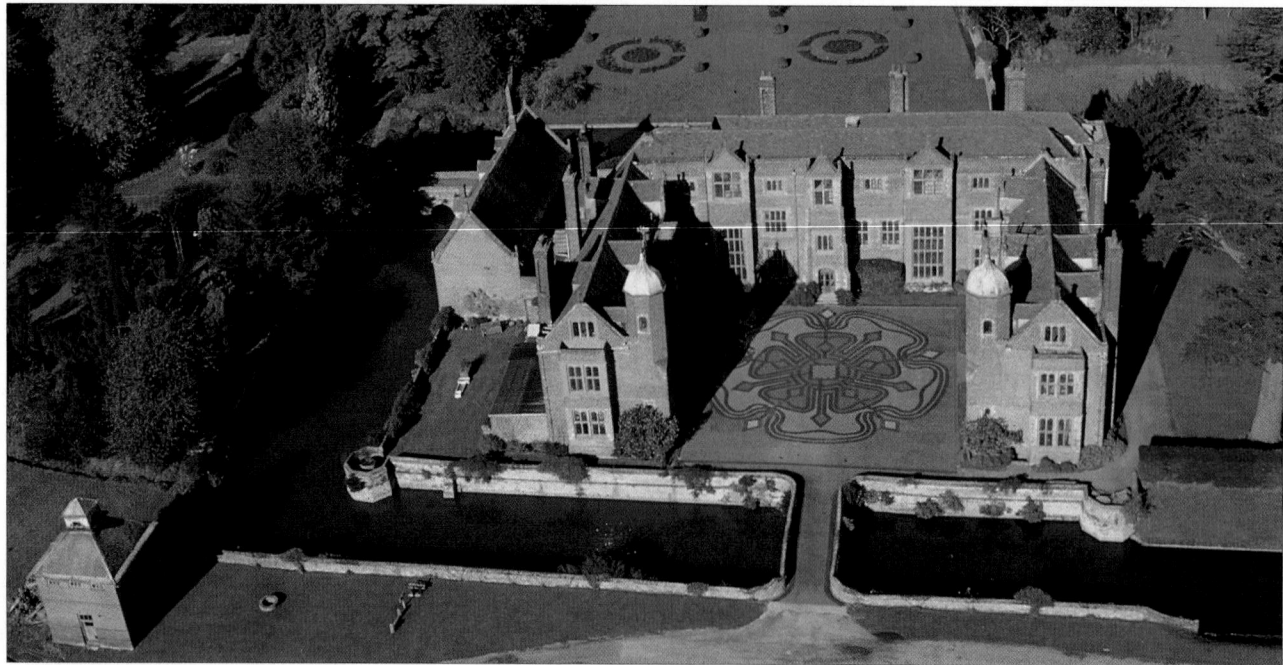

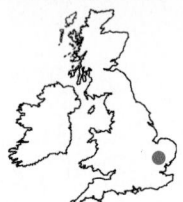

Owner:
Patrick Phillips Esq

CONTACT

Mrs J G Phillips
Kentwell Hall
Long Melford
Suffolk
CO10 9BA

Tel: 01787 310207

Fax: 01787 379318

LOCATION

OS Ref. TL864 479

Off the A134.
4m N of Sudbury, 14m S of
Bury St. Edmunds
1m NNW of
Long Melford off A134.

Rail: Sudbury Station 4m
Colchester Station 20m.

Air: Stansted 30m.
Airstrip at Kentwell
suitable for light aircraft
and microlites.

Taxi: Sudbury Town Taxis
01787 377366.

CONFERENCE/FUNCTION		
ROOM	SIZE	MAX CAPACITY
Great Hall	40' x 24'	120
Main Dining Room	24' x 24'	75
Drawing Rm	35' x 24'	75
Library	36' x 20'	20
Overcroft	120' x 22'	300

KENTWELL HALL
Long Melford

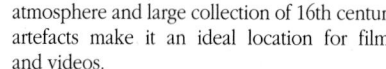

KENTWELL HALL is a beautiful redbrick Tudor Manor House surrounded by a broad moat.

Built by the Clopton Family, from wealth made in the wool trade, Kentwell has an air of timeless tranquillity. The exterior is little altered in 450 years. The interior was remodelled by Hopper in 1825 and his work has been embellished and enhanced in restoration by the present owners. Hopper's interiors, notably the Great Hall and Dining Room, emphasise their Tudor provenance, but the Drawing Room and Library are simply and restrainedly classical; all are eminently habitable.

Kentwell, as well as being a family home, conveys a deep feeling of the Tudor period with the service areas: great kitchen, bakery, dairy and forge always fully equipped in 16th century style. Kentwell's unique 16th century atmosphere and large collection of 16th century artefacts make it an ideal location for films and videos.

The gardens are part of Kentwell's delight. Intimate yet spacious, you are seldom far from a moat, clipped yews (some 30ft high) or mellow brick wall. There is a fine walled garden with original 17th century layout and a well established large Herb Garden and Potager.

The farm is run organically and is set around timber-framed buildings and stocked with rare breed farm animals.

Home to the award winning **'Re-creations of Tudor Domestic Life'** when visitors meet numerous 'Tudors' with dress, speech, activities and locations appropriate for the 16th century. These take place on selected weekends between April and September.

❖

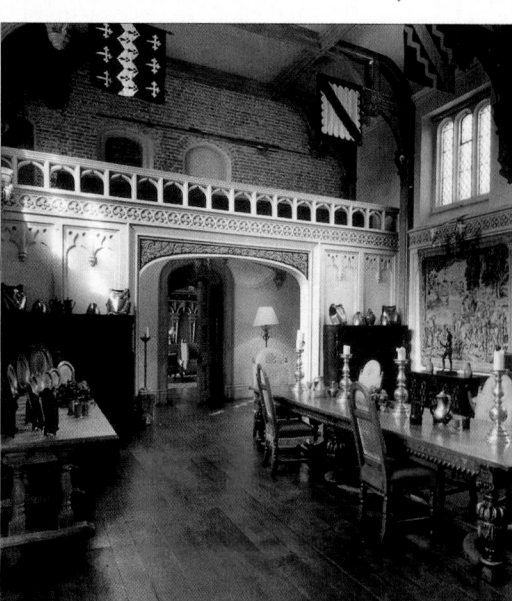

🏛 ℹ Corporate events include conferences and 'company days', specially devised one-day programme of fun, stimulation and challenges. A wide range of Tudor activities can be arranged for visitors, including longbow shooting, working bakery, dairy and still-room, spinning, etc. or even clay pigeon shooting in the Park. No photography in house.

🍴 Genuine Tudor-style banquets, wedding receptions, formal but friendly luncheons and dinners.

♿ Visitors may alight at house, with prior notice. WC.

☕ Home-made food. The Undercroft comfortably seats 96. Overcroft can accommodate up to 300.

P Ample.

🏫 There is a highly developed schools programme dealing with 700 parties per year. Schools can visit a re-creation of Tudor life, re-create Tudor life themselves for the day or take one of the tours conducted by experienced guides on the House, Garden, Farm or aspects of each.

🐕 No dogs.

OPENING TIMES

House, Gardens & Farm

- 22 April - 10 June: Suns only except:
  17 - 20 April: daily and
  Half-term: 29 May - 1 June.
  12 noon - 5pm.
- 11 July - 21 September
  daily 12 noon - 5pm.
- 30 Sept - 28 Oct
  Suns only, 12 noon - 5pm
- 21 - 26 Oct
  daily: 12 noon - 5pm.

Gardens & Farm only

- 4 March - 8 April: Suns only,
  10am - 5pm.

🎭 **The Great Annual Re-creation**

- 17 June - 8 July:
  Sats & Suns only & Fri,
  6 July, 11am - 5pm.

Other Re-creations

- 13 - 16 Apr: Easter
- 5 - 6 May: May Day
- 19 - 20 May: Land Girls
- 26 - 28 May: Whitsun
- 4 - 5 Aug: World War II
- 24 - 27 Aug: High Summer
- 22 - 23 Sept: Michaelmas
- 13 - 14 Oct: World War II
  All 11am - 6pm,
  sometimes 5pm.

Special Prices apply.

ADMISSION

House, Gardens & Farm
Adult £5.70
Child (5-15yrs) £3.40
OAP.........................£4.90

Gardens & Farm only
Adult £3.60
Child (5-15yrs) £2.30
OAP.........................£3.20

Great Annual Re-creation
Adult £12.00
Child (5-15yrs) £9.00
OAP.......................£10.50

THE ANCIENT HOUSE

Tel: 01628 825920 or 825925 (bookings)

Clare, Suffolk CO10 8NY

Owner: Leased to the Landmark Trust by Clare Parish Council

Contact: The Landmark Trust

A 14th century house extended in the 15th and 17th centuries, decorated with high relief pargetting. Half of the building is managed by the Landmark Trust, which lets buildings for self-catering holidays. The other half of the house is run as a museum. Full details of The Ancient House and 170 other historic buildings available for holidays are featured in The Landmark Handbook (price £9.50 refundable against booking), from The Landmark Trust, Shottesbrooke, Maidenhead, Berkshire SL6 3SW.

Location: OS Ref. TL769 454. Village centre, on A1092 8m WNW of Sudbury.

Opening Times: By appointment only and for Clare Arts Festival, week commencing 16 Jun.

Admission: Museum: Contact 01787 277662 for details.

BELCHAMP HALL

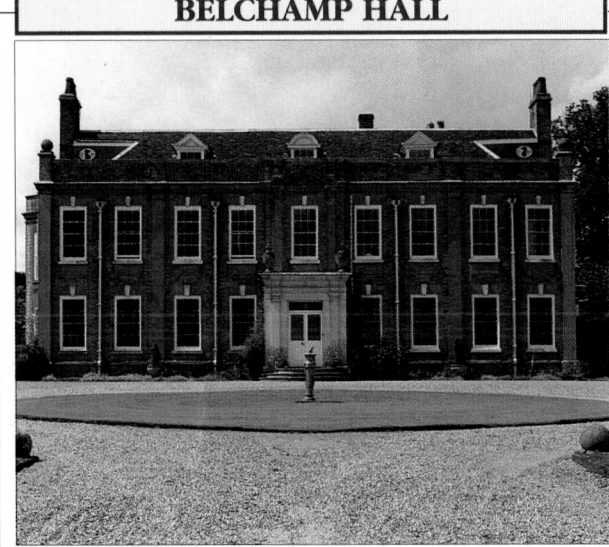

BELCHAMP WALTER, SUDBURY, SUFFOLK CO10 7AT
Owner/Contact: Mr C F V Raymond

Tel: 01787 881961 **Fax:** 01787 880729

Superb Queen Anne house on a site belonging to the Raymond family since 1611. Historic portraits and period furniture. Suitable for receptions and an ideal film location, often seen as Lady Jane's house in *Lovejoy*. Gardens including a cherry avenue, follies, a sunken garden, walled garden and lake. Medieval church with 15th century wall paintings.

Location: OS Ref. TL827 407. 5m SW of Sudbury, opposite Belchamp Walter Church.

Opening Times: By appointment only: May - Sept: Tues, Thurs & BHs, 2.30 - 6pm.

Admission: Adult £4, Child £1.75. No reduction for groups.

No photography in house. By arrangement. Obligatory. Guide dogs only.

CHRISTCHURCH MANSION

Tel: 01473 253246 **Fax:** 01473 281274

Christchurch Park, Ipswich, Suffolk IP4 2BD

Owner/Contact: Ipswich Borough Council

A fine Tudor house set in beautiful parkland.

Location: OS Ref. TM165 450. Christchurch Park, near centre of Ipswich.

Opening Times: All year: Tue - Sat, 10am - 5pm (dusk in winter). Suns, 2.30 - 4.30pm (dusk in winter). Also open BH Mons. Closed 24 - 26 Dec, 1/2 Jan and Good Fri.

Admission: Free.

EAST BERGHOLT PLACE GARDEN

Tel/Fax: 01206 299224

East Bergholt, Suffolk CO7 6UP

Owner: Mr & Mrs R L C Eley   **Contact:** Sara Eley

Fifteen acres of garden and arboretum originally laid out at the beginning of the century by the present owner's great-grandfather. A wonderful collection of fine trees and shrubs, many of which are rarely seen growing in East Anglia and originate from the famous plant hunter George Forrest. Particularly beautiful in the spring when the rhododendrons, magnolias and camellias are in flower. There is a specialist plant centre in the Victorian walled garden.

Location: OS Ref. TM084 343. 2m E of A12 on B1070, Manningtree Rd, on the edge of East Bergholt.

Opening Times: Mar - Sept: daily, 10am - 5pm. Closed Easter Sun.

Admission: Adult £2.50, Child Free. (Proceeds to garden up-keep).

By arrangement.

EUSTON HALL

Tel: 01842 766366 **Fax:** 01842 766764

Estate Office, Euston, Thetford, Norfolk IP24 2QP

Owner: The Duke of Grafton   **Contact:** Mrs L Campbell

18th century house contains a famous collection of paintings including works by Stubbs, Van Dyck, Lely and Kneller. The Pleasure Grounds were laid out by John Evelyn and William Kent. 17th century parish church in Wren style. River walk, watermill and picnic area.

Location: OS Ref. TL897 786. 12m N of Bury St Edmunds, on A1088. 2m E of A134.

Opening Times: 7 Jun - 27 Sept: Thurs 2.30 - 5pm. Also Suns 24 Jun & 2 Sept: 2.30 - 5pm.

Admission: Adult £3, Child 50p, OAP £2.50. Groups (12+): £2.50pp.

Grounds suitable.

FLATFORD BRIDGE COTTAGE

Tel: 01206 298260 **Fax:** 01206 299193

Flatford, East Bergholt, Colchester, Essex CO7 6OL

Owner: The National Trust   **Contact:** The Property Manager

Just upstream from Flatford Mill, the restored thatched cottage houses a display about John Constable, several of whose paintings depict this property. Facilities include a tea garden, shop, boat hire, an Information Centre and countryside walks.

Location: OS Ref. TM077 332. On N bank of Stour, 1m S of East Bergholt B1070.

Opening Times: Mar & Apr: Wed - Sun, 11am - 5.30pm. May - end Sept: daily, 10am - 5.30pm. Oct: daily, 11am - 5.30pm. Nov & Dec: Wed - Sun, 11am - 3.30pm. Jan & Feb 2002: Sats & Suns only, 11am - 3.30pm. Closed Christmas & New Year.

Admission: Guided walks £1.90, accompanied child Free.

Tea garden & shop accessible. WC. Charge applies. Guide dogs only.

FRAMLINGHAM CASTLE

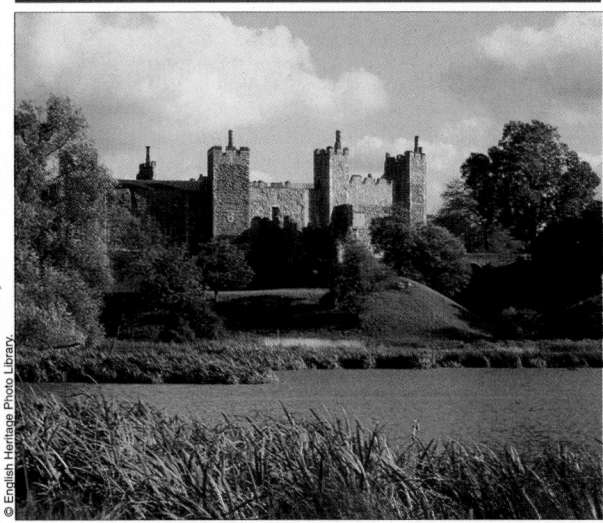

© English Heritage Photo Library.

FRAMLINGHAM, SUFFOLK IP8 9BT
Owner: English Heritage   Contact: The Custodian

Tel: 01728 724189

A superb 12th century castle which, from the outside, looks almost the same as when it was built. From the continuous curtain wall linking 13 towers, there are excellent views of Framlingham and the charming reed-fringed mere. At different times the castle has been a fortress, an Elizabethan prison, a poor house and a school. The many alterations over the years have led to a pleasing mixture of historic styles.

Location: OS Ref. TM287 637. In Framlingham on B1116. NE of town centre.

Opening Times: 1 Apr - 31 Oct: daily 10am - 6pm (5pm in Oct). 1 Nov - 31 Mar: daily 10am - 4pm. Closed 24 - 26 Dec & 1 Jan.

Admission: Adult £3.50, Child £1.80, Conc. £2.60, Family £8.80. 15% discount for groups (11+).

Ground floor & grounds suitable. WCs. Tel. for details.

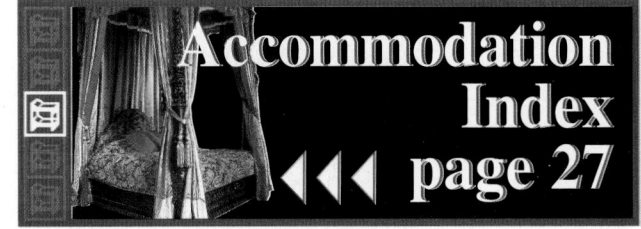

GAINSBOROUGH'S HOUSE

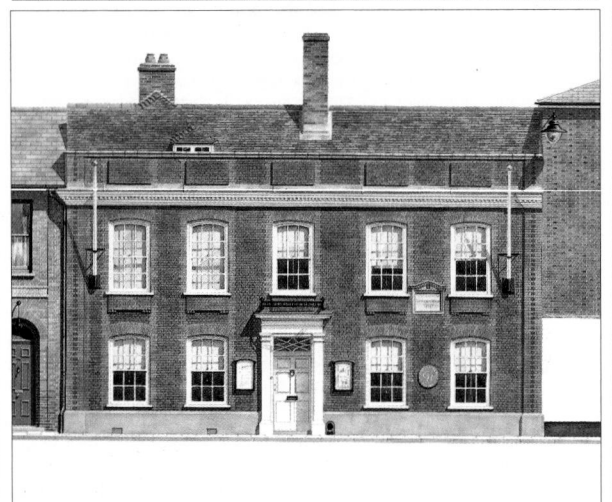

46 GAINSBOROUGH ST, SUDBURY, SUFFOLK CO10 2EU

Owner: *Gainsborough's House Society*   **Contact:** *Rosemary Woodward*

Tel: 01787 372958   **Fax:** 01787 376991   **e-mail:** mail@gainsborough.org

Birthplace of Thomas Gainsborough RA (1727-88). Georgian-fronted town house, with attractive walled garden, displays more of the artist's work than any other gallery. The collection is shown together with 18th century furniture and memorabilia. Varied programme of contemporary exhibitions organised throughout the year includes: fine art, craft, photography, printmaking, sculpture and highlights the work of East Anglian artists.

Location: OS Ref. TL872 413. 46 Gainsborough Street, Sudbury town centre.

Opening Times: All year: Tue - Sat, 10am - 5pm, Suns & BH Mons, 2 - 5pm. Closes at 4pm Nov - Mar. Closed: Mons, Good Fri and Christmas to New Year.

Admission: Adult £3, Child/Student £1.50, OAP £2.50.

ℹ️ No photography.   📷 ♿ Ground floor suitable. WCs.
🅿️ No parking.   🎭 ❄️ Ⓦ

HADLEIGH GUILDHALL   **Tel:** 01473 827752

Hadleigh, Suffolk IP7 5DT

Owner: Hadleigh Market Feoffment Charity   **Contact:** Jane Haylock

Fine timber framed guildhall, one of the least known medieval buildings in Suffolk.

Location: OS Ref. TM025 425. S side of churchyard.

Opening Times: Jun - end Sept: Building: Thurs & Suns; Garden: daily (except Sats), 2 - 5pm

Admission: £1.50, Conc. £1. Garden only: Free.

HAUGHLEY PARK 🏛️   **Tel:** 01359 240701

Stowmarket, Suffolk IP14 3JY

Owner/Contact: R J Williams Esq

Jacobean manor house, garden and woodland walks.

Location: OS Ref. TM005 618. 4m W of Stowmarket signed off A14.

Opening Times: Garden only: May - Sept: Tues & last Sun in Apr & 1st Sun in May, 2 - 5.30pm. House open by prior appointment on above Tues only (tel: 01359 240701).

Admission: Adult £2, Child £1.

Website Index page 39 ◀◀◀

HELMINGHAM HALL GARDENS 🏛️

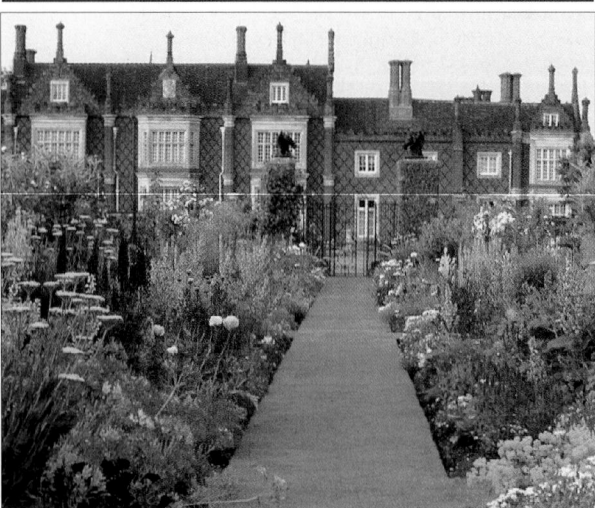

STOWMARKET, SUFFOLK IP14 6EF

Owner: *The Lord & Lady Tollemache*   **Contact:** *Ms Jane Tresidder*

Tel: 01473 890363   **Fax:** 01473 890776

The Tudor Hall surrounded by its wide moat is set in a 400 acre deer park. Two superb gardens, one surrounded by its own moat and walls extends to several acres and has wide herbaceous borders and an immaculate kitchen garden. The second enclosed within yew hedges, has a special rose garden with a herb and knot garden containing plants grown in England before 1750.

Location: OS Ref. TM190 578. B1077, 9m N of Ipswich, 5m S of Debenham.

Opening Times: Gardens only: 29 Apr - 9 Sept: Suns, 2 - 6pm. Groups: by appointment only on Weds, 2 - 5pm. (We can also accept individual bookings on a Wed if a group is booked.)

Admission: Adult £3.75, Child (5-15yrs) £2. Groups (30+) £3.25. Weds: £3.75pp.

📷 🌳 ♿ Grounds suitable. WCs.   🐕 🖼️ By arrangement.   🅿️
🐾 In grounds, on leads.   Ⓦ

HENGRAVE HALL CENTRE

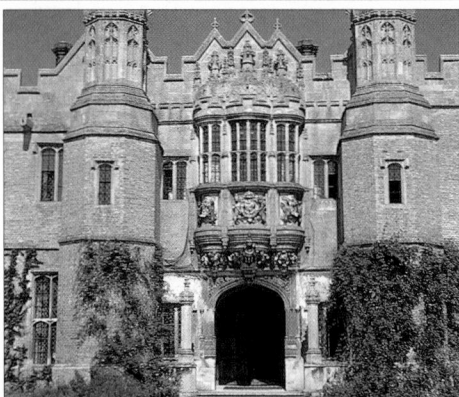

BURY ST EDMUNDS, SUFFOLK IP28 6LZ

Owner: *Religious of the Assumption*   **Contact:** *Mr J H Crowe*

Tel: 01284 701561   **Fax:** 01284 702950

e-mail: co-ordinator@hengravehallcentre.org.uk

Hengrave Hall is a unique Tudor house of stone and brick, built between 1525 and 1538 by Sir Thomas Kytson, Warden of the Mercers' Company. Former home to the Kytson and Gage families, it was visited by Elizabeth I on her Suffolk Progress in 1578. Set in 45 acres of cultivated grounds, the Hall is now run as a Conference and Retreat Centre by the Hengrave Community of Reconciliation. The Hall has many important and distinctive features, including beautiful stained glass and the magnificent Oriel Window and Frieze incorporating the Garter Arms and other Coats of Arms which were comprehensively restored in summer 2000. The ancient church with Saxon tower adjoins the Hall and continues to be used for daily prayer.

Location: OS Ref. TL824 686. 3¹/₂ m NW of Bury St Edmunds on the A1101.

Opening Times: Please telephone the Warden for conference facilities (day and residential); tours (by appointment); retreats; programme of events; schools' programme. Special group rates.

ℹ️ Children's playground.   📷 🍽️ 🌳 ♿ 🖼️ 🏺 By arrangement.
🖼️ ❄️ 🍴 Tel. for details.   Ⓦ

ICKWORTH HOUSE & PARK

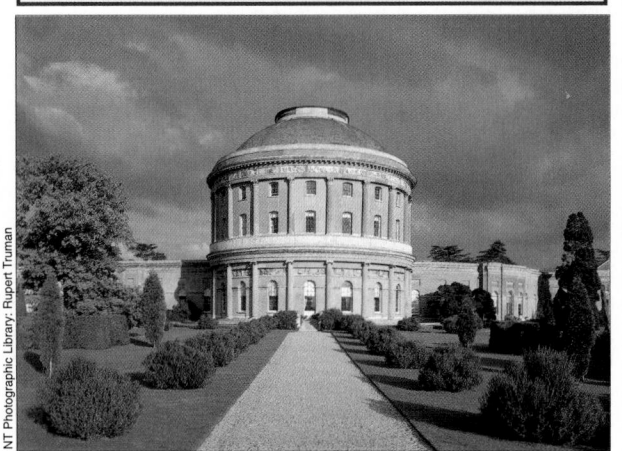

NT Photographic Library: Rupert Truman

THE ROTUNDA, HORRINGER, BURY ST EDMUNDS IP29 5QE

Owner: The National Trust   *Contact:* The Property Manager

Tel: 01284 735270 **Fax:** 01284 735175 **e-mail:** arorec@smtp.ntrust.org.uk

One of the most unusual houses in East Anglia. The huge Rotunda of this 18th century Italianate house dominates the landscape. Inside are collections of Georgian silver, Regency furniture, Old Master paintings and family portraits.

Location: OS155 Ref. TL816 611. In Horringer, 3m SW of Bury St Edmunds on W side of A143.

Opening Times: House: 24 Mar - 28 Oct: daily except Mons & Thurs (open BH Mons), 1 - 5pm, last admission 4.30pm (closes 4.30pm in Oct). Garden: 24 Mar - 28 Oct: daily; 29 Oct - end Mar 2002: Mon - Fri, 10am - 5pm, last admission 4.30pm. 1 Nov - end Mar 2002: 10am - 4pm. Park: daily, 7am - 7pm. Note: Garden & Park closed 25 Dec.

Admission: Adult £5.70, Child £2.50. Family discounts. Park & Garden only (includes access to shop & restaurant): Adult £2.50, Child 80p. Groups (must book): Adult £4.70, Child £2. No group discounts on Suns & BH Mons.

Partially suitable. Licensed. By arrangement. In park, on leads. Tel. for details.

KENTWELL HALL

See page 276 for full page entry.

LANDGUARD FORT

Tel: 01394 277767

Felixstowe, Suffolk

Owner: English Heritage   **Contact:** The Custodian

Impressive 18th century fort with later additions built on a site originally fortified by Henry VIII and in use until after World War II. There is also a museum (not EH).

Location: OS Ref. TM284 318. 1m S of Felixstowe at extreme S end of dock area.

Opening Times: 23 Apr - 29 Oct: Suns & BHs, 10.30am - 5pm. 6 Jun - 16 Sept: Tues, Weds & Sats, 1 - 5pm (2000/2001 openings). Please telephone for 2001 - 2002 details.

Admission: Adult £2, Child £1, Conc. £1.50.

LAVENHAM: THE GUILDHALL OF CORPUS CHRISTI   **Tel:** 01787 247646

The Market Place, Lavenham, Sudbury CO10 9QZ   e-mail: almjtg@smtp.ntrust.org.uk

Owner: The National Trust   **Contact:** The Property Manager

This splendid 16th century timber-framed building dominates the Market Place of the picturesque town of Lavenham with its many historic houses and wonderful church. Inside are exhibitions on local history, farming and industry, as well as the story of the medieval woollen cloth trade. There is also a walled garden with dye plants.

Location: OS155 Ref. TL915 942. 6m NNE of Sudbury. Village centre. A1141 and B1071.

Opening Times: Mar & Nov: Sats & Suns, 11am - 4pm. Apr - end Oct: daily, 11am - 5pm (closed Good Fri). The building or parts of it, may be closed occasionally for community use.

Admission: Adult £3, accompanied child Free. Groups: £2.50. School parties (by arrangement) 60p per child.

Shop & tearoom suitable.

LEISTON ABBEY

Tel: 01223 582700 (Regional Office)

Leiston, Suffolk

Owner: English Heritage   **Contact:** The East of England Regional Office

The remains of this abbey for Premonstratensian canons, including a restored chapel, are amongst the most extensive in Suffolk.

Location: OS Ref. TM445 642. 1m N of Leiston off B1069.

Opening Times: Any reasonable time.

Admission: Free.

LITTLE HALL

Tel: 01787 247179   **Fax:** 01787 248341

Market Place, Lavenham, Suffolk CO10 9QZ

Owner: Suffolk Building Preservation Trust   **Contact:** R Attew

Little Hall, a Grade II Listed Building with a Crown Post roof, reveals five centuries of change. Its history mirrors the rise and fall of Lavenham's cloth trade. Restored by the Gayer-Anderson twins in the 1930s.

Location: OS Ref. TL917 494. Market Place, Lavenham. 50yds E of Guildhall.

Opening Times: 1 Apr - end Oct: Weds, Thurs, Sats, Suns, 2 - 5pm. BHs: 11am - 5.30pm.

Admission: Adult £1.50, Child Free.

MANOR HOUSE MUSEUM

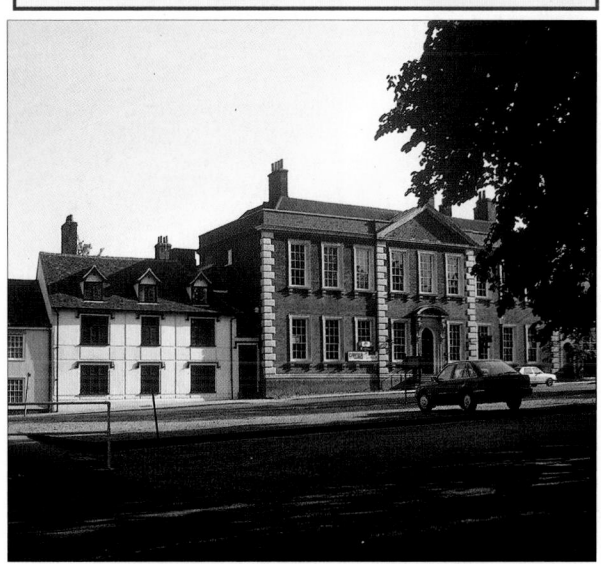

HONEY HILL, BURY ST EDMUNDS, SUFFOLK IP33 IHF

Owner: St Edmundsbury Borough Council   *Contact:* The Manager

Tel: 01284 757076 **Fax:** 01284 757079

A Georgian town house, built by the Earl of Bristol for his wife Elizabeth between 1736 and 1737 as her town house in which she would entertain her friends during the day and into the evening, before returning to Ickworth House, the family seat. Extensively restored in the '80s it now houses a collection of clocks, watches and wooden time pieces, a collection of costume, local and international artists. Also a friendly ghost.

Location: OS Ref. TL858 640. Bury town centre off A14. Just S of Abbey grounds.

Opening Times: Please telephone for details.

Admission: Please telephone for details.

Tel. for details.

MELFORD HALL

Tel: 01787 880286

Long Melford, Sudbury, Suffolk CO10 9AA

Owner: The National Trust   **Contact:** The Administrator

A turreted brick Tudor mansion, little changed since 1578 with the original panelled banqueting hall, an 18th century drawing room, a Regency library and Victorian bedrooms, showing fine furniture and Chinese porcelain.

Location: OS Ref. TL867 462. In Long Melford off A134, 14m S of Bury St Edmunds, 3m N of Sudbury.

Opening Times: Apr & Oct: Sat, Sun & BH Mon, 2 - 5.30pm. May - Sept: Wed - Sun & BH Mon, 2 - 5.30pm. Last admission 5pm.

Admission: £4.40. Groups (pre-arranged) £3.30. Wed - Sat only, write with SAE to Senior Visitor Reception Assistant.

Stairlift to 1st floor. WC. In car park & park walk only, on leads.

MOYSES HALL MUSEUM

Tel: 01284 757069

e-mail: maggie.goodger@stedsbc.gov.uk

Cornhill, Bury St Edmunds, Suffolk IP33 1DX

Owner: St Edmundsbury Borough Council   **Contact:** The Gallery Supervisor

Very early 12th century flint house, now a museum of local history.

Location: OS Ref. TL853 644. Town centre off A14. 300 yds NW of Abbey grounds.

Opening Times: Museum will be closed for much of 2001 for redevelopment work. Please telephone or e-mail for details of re-opening.

Admission: Please telephone or e-mail for details.

ORFORD CASTLE

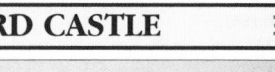

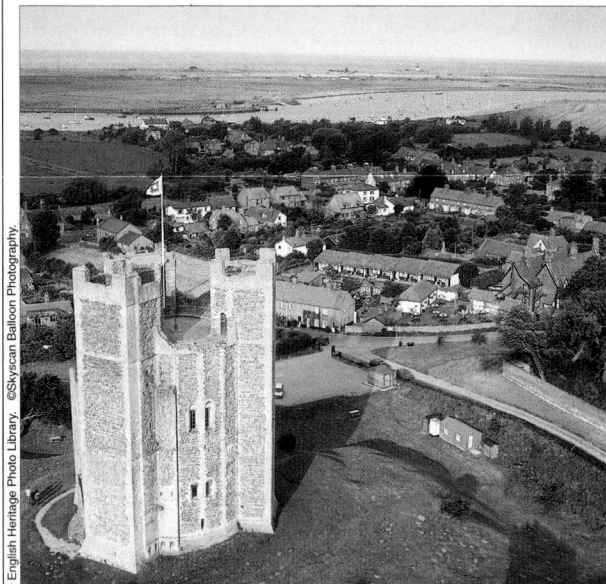

©Skyscan Balloon Photography. © English Heritage Photo Library.

ORFORD, WOODBRIDGE, SUFFOLK IP12 2ND

Owner: English Heritage   ***Contact:*** *The Custodian*

Tel: 01394 450472

A royal castle built by Henry II for coastal defence in the 12th century. A magnificent keep survives almost intact with three immense towers reaching to 30m (90ft). Fine views over Orford and the surrounding countryside.

Location: OS169 Ref. TM419 499. In Orford on B1084, 20m NE of Ipswich.

Opening Times: 1 Apr - 31 Oct: daily 10am - 6pm (5pm in Oct). 1 Nov - 31 Mar: Wed - Sun, 10am - 4pm. Closed 1 - 2pm. Closed 24 - 26 Dec & 1 Jan.

Admission: Adult £3.10, Child £1.60, Conc. £2.30. 15% discount for groups (11+).

Tel. for details.

OTLEY HALL

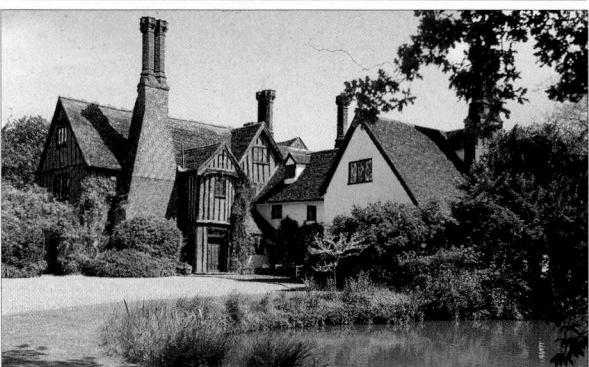

OTLEY, IPSWICH, SUFFOLK IP6 9PA

Owner: Mr Nicholas & Mrs Ann Hagger   ***Contact:*** *Mrs Chris Buckle (Administrator)*

Tel: 01473 890264 **Fax:** 01473 890803

A stunning 15th century Moated Hall (Grade I), set in gardens and grounds of 10 acres, frequently described as "one of England's loveliest houses". Rich in history and architectural detail. Features of particular note are richly carved beams, superb linenfold, c1559 wall paintings, herringbone brickwork and vine-leaf pargetting. From around 1401 Otley Hall was the home of the Gosnold family for some 300 years. Bartholomew Gosnold voyaged to the New World in 1602 and named Cape Cod and Martha's Vineyard. He returned in 1607 to found the Jamestown settlement, the first English-speaking settlement in the US, 13 years before the Mayflower landed. The account of the 1602 voyage is thought to have provided the geography for Shakespeare's *Tempest*. The gardens are formal and informal, with canal, mount, nutteries, rose garden, woodland, and historically accurate Tudor features including a knot and herb garden, designed by Sylvia Landsberg (author of *The Medieval Garden*). The new Millennium Garden is a gravel garden with a Mediterranean theme.

Location: OS Ref. TM207 563. 7m N of Ipswich, off the B1079.

Opening Times: Every BH Sun & Mon, 12.30 - 6pm. Gardens: Mons & Weds only from 16 Apr - 24 Sept, 2 - 5pm.

Admission: Adult £4.50, Child £2.50. Garden days: Adult £3, Child £1, OAP £2.60. Coach parties welcome all year by appointment for private guided tours.

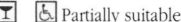 Partially suitable. 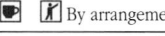 By arrangement.

PAKENHAM WATERMILL   **Tel:** 01359 270570

Mill Road, Pakenham, Bury St Edmunds, Suffolk

Owner: Suffolk Building Preservation Trust   **Contact:** Roger Gillingham

Fine 18th century working watermill.

Location: OS Ref. TL937 694. Signposted from A143 Ixworth bypass.

Opening Times: 1 Apr - 30 Sept: Weds, Sats, Suns & BHs, 2 - 5.30pm.

Admission: Adult £2, Child £1.20, OAP £1.75.

ST EDMUNDSBURY CATHEDRAL   **Tel:** 01284 754933 **Fax:** 01284 768655

Angel Hill, Bury St Edmunds, Suffolk IP33 1LS   **e-mail:** cathedral@btconnect.com

Owner: The Church of England   **Contact:** Sarah Friswell

At the heart of Christian worship since Saxon times, evidence of previous churches is visible. The elegant, English Perpendicular 16th century Nave of St James' survived its patron, the once great, now ruined Abbey of St Edmund, to become the Cathedral of Suffolk in 1914. It was skilfully extended with Quire and Crossing in the 1960s and a magnificent gothic-style lantern tower, Transept and Apostles' Chapel, will complete the Cathedral to mark the millennium. Dedicated to St James, Patron Saint of Pilgrims, is subtly reflected in architectural hints of Spain.

Location: OS Ref. TL857 642. Bury St Edmunds town centre.

Opening Times: All year: daily 8.30am - 6pm, Jun - Aug: 8.30am - 7pm.

Admission: Donation invited.

SAXTEAD GREEN POST MILL   **Tel:** 01728 685789

Post Mill Bungalow, Saxtead Green, Woodbridge, Suffolk IP13 9QQ

Owner: English Heritage   **Contact:** The Custodian

The finest example of a Suffolk Post Mill. Still in working order, you can climb the wooden stairs to the various floors, full of fascinating mill machinery. Ceased production in 1947.

Location: OS Ref. TM253 645. 2^1/$_2$ m NW of Framlingham on A1120.

Opening Times: 1 Apr - 31 Oct: Mon - Sat, 10am - 6pm (5pm in Oct). Closed 1 - 2pm.

Admission: Adult £2.20, Child £1.10, Conc. £1.70.

SHRUBLAND PARK GARDENS   **Tel:** 01473 830221 **Fax:** 01473 832202

Ipswich, Suffolk IP6 9QQ

Owner/Contact: Lord de Suamarez

One of the finest examples of an Italianate garden in England, designed by Sir Charles Barry.

Location: OS Ref. TM125 525. 6m N of Ipswich to the E of A14/A140.

Opening Times: 15 Apr - 23 Sept: Suns & BH Mons, 2 - 5pm.

Admission: Adult £3, Child/OAP £2.

SOMERLEYTON HALL & GARDENS

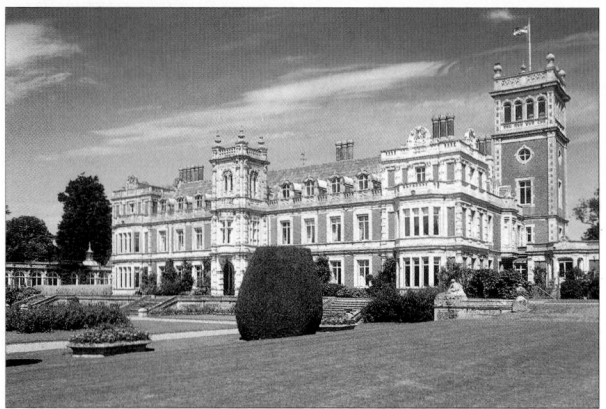

SOMERLEYTON, LOWESTOFT, SUFFOLK NR32 5QQ

Owner/Contact: The Rt Hon Lord Somerleyton GCVO

Tel: 01502 730224 office or 01502 732950 (Entrance Gate) **Fax:** 01502 732143

Splendid early Victorian mansion built in Anglo-Italian style by Sir Morton Peto, with lavish architectural features, magnificent carved stonework and fine state rooms. Paintings by Landseer, Wright of Derby and Stanfield, wood carvings by Willcox of Warwick and Grinling Gibbons. Somerleyton's 12-acre gardens are justly renowned with beautiful borders, specimen trees and the 1846 yew hedge maze which ranks amongst the finest in the country. Special features include glasshouses by Paxton, 300ft pergola, walled garden, Vulliamy tower clock, Victorian ornamentation.

Location: OS134 Ref. TM493 977. 5m NW of Lowestoft on B1074, 7m SW of Great Yarmouth off A143.

Opening Times: Easter Sun - Sept: Thurs, Suns, BHs. Jul & Aug: Tue - Thur, Suns & BHs. Gardens: 12.30 - 5.30pm. Hall: 1 - 5pm. Closed all other dates except by appointment. Private group tours by arrangement.

Admission: Adult £5.50, Child £2.60, OAP £5, Family (2+2) £14.80. Groups: Adult £4.80, Child/Student £2.40. Prices and opening times subject to review.

No photography in house. Receptions/functions/conferences. By arrangement.

SOUTH ELMHAM HALL

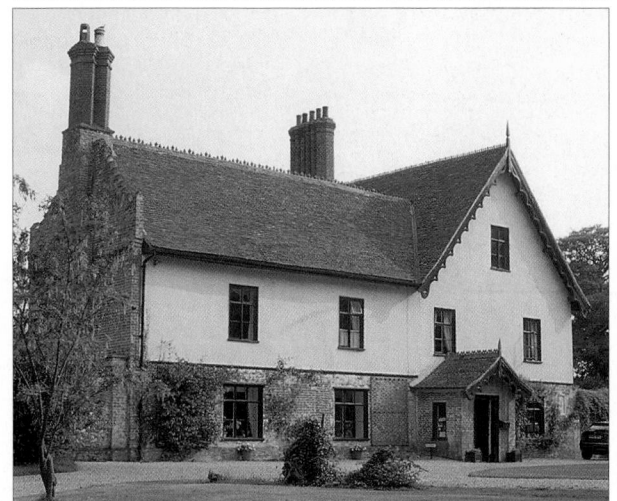

ST CROSS, HARLESTON, NORFOLK IP20 0PZ

Owner: John Sanderson **Contact:** *Jo & John Sanderson*

Tel: 01986 782526 **Fax:** 01986 782203 **e-mail:** john@southelmham.co.uk

A Grade I listed medieval manor house set inside moated enclosure. Originally built by the Bishop of Norwich around 1270. Much altered in the 16th century. Self guided trail through former deer park to South Elmham Minster, a ruined Norman chapel with Saxon origins.

Location: OS30 Ref. TM778 324. Between Harleston and Bungay from the A143 take the B1062.

Opening Times: Minster, Walks (free) & Café: Easter - 31 Oct: Suns, Thurs, Fris & BH Mons. 1 Nov - Easter: Suns only, 10.30am - 5pm. Hall: Thurs, some Suns & BH Mons. 1 May - 30 Sept: Guided tours only, 2pm.

Admission: House: Adult £6, Child £3. Groups (12 - 50): Adult £4, Child £2.50.

⬚ ⛁ &WC. ▣ 🏃Obligatory. ▦ 🅿Limited for coaches. 🐕In grounds, on leads. 🔔Licence applied for. ❄ Ⓦ

THE TIDE MILL

Tel: 01473 626618

Woodbridge, Ipswich, Suffolk

Owner/Contact: Geoff Gostling

First recorded in 1170, now fully restored, machinery demonstrated at low tide. Ring for wheel turning times.

Location: OS Ref. TM275 487. By riverside ¼ m SE of Woodbridge town centre. 1¼ m off A12.

Opening Times: Easter, then May - Sept: daily. Apr & Oct: Sats & Suns only, 11am - 5pm.

Admission: Adult £1.50, Child Free, Conc. £1.

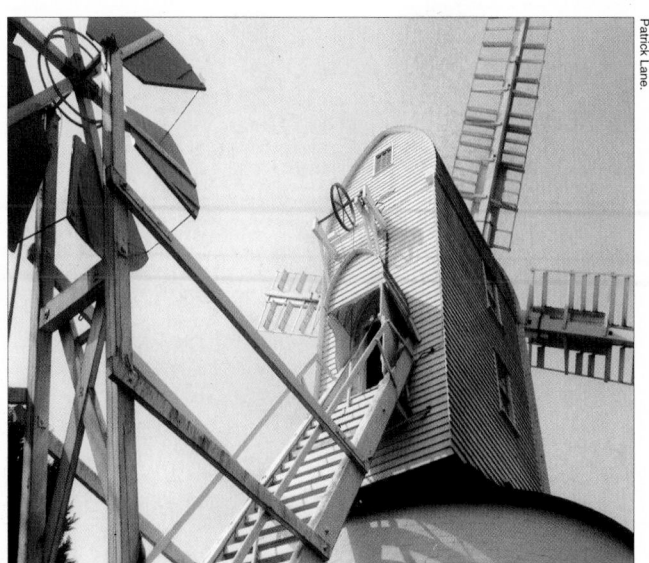

Patrick Lane.

Saxtead Green Post Mill, Suffolk.

WINGFIELD OLD COLLEGE & GDNS 🏛

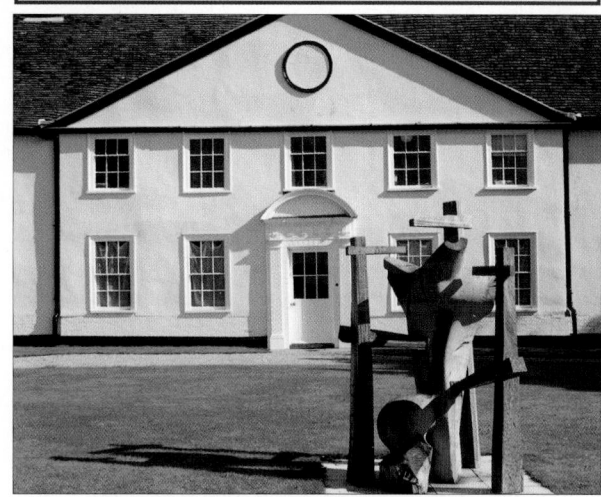

WINGFIELD, Nr STRADBROKE, SUFFOLK IP21 5RA

Owner: Mr & Mrs Ian Chance **Contact:** *Mrs H Chance*

Tel: 01379 384888 **Fax:** 01379 388082

Delightful family home with walled gardens. Lovely old Suffolk house with spectacular medieval great hall, contemporary art in the new College Yard Visual Arts Visitor Centre, garden sculpture, collections of ceramics and textiles, 4 acres of gardens with topiary, ponds and old roses, in unspoilt Suffolk countryside. Steeped in history, this "oasis of arts and heritage" offers an afternoon of discovery and relaxation. Children's play garden. Teas in College Yard. Open in 2001 – newly restored Walled Arts Garden.

Location: OS Ref. TM230 767. Signposted off B1118 (2m N of Stradbroke) and B1116 at Fressingfield.

Opening Times: 14 Apr - 30 Sept: Sats & Suns, 2 - 6pm.

Admission: Adult £3.60, Child/Student £1.50, OAP £3, Family £8.50 (2000 prices).

⛁ ⛁ Wedding receptions. & ▣ 🏃 By arrangement for groups. 🅿 ▦ 🐕 Guide dogs only.

WYKEN HALL GARDENS

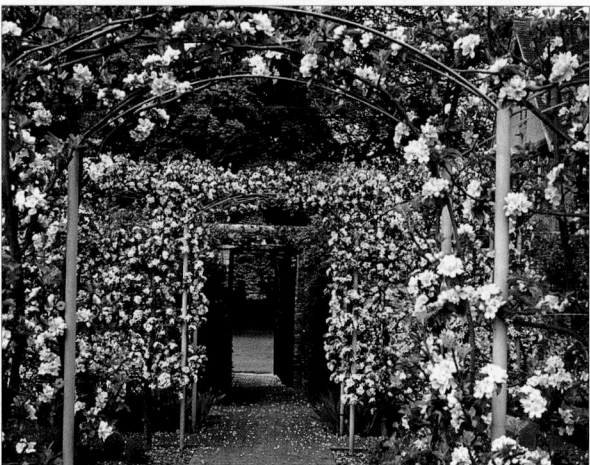

STANTON, BURY ST EDMUNDS, SUFFOLK IP31 2DW

Owner: Sir Kenneth & Lady Carlisle **Contact:** *Mrs Barbara Hurn*

Tel: 01359 250287 **Fax:** 01359 252256

The Elizabethan manor house is surrounded by a romantic, plant-lover's garden with maze, knot and herb garden and rose garden featuring old roses. A walk through ancient woodlands leads to Wyken Vineyards, winner of EVA Wine of the Year. In the 16th century barn, the Vineyard Restaurant serves our wines along with a varied menu from fresh local produce. It is a 'Bib Gourmand' in the Michelin Guide and features also in The Good Food Guide.

Location: OS Ref. TL963 717. 9m NE of Bury St. Edmunds 1m E of A143. Follow brown tourist signs to Wyken Vineyards from Ixworth.

Opening Times: 14 Jan - 24 Dec: Wed - Sun & BH Mons, 10am - 6pm. Also Fris & Sats dinner from 7pm. Garden closed on Sats. Gardens only: 1 Apr - 1 Oct.

Admission: Gardens: Adult £2.50, Child (under 12yrs) Free, Conc. £2. Groups by appointment.

⬚ & Grounds suitable. WC. ⛁ Licensed. 🐕 In grounds, on leads. ❄

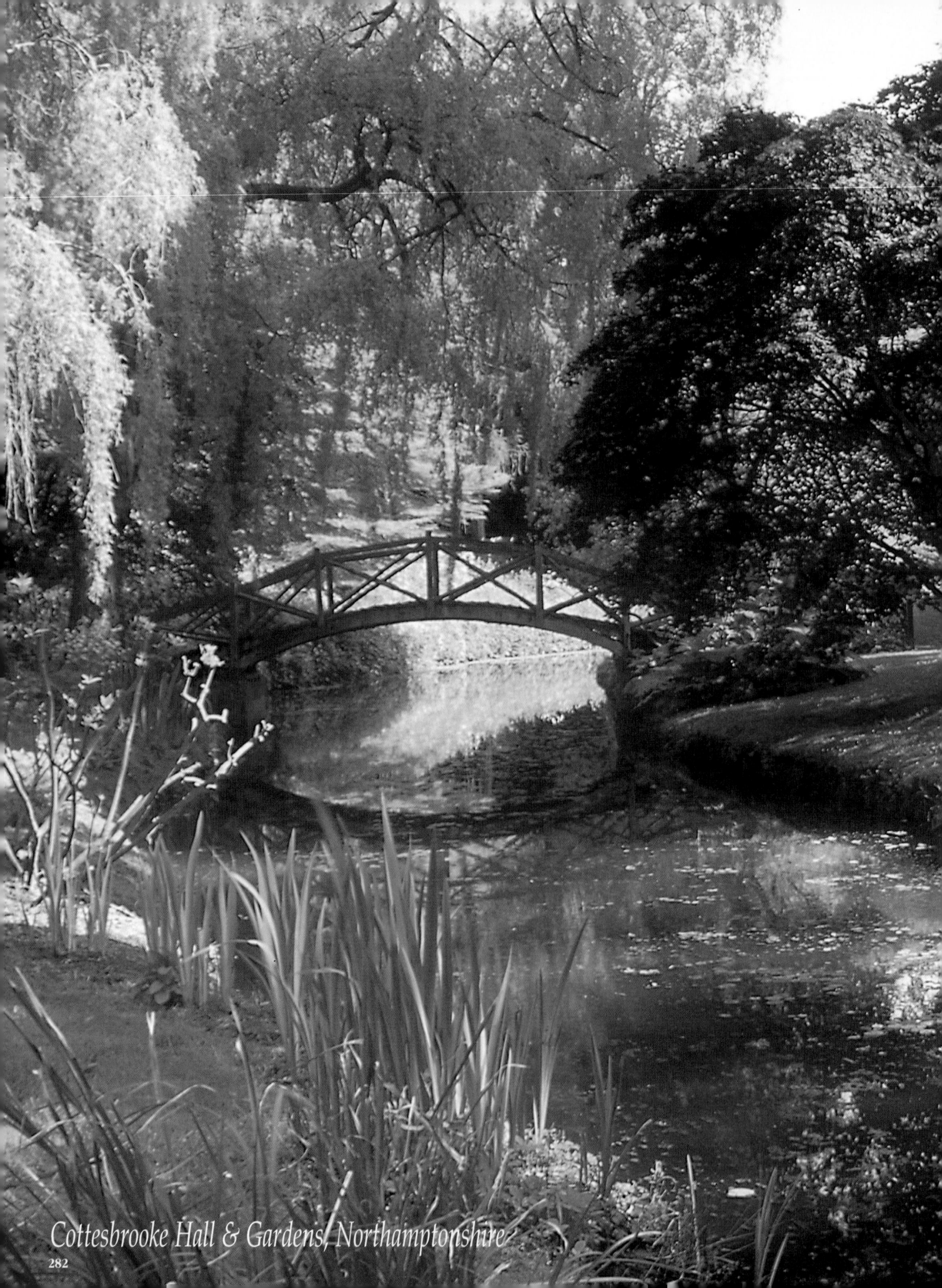

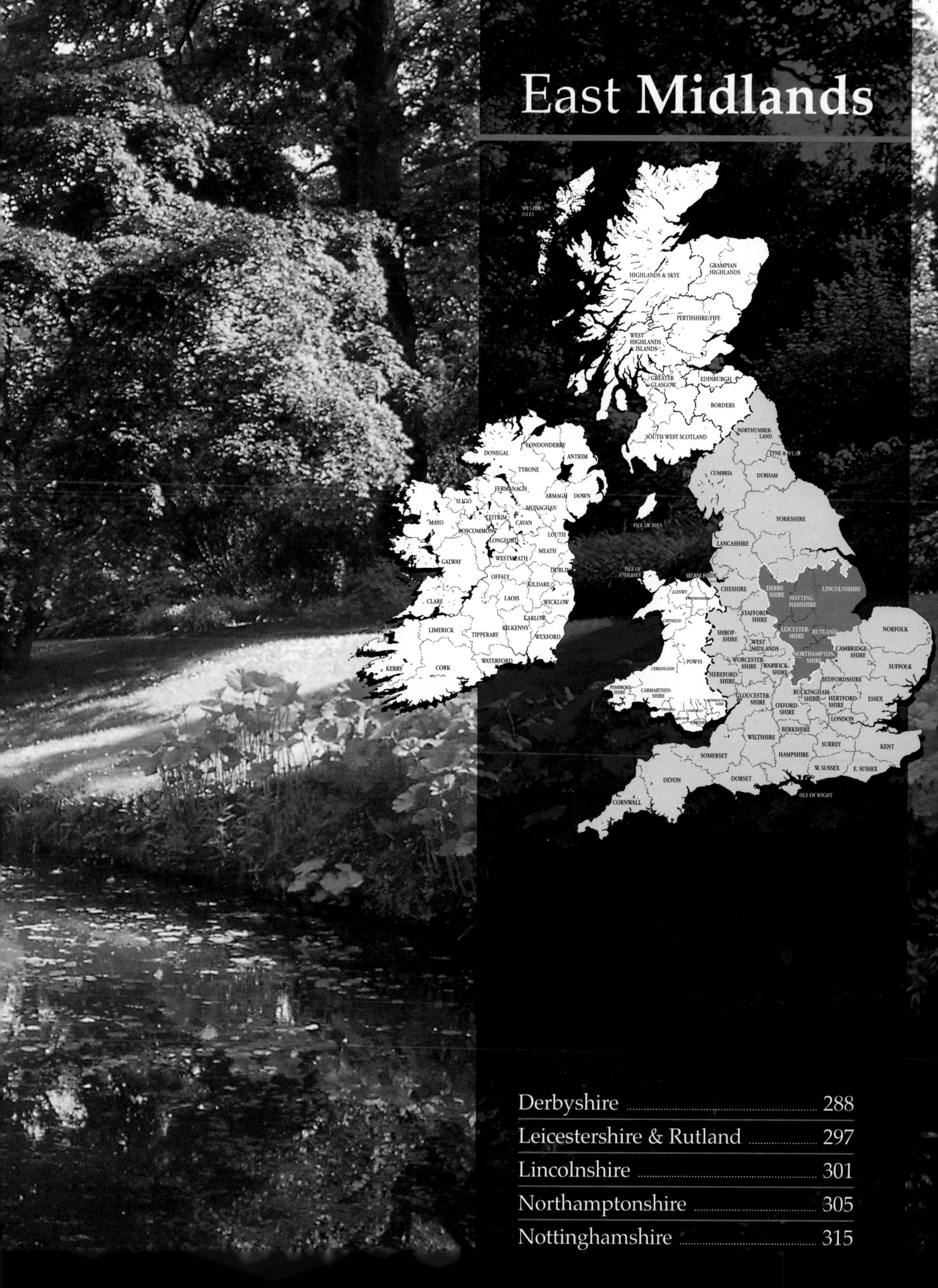

East Midlands

Cottesbrooke Hall and Gardens

"My family and I consider that we are especially fortunate to live at Cottesbrooke, both in the house and for its surroundings."

Captain John Macdonald-Buchanan

Cottesbrooke Hall nestles in rolling open countryside in the northern corner of Northamptonshire, some 10 miles to the north of Northampton. This architecturally exquisite house, built in the reign of Queen Anne for Sir John Langham, 4th Baronet, happily remains delightfully untouched by the vagaries of future architectural styles.

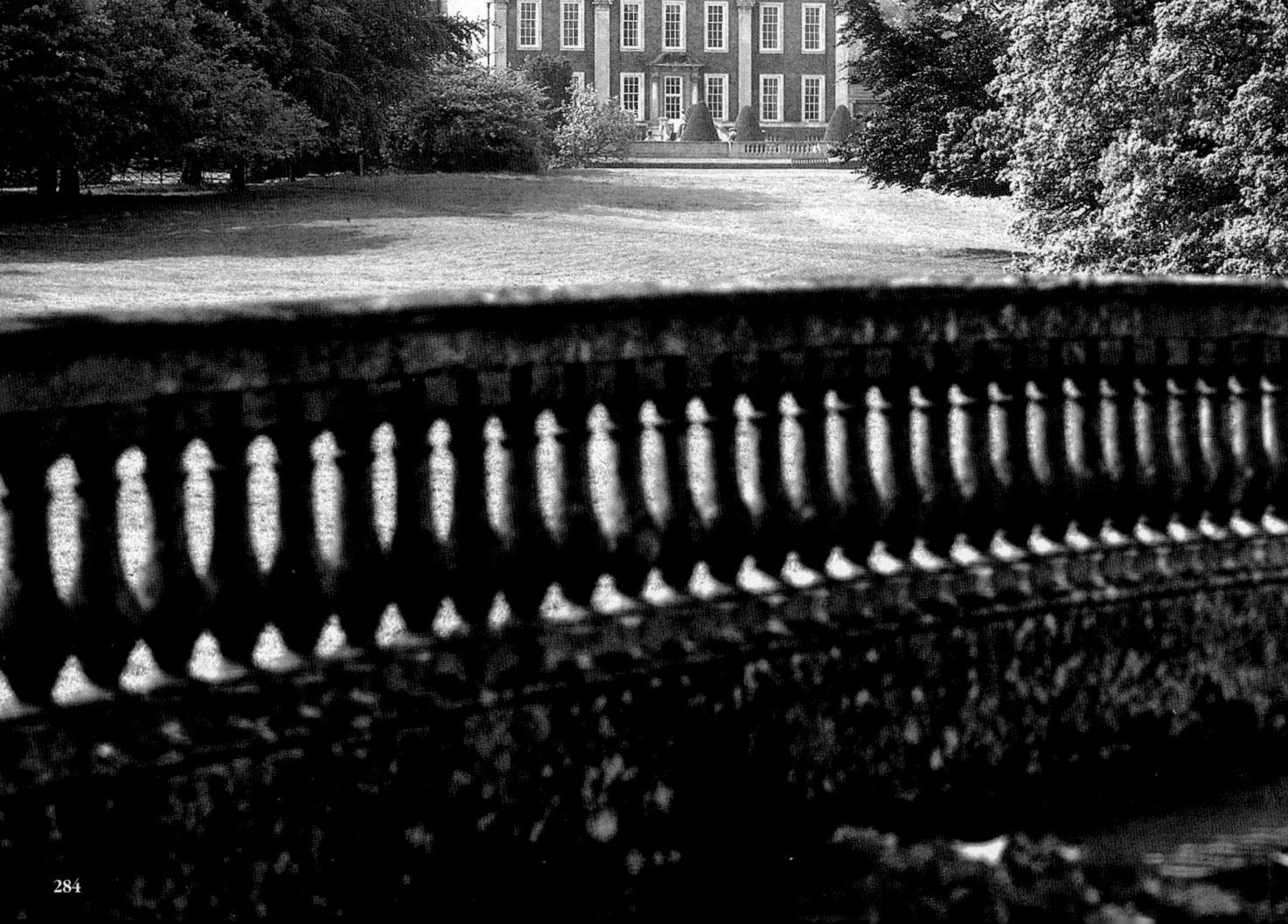

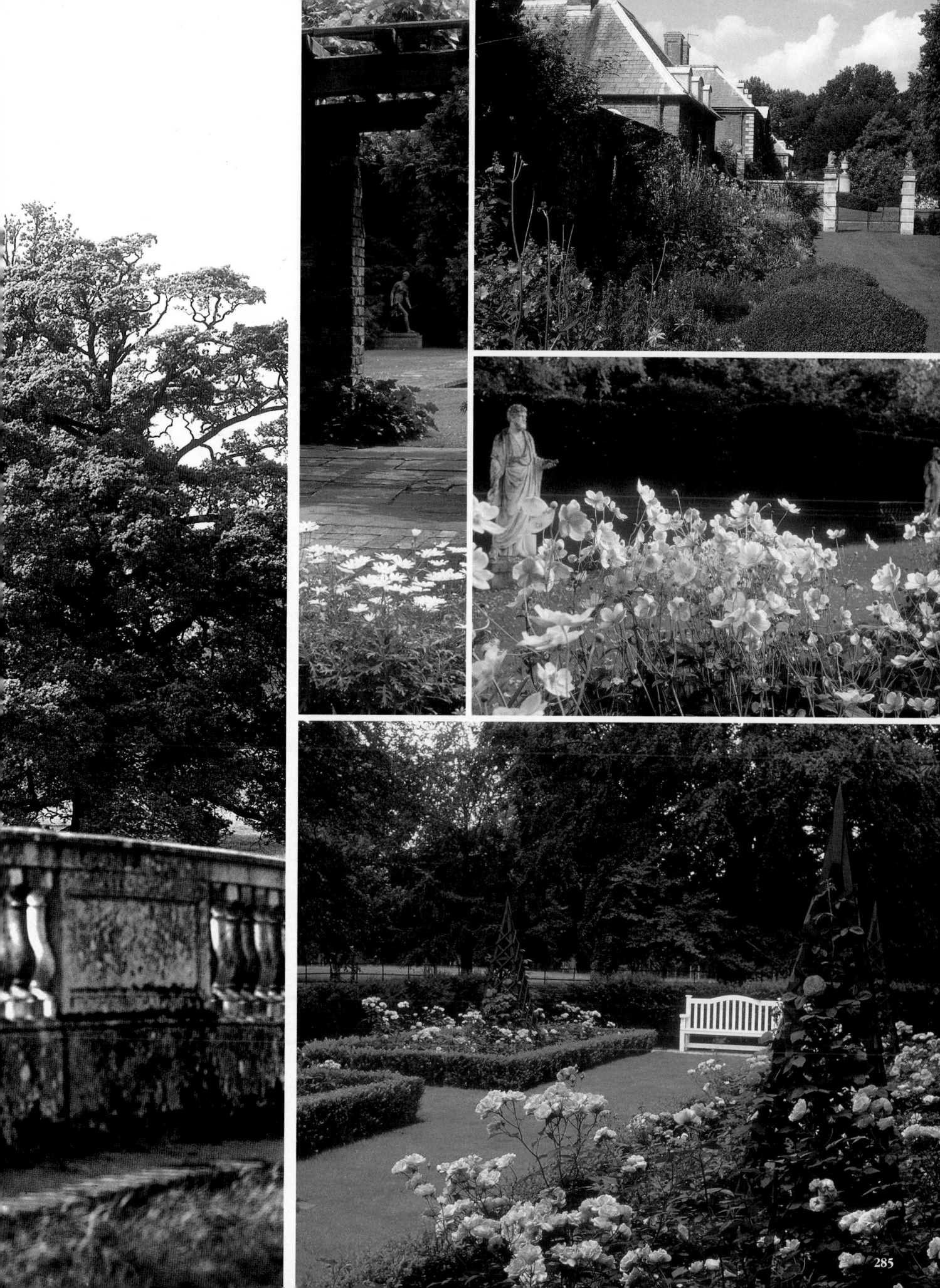

285

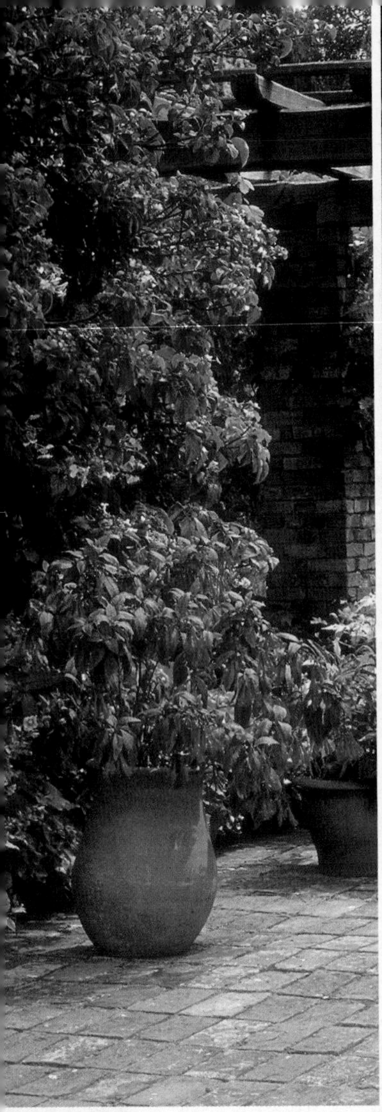

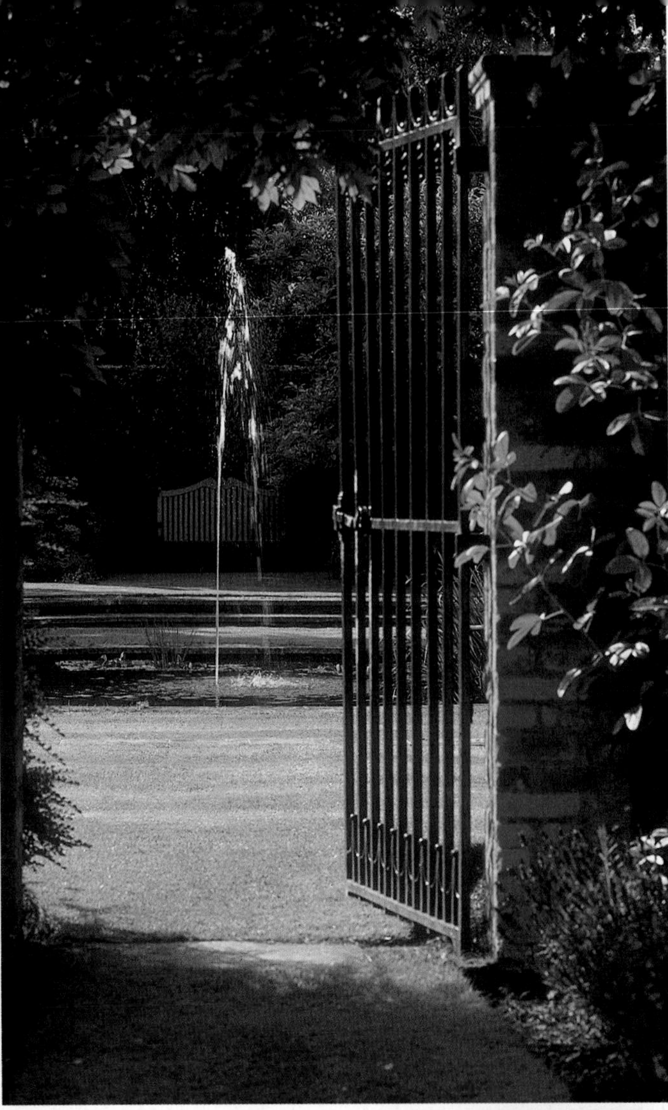

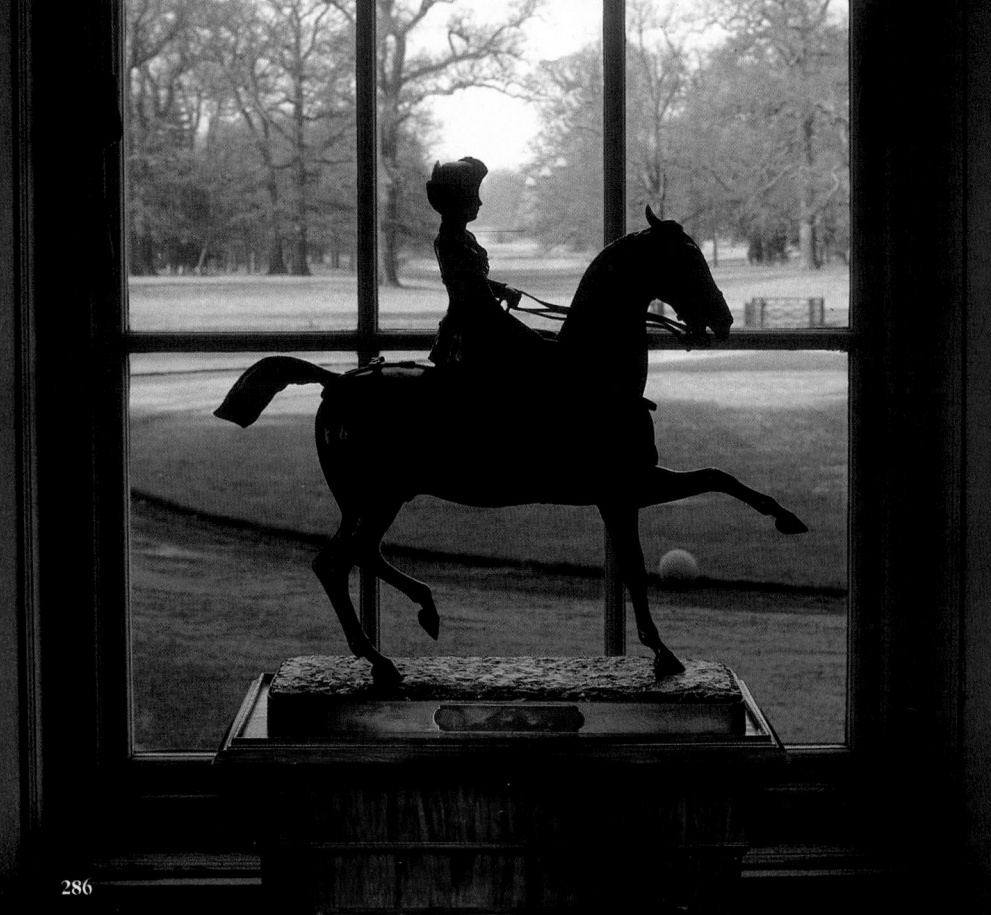

It is thought that the original architect is most likely to have been Francis Smith of Warwick, but it remains a matter for speculation. Built of fine rose-pink brick enriched with pale Ketton stone, the plan of Cottesbrooke today includes a central block containing the principal rooms, with two wings or pavilions connected by blank quadrant walls, serving as arcades. The interior contains wonderful 18th century English and French furniture as well as fine English, Continental and Chinese porcelain. However, it is the 'Woolavington Collection', a collection of sporting and equestrian paintings, for which the house is renowned – considered the finest in Britain.

Regrettably, few records remain to tell the early history of the 18th century landscaping of the park vistas, lakes and garden at Cottesbrooke. However, a striking feature of the house is the way it is sited on an axis looking towards the Anglo-Saxon Brixworth Church, whose spire can be seen three miles away. It seems likely that the south side of the house was built to incorporate the spire as a focal point in the initial landscaping scheme for the Hall.

Today the true distinction of the garden at Cottesbrooke belongs almost entirely to the 20th century. A number of distinguished landscape designers have been involved. These include the Arts & Crafts architect Edward Weir Schultz, Sir Geoffrey Jellicoe before the Second World War, and Dame Sylvia Crowe afterwards.

Between 1911 and 1914 Schultz laid out a Rose Garden with an elaborate pergola south-west of the house. After World War I, the late Hon Lady Macdonald-Buchanan's time, many changes took place and it was she who gave the garden its present character. She removed the pergola in the present Pool Garden and commissioned an elegant pillared pavilion designed by Dame Sylvia Crowe.

There are several notable areas in the gardens. Firstly, the Forecourt – the formal garden to the south front and designed by Sir Geoffrey Jellicoe. It is from here the visitor can enjoy two of the magnificent vistas to the south and south-east of the Hall. To the west is the Statue Walk, more sombre in character – a wide grassy walk leads past a yew hedge, breaking out occasionally into buttresses dominated by its fine early 18th century statues by Peter Scheemakers and formerly at Stowe Park.

Altogether different in character is the Wild Garden leading away from the Hall which, with its acers and rhododendrons, becomes the highlight of the garden in the Spring and Autumn. As with every other aspect of Cottesbrooke, the visitor can wander at leisure through a tranquil scene, managed and maintained with the perfectionist standards of its loving owners.

For further details about *Cottesbrooke Hall and Gardens* see entry in East Midlands Region → Northamptonshire.

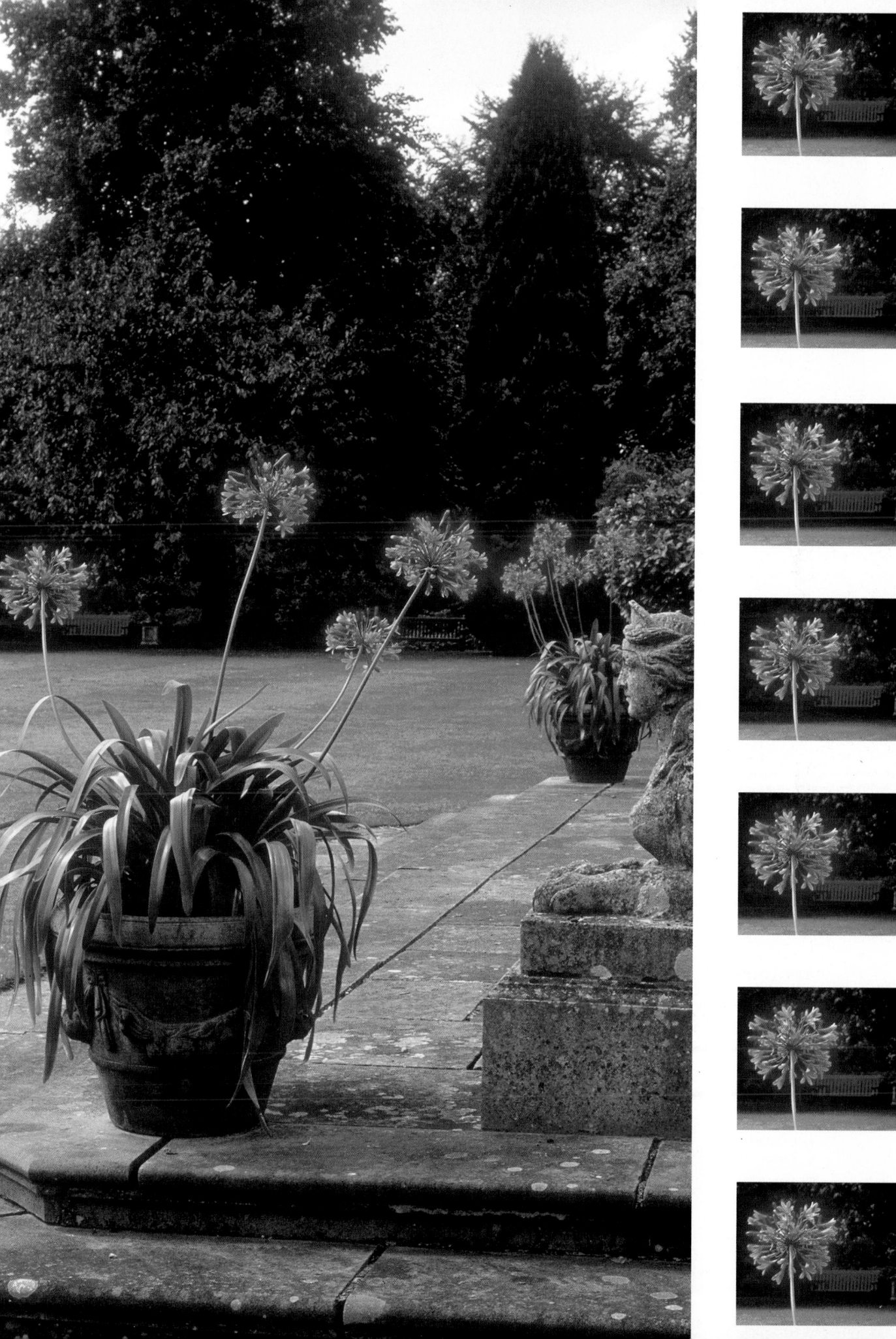

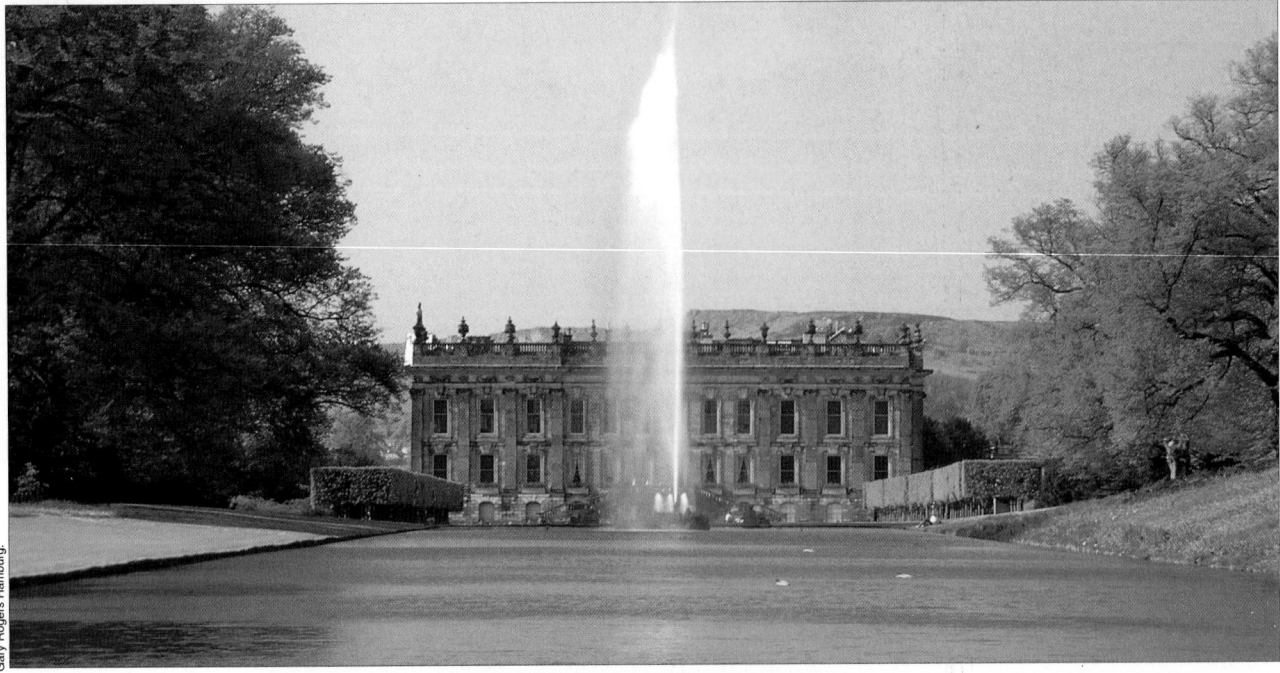

Gary Rogers Hamburg.

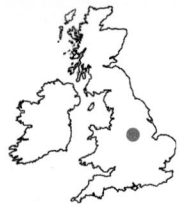

Owner: Trustees of the Chatsworth Settlement. Home of the Duke & Duchess of Devonshire

CONTACT

Mr John Oliver
Chatsworth
Bakewell
Derbyshire
DE45 1PP

Tel: 01246 582204
01246 565300

Fax: 01246 583536

e-mail: visit@
chatsworth-house.co.uk

LOCATION

OS Ref. SK260 703

From London
3 hrs M1/J29,
signposted via
Chesterfield.

3m E of Bakewell,
off B6012,
10m W of Chesterfield.

Rail: Chesterfield
Station, 11m.

Bus: Chesterfield -
Baslow, 1¹/₂ m.

CONFERENCE/FUNCTION		
ROOM	SIZE	MAX CAPACITY
Hartington Rm.		70
Coffee Rm.		24

CHATSWORTH
Bakewell

The great Treasure House of Chatsworth was first built by Bess of Hardwick in 1552 and has been lived in by the Cavendish family, the Dukes of Devonshire, ever since. The House today owes its appearance to the 1st Duke who remodelled the building at the end of the 17th century, while the 6th Duke added a wing 130 years later. Visitors can see 26 rooms including the run of 5 virtually unaltered 17th century State Rooms and Chapel. There are painted ceilings by Verrio, Thornhill and Laguerre, furniture by William Kent and Boulle, tapestries from Mortlake and Brussels, a library of over 17,000 volumes, sculpture by Cibber and Canova, old master paintings by Rembrandt, Hals, Van Dyck, Tintoretto, Veronese, Landseer and Sargent; the collection of neo-classical sculpture, Oriental and European porcelain and the dazzling silver collection, including an early English silver chandelier. The present Duke has added to the collection. In 2001 the special exhibition in the House will be devoted to 20th century works of art collected by the present Duke and Duchess, including work by Epstein, Freud, Sickert and Gwen John. In 1996 and 1999 Chatsworth was voted the public's favourite house winning the NPI National Heritage Gold Award.

GARDEN

The 105 acre garden was created during three great eras in garden and landscape design. The 200 metre Cascade, the Willow Tree fountain and the Canal survive from the 1st Duke's formal garden. 'Capability' Brown landscaped the garden and park in the 1760s. The 6th Duke's gardener, Sir Joseph Paxton, built rockeries and designed a series of glasshouses. He also created the Emperor fountain, the tallest gravity-fed fountain in the world. More recent additions include the Rose, Cottage and Kitchen gardens, the Serpentine Hedge and the Maze. In 1999, a new water sculpture, Revelation, was unveiled.

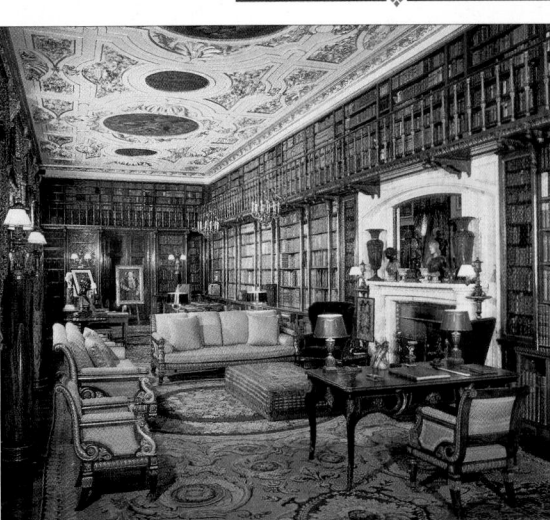

i / shop Farmyard and Adventure Playground. Guide book translations and audio guides in French, German, Italian, Spanish and Japanese.

♿ No wheelchairs in house, but welcome in garden (3 electric, 7 standard available). WCs. Special leaflet.

T New rooms available for conferences and private functions. Contact Head of Catering.

🍴 Restaurant (max 300); home-made food. Menus on request.

🚶 Private tours of house or Greenhouses and Behind the Scenes Days, by arrangement only (extra charges apply). Tape recorded tour may be hired at entrance. Groups please pre-book.

P Cars 100 yds, Coaches 25 yds from house.

👶 Guided tours, packs, trails and school room. Free preliminary visit recommended.

❄

OPENING TIMES

SUMMER
21 March - 28 October.

Daily: 11am - 4.30pm.

WINTER
Closed.

The Park is open free throughout the year.

ADMISSION

House & Garden
Adult £7.00
Child £3.00
OAP/Student...........£5.75
Family £17.25
Pre-booked groups
Adult £6.25
School (no tour).......£3.00
School (w/tour)........£3.50
OAP/Student...........£5.00
Garden only
Adult £4.00
Child £1.75
OAP/Student...........£3.00
Family £9.50
Scots Suite
Adult £1.00
Child £0.50

Car Park £1.00

**Farmyard &
Adventure Playground**
All............................£3.50
Groups (5+)............£3.00
OAP/School £2.90

SPECIAL EVENTS

• **MAY 12 - 13:**
International Horse Trials.

• **MAY 19 - 20:**
Angling Fair.

• **SEPT 1 - 2:**
Country Fair.

East Midlands
England

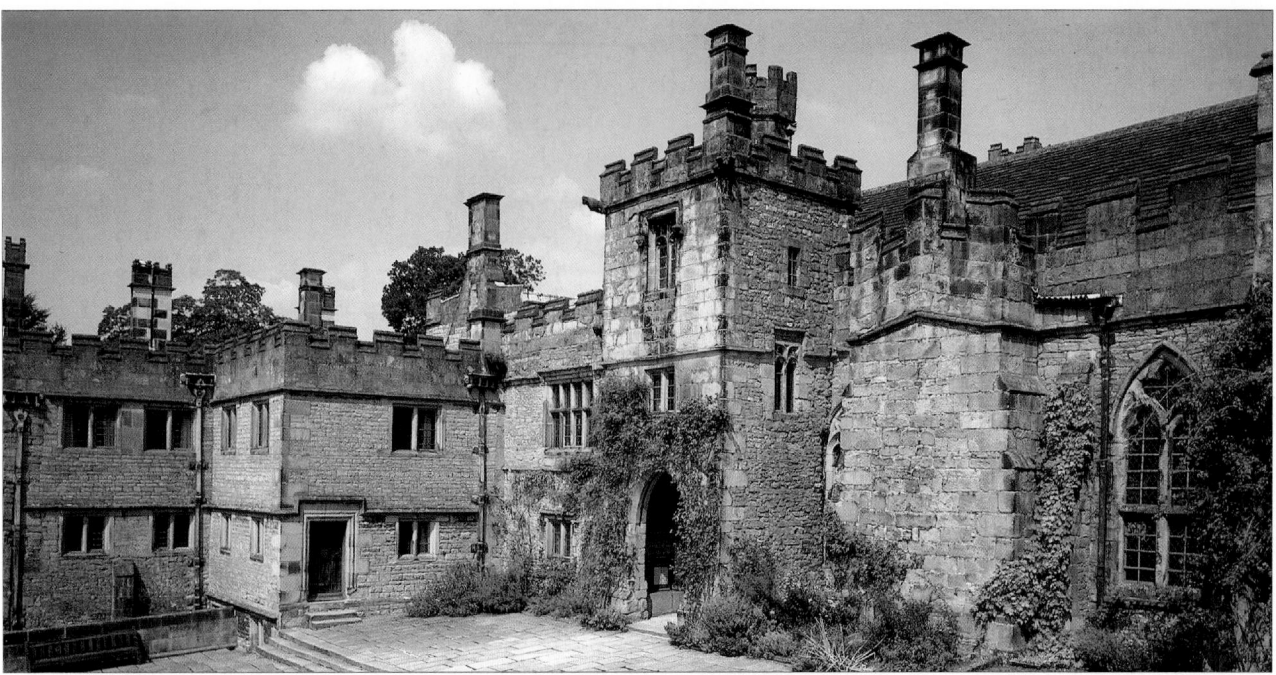

HADDON HALL
Bakewell

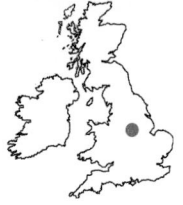

Owner:
Lord Edward Manners

CONTACT

Janet O'Sullivan
Estate Office
Haddon Hall
Bakewell
Derbyshire
DE45 1LA

Tel: 01629 812855

Fax: 01629 814379

e-mail: info@
haddonhall.co.uk

LOCATION

OS Ref. SK234 663

From London 3 hrs
Sheffield ¹/₂ hr
Manchester 1 hr
Haddon is on the
E side of A6 1¹/₂ m
S of Bakewell.
M1/J30.

Rail: Chesterfield
Station, 12m.

Bus: Chesterfield
Bakewell.

William the Conqueror's illegitimate son, Peverel, and his descendants held Haddon for a hundred years before it passed into the hands of the Vernons. Over the following four centuries, the existing medieval and Tudor manor house developed from its Norman origins. In the late 16th century, the estate passed through marriage to the Manners family, later to become Dukes of Rutland, in whose possession it has remained ever since.

Little has been added since the reign of Henry VIII, whose elder brother, Arthur, was a frequent guest of the Vernons. He would have been quite familiar with the house as it stands today – the Great Hall, kitchens and Chapel all dating from the 14th century. Incredibly, despite its time worn steps, no other medieval house has so triumphantly withstood the passage of time. *Jane Eyre* (1996), *The Prince and the Pauper* (1996) and *Elizabeth* (1997) were filmed at Haddon.

GARDENS

The award-winning terraced Rose Gardens are planned for year-round colour. Over 150 varieties of rose and clematis, many over 70 years old, provide colour and scent throughout the summer.

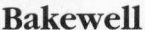

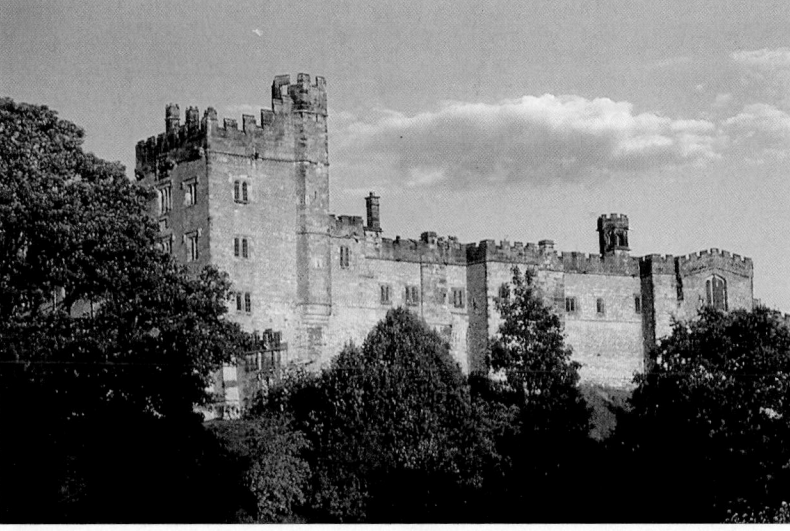

OPENING TIMES

SUMMER
1 April - 30 September
(closed Sun 15 July).

Daily: 10.30am - 5.45pm.
Last admission 5pm.

October: Mon - Thur
10.30am - 4.30pm
Last admission 4pm.

WINTER
November - 31 March
Closed.

ADMISSION

SUMMER
Adult £5.90
Child (5 -15yrs).........£3.00
Conc........................£5.00
Family (2+3) £15.00

Groups (20+)
Adult £5.00
Child (5 -15yrs).........£2.75
Conc........................£4.25

SPECIAL EVENTS

Please telephone for details.

🛍 ℹ️ Recent productions testify to Haddon's suitability as a film location: *Jane Eyre* (1996) Rochester Films; *Prince and the Pauper* (1996) BBC; *Elizabeth I* (1997).

♿ Not suitable, steep approach, varying levels of house.

🍴 Self-service restaurant (max 75). Home-made food.

👥 Special tours £25 extra for groups of 15, 7 days' notice.

🅿 Ample, 450 yds from house. 50p per car.

👤 Tours of the house bring alive Haddon Hall of old. Costume room also available, very popular!

🐕 Guide dogs only.

East Midlands England

BAKEWELL OLD HOUSE MUSEUM   **Tel:** 01629 815294

Cunningham Place, Bakewell DE45 1DD
Owner: Bakewell District Historical Society   **Contact:** The Secretary
A rare and curious Peakland house built by Ralf Gell in 1534.
Location: OS Ref. SK215 685. 100 yds W of Bakewell Parish Church.
Opening Times: Please contact for details.
Admission: Adult £2.50, Child £1, Child under 5yrs free.

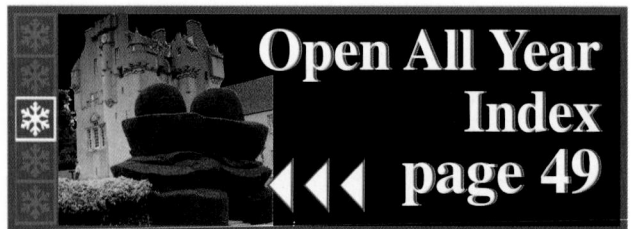

Open All Year
Index
◀◀◀ page 49

BOLSOVER CASTLE

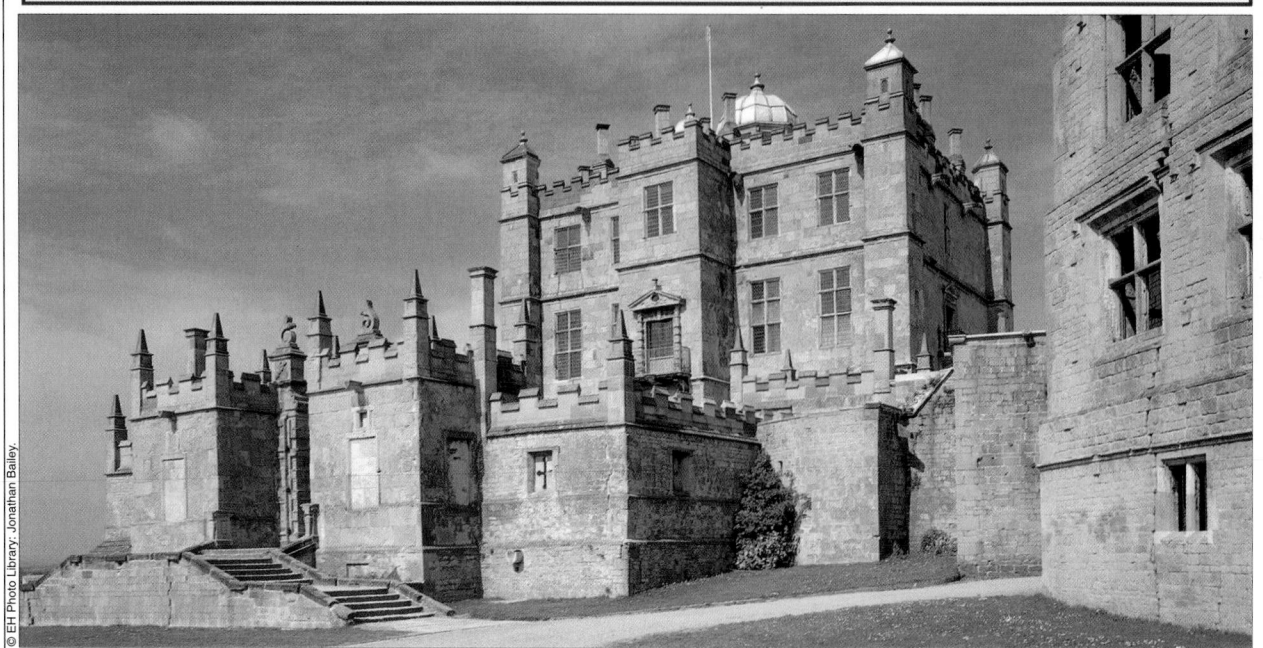

© EH Photo Library, Jonathan Bailey

CASTLE STREET, BOLSOVER, DERBYSHIRE S44 6PR

Owner: *English Heritage*   **Contact:** *The Custodian*

Tel: 01246 822844

An enchanting and romantic spectacle, situated high on a wooded hilltop dominating the surrounding landscape. Built on the site of a Norman castle, this is largely an early 17th century mansion. Most delightful is the 'Little Castle', a bewitching folly with intricate carvings, panelling and wall painting. See the restored interiors of the Little Castle and the working Venus Fountain and statuary. There is also an impressive 17th century indoor Riding House built by the Duke of Newcastle. Enjoy the Visitor and Discovery Centre. Bolsover is now available for civil weddings, receptions and corporate hospitality.

Location: OS120, Ref. SK471 707. Off M1/J29, 6m from Mansfield. In Bolsover 6m E of Chesterfield on A632.

Opening Times: 1 Apr - 31 Oct: daily, 10am - 6pm (5pm in Oct). 1 Nov - 31 Mar: Wed - Sun, 10am - 4pm. Closed 24 - 26 Dec & 1 Jan.

Admission: Adult £5, Child £2.50, Conc. £3.80, Family £12.50. 15% discount for groups (11+).

  Grounds suitable. WC. 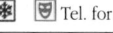 Tel. for details.

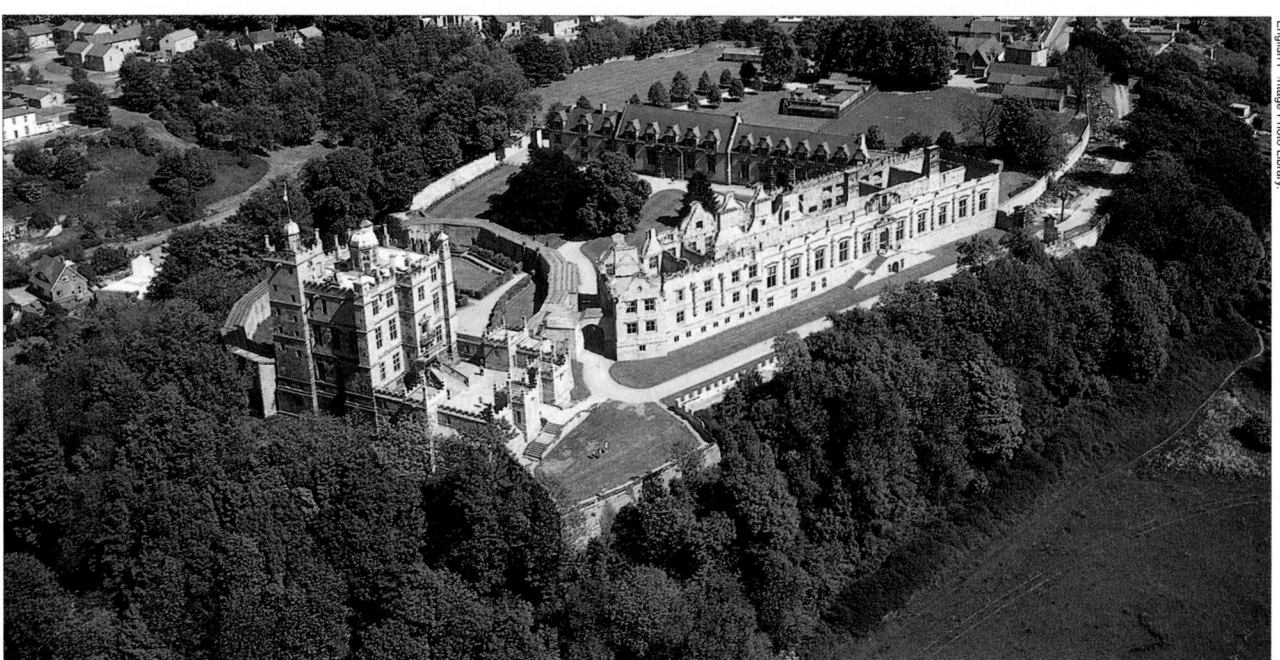

English Heritage Photo Library

Bolsover Castle, Derbyshire.

East Midlands England

CALKE ABBEY

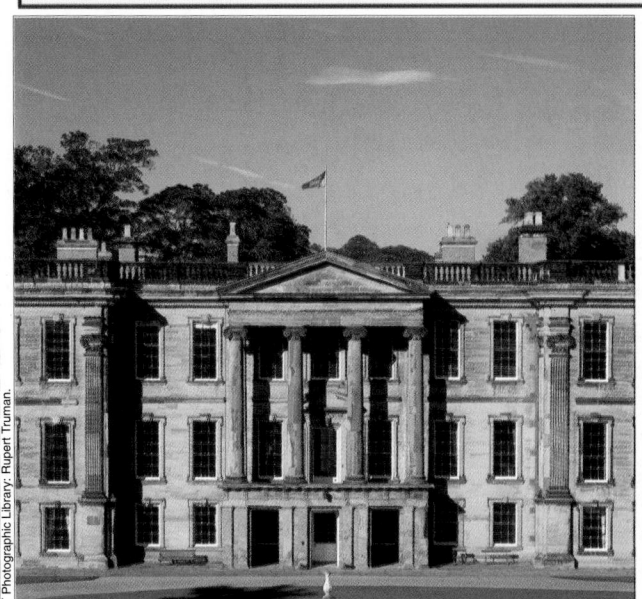

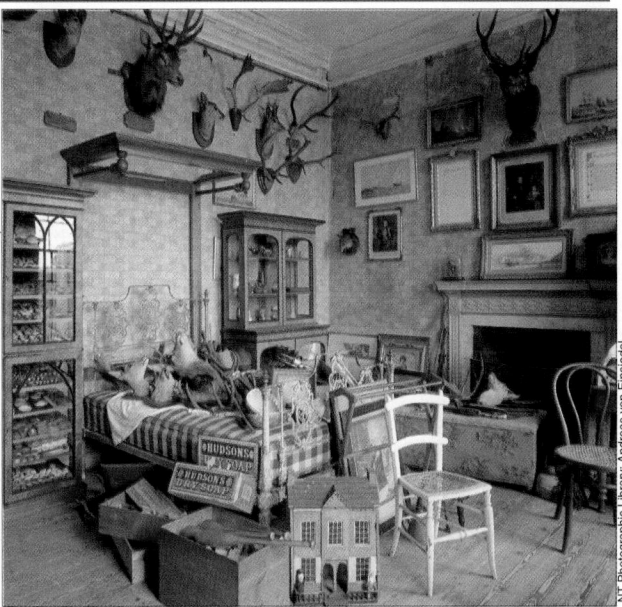

NT Photographic Library: Rupert Truman.

NT Photographic Library: Andreas von Einsiedel.

TICKNALL, DERBYSHIRE DE73 1LE

Owner: The National Trust   *Contact:* The Property Manager

Tel: 01332 863822 **Fax:** 01332 865272

The house that time forgot, this baroque mansion, built 1701 - 3 for Sir John Harpur and set in a landscaped park. Little restored, Calke is preserved by a programme of conservation as a graphic illustration of the English country house in decline; it contains the family's collection of natural history, a magnificent 18th century state bed and interiors that are virtually unchanged since the 1880s. Walled garden, pleasure grounds and recently restored orangery. Early 19th century Church. Historic parkland with Portland sheep and deer. Staunton Harold Church is nearby.

Location: OS128 Ref. SK356 239. 10m S of Derby, on A514 at Ticknall between Swadlincote and Melbourne.

Opening Times: House, Garden & Church: 31 Mar - 4 Nov: Sat - Wed & BH Mons (closed Good Fri). House & Church: 1 - 5.30pm (last admission 5pm), Garden: 11am - 5.30pm (last adm. 5pm). Park: Most days until 9pm or dusk if earlier. Ticket office from 11am. Closed Sat 11 Aug for concert. Shop & Restaurant only: 10 Nov - 23 Dec & Jan - Mar 2002: Sats & Suns, 11am - 4pm.

Admission: All sites: Adult £5.20, Child £2.60, Family £13. Garden only: £2.50. Discount for pre-booked groups.

House suitable. Braille guide. Wheelchairs. WCs. Licensed. By arrangement. In park, on leads only.

CARNFIELD HALL

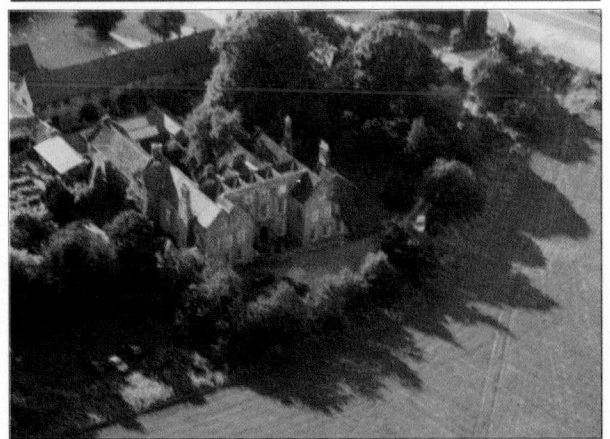

SOUTH NORMANTON, Nr ALFRETON, DERBYSHIRE DE55 2BE

Owner/Contact: J B Cartland

Tel: 01773 520084

Unspoilt Elizabethan 'Mansion House'. Panelled rooms, two 17th century staircases, great chamber. From 1502 the seat of the Revell, Wilmot and Cartland families. Atmospheric interior with three centuries of portraits, furniture, china, needlework, costumes, royal relics and manorial documents. Guided tours by the owner. Fine fan and costume collection, if booked for groups in advance, and candlelit evening visits in winter. Old walled garden

Location: OS Ref. SK425 561. 1½ m W of M1/J28 on B6019. Alfreton Station 5 mins walk.

Opening Times: Spring & Summer BHs including Good Fri & Mon; Easter – 30 Sept: most weekends; 2 - 5 Jul & Aug: Most Tues & Thurs; 2 - 5pm. By appointment throughout the year (including evenings) for groups (4-22). Winter: Some weekends if fine, 2 - 4pm. NB. Times may vary. Please telephone to confirm dates and times.

Admission: Adult £4, Child (8-16yrs) £2, Conc. £3. Groups: Adult £3.50, Child (8-16yrs) £1.50, Conc. £2.50. Groups must book. No reduction for evening visits.

No photography in Hall. Grounds suitable. WCs. Licensed. Obligatory. In grounds, on leads only.

CATTON HALL

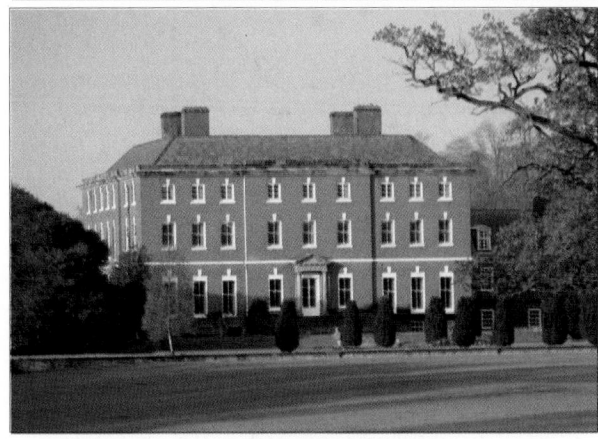

CATTON, WALTON-ON-TRENT, SOUTH DERBYSHIRE DE12 8LN

Owner/Contact: Robin & Katie Neilson

Tel: 01283 716311 **Fax:** 01283 712876 **e-mail:** kneilson@catton-hall.com

Catton, built in 1745, has been in the hands of the same family since 1405 and is still lived in by the Neilsons as their private home. This gives the house, with its original collection of 17th and 18th century portraits, pictures and antique furniture, a unique, relaxed and friendly atmosphere. Catton is available for corporate entertaining throughout the year. With its spacious reception rooms and luxury accommodation it is ideal for exclusive business meetings, lunches, dinners and for exhibitors and visitors to Birmingham. The 100 acres of parkland alongside the River Trent are ideal for all types of corporate and public events.

Location: OS Ref. SK206 154. 2m E of A38 at Alrewas between Lichfield & Burton-on-Trent (8m from each). Birmingham NEC 20m.

Opening Times: By arrangement only: Conferences/meetings, product launches, wedding receptions, team building, activity days, motorised sports, off road driving, shooting, falconry. Tours: Apr - Oct: Mons only, 1.30pm & 3pm. Groups by appointment only.

Conference facilities. By arrangement. By arrangement. 3 x four posters, 5 twin, all en-suite.

CHATSWORTH
See page 288 for full page entry.

HADDON HALL
See page 289 for full page entry.

CROMFORD MILL (SIR RICHARD ARKWRIGHT'S) Tel/Fax: 01629 823256

Cromford, Nr Matlock, Derbyshire DE4 3RQ   **Contact:** The Visitor Services Dept.
Built in 1771, Cromford Mill is the world's first successful water powered cotton spinning mill, set in the beautiful Derwent Valley surrounded by limestone tors and rolling hills. There is a wholefood restaurant on site with shops, free car parking and friendly staff. A tour guide will explain the story of this important historic site and describe the development plans for the future.
Location: OS Ref. SK296 569. 3m S of Matlock, 17m N of Derby just off A6.
Opening Times: All year except Christmas Day, 9am - 5pm.
Admission: Free entry. Guided tours: Adult £2, Conc. £1.50.

[icons] Partially suitable. WCs. In grounds, on leads.

ELVASTON CASTLE COUNTRY PARK   **Tel:** 01332 571342 **Fax:** 01332 758751

Borrowash Road, Elvaston, Derbyshire DE72 3EP
Owner: Derbyshire County Council   **Contact:** The Park Manager
200 acre park landscaped in 19th century. Walled garden. Estate museum with exhibitions of traditional crafts.
Location: OS Ref. SK407 330. 5m SE of Derby, 2m from A6 or A52.
Opening Times: Please contact park for details.
Admission: Museum: Adult £1.20, Child 60p, Family (2+2) £3. Park and Gardens free. Car park: Midweek 70p, weekends/BHs £1.30, Coaches £7.50.

[icons] Ground floor & grounds suitable. WCs. By arrangement. In grounds, on leads.

HARDSTOFT HERB GARDEN   **Tel:** 01246 854268

Hall View Cottage, Hardstoft, Chesterfield, Derbyshire S45 8AH
Owner: Mr Stephen Raynor/L M Raynor   **Contact:** Mr Stephen Raynor
Consists of four display gardens with information boards and well labelled plants.
Location: OS Ref. SK436 633. On B6039 between Holmewood & Tibshelf, 3m from J29 on M1.
Opening Times: 15 Mar - 15 Sept: daily (except Tues) 10am - 5pm. Closed Sunday follwing Aug BH weekend.
Admission: Adult £1, Child Free.

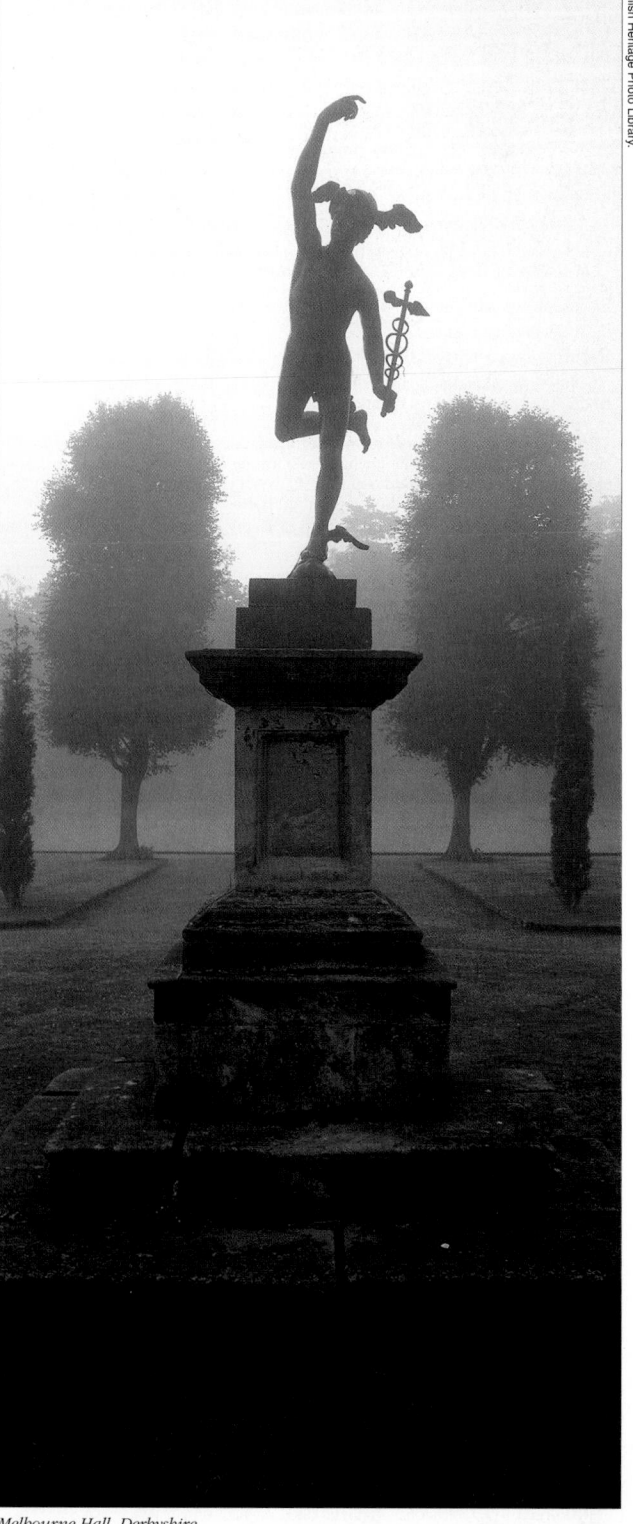

Melbourne Hall, Derbyshire.

EYAM HALL

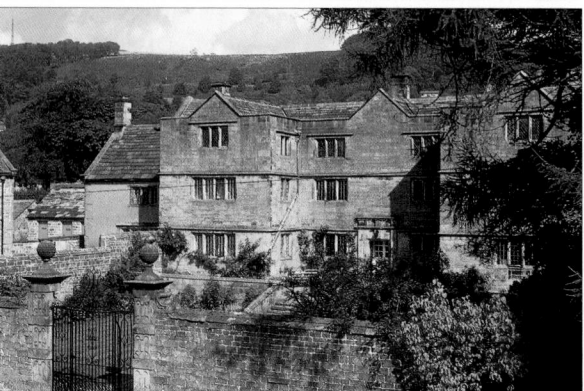

EYAM, HOPE VALLEY, DERBYSHIRE S32 5QW

Owner: Mr R H V Wright   *Contact: Mrs Nicola Wright*

Tel: 01433 631976   **Fax:** 01433 631603   **e-mail:** nicwri@globalnet.co.uk

This small but charming manor house in the famous plague village has been the home of the Wright family since 1671. The present family opened the house to the public in 1992, but it retains the intimate atmosphere of a much-loved private home. The Jacobean staircase, fine tapestries, family portraits and costumes and an impressive tester bed are among its interior treasures. Craft centre, buttery and shops in a historic farmyard, with crafts people at work and authentic local products for sale. Now licensed for Civil wedding ceremonies.
Location: OS119 Ref. SK216 765. Approx 10m from Sheffield, Chesterfield and Buxton. Eyam is off A623 between Stockport and Chesterfield. Eyam Hall is in the centre of the village, past the church.
Opening Times: Jun, Jul & Aug: Tue - Thur, Suns & BH Mons, 11am - 4pm. Victorian Christmas tours, school tours (booked groups only) please telephone for details.
Admission: Adult £4.25, Child £3.25, Conc. £3.75. Family (2+4) £13.50. Group rates available. Craft Centre & Buttery: All year: daily, except Mons, 10.30am - 5pm.

[i] Craft centre. [icons] Partially suitable. WC. Licensed.
Obligatory. [P] In grounds, on leads. Guide dogs only in house.
Tel. for details.

HARDWICK HALL & STAINSBY MILL

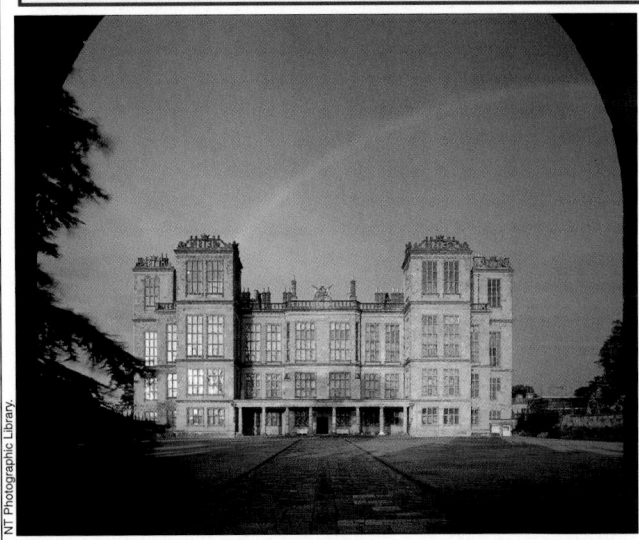
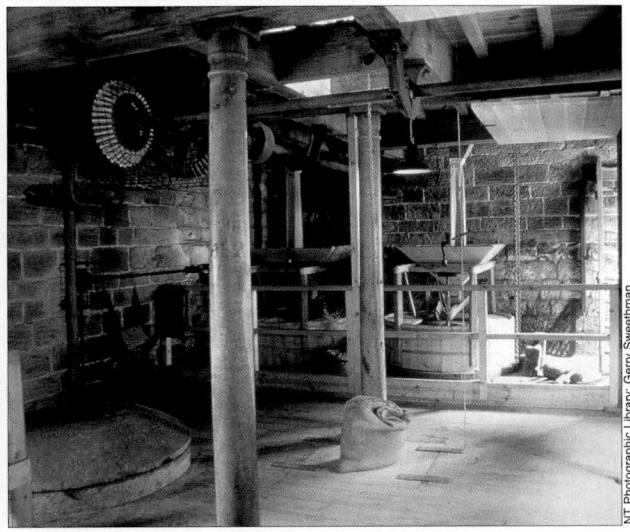

DOE LEA, CHESTERFIELD, DERBYSHIRE S44 5QJ

Owner: The National Trust   *Contact:* The Property Manager

Tel: 01246 850430 **Fax:** 01246 854200 **Shop/Restaurant:** 01246 854088

Hardwick Hall: A late 16th century 'prodigy house' designed by Robert Smythson for Bess of Hardwick. The house contains outstanding contemporary furniture, tapestries and needlework including pieces identified in an inventory of 1601; a needlework exhibition is on permanent display. Walled courtyards enclose fine gardens, orchards and a herb garden. The country park contains Whiteface Woodland sheep and Longhorn cattle.

Location: OS120 Ref. SK456 651. $7^1/2$ m NW of Mansfield, $9^1/2$ m SE of Chesterfield: approach from M1/J29 via A6175.

Opening Times: Hall: 31 Mar - 28 Oct: Weds, Thurs, Sats, Suns & BH Mons, 12.30 - 5pm (closed Good Fri). Last adm. to Hall 4.30pm. Garden: 31 Mar - 28 Oct: daily 12 noon - 5.30pm. Restaurant: open as per Hall: 12 noon - 2pm lunches, 2 - 4.45pm teas.

Admission: Hall & Garden: Adult £6.20, Child £3.10, Family £15.50. Garden only:

Adult £3.30, Child £1.60, Family £8.20. Pre-booking for groups essential, discount for groups of 15+. Timed tickets on busy days, inc NT members. Joint ticket available (Old and New Hall).

Hardwick Estate - Stainsby Mill is an 18th century water-powered corn mill in working order.

Location: OS120 Ref. SK455 653. From M1/J29 take A6175, signposted to Clay Cross then first left and left again to Stainsby Mill.

Opening Times: 31 Mar - 31 May, 1 Oct - 4 Nov: Weds, Thurs, Sats, Suns & BH Mons; 1 Jun - 30 Sept: Wed - Sun & BH Mons, 11am - 4.30pm, last admission 4pm.

Admission: Adult £2, Child £1, Family £5. No discounts for groups. School Groups: Weds & Thurs (plus Fri: Jun - Sept), for information send SAE to Property Manager at Hardwick Hall.

🖼 ♿Hall limited, garden suitable. 🍴Licensed. 🐕In park, on leads.

HARDWICK OLD HALL ▦

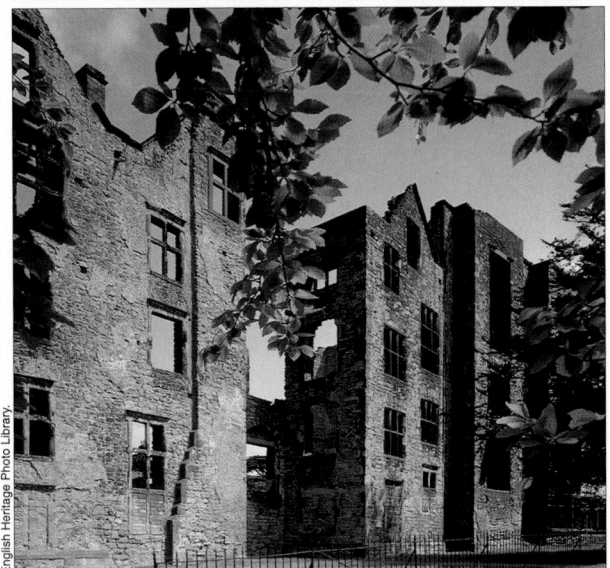

DOE LEA, Nr CHESTERFIELD, DERBYSHIRE S44 5QJ

Owner: National Trust, managed by English Heritage   *Contact:* The Custodian

Tel: 01246 850431

This large ruined house, finished in 1591, still displays Bess of Hardwick's innovative planning and interesting decorative plasterwork. The views from the top floor over the country park and 'New' Hall are spectacular.

Location: OS120 Ref. SK463 638. $7^1/2$ m NW of Mansfield, $9^1/2$ m SE of Chesterfield, off A6175, from M1\J29.

Opening Times: 1 Apr - 31 Oct: Wed - Sun, 10am - 6pm (5pm in Oct).

Admission: Adult £2.75, Child £1.40, Conc. £2.10. 15% discount for groups (11+).

🐕 On leads.

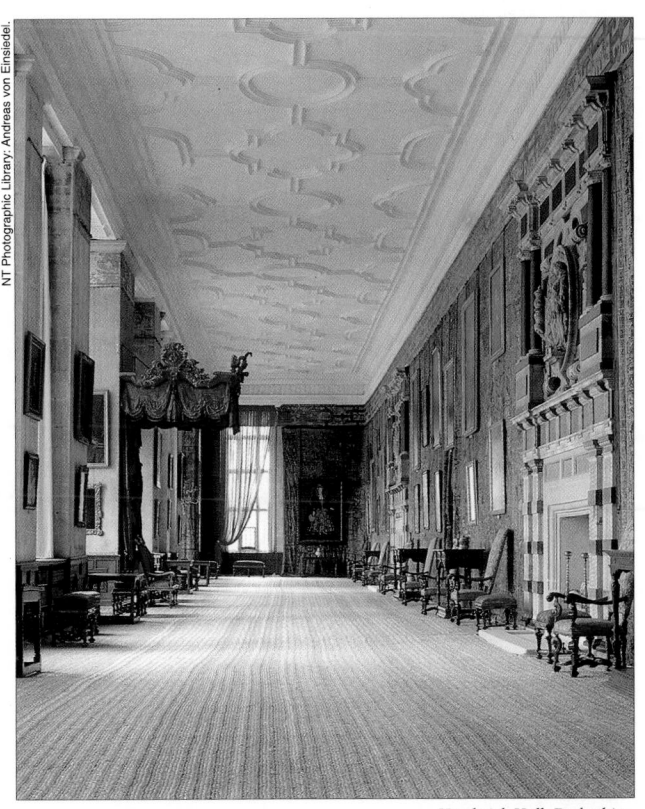

Hardwick Hall, Derbyshire.

KEDLESTON HALL

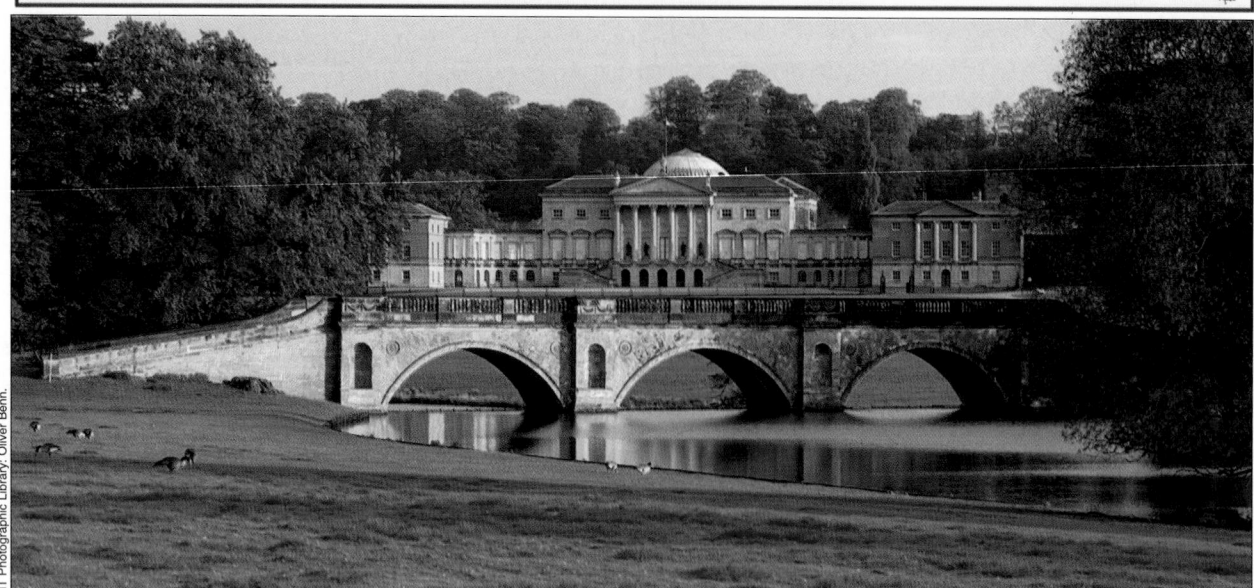

NT Photographic Library: Oliver Benn.

DERBY, DERBYSHIRE DE22 5JH

Owner: *The National Trust*   **Contact:** *The Property Manager*

Tel: 01332 842191   **Fax:** 01332 841972

Experience the age of elegance in this neo-classical house built between 1759 and 1765 for the Curzon family and little altered since. Set in 800 acres of parkland with an 18th century pleasure ground, garden and woodland walks – a day at Kedleston is truly an experience to remember. The influence of the architect Robert Adam is everywhere, from the Park buildings to the decoration of the magnificent state rooms. Groups are welcome and an introductory talk can be arranged.

Location: OS Ref. SK312 403. 5m NW of Derby, signposted from roundabout where A38 crosses A52 Derby ring road.

Opening Times: House: 31 Mar - 4 Nov: Sat - Wed, 12 - 4.30pm. Last adm. 4pm.

Park & Gardens: 11am - 6pm. Restaurant: 11am - 5pm. Shop: 11.30am - 5.30pm. Park only: Thur & Fri, 11am - 6pm, Vehicle charge. Park, Shop & Restaurant: Nov - 23 Dec: Sats & Suns, 12 noon - 4pm.

Admission: Adult £5.10, Child £2.50, Family £12.70. Garden & Park: Adult £2.30, Child £1. Discount for groups, please telephone.

🖼   ♿ Stairclimber & Batricar.   🍴 Licensed.   🐕 In grounds, on leads.
🔔   Ⓣ Tel. for details.

LEA GARDENS

Tel: 01629 534380/534260   **Fax:** 01629 534260

Lea, Matlock, Derbyshire DE4 5GH

Owner/Contact: Mr & Mrs J Tye

The gardens are sited on the remains of a medieval millstone quarry and cover 4 acres within a wooded hillside. A unique collection of rhododendrons, azaleas, kalmias.

Location: OS Ref. SK324 570. On W side of small lane 600yds SW of Lea village & ¹/₂ m N of Holloway. 1¹/₂ m NE of A6, 2¹/₂ m SE of Matlock.

Opening Times: 20 Mar - 30 Jun: 10am - 5.30pm.

Admission: Adult £3, Child 50p, Season ticket £5.

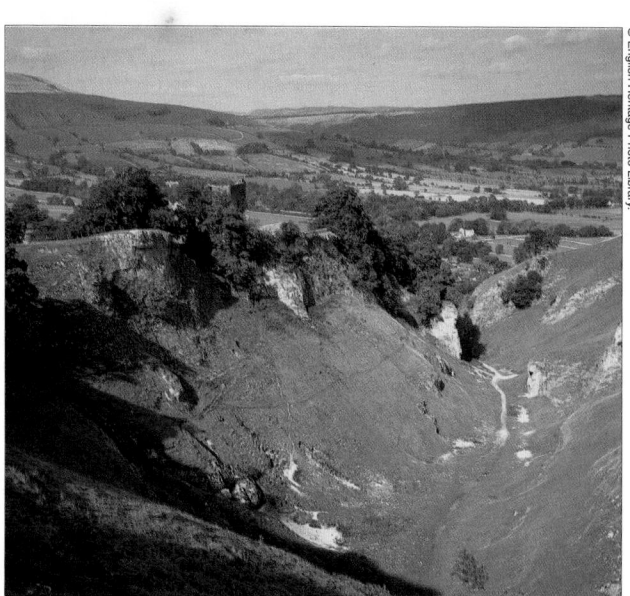

Peveril Castle, Derbyshire.

MELBOURNE HALL & GARDENS 🏛

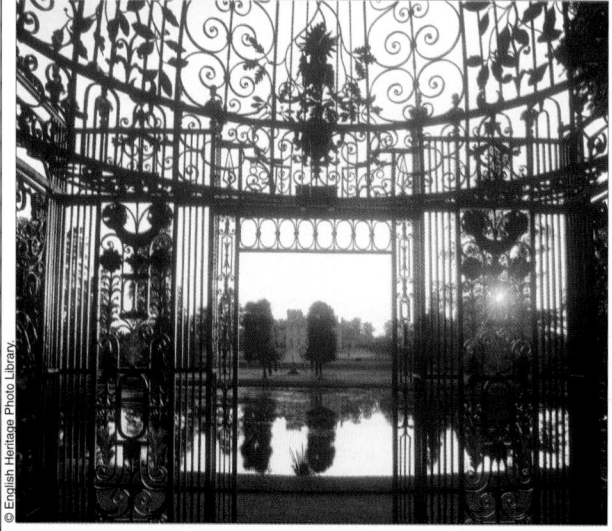

© English Heritage Photo Library.

MELBOURNE, DERBYSHIRE DE73 1EN

Owner: *Lord & Lady Ralph Kerr*   **Contact:** *Mrs Gill Weston*

Tel: 01332 862502   **Fax:** 01332 862263

This beautiful house of history, in its picturesque poolside setting, was once the home of Victorian Prime Minister William Lamb. The fine gardens, in the French formal style, contain Robert Bakewell's intricate wrought iron arbour and a fascinating yew tunnel.

Location: OS Ref. SK389 249. 8m S of Derby. From London, exit M1/J24.

Opening Times: Hall: Aug only (not first 3 Mons) 2 - 5pm. Last admission 4.15pm. Gardens: 1 Apr - 30 Sept: Weds, Sats, Suns, BH Mons, 1.30 - 5.30pm.

Admission: Hall: Adult £3, Child £1.50, OAP £2.50. Gardens: Adult £3, Child/OAP £2. Hall & Gardens: Adult £5, Child £3, OAP £4.

ⓘ Crafts. No photography in house.   🖼   ♿ Partially suitable.   📷
🎧 Obligatory.   Ⓟ Limited. No coach parking.   🐕 Guide dogs only.

PEVERIL CASTLE

Tel: 01433 620613

Market Place, Castleton, Hope Valley S33 8WQ

Owner: English Heritage   **Contact:** The Custodian

There are breathtaking views of the Peak District from this castle, perched high above the pretty village of Castleton. The great square tower stands almost to its original height. Formerly known as Peak Castle.

Location: OS110 Ref. SK150 827. S side of Castleton, 15m W of Sheffield on A6187.

Open: 1 Apr - 31 Oct: daily, 10am - 6pm (5pm in Oct). 1 Nov - 31 Mar, Wed - Sun, 10am - 4pm. Closed 24 - 26 Dec & 1 Jan.

Admission: Adult £2.30, Child £1.20, Conc. £1.70. 15% discount for groups (11+).

 Tel: for details.

RENISHAW HALL

See opposite for quarter page entry.

REVOLUTION HOUSE

Tel: 01246 345727

High Street, Old Whittington, Chesterfield, Derbyshire S41 9LA

Contact: Ms A M Knowles

Originally the Cock and Pynot ale house, now furnished in 17th century style.

Location: OS Ref. SK384 749. 3m N of Chesterfield on B6052 off A61.

Opening Times: Good Fri - end Oct: daily, 10am - 4pm. Special opening over Christmas period.

Admission: Free.

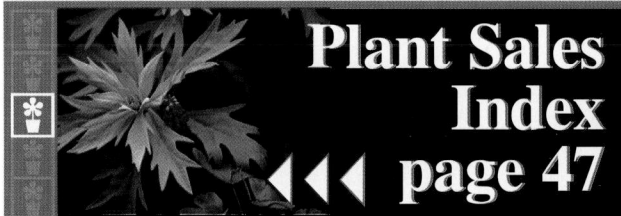

Plant Sales Index ◀◀◀ page 47

RENISHAW HALL ✗No

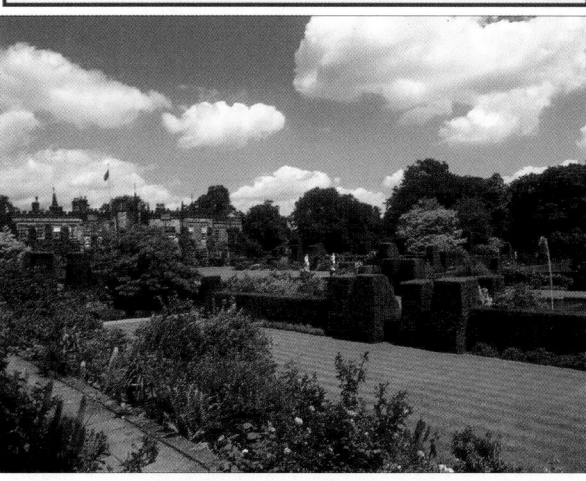

SHEFFIELD, DERBYSHIRE S31 9WB

Owner: Sir Reresby Sitwell Bt DL   **Contact:** The Administrator

Tel: 01246 432310   **Fax:** 01246 430760
e-mail: info@renishawhall.free-online.co.uk

Home of Sir Reresby and Lady Sitwell. Seven acres of Italian style formal gardens stand in 300 acres of mature parkland, encompassing statues, shaped yew hedges, a water garden and lakes. The Sitwell museum and art gallery (display of Fiori de Henriques sculptures) are located in the Georgian stables alongside craft workshops and café, furnished with contemporary art.

Location: OS Ref. SK435 786. 3m from M1/J30, equidistant from Sheffield & Chesterfield.

Opening Times: 6 Apr - 30 Sept: Fri - Sun & BHs, 10.30am - 4.30pm. Also Thurs in Jul & Aug.

Admission: House: by written application only. Garden only: Adult £3, Conc. £2.50. Museum & Art Exhib: Adult £3, Conc. £2.50. Garden, Museum & Art Exhibition: Adult £5, Conc. £3.50.

Conferences. By arrangement. In grounds, on leads.

SUDBURY HALL & NATIONAL TRUST MUSEUM OF CHILDHOOD

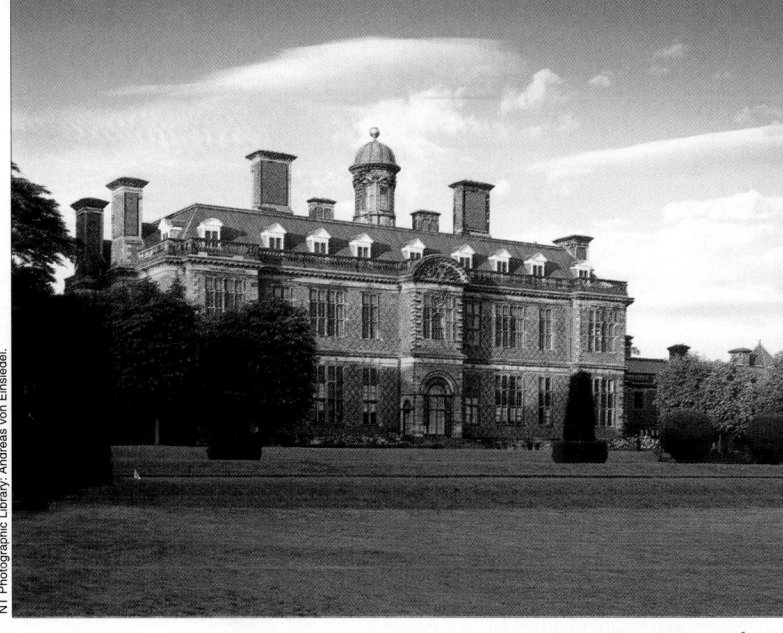

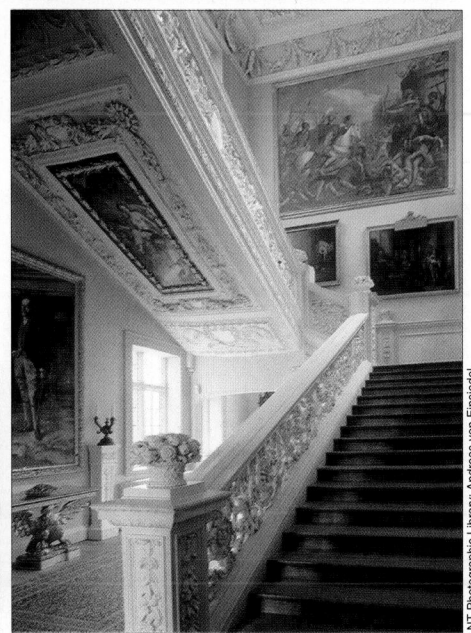

NT Photographic Library: Andreas von Einsiedel.

ASHBOURNE, DERBYSHIRE DE6 5HT

Owner: The National Trust   **Contact:** The Property Manager

Tel: 01283 585305   **Fax:** 01283 585139

One of the most individual of late 17th century houses, begun by George Vernon c1660. The rich decoration includes wood carvings by Gibbons and Pierce, superb plasterwork, mythological decorative paintings by Laguerre. The great staircase is one of the finest of its kind in an English house. Also National Trust Museum of Childhood in 19th century service wing of the Hall. The museum contains fascinating and innovative displays about children from the 18th century onwards. There are chimney climbs for adventurous 'sweep-sized' youngsters, and Betty Cadbury's fine collection of toys and dolls is on show.

Location: OS128 Ref. SK160 323. 6m E of Uttoxeter at the junction of A50 Derby - Stoke & A515 Ashbourne.

Opening Times: 31 Mar - 4 Nov: Wed - Sun & BH Mons, 1 - 5.30pm. Last admission. 30 mins before closing. Grounds: 12 noon - 6pm. Museum: As house.

Admission: Hall: Adult £3.80, Child £1.90, Family £9.50. Groups by prior arrangement. Museum: As house. Hall & Museum: Adult £6.10, Child £3, Family £15.20.

Limited, braille guide. WC. Licensed. Car park only.

SUTTON SCARSDALE HALL

Tel: 01604 735400 (Regional Office)

Chesterfield, Derbyshire

Owner: English Heritage

Contact: The East Midlands Regional Office

The dramatic hilltop shell of a great early 18th century baroque mansion.

Location: OS Ref. SK441 690. Between Chesterfield & Bolsover, 1^1/$_2$ m S of Arkwright Town.

Opening Times: 10am - 6pm (5pm Oct - Mar).

Admission: Free.

WINGFIELD MANOR

Tel: 01773 832060

Garner Lane, South Wingfield, Derbyshire DE5 7NH

Owner: Mr S Critchlow (managed by English Heritage)

Contact: The Custodian

Huge, ruined, country mansion built in the mid-15th century. Mary Queen of Scots was imprisoned here in 1569, 1584 and 1585.

Location: OS Ref. SK374 548. S side of B5035, ^{1}/$_2$ m S of South Wingfield village. Access by 600yd drive (**no vehicles**). From M1 J28, W on A38, A615 (Matlock road) at Alfreton and turn onto B5035 after 1^1/$_2$m.

Opening Times: 1 Apr - 30 Sept: Wed - Sun, 10am - 6pm. 1 - 31 Oct: Wed - Sun, 10am - 5pm. 1 Nov - 31 Mar: 10am - 4pm. Closed 24 - 26 Dec & 1 Jan. Closed 1 - 2pm in winter. The Manor incorporates a working farm. Visitors are requested to respect the privacy of the owners, to keep to visitor routes and refrain from visiting outside official opening times.

Admission: Adult £3, Child £1.50, Conc. £2.30.

TISSINGTON HALL

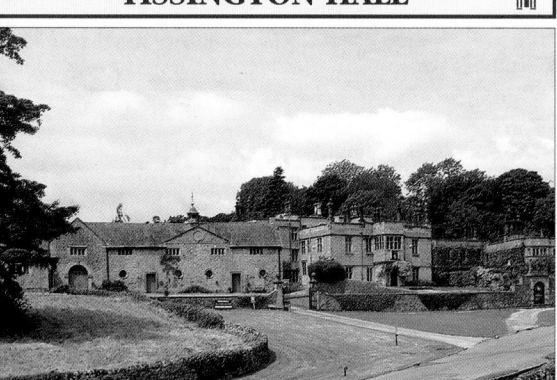

ASHBOURNE, DERBYSHIRE DE6 1RA

Owner/Contact: Sir Richard FitzHerbert Bt

Tel: 01335 352200 **Fax:** 01335 352201 **e-mail:** tisshall@dircon.co.uk

Home of the FitzHerbert family for over 500 years. The Hall stands in a superbly maintained estate village, and contains wonderful panelling and fine old masters. A 10 acre garden and arboretum. Schools very welcome. Award-winning Old Coach House Tearoom, open daily 11am - 5pm for lunch and tea.

Location: OS Ref. SK175 524. 4m N of Ashbourne off A515 towards Buxton.

Opening Times: 10 Jul - 17 Aug: Tue - Fri, 1.30 - 4.30pm. 20 - 31 Aug: Mon - Fri, 1.30 - 4.30pm. Groups & societies welcome by appointment throughout the year. Corporate days and events also available, contact: The Estate Office on 01335 352200

Admission: Hall & Gardens: Adult £5.50, Child (10-16yrs) £2.50, Conc. £4.50, Gardens only: Adult £2, Child £1.

ℹ No photography in house. ♿ Partially suitable. WCs at tearooms.
☕ Tearoom adjacent to Hall. 🎫 Obligatory. 🅿 Limited. 🚫
🐕 Guide dogs only. ❄ ⓘⓦ

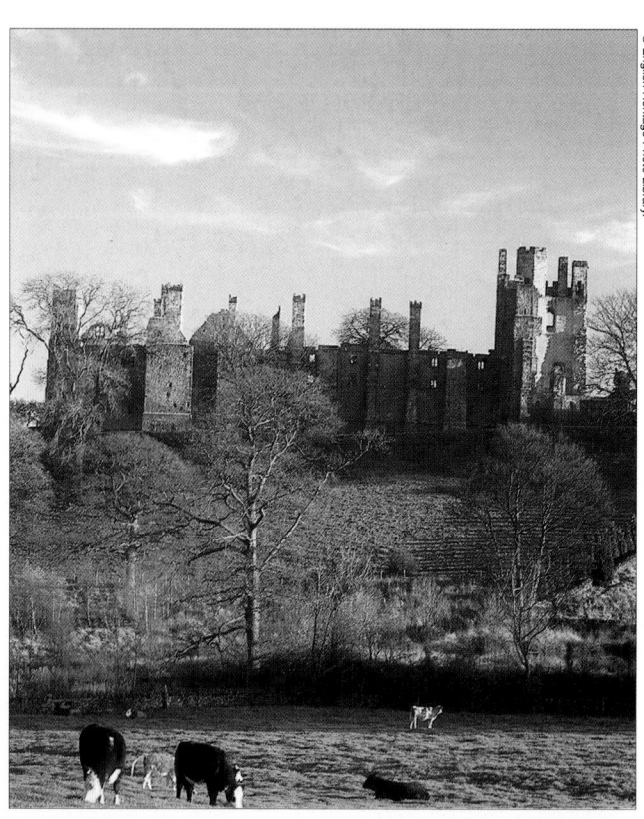

Wingfield Manor, Derbyshire.

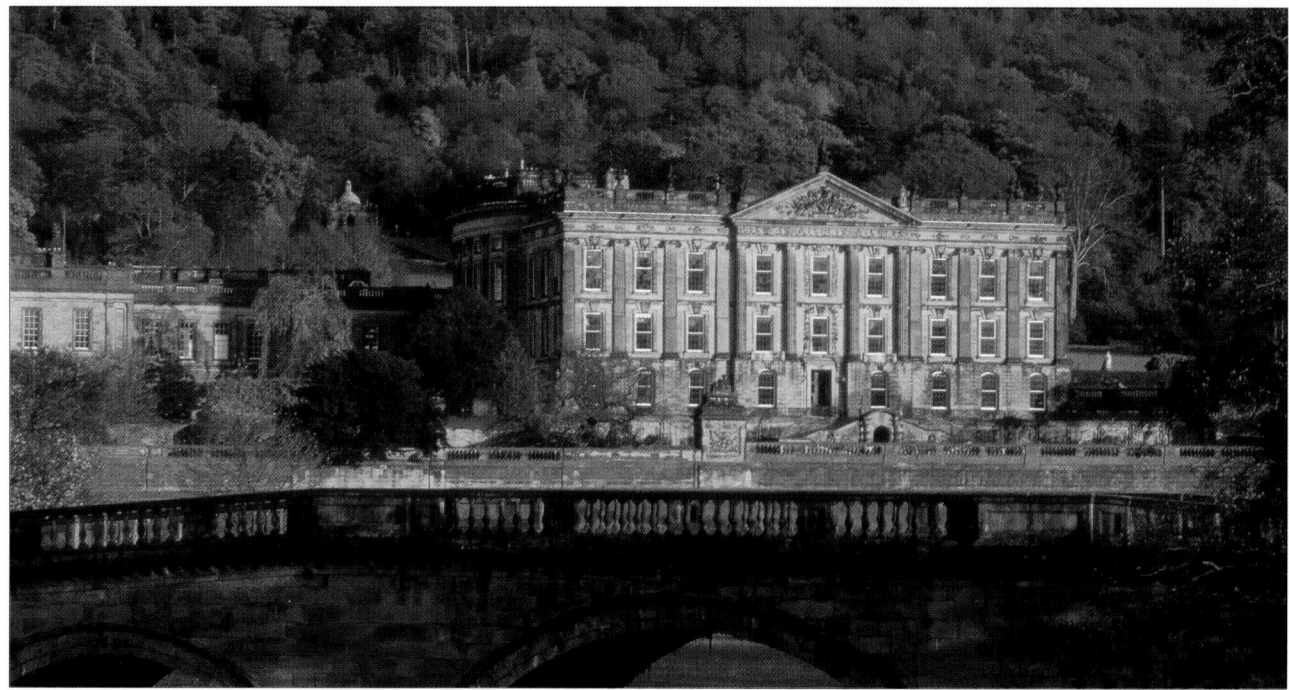

Chatsworth, Derbyshire.

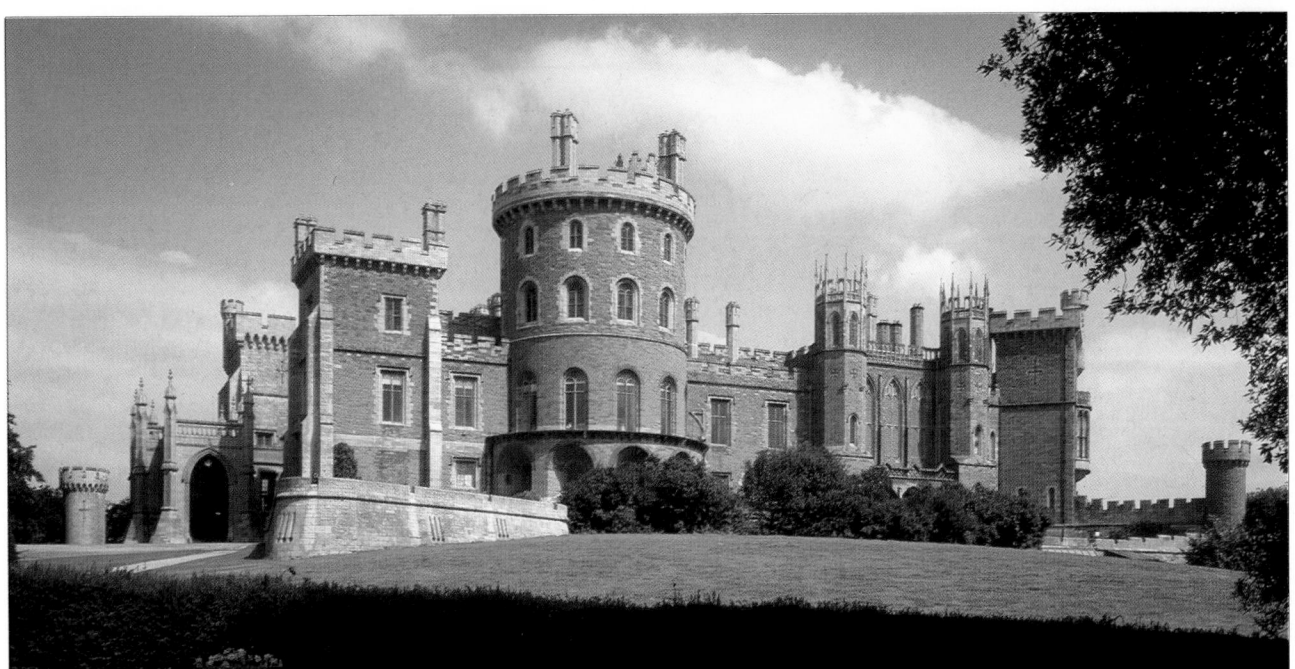

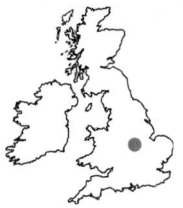

Owner: His Grace
The Duke of Rutland

CONTACT

Andrew Norman
Castle Estate Office
Belvoir Castle
Grantham
Lincolnshire
NG32 1PD

Tel: 01476 870262
Fax: 01476 870443

e-mail: info@
belvoircastle.com

LOCATION

OS Ref. SK820 337

A1 from London 110m
York 100m
Grantham 7m.
A607 Grantham-Melton
Mowbray.

Air: East Midlands
International.

Rail: Grantham
Station 7m

Bus: Melton Mowbray -
Vale of Belvoir via
Castle Car Park.

BELVOIR CASTLE
Grantham

BELVOIR CASTLE, home of the Duke and Duchess of Rutland, commands a magnificent view over the Vale of Belvoir. The name Belvoir, meaning beautiful view, dates back to Norman times, when Robert de Todeni, Standard Bearer to William the Conqueror, built the first castle on this superb site. Destruction caused by two Civil Wars and by a catastrophic fire in 1816 have breached the continuity of Belvoir's history. The present building owes much to the inspiration and taste of Elizabeth, 5th Duchess of Rutland and was built after the fire.

Inside the Castle are notable art treasures including works by Poussin, Holbein, Rubens, and Reynolds, Gobelin and Mortlake tapestries, Chinese silks, furniture, fine porcelain and sculpture.

The Queen's Royal Lancers' Museum at Belvoir has a fascinating exhibition of the history of the Regiment, as well as a fine collection of weapons, uniforms and medals.

GARDENS

The Statue Gardens are built into the hillside below the castle and take their name from the collection of 17th century sculptures on view. The garden is planted so that there is nearly always something in flower.

The Duchess' private Spring Gardens are available for viewing throughout the year by pre-booked groups of 15 persons or more. Details from the Estate Office.

OPENING TIMES

SUMMER
April: 13 - 17, 22, 29
May - Sept: Daily
October - Sundays only
11am - 5pm.

WINTER
Groups welcome by appointment.

ADMISSION

Adult £6.00
Child (5-16yrs)..........£3.50
OAP/Student £5.50
Family (2+2) £16.00

Groups (20-200)
Adult £5.50
Child (5-16yrs)..........£3.00
OAP/Student...........£5.00

Spring Garden Tours (15+)
Adult £5.00
OAP/Student...........£4.50

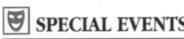

Suitable for exhibitions, product launches, conferences, filming, photography welcomed (permit £2).

Banquets, private room available.

Ground floor and restaurant accessible. Please telephone for advice. WC.

Licensed restaurant. Groups catered for.

By prior arrange- ment Additional charge of £1pp. Tour time: 1¹/₄ hrs.

Ample. Coaches can take passengers to entrance by arrangement but should report to the main car park and ticket office on arrival.

Guided tours. Teacher's pack. Education room. Picnic area and adventure playground.

Guide dogs only.

SPECIAL EVENTS

Please telephone for details of special events.

CONFERENCE/FUNCTION		
ROOM	SIZE	MAX CAPACITY
State Dining Room	52' x 31'	130
Regents Gallery	131' x 16'	300
Old Kitchen	45' x 22'	100

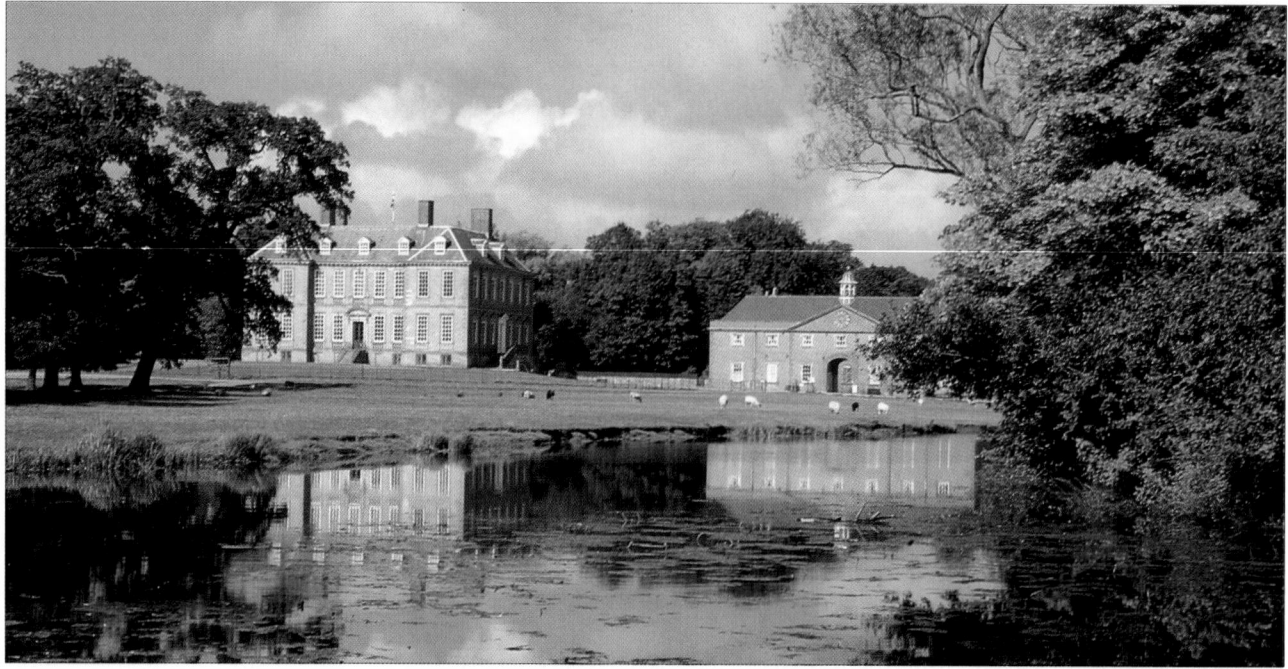

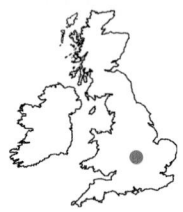

Owner: The Lady Braye

CONTACT

Lt Col E H L Aubrey-
Fletcher
Stanford Hall
Lutterworth
Leicestershire
LE17 6DH

Tel: 01788 860250

Fax: 01788 860870

e-mail: stanford.hall
@virginnet.co.uk

LOCATION

OS Ref. SP587 793

M1/J18 6m,
M1/J19 (from/to
the N only) 2m,
M6 exit/access at
A14/M1(N)J 2m,
A14 2m.

Follow Historic
House signs.

Rail: Rugby Station
7$^{1}/_{2}$ m.

Air: Birmingham
Airport 27m.

Taxi: Fone-A-Car.
01788 543333.

CONFERENCE/FUNCTION

ROOM	SIZE	MAX CAPACITY
Ballroom	39' x 26'	100
Old Dining Rm	30' x 20'	70
Crocodile Room	39' x 20'	60

STANFORD HALL
Nr Rugby

STANFORD has been the home of the Cave family, ancestors of the present owner, Lady Braye, since 1430. In the 1690s, Sir Roger Cave commissioned the Smiths of Warwick to pull down the old Manor House and build the present Hall, which is an excellent example of their work and of the William and Mary period.

As well as over 5000 books, the handsome Library contains many interesting manuscripts, the oldest dating from 1150. The splendid pink and gold Ballroom has a fine coved ceiling with four *trompe l'oeil* shell corners. Throughout the house are portraits of the family and examples of furniture and objects which they collected over the centuries. There is also a collection of Royal Stuart portraits, previously belonging to the Cardinal Duke of York, the last of the male Royal Stuarts. An unusual collection of family costumes is displayed in the Old Dining Room, which also houses some early Tudor portraits and a fine Empire chandelier.

The Hall and Stables are set in an attractive Park on the banks of Shakespeare's Avon. There is a walled Rose Garden behind the Stables. An early ha-ha separates the North Lawn from the mile-long North Avenue.

❖

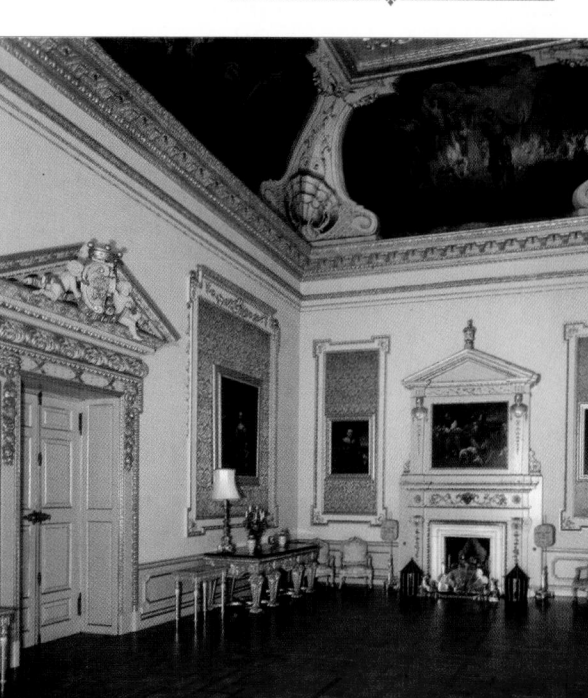

Craft centre (most Suns). No photography in house. Available for corporate days, clay pigeon shoots, filming, photography, small conferences and fashion shows. Parkland, helicopter landing area, lecture room, Blüthner piano.

Available for lunches, dinners and wedding receptions using outside caterers.

Visitors may alight at the entrance. WC.

Homemade teas, lunch, and supper. Groups (70 max.) must book.

Tour time: $^{3}/_{4}$ hr in groups of approx 25.

1,000 cars and 6 - 8 coaches. Free meals for coach drivers, coach parking on gravel in front of house.

£1.80 per child. Guide provided by prior arrangement, nature trail with guide book & map, motorcycle museum.

In park, on leads.

OPENING TIMES

SUMMER

7 April - 30 September:

Sats & BH Tues,
House: 1.30 - 5.30pm.
Museum closed.

Suns & BH Mons:
House & Museum:
1.30 - 5.30pm

Last admissions 5pm.

NB. On BH Mons & event days: grounds open at 12 noon.

House open any day or evening for pre-booked groups.

WINTER

October - Easter
Closed to public. Available during October for corporate events.

ADMISSION

House & Grounds

Adult	£4.20
Child (4-15yrs)	£2.00
Groups (20+)	
Adult	£3.90
Child (4-15yrs)	£1.80

Grounds only

Adult	£2.50
Child (4-15yrs)	£1.00

Motorcycle Museum

Adult	£1.00
Child (4-15yrs)	£0.35
School Group	
Adult	FREE
Child (4-15yrs)	£0.20

SPECIAL EVENTS

Please telephone for details of special events.

ABBEY PUMPING STATION

Tel: 0116 2995111 **Fax:** 0116 2995125

Corporation Road, Leicester LE4 5PX

Owner: Leicester City Council **Contact:** Stuart Warburton

A Victorian sewage pumping station with four massive beam engines still working by steam. Exhibitions include: 'Flushed with Pride' which explores the history, science and technology of public health, 'Fun at the Flicks' and ' Transport of Delight'. Series of special events and steam rallies/days throughout the year.

Location: OS Ref. SK589 067. 2 M N of city centre situated on River Soar riverside walk and 400m E of A6. 5 mins from Belgrave Hall.

Opening Times: Please contact Abbey Pumping Station for details.

Admission: Free except for special events.

⬜ 🍴 ♿ Partially suitable. 🎥 On event days. 🚶 By arrangement. 🅿 🏛
🐕 Guide dogs only. ❄ 🛡 Tel. for details.

ASHBY-DE-LA-ZOUCH CASTLE ⚎

Tel: 01530 413343

South Street, Ashby-de-la-Zouch, Leicestershire LE65 1BR

Owner: English Heritage **Contact:** The Custodian

The impressive ruins of this late medieval castle are dominated by a magnificent tower, over 80 feet high, which was split in two during the Civil War. Panoramic views.

Location: OS Ref. SK363 167. In Ashby de la Zouch, 12m S of Derby on A511. SE of town centre.

Opening Times: 1 Apr - 31 Oct: daily, 10am - 6pm (5pm in Oct). 1 Nov - 31 Mar: Wed - Sun, 10am - 4pm. Closed 24 - 26 Dec & 1 Jan.

Admission: Adult £2.75, Child £1.40, Conc. £2.10.

♿ Grounds suitable. 🅿 🐕 On leads. ❄ 🛡 Tel. for details.

BELGRAVE HALL & GARDENS

Tel: 0116 2666590 **Fax:** 0116 2613063

Church Road, off Thurcaston Road, Leicester LE4 5PE

Owner: Leicester City Council **Contact:** Emma Martin

Belgrave Hall and Gardens, famed for its ghost story, is a period house with period decoration ranging from 1750 - 1900. The three story house is open throughout, and a series of special events is organised throughout the year using themes and living interpretation. Includes period Victorian formal gardens. Displays include the Gimson Collection.

Location: OS Ref. SK593 072. 2m N of city centre, on riverside walk and off the A6/A46 Loughborough Road.

Opening Times: Please contact Belgrave Hall for details.

Admission: Free.

⬜ 🍴 ♿ Partially suitable. WC. Staff with sign language skills. 🚶 By arrangement.
🅿 Limited (on street). 🏛 🐕 Guide dogs only. ❄ 🛡 Tel. for details.

BELVOIR CASTLE 🏛

See page 297 for full page entry.

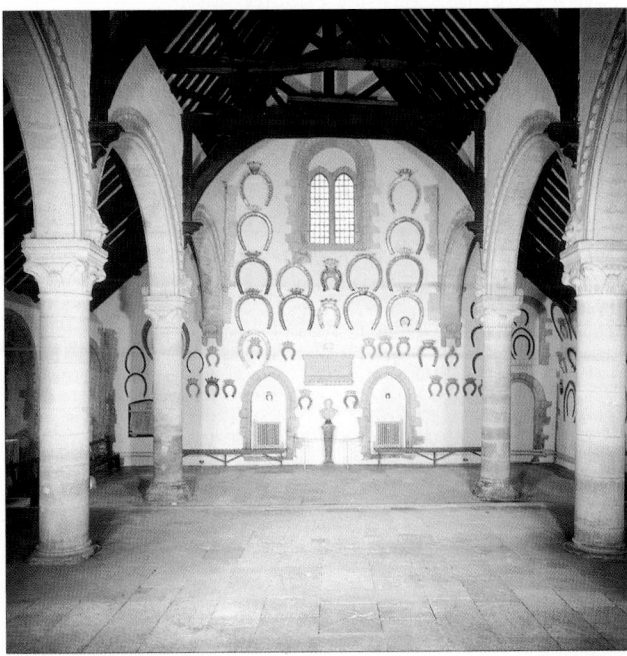

Oakham Castle, Leicestershire & Rutland.

BOSWORTH BATTLEFIELD

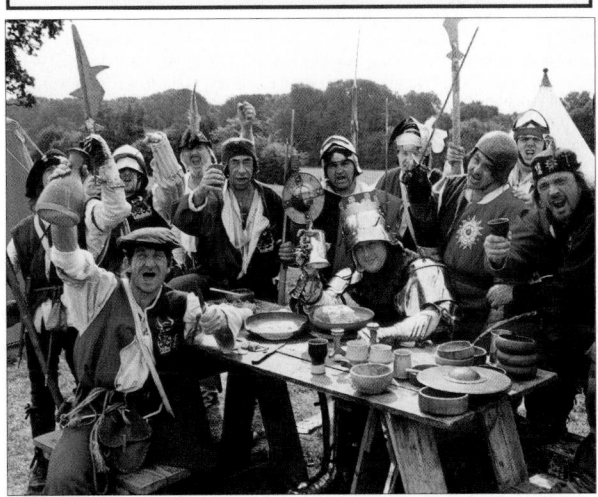

VISITOR CENTRE & COUNTRY PARK, SUTTON CHENEY, MARKET BOSWORTH CV13 0AD

Owner: Leicestershire City Council *Contact: Ranger*

Tel: 01455 290429 **Fax:** 01455 292841 **e-mail:** countryparks@leics.gov.uk

Historic site of the Battle of Bosworth Field 1485, where King Richard III lost his crown and his life to the future Henry VII. Visitor Centre, film theatre, battle trail, picnic areas and car parks. Summer event programme: Medieval Spectacular 18th & 19th Aug 2001 (including battle re-enactment).

Location: OS Ref. SK404 001. Bounded by A5, A444, A447, B585. Clearly signposted from all these roads.

Opening Times: 1 Apr - 31 Oct: Mon - Sat, 11am - 5pm. Sun & BHs, 11am - 6pm. Nov & Dec: Suns, 11am - dusk. Mar: Sats & Suns, 11am - 5pm.

Admission: Adult £3, Child/Conc. £1.90, Family (2+3) £7.95. Groups (20+): Adult £2.30, Child/Conc. £1.60. (Opening times and charges subject to review.)

⬜ 🍴 ♿ Partially suitable. 🍷 Licensed. 🚶 By arrangement. 🅿 🏛
❄ 🛡 🚻

BRADGATE PARK & SWITHLAND WOOD COUNTRY PARK

Bradgate Park, Newtown Linford, Leics **Tel:** 0116 2362713

Owner: Bradgate Park Trust **Contact:** M H Harrison

Includes the ruins of the brick medieval home of the Grey family and childhood home of Lady Jane Grey. Also has a medieval deer park.

Location: OS Ref. SK534 102. 7m NW of Leicester, via Anstey & Newtown Linford. Country Park gates in Newtown Linford. 1¼ m walk to the ruins.

Opening Times: All year during daylight hours.

Admission: No charge. Car parking charges.

DONINGTON-LE-HEATH MANOR HOUSE

Tel: 01530 831259

Manor Road, Donington-le-Heath, Leicestershire LE67 2FW

Owner/Contact: Leicestershire County Council

Medieval manor c1280 with 16th-17th century alterations.

Location: OS Ref. SK421 126. ½ m SSW of Coalville. 4½ m W of M1/J22, by A511.

Opening Times: Apr - Sept: daily, 11am - 5pm. Oct - Mar: daily 11am - 3pm.

Admission: Free.

THE GUILDHALL

Tel: 0116 2532569 **Fax:** 0116 2539626

Guildhall Lane, Leicester LE1 5FQ

Owner: Leicester City Council **Contact:** Nicholas Ladlow

Magnificent timber-framed medieval building c1390. First used by the Corpus Christi Guild. Became town hall until 1876, includes 17th century town library and Victorian police cells. The great hall provides a unique setting for a varied programme of music, storytelling and theatre.

Location: OS Ref. SK584 044. Adjacent to High Street, Cathedral and St Nicholas Place.

Opening Times: Please contact The Guildhall for details.

Admission: Free.

⬜ ♿ Partially suitable. 🚶 Obligatory. 🅿 No parking. 🏛
🐕 Guide dogs only. ❄ 🛡 Tel. for details. 🚻

JEWRY WALL MUSEUM & SITE　　　　**Tel:** 0116 2473021　**Fax:** 0116 2512257

St Nicholas Circle, Leicester LE1 4LB

Owner: Leicester City Council　　　　　　**Contact:** John Lucas

Jewry Wall Museum focuses on the archaeology and history of Leicestershire from prehistoric times to 1485. Inside you can see the skeleton of the Saxon 'Glen Parva Lady' alongside fine mosaics, wall paintings and other legacies of the Roman settlement. The new 'Making of Leicester' exhibition uncovers the secrets of Leicester's past. After visiting the museum, explore the site of the Roman baths and wonder at the massive 2nd century Jewry Wall.

Location: OS Ref. SK581 044. On St Nicholas Circle, at W end of High Street, opposite the Holiday Inn, next to St Nicholas Church.

Opening Times: Please contact Jewry Wall Museum for details.

Admission: Free.

▢ ⅏ Partially suitable. WC. 🚶 By arrangement. 🅿 No parking. ▦
🐾 Guide dogs only. ❄

KIRBY MUXLOE CASTLE ⌗　　　　　　**Tel:** 01162 386886

Kirby Muxloe, Leicestershire LE9 9MD

Owner: English Heritage　　　**Contact:** East Midlands Regional Office (01604 735400)

Picturesque, moated, brick built castle begun in 1480 by William Lord Hastings. It was left unfinished after Hastings was executed in 1483.

Location: OS Ref. SK524 046. 4m W of Leicester off B5380.

Opening Times: 1 Apr - 31 Oct: weekends & BH Mons only, 12 noon - 5pm.

Admission: Adult £2, Child £1, Conc. £1.50.

LYDDINGTON BEDE HOUSE ⌗　　　　　**Tel:** 01572 822438

Blue Coat Lane, Lyddington, Uppingham, Rutland LE15 9LZ

Owner: English Heritage　　　　　　**Contact:** The Custodian

Set among golden-stone cottages, the Bede House was originally a medieval palace of the Bishops of Lincoln. It was later converted into an alms house.

Location: OS Ref. SP875 970. In Lyddington, 6m N of Corby, 1m E of A6003.

Opening Times: 1 Apr - 31 Oct: daily, 10am - 6pm (5pm in Oct).

Admission: Adult £2.75, Child £1.40, Conc. £2.10.

NEW WALK MUSEUM　　　　　**Tel:** 0116 2554100　**Fax:** 0116 2473005

New Walk, Leicester LE1 7EA

Owner: Leicester City Council　　　　　　**Contact:** John Martin

Leicester's first public museum, opened in 1849, houses six permanent exhibitions: The Ancient Egypt Gallery, Natural History (including dinosaurs), German Expressionist, Victorian and European Art Galleries, Decorative Art Gallery and The Royal Leicestershire Regiment Gallery. The Discovery Room invites younger visitors to try on replica clothes, handle real objects and explore the natural world.

Location: OS Ref. SK591 039. Museum Sq, 150m W of Waterloo Way, 250m SW of station.

Opening Times: Please contact New Walk Museum for details.

Admission: Free.

▢ 🍵 ⅏ 🚶 By arrangement. 🅿 Limited. ▦ 🐾 Guide dogs only. ▲ ❄

NEWARKE HOUSES MUSEUM　　　**Tel:** 0116 2473222　**Fax:** 0116 2470403

The Newarke, Leicester LE2 7BY

Owner: Leicester City Council　　　　　　**Contact:** Philip French

Over 500 years of Leicester's social history can be traced through a visit to Newarke Houses. Everyday life at home and at work is represented in displays of domestic equipment, clocks, toys and furniture. Visit the 1940s village grocer's shop, the reconstructed Victorian street scene and workshops of various local trades. Items belonging to Daniel Lambert, Leicester's largest man, can be seen in the museum. Don't forget to visit the beautiful gardens to the rear of the museum.

Location: OS Ref. SK584 041. Just SW of city centre ring road.

Opening Times: Please contact Newarke Houses Museum for details.

Admission: Free.

ℹ Photography in house by permission only. ▢ ⅏ Not suitable.
🚶 By arrangement. 🅿 No parking. ▦ 🐾 Guide dogs only. ❄

OAKHAM CASTLE　　　　　　　　**Tel:** 01572 758440

Rutland County Museum, Catmos St, Oakham, Rutland LE15 6HW

Owner: Rutland County Council　　　　　　**Contact:** Mr T Clough

Exceptionally fine Norman Great Hall of a late 12th century fortified manor house, with contemporary musician sculptures. Bailey earthworks and remains of earlier motte. The hall contains over 200 unique horseshoes forfeited by royalty and peers of the realm to the Lord of the Manor from Edward IV onwards.

Location: OS Ref. SK862 088. Near town centre, E of the church.

Opening Times: Late Mar - late Oct (BST): Mon - Sat, 10am - 1pm, 1.30 - 5pm. Sun, 1 - 5pm. Late Oct - Late Mar (GMT): As above, but closing at 4pm. Closed on Good Fri, on court Mons (normally once a month), and at Christmas.

Admission: Free.

▢ ⅏ Great Hall suitable. 🅿 For disabled, on request. ▲ ❄ 🐾

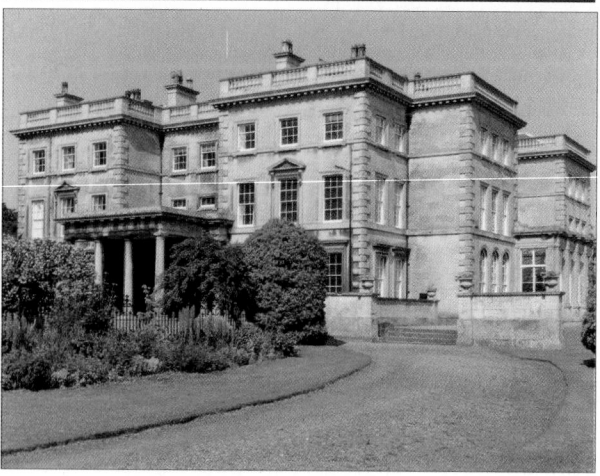

PRESTWOLD HALL

LOUGHBOROUGH, LEICESTERSHIRE LE12 5SQ

Owner: E J Packe-Drury-Lowe　　　**Contact:** Henry Weldon

Tel: 01509 880236　**Fax:** 01509 889060　**e-mail:** henryweldon@hotmail.com

A magnificent private house, largely remodelled in 1843 by William Burn. For the past 350 years it has been the home of the Packe family and contains fine Italian plasterwork, 18th century English and European furniture and a collection of family portraits. The house is not open to the general public but offers excellent facilities as a conference centre, corporate entertainment and wedding venue. Up to 150 guests can be seated and the 20 acres of gardens provide a perfect setting for larger events using marquees. Excellent chefs provide a selection of varied menus complemented by a well stocked wine cellar. Activity days, clay pigeon shooting, motor sports and archery can also be organised on request.

Location: OS Ref. SK578 215. At the heart of the Midlands, 3m E of Loughborough on B675. 5m W of A46 via B676.

Admission: Corporate entertaining venue, conference centre and function venue by arrangement only.

ℹ Conferences. 🍵 ⅏ Ground floor & grounds suitable. WC. ▲ ❄

STANFORD HALL 🏛　　　　　　　　　See page 298 for full page entry.

STAUNTON HAROLD CHURCH 🌿　　**Tel:** 01332 863822　**Fax:** 01332 865272

Staunton Harold Church, Ashby-de-la-Zouch, Leicestershire

One of the very few churches to be built during the Commonwealth, erected by Sir Robert Shirley, an ardent Royalist. The interior retains its original 17th century cushions and hangings, and includes fine panelling and painted ceilings.

Location: OS Ref. SK379 208. 5m NE of Ashby-de-la-Zouch, W of B587.

Opening Times: 31 Mar - 30 Sept: Wed - Sun & BH Mons (closed Good Fri), 1 - 5pm or sunset if earlier. Oct: Sats & Suns only, 1 - 5pm.

Admission: £1 donation.

⅏ Partially suitable. ▦ At hall.

WARTNABY GARDENS　　　　　　　**Tel:** 01664 822296　**Fax:** 01664 822231

Melton Mowbray, Leicestershire LE14 3HY

Owner: Lord and Lady King

This garden has delightful little gardens within it, including a white garden, a sunken garden and a purple border of shrubs and roses, and there are good herbaceous borders, climbers and old-fashioned roses. A large pool has an adjacent bog garden with primulas, ferns, astilbes and several varieties of willow. There is an arboretum with a good collection of trees and shrub roses, and alongside the drive is a beech hedge in a Grecian pattern. Greenhouses, a fruit and vegetable garden with rose arches and cordon fruit.

Location: OS Ref. SK709 228. 4m NW of Melton Mowbray. From A606 turn W in Ab Kettleby for Wartnaby.

Opening Times: Suns, 29 Apr, 20 May & 24 June: 11am - 4pm. Plant sales: 29 Apr & 20 May. Groups by appointment at other times (except Weds). Plant Fair: 24 June.

Admission: Adult £2.50, Child Free.

⅏ ▦ By arrangement. 🅿 Limited for coaches. 🐾 In grounds on leads.
❄ 🛡

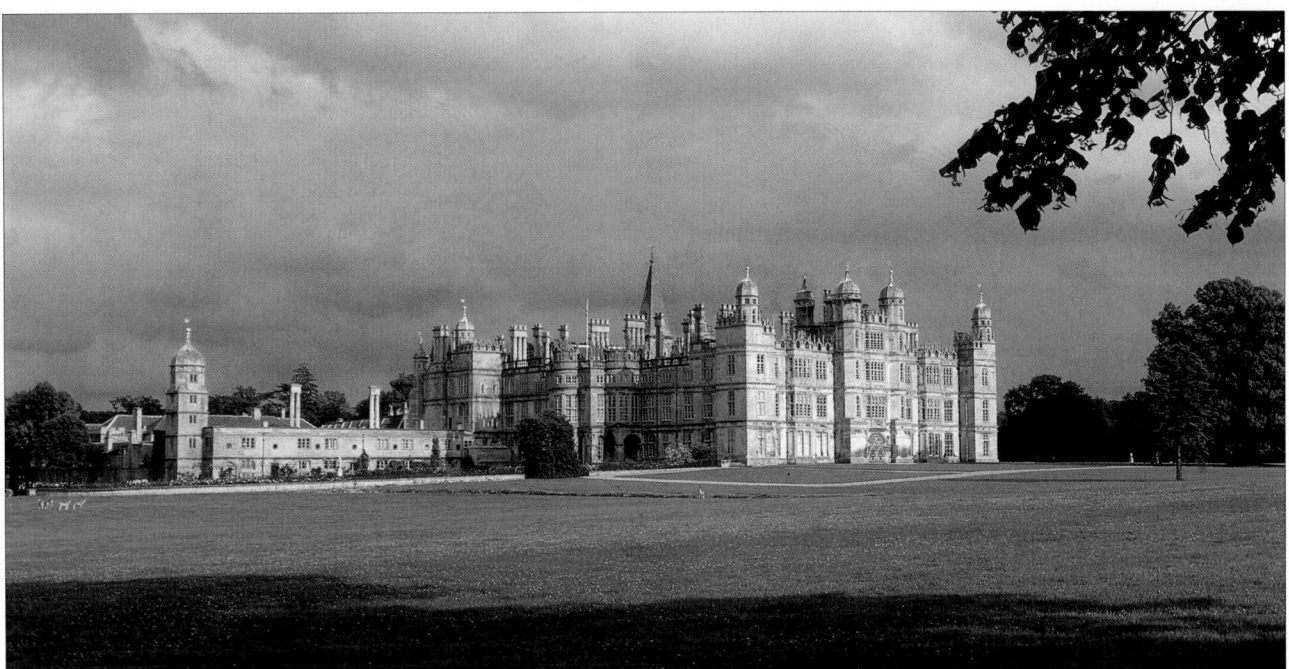

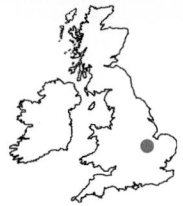

BURGHLEY HOUSE
Stamford

BURGHLEY HOUSE, home of the Cecil family for over 400 years, was built as a country seat during the latter part of the 16th century by Sir William Cecil, later Lord Burghley, principal adviser and Lord Treasurer to Queen Elizabeth.

The House was completed in 1587 and there have been few alterations to the architecture since that date thus making Burghley one of the finest examples of late Elizabethan design in England. The interior was remodelled in the late 17th century by John, 5th Earl of Exeter who was a collector of fine art on a huge scale, establishing the immense collection of art treasures at Burghley. Burghley is truly a 'Treasure House', containing one of the largest private collections of Italian art, unique examples of Chinese and Japanese porcelain and superb items of 18th century furniture. The remodelling work of the 17th century means that examples of the work of the principal artists and craftsmen of the period are to be found at Burghley: Antonio Verrio, Grinling Gibbons and Louis Laguerre all made major contributions to the beautiful interiors.

PARK AND GARDENS

The house is set in a 300-acre deer park landscaped by 'Capability' Brown. A lake was created by him and delightful avenues of mature trees feature largely in his design. The park is home to a large herd of Fallow deer, established in the 16th century. The Sculpture Garden contains many specimen trees and shrubs and is a display area for a number of dramatic art works by contemporary sculptors. The sculptures are varied in style, but their placement is designed to provoke thought and accentuate the beauty of the surroundings. The private gardens around the house are open in April for the display of spring bulbs. Please telephone for details.

Owner:
Burghley House
Preservation Trust Ltd

CONTACT

David Parratt
Burghley House
Stamford
Lincolnshire
PE9 3JY

Tel: 01780 752451

Fax: 01780 480125

e-mail: burghley@
burghley.co.uk

LOCATION

OS Ref. TF048 062

Burghley House
is 1m SE of Stamford.
From London, A1 2hrs.

Visitors entrance
is on B1443.

Rail: Stamford Station
1½ m.

Taxi: Direct Line:
01780 481481.

OPENING TIMES

SUMMER

1 April - 7 October
(closed 1 September).
Daily: 11am - 4.30pm.

NB. The house is viewed by guided tour except on Sat and Sun afternoons when there are stewards throughout the house and visitors may wander.

WINTER

8 October - 1 April
closed to the
general public.

The Park and Sculpure Gardens are open all year and entry is free of charge.

ADMISSION

Adult	£6.80
Child*	£3.30
OAP	£6.30
Groups (20+)	
Adult	£5.90
School groups (up to 14 yrs)	£3.10

* (5 - 12 years) one child Free with every paying adult, otherwise £3.30.

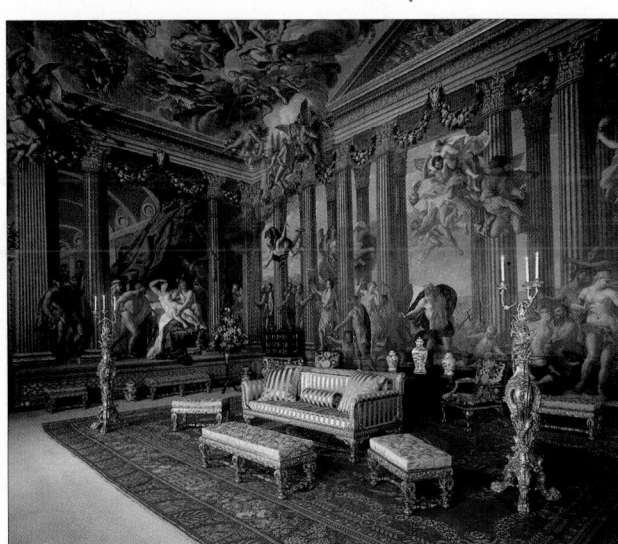

Suitable for a variety of events, large park, golf course, helicopter landing area, cricket pitch. No photography in house.

Visitors may alight at the entrance. WC. Chair lift to Orangery Coffee Shop, house tour involves two staircases one of which has a chairlift.

Restaurant/tearoom. Groups can book in advance.

Obligatory, except Sats & Suns after 1pm. Tour time: 1½ hrs at ½ hr intervals. Max. 25.

Ample. Free refreshments for coach drivers.

Welcome. Guide provided.

No dogs in house.

CONFERENCE/FUNCTION

ROOM	SIZE	MAX CAPACITY
Great Hall	70' x 30'	150
Orangery	100' x 20'	120

AUBOURN HALL

Tel: 01522 788270 **Fax:** 01522 788199

Lincoln LN5 9DZ

Owner/Contact: Lady Nevile

Late 16th century house with important staircase and panelled rooms. Garden.

Location: OS Ref. SK928 628. 6m SW of Lincoln. 2m SE of A46.

Opening Times: Aubourn Hall will not be opened on a regular basis during 2001. The garden will be opened on occasional Sundays.

Admission: Adult £3, OAP £2.50.

AYSCOUGHFEE HALL MUSEUM & GARDENS

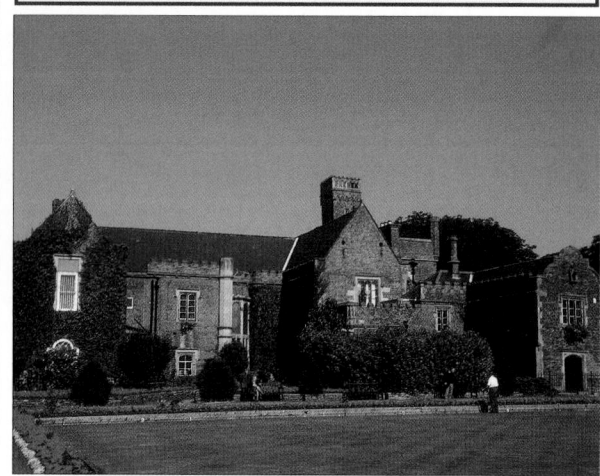

CHURCHGATE, SPALDING, LINCOLNSHIRE PE11 2RA

Owner: South Holland District Council *Contact:* Mrs S Sladen

Tel: 01775 725468 **Fax:** 01775 762715

A late Medieval wool merchant's house surrounded by five acres of walled gardens. The Hall contains the Museum of South Holland Life and has galleries on local villages, the history of Spalding, agriculture and horticulture. There is also a gallery dedicated to Matthew Flinders, the district's most famous son. Many specimens from the Ashley Maples bird collections are on display.

Location: OS Ref. TF240 230. E bank of the River Welland, 5 mins walk from Spalding town centre.

Opening Times: All year: Mon - Fri, 9am - 5pm, Sats, 10am - 5pm. Suns & BHs, 11am - 5pm. Closed weekends in Nov - Feb.

Admission: Free.

ℹ️ TIC located in Hall. 📷 ♿ Partially suitable. 🛍️ 👤 By arrangement.
🅿️ Limited for coaches. 🍴
🐕 In grounds, on leads. Guide dogs only in Hall ❄️

BELTON HOUSE

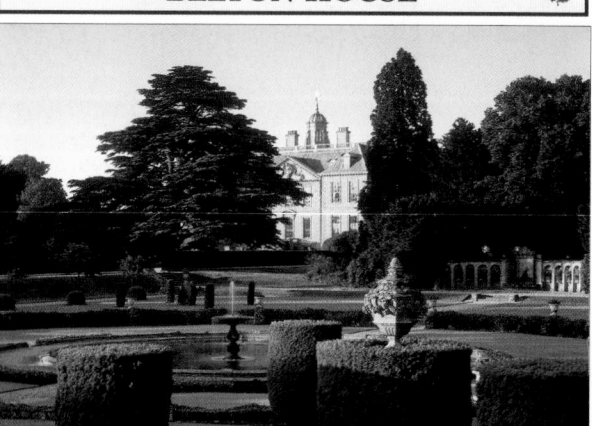

GRANTHAM, LINCOLNSHIRE NG32 2LS

Owner: The National Trust *Contact:* The Property Manager

Tel: 01476 566116 / 592900 **Fax:** 01476 579071

The crowning achievement of Restoration country house architecture, built 1685 - 88 for Sir John Brownlow, and altered by James Wyatt in the 1770s. Plasterwork ceilings by Edward Goudge and fine wood carvings of the Grinling Gibbons school. The rooms contain portraits, furniture, tapestries, oriental porcelain, silver and silver gilt. Gardens with orangery, landscaped park with lakeside walk, woodland adventure playground, and Bellmount Tower. Fine church with family monuments.

Location: OS Ref. SK929 395. 3m NE of Grantham on A607. Signed off the A1.

Opening Times: House: 31 Mar - 4 Nov: House: Wed - Sun & BH Mons (closed Good Fri), 1 - 5.30pm. Garden & Park: 11am - 5.30pm. Last admission to house, garden & park 5pm.

Admission: Adult £5.40, Child £2.70, Family £13.50. Groups (15+): Adult £4.40, Child £2.20.

📷 ♿ Partially suitable. Please telephone for arrangements. 🍴 Licensed.
🅿️ 🍴 🔔

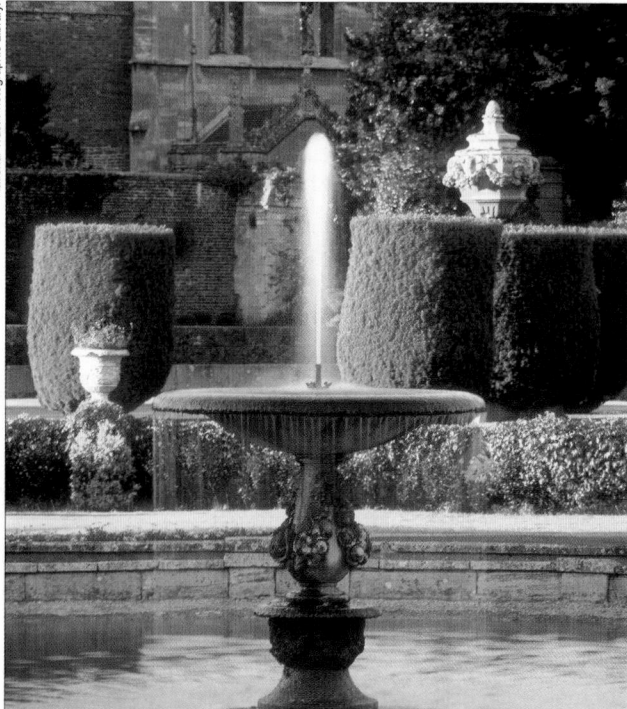

Belton House, Lincolnshire.

BURGHLEY HOUSE

See page 301 for full page entry

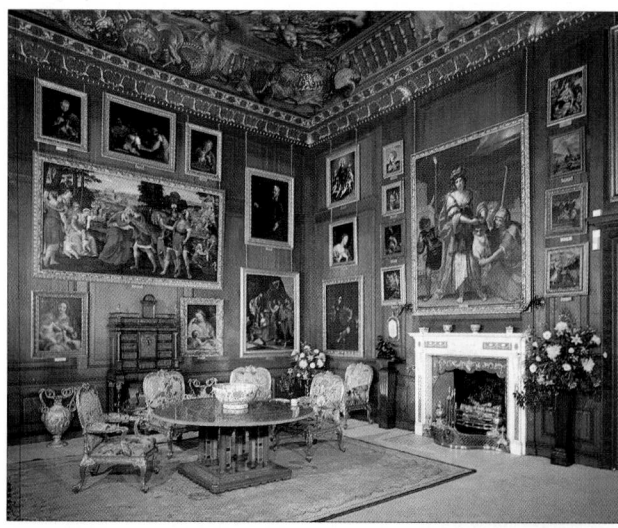

Burghley House, Lincolnshire.

DODDINGTON HALL

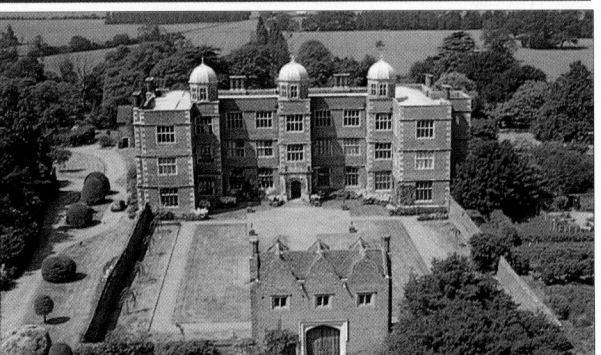

LINCOLN LN6 4RU

Owner: Mr & Mrs A Jarvis　*Contact:* The House Manager

Tel: 01522 694308　**Fax:** 01522 685259

e-mail: estateoffice@doddingtonhall.free-online.co.uk

Magnificent Smythson mansion was completed in 1600 and stands today with its contemporary walled gardens and gatehouse. The Hall is still very much the home of the Jarvis family and has an elegant Georgian interior with a fine collection of porcelain, furniture, paintings and textiles representing 400 years of unbroken family occupation. The beautiful gardens contain a superb layout of box-edged parterres, sumptuous borders that provide colour all seasons, and a wild garden with a marvellous succession of spring bulbs and flowering shrubs set among mature trees. Sandford Award winning schools project, and a nature trail into the nearby countryside.

Location: OS Ref. SK900 701. 5m W of Lincoln on the B1190, signposted off the A46 Lincoln bypass.

Opening Times: Gardens only: 4 Feb - 30 Apr: Suns, 2 - 6pm. House & Garden: May - Sept: Weds, Suns & BH Mons, 2 - 6pm.

Admission: House & Garden: Adult £4.50, Child £2.25, Family £12.50. 10% group discount on open days. Garden only half price.

ℹ️ No photography. No stilettos. 📷 ⛲Occasional. ♿Gardens. WC. ▭
🎟️ By arrangement. 🚩 🅿️ 🦮Guide dogs only. 📧 Tel. for details. ⓗ

GAINSBOROUGH OLD HALL ⌗　　　　**Tel:** 01427 612669

Parnell Street, Gainsborough, Lincolnshire DN21 2NB

Owner: English Heritage　　　　**Contact:** The Custodian

A large medieval house with a magnificent Great Hall and suites of rooms. A collection of historic furniture and a re-created medieval kitchen are on display.

Location: OS Ref. SK815 895. In centre of Gainsborough, opposite library.

Opening Times: Easter Sun - 31 Oct: Mon - Sat, 10am - 5pm. Suns, 2 - 5.30pm. 1 Nov - Easter Sat: Mon - Sat, 10am - 5pm (closed Good Fri, 24 - 26 Dec & 1 Jan).

Admission: Adult £2.50, Child £1, Conc. £1.50 (2000/2001 prices).

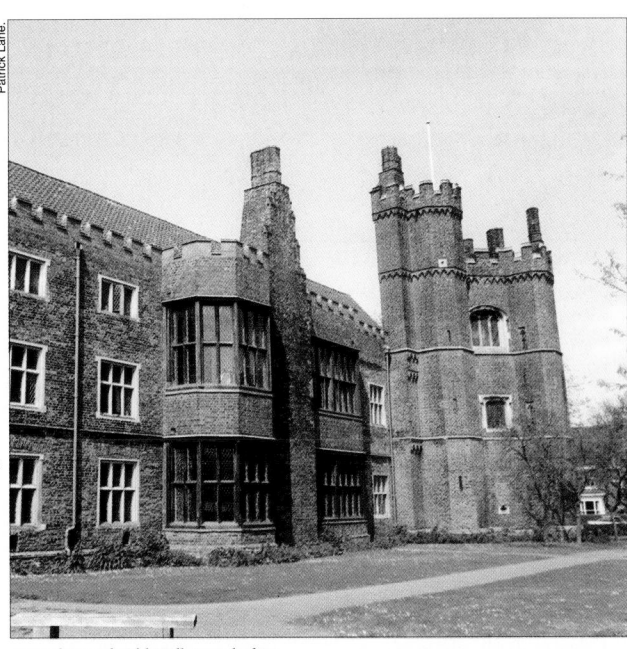

Gainsborough Old Hall, Lincolnshire.

GRIMSTHORPE CASTLE, PARK & GARDENS

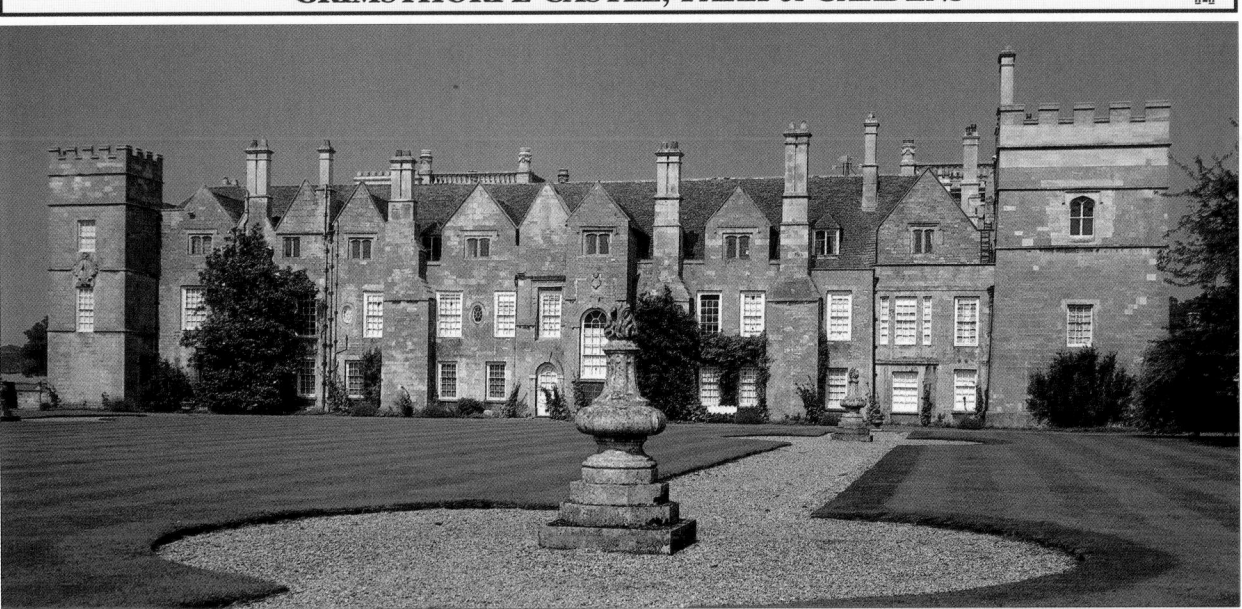

GRIMSTHORPE, BOURNE, LINCOLNSHIRE PE10 0NB

Owner: Grimsthorpe and Drummond Castle Trust Ltd　*Contact:* Ray Biggs

Tel: 01778 591205　**Fax:** 01778 591259　**e-mail:** ray@grimsthorpe.co.uk

Home of the Willoughby de Eresby family since 1516. Examples of 13th century architecture, Tudor period and Sir John Vanbrugh's last major work. State Rooms and picture galleries contain magnificent contents and paintings. 3,000 acre landscaped park, with lakes, ancient woods, nature trail, woodland adventure playground, red deer herd, formal and woodland gardens, unusual ornamental vegetable garden, family cycle trail, events programme. Landrover tours with park ranger.

Location: OS Ref. TF040 230. 4m NW of Bourne on A151, 8m E of Colsterworth roundabout off A1.

Opening Times: 1 Apr - 30 Sept: Suns, Thurs & BHs. Aug: daily except Fris & Sats.

Park & Gardens: 11am - 6pm. Castle: 1 - 4.30pm (last admission). Tearoom: open from 11am (last orders 5.15pm).

Admission: Park & Garden: Adult £3, Child £1.50, Conc. £2, Family (2+2) £7.50. Castle, Park & Garden: Adult £6.50, Child £3.25, Conc. £4.75, Family (2+2) £16.25. Special charges may be made for special events. Group rates on application.

ℹ️ No photography in house. 📷　🍽️ Conferences (up to 70), inc catering
♿ Partially suitable. WC. ▭ Licensed. 🎟️ Obligatory except Suns.
🅿️ Limited for coaches. 🚩 🦮 In grounds, on leads. 📧 Tel. for details. ⓗ

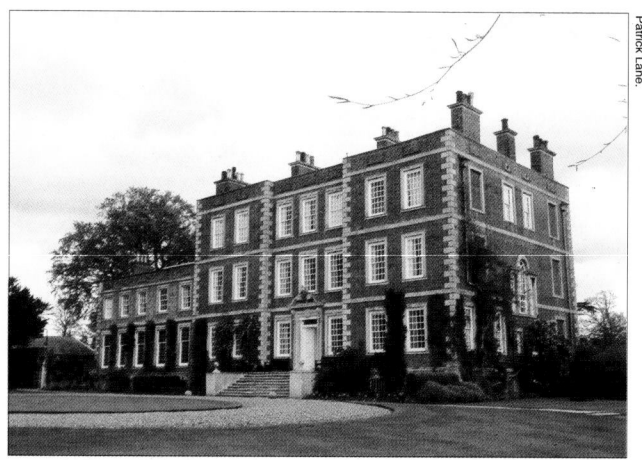

Gunby Hall, Lincolnshire.

GUNBY HALL ✤

Tel: 01909 486411 **Fax:** 01909 486377

Gunby, Spilsby, Lincolnshire PE23 5SS

Owner: The National Trust   **Contact:** Regional Office

A red brick house with stone dressings, built in 1700 and extended in 1870s. Within the house, there is good early 18th century wainscoting and a fine oak staircase, also English furniture and portraits by Reynolds. Also of interest is the contemporary stable block, a walled kitchen and flower garden, sweeping lawns and borders and an exhibition of Field Marshall Sir Archibald Montgomery-Massingberd's memorabilia. Gunby was reputedly Tennyson's 'haunt of ancient peace'.

Location: OS122 Ref. TF466 672. 2¹/₂ m NW of Burgh Le Marsh, 7m W of Skegness. On S side of A158 (access off roundabout).

Opening Times: Ground floor of house & garden: 4 Apr - end Sept: Weds, 2 - 6pm. Last admission 5.30pm. Closed BHs. Garden also open Thurs, 2 - 6pm. House & garden also open Tues, Thurs & Fris by written appointment to J D Wrisdale at above address.

Admission: House & Garden: Adult £3.60, Child £1.80, Family £9. Garden only: Adult £2.50, Child £1.20, Family £6.20. No reduction for groups. Access roads unsuitable for coaches which must park in layby at gates ¹/₂ m from Hall.

♿ Grounds suitable.   🐕 In grounds, on leads.

HARLAXTON MANOR

Tel: 01476 403000 **Fax:** 01476 403030

Harlaxton, Grantham, Lincolnshire NG32 1AG

Owner: University of Evansville   **Contact:** Mrs F Watkins

Neo-Elizabethan house. Grandiose and imposing exterior by Anthony Salvin. Internally an architectural tour de force with various styles and an unparalleled Cedar Staircase.

Location: OS Ref. SK895 323. 3m W of Grantham (10 mins from A1) A607. SE of the village.

Opening Times: House: Sun 3 Jun & Sun 1 Jul: 11am - 5pm. House open at other times for group tours by appointment only.

Admission: House open days: Adult £4.50, Child £2, OAP £4.

HECKINGTON WINDMILL

Tel: 01529 461919

Heckington, Sleaford, Lincolnshire

Britain's last surviving eight sail windmill. **Location:** OS Ref. TF145 436. W side of B1394, S side of Heckington village.

Opening Times: Nov - Easter: Suns only, 2 - 5pm. Easter - 15 Jul: Thur - Sun & BH Mons, 12 noon - 5pm. 16 Jul - 2 Sept: daily, 12 noon - 5pm. 8 Sept - 28 Oct: Sats & Suns only, 2 - 5pm. Closed 23 & 30 Dec.

Admission: Ground floor: Free. Mill: Adult £1.50, Child 75p.

LEADENHAM HOUSE

Tel: 01400 273256 **Fax:** 01400 272237

Leadenham House, Lincolnshire LN5 0PU

Owner: Mr P Reeve   **Contact:** Mr and Mrs P Reeve

Late eighteenth century house in park setting.

Location: OS Ref. SK949 518. Entrance on A17 Leadenham bypass (between Newark and Sleaford).

Opening Times: 8 - 12 May, 4 - 9, 11 - 16 & 18 - 21 Jun & 2 - 6 Jul. Also Spring & Aug BHs: 2 - 5pm.

Admission: £3. Groups by prior arrangement only.

ℹ️ No photography. ♿ ✖️

LINCOLN CASTLE

Tel: 01522 511068

Castle Hill, Lincoln LN1 3AA   **Contact:** The Manager

Built by William the Conqueror in 1068. Informative exhibition of the 1215 Magna Carta.

Location: OS Ref. SK975 718. Opposite west front of Lincoln Cathedral.

Opening Times: BST: Sats, 9.30am - 5.30pm, Suns, 11am - 5.30pm. GMT: Mon - Sat: 9.30am - 4pm, Suns, 11am - 4pm. Closed Christmas Day, Boxing Day & New Year's Day.

Admission: Adult £2.50, Child £1, Family (2+3) £6.50.

LINCOLN CATHEDRAL

Tel: 01522 544544 **e-mail:** roybentham@aol.com

Lincoln LN2 1PZ   **Contact:** Communications Office

Medieval Gothic Cathedral of outstanding historical and architectural merit. Schools centre.

Location: OS Ref. SK978 718. At the centre of Uphill, Lincoln.

Opening Times: All year: May - Aug: 7.15am - 8pm, Suns, 7.15am - 6pm. Sept - May: 7.15am - 6pm, Suns, 7.15am - 5pm. Tours daily: Jan - Apr & Oct - Dec: 11am & 2pm. May - Sept: 11am, 1pm & 3pm. Roof tours available. Booked tours throughout the year.

Admission: £3.50, Child up to 14yrs Free, Conc. £3.

LINCOLN MEDIEVAL BISHOPS' PALACE ⊞

Tel: 01522 527468

Minster Yard, Lincoln LN2 1PU

Owner: English Heritage   **Contact:** The Custodian

In the shadow of Lincoln Cathedral are the remains of this medieval palace of the Bishops of Lincoln. Climb the stairs to the Alnwick Tower, explore the undercroft and see one of the most northerly vineyards in Europe.

Location: OS121 Ref. SK981 717. S side of Lincoln Cathedral, in Lincoln.

Opening Times: 1 Apr - 31 Oct: daily, 10am - 6pm (5pm in Oct). 1 Nov - 31 Mar: weekends only, 10am - 4pm. Closed 24 - 26 Dec & 1 Jan. Open daily for Lincoln Christmas Market.

Admission: Adult £2.50, Child £1.30, Conc. £1.90. 15% discount for groups (11+).

❄️ 🛡️ Tel. for details.

SIBSEY TRADER WINDMILL ⊞

Tel: 01604 735400

Sibsey, Boston, Lincolnshire

Owner: English Heritage   **Contact:** The East Midlands Regional Office

An impressive old mill built in 1877, with its machinery and six sails still intact. Flour milled on the spot can be bought here.

Location: OS Ref. TF345 511. ¹/₂ m W of village of Sibsey, off A16, 5m N of Boston.

Opening Times: Mill can be seen in action during the year, please telephone for details.

Admission: Adult £1.80, Child 90p, Conc. £1.40.

TATTERSHALL CASTLE ✤

Tel/Fax: 01526 342543

Tattershall, Lincoln, Lincolnshire LN4 4LR

Owner: The National Trust   **Contact:** The Custodian

A vast fortified tower built c1440 for Ralph Cromwell, Lord Treasurer of England. The Castle is an important example of an early brick building, with a tower containing state apartments, rescued from dereliction and restored by Lord Curzon 1911-14. Four great chambers, with ancillary rooms, contain late gothic fireplaces and brick vaulting. There are tapestries and information displays in turret rooms.

Location: OS122 Ref. TF209 575. On S side of A153, 15m NE of Sleaford, 10m SW of Horncastle.

Opening Times: 1 Apr - 4 Nov: daily except Thurs & Fris, 10.30am - 5.30pm. 10 Nov - 16 Dec: Sats & Suns, 12 noon - 4pm.

Admission: Adult £3, Child £1.50, Family £7.50. Child Free Jul/Aug. Discount for groups.

♿ Ground floor. WC.   🐕 Car park only.   🎧 Free.   🔔

WOOLSTHORPE MANOR ✤

Tel/Fax: 01476 860338

23 Newton Way, Woolsthorpe-by-Colsterworth, Grantham NG33 5NR

Owner: The National Trust   **Contact:** The Custodian

This small 17th century farmhouse was the birthplace and family home of Sir Isaac Newton. Some of his major work was formulated here, during the Plague years (1665 - 67); an early edition of the *Principia* is on display. The orchard has a descendant of the famous apple tree. Science Discovery Centre and exhibition of Sir Isaac Newton's work.

Location: OS130 Ref. SK924 244. 7m S of Grantham, ¹/₂ m NW of Colsterworth, 1m W of A1.

Opening Times: House & Science Discovery Centre: 31 Mar - 4 Nov: Wed - Sun & BH Mons (closed Good Fri), 1 - 5.30pm. Last admission 5pm. Also Science Discovery Centre: 3/4, 10/11, 17/18 & 24/25 Mar (Sats & Suns) & 8/9 & 15/16 Dec: 1 - 5pm.

Admission: Adult £3.30, Child £1.60, Family £8.20, no reduction for groups which must book in advance. Science Discovery Centre on special opening days: Adult £2, Child £1, Family £5.

♿ Ground floor suitable.   🅿️ Limited.   🐕 Car park only.

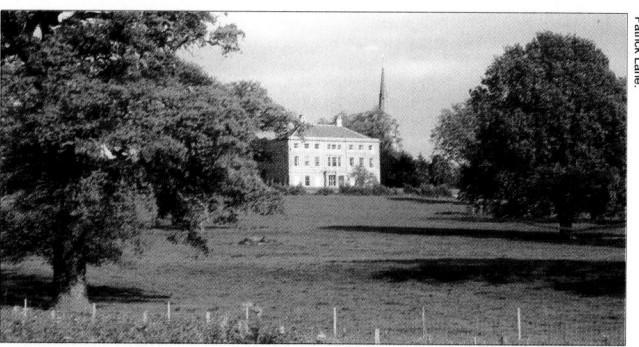

Leadenham House, Lincolnshire.

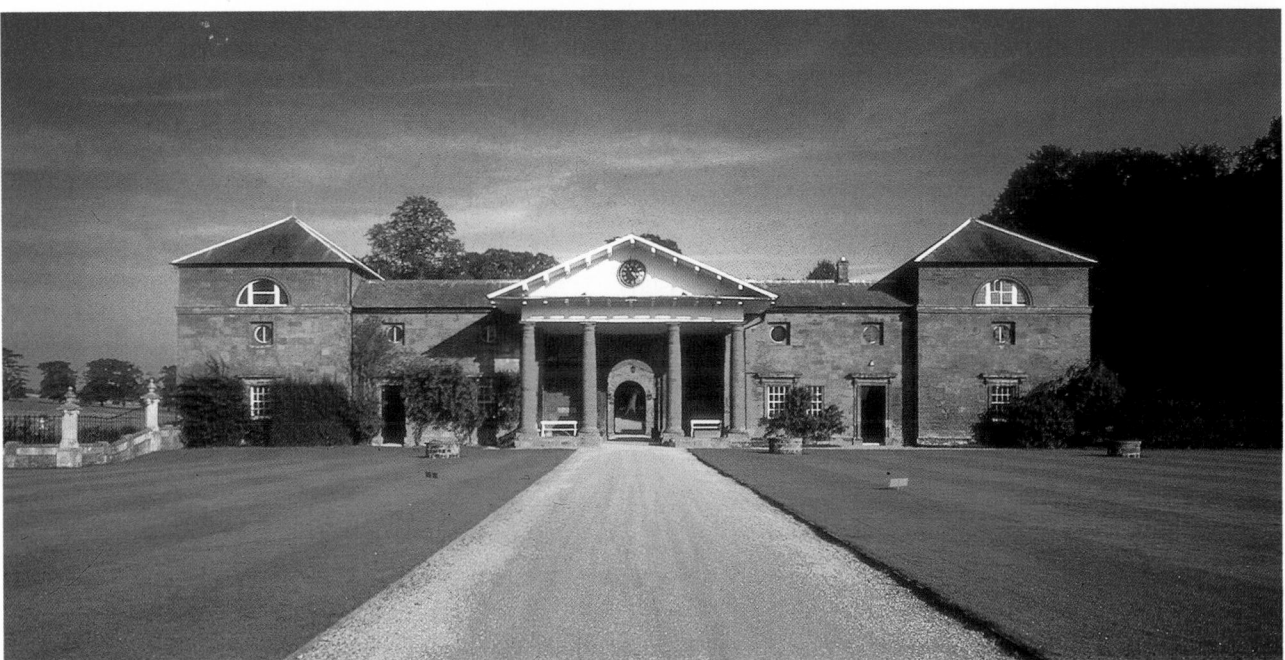

The Stable Block

ALTHORP
Northampton

The history of Althorp is the history of a family. The Spencers have lived and died here for nearly five centuries and twenty generations.

Since the death of Diana, Princess of Wales, Althorp has become known across the world, but before that tragic event, connoisseurs had heard of this most classic of English stately homes on account of the magnificence of its contents and the beauty of its setting.

Next to the mansion at Althorp lies the honey-coloured stable block, a truly breathtaking building which at one time accommodated up to 100 horses and 40 grooms. The stables are now the setting for the Exhibition celebrating the life of Diana, Princess of Wales and honouring her memory after her death. The freshness and modernity of the facilities are a unique tribute to a woman who captivated the world in her all-too-brief existence.

All visitors are invited to view the House, Exhibition and Grounds as well as the Island in the Round Oval where Diana, Princess of Wales is laid to rest.

Please contact the dedicated booking line (24 hour service) Tel: 0870 1679000 or www.althorp.com

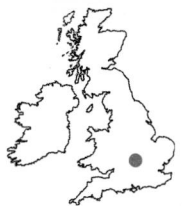

Owner:
The Earl Spencer

CONTACT

Visitor Manager
Althorp
Northampton
NN7 4HQ

Tel: 01604 770107

Fax: 01604 770042

Dedicated booking line: 0870 1679000

LOCATION

OS Ref. SP682 652

From the M1/J16, 7m J18, 10m.
Situated on A428 Northampton - Rugby.
London on average 85 mins away.

Rail: 5m from Northampton station. 14m from Rugby station.

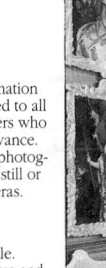 **i** Information leaflet issued to all ticket holders who book in advance. No indoor photography with still or video cameras.

Café.

Suitable. Visitor Centre and ground floor of house accessible. WCs.

P Limited for coaches.

Guide dogs only.

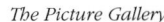

The Picture Gallery

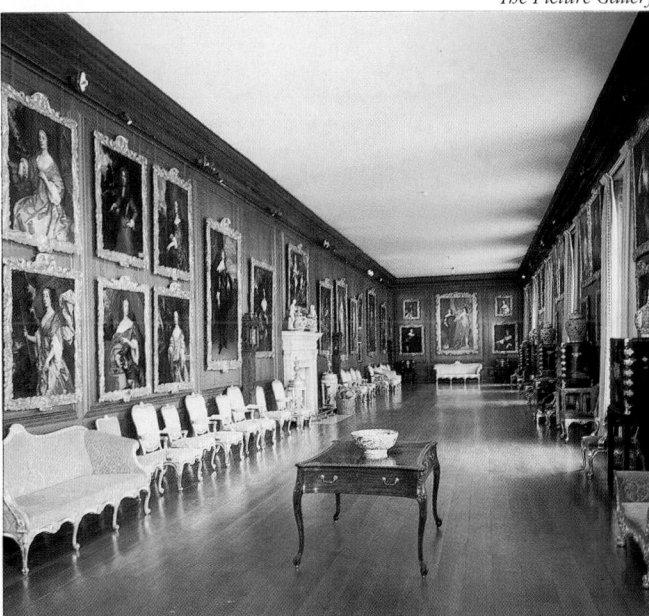

OPENING TIMES

SUMMER
1 July - 30 August
Daily, 9am - 5pm.

Last admission 4pm.

At the time of booking visitors will be asked to state a preference for a morning or an afternoon visit.

Pre-booking recommended.

WINTER
Closed.

ADMISSION

House & Garden (Pre-booked)
Adult £10.00
Child* (5-17yrs) £5.00
OAP.......................£8.00

(Paying at gate subject to availability)
Adult £11.00
Child* (5-17yrs) £5.00
OAP.......................£9.00

* under 5yrs Free.

There is a supplement to view the upstairs rooms of the House.

Group visits by arrangement only.

All the profits from visitor activity at Althorp are donated to the **Diana, Princess of Wales Memorial Fund**.

Numbers are limited each day. Advance booking is recommended.

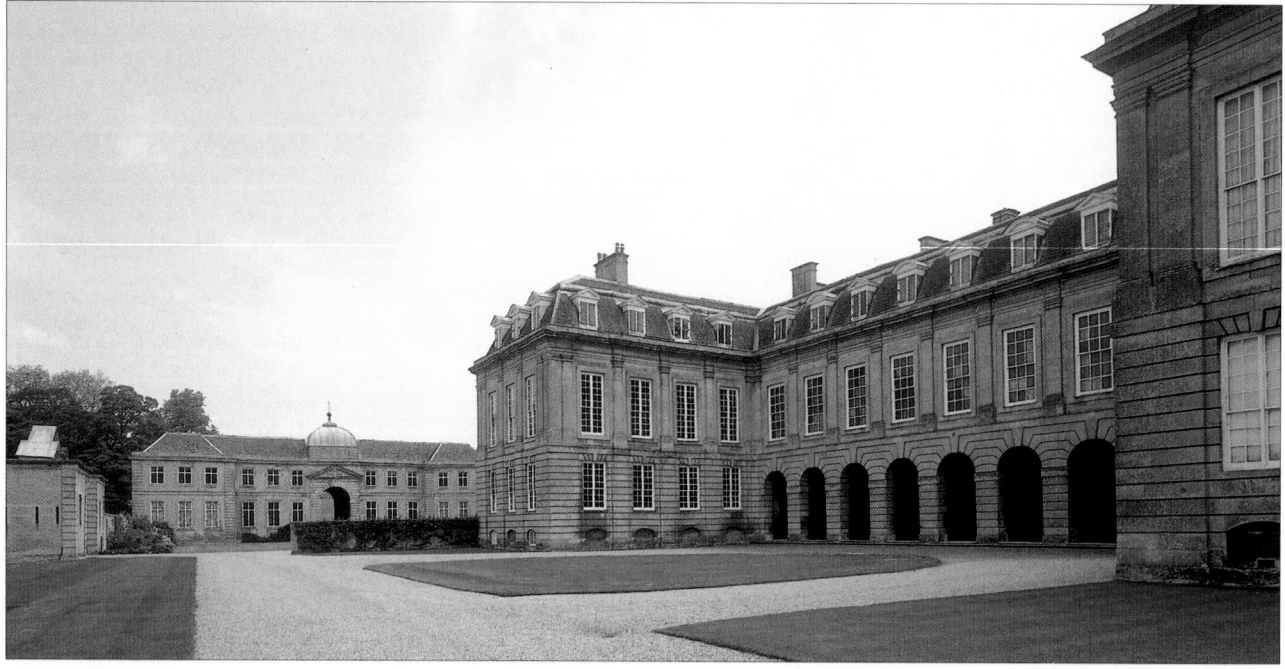

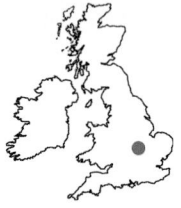

Owner:
His Grace The Duke
of Buccleuch &
Queensberry KT

CONTACT

Gareth Fitzpatrick
The Living Landscape Trust
Boughton House
Kettering
Northamptonshire
NN14 1BJ

Tel: 01536 515731

Fax: 01536 417255

e-mail:
llt@boughtonhouse.org.uk

LOCATION

OS Ref. SP900 815

3m N of
Kettering on
A43 - junction
from A14.

Signposted through
Geddington.

CONFERENCE/FUNCTION		
ROOM	SIZE	MAX CAPACITY
Lecture		100
Seminar Rm		25
Conference facilities available in stable block adjacent to House		

BOUGHTON HOUSE
Kettering

BOUGHTON HOUSE is the Northamptonshire home of the Duke of Buccleuch and Queensberry KT, and his Montagu ancestors since 1528. A 500 year old Tudor monastic building gradually enlarged around seven courtyards until the French style addition of 1695, which has lead to Boughton House being described as 'England's Versailles'.

The house contains an outstanding collection of 17th and 18th century French and English furniture, tapestries, 16th century carpets, porcelain, painted ceilings and notable works by El Greco, Murillo, Caracci and 40 Van Dyck sketches. There is an incomparable Armoury and Ceremonial Coach.

Beautiful parkland with historic avenues, lakes, picnic area, gift shop, adventure woodland play area, plant centre and tearoom. Boughton House is administered by The Living Landscape Trust, which was created by the present Duke of Buccleuch to show the relationship between the historic Boughton House and its surrounding, traditional, working estate.

For information on the groups visit programme and educational services, including fine arts courses run in conjunction with Sotheby's Institute, please contact The Living Landscape Trust. Our newly developed Internet website gives information on Boughton House and The Living Landscape Trust, including a 'virtual' tour, together with full details of our schools' educational facilities (Sandford Award winner 1988, 1993 and 1998).

Silver award winner of the 1st Historic House Awards, given by AA and NPI, in co-operation with the Historic Houses Association, for the privately-owned historic house open to the public which has best preserved its integrity, character of its architecture and furniture, while remaining a lived-in family home.

Parkland available for film location and other events. Stable block contains 100 seats and lecture theatre. No inside photography. No unaccompanied children. Browse our web site for a 'virtual' tour of the house

Access and facilities, no charge for wheelchair visitors. WCs.

Tearoom seats 80, groups must book. Licensed.

By arrangement.

Heritage Education Trust Sandford Award winner 1988, 1993 & 1998. School groups free, teachers' pack.

No dogs in house and garden, welcome in Park on leads.

By arrangement.

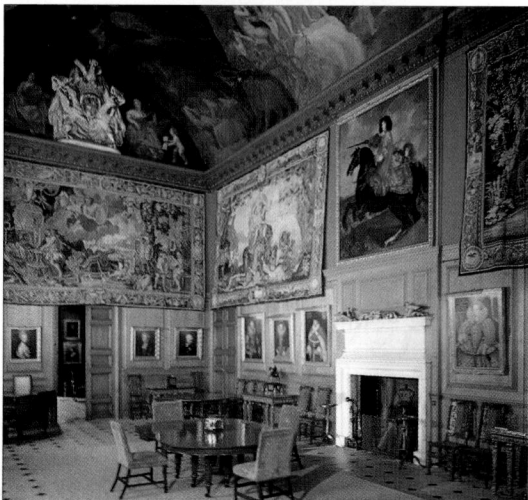

OPENING TIMES

SUMMER

House
1 August - 1 September
Daily, 2 - 4.30pm.

Grounds
1 May - 1 September
Daily:
(except Fris, May - July)
1 - 5pm.

During August opening staterooms on view strictly by prior appointment which can be made by telephone, fax or e-mail. For conservation reasons, numbers are restricted.

Opening of the Woodland Adventure Play Area is subject to weather conditions for reasons of health and safety.

WINTER

Daily by appointment throughout the year for educational groups - contact for details.

ADMISSION

SUMMER

House & Grounds
Adult £6.00
Child/Conc. £5.00

Grounds
Adult £1.50
Child/Conc. £1.00

Wheelchair visitors free.
HHA Friends are admitted Free in August.

WINTER

Group rates available – contact for further details.

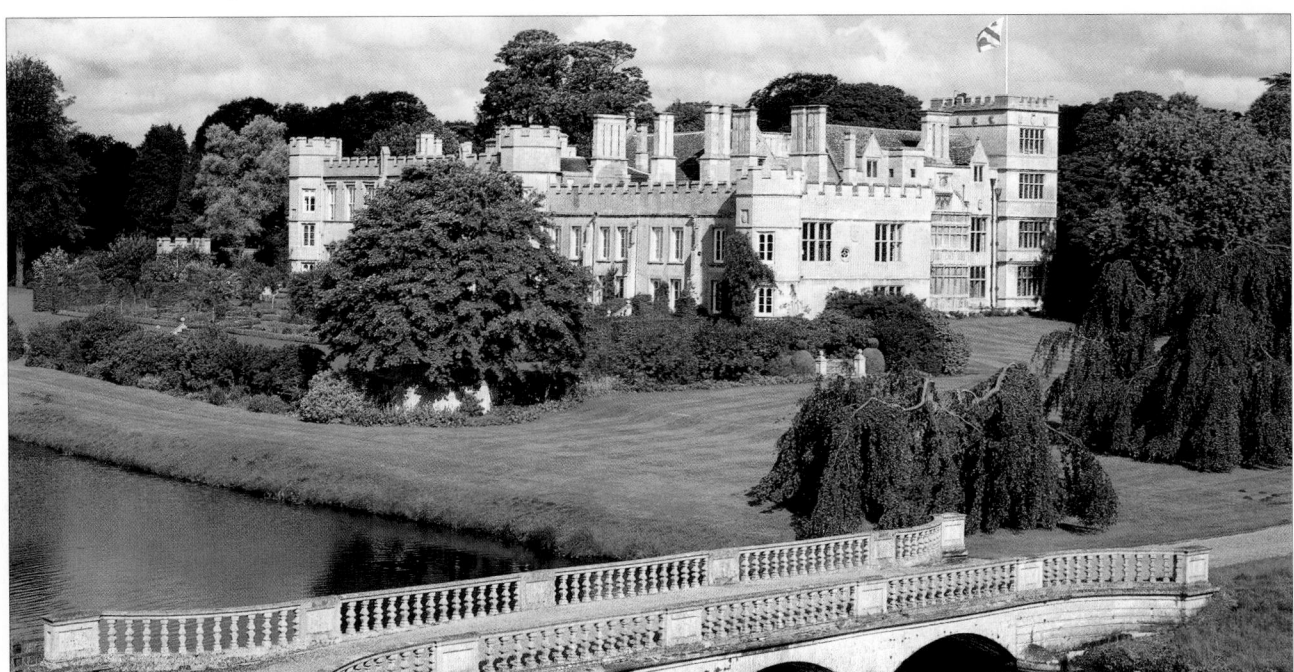

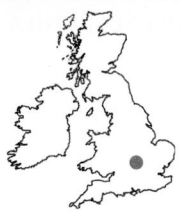

Owner:
E Brudenell Esq

CONTACT

The House Keeper
Deene Park
Corby
Northamptonshire
NN17 3EW

Tel: 01780 450278
or 01780 450223

Fax: 01780 450282

LOCATION

OS Ref. SP950 929

6m NE of
Corby off A43.
From London via M1/J15
then A43.
or via A1, A14,
A43 - 2 hrs.

From Birmingham
via M6, A14, A43, 90 mins.

Rail: Kettering Station
20 mins.

DEENE PARK
Corby

A very interesting house which developed over six centuries from a typical medieval manor around a courtyard into a Tudor and Georgian mansion. Many rooms of different periods are seen by visitors who enjoy the impressive yet intimate ambience of the family home of the Brudenells, seven of whom were Earls of Cardigan. The most flamboyant of them was the 7th Earl who led the Light Brigade charge at Balaklava and of whom there are some historic relics and pictures.

The present owner is Mr Edmund Brudenell

who has carefully restored the house from its dilapidated condition at the end of the last war and also added considerably to the furniture and picture collection.

The gardens have been made over the last thirty years, with long, mixed borders of shrubs, old fashioned roses and flowers, a recent parterre designed by David Hicks and long walks under fine old trees by the water.

The car park beside the big lake is a good place for picnics.

'Have you seen the new Millennium Column at Deene?'

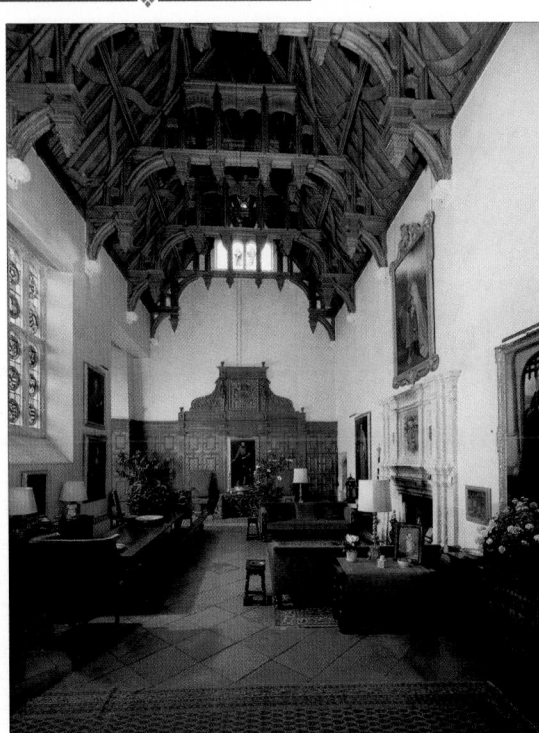

Suitable for indoor and outdoor events, filming, specialist lectures on house, its contents, gardens and history.
No photography in house.

Including buffets, lunches and dinners.

Partially suitable. Visitors may alight at the entrance, access to ground floor and garden. WC.

Special rates for groups, bookings can be made in advance, menus on request.

By arrangement.

Tours inclusive of admittance, tour time 90 mins. Owner will meet groups if requested.

Unlimited for cars, space for 3 coaches 10 yards from house.

In car park only.

Residential conference facilities by arrangement.

OPENING TIMES

SUMMER

June - August
Suns, 2 - 5pm

Open Suns & Mons for Easter, early and late Spring BHs & August BH
2 - 5pm.

Open at all other times by arrangement, including pre-booked parties.

WINTER

House and Gardens closed to casual visitors. Open at all other times by arrangement for groups.

ADMISSION

SUMMER
House & Gardens
  Adult £5.00
  Child (10-14yrs)........£2.50
  Child (under 10).... Free*
Gardens only
  Adult £3.00
  Child (10-14yrs)........£1.50
  Child (under 10).... Free*
Groups (20+)
  Weekdays...............£4.00
  (Min £80)
  Weekends & BHs £5.00
  (Min £100)

* Child up to 10yrs free with an accompanying adult.

WINTER
Groups visits only by prior arrangement.

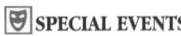 **SPECIAL EVENTS**

Telephone for details.

CONFERENCE/FUNCTION

ROOM	SIZE	MAX CAPACITY
Great Hall	–	150
Tapestry Rm	–	75
East Room	–	18

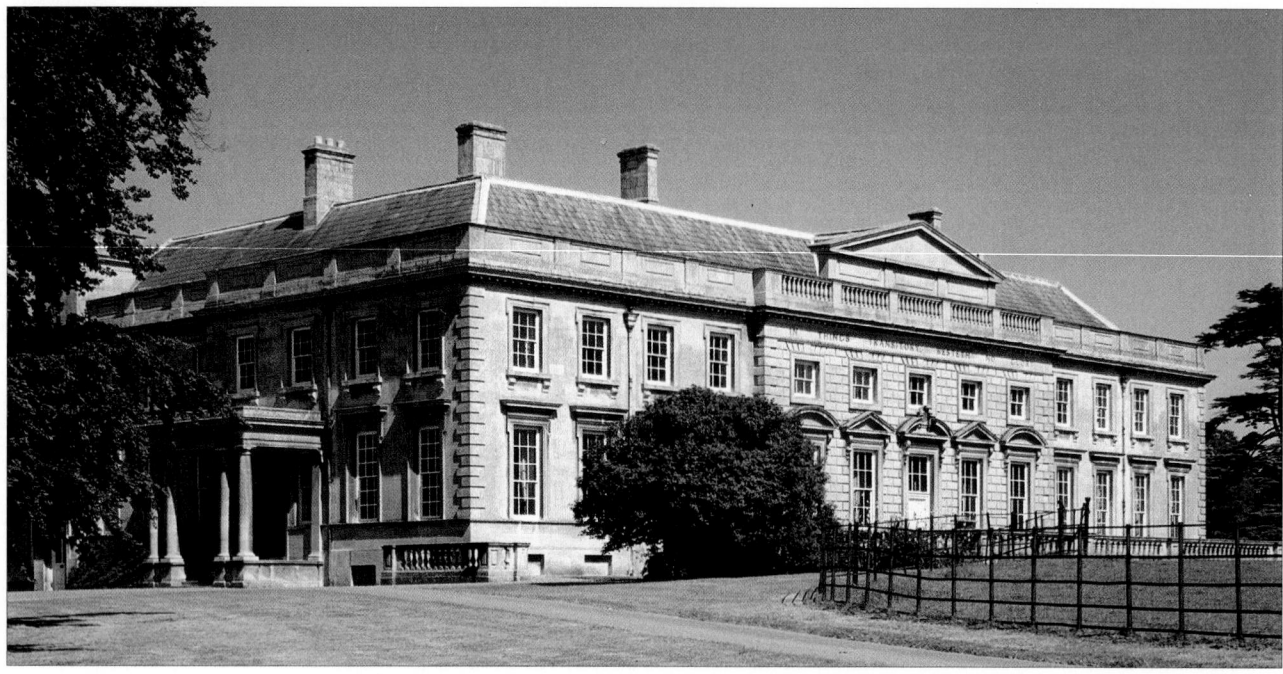

LAMPORT HALL & GARDENS
Northampton

Home of the Isham family from 1560 to 1976. The 17th and 18th century façade is by John Webb and the Smiths of Warwick and the North Wing of 1861 by William Burn.

The Hall contains a wealth of outstanding furniture, books and paintings including portraits by Van Dyck, Kneller, Lely and others. The fine rooms include the High Room of 1655 with magnificent plasterwork, the 18th century library with books from the 16th century, the early 19th century Cabinet Room containing rare Venetian cabinets with mythological paintings on glass and the Victorian Dining Room where refreshments are served.

The first floor has undergone lengthy restoration allowing further paintings and furniture to be displayed as well as a photographic record of Sir Gyles Isham, a Hollywood actor, who initiated the restoration.

The tranquil gardens were laid out in 1655 although they owe much to Sir Charles Isham, the eccentric 10th Baronet who, in the mid-19th century, created the Italian Garden and the Rockery where he introduced the first garden gnomes to England. There are also box bowers, a rose garden and lily pond and extensive walks, borders and lawns all surrounded by a spacious park.

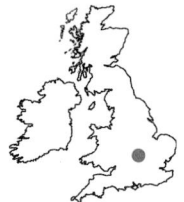

Owner:
Lamport Hall Trust

CONTACT

George Drye
Executive Director
Lamport Hall
Northampton
NN6 9HD

Tel: 01604 686272

Fax: 01604 686224

LOCATION

OS Ref. SP759 745

From London via M1/J15, 1¼ hours. Entrance on A508, 8m N of Northampton at junction with B576. 3½ m S of A14 (A1/M1 link).

Rail: Kettering Station 9m. Northampton 8m.

Bus: From Northampton and Market Harborough.

Conferences, garden parties, activity days, clay pigeon shoots, equestrian events, fashion shows, air displays, archery, rallies, filming, parkland, grand piano, 2 exhibition rooms. Lectures on history of property and gardens. Lecture/meeting rooms. No unaccompanied children. No photography in house.

Special functions, buffets, lunches and dinners, wedding receptions.

Visitors may alight at the entrance, access to ground floor and gardens.

Dining/tearoom. Groups can book in advance. Licensed.

At no additional cost, by prior arrangement, max 70 people, tour time 1¼ hours. On non-fair days.

100 cars & 3 coaches, 20 yds from property. Use main entrance only (on A508).

Work room, specialist advisory teacher study packs. Further information contact Education Officer or the Trust Office.

In grounds, on leads.

Tel. for details.

Tel. for further information.

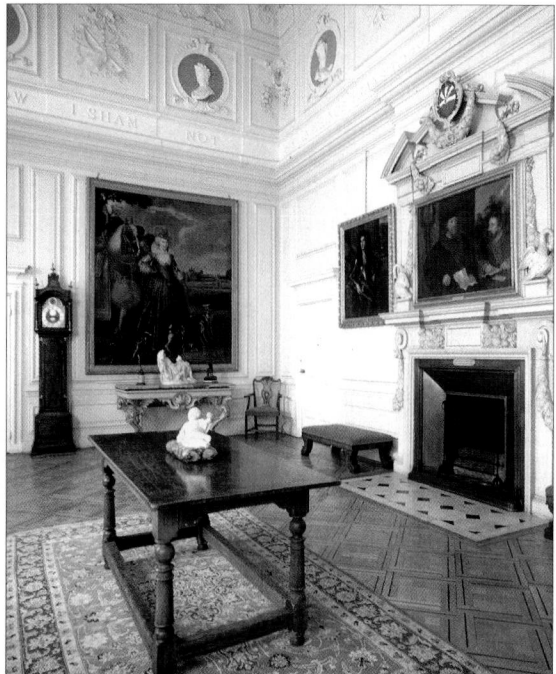

CONFERENCE/FUNCTION

ROOM	SIZE	MAX CAPACITY
Dining Rm	31' x 24' 6"	70

OPENING TIMES

SUMMER

Easter - 7 October
Suns and BH Mons
2.15 - 5.15pm.
Last admission/tour 4pm.

August: Mon - Sat
open for only one
tour at 2.30pm.

20 & 21 October
2.15 - 5.15pm.

Tours on other days by
prior arrangement.

WINTER

Group visits only by
arrangement.

ADMISSION

SUMMER
House & Garden

Adult £4.00
Child (5-16yrs)..........£2.00
OAP.........................£3.50

Group*
Adult £4.00

* Min. payment £135.00
  excluding refreshments

WINTER

Group visits only by
prior arrangement.

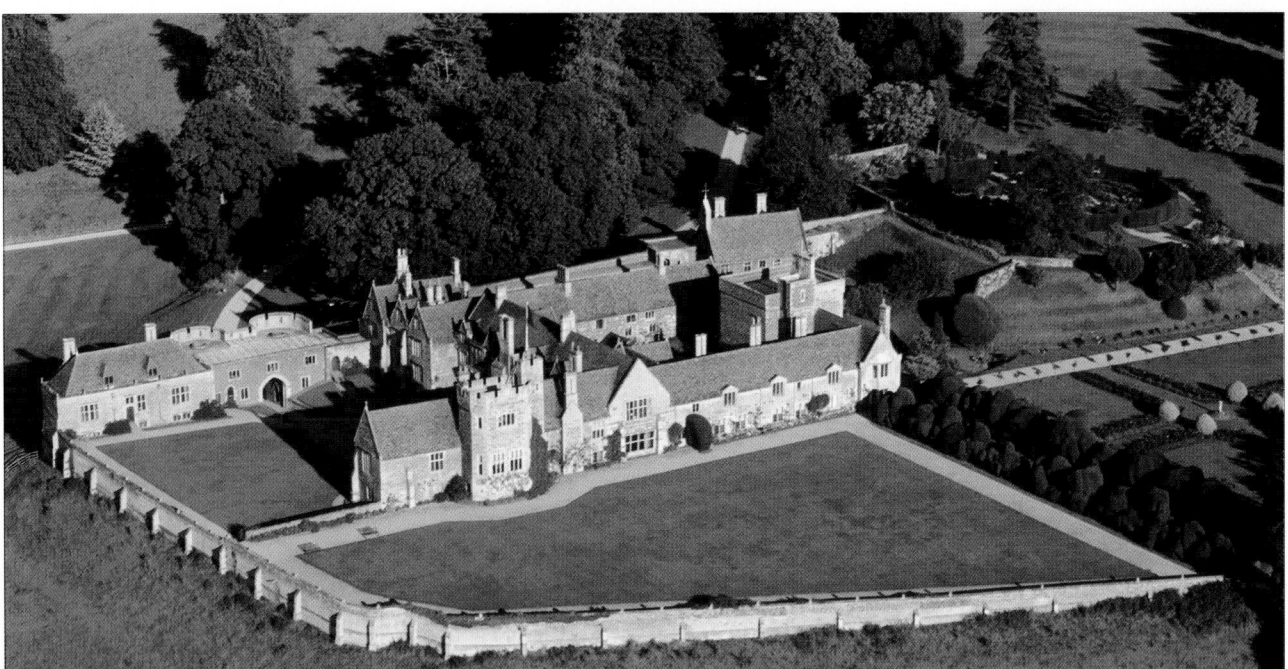

ROCKINGHAM CASTLE
Nr Corby

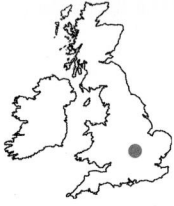

Owner:
James Saunders Watson Esq

CONTACT

Administrator
Rockingham Castle
Market Harborough
Leicestershire
LE16 8TH

Tel: 01536 770240

Fax: 01536 771692

e-mail: rockinghamcastle@
lineone.net

LOCATION

OS Ref. SP867 913

2m N of Corby.
9m E of
Market Harborough.
14m SW of
Stamford on A427.
8m from
Kettering on A6003.

Vehicle entrance on A6003
just S of junction
with A6116.

A Royal castle until 1530, since then home of the Watson family. Rockingham Castle was built by William the Conqueror on the site of an earlier fortification and was regularly used by the early Kings of England until the 16th century, when it was granted by Henry VIII to Edward Watson whose family still live there today.

The house itself is memorable not so much as representing any particular period, but rather a procession of periods. The dominant influence in the building is Tudor within the Norman walls, but practically every century since the 11th has left its mark in the form of architecture, furniture or works of art. The castle has a particularly fine collection of English 18th, 19th and 20th century paintings, and Charles Dickens, who was a frequent visitor, was so captivated by Rockingham that he used it as a model for Chesney Wold in *Bleak House*.

The castle stands in 12 acres of formal and wild garden and commands a splendid view of five counties. Particular features are the 400 year old elephant hedge and the rose garden marking the foundations of the old keep. See Special Exhibition: "450 years a royal castle, 450 years a family home".

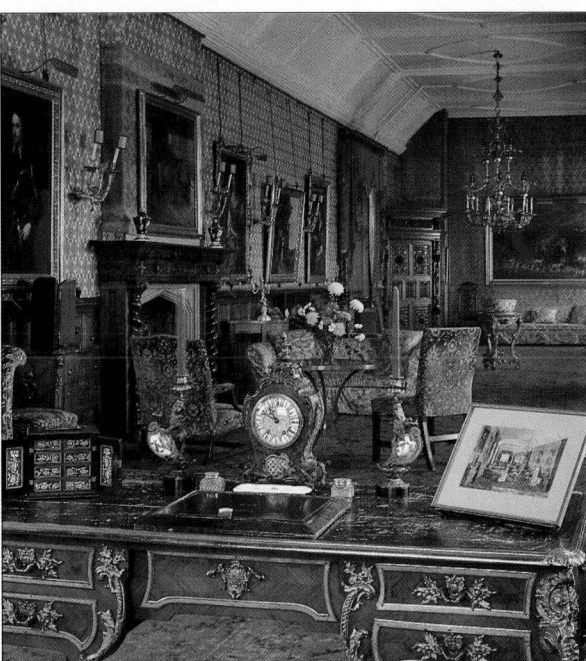

Concerts, conferences, fashion shows, product launches, receptions, seminars, air displays, clay pigeon shoots, archery, equestrian events, fairs, garden parties, filming. Exhibition celebrating 900 years of life in the castle. Parkland and cricket pitch. Strip for light aircraft 4m. No photography in Castle.

Table licence.

Visitors may alight at entrance, ramps provided.

Home-made cream teas and light lunches.

All pre-booked parties have guided tour, except on open-days at no additional cost.

Unlimited.

Winner of 3 Sandford Awards for Heritage Education, special pack designed with National Curriculum. Tours for schools. £1.80 per head (min. charge £40.00). 1 adult free/15 children.

OPENING TIMES

SUMMER
1 April - 30 September
Thurs, Suns, BH Mons & Tues following and all Tues in August: 1 - 5pm.
Grounds open 11.30am on Suns & BHs. 1pm on other open days.
Refreshments available on open days.
Groups at any time by appointment.

WINTER
By appointment for booked parties and schools.

ADMISSION

House & Garden
Adult £4.50
Child (up to 16 yrs) ...£3.00
Conc.......................£4.00
Family (2+2) £12.50

Groups (Min. charge £80.00)
Adult £4.00
Child (up to 16 yrs)....£3.00

Grounds only
...............................£3.00

Schools (min. charge £40.00)
Each child..............£1.80
1 adult Free with every 15 children.

Groups and school parties can be accommodated on most days by arrangement. Children qualify 5 - 16, Under 5s Free.

Prices may vary for special events held in grounds.

SPECIAL EVENTS

Please telephone for details.

CONFERENCE/FUNCTION		
ROOM	SIZE	MAX CAPACITY
Great Hall	37'6" x 22'	100
Panel Room	36' x 23'	100
Long Gallery	87' x 16'6"	100
Walkers House 1	31' x 17'6"	60
Walkers House 2	24' x 18'	50

ALTHORP　　　　　See page 305 for full page entry.

BOUGHTON HOUSE 　　　　　See page 306 for full page entry.

CANONS ASHBY　　　**Tel:** 01327 860044　**Fax:** 01327 860168
e-mail: ecaxxx@smtp.ntrust.org.uk

Canons Ashby, Daventry, Northamptonshire NN11 3SD
Owner: The National Trust　　　　　**Contact:** The Property Manager
Home of the Dryden family since the 16th century, this Elizabethan manor house was built c1550, added to in the 1590s, and altered in the 1630s and c1710; largely unaltered since. Within the house, Elizabethan wall paintings and outstanding Jacobean plasterwork are of particular interest. A formal garden includes terraces, walls and gate piers of 1710. There is also a medieval priory church and a 70 acre park.
Location: OS152 Ref. SP577 506. Access from M40/J11, or M1/J16. Signposted from A5 2m S of Weedon crossroads. Then 7m to SW.
Opening Times: House: 31 Mar - 4 Nov: Sat - Wed including BH Mons (closed Thurs & Fris) 1 - 5.30pm/dusk. Last admissions 5pm. Park, Gardens & Church open as house, 12 noon - 5.30pm; Oct - 4 Nov: 12 noon - 4.30pm, access through garden. Shop: 12.30 - 5pm; Tea Room 12 noon - 5pm.
Admission: Adult £5, Child £2.50, Family £12.50. Discount for booked groups, contact Property Manager.

　Suitable, some steps. WC.　　In grounds, on leads.

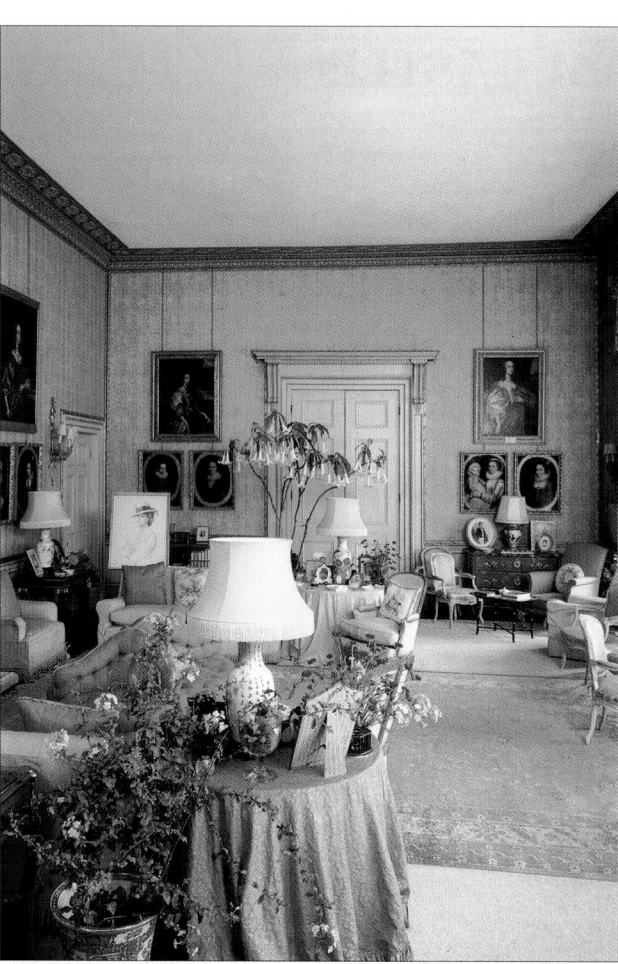

Deene Park, Northamptonshire.

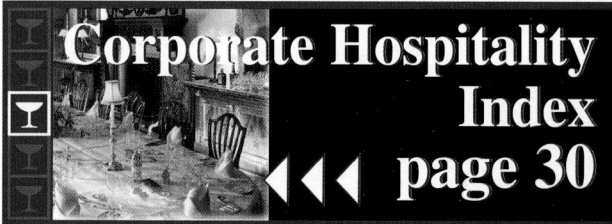

Corporate Hospitality Index ◀◀◀ page 30

CASTLE ASHBY

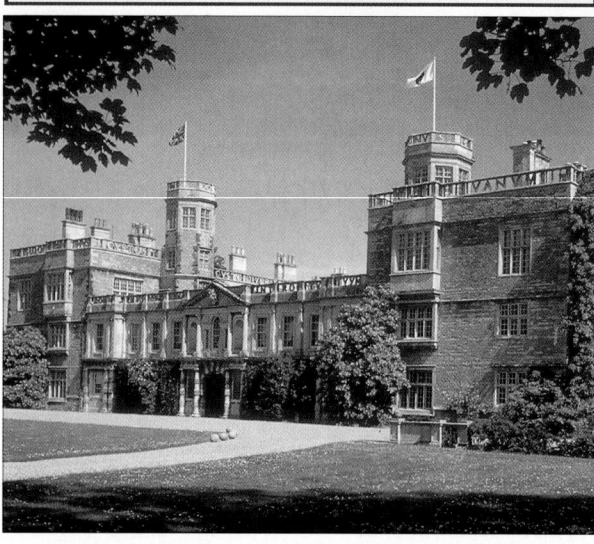

CASTLE ASHBY HOUSE, CASTLE ASHBY, NORTHAMPTON NN7 1LQ
Owner: *7th Marquess of Northampton*　　**Contact:** *Andrea Fowkes*

Tel: 01604 696696　**Fax:** 01604 696516　**e-mail:** andreafowkes@castleashby.co.uk
Castle Ashby is the ancestral home of the 7th Marquess of Northampton, and was built in 1574 to entertain Queen Elizabeth. The castle itself has 26 exquisite bedrooms, including the State Suite, and is available on an exclusive basis for private events. The extensive gardens are open throughout the year and offer a combination of styles.
Location: OS Ref. SP862 582. 55m N of London, between Bedford and Northampton, off A428.
Opening Times: House not open to the public but available for private events. Gardens: All year, 10am - dusk.
Admission: Please telephone for details.

　Private & corporate events.

COTON MANOR GARDEN

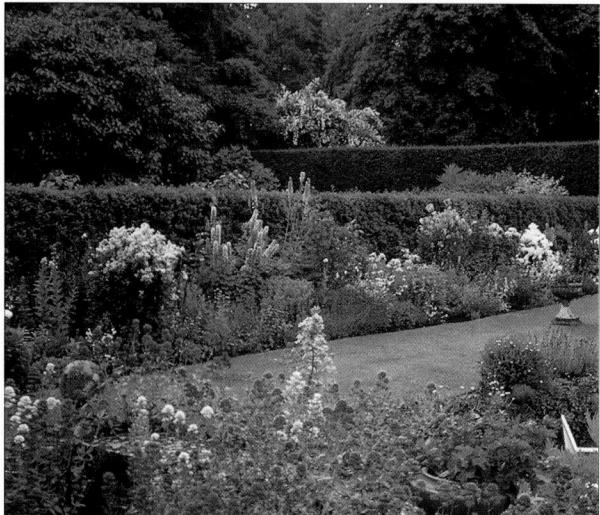

GUILSBOROUGH, NORTHAMPTONSHIRE NN6 8RQ
Owner: *Ian & Susie Pasley-Tyler*　　**Contact:** *Sarah Ball*

Tel: 01604 740219　**Fax:** 01604 740838
e-mail: pasleytyler@cotonmanor.fsnet.co.uk
Traditional English garden laid out on different levels surrounding a 17th century stone manor house. Many herbaceous borders, with extensive range of plants, old yew and holly hedges, rose garden, water garden and fine lawns set in 10 acres. Also wild flower meadow and bluebell wood.
Location: OS Ref. SP675 716. 9m NW of Northampton, between A5199 (formerly A50) and A428.
Opening Times: 1 Apr - 30 Sept: Wed - Sun & BHs, 12 noon - 5.30pm.
Admission: Adult £3.50, Child £2, Conc. £3. Groups: £3.

　　　Grounds suitable. WC.　　　　By arrangement.　　**P**

East Midlands
England

COTTESBROOKE HALL & GDNS

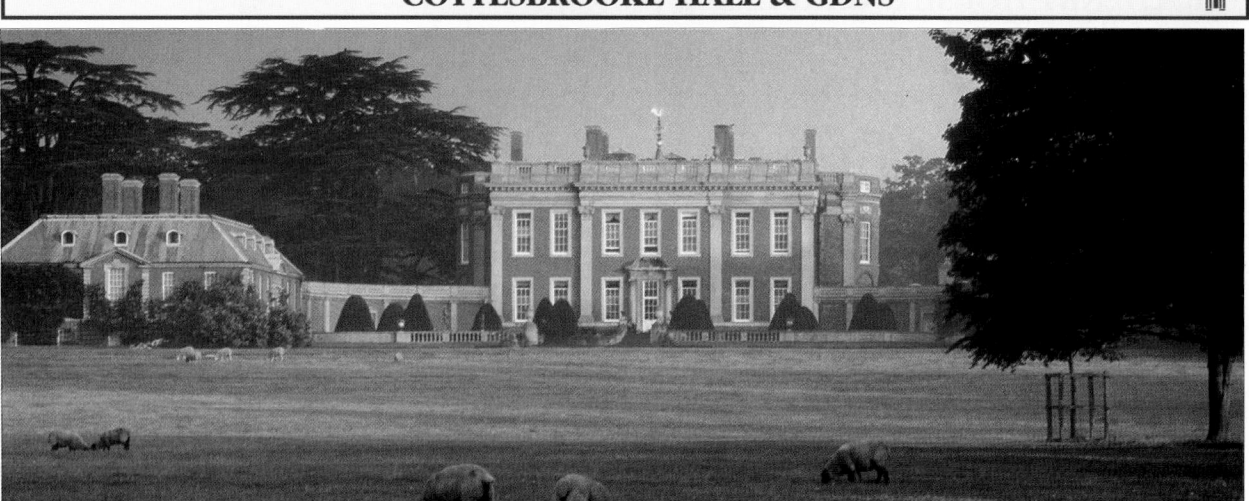

COTTESBROOKE, NORTHAMPTONSHIRE NN6 8PF

Owner: *Capt & Mrs John Macdonald-Buchanan* **Contact:** *The Administrator*

Tel: 01604 505808 **Fax:** 01604 505619 **e-mail:** hall@cottesbrooke.co.uk

Architecturally magnificent house built in the reign of Queen Anne. The identity of the original architect remains a mystery but the house has stayed essentially the same since that time. Renowned picture collection, particularly of sporting and equestrian subjects. Fine English and Continental furniture and porcelain. House reputed to be the pattern for Jane Austen's *Mansfield Park.*

Celebrated gardens of great variety including herbaceous borders, water and wild gardens, fine old cedars and specimen trees. Magnolia, cherry and acer collections and several fine vistas across the Park. Notable planting of containers. A number of distinguished landscape designers have been involved including Rober Weir Schultz, the late Sir Geoffrey Jellicoe and the late Dame Sylvia Crowe.

Location: OS Ref. SP711 739. 10m N of Northampton near Creaton on A5199 (formerly A50), near Brixworth on A508 or Kelmarsh on A14.

Opening Times: House & Gardens: Easter - end Sept: Thurs & BH Suns & Mons & May - Sept: 1st Sun in each month, 2 - 5.30pm. Gardens only: 1 Jun - end Sept: Tue - Fri & BH Suns & Mons & May - Sept: 1st Sun in each month, 2 - 5.30pm.

Admission: House & Gardens: Adult £4.50. Gardens only: Adult £3, Child half price. RHS members Free. Private groups welcome (except weekends) by prior arrangement.

ℹ No photography in house. Craft Fairs & Open Air Concerts. Filming outside.

Unusual plants.

Banqueting facilities, corporate hospitality and catering for functions.

Gardens suitable. WC. Obligatory. P Ⓦ

DEENE PARK 🏛   *See page 307 for full page entry.*

EDGCOTE HOUSE

Edgcote, Banbury, Oxfordshire OX17 1AG
Owner/Contact: Christopher Courage
Early Georgian house with good rococo plasterwork.
Location: OS Ref. SP505 480. 6m NE of Banbury off A361.
Opening Times: By written appointment only.

ELEANOR CROSS ⚎   **Tel:** 01604 735400 (Regional Office)

Geddington, Kettering, Northamptonshire
Owner: English Heritage   **Contact:** The East Midlands Regional Office
One of a series of famous crosses, of elegant sculpted design, erected by Edward I to mark the resting places of the body of his wife, Eleanor, when brought for burial from Harby in Nottinghamshire to Westminster Abbey in 1290.
Location: OS Ref. SP896 830. In Geddington, off A43 between Kettering and Corby.
Opening Times: Any reasonable time.

HADDONSTONE SHOW GARDEN   **Tel:** 01604 770711 **Fax:** 01604 770027

The Forge House, East Haddon, Northampton NN6 8DB
      e-mail: info@haddonstone.co.uk
Owner: Haddonstone Ltd   **Contact:** Marketing Director
See Haddonstone's classic garden ornaments in the beautiful setting of the walled manor gardens – including urns, troughs, fountains, statuary, bird baths, sundials and balustrading. The garden is on different levels with shrub roses, conifers, clematis and climbers. The newly opened Jubilee garden features a pavilion, temple and Gothic grotto.
Location: OS Ref. SP667 682. 7m NW of Northampton off A428. Signposted.
Opening Times: Mon - Fri, 9am - 5.30pm. Closed weekends, BHs & Christmas period.
Admission: Free. Groups by appointment only. Not suitable for coach groups.

 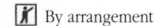 By arrangement. Limited. 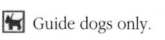 Guide dogs only.

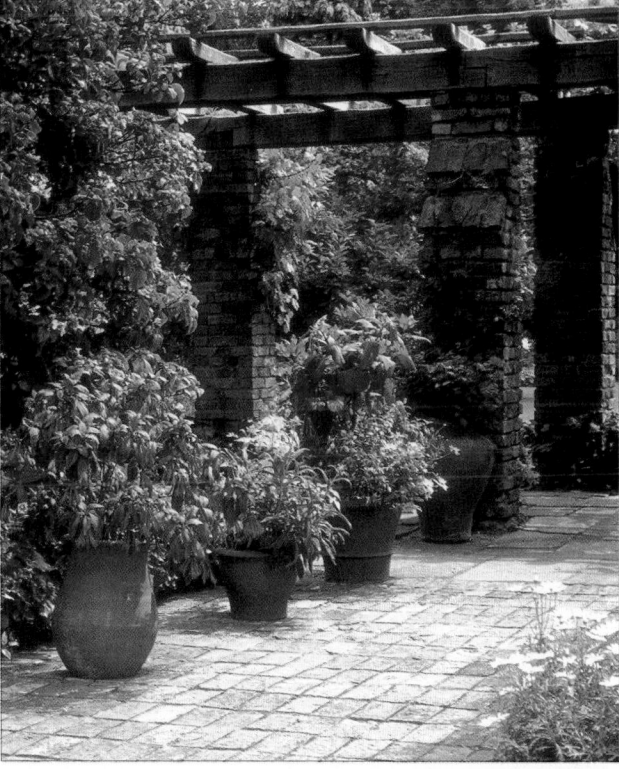

Cottesbrooke Gardens, Northamptonshire.

HOLDENBY HOUSE & GARDENS

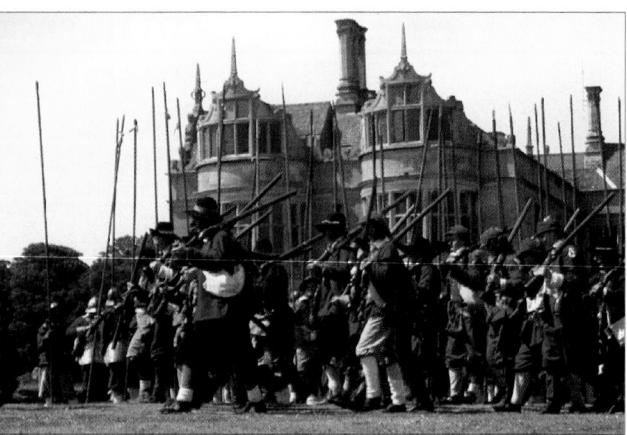

Kirby Hall, re-enactment, Northamptonshire.

HOLDENBY, NORTHAMPTONSHIRE NN6 8DJ

Owner: *James Lowther Esq*   **Contact:** *Mrs Sarah Maughan*

Tel: 01604 770074   **Fax:** 01604 770962

On a hill across the fields from Althorp stands Holdenby. Once the largest house in England it was built to entertain Queen Elizabeth I and subsequently became the palace and prison of her successor Charles I. Now a family home, the house provides a splendid backdrop to the beautiful gardens re-created by Rosemary Verey and Rupert Golby, the rare breeds of farm animals, reconstructed 17th century farmstead and, overhead, our magnificent birds of prey soaring over the scene of so much history.

Location: OS Ref. SP693 681. M1/J15a. 7m NW of Northampton off A428 and A5199.

Opening times: Gardens & Falconry demonstrations: 1 Apr - end Sep: Suns, 1 - 5pm; Jul & Aug: daily (except Sats), 1 - 5pm. House: 16 Apr, 28 May, 27 Aug and by appointment. Events all BHs, 1 - 6pm.

Admission: Garden & Falconry: Adult £3, Child (3-15yrs) £1.75, OAP £2.50. House: Adult £5, Child £3, OAP £4.50. Events: Adult £4, Child £2, OAP £3.50.

ℹ️ Children's play area.   📷   ⛧   ⟟   ♿ Partially suitable. WC.

☕ Home-made teas. Groups must book. 🚶 By arrangement.   🅿️

🏆 Sandford Award-winner.   🐕 In grounds, on leads.   🛡️ Tel. for details.

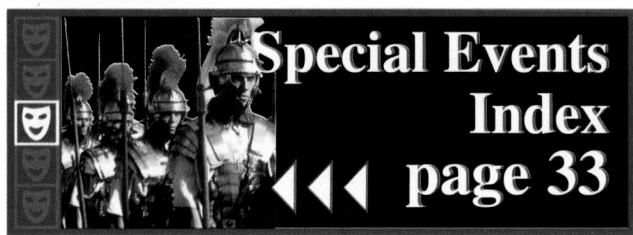

Special Events Index ◀◀◀ page 33

KELMARSH HALL

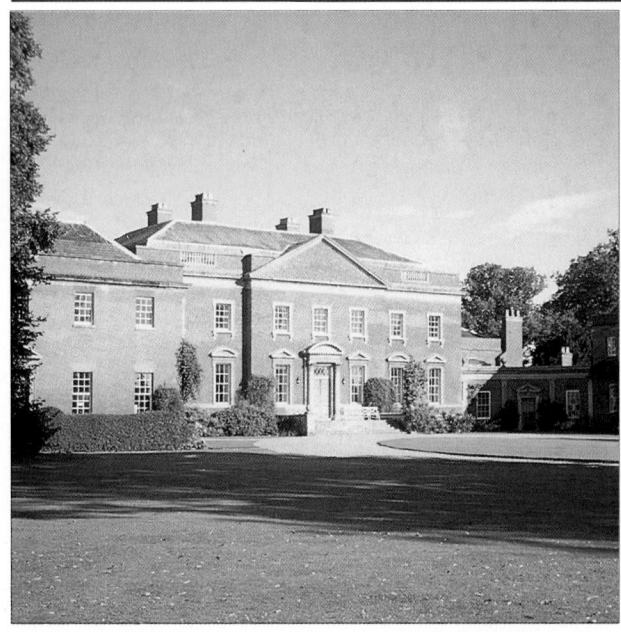

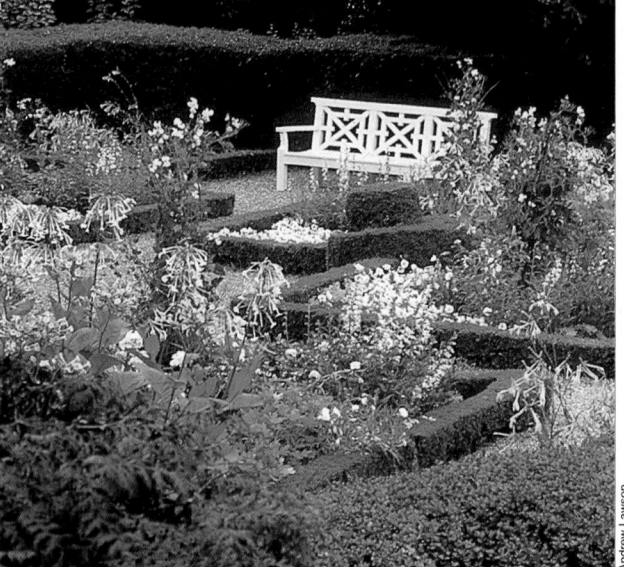

Andrew Lawson.

KELMARSH, NORTHAMPTONSHIRE NN6 9LU

Owner: *The Kelmarsh Trust*   **Contact:** *General Manager*

Tel/Fax: 01604 686543

Built in 1732 to a James Gibbs design, Kelmarsh Hall is surrounded by its working estate, grazed parkland and beautiful gardens. In 1928 the Palladian house was occupied and decorated by Nancy Lancaster, and the Great Hall, Chinese Room and other rooms still bear her creative touch that has become known as the English Country House style. The gardens, with schemes and designs also by Geoffrey Jellicoe and Norah Lindsay, now have a unique place in garden history. Gifted to the Kelmarsh Trust by the Lancaster family the house, gardens and estate are now available for study, group and general visits.

Location: OS Ref. SP736 795. 500 metres N of A14 - A508 junction.

Opening Times: House: 15 Apr - 27 Aug: Suns & BH Mons, 2.30 - 5pm. Gardens: 15 Apr - 30 Aug: Tues, Thurs, Suns & BH Mons, 2.30 - 5pm. Sept: Tues & Thurs only.

Admission: House & Grounds: Adult £3.50, Child £2, Conc. £3. Garden only: £2. Group visits all year by arrangement.

ℹ️ No photography in house.   ♿ Partially suitable. WC.   ☕ On Suns only.

🚶 Obligatory.   🅿️ Limited for coaches.   🏆   🐕 In grounds, on leads.

KIRBY HALL   Tel: 01536 203230

Deene, Corby, Northamptonshire NN17 5EN

Owner: English Heritage   **Contact:** The Custodian

Outstanding example of a large, stone-built Elizabethan mansion, begun in 1570 with 17th century alterations. There are fine gardens with topiary, home to peacocks. Jane Austen's *Mansfield Park* was filmed at Kirby Hall in 1998. Venue for *History in Action*, Europe's largest multi-period historical festival.

Location: OS141 Ref. SP926 927. On unclassified road off A43, Corby to Stamford road, 4m NE of Corby. 2m W of Deene Park.

Opening Times: 1 Apr - 31 Oct: daily 10am - 6pm (5pm in Oct). 1 Nov - 31 Mar: Sats & Suns, 10am - 4pm. Closed 24 - 26 Dec & 1 Jan.

Admission: Adult £3, Child £1.50, Conc. £2.30.

   Tel. for details.

LAMPORT HALL & GARDENS   See page 308 for full page entry.

LYVEDEN NEW BIELD   Tel: 01832 205358

Nr Oundle, Peterborough PE8 5AT

Owner: The National Trust   **Contact:** The Custodian

An incomplete Elizabethan garden house and moated garden. Begun in 1595 by Sir Thomas Tresham to symbolise his Catholic faith, Lyveden remains virtually unaltered since work stopped when Tresham died in 1605.

Location: OS141 Ref. SP983 853. 4m SW of Oundle via A427, 3m E of Brigstock, off Harley Way. Access by foot along a 1/2 m farm track.

Opening Times: All year: 9am - 5pm. Groups by arrangement with Custodian: Lyveden New Bield Cottage, Oundle, Peterborough PE8 5AT. Elizabethan water gardens and visitor information room open Apr - Nov: daily except Mons & Tues.

Admission: £2.

Limited.   On leads.

THE MENAGERIE

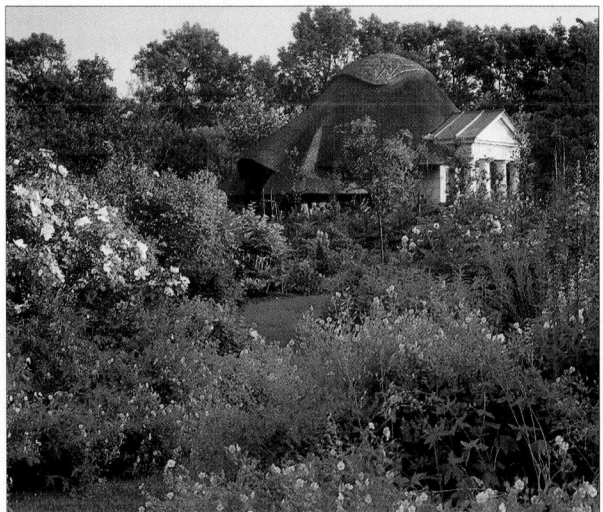

HORTON, NORTHAMPTON NN7 2BX

Owner: Mr A Myers   *Contact: Mr Neill Case (Head Gardener)*

Tel: 01604 870957

Folly built in the 1750s for the 2nd Earl of Halifax by the architect and astronomer Thomas Wright of Durham. The north front of the house has just been restored. The gardens, where Lord Halifax's animals were once kept, were created by the late Ian Kirby and include formal ponds, wetland and bog area, herbaceous border, two thatched arbours, one gothic and one circular and classical which is now a chapel. The whole grotto is covered in shells and minerals and devoted to Orpheus playing to the animals in the underworld.

Location: OS Ref. SP822 534. 5m SE of Northampton. Entry by field gate on E of A526.

Opening Times: Grotto & Gardens open to groups (20+) by arrangement £5. Gardens: Apr - Sept: Mons & Thurs, 2 - 5pm. Last Sun of each month 2 - 6pm.

Admission: Adult £3.50, Child £1.50.

  Grounds suitable.

NORTHAMPTON CATHEDRAL   Tel: 01604 714556   Fax: 01604 712066

Cathedral House, Kingsthorpe Road, Northampton NN2 6AG

Partly 19th century Pugin.   **Contact:** Cathedral Administrator, Canon D McSwenney

Location: OS Ref. SP753 617. 3/4 m N of town centre.

Opening Times: Daily, 10am - 7pm. Sun Service: 7pm (Sat) 8.30am, 10.30am 5.15pm. Weekday services: 9.30am and 7pm.

Admission: Guided visit by prior application.

THE PREBENDAL MANOR HOUSE

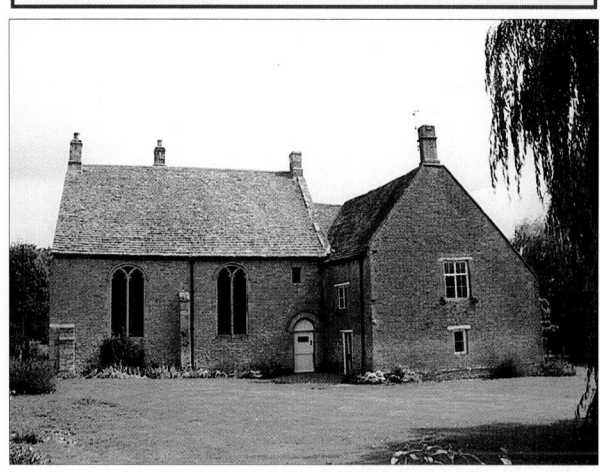

NASSINGTON, PETERBOROUGH PE8 6QG

Owner/Contact: Mrs J Baile

Tel: 01780 782575   **e-mail:** info@prebendal-manor.demon.co.uk

Grade I listed and dating from the early 13th century, it is the oldest manor in Northamptonshire and one of the longest continually occupied houses in the country. The manor still retains many fine original medieval features and included in the visit are the 15th century dovecote, tithe barn museum and medieval fish ponds. Designed by Michael Brown and unique to the area and encompassing 5 acres are the 14th century re-created medieval gardens.

Location: OS Ref. TL063 962. 6m N of Oundle, 9m W of Peterborough, 7m S of Stamford.

Opening times: May, Jun & Sept: Suns, Weds & BH Mons. Jul/Aug: Suns, Weds & Thurs. 1 - 5.30pm. Closed Christmas.

Admission: Adult £4, Child £1.20. Groups (20 - 50) outside normal opening times by arrangement: Adult £3.50, Child £1.

No photography.   Partially suitable.
Lunches & home-made teas.   Limited.   Free.
Guide dogs only.

ROCKINGHAM CASTLE   See page 309 for full page entry.

RUSHTON TRIANGULAR LODGE   Tel: 01536 710761

Rushton, Kettering, Northamptonshire NN14 1RP

Owner: English Heritage   **Contact:** The Custodian

This extraordinary building, completed in 1597, symbolises the Holy Trinity. It has three sides, 33 ft wide, three floors, trefoil windows and three triangular gables on each side.

Location: OS Ref. SP830 831. 1m W of Rushton, on unclassified road 3m from Desborough on A6.

Opening Times: 1 Apr - 31 Oct: daily, 10am - 6pm (5pm in Oct).

Admission: Adult £1.75, Child 90p, Conc. £1.30.

SOUTHWICK HALL   Tel: 01832 274064

Nr Oundle, Peterborough PE8 5BL

Owner: Christopher Capron Esq   **Contact:** W J Richardson

A family home since 1300, retaining medieval building dating from 1300, with Tudor rebuilding and 18th century additions. Exhibitions: Victorian and Edwardian Life, collections of agricultural and carpentry tools and local archaeological finds.

Location: OS152 Ref. TL022 921. 3m N of Oundle, 4m E of Bulwick.

Opening Times: 15/16 Apr, 6/7 & 27/28 May, 26/27 Aug, also Weds May - Aug: 2 - 5pm (last admission 4.30pm).

Admission: Adult £3.50, Child £2, OAP £3.

Partially suitable. WC.   By arrangement.   In grounds on leads.

STOKE PARK PAVILIONS

Tel: 01604 862172

Stoke Bruerne, Towcester, Northamptonshire NN12 7RZ

Owner: A S Chancellor Esq   **Contact:** Mrs C Cook

The two Pavilions, dated c1630 and attributed to Inigo Jones, formed part of the first Palladian country house built in England by Sir Francis Crane. The central block, to which the Pavilions were linked by quadrant colonnades, was destroyed by fire in 1886. The grounds include extensive gardens and overlook the former park, now farmland.

Location: OS Ref. SP740 488. 7m S of Northampton.

Opening Times: Aug: daily, 3 - 6pm. Other times by appointment only.

Admission: Adult £3, Child £1.

♿ Grounds suitable.   🅿 Limited.   🐾 In grounds, on leads.   ❋

WAKEFIELD LODGE

Tel: 01327 811493

Potterspury, Northamptonshire NN12 7QX

Owner/Contact: J H Richmond-Watson

Georgian Hunting Lodge with deer park.

Location: OS Ref. SP739 425. 4m S of Towcester on A5.

Opening Times: House: 30 Apr - 8 Jun: Mon - Fri (closed BHs).

Admission: £5.

ℹ No photography.   📷   ♿ Not suitable.   🚻 🍴 🅺 Obligatory.   🅿 Limited for coaches.   🦮 Guide dogs only.

SULGRAVE MANOR

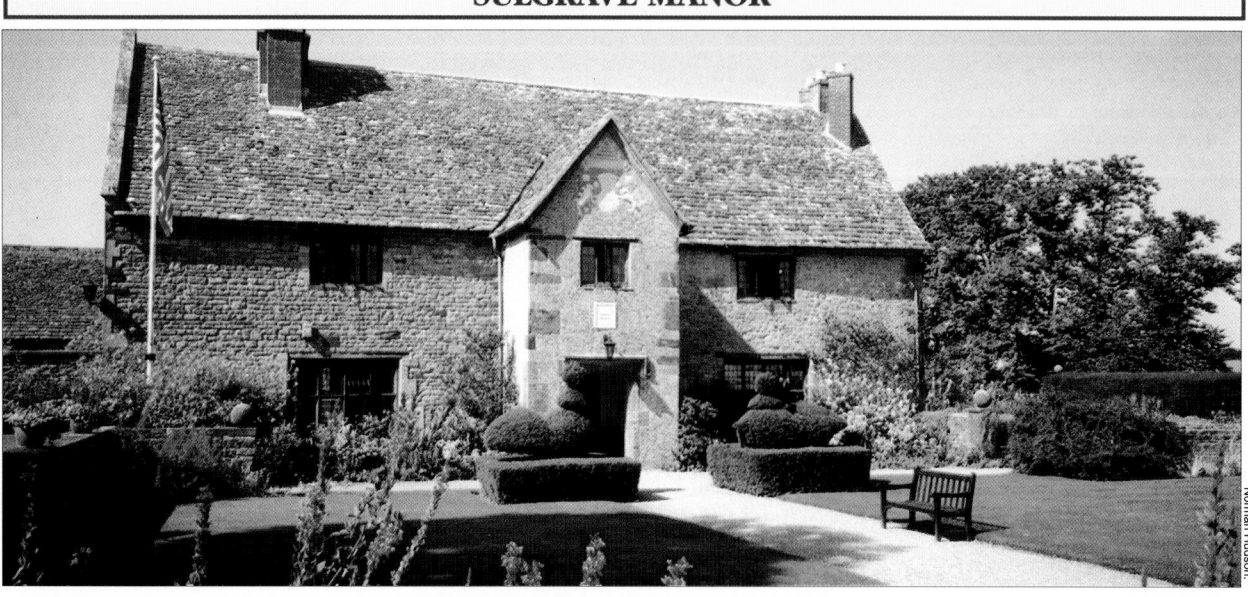

Norman Hudson.

MANOR ROAD, SULGRAVE, BANBURY, OXON OX17 2SD

Owner: *Sulgrave Manor Board*   **Contact:** *Martin Sirot-Smith*

Tel: 01295 760205   **Fax:** 01295 768056   **e-mail:** sulgrave-manor@talk21.com

A delightful 16th century Manor House that was the home of George Washington's ancestors. Today it presents a typical wealthy man's home and gardens of Elizabethan times. Restored with scholarly care and attention to detail that makes a visit both a pleasure and an education. '*A perfect illustration of how a house should be shown to the public*' – Nigel Nicholson, *Great Houses of Britain*. New Courtyard development with fine visitor/education facilities.

Location: OS152 Ref. SP561 457. Off Banbury - Northampton road (B4525) 5m from M40/J11. 15m from M1/J15A.

Opening Times: 1 Apr - 31 Oct: daily except Weds. W/days 2 - 5.30pm, W/ends 10.30am - 1pm & 2 - 5.30pm. Nov, Dec & Mar: W/ends only, 10.30am - 1pm & 2 - 4.30pm. Also open 27 - 30 Dec. Closed 25 - 26 & 31 Dec & Jan. Open by appointment for groups and school groups out of normal hours.

Admission: Adult £4, Child £2, Conc. £4. Groups: Adult £3.50, Child £1.75, Conc. £3.50. Special Events: Adult £4.50, Child £2.25, Family £12. Groups: Adult £4, Child £2. Gardens only: £2. All visitors on non-event days are taken round the Manor House in regularly organized guided tours.

ℹ No photography in house.   📷 🍴 🍽   ♿ Partially suitable.   🛍 🅺 Obligatory.   🅿 🚃 🐾 In grounds, on leads.   🔔 ❋   📧 Tel. for details.   🆃🆆

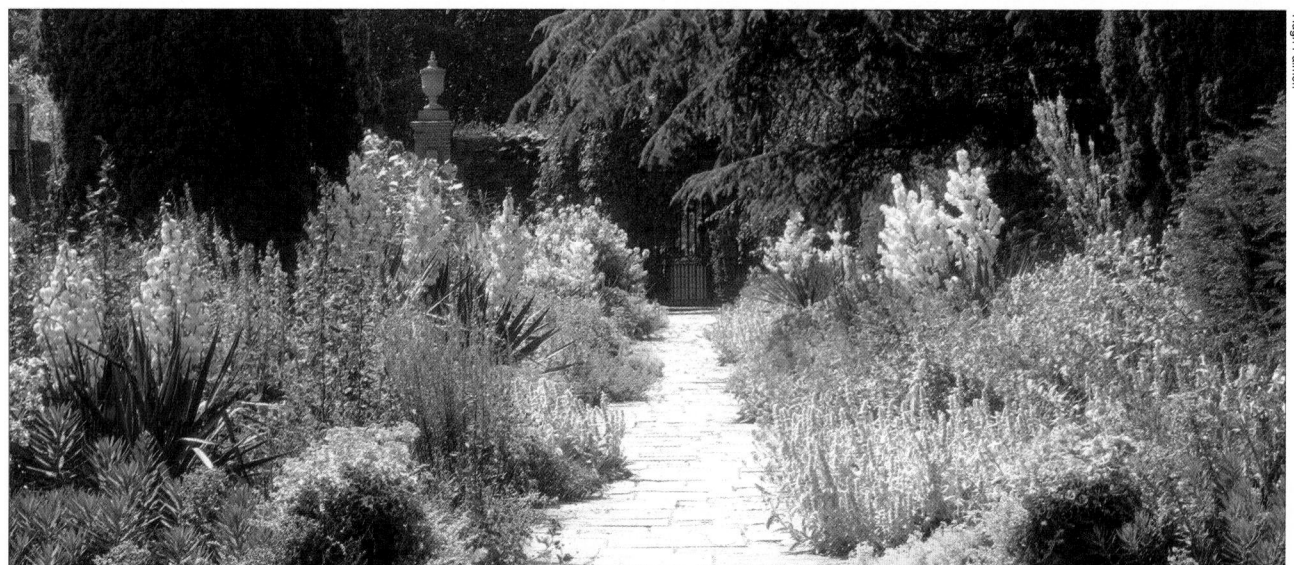

Hugh Palmer.

Cottesbrooke Gardens, Northamptonshire.

East Midlands
England

BREWHOUSE YARD MUSEUM
Tel: 0115 9153600 **Fax:** 0115 9153601

THE MUSEUM OF NOTTINGHAM LIFE

Castle Boulevard, Nottingham NG7 1FB

Owner/Contact:

Set in a group of 18th century cottages, the museum presents a realistic glimpse of life in Nottingham over the past 200 years.

Location: OS Ref. SK570 393. 500yds SW of City Centre.

Opening Times: Daily, 10am - 4.30pm (Nov - Feb: closed Fris).

Admission: Weekdays: Free. Weekends & BHs: Adult £1.50, Conc. 80p, Family £3.80.

CARLTON HALL
Tel: 01636 821421 **Fax:** 01636 821554

Carlton-on-Trent, Nottinghamshire NG23 6LP

Owner/Contact: Lt Col & Mrs Vere-Laurie

Mid 18th century house by Joseph Pocklington of Newark. Stables attributed to Carr of York. Family home occupied by the same family since 1832.

Location: OS Ref. SK799 640. 7m N of Newark off A1. Opposite the church.

Opening Times: By appointment only.

Admission: Hall and Garden £3.50. Minimum charge for a group £35.

⊤ Conferences. &. Not suitable. 🐕 In grounds, on leads. Guide dogs in house. ❄

CASTLE MUSEUM & ART GALLERY
Tel: 0115 9153700 **Fax:** 0115 9153653

Nottingham NG1 6EL
Contact: Janet Owen

17th century ducal mansion, home to a museum and art gallery.

Location: OS Ref. SK569 395. SW of the city centre on hilltop.

Opening Times: Daily (closed Fris from Nov-Feb): 10am - 5pm. Closed 24, 25 Dec & 1 Jan.

Admission: Weekdays Free. Weekends: Adult £2, Conc. £1 (2000 times & prices).

CLUMBER PARK 🌳
Tel: 01909 476592 **Fax:** 01909 500721

Clumber Park, Worksop, Nottinghamshire S80 3AZ

Owner: The National Trust
Contact: Claire Herring, Property Manager

Historic parkland with peaceful woods, open heath and rolling farmland around a serpentine lake.

Location: OS120 Ref SK626 746. 4$^{1}/_{2}$m SE of Worksop, 6$^{1}/_{2}$m SW of Retford, just off A1/A57 via A614. 11m from M1/J30.

Opening Times: Park: All year during daylight hours, except 14 Jul & 18 Aug. Walled Kitchen Garden: Apr - end Sept: Weds & Thurs, 10.30am - 5.30pm, Sats, Suns & BH Mons, 10.30am - 6pm. Chapel: Apr - end Sept: Mon - Fri, 10.30am - 5.30pm, Sats & Suns, 10.30am - 6pm. Oct - 11 Jan 2001: daily, 10.30am - 4pm. Closed 12 Jan - end Mar for conservation cleaning.

Admission: Pedestrians: Free, NT Members: Free, Cars £3, Caravans/mini-coaches £4.30. Coaches Free weekday, £7 weekends & BH Mons. Walled kitchen garden 70p.

🏠 🍴 ⊤ &. Partially suitable. Wheelchairs available. 🍽 P 🎁
🐕 In grounds on leads. ❄

Gardener's World Mar. 2002

GREEN'S MILL
Tel: 0115 9156878

Windmill Lane, Sneinton, Nottingham NG2 4QB

Owner/Contact:

This fully operational windmill was once owned and operated by George Green, mathematician and physicist.

Location: OS Ref. SK585 398. $^{1}/_{2}$ m due E of City Centre, between A612 and B686.

Opening Times: Wed - Sun & BH Mons, 10am - 4pm.

Admission: Free.

HODSOCK PRIORY GARDEN
Tel: 01909 591204 **Fax:** 01909 591578

Blyth, Nr Worksop, Nottinghamshire S81 0TY

Owner: Sir Andrew & Lady Buchanan
Contact: Lady Buchanan

Sensational snowdrops, winter flowering plants and shrubs, woodland walk.

Location: OS Ref. SK612 853. W of B6045 Worksop/Blyth road, 1m SW of Blyth, less than 2m from A1.

Opening Times: Snowdrop period only: daily, 10am - 4pm. Please telephone for details.

Admission: Adult £3, accompanied Child (6-16yrs) 50p.

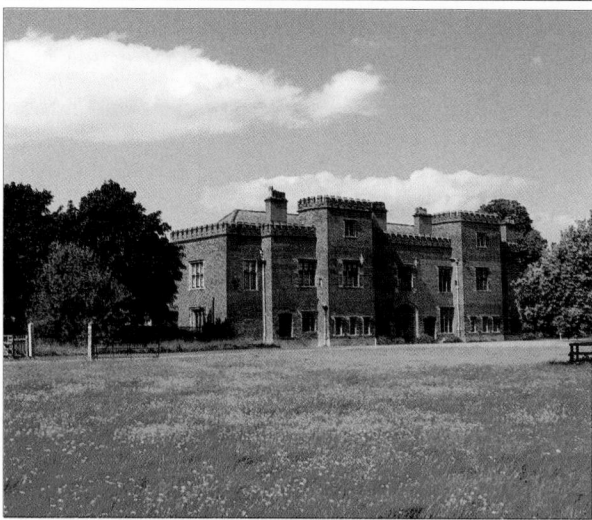

HOLME PIERREPONT HALL 🏛

HOLME PIERREPONT, Nr NOTTINGHAM NG12 2LD

Owner: Mr & Mrs Robin Brackenbury
Contact: Robert Brackenbury

Tel: 0115 933 2371

This charming late medieval manor house is set in thirty acres of Park and Gardens with regional furniture and family portraits. The recently restored Ball Room, Dining Room and Long Gallery which seats 100 people are available, on an exclusive basis, for business events and wedding receptions. Filming welcome.

Location: OS Ref. SK628 392. 5m ESE of central Nottingham. Follow signs to the National Water Sports Centre and continue for 1$^{1}/_{2}$ m.

Opening Times: Easter, Spring & Summer BHs (Suns & Mons). Jun: Thurs, Jul: Weds & Thurs. Aug: Tue - Thurs, 2 - 5.30pm. Private functions at other times by arrangement.

Admission: Adult £3.50, Child £1.50. Gardens only £1.50.

&. Partially suitable. WC. ⊤ Business & charity functions, wedding receptions.
🍽 🐕 In grounds on leads. 🔔 ❄ 🛡 🅦

MUSEUM OF COSTUME & TEXTILES
Tel: 0115 9153500

Castle Gate, Nottingham NG1 6AF

Costume displays from 1790 to the mid-20th century are beautifully presented in period rooms.

Location: OS Ref. SK570 395. Just SW of City Centre.

Opening Times: Wed - Sun & BH Mons, 10am - 4pm.

Admission: Free.

NEWARK TOWN HALL
Tel: 01636 680333 **Fax:** 01636 680350

Market Place, Newark, Nottinghamshire NG24 1DU

Owner: Newark Town Council
Contact: The Curator

A fine Georgian Grade I listed Town Hall containing a museum of the town's treasures. Disabled access – lift and WC.

Location: OS Ref. SK570 395. Close to A46 and A1.

Opening Times: Mon - Fri, 10.30am - 1pm & 2 - 4.30pm. Sats, 2 - 4.30pm (Apr - Oct). Closed BHs.

Admission: Free.

NEWSTEAD ABBEY
Tel: 01623 455900 **Fax:** 01623 455904

Newstead Abbey Park, Nottinghamshire NG15 8GE
Contact: Julie DeLong

Historic home of the poet, Lord Byron, set in grounds of over 300 acres. Mementoes of Byron and period rooms from medieval to Victorian times.

Location: OS Ref. SK540 639. 12m N of Nottingham 1m W of the A60 Mansfield Rd.

Opening Times: 1 Apr - 30 Sept: 12 noon - 5pm, last adm. 4pm. Grounds: All year except last Fri in Nov. Apr - Sept: 9am - 7.30pm. Oct - Mar: 9am - 5pm.

Admission: House & Grounds: Adult £4, Child £1.50, Conc. £2. Grounds only: Adult £2, Conc. £1.50 (2000 prices).

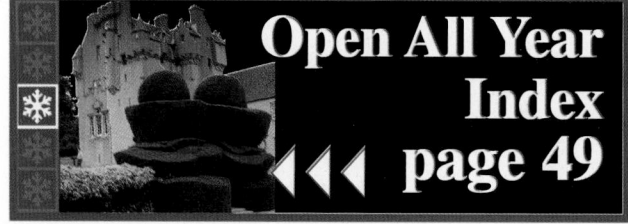

Open All Year

Index
◀◀◀ **page 49**

NORWOOD PARK

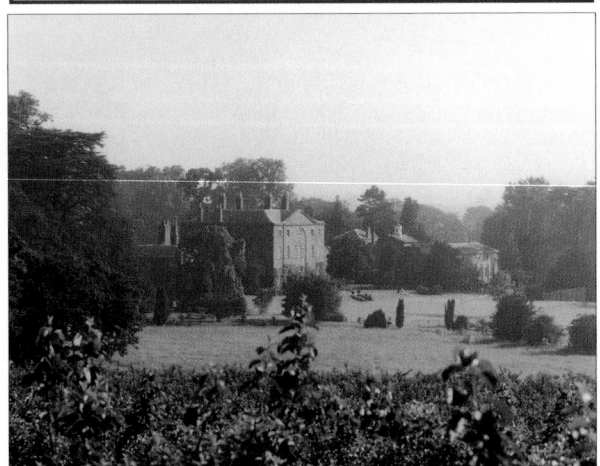

SOUTHWELL, NOTTINGHAMSHIRE NG25 0PF

Owner: Sir John & Lady Starkey   *Contact:* Sarah Dodd, Events Manager

Tel: 01636 815649 **Fax:** 01636 815702 **e-mail:** events@norwoodpark.org.uk

Delightful Georgian country house and stables set in a medieval deer park, with ancient oaks, fishponds and eyecatcher Temple, overlooking apple orchards and cricket ground. Perfect venue for all manner of business or social occasion. Combination of reception/meeting/dining rooms available in the house for smaller groups. Unique Stables Gallery complex adjacent to the house, ideal for fairytale wedding receptions, corporate dances and promotions for larger groups. Idyllic and versatile grounds for activity days, promotional work and filming. USA designed 9-hole golf course and practice area in the magnificent parkland available for event days.

Location: OS Ref. SK688 545. 3/4 m W of Southwell.

Opening Times: All year by appointment only.

Admission: Please telephone for information.

ⓘOutdoor activity days. 👕Events/weddings. ♿Partially suitable. 🖥By arrangement. 🎬By arrangement. 🅿Limited for coaches. 🐾In grounds, on leads. 🛏Honeymoon suite only. 🔔❄ⓦ

PAPPLEWICK HALL 🏛   **Tel:** 0115 963 3491 **Fax:** 0115 964 2767

Papplewick, Nottinghamshire NG15 8FE

Owner: Dr R Godwin-Austen

A beautiful stone built classical house set in a park with woodland garden laid out in the 18th century. The house is notable for its very fine plasterwork and elegant staircase. Grade I listed.

Location: OS Ref. SK548 518. Halfway between Nottingham & Mansfield, 3m E of M1/J27 on B683.

Opening Times: By appointment and 1st, 3rd & 5th Wed in each month, 2 -5pm.

Admission: Adult £5. Groups (10+): £4.

ⓘNo photography. 🎬Obligatory. 🅿Limited for coaches. 🐾In grounds on leads. ❄

RUFFORD ABBEY ⊞   **Tel:** 01623 822944

Ollerton, Nottinghamshire NG22 9DF

Owner: English Heritage   **Contact:** Nottinghamshire County Council

The remains of a 17th century country house; displaying the ruins of a 12th century Cistercian Abbey. It is set in what is now Rufford Country Park.

Location: OS Ref. SK645 646. 2m S of Ollerton off A614.

Opening Times: 1 Apr - 31 Oct: Daily, 10am - 5pm. 1 Nov - 31 Mar: daily, 10am - 4pm. (Closed 24 - 26 Dec & 1 Jan).

Admission: Free - parking charge applies.

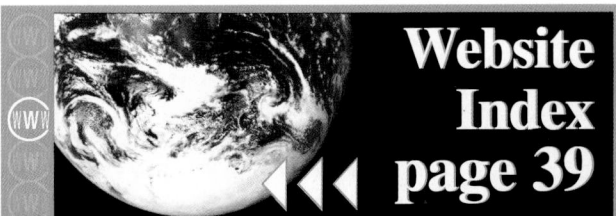

Website Index page 39

SUTTON BONINGTON HALL

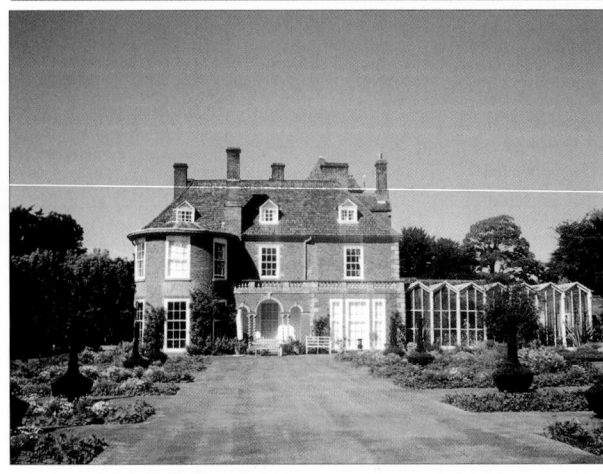

Nr LOUGHBOROUGH, NOTTINGHAM LE12 5PF

Owner: Lady Anne Elton   *Contact:* Mr & Mrs Henry Weldon

Tel: 01509 672355 **Fax:** 01509 889060 **e-mail:** henryweldon@hotmail.com

Sutton Bonington Hall, home of the Paget family since 1750, is a magnificent example of Queen Anne architecture, with an early conservatory (1810), and fine Queen Anne furniture. Sutton Bonington is not open to the general public, but offers excellent facilities for small conferences, corporate dinners and weddings. Extensive formally laid-out gardens can accommodate marquees for larger events. Seven luxurious bedrooms (all en-suite) can accommodate up to 14 guests in style.

Location: SK505 255. 1m E of A6, 5m N of Loughborough. In the heart of the Midlands, a short distance from Nottingham, Derby, Leicester, M1 and East Midlands airport.

Opening Times: By arrangement.

Admission: Corporate/private entertainment and wedding venue by arrangement only. Residential rooms by prior reservation only.

👕 ♿Partially suitable. 🅿Ample for cars. 🐾In grounds, on leads. 🛏7 doubles. 🔔❄

THRUMPTON HALL

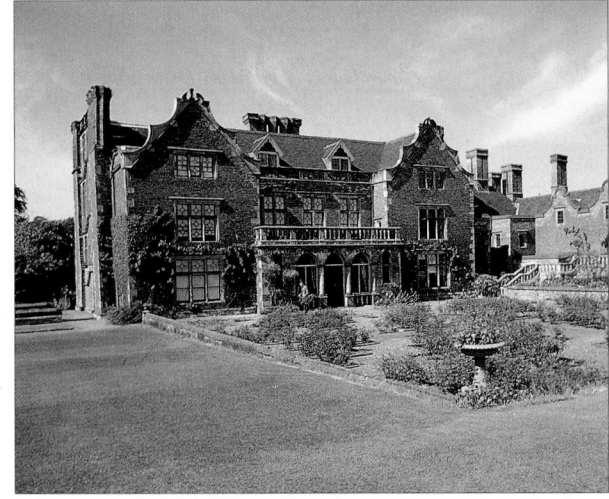

THRUMPTON, NOTTINGHAM NG11 0AX

Owner/Contact: The Hon Mrs R Seymour

Tel: 01159 830333 **Fax:** 01159 831309

Fine Jacobean house, built in 1607 incorporating an earlier manor house. Priest's hiding hole, magnificent carved Charles II staircase, carved and panelled saloon. Other fine rooms containing beautiful 17th and 18th century furniture and many fine portraits. Large lawns separated from landscaped park by ha-ha and by lake in front of the house. The house is still lived in as a home and the owner will show parties around where possible. Dining room with capacity for 52 with silver service or buffet. Free access and meal for coach drivers.

Location: OS Ref. SK508 312. 7m S of Nottingham, 3m E M1/J24, 1m from A453.

Opening Times: By appointment. Parties of 20+ 10.30am - 7.30pm.

Admission: Adult £5, Child £2.50.

📷 👕Wedding receptions. ♿Ground floor & grounds suitable. WC. 🍴 🐾In grounds on leads. ❄

UPTON HALL 🏛

Tel: 01636 813795

Upton, Newark, Nottinghamshire NG23 5TE
Owner: British Horological Institute   **Contact:** The Director
Location: OS Ref. SK735 544. A612 between Newark and Southwell.
Opening Times: Please telephone for details.
Admission: Adult £2.50, Child £1, (under 11yrs free), OAP £2.

WINKBURN HALL

Tel: 01636 636465 **Fax:** 01636 636717

Winkburn, Newark, Nottinghamshire NG22 8PQ   **e-mail:** any@alderton.co.uk
Owner/Contact: Richard Craven-Smith-Milnes Esq
A fine William and Mary house.
Location: OS Ref. SK711 584. 8m W of Newark 1m N of A617.
Opening Times: Throughout the year by appointment only.
Admission: £4.50.

WOLLATON HALL NATURAL HISTORY MUSEUM

Tel: 0115 915 3900

Wollaton Park, Nottingham NG8 2AE
Owner: Nottingham City Council   **Contact:** Phil Hackett
Tudor building set in 500 acres of parkland and home to the Natural History Museum.
Location: OS Ref. SK532 392. Wollaton Park, Nottingham. 3m W of city centre.
Opening Times: Summer: 11am - 5pm. Winter: 11am - 4pm. Closed Fridays from Nov - Mar.
Admission: Weekdays Free. Weekends & BHs Adult: £1.50, Child 80p. Joint ticket for Wollaton Hall & Industrial Museum. Grounds £1/car (free for orange badge holders). (2000 times and prices.)

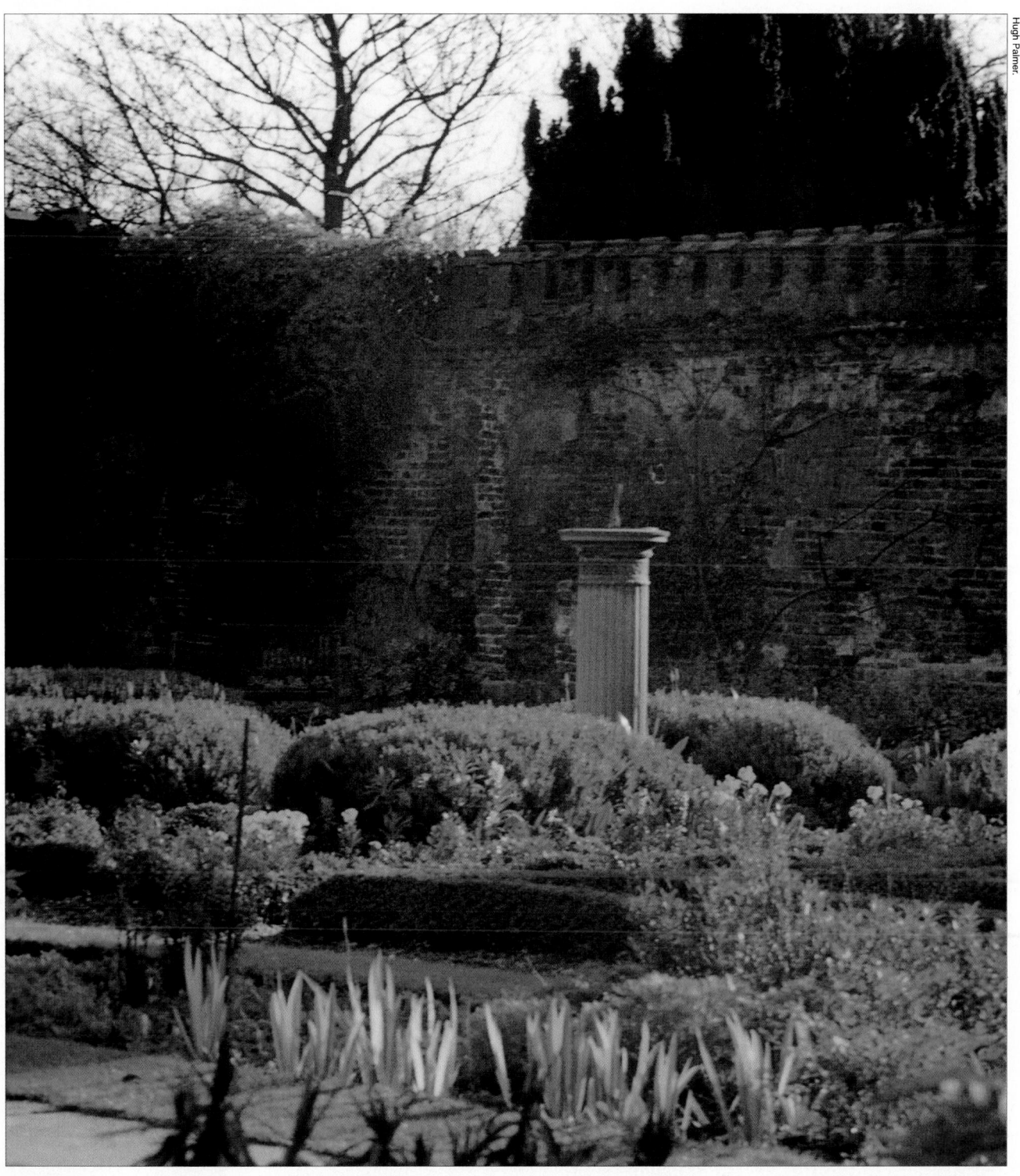

Hugh Palmer.

Holme Pierrepont Hall, Nottinghamshire.

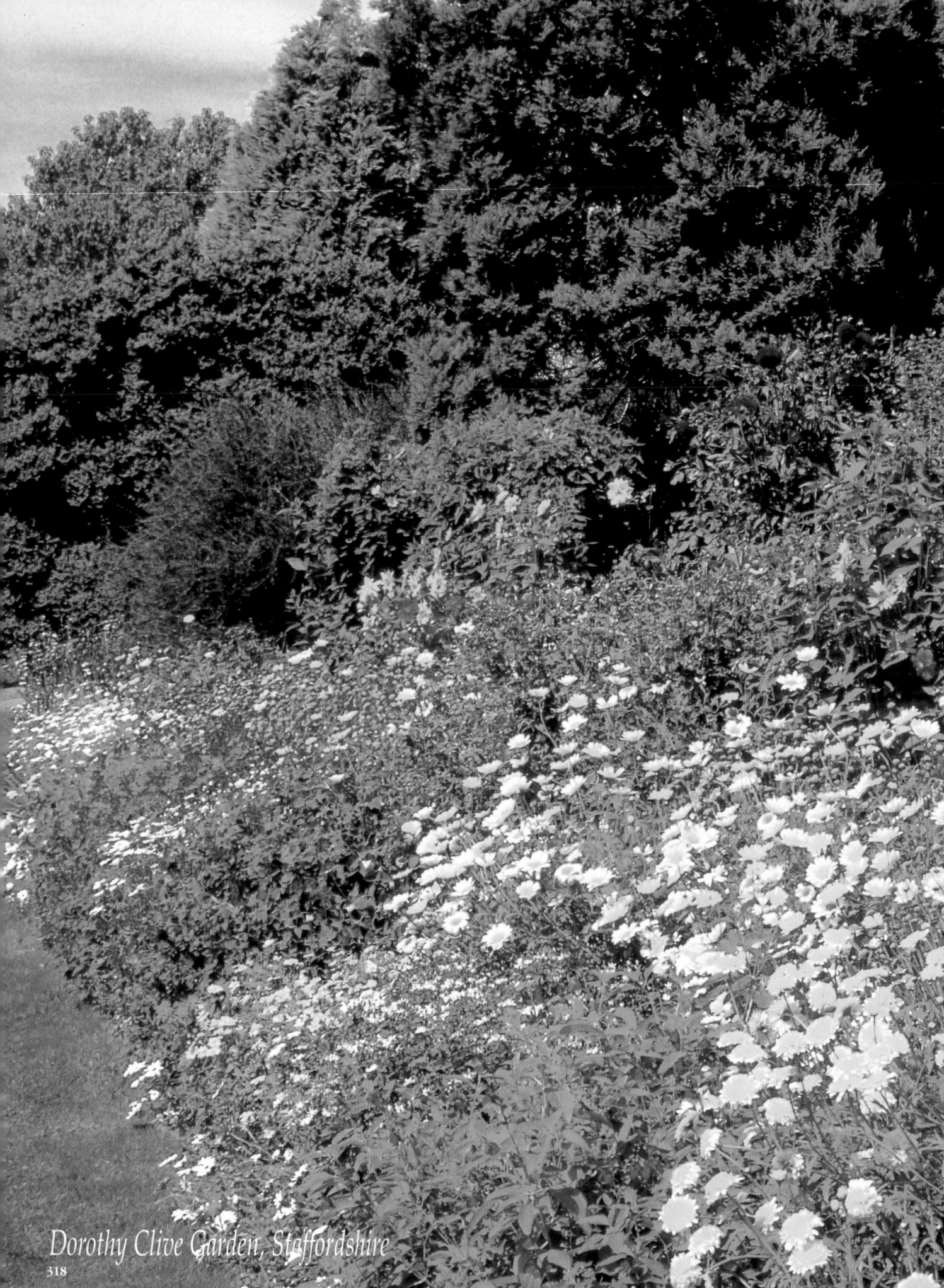

Dorothy Clive Garden, Staffordshire

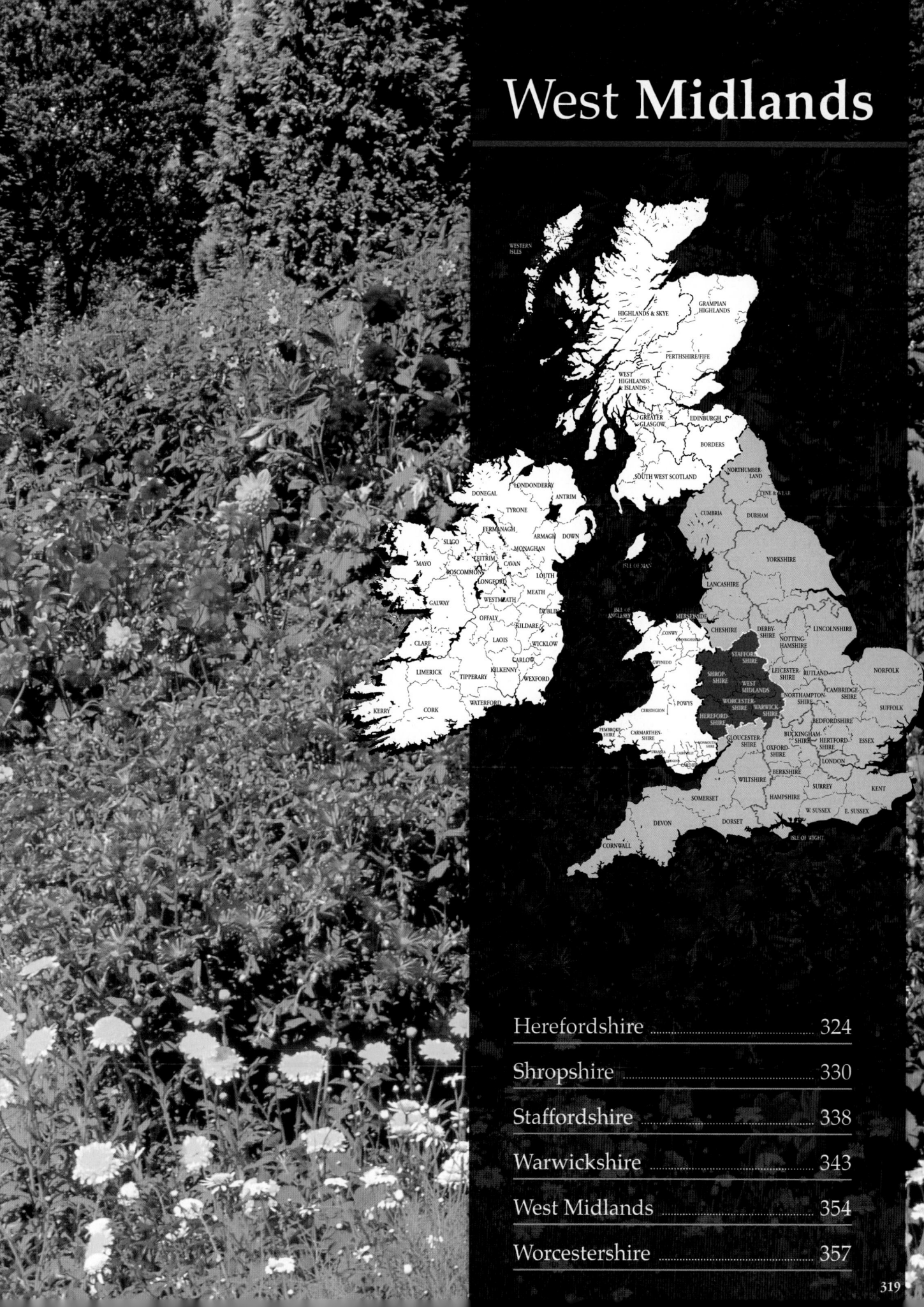

West Midlands

319

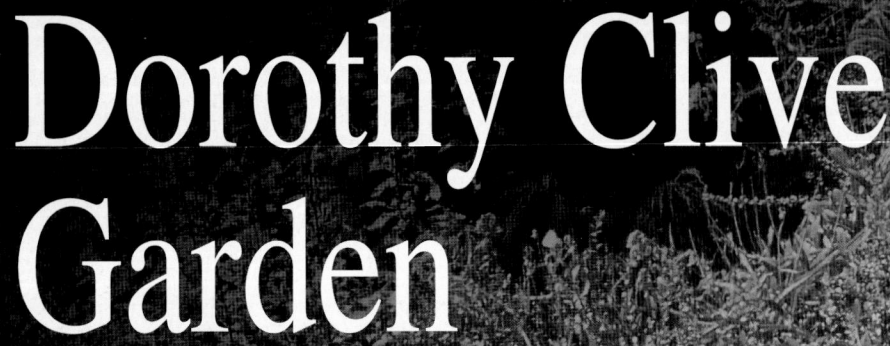

Dorothy Clive Garden

"A woodland garden, tranquil, silent; ever verdant, and in its seasonal splendour, elevating even the most grounded of human spirits."

The Dorothy Clive Garden at Willoughbridge near Market Drayton, is today owned by the Willoughbridge Garden Trust.

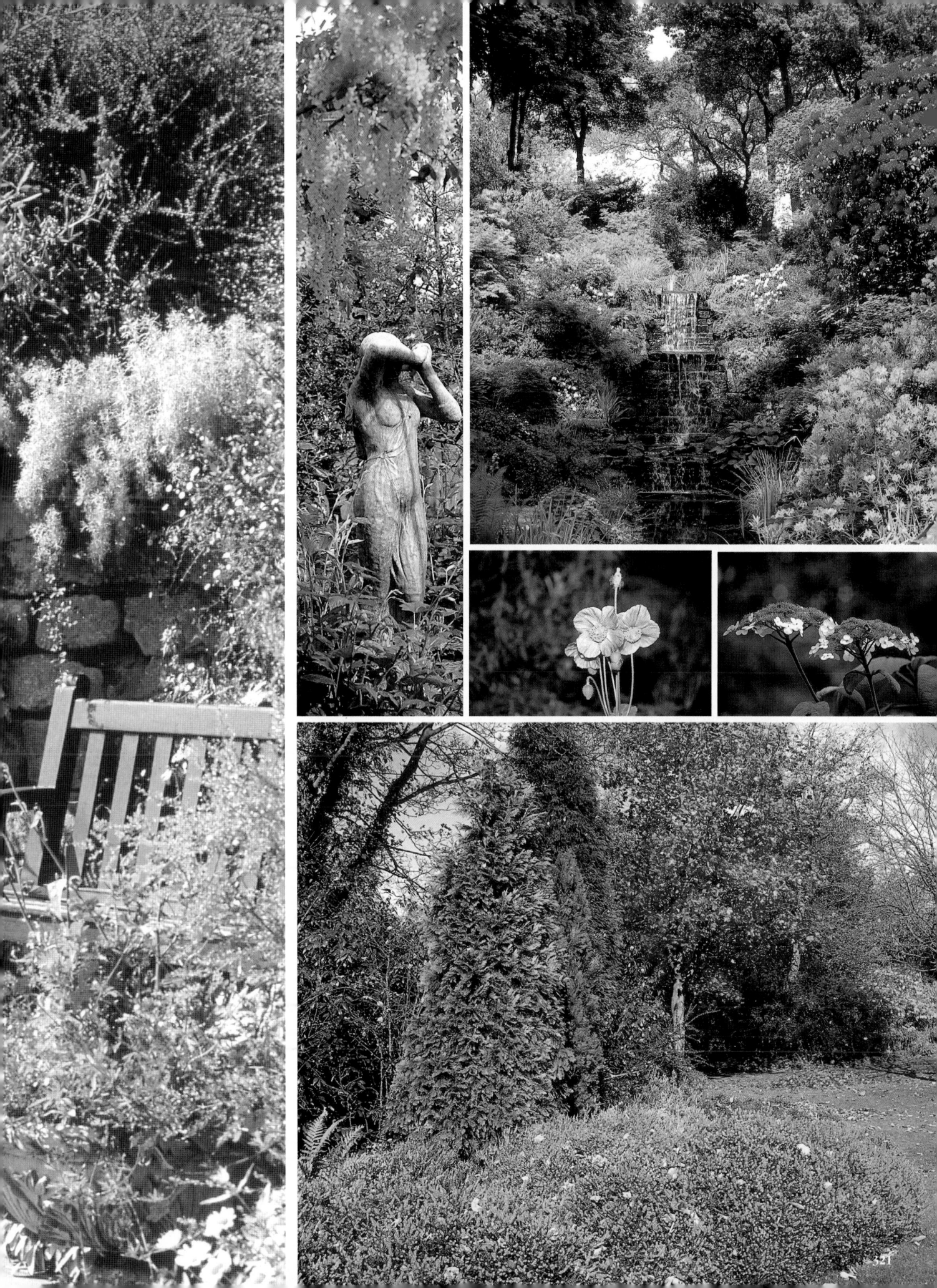

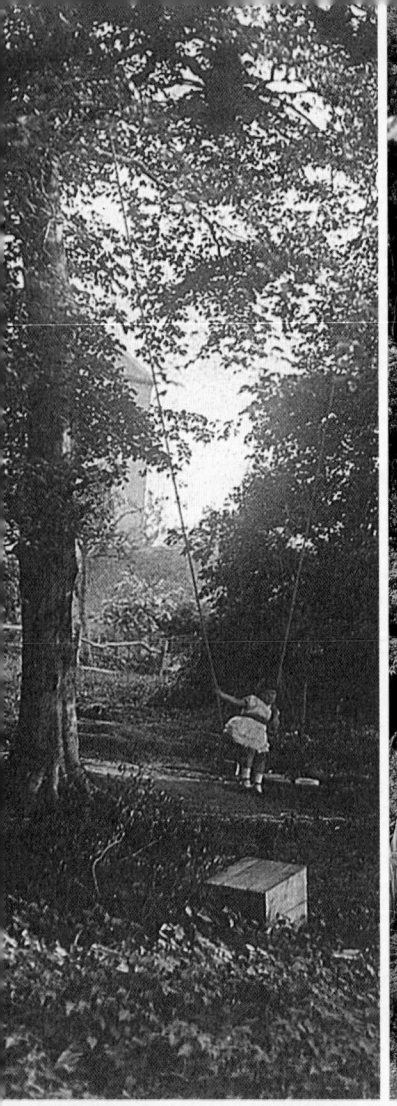

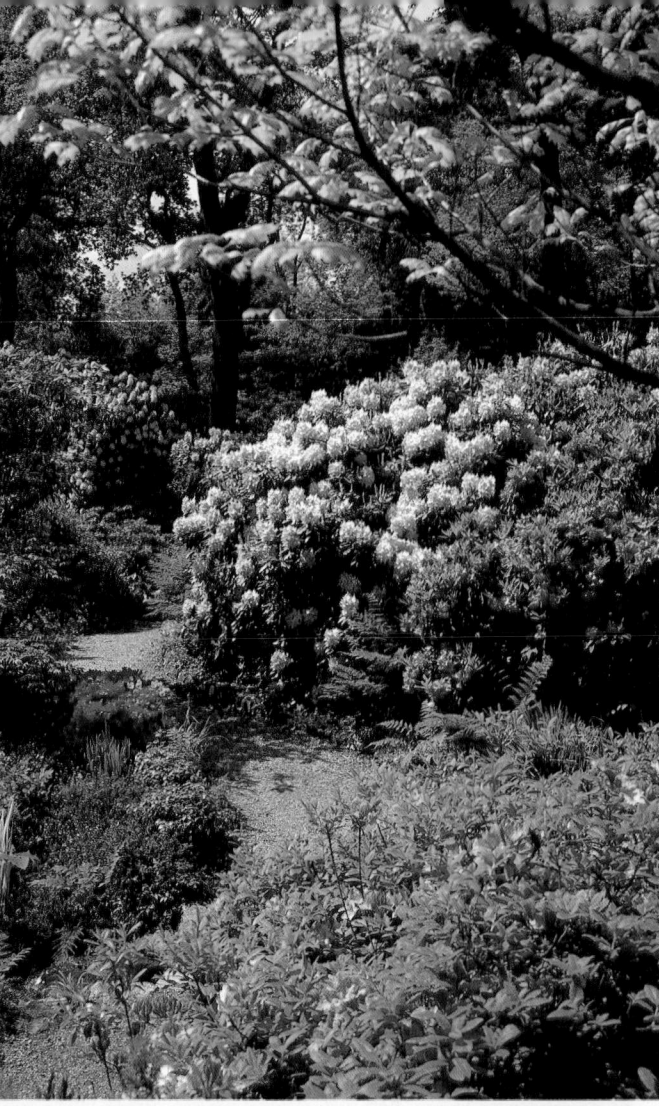

Set on the side of a hill, with some steep winding paths to tackle, this well stocked plantsman's garden is divided into two distinct parts. Above the house is the wonderfully naturally planted hillside garden, below it is more open and highly cultivated.

The garden was created by Col Harry Clive for his wife Dorothy in 1939. Col and Mrs Clive lived at Elds Gorse, the large house on the west side of the garden, visible from the road, and from the garden in winter when the trees have lost their leaves. During the last years of her life Dorothy, due to ill health, was restricted to monotonous daily circuits around the lawn. Col Clive therefore decided to transform a wooded and defunct quarry nearby into what is now a superb woodland garden.

Bowl-shaped, the woodland garden is filled with a mass of hybrid and unusual rhododendrons, and deciduous and evergreen azaleas. Sheltered from the wind, it is the ideal site for rhododendrons to grow. Weaving along paths in late spring, the top of this steep-sided dell is a riot of colour. Blood red *Rhododendron thomsonii*, pale yellow *R campyloarpum elatum* and groups of pink, orange and red Exbury and Knaphill azaleas flower magnificently.

The peak months for viewing this garden are May, June and the autumn. Native and specimen trees which have been planted in the hillside garden provide wonderful strong autumn colour. The clever tree planting also shelters the more tender and unusual shrubs – these in turn are underplanted with spring bulbs such as the cyclamen flowered daffodil and the *Narcissus cyclamineus* which has naturalised.

Following his wife's death in 1942 Col Clive built a bungalow below the dell and turned his energies to cultivating the field which sloped away below. He did not live to see this part of the garden completed, but the Willoughbridge Garden Trust was formed and the garden's future was secured.

This beautiful and thoughtfully planted garden is a wonderful lesson in how to lay out a rewarding but 'labour saving' garden and it is a delight to visit.

For further details about *Dorothy Clive Garden* see entry in West Midlands Region ➔ Staffordshire.

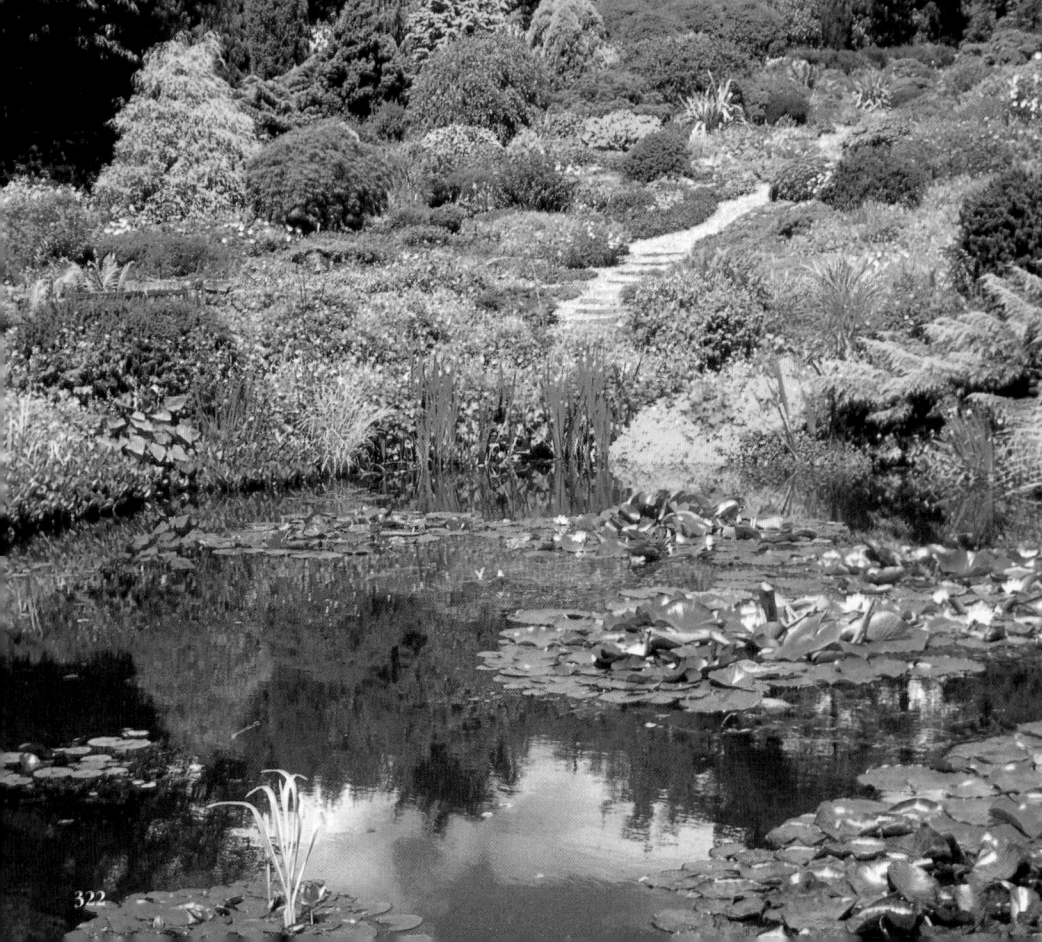

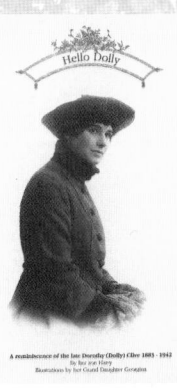

Hello Dolly

A reminiscence of the late Dorothy (Dolly) Clive 1883 - 1942
by her son Harry
Illustrations by her Grand Daughter Georgina

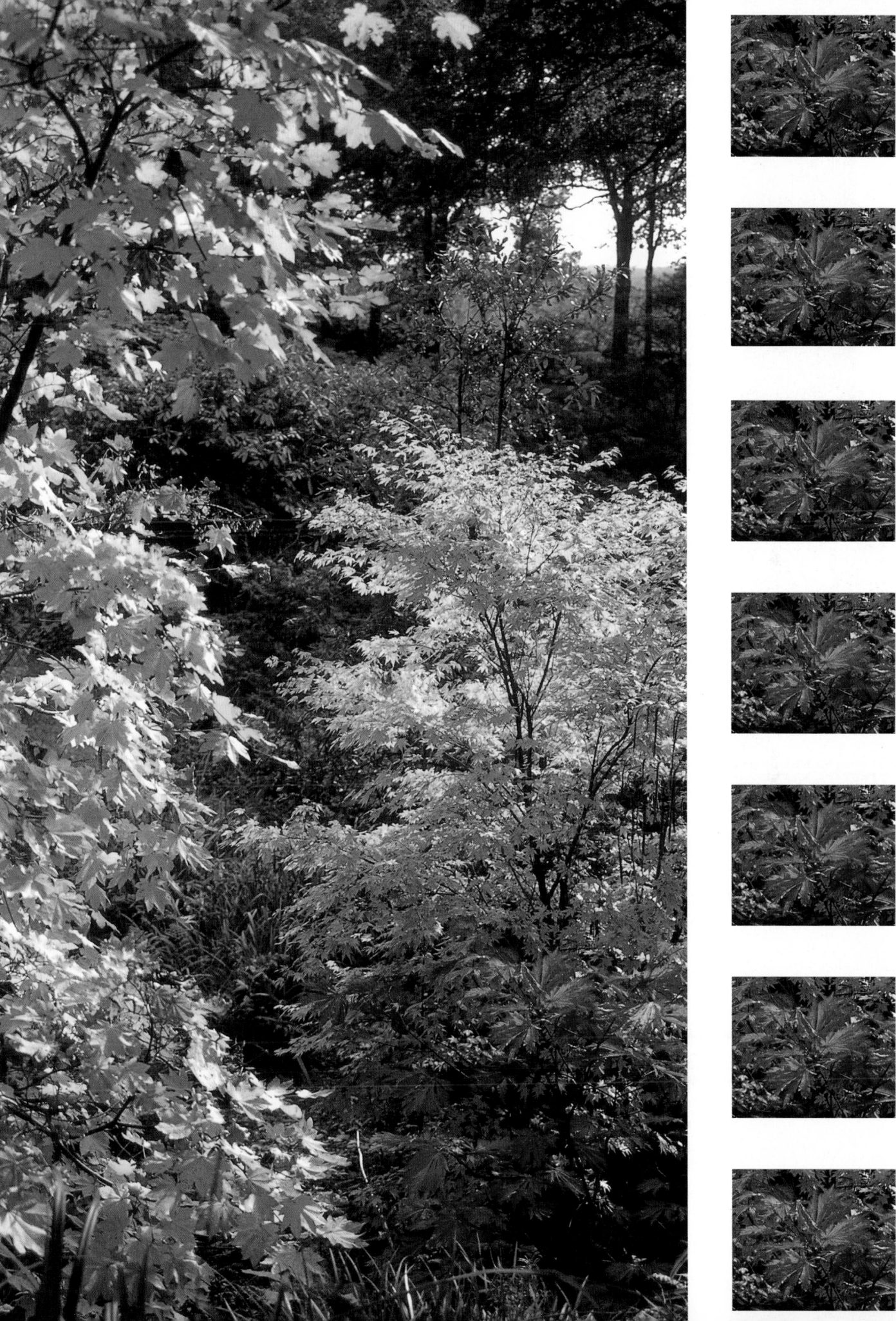

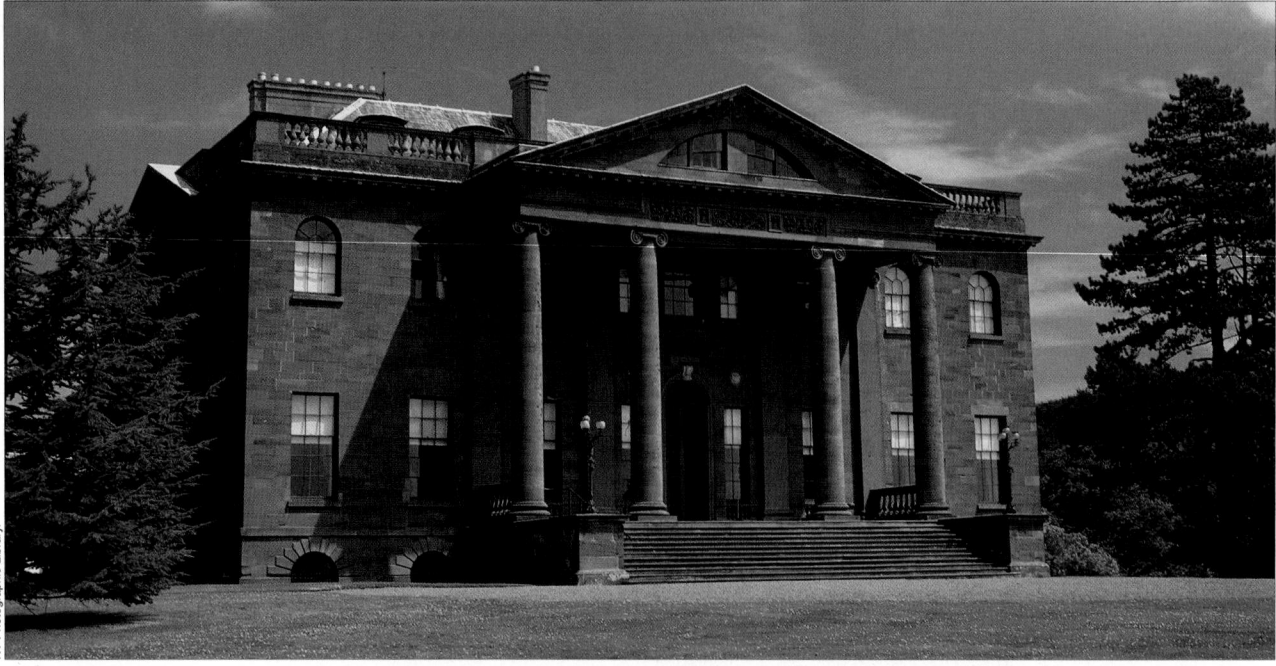

NT Photographic Library.

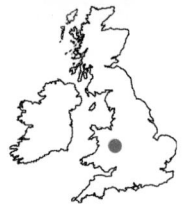

Owner: The National Trust

CONTACT

The Property Manager
Berrington Hall
Nr Leominster
Herefordshire
HR6 0DW

Tel: 01568 615721

Fax: 01568 613263

Information Line:
01684 855367

Restaurant:
01568 610134

e-mail: berrington
@smtp.ntrust.org.uk

LOCATION

OS137 SP510 637

3m N of Leominster, 7m S
of Ludlow on
W side of A49.

Rail: Leominster 4m.

BERRINGTON HALL
Nr Leominster

BERRINGTON HALL is the creation of Thomas Harley, the 3rd Earl of Oxford's remarkable son, who made a fortune from supplying pay and clothing to the British Army in America and became Lord Mayor of London in 1767 at the age of thirty-seven. The architect was the fashionable Henry Holland. The house is beautifully set above the wide valley of a tributary of the River Lugg, with views west and south to the Black Mountains and Brecon Beacons. This was the site advised by 'Capability' Brown who created the lake with its artificial island. The rather plain neo-classical exterior with a central portico gives no clue to the lavishness of the interior. Plaster ceilings now decorated in muted pastel colours adorn the principal rooms. Holland's masterpiece is the staircase hall rising to a central dome. The rooms are set off with a collection of French furniture, including pieces which belonged to the Comte de Flahault, natural son of Talleyrand, and Napoleon's step-daughter Hortense.

In the dining room, vast panoramic paintings of battles at sea, three of them by Thomas Luny, are a tribute to the distinguished Admiral Rodney.

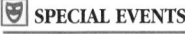

NT Photographic Library.

OPENING TIMES

House

1 Apr - 31 Oct:
Daily except Thurs & Fris.
(open Good Fri)
1 - 5pm.
(4.30pm in Oct).

Garden

1 Apr - 31 Oct:
Daily except Thurs & Fris.
(open Good Fri)
12 noon - 5pm.
(4.30pm in Oct).

Park Walk

1 Jul - 31 Oct:
Daily except Thurs & Fris.
12 noon - 5pm
(4.30pm in Oct).

ADMISSION

Adult £4.30
Child (5-12yrs) £2.15
Family (2+3) £10.75

Groups (15-25)*
Reduced rate available.

Garden Ticket......... £2.15

Groups must pre-book. Two
groups can visit at a time.

SPECIAL EVENTS

Please telephone for details of
special events.

No photography in the house. Groups by arrangement only.

Single seater batricar, stairclimber; pre-booking essential. Audio tours for the visually impaired

Licensed restaurant: open as house: 12.30 - 5.30pm (4.30pm in Oct).

By arrangement only. Tour time: 1 hr.

Ample for cars. Parking for coaches limited; instructions given when booking is made.

Children's quizzes. Play area in walled garden.

Guide dogs only.

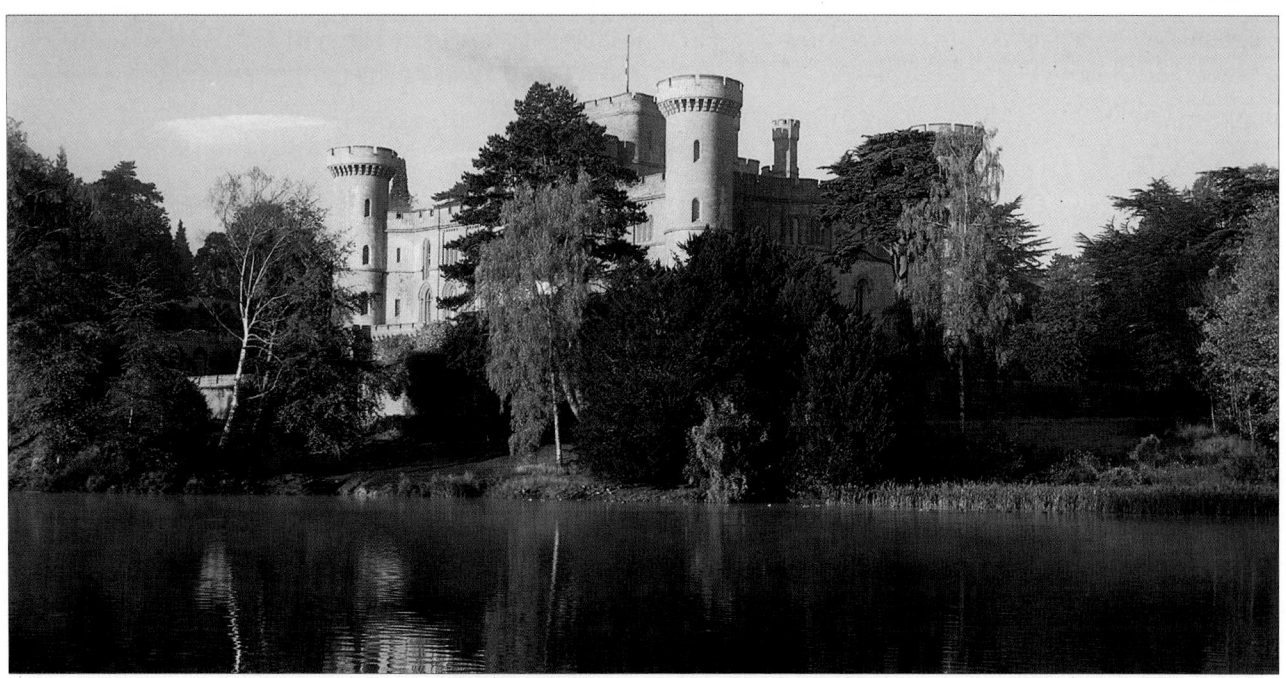

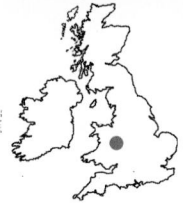

Owner:
Mr J & The Hon
Mrs Hervey-Bathurst

CONTACT

Simon Foster
Portcullis Office
Eastnor Castle
Nr Ledbury
Herefordshire HR8 1RL

Tel: 01531 633160

Fax: 01531 631776

e-mail: enquiries@
eastnorcastle.com

LOCATION

OS Ref. SO735 368

2m SE of Ledbury on the
A438 Tewkesbury road.
Alternatively M50/J2 &
from Ledbury take the
A449/A438.

Tewkesbury 20 mins, Malvern
20 mins, Gloucester 25 mins
Hereford 25 mins, Worcester
30mins, Cheltenham 30 mins
B'ham 1 hr, London 2¼ hrs.

Taxi: Meredith Taxis
01531 632852
Clive Fletcher 0589 299283

CONFERENCE/FUNCTION

ROOM	SIZE	MAX CAPACITY
Library	18 x 8m	120
Great Hall	16 x 8m	150
Dining Rm	11 x 7m	80
Gothic Rm	11 x 7m	80
Octagon Rm	9 x 9m	50

EASTNOR CASTLE
Ledbury

Encircled by the Malvern Hills and surrounded by a famous arboretum and lake, this fairytale castle looks as dramatic inside as it does outside.

The atmosphere Everyone is struck by it. The vitality of a young family brings the past to life and the sense of warmth and optimism is tangible. Eastnor, however grand, is a home.

'Sleeping' for the past fifty years, the Castle has undergone a triumphant renaissance – 'looking better than it probably ever has', *Country Life* 1993.

Hidden away in attics and cellars since 1939, many of the castle's treasures are now displayed for the first time – early Italian Fine Art, 17th century Venetian furniture and Flemish tapestries, mediaeval armour and paintings by Van Dyck, Romney, Wootton and Watts, photographs by Julia Margaret Cameron. Drawing Room by Pugin.

'The princely and imposing pile' as it was described in 1812 when it was being built to pitch the owner into the aristocracy, remains the home of his descendants. The castle contains letters diaries, clothes and furnishings belonging to friends and relations who include: Horace Walpole, Elizabeth Barrett Browning, Tennyson, Watts, Julia Margaret Cameron and Virginia Woolf.

Encircled by the Malvern Hills, the medieval beauty of the estate remains unchanged.

GARDENS
Castellated terraces descend to a 21 acre lake with a restored lakeside walk. The arboretum holds a famous collection of mature specimen trees. There are spectacular views of the Malvern hills across a 300 acre deer park, once part of a mediaeval chase and now designated a Site of Special Scientific Interest.

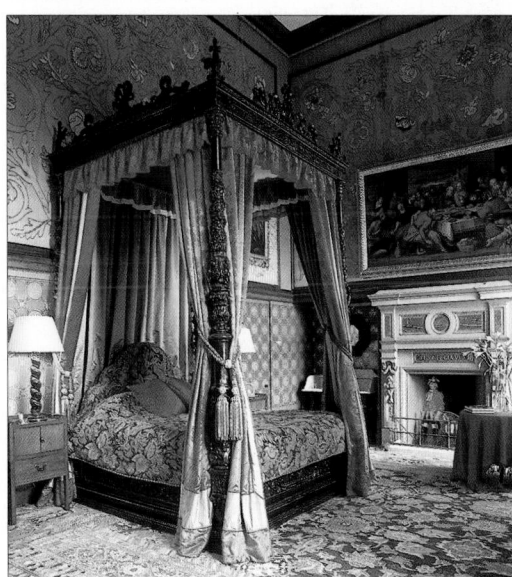

Plant Centre.

Maze, off-road driving, clay-pigeon shooting, quad bikes, archery and falconry. Survival training, team building activity days. Product launches, fashion shows, concerts, charity events, craft fairs, television and feature films. No photography in castle.

Wedding receptions. Catering for booked events.

Partially suitable. Visitors may alight at the castle. Priority parking.

Home-made food, menus on request, groups must book.

By arrangement.

Ample 10 - 200 yds from castle. Coaches phone in advance to arrange parking & catering. Free meal for drivers.

Welcome. Guides available if required. Children's fun worksheets.

On leads in Castle and grounds.

Luxury accommodation within castle for small groups. 1 single room and 10 double. Ensuite available.

OPENING TIMES

SUMMER
15 April - 7 October:
Suns & BH Mons.
July - August: Sun - Fri
11am - 5pm.

NB. Groups by appointment at other times when the castle is closed to casual visitors.

ADMISSION

SUMMER
Castle & Grounds
Adult £5.00
Child (5-15yrs)..........£3.00
OAP.......................£4.75
Family (2+2) £13.00
Groups* (with guide)
Adult £7.50
Groups* (without guide)
Adult £4.50
* Min. payment for 20 people.

Grounds only
Adult £3.00
Child (5-15yrs)..........£2.00
OAP.......................£2.75

Season Ticket
Adult £15.00
Child (5-15yrs)..........£9.00
OAP.......................£14.25
Family £39.00
Please telephone for admission prices for special events.

WINTER
By appointment.

SPECIAL EVENTS

- **MAY 6/7**
  Spring Country Crafts Fair.
- **MAY 28**
  Steam Fair & Country Show with Fred Dibnah.
- **JUL 1**
  Wood Festival.
- **JUL 14/15**
  Medieval Jousting and Hot Air Balloon Festival.
- **AUG 26/27**
  Children's Fun Week
- **OCT 6/7**
  Festival of Fine Food and Drink.

ABBEYDORE COURT GARDENS

Tel/Fax: 01981 240419

Abbey Dore, Hereford HR2 0AD

Owner/Contact: Mrs C L Ward

6 acre rambling garden, intersected by the River Dore. Shrubs and herbaceous perennials, rock garden and ponds.

Location: OS Ref. SO387 309. 3 m W of A465 midway Hereford - Abergavenny.

Opening Times: Apr - Sept: daily except Weds & Fris, 11am - 6pm.

Admission: Adult £2.50, Child 50p.

BERRINGTON HALL

See page 324 for full page entry.

CONINGSBY HOSPITAL, MUSEUM & GARDENS

Tel: 01432 267821

Widemarsh Street, Hereford HR4 9HN

Contact: Mr D G Harding

Built in 1614 on the site of a Knights-Hospitallers Place.

Location: OS Ref. SO512 404. East side of Widemarsh Street. 500 yards N of City Centre.

Opening Times: Tue - Thur, weekends & BHs, 2 - 5pm.

Admission: Adult £2, Child/Conc. £1. Groups rates for educational visits.

BROCKHAMPTON ESTATE & LOWER BROCKHAMPTON

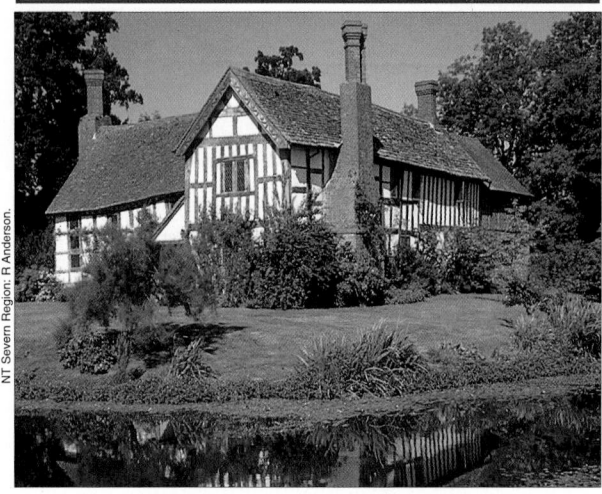

BRINGSTY, WORCESTERSHIRE WR6 5UH

Owner: The National Trust   *Contact:* The Administrator

Tel: 01885 488099

A late 14th century moated manor house, with an attractive detached half-timbered 15th century gatehouse, a rare example of this type of structure. Also, the ruins of a 12th century chapel. Woodland walks including sculpture trail. Easy access for all, long and short waymarked walks.

Location: OS149, Ref. SO682 546. 2m E of Bromyard N side of A44, reached by narrow road through 1¹/₂ m of woods and farmland.

Opening Times: Medieval Hall, parlour, minstrel gallery, information room, gatehouse and chapel: 1 Apr - end Oct: Wed - Sun & BH Mons, 12.30 - 5pm. Weekends Jul & Aug: 10.30am - 5pm. Last admission ¹/₂ hr before closing. Estate: All year: daily during daylight hours.

Admission: Adult £2.70, Child £1.35, Family £6.75. Car park £1.50.

 Partially suitable.

CROFT CASTLE

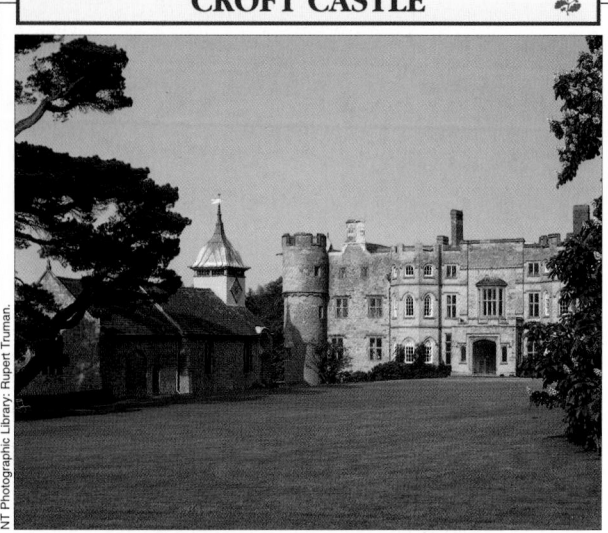

LEOMINSTER, HEREFORDSHIRE HR6 9PW

Owner: The National Trust   *Contact:* The House Manager

Tel: 01568 780246 **e-mail:** croft@smtp.ntrust.org.uk

Home of the Croft family since Domesday (with a break of 170 years from 1750). Walls and corner towers date from 14th and 15th centuries, interior mainly 18th century when fine Georgian-Gothic staircase and plasterwork ceilings were added; splendid avenue of 350 year old Spanish chestnuts. Iron Age Fort (Croft Ambrey) may be reached by footpath. The walk is uphill (approx. 40 mins).

Location: OS137 Ref. SO455 655. 5m NW of Leominster, 9m SW of Ludlow, approach from B4362.

Opening times: Castle: 31 Mar - 29 Apr: Sats & Suns, Good Fri & BH Mons; 2 May - 30 Sept: daily except Mons & Tues (open BH Mons); 6 Oct - 4 Nov: Sats & Suns. 1 - 5pm (closes 4.30pm in Oct & Nov). Park & Croft Ambrey: daily.

Admission: Adult £3.90, Child £1.95. Family £10. Grounds only: Car park £2 per car, £10 per coach.

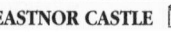

EASTNOR CASTLE

See page 325 for full page entry.

GOODRICH CASTLE

Tel: 01600 890538

Ross-on-Wye, Herefordshire HR9 6HY

Owner: English Heritage   **Contact:** The Custodian

This magnificent red sandstone castle is remarkably complete with a 12th century keep and extensive remains from 13th & 14th centuries. From the battlements there are fine views over the Wye Valley to Symonds Yat. Marvel at the maze of small rooms and the 'murder holes'.

Location: OS162, Ref. SO579 199. 5m S of Ross-on-Wye, off A40.

Opening Times: 1 Apr - 31 Oct: daily, 10am - 6pm (5pm in Oct). 1 Nov - 31 Mar: daily, 10am - 4pm. Closed 1 - 2pm in winter. Closed 24 - 26 Dec & 1 Jan.

Admission: Adult £3.60, Child £1.80, Conc. £2.70. Family ticket £9. 15% discount for groups (11+).

Tel. for details.

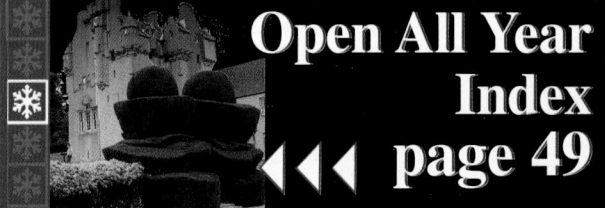

Open All Year
Index
page 49

HAMPTON COURT

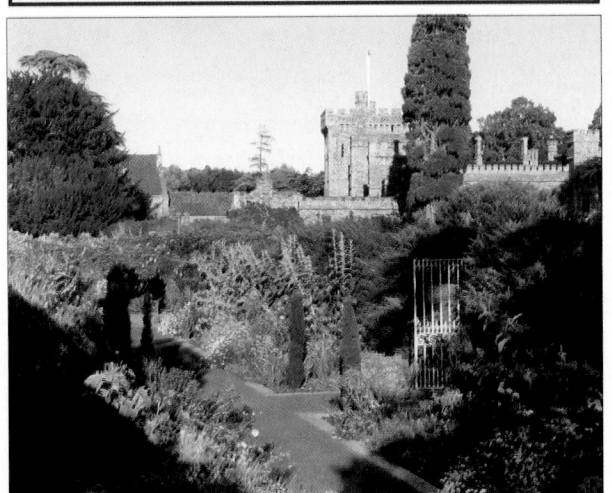

HOPE UNDER DINMORE, LEOMINSTER, HEREFORDSHIRE HR6 0PN

Owner: *Charity*   **Contact:** *Ed Waghorn*

Tel: 01568 7977777   **Fax:** 01568 797472

e-mail: vankampengardens@hamptoncourt.org.uk

The Van Kampen Gardens at Hampton Court, Herefordshire are extensive new gardens in the historic grounds of a medieval fortified manor house. There is a walled organic garden, flower gardens, canals, pavilions, a maze and a secret tunnel, a hermit's grotto, waterfalls and a flooded sunken garden. There are beautiful parkland views and river walks. An organic teashop serves light lunches, tea and cake from a conservatory designed by Joseph Paxton.

Location: OS Ref. SO520 525. On the A417 near to the junction with the A49.

Opening times: 13 Apr - 28 Oct: Wed - Sun & BH Mons, 11am - 5pm. Groups by prior arrangement.

Admission: Adults £4, Child (6-13yrs) £2, OAP £3.50.

⬜ 🚻 💷 ♿ 🎫By arrangement. **P** 🦮Guide dogs only.
🛡️Tel. for details. Ⓦ

HEREFORD CATHEDRAL

Hereford HR1 2NG

Tel: 01432 374202   **Fax:** 01432 374220

e-mail: visits@herefordcathedral.co.uk

Contact: Mr D Harding - The Visits Manager

Location: OS Ref. SO510 398. Hereford city centre on A49.

Opening Times: 7.30am - 5pm. Sun services: 8am, 10am, 11.30am & 3.30pm. Weekday services: 8am and 5.30pm.

Admission: Admission only for Mappa Mundi and Chained Library Exhibition: Adult £4, OAP/Student/Unemployed £3.50, Child under 5yrs Free. Family ticket (2+3) £10.00.

HERGEST COURT

Tel/Fax: 01544 230160

c/o Hergest Estate Office, Kington HR5 3EG

Owner/Contact: W L Banks

The ancient home of the Vaughans of Hergest, dating from the 13th century.

Location: OS Ref. SO283 554. 1m W of Kington on unclassified road to Brilley.

Opening Times: Strictly by appointment only through Estate Office.

Admission: Adult £4, Child £1.50. Groups: Adult £3.50, Child £1.

♿ Not suitable.   **P** Limited.   🦮 Guide dogs only.   ❄

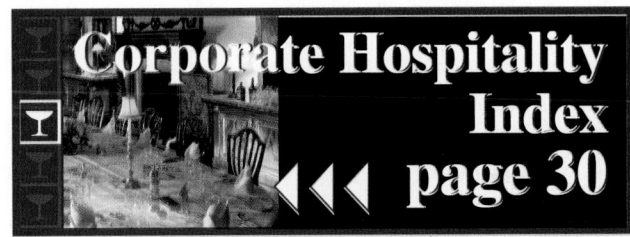

Corporate Hospitality Index ◀◀◀ page 30

HELLENS

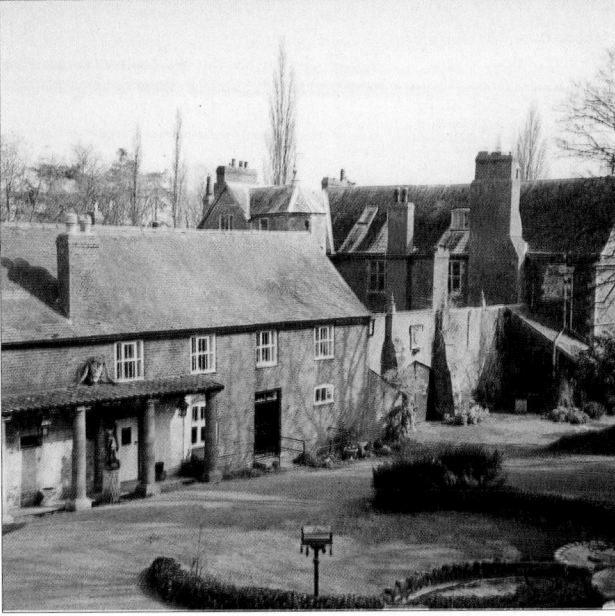

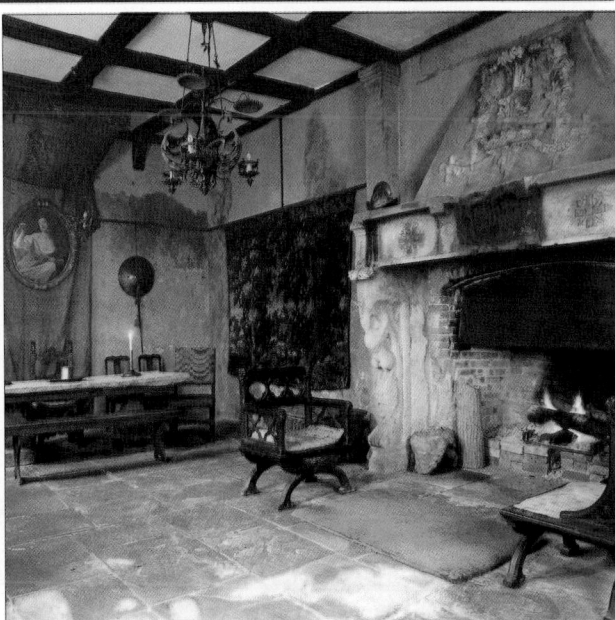

MUCH MARCLE, LEDBURY, HEREFORDSHIRE HR8 2LY

Owner: *Pennington-Mellor-Munthe Charity Trust*   **Contact:** *The Administrator*

Tel: 01531 660504

Built as a monastery and then a stone fortress in 1292 by Morhimes, Earl of March, with Tudor, Jacobean and Stuart additions and lived in ever since by descendants of the original builder. Visited by the Black Prince, Bloody Mary and the 'family ghost'. Family paintings, relics and heirlooms from the Civil War and possessions of the Audleys, Walwyns and Whartons as well as Anne Boleyn. Also beautiful 17th century woodwork carved by the 'King's Carpenter', John Abel. All those historical stories incorporated into guided tours, revealing the loves and lives of those who lived and died here. Goods and chattels virtually unchanged.

Location: OS149 Ref. SO661 332. Off A449 at Much Marcle. Ledbury 4m, Ross-on-Wye 4m.

Opening Times: Good Fri - 2 Oct: Weds, Sats, Suns & BH Mons. Guided tours only at 2pm, 3pm & 4pm. Other times only by arrangement with the Administrator.

Admission: Adult £3.50, Child £1.50.

ℹ️No photography inside house. 💷 ♿Partially suitable. 🎫Obligatory.
🚻 **P** 🦮In grounds, on leads. 🛡️ Tel. for details.

West Midlands England

HERGEST CROFT GARDENS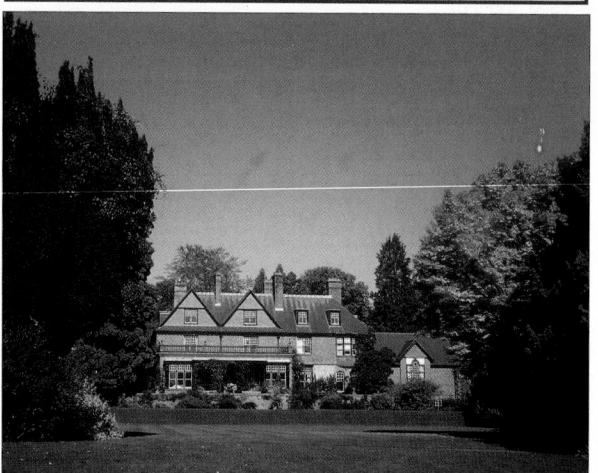

KINGTON, HEREFORDSHIRE HR5 3EG
Owner: *W L Banks*   **Contact:** *Gill Wilson*

Tel/Fax: 01544 230160   **e-mail:** banks@hergest.kc3.co.uk
From spring bulbs to autumn colour, this is a garden for all seasons. An old-fashioned kitchen garden has spring and summer borders and roses. Over 59 Champion trees and shrubs grow in one of the finest collections in the British Isles. Holds National Collection of birches, maples and zelkovas. Park Wood is a hidden valley with rhododendrons up to 30 ft tall.
Location: OS Ref. SO281 565. On W side of Kington. 1/2 m off A44, left at Rhayader end of bypass. Turn right and gardens are 1/4 m on left. Signposted from bypass.
Opening Times: 1 Apr - 31 Oct: 1.30 - 6pm. Season tickets and groups by arrangement throughout the year. Winter by appointment.
Admission: Adult £4, Child (under 16yrs) Free. Groups (20+) £3.50. Guided groups (20+) £5.50 (must book). Season ticket £15.

ⓘ Gift sales. ✿ Rare plants. ☕ ⋔ In grounds, on leads. ❅ 🅦 📞 Tel. for details.

KINNERSLEY CASTLE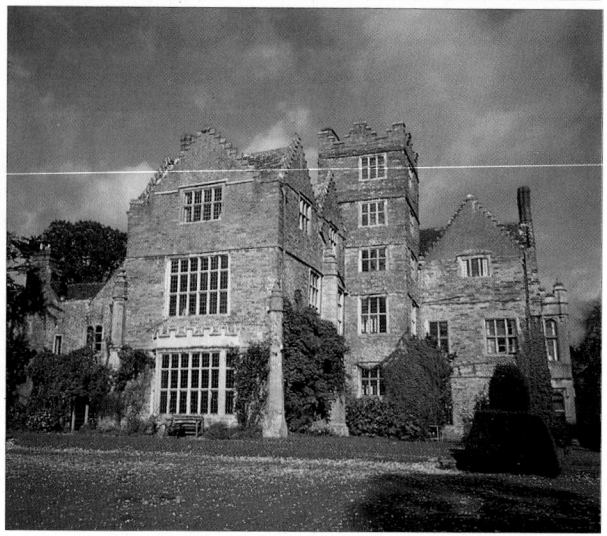

KINNERSLEY, HEREFORDSHIRE HR3 6QF
Contact: *Caius Hawkins / Ekatherina Henning*

Tel: 01544 327507   **Fax:** 01544 327663   **e-mail:** castle@kinnersley.com
Welsh border castle remodelled by Roger Vaughan in the 1580s. Still a family home, it has housed among others the de Kinnardsleys, the de la Beres and parliamentary general Sir Thomas Morgan. Shows some fine plasterwork and panelling. Gardens boast one of the largest ginkgo trees in the UK. Many yew hedges and a walled kitchen garden. Will be hosting open air theatrical events this summer.
Location: OS Ref. SO346 496. 4m W of Weobley on A4112, 15m W of Hereford.
Opening Times: Please contact the property or the local TIC.
Admission: Castle & Gardens: Adult £2.50, Child £1.50, Conc. £2. Groups: £2. Groups by arrangement throughout the year.

☕ Teas by arrangement. 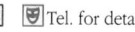 Tel. for details. 🅦

HOW CAPLE COURT GARDENS
Tel: 01989 740626 **Fax:** 01989 740611
How Caple, Hereford HR1 4SX
Owner/Contact: Mr & Mrs Roger Lee
Exciting 11 acre garden overlooking River Wye.
Location: OS Ref. SO613 306. In NE end of How Caple. 1m W of the B4224 Ross-on-Wye/Fownhope Road.
Opening Times: Easter - end Sept: daily 10am - 5pm.
Admission: Adult £2.50.

LONGTOWN CASTLE
Tel: 0121 625 6820 (Regional Office)
Abbey Dore, Herefordshire
Owner: English Heritage   **Contact:** The West Midlands Regional Office
An unusual cylindrical keep built c1200 with walls 15ft thick. There are magnificent views of the nearby Black Mountains.
Location: OS Ref. SO321 291. 4m WSW of Abbey Dore.
Opening Times: Any reasonable time.
Admission: Free.

MOCCAS COURT
Tel: 01981 500381
Moccas, Herefordshire HR2 9LH
Owner: Trustees of the Baunton Trust   **Contact:** Ivor Saunders
18th century Adam interiors, 'Capability' Brown park.
Location: OS149 Ref. SO359 434. 1m N of B4352, 3 1/2 m SE of Bredwardine.
Opening Times: Apr - Sept: Thurs, 2 - 6pm.
Admission: £2.

OLD SUFTON
Tel: 01432 870268/850328 **Fax:** 01432 850381
Mordiford, Hereford HR1 4EJ
Owner: Trustees of Sufton Heritage Trust   **Contact:** Mr & Mrs J N Hereford
A 16th century manor house which was altered and remodelled in the 18th and 19th centuries and again in this century. The original home of the Hereford family (see Sufton Court) who have held the manor since the 12th century.
Location: OS Ref. SO575 384. Mordiford, off B4224 Mordiford - Dormington road.
Opening Times: By written appointment to Sufton Court or by fax.
Admission: Adult £2, Child 50p.

♿ Partially suitable. Obligatory.   ❅

Berrington Hall, Herefordshire.

NT Photographic Library

ROTHERWAS CHAPEL

Tel: 0121 625 6820 (Regional Office)

Hereford, Herefordshire

Owner: English Heritage

Contact: The West Midlands Regional Office

This Roman Catholic chapel, dating from the 14th and 16th centuries, is testament to the past grandeur of the Bodenham family and features an interesting mid-Victorian side chapel and High Altar.

Location: OS Ref. SO537 383. 1½ m SE of Hereford 500yds N of B4399.

Opening Times: Any reasonable time. Keykeeper at nearby filling station.

Admission: Free.

SUFTON COURT

Tel: 01432 870268/850328 **Fax:** 01432 850381

Mordiford, Hereford HR1 4LU

Owner: J N Hereford

Contact: Mr & Mrs J N Hereford

Sufton Court is a small Palladian mansion house. Built in 1788 by James Wyatt for James Hereford. The park was laid out by Humphrey Repton whose 'red book' still survives. The house stands above the rivers Wye and Lugg giving impressive views towards the mountains of Wales.

Location: OS Ref. SO574 379. Mordiford, off B4224 on Mordiford to Dormington road.

Opening Times: 15 - 28 May & 14 - 27 Aug: 2 - 5pm.

Admission: Adult £2, Child 50p.

Partially suitable. Obligatory. Only small coaches.

In grounds, on leads.

THE WEIR

Tel: 01981 590509

Swainshill, Hereford, Herefordshire

Owner: The National Trust

Contact: Regional Office

Delightful riverside garden particularly spectacular in early spring, with fine view over the River Wye and Black Mountains.

Location: OS Ref. SO435 421. 5m W of Hereford on S side of A438.

Opening Times: 20 Jan - 11 Feb: Sats & Suns, 11am - 4pm. 14 Feb - 31 Oct: Wed - Sun, Good Fri & BH Mons, 11am - 6pm.

Admission: £2.50.

Not suitable. No parking.

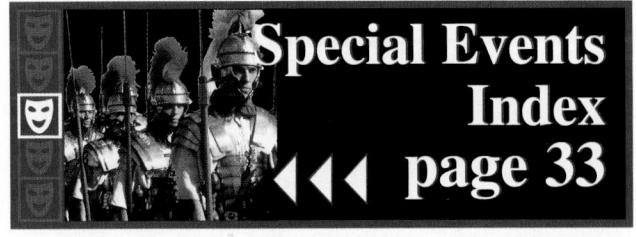

Special Events
Index
◀◀◀ page 33

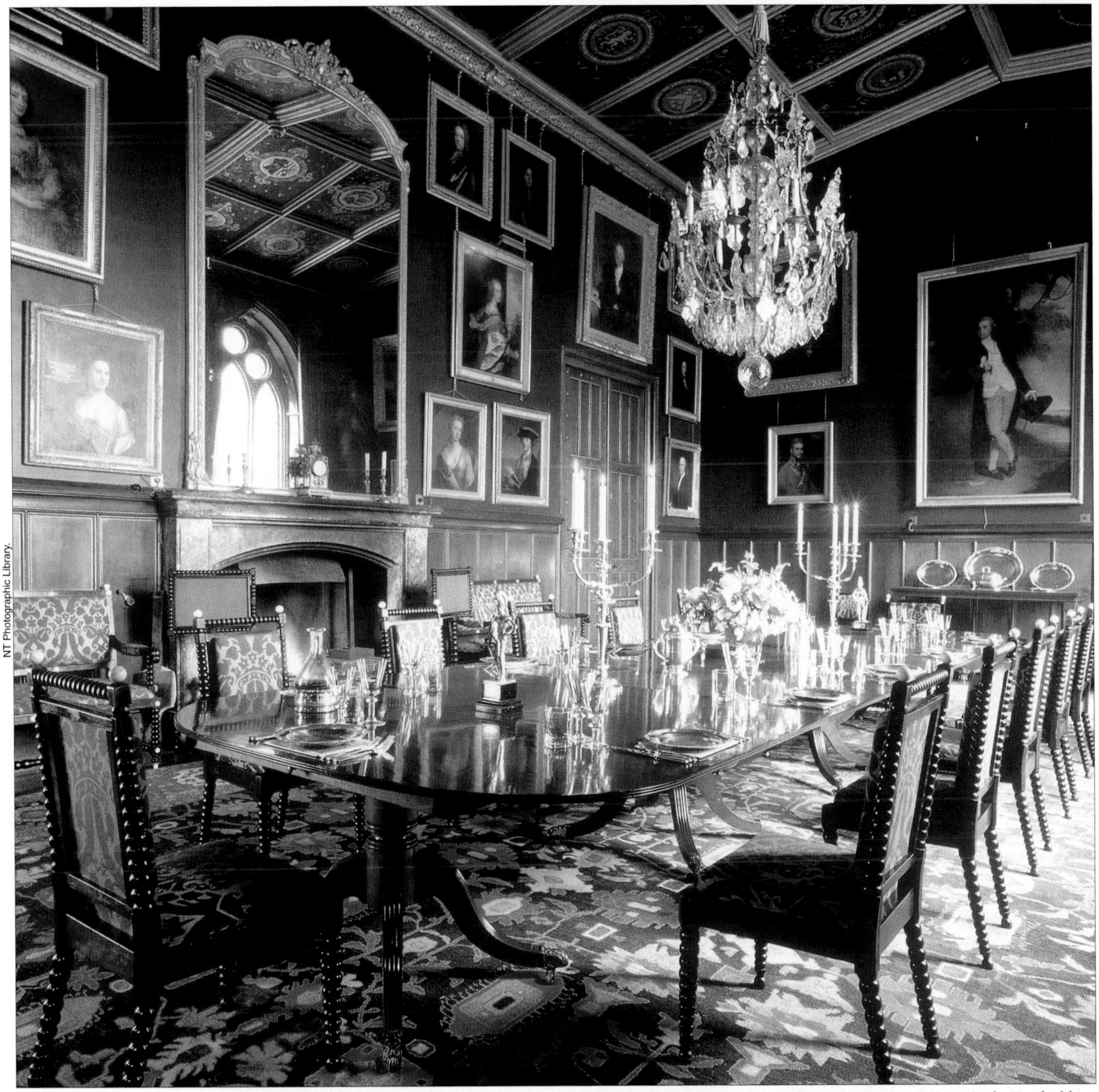

NT Photographic Library

The Dining Room at Eastnor Castle, Herefordshire.

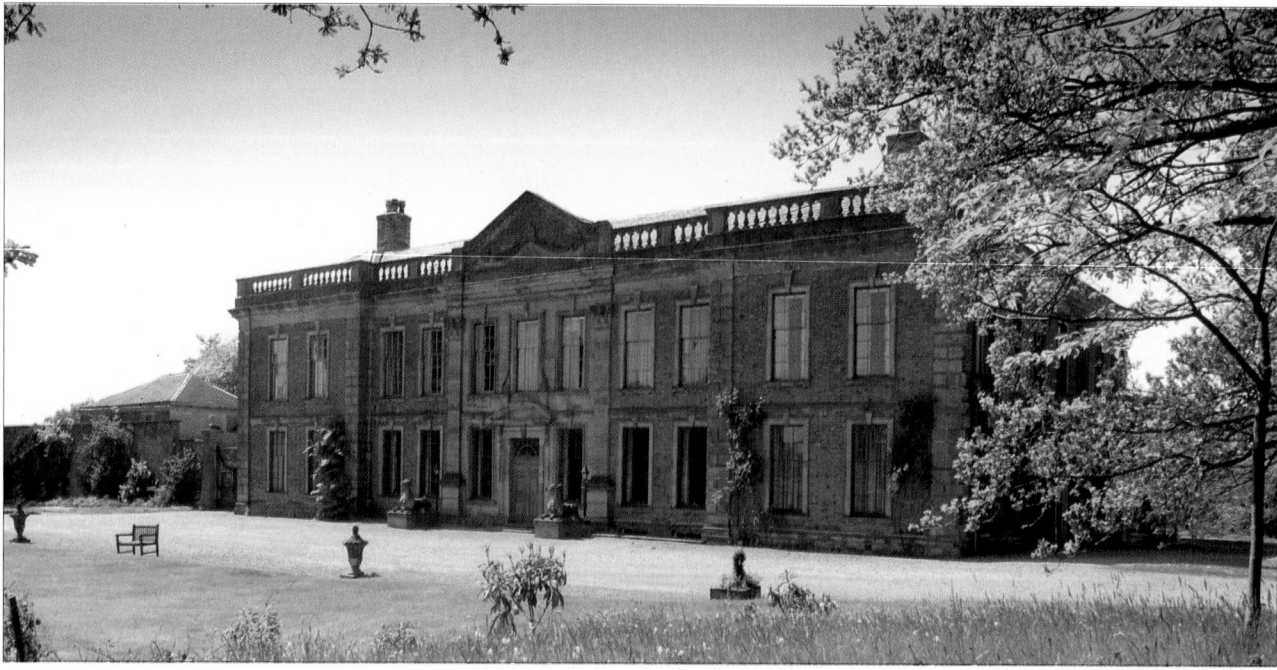

OAKLEY HALL
Market Drayton

OAKLEY HALL is situated in magnificent countryside on the boundary of Shropshire and Staffordshire. The present Hall is a fine example of a Queen Anne mansion house and was built on the site of an older dwelling mentioned in the Domesday Survey of 1085. Oakley Hall was the home of the Chetwode family until it was finally sold in 1919.

GARDENS

Set in 100 acres of rolling parkland, the Hall commands superb views over the surrounding countryside and the gardens include wild areas in addition to the more formal parts.

Oakley Hall is a privately owned family house and since it is not open to the general public it provides a perfect location for exclusive private or corporate functions. The main hall can accommodate 120 people comfortably and has excellent acoustics for concerts. The secluded location and unspoilt landscape make Oakley an ideal setting for filming and photography.

The surrounding countryside is rich in historical associations. St Mary's Church at Mucklestone, in which parish the Hall stands, was erected in the 13th century and it was from the tower of this Church that Queen Margaret of Anjou observed the Battle of Blore Heath in 1459. This was a brilliant victory for the Yorkist faction in the Wars of the Roses and the blacksmith at Mucklestone was reputed to have shod the Queen's horse back to front in order to disguise her escape.

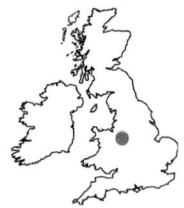

Owner:
Mr & Mrs F Fisher

CONTACT

Mrs Ann E Fisher
Oakley Hall
Market Drayton
Shropshire
TF9 4AG

Tel: 01630 653472

Fax: 01630 653282

Wedding Enquiries:
Mrs D Hastie
Tel: 01244 572021

LOCATION

OS Ref. SJ701 367

From London 3hrs:
M1, M6/J14, then A5013 to
Eccleshall, turn right at
T-junction, 200 yards, then
left onto B5026.
Mucklestone is 1³/₄ m from
Loggerheads on B5026. 3m
NE of Market Drayton
N of the A53,
1¹/₂ m W of Muckle-
stone, off B5145.

CONFERENCE/FUNCTION		
ROOM	SIZE	MAX CAPACITY
Hall	50' x 30'	100
Dining Rm	40' x 27'	60
Ballroom	40' x 27'	60

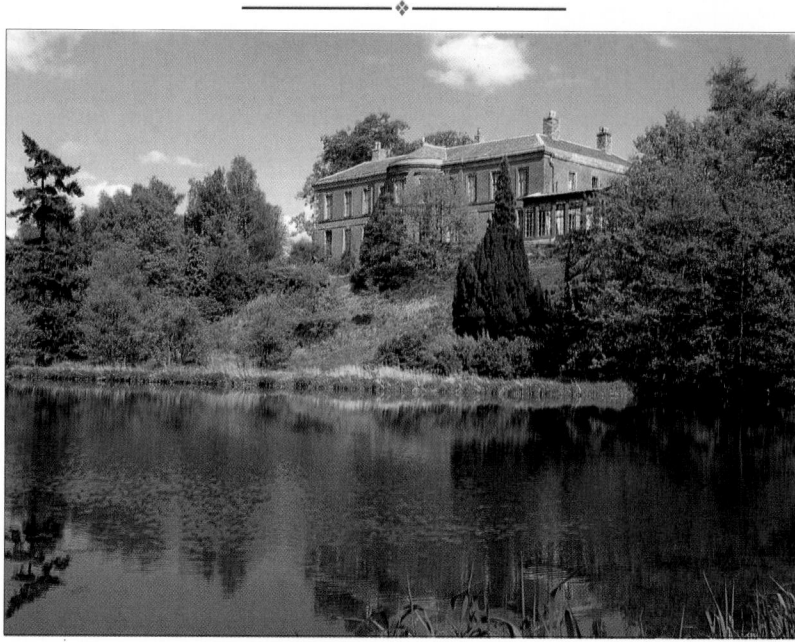

OPENING TIMES

ALL YEAR

Not open to the public. The house is available all year round for private or corporate events.

ADMISSION

Please telephone for details.

ℹ️ Concerts, conferences (see left for rooms available). Slide projector, word processor, fax and secretarial assistance are all available by prior arrangement, fashion shows, product launches, seminars, clay pigeon shooting, garden parties and filming. Grand piano, hard tennis court, croquet lawn, horse riding. No stiletto heels.

🍴 Wedding receptions, buffets, lunches and dinners can be arranged for large or small groups, using high quality local caterers.

♿ Visitors may alight at the entrance to the Hall, before parking in allocated areas. WCs.

🚶 By prior arrangement groups will be met and entertained by members of the Fisher family.

🅿️ 100 cars, 100/200 yds from the Hall.

🛏️ 3 double with baths.

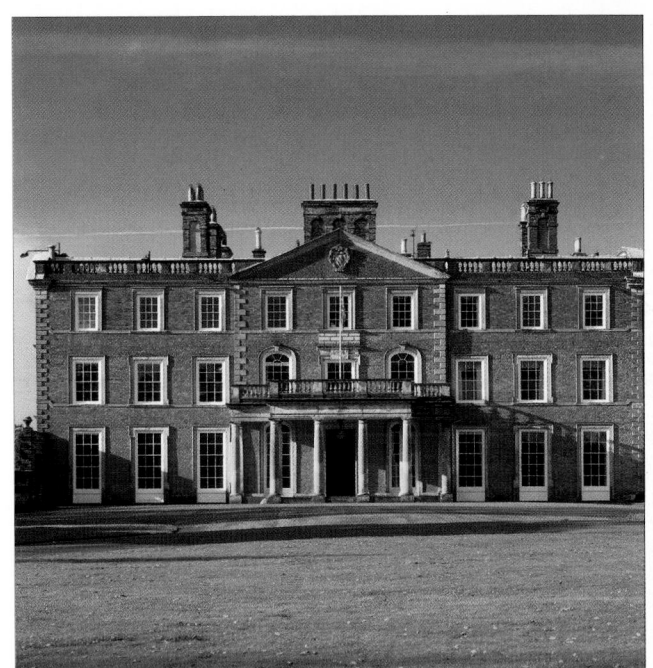

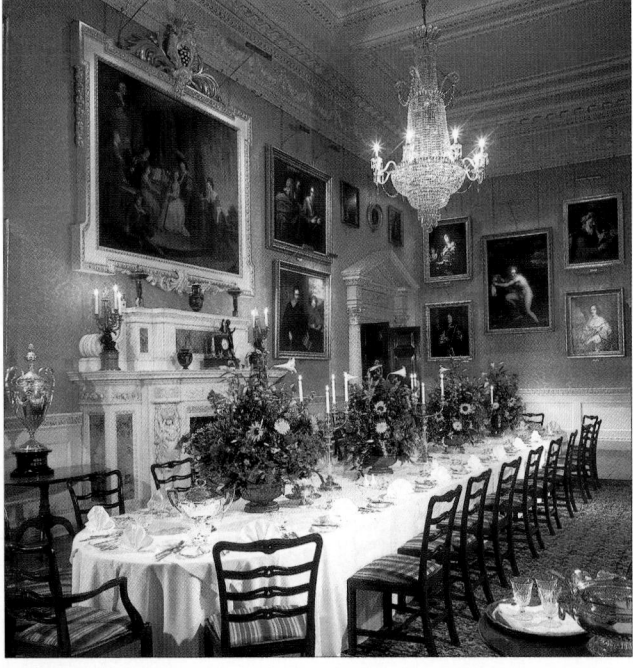

WESTON PARK
Nr Shifnal

WESTON PARK is a magnificent Stately Home and Parkland situated on the Staffordshire/ Shropshire border. The former home of the Earls of Bradford, the Park is now held in trust for the nation by The Weston Park Foundation.

Built in 1671 by Lady Elizabeth Wilbraham, this warm and welcoming house boasts a superb collection of paintings, including work by Van Dyck, Gainsborough and Stubbs, furniture and *objets d'art*, providing continued interest and enjoyment for all of its visitors.

Step outside to enjoy the 1,000 acres of glorious Parkland, designed by the legendary 'Capability' Brown - meander through the formal gardens,

take one of a variety of woodland walks and then relax in The Stables Restaurant. Take time to browse through the Gift Shop, completing your day with a delicious ice-cream from the Ice-Cream Parlour.

With the exciting Woodland Adventure Playground, Pets Corner and Deer Park, as well as the Miniature Railway, there is so much for children to do.

Weston Park has a long-standing reputation for staging outstanding events. The exciting and varied programme of entertainment includes Balloon Festivals, Music Festivals, Opera Evenings and Battle Re-enactments.

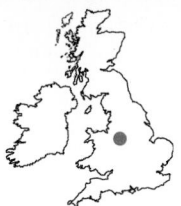

Owner:
The Weston Park Foundation

CONTACT

Alison Robbins
Weston Park
Weston-under-Lizard
Nr Shifnal
Shropshire
TF11 8LE

Tel: 01952 852100

Fax: 01952 850430

e-mail: enquiries@ weston-park.com

LOCATION

OS Ref. SJ808 107

Birmingham 40 mins. Manchester 1 hr. Motorway access M6/J12 or M54/J3. House situated on A5 at Weston-under-Lizard.

Rail: Nearest Railway Stations: Wolverhampton, Stafford or Telford.

Air: Birmingham, West Midlands, Manchester.

CONFERENCE/FUNCTION

ROOM	SIZE	MAX CAPACITY
Dining Rm	52' x 23'	120
Orangery	51' x 20'	120
Music Rm	50' x 20'	80
The Old Stables	58' x 20'	60
Conference Room	40' x 7'6"	60

OPENING TIMES

OPENING TIMES

Easter weekend:
14 - 16 April.

21 April - 30 June:
weekends.

1 July - 31 August:
Daily.

Every weekend in September until 16 September, then closed.

House: 1 - 5pm
Last admission 4.30pm.

Park: 11am - 7pm
Last admission 5pm.

NB. Visitors are advised to telephone first to check this information.

ADMISSION

Park & Gardens
Adult £2.50
Child (3 - 16yrs).........£2.00
OAP.........................£1.50

House
Adult £2.00
Child (3 - 16yrs).........£1.50
OAP.........................£1.00

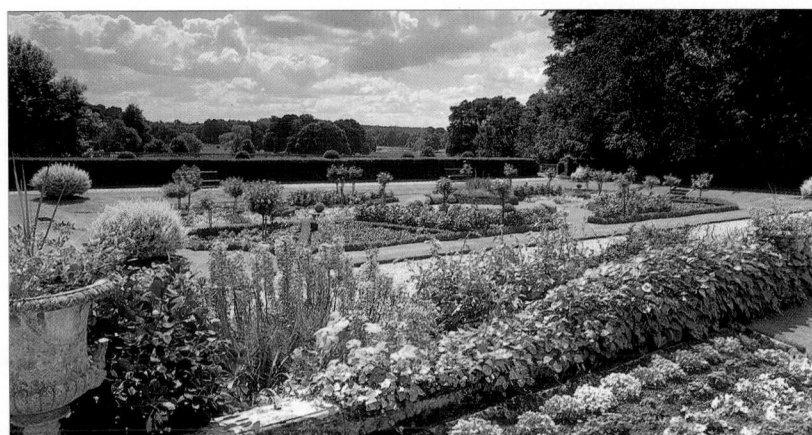

 House available on an exclusive use basis. Conferences, product launches, outdoor concerts and events, filming location. Helipad and airstrip. Sporting activities organised for private groups eg. clay pigeon shooting, archery, hovercrafts, rally driving. Interior photography by prior arrangement only.

Gift Shop.

Full event organisation service. Residential parties, special dinners, wedding receptions. Dine and stay arrangements in the house on selected dates.

House and part of the grounds. WCs.

The Stables bar and restaurant provide meals and snacks. Licensed.

Ample 100 yds away. Private booked groups may park vehicles at front door.

Tues, Weds and Thurs in the latter half of Jun and all Jul. Must book. Teachers' guidance notes and National Curriculum related workpacks available.

Weston Park offers 28 delightful bedrooms with bathrooms, 20 doubles, 4 twins, 4 singles. On an exclusive only basis.

In grounds, on leads.

Telephone for details.

ACTON BURNELL CASTLE ⊞

Tel: 0121 625 6820 (Regional Office)

Acton Burnell, Shrewsbury, Shropshire
Owner: English Heritage　　　　**Contact:** The West Midlands Regional Office
The warm red sandstone shell of a fortified 13th century manor house.
Location: OS Ref. SJ534 019. In Acton Burnell, on unclassified road 8m S of Shrewsbury.
Opening Times: Any reasonable time.
Admission: Free.

ADCOTE SCHOOL

Tel: 01939 260202 **Fax:** 01939 261300

Little Ness, Shrewsbury, Shropshire SY4 2JY
Owner: Adcote School Educational Trust Ltd　　　　**Contact:** Mrs A Read
Adcote is a Grade I listed building designed by Norman Shaw, and built to a Tudor design in 1879. Its features include a Great Hall, Minstrels' Gallery, William De Morgan tiled fireplaces and stained glass windows. Landscaped gardens include many fine trees.
Location: OS Ref. SJ418 294. 7m NW of Shrewsbury. 2m NE of A5.
Opening Times: By appointment only.
Admission: Free, but the Governors reserve the right to make a charge.

🔔 ❄

ATTINGHAM PARK 🌿

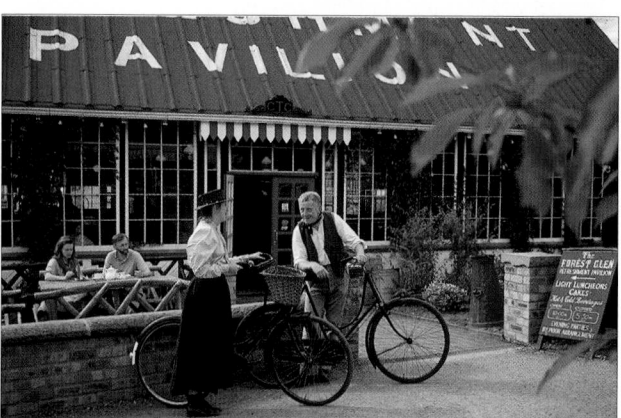

SHREWSBURY, SHROPSHIRE SY4 4TP
Owner: The National Trust　　*Contact: The Property Manager*
Infoline: 01743 708123　**Tel:** 01743 708162　**Fax:** 01743 708175
One of the great houses of the Midlands. An elegant late 18th century mansion by George Steuart, with a Picture Gallery by Nash. It has magnificent Regency interiors with exceptional collections of ambassadorial silver, Italian neo-classical furniture and Grand Tour paintings. The park was landscaped by Repton in 1797.
Location: OS127 Ref. SJ837 083. 4m SE of Shrewsbury on N side of B4380 in Atcham village.
Opening Times: 30 Mar - 28 Oct: daily (closed Wed & Thur), 1 - 4.30pm, last admission to house 4pm. Deer Park & Grounds: daily, closed 25 Dec. Mar - end Oct: 9am - 8pm. Nov - Feb 2001: 9am - 5pm. Introductory talks from 1pm.
Admission: House & Grounds: Adult £4.30, Child £2.15, Family £10.75. Park & Grounds only: Adult £2, Child £1. Booked groups (15+): Adult £3.90, Child £1.95.

ℹ No photography in house.　📷　♿　▣ Licensed.
🖼 By arrangement.　🅿　🎫　🐾 In grounds on leads.　❄

Ironbridge Gorge Museums, Shropshire.

BENTHALL HALL 🌿

Tel: 01952 882159

Benthall, Nr Broseley, Shropshire TF12 5RX
Owner: The National Trust　　　　**Contact:** Mr R Benthall
A 16th century stone house with mullioned windows and moulded brick chimneys.
Location: OS Ref. SJ658 025. 1m NW of Broseley (B4375), 4m NE of Much Wenlock, 1m SW of Ironbridge.
Opening Times: 1 Apr - 30 Sept: Weds, Suns & BH Mons 1.30 - 5.30pm. Last adm. 5pm. Groups at other times by prior arrangement.
Admission: Adult: £3.50, Child: £1.75. Garden: £2.25. Reduced rates for groups.

♿ Ground floor suitable. WC.　🖼 By arrangement.　🅿 Limited.

BOSCOBEL HOUSE & THE ROYAL OAK ⊞

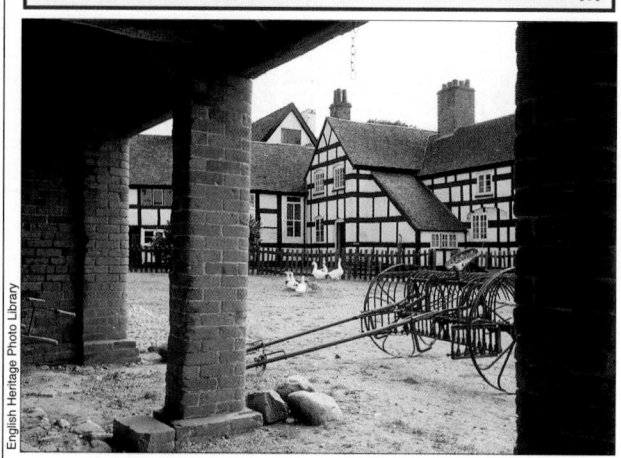

BREWOOD, BISHOP'S WOOD, SHROPSHIRE ST19 9AR
Owner: English Heritage　　*Contact: The Custodian*
Tel: 01902 850244
This 17th century hunting lodge was destined to play a part in Charles II's escape from the Roundheads. A descendant of the Royal Oak, which sheltered the fugitive King from Cromwell's troops after the Battle of Worcester in 1651, still stands in the fields near Boscobel House. 2001 will be the 350th anniversary of this event. The timber-framed house where the King slept in a tiny 'sacred hole' has been fully restored and furnished in Victorian period and there are panelled rooms and secret hiding places. There is an exhibition in the house as well as the farmyard and smithy.
Location: OS127 Ref. SJ837 083. On unclassified road between A41 & A5. 8m NW of Wolverhampton.
Opening Times: 1 Apr - 30 Sept: daily: 10am - 6pm (5pm in Oct). 1 - 30 Nov: Wed - Sun, 10am - 4pm. 1 - 31 Dec: Sats & Suns, 10am - 4pm. Closed 1 Jan - 31 Mar. Last admission 45 mins before closing.
Admission: Adult £4.40, Child £2.20, Conc. £3.30, Family £11. 15% discount on groups (11+).

♿ Grounds suitable. WC.　🍴　🖼 Obligatory.　🚫　❄　🛡 Tel. for details.

BUILDWAS ABBEY ⊞

Tel: 01952 433274

Iron Bridge, Telford, Shropshire TF8 7BW
Owner: English Heritage　　　　**Contact:** The Custodian
Extensive remains of a Cistercian abbey built in 1135, set beside the River Severn against a backdrop of wooded grounds. The remains include the church which is almost complete except for the roof.
Location: OS Ref. SJ642 044. On S bank of River Severn on A4169, 2m W of Ironbridge.
Opening Times: 1 Apr - 31 Oct: daily, 10am - 6pm (5pm in Oct).
Admission: Adult £2, Child £1, Conc. £1.50.

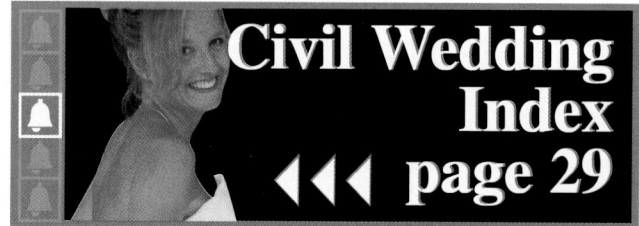

BURFORD HOUSE GARDENS

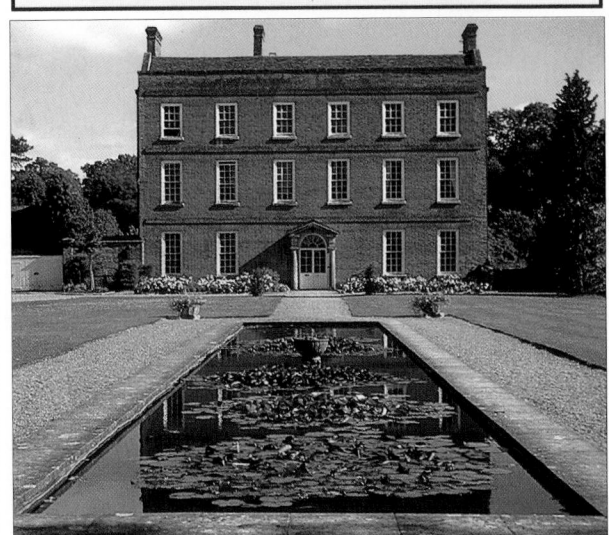

TENBURY WELLS, WORCESTERSHIRE WR15 8HQ

Owner: *Treasures of Tenbury Ltd*   **Contact:** *Charles Chesshire*

Tel: 01584 810777 **Fax:** 01584 810673

Seven acre garden in beautiful riverside setting, home to the national clematis collection, with over 300 varieties, and 2,000 varieties of other plants. New designs include a wildflower garden, bamboo and grass garden. Also visit Treasures Garden Centre, Burford House Gallery, Home & Garden shop, café-bar, Mulu Exotic Plants and Jungle Giants Bamboos.

Location: OS Ref. SO585 680. 1m W of Tenbury Wells on the A456, 8m from Ludlow.

Opening Times: All year: daily, 10am - 5pm.

Admission: Adult £3.50, Child £1. Groups (10+): £3.

Licensed. By arrangement. Guide dogs only.

CLUN CASTLE

Tel: 0121 625 6820 (Regional Office)

Clun, Ludlow, Shropshire

Owner: English Heritage   **Contact:** The West Midlands Regional Office

Remains of a four-storey keep and other buildings of this border castle are set in outstanding countryside. Built in the 11th century.

Location: OS Ref. SO299 809. In Clun, off A488, 18m W of Ludlow. 9m W of Craven Arms.

Opening Times: Any reasonable time.

Admission: Free.

COLEHAM PUMPING STATION

Tel: 01743 362947 **Fax:** 01743 358411

Longden Coleham, Shrewsbury, Shropshire SY3 7DN

Owner: Shrewsbury & Atcham Borough Council   **Contact:** Mary White

Two Renshaw beam engines of 1901 are being restored to steam by members of Shrewsbury Steam Trust. 2001 is the centenary year of Coleham Pumping Station.

Location: OS Ref. SJ497 122. Shrewsbury town centre, near the River Severn.

Opening Times: 28 & 29 Apr: special centenary celebrations. Also Apr - Sept: 4th Sun in each month, 10am - 4pm. Plus occasional other days. Details: 01743 361196.

Admission: Adult £1, Child 50p, Student £1.

Partially suitable. By arrangement. No parking. Guide dogs only.

COMBERMERE ABBEY

Tel: 01948 662880 **Fax:** 01948 660940

Whitchurch, Shropshire SY13 4AJ   **e-mail:** cottages@combermereabbey.co.uk

Owner: Mrs S Callander Beckett   **Contact:** Mrs Carol Sheard

Combermere Abbey, originally a Cistercian Monastery, and remodelled as a Gothic house in 1820 sits in a magnificent 1000 acre private parkland setting. Host to many remarkable historical personalities, the splendid 17th century Library and elegant Porter's Hall are licensed for weddings, receptions, concerts and lectures. Excellent accommodation is available on the Estate.

Location: OS Ref. SJ590 440. 5m E of Whitchurch, off A530.

Opening Times: By arrangement for groups.

Admission: Groups £7 per person inclusive of refreshments.

No photography. Not suitable. By arrangement. By arrangement. Limited.

DAVENPORT HOUSE

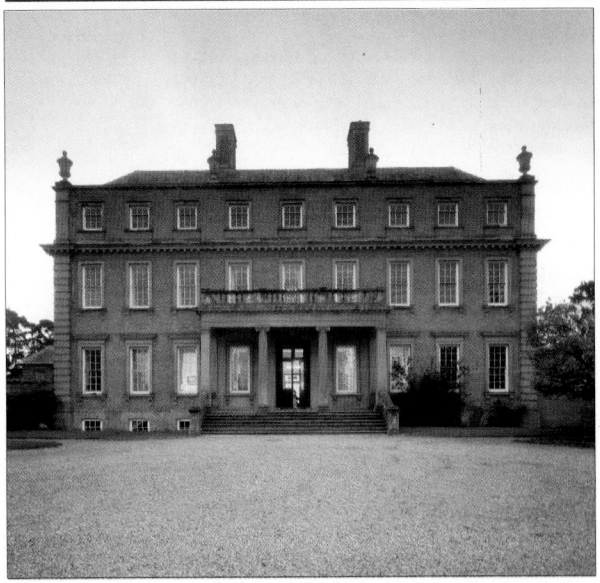

WORFIELD, Nr BRIDGNORTH, SHROPSHIRE WV15 5LE

Owner/Contact: *Roger Murphy*

Tel: 01746 716221 / 716345 **Fax:** 01746 716021

A Grade I listed country house of 1726 by the architect Francis Smith of Warwick. The house sits within an extensive estate and is a popular regional venue for wedding receptions, civil marriage ceremonies and corporate and social group entertainment. Open to the public as a restaurant Wednesday evenings, advance booking only.

Location: OS Ref. SO756 955. Worfield village, drive entrance by war memorial.

Opening Times: Available for weddings and other functions throughout the year.

Admission: Please telephone for details.

Partially suitable. Licensed.

DUDMASTON

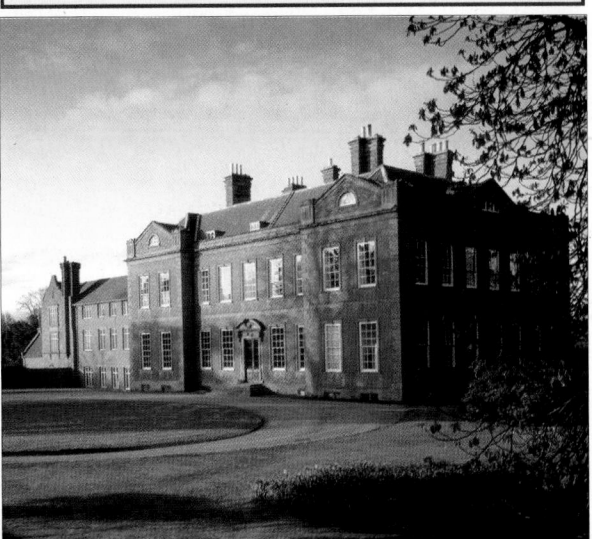

Michael Caldwell.

QUATT, BRIDGNORTH, SHROPSHIRE WV15 6QN

Owner: *The National Trust*   **Contact:** *The Administrator*

Tel: 01746 780866 **Fax:** 01746 780744 **e-mail:** mduefe@smtp.ntrust.org.uk

Late 17th century manor house. Contains furniture and china, Dutch flower paintings, watercolours, botanical art and modern pictures and sculpture, family and natural history. 9 acres of lakeside gardens and Dingle walk. Two estate walks 5 1/2 m and 3 1/2 m starting from Hampton Loade car park.

Location: OS Ref. SO748 888. 4m SE of Bridgnorth on A442.

Opening Times: 1 Apr - 30 Sept: House; Tues, Weds, Suns & BH Mons, 2 - 5.30pm. Mons booked groups by arrangement. Garden; Mon - Wed & Suns, 12 noon - 6pm. Tearoom: 11.30am - 5.30pm. Last admission to house 5pm.

Admission: House & Garden: Adult £3.85, Child £2.30, Family £9. Groups £3. Garden only: £2.80.

Countryside walks. In grounds, on leads.

HAUGHMOND ABBEY

Tel: 01743 709661

Upton Magna, Uffington, Shrewsbury, Shropshire SY4 4RW

Owner: English Heritage   **Contact:** The Custodian

Extensive remains of a 12th century Augustinian abbey, including the Chapter House which retains its late medieval timber ceiling, and including some fine medieval sculpture.

Location: OS Ref. SJ542 152. 3m NE of Shrewsbury off B5062.

Opening Times: 1 Apr - 31 Oct: daily, 10am - 6pm (5pm in Oct).

Admission: Adult £2, Child £1, Conc. £1.50.

HAWKSTONE HALL & GARDENS

Tel: 01630 685242   **Fax:** 01630 685565

Marchamley, Shrewsbury SY4 5LG

Owner: The Redemptorists   **Contact:** Guest Mistress

Grade I Georgian mansion and restored gardens set in spacious parkland.

Location: OS Ref. SJ581 299. Entrance 1m N of Hodnet on A442.

Opening Times: 5 - 31 Aug, daily, 2 - 5pm.

Admission: Adult £3.50, Child £1.

HODNET HALL GARDENS

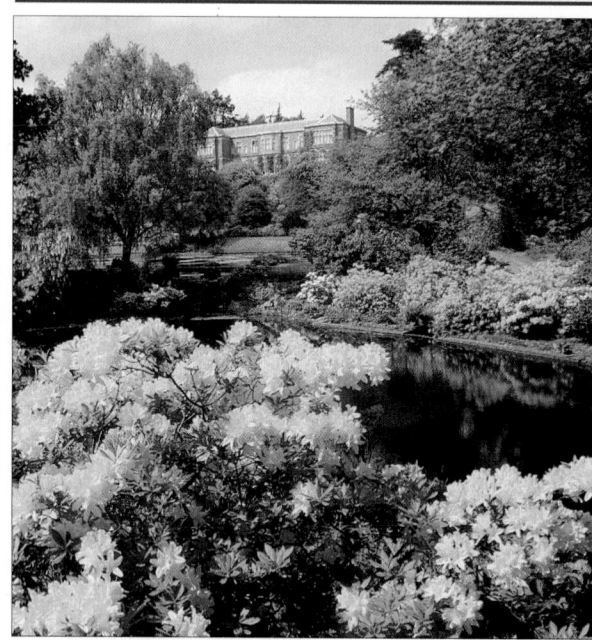

HODNET, MARKET DRAYTON, SHROPSHIRE TF9 3NN

Owner: Mr and the Hon Mrs A Heber-Percy   *Contact: Mrs M A Taylor*

Tel: 01630 685202   **Fax:** 01630 685853

Beautiful woodland walks through trees and shrubs in 60 acres of flowering lakeside gardens. Tearooms serve light lunches and afternoon teas. Gift shop.

Location: OS Ref. SJ613 286. 12m NE of Shrewsbury on A53; M6/J15, M54/J3.

Opening Times: 1 Apr - 30 Sept: Tue - Sun & BH Mons, 12 noon - 5pm.

Admission: Adult £3.25, Child £1.20, OAP £2.75. Reduced rates for groups.

Kitchen garden sales.   For groups.   On leads.

IRON BRIDGE

Tel: 0121 625 6820 (Regional Office)

Ironbridge, Shropshire

Owner: English Heritage   **Contact:** The West Midlands Regional Office

The world's first iron bridge and Britain's best known industrial monument. Cast in Coalbrookdale by local ironmaster, Abraham Darby, it was erected across the River Severn in 1779. Iron Bridge is a World Heritage Site.

Location: OS Ref. SJ672 034. In Ironbridge, adjacent to A4169.

Opening Times: Any reasonable time.

Admission: Free crossing.

IRONBRIDGE GORGE MUSEUMS

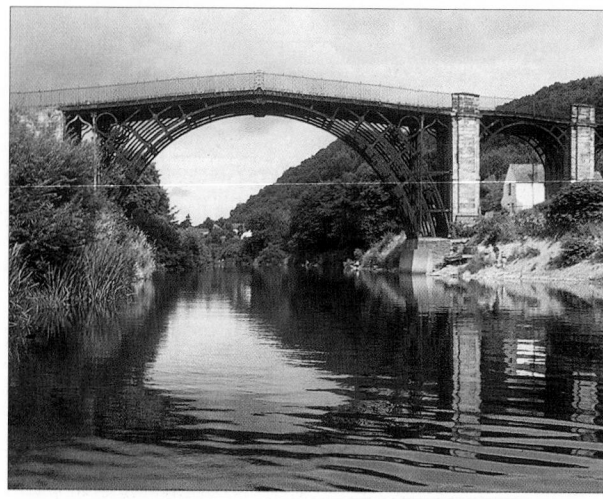

IRONBRIDGE, TELFORD, SHROPSHIRE TF8 7AW

Owner: Independent Museum   *Contact: Visitor Information*

Tel: 01952 432166 (7 day line) or 433522   **Fax:** 01952 432204

Freephone: 0800 590258 for a **free** colour guide.

Scene of pioneering events which led to the Industrial Revolution. The Ironbridge Gorge is home to nine unique museums set in six square miles of stunning scenery. These include Jackfield Tile Museum, Coalport China Museum and a recreated Victorian Town where you can chat to locals as they go about their daily business. You'll need two days here.

Location: OS Ref. SJ666 037. Telford, Shropshire via M6/M54.

Open: All year: daily from 10am - 5pm (closed 24/25 Dec & 1 Jan). Please telephone for winter details before visit.

Admission: Passport ticket which allows admission to all museums; Adult £10, Child/Student £6, OAP £9, Family £30. Prices valid until 31 March 2001. Group discounts available.

Licensed.   Guide dogs only.

LANGLEY CHAPEL

Tel: 0121 625 6820 (Regional Office)

Acton Burnell, Shrewsbury, Shropshire

Owner: English Heritage   **Contact:** The West Midlands Regional Office

A delightful medieval chapel, standing alone in a field, with a complete set of early 17th century wooden fittings and furniture.

Location: OS Ref. SJ538 001. 1$\frac{1}{2}$ m S of Acton Burnell, on unclassified road 4m E of the A49, 9$\frac{1}{2}$ m S of Shrewsbury.

Opening Times: Open any reasonable time. Closed 24- 26 Dec & 1 Jan.

Admission: Free.

LILLESHALL ABBEY

Tel: 0121 625 6820 (Regional Office)

Oakengates, Shropshire

Owner: English Heritage   **Contact:** The West Midlands Regional Office

Extensive ruins of an abbey of Augustinian canons including remains of the 12th and 13th century church and the cloister buildings. Surrounded by green lawns and ancient yew trees.

Location: OS Ref. SJ738 142. On unclassified road off the A518, 4m N of Oakengates.

Opening Times: Any reasonable time.

Admission: Free.

LONGNER HALL

Tel: 01743 709215

Uffington, Shrewsbury, Shropshire SY4 4TG

Owner: Mr R L Burton   **Contact:** Mrs R L Burton

Designed by John Nash in 1803, Longner Hall is a Tudor Gothic style house set in a park landscaped by Humphry Repton. The home of one family for over 700 years. Longner's principal rooms are adorned with plaster fan vaulting and stained glass.

Location: OS Ref. SJ529 110. 4m SE of Shrewsbury on Uffington road, $\frac{1}{4}$ m off B4380, Atcham.

Opening Times: Apr - Oct: Tues & BH Mons, 2 - 5pm. Tours at 2pm & 3.30pm. Groups at any time by arrangement.

Admission: Adult £5, Child/OAP £3.

No photography in house.   Partially suitable.   By arrangement for groups.   Obligatory.   Limited for coaches.   By arrangement.   Guide dogs only.

LUDLOW CASTLE

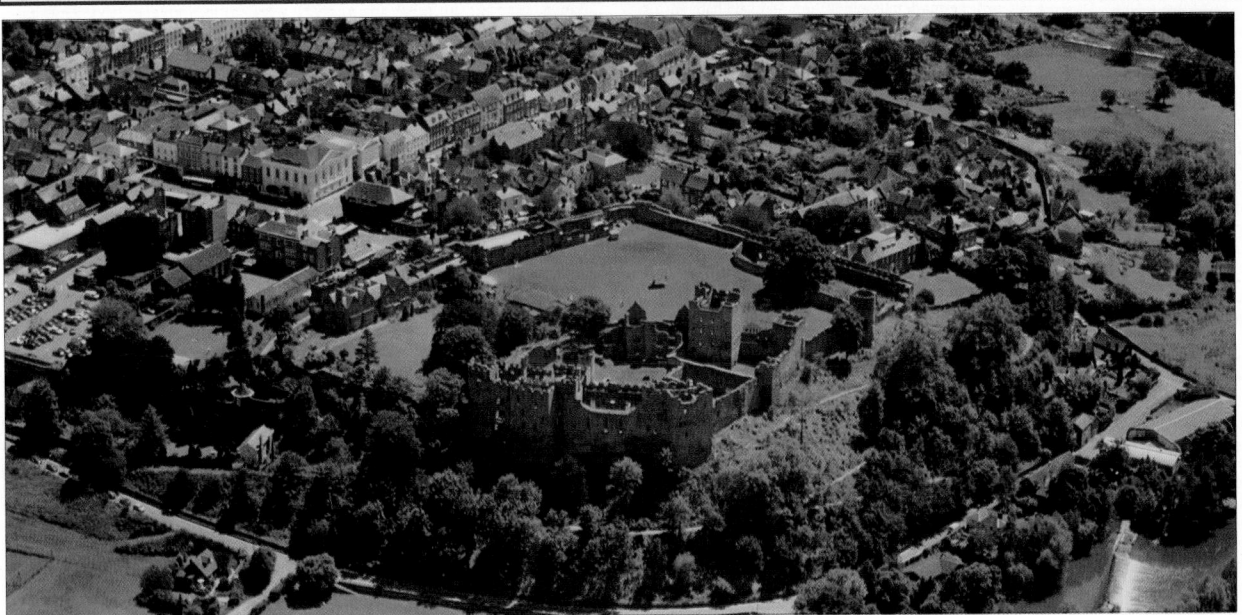

CASTLE SQUARE, LUDLOW, SHROPSHIRE SY8 1AY

Owner: *The Earl of Powis & The Trustees of the Powis Estate*   **Contact:** *Helen J Duce*

Tel: 01584 873355

900 year old castle of the Marches, dates from 1086 and greatly extended over the centuries to a fortified Royal Palace. Ludlow Castle became a seat of government with the establishment of the Council for Wales and the Marches. Privately owned by the Earls of Powis since 1811. A magnificent ruin set in the heart of Ludlow and surrounding countryside.

Location: OS Ref. SO509 745. Shrewsbury 28m, Hereford 26m. A49 centre of Ludlow.

Opening Times: Jan: weekends only, 10am - 4pm, Feb - Mar & Oct - Dec: 10am - 4pm. Apr - Jul & Sept: 10am - 5pm. Aug: 10am - 7pm. Last adm. 30mins before closing. Closed 25 Dec.

Admission: Adult £3, Child £1.50, Conc. £2.50, Family £8.50. 10% reduction for groups (10+).

Partially suitable. WC.   Not available.

No parking.   In grounds on leads.

SPECIAL EVENTS

APR 16: Easter Egg Hunt
MAY 13: Vintage Vehicle Display
MAY 26 - 28: Festival of Crafts
JUN 23 - JUL 8: Ludlow Festival
SEPT 7 - 9: Food & Drink Fair
NOV 24 - 25: Medieval Christmas Fayre
Weds during summer school holidays: Birds of Prey & costumed tour guide.

MAWLEY HALL

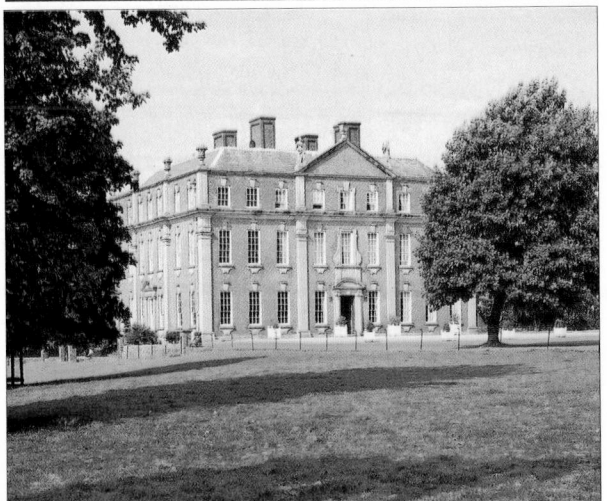

CLEOBURY MORTIMER, DY14 8PN

Owner: *R Galliers-Pratt Esq*   **Contact:** *Mrs R Sharp*

Tel: 01299 270869 **Fax:** 01299 270022 **e-mail:** administration@mawley.com

Built in 1730 and attributed to Francis Smith of Warwick, Mawley is set in 18th century landscaped parkland with extensive gardens and walks down to the River Rea. Magnificent plasterwork and a fine collection of English and Continental furniture and porcelain.

Location: OS137 Ref. SO688 753. 1m N of Cleobury Mortimer on the A4117 and 7m W of Bewdley.

Opening Times: 12 Apr - 15 Jul: Mons & Thurs, 3 - 5pm and throughout the year by appointment.

Admission: Adult £5, Child/OAP £3.

Lunches, dinners & functions in association with Sean Hill of the Michelin starred restaurant, The Merchant House, in Ludlow.

By arrangement.   In grounds, on leads.

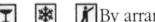

MORETON CORBET CASTLE

Tel: 0121 625 6820 (Regional Office)

Moreton Corbet, Shrewsbury, Shropshire

Owner: English Heritage   **Contact:** The West Midlands Regional Office

A ruined medieval castle with the substantial remains of a splendid Elizabethan mansion, captured in 1644 from Charles I's supporters by Parliamentary forces.

Location: OS Ref. SJ562 232. In Moreton Corbet off B5063, 7m NE of Shrewsbury.

Opening Times: Any reasonable time.

Admission: Free.

MORVILLE HALL

Tel: 01743 708100

Bridgnorth, Shropshire WV16 5NB

Owner: The National Trust   **Contact:** Dr & Mrs C Douglas

An Elizabethan house of mellow stone, converted in the 18th century and set in attractive gardens.

Location: OS Ref. SO668 940. Morville, on A458 3m W of Bridgnorth.

Opening Times: By written appointment only with the tenants.

Obligatory.

OAKLEY HALL

See page 330 for full page entry.

PREEN MANOR GARDENS

Tel: 01694 771207

Church Preen, Church Stretton, Shropshire SY6 7LQ

Owner: Mr & Mrs P Trevor-Jones   **Contact:** Mrs P Trevor-Jones

Six acre garden on site of Cluniac monastery, with walled, terraced, wild, water, kitchen and chess gardens. 12th century monastic church with a yew tree reputedly the oldest in Europe.

Location: OS Ref. SO544 981. 10m SSE of Shrewsbury. 7m NE of Church Stretton, 6m SW of Much Wenlock.

Opening Times: Refer National Gardens Scheme Yellow Book. Coach parties Jun & Jul by appointment only.

Admission: Adult £3, Child 50p.

Fred Dibnah Mar. 2002

ROWLEY'S HOUSE MUSEUM

Tel: 01743 361196   **Fax:** 01743 358411
e-mail: museums@shrewsbury-atcham.gov.uk

Barker Street, Shrewsbury, Shropshire SY1 1QH

Owner: Shrewsbury and Atcham Borough Council   **Contact:** Mrs M White

Impressive timber-framed building and attached 17th century brick mansion with costume, archaeology and natural history, geology, local history and temporary exhibitions.

Location: OS Ref. SJ490 126. Barker Street.

Opening Times: 9 Jan - Easter: Tue - Sat, 10am - 4pm. Easter - end Sept: Tue - Sat, 10am - 5pm. Also Suns, BHs & summer Mons, 10am - 4pm. Oct - Easter 2002: Tue - Sat, 10am - 4pm. Closed Christmas & New Year period.

Admission: Free.

ℹ️ No photography.   📷   ♿ Not suitable.   🅿️ No parking.   ▥
🐕 Guide dogs only.   ✳️

SHIPTON HALL 🏛️

Tel: 01746 785225   **Fax:** 01746 785125

Much Wenlock, Shropshire TF13 6JZ

Owner: Mr J N R Bishop   **Contact:** Mrs M J Bishop

Built around 1587 by Richard Lutwyche who gave the house to his daughter Elizabeth on her marriage to Thomas Mytton. Shipton remained in the Mytton family for the next 300 years. The house has been described as 'an exquisite specimen of Elizabethan architecture set in a quaint old fashioned garden, the whole forming a picture which as regards both form and colour, satisfies the artistic sense of even the most fastidious'. The Georgian additions by Thomas F Pritchard include some elegant rococo interior decorations and some noteworthy Tudor and Jacobean panelling. Family home. In addition to the house visitors are welcome to explore the gardens, the dovecote and the parish church which dates back to Saxon times.

Location: OS Ref. SO563 918. 7m SW of Much Wenlock on B4378. 10m W of Bridgnorth.

Opening Times: Easter - end Sept: Thurs, 2.30 - 5.30pm. Also Suns and Mons of BH, 2.30 - 5.30pm. Groups of 20+ at any time of day or year by prior arrangement.

Admission: Adult £4, Child £2. Discount of 10% for groups (20+).

♿ Not suitable.   🍽️ By arrangement for groups (20+).   📷 Obligatory.
🐕 Guide dogs only.   ✳️

SHREWSBURY ABBEY

Tel: 01743 232723   **Fax:** 01743 240172

Shrewsbury, Shropshire SY2 6BS   **Contact:** Mr Terence Hyde

Benedictine Abbey founded in 1083, tomb of Roger de Montgomerie and remains of tomb of St Winefride, 7th century Welsh saint. The Abbey was part of the monastery and has also been a parish church since the 12th century. Now made popular by Ellis Peters author of 'Brother Cadfael' novels. Historical exhibition from Saxon times to present.

Location: OS Ref. SJ499 125. Signposted from Shrewsbury bypass (A5 and A49). 500yds E of town centre, across English Bridge.

Opening Times: 25 Mar - 27 Oct: 9.30am - 5.30pm. 28 Oct - 23 Mar: 10.30am - 3pm.

Admission: Donation. Guided tours £10 per pre-arranged group.

SHREWSBURY CASTLE & SHROPSHIRE REGIMENTAL MUSEUM

Castle Street, Shrewsbury SY1 2AT   **Tel:** 01743 358516   **Fax:** 01743 358411
e-mail: museums@shrewsbury-atcham.gov.uk

Owner: Shrewsbury & Atcham Borough Council   **Contact:** Steve Martin

Norman Castle with 18th century work by Thomas Telford. Free admission to attractive floral grounds. The main hall houses the Shropshire Regimental Museum and displays on the history of the castle.

Location: OS Ref. SJ495 128. Town centre, adjacent BR and bus stations.

Opening Times: Main building & Museum: 7 Feb - Easter: Wed - Sat, 10am - 4pm. Easter - end Sept: Tue - Sat, 10am - 5pm. Also Suns & BHs, 10am - 4pm. Details of winter openings on request. Grounds: daily.

Admission: Museum: Adult £2, OAP £1, Shrewsbury residents, under 18s, Students & members of the regiments Free. Grounds: Mon - Sat, Free, Suns, charged as above.

ℹ️ No photography.   📷   ♿   🅿️ No parking.   ▥ Guide dogs only.   🔔

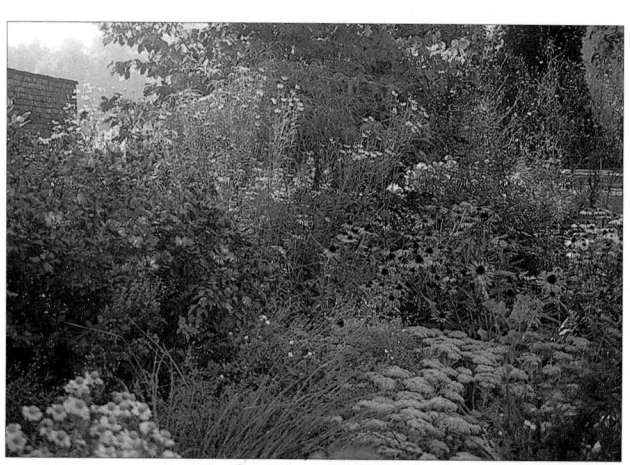

Burford House Gardens, Shropshire.

STOKESAY CASTLE ⌗

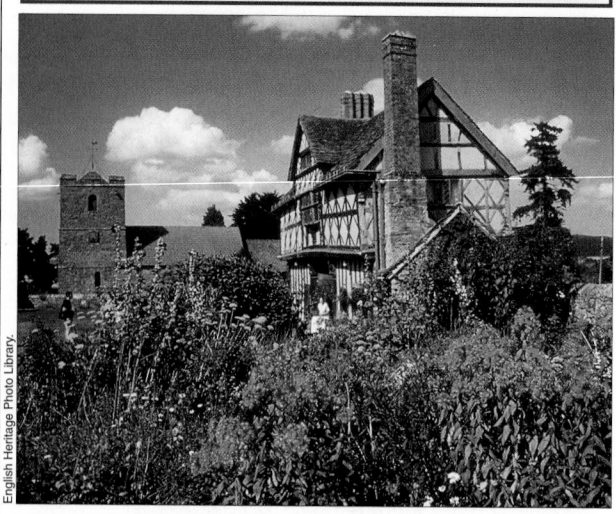

Nr CRAVEN ARMS, SHROPSHIRE SY7 9AH

Owner: *English Heritage*   **Contact:** *The Custodian*

Tel: 01588 672544

This perfectly preserved example of a 13th century fortified manor house gives us a glimpse of the life and ambitions of a rich medieval merchant. Lawrence of Ludlow built this country house to impress the landed gentry. Lawrence built a magnificent Great Hall where servants and guests gathered on feast days, but the family's private quarters were in the bright, comfortable solar on the first floor. From the outside the castle forms a picturesque grouping of castle, parish church and timber-framed Jacobean gatehouse set in the rolling Shropshire countryside.

Location: OS137 Ref. SO436 817. 7m NW of Ludlow off A49. 1m S of Craven Arms off A49.

Opening Times: 1 Apr - 31 Oct: daily, 10am - 6pm (5pm in Oct). 1 Nov - 31 Mar: Wed - Sun, 10am - 4pm. Closed 1 - 2pm in Winter. Closed 24 - 26 Dec & 1 Jan.

Admission: Adult £4, Child £2, Conc. £3, Family £10. Groups of 11+ 15% discount.

♿ Great Hall & gardens only. WC.   🍽️   🅿️   ✳️   📞 Tel. for details.

WALCOT HALL

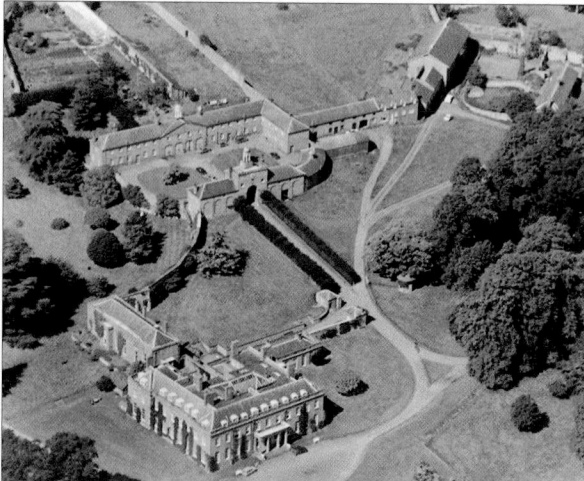

LYDBURY NORTH, Nr BISHOP'S CASTLE, SHROPSHIRE SY7 8AZ

Owner: *C R W Parish*   **Contact:** *Lesley Higgs, Marketing Manager*

Tel: 01584 874520   **Fax:** 01584 872679   **e-mail:** enquiries@walcothall.com

Georgian home of Lord Clive of India who commissioned Sir William Chambers to re-design it and the stable block, in 1763. His son added the free-standing Ballroom and developed 30 acres of arboretum and pools to the rear, with mile-long lakes in the front. Suitable for film locations, balls, corporate events, receptions, parties and shows.

Location: OS Ref. SO348 850. On the edge of the Clun Forest. 3m SE of Bishop's Castle on B4385; 1/2 m outside Lydbury North. The drive is adjacent to the Powis Arms Pub.

Opening Times: House & Garden: BHs, Suns & Mons (except Christmas and New Year), 2.15 - 4.30pm. All other times by appointment.

Admission: Adult £3, Child (under 15yrs) Free. Teas by arrangement.

♿ House suitable. WC.   🍽️ By arrangement.   🐕 On leads.
🏠 Holiday apartments, sleeping 2 - 32 people.   ✳️

WENLOCK GUILDHALL

Tel: 01952 727509

Much Wenlock, Shropshire TF13 6AE

Owner/Contact: Much Wenlock Town Council

16th century half-timbered building has an open-arcade market area.

Location: OS127 Ref. SJ624 000. In centre of Much Wenlock, next to the church.

Opening Times: 1 Apr - 30 Sept: Mon - Sat, 10.30am - 1pm & 2 - 4pm. Suns: 2 - 4pm.

Admission: Adult 50p, Child Free.

WENLOCK PRIORY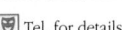

Tel: 01952 727466

Much Wenlock, Shropshire TF13 6HS

Owner: English Heritage **Contact:** The Custodian

A prosperous, powerful priory at its peak in the Middle Ages. A great deal of the structure still survives in the form of high, romantic ruined walls and it is the resting place of St Milburga the first Abbess. A monastery was first founded at Wenlock in the 7th century, and little more is known of the site until the time of the Norman Conquest when it became a Cluniac monastery. These majestic ruins of the priory church are set in green lawns and topiary, and there are substantial remains of the early 13th century church and Norman Chapter House.

Location: OS127 Ref. SJ625 001. In Much Wenlock.

Opening Times: 1 Apr - 31 Oct: daily: 10am - 6pm (5pm in Oct). 1 Nov - 31 Mar: Wed - Sun, 10am - 4pm (closed 1 - 2pm in winter). Closed 24 - 26 Dec & 1 Jan.

Admission: Adult £2.85, Child £1.40, Conc. £2.10. 15% discount for groups (11+).

P ❄ Tel. for details.

WESTON PARK

See page 331 for full page entry.

WILDERHOPE MANOR

Tel: 01694 771363

Longville, Much Wenlock, Shropshire TF13 6EG

Owner: The National Trust **Contact:** The Warden

This limestone house stands on southern slope of Wenlock Edge in remote country with views down to Corvedale. Dating from 1586, it is unaltered but unfurnished. Features include remarkable wooden spiral stairs, unique bow rack and fine plaster ceilings.

Location: OS Ref. SO545 929. 7m SW of Much Wenlock. 7m E of Church Stretton, 1/2 m S of B4371.

Opening Times: Apr - Sept: Weds & Sats, 2 - 4.30pm. Oct - Mar: Sats only, 2 - 4.30pm.

Admission: £1. No reduction for groups. Steep access to house.

WOLLERTON OLD HALL GARDEN

Tel: 01630 685760 **Fax:** 01630 685583

Wollerton, Market Drayton, Shropshire TF9 3NA

Owner: Mr & Mrs J D Jenkins **Contact:** Mrs Di Oakes

Three acre plantsman's garden created around a 16th century house (not open).

Location: OS Ref. SJ623 296. 14m NE of Shrewsbury off A53 between Hodnet and Market Drayton.

Opening Times: 13 Apr - 28 Sept: Fris, Suns & BHs (Fris only in Sept), 12 noon - 5pm. Groups (25+) by appointment at other times.

Admission: Adult £3.50, Child £1.

Gardener's World Mar 2002

WROXETER ROMAN CITY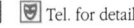

Tel: 01743 761330

Wroxeter, Shrewsbury, Shropshire SY5 6PH

Owner: English Heritage **Contact:** The Custodian

The part-excavated centre of the fourth largest city in Roman Britain, originally home to some 6,000 men and several hundred houses. Impressive remains of the 2nd century municipal baths. There is a site museum in which many finds are displayed, including those from recent work by Birmingham Field Archaeological Unit.

Location: OS Ref. SJ568 088. At Wroxeter, 5m E of Shrewsbury, on B4380.

Opening Times: 1 Apr - 31 Oct: daily 10am - 6pm (5pm in Oct). 1 Nov - 31 Mar: Wed - Sun, 10am - 4pm (closed for lunch 1 - 2pm in winter). Closed 24 - 26 Dec & 1 Jan.

Admission: Adult £3.50, Child £1.80, Conc. £2.60, Family £8.80.

♿ P ❄ Tel. for details.

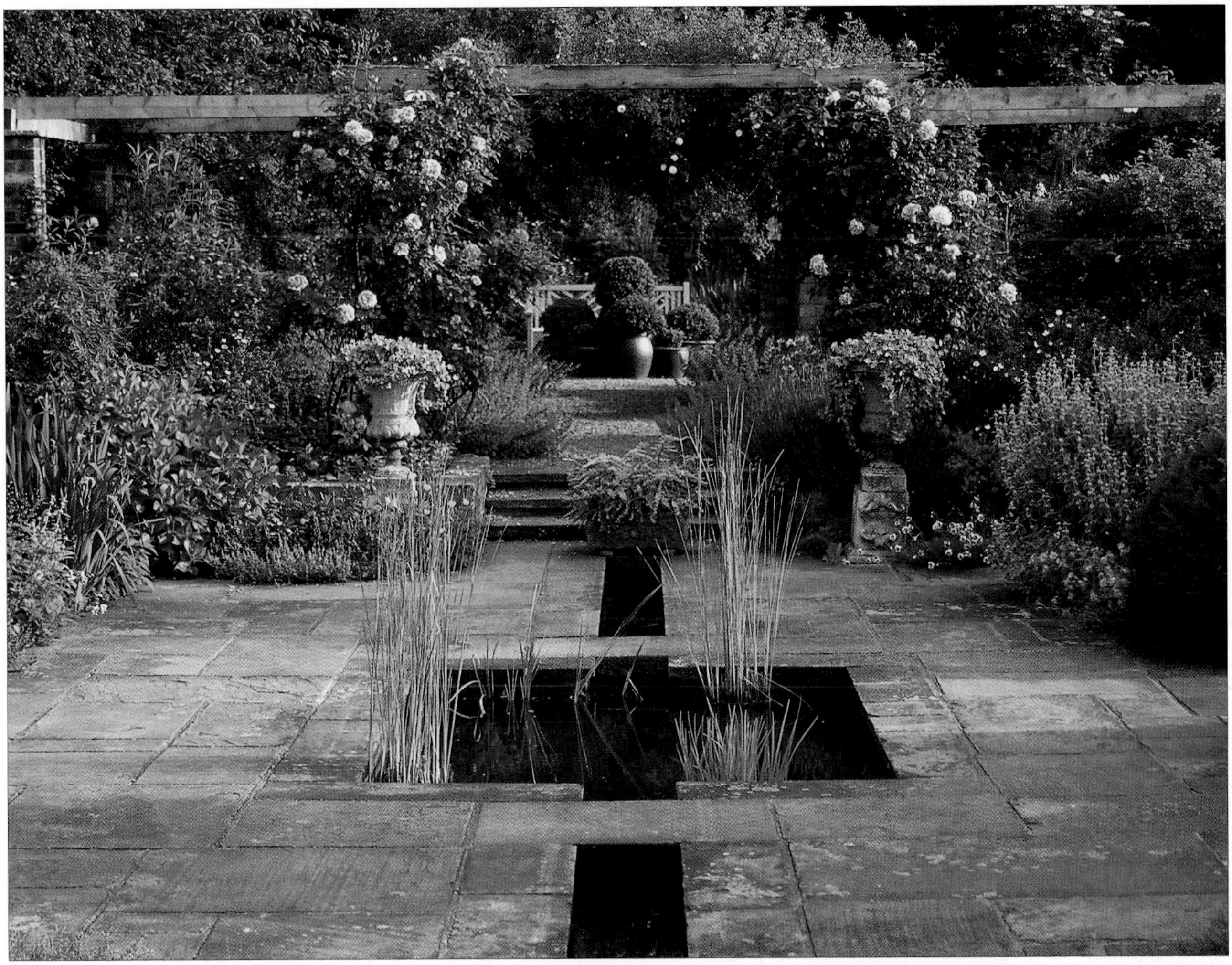

Wollerton Old Hall Garden, Shropshire.

West Midlands England

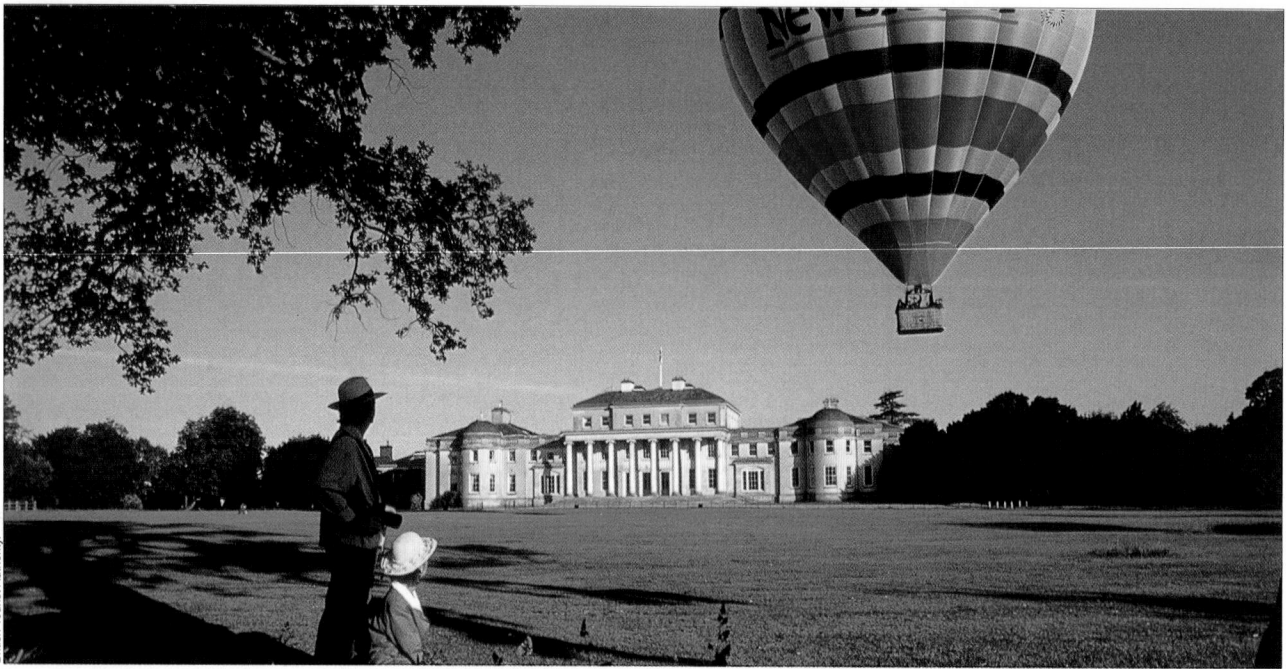

British Tourist Authority

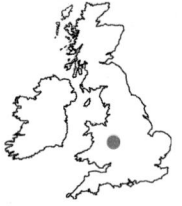

Owner:
The National Trust

CONTACT

Sales and
Marketing Office
Shugborough
Milford
Stafford
ST17 0XB

Tel: 01889 881388

Fax: 01889 881323

e-mail: shugborough.
promotions@staffordshire.
gov.uk

LOCATION

OS Ref. SJ992 225

10mins from M6/J13 on
A513 Stafford/
Lichfield Road.

Rail: Stafford 6m.

Taxi: Anthony's
01785 252255

CONFERENCE/FUNCTION		
ROOM	SIZE	MAX CAPACITY
Banqueting Hall	15 x 6.5m	65
Saloon	15 x 6m	80
Conference Suite	6 x 6m	35
Granary	5.5 x 9.5m	60
Blue Drawing Rm	6.5 x 8m	20
Tower of the Winds	6.5 x 6.5m	20

SHUGBOROUGH
Stafford

SHUGBOROUGH is the magnificent 900-acre ancestral home of the 5th Earl of Lichfield, who is known world-wide as Patrick Lichfield the leading photographer.

The 18th century mansion house contains a fine collection of ceramics, silver, paintings and French furniture. Part of the house is still lived in by the Earl and his family.

Visitors can enjoy the splendid 18-acre Grade I Historic Garden with its Edwardian Rose Garden and terraces. A unique collection of neo-classical monuments by James Stuart can be found in the parkland which also includes walks and trails.

Other attractions include the County Museum which is housed in the original servants' quarters. The working laundry, kitchens and

brewhouse have all been lovingly restored and are staffed by costumed guides who show how the servants lived and worked over 100 years ago.

Shugborough Park Farm is a Georgian working farm which features an agricultural museum, restored working corn mill and is also a rare breeds centre. In the farmhouse kitchen visitors can see bread baked in brick ovens and in the dairy, cheese and butter being made.

Throughout the year a lively collection of themed tours are in operation for the coach market and an award-winning educational programme for schools. From April to December an exciting events programme is in operation.

Shugborough is an ideal venue for weddings, conferences, corporate activity days and product launches.

Private and corporate entertainment, conferences, product launches and dinner parties. Filming and event location. Over 900 acres of parkland and gardens available for hire. Themed activities. No photography in house.

Catering for special functions/ conferences.

Visitors may alight at entrance before parking. WCs. Stairclimber to house. Batricars available. Disabled-friendly picnic tables available. Taped tours.

Licensed tearoom/café seating 95, also tearoom at Farm seats 30. Prior notice for large groups.

Tour time 1hr. Themed tours as required. Groups of 15+. Please telephone for details.

Ample car and coach parking. Discounted vouchers for coach drivers' meals available.

Award-winning educational packages. Curriculum-related. Contact Sales & Development Officer.

In grounds, on leads.

Civil Wedding Licence.

OPENING TIMES

31 March - 30 September
Daily: 11am - 5pm except
Mondays (open holiday
Mondays).

Pre-booked parties
throughout the year.

ADMISSION

Each attraction
Adults......................£4.50
Conc*.....................£3.00

Voyager Tickets
(all 3 sites)
Adult.......................£9.00
Conc*.....................£6.00
Family....................£22.00

Gardens and Parkland
Cars........................£2.00
Coaches..................Free

* Concessions for children (under 5yrs Free), OAPs, Students, registered unemployed & groups.

** NT Members free admission to Mansion House, Museum and Farm.

SPECIAL EVENTS

- **APR 21/22:**
Gamekeepers' Fair.
- **MAY 26/27/28:**
Spring Craft Fair.
- **JUNE 30, JULY 1:**
Gardeners' Weekend.
- **AUGUST 5:**
Victorian Street Market.
- **AUGUST 25/26/27:**
Summer Craft Fair.
- **SEPTEMBER 9**
Heavy Horse and Harvest.
- **DEC 4 - 7: (2001)**
Shugborough Victorian
Christmas Evening.

THE ANCIENT HIGH HOUSE

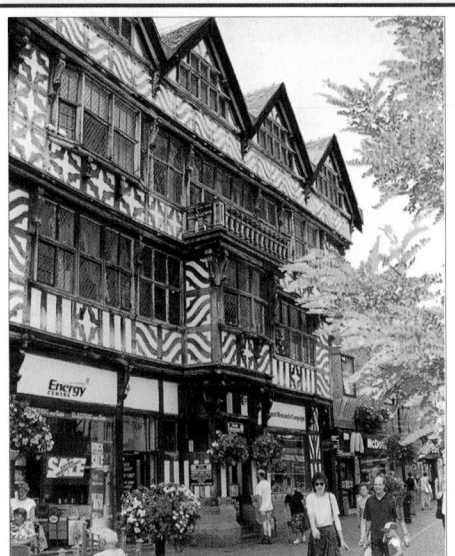

GREENGATE STREET, STAFFORD ST16 2JA

Owner: Stafford Borough Council   *Contact:* K Stringer

Tel: 01785 619131   **Fax:** 01785 619132   **e-mail:** ahh@staffordbc.gov.uk

This building is the largest timber-framed town house in England. Built in 1595 by the Dorrington family, this house is still very impressive on Stafford's skyline. It was lived in by Richard Sneyd, a member of one of Staffordshire's greatest families when King Charles I stayed here in 1642. It is now a registered museum with displays set out as period room settings which present aspects of the house's history. The Staffordshire Yeomanry Museum is on the top floor.

Location: OS Ref. SJ922 232. Town centre.

Opening Times: All year: Mon - Sat, 10am - 5pm. Check BHs.

Admission: Please telephone for details.

 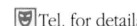 Not suitable. Guide dogs only. Tel. for details.

BIDDULPH GRANGE GARDEN

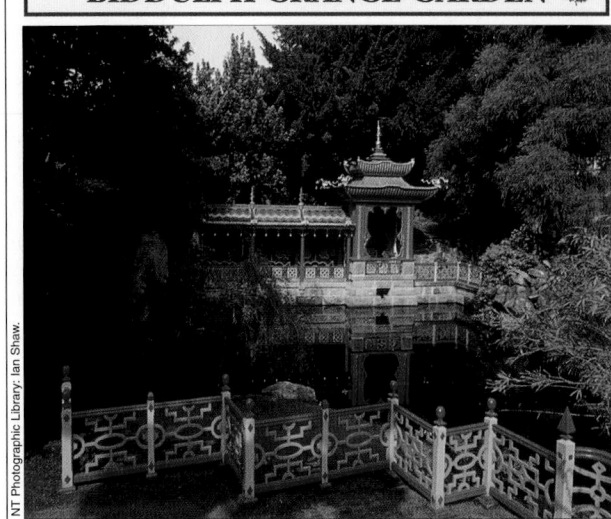

NT Photographic Library: Ian Shaw.

GRANGE ROAD, BIDDULPH, STOKE-ON-TRENT ST8 7SD

Owner: The National Trust   *Contact:* The Garden Office

Tel: 01782 517999   **Fax:** 01782 510624

A rare and exciting survival of a High Victorian garden, restored by the National Trust. The garden is divided into a series of themed gardens within a garden, with a Chinese temple, Egyptian court, pinetum, dahlia walk, glen and many other settings. Difficult uneven levels, unsuitable for wheelchairs.

Location: OS Ref. SJ891 592. E of A527, 3½ m SE of Congleton, 8m N of Stoke-on-Trent.

Opening Times: 28 Mar - 4 Nov: Wed - Fri, 12 noon - 6pm. Sats, Suns & BH Mons, 11am - 6pm. Closed Good Fri. 10 Nov - 17 Dec: Sats & Suns, 12 noon- 4pm or dusk if earlier.

Admission: Adult £4.40, Child £2.30, Family (2+2) £11. Nov and Dec: Adult £2, Child £1, Family £5. Joint ticket with Little Moreton Hall: Adult £6.75, Child £3.30, Family £16.50.

 Unsuitable for wheelchairs. In car park, on leads.

BARLASTON HALL

Tel: 01782 372749   **Fax:** 01782 372391

Barlaston, Staffordshire ST12 9AT

Owner/Contact: Mr & Mrs James Hall

Barlaston Hall is a mid-18th century Palladian villa, attributed to Sir Robert Taylor. Extensively restored during the 1990s with the help of English Heritage. The four public rooms open to visitors contain some fine examples of 18th century plasterwork.

Location: OS Ref. SJ895 391. ½ m E of A34 between Stoke and Stafford.

Opening Times: By appointment to groups of 10-30. Admission includes refreshments. Please write to the above address or fax giving details of numbers, possible dates and a contact telephone number. Recorded message with other opening times on above number.

Admission: Pre-arranged groups: £3.50.

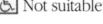 No photography.   Not suitable. Limited.

CHILLINGTON HALL

Tel: 01902 850236   **Fax:** 01902 850768

Codsall Wood, Wolverhampton, Staffordshire WV8 1RE

Owner/Contact: Mr & Mrs J W Giffard   **e-mail:** mrsplod@globalnet.co.uk

Georgian red brick house with fine saloon by Soane set in 'Capability' Brown park having one of the largest lakes created by Brown. Extensive woodland walks.

Location: OS Ref. SJ864 067. 2m S of Brewood off A449. 4m NW of M54/J2.

Opening Times: Easter Sun; Suns prior to both May BHs; Jul: Thurs; Aug: Thurs, Fris & Suns, 2 - 5pm.

Admission: Adult £3, Child £1.50. Grounds only: half price.

Partially suitable. Obligatory. In grounds, on leads.

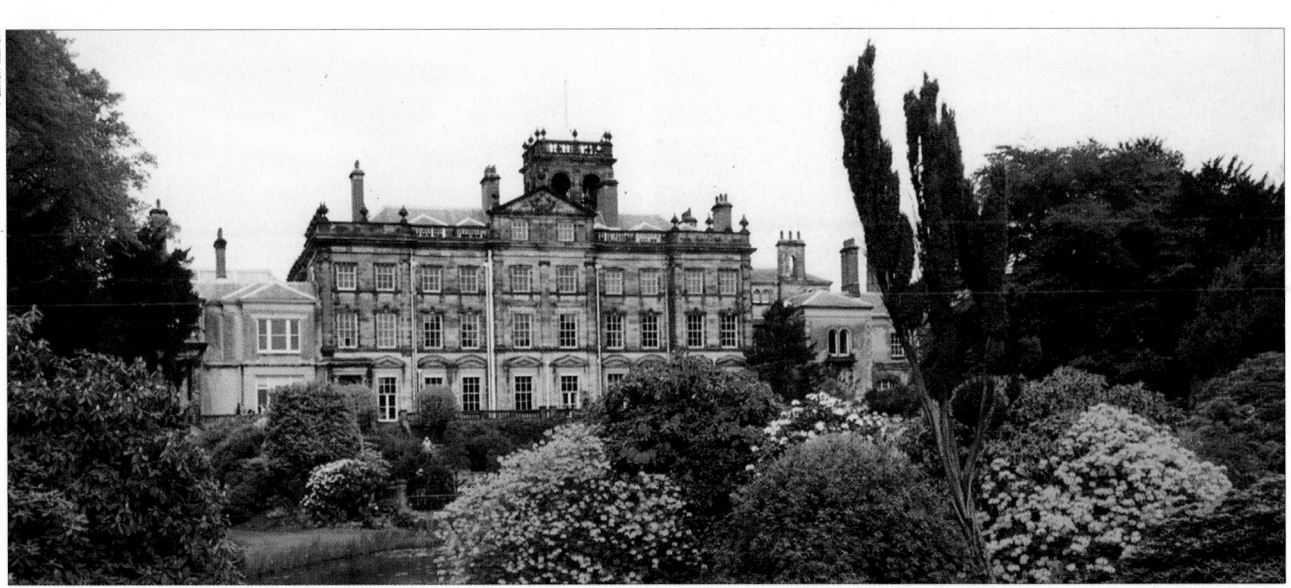

Patrick Lane.

Biddulph Grange Garden, Staffordshire.

THE DOROTHY CLIVE GARDEN

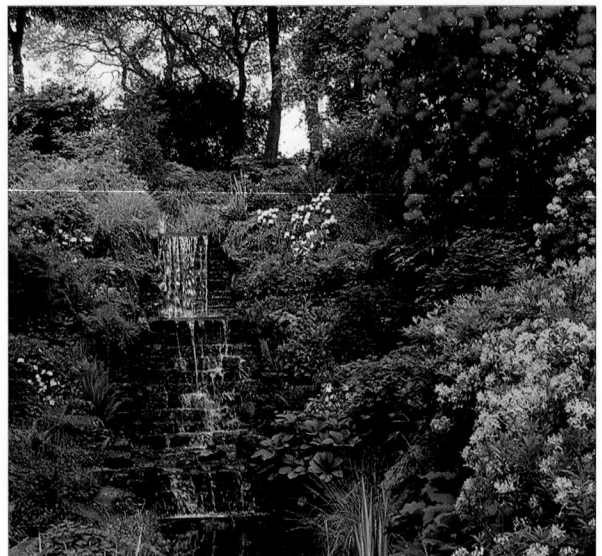

WILLOUGHBRIDGE, MARKET DRAYTON, SHROPSHIRE TF9 4EU

Owner: Willoughbridge Garden Trust   *Contact: Mrs M Grime*

Tel: 01630 647237 **Fax:** 01630 647902

The Dorothy Clive Garden accommodates a wide range of choice and unusual plants providing year round interest. Features include a quarry with spectacular waterfall, flower borders, a scree and water garden. Tearoom serving home-baked hot and cold snacks throughout the day.

Location: OS Ref. SJ753 400. A51, 2m S of Woore, 3m from Bridgemere.

Opening Times: 1 Apr - 31 Oct: daily, 10am - 5.30pm.

Admission: Adult £3.20, Child (11-16yrs) £1, (under 11yrs Free), OAP £2.70. Groups (20+) £2.70.

 In grounds on leads.

FORD GREEN HALL

Tel: 01782 233195 **Fax:** 01782 233194

e-mail: ford-green-hall@stoke.gov.uk

Ford Green Road, Smallthorne, Stoke-on-Trent ST6 1NG

Owner: Stoke-on-Trent City Council   **Contact:** Angela Graham

A 17th century house, home to the Ford family for two centuries. The hall has been designated a museum with an outstanding collection of original and reproduction period furniture, ceramics and textiles. There is a Tudor-style garden. The museum has an award-winning education service and regular events.

Location: OS Ref. SJ887 508. NE of Stoke-on-Trent on B551, signposted from A500.

Opening Times: All year: (closed 25 Dec - 1 Jan), Sun - Thurs, 1 - 5pm.

Admission: Adult £1.50, Conc. £1. Special group packages (must book, min 10).

 Partially suitable. WC. 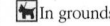 In grounds, on leads.
Telephone for details

SAMUEL JOHNSON BIRTHPLACE MUSEUM

Tel: 01543 264972

Breadmarket Street, Lichfield, Staffordshire WS13 6LG   **Fax:** 01543 414779

Owner: Lichfield City Council   **Contact:** Annette French

The house where Samuel's father had a bookshop is now a museum with many of Johnson's personal belongings.

Location: OS Ref. SK115 094. Breadmarket Street, Lichfield.

Opening Times: Daily: 10.30am - 4.30pm. Closed Suns, Nov - Jan.

Admission: Adult £2, Child/Conc. £1.10, Family £5.40. Groups: £1.10. (2000 prices).

LICHFIELD CATHEDRAL

Tel: 01543 306240 **Fax:** 01543 306109

Lichfield, Staffordshire WS13 7LD   **e-mail:** enquiries@lichfield-cathedral.org

Contact: Canon A Barnard

The only medieval cathedral with three spires, in the heart of an historic city. Meet a living Christian community, 1300 years old. See the 8th century illuminated 'Lichfield Gospels' manuscript; superb 16th century Flemish glass; sculpture by Chantrey & Epstein, modern silver collection and half-timbered buildings of Vicars' Close.

Location: OS Ref. SK115 097. Approach from A38 and A51, N from M42 and M6. N of city centre.

Opening Times: All year: daily.

Admission: Suggested donation, £3 per adult.

MOSELEY OLD HALL

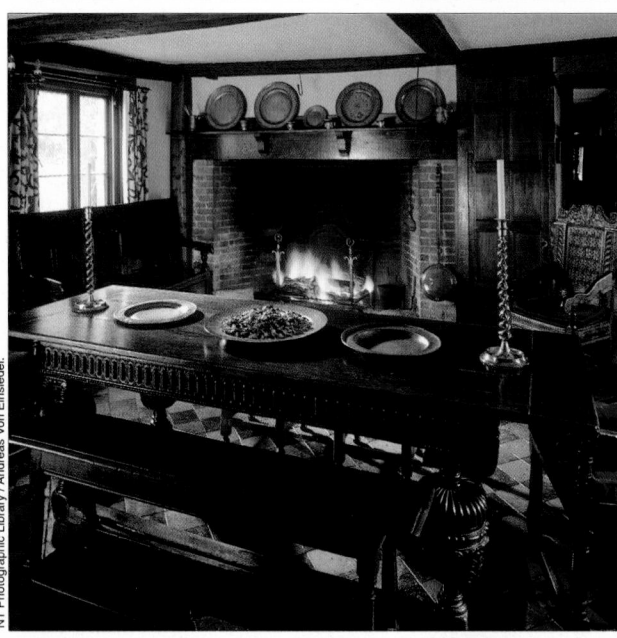

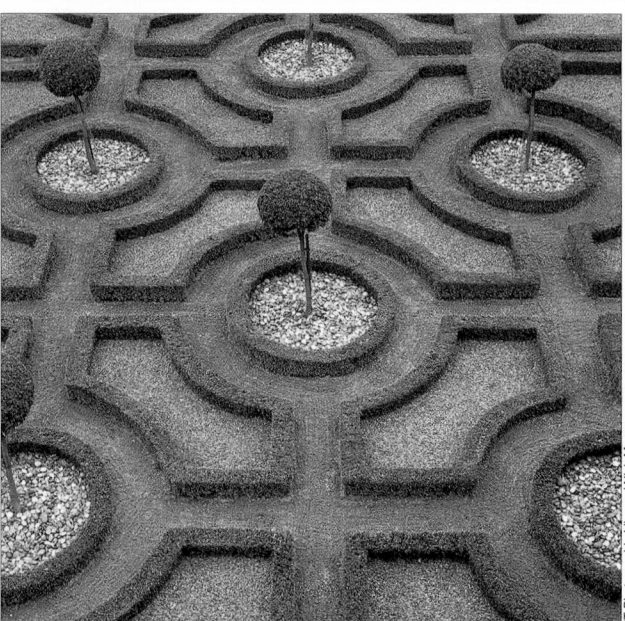

FORDHOUSES, WOLVERHAMPTON WV10 7HY

Owner: The National Trust   **Contact:** *The Property Manager*

Tel/Fax: 01902 782808

An Elizabethan house with later alterations. Charles II hid here after the Battle of Worcester. The bed in which he slept is on view as well as the hiding place he used. An exhibition retells the story of the King's dramatic escape from Cromwell's troops, and there are optional, free guided tours. The garden has been reconstructed in 17th century style with formal box parterre, only 17th century plants are grown. The property is a Sandford Education Award Winner.

Location: OS Ref. SJ932 044. 4m N of Wolverhampton between A449 and A460.

Opening Times: 24 Mar - 4 Nov: Sats, Suns, Weds, BH Mons & following Tues. 11 Nov - 16 Dec: Suns (guided tour only). Times: Mar - end Oct: 1.30 - 5.30pm (garden & tearoom from 1pm). BH Mons: 11am - 5pm. Nov & Dec: 1.30 - 4pm. 4 Mar: special opening. Pre-booked groups at other times including evening tours.

Admission: Adult £4.10, Child £2.05, Family £10.25.

Ground floor & grounds suitable. WC.
Tearoom in 18th century barn.   Guide dogs only.

SANDON HALL

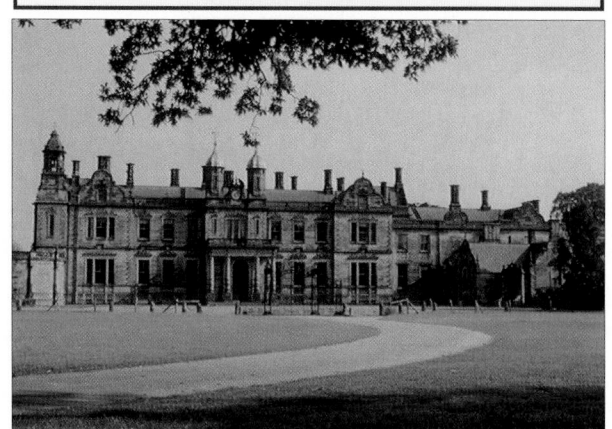

SANDON, STAFFORDSHIRE ST18 OBZ

Owner: *The Earl of Harrowby*   **Contact:** *Michael Bosson*

Tel/Fax: 01889 508004   **e-mail:** info@sandonhall.co.uk

Ancestral seat of the Earls of Harrowby, conveniently located in the heart of Staffordshire. The imposing neo-Jacobean house was rebuilt by William Burn in 1854. Set amidst 400 acres of glorious parkland, Sandon, for all its grandeur and elegance, is first and foremost a home. The family museum which opened in 1994 has received considerable acclaim, and incorporates several of the State Rooms. The 50 acre landscaped gardens feature magnificent trees and are especially beautiful in May and autumn.

Location: OS Ref. SJ957 287. 5m NE of Stafford on the A51, between Stone and Lichfield, easy access from M6/J14.

Opening Times: All year: for events, functions and for pre-booked visits to the museum and gardens. Evening tours by special arrangement. Closed Christmas Day, Boxing Day and New Year's Day.

Admission: Museum: Adult £4, Child £3, OAP £3.50. Gardens: Adult £1.50, Child £1, OAP £1. NB. Max group size 22 or 45 if combined Museum and Gardens.

Grounds suitable. By arrangement. In grounds, on leads.

STAFFORD CASTLE & VISITOR CENTRE

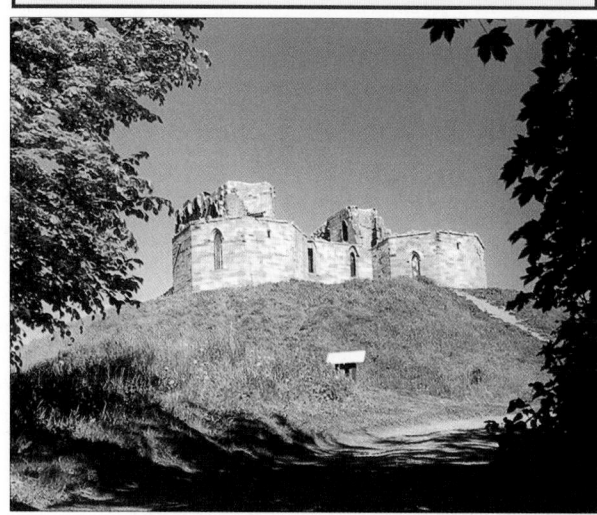

NEWPORT ROAD, STAFFORD ST16 1DJ

Owner: *Stafford Borough Council*   **Contact:** *N Thomas*

Tel/Fax: 01785 257698

This impressive site was once a Norman motte and bailey castle. Earl Ralph, a founder member of the Order of the Garter, spent part of his fortune building a stone keep in 1348. During the Civil War, the castle was successfully defended, but eventually demolished. The current building was erected in the early 19th century and fell into ruin through this century. The Visitor Centre displays artefacts found during recent excavations. An imaginative audio-visual presentation describes the castle's mixed fortunes.

Location: OS Ref. SJ904 220. On N side of A518, 1½ m WSW of town centre.

Opening Times: Apr - Oct: Tue - Sun, 10am - 5pm. Nov - Mar: Tue - Sun, 10am - 4pm.

Admission: Please telephone for details.

Grounds suitable. WC. In grounds, on leads. Tel. for details.

SHUGBOROUGH    See page 338 for full page entry.

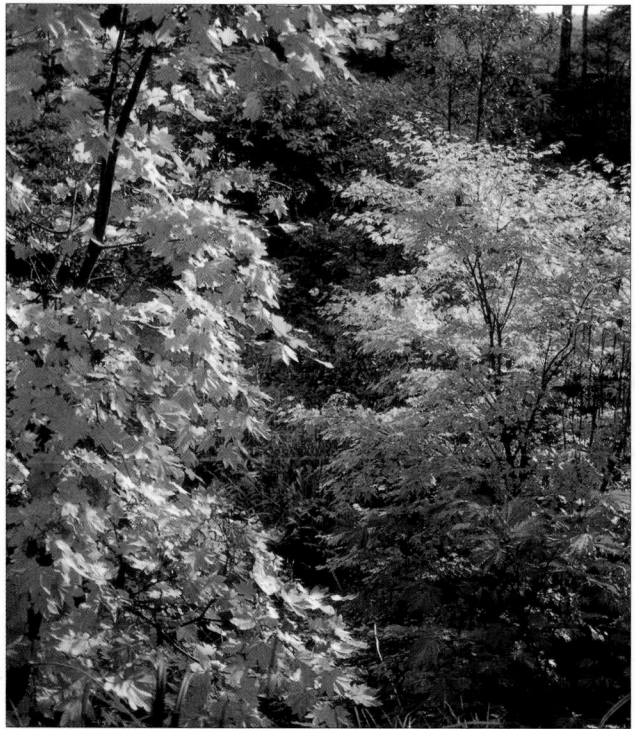

Dorothy Clive Garden, Staffordshire.

TAMWORTH CASTLE   **Tel:** 01827 709626   **Fax:** 01827 709630

The Holloway, Tamworth, Staffordshire B79 7LR

Owner: Tamworth Borough Council   **Contact:** Mrs Esme Ballard

Dramatic Norman castle with 15 rooms open to the public, spanning 800 years of history. Attractive town centre park with floral terraces.

Location: OS Ref. SK206 038. Town centre off A51.

Opening Times: All year: Mon - Sat, 10am - 5.30pm. Suns, 2 - 5.30pm. Last adm. 4.30pm. Please check opening times after 1 Nov. (2000 dates.)

Admission: Please telephone for 2001 prices.

TUTBURY CASTLE   **Tel:** 01283 812129

Tutbury, Staffordshire

Owner: The Duchy of Lancaster   **Contact:** Lesley Smith

Remains of a large motte and bailey castle overlooking the Dove Valley. Also recreated Tudor Garden/Herbery. Now possible to go into castle. Often costumed guides.

Location: OS Ref. SK210 291. W side of Tutbury off A50 Tutbury - Barton road.

Opening Times: Apr - Oct: Wed - Suns, 11am - 5pm.

Admission: Adult £3, Child/OAP £1.50.

WALL ROMAN SITE (Letocetum)   **Tel:** 01543 480768

Watling Street, Nr Lichfield, Staffordshire WS14 0AW

Owner: English Heritage   **Contact:** The Custodian

The remains of a staging post alongside Watling Street. Foundations of an Inn and a Bath House can be seen and there is a display of finds in the site museum.

Location: OS139 Ref. SK099 067. Off A5 at Wall, nr Lichfield.

Opening Times: 1 Apr - 31 Oct: daily, 10am - 6pm (5pm in Oct).

Admission: Adult £2.40, Child £1.20, Conc. £1.80. 15% discount for groups (11+). (2000 prices.)

Tel. for details.

IZAAK WALTON'S COTTAGE

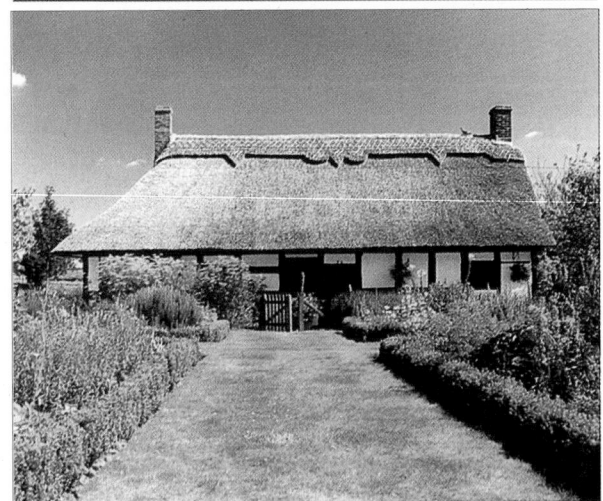

WORSTON LANE, SHALLOWFORD, Nr STAFFORD ST15 0PA

Owner: Stafford Borough Council   *Contact:* S Bailey

Tel/Fax: 01785 760278

Thatched, timber-framed cottage in the heart of the Staffordshire countryside. Bequeathed by Izaak Walton, author of the *Compleat Angler*, it has displays on the history of angling. Ground floor rooms are set out in 17th century style.

Location: OS Ref. SJ876 293. Shallowford, nr Great Bridgeford, 6m N of Stafford.

Opening Times: Apr - Oct: Wed - Sun & BHs, 1 - 5pm.

Admission: Please telephone for details.

[icons] By arrangement. P Guide dogs only.

SPECIAL EVENTS:
Events programme during the summer. Please telephone for details.

WHITMORE HALL

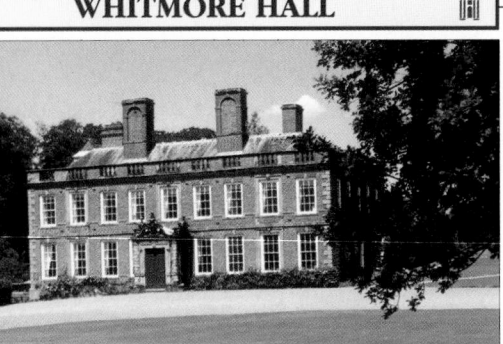

WHITMORE, NEWCASTLE-UNDER-LYME ST5 5HW

Owner: Mr Guy Cavenagh-Mainwaring   *Contact:* Mr Michael Cavenagh-Thornhill

Tel: 01782 680478 **Fax:** 01782 680906

Whitmore Hall is a Grade I listed building, designated as a house of outstanding architectural and historical interest, and is a fine example of a small Carolinian manor house, although parts of the hall date back to a much earlier period. The hall has beautifully proportioned light rooms, curving staircase and landing. There are some good family portraits to be seen with a continuous line, from 1624 to the present day. It has been the family seat, for over 900 years, of the Cavenagh-Mainwarings who are direct descendants of the original Norman owners. The interior of the hall has recently been refurbished and is in fine condition. The grounds include a beautiful home park with a lime avenue leading to the house, as well as landscaped gardens encompassing an early Victorian summer house. One of the outstanding features of Whitmore is the extremely rare example of a late Elizabethan stable block, the ground floor is part cobbled and has nine oak-carved stalls.

Location: OS Ref. SJ811 413. On A53 Newcastle - Market Drayton Road, 3m from M6/J15.

Opening Times: 1 May - 31 Aug: Tues, Weds, 2 - 5pm. Groups of 15+ by arrangement outside normal opening days. (between 1 Apr - 31 Aug). Teas arranged for groups over 15.

Admission: Adult £3, Child 50p.

[icon] Ground floor & grounds suitable. P [icon]

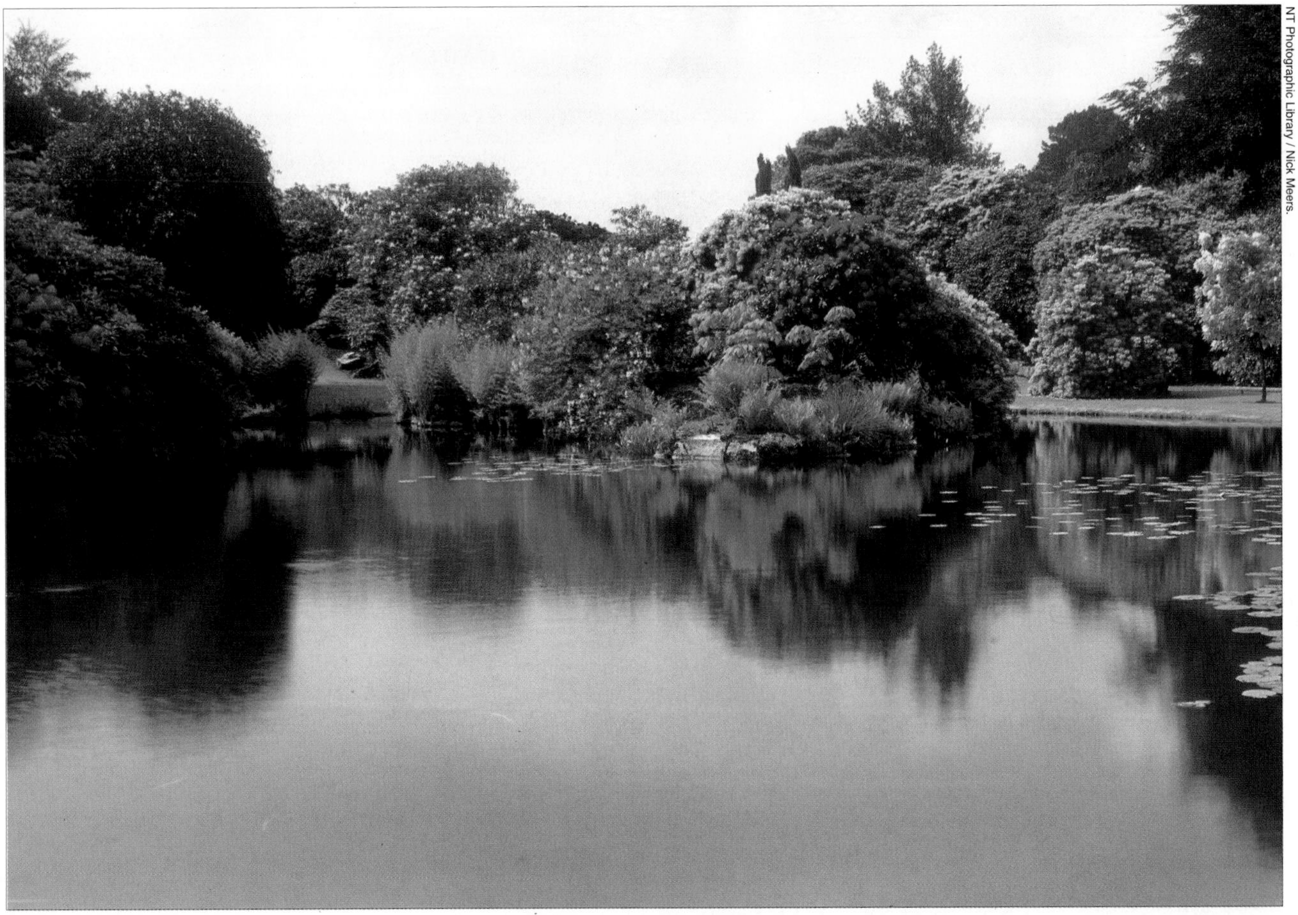

Shugborough, Staffordshire.

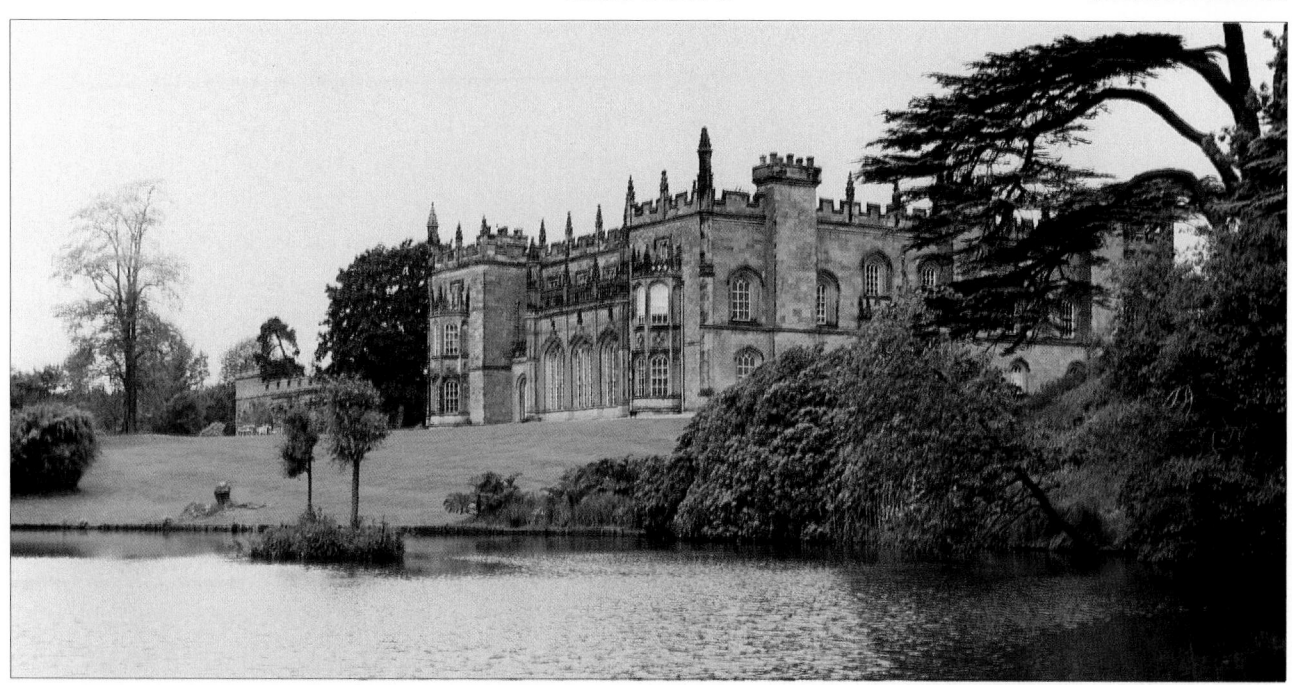

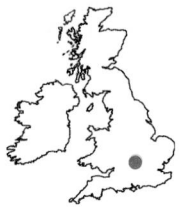

Owner:
The Viscount Daventry

CONTACT

Colonel CMG Hendy OBE
Arbury Hall
Nuneaton
Warwickshire CV10 7PT

Tel: 024 7638 2804

Fax: 024 7664 1147

LOCATION

OS Ref. SP335 893

London, M1, M6/J3
(A444 to Nuneaton),
2m SW of Nuneaton.
1m W of A444.

Chester A51, A34, M6
(from J14 to J3), 2¹/₂ hrs.
Nuneaton 10 mins.

London 2 hrs, Birmingham
¹/₂ hr, Coventry 20 mins.

Bus: Nuneaton 3m.

Rail: Nuneaton Station 3m.

Air: Birmingham
International 17m.

CONFERENCE/FUNCTION		
ROOM	SIZE	MAX CAPACITY
Dining Room	35' x 28'	120
Saloon	35' x 30'	70
Long Gallery	48' x 11'	40
Stables Tearooms	31' x 18'	80

ARBURY HALL
Nuneaton

ARBURY HALL has been the seat of the Newdegate family for over 400 years and is the ancestral home of Viscount Daventry. This Tudor/Elizabethan House was gothicised by Sir Roger Newdegate in the 18th century and is regarded as the 'Gothic Gem' of the Midlands. The Hall contains a fine collection of both oriental and Chelsea porcelain, portraits by Lely, Reynolds, Devis and Romney and furniture by Chippendale and Hepplewhite. The principal rooms, with their soaring fan vaulted ceilings and plunging pendants and filigree tracery, stand as a most breathtaking and complete example of early Gothic Revival architecture and provide a unique and fascinating venue for corporate entertaining, product launches, receptions, fashion shoots and activity days. Exclusive use of this historic Hall, its gardens and parkland is offered to clients. The Hall stands in the middle of beautiful parkland with landscaped gardens of rolling lawns, lakes and winding wooded walks. Spring flowers are profuse and in June rhododendrons, azaleas and giant wisteria provide a beautiful environment for the visitor.

George Eliot, the novelist, was born on the estate and Arbury Hall 'and Sir Roger Newdegate were immortalised in her book 'Scenes of Clerical Life'.

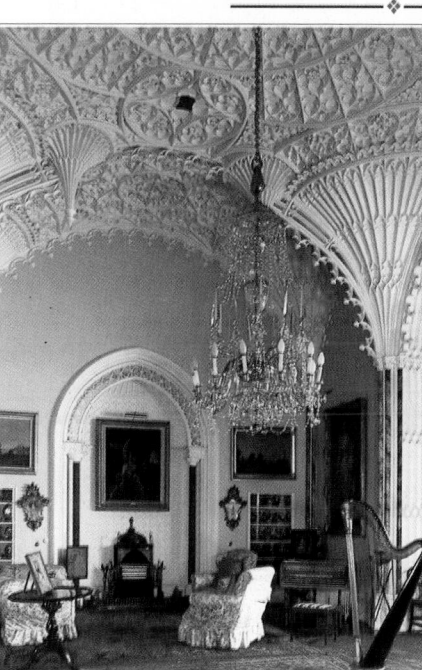

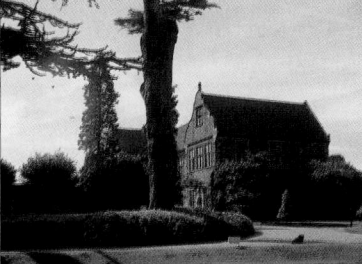

Corporate hospitality, film location, small conferences, product launches and promotions, marquee functions, clay pigeon shooting, archery and other sporting activities, grand piano in Saloon, helicopter landing site. No cameras or video recorders.

Exclusive lunches and dinners for corporate parties in dining room, max. 50, buffets 120.

Visitors may alight at the Hall's main entrance. Parking in allocated areas. Ramp access to main hall.

By arrangement for groups.

Obligatory. Tour time: 1hr.

200 cars and 3 coaches 250 yards from house. Follow tourist signs. Approach map available for coach drivers.

Welcome, must book. School room available.

In gardens on leads. Guide dogs only in house.

OPENING TIMES

ALL YEAR

Open all year on Tues, Weds & Thurs only, for corporate events.

Pre-booked visits to the Hall and Gardens for groups of 25+ on Tues, Weds & Thurs (until 4pm) from Easter to the end of September.

Hall & Gardens open 2 - 5pm on BH weekends only (Suns & Mons) Easter - September.

ADMISSION

SUMMER

Hall & Gardens
Adult £5.00
Child (up to 14 yrs.)...£3.00
Family (2+2) £12.00

Gardens Only
Adult £4.00
Child (up to 14 yrs.)...£3.00

Groups (25+)
Adult £4.50

Special rates for pre-booked groups of 25+.

SPECIAL EVENTS

Please telephone for details.

West Midlands England

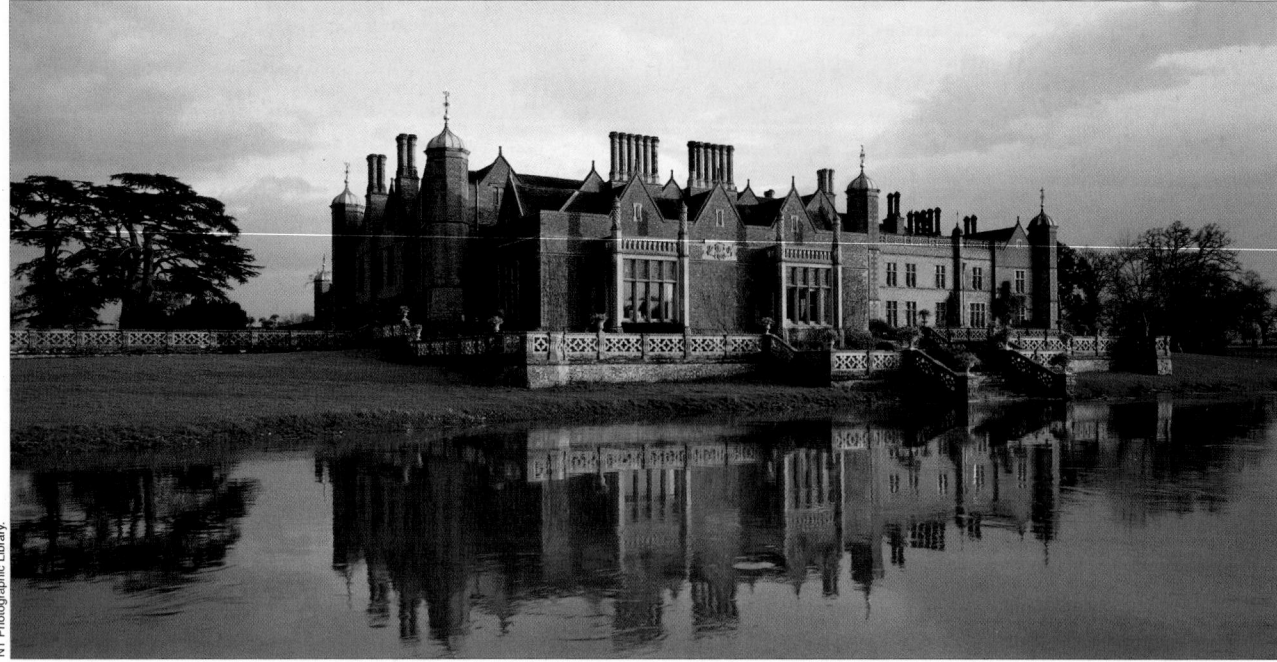

NT Photographic Library.

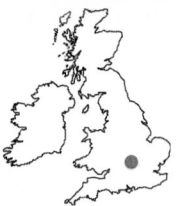

Owner: The National Trust

CONTACT

Linda Griffin
Charlecote Park
Warwick
CV35 9ER

Tel: 01789 470277

Fax: 01789 470544

e-mail: charlecote@
smtp.ntrust.org.uk

LOCATION

OS151 Ref. SP263 564

1m W of
Wellesbourne, 5m E of
Stratford-upon-Avon.

Rail: Stratford & Warwick.

Air: Birmingham.

CHARLECOTE PARK
Wellesbourne

Owned by the Lucy family since 1247, Sir Thomas Lucy built the house in 1558. Now, much altered, it is shown as it would have been a century ago, complete with Victorian kitchen, brewhouse and family carriages in the coach house and (new in 2000) two bedrooms, a dressing room and the main staircase. A video of Victorian life can be viewed. The formal gardens and informal parkland lie to the north and west of the house, Red Fallow Deer can be seen in the parkland also Jacob Sheep which were brought to Charlecote in 1756 by Sir Thomas Lucy. It is reputed that William Shakespeare was apprehended for poaching c1583 and Sir Thomas Lucy is said to be the basis of Justice Shallow in Shakespeare's '*Merry Wives of Windsor*'.

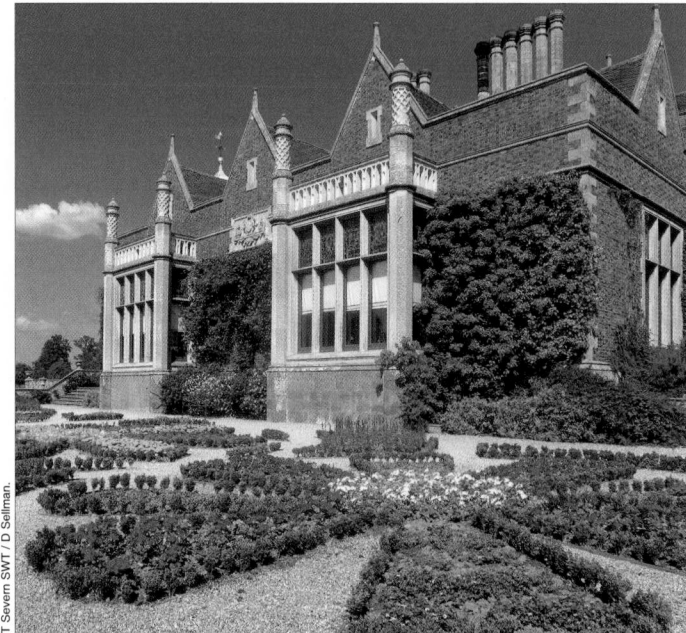

NT Severn SWT / D Sellman.

OPENING TIMES

House & Grounds
24 Mar - 4 Nov: daily except Weds & Thurs.
Open Good Fri.
Jul & Aug: daily except Thurs.
House: 12 noon - 5pm.
Grounds: 11am - 6pm.

Grounds only
3 Feb - 18 Mar: Sats & Suns, 1 - 4.30pm including Brewhouse, Victorian Kitchens & Carriage Collection.

Park, Shop & Tearoom
3 Feb - 18 Mar: Sats & Suns, 1 - 4.30pm.

ADMISSION

Adult £5.60
Child (5-16).............£2.80
Family £14.00
Groups
Adult £4.60
Under 5s Free.
Grounds only............£3.00

ℹ️ Children's play area.

🛍️

🍸

♿ Wheelchairs, braille guide.

🍽 Licensed.

🍴 Licensed. Open as grounds: 11am - 5.30pm.

🎭 Evening guided tours for booked groups May - Sept: Tues, 7.30 - 9.30pm (£6.50 including NT members). Minimum charge £150.

🅿️ Limited for coaches.

🛏 By arrangement. Resource book.

🐕 On leads, in car park only.

🎭 Tel. for details.

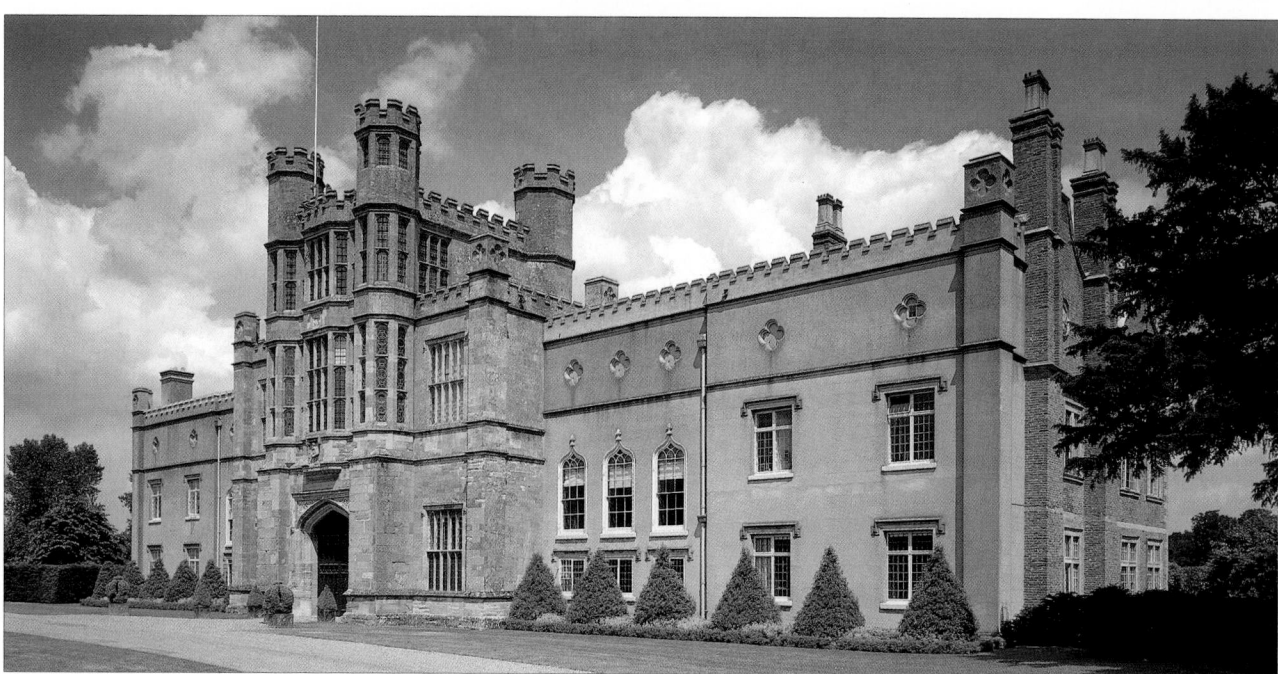

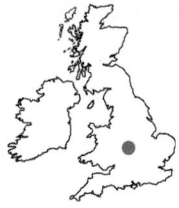

Owner:
Mrs C Throckmorton

CONTACT

Mr A McLaren
Coughton Court
Alcester
Warwickshire
B49 5JA

Tel: 01789 400777

Fax: 01789 765544

Visitor Information:
01789 762435

e-mail: carol@
throckmortons.co.uk

LOCATION

OS Ref. SP080 604

Located on A435,
2m N of Alcester,
8m NW of
Stratford-on-Avon.
18m from Birmingham City
Centre.

Rail: Birmingham
International

Air: Birmingham
International

CONFERENCE/FUNCTION		
ROOM	SIZE	MAX CAPACITY
Dining Rm	45' x 27'	60
Saloon	60' x 36'	100

The Saloon, which has particularly
good acoustics, is often used for music
recording.

COUGHTON COURT
Alcester

COUGHTON COURT has been the home of the Thockmortons since the 15th century and the family still live here today. The magnificent Tudor gatehouse was built around 1530 with the north and south wings completed 10 or 20 years later. The gables and the first storey of these wings are of typical mid-16th century half-timbered work.

Of particular interest to visitors is the Thockmorton family history from Tudor times to the present generation. On view are family portraits through the centuries with other family memorabilia and recent photographs. Also furniture, tapestries and porcelain.

A long-standing Roman Catholic theme runs through the family history as the Thockmortons have maintained their Catholic religion until the present day. The house has a strong connection with the Gunpowder Plot and also suffered damage during the Civil War. Exhibitions on the Gunpowder Plot as well as Children's Clothes (included in price).

Gardens

The house stands in 25 acres of gardens and grounds along with two churches and a lake. A formal garden was constructed in 1992 with designs based on an Elizabethan knot garden in the courtyard. A new $1^1/2$ acre garden in the old walled garden opened in 1996. Visitors can also enjoy a specially created walk beside the River Arrow and a new bog garden opened in 1997.

Receptions, special dinners, filming, buffets, business meetings, fairs and garden parties. The excellent acoustics of the Saloon make it ideal for concerts, especially chamber music. Marquees can be erected on the large lawn area, grand piano. No photography or stiletto heels in house.

Buffet or sit-down meals can be provided by arrangement, in the Dining Room and Saloon. In-house catering can be arranged for other events. Wedding receptions welcome.

Ground floor of house and gardens. WC.

Licensed restaurant, 11am - 5.30pm. Capacity 100 inside and 60 outside.

By arrangement.

Unlimited for cars plus 4 coaches.

Car park only.

House

17 - 31 March: Sats & Suns
Apr - Sept: Wed - Sun
11.30am - 5pm
(BH Mons open 11am).

Also open BH Mon & Tue plus Tues in Aug (Closed Good Fri & Sat 23 Jun).

October: Sats & Suns (closes 28 Oct for winter).

Gardens, Restaurant, Gift Shop & Plant Centre: 11am - 5.30 on house open days.

Last admission to House and Gardens including Walled Garden, 4.30pm.

Grounds

As house: 11am - 5.30pm.

ADMISSION

House & Gardens

Adult £6.95
Child* (5-15yrs) £3.45
Family (2+4)...........£21.50
Booked Groups (15+)
Adult £5.60
Child £2.80

Gardens only

Adult £5.10
Child* (5-15yrs) £2.55
Family (2+4)...........£15.75
Groups (15+)
per person £4.10

*under 5yrs Free.
NT members Free
admission to house,
£2.50 charge to walled garden.

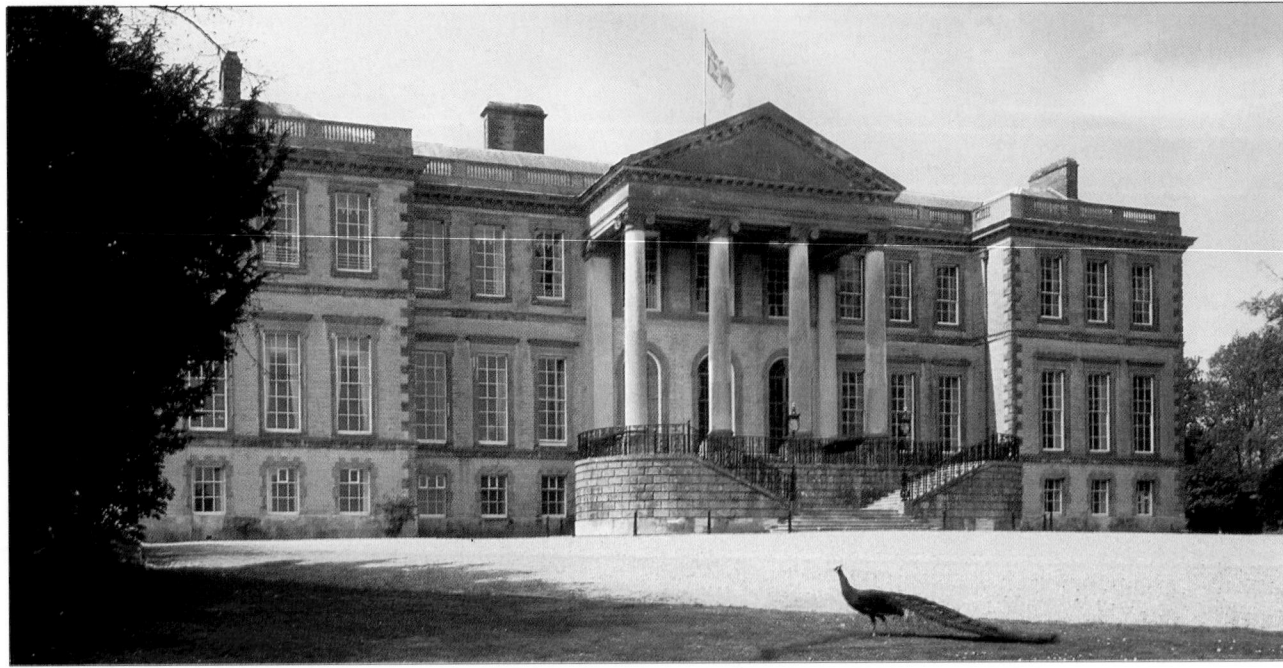

RAGLEY HALL
Alcester

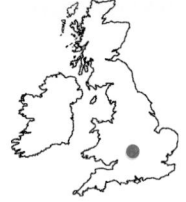

Owner:
The Marquess of Hertford

CONTACT

Mrs Julie Timms
Ragley Hall
Alcester
Warwickshire
B49 5NJ

Tel: 01789 762090

Fax: 01789 764791

e-mail:
ragley.hall@virginnet.co.uk

LOCATION

OS Ref. SP073 555

Off A46/A435 1m SW of
Alcester.
From London 100m, M40
via Oxford and
Stratford-on-Avon.

Rail: Evesham
Station 9m.

Air: Birmingham
International 20m.

Taxi: 007 Taxi
01789 414007

RAGLEY HALL, home of the Marquess and Marchioness of Hertford and their family, was designed by Robert Hooke in 1680 and is one of the earliest and loveliest of England's great Palladian houses. The perfect symmetry of its architecture remains unchanged except for the massive portico added by Wyatt in 1780.

In 1750, when Francis Seymour owned Ragley, James Gibbs designed the magnificent baroque plasterwork of the Great Hall. On completion, Francis filled the Hall with French and English furniture and porcelain and had portraits of himself and his sons painted by

Sir Joshua Reynolds. Notable also is the mural, by Graham Rust, in the south Staircase Hall which was completed in 1983.

PARK, GARDENS & GROUNDS

Ragley is a working estate with more than 6000 acres of land, the house is situated in 27 acres of gardens that were designed by 'Capability' Brown, and include the beautiful Rose Garden. Near to the hall are the working stables, housing a carriage collection dating back to 1760 and a display of assorted historical equestrian equipment. For children there is the adventure playground and maze situated by the lake.

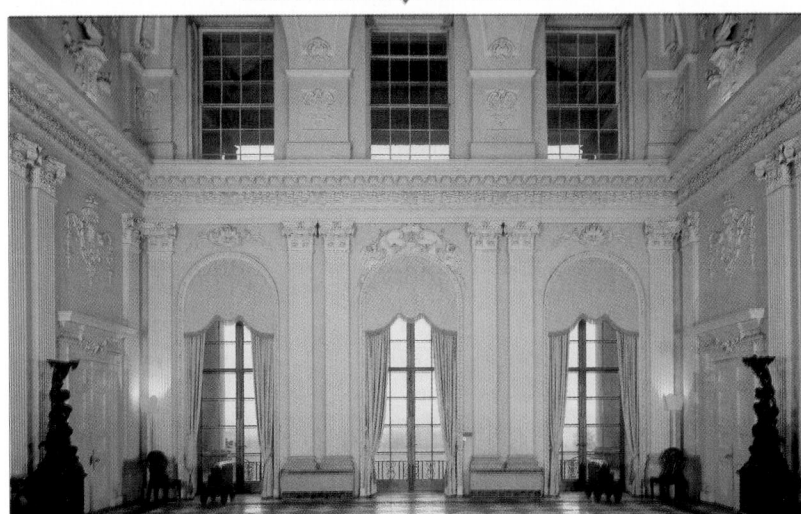

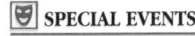

CONFERENCE/FUNCTION

ROOM	SIZE	MAX CAPACITY
Great Hall	70' x 40'	150
Red Saloon	30' x 40'	40
Green Drawing Rm	20' x 30'	30
Hertford	45' x 22'	60
Seymour	25' x 23'	30

Product launches, dinners and activity days, film and photographic location, park, lake and picnic area, marquee. No photography or camcorders in the house.

Private and corporate entertainment, wedding receptions, conferences, seminars. Telephone for details.

Visitors may alight at entrance. Parking in allocated areas. WCs. Lifts.

Licensed tearooms 11am - 5pm. Groups must book.

Licensed.

By arrangement.

Coach drivers admitted free and receive info pack and luncheon voucher. Please advise of group visits.

Welcome, £2.50 per head. Teachers' packs and work modules on request. Adventure Wood and Woodland Walk.

In grounds, on leads.

OPENING TIMES

9 April - 30 September
(House, Park & Gardens
are closed Good Friday).

House
Thurs, Fris & Suns,
12.30 - 5pm
(last adm. 4.30pm),
Sats, 11am - 3.30pm
(last adm. 3.00pm).
BH Mons, 11am - 5pm
(last adm. 4.30pm).

Park & Gardens
Thur - Sun & BH Mons
10am - 6pm
(last adm. 4.45pm).
Also open daily
9 - 22 Apr
24 May - 3 Jun
19 Jul - 2 Sept.

ADMISSION

House Park & Garden
Adult £5.50
Child (5-16yrs) £4.00
OAP......................£5.00
Disabled Badge
Holders £5.00
Groups* (20-100)
Adult £4.50
Schools £2.50
OAP......................£4.50

Park & Garden
Adult £4.50
Child (5-16yrs) £3.50
OAP......................£4.00
Disabled Badge
Holders £4.00
Groups* (20-100)
Adult £3.50
Schools £2.50
OAP......................£3.50

* Groups of 20+ must book and confirm in writing prior to visit.

Season tickets available.

SPECIAL EVENTS

See Special Events Index.

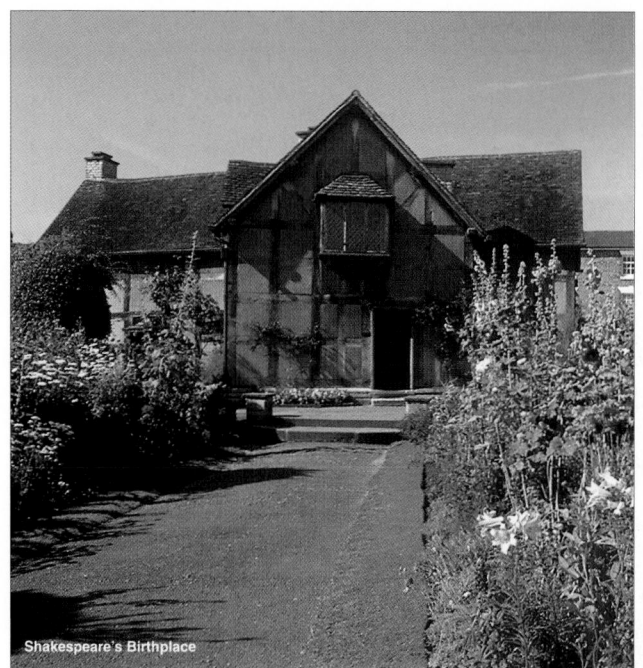

Shakespeare's Birthplace

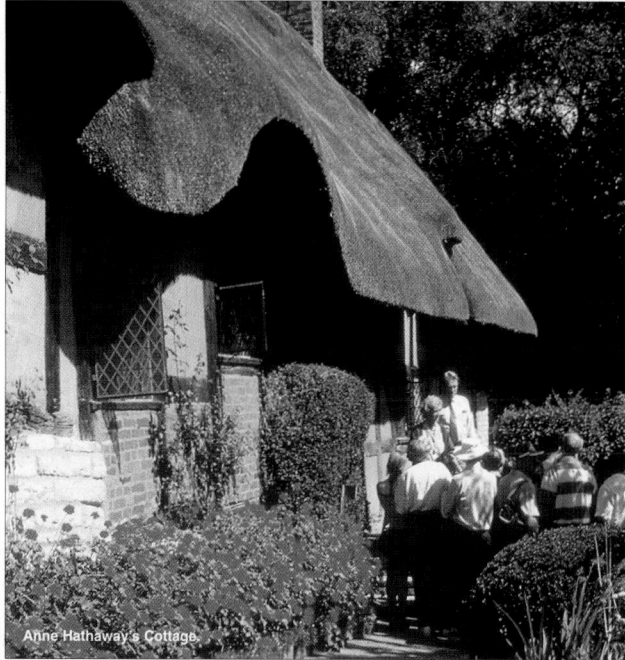

Anne Hathaway's Cottage

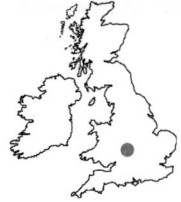

Owner:
The Shakespeare
Birthplace Trust

CONTACT

Tracey Powell
Marketing &
Publicity Manager
The Shakespeare
Birthplace Trust
Henley Street
Stratford-upon-Avon
CV37 6QW

Tel: 01789 204016
(General enquiries)

Tel: 01789 201806
(Group Visits)

Fax: 01789 296083

e-mail: info@
shakespeare.org.uk

LOCATION

OS Refs:
Birthplace - **SP201 552**
New Place - **SP201 548**
Hall's Croft - **SP200 546**
Hathaway's - **SP185 547**
Arden's - **SP166 582**

Direct rail services from
London (Paddington)

2 hrs from London
45 mins from
Birmingham by car.

4m from M40/J15
and well signed from
all approaches.

THE SHAKESPEARE HOUSES
Stratford-upon-Avon

Step back in time to enjoy these beautifully preserved Tudor homes connected with William Shakespeare and his family; the architectural character, period furniture, special collections, attractive gardens, grounds and walks and craft displays.

In Town: Shakespeare's Birthplace: Step into the house where William Shakespeare was born in 1564 and re-enter the Tudor World. Newly refurbished, the house now offers visitors a fascinating insight into life as it was when Shakespeare was a child. See the Shakespeare Exhibition which provides an introduction to his life and background and the traditional English garden.

Nash's House and New Place: The site and grounds of Shakespeare's home from 1597 until his death, with its Elizabethan-style garden, is approached through Nash's House adjoining, which contains exceptional furnishings and displays of the history of Stratford.

Hall's Croft: A delightful Elizabethan town house, once the home of Dr Hall, Shakespeare's physician son-in-law. Exceptional furniture and paintings and exhibition on Tudor medicine. Fine walled garden. Meals and refreshments available which can also be served in the beautiful garden.

Out of Town: Anne Hathaway's Cottage: This famous, picturesque thatched cottage was Anne's home before her marriage to Shakespeare. Cottage garden and Shakespeare Tree Garden as well as a garden shop and attractive Shottery Brook and Jubilee Walks. Summer tea garden.

Mary Arden's House and The Shakespeare Countryside Museum: Tudor farmstead, home of Shakespeare's mother, with outbuildings and nearby Glebe Farm containing exhibits illustrating country life over 400 years. Gypsy caravans, dovecote, duck pond, rare breeds, field walk, and falconry displays. Refreshments and picnic area.

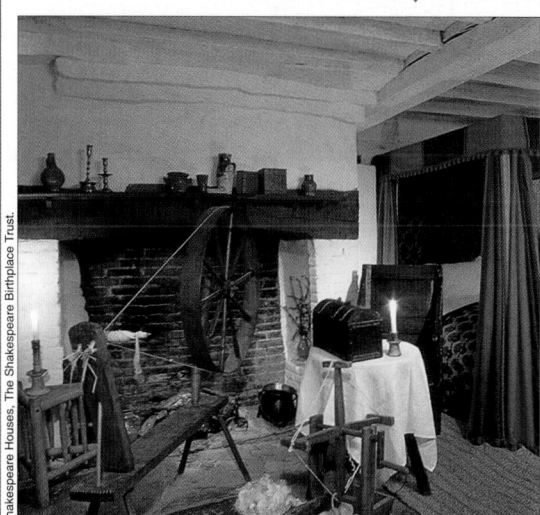

© Shakespeare Houses, The Shakespeare Birthplace Trust.

ℹ️ Regular Guide Friday, guided bus tour service connecting the town houses with Anne Hathaway's Cottage and Mary Arden's House, does not include admission to houses. No photography inside properties.

🛍️ Shops at Shakespeare's Birthplace, Hall's Croft, Anne Hathaway's Cottage and Mary Arden's House.

🍽️ Available, details upon request.

♿ WCs. Naturally difficult levels but much for disabled to enjoy at Mary Arden's House, ground floor & gardens accessible.

🍴 Available on site or close by.

🚶 By special arrangement.

🅿️ The Trust provides a free coach terminal for delivery and pick-up of groups, maximum stay 30 mins at Shakespeare's Birthplace. Parking at Anne Hathaway's Cottage and Mary Arden's House.

🐕 Available for all houses. For information 01789 201804.

🐕 Guide dogs only.

OPENING TIMES

SUMMER
20 March - 19 October

**Birthplace & Anne
Hathaway's**
Mon - Sat: 9am - 5pm.
Suns: 9.30am - 5pm

**Nash's House/New Place,
Hall's Croft &
Mary Arden's House**
Mon - Sat: 9.30am - 5pm.
Suns: 10am - 5pm

WINTER
20 October - 19 March

**Birthplace & Anne
Hathaway's**
Mon - Sat: 9.30am - 4pm.
Suns: 10am - 4pm

**Nash's House/New Place,
Hall's Croft &
Mary Arden's House**
Mon - Sat: 10am - 4pm.
Suns. 10.30am - 4pm

Closed 23 - 26 December. Open evenings out of hours by special arrangement.

ADMISSION

Shakespeare's Birthplace
Adult....................................£5.50
Child....................................£2.50
Conc. £5.00
Family (2+3)................£14.00

**New Place/Nash's
House or Hall's Croft**
Adult....................................£3.50
Child....................................£1.70
Conc. £3.00
Family (2+3)..................£8.50

Anne Hathaway's Cottage
Adult....................................£4.20
Child....................................£1.70
Conc. £3.70
Family (2+3)................£10.00

Mary Arden's House
Adult....................................£5.00
Child....................................£2.50
Conc. £4.50
Family (2+3)................£12.50

3 in-town houses
Adult....................................£8.50
Child....................................£4.20
Conc. £7.50
Family (2+3)................£20.00

All five houses
Adult..................................£12.00
Child....................................£6.00
Conc. £11.00
Family................................£29.00

Accompanied groups
20+, 10% discount.

West Midlands England

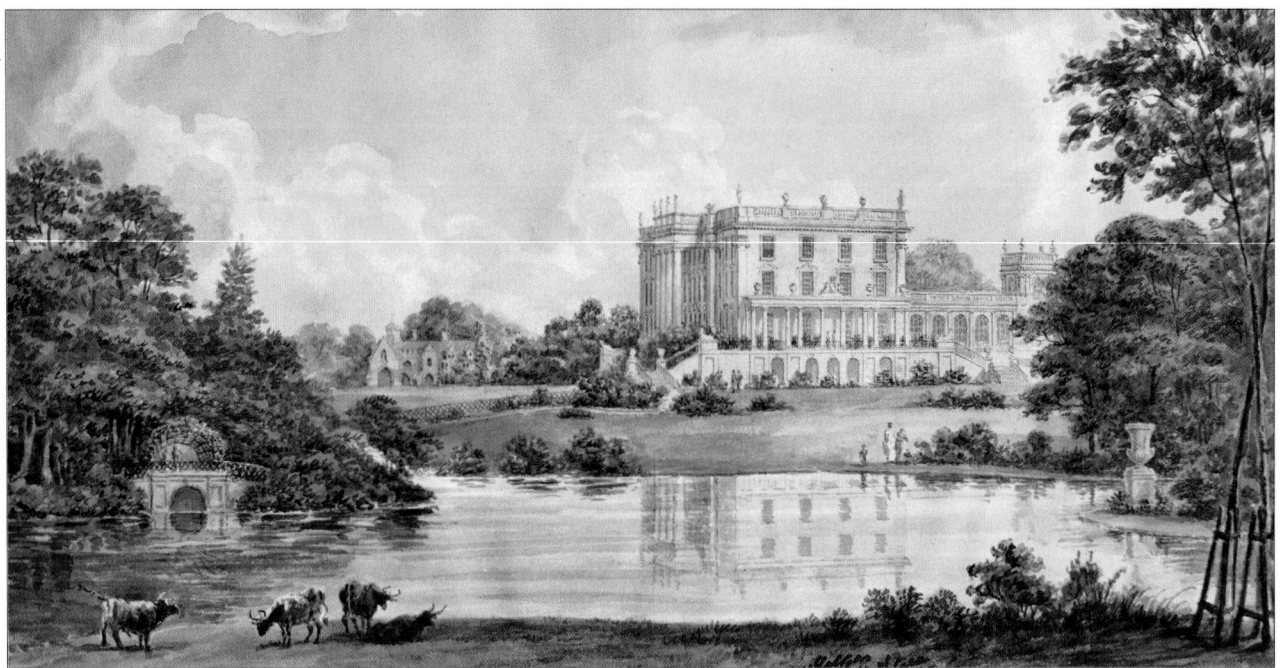

STONELEIGH ABBEY
Kenilworth

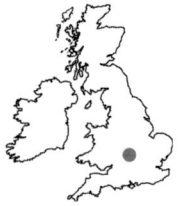

Owner:
Stoneleigh Abbey Ltd

CONTACT

Shahab Seyfollahi
The Estate Office
Stoneleigh Abbey
Kenilworth
Warwickshire
CV8 2LF

Tel: 01926 858585

Fax: 01926 850724

e-mail: enquiries
@stoneleighabbey.org

LOCATION

OS Ref. SP318 712

Off A46/B4115, 2m W of
Kenilworth. From London
100m, M40 to Warwick.

Rail: Coventry station 5m,
Leamington Spa
station 5m.

Air: Birmingham
International 20m.

Stoneleigh Abbey has been the subject of a major restoration programme funded by the Heritage Lottery Fund, English Heritage and the European Regional Development Fund.

The Abbey was founded in the reign of Henry II and after the Dissolution was granted to the Duke of Suffolk. The estate then passed into the ownership of the Leigh family who remained for 400 years. The estate is now managed on behalf of the nation by a charitable trust.

Visitors will experience a wealth of architectural styles spanning more than 600 years: the magnificent state rooms and chapel of the 18th century Baroque West Wing; a medieval Gatehouse, the Gothic Revival style Regency Stables, the first two bays of which have been fully restored using the same methods and materials employed in their original construction.

The River Avon flows through the estate's 690 acres of grounds and parkland which displays the influences of Humphry Repton and other major landscape architects. Repton designed an expanse of the river to form a lake in which the beauty of the Abbey was reflected. After World War II the lake was used as landfill. The Trust is extremely pleased to have been able to restore the lake and is indebted to Case United Kingdom for generously providing the resources and manpower to achieve this important goal.

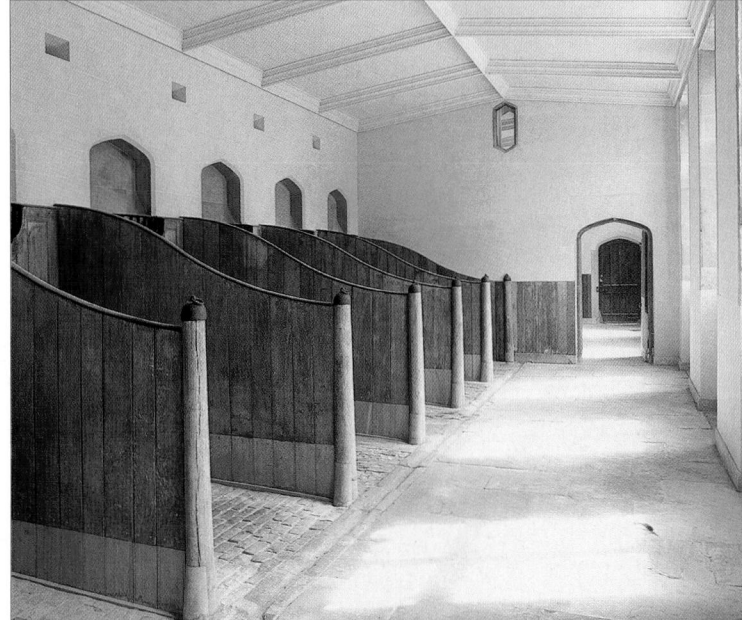

 Production launches, dinners, weddings, corporate entertaining, film and photographic locations.

 Suitable.

By arrangement.

 In grounds, on leads.

 Parkland only.

Tel. for details.

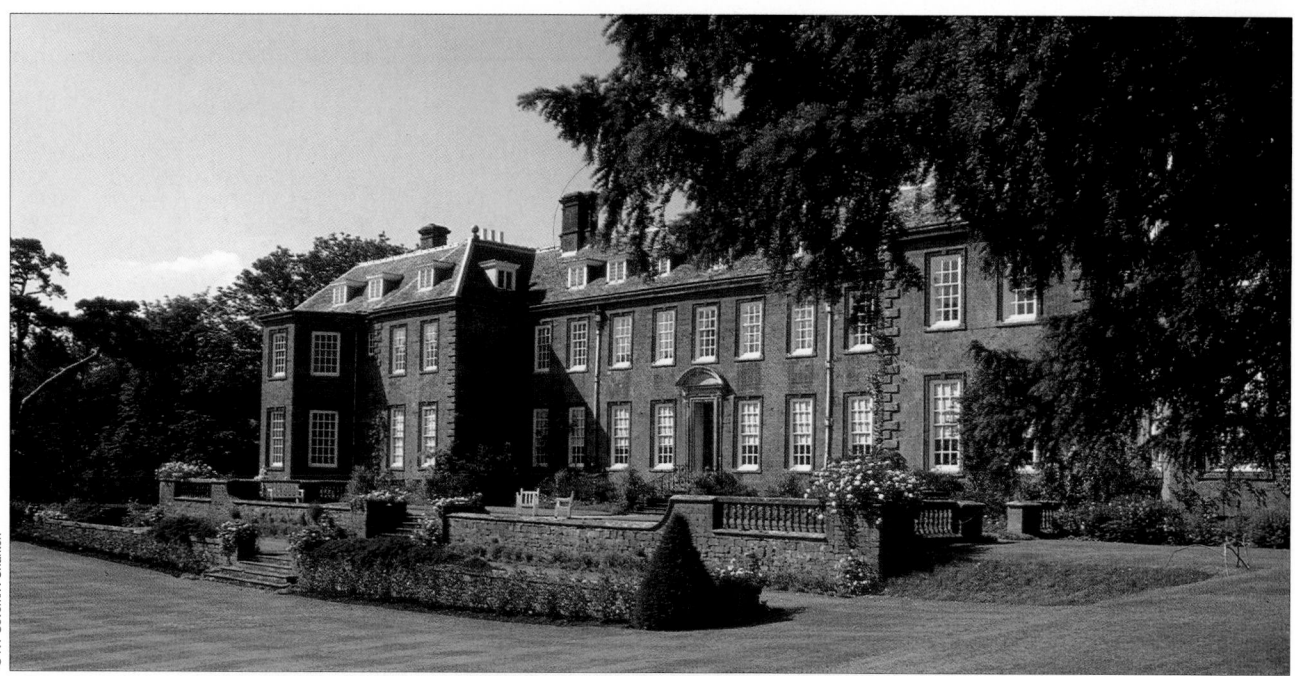

© NT Severn/R Charlton

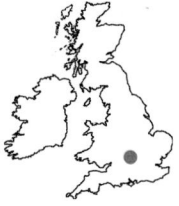

Owner:
The National Trust

CONTACT

The Property Manager
Upton House
Banbury
Oxfordshire
OX15 6HT

Tel: 01295 670266

Infoline: 01684 855365

e-mail: upton_house
@smtp.ntrust.org.uk

LOCATION

OS151 Ref. SP371 461

On A422, 7m NW
of Banbury. 12m SE of
Stratford-upon-Avon

Rail: Banbury
Station, 7m.

UPTON HOUSE
Banbury

UPTON HOUSE stands less than a mile to the south of the battlefield of Edgehill and there has been a house on this site since the Middle Ages. The present house was built at the end of the 17th century and remodelled 1927 - 29 for the 2nd Viscount Bearsted.

He was a great collector of paintings, china and many other valuable works of art, and adapted the building to display them. The paintings include works by El Greco, Bruegel, Bosch, Memling, Guardi, Hogarth and Stubbs. The rooms provide an admirable setting for the china collection which includes Chelsea figures and superb examples of beautifully decorated Sèvres porcelain. The set of 17th century Brussels tapestries depict the Holy Roman Emperor Maximilian I's boar and stag hunts.

Artists and Shell Exhibition of Paintings and Posters commissioned by Shell for use in its publicity 1921 - 1949, while the 2nd Viscount Bearsted was chairman of the company, founded by his father.

GARDEN

The outstanding garden is of interest throughout the season with terraces descending into a deep valley from the main lawn. There are herbaceous borders, the national collection of asters, over an acre of kitchen garden, a water garden laid out in the 1930s and pools stocked with ornamental fish.

Over a mile from the house, but just visible from the west end of the terrace on the garden front, is the lower lake which was formed in the mid-18th century after the fashion of 'Capability' Brown. A small temple with Doric columns and pediment sits in the centre of the one straight edge.

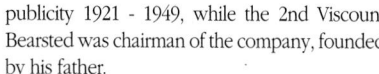

© NT Severn/R Charlton

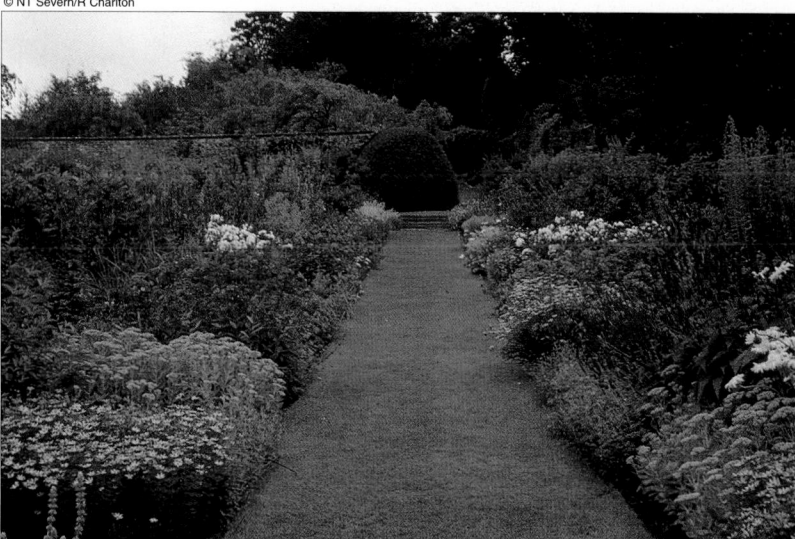

OPENING TIMES

SUMMER
31 March - 31 October
Sat - Wed including
BH Mons & Good Fri,
1 - 5pm. Last admission
4.30pm.

Closed Thurs & Fris

ADMISSION

Adult £5.50
Child £2.75
Family £13.75

Garden
Adult £2.70

Parent & baby room. No indoor photography.

Wheelchair available. Access to all ground floor rooms. WC. Motorised buggy to /from lower garden.

Tour time 1½ - 2hrs. Groups (15+) must pre-book. Evening tours by written appointment (no reduction).

Coaches park in the main car park.

SPECIAL EVENTS

- **ALL YEAR:**
Fine arts study tours, jazz concerts and other events, please send SAE or telephone for details

West Midlands England

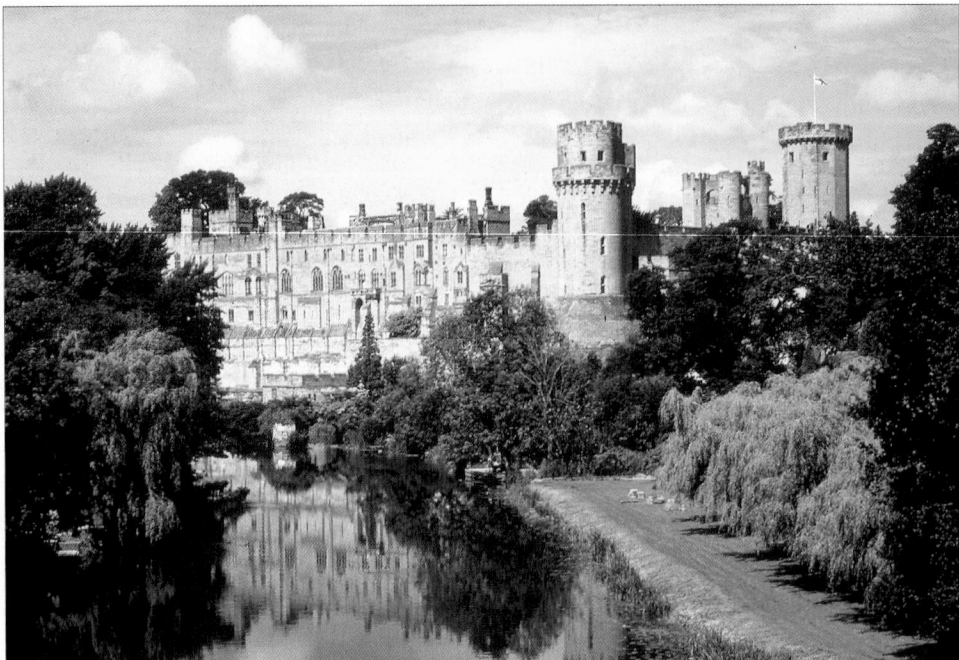

WARWICK CASTLE
Warwick

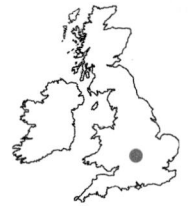

CONTACT

Sales Office
Warwick Castle
Warwick
CV34 4QU

Tel: 01926 495421 (Admin)
01926 406600 (Info)

Fax: 01926 401692

LOCATION

OS Ref. SP284 648

2m from M40/J15.
Birmingham 35 mins
Leeds 2 hrs 5 mins
London, 1 hr 30 mins
Vehicle entrance from A429
1/2 m SW of town centre.

Rail: Intercity from London
Euston to Coventry.
Direct service Chiltern Line
from Marylebone &
Paddington to Warwick.

Over a thousand years of secrets hide in the shadows of Warwick Castle. Murder, mystery, intrigue and scandal: the Castle has witnessed it all, and now reveals the secret life of England as you have never seen it before.

From the days of William the Conqueror to the reign of Queen Victoria, the Castle has provided a backdrop for many turbulent times.

Here you can join a mediaeval household in our Kingmaker attraction, watching them prepare for the final battle of the Earl of Warwick. Enter the eerie Ghost Tower, where it is said that the unquiet spirit of Sir Fulke Greville, murdered most foully by a manservant, still roams.

Descend into the gloomy depths of the Dungeon and Torture Chamber, then step forward in time and marvel at the grandeur of the Great Hall and in 'Death or Glory', our

Armoury attraction, you can feel the weight of a sword and try on a helmet. The 14th century Great Hall lies at the heart of the Castle and here you can see the death mask of Oliver Cromwell and Bonnie Prince Charlie's shield.

Witness the perfect manners and hidden indiscretions of Daisy, Countess of Warwick and her friends at the Royal Weekend Party 1898 or stroll through the 60 acres of grounds and gardens, landscaped by 'Capability' Brown, which surround the Castle today.

Besides the secrets, there are a host of special events to enjoy throughout the year, with a unique opportunity to witness mediaeval life at the Mediaeval Festival (12 May to 9 September).

Warwick Castle really is one of the best days out in history.

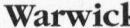

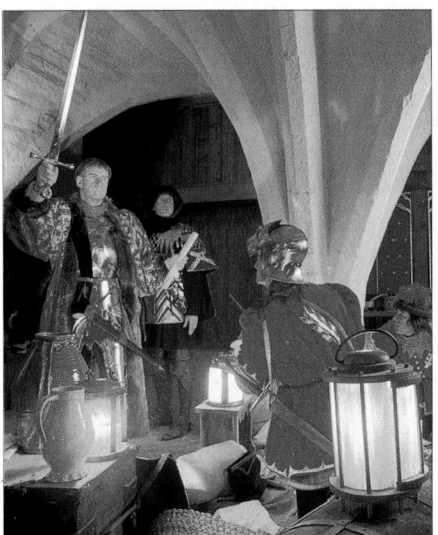

i Corporate events, receptions, Kingmaker's Feasts and Highwayman's Supper. Guide books available in French, German, Japanese, Spanish and Italian.

Four shops.

Parking spaces in Stables Car Park, free admission for registered blind and visitors in wheelchairs.

Available, ranging from cream teas to three-course hot meals. During the summer there is an open air barbecue and refreshment pavilion in the grounds (weather permitting).

For groups (must be pre-booked). Guides in every room.

P Limited free car parking in main car park. Free coach parking, free admission and refreshment voucher for coach driver.

Ideal location, being a superb example of military architecture dating back to the Norman Conquest and with elegant interiors up to Victorian times. Group rates apply. To qualify for group rates, groups must book in advance. Education packs available.

Registered assistance dogs only.

Tel. for details.

OPENING TIMES

SUMMER
April - October
10am - 6pm
Last admission 5.30pm.

WINTER
November - March
10am - 5pm
Last admission 4.30pm.

ADMISSION

11 Sept 2000 - 28 Feb 2001

Adult £9.75
Child (4 - 16yrs) £5.95
Student................... £7.45
OAP £7.00
Family (2+2) £28.00

Groups (20+)
Adult £7.95
Child(4 - 16yrs)........ £5.20
Student................... £6.95
OAP £6.40

**Call the Warwick Castle
Information Line on:
01926 406600
for the latest
admission prices.**

CONFERENCE/FUNCTION		
ROOM	SIZE	MAX CAPACITY
Great Hall	61' x 34'	130
State Dining Room	40' x 25'	32
Undercroft	46' x 26'	120
Coach House	44' x 19'	70
Marquees		2000

ARBURY HALL See page 343 for full page entry.

CHARLECOTE PARK See page 344 for full page entry.

COUGHTON COURT See page 345 for full page entry.

BADDESLEY CLINTON

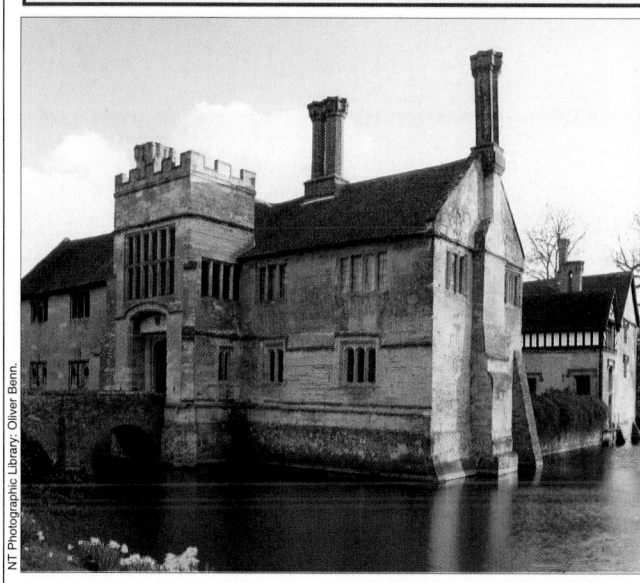

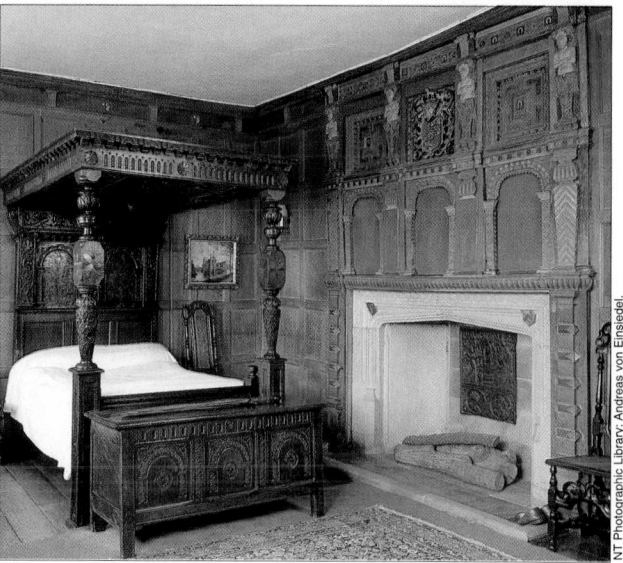

RISING LANE, BADDESLEY CLINTON, KNOWLE, SOLIHULL B93 0DQ

Owner: *The National Trust*   **Contact:** *The Property Manager*

Tel: 01564 783294   **Fax:** 01564 782706   **e-mail:** baddesley@smtp.ntrust.org.uk

A romantically sited medieval moated manor house, dating from 14th century; little changed since 1634; family portraits, priest holes; garden; ponds and lake walk. Make a day of it! Revised opening times and substantial discounts on joint ticket prices make a combined visit to Baddesley Clinton and Packwood House even more attractive, especially since both properties are only two miles apart.

Location: OS139, Ref. SP199 715. ³/₄ m W of A4141 Warwick/Birmingham road at Chadwick End.

Opening Times: House: 28 Feb - 28 Oct: Wed - Sun & BH Mons (closed Good Fri). Feb - Apr & Oct: 1.30 - 5pm; May - end Sept: 1.30 - 5.30pm.

Grounds: 28 Feb - 16 Dec: Wed - Sun, Good Fri & BH Mons. Feb - Apr & Oct: 12 noon - 5pm; May - end Sept: 12 noon - 5.30pm; Nov - 16 Dec: 12 noon - 4.30pm.

Admission: Adult £5.60, Child £2.80, Family £14. Garden only: Adult £2.80, Child £1.40. Groups: £4.50. Guided tours (out of hours) £9.

Combined ticket with Packwood House: Adult £8, Child £4, Family £20. Garden only: Adult £4, Child £2. Groups £8.

Partially suitable. WC. Licensed. By arrangement. Guide dogs only. Tel. for details.

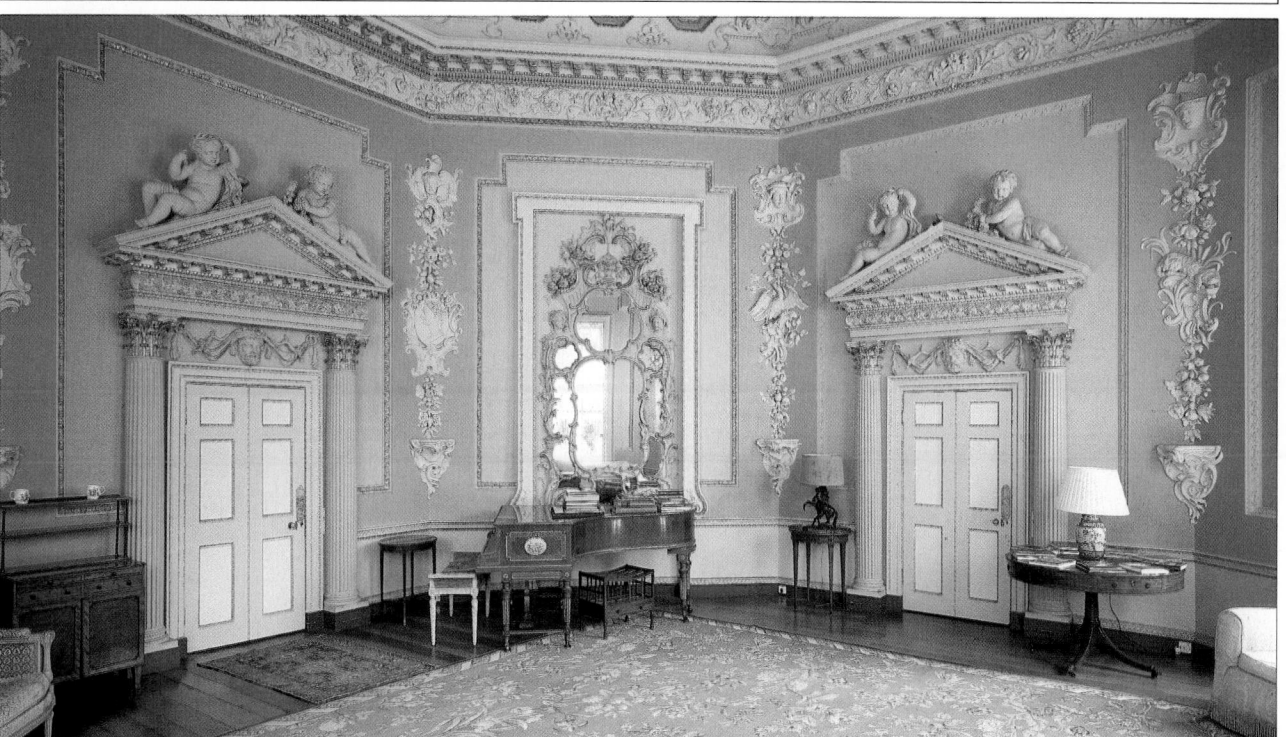

West Midlands
England

FARNBOROUGH HALL

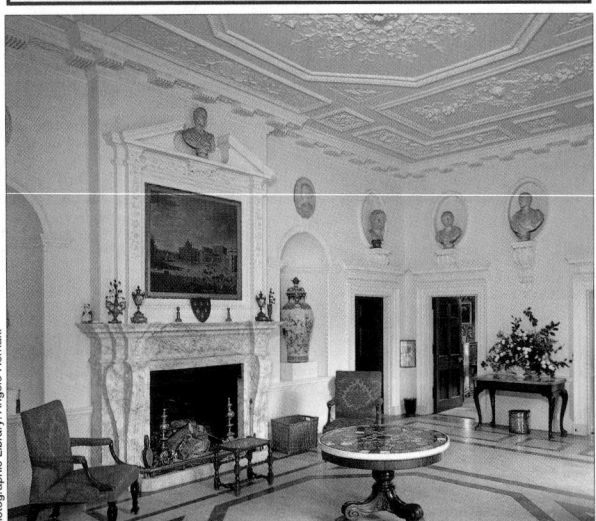

BANBURY, OXFORDSHIRE OX17 1DU

Owner: The National Trust   *Contact:* Mr G Holbech

Tel: 01295 690002

A classical mid-18th century stone house, home of the Holbech family for 300 years; notable plasterwork, the entrance hall, staircase and 2 principal rooms are shown; the grounds contain charming 18th century temples, a $^2/_3$ mile terrace walk and an obelisk.

Location: OS151, Ref. SP430 490. 6m N of Banbury, $^1/_2$ m W of A423.

Opening Times: House, grounds and terrace walk: Apr - end Sept: Weds & Sats also 6/7 May, 2 - 6pm. Terrace walk only, Thurs & Fris, 2 - 6pm, closed Good Fri. Last admission to house 5.30pm.

Admission: House, grounds & terrace walk: Adult £3.40. Garden & terrace walk: £1.70. Terrace walk only (Thurs & Fris) £1.

House & grounds, but steep terrace walk.   In grounds, on leads.

THE HILLER GARDEN   **Tel:** 01789 490991 **Fax:** 01789 490439

Dunnington Heath Farm, Alcester, Warwickshire B49 5PD

Owner: Mr & Mrs R Beach   **Contact:** Mr David Carvill

2 acre garden of unusual herbaceous plants and over 200 rose varieties.

Location: OS Ref. SP066 539. $1^1/_2$ m S of Ragley Hall on B4088 (formerly A435).

Opening Times: All year: daily 10am - 5pm.

Admission: Free.

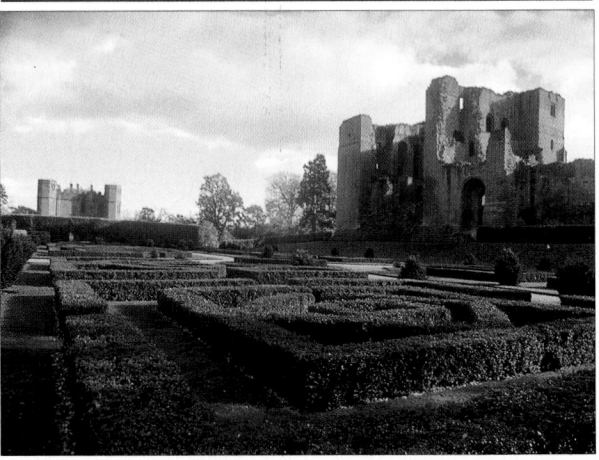

The Obelisk, Farnborough Hall, Warwickshire.

HONINGTON HALL

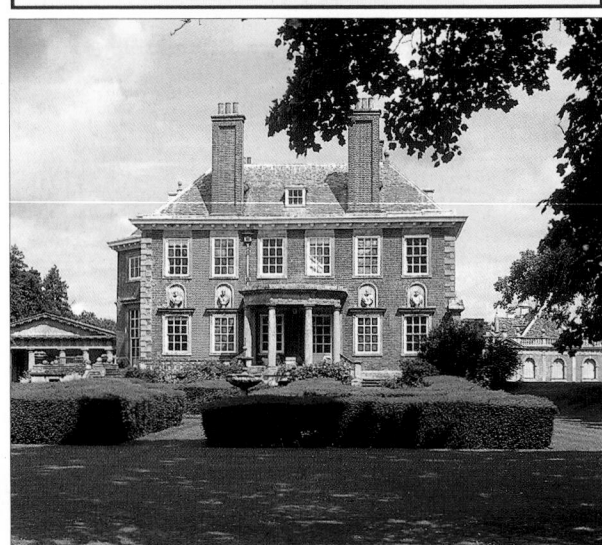

SHIPSTON-ON-STOUR, WARWICKSHIRE CV36 5AA

Owner/Contact: Benjamin Wiggin Esq

Tel: 01608 661434 **Fax:** 01608 663717

This fine Caroline manor house was built in the early 1680s for Henry Parker in mellow brickwork, stone quoins and window dressings. Modified in 1751 when an octagonal saloon was inserted. The interior was also lavishly restored around this time and contains exceptional mid-Georgian plasterwork. Set in 15 acres of grounds.

Location: OS Ref. SP261 427. 10m S of Stratford-upon-Avon. $1^1/_2$ m N of Shipston-on-Stour. Take A3400 towards Stratford, then signed right to Honington.

Opening Times: Jun - Aug: Weds only. BH Mon, 2.30 - 5pm. Groups at other times by appointment.

Admission: Adult £3.50, Child £1.75.

Not suitable.   Obligatory.

KENILWORTH CASTLE

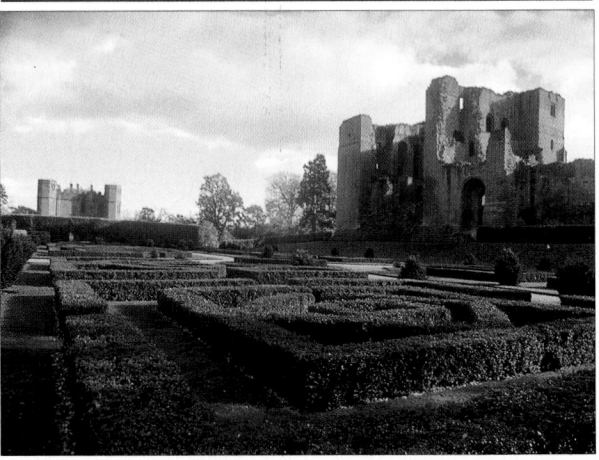

KENILWORTH, WARWICKSHIRE CV8 1NE

Owner: English Heritage   *Contact:* The Custodian

Tel: 01926 852078

Kenilworth is the largest castle ruin in England, the former stronghold of great Lords and Kings. Its massive walls of warm red stone tower over the peaceful Warwickshire landscape. The Earl of Leicester entertained Queen Elizabeth I with 'Princely Pleasures' during her 19 day visit. He built a new wing for the Queen to lodge in and organised all manner of lavish and costly festivities. The Great Hall, where Gloriana dined with her courtiers, still stands and John of Gaunt's Hall is second only in width and grandeur to Westminster Hall. Climb to the top of the tower beside the hall and you will be rewarded by fine views over the rolling wooded countryside. New exhibition, interactive castle model and café in Leicester's Barn.

Location: OS140 Ref. SP278 723. In Kenilworth, off A452, W end of town.

Opening Times: 1 Apr - 31 Oct: daily, 10am - 6pm (5pm in Oct). 1 Nov - 31 Mar: daily 10am - 4pm. Closed 24 - 26 Dec & 1 Jan.

Admission: Adult £4, Child £2, Conc. £3, Family £10. 15% discount for groups (11+).

   Tel. for details.

LORD LEYCESTER HOSPITAL

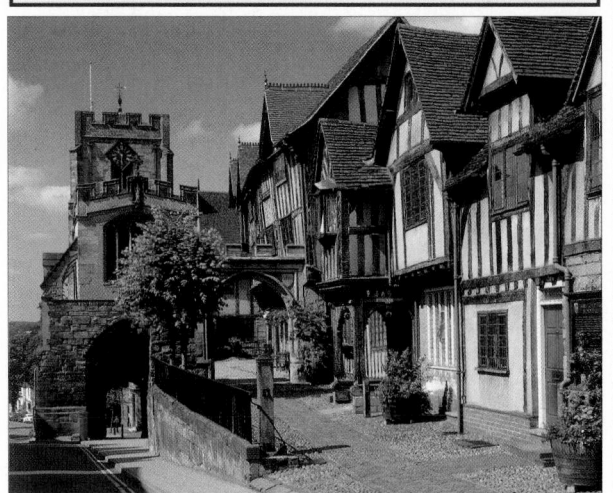

HIGH STREET, WARWICK · CV34 4BH

Owner: The Governors   *Contact:* The Master

Tel/Fax: 01926 491422

This magnificent range of 14th century half-timbered buildings was adapted into almshouses by Robert Dudley, Earl of Leycester, in 1571. The Hospital still provides homes for ex-servicemen and their wives. The Guildhall, Great Hall, Chapel, Brethren's Kitchen and galleried Courtyard are still in everyday use. The Queen's Own Hussars regimental museum is here. The historic Master's Garden, featured in BBC TV's Gardener's World, has been restored and a new Knot Garden created for the Millennium.

Location: OS Ref. 280 648. 1m N of M40/J15 on the A429 in town centre.

Opening Times: All year: Tue - Sun & BHs, 10am - 5pm (4pm in winter). Garden: Apr - Sept: 10am - 4pm.

Admission: Adult £3, Child £2, Conc. £2.50. 5% discount for adult groups (20+).

⬜ ♨ 🍽 ♿ Partially suitable. 📷 🍴 🔑 By arrangement.
🅿 Limited 📖 🐕 Guide dogs only. ✳

MIDDLETON HALL   **Tel:** 01827 283095 **Fax:** 01827 285717

Middleton, Tamworth, Staffordshire B78 2AE

Owner: Middleton Hall Trust   **Contact:** Mrs B Ellerslie

Hall (1285 - 1824). Former home of Hugh Willoughby (Tudor explorer), Francis Willughby and John Ray (17th century naturalists).

Location: OS Ref. SP193 982. A4091, S of Tamworth.

Opening Times: Easter - 30 Sept: Suns, 2 - 5pm, BH Mons, 11am - 5pm.

Admission: Adult £2, OAP £1.

RAGLEY HALL 🏛   See page 346 for full page entry.

THE SHAKESPEARE HOUSES   See page 347 for full page entry.

STONELEIGH ABBEY 🏛   See page 348 for full page entry.

UPTON HOUSE 🌿   See page 349 for full page entry.

WARWICK CASTLE 🏛   See page 350 for full page entry.

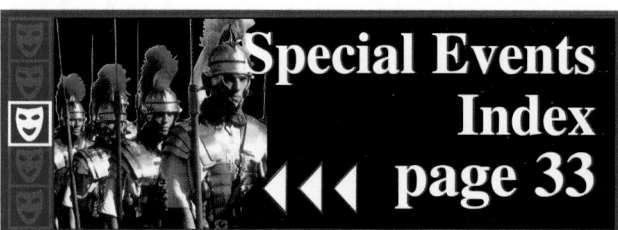

Special Events Index ◀◀◀ page 33

PACKWOOD HOUSE

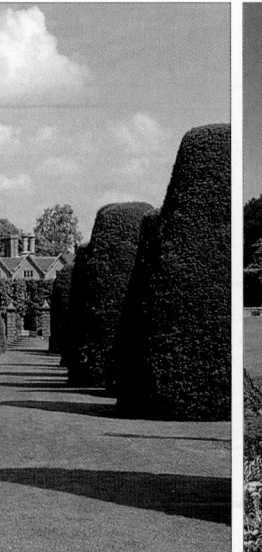
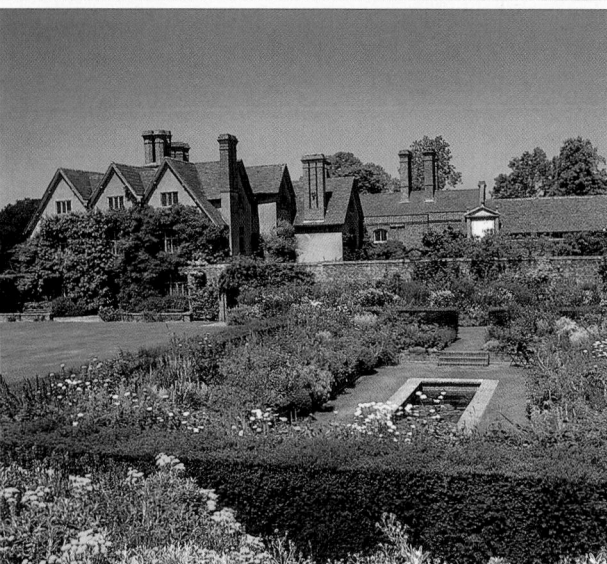

LAPWORTH, SOLIHULL B94 6AT

Owner: The National Trust   *Contact:* The Property Manager

Tel: 01564 783294 **Fax:** 01564 782706 **e-mail:** baddesley@smtp.ntrust.org.uk

Originally a 16th century house, Packwood has been much altered over the years and today is the vision of Graham Baron Ash who recreated a Jacobean house in the 1920s and '30s. A fine collection of 16th century textiles and furniture. Important gardens with renowned herbaceous border and famous yew garden based on the Sermon on the Mount. Make a day of it! Revised opening times and substantial discounts on joint ticket prices make a combined visit to Baddesley Clinton and Packwood House even more attractive, especially since both properties are only two miles apart.

Location: OS139, Ref. 174 722. 2m E of Hockley Heath (on A3400), 11m SE of central Birmingham.

Opening Times: House: 28 Mar 28 Oct: Wed - Sun, Good Fri & BH Mons, 12 noon - 4.30pm. NB: on busy days entry may be by timed ticket. Garden: 3 - 25 Mar: Sats & Suns. 28 Mar - 28 Oct: Wed - Sun, Good Fri & BH Mons. Mar, Apr & Oct: 11am - 4.30pm; May - end Sept: 11am - 5.30pm. Park & Woodland Walks: All year: daily.

Admission: Adult £5, Child £2.50, Family £12.50, Garden only: Adult £2.50, Child £1.25. Groups £4. Guided tours (out of hours) £8.

Combined ticket with Baddesley Clinton: Adult £8, Child £4, Family £20. Garden only: Adult £4, Child £2. Groups £8.

⬜ ♨ 📷 ♿ Partially suitable. WC. 🔑 By arrangement. 🅿 📖
🐕 Guide dogs only. ✳ ☎ Tel. for details.

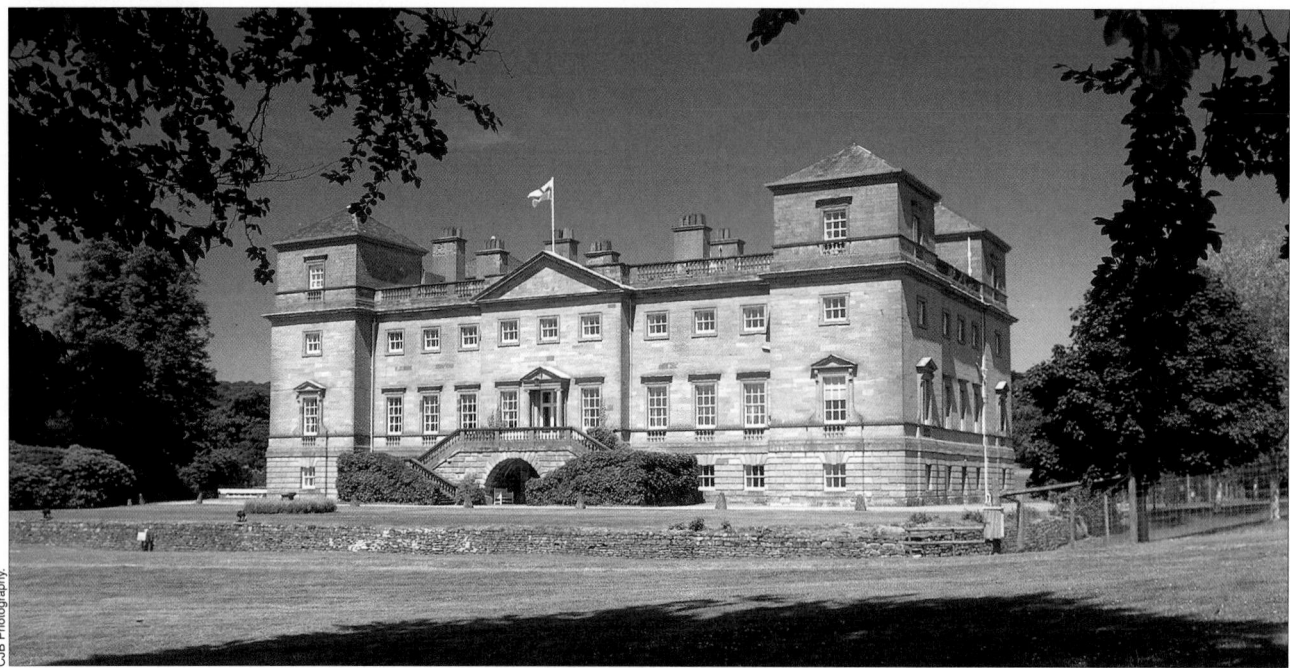

CJB Photography.

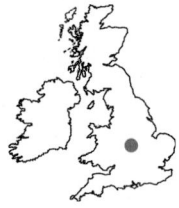

Owner: Viscount Cobham

CONTACT

Mrs Lesley Haynes
Hagley Hall
Hagley
Worcestershire
DY9 9LG

Tel: 01562 882408

Fax: 01562 882632

LOCATION

OS Ref. SO920 807

Easily accessible from all
areas of the country.
1/4 m S of A456 at Hagley.

Close to the M42, M40, M6
and only 5m from
M5/J3/J4.

Birmingham City
Centre 12m.

Rail: Railway Station and
the NEC 25 mins.

Air: Birmingham
International Airport
25 mins.

HAGLEY HALL
Stourbridge

HAGLEY HALL is set in a 350-acre landscaped park yet is only 25 minutes from Birmingham city centre, the NEC and ICC and close to the motorway network of M5, M6, M40 and M42.

The house is available throughout the year on an exclusive basis for conferences, product launches, presentations, lunches, dinners, country sporting days, team building activities, themed evenings, murder mysteries, concerts, filming and wedding receptions.

Hagley's high standards of catering are now available at other venues as well as at Hagley Hall.

The elegant Palladian house, completed in 1760, contains some of the finest examples of Italian plasterwork. Hagley's rich rococo decoration is a remarkable tribute to the artistic achievement of great 18th century amateurs and is the much loved home of the 11th Viscount Cobham.

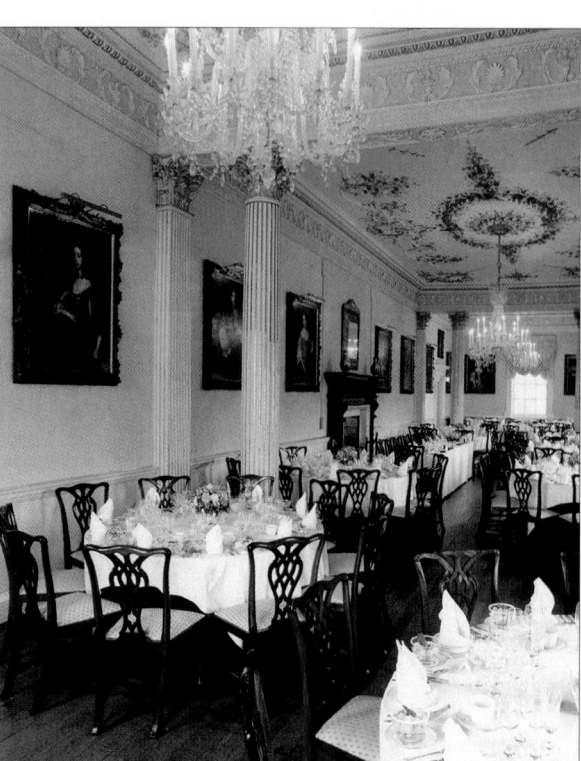

i Available on an exclusive basis for conferences, presentations, lunches, dinners, product launches, themed evenings, murder mysteries, concerts, wedding receptions. Extensive parkland for country sporting days, team-building activities, off-road driving and filming.

T As well as in-house catering, Hagley also offers a unique catering service at the venue of your choice.

♿ Visitors may alight at the entrance. No WC.

☕ Teas available during opening times.

🚶 Obligatory. Please book parties in advance, guided tour time of house 1 hr. Colour guide - book.

P Unlimited for coaches and cars.

🎒 By arrangement.

🐕 Guide dogs only.

🔔

❄

OPENING TIMES

House

3 January - 25 January
29 January - 2 February
5 - 16 February
19 - 25 February
27 May - 1 June
26 - 31 August
Daily except Saturdays.

13 - 20 April
Daily, 2 - 5pm.

Please telephone prior
to visit to ensure the house
is open.

ADMISSION

House

Adult	£3.50
Child (under 14 yrs)	£1.50
OAP	£2.50
Student	£2.50

CONFERENCE/FUNCTION

ROOM	SIZE	MAX CAPACITY
Gallery	85' x 17'	130
Crimson Rm	23' x 31'	40
The Saloon	34' x 27'	70
Westcote	31' x 20'	60

ASTON HALL

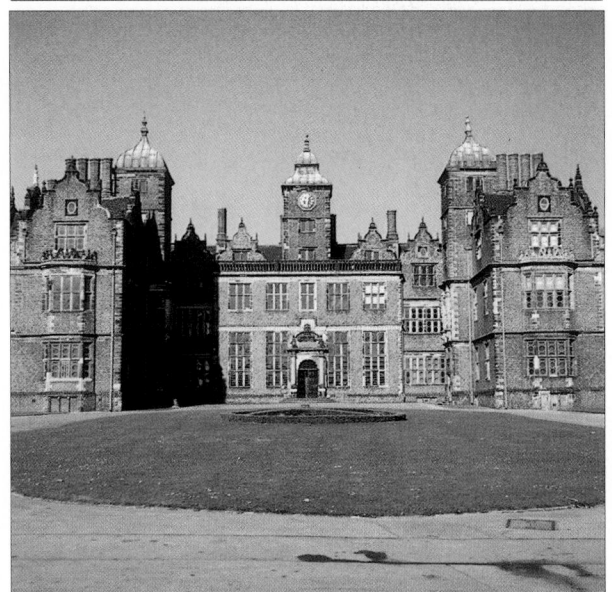

TRINITY ROAD, BIRMINGHAM, WEST MIDLANDS B6 6JD

Owner: Birmingham City Council **Contact:** *Curator/Manager*

Tel: 0121 327 0062 **Fax:** 0121 327 7162

A large Jacobean mansion built 1618 - 1635 from plans by John Thorpe. The Hall is brick-built with a fairytale skyline of gables and turrets. The interior has period rooms from the 17th, 18th and 19th centuries and a splendid long gallery measuring 136ft. A large kitchen and servants' rooms are also on display.

Location: OS139, Ref. SP080 899. 3m NE of Birmingham,^{1}/4 m from A38(M).

Opening times: 13 Apr - 28 Oct: daily 2 - 5pm. Parkland open all year round.

Admission: Free.

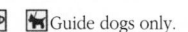 Ground floor & grounds suitable.   Guide dogs only.

THE BIRMINGHAM BOTANICAL GARDENS AND GLASSHOUSES

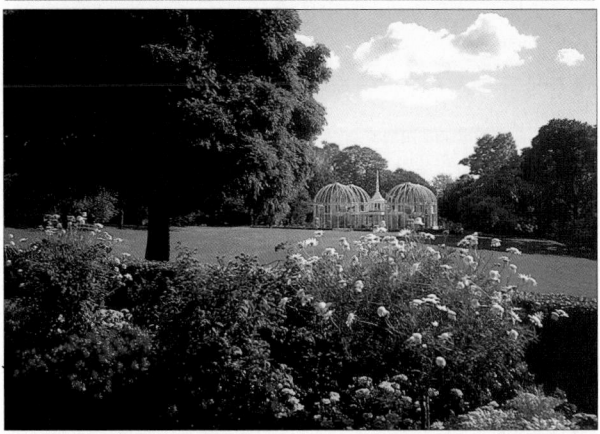

WESTBOURNE ROAD, EDGBASTON, BIRMINGHAM B15 3TR

Owner: Birmingham Botanical & Horticultural Society **Contact:** *Mrs H Champion*

Tel: 0121 454 1860 **Fax:** 0121 454 7835
e-mail: admin@bham-bot-gdns.demon.co.uk

Tropical, Mediterranean and Desert Glasshouses contain a wide range of exotic and economic flora. 15 acres of beautiful gardens with the finest collection of plants in the Midlands. Home of the National Bonsai Collection. Children's adventure playground, aviaries and gallery.

Location: OS Ref. SP048 855. 2m W of city centre. Follow signs to Edgbaston then brown tourist signs.

Opening times: Daily: 9am - Dusk (7pm latest except pre-booked groups). Suns opening time 10am.

Admission: Adult £4.80 (£5.20 on summer Suns & BHs), Child (under 5yrs) Free, Conc. £2.60, Family £12.50 (£13.50, Suns & BHs). Reduced rates for groups of 10+ (prices from April 2001).

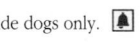 Licensed.   Guide dogs only.   Tel. for details.

BLAKESLEY HALL

Tel: 0121 803 1675

Blakesley Road, Yardley, Birmingham B25 8RN
Owner: Birmingham City Council   **Contact:** Curator/Manager
Blakesley Hall has been awarded a grant by the Heritage Lottery Fund and will be closed during 2001 for development. For further details telephone 0121 303 1675.
Location: OS139, Ref. SP130 862. 6m E of Birmingham city centre off A4040 from A45.
Opening times: Closed for 2001.

CASTLE BROMWICH HALL GARDENS

Tel/Fax: 0121 749 4100
e-mail: enq@cbhgt.swinternet.co.uk

Chester Road, Castle Bromwich, Birmingham B36 9BT
Owner: Castle Bromwich Hall Gardens Trust   **Contact:** The Secretary
A unique example of 17th and 18th century formal garden design within a 10 acre walled area, comprising historic plants, vegetables, herbs and fruit, with a 19th century holly maze. Classical patterned parterres can be seen at the end of the holly walk, together with restored green house and summer house.
Location: OS Ref. SP142 898. Off B4114, 4m E of Birmingham city centre, 1m from M6/J5 (exit northbound only). Southbound M6/J6 and follow A38 & A452.
Opening Times: Apr - end Oct: Tue - Thur, 1.30 - 4.30pm. Sats, Suns & BHs 2 - 6pm. Closed Mons & Fris including Good Fri.
Admission: Adult £3, Child £1, OAP £2.

Daily.   Limited for coaches.   In grounds, on leads.   Tel. for details.

COVENTRY CATHEDRAL

Tel: 02476 227597 **Fax:** 02476 631448

7 Priory Row, Coventry CV1 5ES   **e-mail:** information@coventrycathedral.org
Owner: Provost & Canons of Coventry Cathedral   **Contact:** The Visits Secretary
The remains of the medieval Cathedral, bombed in 1940, stand beside the new Cathedral by Basil Spence, consecrated in 1962. Modern works of art include a huge tapestry by Graham Sutherland, a stained glass window by John Piper and a bronze sculpture by Epstein. '*Reconciliation*' statue by Josefina de Vasconcellos.
Location: OS Ref. SP336 790. City centre.
Opening Times: Cathedral: Easter - Oct: from 8.30am - 6pm. Nov - Easter: 9.30am - 5pm. Visitors Centre: Easter - Oct: Mon - Sat, 10am - 4pm. Nov - Easter: Mon - Sat, 11am - 3pm.
Admission: Cathedral: £2 donation. Visitor Centre: Adult £2, Child/Conc. £1. Groups (10+): Adult £1.50, Child/Conc. £1. Groups must book in advance.

Photo permit required   Partially suitable. WC.   By arrangement. No parking.   By arrangement.   Guide dogs only.

HAGLEY HALL

See page 354 for full page entry.

HALESOWEN ABBEY

Tel: 0121 625 6820 (Regional Office)

Halesowen, Birmingham, West Midlands
Owner: English Heritage   **Contact:** The West Midlands Regional Office
Remains of an abbey founded by King John in the 13th century, now incorporated into a 19th century farm. Parts of the church and the monks' infirmary can still be made out.
Location: OS Ref. SO975 828. Off A456 Kidderminster road, ^{1}/2m W of M5/J3, 6m W of Birmingham city centre.
Opening Times: 21/22 Jul only: 10am - 6pm.
Admission: Adult £2, Child £1.50, Conc. £1.

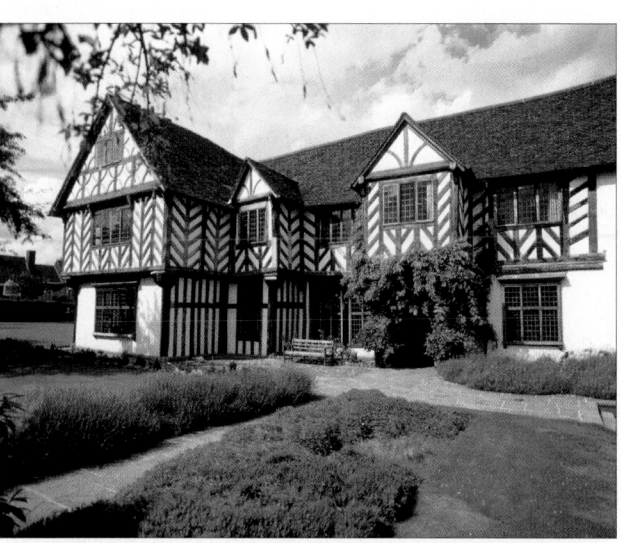

Blakesley Hall, West Midlands.

West Midlands England

MUSEUM OF THE JEWELLERY QUARTER

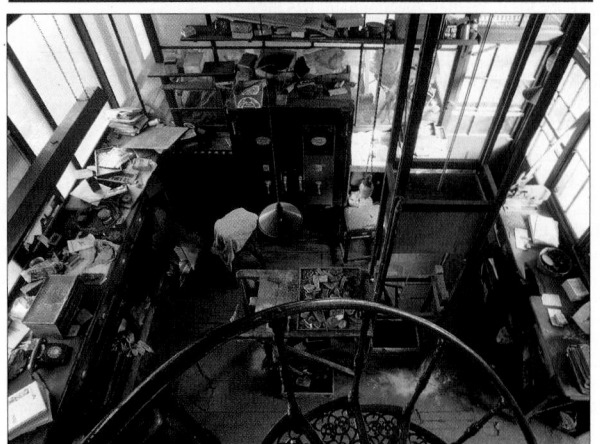

75 - 79 VYSE STREET, HOCKLEY, BIRMINGHAM B18 6HA

Owner: *Birmingham City Council*   **Contact:** *The Curator*

Tel: 0121 554 3598 **Fax:** 0121 554 9700

Built around the preserved workshops and offices of Smith and Pepper, a Birmingham jewellery firm. This lively working Museum offers a fascinating insight into the city's historic jewellery trade. Enjoy a tour of the factory with one of our knowledgeable guides and meet skilled jewellers at work. You can also explore the displays which tell the story of the Quarter and the jeweller's craft, practiced in this distinctive part of Birmingham for over 200 years. The museum is available for private evening bookings with catering provision if required.

Location: OS Ref. SP060 880. ³/4 m NW of city centre, just within A4540 (ring road).

Opening Times: Mon - Fri, 10am - 4pm. Sats, 11am - 5pm. Closed Suns.

Admission: Adult £2.50, Conc. £2, Family (2+3) £6.50. 10% discount for booked groups (10+).

ⓘ Temporary exhibitions. 📷 ♿ 🎦 ⚔ 🅿 On street parking only. 🏠 🐕 Guide dogs only. ❄ 🛡 Tel. for details.

RYTON ORGANIC GARDENS   **Tel:** 024 7630 3517 **Fax:** 024 7663 9229

Ryton-on-Dunsmore, Coventry, West Midlands CV8 3LG

Owner: HDRA - The Organic Organisation   **Contact:** Sally Furness

Beautiful and informative gardens including herbs, shrubs, flowers, rare and unusual vegetables, all organically grown.

Location: OS Ref. SP400 745. 5m SE of Coventry off A45 on the road to Wolston.

Opening Times: Daily (closed Christmas week): 9am - 5pm.

Admission: Adult £3 (no concessions), accompanied child free. Groups (14+) £2.50 plus 50p for garden tour.

SELLY MANOR   **Tel:** 0121 472 0199 **Fax:** 0121 471 4101

Maple Road, Bournville, West Midlands B30 1UB   e-mail: gillianellis@bvt.org.uk

Owner: Bournville Village Trust   **Contact:** Gillian Ellis

A beautiful half-timbered manor house in the heart of the famous Bournville village. The house has been lived in since the 14th century and was rescued from demolition by George Cadbury. It houses furniture dating back several centuries and is surrounded by a delightful typical Tudor garden.

Location: OS Ref. SP045 814. N side of Sycamore Road, just E of Linden Road (A4040). 4m SSW of City Centre.

Opening Times: All year: Tue - Fri, 10am - 5pm. Apr - Sept: Sats, Suns & BHs, 2 - 5pm. Closed Mons.

Admission: Adult £2, Child 50p, Conc. £1.50, Family £4.50.

📷 ♿ Partially suitable. WC. 🎦 By arrangement. 🅿 Limited. 🏠 🐕 Guide dogs only. 🔔 ❄

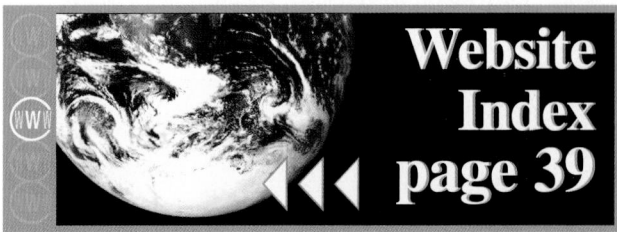

Website Index ◀◀◀ page 39

SOHO HOUSE

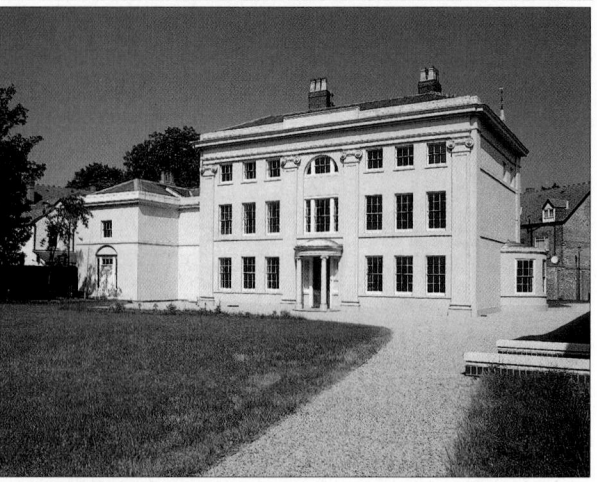

SOHO AVENUE, HANDSWORTH, BIRMINGHAM B18 5LB

Owner: *Birmingham City Council*   **Contact:** *Reception*

Tel: 0121 554 9122 **Fax:** 0121 554 5929

The elegant home of the industrial pioneer Matthew Boulton from 1766 to 1809, Soho House has been carefully restored. Special features include an early 19th century hot air heating system. Period rooms and displays on Boulton's businesses, family and associates as well as the architectural development of the house.

Location: OS Ref. SP054 893. S side of Soho Avenue, just SW of Soho Hill/Soho Road (A41). 2m NW of city centre. Follow signs for Handsworth then brown tourist signs.

Opening Times: Tue - Sat, 10am - 5pm. Suns, 12 noon - 5pm. Closed Mons except BHs.

Admission: Adult £2.50, Conc. £2, Family £6.50. 10% discount for booked groups.

ⓘ Meeting room. 📷 ♿ 🎦 🎭 By arrangement. 🅿 Limited for cars. 🏠 🐕 Guide dogs only. ❄

WIGHTWICK MANOR

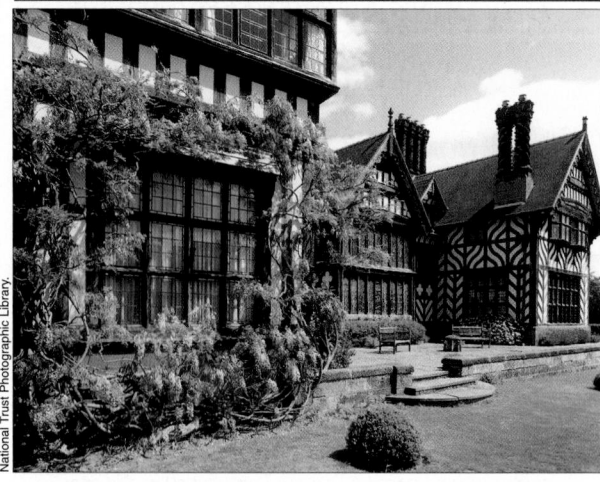

National Trust Photographic Library

WIGHTWICK BANK, WOLVERHAMPTON, WEST MIDLANDS WV6 8EE

Owner: *The National Trust*   **Contact:** *The Property Manager*

Tel: 01902 761108 **Fax:** 01902 764663

Begun in 1887, the house is a notable example of the influence of William Morris, with many original Morris wallpapers and fabrics. Also of interest are pre-Raphaelite pictures, Kempe glass and De Morgan ware. The 17 acre Victorian/Edwardian garden designed by Thomas Mawson has formal beds, pergola, yew hedges, topiary and terraces, woodland and two pools.

Location: OS Ref. SO869 985. 3m W of Wolverhampton, up Wightwick Bank (A454), beside the Mermaid Inn.

Opening Times: 1 Mar - 31 Dec: Thurs & Sats, 1.30 - 5pm (last entry 4.30pm). Admission by timed ticket. Guided groups through ground floor, freeflow upstairs. Min. tour time approx. 1 hr 30 mins. Also open BH Sats, Suns & Mons, 1.30 - 5pm (last entry 4.30pm) - ground floor only, no guided tours. booked groups Weds & Thurs. Garden: Weds & Thurs, 11am - 6pm; Sats, BH Mons, 11am - 6pm.

Admission: Adult £5.50, Child £2.75. Garden only: £2.40, Child Free.

📷 ♿ Ground floor & grounds suitable. 🎦 🏠 🐕 In grounds, on leads.

AVONCROFT MUSEUM OF HISTORIC BUILDINGS

Tel: 01527 831886
Fax: 01527 876934

Stoke Heath, Bromsgrove, Worcestershire B60 4JR

Owner: Council of Management
Contact: Dr Simon Penn

Historic buildings rescued and restored in 15 acres of Worcestershire countryside.

Location: OS Ref. SO954 684. 2m S of Bromsgrove just SE of A38 by-pass.

Opening Times: Mar & Nov: Tue - Thur, Sats & Suns 10.30am - 4pm. Apr - Jun & Sept - Oct: daily except Mons, 10.30am - 4.30pm. Jul & Aug: daily 10.30am - 5pm. (5.30pm Sat & Suns).

Admission: Adult £5, Child £2.50, OAP £4, Family (2+3) £13.50. Booked groups at reduced rates.

BROADWAY TOWER COUNTRY PARK

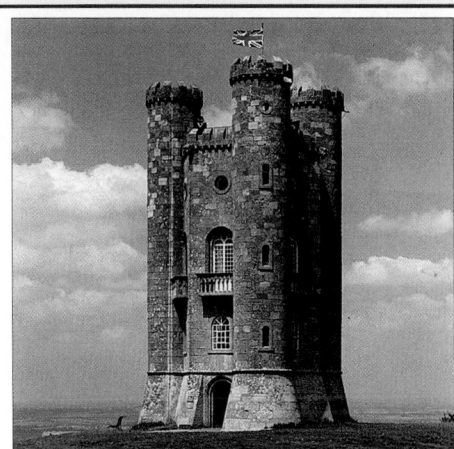

BROADWAY, WORCESTERSHIRE WR12 7LB

Owner: Broadway Tower Country Park Ltd   *Contact:* Annette Gorton

Tel: 01386 852390 **Fax:** 01386 858038 **e-mail:** broadway-tower@clara.net

Broadway Tower is a unique historic building on top of the Cotswold ridge, having been built by the 6th Earl of Coventry in the late 1790s. Its architecture, the fascinating views as well as its exhibitions on famous owners and occupants (including William Morris) make the Tower a "must" for all visitors to the Cotswolds. The Tower is surrounded by 35 acres of parkland with animal enclosures, picnic/BBQ facilities and adventure playground. A complete family day out.

Location: OS Ref. SP115 362. $^1/_2$ m SW of the A44 Evesham to Oxford Rd. $1^1/_2$ m E of Broadway.

Opening Times: 27 Mar – 31 Oct: daily, 10.30am - 5pm. Nov - Mar: Sats & Suns (weather permitting), 11am - 3pm.

Admission: Adult £4, Child £2.30, Conc. £3, Family (2+3) £11.50. Group rate on request. Passport Ticket: (free adm. for 1 yr) Adult £12, Child/Conc. £9, Family £34.50. Tower: Adult £3, Child £1.50.

 Wedding receptions. WC. P Licensed. In grounds, on leads.

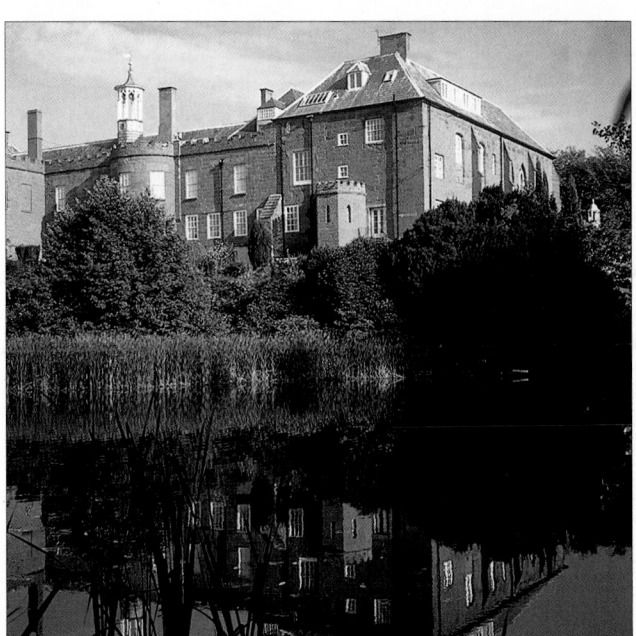

Hartlebury Castle, Worcestershire.

THE COMMANDERY

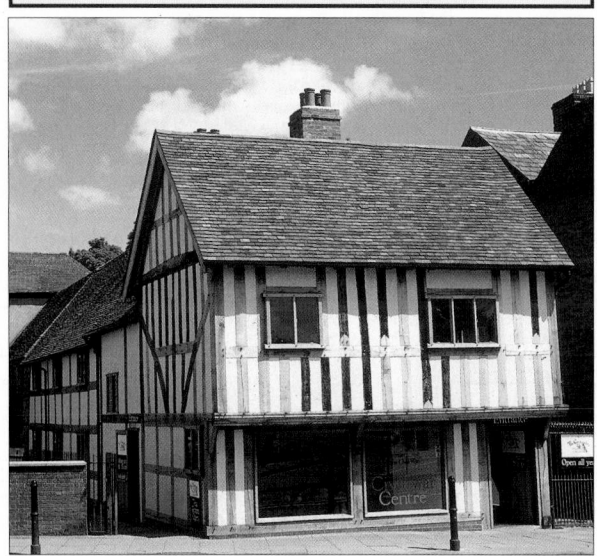

SIDBURY, WORCESTER WR1 2HU

Owner: Worcester City Council   *Contact:* Amanda Lunt

Tel: 01905 361821 **Fax:** 01905 361822

A complex of mainly timber-framed buildings, the Commandery was originally founded as a monastic institution and served as the Royalist headquarters at the Battle of Worcester in 1651. Today it houses fascinating exhibitions including 'Civil War', 'The Commandery Chronicle' and plays host to a varied events programme.

Location: OS Ref. SO853 544. Worcester city centre. 350 yds SE of cathedral.

Opening Times: All year: Mon - Sat, 10am - 5pm; Suns, 1.30 - 5pm.

Admission: Adult £3.70, Child/Conc. £2.60, Family £9.90. Groups (20-100): Adult £2.70, Child/Conc. £2.10.

Partially suitable. By arrangement. Limited. Guide dogs only.

CROOME PARK

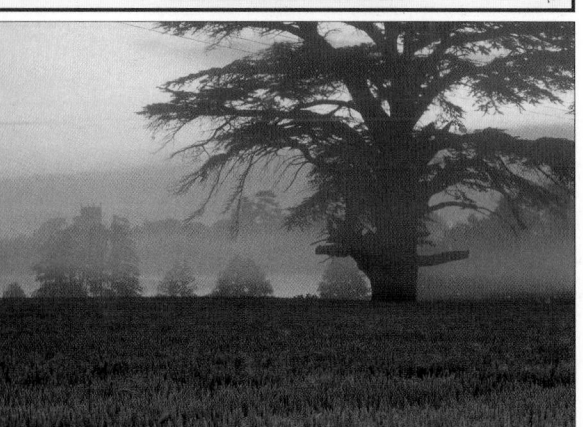

SEVERN STOKE, WORCESTERSHIRE WR8 9JS

Owner: The National Trust   *Contact:* The Property Manager

Tel: 01905 371006 **Fax:** 01905 371090 **e-mail:** croome@smtp.ntrust.org.uk

Croome was 'Capability' Brown's first complete landscape, making his reputation and establishing a new parkland aesthetic which became universally adopted over the next fifty years. The elegant park buildings and other structures are mostly by Robert Adam and James Wyatt. The Trust acquired most of the park in 1996 with substantial grant aid from the Heritage Lottery Fund. The Trust has embarked on a ten year restoration plan, including dredging the water features, clearance and replanting of the gardens and parkland. Royal & Sun Alliance is making a major financial contribution towards the cost of this restoration.

Location: OS150 Ref. SO887 452. 8m S of Worcester and E of A38 and M5, 6m W of Pershore and A44.

Opening Times: 31 Mar - 29 Apr: Sats, Suns, Good Fri & BH Mon, 11am - 5pm. 1 May - 30 Sept: Fri - Mon, 11am - 5pm. 1 Oct - 4 Nov: Sat - Sun, 11am - 5pm. Church: as gardens. Open in association with the Churches Conservation Trust, who own the church. Last admission 4.30pm.

Admission: Adult £3, Child £1.50, Family £7.50.

THE ELGAR BIRTHPLACE MUSEUM

Tel/Fax: 01905 333224

Crown East Lane, Lower Broadheath, Worcester WR2 6RH

Owner: The Elgar Foundation   **Contact:** The Museum Services Manager

A fascinating insight into Elgar's life and music, family and friends. Photographs and memorabilia are displayed in the country cottage where the composer was born. Letters, manuscripts, concert programmes and other treasures from this unique collection feature in the new Elgar Centre's major exhibition, exploring his musical development and inspirations.

Location: OS Ref. SO807 556. 3m W of Worcester, signposted from A44 Worcester/Leominster road.

Opening Times: Daily, 11am - 5pm (last admission 4.15pm). Closed for four weeks in winter (telephone for details).

Admission: Adult £3.50, Child £1.50, OAP £2.60, Student £1.75, Family £8.50. Booked groups (10+): Adult £3, Child £1, OAP £2, Student £1.25.

No inside photography. Partially suitable. WC. Limited for coaches. In grounds, on leads. Tel. for details.

THE GREYFRIARS

Tel: 01905 23571 **e-mail:** greyfriars@smtp.ntrust.org.uk

Worcester WR1 2LZ

Owner: The National Trust   **Contact:** The Custodian

Built in 1480, with early 17th and late 18th century additions, this timber-framed house was rescued from demolition at the time of the Second World War and has been restored and refurbished; interesting textiles and furnishings add character to the panelled rooms; an archway leads through to a delightful garden.

Location: OS150, Ref. SO852 546. Friar Street, in centre of Worcester.

Opening Times: 16 Apr - 25 Oct: Weds, Thurs & BH Mons, 2 - 5pm. Also open: 29/30 Nov & 1 Dec: Street Fayre.

Admission: Adult £2.80, Child £1.40, Family £7.

HARTLEBURY CASTLE

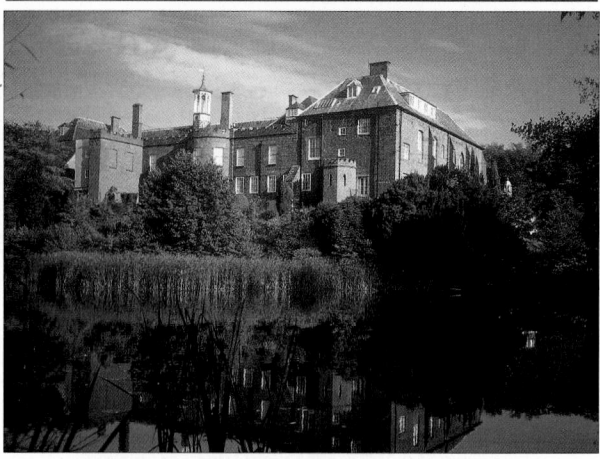

HARTLEBURY, NR KIDDERMINSTER DY11 7XZ

Owner: The Church Commissioners   *Contact:* The County Museum

Tel: 01299 250416 **Fax:** 01299 251890 **e-mail:** museum@worcestershire.gov.uk

Hartlebury Castle has been home to the Bishops of Worcester for over a thousand years. The three principal State Rooms – the medieval Great Hall, the Saloon and the unique Hurd Library – contain period furniture, fine plasterwork and episcopal portraits. In the former servants' quarters in the Castle's North Wing, the County Museum brings to life the past inhabitants of the county, from Roman times to the twentieth century. A wide range of temporary exhibitions and events are held each year, and detailed listings are available from the Museum.

Location: OS Ref. SO389 710. N side of B4193, 2m E of Stourport, 4m S of Kidderminster.

Opening Times: 1 Feb - 30 Nov. County Museum: Mon - Thur, 10am - 5pm. Fris & Suns, 2 - 5pm. Closed Good Fri and Sats. Staterooms: Tue - Thur, 10am - 5pm.

Admission: Combined ticket (Museum & State rooms): Adult £2.20, Child/OAP £1.10. Family (2+3) £6 (2000 prices).

Ground floor & grounds. WC. By arrangement for groups. Guide dogs only.

HANBURY HALL

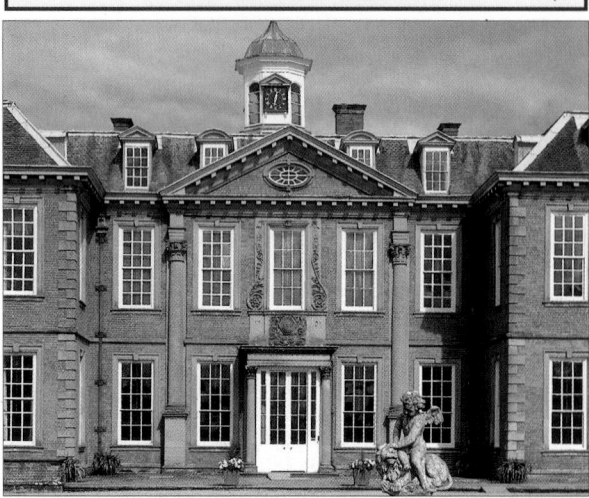

DROITWICH, WORCESTERSHIRE WR9 7EA

Owner: The National Trust   *Contact:* The Property Manager

Tel: 01527 821214 **Fax:** 01527 821251 **e-mail:** hanbury@smtp.ntrust.org.uk

Set in 400 acres of parkland and gardens, this delightful William and Mary house was home to the Vernon family for three centuries. The permanent home of the Watney collection of fine porcelain and Dutch flower paintings, Hanbury Hall also boasts magnificent staircase and ceiling paintings by Sir James Thornhill. Restored 18th century garden, orangery and ice house.

Location: OS150, Ref. SO943 637. 4¹/₂ m E of Droitwich, 4m SE M5/J5.

Opening Times: 1 Apr - 31 Oct: Sun - Wed, 1.30- 5.30pm (open Good Fri). Last adm. 5.30pm or dusk if earlier. Gardens, shop & tearoom open at 12 noon.

Admission: House & Garden: Adult £3, Child £1.50, Family £7.50. Special rates for groups by prior arrangement. New for 2001: Reduced admission rate to celebrate Hanbury's tercentenary.

Ground floor & grounds suitable. WC. For pre-booked groups. Guide dogs only.

HARVINGTON HALL

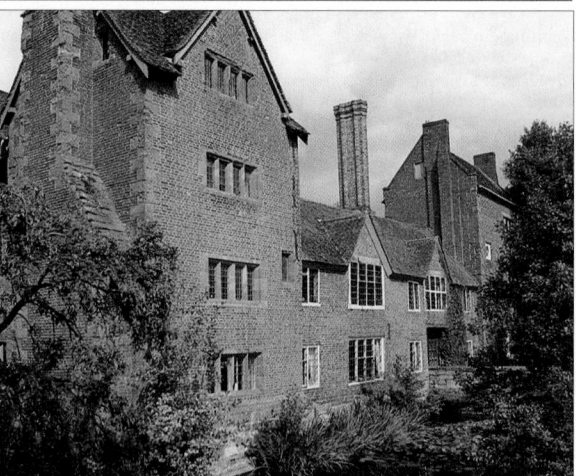

HARVINGTON, KIDDERMINSTER, WORCESTERSHIRE DY104LR

Owner: Roman Catholic Archdiocese of Birmingham   *Contact:* The Administrator

Tel: 01562 777846 **Fax:** 01562 777190 **e-mail:** thehall@harvington.fsbusiness.co.uk

Harvington Hall is a moated, medieval and Elizabethan manor house. Many of the rooms still have their original Elizabethan wall paintings and the Hall contains the finest series of priest-holes in the country. A full programme of events throughout the year including outdoor plays, craft fairs, living history weekends and a pilgrimage is available.

Location: OS Ref. SO839 710. On minor road, ¹/₂ m NE of A450/A448 crossroads at Mustow Green. 3m SE of Kidderminster.

Opening Times: Mar & Oct: Sats & Suns; Apr - Sept: Wed - Sun & BH Mons (closed Good Fri), 11.30am - 5pm. Open throughout the year for pre-booked groups and schools. Occasionally the Hall may be closed for a private function.

Admission: Adult £3.80, Child £2.50, OAP £3, Family £10.50. Garden: £1.

Partially suitable. Licensed. Limited for coaches. Guide dogs only. Tel. for details.

HAWFORD DOVECOTE

Tel: 01684 855300

Hawford, Worcestershire
Owner: The National Trust **Contact:** Regional Office
A 16th century half-timbered dovecote.
Location: OS Ref. SO846 607. 3m N of Worcester, 1/2 m E of A449.
Opening Times: Apr - 31 Oct: daily 9am - 6pm or sunset if earlier. Closed Good Fri, other times by prior appointment.
Admission: 60p.

LEIGH COURT BARN

Tel: 0121 625 6820 - Regional Office

Worcester
Owner: English Heritage **Contact:** The West Midlands Regional Office
Magnificent 14th century timber-framed barn built for the monks of Pershore Abbey. It is the largest of its kind in Britain.
Location: OS Ref. SO784 534. 5m W of Worcester on unclassified road off A4103.
Opening Times: 1 Apr - 30 Sept: Thur - Sun, 10am - 6pm.
Admission: Free.

LITTLE MALVERN COURT

Tel: 01684 892988 **Fax:** 01684 893057

Nr Malvern, Worcestershire WR14 4JN
Owner: Trustees of the late T M Berington **Contact:** Mrs T M Berington
Prior's Hall, associated rooms and cells, c1480, of former Benedictine Monastery. Formerly attached to, and forming part of the Little Malvern Priory Church which may also be visited. It has an oak-framed roof, 5-bay double-collared roof, with two tiers of cusped windbraces. Library. Collections of religious vestments, embroideries and paintings. Gardens: 10 acres of former monastic grounds with spring bulbs, blossom, old fashioned roses and shrubs.
Location: OS130, Ref. SO769 403. 3m S of Great Malvern on Upton-on-Severn Rd (A4104).
Opening Times: 18 Apr - 19 Jul: Weds & Thurs, 2.15 - 5pm. Last admission 4.30pm.
Admission: House & Garden: Adult £4.60, Child £2.50, Garden only: Adult £3.60, Child £1.50.

Garden partially suitable.

MADRESFIELD COURT

Tel: 01684 573614 **Fax:** 01684 569197

Madresfield, Malvern WR13 5AU **e-mail:** madresfield@clara.co.uk
Owner: The Trustees of Madresfield Estate **Contact:** Mr Peter Hughes
Elizabethan and Victorian house with medieval origins. Fine contents. Extensive gardens and arboretum.
Location: OS Ref. SO809 474. 6m SW of Worcester. 1¹/₂ m SE of A449. 2m NE of Malvern.
Opening Times: Guided tours between mid-Apr and Jul on specified dates which are available from the Estate Office, Madresfield, Malvern, Worcs WR13 5AH, tel: 01684 573614. All visitors must join a guided tour and pre-booking is advisable to avoid disappointment.
Admission: £6.

Not suitable. Obligatory.

SPETCHLEY PARK GARDEN

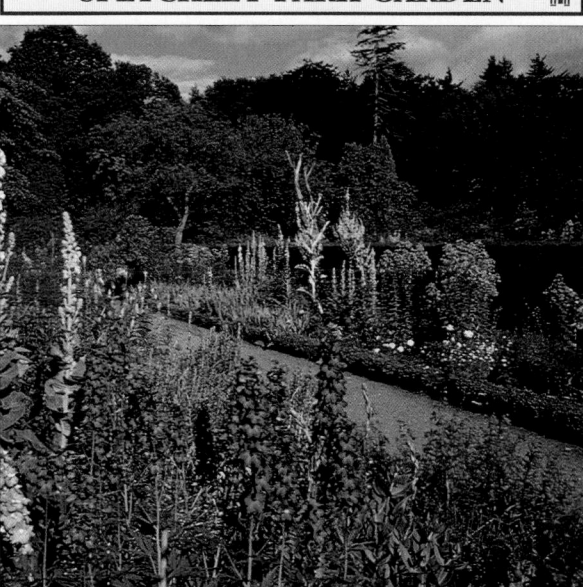

Jerry Harpur.

SPETCHLEY, WORCESTER WR5 1RS
Owner: *Spetchley Garden Charitable Trust* **Contact:** *Mr R J Berkeley*

Tel: 01905 345213/345224 **Fax:** 01453 511915
This lovely 30 acre private garden contains a large collection of trees, shrubs and plants, many rare or unusual. A garden full of secrets, every corner reveals some new vista, some treasure of the plant world. The exuberant planting and the peaceful walks make this an oasis of beauty, peace and quiet. Deer Park close by.
Location: OS Ref. SO895 540. 2m E of Worcester on A422. Leave M5/J6 or J7.
Opening Times: 1 Apr - 30 Sept: Tue - Fri & BH Mons, 11am - 5pm. Suns, 2 - 5pm. Closed all Sats and all other Mons.
Admission: Adult £3.40, Child £1.70. Groups: Adult £3.20, Child £1.60.

Grounds suitable. P

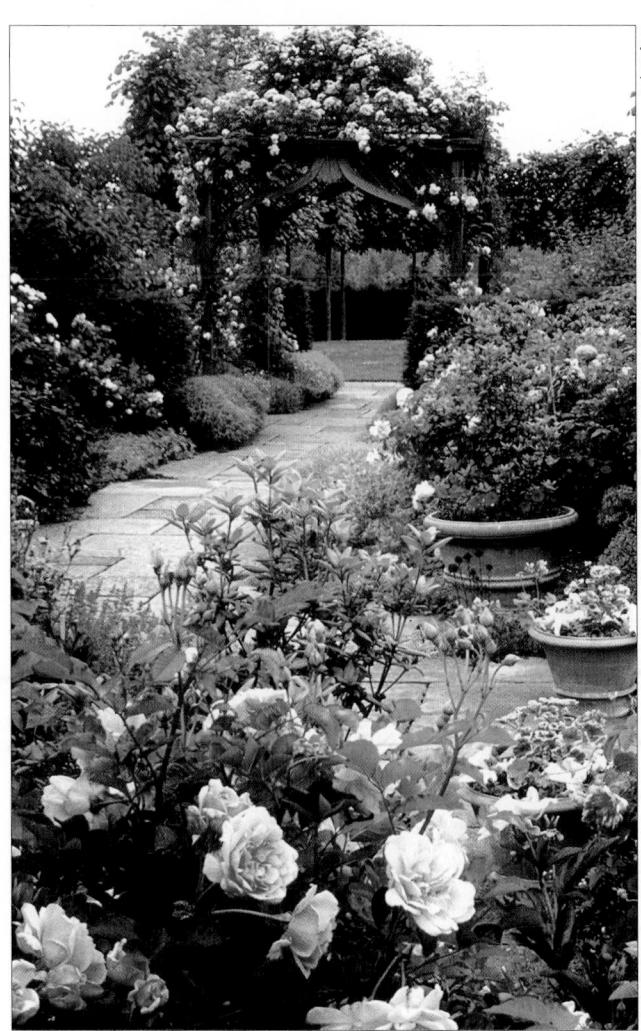

Little Malvern Court, Worcestershire.

THE TUDOR HOUSE

Tel: 01684 592447/594522

16 Church Street, Upton-on-Severn, Worcestershire WR8 0HT
Owner: Mrs Lavender Beard **Contact:** Mrs Wilkinson
Upton past and present, exhibits of local history.
Location: OS Ref. SO852 406. Centre of Upton-on-Severn, 7m SE of Malvern by B4211.
Opening Times: Apr - Oct: daily, 2 - 5pm (Suns until 4pm). Winter Suns only, 2 - 4pm.
Admission: Adult £1, Conc. 50p, Family £2.

WICHENFORD DOVECOTE

Tel: 01684 855300

Wichenford, Worcestershire
Owner: The National Trust **Contact:** Regional Office
A 17th century half-timbered dovecote.
Location: OS Ref. SO788 598. 5¹/₂ m NW of Worcester, N of B4204. Behind the barns.
Opening Times: Apr - 31 Oct: daily, 9am - 6pm or sunset if earlier. Closed Good Fri, other times by appointment.
Admission: 60p.

West Midlands England

WITLEY COURT

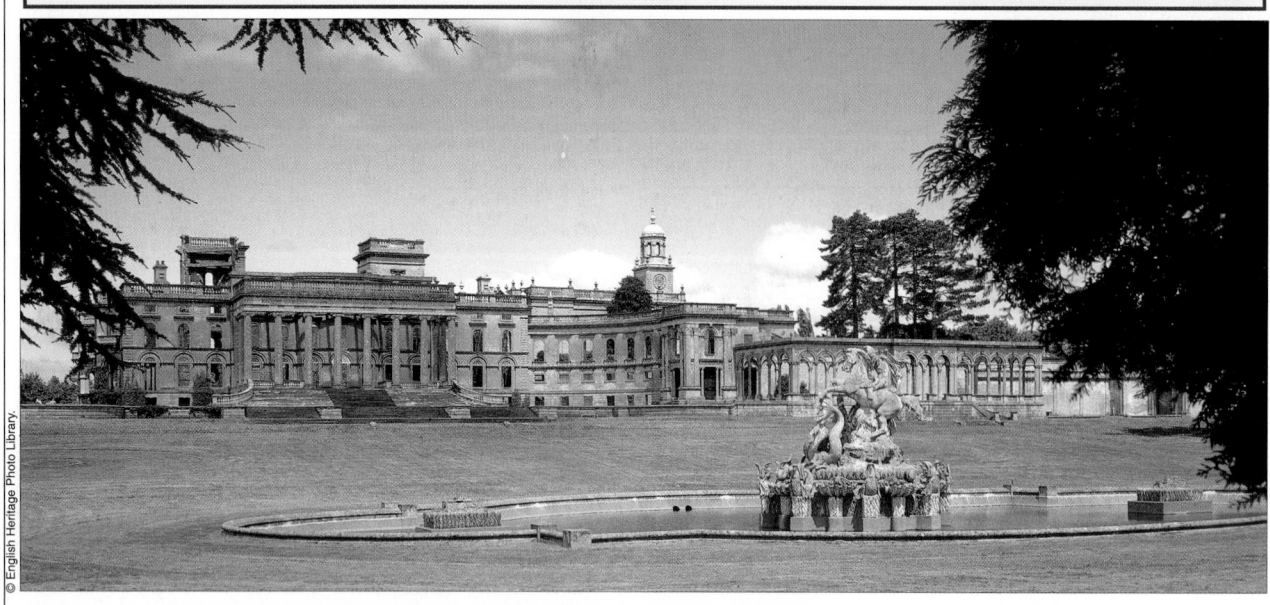

© English Heritage Photo Library.

GREAT WITLEY, WORCESTER WR6 6JT

Owner: *English Heritage* ***Contact:*** *The Custodian*

Tel: 01299 896636

The spectacular ruins of a once great house. An earlier Jacobean manor house, converted in the 19th century into an Italianate mansion, with porticoes by John Nash. The adjoining church, by James Gibbs, has a remarkable 18th century baroque interior. The gardens, William Nesfield's 'Monster Work' were equally elaborate and contained immense fountains, which survive today. The largest is the Perseus and Andromeda Fountain, which will be fired on Easter Sun & Mon; early May BH, Sun & Mon and late May BH, Sun & Mon. The landscaped grounds, fountains and woodlands are being restored to their former glory. The historic parkland will contain the Jerwood Foundation Sculpture Park, eventually consisting of 40 modern British sculptures.

Location: OS150, Ref. SO769 649. 10m NW of Worcester on A443.

Opening Times: 1 Apr - 31 Oct: daily, 10am - 6pm (5pm in Oct). 1 Nov - 31 Mar: Wed - Sun, 10am - 4pm. Closed 24 - 26 Dec & 1 Jan.

Admission: Adult £3.80, Child £1.90, Conc. £2.90, Family £9.50. 15% discount for groups of 11+.

i Visitor welcome point.   Grounds suitable. WC. ⚐ P ❄
🛡 Tel. for details.

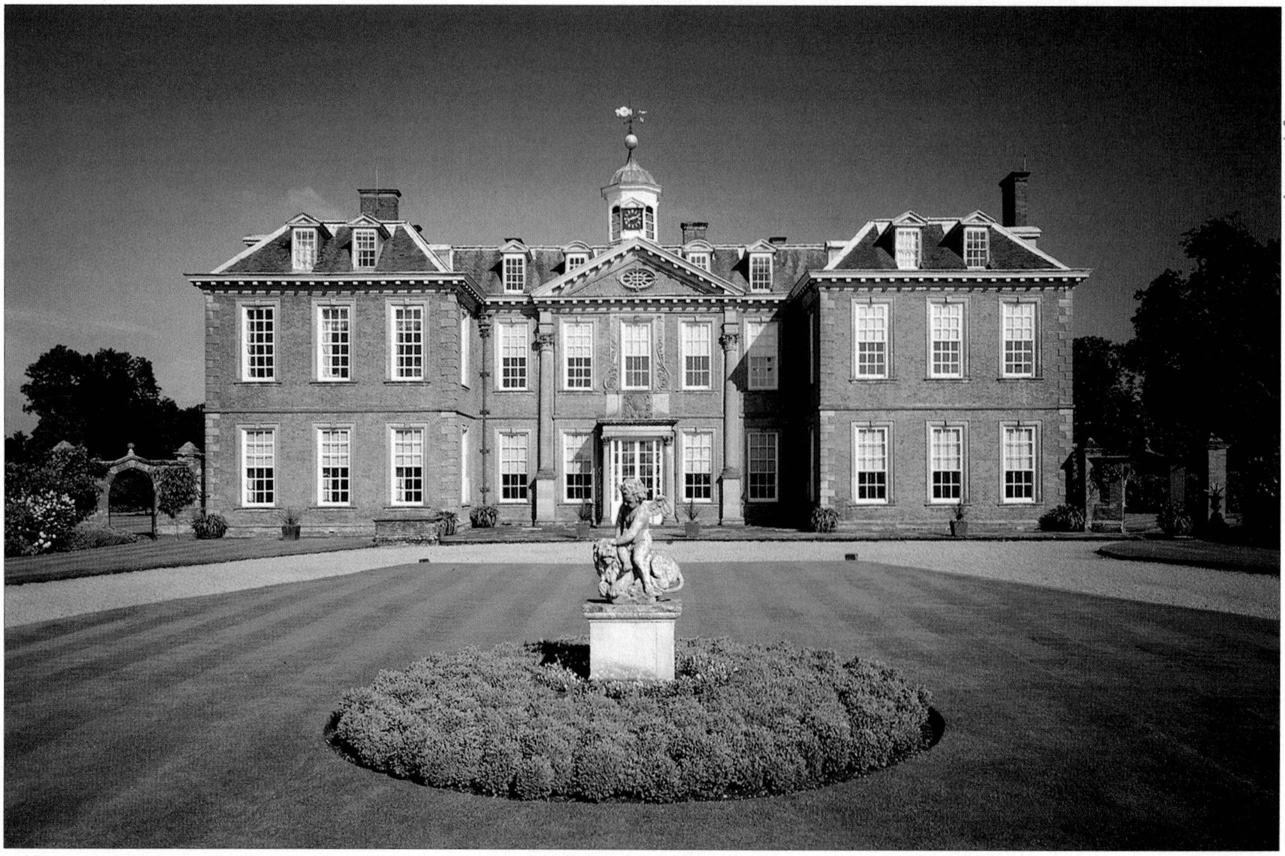

National Trust Photographic Library.

Hanbury Hall, Worcestershire.

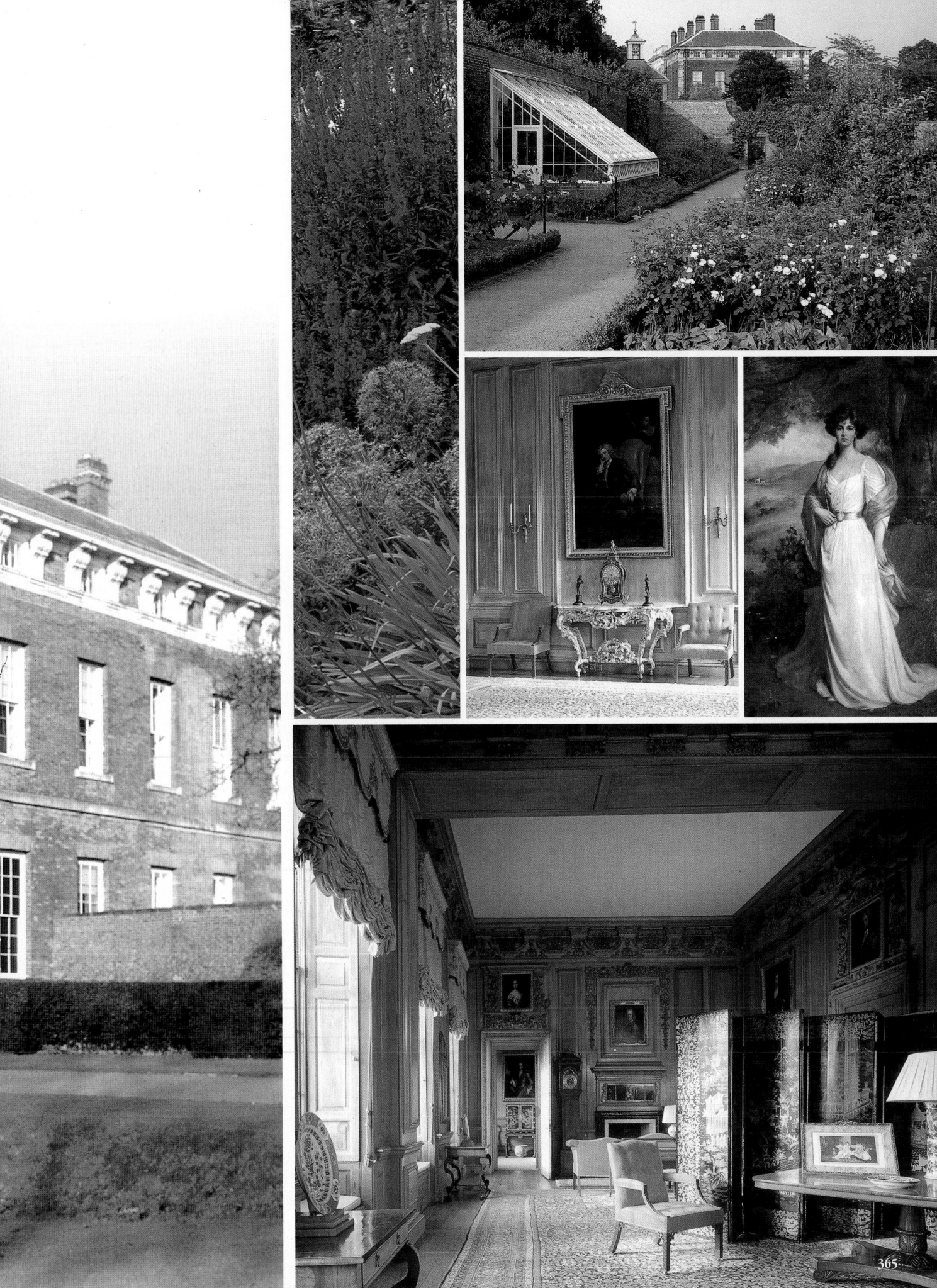

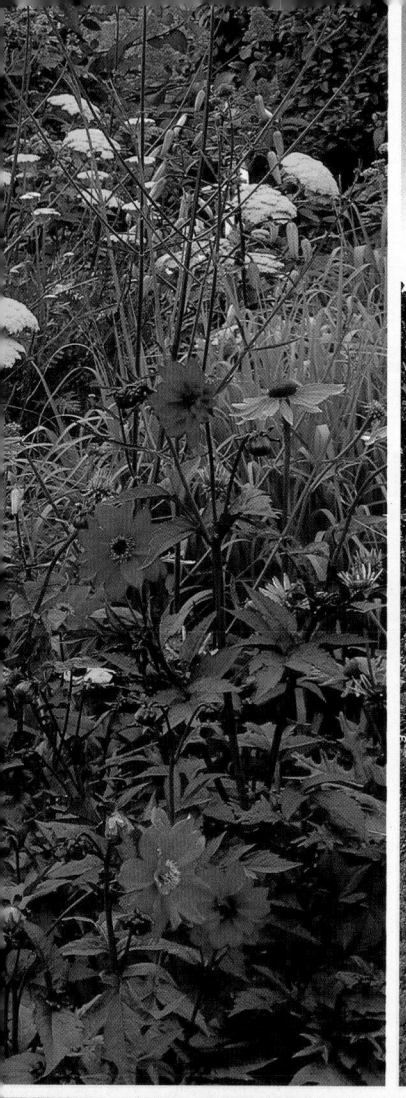

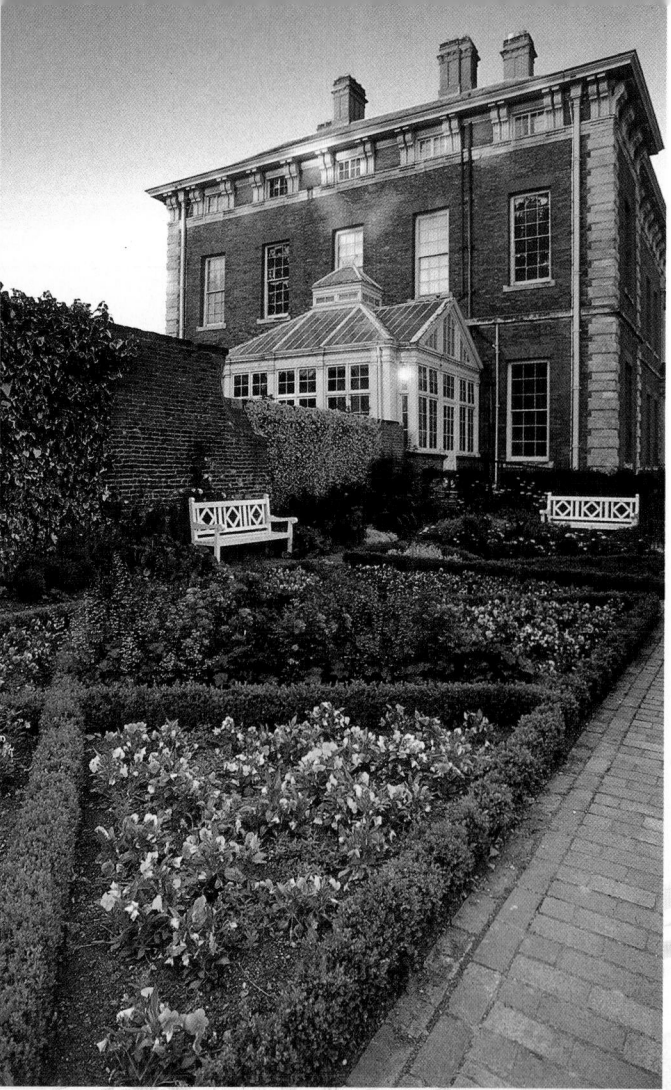

Beningbrough Hall, elegant and graceful, stands at the far end of an avenue of limes. Built of small, locally made, bright red bricks, and flanked by pavilions with cupola roofs, with interiors richly carved and finished, this handsome baroque house has changed little since it was built in the early 18th century. Set among water meadows, bordering the River Ouse, in the Vale of York – the scene is truly idyllic.

Yet although Beningbrough is one of the most remarkable baroque houses in England, it is also an enigma. Almost nothing is known of its building history, and all estate records have been lost.

What the visitor today sees at Beningbrough is therefore very much an attempt by the National Trust to recreate the spirit of a house and garden, rather than a restoration of its precise appearance at the time it was built. The result is a masterpiece.

The National Trust acquired Beningbrough in June 1958 on the death of the last private owner, Lady Chesterfield. However, the Trust's early years at Beningbrough were not easy. The second of six major houses accepted by them between 1957 and 1977 without any endowment to cover running costs – Beningbrough was very soon in dire financial straits. By the mid-1970s its future had become critical. With no money and few visitors, something radical had to be done.

In 1977 the Trust embarked upon a major restoration programme. Rooms were taken back to the soft whites and pale greys typical of early 18th century interiors and furnished with fine walnut pieces and porcelain, as a result of bequests and gifts to the Trust. Walls have been hung with over 100 portraits from the National Portrait Gallery.

By 1997 the gardens, too, were decaying quietly. Today the seven acres of gardens stretching from the south front of the house contain a mix of period and other features. The walled garden, which must have been a model kitchen garden in the 19th century, is now planted for a more labour-saving treatment, but the walls continue to shelter a range of apples, figs and pears, and the original pear arch has been retained as a centrepiece. To the west of the Walled Garden are more intricate planting schemes, with huge double borders having been redesigned to reflect the Edwardian theme of cool midsummer tints.

In capturing the 'spirit' of the place, the Trust has recreated a house and garden of great charm and tranquility, and a wonderful spot to visit.

For further details about *Beningbrough Hall* see entry in Yorkshire and Humber Region.

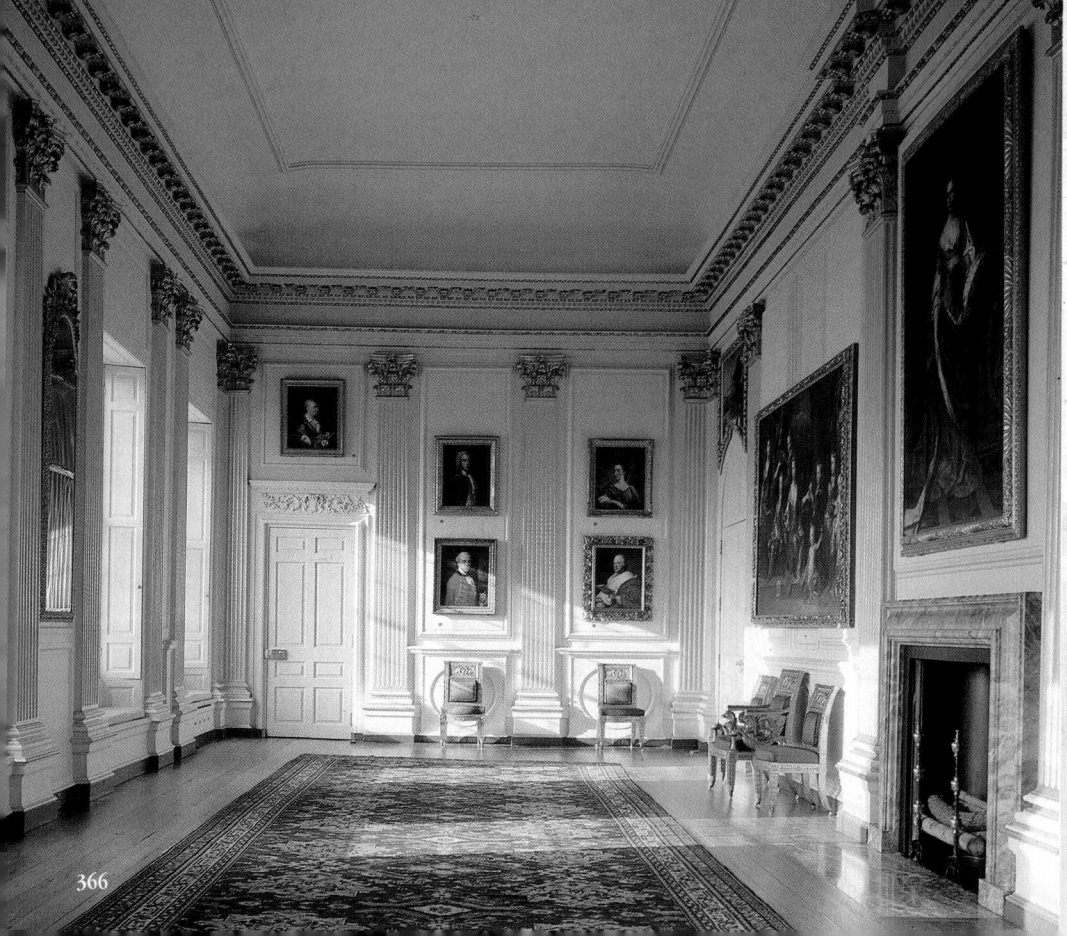

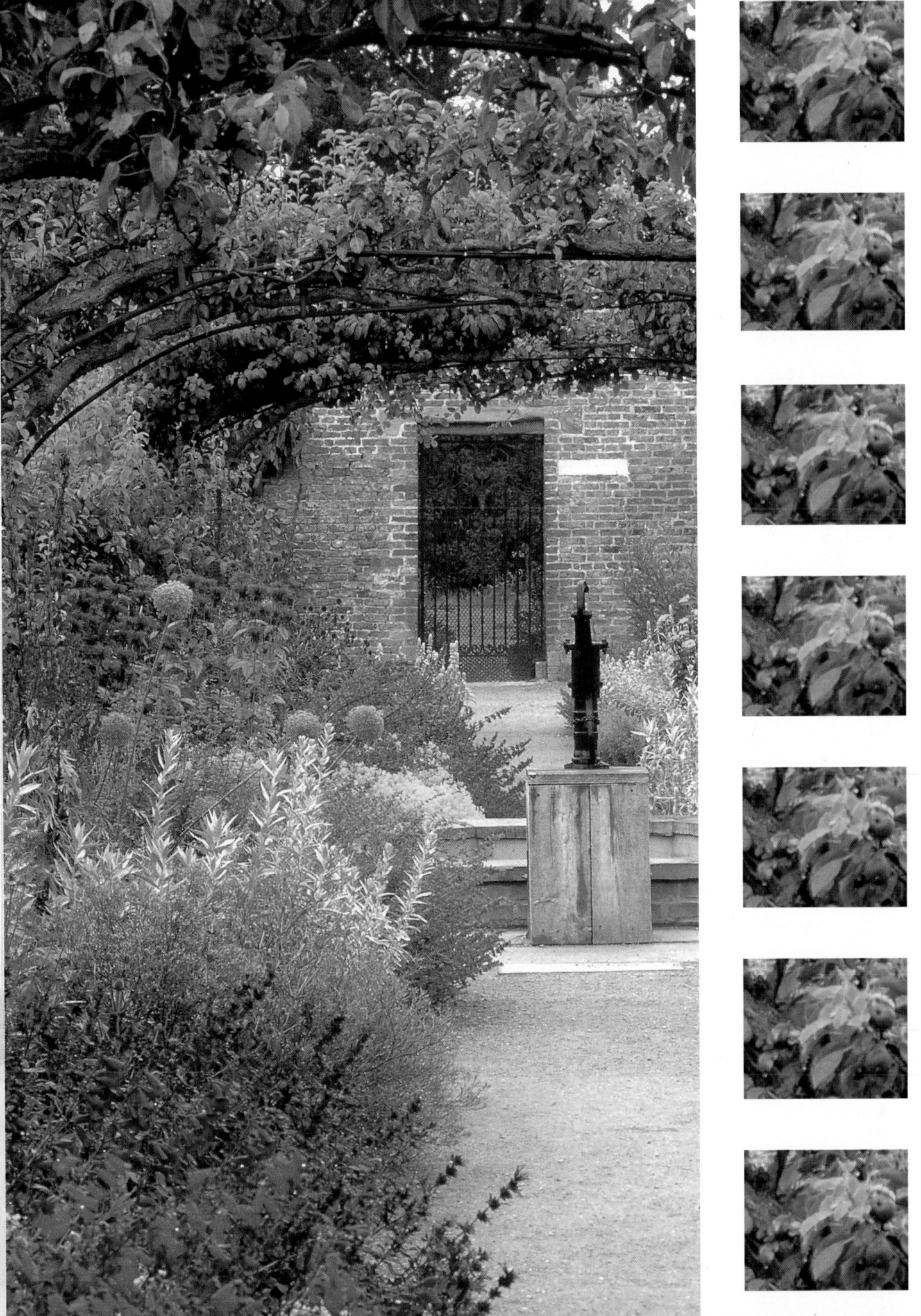

Yorkshire
England

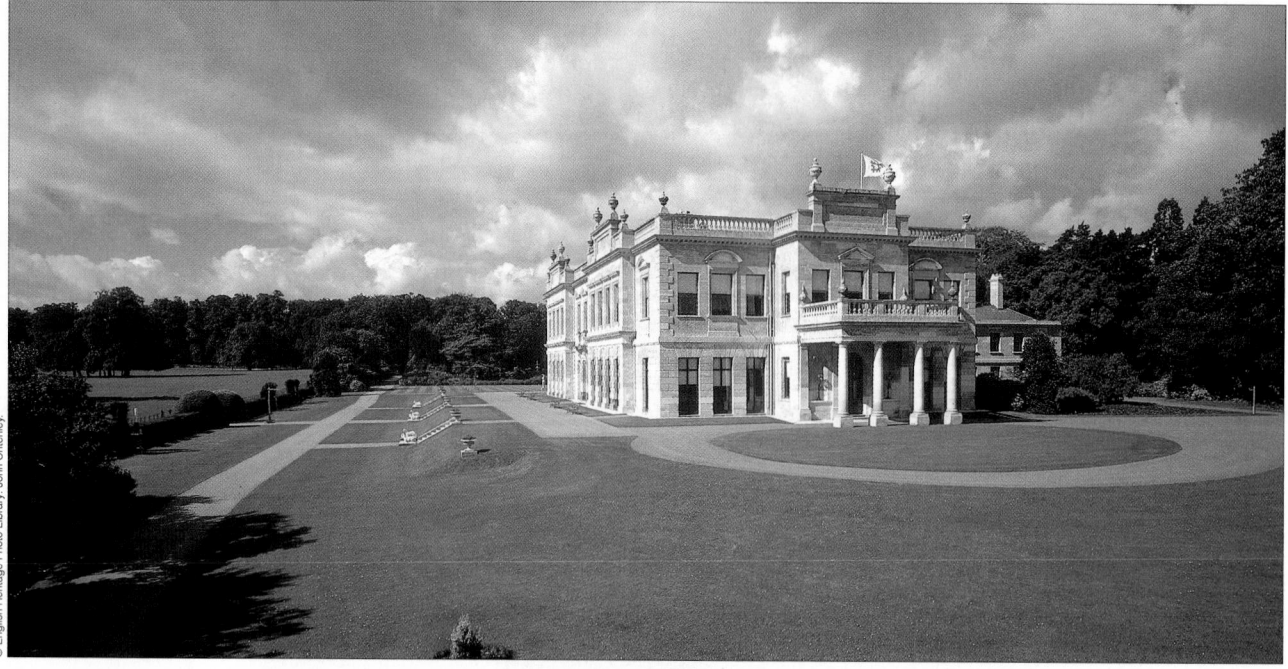

© English Heritage Photo Library: John Critchley

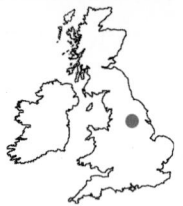

Owner: English Heritage

CONTACT

The Custodian
Brodsworth Hall
Brodsworth
Nr Doncaster
Yorkshire
DN5 7XJ

Tel: 01302 722598

Fax: 01302 337165

LOCATION

OS Ref. SE505 070

In Brodsworth, 5m NW of
Doncaster off A635. Use
A1(M)/J37.

Rail: Doncaster.

BRODSWORTH HALL & GDNS
Nr Doncaster

BRODSWORTH HALL is a rare example of a Victorian country house that has survived largely unaltered with much of its original furnishings and decorations intact. Designed and built in the 1860s it remains an extraordinary time capsule. The now faded grandeur of the reception rooms speaks of an opulent past whilst the cluttered servants wing, with its great kitchen from the age of Mrs Beeton, recalls a vanished way of life. Careful conservation by English Heritage has preserved the patina of time throughout the house to produce an interior that is both fascinating and evocative. The Hall is set within beautifully restored Victorian gardens rich in features which are a delight in any season.

© English Heritage Photo Library

Exhibitions about the family and their love of yachting, the servants and the gardens.

Most of house is accessible. WCs.

Seating for 70.

Groups must book. Booked coach parties: 10am - 1pm.

220 cars and 3 coaches. Free.

Education Centre. Free if booked in advance.

No dogs in gardens.

OPENING TIMES

SUMMER

31 March - 4 November
Tue - Sun, & BHs.

House: 1 - 6pm
(last admission 1 hour
before closing).

Gardens: 12 noon - 6pm.

WINTER

**Gardens, Shop &
Tearoom only**
10 November - 26 March
Sats & Suns: 11am - 4pm.

ADMISSION

SUMMER

House
Adult	£5.00
Child* (5-15yrs)	£2.50
Conc.	£3.80

Groups (11+) 15% discount

Free admission for tour
leaders and coach drivers.

Gardens
Adult	£2.60
Child* (5-15yrs)	£1.30
Conc.	£2.00

WINTER
Adult	£1.60
Child* (5-15yrs)	£0.80
Conc.	£1.20

* Under 5yrs Free

SPECIAL EVENTS

Please telephone for details.

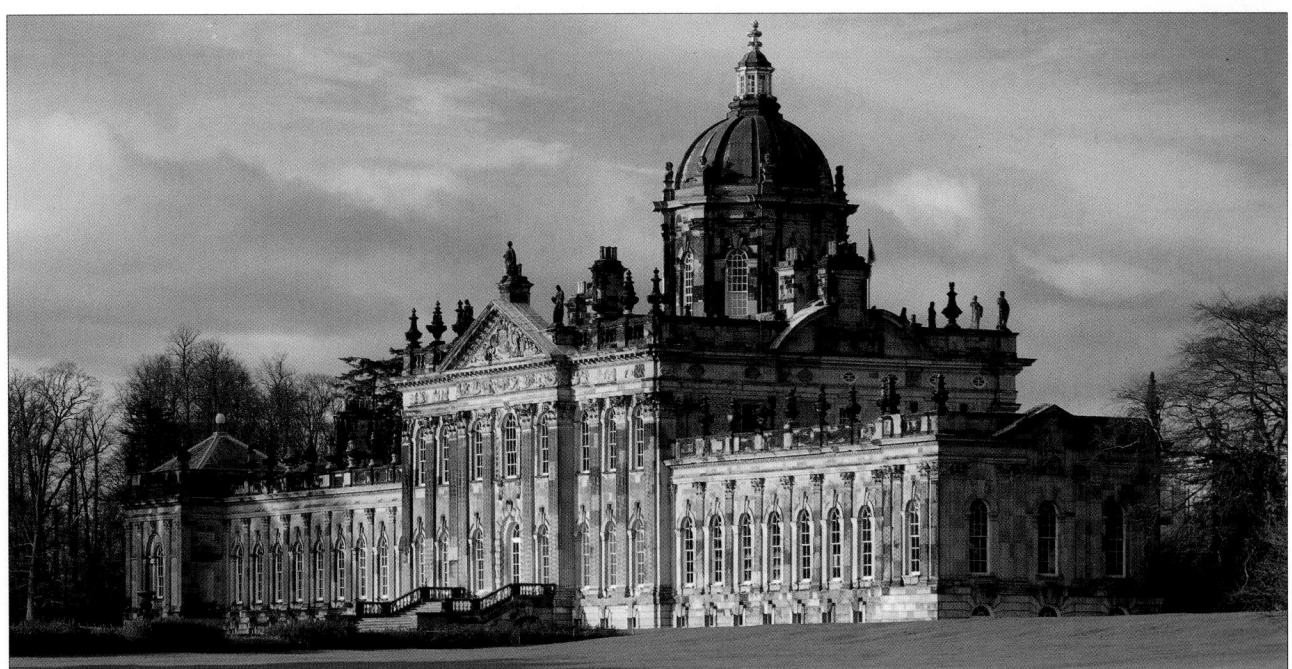

CASTLE HOWARD
York

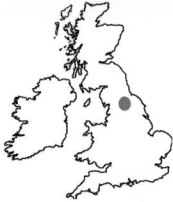

Owner:
The Hon Simon Howard

CONTACT

Mrs M E Carmichael
Castle Howard
York, North Yorks,
YO60 7DA

Tel: 01653 648444

Fax: 01653 648501

e-mail:
house@castlehoward.co.uk

LOCATION

OS Ref. SE716 701

Approaching from S, A64 to
Malton, on entering Malton,
take Castle Howard road
via Coneysthorpe village.
Or from A64 following
signs to Castle Howard via
the Carrmire Gate 9' wide
by 10' high.

York 15m (20 mins), A64.
From London: M1/J32,
M18 to A1(M) to A64,
York/Scarborough Road,
3¹/₂ hrs.

Train: London Kings
Cross to York 1hr. 50
mins. York to Malton
Station 30 mins.

Bus: Service and tour
buses from York Station.

CONFERENCE/FUNCTION		
ROOM	SIZE	MAX CAPACITY
Long Gallery	197' x 24'	280
Grecian Hall	40' x 40'	160

In a dramatic setting between two lakes with
extensive gardens and impressive fountains,
this 18th century Palace was designed by
Sir John Vanbrugh in 1699. Undoubtedly the
finest private residence in Yorkshire it was built
for Charles Howard, 3rd Earl of Carlisle, whose
descendants still live here.

With its painted and gilded dome reaching 80ft
into the Yorkshire sky, this impressive house
has collections of antique furniture, porcelain
and sculpture, while its fabulous collection of
paintings is dominated by the famous Holbein
portraits of Henry VIII and the Duke of Norfolk.

GARDENS

Designed on a heroic scale covering 1,000
acres. The gardens include memorable sights
like the Temple of the Four Winds and the
Mausoleum, the New River Bridge and the
recently restored waterworks of the South
Lake, Cascade, Waterfall and Prince of Wales
Fountain. The walled garden has collections of
old and modern roses.

Ray Wood, acknowledged by the Royal Botanic
Collection, Kew, as a "rare botanical jewel"
has a unique collection of rare trees, shrubs,
rhododendrons, magnolias and azaleas.

Suitable for concerts, craft fairs, fashion shows,
clay pigeon shooting, equestrian events, garden parties,
filming, product launches. Helicopter landing. Firework
displays.

Booked private parties and receptions, min. 25.

Transport equipped for wheelchairs. Chairlift in house
to main floor. WCs.

Two cafeterias.

Guides posted throughout house. Private garden tours
and lectures by arrangement covering house, history, contents
and garden.

400 cars, 20 coaches.

1:10 teacher/pupil ratio required. Special interest: 18th
century architecture, art, history, wildlife, horticulture.

OPENING TIMES

SUMMER

16 March - 4 November
Daily, 11am - 4.30pm.

Last admission 4.30pm.

NB. Grounds, Rose
Gardens, Plant Centre
and Stable Courtyard
Complex open 10am.

WINTER

November - mid March

Grounds open most days
November, December and
January - telephone
for confirmation.

ADMISSION

SUMMER

House & Garden

Adult £7.50

Child (4-16yrs) £4.50

OAP £6.75

Groups (12+)

Adult £6.50

Child (4-16yrs) £4.00

OAP £6.00

Garden only

Adult £4.50

Child* £2.50

WINTER

Grounds only.

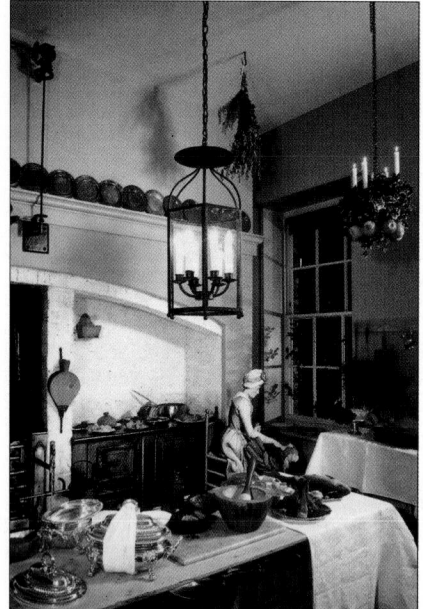
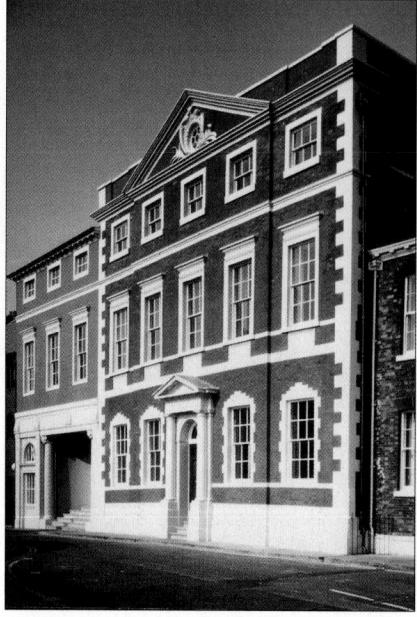
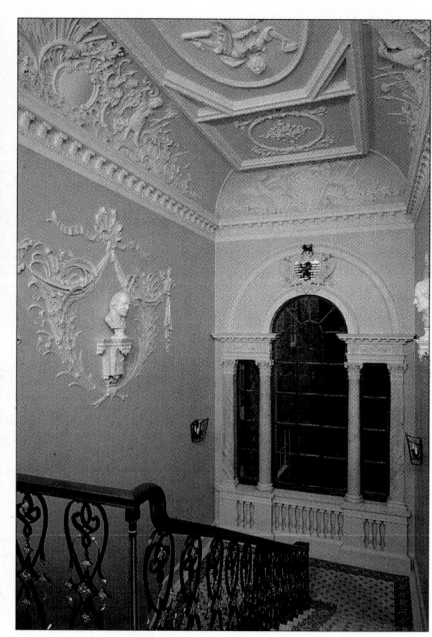

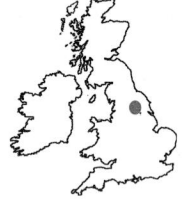

Owner:
York Civic Trust

CONTACT

Mr Peter Brown
Fairfax House
Castlegate
York
YO1 9RN

Tel: 01904 655543

Fax: 01904 652262

LOCATION

OS Ref. SE605 515

In centre of York between
Castle Museum and
Jorvik Centre.

London 4 hrs by car,
2 hrs by train.

Rail: York Station,
10 mins walk.

Taxi: Station Taxis
01904 623332.

FAIRFAX HOUSE
York

FAIRFAX HOUSE was acquired and fully restored by the York Civic Trust in 1983/84. The house, described as a classic architectural masterpiece of its age and certainly one of the finest townhouses in England, was saved from near collapse after considerable abuse and misuse this century, having been converted into a cinema and dance hall.

The richly decorated interior with its plasterwork, wood and wrought-iron, is now the home for a unique collection of Georgian furniture, clocks, paintings and porcelain.

The Noel Terry Collection, gift of a former treasurer of the York Civic Trust, has been described by Christie's as one of the finest private collections formed this century. It enhances and complements the house and helps to create that special 'lived-in' feeling, providing the basis for a series of set-piece period exhibitions which bring the house to life in a very tangible way.

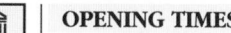

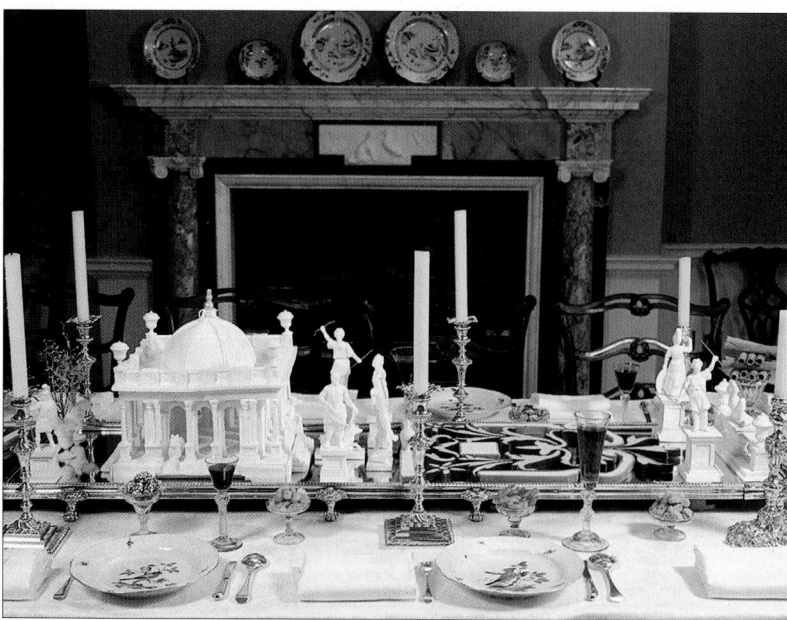

ℹ️ Suitable for filming. No photography in house. Liveried footmen, musical & dancing performances can be arranged.

🛍️

🍽️ Max. 28 seated. Groups up to 50: buffet can be provided.

♿ Visitors may alight at entrance prior to parking. No WCs except for functions.

🚶 A guided tour can be arranged at a cost of £5. Evening and daytime guided tours, telephone for details. Available in French and German. Tour time: 1¹/₂ hrs.

🅿️ 300 cars, 50 yds from house. Coach park is ¹/₂ m away, parties are dropped off; drivers please telephone for details showing the nearest coach park and approach to the house.

❄️

OPENING TIMES

SUMMER

17 February - 6 January

Mon - Thur: 11am - 5pm.

Fris: Guided tours only at 11am and 2pm.

Sats: 11am - 5pm.

Suns: 1.30 - 5pm.

Last admission 4.30pm.

WINTER

Closed

7 January - 16 February & 24 - 26/31 December.

ADMISSION

Adult £4.00

Child (5 -16yrs).........£1.50

Conc. £3.50

Groups*

Adult £3.00

Child (5 -16yrs).........£1.00

Conc. £3.00

* Min payment 15 persons.

🎭 SPECIAL EVENTS

• **MAR 1 - JUN 1:**
'Obsession' - The Collector and their Collections.

• **SEPT 1 - NOV 20:**
'Cutting Edge' - Evolution of of Cutlery and Place Settings.

• **DEC 3 - JAN 6:**
Annual exhibition on the 'Keeping of Christmas'. Information extracted from the family papers helps re-create, in a very tangible way, the ritual and decoration of Christmas celebrations in Fairfax House from 1760 -1840. Booked parties can be given mulled wine and mince pies at end of the tour.

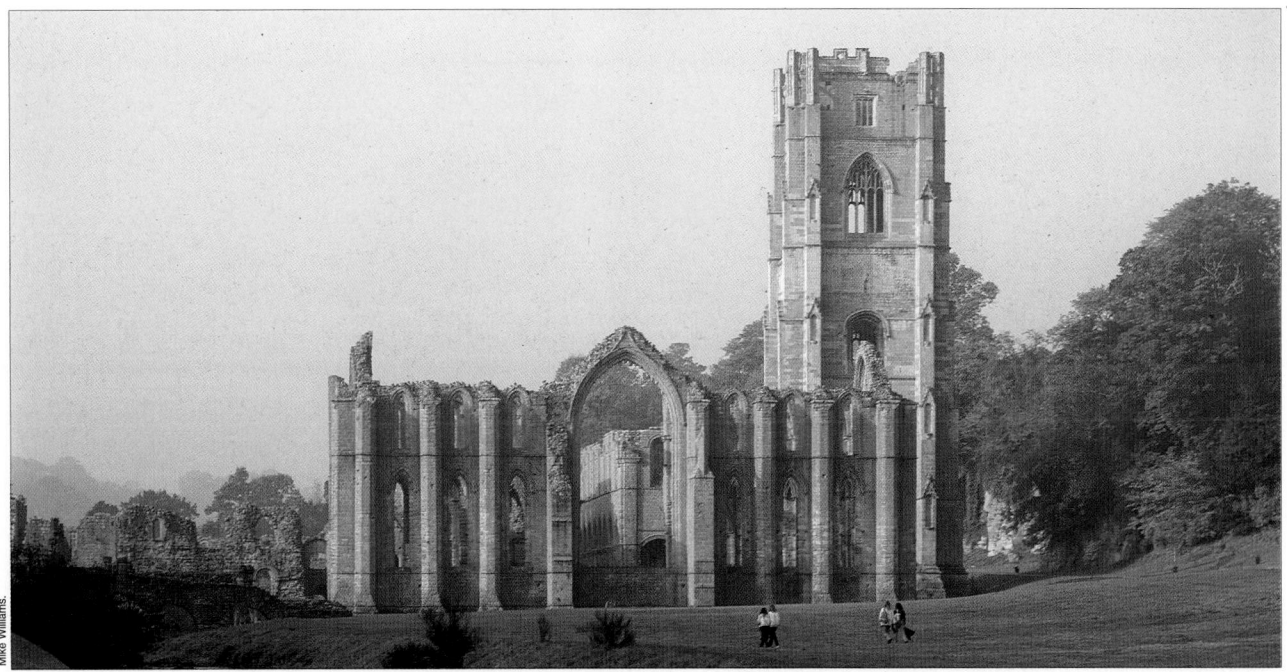

Mike Williams.

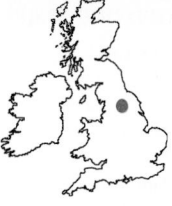

Owner:
The National Trust

CONTACT

The National Trust
Fountains Abbey
and Studley Royal
Ripon
North Yorkshire
HG4 3DY

Tel: 01765 608888

Fax: 01765 608889

LOCATION

OS Ref. SE275 700

Abbey entrance;
4m W of Ripon off B6265.
8m W of A1.

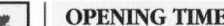

FOUNTAINS ABBEY & STUDLEY ROYAL
Ripon

One of the most remarkable sites in Europe, sheltered in a secluded valley, Fountains Abbey and Studley Royal, a World Heritage Site, encompasses the spectacular remains of a 12th century Cistercian abbey, an Elizabethan mansion, and one of the best surviving examples of a Georgian green water garden. Elegant ornamental lakes, avenues, temples and cascades provide a succession of unforgettable eye-catching vistas in an atmosphere of peace and tranquillity. St Mary's Church, built by William Burges in the 19th century, provides a dramatic focal point to the medieval deer park with over 500 deer.

Fountains Mill opens Summer 2001. Over eight centuries of various industrial activity will be revealed. Considered to be one of the finest surviving examples of a monastic water mill in Britain.

The Abbey is maintained by English Heritage. St Mary's Church is owned by English Heritage and managed by the National Trust.

OPENING TIMES

April - September
Daily: 10am - 7pm.

January - March &
October - December
Daily: 10am - 5pm.

Last admission 1 hr
before closing.

Closes at 4pm on
6/7 July.

Closed 24/25 December,
and Fris in November -
January.

ADMISSION

Adult £4.50
Child (5-16yrs)...........£2.30
Family £11.00

Groups (15-30)
Adult £3.90
Child (5-16yrs)...........£2.10

Groups (31+)
Adult £3.50
Child (5-16yrs)...........£1.90

Under 5s Free.

Group discount
applicable only with
prior booking.

Group visits and disabled
visitors, please telephone
in advance, 01765 601005.

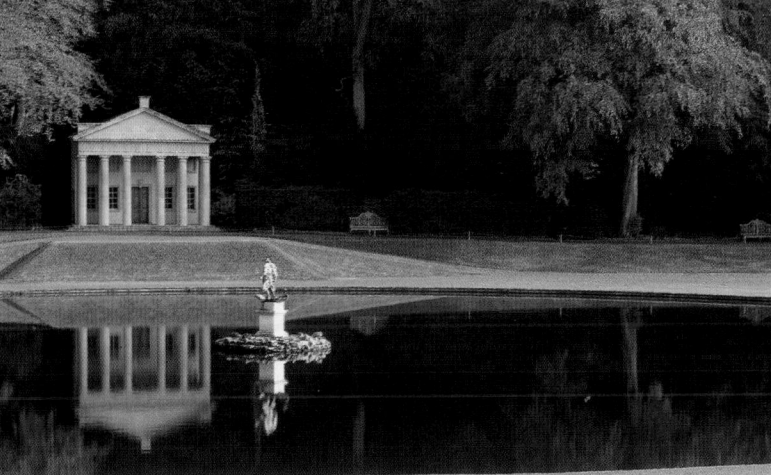

Events held throughout the year. Exhibitions. Seminar facilities. Outdoor concerts, meetings, activity days, walks.

Two shops.

Dinners and dances.

Free batricars & wheelchairs, please book, tel. 01765 601005. 3-wheel Batricars not permitted due to terrain. Tours for visually impaired, please book. WC.

Groups please book, discounted rates. Licensed.

Licensed.

Free, but seasonal. Groups, please use Visitor Centre entrance.

Drivers must book groups. Limited for coaches.

In grounds, on leads.

Tel. for details.

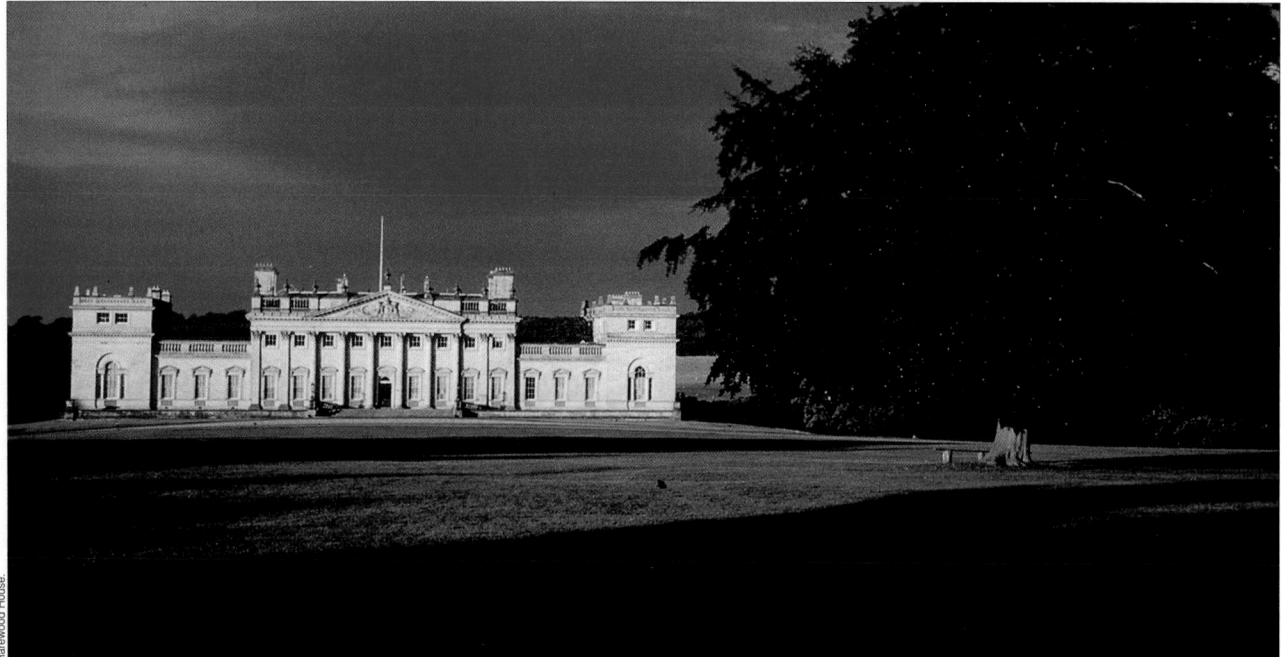

Harewood House.

HAREWOOD HOUSE
Leeds

Designed in 1759 by John Carr, Harewood House is the Yorkshire home of the Queen's cousin, the Earl of Harewood. His mother, HRH Princess Mary, Princess Royal - daughter of King George V - lived at Harewood for 35 years and much of her fascinating Royal memorabilia is still displayed throughout her former rooms.

The House, renowned for its stunning architecture and exquisite Adam interiors, contains a rich collection of Chippendale furniture, fine porcelain and outstanding art collections from Italian Renaissance masterpieces and Turner watercolours to 18th century and 20th century works. Also now on permanent display, is the opulent Chippendale State Bed - newly restored to its former glory and unseen for 150 years.

In the 1000 acres of parkland, landscaped by 'Capability' Brown are lakeside and woodland walks, magnificent collections of Rhododendron (April - June) and Sir Charles Barry's parterre Terrace which offers excellent views of the surrounding countryside beyond.

The hugely popular Bird Garden is home to around 100 rare and endangered species from Africa, America and Australia, as well as popular favourites - penguins, flamingos and owls.

Throughout the season are a host of special events including open-air concerts, theatre performances, craft festivals, car rallies and much more. During 2001, the dedicated Watercolour Rooms and Terrace Gallery will feature a changing programme of exhibitions from works by JMW Turner to historical and contemporary portraiture.

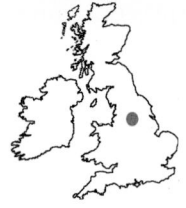

Owner: The Earl of Harewood

CONTACT

Mary Stuart
Moor House
Harewood Estate
Harewood
Leeds
West Yorkshire
LS17 9LQ

Tel: 0113 2181010
Fax: 0113 2181002
e-mail: business@
harewood.org

LOCATION

OS Ref. SE311 446

A1 N or S to Wetherby.

A659 via Collingham, Harewood is on A61 between Harrogate and Leeds. Easily reached from A1, M1, M62 and M18. Half an hour from York.

15 mins from centre of Leeds or Harrogate.

Rail: Leeds Station 7m.

Bus: No. 36 from Leeds or Harrogate.

CONFERENCE/FUNCTION		
ROOM	SIZE	MAX CAPACITY
State Dining Rm.		32
Gallery		96
Courtyard Suite		120
Courtyard Marquee	20' x 24'	400

Marquees can be accommodated, concerts and product launches. No photography in the house.

Ideal for corporate entertaining including drinks receptions, buffets and wedding receptions. Specific rooms available for corporate entertaining plus Courtyard Suite for conferences/product launches.

Visitors may alight at entrance. Parking in allocated areas. Most facilities accessible. Wheelchair available at House and Bird Garden. WC. Special concessions apply to disabled groups. Some steep inclines.

Licensed.   Licensed.

Cars 400 yds from house. 50+ coaches 500 yds from house. Drivers to verify in advance.

By arrangement. Audio tour of house £1.50. Lectures by arrangement.

Dogs on leads in grounds, guide dogs only in house.

Civil Wedding Licence.

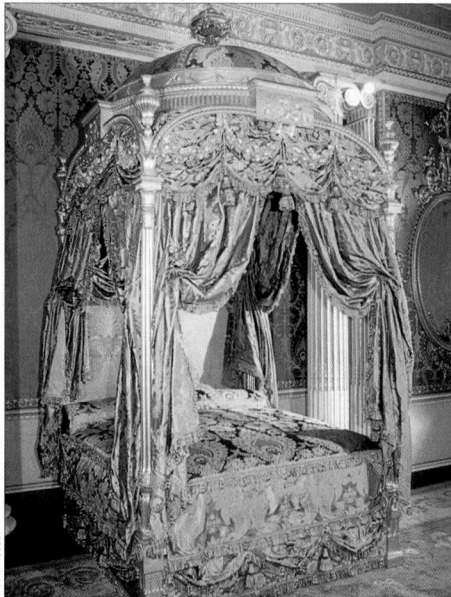

Harewood House.

OPENING TIMES

SUMMER
14 Mar - 4 Nov 2001
closed 8 June

House
Daily from 11am - 4.30pm.

Bird Garden & Grounds
Daily from 10am.

Café
10.30am - 4.30pm.

WINTER
House closed: Nov - Mar.
Grounds & Gardens:
Nov/Dec, open weekends
(ring to confirm times).

ADMISSION

All attractions

Adult	£7.50
Child (4-15yrs)	£5.00
Student	£5.00
OAP	£6.75
Family (2+3)	£26.00

Groups (15+)

Adult	£6.25
OAP	£5.75

Bird Garden & Grounds

Adult	£6.25
Child (4-15yrs)	£3.50
Student	£3.50
OAP	£5.25
Family (2+3)	£19.00

SPECIAL EVENTS

- **MAY 26 - 28:**
  Live Crafts.

- **JUN 17:**
  Vintage & Classic Car Rally.

- **JUL 13 - 15**
  Food Lovers Fair.

- **JUL 28 - 30**
  Leeds Championship Dog Show.

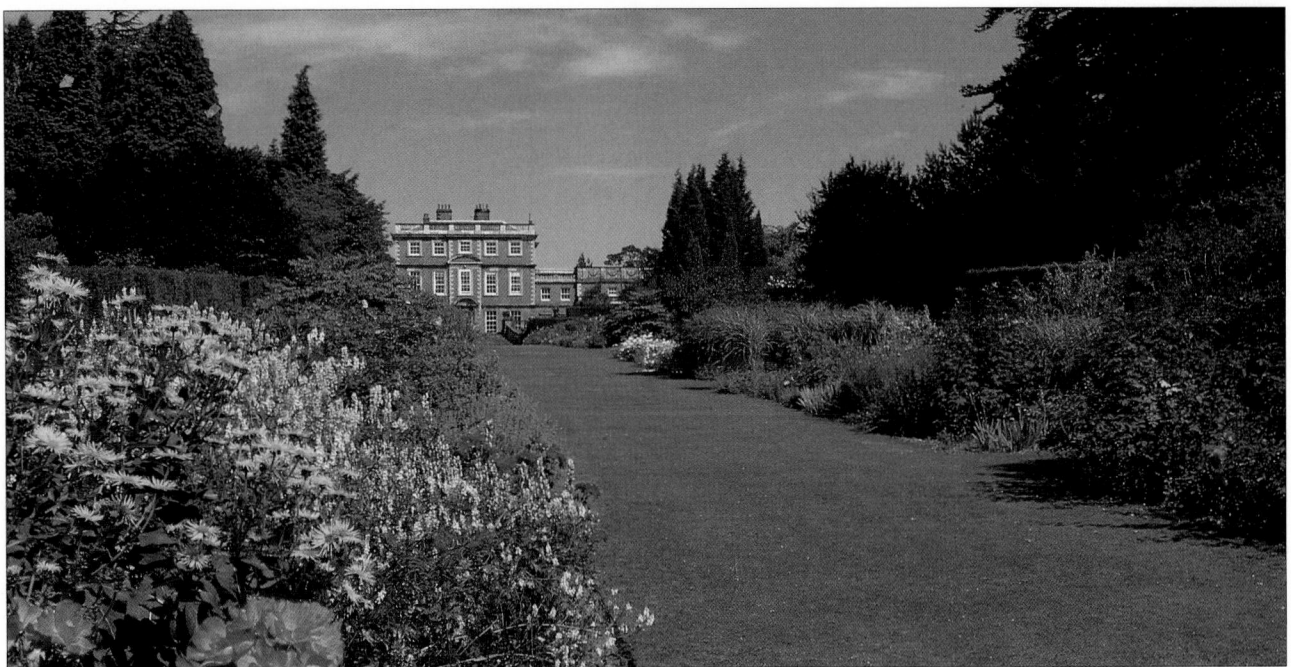

NEWBY HALL & GARDENS
Ripon

NEWBY HALL, the Yorkshire home of the Compton family, is a late 17th century house built in the style of Sir Christopher Wren. William Weddell, an ancestor of Mr Compton, made the Grand Tour in the 1760s, and amongst the treasures he acquired were magnificent classical statuary and a superb set of Gobelin Tapestries. To house these treasures, Weddell commissioned Robert Adam to create the splendid domed Sculpture Gallery and Tapestry Room that we see today. The Regency dining room and billiard room were added later. There is much fine Chippendale furniture and in recent years Mrs Robin Compton restored the decoration of the house, painstakingly researching colour and decor of the Adam period.

GARDENS

25 acres of glorious gardens contain rare and beautiful shrubs and plants. Newby's famous double herbaceous borders, flanked by great bastions of yew hedges, sweep down to the River Ure. Formal gardens such as the Autumn and Rose Gardens – each with splashing fountains – a Victorian rock garden, the tranquillity of Sylvia's Garden, pergolas and even a tropical garden, make Newby a 'Garden for all Seasons'. Newby holds the National Collection of the Genus Cornus and in 1987 won the Christie's/ HHA Garden of the Year Award. The gardens also incorporate an exciting children's adventure garden and miniature railway.

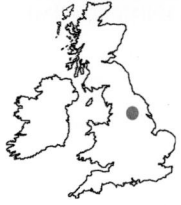

Owner:
Mr Richard Compton

CONTACT

The Opening Administrator
Newby Hall
Ripon
North Yorkshire
HG4 5AE

Tel: 01423 322583

Fax: 01423 324452

e-mail:
info@newbyhall.com

LOCATION

OS Ref. SE348 675

Midway between London and Edinburgh, 4m W of A1, towards Ripon. S of Skelton 2m NW of (A1) Boroughbridge. 4m SE of Ripon.

Taxi: Ripon Taxi Rank 01765 601283.

Bus: On Ripon - York route.

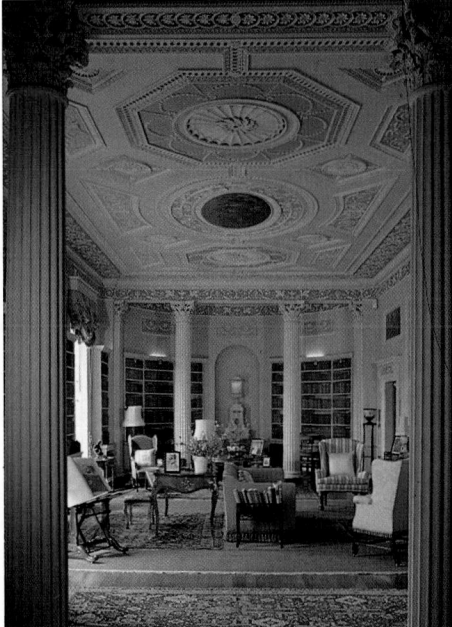

Suitable for filming and for special events, craft and country fairs, vehicle rallies etc, promotions and lectures. No indoor photography. Allow a full day for viewing house and gardens.

Wedding receptions & special functions.

5 wheelchairs available. Access to ground floor of house and key areas in gardens. WC.

Garden restaurant, teas, hot and cold meals. Booked groups in Grantham Room. Menus/rates on request.

Ample. Hard standing for coaches.

Welcome. Rates on request. Grantham Room for use as wet weather base subject to availability. Woodland discovery walk, adventure gardens and train rides on 10¼" gauge railway.

Guide dogs only.

SPECIAL EVENTS

• **MAY 13:**
Spring Plant Fair.

• **JUN 8 - 10 & AUG 24 - 27:**
Rainbow Craft Fair.

• **JUL 15:**
Historic Vehicle Rally.

See Special Events Index for full details

OPENING TIMES

SUMMER

House
1 April - end September
Daily except Mons but open BH Mons,
12 noon - 5pm
Last admission 4.30pm.

Garden
1 April - end September
Daily except Mons but open BH Mons.
11am - 5.30pm
Last admission 5pm.

WINTER
October - end March
Closed.

ADMISSION

House & Garden
Adult £6.80
Child (4-16yrs)..........£4.00
OAP.........................£5.80
Disabled.................£4.00
Group (15+)
Adult £5.50
Child (4-16yrs) £3.70

Garden only
Adult £5.00
Child (4-16yrs)..........£3.50
OAP.........................£4.00
Disabled.................£3.50
Group (15+)
Adult £4.00
Child (4-16yrs) £3.00

Additional charge for train.

CONFERENCE/FUNCTION		
ROOM	SIZE	MAX CAPACITY
Grantham Room	90' x 20'	200

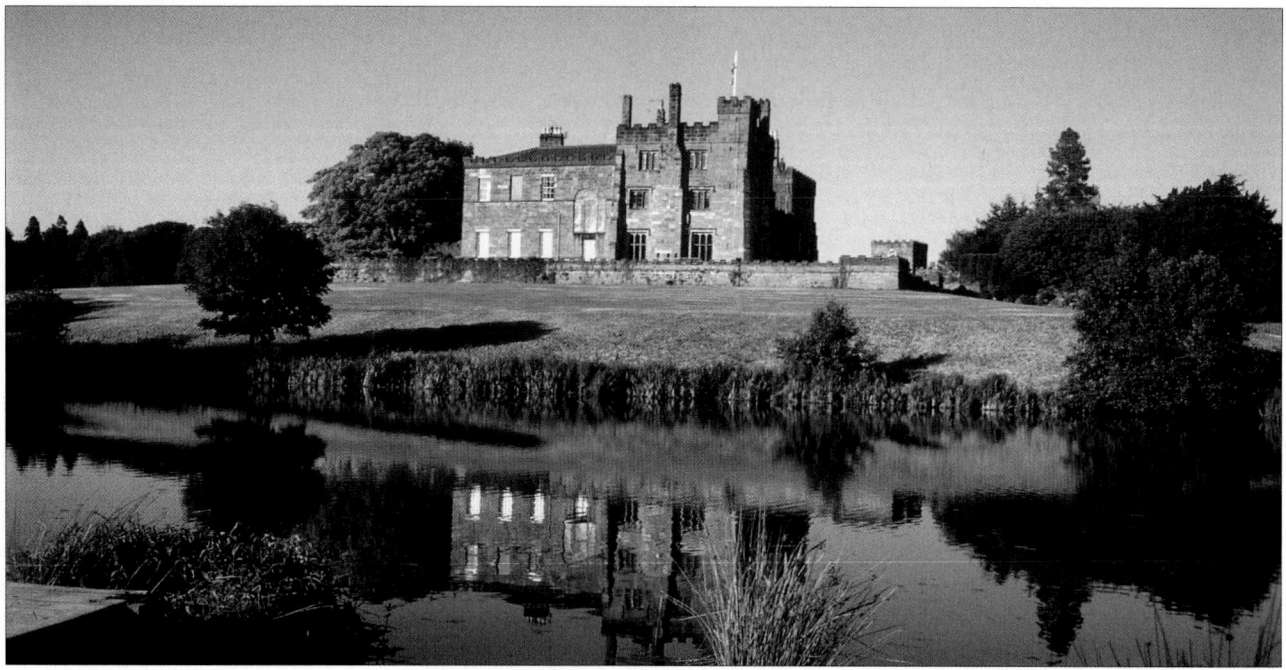

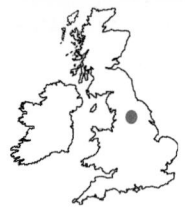

RIPLEY CASTLE
Harrogate

RIPLEY CASTLE has been the home of the Ingilby family for twenty-six generations and Sir Thomas and Lady Ingilby together with their five children continue the tradition. The guided tours are amusing and informative, following the lives and loves of one family for over 670 years and how they have been affected by events in English history. The Old Tower dates from 1555 and houses splendid armour, books, panelling and a Priest's Secret Hiding Place, together with fine paintings, china, furnishings and chandeliers collected by the family over the centuries. The extensive Victorian Walled Gardens have been transformed and are a colourful delight

through every season. In the Spring you can appreciate 150,000 flowering bulbs which create a blaze of colour through the woodland walks, and also the National Hyacinth Collection whose scent is breathtaking. The restored Hot Houses have an extensive tropical plant collection, and in the Kitchen Gardens you can see an extensive collection of rare vegetables from the Henry Doubleday Research Association.

Ripley village on the Castle's doorstep is a model estate village with individual charming shops, an art gallery, delicatessen and Farmyard Museum.

Owner:
Sir Thomas Ingilby Bt

CONTACT

Tours: Wendy McNae
Meetings/Dinners:
Chloë Drummond
Ripley Castle
Ripley
Harrogate
North Yorkshire
HG3 3AY

Tel: 01423 770152

Fax: 01423 771745

e-mail: enquiries@
ripleycastle.co.uk

LOCATION

OS Ref. SE283 605

W edge of village. Just off A61, 3½ m N of Harrogate, 8m S of Ripon. M1 18m S, M62 20m S.

Rail: London - Leeds/York 2hrs. Leeds/York - Harrogate 30mins.

Taxi: Blueline taxis Harrogate (01423) 503037.

CONFERENCE/FUNCTION		
ROOM	SIZE	MAX CAPACITY
Morning Rm	27' x 22'	80
Large Drawing Rm	30 'x 22'	80
Library	31 x 19'	75
Tower Rm	33' x 21'	75
Map Rm	19' x 14'	20
Dining Rm	23' x 19'	30

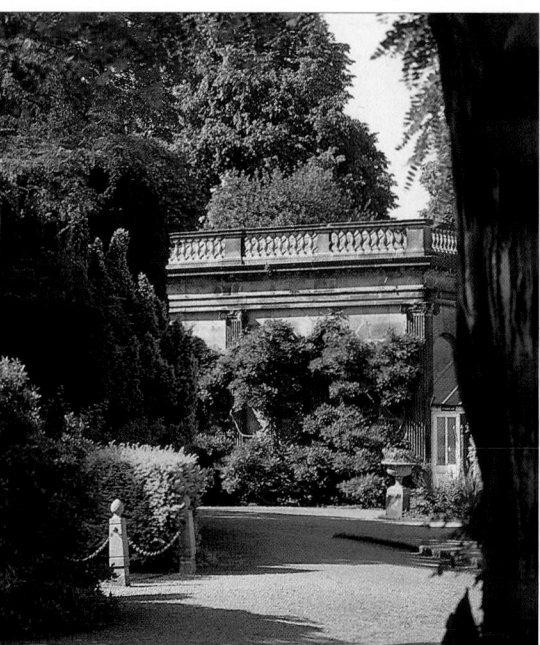

No photography inside castle unless by prior written consent. Parkland for outdoor activities & concerts. Murder mystery weekends.

VIP lunches & dinners (max. 66): unlimited in marquees. Full catering service, wedding receptions, banquets and medieval banquets.

5/7 rooms accessible. Gardens accessible (not Tropical Collection). WCs. Parking 50 yds.

The Castle Tearooms (seats 56) in Castle courtyard. Licensed. Pub lunches or dinner at hotel (100 yds). Groups must book.

Obligatory. Tour time 75 mins.

290 cars - 300 yds from castle entrance. Coach park 50 yds. Free.

Welcome by arrangement, between 10.30am - 7.30pm. Educational Fact Pack.

Guide dogs only.

Boar's Head Hotel (RAC***) 100 yds. Owned and managed by the estate.

Civil Wedding Licence.

Open all year.

OPENING TIMES

SUMMER
Castle & Gardens
January - May,
September - December:
Tues, Thurs, Sats & Suns:
10.30am - 3pm.

June - August:
Daily: 10.30am - 3pm.

Gardens
Daily, 10am - 5pm.

WINTER
December - May &
September - December:
Tues, Thurs, Sats & Suns.
10.30am - last guided tour 3pm.

ADMISSION

ALL YEAR
Castle & Gardens
Adult £5.50
Child (5-16yrs)..........£3.00
OAP.........................£4.50
Groups (15+)
Adult £4.50
Child (5-16yrs)..........£2.50

Gardens only
Adult £3.00
Child (5-16yrs)..........£1.50
OAP.........................£2.50
Groups (15+)
Adult £2.50

 SPECIAL EVENTS

- **APR 5 - 8:**
Galloway Antiques Fair
- **JUNE 7 - 10:**
Grand Summer Sale
- **JULY 12 - 15:**
Galloway Antiques Fair

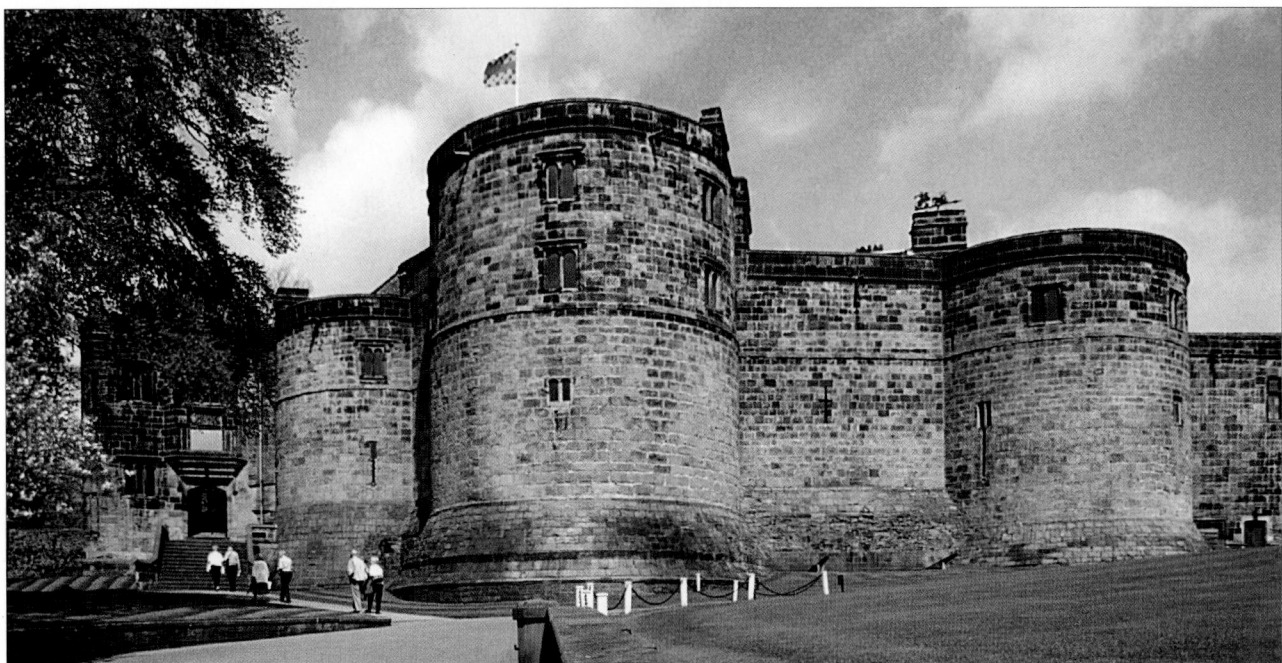

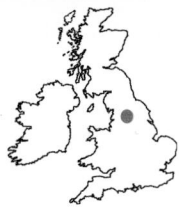

SKIPTON CASTLE
Skipton

Guardian of the gateway to the Yorkshire Dales for over 900 years, this is one of the most complete and well-preserved medieval castles in England. From 1310 stronghold of the Cliffords, two Lords of Skipton went out from here to die on Roses battlefields. In the Civil War this was the last Royalist bastion in the North, falling after a three year siege.

Every phase of this turbulent history has left its mark, from the Norman entrance arch and gateway towers to the beautiful early Tudor courtyard built in the heart of the castle by 'The Shepherd Lord'; it was there in 1659, that Lady Anne Clifford planted a yew tree (in whose shade you can sit today) to mark the completion of her repairs after the Civil War. Thanks to her, and to Cromwell, who permitted them on condition that the roofs should not be able to support cannon – the castle is still fully roofed,

making a visit well worthwhile at any time of year. A delightful picnic area has been created on the Chapel Terrace with views over the town and woods.

The gatehouse of the castle contains the Shell Room, decorated in 1620 with shells and Jamaican coral said to have been brought home by Lady Anne's father, George Clifford, 3rd Earl of Cumberland, Champion to Queen Elizabeth and one of her Admirals against the Armada; he lies beneath a splendid tomb in Skipton's parish church, a few yards from the castle gates.

On leaving the castle, the visitor is at once in the town's bustling High Street, with its four market days every week (and lots of other good shopping) and a great variety of pubs and restaurants. Close by, the Leeds and Liverpool canal presents a lively scene.

CONTACT

Judith Parker
Skipton Castle
Skipton
North Yorkshire
BD23 1AQ

Tel: 01756 792442

Fax: 01756 796100

e-mail: info@
skiptoncastle.co.uk

LOCATION

OS Ref. SD992 520

In the centre of Skipton, at the N end of High Street.

Skipton is 20m W of Harrogate on the A59 and 26m NW of Leeds on A65.

Rail: Regular services from Leeds & Bradford.

OPENING TIMES

ALL YEAR
(closed 25 December)

Mon - Sat: 10am - 6pm
Suns: 12 noon - 6pm
(October - February 4pm)

ADMISSION

Adult £4.40
Child (0 - 4yrs) .... Free
Child (5-17yrs) £2.20
OAP £3.80
Student (with ID) £3.80
Family (2+3) £11.90
Groups (15+)
Adult £3.60
Child (0-17yrs) £2.20

Includes illustrated tour sheet in a choice of eight languages, plus free badge for children.

Groups welcome:
Guides available for booked groups at no extra charge.

 Not suitable.

Tearoom. Indoor and outdoor picnic areas.

By arrangement.

Large public coach and car park off nearby High Street. Coach drivers' rest room at Castle.

Welcome. Guides available. Teachers free.

In grounds on leads.

SPECIAL EVENTS

Please telephone for details.

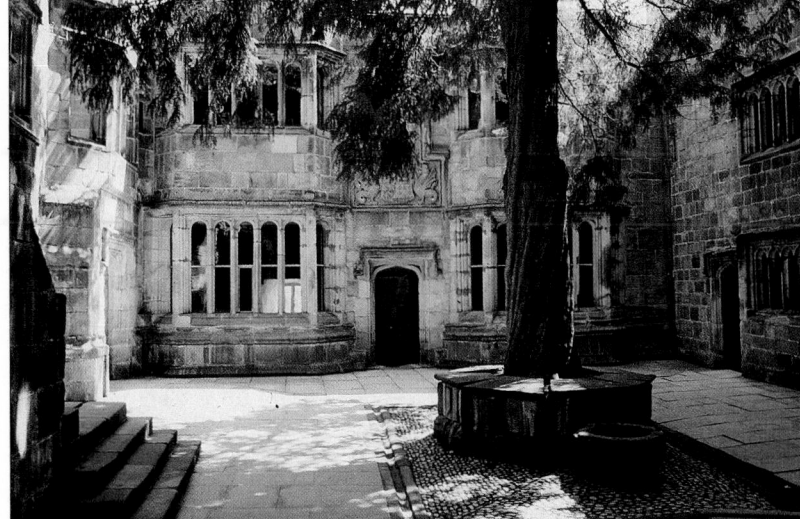

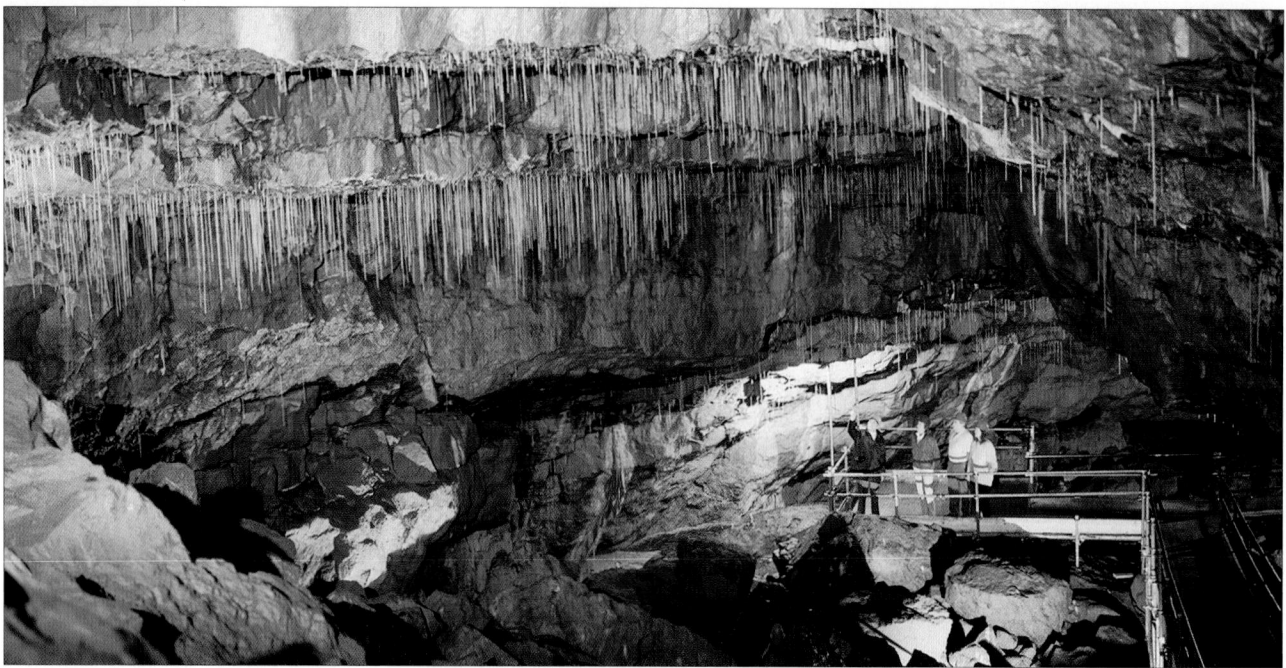

WHITE SCAR CAVE
Ingleton

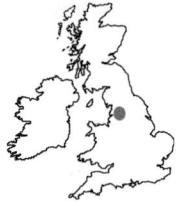

Owner: White Scar Caves Ltd

CONTACT

John Connaughton
White Scar Cave
Ingleton
North Yorkshire
LA6 3AW

Tel: 01524 241244

Fax: 01524 241700

e-mail: wsb@
oyez.freeserve.co.uk

LOCATION

OS Ref. SD713 745

1½ m from Ingleton on B6255 road to Hawes.

WHITE SCAR CAVE is the longest show cave in Britain. The guided tour covers one mile, and takes about 80 minutes. The highlight of the tour is the impressive 200,000 year old Battlefield Cavern. Over 330 feet long, with its roof soaring in places to 100 feet, this is one of the largest caverns in Britain. It contains thousands of delicate stalactites, which hang from the roof in great clusters.

The tour begins near the original entrance found by Christopher Long, the student who discovered the cave in 1923. The path winds its way past cascading waterfalls, between massive banks of flowstone, and through galleries decorated with cream- and carrot-coloured stalactites and stalagmites. Under the steel-grid walkways you can see the stream rushing and foaming on its way. Your guide will show you curious cave formations, including the Devil's Tongue, the Arum Lily and the remarkably lifelike Judge's Head.

There is electric lighting throughout, and the principal features are floodlit. White Scar Cave is part of a Site of Special Scientific Interest. It enjoys a spectacular location in the Yorkshire Dales National Park on the slopes of Ingleborough Hill (2372 ft).

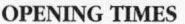

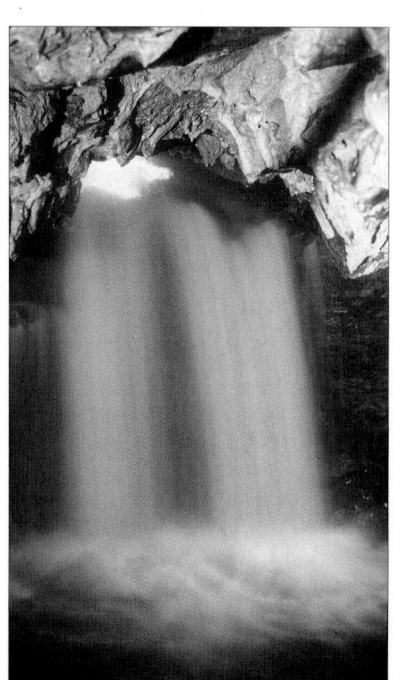

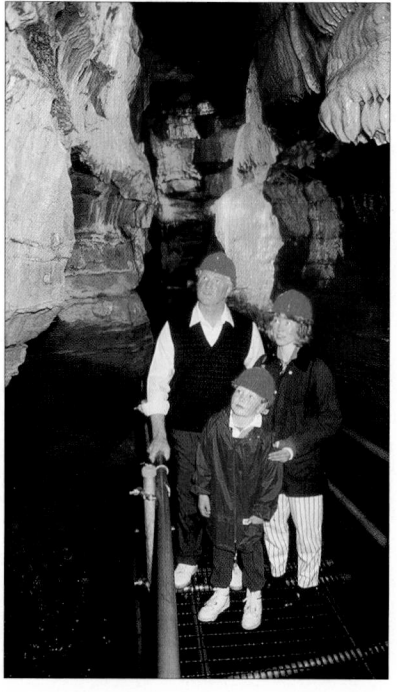

OPENING TIMES

ALL YEAR
Daily: 10am
Last tour at 5.30pm.
Closed 25 December.

ADMISSION

Adult £6.25
Child......................£3.45
Family £17.50

Groups (12+)
Adult £5.00
Child £2.70

ℹ️ Member of the International Show Caves Association.

🛍️

♿ Partially suitable.

☕

🚶 Obligatory.

🅿️

📋 Fact sheets.

🐕 In grounds on leads.

❄️

ALDBOROUGH ROMAN TOWN

Tel: 01423 322768

High Street, Boroughbridge, North Yorkshire YO5 9ES

Owner: English Heritage   **Contact:** The Custodian

The principal town of the largest Roman tribe in Britain. The delightfully located remains include Roman defences and two mosaic pavements, a small museum displays finds.

Location: OS99 Ref. SE405 661. Close to Boroughbridge off A1.

Opening Times: 1 Apr - 30 Sept: daily, 10am - 6pm. 1 - 31 Oct: daily, 10am - 5pm. Closed 1 - 2pm.

Admission: Adult £1.80, Child 90p, Conc. £1.40. 15% discount for groups (11+).

ARCHAEOLOGICAL RESOURCE CENTRE

Tel: 01904 643211   **Fax:** 01904 627097   **e-mail:** arc@jvcyork.demon.co.uk

St Saviour's Church, St Saviourgate, York YO1 8NN

Owner: York Archaeological Trust   **Contact:** Nicola Bexon

Housed in the restored medieval church of St Saviour, the ARC offers a glimpse behind the scenes of a leading archaeological unit. Led by experienced archaeologists, visitors take part in hands-on activities with real finds, investigating a section of a layer from an archaeological dig and even examining Viking-Age artefacts.

Location: OS99 Ref. SE606 519. Central York, close to the Shambles.

Opening Times: School holidays: Mon - Sat, 11am - 3.30pm. Term time (pre-booked groups only): Mon - Fri, 10am - 3.30pm. Closed last two weeks of Dec & first week of Jan.

Admission: £3.60. Pre-booked groups (15+) £3.20. (valid to 30/4/01)

   Partially suitable.   Obligatory.   None.   Guide dogs only.

ASKE HALL

See right.

BAGSHAW MUSEUM

Tel: 01924 326155   **Fax:** 01924 326164

Wilton Park, Batley, Yorkshire WF17 0AS

Owner: Kirklees Cultural Services   **Contact:** Melanie Brook

Travel through Asia, Africa and the Americas.

Location: OS Ref. SE235 257. From M62/J27 follow A62 to Huddersfield. At Birstall, follow tourist signs. Bagshaw Museum is approached through a small housing estate.

Opening Times: Mon - Fri, 11am - 5pm. Sats & Suns, 12 noon - 5pm. Pre-booked groups and school parties welcome.

Admission: Free.

BAYSGARTH HOUSE MUSEUM

Tel: 01652 632318

Caistor Road, Barton-on-Humber, North Lincolnshire DN18 6AH

Owner: North Lincolnshire Council   **Contact:** Mr D J Williams

18th century town house and park. Displays of porcelain and local history.

Location: OS Ref. TA035 215. Caistor Road, Barton-on-Humber.

Opening Times: Please contact for details.

Admission: Please contact for details.

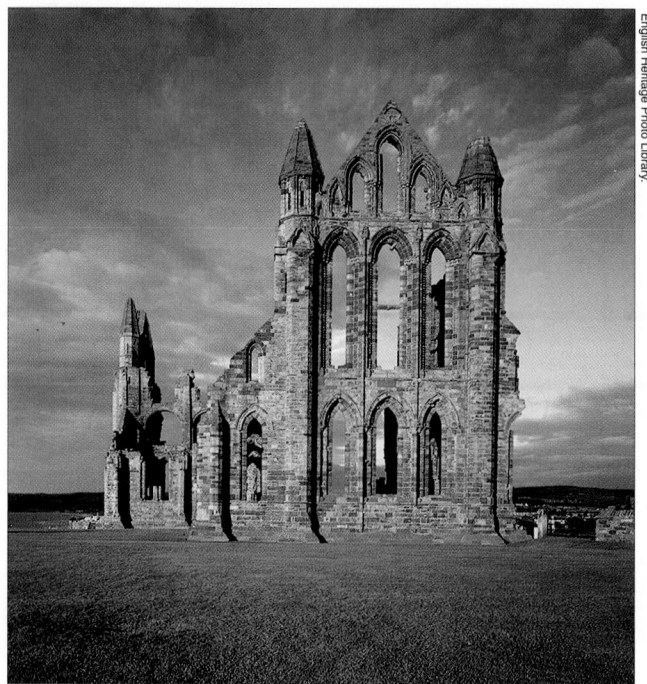

Whitby Abbey, Yorkshire.

English Heritage Photo Library.

ASKE HALL

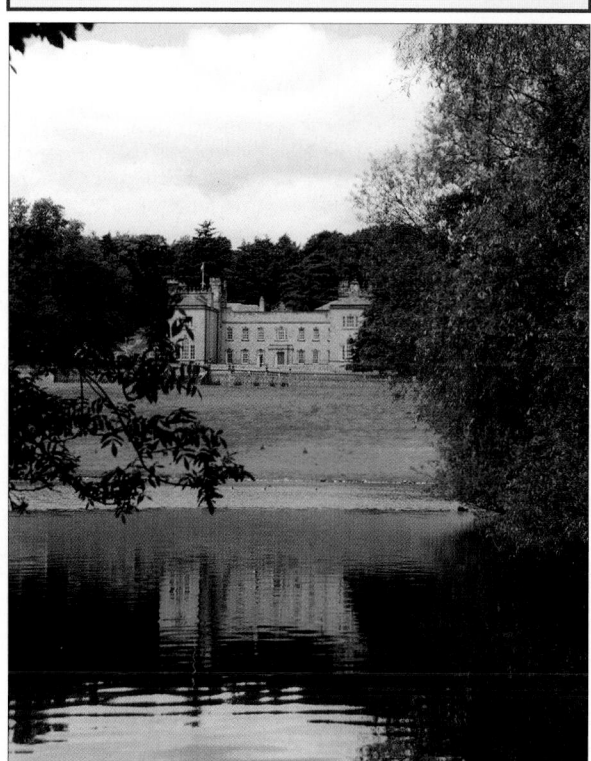

RICHMOND, NORTH YORKSHIRE DL10 5HJ

Owner: **The Marquess of Zetland**   *Contact:* **Mhairi Mercer**

Tel: 01748 850391   **Fax:** 01748 823252

Nestling in 'Capability' Brown landscaped parkland, Aske has been the family seat of the Dundas family since 1763. This Georgian treasure house boasts exquisite 18th century furniture, paintings and porcelain, including work by Robert Adam, Chippendale, Gainsborough, Raeburn and Meissen.

Aske is an architectural kaleidoscope. There is the original 13th century pele tower and remodelled Jacobean tower. John Carr's stable block, built in 1765, was later converted into a chapel with Italianate interior. A coach house with clock tower houses the family's carriage. There are follies and a lake as well as the new three tier terraced garden.

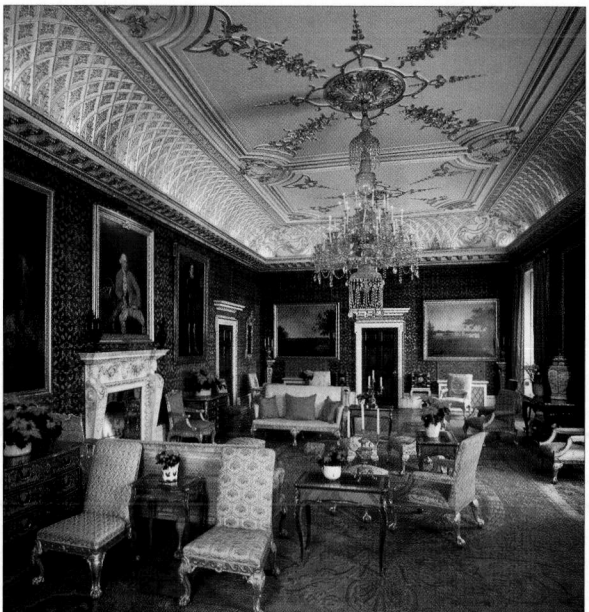

Location: OS Ref. NZ179 035. 2m SW of A1 at Scotch Corner, 1m from the A66, on the Gilling West road (B6274).

Opening Times: All year: for groups (15+) by appointment only.

Admission: House & grounds: Adult £6.50, Child £4.

Conferences. No photography in house.   Partially suitable. By arrangement.   In grounds on leads. Telephone for programme of special events.

BENINGBROUGH HALL & GARDENS

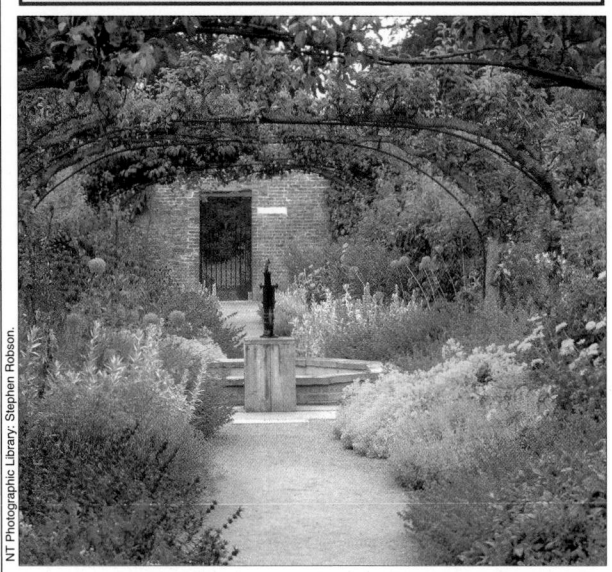

NT Photographic Library; Stephen Robson.

BENINGBROUGH, NORTH YORKSHIRE YO30 1DD

Owner: The National Trust   *Contact:* The Visitor Services Manager

Tel: 01904 470666 **Fax:** 01904 470002

Imposing 18th century house with over 100 portraits from the National Portrait Gallery. Walled garden, children's playground, Victorian laundry. Herbaceous borders and parkland.

Location: OS Ref. SE516 586. 8m NW of York, 3m W of Shipton, 2m SE of Linton-on-Ouse, follow signposted route.

Opening Times: 31 Mar - 31 Oct: Sat - Wed & Good Fri also Fris in Jul & Aug. House: 12 noon - 5pm. Last admission 4.30pm. Grounds: 11am - 5.30pm.

Admission: House & Garden: Adult £5.20, Child £2.60, Family £13. Garden: Adult £3.60, Child £1.80, Family £9.

Partially suitable. WC.

BISHOPS' HOUSE
Tel: 0114 278 2600

Meersbrook Park, Norton Lees Lane, Sheffield, Yorkshire S8 9BE

Owner: Sheffield Galleries & Museums Trust   **Contact:** Ms K Streets

A beautiful 16th century timber-framed house, the oldest surviving building of its type in Sheffield.

Location: OS Ref. SK348 843. A61, 2m S of city centre E of the Chesterfield Road.

Opening Times: Sat, 10am - 4.30pm. Sun, 11am - 4.30pm. Mon - Fri: 10am - 3pm for pre-booked groups only.

Admission: Free.

BOLLING HALL MUSEUM
Tel: 01274 723057

Bowling Hall Road, Bradford, Yorkshire BD4 7LP

Owner: City of Bradford Metropolitan District Council   **Contact:** Jane Whittaker

Medieval tower with 17th century additions.

Location: OS Ref. SE174 315. 1$^{1}/_{2}$ m SE of Bradford centre, $^{1}/_{4}$ m SE of A650.

Opening Times: Please telephone for details.

Admission: Free.

Bolling Hall Museum, Yorkshire.

BOLTON ABBEY

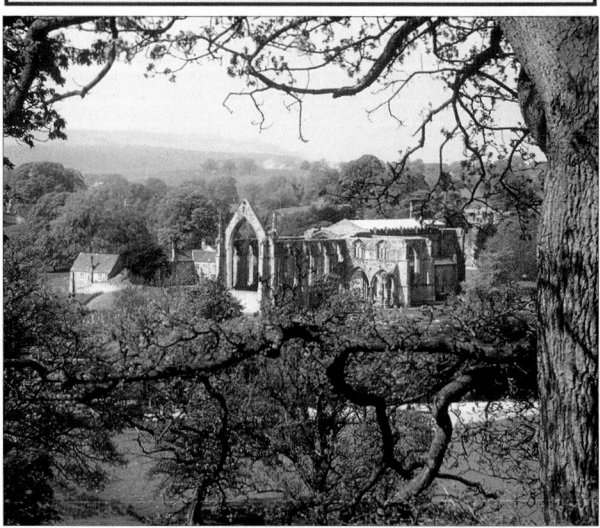

SKIPTON, NORTH YORKSHIRE BD23 6EX

Owner: Trustees of the Chatsworth Settlement   *Contact:* Tourism Manager

Tel: 01756 710533 **Fax:** 01756 710535

Wordsworth, Turner and Landseer were inspired by this romantic and varied landscape. The Estate, centred around Bolton Priory (founded 1154), is the Yorkshire home of the Duke and Duchess of Devonshire and provides 80 miles of footpaths to enjoy some of the most spectacular landscape in England.

Location: OS Ref. SE074 542. On B6160, N from the junction with A59 Skipton - Harrogate road, 23m from Leeds.

Opening Times: All year.

Admission: £3.50 per car, £2 for disabled (car park charge only).

Licensed. Licensed. In grounds, on leads. Devonshire Arms Country House Hotel & Devonshire Fell Hotel nearby.

BOLTON CASTLE

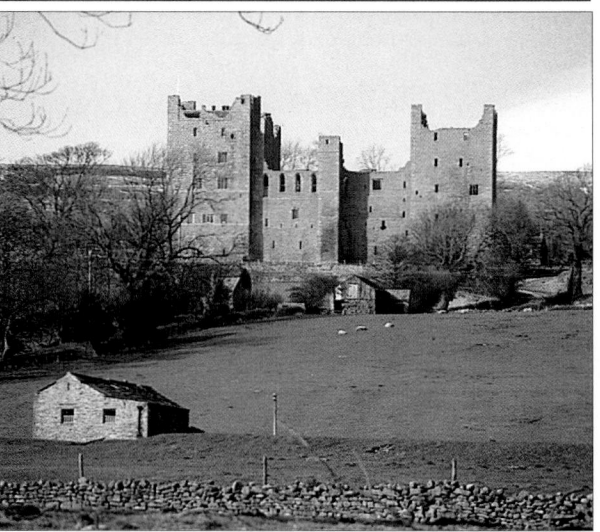

Patrick Lane.

LEYBURN, NORTH YORKSHIRE DL8 4ET

Owner/Contact: Hon Mr & Mrs Harry Orde-Powlett

Tel: 01969 623981 **Fax:** 01969 623332 **e-mail:** harry@boltoncastle.co.uk

A fine medieval castle that overlooks beautiful Wensleydale. Bolton Castle celebrated its 600th anniversary in 1999. Set your imagination free as you wander round this fascinating castle, which once held Mary Queen of Scots prisoner for 6 months and succumbed to a bitter Civil War siege. Don't miss the beautiful medieval garden and vineyard.

Location: OS Ref. SE034 918. Approx 6m from Leyburn. 1m NW of Redmire.

Opening Times: All year: daily, 10am - 5pm or dusk. Please telephone to confirm times from 14 Dec - 14 Feb.

Admission: Adult £4, Conc. £3. Groups: Adult £3, Conc. £2.

Wedding receptions. Partially suitable. In grounds, on leads.

BRAMHAM PARK

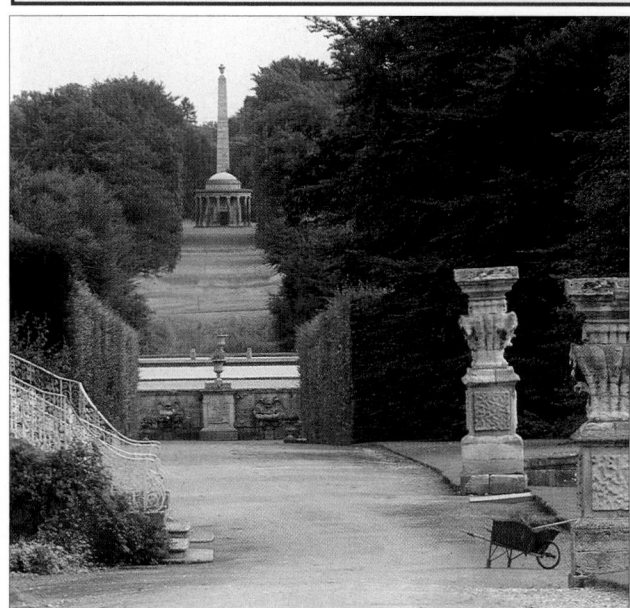

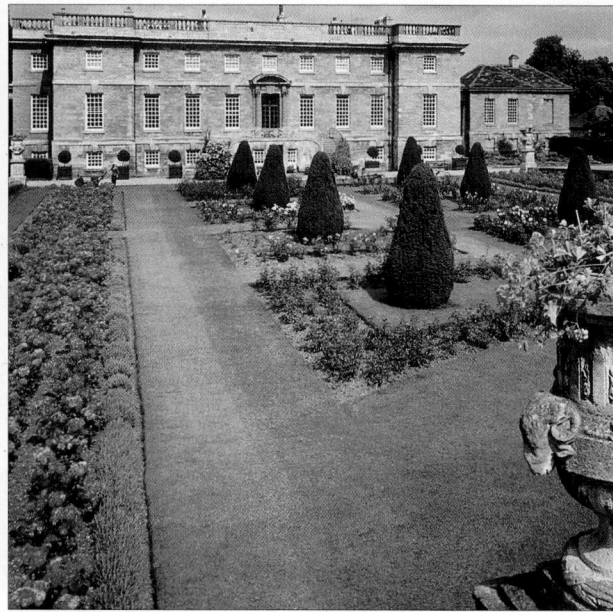

WETHERBY, WEST YORKSHIRE LS23 6ND

Owner: George Lane Fox   *Contact:* Estate Office

Tel: 01937 846005 **Fax:** 01937 846006

This Queen Anne house is 5 miles south of Wetherby on the A1, 10 miles from Leeds and 15 miles from York. The grand design of the gardens (66 acres) and pleasure grounds (100) are the only example of a formal, early 18th century landscape in the British Isles. Unexpected views and grand vistas, framed by monumental hedges and trees, delight the visitor, while temples, ornamental ponds and cascades focus the attention. The profusion of spring and summer wild flowers give a constant variety of colour and include many rare species.

Location: OS Ref. SE410 416. Half way from London to Edinburgh, 1m W of A1,

5m S of Wetherby, 10m NE of Leeds, 15m SW of York.

Opening Times: Gardens: 1 Apr - 30 Sept: daily, 10.30am - 5.30pm. Closed 7 - 10 Jun. House: by appointment for groups (6+).

Admission: Garden only: Adult £4, Child under 5yrs Free, Child (under 16yrs)/ OAP £2.

Grounds suitable. WC. In grounds, on leads.

🛡 **SPECIAL EVENTS**

JUN 7 - 10: Bramham International Horse Trials & Yorkshire Country Fair.

BROCKFIELD HALL 🏛

Tel: 01904 489298

Warthill, York YO19 5XJ

Owner/Contact: Lord Martin Fitzalan Howard

Late Georgian house.

Location: OS Ref. SE664 550. 5m E of York off A166 or A64.

Opening Times: Aug: daily except Mons, 1 - 4pm. Tours by arrangement.

Admission: Adult £3.50, Child £1.

BRODSWORTH HALL & GARDENS ⛲   See page 368 for full page entry.

BRONTË PARSONAGE MUSEUM

Tel: 01535 642323 **Fax:** 01535 647131

e-mail: bronte@bronte.prestel.co.uk

Church St, Haworth, Keighley, West Yorkshire BD22 8DR

Owner: The Brontë Society   **Contact:** The Administrator

Georgian Parsonage, former home of the Brontë family, now a museum with rooms furnished as in the sisters' day and displays of their personal treasures.

Location: OS Ref. SE029 373. 8m W of Bradford, 3m S of Keighley.

Opening Times: Apr - Sept: 10am - 5.30pm, Oct - Mar: 11am - 5pm. Daily except 24 - 27 Dec & 8 Jan - 2 Feb 2001. Last admission ½ hour before closing.

Admission: Adult £4.50, Child £1.40, Conc. £3.30, Family £10. Discounts for booked groups.

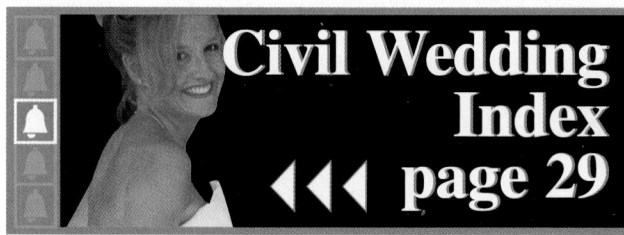

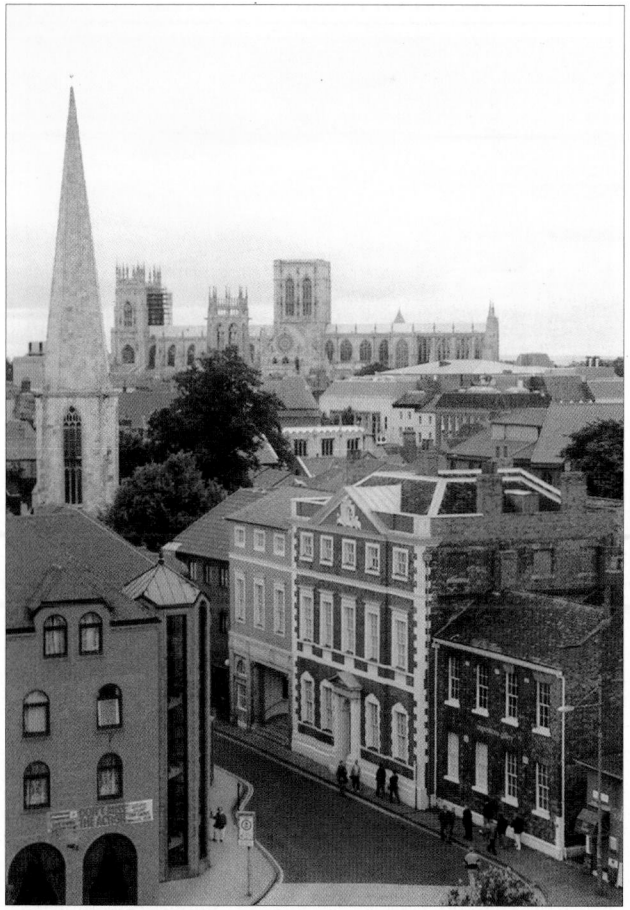

Patrick Lane.

View of York Minster (showing Fairfax House in the foreground), Yorkshire.

BROUGHTON HALL

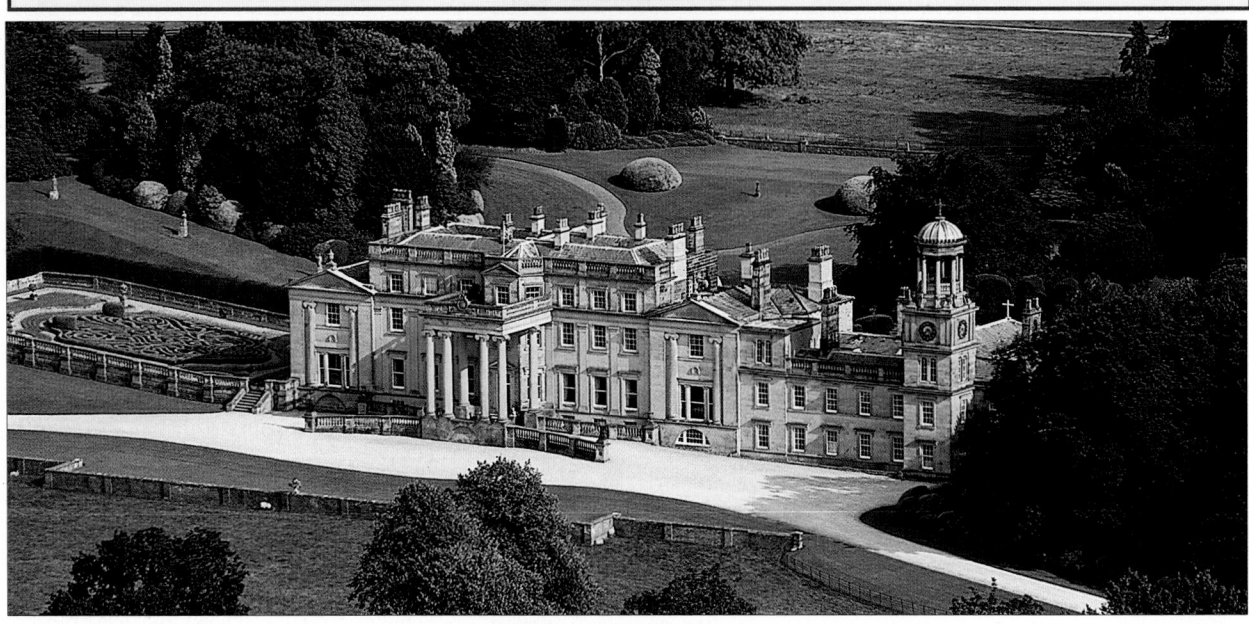

SKIPTON, YORKSHIRE BD23 3AE

Tel: 01756 799608 **Fax:** 01756 700357
e-mail: tempest@broughtonhall.co.uk   **e-mail:** infor@ruralsolutions.co.uk

Owner: *The Tempest Family*   **Contact:** *The Estate Office*

The Hall was built in 1597 by the Tempest family and it continues to be their private home which provides it with a very special atmosphere. The building is Grade I listed and set in 3000 acres of parkland and rolling countryside. It is available to groups for tours by prior arrangement throughout the year and also as a prestigious venue for business promotions and functions. The grounds were designed by Nesfield in 1855 including fine Italianate gardens, gazebo, fountains and balustrades. The magnificent conservatory is a particular feature. Filming often takes place at Broughton with its wide diversity of settings and locations and the owners appreciate and understand production requirements.

Separate from the Hall is the Broughton Hall Business Park formed from listed Estate buildings housing 40 companies employing 500 people in quality office accommodation.

Location: OS Ref. SD943 507. On A59, 3m W of Skipton midway between the Yorkshire and Lancashire centres. Good air and rail links.

Open: Year round tours for groups by arrangement.

Admission: £5.

 By arrangement.

BURTON AGNES HALL

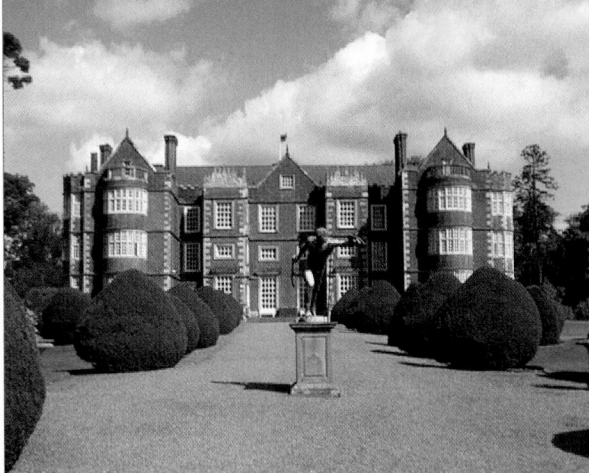

DRIFFIELD, YORKSHIRE YO25 0ND

Owner: *Burton Agnes Hall Preservation Trust Ltd*   **Contact:** *Mrs Susan Cunliffe-Lister*

Tel: 01262 490324 **Fax:** 01262 490513

A lovely Elizabethan Hall containing treasures collected by the family over four centuries from the original carving and plasterwork to modern and Impressionist paintings. The Hall is surrounded by lawns and topiary yew. The old walled garden contains a maze, potager, jungle garden, campanula collection and colour gardens incorporating giant game boards. Children's corner.

Location: OS Ref. TA103 633. Off A166 between Driffield and Bridlington.

Opening Times: 1 Apr - 31 Oct: daily, 11am - 5pm.

Admission: House & Gardens: Adult £4.80, Child £2.40, OAP £4.30. Gardens only: Adult £2.40, Child £1, OAP £2.20. 10% reduction for groups of 30+.

 Ground floor & grounds. Café. Ice-cream parlour.

Registered Charity No. 272796.

BURTON AGNES MANOR HOUSE   **Tel:** 01904 601901

Burton Agnes, Bridlington, Humberside

Owner: English Heritage   **Contact:** The North Regional Office

A rare example of a Norman house, altered and encased in brick in the 17th & 18th centuries.

Location: OS Ref. TA103 633. Burton Agnes village, 5m SW of Bridlington on A166.

Opening Times: Please telephone for details.

Admission: Free.

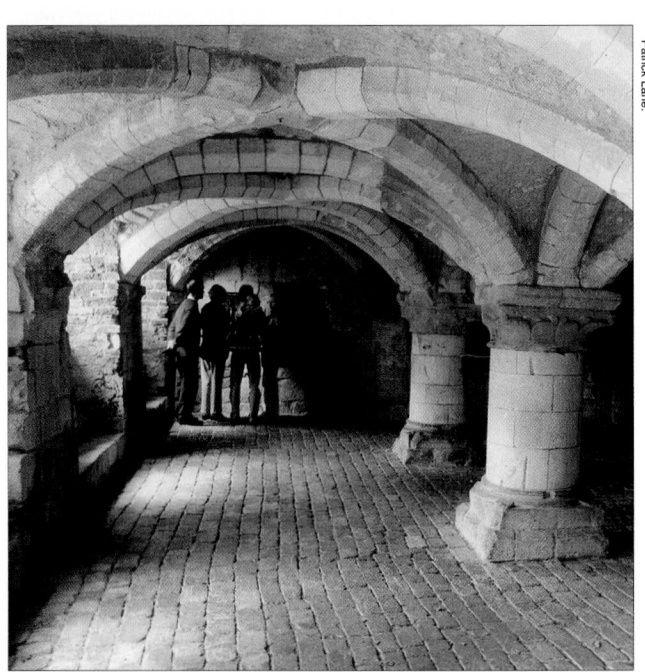

Burton Agnes Manor House, Yorkshire.

Patrick Lane.

BURTON CONSTABLE HALL

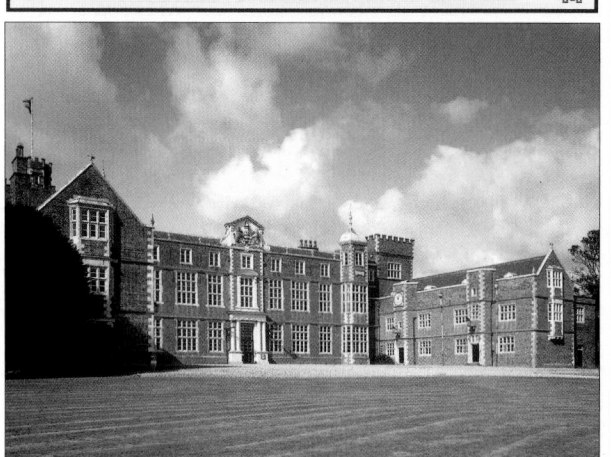

SKIRLAUGH, EAST YORKSHIRE HU11 4LN

Owner: Burton Constable Foundation   *Contact: Mrs P Connelly*

Tel: 01964 562400 **Fax:** 01964 563229 **e-mail:** enquiries@burtonconstable.com

Built in the 16th century and set in 300 acres of parkland landscaped by 'Capability' Brown, Burton Constable Hall is the magnificent ancestral home of the Constable family. Superb interiors containing paintings, prints and fine English furniture. 30 rooms open to view including a unique 'Cabinet of Curiosities', a fascinating Lamp Room and servants' corridors.

Location: OS Ref. TA193 369. 14m E of Beverley via A165 Bridlington Road, follow Historic House signs. 7m NE of Hull via B1238 to Sproatley then follow Historic House signs.

Opening Times: Easter Sun - 31 Oct: Sat - Thur. Grounds & tearoom open 12 noon. Hall: 1 - 5pm.

Admission: Hall & Grounds: Adult £4, Child £1.50, OAP £3.70, Family £9. Grounds only: Adult £1, Child 50p. Groups (30+): special rates available.

ⓘ No photography in house. 📷 ♿ 💼 🎟 By arrangement. 🅿 🎦
🐕 In grounds on leads. ♿

Registered Charity No. 1010121

BYLAND ABBEY 🏛   **Tel:** 01347 868614

Coxwold, Helmsley, North Yorkshire YO6 4BD

Owner: English Heritage   **Contact:** The Custodian

Hauntingly beautiful ruin, set in peaceful meadows in the shadow of the Hambleton Hills. It illustrates later development of Cistercian churches, including a beautiful floor of mosaic tiles.

Location: OS100 Ref. SE549 789. 2m S of A170 between Thirsk and Helmsley, NE of Coxwold village.

Opening Times: 1 Apr - 30 Sept: daily 10am - 6pm. 1 - 31 Oct: daily, 10am - 5pm. Closed 1 - 2pm.

Admission: Adult £1.70, Child 90p, Conc. £1.30. 15% discount for groups (11+).

♿ 🅿 Limited. 🎦 🐕 On leads. ♿ Tel. for details.

CANNON HALL MUSEUM, PARK & GARDENS   **Tel:** 01226 790270

Cawthorne, Barnsley, South Yorkshire S75 4AT   Fax: 01226 792117
e-mail: cannonhall@barnsley.gov.uk

Owner: Barnsley Metropolitan Borough Council   **Contact:** The Keeper

Late 17th century house, remodelled in the 1760s by John Carr. Contains decorative arts collections including fine furniture and paintings. Moorcroft pottery and Glass galleries. Also the Regimental Museum of the 13th/18th Hussars. Surrounding 18th century park landscaped by Richard Woods, with Walled Garden. Events and education programme.

Location: OS Ref. SE272 084. 6m NW of Barnsley of A635.

Opening Times: 1 Nov - 31 Mar: Sats, 10.30am - 5pm. Suns, 12 noon - 5pm. 1 Apr - 31 Oct: Tue - Sat, 10.30am - 5pm. Suns, 12 noon - 5pm. Last admission 4.15pm. Closed Christmas and New Year's Day. Open BH Mons.

Admission: Adults £1, Child/Conc. 50p, (2000 prices, subject to change.). Group discount (10+).

📷 🍽 ♿ Partially suitable. WC. 💼 Seasonal. 🅿 🎦
🐕 In grounds, on leads. ❄ ♿ Please telephone for details.

CASTLE HOWARD 🏛   See page 369 for full page entry.

CAWTHORNE VICTORIA JUBILEE MUSEUM   **Tel:** 01226 790545/790246

Taylor Hill, Cawthorne, Barnsley, Yorkshire S75 4HQ

Owner: Cawthorne Village   **Contact:** Mrs Mary Herbert

A quaint and eccentric collection with something for everyone in a half-timbered building. Museum has a ramp and toilet for disabled visitors. School visits welcome.

Location: OS Ref. SE285 080. 4m W of Barnsley, just off the A635.

Opening Times: Palm Sun - end Oct: Sats, Suns & BH Mons, 2 - 5pm. Groups by appointment throughout the year.

Admission: Adult 50p, Child 20p.

CLIFFE CASTLE   **Tel:** 01535 618231

Keighley, West Yorkshire BD20 6LH

Owner: City of Bradford Metropolitan District Council   **Contact:** Jane Whittaker

Typical Victorian manufacturer's mansion of 1878 with tall tower and garden. Now a museum.

Location: OS Ref. SE057 422. 3/4 m NW of Keighley off the A629.

Opening Times: Please telephone for details.

Admission: Free.

CLIFFORD'S TOWER 🏛   **Tel:** 01904 646940

Clifford Street, York, Yorkshire YO1 1SA

Owner: English Heritage   **Contact:** The Custodian

A 13th century tower on one of two mottes thrown up by William the Conqueror to hold York. There are panoramic views of the city from the top of the tower.

Location: OS105 Ref. SE 605 515. York city centre.

Opening Times: 1 Apr - 30 Sept: daily, 10am - 6pm (Aug: 9.30am - 7pm). 1 - 31 Oct: daily, 10am - 5pm. 1 Nov - 31 Mar: daily, 10am - 4pm. Closed 24/25 Dec.

Admission: Adult £2, Child £1, Conc. £1.50. Family ticket £5. 15% discount available for groups (11+).

📷 ♿ Not suitable. 🎦 🐕 In grounds, on leads. ❄

CLIFTON PARK MUSEUM   **Tel:** 01709 823635

Clifton Park, Rotherham, Yorkshire S65 2AA

Owner: Rotherham Metropolitan Borough Council.   **Contact:** Guy Kilminster

Furnished period rooms and one of the best collections of Rockingham porcelain in the country in an 18th century house set within a delightful park.

Location: OS Ref. SK435 926.

Opening Times: Mon - Thur & Sats, 10am - 5pm. Suns, 1.30 - 5pm (Apr - Sept) & 1.30 - 4.30pm (Oct - Mar).

Admission: Free.

❄ 🚌

CONISBROUGH CASTLE 🏛   **Tel:** 01709 863329

Conisbrough, Yorkshire

Owner: English Heritage   **Contact:** The Administrator

The oldest circular keep in England and one of the finest medieval buildings.

Location: OS111 Ref. SK515 989. 4 1/2 m SW of Doncaster.

Opening Times: 1 Apr - 30 Sept: daily 10am - 5pm (6pm at weekends & BHs). 10 Oct - 31 Mar: daily, 10am - 4pm.

Admission: Adults £2.80, Child £1, Conc. £1.80, Family £6.75.

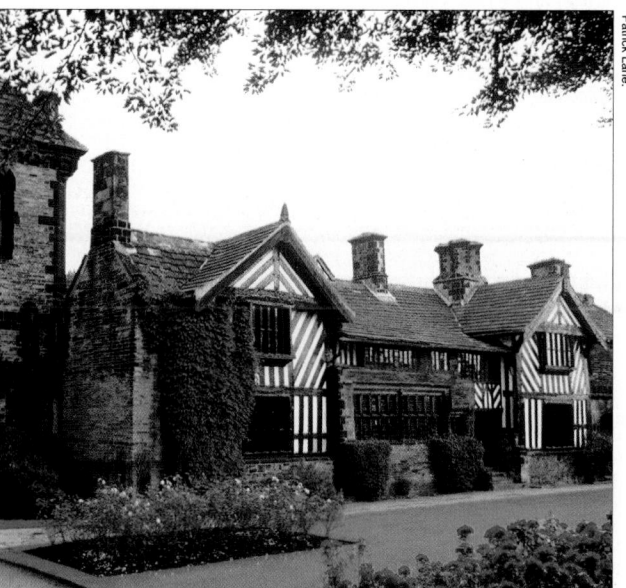

Patrick Lane.

Shibden Hall, Yorkshire.

CONSTABLE BURTON HALL GARDENS

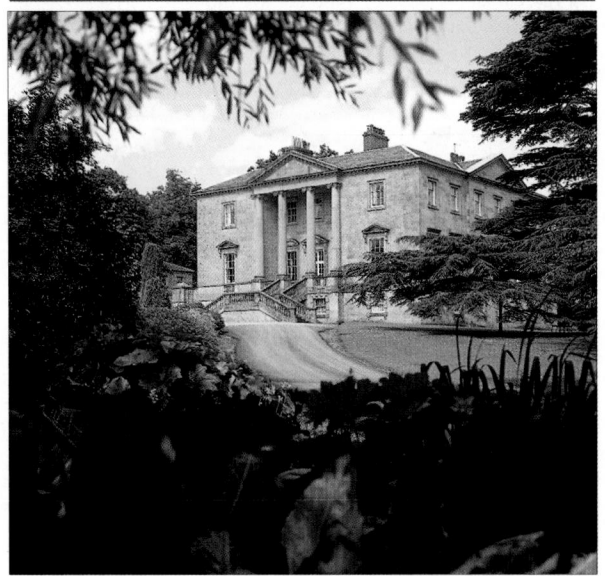

LEYBURN, NORTH YORKSHIRE DL8 5LJ

Owner/Contact: M C A Wyvill Esq

Tel: 01677 450428   **Fax:** 01677.450622

A delightful terraced woodland garden of lilies, ferns, hardy shrubs, roses and wild flowers, attached to a beautiful Palladian house designed by John Carr (not open). Garden trails, rockery with an interesting collection of alpines. Stream garden with large architectural plants and reflection ponds. Impressive spring display of daffodils, aconites and snowdrops.

Location: OS Ref. SE164 913. 3m E of Leyburn off the A684.

Opening Times: Garden only: 24 Mar - 14 Oct: daily, 9am - 6pm.

Admission: Adult £2.50, Child (under 16yrs) 50p, OAP £2.

Tel. for details.

DUNCOMBE PARK

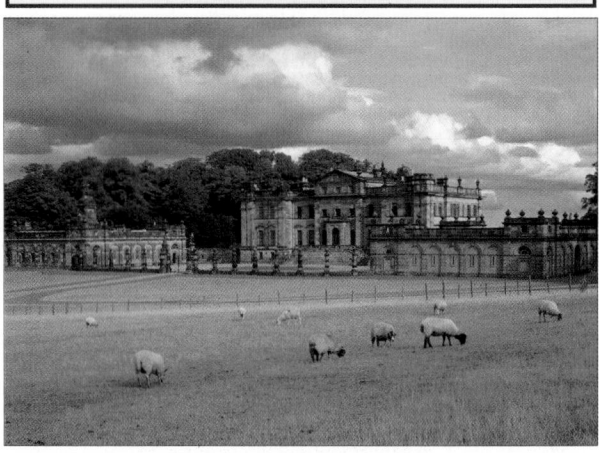

HELMSLEY, YORK YO62 5EB

Owner/Contact: Lord & Lady Feversham

Tel: 01439 770213   **Fax:** 01439 771114   **e-mail:** sally@duncombepark.com

Lord and Lady Feversham's restored family home in the North York Moors National Park. Built on a virgin plateau overlooking Norman Castle and river valley, it is surrounded by 35 acres of beautiful 18th century landscaped gardens and 400 acres of parkland with national nature reserve and veteran trees.

Location: OS SE604 830. Entrance just off Helmsley Market Square, signed off A170 Thirsk - Scarborough road.

Opening Times: 13 Apr - 28 Oct: Sun - Thur. House & Gardens: 10.30am - 6pm (last admission 4pm). Parkland, tearoom, shop & walks: 10.30am - 5.30pm (last orders in tearoom 5.15pm).

Admission: House & Gardens: Adult £6, Child £3, Conc. £5, Family (2+2) £13.50 Groups (15+): £4.50. Gardens & Parkland: Adult £4, Child (10-16yrs) £2. Parkland: Adult £2, Child (10-16yrs) £1. Season ticket (2+2) £20.

Country walks, nature reserve, orienteering, conferences.

Banqueting facilities. Partially suitable. Licensed. Obligatory. In park on leads. Tel. for details.

CRAKEHALL WATERMILL   **Tel:** 01677 423240

Little Crakehall, Nr Bedale, North Yorkshire DL8 1HU

Owner/Contact: Mrs Gill

Site of a mill since 1086, still milling stone-ground wholemeal flour.

Location: OS Ref. SE244 902. ½ m from village centre.

Opening Times: Easter - End September: Closed Mons & Tues. Please telephone for details.

Admission: Adult £1, Child/OAP 60p (2000 prices).

DANBY WATERMILL   **Tel:** 01287 660330

Danby, Whitby, Yorkshire YO21 2JL

Owner/Contact: Frank & Brenda Palmer

350 year old watermill restored to working order.

Location: OS Ref. NZ708 082. ½ m S of village.

Opening Times: Please contact for details.

Admission: Adult £1.50, Child/OAP 75p (2000 prices).

EASBY ABBEY   **Tel:** 01904 601901

Nr Richmond, North Yorkshire

Owner: English Heritage   **Contact:** The Custodian

Substantial remains of the medieval abbey buildings stand by the River Swale near Richmond.

Location: OS92 Ref. NZ185 003. 1m SE of Richmond off B6271.

Opening Times: Any reasonable time.

Admission: Free.

EAST RIDDLESDEN HALL   **Tel:** 01535 607075 **Fax:** 01535 691462

Bradford Road, Keighley, West Yorkshire BD20 5EL

Owner: The National Trust   **Contact:** Assistant Property Manager

Homely 17th century merchant's house with beautiful embroideries and textiles, Yorkshire carved oak furniture and fine ceilings. Delightful garden with lavender and herbs. Also wild garden with old varieties of apple trees. Magnificent Great Barn with timber structure. Handling collection Events.

Location: OS104 SE079 421. 1m NE of Keighley on S side of B6265 in Riddlesden. 50yds from Leeds/Liverpool Canal. Bus: Frequent services from Skipton, Bradford and Leeds. Railway station at Keighley 2m.

Opening Times: 31 Mar - 4 Nov: daily except Mons, Thurs & Fris (open Good Fri, BH Mons & Mons in Jul & Aug), 12 noon - 5pm, Sats, 1 - 5pm.

Admission: Adult £3.50, Child £1.80, Family £8.80.

Partially suitable. WC. Limited for coaches, please book. Tel. for details.

ELSHAM HALL COUNTRY & WILDLIFE PARK & BARN THEATRE

Elsham, Brigg, Lincolnshire DN20 0QZ   **Tel:** 01652 688698 **Fax:** 01652 688240

Owner: Elwes Trust   **Contact:** Robert Elwes

Winner of Ten Awards for Tourism. Attractions include Falconry Centre, the Mini Zoo, Georgian Courtyard, Craft Workshops, Arboretum, Theatre and Conference Centre, Clocktower Museum, Garden Centre and beautiful lakeside gardens with Carp and Trout Lakes.

Location: OS Ref. TA030 120. 10 mins from M180/J5, Humber Bridge turn-off.

Opening Times: Easter - mid Sept: daily, closed Mons (except on Bank holidays and during Spring/Summer Holidays) 11am - 5pm. Theatre & Craft Centre open separately.

Admission: Adult £3.95, Child £2.50 (3+), OAP £3.75. Group rates for groups (20+).

Medieval banquets. Licensed. By arrangement. Guide dogs only.

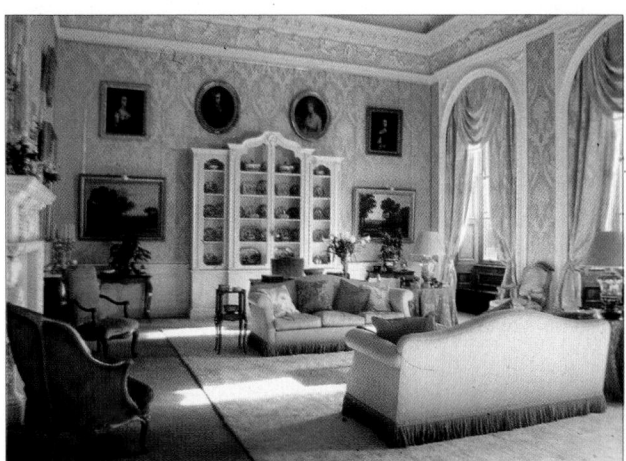

Duncombe Park, Yorkshire.

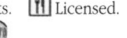

EPWORTH OLD RECTORY

Tel: 01427 872268

1 Rectory Street, Epworth, Doncaster, South Yorkshire DN9 1HX

e-mail: epworth@oldrectory63.freeserve.co.uk

Owner: World Methodist Council　　**Contact:** A Milson (Curator/Warden)

1709 Queen Anne period house, John and Charles Wesley's boyhood home. Portraits, period furniture, Methodist memorabilia. Garden, picnic facilities, cinematic presentation.

Location: OS Ref. SE785 036. Epworth lies on A161, 3m S M180/J2. 10m N of Gainsborough. When in Epworth follow the Wesley Trail information boards.

Opening Times: 1 Mar - 31 Oct. Mar, Apr & Oct: Mon - Sat, 10am - 12 noon & 2 - 4pm, Suns, 2 - 4pm. May - Sept: Mon - Sat, 10am - 4.30pm, Suns, 2 - 4.30pm.

Admission: Adult £2.50, Children in full-time education £1, OAP £2, Family £6. (2000 prices)

⬚ 🏛Ground floor & grounds suitable. 🖥By arrangement. 🎟Obligatory. Ⓟ Limited. 🍴 🐕Guide dogs only. 🛏2 twins.

FAIRFAX HOUSE 🏛

See page 370 for full page entry.

FOUNTAINS ABBEY & STUDLEY ROYAL 🏵

See page 371 for entry.

HANDS ON HISTORY

Tel: 01482 613902　**Fax:** 01482 613710

Market Place, Hull HU1 1EP

Owner: Hull City Council　　**Contact:** S R Green

Housed in the Old Grammar School this history resource centre offers hands on activities for the public and schools alike.

Location: OS Ref. TA099 285. 50 yds SW of the Church at centre of the Old Town.

Opening Times: School holidays and weekends open to the public. Please phone for details.

Admission: Free.

HAREWOOD HOUSE

See page 372 for full page entry.

HARLOW CARR BOTANICAL GARDENS

Tel: 01423 565418　**Fax:** 01423 530663

Crag Lane, Harrogate, North Yorkshire HG3 1QB

e-mail: admin@harlowcarr.fsnet.co.uk

Owner: Northern Horticultural Society　　**Contact:** Admin Manager

68 acre headquarters of the Northern Horticultural Society. Vegetable, fruit and flower trials; rock, foliage, winter and heather gardens; alpines and herbaceous beds.

Location: OS Ref. SE285 543. Off Otley Rd (B6162). 1 1/2 m W from town centre.

Opening Times: Daily from 9.30am. Last admission 6pm or dusk if earlier.

Admission: Adult £4.50, Child (11-16yrs) £1, Child (under 11yrs) Free, OAPs/Groups (20+): £3.50.

HELMSLEY CASTLE

Tel: 014397 70442

Helmsley, North Yorkshire YO6 5AB

Owner: English Heritage　　**Contact:** The Custodian

Close to the market square, with a view of the town, is this 12th century castle. Spectacular earthworks surround a great ruined Norman keep. Exhibition and tableau on the castle's history.

Location: OS100 SE611 836. In Helmsley town.

Opening Times: 1 Apr - 30 Sept: daily, 10am - 6pm. 1 - 31 Oct, daily, 10am - 5pm. 1 Nov - 31 Mar: Wed - Sun, 10am - 4pm (closed 1 - 2pm). Closed 24 - 26 Dec.

Admission: Adult £2.40, Child £1.20, Conc £1.80. 15% discount for groups (11+).

🖼 ❄ 🎗 Tel. for details.

HELMSLEY WALLED GARDEN

Tel/Fax: 01439 771427

Cleveland Way, Helmsley, North Yorkshire YO6 5AH

Owner: Helmsley Walled Garden Ltd　　**Contact:** Paul Radcliffe/Lindsay Tait

A 5 acre walled garden under restoration. Orchid house being re-built. Plant sales area and café conservatory.

Location: OS100 SE611 836. 25m N of York, 15m from Thirsk. In Helmsley follow signs to Cleveland Way.

Open: 1 Apr - 31 Oct: daily, 10.30am - 5pm. Nov - Mar: Sats/Suns, 12 noon - 4pm.

Admission: Adult £2.50, Child Free, Conc. £1.50.

HOVINGHAM HALL

Tel: 01653 628206　**Fax:** 01653 628668

York, North Yorkshire YO62 4LU

Owner: Sir Marcus Worsley　　**Contact:** Mrs Lamprey

Palladian house built c1760 by Thomas Worsley to his own design. Unique entry by huge riding school. Visitors see family portraits and rooms in everyday use; also extensive gardens with magnificent yew hedges, dovecot and private cricket ground, said to be the oldest in England.

Location: OS Ref. SE666 756. 18m N of York on Malton/Helmsley Road (B1257).

Opening Times: Apr - 30 Sept: 11am - 7pm by appointment only.

Admission: Adult £4. Groups(15+): £60 min. charge.

ⓘNo photography in house. 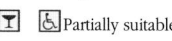Partially suitable. Obligatory. Ⓟ 🐕Guide dogs only.

JERVAULX ABBEY

Tel: 01677 460391

Ripon, Yorkshire HG4 4PH

Owner/Contact: Mr I S Burdon

Extensive ruins of a former Cistercian abbey.

Location: OS100 Ref. SE169 858. Beside the A6108 Ripon - Leyburn road, 5m SE of Leyburn and 5m NW of Masham.

Opening Times: Daily during daylight hours. Visitor centre: Mar - end Nov: daily, 10am - 5pm.

Admission: Adult £2, Child £1.50.

KIPLIN HALL 🏛

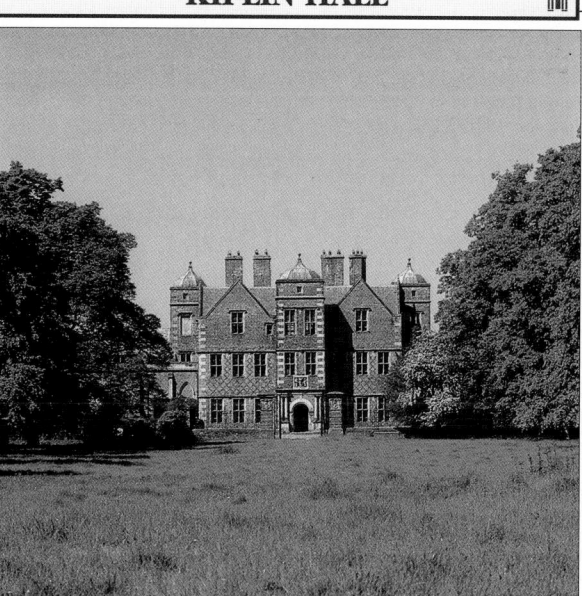

KIPLIN, Nr SCORTON, RICHMOND, NORTH YORKSHIRE DL10 6AT

Owner: Kiplin Hall Trustees　*Contact:* The Administrator

Tel/Fax: 01748 818178

A Grade I Jacobean House built in 1620 by George Calvert, First Lord Baltimore, founder of the State of Maryland, USA, it contains a fascinating collection of paintings and furniture collected by different families over four centuries. Some rooms are undergoing major refurbishment and visitors should contact the Administrator for details of what can be viewed.

Location: OS Ref. SE274 976. Signposted from Scorton - Northallerton road (B6271).

Opening Times: 1 Jul - 2 Sept: daily except Mons, 2 - 5pm. Open at other times of the year by appointment with the Administrator.

Admission: Adult £3.50, Child £1.75, Conc. £2. Groups by arrangement.

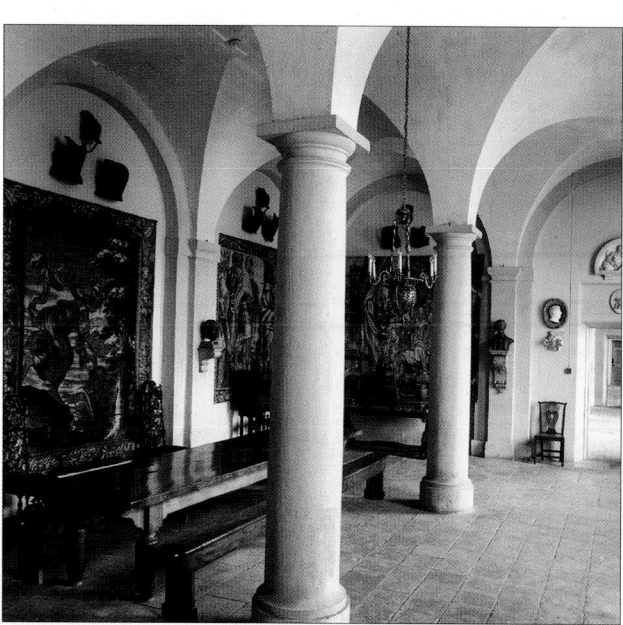

Hovingham Hall, Yorkshire.

KIRKHAM PRIORY

Tel: 01653 618768

Kirkham, Whitwell-on-the-Hill, Yorkshire YO6 7JS
Owner: English Heritage   **Contact:** The Custodian
The ruins of this Augustinian priory include a magnificent carved gatehouse.
Location: OS100 Ref. SE735 657. 5m SW of Malton on minor road off A64.
Opening Times: 1 Apr - 30 Sept: daily, 10am - 6pm. 1 - 31 Oct: daily, 10am - 5pm.
Admission: Adult £1.70, Child 90p, Conc. £1.30. 15% discount for groups (11+).

🏛 ♿ **P**Limited. 🔲 🐕On leads.

KNARESBOROUGH CASTLE

Tel: 01423 556188 **Fax:** 01423 556130

Knaresborough, North Yorkshire HG5 8AS   **e-mail:** lg12@harrogate.gov.uk
Owner: Duchy of Lancaster   **Contact:** Ms Vanessa Hirst
Ruins of 14th century castle standing high above the town. Local history museum housed in Tudor Courthouse. Gallery devoted to the Civil War.
Location: OS Ref. SE349 569. 5m E of Harrogate, off A59.
Opening Times: Easter BH - 30 Sept: daily, 10.30am - 5pm.
Admission: Adult £2, Child/OAP £1.50, Family £5.50, Groups (10+) £1.50.

LEDSTON HALL

Tel: 01423 523423 **Fax:** 01423 521373

Hall Lane, Ledston, Castleford, West Yorkshire WF10 2BB
Owner/Contact: James Hare
17th century mansion with some earlier work.
Location: OS Ref. SE437 289. 2m N of Castleford, off A656.
Opening Times: Exterior only: May - Aug, Mon - Fri, 9am - 4pm. Other days by appointment.
Admission: Free.

LING BEECHES GARDEN

Tel: 0113 2892450

Ling Lane, Scarcroft, Leeds, Yorkshire LS14 3HX
Owner/Contact: Mrs A Rakusen
A 2 acre woodland garden designed by the owner.
Location: OS Ref. SE354 413. Off A58 midway between Leeds & Wetherby. At Scarcroft turn into Ling Lane, signed to Wike on brow of hill.
Opening Times: Twice a year for Northern Horticultural Society (telephone for details). Also by appointment.
Admission: Adult £2.50, Child Free.

LONGLEY OLD HALL

Tel: 01484 430852 **e-mail:** robingallagher@debrett.net

Longley, Huddersfield HD5 8LB
Owner: Christine & Robin Gallagher   **Contact:** Christine Gallagher
This timber framed Grade II* manor house dates from the 15th century and was owned by the Rambden family, the Lords of the Manors of Huddersfield and Almondbury, for 400 years. 2001 will see the end of the main restoration work and the start of the Elizabethan Garden.
Location: OS Ref. SE157 117. 1 1/2 m SE of Huddersfield centre towards Castle Hill.
Opening Times: By appointment.
Admission: Please contact for details.

🍽 ♿Not suitable. Obligatory. By arrangement. **P**Limited for coaches. ❄

LOTHERTON HALL

Tel: 0113 2813259 **Fax:** 0113 2812100

Aberford, West Yorkshire LS25 3EB
Owner: Leeds City Council   **Contact:** Adam White
Late Victorian and Edwardian country house of great charm and character.
Location: OS92 Ref. SE450 360. 2 1/2 m E of M1 J47 on B2177 the Towton Road.
Opening Times: 1 Apr - 31 Oct: Tue - Sat, 10am - 5pm, Suns, 1 - 5pm. 1 Nov - 31 Dec & Mar: Tue - Sat, 10am - 4pm, Suns, 12 noon - 4pm. Closed Jan & Feb.
Admission: Adult £2, Child 50p, Conc. £1. Groups: £1. Parking: £5 includes 1 yrs free admission to house. Day ticket: £2.

MARKENFIELD HALL

Tel: 01609 780306 **Fax:** 01609 777510

Nr Ripon, North Yorkshire HG4 3AD
Owner: The Lady Grantley   **Contact:** Strutt & Parker
Fine example of a moated English Manor House (14th and 15th century).
Location: OS Ref. SE294 672. Local access from gate on W side A61, 3m S of Ripon.
Opening Times: Groups by appointment only.
Admission: Please contact for details.

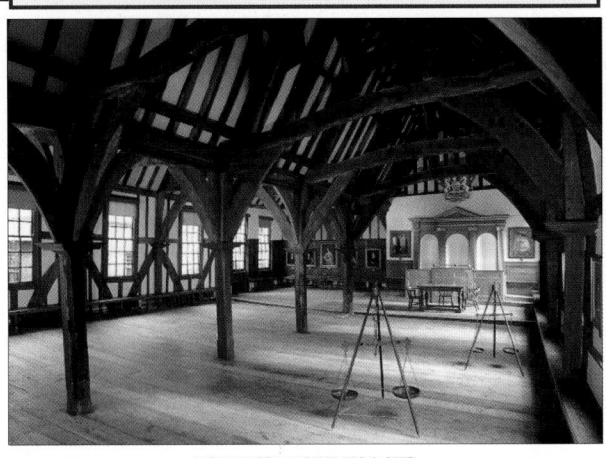

MERCHANT ADVENTURERS' HALL

FOSSGATE, YORK YO1 9XD
Owner: The Company of Merchant Adventurers   *Contact: The Clerk*

Tel/Fax: 01904 654818 **e-mail:** The.Clerk@mahall-york.demon.co.uk
The finest medieval guild hall in Europe, built in 1357/62 and substantially unaltered. In it the Merchants transacted their business, as their successors still do today. On the ground floor was their hospice, where they cared for the poor, and their private chapel, a unique survival in England. There are good collections of early portraits, furniture, silver and other objects used by the Merchants over the centuries, when their wealth and influence helped to make York the second city in England after London.
Location: OS Ref. SE606 518. Main entrance in Piccadilly, other entrance in Fossgate.
Opening Times: 2 Jan - 8 Apr, 6 Oct - 30 Mar: Mon - Sat, 9am - 3.30pm (closed Suns). 9 Apr - 5 Oct: Mon - Sat, 9am - 5pm, Suns, 12 noon - 4pm. Closed 24 Dec - 1 Jan 01.
Admission: Adult £2, Child (7-17yrs) 70p, Child under 7 Free, Conc. £1.70. Group rates available by prior arrangement.

🍽Wedding receptions. ♿Ground floor & grounds suitable. WCs. 🎦By arrangement. 🔲 🐕In grounds, on leads. 🔔 ❄ Ⓦ

MIDDLEHAM CASTLE

Tel: 01969 623899

Middleham, Leyburn, Yorkshire DL8 4RJ
Owner: English Heritage   **Contact:** The Custodian
This childhood home of Richard III stands controlling the river that winds through Wensleydale. There is a massive 12th century keep with splendid views of the surrounding countryside from the battlements.
Location: OS99 Ref. SE128 875. At Middleham, 2m S of Leyburn of A6108.
Opening Times: 1 Apr - 30 Sept: daily, 10am - 6pm. 1 - 31 Oct, daily, 10am - 5pm. 1 Nov - 31 Mar: Wed - Sun, 10am - 4pm (closed 1 - 2pm). Closed 24 - 26 Dec.
Admission: Adult £2.40, Child £1.20, Conc. £1.80. 15% discount for groups (11+).

ℹ Exhibition. 🏛 ♿Grounds suitable. 🔲 🐕In grounds, on leads. ❄ Ⓥ Tel. for details.

MOTHER SHIPTON'S CAVE & PETRIFYING WELL

Tel: 01423 864600

Prophecy House, Knaresborough, North Yorkshire HG5 8DD
                    Contact: Mr McBratney, General Manager
The cave and well lie at the heart of the Mother Shipton Estate - a relic of the ancient forest of Knaresborough.
Location: OS Ref. SE346 565. Access from A59 at S end of bridge then by riverside footpath.
Opening Times: 12 Feb - Sunday 2 Dec: daily 9.30am - 5pm. Also open weekends from 3 Dec - 11 Feb (2002).
Admission: Adult £4.95, Child £3.95 (under 5yrs Free), OAP £4.45, Family (2+2) £13.85. (2000 prices.)

MOUNT GRACE PRIORY

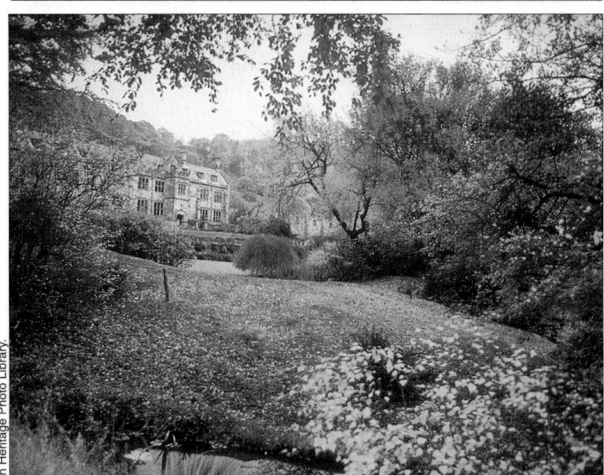

© English Heritage Photo Library.

SADDLE BRIDGE, NORTH YORKSHIRE DL6 3JG

Owner: *National Trust*   **Managed by:** *English Heritage*   **Contact:** *The Custodian*

Tel: 01609 883494

Hidden in tranquil wooded countryside at the foot of the Cleveland Hills, one of the loveliest settings of any English priory, and the best preserved Carthusian monastery in England. Monks lived as hermits in their cells and one cell, recently restored, is furnished to give a clear picture of their austere routine of work and prayer. Visitors enter through the manor built by Thomas Lascelles in 1654 on the site of the monastery guest house. It was rebuilt at the turn of the century using traditional techniques, typical of the Arts and Crafts movement.

Location: OS Ref. SE449 985. 12m N of Thirsk, 7m NE of Northallerton on A19.

Opening Times: 1 Apr - 30 Sept: daily, 10am - 6pm. 1 - 31 Oct: daily, 10am - 5pm. 1 Nov - 31 Mar: Wed - Sun, 10am - 4pm (closed 1 - 2pm). Closed 24 - 26 Dec.

Admission: Adult £2.90, Child £1.50, Conc. £2.20. 15% discount for groups (11+).

 Ground floor & grounds suitable. 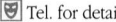 Tel. for details.

THE MUSEUM OF SOUTH YORKSHIRE LIFE   **Tel:** 01302 782342

Cusworth Hall, Cusworth Lane, Doncaster, South Yorkshire DN5 7TU

Owner: Doncaster Metropolitan Borough Council   **Contact:** Mr F Carpenter, Curator

A magnificent Grade I country house set in a landscaped parkland and built in 1740, with a chapel and other rooms designed by James Paine, the house is now the home of a museum showing the changing home, work and social conditions of the region over the last 250 years. Regular events and activities.

Location: OS Ref. SE547 039. A1(M)/J37, then A635 and right into Cusworth Lane.

Opening Times: Mon - Fri, 10am - 5pm. Sats, 11am - 5pm, Suns, 1 - 5pm. Closes at 4pm Dec & Jan.

Admission: Free.

NEWBURGH PRIORY   **Tel:** 01347 868435

Coxwold, York YO61 4AS

Owner/Contact: Sir George Wombwell Bt

Augustinian priory founded in 1145 converted into Tudor mansion, and again later in 18th century. Beautiful water garden.

Location: OS Ref. SE541 764. 7m SE Thirsk. 1/2 m SE of Coxwold.

Opening Times: Apr - end Jun: Weds & Suns: House: 2.30 - 4.45pm, Garden: 2 - 6pm. Guided tours approx 60 mins.

Admission: Gardens only: £2, Child Free. House & Grounds: £4. Child £1.

NEWBY HALL & GARDENS   See page 373 for full page entry.

NORMANBY HALL   See opposite for half page entry.

NORMANBY HALL

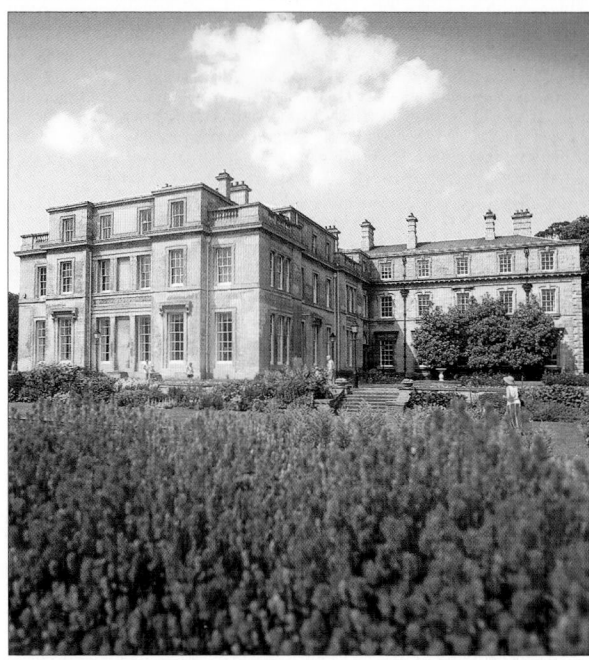

NORMANBY, SCUNTHORPE, NORTH LINCOLNSHIRE DN15 9HU

Owner: *North Lincolnshire Council*   **Contact:** *Park Manager*

Tel: 01724 720588 **Fax:** 01724 721248

The restored working Victorian Walled Kitchen Garden is growing produce for the 'big house' as it would have done 100 years ago. Victorian varieties of fruit and vegetables are grown using organic and Victorian techniques. Set in 300 acres of Park, visitors may also see the Regency Mansion, designed by Sir Robert Smirke, which the Garden was built to serve.

The ground floor rooms of the Hall are displayed in Regency style, while those upstairs reflect the changing styles of the Victorian and Edwardian eras. Costume from the Museum Service's collections is also exhibited.

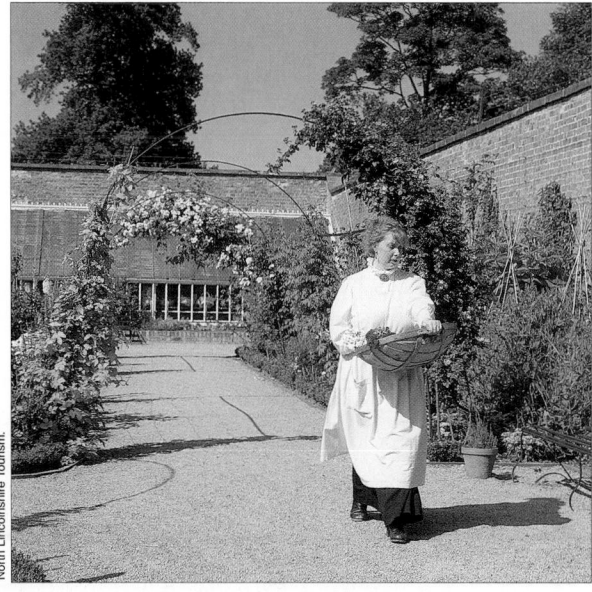

North Lincolnshire Tourism.

Location: OS Ref. SE886 166. 4m N of Scunthorpe off B1430. Follow signs for M181 & Humber Bridge. Tours by arrangement.

Opening Times: Hall & Farming Museum: 26 Mar - 30 Sept: 1 - 5pm. Park: daily, 9am - dusk. Walled Garden: daily, 10.30am - 5pm (4pm in winter). Last admission at all venues 1/2 hour before closing.

Admission: Summer Season: Adult £2.90, Conc. £1.90, Family (2+3) £8. Discounts for North Lincolnshire residents. Winter Season: £2.20 per car. (2000 rates).

All details correct at time of going to press. For up to date information, please contact Normanby Hall Country Park.

Wedding receptions. Ground floor & grounds. WC. By arrangement. In grounds, on leads. Tel. for details.

NORTON CONYERS

Tel/Fax: 01765 640333

Nr Ripon, North Yorkshire HG4 5EQ   **e-mail:** norton.conyers@ripon.org

Owner: Sir James and Lady Graham   **Contact:** Lady Graham

Visited by Charlotte Brontë in 1839, Norton Conyers is an original of the 'Thornfield Hall' in *Jane Eyre* and a family legend was an inspiration for the mad Mrs Rochester. Building is late medieval with Stuart and Georgian additions. Friendly atmosphere, resulting from 377 years of occupation by the same family. 18th century walled garden near house, with orangery and herbaceous borders. Small plant sales area specialising in unusual hardy plants. Pick your own fruit in season.

Location: OS Ref. SF319 763. 4m N of Ripon. 3^1/$_2$m from the A1.

Opening Times: House & Garden: Easter Sun & Mon. BH Suns & Mons. Suns 13 May - 9 Sept. Daily 9 - 14 Jul. House: 2 - 5pm. Garden 11.30am - 5pm.

Admission: House: Adult £4, Child (10-16yrs)/Conc. £3. Reduced rate for two or more children. Garden: Free (donations welcome), but charges are made at charity openings.

ℹ️ No photography. No stilettos in house.   📷 🍴 ♿ Partially suitable. WC. 🚶 By arrangement.   🅿️ 🐕 In grounds, on leads.

NOSTELL PRIORY

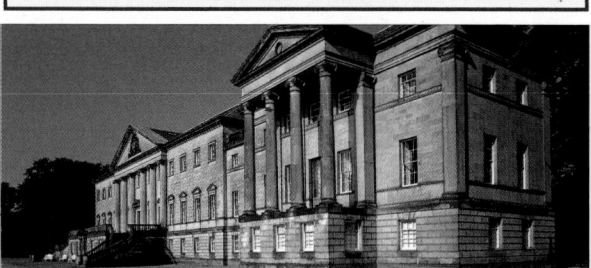

DONCASTER ROAD, WAKEFIELD, WEST YORKSHIRE WF4 1QE

Owner: The National Trust   *Contact: The Property Manager*

Tel: 01924 863892   **Fax:** 01924 865282

After a closed period of 18 months during which Nostell Priory, one of Yorkshire's finest jewels, benefited from substantial building works, redecoration and upgrading. The present house is an 18th century architectural masterpiece by James Paine built on the site of a medieval priory for Sir Rowland Winn, 4th Baronet, in 1733. Later, Robert Adam was commissioned to complete the State Rooms which are amongst the finest examples of his interiors. The Priory houses one of England's finest collections of Chippendale furniture, designed specially for the house by the great cabinet maker who was once apprentice on the estate. Nostell Priory's other treasures include an outstanding art collection with works by Pieter Breughel the younger and Angelica Kaufmann and the remarkable 18th century dolls house, complete with its original fittings and Chippendale furniture. In the grounds are delightful lakeside walks with a stunning collection of rhododendrons and azaleas in late spring. New attractions for this year include a new shop and guidebook, restoration of the Adam library and opening of the domestic areas of the house which include the Servant's Hall and unrestored Great Kitchen which houses an exhibition of recent works.

Location: OS Ref. SE403 175. 6m SE of Wakefield, off A638.

Opening Times: House: 31 Mar - 4 Nov: Wed - Sun & BH Mons, 1 - 5.30pm. 10 Nov - 9 Dec: Sats & Suns, 12 noon - 4.30pm. Grounds: as house, 11am - 6pm.

Admission: House & Gardens: Adult £4.50, Child £2.20, Family £11. Grounds only: Adult £2.50, Child £1.20. Guided tours for booked groups only, outside normal opening times: £250 min charge. Shop: Wed - Sun: 11am - 6pm.

ℹ️ Baby facilities.   🍴 📷 ♿ Partially suitable. WC. 🖥️ 🚶 By arrangement. 🅿️ 🚌 🐕 In grounds, on leads.   🔔 ✉️ Send SAE for details. 🆎

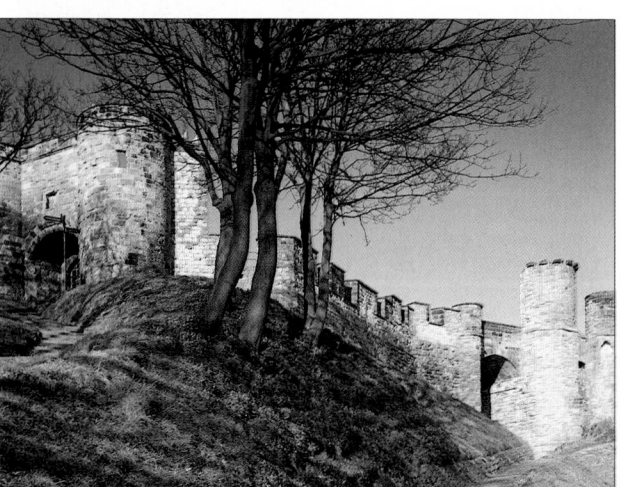

Scarborough Castle, Yorkshire.

NUNNINGTON HALL

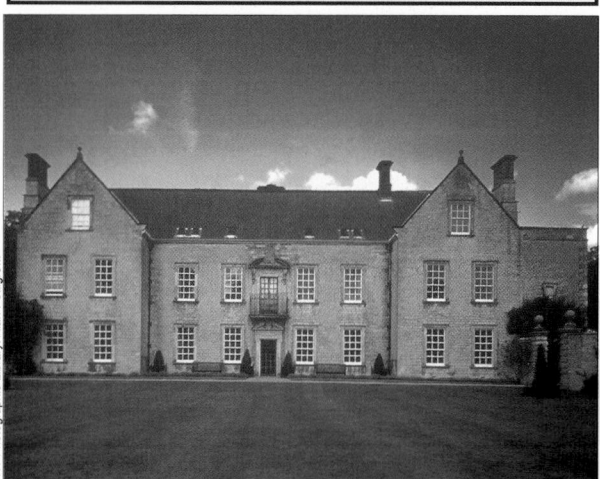

NUNNINGTON, NORTH YORKSHIRE YO62 5UY

Owner: The National Trust   *Contact: The Visitor Manager*

Tel: 01439 748283   **Fax:** 01439 748284

The sheltered walled garden on the bank of the River Rye with its delightful mixed borders, orchards of traditional Ryedale fruit varieties and spring flowering meadows, complements this mellow 17th century manor house. From the magnificent oak-panelled hall, follow three staircases to discover family rooms, the nursery, the haunted room and the attics, with their fascinating Carlisle collection of miniature rooms fully furnished to reflect different periods.

Location: OS Ref. SE670 795. In Ryedale, 4^1/$_2$ m SE of Helmsley, 1^1/$_2$ m N of B1257.

Opening Times: 31 Mar - 4 Nov: Wed - Sun & BH Mons. 1 Jun - 31 Aug: daily except Mons (open BH Mons). Apr - Oct: 1.30 - 4.30pm. 1 May - end Sept: 1.30 - 5pm.

Admission: House and Garden: Adult £4.50, Child £2. Family (2+3) £11. Garden only: Adult £2, Child Free. Groups (15+): £4.

📷 ♿ Ground floor & grounds suitable. WC. 🖥️ 12.30 - 5pm. 🐕 Guide dogs only. 🆎

OAKWELL HALL COUNTRY PARK

Tel: 01924 326240   Fax: 01924 326249

Nutter Lane, Birstall, Batley, West Yorkshire WF17 9LG

Owner: Kirklees Cultural Services

Location: OS99 Ref. SE217 271. On A652 in Birstall. Take J27/A62 towards Huddersfield to Birstall.

Opening Times: All year: Mon - Fri, 11am - 5pm. Sats & Suns, 12 noon - 5pm.

Admission: Adult £1.20, Child 50p, Family £2.50. Discounts available for booked groups. Admission charge seasonal - 2000 prices.

OLD SLENINGFORD HALL

Tel: 01765 635229   Fax: 01765 635485

Ripon, North Yorkshire HG4 3JD   **e-mail:** oldslen@fsnet.co.uk

Contact: Mrs Ramsden

Unusual garden with extensive lawns, interesting trees, lake and islands watermill in walled kitchen garden and Victorian fernery.

Location: OS99 Ref. SE265 768. From Ripon on A6108. After North Stainley take 2nd left, follow signs to Mickley for 1m from main road.

Opening Times: Spring BH Sun & Mon, Whit BH Sun & Mon. Also all year by appointment.

Admission: Adult £2.50, Child 50p.

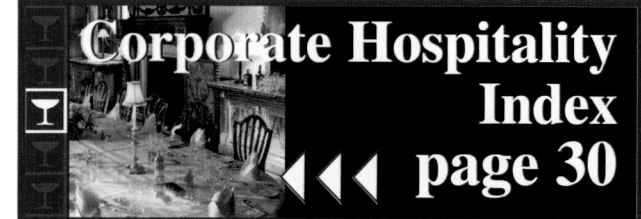

ORMESBY HALL

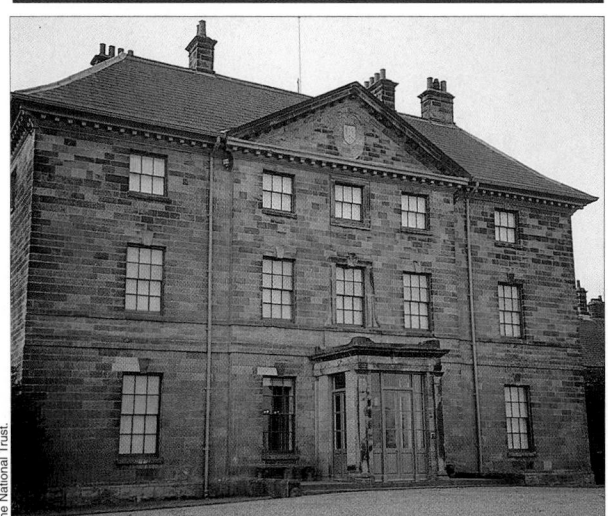

The National Trust.

CHURCH LANE, ORMESBY, MIDDLESBROUGH TS7 9AS

Owner: The National Trust   *Contact: The House Manager*

Tel: 01642 324188 **Fax:** 01642 300937 **e-mail:** yorkor@smtp.ntrust.org.uk

A mid 18th century house with opulent decoration inside, including fine plaster-work by contemporary craftsmen. A Jacobean doorway with a carved family crest survives from the earlier house on the site. The stable block, attributed to Carr of York, is a particularly fine mid 18th century building with an attractive courtyard leased to the Mounted Police; also an attractive garden with holly walk.

Location: OS Ref. NZ530 167. 3m SE of Middlesbrough.

Opening Times: 1 Apr - 4 Nov: daily except Mons, Fris & Sats (open Good Fri & BH Mons), 2 - 5pm. Garden tours, last Thur of each month (please enquire for further details).

Admission: House, garden, railway and exhibitions: Adult £3.50, Child £1.70, Family £8.50. Garden, railway and exhibitions: Adult £2.20, Child £1.

Ground floor & grounds suitable. WC.

PARCEVALL HALL GARDENS   **Tel:** 01756 720311

Skyreholme, Skipton, Yorkshire BD23 6DE   **Contact:** Jo Makin (Administrator)

Owner: Walsingham College (Yorkshire Properties) Ltd.

Location: OS Ref. SE068 613. E side of Upper Wharfedale, 1½ m NE of Appletreewick. 12m NNW of Ilkley by B6160 and via Burnsall.

Opening Times: 1 Apr - 31 Oct: 10am - 6pm.

Admission: £3, Child 50p. (Prices subject to increase in 2001.)

PICKERING CASTLE   **Tel:** 01751 474989

Pickering, Yorkshire YO18 7AX

Owner: English Heritage   **Contact:** The Custodian

A splendid motte and bailey castle, once a royal ranch. It is well preserved, with much of the original walls, towers and keep, and there are spectacular views over the surrounding countryside. There is an exhibition on the castle's history.

Location: OS100 Ref. SE800 845. In Pickering, 15m SW of Scarborough.

Opening Times: 1 Apr - 30 Sept: daily, 10am - 6pm. 1 - 31 Oct: daily, 10am - 5pm. 1 Nov - 31 Mar: Wed - Sun, 10am - 4pm (closed 1 - 2pm). Closed 24 - 26 Dec.

Admission: Adult £2.40, Child £1.20, Conc. £1.80. 15% discount for groups (11+).

Partially suitable. Limited. In grounds, on leads.

PLUMPTON ROCKS   **Tel:** 01423 863950

Plumpton, Knaresborough, North Yorkshire HG5 8NA

Owner: Edward de Plumpton Hunter   **Contact:** Robert de Plumpton Hunter

Grade II* listed garden extending to over 30 acres including an idyllic lake, dramatic millstone grit rock formation, romantic woodland walks winding through bluebells and rhododendrons. Declared by English Heritage to be of outstanding interest. Painted by Turner. Described by Queen Mary as 'Heaven on earth'.

Location: OS Ref. SE355 535. Midway between Harrogate and Wetherby on the A661, 1m SE of A661 junction with the Harrogate southern bypass.

Opening Times: Mar - Oct: Sat, Sun & BHs, 11am - 6pm.

Admission: Adult £1.50, Child/OAP £1, Student £1.50.

Not suitable. By arrangement. Limited for coaches. In grounds, on leads.

RED HOUSE MUSEUM   **Tel:** 01274 335100   **Tel:** 01274 335105

Oxford Road, Gomersal, Cleckheaton BD19 4JP

Owner: Kirklees Cultural Services

Location: OS Ref. SE210 260. On A651 in Gomersal. M62/J27, follow A62 towards Huddersfield to Birstall, follow brown tourist signs.

Opening Times: All year: Mon - Fri, 11am - 5pm. Sats & Suns, 12 noon - 5pm.

Admission: Free.

RICHMOND CASTLE

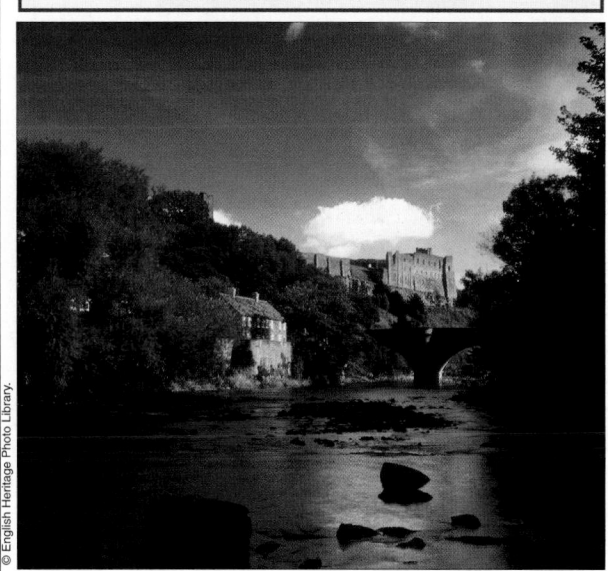

© English Heritage Photo Library.

RICHMOND, NORTH YORKSHIRE DL10 4QW

Owner: English Heritage   *Contact: The Custodian*

Tel: 01748 822493

A splendid medieval fortress, with a fine 12th century keep and 11th century remains of the curtain wall and domestic buildings. There are magnificent views from the 100 feet high keep. Exciting new interactive exhibition brings the history of the site alive.

Location: OS92 Ref. NZ174 006. In Richmond.

Opening Times: 1 Apr - 30 Sept: daily, 10am - 6pm. 1 - 31 Oct: daily, 10am - 5pm. 1 Nov - 31 Mar: daily, 10am - 4pm (closed 1 - 2pm). Closed 24- 26 Dec.

Admission: Adult £2.70, Child £1.40, Conc. £2. 15% discount for groups (11+).

New interactive exhibition. Partially suitable. In grounds, on leads. Tel. for details.

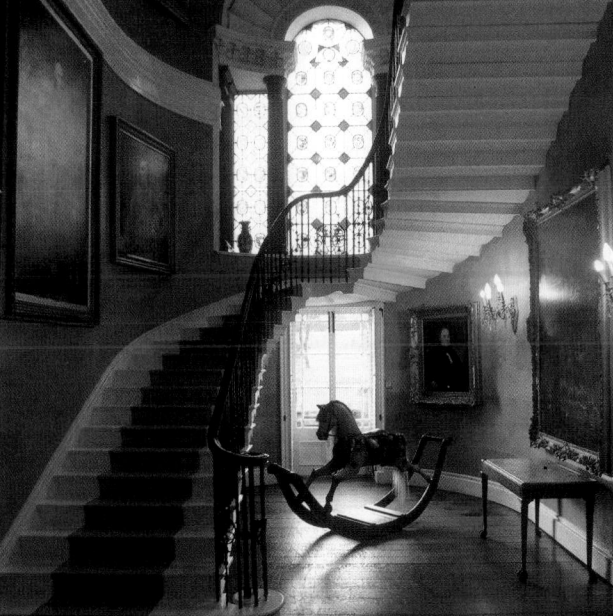

Ripley Castle, Yorkshire.

RIEVAULX ABBEY

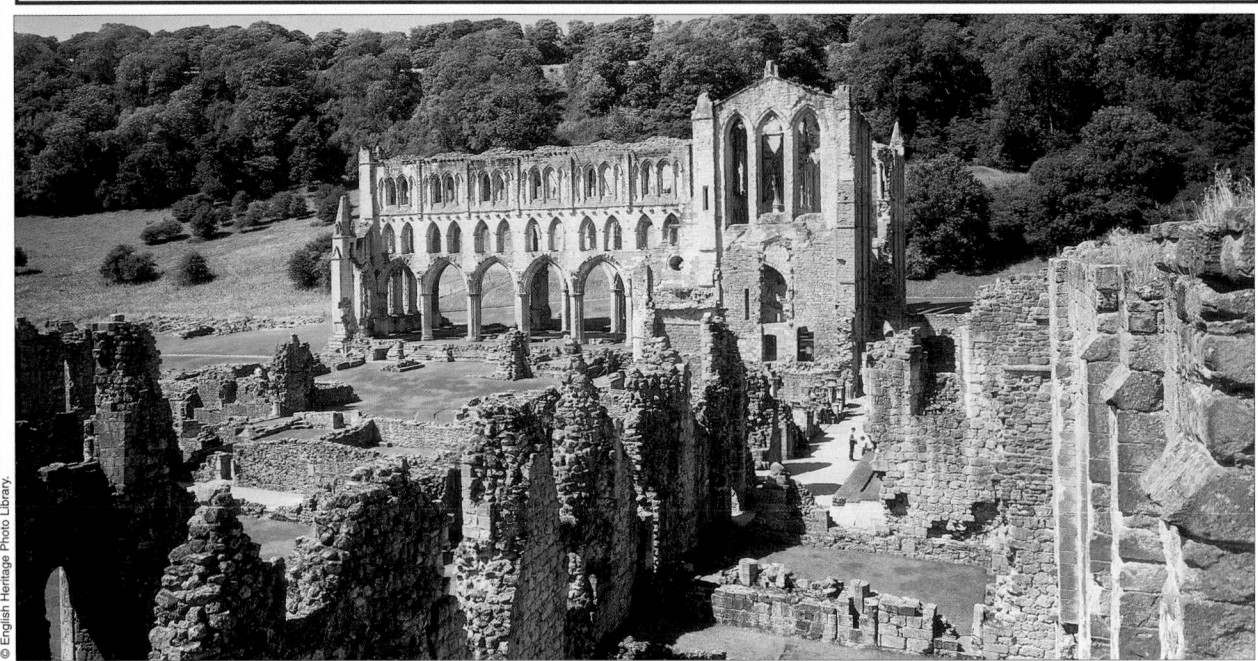

© English Heritage Photo Library.

RIEVAULX, Nr HELMSLEY, NORTH YORKSHIRE YO6 5LB

Owner: English Heritage   *Contact:* The Custodian

Tel: 01439 798228

In a deeply wooded valley by the River Rye you can see some of the most spectacular monastic ruins in England, dating from the 12th century. The church has the earliest large Cistercian nave in Britain. A fascinating exhibition shows how successfully the Cistercians at Rievaulx ran their many businesses and explains the part played by Abbot Ailred, who ruled for twenty years. New interactive museum, exhibition and interactive display.

Location: OS100 Ref. SE577 849. 2¼ m W of Helmsley on minor road off B1257.
Opening Times: 1 Apr - 30 Sept: daily, 10am - 6pm (Aug: 9.30am - 7pm). 1 - 31 Oct: daily, 10am - 5pm. 1 Nov - 31 Mar: daily, 10am - 4pm. Closed 24- 26 Dec.
Admission: Adult £3.50, Child £1.80, Conc. £2.60. 15% discount for groups (11+).

Partially suitable.   P   On leads.   Tel. for details.

RIEVAULX TERRACE & TEMPLES

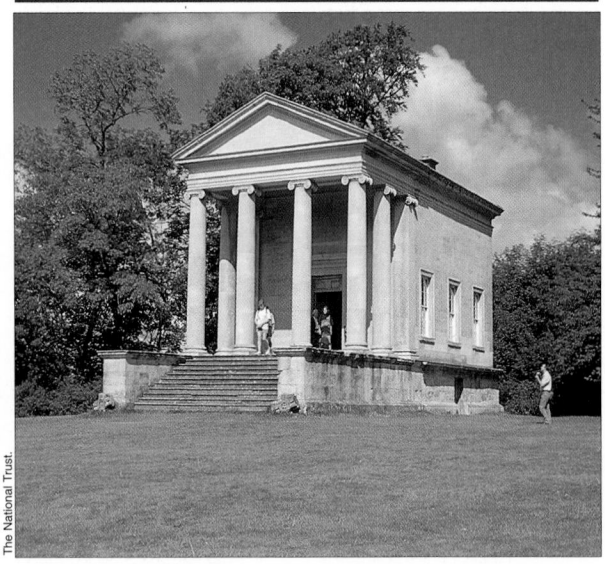

The National Trust.

RIEVAULX, HELMSLEY, NORTH YORKSHIRE YO62 5LJ

Owner: The National Trust   *Contact:* The Visitor Manager

Tel: 01439 748283   **Fax:** 01439 748284

A ½ m long grass-covered terrace and adjoining woodlands with vistas over Rievaulx Abbey (English Heritage) and Rye valley to Ryedale and the Hambleton Hills. There are two mid-18th century temples: the Ionic Temple has elaborate ceiling paintings and fine 18th century furniture. Note: no access to property Nov - end Mar.

Location: OS Ref. SE579 848. 2¼ m NW of Helmsley on B1257. E of the Abbey.
Opening Times: 31 Mar - 4 Nov. Oct & Nov: daily, 10.30am - 4pm. Mar - Sept: daily, 10.30am - 5pm. Open Good Fri & BH Mons.
Admission: Adult £3.30, Child £1.50, Family (2+3) £8. Groups (15+): £2.80.

Grounds suitable.   In grounds, on leads.

RIPLEY CASTLE   See page 374 for full page entry.

RIPON CATHEDRAL   **Tel:** 01765 604108 (information on tours etc.)

Ripon, Yorkshire HG4 1QR
Contact: Canon Keith Punshon
One of the oldest crypts in Europe (672). Marvellous choir stalls and misericords (500 years old). Almost every type of architecture. Treasury.
Location: OS Ref. SE314 711. 5m W signposted off A1, 12m N of Harrogate.
Opening Times: All year: 8am - 6pm.
Admission: Donations. £2 per head pre-booked guided tours.

RIPON WORKHOUSE   **Tel:** 01765 690799

Allhallowgate, Ripon, Yorkshire
Contact: Mr D Gowling
The workhouse shows restored vagrants' wards and the treatment of paupers.
Location: OS Ref. SE312 712 Close to Market Square.
Opening Times: 7 Apr - 28 Oct: daily, 11am - 4pm.
Admission: Adult £1.25, Child (6 - 16yrs) 75p, Child under 6yrs Free, Conc./Student £1.

ROCHE ABBEY   **Tel:** 01709 812739

Maltby, Rotherham, South Yorkshire S66 8NW
Owner: English Heritage   **Contact:** The Custodian
This Cistercian monastery, founded in 1147, lies in a secluded landscaped valley sheltered by limestone cliffs and trees. Some of the walls still stand to their full height and excavation has revealed the complete layout of the abbey.
Location: OS111 Ref. SK544 898. 1m S of Maltby off A634.
Opening Times: 1 Apr - 30 Sept: daily, 10am - 6pm. 1 - 31 Oct: daily, 10am - 5pm.
Admission: Adult £1.70, Child 90p, Conc. £1.30. 15% discount for groups (11+).

Partially suitable.   P Limited.   In grounds, on leads.   Tel. for details.

RYDALE FOLK MUSEUM

Tel: 01751 417367

Hutton Le Hole, York, North Yorkshire YO6 6UA

Owner: The Crosland Foundation   **Contact:** Martin Watts

13 historic buildings showing the lives of ordinary folk from earliest times to the present day.

Location: OS Ref. SE705 902. Follow signs from Hutton Le Hole. 3m N of Kirby Moorside.

Opening Times: 11 Mar - 4 Nov: 10am - 5.30pm last admission 4.30pm.

Admission: Adult £3.25, Child £1.75, Conc. £2.75 (2000 prices).

ST WILLIAM'S COLLEGE

Tel: 01904 557233 **Fax:** 01904 557234

5 College Street, York, Yorkshire YO1 2JF

Owner: The Dean and Chapter of York   **Contact:** Sandie Clarke

15th century medieval home of Minster Chantry Priests. Three large medieval halls, available for functions, conferences, weddings, medieval banquets, etc. Halls open to view when not in use. Information Centre.

Location: OS Ref. SE605 522. College Street, York. Adjoining E end of York Minster.

Opening Times: 10am - 5pm.

Admission: Adult 60p, Child 30p. For further details please telephone.

SCAMPSTON HALL

Tel: 01944 758224 **Fax:** 01944 758700

Scampston, Malton, North Yorkshire YO17 8NG   **e-mail:** info@scampston.co.uk

Owner/Contact: Sir Charles Legard Bt

Opened for the first time in 1997, this country house has remained in the same family since it was built towards the end of the 17th century. The house was extensively remodelled in 1801 by the architect Thomas Leverton and has fine Regency interiors. It houses an important collection of works of art including pictures by Gainsborough, Marlow, Scott and Wilson. The park was laid out under the guidance of 'Capability' Brown and includes 10 acres of lakes and a Palladian bridge. The garden features a recently restored 19th century walk in rock and water garden with a collection of alpines, some of which are available for sale.

Location: OS100 Ref. SE865 755. 5m E of Malton, off A64.

Opening Times: 27 May - 10 Jun & 22 Jul - 5 Aug (closed Sats), 1.30 - 5pm. Last admission 4.30pm.

Admission: House & Garden: £5, Garden £2, no concessions. Groups and coaches by appointment only. Prices for groups by arrangement. Friends of the HHA admitted free.

Not suitable. Guided tours only.

SCARBOROUGH CASTLE

Tel: 01723 372451

Castle Road, Scarborough, North Yorkshire YO11 1HY

Owner: English Heritage   **Contact:** The Custodian

Spectacular coastal views from the walls of this enormous 12th century castle. The buttressed castle walls stretch out along the cliff edge and remains of the great rectangular stone keep still stand to over three storeys high. There is also the site of a 4th century Roman signal station. The castle was frequently attacked, but despite being blasted by cannons of the Civil War and bombarded from the sea during World War I, it is still a spectacular place to visit.

Location: OS101, Ref. TA050 893. Castle Road, E of town centre.

Opening Times: 1 Apr - 30 Sept: daily, 10am - 6pm (7pm in Aug). 1 - 31 Oct: daily, 10am - 5pm. 1 Nov - 31 Mar: Wed - Sun, 10am - 4pm (closed 1 -2 pm). Closed 24 - 26 Dec.

Admission: Adult £2.40, Child £1.20, Conc. £1.80. 15% discount for groups (11+).

Partially suitable. Inclusive. In grounds, on leads. Tel. for details.

SEWERBY HALL & GARDENS

Tel: 01262 673769 **Fax:** 01262 673090
e-mail: museum@pop3.poptel.org.uk

Church Lane, Sewerby, Bridlington, East Yorkshire Y015 1EA

Owner: East Riding of Yorkshire Council   **Contact:** Customer Service Officer

Sewerby Hall and Gardens, set in 50 acres of parkland, dates back to 1715. The Georgian house contains: 19th century orangery; history/archaeology displays; art galleries and an Amy Johnson Room. The Grounds include: walled gardens, woodland, children's zoo and play area, golf and putting.

Location: OS Ref. TA203 690. 2m N of Bridlington in Sewerby village.

Opening Times: Hall: 17 Feb - 27 Mar, Sat - Tues, 11am - 4pm; 31 Mar - 28 Oct, Daily 10am - 6pm; 29 Oct - 23 Dec, Sat - Tues, 11am - 4pm. Gardens only: daily, dawn - dusk.

Admission: Please telephone for admission prices.

Licensed. In grounds, on leads. Guide dogs in hall. Tel. for details.

SHANDY HALL

Tel/Fax: 01347 868465

Coxwold, York YO61 4AD

Owner: The Laurence Sterne Trust   **Contact:** Mrs J Monkman

Built as a timber-framed hall in the 15th century.

Location: OS Ref. SE531 773. W end of Coxwold village, 4m E of A19 & 20m N of York, via Easingwold.

Opening Times: 1 May - 30 Sept: Weds, 2 - 4.30pm. Suns, 2.30 - 4.30pm. Other times by appointment. Garden: 1 May - 30 Sept: Sun - Fri, 11am - 4.30pm.

Admission: Hall & Garden: Adult £3.50, Child £1.50. Garden only: Adult £2.50, Child £1.

SHIBDEN HALL

Tel: 01422 352246 **Fax:** 01422 348440

Lister's Road, Halifax, West Yorkshire HX3 6XG

Owner: Calderdale MBC   **Contact:** Valerie Stansfield

A half-timbered manor house, the home of Anne Lister set in a landscaped park. Oak furniture, carriages and an array of objects make Shibden an intriguing place to visit.

Location: OS Ref. SE106 257. 1½ m E of Halifax off A58.

Opening Times: 1 Mar - 30 Nov: Mon - Sat, 10am - 5pm. Suns, 12 noon - 5pm. Last admission 4.30pm. Dec - Feb: Mon - Sat, 10am - 4pm. Suns, 12 noon - 4pm.

Admission: Adult £2.50, Child/Conc. £1.50, Family £6.

Ground floor & grounds suitable. P Guide dogs only.

SION HILL HALL

Tel: 01845 587206 **Fax:** 01845 587486
e-mail: enquiries.sionhall@virgin.net

Kirby Wiske, Thirsk, North Yorkshire YO7 4EU

Owner: H W Mawer Trust   **Contact:** R M Mallaby
Falconry Centre: 01845 587522 **Fax:** 01845 523735
Antique Centre/Tearoom: 01845 587071

Sion Hill Hall was designed in 1912 by the renowned York Architect Walter H Brierley, 'the Lutyens of the North'. With its fine lines, unique character and superb layout, the Hall was designated by the Royal Institute of British Architects as being of Outstanding Architectural Merit. Sion Hill contains the H W Mawer collection of fine furniture, porcelain, paintings and clocks in superb room settings. Additionally the Edwardian kitchen has been recently restored to its former splendour. Member of the Herriot Country Attractions Group.

Location: OS Ref. SE373 844. 6m S of Northallerton off A167, 4m W of Thirsk, 6m E of A1 via A61.

Opening Times: Hall: 13 (Good Fri), 15, 16, 22 & 29 Apr. Also May - end Sept: Weds, Thurs, Suns & BH Mons, 1 - 5pm, last entry 4pm. Groups welcome by prior arrangement at other times.

Admission: Non-guided tours: Adult £4.50, Child under 12yrs Free (if accompanied by an adult), Conc. £4. Guided tours: £5.75 per person.

Partially suitable. WC. P In grounds, on leads.

SKIPTON CASTLE

See page 375 for full page entry.

See page 375 for full page entry.

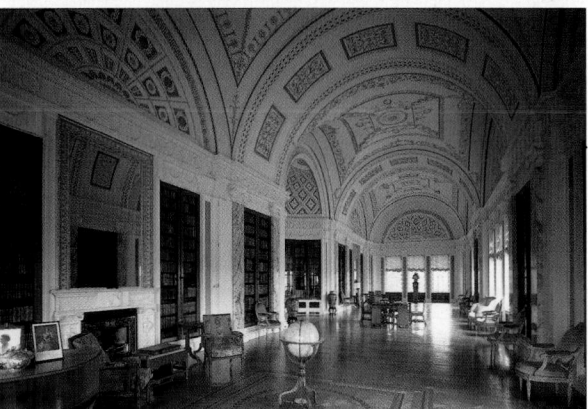

SLEDMERE HOUSE

SLEDMERE, DRIFFIELD, EAST YORKSHIRE YO25 3XG

Owner: Sir Tatton Sykes Bt   *Contact: Mrs Anne Hines*

Tel: 01377 236637 **Fax:** 01377 236500

Sledmere House is the home of Sir Tatton Sykes, 8th Baronet. There has been a manor house at Sledmere since medieval times. The present house was designed and built by Sir Christopher Sykes, 2nd Baronet, a diary date states *"June 17th, 1751 laid the first stone of the new house at Sledmere."* Sir Christopher employed a fellow Yorkshireman, Joseph Rose, the most famous English plasterer of his day, to execute the decoration of Sledmere. Rose's magnificent work at Sledmere was unique in his career. A great feature at Sledmere is the 'Capability' Brown parkland and the beautiful 18th century walled rose gardens. Also worthy of note is the recently laid out knot-garden, all accessible by wheelchair.

Location: OS Ref. SE931 648. Off the A166 between York & Bridlington. ½ hr drive from York, Bridlington & Scarborough.

Opening Times: 13 - 17 Apr & 6 May - 30 Sept: closed Mons & Sats but open BHs: 11.30am - 4.30pm. Famous pipe organ played Weds, Fris & Suns.

Admission: House & Gardens: Adult £4.50, Child £2, OAP £4. Gardens & Park: Adult £2, Child £1.

No photography in house. Licensed. By arrangement. P In grounds on leads. Guide dogs in house.

SPOFFORTH CASTLE

Tel: 01904 601901

Harrogate, Yorkshire

Owner: English Heritage   **Contact:** The Northern Regional Office

This manor house has some fascinating features including an undercroft built into the rock. It was once owned by the Percy family.

Location: OS Ref. SE360 511. $3^1/_2$ m SE of Harrogate on minor road off A661 at Spofforth.

Opening Times: 1 Apr - 30 Sept: daily, 10am - 6pm. 1 - 31 Oct: daily, 10am - 6pm or dusk if earlier. 1 Nov - 31 Mar: 10am - 4pm.

Admission: Free.

STOCKELD PARK

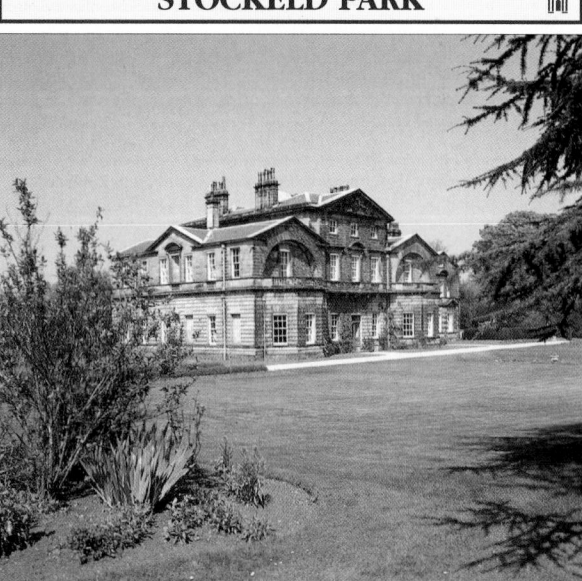

WETHERBY, YORKSHIRE LS22 4AH

Owner: Mr and Mrs P G F Grant   *Contact: Mrs L A Saunders*

Tel: 01937 586101 **Fax:** 01937 580084

Stockeld is a beautifully proportioned Palladian villa designed by James Paine in 1763, featuring a magnificent cantilevered staircase in the central oval hall. Stockeld is still very much a family home, with a fine collection of 18th and 19th century furniture and paintings. The house is surrounded by lovely gardens of lawns, large herbaceous and shrub borders, fringed by woodland, and set in 100 acres of fine parkland in the midst of an extensive farming estate.

Location: OS Ref. SE376 497. York 12m, Harrogate 5m, Leeds 12m.

Opening Times: 19 Apr - 11 Oct: Thurs only, 2 - 5pm. Groups please book.

Admission: Adult £4.50. Group prices on application.

House only. Obligatory.

STUDLEY ROYAL: ST MARY'S CHURCH

Tel: 01765 608888

Ripon, Yorkshire

Owner: English Heritage   **Contact:** The Custodian

A magnificent Victorian church, designed by William Burges in the 1870s, with a highly decorated interior. Coloured marble, stained glass, gilded and painted figures and a splendid organ.

Location: OS Ref. SE278 703. $2^1/_2$ m W of Ripon off B6265, in grounds of Studley Royal estate.

Opening Times: 1 Apr - 30 Sept: daily, 1 - 5pm.

Admission: Free.

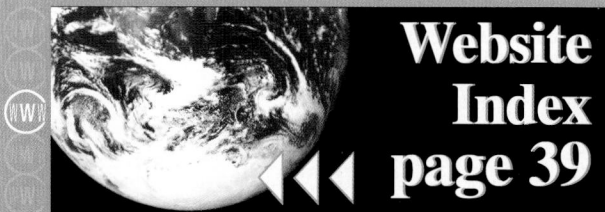

Website Index page 39

SUTTON PARK

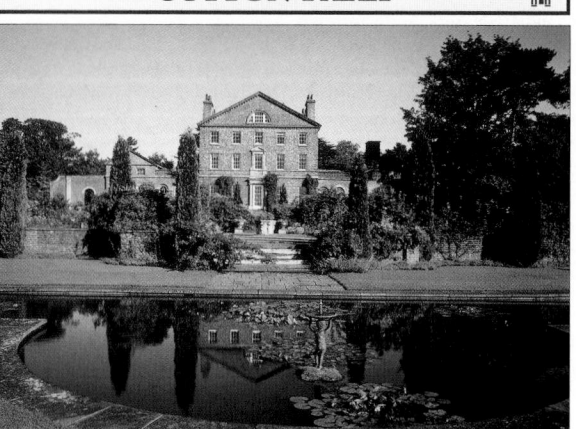

SUTTON-ON-THE-FOREST, NORTH YORKSHIRE YO61 1DP

Owner: Sir Reginald & Lady Sheffield   *Contact: Mrs A Wilkinson*

Tel: 01347 810249/811239 **Fax:** 01347 811251 **e-mail:** suttonpark@fsbdial.co.uk

The Yorkshire home of Sir Reginald and Lady Sheffield. Charming example of early Georgian architecture. Magnificent plasterwork by Cortese. Rich collection of 18th century furniture, paintings, porcelain, needlework, beadwork. All put together with great style to make a most inviting house. Award winning gardens attract enthusiasts from home and abroad.

Location: OS Ref. SE583 646. 8m N of York on B1363 York - Helmsley Road.

Opening Times: House: 1 Apr - 30 Sept: Suns & Weds, also Good Fri - Easter Mon & BH Mons, 1.30 - 5pm. Tearoom: as house, 12 noon - 5pm. Private Groups: Any other day of the week by appointment. House open Oct - Mar for private groups only. Gardens: 1 Apr - 30 Sept, daily, 11am - 5pm.

Admission: House & Garden: Adult £5, Child £2.50, Conc. £4. Gardens only: Adult £2.50, Child 50p, Conc. £1.50. Coach parties: £4.50. Gardens only £2. Private Groups (15+): £5.50. Caravans: £4.50 per night.

No photography. Hosted lunches & dinners. Partially suitable. Obligatory. Limited for coaches.   3 double with ensuite bathrooms. Tel. for details.

TEMPLE NEWSAM HOUSE

Tel: 0113 2647321 **Fax:** 0113 2602285

Leeds LS15 0AE

Owner: Leeds City Council   **Contact:** Denise Lawson

A Tudor-Jacobean mansion with over thirty rooms open to the public.

Location: OS Ref. SE358 321. 5m E of city centre, off A63 Selby Road. M1/J46.

Opening Times: 1 Apr - 31 Oct: Tue - Sat, 10am - 5pm. Suns, 1 - 5pm. 1 Nov - 31 Dec & Mar: Tue - Sat, 10am - 4pm, Suns, 12 noon - 4pm. Last admission $3/_4$ hr before closing time. Closed Jan & Feb.

Admission: Adult £2, Child 50p, Conc. £1. Groups (10+): Adult £1, Child 50p.

THORNTON ABBEY

Tel: 01904 601901

Scunthorpe, Humberside

Owner: English Heritage   **Contact:** The Yorkshire Regional Office

The magnificent brick gatehouse of this ruined Augustine priory stands three storeys high.

Location: OS Ref. TA115 190. 18m NE of Scunthorpe on minor road N of A180.

Opening Times: 1 Apr - 30 Sept: 1st & 3rd Suns, 12 - 6pm. 1 Oct - 31 Mar: 3rd Suns, 12 - 4pm.

Admission: Free.

THORP PERROW ARBORETUM & THE FALCONS OF THORP PERROW

Tel/Fax: 01677 425323

Bedale, North Yorkshire DL8 2PR   **e-mail:** louise@thorpperrow.freeserve.co.uk

Owner: Sir John Ropner Bt   **Contact:** Louise McNeill

85 acres of woodland walks. One of the largest collections of trees and shrubs in the north of England, including a 16th century medieval spring wood and 19th century pinetum. The Falcons of Thorp Perrow, an additional attraction which opened spring 2000. Various trails available, playground with mini beast station, tearoom and plant centre.

Location: OS Ref. SE258 851. Bedale - Ripon road, S of Bedale, 4m from Leeming Bar on A1.

Opening Times: All year: dawn - dusk.

Admission: Arboretum: Adult £3.50, Child £2, OAP £2.50, Family (2+2) £10, (2+4) £14. Arboretum & Falcons: Adult £7, Child £4, OAP £5, Family (2+2) £20, (2+4) £28.

Picnic area. Children's playground. By arrangement. Limited for coaches. In grounds, on leads.   Tel. for details.

TREASURER'S HOUSE

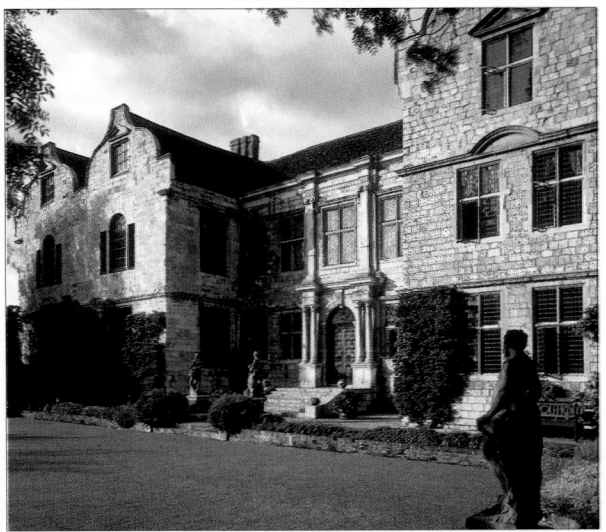

MINSTER YARD, YORK, NORTH YORKSHIRE YO1 7JH

Owner: *The National Trust* **Contact:** *The Property Manager*

Tel: 01904 624247 **Fax:** 01904 647372 **e-mail:** yorkth@smtp.ntrust.org.uk

An elegant townhouse situated in the tranquil surroundings of the Minster Close. A series of period rooms is the setting for a fine collection of furniture and paintings given to the National Trust by Yorkshire industrialist Frank Green, who lived here from 1897 to 1930. Introductory video and exhibition.

Location: OS Ref. SE604 523. The N side of York Minster. Entrance on Chapter House St.

Opening Times: 31 Mar - 31 Oct: daily except Fris, 11am - 5pm. Last adm. 4.30pm.

Admission: Adult £3.70, Child £2. Family £9.50. Booked groups (15+): Adult £3, Child £1.50.

 Partially suitable. WC. Licensed. Licensed. None. In grounds, on leads.

WHITBY ABBEY

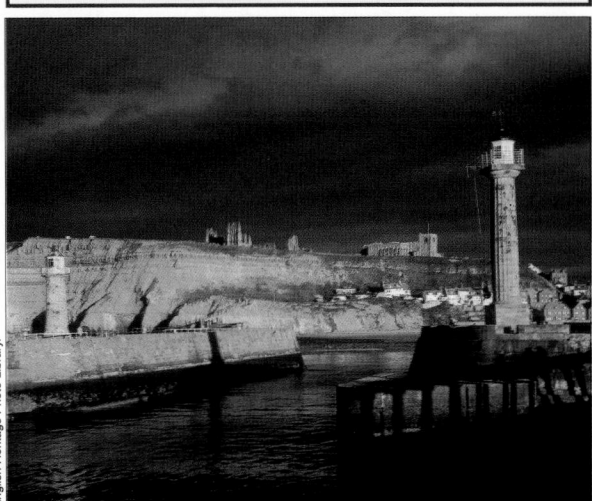

© English Heritage Photo Library.

WHITBY, NORTH YORKSHIRE YO22 4JT

Owner: *English Heritage* **Contact:** *The Custodian*

Tel: 01947 603568

An ancient holy place, once a burial place of kings and an inspiration for saints. A religious community was first established at Whitby in 657 by Abbess Hilda and was the home of Caedmon, the first English poet. The remains we can see today are of a Benedictine church built in the 13th and 14th centuries, and include a magnificent three-tiered choir and north transept. It is perched high above the picturesque harbour town of Whitby.

Location: OS94, Ref. NZ904 115. On cliff top E of Whitby.

Opening Times: 1 Apr - 30 Sept: daily 10am - 6pm. 1 - 31 Oct: daily, 10am - 5pm. 1 Nov - 31 Mar: daily, 10am - 4pm. Closed 24 - 26 Dec.

Admission: Adult £1.80, Child 90p, Conc. £1.40. 15% discounts for groups (11+).

Ground floor suitable. In grounds, on leads. Tel. for details.

WAKEFIELD CATHEDRAL **Tel:** 01924 373923 **Fax:** 01924 215054

Northgate, Wakefield, West Yorkshire WF1 1HG

Owner: Church of England **Contact:** Mr F Arnold, Head Verger

Built on the site of a previous Saxon church, this 14th century Parish Church became a cathedral in 1888 and was extended by Pearson and completed by his son. It also boasts, at 247ft, the highest spire in Yorkshire.

Location: OS Ref. SE333 208. Wakefield city centre. M1/ J39-41, M62/J29W, J30 E.

Opening Times: Mon - Sat: 8am - 5pm. Suns: between services only. Sunday Services: Holy Communion: 8am. Parish Eucharist: 9.15am. Solemn Eucharist: 11am. Choral Evensong (Winter): 4pm. Choral Evensong (Summer): 6.30pm. Daily Services: Holy Communion: Daily, 8am plus 10.30am on Weds & Sats and 12.30pm on Fris. Choral Evensong: Thurs, 6.30pm. Said Evensong: Mons, Tues, Fris & Sats, 5pm. Weds (girls' choir) Choral Evensong 6pm.

Admission: Free admission. Donations welcome.

WENTWORTH CASTLE GARDENS **Tel:** 01226 731269

Lowe Lane, Stainborough, Barnsley, Yorkshire S75 3ET

Owner: Barnsley MBC **Contact:** Chris Margrave

300 years old, these gardens are the only Grade I listed gardens in South Yorkshire, 28 listed buildings and monuments and the National Collections of rhododendrons, magnolias and williamsii camellias.

Location: OS Ref. SE320 034. 5km W of Barnsley, M1/J36 via Birdwell & Rockley Lane then Lowe Lane.

Opening Times: Mid April - end June, mainly by guided tours. Please telephone 01226 731269 for a recorded message.

Admission: £2.50, Conc. £1.50.

WHITE SCAR CAVE **See page 376 for full page entry.**

WILBERFORCE HOUSE **Tel:** 01482 613902 **Fax:** 01482 613710

High Street, Hull, Yorkshire HU1 1NQ

Owner: Hull City Council **Contact:** S R Green

Built c1660 the house is a museum to the memory of William Wilberforce.

Location: OS Ref. TA102 286. High Street, Hull.

Opening Times: Mon - Sat, 10am - 5pm. Suns, 1.30 - 4.30pm. Closed Good Fri & Christmas Day.

Admission: Free.

WORTLEY HALL **Tel:** 0114 2882100 **Fax:** 0114 2830695

Wortley, Sheffield, Yorkshire S35 7DB

Owner: Labour, Co-operative & Trade Union Movement **Contact:** John Howard

15 acres of formal Italianate gardens surrounded by 11 acres of informal pleasure grounds.

Location: OS Ref. SK313 995. 10kms S of Barnsley in Wortley on A629.

Opening Times: Gardens: All year except 7 - 14 Aug & 6 - 13 Nov.

Admission: Free. Groups must book for gardeners' tour, £1.50.

YORK MINSTER **Tel:** 01904 557216 **Fax:** 01904 557218

Deangate, York YO1 7HH

Owner: Dean and Chapter of York **Contact:** Dorothy Lee, Visitors' Officer

Large gothic church housing the largest collection of medieval stained glass in England.

Location: OS Ref. SE603 522. Centre of York.

Opening Times: Nov - Mar: 7am - 6pm, Apr: 7am - 6.30pm, May: 7am - 7.30pm, Jun - Aug: 7am - 8.30pm, Sept: 7am - 8pm, Oct: 7am - 7pm, daily.

Admission: By donation. Tour companies £3 per person, Child (6-16yrs) £1.

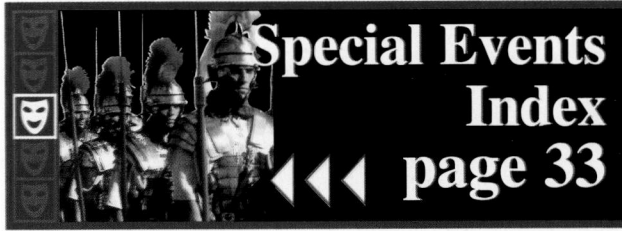

Special Events Index ◄◄◄ page 33

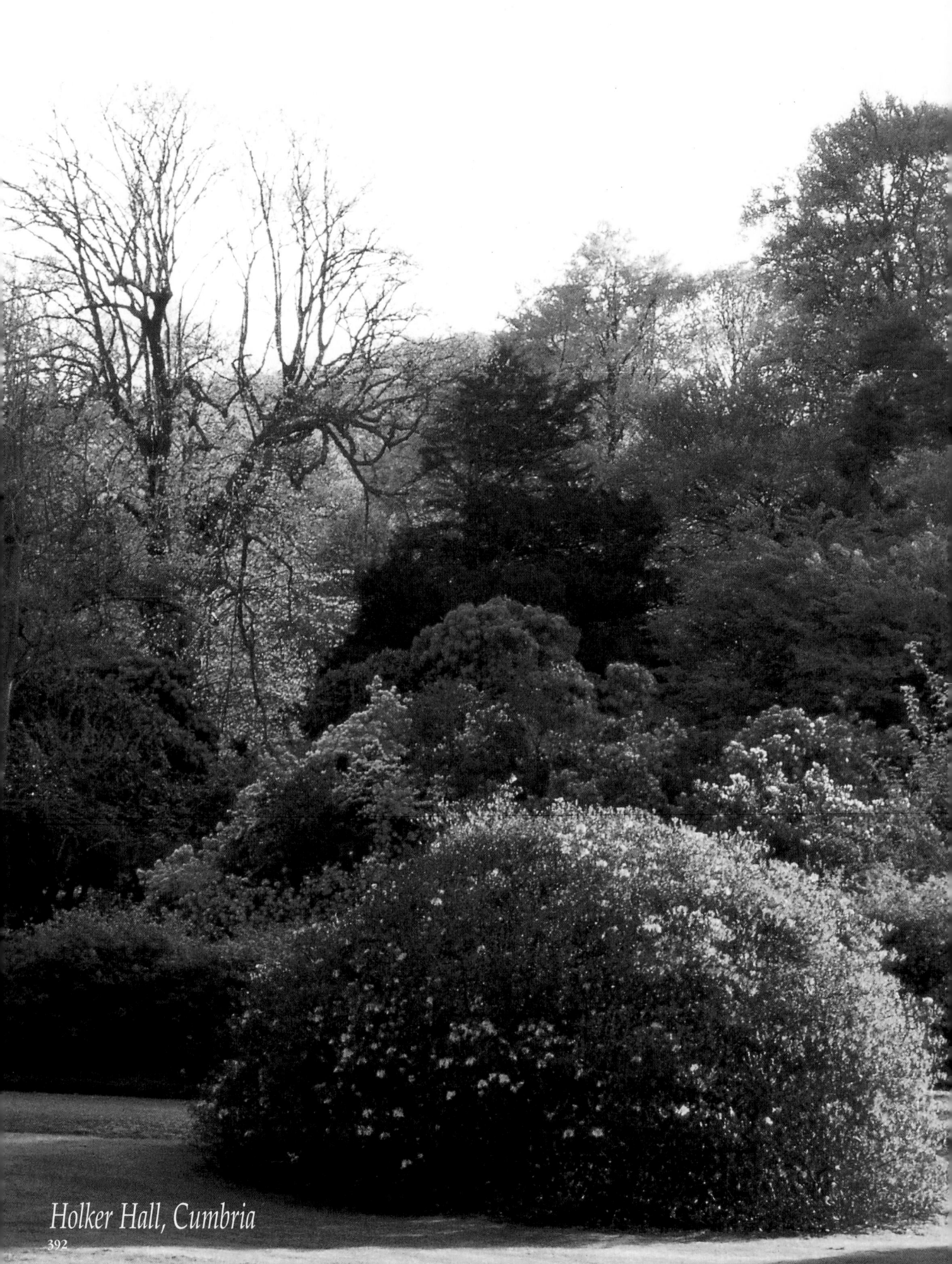

Holker Hall, Cumbria

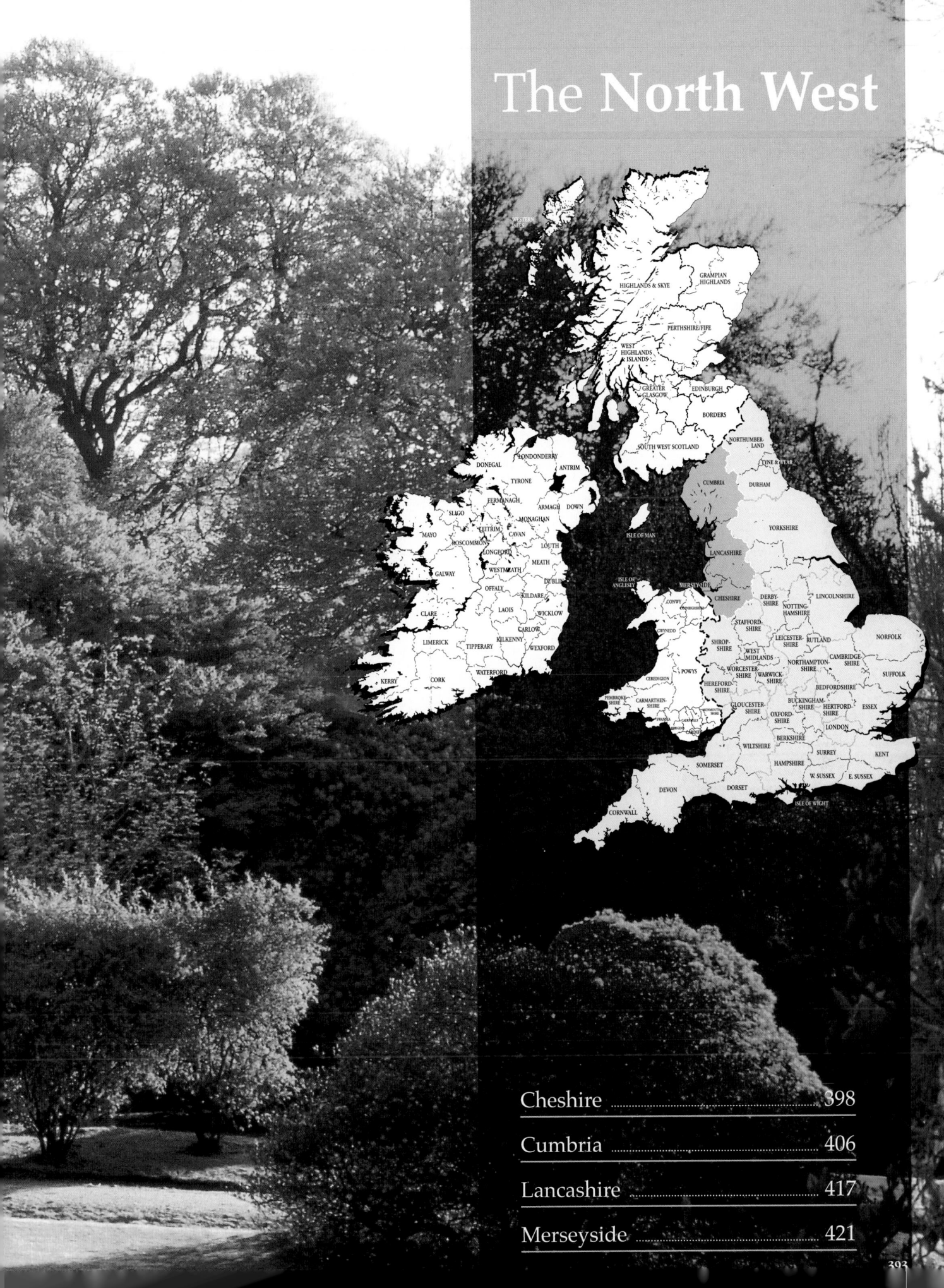

The North West

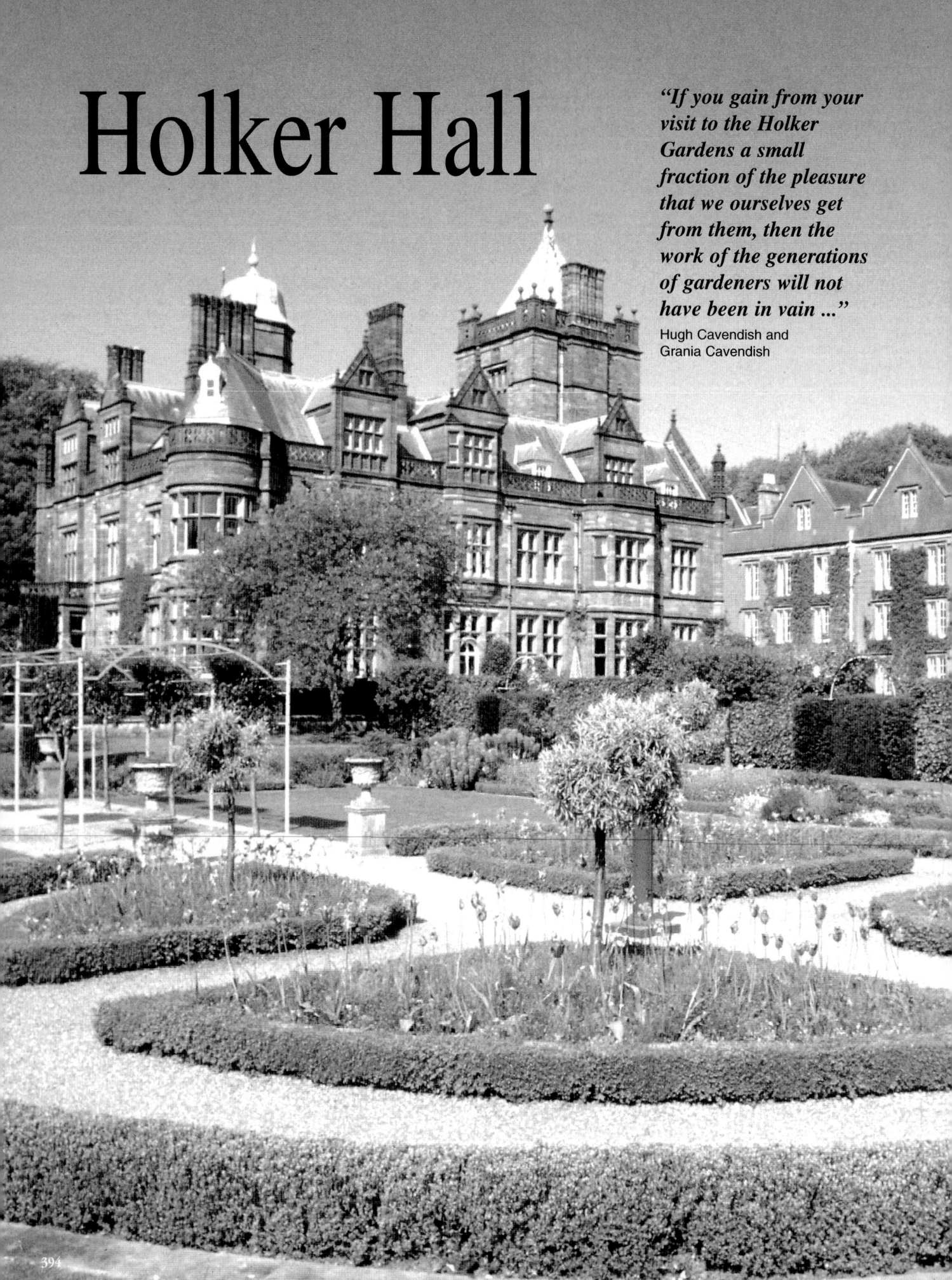

Holker Hall

"If you gain from your visit to the Holker Gardens a small fraction of the pleasure that we ourselves get from them, then the work of the generations of gardeners will not have been in vain ..."

Hugh Cavendish and
Grania Cavendish

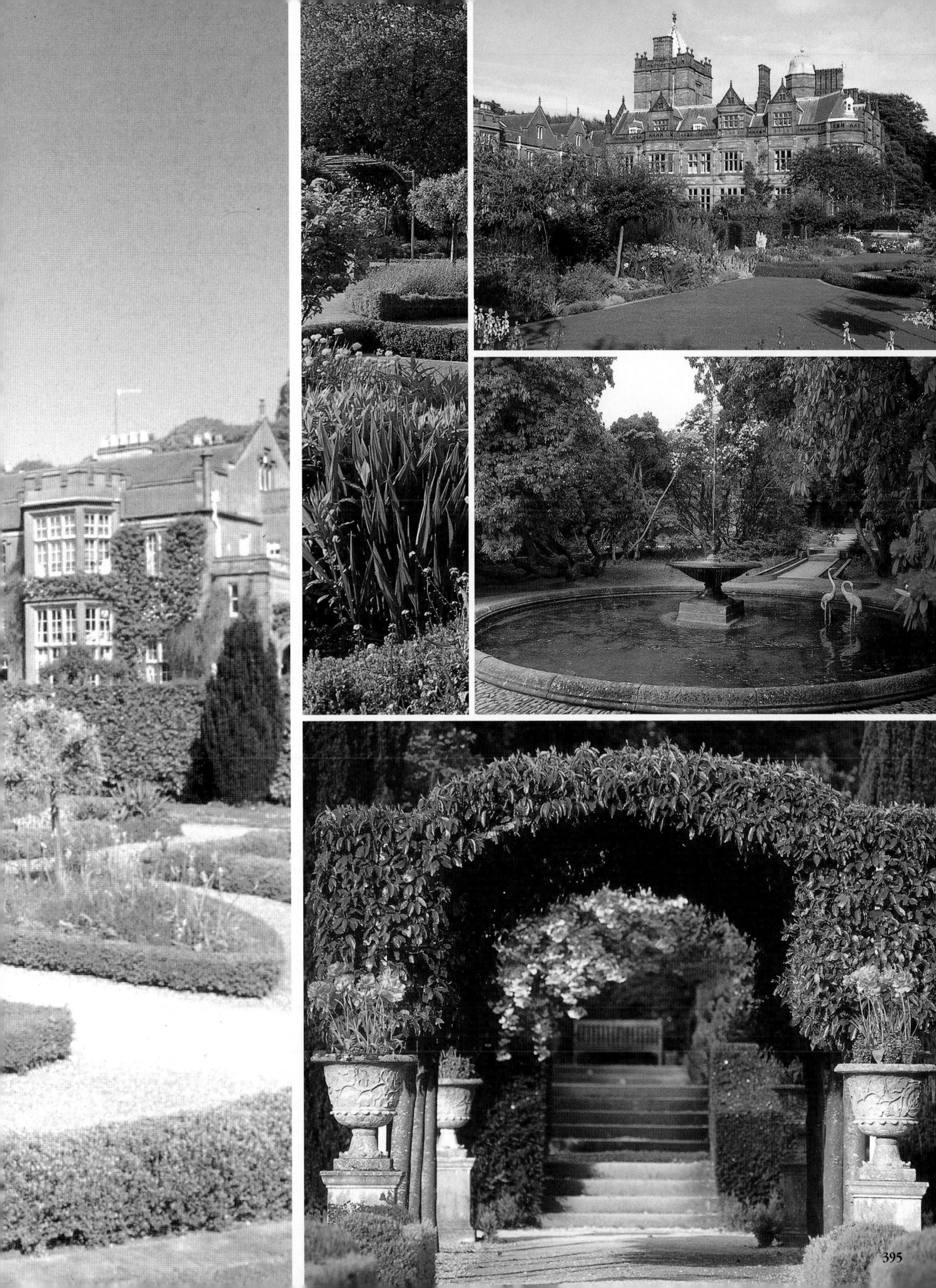

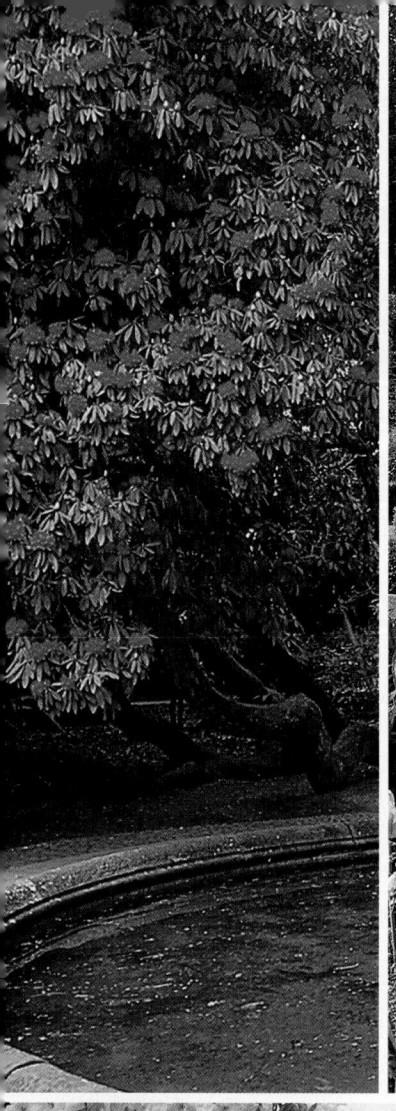

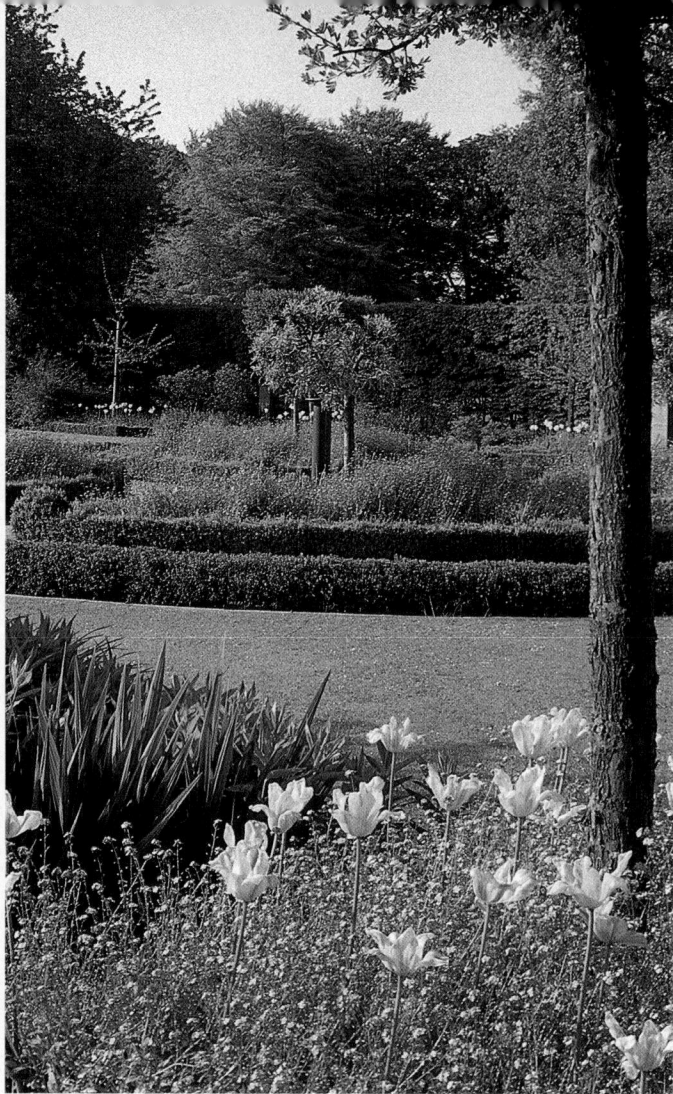

Only a short distance from the sea, Holker Hall is magnificently situated on the wooded slopes of the Cartmel peninsula which juts out from the north into Morecombe Bay. Despite its grand scale, this handsome rose coloured neo-Elizabethan mansion and its gardens provide a soft and gentle contrast to the ruggedness of the Lakeland countryside to the north.

The earliest records of a house on the present site date back to the beginning of the 16th century. From then until the present day it has been home to three families: the Prestons, the Lowthers and Cavendishes. The estate has never been bought or sold, but has passed by inheritance through the family line, with each generation leaving its impressions, either by planning and altering the landscape or by changing the house by adding, refacing, embellishing or even rebuilding – as was necessary after the disastrous fire of 1871.

The present appearance of Holker, and the New Wing built by the 7th Duke of Devonshire, is chiefly the work in the 1870s of the Lancashire architects Paley and Austin. Through their work, Holker Hall exhibits all the grandeur, confidence, spaciousness and prosperity of the late Victorian age. Yet despite its sheer scale, Holker is still very much the family home and one which Lord and Lady Cavendish are delighted to share with thousands of visitors each year.

The immaculately kept gardens (25 acres in all) are part woodland, part formal and essentially Victorian in character, though never heavy or oppressive. The 200 acre 'natural' parkland is in fact the result of the late 18th century planting of Lord George Cavendish. In the early 19th century several new features were added: an arboretum, a conservatory, balustraded terraces by the house, and a large walled kitchen garden.

However, Lord and Lady Cavendish have sought not only to conserve the historic. Changes and additions are still being made to the gardens, with great liveliness and confidence: the shelter belt of trees, planted in the last 20 years, gives protection between park and garden; and the old croquet lawn planted as a garden 'room' is one of the formal highlights of a visit.

The Cascade, inspired by an ancient water garden in Rajasthan, creates movement among the spectacular Rhud as water flows over a zig-zag pattern picked out in slate. In the year 2000 a new Sunken Garden was completed where the former Rose Garden was situated, which has been redesigned and replanted.

In the Woodland Garden you will find recently planted specimen trees and shrubs mixed with ancient conifers, dogwoods and magnolias, all of which love the acid soil and high rainfall. This has made it one of the most interesting and worthwhile gardens to visit in the north of England.

For further details about *Holker Hall* see entry in North West Region → Cumbria.

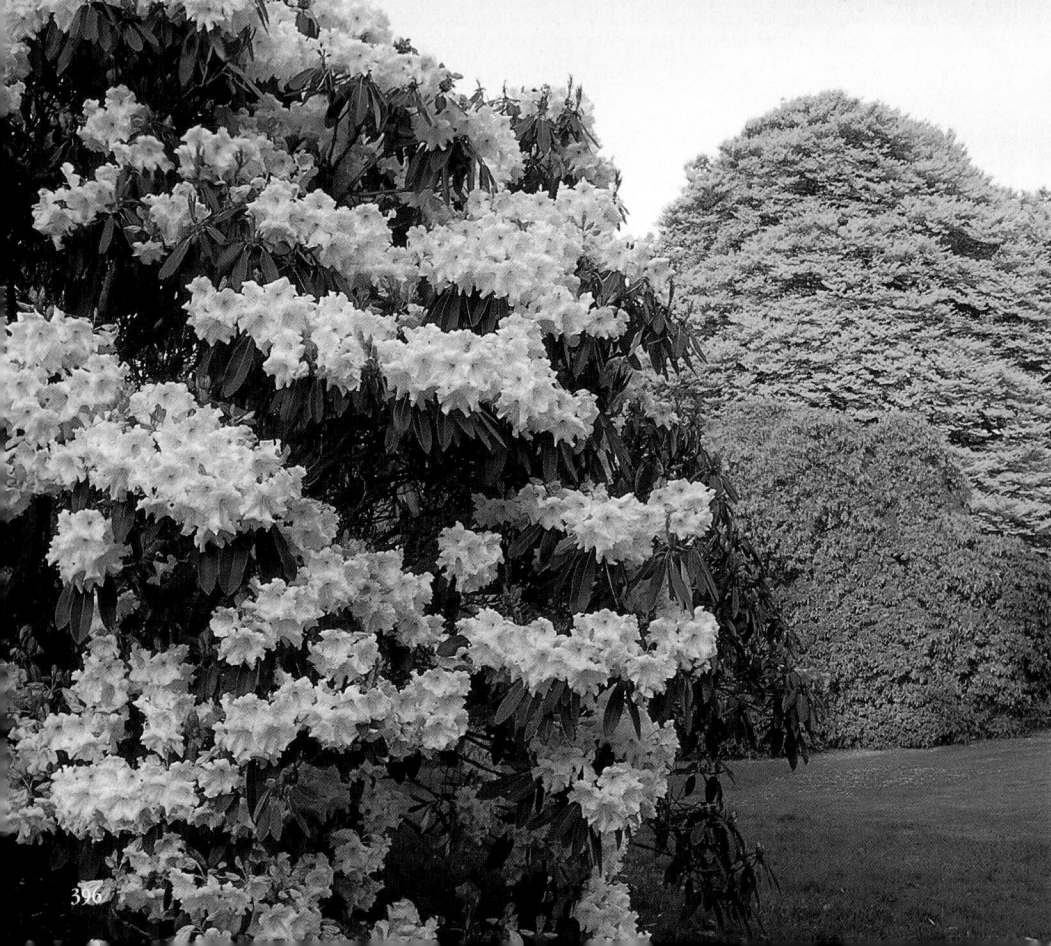

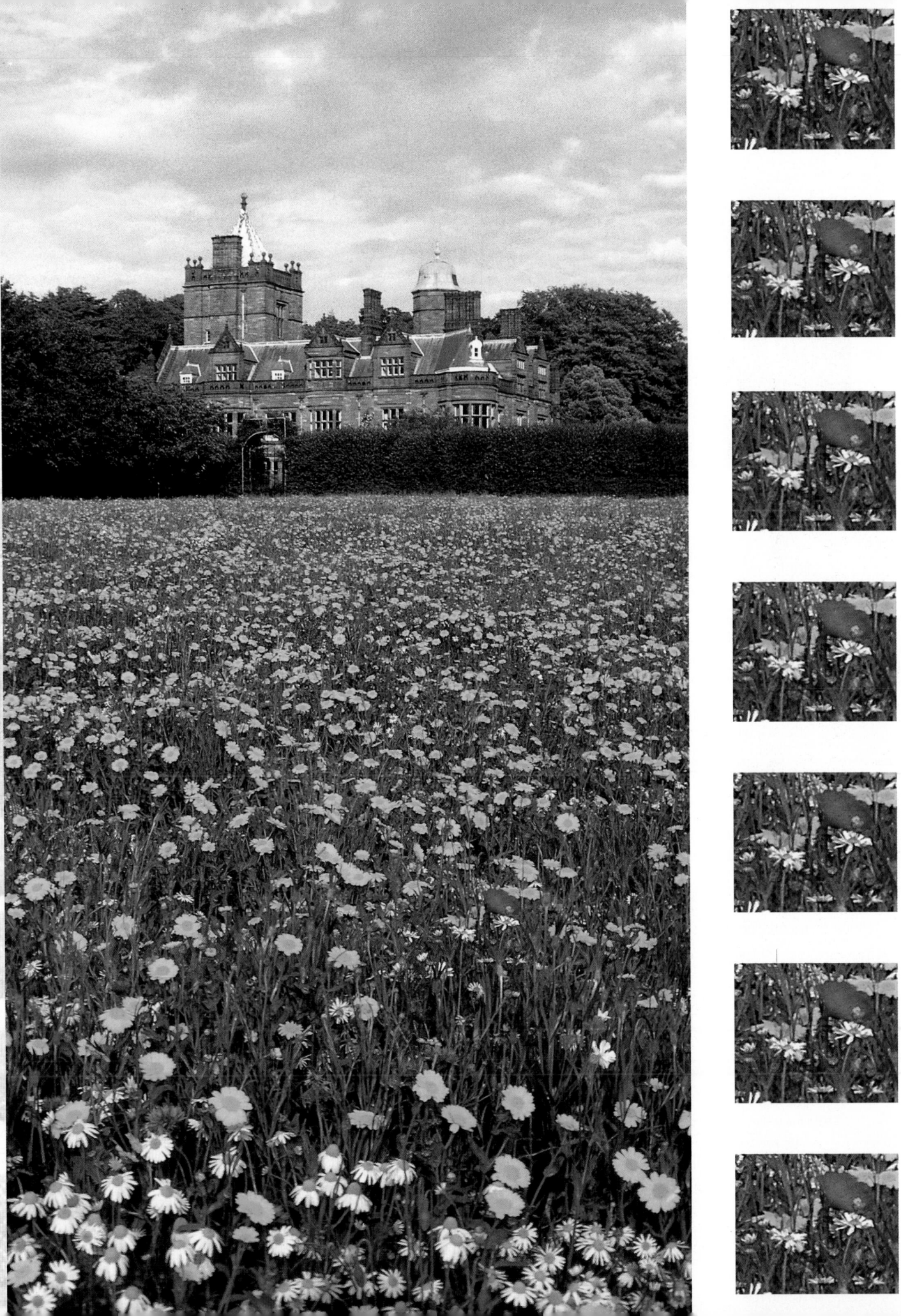

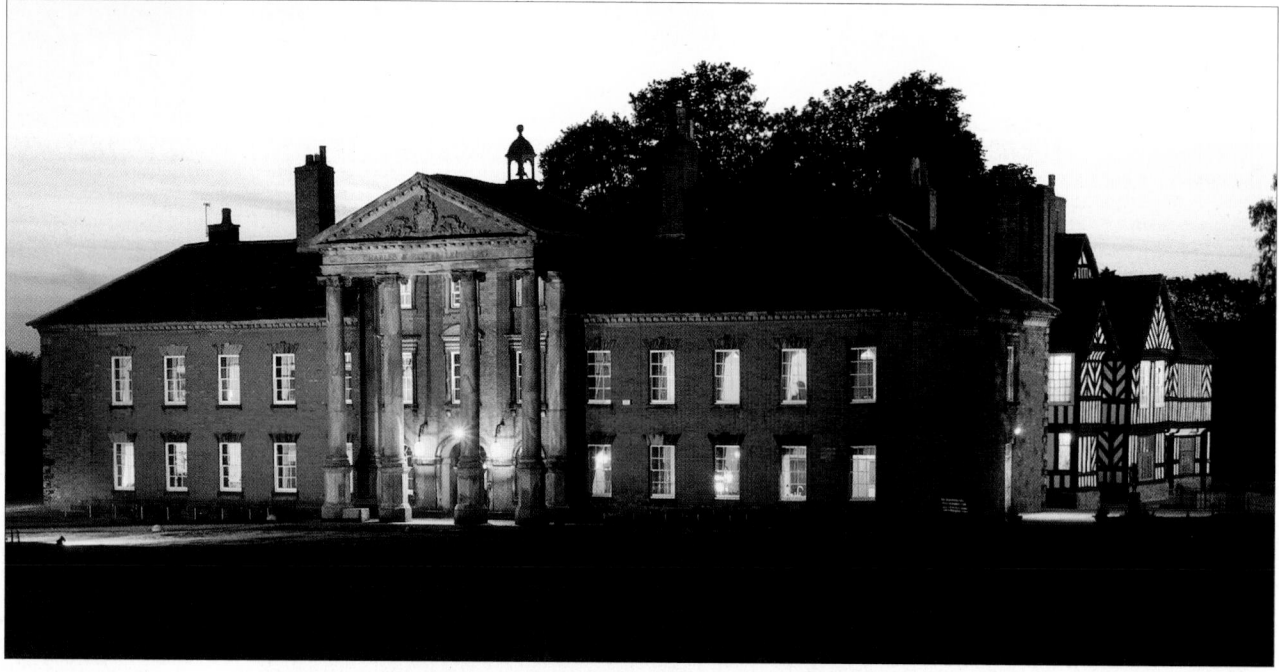

ADLINGTON HALL
Macclesfield

ADLINGTON HALL, the home of the Leghs of Adlington from 1315 to the present day, was built on the site of a Hunting Lodge which stood in the Forest of Macclesfield in 1040. Two oaks, part of the original building, remain with their roots in the ground and support the east end of the Great Hall, which was built between 1480 and 1505.

The Hall is a manor house, quadrangular in shape, and was once surrounded by a moat. Two sides of the Courtyard and the east wing were built in the typical 'Black and White' Cheshire style in 1581. The south front and west wing (containing the Drawing Room and Dining Room) were added between 1749 and 1757 and are built of red brick with a handsome stone portico with four Ionic columns on octagonal pedestals. Between the trees in the Great Hall stands an organ built by 'Father' Bernard Smith (c1670-80). Handel subsequently played on this instrument, and now fully restored, it is the largest 17th century organ in the country.

GARDENS

The gardens were landscaped in the style of 'Capability' Brown in the middle of the 18th century. Visitors may walk round the 'wilderness' area, among the follies to be seen are 'Temple to Diana', a 'Shell Cottage', Chinese bridge and T'ing house. There is a fine yew walk and a lime avenue planted in 1688. Old fashioned rose garden and yew maze recently planted. New for 2000 is a herbaceous border and woodlands area to enhance the North Lodge entrance.

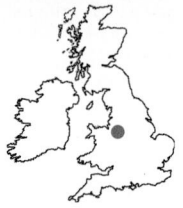

Owner:
Mrs C J C Legh

CONTACT

Corporate Enquiries:
Julian Langlands-Perry
or Tessa Quayle
The Estate Office
Adlington Hall
Macclesfield
Cheshire
SK10 4LF

Tel: 01625 829206

Fax: 01625 828756

e-mail: enquiries@
adlingtonhall.com

Hall Tours:
Gwyn & Barbara Martin

Tel: 01625 820875

LOCATION

OS Ref. SJ905 804

5m N of
Macclesfield, A523,
13m S of Manchester.
London 178m.

Rail: Macclesfield
& Wilmslow stations 5m.

Air: Manchester
Airport 8m.

CONFERENCE/FUNCTION		
ROOM	SIZE	MAX CAPACITY
Great Hall	11 x 8m	120
Dining Rm	10.75 x 7m	90
Courtyard	27 x 17m	300

Open to the public in
June & July:
Mon & Wed, 2 - 5pm.

Also by prior arrangement
for groups throughout the
year. Please contact for
details.

ADMISSION

Hall & Gardens

Adult	£4.50
Child	£1.75
Student	£1.75
Groups of 20+	£4.00

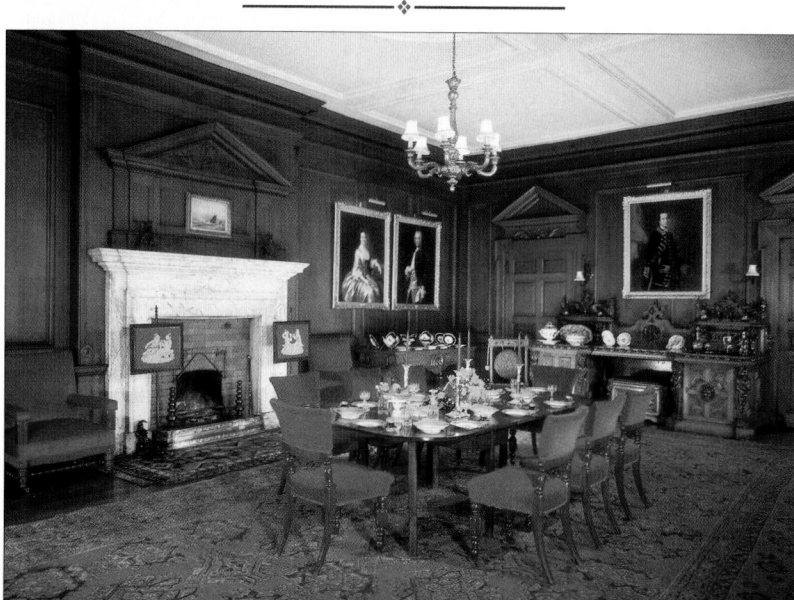

ℹ️ Suitable for corporate events, product launches, business meetings, conferences, concerts, fashion shows, garden parties, rallies, clay-pigeon shooting and filming.

The Great Hall and Dining Room are available for corporate entertaining. Catering can be arranged.

♿ Visitors may alight at entrance to Hall. WCs.

☕ By arrangement.

🅿️ For 100 cars and 4 coaches, 100 yds from Hall.

 Schools welcome. Guide can be provided.

 No dogs.

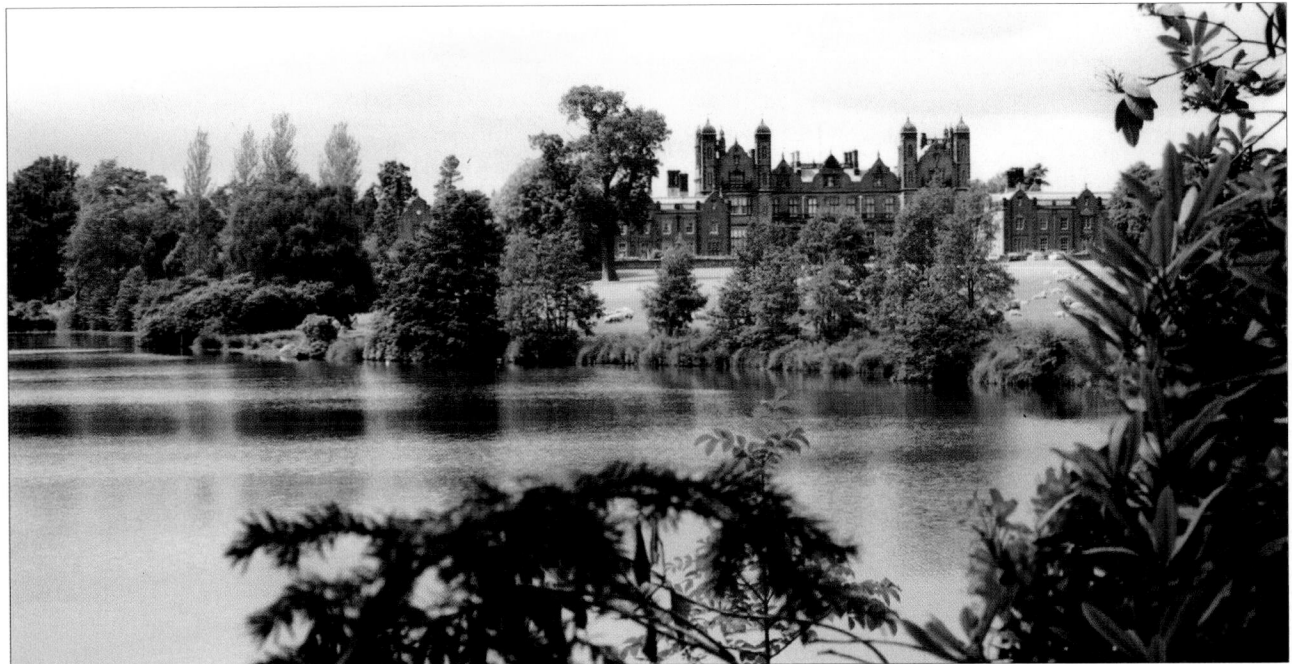

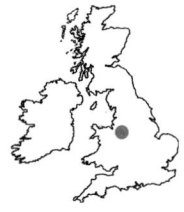

CAPESTHORNE HALL
Macclesfield

CAPESTHORNE HALL, set in 100 acres of picturesque Cheshire parkland, has been touched by nearly 1,000 years of English history - Roman legions passed across it, titled Norman families hunted on it and, during the Civil War, a Royalist ancestress helped Charles II to escape after the Battle of Worcester. The Jacobean-style Hall has a fascinating collection of fine art, marble sculptures, furniture and tapestries. Originally designed by the Smiths of Warwick it was built between 1719 and 1732. It was altered by Blore in 1837 and partially rebuilt by Salvin in 1861 following a disastrous fire.

The present Squire is William Bromley-Davenport, Lord Lieutenant of Cheshire, whose ancestors have owned the estate since Domesday times when they were appointed custodians of the Royal Forest of Macclesfield.

In the grounds near the family Chapel the 18th century Italian *Milanese Gates* open onto the herbaceous borders and maples which line the beautiful lakeside gardens. But amid the natural spectacle and woodland walks, Capesthorne still offers glimpses of its man-made past... the remains of the Ice House, the Old Boat House and the curious Swallow Hole.

Facilities at the Hall can be hired for corporate occasions and family celebrations including Civil wedding ceremonies.

❖

Owner:
Mr & Mrs Bromley-Davenport

CONTACT

Gwyneth Jones,
Hall Manager
Capesthorne Hall
Siddington
Macclesfield
Cheshire
SK11 9JY

Tel: 01625 861221

Fax: 01625 861619

LOCATION

OS Ref. SJ840 727

5m W of Macclesfield.

30 mins S of Manchester on A34.

Near M6, M63 and M62.

Airport: Manchester International 20 mins.

Rail: Macclesfield 5m (2 hrs from London).

Taxi: 01625 533464.

CONFERENCE/FUNCTION

ROOM	SIZE	MAX CAPACITY
Theatre	45' x 19'	155
Garden Room	52' x 20'	80
Saloon	40' x 25'	80
Queen Anne Room	34' x 25'	80
Board Room		10

ℹ Available for corporate functions, meetings, product launches, promotions, exhibitions, presentations, seminars, activity days, Civil weddings and receptions, family celebrations, still photography, fishing, clay shooting, car rallies, garden parties, barbecues, firework displays, concerts, antique, craft, country and game fairs. No photography in Hall.

🍽 Catering can be provided for groups (full menus on request). Function rooms available for wedding receptions, corporate hospitality, meetings and other special events. 'The Butler's Pantry' serves tea, coffee and ices.

♿ Compacted paths, ramps. WCs.

👤 For up to 50. Tours are by staff members or Hall Manager. Tour time 1 hr.

P 100 cars/20 coaches on hard-standing and unlimited in park, 50 yds from house. Rest room and free refreshment for coach drivers.

🐕 Guide dogs in Hall. Under control in Park.

🔔 Civil Wedding Licence. ❄

OPENING TIMES

SUMMER
April - October
BHs, Weds & Suns.

House, Gardens & Chapel
Open at 1.30pm.
Last admission 3.30pm.

Gardens & Chapel
12 noon - 6pm.

Groups welcome by appointment.

Caravan Park also open Easter - end September.

Corporate enquiries:
March - December.

ADMISSION

Hall & Gardens
Adult £6.50
Child (5-18yrs) £3.00
OAP..........................£5.50
Family £12.00

Gardens & Chapel
Adult £4.00
Child (5-18yrs) £2.00
OAP..........................£3.00

Transfers to Hall
Adult/OAP £3.50
Child (5-18yrs) £1.50

Groups (25+) please telephone for details.

Caravans
Up to 2 people £11.50 pn
Over 2 people £13.50 pn

SPECIAL EVENTS

• **APR 7 - 8 & SEPT 15 - 16:**
Rainbow Craft Fair

See the Special Events Section or telephone for more details and other special events.

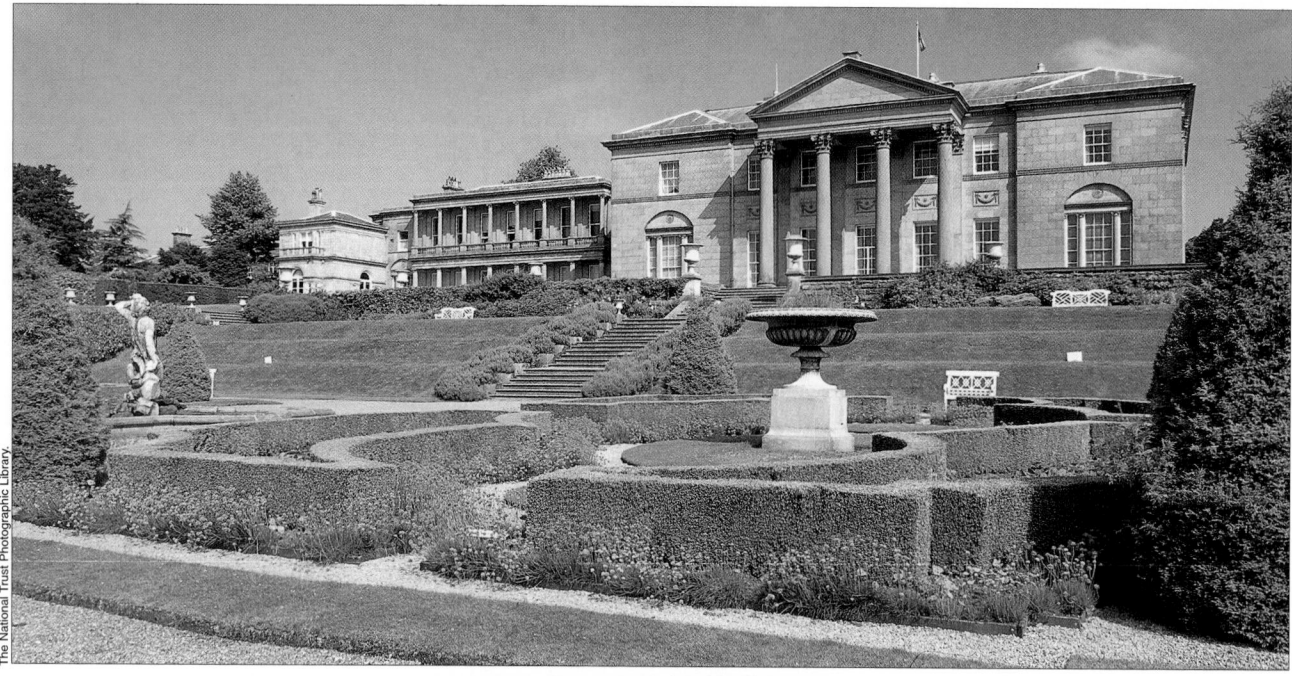

The National Trust Photographic Library.

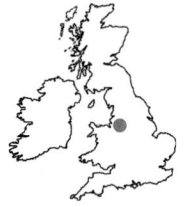

Owner:
The National Trust

CONTACT

Conferences, exhibitions, social occasions
Sheila Hetherington
Sales & Booking Officer
01625 534406

Party Visits
Janet Gidman
Tatton Park
Knutsford
Cheshire WA16 6QN

Tel: 01625 534400/534428

Fax: 01625 534403

LOCATION

OS Ref. SJ745 815

From M56/J7 follow signs.
From M6/J19, signed on
A56 & A50.

Rail: Knutsford or
Altrincham Station,
then taxi.

Air: Manchester Airport 6m.

CONFERENCE/FUNCTION

ROOM	SIZE	MAX CAPACITY
Tenants' Hall	125' x 45'	330 - 400
Foyer	23' x 20'	50 - 100

Tenants' Hall Event Wing – total of 8,000 sq.ft. available

Lord Egerton's Apartment	20' x 16'	16 - 40
	24' x 18'	19 - 40
Stable Block	31' x 20'	80

TATTON PARK
Knutsford

TATTON is one of the most splendid historic estates in the United Kingdom. The 1000 acres of parkland are home to herds of red and fallow deer and provide the setting for a Georgian Mansion, over 50 acres of Gardens, Tudor Old Hall and a working Farm. These attractions, plus private functions and a superb events programme attract over 700,000 visits each year.

Archaeologists have found evidence of occupation at Tatton since 8000 BC with the discovery of flints in the park. There is also proof of people living here in the Iron Age, Roman times, Anglo-saxon and medieval periods.

The neo-Classical Mansion by Wyatt is the jewel in Tatton's crown and was built in stages from 1780 - 1813. The Egerton family collection of Gillow furniture, Baccarat glass, porcelain and paintings by Italian and Dutch masters is found in the splendid setting of the magnificent staterooms. In stark contrast, the Victorian kitchens and cellars provide fascinating insight into life as it would have been 'downstairs'.

The Gardens extend over 50 acres and feature rare species of plants, shrubs and trees, and in fact are considered to be one of the most important gardens within the National Trust. Features include: a conservatory by Wyatt, Fernery by Paxton, plus the Japanese and Italian terraced gardens. The rare collection of plants including rhododendrons, tree ferns, bamboo and pines are the result of 200 years of collecting by the Egerton family.

The Home Farm has traditional breeds of animal including rare sheep and cattle, pigs and horses plus estate workshops. The Tudor Old Hall shows visitors how life would have been at Tatton Park over centuries past for the estate workers. Tours start in the smoky 16th century great hall lit by flickering candles and end in the 1950s home of an estate employee.

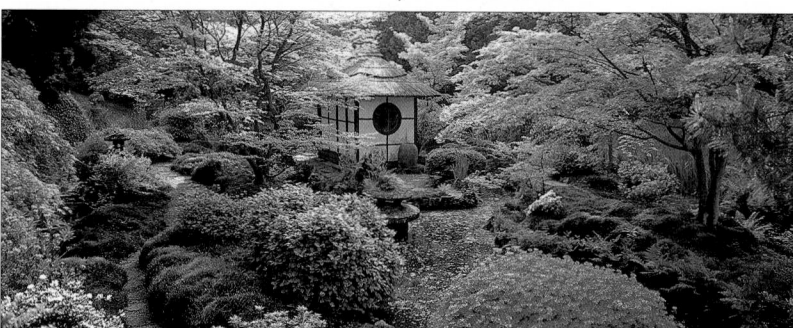

📷 ❄ ⓘ Conferences, trade exhibitions, presentations, product launches, concerts and fashion shows. Special family days. Spotlights, stages, dance floor, PA system. The Tenants' Hall seats up to 400 for presentations.

🍴 Telephone for details. Dinners, dances, weddings.

♿ Upstairs in Mansion, Old Hall & areas of farm not accessible. Wheelchairs & electric vehicles available. WCs.

☕ 🍴 Self-service. Tuck shop.

🚶 By arrangement.

🅿 200-300 yds away. Meal vouchers for coach drivers.

👨‍🏫 Award-winning educational programmes, please book. Environmental days, Orienteering, adventure playground.

🐕 In grounds, on leads.

🔔 Civil Wedding Licence.

❄

SUMMER

31 March - 30 September

Park: All year, daily 10am - 7pm, last entry 6pm

Gardens: All year: Tue - Sun (open BH Mons), 10.30am - 6pm, last entry 5pm

Mansion: Apr - Oct: Tue - Sun 1 - 5pm. (12 noon - 12.30pm guided tours by timed ticket limited number per tour)

Tudor Old Hall: Apr - Oct: Guided tours: Tue - Fri, 3pm & 4pm. Sats & Suns, hourly, 12 noon - 4pm.

Restaurant: Daily, 10.30am - 5pm.

Gift, Garden & Housekeeper's Store: Apr - Oct: Tue - Sun, 11.30am - 5pm.

Farm: Apr - Sept: Tue - Sun.

WINTER

Special openings in Oct & Dec: Mansion & Farm.
1 Oct - 31 Mar 2002

Park: Tue - Sun, 11.30am - 5pm, last entry 4pm.

Farm: Suns only, 11.30am - 4pm, last admission 3pm.

Gardens: Tue - Sun, 11am - 5pm, last entry 4pm.

ADMISSION

Any two attractions

	Single	Group*
Adult	£4.60	£3.70
Child**	£2.60	£2.10

Mansion, Gardens, Tudor Old Hall, Farm

Adult	£3.00	£2.40
Child**	£2.00	£1.60
Family	£8.00	

(50% reduction for NT members to Tudor Old Hall & Farm.)

Parking

Per car	£3.50
Coaches	Free

*Min. 12 ** Aged 4 - 15yrs.
OAP rate as Adult
Tours available outside normal openings phone for details.

SPECIAL EVENTS

Please telephone for details.

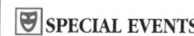

ADLINGTON HALL   See page 398 for full page entry.

ARLEY HALL & GARDENS

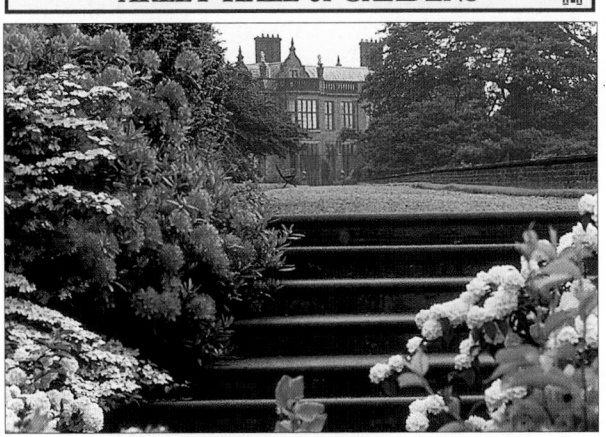

ARLEY, Nr NORTHWICH, CHESHIRE CW9 6NA

Owner: Viscount Ashbrook   *Contact: Estate Secretary*

Tel: 01565 777353 / 777284 **Fax:** 01565 777465
e-mail: enquiries@arleyestate.zuunet.co.uk

Set amongst beautiful parkland, Arley Hall, home to Viscount and Viscountess Ashbrook, offers visitors a delightful family hall and glorious gardens. The Hall can be used for all types of corporate entertaining and events and is licensed for weddings. The gardens, a plantsman's paradise, rank amongst the finest in England with many features. Special events throughout the year.

Location: OS Ref. SJ675 809. Knutsford 5m, NW Northwich 5m, N M6/J19 & 20 5m M56/J9 & 10, 5m.

Opening Times: 13 Apr - 30 Sept: Tue - Sun & BH Mons, 11am - 5pm. Hall: please telephone for open days, 12 noon - 5pm.

Admission: Gardens, Grounds & Chapel: Adult £4.40, Child £2.20, OAP £3.80, Family £11. Groups: Adult £3.75, Child £2, OAP £3.25. Season ticket £19.50, Family season ticket £50 (2+2). Hall & Gardens: Adult £6.90, Child £3.70, OAP £5.80, Family £17.50. Hall: Disabled Adult £1.50, Disabled Child £75p. Groups: Adult £6, Child £3.25, OAP £5.

 Photography in gardens only.   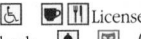 Licensed. 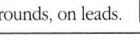 By arrangement. In grounds, on leads.

BRAMALL HALL

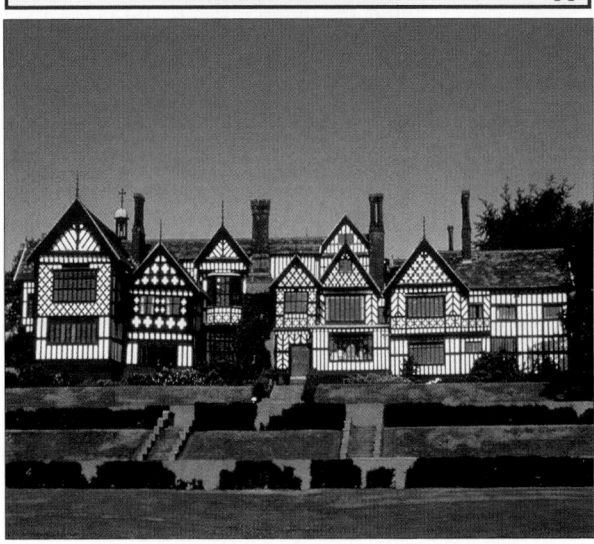

BRAMHALL PARK, BRAMHALL, STOCKPORT SK7 3NX

Owner: Stockport MBC   *Contact: Ruth Maddocks*

Tel: 0161 485 3708 **Fax:** 0161 486 6959

Surrounded by 70 acres of beautiful parkland, Bramall Hall is a superb example of a Cheshire black and white timber-framed manor house, dating from the 14th century. The house has beautiful Tudor rooms with splendid Victorian additions. Extensive events programme and ideal for weddings.

Location: OS117, Ref. SJ886 863. 4m S of Stockport, off A5102.

Opening Times: Good Fri - 30 Sept: Mon - Sat, 1 - 5pm, Suns & BHs, 11am - 5pm. 1 Oct - 1 Jan: Tue - Sat, 1 - 4pm, Suns & BHs, 11am - 4pm. Closed 25/26 Dec. 2 Jan - 4 Apr: Sats & Suns, 12 noon - 4pm.

Admission: Adult £3.50, Child/Conc. £2. Group prices on request.

Partially suitable. By arrangement. Limited for coaches. In grounds on leads. Tel for details.

CAPESTHORNE HALL   See page 399 for full page entry.

BEESTON CASTLE   **Tel:** 01829 260464

Beeston, Tarporley, Cheshire CW6 9TX

Owner: English Heritage   **Contact:** The Custodian

Standing majestically on sheer, rocky crags which fall sharply away from the castle walls, Beeston has possibly the best views of the surrounding countryside of any castle in England.

Location: OS117, Ref. SJ537 593. 11m SE of Chester on minor road off A49, or A41. 2m SW of Tarporley.

Opening Times: 1 Apr - 30 Sept: 10am - 6pm. 1 - 31 Oct: daily, 10am - 5pm. 1 Nov - 31 Mar: daily, 10am - 4pm. Closed 24 & 25 Dec.

Admission: Adult £2.90, Child £1.50, Conc. £2.20. 15% discount for groups (11+).

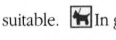 Exhibition. 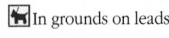 Not suitable. In grounds on leads. 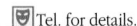 Tel. for details.

CHESTER CATHEDRAL   **Tel:** 01244 324756 **Fax:** 01244 341110

12 Abbey Square, Chester, Cheshire CH1 2HU   **Contact:** Mr N Fry

Founded in 1092 as a Benedictine monastery, it became an Anglican cathedral in 1541. All styles of architecture are represented as well as spectacular medieval woodwork.

Location: OS Ref. SJ406 665. Chester city centre.

Opening Times: 7.30am - 6.30pm, daily.

Admission: Donation.

CHESTER ROMAN AMPHITHEATRE   **Tel:** 0161 242 1400

Vicars Lane, Chester, Cheshire

Owner: English Heritage   **Contact:** The North Regional Office

The largest Roman amphitheatre in Britain, partially excavated. Used for entertainment and military training by the 20th Legion, based at the fortress of Deva.

Location: OS Ref. SJ404 660. On Vicars Lane beyond Newgate, Chester.

Opening Times: Any reasonable time.

Admission: Free.

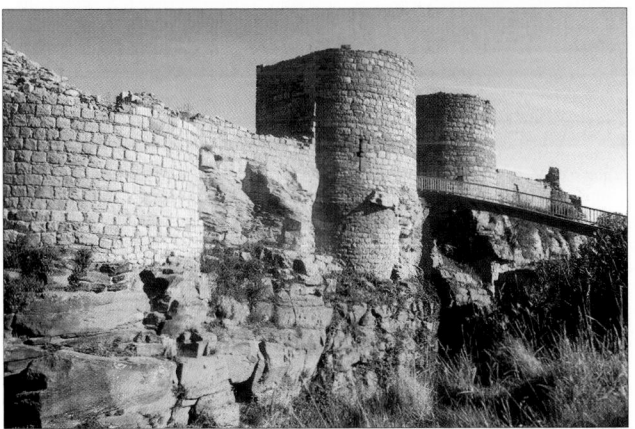

Beeston Castle, Cheshire.

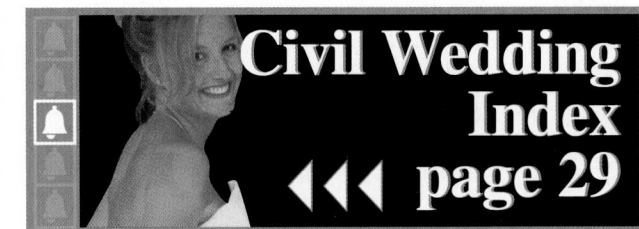

Civil Wedding Index ◀◀◀ page 29

CHOLMONDELEY CASTLE GARDEN

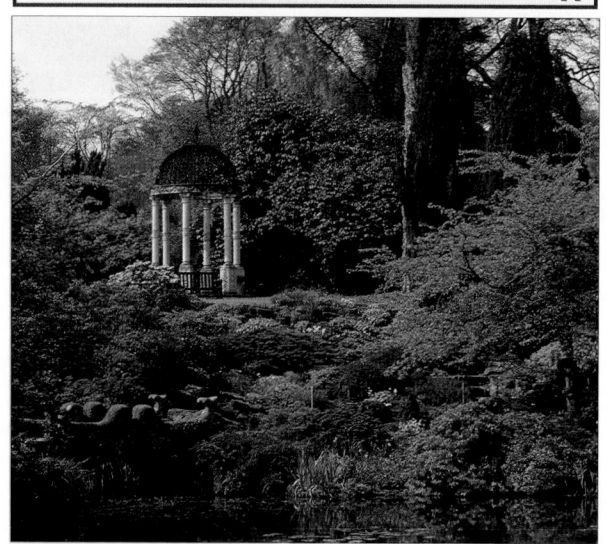

MALPAS, CHESHIRE SY14 8AH

Owner: The Marchioness of Cholmondeley　　*Contact:* The Secretary

Tel/Fax: 01829 720383

Extensive ornamental gardens dominated by romantic Gothic Castle built in 1801 of local sandstone. Beautiful temple water garden, rose garden and many mixed borders. Lakeside picnic area, children's play areas, rare breeds of farm animals, including Llamas. Ancient private chapel in the park.

Location: OS Ref. SJ540 515. Off A41 Chester/Whitchurch Rd. & A49 Whitchurch/Tarporley Road. 7m N of Whitchurch.

Opening Times: 1 Apr - 30 Sept: Weds, Thurs, Suns & BH Mons, 11.30am - 5.30pm, last entry 5pm. Closed Good Fri. Groups (25+): other days by prior arrangement at reduced rates.

Admission: Adult £3, Child £1.50.

🖻 ⚐ ▼ 🖢 Limited suitability. WCs. ▣ 🐕 In grounds on leads only. ❄

DUNHAM MASSEY

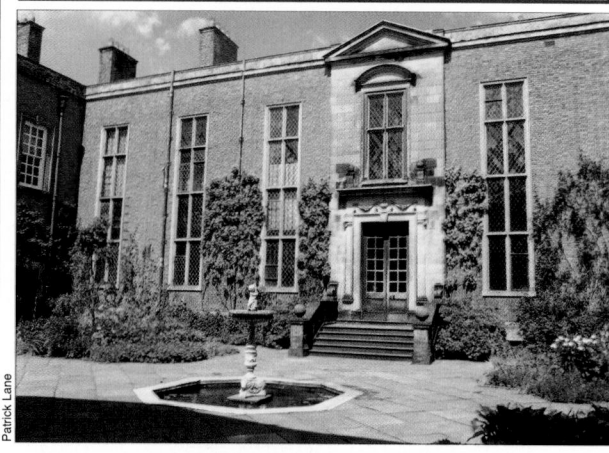

Patrick Lane

ALTRINCHAM, CHESHIRE WA14 4SJ

Owner: The National Trust　　*Contact:* The Property Manager

Tel: 0161 941 1025 **Fax:** 0161 929 7508

Originally an early Georgian house, Dunham Massey has sumptuous interiors, with collections of walnut furniture, paintings and magnificent Huguenot silver. The richly planted garden contains waterside plantings, late flowering azaleas, an orangery and Elizabethan mount. The surrounding deer park escaped the attentions of 18th century landscape gardeners and contains some notable specimen trees.

Location: OS Ref. SJ735 874. 3m SW of Altrincham off A56. M56/J7.

Opening Times: House: 31 Mar - 4 Nov: Sat - Wed, 12 noon - 5pm (11am - 5pm BH Sun & Mon; Oct & Nov: 12 noon - 4pm). Garden: 31 Mar - 4 Nov: daily, 11am - 5.30pm (4.30pm in Oct & Nov). Last admission normally ^{1}/$_2$ hr before closing. Park open daily throughout the year.

Admission: House & Garden: Adult £5, Child £2.50, Family £12.50 (2 adults + children). House or Garden only: Adult £3.20, Child £1.60. Car entry: £3 per car. Coach /minibus entry: £5 (free to booked parties). Motorcycle: £1. Booked Groups: £4 for 15 or more paying adults, not available Suns & BHs.

ℹ No photography in house.　🖻 ⚐ 🖢 Partially suitable. WC. Batricars.
🍴 Licensed. 🐾 Optional. No extra charge. ▣ 🎦 🐕 In grounds, on leads. ❄

DORFOLD HALL

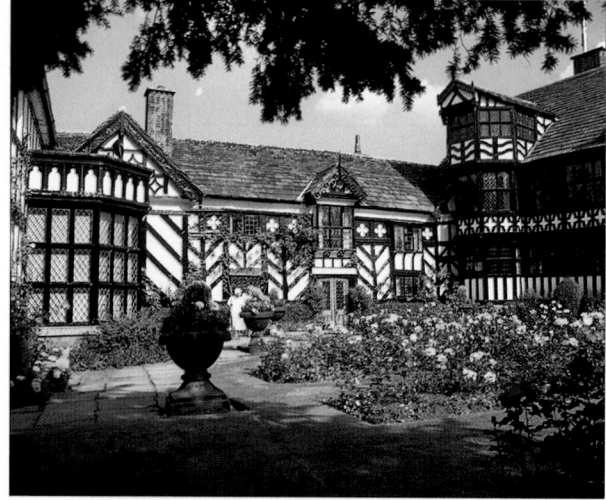

ACTON, Nr NANTWICH, CHESHIRE CW5 8LD

Owner/Contact: Richard Roundell

Tel: 01270 625245 **Fax:** 01270 628723

Jacobean country house built in 1616 for Ralph Wilbraham. Family home of Mr & Mrs Richard Roundell. Beautiful plaster ceilings and oak panelling. Attractive woodland gardens and summer herbaceous borders.

Location: OS Ref. SJ634 525. 1m W of Nantwich on the A534 Nantwich - Wrexham road.

Opening Times: Apr - Oct: Tues only and BH Mons, 2 - 5pm.

Admission: Adult £4.50, Child £3.

🐾 Obligatory.　▣ Limited. Narrow gates with low arch prevent coaches.
🐕 In grounds on leads.

GAWSWORTH HALL

MACCLESFIELD, CHESHIRE SK11 9RN

Owner: Mr and Mrs T Richards　　*Contact:* Mr T Richards

Tel: 01260 223456 **Fax:** 01260 223469 **e-mail:** gawsworth@lineone.net

Fully lived-in Tudor half-timbered manor house with Tilting Ground. Former home of Mary Fitton, Maid of Honour at the Court of Queen Elizabeth I, and the supposed 'Dark Lady' of Shakespeare's sonnets. Pictures, sculpture and furniture. Open air theatre with covered grandstand - June, July and August, please telephone for details. Situated halfway between Macclesfield and Congleton in an idyllic setting close to the lovely medieval church.

Location: OS Ref. SJ892 697. 3m S of Macclesfield on the A536 Congleton to Macclesfield road.

Opening Times: Easter - 7 Oct: Apr, May & Sept: Sun - Wed, 2 - 5pm plus special events & BH weekends. Jun, Jul & Aug: daily, 2 - 5pm.

Admission: Adult £4.50, Child £2.25.

🖻 ▣ 🐕 Guide dogs in garden only. 🔔 🛡 Tel. for details.

North West England

HARE HILL

Over Alderley, Macclesfield, Cheshire SK10 4QB

Owner: The National Trust   **Contact:** The Head Gardener

A woodland garden surrounding a walled garden with pergola, rhododendrons and azaleas: parkland: link path to Alderley Edge (2m).

Location: OS Ref. SJ875 765. Between Alderley Edge and Prestbury, turn N at B5087, Greyhound Road.

Opening Times: 1 Apr - 30 Oct: Weds, Thurs, Sats, Suns & BH Mons, 10am - 5.30pm. Special opening to see rhododendrons & azaleas: 10 - 30 May: daily, 10am - 5.30pm. Closed Nov - Mar.

Admission: £2.50. Entrance per car £1.50 refundable on entry to garden. Groups by written appointment c/o Garden Lodge at address above.

Gravel paths - strong companion advisable.   Not in garden, elsewhere on leads.

LITTLE MORETON HALL

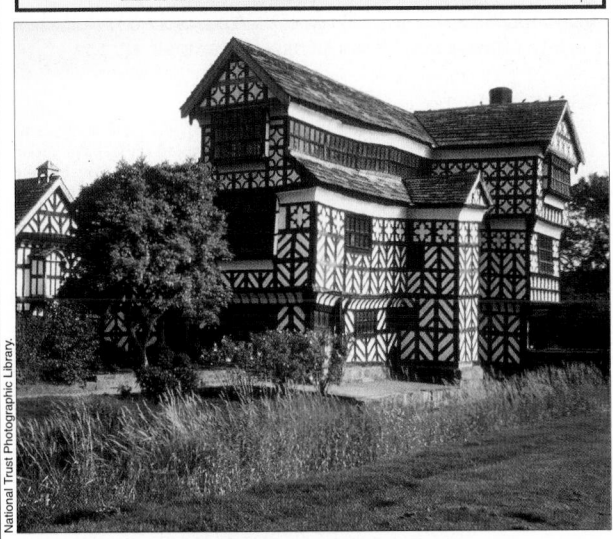

National Trust Photographic Library

CONGLETON, CHESHIRE CW12 4SD

Owner: *The National Trust*   **Contact:** *The Property Manager*

Tel: 01260 272018   **Fax:** 01260 292802

Begun in 1450 and completed 130 years later, Little Moreton Hall is regarded as the finest example of a timber-framed moated manor house in the country. The drunkenly reeling South Front topped by its Elizabethan Long Gallery opens onto a cobbled courtyard and the main body of the Hall. The Chapel, Great Hall, wall paintings and Knot Garden are of particular interest.

Location: OS Ref. SJ833 589. 4m SW of Congleton on E side of A34.

Opening Times: 31 Mar - 4 Nov: daily (includes BH Mons & Good Fri), 11.30am - 5pm. 10 Nov - 22 Dec: weekends only, 11.30am - 4pm.

Admission: Adult £4.40, Child £2.20, Family £11. Groups: £3.50 (must book). Joint ticket with Biddulph Grange Garden £6.75, Child £3.30, Family £16.50.

Braille guide, wheelchair & electric vehicle. WCs.   Car park only.

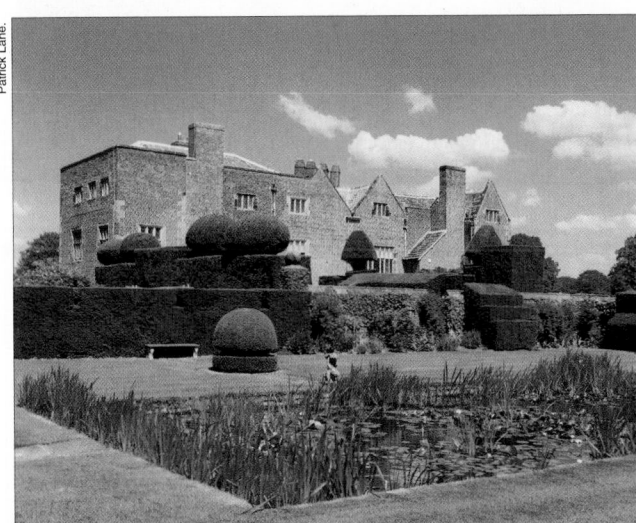

Patrick Lane.

Peover Hall, Cheshire.

LYME PARK

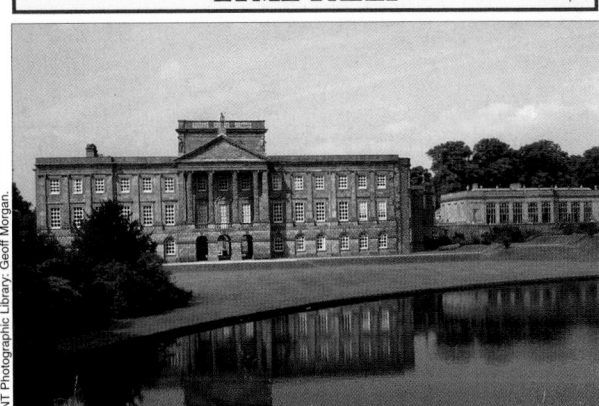

NT Photographic Library: Geoff Morgan.

DISLEY, STOCKPORT, CHESHIRE SK12 2NX

Owner: *The National Trust*   **Contact:** *The Property Manager*

Tel: 01663 762023   **Fax:** 01663 765035   **e-mail:** mlyrec@smtp.ntrust.org.uk

Legh family home for 600 years. Part of the original Elizabethan house survives with 18th and 19th century additions by Giacomo Leoni and Lewis Wyatt. Four centuries of period interiors – Mortlake tapestries, Grinling Gibbons carvings, unique collection of English clocks. Historic gardens with conservatory by Wyatt, a lake and a 'Dutch' garden. A 1,400 acre medieval deer park, home to red and fallow deer. Exterior featured as 'Pemberley' in BBC's *Pride and Prejudice*.

Location: OS Ref. SJ966 843. Off the A6 at Disley. 6¹/₂ m SE of Stockport.

Opening Times: Park: Apr - Oct: daily, 8am - 8.30pm; Nov - Mar 8am - 6pm. Gardens: 30 Mar - 30 Oct: Fri - Tue, 11am - 5pm, Wed & Thur 1 - 5pm. Nov - 18 Dec: Sats & Suns, 12 noon - 3pm. House: 30 Mar - 30 Oct: Fri - Tue, 1 - 5pm (last admission 4.30pm) (BH Mons, 11am - 5pm). Shop & Tearoom: 30 Mar - 30 Oct: daily, 11am - 5pm. Nov - Mar: Sats & Suns, 12 noon - 4pm.

Admission: House & Garden: £5, House only: £4, Garden only: £2.50, Park only: £3.50 per car. Combined Family Ticket: £15. NT members Free.

No photography in house.   Partially suitable. WC.   Licensed.   By arrangement.   In park, close control. Guide dogs only in house & garden.

MACCLESFIELD MUSEUMS   **Tel:** 01625 613210 **Fax:** 01625 617880

Roe Street, Macclesfield SK11 6UT   **e-mail:** postmaster@silk-macc.u-net.com

Owner: Macclesfield Museums Trust   **Contact:** Louanne Collins

Silk museum housed in Georgian Sunday School. Development of the silk industry is told through an award-winning audio-visual programme, exhibitions, models and costume. Nearby Paradise Mill houses 26 hand jacquard silk looms. Tours with knowledgeable guides, demonstrations of weaving, shows life in the 1930s.

Location: OS Ref. SJ917 733. Centre of Macclesfield.

Opening Times: Silk Museum: Mon - Sat, 11am - 5pm, BHs & Suns, 1 - 5pm (closed Good Fri, 25, 26 Dec, 1 Jan & Suns Jan - Mar). Paradise Mill: Tue - Sun, 1 - 5pm, Nov - Mar, 1 - 4pm (closed 23 Dec - 2 Jan 2001 & Suns Nov - Mar).

Admission: Adult £2.85, Child/Conc. £2, Family £7.60. Joint ticket: Adult £5, Conc. £2.90, Family £10.90. Special evening rates (2000 prices).

Licensed.   By arrangement.   Guide dogs only.

NESS BOTANIC GARDENS   **Tel:** 01513 530123 **Fax:** 01513 531004

Ness, Neston, Cheshire CH64 4AY   **e-mail:** ejs@liv.ac.uk

Owner: University of Liverpool   **Contact:** Dr E J Sharples

Location: OS Ref. SJ302 760 (village centre). Off A540. 10m NW of Chester. 1¹/₂ m S of Neston.

Opening Times: 1 Mar - 31 Oct: 9.30am - 5pm (last entry). Nov - Feb: 9.30am - 4pm.

Admission: Charge for Adults & Conc. Accompanied child (under 18yrs) Free. 10% discount for groups. Please telephone for details.

NETHER ALDERLEY MILL   **Tel:** 01625 523012 **Fax:** 01625 527139

Congleton Road, Nether Alderley, Macclesfield, Cheshire SK10 4TW

Owner/Contact: The National Trust

A fascinating overshot tandem wheel watermill, dating from the 15th century, with a stone-tiled low pitched roof. The machinery is in full working order, and grinds flour occasionally for demonstrations.

Location: OS Ref. SJ844 763. 1¹/₂ m S of Alderley Edge, on E side of A34.

Opening Times: Apr, May & Oct: Weds, Suns & BH Mons, 1 - 4.30pm. Jun - Sept: daily (except Mons but open BH Mons), 1 - 5pm.

Admission: Adult £2, Child £1. Groups by prior arrangement (max. 20).

Not suitable.   By arrangement.

North West England

NORTON PRIORY WALLED GARDEN & MUSEUM   Tel: 01928 569895

Tudor Road, Manor Park, Runcorn, Cheshire WA7 1SX

Owner/Contact: The Norton Priory Museum Trust

Site of medieval priory set in beautiful woodland gardens.

Location: OS Ref. SJ545 835. 3m from M56/J11. 2m E of Runcorn.

Opening Times: Garden: 1 Mar - 31 Oct, every afternoon. Museum: all year.

Admission: Adult £3.75, Child/Conc. £2,50. Family £9.80, Groups £2.20.

W/chairs, braille guide, audio tapes & WC. By arrangement. In grounds, on leads. Telephone for details.

PECKFORTON CASTLE   Tel: 01829 260930   Fax: 01829 261230

Stonehouse Lane, Nr Tarporley CW6 9TN

Owner/Contact: Mrs Graybill

The only intact medieval style castle in Britain. Built mid-1800s, designed by Anthony Salvin.

Location: OS Ref. SJ533 581. Access by gateway on W side of minor road ³/₄ m S of Beeston village, ³/₄ m N of Peckforton village. 12m E of Chester.

Opening Times: Private functions and weddings only. No public access.

PEOVER HALL

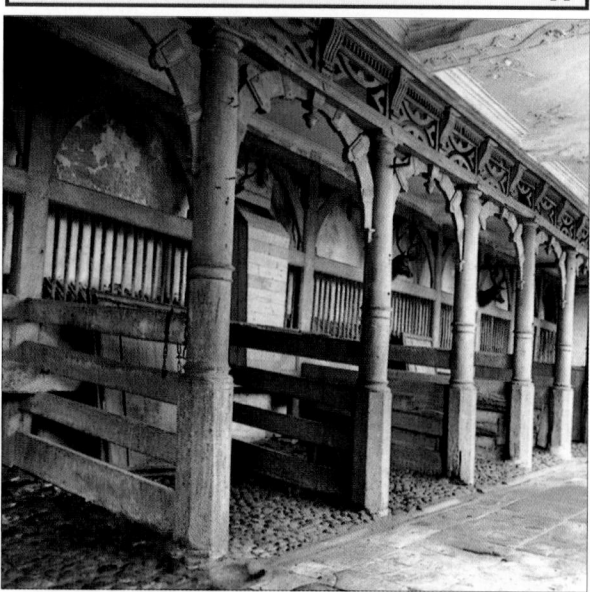

OVER PEOVER, KNUTSFORD WA16 9HN

Owner: *Randle Brooks*   **Contact:** *I Shepherd*

Tel: 01565 632358

An Elizabethan house dating from 1585. Fine Carolean stables. Mainwaring Chapel, 18th century landscaped park. Large garden with topiary work, also walled and herb gardens.

Location: OS Ref. SJ772 734. 4m S of Knutsford off A50 at Whipping Stocks Inn.

Opening Times: Apr - Oct: House, Stables & Gardens: Mons except BHs, 2 - 5pm. Tours of the House at 2.30 & 3.30pm. Stables & Gardens only: Thurs, 2 - 5pm.

Admission: House, Stables & Gardens: Adult £3, Child £2. Stables & Gardens only: £2.

Mondays only. Obligatory.

QUARRY BANK MILL & STYAL COUNTRY PARK

Styal, Wilmslow, Cheshire SK9 4LA   **Tel:** 01625 527468   **Fax:** 01625 539267

Owner: The National Trust   **Contact:** The Property Manager

Location: OS Ref. SJ835 830. 1¹/₂ m N of Wilmslow off B5166. 2¹/₂ m from M56/J5.

Opening Times: Mill: Apr - end Sept: daily, 11am - 6pm, last admission 4.30pm. Oct - Mar: daily except Mons, 11am - 5pm, last admission 3.30pm. Apprentice House & garden: daily except Mons (but open BH Mons),Tue - Fri, 2 - 4.30pm, Sats, Suns & Aug: 11am - 6pm.

Admission: Adult £6, Child/Conc. £3.70, Family £16. Mill only: Adult £4.80, Child/ Conc. £3.40, Family £14.00. Apprentice House & Garden: Adult £3.80, Child/Conc. £2.70, Family £12. Advance bookings essential for groups (10+).

RODE HALL

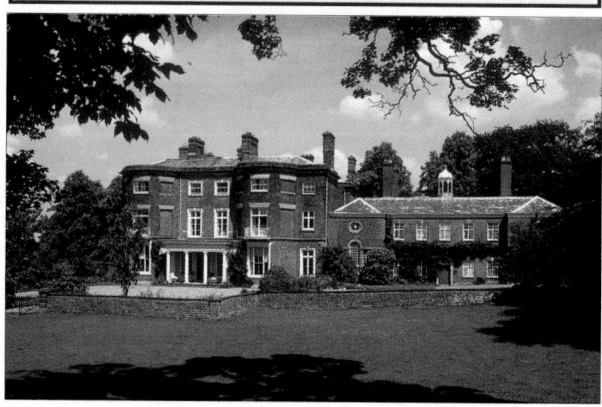

CHURCH LANE, SCHOLAR GREEN, CHESHIRE ST7 3QP

Owner/Contact: *Sir Richard Baker Wilbraham Bt*

Tel: 01270 873237   **Fax:** 01270 882962

The Wilbraham family have lived at Rode since 1669; the present house was constructed in two stages, the earlier two storey wing and stable block around 1705 and the main building was completed in 1752. Later alterations by Lewis Wyatt and Darcy Braddell were undertaken in 1812 and 1927 respectively. The house stands in a Repton landscape and the extensive gardens include a woodland garden, with a terraced rock garden and grotto, which has many species of rhododendrons, azaleas, hellebores and climbing roses following snowdrops and daffodils in the early spring. The formal rose garden was designed by W Nesfield in 1860 and there is a large walled kitchen garden which is at its best from the middle of June. The icehouse in the park has recently been restored.

Location: OS Ref. SJ819 573. 5m SW of Congleton between the A34 and A50. Kidsgrove railway station 2m NW of Kidsgrove.

Opening Times: 4 Apr - 26 Sept: Weds & BHs (closed Good Fri) and by appointment. Garden only: Tues & Thurs, 2 - 5pm. Snowdrop Walk: 4 - 18 Feb: 12 noon - 4pm.

Admission: House, Garden & Kitchen Garden: Adult £4, OAP £2.50. Garden & Kitchen Garden: Adult £2.50, OAP £1.50. Snowdrop Walk: £2.50.

Home-made teas. On leads.

TABLEY HOUSE

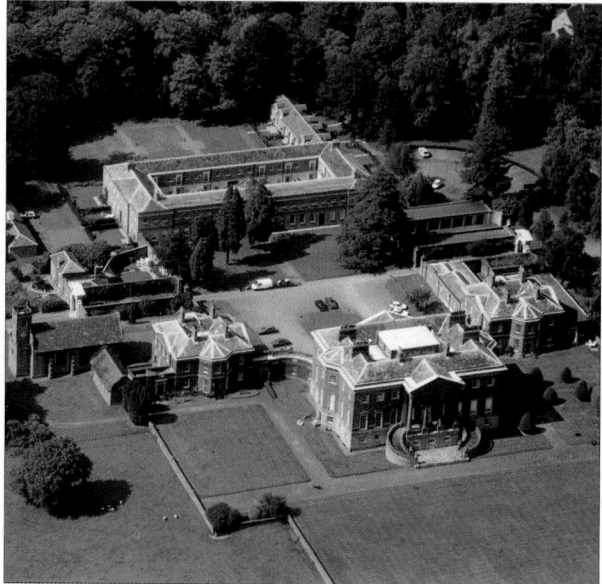

KNUTSFORD, CHESHIRE WA16 0HB

Owner: *Victoria University of Manchester*   **Contact:** *The Administrator*

Tel: 01565 750151   **Fax:** 01565 653230

The finest Palladian mansion in the North West of England, Grade I, by John Carr of York completed 1767 for the Leicester family who lived at Tabley for over 700 years. The first collection of English paintings ever made, furniture and memorabilia, can be seen in the State Rooms. Private chapel 1678 re-erected due to brine pumping.

Location: OS Ref. SJ725 777. M6/J19, A556 S on to A5033. 2m W of Knutsford.

Opening Times: Apr - end Oct inclusive: Thurs, Fris, Sats, Suns & BHs, 2 - 5pm.

Admission: Adult £4. Child £1.50. Groups by arrangement.

         Registered Charity 1047299.

TATTON PARK 🌿   See page 400 for full page entry.

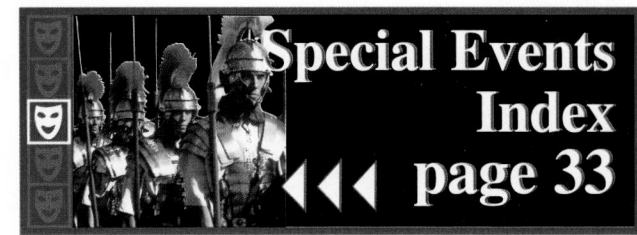

Special Events Index ◀◀◀ page 33

WOODHEY CHAPEL   **Tel:** 01270 524215

Faddiley, Nr Nantwich, Cheshire CW5 8JH   **Contact:** Mr Robinson, The Curator

Owner: The Trustees of Woodhey Chapel

Small private chapel that has been recently restored.

Location: OS Ref. SJ573 528. Proceeding W from Nantwich on A534, turn left 1m W of the Faddiley - Brindley villages onto narrow lane, keep ahead at next turn, at road end obtain key from farmhouse.

Opening Times: Apr - Oct: Sats & BHs, 2 - 5pm, or apply for key at Woodhey Hall.

Admission: £1.

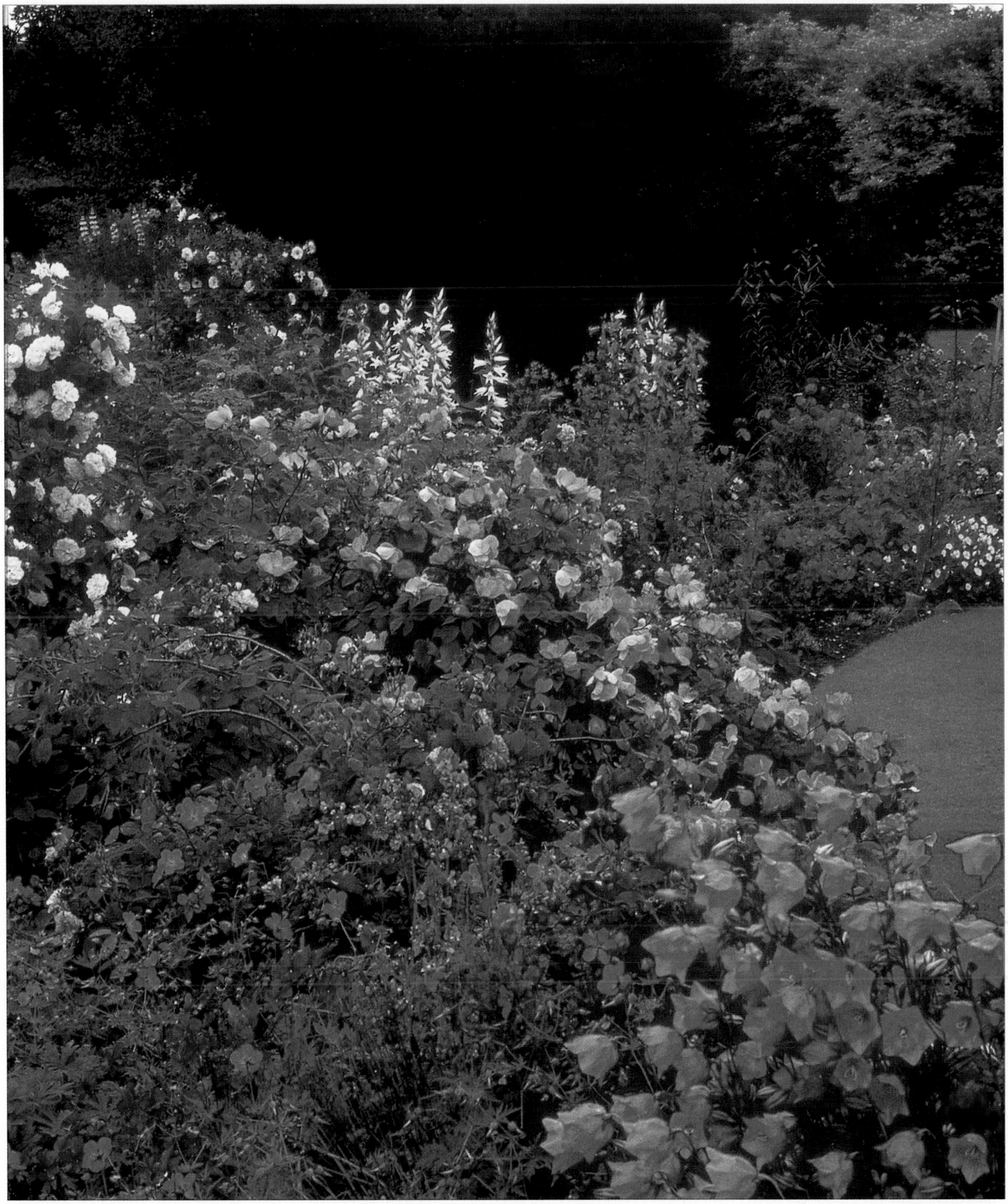

Arley Hall, Cheshire.

North West England

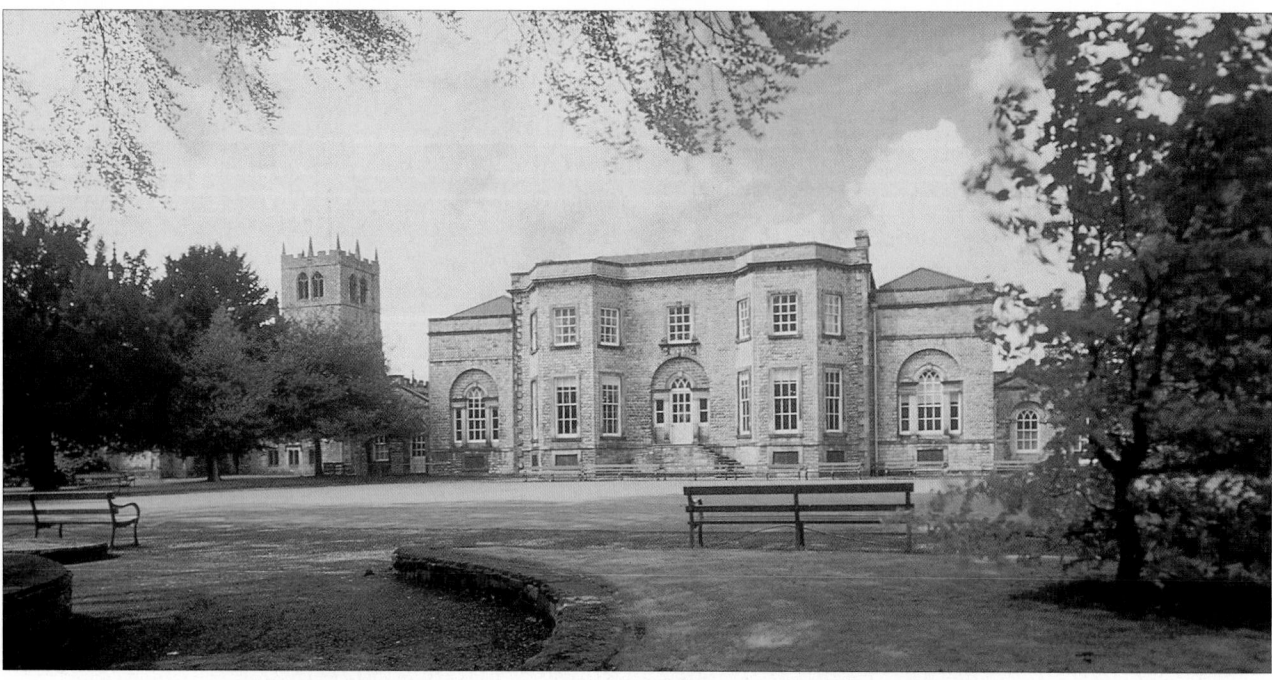

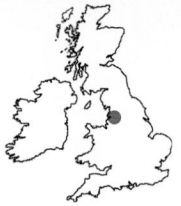

Owner: Lake District Art Gallery & Museum Trust

CONTACT

Sandy Kitching
Abbot Hall Art Gallery
Kendal
Cumbria
LA9 5AL

Tel: 01539 722464

Fax: 01539 722494

e-mail: info@
abbothall.org.uk

LOCATION

OS Ref. SD516 922

10mins from M6/J36.
Follow brown museum
signs to South Kendal.

Rail: Oxenholme.

Air: Manchester.

ABBOT HALL ART GALLERY
Kendal

Abbot Hall is a jewel of a building in a beautiful setting on the banks of the River Kent, surrounded by a park and overlooked by the ruins of Kendal Castle. This is one of Britain's finest small art galleries and a wonderful place in which to see and enjoy changing exhibitions in the elegantly proportioned rooms of a Grade I Listed Georgian building. The collection includes works by Romney, Ruskin, Turner and Freud. The adjacent Museum of Lakeland Life is a popular family attraction with a Victorian street scene, farmhouse rooms, Arthur Ransome room and displays of Arts and Crafts Movement furniture and fabrics.

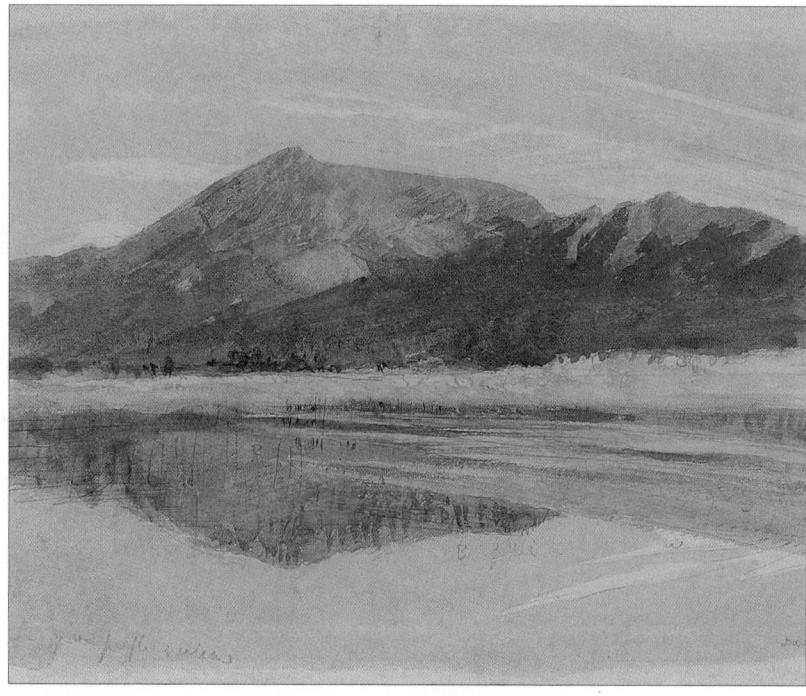

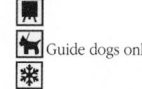

ℹ No photography. No mobile phones.

♿ Chairlifts in split level galleries. WCs.

Licensed.

By arrangement.

P Ample. Free.

Guide dogs only.

OPENING TIMES

8 February - 21 December:
Daily, 10.30am - 5pm,
reduced hours in winter.

ADMISSION

Adult	£3.00
Child	£1.50
Student	£1.50
OAP	£2.80
Family	£7.50
Groups	£2.50

Friends of the Trust
membership available.

All ages welcome.

SPECIAL EVENTS

• **FEB 8 - MAR 18:**
Andy Goldsworth -
Photographic Works.

• **MAR 27 - JUN 3:**
Li Yuan-chia

• **JUN 12 - OCT 7:**
Paula Rego

• **OCT 16 - DEC 21:**
Hughie O'Donoghue
Carborundum Prints:
Process and Content.

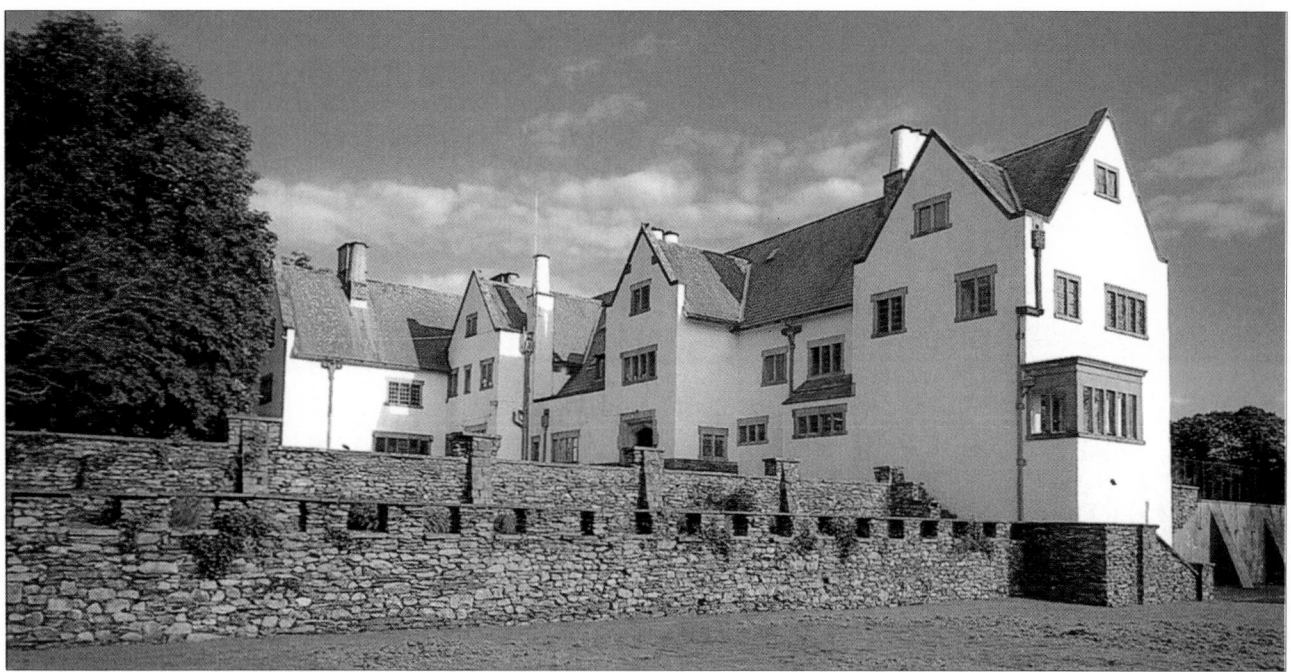

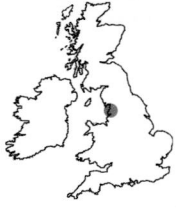

Owner: Lake District Art Gallery & Museum Trust

CONTACT

Sandy Kitching
Blackwell
The Artistic House
Bowness on Windermere
Cumbria
LA23 3JR

Tel: 01539 722464

Fax: 01539 722494

e-mail: info@ blackwell.org.uk

LOCATION

OS Ref. SD400 945

1¹/₂ m S of Bowness just off the A5074 on the B5360.

Rail: Windermere.

Air: Manchester.

BLACKWELL - THE ARTISTIC HOUSE
Bowness on Windermere

Blackwell is a superb example of an Arts and Crafts Movement house situated in the Lake District. Completed in 1900, it sits in an elevated position overlooking Lake Windermere. Blackwell is the most important, and the largest, surviving early example of work by the architect Mackay Hugh Baillie Scott. Changing exhibitions of the highest quality applied arts and crafts can be seen in the setting of the Arts and Crafts Movement architecture itself.

In this treasure trove of 1890s Arts and Crafts design are fine examples of the decorative arts, drawn from natural forms. Lakeland birds and local wild flowers, trees and berries can be seen in the many original stained glass windows, pristine oak panelling and plasterwork. These rooms were designed for relaxation and everywhere you turn you will find inglenooks and places to sit and enjoy the views and garden terraces.

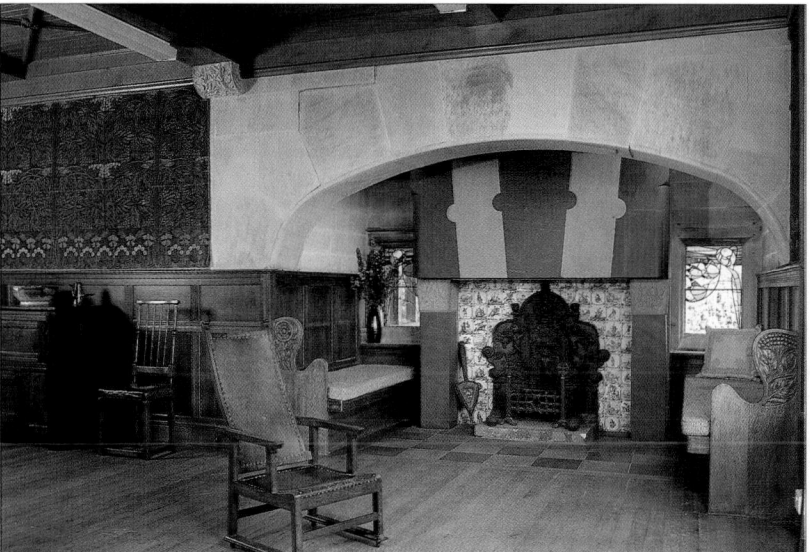

OPENING TIMES

New attraction
6 July - 21 December 2001:
Daily, 10am - 5pm,
reduced hours in winter.

ADMISSION

Please contact for details.

Note: Concessions and Friends of the Trust/ Friends of Blackwell membership available.

All ages welcome.

SPECIAL EVENTS

- **JUL 6 - SEPT 23:**
  Magdalene Odundo - Ceramic Vessels.

- **OCT 4 - DEC 21:**
  Kokten Korgei - Contemporary Crafts from Japan

ℹ️ No photography. No mobile phones.

🏃 By arrangement.

🅿️ Limited for cars and coaches.

♿ Partially suitable. WCs.

🐕 Guide dogs only.

☕ Licensed.

North West England

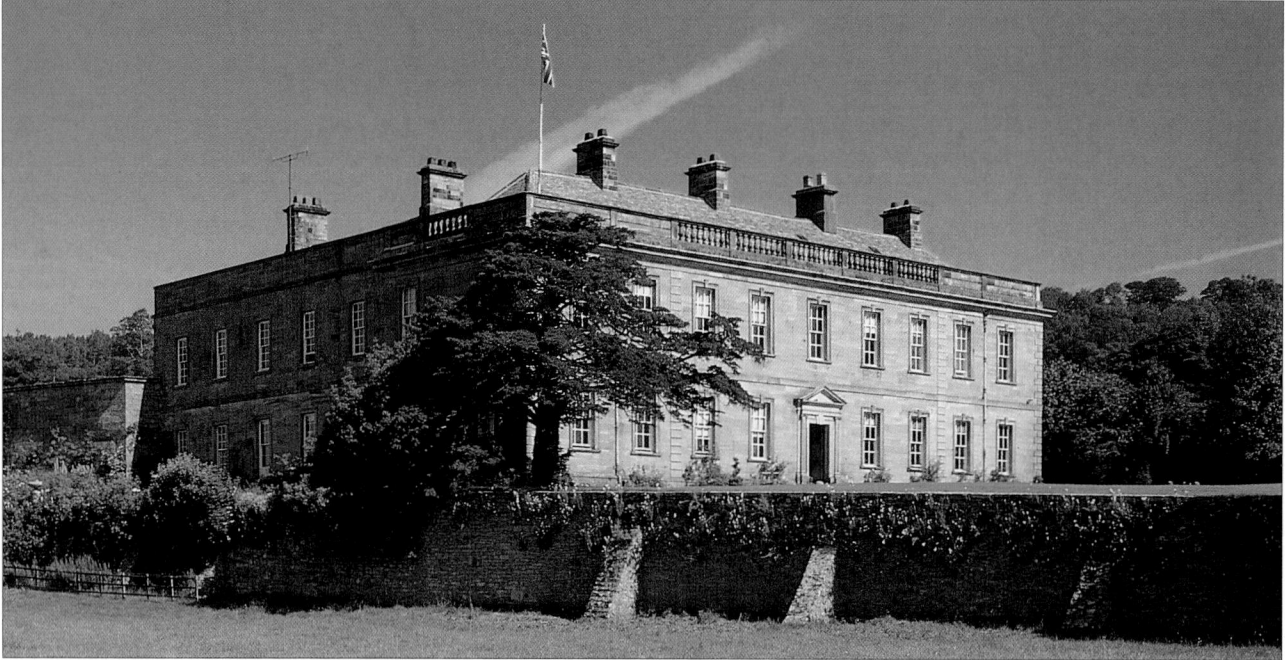

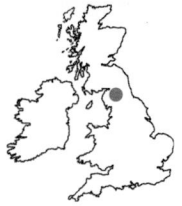

Owner:
Robert Hasell McCosh Esq

CONTACT

Bryan McDonald
Administrator
Dalemain Estate Office
Dalemain
Penrith
Cumbria
CA11 0HB

Tel: 017684 86450

Fax: 017684 86223

LOCATION

OS Ref. NY477 269

On A592 1m S of A66.
4m SW of Penrith.
From London, M1,
M6/J40: 4 hrs.

From Edinburgh,
A73, M74,
M6/J40: 2¹/₂ hrs.

Rail: Penrith 4m.

Taxi: Lakeland Taxis:
Penrith 01768 865722.

DALEMAIN
Penrith

DALEMAIN is a fine mixture of mediaeval, Tudor and early Georgian architecture. The imposing Georgian façade strikes the visitor immediately but in the cobbled courtyard the atmosphere of the north country Tudor manor is secure. The present owner's family have lived at Dalemain since 1679 and have collected china, furniture and family portraits. Visitors can see the grand Drawing Rooms with 18th century Chinese wallpaper and fine oak panelling, also the Nursery and Housekeeper's Room. The Norman pele tower contains the regimental collection of the Westmorland and Cumberland Yeomanry. The house is full of the paraphernalia of a well established family house which is still very much lived in by the family.

The 16th century Great Barn holds a collection of agricultural bygones and a Fell Pony Museum. Do not miss Mrs Mouse's house on the back stairs or the Nursery with toys from all ages. Something of interest for all the family. Location for ITV's production of *Jane Eyre*.

GARDENS

The Gardens have a long history stretching back to a mediaeval herb garden. Today a knot garden remains, with a fine early Roman fountain and box hedges enclosing herb beds.

The imposing terrace wall supports a full and colourful herbaceous border during the summer months. Visitors can enjoy the fine views of the park and the woodland and riverside walks. The gardens have been featured on television's *Gardener's World* and also in *Country Life*. Deer Park.

❖

Fashion shows, archery, clay pigeon shooting, garden parties, rallies, filming, caravan rallies, antique fairs and children's camps. Business meetings and conferences. Grand piano available. Deer Park. Lectures on the house, gardens and history by arrangement (max 50). No photography in house. Moorings available on Ullswater.

Corporate events: telephone for details.

Visitors may drive into the Courtyard and alight near the gift shop. Electric scooter for visiting the gardens. Admission free for visitors in wheelchairs. WCs.

Licensed (in Mediaeval Hall). Seats 50. Groups must book for lunches/high teas. Free admission.

1 hr tours. German and French translations in every room. Garden tour for groups extra.

P 50 yds from house. Free.

Welcome. Guides can be arranged. Interest includes Military, Country Life, Agricultural and Fell Pony Museums, also country walk past Dacre Castle to St Andrew's Church, Dacre where there is a fine Laurence Whistler window.

Guide dogs in house only. Strictly no dogs in garden but allowed in grounds.

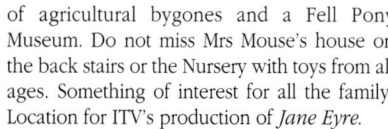

OPENING TIMES

SUMMER
25 March - 7 October
Sunday - Thursday

House: 11am - 4pm.

Gardens, restaurant, tearoom, gift shop, plant sales & museums: 10.30am - 5pm.

NB. Groups (12+) please book.

WINTER
October - Easter open by special arrangement with the Administrator.

ADMISSION

House & Garden

Adult £5.00
Child (6-16yrs)..........£3.00
Family £13.00

Gardens only

Adult £3.00
Child (6-16yrs) ....Free

Groups (12+)

Adult £4.00
Child (6-16yrs) £3.00

All prices include VAT.

SPECIAL EVENTS

• **JUL 21 - 22:**
Dalemain Rainbow Craft Fair.

• **AUG:**
Cumbrian Classic Car Show. Please telephone for further details.

CONFERENCE/FUNCTION		
ROOM	SIZE	MAX CAPACITY
Dining Room		40
Old Hall		50

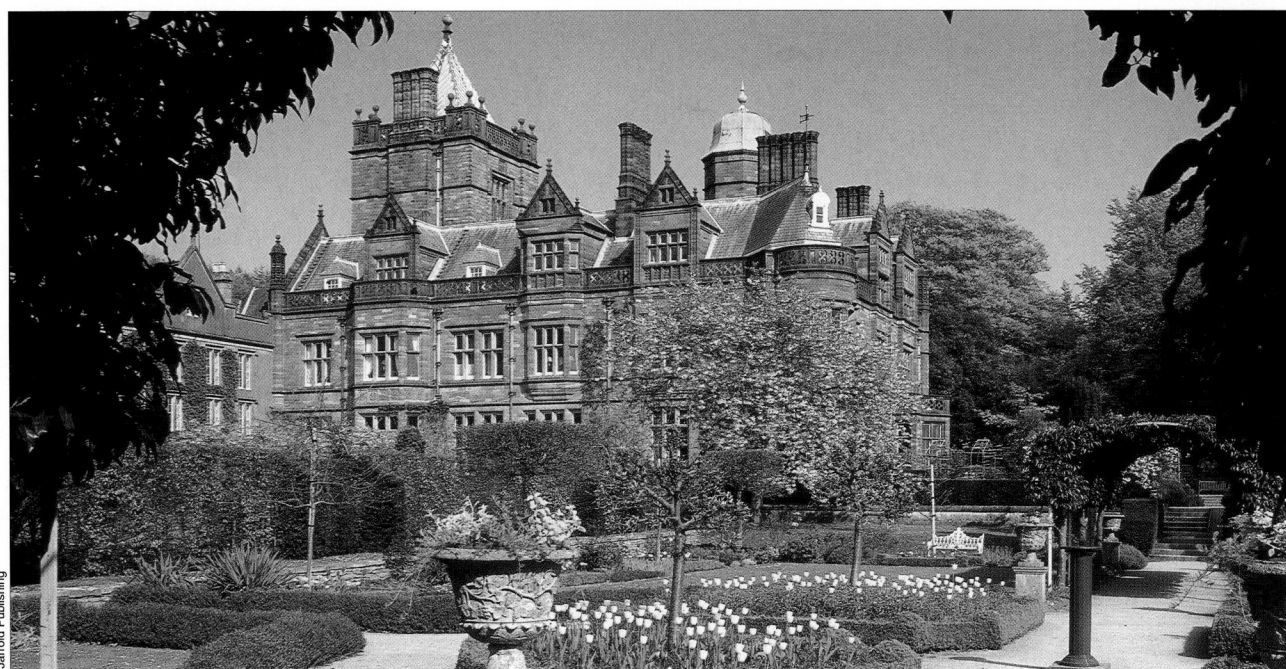

Jarrold Publishing

HOLKER HALL & GARDENS
Cark-in-Cartmel

HOLKER HALL, home of Lord and Lady Cavendish, shows the confidence, spaciousness and prosperity of Victorian style on its grandest scale. The New Wing, built by the 7th Duke of Devonshire (1871-4), replaced a previous wing totally destroyed by fire. Workmanship throughout is of the highest quality, particularly the detailed interior carving and linenfold panelling.

Despite this grand scale, Holker is very much a family home. Visitors can wander freely throughout the New Wing. Photographs, beautiful floral displays and bowls of scented pot pourri create the warm and friendly atmosphere so often remarked upon by visitors. Varying in period and style, Louis XV pieces happily mix with the Victorian. Pictures range from an early copy of the famous triple portrait of Charles I by Van Dyck to a modern painting by Douglas Anderson.

GARDENS

Christie's/HHA Garden of the Year (1991), includes formal and woodland areas covering 24 acres. Designated "*amongst the best in the world in terms of design and content*" by the *Good Gardens Guide*. This wonderful Italianate-cum-English garden includes a lime-stone cascade, a fountain, a sunken garden and many rare and beautiful plants and shrubs. The gardens featured in BBC 2's *Gardeners' World*. Holker is home to the Holker Garden Festival 1 - 3 June.

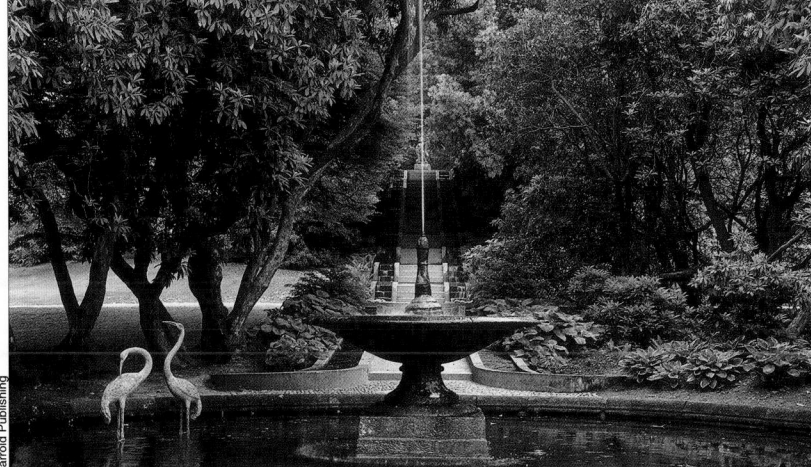

Jarrold Publishing

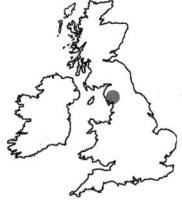

Owner: Lord Cavendish of Furness

CONTACT

Holker Hall & Gardens
Cark-in-Cartmel
Grange-over-Sands
Cumbria
LA11 7PL

Tel: 01539 558328

Fax: 01539 558838

e-mail: publicopening@ holker.co.uk

LOCATION

OS Ref. SD359 773

Close to Morecambe Bay, 5m W of Grange-over-Sands by B5277. From Kendal, A6, A590, B5277, B5278: 16m.

Motorway: M6/J36.

Bus: From Grange-over-Sands.

Rail: Cark Station.

Taxi: Parkers Motors, Grange-over-Sands.

Air: Blackpool/ Manchester.

CONFERENCE/FUNCTION

ROOM	SIZE	MAX CAPACITY
Burlington	16 x 6m	100
Cavendish	14.5 x 7.5m	120

OPENING TIMES

SUMMER
1 April - 31 October
Daily except Sats
10am - 6pm.

Last admission 4.30pm.

WINTER
1 November - 31 March
Closed.

ADMISSION

SUMMER
House & Garden

Adult £6.50
Child* £3.95

Groups (20-100)
Adult £4.50
Child* £3.00
OAP.........................£4.00

* Under 6yrs Free.

SPECIAL EVENTS

• **JUN 1 - 3:**
Holker Garden Festival. Magnificent horticultural displays & floral art combined with countryside displays and festival gardens. Family & children entertainment, craft demonstrations etc.
Tel: 01539 558838
Fax: 01539 558776

• **AUG:**
MG Rally. Post and Pre 1955 MGs in concours and driving trials. Discounted admission to MG drivers. Competition entries on the day.

Please telephone for further details.

Suitable for filming and photography. Deer Park. Lakeland Motor Museum, adventure playground and exhibitions. No photography in house. Guide book translations in French, Spanish, German, Dutch & Japanese.

Wedding receptions.

Visitors alight at entrance. Ramps and unisex WCs.

The Courtyard Café (max 200).

Pre-booked tours at additional cost from 50p each.

150 yds from Hall. Plus grass car parking.

New programme of educational packages available in 2001 focusing on KS1 & 2 and tailor-made courses.

In grounds on leads. No dogs in the gardens.

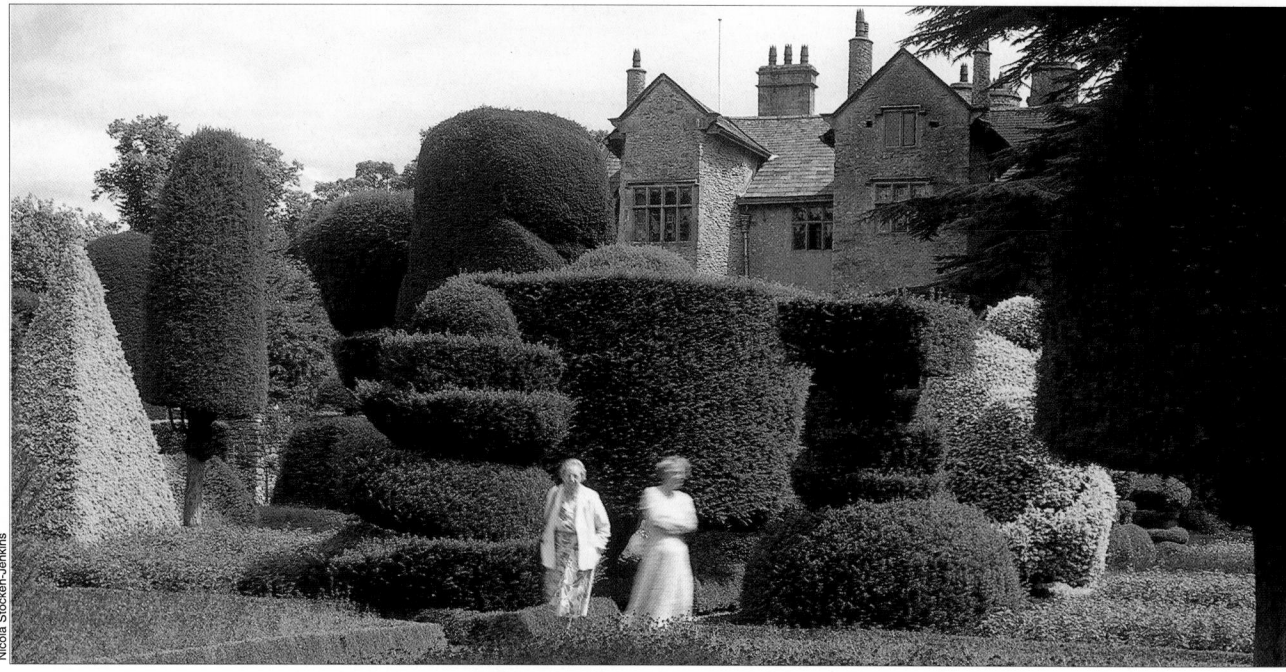

Nicola Stocken-Jenkins

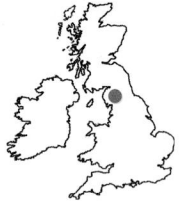

Owner: C H Bagot

CONTACT

Peter Milner
Levens Hall
Kendal
Cumbria
LA8 0PD

Tel: 01539 560321

Fax: 01539 560669

e-mail: email@
levenshall.fsnet.co.uk

LOCATION

OS Ref. SD495 851

5m S of Kendal on the A6.
Exit M6/J36.

Rail: Oxenholme 5m.

Air: Manchester.

LEVENS HALL
Kendal

LEVENS HALL is an Elizabethan mansion built around a 13th century pele tower. The much loved home of the Bagot family, visitors comment on the warm and friendly atmosphere. Fine panelling and plasterwork, period furniture, Cordova leather wall coverings, paintings by Rubens, Lely and Cuyp, the earliest English patchwork and Wellingtoniana combine with other beautiful objects to form a fascinating collection.

The world famous Topiary Gardens were laid out by Monsieur Beaumont from 1694 and his design has remained largely unchanged to this day. Over ninety individual pieces of topiary, some over nine metres high, massive beech hedges and colourful seasonal bedding provide a magnificent

visual impact. Past winner of the HHA/Christie's Garden of the Year Award. During 2001, the 'Year of the Artist', Julia Barton will be displaying a residency exhibition, adopting a contemporary approach to topiary and plant sculpture. Monty Don wrote in The Observer that the gardens at Levens are 'Considered to be in the top ten UK gardens'. Levens Hall provided the interior of Hamley Hall in the recent highly acclaimed BBC production of 'Wives and Daughters' by Elizabeth Gaskell.

On Sundays and Bank Holidays 'Bertha', a full size Showman's Engine, is in steam. Delicious home-made lunches and teas are available, together with the award winning Levens beer 'Morocco Ale', in the Bellingham Buttery.

❖

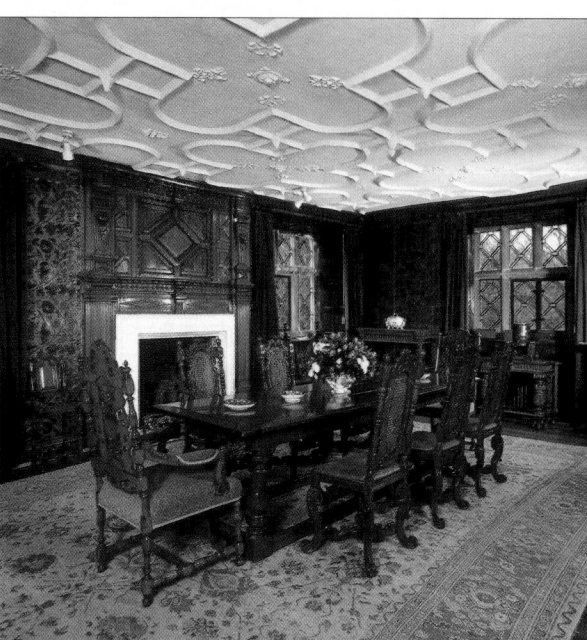

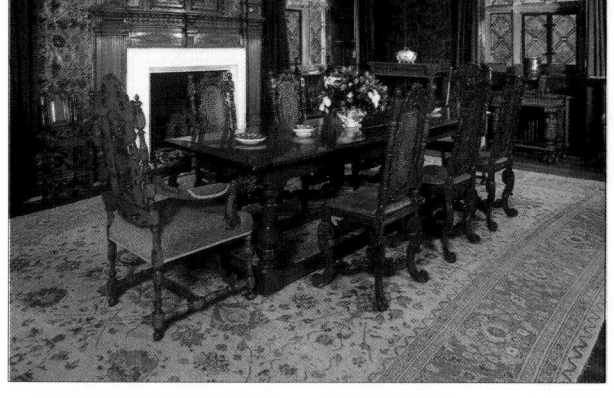

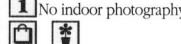 No indoor photography.

 Partially suitable. WC. Wheelchair loan - gardens only suitable.

Licensed.

By arrangement.

 Guide dogs only.

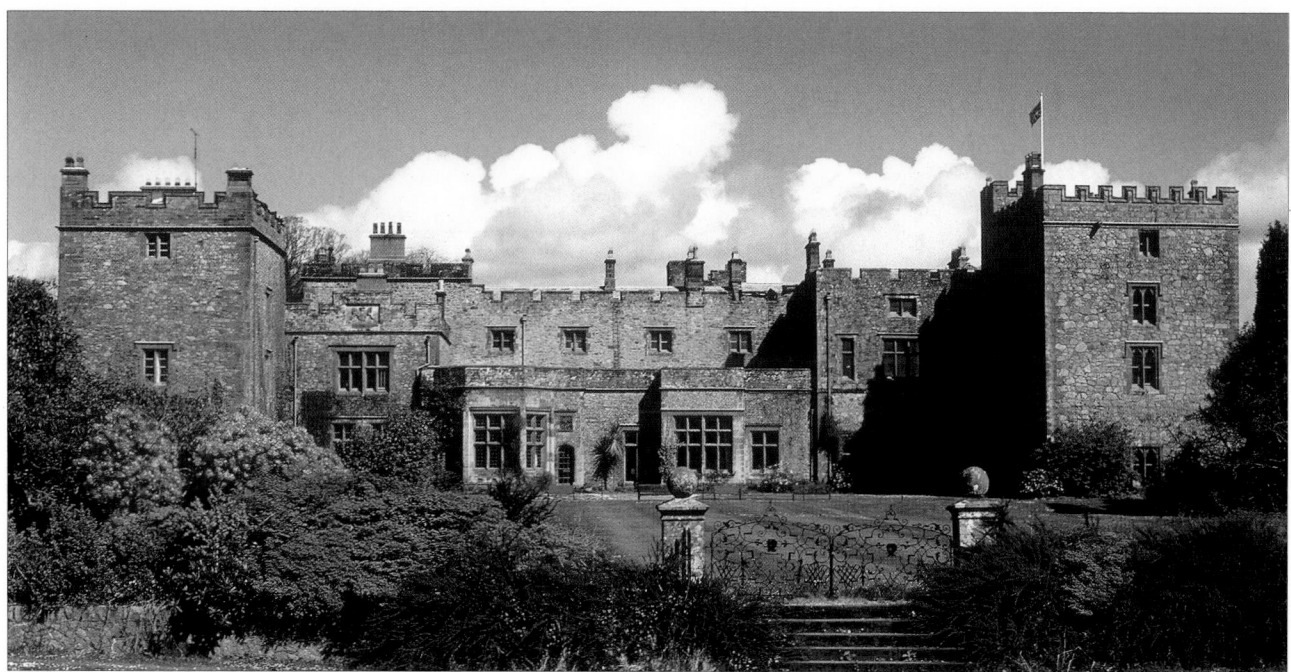

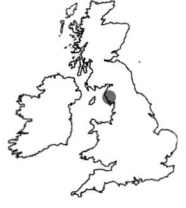

Owner: Mrs Phyllida
Gordon-Duff-Pennington

CONTACT

Peter Frost-Pennington
Muncaster Castle
Ravenglass
Cumbria
CA18 1RQ

Tel: 01229 717614
Fax: 01229 717010

e-mail: info@
muncastercastle.co.uk

LOCATION

OS Ref. SD103 965

On the A595 1m S of
Ravenglass, 19m S of
Whitehaven.

From London 6 hrs,
Chester 2^1/$_2$ hrs, Edinburgh
3^1/$_2$ hrs, M6/J36, A590,
A595 (from S). M6/J40,
A66, A595(from E).
Carlisle, A595 (from N).

Rail: Ravenglass
(on Barrow-in-Furness-
Carlisle Line) 1^1/$_2$ m.

Air: Manchester 2^1/$_2$ hrs.

CONFERENCE/FUNCTION

ROOM	SIZE	MAX CAPACITY
Drawing Rm	–	120
Dining Rm	–	50
Family Dining Rm	–	60
Great Hall	–	110
Old Laundry	–	120
Library	–	40

MUNCASTER CASTLE
GARDENS & OWL CENTRE, Ravenglass

MUNCASTER CASTLE has been owned by the Pennington family since 1208. It has grown from the original pele tower built on Roman foundations to the impressive structure visible today. Outstanding features are the Great Hall and Salvin's Octagonal Library and the Drawing Room with its barrel ceiling.

The castle contains many treasures including beautiful furniture, exquisite needlework panels, tapestries and oriental rugs. The family silver is very fine and is accompanied in the Dining Room by the Ongley Service, the most ornamental set of porcelain ever created by the Derby factory, Florentine 16th century bronzes and an alabaster lady by Giambologna can be seen. The family are actively involved in entertaining their many visitors.

The woodland gardens cover 77 acres and command spectacular views of the Lakeland Fells, with many delightful walks. From mid-March to June the rhododendrons, azaleas, camellias and magnolias are at their best.

The Owl Centre boasts a fine collection of owls from all over the world. 'Meet the Birds' occurs daily at 2.30pm (11Mar to 4 Nov), when a talk is given on the work of the centre. Weather permitting, the birds fly free.

NEW – shrink to 2 inches tall and see if you can survive the dangers of meadowland by getting through the MeadowVole Maze without getting eaten. Great for kids of all ages!

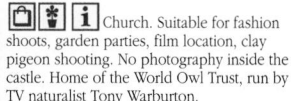

Church. Suitable for fashion shoots, garden parties, film location, clay pigeon shooting. No photography inside the castle. Home of the World Owl Trust, run by TV naturalist Tony Warburton.

Wedding receptions. For catering and functions in the castle Tel: 01229 717614.

By prior arrangement visitors alight near Castle. Wheelchairs for loan. WCs. Special audio tour tapes for the partially sighted/those with learning difficulties. Allocated parking.

Creeping Kate's Kitchen (licensed) (max 80) – full menu. Groups can book: 01229 717432 to qualify for discounts.

Individual audio tour (40mins) included in price. Private tours with a personal guide (family member possible) can be arranged at additional fee. Lectures by arrangement.

500 cars 800 yds from House; coaches may park closer.

Guides available. Historical subjects, horticulture, conservation, owl tours.

In grounds, on leads.

OPENING TIMES

Castle
11 March - 4 November
Daily (closed Sat),
12 noon - 5pm.

Gardens & Owl Centre
All year: daily:
10.30am - 6pm or dusk if earlier.

'Meet the Birds'
11 March - 4 November
Daily at 2.30pm.

'Heron Happy Hour'
Feeding of wild herons.
11 March - 4 November
Daily at 4.30pm.

Winter
Castle closed. Open by appointment for groups.

ADMISSION

Castle, Gardens & Owl Centre
Adult £6.50
Child (5-15yrs)..........£4.00
Under 5yrs...............Free
Family (2+2) £18.00
Groups
Adult £5.50
Child (5-15yrs)..........£3.00

Season Tickets
Adult £5.00
Family £32.50

Gardens & Owl Centre and MeadowVole Maze
Adult £5.00
Child (5-15yrs)..........£3.00
Under 5yrs...............Free
Family (2+2) £15.00
Groups
Adult £4.50
Child (5-15yrs)..........£2.00

ACORN BANK GDN & WATERMILL

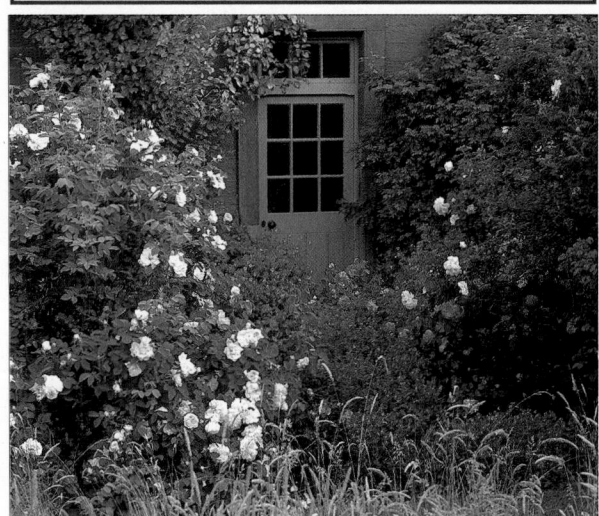

TEMPLE SOWERBY, PENRITH, CUMBRIA CA10 1SP

Owner: The National Trust   *Contact:* The Custodian

Tel: 01768 361893   **e-mail:** racorn@smtp.ntrust.org.uk

A one hectare garden protected by fine oaks under which grow a vast display of daffodils. Inside the walls there are orchards containing a variety of fruit trees surrounded by mixed borders with shrubs, herbaceous plants and roses, while the impressive herb garden has the largest collection of culinary and medicinal plants in the north. A circular woodland walk runs beside the Crowdundle Beck to Acorn Bank Watermill, which although under restoration, is open to visitors. The house is open only during some events.

Location: Gate: OS Ref. NY612 281. Just N of Temple Sowerby, 6m E of Penrith on A66.

Opening Times: 31 Mar - 4 Nov: daily, 10am - 5pm. Last admission 4.30pm.

Admission: Adult £2.50, Child £1.20, Family £6.20. Pre-arranged groups £1.80.

◻   ♿Grounds only. WCs.   ✖

BROUGH CASTLE

Tel: 0161 242 1400

Brough, Cumbria

Owner: English Heritage   **Contact:** The North Regional Office

This ancient site dates back to Roman times. The 12th century keep replaced an earlier stronghold destroyed by the Scots in 1174.

Location: OS Ref. NY791 141. 8m SE of Appleby S of A66. South part of the village.

Opening Times: Any reasonable time.

Admission: Free.

BROUGHAM CASTLE

Tel: 01768 862488

Penrith, Cumbria CA10 2AA

Owner: English Heritage   **Contact:** The Custodian

These impressive ruins on the banks of the River Eamont include an early 13th century keep and later buildings. You can climb to the top of the keep and survey the domain of its eccentric one-time owner Lady Anne Clifford, who restored the castle in the 17th century. There is a small exhibition of Roman tombstones from the nearby fort.

Location: OS Ref. NY537 290. $1^{1}/_{2}$ m SE of Penrith, between A66 & B6262.

Opening Times: 1 Apr - 30 Sept: daily, 10am - 6pm. 1 - 31 Oct: daily, 10am - 5pm.

Admission: Adult £2.10, Child £1.10, Conc. £1.60. 15% discount for groups (11+).

◻   ♿Grounds suitable.   ℗Limited.   ▥   In grounds, on leads.   ◿Tel. for details.

BEATRIX POTTER GALLERY

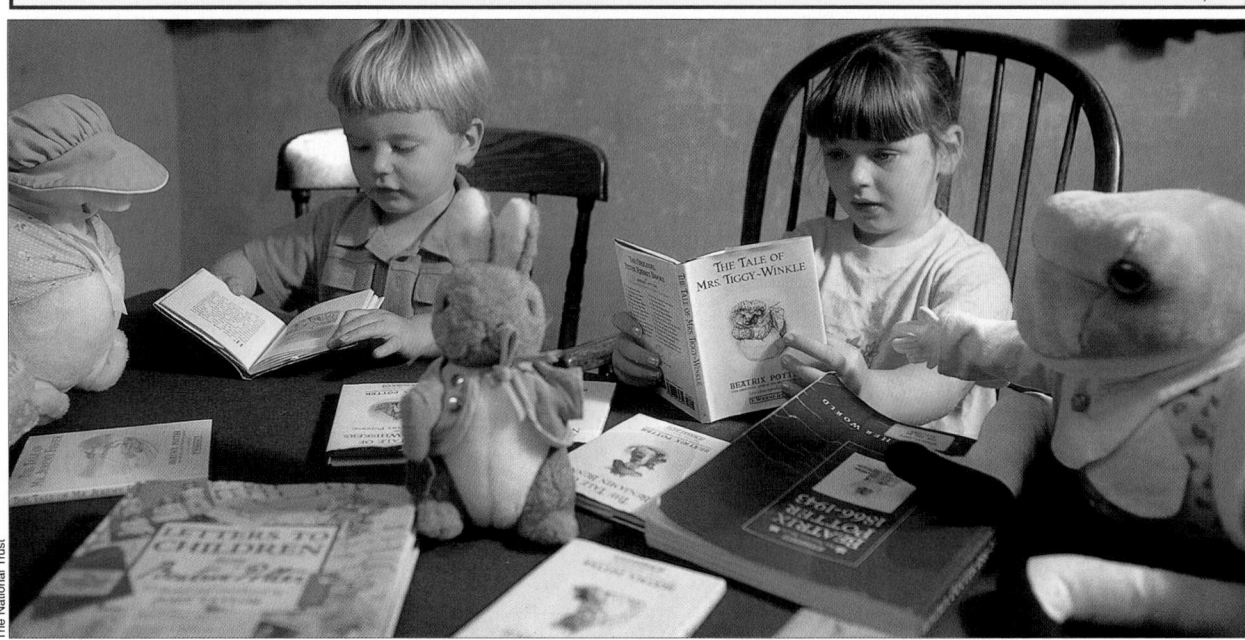

The National Trust

MAIN STREET, HAWKSHEAD, CUMBRIA LA22 0NS

Owner: The National Trust   *Contact:* The Custodian

Tel: 01539 436355

An annually changing exhibition of original sketches and watercolours painted by Beatrix Potter for her children's stories. Each year the new exhibition delights young and old as they discover the amazing delicacy and charm of her work. One of many historic buildings in this picturesque village, the gallery was once the office of Beatrix Potter's husband, William Heelis, and the interior remains substantially unaltered since his day. The gallery is ideally matched with a visit to Beatrix Potter's house, Hill Top, two miles away, where she wrote and illustrated many of her children's stories.

Location: OS Ref. SD352 982. 5m SSW of Ambleside. In the Square.

Opening Times: 1 Apr - 1 Nov: Sun - Thur (closed Fris & Sats except Good Fri) 10.30am - 4.30pm. Last admission 4pm. Admission is by timed ticket (incl. NT members).

Admission: Adult £3, Child £1.50. No reduction for groups.

◻   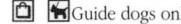Guide dogs only.

CARLISLE CASTLE

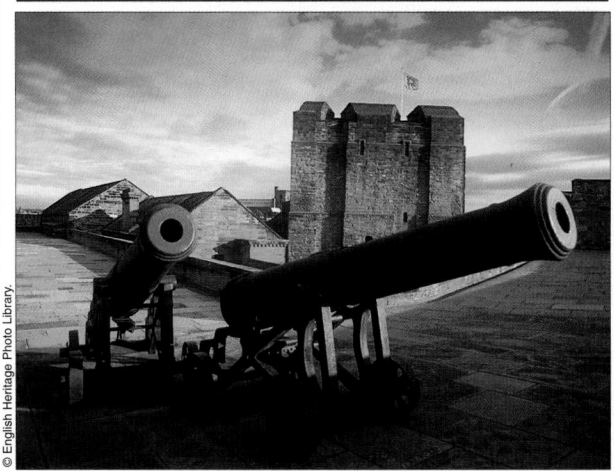

© English Heritage Photo Library.

CARLISLE, CUMBRIA CA3 8UR

Owner: *English Heritage*   **Contact:** *The Custodian*

Tel: 01228 591922

This impressive medieval castle, where Mary Queen of Scots was once imprisoned, has a long and tortuous history of warfare and family feuds. A portcullis hangs menacingly over the gatehouse passage, there is a maze of passages and chambers, endless staircases to lofty towers and you can walk the high ramparts for stunning views. There is also a medieval manor house in miniature: a suite of medieval rooms furnished as they might have been when used by the castle's former constable. The castle is also the home of the Museum of the King's Own Border Regiment (included in the admission price).

Location: OS85 Ref. NY397 563. In Carlisle town, at N end of city centre.

Open: 1 Apr - 30 Sept: daily, 9.30am - 6pm. 1 - 31 Oct: daily, 10am - 5pm. 1 Nov - 31 Mar: daily, 10am - 4pm. Closed 24 - 26 Dec.

Admission: Adult £3.10, Child £1.60, Conc £2.30. 15% discount for groups (11+).

Partially suitable, wheelchairs available. By arrangement. No parking. Dogs on leads. Tel. for details.

CARLISLE CATHEDRAL   **Tel:** 01228 548151 **Fax:** 01228 547049

Carlisle, Cumbria CA3 8TZ   **e-mail:** office@carlislecathedral.org.uk

Contact: Ms C Baines

Fine sandstone Cathedral, founded in 1122. Medieval stained glass. Gift shop. Restaurant.

Location: OS Ref. NY399 559. Carlisle city centre, 2m from M6/J43.

Opening Times: Mon - Sat: 7.45am - 6.15pm, Suns, 7.45 - 5pm. Closes 4pm between Christmas Day & New Year. Sun services: 8am, 10.30am & 3pm. Weekday services: 8am, 5.30pm & a 12.30 service on Weds, Fris and Saints' Days.

Admission: Donation.

CONISHEAD PRIORY & MANJUSHRI BUDDHIST TEMPLE

Ulverston, Cumbria LA12 9QQ   **Tel:** 01229 584029 **Fax:** 01229 580080

Owner: Manjushri Mahayana Buddhist Centre   **Contact:** Mr D Coote

A Georgian gothic mansion on site of a medieval Augustinian Priory.

Location: OS Ref. SD300 750. 2m S of Ulverston on Bardsea Coast Rd A5087.

Opening Times: Easter - Oct, w/e & BHs, 2 - 5pm. Closed 9 - 25 June & 21 July - 20 Aug.

Admission: Free. House tours and audio visual: Adult £2, Child 75p, OAP £1.

DALEMAIN   **See page 408 for full page entry.**

DOVE COTTAGE & WORDSWORTH MUSEUM   **Tel:** 01539 435544

Grasmere, Cumbria LA22 9SH   **Fax:** 01539 435748

See full page advertisement on page 24   **e-mail:** enquiries@wordsworth.org.uk

Owner: Wordsworth Trust   **Contact:** Enquiries

Wordsworth's home 1799 - 1808, Dove Cottage is beautifully preserved. Visitors are offered guided tours. The garden is open, weather permitting. The award-winning Wordsworth Museum displays a permanent exhibition and a programme of special exhibitions and events.

Location: OS Ref. NY342 070. Immediately S of Grasmere village on A591. Main car/coach park next to Dove Cottage Tea Rooms.

Opening Times: All year: daily, 9.30am - 5pm. Closed 10 Jan - 6 Feb (inc) & 24 - 26 Dec.

Admission: Adult £5, Child £2.50, Student £4.20, OAP £4.70 (2000 prices). Pre-arranged groups (15-60): Adult £4.40, Child £2.20. Reciprocal discount ticket with Rydal Mount and Wordsworth House, Cockermouth.

No photography. Partially suitable. WC. Obligatory. Limited. Guide dogs only. Please tel. for details.

FELL FOOT PARK   **Tel:** 01539 531273 **Fax:** 01539 530049

Newby Bridge, Ulverston LA12 8NN   **e-mail:** rffoot@smtp.ntrust.org.uk

Owner: The National Trust   **Contact:** The Property Manager

This Victorian park, restored to its former glory, offers substantial access to the lakeshore of Windermere where there are leisure facilities in season. Fine picnic areas and boat hire make this property particularly rewarding for families.

Location: OS96, Ref. SD381 869. At the extreme S end of Lake Windermere on E shore, entrance from A592.

Opening Times: Daily, 9am - 7pm or dusk if earlier. Facilities & Shop: 25 Mar - 28 Oct: daily, 11am - 4.30pm.

Admission: Car park: £2 (up to 2hrs), £5 (all day).Coaches £10 by arrangement.

Partially suitable. Charge. On leads. Tel. for details.

FURNESS ABBEY   **Tel:** 01229 823420

Barrow-in-Furness, Cumbria LH13 0TJ

Owner: English Heritage   **Contact:** The Custodian

Hidden in a peaceful green valley are the beautiful red sandstone remains of the wealthy abbey founded in 1123 by Stephen, later King of England. This abbey first belonged to the Order of Savigny and later to the Cistercians. There is a museum and exhibition.

Location: OS96, Ref. SD218 717. 1¹/₂ m NE of Barrow-in-Furness.

Opening Times: 1 Apr - 30 Sept: daily, 10am - 6pm. 1 - 31 Oct:, daily, 10am - 5pm. 1 Nov - 31 Mar: Wed - Sun, 10am - 4pm. Closed 1 - 2pm in winter. Closed 24 - 26 Dec.

Admission: Adult £2.70, Child £1.40, Conc. £2. 15% discount for groups (11+).

Grounds suitable. Inclusive. In grounds, on leads. Tel. for details.

HARDKNOTT ROMAN FORT   **Tel:** 0161 242 1400

Ravenglass, Cumbria

Owner: English Heritage   **Contact:** The Regional Office

This fort, built between AD120 and 138, controlled the road from Ravenglass to Ambleside.

Location: OS Ref. NY218 015. At the head of Eskdale. 9m NE of Ravenglass, at W end of Hardknott Pass.

Opening Times: Any reasonable time. Access may be hazardous in winter.

Admission: Free.

HERON CORN MILL & MUSEUM OF PAPERMAKING   **Tel:** 015395 65027

Fax: 015395 65033 **e-mail:** ntstobbs@virgin.net

c/o Henry Cooke, Waterhouse Mills, Beetham, Milnthorpe LA7 7AR

Owner: Heron Corn Mill Beetham Trust   **Contact:** Mr Neil Stobbs

Location: OS Ref. SD497 800. At Beetham. 1m S of Milnthorpe on the A6.

Opening Times: Easter: 1 Apr - 30 Sept: Tue - Sun & BH Mon, 11am - 5pm.

Admission: Adult £1.50, Child/OAP £1, Family (2+2) £4.50, Coach parties/groups 10% discount if pre-booked.

HILL TOP   **Tel:** 01539 436269 **e-mail:** rpmht@smtp.ntrust.org.uk

Near Sawrey, Ambleside, Cumbria LA22 0LF

Owner: The National Trust   **Contact:** The Property Manager

Beatrix Potter wrote many '*Peter Rabbit*' books in this little 17th century house, which contains her furniture and china. There is a traditional cottage garden attached.

Location: OS Ref. SD370 955. 2m S of Hawkshead, in hamlet of Near Sawrey, behind the Tower Bank Arms.

Opening Times: Mar - May: 11am - 4.30pm. June - Aug, 10.30am - 5pm. Sept & Oct, 11am - 4.30pm. Last admission 30mins before closing. Booking prior to visit essential to guarantee entry.

Admission: Adult £4, Child £2, Family £9.75. No reduction for groups.

HOLEHIRD
Tel: 01539 446008 **e-mail:** george.feather@care4free.net

Patterdale Road, Windermere, Cumbria LA23 1NP

Owner: Lakeland Horticultural Society **Contact:** The Hon Secretary

Over 4 acres of hillside gardens overlooking Troutbeck Valley, including a walled garden and national collection of astilbes, hydrangeas and polystichum ferns. All of the work in the gardens is done by volunteers.

Location: OS Ref. NY410 008. On A592, 3/4 m N of junction with A591. 1/2 m N of Windermere. 1m from Townend.

Opening Times: All year: dawn to dusk.

Admission: Free. Donation appreciated (at least £2 suggested).

HOLKER HALL 🏛

See page 409 for full page entry.

LANERCOST PRIORY ⊞
Tel: 01697 73030

Brampton, Cumbria CA8 2HQ

Owner: English Heritage **Contact:** The Custodian

This Augustinian priory was founded c1166. The nave of the church, which is intact and in use as the local parish church, contrasts with the ruined chancel, transepts and priory buildings.

Location: OS86, Ref. NY556 637. 2m NE of Brampton. 1m N of Naworth Castle.

Opening Times: 1 Apr - 30 Sept: daily, 10am - 6pm. 1 - 31 Oct: daily, 10am - 5pm.

Admission: Adult £2.10, Child £1.10, Conc. £1.60. Groups: 15% discount for groups (11+).

📷 ♿Ground floor suitable. 🎧Inclusive. 🅿Limited. 🔲 ✂
🐕 Tel. for details.

LEVENS HALL 🏛

See page 410 for full page entry.

HUTTON-IN-THE-FOREST 🏛

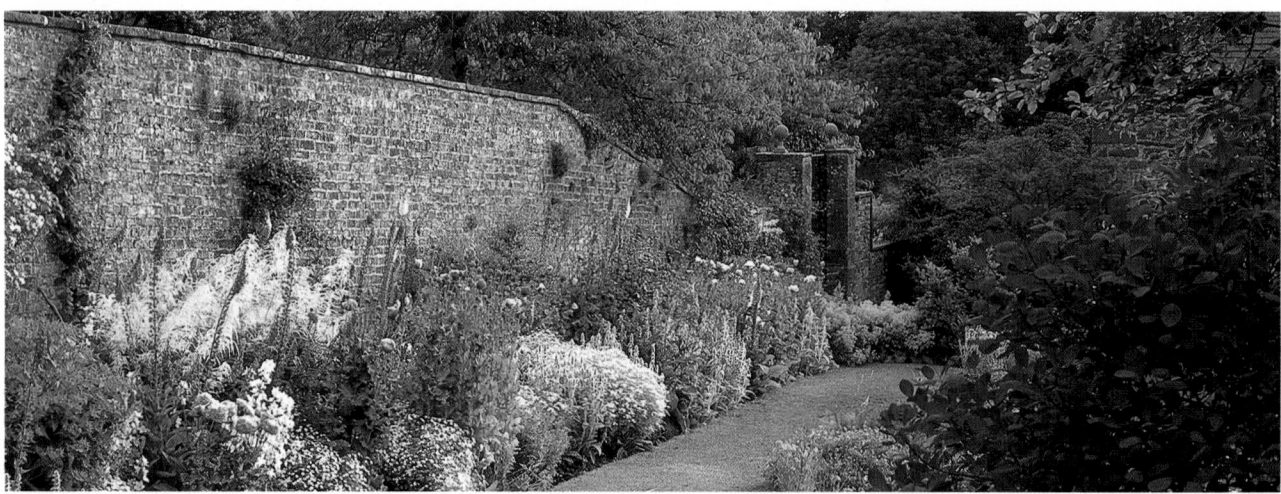

PENRITH, CUMBRIA CA11 9TH

Owner: Lord Inglewood *Contact: Edward Thompson*

Tel: 01768 484449 **Fax:** 01768 484571 **e-mail:** hutton-in-the-forest@talk21.com

The home of Lord Inglewood's family since 1605. Built around a medieval pele tower with 17th, 18th and 19th century additions. Fine collections of furniture and paintings, ceramics and tapestries. Outstanding grounds with terraces, topiary, walled garden, dovecote and woodland walk through magnificent specimen trees.

Location: OS Ref. NY460 358. 6m NW of Penrith & 2 1/2 m from M6/J41 on B5305.

Opening Times: 12 Apr - 30 Sept: Thur - Fri, Suns & BH Mons. 12.30 - 4pm (last entry).

Tearoom: As house: 11am - 4.30pm. Grounds: daily except Sats, 11am - 5pm.

Admission: House, Gardens & Grounds: Adult £4.50, Child £2.50, Family £12. Gardens & Grounds: Adult £2.50, Child Free.

ℹ Picnic area. 📷Gift stall. 🍵By arrangement. ♿Partially suitable. 🍴
👣Obligatory (except Jul/Aug & BHs). 🔲

Acorn Bank Garden & Watermill, Cumbria

MIREHOUSE

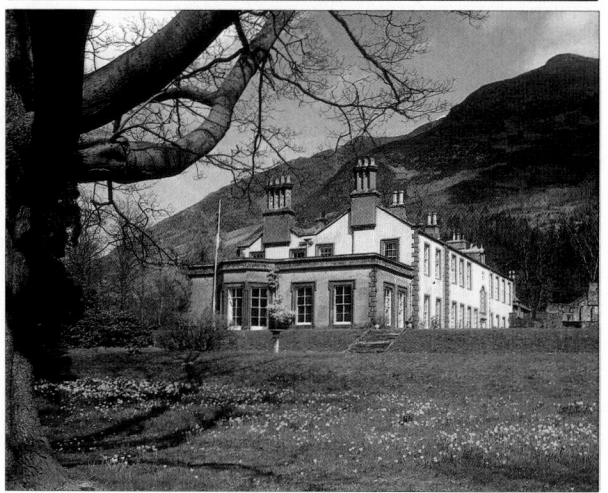

KESWICK, CUMBRIA CA12 4QE

Owner: *James Fryer-Spedding* ***Contact:*** *Clare Spedding*

Tel/Fax: 017687 72287 **e-mail:** info@mireho.freeserve.co.uk

'The Best Heritage Property for Families in the UK' 1999 NPI Award. Our visitors particularly appreciate the spectacular setting between mountain and lake, the extraordinary literary and artistic connections, varied gardens, walks, natural playgrounds, live classical music and the personal attention of members of the family. The tearoom is known for generous Cumbrian cooking.

Location: OS Ref. NY235 284. Beside A591, 3¹/₂ m N of Keswick. Good bus service.

Opening Times: 1 Apr - 31 Oct: Gardens & Tearoom: daily, 10am - 5.30pm. House: Suns & Weds (also Fris in Aug), 2 - 4.30pm (last entry). At other times for groups by appointment.

Admission: House & Garden: Adult £4, Child £2, Family £11.75. Gardens only: Adult £2, Child £1. 10% discount for groups (20+), booked in advance.

ℹ️ No photography in house. ♿ 💷 🖼 By arrangement. 🅿️ Limited. 🏛 🐕 In grounds on leads. ❄️ Booked groups only.

THE QUAKER TAPESTRY EXHIBITION CENTRE   **Tel/Fax:** 01539 722975

Friends Meeting House, Stramongate, Kendal, Cumbria LA9 4BH

e-mail: info@quaker-tapestry.co.uk

Owner: Trustees of the Quaker Tapestry   **Contact:** Bridget Guest

This unique exhibition of 77 panels of community embroidery delights visitors of all ages. Explore the Quaker journey from 17th century to the present day as you uncover over 300 years of social history, beautifully illustrated by 4000 men, women and children from 15 countries.

Location: OS Ref. SD517 927. Centre of Kendal, access from either Stramongate or New Road.

Opening Times: Apr - Oct: Mon - Sat, 10am - 5pm, last admission 4.15pm. Nov - Dec: Mon - Fri.

Admission: Adult £4, Child £1, Conc. £2.50.

ℹ️ No indoor photography. Demonstrations. 📷 ♿ 💷 For group visits (20+). 🎨 By arrangement. 🎧 🅿️ Limited. 🏛 🐕 Guide dogs only. 🆘

RYDAL MOUNT & GARDENS 🏛   **Tel:** 01539 433002 **Fax:** 01539 431738

Ambleside, Cumbria LA22 9LU   **e-mail:** Rydalmount.aol.com

Owner: Rydal Mount Trustees   **Contact:** Peter & Marian Elkington

See full page advertisement on page 24

The historic house of William Wordsworth from 1813 until his death in 1850, now the family home of his descendants. It contains family portraits and his personal possessions. The extensive garden, landscaped by the poet, includes terraces, rare shrubs, trees and the poet's summerhouse which overlooks beautiful Rydal Water.

Location: OS Ref. NY364 063. 1¹/₂ m N of Ambleside on A591 Grasmere Road.

Opening Times: Mar - Oct: Daily, 9.30am - 5pm. Nov - Feb: Daily except Tues, 10am - 4pm.

Admission: Adult £4, Child £1.25, Student £3, OAP £3.25. Pre-arranged groups £2.75. Garden only: £1.75. Free parking. Reciprocal discount ticket with Dove Cottage and Wordsworth House.

ℹ️ No inside photography. 📷 ♿ Partially suitable. 🎨 By arrangement. 🅿️ Limited. 🏛 🐕 In grounds, on leads. Guide dogs only in house. ❄️ 🆘

MUNCASTER CASTLE 🏛   **See page 411 for full page entry.**

MUNCASTER WATER MILL   **Tel:** 01229 717232

Ravenglass, Cumbria CA18 1ST

Owner: Lake District Estates   **Contact:** E & P Priestly

Working old manorial mill with 13ft overshot wheel and all milling equipment.

Location: OS Ref. SD094 977. 1m N of Ravenglass on A595.

Opening Times: Easter - Oct: daily 10am - 5pm. Nov - Mar: weekends only, 11am - 4pm.

Admission: Adult £2, Child 50p, Family (2+3) £5. Groups by arrangement.

NAWORTH CASTLE   **Tel:** 01697 73229 **Fax:** 01697 73679

Brampton, Cumbria CA8 2HF   **e-mail:** philip@naworth.co.uk

Owner: Philip Howard   **Contact:** Colleen Hall

Cumbria's premier function venue for weddings and corporate events.

Location: OS Ref. NY560 626. ¹/₂ m off main A69 Carlisle - Newcastle road. 3m E of Brampton. Carlisle 12m, Newcastle 46m, M6 9m.

Opening Times: All year by appointment only.

🍴 🔔

PENRITH CASTLE ⬜   **Tel:** 0161 242 1400

Penrith, Cumbria

Owner: English Heritage   **Contact:** The North Regional Office

This 14th century castle, set in a park on the edge of the town, was built to defend Penrith against repeated attacks by Scottish raiders.

Location: OS Ref. NY513 299. Opposite Penrith railway station. W of the town centre. Fully visible from the street.

Opening Times: Park opening hours.

Admission: Free.

SIZERGH CASTLE & GARDEN 🌿

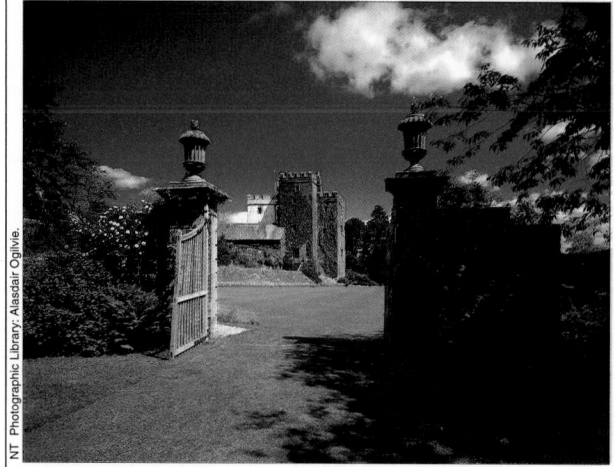

NT Photographic Library: Alasdair Ogilvie.

Nr KENDAL, CUMBRIA LA8 8AE

Owner: *The National Trust*   ***Contact:*** *The House Manager*

Tel: 01539 560070 **Fax:** 01539 561621

The Strickland family have lived here for more than 750 years. The impressive 14th century pele tower was extended in Tudor times, with some of the finest Elizabethan carved overmantels in the country. Contents include good English and French furniture and family portraits. A visit culminates in the important and impressive Inlaid Chamber. The castle is surrounded by gardens of beauty and interest, including the Trust's largest limestone rock garden; good autumn colour. Large estate; walks leaflet available in shop.

Location: OS Ref. SD498 878. 3¹/₂ m S of Kendal, NW of the A590/A591 interchange.

Opening Times: Castle: 1 Apr - 31 Oct: Sun - Thur, 1.30 - 5.30pm. Garden: As house: 12.30 - 5.30pm. Last admission 5pm.

Admission: Adult £4.80, Child £2.40, Family £12. Garden only: £2.40. Groups (15+): £3.80 by arrangement (not on BHs).

📷 ♿ Partially suitable. 💷 🎨

North West England

STAGSHAW GARDEN ⚜

Tel / Fax: 015394 46027

Ambleside, Cumbria LA22 0HE

Owner: The National Trust   **Contact:** Windermere & Troutbeck Property Office

This woodland garden was created by the late Cubby Acland, Regional Agent for the National Trust. It contains a fine collection of azaleas and rhododendrons, planted to give good blends of colour under the thinned oaks on the hillside; also many trees and shrubs, including magnolias, camellias and embothriums.

Location: OS Ref 200. NY380 029. $^1/_2$ m S of Ambleside on A591.

Opening Times: 1 Apr - end Jun: daily, 10am - 6.30pm. Jul - end Oct: by appointment.

Admission: £1.50, no reduction for groups.

♿ Not suitable. 🅿 No parking. 🐾

STEAM YACHT GONDOLA ⚜

Tel/Fax: 015394 63856

(NT Gondola Bookings) National Trust Office, The Hollens, Grasmere, LA22 9QZ

Owner: The National Trust   **Contact:** The Manager

The Steam Yacht Gondola, first launched in 1859 and now completely renovated by the Trust, provides a steam-powered passenger service, carrying 86 passengers in opulently upholstered saloons. A superb way to see Coniston's scenery.

Location: OS Ref. SD305 975. Coniston ($^1/_2$ m to Coniston Pier).

Opening Times: Sails from Coniston Pier daily at 11am, 1 Apr - 31 Oct. The Trust reserves the right to cancel sailings in the event of high winds or lack of demand. Piers at Coniston and Brantwood (not NT). Open until 21 Dec for private bookings.

Admission: Ticket prices & timetable on application and published locally. Family ticket available. No reduction for NT members as Gondola is an enterprise and not held solely for preservation. Groups & private charters by prior arrangement.

♿ Not suitable. 🐾 Dogs on leads, outside saloons, 50p any journey.

STOTT PARK BOBBIN MILL ⚏

Tel: 01539 531087

Low Stott Park, Ulverston, Cumbria LA12 8AX

Owner: English Heritage   **Contact:** The Custodian

When this working mill was built in 1835 it was typical of the many mills in the Lake District which grew up to supply the spinning and weaving industry in Lancashire but have since disappeared. A remarkable opportunity to see a demonstration of the machinery and techniques of the Industrial Revolution. There is a working Static Steam Engine on Tuesdays to Thursdays.

Location: OS96 Ref. SD373 883. Near Newby Bridge on A590.

Opening Times: 1 Apr - 30 Sept: daily, 10am - 6pm. 1 - 31 Oct: daily, 10am - 5pm. Last admission 1hr before closing.

Admission: Adult £3.10, Child £1.60, Conc. £2.30. Groups: discount for groups (11+).

📷 ♿ Ground floor suitable. WC. 🍴 Inclusive. 🅿 ☕ 🐾

HELENA THOMPSON MUSEUM

Tel: 01900 326255

Park End Road, Workington, Cumbria CA14 4DE

Owner: Allerdale Borough Council   **Contact:** Heritage & Arts Unit

The museum is housed in a fine listed mid-Georgian building. Displays include pottery, silver, glass, furniture and dress collection.

Location: OS Ref. NY007 286. Corner of A66, Ramsey Brow & Park End Road.

Opening Times: Apr - Sept: Mon - Sat, 10.30am - 4pm. Nov - Mar: Mon - Sat, 11am - 3pm.

Admission: Free.

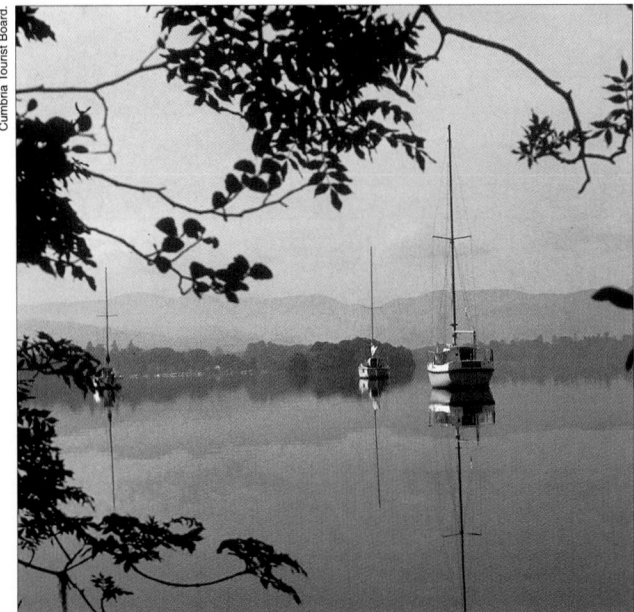

Lake Windermere, Cumbria.

Cumbria Tourist Board.

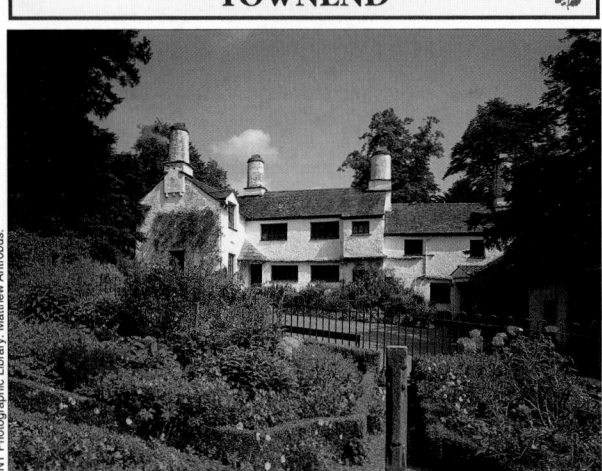

TOWNEND ⚜

NT Photographic Library: Matthew Antrobus.

TROUTBECK, WINDERMERE, CUMBRIA LA23 1LB

Owner: *The National Trust*   **Contact:** *The Administrator*

Tel: 01539 432628

An exceptional relic of Lake District life during past centuries. Originally a 'statesman' (wealthy yeoman) farmer's house, built about 1626. Townend contains carved woodwork, books, papers, furniture and fascinating implements of the past which were accumulated by the Browne family who lived here from 1626 until 1943. Regular 'Living History' programme - Meet George Browne c1900.

Location: OS Ref. NY407 020. 3m SE of Ambleside at S end of Troutbeck village. 1m from Holehird, 3m N of Windermere.

Opening Times: 2 Apr - 31 Oct: Tue - Fri, Suns & BH Mons, 1 - 5pm or dusk if earlier. Last admission 4.30pm.

Admission: Adult £3, Child £1.50, Family £7.50. No reduction for groups which must be pre-booked. Townend and village unsuitable for coaches; 12 - 15 seater mini-buses are acceptable; permission to take coaches to Townend must be obtained from the Transportation and Highways Dept, Cumbria CC, Carlisle, Cumbria.

♿ Unsuitable for wheelchairs. Braille guide. 🐾

WORDSWORTH HOUSE ⚜

Tel: 01900 824805

Main Street, Cockermouth, Cumbria CA13 9RX   **e-mail:** rwordh@smtp.ntrust.org.uk

Owner: The National Trust   **Contact:** The Custodian

See full page advertisement on page 24   **e-mail:** wordh@smpt.ntrust.org.uk

A Georgian town house where William Wordsworth was born in 1770 in the ancient market town of Cockermouth. Several rooms contain some of the poet's personal effects. His childhood garden, with terraced walk attractively restored, with views over the River Derwent referred to in 'The Prelude'. Kitchen garden under restoration.

Location: OS Ref. NY118 307. Main Street, Cockermouth.

Opening Times: 2 Apr - 2 Nov: weekdays only, plus all BH Sats and Sats in Jun, Jul & Aug, 10.30am - 4.30pm. Last admission 4pm.

Admission: Adult £3, Child £1.50, Family £7.50. Pre-booked groups £2.20. Reciprocal discount ticket with Dove Cottage and Rydal Mount.

📷 ♿ By arrangement only. ☕ 🅿 No parking. 🐾 🌐

WORKINGTON HALL

Tel: 01900 326408

Ramsey Brow, Workington, Cumbria

Owner: Allerdale Borough Council   **Contact:** Allerdale Borough Council Tourism Dept.

Refuge for Mary Queen of Scots during her last night of freedom in May 1568, this was one of the finest Manor houses in the region. Now a ruin.

Location: OS Ref. NY007 288. In public park on N side of A66

Opening Times: Easter - Oct: Tue - Fri & BHs, 10am - 1pm & 2 - 5pm, Sats & Suns 2 - 5pm.

Admission: Adult 85p, Conc. 55p, Family (2+2/1+3) £2.25.

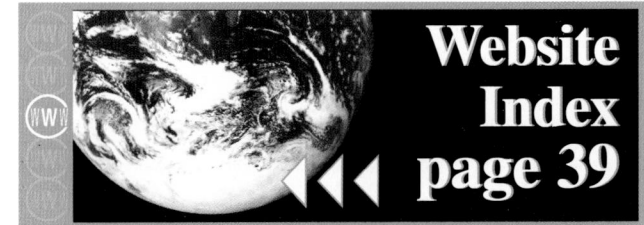

Website Index page 39 ◀◀◀

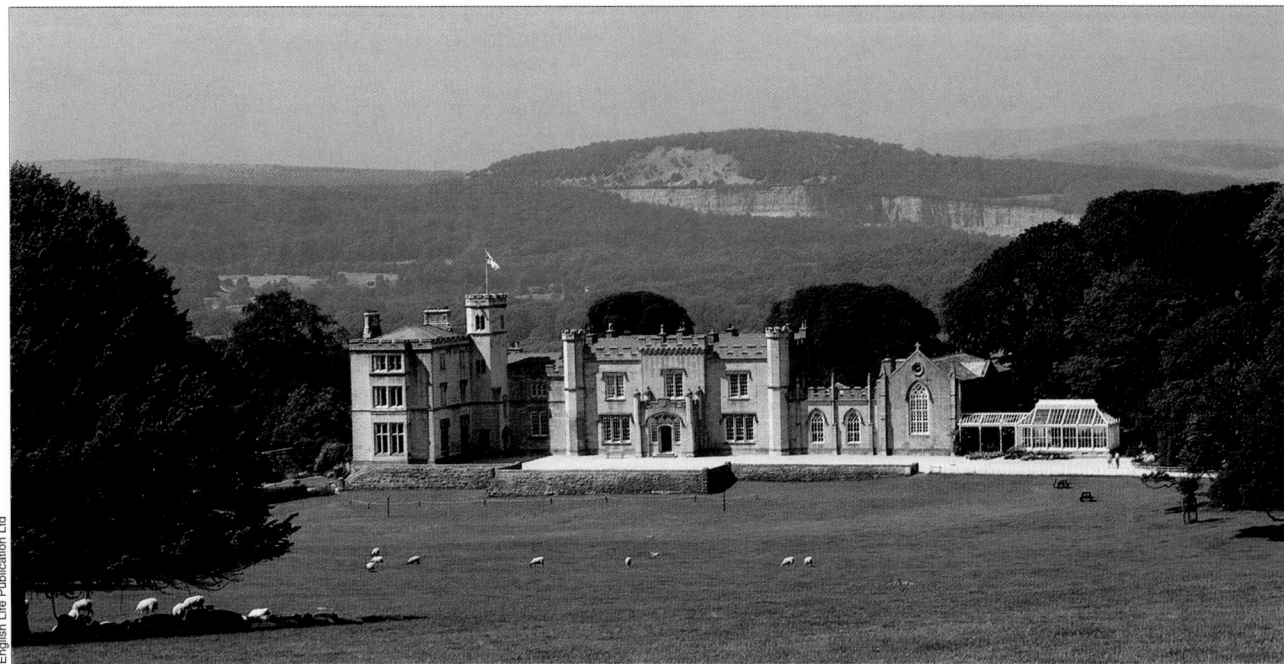

English Life Publication Ltd

LEIGHTON HALL
Carnforth

LEIGHTON HALL is one of the most beautifully sited houses in the British Isles, situated in a bowl of parkland, with the whole panorama of the Lakeland Fells rising behind. The hall's neo-gothic façade was superimposed on an 18th century house, which, in turn, had been built on the ruins of the original medieval house. The present owner is descended from Adam d'Avranches who built the first house in 1246.

The whole house is lived in by the Reynolds family and emphasis is put on making visitors feel welcome in a family home.

Connoisseurs of furniture will be particularly interested in the 18th century pieces by Gillow of Lancaster. Mr Reynolds is directly descended from the founder of Gillow and Company, hence the strong Gillow connection with the house. Also on show are some fine pictures, clocks, silver and *objets d'art.*

GARDENS
The main garden has a continuous herbaceous border and rose covered walls, while the Walled Garden contains flowering shrubs, a herb garden, an ornamental vegetable garden and a maze. Beyond is the Woodland Walk, where wild flowers abound from early Spring.

A varied collection of Birds of Prey is on display in the Bird Garden, and flown each afternoon that the hall is open, weather permitting.

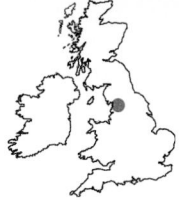

Owner:
Richard Gillow
Reynolds Esq

CONTACT
Mrs C S Reynolds
Leighton Hall
Carnforth
Lancashire
LA5 9ST

Tel: 01524 734474

Fax: 01524 720357

e-mail: leightonhall@
yahoo.co.uk

LOCATION
OS Ref. SD494 744
9m N of Lancaster,
10m S of Kendal,
3m N of Carnforth.
1¹/₂ m W of A6.
3m from M6/A6/J35,
signed from J35A.

Rail: Lancaster
Station 9m.

Air: Manchester
Airport 65m.

Taxi: Carnforth Radio
Taxis, Carnforth 732763.

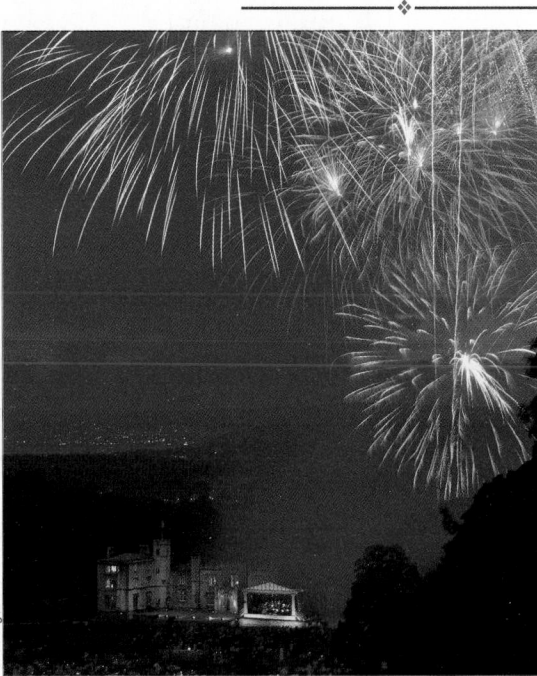

Performing Arts

CONFERENCE/FUNCTION		
ROOM	SIZE	MAX CAPACITY
Music Room	24' x 21'6"	80
Dining Rm		30
Other		80

Product launches, seminars, filming, garden parties, conferences, rallies, overland driving, archery and clay pigeon shoots, grand piano. No photography in house. Large collection of birds of prey on display in the afternoon, some of which fly at 3.30pm, weather permitting.

Buffets, lunches, dinners and wedding receptions.

Partially suitable. WC. Visitors may alight at the entrance.

Groups must book, menus on request.

Obligatory. By prior arrangement owner may meet groups, tour time: 45 mins. House and flying display tour time: 2 hrs. Lectures on property, its contents, gardens and history.

Ample.

School programme 10am-2pm daily May-Sept except Mons & Sats. Birds of prey flown for schools at 12pm. Schools Visit Programme won the Sandford Award for Heritage Education in 1983 and in 1989.

In grounds, on leads.

OPENING TIMES
SUMMER
1 May - 30 September
Daily except Mons & Sats
2 - 5pm. Open BH Mons.

August only:
12.30 - 5pm.
NB. Booked groups (25+)
at any time by
arrangement.

WINTER
1 October - 30 April
Open to booked
groups (25+).

ADMISSION
SUMMER
House, Garden & Birds
Adult £4.50
Child (5-12yrs)..........£3.00
OAP.......................£4.00
Groups (Min. payment £80)
Adult £3.50
Child (5-12yrs)..........£3.00
Family (2+3) £13.00
School £2.75

Children under 5yrs Free

Grounds only
(after 4.30pm)
Per person £1.50

WINTER
As above but groups by
appointment only.

SPECIAL EVENTS
- **JUL 6:**
  Concert & Fireworks:
  'Last Night of the Proms'.
- **JUL 22:**
  Classic Car Rally.
- **AUG 3 - 4:**
  Shakespeare in the Garden:
  'Henry V'.
- **SEPT 8 - 9:**
  Rainbow Craft Fair.
- **OCT 13:**
  Teddy Bear Fair.
- **OCT 14:**
  Dolls House & Miniaturist Fair.

North West England

ASTLEY HALL

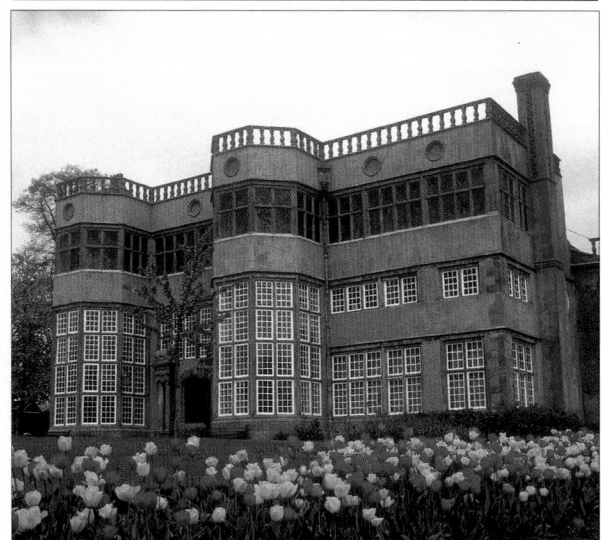

ASTLEY PARK, OFF HALL GATE, CHORLEY PR7 1NP

Owner: Chorley Borough Council *Contact: Dr Nigel Wright*

Tel: 01257 515555 **Fax:** 01257 515556 **e-mail:** astleyhall@lineone.net

A charming house, dating back to 1580, with additions in the 1660s and 1820s. Interiors include sumptuous plaster ceilings, fine 17th century oak furniture and tapestries, plus displays of fine and decorative art. Set in parkland.

Location: OS Ref. SD574 183. 2m W of Chorley, off A581 Chorley - Southport road. 5 mins from M61/J8.

Opening Times: Easter - end Oct: Tue - Sun, 12 noon - 5pm. Plus BH Mons. Nov - Easter: weekends only, 12 noon - 4pm. Closed Christmas & New Year.

Admission: Adult £2.90, Child/Conc. £1.90. Groups: Adult £2.30, Child/Conc. £1.30.

No photography. Partially suitable. Braille guide. By arrangement. Guide dogs only.

BLACKBURN CATHEDRAL

Tel: 01254 51491 **Fax:** 01254 689666

Cathedral Close, Blackburn, Lancashire BB1 5AA **Contact:** Mrs Alison Feeney

On an historic Saxon site in town centre. The 1826 Parish Church dedicated as the Cathedral in 1977 with new extensions to give a spacious and light interior. The distinctive 'crowning glory' Lantern Tower was rebuilt in 1998 with 56 panels of newly-designed symbolic stained glass to give a new and unique magnificence by day and night. Other features include a fine Walker organ, 12 peal bells and a 'corona' (crown of thorns) above the central altar.

Location: OS Ref. SD684 280. 9m E of M6/J31, via A59 and A677. City centre.

Opening Times: Daily, 9am - 5pm. Sun services: at 8am, 9.15am, 10.30am and 4pm.

Admission: Free. Donations invited.

Wheelchair access. Wed & Fri, 10am - 2.30pm or Sats by arrangement. By arrangement. Nearby shopping centre.

BROWSHOLME HALL

Tel: 01254 826719 **Fax:** 01254 826739

Clitheroe, Lancashire BB7 3DE

Owner/Contact: Mr R R Parker

Built in 1507 and set in a landscaped park, the ancestral home of the Parker family.

Location: OS Ref. SD683 452. 5m NW of Clitheroe off B6243.

Opening Times: Spring Bank Hol. weekend. 1 - 14 July (except Mons). 14 Aug - Aug BH Mon (except other Mons), 2 - 4.30pm. Groups at other times by appointment.

Admission: Adult £4, Child £1. Pre-arranged groups: Adult £3.70, Child £2.

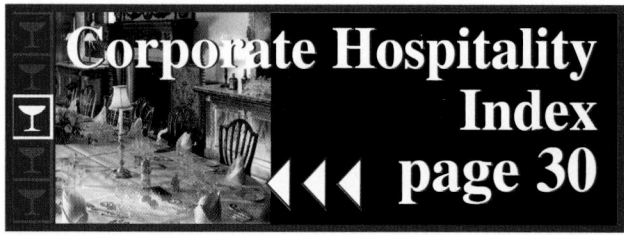

Corporate Hospitality Index ◀◀◀ ◀ page 30

GAWTHORPE HALL

Tel: 01282 771004 **Fax:** 01282 770178

Padiham, Nr Burnley, Lancashire BB12 8UA

Owner: The National Trust **Contact:** The Property Manager

The house was built in 1600-05, and restored by Sir Charles Barry in the 1850s. Barry's designs have been re-created in the principal rooms. Gawthorpe was the home of the Shuttleworth family, and the Rachel Kay-Shuttleworth textile collections are on display in the house, private study by arrangement. Collection of portraits on loan from the National Portrait Gallery.

Location: OS Ref. SD806 340. M65/J8. On E outskirts of Padiham, 3/4 m to house on N of A671. Signed to Clitheroe, then signed from 2nd set of traffic lights.

Opening Times: Hall: 31 Mar - 31 Oct: daily except Mons & Fris, open Good Fri & BH Mons, 1 - 5pm. Last adm. 4.30pm. Garden: All year: daily, 10am - 6pm.

Admission: Hall: Adult £3, Child £1.30, Conc. £1.50, Family £8 (prices may change). Garden: Free. Groups must book.

Prior warning of visit essential. In grounds on leads.

HALL I'TH'WOOD

Tel: 01204 332370

off Green Way, Tonge Moor, Bolton BL1 8UA

Owner: Bolton Metropolitan Borough Council **Contact:** W H Farrell

Late medieval manor house with 17/18th century furniture, paintings and decorative art.

Location: OS Ref. SD724 116. 2m NNE of central Bolton. 1/4 m N of A58 ring road between A666 and A676 crossroads.

Opening Times: Please contact for details.

Admission: Adult £3, Conc. £1.50.

HOGHTON TOWER

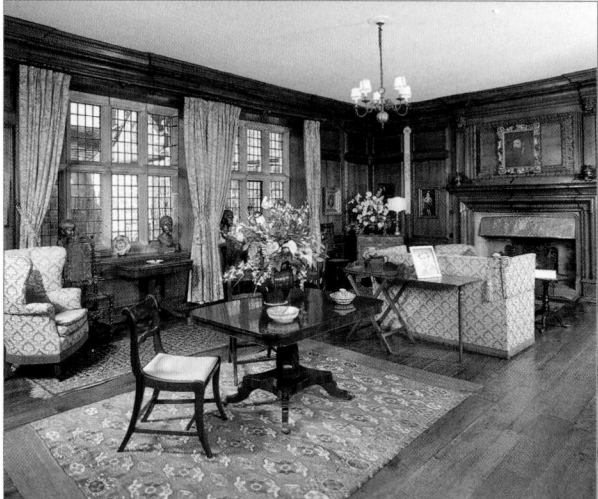

HOGHTON, PRESTON, LANCASHIRE PR5 0SH

Owner: Sir Bernard de Hoghton Bt *Contact: Office*

Tel: 01254 852986 **Fax:** 01254 852109

Hoghton Tower, home of 14th Baronet, is one of the most dramatic looking houses in northern England. Three houses have occupied the hill site since 1100 with the present house re-built by Thomas Hoghton between 1560 - 1565. Rich and varied historical events including the Knighting of the Loin 'Sirloin' by James I in 1617.

Location: OS Ref. SD622 264. M65/J3. Midway between Preston & Blackburn on A675.

Opening Times: Jul, Aug & Sept: Mon - Thur, 11am - 4pm. Suns, 1 - 5pm. BH Suns & Mons excluding Christmas & New Year. Group visits by appointment all year.

Admission: House tours: Adult £3, Child/Conc. £2, Family £8. Gardens, Shop & Tearoom only: £2. Private tours by arrangement (25 min) £6, OAP £5.

Conferences, wedding receptions. Not suitable. Obligatory.

LEIGHTON HALL

See page 417 for full page entry.

MANCHESTER CATHEDRAL

Tel: 0161 833 2220 **Fax:** 0161 839 6226

Manchester M3 1SX

In addition to regular worship and daily offices, there are frequent professional concerts, day schools, organ recitals, guided tours and brass-rubbing. The cathedral contains a wealth of beautiful carvings and has the widest medieval nave in Britain.

Location: OS Ref. SJ838 988. Manchester.

Opening Times: Daily.

Admission: Donations welcome.

MARTHOLME

Great Harwood, Blackburn, Lancashire BB6 7UJ

Owner: Mr & Mrs T H Codling   **Contact:** Miss P M Codling

Part of medieval manor house with 17th century additions and Elizabethan gatehouse.

Location: OS Ref. SD753 338. 2m NE of Great Harwood off A680 to Whalley.

Opening Times: Groups (8+) by written appointment only.

Admission: £3.50.

ROSSENDALE MUSEUM

Tel: 01706 217777 or 01706 226509

Whitaker Park, Rawtenstall, Rossendale, Lancashire BB4 6RE

Owner: Rossendale Borough Council   **Contact:** Mrs S Cruise

Former 19th century mill owner's house set in Whitaker Park. Displays include fine and decorative arts and furniture.

Location: OS Ref. SD805 226. Off A681, ¹/₄ m from Rawtenstall Centre.

Opening Times: Apr - Oct: Mon - Fri, 1 - 5pm, Sats, 10am - 5pm, Suns, 12 noon - 5pm. Nov - Mar: Mon - Fri, 1 - 5pm, Sats, 10am - 4pm, Suns, 12 noon - 4pm. BHs, 1 - 5pm. Closed Christmas Day, Boxing Day and New Year's Day.

Admission: Free.

SAMLESBURY HALL

Tel: 01254 812010 **Fax:** 01254 812174

Preston New Road, Samlesbury, Preston PR5 0UP

Owner: Samlesbury Hall Trust   **Contact:** Mr David Hornby

Built in 1325, the hall is an attractive black and white timbered manor house set in extensive grounds.

Location: OS Ref. SD623 305. N side of A677, 4m WNW of Blackburn.

Opening Times: All year: daily except Mons: 11am - 4.30pm. Closed over Christmas and New Year.

Admission: Adult £2.50, Child £1.

SMITHILLS HALL MUSEUM

Tel: 01204 332377

Smithills Dean Road, Bolton BL1 7NP

Owner: Bolton Metropolitan Borough Council   **Contact:** Linda McKay

14th century fortified manor house with Tudor panelling. Stuart furniture. Stained glass.

Location: OS Ref. SD699 119. 2m NW of central Bolton, ¹/₂ m N of A58 ringroad.

Opening Times: Please contact for details.

Admission: Adult £3, Conc. £1.50.

STONYHURST COLLEGE

Tel: 01254 826345 **Fax:** 01254 826732

Stonyhurst, Clitheroe, Lancashire BB7 9PZ   **Contact:** Miss F Ahearne

The original house dates from the late 16th century. Set in extensive grounds.

Location: OS Ref. SD690 391. 4m SW of Clitheroe off B6243.

Opening Times: House: 16 Jul - 27 Aug: Sat - Thur (including Aug BH Mon), 1 - 5pm. Grounds & Gardens: 1 Jul - 27 Aug: Sat - Thur (including Aug BH Mon), 1 - 5pm.

Admission: House & Grounds: Adult £4.50, Child (4-14yrs)/OAP £3.50. Grounds only £1.

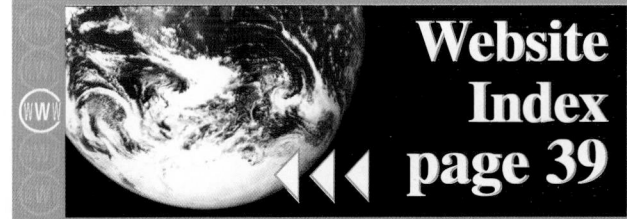

Website Index page 39

RUFFORD OLD HALL

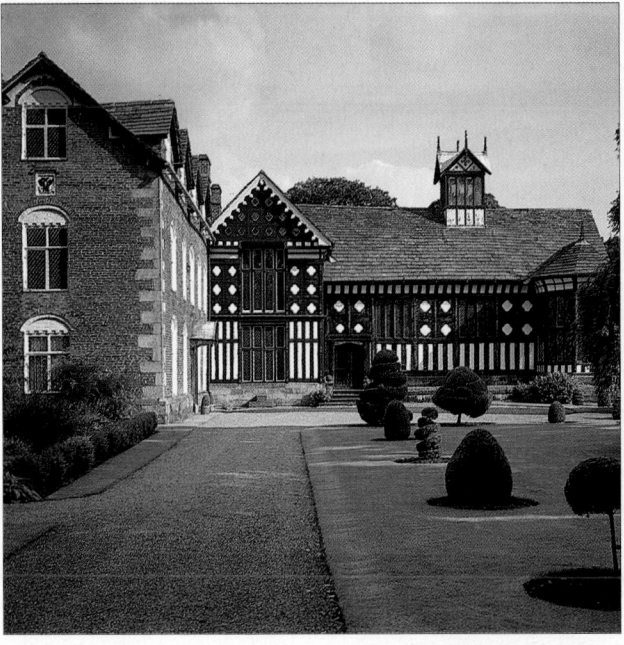

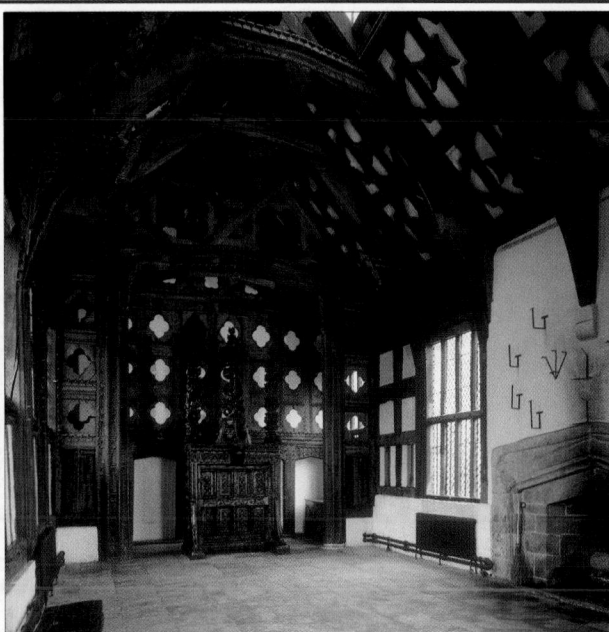

RUFFORD, Nr ORMSKIRK, LANCASHIRE L40 1SG

Owner: *The National Trust*   **Contact:** *The Property Manager*

Tel: 01704 821254

There is a legend that William Shakespeare performed here for the owner Sir Thomas Hesketh in the Great Hall of this, one of the finest 16th century buildings in Lancashire. The playwright would have delighted in the magnificent hall with its intricately carved movable wooden screen. Built in 1530, it established the Hesketh family seat for the next 250 years. In the Carolean Wing, altered in 1821, there are fine collections of 16th and 17th century oak furniture, arms, armour and tapestries. An audio tour is available to guide visitors around the house. The attractive garden includes sculpture and topiary.

Location: OS Ref. SD463 160. 7m N of Ormskirk, in village of Rufford on E side of A59.

Opening Times: 31 Mar - 4 Nov: Sat - Wed, 1 - 5pm. Last admission 4.30pm. Garden: same days as house, 12 noon - 5.30pm.

Admission: House & Garden: Adult £3.80, Child £1.90, Family £9.50. Garden only: £2. Pre-booked groups £2.60 (no groups on Suns & BH Mons).

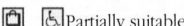 Partially suitable. In grounds, on leads.

TOWNELEY HALL ART GALLERY & MUSEUMS

Burnley BB11 3RQ   **Tel:** 01282 424213 **Fax:** 01282 436138
Owner: Burnley Borough Council   **Contact:** Miss Susan Bourne
House dates from the 14th century with 17th and 19th century modifications. Collections
include oak furniture, 18th and 19th century paintings. There is a Museum of Local Crafts
and Industries and a Natural History Centre with an aquarium in the grounds.
Location: OS Ref. SD854 309. ¹/₂ m SE of Burnley on E side of Todmorden Road (A671).
Opening Times: All year: Mon - Fri, 10am - 5pm. Suns, 12 noon - 5pm. Closed Sats. Closed
Christmas - New Year.
Admission: Free. Guided tours: Tues, Weds & Thurs afternoons or as booked for parties.

⬜ ♿Ground floor & grounds suitable. WC. ▣ 🕴 🛡 Tel. for details.
❄ (W)

TURTON TOWER

                 Tel: 01204 852203 **Fax:** 01204 853759
Chapeltown Road, Turton BL7 0HG
Owner: Lancashire County Council   **Contact:** Martin Robinson-Dowland
Country house based on a medieval tower, extended in the 16th, 17th and 19th centuries.
Location: OS Ref. SD733 153. On B6391, 4m N of Bolton.
Opening Times: Feb & Nov: Suns, 1 - 4pm. Mar & Oct: Sat - Wed, 1 - 4pm. Apr: Sat - Wed,
2 - 5pm. May - Sept: Mon - Thur, 10am - 12 noon, 1 - 5pm. Sats & Suns 1 - 5pm.
Admission: Adult £3, Child/OAP £1.50, Family £8. Season ticket available.

WARTON OLD RECTORY ⌗

                 Tel: 0161 242 1400
Warton, Carnforth, Lancashire
Owner: English Heritage   **Contact:** The Regional Office
A rare medieval stone house with remains of the hall, chambers and domestic offices.
Location: OS Ref. SD499 723. At Warton, 1m N of Carnforth on minor road off A6.
Opening Times: Any reasonable time.
Admission: Free.

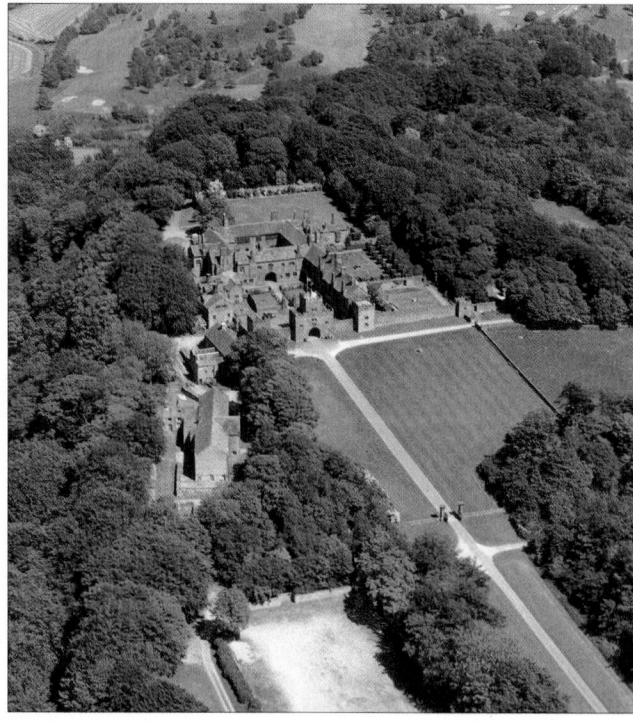

Hoghton Tower, Lancashire.

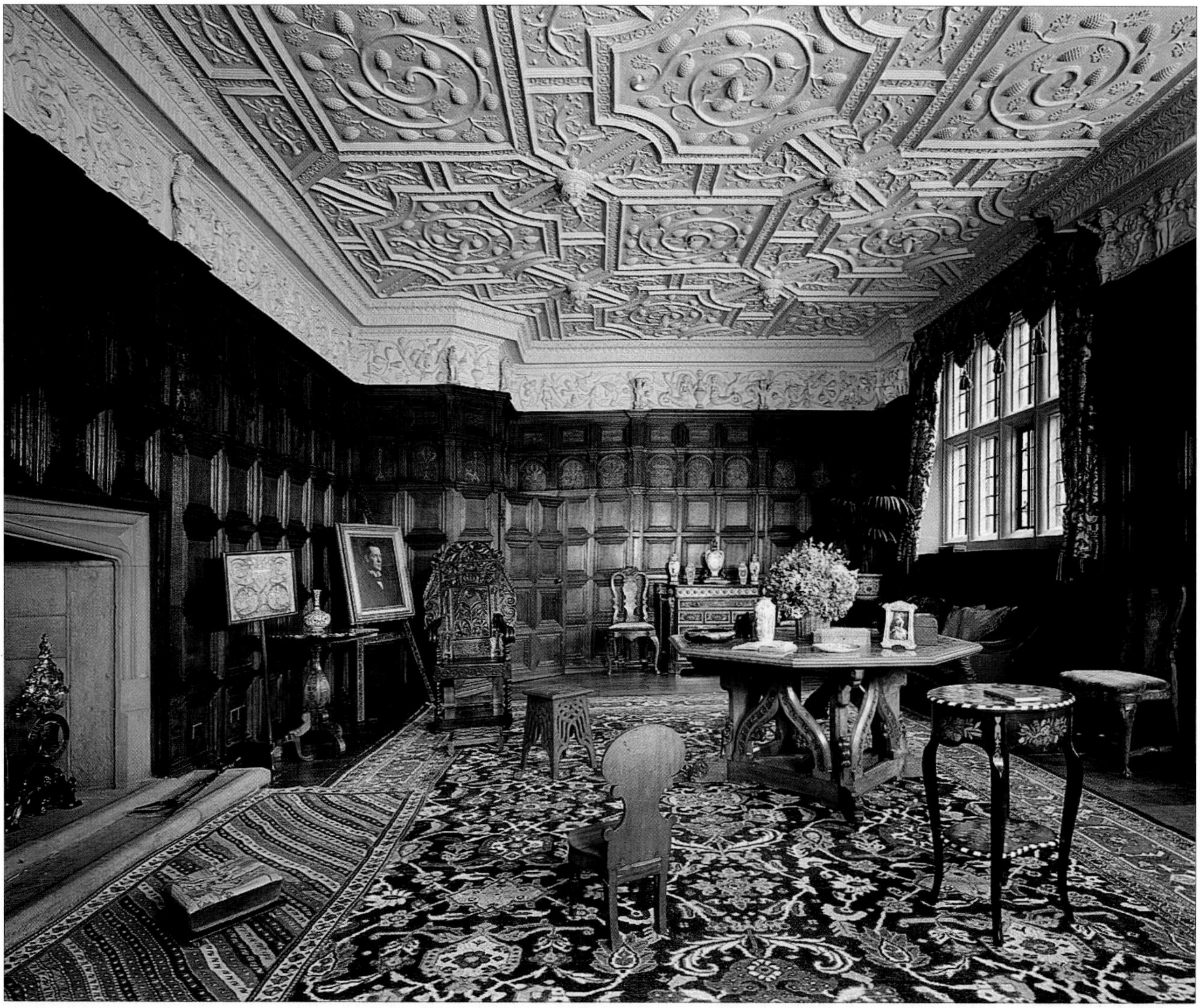

Gawthorpe Hall, Lancashire.

BLUECOAT ARTS CENTRE

Tel: 0151 709 5297 **Fax:** 0151 707 0048
e-mail: admin@bluecoatartscentre.com

Bluecoat Chambers, School Lane, Liverpool L1 3BX

Owner: Bluecoat Arts Centre Ltd   **Contact:** Building Manager

Built in 1717, the Bluecoat is of outstanding historical and architectural interest, with Grade I listed building status, and is a popular tourist attraction in the heart of Liverpool. The oldest building in the city centre, and now, arguably the oldest arts centre in Britain, it is one of the most exciting arts venues in the region with an impressive Queen Anne style façade and walled garden. The unique mix of exhibitions and performances, café and shops, including local history, books and crafts and collectors' fairs offers visitors an alternative experience in the city.

Location: OS Ref. SJ346 902. $^1/_4$ m S of Lime Street station.

Opening Times: Mon - Sat, 9.30am - 6pm (unless there is an evening performance, outside hire or exhibition opening). Gallery closed Mons.

Admission: Free admission to Building and Gallery, with varying prices for the Performing Arts events.

Partially suitable. WC.

CROXTETH HALL & COUNTRY PARK   **Tel:** 0151 228 5311 **Fax:** 0151 228 2817

Liverpool, Merseyside L12 0HB

Owner: Liverpool City Council   **Contact:** Mrs Irene Vickers

Ancestral home of the Molyneux family. 500 acres country park. Special events and attractions most weekends.

Location: OS Ref. SJ408 943. 5m NE of Liverpool city centre.

Opening Times: Parkland: daily throughout the year. Hall, Farm & Garden: daily, 11am - 5pm during main season. Telephone for exact dates.

Admission: Parkland: Free. Hall, Farm & Garden: prices on application.

LIVERPOOL CATHEDRAL

Tel: 0151 709 6271 **Fax:** 0151 709 1112

Liverpool, Merseyside L1 7AZ

Owner: The Dean and Chapter   **Contact:** Canon Noel Vincent

Sir Giles Gilbert Scott's greatest creation. Built this century from local sandstone with superb glass, stonework and major works of art, it is the largest cathedral in Britain and has a fine musical tradition, a tower offering panoramic views, and an award-winning refectory. There is a unique collection of church embroidery, and SPCK shop with a full range of souvenirs, cards and religious books.

Location: OS Ref. SJ354 893. Central Liverpool, $^1/_2$ m S of Lime Street Station.

Opening Times: 8am - 6pm. Sun services: 8am, 10.30am, 3pm, 4pm. Weekdays: 8am & 5.30pm. Sats: 8am & 3pm.

Admission: Donation. Lift to Tower and Embroidery Exhibition: £2.

Grounds suitable. WC. Guide dogs only.

LIVERPOOL METROPOLITAN CATHEDRAL OF CHRIST THE KING

Liverpool, Merseyside L3 5TQ   **Tel:** 0151 709 9222 **Fax:** 0151 708 7274
e-mail: met.cathedral@cwcom.net

Owner: Roman Catholic Archdiocese of Liverpool   **Contact:** Rt Rev P Cookson

Modern circular cathedral with spectacular glass by John Piper and numerous modern works of art. Extensive earlier crypt by Lutyens. Grade II* listed.

Location: OS Ref. SJ356 903. Central Liverpool, $^1/_2$ m E of Lime Street Station.

Opening Times: 8am - 6pm (closes 5pm Suns in Winter). Sun services: 8.30am, 10am, 11am, 3pm & 7pm. Weekday services: 8am, 12.15pm, 5.15pm & 5.45pm. Sats, 9am & 6.30pm.

Admission: Donation.

Except crypt. WCs. By arrangement. Ample for cars. Guide dogs only.

MEOLS HALL

Tel: 01704 228326 **Fax:** 01704 507185

Churchtown, Southport, Merseyside PR9 7LZ

Owner: Robert Hesketh Esq   **Contact:** Pamela Whelan

17th century house with subsequent additions. Interesting collection of pictures and furniture.

Location: OS Ref. SD365 184. 3m NE of Southport town centre in Churchtown. SE of A565.

Opening Times: 14 Aug - 14 Sept: daily, 2 - 5pm.

Admission: Adult £3, Child £1. Groups £8.50 (inclusive of afternoon tea).

PORT SUNLIGHT VILLAGE & HERITAGE CENTRE

Tel: 0151 6446466 **Fax:** 0151 6458973

95 Greendale Road, Port Sunlight CH62 4XE   **Contact:** The Centre

Port Sunlight is a picturesque 19th century garden village on the Wirral.

Location: OS Ref. SJ340 845. Follow signs from M53/J4 or 5 or follow signs on A41.

Opening Times: All year, 10am - 4pm in summer; 11am - 4pm in winter.

Admission: Adult 60p, Child 30p, Conc. 50p. Group rates on application.

SPEKE HALL GARDEN & ESTATE   **Tel:** 0151 427 7231 **Fax:** 0151 427 9860

The Walk, Liverpool L24 1XD   **Info Line:** 0345 585702 (local rate)

Owner: The National Trust   **Contact:** The Property Manager

One of the most famous half-timbered houses in the country.

Location: OS Ref. SJ419 825. North bank of the Mersey, 6m SE of city centre. Follow signs for Liverpool airport.

Opening Times: House: 28 Mar - 29 Oct: daily except Mons & Tues (open BH Mons), 1 - 5.30pm. 4 Nov - 10 Dec: Sats & Suns, 1 - 4.30pm. Woodland & Garden: 28 Mar - 29 Oct: Daily except Mons (open BH Mons) from 12 noon. Nov - Mar 2000: daily except Mons, 12 noon - 4pm. Closed Good Fri, 24/25/26/31 Dec & 1 Jan. Last admission 30 mins before close.

Admission: Estate: £2.50 per car (refunded when when garden or house ticket purchased). Garden: £2pp. House & Garden: £4.50. Family £12.

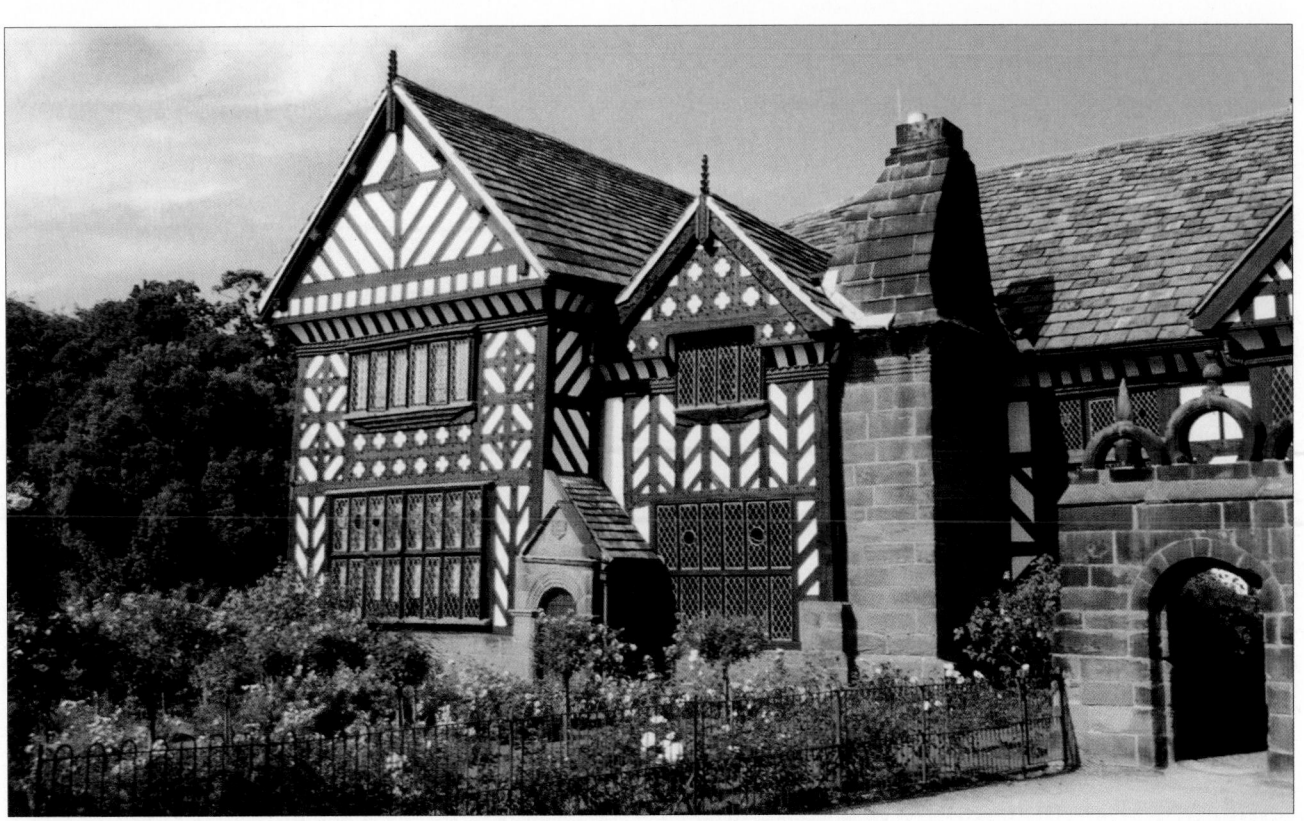

Speke Hall, Merseyside.

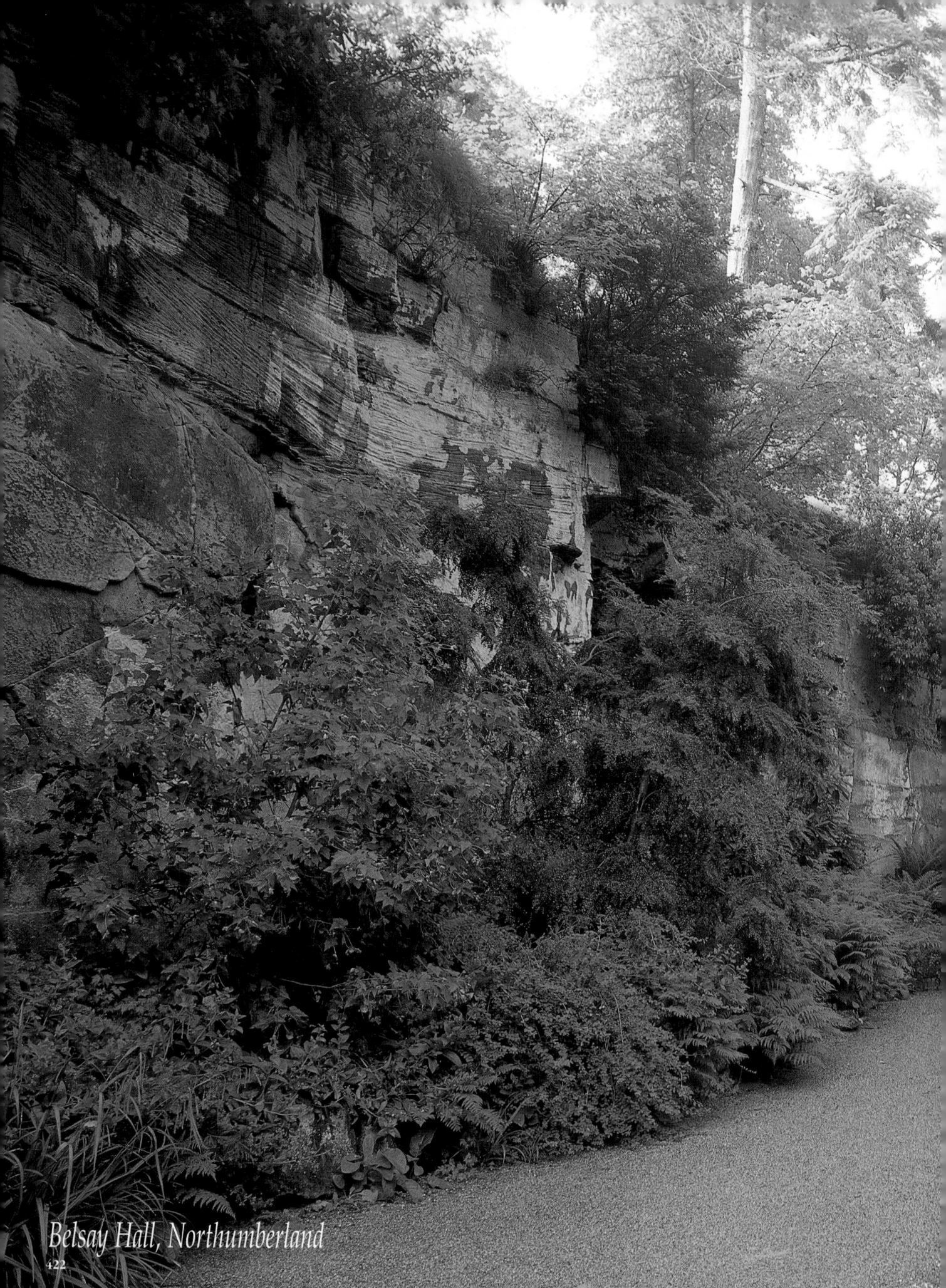

Belsay Hall, Northumberland

North East

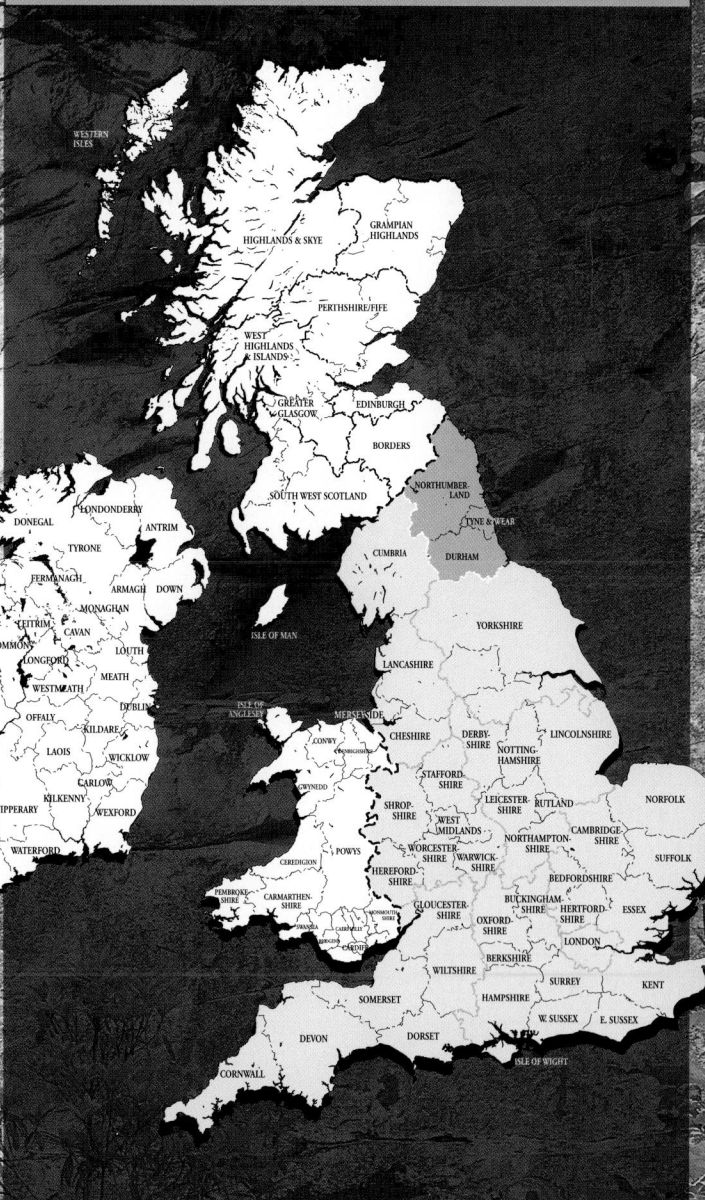

Belsay Hall

"At Belsay, a 12th century castle, 17th century manor house and an early 19th century hall, are surrounded by 30 acres of landscaped grounds. These contain a number of period garden features, one of them unique. The architectural style, period and surrounding terrain of a house inevitably influence the design of its garden. At Belsay, it was a by-product of the actual building of the house which triggered the creation of the extraordinary quarry garden that can be seen today.

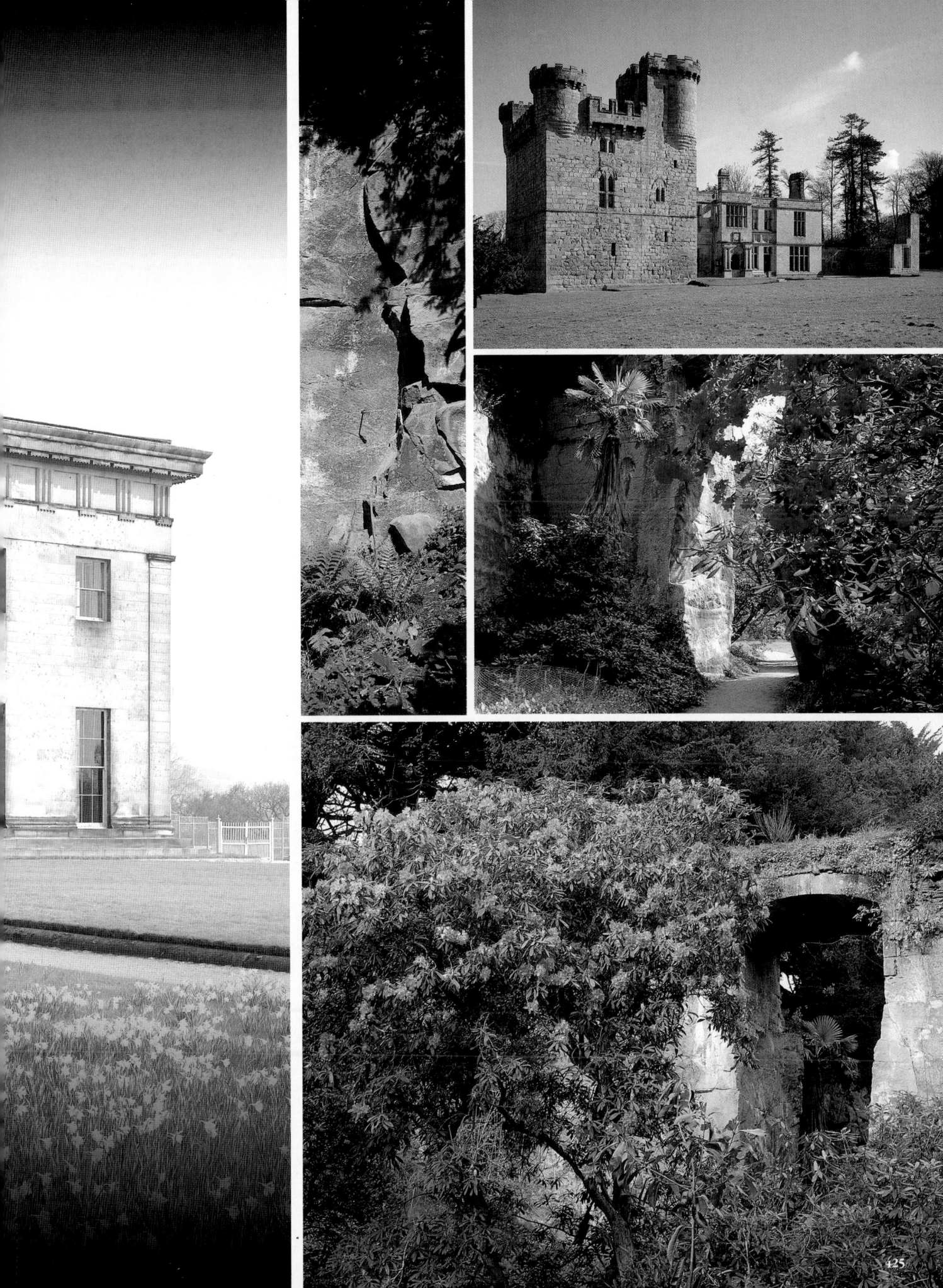

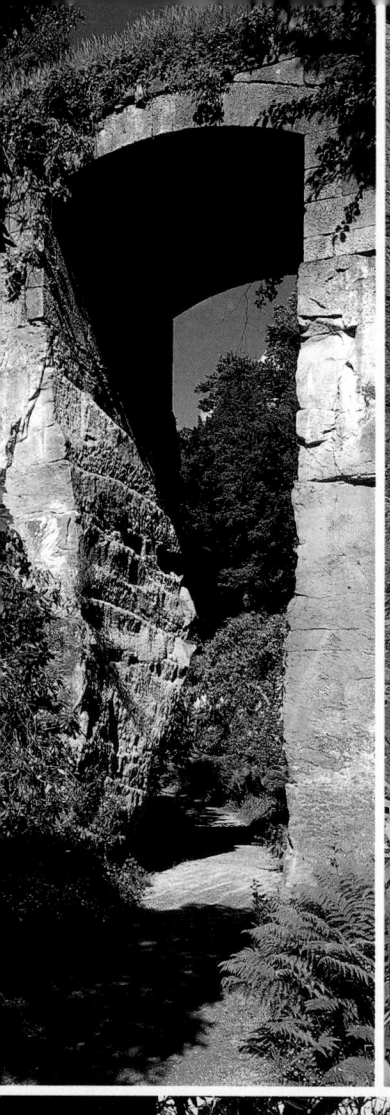

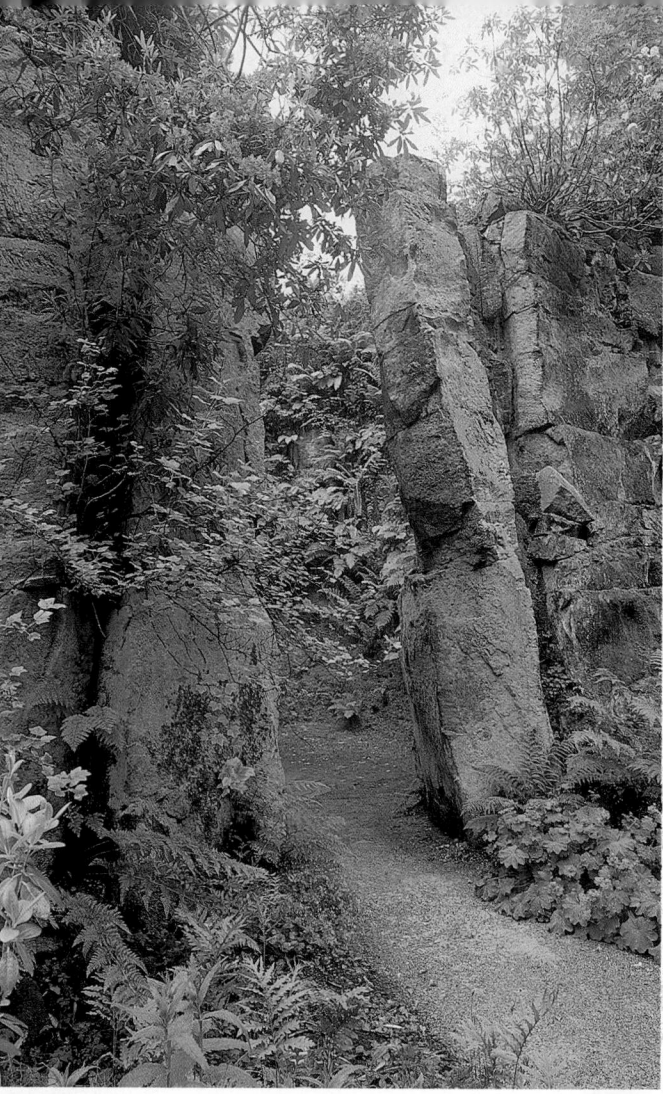

Belsay Hall is a Greek Revival mansion built, between 1810 and 1817, by its owner Sir Charles Monck, a keen classicist and talented draughtsman. Exactly 100' square, harsh and symmetrical in style, it was built of stone quarried from the grounds. The resulting ravine left by the quarrying was transformed by Sir Charles into a unique landscape inspired by the theories of the Picturesque.

The Picturesque was a reaction to the softness of the landscapes of 'Capability' Brown – it sought to be much rougher, exciting and dramatic. The quarry garden at Belsay is the prime example of this style. A man-made landscape, finished to look natural, then planted with exotic plants in such a way to make them seem natural too.

Other Picturesque scenes can be found, but it is the Quarry Garden's sheer scale and treatment which puts it in a class of its own, and it is this that enchants visitors to Belsay.

You are drawn into the Quarry Garden along a narrow, weaving path. This narrowing corridor is flanked on either side by sheer rock faces – sombre, raw and uncompromising. The ravine's height is exaggerated by the line of yews and Scots pines towering 70' above. The atmosphere is secluded and still. Glossy and feathery ferns grow out of rocky crevices at unusual angles. The two rock faces are finally linked by a great arch and beyond this the quarry opens out into a clearing, ringed by cliffs and rock pinnacles. In this sunnier more open space rhododendrons, up to 30'-40' high, flower in vivid and spectacular profusion in the early spring.

The path eventually emerges into pasture land, with the remains of the 12th century castle forming a wonderful eye-catcher. To emerge from the shade and damp of the ravine into the open meadows is an extraordinarily refreshing finale to this spectacular and captivating walk.

English Heritage have, at Belsay, buildings and gardens which are the very essence of the early 19th century Romantic taste for primitive style and wild nature – they provide a memorable and exhilarating visit and are deservedly listed Grade I in the Register of Gardens. ✳

For further details about *Belsay Hall* see entry in North East Region ➔ Northumberland.

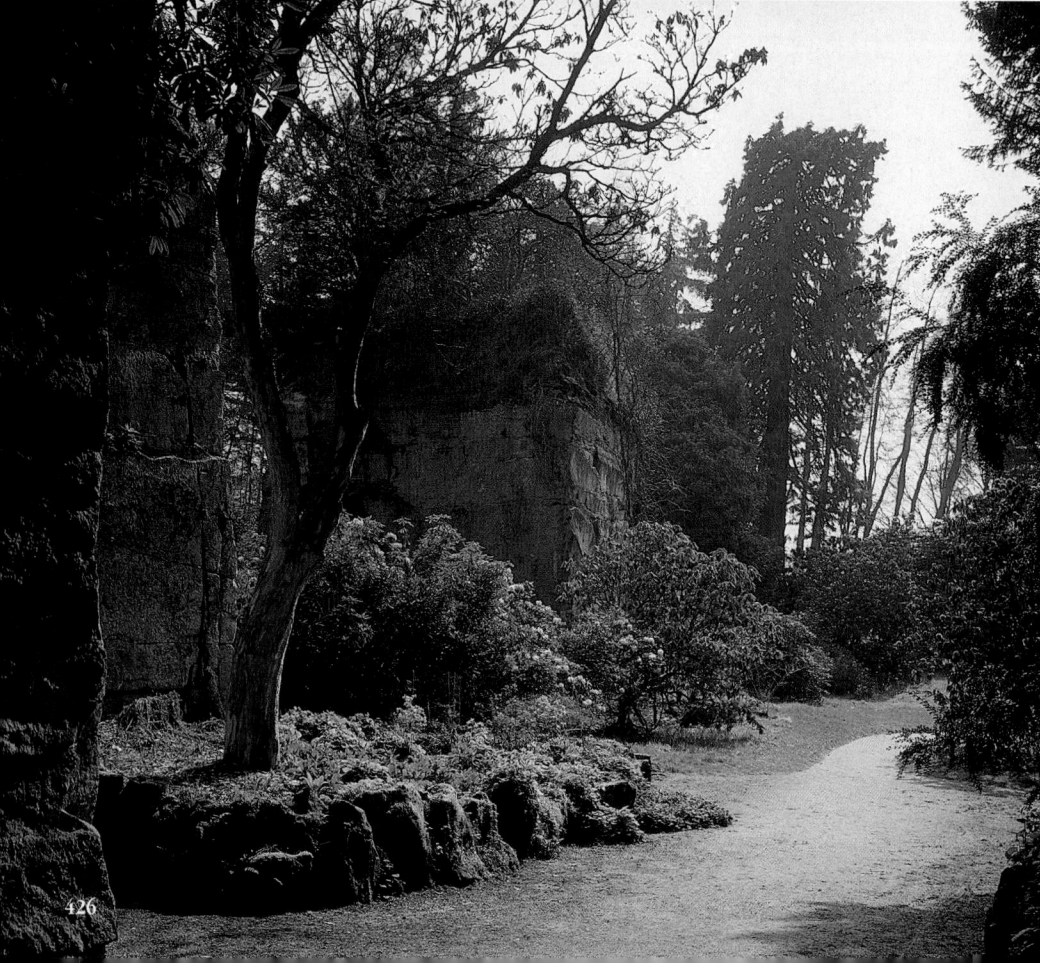

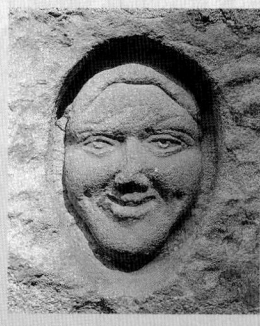

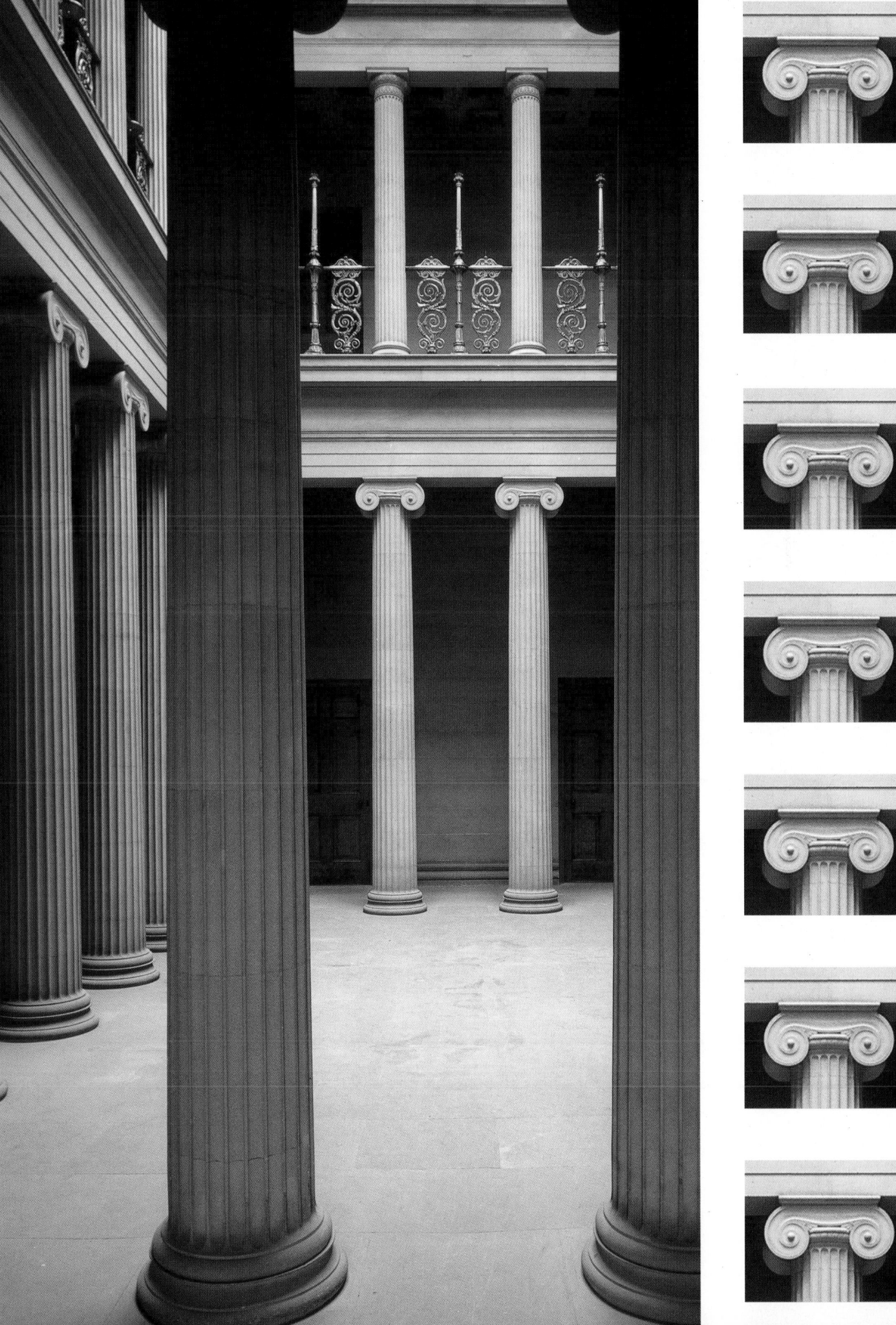

North East England

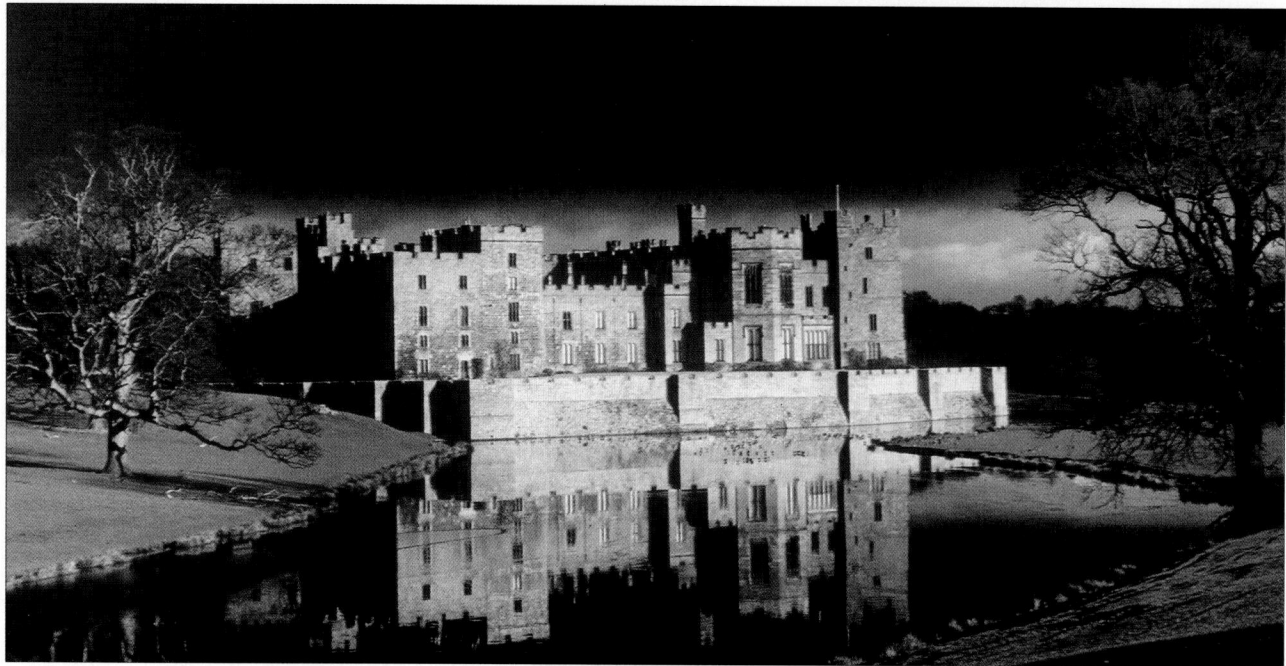

Lord Barnard

RABY CASTLE
Darlington

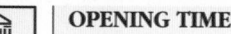

Raby is without doubt one of the most impressive lived in castles in England. Built mainly in the 14th century by the Nevill family on the site of an earlier manor house, it remained in their ownership until 1569. Since 1626 to the present day it has been the home of the Vane family. It was the childhood home of Cicely, Rose of Raby, mother of Kings Edward IV and Richard III, scene of the Plotting of the Rising of the North and a Parliamentary stronghold during the Civil War.

Despite its medieval exterior, Raby houses a fabulous art collection and sumptuous interiors. Treasures include one of the nation's most important collections of Meissen porcelain, tapestries, furniture, furnishings and paintings by De Hooch, Herring, Reynolds, Teniers, and Van Dyck.

Raby Castle is situated amidst a 200-acre Deer Park in the foothills of the North Pennines, where Red and Fallow Deer and Longhorn Cattle graze. Beautiful walled gardens with formal lawns, rose gardens and ornamental pond frame picturesque views of the Castle. The 18th century stable block contains a horse-drawn carriage collection and an Adventure Playground near the Stable Tearooms and Gift Shop means that Raby has something for everyone to enjoy.

Owner: The Lord Barnard

CONTACT

Miss C Turnbull
Raby Estate Office
Staindrop
Darlington
Co. Durham
DL2 3NF

Tel: 01833 660207
01833 660202

Fax: 01833 660835

e-mail: rabyestate@rabycastle.com

LOCATION

OS Ref. NZ129 218

On A688, 1m N of Staindrop. 8m NE of Barnard Castle, 12m WNW of Darlington.

Rail: Darlington Station, 12m.

Air: Teesside Airport, 20m.

 Raby Castle beef, lamb, venison and game are available. Soft fruit available in season. No photography or video filming is permitted, slides are on sale.

Partially suitable. WC.

Licensed.

By arrangement. Tour time: 1 1/2 hrs.

Suitable for up to 60 children.

Guide dogs welcome, others on leads in park & gardens only.

Tel. for details.

OPENING TIMES

SUMMER

Castle

Easter & BH weekends
Sat - Wed, 1- 5pm.

May & September:
Weds & Suns only, 1 - 5pm.

June, July & August:
Daily except Sats, 1 - 5pm.

Guided tours by arrangement Easter - end September:
Mon - Fri, mornings only.

Park & Gardens
On Castle open days:
11am - 5.30pm.

WINTER
October - Easter Closed.

ADMISSION

Castle, Park & Gardens
Adult £5.00
Child (5-15yrs) £2.00
OAP/Student...........£4.00
Family (2+3)...........£12.00
Groups (min 20)
Adult £4.00
Child (5-15yrs)..........£1.75
OAP/Student...........£3.50

Guided Tour
(includes tea/coffee
reception) £7.50

Park & Gardens
Adult £3.00
Child (5-15yrs) £2.00
OAP/Student £2.00
Groups (min 20)
Adult £2.00
Child (5-15yrs)..........£1.75
OAP/Student...........£1.75

AUCKLAND CASTLE

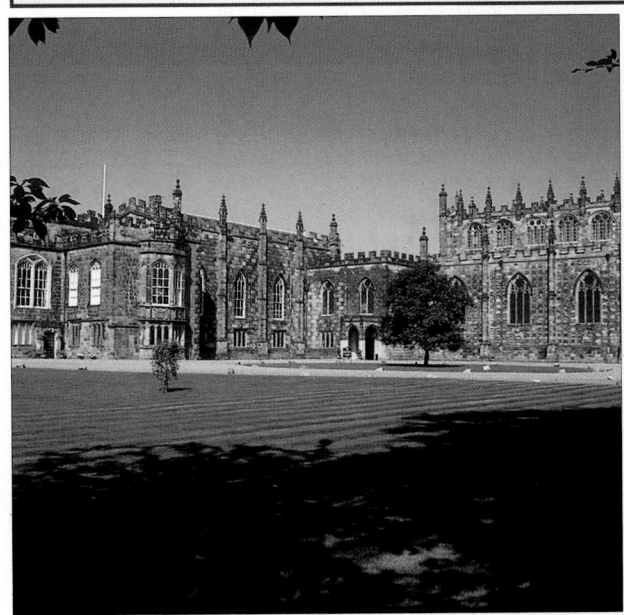

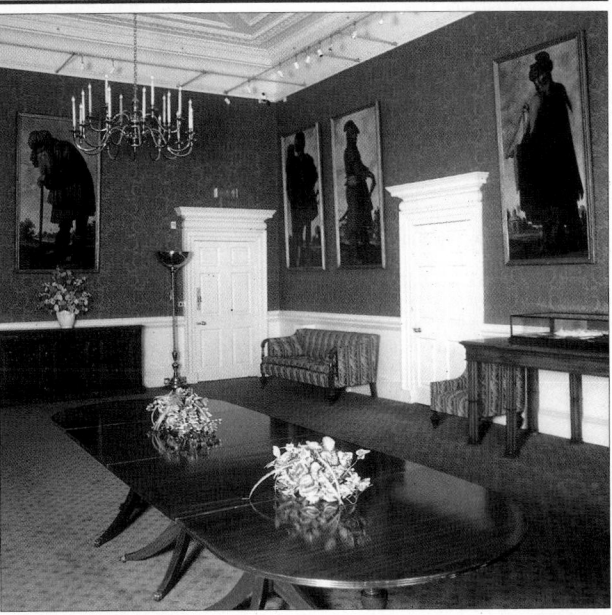

BISHOP AUCKLAND, CO. DURHAM DL14 7NR

Owner: Church Commissioners *Contact: The Manager*

Tel: 01388 601627 **Fax:** 01388 609323 **e-mail:** auckland.castle@zetnet.co.uk

Principal country residence of the Bishops of Durham since Norman times and now the official residence of the present day Bishops. The Chapel, reputedly the largest private chapel in Europe, was originally the 12th century banquet hall. Chapel and State Rooms including the Throne Room, Long Dining Room and King Charles Dining Room are open to the public. Exhibition in the medieval kitchens dedicated to the life of St Cuthbert and the history of the Durham diocese. Access to the adjacent Bishop's Park with its 18th century Deer House.

Location: OS Ref. NZ214 303. Bishop Auckland, N end of town centre.
Opening Times: 4 May - 15 Jul: Fris & Suns. 16 Jul - 31 Aug: daily except Sats. Sept: Fris & Suns. 2 - 5pm. Also open BH Mons & special event days.
Admission: Adult £3.50, Child/Conc. £2.50. Child (under 12yrs) Free. Special openings for groups (15+): £4.50pp.

Exhibitions. No indoor photography.   Wedding receptions, functions.   Guide dogs only.

AUCKLAND CASTLE DEER HOUSE

Tel: 0191 2691200

Bishop Auckland, Durham

Owner: English Heritage   **Contact:** The North Regional Office

A charming building erected in 1760 in the Park of the Bishops of Durham so that the deer could shelter and find food.

Location: OS Ref. NZ216 305. In Bishop Auckland Park, just N of town centre on A689. About 500 yds N of the castle.

Opening Times: Park opening times – see Auckland Castle.

Admission: Free.

BARNARD CASTLE

Tel: 01833 638212

Barnard Castle, Castle House, Durham DL12 9AT

Owner: English Heritage   **Contact:** The Custodian

The substantial remains of this large castle stand on a rugged escarpment overlooking the River Tees. Parts of the 14th century Great Hall and the cylindrical 12th century tower, built by the Baliol family can still be seen. New sensory garden.

Location: OS92 Ref. NZ049 165. In Barnard Castle.

Opening Times: 1 Apr - 30 Sept: daily, 10am - 6pm. 1 - 31 Oct: daily, 10am - 5pm. 1 Nov - 31 Mar: Wed - Sun, 10am - 4pm. Closed 24 - 26 Dec. Closed 1 - 2pm.

Admission: Adult £2.40, Child £1.20, Conc. £1.80. 15% discount for groups (11+).

Grounds suitable. Inclusive. No parking.
In grounds, on leads. Tel. for details.

BINCHESTER ROMAN FORT

Tel: 0191 3834212

Bishop Auckland, Co. Durham

e-mail: archaeology@durham.gov.uk

Owner: Durham County Council   **Contact:** Niall Hammond

Once the largest Roman fort in Co Durham, the heart of the site has been excavated.

Location: OS92 Ref. NZ210 312. 1½ m N of Bishop Auckland, signposted from A690 Durham - Crook and from A688 Spennymoor - Bishop Auckland roads.

Opening Times: Easter weekend & 1 May - 30 Sept: daily, 11am - 5pm.

Admission: Please contact for details.

THE BOWES MUSEUM

Tel: 01833 690606

Barnard Castle, Durham DL12 8NP

Owner: The Bowes Museum Ltd

A stunning French-style château containing the largest collection of French paintings in the country.

Location: OS Ref. NZ055 164. ¼ m E of Market Place in Barnard Castle.

Opening Times: All year: Daily, 11am - 5pm.

Admission: Adult £3.90, Child/OAP £2.90, Family £12. Prices and opening times subject to review, please check with museum in advance.

CROOK HALL & GARDENS

Tel: 0191 3848028

Sidegate, Durham DH1 5SZ

Owner: Keith & Maggie Bell   **Contact:** Mrs Maggie Bell

Medieval manor house set in rural landscape on the edge of Durham city.

Location: OS Ref. NZ274 432. ½ m N of city centre.

Opening Times: Easter weekend, BHs & Suns in May; Jun, Jul & Aug: daily except Sats, 1 - 5pm.

Admission: Adult £3.75, Child/OAP £2.75, Family £9.

DERWENTCOTE STEEL FURNACE

Tel: 0191 2691200

Newcastle, Durham

Owner: English Heritage   **Contact:** The Custodian

Built in the 18th century it is the earliest and most complete authentic steel making furnace to have survived.

Location: OS Ref. NZ131 566. 10m SW of Newcastle N of the A694 between Rowland's Gill and Hamsterley.

Opening Times: 1 Apr - 30 Sept: 1 - 5pm, 1st & 3rd Sun of every month.

Admission: Free.

DURHAM CASTLE

Tel: 0191 3743863 **Fax:** 0191 3747470

Palace Green, Durham DH1 3RW   **Contact:** Mrs Julie Marshall

Durham Castle, founded in the 1070s, with the Cathedral is a World Heritage Site.

Location: OS Ref. NZ274 424. City centre, adjacent to cathedral.

Opening Times: Mar - Sept: 10am - 12 noon & 2 - 4.30pm. Oct - Mar: 2 - 4pm.

Admission: Adult £3, Child £2, Family £6.50. Guide book £2.50.

DURHAM CATHEDRAL

Tel: 0191 3864266 **Fax:** 0191 3864267

Durham DH1 3EH   **e-mail:** enquiries@durhamcathedral.co.uk

Contact: Miss A Heywood

A World Heritage Site. Norman architecture. Burial place of St Cuthbert and the Venerable Bede.

Location: OS Ref. NZ274 422. Durham city centre.

Opening Times: Summer: 21 Jun - 21 Sept. 9.30am - 8pm. Open only for worship and private prayer: All year: Mon - Sat, 7.30am - 9.30am and Suns, 7.45am - 12.30pm. The Cathedral is closed to visitors during evening recitals and concerts.

Admission: Cathedral: £3 donation. Tower: Adult £2, Child (under 16) £1, Family £5. Monk's Dormitory: Adult 80p, Child 20p, Family £1.50. AV: Adult 80p, Child 20p, Family £1.50.

EGGLESTONE ABBEY

Tel: 0191 2691200

Durham

Owner: English Heritage   **Contact:** The North Regional Office

Picturesque remains of a 12th century abbey, located in a bend of the River Tees. Substantial parts of the church and abbey buildings remain.

Location: OS Ref. NZ062 151. 1$^{1}/_{2}$ m SE of Barnard Castle on minor road off B6277.

Opening Times: Any reasonable time.

Admission: Free.

ESCOMB CHURCH

Escomb, Bishop Auckland DL14 7ST   **Contact:** Mrs E Kitching (01388 662265)

Owner: Church of England   or The Vicar (01388 602861)

Saxon church dating from the 7th century built of stone from Binchester Roman Fort.

Location: OS Ref. NZ189 302. 3m W of Bishop Auckland.

Opening Times: Summer: 9am - 8pm. Winter: 9am - 4pm. Key available from 22 Saxon Green, Escomb.

Admission: Free.

FINCHALE PRIORY

Tel: 0191 3863828

Finchdale Priory, Brasside, Newton Hall DH1 5SH

Owner: English Heritage   **Contact:** The Custodian

These beautiful 13th century priory remains are located beside the curving River Wear.

Location: OS85 Ref. NZ297 471. 4$^{1}/_{2}$ m NE of Durham.

Opening Times: 1 Apr - 30 Sept: daily, 10am - 6pm. 1 - 31 Oct: daily, 10am - 5pm.

Admission: Adult £1.40, Child 70p, Conc. £1.10. 15% discount for groups (11+).

PIERCEBRIDGE ROMAN FORT

Tel: 01325 460532

Piercebridge, Co. Durham

Owner: Darlington Borough Council   **Contact:** Heritage Manager

Visible Roman remains include the east gate and defences, courtyard building and Roman road. Also remains of a bridge over the Tees.

Location: OS85 Ref. NZ211 157. Through narrow stile and short walk down lane opposite car park off A67 NE of the village. Bridge via signposted footpath from George Hotel car park.

Opening Times: At all times.

Admission: Free.

RABY CASTLE

See page 428 for full page entry.

ROKEBY PARK

Tel: 01833 637334

Nr Barnard Castle, Co Durham DL12 9RZ

Owner: Trustees of Mortham Estate   **Contact:** Mrs P I Yeats (Curator)

Rokeby, a fine example of a 18th century Palladian-style country house.

Location: OS Ref. NZ082 142. Between A66 & Barnard Castle.

Opening Times: May BH Mon then each Mon & Tue from Spring BH until the first Tue in Sept. Groups (25+) on other days by appointment.

Admission: Adult £5, Child £1.50, OAP £4.50. Group prices on request.

THE WEARDALE MUSEUM

Tel: 01388 517433

Ireshopeburn, Co. Durham DL13 1EY   **Contact:** D T Heatherington

Small folk museum in minister's house. Includes 1870 Weardale cottage room, Wesley room and local history displays.

Location: OS Ref. NZ872 385. Adjacent to 18th century Methodist Chapel.

Opening Times: Easter & May - Sept: Wed - Sun & BH, 2 - 5pm. Aug: daily, 2 - 5pm.

Admission: Adult £1, Child 30p.

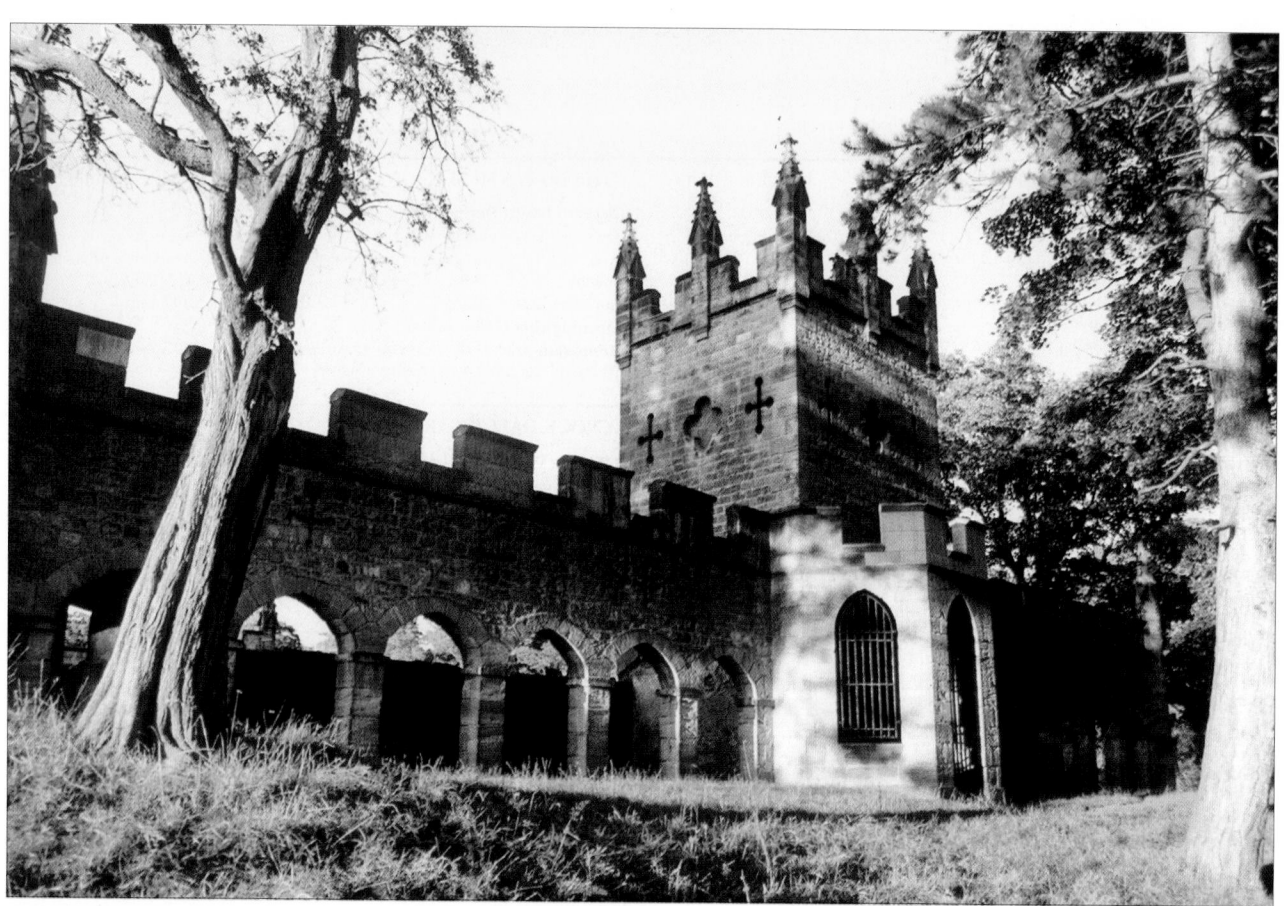

Patrick Lane.

Auckland Castle Deer House, Co Durham.

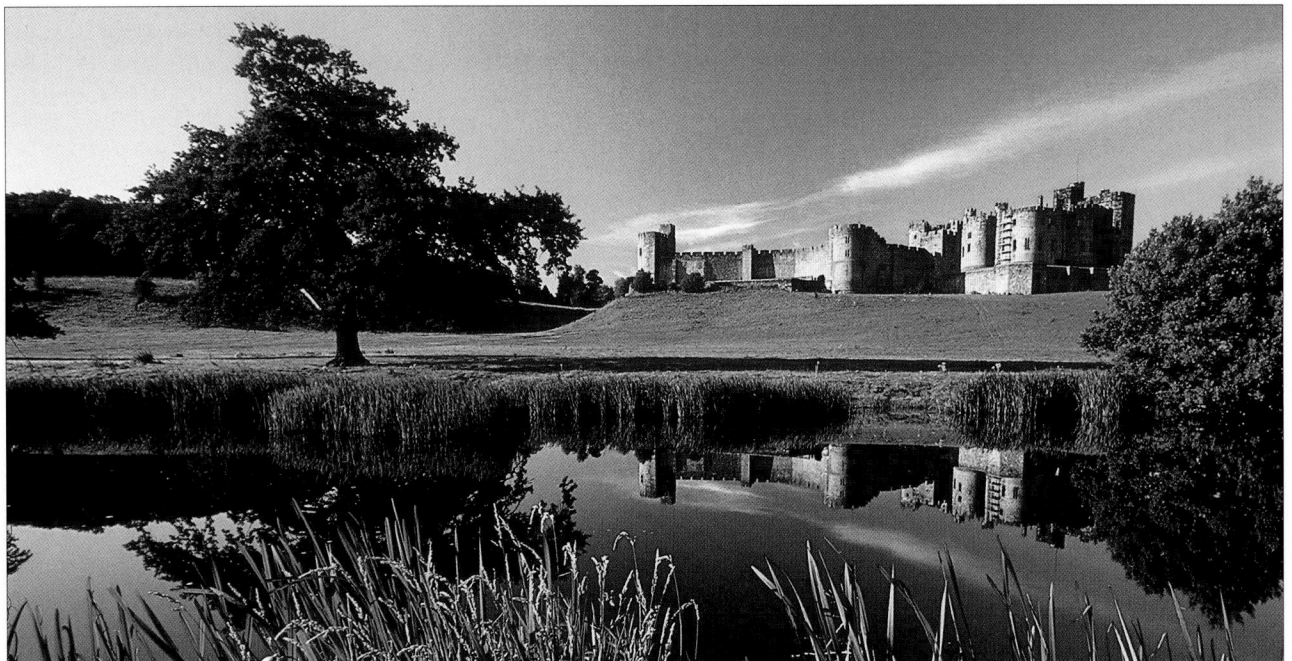

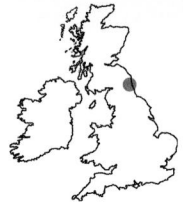

ALNWICK CASTLE
Alnwick

Described by the Victorians as the 'Windsor of the North', Alnwick Castle is the main seat of the Duke of Northumberland, whose family, the Percys, have lived here since 1309.

This Border stronghold has survived many battles, but now peacefully dominates the picturesque market town of Alnwick, overlooking landscape designed by 'Capability' Brown. The stern medieval exterior belies the treasure house within, furnished in palatial Renaissance style, with painting by Titian, Van Dyck and Canaletto, fine furniture and an exquisite collection of china.

The Regimental Museum of the Northumberland Fusiliers is housed in the Abbot's Tower of the Castle, while the Postern Tower contains an exhibition of the Duke's collection of archaeology. In the Constable's Tower is an exhibition of the Percy Tenantry Volunteers 1798 - 1814.

Other attractions include the Percy State Coach, dungeon, gun terrace and the grounds which offer peaceful walks and superb views over the surrounding countryside.

Alnwick Castle Guest Hall is one of the chief buildings of Anthony Salvin's 19th century restoration. Built as a magnificent coach house, it has throughout its history served as a venue for entertainment. This splendid Guest Hall is available for conferences, entertaining, wedding receptions, concerts, dinner dances and theatre productions. Please note that the Guest Hall is **not** open to Castle visitors.

Owner:
His Grace the Duke
of Northumberland

CONTACT

Alnwick Castle
Estate Office
Alnwick
Northumberland
NE66 1NQ

Tel: 01665 510777

Info: 01665 511100

Fax: 01665 510876

e-mail: enquiries@
alnwickcastle.com

LOCATION

OS Ref. NU187 135

In Alnwick 1¹/₂ m W of A1.

From London 6 hrs,
Edinburgh 2 hrs,
Chester 4 hrs,
Newcastle 40mins
North Sea ferry
terminal 30mins.

Bus: From bus station
in Alnwick.

Rail: Alnmouth Station 5m.
Kings Cross, London 3¹/₂hrs

Air: Newcastle 40mins.

CONFERENCE/FUNCTION		
ROOM	SIZE	MAX CAPACITY
The Guest Hall	100' x 30'	300

OPENING TIMES

SUMMER

1 April - 26 October
Daily, 11am - 5pm,
last admission 4.15pm.

Private functions by
arrangement.

ADMISSION

SUMMER
House & Garden

Adult......................£6.75
Child (5-16yrs) £3.50
Conc. £5.75
Family (2+2)........ £15.50

Pre-booked Groups (14+)
Adult......................£5.75
Child (5-16yrs) £3.00
Conc. £5.50

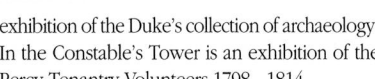

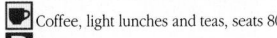

Conference facilities. Fashion shows, fairs, filming, parkland for hire. No photography inside the castle. No un-accompanied children.

Wedding receptions.

Not suitable. By arrangement.

Coffee, light lunches and teas, seats 80.

70 cars and 4 coaches.

Guidebook and worksheet, special rates for children and teachers.

Guide dogs only.

North East England

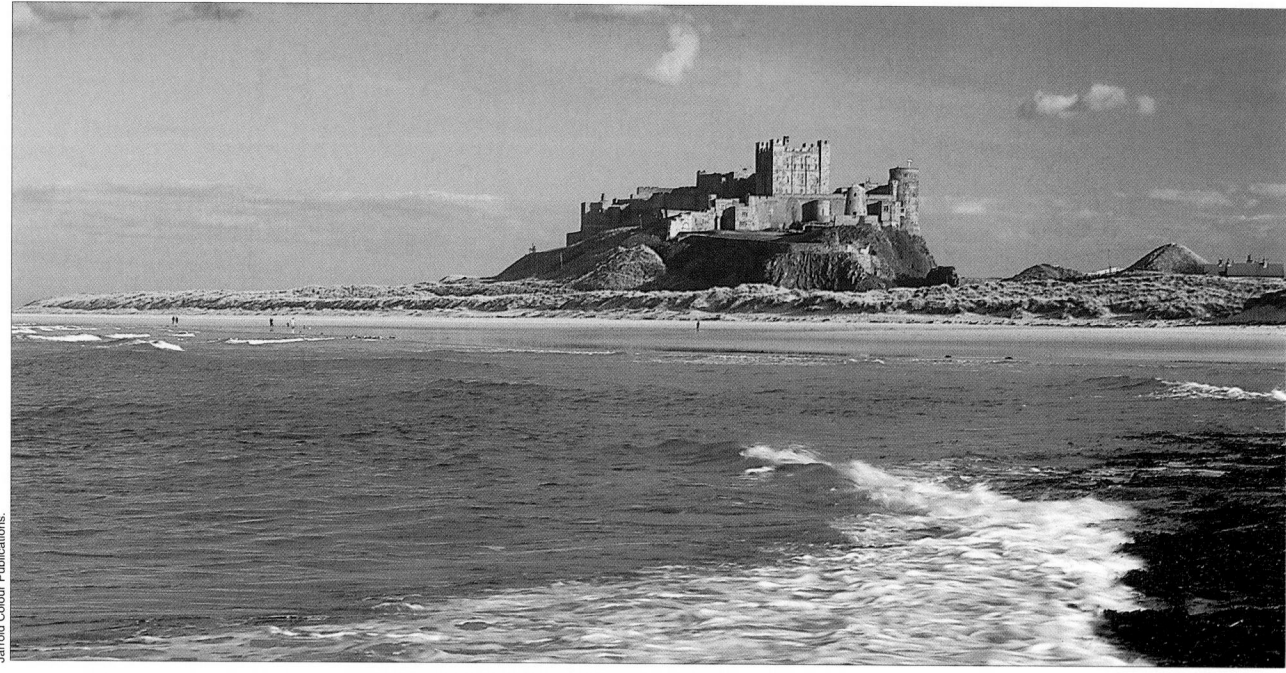

Jarrold Colour Publications.

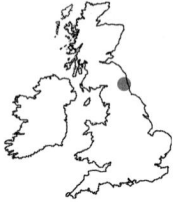

Owner:
Trustees Lord Armstrong
dec'd.

CONTACT

P Bolam
R G Bolam & Son
Townfoot
Rothbury
Northumberland
NE65 7SP

Tel: 01669 620314

Fax: 01669 621236

LOCATION

OS Ref. NU184 351

42m N of
Newcastle-upon-Tyne.
20m S of Berwick upon
Tweed. 6m E of Belford by
B1342 from A1 at Belford.

Bus: Bus service
200 yards.

Rail: Berwick-upon-
Tweed 20m.

Taxi: J Swanston
01289 306124.

Air: Newcastle-upon-
Tyne 45m.

BAMBURGH CASTLE
Bamburgh

BAMBURGH CASTLE is the home of the Armstrong family. The earliest reference to Bamburgh shows the craggy citadel to have been a royal centre by AD 547. Recent archaeological excavation has revealed that the site has been occupied since prehistoric times.

The Norman Keep has been the stronghold for nearly nine centuries, but the remainder has twice been extensively restored, initially by Lord Crewe in the 1750s and subsequently by the 2nd Lord Armstrong at the beginning of the 20th century. This Castle was the first to succumb to artillery fire – that of Edward IV.

The public rooms contain many exhibits,

including the loan collections of armour from HM Tower of London, the John George Joicey Museum, Newcastle-upon-Tyne and other private sources, which complement the castle's armour. Porcelain, china, jade, furniture from many periods, oils, water-colours and a host of interesting items are all contained within one of the most important buildings of Britain's national heritage.

VIEWS

The views from the ramparts are unsurpassed and take in Holy Island, the Farne Islands, one of Northumberland's finest beaches and, landwards, the Cheviot Hills.

OPENING TIMES

April - October
Daily, 11am - 5pm.
Last entry 4.30pm.

Tours by arrangement
at any time.

ADMISSION

SUMMER
Adult £4.50
Child (6 - 16yrs) £1.50
OAP.........................£3.50
Groups *
Adult £3.00
Child (6 - 16yrs) £1.00
OAP.........................£2.00

* Min payment £30

WINTER
Group rates only quoted.

Filming. No photography in house.

Limited access. WC.

Tearooms for light refreshments. Groups can book.

By arrangement at any time, min charge out of hours £30.

100 cars, coaches park on tarmac drive at entrance.

Welcome. Guide provided if requested, educational pack.

Guide dogs only.

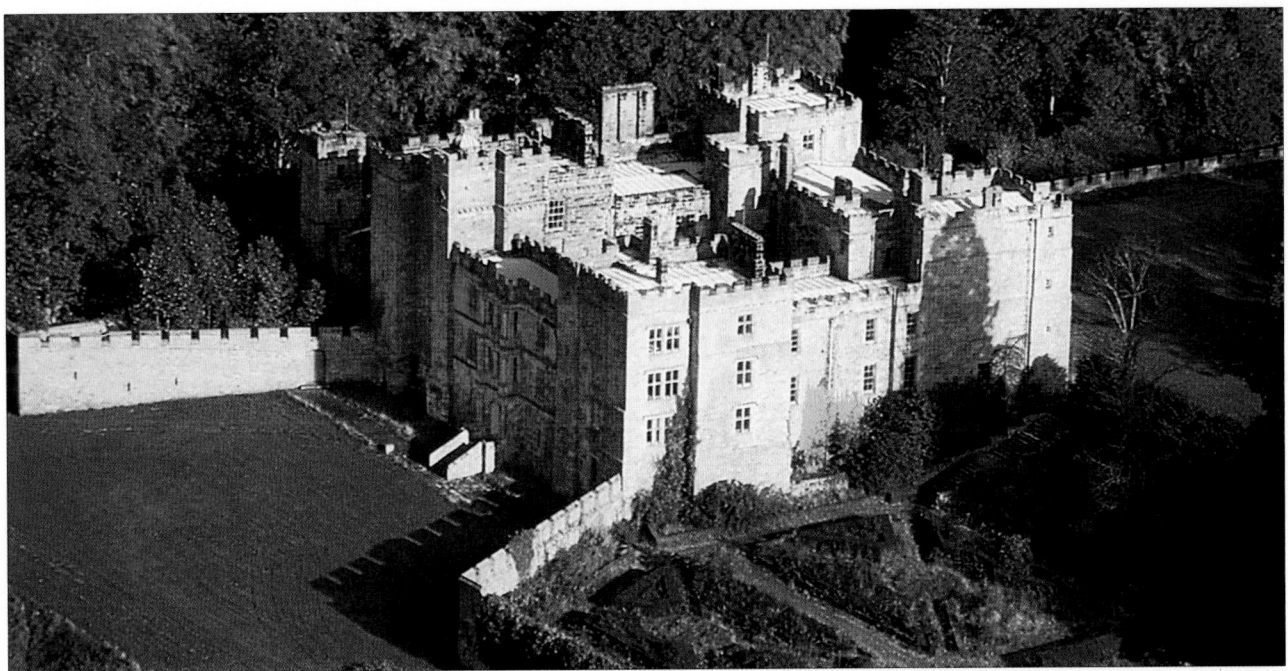

CHILLINGHAM CASTLE
Nr Alnwick

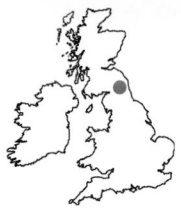

This remarkable castle, the home of Sir Humphry Wakefield Bt, with its alarming dungeons has, since the 1200s, been continuously owned by the family of the Earls Grey and their relations. You will see active restoration of complex masonry, metalwork and ornamental plaster as the great halls and state rooms are gradually brought back to life with antique furniture, tapestries, arms and armour as of old and even a torture chamber.

At first a 12th century stronghold, Chillingham became a fully fortified castle in the 14th century. Wrapped in the nation's history it occupied a strategic position as a fortress during Northumberland's bloody border feuds, often besieged and at many times enjoying the patronage of royal visitors. In Tudor days there were additions but the underlying medieval character has always been retained. The 18th and 19th centuries saw decorative refinements and extravagances including the lake, garden and grounds laid out by Sir Jeffrey Wyatville, fresh from his triumphs at Windsor Castle.

GARDENS

With romantic grounds, the castle commands breathtaking views of the surrounding countryside. As you walk to the lake you will see, according to the season, drifts of snowdrops, daffodils or bluebells and an astonishing display of rhododendrons. This emphasises the restrained formality of the Elizabethan topiary garden, with its intricately clipped hedges of box and yew. Lawns, the formal gardens and woodland walks are all fully open to the public.

Owner:
Sir Humphrey Wakefield Bt

CONTACT

Anne Benson
Chillingham Castle
Northumberland
NE66 5NJ

Tel: 01668 215359

Fax: 01668 215463

e-mail: enquiries@
chillingham-castle.com

LOCATION

OS Ref. NU062 258

45m N of Newcastle
between A697 & A1.
2m S of B6348 at Chatton.
6m SE of Wooler.

Rail: Alnmouth or
Berwick.

CONFERENCE/FUNCTION		
ROOM	SIZE	MAX CAPACITY
King James I Room		
Great Hall		100
Minstrels' Hall		60
2 x Drawing Room		
Museum		
Tea Room		35
Lower Gallery		
Upper Gallery		

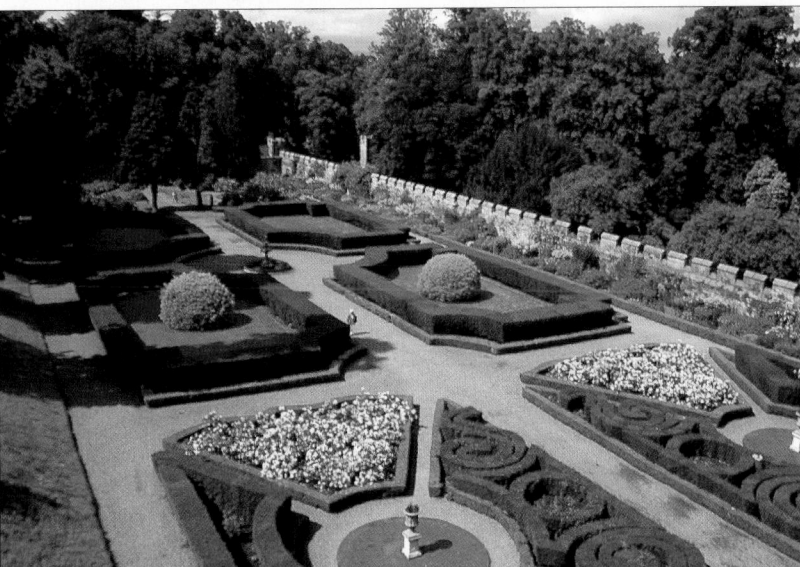

OPENING TIMES

SUMMER
Easter
1 May - 30 September
Daily except Tues
12 noon - 5pm.

July - August,
Daily: 12 noon - 5pm.

WINTER
October - April: Groups
any time by appointment.
All function activities
available.

ADMISSION

SUMMER

Adult	£4.50
OAP	£4.00
Child (3-13)	£0.50
Groups (10+)	
Per person	£3.80
Tour	£25.00

 Corporate entertainment, lunches, drinks, dinners, wedding ceremonies and receptions.

Partially suitable.

Booked meals for up to 100 people.

By arrangement.

P Avoid Lilburn route, coach parties welcome by prior arrangement. Limited for coaches.

Apartments.

Civil Wedding Licence.

ALNWICK CASTLE

See page 431 for full page entry.

AYDON CASTLE

Tel: 01434 632450

Corbridge, Northumberland NE45 5PJ

Owner: English Heritage   **Contact:** The Custodian

One of the finest fortified manor houses in England, dating from the late 13th century. Its survival, intact, can be attributed to its conversion to a farmhouse in the 17th century.

Location: OS87 Ref. NZ002 663. 2m NE of Corbridge, on minor road off B6321 or A68.

Opening Times: 1 Apr - 30 Sept: daily, 10am - 6pm. 1- 31 Oct: daily, 10am - 5pm.

Admission: Adult £2.10, Child £1.10, Conc. £1.60. 15% discount for groups (11+).

Ground floor & grounds suitable.   Limited.   In grounds, on leads.   Tel. for details.

BAMBURGH CASTLE

See page 432 for full page entry.

BELSAY HALL, CASTLE & GARDENS

See opposite for half page entry.

BERWICK BARRACKS

Tel: 01289 304493

The Parade, Berwick-upon-Tweed, Northumberland TD15 1DF

Owner: English Heritage   **Contact:** The Custodian

Among the earliest purpose built barracks, these have changed very little since 1717. They house an exhibition 'By Beat of Drum', which recreates scenes such as the barrack room from the life of the British infantryman, the Museum of the King's Own Scottish Borderers and the Borough Museum with fine art, local history exhibition and other collections. Guided tours available.

Location: OS75 Ref. NT994 535. On the Parade, off Church Street, Berwick town centre.

Opening Times: 1 Apr - 30 Sept: daily, 10am - 6pm. 1 - 31 Oct: daily, 10am - 5pm. 1 Nov - 31 Mar: Wed - Sun, 10am - 4pm. Closed 24 - 26 Dec.

Admission: Adult £2.70, Child £1.40, Conc. £2. 15% discount for groups (11+).

Ground floor & grounds suitable.   Limited.   In grounds, on leads.   Tel. for details.

BERWICK RAMPARTS

Tel: 0191 269 1200

Berwick-upon-Tweed, Northumberland

Owner: English Heritage   **Contact:** The Northern Regional Office

A remarkably complete system of town fortifications consisting of gateways, ramparts and projecting bastions built in the 16th century.

Location: OS Ref. NT994 535. Surrounding Berwick town centre on N bank of River Tweed.

Opening Times: Any reasonable time.

Admission: Free.

BRINKBURN PRIORY

Tel: 01665 570628

Long Framlington, Morpeth, Northumberland NE65 8AF

Owner: English Heritage   **Contact:** The Custodian

This late 12th century church is a fine example of early gothic architecture, almost perfectly preserved, and is set in a lovely spot beside the River Coquet.

Location: OS81, Ref. NZ116 984. 4^{1}/2 m SE of Rothbury off B6344 5m W of A1.

Opening Times: 1 Apr - 30 Sept: daily, 10am - 6pm. 1 - 31 Oct, daily, 10am - 5pm.

Admission: Adult £1.70, Child 90p, Conc. £1.30. 15% discount for groups (11+).

Not suitable.   Limited.   On leads.   Tel. for details.

CAPHEATON HALL

Tel: 01830 530253

Newcastle-upon-Tyne NE19 2AB

Owner/Contact: J Browne-Swinburne

Built for Sir John Swinburne in 1668 by Robert Trollope, an architect of great and original talent.

Location: OS Ref. NZ038 805. 17m NW of Newcastle off A696.

Opening Times: By written appointment only.

Admission: Adult £3.

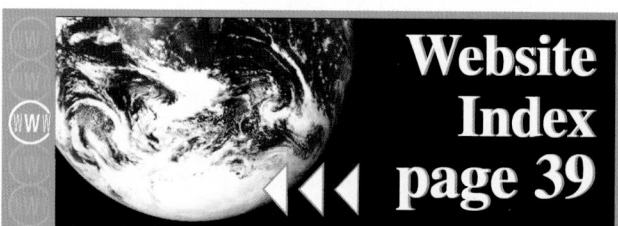

Website Index page 39

BELSAY HALL, CASTLE & GARDENS

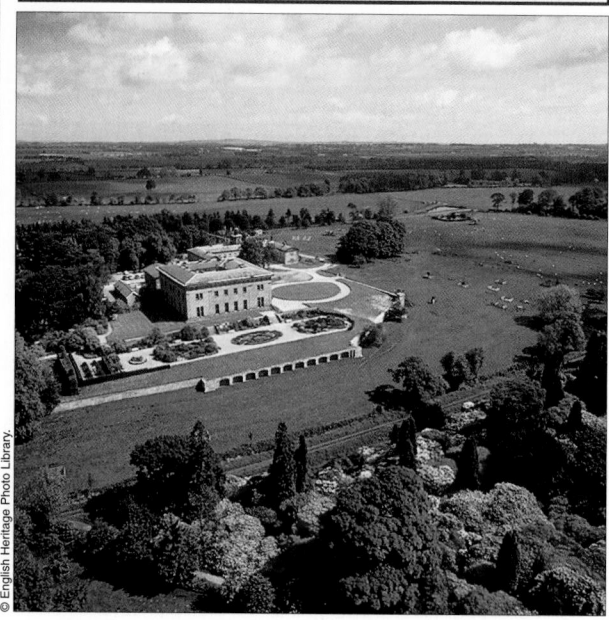

BELSAY, Nr PONTELAND, NORTHUMBERLAND NE20 0DX

Owner: *English Heritage*   **Contact:** *The Custodian*

Tel: 01661 881636   **Fax:** 01661 881043

Belsay is one of the most remarkable estates in Northumberland's border country. The buildings, set amidst 30 acres of magnificent landscaped gardens, have been occupied by the same family for nearly 600 years. The gardens, created largely in the 19th century, are a fascinating mix of the formal and the informal with terraced gardens, a rhododendron garden, magnolia garden, mature woodland and even a winter garden. The buildings comprise a 14th century castle, a manor house and Belsay Hall, an internationally famous mansion designed by Sir Charles Monck in the 19th century in the style of classical buildings he had encountered during a tour of Greece.

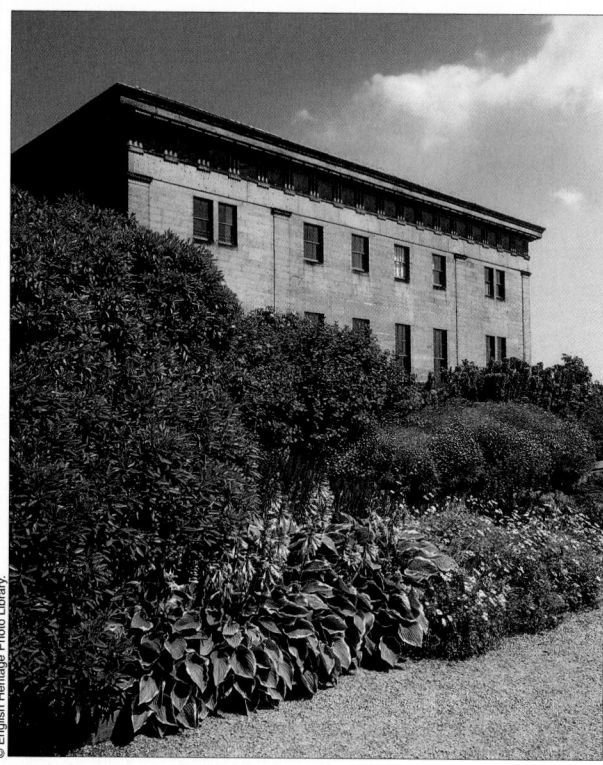

Location: OS87, Ref. NZ088 785. In Belsay 14m (22.4 km) NW of Newcastle on SW of A696. 7m NW of Ponteland. Nearest airport and station is Newcastle.

Opening Times: 1 Apr - 30 Sept: daily, 10am - 6pm. 1 - 31 Oct: daily, 10am - 5pm. 1 Nov - 31 Mar: daily, 10am - 4pm.

Admission: Adult £3.90, Child £2.90, Conc. £2. 15% discount for groups (11+).

Partially suitable. WC.   During summer & weekends Apr - Oct.   In grounds, on leads.   Tel. for details.

CHERRYBURN – THOMAS BEWICK BIRTHPLACE Tel: 01661 843276

Station Bank, Mickley, Stocksfield, Northumberland NE43 7DD

Owner: The National Trust **Contact:** The Administrator

Birthplace of Northumbria's greatest artist, wood engraver and naturalist, Thomas Bewick, b.1753. The Museum explores his famous works and life with occasional demonstrations of wood block printing in the printing house. Farmyard animals, picnic area, garden.

Location: OS Ref. NZ075 627. 11m W of Newcastle on A695 (400yds signed from Mickley Square). 1½ m W of Prudhoe.

Opening Times: 1 Apr - 31 Oct: daily except Tues & Weds, 1 - 5.30pm. Last admission 5pm.

Admission: Adult £3. No group rate.

Some steps. WC. Morning coffee for booked groups. Tel. for details.

CHILLINGHAM CASTLE See page 433 for full page entry.

CHIPCHASE CASTLE Tel: 01434 230203 Fax: 01434 230740

Wark, Hexham, Northumberland NE48 3NT

Owner/Contact: Mrs P J Torday

The castle overlooks the River North Tyne and is set in formal and informal gardens. One walled garden is used as a nursery specialising in unusual perennial plants.

Location: OS Ref. NY882 758. 10m NW of Hexham via A6079 to Chollerton. 2m SE of Wark.

Opening Times: Castle: 1 - 28 Jun: daily 2 - 5pm. Tours by arrangement at other times. Castle Gardens & Nursery: Easter - 31 Jul, Thur - Sun & BH Mons, 10am - 5pm.

Admission: Castle £4, Garden £1.50, concessions available. Nursery Free.

Not suitable. Obligatory.

CHESTERS ROMAN FORT & MUSEUM

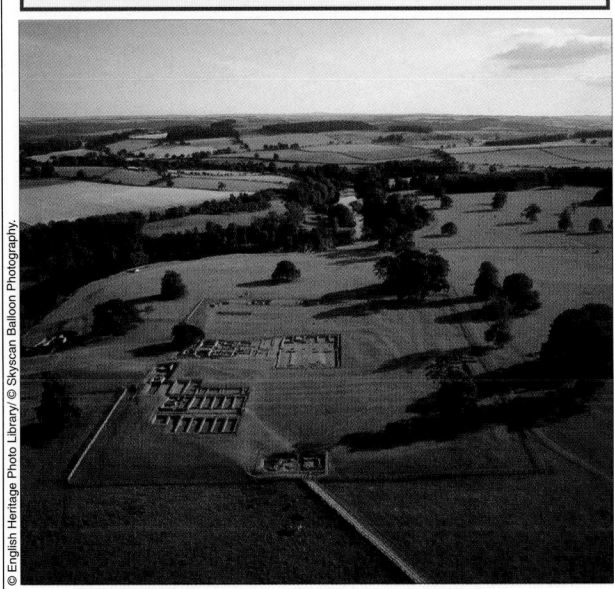

© English Heritage Photo Library/ © Skyscan Balloon Photography.

CHOLLERFORD, Nr HEXHAM, NORTHUMBERLAND NE46 4EP

Owner: English Heritage *Contact: The Custodian*

Tel: 01434 681379

The best preserved example of a Roman cavalry fort in Britain, including remains of the bath house on the banks of the River North Tyne. The museum houses a fascinating collection of Roman sculpture and inscriptions.

Location: OS87, Ref. NY913 701. 1½ m from Chollerford on B6318.

Opening Times: 1 Apr - 30 Sept: daily, 9.30am - 6pm. 1 - 31 Oct: daily, 10am - 5pm. 1 Nov - 31 Mar: daily, 10am - 4pm. Closed 24 - 26 Dec.

Admission: Adult £2.90, Child £1.50, Conc. £2.20. 15% discount for groups (11+).

Grounds suitable. WC. Summer only. In grounds, on leads. Tel. for details.

CORBRIDGE ROMAN SITE Tel: 01434 632349

Corbridge, Northumberland NE45 5NT

Owner: English Heritage **Contact:** The Custodian

A fascinating series of excavated remains, including foundations of granaries with a grain ventilation system. From artefacts found, which can be seen in the site museum, we know a large settlement developed around this supply depot.

Location: OS87 Ref. NY983 649. ½ m NW of Corbridge on minor road, signposted for Corbridge Roman Site.

Opening Times: 1 Apr - 30 Sept: daily, 10am - 6pm. 1 - 31 Oct: daily, 10am - 5pm. 1 Nov - 31 Mar: Wed - Sun, 10am - 4pm. Closed 1 - 2pm during winter & 24 - 26 Dec.

Admission: Adult £2.90, Child £1.50, Conc. £2.20. 15% discount for groups (11+).

Partially suitable. Inclusive. Limited for coaches. In grounds, on leads. Tel. for details.

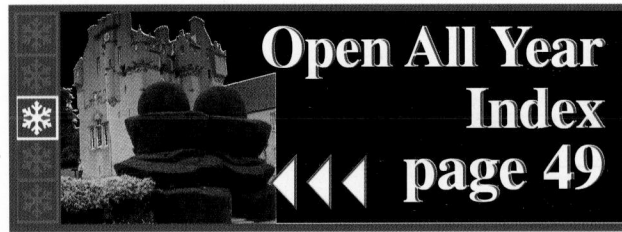

Open All Year
Index
◀◀◀ page 49

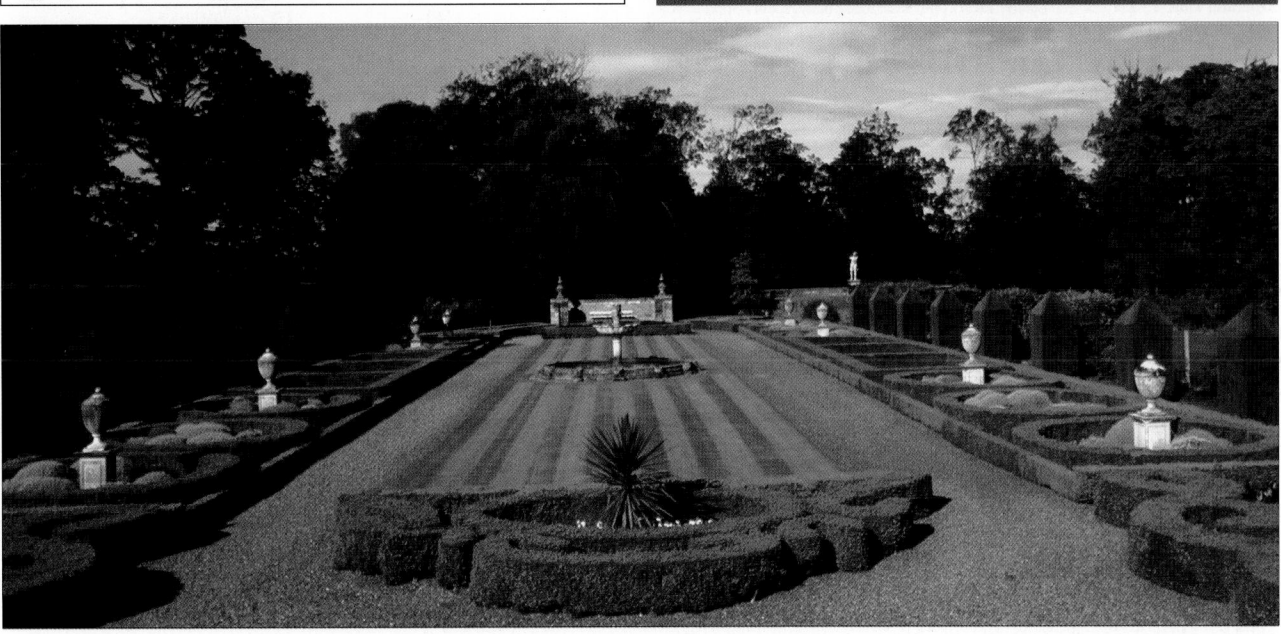

Seaton Delaval Hall, Northumberland.

CRAGSIDE

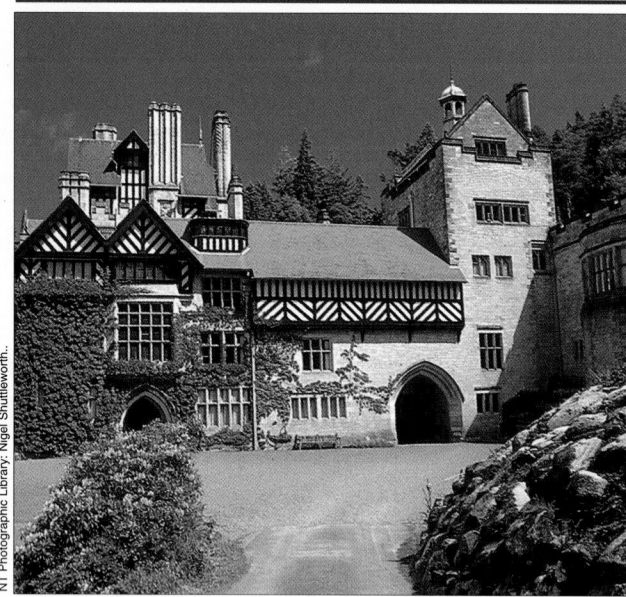

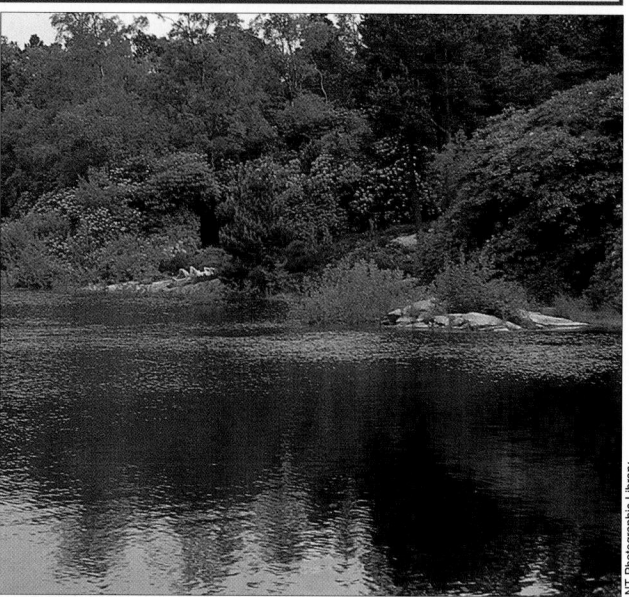

ROTHBURY, MORPETH, NORTHUMBERLAND NE65 7PX
Owner: *The National Trust*   **Contact:** *Property Manager*

Tel: 01669 620150 **Fax:** 01669 620066

Built for the 19th century's greatest gun-maker and innovator, 1st Lord Armstrong, Cragside became one of the most modern and surprising houses for its time in the country. In the 1880s, the house had hot and cold running water, central heating, telephones, a Turkish bath suite and a passenger lift but - most remarkable of all - it was the first house in the world to be lit by hydro-electricity. No wonder it was described as 'The Palace of a Modern Magician'. Children will love exploring the 1000-acre forest garden, which contains one of Europe's largest rock gardens, a formal garden, lakes and an exciting Adventure Play Area (new for 2001). Allow a whole day!

Location: OS Ref. NU073 022. ¹/₂ m NE of Rothbury on B6341.

Opening Times: House: 31 Mar - 4 Nov: daily except Mons (open BH Mons), 1 - 5.30pm. Last admission 4.30pm. Estate & Formal Garden: 31 Mar - 4 Nov: daily except Mons (open BH Mons), 10.30am - 7pm. Last admission 5pm. 7 Nov - 16 Dec: Estate, Garden, Shop & Restaurant: Wed - Sun, 11am - 4pm (house closed).

Admission: House, Estate & Gardens: Adult £6.70, Child (5-17yrs) £3.40, Family (2+3) £16.80. Groups (15+) £5.70. Estate & Formal Garden: Adult £4.20, Child (5-17yrs) £2.10, Family (2+3) £10.50. Groups (15+) £3.50.

  Partially suitable.

DUNSTANBURGH CASTLE
Tel: 01665 576231

c/o 14 Queen Street, Alnwick, Northumberland NE66 1RD
Owner: The National Trust   **Guardian:** English Heritage   **Contact:** The Custodian

An easy, but bracing, coastal walk leads to the eerie skeleton of this wonderful 14th century castle sited on a basalt crag, rearing up more than 100 feet from the waves crashing on the rocks below. The surviving ruins include the large gatehouse, which later became the keep, and curtain walls.

Location: OS75 Ref. NU258 220. 8m NE of Alnwick.

Opening Times: 1 Apr - 30 Sept: daily, 10am - 6pm. 1 - 31 Oct, daily, 10am - 5pm. 1 Nov - 31 Mar: Wed - Sun, 10am - 4pm. Closed 24 - 26 Dec.

Admission: Adult £1.90, Child £1, Conc. £1.40. 15% discount for groups (11+).

Not suitable. No parking. In grounds, on leads.

EDLINGHAM CASTLE
Tel: 0191 269 1200

Edlingham, Alnwick, Northumberland
Owner: English Heritage   **Contact:** The Northern Regional Office

Set beside a splendid railway viaduct this complex ruin has defensive features spanning the 13th and 15th centuries.

Location: OS Ref. NU115 092. At E end of Edlingham village, on minor road off B6341 6m SW of Alnwick.

Opening Times: Any reasonable time.

Admission: Free.

ETAL CASTLE
Tel: 01890 820332

Cornhill-on-Tweed, Northumberland
Owner: English Heritage   **Contact:** The Custodian

A 14th century castle located in the picturesque village of Etal. Award-winning exhibition about the castle, Border warfare and the Battle of Flodden.

Location: OS75 Ref. NT925 394. In Etal village, 10m SW of Berwick.

Opening Times: 1 Apr - 30 Sept: daily, 10am - 6pm. 1 - 31 Oct: daily, 10am - 5pm.

Admission: Adult £2.90, Child £1.40, Conc. £2. 15% discount for groups (11+).

Partially suitable. WC. Inclusive. Limited. In grounds, on leads. Tel. for details.

HERTERTON HOUSE GARDENS
Tel: 01670 774278

Hartington, Cambo, Morpeth, Northumberland NE61 4BN
Owner/Contact: C J "Frank" Lawley

One acre of formal garden in stone walls around a 16th century farmhouse, including a small topiary garden, physic garden, flower garden, fancy garden and gazebo.

Location: OS Ref. NZ022 881. 2m N of Cambo, just off B6342.

Opening Times: 1 Apr - 30 Sept: Mons, Weds, Fri - Sun, 1.30 - 5.30pm.

Admission: Adult £2.40, Child (5-15yrs) £1. Groups by arrangement.

Not suitable. By arrangement. Limited for coaches. Guided tours for adult students only.

HOUSESTEADS ROMAN FORT
Tel: 01434 344363

Nr Haydon Bridge, Northumberland NE47 6NN
Owner: The National Trust **Guardian:** English Heritage **Contact:** The Custodian

Perched high on a ridge overlooking open moorland, this is the best known part of the Wall. The fort covers five acres and there are remains of many buildings, such as granaries, barrack blocks and gateways. A small exhibition displays altars, inscriptions and models.

Location: OS87 Ref. NY790 687. 2m NE of Bardon Mill.

Opening Times: 1 Apr - 30 Sept: daily, 10am - 6pm. 1 - 31 Oct: daily, 10am - 5pm. 1 Nov - 31 Mar: daily, 10am - 4pm. Closed 24 - 26 Dec.

Admission: Adult £2.90, Child £1.50, Conc. £2.20. 15% discount for groups (11+).

Not suitable. Charge. In grounds, on leads. Tel. for details.

HOWICK HALL GARDENS
Tel/Fax: 01665 577285

Howick, Alnwick, Northumberland NE66 3LB **e-mail:** howickarb@compuserve.com
Owner: Howick Trustees Ltd   **Contact:** Lord Howick

Romantically landscaped grounds surrounding the house in a little valley, with rare rhododendrons and flowering shrubs and trees.

Location: OS Ref. NU249 175. 6m NE of Alnwick. 1m E of B1339.

Opening Times: Apr - Oct: daily 1 - 6pm.

Admission: Adult £2, Child/OAP £1, Student (up to 16yrs) £1. Season tickets available.

Grounds partly suitable. WC. Limited.

KIRKLEY HALL GARDENS

Tel: 01661 860808 **Fax:** 01661 860047

Ponteland, Northumberland NE20 0AQ **Contact:** J Guy

Over 9 acres of beautiful gardens incorporating a Victorian walled garden, woodland walks, sunken garden and wildlife areas and ponds.

Location: OS Ref. NZ150 772. 10m from the centre of Newcastle upon Tyne. 2 1/2 m N of Ponteland on byroad to Morpeth.

Opening Times: 1 Apr - 30 Sept: daily, 10am - 5pm.

Admission: Free.

THE LADY WATERFORD HALL & MURALS

Ford, Berwick-upon-Tweed TD15 2QA **Tel:** 01890 820524 **Fax:** 01890 820384

Owner: Ford & Etal Estates **Contact:** The Caretaker

Commissioned in 1860 the walls of this beautiful building are decorated with beautiful murals depicting Bible stories.

Location: OS Ref. NT945 374. On the B6354, 9m from Berwick-upon-Tweed, midway between Newcastle-upon-Tyne and Edinburgh, close to the A697.

Opening Times: 1 Apr - 29 Oct: daily, 10.30am - 12.30pm & 1.30 - 5.30pm. By arrangement with the caretaker during winter months.

Admission: Adult £1.50, Child Free (over 12yrs 50p), Conc. £1. Groups by arrangement.

LINDISFARNE CASTLE

Tel: 01289 389244

Holy Island, Berwick-upon-Tweed, Northumberland TD15 2SH

Owner: The National Trust **Contact:** The Administrator

Built in 1550 to protect Holy Island harbour from attack, the castle was restored and converted into a private house for Edward Hudson by Sir Edwin Lutyens in 1903. Small walled garden was designed by Gertrude Jekyll. 19th century lime kilns in field by the castle.

Location: OS Ref. NU136 417. On Holy Island, 3/4 m E of village, 6m E of A1 across causeway. Usable at low tide.

Opening Times: 31 Mar - 31 Oct: daily except Fris (but open Good Fri), 12 noon - 3pm, but earlier or later as the tide allows. Last admission 1/2 before close. Admission to garden only when gardener in attendance. Holy Island is cut off by the tide from 2 hours before and 3 1/2 hours after high tide. Visitors are advised to check tide times before visiting.

Admission: £4, Family £10. No group rate. Groups (15+) must pre-book.

NT Shop (in Main St.) Not suitable. No parking. In grounds, on leads.

LINDISFARNE PRIORY

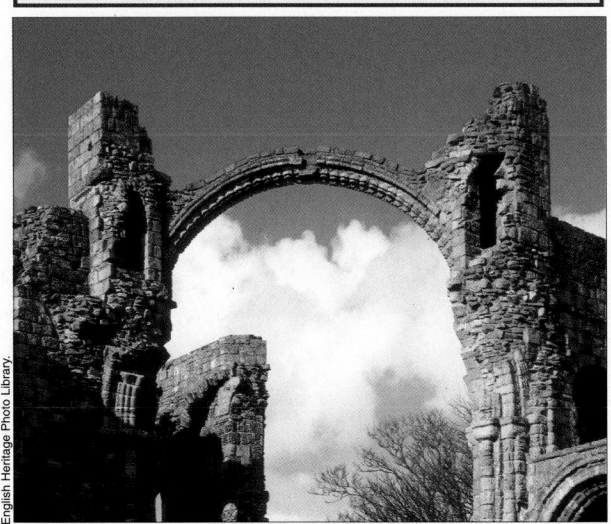

English Heritage Photo Library

HOLY ISLAND, BERWICK-UPON-TWEED TD15 2RX

Owner: English Heritage *Contact: The Custodian*

Tel: 01289 389200

The site of one of the most important early centres of Christianity in Anglo-Saxon England. St Cuthbert converted pagan Northumbria, and miracles occurring at his shrine established this 11th century priory as a major pilgrimage centre. The evocative ruins, with the decorated 'rainbow' arch curving dramatically across the nave of the church, are still the destination of pilgrims today. The story of Lindisfarne is told in an exhibition which gives an impression of life for the monks, including a reconstruction of a monk's cell.

Location: OS75 Ref. NU126 418. On Holy Island, check tide times.

Opening Times: 1 Apr - 30 Sept: daily, 10am - 6pm. 1 - 31 Oct: daily, 10am - 5pm. 1 Nov - 31 Mar: daily, 10am - 4pm. Closed 24 - 26 Dec.

Admission: Adult £2.90, Child £1.50, Conc. £2.20. 15% discount for groups (11+).

Partially suitable. Charge. Restricted. Tel. for details.

MELDON PARK

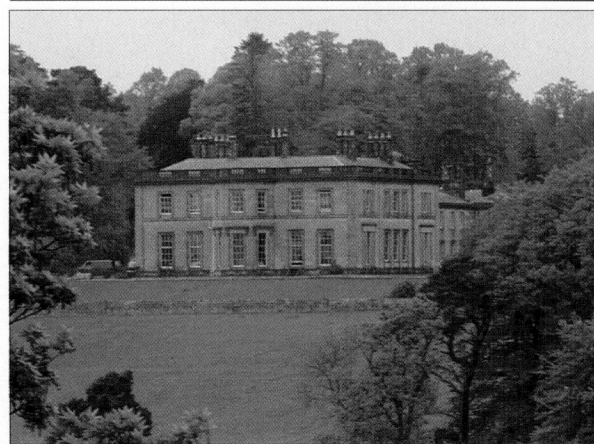

MORPETH, NORTHUMBERLAND NE61 3SW

Owner/Contact: M Cookson

Tel: 01670 772661

Isaac Cookson III purchased the Meldon land in 1832. John Dobson, the famous architect, was commissioned to build a house by Isaac Cookson and he recommended the present site. The entrance is through an Ionic porch having two rows of columns to the front door. Once inside you are in the main hall which has an enormous staircase lit by a large window to the north. Between the two World Wars Edwin Lutyens was employed to enrich the Hall, which included mahogany balustrades and 18th century decorations. The garden has a wonderful collection of rhododendrons best seen in early June, an old-fashioned kitchen garden and greenhouses.

Location: OS Ref. NZ105 856. 7m W of Morpeth on B6343. 5m N of Belsay. 7m W of Morpeth.

Opening Times: 26 May - 24 Jun, 2 - 5pm & Aug BH weekend, 2 - 5.30pm.

Admission: Adult £3, Child £1.50, OAP £2.

No photography. Sundays only. By arrangement. P

Guide dogs only.

NORHAM CASTLE

Tel: 01289 382329

Norham, Northumberland

Owner: English Heritage **Contact:** The Custodian

Set on a promontory in a curve of the River Tweed, this was one of the strongest of the Border castles, built c1160.

Location: OS75 Ref. NT907 476. 6m SW of Berwick.

Opening Times: 1 Apr - 30 Sept: daily, 10am - 6pm. 1 - 31 Oct: daily, 10am - 5pm.

Admission: Adult £1.90, Child £1, Conc. £1.40. 15% discount for groups (11+).

Partially suitable. P On leads. Tel. for details.

PRESTON TOWER

Tel: 01665 589227

Chathill, Northumberland NE67 5DH

Owner/Contact: Major T Baker Cresswell

The Tower was built by Sir Robert Harbottle in 1392 and is one of the few survivors of 78 pele towers listed in 1415. The tunnel vaulted rooms remain unaltered and provide a realistic picture of the grim way of life under the constant threat of "Border Reivers". Two rooms are furnished in contemporary style and there are displays of historic and local information. Visitors are welcome to walk in the grounds which contain a number of interesting trees and shrubs. A woodland walk to the natural spring from which water is now pumped up to the Tower for the house and cottages.

Location: OS Ref. NU185 253. Follow Historic Property signs on A1 7m N of Alnwick.

Opening Times: Daylight hours all year.

Admission: Adult £1, Child/Conc./Groups 50p.

Grounds suitable.

PRUDHOE CASTLE

Tel: 01661 833459

Prudhoe, Northumberland NE42 6NA

Owner: English Heritage **Contact:** The Custodian

Set on a wooded hillside overlooking the River Tyne are the extensive remains of this 12th century castle including a gatehouse, curtain wall and keep. Small exhibition and video presentation.

Location: OS88 Ref. NZ092 634. In Prudhoe, on minor road N from A695.

Opening Times: 1 Apr - 30 Sept: daily, 10am - 6pm. 1 - 31 Oct: daily, 10am - 5pm.

Admission: Adult £1.90, Child £1, Conc. £1.40. 15% discount for groups (11+).

Partially suitable. P Limited. In grounds, on leads.

Tel. for details.

North East England

SEATON DELAVAL HALL

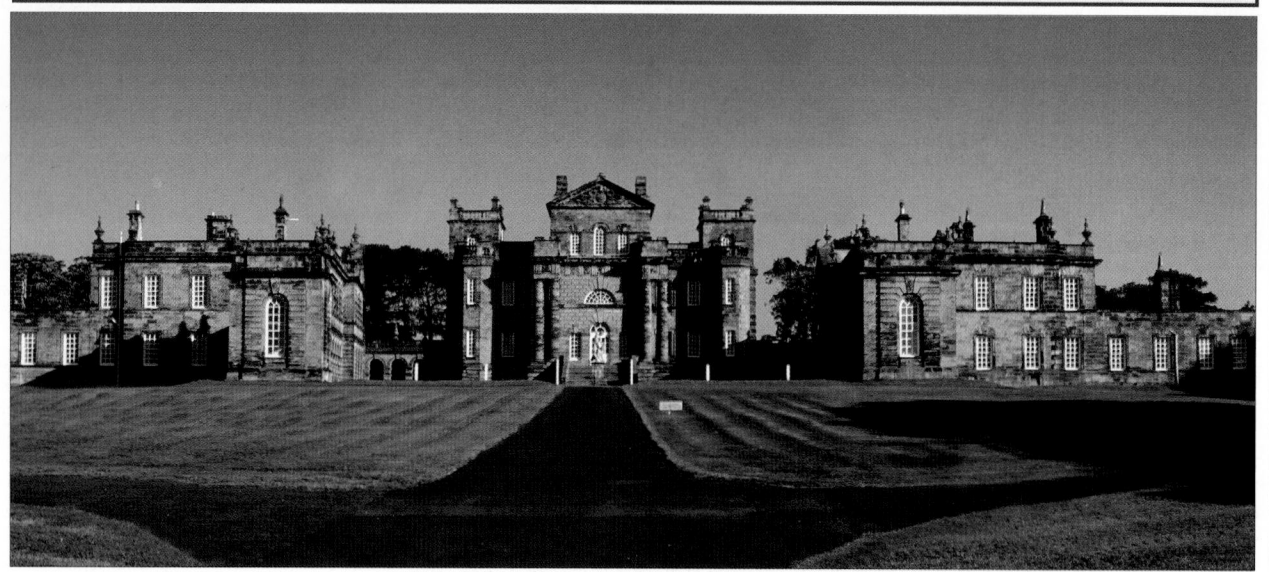

SEATON SLUICE, WHITLEY BAY, NORTHUMBERLAND NE26 4QR

Owner: Lord Hastings　　*Contact:* Mrs Mills

Tel: 0191 2371493/0191 2370786

The home of Lord and Lady Hastings, half a mile from Seaton Sluice, is the last and most sensational mansion designed by Sir John Vanbrugh, builder of Blenheim Palace and Castle Howard. It was erected 1718 - 1728 and comprises a high turreted block flanked by arcaded wings which form a vast forecourt. The centre block was gutted by fire in 1822, but was partially restored in 1862 and again in 1959 - 1962 and 1999 - 2000. The remarkable staircases are a visual delight, and the two surviving rooms are filled with family pictures and photographs and royal seals spanning three centuries as well as various archives. This building is used frequently for concerts and charitable functions. The East Wing contains immense stables in ashlar stone of breathtaking proportions. Nearby are the Coach House with farm and passenger

vehicles, fully documented, and the restored ice house with explanatory sketch and description. There are beautiful gardens with herbaceous borders, rose garden, rhododendrons, azaleas, laburnum walk, statues, and a spectacular parterre by internationally famous Jim Russell, also a unique Norman Church.

Location: OS Ref. NZ322 766. $^1/_2$ m from Seaton Sluice on A190, 3m from Whitley Bay.

Opening Times: May & Aug BH Mons; Jun - 30 Sept: Weds & Suns, 2 - 6pm.

Admission: Adult £3, Child £1, Conc. £2.50. Groups (20+): Adult £2.50, Child £1, Student £1.

⬜ ♿Partially suitable. WC. ▣ **P**Free. 🐾In grounds, on leads.

WALLINGTON 🌿

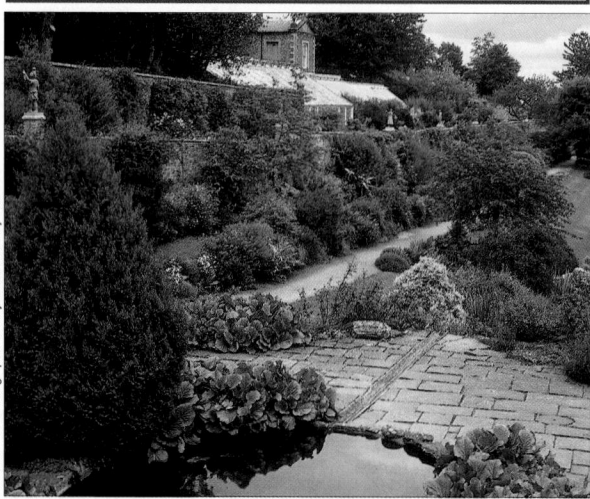

National Trust Photographic Library/ Marianne Majerus.

CAMBO, MORPETH, NORTHUMBERLAND NE61 4AP

Owner: The National Trust　　*Contact:* The House Manager

Tel: 01670 774283 **Fax:** 01670 774420

A beautiful walled garden, Edwardian conservatory, woodland walks and ornamental ponds make a delightful setting for the Trevelyan's historic home. The house at Wallington dates from 1688 and boasts fine interiors, a superb collection of ceramics and William Bell-Scott's famous paintings of Northumbrian history but still retains the atmosphere of a much loved family home.

Location: OS Ref. NZ030 843. Near Cambo, 6m NW of Belsay (A696).

Opening Times: House: 31 Mar - 30 Sept: daily (except Tues), 1 - 5.30pm. 1 Oct - 4 Nov: daily (except Tues), 1 - 4.30pm. Gardens: daily, 10am - 7pm (summer). Grounds: all year.

Admission: House, Garden & Grounds: Adult £5.50, Child £2.75, Family £13.75, Group: £5. Garden & Grounds: Adult £4, Child £2, Groups £3.50.

ℹ️No photography in house. ⬜ 🚻 🍽 ♿ ▣ 🎨By arrangement. **P** 🏛🐾In grounds on leads. 🔔 ❋ 🖥Please telephone for details.

WARKWORTH CASTLE ⊞

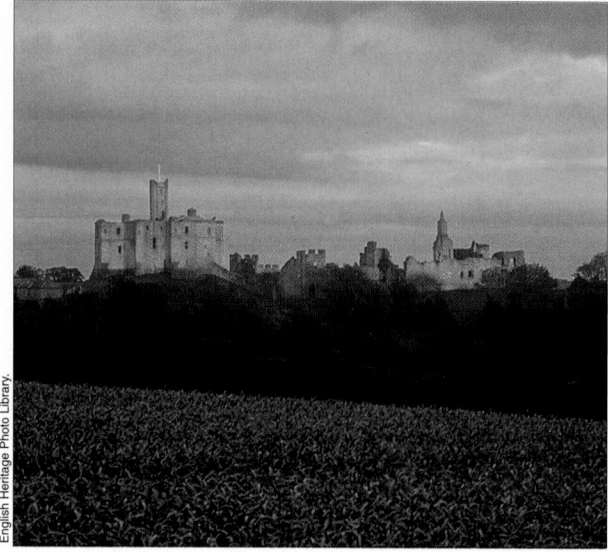

English Heritage Photo Library.

WARKWORTH, MORPETH, NORTHUMBERLAND NE66 0UJ

Owner: English Heritage　　*Contact:* The Custodian

Tel: 01665 711423

The great towering keep of this 15th century castle, once the home of the mighty Percy family, dominates the town and River Coquet. Warkworth is one of the most outstanding examples of an aristocratic fortified residence. Upstream by boat from the castle lies Warkworth Hermitage, cutting into the rock of the river cliff (separate charge applies).

Location: OS81 Ref. NU247 057. 7m S of Alnwick on A1068.

Opening Times: 1 Apr - 30 Sept: daily, 10am - 6pm. 1 - 31 Oct: daily, 10am - 5pm. 1 Nov - 31 Mar: daily, 10am - 4pm (closed 1 - 2pm). Closed 24 - 26 Dec.

Admission: Adult £2.50, Child £1.30, Conc. £1.90. 15% discount for groups (11+).

⬜ ♿Grounds suitable. 🎧 **P** 🏛🐾On leads. ❋ 🖥Tel. for details.

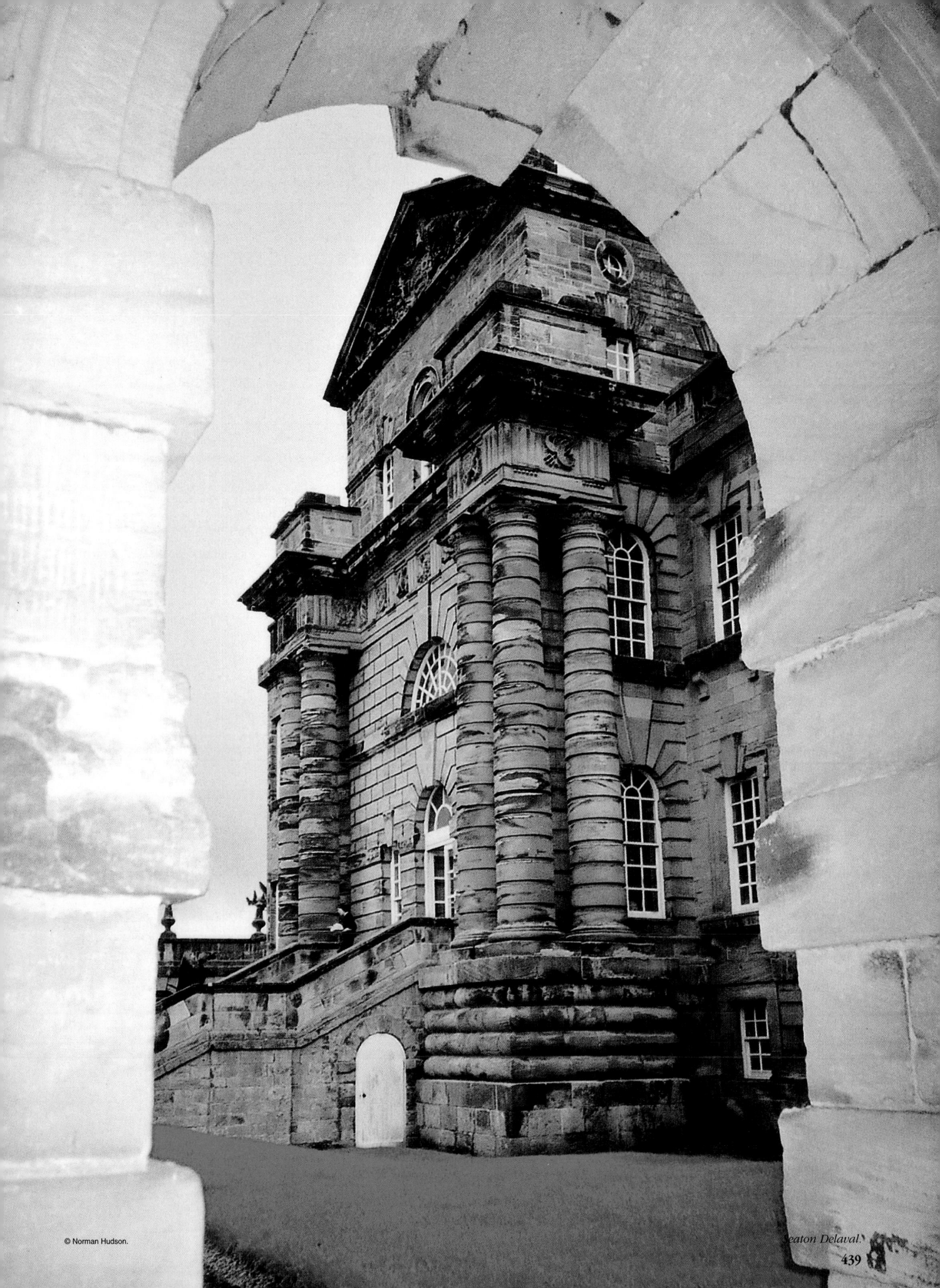

© Norman Hudson.

Seaton Delaval.

439

ARBEIA ROMAN FORT

Tel: 0191 456 1369 **Fax:** 0191 427 6862

Baring Street, South Shields, Tyne & Wear NE33 2BB
Owner: South Tyneside Metropolitan Borough Council   **Contact:** The Curator
Managed by: Tyne & Wear Museums
Extensive remains of 2nd century Roman fort, including fort defences, stone granaries, gateways and latrines. Full-scale reconstruction of Roman gateway and museum featuring finds including weapons, jewellery and tombstones. Watch excavations throughout the year.
Location: OS Ref. NZ365 679. Near town centre and Metro Station.
Opening Times: Easter - Oct: Mon - Sat: 10am - 5.30pm, Suns, 1 - 5pm. Open BH Mons. Winter: Mon - Sat, 10am - 4pm. Closed Christmas Day, Boxing Day, New Year's Day, Good Friday.
Admission: Free, except for Timequest Gallery: Adult £1.50, Conc. 80p.

BEDE'S WORLD MUSEUM

Tel: 0191 489 2106 **Fax:** 0191 428 2361

Church Bank, Jarrow, Tyne & Wear NE32 3DY
Managed by: Jarrow 700AD Ltd   **Contact:** Miss M Harte
A new museum telling the story of the Venerable Bede and Anglo-Saxon Northumbria.
Location: OS Ref. NZ339 652. Just off A19, S end of Tyne Tunnel.
Opening Times: Apr - Oct: Mon - Sat, 10am - 5.30pm, Suns, 12 noon - 5.30pm. Nov - Mar: Mon - Sat, 10am - 4.30pm, Suns, 12 noon - 4.30pm. Also open BH Mons.
Admission: Adult £4.50, Conc. £2.50, Family £9. Groups by arrangement.

BESSIE SURTEES HOUSE ⬚

Tel: 0191 269 1200

41 - 44 Sandhill, Newcastle, Tyne & Wear
Owner: English Heritage   **Contact:** The Custodian
Two 16th and 17th century merchants' houses stand on the quayside near the Tyne Bridge. One is a rare example of Jacobean domestic architecture. 3 rooms open.
Location: OS Ref. NZ252 639. 41- 44 Sandhill, Newcastle.
Opening Times: Weekdays only: 10am - 4pm. Closed BHs, 24 - 26 Dec and 1 Jan.
Admission: Free.

CATHEDRAL CHURCH OF ST NICHOLAS

Newcastle-upon-Tyne, Tyne & Wear NE1 1PF Tel: 0191 232 1939 **Fax:** 0191 230 0735
e-mail: stnicholas@aol.com   **Contact:** Rev Canon Peter Strange
Mostly 14th century surmounted by 15th century lantern spire, one medieval window, two Renaissance memorials, one large 15th century Flemish brass.
Location: OS Ref. NZ250 640. City centre, 1/2 m from A167 signposted from Swan House roundabout.
Opening Times: Suns: 7am - 12 noon, 4 - 7pm. Mon - Fri: 7am - 6pm. Sats: 8.30am - 4pm. BHs, 8am - 12 noon.

 📷 ♿ ☕ 🍴 By arrangement. 🅿 No parking. 🐑 🐕 Guide dogs only. ❄ (IW)

GIBSIDE ❧

Tel: 01207 542255

Nr Rowlands Gill, Burnopfield, Newcastle-upon-Tyne NE16 6BG
Owner: The National Trust   **Contact:** The Property Manager
Gibside is one of the finest 18th century designed landscapes in the north of England. The Chapel was built to James Paine's design soon after 1760. Outstanding example of Georgian architecture approached along a terrace with an oak avenue. Walk along the River Derwent through woodland.
Location: OS Ref. NZ172 583. 6m SW of Gateshead, 20m NW of Durham. Entrance on B6314 between Burnopfield and Rowlands Gill.
Opening Times: Grounds: 1 Apr - 31 Oct: daily except Mons (open BH Mons), 10am - 6pm. Last admission 4.30pm. 1 Nov - 31 Mar: 10am - sunset. Last admission 1 hour before sunset. Chapel: 1 Apr - 31 Oct: as grounds, otherwise by arrangement.
Admission: Chapel and Grounds: Adult £3, Child half price. Booked groups £2.60.

NEWCASTLE CASTLE GARTH

Tel: 0191 232 7938

Castle Keep, Castle Garth, Newcastle-upon-Tyne NE1 1RQ
Owner: Newcastle City Council   **Contact:** Paul MacDonald
The Keep originally dominated the castle bailey. The 'new' castle was founded in 1080.
Location: OS Ref. NZ251 638. City centre between St Nicholas church and the high level bridge.
Opening Times: All year: daily, 9.30am - 5pm.
Admission: Adult £1.50, Child/Conc. 50p.

ST PAUL'S MONASTERY ⬚

Tel: 0191 489 2106

Jarrow, Tyne & Wear
Owner: English Heritage   **Contact:** The Custodian
The home of the Venerable Bede in the 7th and 8th centuries, partly surviving as the chancel of the parish church. It has become one of the best understood Anglo-Saxon monastic sites.
Location: OS Ref. NZ339 652. In Jarrow, on minor road N of A185.
Opening Times: Any reasonable time.
Admission: Free.

SOUTER LIGHTHOUSE ❧

Tel: 0191 529 3161

Coast Road, Whitburn, Tyne & Wear SR6 7NR
Owner: The National Trust   **Contact:** The Property Manager
Shore-based lighthouse and associated buildings, built in 1871, the first to be powered by an alternating electric current.
Location: OS Ref. NZ408 641. 2 1/2 m S of South Shields on A183. 5m N of Sunderland.
Opening Times: 1 Apr - 31 Oct: daily except Fris (open Good Fri), 11am - 5pm. Last admission 4.30pm. Open after 31 Oct for events & activities – contact property for details.
Admission: Adult £2.80, Child half price. Booked Groups: £2.30. Family £7.

TYNEMOUTH PRIORY & CASTLE ⬚

Tel: 0191 257 1090

North Pier, Tynemouth, Tyne & Wear NE30 4BZ
Owner: English Heritage   **Contact:** The Custodian
The castle walls and gatehouse enclose the substantial remains of a Benedictine priory founded c1090 on a Saxon monastic site. Their strategic importance has made the castle and priory the target for attack for many centuries. In World War I, coastal batteries in the castle defended the mouth of the Tyne.
Location: OS88 Ref. NZ374 695. In Tynemouth.
Opening times: 1 Apr - 30 Sept: daily, 10am - 6pm. 1 - 31 Oct: daily, 10am - 5pm. 1 Nov - 31 Mar: Wed - Sun, 10am - 4pm (closed 1 - 2 pm).
Admission: Adult £1.90, Child £1, Conc. £1.40. 15% discount for groups (11+).

📷 ♿ Grounds suitable. ⚔ By arrangement. ▮ 🐎 In grounds, on leads. ❄ ⛨ Tel. for details.

WASHINGTON OLD HALL ❧

Tel: 0191 416 6879 **Fax:** 0191 419 2065

The Avenue, Washington Village, District 4, Washington, Tyne & Wear NE38 7LE
Owner: The National Trust   **Contact:** The Property Manager
Jacobean manor house incorporating portions of 12th century house of the Washington family. Displays of George Washington commemoratives. Small Jacobean knot garden.
Location: OS Ref. NZ312 566. In Washington on E side of The Avenue. 5m W of Sunderland (2m from A1), S of Tyne Tunnel, follow signs for Washington District 4 and then village.
Opening Times: 1 Apr - 31 Oct: Sun - Wed. Closed Thur - Sat (open Good Fri), 11am - 5pm. Last admission 4.30pm.
Admission: Adult £2.80, Child half-price, Family £7. Groups (15+) by arrangement only: £2.30.

📷 ▮ Conferences. ♿ Ground floor & grounds suitable. ☕ ⚔ By arrangement. 🅿 Limited. 🐎 In grounds, on leads. 🔔

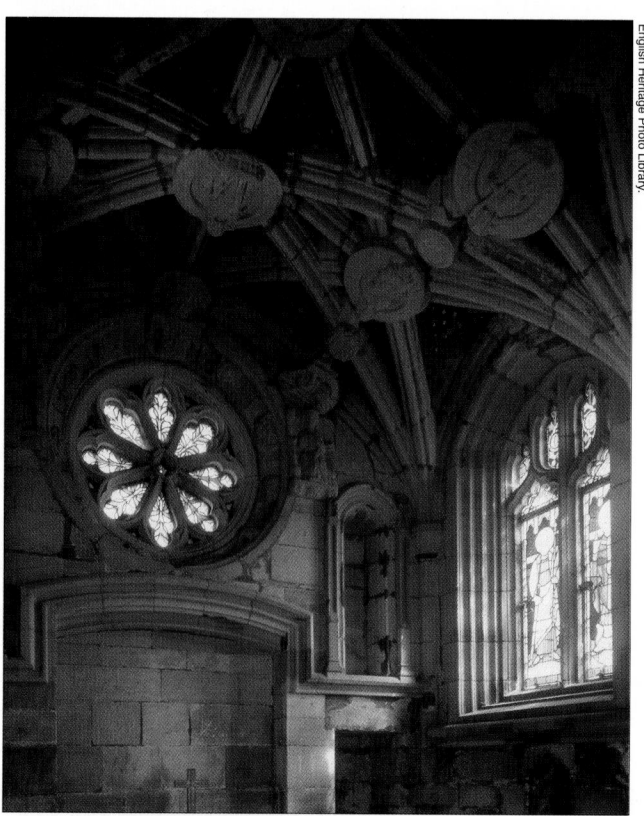

Tynemouth Priory & Castle, Tyne & Wear.

English Heritage Photo Library

THE REGIONS OF
SCOTLAND

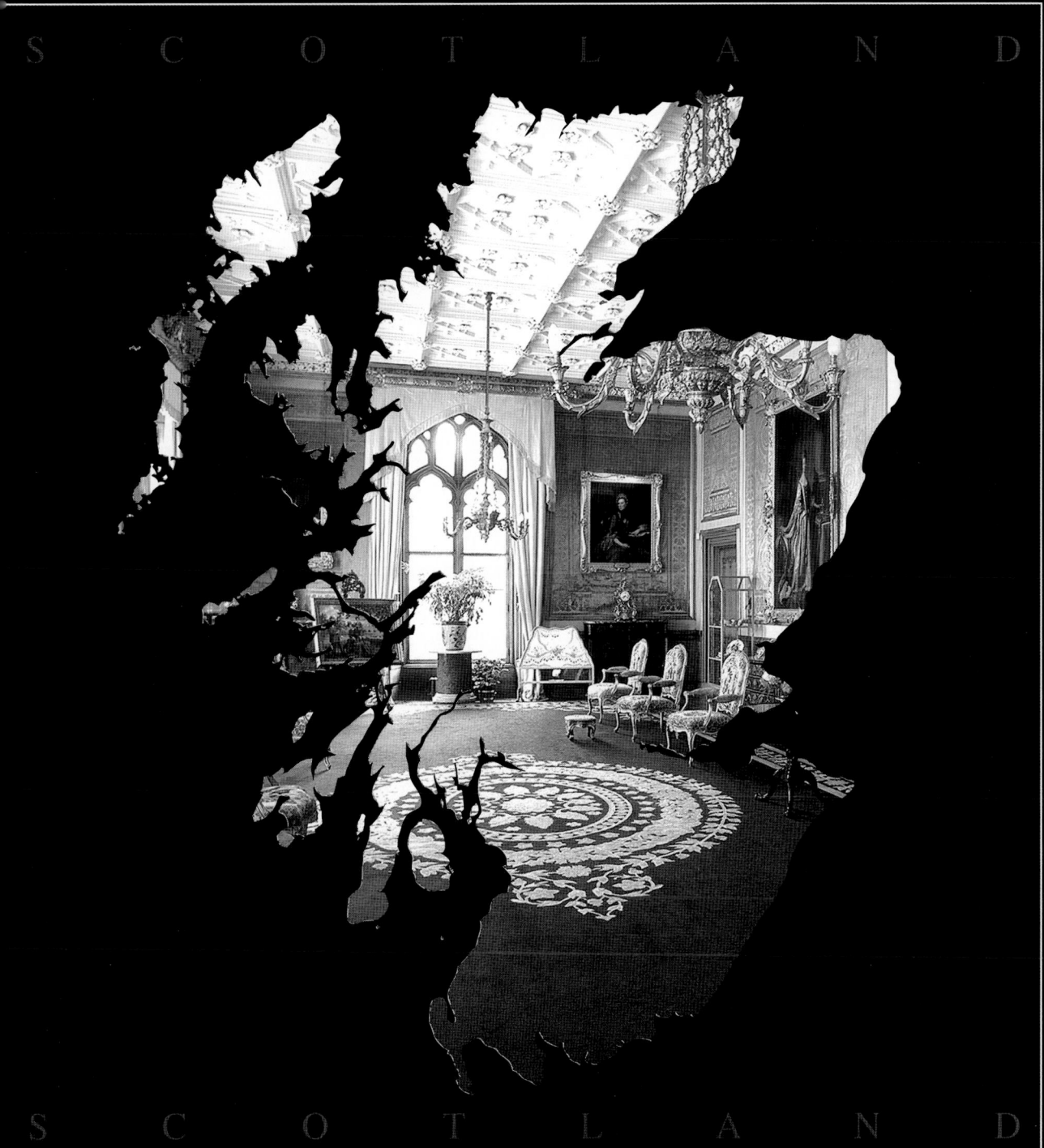

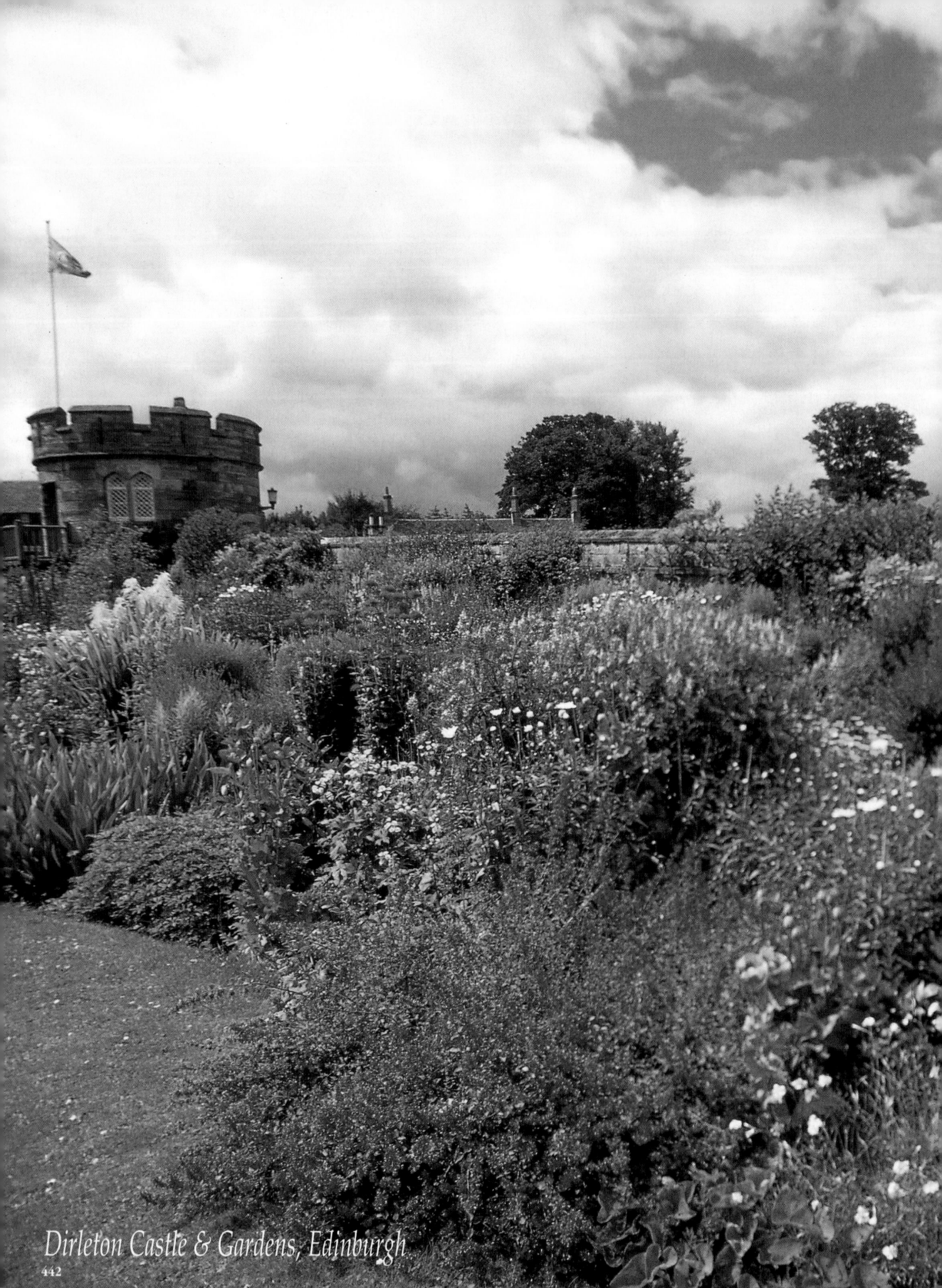

Dirleton Castle & Gardens, Edinburgh

442

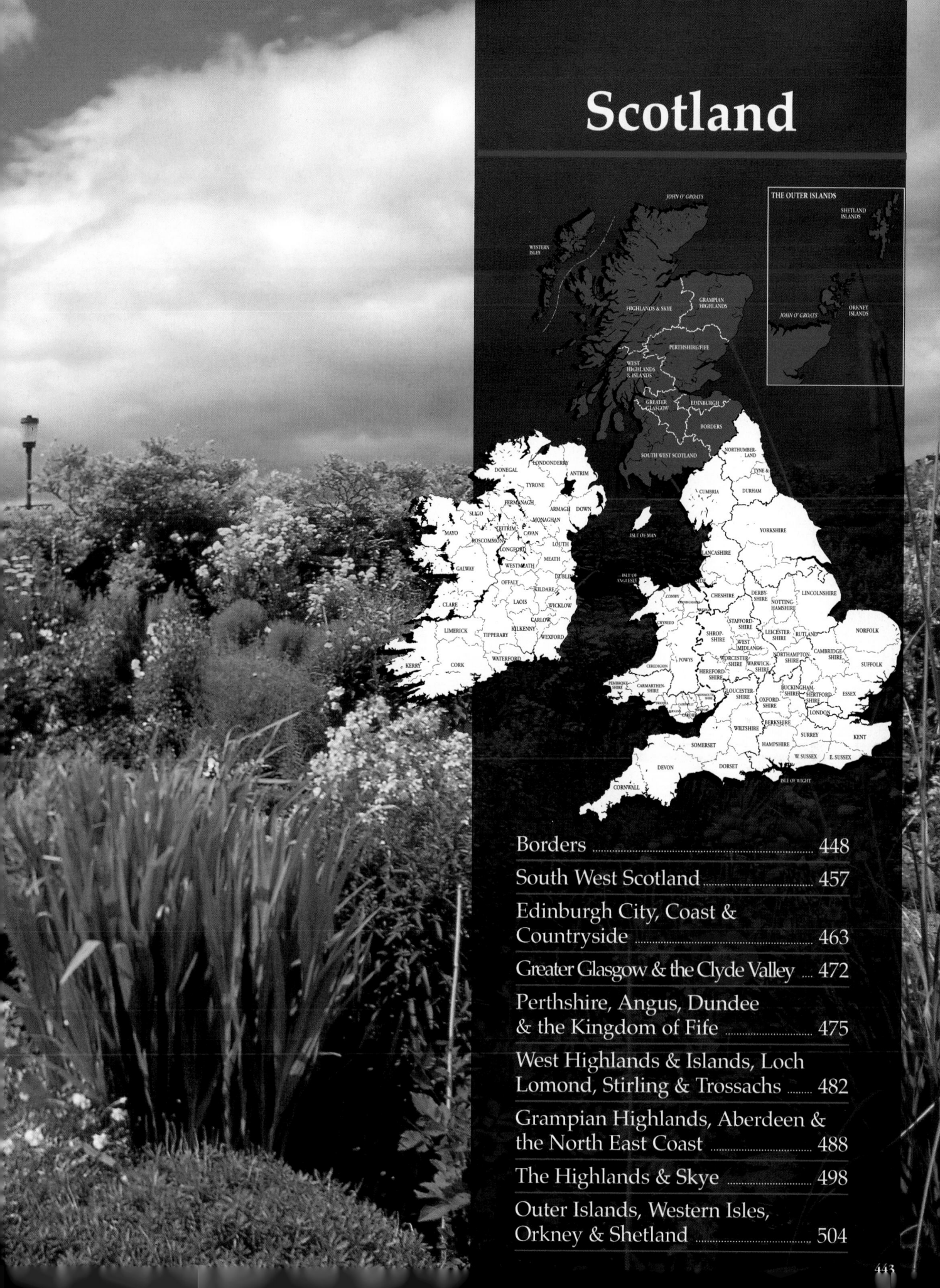

Scotland

THE OUTER ISLANDS

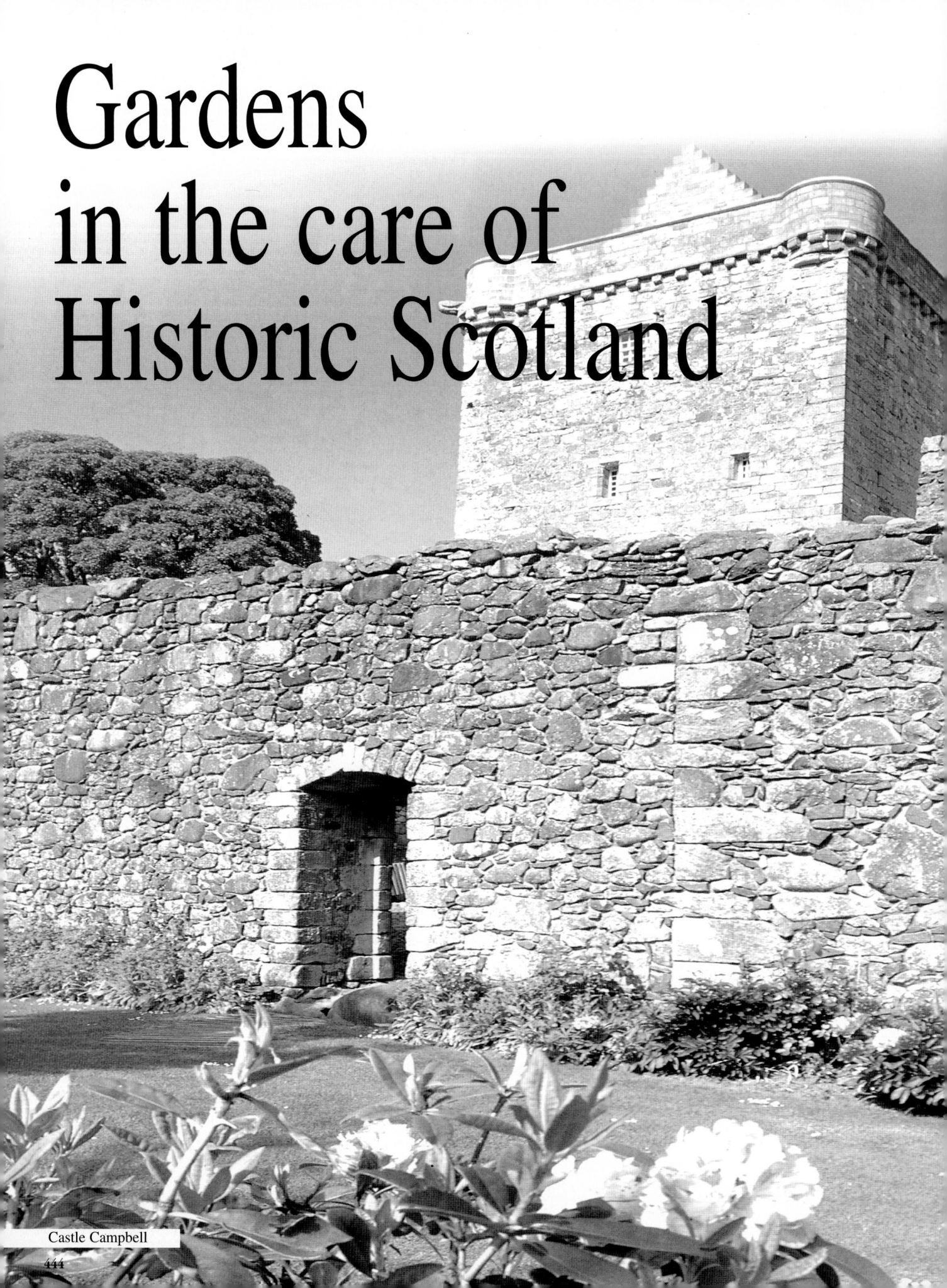

Gardens
in the care of
Historic Scotland

Castle Campbell

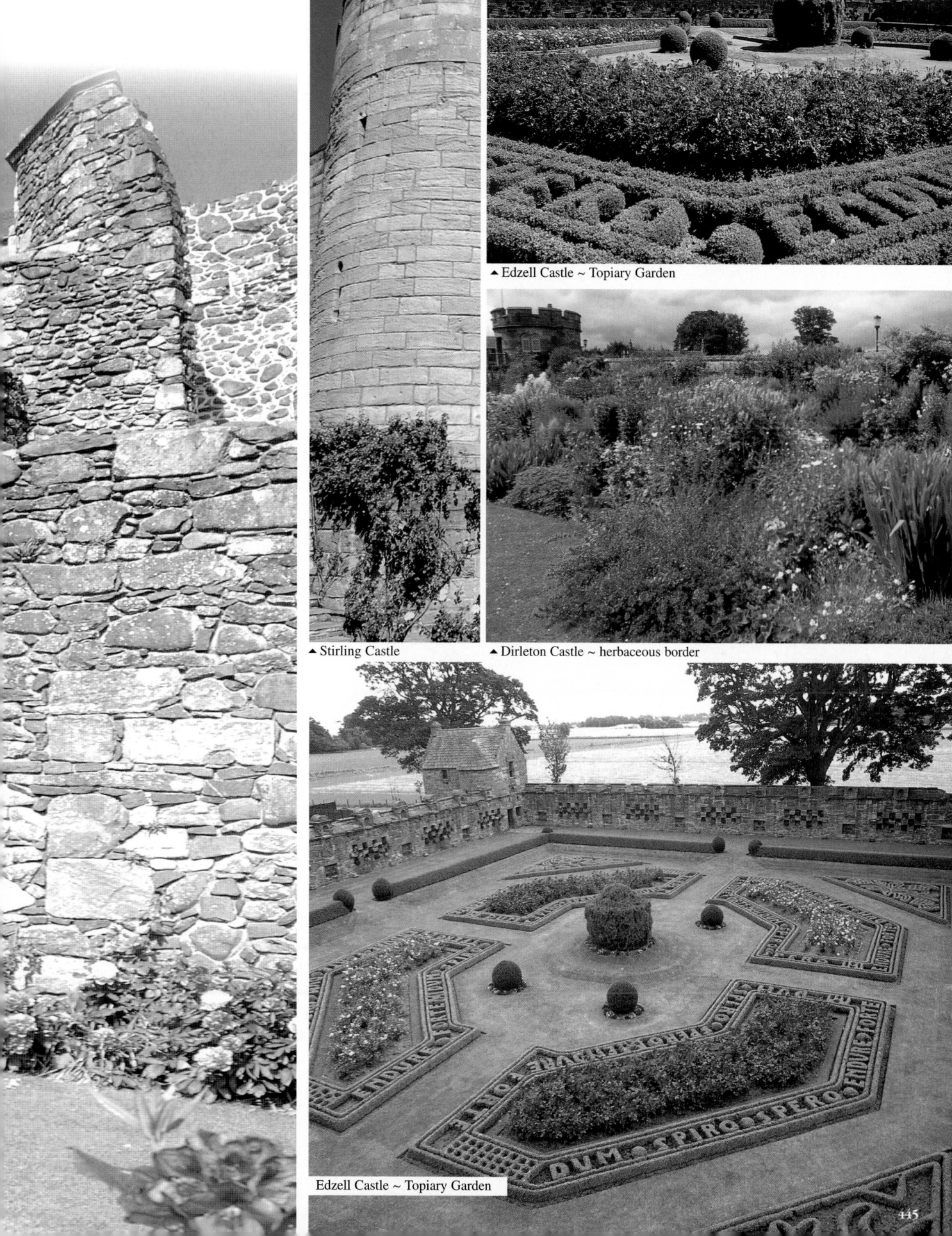

▲ Edzell Castle ~ Topiary Garden

▲ Stirling Castle

▲ Dirleton Castle ~ herbaceous border

Edzell Castle ~ Topiary Garden

445

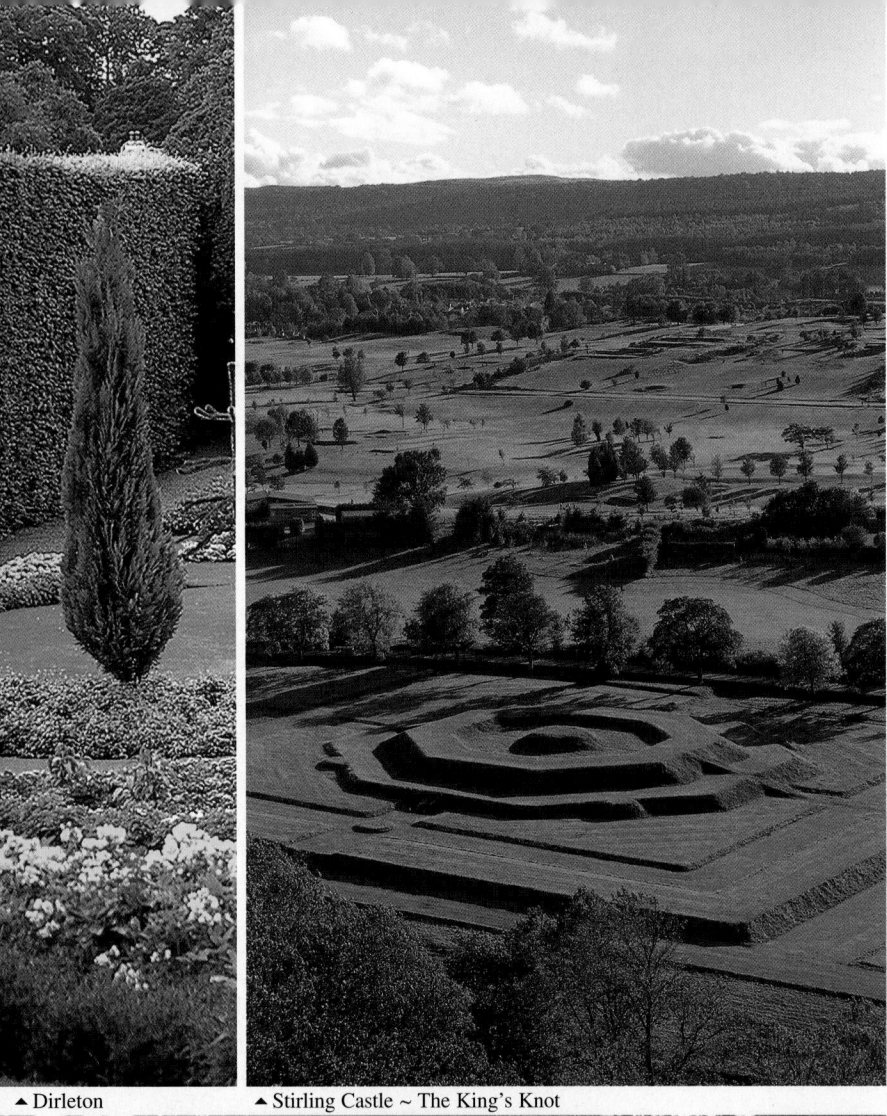

▲ Dirleton   ▲ Stirling Castle ~ The King's Knot

The gardens in the care of Historic Scotland vary in spirit, character and history – all have their own charm.

Edzell, Aberdour, Dirleton Castle and Stirling Castle, the nearby wild splendour of Castle Campbell, make an ideal itinerary for a garden lovers' tour.

Edzell

"... delicat gardine with walls sumptuously built of hewen stone polisht, with pictures and coats of armes in the walls."
Oucterlony of Guinde, c1700

Built for Sir David Lindsay, Lord Edzell, about 1604 and recreated in the 1930s, the walled garden at Edzell features extraordinary carvings depicting the Planetary Deities, Liberal Arts and Cardinal Virtues. Visitors see decorative hedges shaped and trimmed into the Fleur de Lys, Scottish Thistle and English Rose. Sir David intended his garden to stimulate both mind and senses, and it does.

Dirleton Castle

"... some of the best examples of modern flower gardening, together with others of a style some two centuries old."
Journal account, 1865

The gardens at Dirleton emphasise the attractiveness of this castle. The castle's buildings divide into three distinct periods ranging from the 1200s to the 1500s, through the hands of three families: the de Vauxs, Halyburtons and Ruthvens. The terraced garden to the west of the castle was devised and laid out by William Ruthven, the Earl of Gowrie, in the late 1500s. A sunken bowling green probably started life as a formal parterre surrounded by yew hedges. Beyond lay lawns planted with specimen trees, leading to a well-preserved beehive doocot, which provided winter meat. Historic Scotland has also recreated the Victorian garden devised by the castle's owners in the 1860s. The castle is approached by passing along officially the world's longest herbaceous borders which are some of the most magnificent to be seen.

Aberdour

"I was lead in through the garden which was so fragrant and delightful that I thought I was still in England."
Anne Murray, 1650

Aberdour is a wonderful example of how a medieval castle could be extended and modified over several centuries. A castle stood on the site from as early as the 13th century but first known mention of a garden is not until 1540. The walled garden was converted into a bowling green by 1668, a use which continued at least until 1745, and the area still abounds with plants which, when in season, provide cuttings for sale.

Castle Campbell

Castle Campbell sits above the small village of Dollar. This spectacularly sited 15th century fortress was the lowland stronghold of the Campbells. Stunning views from the parapet walk look down on the rushing waters of the Burn of Care and Burn of Sorrow. Evidence of a formal garden remains at Castle Campbell and the entrance is dominated by the ancient 'Maiden Tree', but its wilderness setting close to Stirling makes it a particularly beautiful and accessible site.

Stirling Castle

In the 16th century Stirling Castle reflected Scotland's cultural ascendancy. Vast formal gardens were created by James IV and V, and these attracted lavish attention for many years after. Visitors in the Queen Anne rose garden can still look down and see the ghostly relief map beyond the castle walls, clearly showing the 1620s layout of what is known as the King's Knot.

Historic Scotland has 300 properties in its care, and its gardens are a rich jewel in its crown, offering hours of enjoyment.

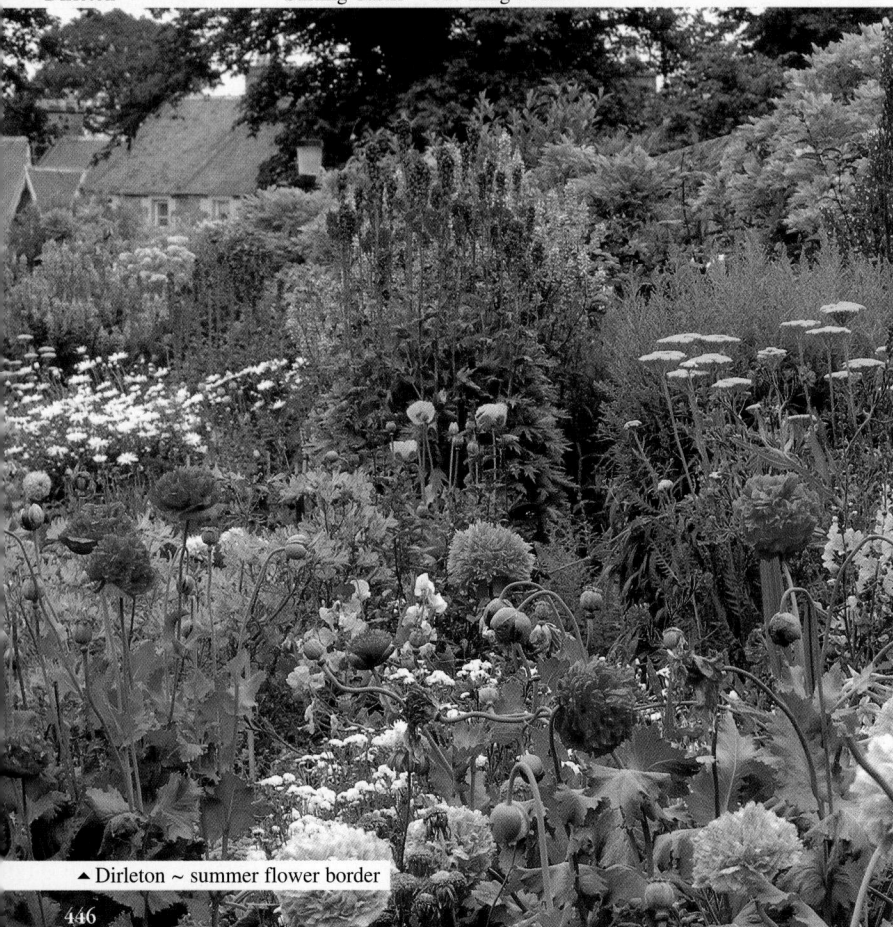

▲ Dirleton ~ summer flower border

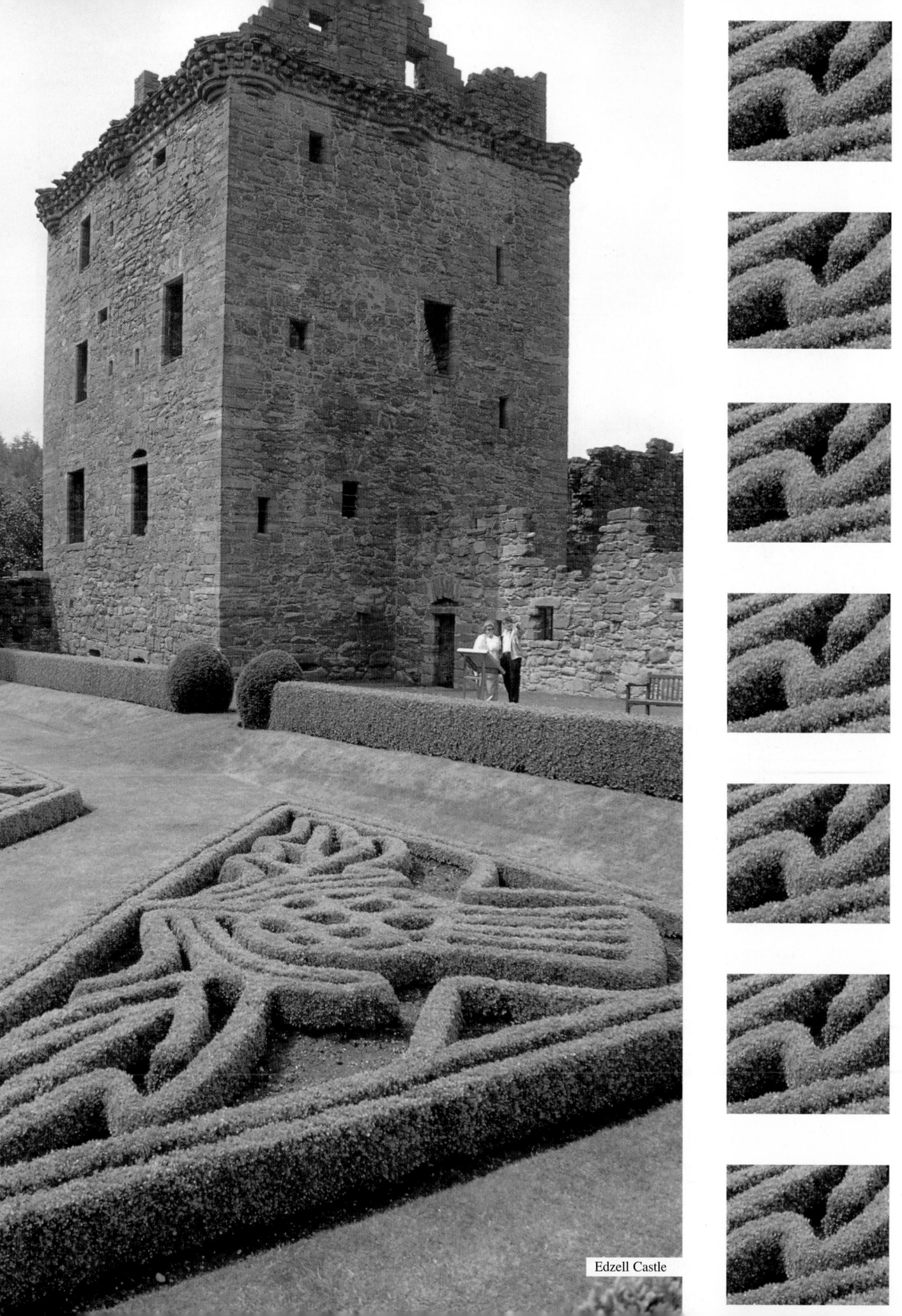

Edzell Castle

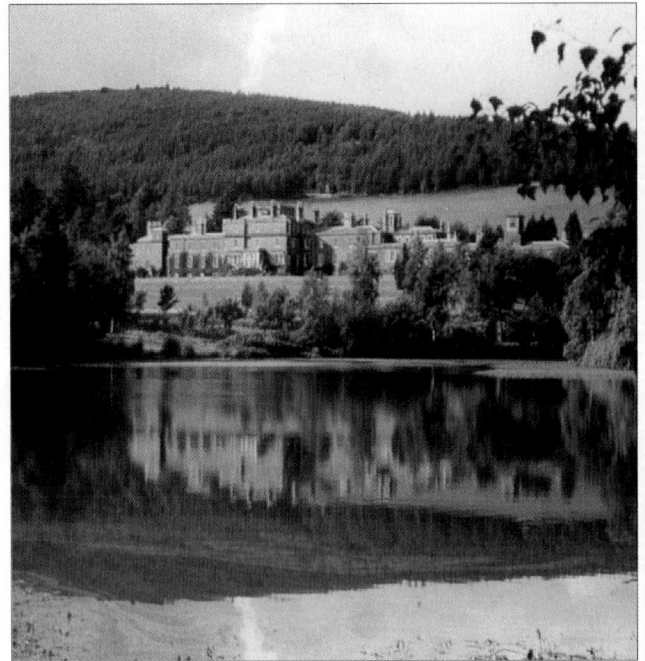

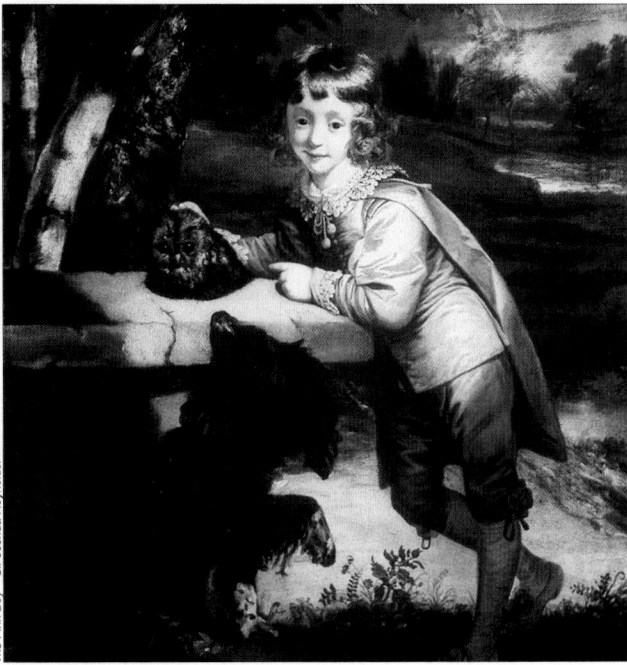

'The Pink Boy' - Sir Joshua Reynolds.

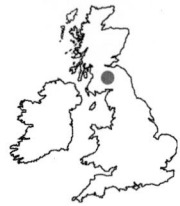

Owner: His Grace the Duke of Buccleuch & Queensberry KT

CONTACT

Buccleuch Heritage Trust
Bowhill House &
Country Park
Bowhill
Selkirk
TD7 5ET

Tel/Fax: 01750 22204

e-mail:
bht@buccleuch.com

LOCATION

OS Ref. NT426 278

3m W of Selkirk off A708
Moffat Road,
A68 from Newcastle,
A7 from Carlisle
or Edinburgh.

Bus: 3m Selkirk.

Taxi: 01750 20354.

BOWHILL HOUSE & COUNTRY PARK
Selkirk

Scottish Borders home of the Duke and Duchess of Buccleuch, dating mainly from 1812 and christened 'Sweet Bowhill' by Sir Walter Scott in his *Lay of the Last Minstrel*.

Many of the works of art were collected by earlier Montagus, Douglases and Scotts or given by Charles II to his natural son James, Duke of Monmouth and Buccleuch. Paintings include Canaletto's *Whitehall*, works by Guardi, Claude, Ruysdael, Gainsborough, Raeburn, Reynolds, Van Dyck and Wilkie. Superb French furniture, Meissen and Sèvres porcelain, silver and tapestries.

Historical relics include Monmouth's saddle and execution shirt, Sir Walter Scott's plaid and some proof editions, Queen Victoria's letters and gifts to successive Duchesses of Buccleuch, her Mistresses of the Robes.

There is also a completely restored Victorian Kitchen, 19th century horse-drawn fire engine, 'Bowhill Little Theatre', a lively centre for the performing arts and where, prior to touring the house, visitors can see 'The Quest for Bowhill', a 20 minute audio-visual presentation by Dr Colin Thompson.

Conference centre, arts courses, literary lunches, education service, visitor centre. Shop, tearoom, adventure playground, woodland walks, nature trails, picnic areas. Garden and landscape designed by John Gilpin.

Fashion shows, air displays, archery, clay pigeon shooting, equestrian events, charity garden parties, shows, rallies, filming, lecture theatre. House is open by appointment outside public hours to groups led by officials of a recognised museum, gallery or educational establishment. No photography inside house.

Inside caterers normally used but outside caterers considered.

Visitors may alight at entrance. WC. Wheelchair visitors free.

Groups can book in advance (special rates), menus on request.

For groups. Tour time 1¼ hrs.

60 cars and 6 coaches within 50yds of house.

Welcome. Projects in Bowhill House and Victorian kitchen, Education Officers (service provided free of charge), schoolroom, ranger-led nature walks, adventure playground. Heritage Education Trust Sandford Award winner 1993 and 1998.

On leads.

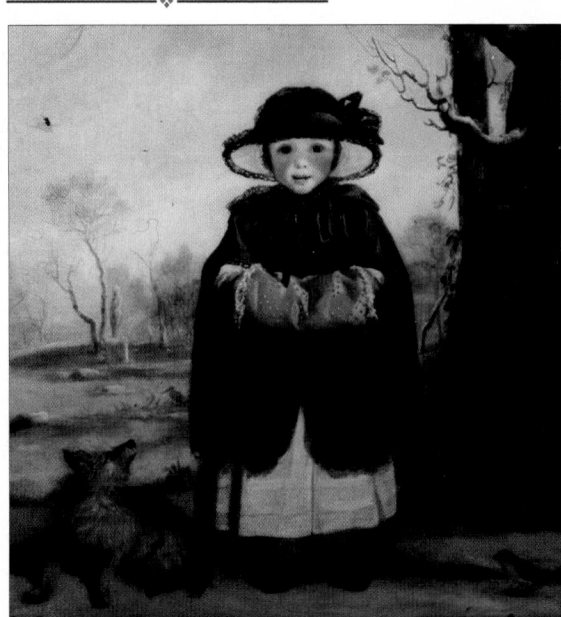

'Winter' - Sir Joshua Reynolds.

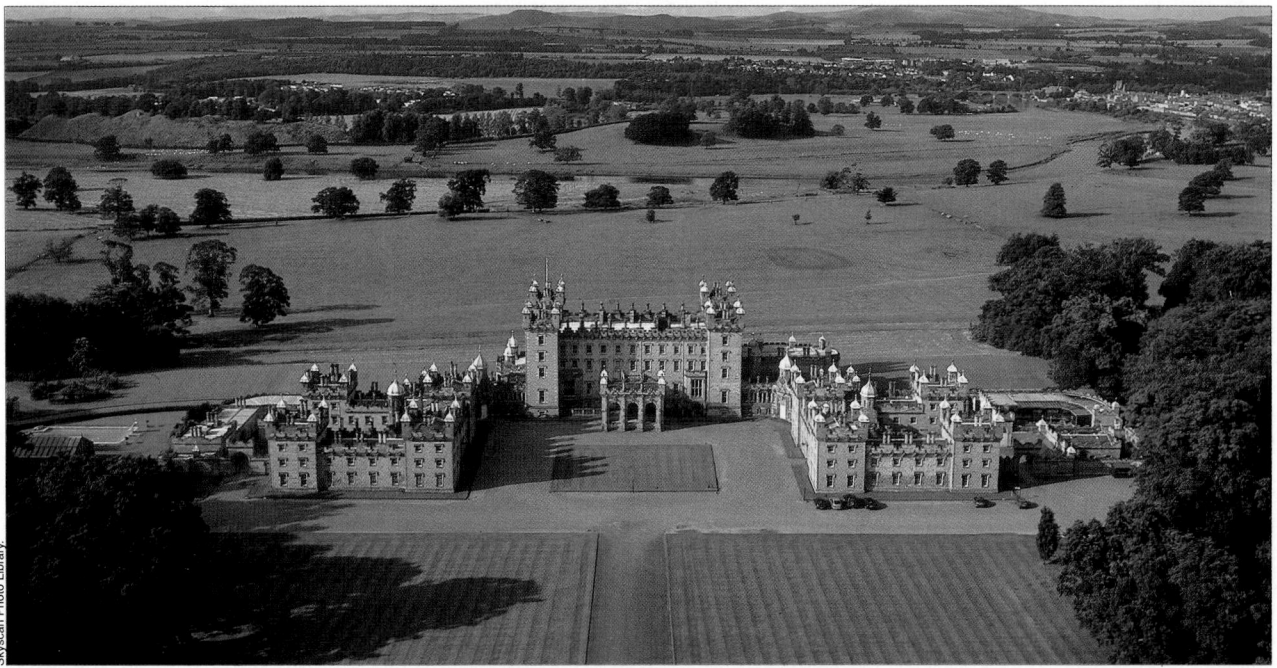

Skyscan Photo Library.

FLOORS CASTLE
Kelso

FLOORS CASTLE, home of the Duke and Duchess of Roxburghe, is situated in the heart of the Scottish Border Country. It is reputedly the largest inhabited castle in Scotland. Designed by William Adam, who was both masterbuilder and architect, for the first Duke of Roxburghe, building started in 1721.

It was the present Duke's great-great-grand-father James, the 6th Duke, who embellished the plain Adam features of the building. In about 1849 Playfair, letting his imagination and talent run riot, transformed the castle, creating a multitude of spires and domes.

The apartments now display the outstanding collection of French 17th and 18th century furniture, magnificent tapestries, Chinese and European porcelain and many other fine works of art. Many of the treasures in the castle today were collected by Duchess May, American wife of the 8th Duke.

The castle has been seen on cinema screens worldwide in the film *Greystoke*, as the home of Tarzan, the Earl of Greystoke.

Gardens
The extensive parkland and gardens overlooking the Tweed provide a variety of wooded walks. The walled garden contains splendid herbaceous borders and in the outer walled garden a parterre to commemorate the Millennium can be seen. An excellent children's playground and picnic area are very close to the castle.

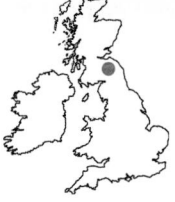

Owner: His Grace the Duke of Roxburghe

CONTACT

Philip Massey
Director of Operations
Roxburghe Estates Office
Kelso
Roxburghshire
Scotland
TD5 7SF

Tel: 01573 223333

Fax: 01573 226056

LOCATION

OS Ref. NT711 347

From South A68, A698.

From North A68, A697/9
In Kelso follow signs.

Bus: Kelso Bus Station 1m.

Rail: Berwick 20m.

OPENING TIMES

SUMMER
13 April - 28 October
Daily: 10am - 4.30pm.

Last admission 4pm.

WINTER
November - March
Closed to the general public, available for events.

ADMISSION

SUMMER

Adult	£5.50
Child (5 - 15yrs)	£3.25
OAP/Student	£4.75
Family	£12.00

Groups (min 20)	
Adult	£4.25
Child (5 - 15yrs)	£2.75
OAP/Student	£4.00

Grounds only	
	£3.00
Groups	£2.50

Under 5yrs Free.

SPECIAL EVENTS

- **AUG 26:**
  Family Day with Massed Pipe Bands.

CONFERENCE/FUNCTION

ROOM	SIZE	MAX CAPACITY
Dining Rm	18m x 7m	150
Ballroom	21m x 8m	150

Gala dinners, conferences, product launches, 4 x 4 driving, incentive groups, highland games and other promotional events. Extensive park, helicopter pad, fishing, clay pigeon and pheasant shooting. No photography inside the castle.

Visitors may alight at the entrance. WC.

Self-service, licensed, seats 125 opens 10am.

By arrangement for up to 100. Tour time 1¼ hrs.

Unlimited for cars, 100 yds away, coach park 50 yds. Coaches can be driven to the entrance, waiting area close to restaurant exit. Lunch or tea for coach drivers.

Welcome, guide provided. Playground facilities.

Guide dogs only.

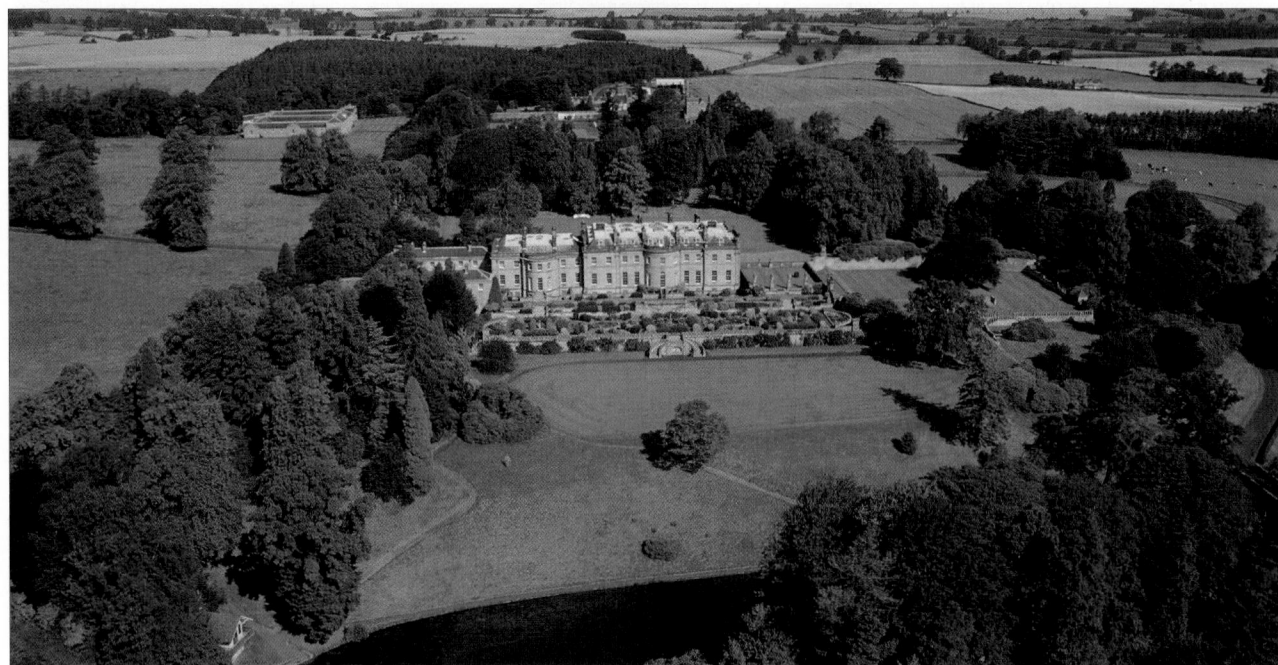

Borders
Scotland

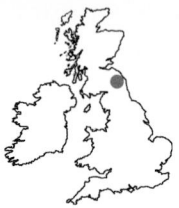

Owner: The Lord Palmer

CONTACT

The Lord or Lady Palmer
Manderston
Duns
Berwickshire
Scotland
TD11 3PP

Tel: 01361 883450
Secretary: 01361 882636

Fax: 01361 882010

e-mail: palmer@
manderston.co.uk

LOCATION

OS Ref. NT810 544

From Edinburgh
47m, 1hr.
1½ m E of Duns on
A6105.

Bus: 400 yds.

Rail: Berwick Station 12m.

Taxi: Chirnside 818216.

Airport: Edinburgh or
Newcastle both
60m or 80 mins.

CONFERENCE/FUNCTION		
ROOM	SIZE	MAX CAPACITY
Dining Rm	22 'x 35'	100
Ballroom	34' x 21'	150
Hall	22' x 38'	130
Drawing Rm	35' x 21'	150

MANDERSTON
Duns

MANDERSTON, together with its magnificent stables, stunning marble dairy and 56 acres of immaculate gardens, forms an ensemble which must be unique in Britain today.

The house was completely rebuilt between 1903 and 1905, with no expense spared.

Visitors are able to see not only the sumptuous State Rooms and bedrooms, decorated in the Adam manner, but also all the original domestic offices, in a truly 'upstairs downstairs' atmosphere. Manderston boasts a unique and recently restored silver staircase.

There is a special museum with a nostalgic display of valuable tins made by Huntley and Palmer from 1868 to the present day. Winner of the AA/NPI Bronze Award UK 1994.

GARDENS

Outside, the magnificence continues and the combination of formal gardens and picturesque landscapes is a major attraction: unique amongst Scottish houses.

The stables, still in use, have been described by *Horse and Hound* as "probably the finest in all the wide world."

❖

Corporate & incentives venue. Ideal retreat: business groups, think-tank weekends. Fashion shows, air displays, archery, clay pigeon shooting, equestrian events, garden parties, shows, rallies, filming, product launches and marathons. Two airstrips for light aircraft, approx 5m, grand piano, billiard table, fox-hunting, pheasant shoots, sea angling, salmon fishing, stabling, cricket pitch, tennis court, lake. Nearby: 9-hole golf course, indoor swimming pool, squash court. No photography in house.

Available. Buffets, lunches and dinners. Wedding receptions.

Special parking available outside the House.

Tearoom (open as house) with waitress service. Can be booked in advance, menus on request.

Included. Available in French. Guides in rooms. If requested, the owner may meet groups. Tour time 1¼ hrs.

400 cars 125yds from house, 30 coaches 5yds from house. Appreciated if group fees are paid by one person.

Welcome. Guide can be provided. Biscuit Tin Museum of particular interest.

Grounds only, on leads.

5 twin, 4 double and 1 single.

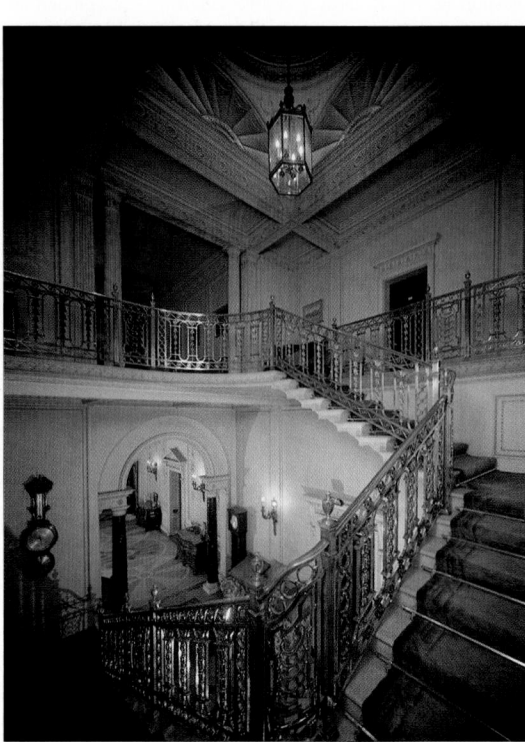

OPENING TIMES

SUMMER
Mid-May - end September
Thurs & Suns
2 - 5pm.

BH Mons, late May
& August
2 - 5pm.

Groups welcome all year
by appointment.

WINTER
September - May
Group visits welcome
by appointment.

ADMISSION

(2000 prices -
subject to alteration)

House & Grounds
Adult £6.00
Child £3.00
Groups (20+ on open days)
Per person £5.00

Grounds only
Including Stables &
Marble Dairy
Adult £3.50
Child £1.50

On days when the house is closed to the public, groups viewing by appointment will have personally conducted tours. The Gift Shop will be open. On these occasions reduced party rates (except for school children) will not apply. Group visits (20+) other than open days are £6 (minimum £120). Cream teas on open days only.

ABBOTSFORD HOUSE

Tel: 01896 752043 **Fax:** 01896 752916

Melrose, Roxburghshire TD6 9BQ

Sir Walter Scott purchased the Cartley Hall farmhouse on the banks of the Tweed in 1812. Together with his family and servants he moved into the farm which he renamed Abbotsford. Scott had the old house demolished in 1822 and replaced it with the main block of Abbotsford as it is today. Scott was a passionate collector of historic relics including an impressive collection of armour and weapons and over 9,000 rare volumes in his library.

Location: OS Ref. NT508 343. 35m S of Edinburgh. Melrose 3m, Galashiels 2m.

Opening Times: 18 Mar - 31 Oct: Mon - Sat, & Suns (Jun - Sept only) 10am - 5pm. Also Suns in Mar - May & Oct, 2 - 5pm. Other dates by arrangement.

Admission: Adult £4, Child £2. Groups: Adult £3, Child £1.50.

☐ 🚻House suitable. WC. 🐕 🦮Guide dogs only.

AIKWOOD TOWER & JAMES HOGG EXHIBITION

Tel: 01750 52253 **Fax:** 01750 52261 **e-mail:** steel@aikwoodscottishborders.com

Ettrick Valley, Nr Selkirk TD7 5HJ

Owner: Lord & Lady Steel of Aikwood **Contact:** Judy Steel

A fine 16 century peel tower and exhibition of James Hogg.

Location: OS Ref. NT419 260. SE side of B7009, 4m SW of Selkirk.

Opening Times: May - Sept: Tues, Thurs & Suns, 2 - 5pm.

Admission: £2.

AYTON CASTLE

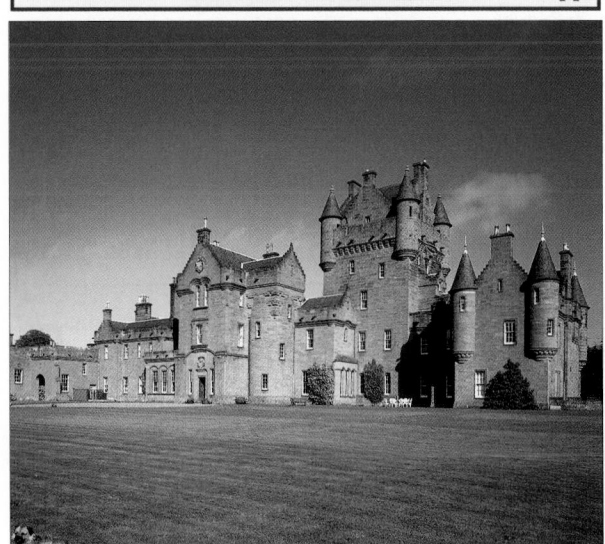

AYTON, EYEMOUTH, BERWICKSHIRE TD14 5RD

Owner: D I Liddell-Grainger of Ayton   *Contact:* The Curator

Tel: 018907 81212 or 018907 81550

Built in 1846 by the Mitchell-Innes family and designed by the architect James Gillespie Graham. Over the last ten years it has been fully restored and is now a family home. It is a unique restoration project and the quality of the original and restored workmanship is outstanding. The castle stands on an escarpment surrounded by mature woodlands containing many interesting trees and has been a film-making venue due to this magnificent setting.

Location: OS Ref. NT920 610. 7m N of Berwick-on-Tweed on Route A1.

Opening Times: 6 May - 30 Sept: Suns, 2 - 5 pm or by appointment.

Admission: Adult £3, Child (under 15yrs) Free.

🍴 🔑Obligatory. 🅿 🐕In grounds, on leads. ❄

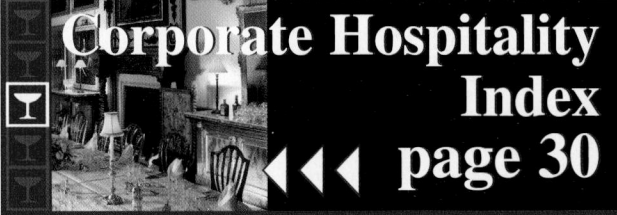

BOWHILL HOUSE & COUNTRY PARK

See page 448 for full page entry.

BUGHTRIG GARDEN

Tel: 01890 840678 **Fax:** 01890 840509

Bughtrig, Coldstream, Berwickshire TD12 4JP

Owner: Major General C A & the Hon Mrs Ramsay **Contact:** The Secretary

Bughtrig is a classic Georgian family house c1785 with later additions. The formal garden is hedged and close to the house, surrounded by fine specimen trees which provide remarkable shelter. Its 2½ acres contain an interesting combination of herbaceous plants, roses, shrubs, annuals, fruit, vegetables and a tree nursery. Small picnic area.

Location: OS Ref. NT797 447. ¼ m E of Leitholm Village on B6461.

Opening Times: Garden: Jun - Sept: daily, 11am - 5pm. House: by appointment only.

Admission: Adult £2, Child (under 18yrs) £1. Rates for House or accommodation by arrangement.

🚻Partially suitable. 🅿Limited. 🐕Guide dogs only. 🛏4 twin bedrooms/3 bathrooms. ❄

DAWYCK BOTANIC GARDEN

Tel: 01721 760254 **Fax:** 01721 760214

Stobo, Peeblesshire EH45 9JU **Contact:** The Curator

Renowned historic arboretum. Amongst mature specimen trees – some over 40 metres tall – are a variety of flowering trees, shrubs and herbaceous plants. Explore the world's first Cryptogamic Sanctuary and Reserve for 'non-flowering' plants.

Location: NT168 352. 8m SW of Peebles on B712.

Opening Times: 1 Mar - 31 Oct: daily, 9.30am - 6pm.

Admission: Adult £3, Child £1, Family £7, Conc. £2.50, Group discounts available.

DRUMLANRIG'S TOWER

Tel: 01450 373457 **Fax:** 01450 378506

Tower Knowe, Hawick TD9 9EN **e-mail:** hawickmuseum@hotmail.com

Owner: Scottish Borders Council **Contact:** The Curator

An 18th century town house containing the remains of a fortified tower of the 1550s.

Location: OS Ref. NT502 144. In Hawick town centre at W end of the High Street.

Opening Times: Please contact for details: open all year.

Admission: Adult £2, Conc. £1. 10% group discount. Free for local residents. Free for under 16s if accompanied.

DRYBURGH ABBEY

Tel: 01835 822381

St Boswells, Melrose

Owner: Historic Scotland **Contact:** The Steward

The ruins of Dryburgh Abbey are remarkably complete. The burial place of Sir Walter Scott and Field Marshal Earl Haig. Perhaps the most beautiful of all the Border abbeys.

Location: OS Ref. NT591 317. 5m SE of Melrose off B6356. 1½ m N of St Boswells.

Opening Times: 1 Apr - 30 Sept: daily, 9.30am - 6.30pm. Last ticket 6pm. 1 Oct - 31 Mar: Mon - Sat, 9.30am - 4.30pm, Suns, 2 - 4.30pm, last ticket 4pm.

Admission: Adult £2.80, Child £1, Conc. £2.

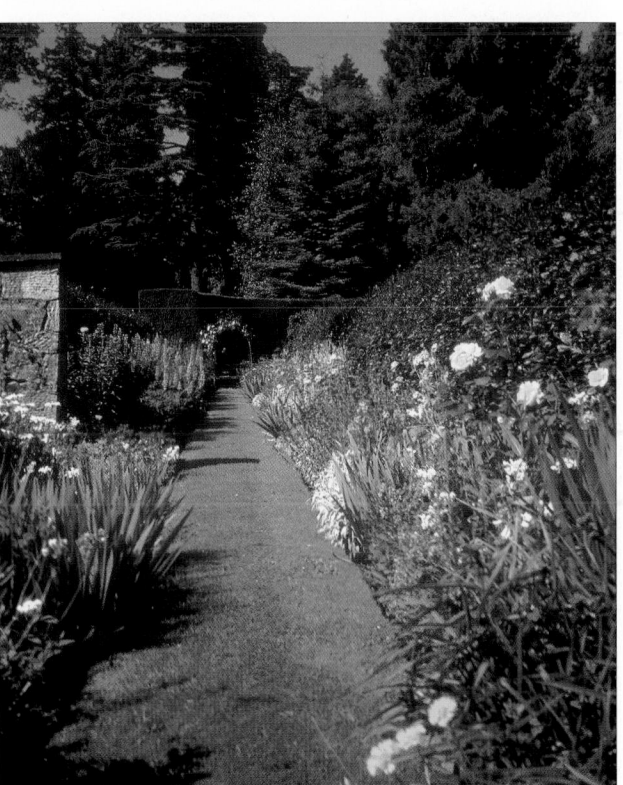

Bughtrig Garden, Borders.

DUNS CASTLE

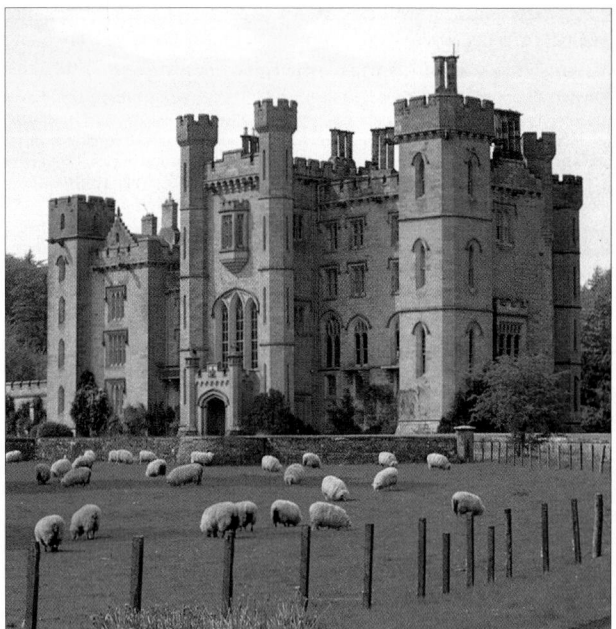
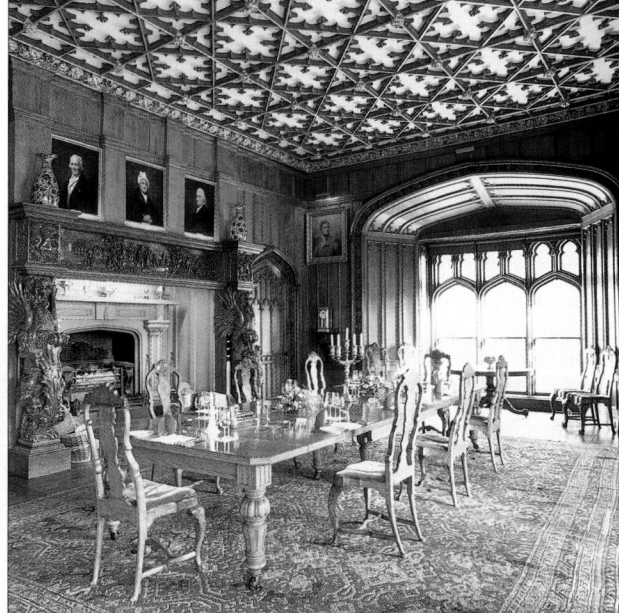

DUNS, BERWICKSHIRE TD11 3NW

Owner: *Alexander Hay of Duns*   **Contact:** *Mrs Aline Hay*

Tel: 01361 883211   **Fax:** 01361 882015   **e-mail:** aline_hay@lineone.net

This historical 1320 pele tower has been home to the Hay family since 1696, and the current owners Alexander and Aline Hay offer it as a welcoming venue for individuals, groups and corporate guests to enjoy. They have renovated it to produce the highest standards of comfort while retaining all the character of its rich period interiors. Wonderful lakeside and parkland setting.

Location: OS Ref. NT777 544. 10m off A4. Rail: Berwick station 16m. Airports: Newcastle & Edinburgh, 1 hr.

Opening Times: Not open to the public except by arrangement and for individuals, groups and companies for day or residential stays. Available all year.

Admission: Rates for private and corporate visits, wedding receptions, filming by arrangement.

4 x 4-poster, 3 x double, 3 x twin (all with bathrooms), 2 single.

FERNIEHIRST CASTLE

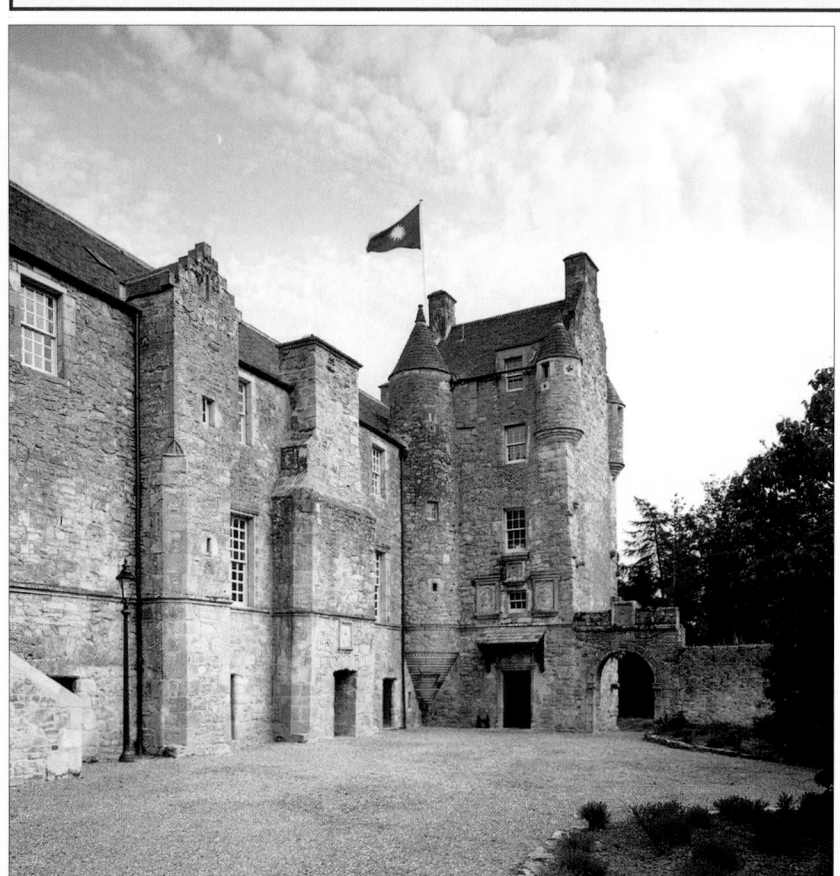

JEDBURGH, ROXBURGHSHIRE TD8 6NX

Owner: *The Marquess of Lothian*   **Contact:** *Mrs J Fraser*

Tel: 01835 862201   **Fax:** 01835 863992

Ferniehirst Castle – Scotland's Frontier Fortress. Ancestral home of the Kerr family. Restored (1984/1987) by the 12th Marquess of Lothian. Unrivalled 16th century Border architecture. Grand Apartment and Turret Library. A 16th century Chamber Oratory. The Kerr Chamber – Museum of Family History. A special tribute to Jedburgh's Protector to Mary Queen of Scots – Sir Thomas Kerr. Riverside walk by Jed Water. Archery Field opposite the Chapel where sheep of Viking origin still graze as they did four centuries ago.

Location: OS Ref. NT653 181. 2m S of Jedburgh on the A68.

Opening Times: Jul: Tue - Sun (closed Mons), 11am - 4pm.

Admission: Adult £3, Child £1.50. Groups (max. 50) by prior arrangement (01835 862201).

Partially suitable. WCs.

Guided tours only, groups by arrangement.

Ample for cars and coaches.

In grounds, on leads.

FLOORS CASTLE

See page 449 for full page entry.

HALLIWELL'S HOUSE MUSEUM

Tel: 01750 20096 **Fax:** 01750 23282

Halliwell's Close, Market Place, High Street, Selkirk

Owner: Scottish Borders Council   **Contact:** Ian Brown

Re-creation of buildings, formerly used as a house and ironmonger's shop.

Location: OS Ref. NT472 286. In Selkirk town centre.

Opening Times: Easter - 31 Oct: Mon - Sat, 10am - 5pm, Suns, 2 - 4pm. Jul & Aug: Mon - Sat, 9.30am - 5.30pm, Suns, 2 - 5pm.

Admission: Free.

HARMONY GARDEN

Tel: 01721 722502 **Fax:** 01721 724700

St Mary's Road, Melrose TD6 9LJ

Owner: The National Trust for Scotland   **Contact:** Head Gardener

A tranquil garden offering herbaceous and mixed borders, lawns, vegetable and fruit areas. Fine views of Melrose Abbey and the Eildon Hills. Garden set around 19th century house (not open to visitors).

Location: OS Ref. NT549 342. In Melrose, opposite the Abbey.

Opening Times: 1 Apr - 30 Sept: Mon - Sat, 10am - 5.30pm, Suns, 1.30 - 5.30pm.

Admission: £2 (honesty box).

🅿 No parking. ⬛ ⬛

HERMITAGE CASTLE

Tel: 01387 376222

Liddesdale, Newcastleton

Owner: In the care of Historic Scotland   **Contact:** The Steward

Eerie fortress at the heart of the bloodiest events in the history of the Borders. Mary Queen of Scots made her famous ride here to visit her future husband.

Location: OS Ref. NY497 961. In Liddesdale 5^1/$_2$ m NE of Newcastleton, B6399.

Opening Times: 1 Apr - 30 Sept: daily, 9.30am - 6.30pm, last ticket 6pm.

Admission: Adult £2, Child 75p, Conc. £1.50.

THE HIRSEL GARDENS, COUNTRY PARK & HOMESTEAD MUSEUM

Coldstream, Berwickshire TD12 4LP   **Tel/Fax:** 01890 882834

Owner: Lord Home of the Hirsel   **Contact:** Peter Goodall, Hirsel Estate Office

Wonderful spring flowers and rhododendrons. Homestead museum and crafts centre. Displays of estate life and adaption to modern farming.

Location: OS Ref. NT838 393. Immediately W of Coldstream off A697.

Opening Times: Please contact property for details.

Admission: Please contact property for details.

JEDBURGH ABBEY

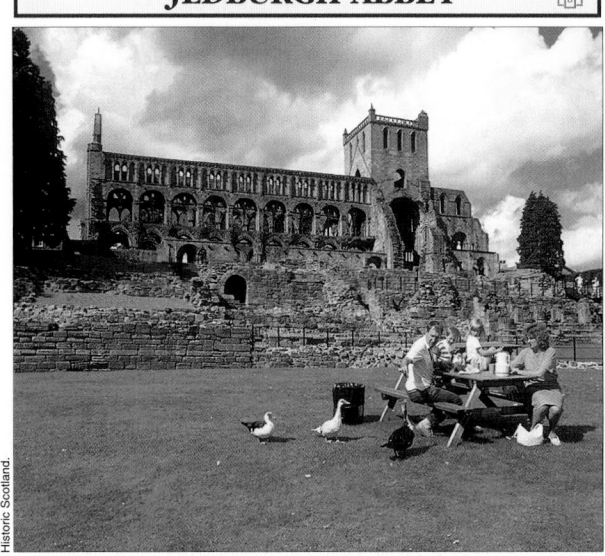

Historic Scotland.

4/5 ABBEY BRIDGEND, JEDBURGH TD8 6JQ

Owner: In the care of Historic Scotland   *Contact:* The Steward

Tel: 01835 863925

Founded by David I c1138 for Augustinian Canons. The church is mostly in the Romanesque and early Gothic styles and is remarkably complete. The award-winning visitor centre contains the priceless 12th century 'Jedburgh Comb' and other artefacts found during archaeological excavations.

Location: OS Ref. NT650 205. In Jedburgh on the A68.

Opening Times: Apr - Sept: daily, 9.30am - 6.30pm. Oct - Mar: Mon - Sat, 9.30am - 4.30pm, Suns, 2 - 4.30pm. Last ticket 30 mins before closing. 10% discount for groups (10+).

Admission: Adult £3.30, Child £1.20, Conc. £2.50.

ℹ️ Picnic area. 📷 ♿ Partially suitable. WC. 🅿 ⬛ Free when booked. 🐕 Guide dogs only. ❄

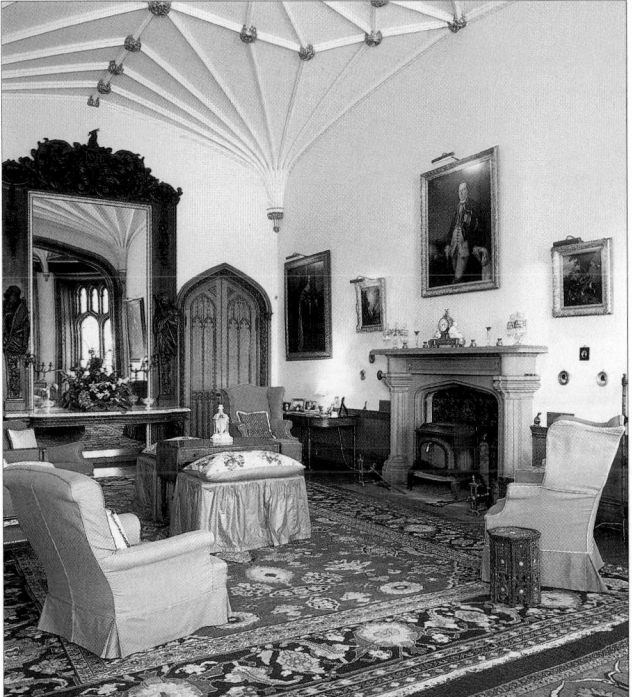

Duns Castle, Borders.

MANDERSTON

See page 450 for full page entry.

MARY QUEEN OF SCOTS' HOUSE

Tel/Fax: 01835 863331

Jedburgh, Roxburghshire   **e-mail:** hawickmuseum@hotmail.com

Owner: Scottish Borders Council   **Contact:** The Curator

16th century fortified bastel house. Telling the story 'Scotland's tragic Queen'.

Location: OS Ref. NT652 206. In Queen Street between High Street and A68.

Opening Times: Mar - Nov: Mon - Sat, 10am - 4.30pm, Suns, 12 noon - 4.30pm. Jun - Aug: Suns, 10am - 4pm.

Admission: Adult £2, Accompanied child (under 16yrs) Free, Conc. £1. 10% group discount. Free for local residents.

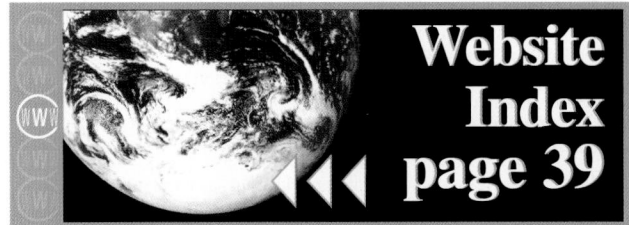

Website Index page 39

MELLERSTAIN HOUSE

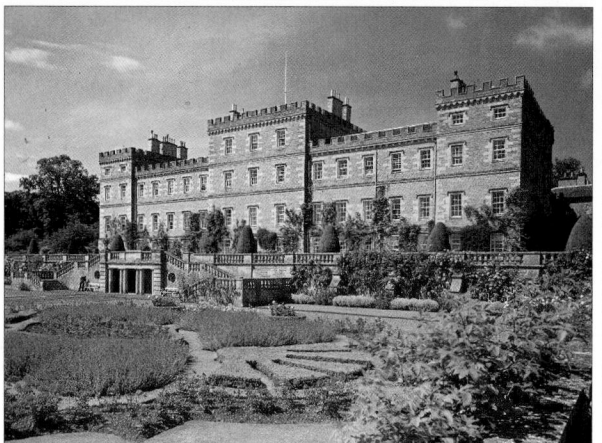

MELLERSTAIN, GORDON, BERWICKSHIRE TD3 6LG
Owner: The Earl of Haddington   *Contact:* Mr A Ashby

Tel: 01573 410225 **Fax:** 01573 410636 **e-mail:** mellerstain.house@virgin.net

One of Scotland's great Georgian houses and a unique example of the work of the Adam family; the two wings built in 1725 by William Adam, the large central block by his son, Robert 1770-78. Rooms contain fine plasterwork, colourful ceilings and marble fireplaces. The library is considered to be Robert Adam's finest creation. Many fine paintings and period furniture.

Location: OS Ref. NT648 392. From Edinburgh A68 to Earlston, turn left 5m, signed.

Opening Times: Easter weekend (4 days), 1 May - 30 Sept: daily except Sats, 12.30 - 5pm. Groups at other times by appointment. Last admission 4.30pm. Tearoom & shops: daily, except Sats, 11.30am - 5.30pm.

Admission: Adult £5, Child £2, Conc. £4.50. Groups (20+) £4.50. Grounds only: £2.

ⓘ No photography or video cameras.   📷 🎁 🍴 ♿ Partially suitable.   🍽 Licensed. 🍴 Licensed. 🅺 By arrangement. 🅿   🐕 In grounds, on leads, Guide dogs only in house. 🛡 Tel. for details. 🆔

MELROSE ABBEY

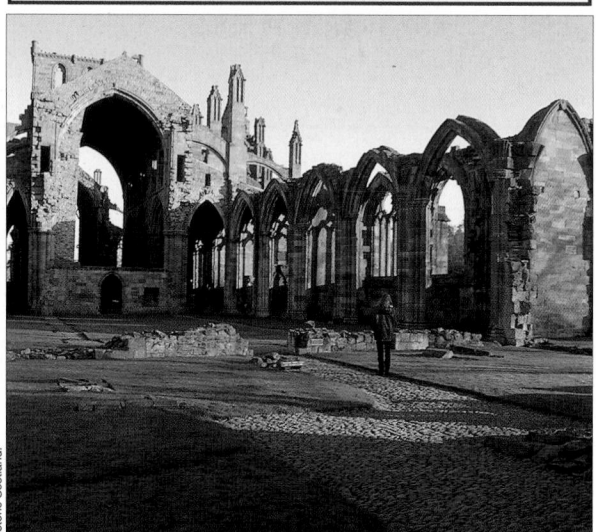

Historic Scotland.

MELROSE, ROXBURGHSHIRE TD6 9LG
Owner: Historic Scotland   *Contact:* The Steward

Tel: 01896 822562

The Abbey was founded about 1136 by David I as a Cistercian Abbey and at one time was probably the richest in Scotland. Richard II's English army largely destroyed it in 1385 but it was rebuilt and the surviving remains are mostly 14th century. Burial place of Robert the Bruce's heart. Local history displays.

Location: OS Ref. NT549 342. In the centre of Melrose off the A68 or A7.

Opening Times: Apr - Sept: daily, 9.30am - 6.30pm. Oct - Mar: Mon - Sat, 9.30am - 4.30pm, Suns, 2 - 4.30pm. Last ticket 30 mins before closing.

Admission: Adult £3.30, Child £1.20, Conc. £2.50. 10% discount for groups (10+).

ⓘ Picnic area.   📷 ♿ Tape for visitors with learning difficulties.   🎧 🅿   🐕 Pre-booked visits free.   🦮 Guide dogs only. ✳

MERTOUN GARDENS 🏛   **Tel:** 01835 823236 **Fax:** 01835 822474

St Boswells, Melrose, Roxburghshire TD6 0EA

Owner: His Grace the Duke of Sutherland   **Contact:** Mrs Barnsley

26 acres of beautiful grounds. Walled garden and well-preserved circular dovecote.

Location: OS Ref. NT617 318. Entrance off B6404 2m NE of St Boswells.

Opening Times: Apr - Sept: weekends & Public Holiday Mons only, 2 - 6pm. Last admission 5.30pm.

Admission: Adult £2, Child 50p, OAP £1.50. Groups by arrangement: 10% reduction.

🅺 By arrangement.   🅿 🚫

MONTEVIOT HOUSE GARDEN   **Tel:** 01835 830380 (mornings only)

Jedburgh, Roxburghshire TD8 6UQ   **Fax:** 01835 830288

       Contact: The Administrator

The river garden planted with herbaceous shrub borders, has a beautiful view of the River Teviot. A semi-enclosed rose garden with a collection of hybrid teas, floribunda and shrub roses. The pinetum is full of unusual trees and nearby a water garden of islands is linked by bridges.

Location: OS Ref. NT648 247. 3m N of Jedburgh. S side of B6400 (to Nisbet). 1m E of A68.

Opening Times: Apr - Oct: daily, 12 noon - 5pm. Coach parties by prior arrangement.

Admission: Adult £2, Child (under 14yrs) Free.

🚻 ♿ Partially suitable. Parking & WCs.   🅺 By arrangement.   🅿 🐕 In grounds, on leads.

NEIDPATH CASTLE 🏛   **Tel/Fax:** 01721 720333

Peebles, Scottish Borders EH45 8NW

Owner: Wemyss and March Estates   **Contact:** The Custodian

Authentic 14th century castle converted to tower house (17th century) home of Fraser, Hay and Douglas families. Pit prison, Laigh Hall with displays, Great Hall with 'Life of Mary Stuart - Queen of Scots' in Batik wall hangings. Wonderful setting in wooded gorge of River Tweed. Popular film location (7 to date).

Location: OS Ref. NT237 405. In Tweeddale 1m W of Peebles on A72.

Opening Times: Easter week. Both May BHs: Fri - Mon. 29 Jun - 9 Sept: Mon - Sat, 11am - 6pm, Suns, 1 - 5pm. Group bookings available outside listed opening hours.

Admission: Adult £3, Child £1, Conc. £2.50, Family (2+3) £7.50. 10% discount for groups in season (20+). School rate available, 1 teacher free for every 10 children.

📷 ♿ Ground floor & grounds suitable.   🅿 🐕 In grounds, on leads.

OLD GALA HOUSE   **Tel:** 01750 20096

Scot Crescent, Galashiels TD1 3JS

Owner: Scottish Borders Council

Dating from 1583, the former house of the Lairds of Gala. Particularly memorable is the painted ceiling dated 1635.

Location: OS Ref. NT492 357. S of town centre, signed from A7.

Opening Times: Apr - Sept: Tue - Sat, 10am - 4pm. Jul & Aug: Mon - Sat, 10am - 4pm, Suns, 2 - 4pm. Oct: Tue - Sat, 1 - 4pm.

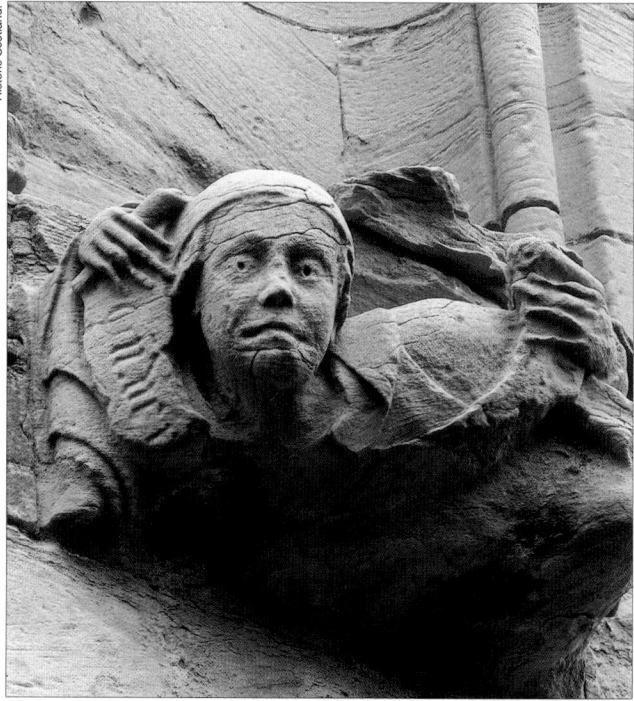

Historic Scotland.

Melrose Abbey, Borders.

PAXTON HOUSE & COUNTRY PARK

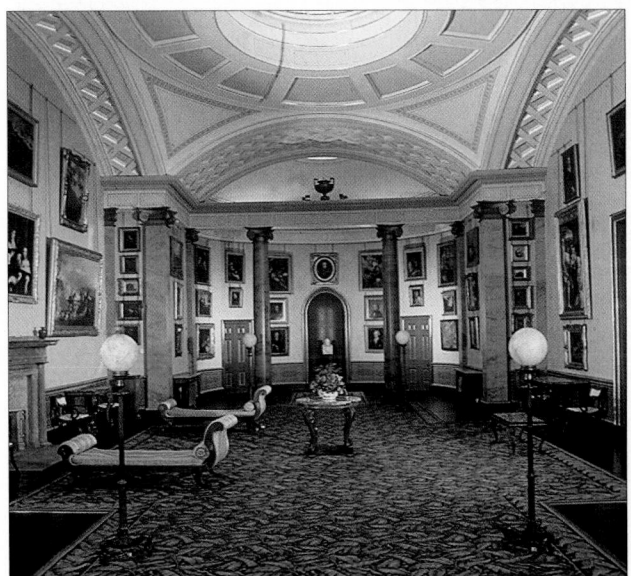

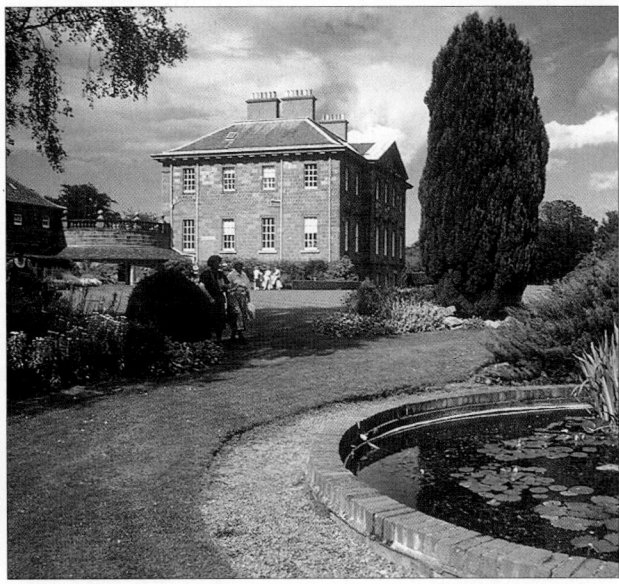

BERWICK-UPON-TWEED TD15 1SZ

Owner: *The Paxton Trust*   **Contact:** *Jacky Miller*

Tel: 01289 386291 **Fax:** 01289 386660 **e-mail:** info@paxtonhouse.com

Highly Commended by the Scottish Tourist Board 1999

Award-winning country house and country park built from 1758-62 to the design of John and James Adam for Patrick Home, Laird of Wedderburn. The house boasts the pre-eminent collection of Chippendale furniture in Scotland, the largest picture gallery in a Scottish country house built by Robert Reid in 1814, now acting as the first outstation of the National Galleries of Scotland, and a fine collection of regency furniture by William Trotter of Edinburgh. The estate has woodland trails, riverside walks, gardens, park land, red squirrel hide, highland cattle and croquet. There are shops, a stables tearoom, a function suite and a temporary exhibition programme.

Location: OS Ref. NT931 520. 3m off the A1 Berwick-upon-Tweed on B6461.

Opening Times: 1 Apr - 31 Oct: Grounds: 10am - sunset. House: 11am - 5pm. Last house tour 4.15pm. Open to groups/schools all year by appointment.

Admission: Adult £5, Child £2.50, OAP £4.75, Student £4. Groups (pre-arranged, 12+). Adult £4, Child £1.50, OAP £4. Grounds only: Adult £2.25, Child £1.

ⓘ No photography. 📷 ✳ 🅣 Conferences, wedding receptions. ♿ Partially suitable. ▣ 🍽 Licensed. 🅚 Obligatory. 🅿 ▥ 🐕 In grounds, on leads. ❄ 🛡 Tel for details. 🆆

PRIORWOOD GARDEN & DRIED FLOWER SHOP ♨

Melrose TD6 9PX   **Tel:** 01896 822493

Owner: The National Trust for Scotland   **Contact:** Mrs Cathy Ross

Overlooked by the Abbey's 15th century ruins is this unique garden, where most of the plants are suitable for drying. With the aid of volunteers, Priorwood Garden markets a wide variety of dried flower arrangements through its own dried flower shop.

Location: OS Ref. NT549 341. In the Border town of Melrose, beside the Abbey.

Opening Times: 1 Apr - 30 Sept: Mon - Sat, 10am - 5.30pm. Suns, 1.30 - 5.30pm. 1 Oct - 24 Dec: Mon - Sat, 10am - 4pm, Suns, 1.30 - 4pm.

Admission: Honesty box £2.

📷 ♿ Grounds suitable. WC. 🅿 No parking. 🐕 Guide dogs only. 🆆

ROBERT SMAIL'S PRINTING WORKS ♨

Tel: 01896 830206

High Street, Innerleithen, Perthshire EH44 6HA

Owner: The National Trust for Scotland   **Contact:** Edward Nicol

A printing time-capsule featuring a completely restored Victorian printing works. Visitors can experience the almost forgotten craft of hand typesetting. They will discover the secrets of the printing works from the archive-based posters and see the fully restored machines in action. The buildings also contain the Victorian office with its acid-etched windows, reconstructed waterwheel and many historic items which provide an insight into the history of the Border town of Innerleithen.

Location: OS Ref. NT333 366. In High Street, Innerleithen, 30m S of Edinburgh.

Opening Times: 13 - 16 Apr; 1 May - 30 Sept: Mon - Sat, 10am - 1pm & 2 - 5pm, Suns, 2 - 5pm. W/ends in Oct: Sats: 10am - 1pm & 2 - 5pm, Suns, 2 - 5pm. Last admission 45 mins before closing morning or afternoon.

Admission: Adult £2.50, Conc. £1.70, Family £7. Groups: Adult £2, Child/School £1.

📷 ♿ Ground floor suitable. 🅿 No parking. 🚻 🆆

SMAILHOLM TOWER ⌂

Tel: 01573 460365

Smailholm, Kelso

Owner: In the care of Historic Scotland   **Contact:** The Steward

Set on a high rocky knoll this well preserved 16th century tower houses an exhibition of tapestries and costume dolls depicting characters from Sir Walter Scott's *Minstrelsy of the Scottish Borders.*

Location: OS Ref. NT638 347. Nr Smailholm Village, 6m W of Kelso on B6937.

Opening Times: 1 Apr - 30 Sept: daily, 9.30am - 6.30pm. Last tickets ½ hour before closing.

Admission: Adult £2, Child 75p, Conc. £1.50.

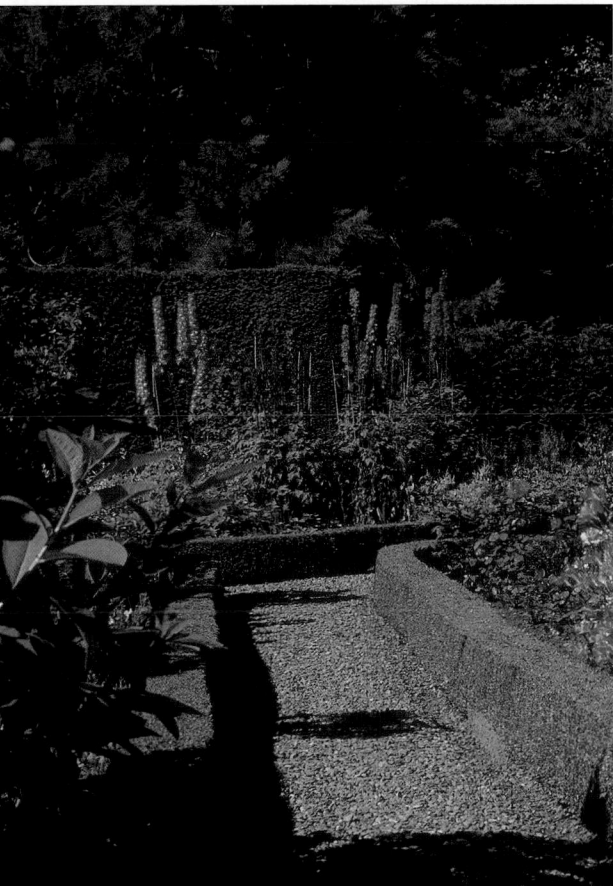

Bughtrig Garden, Borders.

THIRLESTANE CASTLE

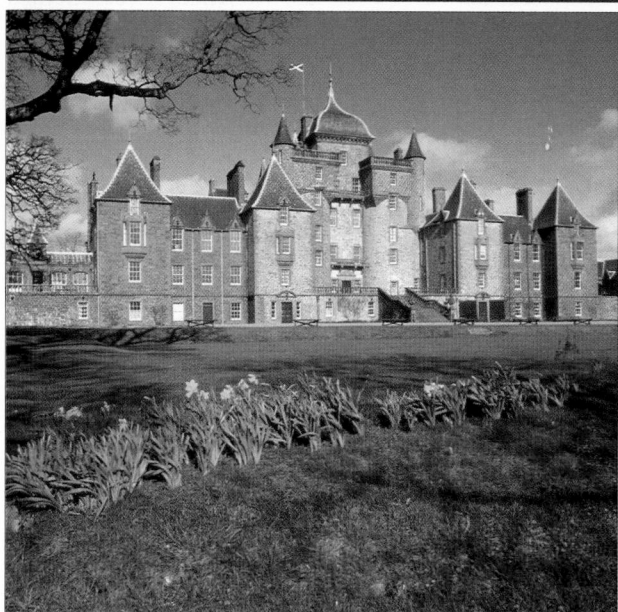
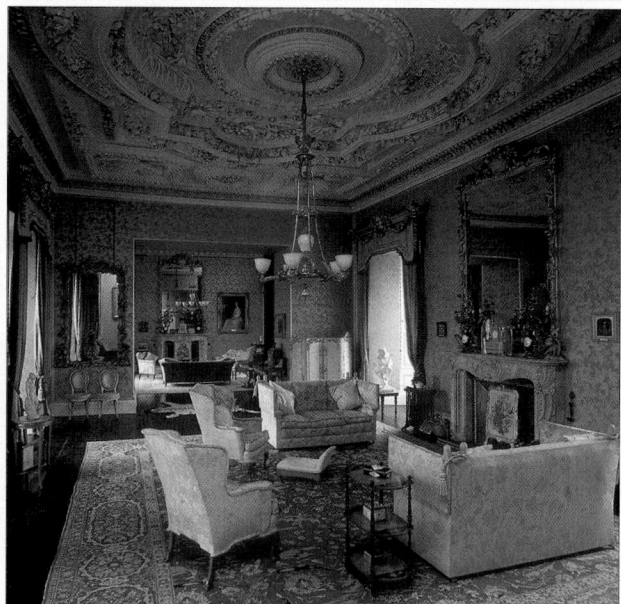

LAUDER, BERWICKSHIRE TD2 6RU

Owner: Thirlestane Castle Trust   *Contact: Peter Jarvis*

Tel: 01578 722430 **Fax:** 01578 722761
e-mail: admin@thirlestanecastle.co.uk

One of the seven 'Great Houses of Scotland', Thirlestane Castle was the ancient seat of the Earls and Duke of Lauderdale and is still home to the Maitlands. Standing in beautiful Border countryside, Thirlestane has exquisite 17th century plasterwork ceilings, a fine portrait collection, historic toys, kitchens and country life exhibitions. Facilities include free parking, audio visual display, gift shop, café, adventure playground and woodland picnic tables. Four star STB award; Registered Museum. The state rooms are available for banquets, dinners and receptions. Non-destructive events can be held in the grounds which overlook the Leader Valley and Lammermuir Hills.

Location: OS Ref. NT540 473. Off A68 at Lauder, 28m S of Edinburgh.

Opening Times: 1 Apr - 31 Oct: daily except Sats, 10.30am - 4.15pm (last admission).

Admission: Adult £5.20, Child £3. Family £13. Groups (30+): Adult £4.50, Child £3.

⬜ 🍴 ♿Not suitable. ☕ ✗By arrangement. 🅿 🏛
🐕In grounds, on leads. 🆔

TRAQUAIR

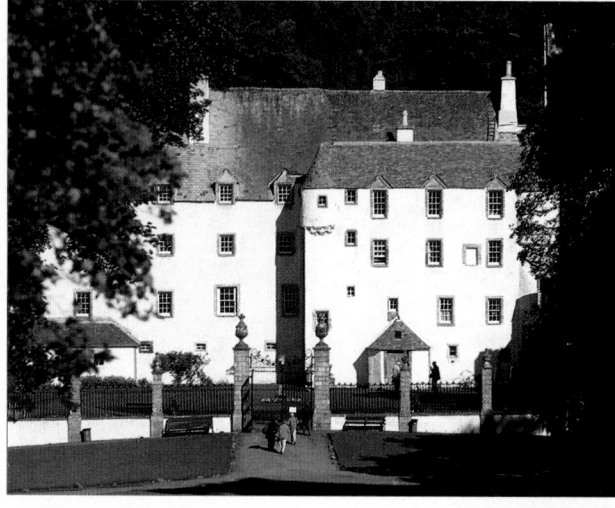
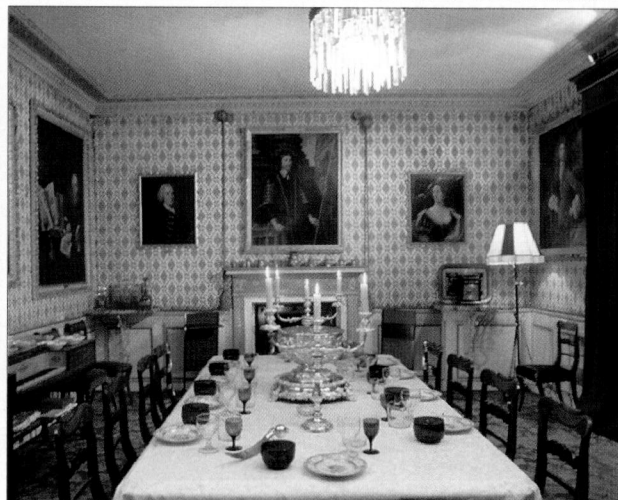

INNERLEITHEN, PEEBLESSHIRE EH44 6PW

Contact: Ms C Maxwell Stuart

Tel: 01896 830323 **Fax:** 01896 830639
e-mail: enquiries@traquair.co.uk

Traquair, situated amidst beautiful scenery and close by the River Tweed, is the oldest inhabited house in Scotland - visited by twenty-seven kings. Originally a Royal hunting lodge, it was owned by the Scottish Crown until 1478 when it passed to a branch of the Royal Stuart family whose descendants still live in the house today. Nearly ten centuries of Scottish political and domestic life can be traced from the collection of treasures in the house. It is particularly rich in associations with the Catholic Church in Scotland, Mary Queen of Scots and the Jacobite Risings.

There is an 18th century working brewery in one of the wings of the house where the famous Traquair House Ales are produced. Maze, Craft Workshops, Children's Adventure Playground.

Location: OS Ref. NY330 354. On B709 near junction with A72. Edinburgh 1hr, Glasgow 1½ hrs, Carlisle 1½ hrs, Newcastle 1½ hrs.

Opening Times: 14 Apr - 31 Oct: daily, 12.30 - 5.30pm. Jun, Jul & Aug: 10.30am - 5.30pm. Last admission 5pm. Restaurant: open from 11am. Jun, Jul & Aug open from 10.30am.

Admission: House & Garden: Adult £5.30, Child (under 15yrs) £2.80. Groups: Adult £4.80, Child (under 15yrs) £2. Garden only: Adult £2, Child (under 15yrs) £1. Winter: Groups: £7, includes glass of wine/whisky/Traquair Ale and shortbread (min charge £116).

⬜ ℹNo photography in house. 🍴 ♿ ☕Licensed, self-service.
✗Outside opening hours. 🅿Coaches please book. 🐕In grounds on leads.
🛏2 four-poster suites, B&B. 🆔

🛡 **SPECIAL EVENTS**
- **APR 15:** Easter Egg Extravaganza.   • **MAY 26/27:** Scottish Beer Festival.
- **AUG 4/5:** Traquair Fair.

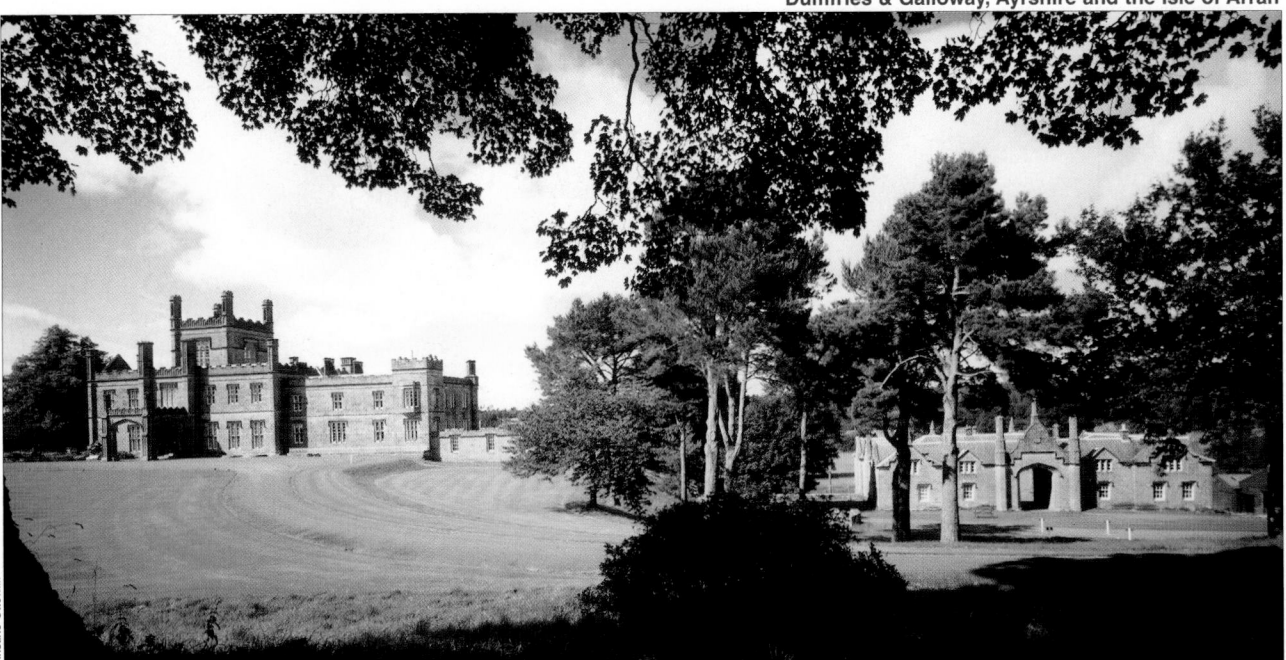

Christine Ottewill.

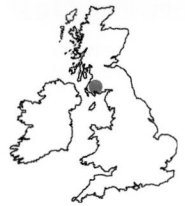

Owner: James Hunter Blair

CONTACT

James Hunter Blair
Blairquhan Castle
Maybole
Ayrshire
KA19 7LZ

Tel: 01655 770239

Fax: 01655 770278

e-mail: enquiries@
blairquhan.co.uk

LOCATION

OS Ref. NS366 055

From London M6 to
Carlisle, A75 to
Crocketford, A712 to
A713 nr New Galloway,
B741 to Straiton, B7045 to
Ayr. Turn left ¹/₄ m beyond
village. 6m SE of Maybole
off B7045.

Rail: Maybole 7m.

Air: Prestwick Airport,
15m. Direct flights to
London, Belfast & Dublin.
Executive Travel: contact
01655 882666.

BLAIRQUHAN CASTLE
Maybole

BLAIRQUHAN is the home of James Hunter Blair, the great-great-grandson of Sir David Hunter Blair, 3rd Baronet for whom it was designed by William Burn and built in 1821-24.

All the Regency furniture bought for the house remains, and the house has not been altered except discreetly to bring it up-to-date. There are ten double bedrooms including four four-poster beds, with en-suite bathrooms, five singles, and many public rooms which can be used for conferences and every sort of occasion.

The castle is approached by a 3 mile private drive along the River Girvan and is situated in one of the most charming parts of south west Scotland. There is a well-known collection of pictures. It is particularly suitable for conferences because the house is entirely at your disposal.

A five minute walk from the Castle are the walled gardens, laid out around the 1800s and recently replanned and replanted.

Blairquhan is only 50 miles from Glasgow. It is within about half an hour's drive of the world-famous golf courses of Prestwick, Troon and Turnberry, the last two of which are venues for the British Open Golf Championships.

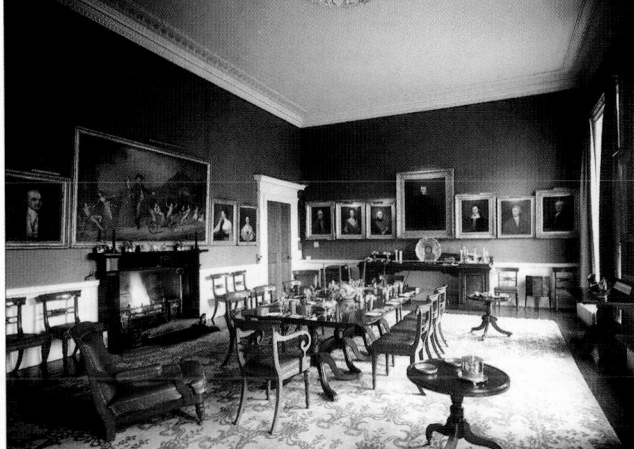

Christine Ottewill.

OPENING TIMES

SUMMER
14 July - 12 August
Daily (except Mons)
1.30 - 4.15pm
(Last admission).

Open at all other times
by appointment.

WINTER
Open by appointment.

ADMISSION

House & Garden

Adult £5.00
Child (6-16yrs)..........£3.00
Conc......................£4.00

Groups*
Negotiable

* Minimum payment £20.

SPECIAL EVENTS

- **EVENTS EVERY WEEKEND INCLUDING:**
  Model aeroplane flying
  Battle re-enactments
  Kite-flying
  Highland Dancing
  Music

CONFERENCE/FUNCTION		
ROOM	SIZE	MAX CAPACITY
Drawing Rms	1200 sq ft	100
Dining Rm	750 sq ft	100
Library	400 sq ft	25
Saloon	600 sq ft	100
Meeting Rm	255 sq ft	50

Tree trail, fashion shows, shooting, equestrian events, garden parties, shows, rallies, filming, grand piano, snooker, fishing. Slide projector, overhead projector, screen, and secretarial assistance for meetings. No photography in castle.

Wedding receptions.

Two main floors suitable. WC.

Teas, lunches, buffets and dinners. Groups can book in advance, special rates for groups.

By arrangement. Also available in French.

Unlimited.

Guide and schoolroom provided, cost negotiable.

10 doubles (4 4-posters) with bathrooms en-suite, 5 singles. The Dower House at Milton has 10 doubles, 1 single, 6 bathrooms. 7 holiday cottages on the Estate.

In grounds on leads.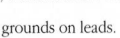

South West Scotland

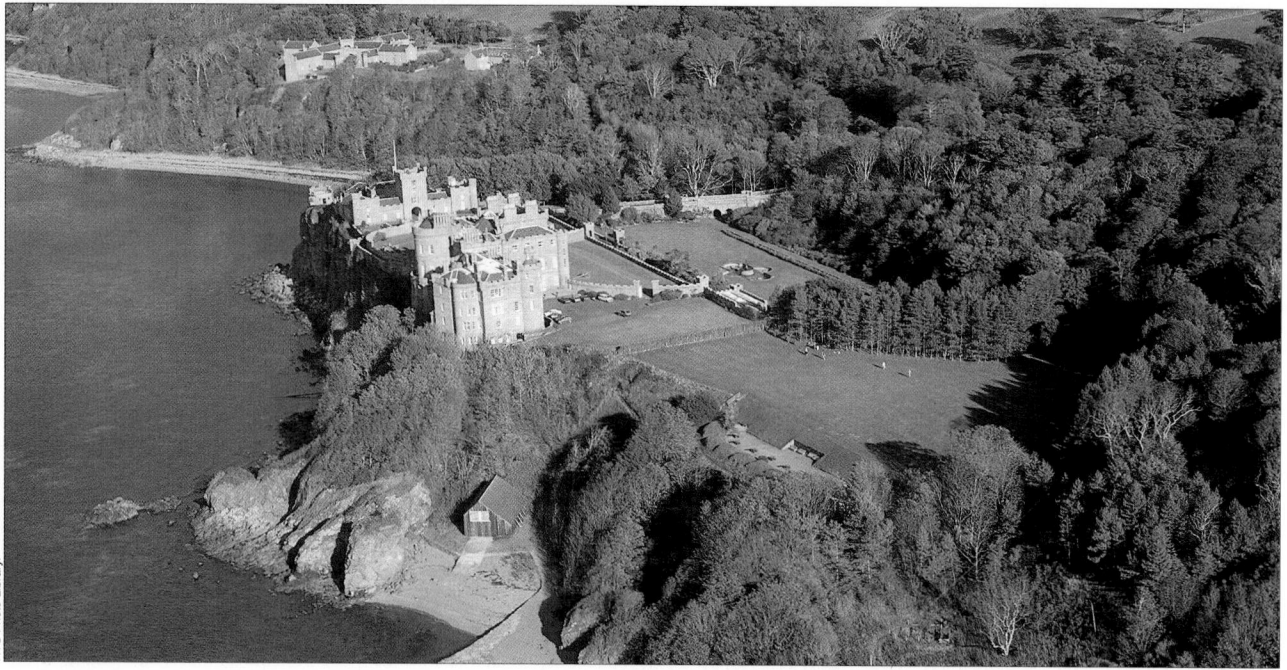

NTS Photo Library.

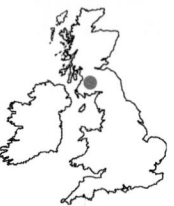

Owner: The National Trust for Scotland

CONTACT

Jonathan Cardale
Culzean Castle &
Country Park
Maybole
KA19 8LE

Tel: 01655 884455

Fax: 01655 884503

e-mail: culzean@
nts.org.uk

LOCATION

OS Ref. NS240 100

12m SW of Ayr, on A719,
4m W of Maybole.

CULZEAN CASTLE & COUNTRY PARK
Maybole

One of Scotland's major attractions – a perfect day out for all the family. Robert Adam's romantic 18th century masterpiece – a real 'castle in the air' – is perched on a cliff high above the the Firth of Clyde. The interior, with its spectacular oval staircase and circular saloon, has been restored to the original elegant colour scheme. Gifted to the Trust by the 5th Marquess of Ailsa and the Kennedy family in 1945, the top floor was given to General Eisenhower as a Scottish holiday home. Today the Eisenhower Apartments offer country house style accommodation for that special occasion.

Culzean was Scotland's first country park and has been described as 'the most magnificent in Britain'. The 560 acres include 5km of coastline, woodland walks, ponds, a deer park, gardens, picnic areas and a new children's playground. Fascinating restored buildings include the Gas House, Ruined Arch and Viaduct, Ice House, Camellia House and unique Pagoda. The Victorian Vinery has recently been rebuilt in the Walled Garden. A new exhibition in the Visitor Centre tells the history of the castle and estate and 50 years of the Trust's conservation work. Three exciting shops offer an exclusive range of gifts and souvenirs and the self-service restaurant provides snacks and full meals.

❖

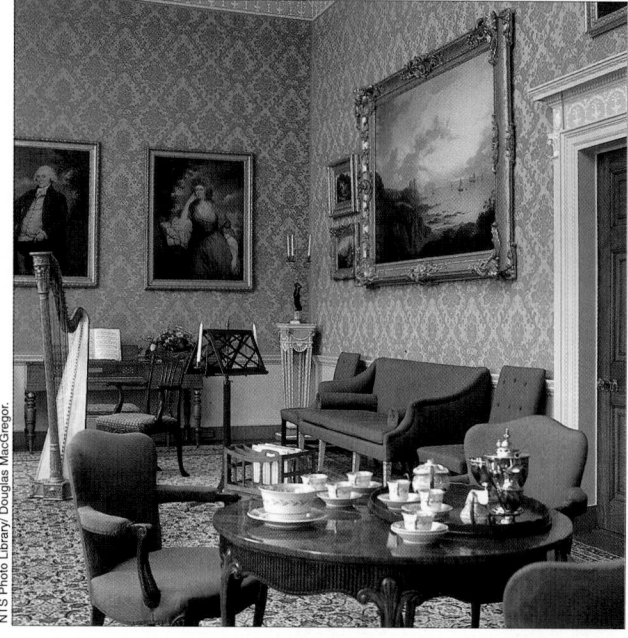

NTS Photo Library/ Douglas MacGregor.

Suitable.

Licensed.

By arrangement.

In grounds on leads.

Contact for details.

Tel. for details.

OPENING TIMES

Castle, Visitor Centre, Restaurants & Shop
1 Apr - 31 Oct: daily,
11am - 5.30pm.
Last entry to Castle 4.30pm.
Walled Garden closes 5pm.

Visitor Centre, Restaurant, Home Farm Shop & Country Park Shop: also open weekends in Jan, Feb, Mar, Nov & Dec:
12 noon - 4pm.

Castle: also open weekends in Mar, Nov & Dec: guided tours every 30mins, 12 noon - 2.30pm.

Country Park
All year: daily 9.30am - sunset.

ADMISSION

Castle, Grounds & Country Park
Adult £8.00
Conc. £6.00
Family £20.00
Groups
  Adult £6.50

Country Park only
Adult £4.00
Conc. £3.00
Family £10.00
Groups
  Adult £3.50

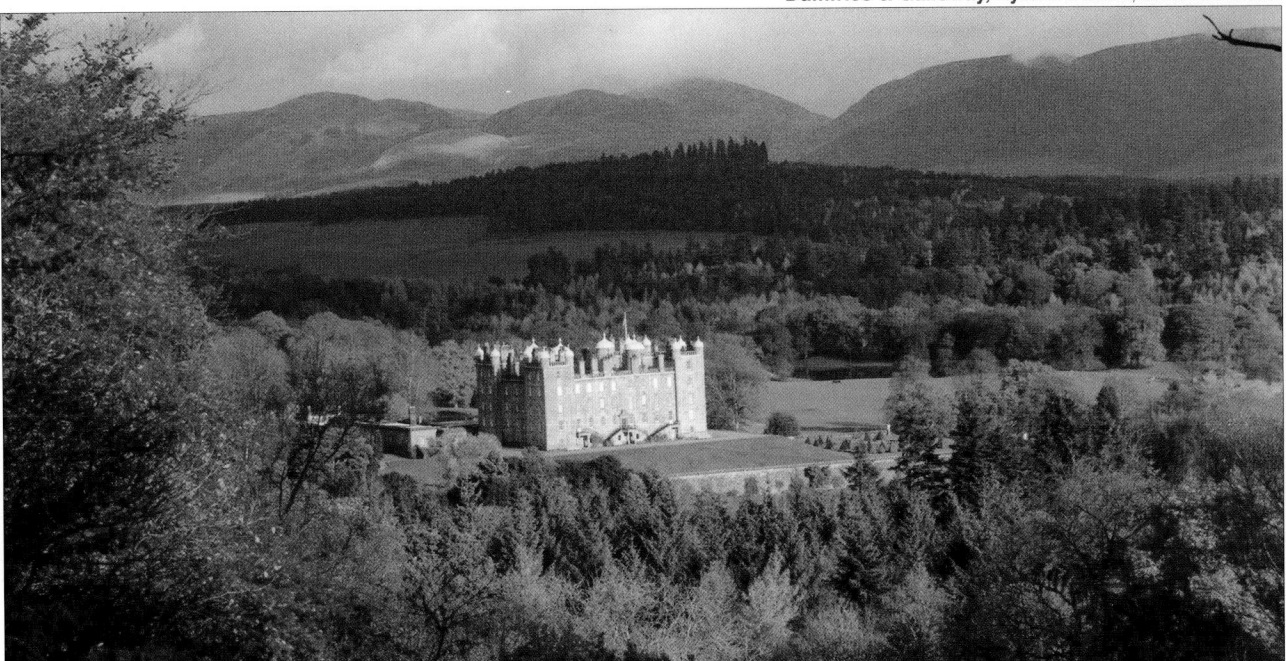

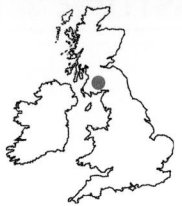

Owner: His Grace the
Duke of Buccleuch &
Queensberry KT

CONTACT

Claire Fisher
Drumlanrig Castle
Thornhill
Dumfriesshire
DG3 4AQ

Tel: 01848 330248

Fax: 01848 331682

Countryside Service:
01848 331555

e-mail: bre@
drumlanrigcastle.org.uk

LOCATION

OS Ref. NX851 992

18m N of Dumfries,
3m NW of Thornhill
off A76.
16m from M74 at
Elvanfoot.
Approx. 1½ hrs
by road from Edinburgh,
Glasgow and Carlisle.

DRUMLANRIG CASTLE
Thornhill

DRUMLANRIG CASTLE, Gardens and Country Park, the home of the Duke of Buccleuch and Queensberry KT was built between 1679 and 1691 by William Douglas, 1st Duke of Queensberry. Drumlanrig is rightly recognised as one of the first and most important buildings in the grand manner in Scottish domestic architecture. James Smith, who made the conversion from a 15th century castle, made a comparable transformation at Dalkeith a decade later.

The castle, of local pink sandstone, offers superb views across Nithsdale. It houses a renowned art collection, including work by Leonardo, Holbein, and Rembrandt, as well as cabinets made for Louis XIV's Versailles, relics of Bonnie Prince Charlie and a 300 year old silver chandelier.

The story of Sir James Douglas, killed in Spain while carrying out the last wish of Robert Bruce, pervades the castle in the emblem of a winged heart. Douglas family historical exhibition. Working forge. The gardens, now being restored to the plan of 1738, add to the overall effect. The fascination of Drumlanrig as a centre of art, beauty and history is complemented by its role in the Queensberry Estate, a model of dynamic and enlightened land management.

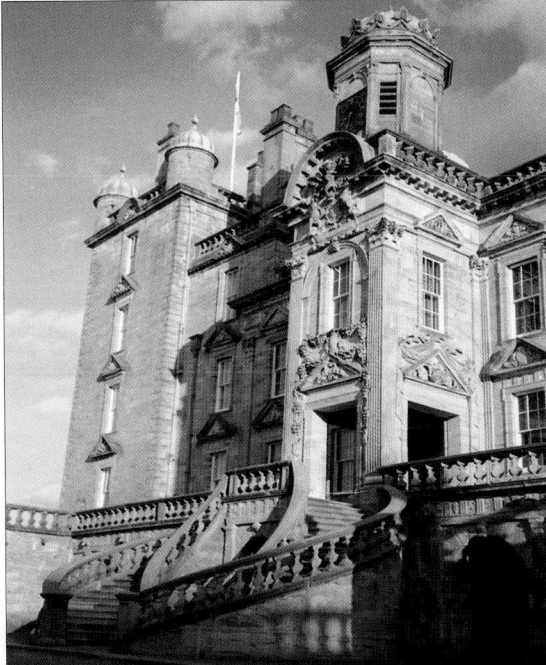

❖

No photography inside the castle.

Suitable. WC. Please enquire about facilities before visit.

Licensed.

Snacks, lunches and teas during opening hours.

Adjacent to the castle.

Children's quiz and worksheets. Ranger-led activities, including woodlands and forestry. Adventure playground. School groups welcome throughout the year by arrangement.

In grounds on leads.

❄

OPENING TIMES

SUMMER

Castle
14 - 16 April
28 April - 12 August
25 - 31 August:
Weekdays: 11am - 4pm,
Suns, 12 noon - 4pm.

1 - 30 September groups
by appointment only.

**Country Park, Gardens
& Adventure Woodland**
14 April - 30 September:
daily, 11am - 5pm.

WINTER
By appointment only.

ADMISSION

Castle and Country Park

Adult £6.00
Child £2.00
OAP/Student...........£4.00
Family (2+4) £14.00
Disabled in
wheelchairs ....Free

Pre-booked groups (20+)
Adult £4.00
Child £2.00
Outside normal opening
times..........................£8.00

Country Park only
Adult £3.00
Child £2.00

CONFERENCE/FUNCTION

ROOM	SIZE	MAX CAPACITY
Visitors' Centre	6m x 13m	50

South West Scotland

ARDWELL GARDENS
Tel: 01776 860227

Ardwell, Nr Stranraer, Dumfries and Galloway DG9 9LY
Owner: Mr Francis Brewis   **Contact:** Mrs Terry Brewis
The gardens include a formal garden, wild garden and woodland.
Location: OS Ref. NX102 455. A716 10m S of Stranraer.
Opening Times: 1 Apr - 30 Sept: daily, 10am - 5pm.
Admission: Adult £2, Child/Conc. £1.

BACHELORS' CLUB
Tel: 01292 541940

Sandgate Street, Tarbolton KA5 5RB
Owner: The National Trust for Scotland   **Contact:** The Manager
17th century thatched house in which poet Robert Burns and friends formed a debating society in 1780. Burns' mementos and relics, period furnishings.
Location: OS Ref. NS430 270. In Tarbolton, B744, 7¹/₂ m NE of Ayr, off B743.
Opening Times: 1 Apr - 30 Sept: daily, 1.30 - 5.30pm. Weekends in Oct: 1.30 - 5.30pm. Last admission 5pm.
Admission: Adult £2.50, Conc. £1.70, Family £7. Groups: Adult £2, School £1.

♿ Ground floor suitable.   ⛄   [IW]

BARGANY GARDENS
Tel: 01465 871249   **Fax:** 01465 871282

Girvan, Ayrshire KA26 9QL
Owner/Contact: Mr John Dalrymple Hamilton
Lily pond, rock garden and a fine collection of hard and softwood trees.
Location: OS Ref. NS250 001. 4m ENE of Girvan by B734. After 2¹/₂ m keep ahead on to minor road to Old Dailly.
Opening Times: Weekends & Mons in May only, 10am - 6pm.
Admission: £2 per head, Child Free. Buses by arrangement.

BLAIRQUHAN CASTLE 🏛
See page 457 for full page entry.

BRODICK CASTLE & COUNTRY PARK 🏰

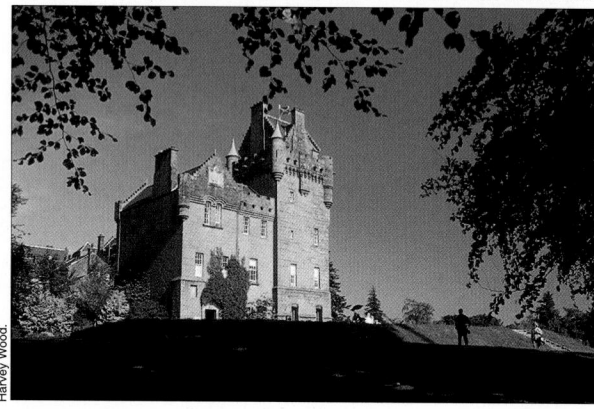

ISLE OF ARRAN KA27 8HY
Owner: The National Trust for Scotland   *Contact: Administrator*
Tel: 01770 302202   **Fax:** 01770 302312

This is a castle you will never forget! The tall, stately building beckons you with the glow of its warm red sandstone. The setting is staggering, fronted by the sea, bedecked with gardens and overlooked by the majestic mountain of Goatfell. The castle was built on the site of a Viking fortress and dates from the 13th century. The contents are magnificent and include superb silver, porcelain, paintings and sporting trophies. The woodland garden ranks as one of Europe's finest.
Location: OS Ref. NS010 360. Isle of Arran. Ferries from Ardrossan & Claonaig and Kintyre. Ferry enquiries: 01475 650100.
Opening Times: Castle: 1 Apr - 30 Jun & 1 Sept - 31 Oct: daily, 11am - 4.30pm, (last admission 4pm). 1 Jul - 31 Aug: daily, 11am - 5pm (last admission 4.30pm). Reception Centre and shop: (dates as castle) 10am - 5pm; restaurant: 11am - 5pm. Shop & Restaurant: weekends in Nov & Dec: 11am - 3pm. Walled Garden: All year: daily, 9.30am - 5pm. Country Park: All year, daily 9.30am - sunset. Goatfell open all year.
Admission: Castle & Garden: Adult £6, Conc. £4.50, Family £16.50. Groups: Adult £4.80, Child/ School £1. Garden & Country Park: Adult £2.50, Conc. £1.70. Groups: Adult £2, Child/School £1. Garden only: Family £7.

📷   ♿ Suitable. WC.   🍴 Licensed.   🐕 In grounds, on leads.   ⛄   [IW]

BROUGHTON HOUSE & GARDEN
Tel/Fax: 01557 330437

High Street, Kirkcudbright DG6 4JX
Owner: The National Trust for Scotland   **Contact:** Frances Scott
This fascinating 18th century house in the pleasant coastal town of Kirkcudbright was the home and studio from 1901 - 1933 of the artist E A Hornel, one of the 'Glasgow Boys'. It contains many of his works, along with paintings by other contemporary artists, and an extensive collection of rare Scottish books, including valuable editions of Burns' works.
Location: OS Ref. NX684 509. Off A711 / A755, in Kirkcudbright, at 12 High St.
Opening Times: House & Garden: 1 - 12 Apr; 17 Apr - 30 Jun & 1 Sept - 31 Oct: daily, 1 - 5.30pm. 13 - 16 Apr & 1 Jul - 31 Aug: daily, 11am - 5.30pm (last entry 4.45pm). Garden only: 24/25 Feb & 1 - 30 Nov: Mon - Fri, 11am - 4pm.
Admission: Adult £3.50, Conc. £2.50, Family £9.50. Groups: Adult £3, Child/School £1.

♿ Not suitable.   👤 By arrangement.   🅿 Limited.   ⛄   [IW]

BURNS' COTTAGE
Tel: 01292 441215

Alloway, Ayrshire KA7 4PY
Contact: J Manson
Thatched cottage, birthplace of Robert Burns in 1759, with adjacent museum.
Location: OS Ref. NS335 190. 2m SW of Ayr.
Opening Times: Apr - Oct: daily, 9am - 6pm. Nov - Mar: daily, 10am - 4pm (Suns, 12 noon - 4pm).
Admission: Adult £2.80, Child/OAP £1.40, Family £8. Admission charge includes entry to Burns' Monument and Gardens.

⛄

CAERLAVEROCK CASTLE

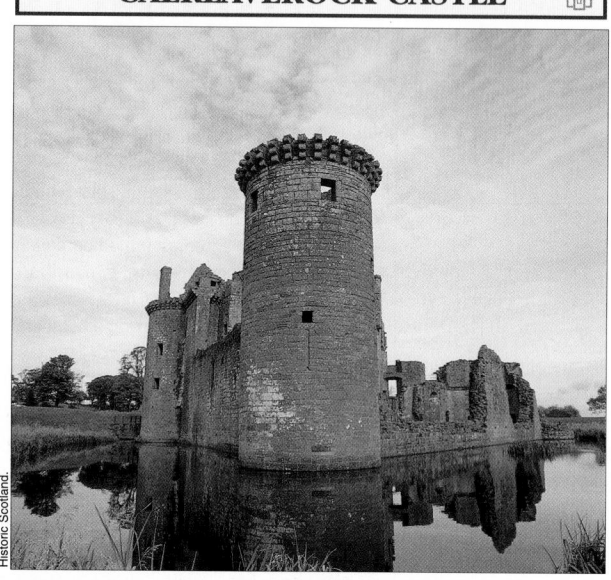

Historic Scotland.

GLENCAPLE, DUMFRIES DG1 4RU
Owner: In the care of Historic Scotland   *Contact: The Steward*
Tel: 01387 770244

One of the finest castles in Scotland on a triangular site surrounded by moats. Its most remarkable features are the twin-towered gatehouse and the Renaissance Nithsdale lodging. The site of two famous sieges. Children's park, replica siege engines and nature trail to site of earlier castle.
Location: OS84 NY025 656. 8m S of Dumfries on the B725.
Opening Times: Apr - Sept: daily, 9.30am - 6.30pm. Oct - Mar: Mon - Sat, 9.30am - 4.30pm, Suns, 2 - 4.30pm. Last ticket sold 30 mins before closing.
Admission: Adult £2.80, Child £1, Conc. £2. 10% discount for groups (10+).

📷   ♿ Partially suitable. WCs.   🅿 Limited for coaches.   🎟 Free if pre-booked.   🐕 In grounds, on leads.   ⛄

CARDONESS CASTLE 🏰
Tel: 01557 814427

Gatehouse of Fleet
Owner: In the care of Historic Scotland   **Contact:** The Steward
Well preserved ruin of a four storey tower house of 15th century standing on a rocky platform above the Water of Fleet. Ancient home of the McCullochs. Very fine fireplaces.
Location: OS Ref. NX591 553. 1m SW of Gatehouse of Fleet, beside the A75.
Opening Times: 1 Apr - 30 Sept: daily, 9.30am - 6.30pm. Last ticket 6pm. 1 Oct - 31 Mar: Sats, 9.30am - 4.30pm, Suns, 2 - 4.30pm. Last ticket 4pm.
Admission: Adult £2, Child 75p, Conc. £1.50.

THOMAS CARLYLE'S BIRTHPLACE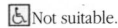

Tel: 01576 300666

Ecclefechan, Dumfriesshire DG11 3DG

Owner: The National Trust for Scotland   **Contact:** The Manager

Thomas Carlyle was born here in The Arched House in 1795, the year before Burns died. Carlyle was a brilliant essayist, historian, social reformer, visionary and literary giant. When he was 14 he walked the 84 miles to Edinburgh University - taking three days. Upstairs is the bedroom in which Carlyle was born. There is also a little museum with a notable collection of photographs, manuscripts and other documents.

Location: OS Ref. NY193 745. Off M74, 6m SE of Lockerbie. In Ecclefechan village.

Opening Times: 1 Apr - 30 Sept: Fri - Mon, 1.30 - 5.30pm. Last admission 5pm.

Admission: Adult £2.50, Conc. £1.70, Family £7. Groups: Adult £2, Child/School £1.

♿ Not suitable.   By arrangement.   P Limited.   ✕   (tw)

CASTLE KENNEDY GARDENS

Tel: 01776 702024   **Fax:** 01776 706248

Stair Estates, Rephad, Stranraer, Dumfries and Galloway DG9 8BX

Owner: The Earl & Countess of Stair   **Contact:** The Earl of Stair

75 acres of gardens, originally laid out in 1730, includes rhododendrons, pinetum, walled garden and circular lily pond.

Location: OS Ref. NX109 610. 3m E of Stranraer on A75.

Opening Times: Apr - Sept: daily.

Admission: Adult £3, Child £1, OAP £2 (2000 prices).

CRAIGDARROCH HOUSE

Tel: 01848 200592

Moniaive, Dumfriesshire DG3 4JB

Owner/Contact: Mr Alexander Sykes

Location: OS Ref. NX741 909. S side of B729, 2m W of Moniaive, 19m WNW of Dumfries.

Opening Times: Jul: daily, 2 - 4pm.

Admission: £2.

CRAIGIEBURN GARDEN

Tel: 01683 221250

Craigieburn House, Nr Moffat, Dumfriesshire DG10 9LF   **e-mail:** ajmw1@aol.com

Owner/Contact: Janet Wheatcroft

A plantsman's garden with a huge range of rare and unusual plants surrounded by natural woodland.

Location: OS Ref. NT117 053. NW side of A708 to Yarrow & Selkirk, 2½ m E of Moffat.

Opening Times: Easter - Sept: Sats & Suns (open for charity).

Admission: Adult £2, Child Free.

CROSSRAGUEL ABBEY

Tel: 01655 883113

Maybole, Strathclyde

Owner: In the care of Historic Scotland   **Contact:** The Steward

Founded in the early 13th century by the Earl of Carrick. Remarkably complete remains include church, cloister, chapter house and much of the domestic premises.

Location: OS Ref. NS275 083. 2m S of Maybole on the A77.

Opening Times: 1 Apr - 30 Sept: daily, 9.30am - 6.30m. Last ticket 6pm.

Admission: Adult £2, Child 75p, Conc. £1.50.

CULZEAN CASTLE & COUNTRY PARK   See page 458 for full page entry.

DALGARVEN MILL MUSEUM

Tel: 01294 552448

Dalry Road, Kilwinning, Ayrshire K13 6PL

Owner: Dalgarven Mill Trust   **Contact:** The Administrator

Water-driven flour mill and Ayrshire country life & costume museum.

Location: OS Ref. NS295 460. On A737 2m from Kilwinning.

Opening Times: All year: Summer: Easter - end Oct: Tue - Sat, 10am - 5pm. Suns, 11am - 5pm. Winter: Tue - Sat, 10am - 4pm. Suns, 11am - 5pm. Closed Mons.

Admission: Charges.

DEAN CASTLE COUNTRY PARK

Tel: 01563 574916

Dean Road, Kilmarnock, East Ayrshire KA3 1XB

Owner: East Ayrshire Council   **Contact:** Andrew Scott-Martin

Set in 200 acres of Country Park. Visits to castle by guided tour only.

Location: OS Ref. NS437 395. Off A77. 1¼ m NNE of town centre.

Opening Times: Country Park & Visitor Centre: All year. Castle: Easter - end Oct: daily, 12 noon - 5pm (last tour 4.15pm). Oct - Easter: weekends only, 12 noon - 4pm (last tour 3.15pm).

Admission: Free (group charge on application).

DRUMLANRIG CASTLE   See page 459 for full page entry.

DUNDRENNAN ABBEY

Tel: 01557 500262

Kirkcudbright

Owner: Historic Scotland   **Contact:** The Steward

Mary Queen of Scots spent her last night on Scottish soil in this 12th century Cistercian Abbey founded by David I. The Abbey stands in a small and secluded valley.

Location: OS Ref. NX749 475. 6½ m SE of Kirkcudbright on the A711.

Opening Times: 1 Apr - 30 Sept: daily, 9.30am - 6.30pm. Last ticket 6pm. 1 Oct - 31 Mar: Sats, 9.30am - 4.30pm, Suns, 2 - 4.30pm.

Admission: Adult £1.80, Child 75p, Conc. £1.30.

GALLOWAY HOUSE GARDENS

Tel: 01988 600680

Garlieston, Newton Stewart, Wigtownshire DG8 8HF

Owner: Galloway House Gardens Trust   **Contact:** D Marshall

Created in 1740 by Lord Garlies, currently under restoration.

Location: OS Ref. NX478 453. 15m S of Newton Stewart on B7004.

Opening Times: 1 Mar - 31 Oct: 9am - 5pm.

Admission: £1 per person.

GILNOCKIE'S TOWER

Tel: 01387 371876

Hollows, Canonbie, Dumfriesshire

Owner/Contact: Edward Armstrong

16th century tower house, occupied by the Clan Armstrong Centre.

Location: OS Ref. NY383 787. 2m N of Canonbie on minor road E of A7 just N of Hollows.

Opening Times: Summer months by guided tours: 10am & 2.30pm (closed 11.45am - 2pm). Winter months open by appointment.

Admission: Adult £3, Child (under 14yrs) £1.50.

GLENLUCE ABBEY

Tel: 01581 300541

Glenluce

Owner/Contact: In the care of Historic Scotland

A Cistercian Abbey founded in 1190. Remains include a 16th century Chapter House.

Location: OS Ref. NX185 587. 2m NW of Glenluce village off the A75.

Opening Times: 1 Apr - 30 Sept: daily 9.30am - 6.30pm. Last ticket 6pm. 1 Oct - 31 Mar: Sats, 9.30am - 4.30pm, Suns, 2 - 4.30pm. Last ticket 4pm.

Admission: Adult £1.80, Child 75p, Conc. £1.30.

GLENWHAN GARDENS

Tel: 01581 400222   **Fax:** 01581 400295

Dunragit, Stranraer, Wigtownshire DG9 8PH

Contact: Tessa Knott

Beautiful 12 acre garden overlooking Luce Bay and the Mull of Galloway.

Location: OS Ref. NX150 580. N side of A75, 6m E of Stranraer.

Opening Times: 1 Apr - 30 Sept: daily, 10am - 5pm or by appointment at other times.

Admission: Adult £3, Child £1, Conc. £2.50.

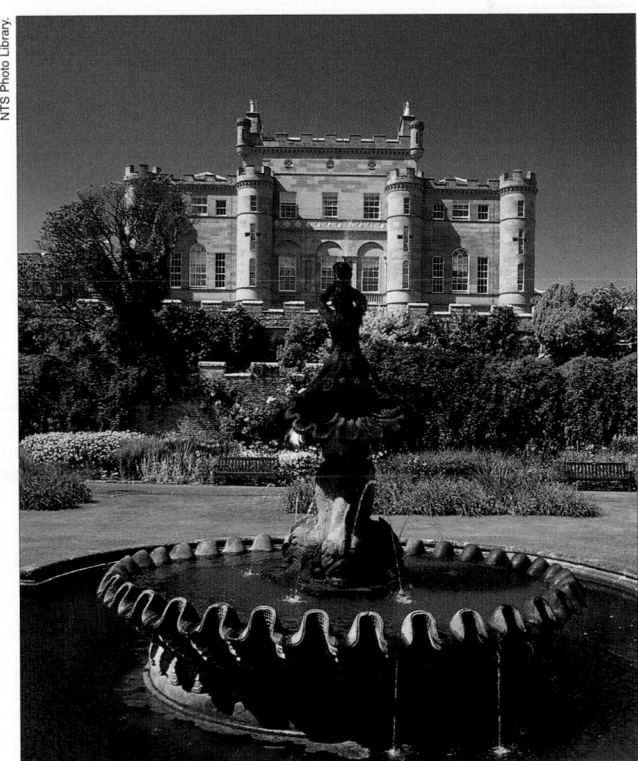

NTS Photo Library.

Culzean Castle, South West Scotland.

LOGAN BOTANIC GARDEN

Tel: 01776 860231 **Fax:** 01776 860333

Port Logan, Stranraer, Wigtownshire DG9 9ND

Owner: Royal Botanic Garden Edinburgh   **Contact:** The Curator

Scotland's most exotic garden. Take a trip to the south west of Scotland and experience the southern hemisphere!

Location: OS Ref. NX097 430. 14m S of Stranraer on B7065.

Opening Times: 1 Mar - 31 Oct: daily, 9.30am - 6pm.

Admission: Adult £3, Child £1, Conc. £2.50, Family £7. Group discount available.

MACLELLAN'S CASTLE

Tel: 01557 331856

Kirkcudbright

Owner: In the care of Historic Scotland   **Contact:** The Steward

Castellated mansion, built in 1577 using stone from an adjoining ruined monastery by the then Provost. Elaborately planned with fine architectural details, it has been a ruin since 1752.

Location: OS Ref. NX683 511. Centre of Kirkcudbright on the A711.

Opening Times: 1 Apr - 30 Sept: daily, 9.30am - 6.30pm. Last ticket 6pm.

Admission: Adult £1.80, Child 75p, Conc. £1.30.

NEW ABBEY CORN MILL

Tel: 01387 850260

New Abbey Village

Owner: Historic Scotland   **Contact:** The Custodian

This carefully renovated 18th century water-powered oatmeal mill is in full working order and regular demonstrations are given for visitors in the summer.

Location: OS Ref. NX962 663. 8m S of Dumfries on the A710. Close to Sweetheart Abbey.

Opening Times: 1 Apr - 30 Sept: daily, 9.30am - 6.30pm. Last ticket 6pm. 1 Oct - 31 Mar: Mon - Wed & Sat, 9.30am - 4.30pm, Thurs, 9.30am - 12 noon, Fris closed, Suns, 2 - 4.30pm. Last ticket 4pm.

Admission: Adult £2.50, Child £1, Conc. £1.90. Joint entry ticket with Sweetheart Abbey: Adult £3, Child £1.20, Conc. £2.25.

RAMMERSCALES

Tel: 01387 810229/810361 **Fax:** 01387 810940

Lockerbie, Dumfriesshire DG11 1LD

Owner/Contact: Mr M A Bell Macdonald

Georgian house.

Location: OS Ref. NY080 780. W side of B7020, 3m S of Lochmoben.

Opening Times: Last week in Jul, 1st three weeks in Aug: daily (excluding Sats), 2 - 5pm.

Admission: £5.

SHAMBELLIE HOUSE MUSEUM OF COSTUME

New Abbey, Dumfries DG2 8HQ   **Tel:** 01387 850375 **Fax:** 01387 850461

Owner: National Museums of Scotland   **Contact:** Sheila Watt

Shambellie House is a modest country house designed by David Bryce in 1856 for William Stewart. It is set in woodland just outside the village of New Abbey. Shambellie offers visitors the chance to see period clothes in appropriate room settings, with accessories, furniture and decorative art.

Location: OS Ref. NX960 665. On A710, 7m outside Dumfries on Solway coast road.

Opening Times: 1 Apr - 31 Oct: daily, 11am - 5pm.

Admission: Adult £2.50, Child Free, Conc. £1.50. Season ticket for all National Museums of Scotland sites: Adult £8, Conc. £5, Family £15.

📷   ℹ️ No photography in house.   🍴 ♿ Not suitable.   📹
🚶 By arrangement.   🅿️ Limited.   🏛️ 🐕 In grounds, on leads.

SORN CASTLE

Tel: 01290 551555

Ayrshire KA5 6HR

Owner/Contact: Mrs R G McIntyre

14th century castle. Enlarged several times, most recently in 1908.

Location: OS Ref. NS555 265. 4m E of Mauchline on B743.

Opening Times: 14 Jul - 11 Aug: daily, 2 - 4pm.

Admission: Adult £3.50.

SOUTER JOHNNIE'S COTTAGE

Tel: 01655 760603

Main Road, Kirkoswald KA19 8HY

Owner: The National Trust for Scotland   **Contact:** Ms Jan Gibson

The home of John Davidson, original 'Souter' (cobbler) of Robert Burns' famous narrative poem *Tam O' Shanter*. Burns mementos and restored cobbler's workshop. Life-sized stone figures in adjacent 'ale-house'.

Location: OS Ref. NS240 070. On A77, in Kirkoswald village, 4m SW of Maybole.

Opening Times: 1 Apr - 30 Sept: daily, 11.30am - 5pm. Weekends in Oct: 11.30am - 5pm (last admission 4.30pm).

Admission: Adult £2.50, Conc. £1.70, Family £7. Groups: Adult £2, Child/School £1.

♿ House suitable.   🅿️ Limited.

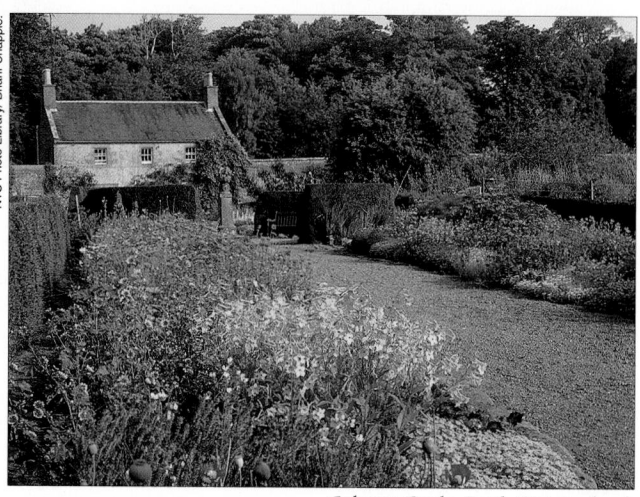

Culzean Castle, South West Scotland.

STRANRAER CASTLE

Tel: 01776 705088 **Fax:** 01776 705835

Stranraer, Galloway

Owner: Dumfries & Galloway Council   **Contact:** John Pickin

Much altered 16th century L-plan tower house, now a museum telling the history of the castle.

Location: OS Ref. NX061 608. In Stranraer, short distance SW of junction between A77 & B737, 1/4 m short of the harbour.

Opening Times: Easter - mid-Sept: Mon - Sat, 10am - 1pm & 2 - 5pm.

Admission: Adult £1.20, Conc. 60p, Family £3.

SWEETHEART ABBEY

Tel: 01387 850397

New Abbey Village

Owner: In the care of Historic Scotland   **Contact:** The Steward

Cistercian abbey founded in 1273 by Devorgilla, in memory of her husband John Balliol. A principal feature is the well-preserved precinct wall enclosing 30 acres.

Location: OS Ref. NX965 663. In New Abbey Village, on A710 8m S of Dumfries.

Opening Times: 1 Apr - 30 Sept: daily, 9.30am - 6.30pm. Last ticket 6pm. 1 Oct - 31 Mar: Mon - Wed & Sat, 9.30am - 4.30pm, Thurs, 9.30am - 12 noon, Fris closed, Suns, 2 - 4.30pm. Last ticket 4pm.

Admission: Adult £1.50, Child 50p, Conc. £1.10. Joint entry ticket with New Abbey Corn Mill: Adult £3, Child £1.20, Conc. £2.25.

THREAVE CASTLE

Tel: 01831 168512

Castle Douglas

Owner: The National Trust for Scotland   **Contact:** Historic Scotland

Built by Archibald the Grim in the late 14th century, early stronghold of the Black Douglases. Around its base is an artillery fortification built before 1455 when the castle was besieged by James II. Ring the bell and the custodian will come to ferry you over. Long walk to property. Owned by The National Trust for Scotland but under the guardianship of Historic Scotland.

Location: OS Ref. NX739 623. 2m W of Castle Douglas on the A75.

Opening Times: 1 Apr - 30 Sept: daily, 9.30am - 6.30pm. Last ticket 6pm.

Admission: Adult £2, Child 75p, Conc. £1.50. Charges include ferry trip.

THREAVE GARDEN & ESTATE

Tel: 01556 502575 **Tel:** 01556 502683

Castle Douglas DG7 1RX

Owner: The National Trust for Scotland   **Contact:** Trevor Jones

The garden has a wide range of features and a good collection of plants. There are peat and woodland garden plants and a colourful rock garden. Summer months bring a superb show from the herbaceous beds and borders. The heather gardens give a splash of colour, along with bright berries in the autumn. Truly a garden for all seasons.

Location: OS Ref. NX752 605. Off A75, 1m SW of Castle Douglas.

Opening Times: Estate & garden: All year: daily, 9.30am - sunset. Walled garden & glasshouses: all year: daily, 9.30am - 5pm. Visitor Centre, Exhibition, Countryside Centre, Shop & Restaurant: 1 - 31 Mar & 1 Nov - 23 Dec: Wed - Sun, 10am - 4pm. 1 Apr - 31 Oct: daily, 9.30am - 5.30pm.

Admission: Adult £4.50, Conc. £3.50, Family £12.50. Groups: Adult £3.60.

📷   ♿ Grounds suitable. WC.   🍴 ❄️ 🅒

WHITHORN PRIORY

Tel: 01988 500700

Whithorn

Owner: In the care of Historic Scotland   **Contact:** The Project Manager

The site of the first Christian church in Scotland. Founded as 'Candida Casa' by St Ninian in the early 5th century it later became the cathedral church of Galloway.

Location: OS Ref. NX445 403. At Whithorn on the A746.

Opening Times: Please telephone for details.

Admission: Joint ticket gives entry to Priory, Priory Museum and archaeological dig.

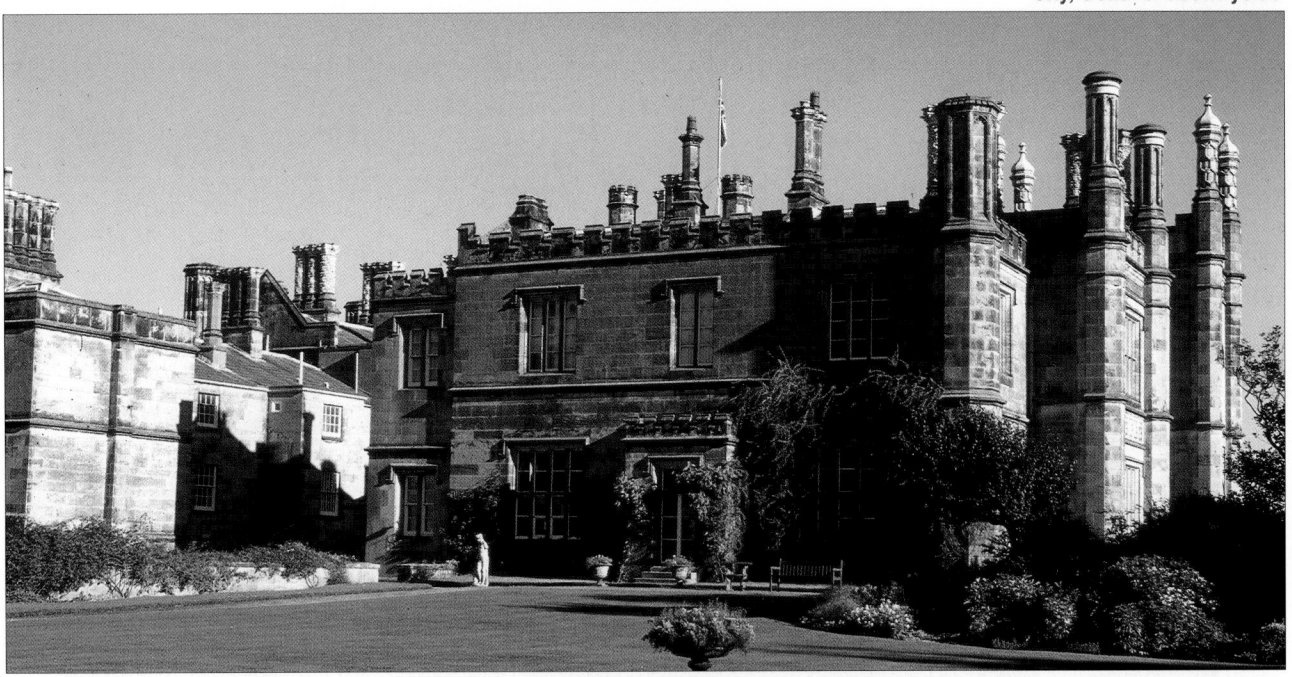

DALMENY HOUSE
South Queensferry

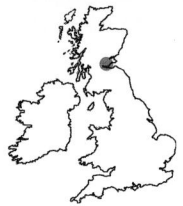

DALMENY HOUSE rejoices in one of the most beautiful and unspoilt settings in Great Britain, yet it is only seven miles from Scotland's capital, Edinburgh, fifteen minutes from Edinburgh airport and less than an hour's drive from Glasgow. It is an eminently suitable venue for group visits, business functions, meetings and special events, including product launches. Outdoor activities such as off-road driving, also feature strongly.

Dalmeny Estate, the family home of the Earls of Rosebery for over 300 years, boasts superb collections of porcelain and tapestries, fine paintings by Gainsborough, Raeburn, Reynolds and Lawrence, together with the exquisite Mentmore Rothschild collection of 18th century French furniture. There is also the Napoleonic collection, assembled by the 5th Earl of Rosebery, Prime Minister, historian and owner of three Derby winners.

The Hall, Library and Dining Room will lend a memorable sense of occasion to corporate receptions, luncheons and dinners. A wide range of entertainment can also be provided, from piano recitals to a floodlit pipe band Beating the Retreat.

Owner: The Earl of Rosebery

CONTACT

The Administrator
Dalmeny House
South Queensferry
Edinburgh
EH30 9TQ

Tel: 0131 331 1888

Fax: 0131 331 1788

e-mail: events@ dalmeny.co.uk

LOCATION

OS Ref. NT167 779

From Edinburgh A90, B924, 7m N, A90 ¹/₂ m.

On south shore of Firth of Forth.

Bus: From St Andrew Square to Chapel Gate 1m from House.

Rail: Dalmeny railway station 3m.

Taxi: Queensferry Fare Radio Cabs 0131 331 1041.

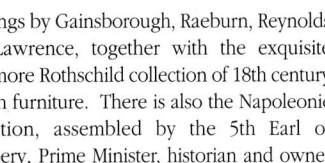

OPENING TIMES

SUMMER

July and August
Sun - Tue, 2 - 5.30pm.
Last admission 4.30pm.

WINTER

Open at other times by appointment only.

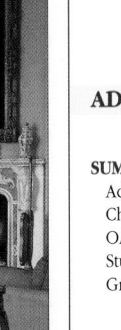

ADMISSION

SUMMER

Adult	£4.00
Child (10-16yrs)	£2.00
OAP	£3.50
Student	£3.00
Groups (20+)	£3.00

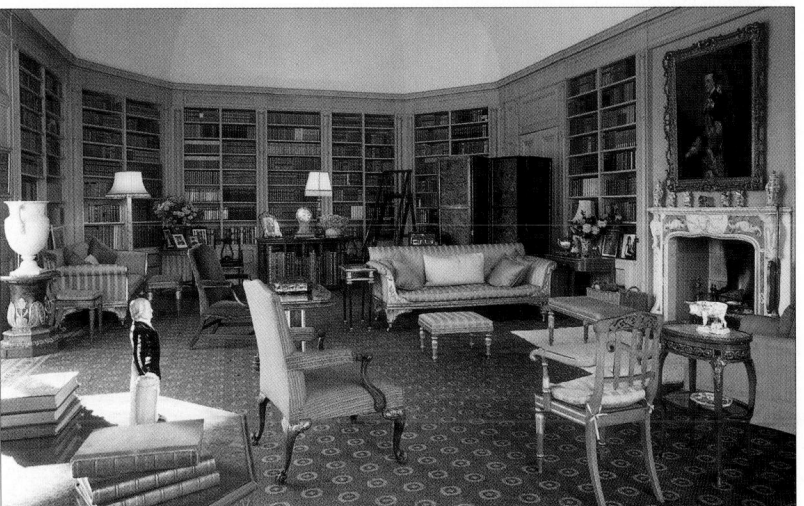

 Fashion shows, product launches, archery, clay pigeon shooting, equestrian events, shows, filming, background photography, small meetings and special events. Lectures on House, contents and family history. Screen and projector. Helicopter landing area. House is centre of a 4¹/₂ m shore walk from Forth Rail Bridge to small foot passenger ferry at Cramond (ferry 9am - 1pm, 2 - 7pm in summer, 2 - 4pm winter, closed Fri). No fires, picnics or photography.

Conferences and functions, buffets, lunches, dinners.

Partially suitable. Visitors may alight at entrance. WC.

Teas and lunches, groups can book in advance.

Obligatory. Special interest tours can be arranged outside normal opening hours.

 60 cars, 3 coaches. Parking for functions in front of house.

No dogs.

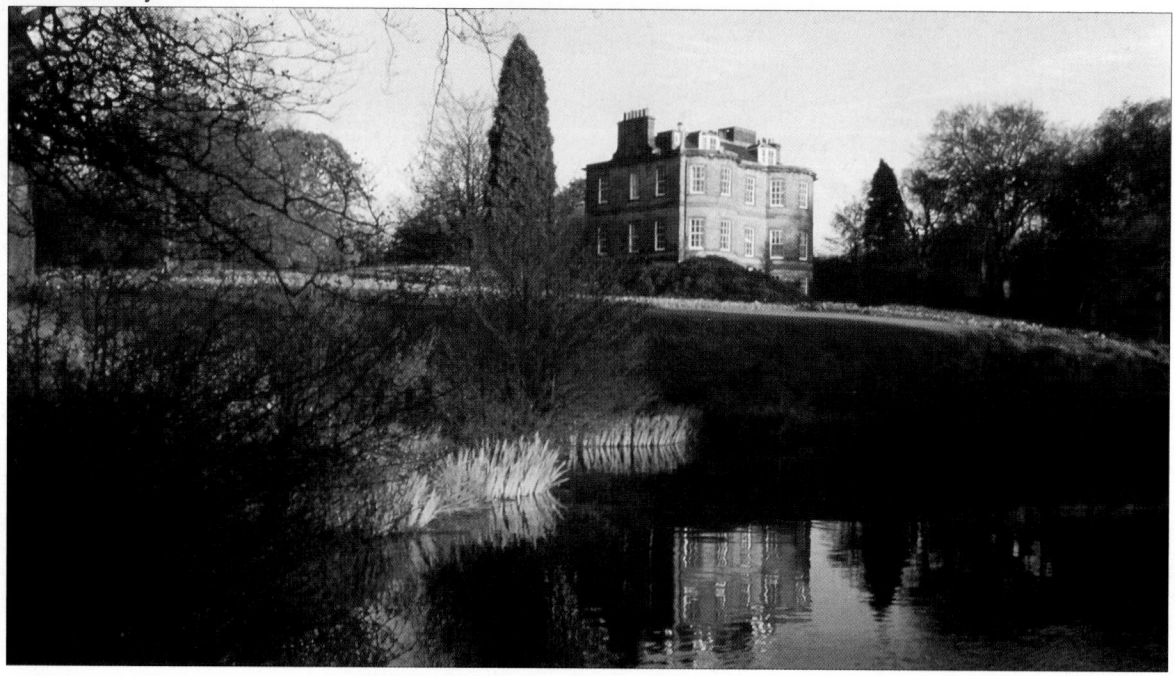

HARBURN HOUSE
Nr Livingston

HARBURN HOUSE offers its guests the perfect alternative to a first class hotel. This privately owned Georgian mansion, surrounded by its own 3000 acre sporting and leisure estate, is ideally situated offering unparalleled accessibility.

Harburn is essentially small and very personal. It is therefore frequently taken over exclusively for conferences, incentive travel, training seminars and product launches, etc. In this way guests may enjoy the luxury of a five star hotel, combined with the comfort and privacy of their own home.

The policies and lawns of Harburn are ideal for larger events and these can be complemented by our own fully lined and floored marquee.

A stay at Harburn is a very relaxed and informal affair. The staff are first class and the atmosphere is one of a private house party.

The estate provides the full range of sporting and leisure activities including, golf, game shooting, fishing, clay pigeon shooting, tennis, riding and archery to name but a few.

The complete privacy and outstanding scenery, so accessible to the major cities and beauty spots, makes Harburn the ultimate choice for the discerning event or conference organiser.

❖

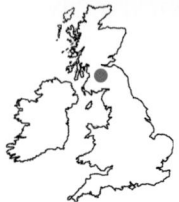

Owner: Humphrey & Rozi Spurway

CONTACT

Rozi Spurway
Harburn House
Harburn
West Calder
West Lothian
EH55 8RN

Tel: 01506 461818

Fax: 01506 416591

e-mail: information@harburnhouse.com

LOCATION

OS Ref. NT045 608

Off B7008, $2^1/_2$ m S of A71. 2m N of A70. 20m SW of Edinburgh. Almost equidistant between Glasgow and Edinburgh, within 1hr of Perth, Stirling, Dundee and the Border country.

CONFERENCE/FUNCTION		
ROOM	SIZE	MAX CAPACITY
Conference Room	30' x 18'	20
Drawing Rm	30' x 18'	40
Dining Rm	30' x 18'	40
Library	14' x 12'	15
Morning Rm	16' x 15'	20
Whole house		80
Marquee	120' x 40'	500

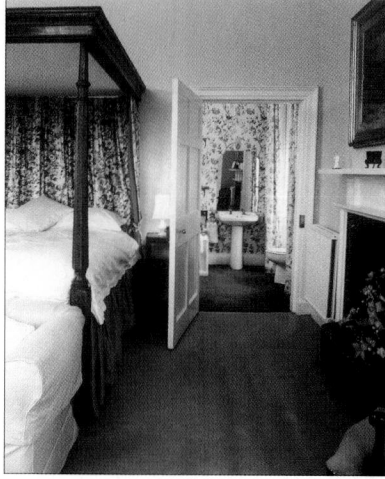

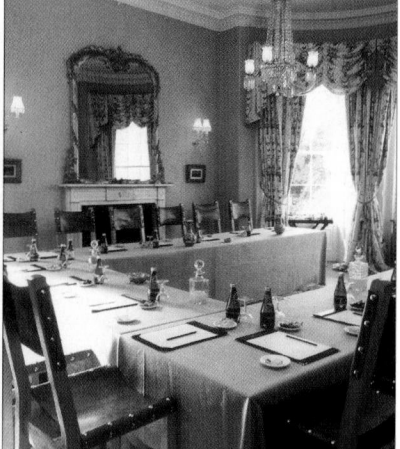

ℹ️ Filming, conferences, activity days, product launches, golf, riding, fishing, archery, buggies, game shooting, falconry, etc. Golf and Country Club nearby.

🍽️ High quality in-house catering by our own top chef and fully trained staff. Prices and menus on request. Wedding receptions.

♿ Ground floor bedroom, dining room and drawing room.

🅿️ Parking for 300 cars and 10 coaches in summer, 100+/10 in winter. Follow one way system and 20 mph speed limit, vehicles should not park on grass verges.

🐕 On leads.

🛏️ 20 bedrooms, all with their own bathrooms, exclusive to one group at a time.

❄️

OPENING TIMES

All year by appointment for exclusive use of house and grounds.

ADMISSION

The exclusive use of House and Grounds for activity days (without accommodation).

Per day from £700.00

Accommodation Rates
On application

Day Delegate Rate
Per person..............£45.00

24 hour rate
Per person............£130.00

VAT is not included in the above rates.

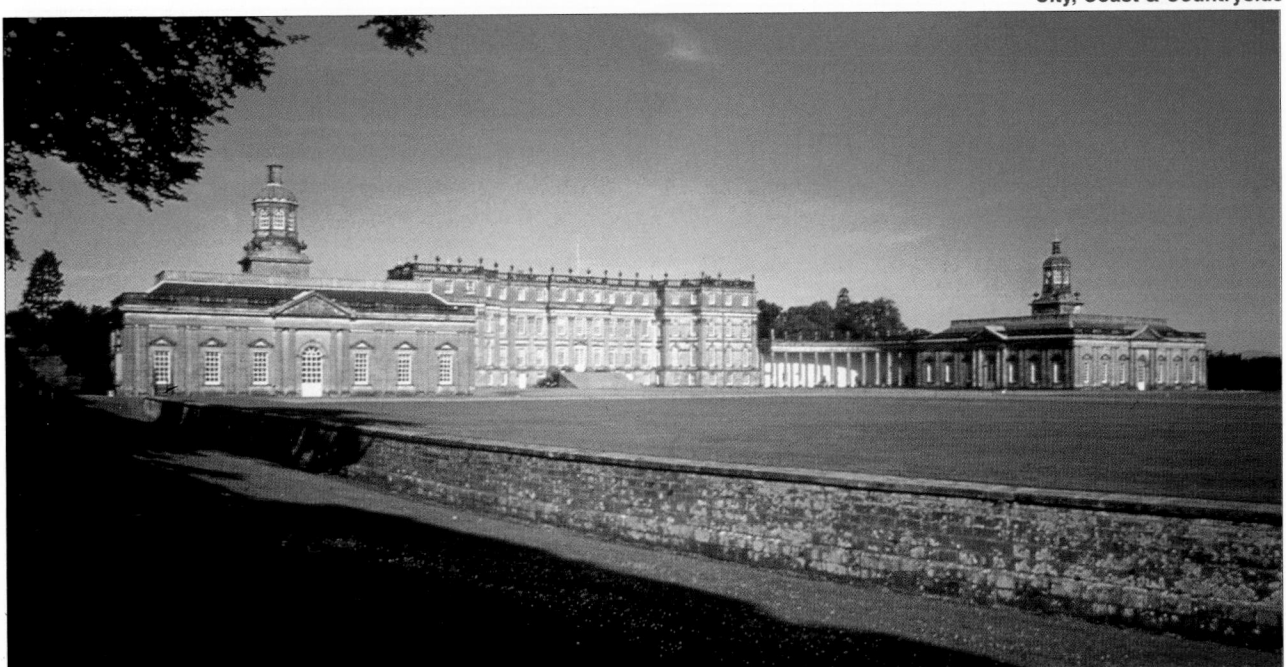

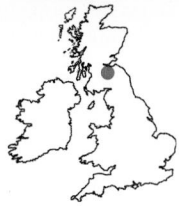

Owner: Hopetoun House Preservation Trust

CONTACT

Lois Bayne Jardine
Hopetoun House
South Queensferry
Edinburgh
West Lothian
EH30 9SL

Tel: 0131 331 2451

Fax: 0131 319 1885

LOCATION

OS Ref. NT089 790

2¹/₂ m W of Forth Road Bridge.

12m W of Edinburgh (25 mins. drive).

34m E of Glasgow (50 mins. drive).

HOPETOUN HOUSE
Edinburgh

HOPETOUN HOUSE is a unique gem of Europe's architectural heritage and undoubtedly 'Scotland's Finest Stately Home'. Situated on the shores of the Firth of Forth, it is one of the most splendid examples of the work of Scottish architects Sir William Bruce and William Adam. The interior of the house, with opulent gilding and classical motifs, reflects the aristocratic grandeur of the early 18th century, whilst its magnificent parkland has fine views across the Forth to the hills of Fife. The house is approached from the Royal Drive, used only by members of the Royal Family, notably King George IV in 1822 and Her Majesty Queen Elizabeth II in 1988.

Hopetoun is really two houses in one, the oldest part of the house was designed by Sir William Bruce and built between 1699 and 1707. It shows some of the finest examples in Scotland of carving, wainscotting and ceiling painting. In 1721 William Adam started enlarging the house by adding the magnificent façade, colonnades and grand State apartments which were the focus for social life and entertainment in the 18th century.

The house is set in 100 acres of rolling parkland including fine woodland walks, the red deer park, the spring garden with a profusion of wild flowers, and numerous picturesque picnic spots.

Hopetoun has been home of the Earls of Hopetoun, later created Marquesses of Linlithgow, since it was built in 1699 and in 1974 a charitable trust was created to preserve the house with its historic contents and surrounding landscape for the benefit of the public for all time.

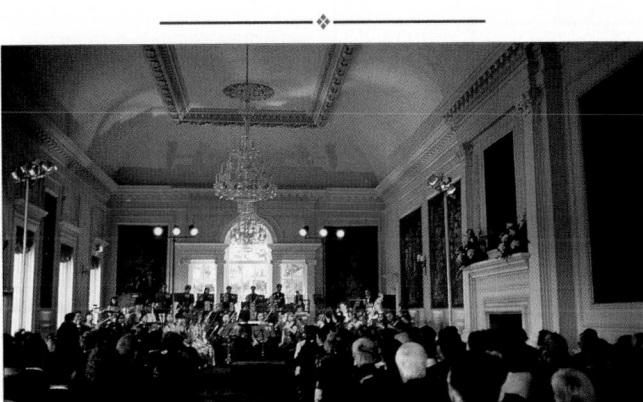

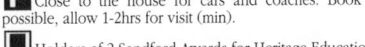

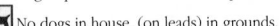

Private functions, special events, antiques fairs, concerts, Scottish gala evenings, conferences, grand piano, boules (petanque) piste, croquet lawn, helicopter landing. No smoking or flash photography in house.

Receptions, gala dinners.

Restaurant and exhibitions on ground floor. WC.

Licensed. Groups (up to 250) can book in advance, menus on request tel: 0131 331 4305.

By arrangement. Foreign language guides are usually available.

Close to the house for cars and coaches. Book if possible, allow 1-2hrs for visit (min).

Holders of 2 Sandford Awards for Heritage Education. Special tours of house and/or grounds for different age/interest groups. Teachers' information pack.

No dogs in house, (on leads) in grounds.

OPENING TIMES

SUMMER

1 April - 30 September: daily, 10am - 5.30pm
Last admission 4.30pm.

WINTER

By appointment only for groups of 15+.

ADMISSION

Adult £5.30
Child (5-16yrs)........£2.70
Conc......................£4.70
Groups
  Adult £4.70
  Child (5-16yrs)........£2.20

Under 5yrs Free.

Winter prices on request.

Admission to Shop & Adam Stables Restaurant Free.

SPECIAL EVENTS

• **MAR 9 - 11**
  Antiques Fair.

• **APR 7 - 12**
  Sotheby's Spring Sale.

• **JUN 1 - 2**
  Hopetoun Carriage Driving Event.

• **JUN 3**
  Dolls House & Miniatures Fair.

• **OCT 12 - 14**
  Antiques Fair.

• **NOV 23 - 25**
  Hopetoun's Present Event Shopping Fair.

CONFERENCE/FUNCTION		
ROOM	SIZE	MAX CAPACITY
Ballroom	92' x 35'	300
Tapestry Rm	37' x 24'	100
Red Drawing Rm	44' x 24'	100
State Dining Rm	39' x 23'	20

AMISFIELD MAINS

Tel: 01875 870201 **Fax:** 01875 870620

Nr Haddington, East Lothian EH41 3SA

Owner: Wemyss and March Estates Management Co Ltd   **Contact:** M Andrews

Georgian farmhouse with gothick barn and cottage.

Location: OS Ref. NT526 755. Between Haddington and East Linton on A1 Edinburgh-Dunbar Road.

Opening Times: Exterior only: By appointment, Wemyss and March Estates Office, Longniddry, East Lothian EH32 0PY.

Admission: Please contact for details.

ARNISTON HOUSE

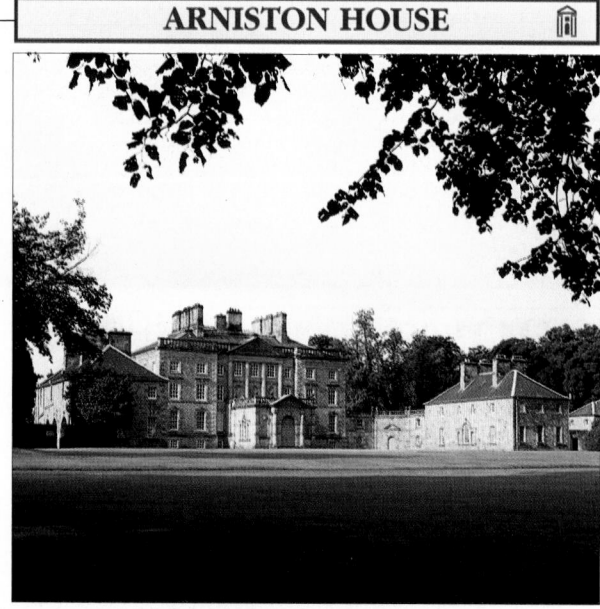

GOREBRIDGE, MIDLOTHIAN EH23 4RY

Owner: Mrs A Dundas-Bekker   Contact: Miss H Dundas-Bekker

Tel/Fax: 01875 830515

Magnificent William Adam mansion started in 1726. Fine plasterwork, Scottish portraiture, period furniture and other fascinating contents. Beautiful country setting beloved by Sir Walter Scott.

Location: OS Ref. NT326 595. Off B6372, 1m from A7, Temple direction.

Opening Times: Apr, May & Jun: Tues. Guided tours at 2pm & 3.30pm. 1 Jul - 13 Sept: Sun, Tue & Thur, 2 - 5pm. Guided tours at $^1\!/_2$ hourly intervals. Pre-arranged groups (10-50) accepted throughout the rest of the year.

Admission: Adult £4, Child £1.50 (under school age Free).

 Obligatory.   In grounds, on leads.   ❊   ⓘⓦ

BEANSTON

Tel: 01875 870201 **Fax:** 01875 870620

Nr Haddington, East Lothian EH41 3SB

Owner: Wemyss and March Estates Management Co. Ltd   **Contact:** M Andrews

Georgian farmhouse with Georgian orangery.

Location: OS Ref. NT546 763. Between Haddington and East Linton on A1 Edinburgh-Dunbar Road.

Opening Times: Exterior only: By appointment, Wemyss and March Estates Office, Longniddry, East Lothian EH32 0PY.

Admission: Please contact for details.

BIEL

Tel: 01620 860355

Dunbar, East Lothian EH42 1SY

Owner/Contact: C G Spence

Originally a fortified tower, considerably added to over time.

Location: OS Ref. NT635 759. 5m from Dunbar on the A1 towards Edinburgh.

Opening Times: By appointment.

Admission: Contribution to charity.

BLACKNESS CASTLE

Tel: 01506 834807

Blackness

Owner: In the care of Historic Scotland   **Contact:** The Steward

One of Scotland's most important strongholds. Built in the 14th century and massively strengthened in the 16th century as an artillery fortress, it has been a Royal castle and a prison armaments depot and film location for *Hamlet*. It was restored by the Office of Works in the 1920s. It stands on a promontory in the Firth of Forth.

Location: OS Ref. NT055 803. 4m NE of Linlithgow on the Firth of Forth, off the A904.

Opening Times: 1 Apr - 30 Sept: daily, 9.30am - 6.30pm, last ticket 6pm. 1 Oct - 31 Mar: Mon - Sat, 9.30am - 4.30pm, last ticket 4pm. Closed Thur pm, Fri & Sun in winter.

Admission: Adult £2, Child 75p, Conc. £1.50.

CRAIGMILLAR CASTLE

Tel: 0131 661 4445

Edinburgh

Owner: In the care of Historic Scotland   **Contact:** The Steward

Mary Queen of Scots fled to Craigmillar after the murder of Rizzio and it was here that the plot was hatched for the murder of her husband Lord Darnley. This handsome structure with courtyard and gardens covers an area of one and a quarter acres. Built around an L-plan tower house of the early 15th century including a range of private rooms linked to the hall of the old tower.

Location: OS Ref. NT285 710. 2$^1\!/_2$ m SE of Edinburgh off the A68.

Opening Times: 1 Apr - 30 Sept: daily, 9.30am - 6.30pm, last ticket 6pm. 1 Oct - 31 Mar: Mon - Sat, 9.30am - 4.30pm, Suns, 2 - 4.30pm, last ticket 4pm. Closed Thur pm & Fri in winter.

Admission: Adult £2, Child 75p, Conc. £1.50.

CRICHTON CASTLE

Tel: 01875 320017

Pathhead

Owner: In the care of Historic Scotland   **Contact:** The Steward

A large and sophisticated castle with a spectacular façade of faceted stonework in an Italian style added by the Earl of Bothwell between 1581 and 1591 following a visit to Italy. Mary Queen of Scots attended a wedding here.

Location: OS Ref. NT380 612. 2$^1\!/_2$ m SSW of Pathhead off the A68.

Opening Times: 1 Apr - 30 Sept: daily, 9.30am - 6.30pm, last ticket 6pm.

Admission: Adult £2, Child 75p, Conc. £1.50.

DALKEITH COUNTRY PARK

Tel: 0131 663 5684

Dalkeith, Midlothian EH22 2NJ   **e-mail:** cameron@dalkeith.freeserve.co.uk

Contact: J C Manson

Extensive grounds of Dalkeith Palace. 18th century bridge and orangery. Interpretation area.

Location: OS Ref. NT333 679. 7m SE of Edinburgh.

Opening Times: Mar - Oct: 10am - 6pm.

Admission: Adult/Child £2, Family £7, Groups £1.50.

DALMENY HOUSE

See page 463 for full page entry.

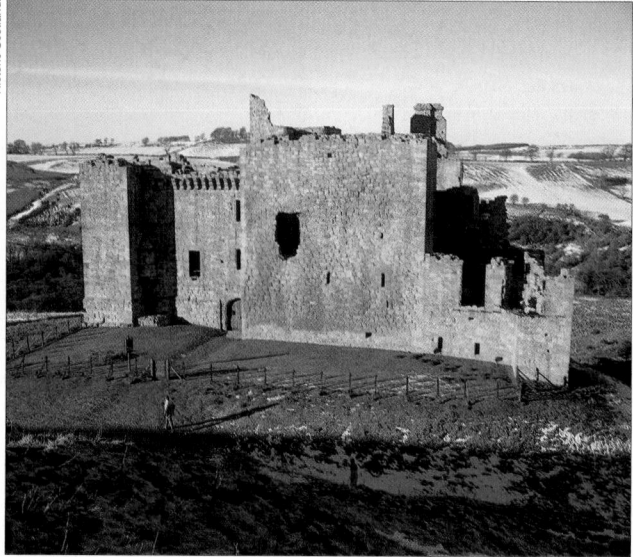

Crichton Castle, Edinburgh.

DIRLETON CASTLE & GARDEN

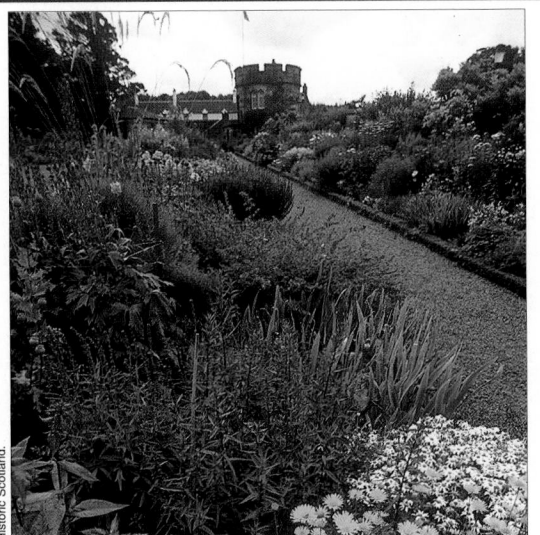

DIRLETON, EAST LOTHIAN EH39 5ER

Owner: *In the care of Historic Scotland*   **Contact:** *The Steward*

Tel: 01620 850330

The oldest part of this romantic castle dates from the 13th century, when it was built by the De Vaux family. The renowned gardens, first laid out in the 16th century, now include a magnificent Arts and Crafts herbaceous border (the longest in the world) and a re-created Victorian Garden. In the picturesque village of Dirleton.

Location: OS Ref. NT516 839. In Dirleton, 7m W of North Berwick on the A198.

Opening Times: Apr - Sept: daily, 9.30am - 6.30pm. Oct - Mar: Mon - Sat, 9.30am - 4.30pm, Suns, 2 - 4.30pm. Last ticket 30 mins before closing.

Admission: Adult £2.80, Child £1, Conc. £2. 10% discount for groups (10+).

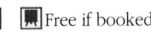 Partially suitable. 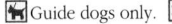 Free if booked. 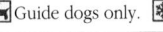 Guide dogs only. ❋

DUNGLASS COLLEGIATE CHURCH   **Tel:** 0131 668 8800

Cockburnspath

Owner: In the care of Historic Scotland

Founded in 1450 for a college of canons by Sir Alexander Hume. A handsome cross-shaped building with vaulted nave, choir and transepts.

Location: OS Ref. 67 NT766 718. 1m NW of Cockburnspath. SW of A1.

Opening Times: All year.

Admission: Free.

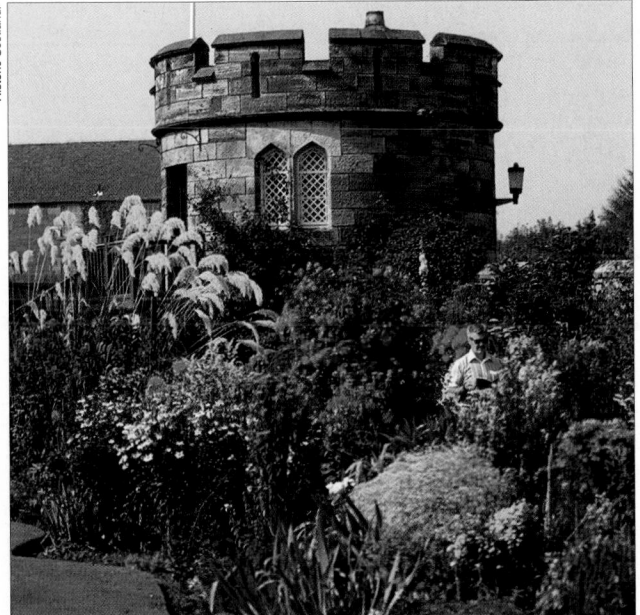

Crichton Castle, Edinburgh.

EDINBURGH CASTLE

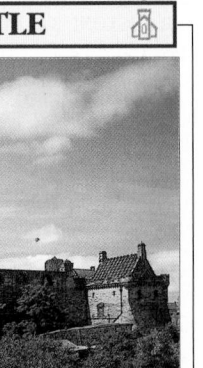

CASTLEHILL, EDINBURGH EH1 2NG

Owner: *Historic Scotland*   **Contact:** *Barbara Smith*

Tel: 0131 225 9846   **Fax:** 0131 220 4733

Scotland's most famous castle, dominating the capital's skyline and giving stunning views of the city and countryside. Home to the Scottish crown jewels, the Stone of Destiny and Mons Meg. Other highlights include St Margaret's Chapel, the Great Hall and the Scottish National War Memorial.

Location: OS Ref. NT252 736. At the top of the Royal Mile in Edinburgh.

Opening Times: Apr - Sept: daily, 9.30am - 6pm. Oct - Mar: daily, 9.30am - 5pm. Last ticket 45 mins before closing.

Admission: Adult £7.50, Child £2, Conc. £5.50. Pre-booked school visits available free, except May - Aug.

 Private evening hire.
Partially suitable. WCs. Courtesy vehicle. Licensed.
In 6 languages. Ample (except Jun-Oct). Guide dogs. ❋

THE GEORGIAN HOUSE

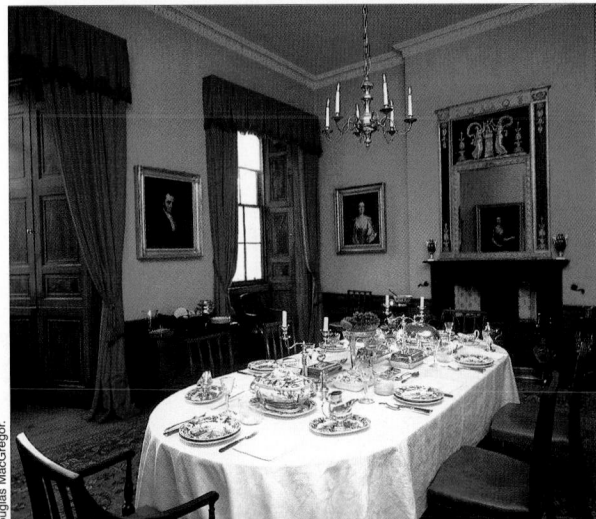

7 CHARLOTTE SQUARE, EDINBURGH EH2 4DR

Owner: *The National Trust for Scotland*   **Contact:** *Jacqueline Wright*

Tel/Fax: 0131 226 3318

The north side of Charlotte Square is Robert Adam's masterpiece of urban architecture - a splendid example of the neo-classical 'palace front'. The three floors of No.7, The Georgian House, are delightfully furnished as they would have been around 1796. There is a fascinating array of china and silver, pictures and furniture, gadgets and utensils from the decorative to the purely functional.

Location: OS Ref. NT247 740. In Edinburgh's city centre, NW of Princes St.

Opening Times: 1 Mar - 31 Oct: Mon - Sat, 10am - 5pm, Suns, 2 - 5pm (last admission 4.30pm); 1 Nov - 24 Dec: Mon - Sat, 11am - 4pm, Suns, 2 - 4pm (last entry 3.30pm). Shop: As house, but opens at 11am.

Admission: Adult £5, Conc. £4, Family £14. Groups: Adult £4.

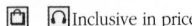 Inclusive in price. 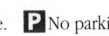 No parking.

GLADSTONE'S LAND

Tel: 0131 226 5856 **Fax:** 0131 226 4851

477b Lawnmarket, Royal Mile, Edinburgh EH1 2NT

Owner: The National Trust for Scotland   **Contact:** Pat Wigston

Gladstone's Land was the home of a prosperous Edinburgh merchant in the 17th century. On the Royal Mile, near the Castle, it is decorated and furnished with great authenticity to give visitors an impression of life in Edinburgh's Old Town some 300 years ago. Features of the 6-storey building are the painted ceilings and the reconstructed shop both complete with replicas of 17th century goods.

Location: OS Ref. NT255 736. In Edinburgh's Royal Mile, near the castle.

Opening Times: House & Shop: 1 Apr - 31 Oct: Mon - Sat, 10am - 5pm, Suns, 2 - 5pm, last admission 4.30pm.

Admission: Adult £3.50, Conc. £2.50, Family £9.50. Groups: Adult £3. Group visits must be booked.

Ground floor suitable. No parking.

GOSFORD HOUSE

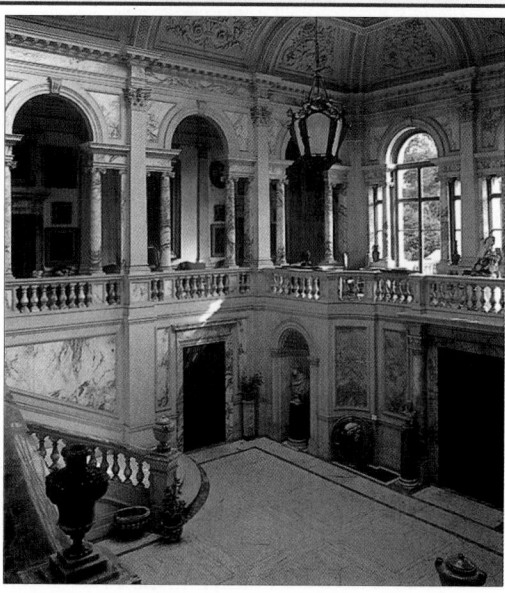

LONGNIDDRY, EAST LOTHIAN EH32 0PX

Owner/Contact: The Earl of Wemyss

Tel: 01875 870201

Though the core of the house is Robert Adam, the family home is in the South Wing built by William Young in 1890. This contains the celebrated Marble Hall and a fine collection of paintings and works of art. The house is set in extensive policies with an 18th century Pleasure Garden and Ponds. Greylag geese and swans abound.

Location: OS Ref. NT453 786. Off A198 2m NE of Longniddry.

Opening Times: 4 Jul - 5 Aug (inclusive): Wed - Sun, 2 - 5pm.

Admission: Adult £5, Child £1.

In grounds, on leads.

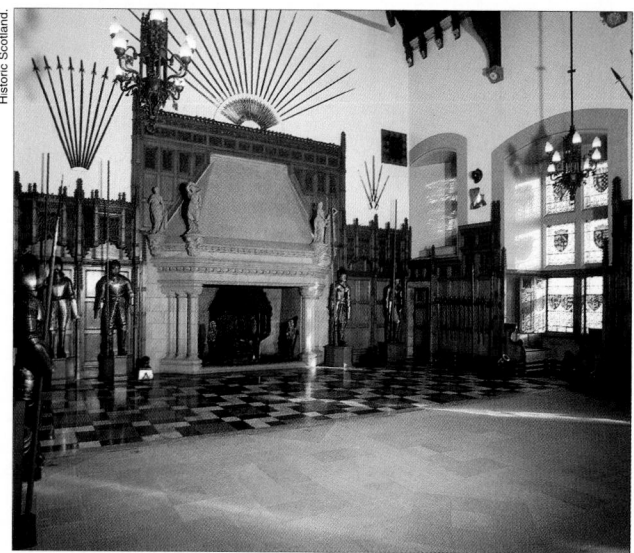

Historic Scotland.

Edinburgh Castle.

GREYWALLS

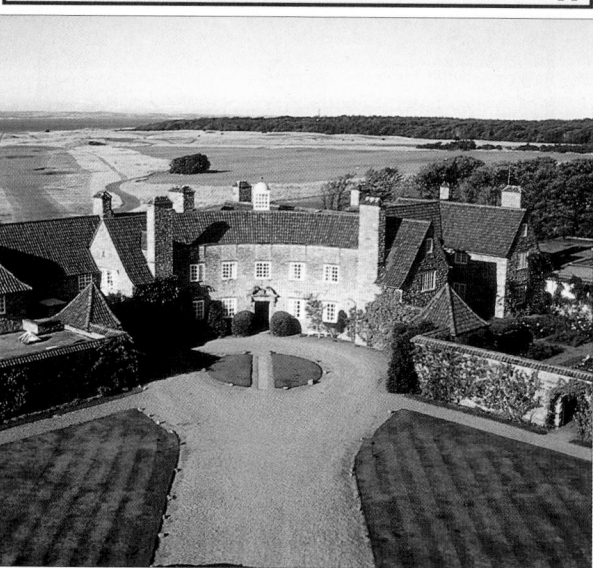

MUIRFIELD, GULLANE, EAST LOTHIAN EH31 2EG

Owner: Giles Weaver   *Contact:* Mrs Sue Prime

Tel: 01620 842144 **Fax:** 01620 842241 **e-mail:** hotel@greywalls.co.uk

Stunning Edwardian Country House Hotel only 30 minutes from the centre of Edinburgh. Close to wonderful golf courses and beaches. Designed by Sir Edwin Lutyens with secluded walled gardens attributed to Gertrude Jekyll. Greywalls offers the delights of an award-winning menu and an excellent wine list in this charming and relaxed environment. There is a welcome whether you stay or simply spend a peaceful few hours in this oasis of calm.

Location: OS Ref. NT490 835. Off A198, 5m W of North Berwick, 30 mins from Edinburgh.

Opening Times: Apr - Oct.

HAILES CASTLE

Tel: 0131 668 8800

East Linton

Owner: In the care of Historic Scotland

Beautifully-sited ruin incorporating a fortified manor of the 13th century. It was extended in the 14th and 15th centuries. There are two vaulted pit prisons.

Location: OS Ref. NT575 758. 1½m SW of East Linton. 4m E of Haddington. S of A1.

Opening Times: All year.

Admission: Free.

HARBURN HOUSE

See page 464 for full page entry.

HARELAW FARMHOUSE

Tel: 01875 870201 **Fax:** 01875 870620

Nr Longniddry, East Lothian EH32 0PH

Owner: Wemyss and March Estates Management Co Ltd   **Contact:** M Andrews

Early 19th century 2-storey farmhouse built as an integral part of the steading. Dovecote over entrance arch.

Location: OS Ref. NT450 766. Between Longniddry and Drem on B1377.

Opening Times: Exteriors only: By appointment, Wemyss and March Estates Office, Longniddry, East Lothian EH32 0PY.

Admission: Please contact for details.

HOPETOUN HOUSE

See page 465 for full page entry

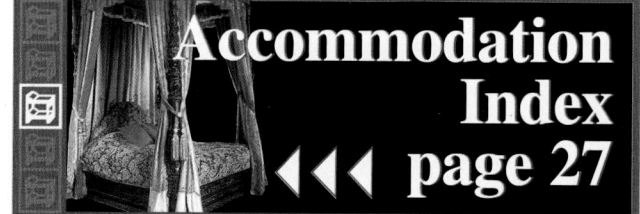

Accommodation Index ◀◀◀ **page 27**

HOUSE OF THE BINNS

Tel: 01506 834255

Linlithgow, West Lothian EH49 7NA

Owner: The National Trust for Scotland   **Contact:** Tam & Kathleen Dalyell

A 17th century house, the home of the Dalyells, one of Scotland's great families, since 1612. Here in 1681, General Tam Dalyell raised the Royal Scots Greys Regiment, named after the colour of their uniforms. The house contains fine Italian-style plasterwork and an outstanding collection of family paintings.

Location: OS Ref. NT051 786. Off A904, 15m W of Edinburgh. 3m E of Linlithgow.

Opening Times: House: 1 May - 30 Sept: daily except Fris, 1.30 - 5.30pm, last admission 5pm. Parkland: 1 Apr - 31 Oct: daily, 10am - 7pm. 1 Nov - 31 Mar: daily, 10am - 4pm, last admission 30mins before close.

Admission: House & Parkland: Adult £4, Conc. £3, Family £11. Groups: Adult £3.20, Child/School £1. Group visits must be booked. Members of the Royal Scots Dragoon Guards admitted Free.

⎣ Partially suitable. WCs. **P** Limited. **!** Obligatory. ⛺ Guide dogs only.
❋ ⓣⓦ

INVERESK LODGE GARDEN

Tel: 01721 722502 **Fax:** 01721 724700

24 Inveresk Village, Musselburgh, East Lothian EH21 7TE

Owner: The National Trust for Scotland   **Contact:** Head Gardener

Small garden in grounds of 17th century house, with large selection of plants. House closed.

Location: OS Ref. NT348 718. A6124, S of Musselburgh, 6m E of Edinburgh.

Opening Times: 1 Apr - 31 Oct: Mon - Fri, 10am - 6pm, Sats & Suns, 12 noon - 6pm; 1 Nov - 31 Mar: Mon - Fri, 10am - 4.30pm, Suns, 2 - 5pm.

Admission: £2 (honesty box).

⎣ Grounds suitable. **P** Limited. ⛺ No dogs in the garden.
P Cars to be parked by garden wall only. ❋ ⓣⓦ

LAURISTON CASTLE

Tel: 0131 336 2060 **Fax:** 0131 312 7165

Cramond Road South, Edinburgh EH4 5QD

Owner: City of Edinburgh Council   **Contact:** Robin Barnes

A beautiful house overlooking the Firth of Forth. The oldest part is a 16th century tower house.

Location: OS Ref. NT203 761. Between Davidsons Mains and Cramond, NW Edinburgh.

Opening Times: 1 Apr - 31 Oct: daily except Fris, 11.20am, 12.20pm, 2.20pm, 3.20pm, 4.20pm. 1 Nov - 31 Mar: Sats & Suns, 2 - 4pm. Admission by guided tour only. Booking only required for groups of 10+.

Admission: Adult £4.50, Conc. £3.

LENNOXLOVE HOUSE

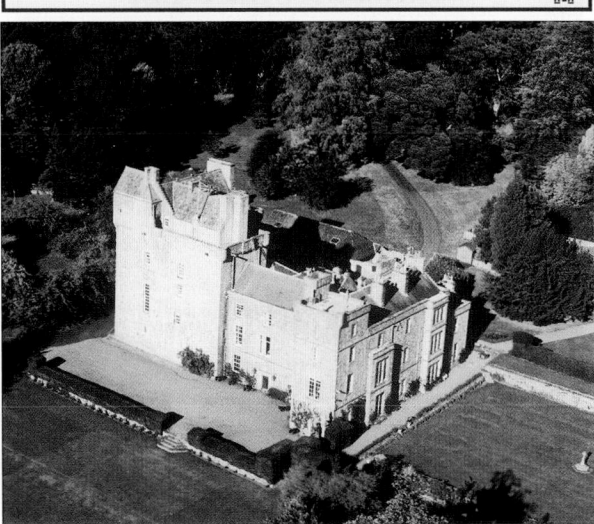

HADDINGTON, EAST LOTHIAN EH41 4NZ

Owner: Lennoxlove House Ltd   Contact: House Administrator

Tel: 01620 823720 **Fax:** 01620 825112 **e-mail:** lennoxlove@compuserve.com

Home of the Duke of Hamilton. The 14th century keep houses a death mask said to be that of Mary Queen of Scots, a silver casket which once contained incriminating letters that helped send Mary to her death, and a sapphire ring given to her by Lord John Hamilton. The 17th century part of the house contains the Hamilton Palace collection of pictures, furniture and porcelain arranged in classic stately home style.

Location: OS Ref. NT515 721. 20m SE of Edinburgh, near Haddington.

Opening Times: Easter - end Oct: Wed, Thur, Sat & Sun, 2 - 4.30pm. Guided tours. Please check if house is open on a Sat before arriving.

Admission: Adult £4, Child £2. Group charges on application.

ⓘ No photography in house. ⎣ **T** Weddings, gala dinners.
▣ **!** Obligatory. **P** ⓣⓦ

LIBERTON HOUSE

Tel: 0131 467 7777 **Fax:** 0131 467 7774
e-mail: mail@nicholas-groves-raines-architects.co.uk

73 Liberton Drive, Edinburgh EH16 6NP

Owner/Contact: Nicholas Groves-Raines

Built around 1600 for the Littles of Liberton, this harled L-plan house has been carefully restored by the current architect owner using original detailing and extensive restoration of the principal structure. Public access restricted to the Great Hall and Old Kitchen. The restored garden layout suggests the original and there is a late 17th century lectern doocot by the entrance drive.

Location: OS Ref. NT267 694. 73 Liberton Drive, Edinburgh.

Opening Times: 1 Mar - 31 Oct: 10am - 4.30pm, by prior appointment only.

Admission: Free.

⎣ Not suitable. **P** Limited. ⛺

LINLITHGOW PALACE

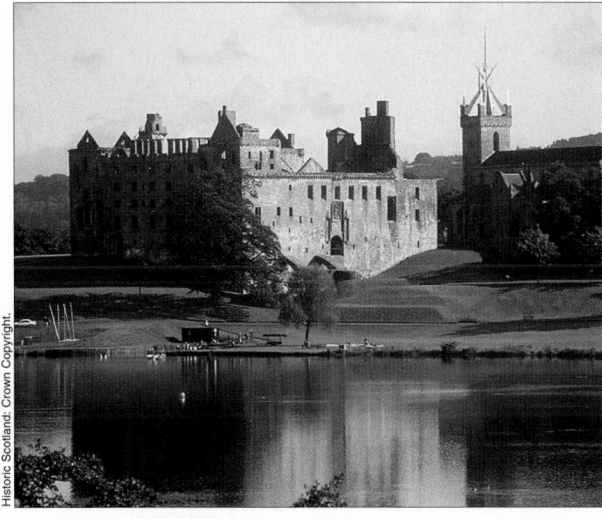

Historic Scotland: Crown Copyright.

LINLITHGOW, WEST LOTHIAN EH49 7AL

Owner: Historic Scotland   Contact: The Steward

Tel: 01506 842896

The magnificent remains of a great royal palace set in its own park and beside Linlithgow Loch. A favoured residence of the Stewart monarchs, James V and his daughter Mary Queen of Scots were born here. Bonnie Prince Charlie stayed here during his bid to regain the British crown.

Location: OS Ref. NT003 774. In the centre of Linlithgow off the M9.

Opening Times: Apr - Sept: daily, 9.30am - 6.30pm. Oct - Mar: Mon - Sat, 9.30am - 4.30pm, Suns, 2 - 4.30pm. Last ticket 30 mins before closing.

Admission: Adult £2.80, Child £1, Conc. £2. 10% discount for groups (10+).

ⓘ Picnic area. 📷 **T** Private evening hire. ⎣ Partially suitable.
! By arrangement. **P** Cars only. ▪ Free if booked.
⛺ In grounds, off leads. ❋

NEWLISTON

Tel: 0131 333 3231 **Fax:** 0131 335 3596

Kirkliston, West Lothian EH29 9EB

Owner/Contact: Mrs Caroline Maclachlan

Late Robert Adam house. Costumes on display. 18th century designed landscape, rhododendrons, azaleas and water features. On Sundays tea is in the Edinburgh Cookery School in the William Adam Coach House. Also on Sundays there is a ride-on steam model railway from 2 - 5pm. An inventory of chattels not on public display can be inspected and such chattels can be viewed by request when the house is open to the public.

Location: OS Ref. NT110 735. 8m W of Edinburgh, 3m S of Forth Road Bridge, off B800.

Opening Times: 2 May - 3 Jun: Wed - Sun, 2 - 6pm. Also by appointment.

Admission: Adult £1.50, Child/OAP 50p, Student £1.

⎣ Grounds suitable. ▣ ⛺ In grounds, on leads. ❋

THE PALACE OF HOLYROODHOUSE

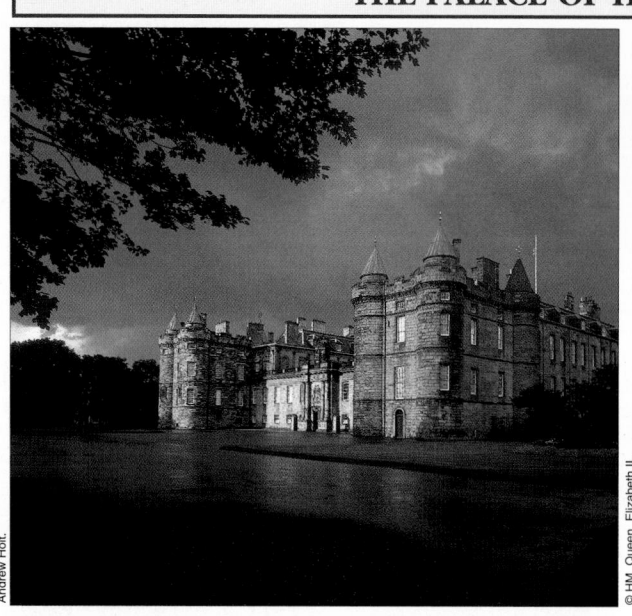

Andrew Holt.

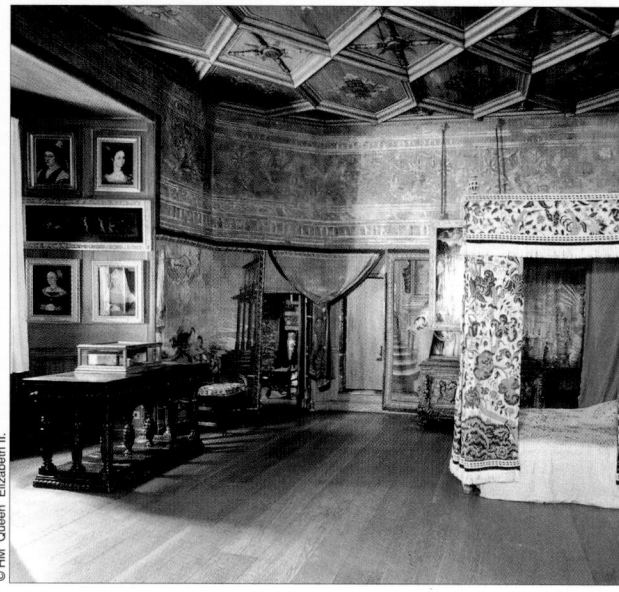

© HM Queen Elizabeth II.

EDINBURGH EH8 8DX

Owner: HM The Queen   *Contact:* The Superintendent

Tel: 0131 556 1096 **Fax:** 0131 557 5256

The Palace of Holyroodhouse, Buckingham Palace and Windsor Castle are the Official residences of the Sovereign and are used by The Queen as both a home and office. The Queen's personal standard flies when Her Majesty is in residence. Furnished with works of art from the Royal Collection, these buildings are used extensively by The Queen for State ceremonies and Official entertaining. They are opened to the public as much as the commitments allow. At the end of the Royal Mile stands the Palace of Holyroodhouse. Set against the spectacular backdrop of Arthur's Seat, Holyroodhouse has evolved from a medieval fortress into a baroque residence. The Royal Apartments, an extensive suite of rooms, epitomise the elegance and grandeur of this ancient and noble house, and contrast with the

historic tower apartments of Mary, Queen of Scots', which are steeped in intrigue and sorrow. These intimate rooms where she lived on her return from France in 1561, witnessed the murder of David Rizzio, her favourite secretary, by her jealous husband, Lord Darnley and his accomplices.

Location: OS Ref. NT269 739. Central Edinburgh, E end of Royal Mile.

Opening Times: Apr - Oct: daily, 9.30am - 5.15pm. Nov - Mar: daily, 9.30am - 3.45pm. 25 - 26 Dec & 13 Apr and during Royal visits. Opening arrangements may change at short notice.

Admission: Adult £6.50, Child (up to 17yrs) £3.30, Over 60yrs £5, Family (2+2) £16.30.

🖼 ♿Suitable. 🅿 🍴 🐕Guide dogs only. ❄ Ⓦ

PARLIAMENT HOUSE

Tel: 0131 225 2595

Parliament Square, Royal Mile, Edinburgh   **Contact:** Reception Desk at Door 11

Supreme Court for Scotland, adjacent exhibition detailing the history of Parliament House and its important features.

Location: OS Ref. NT258 736. In the centre of Edinburgh's Royal Mile.

Opening Times: All year: Mon - Fri, 9am - 5pm.

Admission: Free.

PRESTON MILL

Tel: 01620 860426

East Linton, East Lothian EH40 3DS

Owner: The National Trust for Scotland   **Contact:** Property Manager

For centuries there has been a mill on this site and the present one operated commercially until 1957. While the interior of the mill is exciting, the exterior is extremely evocative and much favoured by artists who come from near and far to paint the attractive old buildings, with their red pantile roofs, fringed by the tranquillity of the mill pond with its ever present ducks.

Location: OS Ref. NT590 770. Off the A1, in East Linton, 23m E of Edinburgh.

Opening Times: 13 Apr - 30 Sept: Mon - Sat, 11am - 1pm and 2 - 5pm, Suns, 1.30 - 5pm. Weekends in Oct: 1.30 - 4pm (last admission 20mins before closing, morning and afternoon).

Admission: Adult £2.50, Conc. £1.70, Family £7. Group: Adult £2, Child/School £1. Group visits must book.

ℹ ♿Grounds suitable. WC. 🅿Limited. 🐕Guide dogs only. Ⓦ

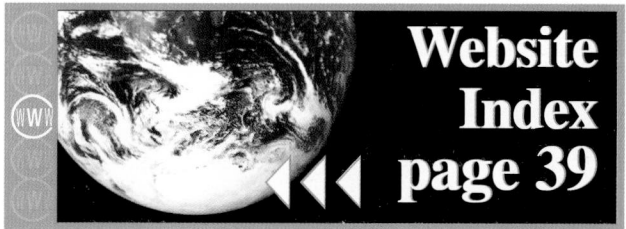

Website Index page 39

ROSSLYN CHAPEL

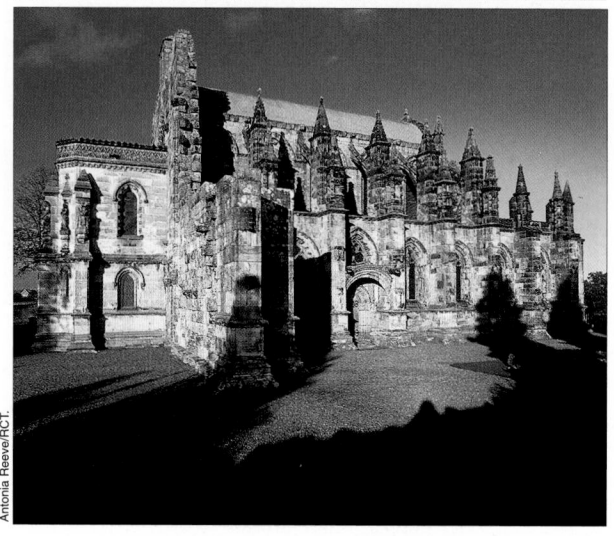

Antonia Reeve/RCT.

ROSLIN, MIDLOTHIAN EH25 9PU

Owner: The Earl of Rosslyn   *Contact:* Stuart Beattie

Tel: 0131 440 2159 **Fax:** 0131 440 1979 **e-mail:** rosslynch@aol.com

This most remarkable of churches was founded in 1446 by William St Clair, Prince of Orkney. Set in the woods of Roslin Glen and overlooking the River Esk, the Chapel is renowned for its richly carved interior and world famous apprentice pillar. Visitors to the chapel can enjoy a walk in some of Scotland's most romantic scenery. As Sir Walter Scott wrote,'*A morning of leisure can scarcely be anywhere more delightfully spent than in the woods of Rosslyn*'. The chapel is available for weddings throughout the year.

Location: OS Ref. NT275 630. 6m S of Edinburgh off A701. Follow B7006.

Opening Times: All year: Mon - Sat, 10am - 5pm, Suns, 12 noon - 4.45pm.

Admission: Adult £4, Child £1, Conc. £3.50. 10% discount for groups (20-40).

🖼 ♿Chapel. Grounds suitable. WC. 📷 🅿Limited for coaches. ❄ Ⓦ

ROYAL BOTANIC GARDEN EDINBURGH

Tel: 0131 552 7171
Fax: 0131 248 2901
Contact: Press Office

20A Inverleith Row, Edinburgh EH3 5LR
Scotland's premier garden. Discover the wonders of the plant kingdom in over 70 acres of beautifully landscaped grounds.
Location: OS Ref. NT249 751. Off A902, 1m N of city centre.
Opening Times: Daily (except 25 Dec & 1 Jan): open from 9.30am. Closing: Feb 5pm; Mar 6pm; Apr - Aug 7pm; Sept 6pm; Oct 5pm; Nov - Jan 4pm.
Admission: Free. Donations welcome.

ST GILES' CATHEDRAL

Tel: 0131 225 9442 **Fax:** 0131 220 4763

Royal Mile, Edinburgh EH1 1RE
Owner: St Giles' Cathedral
Contact: Jan-Andrew Henderson
St Giles' Cathedral dates from the 12th century and is central to Scotland's turbulent history. This beautiful building was the church of John Knox during the Reformation.
Location: OS Ref. NT258 736. In the centre of Edinburgh's Royal Mile.
Opening Times: Easter - Mid Sept: Mon - Fri, 9am -7pm, Sats, 9am - 5pm, Suns, 1 - 5pm. Mid Sept - Easter: Mon - Sat, 9am - 5pm, Suns, 1 - 5pm.
Admission: Admission free - donation of £1 per head suggested.

ST MARY'S CATHEDRAL

Tel: 0131 225 6293 **Fax:** 0131 225 3181
e-mail: office@cathedral.net
Contact: Cathedral Secretary

Palmerston Place, Edinburgh EH12 5AW
Neo-gothic grandeur in the classical new town.
Location: OS Ref. NT241 735. $^1/_2$ m W of west end of Princes Street.
Opening Times: 7.30am - 6pm. Sun services: 8am, 10.30am and 3.30pm. Weekday services: 7.30am, 1.05pm and 5.30pm. Sat service: 7.30am.
Admission: Free.

SCOTTISH NATIONAL PORTRAIT GALLERY

Tel: 0131 624 6200
Contact: Catriona Black

1 Queen Street, Edinburgh EH2 1JD
Unique visual history of Scotland.
Location: OS Ref. NT256 742. At E end of Queen Street, 300yds N of Princes Street.
Opening Times: All year: Mon - Fri, 10am - 5pm. Suns, 12 noon - 5pm. Closed 25 & 26 Dec.
Admission: Free

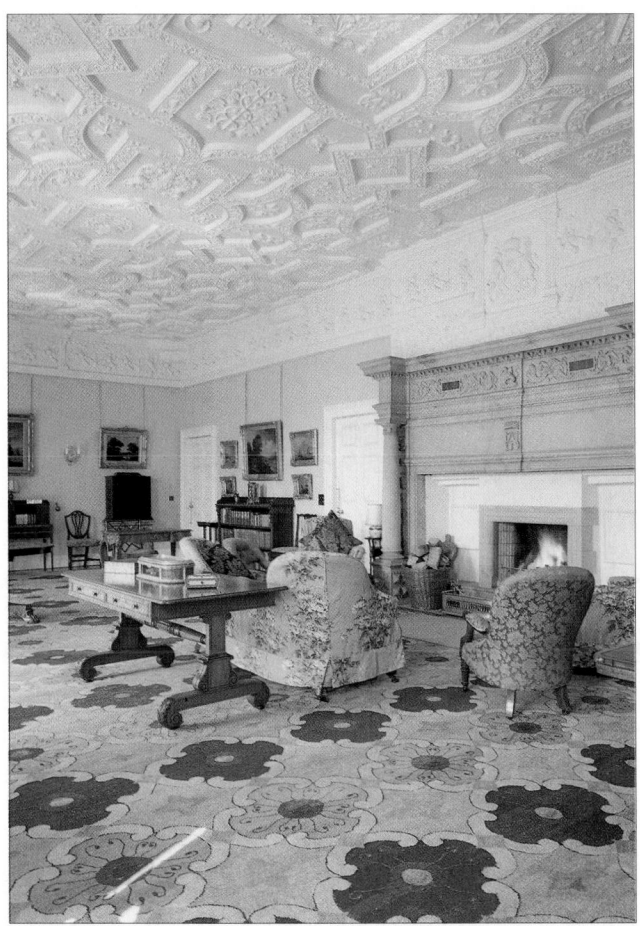

Winton House, Edinburgh.

TANTALLON CASTLE

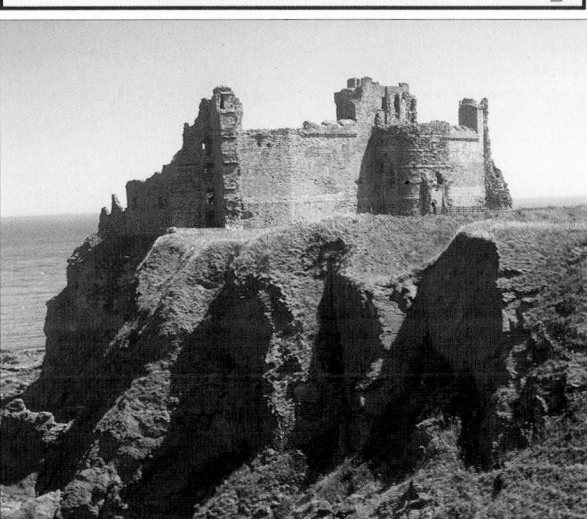

Crown Copyright.

BY NORTH BERWICK, EAST LOTHIAN EH39 5PN
Owner: *In the care of Historic Scotland*   **Contact:** *The Steward*

Tel: 01620 892727
Set on the edge of the cliffs, looking out to the Bass Rock, this formidable castle was a stronghold of the powerful Douglas family. The castle has earthwork defences and a massive 80-foot high 14th century curtain wall. Interpretive displays include a replica gun.
Location: OS67 Ref. NT595 850. 3m E of North Berwick off the A198.
Opening Times: Apr - Sept: daily, 9.30am - 6.30pm. Oct - Mar: Mon - Sat, 9.30am - 6.30pm (but closed Thur pm & all day Fri), Suns, 2 - 4.30pm.
Admission: Adult £2.80, Child £1, Conc. £2. 10% discount for groups (10+).

ℹ️ Picnic area. 📷 ♿ Partially suitable. 🅿️ 🚌 Booked school visits free. 🐕 In grounds, on leads. ❄️

WINTON HOUSE

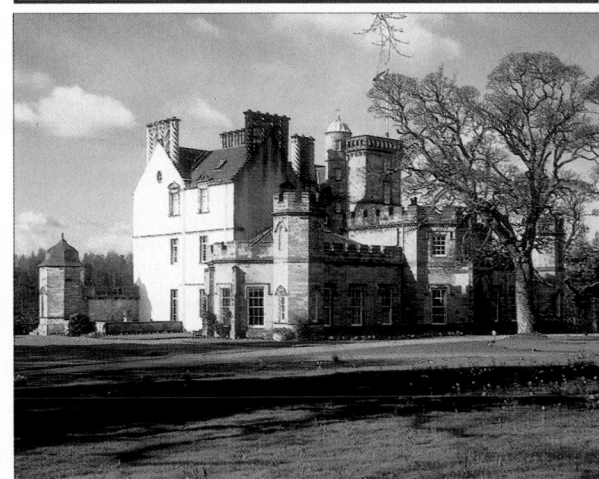

PENCAITLAND, TRANENT, EAST LOTHIAN EH34 5AT
Owner: *The Winton Trust*   **Contact:** *Barbara Smith*

Tel: 01620 824986 **Fax:** 01620 823961 **e-mail:** enquiries@wintonhouse.co.uk
A masterpiece of the Scottish Renaissance with famous stone twisted chimneys and magnificent plaster ceilings. A family home, still after 500 years with many treasures inside, including paintings by some of Scotland's most notable artists, and fine furniture. New Loch. Specimen trees and terraced gardens.
Location: OS Ref. NT439 695. 14m SE of Edinburgh off the A1 at Tranent. Lodge gates S of New Winton (B6355) and in Pencaitland (A6093).
Opening Times: 2/3 Jun; 7/8 Jul; 4/5 Aug: 12.30 - 4.30pm. Other times by prior arrangement.
Admission: Adult £4.50, Child £2, Conc. £3.80, Family £11.50 Groups should pre-book (10+).

ℹ️ Filming, product launches. Pottery. 🍽️ ♿ Suitable. WCs. 📷 🎧 Obligatory. 🅿️ 🐕 In grounds, on leads. 🛏️ ❄️ 📷 Tel. for details. 🅲

BOTANIC GARDENS
Tel: 0141 334 2422　**Fax:** 0141 339 6964

730 Great Western Road, Glasgow G12 0UE
Owner: Glasgow City Council　　**Contact:** The General Manager
Location: OS Ref. NS568 674.
Opening Times: All year: 7am - dusk. Glasshouse: Daily, 10am - 4.15pm (Winter), 10am - 4.45pm (Summer).
Admission: Free.

BOTHWELL CASTLE
Tel: 01698 816894

Uddingston, Strathclyde
Owner: In the care of Historic Scotland　　**Contact:** The Steward
The largest and finest 13th century stone castle in Scotland, much fought over during the Wars of Independence. Part of the original circular keep survives, but most of the castle dates from the 14th and 15th centuries. In a beautiful setting overlooking the Clyde.
Location: OS Ref. NS688 593. 1m NW of Bothwell. At Uddingston off the B7071.
Opening Times: 1 Apr - 30 Sept: daily, 9.30am - 6.30pm, last ticket 6pm. 1 Oct - 31 Mar: Mon - Sat, 9.30am - 4.30pm, Suns, 2 - 4.30pm, last ticket 4pm. Closed Thur pm & Fri & Sun mornings in winter.
Admission: Adult £2, Child 75p, Conc £1.50.

BURRELL COLLECTION
Tel: 0141 287 2550

Pollok Country Park, 2060 Pollokshaws Road, Glasgow G2 3EH
Owner: Glasgow Museums　　**Contact:** Mr Mark McTee
An internationally renowned, outstanding collection of art.
Location: OS Ref. NS560 615.
Opening Times: All year: Mon - Thur & Sats, 10am - 5pm. Fri & Sun, 11am - 5pm. Closed Christmas Day, Boxing Day & 1 & 2 Jan.
Admission: Free.

CHATELHERAULT HUNTING LODGE　**Tel:** 01698 426213　**Fax:** 01698 421532

Ferniegair, Hamilton ML3 7UE
Owner: South Lanarkshire Council　　**Contact:** Alison Reid
Built for James, 5th Duke of Hamilton, designed by William Adam, completed around 1744. Set in 500 acre country park.
Location: OS Ref. NS737 540. W side of A72, 1½ m SE of Hamilton.
Opening Times: Mon - Sat, 10am - 5pm. Suns, 12 noon - 5pm (Easter Sun - end Sept, 5pm). Closed Christmas and New Year.
Admission: Free.

COLZIUM HOUSE & WALLED GARDEN
Tel/Fax: 01236 828156

Colzium-Lennox Estate, off Stirling Road, Kilsyth G65 0RZ
Owner: North Lanarkshire Council　　**Contact:** Charlie Whyte
A walled garden with an extensive collection of conifers, rare shrubs and trees. Kilsyth Heritage Museum, curling pond, picnic tables, woodland walks.
Location: OS Ref. NS762 786. Off A803 Banknock to Kirkintilloch Road. ½ m E of Kilsyth.
Opening Times: House: All year, daily, 9am - 4pm (closed 25 Dec & 1 Jan). Walled garden: Apr - Sept: daily, 12 noon - 7pm; Oct - Mar: Sats & Suns, 12 noon - 4pm.
Admission: Free.

COREHOUSE
Tel: 01555 663126 or 0131 667 1514

Lanark ML11 9TQ
Owner: The Trustees of the late Lt Col A J E Cranstoun MC　　**Contact:** Estate Office
Designed by Sir Edward Blore and built in the 1820s, Corehouse is a pioneering example of the Tudor Architectural Revival in Scotland.
Location: OS Ref. NS882 416. On S bank of the Clyde above the village of Kirkfieldbank.
Opening Times: 1 Aug - 2 Sept: Wed - Sun; Guided tours. Weekdays: 1 & 2pm, Weekends: 12 noon & 4pm. Closed Mons & Tues.
Admission: Adult £4, Child (under 14yrs) £2, OAP £2.

CRAIGNETHAN CASTLE
Tel: 01555 860364

Lanark, Strathclyde
Owner: Historic Scotland　　**Contact:** The Steward
In a picturesque setting overlooking the River Nethan and defended by a wide and deep ditch with an unusual caponier, a stone vaulted artillery chamber, unique in Britain.
Location: OS Ref. NS815 463. 5½ m WNW of Lanark off the A72. ½ m footpath to W.
Opening Times: 1 Apr - 30 Nov: daily, 9.30am - 6.30pm.
Admission: Adult £2, Child 75p, Conc. £1.50.

GLASGOW CATHEDRAL
Tel: 0141 552 6891

Glasgow
Owner: Historic Scotland　　**Contact:** The Steward
The only Scottish mainland medieval cathedral to have survived the Reformation complete. Built over the tomb of St Kentigern. Notable features in this splendid building are the elaborately vaulted crypt, the stone screen of the early 15th century and the unfinished Blackadder Aisle.
Location: OS Ref. NS603 656. E end of city centre. In central Glasgow.
Admission: Free.

GREENBANK GARDEN
Tel: 0141 639 3281

Clarkston, Glasgow G76 8RB
Owner: The National Trust for Scotland　　**Contact:** Mr Jim May
Be allured by the beautiful bronze water nymph 'Foam' whose exquisite form complements the circular pool and surrounding greenery. There are several small gardens including a parterre layout illustrating different aspects of gardening. The larger borders contain a wide range of shrub roses and perennial and annual flowers.
Location: OS Ref. NS563 566. Flenders Road, off Mearns Road, Clarkston. Off M77 and A726, 6m S of Glasgow city centre.
Opening Times: Garden & Grounds: All year: daily, 9.30am - sunset. Shop & tearoom: 1 Apr - 31 Oct: daily, 11am - 5pm. 1 Nov - 31 Mar: Sats & Suns, 2 - 4pm. House: 1 Apr - 31 Oct: Suns only & during special events (subject to functions in progress).
Admission: Adult £3.50, Conc. £2.50, Family £9.50. Groups: Adult £3.

Grounds suitable. WC.　In grounds, on leads. No dogs in garden.

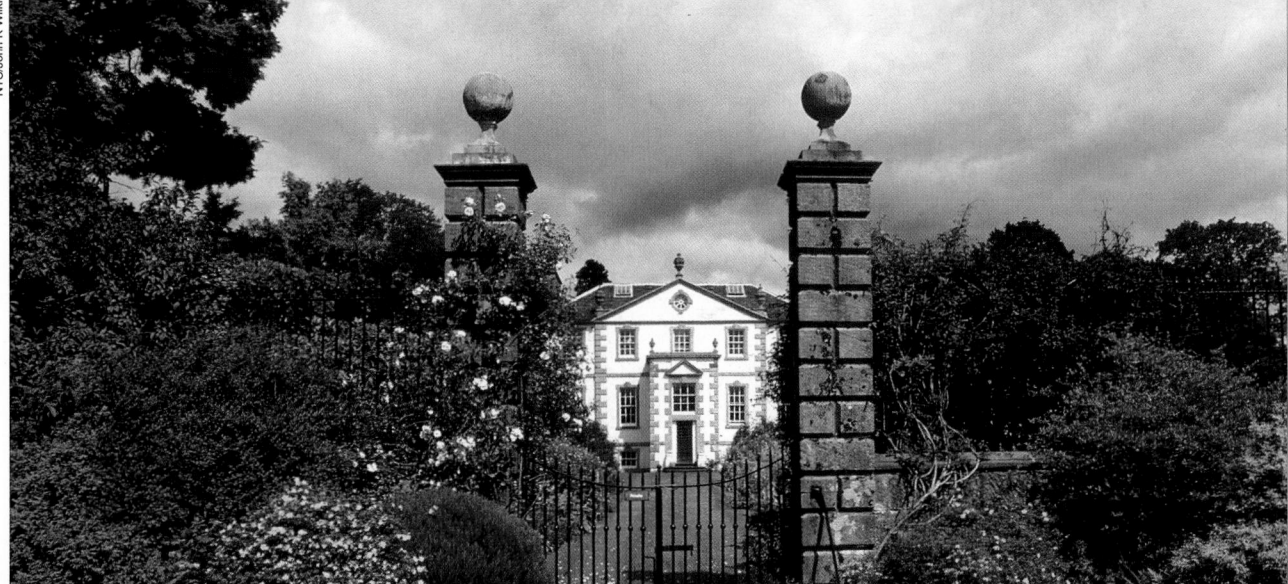

Greenbank Garden, Glasgow.

HOLMWOOD HOUSE ♛

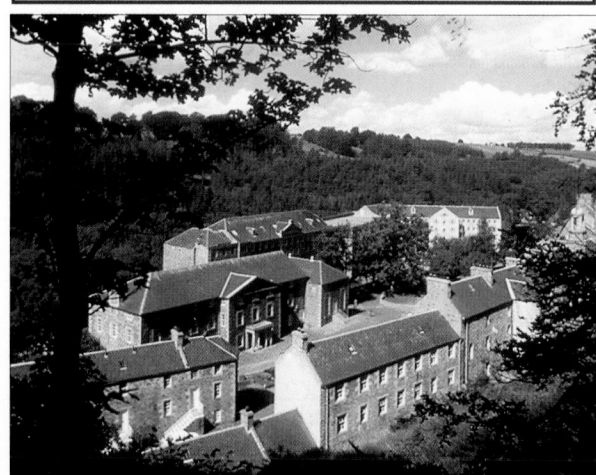

The National Trust for Scotland.

61 NETHERLEE ROAD, CATHCART, GLASGOW G44 3YG

Owner: The National Trust for Scotland   *Contact:* The Property Manager

Tel: 0141 637 2129

This unique villa has been described as Alexander 'Greek' Thomson's finest domestic design. It was built in 1857-8 for James Couper who owned Millholm Paper Mills. The architectural style of the house is classical Greek and many rooms are richly ornamented in wood, plaster and marble. Conservation work continuing to reveal this decoration.

Location: OS Ref. NS580 593. Netherlee Road, off Clarkston road (off A77 and B767).

Opening Times: 1 Apr - 31 Oct: daily, 1.30 - 5.30pm. Access may be restricted at peak times and at the discretion of the property. Groups must book.

Admission: Adult £3.50, Conc. £2.50, Family £9.50. Groups: Adult £3, Child/School £1.

ℹ️ No photography in house.   🅿️ Limited for coaches.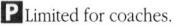

HUTCHESONS' HALL ♛   **Tel:** 0141 552 8391   **Fax:** 0141 552 7031

158 Ingram Street, Glasgow G1 1EJ

Owner: The National Trust for Scotland   **Contact:** Carla Sparrow

Described as one of Glasgow city centre's most elegant buildings, the Hall by David Hamilton, replaced the earlier 1641 hospice founded by George and Thomas Hutcheson. Reconstructed in 1876, the building is now 'A-Listed' as being of national importance. New 'Glasgow Style' exhibition & shop now open.

Location: OS Ref NS594 652. Glasgow city centre, near SE corner of George Square.

Opening Times: Gallery, Shop & Hall: All year, Mon - Sat (except Public Holidays & 24 Dec - 8 Jan): 10am - 5pm. (Hall on view subject to functions in progress).

Admission: Free.

ℹ️ Conferences.   📷   🍴 Up to 120.   ♿ Stairlift. WC.   🏃 By arrangement.   ❄️

KELBURN 🏛   **Tel:** 01475 568685/568204

Fairlie, Nr Largs, Ayrshire KA29 0BE

Owner/Contact: The Earl of Glasgow

The home of the Boyle family, later the Earls of Glasgow since the 13th century.

Location: OS Ref NS210 580. A78 to Largs, 2m S of Largs.

Opening Times: Castle: Jul & Aug and first week in Sept.

Admission: Castle: Adult: £1.50, Student £1.20. Country Centre: Adult £ 4.50, Child £3, Groups (12+): Adult: £3, Child/OAPs £2, Family (2+3) £13.00.

Open All Year
Index
◀◀◀ **page 49**

DAVID LIVINGSTONE CENTRE ♛   **Tel:** 01698 823140

165 Station Road, Blantyre, Glasgow G72 9BT

Owner: The National Trust for Scotland   **Contact:** Karen Carruthers

Scotland's most famous explorer and missionary was born here in 1813 and today the Centre commemorates his life and work. Livingstone's childhood home - consisting of just one room - remains much as it would have done in his day and gives a fascinating insight into the living conditions endured by industrial workers in the 19th century. The museum contains a wide range of his personal belongings and travel aids.

Location: OS Ref NS690 575. In Blantyre town centre.

Opening Times: Museum & Shop: 8 Jan - 31 Mar & 1 Nov - 23 Dec: Mon - Sat, 10.30am - 4.30pm, Suns, 12.30 - 4.30pm. 1 Apr - 31 Oct: Mon - Sat, 10am - 5.30pm, Suns, 12.30 - 5.30pm.

Admission: Adult £3, Conc. £2, Family £8. Group: Adult £2.50.

📷 ♿ 🅿️ ⓦ

MOTHERWELL HERITAGE CENTRE   **Tel:** 01698 251000

High Road, Motherwell ML1 3HU

Owner: North Lanarkshire Council   **Contact:** The Manager

Multimedia exhibition and other displays of local history. STB Commended attraction.

Location: OS Ref. NS750 570.

Opening Times: All year: Wed - Sat, 10am - 5pm. Suns, 12 noon - 5pm. (closed 25/26 Dec & 1 Jan).

Admission: Free.

NEW LANARK

NEW LANARK MILLS, LANARK, S. LANARKSHIRE ML11 9DB

Owner: New Lanark Conservation Trust   *Contact: Richard Evans*

Tel: 01555 661345   **Fax:** 01555 665738   **e-mail:** visit@newlanark.org

Surrounded by native woodlands and close to the famous Falls of Clyde, this cotton mill village was founded in 1785 and became famous as the site of Robert Owen's radical reforms. Now beautifully restored as both a living community and attraction, the fascinating history of the village is interpreted in an award-winning Visitor Centre. Accommodation is available in the New Lanark Mill Hotel and Waterhouses, a stunning conversion from an original 18th century mill. New Lanark is now a nominated World Heritage Site.

Location: OS Ref. NS880 426. 1m S of Lanark.

Opening Times: All year: daily, 11am - 5pm (closed 25 Dec & 1/2 Jan).

Admission: Visitor Centre: Adult £3.95, Child/OAP £2.95. Groups: 1 free/10 booked.

ℹ️ Conference facilities.   📷   🍴
♿ Partially suitable. WC. Visitor Centre is wheelchair friendly.   🍴
🏃 By arrangement.   🅿️ 5 min walk.   🐕 In grounds, on leads.   📷 ❄️ ⓦ

NEWARK CASTLE 🏰   **Tel:** 01475 741858

Port Glasgow, Strathclyde

Owner: In the care of Historic Scotland   **Contact:** The Steward

The oldest part of the castle is a tower built soon after 1478 with a detached gatehouse, by George Maxwell. The main part was added in 1597 - 99 in a most elegant style. Enlarged in the 16th century by his descendent, the wicked Patrick Maxwell who murdered two of his neighbours.

Location: OS Ref. NS329 744. In Port Glasgow on the A8.

Opening Times: 1 Apr - 30 Sept: daily, 9.30am - 6.30pm. Last ticket 6pm.

Admission: Adult £2, Child 75p, Conc. £1.50.

POLLOK HOUSE

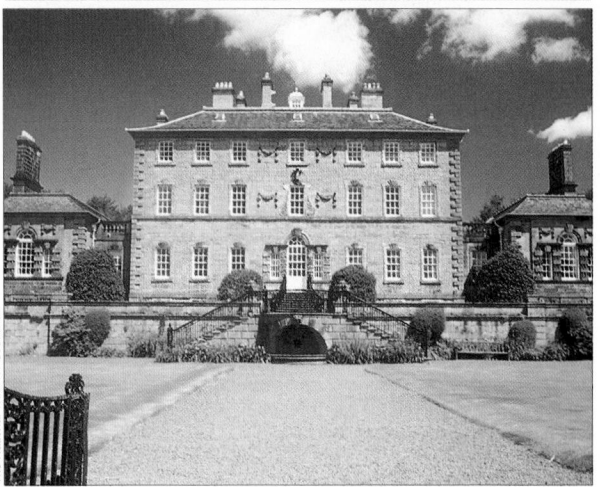

POLLOK COUNTRY PARK, POLLOKSHAWS ROAD, GLASGOW G43 1AT

Owner: Glasgow City Council (Managed by The National Trust for Scotland)
Contact: The Property Manager

Tel: 0141 616 6410

The Maxwell family have lived at Pollok since the 13th century. Three earlier castles here were replaced by the present house (c1740) after consultation with William Adam. The house now contains an internationally famed collection of paintings as well as porcelain and furnishings appropriate to an Edwardian house.

Location: OS Ref. NS550 616. In Pollok Country Park, off M77/J1, follow signs for Burrell Collection.

Opening Times: House, Shop & Restaurant: 1 Apr - 31 Oct: daily, 10am - 5pm. 1 Nov - 31 Mar: daily, 11am - 4pm. Closed 25, 26 Dec & 1, 2 Jan.

Admission: Adult £4, Conc. £3, Family £11. Groups: Adult £3.20, Child/School £1. 1 Nov - 31 Mar: Free.

ℹ️ No photography in house. 📷 🍸 ♿ Partially suitable. 🍽️ 🅿️ 🏛️ ❄️ 🕸️

THE TENEMENT HOUSE

Tel: 0141 333 0183

145 Buccleuch Street, Glasgow G3 6QN
Owner: The National Trust for Scotland   **Contact:** Miss Lorna Hepburn

A typical Victorian tenement flat of 1892, and fascinating time capsule of the first half of the 20th century. It was the home of an ordinary Glasgow shorthand typist, who lived up this 'wally close' for more than 50 years. It is exceptional as the gaslit flat retains many of its original fittings and items such as her mother's sewing machine.

Location: OS Ref. NS583 662. Garnethill (three streets N of Sauchiehall Street, near Charing Cross), Glasgow.

Opening Times: 1 Mar - 31 Oct; daily, 2 - 5pm, last admission 4.30pm. Weekday morning visits by educational and other groups (max 15) by advance booking only.

Admission: Adult £3.50, Conc. £2.50, Family £9.50. Groups: Adult £3, Child/School £1.

♿ Not suitable. 🅿️ Very restricted. 🕸️

THE TOWER OF HALLBAR

Tel: 020 7930 8030 **Fax:** 020 7930 2295

Braidwood Road, Braidwood, Lanarkshire   **e-mail:** aniela@vivat.demon.co.uk
Owner: The Vivat Trust   **Contact:** Miss Aniela Waitt

A 16th century defensive tower and Bothy set in ancient orchards and meadowland. Converted into self-catering holiday accommodation and furnished and decorated in keeping with its history, by The Vivat Trust. Hallbar sleeps up to seven people, including facilities for a disabled person and their carer.

Location: OS Ref. NS834 471. 45mins outsite Glasgow, on B7056 in Braidwood.

Opening Times: All year: Sats afternoon only, 2 - 3pm, by appointment. Also four open days a year.

Admission: Free.

♿ Partially suitable. 🎨 By arrangement. 🅿️ Limited. 🐕 In grounds, on leads. 🛏️ 3 single, 1 twin & 1 double. ❄️ 🕸️

WEAVER'S COTTAGE

Tel: 01505 705588

Shuttle Street, Kilbarchan, Renfrew PA10 2JG
Owner: The National Trust for Scotland   **Contact:** Grace Murray

Typical cottage of an 18th century handloom weaver contains looms, weaving equipment and domestic utensils. Attractive cottage garden. Regular weaving demonstrations.

Location: OS Ref. NS402 633. Off A740 (off M8) and A737, at The Cross, Kilbarchan, (nr Johnstone, Paisley) 12m SW of Glasgow.

Opening Times: 1 Apr - 30 Sept: daily, 1.30 - 5.30pm. Weekends in Oct: 1.30 - 5.30pm. (last admission 5pm).

Admission: Adult £2.50, Conc. £1.70, Family £7. Groups: Adult £2, Child/School £1.

🕸️

ST MARY'S EPISCOPAL CATHEDRAL **Tel:** 0141 339 6691 **Fax:** 0141 334 5669

e-mail: cathedral@glasgow.anglican.org
300 Great Western Road, Glasgow G4 9JB   **Contact:** Rev Griff Dines

Fine Gothic Revival church by Sir George Gilbert Scott, with outstanding contemporary murals by Gwyneth Leech. Regular concerts and exhibitions.

Location: OS Ref. NS578 669. ¹/₄ m after the Dumbarton A82 exit from M8 motorway.

Opening Times: Mon - Fri, 9.30am - 5pm, Sat, 9.30am - 12 noon. Sun services: 8.30am, 10am, 12 noon & 6.30pm. Weekday services: please telephone. The Cathedral will be closed for restoration from Nov 2000 - Nov 2001. Please call for details of services.

SUMMERLEE HERITAGE PARK

Tel: 01236 431261

Heritage Way, Coatbridge, North Lanarkshire ML5 1QD
Owner: North Lanarkshire Council   **Contact:** The Manager

STB 'Commended' attraction. 22 acres of industrial heritage including Scotland's only remaining electric tramway; a re-created addit mine and mine workers' cottages.

Location: OS Ref. NS730 650.

Opening Times: All year. Summer, 10am - 5pm. Winter: 10am - 4pm (closed 25/26 Dec & 1/2 Jan).

Admission: Free. Tram ride: Adult 70p, Child 35p.

Website Index ◀◀ page 39

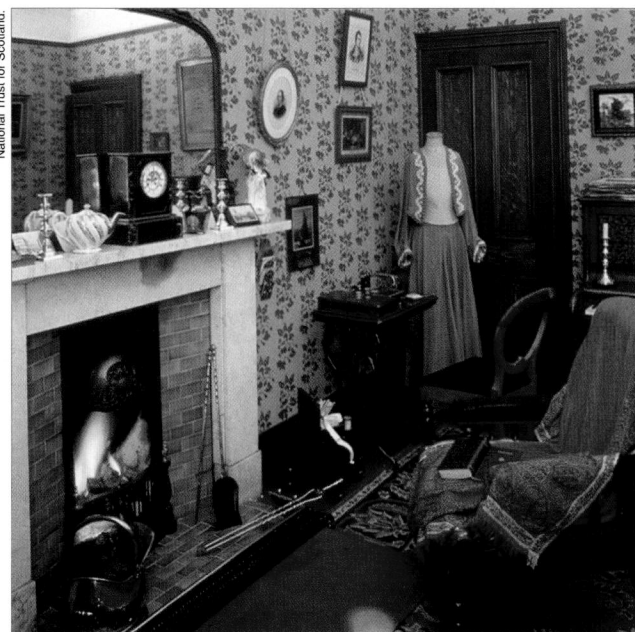

The Tenement House, Glasgow.

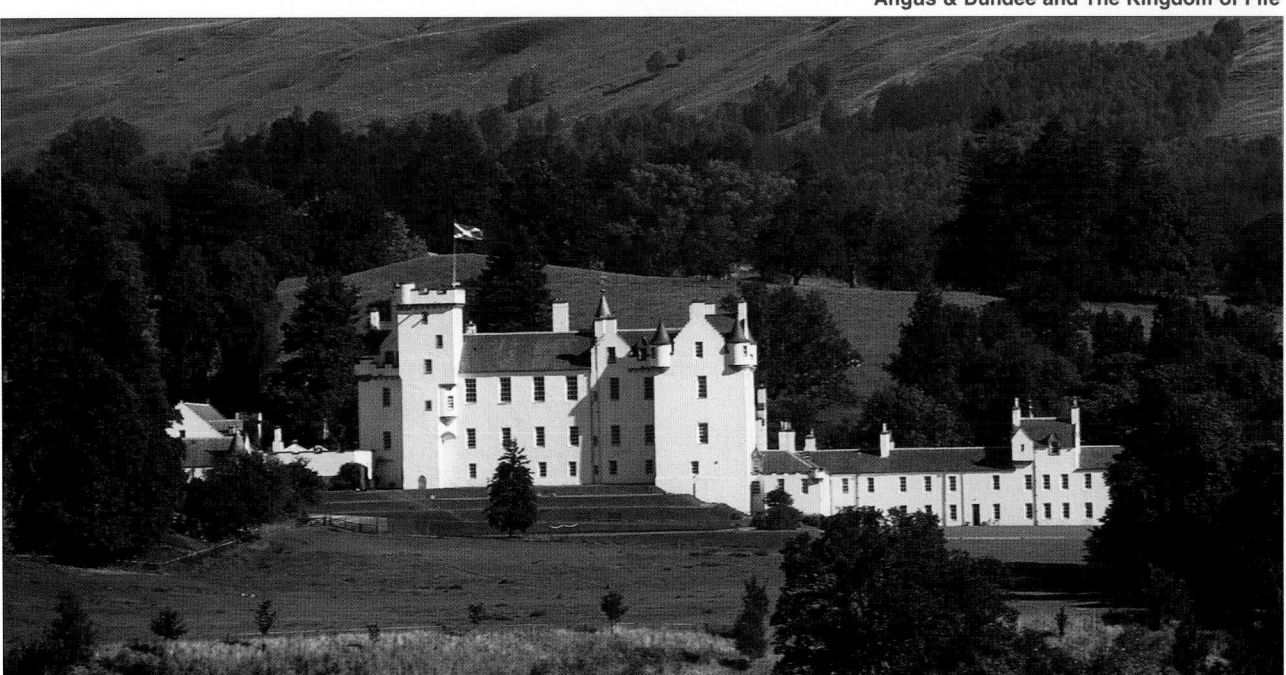

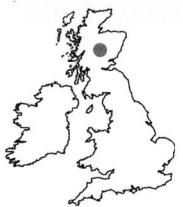

BLAIR CASTLE
Pitlochry

BLAIR CASTLE has been the ancient home and fortress of the Earls and Dukes of Atholl for over 725 years. Its central location makes it easily accessible from all major Scottish centres in less than two hours.

The castle has known the splendour of Royal visitations, submitted to occupation by opposing forces on no less than four occasions, suffered siege and changed its architectural appearance to suit the taste of successive generations.

Today 32 rooms of infinite variety display beautiful furniture, fine collections of paintings, arms, armour, china, costumes, lace and embroidery, Jacobite relics and other unique treasures giving a stirring picture of Scottish life

from the 16th to 20th centuries.

The Duke of Atholl has the unique distinction of having the only remaining private army in Europe - The Atholl Highlanders.

GARDENS

Blair Castle is set in extensive parklands. Near the car and coach parks, there is a picnic area, a deer park and a unique two acre plantation of large trees known as 'Diana's Grove.' It has been said that "it is unlikely that any other two acres in the world contain such a number of different conifers of such heights and of such small age." A restored 18th century garden re-opened to visitors in 1996.

Owner: Blair Castle Charitable Trust

CONTACT

Geoff G Crerar
Tourism Administrator
Blair Castle
Blair Atholl
Pitlochry
Perthshire
PH18 5TL

Tel: 01796 481207

Fax: 01796 481487

e-mail: office@ blair-castle.co.uk

LOCATION

OS Ref. NN880 660

From Edinburgh 80m, M90 to Perth, A9, follow signs for Blair Castle, 1½ hrs. Trunk Road A9 2m.

Bus: Bus stop 1m in Blair Atholl.

Train: 1m, Blair Atholl Euston-Inverness line.

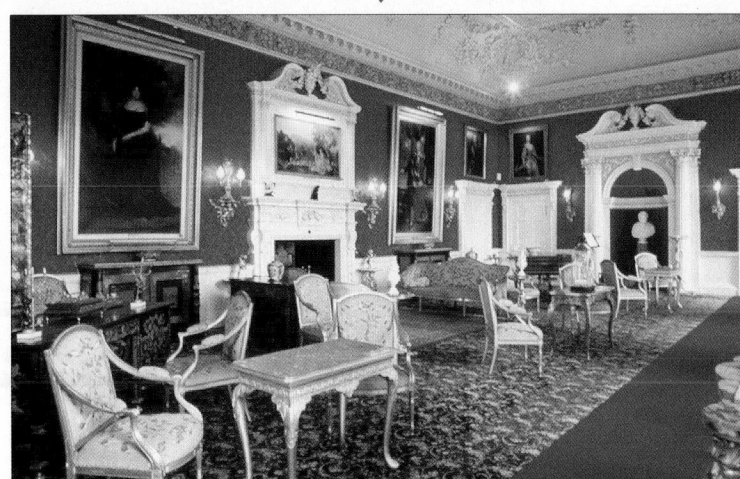

OPENING TIMES

SUMMER
1 April - 26 October
Daily, 10am - 6pm
Last admission 5pm.
(Jul & Aug: opens 9.30am).
At other times by special arrangement.

WINTER
Access by arrangement.

ADMISSION

House & Grounds

Adult	£6.25
Child (5-16yrs)	£4.00
OAP/Student	£5.25
Family	£18.00
Disabled	£2.00

Groups (12-40) (Please book)

Adult	£5.00
Child (5-16yrs)	£4.00
Primary School	£3.00
OAP	£4.50
Student	£4.00
Disabled	£2.00

Grounds only

Adult	£2.00
Child	£1.00
OAP/Student	£2.00
Family	£5.00
Disabled	Free

SPECIAL EVENTS

- **APR 20 - 22:**
Needlework & Lace Exhibition.

- **MAY 26:**
Atholl Highlanders' Parade.

- **MAY 27:**
Atholl Gathering & Highland Games.

- **JUL 5:**
Charity Day in Aid of McMillan Cancer Research.

- **JUL 16 - 22:**
Contemporary Textile Art Exhibition by Northern Fringes.

- **AUG 23 - 26:**
Bowmore Blair Castle Int'l Horse Trials & Country Fair.

- **OCT 27:**
Glenfiddich Piping Championships.

FUNCTION		
ROOM	SIZE	MAX CAPACITY
Ballroom	89' x 35'	400
State Dining Rm	36' x 25'	200
Exhibition Hall	55' x 27'	90

ℹ️ Fashion shows, garden parties, equestrian events, shows, rallies, filming, highland and charity balls, piping championships, grand piano, helicopter pad, cannon firing by Atholl Highlanders, resident piper, needlework displays. No smoking.

🍽️ Buffets, dinners, wedding receptions and banquets.

♿ Visitors may alight at the entrance. WC & wheelchair.

🍴 Non-smoking. Seats up to 125.

🚻 In English, German and French at no extra cost. Max group size 25, tour time 1½ hrs (max).

🅿️ 200 cars, 20 coaches. Coach drivers/couriers free, plus free meal and shop voucher, information pack.

🚶 Nature walks, deer park, children's games & pony trekking.

🐕 Grounds only.

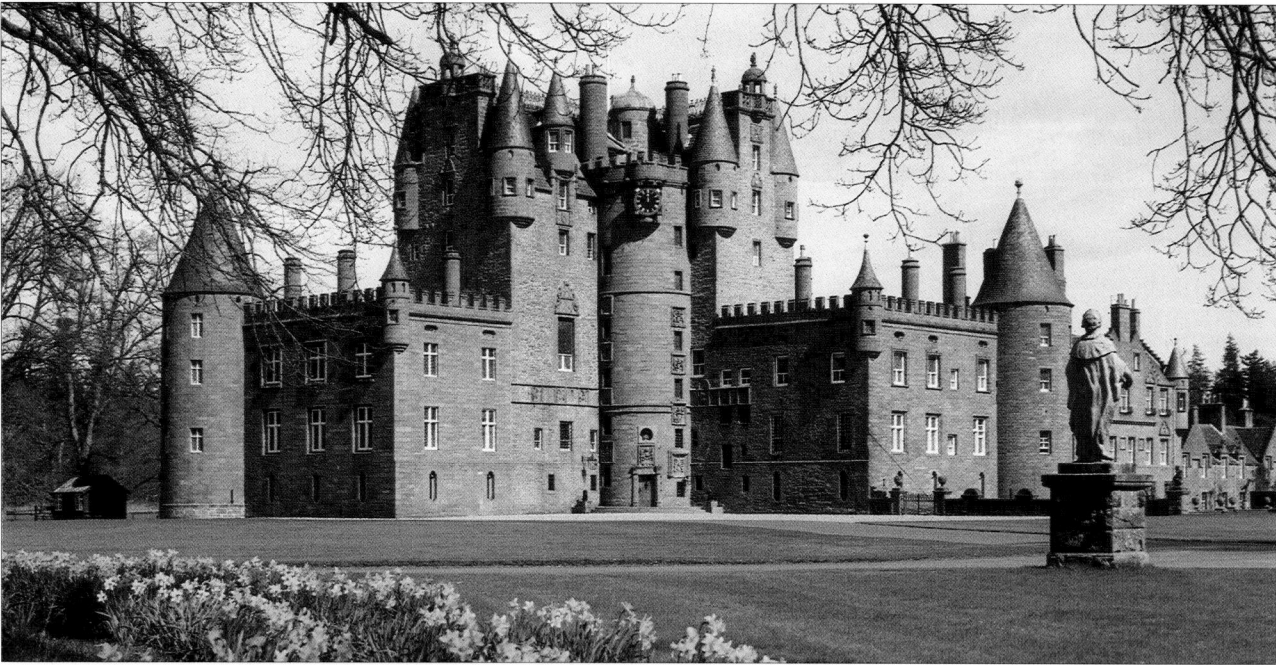

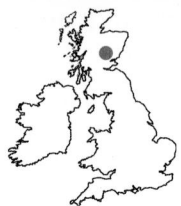

GLAMIS CASTLE
by Forfar

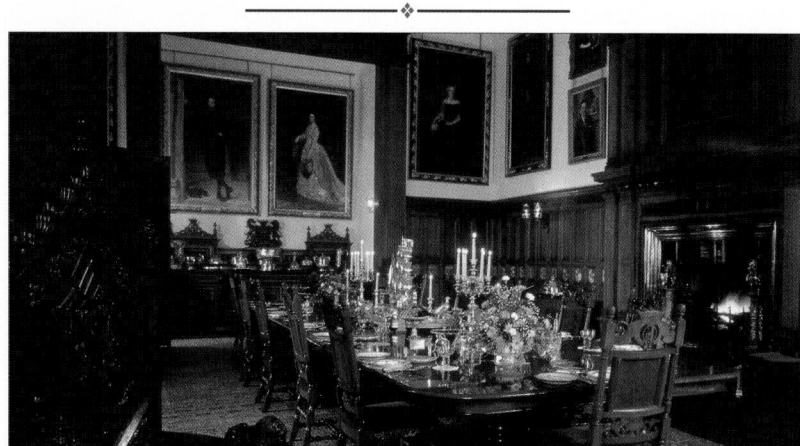

GLAMIS CASTLE is the family home of the Earls of Strathmore and Kinghorne and has been a royal residence since 1372. It is the childhood home of Her Majesty Queen Elizabeth The Queen Mother, the birthplace of Her Royal Highness The Princess Margaret and the legendary setting of Shakespeare's play *Macbeth*. Although the castle is open to visitors it remains a family home lived in and loved by the Strathmore family.

The castle, a five-storey 'L' shaped tower block, was originally a royal hunting lodge. It was remodelled in the 17th century and is built of pink sandstone. It contains the Great Hall, with its magnificent plasterwork ceiling dated 1621, a beautiful family Chapel constructed inside the Castle in 1688, an 18th century billiard room housing what is left of the extensive library once at Glamis, a 19th century dining room containing family portraits and the Royal Apartments which have been used by Her Majesty Queen Elizabeth The Queen Mother.

The castle stands in an extensive park, landscaped towards the end of the 18th century, and contains the beautiful Italian Garden and the Pinetum which reflect the peace and serenity of the castle and grounds.

Owner: The Earl of Strathmore & Kinghorne

CONTACT

Lt Col P J Cardwell Moore
(The Administrator)
Estates Office
Glamis Castle
Glamis
by Forfar
Angus
DD8 1RJ

Tel: 01307 840393

Fax: 01307 840733

e-mail: glamis@great-houses-scotland.co.uk

LOCATION

OS Ref. NO386 480

From Edinburgh M90, A94, 81m.
From Forfar A94, 6m.
From Glasgow 93m.

Motorway: M90.

Rail: Dundee Station 12m.

Air: Dundee Airport 12m.

Taxi: K Cabs 01575 573744.

CONFERENCE/FUNCTION		
ROOM	SIZE	MAX CAPACITY
Dining Rm	84 sq.m.	120
Restaurant	140 sq.m.	100
16th century Kitchens		50

ℹ️ Fashion shoots, archery, clay pigeon shooting, equestrian events, shows, rallies, filming, product launches, highland games, new cricket pavilion, grand piano. No photography in the castle.

📷 Shopping complex. ❀

🍽 The State Rooms are available for grand dinners, lunches and wedding receptions.

♿ Disabled visitors may alight at entrance. Those in wheelchairs will be unable to tour the castle but may visit the two exhibitions. WC.

🍴 Morning coffees, light lunches, afternoon teas. Self-service, licensed restaurant.

All visits are guided, tour time 50 - 60 mins. Tours leave every 10 - 15 mins. Tours in French, German, Italian and Spanish by appointment at no additional cost. Three exhibitions.

🅿 500 cars and 20 coaches 200 yds from castle. Coach drivers and couriers admitted free. Beware narrow gates; they are wide enough to take buses (10ft wide).

One teacher free for every 10 children. Nature trail, family exhibition rooms, dolls' house, play park. Glamis Heritage Education Centre in Glamis village. Education pack. Winner of Sandford Award in 1997.

🐕 In grounds, on leads. ❄️

OPENING TIMES

31 March - 28 October
Daily, 10.30am - 5.30pm.

(July - August opens 10am).

Last admission 4.45pm.

Groups welcome by appointment at other times.

WINTER

By arrangement.

ADMISSION

SUMMER
House & Grounds

Adult £6.20
Child (5-16yrs)* £3.10
OAP/Student...........£4.70
Family £16.50

Groups (20+)
Adult £5.20
Child (5-16yrs)* £2.60
OAP/Student...........£4.20

Grounds only
Adult £3.10
Child (5 - 16yrs)*......£1.60
OAP/Student...........£1.60
Disabled ....Free

*Under 5yrs Free.

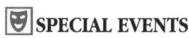 **SPECIAL EVENTS**

Please telephone for details.

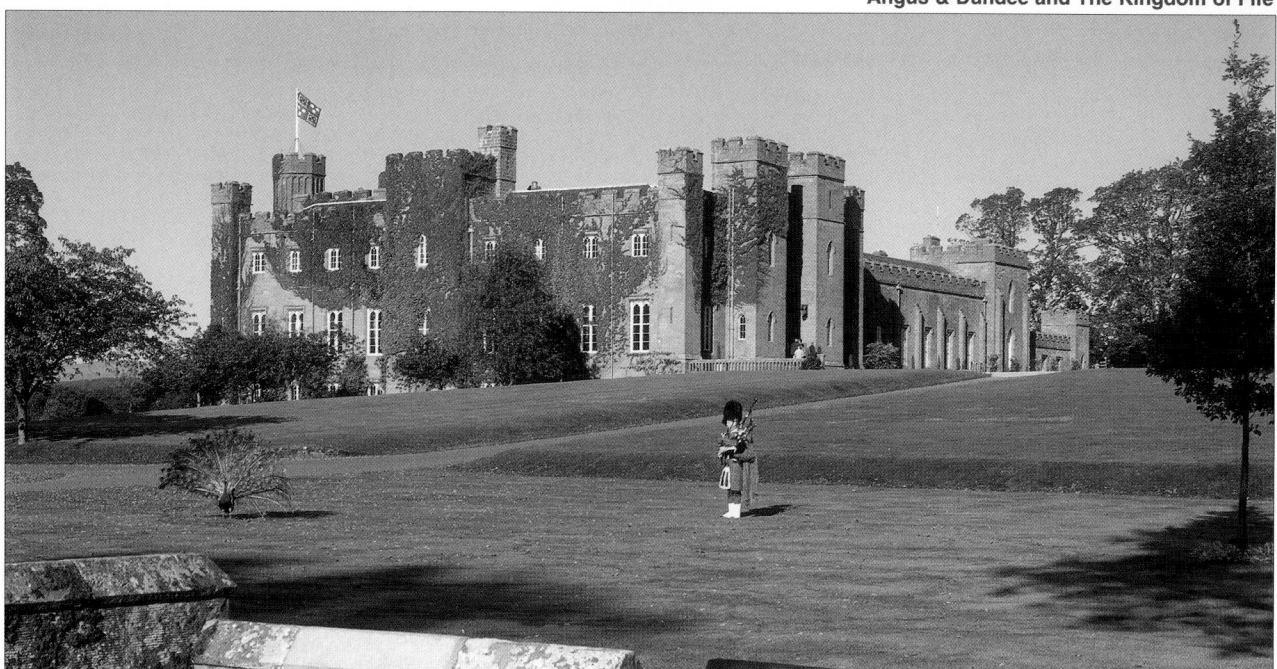

SCONE PALACE & GROUNDS
Perth

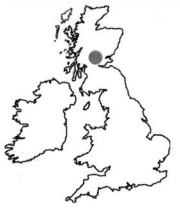

Owner: The Earl of Mansfield

CONTACT

The Administrator
Scone Palace
Perth
PH2 6BD

Tel: 01738 552300

Fax: 01738 552588

e-mail: visits@
scone-palace.co.uk

LOCATION

OS Ref. NO114 266

From Edinburgh Forth Bridge M90, A93 1 hr.

Bus: Regular buses from Perth (including open-top tours).

Rail: Perth Station 3m.

Motorway: M90 from Edinburgh.

Taxi: 01738 636777.

SCONE PALACE, on the outskirts of Perth, sits on one of Scotland's most historic sites. The crowning place of Scottish kings including Macbeth and Robert the Bruce, and until its infamous removal by Edward I, home of the Stone of Destiny on the Moot Hill.

The Palace was built on the ruins of the old Abbey and Bishop's Palace which were destroyed in the Reformation. After a brief spell under the Gowrie family, in 1600 Scone passed to the Murray family who continue to own and live in it. Extensively rebuilt by the 3rd Earl around 1804, Scone now houses unique collections of Vernis Martin, French furniture, clocks, 16th century needlework (including pieces by Mary Queen of Scots), ivories, *objets d'art* and one of the country's finest porcelain collections.

Winner of a 2000 Sandford Award from the Heritage Education Trust for education services.

GARDENS

The grounds of the Palace house magnificent collections of shrubs, with woodland walks through the pinetum containing David Douglas' original fir and are home to the Murray Star Maze. There are Highland cattle and peacocks to admire and an adventure play area for children. Like the Palace, the grounds and wooded parklands that stretch down to the River Tay are available for a variety of events, including corporate and private entertaining.

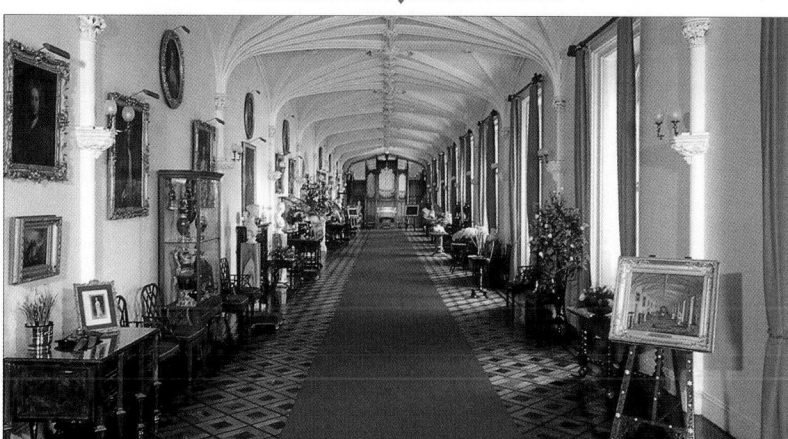

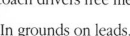 Receptions, fashion shows, war games, archery, clay pigeon shooting, equestrian events, garden parties, shows, rallies, filming, shooting, fishing, floodlit tattoos, product launches, highland games, parkland, cricket pitch, helicopter landing, croquet, racecourse, polo field, firework displays, adventure playground.

Grand dinners in state rooms, buffets, receptions, wedding receptions, cocktail parties.

Ramp at front door. All state rooms on one level, wheelchair access to restaurants. Visitors may alight at entrance. WC.

Licensed. Teas, lunches & dinners, can be booked, menus upon request, special rates for groups.

By arrangement. Guides in rooms, tour time 45 mins. French and German guides available by appointment.

Welcome.

300 cars and 15 coaches, groups please book, couriers and coach drivers free meal and admittance.

In grounds on leads.

OPENING TIMES

SUMMER

1 April - 31 October
Daily: 9.30am - 5.15pm.

Last admission 4.45pm.

Evening tours by appointment.

WINTER

By appointment only.

ADMISSION

SUMMER

Palace & Garden

Adult	£5.90
Child (5-16)	£3.40
Conc	£5.10
Family	£17.00

Groups (20+)

Adult	£5.10
Child (5-16)	£2.80
Conc	£4.40

Grounds only

Adult	£2.90
Child (5-16)	£1.50
Conc	£2.50

Under 5s Free
Private Tour £30 supplement.

WINTER

On application.

SPECIAL EVENTS

- **MAY - SEPT (Monthly):** Horse Trials.
- **APR - SEPT:** Perth Races (01738 551597).
- **JUL 7/8:** Game Conservancy Scottish Fair.
- **AUG 3/4** (to be confirmed) Perth Agricultural Show.

CONFERENCE/FUNCTION

ROOM	SIZE	MAX CAPACITY
Long Gallery	140' x 20'	200
Queen Victoria's Rm	20' x 20'	20
Drawing Rm	48' x 25'	80

ABERDOUR CASTLE

Tel: 01383 860519

Aberdour, Fife

Owner: In the care of Historic Scotland   **Contact:** The Steward

A 14th century castle built by the Douglas family. The gallery on the first floor gives an idea of how it was furnished at the time. The castle has a 14th century tower extended in the 16th and 17th centuries, a delightful walled garden and a circular dovecote.

Location: OS Ref. NT193 854. In Aberdour 5m E of the Forth Bridge on the A921.

Opening Times: 1 Apr - 30 Sept: daily, 9.30am - 6.30pm, last ticket 6pm. 1 Oct - 31 Mar: Mon - Sat, 9.30am - 4.30pm, Suns, 2 - 4.30pm, last ticket 4pm. Closed Thur pm & Fris in winter.

Admission: Adult £2, Child 75p, Conc. £1.50.

ALLOA TOWER

Tel: 01259 211701

Alloa Park, Alloa, Clackmannanshire FK10 1PP

Owner: The National Trust for Scotland   **Contact:** The Manager

Alloa Tower is a beautifully restored and furnished 14th century Tower House with an unusual 18th century interior. It contains several rare medieval features including the original oak-beamed roof, groin vaulting and interior well. Alloa Tower was the ancestral home of the Erskines, Earls of Mar, and contains a superb collection of family portraits, including works on loan from the present Earl.

Location: OS Ref. NS886 925. On A907, in Alloa.

Opening Times: 1 Apr - 30 Sept: daily, 1.30 - 5.30pm. Weekends in Oct, 1.30 - 5.30pm, last admission 5pm.

Admission: Adult £3, Conc. £2, Family £8. Groups: Adult £2.50, Child/ School £1. 25% discount to Clackmannanshire residents.

Partially suitable. WC.

ANGUS FOLK MUSEUM

Tel: 01307 840288

Kirkwynd, Glamis, Forfar, Angus DD8 1RT   **Fax:** 01307 840233

Owner: The National Trust for Scotland   **Contact:** Kathleen Ager

Where will you find cruisie lamps, pirn winders, cloutie rugs, bannock spades and a thrawcrook? All these fascinating items, and many more, are to be found in the Angus Folk Museum, one of Scotland's finest. The domestic section is housed in six charming 18th century cottages in Kirkwynd, and the agricultural collection is in the farmsteading opposite. The displays inside the building explain and illustrate changes in the Angus countryside in the last 200 years.

Location: OS Ref. NO385 467 Off A94, in Glamis, 5m SW of Forfar.

Opening Times: 1 Apr - 30 Jun & 1 - 30 Sept; daily, 11am - 5pm. 1 Jul - 31 Aug: daily, 10am - 5pm. Weekends in Oct: 11am - 5pm (last admission 4.30pm).

Admission: Adult £3, Conc. £2, Family £8. Groups: Adult £2.50, Child/School £1.

Partially suitable. WC. Limited.

ARBROATH ABBEY

Tel: 01241 878756

Arbroath, Tayside

Owner: In the care of Historic Scotland   **Contact:** The Steward

The substantial ruins of a Tironensian monastery, notably the gate house range and the abbot's house. Arbroath Abbey holds a very special place in Scottish history. Scotland's nobles swore their independence from England in the famous 'Declaration of Arbroath' in 1320. New visitor centre opening in 2001.

Location: OS Ref. NO644 414. In Arbroath town centre on the A92.

Opening Times: 1 Apr - 30 Sept: daily 9.30am - 6.30pm, last ticket 6pm. 1 Oct - 31 Mar: Mon - Sat, 9.30am - 4.30 pm, Suns, 2 - 4.30pm, last ticket 4pm.

Admission: Adult £2, Child 75p, Conc. £1.50. Prices will change when visitor centre opens.

BALGONIE CASTLE

Tel: 01592 750119 **Fax:** 01592 753103

Markinch, Fife KY7 6HQ

Owner/Contact: The Laird of Balgonie

14th century tower, additions to the building up to 1702. Still lived in by the family. 14th century chapel for weddings.

Location: OS Ref. NO313 006. ½ m S of A911 Glenrothes - Leven road at Milton of Balgonie on to B921.

Opening Times: All year: daily, 10am - 5pm.

Admission: Adult £3, Child £1.50, OAP £2.

BALHOUSIE CASTLE (BLACK WATCH MUSEUM)

Tel: 0131 310 8530

Hay Street, North Inch Park, Perth PH1 5HR

Owner: MOD   **Contact:** Major Proctor

Regimental museum housed in the castle.

Location: OS Ref. NO115 244. ½ m N of town centre, E of A9 road to Dunkeld.

Opening Times: May - Sept: Mon - Sat, 10am - 4.30pm. Oct - Apr: Mon - Fri, 10am - 3.30pm. Closed 23 Dec - 3 Jan & last Sat in Jun.

Admission: Free.

J M BARRIE'S BIRTHPLACE

Tel: 01575 572646

9 Brechin Road, Kirriemuir, Angus DD8 4BX

Owner: The National Trust for Scotland   **Contact:** Karen Gilmour or Mrs Sheila Philip

'Do you believe in fairies?' The creator of the eternal magic of *Peter Pan*, J M Barrie, was born here in 1860. He was the ninth of ten children born to David Barrie, a handloom weaver and his wife Margaret Ogilvy. See the imaginative exhibition about this famous novelist and dramatist with life-size figures, miniature stage sets, dioramas, theatre posters and stage costumes, while a darting light, 'Tinkerbell', moves around the room!

Location: OS Ref. NO388 542. On A926/B957, in Kirriemuir, 6m NW of Forfar.

Opening Times: 1 Apr - 30 Sept: Mon - Sat, 11am - 5.30pm, Suns, 1.30 - 5.30pm. Weekends in Oct: Sats, 11am - 5.30pm, Suns, 1.30pm - 5.30pm, last adm. 5pm.

Admission: Adult £3, Conc. £2, Family £8. Groups: Adult £2.50, Child/School £1.

Stairlift. No parking.

BARRY MILL

Tel: 01241 856761

Barry, Carnoustie, Angus DD7 7RJ

Owner: The National Trust for Scotland   **Contact:** Peter Ellis

19th century meal mill. Demonstrations and displays. Waymarked walks. Picnic area.

Location: OS Ref. NO533 349. N of village between A92 & A930, 2m W of Carnoustie.

Opening Times: 1 Apr - 30 Sept; daily, 11am - 5pm. Weekends in Oct: 11am - 5pm.

Admission: Adult £3, Conc £2, Family £8. Groups: Adult £2.50, Child/School £1.

BLAIR CASTLE

See page 475 for full page entry.

BOLFRACKS GARDEN

Tel: 01887 820207

Aberfeldy, Perthshire PH15 2EX

Owner/Contact: Mr J D Hutchison

A garden of approximately 4 acres with splendid views over the River Tay to the hills beyond. A walled garden contains a wide collection of trees, shrubs and perennials. Also a burn garden with rhododendrons, azaleas, meconopsis, primulas etc. with peat wall arrangements. Lots of bulbs and good autumn colour.

Location: OS Ref. NN822 481. 2m W of Aberfeldy on A827 towards Kenmore.

Opening Times: 1 Apr - 31 Oct: daily, 10am - 6pm.

Admission: Adult £2.50, Child (under 16 yrs) Free.

BRANKLYN GARDEN

Tel: 01738 625535

Dundee Road, Perth PH2 7BB

Owner: The National Trust for Scotland   **Contact:** Steve McNamara

Small but magnificent garden with an impressive collection of rare and unusual plants. Among the most breathtaking is the Himalayan blue poppy, *Meconopsis x sheldonii*. There is a rock garden with purple maple and the rare golden *Cedrus*. Seasonal highlights in May and June are the alpines and rhododendrons and in autumn the fiery red *Acer palmatum*.

Location: OS Ref. NO125 225. On A85 at 116 Dundee Road, Perth.

Opening Times: 1 Mar - 31 Oct; daily, 9.30am - sunset.

Admission: Adult £3, Conc. £2, Family £8. Groups: Adult £2.50, Child/School £1.

Grounds suitable, but limited access.

CAMBO GARDENS

Tel: 01333 450054 **Fax:** 01333 450987

Cambo Estate, Kingsbarns, St Andrews, Fife KY16 8QD

Owner: Mr & Mrs T P N Erskine   **Contact:** Catherine Erskine

Enchanting Victorian walled garden designed around the Cambo Burn. Snowdrops, lilac and roses are specialities. Ornamental potager, autumn borders. Garden supplies mansion house (not open) with fruit, vegetables and flowers. Woodland walks to sandy beach.

Location: OS Ref. NO603 114. 3m N of Crail. 7m SE of St Andrews on A917.

Opening Times: All year: daily except Christmas and New Year, 10am - dusk.

Admission: Adult £2.50, Child Free.

Conferences. Mail order snowdrops in the green. Limited for coaches. In grounds, on leads. 2 doubles & self-catering apartments/cottages.

CASTLE MENZIES

Tel: 01887 820982

Weem, Aberfeldy, Perth PH15 2JD

Owner: Menzies Charitable Trust   **Contact:** The Administrator

Magnificent example of a 16th century 'Z' plan fortified tower house, seat of the Chiefs of Clan Menzies for over 400 years. 'Bonnie Prince Charlie' was given hospitality here in 1746. Visitors can explore the whole building, together with part of 19th century addition. Small clan museum and gift shop.

Location: OS Ref. NN838 497. 1½ m from Aberfeldy on B846.

Opening Times: 31 Mar - 13 Oct: Mon - Sat, 10.30am - 5pm, Suns, 2 - 5pm, last entry 4.30pm.

Admission: Adult £3.50, Child £2, Conc. £3, Groups (20+): Adult £3.

Ground floor suitable. WC. Guide dogs only.

CHARLETON HOUSE

Tel: 01333 340249 **Fax:** 01333 340583

Colinsburgh, Leven, Fife KY9 1HG

Location: OS Ref. NO464 036. Off A917. 1m NW of Colinsburgh. 3m NW of Elie.

Opening Times: Sept: 12 noon - 3pm. Admission every ½ hr with guided tours only.

Admission: £6.

Obligatory.

CULROSS PALACE

Tel: 01383 880359 **Fax:** 01383 882675

Culross, Fife KY12 8JH

Owner: The National Trust for Scotland   **Contact:** Property Manager

Relive the domestic life of the 16th and 17th centuries at this Royal Burgh fringed by the River Forth. Here the old buildings and cobbled streets create a time warp for visitors as they explore the old town. Enjoy too the Palace, dating from 1597 and the medieval garden.

Location: OS Ref. NS985 860. Off A985. 12m W of Forth Road Bridge and 4m E of Kincardine Bridge, Fife.

Opening Times: Palace, Study & Town House: 1 - 12 Apr, 17 Apr - 31 May & 1 - 30 Sept: daily, 12.30 - 4.30pm; 13 - 16 Apr & 1 Jun - 31 Aug: daily, 10am - 5pm; weekends in Oct: 12.30 - 4.30pm. (last admission to Palace 1 hour before closing, to Town House & Study 15mins before closing). Groups at other times by appointment.

Admission: Combined ticket: Adult £5, Conc. £4, Family £14. Groups: Adult £4, Child/School £1.

WC. By arrangement.

DRUMMOND CASTLE GARDENS

See below.

DUNFERMLINE ABBEY & PALACE

Tel: 01383 739026

Dunfermline, Fife

Owner: In the care of Historic Scotland   **Contact:** The Steward

The remains of the Benedictine abbey founded by Queen Margaret in the 11th century. The foundations of her church are under the 12th century Romanesque-style nave. Robert the Bruce was buried in the choir. Substantial parts of the Abbey buildings remain, including the vast refectory.

Location: OS Ref. NY090 873. In Dunfermline off the M90.

Opening Times: 1 Apr - 30 Sept: daily, 9.30am - 6.30pm, last ticket 6pm. 1 Oct - 31 Mar: Mon - Sat, 9.30am - 4.30pm, Suns, 2 - 4.30pm, last ticket 4pm. Closed Thur pm and Fris in winter.

Admission: Adult £2, Child 75p, Conc. £1.50.

DUNNINALD

Tel: 01674 674842 **Fax:** 01674 674860

Montrose, Angus DD10 9TD

Owner/Contact: J Stansfeld

This house, the third Dunninald built on the estate, was designed by James Gillespie Graham in the gothic Revival style, and was completed for Peter Arkley in 1824. It has a superb walled garden and is set in a planned landscape dating from 1740. It is a family home.

Location: OS Ref. NO705 543 2m S of Montrose, between A92 and the sea.

Opening Times: 30 Jun - 29 Jul: Tue - Sun, 1 - 5pm. Garden: from 12 noon.

Admission: Adult £4, Child £2.50, Conc. £2.50. Garden only: £2.

 No photography in house.   Not suitable.   Obligatory.   In grounds, on leads.

EDZELL CASTLE AND GARDEN

Tel: 01356 648631

Edzell, Angus

Owner: In the care of Historic Scotland   **Contact:** The Steward

The beautiful walled garden at Edzell is one of Scotland's unique sights, created by Sir David Lindsay in 1604. The 'Pleasance' is a delightful formal garden with walls decorated with sculptured stone panels, flower boxes and niches for nesting birds. The fine tower house, now ruined, dates from the last years of the 15th century. Mary Queen of Scots held a council meeting in the castle in 1562 on her way north as her army marched against the Gordons.

Location: OS Ref. NO585 691. At Edzell, 6m N of Brechin on B966. 1m W of village.

Opening Times: 1 Apr - 30 Sept: daily, 9.30am - 6.30pm, last ticket 6pm. 1 Oct - 31 Mar: Mon - Sat, 9.30am - 4.30pm, Suns, 2 - 4.30pm, last ticket 4pm. Closed Thur pm and Fris in winter.

Admission: Adult £2.80, Child £1, Conc. £2.

ELCHO CASTLE

Tel: 01738 639998

Perth

Owner: In the care of Historic Scotland

This handsome and complete fortified mansion of 16th century date has four projecting towers. The original wrought-iron grilles to protect the windows are still in place.

Location: OS Ref. NO164 211. On the Tay, 3m SE of Perth.

Opening Times: 1 Apr - 30 Sept: daily, 9.30am - 6.30pm, last ticket 6pm.

Admission: Adult £2, Child 75p, Conc. £1.50.

DRUMMOND CASTLE GARDENS

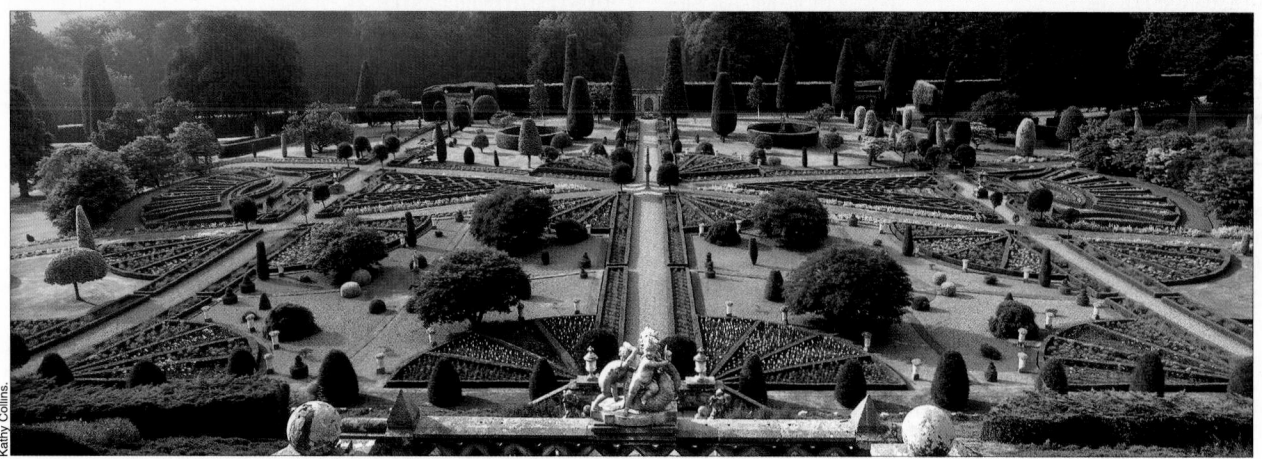

Katty Collins.

MUTHILL, CRIEFF, PERTHSHIRE PH5 2AA

Owner: Grimsthorpe & Drummond Castle Trust   *Contact: Pat Keith*

Tel: 01764 681257 **Fax:** 01764 681550 **Weekends:** 01764 681433

e-mail: the.gardens@drummondcastle.sol.co.uk

Scotland's most important formal gardens, among the finest in Europe. A mile of beech-lined avenue leads to a formidable ridge top tower house. Enter through the woven iron yett to the terraces and suddenly revealed is a magnificent Italianate parterre, celebrating the saltire and family heraldry, surrounding the famous multiplex sundial by John Milne, master mason to Charles I. First laid out in the early 17th century by John Drummond, the 2nd Earl of Perth and renewed in the early 1950s by Phyllis Astor, Countess of Ancaster.

Location: OS Ref. NN844 181. 2m S of Crieff off the A822.

Opening Times: Easter weekend, then 1 May - 31 Oct: 2 - 6pm, last entry 5pm.

Admission: Adult £3, Child £1.50, OAP £2.

Partially suitable. WC. By arrangement.   In grounds, on leads.

SPECIAL EVENTS
AUG 5: Open Day, entertainments, teas, raffle.

FALKLAND PALACE

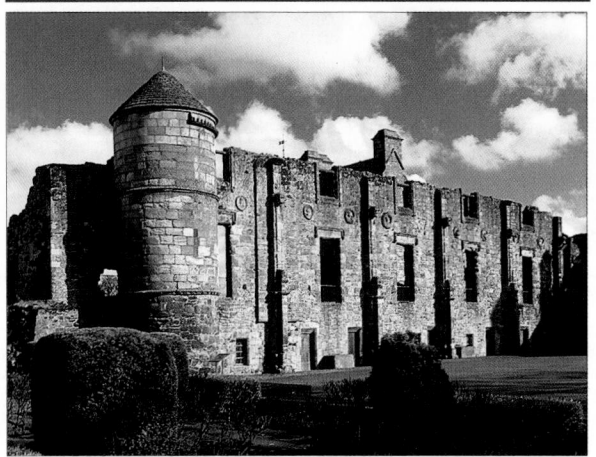

FALKLAND KY15 7BU

Owner: *The National Trust for Scotland*   ***Contact:*** *Mrs Margaret Marshall*

Tel: 01337 857397   **Fax:** 01337 857980

The Royal Palace of Falkland, set in the heart of a unique medieval village, was the country residence and hunting lodge of eight Stuart monarchs, including Mary Queen of Scots. Built between 1502 and 1541, the Palace is an extremely fine example of Renaissance architecture. It includes the exceptionally beautiful Chapel Royal, and is surrounded by internationally known gardens, laid out in the 1950s. The Royal Tennis Court, reputedly the world's oldest, is still used today.

Location: OS Ref. NO253 075. A912, 11m N of Kirkcaldy.

Opening Times: Palace & Garden: 1 Apr - 31 May & 1 Sept - 31 Oct: Mon - Sat, 11am - 5.30pm, Suns, 1.30 - 5.30pm. 1 Jun - 31 Aug: Mon - Sat, 10am - 5.30pm, Suns, 1.30 - 5.30. Last admission to Palace 4.30pm, to Garden 5pm. Groups at other times by appointment. Town Hall: as Palace.

Admission: Palace & Garden: Adult £5, Conc. £4, Family £14. Groups: Adult £4, Child/School £1. Garden only: Adult £2.50, Conc. £1.70, Family £7. Groups: Adult £2, Child/School £1. Members of Scots Guards' Association admitted Free.

Grounds suitable.

HOUSE OF DUN

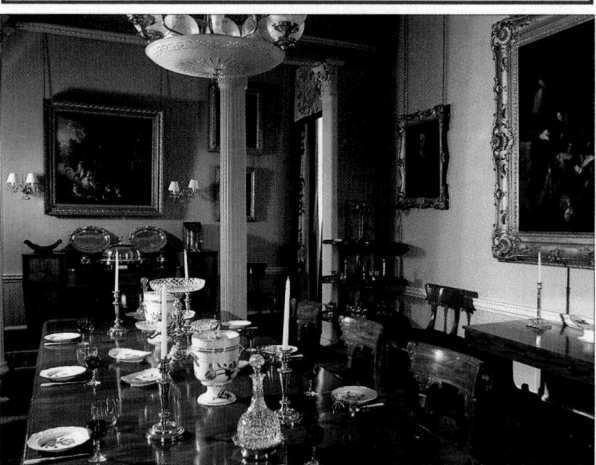

MONTROSE, ANGUS DD10 9LQ

Owner: *The National Trust for Scotland*   ***Contact:*** *The Manager*

Tel: 01674 810264   **Fax:** 01674 810722

This beautiful Georgian house, overlooking the Montrose Basin, was designed by William Adam and built in 1730 for David Erskine, Lord Dun. Lady Augusta Kennedy-Erskine was the natural daughter of William IV and Mrs Jordan and House of Dun contains many royal mementos. The house features superb plasterwork by Joseph Enzer.

Location: OS Ref. NO670 599. 3m W Montrose on A935.

Opening Times: House & shop: 13 - 16 Apr; 1 May - 30 Jun & 1 -30 Sept: daily, 1.30 - 5.30pm; 1 Jul - 31 Aug: daily, 11am - 5.30pm; weekends in Oct, 1.30 - 5.30pm (last admission 5pm). Restaurant opens at 11am. Gardens & Grounds: All year, daily, 9.30am - sunset.

Admission: House & Gardens: Adult £6, Conc. £4.50, Family £16.50. Groups: Adult £4.80, Child/ School £1. Gardens only: £1.

Conferences.   Ground floor & basement suitable. WC.   In grounds, on leads. Special dog walk.

GLAMIS CASTLE

See page 476 for full page entry.

GLENEAGLES

Tel: 01764 682388

Auchterarder, Perthshire PH3 1PJ

Owner: Gleneagles 1996 Trust   **Contact:** J Martin Haldane of Gleneagles

Gleneagles has been the home of the Haldane family since the 12th century. The 18th century pavilion is open to the public by written appointment.

Location: OS Ref. NS931 088. Auchterarder.

Opening Times: By written appointment only.

HILL OF TARVIT MANSIONHOUSE

Tel/Fax: 01334 653127

Cupar, Fife KY15 5PB

Owner: The National Trust for Scotland   **Contact:** The Manager

This fine house was rebuilt in 1906 by Sir Robert Lorimer, the renowned Scottish architect, for a Dundee industrialist, Mr F B Sharp. The house still presents a perfect setting for Mr Sharp's notable collection of superb French, Chippendale and vernacular furniture. Fine paintings by Raeburn and Ramsay and a number of eminent Dutch artists are on view together with Chinese porcelain and bronzes. Don't miss the restored Edwardian laundry behind the house which is set in the midst of a delightful garden.

Location: OS Ref. NO379 118. Off A916, 2^1/$_2$ m S of Cupar, Fife.

Opening Times: House: 13 - 16 Apr; 1 May - 30 Jun & 1 - 30 Sept: daily, 1.30 - 5.30pm; 1 Jul - 31 Aug: daily, 11am - 5.30pm; weekends in Oct, 1.30 - 5.30pm (last admission 4.45pm). Tearoom opens at 12.30pm when house opens at 1.30pm. Garden & Grounds: All year, daily, 9.30am - sunset.

Admission: House & Garden: Adult £5, Conc. £4, Family £14. Groups: Adult £4, Child/School £1. Garden only: £2, Conc. £1 (honesty box).

Ground floor & grounds suitable. WC.   By arrangement.   P

HUNTINGTOWER CASTLE

Tel: 01738 627231

Perth

Owner: In the care of Historic Scotland   **Contact:** The Steward

The splendid painted ceilings are especially noteworthy in this castle, once owned by the Ruthven family. Scene of a famous leap between two towers by a daughter of the house who was nearly caught in her lover's room. The two towers are still complete, one of 15th - 16th century date, the other of 16th century origin. Now linked by a 17th century range.

Location: OS Ref. NO084 252. 3m NW of Perth off the A85.

Opening Times: 1 Apr - 30 Sept: daily, 9.30am - 6.30pm, last ticket 6pm. 1 Oct - 31 Mar: Mon - Sat, 9.30am - 4.30pm, Suns, 2 - 4.30pm, last ticket 4pm. Closed Thur pm & Fris in winter.

Admission: Adult £2, Child 75p, Conc. £1.50.

INCHCOLM ABBEY

Tel: 01383 823332

Inchcolm, Fife

Owner: In the care of Historic Scotland   **Contact:** The Steward

Known as the 'Iona of the East'. This is the best preserved group of monastic buildings in Scotland, founded in 1123. Includes a 13th century octagonal chapter house.

Location: OS Ref. NT190 826. On Inchcolm in the Firth of Forth. Reached by ferry from South Queensferry (30 mins). Tel 01383 823332 for times.

Opening Times: 1 Apr - 30 Sept: daily, 9.30am - 6.30pm, last ticket 6pm.

Admission: Adult £2.80, Child £1, Conc. £2. Additional charge for ferries.

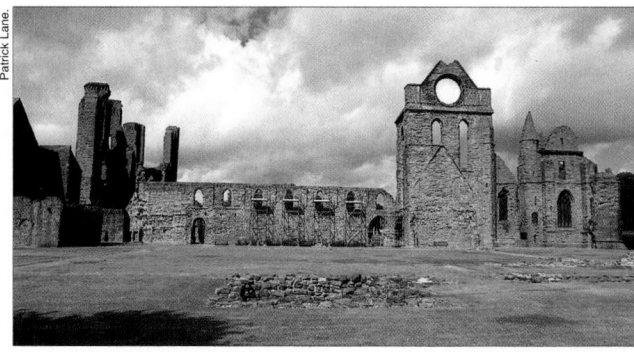

Arbroath Abbey, Perthshire.

KELLIE CASTLE & GARDEN

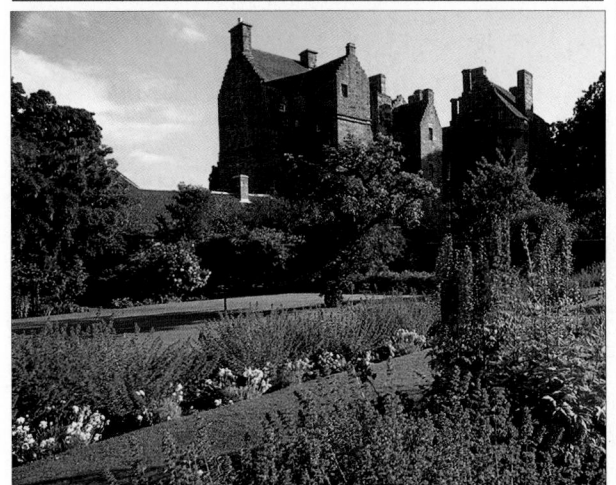

PITTENWEEM, FIFE KY10 2RF

Owner: The National Trust for Scotland   *Contact:* The Property Manager

Tel: 01333 720271   **Fax:** 01333 720326

This very fine example of domestic architecture in Lowland Scotland dates from the 14th century and was sympathetically restored by the Lorimer family in the late 19th century. The castle contains magnificent plaster ceilings and painted panelling as well as fine furniture designed by Sir Robert Lorimer. Of particular interest are the Victorian nursery and the old kitchen. The late Victorian garden features a fine collection of old-fashioned roses and herbaceous plants which are cultivated organically.

Location: OS Ref. NO519 051. On B9171, 3m NW of Pittenweem, Fife.

Opening Times: Castle: 13 Apr - 30 Sept: daily, 1.30 - 5.30pm, weekends in Oct, 1.30 - 5.30pm (last admission 4.45pm). Garden: All year, daily, 9.30am - sunset.

Admission: House & Garden: Adult £5, Conc. £4, Family £14. Groups: Adult £4, Child/ School £1. Garden only: £2, Conc. £1 (honesty box).

 Ground floor & grounds suitable.

LOCH LEVEN CASTLE

Tel: 0388 040483

Loch Leven, Kinross

Owner: In the care of Historic Scotland   **Contact:** The Steward

Mary Queen of Scots endured nearly a year of imprisonment in this 14th century tower before her dramatic escape in May 1568. During the First War of Independence it was held by the English, stormed by Wallace and visited by Bruce.

Location: OS Ref. NO138 018. On island in Loch Leven reached by ferry from Kinross off the M90.

Opening Times: 1 Apr - 30 Sept: daily, 9.30am - 6.30pm, last ticket 6pm.

Admission: Adult £3.30, Child £1.20, Conc. £2.50. Prices include ferry trip.

MEGGINCH CASTLE GARDENS

Tel: 01821 642222 **Fax:** 01821 642708

Errol, Perthshire PH2 7SW

Owner: Captain Drummond of Megginch and Lady Strange

15th century castle, 1,000 year old yews, flowered parterre, double walled kitchen garden, topiary, astrological garden, pagoda dovecote in courtyard. Part used as a location for the film *Rob Roy*.

Location: OS Ref. NO241 245. 8m E of Perth on A90.

Opening Times: Apr - Oct: Weds. Aug: daily, 2.30 - 6pm. (2000 details.)

Admission: Adult £2.50, Child £1. (2000 details.)

Partially suitable. By arrangement. Limited for coaches. In grounds, on leads.

MEIGLE SCULPTURED STONE MUSEUM

Tel: 01828 640612

Meigle

Owner: In the care of Historic Scotland

A remarkable collection of 25 sculptured monuments of the Celtic Christian period. This is one of the finest collections of Dark Age sculpture in Western Europe.

Location: OS Ref. NO287 446. In Meigle on the A94.

Opening Times: 1 Apr - 30 Sept: daily, 9.30am - 6.30pm, last ticket 6pm.

Admission: Adult £2, Child 75p, Conc. £1.50.

MONZIE CASTLE

Tel: 01764 653110

Crieff, Perthshire PH7 4HD

Owner/Contact: Mrs C M M Crichton

Built in 1791. Destroyed by fire in 1908 and rebuilt and furnished by Sir Robert Lorimer.

Location: OS Ref. NN873 244. 2m NE of Crieff.

Opening Times: 12 May - 10 Jun: daily, 2 - 5pm. By appointment at other times.

Admission: Adult £3, Child £1. Groups: Adult £2.50.

PITTENCRIEFF HOUSE MUSEUM

Tel: 01383 313838

Dunfermline, Fife

Owner: Fife Council   **Contact:** Ms Lin Collis

A temporary exhibition programme.

Location: OS Ref. NN087 873. In Dunfermline, S of A994 in Pittencrieff Park.

Opening Times: All year. May - Sept: 11am - 5pm. Oct - Apr: 11am - 4pm.

Admission: Free.

ST ANDREWS CASTLE

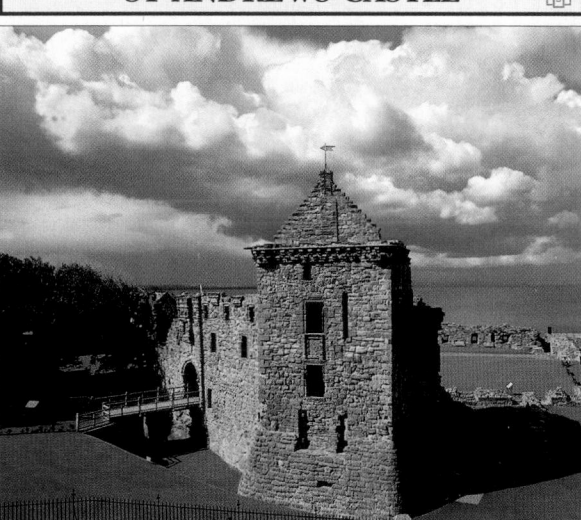

THE SCORES, ST ANDREWS, KY16 9AR

Owner: Historic Scotland   *Contact:* The Steward

Tel: 01334 477196

This was the castle of the Bishops of St Andrews and has a fascinating mine and counter-mine, rare examples of medieval siege techniques. There is also a bottle dungeon hollowed out of solid rock. Cardinal Beaton was murdered here and John Knox was sent to the galleys when the ensuing siege was lifted.

Location: OS Ref. NO513 169. In St Andrews on the A91.

Opening Times: Apr - Sept: daily, 9.30am - 6.30pm. Oct - Mar: Mon - Sat, 9.30am - 4.30pm; Suns, 2 - 4.30pm. Last ticket 30 mins before closing. Joint ticket with St Andrews Cathedral available.

Admission: Adult £2.80, Child £1, Conc. £2. 10% discount for groups (10+). Free pre-booked school visits.

Visitor centre. Private evening hire. Partially suitable. WCs. By arrangement. On street. Free if booked. Guide dogs.

SCONE PALACE GROUNDS

See page 477 for full page entry.

STOBHALL GARDENS & CHAPEL

Tel: 01821 640332

Stobhall, Guildtown, Perthshire PH2 6DR

Owner: The Earl of Perth   **Contact:** J Stormonth-Darling

Dramatic shrub gardens surround this unusual and charming cluster of historic buildings in a magnificent situation overlooking the River Tay. Access to 14th century chapel with its unique painted ceiling (1630).

Location: OS Ref. NO132 343. 8m N of Perth on A93.

Opening Times: 26 May - 24 Jun: 1 - 5pm. Also 21 & 28 Oct: 2 - 5pm.

Admission: Adult £2, Child £1.

Partially suitable. WC. Limited. Schools welcome if suitably accompanied. No education programme. Guide dogs only.

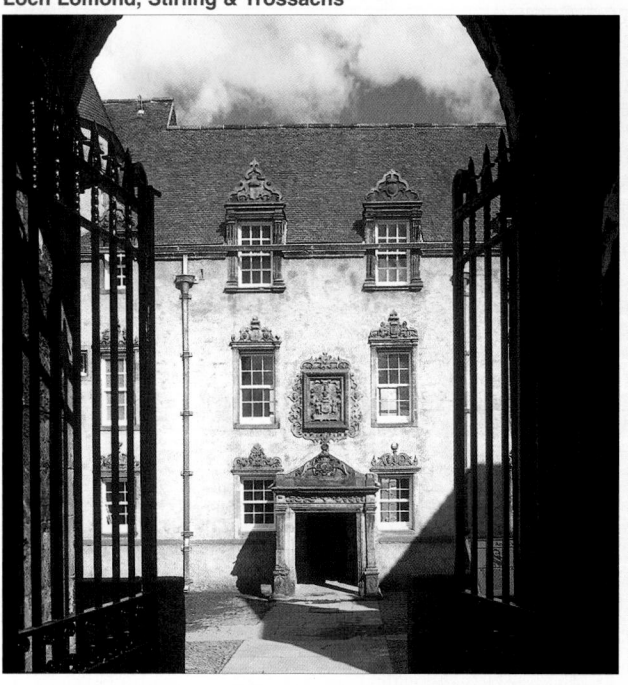

Historic Scotland.

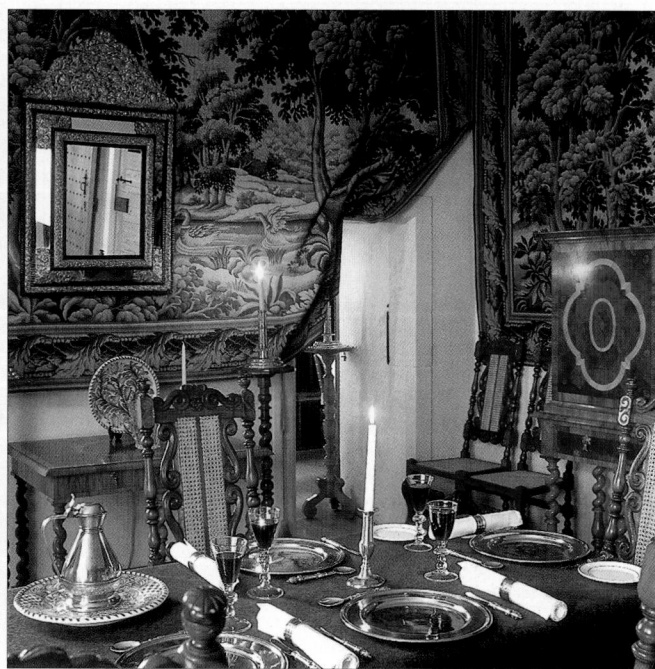

ARGYLL'S LODGING
Stirling

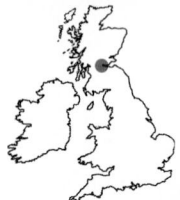

Owner: Historic Scotland

CONTACT

Neil Young
Argyll's Lodging
Castle Wynd
Stirling
FK8 1EJ

Tel: 01786 431319

Fax: 01786 448194

LOCATION

OS Ref. NS793 938

At the top and on
E side of Castle
Wynd in Stirling.

Train: Stirling.

Air: Edinburgh or
Glasgow.

ARGYLL'S LODGING, the residence of the Earls of Argyll in Stirling, is the finest and most complete surviving example in Scotland of a 17th century town residence. Set back behind a screen wall on the upper approaches to Stirling Castle, its fine architecture marks it out as a town house intended for the household of a great nobleman serving the Royal Stewart Court within the Castle. The principal rooms within the lodging – including the Laigh Hall, Dining Room, Drawing Room and Bedchamber – have recently been restored and furnished as they would have been when the 9th Earl of Argyll lived there in 1680. The Earl was executed for treason in 1685.

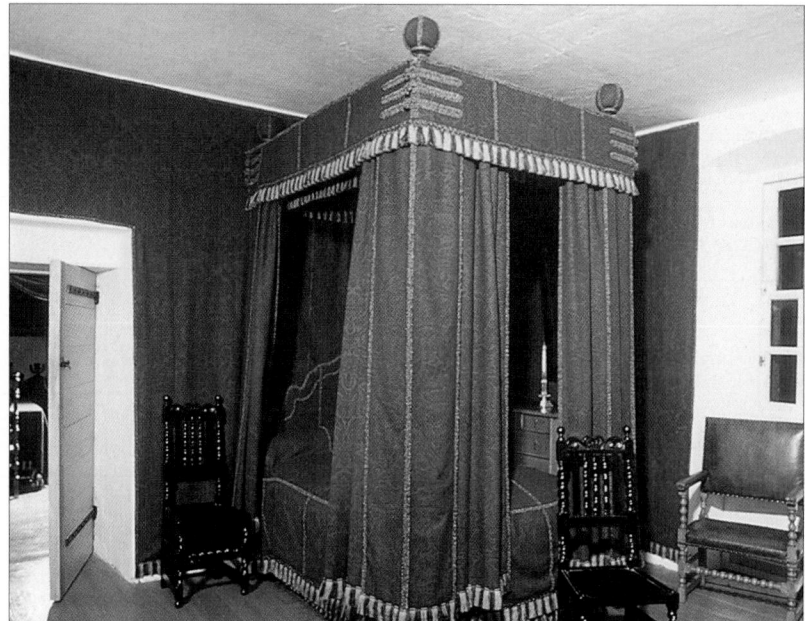

OPENING TIMES

April - September:
Daily: 9.30am - 6pm.

October - March:
Daily: 9.30am - 5pm.

ADMISSION

Adult £3.00
Child* £1.20
Conc.......................£2.25

*up to 16 years

FUNCTION

ROOM	SIZE	MAX CAPACITY
Laigh Hall	11 x 6m	60 for reception
High Dining Room	11 x 6m	26 for dinner
Both rooms: 120 for receptions		

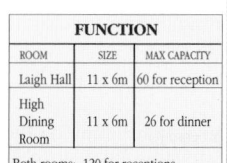

Interpretation scheme includes computer animations; joint ticket with Stirling Castle available.

Evening receptions/dinners.

Partially suitable. No wheelchair access to upper floor.

Ample parking for coaches and cars on Stirling Castle Esplanade.

Free pre-booked school visits scheme.

Guide dogs only.

482

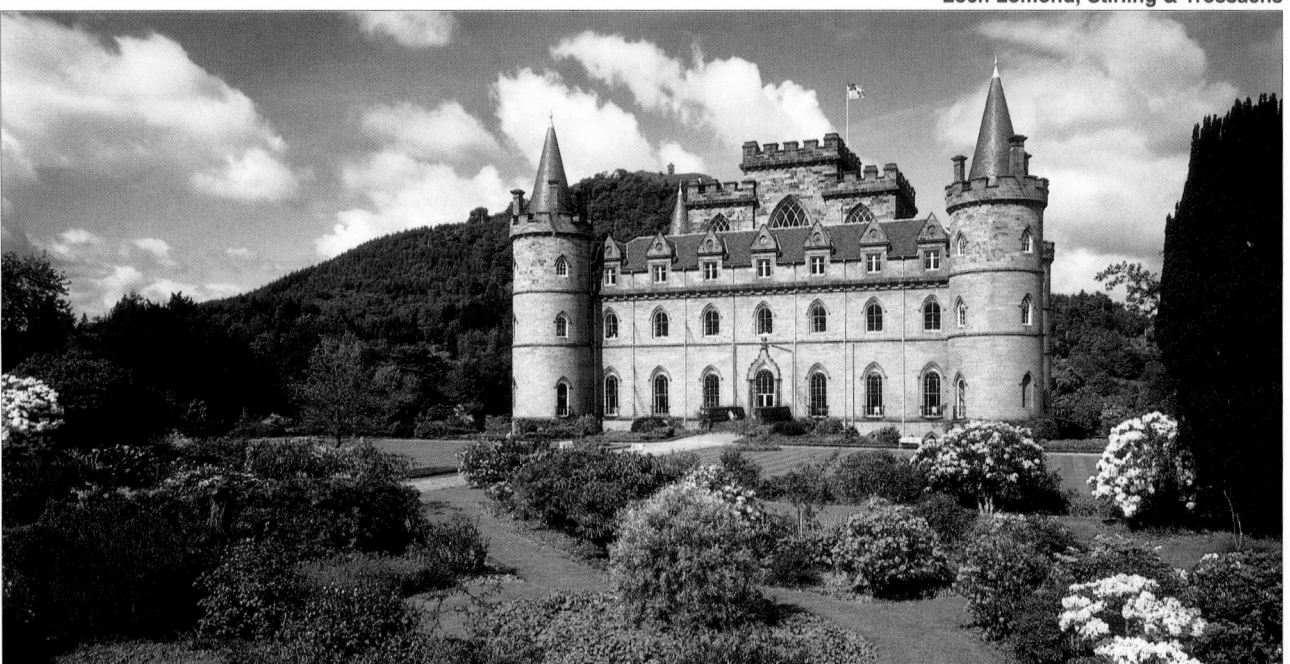

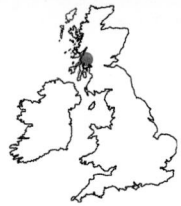

INVERARAY CASTLE
Inveraray

The Duke of Argyll's family have lived in Inveraray since the early 15th century. The present Castle was built between 1745 and 1790.

The ancient Royal Burgh of Inveraray lies about 60 miles north west of Glasgow by Loch Fyne in an area of spectacular natural beauty combining the ruggedness of highland scenery with the sheltered tidal loch 90 miles from the open sea.

The Castle is the home of the Duke and Duchess of Argyll. Its fairytale exterior belies the grandeur of its gracious interior. The building was designed by Roger Morris and decorated by Robert Mylne, the clerk of works being William

Adam, father of Robert and John, who did much of the laying out of the present Royal Burgh, an unrivalled example of an early planned town.

Visitors may see the famous Armoury Hall containing some 1300 pieces, French tapestries made especially for the Castle, fine examples of Scottish, English and French furniture together with a wealth of other works of art including china, silver and family artifacts, all of which form a unique collection spanning the generations which are identified by a magnificent genealogical display in the Clan Room.

Owner: Trustees of the 10th Duke of Argyll

CONTACT

The Factor
Dept HHD
Argyll Estates Office
Cherry Park
Inveraray
Argyll
PA32 8XE

Tel: 01499 302203

Fax: 01499 302421

e-mail: enquiries@ inveraray-castle.com

LOCATION

OS Ref. NN100 090

From Edinburgh 2¹/₂ - 3 hrs via Glasgow.

Just NE of Inveraray on A83. W shore of Loch Fyne.

Bus: Bus route stopping point within ¹/₂ m.

OPENING TIMES

7 April - 14 October

April, May, June, September & October:
Mon -Thur & Sats:
10am - 1pm & 2 - 5.45pm
Fris: Closed
Suns: 1 - 5.45pm.

July & August
Daily: 10am - 5.45pm
(including Friday)
Suns: 1 - 5.45pm.

Last admissions
12.30 & 5pm.

WINTER
Closed.

ADMISSION

House only

Adult £5.50
Child (under 16yrs) ...£3.50
OAP/Student...........£4.50
Family (2+2)...........£14.00
Groups (20+)
.... 20% discount

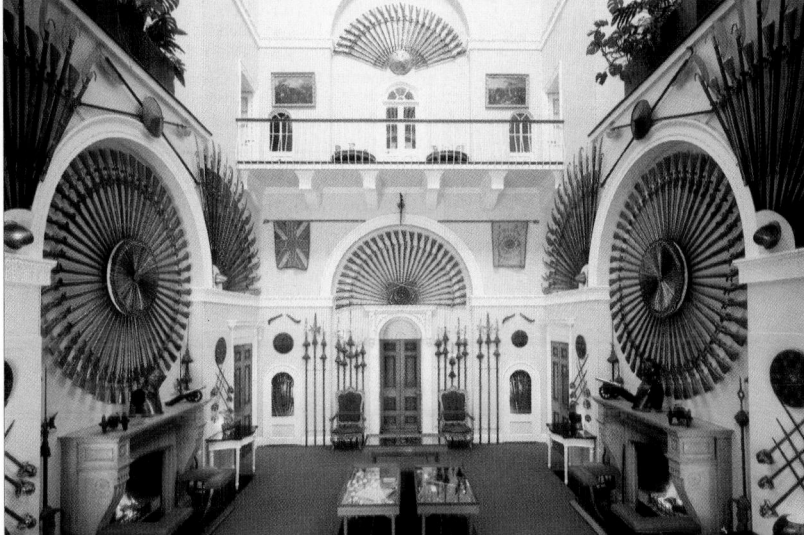

No photography. Guide books in French, Italian, Japanese and German translations.

Visitors may alight at the entrance. 2 wheelchair ramps to castle. All main public rooms suitable but two long flights of stairs to the smaller rooms upstairs. WCs.

Seats up to 50. Licensed. Menus available on request. Groups book in advance. Tel: 01786 813317.

Available for up to 100 people at no additional cost. Groups please book. Tour time: 1 hr.

100 cars. Separate coach park close to Castle

£1.50 per child. A guide can be provided. Areas of interest include a nature walk.

In grounds, on leads. Guide dogs only inside Castle.

ACHAMORE GARDENS
Tel: 01583 505254/505267

Isle of Gigha, Argyll PA41 7AD
Owner: Mr and Mrs Derek Holt **Contact:** Mr William Howden
Gardens only open. Sub-tropical gardens created by Sir James Horlick who bought Gigha in 1944.
Location: OS Ref. NR650 500. Off the Mull of Kintyre. Ferry from Tayinloan.
Opening Times: Dawn until dusk every day.
Admission: Adult £2, Child £1.

ANGUS'S GARDEN
Tel: 01866 822375 **Fax:** 01866 822652

Barguillean, Taynuilt, Argyll, West Highlands PA35 1HY
Owner: Mr Sam MacDonald **Contact:** Mr Sam MacDonald
Memorial garden of peace, tranquillity and reconciliation.
Location: OS Ref. NM999 298.
Opening Times: All year: daily, 9am - 5pm.
Admission: £2.

ARDENCRAIG GARDENS
Tel: 01700 504225 **Fax:** 01700 504225

Ardencraig, Rothesay, Isle of Bute, West Highlands PA20 9BP
Owner: Argyll and Bute Council **Contact:** Allan Macdonald
Walled garden, greenhouses, aviaries.
Location: OS Ref. NS105 645. 2m from Rothesay.
Opening Times: May - Sept: Mon - Fri, 10am - 4.30pm, Sats & Suns, 1 - 4.30pm.

ARDKINGLAS ESTATE
Tel: 01499 600261 **Fax:** 01499 600241
e-mail: ardkinglas@btinternet.com

Cairndow, Argyll PA26 8BH
Owner: S J Noble **Contact:** The Estate Manager
Location: OS Ref. NN179 106. Head of Loch Fyne, just off the A83 at Cairndow, 10m W of Arrochar. About 1hr from Glasgow.
Opening Times: Woodland Garden & woodland trails: All year: dawn - dusk. Tree Shop: All year: daily.
Admission: Garden: Adult £2.

ARDUAINE GARDEN

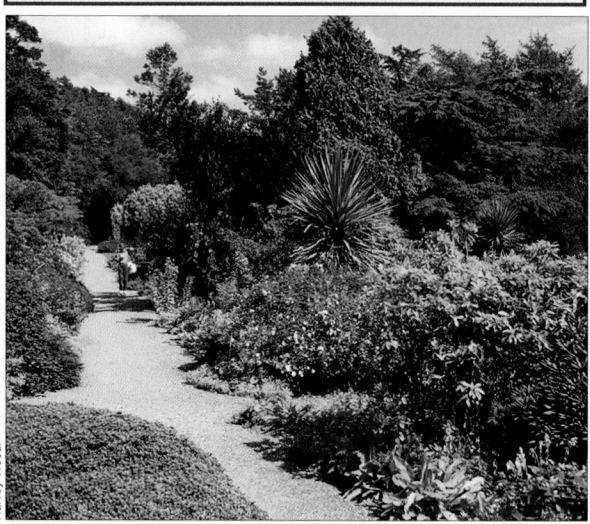

ARDUAINE, BY OBAN, ARGYLL PA34 4XQ
Owner: The National Trust for Scotland *Contact: Maurice Wilkins*

Tel/Fax: 01852 200366

A haven of tranquillity nestling on the west coast, Arduaine Garden is most spectacular in the late spring and early summer when the rhododendrons and azaleas are at their glorious best. With informal perennial borders giving a delightful display of colour throughout the season, the garden offers pleasant surroundings for a relaxing walk through the woodland garden to the coastal viewpoint, or simply an opportunity to sit and enjoy the peaceful atmosphere of the water garden.
Location: OS Ref. NM798 105. On A816, 20m S of Oban and 17m N of Lochgilphead.
Opening Times: All year: daily, 9.30am - sunset.
Admission: Adult £3, Conc. £2, Family £8. Groups: Adult £2.50. Child/School £1.

By arrangement. P Guide dogs only.

ARGYLL'S LODGING
See page 482 for full page entry.

AUCHINDRAIN TOWNSHIP
Tel: 01499 500235

Auchindrain, Inveraray, Argyll PA32 8XN
Owner: Auchindrain Trust **Contact:** Peter Fairweather
Open-air museum of an original West Highland township.
Location: OS Ref. NN050 050. On A83, 6m SW of Inveraray.
Opening Times: Please contact for details.
Admission: Please contact for details.

BALLOCH CASTLE COUNTRY PARK
Tel: 01389 758216 **Fax:** 01389 720922

Balloch, Dunbartonshire G83 8LX
Contact: Loch Lomond Park Authority Ranger Service
A 200 acre country park on the banks of Loch Lomond.
Location: OS Ref. NS390 830. SE shore of Loch Lomond, off A82 for Balloch or A811 for Stirling.
Opening Times: Visitor Centre: Easter - Oct: daily, 10am - 5.30pm. Country Park: All year: dawn - dusk.
Admission: Free for both Visitor Centre and Country Park.

BANNOCKBURN HERITAGE CENTRE
Tel: 01786 812664
Fax: 01786 810892

Glasgow Road, Stirling FK7 0LJ
Owner: The National Trust for Scotland **Contact:** Judith Fairley
In 1314 from this battlefield the Scots 'sent them homeward to think again', when Edward II's English army was soundly defeated by King Robert the Bruce. Inside the Heritage Centre there is a life-size statue of William Wallace, Bruce on his throne, a display enriched with replicas, vignettes of Scottish life and a panorama of historical characters.
Location: OS Ref. NS810 910. Off M80 & M9/J9, 2m S of Stirling.
Opening Times: Site: All year: daily. Heritage Centre shop & café: 1 - 31 Mar and 1 Nov - 23 Dec: daily, 10.30am - 4pm. 1 Apr - 31 Oct: daily, 10am - 5.30pm (last audio-visual show ¹/₂ hr before closing).
Admission: Adult £2.50, Conc. £1.70, Family £7. Groups: Adult £2, Child/School £1.

In grounds, on leads.

BONAWE IRON FURNACE
Tel: 01866 822432

Taynuilt, Argyll
Owner: In the care of Historic Scotland **Contact:** The Steward
Founded in 1753 by Cumbrian iron masters this is the most complete remaining charcoal fuelled ironworks in Britain. Displays show how iron was once made here.
Location: OS Ref. NN005 310. By the village of Taynuilt off the A85.
Opening Times: 1 Apr - 30 Sept: daily, 9.30am - 6.30pm, last ticket 6pm.
Admission: Adult £2.50, Child £1, Conc. £1.90.

CASTLE CAMPBELL
Tel: 01259 742408

Dollar Glen, Central District
Owner: The National Trust for Scotland **Contact:** Historic Scotland
Known as 'Castle Gloom' this spectacularly sited 15th century fortress was the lowland stronghold of the Campbells. Stunning views from the parapet walk.
Location: OS Ref. NS961 993. At head of Dollar Glen, 10m E of Stirling on the A91.
Opening Times: 1 Apr - 30 Sept: daily, 9.30am - 6.30pm, last ticket 6pm. 1 Oct - 31 Mar: Mon - Sat, 9.30am - 4.30pm (closed Thurs pm & Fris all day) Suns, 2 - 4.30pm, last ticket 4pm.
Admission: Adult £2.80, Child £1, Conc. £2.

CASTLE STALKER
Tel: 01883 622768 **Fax:** 01883 626238

Portnacroish, Appin, Argyll PA38 4BA
Owner: Mrs M Allward **Contact:** Messrs R & A Allward
Early 15th century tower house and ancient seat of the Stewarts of Appin. Picturesquely set on a rocky islet approx 400 yds off the mainland on the shore of Loch Linnhe. Reputed to have been used by James IV as a hunting lodge. Garrisoned by Government troops during the 1745 rising. Restored from a ruin by the late Lt Col Stewart Allward following acquisition in 1965 and now retained by his family.
Location: OS Ref. NM930 480. Approx. 20m N of Oban on the A828. On islet ¹/₄ m off-shore.
Opening Times: Apr - Sept for 25 days. Telephone for details. Times variable depending on tides and weather.
Admission: Adult £6, Child £3.

Not suitable for coach parties. Not suitable.

DOUNE CASTLE

Tel: 01786 841742

Doune

Owner: Earl of Moray (leased to Historic Scotland)   **Contact:** The Steward

A formidable 14th century courtyard castle, built for the Regent Albany. The striking keep-gatehouse combines domestic quarters including the splendid Lord's Hall with its carved oak screen, musicians' gallery and double fireplace.

Location: OS Ref. NN720 020. In Doune, 8m S of Callendar on the A84.

Opening Times: 1 Apr - 30 Sept: daily, 9.30am - 6.30pm. 1 Oct - 31 Mar: Mon - Wed & Sats, 9.30am - 4.30pm, Thurs, 9.30am - 12 noon, Fris, closed, Suns, 2 - 4.30pm, last admission 1/2 hr before closing.

Admission: Adult £2.50, Child £1, Conc. £1.90.

DUART CASTLE

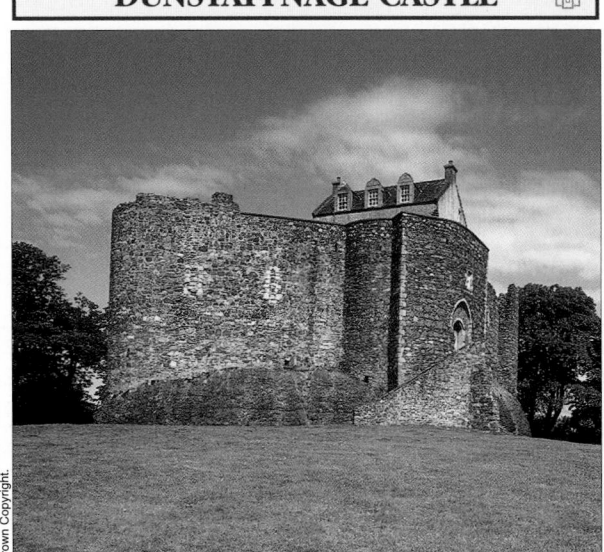

ISLE OF MULL, ARGYLL PA64 6AP

Owner/Contact: Sir Lachlan Maclean Bt

Tel: 01680 812309 or 01577 830311 **e-mail:** duartguide@isle-of-mull.demon.co.uk

Duart Castle has been a Maclean stronghold since the 12th century. The keep was built by Lachlan Lubanach, 5th Chief, in 1360. Burnt by the English in 1758, the castle was restored in 1912 and today is still the home of the Chief of the Clan Maclean. It has a spectacular position overlooking the Sound of Mull.

Location: OS Ref. NM750 350. Off A849 on the east point of the Isle of Mull.

Opening Times: 1 May - 14 Oct: 10.30am - 6pm.

Admission: Adult £3.80, Child £1.90, Conc. £3, Family £9.50.

Not suitable. By arrangement. In grounds, on leads.

DUMBARTON CASTLE

Tel: 01389 732167

Dumbarton, Strathclyde

Owner: Historic Scotland   **Contact:** The Steward

Location: OS Ref. NS401 744. In Dumbarton on the A82.

Opening Times: 1 Apr - 30 Sept: daily, 9.30am - 6.30pm, last ticket 6pm. 1 Oct - 31 Mar: Mon - Wed & Sats, 9.30am - 4.30pm, Thurs, 9.30am - 12 noon, Fris closed, Suns, 2 - 4.30pm, last ticket 4pm.

Admission: Adult £2, Child 75p, Conc £1.50.

DUNBLANE CATHEDRAL

Tel: 01786 823388

Dunblane

Owner: Historic Scotland   **Contact:** The Steward

One of Scotland's noblest medieval churches. The lower part of the tower is Romanesque but the larger part of the building is of the 13th century. It was restored in 1889 - 93 by Sir Rowand Anderson.

Location: OS Ref. NN782 015. In Dunblane.

Opening Times: All year.

Admission: Free.

DUNSTAFFNAGE CASTLE

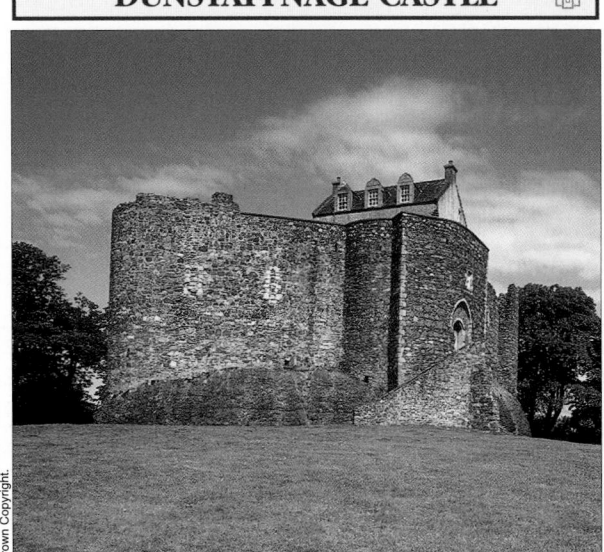

Crown Copyright.

BY OBAN, ARGYLL PA37 1PZ

Owner: In the care of Historic Scotland   *Contact: The Steward*

Tel: 01631 562465

A very fine 13th century castle built on a rock with a great curtain wall. The castle's colourful history stretches across the Wars of Independence to the 1745 rising. The castle was briefly the prison of Flora Macdonald. Marvellous views from the top of the curtain wall. Close by are the remains of a chapel with beautiful architectural detail.

Location: OS49 NM882 344. By Loch Etive, 3 1/2 m from Oban on the A85.

Opening Times: Apr - Sept: daily, 9.30am - 6.30pm, last ticket 1/2 hr before closing. Oct - Mar: Mon - Sat, 9.30am - 4.30pm; Suns, 2 - 4.30pm.

Admission: Adult £2, Child 75p, Conc. £1.50. 10% discount for groups (10+).

Partially suitable. By arrangement. Free pre-booked school visits. In grounds, on leads.

GLENCOE

Tel: 01855 811307/811729 (during closed season) **Fax:** 01855 811772

Ballachulish, Argyll PA39 4HX

Owner: The National Trust for Scotland   **Contact:** Derrick Warner

This is a breathtaking, dramatic glen with jagged peaks incised on either side by cascading water. In 1692 many of the MacDonald clan were massacred by soldiers of King William's army, to whom they had given hospitality. Wildlife abounds and herds of red deer, wildcat and golden eagle enjoy this wilderness area.

Location: OS Ref. NN100 590. Off A82, 17m S of Fort William.

Opening Times: Please contact property for details.

Admission: Please contact property for details.

Ground floor suitable. WC. Guide dogs only.

THE HILL HOUSE

Tel: 01436 673900 **Fax:** 01436 674685

Upper Colquhoun Street, Helensburgh G84 9AJ

Owner: The National Trust for Scotland   **Contact:** Mrs Anne Ellis

Certainly the finest domestic creation of the famous Scottish architect and artist, Charles Rennie Mackintosh. He set this 20th century masterpiece high on a hillside overlooking the Firth of Clyde. Mackintosh also designed furniture, fittings and decorative schemes to complement the house, and suggested a layout for the garden which has been renovated by the Trust.

Location: OS Ref. NS300 820. Off B832, between A82 & A814, 23m NW of Glasgow.

Opening Times: 1 Apr - 31 Oct: daily, 1.30 - 5.30pm (last admission 5pm). Tearoom: 1.30 - 4.30pm. Access may be restricted at peak times and at the discretion of the Property Manager. Groups must pre-book.

Admission: Adult £6, Conc. £4.50, Family £16.50. Groups must book.

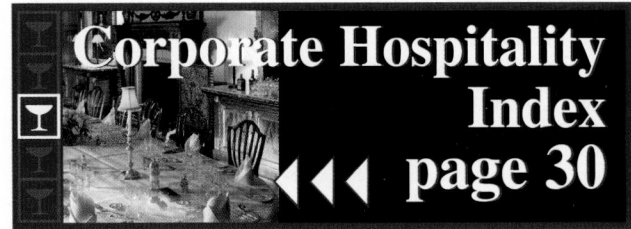

INCHMAHOME PRIORY

Tel: 01877 385294

Port of Menteith

Owner: In the care of Historic Scotland   **Contact:** The Steward

A beautifully situated Augustinian priory on an island in the Lake of Menteith founded in 1238 with much of the building surviving. The five year old Mary Queen of Scots was sent here for safety in 1547.

Location: OS Ref. NN574 005. On an island in Lake of Menteith. Reached by ferry from Port of Menteith, 4m E of Aberfoyle off A81.

Opening Times: 1 Apr - 30 Sept: daily, 9.30am - 6.30pm, last ticket 6pm.

Admission: Adult £3.30, Child £1.20, Conc. £2.50. Charge includes ferry trip.

INVERARAY CASTLE

See page 483 for full page entry.

INVERARAY JAIL

Tel: 01499 302381   **Fax:** 01499 302195

Church Square, Inveraray, Argyll PA32 8TX   **e-mail:** inverarayjail@btclick.com

Owner: Visitor Centres Ltd   **Contact:** J Linley

A living 19th century prison! Uniformed prisoners and warders, life-like figures, imaginative exhibitions, sounds, smells and trials in progress, bring the 1820 courtroom and former county prison back to life. See the 'In Prison Today' exhibition.

Location: OS Ref. NN100 090. Church Square, Inveraray, Argyll.

Opening Times: Apr - Oct: 9.30am - 6pm, last adm. 5pm. Nov - Mar: 10am - 5pm, last adm. 4pm.

Admission: Adult £4.90, Child £2.40, OAP £3.10, Family £13.40. Groups (10+): £3.90, OAP £2.60 (from 2 Apr 2001).

IONA ABBEY & NUNNERY

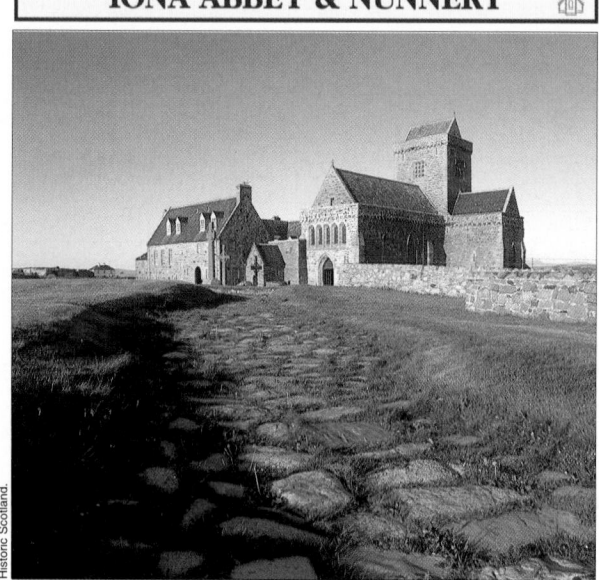

IONA, WEST HIGHLANDS

Owner: In the care of Historic Scotland   *Contact: Chris Calvert*

Tel/Fax: 01681 700512   **e-mail:** hs.ionaabbey@scotland.gov.uk

One of Scotland's most historic and venerated sites, Iona Abbey is a celebrated Christian centre and the burial place for many Scottish kings. The abbey and nunnery grounds house one of the most comprehensive collections of Christian carved stones in Scotland, dating from 600AD to the 1600s. Includes the Columbia Centre, Fionnphort exhibition and giftshop.

Location: OS Ref. NM270 240. Ferry service from Fionnphort, Mull.

Opening Times: All year, daily.

Admission: Adult £2.80, Child (under 16) £1.20, Conc. £2. Columba Centre, exhibition & giftshop: Free.

KILCHURN CASTLE

Tel: 01786 431323

Loch Awe, Dalmally, Argyll

Owner: In the care of Historic Scotland   **Contact:** The Steward

A square tower, built by Sir Colin Campbell of Glenorchy c1550, it was much enlarged in 1693 to give the building, now a ruin, its present picturesque outline. Spectacular views of Loch Awe.

Location: OS Ref. NN133 276. At the NE end of Loch Awe, 2¹/₂ m W of Dalmally.

Opening Times: Ferry service operates in the summer. Tel: 01838 200440 for times.

Admission: Adult £4, Child £2, Conc.£3, Family £10.

MOUNT STUART

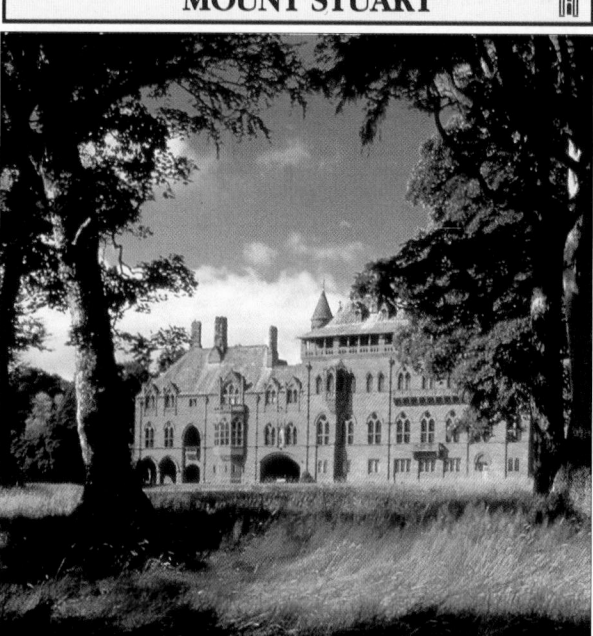

ISLE OF BUTE PA20 9LR

Owner: The Mount Stuart Trust   *Contact: The Administrator*

Tel: 01700 503877   **Fax:** 01700 505313   **e-mail:** contactus@mountstuart.com

Spectacular High Victorian Gothic house, ancestral home of the Marquesses of Bute. Splendid interiors, art collection and architectural detail. Set in 300 acres of stunning woodlands, mature pinetum, arboretum and exotic gardens. Countryside Ranger Service. Scottish Tourism Oscar winner.

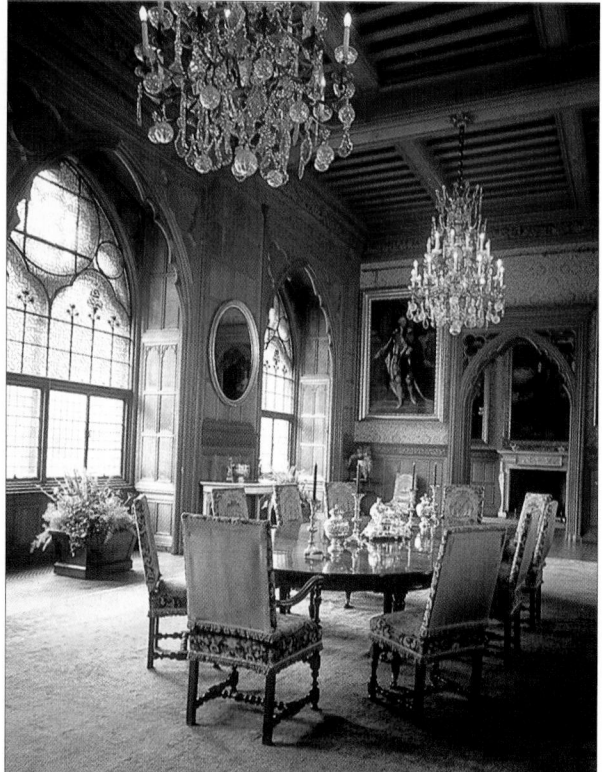

Location: OS Ref. NS100 600. 5m S of Rothesay Pierhead, local bus service to house. Frequent ferry service from Wemyss Bay, Renfrewshire & Colintraive, Argyll. 1 hr from Glasgow Airport.

Opening Times: May - Sept: daily (except Tues & Thurs). House: 11am - 5pm. Gardens: 10am - 6pm.

Admission: House & Garden: Adult £6, Child £2.50, Family £15, Season £15. Gardens: Adult £3.50, Child £2, Family £9. Conc. & group rates given. Pre-booked guided tours available. (2000 prices.)

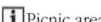 Picnic area.   By arrangement.

ROTHESAY CASTLE

Tel: 01700 502691

Rothesay, Isle of Bute

Owner: In the care of Historic Scotland   **Contact:** The Steward

A favourite residence of the Stuart Kings, this is a wonderful example of a 13th century circular castle of enclosure with 16th century forework containing the Great Hall. Attacked by Vikings in its earlier days.

Location: OS Ref. NS088 646. In Rothesay, Isle of Bute. Ferry from Wemyss Bay on the A78.

Opening Times: 1 Apr - 30 Sept: daily, 9.30am - 6.30pm, last ticket 6pm. 1 Oct - 31 Mar: Mon - Wed & Sats, 9.30am - 4.30pm, Thurs 9.30am - 12 noon, Fris closed, Suns, 2 - 4.30pm, last ticket 4pm.

Admission: Adult £2, Child 75p, Conc. £1.50.

ST BLANE'S CHURCH

Tel: 0131 668 8800

Kingarth, Isle of Bute

Owner: In the care of Historic Scotland

This 12th century Romanesque chapel stands on the site of a 12th century Celtic monastery.

Location: OS Ref. NS090 570. At the S end of the Isle of Bute.

Opening Times: All year: daily.

Admission: Free.

STIRLING CASTLE

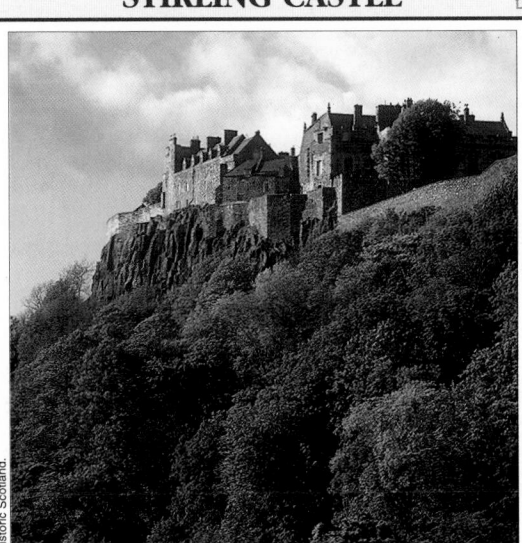

Historic Scotland.

CASTLE WYND, STIRLING FK8 1EJ

Owner: Historic Scotland   *Contact: Neil Young*

Tel: 01786 450000   **Fax:** 01786 464678

Stirling Castle has played a key role in Scottish history, dominating the North–South and East–West routes through Scotland. The battles of Stirling Bridge and Bannockburn were fought in its shadow and Mary Queen of Scots lived here as a child. Marvellous Renaissance architecture and restored Great Hall.

Location: OS Ref. NS790 941. At the top of Castle Wynd in Stirling.

Opening Times: Apr - Sept: 9.30am - 6pm. Oct - Mar: 9.30am - 5pm, last ticket 45 mins before closing.

Admission: Adult £6.50, Child £2, Conc. £5. 10% discount for groups (10+). Free booked school visits, except May - August.

[i] Picnic area. Joint ticket with Argyll's Lodging.   [T] Private hire. Partially suitable. WC. Licensed. [P] Guide dogs.

TOROSAY CASTLE & GARDENS

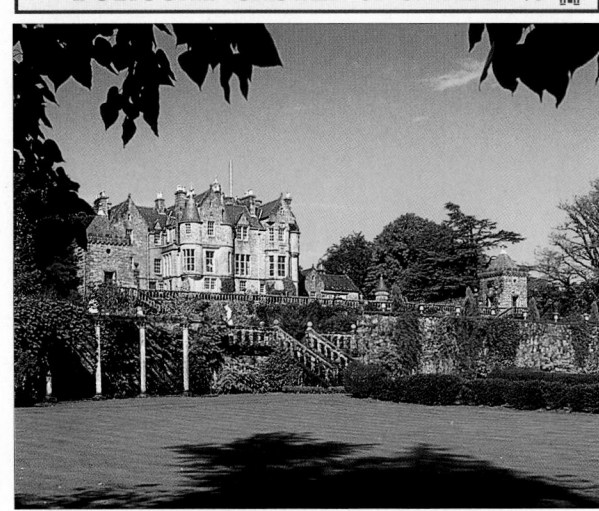

CRAIGNURE, ISLE OF MULL PA65 6AY

Owner/Contact: Mr Chris James

Tel: 01680 812421   **Fax:** 01680 812470   **e-mail:** torosay@aol.com

Torosay Castle and Gardens set on the magnificent Island of Mull, was completed in 1858 by the eminent architect David Bryce in the Scottish baronial style, and is surrounded by 12 acres of spectacular gardens which offer an exciting contrast between formal terraces, impressive statue walk and informal woodland, also rhododendron collection, alpine, walled, bog and oriental gardens. The house offers family history, portraits, scrapbooks and antiques in an informal and relaxed atmosphere.

Location: OS Ref. NM730 350. 1½ m SE of Craignure by A849.

Opening Times: House: Easter - mid-Oct: daily, 10.30am - 5.30pm, last admission 5pm. Gardens: All year: daily, 9am - 7pm or daylight hours in winter.

Admission: Adult £4.50, Child £1.50, Conc. £3.50. Groups: Adult £3.50, Child £1, Conc. £3.50.

 Grounds suitable. WC. In grounds, on leads.

YOUNGER BOTANIC GARDEN BENMORE

Tel: 01369 706261
Fax: 01369 706369

Dunoon, Argyll PA23 8QU

Contact: The Curator

A botanical paradise. Enter the magnificent avenue of giant redwoods and follow trails through the Formal Garden and hillside woodlands with its spectacular outlook over the Holy Loch and the Eachaig Valley.

Location: OS Ref. NS150 850. 7m N of Dunoon on A815.

Opening Times: 1 Mar - 31 Oct: daily, 9.30am - 6pm.

Admission: Adult £3, Child £1, Conc. £2.50, Family £7. Group discounts available.

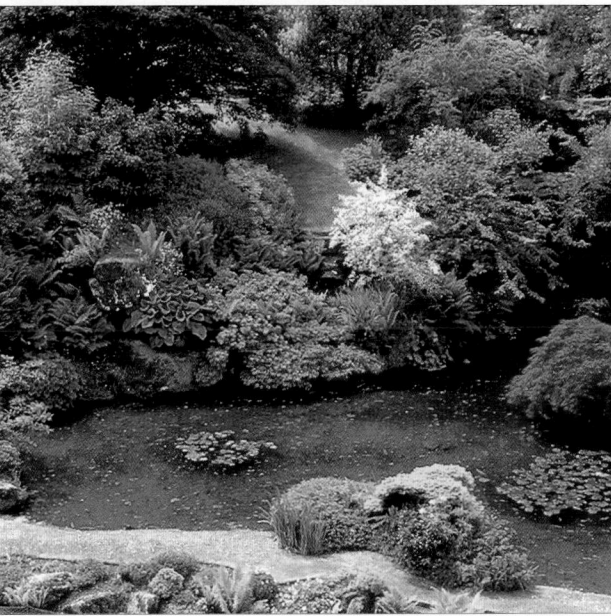

Mount Stuart, West Highlands.

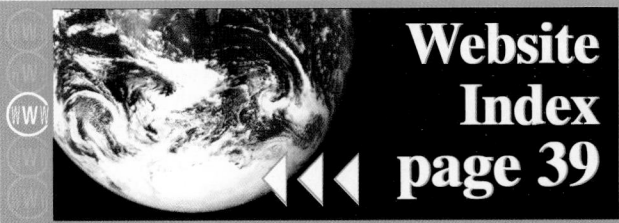

Website Index page 39

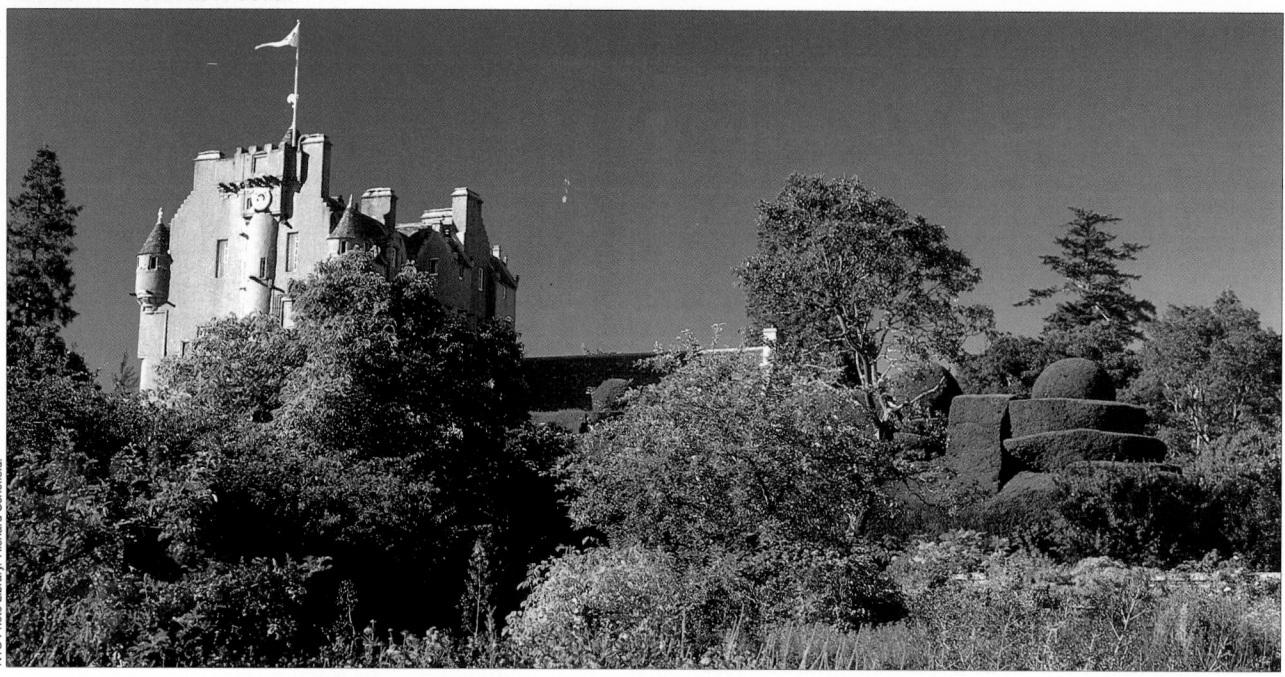

NTS Photo Library/ Richard Schofield

CRATHES CASTLE & GDN
Banchory

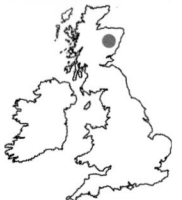

Owner: The National
Trust for Scotland

CONTACT

The Property
Administrator
Crathes Castle
Banchory
AB31 3QJ

Tel: 01330 844525

Fax: 01330 844797

e-mail: crathes@nts.org.uk

LOCATION

OS Ref. NO733 969

On A93, 3m E of Banchory
and 15m W of Aberdeen.

Part of Aberdeenshire's Castle Trail: fairytale-like turrets, gargoyles of fantastic design, superb painted ceilings and the ancient Horn of Leys given in 1323 to Alexander Burnett by King Robert the Bruce, are just a few of the exciting features at this most picturesque castle. The building of the castle began in 1553 and took 40 years to complete. Just over 300 years later, Sir James and Lady Burnett began developing the walled garden and created not just one but eight superb gardens which now provide a riot of colour throughout the summer.

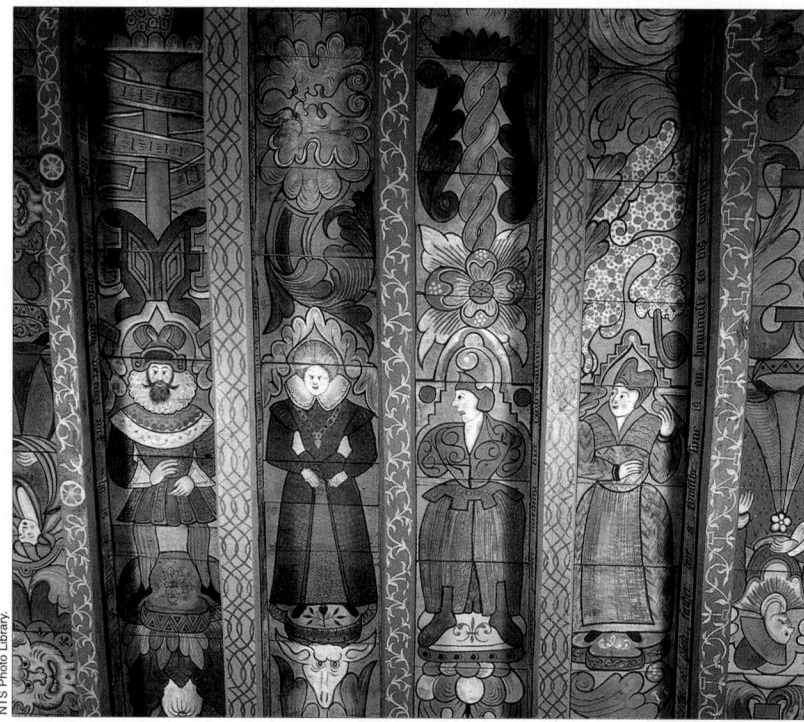

NTS Photo Library.

OPENING TIMES

**Castle, Visitor Centre
& Shop**

1 Apr - 30 Sept: daily,
10.30am - 5.30pm.

1 - 31 Oct: daily,
10.30am - 4.30pm
(last admission to Castle
45mins before closing).

Other times by
appointment.

Plant sales: same dates,
except weekends only
in October.

Licensed Restaurant:
10 Jan - 31 Mar & 1 Nov -
23 Dec: Wed - Sun,
10.30am - 4pm;
1 Apr - 31 Oct: daily,
10.30am - 5.30pm.

To help you to enjoy your
visit, admission to the
Castle is by timed ticket
and entry may be delayed.

Garden & Grounds

All year: daily,
9am - sunset.
Grounds may be closed at
short notice on very busy
days due to the limited
capacity for car parking.

ADMISSION

Castle & Garden

Adult £7.00
Conc.......................£5.00
Family £19.00

Groups
Adult £5.20
Child/School..........£1.00

Car Park £1.00

**Castle or Walled Garden
only**

Adult £4.50
Conc.......................£3.00

🛍
❄️
🍷
♿ Partially suitable.
☕

🍴 Licensed.

🅿

✳️

🎭 Tel. for details.

ARBUTHNOTT HOUSE

Tel: 01561 361226 **Fax:** 01561 320476

Arbuthnott, Laurencekirk AB30 1PA

e-mail: keith@arbuthnott.co.uk

Owner: The Viscount of Arbuthnott **Contact:** The Master of Arbuthnott

Arbuthnott family home for 800 years with formal 17th century walled garden on unusually steep south facing slope. Well maintained grass terraces, herbaceous borders, shrubs and greenhouses.

Location: OS Ref. NO796 751. Off B967 between A90 and A92, 25m S of Aberdeen.

Opening Times: House: 15/16 Apr, 27/28 May, 10/11 Jun, 5/6 & 26/27 Aug. Guided tours: 2 - 5pm. Garden: All year: 9am - 5pm.

Admission: House: £3. Garden: £2.

Ground floor suitable. Obligatory. P ✕ ❄

BALFLUIG CASTLE

Tel: 020 7624 3200

Alford, Aberdeenshire AB33 8EJ

Owner/Contact: Mark Tennant of Balfluig

Small 16th century tower house in farmland, restored in 1967.

Location: OS Ref. NJ586 151. Alford, Aberdeenshire.

Opening Times: Please write to M I Tennant Esq, 30 Abbey Gardens, London NW8 9AT. Occasionally let by the week for holidays. Scottish Tourist Board ***.

Not suitable. ✕ 🛏 1 single, 4 double. ❄

BALMORAL CASTLE (GROUNDS & EXHIBITIONS)

Tel: 013397 42334/42335 **Fax:** 013397 42034

Balmoral, Ballater, Aberdeenshire AB35 5TB

e-mail: info@balmoralcastle.com

Owner: Her Majesty The Queen **Contact:** Captain Roger Wilson

Holiday home of The Royal Family, bought by Prince Albert in 1852. Grounds, gardens and exhibition of paintings and works of art in the Ballroom. Exhibition of royal heraldry, commemorative china and a display of native wildlife in their natural habitat in the Carriage Hall. Display of carriages and Upper Deeside Art Society exhibition on view in the Stables.

Location: OS Ref. NO256 951. Off A93 between Ballater and Braemar. 50m W of Aberdeen.

Opening Times: 12 Apr - 31 Jul: daily, 10am - 5pm (last recommended admission 4pm).

Admission: Adult £4.50, Child (5-16yrs) £1, OAP £3.50.

BALVENIE CASTLE

Tel: 01340 820121

Dufftown

Owner: In the care of Historic Scotland **Contact:** The Steward

Picturesque ruins of 13th century moated stronghold originally owned by the Comyns. Visited by Edward I in 1304 and by Mary Queen of Scots in 1562. Occupied by Cumberland in 1746.

Location: OS Ref. NJ326 408. At Dufftown on A941.

Opening Times: 1 Apr - 30 Sept: daily, 9.30am - 6.30pm, last ticket 6pm.

Admission: Adult £1.50, Child 50p, Conc. £1.10.

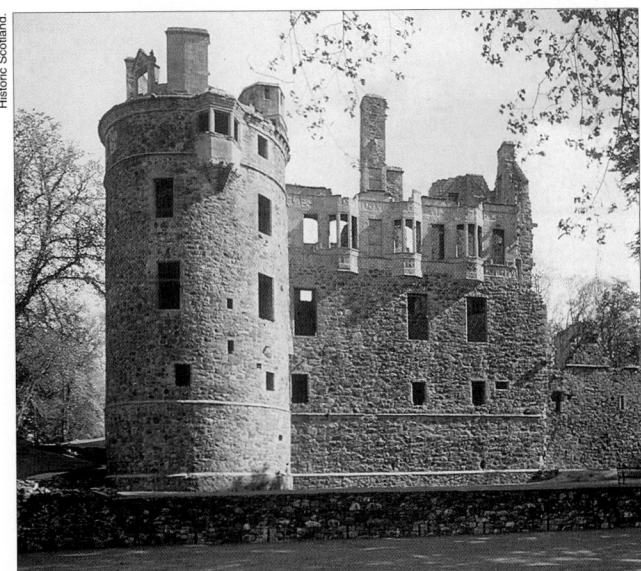

Historic Scotland.

Huntly Castle, Grampian Highlands.

BRAEMAR CASTLE

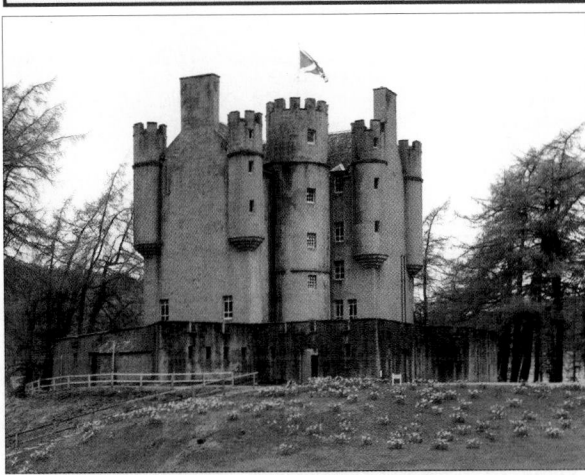

BRAEMAR, ABERDEENSHIRE AB35 5XR

Owner: Capt A A C Farquharson of Invercauld *Contact: Bruce & Carrol McCudden*

Tel/Fax: 013397 41219 **e-mail:** invercauld@freenet.com

Braemar Castle has been the ancestral home of the Clan Farquharson for over 200 years. The 'Black' Colonel of Inverey, the enemy clan leader, attacked and burned the castle in 1689 and after being rebuilt was garrisoned by Hanoverian troops for some 60 years after the 1745 Jacobite rebellion. In some of the rooms you can see the 'graffiti' of the English soldiers. Nowadays, the castle is peaceful, and this family home attracts thousands of visitors each year to see the impressive selection of furnished rooms covering decades of the Farquharson history. A massive iron yett leads you to the pit dungeon, which was a gruesome place in years gone by.

Location: OS Ref. NO156 924. ¹/₂ m NE of Braemar on A93.

Opening Times: 1 Apr - 31 Oct: Sat - Thur (plus Fris during Jul & Aug), 10am - 6pm (last entry 5.30pm).

Admission: Adult £3, Child £1, Conc. £2.50.

ℹ Picnic area. 📷 Not suitable. By arrangement. P 🍴
🐕 In grounds on leads.

BRODIE CASTLE

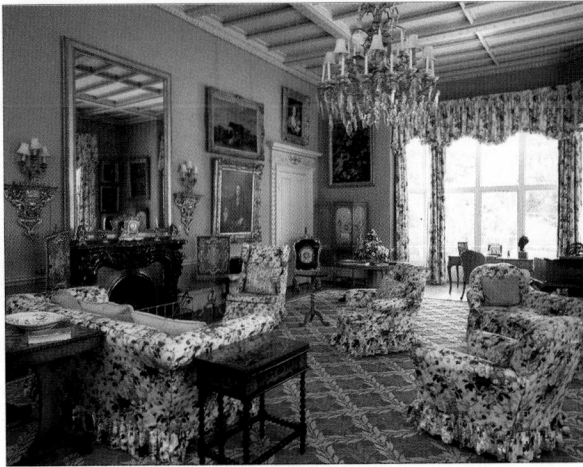

FORRES, MORAY IV36 0TE

Owner: The National Trust for Scotland *Contact: Dr Stephanie Blackden*

Tel: 01309 641371 **Fax:** 01309 641600

This imposing Castle stands in rich Morayshire parkland. The lime harled building is a typical 'Z' plan tower house with ornate corbelled battlements and bartizans, with 17th & 19th century additions. The interior has unusual plaster ceilings, a major art collection, porcelain and fine furniture. There is a woodland walk by a large pond with access to wildlife observation hides. In springtime the grounds are carpeted with many varieties of daffodils for which Brodie Castle is rightly famous.

Location: OS Ref. NH980 577. Off A96 4¹/₂ m W of Forres and 24m E of Inverness.

Opening Times: Castle & Shop: 1 Apr - 30 Sept: Mon - Sat, 11am - 5.30pm, Suns, 1.30 - 5.30pm; weekends in Oct, Sats, 11am - 5.30pm, Suns, 1.30 - 5.30pm (last admission 4.30pm). Tearoom closes at 4.30pm. Other times by appointment. Grounds: All year: daily, 9.30am - sunset.

Admission: Adult £6, Conc. £4.50, Family £16.50. Groups: Adult £4.80, Child/Schools £1. Grounds only: £1 honesty box.

   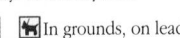 🐕 In grounds, on leads.

Grampian
Scotland

CANDACRAIG GARDEN & GALLERY   Tel: 01975 651226 Fax: 01975 651391

Candacraig Gardens, Strathdon AB36 8XT
Owner/Contact: Harry Young
1820s B listed walled display garden, art gallery and specialist plant nursery. Wedding ceremonies conducted in beautiful Victorian Gothic marriage room.
Location: OS Ref. NJ339 110. On A944 1½ m SW of Strathdon, 20m from Alford.
Opening Times: 1 May - 30 Sept: daily, 10am - 6pm.
Admission: Donation box. Pre-arranged groups: Adult £1, Child Free.

CASTLE FRASER & GARDEN

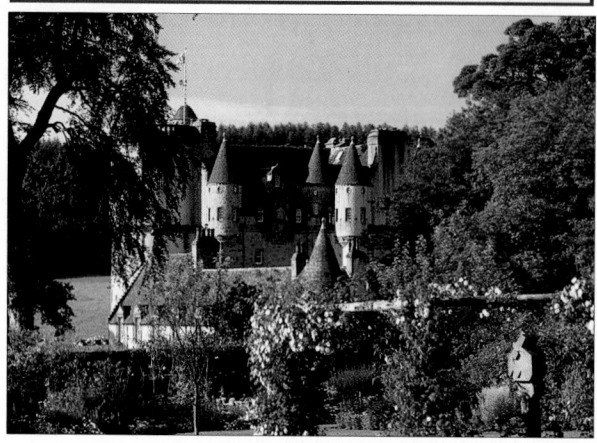

SAUCHEN, INVERURIE AB51 7LD
Owner: The National Trust for Scotland   *Contact:* Eric Wilkinson

Tel: 01330 833463

Over 400 years of history could be told if the stout walls of Castle Fraser could speak. Begun in 1575 by the 6th Laird, Michael Fraser, the two low wings contribute to the scale and magnificence of the towers rising above them, combining to make this the largest and most elaborate of the Scottish castles built on the 'Z' plan. The stunning simplicity of the Great Hall, which occupies the entire first floor of the main block, with its striking fireplace, almost 3 metres wide, immediately creates for the visitor the atmosphere of past centuries.
Location: OS Ref. NJ723 125. Off A944, 4m N of Dunecht & 16m W of Aberdeen.
Opening Times: Castle: 13 Apr - 31 May & 1 - 30 Sept: daily, 1.30 - 5.30pm. 1 Jun - 31 Aug: daily, 11am - 5.30pm; weekends in Oct, 1.30 - 5.30pm (last admission 4.45pm). Shop & Café: open at 12.30pm when Castle opens at 1.30pm. Garden: All year: daily, 9.30am - 6pm. Grounds: All year: daily, 9.30am - sunset.
Admission: Castle & Garden: Adult £6, Conc. £4.50, Family £16.50. Groups: Adult £4.80. Child/School £1. Garden & grounds only: Adult £2, Conc. £1.30, Family £6. Groups: Adult £1.60, Child/School £1. Car Park: All year: £1.

CORGARFF CASTLE   Tel: 013398 83635

Strathdon
Owner: In the care of Historic Scotland   **Contact:** The Steward
A 16th century tower house converted into a barracks for Hanoverian troops in 1748. Its last military use was to control the smuggling of illicit whisky between 1827 and 1831. Still complete and with star-shaped fortification.
Location: OS Ref. NJ255 086. 8m W of Strathdon on A939. 14m NW of Ballater.
Opening Times: 1 Apr - 30 Sept: daily, 9.30am - 6.30pm. 1 Oct - 31 Mar: Sats, 9.30am - 4.30pm. Suns, 2 - 4.30pm, last admission ½ hr before closing.
Admission: Adult £2.80, Child £1, Conc. £2.

CRATHES CASTLE & GARDEN   See page 488 for full page entry.

CRAIGSTON CASTLE   Tel: 01888 551228/551640

Turriff, Aberdeenshire AB53 5PX
Owner: William Pratesi Urquhart   **Contact:** Mrs Fiona Morrison
Built in 1607 to John Urquhart Tutor of Cromarty's individualistic plan. An arch and ornate sculptured balcony joins two towers, one noticeably wider than the other, to accommodate the Laird's private apartments. The largely unchanged interior, still lived in by the Urquhart family, includes carved portraits of the Scottish Kings.
Location: OS Ref. NJ762 550. On B9105, 4½ m NE of Turriff.
Opening Times: 22 Jul - 5 Aug: daily (closed Mons & Tues), 10am - 4pm. 25 Aug - 9 Sept: daily (closed Mons & Tues), 10am - 4pm. Groups throughout the year by appointment. (2000 details.)
Admission: Adult £3.50, Child £1, OAP £3, Student £1.50. (2000 details.)

 Not suitable. Obligatory. 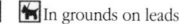 In grounds on leads.

CRUICKSHANK BOTANIC GARDEN   Tel: 01224 272704 Fax: 01224 272703

St Machar Drive, Aberdeen AB24 3UU
Owner: University of Aberdeen   **Contact:** R B Rutherford
Extensive collection of shrubs, herbaceous and alpine plants and trees. Rock and water gardens.
Location: OS Ref. NJ938 084. In old Aberdeen.
Opening Times: All year: Mon - Fri, 9am - 4.30pm. May - Sept: Sats & Suns, 2 - 5pm.
Admission: Free.

DALLAS DHU DISTILLERY   Tel: 01309 676548

Forres
Owner: In the care of Historic Scotland   **Contact:** The Steward
A completely preserved time capsule of the distiller's craft. Wander at will through this fine old Victorian distillery then enjoy a dram. Visitor centre, shop and audio-visual theatre.
Location: OS Ref. NJ035 566. 1m S of Forres off the A940.
Opening Times: 1 Apr - 30 Sept: daily, 9.30am - 6.30pm, last ticket 6pm. 1 Oct - 31 Mar: Mon - Sat, 9.30am - 4.30pm, Suns, 2 - 4.30pm, last ticket 4pm. Closed Thurs pm and Fris in winter.
Admission: Adult £3, Child £1, Conc. £2.30.

DELGATIE CASTLE

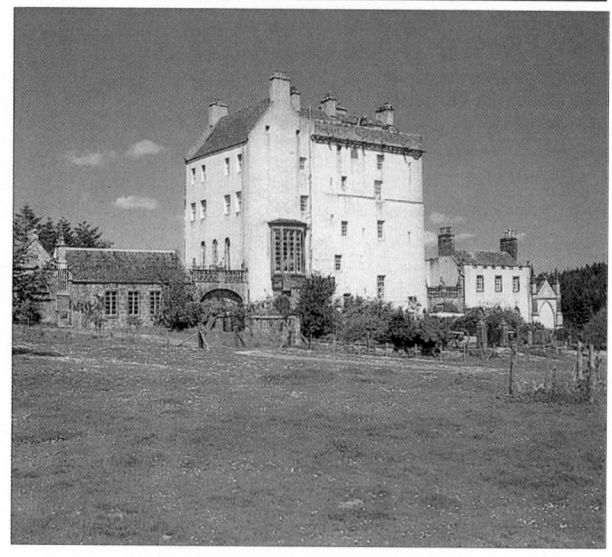

TURRIFF, ABERDEENSHIRE AB53 5TD
Owner: Delgatie Castle Trust   *Contact:* Mrs Joan Johnson

Tel/Fax: 01888 563479 **e-mail:** jjohnson@delgatie-castle.freeserve.co.uk

11th century castle which has largely remained in the Hay family for the last 650 years and is now officially the Clan Hay centre. Mary Queen of Scots stayed here in 1562. Her bed-chamber is on view. Painted ceilings dated 1592 and 1597. Widest turnpike stair of its kind in Scotland. Lake and woodland walks.
Location: OS Ref. NJ754 506. Off A947 Aberdeen to Banff Road.
Opening Times: 2 Apr - 25 Oct: 10am - 5pm.
Admission: Adult £3, Child/OAP £2.

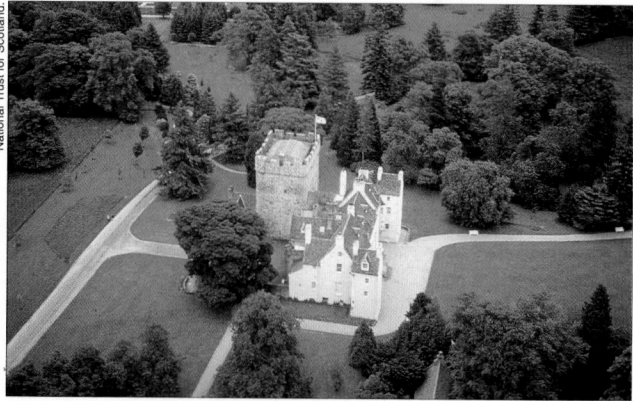

Drum Castle, Grampian Highlands.

DRUM CASTLE

Tel: 01330 811204

Drumoak, by Banchory AB31 3EY
Owner: The National Trust for Scotland   **Contact:** The Property Manager
The combination over the years of a 13th century square tower, a very fine Jacobean mansion house and the additions of the Victorian lairds make Drum Castle unique among Scottish castles. Owned for 653 years by one family, the Irvines, every stone and every room is steeped in history. Superb furniture and paintings provide a visual feast for visitors. In the 16th century chapel, the stained glass windows, the font copied from the Saxon one in Winchester Cathedral and the Augsburg silver Madonna, all add immense interest for visitors.
Location: OS Ref. NJ796 004. Off A93, 3m W of Peterculter and 10m W of Aberdeen.
Opening Times: Castle: 13 Apr - 31 May & 1 - 30 Sept: daily, 1.30 - 5.30pm. 1 Jun - 31 Aug: daily, 11am - 5.30pm; weekends in Oct: 1.30 - 5.30pm (last admission 4.45pm). Garden: same dates, daily, 10am - 6pm. Grounds: All year, daily, 9.30am - sunset.
Admission: Castle & Garden: Adult £6, Conc. £4.50, Family £16.50. Groups: Adult £4.80, Child/ School £1. Garden & Grounds only: £1.

DRUMMUIR CASTLE

Tel: 01542 810332 **Fax:** 01542 810302

Drummuir, by Keith, Banffshire AB55 5JE
Owner: The Gordon-Duff Family   **Contact:** Liz Robson
Castellated Victorian Gothic-style castle built in 1847 by Admiral Duff. 60ft high lantern tower with fine plasterwork. Family portraits, interesting artefacts and other paintings. Organic walled garden and plant sales.
Location: OS Ref. NO881 839. Midway between Keith (5m) and Dufftown, off the B9014.
Opening Times: 25/26 Aug, 1/2 & 5 - 26 Sept: Tours at 2pm & 3pm.
Admission: Adult £2, Child £1.50. Pre-arranged groups: Adult £2, Child £1.50.

Obligatory. P In grounds on leads.

DUFF HOUSE

Tel: 01261 818181 **Fax:** 01261 818900

Banff, AB45 3SX
Contact: The Chamberlain
One of the most imposing and palatial houses in Scotland.
Location: OS Ref. NJ691 634. Banff. 47m NW of Aberdeen on A947.
Opening Times: 1 Apr - 31 Oct: daily, 11am - 5pm. 1 Nov - 31 Mar: Thur - Sun, 11am - 4pm.
Admission: Adult £3.50, Conc. £2.50, Family £8.50. Groups (10+): £2.50.

DUNNOTTAR CASTLE

Tel: 01569 762173

The Lodge, Stonehaven AB39 2TL   **Contact:** P McKenzie
Spectacular ruin. Impregnable fortress to the Earls Marischals of Scotland.
Location: OS Ref. NO881 839. Just off A92. 1½ m SE of Stonehaven.
Opening Times: Easter weekend - 11 Oct: Mon - Sat, 9am - 6pm. Suns, 2 - 5pm. 1 Nov - Easter weekend: Mon - Fri, 9am - sunset (closed weekends). Last admission: 30 mins before closing.
Admission: Adult £3.50, Child £1.

DUTHIE PARK & WINTER GARDENS   **Tel:** 01224 585310 **Fax:** 01224 210532

Polmuir Road, Aberdeen, Grampian Highlands AB11 7TH
Owner: Aberdeen City Council   **Contact:** Alan Findlay
45 acres of parkland and gardens. Glasshouses.
Location: OS Ref. NJ97 044. Just N of River Dee, 1m S of city centre.
Opening Times: All year: daily from 9.30pm.
Admission: Free.

ELGIN CATHEDRAL

Tel: 01343 547171

Elgin
Owner: Historic Scotland   **Contact:** The Steward
When entire this was perhaps the most beautiful of Scottish cathedrals, known as the Lantern of the North. 13th century, much modified after almost being destroyed in 1390 by Alexander Stewart, the infamous 'Wolf of Badenoch'. The octagonal chapterhouse is the finest in Scotland. You can see the Bishop's home at Spynie Palace, 2m north of the town.
Location: OS Ref. NJ223 630. In Elgin on the A96.
Opening Times: 1 Apr - 30 Sept: daily, 9.30am - 6.30pm, last ticket 6pm. 1 Oct - 31 Mar: Mon - Sat, 9.30am - 4.30pm, Suns, 2 - 4.30pm, last ticket 4pm. Closed Thurs pm & Fris in winter.
Admission: Adult £2.80, Child £1, Conc. £2. Joint entry ticket with Spynie Palace: Adult £3.30, Child £1.20, Conc. £2.80.

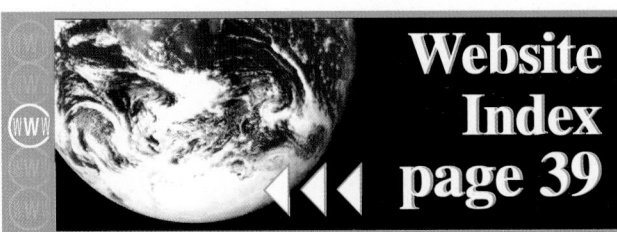

Website Index page 39

FASQUE

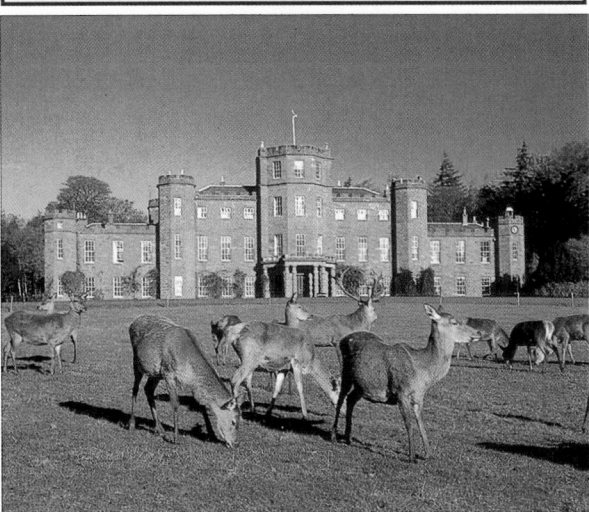

FETTERCAIRN, LAURENCEKIRK, KINCARDINESHIRE AB30 1DN
Owner: *Charles Gladstone* **Contact:** *Scott Traynor*
Tel/Fax: 01561 340569
Fasque is a spectacular example of a Victorian 'Upstairs-Downstairs' stately home. Bought by Sir John Gladstone in 1829, it was home to William Gladstone, four times Prime Minister, for much of his life. In front of the house red deer roam in the park, and behind the hills rise dramatically towards the Highlands. Inside very little has changed since Sir John's days. Fasque is not a museum, but rather an unspoilt old family home.
Location: OS Ref. NO648 755. On the B974, 1m N of Fettercairn, 4m from A90. Aberdeen/ Dundee 35m.
Opening Times: 1 May - 30 Sept: daily, 11am - 5.30pm. Groups by arrangement any time.
Admission: Adult £4, Child £1.50, OAP £3.

By arrangement. P Tel. for details.

FYVIE CASTLE

TURRIFF, ABERDEENSHIRE AB53 8JS
Owner: *The National Trust for Scotland*   **Contact:** *The Property Manager*
Tel: 01651 891266   **Fax:** 01651 891107
The south front of this magnificent building employs a plethora of crow-stepped gables, turrets, sculpted dormers and finials in the form of musicians, to create a marvellous façade. The five towers of the castle bear witness to the five families who have owned it. Fyvie Castle boasts the finest wheel stair in Scotland and there is a superb collection of arms and armour and paintings, including works by Batoni, Raeburn, Romney, Gainsborough, Opie and Hoppner.
Location: OS Ref. NJ763 393. Off A947, 8m SE of Turriff, and 25m N of Aberdeen.
Opening Times: Castle: 13 Apr - 31 May and 1 - 30 Sept: daily, 1.30 - 5.30pm; 1 Jun - 31 Aug: daily, 11am - 5.30pm; weekends in Oct: 1.30 - 5.30pm (last admission 4.45pm). Tearoom & Shop: open at 12.30pm when Castle opens at 1.30pm. Grounds: All year, daily, 9.30am - sunset.
Admission: Adult £6, Conc. £4.50, Family £16.50. Groups: Adult £4.80, Child/ School £1.

HADDO HOUSE

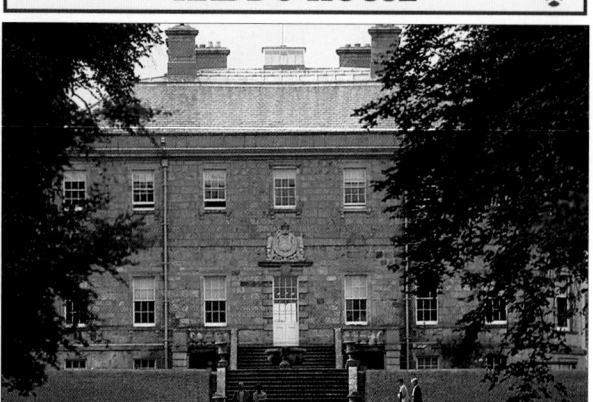

TARVES, ELLON, ABERDEENSHIRE AB41 0ER

Owner: The National Trust for Scotland   *Contact: Craig Ferguson*

Tel: 01651 851440   **Fax:** 01651 851888

This appealing house was designed by William Adam in 1731 for William, 2nd Earl of Aberdeen. Much of the splendid interior is 'Adam Revival' carried out about 1880 for John, 7th Earl and 1st Marquess of Aberdeen and his Countess, Ishbel. It is arguably the most elegant house in the north east, a classic English-style stately home transplanted to Scotland. Features of the house include the Italianate sweeping twin staircases at the front of the house, the atmospheric library and the subtlety of the great curving corridor.

Location: OS Ref. NJ868 348. Off B999, 4m N of Pitmedden, 10m NW of Ellon.

Opening Times: House: 13 - 16 Apr & 1 May - 30 Sept: daily, 1.30 - 5.30pm; weekends in Oct: 1.30 - 5.30pm (last admission 4.45pm). Shop & Tearoom: same dates, 11am - 5.30pm. Shop also open weekends in Mar. & Apr, 11am - 5.30pm. Tearoom: open weekends in Mar & daily in Apr, 11am - 5.30pm. Garden: 1 Apr - 31 Oct: daily, 9.30am - 6pm; 1 Nov - 31 Mar: daily, 9.30am - 4pm. Country Park: All year, daily, 9.30am - sunset.

Admission: Adult £6, Conc. £4.50, Family £16.50. Groups: Adult £4.80, Child/School £1.

HUNTLY CASTLE

Tel: 01466 793191

Huntly

Owner: In the care of Historic Scotland   **Contact:** The Steward

Known also as Strathbogie Castle, this glorious ruin stands in a beautiful setting on the banks of the River Deveron. Famed for its fine heraldic sculpture and inscribed stone friezes.

Location: OS Ref. NJ532 407. In Huntly on the A96. N side of the town.

Opening Times: 1 Apr - 30 Sept: daily, 9.30am - 6.30pm, last ticket 6pm. 1 Oct - 31 Mar: Mon - Sat, 9.30am - 4.30pm, Suns, 2 - 4.30pm, last ticket 4pm. Closed Thur pm & Fris in winter.

Admission: Adult £2.80, Child £1, Conc £2.

KILDRUMMY CASTLE

Tel: 01975 571331

Alford, Aberdeenshire

Owner: In the care of Historic Scotland   **Contact:** The Steward

Though ruined, the best example in Scotland of a 13th century castle with a curtain wall, four round towers, hall and chapel of that date. The seat of the Earls of Mar, it was dismantled after the first Jacobite rising in 1715.

Location: OS Ref. NJ455 164. 10m W of Alford on the A97. 16m SSW of Huntley.

Opening Times: 1 Apr - 30 Sept: daily, 9.30am - 6.30pm, last ticket 6pm.

Admission: Adult £2, Child 75p, Conc. £1.50.

KILDRUMMY CASTLE GARDEN

Tel: 01975 571203 / 571277

Kildrummy, Aberdeenshire   **Contact:** Alastair J Laing

Ancient quarry, shrub and alpine gardens renowned for their interest and variety. Water gardens below ruined castle.

Location: OS Ref. NJ455 164. On A97 off A944 10m SW of Alford. 16m SSW of Huntley.

Opening Times: Apr - Oct: daily, 10am - 5pm.

Admission: Adult £2, Child free.

Plant Sales Index ◄◄◄ page 47

LEITH HALL

Tel: 01464 831216   **Fax:** 01464 831594

Huntly, Aberdeenshire AB54 4NQ

Owner: The National Trust for Scotland   **Contact:** The Property Manager

This mansion house is built around a courtyard and was the home of the Leith family for almost 400 years. With an enviable family record of military service over the centuries, the house contains a unique collection of military memorabilia displayed in an exhibition 'For Crown and Country'. The graciously furnished rooms are a delight to wander through and present a fine impression of the lifestyle of the Leith family.

Location: OS Ref. NJ541 298. B9002, 1m W of Kennethmont, 7m S of Huntley.

Opening Times: House & tearoom: 13 - 16 Apr & 1 May - 30 Sept: daily, 1.30 - 5.30pm; weekends in Oct: 1.30 - 5.30pm (last admission 4.45pm). Garden & Grounds: All year, daily, 9.30am - sunset.

Admission: Adult £6, Conc. £4.50, Family £16.50. Groups: Adult £4.80, Child/School £1. Gardens & grounds only: Adult £2, Conc. £1.30, Family £6. Groups: Adult £1.60, Child/School £1.

Partially suitable. WC.

MONYMUSK WALLED GARDEN

Tel: 01467 651543

Home Farm, Monymusk, Aberdeen AB51 7HL

Owner/Contact: Mrs E Whyte

Mainly herbaceous plants in walled garden setting.

Location: OS Ref. NJ692 152. N side of B993, ¹/₂ m E of Monymusk village.

Opening Times: Nov - Mar: Mons, Weds, Fris & Sats, 10am - 3pm, Suns, 12 noon - 3pm. Apr - Oct: Mon - Sat, 10am - 5pm, Suns, 12 noon - 5pm.

Admission: Donations welcome.

PITMEDDEN GARDEN

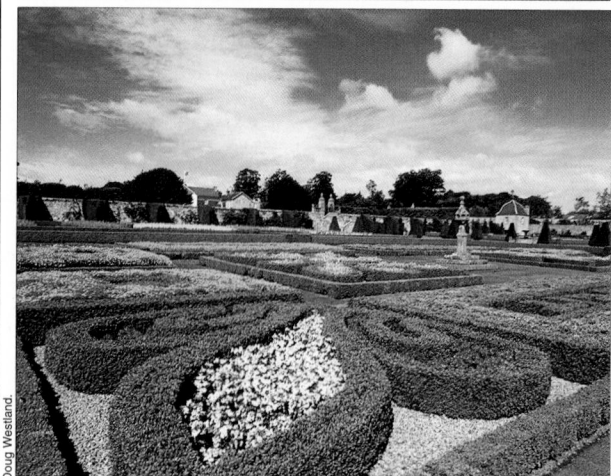

Doug Westland.

ELLON, ABERDEENSHIRE AB41 0PD

Owner: The National Trust for Scotland   *Contact: The Property Manager*

Tel: 01651 842352   **Fax:** 01651 843188

The centrepiece of this property is the Great Garden which was originally laid out in 1675 by Sir Alexander Seton, 1st Baronet of Pitmedden. The elaborate designs, inspired by the garden at the Palace of Holyroodhouse in Edinburgh, have been painstakingly recreated for the enjoyment of visitors. The 100 acre estate contains the very fine Museum of Farming Life, which presents a vivid picture of the lives and times of bygone days when the horse was the power in front of the plough and farm machinery was less complicated than it is today.

Location: OS Ref. NJ885 280. On A920 1m W of Pitmedden village and 14m N of Aberdeen.

Opening Times: Garden, Visitor Centre, museum & tearoom: 1 May - 30 Sept: daily, 10am - 5.30pm (last admission 5pm). Grounds: All year, daily.

Admission: Adult: £5, Conc. £4, Family £14. Groups: Adult £4, Child/School £1.

PLUSCARDEN ABBEY

Tel: 01343 890257   **Fax:** 01343 890258
e-mail: monks@pluscardenabbey.org

Nr Elgin, Moray IV30 8UA   **Contact:** Father Giles

Valliscaulian, founded 1230.

Location: OS Ref. NJ142 576. On a minor road 6m SW of Elgin. Follow B9010 for first mile.

Opening Times: All year: 4.45am - 8.30pm. Shop open 8.30am - 5pm.

Admission: Free.

PROVOST SKENE'S HOUSE

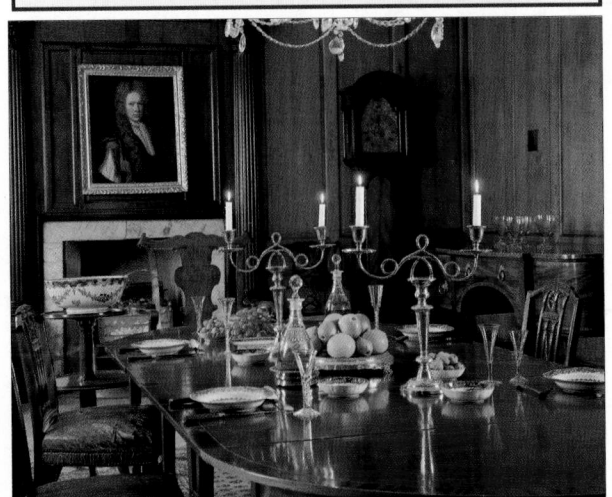

45 GUEST ROW, OFF BROAD STREET, ABERDEEN AB10 1AS

Owner: *Aberdeen City Council*   **Contact:** *Christine Rew*

Tel: 01224 641086 **Fax:** 01224 632133

Built in the 16th century, Provost Skene's House is one of Aberdeen's few remaining examples of early burgh architecture. Splendid room settings include a suite of Georgian rooms, an Edwardian nursery, magnificent 17th century plaster ceilings and wood panelling. Costume gallery features changing displays of historic dress. The painted gallery houses the most important cycle of religious painting in North East Scotland.

Location: OS Ref. NJ943 064. Aberdeen city centre, off Broad Street.

Opening Times: All year: Mon - Sat, 10am - 5pm, Suns, 1 - 4pm (closed 25/26/31 Dec & 1/2 Jan).

Admission: Free.

i No photography in house. 📷 🍽 Small functions. ♿ Not suitable. 🖥
🏃 By arrangement. P Nearby. 🏛 🐕 Guide dogs only. ❄ (IW)

ST MACHAR'S CATHEDRAL TRANSEPTS 🏛   **Tel:** 0131 668 8800

Old Aberdeen

Owner: In the care of Historic Scotland

The nave and towers of the Cathedral remain in use as a church, and the ruined transepts are in care. In the south transept is the fine altar tomb of Bishop Dunbar (1514 - 32).

Location: OS Ref. NJ939 088. In old Aberdeen. 1/2 m N of King's College.

Admission: Free.

SPYNIE PALACE 🏛   **Tel:** 01343 546358

Elgin

Owner: In the care of Historic Scotland   **Contact:** The Steward

Spynie Palace was the residence of the Bishops of Moray from the 14th century to 1686. The site is dominated by the massive tower built by Bishop David Stewart (1461-77) and affords spectacular views across Spynie Loch.

Location: OS Ref. NJ231 659. 2m N of Elgin off the A941.

Opening Times: 1 Apr - 30 Sept: daily, 9.30am - 6.30pm. 1 Oct - 31 Mar: Sats, 9.30am - 4.30pm, Suns, 2 - 4.30pm. Last ticket 30 mins before closing.

Admission: Adult £2, Child 75p, Conc. £1.50. Joint entry ticket with Elgin Cathedral: Adult £3.30, Child £1.20, Conc. £2.50.

TOLQUHON CASTLE 🏛   **Tel:** 01651 851286

Aberdeenshire

Owner: In the care of Historic Scotland   **Contact:** The Steward

Tolquhon was built for the Forbes family. The early 15th century tower was enlarged between 1584 and 1589 with a large mansion around the courtyard. Noted for its highly ornamented gatehouse and pleasance.

Location: OS Ref. NJ874 286. 15m N of Aberdeen on the A920. 6m N of Ellon.

Opening Times: 1 Apr - 30 Sept: daily, 9.30am - 6.30pm. 1 Oct - 31 Mar: Sats, 9.30am - 4.30pm, Suns, 2 - 4.30pm. Last ticket 30 mins before closing.

Admission: Adult £2, Child 75p, Conc. £1.50.

National Trust for Scotland.

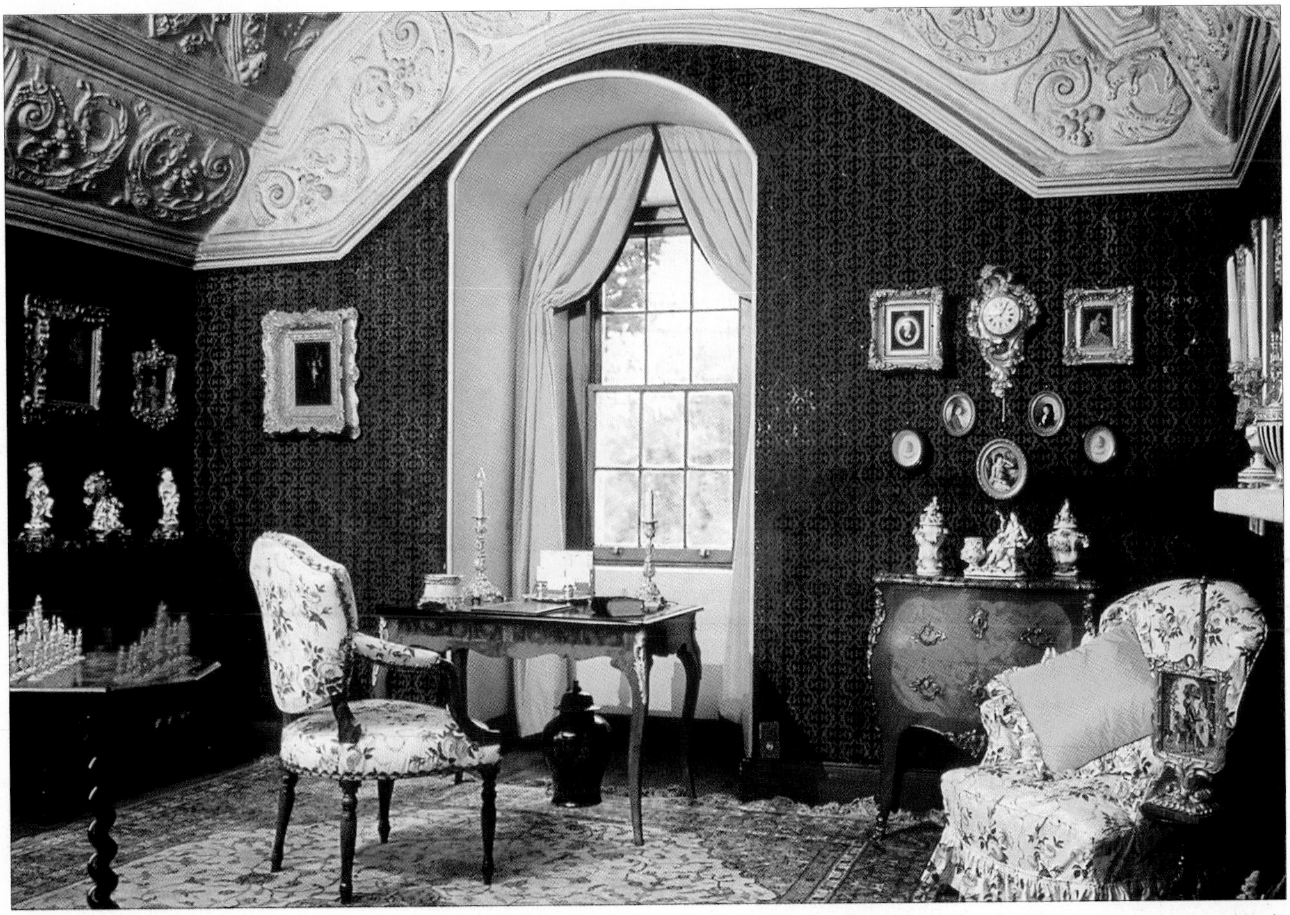

Brodie Castle, Grampian Highlands.

Cawdor Castle

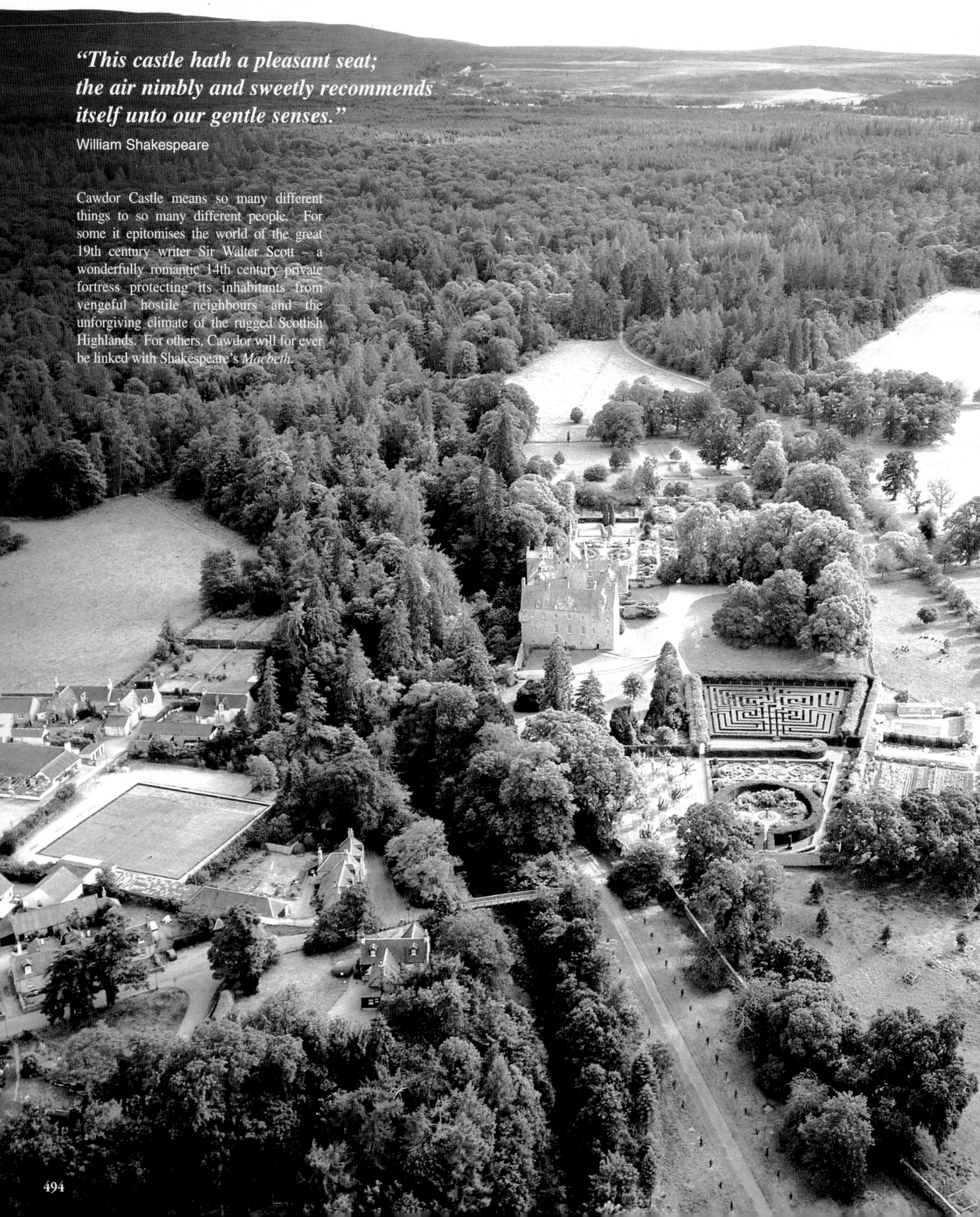

*"This castle hath a pleasant seat;
the air nimbly and sweetly recommends
itself unto our gentle senses."*

William Shakespeare

Cawdor Castle means so many different things to so many different people. For some it epitomises the world of the great 19th century writer Sir Walter Scott – a wonderfully romantic 14th century private fortress protecting its inhabitants from vengeful hostile neighbours and the unforgiving climate of the rugged Scottish Highlands. For others, Cawdor will for ever be linked with Shakespeare's *Macbeth*.

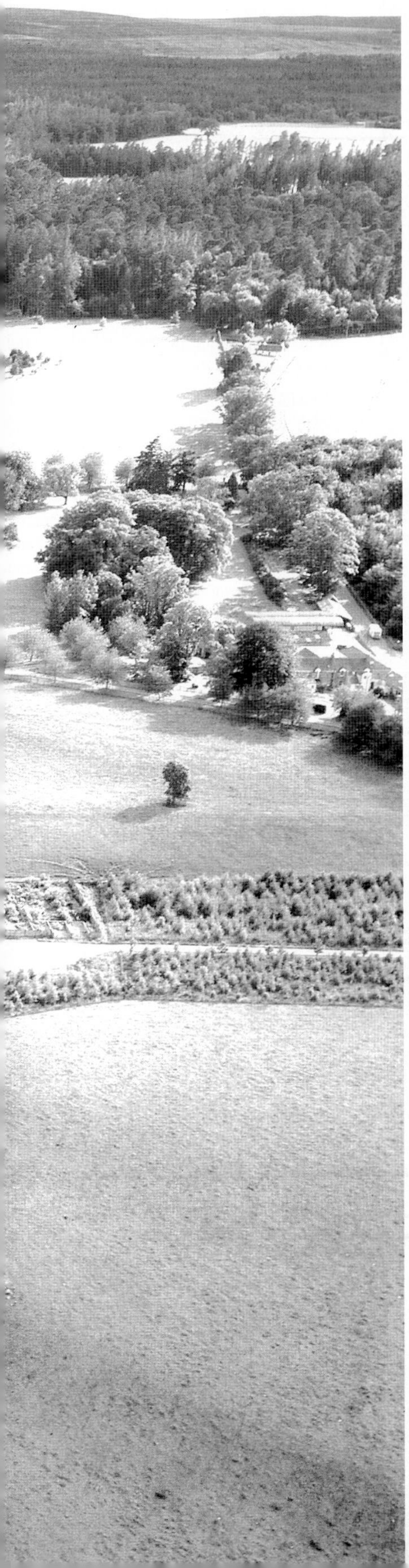

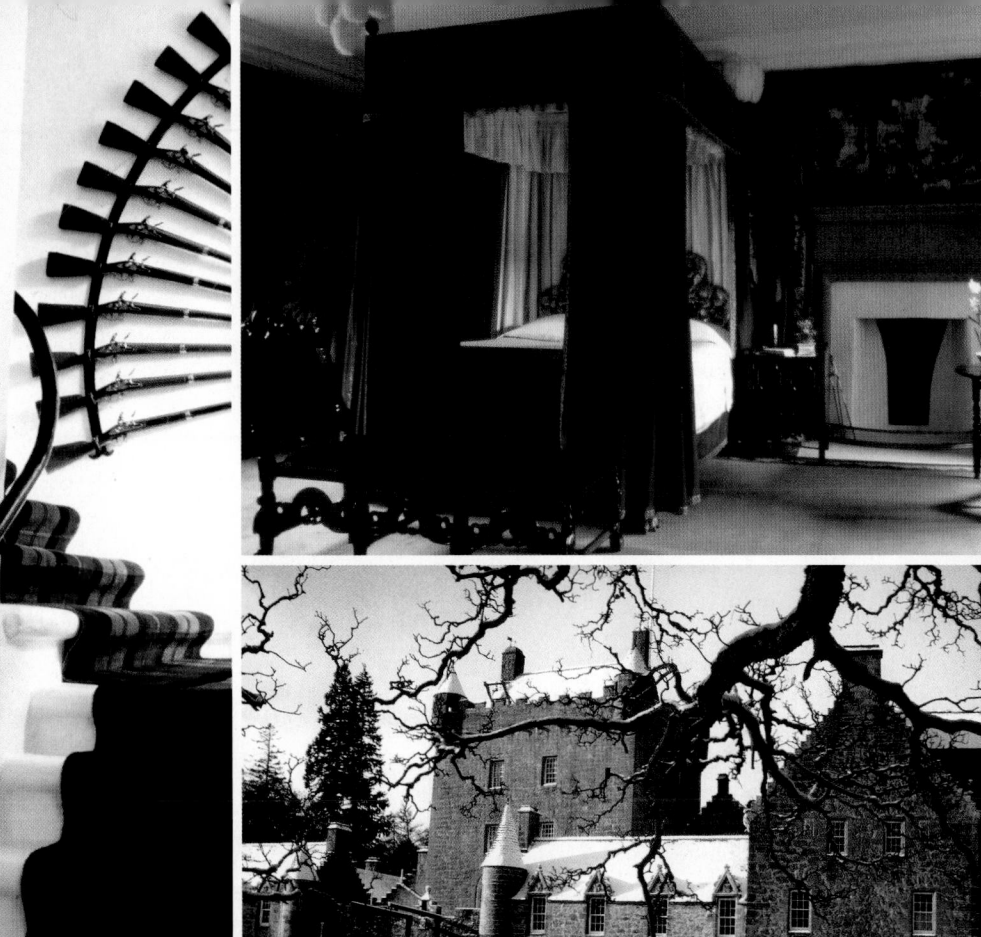
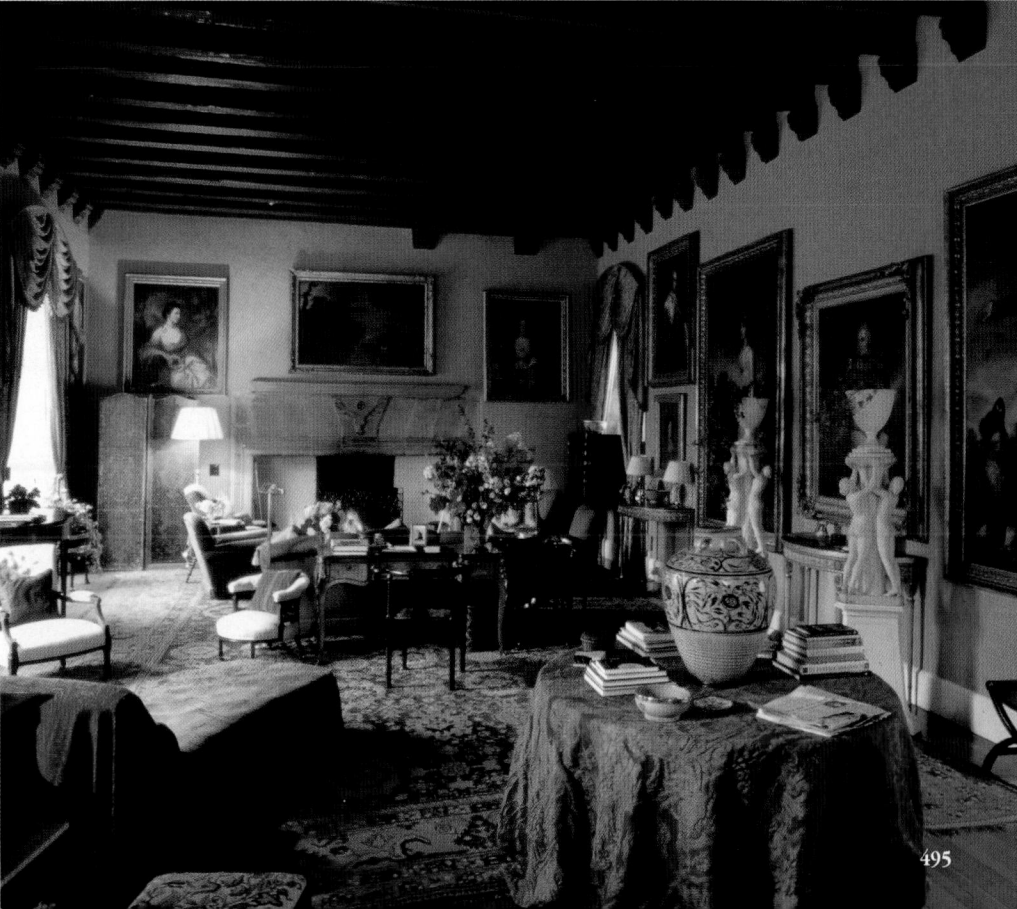

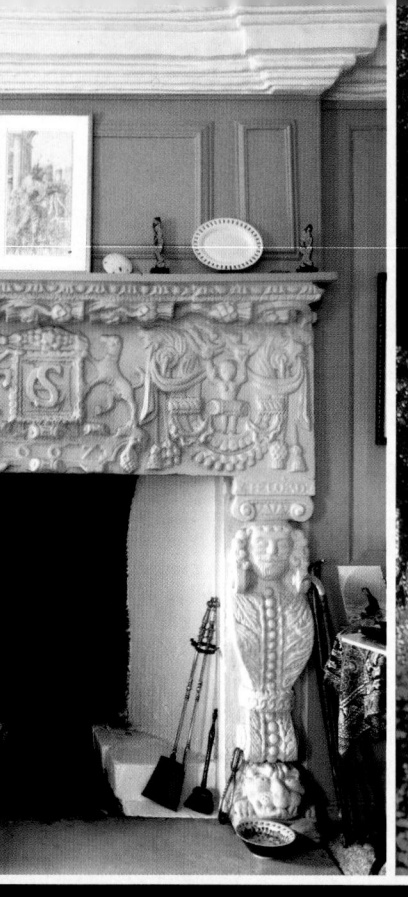

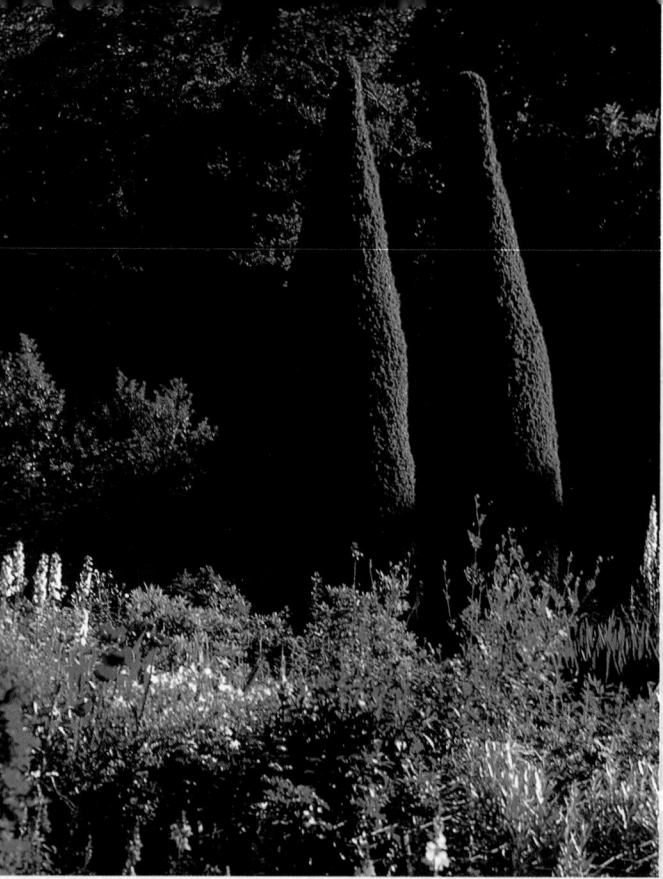

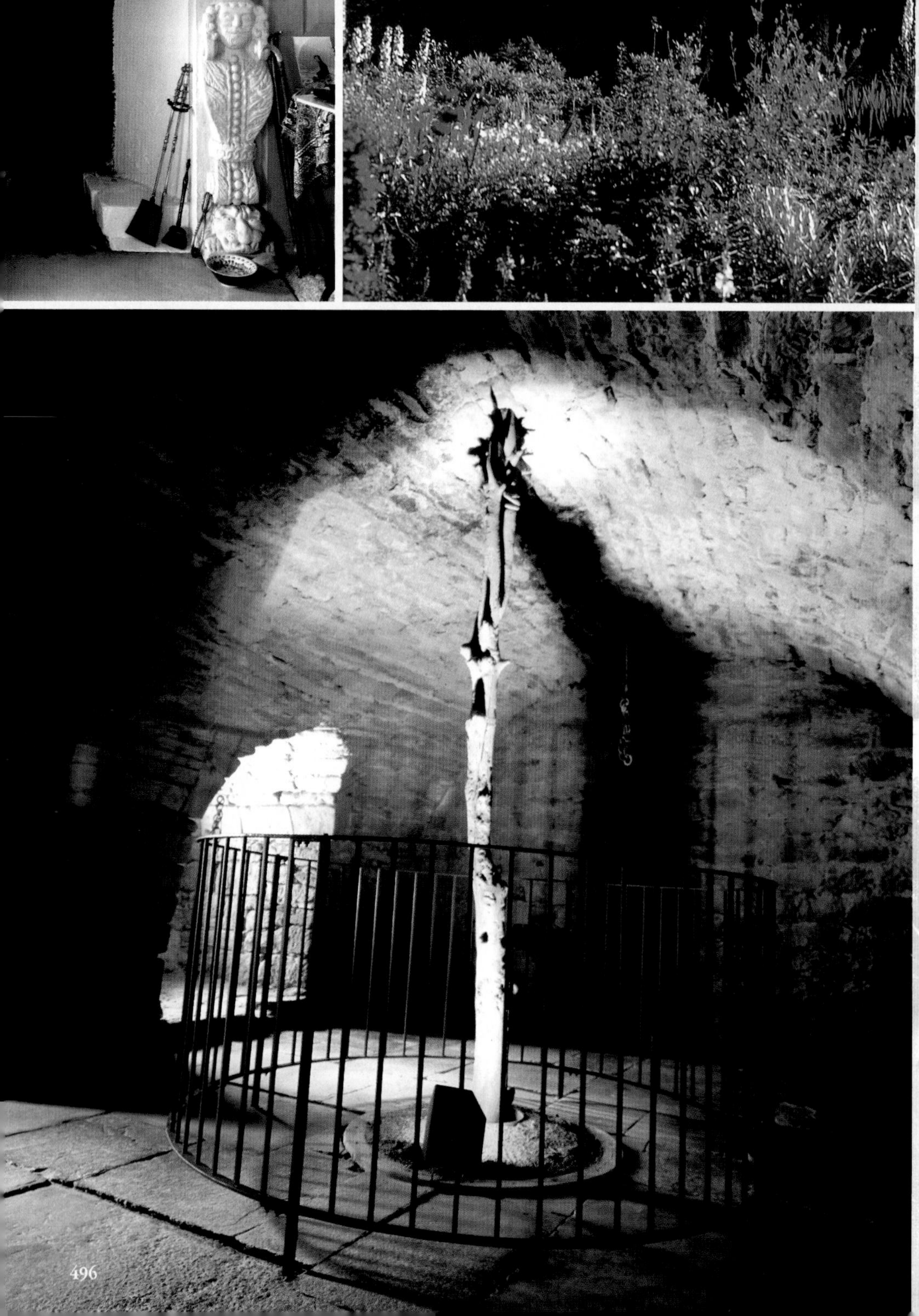

Above all, Cawdor Castle is an exciting and unusual building to visit – built on superstition, its massive, severe exterior belies an intimate interior that gives the visitor to Cawdor a welcoming and surprisingly personal and friendly tour of the Cawdor family home.

Calder and Cawdor are different spellings of the same name which means, roughly, the woodland stream. The foundations of the present castle are thought to date from around 1370, when the choice of site was decided through a mixture of tradition and superstition. A donkey is said to have led the way to a high, rocky position with water nearby. The fortified tower was then built around a living holly tree, a symbol of life and luck and, as some people believed, a protection against fiends, lightning and fairies. Whatever the reasons, the tree soon died on being deprived of light, but it remains standing in the vaulted ground floor Guard Room.

The family history of the Thanes of Cawdor over the last 600 years is, as one would imagine, a bloody and colourful story. A story of kidnappings, successful marriage alliances, courage and valour – something which has passed down to this century. Discounting minor honours, foreign and civil decorations, 12 men of the clan won a total of 24 awards for valour: six Military Crosses, 15 Distinguished Service Orders and three Victoria Crosses. The late Lord Cawdor (who died in 1993) was, like many of his ancestors, cast in the same mould – a rainbow of knowledge, anger, wit, courage and silence.

The interior of Cawdor has well-proportioned rooms, stunning stone fireplaces and striking décor. Much of this style is owed to the occupation by the 1st and 2nd Earls Cawdor of the castle in the 19th century. Following a devastating fire, the interior was redecorated and made more comfortable for modern living. Good furniture, family portraits and pictures abound at Cawdor and are cleverly mixed with modern works of art bought by the family. There is also a fine display of tapestries in the Tapestry Room and the Tower Sitting Room.

The gardens at Cawdor also have a family feel to them, where plants are chosen out of affection rather than affectation. The Flower Garden is a particularly lovely spot to visit between Spring and Summer. The Walled Garden has been restored with a Holly Maze and there is also a Paradise Garden, Knot Garden and Thistle Garden.

Cawdor will provide a wonderfully memorable highlight to a visit to the Scottish Highlands – and one to which the visitor is sure to want to return.

For further details about *Cawdor Castle* see entry in Scotland ➔ Highlands & Skye..

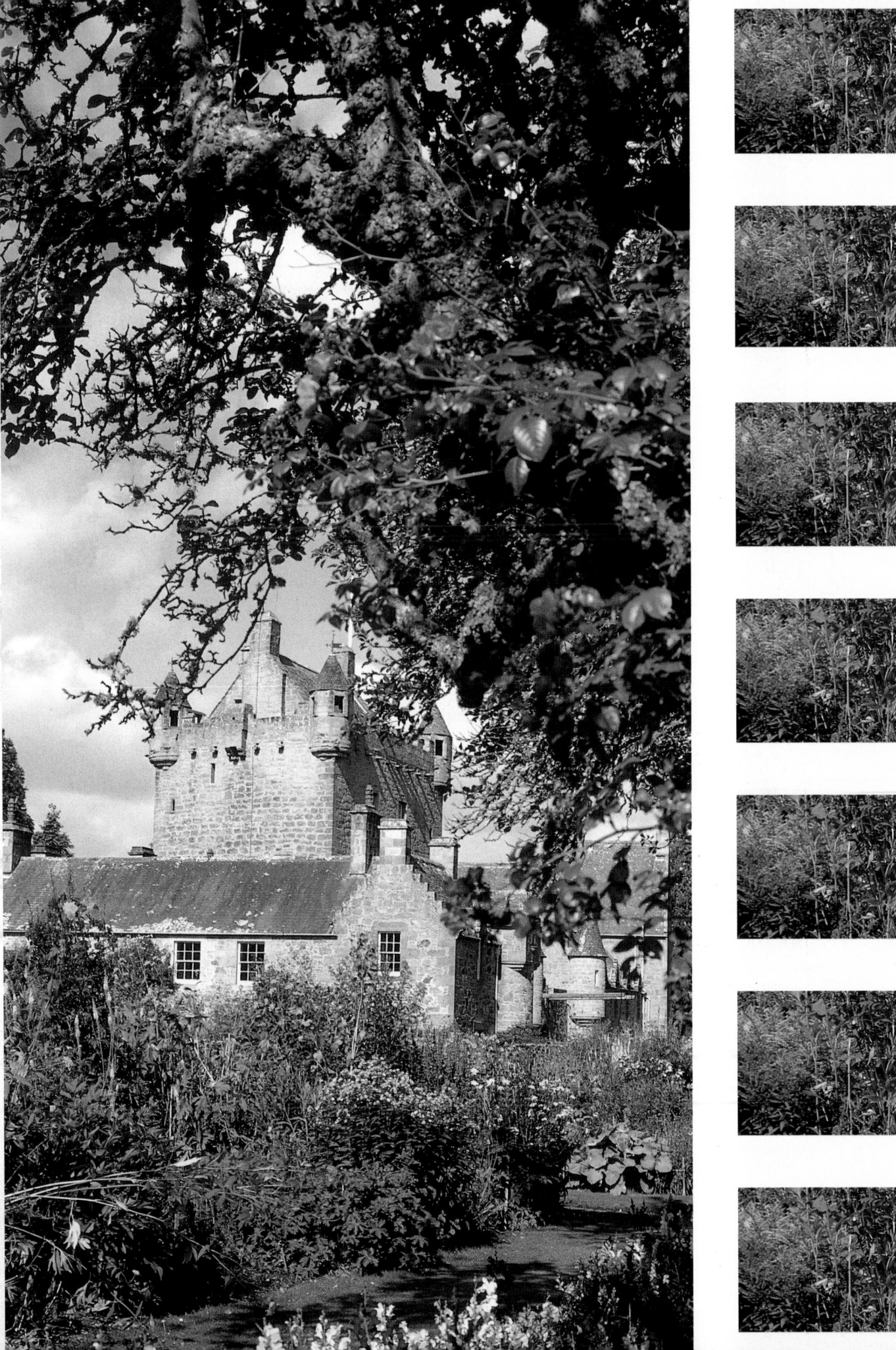

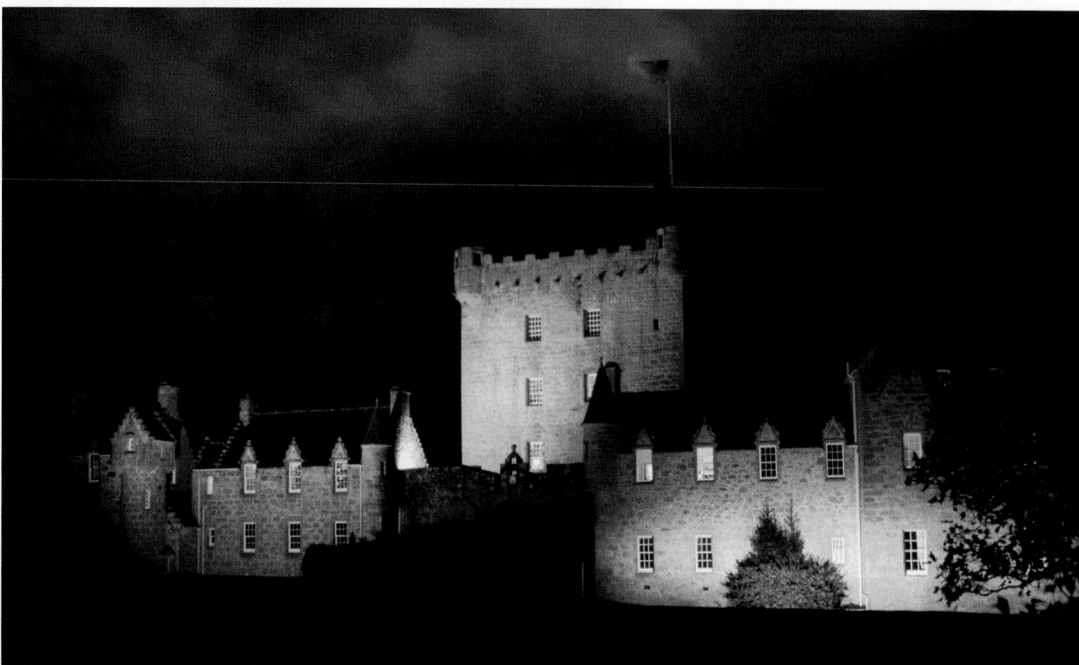

CAWDOR CASTLE
Nairn

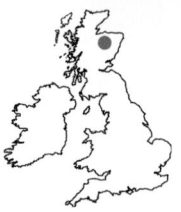

Owner: The Dowager Countess Cawdor

CONTACT

The Secretary
Cawdor Castle
Nairn
Scotland
IV12 5RD

Tel: 01667 404615

Fax: 01667 404674

e-mail: info@ cawdorcastle.com

LOCATION

OS Ref. NH850 500

From Edinburgh
A9, 3^1/$_2$ hrs,
Inverness 20 mins,
Nairn 10 mins.
Main road: A9, 14m.

Rail: Nairn Station 5m.

Bus: Inverness to Nairn bus route 200 yds.

Taxi: Cawdor Taxis 01667 404315.

Air: Inverness Airport 5m.

CONFERENCE/FUNCTION		
ROOM	SIZE	MAX CAPACITY
Cawdor Hall		40

This splendid romantic castle dating from the late 14th century was built as a private fortress by the Thanes of Cawdor, and remains the home of the Cawdor family to this day. The ancient medieval tower was built around the legendary holly tree.

Although the house has evolved over 600 years, later additions mainly of the 17th century were all built in the Scottish vernacular style with slated roofs over walls and crow-stepped gables of mellow local stone. This style gives Cawdor a strong sense of unity, and the massive, severe exterior belies an intimate interior that gives the place a surprisingly personal, friendly atmosphere.

Good furniture, fine portraits and pictures, interesting objects and outstanding tapestries are arranged to please the family rather than to echo fashion or impress. Memories of Shakespeare's *Macbeth* give Cawdor an elusive, evocative quality that delights visitors.

GARDENS

The flower garden also has a family feel to it, where plants are chosen out of affection rather than affectation. This is a lovely spot between spring and late summer. The walled garden has been restored with a holly maze, paradise garden, knot garden and thistle garden. The wild garden beside its stream leads into beautiful trails through a spectacular mature mixed woodland, through which paths are helpfully marked and colour-coded.

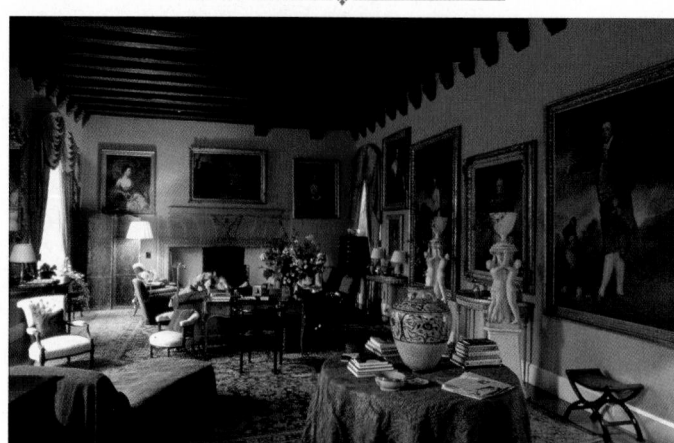

SUMMER

1 May - 14 October
Daily: 10am - 5.30pm.

Last admission 5pm.

WINTER

15 October - 30 April
Closed.

ADMISSION

SUMMER
House & Garden

Adult £5.90
Child (5-15yrs)..........£3.00
OAP/Student...........£4.90
Family (2+5)...........£17.00

Groups (20+)
Adult £5.10
Child (5-15yrs)..........£2.60
OAP/Student...........£4.90

Garden only
Per person £3.00

SPECIAL EVENTS

• **JUN 2 - 3:**
Special Gardens Weekend: Guided tours of gardens and Cawdor Big Wood.

ⓘ 9 hole golf course, putting green, golf clubs for hire, Conferences, whisky tasting, musical entertainments, specialised garden visits. No photography, video taping or tripods inside.

Gift, book and wool shops.

Lunches, sherry or champagne receptions.

Visitors may alight at the entrance. WC. Only ground floor accessible.

Licensed buttery, May-Oct, groups should book.

Ⓟ 250 cars and 25 coaches. Two weeks' notice for group catering, coach drivers/couriers free.

£2.60 per child. Room notes, quiz and answer sheet can be provided. Ranger service and nature trails.

Guide dogs only.

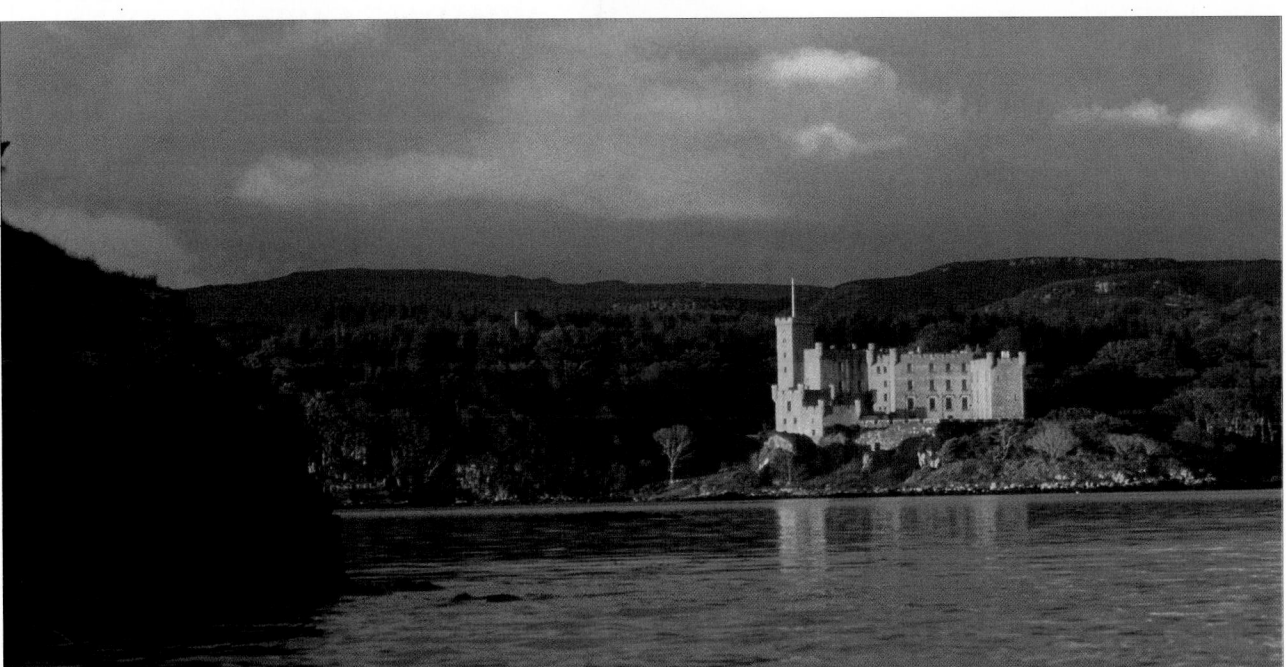

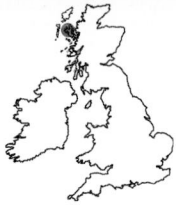

Owner: John Macleod of Macleod

CONTACT

The Administrator
Dunvegan Castle
Isle of Skye
Scotland
IV55 8WF

Tel: 01470 521206

Fax: 01470 521205

Seal Tel: 01470 521500

e-mail: info@
dunvegancastle.com

LOCATION

OS Ref. NG250 480

1m N of village. NW corner of Skye.

From Inverness A82 to Invermoriston, A887 to Kyle of Lochalsh 82m. From Fort William A82 to Invergarry, A87 to Kyle of Lochalsh 76m.

Kyle of Lochalsh to Dunvegan 45m via Skye Bridge (toll).

Ferry: To the Isle of Skye, 'roll-on, roll-off', 30 minute crossing.

Rail: Inverness to Kyle of Lochalsh 3 - 4 trains per day -'45m.

Bus: Portree 25m, Kyle of Lochalsh 45m.

DUNVEGAN CASTLE
Isle of Skye

DUNVEGAN is unique. It is the only Great House in the Western Isles of Scotland to have retained its family and its roof. It is the oldest home in the whole of Scotland continuously inhabited by the same family – the Chiefs of the Clan Macleod. A Castle placed on a rock by the sea - the curtain wall is dated before 1200 AD – its superb location recalls the Norse Empire of the Vikings, the ancestors of the Chiefs.

Dunvegan's continuing importance as a custodian of the Clan spirit is epitomised by the famous Fairy Flag, whose origins are shrouded in mystery but whose ability to protect both Chief and Clan is unquestioned. To enter Dunvegan is to arrive at a place whose history combines with legend to make a living reality.

GARDENS
The gardens and grounds extend over some ten acres of woodland walks, peaceful formal lawns and a water garden dominated by two spectacular natural waterfalls. The temperate climate aids in producing a fine show of rhododendrons and azaleas, the chief glory of the garden in spring. One is always aware of the proximity of the sea and many garden walks finish at the Castle Jetty, from where traditional boats make regular trips to view the delightful Seal Colony.

❖

 Gift and craft shop. Boat trips to seal colony. Pedigree Highland cattle. No photography in castle.

Visitors may alight at entrance. WC.

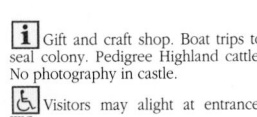 Licensed restaurant, (cap. 70) special rates for groups, menus upon request. Tel: 01470 521310. Open late peak season for evening meals.

By appointment in English or Gaelic at no extra charge. If requested owner may meet groups, tour time 45mins.

P 120 cars and 10 coaches. Do not attempt to take passengers to Castle Jetty (long walk). If possible please book. Seal boat trip dependent upon weather.

Welcome by arrangement. Guide available on request.

In grounds only, on lead.

4 self-catering units, 3 of which sleep 6 and 1 of which sleeps 7.

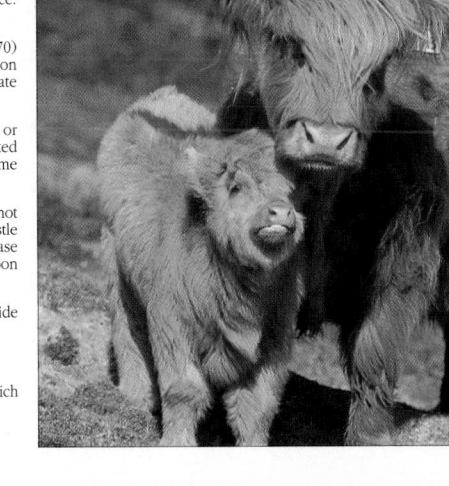

OPENING TIMES

SUMMER

20 March - 31 October
Daily: 10am - 5.30pm.
Last admission 5pm.

WINTER

November - March
Daily: 11am - 4pm.
Last admission 3.30pm.

Closed Christmas Day, Boxing Day, New Year's Day and 2 January.

ADMISSION

2000 prices

SUMMER

Castle & Gardens
Adult £5.50
Child* (5 -15yrs) £3.00
Conc........................£4.80
Family (2+3) £15.00

Groups (10+)
.............................£5.00

Gardens only
Adult £3.80
Child* (5 -15yrs) £2.00

Seal Boats
Adult £4.00
Child* (5 -15yrs) £2.50

*Child under 5yrs Free.

WINTER

11am - 4pm.
No boat trips.

ATTADALE GARDENS

Tel: 01520 722217 **Fax:** 01520 722546

By Strathcarron, Ross-shire IV54 8YX

e-mail: cottages@attadale.com

Owner/Contact: Mr & Mrs Ewen Macpherson

The garden and woodland walks were planted by the Schroder family from 1890 onwards with species rhododendrons, azaleas and southern hemisphere plants made possible by the warm gulf stream. Outstanding water garden.

Location: OS Ref. NG920 400. On A890 between Strathcarron and South Strome. 12m N of A87.

Opening Times: 1 Apr - 31 Oct: Mon - Sat, 10am - 5.30pm.

Admission: Adult £2, Child £1. Coaches/guided tours by prior arrangement.

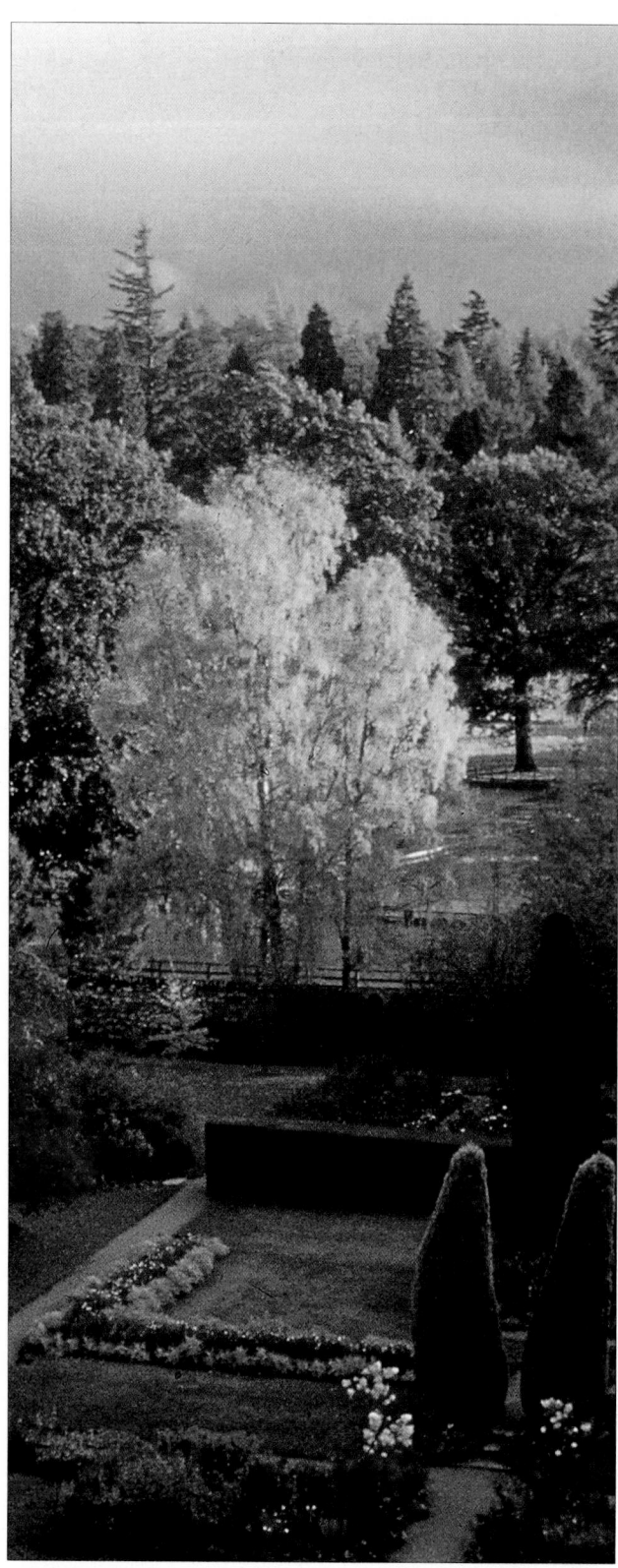

Cawdor Castle, Highlands & Skye.

ARMADALE CASTLE GARDENS & MUSEUM OF THE ISLES

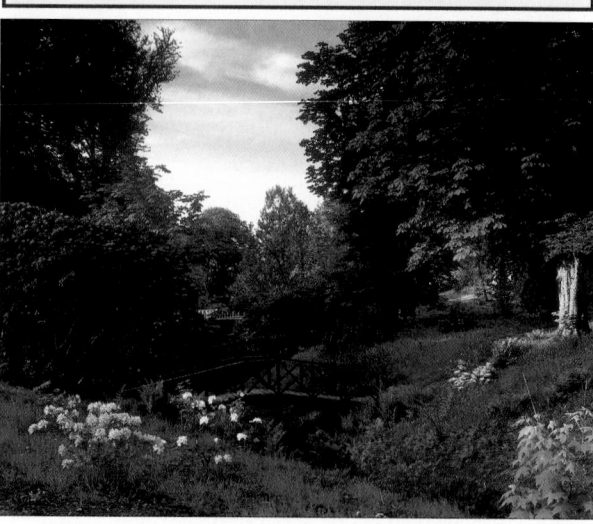

ARMADALE, SLEAT, ISLE OF SKYE IV45 8RS

Owner/Contact: Clan Donald Lands Trust

Tel: 01471 844305 **Fax:** 01471 844275

40 acre gardens with sea views to Knoydart across the Sound of Sleat. Sheltered and due to the warming effect of the gulf stream allowing exotic trees, shrubs and flowers to grow. Enjoy a complete experience to Armadale by visiting the Museum of the Isles within the gardens.

Location: OS Ref. NG630 020. 1m from Armadale - Mallaig ferry terminal and approximately 21m S of Skye Bridge.

Opening Times: Apr - Oct: 9.30am - 5.30pm.

Admission: Adult £3.90, Child/Conc. £2.85. Booked Groups (min 8): £2.50.

 Licensed. Licensed. By arrangement. P
In grounds, on leads. Self-catering cottages.

BALLINDALLOCH CASTLE

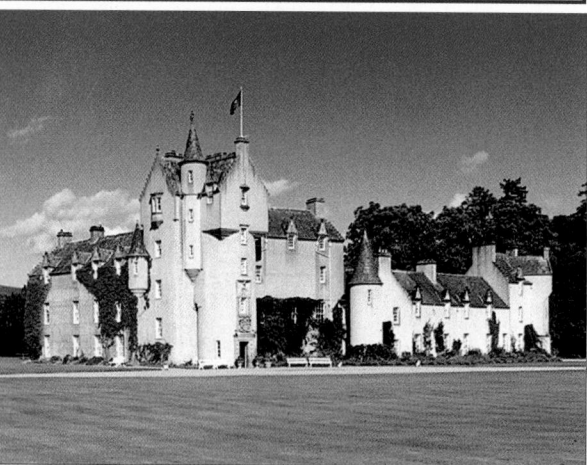

GRANTOWN-ON-SPEY, BANFFSHIRE AB37 9AX

Owner: Mr & Mrs Russell *Contact: Mrs Clare Russell*

Tel: 01807 500206 **Fax:** 01807 500210 **e-mail:** enquiries@ballindallochcastle.co.uk

Ballindalloch is a much loved family home and one of the few castles lived in continuously by its original owners, the Macpherson-Grants, since 1546. Filled with family memorabilia and a magnificent collection of 17th century Spanish paintings, it is home to the famous breed of Aberdeen Angus cattle. Beautiful rock and rose garden, river walks.

Location: OS Ref. NJ178 366. 14m NE of Grantown-on-Spey on A95, 22m S of Elgin on A95.

Opening Times: 15 Apr - 30 Sept: 10.30am - 5.30pm. Coaches welcome all year by appointment.

Admission: House & Grounds: Adult £5.20, Child (5-16) £2.50, Conc. £4.50, Family (2+3) £13. Grounds only: Adult £2, Child £1. Groups: (20+) Adult £4.50, Child £2.

Ground floor & grounds. WC. P Audio-visual.
In grounds, on leads in dog walking area.

CAWDOR CASTLE

See page 498 for full page entry.

CROMARTY COURTHOUSE

Tel: 01381 600418 **Fax:** 01381 600408

Church Street, Cromarty IV11 8XA

Contact: David Alston

18th century town courthouse, visitor centre and museum.

Location: OS Ref. NH790 680. 25m N of Inverness.

Opening Times: Apr - Oct: 10am - 5pm. Nov, Dec & Mar: 12 noon - 4pm.

Admission: Adult £3, Conc. £2, Family (2+4) £8.

CULLODEN

Tel: 01463 790607 **Fax:** 01463 794294

Culloden Moor, Inverness IV1 2ED

Owner: The National Trust for Scotland

Contact: Ross Mackenzie

No name in Scottish history evokes more emotion than that of Culloden, the bleak moor which in 1746 saw the hopes of the young Prince Charles Edward Stuart crushed, and the end of the Jacobite Rising, the 'Forty-Five'. The Prince's forces, greatly outnumbered by those of the brutal Duke of Cumberland, nevertheless went into battle with a courage which has passed into legend.

Location: OS Ref. NH745 450. On B9006, 5m E of Inverness.

Opening Times: Site: All year: daily. Visitor Centre & Shop: 15 Jan - 31 Mar & 1 Nov - 31 Dec (closed 24 - 26 Dec): daily, 10am - 4pm. 1 Apr - 31 Oct: daily, 9am - 6pm (last admission 30 mins before closing). Restaurant & audio-visual show close 30 mins earlier.

Admission: Visitor Centre & Old Leanach Cottage: Adult £4, Conc. £3, Family £11. Groups: Adult £3.20, Child/School £1.

i Visitor centre. 📷 ♿ 🍴 🎧 Audio-visual. In dog walking area only.

DOCHFOUR GARDENS

Tel: 01463 861218 **Fax:** 01463 861366

Dochgarroch, Inverness IV3 6JY

Owner: Dochfour Estate

Contact: Miss J Taylor

Victorian terraced garden near Inverness with panoramic views over Loch Dochfour. Magnificent specimen trees, naturalised daffodils, rhododendrons, water garden, yew topiary.

Location: OS Ref. NH620 610. 6m SW of Inverness on A82 to Fort William.

Opening Times: Gardens: Apr - Sept, Mon - Fri, 10am - 4pm. House not open.

Admission: Garden walk - £1.50.

THE DOUNE OF ROTHIEMURCHUS

Tel: 01479 812345

By Aviemore PH22 1QH

Owner: J P Grant of Rothiemurchus

Contact: Rothiemurchus Visitor Centre

The family home of the Grants of Rothiemurchus was nearly lost as a ruin and has been under an ambitious repair programme since 1975. This exciting project may be visited on selected Mondays throughout the year. Book with the Visitor Centre for a longer 2hr 'Highland Lady' tour which explores the haunts of Elizabeth Grant of Rothiemurchus, born 1797, author of *Memoirs of a Highland Lady*, who vividly described the Doune and its surroundings from the memories of her childhood.

Location: OS Ref. NH900 100. 2m S of Aviemore on E bank of Spey river.

Opening Times: House: selected Mons. Grounds: May - Aug: Mon, 10am - 12.30pm & 2 - 4.30pm, also 1st Mon in the month during winter.

Admission: House £5. Grounds only: £1. Booking essential.

i Visitor Centre. 📷 🎫 Obligatory. P Limited. In grounds, on leads.

DUNROBIN CASTLE

See below.

DUNVEGAN CASTLE

See page 499 for full page entry.

DUNROBIN CASTLE

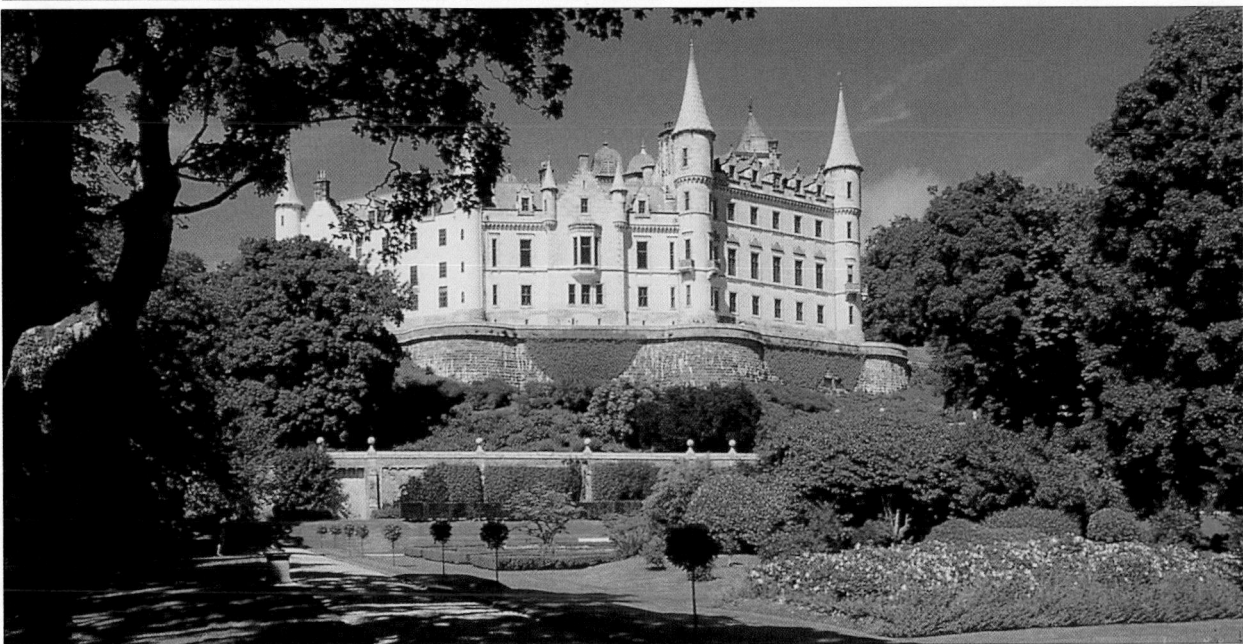

GOLSPIE, SUTHERLAND KW10 6SF

Owner: The Sutherland Trust   *Contact:* Keith Jones, Curator

Tel: 01408 633177 **Fax:** 01408 634081 **e-mail:** dunrobin.est@btinternet.com

Dates from the 13th century with additions in the 17th, 18th and 19th centuries. Wonderful furniture, paintings, library, ceremonial robes and memorabilia. Victorian museum in grounds with a fascinating collection including Pictish stones. Set in fine woodlands overlooking the sea. Magnificent formal gardens, one of few remaining French/Scottish formal parterres. Falconry display.

Location: OS Ref. NC850 010. 50m N of Inverness on A9. 1m NE of Golspie.

Opening Times: 1 Apr - 31 May & 1 - 15 Oct: Mon - Sat, 10.30am - 4.30pm. Suns, 12 noon - 4.30pm. 1 Jun - 30 Sept: Mon - Sat, 10.30am - 5.30pm. Suns, 12 noon - 5.30pm (Jul & Aug: Suns, opens at 10.30am).

Admission: Adult £6, Child/Conc. £4.50. Groups: Adult £5.50, Child/Conc £4.50. Family (2+2) £17.

   By arrangement.

EILEAN DONAN CASTLE

Tel: 01599 555202 **Fax:** 01599 555262

Dornie, Kyle of Lochalsh, Wester IV40 8DX   **e-mail:** info@eileandonancastle.com

Contact: Rod Stenson – Castle Keeper

Location: OS Ref. NG880 260. On A87 8m E of Skye Bridge.

Opening Times: Mar & Nov: 10am - 3.30pm. Apr - Oct: 10am - 5.30pm.

Admission: Adult £3.95, Conc. £3.20.

INVEREWE GARDEN

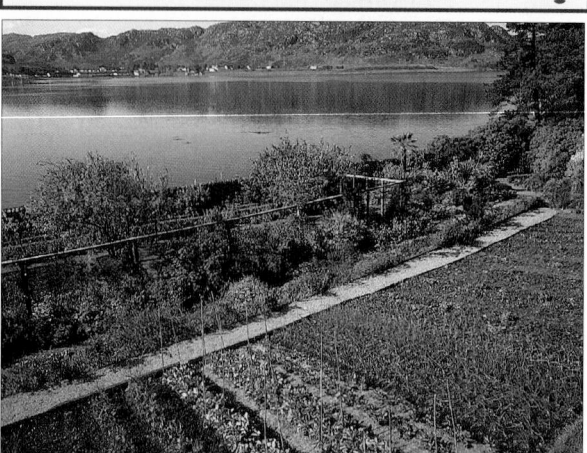

POOLEWE, ROSS & CROMARTY IV22 2LQ

Owner: *The National Trust for Scotland*   **Contact:** *Keith Gordon*

Tel: 01445 781200 **Fax:** 01445 781497

Where in Scotland will you see the tallest Australian gum trees in Britain, sweetly scented Chinese rhododendrons, exotic trees from Chile and Blue Nile lilies from South Africa, all growing on a latitude more northerly than Moscow? The answer is Inverewe: you are in Wester Ross, you are also in a sheltered garden, blessed by the North Atlantic Drift. In a spectacular lochside setting among pinewoods, Osgood Mackenzie's Victorian dreams have produced a glorious 50 acre mecca for garden lovers.

Location: OS Ref. NG860 820. On A832, by Poolewe, 6m NE of Gairloch, Highland.

Opening Times: Garden: 15 Mar - 31 Oct: daily, 9.30am - 9pm. 1 Nov - 14 Mar: daily, 9.30am - 5pm. Visitor Centre & shop: 15 Mar - 31 Oct: daily, 9.30am - 5.30pm. Restaurant: 10am - 5pm. Guided garden walks: 15 Apr - 15 Sept: Mon - Fri at 1.30pm.

Admission: Adult £5, Conc. £4, Family £14. Groups: Adult £4, Child/School £1.

ⓘ Visitor centre.   📷   ♿ Grounds suitable. WC.   🍴 Licensed.   Ⓟ No shade for dogs.   🦮 Guide dogs only.   ❄   (W)

FORT GEORGE

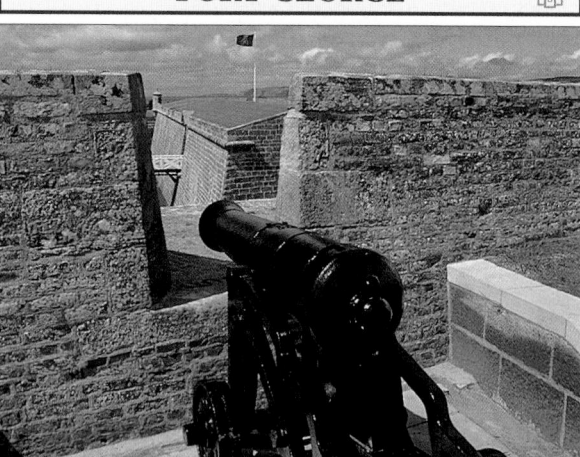

ARDERSIER BY INVERNESS IV1 2TD

Owner: *In the care of Historic Scotland*   **Contact:** *Tommy Simpson*

Tel: 01667 462777 **Fax:** 01667 462698

Built following the Battle of Culloden to subdue the Highlands, Fort George never saw a shot fired in anger. One of the most outstanding artillery fortifications in Europe with reconstructed barrack room displays. The Queen's Own Highlanders' Museum.

Location: OS Ref. NH762 567. 11m NE of Inverness off the A96 by Ardersier.

Opening Times: Apr - Sept: daily, 9.30am - 6.30pm. Oct - Mar: Mon - Sat, 9.30am - 4.30pm; Suns, 2 - 4.30pm. Last ticket sold 45 mins before closing.

Admission: Adult £4.50, Child £1.50, Conc. £3.50. 10% discount for groups (10+).

ⓘ Picnic tables.   📷   🍴 Private evening hire.   ♿ Wheelchairs available. WCs.   🍴 In summer.   Ⓟ   🍴 Free if pre-booked.   🦮 In grounds, on leads.   ❄

URQUHART CASTLE

Tel: 01456 450551

Drumnadrochit, Loch Ness

Owner: In the care of Historic Scotland   **Contact:** The Steward

The remains of one of the largest castles in Scotland dominate a rocky promontory on Loch Ness. Most of the existing buildings date from the 16th century. New visitor centre opening autumn 2001.

Location: OS Ref. NH531 286. On Loch Ness, 1¹/₂ m S of Drumnadrochit on A82.

Opening Times: 1 Apr - 30 Sept: daily, 9.30am - 6.30pm, last ticket 5.45pm. 1 Oct - 31 Mar: daily, 9.30am - 4.30pm, last ticket 3.45pm.

Admission: Adult £3.80, Child £1.20, Conc. £2.80.

GLENFINNAN MONUMENT

Tel/Fax: 01397 722250

Inverness-shire PH37 4LT

Owner: The National Trust for Scotland   **Contact:** Mrs Lillias Grant

The monument, situated on the scenic road to the Isles, is set amid superb Highland scenery at the head of Loch Shiel. It was erected in 1815 in tribute to the clansmen who fought and died in the Jacobite cause. Prince Charles Edward Stuart's standard was raised near here in 1745. Despite its inspired beginnings, the campaign came to a grim conclusion on the Culloden battlefield in 1746.

Location: OS Ref. NM906 805. On A830, 18m W of Fort William, Lochaber.

Opening Times: Site: All year: daily. Monument & Visitor Centre: 1 Apr - 18 May & 1 Sept - 31 Oct: daily, 10am - 5pm. 19 May - 31 Aug: daily, 9.30am - 6pm. Glenfinnan Games: 18 August.

Admission: Adult £1.50, Conc. £1 (includes parking).

ⓘ Visitor centre.   📷   ♿ Grounds suitable. WC.   🍴   Ⓟ   🦮 In grounds, on leads.   ❄   🛡   (W)

HUGH MILLER'S COTTAGE

Tel: 01381 600245

Cromarty IV11 8XA

Owner: The National Trust for Scotland   **Contact:** Ms Frieda Gostwick

Furnished thatched cottage of c1698, birthplace of eminent geologist and writer Hugh Miller. Exhibition and video.

Location: OS Ref. NH790 680. Via Kessock Bridge & A832, in Cromarty, 22m NE of Inverness.

Opening Times: 1 May - 30 Sept: Mon - Sat, 11am - 1pm & 2 - 5pm. Suns, 2 - 5pm. Last entry 4.30pm.

Admission: Adult £2.50, Conc. £1.70, Family £7. Groups: Adult £2, Child/School £1.

♿ Not suitable.   Ⓟ Public parking at shore.   🦮 Guide dogs only.   (W)

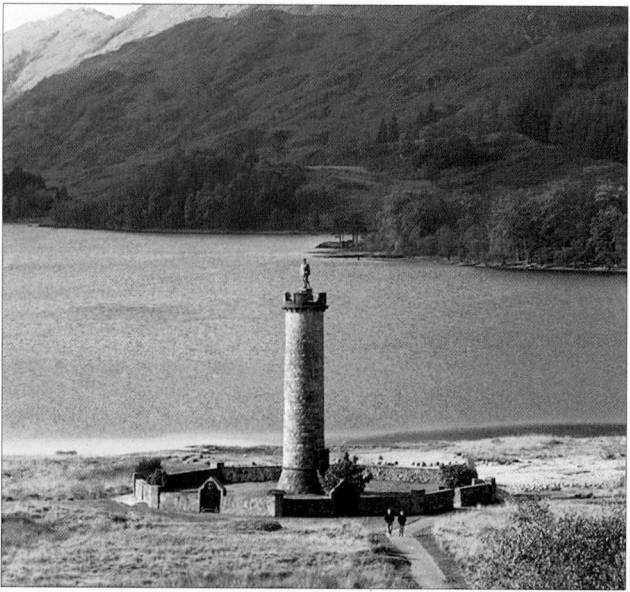

Glenfinnan Monument, Highlands & Skye.

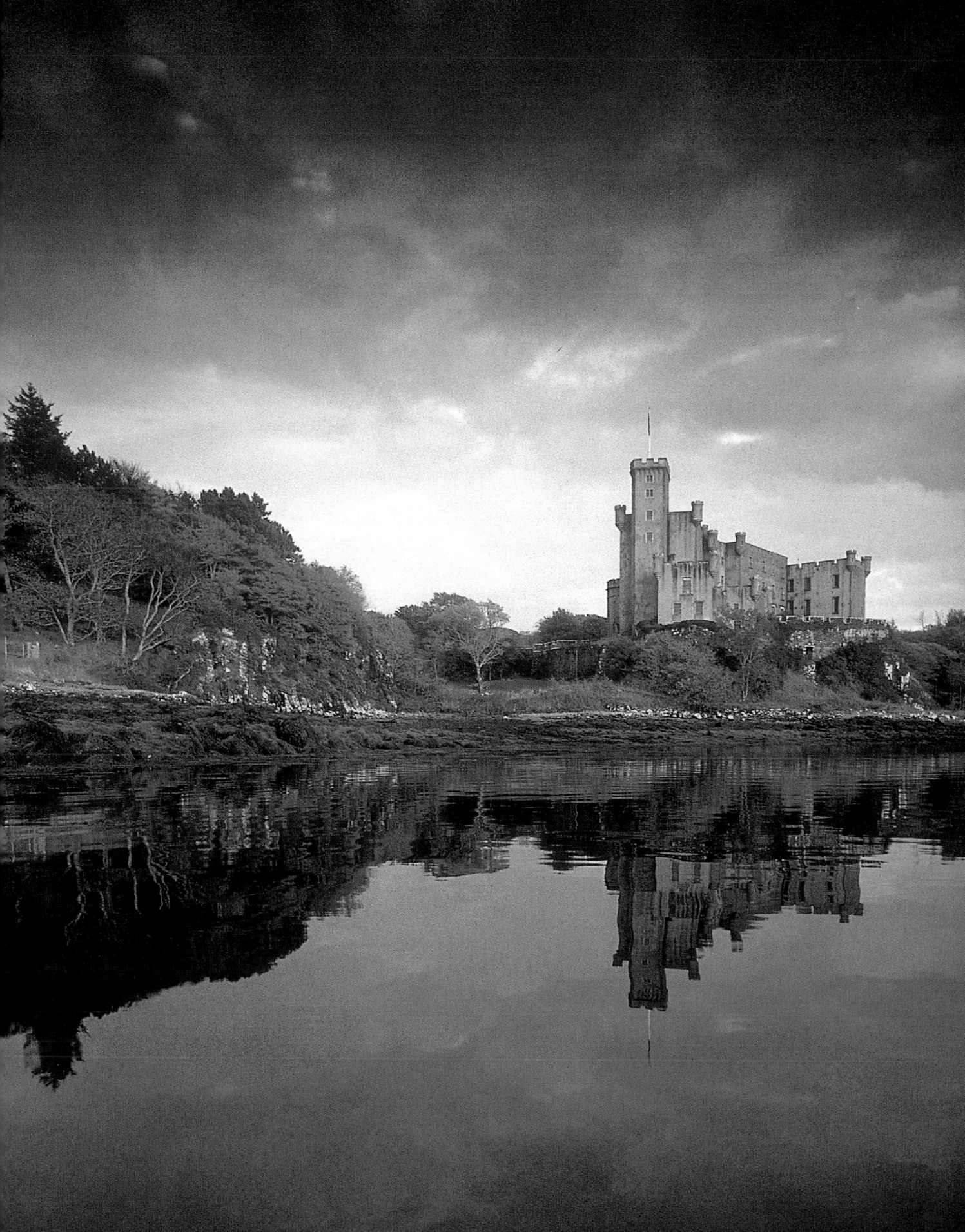

Dunvegan Castle, Highlands & Skye.

BALFOUR CASTLE

Tel: 01856 711282   **Fax:** 01856 711283

Shapinsay, Orkney Islands KW17 2DY   **e-mail:** balfourcastle@btinternet.com

Owner/Contact: Mrs Lidderdale

Built in 1848.

Location: OS Ref. HY475 164 on Shapinsay Island, 3½ m NNE of Kirkwall.

Opening Times: Mid-May – mid-Sept: Weds. 2.30 - 5.30pm.

Admission: £15 including boat fare, guided tour, gardens & afternoon tea. Child £7.50.

BISHOP'S & EARL'S PALACES

Tel: 01856 875461

Kirkwall, Orkney

Owner: In the care of Historic Scotland   **Contact:** The Steward

The Bishop's Palace is a 12th century hall-house with a round tower built by Bishop Reid in 1541-48. The adjacent Earl's Palace built in 1607 has been described as the most mature and accomplished piece of Renaissance architecture left in Scotland.

Location: Bishop's Palace: OS Ref. HY447 108. Earl's Palace: OS Ref. HY448 108. In Kirkwall on A960.

Opening Times: 1 Apr - 30 Sept: daily, 9.30am - 6.30pm, last ticket 6pm.

Admission: Adult £2, Child 75p, Conc. £1.50. Joint entry ticket available for all the Orkney monuments: Adult £11, Child £3.50, Conc. £8.

BLACK HOUSE

Tel: 01851 710395

Arnol, Isle of Lewis

Owner: In the care of Historic Scotland   **Contact:** The Steward

A traditional Lewis thatched house, fully furnished, complete with attached barn, byre and stockyard. A peat fire burns in the open hearth. New visitor centre open and restored 1920s croft house.

Location: OS Ref. NB320 500. In Arnol village, 11m NW of Stornoway on A858.

Opening Times: 1 Apr - 30 Sept: Mon - Sat, 9.30am - 6.30pm, last ticket 6pm. 1 Oct - 31 Mar: Mon - Thur & Sat, 9.30am - 4.30pm, last ticket 4pm.

Admission: Adult £2.80, Child £1, Conc. £2.

BROCH OF GURNESS

Tel: 01831 579478

Aikerness, Orkney

Owner: In the care of Historic Scotland   **Contact:** The Steward

Protected by three lines of ditch and rampart, the base of the broch is surrounded by a warren of Iron Age buildings.

Location: OS Ref. HY383 268. At Aikerness, about 14m NW of Kirkwall on A966.

Opening Times: 1 Apr - 30 Sept: daily, 9.30am - 6.30pm, last ticket 6pm.

Admission: Adult £2.80, Child £1, Conc. £2. Joint entry ticket available for all Orkney monuments: Adult £11, Child £3.50, Conc. £8.

CALANAIS STANDING STONES

Tel: 01851 621422

Calanais, Stornoway, Lewis, Outer Islands

Owner: In the care of Historic Scotland

A cross-shaped setting of standing stones, unique in Scotland.

Location: OS Ref. NB213 330. 12m W of Stornaway off A859.

Opening Times: Visitor Centre: please telephone for opening times and admission costs.

CARRICK HOUSE

Tel: 01857 622260

Carrick, Eday, Orkney KW17 2AB

Owner: Mr & Mrs Joy   **Contact:** Mrs Rosemary Joy

17th century house of 3 storeys, built by John Stewart, Lord Kinclaven Earl of Carrick younger brother of Patrick, 2nd Earl of Orkney in 1633.

Location: OS Ref. NT227 773. N of island of Eday on minor roads W of B9063 just W of the shore of Calf Sound. Regular ferry service.

Opening Times: Mid-Jun - mid-Sept: Sun afternoons, also guided tours of the house, 2pm onwards. Other times by arrangement.

Admission: Adult £2, Child £1.

JARLSHOF PREHISTORIC & NORSE SETTLEMENT

Shetland

Tel: 01950 460112

Owner: In the care of Historic Scotland   **Contact:** The Steward

Over 3 acres of remains spanning 3,000 years from the Stone Age. Oval-shaped Bronze Age houses, Iron Age broch and wheel houses. Viking long houses, medieval farmstead and 16th century laird's house.

Location: OS Ref. HY401 096. At Sumburgh Head, 22m S of Lerwick on the A970.

Opening Times: 1 Apr - 30 Sept: daily, 9.30am - 6.30pm. Last adm. ½ hr before closing.

Admission: Adult £2.80, Child £1, Conc. £2.

KIESSIMUL CASTLE

Tel: 01871 810449

Castlebray, Isle of Barra, Western Isles HF9 5XD

Owner/Contact: Ian Allen MacNeil of Barra

Home of the Chief of the MacNeil clan. Dating from the 13th century, the castle has been restored to its 17th century condition.

Location: OS Ref. NL670 990. Just S of Castlebay on Barra, by boat S of A888 in Castlebay.

Opening Times: Apr - Sept: Mon Wed & Sat, 2 - 5pm wind and tide permitting. Please telephone to check.

Admission: Boat and entrance to castle: Adult £3, Child 50p.

MAES HOWE

Tel: 01856 761606

Orkney

Owner: In the care of Historic Scotland   **Contact:** The Steward

This world-famous tomb was built in Neolithic times, before 2700 BC. The large mound covers a stone-built passage and a burial chamber with cells in the walls. Runic inscriptions tell of how it was plundered of its treasures by Vikings.

Location: OS Ref. NY318 128. 9m W of Kirkwall on the A965.

Opening Times: 1 Apr - 30 Sept: daily, 9.30am - 6.30pm. 1 Oct - 31 Mar: daily, 9.30am - 5pm except Thurs pm, Fris and Suns am.

Admission: Adult £2.80, Child £1, Conc. £2. Joint entry ticket available for all Orkney monuments: Adult £11, Child £3.50, Conc. £8. Admission, shop and refreshments at nearby Tormiston Mill.

RING OF BRODGAR STONE CIRCLE & HENGE

Tel: 0131 668 8800

Stromness, Orkney

Owner/Contact: In the care of Historic Scotland

A magnificent circle of upright stones with an enclosing ditch spanned by causeways. Of late Neolithic date.

Location: OS Ref. HY294 134. 5m NE of Stromness.

Opening Times: Any reasonable time.

Admission: Free.

ST MAGNUS CATHEDRAL

Tel: 01856 874894

Broad Street, Kirkwall, Orkney

Owner: Orkney Islands Council   **Contact:** Mr J Rousay

Location: OS Ref. HY449 108. Centre of Kirkwall.

Opening Times: 1 Apr - end Sept: Mon - Sat, 9am - 6pm, Suns, 2 - 6pm. 1 Oct - end Mar: Mon - Sat, 9am - 1pm & 2 - 5pm.

Admission: Free.

SKARA BRAE & SKAILL HOUSE

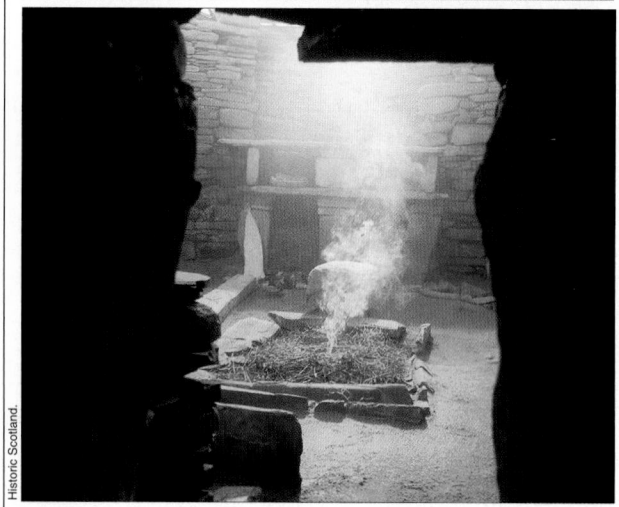

Historic Scotland.

SANDWICK, ORKNEY

Owner: Historic Scotland/Major M R S Macrae   *Contact:* The Steward

Tel: 01856 841815

Skara Brae is one of the best preserved groups of Stone Age houses in Western Europe. Built before the Pyramids, the houses contain stone furniture, hearths and drains. New visitor centre and replica house with joint admission with Skaill House – 17th century home of the Laird who excavated Skara Brae.

Location: OS6 HY231 188. 19m NW of Kirkwall on the B9056.

Opening Times: Apr - Sept: daily, 9.30am - 6.30pm. Oct - Mar: Mon - Sat, 9.30am - 4.30pm, Suns, 2 - 4.30pm.

Admission: Apr - Sept: Adult £4.50, Child £1.30, Conc. £3.30. Oct - Mar: Adult £3.50, Child £1.20, Conc. £2.60. 10% discount for groups (10+). Joint ticket with other Orkney sites available.

Visitor centre. Partially suitable. WCs. Licensed. Free school visits when booked. Guide dogs only.

TANKERNESS HOUSE

Tel: 01856 873191   **Fax:** 01856 871560

Broad Street, Kirkwall, Orkney

Owner: Orkney Islands Council   **Contact:** Bryce S Wilson

A fine vernacular 16th century town house contains Museum of Orkney.

Location: OS Ref. HY446 109. In Kirkwall opposite W end of cathedral.

Opening Times: Oct - Apr: Mon - Sat, 10.30am - 12.30pm & 1.30 - 5pm. May - Sept: Mon - Sat, 10.30am - 5pm, Suns, 2 - 5pm. Gardens always open.

Admission: Free.

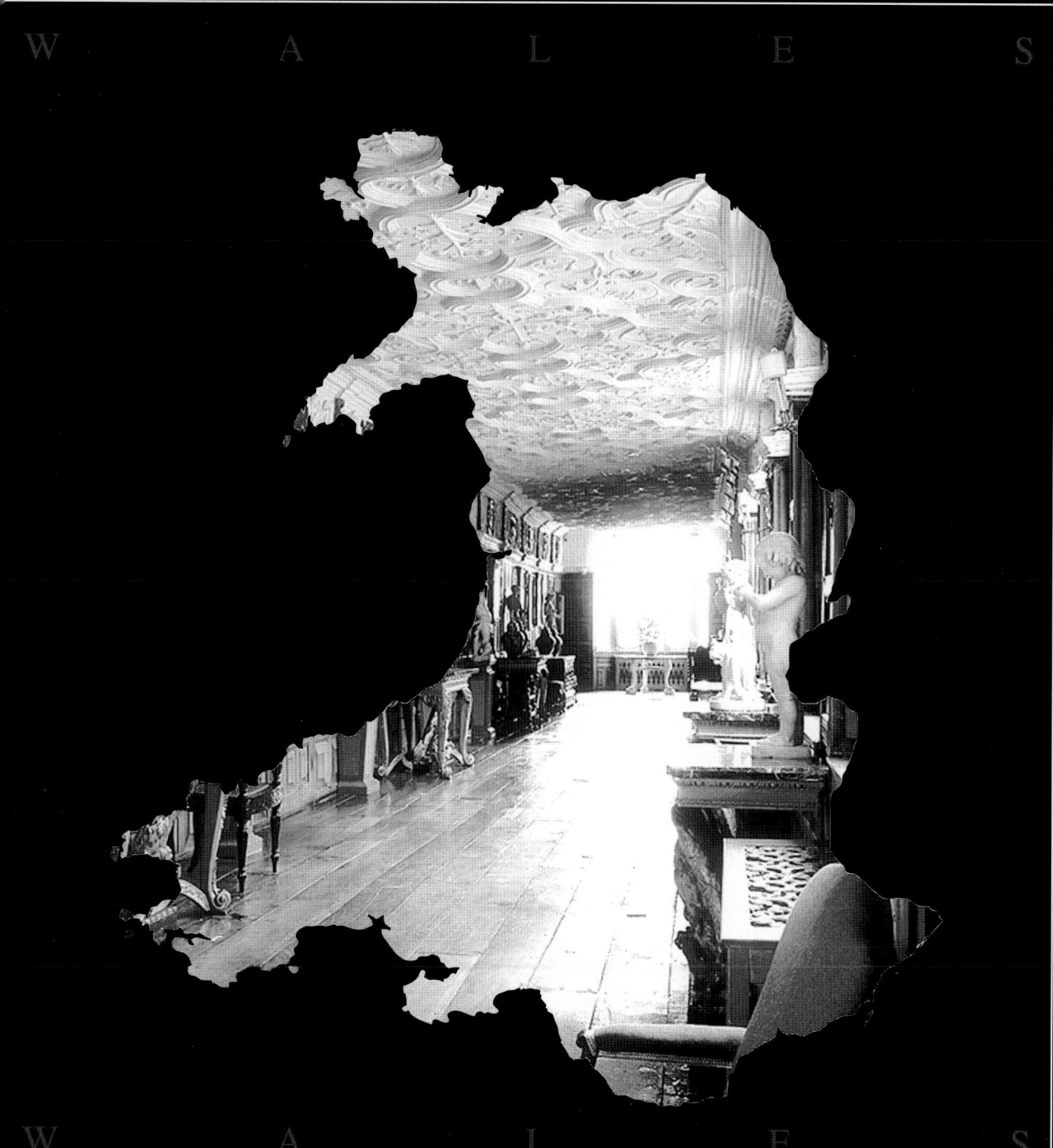

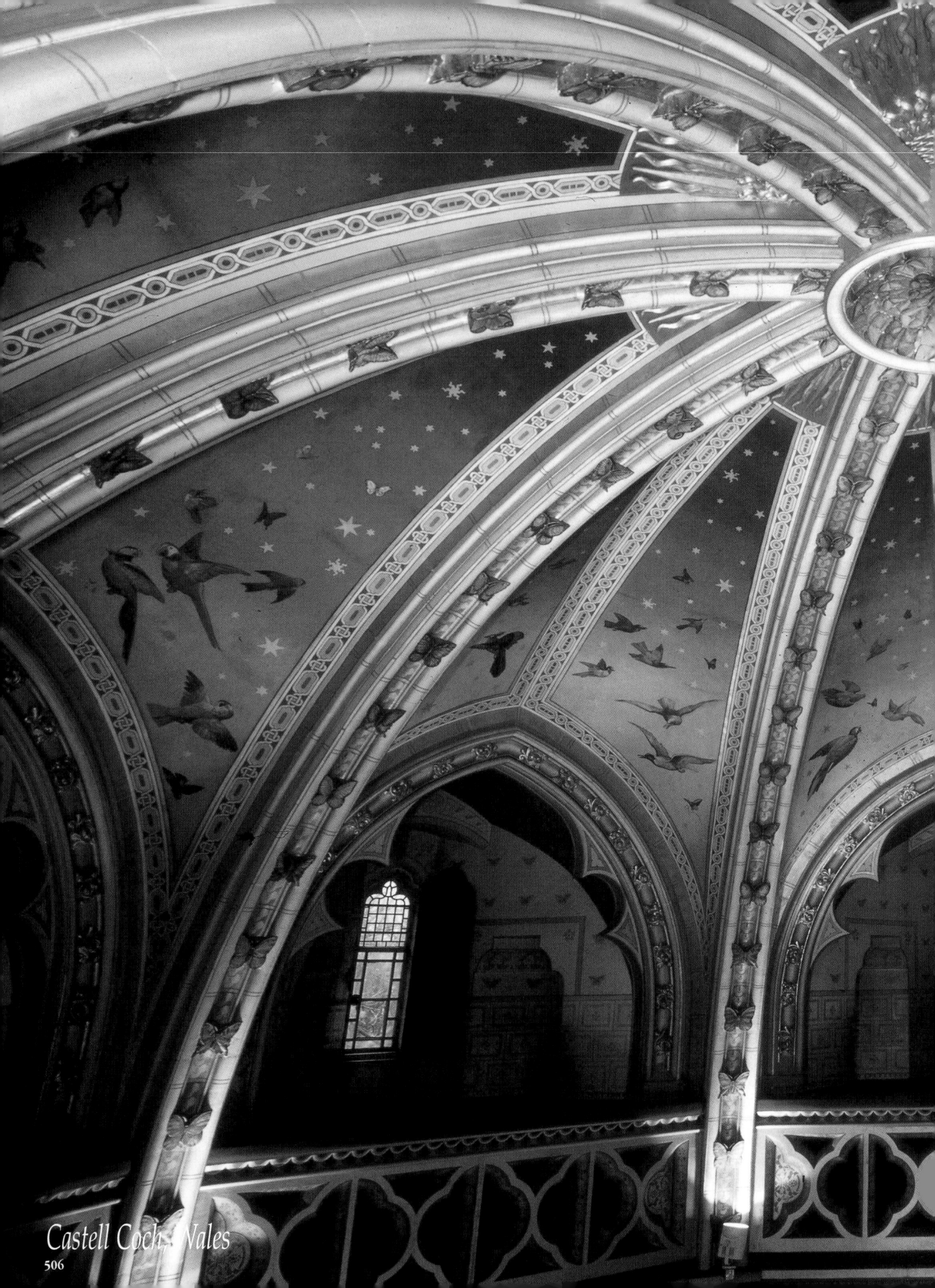

Castell Coch, Wales

Wales

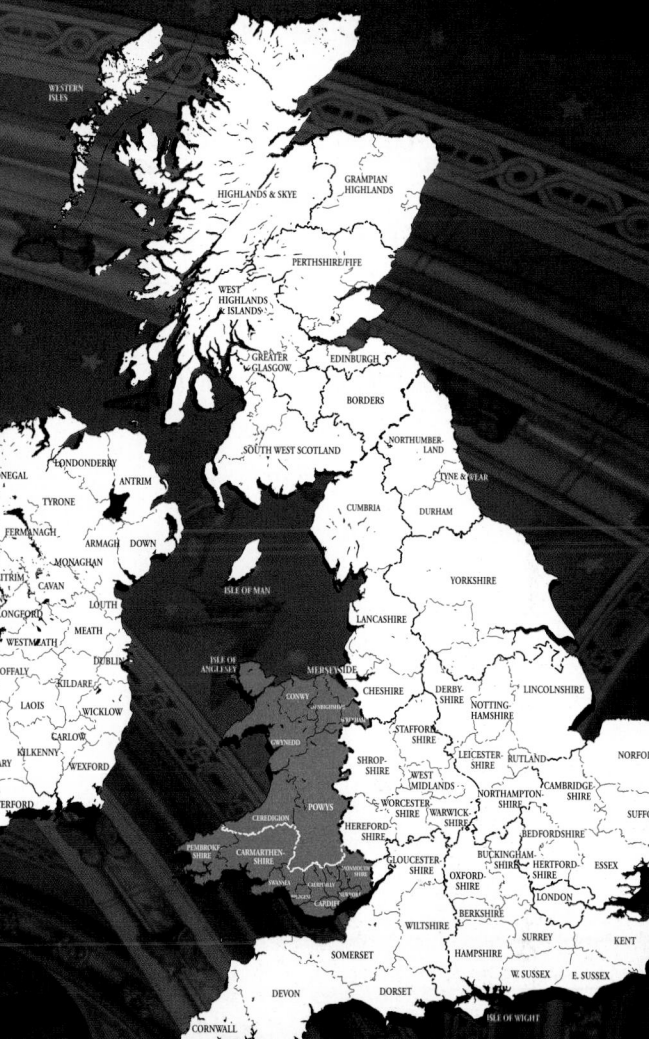

Castell Coch

"A castle of dreams and romance."

With the sharp conical roofs of its towers rising theatrically from the beech woods of Fforest Fawr, Castell Coch – the Red Castle – is an irresistibly striking landmark to those who chance to travel along one of the major roads north of Cardiff.

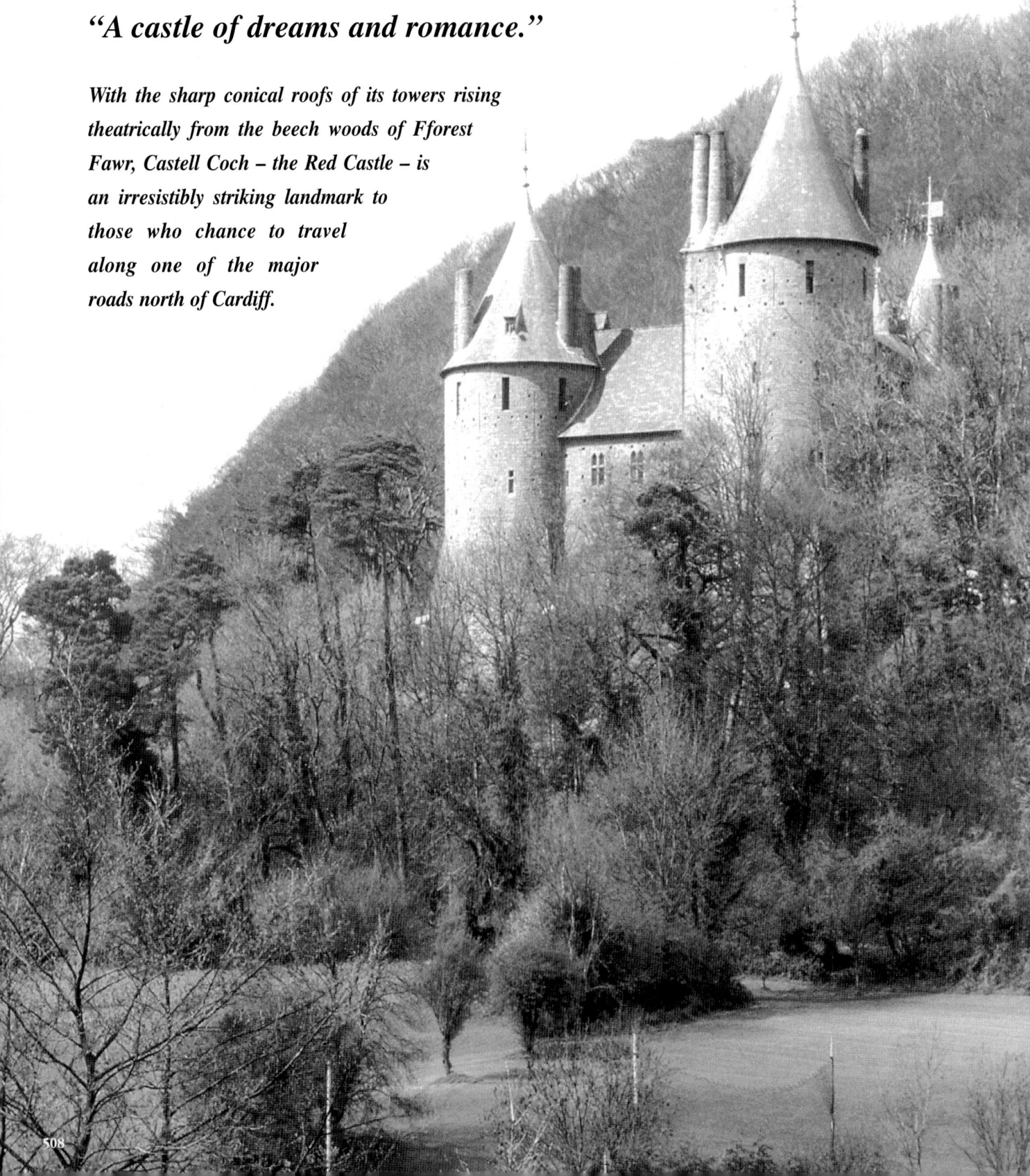

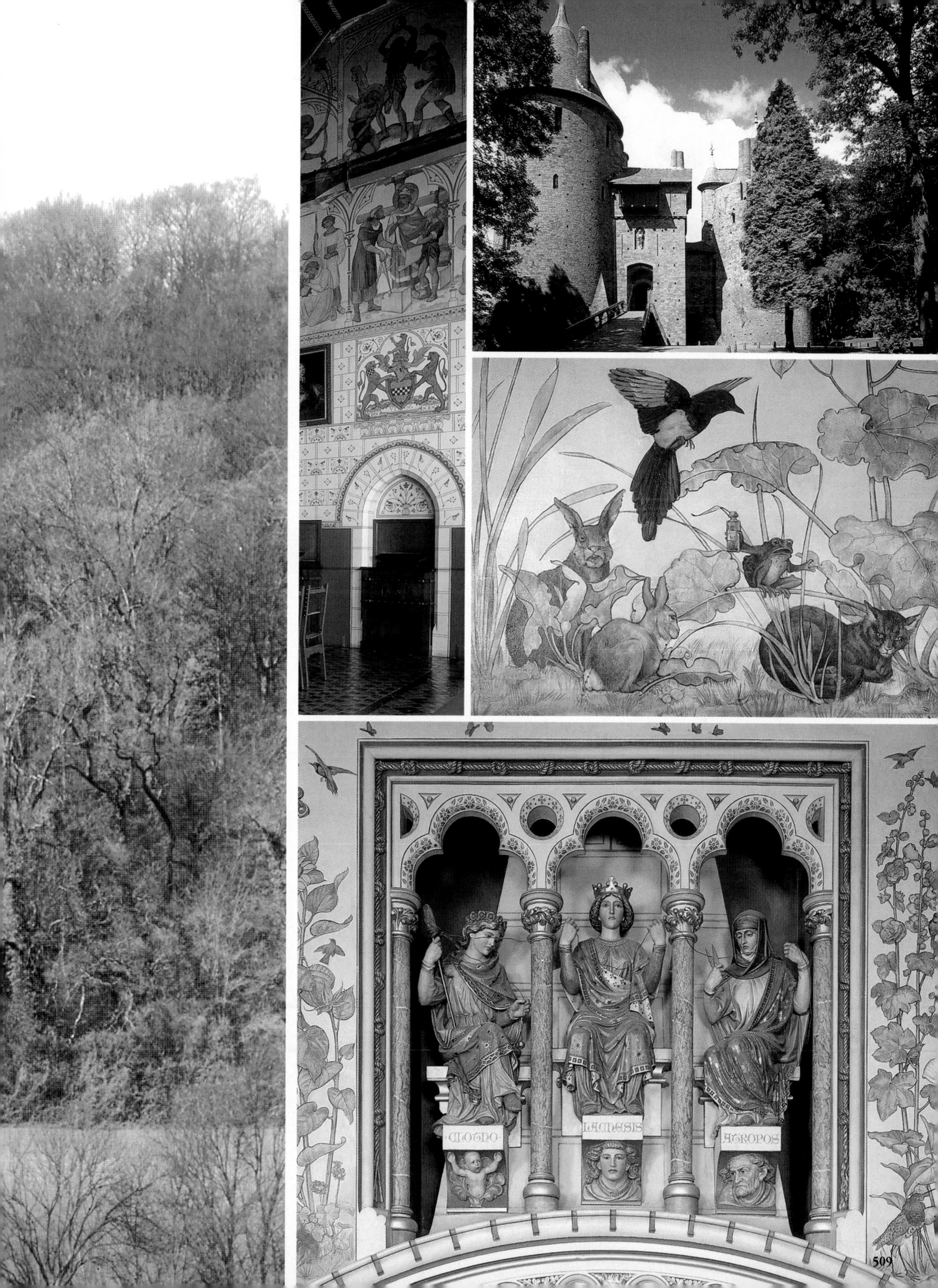

509

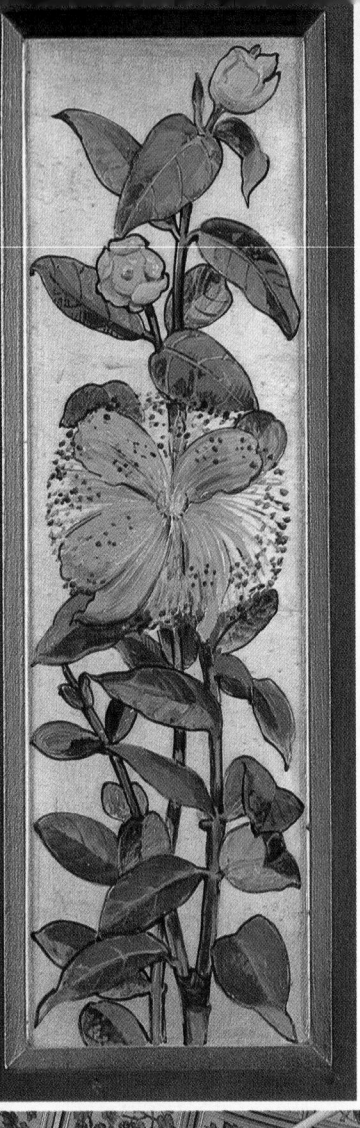

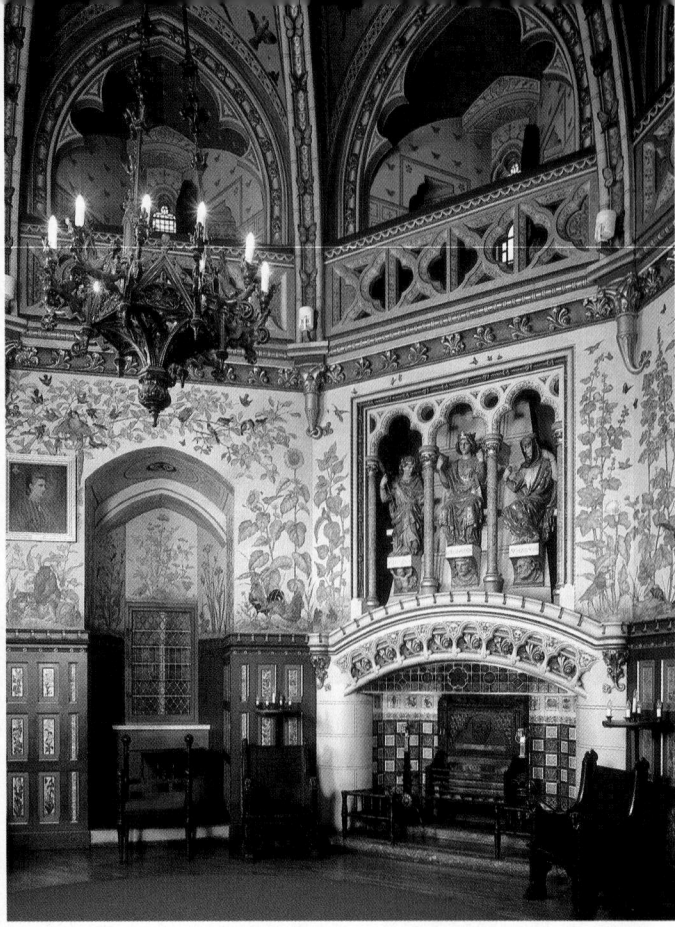

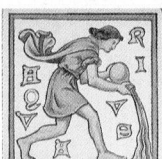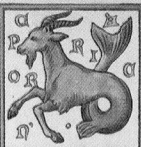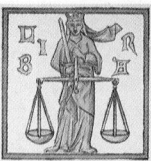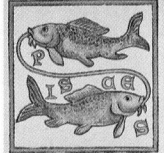

Castell Coch stands proudly on the hillside, a dazzling architectural tour de force of the High Victorian era, a fairytale, romanticised and dream-like castle with sumptuous Gothic fantasy interiors.

However the extravagant building we see today would not have been created had it not been for a highly successful Victorian partnership. The patron – the eccentric academic John Patrick Crichton Stuart (1847 – 1900) 3rd Marquis of Bute, the richest industrialist in the British Isles, and the 'pre-Raphaelite' architect – William Burges (1827 – 81). These men could hardly have been more different: Bute serious and reclusive; Burges raffish and clubbable, but since both were instinctive antiquarians, learned travellers and erudite aesthetes, their relationship blossomed.

Both men were deeply intoxicated with the spirit of Romanticism and fantasists of Victorian medievalism. Together, Bute and Burges were to produce two of the most remarkable expressions of this form to be seen anywhere in the British Isles – here at Castell Coch and at Cardiff Castle.

Viewing the extravagant Victorian mantle of Castell Coch today, it is easy to forget that it is built on the remains of a medieval castle. In Burges's report to Lord Bute of 1872, he wrote:

"There are two courses open with regard to the ruins; – one is to leave them as they are and the other to restore them so as to make a Country residence for your occasional occupation in the Summer."

Bute chose to rebuild and the work of construction at Castell Coch began in earnest in the summer of 1875, though regrettably Burges died in 1881 before the project was fully completed. It would, in fact, take a further 10 years before the assembled team of craftsmen were able to realise the dreams of Lord Bute. Working from detailed interior drawings prepared by Burges before his death, as well as a domed model of the decorative scheme in Lady Bute's bedroom, little of the intensity of Burges's plans have been lost. The interiors dazzle with rich ruby reds, blues and gold; the exterior has an almost Wagnerian splendour about it.

Today this fabulous masterpiece of Victorian medieval escapism is cared for on behalf of the State by Cadw: Welsh Historic Monuments. It is a beguiling jewel, and very much worth a visit.

For further details about *Castell Coch* see entry in South Wales Region.

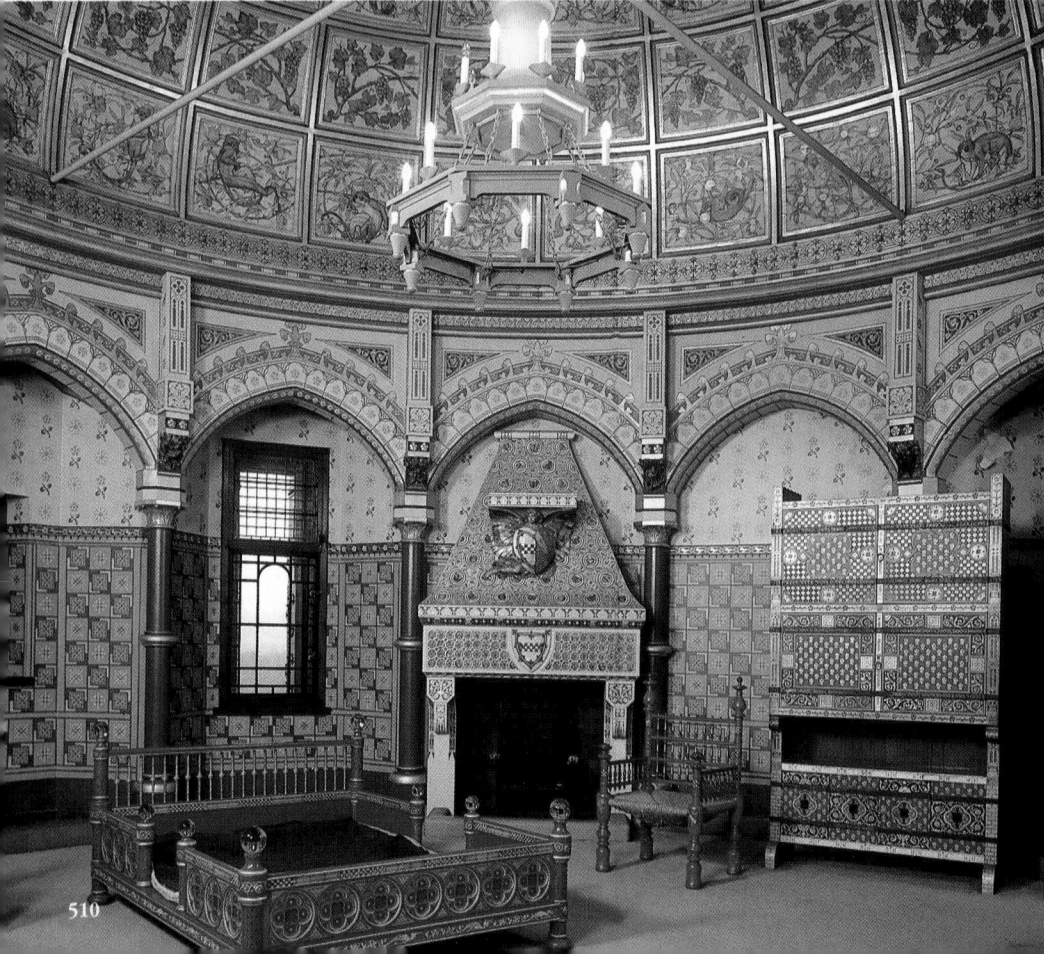

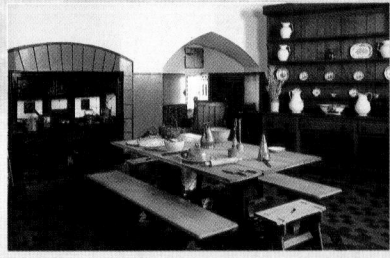

510

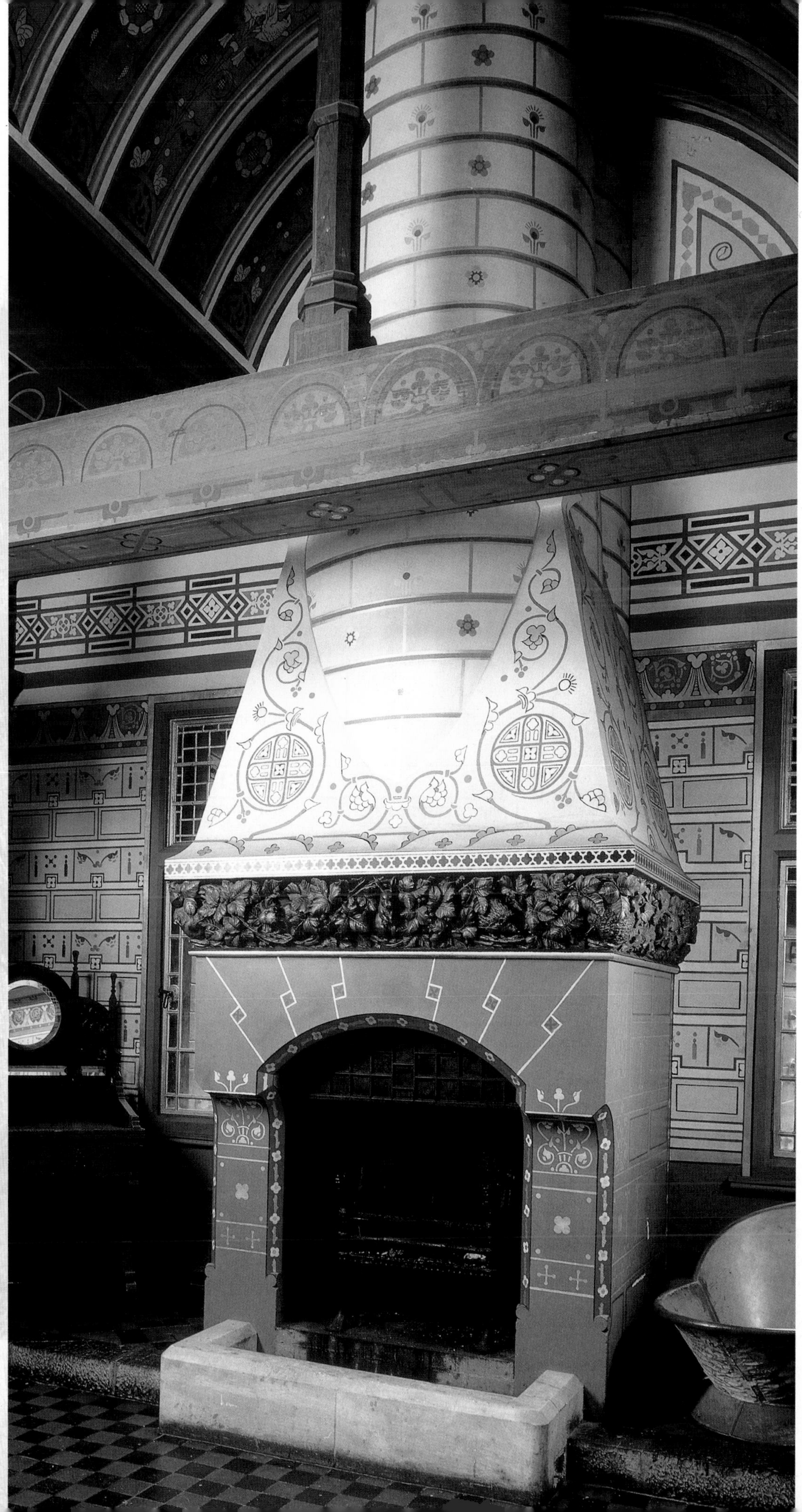

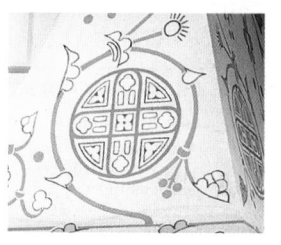

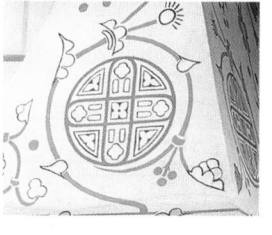

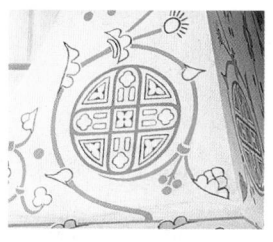

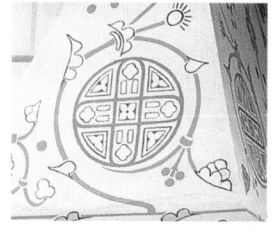

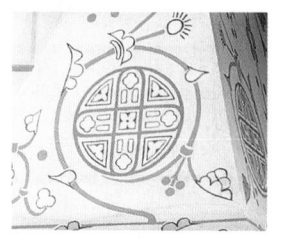

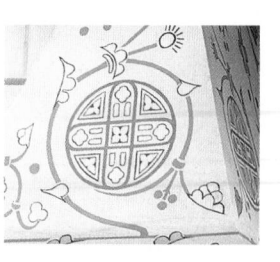

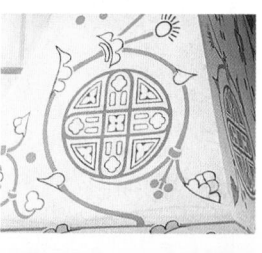

ABERCONWY HOUSE

Tel: 01492 592246 **Fax:** 01492 585153

Castle Street, Conwy LL32 8AY

Owner: The National Trust   **Contact:** The Custodian

Dating from the 14th century, this is the only medieval merchant's house in Conwy to have survived the turbulent history of this walled town for nearly six centuries. Furnished rooms and an audio-visual presentation show daily life from different periods in its history.

Location: OS Ref. SH781 775. At junction of Castle Street and High Street.

Opening Times: 31 Mar - 4 Nov: daily except Tues, 11am - 5pm. Last adm. 30mins before close.

Admission: Adult £2, Child £1, Family (2+2) £5. Pre-booked groups (15+) £1.80. National Trust members Free.

No indoor photography.   Open all year.   By arrangement.   In town car parks only.   Guide dogs only.

BEAUMARIS CASTLE

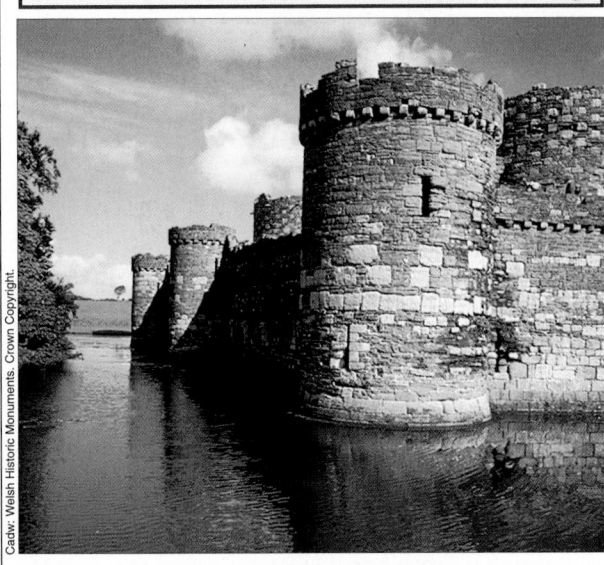

BEAUMARIS, ANGLESEY LL58 8AP

Owner: *In the care of Cadw*   **Contact:** *The Custodian*

Tel: 01248 810361

The most technically perfect medieval castle in Britain, standing midway between Caernarfon and Conwy, commanding the old ferry crossing to Anglesey. A World Heritage Listed Site.

Location: OS Ref. SH608 762. 5m NE of Menai Bridge (A5) by A545. 7m from Bangor.

Opening Times: 27 Mar - 26 May: 9.30am - 5pm. 27 May - 1 Oct: 9.30am - 6pm. 2 - 29 Oct: 9.30am - 5pm. 30 Oct - 31 Mar: Mon - Sat, 9.30am - 4pm, Suns, 11am - 4pm. Closed 24 - 26 Dec & 1 Jan.

Admission: Adult £2.20, Child/Conc. £1.70, Family £6.10.

    Guide dogs only.

Cadw: Welsh Historic Monuments. Crown Copyright.

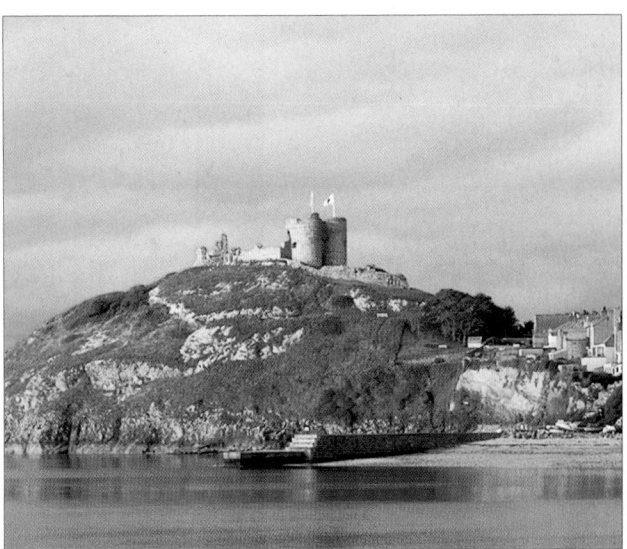

Criccieth Castle, North Wales.

BODELWYDDAN CASTLE

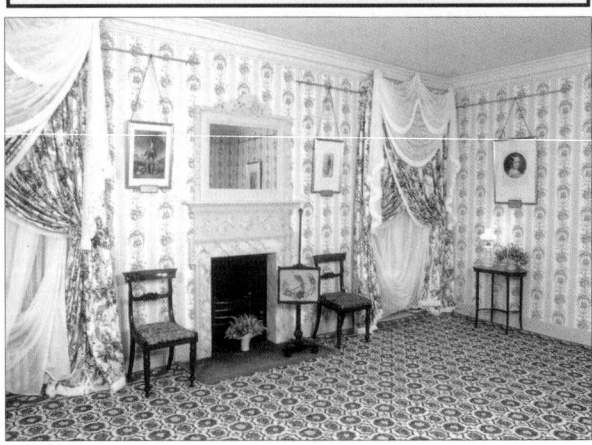

BODELWYDDAN, DENBIGHSHIRE LL18 5YA

Owner: *Denbighshire County Council*   **Contact:** *Piers Norbury*

Tel: 01745 584060 **Fax:** 01745 584563

This magnificently restored Victorian mansion set in rolling parkland, displays extensive collections from the National Portrait Gallery, furniture from the Victoria and Albert Museum and John Gibson sculpture from the Royal Academy. There are exhibitions of Victorian Amusements and Inventions and a programme of temporary exhibitions takes place throughout the year.

Location: OS Ref. SH999 749. Follow signs off A55 expressway. 2m W of St Asaph, opposite Marble Church.

Opening Times: Apr - Oct: daily except Fri, 11am - 5pm. Nov - Mar: daily except Mon & Fri, 11am - 3.30pm. Last admission to site 1hr before closing. Note: minimum opening times - please telephone for further details.

Admission: Adult £4, Child (under 16yrs) £2.50 (under 5yrs Free), Conc. £3.50, Family (2+2) £10. Group: Adult £3.50, Child (under 16yrs) £2.15, Conc. £3. Season Ticket: Adult £12.60, Child/Student/Disabled £8.40, OAP/UB40 £10.50, Family (2+2) £27.30.

Partially suitable. WCs.   By arrangement.   Guide dogs only.

BODNANT GARDEN

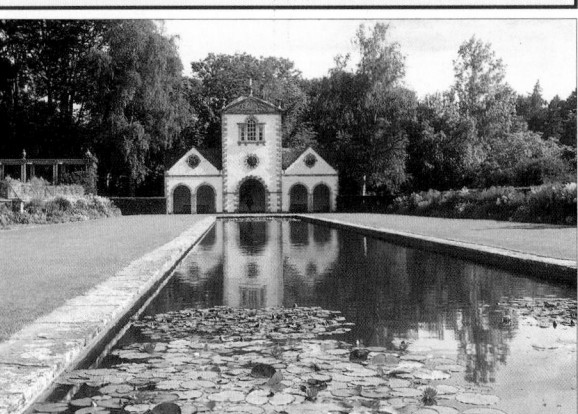

TAL-Y-CAFN, COLWYN BAY LL28 5RE

Owner: *The National Trust*   **Contact:** *General Manager & Head Gardener*

Tel: 01492 650460 **Fax:** 01492 650448

Bodnant Garden is one of the finest gardens in the country not only for its magnificent collections of rhododendrons, camellias and magnolias but also for its idyllic setting above the River Conwy with extensive views of the Snowdonia range. Visit in early Spring and be rewarded by the sight of masses of golden daffodils and other spring bulbs, as well as the beautiful blooms of the magnolias, camellias and flowering cherries. The spectacular rhododendrons and azaleas will delight from mid-April until late May, whilst the famous original Laburnum Arch is an overwhelming mass of yellow bloom from mid-May to mid-June. The herbaceous borders, roses, hydrangeas, clematis and water lilies flower from the middle of June until September. This 32-ha garden has many interesting features including the Lily Terrace, pergola, Canal Terrace, Pin Mill and the Dell Garden.

Location: OS Ref. SH801 723. 8 miles S of Llandudno and Colwyn Bay, off A470. Signposted from A55.

Opening Times: 17 Mar - 31 Oct: daily, 10am - 5pm.

Admission: Adult £5, Child £2.50. Groups (20+) £4.50. Refreshment Pavilion: Daily from 11am (Entrance fee does not have to be paid for the Pavilion).

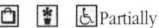 Partially suitable. WCs.   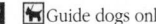 Guide dogs only.

BODRHYDDAN

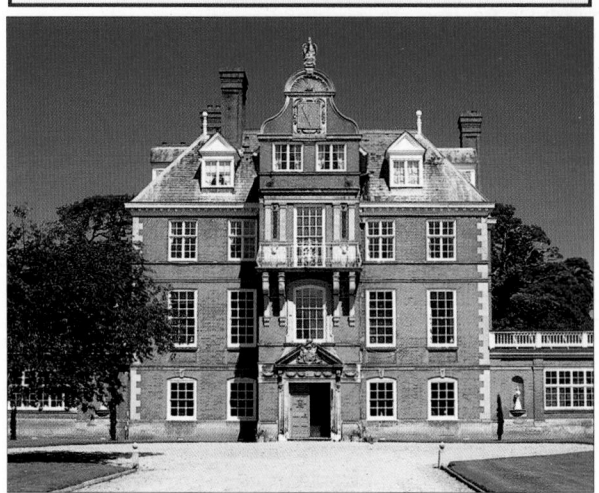

RHUDDLAN, CLWYD LL18 5SB

Owner/Contact: *Colonel The Lord Langford OBE DL*

Tel: 01745 590414

The home of Lord Langford and his family, Bodrhyddan is basically a 17th century house with 19th century additions by the famous architect, William Eden Nesfield, although traces of an earlier building exist. The house has been in the hands of the same family since it was built over 500 years ago. There are notable pieces of armour, pictures, period furniture, a 3,000 year old mummy, a formal parterre, a woodland garden and attractive picnic areas. Bodrhyddan is a Grade I listing, making it one of few in Wales to remain in private hands.

Location: OS Ref. SJ045 788. On the A5151 midway between Dyserth and Rhuddlan, 4m SE of Rhyl.

Opening Times: Jun - Sept inclusive: Tues & Thurs, 2 - 5.30pm.

Admission: House & Gardens: Adult £4, Child £2. Gardens only: Adult £2, Child £1.

Receptions by special arrangement. Partially suitable. Obligatory.

BRYN BRAS CASTLE   **Tel/Fax:** 01286 870210

Llanrug, Caernarfon, Gwynedd LL55 4RE

Owner: Mr & Mrs N E Gray-Parry   **Contact:** Marita Gray-Parry

Built in the Neo-Romanesque style in 1830, on an earlier structure and probably designed by Thomas Hopper. Elegantly romantic family home with fine stained-glass, panelling, interesting ceilings and richly carved furniture. The castle stands in the beautiful Snowdonian range and the extensive gardens include herbaceous borders, walled knot garden, woodland walks, stream and pools, $^1/_4$ m mountain walk with superb views of Snowdon, Anglesey and the sea. Picnic area.

Location: OS Ref. SH543 625. $^1/_2$ m off A4086 at Llanrug, $4^1/_2$ m E of Caernarfon.

Opening Times: Only for groups by prior appointment.

Admission: By arrangement. No young children please.

Self-catering apartments for twos within castle.

CAERNARFON CASTLE

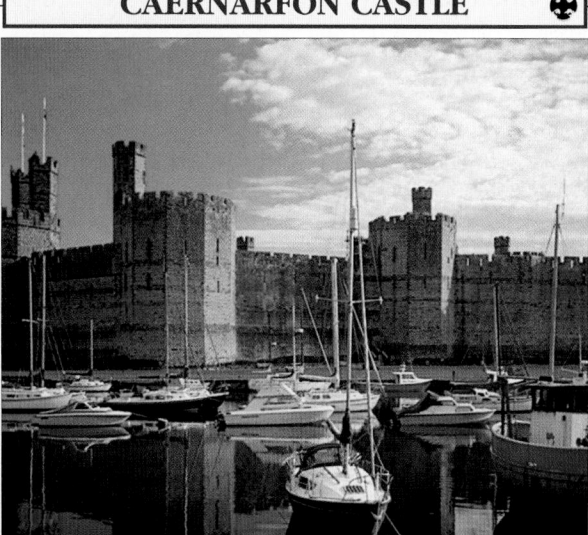

Cadw: Welsh Historic Monuments. Crown Copyright.

CASTLE DITCH, CAERNARFON LL55 2AY

Owner: *In the care of Cadw*   ***Contact:*** *The Custodian*

Tel: 01286 677617

The most famous, and perhaps the most impressive castle in Wales. Taking nearly 50 years to build, it proved the costliest of Edward I's castles. A World Heritage Listed Site.

Location: OS Ref. SH477 626. In Caernarfon, just W of town centre.

Opening Times: 27 Mar - 26 May: 9.30am - 5pm. 27 May - 1 Oct: 9.30am - 6pm. 2 - 29 Oct: 9.30am - 5pm. 30 Oct - 31 Mar: Mon - Sat, 9.30am - 4pm, Suns, 11am - 4pm. Closed 24 - 26 Dec & 1 Jan.

Admission: Adult £4.20, Child/Conc. £3.20, Family £11.60.

Guide dogs only.

CHIRK CASTLE

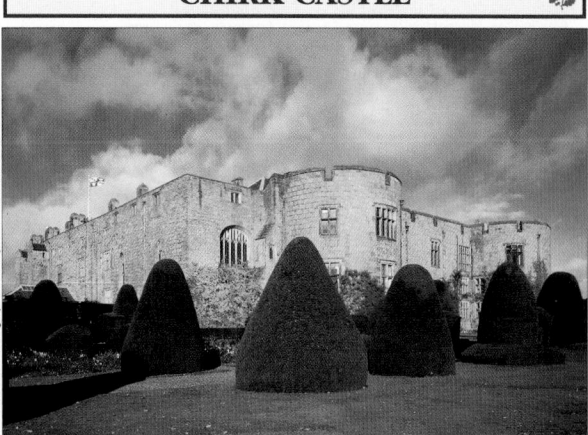

National Trust Photographic Library: Matthew Antrobus.

CHIRK LL14 5AF

Owner: *The National Trust*   ***Contact:*** *The Property Manager*

Tel: 01691 777701   **Fax:** 01691 774706

700 year old Chirk Castle, a magnificent marcher fortress, commands fine views over the surrounding countryside. Rectangular with a massive drum tower at each corner, the castle has beautiful formal gardens with clipped yews, roses and a variety of flowering shrubs. Voted best National Trust garden in 1999. The dramatic dungeon is a reminder of the castle's turbulent history, whilst later occupants have left elegant state rooms, furniture, tapestries and portraits. The castle was sold for five thousand pounds to Sir Thomas Myddelton in 1595, and his descendants continue to live in part of the castle today.

Location: OS Ref. SJ269 380. 8m S of Wrexham off A483, 2m from Chirk village.

Opening Times: 28 Mar - 28 Oct: daily (except Mons & Tues) & BH Mons. Castle: Mar - Sept: 12 noon - 5pm. Oct: 12 noon - 4pm. Last admission $^1/_2$ hr before close. Garden: Mar - Sept: 11am - 6pm. Oct: 11am - 5pm. Last admission 1hr before closing.

Admission: Adult £5, Child £2.50, Family (2+3) £12.50. Pre-booked groups (15+) £4. Garden only: Adults £2.80, Child £1.40.

No indoor photography. Licensed. By arrangement. Guide dogs only.

North Wales

COCHWILLAN OLD HALL
Tel: 01248 355853

Talybont, Bangor, Gwynedd LL57 3AZ
Owner: R C H Douglas Pennant   **Contact:** Mrs G Lloyd

A fine example of medieval architecture with the present house dating from 1450. It was probably built by William Gryffydd who fought for Henry VII at Bosworth. Once owned in the 17th century by John Williams who became Archbishop of York. The house was restored from a barn in 1971.

Location: OS Ref. SH606 695. 3½ m SE of Bangor. 1m SE of Talybont off A55.
Opening Times: By appointment.
Admission: Please telephone for details.

CONWY CASTLE
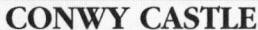

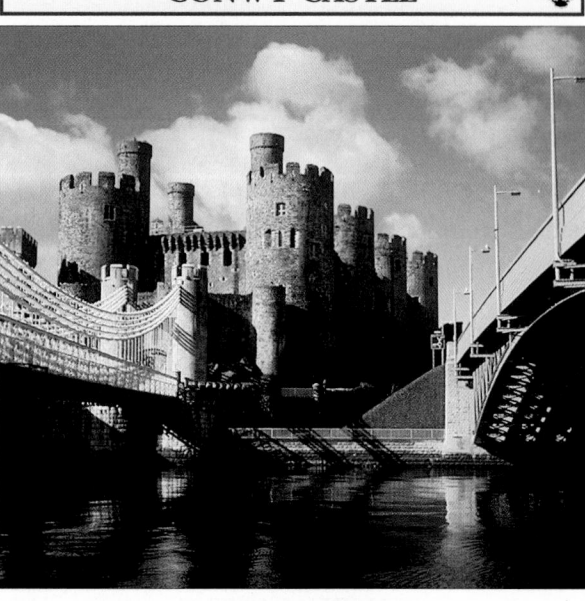

Cadw: Welsh Historic Monuments. Crown Copyright.

CONWY LL32 8AY
Owner: In the care of Cadw   *Contact:* The Custodian

Tel: 01492 592358
Taken together the castle and town walls are the most impressive of the fortresses built by Edward I, and remain the finest and most impressive in Britain. A World Heritage Listed Site.

Location: OS Ref. SH783 774. Conwy by A55 or B5106.
Opening Times: 27 Mar - 26 May: 9.30am - 5pm. 27 May - 1 Oct: 9.30am - 6pm. 2 - 29 Oct: 9.30am - 5pm. 30 Oct - 31 Mar: Mon - Sat, 9.30am - 4pm, Suns, 11am - 4pm. Closed 24 - 26 Dec & 1 Jan.
Admission: Adult £3.50, Child/OAP £2.50, Family £9.50.

By arrangement. Guide dogs only.

CRICCIETH CASTLE
Tel: 01766 522227

Castle Street, Criccieth, Gwynedd LL52 0DP
Owner: In the care of Cadw   **Contact:** The Custodian

Overlooking Cardigan Bay, Criccieth Castle is the most striking of the fortresses built by the native Welsh Princes. Its inner defences dominated by a powerful twin-towered gatehouse.
Location: OS Ref. SH500 378. A497 to Criccieth from Porthmadog or Pwllheli.
Opening Times: 1 Apr - 26 May: 9.30am - 5pm. 27 May - 24 Sept: 9.30am - 6pm.
Admission: Adult £2.20, Child/Conc. £1.70, Family £6.10.

Guide dogs only.

CYMER ABBEY
Tel: 01341 422854

Dolgellau, Gwynedd
Owner: In the care of Cadw   **Contact:** The Custodian

The modest little Abbey at Cymer, with its simple church, stands amid remote and beautiful countryside. Situated near the head of the Mawddach estuary.
Location: OS Ref. SH722 195. 2m NW of Dolgellau on A470.
Opening Times: Early Apr - end Oct: 9.30am - 6.30pm. End Oct - end Mar: 9.30am - 4pm. Closed 24 - 26 Dec & 1 Jan.
Admission: Adult £1.20, Conc. 70p, Family £3.10.

Limited. Guide dogs only.

DENBIGH CASTLE
Tel: 01745 813385

Denbigh, Clwyd
Owner: In the care of Cadw   **Contact:** The Custodian

Crowning the summit of a prominent outcrop dominating the Vale of Clwyd, the principal feature of this spectacular site is the great gatehouse dating back to the 11th century. Some of the walls can still be walked by visitors.
Location: OS Ref. SJ052 658. Denbigh via A525 or B5382.
Opening Times: Early Apr - late Oct: Mon - Fri, 10am - 5.30pm. Sats & Suns, 9.30am - 5.30pm. Winter: open site.
Admission: Castle: Adult £2, Child/Conc. £1.50, Family £5.50.

Guide dogs only.

DOLWYDDELAN CASTLE
Tel: 01690 750366

Blaenau Ffestiniog, Gwynedd
Owner: In the care of Cadw   **Contact:** The Custodian

Standing proudly on a ridge, this stern building remains remarkably intact and visitors cannot fail to be impressed with the great solitary square tower, built by Llewelyn the Great in the early 13th century.
Location: OS Ref. SH722 522. A470(T) Blaenau Ffestiniog to Betws-y-Coed, 1m W of Dolwyddelan.
Opening Times: Early Apr - late Oct: daily, 9.30am - 6.30pm. Late Oct - late Mar: Mon - Sat, 9.30am - 4pm, Suns, 11am - 4pm. Closed 24 - 26 Dec & 1 Jan.
Admission: Adult £2, Child/Conc. £1.50, Family £5.50.

Guide dogs only.

ERDDIG

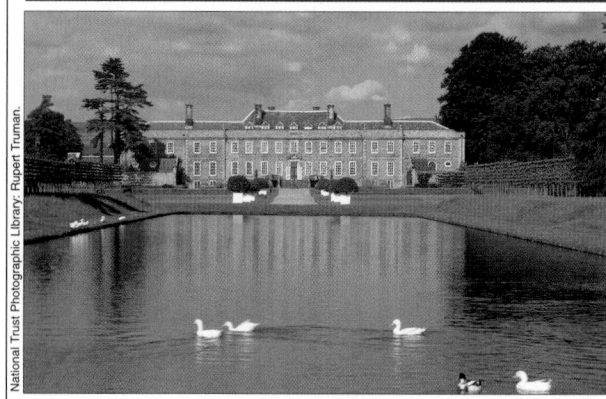

National Trust Photographic Library: Rupert Truman.

Nr WREXHAM LL13 0YT
Owner: The National Trust   *Contact:* Sally Smith

Tel: 01978 355314   **Fax:** 01978 313333   **Info Line:** 01978 315151
One of the most fascinating houses in Britain, not least because of the unusually close relationship that existed between the family of the house and their servants. The beautiful and evocative range of outbuildings includes kitchen, laundry, bakehouse, stables, sawmill, smithy and joiner's shop, while the stunning state rooms display most of their original 18th & 19th century furniture and furnishings, including some exquisite Chinese wallpaper. The large walled garden has been restored to its 18th century format design with Victorian parterre and yew walk, and also contains the National Ivy Collection. There is an extensive park with woodland walks.

Location: OS Ref. SJ326 482. 2m S of Wrexham.
Opening Times: 31 Mar - 4 Nov: daily except Thurs & Fris, open Good Fri. House: 12 noon - 5pm. Garden: 11am - 6pm (10am - 6pm during Jul & Aug). From 1 Oct: House: 12 noon - 4pm, Garden: 11am - 5pm. Last admission 1 hr before closing.
Admission: All-inclusive ticket: Adult £6, Child £3, Family (2+3) £15. Pre-booked group (15+) £5. Below stairs (including outbuildings & Garden): Adult £4, Child £2, Family (2+3) £10, Pre-booked groups (15+) £3.20. NT members Free.

Partially suitable. WCs. Licensed. AV presentation. Guide dogs only.

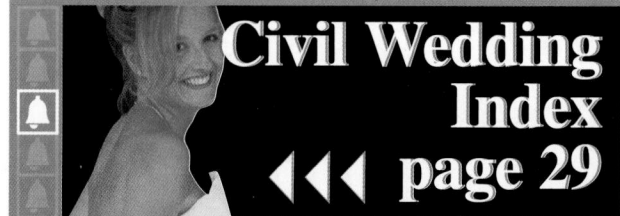

FFERM

Tel/Fax: 01352 770217

Pontblyddyn, Mold, Flintshire

Owner/Contact: Dr M Jones-Mortimer

17th century farmhouse. Viewing is limited to 7 persons at any one time. Prior booking is recommended. No toilets or refreshments.

Location: OS Ref. SJ279 603. Access from A541 in Pontblyddyn, 3^1/$_2$ m SE of Mold.

Opening Times: 2nd Wed in every month, 2 - 5pm. Pre-booking is recommended.

Admission: £4.

GLANSEVERN HALL GARDENS

Tel: 01686 640200   **Fax:** 01686 640829

Berriew, Welshpool, Powys SY21 8AH

Owner: Mr G and Miss M Thomas   **Contact:** Mr & Mrs R N Thomas

A classic Greek revival house romantically positioned on banks of River Severn. Over 18 acres of mature gardens notable for variety of unusual tree species. Also much new planting. Lakeside and woodland walks, water and rock gardens, grotto, walled rose garden.

Location: OS Ref. SJ195 001. On A483, 5m S of Welshpool, 1m SE of Berriew.

Opening Times: May - Sept: Fris, Sats and BH Mons, 12 noon - 6pm. Groups by appointment on other days.

Admission: Adult £3, Child (under 16) Free.

 Grounds suitable.   In grounds, on leads.

GWYDIR CASTLE

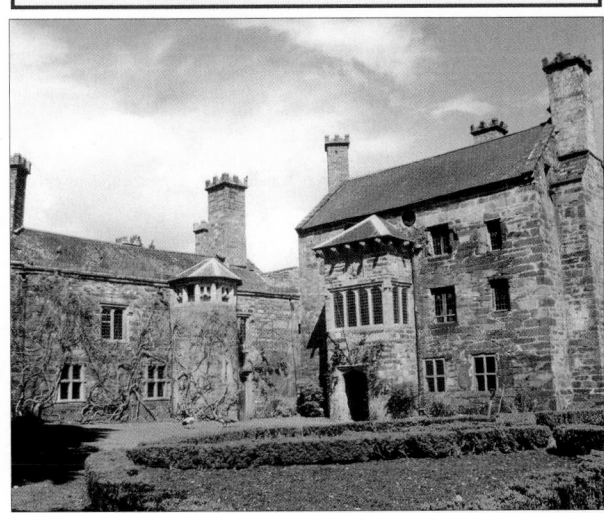

LLANRWST, GWYNEDD LL26 0PN

Owner/Contact: Mr & Mrs Welford

Tel/Fax: 01492 641687

Gwydir Castle is situated in the beautiful Conwy Valley and is set within a Grade I listed, 10 acre garden. Built by the illustrious Wynn family c1500, Gwydir is a fine example of a Tudor courtyard house, incorporating re-used medieval material from the dissolved Abbey of Maenan. Further additions date from c1600 and c1826. The important 1640s panelled Dining Room has now been reinstated, following its repatriation from the New York Metropolitan Museum.

Location: OS Ref. SH795 610. ^{1}/$_2$ m W of Llanrwst on A5106.

Opening Times: 1 Mar - 31 Oct: daily, 10am - 5pm. Limited openings at other times. Occasional weddings on Sats.

Admission: Adult £3, Child £1.50. Group discount 10%.

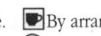 Partially suitable.   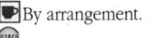 By arrangement.   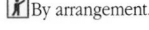 By arrangement.
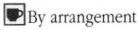 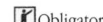 2 doubles.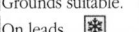

HARLECH CASTLE

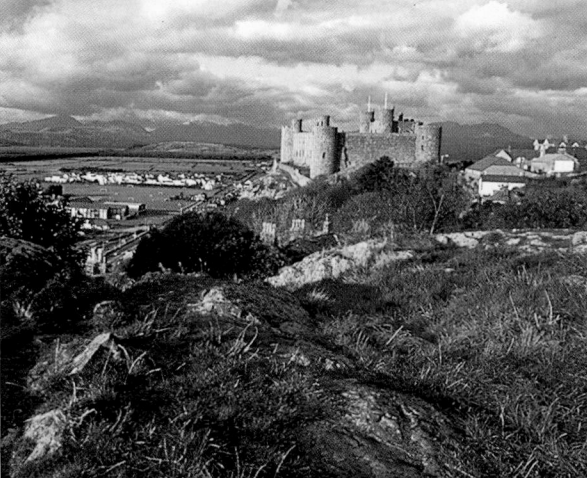

HARLECH LL46 2YH

Owner: In the care of Cadw   *Contact: The Custodian*

Tel: 01766 780552

Set on a towering rock above Tremadog Bay, this seemingly impregnable fortress is the most dramatically sited of all the castles of Edward I. A World Heritage Listed Site.

Location: OS Ref. SH581 312. Harlech, Gwynedd on A496 coast road.

Opening Times: 27 Mar - 26 May: 9.30 - 5pm. 27 May - 1 Oct: 9.30am - 6pm. 2 - 29 Oct: 9.30am - 5pm. 30 Oct - 31 Mar: Mon - Sat, 9.30am - 4pm, Suns, 11am - 4pm. Closed 24 - 26 Dec & 1 Jan.

Admission: Adult £3, Child/OAP £2, Family £8.

 Guide dogs only.

HARTSHEATH

Tel/Fax: 01352 770217

Pontblyddyn, Mold, Flintshire

Owner/Contact: Dr M Jones-Mortimer

18th and 19th century house set in parkland. Viewing is limited to 7 persons at any one time. Prior booking is recommended. No toilets or refreshments.

Location: OS Ref. SJ287 602. Access from A5104, 3^1/$_2$ m SE of Mold between Pontblyddyn and Penyffordd.

Opening Times: 1st, 3rd & 5th Wed in every month, 2 - 5pm.

Admission: £4.

ISCOYD PARK

Nr Whitchurch, Shropshire SY13 3AT

Owner/Contact: Mr P C Godsal

18th century Grade II* listed redbrick house in park.

Location: OS Ref. SJ504 421. 2m W of Whitchurch on A525.

Opening Times: By written appointment only.

GYRN CASTLE

Tel/Fax: 01745 853500

Llanasa, Holywell, Flintshire CH8 9BG

Owner/Contact: Sir Geoffrey Bates BT

Dating, in part, from 1700, castellated 1820. Large picture gallery, panelled entrance hall. Pleasant woodland walks and fantastic views to the River Mersey and the Lake District.

Location: OS Ref. SJ111 815. 26m W of Chester, off A55, 4^1/$_2$ m SE of Prestatyn.

Opening Times: All year by appointment.

Admission: £4. Discount for groups.

Grounds suitable. By arrangement. Obligatory. Limited for coaches. On leads.

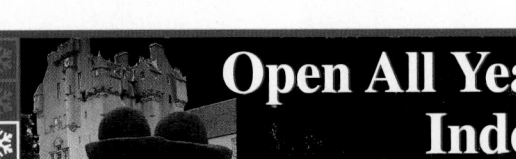

Open All Year Index page 49 ◀◀◀

North Wales

PENRHYN CASTLE

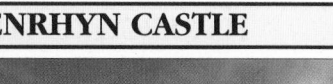

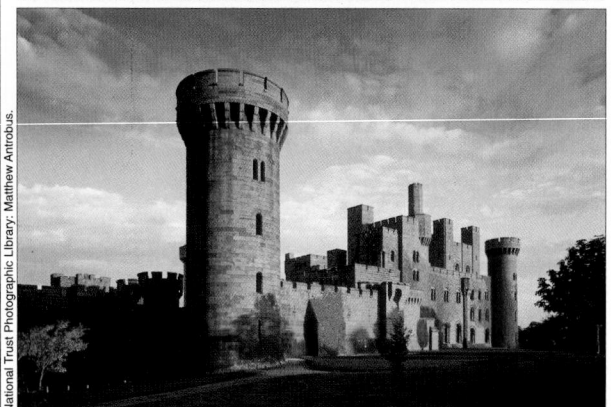

BANGOR LL57 4HN

Owner: The National Trust **Contact:** *The Property Manager*

Tel: 01248 353084

This dramatic neo-Norman fantasy castle sits between Snowdonia and the Menai Strait. Built by Thomas Hopper between 1820 and 1845 for the wealthy Pennant family, who made their fortune from Jamaican sugar and Welsh slate. The castle is crammed with fascinating things such as a 1-ton slate bed made for Queen Victoria, elaborate carvings, mock-Norman furniture and an outstanding collection of paintings. With a countryside exhibition, industrial railway and railway model museums and a superb doll museum. Its grounds include parkland, an extensive exotic tree and shrub collection and a Victorian walled garden. New in 2001: Victorian kitchens fully restored and open to the public for the first time.

Location: OS Ref. SH602 720. 1m E of Bangor, at Llandygai on A5122.

Opening Times: 28 Mar - 2 Nov: daily except Tues. Castle: 12 noon - 5pm (Jul & Aug: 11am - 5pm). Grounds: 11am - 5pm (Jul & Aug: 10am - 5.30pm). Last audio tour 4pm. Last admission 4.30pm.

Admission: All inclusive ticket: Adult £6, Child £3, Family (2+2) £15. Pre-booked groups (15+) £5. Garden & Stableblock Exhibitions only: Adult £4, Child £2. Audio tour: 50p (including NT members). NT members Free.

Licensed.

PLAS BRONDANW GARDENS

Tel: 01766 770228

Plas Brondanw, Llanfrothen, Gwynedd LL48 6SW

Italianate gardens with topiary.

Owner: Trustees of the Second Portmeirion Foundation

Location: OS Ref. SH618 423. 3m N of Penrhyndeudraeth off A4085, on Croesor Road.

Opening Times: All year: daily 9am - 5pm.

Admission: Adult £1.50, Child 25p, Group £1 (if pre-booked).

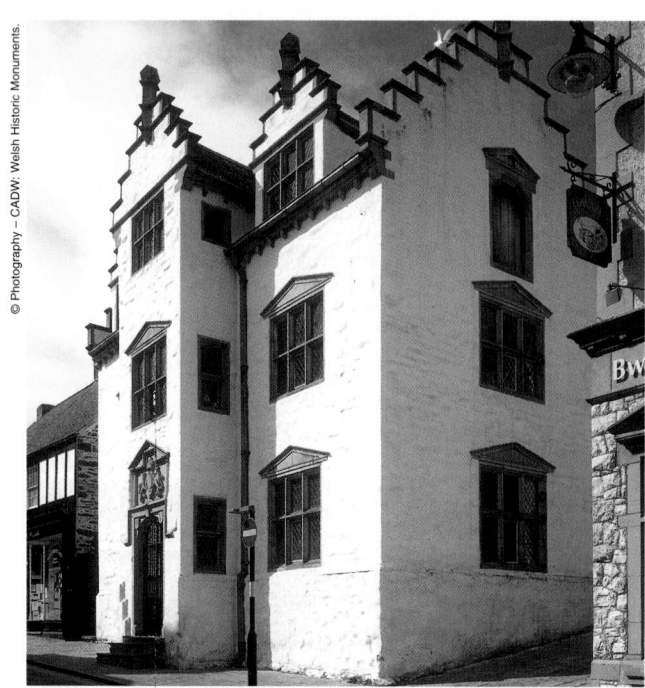

PLAS MAWR

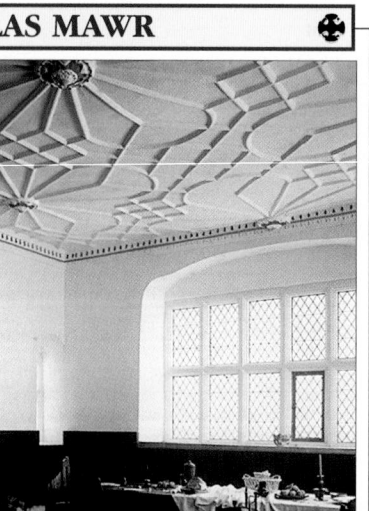

HIGH STREET, CONWY LL32 8EF

Owner: In the care of Cadw **Contact:** *The Custodian*

Tel: 01492 580167

The best preserved Elizabethan town house in Britain, the house reflects the status of its builder Robert Wynn. A fascinating and unique place allowing visitors to sample the lives of the Tudor gentry and their servants, Plas Mawr is famous for the quality and quantity of its decorative plasterwork.

Location: OS Ref. SH779 777. Conwy by A55 or B5106.

Opening Times: 1 Apr - 26 May: 9.30am - 5pm. 27 May - 3 Sept: 9.30am - 6pm. 4 Sept - 1 Oct: 9.30am - 5pm. 2 - 29 Oct: 9.30am - 4pm. Closed on Mons except BHs.

Admission: Adult £4, Child/OAP £3, Family £11.

Limited. Guide dogs only.

PLAS NEWYDD

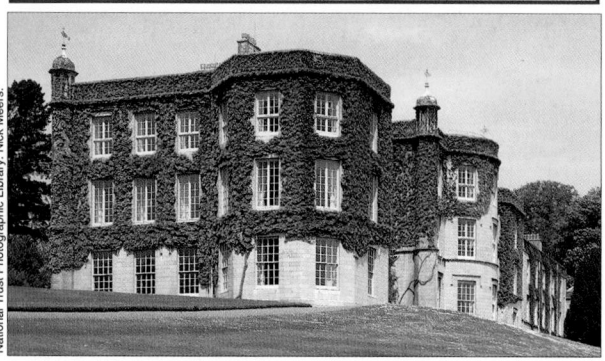

LLANFAIRPWLL, ANGLESEY LL61 6DQ

Owner: The National Trust **Contact:** *The Property Manager*

Tel: 01248 714795 **Fax:** 01248 713673 **e-mail:** ppnmsn@smtp.ntrust.org.uk

Set amidst breathtaking beautiful scenery and with spectacular views of Snowdonia. Fine spring garden and Australasian arboretum with an understorey of shrubs and wildflowers. Summer terrace, and , later, massed hydrangeas and Autumn colour. A woodland walk gives access to a marine walk on the Menai Strait. Rhododendron garden open April - early June only. Elegant 18th century house by James Wyatt, famous for its association with Rex Whistler whose largest painting is here. Military museum contains relics of 1st Marquess of Anglesey and Battle of Waterloo. A historic cruise, a boat trip on the Menai Strait operates from the property weather and tides permitting (additional charge). New for 2001 – 5 seater buggy to rhododendron garden and woodland walk.

Location: OS Ref. SH521 696. 2m S of Llanfairpwll and A5.

Opening Times: 31 Mar - 31 Oct: Sat - Wed. House: 12 noon - 5pm. Garden: 11am - 5.30pm. Last admission $1/2$ hr before closing.

Admission: House & Garden: Adult £4.50, Child £2.25 (under 5s Free), Family (2+3) £11. Groups (15+) £3.70. Garden only: Adult £2.50, Child £1.25.

No indoor photography.

Partially suitable. WCs. Minibus from car park to house.

Licensed. Award winning. By arrangement.

Tel for details.

Plas Mawr, North Wales.

PLAS YN RHIW ※

Tel/Fax: 01758 780219

Rhiw, Pwllheli LL53 8AB

Owner: The National Trust　　　　**Contact:** The Custodian

A small manor house, with garden and woodlands, overlooking the west shore of Porth Neigwl (Hell's Mouth Bay) on the Llyn Peninsula. The house is part medieval, with Tudor and Georgian additions, and the ornamental gardens have flowering trees and shrubs, divided by box hedges and grass paths, rising behind to the snowdrop wood.

Location: OS Ref. SH237 282. 12m SW of Pwllheli, 3m S of the B4413 to Aberdaron. No access for coaches.

Opening Times: 31 Mar - 14 May: daily except Tues & Weds. 16 May - 30 Sept: daily except Tues. 1 - 31 Oct: Sats & Suns only, 12 noon - 5pm.

Admission: Adult £3.20, Child £1.60, Family (2+3) £8. Guided tour for pre-booked groups additional £1.40 (including NT members). Gardens only: Adult £2, Child £1, Family (2+3) £5.

🖼 🚻 ♿Partially suitable. WCs. 🎦By arrangement. 🅿Limited.
🐕Guide dogs only.

PORTMEIRION

Tel: 01766 770000　**Fax:** 01766 771331

Portmeirion, Gwynedd LL48 6ET

e-mail: info@portmeirion-village.com

Owner: The Portmeirion Foundation　　　　**Contact:** Mr R Llywelyn

Portmeirion was built by Clough Williams-Ellis as an 'unashamedly romantic' village resort. All the houses form part of the hotel with rooms and suites within comfortable walking distance from the main building on the quayside. The curvilinear dining room overlooking the estuary serves fresh local produce in elegant surroundings.

Location: OS Ref. SH590 371. Off A487 at Minffordd between Penrhyndeudraeth and Porthmadog.

Opening Times: All year (except Christmas Day): daily, 9.30am - 5.30pm.

Admission: Adult £5, Child £2.50, OAP £4, Family (2+2) £12.50.

ℹConference facilities. 🖼 🚻 🍽 ♿Partially suitable. 🍺🍴Licensed. 🅿
🍽 🛏40 double. Ensuite. 🔔 ❄ 🗝

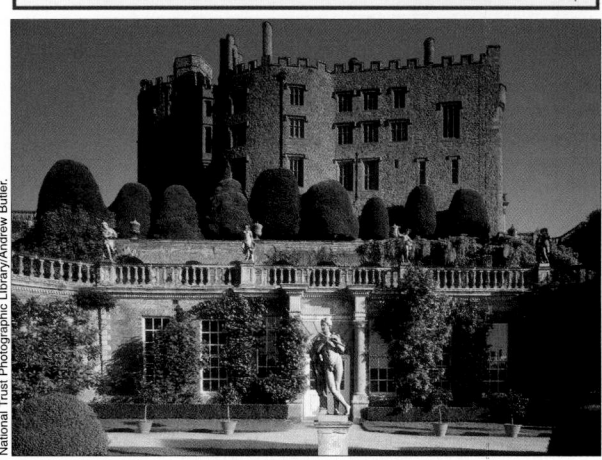

POWIS CASTLE & GARDEN ※

Nr WELSHPOOL SY21 8RF

Owner: The National Trust　*Contact:* Amanda Whitmore

Tel: 01938 554338/551920 **Fax:** 01938 554336 **e-mail:** gpcajw@smtp.ntrust.org.uk

The world-famous garden, overhung with enormous clipped yew trees, shelters rare and tender plants in colourful herbaceous borders. Laid out under the influence of Italian and French styles, the garden retains its original lead statues and, an orangery on the terraces. Perched on a rock above the garden terraces, the medieval castle contains one of the finest collections of paintings and furniture in Wales.

Location: OS Ref. SJ195 001. 1m W of Welshpool, 1m SE of Berriew, car access on A483.

Opening Times: Castle & Museum: 31 Mar - 4 Nov: daily except Mons & Tues (Jul & Aug: daily except Mons), but open BH Mons, 1 - 5pm. Garden: as Castle, 11am - 6pm. Shop & Tearoom: Also open 9 Nov - 16 Dec, Fri - Sun, 11am - 4pm.

Admission: All inclusive: Adult £7.50, Child £3.75, Family £18.75. Groups: (15+ booked): £6.50. Garden only: Adult £5, Child £2.50, Family £12.50. Groups (15+ booked): £4. No groups rates on Suns or BH Mons. NT members & under 5s Free.

ℹNo indoor photography. 🖼 🚻 ♿Partially suitable. 🍺Licensed.
🎦By arrangement. 🅿Limited for coaches. 🐕Guide dogs only.

RHUDDLAN CASTLE ✤

Tel: 01745 590777

Castle Gate, Castle Street, Rhuddlan LL18 5AD

Owner: In the care of Cadw　　　　**Contact:** The Custodian

Guarding the ancient ford of the River Clwyd, Rhuddlan was the strongest of Edward I's castles in North-East Wales. Linked to the sea by an astonishing deep water channel nearly 3 miles long, it still proclaims the innovative genius of its architect.

Location: OS Ref. SJ025 779. SW end of Rhuddlan via A525 or A547.

Opening Times: Apr - Sept: daily, 10am - 5pm.

Admission: Adult £2, Child/OAP £1.50, Family £5.50.

🅿 🐕Guide dogs only. 🗝

RUG CHAPEL & LLANGAR CHURCH ✤

Tel: 01490 412025

c/o Coronation Cottage, Rug, Corwen LL21 9BT

Owner: In the care of Cadw　　　　**Contact:** The Custodian

Prettily set in a wooded landscape, Rug Chapel's exterior gives little hint of the wonders within. Nearby the attractive medieval Llangar Church still retains its charming early Georgian furnishings.

Location: Rug Chapel: OS Ref. SJ065 439. Off A494, 1m N of Corwen. Llangar Church: OS Ref. SJ064 423. Off B4401, 1m S of Corwen (obtain key at Rug).

Opening Times: Rug Chapel: 21 Apr - 24 Sept:10am - 2pm & 3 - 5pm. Closed Mons & Tues except BHs. Llangar Church: Interior access between 2 - 3pm, Apr - Sept through the Custodian at Rug Chapel. Both sites closed in winter.

Admission: Adult £2, Child/Conc. £1.50, Family £5.50.

♿ 🎦By arrangement. 🅿 🏛 🐕Guide dogs only. 🗝

Rhuddlan Castle, North Wales.

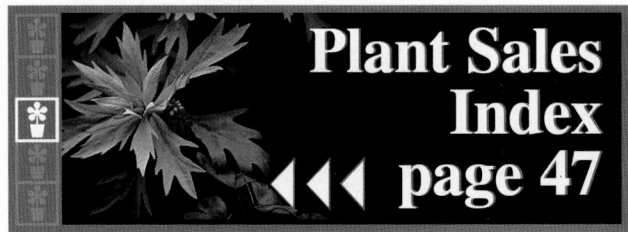

Plant Sales Index
◀◀◀ page 47

ST ASAPH CATHEDRAL
Tel: 01745 583597

St Asaph, Denbighshire LL17 0RL
Contact: The Dean

Britain's smallest ancient cathedral founded in 560AD by Kentigern, a religious community enclosed in a 'llan', hence Llanelwy. Present building dates from 13th century. Post reformation period, close association with the translators of the Welsh Prayer Book and Bible. A copy of the William Morgan Bible of 1588 can be seen. The Translators' Memorial, erected in 1888, stands outside. Within, a 17th century Spanish Madonna in ivory, stained glass, an exhibit of literary treasures, the only recumbent effigy, from 1268 - 93, an iron chest (1738) and four painted angels in the choir roof are just some of the things of interest. Housing an original Hill organ and home to the International North Wales Music Festival yearly, in September.

Location: OS Ref. SJ039 743. In St Asaph, S of A55.

Opening Times: Summer: 7.30am - 6pm. Winter: 7.30am - dusk. Sun services: 8am, 11am, 3.30pm.

⬚ &Ground floor suitable. 🐕Guide dogs only. ❋

TOWER 🏠
Tel: 01352 700220

Nercwys, Mold, Flintshire CH7 4EN
Owner/Contact: Wendy Wynne-Eyton

This Grade I listed building is steeped in Welsh history and bears witness to the continuous warfare of the time. A fascinating place to visit or for overnight stays.

Location: OS Ref. SJ240 620. 1m S of Mold.

Opening Times: Summer: BHs plus most of May. Please telephone for exact dates and times. Groups welcome at other times by appointment.

Admission: Adult £3, Child £2.

TREWERN HALL
Tel: 01938 570657

Trewern, Welshpool, Powys SY21 8DT
Owner: Chapman Family
Contact: Mr John Chapman/Mrs Edna Chapman

Trewern Hall is a Grade II* listed building standing in the Severn Valley. It has been described as 'one of the most handsome timber-framed houses surviving in the area'. The porch contains a beam inscribed RF1610, though it seems likely that parts of the house are earlier. The property has been in the ownership of the Chapman family since 1918.

Location: OS Ref. SJ269 113. Off A458 Welshpool - Shrewsbury Road, 4m from Welshpool.

Opening Times: Last week in Apr. May: Mon - Fri, 2 - 5pm.

Admission: Adult £2, Child/Conc. £1. (2000 prices).

&Not suitable. No parking. 🚫

VALLE CRUCIS ABBEY ✠
Tel: 01978 860326

Llangollen, Clwyd
Owner: In the care of Cadw
Contact: The Custodian

Set in a beautiful valley location, Valle Crucis Abbey is the best preserved medieval monastery in North Wales, enhanced by the only surviving monastic fish pond in Wales.

Location: OS Ref. SJ205 442. B5103 from A5, 2m NW of Llangollen, or A542 from Ruthin.

Opening Times: 21 Apr - 24 Sept: 10am - 5pm. Winter: open site.

Admission: Adult £2, Child/Conc. £1.50. Family £5.50.

& P 🐕Guide dogs only. ❋ (NW)

WERN ISAF
Tel: 01248 680437

Penmaen Park, Llanfairfechan LL33 0RN
Owner/Contact: Mrs P J Phillips

This Arts and Crafts house was built in 1900 by the architect H L North as his family home and it contains much of the original furniture and William Morris fabrics. It is situated in a woodland garden and is at its best in the Spring. It has extensive views over the Menai Straits and Conwy Bay. One of the most exceptional houses of its date and style in Wales.

Location: OS Ref. SH685 752.

Opening Times: 3 - 30 Mar: daily except Mons, 12 noon - 4pm. Please telephone for details.

Admission: £1

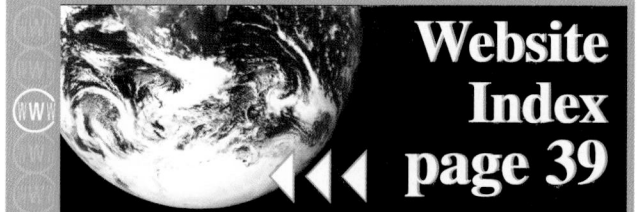

Website Index page 39 ◀◀◀

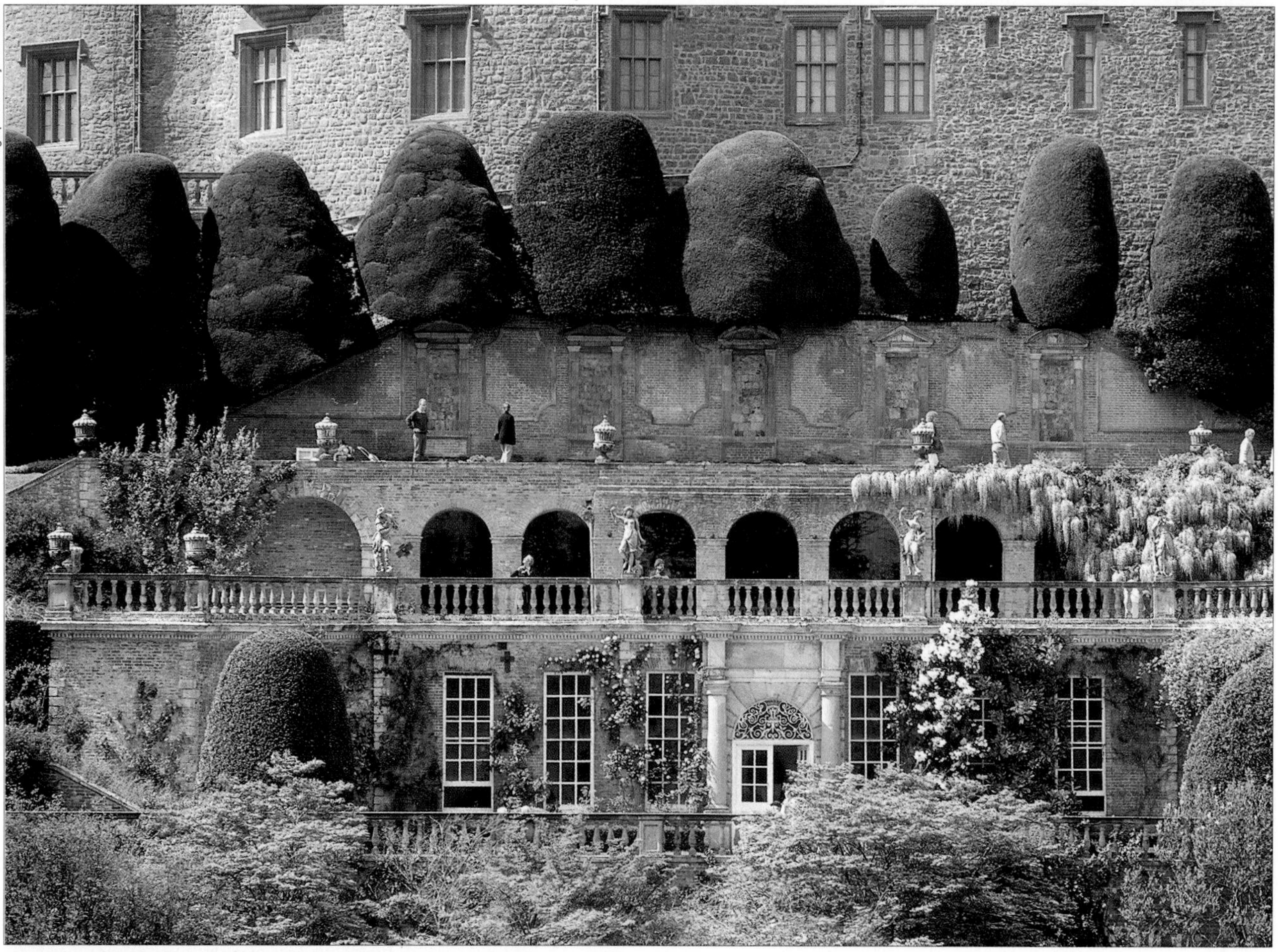

Powis Castle & Garden, North Wales.

NT Photographic Library: Ian Shaw.

ABERDULAIS FALLS

Tel: 01639 636674

Aberdulais, Vale of Neath SA10 8EU

Owner: The National Trust

Contact: The Property Warden

For over 300 years this famous waterfall has provided the energy to drive the wheels of industry, from the first manufacture of copper in 1584 to present day remains of the tinplate works. It has also been visited by famous artists such as J M W Turner in 1796. The site today houses a unique hydro-electrical scheme which has been developed to harness the waters of the Dulais river.

Location: OS Ref. SS772 995. On A4109, 3m NE of Neath. 4m from M4/J43, then A465.

Opening Times: Mar: Sats & Suns only, 11am - 4pm. 1 Apr - 28 Oct: Mon - Fri, 10am - 5pm, Sats, Suns & BHs 11am - 6pm. Shop: as property. 2 Nov - 23 Dec: Fri - Sun, 11am - 4pm (closed 2pm on 23 Dec).

Admission: Adult £3, Child £1.50, Family £7.40. Groups (15+): Adult £2.40, Child £1.20. National Trust members Free.

Light refreshments (summer only) Limited.

ABERGLASNEY GARDENS

Tel/Fax: 01558 668998

Llangathen, Carmarthenshire SA32 8QH

e-mail: info@aberglasney.org.uk

Contact: Booking Department

In a sheltered glade of the beautiful Towy Valley stands Aberglasney and its gardens. What sets this property apart from others are the extraordinary, enigmatic structures within the gardens. The restoration project has already restored the structures and will bring both the house and gardens back to their former glory.

Location: OS Ref. SN581 221. 4m W of Llandeilo, 10m E of Carmarthen.

Opening Times: 1 Apr - 31 Oct: daily, 10am - 6pm. 1 Nov - 31 Mar: please telephone for opening times.

Admission: Adult £3.95, Child £1.95, OAP £3.45. Booked groups (10+): Adult £3.45, Child £1.45, OAP £2.95.

Partially suitable. WC. Licensed. By arrangement. Limited for coaches. Guide dogs only.

BLAENAVON IRONWORKS

Tel: 01495 792615

Winter Bookings: 01633 648082

Nr Brecon Beacons National Park, Blaenavon, Gwent

Owner: In the care of Cadw

Contact: The Custodian

The famous ironworks at Blaenavon were a milestone in the history of the Industrial Revolution. Visitors can view much of the ongoing conservation work as well as 'Stack Square' - a rare survival of housing built for pioneer ironworkers.

Location: OS Ref. SO248 092. Via A4043 follow signs to Big Pit Mining Museum and Blaenavon Ironworks. Abergavenny 8m. Pontypool 8m. From carpark, cross road, then path to entrance gate.

Opening Times: Easter - end Oct: 9.30am - 4.30pm. For opening times outside this period call the above number or 029 2050 0200.

Admission: Adult £1.50, Child/Conc. £1, Family £4.

Partially suitable. By arrangement. Guide dogs only.

CAE HIR GARDENS

Tel: 01570 470839

Cae Hir, Cribyn, Lampeter, Cardiganshire SA48 7NG

Owner/Contact: Mr W Akkermans

This transformed 19th century smallholding offers a succession of pleasant surprises and shows a quite different approach to gardening.

Location: OS Ref. SN521 520. W on A482 from Lampeter, after 5m turn S on B4337. Cae Hir is 2m on left.

Opening Times: Daily, excluding Mons (open BH Mons), 1 - 6pm.

Admission: Adult £2.50, Child 50p, OAP £2. Groups: (20+) £2.

CAERLEON ROMAN BATHS & AMPHITHEATRE

Tel: 01633 422518

High Street, Caerleon NP6 1AE

Owner: In the care of Cadw

Contact: The Custodian

Caerleon is the most varied and fascinating Roman site in Britain – incorporating fortress and baths, well-preserved amphitheatre and a row of barrack blocks, the only examples currently visible in Europe.

Location: OS Ref. ST340 905. 4m ENE of Newport by B4596 to Caerleon, M4/J25.

Opening Times: 27 Mar - 29 Oct: 9.30am - 5pm. 30 Oct - 31 Mar: Mon - Sat, 9.30am - 5pm, Suns, 1 - 5pm. Closed 24 - 26 Dec & 1 Jan.

Admission: Adult £2, Child/Conc. £1.50, Family £5.50.

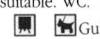 Guide dogs only.

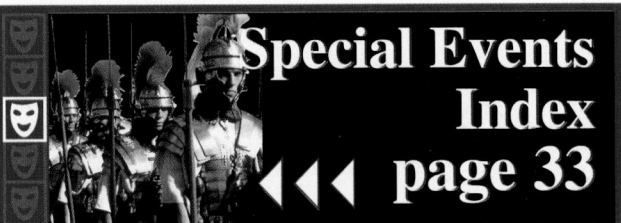

Special Events Index ◀◀◀ page 33

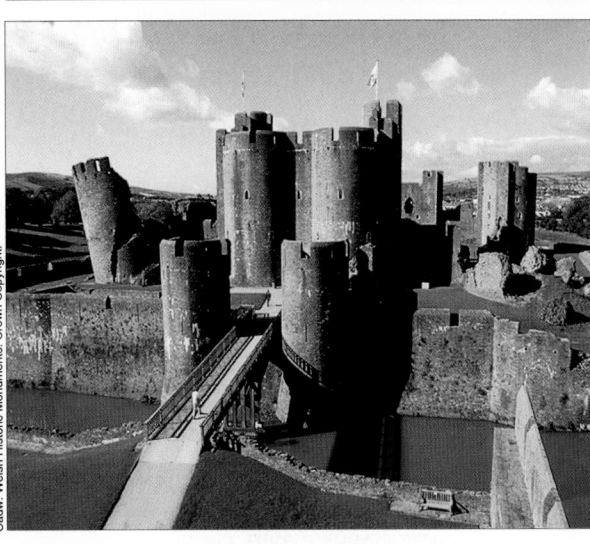

Cadw: Welsh Historic Monuments. Crown Copyright.

CAERPHILLY CF8 1JL

Owner: In the care of Cadw   *Contact: The Custodian*

Tel: 029 2088 3143

Often threatened, never taken, this vastly impressive castle is much the biggest in Wales. 'Red Gilbert' de Clare, Anglo-Norman Lord of Glamorgan, flooded a valley to create the 30 acre lake, setting his fortress on 3 artificial islands. Famous for its leaning tower, its fortifications are scarcely rivalled in Europe.

Location: OS Ref. ST156 871. Centre of Caerphilly, A468 from Newport, A470, A469 from Cardiff.

Opening Times: 27 Mar - 26 May: 9.30am - 5pm. 27 May - 1 Oct: 9.30am - 6pm. 2 - 29 Oct: 9.30am - 5pm. 30 Oct - 31 Mar: Mon - Sat, 9.30am - 4pm, Suns, 11am - 4pm. Closed 24 - 26 Dec & 1 Jan.

Admission: Adult £2.50, Child/Conc. £2, Family £7.

Limited. Guide dogs only.

CARDIFF CASTLE

Tel: 029 2087 8100   **Fax:** 029 2023 1417

Castle Street, Cardiff CF10 3RB

Owner: City and County of Cardiff

Contact: Mrs Jean Brown

2000 years of history, including Roman Walls, Norman Keep and Victorian interiors.

Location: OS Ref. ST181 765. Cardiff city centre, signposted from M4.

Opening Times: 1 Mar - 30 Oct: daily, 9.30am - 6pm, last entry 5pm. Nov - Feb: daily, 9.30am - 4.30pm, last entry 3.15pm. Closed Christmas and New Year.

Admission: Adult £5, Child/OAP £3 (2000 prices).

CAREW CASTLE & TIDAL MILL

Tel/Fax: 01646 651782

Tenby, Pembrokeshire SA70 8SL

Owner: Pembrokeshire Coast National Park

Contact: Mr G M Candler

A magnificent Norman castle which later became an Elizabethan country house. Royal links with Henry Tudor and the setting for the Great Tournament of 1507. The Mill is one of only four restored tidal mills in Britain. Introductory slide programme, automatic 'talking points' and special exhibition on *'The Story of Milling'*.

Location: OS Ref. SN046 037. $^1/_2$ m N of A477, 5m E of Pembroke.

Opening Times: Easter - end Oct: daily, 10am - 5pm.

Admission: Adult £2.75, Child/OAP £1.80, Family £7.30 (prices under review).

Partially suitable. WC. By arrangement. In grounds on leads.

CARREG CENNEN CASTLE

Tel: 01558 822291

Tir-y-Castell Farm, Llandeilo

Owner: In the care of Cadw

Contact: The Custodian

Spectacularly crowning a remote crag 300 feet above the River Cennen, the castle is unmatched as a wildly romantic fortress sought out by artists and visitors alike. The climb from Rare Breeds Farm is rewarded by breathtaking views and the chance to explore intriguing caves beneath.

Location: OS Ref. SN668 190. Minor roads from A483(T) to Trapp village. 5m SE of A40 at Llandeilo.

Opening Times: early Apr - late Oct: 9.30am - 7.30pm. Late Oct - late Mar: 9.30am - dusk. Closed 25 Dec.

Admission: Adult £2.50, Child/Conc. £2, Family £7.

Guide dogs only.

South Wales

CASTELL COCH

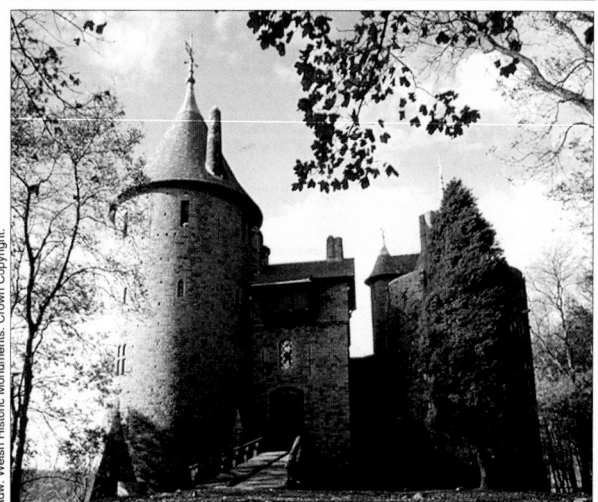

Cadw: Welsh Historic Monuments. Crown Copyright.

TONGWYNLAIS, CARDIFF CF4 7JS
Owner: In the care of Cadw **Contact:** *The Custodian*

Tel: 029 2081 0101

A fairytale castle in the woods, Castell Coch embodies a glorious Victorian dream of the Middle Ages. Designed by William Burges as a country retreat for the 3rd Lord Bute, every room and furnishing is brilliantly eccentric, including paintings of Aesop's fables on the drawing room walls.

Location: OS Ref. ST131 826. M4/J32, A470 then signposted. 5m NW of Cardiff city centre.

Opening Times: 27 Mar - 26 May: 9.30am - 5pm. 27 May - 1 Oct: 9.30am - 6pm. 2 - 29 Oct: 9.30am - 5pm. 30 Oct - 31 Mar: Mon - Sat, 9.30am - 4pm, Suns, 11am - 4pm. Closed 24 - 26 Dec & 1 Jan. Teashop: Summer: daily. Winter: weekends.

Admission: Adult £2.50, Child/Conc. £2, Family £7.

   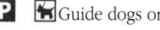   Guide dogs only.

CHEPSTOW CASTLE
Tel: 01291 624065

Chepstow, Gwent

Owner: In the care of Cadw **Contact:** The Custodian

This mighty fortress has guarded the route from England to South Wales for more than nine centuries. So powerful was this castle that it continued in use until 1690, being finally adapted for cannon and musket after an epic civil war siege. This huge, complex, grandiosely sited castle deserves a lengthy visit.

Location: OS Ref. ST533 941. Chepstow via A465, B4235 or A48. 1 1/2 m N of M4/J22.

Opening Times: 27 Mar - 26 May: 9.30am - 5pm. 27 May - 1 Oct: 9.30am - 6pm. 2 - 29 Oct: 9.30am - 5pm. 30 Oct - 31 Mar: Mon - Sat, 9.30am - 4pm, Suns, 11am - 4pm. Closed 24 - 26 Dec & 1 Jan.

Admission: Adult £3, Child/OAP £2, Family £8.

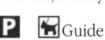 Partially suitable. Guide dogs only.

CILGERRAN CASTLE
Tel: 01239 615007

Cardigan, Dyfed

Owner: In the care of Cadw **Contact:** The Custodian

Perched high up on a rugged spur above the River Teifi, Cilgerran Castle is one of the most spectacularly sited fortresses in Wales. It dates from the 11th - 13th centuries.

Location: OS Ref. SN195 431. Main roads to Cilgerran from A478 and A484. 3 1/2 m SSE of Cardigan.

Opening Times: Late Mar - late Oct: 9.30am - 6.30pm. Late Oct - late Mar: 9.30am - 4pm. Closed 24 Dec & 1 Jan.

Admission: Adult £2, Child/OAP £1.50, Family £5.50.

 Guide dogs only.

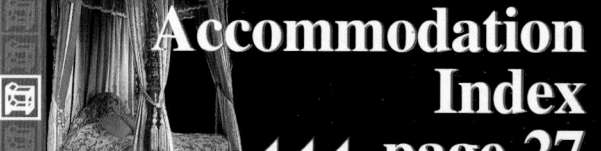

CLYNE GARDENS
Tel: 01792 401737

Mill Lane, Blackpill, Swansea SA3 5BD

Owner: City and County of Swansea **Contact:** Steve Hopkins

50 acre spring garden, large rhododendron collection, 4 national collections, extensive bog garden, native woodland.

Location: OS Ref. SS614 906. S side of Mill Lane, 500yds W of A4067 Mumbles Road, 3m SW of Swansea.

Opening Times: All year: daily.

Admission: Free.

COLBY WOODLAND GARDEN
Tel: 01834 811885/01492 860123

Amroth, Narbeth, Pembrokeshire SA67 8PP

Owner: The National Trust **Contact:** The Centre Manager

An attractive woodland garden. There are walks through secluded valleys along open woodland pathways. Nearby is the coastal resort of Amroth.

Location: OS Ref. SN155 080. 1/2 m inland from Amroth beside Carmarthen Bay. Signs from A477.

Opening Times: 1 Apr - 4 Nov: daily, 10am - 5pm. Walled Garden: 1 Apr - 31 Oct: 11am - 5pm.

Admission: Adult £2.80, Child £1.40, Family £7. Groups: by arrangement (15+): Adult £2.30, Child £1.15. National Trust members Free.

Gallery events.

CRESSELLY
Fax: 01646 687045

Kilgetty, Pembrokeshire SA68 0SP

Owner/Contact: H D R Harrison-Allen Esq MFH

Home of the Allen family for 250 years. The house is of 1770 with matching wings of 1869 and contains good plasterwork and fittings of both periods. The Allens are of particular interest for their close association with the Wedgwood family of Etruria and a long tradition of foxhunting.

Location: OS Ref. SN065 065. In the Pembrokeshire National Park, W of the A4075 between Canaston Bridge and Carew in Cresselly village.

Opening Times: 30 days between May & Sept. Please write or fax for details.

Admission: Adult £3.50, no children under 12.

 Ground floor only. Obligatory. Coaches by arrangement.

CYFARTHFA CASTLE MUSEUM
Tel/Fax: 01685 723112

Brecon Road, Merthyr Tydfil, Mid Glamorgan CF47 8RE

Owner: Merthyr Tydfil County Borough Council **Contact:** Mrs Claire Dovey-Evans

Castle originates from 1824/1825, now a museum and school.

Location: OS Ref. S0041 074. NE side of A470 to Brecon, 1/2 m NW of town centre.

Opening Times: 1 Apr - 1 Oct: Mon - Sun, 10am - 5.30pm. Winter: Tue - Fri, 10am - 4pm, Sat & Sun, 12 noon - 4pm.

Admission: Adult £2, Conc. £1.

 Conference facilities. By appointment. Guide dogs only.

DINEFWR
Tel: 01558 823902 **Fax:** 01558 822036

Llandeilo SA19 6RT **e-mail:** gdroff@smtp.ntrust.org.uk

Owner: The National Trust **Contact:** The House Manager

A deeply historic site with particular connections to the medieval Princes of Wales. An 18th century part 'naturalistic', part designed landscape parkland, with deer herd and White Park cattle, surrounds a 17th century mansion. Access to Dinefwr Castle (Cadw).

Location: OS Ref. SN615 225. On outskirts of Llandeilo. M4 from Swansea to Pont Abraham. A48 to Cross Hands and A476 to Llandeilo. Entrance by police station (A40).

Opening Times: House, Garden, Deer Park: 31 Mar - 4 Nov: daily except Tues & Weds, 11am - 5pm. Parkland: All year: 11am - 5pm (Nov - Mar: daily during daylight hours).

Admission: House & Park: Adult £3, Child £1.50, Family £7.50. Groups: (pre-booked 15+) £2.40. Park only (charges apply between 1 Apr - 29 Oct): Adult £2, Child £1, Family £5. National Trust members Free.

 By arrangement. Limited for coaches. In grounds on leads.

THE DINGLE
Tel: 01437 764370 **Fax:** 01437 768844

Dingle Lane, Crundale, Haverfordwest, Pembrokeshire SA62 4DJ

Owner/Contact: Andrew Barton

18th century country gentleman's home, surrounded by gardens. Gardens only open.

Location: OS Ref. SM973 175. 2m NE of Haverfordwest 600yds SE of B4329.

Opening Times: 10am - 6pm.

Admission: Gardens: Adult £2, Child £1. Nursery & tearooms Free.

DYFFRYN GARDENS

Tel: 029 2059 3328 **Fax:** 029 2059 1966

St Nicholas, Cardiff CF5 6SU

Owner: The Vale of Glamorgan Council **Contact:** Miss G Donovan

Grade I listed Edwardian garden. 55 acres of landscaped gardens, beautiful at all times of year. Numerous small theme gardens, arboretum and extensive lawns.

Location: OS Ref. ST095 723. 3m NW of Barry, J33/M4. 1½ m S of St Nicholas on A48.

Opening Times: Summer: daily, 10am - 8pm. Winter: daily, 10am - 5pm

Admission: Adult £3. Please telephone for details of concessions and tours.

FONMON CASTLE

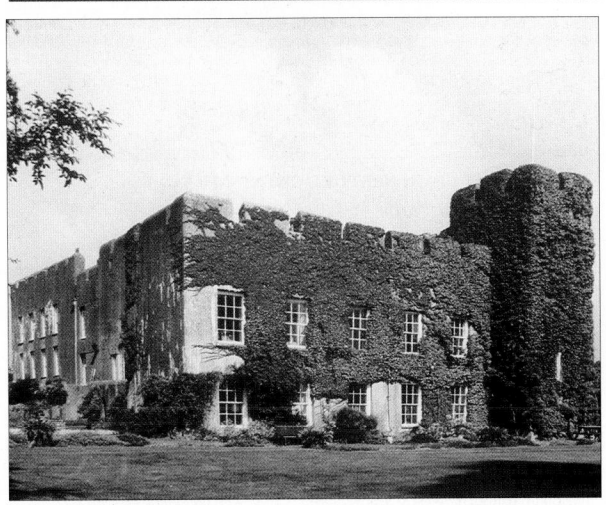

RHOOSE, BARRY, SOUTH GLAMORGAN CF62 3ZN

Owner: Sir Brooke Boothby Bt *Contact: Sophie Katzi*

Tel: 01446 710206 **Fax:** 01446 711687 **e-mail:** fonmon_castle@msn.com

Occupied as a home since the 13th century, this medieval castle has the most stunning Georgian interiors and is surrounded by extensive gardens. Available for weddings, concerts, corporate entertainment and multi-activity days.

Location: OS Ref. ST047 681. 15m W of Cardiff, 1m W of Cardiff airport.

Opening Times: 1 Apr - 30 Sept: Tues & Weds, 2 - 5pm (last tour 4pm). Other times by appointment. Groups: by appointment.

Admission: Adult £4, Child Free.

ⓘConferences. ☕By arrangement (up to 120). ♿Partially suitable. WC. 🅿 🐕Guide dogs only. 🔔 ❄

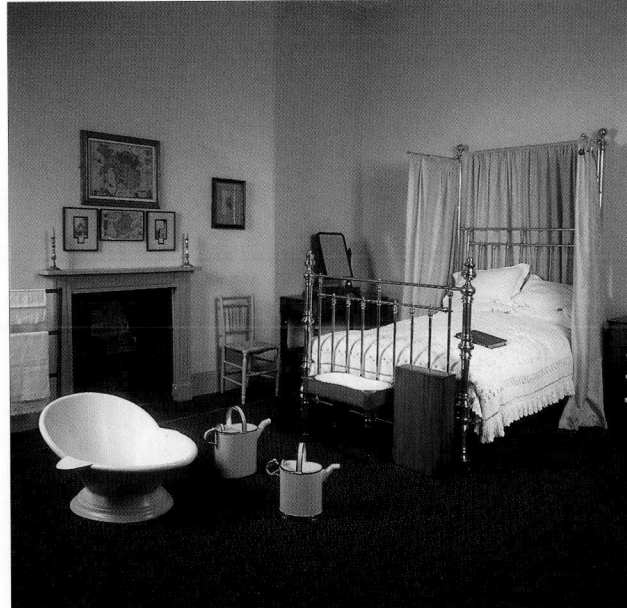

The Judge's Lodging, South Wales.

THE JUDGE'S LODGING

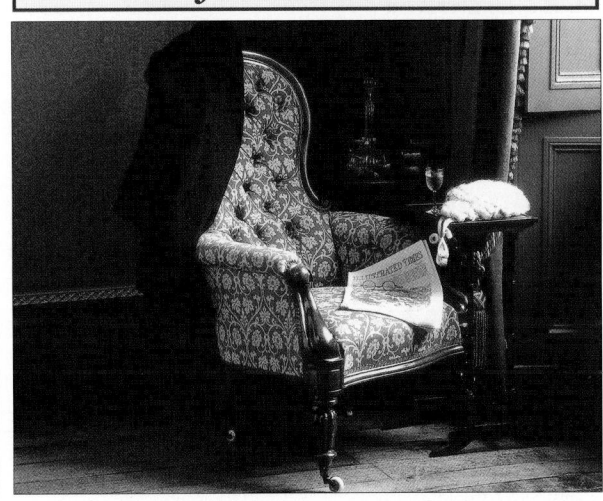

BROAD STREET, PRESTEIGNE, POWYS LD8 2AD

Owner: Powys County Council *Contact: Gabrielle Rivers*

Tel: 01544 260650 **Fax:** 01544 260652 **e-mail:** gaby@lodging.fsnet.co.uk

This stunningly restored Judge's Lodging captures the 'upstairs, downstairs' heyday of a most unusual Victorian household - by gaslight, lamp and candle. An 'eavesdropping' audio tour features actor Robert Hardy - A Victorian Revelation. Interpret Britain Award winner 1998 and Britain's 'Local Museum of the Year', *The Good Guide to Britain 1999*.

Location: OS Ref. SO314 644. In town centre, off A44 and A4113. Easy reach from Herefordshire and mid-Wales.

Opening Times: 1 Mar - 31 Oct: daily, 10am - 6pm. 1 Nov - 22 Dec: Wed - Sun, 10am - 4pm. Bookings by arrangement accepted all year.

Admission: Adult £3.75, Child/Conc. £2.75. Groups (10-80): Adult £3,Child/Conc. £2.25, Family £11.

📷 ☕ ♿Partially suitable (access via lift). 🎧 🅿In town. 🏛 🐕Guide dogs only. ❄ 🚻

KIDWELLY CASTLE ✠

Tel: 01554 890104

Kidwelly, West Glamorgan SA17 5BG

Owner: In the care of Cadw **Contact:** The Custodian

A chronicle in stone of medieval fortress technology this strong and splendid castle developed during more than three centuries of Anglo-Welsh warfare. The half-moon shape stems from the original 12th century stockaded fortress, defended by the River Gwendraeth on one side and a deep crescent-shaped ditch on the other.

Location: OS Ref. SN409 070. Kidwelly via A484. Kidwelly Rail Station 1m.

Opening Times: 27 Mar - 26 May: 9.30am - 5pm. 27 May - 1 Oct: 9.30am - 6pm. 2 - 29 Oct: 9.30am - 5pm. 30 Oct - 31 Mar: Mon - Sat, 9.30am - 4pm, Suns, 11am - 4pm. Closed 24 - 26 Dec & 1 Jan.

Admission: Adult £2.20, Child/OAP £1.70, Family £6.10.

♿ 🚶By arrangement. 🎧 🅿 🐕Guide dogs only. ❄ 🚻

LAMPHEY BISHOP'S PALACE ✠

Tel: 01646 672224

Lamphey, Dyfed

Owner: In the care of Cadw **Contact:** The Custodian

Lamphey marks the place of the spectacular Bishop's Palace but it reached its height of greatness under Bishop Henry de Gower who raised the new Great Hall. Today the ruins of this comfortable retreat reflect the power enjoyed by the medieval bishops.

Location: OS Ref. SN018 009. A4139 from Pembroke or Tenby. N of village (A4139).

Opening Times: Daily, 10am - 5pm. Closed 25 Dec.

Admission: Adult £2, Child/Conc. £1.50, Family £5.50.

🎧 🅿 🐕Guide dogs only. ❄ 🚻

LAUGHARNE CASTLE ✠

Tel: 01994 427906

King Street, Laugharne SA33 4SA

Owner: In the care of Cadw **Contact:** The Custodian

Picturesque Laugharne Castle stands on a low ridge overlooking the wide Taf estuary, one of a string of fortresses controlling the ancient route along the South Wales coast.

Location: OS Ref. SN303 107. 4m S of A48 at St Clears via A4066.

Opening Times: Apr - Sept: daily, 10am - 5pm.

Admission: Adult £2, Child/Conc. £1.50, Family £5.50.

🐕Guide dogs only. 🚻

LLANCAIACH FAWR MANOR   Tel: 01443 412248 Fax: 01443 412688

Nelson, Treharris CF46 6ER

Owner: Caerphilly County Borough Council   **Contact:** The Administrator

Tudor fortified manor dating from 1530 with Stuart additions.

Location: OS Ref. ST114 967. S side of B4254, 1m N of A472 at Nelson.

Opening Times: All year: weekdays, 10am - 5pm. weekends, 10am - 6pm. Last admission 1½ hours before closing. Nov - Feb: closed Mons. Closed Christmas week.

Admission: Adult £4.50, Child/Conc. £3, Family £12.

LLANDAFF CATHEDRAL   Tel: 029 2056 4554

Llandaff, Cardiff, Glamorgan CF5 2YF

Contact: The Cathedral Office

Oldest cathedral in the British Isles. Epstein's *'Christ in Majesty'* and Rosetti's *'Seed of David'*.

Location: OS Ref. ST155 781. 2½ m NW of city centre, ¼ m W of A48 ring road.

Opening Times: Daily: 7am - 7pm. Sun services: 8am, 9am, 11am, 12.15pm (Holy Eucharist), 3.30pm Choral Evensong and 6.30pm Parish Evensong. Weekday evening service: 6pm, (Wed 5.30pm).

Admission: Donation.

MARGAM PARK   Tel: 01639 881635 Fax: 01639 895897

Port Talbot, Glamorgan SA13 2TJ

Owner: Neathport Talbot County Borough Council   **Contact:** Mr Ray Butt

Margam Orangery is the largest of its kind in Britain. Castle and Abbey ruins, 850 acres of parkland and forest, with waymarked signs.

Location: OS Ref. SS804 865. NE side of A48, 1m SE of M4/J38, 4m SE of Port Talbot.

Opening Times: Summer: daily, 10am - 5pm, last entry 4pm. Winter: Wed - Sun, 10am - 5pm, last entry 3pm.

Admission: Adult £3.85, Child £2.85, Family (2+4) £11.85.

MUSEUM OF WELSH LIFE   Tel: 029 2057 3500 Fax: 029 2057 3490

St Fagans, Cardiff CF5 6XB

St Fagans Castle, a 16th century building built within the walls of a 13th century castle.

Location: OS Ref. ST118 772. 4m W of city centre, 1½m N of A48, 2m S of M4/J33 off A4232.

Opening Times: All year: daily, 10am - 5pm.

Admission: Summer: Adult £5.50, Child (under 18) Free, Over 60s & unemployed Free, Conc. £3.90. Winter: Adult £4.50 Child (under 18) Free, Over 60s & unemployed Free, Conc. £2.65.

THE NATIONAL BOTANIC GARDEN OF WALES   Tel: 01558 668768

Port Talbot, Glamorgan SA13 2TJ   **Tel:** 01558 667134 **Fax:** 01558 667138

Owner: The National Botanic Garden of Wales   **Contact:** Ian Ball

The first national botanic garden to be created in the United Kingdom for more than two hundred years.

Location: OS159 Ref. SN518 175. ½ m off A48 (M4), 4½ m NW Cross Hands.

Opening Times: Please contact property for details.

Admission: Please contact property for details.

OXWICH CASTLE 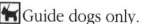   Tel: 01792 390359

c/o Oxwich Castle Farm, Oxwich SA3 1NG

Owner: In the care of Cadw   **Contact:** The Custodian

Beautifully sited in the lovely Gower peninsula, Oxwich Castle is a striking testament to the pride and ambitions of the Mansel dynasty of Welsh gentry.

Location: OS159 Ref. SS497 864. A4118, 11m SW of Swansea, in Oxwich village.

Opening Times: Apr - Sept: daily, 10am - 5pm.

Admission: Adult £2, Child/OAP £1.50, Family £5.50.

  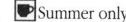Guide dogs only.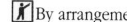

PEMBROKE CASTLE   Tel: 01646 681510 Fax: 01646 622260

Pembroke, Dyfed SA71 4LA

Owner: Trustees of Pembroke Castle   **Contact:** I B Ramsden

Early 13th century Norman castle. Birthplace of Henry VII the first Tudor monarch. Exhibitions and video. Brass Rubbing Centre. Stroll around its idyllic millpond and town walls to complete the day.

Location: OS Ref. SM983 016. W end of the main street in Pembroke.

Opening Times: 1 Apr - 30 Sept: daily, 9.30am - 6pm. Mar & Oct: daily, 10am - 5pm. Nov - Feb: daily, 10am - 4pm. Closed Christmas Day, Boxing Day and New Year's Day.

Admission: Adult £3, Child/Conc. £2. Groups (20+): Adult £2.60, OAP £1.70.

 Summer only. 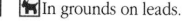By arrangement. In grounds on leads.

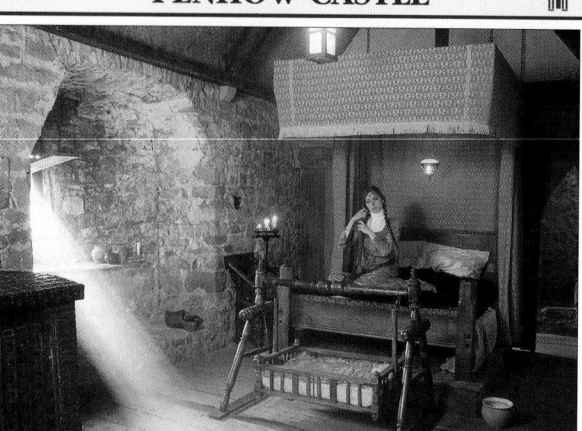

PENHOW CASTLE

Nr NEWPORT, GWENT NP6 3AD

Owner: Stephen Weeks Esq   *Contact: The Administrator*

Tel: 01633 400800 **Fax:** 01633 400990 **e-mail:** admin@penhowcastle.com

Wales' oldest lived-in Castle, the first home in Britain of the Seymour family. Now lovingly restored by the present owner, visitors explore the varied period rooms from battlements to kitchens. Discover the Norman bedchamber, 15th century Great Hall with minstrels' gallery, elegant panelled Carolean dining room, guided by the acclaimed 'Time Machine' audio tours included in the admission; also in French and German. Penhow holds 8 awards for careful restoration and imaginative interpretation. Exciting children's tours and school visits.

Location: OS Ref. ST423 908. Midway between Chepstow and Newport on the A48. Use M4/J24.

Opening Times: Summer: Good Fri - 30 Sept: Wed - Sun & BHs. Aug: daily, 10am - 5.15pm (last adm.) Winter: Weds, 10am - 4pm. Selected Suns, 1 - 4pm. Evening Candlelit Tours all year by arrangement. Christmas Tours: 15 Nov - 5 Jan.

Admission: Adult £3.80, Child £2.60, Family (2+2) £10.20. Groups: by arrangement all year, 10% discount for 20+.

Not suitable. By arrangement. Limited. Guide dogs only. 1 double.

PENPERGWM LODGE   Tel/Fax: 01873 840208

Abergavenny, Gwent   **e-mail:** penpergwmplants@dial.pipex.com

Owner/Contact: Mrs Catriona Boyle

3 acre terraced garden including rose and vine walks.

Location: OS Ref. SO335 104. ¼ m N of B4598 to Usk, 3m SE of Abergavenny.

Opening Times: Mar - Oct: Thur - Sun, 2 - 6pm.

Admission: Adult £2, Child Free.

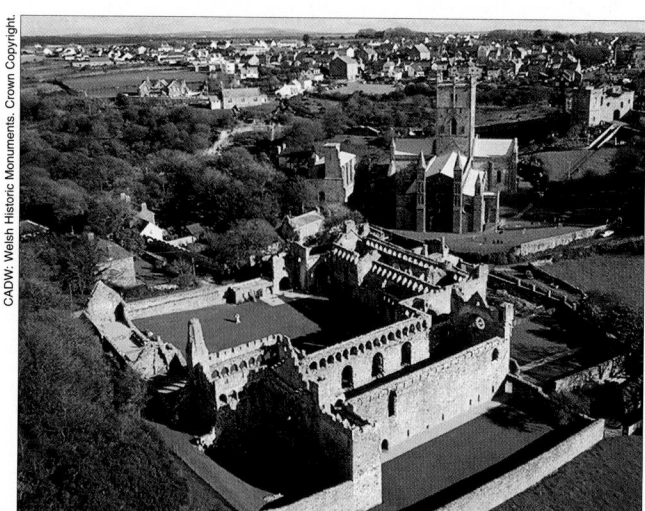

St Davids Bishop's Palace, South Wales.

CADW: Welsh Historic Monuments. Crown Copyright.

PICTON CASTLE

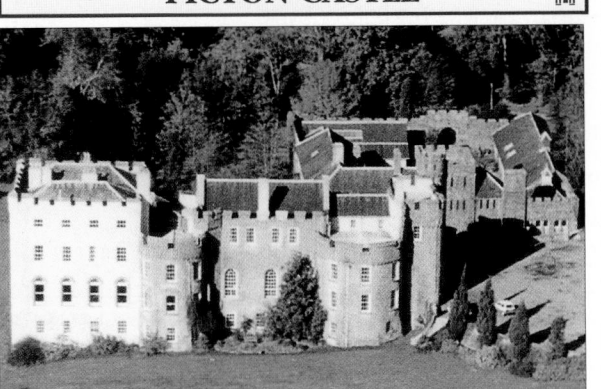

HAVERFORDWEST, PEMBROKESHIRE SA62 4AS

Owner: *Picton Castle Trust*   ***Contact:*** *D Pryse Lloyd*

Tel/Fax: 01437 751326 **e-mail:** pct@pictoncastle.freeserve.co.uk

Built in the 13th century by Sir John Wogan, his direct descendants still use the castle as their family home, carrying the family name of Philipps. Retaining its external appearance, the castle was remodelled inside, above the undercroft in the 1750s and extended around 1800. The woodland and walled gardens cover 40 acres and are part of The Royal Horticultural Society access scheme for beautiful gardens. There is a unique collection of rhododendrons and azaleas, mature trees, unusual shrubs, wild flowers and a large collection of herbs as featured on television. The Picton Gallery is used for nationally acclaimed exhibitions. Events include spring and autumn plant sales.

Location: OS Ref. SN011 135. 4m E of Haverfordwest, 2m S of A40.

Opening Times: Castle: Apr - Sept. Closed Mon & Sat except BHs, open all other afternoons for guided tours. Garden & Gallery: Apr - Oct: Tue - Sun, 10.30am - 5pm.

Admission: Castle, Garden & Gallery: Adult £4.95, Child £1.95, OAP £4.75. Garden & Gallery: Adult £3.95, Child £1.95, OAP £3.75. Groups (20+): reduced prices by prior arrangement.

ℹ️ No indoor photography. 🖼️ 🎁 🍴 ♿ 🍽️ Licensed. 🚶 Obligatory. 🅿️ 🐕 In grounds, on leads. 🔔 ♿ 🆆

RAGLAN CASTLE ✚

Tel: 01291 690228

Raglan NP5 2BT

Owner: In the care of Cadw   **Contact:** The Custodian

Undoubtedly the finest late medieval fortress-palace in Britain, it was begun in the 1430s by Sir William ap Thomas who built the mighty 'Yellow Tower'. His son William Lord Herbert added a palatial mansion defended by a gatehouse and many towered walls. The high quality is still obvious today.

Location: OS Ref. SO415 084. Raglan, NE of Raglan village off A40 (eastbound) and sign-posted.

Opening Times: 27 Mar - 26 May: 9.30am - 5pm. 27 May - 1 Oct: 9.30am - 6pm. 2 - 29 Oct: 9.30am - 5pm. 30 Oct - 31 Mar: Mon - Sat, 9.30am - 4pm, Suns, 11am - 4pm. Closed 24 - 26 Dec & 1 Jan.

Admission: Adult £2.40, Child/Conc. £1.90, Family £6.70.

🖼️ ♿ 🅿️ 🐕 Guide dogs only. ❄️ 🆆

ST DAVIDS BISHOP'S PALACE ✚

Tel: 01437 720517

St Davids, SA62 6PE

Owner: In the care of Cadw   **Contact:** The Custodian

The city of St Davids boasts not only one of Britain's finest cathedrals but also the most impressive medieval palace in Wales. Built in the elaborate 'decorated' style of gothic architecture, the palace is lavishly encrusted with fine carving.

Location: OS Ref. SM750 254. A487 to St Davids, minor road past the Cathedral.

Opening Times: 27 Mar - 26 May: 9.30am - 5pm. 27 May - 1 Oct: 9.30am - 6pm. 2 - 29 Oct: 9.30am - 5pm. 30 Oct - 31 Mar, Mon - Sat, 9.30am - 4pm, Suns, 12 noon - 2pm. Closed 24 - 26 Dec & 1 Jan.

Admission: Adult £2, Child/Conc. £1.50, Family £5.50.

♿ 🅿️ 🐕 Guide dogs only. ❄️ 🆆

ST DAVIDS CATHEDRAL

Tel: 01437 720691 **Fax:** 01437 721885

St Davids, Dyfed SA62 6QW   **Contact:** Mr R G Tarr

St Davids is Britain's smallest city by Royal Charter, March 1994. Premier cathedral of church in Wales. Over eight centuries old. Many unique and 'odd' features.

Location: OS Ref. SM751 254. 5-10 mins walk from car/coach parks; signs for pedestrians.

Opening Times: Daily: 7.30am - 6.30pm. Suns: 12.30 - 5.30pm, may be closed for services in progress. Sun services: 8am, 9.30am, 11.15am & 6pm. Weekday services: 8am & 6pm. Weds extra service: 10am.

Admission: Donations. Guided tours (Adult £3, Child £1.20) must be booked in advance.

STRATA FLORIDA ABBEY ✚

Tel: 01974 831261

Ystrad Meurig, Pontrhydfendigaid SY25 6BT

Owner: In the care of Cadw   **Contact:** The Custodian

Remotely set in the green, kite-haunted Teifi Valley with the lonely Cambrian mountains as a backdrop, the ruined abbey has a wonderful doorway with Celtic spiral motifs and preserves a wealth of beautiful medieval tiles.

Location: OS Ref. SN746 658. Minor road from Pontrhydfendigaid 14m SE of Aberystwyth by the B4340.

Opening Times: 21 Apr - 24 Sept: daily, 10am - 5pm. Winter: open site.

Admission: Adult £2, Child/Conc. £1.50, Family £5.50.

♿ 🅿️ 🐕 Guide dogs only. ❄️ 🆆

TINTERN ABBEY ✚ *Watercolour Challenge* **Tel:** 01291 689251

Tintern NP6 6SE

Owner: In the care of Cadw   **Contact:** The Custodian

Tintern is the best preserved abbey in Wales and ranks among Britain's most beautiful historic sites. Elaborately decorated in 'gothic' architecture style this church stands almost complete to roof level. Turner sketched and painted here, while Wordsworth drew inspiration from the surroundings.

Location: OS Ref. SO533 000. Tintern via A466, from M4/J22. Chepstow 6m.

Opening Times: 27 Mar - 26 May: 9.30am - 5pm. 27 May - 1 Oct: 9.30am - 6pm. 2 - 29 Oct 9.30am - 5pm. 30 Oct - 31 Mar: Mon - Sat, 9.30am - 4pm, Suns, 11am - 4pm. Closed 24 - 26 Dec & 1 Jan.

Admission: Adult £2.40, Child/Conc. £1.90, Family £6.70.

🖼️ ♿ 🎧 🅿️ 🐕 Guide dogs only. ❄️ 🆆

TREDEGAR HOUSE & PARK

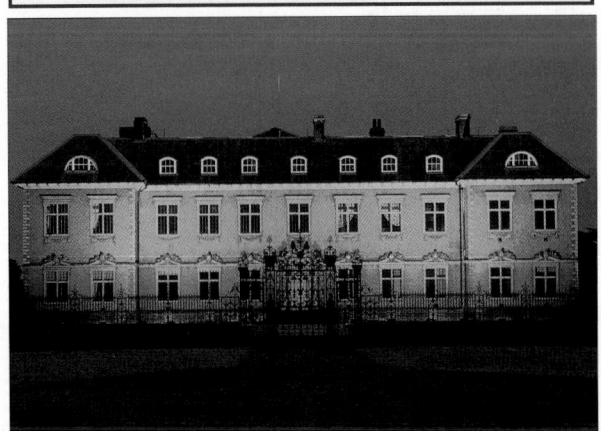

NEWPORT, SOUTH WALES NP1 9YW

Owner: *Newport County Borough Council*   ***Contact:*** *The Manager*

Tel: 01633 815880 **Fax:** 01633 815895 **e-mail:** tredegar.house@newport.gov.uk

South Wales' finest country house, ancestral home of the Morgan family. Parts of a medieval house remain, but Tredegar owes its reputation to lavish rebuilding in the 17th century. Visitors have a lively and entertaining tour through 30 rooms, including glittering State Rooms and 'below stairs'. Set in 90 acres of parkland with formal gardens. Winner of Best Public Park and Garden in Great Britain 1997. Craft workshops.

Location: OS Ref. ST290 852. M4/J28 signposted. From London 2¹/₂ hrs, from Cardiff 20 mins. 2m SW of Newport town centre.

Opening Times: Easter - Sept: Wed - Sun & BHs, 11.30am - 4pm. Evening tours & groups by appointment. Nov - Mar: Groups only by appointment.

Admission: Adult £4.75, Child £2.25, Conc. £3.65, Family £12.95. Special discounts for Newport residents (2000 prices).

ℹ️ Conferences. No photography in house. 🖼️ 🍴 ♿ Partially suitable. WC. 🍽️ 🚶 Obligatory. 🅿️ 🐕 In grounds, on leads. 🔔 ♿ Tel. for details.

TREOWEN

Tel/Fax: 01600 712031

Wonastow, Nr Monmouth NP5 4DL   **e-mail:** john.wheelock@virgin.net

Owner: R A & J P Wheelock   **Contact:** John Wheelock

Early 17th century mansion built to double pile plan with magnificent well-stair to four storeys.

Location: OS Ref. SO461 111. 3m WSW of Monmouth.

Opening Times: May, Jun, Aug & Sept: Fris. Also Sat & Sun on 12/13 & 19/20 May and 15/16, 22/23 & 29/30 Sept: 10am - 4pm.

Admission: £4. £2.50 if appointment made. Groups by appointment only.

🍴 🏠 Entire house let, self-catering. Sleeps 24+. 🔔 🆆

TRETOWER COURT & CASTLE ✠

Tel: 01874 730279

Tretower, Crickhowell NP8 2RF

Owner: In the care of Cadw   **Contact:** The Custodian

A fine fortress and an outstanding medieval manor house, Tretower Court and Castle range around a galleried courtyard, now further enhanced by a beautiful recreated medieval garden.

Location: OS Ref. SO187 212. Signposted in Tretower Village, off A479, 3m NW of Crickhowell.

Opening Times: 1 - 26 Mar: 10am - 4pm. 27 Mar - 26 May: 10am - 5pm. 27 May - 3 Sept: 10am - 6pm. 4 Sept - 29 Oct: 10am - 5pm.

Admission: Adult £2.20, Child/Conc. £1.70, Family £6.10.

♿ 🎧 🅿 🐕 Guide dogs only. ⓦ

TUDOR MERCHANT'S HOUSE

Tel: 01834 842279

Quay Hill, Tenby SA70 7BX

Owner: The National Trust   **Contact:** The Custodian

A late 15th century town house, characteristic of the building tradition of south west Wales. The ground-floor chimney at the rear of the house is a fine vernacular example, and the original scarfed roof-trusses survive. The remains of early frescoes can be seen on three interior walls. Access to small herb garden, weather permitting. Furniture and fittings re-create the atmosphere from the time when a Tudor family was in residence.

Location: OS Ref. SN135 004. Tenby. W of alley from NE corner of town centre square.

Opening Times: 1 Apr - 30 Sept: daily except Weds, 10am - 5pm; Suns, 1 - 5pm. 1 Oct - 4 Nov: daily except Weds & Sats, 10am - 3pm; Suns, 12 noon - 3pm.

Admission: Adult £1.80, Child 90p. Groups: Adult £1.40, Child 70p. NT members Free.

ℹ️ No indoor photography. 🅿 No parking. 🖼 🐕 Guide dogs only.

USK CASTLE

Tel: 01291 672563

Usk, Monmouthshire NP15 1SD

Owner/Contact: J H L Humphreys

Romantic, ruined castle overlooking the picturesque town of Usk. Inner and outer baileys, towers and earthwork defences. Surrounded by enchanting gardens (open under NGS) incorporating The Castle House, the former medieval gatehouse lived in by owner.

Location: OS Ref. SO376 011. Off Monmouth Road in Usk, opposite fire station.

Opening Times: Castle ruins: daily, 11am - 5pm. Groups by appointment. Gardens & Castle House: Jun & BHs: 2 - 5pm, prior arrangement advised.

Admission: Castle ruins: Adult £2, Child Free. Gardens & Castle House: Adult £5, Child £2.

🍸 ♿ Partially suitable. 🎟 By arrangement. 🅿 Limited. 🐕 In grounds, on leads. ❄ ⓦ

WEOBLEY CASTLE ✠

Tel: 01792 390012

Weobley Castle Farm, Llanrhidian SA3 1HB

Owner: In the care of Cadw   **Contact:** The Custodian

Perched above the wild northern coast of the beautiful Gower peninsula, Weobley Castle was the home of the Knightly de Bere family. Its rooms include a fine hall and private chamber as well as numerous 'garderobes' or toilets and an early Tudor porch block.

Location: OS Ref. SN477 928. B4271 or B4295 to Llanrhidian Village, then minor road for 1½ m.

Opening Times: Apr - early Oct: 9.30am - 6pm. 2 - 29 Oct: 9.30am - 5pm. Late Oct - late Mar: 9.30am - 4pm. Closed 24 - 26 Dec & 1 Jan.

Admission: Adult £2, Child/Conc. £1.50, Family £5.50.

🅿 🐕 Guide dogs only. ❄ ⓦ

WHITE CASTLE ✠

Tel: 01600 780380

Llantillio Crossenny, Gwent

Owner: In the care of Cadw   **Contact:** The Custodian

With its high walls and round towers reflected in the still waters of its moat, White Castle is the ideal medieval fortress. It was rebuilt in the mid-13th century by the future King Edward I to counter a threat from Prince Llywelyn the Last.

Location: OS Ref. SO380 167. By minor road 2m NW from B4233 at A7 Llantilio Crossenny. 8m ENE of Abergavenny.

Opening Times: 21 Apr - 24 Sept: 10am - 5pm. Winter: Open site.

Admission: Adult £2, Conc. £1.50, Family £5.50.

🅿 🐕 Guide dogs only. ❄ ⓦ

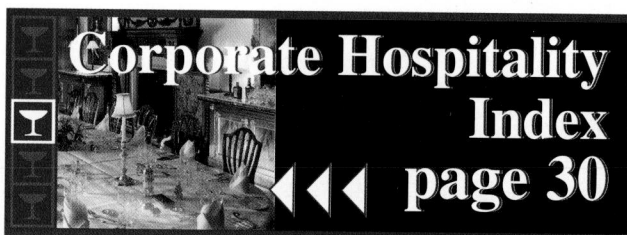

Corporate Hospitality Index ◀◀◀ page 30

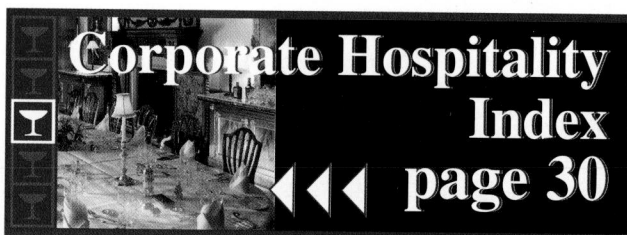

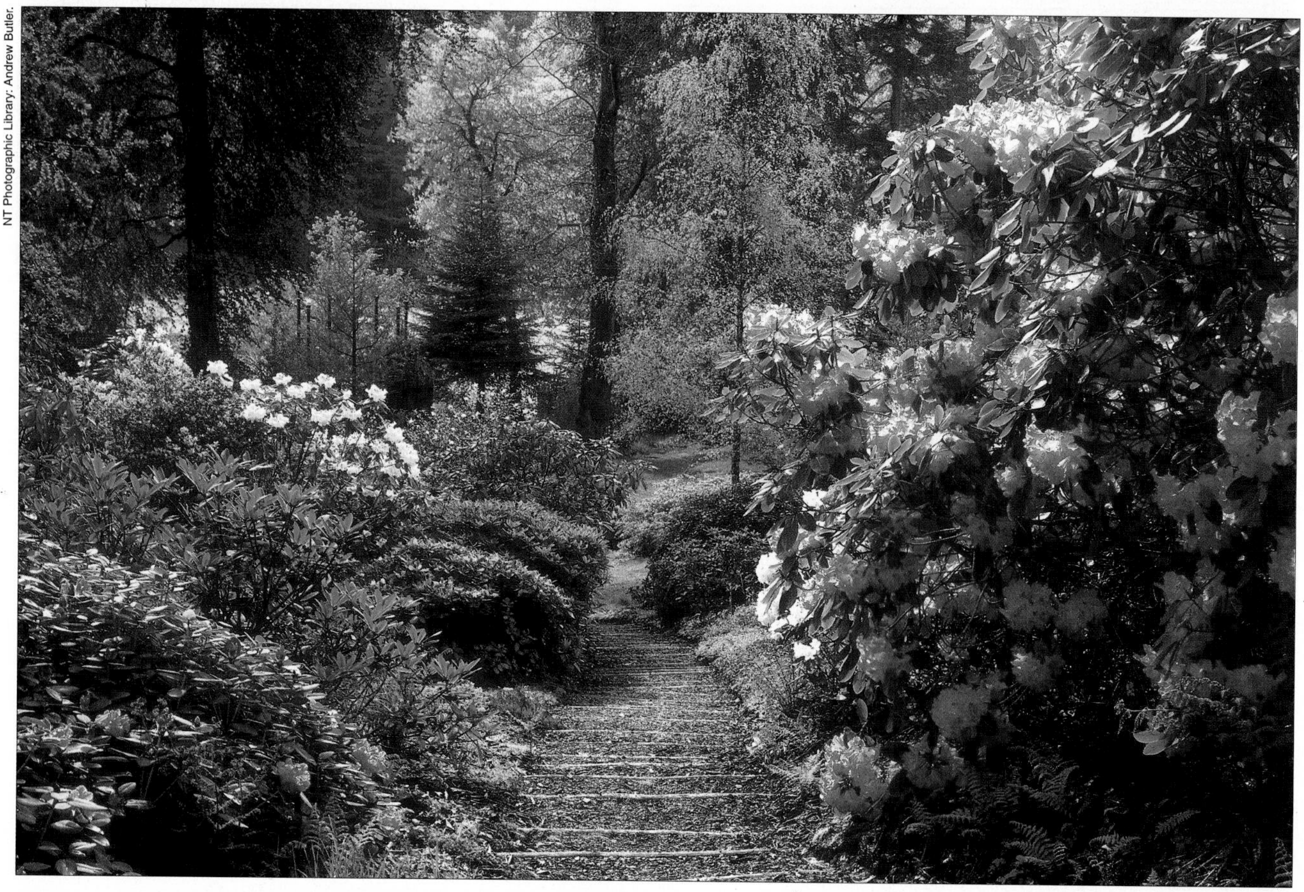

Colby Woodland Garden, South Wales

IRELAND

IRELAND

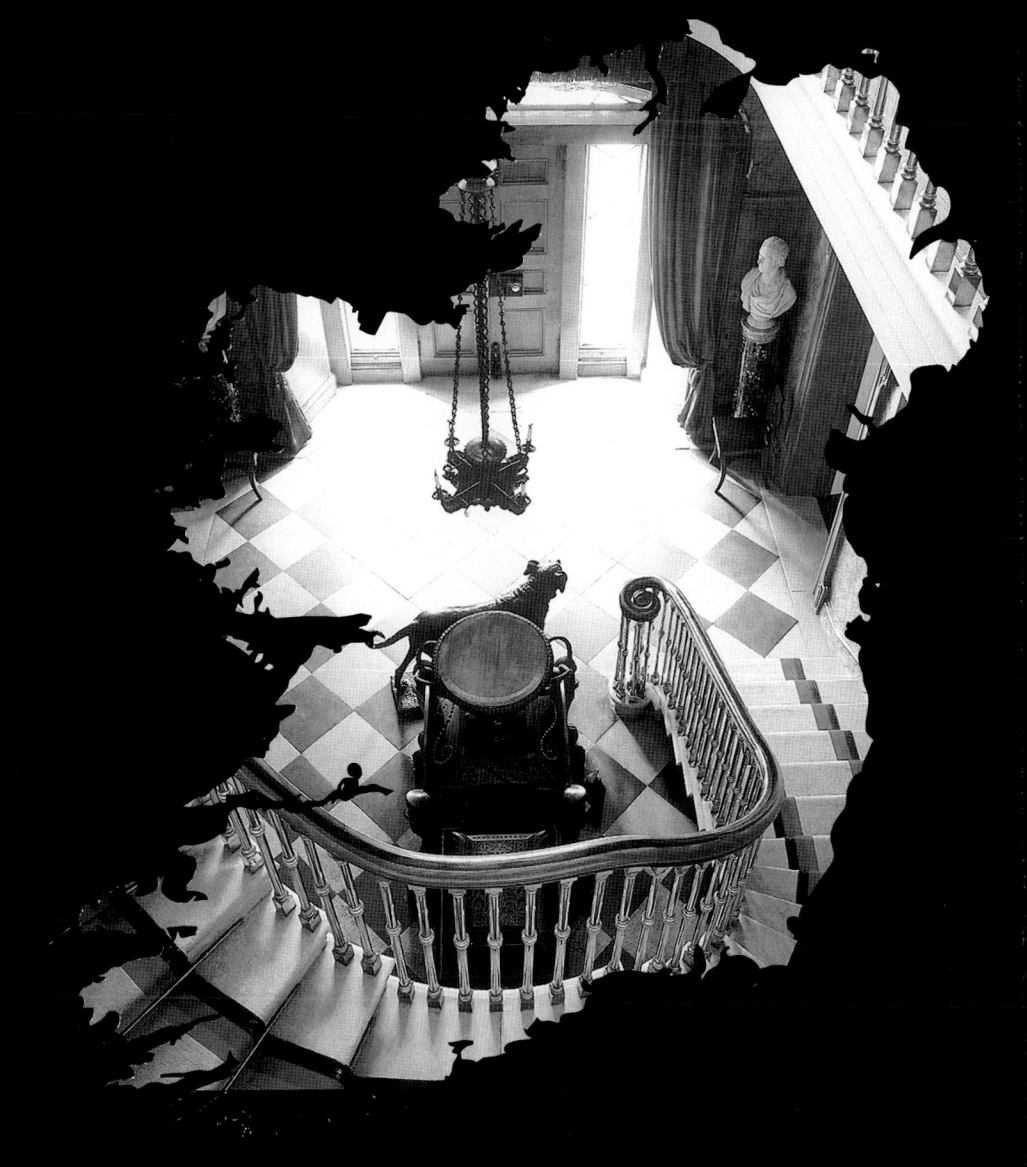

IRELAND

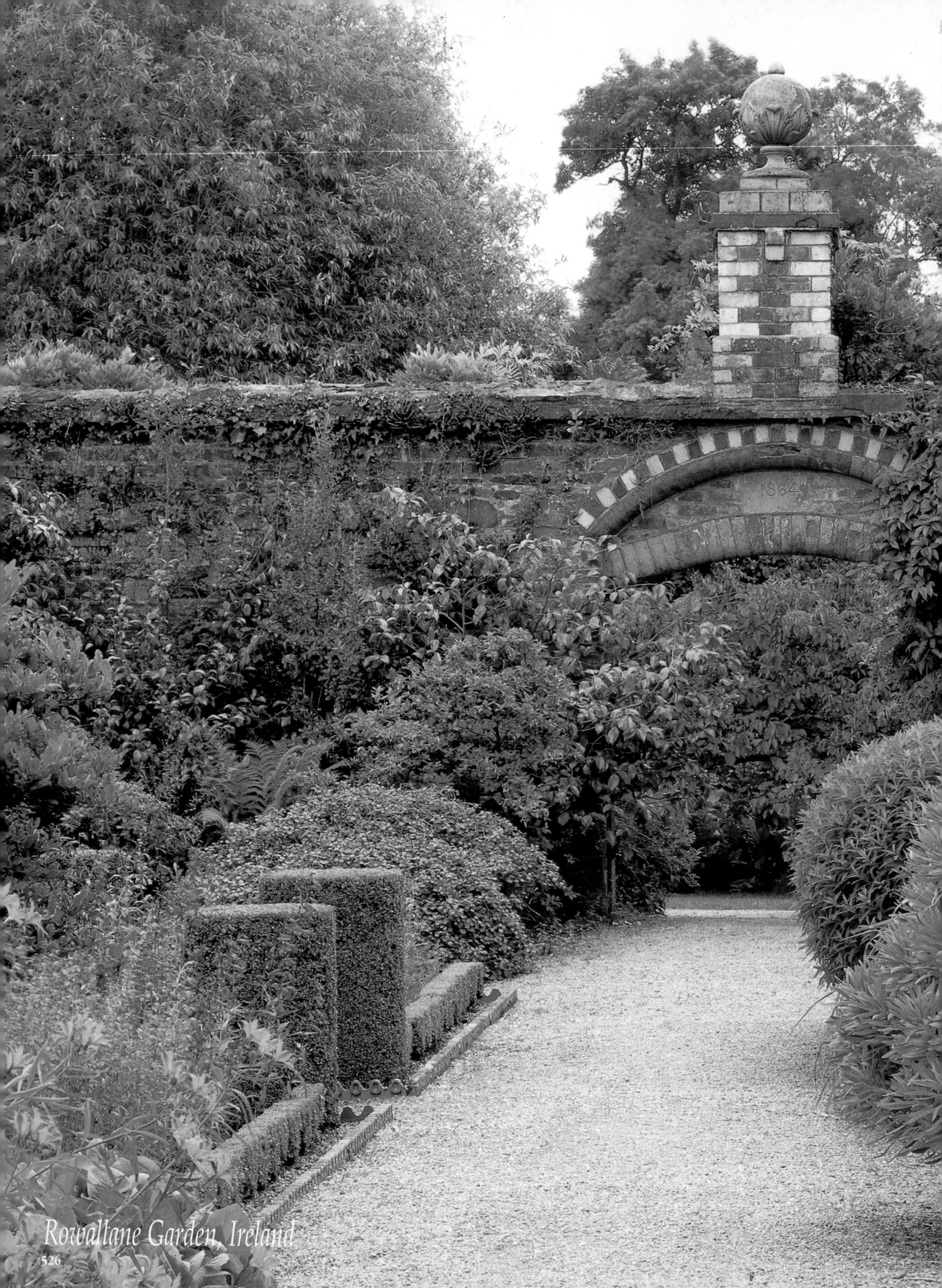

Rowallane Garden, Ireland

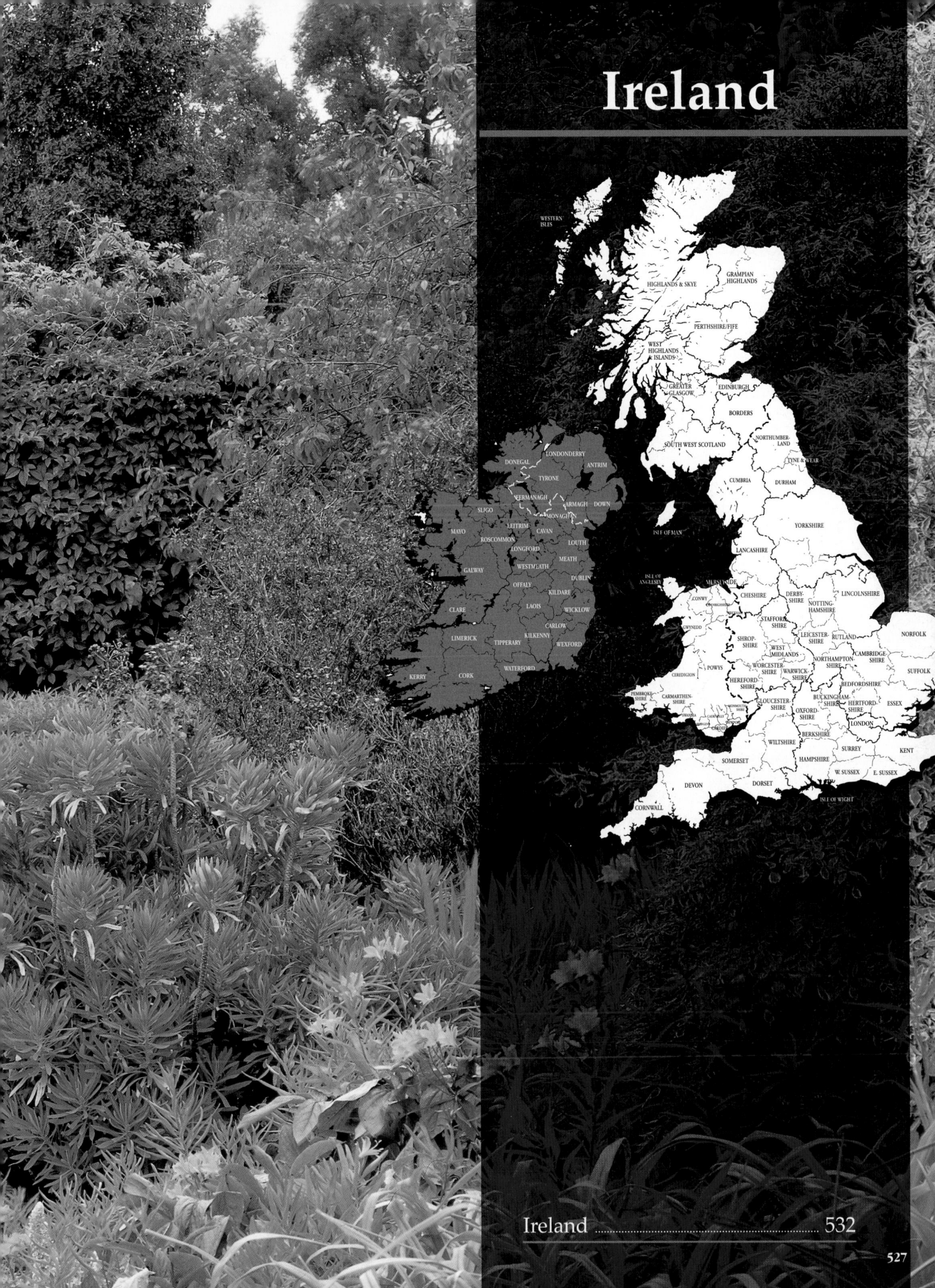

Ireland

Rowallane Garden

"As with the first act of any good play, you soon become enthralled, as each turn reveals a different scene."

a visitor to Rowallane

Rowallane is a garden for all seasons and for all people, with appeal both for the connoisseur of rare plants and for those who just like to wander through a beautiful landscape. Eleven miles south of Belfast and one mile south of Saintfield, it nestles in the rolling hills of Co Down.

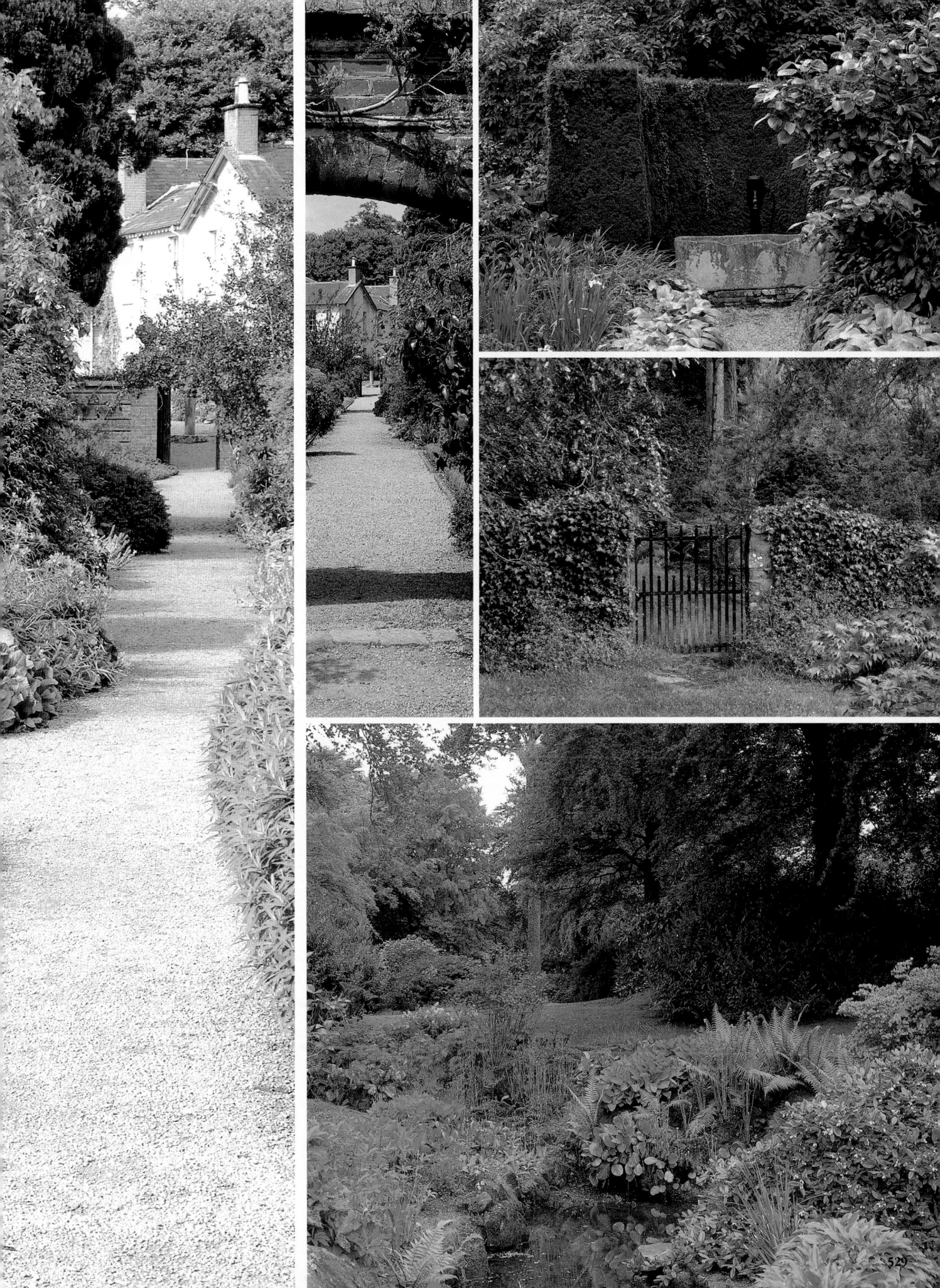

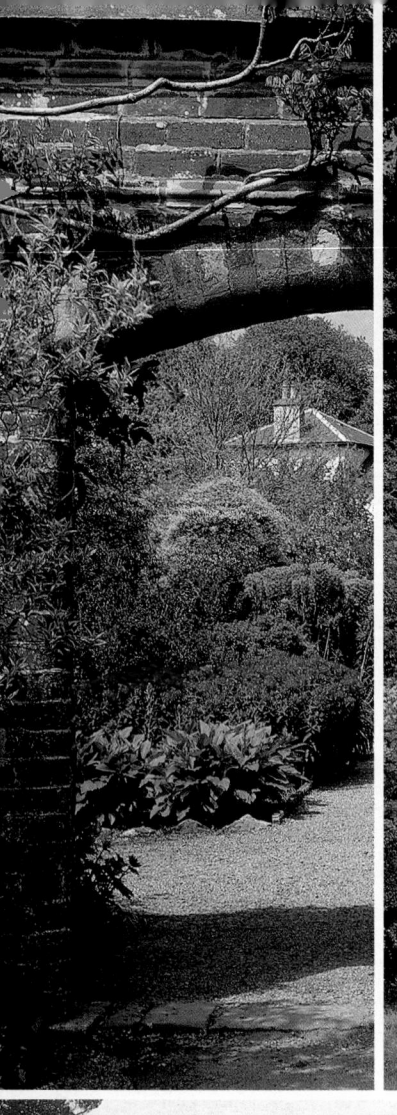

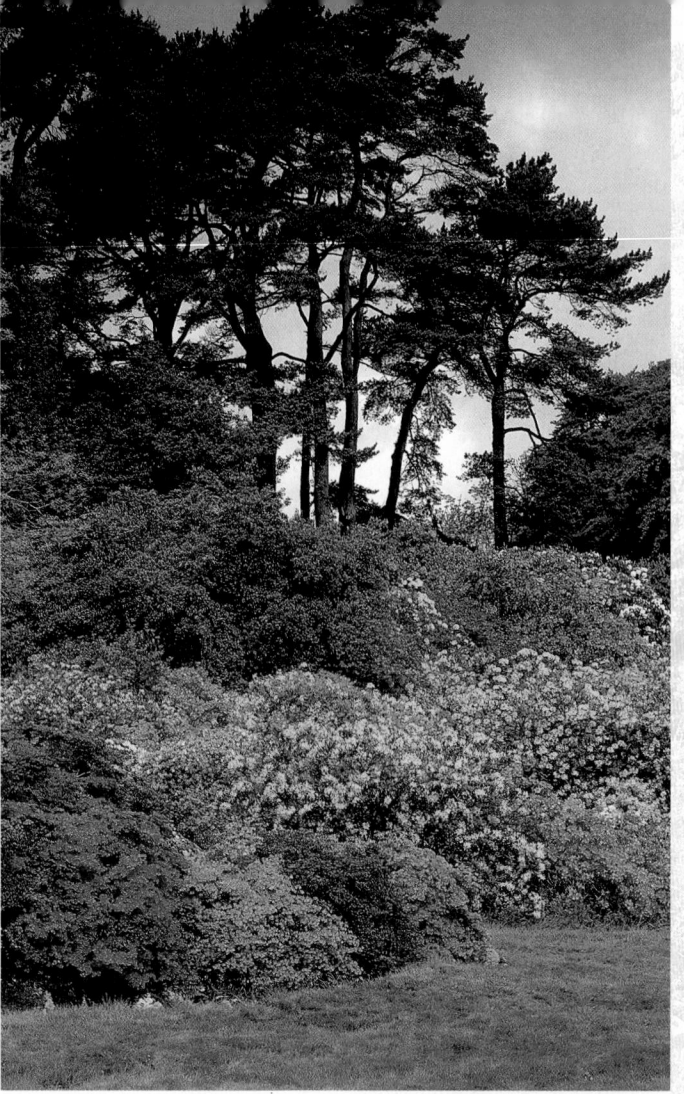

Formerly the farm belonging to the Reverend John Moore who acquired it in the 1860s, Rowallane has become one of the foremost gardens in the British Isles in this century – and a rare jewel in the National Trust's collections of gardens. Unlike gardens such as Mount Stewart it was never 'landscaped' but dropped in around natural outcrops of whinstone rock and dry stone walled fields.

The 52 acres of gardens that can be visited today are the work of the Reverend Hugh Moore, who began the task some 130 years ago, and his nephew Hugh Armytage Moore, who continued the work. In the past 20 years, the gardens have been cared for and maintained by Mike Snowden, the National Trust's Head Gardener.

Although late spring may find Rowallane at its most spectacular, it is an enthralling place to visit in high summer, when part of its attraction is the fine herbaceous display in the Walled Garden. Sheltered by high walls, the visitor can enjoy wonderfully lush plantings. Great drifts of Himalayan Poppies, in particular the scintillating turquoise blue Meconopsis x grandis. Also to be found is a National Collection of penstemons, alongside phlox and the soft yellow Japanese Kirengeshoma palmata which provide colour in the late summer.

Autumn is also a magnificent time for the garden – rich reds, russets, golds and browns form banks or single flames of colour, whilst a heavy frost or a fall of crisp snow still highlight the fine evergreens and the colourful bark and fruit of deciduous trees planted for winter interest as well as their summer colour. However, the garden is perhaps best loved for its spectacular arrangement and variety of rhododendrons and azaleas. These thrive on the high rainfall and acid thin soil of the region. Some of these plants are well over 60 years old; they have been planted with the expert eye of shade, colour and form, sometimes in groups of over 50 or more – this is no timid planting scheme.

The trees at Rowallane are superb – quietly setting the mood and structure of this plantsman's garden. Monterey, Scots, Bishop and Umbrella Pines, redwood, Wellingtonia, cypresses, multi-stemmed Western Red Cedar, and Douglas Fir are just some of the species.

The joy of Rowallane is not only its trees and its rainbow rhododendrons. Like any great garden, it is a continuing story and a gardener's garden. Through the efforts of Mike Snowden visitors can enjoy walking through meadows of pig-nut, wild orchids and meadow buttercup, or wooded areas with bluebells, cuckoo-pint and wood anemones.

For any keen plantsman a first visit to Rowallane would be a revelation – take a notebook and take time to stroll through this wonderfully captivating garden in Northern Ireland – you will not be disappointed.

For further details about *Rowallane Garden* see entry in Ireland.

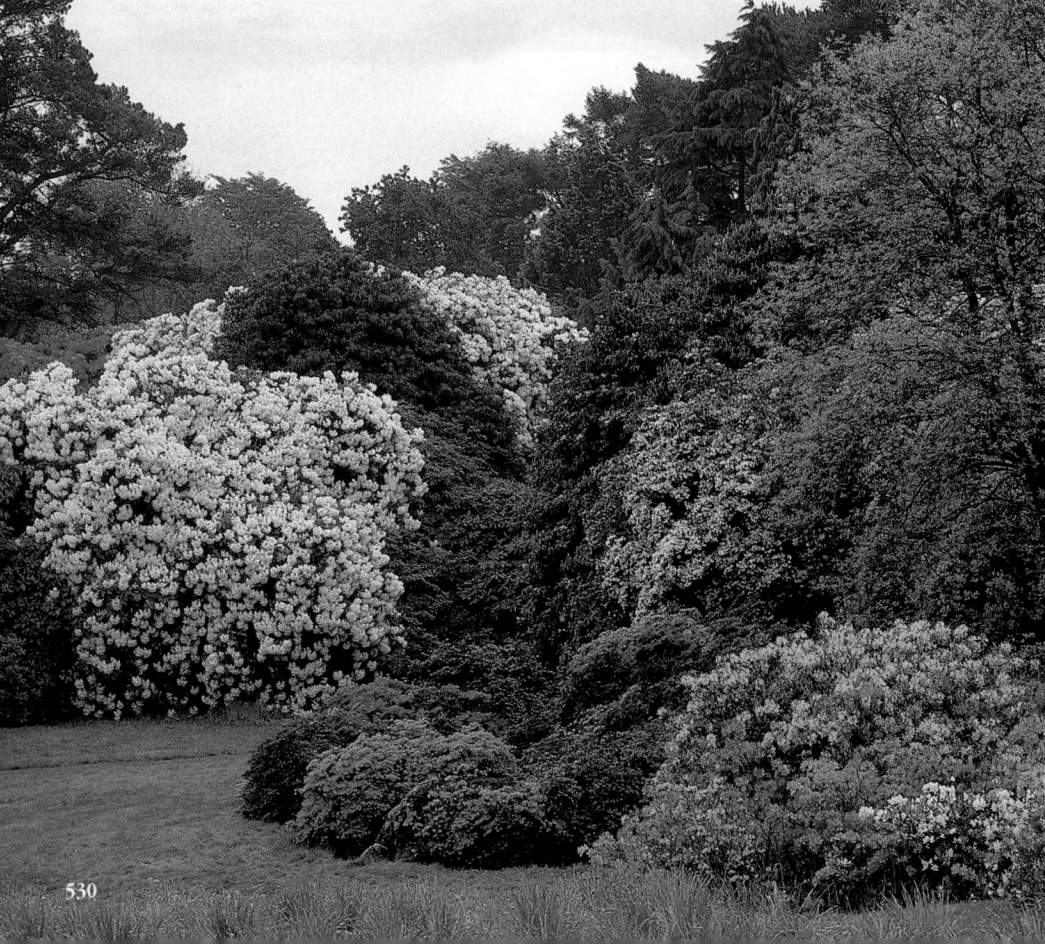

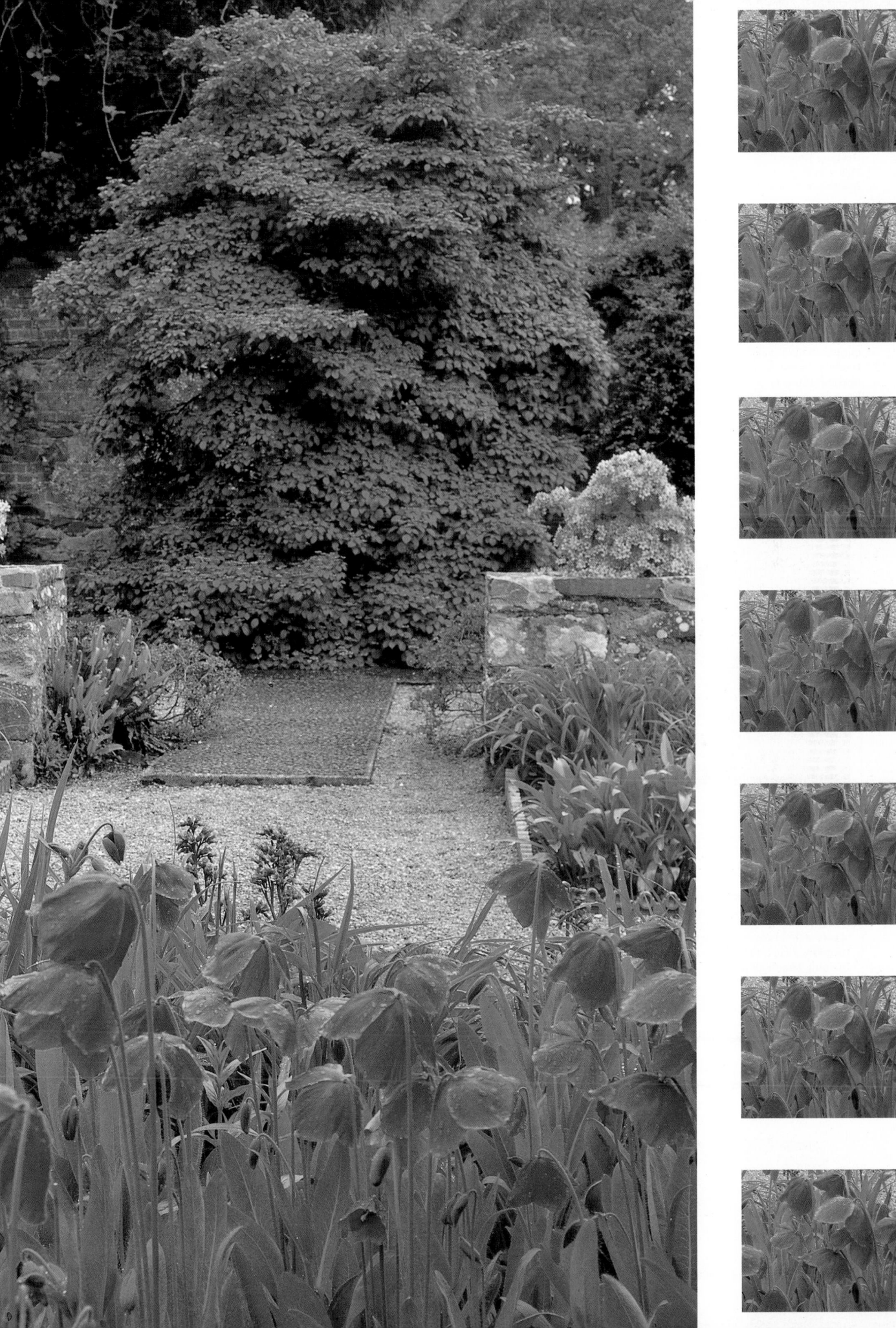

ANNES GROVE GARDENS

Tel: +353 22 26145

Castletownroche, Co Cork
Owner/Contact: Mr P Annesley
The gardens around the 18th century house contain magnolias, eucryphias and hoherias of unusual size. Winding paths and riverside walks.
Location: 1.6 km N of Castletownroche.
Opening Times: 17 Mar - 30 Sept: Mon - Sat, 10am - 5pm; Suns, 1 - 6pm. Other times by arrangement.
Admission: Adult £3, Child £1.50, Conc. £2.

ANTRIM CASTLE GARDENS

Tel: 028 9442 8000 **Fax:** 028 9446 0360

Randalstown Road, Antrim BT41 4LH
e-mail: clotworthy@antrim.gov.uk
Owner: Antrim Borough Council
Contact: Kate Wimpress
Situated adjacent to Antrim Town, the Sixmilewater River and Lough Neagh's shore, these recently restored, 17th century Anglo-Dutch water gardens are maintained in a manner authentic to the period. The gardens comprise of ornamental canals, round pond, ancient motte and a parterre garden planted with 17th century plants - many with culinary or medicinal uses. An interpretative display introducing the history of the gardens and the process of their restoration, along with a scale model of former Antrim Castle is located in the reception of Clotworthy Arts Centre.
Location: Outside Antrim town centre off A26 on A6.
Opening Times: All year: Mon - Fri, 9.30am - 9.30pm (dusk if earlier). Sats, 10am - 5pm. July & Aug: also open Suns, 2 - 5pm.
Admission: Free. Charge for guided group tours (by arrangement only).

ARDGILLAN CASTLE GARDEN

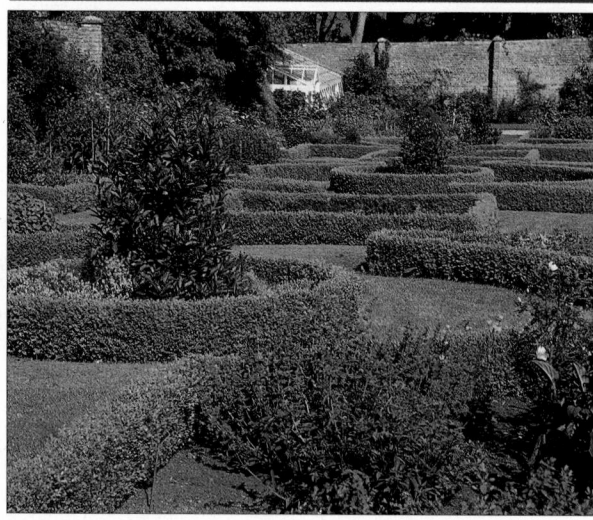

BALBRIGGAN, Co DUBLIN
Owner: Fingal County Council *Contact:* Brenda Kenny

Tel: +353 1 849 2212 **Fax:** +353 1 849 2786
"Flúirse talamh is mara" – Rich in land and sea – part of the Fingal Region of North County Dublin crest and nowhere more true than in Ardgillan Demesne. 194 acres of parkland and gardens surround this early 18th century house.
Location: 30km N of Dublin, off the N1.
Opening Times: All year: Jul & Aug: daily. 1 Apr - end May & Sept: Tue - Sun & Public Hols, 11am - 6pm. 1 Oct - 31 Mar: Tue - Sun & Public Hols, 11am - 4.30pm. Closed 23 Dec - 1 Jan.
Admission: Castle by guided tour only: Adult £3, Conc. £2, Family £6.50. Groups: (10+) £2.

[i] No photography.
[K] Castle: Obligatory. Gardens: Thurs in Jun/Jul/Aug at 3pm.
In grounds, on leads.

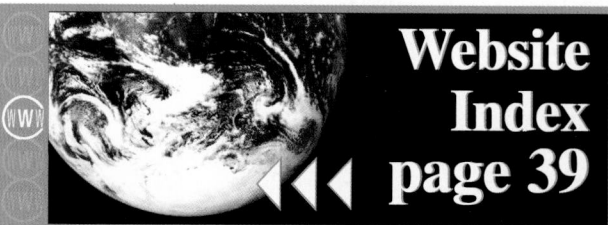

Website Index
◀◀ page 39

Admission prices for properties in Northern Ireland are given in £ Sterling.
Admission prices for properties in the Republic of Ireland are given in Irish Punt.

ARDRESS

Tel/Fax: 028 3885 1236 **e-mail:** uagest@smtp.ntrust.org.uk

64 Ardress Road, Portadown, Co Armagh BT62 1SQ
Owner: The National Trust
Contact: The Custodian
A 17th century farmhouse with elegant 18th century additions by owner-architect George Ensor. Includes a farmyard, popular with children, with rare breeds and traditional farm implements. House tours include the Adam-style drawing room, fine furniture and pictures. Also an attractive garden with woodland and riverside walks amid apple orchards.
Location: On B28, 5m from Moy, 5m from Portadown, 3m from M1/J13.
Opening Times: 13 - 17 Apr: daily, 2 - 6pm. Apr, May & Sept: Weekends & BHs, 2 - 6pm. Jun & Aug: daily except Tue, 2 - 6pm.
Admission: House tour & Farmyard: Adult £2.70, Child £1.35, Family £6.75. Groups £2.20. Farmyard only: Adult £2.40, Child £1.20, Family £6.

Ground floor suitable. WC. Obligatory. [P]

THE ARGORY

Tel: 028 8778 4753 **Fax:** 028 8778 9598

Moy, Dungannon, Co Tyrone BT71 6NA
e-mail: uagest@smtp.ntrust.org.uk
Owner: The National Trust
Contact: The Property Manager
The Argory is a handsome 19th century Victorian house furnished as it was in 1900, providing an excellent illustration of Victorian/Edwardian interior taste and interests. Includes the 1824 Bishop's barrel organ, still in working order. Imposing stableyard with horse carriages, harness room, acetylene gas plant, laundry and children's playground. It is set in 130 hectares of wooded countryside overlooking the River Blackwater. Variety of garden, woodland or riverside walks suitable for all ages. Note: In Autumn 2001 a major restoration will start, house tours may not be on offer during September.
Location: On Derrycaw road, 4m from Moy, 3m from M1/J13 or J14 (coaches J13).
Opening Times: 13 - 17 Apr: daily, 2 - 6pm. Apr, May & Sept: Weekends & BHs, 2 - 6pm (BHs, 1 - 6pm). Jun & Aug: daily except Tues, 2 - 6pm. Grounds only: 4 & 11 Feb; Mar: Suns, 2 - 5pm.
Admission: House: Adult £3, Child £1.50, Family £7.50. Groups £2.55. Groups outside normal hours £2.55. Car park: £1.50.

Ground floor suitable. WC. Obligatory. [P] £1.50.

BALLINDOOLIN HOUSE & GARDEN

Tel: +353 405 31430 **Fax:** +353 405 32377

Carbery, Co Kildare
e-mail: sundial@iol.ie
Owner: R Molony
Contact: Esther Molony
Large Georgian country house and farmyards surrounded by extensive gardens and ancient woods.
Location: 5.6km N of Edenderry on the R401 to Kinnegad.
Opening Times: 1 May - 30 Sept: Tue - Sun, 12 noon - 6pm.
Tyrrells Restaurant: All year, tel. +353 405 32400.
Admission: House: £2.50. Garden: Adult £4, Child £2. Under 5s Free.
Booked groups (20+): House: £2. Garden: Adult £3, Child £1.50. Under 5s Free.

[i] No photography in house. Partially suitable. WC.
Obligatory for house. [P] Guide dogs only. Restaurant only.

BALLINLOUGH CASTLE GARDENS

Tel: +353 46 33135 **Fax:** +353 46 33331

Ballinlough Castle, Clonmellon, Co Westmeath
Owner: Sir John & Lady Nugent
Contact: Sir John Nugent
Set in the lakeland county of Westmeath the gardens comprise of herbaceous borders, roses, fruit and much more.
Location: On N52 half-way between Clonmellon and Delvin. Signed from Athboy.
Opening Times: 1 May - 30 Sept: Tue - Sat, 11am - 6pm. Suns & BHs, 2 - 6pm. Gardens: closed 1st two weeks in Aug.
Admission: Adult £4, Child £1, Conc. £3. Groups (10+): £3.

BALLYWALTER PARK

Tel: 028 4275 8264 **Fax:** 028 4275 8818

Nr Newtownards, Co Down BT22 2PP
e-mail: enquiries@dunleath-estates.co.uk
Owner: Lord & Lady Dunleath
Contact: The Secretary, The Estate Office
Victorian mansion, situated in 40 acres of landscaped grounds, built in the mid-19th century by Charles Lanyon, with Edwardian additions by W J Fennell. Currently undergoing major restoration works. Self-catered (4 star) listed gatelodge overlooking beach available for holiday lets (sleeps four).
Location: 1km S of Ballywalter village.
Opening Times: Please telephone for access, due to major restoration work.
Admission: House or Gardens: Adult £4, Child/Conc. £3. House and gardens: Adult £7, Conc. £5.50. Groups (Max. 50): Adult £4, Child/Conc. £2.

[i] No photography indoors. Pick-your-own, Jun - Aug. Obligatory. [P]

BANTRY HOUSE & GARDENS

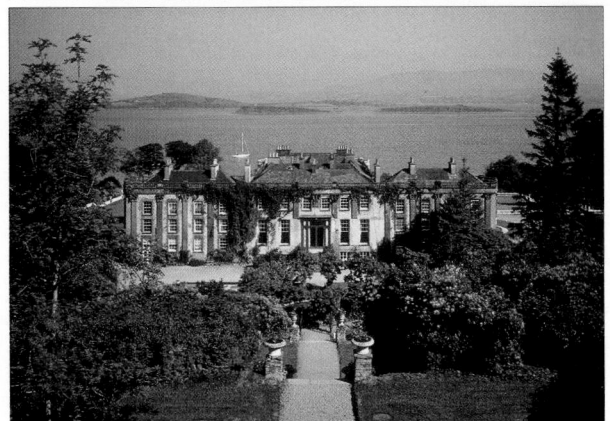

BANTRY, Co CORK

Owner/Contact: Mr & Mrs Egerton Shelswell-White

Tel: +353 27 50047 **Fax:** +353 27 50795 **e-mail:** bantryhouse@eircom.net

Overlooking Bantry Bay, with views to the Cork-Kerry mountains, the house and gardens enjoy one of the most spectacular views in Ireland. Bantry House, home to the White family since 1739, is one of the finest stately homes in Ireland, containing a unique collection of tapestries, furniture, carpets and art treasures, collected mainly by the 2nd Earl in the 19th century. The magnificent gardens and grounds (under restoration) are home to many sub-tropical plants and shrubs – reflecting the best European design and style. Other features within the 45 acre grounds include the renowned 100-stepped 'Stairway to the Sky', the Italian Garden and the largest wisteria circle in the country. Bantry House and Gardens is a member of the Houses, Castles and Gardens of Ireland Scheme.

Location: E outskirts of Bantry town on the main Cork - Killarney coast road (N71).
Opening Times: 1 Mar - end Oct: daily, 9am - 5pm (last admission).
Admission: House & Gardens: Adult £6, Child Free, OAP £4.50, Student £4. Groups (min 20): £4, Child Free. Gardens only: Adult £2, Child Free, Conc. £2.

8 doubles.

BARONS COURT **Tel:** 028 8166 1683 **Fax:** 028 8166 2059

Newtownstewart, Omagh, Co Tyrone BT78 4EZ
Owner: Mount Castle Trust **Contact:** The Agent
The home of the Duke and Duchess of Abercorn, Barons Court was built in the late 18th century and subsequently extensively remodelled by William and Richard Morrison (1819 - 1841), Sir Albert Richardson (1947-49) and David Hicks (1975-76).
Location: 5km SW of Newtownstewart.
Opening Times: By appointment only.
Admission: Adult £4.50, Conc. £3. Groups max. 50.

Partially suitable. WCs. By arrangement.

BENVARDEN GARDEN **Tel:** 028 2074 1331 **Fax:** 028 2074 1955

Dervock, Ballymoney, Co Antrim
Owner/Contact: Mr H J Montgomery
Beautiful walled gardens with woodland walks on the banks of the River Bush.
Location: 10km from Giants' Causeway on B67 Coleraine - Ballycastle road, then follow brown tourist signs.
Opening Times: 1 Jun - 31 Aug: daily (except Mons), 1.30 - 5pm. Other times by arrangement.
Admission: Adult £2.50, Child £1. Group rates on request.

Small museum. By arrangement.

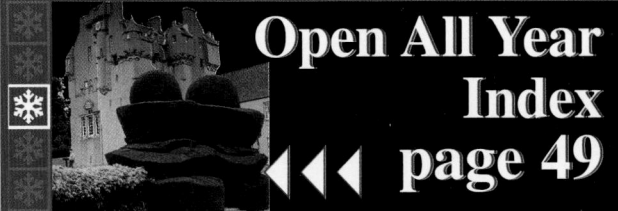

Open All Year
Index
◀◀◀ page 49

BIRR CASTLE DEMESNE **Tel:** +353 509 20336 **Fax:** +353 509 21583
Birr, Co Offaly **e-mail:** info@birrcastle.com
Contact: A Parsons
Discover the largest telescope for over 70 years; constructed here at Birr Castle in the 1840s by the 3rd Earl of Rosse. The telescope looks and moves just as it did over 150 years ago. Magnificent award-winning gardens which feature collections of rare trees, imaginative planting, the tallest box hedges in the world, beautiful landscapes with lake, rivers and waterfalls. At the science centre discover many pioneering achievements of the Parsons family and of other great Irish scientists in the fields of astronomy, photography, engineering, botany and horticulture.
Location: In town of Birr. 130km from Dublin; 90km from Shannon via Limerick.
Opening Times: All year: 9am - 6pm or dusk if earlier. Science Centre: As gardens.
Admission: Adult £5, Child £2.50, Conc. £3.50, Family (2+2) £12. Groups (20+): Adult £4, Child £2.50, Conc. £3.

Partially suitable. WC. By arrangement. Limited for coaches. In grounds, on leads.

BLARNEY CASTLE & ROCK CLOSE **Tel:** +353 21 385252 **Fax:** +353 21 381215
Co Cork **e-mail:** info@blarneyc.iol.ie
Owner: Sir Richard La T Colthurst Bart **Contact:** Mervyn Johnston Esq
Site of the Blarney Stone.
Location: 5m from Cork city, off N20.
Opening Times: May & Sept: Mon - Sat, 9am - 6pm; Suns, 9.30am - 5.30pm. Jun - Aug: Mon - Sat, 9am - 7pm; Suns, 9.30am - 5.30pm, Oct - Apr: Mon - Sat, 9am - 5pm or sundown; Suns, 9.30am - sundown. Closed 24 & 25 Dec.
Admission: Adult £3.50, Child £1, Student/OAP £2.50.

CARRIGGLAS MANOR **Tel:** +353 43 45165 **Fax:** +353 43 41026
Longford
Owner: Mr J G Lefroy **Contact:** Mrs J G Lefroy or Miss Flynn
A romantic Tudor Gothic house. Family occupied. Robinsonia garden.
Location: 4.8km from Longford town on T15/R194.
Opening Times: Please telephone for details.
Admission: Teashop & Shop: Free. Gardens & museum: Adult £2.50, Child (under 7yrs) Free, Conc. £2.
House: £3 extra. Pre-booked groups welcome (10+), Apr - Oct. (2000 prices)

CASTLE COOLE

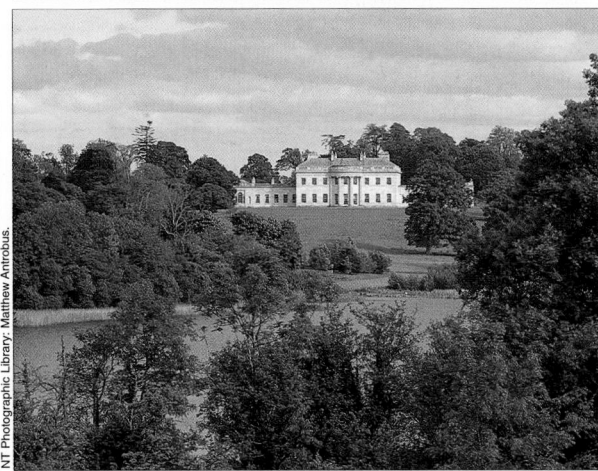

ENNISKILLEN, Co FERMANAGH BT74 6JY
Owner: The National Trust Contact: The Property Manager

Tel: 028 6632 2690 **Fax:** 028 6632 5665 **e-mail:** ucasco@smtp.ntrust.org.uk
Castle Coole is one of the finest neo-classical houses in Ireland, built by James Wyatt in the late 18th century, and sited in a rolling landscape park right on the edge of Enniskillen. Features opulent Regency interior decoration, furnishings and furniture. Guided tour includes ornate state bedroom prepared for George IV in 1821. Also includes stables, Belmore private coach, servants' tunnel, laundry house, dairy and icehouse. The surrounding parkland is ideal for long walks and picnics and includes a children's play area. Tea-room in Tallow House for light refreshments.
Location: On A4, 1m from Enniskillen on A4, Belfast - Enniskillen road.
Opening Times: 13 - 17 Apr: daily. Apr, May & Sept: Sats, Suns & BHs. Jun - Aug: daily (except Thurs), 1 - 6pm. Park: all year, dawn - dusk.
Admission: House tour: Adult £3, Child £1.50, Family £8. Groups: £2.50. Groups after hours £3.50. Park Free.

Partially suitable. WC. In grounds, on leads.

Ireland

CASTLE LESLIE

Tel: +353 47 88109   **Fax:** +353 47 88256

Glaslough, Co Monaghan   **e-mail:** ultan@castle-leslie.ie

Owner/Contact: Samantha Leslie

The present castle was built in 1878. Contains Italian and Spanish furniture, tapestries and carpets. The family home of the Leslies.

Location: 6 km N of Monaghan at Glaslough village.

Opening Times: Open for accommodation and dining throughout the year.

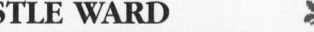

CASTLE WARD

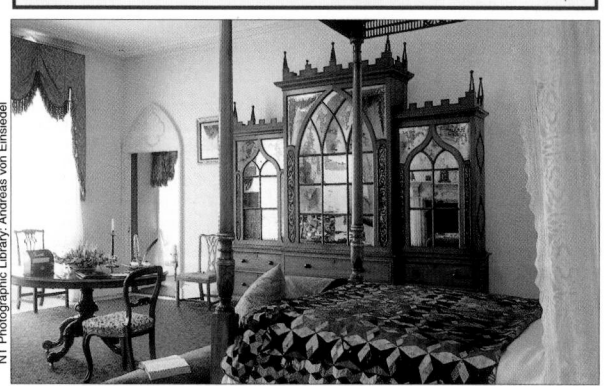

NT Photographic Library: Andreas von Einsiedel

STRANGFORD, DOWNPATRICK, Co DOWN BT30 7LS

Owner: The National Trust *Contact:* The Property Manager

Tel: 028 4488 1204 **Fax:** 028 4488 1729 **e-mail:** ucwest@smtp.ntrust.org.uk

Castle Ward is a beautiful 750 acre walled estate in a stunning location overlooking Strangford Lough. The mid-Georgian mansion is one of the architectural curios of its time, built inside and out in two distinct architectural styles. Due to a difference of opinion between its 18th century owners, Bernard and Anne Ward, the house features Classical styling on one side and Gothic on the other. The picturesque estate also includes a Victorian laundry and children's playroom, water-driven cornmill demonstrations, a disused leadmine and sawmill, which provide a fascinating insight into how the house and estate worked. Paths and horse trails wind their way throughout the estate. Also formal gardens, the Old Castle Ward tower house from 1610, the Temple Water (a man-made lake) and the Strangford Lough Wildlife Centre. Stableyard includes tearoom and a large Trust shop.

Location: On A25, 7m from Downpatrick and 1½ m from Strangford.

Opening Times: House: 13 - 22, 28 & 29 Apr: daily; May, Sept & Oct: Sats, Suns & BHs. Jun - Aug: daily (except Thurs), 1 - 6pm. Estate: All year: dawn - dusk.

Admission: House tour: Adult £3, Child £1.50, Family £7.50. Groups: £2.50 (after hours £3.50). Grounds: £3 per car. £1 if facilities closed, Coach £15 (free if booked for house tour). Horse box £5.

⬜ 🍴 ♿Ground floor & grounds suitable. 💻 🎦Obligatory. 🅿£3.
🐾In grounds, on leads. 🏕Caravan park, holiday cottages, basecamp. 🔔 ❄

CLONALIS HOUSE

Tel: +353 907 20014

Castlerea, Co Rosscommon

Owner: P O'Conor Nash Esq

Ancestral home of the O'Conors of Connaught, descendants of the last High Kings of Ireland.

Location: W of Castlerea town on N60.

Opening Times: 1 Jun - 15 Sept: daily (except Suns), 11am - 5pm. Open all year to groups by arrangement.

Admission: Adult £3.75, Child £1.50, Conc. £2.50.

CRATLOE WOODS HOUSE

Tel: +353 61 327028 **Fax:** +353 61 327031

Cratloe, Co Clare

Owner/Contact: Mr & Mrs G Brickenden

House dates from the 17th century and is the only example of the Irish longhouse which is still a home.

Location: 8 km from Limerick and 16 km from Shannon airport on N7 westbound carriageway. Enter at Red Gate Lodge.

Opening Times: 1 Jun - mid Sept: Mon - Sat, 2 - 6pm. Open other times by arrangement.

Admission: Adult £3, Child £1.50, Conc. £2.50. Special rate for guided tour in morning with lunch, for groups of 20 - 40.

CREAGH GARDENS

Tel/Fax: +353 28 22121

Skibbereen, Co Cork

Owner: Creagh Gardens Trust   **Contact:** Martin Sherry

Woodland glades with varied wild-life. Walled orchard garden with rare breed fowl.

Location: 6 km from Skibbereen on Baltimore Road.

Opening Times: 1 Mar - 31 Oct: daily, 10am - 6pm.

Admission: Adult £3, Child £2.

CROM ESTATE 🍂

Tel/Fax: 028 6773 8118 (Visitor Centre)
028 6773 8174 (Estate)

Newtownbutler, Co Fermanagh BT92 8AP   **e-mail:** ucrvfm@smtp.ntrust.org.uk

Owner: The National Trust   **Contact:** The Visitor Facilities Manager

Crom is one of Ireland's most important nature conservation areas. It is set in 770 hectares of romantic and tranquil islands, woodland and ruins on the shores of Upper Lough Erne. Things to look out for include the spotted flycatcher, curlew, purple hairstreak butterfly, pine marten and fallow deer. Lots of well-maintained nature trails take in the Old Castle, boathouse and summer house. Wildlife exhibition, information point and tearoom for light snacks in visitor centre. Further facilities include jetty for boats, boat hire, award-winning holiday cottages, coarse angling, pike fishing, overnight woodland hide, lecture and conference facilities. The 19th century castle within the estate is private.

Location: 3m from A34, well signposted from Newtownbutler. Jetty at Visitor Centre.

Opening Times: 17 Mar - end Sept: daily, 10am - 6pm; Suns, 12 noon - 6pm.

Admission: £3 per car or boat. Minibus £10, Coach £20.

🍴 💻 🅿 🏠Holiday cottages. 🔔

CURRAGHMORE

Tel: +353 51 387 101 **Fax:** +353 51 387 481

Portlaw, Co Waterford

Owner/Contact: Lord Waterford

Magnificent home of the Marquis of Waterford and his ancestors since 1170.

Location: 14m from Waterford. 8m from Kilmacthomas.

Opening Times: Jan: Mon - Fri, 9am - 1pm. May - Jun & 1 - 15 Jul: Mon - Sat, 9am - 1pm.

Admission: House £4. Grounds & Shell House: £3

DERRYMORE HOUSE 🍂

Tel: 028 3083 8361

Bessbrook, Newry, Co Armagh BT35 7EF

Owner: The National Trust

An elegant late 18th century thatched cottage, built by Isaac Corry, who represented Newry in the Irish House of Commons. Good walks in picturesque park laid out in the style of 'Capability' Brown. Good attraction to break journey between Belfast and Dublin.

Location: On A25, 2m from Newry on road to Camlough.

Opening Times: 14, 16 & 17 Apr: daily; May - Aug: Thur, - Sat, 2 - 5.30pm.

Admission: House tour: Adult £2, Child £1, Family £4.50. Groups: £1.30.

🅿 🐕On leads.

DRIMNAGH CASTLE

Tel: +353 450 2530

Longmile Road, Drimnagh, Dublin 12

Medieval castle with a flooded moat and boasts a barrel-vaulted undercroft.

Location: 5 km SW of Dublin. Buses: 18, 56, 77.

Opening Times: 1 Apr - 1 Oct: Wed, Sat & Sun, 12 noon - 5pm. 1 Oct - 31 Mar: Suns only, 2 - 5pm. Last tour 4.15pm.

Admission: Adult £2.50, Student/OAP £2, Child £1.

DUBLIN WRITERS MUSEUM

Tel: +353 1 8722077 **Fax:** +353 1 8722231

18 Parnell Square, Dublin 1

Owner: Dublin Tourism Enterprises   **Contact:** Eilish Rafferty

The museum features the lives and works of Dublin's literary celebrities over the past 300 years.

Location: City Centre, N of O'Connell Street.

Opening Times: Jan - Dec: Mon - Sat, 10am - 5pm. Suns & BHs, 11am - 5pm. Jun - Aug: late opening Mon - Fri, 10am - 6pm.

Admission: Adult £4, Child (3-11yrs) £2, Conc. £3, Family £11.

DUNKATHEL

Tel: +353 21 821014 **Fax:** +353 21 821023

Glanmire, Co Cork

Owner: The Russell Family   **Contact:** Mr John Russell

House dates from c1790. Contains splendid bifurcated staircase of Bath stone.

Location: 5 km from Cork off N25.

Opening Times: 1 May - mid Oct: Wed - Sun, 2 - 6pm.

Admission: Adult £2, Child £1, Conc. £1.50. Special group rate.

DUNLOE CASTLE HOTEL GARDENS   Tel: +353 64 44111   Fax: +353 64 44583

Beaufort, Killarney, Co Kerry
Owner: The Liebherr Family   **Contact:** Mary Rose Hickey
Collection of trees, shrubs and plants from around the world.
Location: 13 km from Killarney.
Opening Times: May - Oct: Groups and tours by appointment.
Admission: Free. Catalogue £1.

FERNHILL   Tel: +353 1 295 6000

Sandyford, Co. Dublin
Owner/Contact: Mrs Sally Walker
200 year old garden for all seasons. Fine trees, rare shrubs and Victorian kitchen garden.
Location: On the NE slope of the Three Rock mountain, 11 km S of the city centre on the Enniskerry Road. 6 km inland from Dun Laoghaire.
Opening Times: 1 Mar - 30 Sept: Tue - Sat & BH Mons, 11am - 5pm; Suns, 2 - 6pm.
Admission: Adult £3, Child £1, Conc. £2. Groups: £2.50.

FLORENCE COURT

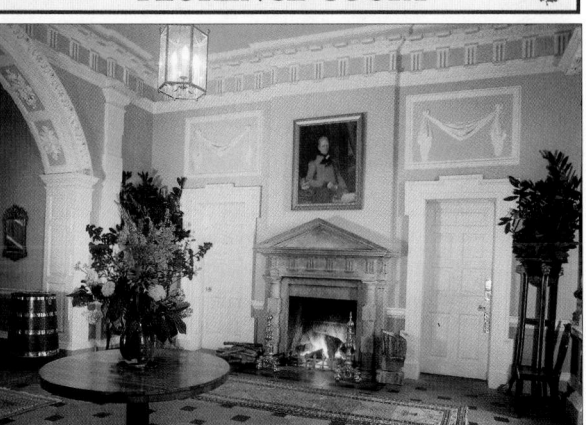

ENNISKILLEN, Co FERMANAGH BT92 1DB

Owner: The National Trust   *Contact:* The Property Manager

Tel: 028 6634 8249   **Fax:** 028 6634 8873   **e-mail:** ufcest@smtp.ntrust.org.uk
Florence Court is a fine mid-18th century house and estate set against the stunning backdrop of the Cuilcagh Mountains. It was the home of the Earls of Enniskillen and is one of the most important houses in Ulster. It is now a popular attraction for all the family. Exquisite rococo ceilings and panels, fine Irish furniture. Original paintings, furniture and artefacts returned in 1998 and 1999. House tour includes service quarters popular with all ages. Water-powered sawmill; ice-house; summer house; beautiful walled garden and lots of walks in grounds. Morning coffee, lunches and afternoon teas in Stables Restaurant, gift shop. Also children's playground and holiday cottage.
Location: 8m SW of Enniskillen via A4 and then A32 to Swanlinbar.
Opening Times: House: Easter (13 - 17 Apr): daily, 1 - 6pm. Apr, May & Sept: Sats, Suns & BHs. Jun - Aug: daily (except Tues), 1 - 6pm. Estate: Apr - Sept: daily, 10am - 7pm, Oct - Mar: daily, 10am - 4pm. Closed 25 Dec.
Admission: House tour: Adult £3, Child £1.50, Family £8. Groups: £2.50. Groups outside opening hours £3.50. Estate: £2 per car.

Ground floor suitable. WC. Obligatory. P In grounds, on leads. Holiday cottage.

THE FRY MODEL RAILWAY   Tel: +353 1 846 3779   Fax: +353 1 846 3723

Malahide Castle Demesne, Malahide, Co Dublin
Owner: Dublin Tourism Enterprises   **Contact:** John Dunne
The Fry Model Railway is a unique collection of handmade models of Irish trains from the beginning of travel to modern times.
Location: 10m N of Dublin.
Opening Times: Apr - Oct: Mon - Sat, 10am - 5pm, Suns & BHs 2 - 6pm. Nov - Mar: Sat, Sun & BHs, 2 - 5pm. Closed 1 - 2pm daily all year.
Admission: Adult £4, Child (3-11yrs) £2, Conc. £3, Family (2+4) £11.

GLIN CASTLE   Tel: +353 68 34173   Fax: +353 68 34364

Glin, Co Limerick   **e-mail:** knight@iol.ie
Owner: The Knight of Glin   **Contact:** Bob Duff
Glin Castle, one of Ireland's most historic properties and home to the FitzGerald family, hereditary Knights of Glin. The castle, with its superb interiors, decorative plasterwork and collections of Irish furniture and paintings stands on the banks of the River Shannon.
Location: Co Limerick.
Opening Times: Tours by appointment only.
Admission: Adult £3.

GRAY'S PRINTING PRESS   Tel: 028 7188 4094

49 Main Street, Strabane, Co Tyrone BT82 8AU
Owner: The National Trust   **Contact:** The Administrator
Historic printworks, featuring 18th century printing press and 19th century hand-printing machines. John Dunlap, printer of the American Declaration of Independence, and James Wilson, grandfather of President Woodrow Wilson, are said to have learned their trade here. Tour includes audio-visual presentation, check in advance for compositor demonstrations. Strabane District Council local history museum in the same building.
Location: In the centre of Strabane.
Opening Times: Apr - Sept: Tue - Sat, 2 - 5pm.
Admission: Tour price: Adult £2, Child £1, Family £4.50. Group £1.30.

HAMWOOD HOUSE   Tel: +353 44 8255210

Dunboyne, Co Meath
Owner: Major and Mrs Hamilton   **Contact:** Mrs Hamilton
Palladian-style house, built in 1779, contains a fine collection of 18th century furniture.
Location: 2m from Dunboyne on Maynooth Rd.
Opening Times: 1 Feb - 31 Mar: Mon - Fri, 10am - 2pm. 1 Apr - 31 Aug: Mon - Fri. 2 - 6pm. 3rd Sun of each month, 2 - 6pm.
Admission: House: Adult £3. Garden: Adult £3. Groups by arrangement.

HEZLETT HOUSE   Tel/Fax: 028 7084 8567   e-mail: undpmx@smtp.ntrust.org.uk

107 Sea Road, Castlerock, Coleraine, Co Londonderry BT51 4TW
Owner: The National Trust   **Contact:** The Custodian
Charming 17th century thatched house with 19th century furnishings. Interesting cruck-truss roof construction viewed from specially exposed attic. One of only a few pre-18th century Irish buildings still surviving. Excellent attraction for visitors en-route from Causeway to Londonderry.
Location: 5m W of Coleraine on Coleraine - Downhill coast road, A2.
Opening Times: Easter (13 - 17 Apr): daily. Apr, May & Sept: Sats, Suns & BHs only. Jun - Aug: daily except Tues, 12 noon - 5pm.
Admission: Adult £2, Child £1, Family £5. Groups £1.50 (outside hours £2.50).

Ground floor suitable. Obligatory. P In grounds, on leads.

HILTON PARK   Tel: +353 47 56007   Fax: +353 47 56033

Hilton Park, Clones, Co Monaghan
Owner/Contact: Mr John Madden
Lakeside pleasure grounds, herb garden, parterre and herbaceous border in rolling parkland.
Location: 3m due S of Clones on L46, Ballyhaise Rd.
Opening Times: By appointment.
Admission: Adult £3.

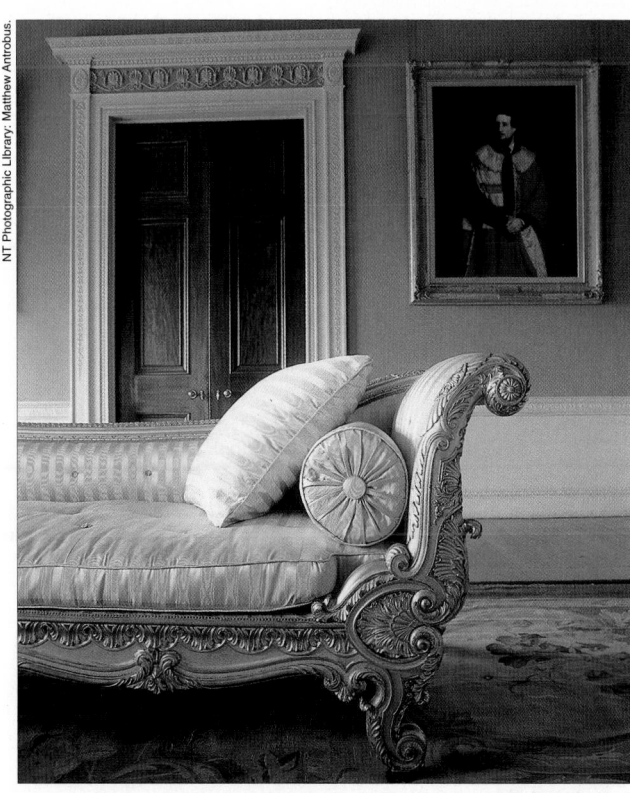

Castle Coole, Ireland.

THE IRISH MUSEUM OF MODERN ART

Tel: + 353 1 612 9900

Royal Hospital, Military Rd, Kilmainham, Dublin 8

Fax: +353 1 612 9999

e-mail: info@modernart.ie

Owner: Irish Museum of Modern Art   **Contact:** Monica Cullinane

The Irish Museum of Modern Art opened in 1991 in the magnificently restored Royal Hospital building and grounds, which include a formal garden, meadow and medieval burial grounds as well as a series of other historic buildings. A series of new galleries, housing exhibitions from important collections worldwide opened in March 2000 and are located in the Deputy Master's House. The museum presents, through its permanent collection and temporary exhibitions, an exciting and innovative range of Irish and international art of the 20th century, alongside strong education and community, national and artists' residency programmes.

Location: Near Heuston Station, 2km from city centre. Buses: 69, 78A, 79, 90.

Opening Times: Tue - Sat, 10am - 5.30pm. Suns, 12 noon - 5.30pm. Guided tours: Weds & Fris at 2.30pm, Suns at 12.15pm. Closed Mons. Other times by appointment.

Admission: Free.

i No inside photography.   On leads in grounds.

JAMES JOYCE MUSEUM

Tel/Fax: +353 1 280 9265

Joyce Tower, Sandycove, Co Dublin

Owner: Dublin Tourism Enterprises   **Contact:** Robert Nicholson

A martello tower containing a museum devoted to the life and works of James Joyce.

Location: Dun Laoghaire, 8m S of Dublin.

Opening Times: Apr - Oct: Mon - Sat, 10am - 5pm. Closed 1 - 2pm. Suns & BHs, 2 - 6pm.

Admission: Adult £4, Child (3 - 11yrs) £2, Conc. £3, Family £11. Group rates on request.

JAPANESE GARDENS & ST FIACHRA GARDEN

Tel: +353 45 521617

Fax: +353 45 522964 **e-mail:** stud@irish-national-stud.ie

Tully, Kildare Town, Co Kildare

Owner: Irish National Stud   **Contact:** Freda O'Connell

Created 1906 - 1910. St Fiachra's Garden created 1999.

Location: 1m from Kildare Town. 30m from Dublin off M/N7.

Opening Times: 12 Feb - 12 Nov: daily 9.30am - 6pm.

Admission: Adult £6, Child (under 12yrs) £3, Conc. £4.50, Family (2+4) £14. One ticket includes National Stud and Japanese Garden & St Fiachra's Garden.

KILLYLEAGH CASTLE

Tel/Fax: 028 4482 8261

e-mail: rowanhamilton.killyleaghcastle@virgin.net

Killyleagh, Downpatrick, Co Down BT30 9QA

Owner/Contact: Lt Col D Rowan-Hamilton

Oldest occupied castle in Ireland. Self-catering towers available to sleep 4-15. Swimming pool and tennis court available. Access to garden.

Location: At the end of the High Street.

Opening Times: By arrangement. Groups (30-50): by appointment.

Admission: Adult £3.50, Child £2. Groups: Adult £2.50, Child £1.50.

i No photography in house. Wedding receptions. Not suitable. Obligatory.

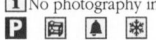

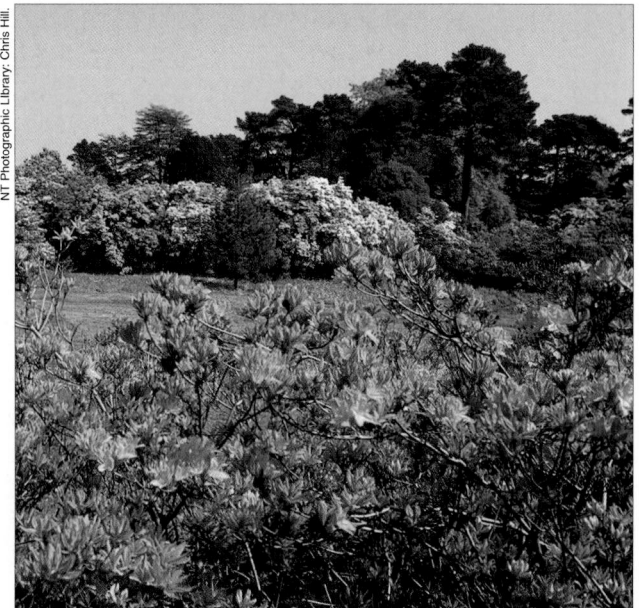

Rowallane, Ireland.

KING HOUSE

Tel: +353 79 63242 **Fax:** +353 79 63243

Boyle, Co Roscommon

e-mail: kinghouse-boyle@hotmail.com

Owner: Roscommon County Council   **Contact:** The Administrator

Four-storey Georgian mansion dating from the early 18th century.

Location: In the centre of Boyle.

Opening Times: Apr - Oct: daily. Late October: weekends, 10am - 6pm. Last admission 5pm.

Admission: Adult £3, Child £2, Conc. £2.50, Family (2+4) £8. Group rates on request.

KYLEMORE ABBEY & GARDEN

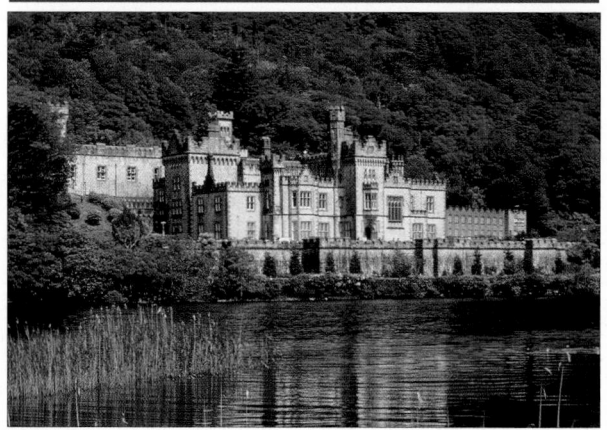

CONNEMARA, CO GALWAY

Owner: *Benedictine Nuns*   **Contact:** *Sister Magdalena OSB*

Tel: +353 95 41146 **Fax:** +353 95 41145 **e-mail:** info@kylemoreabbey.ie

Set in the heart of the Connemara mountains. Kylemore is a premier tourist attraction, international girls' boarding school, a magnificent gothic church, superb restaurant and one of the finest craft shops in Ireland. Victorian Walled Garden, currently undergoing restoration. The walls stretch for up to half a mile to enclose: the kitchen garden, flower or pleasure garden, gardener's cottage, bothy and the glass (hot) house complex. The Benedictine Nuns at Kylemore continue to restore the estate and open it to the education and enjoyment of all who visit.

Location: Between Reccess & Letterfrack, West of Ireland.

Opening Times: Abbey, exhibition, church, lake walk & video: All year (closed Good Fri & Christmas week), 9am - 5.30pm. Garden, Dawros walk, museum, tearoom, shop & exhibition: Easter - Oct:10.30am - 4.30pm.

Admission: Abbey: Adult £3.30, Conc. £2.30, Family £7. Groups (10+): Adult £2.30. Gardens: Adult £4, Conc. £2.75, Family £8.50. Groups (10+): Adult £2.75. Joint ticket: Adult £6.50, Conc. £4.50, Family £14. Groups (10+): £4.50.

 Ground floor & grounds suitable. WC.

LISNAVAGH GARDENS

Tel: +353 503 61104 **Fax:** +353 503 61148

Lisnavagh, Rathvilly, Co Carlow, Ireland

Owner/Contact: Lord and Lady Rathdonnell

Ten acres of outstanding trees and shrubs, mixed borders, rock garden and cruciform yew walk, with panoramic views of the Wicklow Hills and Mount Leinster.

Location: Situated 2m S of Rathvilly. Signposted.

Opening Times: May - July: Suns, 2 - 6pm. Other times by appointment.

Admission: Adult £3, Child £1.50.

LISSADELL HOUSE

Tel: +353 71 63150 **Fax:** +353 71 66906

Ballinfull, Co Sligo

House built in the 1830s by Sir Robert Gore-Booth, and still the family home.

Location: 13km NW of Sligo.

Opening Times: 1 Jun - mid Sept: (except Suns), 10.30am - 11pm & 2 - 5pm. Last admission 12.30pm & 4.30pm. Guided tours.

Admission: Adult £3, Child £1.50. Group: (20+) £2.50.

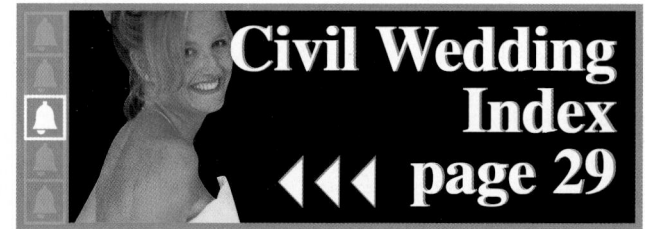

Civil Wedding Index ◀◀◀ page 29

NT Photographic Library: Chris Hill.

LODGE PARK WALLED GARDENS & STEAM MUSEUM

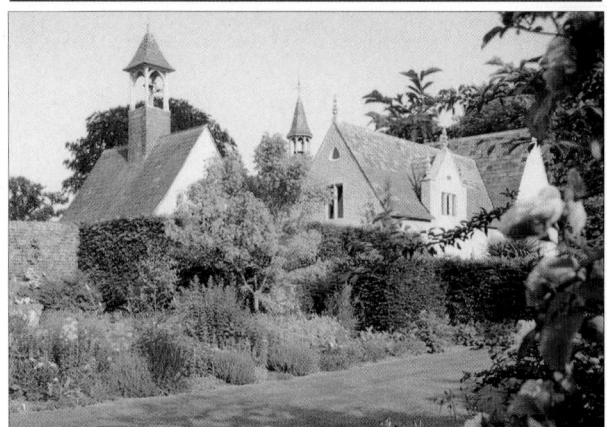

STRAFFAN, CO KILDARE
Owner: Mr R Guinness

Tel: +353 1 6273155 **Fax:** +353 1 6273477 **e-mail:** garden@steam-museum.ie

Lodge Park Walled Garden with brick lined north wall of 18th century origin is a plantsman's delight. From the axis of the long walk it features garden rooms extending to a long rosarie. The Steam Museum building incorporates the roof, windows and other architectural features taken from the c1865 Great Southern & Western Railway Church of St Jude (attributed to the architect Sancton Wood) Inchicore, Dublin. Taken down in 1988 it was rebuilt here, under the consultant architect Mr Percy Le Clerc, and opened by the President of Ireland in 1992 as the Steam Museum. The Richard Guinness model hall displays his collection of historic prototype locomotive models. The Power Hall displays restored stationary engines working in steam. Interactive area for educational use. Memorabilia gallery.

Location: 16m from Dublin, signposted off the N7 road at Kill junction traffic lights.

Opening Times: Easter Sun - May: Suns & BHs, 2.30 - 5.15pm. Jun - Aug: Tue - Sun & BHs, 2 - 5.45pm. Sept: Suns & BHs 2.30 - 5.15pm.

Admission: Adult £3, Conc. £2. Groups (10+) less 10%. Garden only: £2. Tech Student + card Free.

  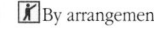 By arrangement.

MOUNT STEWART

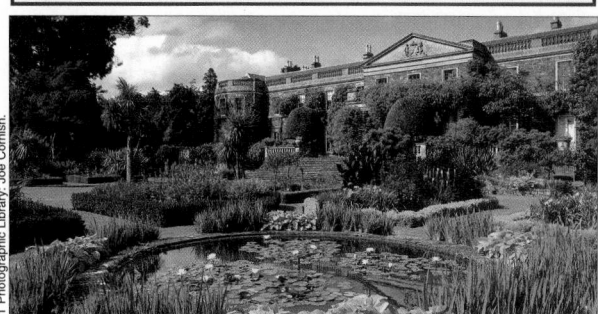

NT Photographic Library: Joe Cornish.

NEWTOWNARDS, Co DOWN BT22 2AD
Owner: The National Trust   *Contact: The Property Manager*

Tel: 028 4278 8387 **Fax:** 028 4278 8569 **e-mail:** umsest@smtp.ntrust.org.uk

Home of the Londonderry family since the early 18th century, Mount Stewart was Lord Castlereagh's house and played host to many prominent political figures. The magnificent gardens planted in the 1920s have made Mount Stewart famous and earned it a World Heritage Site nomination. They feature a series of formal outdoor 'rooms', vibrant parterres, and formal and informal vistas, some with Strangford Lough views. Many rare and unusual plants thrive in the mild climate of the Ards, including eucalyptus, beschorneria, mimosa, and cordyline. The garden is also home to national collections of phormium and libertia. The house includes 'Hambletonian' (*The Independent* rated it in the top 100 British paintings of all time), as well as the full set of chairs used at Congress of Vienna. The Temple of the Winds, a 1785 banqueting hall, is in the grounds. Due to a building programme the shop and tearoom may not be available during 2001.

Location: On A20, 5m from Newtownards on the Portaferry road.

Opening Times: House: 13 - 22 Apr: daily; Apr & Oct: Sats, Suns & BHs; May - Sept: daily, except Tues; 1 - 6pm. Garden: Mar: Suns, 2 - 5pm. 17, 19 Mar: 11am - 6pm. Apr - Sept: daily, 11am - 6pm. Oct: weekends, 11am - 6pm. Nov & 1, 2, 8, 9 Dec: weekends, 2 - 5pm (lake only). Temple of the Winds: Apr - Oct: weekends, 2 - 5pm.

Admission: House tour, Gardens & Temple: Adult £3.50, Child £1.75, Family £8.75. Group £3 (outside normal hours £6). Garden & Temple only: Adult £3, Child £1.50, Family £7.50. Group £2.50. Temple of the Winds only: Adult £1, Child 50p.

   Obligatory.In grounds, on leads.

MALAHIDE CASTLE

Tel: +353 1 846 2184 **Fax:** +353 1 846 2537

Malahide, Co Dublin

Owner: Fingal County Council   **Contact:** Maria Morgan

The castle has changed very little in 800 years, surrounded by parklands.

Location: 10m N of Dublin city.

Opening Times: Apr - Oct: Mon - Sat, 10am - 5pm. Suns & BHs 11am - 6pm. . Nov - Mar: Mon - Fri, 10am - 5pm. Sat, Sun & BH, 2 - 5pm. Closed 12.45 - 2pm daily. Closed for tours 12.45 - 2pm daily.

Admission: Adult £3.15, Child £1.75, Conc. £2.65, Family £8.75 (2000 prices).

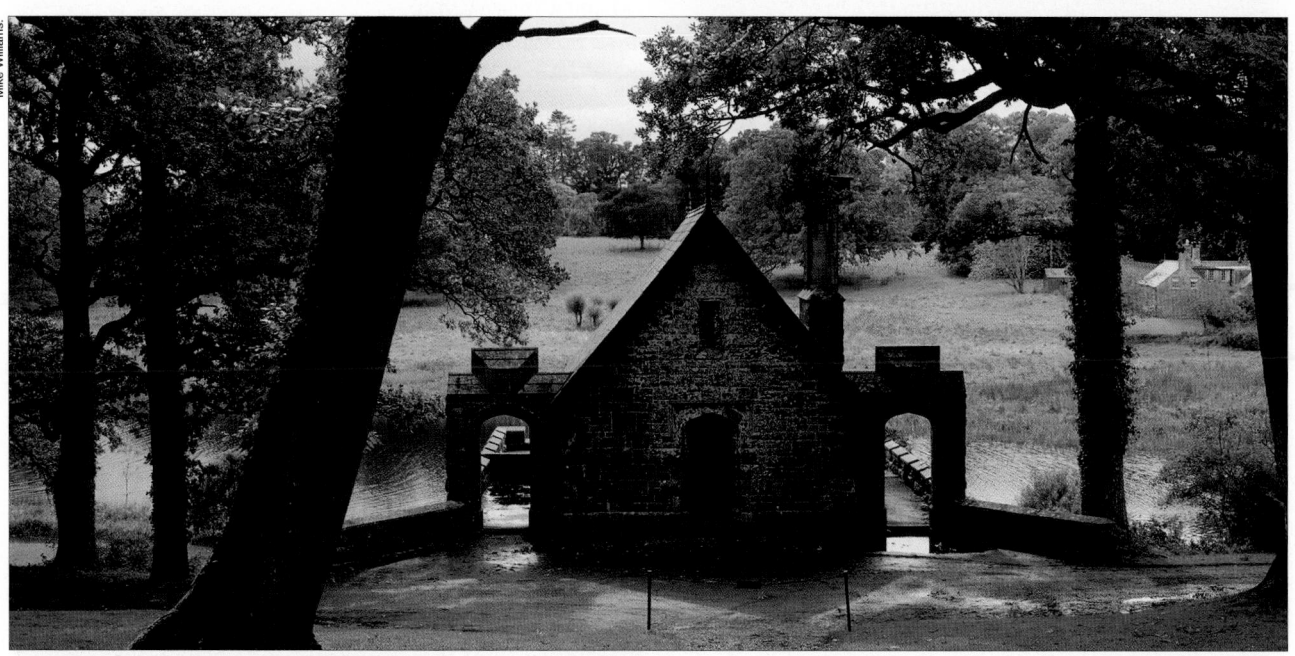

Mike Williams.

Crom Boathouse, Ireland.

MUSSENDEN TEMPLE

Tel/Fax: 028 7084 8728
e-mail: undpmx@smtp.ntrust.org.uk

Castlerock, Co. Londonderry
Owner: The National Trust
The Temple is part of the landscaped Downhill Estate laid out in the 18th century. Woodland glen and cliff top walks.
Location: 1m W of Castlerock.
Opening Times: Downhill Estate: All year: dawn - dusk. Mussenden Temple: Apr - Jun & Sept: weekends & BHs, 12 noon - 6pm. Jul & Aug: daily.
Admission: Grounds open free.

P   On leads.

THE NATIONAL BOTANIC GARDENS

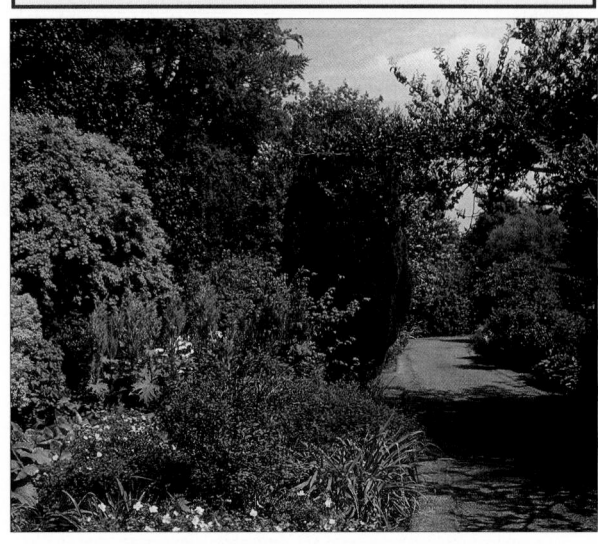

MALAHIDE DEMESNE, MALAHIDE, CO DUBLIN
Owner: Fingal County Council

Tel: +353 1 872 7777   **Fax:** +353 1 8727530
Botanical garden containing over 4,000 species of non-ericaceous plants with a comprehensive collection of southern hemisphere plants, many rare and unusual. The gardens now extend to 9ha including a Walled Garden of 1.6ha, which includes many tender shrub borders, alpine yard, pond and 7 glasshouses.
Location: 13km NE of Dublin City.
Opening Times: Summer: Mon - Sat, 9am - 6pm, Suns, 11am - 6pm. Winter: Mon - Sat, 10am - 4.30pm, Suns, 11am - 4.30pm.
Admission: Adult £2, Child/OAP Free. Groups (10+) £1.50. Guided tours of walled garden £2 (2000 prices).

Partially suitable.   Licensed.   By arrangement.   P
In grounds on leads.

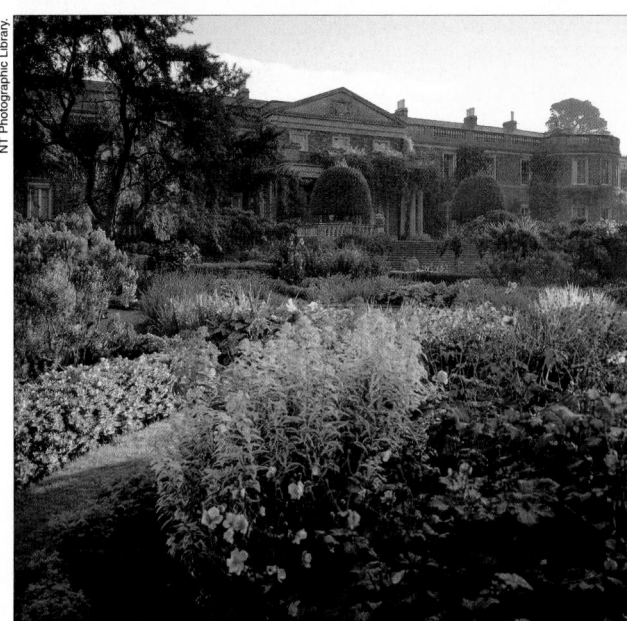

Mount Stewart, Ireland.

NEWBRIDGE HOUSE

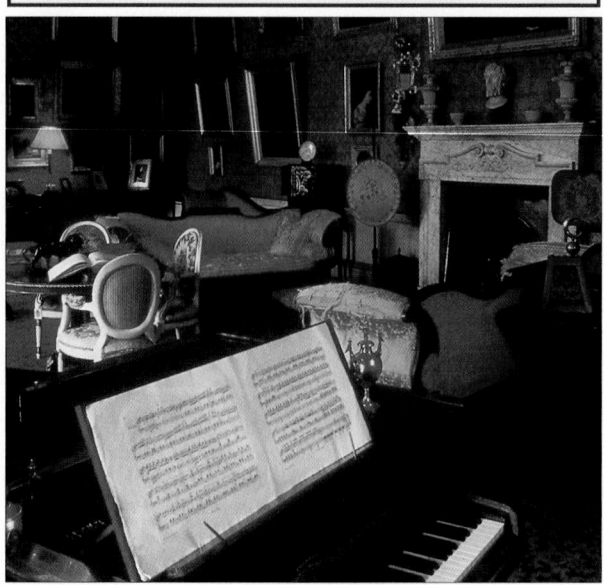

DONABATE, Co DUBLIN
Owner: Fingal County Council   *Contact: Brigid Dunne*

Tel: +353 1 843 6534   **Fax:** +353 1 846 2537
This delightful 18th century manor is set in 350 acres of parkland 12 miles north of Dublin City. It boasts one of the finest Georgian interiors in Ireland. Each room open to the public has its own style of antique and original furniture – indeed the house appears much as it did 150 years ago.
Location: 12m N of Dublin City.
Opening Times: Apr - Sept: Tue - Sat, 10am - 5pm, Suns & BHs, 2 - 6pm (closed Mons). Closed 1 - 2pm daily. Oct - Mar: Sat, Sun & BHs, 2 - 5pm.
Admission: Adult £4, Child £2, Conc. £3, Family £11.

NEWMAN HOUSE
Tel: +353 1 706 7422   **Fax:** +353 1 706 7211

85/86 St Stephen's Green, Dublin
Owner: University College, Dublin   **Contact:** Ruth Ferguson, Curator
Two Georgian houses containing examples of Dublin's finest 18th century plasterwork.
Location: Central Dublin.
Opening Times: Jun, Jul & Aug only. Tue - Fri, 12 noon - 5pm. Sats, 2 - 5pm. Suns, 11am - 2pm.
Admission: Adult £3, Conc. £2.

NUMBER TWENTY-NINE
Tel: +353 1 702 6165   **Fax:** +353 1 702 7796

Lower Fitzwilliam Street, Dublin 2
Owner: Electricity Supply Board & National Museum of Ireland   **Contact:** K Burns
Restored middle-class house of the late 18th century.
Location: Lower Fitzwilliam Street, adjacent Merrion Square.
Opening Times: Tue - Sat, 10am - 5pm. Suns, 2 - 5pm. Closed Mons & 2 weeks before Xmas.
Admission: Adult £2.50, Conc. £1.

PALM HOUSE BOTANIC GARDENS
Tel: 028 9032 4902

Belfast City
Owner: Belfast City Council   **Contact:** Mr Reg Maxwell
Built by Richard Turner who later built the Great Palm House at Kew.
Location: Between Botanic Avenue & Stranmillis Road, South Belfast.
Opening Times: Palm House & Tropical Ravine: Apr - Sept: Mon - Fri, 10am - 12 noon & 1 - 5pm; Sats & Suns, 1 - 5pm. Oct - Mar: Mon - Fri, 10am - 12 noon & 1 - 4pm; Sats & Suns, 1 - 4pm. BHs as Sats & Suns. Park: 8am - sunset.
Admission: Free.

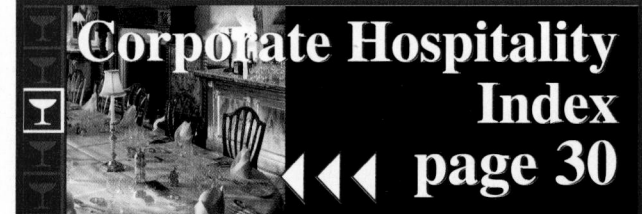

Corporate Hospitality Index ◄◄◄ **page 30**

PATTERSON'S SPADE MILL

Tel/Fax: 028 9443 3619

Templepatrick, Co Antrim BT39 0AP

Owner: The National Trust

Founded in 1919, this is the last surviving water-driven spade mill in Ireland. The original equipment is working for visitors to see, complete with hammers, a turbine and a press. An authentic workshop setting, complete with the smell of oil, metal and wood shavings. Guided tour includes traditional spade-making demonstration, and the history and culture of the humble turf and garden spade. Excellent exhibition in the reception. Good outing from Belfast, or as a stop-off from the M2. Garden spades made in the mill are for sale and make a popular gift. Spades are available by mail order.

Location: On A6 (between Sandyknowes roundabout and Templepatrick roundabout), M2/J4. 1st left at Templepatrick roundabout after exiting motorway.

Opening Times: Easter (13 - 17 Apr): daily; Apr, May – Sept: Sats, Suns & BH Mons; Jun & Aug: daily (except Tues), 2 - 6pm.

Admission: Adult £3, Child £1.25, Family £7.25, Groups £1.75 (outside normal hours £3.50).

POWERSCOURT ESTATE

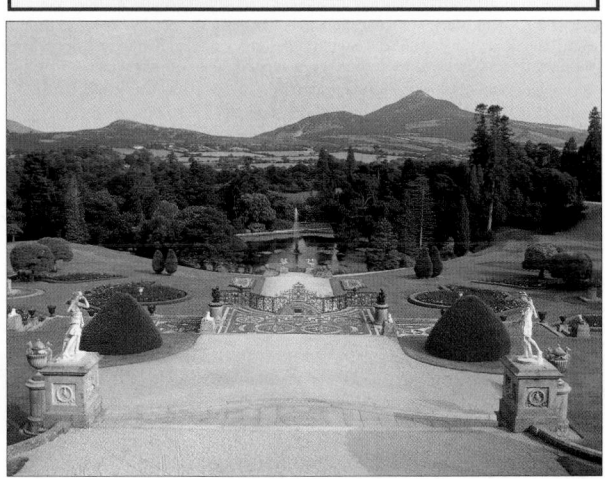

ENNISKERRY, Co WICKLOW

Owner: *The Slazenger Family*   **Contact:** *The Estate office*

Tel: +353 1 204 6000   **Fax:** +353 1 204 6900   **e-mail:** gardens@powerscourt.ie

One of the world's great gardens, situated in the foothills of the Wicklow Mountains. It is a sublime blend of formal gardens, sweeping terraces, statuary and ornamental lakes together with secret hollows, rambling walks, walled gardens and over 200 varieties of trees and shrubs. Powerscourt House incorporates an exhibition on the history of the estate, a terrace café overlooking the gardens and speciality shops, including Interiors Gallery and Garden Pavilion. 5km from the gardens is Powerscourt Waterfall, the highest in Ireland.

Location: 12m S of Dublin City centre, off N11 adjacent to Enniskerry village.

Opening Times: 1 Mar - 31 Oct: daily, 9.30am - 5.30pm. 1 Nov - 28 Feb: daily, 9.30am - dusk. Closed 25/26 Dec.

Admission: House Exhibition & Gardens: Adult £6, Child £3, Conc. £5. Groups: Adult £5, Child £2.80, Conc. £4.30. Special prices for groups (20+).

 Partially suitable. WCs.   Guide dogs only.

POWERSCOURT TOWN HOUSE

Tel: +353 1 679 4144   **Fax:** +353 1 671 7505

South William St, Dublin 2

Owner: Clarendon Properties

Built for the 4th Viscount Powerscourt between 1771 and 1774.

Location: Central Dublin.

Opening Times: All year: Mon - Sat, 10am - 6pm. Suns, 12 noon - 6pm.

Admission: Free.

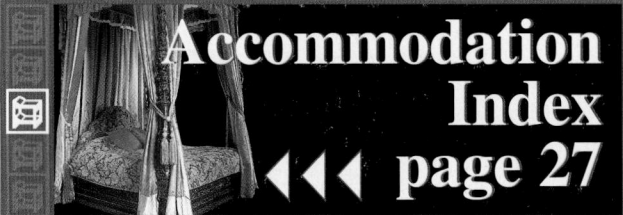

Accommodation Index ◀◀◀ page 27

RAM HOUSE GARDEN

Tel/Fax: +353 402 37238

Ram House, Coolgreany, Gorey, Co Wexford

Owner: Godfrey & Lolo Stevens   **Contact:** Mrs Lolo Stevens

A two acre romantic scented garden. Twice shown on TV and judged 'Best in Co Wexford' in the 2000 Shamrock National Gardens Competition. There are gravel and woodland areas, terraces, pergola, gazebo, mixed borders in soft colours, ponds, lavish planting around a little stream and over 70 varieties of clematis.

Location: In Coolgreany village, 3km off N11 between Arklow and Gorey.

Opening Times: May - Aug: Fri - Sun & BHs, 2.30 - 6pm. Other times and groups by appointment.

Admission: Adult £3, Child £2.

Garden plan & plant list.   Not suitable.   Limited.   Guide dogs only.

RIVERSTOWN HOUSE

Tel: +353 21 4821205

Glanmire, Co Cork

Owner: Mr & Mrs D Dooley   **Contact:** Mrs D Dooley

Georgian House. Plasterwork by Lafranini Bros.

Location: 1m from Glanmire Village, turn right at Riverstown Cross.

Opening Times: May - mid Sept: Wed - Sat, 2 - 6pm. Other times by appointment.

Admission: £3.

ROTHE HOUSE

Tel/Fax: +353 56 22893

Parliament St, Kilkenny

Owner: Kilkenny Archaeological Society   **Contact:** Mary Flood

Built 1594. Various exhibitions. Also houses the County Genealogical Research Service.

Location: Parliament Street, in Kilkenny City.

Opening Times: All year: Mon - Sat, 10.30am - 5pm. Suns, 3 - 5pm.

Admission: Adult £2, Child £1, Conc. £1.50. Groups (20+): Adult £1.50.

ROWALLANE GARDEN

Tel: 028 9751 0131   **Fax:** 028 9751 1242

Saintfield, Ballynahinch, Co Down BT24 7LH   **e-mail:** uroest@smtp.ntrust.org.uk

Owner: The National Trust   **Contact:** The Property Manager

Rowallane is a natural landscape of some 21 hectares, planted with an outstanding collection of trees, shrubs and other plants from many parts of the world, creating a beautiful display of form and colour throughout the year. The garden was established in the 1860s by the Rev John Moore, and carried on by his plant-collecting nephew in the early 1900s. Planting and collecting continue today. In spring the garden features a magnificent display of rhododendrons, azaleas, bulbs, flowering trees and shrubs. Summer brings hypericum, viburnum, shrub roses and fuschias in the walled garden; primulas and heathers in the rock garden and wild flower meadows rich with orchids. The scarlet and gold foliage of autumn gives way to winter, when Rowallane's plentiful supplies of fruit and berries attracts an array of interesting birds.

Location: On A7, 1m from Saintfield on road to Downpatrick.

Opening Times: 17 Mar - end Oct: Mon - Fri, 10.30am - 6pm, Sats & Suns, 12 noon - 6pm. Nov - 16 Mar: Mon - Fri, 10.30am - 5pm. Closed 24 & 25 Dec & 1 Jan.

Admission: Apr - Oct: Adult £3, Child £1.25, Family £6.25. Groups £1.75. Nov - Mar: Adult £1.40, Child 70p. Groups 80p.

 Grounds suitable. WC.   Apr - Aug.   In grounds, on leads.

RUSSBOROUGH

Tel: + 353 45 865239   **Fax:** +353 45 865054

Blessington, Co Wicklow   **Contact:** The Administrator

A beautifully maintained 18th century house housing the Beit collection, fine furniture, tapestries, carpets, porcelain, silver and bronzes.

Location: 30km from Dublin on N81. 3km S of Blessington.

Opening Times: From Easter Sun, Apr & Oct: Sun & BHs, 10.30am - 5.30pm. May - Sept: daily, 10.30am - 5.30pm.

Admission: Main rooms: Adult £4, Conc. £3, Child £2. Upstairs: £2.50

SEAFORDE GARDENS

Tel: 028 44811 225   **Fax:** 028 44811 370

Seaforde, Co Down BT30 8PG

Owner/Contact: Patrick Forde

18th century walled garden and adjoining pleasure grounds, containing many rare and beautiful trees and shrubs; many of them tender. There are huge rhododendrons and the National Collection of Eucryphias. The oldest maze in Ireland is in the centre of the walled garden, which can be viewed from the Mogul Tower. The tropical butterfly house contains hundreds of beautiful highly coloured butterflies; also a collection of parrots, insects and reptiles. The nursery garden contains many interesting plants for sale.

Location: 20m S of Belfast on the main road to Newcastle.

Opening Times: Easter - end Sept: Mon - Sat, 10am - 5pm; Suns, 1 - 6pm. Oct - Mar: Mon - Fri, 10am - 5pm.

By arrangement.

SHAW BIRTHPLACE

Tel: + 353 1 4750854 **Fax:** + 353 1 8722231

33 Synge Street, Dublin 8
Owner: Dublin Tourism Enterprises   **Contact:** Eilish Rafferty
The first home of the Shaw family and the renowned playwright, George Bernard Shaw.
Location: 10 mins from City centre.
Opening Times: May - Oct: Mon - Sat, 10am - 5pm, Suns & BHs 11am - 5pm. Closed 1 - 2pm.
Admission: Adult £4, Child £2, Conc. £3, Family £11.

SPRINGHILL ✤

Tel/Fax: 028 8674 8210 **e-mail:** uspest@smtp.ntrust.org.uk

20 Springhill Road, Moneymore, Co Londonderry BT45 7NQ
Owner: The National Trust   **Contact:** The Property Manager
A charming and atmospheric 17th century 'plantation' house, said by many to be one of the prettiest houses in Ulster. It was home to ten generations of the Conyngham family, originally from Ayr. 50 minutes drive from Belfast or Londonderry, 35 minutes from Coleraine. House tour takes in exceptional library, gun room, nursery, and includes the story of resident ghost. Colourful costume collection, with some Irish 17th century pieces. Beautiful walks in walled gardens and way-marked paths in estate. Excellent tearoom, small shop and children's play area.
Location: 1m from Moneymore on B18 to Coagh, 5m from Cookstown.
Opening Times: Easter (13 - 17 Apr): daily; Apr - Jun & Sept: Sats, Suns and BHs; Jul - Aug: daily except Thurs; 2 - 6pm.
Admission: Adult £3, Child £1.50, Family £6.50, Group £2.50 (outside hours £3.50).

🄯 ♿Partially suitable. WC. 🖵 🅿 🐕In grounds, on leads.

STROKESTOWN PARK HOUSE

Tel: +353 78 33013 **Fax:** +353 78 33712

Strokestown, Co Roscommon
Owner: Westward Group   **Contact:** Declan Jones
The Palladian-style house is complete with its original contents. Houses the National Famine Museum. Recently restored Georgian fruit and vegetable garden.
Location: 114 km from Dublin on N5.
Opening Times: 1 Apr - 31 Oct: daily, 11am - 5.30pm. Tours, other times by appointment.
Admission: £3.50 for one attraction. £6.50 for 2 attractions. £9 for 3 attractions.

TULLYNALLY CASTLE & GARDENS

Tel: +353 44 61159 **Fax:** +353 44 61856

Castlepollard, Co. Westmeath   **e-mail:** tpakenham@tinet.ie
Owner: Thomas & Valerie Pakenham   **Contact:** Valerie Pakenham
Romantic woodland and walled gardens laid out in the early 19th century, with follies, grotto and ornamental lakes. The present owners have added a Chinese garden complete with pagoda and a Tibetan garden of waterfalls and streams, and a local sculptor has carved fantastic shapes from existing trees. The Gothick Revival castle forms a splendid backdrop.
Location: 1m from Castlepollard on Granard Road off N52, or N4 via Mullingar.
Opening Times: Gardens: 1 May - 31 Aug: 2 - 6pm. Castle: 15 Jun - 30 Jul:, 2 - 6pm. Open to groups at other times by appointment. Tearoom: daily, 2 - 6pm.
Admission: Castle & Gardens: Adult £5, Child £2.50. Groups: Adult £4. Gardens only: Adult £3, Child £1.

♿ 🖵 🎥Obligatory. 🐕In grounds, on leads. ❄

WELLBROOK BEETLING MILL ✤

Tel: 028 8674 8210/8675 1735
e-mail: uspest@smtp.ntrust.org.uk

20 Wellbrook Road, Corkhill, Co. Tyrone BT80 9RY
Owner: The National Trust   **Contact:** The Custodian
Wellbrook is an 18th century water-powered beetling mill with the only working beetling engines on show in Northern Ireland. Costumed guides lead visitors through hands-on demonstration of the linen process, from the flax growing next to the car park to watching the beetles pound rolls of linen. Includes new exhibition on the history of linen and its importance to Ireland. Set in picturesque wooded glen with good paths.
Location: 4m from Cookstown, following signs from A505 Cookstown - Omagh road.
Opening Times: Easter (13 - 17 Apr): daily; Apr, Jun & Sept: Sats, Suns & BHs only; Jul & Aug: daily except Tues; 2 - 6pm.
Admission: Adult £2.50, Child £1.25, Family £5. Group: £2 (outside hours £3).

🄯 🅿

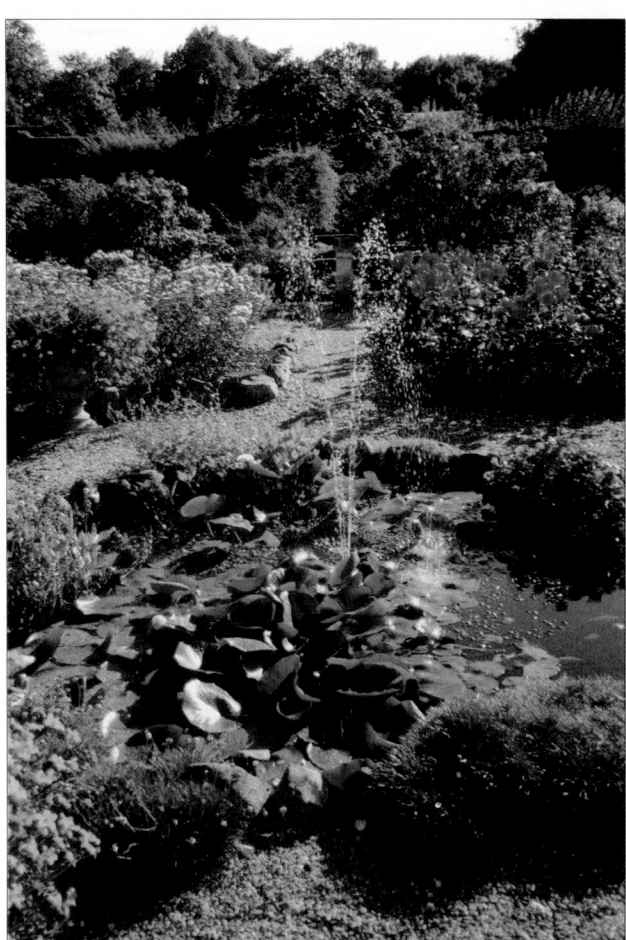

Benvarden Garden, Ireland.

Opening Arrangements at Properties grant-aided by English Heritage

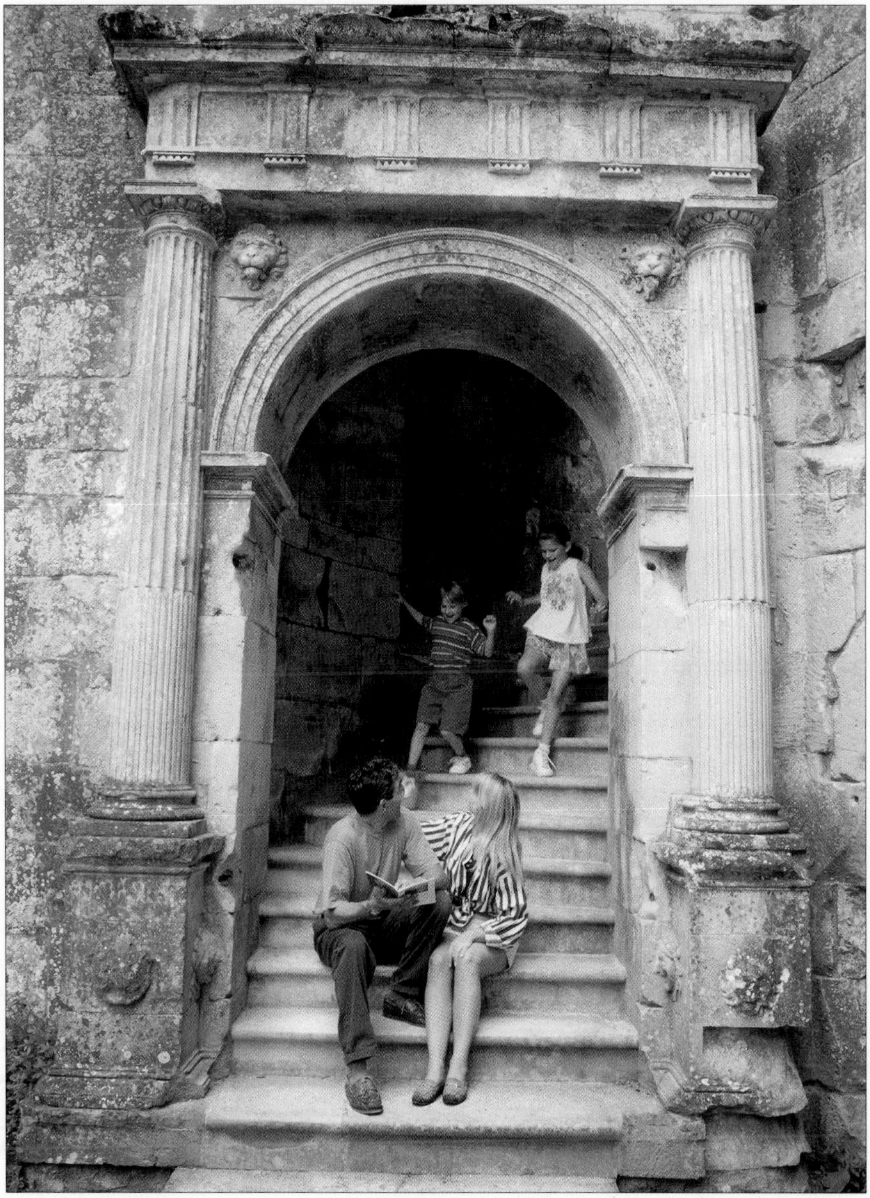

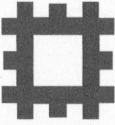

ENGLISH HERITAGE

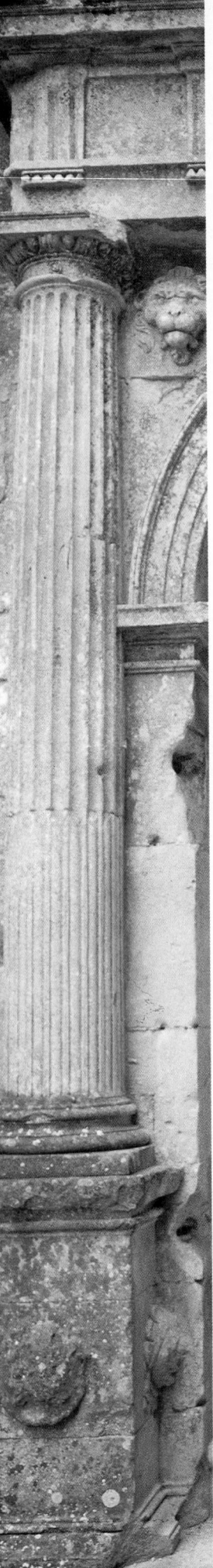

ENGLISH HERITAGE

23 Savile Row, London W1S 2ET

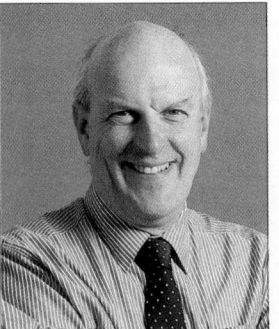

Last year for the first time we published a list of opening arrangements at properties grant-aided by English Heritage. I am pleased to introduce this year's list which has been expanded to make it even more useful to potential visitors and to include National Trust properties which have received grant-aid from English Heritage. Over half the properties are open free but we give details of admission charges where appropriate, as well as a brief description of each property and information on disabled access and parking.

The extent of public access varies from one property to another. The building's size, nature and function are all taken into account. Some buildings, such as town halls, museums or railway stations are regularly open to all by virtue of their use. For other properties, especially those which are family homes or work places, access may need to be arranged in a way which also recognises the vulnerability of the building or the needs of those who live or work in it. Usually this will mean opening 'by appointment' or on an agreed number of days each year. This is made clear by each entry.

Some properties are open 'by written appointment' only. In most cases you should still be able to make initial contact by telephone, but you will be asked to confirm your visit in writing. This is to confirm the seriousness of the visitor's intention as you would for example with a hotel booking. It also provides a form of identification, enabling owners to feel more secure about inviting strangers into their house.

It has always been a condition of grant-aid from English Heritage that the public should have a right to see the buildings to whose repair they have contributed. We therefore welcome feedback from visitors on the quality of their visit to grant-aided properties. In particular, please let us know if you are unable to gain access to any of the buildings on the list on the days or at the times specified, or if you have difficulty in making an appointment to visit and do not receive a satisfactory explanation from the owner. Please contact English Heritage Customer Services at PO Box 569, Swindon SN2 2YR (telephone: 01793 414910; e-mail: customers@english-heritage.org.uk).

Information about public access is also included on our website (www.english-heritage.org.uk). The website is regularly updated to include new properties, any subsequent changes which have been notified to us or any corrections. We suggest that you consult our website for up to date information before visiting. If long journeys or special requirements are involved, we recommend that you telephone the properties in advance, even if no appointment is required.

I hope that you enjoy discovering some of the lesser-known treasures as well as the more well-known buildings we have supported.

Neil Cossons.

Sir Neil Cossons
Chairman

BERKSHIRE

Basildon Park

Lower Basildon, Reading, Berkshire RG8 9NR

Designed in the 18th century by Carr of York and set in parkland in the Thames Valley. Rich interiors with fine plasterwork. Small flower garden, pleasure ground and woodland walks.

Website Address: www.nationaltrust.org.uk
Grant Recipient/Owner: The National Trust
Access contact: Property Manager
Tel: 01189 843040 **Fax:** 01189 841267
Opening Arrangements: House: 31 March to 4 November: daily except Mondays and Tuesdays (but open pm Bank Holiday Mondays and Good Friday) 1 - 5.30pm. Park, garden and woodland walks: as house 12 - 5.30pm. Property closes at 5pm on 17/18 August for concerts. Wheelchair access to ground floor, stairlift to first floor, and garden. Car park 400 metres from property.
Heritage Open Days: No
P Yes. Spaces: 80
♿ Partial. Disabled WC: Yes. Guide Dogs: Yes
£ Yes
Adult: £4.30 (house & gardens). £1.80 (park & gardens).
Child: £2.15 (house & gardens). £0.90 (park & gardens).
Other: £10.50 (family: house & gardens). £4.50 (family: park & gardens). £3.00 (per head for groups of 15+, on application).

Highclere Castle & Park

Highclere, Newbury, Berkshire RG20 9RN

Early Victorian mansion rebuilt by Sir Charles Barry in 1842, surrounded by 'Capability' Brown parkland with numerous listed follies. Family home of the 7th Earl and Countess of Carnarvon.

Website Address: www.highclerecastle.co.uk
Grant Recipient/Owner:
Earl of Carnarvon & Lord Porchester
Access contact: H W Dean & Son
Tel: 01223 351421 **Fax:** 01223 324554
Email Address: agent@hwdean.co.uk
Opening Arrangements: 1 July - 2 September: daily. Wheelchair access to ground floor only. Access enquiries may be made direct to the Castle (01635 253210). Unlimited parking.
Heritage Open Days: No
P See above
♿ Partial. Disabled WC: Yes Guide Dogs: Yes
£ Yes
Adult: £6.50
Child: £3.00
Other: £5.00 (senior citizens and students)

Welford Park

Welford, Newbury, Berkshire RG20 8HU

Red brick country house c1652 and remodelled in 1702, when a third storey was added and the front façade was decorated with Ionic columns. Other alterations were made in the Victorian period.

Grant Recipient/Owner: Mr J H L Puxley
Access contact: Mr J H L Puxley
Tel: 01488 608203
Opening Arrangements: 28 May, 1 - 26 June inclusive and 27 August, 11am - 5pm. Interior of house (4 principal rooms) by prior arrangement only. Admission charges for interior of house only.
Heritage Open Days: No
P Yes. Spaces: 40
♿ Yes. Disabled WC: No. Guide Dogs: Yes
£ Yes
Adult: £3.50
Child: £2.00
Other: £2.00

BUCKINGHAMSHIRE

Abbey Farmhouse

Church Street, Great Missenden, Buckinghamshire HP16 0AZ

Thought to have been the gatehouse to Missenden Abbey. The major part was built in the early 15th century and was converted to a farmhouse probably in the mid 16th century with further 19th century alterations.

Grant Recipient/Owner: Mr N F Pearce
Access contact: Mr N F Pearce
Tel: 01494 862767
Opening Arrangements: By prior arrangement (written appointments preferred). A few days notice will usually be sufficient. Access for wheelchair users to ground floor only.
Heritage Open Days: Yes
P Yes. Spaces: 2
♿ Partial. Disabled WC: No. Guide Dogs: Yes
£ No

Chicheley Hall

Newport Pagnell, Buckinghamshire MK16 9JJ

Built by Sir John Chester between 1719 and 1724 and containing ornate plasterwork, panelling and furniture which was specially made for the house. Home of the 2nd Earl Beatty after the Second World War.

Website Address: www.chicheleyhall.co.uk
Grant Recipient/Owner: Trustees of Mrs Nutting
Access contact: Mrs Valerie Child
Tel: 01234 391252 **Fax:** 01234 391388
Email Address: enquiries@chicheleyhall.co.uk
Opening Arrangements: By prior written arrangement. Wheelchair access to ground floor only.
Heritage Open Days: No
P Yes. Spaces: 60
♿ Partial. Disabled WC: No. Guide Dogs: Yes
£ Yes
Adult: £6.00
Child: £1.50

Chilton House

Chilton, Aylesbury, Buckinghamshire HP18 9LR

Country house, built in the 16th century and remodelled c1740 for Chief Justice Carter based on William Winde's Buckingham House of c1705 in London.

Website Address: www.chiltonhouse.co.uk
Grant Recipient/Owner: Chilton House Ltd
Access contact: Lady Aubrey-Fletcher
Tel: 01844 265200 **Fax:** 01844 265202
Email Address: chiltonhouse@farming.co.uk
Opening Arrangements: By prior arrangement any day 11am - 5pm.
Heritage Open Days: Yes
P Yes. Spaces: 50
♿ Yes. Disabled WC: Yes. Guide Dogs: Yes
£ No

Claydon House

Middle Claydon, nr. Buckingham, Buckinghamshire MK18 2EY

18th century house with fine rococo decoration. A series of great rooms have wood carvings in chinese and gothic styles, and tall windows overlook parkland and a lake. In continuous occupation by the Verney family for over 350 years.

Website Address: www.nationaltrust.org.uk
Grant Recipient/Owner: The National Trust
Access contact: The Custodian
Tel: 01296 730349 **Fax:** 01296 738511
Opening Arrangements: 31 March to 4 November: 1 - 5pm (closed 10 July and Thursdays and Fridays). House closes at 4pm on event days. Wheelchair access to ground floor and all of garden.
Heritage Open Days: Yes
P Yes. Spaces: 30
♿ Partial. Disabled WC: Yes. Guide Dogs: Yes
£ Yes
Adult: £4.30
Child: £2.15
Other: £10.50 (family). £3.60 (groups 15+ Saturdays, Mondays to Wednesdays).

Cliveden Mansion & Clock Tower

Cliveden, Taplow, Maidenhead, Buckinghamshire SL6 0JA

Built by Charles Barry in 1851, once inhabited by Lady Astor now let as a hotel. Series of gardens, each with its own character, featuring roses, topiary, water gardens, a formal parterre, informal vistas, woodland and riverside walks.

Website Address: www.nationaltrust.org.uk
Grant Recipient/Owner: The National Trust
Access contact: Property Manager
Tel: 01628 605069 **Fax:** 01628 66461
Opening Arrangements: House (three rooms) and Octagon Room: April to October Thursdays and Sundays 3 - 5.30pm. Estate and garden: 14 March to 31 December daily 11am - 6pm (closed 10 July and closes at 4pm from 4 November). Woodland car park: open all year daily 11am - 5.30pm (closes at 4pm November to March). Wheelchair access to house (some steps in house) and much of garden.
Heritage Open Days: No
P Yes. Spaces: 300
♿ Partial. Disabled WC: Yes. Guide Dogs: Yes
£ Yes
Adult: £1.00 (house). £5.00 (grounds). £3.00 (car park).
Child: £0.50 (house). £2.50 (grounds). £1.50 (car park).
Other: £12.00 (family: grounds). £7.50 (family: car park).

Freeman Mausoleum

St Mary's Churchyard, Fawley, Buckinghamshire

Built in 1752 for the Freeman family who owned the Fawley Estate. Design by John Freeman based on the mausoleum of Cecilia Metella on the Appian Way in Rome, which he visited while on his Grand Tour. It contains 30 coffin slots with 12 being filled by the Freemans before they sold the Estate in 1850.

Grant Recipient/Owner:
St Mary's Parochial Church Council
Access contact: Mr J B Stuart
Tel: 01491 638782
Opening Arrangements: Mausoleum visible externally at any time, inside can be seen through entrance archway. For full access contact Mr J B Stuart, St Mary's Parochial Church Council, Fawley, Buckinghamshire (tel.01491 638782) for key. Parking on road adjacent to church.
Heritage Open Days: Yes
P Yes. Spaces: 10
♿ Yes. Disabled WC: No. Guide Dogs: Yes
£ No

Hughenden Manor Disraeli Monument

High Wycombe, Buckinghamshire

The home of Prime Minster Benjamin Disraeli from 1848-1881. Hughenden has a red brick 'gothic' exterior. Much of his furniture, books and paintings remain. The garden has been recreated in the spirit of his wife, Mary Anne colourful designs. Park and woodland walks.

Website Address: www.nationaltrust.org.uk
Grant Recipient/Owner: The National Trust
Access contact: Property Manager
Tel: 01494 755575
Opening Arrangements: House: 3 to 31 March: Saturdays and Sundays 1 - 5pm. 1 April to 4 November: Tuesdays to Sundays (open Bank Holiday Mondays, closed Good Friday) 1 - 5pm. Gardens: as house 12 - 5pm. Park and woodlands all year. Wheelchair access to ground floor of house, and terrace.
Heritage Open Days: No
P Yes. Spaces: 100
♿ Partial. Disabled WC: Yes. Guide Dogs: Yes
£ Yes
Adult: £4.30. £1.50 (garden only).
Child: £2.15. £0.75 (garden only).
Other: £10.50 (family). Park & woods free.

Princes Risborough Market House

Market Square, Princes Risborough, Buckinghamshire HA27 0AS

17th/18th century brick building, with slate roof, built on wooden stilts. Originally used to store grain, straw and hay. The market was held under the store room. Now used as a meeting room by town council.

Grant Recipient/Owner:
Princes Risborough Town Council
Access contact: Mr D J Phillips
Tel: 01844 273934
Email Address: dennisphillips@tinyworld.co.uk
Opening Arrangements: Weekdays by prior telephone or written arrangement to Mr D J Phillips, Town Clerk, Princes Risborough Town Council, 3 Barn Road, Longwick, Princes Risborough, Buckinghamshire HP27 9RW (tel. 01844 273934). Short term parking (10 spaces) in High Street, public car park within 100 yards (next to parish church).
Heritage Open Days: Yes
P Yes. Spaces: 10
♿ No
£ No

Stowe House, Buckingham

Buckinghamshire MK18 5EH

Mansion built 1680 and greatly altered and enlarged in the 18th century, surrounded by important 18th century gardens. House and gardens variously worked on by Vanbrugh, Gibbs, Kent and Leoni. Many of the greatest alterations carried out for Viscount Cobham, one of Marlborough's Generals, between 1715 and 1749. Gardens cover 325 acres and contain 6 lakes and 32 garden temples. Kent designed the Elysian Fields in the 1730s, one of the first experiments in 'natural' landscaping, and 'Capability' Brown worked here for 10 years as head gardener and was married in the church in the grounds in 1744. The House is now a public school, the Gardens are owned by the National Trust.

Website Address: www.stowe.co.uk
Grant Recipient/Owner:
The Commercial Director, Stowe School
Access contact: Mr Bob Sharp
Tel: 01280 818282 **Fax:** 01280 818186
Email Address: sses@stowe.co.uk
Opening Arrangements: 24 March - 16 April: Wednesday - Friday 2 - 5pm, Saturday and Sunday 10am - 1pm; 8 July - 31 August: Wednesday and Thursday 2 - 5pm, Friday - Sunday 10am - 1pm; 14-23 December: Friday and Saturday 10am - 1pm; 16 April: Bank Holiday Monday 2 - 5pm.
Heritage Open Days: Yes
P Yes. Spaces: 30
♿ Yes. Disabled WC: Yes. Guide Dogs: Yes
£ Yes
Adult: £3.00
Child: £1.50 (under 16)
Other: £3.00

CAMBRIDGESHIRE

The Black Hostelry

The College, Ely, Cambridgeshire

Built c1291-2 of Carr stone rubble with Barnack, or similar,

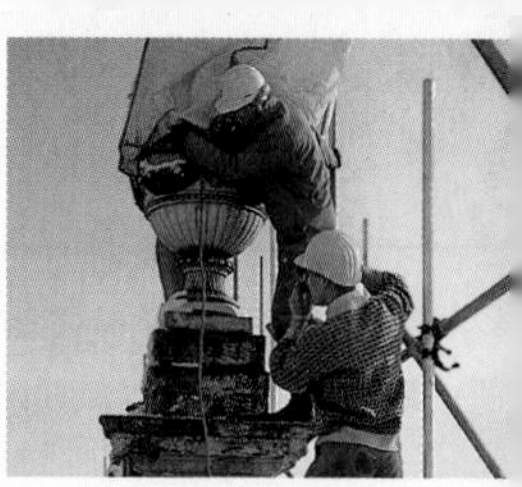
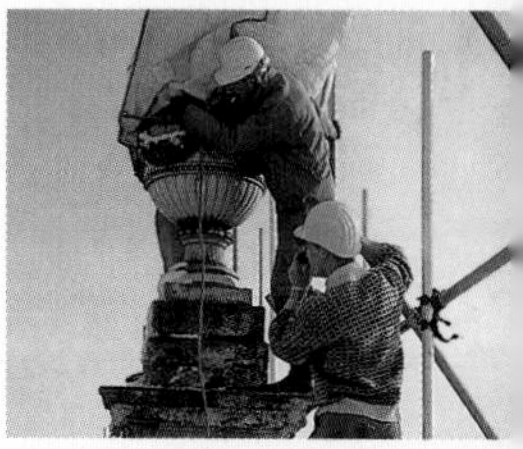
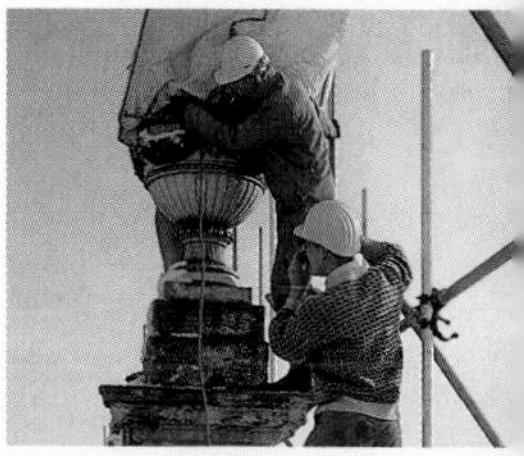
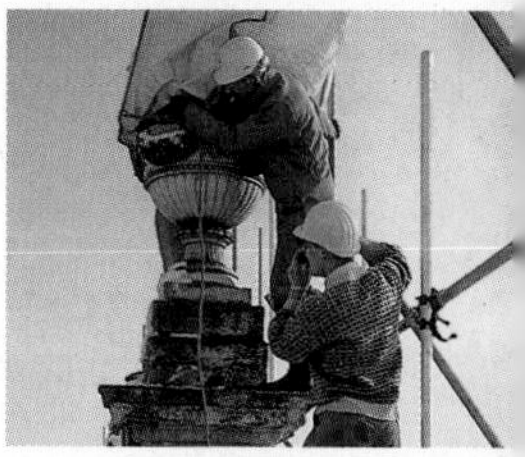
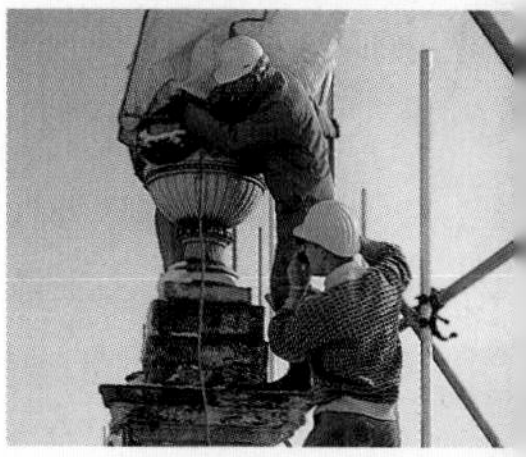
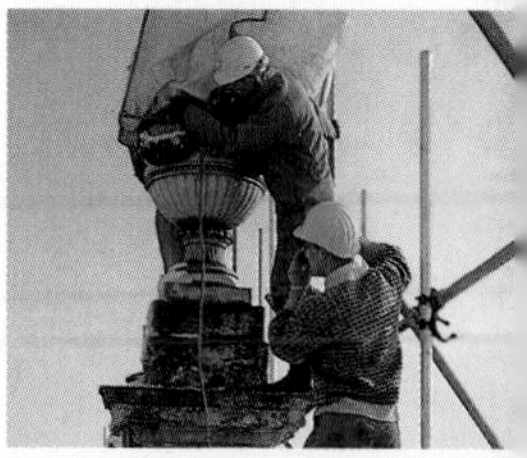
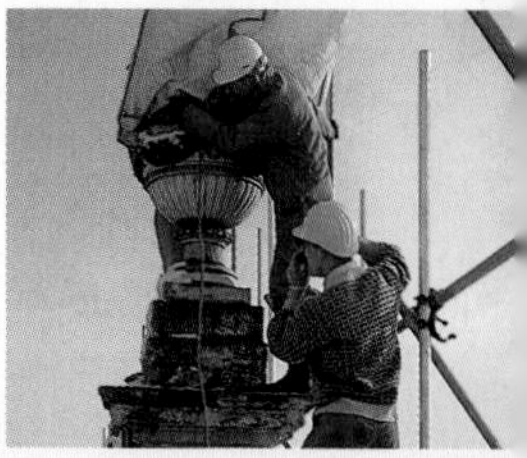

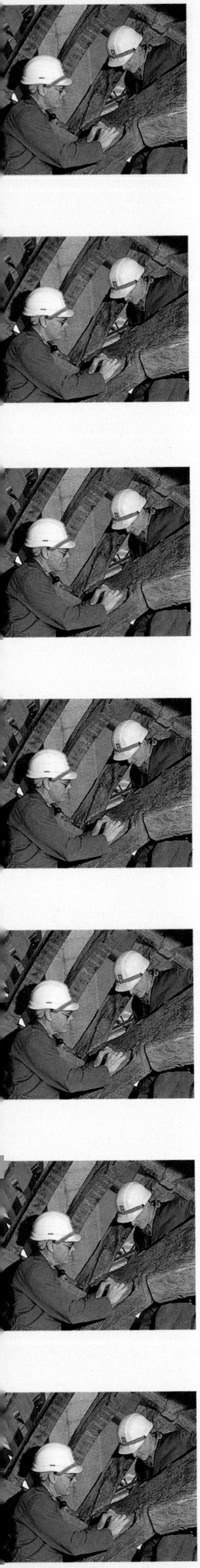

stone dressings, upper storey is timber-framed and plastered on the south and east sides with stone on the west side. Has early 13th century undercroft with ribbed vaults, 13-14th century King Post roof, and 15th century red brick chimney and doorway. Constructed to accommodate visiting monks from other Benedictine monasteries.
Grant Recipient/Owner: The Dean & Chapter of Ely Cathedral
Access contact: The Dean & Chapter of Ely Cathedral
Tel: 01353 667735
Opening Arrangements: By prior written arrangement with the Dean & Chapter of Ely Cathedral, Chapter House, The College, Ely, Cambridgeshire CB7 4DL. Wheelchair access to ground floor only, disabled parking in Cathedral car park by prior arrangement. Parking in town car parks.
Heritage Open Days: No
P See above
♿ Partial. Disabled WC: No. Guide Dogs: Yes
£ No

Buckden Towers
High Street, Buckden, Cambridgeshire PE18 9TA
Victorian house set in 15 acres of gardens and grounds, which include a gatehouse built in 1480.
Grant Recipient/Owner: Claretian Missionaries
Access contact: Mr D J Riddell
Tel: 01480 810344
Opening Arrangements: By prior arrangement. Tea shop open on Saturday and Sunday afternoons in summer.
Heritage Open Days: No
P Yes. Spaces: 50
♿ Yes. Disabled WC: Yes. Guide Dogs: Yes
£ No

Canonry House
The College, Ely, Cambridgeshire
Probably originally 11th/12th century, the ground floor has massive walls and a Norman barrel vault. Much of the original building was demolished in 1770 when current dwelling was built on the south side. Contains part of the 12th century Infirmary.
Grant Recipient/Owner:
The Dean & Chapter of Ely Cathedral
Access contact:
The Dean & Chapter of Ely Cathedral
Tel: 01353 667735
Opening Arrangements: By prior written arrangement with the Dean & Chapter of Ely Cathedral, Chapter House, The College, Ely, Cambridgeshire CB7 4DL. Wheelchair access to ground floor only, disabled parking in Cathedral car park by prior arrangement. Parking in town car parks.
Heritage Open Days: No
P See above
♿ Partial. Disabled WC: No. Guide Dogs: Yes
£ No

The Chapter House
The College, Ely, Cambridgeshire CB7 4DN
Originally part of the chapel of the Infirmary, now the remains of this house the Deanery. Contains part of the arch, ribbed vaulting and arcade of the 12th century chancel.
Grant Recipient/Owner:
The Dean & Chapter of Ely Cathedral
Access contact: The Dean & Chapter of Ely Cathedral
Tel: 01353 667735
Opening Arrangements: By prior written arrangement with the Dean & Chapter of Ely Cathedral, Chapter House, The College, Ely, Cambridgeshire CB7 4DL. Wheelchair access to ground floor only, disabled parking in Cathedral car park by prior arrangement. Parking in town car parks.
Heritage Open Days: No
P See above
♿ Partial. Disabled WC: No. Guide Dogs: Yes
£ No

Elton Hall
Elton, nr. Peterborough, Cambridgeshire PE8 6SH
Grade I historic building and country house. Late 15th century gatehouse built by Sapcote family. Main entrance façade built by Sir Thomas Proby in the 16th century and remodelled by Henry Ashton for 1st Earl of Carysfort in the 19th century. South Garden façade built between 1789 and 1812 in Gothic style.
Grant Recipient/Owner: Mr William Proby
Access contact: Mr W H Proby
Tel: 01832 280468 **Fax:** 01832 280584
Email Address: whp@eltonhall.com
Opening Arrangements: 27/28 May; Wednesdays in June; Wednesdays, Thursdays and Sundays in July and August, plus August Bank Holiday Monday 2 - 5pm. Private groups by arrangement on weekdays April - September. Wheelchair and guide dog access to gardens only.
Heritage Open Days: No
P Yes. Spaces: 500
♿ See above. Disabled WC: No. Guide Dogs: No
£ Yes
Adult: £5. £2.50 (garden only)
Child: Free, if accompanied.

Madingley Post Mill
Mill Farm, Madingley Road, Coton, Cambridgeshire CB3 7PH
Historic post mill with machinery intact.
Grant Recipient/Owner: Mr Matthew Mortlock
Access contact: Mr Matthew Mortlock
Tel: 01954 211047 **Fax:** 01954 210752
Opening Arrangements: Open weekdays and Saturdays between 11am and 4pm by prior telephone arrangement. Parking available in car park of American Cemetery (next door). Wheelchair access only around base of windmill.
Heritage Open Days: No
P See above
♿ Partial. Disabled WC: No. Guide Dogs: Yes
£ No

The Manor
Hemingford Grey, Huntingdon, Cambridgeshire PE18 9BN
Built c1130 and reputedly the oldest continuously inhabited house in Britain, much of the Norman house remains. The house of 'Green Knowe' in the writing of Lucy Boston was based on the Manor.
Grant Recipient/Owner: Mrs Diana Boston
Access contact: Mrs Diana Boston
Tel: 01480 463134 **Fax:** 01480 465026
Email Address: diana_boston@hotmail.com
Opening Arrangements: House: by guided tours at 10am, 12, 2 & 4pm during August (booking advisable), rest of year by prior arrangement. Garden: daily 10am - 6pm (dusk in winter). Parking for disabled visitors at house, otherwise parking in High Street. Wheelchair access to dining room only.
Heritage Open Days: No
P See above
♿ Partial. Disabled WC: No. Guide Dogs: Yes
£ Yes
Adult: £4.00
Child: £1.50
Other: £3.50

The Old Palace
Sue Ryder Care, Ely, Cambridgeshire CB7 4EW
Grade I listed building formerly a bishops palace opposite cathedral, with an Elizabethan promenading gallery, bishops chapel and monks room. 2 acre garden contains the oldest plane tree in Europe.
Grant Recipient/Owner: The Sue Ryder Foundation
Access contact: Mrs Mavis Garner
Tel: 01353 667686 **Fax:** 01353 669425
Email Address: suerely@dialstart.net
Opening Arrangements: Opening arrangements to be confirmed at time of going to print, please check the English Heritage website for current information.
Heritage Open Days: No
P No
♿ Partial. Disabled WC: Yes. Guide Dogs: Yes
£ No

Peckover House
North Brink, Wisbech, Cambridgeshire PE13 1JR
Town house built c1722. Plaster and wood Rococo decoration. Victorian garden includes an orangery, summer houses, fernery and croquet lawn.
Website Address: www.nationaltrust.org.uk
Grant Recipient/Owner: The National Trust
Access contact: Property Manager
Tel: 01945 583463 **Fax:** 01945 583463
Email Address: aprigx@smtp.ntrust.org.uk
Opening Arrangements: House: 31 March to 30 September: Wednesdays, Saturdays, Sundays and Bank Holiday Mondays 12.30 - 5.30pm; 3 October to 4 November 12.30 - 4.00pm. Garden: 31 March to 4 November daily except Fridays 12.30 - 5.30pm. Wheelchair access to garden and reed barn. Self-drive vehicle (telephone to check availability). Parking in courtyard by arrangement. Car park 300 metres from property.
Heritage Open Days: No
P Yes. Spaces: 100
♿ Partial. Disabled WC: No. Guide Dogs: Yes
£ Yes
Adult: £3.80. £2.50 (on garden only days).
Other: £3.00 (groups). Family discount.

Prior Crauden's Chapel
The College, Ely, Cambridgeshire
Private chapel built by Prior Crauden in 1524-5 of Barnack stone ashlar with clunch carved interior, over a 13th century vaulted undercroft. Has windows in the "Decorated" style, octagonal entrance and tower with spiral staircase, richly carved interior and a 14th century mosaic tile floor.
Grant Recipient/Owner:
The Dean & Chapter of Ely Cathedral
Access contact: The Dean & Chapter of Ely Cathedral
Tel: 01353 667735
Opening Arrangements: By prior written arrangement with the Dean & Chapter of Ely Cathedral, Chapter House, The College, Ely, Cambridgeshire CB7 4DL. Wheelchair access to the undercroft only, disabled parking in Cathedral car park by prior arrangement. Parking in town car parks.
Heritage Open Days: No
P See above
♿ Partial. Disabled WC: No Guide Dogs: Yes
£ No

Priory House
Ely, Cambridgeshire
Rebuilt early 14th century by Prior Crauden (1321-1341) of mainly Carr stone rubble with Barnack stone dressings and a considerable amount of brick. Has 12th century undercroft with groined vaults and transverse arches, 14th century pointed arched windows with "Decorated" tracery and early 14th century fireplace.
Grant Recipient/Owner:
The Dean & Chapter of Ely Cathedral
Access contact: The Dean & Chapter of Ely Cathedral
Tel: 01353 667735
Opening Arrangements: By prior written arrangement with the Dean & Chapter of Ely Cathedral, Chapter House, The College, Ely, Cambridgeshire CB7 4DL. Wheelchair access to ground floor only, disabled parking in Cathedral car park by prior arrangement. Parking in town car parks.
Heritage Open Days: No
P See above
♿ Partial. Disabled WC: No. Guide Dogs: Yes
£ No

Queen's Hall
The Gallery, Ely, Cambridgeshire
Built by Prior Crauden c1330 of Carr stone rubble with Barnack, or similar, stone dressings and much brick patching. Has original undercroft with ribbed vaulting, 14th century pointed arched windows with curvilinear tracery and corbels carved in the shape of crouching figures. Reputedly constructed for entertaining Queen Philippa, wife of Edward III.
Grant Recipient/Owner:
The Dean & Chapter of Ely Cathedral
Access contact: The Dean & Chapter of Ely Cathedral
Tel: 01353 667735
Opening Arrangements: By prior written arrangement with the Dean & Chapter of Ely Cathedral, Chapter House, The College, Ely, Cambridgeshire CB7 4DL. Wheelchair access to ground floor only, disabled parking in Cathedral car park by prior arrangement. Parking in town car parks.
Heritage Open Days: No
P See above
♿ Partial. Disabled WC: No. Guide Dogs: Yes
£ No

Sacrewell Watermill
Sacrewell Farm & Country Centre, Sacrewell, Thornhaugh, Peterborough, Cambridgeshire PE8 6HJ
18th century pitch back wheel watermill and millers house, with range of 18th century buildings housing various bygones (domestic, farming and country life).
Website Address: www.peterborough.net/sacrewell
Grant Recipient/Owner: William Scott Abbott Trust
Access contact: Mr M Armitage
Tel: 01780 782254 **Fax:** 01780 782254
Email Address: wsatrust@supanet.com
Opening Arrangements: Daily (except Christmas Day, Boxing Day and New Year's Day) 9.30am - 4pm (winter), 9.30am - 5pm (summer). Wheelchair access to ground floor only. Refreshments available.
Heritage Open Days: No
P Yes. Spaces: 300
♿ Partial. Disabled WC: Yes. Guide Dogs: Yes
£ Yes
Adult: £3.00
Child: £1.50
Other: £2.00 (senior citizens)

Sir John Jacob's Almshouses' Chapel
Church Street, Gamlingay, Cambridgeshire SG19 3JH
Built 1745 of Flemish bond red brick with plain tiled roof, in keeping with adjoining terrace of 10 almshouses constructed 80 years before. Now used as parish council offices.
Grant Recipient/Owner:
The Trustees of Sir John Jacob's Almshouses
Access contact: Mrs L Mayne
Tel: 01767 650310 **Fax:** 01767 650310
Opening Arrangements: Monday and Friday mornings and Wednesday afternoons. Parking in street.

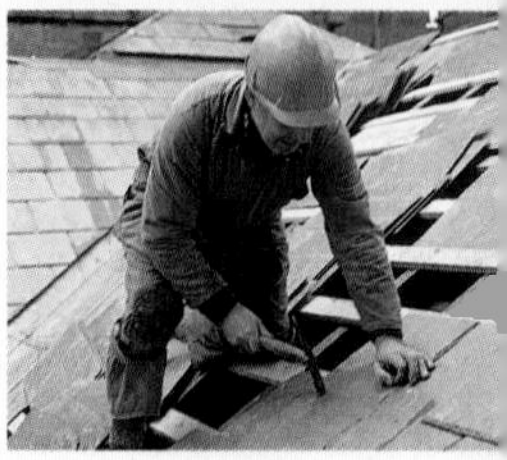

Heritage Open Days: Yes
P See above
♿ Yes. Disabled WC: Yes. Guide Dogs: Yes
£ No

Thomas à Becket Chapel
The Song School, Minster Precincts, Peterborough, Cambridge PE1 1XX
The Chapel was originally built by Abbot Benedict, circa 1180, along with the Norman Arch which gives access to the Cathedral precincts from Cathedral Square. The Chapel and School are now a restaurant called Becket's.
Grant Recipient/Owner:
The Dean & Chapter of Peterborough Cathedral
Access contact:
The Dean & Chapter of Peterborough Cathedral
Tel: 01733 343342 **Fax:** 01733 552465
Opening Arrangements: Open Monday to Saturday from 9.30am - 5pm all the year round.
Heritage Open Days: Yes
P No
♿ Partial. Disabled WC: Yes. Guide Dogs: No
£ No

Thorpe Hall
Sue Ryder Care Centre, Longthorpe, Peterborough, Cambridgeshire PE3 6LW
Built in the 1650s by Peter Mills for Oliver St John, Oliver Cromwell's Lord Chief Justice. Ground floor retains many original features.
Grant Recipient/Owner: Sue Ryder Foundation
Access contact: Mrs P Bartlett
Tel: 01733 330060 **Fax:** 01733 269078
Opening Arrangements: Opening arrangements to be confirmed at time of going to print, please check the English Heritage website for current information.
Heritage Open Days: No
P Yes. Spaces: 30
♿ Yes. Disabled WC: Yes. Guide Dogs: Yes
£ No

The Verger's House & The Old Sacristy
High Street, Ely, Cambridgeshire
The Sacristy is part of a long range of buildings which back onto the High Street on the north side. Originally built by Alan of Walsingham soon after he became sacrist in 1322, but mainly rebuilt in the 19th century.
Grant Recipient/Owner:
The Dean & Chapter of Ely Cathedral
Access contact: The Dean & Chapter of Ely Cathedral
Tel: 01353 667735
Opening Arrangements: By prior written arrangement with the Dean & Chapter of Ely Cathedral, Chapter House, The College, Ely, Cambridgeshire CB7 4DL. Wheelchair access to ground floor only, disabled parking in Cathedral car park by prior arrangement. Parking in town car parks.
Heritage Open Days: No
P See above
♿ Partial. Disabled WC: No. Guide Dogs: Yes
£ No

Wimpole Hall
Arrington, Royston, Cambridgeshire SG8 0BW
18th century house set in extensive wooded park. Interior features work by Gibbs and Soane. The park was landscaped by Bridgeman, Brown and Repton.
Website Address: www.nationaltrust.org.uk
Grant Recipient/Owner: The National Trust
Access contact: Property Manager
Tel: 01223 207257 **Fax:** 01223 207838
Email Address: aweusr@smtp.ntrust.org.uk
Opening Arrangements: Hall: 31 March to 30 July and 2 September to 4 November: daily except Mondays and Fridays (but open Good Friday and Bank Holiday Mondays); August: daily except Mondays (but open Bank Holiday Monday); 11, 18 and 25 November: Sundays only. Times: 1- 5pm (Bank Holiday Mondays 11am -5pm, closes 4pm after 28 October). Garden: 17 March to 2 July, 1 September to 4 November: daily except Mondays and Fridays (but open Good Friday and Bank Holiday Mondays); July and August: daily except Mondays (but open Bank Holiday Mondays); November to March 2002 Saturday and Sunday (open February Half term week). Times: 17 March to 4 November 10.30am to 5pm; 1 November to March 2002 11am to 4pm. Wheelchair access to garden (gravel paths) and restaurant. Disabled visitors may be set down near Hall. Telephone in advance for details.
Heritage Open Days: No
P Yes. Spaces: 500
♿ No. Disabled WC: Yes. Guide Dogs: Yes
£ Yes
Adult: £5.90. £2.50 (garden only).
Child: £2.70
Other: £8.50 (joint ticket with Wimpole Home Farm, adult). £4.90 (group rate). (No group rates on Sundays and Bank Holidays).

CHESHIRE

Bramall Hall
Bramhall Park, Stockport, Cheshire SK7 3NX
Black and white timber-framed manor house dating back to the 14th century, with subsequently several renovations (many during the Victorian period). Contains 14th century wallpaintings, an Elizabethan plaster ceiling and Victorian kitchen and servants quarters.
Grant Recipient/Owner:
Stockport Metropolitan Borough Council
Access contact: Ms Caroline Egan
Tel: 0161 485 3708 **Fax:** 0161 486 6959
Email Address: charlotte.bertin@stockport.gov.uk
Opening Arrangements: Good Friday - end of September: Monday - Saturday 1 - 5pm, Sundays and Bank Holidays 11am - 5pm; October - 1 January: Tuesday - Saturday 1 - 4pm, Sundays and Bank Holidays 11am - 4pm; 2 January - Easter: weekends only 1 - 4pm. Wheelchair access to ground floor only.
Heritage Open Days: No
P Yes. Spaces: 60
♿ Partial. Disabled WC: Yes. Guide Dogs: Yes
£ Yes
Adult: £3.80
Child: £2.00
Other: £2.00

Capesthorne Hall
Macclesfield, Cheshire SK11 9JY
Jacobean style hall with a collection of fine art, sculpture, furniture, tapestry and antiques from Europe, America and the Far East. The Hall dates from 1719 when it was originally designed by the Smith's of Warwick. Altered in 1837 by Blore and rebuilt by Salvin in 1861 following a disastrous fire.
Grant Recipient/Owner:
Mr William Arthur Bromley-Davenport
Access contact: Mrs Gwyneth Jones
Tel: 01625 861221 **Fax:** 01625 861619
Opening Arrangements: April - October: Sundays, Wednesdays and Bank Holidays (except Christmas and New Year). Gardens and Chapel from 12 noon to 5.30pm, Hall from 1.30pm (last admission 3.30pm). Parties on other days by arrangement. Access for wheelchair users to ground floor of Hall, Butler's Pantry and Gardens (compacted paths with some gravel).
Heritage Open Days: No
P Yes. Spaces: 2000
♿ Partial. Disabled WC: Yes. Guide Dogs: Yes
£ Yes
Adult: £6.50
Child: £3.50
Other: £5.50 (senior citizen)

Chester Town Hall
Northgate Street, Chester, Cheshire CH1 2HS
Victorian town hall situated in centre of city, home to the Chester Tapestry, portraits of the Grosvenor family, and World War I memorial dedicated to Chester citizens. There is also a memorial to the Polish air force. One of many stained glass windows, shows the Common Seal of the city.
Grant Recipient/Owner: Chester City Council
Access contact: Ms Rebecca Pinfold
Tel: 01244 402320 **Fax:** 01244 341965
Email Address: r.pinfold@chestercc.gov.uk
Opening Arrangements: Monday to Friday from 8.30am to 7pm. Saturdays by prior arrangement. Please telephone for details of annual open day. Parking in Princess Street.
Heritage Open Days: No
P See above
♿ Yes. Disabled WC: Yes. Guide Dogs: Yes
£ No

Gawsworth Hall
Gawsworth, Cheshire SK11 9RN
Fully lived-in Tudor half-timbered manor house with Tiliting Ground. Former home of Mary Fitton, Maid of Honour at the Court of Queen Elizabeth I, and the supposed 'Dark Lady' of Shakespeare's sonnets. Pictures, sculpture and furniture. Open air theatre with covered grandstand.
Website Address: www.gawsworthhall.com
Grant Recipient/Owner: Mr T Richards
Access contact: Mr T Richards
Tel: 01260 223456 **Fax:** 01260 223469
Email Address: gawsworth@lineone.net
Opening Arrangements: Easter to late September 12 - 5.30pm. Closed Saturdays in April, May, June and September. For confirmation see details on internet/website. Wheelchair and guide dog access to garden only. Disabled parking near house.
Heritage Open Days: No
P Yes. Spaces: 600
♿ See above. Disabled WC: Yes. Guide Dogs: See above
£ Yes
Adult: £4.20
Child: £2.10
Other: £3.00 (for groups of 20+)

Highfields
Audlem, nr. Crewe, Cheshire CW3 0DT
Small half-timbered manor house dating back to c1600.
Grant Recipient/Owner: Mr J B Baker
Access contact: Mrs Susan Baker
Tel: 01630 655479
Opening Arrangements: By prior written arrangement. Wheelchair access to ground floor only, disabled toilet with assistance (down 2 steps).
Heritage Open Days: No
P Yes. Spaces: 20
♿ Partial. Disabled WC: Yes. Guide Dogs: Yes
£ Yes
Adult: £4.00
Child: £2.00
Other: £4.00

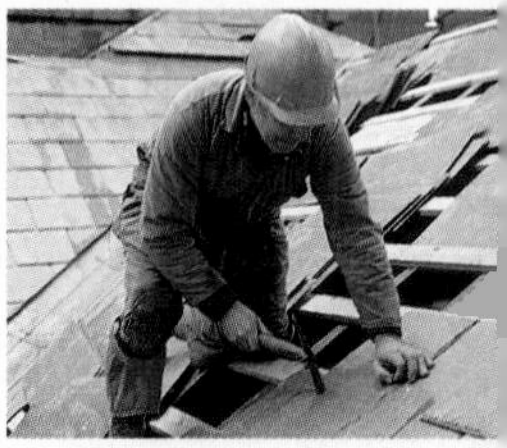

Lightshaw Hall Farm
Lightshaw Lane, Golborne, Warrington, Cheshire WA3 3UJ
16th century timber-framed farmhouse largely rebuilt in the 18th and 19th centuries. Historical evidence suggests there was an estate and probably a house on the site by the end of the 13th century if not before. The west range is supposed to represent the solar apartments of an early post-medieval house. External walls were replaced by bricks in the 18th and 19th centuries. Timber trusses and main roof timbers survive.
Grant Recipient/Owner: Mrs J Hewitt
Access contact: Mrs J Hewitt
Tel: 01942 717429
Opening Arrangements: All year by prior telephone arrangement. Access for wheelchair users to the ground floor only. Video and photographs available for those unable to climb stairs.
Heritage Open Days: No
P Yes. Spaces: 20
♿ Partial. Disabled WC: No. Guide Dogs: Yes
£ No

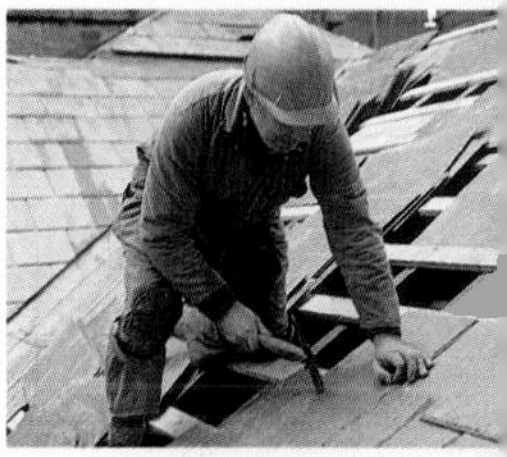

Little Moreton Hall
Congleton, Cheshire CW12 4SD
Begun in 1450 and completed 130 years later, Little Moreton Hall is regarded as one of the most outstanding timber-framed manor houses in the County. The south range, topped by a spectacular long gallery, opens onto a cobbled courtyard. The Chapel, wall paintings and knot garden are of particular interest.
Website Address: www.nationaltrust.org.uk
Grant Recipient/Owner: The National Trust
Access contact: Dean Thomas
Tel: 01260 272018 **Fax:** 01260 292802
Email Address: mlmsca@smtp.ntrust.org.uk
Opening Arrangements: March 31 - 4 November: open Wednesday to Sunday (including Good Friday and Bank Holiday Mondays) 11.30am - 5pm. 10 November to 22 December weekends only 11.30am to 4pm. Wheelchair access to ground floor only.
Heritage Open Days: No
P Yes. Spaces: 90
♿ Partial. Disabled WC: Yes. Guide Dogs: Yes
£ Yes
Adult: £4.40
Child: £2.20
Other: Family tickets.

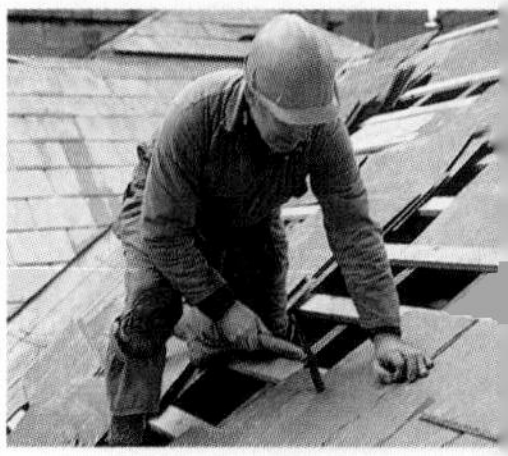

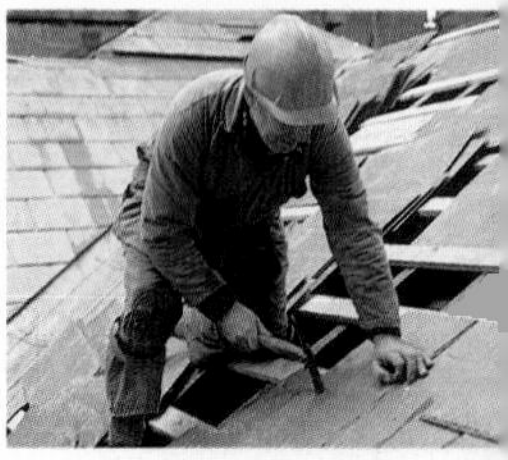

Lyme Park
Disley, Stockport, Cheshire SK12 2NX
Home to the Legh family for 600 years, Lyme Park comprises a 1400 acre medieval deer park, a 17 acre Victorian garden and a Tudor hall which was transformed into an Italianate palace in the 18th century. Location for 'Pemberley' in the BBC TV's production of Pride and Prejudice.
Grant Recipient/Owner:
Stockport Metropolitan Borough Council
Access contact: Mr Kevin Reid
Tel: 01663 762023 **Fax:** 01663 765035
Email Address: mlyrec@smtp.ntrust.org.uk
Opening Arrangements: Hall: 30 March - 30 October, daily except Wednesdays and Thursdays 1 - 5pm. Garden: 30 March - 30 October, Friday - Tuesday 11am - 5pm, Wednesday and Thursday 1 - 5pm; November - 18 December, weekends 12 - 3pm. Park: April - October, daily 8am - 8.30pm; November - March, daily 8am - 6pm. Wheelchair access to garden, first floor of house, parts of park, shop and restaurant.
Heritage Open Days: No
P Yes. Spaces: 1500
♿ Partial. Disabled WC: Yes. Guide Dogs: Yes
£ Yes
Adult: £5.00
Child: £2.50
Other: National Trust members free

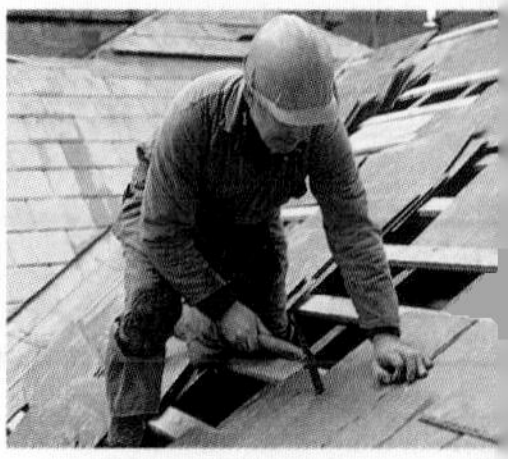

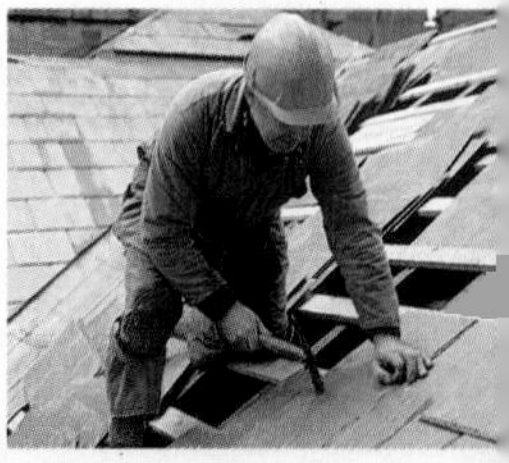

Quarry Bank Mill
Styal, Cheshire SK9 4LA
Georgian cotton mill, now a museum and the only water

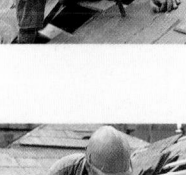

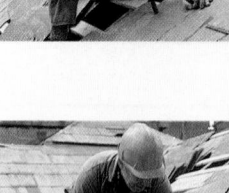

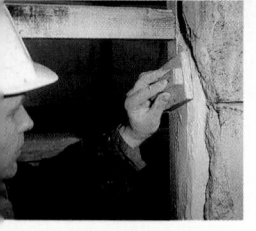

powered cotton mill in the world. Working demonstrations of cotton processing, a giant iron water wheel and two mill engines steaming daily. Restored Apprentice House once housed child workers.
Website Address: www.quarrybankmill.org.uk
Grant Recipient/Owner: The Quarry Bank Mill Trust
Access contact: Mr Josselin Hill
Tel: 01625 527468   **Fax:** 01625 539267
Email Address: enquiries@quarrybankmill.org.uk
Opening Arrangements: Mill: April - September daily 11am - 6pm (last admission 4.30pm), October - March (closed Mondays) 11am - 5pm (last admission 3.30pm); Apprentice House and Garden: Easter and daily during August as Mill, weekends throughout the year as Mill and Tuesdays - Fridays all year 2pm - Mill closing (Mondays closed). Wheelchair access to ground and lower ground floors only.
Heritage Open Days: No
🅿 Yes. Spaces: 350
♿ Partial. Disabled WC: Yes. Guide Dogs: Yes
£ Yes
Adult: £6.00
Child: £3.70
Other: £3.70

Rode Hall

Church Lane, Scholar Green, Cheshire ST7 3QP
Country house built early - mid 18th century, with later alterations. Set in a parkland designed by Repton. Home to the Wilbraham family since 1669.
Grant Recipient/Owner: Sir Richard Baker Wilbraham Bt
Access contact: Sir Richard Baker Wilbraham Bt
Tel: 01270 873237   **Fax:** 01270 882962
Opening Arrangements: Hall and Gardens: 4 April - 26 September, Wednesdays and Bank Holidays (closed Good Friday) 2 - 5pm; Gardens only: Tuesdays and Thursdays 2 - 5pm. Wheelchair access with assistance to ground floor, disabled parking available adjacent to entrance by arrangement.
Heritage Open Days: No
🅿 Yes. Spaces: 200
♿ Partial. Disabled WC: No. Guide Dogs: Yes
£ Yes
Adult: £4.00 House & Garden, £2.50 Garden only.
Other: £2.50 House & Garden (senior citizens), £1.50 Garden only.

St Chad's Church Tower

Wybunbury, Nantwich, Cheshire
Grade II* listed 15th or 16th century church tower, rest of Church demolished in 1977. 96ft high and containing six restored bells, spiral staircase, charity boards and monuments.
Grant Recipient/Owner: Mrs D Lockhart
Access contact: Mrs D Lockhart
Tel: 01270 841481   **Fax:** 01270 842659
Opening Arrangements: Saturday 26 May 2 - 5pm and Heritage Open Days 11am - 4pm. At other times by prior arrangement with Mrs D Lockhart, Wybunbury Tower Preservation Trust, Hawthorn House, 1 Main Road, Wybunbury, Nantwich, Cheshire CW5 7NA (tel.01270 841481) or Mr Sam Wood (tel.01270 841188). Wheelchair access to ground floor only.
Heritage Open Days: Yes
🅿 Yes. Spaces: 20
♿ Partial. Disabled WC: No. Guide Dogs: Yes
£ Yes
Adult: £1.00
Child: 50p

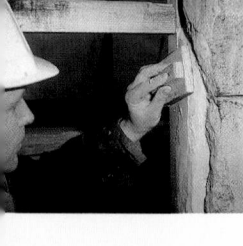

Tatton Park Fernery

Knutsford, Cheshire WA16 6QN
Designed by Joseph Paxton in the 1850s to house the Egerton family's collection of New Zealand ferns and is situated adjacent to a conservatory by Lewis Wyatt.
Website Address: www.tattonpark.org.uk
Grant Recipient/Owner:
Cheshire County Council/ National Trust
Access contact: Mr A J Pellatt
Tel: 01625 534400   **Fax:** 01625 534403
Email Address: tattonpark@cheshire.gov.uk
Opening Arrangements: Fernery open every day except Monday and Christmas Day (open Bank Holidays), 10.30am - 4pm in summer, 11am - 3pm in winter.
Heritage Open Days: No
🅿 Yes. Spaces: 1000
♿ Yes. Disabled WC: Yes. Guide Dogs: Yes
£ Yes
Adult: £3.00
Child: £2.00
Other: £3.50 (car entry)

Watergate House

85 Watergate Street, Chester, Cheshire CH1 2LF
Town house, then headquarters of North Western Command, now offices. Built in 1820 by Thomas Harrison for Henry Potts, Clerk of the Peace.
Grant Recipient/Owner: Ferry Homes Ltd
Access contact: Mrs Hayley Cain

Tel: 01352 713353   **Fax:** 01352 713838
Opening Arrangements: By prior telephone arrangement from 9am - 11am, and 3pm - 6pm.
Heritage Open Days: Yes
🅿 No
♿ No. Disabled WC: No. Guide Dogs: Yes
£ No

CO DURHAM

9 & 10 The College

Durham, DH1 3EH
Independent preparatory school housed in part of the Cathedral Close at Durham. 18th and 19th century buildings, mainly local sandstone with some brickwork. Medieval basement rooms.
Grant Recipient/Owner:
The Dean & Chapter of Durham Cathedral
Access contact: Mr C S S Drew
Tel: 0191 3842935   **Fax:** 0191 3839261
Email Address: head@choristers.durham.sch.uk
Opening Arrangements: During September for 28 days by prior arrangement only.
Heritage Open Days: No
🅿 No
♿ No.
£ No

Croxdale Hall

Durham, County Durham DH6 5JP
18th century re-casing of an earlier Tudor building, containing comfortably furnished mid-Georgian rooms with Rococo ceilings. There is also a private chapel in the north elevation, walled gardens, a quarter-of-a-mile long terrace, an orangery and lakes which date from the mid-18th century.
Grant Recipient/Owner:
Trustees of the Low Butterby Settlement
Access contact: Mrs Caroline Broadfoot
Tel: 0191 3780911   **Fax:** 0191 3783854
Email Address: broadfoot@croxdale99.freeserve.co.uk
Opening Arrangements: By prior arrangement on Tuesdays and Wednesdays from the first Tuesday in May to the second Wednesday in July, 11am - 1pm.
Heritage Open Days: No
🅿 Yes. Spaces: 20
♿ Yes. Disabled WC: Yes. Guide Dogs: Yes
£ Yes
Adult: £5.00
Child: £5.00
Other: £5.00

Durham Castle

Palace Green, Durham, County Durham DH1 3RW
Dating from 1072, the castle was the seat of the Prince Bishops until 1832. Together with the Cathedral, the castle is a World Heritage site. It now houses University College, the Foundation College of Durham University, and is a conference, banqueting and holiday centre in vacations.
Grant Recipient/Owner: University of Durham
Access contact: Bursar
Tel: 0191 374 3800   **Fax:** 0191 374 7470
Email Address: e.a.gibson@dur.ac.uk
Opening Arrangements: Easter - end of September: guided tours daily from 10am - 4pm; 1 October - Easter Monday: Wednesdays, Fridays, Saturdays and Sundays (afternoons only). Access for wheelchair users to courtyard only. Parking in city car parks.
Heritage Open Days: No
🅿 See above
♿ See above. Disabled WC: No. Guide Dogs: Yes
£ Yes
Adult: £3.00
Child: £2.00
Other: £6.50 (family)

Former Stockton & Darlington Railway

Booking Office
48 Bridge Road, Stockton-on-Tees,
Co. Durham TS18 3AX
Original booking office of the Stockton and Darlington Railway. Cottage of plain brick with slate roof facing railway line. A bronze tablet on the gable ends "Martin 1825 the Stockton and Darlington Company booked first passenger, thus marking an epoch in the history of mankind". The first rail of the Railway was laid outside the building. Now used as an administration office and accommodation for single homeless men.
Grant Recipient/Owner: Stockton Church Mission
Access contact: Mr Tom Lane
Tel: 01642 800311   **Fax:** 01642 800322
Opening Arrangements: Monday - Friday 9am - 3pm.
Heritage Open Days: No
🅿 No
♿ No
£ No

Low Butterby Farmhouse

Croxdale & Hett, Co. Durham DH6 5JN
Stone built farmhouse constructed on medieval site incorporating elements of 17th, 18th and 19th century phases of development.
Grant Recipient/Owner: Mr W H T Salvin
Access contact: Mr W H T Salvin
Tel: 01833 690100   **Fax:** 01833 637004
Email Address: williamsalvin@compuserve.com
Opening Arrangements: By prior written or telephone arrangement with Mr W H T Salvin, The Estate Office, Egglestone Abbey, Barnard Castle, Co. Durham DL12 9TN (tel.01833 690100).
Heritage Open Days: No
🅿 Yes. Spaces: 2
♿ No. Disabled WC: No. Guide Dogs: No
£ No

Lumley Castle

Chester-le-Street, Co. Durham DH3 4NX
Large 14th century castle, now a hotel, altered c1570-80 and in 1721 by Sir John Vanbrugh.
Grant Recipient/Owner: Mr H B Morris
Access contact: Mr H B Morris
Tel: 0191 389 1111   **Fax:** 0191 389 1881
Opening Arrangements: Hotel open to the public seven days a week.
Heritage Open Days: No
🅿 Yes. Spaces: 100
♿ No. Disabled WC: No. Guide Dogs: Yes
£ No

The Priest's House

Croxdale Hall, Croxdale, Co. Durham DH6 5JP
18th century stone built cottage with 19th century extension adjacent to and ancillary to the Old Church and Croxdale Hall.
Grant Recipient/Owner: Mr W H T Salvin
Access contact: Mr W H T Salvin
Tel: 01833 690100   **Fax:** 01833 637004
Email Address: williamsalvin@compuserve.com
Opening Arrangements: By prior written or telephone arrangement with Mr W H T Salvin, The Estate Office, Egglestone Abbey, Barnard Castle, Co. Durham DL12 9TN (tel.01833 690100). Wheelchair access only to ground floor.
Heritage Open Days: No
🅿 Yes. Spaces: 2
♿ Partial. Disabled WC: No. Guide Dogs: Yes
£ No

Raby Castle

PO Box 50, Staindrop, Darlington,
County Durham DL2 3AY
Medieval castle, once the seat of the Nevills, it has been home to Lord Barnard's family since 1626. Contains a collection of art and highly decorated interiors. Surrounded by a 200-acre Deer Park and walled gardens.
Website Address: www.rabycastle.com
Grant Recipient/Owner: Lord Barnard TD
Access contact: Miss Catherine Turnbull
Tel: 01833 660207   **Fax:** 01833 660835
Email Address: rabyestate@rabycastle.com
Opening Arrangements: Easter and Bank Holiday weekends: Saturday to Wednesday. May and September: Wednesdays and Sundays only. June, July and August: daily except Saturday. Castle open from 1pm-5pm. Garden and Park from 11am to 5.30pm. Partially suitable for wheelchair users. Guided tours available weekday mornings from Easter to the end of September.
Heritage Open Days: No
🅿 Yes. Spaces: 500
♿ Partial. Disabled WC: Yes. Guide Dogs: Yes
£ Yes
Adult: £5.00 Castle, Park & Gardens; £3.00
Child: £2.00 Castle, Park & Gardens; £2.00
Other: £4.00 Castle, Park & Gardens; £2.00 Park & Gardens; £7.50 (guided tour), £12.00 & £10.00 (season ticket).

Rokeby Hall

Barnard Castle, County Durham DL12 9RZ
Early 18th century Palladian country house with fine needlework pictures.
Grant Recipient/Owner: Trustees of Mortham Estates
Access contact: Mr W H T Salvin
Tel: 01833 690100   **Fax:** 01833 637004
Email Address: williamsalvin@compuserve.com
Opening Arrangements: May Bank Holiday Monday and Spring Bank Holiday Monday and Tuesday, then Mondays and Tuesdays until the second Tuesday in September 2 - 5pm (last admission 4.30pm). Wheelchair access to ground floor only.
Heritage Open Days: No
🅿 Yes. Spaces: 15
♿ Partial. Disabled WC: No. Guide Dogs: No
£ Yes
Adult: £5.00

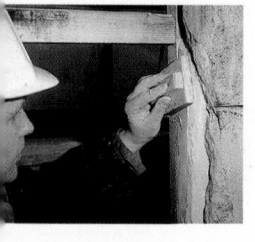
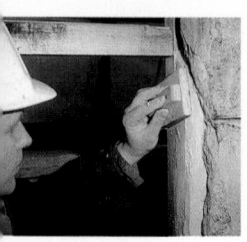
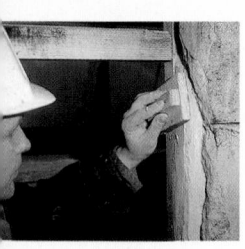
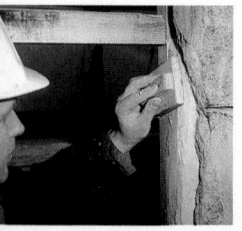

CORNWALL

Antony

Torpoint, Plymouth, Cornwall PL11 2QA
Early 18th century mansion. The main block is faced in lustrous silver-grey stone, flanked by mellow brick pavilions. The ancestral home of the Carew family for nearly 600 years. Set within grounds landscaped by Repton, 'Antony' houses the national collection of day lilies.
Website Address: www.nationaltrust.org.uk
Grant Recipient/Owner: The National Trust
Access contact: Peter Morgan
Tel: 01752 812191 **Fax:** 01752 812191
Opening Arrangements: Antony House and garden: 3 April - 31 May, 4 September - 1 November Tuesday, Wednesdays, Thursdays and Bank Holiday Mondays, also Sundays in June, July and August: 1.30 - 5.30pm. Last admission 4.45pm. Woodland garden (not National Trust): 1 March - 31 October: daily except Mondays and Fridays (but open Bank Holidays) 11am - 5.30pm. No wheelchair access to House. Wheelchair access to: garden: largely accessible, shop, tea room and family history exhibition. Parking available for 2 coaches.
Heritage Open Days: No
P Yes. Spaces: 60
♿ Partial. Disabled WC: Yes. Guide Dogs: Yes
£ Yes
Adult: £4.20 (house & garden). £2.00 (Antony garden only). £3.00 (Woodland garden). £3.60 (combined gardens only).
Child: £2.10 (house & garden). £1.00 (Antony garden only). £1.50 (Woodland garden). £1.80 (combined gardens only).
Other: £10.50 (family). £3.50 (pre-booked group: house & garden). £3.00 (pre-booked groups: combined gardens).

Caerhays Castle & Gardens

Gorran, St Austell, Cornwall PL26 6LY
Built by John Nash in 1808. Set in 60 acres of informal woodland gardens created by J C Williams, who sponsored plant hunting expeditions to China at the turn of the 19th century.
Website Address: www.caerhays.co.uk
Grant Recipient/Owner: Mr F J Williams
Access contact: Miss A B Mayes
Tel: 01872 501144 **Fax:** 01872 501870
Email Address: estateoffice@caerhays.co.uk
Opening Arrangements: House: 19 March - 27 April, Mondays - Fridays 2 - 4pm; Gardens: 12 March - 18 May, Mondays - Fridays 10am - 4pm. Charity openings (Gardens only): Sunday 25 March, Sunday 15 April and Monday 7 May, 10am - 4pm.
Heritage Open Days: No
P Yes. Spaces: 500
♿ Partial. Disabled WC: No. Guide Dogs: Yes
£ Yes
Adult: £3.50 House, £3.50 Gardens, £6.00 combined
Child: £3.50 House, £3.50 Gardens, £6.00 combined.
Other: £4.50 Group guided tour of Gardens.

Cotehele

St Dominick, Saltash, Cornwall PL12 6TA
Cothele, situated on the west bank of the River Tamar, was built mainly between 1485-1627. Home of the Edgcumbe family for centuries. Its granite and slatestone walls contain intimate chambers adorned with tapestries, original furniture and armour.
Website Address: www.nationaltrust.org.uk
Grant Recipient/Owner: The National Trust
Access contact: Lewis Enyon
Tel: 01579 351346 **Fax:** 01579 351222
Email Address: cctlce@smtp.ntrust.org.uk
Opening Arrangements: House and restaurant: 31 March to 4 November daily except Fridays (but open Good Friday) 11am - 5pm; October and November 11am - 4.30pm. Mill: 31 March to 30 June and 1 September to 4 November daily except Fridays (but open Good Friday), July and August daily; March, June and September: 1 - 5.30pm, July and August: 1- 6pm, October and November: 1 - 4.30pm. Garden: all year round daily 10.30am until dusk. Gallery and tea-room on quay: 31 March to 4 November daily 11am - 5pm; gallery 12 - 5pm or dusk; November and December Christmas opening telephone 01579 351494. Wheelchair access to: House: hall and kitchen; garden: area around house; restaurant and shop: ramps available; woodland walks: some paths accessible. Parking space available for coaches.
Heritage Open Days: No
P Yes. Spaces: 100
♿ Partial. Disabled WC: Yes. Guide Dogs: Yes
£ Yes
Adult: £6.20 (house, garden & mill). £3.40 (garden & mill)
Child: £3.10 (house, garden & mill). £1.70 (garden & mill)
Other: £15.50 (family: house, garden & mill). £5.20 (pre-booked groups). £8.50 (family: garden & mill).

Cullacott Farmhouse

Werrington, Launceston, Cornwall PL15 8NH
Grade I listed medieval hall house, built in the 1480s as a long house, and extended 1579. Contains wall paintings of fictive tapestry, Tudor arms, St James of Compostella and remains of representation of St George and the Dragon. Extensively restored 1995-7 but still retains many original features. Now used as holiday accommodation.
Grant Recipient/Owner: Mrs Cole
Access contact: Mrs Cole
Tel: 01566 772631
Opening Arrangements: By prior arrangement.
Heritage Open Days: No
P Yes. Spaces: 20
♿ Partial. Disabled WC: Yes. Guide Dogs: Yes
£ Yes
Adult: £2.00
Child: Free

Godolphin House

Godolphin Cross, Helston, Cornwall, TR13 9RE
Tudor-Stuart mansion of granite round a courtyard. For many generations seat of the Godolphin family who were courtiers from the 16th to the 18th century, the 1st Earl (who was born here) rose to be Queen Anne's Lord Treasurer. Has late Elizabethan stables with wagon collection and a large medieval and other gardens.
Grant Recipient/Owner: Mrs S E Schofield
Access contact: Mrs Joanne Schofield
Tel: 01736 763194 **Fax:** 01736 763194
Email Address: godo@euphony.net
Opening Arrangements: May - June: Thursdays and Sundays 2 - 5pm; July - September: Thursdays, Fridays and Sundays 2 - 5pm; Bank Holiday Mondays (except Christmas) 2 - 5pm. Groups all year by prior arrangement. Wheelchair access to all of the house except one room, but no access to the stables and gardens may be difficult. Parking for 3 coaches.
Heritage Open Days: No
P Yes. Spaces: 100
♿ Partial. Disabled WC: Yes. Guide Dogs: Yes
£ Yes
Adult: £3.00
Child: £1.00

Mount Edgcumbe House & Country Park

Cremyll, Torpoint, Cornwall PL10 1HZ
Grade II former home of the Earls of Mount Edgcumbe in Grade I registered landscape park of 850 acres. Includes 52 listed buildings and 16 acres of formal gardens. 16th - 18th centuries. Spectacular setting above River Tamar and Plymouth Sound. Landscape noted by Horace Walpole and Alexander Pope in 18th century. Used as starting point for D-Day landings by American troops in 1944.
Grant Recipient/Owner:
Mount Edgcumbe Country Park Joint Committee
Access contact: The Manager
Tel: 01752 822236 **Fax:** 01752 822199
Opening Arrangements: Country Park (with listed structures): all year from dawn to dusk. Mount Edgcumbe House and Earls Garden: 4 April - 30 September; Wednesday - Sunday and Bank Holidays 11am - 4.30pm. Wheelchair access to flat areas of garden and most of house.
Heritage Open Days: No
P Yes. Spaces: 120
♿ Partial. Disabled WC: Yes. Guide Dogs: Yes
£ Yes
Adult: £4.50 (house only)
Child: £2.25
Other: £3.50 (concessions & groups)

Prideaux Place

Padstow, Cornwall PL28 8RP
Elizabethan mansion, with various subsequent alterations and additions, built by and still lived in by the Prideaux family. Remodelled in Gothic style in late 18th or early 19th century. Has formal garden, Temple, Gothic dairy and exhibition areas in the stables.
Grant Recipient/Owner: Mr Peter Prideaux-Brune
Access contact: Mr Peter Prideaux-Brune
Tel: 01841 532411 **Fax:** 01841 532945
Opening Arrangements: Easter Sunday - 26 April, 27 May - 4 October: Sunday - Thursday 1.30 - 5pm. Coach parties all year by prior arrangement. Wheelchair access to ground floor, tea-room and grounds.
Heritage Open Days: No
P Yes. Spaces: 40
♿ Partial. Disabled WC: No. Guide Dogs: Yes
£ Yes
Adult: £4.50
Child: £2.00
Other: £4.00 (groups, £4.50 Friday and Saturday).

Southgate Arch

Southgate Street, Launceston, Cornwall PL15 7AR
Only remaining gateway of the three original entrances to the old walled town. Main arch part of original 12th century town wall. Used as a jail for many years, now houses art gallery.
Grant Recipient/Owner: Launceston Town Council
Access contact: Mr P J Freestone
Tel: 01566 773693 **Fax:** 01566 773693
Email Address: ltc@talk21.com
Opening Arrangements: 1 April - 25 December: Mondays, Tuesdays, Wednesdays, Fridays and Saturdays 10am - 4.30pm.
Heritage Open Days: Yes
P No
♿ No. Disabled WC: No. Guide Dogs: Yes
£ No

Tintagel Old Post Office

Tintagel, Cornwall PL34 0DB
Small 14th century manor house is furnished with local oak pieces. One room used in the 19th century as the letter-receiving office for the district is now restored to that period and function.
Website Address: www.nationaltrust.org.uk
Grant Recipient/Owner: The National Trust
Access contact: Sandy Chadwick
Tel: 01840 770024
Opening Arrangements: 31 March to 4 November: daily 11am - 5.30pm; October - 4 November 11am - 4pm. Wheelchair access to: House: ground floor only, garden accessible with help (no ramps) staff will assist. Private car park directly opposite (with lavatories including lavatory for disabled people). National Trust car park 1/4 mile from house.
Heritage Open Days: No
P See above
♿ Partial. Disabled WC: See above. Guide Dogs: Yes
£ Yes
Adult: £2.30
Child: £1.15
Other: £5.70 (family). £1.80 (pre-booked groups).

Tregithew

Manaccan, Helston, Cornwall TR12 6HX
18th century farmhouse, barn and buildings, and horse engine house. Some parts of the property may date back to the 16th century. Panelled parlour, original windows and fireplaces, barrel ceiling in one bedroom and 3 leaded windows.
Grant Recipient/Owner: Mrs B Faull
Access contact: Mrs B Faull
Tel: 01326 231382
Opening Arrangements: By prior written arrangement between June and September.
Heritage Open Days: No
P Yes. Spaces: 2
♿ No.
£ No

CUMBRIA

Brantwood

Coniston, Cumbria LA21 8AD
Brantwood, situated on Coniston Water, was the former home of Victorian writer and artist, John Ruskin, from 1872 to 1900. Displays a collection of paintings by Ruskin and his circle, his furniture, books and personal items. Video, bookshop, craft gallery and restaurant on site. Gardens include the Harbour Walk and Professor's Garden where Ruskin experimented with native flowers and fruit.
Website Address: www.brantwood.org.uk
Grant Recipient/Owner: Brantwood Education Trust Ltd
Access contact: Mr Howard Hull
Tel: 015394 41396 **Fax:** 015394 41263
Email Address: enquiries@brantwood.org.uk
Opening Arrangements: All year: 15 March - 15 November, everyday 11am - 5.30pm; 16 November - 14 March, Wednesday - Sunday 11am - 4.30pm. Open daily during school holidays (except Christmas Day and Boxing Day). Wheelchair access to house, toilets and restaurant only.
Heritage Open Days: No
P Yes. Spaces: 50
♿ Partial. Disabled WC: Yes. Guide Dogs: Yes
£ Yes
Adult: £4.50
Child: £1.00
Other: £3.00 (student)

Coop House

Netherby, nr. Carlisle, Cumbria CA6 5PX
Stands on the bank of the River Esk where 'coops' or traps were set to catch salmon. This summerhouse was built c1765 by Dr Robert Graham as an ornament in the landscape around Netherby Hall and as a place to enjoy the river. By 1980 it was completely derelict.
Website Address: www.landmarktrust.co.uk
Grant Recipient/Owner: The Landmark Trust
Access contact: Ms Victoria Piggott
Tel: 01628 825920 **Fax:** 01628 825417
Email Address: vpiggott@landmarktrust.co.uk
Opening Arrangements: The Landmark Trust is an independent charity, which rescues small buildings of historic or architectural importance from decay or

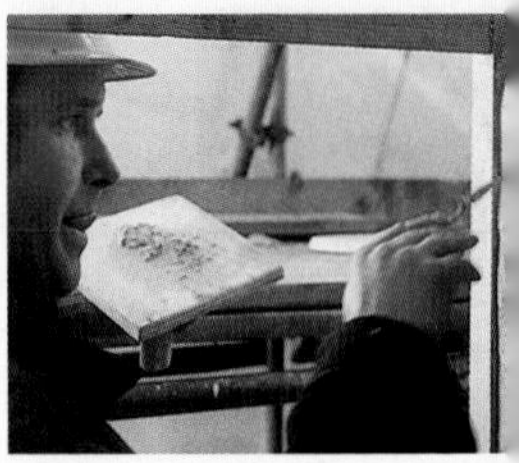
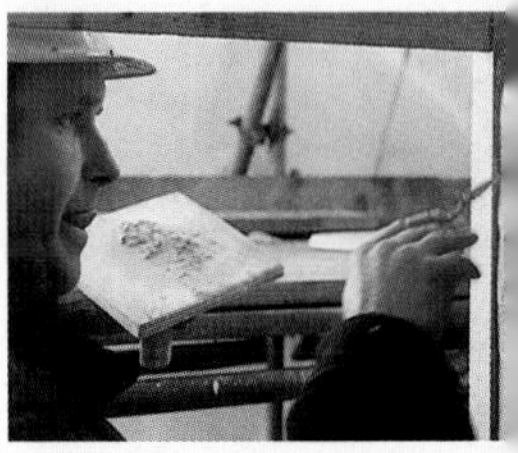
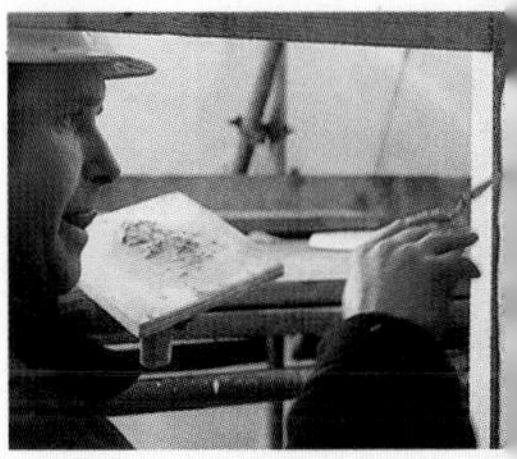
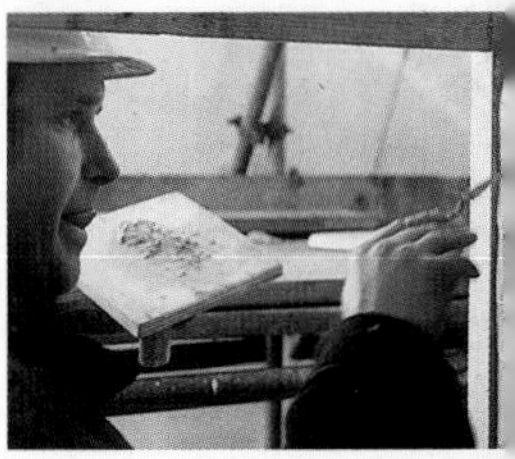
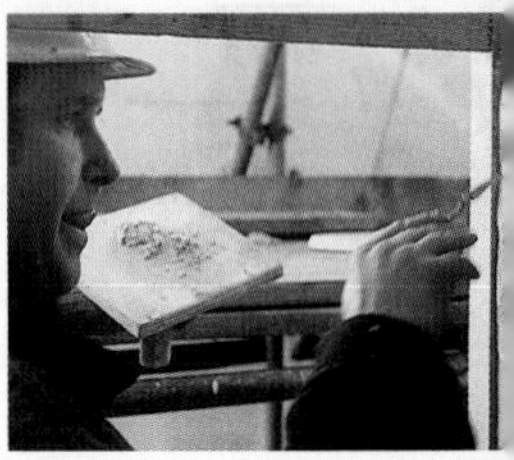
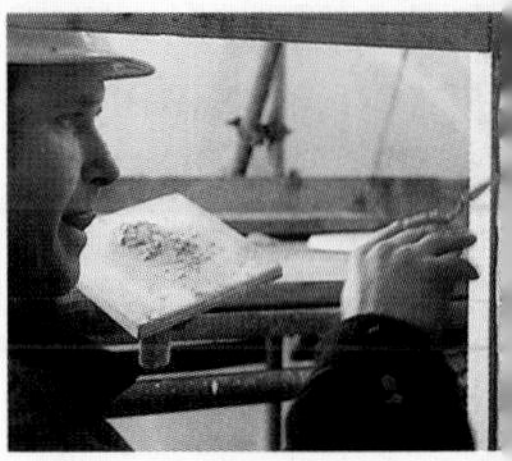
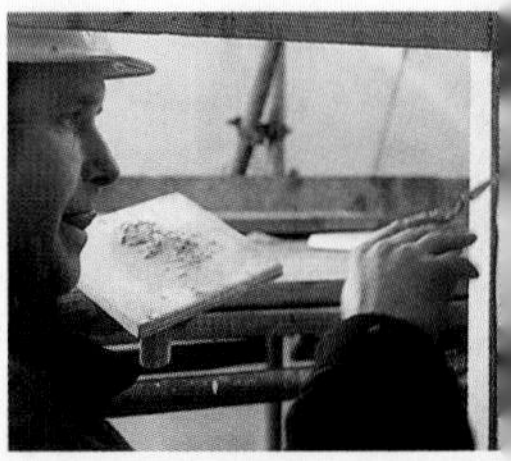

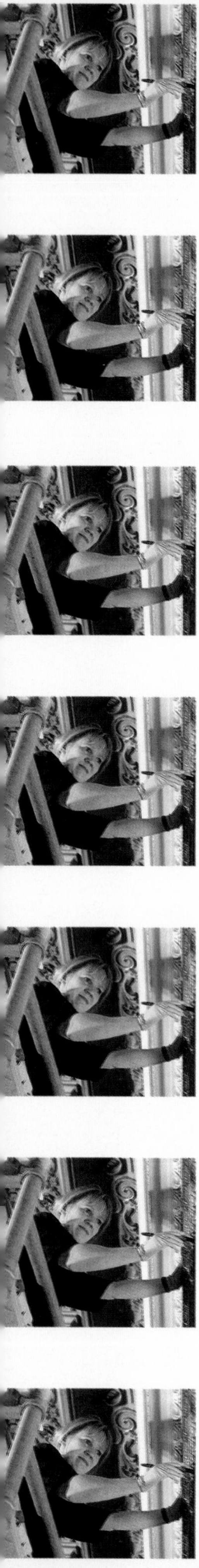

unsympathetic improvement. Landmark's aim is to promote the enjoyment of these historic buildings by making them available to stay in for holidays. Coop House can be rented by anyone, at all times of the year, for periods ranging from a weekend to three weeks. Bookings can be made by telephoning the Booking Office on 01628 825925. As the building is in full-time use for holiday accommodation, it is not normally open to the public. However the public can view the building by prior arrangement by telephoning the access contact (Victoria Piggott on 01628 825920) to make an appointment. Potential visitors will be asked to write to confirm the details
Heritage Open Days: No
P No
♿ No. Disabled WC: No. Guide Dogs: Yes
£ No

Crown & Nisi Prius Court
The Courts, English Street, Carlisle, Cumbria CA3 8NA
Former Crown Court in Carlisle situated at southern entrance to the city. One of a pair of sandstone towers built in the early 19th century as replicas of the medieval bastion. The towers were built to house the civil and criminal courts, used until the 1980s.
Grant Recipient/Owner: Cumbria Crown Court
Access contact: Mr Mike Telfer
Tel: 01228 606116
Opening Arrangements: 16 July - 14 September: Monday - Friday, two tours daily at 11am and 1pm. At other times by prior arrangement with Mr Mike Telfer, Office Superintendent, The Courts, English Street, Carlisle, Cumbria CA3 8NA (tel.01228 606116).
Heritage Open Days: Yes
P No
♿ No. Disabled WC: Yes. Guide Dogs: Yes
£ Yes
Adult: £3.00
Child: £2.00
Other: £2.00

Dalton Castle
Dalton-in-Furness, Cumbria LA22 0EJ
14th century tower in the main street of Dalton-in-Furness, with a local exhibition by the Friends of Dalton Castle and a display about the painter George Romney, a native of Dalton.
Website Address: www.nationaltrust.org.uk
Access contact: Property Manager
Tel: 01524 7011778 **Fax:** 01524 7011778
Email Address: raaspm@smtp.ntrust.org.uk
Opening Arrangements: Easter to the end of September Saturdays 2 - 5pm. On street parking.
Heritage Open Days: No
P See above
♿ No. Disabled WC: No. Guide Dogs: Yes
£ No

Kirkby Hall Wallpaintings
Kirkby-in-Furness, Cumbria LA17 7UX
Chapel in west wing, accessible only from trap door in dairy passage. Wallpaintings in red ochre and black consisting of panels with stylised trees, animals and birds with texts above of the Lord's Prayer, Creed, Ten Commandments and Galations 5, 16-21 from the Great Bible of 1541.
Grant Recipient/Owner: Holker Estates Company Ltd
Access contact: Mr D P R Knight
Tel: 015395 58313 **Fax:** 015395 58966
Email Address: estateoffice@holker.co.uk
Opening Arrangements: By prior written arrangement with the Holker Estate Office, Cark-in-Cartmel, Grange-over-Sands, Cumbria LA11 7PH (tel.015395 58313).
Heritage Open Days: No
P Yes. Spaces: 3
♿ No. Disabled WC: No. Guide Dogs: No
£ No

Muncaster Castle
Ravenglass, Cumbria CA18 1RQ
Large house incorporating medieval fortified tower, remodelled by Anthony Salvin for the 4th Lord Muncaster in 1862-66. Ancestral home of the Pennington family for 800 years containing a panelled Hall and octagonal library. Headquarters of the World Owl Trust.
Website Address: www.muncastercastle.co.uk
Grant Recipient/Owner:
Mrs P R Gordon-Duff-Pennington
Access contact: Mr Peter Frost-Pennington
Tel: 01229 717614 **Fax:** 01229 717010
Email Address: info@muncastercastle.co.uk
Opening Arrangements: 11 March - 4 November: Castle open daily Sunday - Friday (closed Saturdays) 12 noon - 5pm; Gardens, Owl Centre and Maze 10.30am - 6pm. Wheelchair access to ground floor of Castle only but other attractions and facilities are accessible. The hilly nature of the site can create access difficulties so please ask for further information on arrival. Refreshments available.
Heritage Open Days: No
P Yes. Spaces: 150
♿ Partial. Disabled WC: Yes. Guide Dogs: Yes
£ Yes
Adult: £6.50 Castle, Gardens, Owls & Maze; £5.00 Gardens, Owls & Maze only.
Child: £4.00 Castle, Gardens, Owls & Maze; £3.00 Gardens, Owls & Maze.
Other: £18.00 Castle, Gardens, Owls & Maze (family); £15.00 Gardens, Owls & Maze (family).

Orthwaite Hall Barn
Uldale, Wigton, Cumbria CA7 1HL
Grade II* listed agricultural barn. Former house adjoining later Hall, probably late 16th or early 17th century, now used for storage and housing animals.
Grant Recipient/Owner: Mrs S Hope
Access contact: Mr Jonathan Hope
Tel: 016973 71344
Opening Arrangements: By prior telephone arrangement.
Heritage Open Days: No
P Yes. Spaces: 3
♿ No. Disabled WC: No. Guide Dogs: Yes
£ No

Prior Slee Gatehouse
Carlisle Cathedral, Carlisle, Cumbria CA3 8TZ
Dated 1528, the Gatehouse would have replaced an earlier one. It has a large chamber over the gate, with two Tudor fireplaces. Graffiti carved in the stonework is believed to include merchants' marks. One of two integral lodges survives on the north-east side of the building. Now used as residential accommodation.
Grant Recipient/Owner:
The Dean & Chapter of Carlisle Cathedral
Access contact: Mr E T Amos
Tel: 01228 548151 **Fax:** 01228 547049
Email Address: office@carlislecathedral.org.uk
Opening Arrangements: By prior arrangement with Mr E T Amos, The Dean & Chapter of Carlisle Cathedral, 7 The Abbey, Carlisle, Cumbria CA3 8TZ (tel.01228 548151). Parking in nearby City centre car parks. Disabled WC in Cathedral grounds.
Heritage Open Days: No
P See above
♿ No. Disabled WC: No. Guide Dogs: Yes
£ No

Sizergh Castle
nr. Kendal, Cumbria LA8 8AE
Sizergh Castle has been the home of the Strickland family for over 760 years. Its core is the 14th century pele tower, later extended and containing some fine Elizabethan carved wooden chimney-pieces and inlaid chamber. The Castle is surrounded by gardens, including a rock garden.
Website Address: www.nationaltrust.org.uk
Grant Recipient/Owner: The National Trust
Access contact: Property Manager
Tel: 015395 60951 **Fax:** 015395 60951
Email Address: rsizpm@smtp.ntrust.org.uk
Opening Arrangements: Castle: 1 April to 31 October: daily except Fridays and Saturdays 1.30pm - 5.30pm. Garden: 1 April to 31 October: daily except Fridays and Saturdays 12.30 - 5.30pm. Wheelchair access to garden only. Parking for disabled visitors available near the house.
Heritage Open Days: No
P Yes. Spaces: 250
♿ See above. Disabled WC: Yes. Guide Dogs: Yes
£ Yes
Adult: £4.80. £2.40 (garden only).
Child: £2.40
Other: £12.00 (family).

Strickland Hall
Little Strickland, Penrith, Cumbria CA10 3EG
Elizabethan farmhouse, with 17th century alterations. Most notable feature is the Elizabethan plasterwork ceiling in the Lord's Parlour.
Grant Recipient/Owner: W H O'Connor
Access contact: W H O'Connor
Tel: 01931 716 780
Opening Arrangements: By prior written arrangement. Also various open evenings.
Heritage Open Days: No
P Yes. Spaces: 3
♿ Yes. Disabled WC: No. Guide Dogs: Yes
£ No

Wray Castle
Low Wray, Ambleside, Cumbria
A large Gothic mock castle and arboretum. Built in the 1840s over looking the western shore of Lake Windermere.
Website Address: www.nationaltrust.org.uk
Grant Recipient/Owner: The National Trust
Access contact: Property Manager
Tel: 015394 47997 **Fax:** 015394 47997
Opening Arrangements: Castle: July & August, weekdays, entrance hall only 2 - 4pm. Gardens and grounds all year. Telephone the Property Manager for further details.
Heritage Open Days: No
P Yes. Spaces: 20
♿ No
£ No

DERBYSHIRE

Barlborough Hall
Barlborough, Chesterfield, Derbyshire S43 4TL
Built by Sir Francis Rhodes in the 1580s, the Hall is square in plan and stands on a high basement with a small internal courtyard to provide light. Contains Great Chamber, now a chapel, bearing a date of 1584 on the overmantel whilst the porch is dated 1583. Now a private school.
Grant Recipient/Owner:
The Governors of Barlborough Hall School
Access contact: C F A Bogie
Tel: 01246 435138 **Fax:** 01246 435090
Opening Arrangements: Opening arrangements under review at time of going to print, please check the English Heritage website for current information.
Heritage Open Days: No
P Yes. Spaces: 50
♿ No. Disabled WC: No. Guide Dogs: Yes
£ No

Calke Abbey
Ticknall, Derbyshire DE73 1LE
Baroque mansion, built 1701-3 for Sir John Harpur and set in a landscaped park. Little restored, Calke is preserved by a programme of conservation as a graphic illustration of the English house in decline. It contains the natural history collection of the Harpur Crewe family, an 18th century state bed and interiors that are essentially unchanged since the 1880s.
Website Address: www.nationaltrust.org.uk
Grant Recipient/Owner: The National Trust
Access contact: Property Manager
Tel: 01332 863822 **Fax:** 01332 865272
Email Address: eckxxx@smtp.ntrust.org.uk
Opening Arrangements: House, garden and Church: 31 March to 4 November: daily except Thursdays and Fridays. House and Church: 1- 5.30pm (ticket office opens at 11am). Garden: 11am - 5.30pm. Park: most days until 9pm or dusk if earlier. Timed ticket system is in operation. All visitors (including NT members) require a ticket from the ticket office. Wheelchair access to ground floor of house, stables, shop and restaurant.
Heritage Open Days: No
P Yes. Spaces: 75
♿ Partial. Disabled WC: Yes. Guide Dogs: Yes
£ Yes
Adult: £5.20
Child: £2.60
Other: £13.00 (family). £2.50 (garden only).

Caudwell's Mill
Rowsley, Matlock, Derbyshire DE4 2EB
Victorian (1874) Grade II*, complete, 'automatic', water-turbine powered roller flour mill and provender mill. Four floors with a collection of early original milling machinery illustrating the changes over the years in the milling process. Exhibitions, displays and 'hands-on' models. Craftspeople around Stable Courtyard.
Grant Recipient/Owner: The Manager
Access contact: The Manager
Tel: 01629 734374 **Fax:** 01629 734374
Email Address: raymarjoram@compuserve.com
Opening Arrangements: Mill building: 1 March - 31 October daily 10am - 6pm; rest of year weekends 10am - 4.30pm, closed Christmas. Rest of site and shops: daily except 24-26 December and weekdays in January. Introductory film to mill available. Some wheelchair access. Special parking for disabled drivers in the mill yard.
Heritage Open Days: Yes
P Yes. Spaces: 50
♿ Partial. Disabled WC: Yes. Guide Dogs: Yes
£ Yes
Adult: £3.00
Child: £1.00
Other: £2.00 (senior citizens)

Hardwick Hall
Doe Lea, Chesterfield, Derbyshire S44 5QJ
A late 16th century 'prodigy house' designed by Robert Smythson for Bess of Hardwick. Contains an outstanding collection of 16th century furniture, tapestries and needlework. Walled courtyards enclose gardens, orchards and herb garden.
Website Address: www.nationaltrust.org.uk
Grant Recipient/Owner: The National Trust
Access contact: Property Manager
Tel: 01246 850430 **Fax:** 01246 854200
Email Address: ehwxxx@smtp.ntrust.org.uk
Opening Arrangements: 31 March to 28 October: daily except Mondays, Tuesdays and Fridays (but open Bank

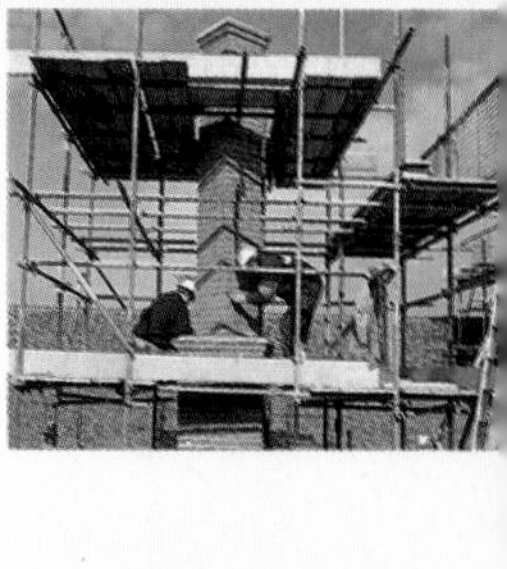

Holiday Mondays) 12.30 - 5pm. Garden: daily 12 - 5.30pm. Parkland: daily. Wheelchair access to ground floor of house, Great Kitchen, shop and garden.
Heritage Open Days: No
P Yes. Spaces: 200
♿ Partial. Disabled WC: Yes. Guide Dogs: Yes
£ Yes
Adult: £6.20
Child: £3.10
Other: £15.50 (family). £3.30 (garden only). £8.30 joint ticket with Hardwick Old Hall (EH property).

Kedleston Hall

Derby, Derbyshire DE22 5JH
A classical Palladian mansion built 1759-65 for the Curzon family and little altered since. Robert Adam interior with state rooms retaining their collection of paintings and original furniture. The Eastern museum houses a range of objects collected by Lord Curzon when Viceroy of India (1899-1905). Set in 800 acres of parkland and 18th century pleasure ground, garden and woodland walks.
Website Address: www.nationaltrust.org.uk
Grant Recipient/Owner: The National Trust
Access contact: Property Manager
Tel: 01332 842191 **Fax:** 01332 841972
Email Address: ekdxxx@smtp.ntrust.org.uk
Opening Arrangements: House: 31 March to 4 November: daily except Thursdays and Fridays 12 - 4.30pm. Garden: as house 11am - 6pm. Park: 31 March to 4 November: daily 11am - 6pm; November to 23 December Saturdays and Sundays 12 - 4pm. Wheelchair access to ground floor of house, garden, restaurant and shop.
Heritage Open Days: No
P Yes. Spaces: 60
♿ Partial. Disabled WC: Yes. Guide Dogs: Yes
£ Yes
Adult: £5.10
Child: £2.50
Other: £12.70 (family). £2.30 (park and garden only). £2.00 (car park charge on Thursdays and Fridays).

Masson Mills

Derby Road, Matlock Bath, Derbyshire DE4 3PY
Built in 1783 as the showpiece mills of Sir Richard Arkwright, they are the oldest continuously occupied mills in the world. Now a working textile museum producing cloth on old looms. Originally water-powered by the River Derwent the water turbines are still in use.
Website Address: www.massonmills.co.uk
Grant Recipient/Owner: Mara Securities Ltd
Access contact: The Co-ordinator
Tel: 01629 581001 **Fax:** 01629 582403
Opening Arrangements: Open all year except Christmas Day and Easter Day: Monday - Friday 10am - 4pm, Saturday 11am - 5pm and Sunday 11am - 4pm.
Heritage Open Days: No
P Yes. Spaces: 200
♿ Partial. Disabled WC: Yes. Guide Dogs: No
£ Yes
Adult: £2.50
Child: £1.50
Other: £2.00

Melbourne Hall & Gardens

Church Square, Melbourne, Derbyshire DE73 1EN
Historic house and formal 18th century garden with yew tunnel and wrought iron arbour by Bakewell. House once home of Victorian Prime Minister William Lamb, who as Viscount Melbourne named the Australian city. A family home since 1628, the hall is lived in by Lord Ralph Kerr (a descendant of the original owner Sir John Coke) and his family.
Grant Recipient/Owner:
Trustees of the Melbourne Garden Charity
Access contact: Mrs Gill Weston
Tel: 01332 862502 **Fax:** 01332 862263
Email Address: melbhall@globalnet.co.uk
Opening Arrangements: Hall: daily during August (except first three Mondays) 2 - 5pm. Gardens: April - September, Wednesdays, Saturdays, Sundays and Bank Holiday Mondays 1.30 - 5.30pm. No specially designed lavatory for disabled people but one cubicle slightly larger than others with handrail.
Heritage Open Days: Yes
P Yes. Spaces: 6
♿ Yes. Disabled WC: See above. Guide Dogs: Yes
£ Yes
Adult: £3.00 Hall, £3.00 Gardens, £5.00 combined.
Child: £1.50 Hall, £2.00 Gardens, £3.00 combined.
Other: £2.50 Hall, £2.00 Gardens, £4.00 combined.

Sudbury Hall

Sudbury, Ashbourne, Derbyshire DE6 5HT
17th century house with rich interior decoration including wood carvings by Laguerre. The Great Staircase (c1676) with white-painted balustrade with luxuriantly carved foliage by Edward Pierce, is one of the finest staircases of its date in an English house. 19th century service wing houses the National Trust Museum of Childhood.
Website Address: www.nationaltrust.org.uk
Grant Recipient/Owner: The National Trust
Access contact: Property Manager
Tel: 01283 585305 **Fax:** 01283 585139
Email Address: esuxxx@smtp.ntrust.org.uk
Opening Arrangements: Hall: 31 March to 4 November: daily except Mondays and Tuesdays (but open Bank Holiday Mondays and closed Good Fridays) 1 - 5.30pm. Grounds: as Hall 12 - 6pm. Wheelchair access to museum, shop and restaurant. Car park is a short distance from the Hall; six-seater volunteer driven buggy available.
Heritage Open Days: No
P Yes. Spaces: 100
♿ Partial. Disabled WC: Yes. Guide Dogs: Yes
£ Yes
Adult: £3.80. £6.10 (Hall & Museum).
Child: £1.90. £3.00 (Hall & Museum).
Other: £9.50 (family). £15.20 (Hall & Museum).

DEVON

Broomham Farm

King's Nympton, Devon EX37 9TS
Late medieval Grade II* listed Devon long-house of stone and cob construction with thatched roof. Contains a smoking room. Currently undergoing renovation.
Grant Recipient/Owner: Mr Clements
Access contact: Miss J Clements
Tel: 01769 572322
Opening Arrangements: By prior telephone arrangement.
Heritage Open Days: No
P Yes. Spaces: 3
♿ No
£ No

Canonsleigh Abbey Gatehouse

Burlescombe, Devon EX16 7JF
15th century Augustinian priory gatehouse. Large double gateway with chamber over. Much contemporary decoration.
Grant Recipient/Owner: Mr Burroughs
Access contact: Mr Burroughs
Opening Arrangements: By prior written arrangement any day from 1 April - 1 October, at least 10 days notice is required. Wheelchair access to ground floor only.
Heritage Open Days: Yes
P Yes. Spaces: 5
♿ Partial. Disabled WC: No. Guide Dogs: Yes
£ No

Castle Drogo

Drewsteignton, Devon EX6 6PB
A granite castle built between 1910 and 1930 for Julius Drewe by Sir Edwin Lutyens. The interior has an interesting kitchen and scullery. Terraced formal gardens.
Website Address: www.nationaltrust.org.uk
Grant Recipient/Owner: The National Trust
Access contact: Alex Raeder
Tel: 01392 881691 **Fax:** 01392 881954
Email Address: dlaarx@smtp.ntrust.org.uk
Opening Arrangements: March: daily except Mondays and Tuesdays, pre-season guided tours only. 31 March to 4 November: daily except Friday (but open Good Friday) 11am - 5.30pm. Special guided tours on Friday 20 July and 31 August 11am, 1pm and 3pm. Garden open all year, daily 10.30 am to dusk. Wheelchair access to: Hall, Library, Chapel and Gun Room, restaurant, shop and garden. Lift with seat (too small for most wheelchairs) to lower ground floor of Castle via 2 steps, to dining and kitchen area. Wheelchairs and buggy service available.
Heritage Open Days: No
P Yes. Spaces: 250
♿ Partial. Disabled WC: Yes. Guide Dogs: Yes
£ Yes
Adult: £5.60 (castle & gardens). £2.80 (garden and grounds).
Child: Free for under 5s. Half adult price for 5-16.
Other: £14.00 (family). £4.70 (booked parties).

Colleton Manor Chapel

Chulmleigh, Devon EX18 7JS
Small chapel over gatehouse, possibly one mentioned in licence of 1381. Stone walls, slate roof, west wall recently rebuilt in stone and cob. Plain interior with Edwardian matchboard panelling and exposed timbers. Still used as a chapel.
Grant Recipient/Owner: Mr Phillips
Access contact: Mr Phillips
Tel: 01769 580240
Opening Arrangements: By prior telephone arrangement. Voluntary donation.
Heritage Open Days: No
P Yes. Spaces: 3
♿ No. Disabled WC: No. Guide Dogs: No
£ See above

The Devon & Exeter Institution Library & Reading Rooms

7 Cathedral Close, Exeter, Devon EX1 1EZ
Building housing the Library and Reading Rooms of the Devon and Exeter Institution since 1813 but was formerly the town house of the Courtenay family and one time home of the Parliamentary General, Sir William Waller. Part of the Tudor house remains at the rear and also the gatehouse range which fronts The Close. In the early 19th century the two lofty libraries were built on the site of the old hall and kitchen.
Grant Recipient/Owner:
Devon & Exeter Institution Library & Reading Rooms
Access contact: Mrs M M Rowe
Tel: 01392 274727
Opening Arrangements: Open Monday - Friday 9am - 5pm. Closed for a week at Easter and Christmas.
Heritage Open Days: No
P No
♿ Yes. Disabled WC: Yes. Guide Dogs: Yes
£ No

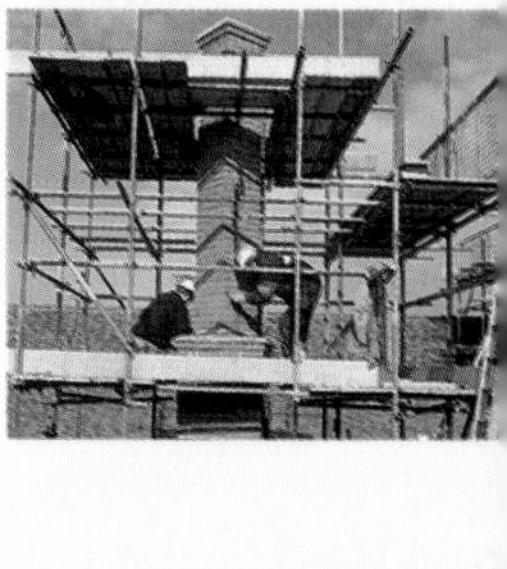

Dunkeswell Abbey

nr. Honiton, Devon EX14 ORP
Ruins of Cistercian abbey.
Grant Recipient/Owner:
Dunkeswell Abbey Preservation Fund
Access contact: Reverend N J Wall
Tel: 01404 891243
Opening Arrangements: Always open. Roadside parking.
Heritage Open Days: No
P See above
♿ Yes. Disabled WC: No. Guide Dogs: Yes
£ No

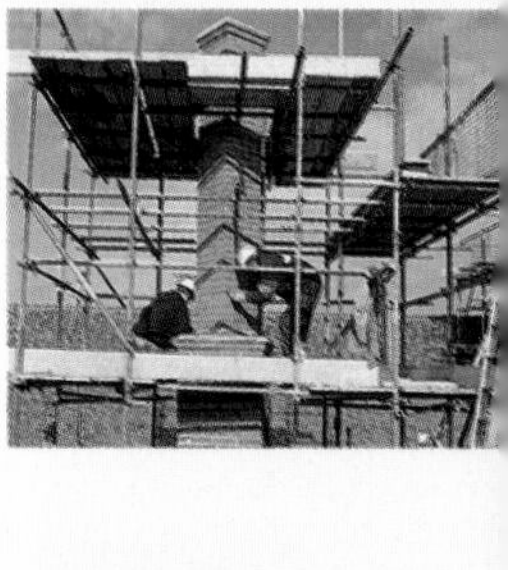

Eastleigh Manor

Eastleigh, Bideford, Devon EX39 4PA
Late 15th or early 16th century manor house, remodelled in late 16th or early 17th century and again c1800. Contains interesting features from each stage of its building history, including a medieval ceiling in one room.
Grant Recipient/Owner: Mr D Grigg
Access contact: Mr D Grigg
Tel: 01271 860418
Opening Arrangements: By prior written arrangement between October and March.
Heritage Open Days: No
P Yes. Spaces: 5
♿ No
£ No

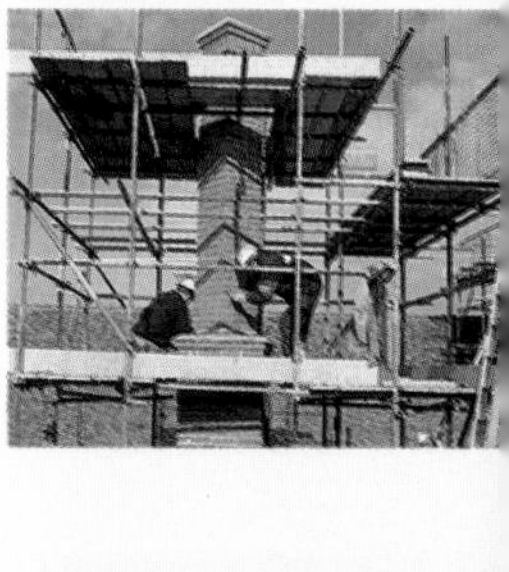

Endsleigh House

Milton Abbot, Tavistock, Devon PL19 0PQ
Built 1811-14 by the 6th Duke of Bedford to the designs of Sir Jeffry Wyatville, the grounds were laid out by Humphry Repton.
Grant Recipient/Owner: Endsleigh Fishing Club Ltd
Access contact: Mr D Bradbury
Tel: 01822 870248 **Fax:** 01822 870502
Opening Arrangements: April - September: Friday - Tuesday 11am - 5pm, plus Wednesdays and Thursdays by prior arrangement.
Heritage Open Days: No
P Yes. Spaces: 20
♿ Yes. Disabled WC: Yes. Guide Dogs: Yes
£ Yes
Adult: £3.00

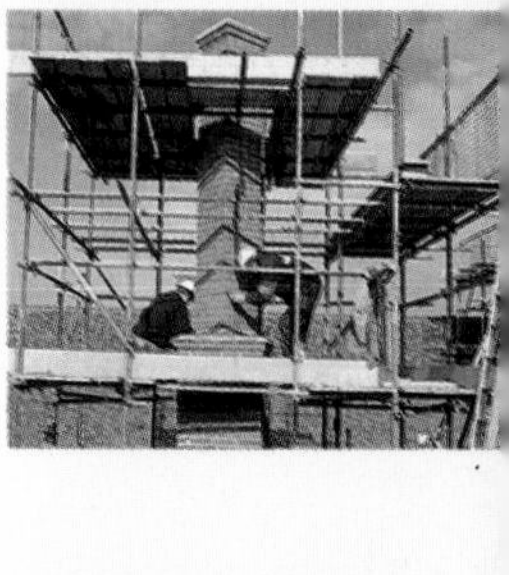

Finch Foundry

Sticklepath, Okehampton, Devon EX20 2NW
19th century water-powered forge, which produced agricultural and mining hand tools. Still in working order with regular demonstrations. The foundry has three water-wheels driving the huge tilt hammer and grindstone.
Website Address: www.nationaltrust.org.uk
Grant Recipient/Owner: The National Trust
Access contact: Alex Raeder
Tel: 01392 881691 **Fax:** 01392 881954
Email Address: dlaarx@smtp.ntrust.org.uk
Opening Arrangements: 31 March to 4 November daily except Tuesdays 11am to 5.30pm. Access to car park is narrow and unsuitable for coaches and wide vehicles. Partial wheelchair access: foundary can be viewed through shop windows; access to workshop and museum is difficult; shop is accessible.
Heritage Open Days: No
P Yes. Spaces: 50
♿ Partial. Disabled WC: No. Guide Dogs: Yes
£ Yes
Adult: £2.90
Child: Free for under 5s. Half adult price for 5-16.

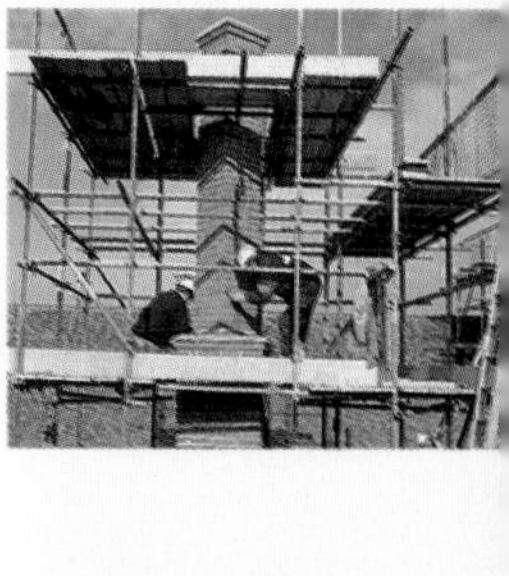

Gittisham Town House

Gittisham, Honiton, Devon EX14 3AJ
Grade II* late 16th century cross passage farmhouse with 17th and 18th century additions. The south side of the

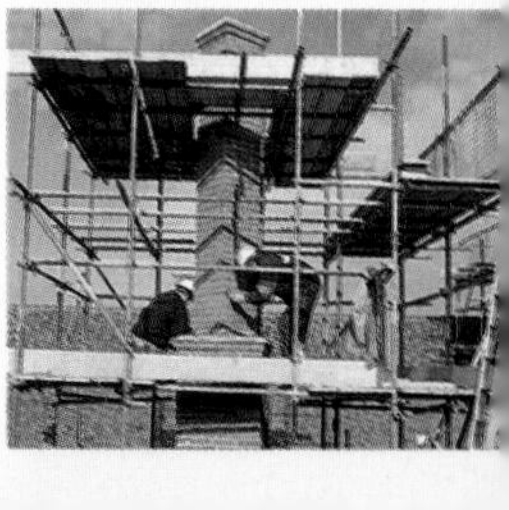

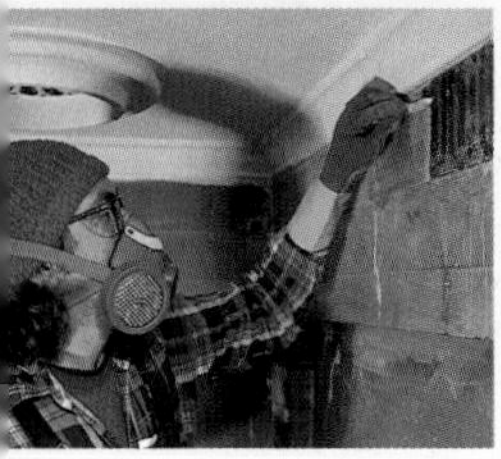
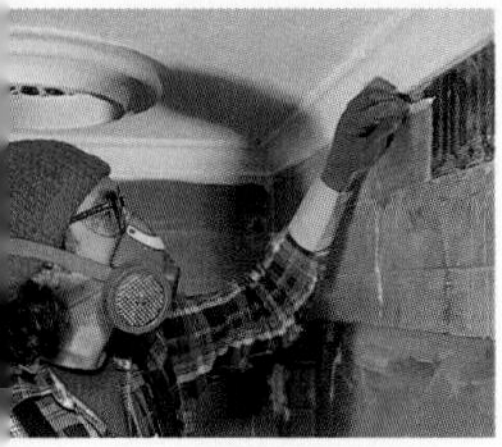
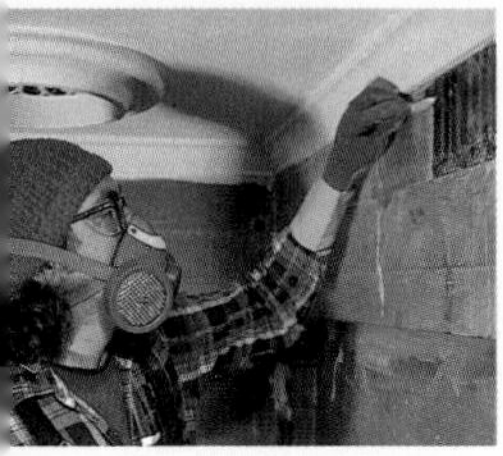
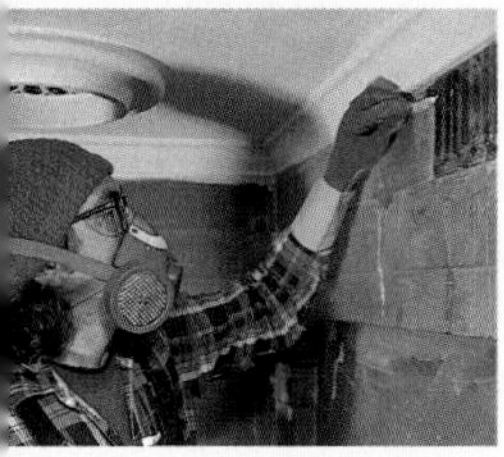
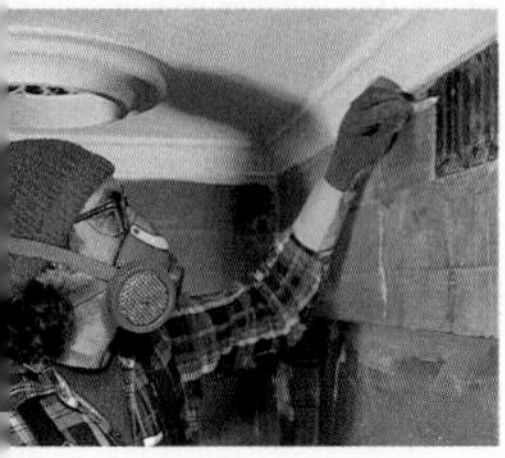
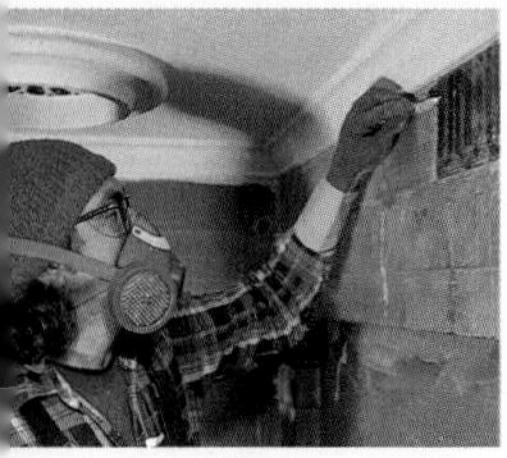
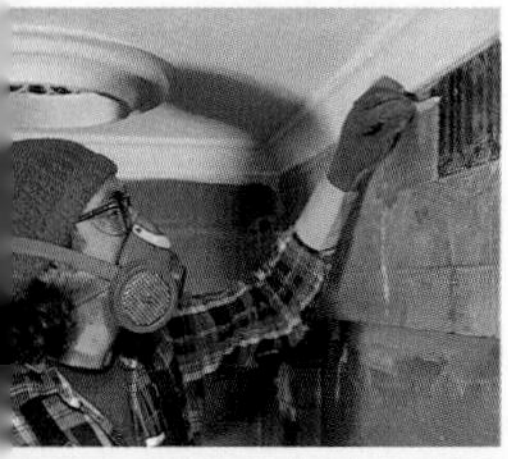

house is bounded by a walled garden.
Grant Recipient/Owner: Mr R J T Marker
Access contact: Andrew Hill
Tel: 01404 851 041 **Fax:** 01404 851 289
Opening Arrangements: By prior written arrangement. Closed Easter and Christmas.
Heritage Open Days: No
P Yes. Spaces: 4
♿ No. Disabled WC: No. Guide Dogs: Yes
£ No

Higher Thornham

Romansleigh, South Molton, Devon EX36 4JS
16th century through passage house, remodelled in the 17th century. Built of stone and cob, with a thatched roof. Beamed ceilings on ground floor and one moulded door frame. Recently renovated using traditional materials.
Grant Recipient/Owner: Mr S W Chudley
Access contact: Mr S W Chudley
Opening Arrangements: By prior written arrangement 1 May - end of September: Monday or Friday 2 - 4.30pm. Dogs not allowed and children must be accompanied by an adult. No photography. Guide dog access to ground floor only.
Heritage Open Days: No
P Yes. Spaces: 2
♿ No. Disabled WC: No. Guide Dogs: Yes
£ Yes
Adult: £4.00
Child: £1.50

Killerton House Chapel

Broadclyst, nr. Exeter, Devon EX5 3LE
The Chapel of the Holy Evangelists was built in 1841 for Sir Thomas Acland. The architect was C R Cockerell RA, better known for designing in the classical tradition than in the Victorian - Neo-Norman style of Killerton Chapel. It is an approximate copy of the Chapel of St Joseph at Glastonbury Abbey.
Website Address: www.nationaltrust.org.uk
Grant Recipient/Owner: The National Trust
Access contact: Alex Raeder
Tel: 01392 881691 **Fax:** 01392 881954
Email Address: dlaarx@smtp.ntrust.org.uk
Opening Arrangements: 10 March to 4 November: daily except Tuesdays 11am to 5.30pm. (Closed Mondays in March and October). Access to the Chapel is free. There is an admission charge to Killerton House and remainder of the grounds. Approach to Chapel is difficult for wheelchairs. Lavatory for disabled people available at Killerton House and car park at entrance to Killerton House.
Heritage Open Days: No
P Yes. Spaces: 20
♿ Partial. Disabled WC: Yes. Guide Dogs: Yes
£ No

Lawrence Castle Haldon Belvedere

Higher Ashton, nr. Dunchideock, Exeter, Devon EX6 7QY
Grade II* listed building built in 1788 as the centrepiece to a 11,600 acre estate. Stands 800ft above sea level overlooking the cathedral city of Exeter, the Exe estuary and the surrounding countryside. Contains a spiral staircase and miniature ballroom.
Website Address: www.haldonbelvedere.co.uk
Grant Recipient/Owner: Mr Ian Turner
Access contact: Mr Ian Turner
Tel: 01392 833668 **Fax:** 01392 833668
Email Address: turner@haldonbelvedere.co.uk
Opening Arrangements: March - October: Sundays and Bank Holidays 2 - 5pm. At other times by prior arrangement. Wheelchair access to ground floor only, disabled parking adjacent to building.
Heritage Open Days: No
P Yes. Spaces: 15
♿ Partial. Disabled WC: No. Guide Dogs: Yes
£ Yes
Adult: £1.50
Child: 75p

Saltram House

Plympton, Plymouth, Devon PL7 1UH
A remarkable survival of a George II mansion, complete with its original contents and set in landscaped park. Robert Adam worked here on two occasions to create the state rooms. Three rooms are decorated with the original Chinese wallpaper. 18th century gardens.
Website Address: www.nationaltrust.org.uk
Grant Recipient/Owner: The National Trust
Access contact: Alex Raeder
Tel: 01392 881691 **Fax:** 01392 881954
Email Address: dlaarx@smtp.ntrust.org.uk
Opening Arrangements: 1 April to 4 November: daily except Friday and Saturday (but open Good Friday) at the following times: 1 April to 30 September 12 - 5pm, last admission 4.15pm; 1 October - 4 November 12 - 4pm, last admission 3.15pm (due to poor light). Garden: 1 February to 31 March: Saturday and Sunday only, 11am - 4pm; 1 April to 4 November as for house 10.30am - 5.30pm. Wheelchair access to: first floor via lift (66cm wide by 86.5cm deep); restaurant, tea room, ticket office over cobbles. Wheelchairs available at house. Parking is 500 metres from house. 30 marked car parking spaces on tarmac, remainder on grass.
Heritage Open Days: No
P Yes. Spaces: 250
♿ Yes. Disabled WC: Yes. Guide Dogs: Yes
£ Yes
Adult: £6.00 (house & garden). £3.00 (garden only).
Child: Free for under 5s. Half adult price for 5-16.
Other: Discount for booked parties. Rates on application.

Tawstock Court Elizabethan Gatehouse

Tawstock, Barnstaple, Devon EX31 3HY
Elizabethan gatehouse at entrance to Tawstock Court, taking the form of two towers joined by a pitched roof covering a small cobbled area. Open on one side, oak doors on the other.
Grant Recipient/Owner:
Governors of St Michael's School
Access contact: Mrs S M Bennett
Tel: 01271 343242 **Fax:** 01271 346771
Opening Arrangements: Easter - August during daylight hours.
Heritage Open Days: No
P Yes. Spaces: 2
♿ No. Disabled WC: No. Guide Dogs: Yes
£ No

Ugbrooke Park

Chudleigh, Devon TQ13 0AD
House and Chapel built c1200 and redesigned by Robert Adam in the 1760s for the 4th Lord Clifford. Chapel and library wing in Adam's characteristic castle style. Set in 'Capability' Brown landscaped park with lakes and 18th century Orangery. Home of the Lords Clifford of Chudleigh for 300 years.
Website Address: www.historichouses.co.uk
Grant Recipient/Owner: Clifford Estate Company Ltd
Access contact: Mrs Lee Martin
Tel: 01626 852179 **Fax:** 01626 853322
Email Address: leececo@netscape.co.uk
Opening Arrangements: 8 July - 6 September: Tuesdays, Wednesdays, Thursdays, Sundays and August Bank Holiday Monday 1.30 - 5.30pm. Group tours and private functions by prior arrangement.
Heritage Open Days: No
P Yes. Spaces: 200
♿ Yes. Disabled WC: Yes. Guide Dogs: Yes
£ Yes
Adult: £4.80
Child: £2.00
Other: £4.50 (senior citizens and groups)

DORSET

Bindon Abbey House

Wool, Dorset
House and chapel built c1794 in gothic style re-using materials from the ruins of Bindon Abbey, with 19th century rear extension. Chapel situated in front part of house on the first floor. Good example of early Gothic Revival.
Grant Recipient/Owner: Mr P Gready
Access contact: Mr S Down
Tel: 01929 400352 **Fax:** 01929 400563
Email Address:s wd@lulworth.com
Opening Arrangements: By prior arrangement with Mr Simon Down at the Lulworth Estate Office, Lulworth Castle, Wareham, Dorset BH20 5QS (tel.01929 400352). Wheelchair access to ground floor only.
Heritage Open Days: No
P Yes. Spaces: 5
♿ Partial. Disabled WC: No. Guide Dogs: Yes
£ No

Highcliffe Castle

Rothesay Drive, Highcliffe-on-Sea, Christchurch, Dorset BH23 4LE
Cliff-top mansion built in the 1830s by Charles Stuart. Constructed in the romantic, picturesque style, much of its stonework is medieval coming from France. Exterior has been restored, interior houses changing exhibitions and the 16th century stained glass Jesse window.
Website Address: www.highcliffecastle.co.uk
Grant Recipient/Owner: Mr B J Kees
Access contact: Mr Mike Allen
Tel: 01425 278807 **Fax:** 01425 280423
Email Address: m.allen@christchurch.gov.uk
Opening Arrangements: Daily 5 May - 28 October, 1 - 5pm (except special events, please phone for details). Although there is currently no wheelchair access to the building, there are toilet facilities for the disabled at the site.
Heritage Open Days: Yes
P Yes. Spaces: 108
♿ No. Disabled WC: Yes. Guide Dogs: Yes
£ Yes
Adult: £1.50

Parnham House & Gardens

Beaminster, Dorset DT8 3NA
Elizabethan manor house built in 1540 and enlarged by John Nash in 1810, situated in 14 acres of formal and informal gardens.
Grant Recipient/Owner: Mr John Makepeace
Access contact: Mr John Makepeace
Tel: 01308 862204 **Fax:** 01308 863806
Opening Arrangements: 1 April - 31 October: Wednesdays only 1pm - 5pm. Wheelchair access to ground floor and gardens only.
Heritage Open Days: No
P Yes. Spaces: 200
♿ Partial. Disabled WC: Yes. Guide Dogs: Yes
£ Yes
Adult: £5.50 (including senior citizens)
Child: £2.50 (5-16)
Other: £2.50 (students)

Woodsford Castle

nr. Dorchester, Dorset
What remains is one side of a quadrangular castle completed in 1370. The grand apartment and lodgings that make up the existing building were the work of Sir Guy de Bryan, a close friend of Edward III. The castle eventually became a farmhouse with an enormous thatched roof replacing the original turrets and crenellations. The castle has a steep staircase inside and outside, steps without railings.
Website Address: www.landmarktrust.co.uk
Grant Recipient/Owner: The Landmark Trust
Access contact: Ms Victoria Piggott
Tel: 01628 825920 **Fax:** 01628 825417
Email Address: vpiggott@landmarktrust.co.uk
Opening Arrangements: The Landmark Trust is an independent charity, which rescues small buildings of historic or architectural importance from decay or unsympathetic improvement. Landmark's aim is to promote the enjoyment of these historic buildings by making them available to stay in for holidays. Woodsford Castle can be rented by anyone, at all times of the year, for periods ranging from a weekend to three weeks. Bookings can be made by telephoning the Booking Office on 01628 825925. As the building is in full-time use for holiday accommodation, it is not normally open to the public. However the public can view the building by prior arrangement by telephoning the access contact (Victoria Piggott on 01628 825920) to make an appointment. Potential visitors will be asked to write to confirm the details of their visit.
Heritage Open Days: No
P Yes. Spaces: 3
♿ No. Disabled WC: No. Guide Dogs: Yes
£ No

EAST RIDING OF YORKSHIRE

Church of Our Lady & St Everilda

Everingham, East Riding of Yorkshire YO42 4JA
Roman Catholic parish church for Everingham, built between 1836 and 1839 to the designs of Agostino Giorgiola. Interior has columned walls and a barrelled ceiling with a semi-dome above the high altar. Also of note are the altar, font and statues and the 1839 organ by William Allen.
Grant Recipient/Owner: Mr N J M Turton
Access contact: Mr N J M Turton
Tel: 01904 627436 **Fax:** 01904 610869
Opening Arrangements: Key available during reasonable hours by telephoning: 01430 861443 or 01759 302226.
Heritage Open Days: No
P Yes. Spaces: 12
♿ No. Disabled WC: No. Guide Dogs: Yes
£ No

Maister House

160 High Street, Kingston-upon-Hull, East Riding of Yorkshire HU1 1NL
Rebuilt in 1743 during Hull's heyday as an affluent trading centre, this house is a typical but rare survivor of a contemporary merchant's residence. The restrained exterior belies the spectacular plasterwork staircase inside. The house is now let as offices.
Website Address: www.nationaltrust.org.uk
Grant Recipient/Owner: The National Trust
Access contact: Gelder & Kitchen Architects
Tel: 01482 324114 **Fax:** 01482 227003
Opening Arrangements: Daily except Saturdays and Sundays (closed Good Friday and all Bank Holidays) 10am - 4pm. Public access is to staircase and entrance hall only. Unsuitable for groups. No WC.
Heritage Open Days: No
P No

[♿] No. Disabled WC: No. Guide Dogs: Yes
[£] Yes
Adult: 80p
Child: 80p
Other: Admission charge includes guidebook.

Old Hall

2-4 Fletchergate, Hedon,
East Riding of Yorkshire HU12 8ER

Grade II* listed building built in 1620 by Sir John Waterland. Contains two panelled rooms and a staircase which have been recently restored. One of the doors in the ground floor room possesses a fine case with a plain frieze and pilasters of the Doric style. Renovation is still ongoing.
Grant Recipient/Owner: Mr George Head
Access contact: Mr George Head
Tel: 01482 899472 **Fax:** 01482 899472
Opening Arrangements: By prior telephone or fax arrangement. Wheelchair access to ground floor only.
Heritage Open Days: Yes
[P] Yes. Spaces: 50
[♿] Partial. Disabled WC: No. Guide Dogs: Yes
[£] No

EAST SUSSEX

Brickwall House

Northiam, Rye, East Sussex TN31 6NL

Jacobean manor house containing a front hall, drawing room and chamber room with leather panels. Previously home of the Frewen family, now a school for dyslexic boys aged 9-17.
Grant Recipient/Owner: Frewen Educational Trust
Access contact: Mr Peter Mold
Tel: 01797 253388 **Fax:** 01797 252567
Email Address: post@frewcoll.demon.co.uk
Opening Arrangements: April 3,4,10,11,13,16,17 & 18; May 7,28 & 30; July 10,11,17,18,24,25 & 31; August 1,7,8,14,15,21,22,27,28 & 29; 1 - 5pm.
Heritage Open Days: No
[P] Yes. Spaces: 40
[♿] Yes. Disabled WC: Yes. Guide Dogs: Yes
[£] Yes
Adult: £3.50

The Flushing Inn

4 Market Street, Rye, East Sussex TN31 7LA

15th century timber-framed building with large recently restored 16th century wallpainting, now a restaurant.
Grant Recipient/Owner: Mr Flynn
Access contact: Mr Flynn
Tel: 01797 223292
Opening Arrangements: Restaurant open Wednesday - Sunday for Lunches and Dinners, Mondays Lunch only and Tuesdays closed. Closed first two weeks in January and October. Unless dining, visiting to view the Fresco is restricted to 10.30 - Noon. Wheelchair access to Fresco with assistance (entrance steps to be negotiated). Parking on street but restricted to 1hr, otherwise public parking elsewhere in Rye.
Heritage Open Days: No
[P] See above
[♿] Partial. Disabled WC: No. Guide Dogs: Yes
[£] No

Glynde Place

Glynde, nr. Lewes, East Sussex BN8 6SX

Elizabethan manor house built in 1589 from local flint and stone from Normandy, then extensively added on to in the 18th century. Contains a collection of Old Masters, family portraits, furniture, embroidery and silver belonging to the family who have lived there for over 400 years.
Grant Recipient/Owner: Viscount Hampden
Access contact: Viscount Hampden
Tel: 01273 858224 **Fax:** 01273 858224
Email Address: info@glyndeplace.co.uk
Opening Arrangements: Sundays and Bank Holidays in May; Sundays and Wednesdays in June and September; Sundays, Wednesdays, Thursdays and Bank Holidays in July and August 2 - 5pm (last admission 4.45pm). House open at other times by prior arrangement. Admission prices for groups if booked in advance. Refreshments available.
Heritage Open Days: No
[P] Yes. Spaces: 150
[♿] No. Disabled WC: No, Guide Dogs: No
[£] Yes
Adult: £4.00
Child: £2.00
Other: £2.50 (groups of 25+ on open days), £5.00 (groups of 25+ at other times).

Great Dixter House & Gardens

Northiam, nr. Rye, East Sussex TN31 6PH

Original medieval hall house built c1450 comprising three rooms, the Great Hall, Parlour and Solar. Bought by Nathanial Lloyd in 1910 who employed Lutyens to restore and extend the property. A Yeoman's hall, originally located in Benenden, was dismantled and re-erected at Great Dixter.
Grant Recipient/Owner: Mr Christopher Lloyd
Access contact: Ms Elaine Francis
Tel: 01797 252878 **Fax:** 01797 252878
Email Address: greatdixter@compuserve.com
Opening Arrangements: 1 April - 28 October: Tuesday - Sunday (and Bank Holiday Mondays) 2 - 5.30pm (last admission 5pm). Wheelchair access to Great Hall and Parlour only.
Heritage Open Days: No
[P] Yes. Spaces: 100
[♿] Partial. Disabled WC: Yes. Guide Dogs: Yes
[£] Yes
Adult: £6.00 House & Garden, £4.50 Garden only.
Child: £1.50 House & Garden, £1.00 Garden only.
Other: Half price for disabled visitors.

Lamb House (Coromandel Lacquer Panels)

3 Chapel Hill, Lewes, East Sussex, BN7 2BB

The incised lacquer panels in the study of Lamb House are a unique surviving example of imported late 17th century Chinese lacquer work that remains as decorative wall panelling. Recently restored.
Grant Recipient/Owner: Prof. Paul Benjamin
Access contact: Prof. Paul Benjamin
Tel: 01273 475657
Opening Arrangements: Weekends only by prior telephone arrangement. Street parking.
Heritage Open Days: No
[P] See above
[♿] Partial. Disabled WC: No. Guide Dogs: No
[£] No

The Royal Pavilion

Brighton, East Sussex BN1 1EE

Former seaside residence of George IV in Indian style with Chinese-inspired interiors. Originally a neo-classical villa by Henry Holland was built on the site in 1787, but this was subsequently replaced by the current John Nash building constructed between 1815-23.
Website Address: www.royalpavilion.brighton.co.uk
Grant Recipient/Owner: Brighton & Hove Council
Access contact: Ms Cara Bowen
Tel: 01273 292810 **Fax:** 01273 292871
Email Address: cara.bowen@brighton-hove.gov.uk
Opening Arrangements: 1 October - 31 May: daily 10am - 5pm (closed Christmas Day and Boxing Day); 1 June - 30 September: daily 10am - 6pm. Admission charges are valid until 31 March 2001, for rates after that date please check with the Royal Pavilion. There is no admission charge for wheelchair users as access is to the ground floor only. Disabled parking is available in the grounds of the Pavilion by prior arrangement.
Heritage Open Days: No
[P] See above
[♿] Partial. Disabled WC: Yes. Guide Dogs: Yes
[£] Yes
Adult: £4.90 (see above), £2.00 (local residents).
Child: £3.00 under 16 (free local residents).
Other: £3.55 (seniors/students/unemployed). £12.80 (family of 2 adults, 4 children), £7.90 (1 adult, 4 children).

ESSEX

Alderford Mill

Alderford Street, Sible Hedingham, Halstead, Essex CO9 3HX

18th century weatherboarded watermill on the River Colne. Internal waterwheel drove two pairs of French Burr millstones. Also contains remains of two pairs of stones which were steam driven, although the engine, boiler and drive mechanism now no longer exist.
Grant Recipient/Owner: Essex County Council
Access contact: Mr M N Hoyle
Tel: 01621 828162 **Fax:** 01621 828764
Opening Arrangements: By prior arrangement with Mr M N Hoyle of Essex County Council Planning Department, County Hall, Chelmsford, Essex CM1 1QH (te.01621 828162). There is limited access to the Mill this year due to on-going restoration work.
Heritage Open Days: No
[P] No
[♿] No. Disabled WC: No. Guide Dogs: No
[£] No

Grange Farm Barns

Little Dunmow, Essex CM6 3HY

Wooden barns, probably 15th century or earlier.
Grant Recipient/Owner: Mr John Kirby
Access contact: Mr John Kirby
Tel: 01371 820205
Opening Arrangements: By prior telephone arrangement.
Heritage Open Days: No
[P] Yes. Spaces: 6
[♿] No. Disabled WC: No. Guide Dogs: Yes
[£] No

Harwich Redoubt Fort

behind 29 Main Road, Harwich, Essex CO12 3LT

180ft diameter circular fort commanding the harbour entrance built in 1808 to defend the port against a Napoleonic invasion. Surrounded by a dry moat, there are 11 guns on the battlements. 18 casements which originally sheltered 300 troops in seige conditions now house a series of small museums.
Website Address: www.harwich-society.com
Grant Recipient/Owner: Harwich Society
Access contact: Mr A Rutter
Tel: 01255 503429 **Fax:** 01255 503429
Email Address: theharwichsociety@quista.net
Opening Arrangements: 1 May - 31 August: daily 10am - 5pm. Rest of year: Sundays only from 10am - 4pm.
Heritage Open Days: Yes
[P] No
[♿] No. Disabled WC: No. Guide Dogs: Yes
[£] Yes
Adult: £1.00
Child: Accompanied children free.
Other: £1.00

Hylands House

Hylands Park, London Road, Widford, Chelmsford, Essex CM2 8WQ

Grade II* listed building, surrounded by 600 acres of landscaped parkland, partly designed by Humphrey Repton. Built c1730, the original house was a red brick Queen Anne style mansion, subsequent owners set about enlarging the property, which produced a neo-classical style house. Internal inspection of the house reveals its Georgian and Victorian features.
Grant Recipient/Owner: Chelmsford Borough Council
Access contact: Ms Linda Pittom
Tel: 01245 606396 **Fax:** 01245 250783
Opening Arrangements: Sundays, Mondays and Bank Holidays (except Christmas Day) throughout the year 11am - 6pm. Group visits by prior arrangement with Ms Linda Pittom, Hylands House Manager, Leisure Services, Chelmsford Borough Council, Civic Centre, Duke Street, Chelmsford, Essex CM1 1JE (tel.01245 606396). Events programme. 4 disabled parking spaces.
Heritage Open Days: Yes
[P] Yes. Spaces: 54
[♿] Yes. Disabled WC: Yes. Guide Dogs: Yes
[£] Yes
Adult: £3.00
Child: Free (under 12)
Other: £2.00

John Webb's Windmill

Fishmarket Street, Thaxted, Essex

Brick tower mill built in 1804 consisting of five floors. Has been fully restored as a working mill. On two floors there is a museum of rural and domestic bygones. There is also a small picture gallery of early photographs of the mill and the surrounding countryside.
Grant Recipient/Owner: Thaxted Parish Council
Access contact: Mr L A Farren
Tel: 01371 830285 **Fax:** 01371 830285
Opening Arrangements: May - September: Saturdays, Sundays and Bank Holidays 2 - 6pm. Conducted parties at other times by prior arrangement with Mr L A Farren, Borough Hill, Bolford Street, Thaxted, Essex CM6 2PY (tel.01371 830285). Wheelchair access to ground floor only. Parking in Thaxted.
Heritage Open Days: Yes
[P] No
[♿] Partial. Disabled WC: No. Guide Dogs: Yes
[£] Yes
Adult: 50p
Child: 25p

Maldon Moot Hall

Maldon, Essex

15th century listed building which once housed a police station and still has the exercise yard, a brickbuilt spiral staircase with brick handrail, courtroom and council chamber. Access to the roof gives good views of the Blackwater estuary and surrounding district.
Grant Recipient/Owner: The Town Clerk
Access contact: The Town Clerk
Tel: 01621 857373 **Fax:** 01621 850793
Email Address: maldontowncouncil@u.genie.co.uk
Opening Arrangements: By prior telephone arrangement with the Town Clerk of Maldon Town Council on 01621 857373. Otherwise open August - end of October Saturday afternoons for visits at 2 and 3.30pm. (This may be extended). Wheelchair access to ground floor only.
Heritage Open Days: Yes
[P] No
[♿] Partial. Disabled WC: No. Guide Dogs: Yes
[£] Yes

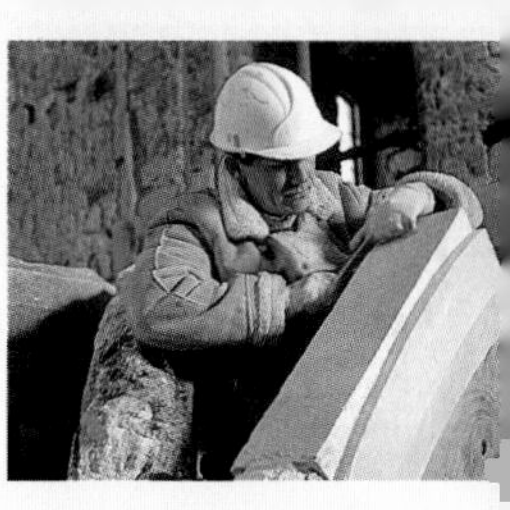
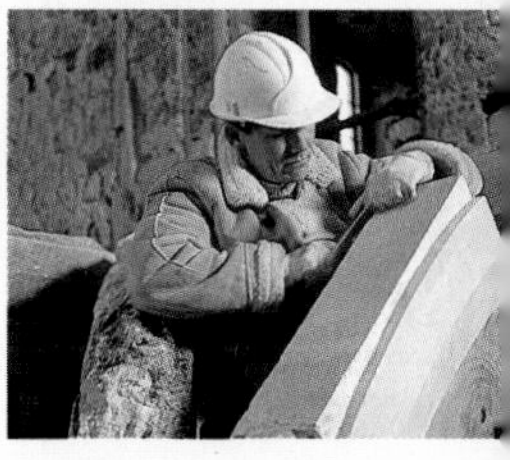
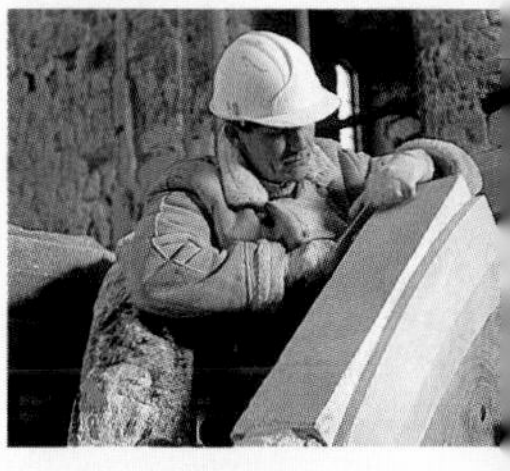
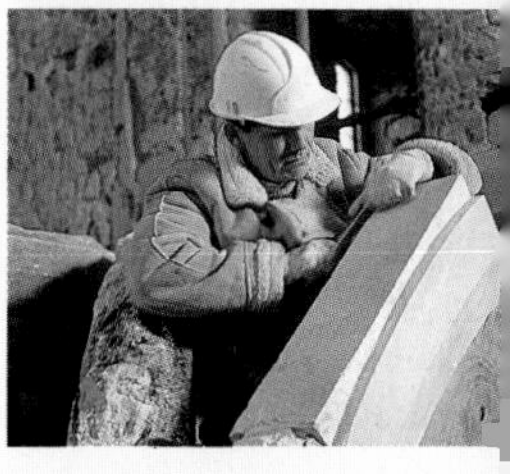
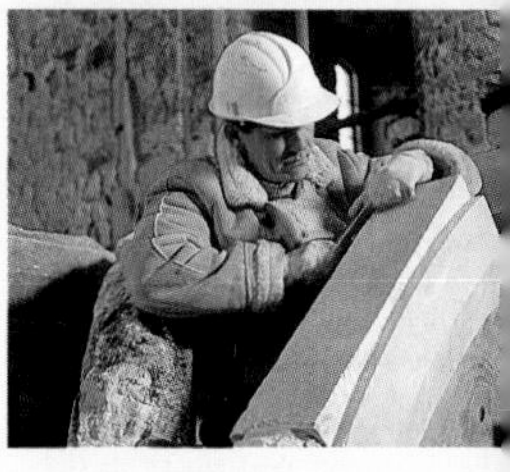
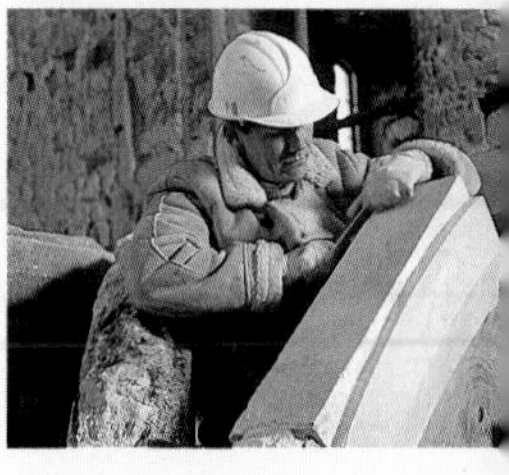
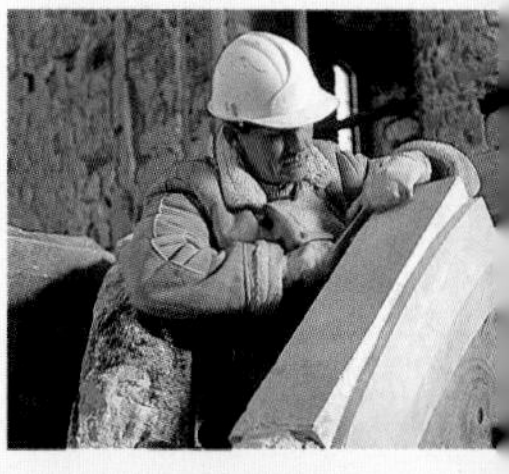

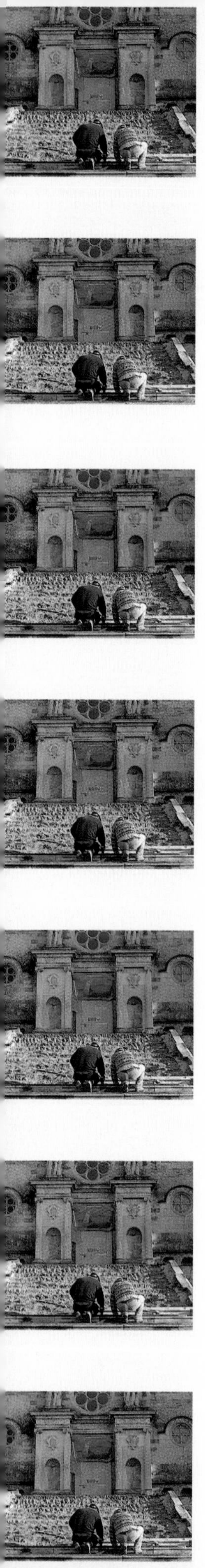

Adult: £1.00
Child: 50p
Other: 50p (senior citizens)

Old Friends Meeting House

High Street, Stebbing, Essex

The Stebbing Meeting House is the earliest Quaker meeting House in Essex. Built circa 1674 it is a particularly fine and complete example and its historical importance is recognised by its Grade II* listing.

Grant Recipient/Owner: The Trustees of the Old Friends Meeting House
Access contact: Mr J B Newbrook
Tel: 01371 856464 **Fax:** 01371 856464
Email Address: jimnewbrook@aol.com
Opening Arrangements: By prior telephone arrangement.
Heritage Open Days: Yes
P Yes. Spaces: 10
♿ Yes. Disabled WC: Yes. Guide Dogs: Yes
£ No

Rainham Hall

The Broadway, Rainham, Essex RM13 9YN

Georgian house built in 1729 to a symmetrical plan and with fine wrought iron gates, carved porch and interior panelling plasterwork.

Website Address: www.nationaltrust.org.uk
Grant Recipient/Owner: The National Trust
Access contact: Thames & Chilterns Regional Office
Tel: 01494 528051 **Fax:** 01494 463310
Opening Arrangements: April to end October: Wednesdays and Bank Holiday Mondays 2 - 6pm. Saturdays by written arrangement (Thames & Chilterns Regional Office, Hughenden Manor, High Wycombe, Buckinghamshire, HP14 4LA). Wheelchair access to ground floor. Guide dogs by prior arrangement. Parking on street (pay and display).
Heritage Open Days: No
P See above
♿ Partial. Disabled WC: Yes. Guide Dogs: See above
£ Yes
Adult: £2.10
Other: No group reductions.

St Mary

Mundon, Essex

Listed Grade I church, now redundant and owned by the Friends of Friendless Churches since 1975. Two-tier timber-framed weatherboarded tower of the 16th century and roughly contemporary north porch. The nave is partly 14th century and retains a complete set of 18th century box pews. The chancel is also Georgian but with simple 19th century fittings. There is a naïve Baroque trompe l'oeil painting of murals on the east wall.

Grant Recipient/Owner: Friends of Friendless Churches
Access contact: Mr Matthew Saunders
Tel: 020 7236 3934 **Fax:** 020 7329 3677
Email Address: ancientmonuments@talk21.com
Opening Arrangements: Open at all reasonable times.
Heritage Open Days: Yes
P No
♿ Partial. Disabled WC: No. Guide Dogs: Yes
£ No

Stansted Windmill

Millside, Stansted Mountfitchet, Essex CM24 8BL

Brick tower mill, built 1787 and a scheduled ancient monument. Ceased working in 1910 but most of the original machinery remains in situ. Given in trust to the village by Lord Blyth in 1935.

Grant Recipient/Owner: Stansted Mountfitchet Council
Access contact: Mrs D P Honour
Tel: 01279 647213 **Fax:** 01279 813160
Opening Arrangements: April - October: first Sunday of each month 2 - 6pm; plus Bank Holiday Sundays and Mondays and every Sunday in August. Parties by prior arrangement with Mrs D P Honour, 59 Blythwood Gardens, Stansted, Essex CM24 8HH (tel.01279 647213). For school groups contact Mrs Minshull (01279 812230). Children must be accompanied. Small souvenir shop.
Heritage Open Days: No
P No
♿ No. Disabled WC: No. Guide Dogs: No
£ Yes
Adult: 50p
Child: 25p
Other: £20.00 (for group guided tour)

Steeple Bumpstead Moot Hall

Steeple Bumpstead, nr. Haverhill, Essex CB9 7DQ

Elizabethan two-storey timber-framed building with jettied upper hall, hipped tiled roof supported by crown post and surmounted by mutilated stone lion at the apex. Originally considered to have been a guildhall but subsequently housed a school founded in 1592. Currently used for meetings and public library.

Grant Recipient/Owner: The Moot Hall (Old School) Trustees
Access contact: Mr P E Bruty
Tel: 01440 730558
Opening Arrangements: Thursdays 2 - 4pm, at other times by prior written arrangement with Mr P E Bruty of the Moot Hall (Old School) Trustees, 5 Blois Road, Steeple Bumpstead, nr. Haverhill, Essex CB9 7BN (tel.01440 730558). Wheelchair and guide dog access to ground floor only. Parking on street.
Heritage Open Days: No
P See above
♿ Partial. Disabled WC: No. Guide Dogs: Yes
£ No

Stock Windmill

Mill Lane, Stock, Ingatestone, Essex

Early 19th century tower mill, modernised in the late 1890s. Five floors, all of which may be visited. The mill has patent sails driving 3 pairs of French Burr millstones. The mill is in working order and occasionally grinds flour.

Grant Recipient/Owner: Essex County Council
Access contact: Mr M Hoyle
Tel: 01621 828162 **Fax:** 01621 828764
Opening Arrangements: April - September: second Sunday of each month 2 - 5pm, plus any reasonable time by prior arrangement for guided visits. Admission charge for guided group visit only.
Heritage Open Days: No
P Yes. Spaces: 6
♿ No. Disabled WC: No. Guide Dogs: Yes
£ Yes
Adult: £2.00 (guided)
Child: £1.50 (guided)
Other: £2.00 (guided)

Thorrington Tide Mill

Brightlingsea Road, Thorrington, Colchester, Essex

Weatherboarded watermill built in 1831 on a creek off the River Colne. The breastshot water wheel is external and drives two pairs of French Burr millstones, a sack hoist and a reel separator. There is provision for a drive from an external portable engine. The mill has been restored and is in working order.

Grant Recipient/Owner: Essex County Council
Access contact: Mr M Hoyle
Tel: 01621 828162 **Fax:** 01621 828764
Opening Arrangements: March - September: last Sunday of each month and Bank Holiday Mondays 2 - 5pm, plus guided group visits at other times by prior arrangement. Admission charge for group guided visits only. Wheelchair access to ground floor with assistance, there is always someone available to help when mill is open. Disabled people may be dropped off at mill door.
Heritage Open Days: No
P Yes. Spaces: 8
♿ Partial. Disabled WC: No. Guide Dogs: Yes
£ Yes
Adult: £2.00 (guided)
Child: £1.50 (guided)
Other: £2.00 (guided)

GLOUCESTERSHIRE

Abbey Gatehouse

Tewkesbury, Gloucestershire

The gatehouse dates from 1500 and was restored in 1849. It has only one very fine room on the first floor. Steep staircase.

Website Address: www.landmarktrust.co.uk
Grant Recipient/Owner: The Landmark Trust
Access contact: Ms Victoria Piggott
Tel: 01628 825920 **Fax:** 01628 825417
Email Address: vpiggott@landmarktrust.co.uk
Opening Arrangements: The Landmark Trust is an independent charity, which rescues small buildings of historic or architectural importance from decay or unsympathetic improvement. Landmark's aim is to promote the enjoyment of these historic buildings by making them available to stay in for holidays. Abbey Gatehouse can be rented by anyone, at all times of the year, for periods ranging from a weekend to three weeks. Bookings can be made by telephoning the Booking Office on 01628 825925. As the building is in full-time use for holiday accommodation, it is not normally open to the public. However the public can view the building by prior arrangement by telephoning the access contact (Victoria Piggott on 01628 825920) to make an appointment. Potential visitors will be asked to write to confirm the details of their visit.
Heritage Open Days: No
P Yes. Spaces: 1
♿ No. Disabled WC: No. Guide Dogs: No
£ No

Acton Court

Latteridge Road, Iron Acton, Gloucestershire BS17 1TJ

Seat of the Poyntzes, an influential courtier family who died out in the 17th century. Their moated medieval manor house has gone, but a Tudor wing survives. This was constructed in 1534 to accommodate King Henry VIII, Queen Anne Boleyn and part of their retinue. The state rooms are unfurnished, but contain important traces of original decoration.

Grant Recipient/Owner: Rosehill Corporation
Access contact: Ms Clare Standen
Tel: 01454 228224
Opening Arrangements: Guided tours by prior arrangement June to mid-September. Please contact Clare Standen for further details. Acton Court will also be open for five weekends in the period June to October. Further details from Clare Standen and on the English Heritage website in the Spring.
Heritage Open Days: No
P Yes. Spaces: 30
♿ No. Disabled WC: No. Guide Dogs: Yes
£ Yes
Adult: £4.00
Child: £3.00

Beach Hall Gazebo

Witcombe Park, Great Witcombe, Gloucestershire

Summerhouse, dated 1697, interior altered in the 19th century. Formerly stood at corner of walled garden.

Grant Recipient/Owner: Mrs Diana Hicks-Beach
Access contact: Mrs M Hicks-Beach
Tel: 01452 863591
Opening Arrangements: By prior arrangement with Mrs M Hicks-Beach, Witcombe Farm, Great Witcombe, Gloucestershire (tel.01452 863591). Donation requested for St. Mary's Church.
Heritage Open Days: No
P Yes. Spaces: 20
♿ Partial. Disabled WC: No. Guide Dogs: Yes
£ No

Berkeley Castle

Berkeley, Gloucestershire GL13 9BQ

Begun in 1117 and in the same family for nearly 850 years. Scene of the murder of Edward II and beseiged by Oliver Cromwell. The State Apartments contain collections of furniture, tapestries, and rare paintings by English and Dutch masters. Part of the Berkeley silver is on display in the Dining Room.

Grant Recipient/Owner: Mr R J Berkeley
Access contact: Mr D Attwood
Tel: 01453 810332
Opening Arrangements: April - May: Tuesday - Sunday 2 - 5pm; June and September: Tuesday - Saturday 11am - 5pm and Sundays 2 - 5pm; July and August: Monday - Saturday 11am - 5pm and Sundays 2 - 5pm; October: Sundays 2 - 4.30pm; Bank Holiday Mondays 11am - 5pm. Last admission half an hour before closing time. Grounds open until 6pm (5.30pm in October).
Heritage Open Days: No
P Yes. Spaces: 150
♿ No. Disabled WC: No. Guide Dogs: Yes
£ Yes
Adult: £5.50
Child: £3.00
Other: £4.50

Chastleton House

Chastleton, Moreton-in-Marsh, Gloucestershire GL56 0SU

Jacobean house filled with a mixture of rare and everyday objects, furniture and textiles collected since 1612. Continually occupied for 400 years by the same family. Emphasis here lies on conservation rather than restoration.

Website Address: www.nationaltrust.org.uk
Grant Recipient/Owner: The National Trust
Access contact: The Custodian
Tel: 01608 674355 **Fax:** 01608 674355
Opening Arrangements: 4 April to 3 November: Wednesdays to Saturdays. Times: April to September 1 - 5pm (last admission 4pm); October and November 1 - 4pm (last admission 3pm). Booking is essential at all times (tel. 01494 755585 between 1.30 - 4.30pm Tuesday to Friday). Wheelchair access to ground floor and parts of garden.
Heritage Open Days: No
P Yes. Spaces: 50
♿ Partial. Disabled WC: Yes. Guide Dogs: Yes
£ Yes
Adult: £5.20
Child: £2.60
Other: £13.00 (family). Groups by written arrangement only.

Chavenage

Tetbury, Gloucestershire GL8 8XP

Elizabethan Manor House (c1576), contains tapestry rooms, furniture and relics from the Cromwellian Period. Has been the home of only two families since the time of Elizabeth I.

Website Address: www.chavenage.com
Grant Recipient/Owner:
Trustees of the Chavenage Settlement
Access contact: Miss Caroline Lowsley-Williams
Tel: 01666 502329 **Fax:** 01453 836778
Email Address: caroline@chavenage.com
Opening Arrangements: May - September: Thursdays, Sundays and Bank Holidays 2 - 5pm; plus Easter Sunday and Monday. Groups at other times by prior arrangement. Limited access for wheelchair users (ground floor only).
Heritage Open Days: No
P Yes. Spaces: 40
♿ Partial. Disabled WC: Yes. Guide Dogs: Yes
£ Yes
Adult: £4.00
Child: £2.00

Court Farm Dovecote

Quenington, Cirencester, Gloucestershire GL7 5BN
Reputed to be dovecote mentioned in 1338, belonging to the Knights Hospitallers, but possibly 17th century. Small round structure of rubble stone with conical stone slate roof with retractable lantern "lid". Contains 600 dove holes stacked at an angle one above another inside wall, above rat rail around which moves revolving ladder on central wooden pin.
Grant Recipient/Owner: Mrs B Gollins
Access contact: Mrs B Gollins
Tel: 01285 750371 **Fax:** 01285 750322
Opening Arrangements: By prior arrangement.
Heritage Open Days: No
P Yes. Spaces: 5
♿ Yes. Disabled WC: No. Guide Dogs: Yes
£ No

East Banqueting House

Calf Lane, Chipping Campden, Gloucestershire
The East Banqueting House stands opposite the West Banqueting House across a broad terrace that ran in front of Sir Baptist Hick's mansion, which was deliberately destroyed by the Royalists in 1645 only 30 years after it had been built. It is elaborately decorated with spiral chimney stacks, finials and ebullient strapwork parapets. Steep staircases.
Website Address: www.landmarktrust.co.uk
Grant Recipient/Owner: The Landmark Trust
Access contact: Ms Victoria Piggott
Tel: 01628 825920 **Fax:** 01628 825417
Email Address: vpiggott@landmarktrust.co.uk
Opening Arrangements: The Landmark Trust is an independent charity, which rescues small buildings of historic or architectural importance from decay or unsympathetic improvement. Landmark's aim is to promote the enjoyment of these historic buildings by making them available to stay in for holidays. East Banqueting House can be rented by anyone, at all times of the year, for periods ranging from a weekend to three weeks. Bookings can be made by telephoning the Booking Office on 01628 825925. As the building is in full-time use for holiday accommodation, it is not normally open to the public. However the public can view the building by prior arrangement by telephoning the access contact (Victoria Piggott on 01628 825920) to make an appointment. Potential visitors will be asked to write to confirm the details of their visit. Parking available in town only.
Heritage Open Days: No
P No
♿ No.
£ No

Ebley Mill

Westward Road, Stroud, Gloucestershire GL5 4UB
19th century riverside textile mill, now restored and converted into offices occupied by Stroud District Council. Has Gothic-style clock tower and block designed by George Bodley.
Website Address: www.stroud.gov.uk
Grant Recipient/Owner: Stroud District Council
Access contact: Mr D Marshall
Tel: 01453 754646 **Fax:** 01453 754934
Email Address: information@stroud.gov.uk
Opening Arrangements: Monday - Thursday 8.45am - 5pm, Fridays 8.45am - 4.30pm (closed Bank Holidays). Tours by prior arrangement.
Heritage Open Days: No
P Yes. Spaces: 30
♿ Yes. Disabled WC: Yes. Guide Dogs: Yes
£ No

Great House Farm

Hasfield, Gloucestershire GL19 4LQ
16th, 17th and 19th century former manor house of stone, timber-frame and brick construction.
Grant Recipient/Owner: Hasfield Estate Trust
Access contact: Mr D Banwell
Tel: 01452 780206
Opening Arrangements: By prior arrangement between 1 April and the end of September.
Heritage Open Days: No
P Yes. Spaces: 6
♿ Yes. Disabled WC: Yes. Guide Dogs: Yes
£ No

Newark Park

Ozleworth, nr. Wotton-under-Edge, Gloucestershire GL12 7PZ
Tudor hunting lodge converted into a castellated county house by James Wyatt.
Website Address: www.ntrustsevern.org.uk
Grant Recipient/Owner: The National Trust
Access contact: South Gloucestershire Office
Tel: 01452 814213
Opening Arrangements: Provisional: April to September Wednesday and Thursdays 2 - 5pm. Viewing arrangements are under review for 2001. Contact South Gloucestershire Office (01452 814213) for confirmation.
Heritage Open Days: No
P Yes. Spaces: 10
♿ No. Disabled WC: No. Guide Dogs: No
£ Yes
Adult: £2.50

Painswick Rococo Garden

Painswick, Gloucestershire GL6 6TH
18th century garden with contemporary buildings situated in a Cotswold combe. Winding woodland walks, formal vistas and early spring show of snowdrops.
Website Address: www.rococogarden.co.uk
Grant Recipient/Owner: Lord Dickinson
Access contact: Mr P R Moir
Tel: 01452 813204 **Fax:** 01452 813204
Email Address: paulmoir@rococogarden.co.uk
Opening Arrangements: Second Wednesday in January - 30 November: Wednesday - Sunday and Bank Holidays 11am - 5pm, plus daily May - September 11am - 5pm. Groups by prior arrangement. Access is possible for wheelchair users but not easy.
Heritage Open Days: No
P Yes. Spaces: 80
♿ Partial. Disabled WC: Yes. Guide Dogs: Yes
£ Yes
Adult: £3.30
Child: £1.75
Other: £3.00 (senior citizens)

St Mary Magdalene Chapel

Hillfield Gardens, London Road, Gloucester, Gloucestershire
Chancel of former church serving the inmates of St Mary Magdalene Hospital, originally a leper hospital, then later almshouses. Medieval graffiti visible on exterior, perhaps mementos of visiting pilgrims. Interior contains south and west doorways rebuilt after the church was demolished in 1861 and tomb of 13th century lady, removed from St Kyneburgh's Chapel near the South Gate in 1550.
Grant Recipient/Owner:
Gloucester Historic Buildings Trust Ltd
Access contact: Mr Malcolm J Watkins
Tel: 01452 396620 **Fax:** 01452 396622
Email Address: culture@gloucester.gov.uk
Opening Arrangements: By prior arrangement with Mr Malcolm J Watkins, Heritage Manager, Cultural Services, Gloucester City Council, Herbert Warehouse, The Docks, Gloucestershire GL1 2EQ (tel.01452 396620), plus part of the Heritage Open Days weekend. Exterior accessible at all reasonable times in public park. Wheelchair access to interior with assistance (entrance steps to be negotiated).
Heritage Open Days: Yes
P No
♿ Partial. Disabled WC: No. Guide Dogs: Yes
£ No

Stancombe Park Temple

Dursley, Gloucestershire GL11 6AU
One in a series of buildings built in the folly gardens at Stancombe Park, in the form of a Greek temple.
Grant Recipient/Owner: Mr N D Barlow
Access contact: Mrs G T Barlow
Tel: 01453 542815
Opening Arrangements: All year by prior telephone arrangement.
Heritage Open Days: No
P Yes. Spaces: 50
♿ No. Disabled WC: No. Guide Dogs: Yes
£ No

Stanley Mill

Kings Stanley, Stonehouse, Gloucestershire GL10 3HQ
Built 1813, with large addition c1825, of Flemish bond red brick with ashlar dressings and Welsh slate roof. Early example of fireproof construction (which survived a major fire in 1884).
Grant Recipient/Owner: Mr Peter Griffiths
Access contact: Mr Mark Griffiths
Tel: 01453 824444
Opening Arrangements: By prior written arrangement. Parking available by prior arrangement.
Heritage Open Days: No
P See above
♿ No. Disabled WC: No. Guide Dogs: No
£ No

Stanway House (Kitchen Court)

Stanway, Gloucestershire
Exterior of Kitchen Court. Courtyard surrounded by domestic buildings including 18th century brewhouse and servants quarters, and 19th century kitchen range. Adjoins Jacobean manor house.
Grant Recipient/Owner:
The Trustees of the Lord Wemyss Trust
Access contact: Lord Neidpath
Tel: 01386 584469 **Fax:** 01386 584688
Email Address: neidpath@btinternet.com
Opening Arrangements: Exterior only. 25 March, 20 May, 30 June, 7 July, and 13 July - 28 September: Mondays - Fridays.
Heritage Open Days: No
P Yes. Spaces: 10
♿ No. Disabled WC: No. Guide Dogs: Yes
£ Yes
Adult: £1.00
Child: Free
Other: £1.00

Sudeley Castle

Winchcombe, nr. Cheltenham, Gloucestershire GL54 5JD
Historic house containing elements from the Tudor, Stuart and Victorian periods. Former home of Queen Katherine Parr and Headquarters of Prince Rupert during the Civil War. Visitors have included Henry VIII, Anne Boleyn, Elizabeth I, Charles I and George III. St Mary's Church, restored by Sir George Gilbert Scott, contains the tomb of Katherine Parr.
Website Address: www.stratford.co.uk/sudeley
Grant Recipient/Owner: The Trustees of Sudeley Castle
Access contact: Mr Timothy Baylis
Tel: 01242 602308 **Fax:** 01242 602959
Email Address: tim.baylis@sudeley.org.uk
Opening Arrangements: Gardens, grounds, shop, exhibition and plant centre: daily 3 March - 28 October 10.30am - 5.30pm; Castle apartments and St Mary's Church: daily 31 March - 28 October 11am - 5pm, restaurant open 10.30am - 5.30pm. Wheelchair access to gardens, shop and restaurant only.
Heritage Open Days: No
P Yes. Spaces: 700
♿ See above. Disabled WC: No. Guide Dogs: Yes
£ Yes
Adult: £6.20 (Castle & Gardens), £4.70 (Gardens & Exhibition).
Child: £3.20 (Castle & Gardens), £2.50 (Gardens & Exhibition).
Other: £5.20 (Castle & Gardens), £3.70 (Gardens & Exhibition).

Wick Court

Overton Lane, Arlingham, Gloucestershire GL2 7JJ
Medieval, 16th and 17th century Grade II* listed manor house with a range of farm buildings enclosed by a moat. The house is now a Farms for City Children centre.
Grant Recipient/Owner: Farms for City Children
Access contact: Ms Heather Tarplee
Tel: 01452 741023 **Fax:** 01452 741023
Opening Arrangements: By prior arrangement.
Heritage Open Days: No
P Yes. Spaces: 20
♿ Partial. Disabled WC: Yes. Guide Dogs: Yes
£ Yes
Adult: £2.50 (guided tour)

GREATER MANCHESTER

1830 Warehouse

Museum of Science & Industry in Manchester, Liverpool Road, Castlefield, Manchester, Greater Manchester M3 4FP
Former railway warehouse, c1830, originally part of the Liverpool Road Railway Station (the oldest surviving passenger railway station in the world) which was the terminus of the Liverpool and Manchester Railway built by George Stephenson and his son Robert. Now part of the Manchester Museum of Science and Industry.
Grant Recipient/Owner:
Museum of Science & Industry in Manchester
Access contact: Ms Kathryn Morgan
Tel: 0161 832 2244 **Fax:** 0161 833 1471
Email Address: marketing@msim.org.uk
Opening Arrangements: Daily (except 24/25/26 December) 10am - 5pm.
Heritage Open Days: No
P Yes. Spaces: 50
♿ Yes. Disabled WC: Yes. Guide Dogs: Yes

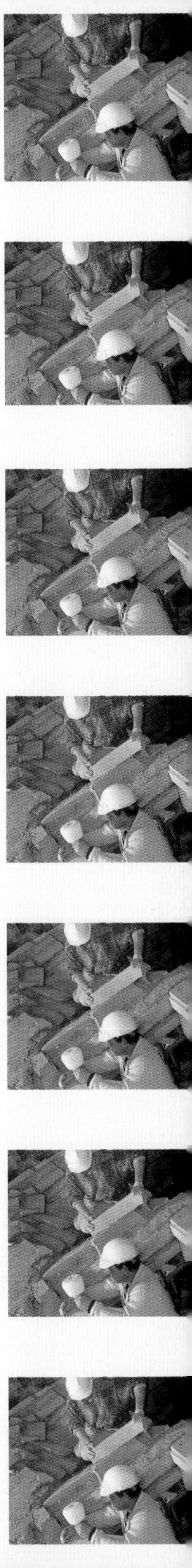

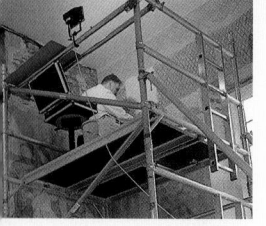
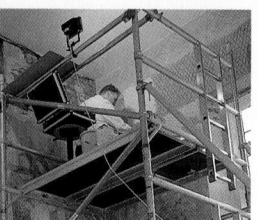
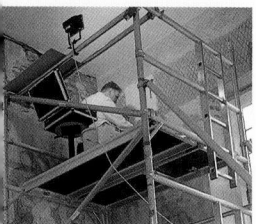
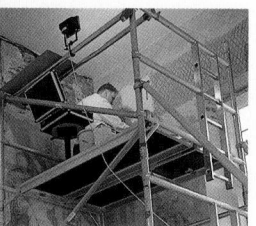
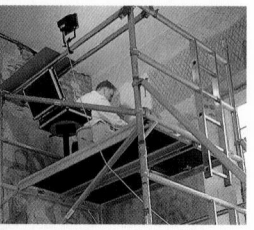
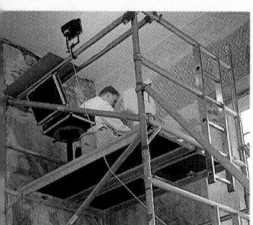
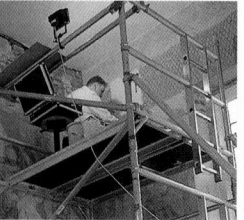

£ Yes
Adult: £6.50
Child: £2.00 for special exhibitions, free to permanent collections.
Other: £3.50 concessions. Group rates also available.

Albion Warehouse

Penny Meadow, Ashton-under-Lyne, Greater Manchester
School, now warehouse. Built 1861-2 by Paull and Ayliffe in Italianate style.
Grant Recipient/Owner: G A Armstrong Ltd
Access contact: G A Armstrong Ltd
Tel: 061 339 5353 **Fax:** 061 339 5353
Opening Arrangements: All year except Christmas Day and New Year's Day.
Heritage Open Days: No
P Yes. Spaces: 80
No. Disabled WC: No. Guide Dogs: Yes
£ No

Alkrington Hall

Middleton, Manchester, Greater Manchester M24 1WD
Grade II* listed building, built 1735, by Giacomo Leoni for Darcy Lever in Classical style. Sub-divided into four dwellings in 1995 but much of the original interior detail survives.
Grant Recipient/Owner: Mr James Pickup
Access contact: Mr James Pickup
Tel: 0161 643 7713
Opening Arrangements: By prior written arrangement with Mr James Pickup, Alkrington Hall East, Middleton, Manchester M24 1WD.
Heritage Open Days: Yes
P Yes. Spaces: 4
Partial. Disabled WC: No. Guide Dogs: No
£ No

Heaton Hall

Heaton Park, Prestwich, Greater Manchester M25 2SW
18th century country house designed by James Wyatt in 1772, containing scrolling plasterwork, wall and ceiling paintings, furniture and paintings. Set in 650 acres of parkland.
Grant Recipient/Owner: Manchester City Council
Access contact: Ms Ruth Shrigley
Tel: 0161 234 1456 **Fax:** 0161 236 2880
Opening Arrangements: Easter - end of October: Wednesday - Sunday 10am - 5.30pm (opening arrangements correct at time of going to print but may change, please contact Manchester City Art Galleries, Room 1025, Lloyd Street, Manchester M60 2LA (tel.0161 234 1456) for current details. Wheelchair access to ground floor only.
Heritage Open Days: No
P Yes. Spaces: 200
Partial. Disabled WC: No. Guide Dogs: Yes
£ No

Manchester Jewish Museum

190 Cheetham Hill Road, Manchester M8 8LW
Grade II* listed building located in the premises of the former Spanish and Portuguese Synagogue, completed in 1874 in Moorish style containing stained-glass windows and distinctive cast-iron fitments.
Website Address: www.manchesterjewishmuseum.com
Grant Recipient/Owner:
Trustees of the Manchester Jewish Museum
Access contact: Mr Don Rainger
Tel: 0161 834 98798 **Fax:** 0161 834 9801
Email Address: info@manchesterjewishmuseum.com
Opening Arrangements: Monday - Thursday 10.30am - 4pm, Sundays 10.30am - 5pm and Fridays by prior arrangement. Closed 1 January; 8, 9 & 15 April; 28 & 29 May; 18, 19 & 27 September; 2, 3, 9 & 10 October; 24-26 December. Early closing (1pm) 17 & 26 September; 1 & 8 October. May participate in the Heritage Open Days weekend on the Sunday, please contact Museum for current information. Groups only by prior arrangement. Wheelchair access to ground floor only. Street parking immediately outside museum.
Heritage Open Days: Yes
P See above
Partial. Disabled WC: No. Guide Dogs: Yes
£ Yes
Adult: £3.50
Child: £2.60
Other: £8.50 (family)

Manchester Law Library

14 Kennedy Street, Manchester M2 4BY
Built in Venetian Gothic style in 1885 to a design by Manchester architect, Thomas Hartas. Has stained glass windows by Evans of Birmingham.
Website Address: www.manchester-law-library.co.uk
Grant Recipient/Owner:
Manchester Incorporated Law Library Society

Access contact: Mrs Julia Bragg
Tel: 0161 236 63128 **Fax:** 0161 236 6119
Email Address: librarian@manchester-law-library.co.uk
Opening Arrangements: By prior telephone or written arrangement.
Heritage Open Days: Yes
P No
No. Disabled WC: No. Guide Dogs: Yes
£ No

Portico Library

57 Mosley Street, Manchester, Greater Manchester M2 3HY
19th century subscription library with Reading Room and Gallery, situated in Manchester city centre. 25,000 volumes, mainly 19th century. Particularly valuable for Victorian studies. Gallery shows mainly art exhibitions of new and established artists' work - local, national and international. Occasionally literary/local history exhibitions also shown.
Grant Recipient/Owner:
The Trustees of the Portico Library
Access contact: Emma Marigliano
Tel: 0161 236 6785 **Fax:** 0161 236 6803
Opening Arrangements: Monday - Friday 9.30am - 4.30pm, except Christmas period - usually 22 December - 2 January. Trial period of Sunday openings currently in operation and for 3rd Sunday of each month. Closed Bank Holidays.
Heritage Open Days: Yes
P No
No. Disabled WC: No. Guide Dogs: Yes
£ No

Smithills Hall

Smithills Dean Road, Bolton, Greater Manchester BL1 7NP
Hall, some parts of which date back to the medieval period. The early East Wing contains collection of mainly 17th century oak furniture. The largely Victorian West Wing has been recently conserved and includes Victorian period rooms, a shop, toilets and refreshments.
Grant Recipient/Owner:
Bolton Metropolitan Borough Council
Access contact: Ms Angela Thomas
Tel: 01204 332212
Opening Arrangements: Easter - end of September: Tuesday - Saturday 11am - 5pm, plus Sundays 2 - 5pm. Groups at other times of the year by prior arrangement with Ms Angela Thomas, Senior Keeper, Bolton Central Museum and Art Gallery, Le Mans Crescent, Bolton, Greater Manchester, BL1 (tel.01204 332212). Access for wheelchair users to lower floor only.
Heritage Open Days: Yes
P Yes. Spaces: 40
Partial. Disabled WC: Yes. Guide Dogs: Yes
£ Yes
Adult: £3.00
Child: £1.50
Other: £1.50 (concessions)

Tonge Hall

Middleton, Manchester, Greater Manchester M24 2JT
Grade II* listed timber-framed hall c1580s with 18th and 19th century alterations. The Hall is a good example of 16th century carpentry and has a distinctive display of quatrefoil panels to front and left elevations.
Grant Recipient/Owner: Mr Norman Wolstonecroft
Access contact: Mr Norman Wolstonecroft
Tel: 0161 643 2995 or 01224 867893
Opening Arrangements: By prior arrangement. Wheelchair access to ground floor only, disabled parking at front door.
Heritage Open Days: Yes
P Yes. Spaces: 100
Partial. Disabled WC: No. Guide Dogs: Yes
£ No

Victoria Baths

Hathersage Road, Manchester, Greater Manchester M13 0FE
Swimming pool complex built 1906, with 2 pools, Turkish and Russian Bath suite, Aerotone and extensive stained glass and tilework. Currently closed awaiting restoration.
Grant Recipient/Owner:
The Manchester Victoria Baths Trust
Access contact: Miss Gill Wright
Tel: 0161 224 2020/8437 **Fax:** 0161 224 0707
Opening Arrangements: Afternoons of Heritage Open Days and at other times by prior arrangement with Miss Gill Wright of the Manchester Victoria Baths Trust, 3 Birch Polygon, Rusholme, Manchester M14 5HX (tel.0161 224 2020/8437). On street parking during the week and use of large adjacent car park at weekends by arrangement. Wheelchair access to ground floor with assistance.
Heritage Open Days: Yes
P Yes. Spaces: 5'
Partial. Disabled WC: No. Guide Dogs: Yes
£ No

HAMPSHIRE

Avington Park

Winchester, Hampshire S021 1DB
Palladian mansion dating back to the 11th century, enlarged in 1670 by the addition of two wings and a classical Portico surmounted by three statues. Visited by Charles II and George IV. Has highly decorated State rooms and a Georgian church in the grounds.
Website Address: www.avingtonpark.co.uk
Grant Recipient/Owner: Mrs Sarah Bullen
Access contact: Mrs Sarah Bullen
Tel: 01962 7792608 **Fax:** 01962 779864
Email Address: sarah@avingtonpark.co.uk
Opening Arrangements: May - September: Sundays and Bank Holidays 2.30 - 5.30pm. At other times by prior arrangement.
Heritage Open Days: Yes
P Yes. Spaces: 150
Yes. Disabled WC: Yes. Guide Dogs: Yes
£ Yes
Adult: £3.50
Child: £1.75

Breach Farm Barn

Sherfield-on-Loddon, Hampshire
15th century barn. Timber frame of 5 bays on a masonry base, with central entrances (projecting slightly on the east side). Cruck construction. Weather-boarded walls. Listed Grade II*.
Grant Recipient/Owner: Mr D Mitchell
Access contact: Mr D Mitchell
Tel: 01962 734275
Opening Arrangements: By prior telephone arrangement at any reasonable time.
Heritage Open Days: No
P Yes. Spaces: 20
Partial. Disabled WC: No. Guide Dogs: Yes
£ No

Breamore Home Farm Tithe Barn

Breamore, nr. Fordingbridge, Hampshire SP6 2DD
Late 16th century tithe barn with dwarf walls supporting a timber-frame and external cladding under a tiled roof with massive timber aisle posts, double doors in the centre of each side and an area of threshing boards.
Grant Recipient/Owner:
Breamore Ancient Buildings Conservation Trust
Access contact: Mr Michael Hulse
Tel: 01725 5128588 **Fax:** 01725 512858
Opening Arrangements: Weekdays by prior arrangement with Mr Michael Hulse of Breamore House.
Heritage Open Days: Yes
P Yes. Spaces: 10
Yes. Disabled WC: No. Guide Dogs: Yes
£ No

The Deanery

The Close, Winchester, Hampshire SO23 9LS
Earliest remains are late 12th or early 13th century, fragments visible in a stairwell cupboard of the Prior's Hall. The hall itself is probably 13th century in origin. Until 1539 the Prior's House, now home of the Dean of Winchester.
Grant Recipient/Owner:
Dean & Chapter of Winchester Cathedral
Access contact: Mrs Judy George
Tel: 01962 857225 **Fax:** 01962 857201
Email Address:
cathedral.office@winchester-cathedral.org.uk
Opening Arrangements: By prior written arrangement with the Cathedral Office, 1 The Close, Winchester, Hampshire SO23 9LS. Open Heritage Open Days 2 - 4pm.
Heritage Open Days: Yes
P No
No. Disabled WC: No. Guide Dogs: No
£ Yes
Adult: £2.50
Child: £1.00
Other: £2.00 (per head for prebooked groups).

Manor Farmhouse

Hambledon, Hampshire PO7 4RW
12th century stone built house with later medieval wing. 17th and 18th century re-fronting of part and minor renovation.
Grant Recipient/Owner: Mr Stuart Mason
Access contact: Mr Stuart Mason
Tel: 023 92632433
Opening Arrangements: By prior arrangement only.
Heritage Open Days: No
P Yes. Spaces: 2
Yes. Disabled WC: No. Guide Dogs: Yes
£ No

St Agatha

Market Way, Portsmouth, Hampshire
Italianate basilica of 1894 built for the Anglo Catholic priest, Fr R Dolling. Highly decorated interior of marble, alabaster, polished granite, carved stone and coloured glass. The apse has a sgraffito mural c1901 by Heywood Summer.
Grant Recipient/Owner: St Agatha's Trust
Access contact: J D Maunder
Tel: 01329 230330   **Fax:** 01329 230330
Opening Arrangements: October - May: Saturdays and Sundays 10am - 2pm; June - September: Saturdays, Sundays and Wednesdays 10am - 3pm. At other times by prior written arrangement with St Agatha's Trust, 9 East Street, Fareham, Hampshire PO16 0BW (tel.01329 230330).
Heritage Open Days: Yes
P Yes. Spaces: 50
♿ Partial. Disabled WC: No. Guide Dogs: Yes
£ No

The Vyne

Sherborne St John, Basingstoke, Hampshire RG24 9HL
Built in the early 16th century for Henry VIII's Lord Chamberlain. The house acquired a classical portico mid 17th century (the first of its kind in England). Tudor chapel with Renaissance glass, Palladian staircase, old panelling and fine furniture. Grounds, containing wild garden, lakes and woodland walks.
Website Address: www.nationaltrust.org.uk
Grant Recipient/Owner: The National Trust
Access contact: Mr Jonathan Ingram
Tel: 01256 881337   **Fax:** 01256 881720
Email Address: svygen@smtp.ntrust.org.uk
Opening Arrangements: House: 31 March to 4 November: daily except Thursdays and Fridays (but open Good Friday) 1 - 5pm (last entry 4.30pm). Grounds: weekends in February and March 11am - 4.30pm; 31 March to 4 November: daily except Thursdays and Fridays (but open Good Friday) 11am - 6pm. Wheelchair access to ground floor. Car park is 140 metres from house. New car park to open late summer (with capacity for 140 cars and 3 coaches) will be located 450 metres from house (buggy service available). Disabled drivers will be able to park by house.
Heritage Open Days: No
P Yes. Spaces: 70
♿ Partial. Disabled WC: Yes. Guide Dogs: Yes
£ Yes
Adult: £5.50
Child: £2.75
Other: £13.75 (family). £4.50 (group rate per head Mondays, Tuesdays and Wednesdays only).

Whitchurch Silk Mill

28 Winchester Street, Whitchurch, Hampshire RG28 7AL
Grade II* watermill built c1800 and has been in continuous use as a silk weaving mill since the 1820s. Now a working museum, the winding, warping and weaving machinery installed between 1890 and 1927 produces traditional silks for theatrical costume, historic houses, fashion and artworks.
Grant Recipient/Owner:
Hampshire Building Preservation Trust Ltd
Access contact: Mill Manager
Tel: 01256 892065   **Fax:** 01256 893882
Opening Arrangements: Mill and shop: Tuesday - Sunday 10.30am - 5pm (last admission 4.15pm). Mill and shop closed Mondays (except Bank Holidays) and between Christmas and New Year. Access for wheelchair users to ground floor of Mill, shop and gardens. Free parking next to Mill, 2 disabled spaces next to shop.
Heritage Open Days: No
P Yes. Spaces: 20
♿ Partial. Disabled WC: Yes. Guide Dogs: Yes
£ Yes
Adult: £3.00
Child: £1.50
Other: £2.50

Woodgreen Village Hall

Hale Road, Woodgreen, Fordingbridge, Hampshire SP6 2BQ
Village hall built in 1930 with murals depicting life in the village covering every wall.
Grant Recipient/Owner:
Woodgreen Village Hall Committee
Access contact: Mrs Angela Sales
Tel: 01725 512288
Opening Arrangements: Any time but advisable to book first (contact Mrs Sales, or Mrs Windel on 01725 512529).
Heritage Open Days: No
P Yes. Spaces: 20
♿ Yes. Disabled WC: Yes. Guide Dogs: Yes
£ Yes

Adult: 50p
Child: 50p
Other: 50p

HEREFORDSHIRE

Chandos Manor

Rushall, Ledbury, Herefordshire HR8 2PA
Farmhouse, probably late C16 with C18 extensions. Timber-frame, partly rendered.
Website Address:
Grant Recipient/Owner: Mr Richard White
Access contact: Mr Richard White
Tel: 01531 660208
Opening Arrangements:
Easter - September: Sundays by prior arrangement.
Heritage Open Days: No
P Yes. Spaces: 12
♿ No. Disabled WC: No. Guide Dogs: Yes
£ No
Adult: Donations to charity.

Chapel Farm

Wigmore, nr. Leominster, Herefordshire HR6 9UQ
Timber-framed farmhouse c1400 of rectangular plan, originally a hall-house with first floor inserted in the 16th century. Contains an open roof with foliate carved windbraces, ornate post-heads and late Elizabethan wall painting. Associated with the Lollards around 1400.
Grant Recipient/Owner: Mr M Pollitt
Access contact: Mr M Pollitt
Opening Arrangements: By prior written arrangement Mondays (except Bank Holidays) May - September 2 - 4.30pm. Maximum 2 persons per visit. No children under 16 and no animals.
Heritage Open Days: No
P Yes. Spaces: 1
♿ No. Disabled WC: No. Guide Dogs: No
£ No

College of the Vicars Choral

Cathedral Close, Hereford, Herefordshire HR1 2NG
College, c1473, of coursed sandstone rubble with a Welsh slate roof and 7 stepped buttress stacks with ashlar chimneys.
Grant Recipient/Owner:
Dean & Chapter of Hereford Cathedral
Access contact: Andrew Eames
Tel: 01432 374200   **Fax:** 01432 374220
Email Address: office@herefordcathedral.co.uk
Opening Arrangements: Sundays (except Palm Sunday, Easter Day and Christmas Day) 11am - 12.30pm and on other days by prior arrangement with the Chapter Clerk, Cathedral Office, 5 College Cloisters, Cathedral Close, Hereford HR1 2NG (tel.01432 374200).
Heritage Open Days: No
P No
♿ Yes. Disabled WC: Yes. Guide Dogs: Yes
£ No

Croft Castle

nr. Leominster, Herefordshire HR6 9PW
Home of the Croft family since Domesday (with a break of 170 years from 1750). Walls and corner towers date from 14th and 15th centuries interior mainly 18th century. The park contains an avenue of 350 year old Spanish chestnuts. The walled garden is independently maintained by the Croft Trust and contains various historic fruit trees and plants.
Website Address: www.ntrustsevern.org.uk
Grant Recipient/Owner: The National Trust
Access contact: Mr David Atkins
Tel: 01568 780246   **Fax:** 01568 780462
Email Address: croft@smtp.ntrust.org.uk
Opening Arrangements: Castle: 31 March to 29 April: Saturday and Sunday, Good Friday and Bank Holiday Monday. 2 May to 30 September: daily except Mondays and Tuesdays (but open Bank Holiday Mondays). 6 October to 4 November: Saturday and Sundays. Times: 1- 5pm (closes 4.30pm in Ocotber and November). Park and Croft Ambrey: daily.
Heritage Open Days: No
P Yes. Spaces: 300
♿ Yes. Disabled WC: Yes. Guide Dogs: No
£ Yes
Adult: £3.90
Child: £1.95
Other: £10.00 (family). £2.00 (parking).

Eastnor Castle

nr. Ledbury, Herefordshire HR8 1RL
Norman-style castellated mansion set in the western slopes of the Malvern Hills. Constructed 1812 - 1820 and designed by Sir Robert Smirke, the castle has 15 state and other rooms fully-furnished and open to visitors. The decoration includes tapestries, paintings, armour and a

drawing room by Augustus Pugin.
Website Address: www.eastnorcastle.com
Grant Recipient/Owner: Mr J Hervey-Bathurst
Access contact: Mr S Foster
Tel: 01531 633160   **Fax:** 01531 631776
Email Address: enquiries@eastnorcastle.com
Opening Arrangements: Easter - end of September: Sundays and Bank Holiday Mondays, plus every day in July and August except Saturdays. Wheelchair access to grounds, tea room and ground floor with assistance (always available).
Heritage Open Days: No
P Yes. Spaces: 150
♿ Partial. Disabled WC: Yes. Guide Dogs: Yes
£ Yes
Adult: £5.00
Child: £3.00
Other: £2.75 (senior citizens)

Hergest Court

Kington, Herefordshire
House dates back to 1267 and was the ancestral home of the Clanvows and Vaughan families. It is an unusual example of a fortified manor in the Welsh Marches. It has literary associations with Sir John Clanvowe and Lewis Glyn Cothi.
Grant Recipient/Owner: Mr W L Banks
Access contact: Mr W L Banks
Tel: 01544 230160   **Fax:** 01544 230160
Email Address: banks@hergest.kc3.co.uk
Opening Arrangements:
By prior arrangement with the Hergest Estate Office, Kington, Herefordshire HR5 3EG (telephone and fax: 01544 230160). Bookings by phone or fax with five days notice. Wheelchair access to ground floor only.
Heritage Open Days: Yes
P Yes. Spaces: 5
♿ Partial. Disabled WC: No. Guide Dogs: Yes
£ Yes
Adult: £5.00

Lower Brockhampton

Brockhampton-by-Bromyard, Herefordshire WR6 5UH
A late 14th century moated manor house with a detached half-timbered 15th century gatehouse. Also, the ruins of a 12th century chapel. Woodland walks.
Website Address: www.ntrustsevern.org.uk
Grant Recipient/Owner: The National Trust
Access contact: Mr Les Rogers
Tel: 01885 488099
Email Address: brockhampton@smtp.ntrust.org.uk
Opening Arrangements:
House: 1 April to 31 October: daily except Mondays and Tuesdays (but open Bank Holiday Mondays). Times: April to October 12.30 - 5pm (closes at 4pm in October). Weekends in July and August 10.30am to 5pm. Wheelchair access to ground floor of house, chapel and estate. Two car parks, 1½ miles and 200 yards from house. Parking for disabled near house.
Heritage Open Days: No
P Yes. Spaces: 60
♿ Partial. Disabled WC: No. Guide Dogs: Yes
£ Yes
Adult: £2.70
Other: £6.75 (family). £1.50 (car park). Estate free to pedestrians.

The Painted Room

Town Council Offices, Church Street, Ledbury, Herefordshire HR8 1DH
The wall paintings, discovered here in 1989, are a unique example of domestic wall painting dating from the Tudor period. They are clearly the work of a commoner, created to imitate the rich tapestries or hangings that would have been found in the homes of the gentry.
Grant Recipient/Owner: Ledbury Town Council
Access contact: Mrs J McQuaid
Tel: 01531 632306   **Fax:** 01531 631193
Email Address: ledburytowncouncil@ledbury.org.uk
Opening Arrangements: Easter - end of September: guided tours Monday - Friday 11.30am - 3pm. Rest of year: Mondays, Tuesdays, Wednesdays and Fridays, if member of staff available. Town centre car parks nearby.
Heritage Open Days: Yes
P See above
♿ No. Disabled WC: No. Guide Dogs: Yes
£ No

St Katharine's Hall and Chapel

High Street, Ledbury, Herefordshire
Part of Hospital founded in 1232 by Bishop Hugh Foliot, the Hall and Chapel were built c1330-40 of local stone rubble with a tiled gabled roof.
Grant Recipient/Owner:
The Trustees of St Katharine's Hospital Charity
Access contact:
Clerk to the Trustees of St Katharine's Hospital Charity
Tel: 01432 374200   **Fax:** 01432 374220

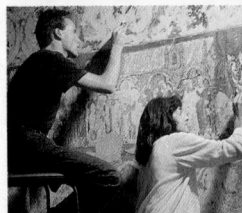
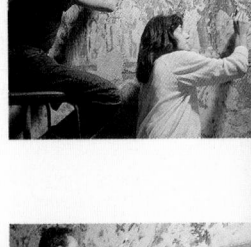
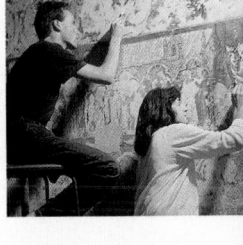
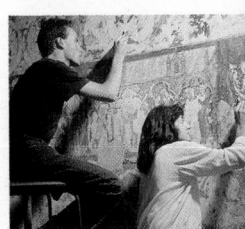
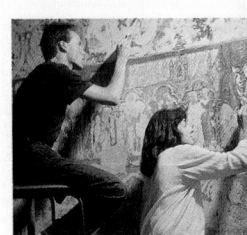
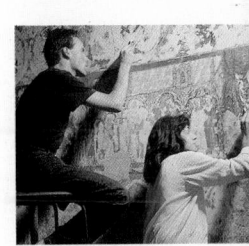
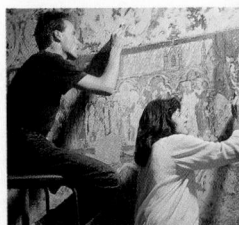

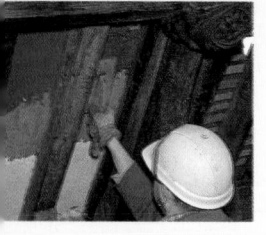

Email Address: office@herefordcathedral.co.uk
Opening Arrangements:
The Hall is normally open during the week. Access to the Chapel is by prior arrangement with the Clerk to the Trustees of St Katharine's Hospital Charity, Cathedral Office, 5 College Cloisters, Hereford HR1 2NG (tel.01432 374200).
Heritage Open Days: No
P No
No. Disabled WC: No. Guide Dogs: No
£ No

HERTFORDSHIRE

Bishop Seth Ward's Almshouse

Market Hill, High Street, Buntingford, Hertfordshire
Almshouses c1684 (possibly by Robert Hooke) for Seth Ward, Bishop of Exeter and Salisbury, mathematician and astronomer and friend of Wren.
Grant Recipient/Owner: Mr R C Woods
Access contact: Mr R C Woods
Tel: 01763 271974 **Fax:** 01763 271974
Opening Arrangements: The exterior and gardens by prior arrangement with Mr R C Woods, Chairman of the Trustees, Bishop Seth Ward's Almshouse Trust, 58 Hare Street Road, Buntingford, Hertfordshire SG9 9HN (tel.01763 271974).
Heritage Open Days: No
P No
No. Disabled WC: No. Guide Dogs: No
£ No

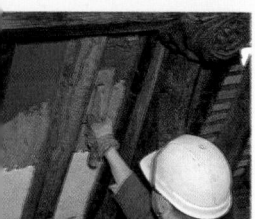

Bridgewater Monument

Aldbury, Hertfordshire
The monument was erected in 1832 to commemorate the Duke of Bridgewater. It is the focal point of Ashridge Estate which runs across the borders of Hertfordshire and Buckinghamshire along the main ridge of the Chilterns.
Website Address: www.nationaltrust.org.uk
Grant Recipient/Owner: The National Trust
Access contact: Property Manager
Tel: 01442 851227 **Fax:** 01442 842062
Opening Arrangements: 1 April to 29 October: Mondays to Thursdays 2 - 5pm, Saturdays, Sundays and Bank Holiday Mondays 2 - 5.30pm, (closed Fridays, but open Good Friday). Full wheelchair access, although some routes difficult in bad weather.
Heritage Open Days: No
P Yes. Spaces: 100
Yes. Disabled WC: Yes. Guide Dogs: Yes
£ Yes
Adult: £1.00
Child: £0.50

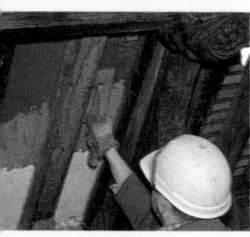

Cromer Windmill

Ardeley, Stevenage, Hertfordshire SG2 7QA
Grade II* postmill dated 1674, last surviving postmill in Hertfordshire. Restored to working order (but not actually working).
Website Address: www.hertsmuseums.org.uk
Grant Recipient/Owner: Ms Cristina Harrison
Access contact: Ms Cristina Harrison
Tel: 01279 843301
Email Address: cristinaharrison@hotmail.com
Opening Arrangements: Open Saturday before National Mill Day, ie. second Sunday in May. Thereafter every Sunday and Bank Holidays, and second and fourth Saturdays until Heritage Open Days 2.30 - 5pm. Wheelchair access to ground floor only but video of upper floors showing all the time. 30 minute video available for schools and other groups. Guided tours. Special parties by prior arrangement with Ms Cristina Harrison, The Forge Museum, High Street, Much Hadham, Hertfordshire SG10 6BS (tel.01279 843301). Refreshments available.
Heritage Open Days: Yes
P Yes. Spaces: 20
Partial. Disabled WC: No. Guide Dogs: Yes
£ Yes
Adult: £1.50
Child: 25p

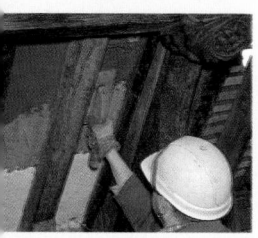

Ducklake House Wallpainting

Springhead, Ashwell, Baldock, Hertfordshire SG7 5LL
16th century wall painting, located on the ground floor, containing classical grotesques holding cartouches.
Grant Recipient/Owner: Mr P W H Saxton
Access contact: Mr P W H Saxton
Opening Arrangements: By prior written arrangement to view the wall painting only. Parking available.
Heritage Open Days: No
P Yes. Spaces: 1
No. Disabled WC: No. Guide Dogs: No
£ No

Knebworth House

Knebworth, nr. Stevenage, Hertfordshire SG3 6PY
Originally a Tudor manor house, rebuilt in gothic style in 1843. Contains rooms in various styles, which include a Jacobean banqueting hall. Set in 250 acres of parkland with 25 acres of formal gardens. Home of the Lytton family since 1490.
Website Address: www.knebworthhouse.com
Grant Recipient/Owner:
Knebworth House Education & Preservation Trust
Access contact: Miss Jacky Wilson
Tel: 01438 812661 **Fax:** 01438 811908
Email Address: info@knebworthhouse.com
Opening Arrangements: 7-22 April, 26 May - 3 June, 7 July - 4 September: daily; 28 April - 20 May, 9 June - 1 July, 8-30 September: weekends and Bank Holidays. Gardens, Park and playground 11am - 5.30pm, House 12 noon - 5pm (last admission 4.30pm). Groups (20+) all year by prior arrangement. Wheelchair access to ground floor only, disabled parking available at front of house on request. Unlimited parking.
Heritage Open Days: No
P See above
Partial. Disabled WC: Yes. Guide Dogs: Yes
£ Yes
Adult: £7.00 (£6.00 group)
Child: £6.50 (£5.50 group)
Other: £6.50 (senior citizens, £5.50 group).

Old Palace

23 Kneeworth Street, Royston, Hertfordshire SG8 5AB
Built 1610 by James I, much altered (half of original building has subsequently been demolished). Has Georgian façade to the rear, the street frontage is in fact the dividing wall of the original building which has been left exposed following demolition of part of the building.
Grant Recipient/Owner: Mr Peter Franks
Access contact: Mr Peter Franks
Opening Arrangements: By prior written arrangement.
Heritage Open Days: No
P Yes. Spaces: 1
No. Disabled WC: No. Guide Dogs: Yes
£ No

Redbournbury Mill

Redbournbury Lane, Redbourn Road, St Albans, Hertfordshire AL3 6RS
18th century watermill in full working order after 10 year restoration programme following 1987 fire.
Supplementary power from Crossley oil engine.
Grant Recipient/Owner: Mr J T James
Access contact: Mrs A L James
Tel: 01582 792874
Email Address: redbrymill@aol.com
Opening Arrangements: 21 March - 3 October: Sundays 2.30 - 5pm, plus Easter, late May and August Bank Holidays. National Mills Weekend, Heritage Open Days and New Year's Day open all day. Special events throughout the year. Private parties by prior arrangement. Wheelchair access to ground floor only. Refreshments available. Milling demonstrations. Organic flour and bread for sale.
Heritage Open Days: Yes
P Yes. Spaces: 30
Partial. Disabled WC: No. Guide Dogs: No
£ Yes
Adult: £1.50
Child: 80p
Other: 80p

Torilla

11 Wilkins Green Lane, Nast Hyde, Hatfield, Hertfordshire AL10 9RT
'Torilla' (house at Nast Hyde) was built by F R S Yorke in 1935 in the international style and features a flat roof, 2 balconies and a large double height living room. Constructed of concrete with large steel framed windows. F R S Yorke was a key figure in the evolution of modern architecture in Britain.
Grant Recipient/Owner: Mr Alan Charlton
Access contact: Mr Alan Charlton
Tel: 01707 259582 **Fax:** 01707 259583
Opening Arrangements: Sunday 20th May and Sunday 19th August, 11am - 5pm. At other times by prior written arrangement.
Heritage Open Days: No
P Yes. Spaces: 5
Partial. Disabled WC: No. Guide Dogs: Yes
£ No

Woodhall Park

Watton-at-Stone, Hertfordshire
Country house, now school. Designed and built by Thomas Leverton in 1785 in neo-Classical style. Normally associated with London houses, this is one of his few country houses. Highly decorated interiors which include

the Print Room with walls covered in engraved paper, reproductions of paintings with frames, ribbons, chains, busts, candelabra and piers with vases.
Grant Recipient/Owner:
Trustees of R M Abel Smith 1991 Settlement
Access contact:
The Trustees of R M Abel Smith 1991 Settlement
Tel: 01920 830286 **Fax:** 01920 830162
Email Address: woodhallest@dial.pipex.com
Opening Arrangements: At all reasonable times, preferably school holidays, by prior arrangement with the Trustees of R M Abel Smith 1991 Settlement, Estate Office, Woodhall Park, Watton-at-Stone, Hertfordshire SG14 3NF (tel.01920 830286). Wheelchair access to ground floor only. During school holidays there is parking for up to 50 cars, but during school terms this is limited to about 10.
Heritage Open Days: No
P Yes. Spaces: 50
Partial. Disabled WC: No. Guide Dogs: Yes
£ No

KENT

Chiddingstone Castle

Chiddingstone, nr. Edenbridge, Kent TN8 7AD
Tudor mansion subsequently twice remodelled by the Streatfeilds whose seat it was. William Atkinson "Master of the picturesque" is responsible for the romantic design, c1805, of the building as it is today. Rescued from dereliction by Denys Bower in the 20th century, now managed by a charitable trust.
Grant Recipient/Owner:
Trustees of the Denys Eyre Bower Bequest
Access contact: Miss M R Eldridge
Tel: 01892 870347
Opening Arrangements: Easter and Spring Bank Holidays, June - September: Wednesday, Thursdays, Fridays and Sundays; 2 - 5.30pm weekdays, Sundays and Bank Holidays 11.30am - 5.30pm (last admission 5pm). Groups (minimum 20) during winter by prior arrangement. Also school groups when Castle is normally closed by prior arrangement. Wheelchair access to ground floor only but this includes everything except the Egyptian collection.
Heritage Open Days: No
P Yes. Spaces: 50
Partial. Disabled WC: Yes. Guide Dogs: Yes
£ Yes
Adult: £4.00
Child: £2.00 (5-15, under 5 free but must be accompanied by an adult).

Church House

72 High Street, Edenbridge, Kent TN8 5AR
Late 14th century timber-framed farmhouse, now houses the Eden Valley Museum.
Grant Recipient/Owner: Mr M Downing
Access contact: Ms Elisabeth Wright
Tel: 01732 868102 **Fax:** 01732 867866
Email Address: eden_tc@thebarn72.freeserve.co.uk
Opening Arrangements: November - March: Tuesdays - Fridays 2 - 4.30pm; April - October: Tuesdays - Fridays and Sundays 2 - 4.30pm, Saturdays 10am - 4.30pm. Private/educational groups by prior arrangement. Wheelchair access to ground floor only (computer link to provide vision of upstairs under development). Free parking in town centre car park 200yds from House.
Heritage Open Days: Yes
P Yes. Spaces: 150
Partial. Disabled WC: Yes. Guide Dogs: Yes
£ Yes
Adult: £1.50
Child: 75p
Other: 75p

Cobham Hall Dairy

Cobham, Kent DA12 3BL
Gothic-style dairy in grounds of Cobham Hall, built by James Wyatt c1790.
Grant Recipient/Owner: Cobham Hall Heritage Trust
Access contact: Mr N G Powell
Tel: 01474 823371 **Fax:** 01474 825904
Opening Arrangements: Easter - end of August: Hall open Wednesdays and Sundays 2 - 5pm (last tour 4.30pm). Please telephone to confirm opening times. At other times (and coach parties) by prior arrangement. Wheelchair access to ground floor only. Self-guided tour of Gardens and Parkland (historical/conservation tour by prior arrangement). Special events.
Heritage Open Days: No
P Yes. Spaces: 100
Partial. Disabled WC: Yes. Guide Dogs: Yes
£ Yes
Adult: £3.50
Child: £2.50
Other: £2.50 (seniors & groups)

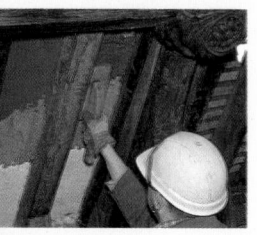

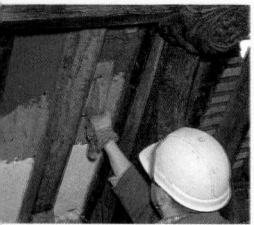

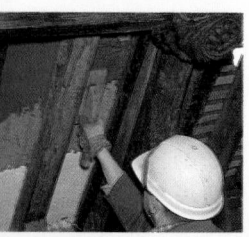

Foord Almshouses

Priestfields, Rochester, Kent ME1 3AF

Main Hall of almshouses built in 1932 of English bond red brick with stone dressings and old tile roof in neo-vernacular style of the 17th century with Baroque reference.

Grant Recipient/Owner:
Trustees of the Foord Almshouses
Access contact: Mr David Hubbard
Tel: 01634 844138
Opening Arrangements: By prior arrangement.
Heritage Open Days: No
P Yes. Spaces: 10
♿ Yes. Disabled WC: Yes. Guide Dogs: Yes
£ No

Gad's Hill Place

Higham-by-Rochester, Kent ME3 7PA

Former home of Charles Dickens, who lived here from 1856 until his death in 1870 whilst writing The Mystery of Edwin Drood. Built c1780 with Dickensian additions, it is now an Independent School and stands in 11 acres of meadowland and gardens.

Grant Recipient/Owner: Gad's Hill School
Access contact: Miss Anne Carter
Tel: 01474 822366 **Fax:** 01474 822977
Opening Arrangements: Easter - October: first Sunday of each month plus Bank Holiday Sundays 2 - 5pm (last admission 4pm). Summer and Christmas Dickens Festivals 11am - 4.30pm. Guided tours at other times by prior arrangement. Access for only certain types of wheelchair, please check with Place for details. Admission charges are provisional at time of going to print, again please check with Place for clarification. Refreshments available.
Heritage Open Days: Yes
P Yes. Spaces: 40
♿ Partial. Disabled WC: Yes. Guide Dogs: Yes
£ Yes
Adult: £2.50 (see above)
Child: £1.50

Herne Windmill

Mill Lane, Herne Bay, Kent CT6 7DR

Kentish smock mill built 1789, worked by wind until 1952 and then by electricity until 1980. Bought by Kent County Council in 1985, which carried out some restoration. Now managed by Friends of Herne Mill on behalf of the County Council. Much of the original machinery is in place, some is run for demonstration and the sails used when the wind conditions permit.

Website Address: www.kentwindmills.co.uk
Grant Recipient/Owner: Kent County Council
Access contact: Mr Ken Cole
Tel: 01227 361326
Opening Arrangements: Easter - end of September: Sundays and Bank Holidays, plus Thursdays in July and August, 2 - 5pm. National Mills Day 11am - 5pm. Wheelchair and guide dog access to ground floor of Mill and meeting room.
Heritage Open Days: No
P Yes. Spaces: 12
♿ Partial. Disabled WC: Yes. Guide Dogs: Yes
£ Yes
Adult: £1.00
Child: 25p (accompanied by adult)

The Hospital of St Thomas the Martyr

Eastbridge, 25 High Street, Canterbury, Kent CT1 2BD

12th century building providing hospitality for pilgrims visiting the shrine of St Thomas Becket at Canterbury Cathedral. Contains two chapels, an undercroft and refectory. Of particular interest is a 12th century fresco of "Our Lord in Glory". Private areas of the Hospital are almshouses for eight people.

Grant Recipient/Owner: Hospital of St Thomas the Martyr, Eastbridge
Access contact: Miss Louise Fittall
Tel: 01227 471688
Opening Arrangements: Monday - Saturday 10am - 4.45pm (except Good Friday, Christmas Day and other occasional Church Festival Days).
Heritage Open Days: No
P No
♿ No. Disabled WC: No. Guide Dogs: Yes
£ Yes
Adult: £1.00
Child: 50p (5-16), under 5s free.
Other: 75p (seniors/students/groups).

Ightham Mote

Ivy Hatch, Sevenoaks, Kent TN15 0NT

Moated manor house covering 650 years of history from medieval times to 1960s. Extended visitor route now includes the newly refurbished north-west quarter with Tudor Chapel, Billiards Room and Drawing Room. Interpretation displays and special exhibition featuring conservation in action.

Website Address:
www.nationaltrust.org.uk/regions/kentesussex
Grant Recipient/Owner: The National Trust
Access contact: The Property Manager
Tel: 01732 810378 **Fax:** 01732 811029
Email Address: kimxxx@smtp.ntrust.org.uk
Opening Arrangements: 1 April - 4 November: daily except Tuesday and Saturday 11am - 5.30pm. Last admission 4.30pm.
Heritage Open Days: No
P Yes. Spaces: 350
♿ Partial. Disabled WC: Yes. Guide Dogs: Yes
£ Yes
Adult: £5.00
Child: £2.50
Other: £12.50 (family), £4.25 (groups). NT members free

Knole

Sevenoaks, Kent TN15 0RP

The largest private house in England, Knole is a fine example of late medieval architecture. It has been the home of the Sackville family since 1603, including four Dukes of Dorset. Knole houses an extensive collection of furnishing and paintings, many in the house since the 17th century, and the prototype of the 'Knole' settee.

Website Address:
www.nationaltrust.org.uk/regions/kentesussex
Grant Recipient/Owner: The National Trust
Access contact: The Property Manager
Tel: 01732 462100 **Fax:** 01732 465528
Email Address: kknxxx@smtp.ntrust.org.uk
Opening Arrangements: 31 March - 4 November: Wednesday - Saturday 12 - 4pm (last admission 3.30pm), Sunday, Bank Holiday Monday and Good Friday 11am - 5pm (last admission 4pm). Garden: May - September: first Wednesday of each month only 12 - 4pm.
Heritage Open Days: No
P Yes. Spaces: 500
♿ Partial. Disabled WC: Yes. Guide Dogs: Yes
£ Yes
Adult: £5.00
Child: £2.50
Other: £12.50 (family), £4.25 (groups). Garden only £1.00, Parking £2.50. NT members free.

Littlebourne Tithe Barn

Church Road, Littlebourne, nr. Canterbury, Kent CT3 1TU

Early 14th century timber-framed aisled barn of 7 and a half bays. Aisled on all four sides with crown-post roof construction, has oak-riven boarding to walls and now thatched in water reed (formerly long straw). The two hipped roof entrances date from 1961.

Grant Recipient/Owner: Canterbury City Council
Access contact: Secretary, Conservation Section
Tel: 01227 862190 **Fax:** 01227 862020
Email Address: conservation@canterbury.gov.uk
Opening Arrangements: Open for events during the year, otherwise at other times by prior arrangement. For details and access, please contact the Conservation Section at Canterbury City Council, Military Road, Canterbury, Kent CT1 1TW (tel.01227 862190).
Heritage Open Days: Yes
P Yes. Spaces: 15
♿ Yes. Disabled WC: Yes. Guide Dogs: Yes
£ No

Nurstead Court

Nurstead Church Lane, Meopham, nr. Gravesend, Kent DA13 9AD

Grade I listed medieval aisled timber-framed hall built 1320, containing massive oak pillars with craved capitals supporting a frame-work of arched braces and tie beams with central crown-post supporting the clay-peg tiled roof. The walls are of knapped flint. Probably built by the Bishop of London, Stephen de Gravesend.

Grant Recipient/Owner: Mrs S M H Edmeades-Stearns
Access contact: Mrs S M H Edmeades-Stearns
Tel: 01474 812121 **Fax:** 01474 815133
Opening Arrangements: Every Wednesday and Thursday in September, plus 3 & 4 October, 2 - 5pm. At other times by prior arrangement.
Heritage Open Days: No
P Yes. Spaces: 30
♿ Yes. Disabled WC: No. Guide Dogs: Yes
£ Yes
Adult: £4.00
Child: £3.00
Other: £3.00 (senior citizens)

Prospect Tower

Belmont Park, Faversham, Kent

This small flint tower stands on the edge of Belmont Park. It was built in 1808 for Lord Harris of Seringapatam as his 'whim', with prize money won in India. The 4th Lord Harris's enthusiasm was cricket. He commandeered the tower as a changing room. Narrow spiral staircase.

Website Address: www.landmarktrust.co.uk
Grant Recipient/Owner: The Landmark Trust
Access contact: Ms Victoria Piggott
Tel: 01628 825920 **Fax:** 01628 825417
Email Address: vpiggott@landmarktrust.co.uk
Opening Arrangements: The Landmark Trust is an independent charity, which rescues small buildings of historic or architectural importance from decay or unsympathetic improvement. Landmark's aim is to promote the enjoyment of these historic buildings by making them available to stay in for holidays. Prospect Tower can be rented by anyone, at all times of the year, for periods ranging from a weekend to three weeks. Bookings can be made by telephoning the Booking Office on 01628 825925. As the building is in full-time use for holiday accommodation, it is not normally open to the public. However the public can view the building by prior arrangement by telephoning the access contact (Victoria Piggott on 01628 825920) to make an appointment. Potential visitors will be asked to write to confirm the details of their visit.
Heritage Open Days: No
P Yes. Spaces: 1
♿ No. Disabled WC: No. Guide Dogs: No
£ No

Roper Gateway

adjacent to 33 St Dunstan's Street, Canterbury, Kent

16th century red brick gateway which originally led to Place House (house of Margaret Roper, daughter of Sir Thomas More). Has a crow stopped gable and a large 4-centred arch with a pair of wooden doors (dating from the 18-19th centuries). Nothing now remains of Place House and the gate now leads to former 19th century brewery buildings. The gateway is clearly visible from St Dunstan's Street.

Grant Recipient/Owner: Canterbury City Council
Access contact: The Secretary Conservation Section
Tel: 01227 862190 **Fax:** 01227 862020
Opening Arrangements: The gateway building can be inspected from St Dunstan's Street and Roper Close. Contact the Conservation Section of Canterbury City Council, Military Road, Canterbury, Kent CT1 1YW (tel.01227 862190) for further information. Parking at West Station.
Heritage Open Days: No
P Yes. Spaces: 100
♿ Yes. Disabled WC: No. Guide Dogs: Yes
£ No

Sissinghurst Tower

Sissinghurst, Cranbrook, Kent TN17 2AB

Red-brick prospect tower and walls - surviving part of an Elizabethan mansion. Surrounded by a world-famous garden. The study where Vita Sackville-West worked and Long Library are open to the public.

Website Address:
www.nationaltrust.org.uk/regions/kentesussex
Grant Recipient/Owner: The National Trust
Access contact: Ms Sarah Cook
Tel: 01580 710700 **Fax:** 01580 710702
Email Address: ksisdc@smtp.ntrust.org.uk
Opening Arrangements: 31 March - 14 October: Tuesday - Friday 1pm - 6.30pm, Saturday, Sunday and Good Friday 10am - 5.30pm. Last admission 30 minutes before close.
Heritage Open Days: No
P Yes. Spaces: 500
♿ Partial. Disabled WC: Yes. Guide Dogs: Yes
£ Yes
Adult: £6.50
Child: £3.00
Other: £16.00 (family)

Somerhill

Tonbridge, Kent TN11 0NJ

Grade I Jacobean mansion with Victorian addition set in 150 acres of parkland. Now used as a school, but original ceilings, panelling and stables have been retained.

Grant Recipient/Owner:
Somerhill Charitable Trust Ltd
Access contact: Diane M Huntingford
Tel: 01732 352124 **Fax:** 01732 363381
Opening Arrangements:
By prior written or telephone arrangement plus the Sunday of the Heritage Open Days weekend. Wheelchair access to ground floor only.
Heritage Open Days: Yes
P Yes. Spaces: 170
♿ Partial. Disabled WC: No. Guide Dogs: Yes
£ No

Willesborough Windmill

Willesborough, Ashford, Kent, TN24 0GQ

Grade II* listed windmill built in 1869 and coaching barn. A 1911 Hornsby 14HP gas oil engine now installed to give auxiliary power. The barn is now enclosed and houses a heritage museum.

Grant Recipient/Owner: Ashford Borough Council
Access contact: Willesborough Windmill Trust

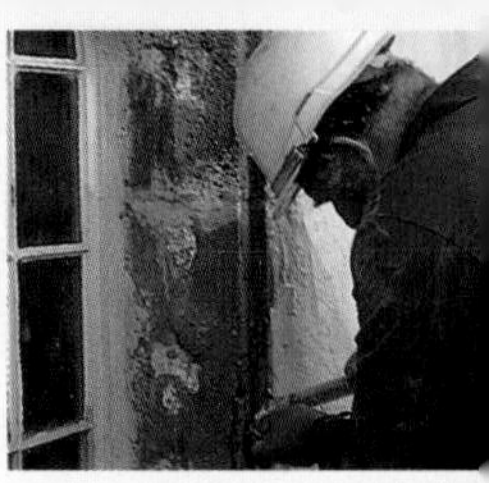
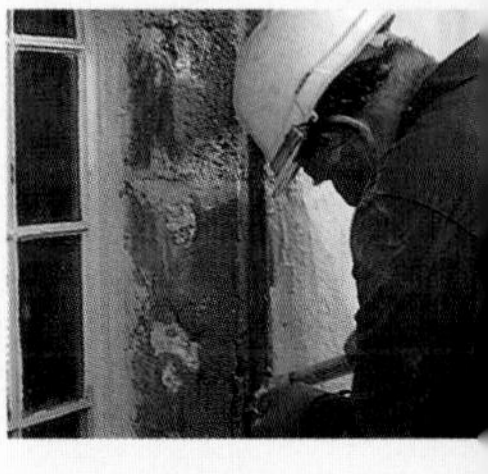
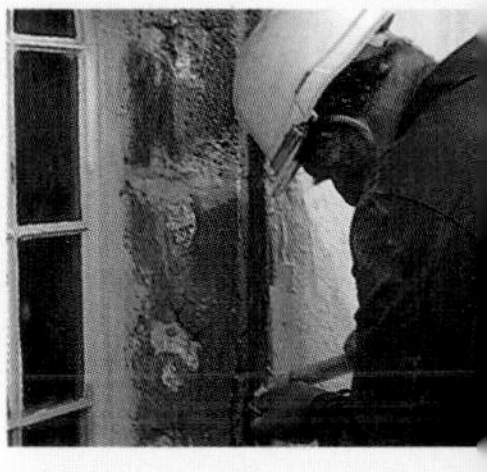
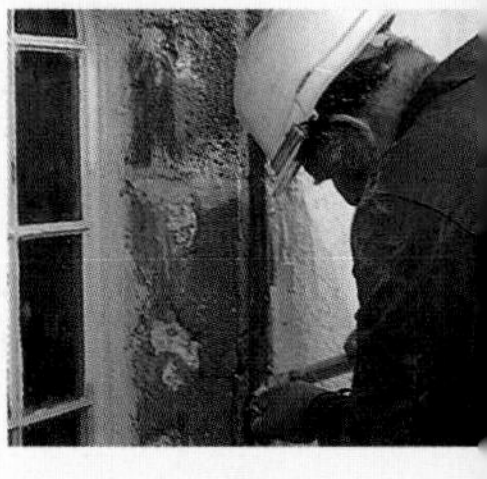
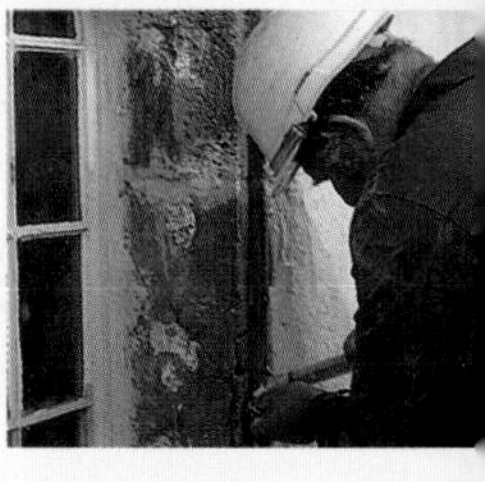
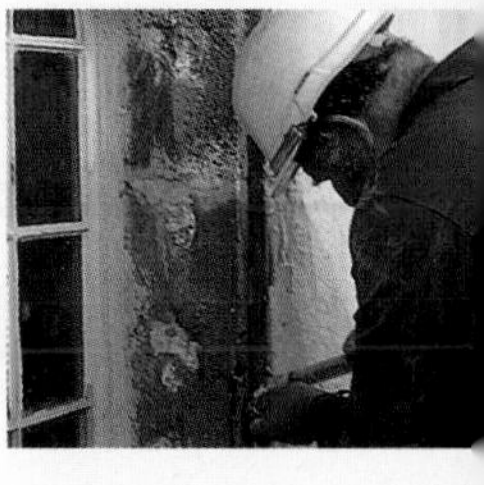
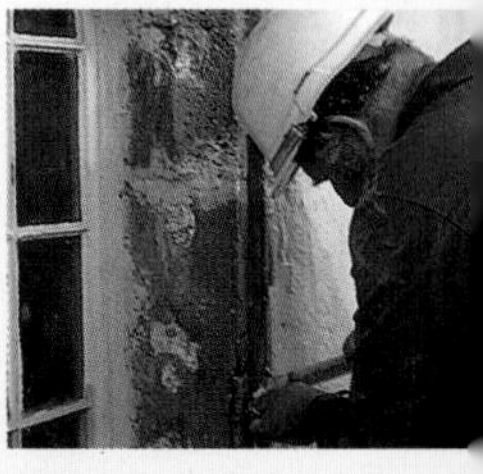

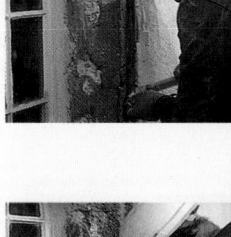

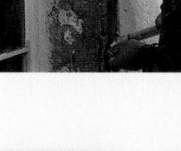

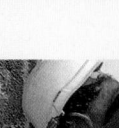

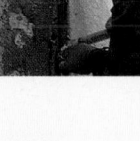

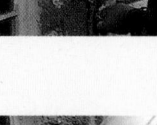

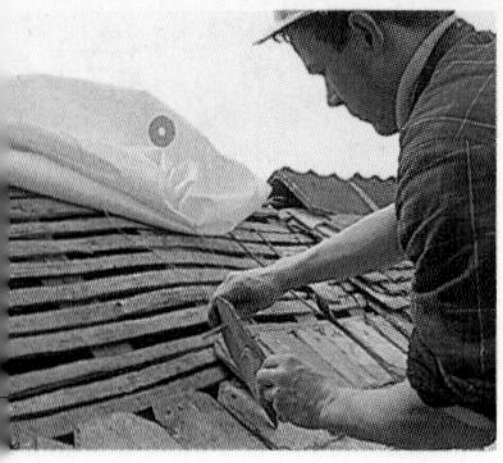
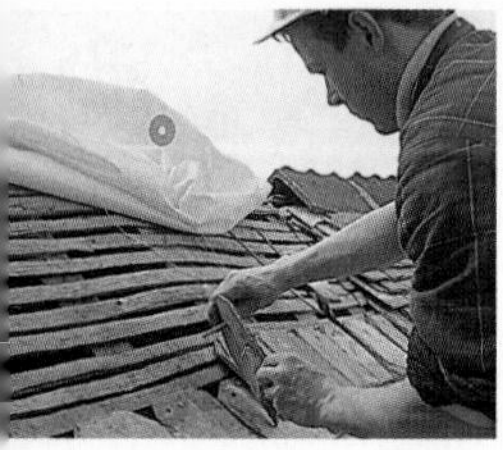
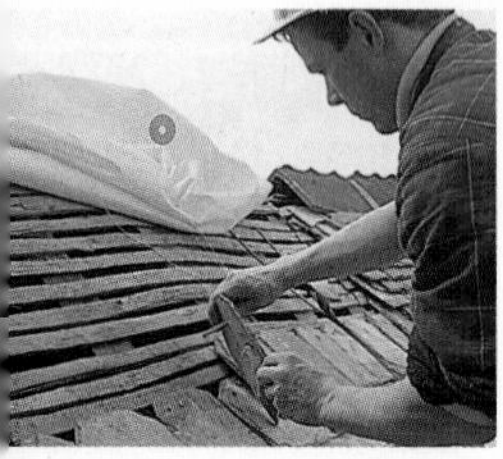
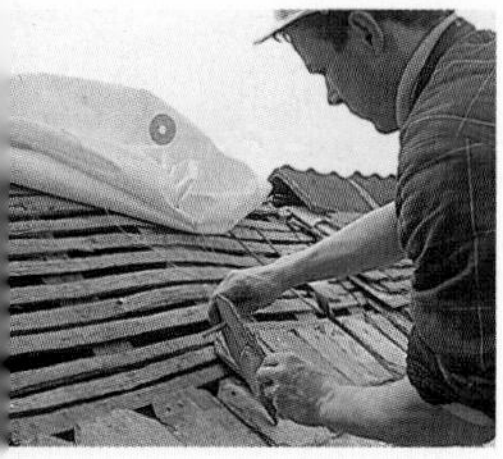
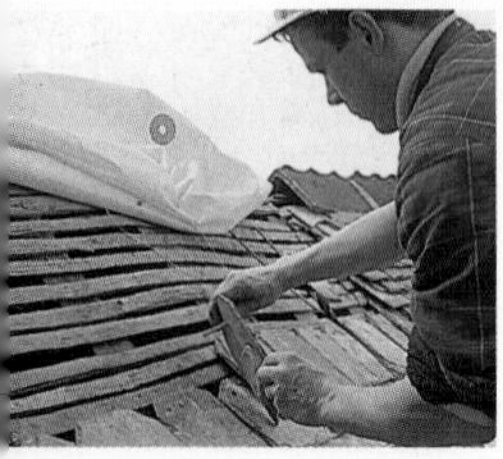
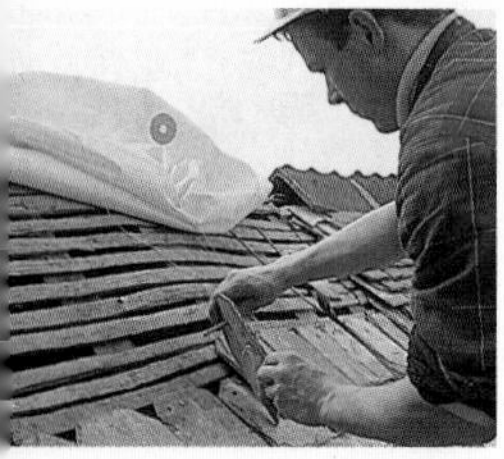
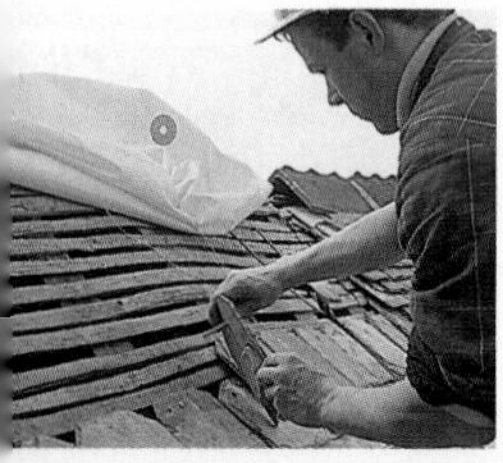

Tel: 01233 661866
Opening Arrangements: April to end September: Saturdays, Sundays and Bank Holiday Mondays 2 -5pm. Wheelchair access to ground floor of mill, all of barn.
Heritage Open Days: Yes
P Yes. Spaces: 30
♿ Partial. Disabled WC: Yes. Guide Dogs: Yes
£ Yes
Adult: £1.00
Child: £0.50
Other: £0.50 (seniors)

LANCASHIRE

Gawthorpe Hall

Padiham, nr. Burnley, Lancashire BB12 8UA
An Elizabethan property in the heart of industrial Lancashire. Restored and refurbished in the mid 19th century by Sir Charles Barry. There are many notable paintings on display loaned to the National Trust by the National Portrait Gallery, and a collection of needlework, assembled by the last family member to live there, Rachel Kay-Shuttleworth.
Website Address: www.nationaltrust.org.uk
Grant Recipient/Owner: The National Trust
Access contact: Property Manager
Tel: 01282 770353 **Fax:** 01282 770353
Email Address: rpmgaw@smtp.ntrust.org.uk
Opening Arrangements: Hall: 1 April to 31 October daily except Mondays and Fridays (but open Good Friday and Bank Holiday Mondays) 1 - 5pm. Garden: all year 10am - 6pm. Wheelchair access to garden only.
Heritage Open Days: No
P Yes. Spaces: 50
♿ See above. Disabled WC: Yes. Guide Dogs: Yes
£ Yes
Adult: £3.00
Child: £1.30
Other: £8.00 (family). Garden free.

Hoghton Tower

Hoghton, Preston, Lancashire PR5 0SH
16th century fortified manor house, ancestral home of the de Hoghton family since William the Conqueror. Associated with many kings and queens (the Banqueting Hall is where James I knighted the Loin of Beef 'Sirloin') and William Shakespeare. Various staterooms open to the public, as well as a Tudor horse-drawn well, dungeons and underground passages.
Grant Recipient/Owner:
Hoghton Tower Preservation Trust
Access contact: Mr John Graver
Tel: 01254 852986 **Fax:** 01254 852109
Opening Arrangements: Guided tours of the house: Bank Holiday Sundays/Mondays (excluding Christmas and New Year); July - September: Monday - Thursday, 11am - 4pm (Sundays 1 - 5pm). Private tours throughout the year by prior arrangement.
Heritage Open Days: No
P Yes. Spaces: 250
♿ No. Disabled WC: No. Guide Dogs: Yes
£ Yes
Adult: £3.00
Child: £2.00
Other: £2.00 (senior citizens & students), £8 (family)

Leighton Hall

Carnforth, Lancashire LA5 9ST
Country House, 1765, probably by J Hird, with earlier remains. Gothic south-east front early 19th century, possibly by Thomas Harrison. Tower at west end of the façade 1870 by Paley and Austin. Ancestral home of the Gillow family with fine furniture, paintings and objets d'art.
Website Address: www.leightonhall.co.uk
Grant Recipient/Owner: Mr Richard Reynolds
Access contact: Mr Richard Reynolds
Tel: 01524 734474 **Fax:** 01524 720357
Email Address: leightonhall@yahoo.co.uk
Opening Arrangements: Daily 1 May - end of September (except Saturdays and non-Bank Holiday Mondays) 2 - 5pm (11.30am - 5pm in August). Groups all year by prior arrangement. The owner reserves the right to close or restrict access to the Hall and grounds for special events (dates to be confirmed). Refreshments available.
Heritage Open Days: No
P Yes. Spaces: 100
♿ Yes. Disabled WC: Yes. Guide Dogs: Yes
£ Yes
Adult: £4.50
Child: £3.00
Other: £4.00 (senior citizen)

Rufford Old Hall

Rufford, nr. Ormskirk, Lancashire L40 1SG
Fine 16th century building with intricately carved movable wooded screen and hammerbeam roof. Owned by the Hesketh family for 250 years, the house contains collections of 16th and 17th century oak furniture, arms, armour and tapestries.
Website Address: www.nationaltrust.org.uk
Grant Recipient/Owner: The National Trust
Access contact: Property Manager
Tel: 01704 821254 **Fax:** 01704 821254
Email Address: rrufoh@smtp.ntrust.org.uk
Opening Arrangements: House: 1 April to 31 October: daily except Thursdays and Fridays (but open Good Friday) 1- 5pm. Garden: as house 12.30pm - 5.30pm. Wheelchair access to garden, tea room and shop.
Heritage Open Days: No
P Yes. Spaces: 130
♿ Partial. Disabled WC: Yes. Guide Dogs: Yes
£ Yes
Adult: £3.80
Child: £1.90
Other: £9.50 (family). £2.00 (garden only).

Stonyhurst College

Stonyhurst, Clitheroe, Lancashire BB7 9PZ
16th century manor house, now home to a Catholic independent boarding and day school. Contains dormitories, library, chapels, school-rooms and historical apartments.
Website Address: www.stonyhurst.ac.uk
Grant Recipient/Owner: Stonyhurst College
Access contact: Miss Frances Ahearne
Tel: 01254 826345 **Fax:** 01254 826732
Opening Arrangements: House: 16 July - 27 August daily (except Friday), plus August Bank Holiday Monday, 1 - 5pm; Gardens: 1 July - 27 August daily (except Friday), plus August Bank Holiday Monday, 1 - 5pm. Limited wheelchair access but assistance is available by prior arrangement. Coach parties by prior arrangement.
Heritage Open Days: No
P Yes. Spaces: 20
♿ Partial. Disabled WC: Yes. Guide Dogs: Yes
£ Yes
Adult: £4.50
Child: £3.50
Other: £3.50

Towneley Hall Art Gallery & Museum

Todmorden Road, Burnley, Lancashire BB11 3RQ
Former home of the Towneley family on outskirts of Burnley, Towneley Hall has been the town's art gallery and museum since 1903. The earliest part of the building dates from c1450. There is a 16th century chapel and Long Gallery, Baroque entrance hall and two reception rooms by Jeffrey Wyat c1820.
Website Address: www.towneleyhall.com
Grant Recipient/Owner: Burnley Borough Council
Access contact: Jackie Sims
Tel: 01282 424213 **Fax:** 01282 436138
Opening Arrangements: Monday - Friday 10am - 5pm, Sunday 12 - 5pm (Saturday closed). Also open Bank Holidays but closed for approximately one week over Christmas and New Year. No parking at site this year due to building works, some rooms may also be closed. Wheelchair access to ground floor only. Refreshments available.
Heritage Open Days: No
P No
♿ Partial. Disabled WC: Yes. Guide Dogs: Yes
£ No

Turton Tower

Chapeltown Road, Turton, nr. Bolton, Lancashire BL7 0HG
Late medieval stone tower house with mainly late 16th and early 19th century alterations and timber-framed additions. Contains period rooms depicting domestic styles in such a building in the 16th, 17th, 19th and early 20th centuries.
Grant Recipient/Owner:
Lancashire County Museums Service
Access contact: Mr Martin Robinson-Dowland
Tel: 01204 8522038 **Fax:** 01204 853759
Email Address: museum@lancashire.co.uk
Opening Arrangements:
February: Sundays 1 - 4pm; March: Saturday - Wednesday 1 - 4pm; April: Saturday - Wednesday 2 - 5pm; May - September: Saturday and Sunday 1 - 5pm, Monday - Thursday 10am - 12 noon and 1 - 5pm; October: Saturday - Wednesday 1 - 4pm; November: Sunday 1 - 4pm. Wheelchair access to ground floor, tea-room and shop. Additional parking for 2 coaches.
Heritage Open Days: No
P Yes. Spaces: 55
♿ Yes. Disabled WC: Yes. Guide Dogs: Yes
£ Yes
Adult: £3.00
Child: £1.50
Other: £1.50

Whalley Abbey

Whalley, Clitheroe, Lancashire BB7 9SS
14th century Cistercian abbey ruins. Exhibition centre on site.
Grant Recipient/Owner:
Blackburn Diocesan Board of Finance
Access contact: Mr John Wilson
Tel: 01254 828400 **Fax:** 01254 828401
Opening Arrangements: Ruins and Gardens: daily Easter - October 11am - 5pm, November - Easter 11am - 4pm. 17th century Retreat House: Open Days and by prior arrangement. Refreshments available. Wheelchair access to most of ruins, coffee shop and exhibition centre.
Heritage Open Days: Yes
P Yes. Spaces: 25
♿ Partial. Disabled WC: Yes. Guide Dogs: Yes
£ Yes
Adult: £2.00
Child: 50p
Other: £1.25 (seniors/students), £4.50 (family), £1.00 (coach 40+).

LEICESTERSHIRE

The Old Rectory

Cossington, Leicestershire LE7 4UU
16th century Closet with plank and muntin walls and oak coffered ceiling with paintings of flowers.
Grant Recipient/Owner: Mrs V H Jones
Access contact: Mrs V H Jones
Tel: 01509 812623 **Fax:** 01509 812110
Opening Arrangements: By prior written arrangement.
Heritage Open Days: No
P Yes. Spaces: 6
♿ No. Disabled WC: No. Guide Dogs: Yes
£ No

Rockingham Castle

Market Harborough, Leicestershire LE16 8TH
Royal castle from William the Conqueror to Henry VIII, since then the home of the Watson family. Castle has remains from practically every century since the 11th. Fine collection of English 18th, 19th and 20th century paintings. Charles Dickens, who was a frequent visitor, used the castle as a model for Chesney Wold in Bleak House.
Website Address: www.rockinghamcastle.com
Grant Recipient/Owner:
Commander L M M Saunders Watson
Access contact: The Administrator
Tel: 01536 770240 **Fax:** 01536 771692
Email Address: rockinghamcastle@liveone.net
Opening Arrangements: 1 April - 30 September: Sundays, Thursdays, Bank Holidays, Tuesdays after Bank Holidays and Tuesdays in August, 1 - 5pm (last admission 4.30pm); grounds open 11.30am Sundays and Bank Holidays, 1pm on other open days. Refreshments available. Wheelchair access to ground floor only.
Heritage Open Days: No
P Yes. Spaces: 500
♿ Partial. Disabled WC: No. Guide Dogs: Yes
£ Yes
Adult: £4.50
Child: £3.00
Other: £4.00, £12.50 (family), also party & school rates.

Stanford Hall

Lutterworth, Leicestershire LE17 6DH
William and Mary house, built by the Smiths of Warwick (begun 1697), for Sir Roger Cave, ancestor of present owner whose family home it is. Visitors see every room on the ground floor (except modern kitchen), the "flying staircase" and two bedrooms. Contents include collection of Royal Stuart paintings.
Grant Recipient/Owner: Lady Braye
Access contact: E H Aubrey-Fletcher
Tel: 01788 860250 **Fax:** 01788 860870
Email Address: stanford.hall@virginnet.co.uk
Opening Arrangements: 7 April - 30 September: Saturdays, Sundays, Bank Holiday Mondays and following Tuesdays, 1.30 - 5.30pm (last admission 5pm). Also groups by prior arrangement any day or evening during this period. Special events. On Bank Holiday Mondays and Event days grounds open 12 noon. Closed October - Easter except for corporate events in October. Wheelchair access to the Park, the Gardens, the Motorcycle Museum, the 1898 Flying Machine, and the ground floor of the Hall if entrance steps can be negotiated.
Heritage Open Days: No
P Yes. Spaces: 1500
♿ Partial. Disabled WC: Yes. Guide Dogs: Yes
£ Yes
Adult: £4.20 House & Grounds, £2.50 Grounds only.
Child: £2.00 House & Grounds, £1.50 Grounds only.
Other: £3.90 Adult, £1.80 Child (groups 20+).

LINCOLNSHIRE

12 Eastgate

Lincoln, Lincolnshire LN2 1QG
Georgian house, located on the north side of the cathedral, based on earlier medieval foundations. Now

occupied by the Dean of Lincoln.
Grant Recipient/Owner:
Dean & Chapter of Lincoln Cathedral
Access contact: Mr William Roberts
Tel: 01522 527637
Opening Arrangements: By prior written arrangement with the Clerk of Works, Lincoln Cathedral, 28 Eastgate, Lincoln LN2 4AA.
Heritage Open Days: No
🅿 No
♿ No. Disabled WC: No. Guide Dogs: Yes
💷 No

12 Minster Yard

Lincoln, Lincolnshire LN2 1PJ
House of early 14th, late 17th and 19th centuries.
Grant Recipient/Owner:
Dean & Chapter of Lincoln Cathedral
Access contact: Mr William Roberts
Tel: 01522 527637
Opening Arrangements: By prior written arrangement with the Clerk of Works, Lincoln Cathedral, 28 Eastgate, Lincoln LN2 4AA.
Heritage Open Days: No
🅿 No
♿ No. Disabled WC: No. Guide Dogs: Yes
💷 No

13/13a Minster Yard

Lincoln, Lincolnshire LN2 1PW
Houses, mid-18th century, with late 18th and 19th century alterations.
Grant Recipient/Owner:
Dean & Chapter of Lincoln Cathedral
Access contact: Mr William Roberts
Tel: 01522 527637
Opening Arrangements: By prior written arrangement with the Clerk of Works, Lincoln Cathedral, 28 Eastgate, Lincoln LN2 4AA.
Heritage Open Days: No
🅿 No
♿ No. Disabled WC: No. Guide Dogs: Yes
💷 No

17 Minster Yard

Lincoln, Lincolnshire LN2 1PX
13th and 14th century building with 15th century additions. Sacked in 1644 and restored 1671-94 and 1704-32 with internal alterations, c1813, by William Fowler. Further additions to the building were made in the late 19th century.
Grant Recipient/Owner:
Dean & Chapter of Lincoln Cathedral
Access contact: Mr William Roberts
Tel: 01522 527637
Opening Arrangements: By prior written arrangement with the Clerk of Works, Lincoln Cathedral, 28 Eastgate, Lincoln LN2 4AA.
Heritage Open Days: No
🅿 No
♿ No. Disabled WC: No. Guide Dogs: Yes
💷 No

18/18a Minster Yard

Lincoln, Lincolnshire LN2 1PX
13th and 14th century building with 17th century additions. Remodelled and extended in 1827 and refronted 1873 by J L Pearson.
Grant Recipient/Owner:
Dean & Chapter of Lincoln Cathedral
Access contact: Mr William Roberts
Tel: 01522 527637
Opening Arrangements: By prior written arrangement with the Clerk of Works, Lincoln Cathedral, 28 Eastgate, Lincoln LN2 4AA.
Heritage Open Days: No
🅿 No
♿ No. Disabled WC: No. Guide Dogs: Yes
💷 No

2/2a Exchequergate

Lincoln, Lincolnshire LN2 1PZ
Late 15th century house, rebuilt 1834-48.
Grant Recipient/Owner:
Dean & Chapter of Lincoln Cathedral
Access contact: Mr William Roberts
Tel: 01522 527637
Opening Arrangements: By prior written arrangement with the Clerk of Works, Lincoln Cathedral, 28 Eastgate, Lincoln LN2 4AA.
Heritage Open Days: No
🅿 No
♿ No. Disabled WC: No. Guide Dogs: Yes
💷 No

22 Minster Yard, Lincoln

Lincolnshire LN2 1PX
Early 18th century house, altered early 19th and divided mid-19th century.
Grant Recipient/Owner:
Dean & Chapter of Lincoln Cathedral
Access contact: Mr William Roberts
Tel: 01522 527637
Opening Arrangements: By prior written arrangement with the Clerk of Works, Lincoln Cathedral, 28 Eastgate, Lincoln LN2 4AA.
Heritage Open Days: No
🅿 No
♿ No. Disabled WC: No. Guide Dogs: Yes
💷 No

3/3a Pottergate

Lincoln, Lincolnshire LN2 1PH
17th century house, now 2 houses, incorporating medieval walling. Remodelled in early 18th century with late 18th and 19th century alterations.
Grant Recipient/Owner:
Dean & Chapter of Lincoln Cathedral
Access contact: Mr William Roberts
Tel: 01522 527637
Opening Arrangements: By prior written arrangement with the Clerk of Works, Lincoln Cathedral, 28 Eastgate, Lincoln LN2 4AA.
Heritage Open Days: No
🅿 No
♿ No. Disabled WC: No. Guide Dogs: No
💷 No

3/3a Vicars Court

Lincoln, Lincolnshire LN2 1PT
Former priests' vicars lodgings, now 2 houses. Begun late 13th century by Bishop Sutton and completed c1309. Altered 15th century, reroofed and altered late 17th and further altered late 17th, 18th and 19th centuries.
Grant Recipient/Owner:
Dean & Chapter of Lincoln Cathedral
Access contact: Mr William Roberts
Tel: 01522 527637
Opening Arrangements: By prior written arrangement with the Clerk of Works, Lincoln Cathedral, 28 Eastgate, Lincoln LN2 4AA.
Heritage Open Days: No
🅿 No
♿ No. Disabled WC: No. Guide Dogs: Yes
💷 No

4 Pottergate

Lincoln, Lincolnshire LN2 1PH
14th and 15th century house, with mid-17th century additions. Altered c1760 and in the 19th century.
Grant Recipient/Owner:
Dean & Chapter of Lincoln Cathedral
Access contact: Mr William Roberts
Tel: 01522 527637
Opening Arrangements: By prior written arrangement with the Clerk of Works, Lincoln Cathedral, 28 Eastgate, Lincoln LN2 4AA.
Heritage Open Days: No
🅿 No
♿ No. Disabled WC: No. Guide Dogs: Yes
💷 No

Belton House & Bellmount Tower

Grantham, Lincolnshire NG32 2LS
Belton was built in 1685-88 and later altered by James Wyatt. The interiors contain fine plasterwork and wood-carving, plus important collections of paintings, furniture, tapestries and silverware. Also formal gardens, orangery and landscape park.
Website Address: www.nationaltrust.org.uk
Grant Recipient/Owner: The National Trust
Access contact: Property Manager
Tel: 01476 566116   **Fax:** 01476 579071
Email Address: ebedxb@smtp.ntrust.org.uk
Opening Arrangements: House: 31 March to 4 November: daily except Mondays and Tuesdays (but open Bank Holiday Mondays and closed Good Friday) 1 - 5.30pm. Garden & Park: as house 11am - 5.30pm (closes 4.30pm on 21 July). Park only: all year on foot only from Lion Lodge gates (no access from this entrance to house, garden or adventure playground). Bellmount Woods: daily access from separate car park. Wheelchair access to ground floor of house, garden, park, restaurant, shop and refreshment kiosk.
Heritage Open Days: No
🅿 Yes. Spaces: 50
♿ Partial. Disabled WC: Yes. Guide Dogs: Yes
💷 Yes
Adult: £5.40
Child: £2.70
Other: £13.50 (family)

Brocklesby Mausoleum

Brocklesby Park, N E Lincolnshire DN41 8PN
Family Mausoleum designed by James Wyatt and built between 1787 and 1794 by Charles Anderson Pelham, who subsequently became Lord Yarborough, as a memorial to his wife Sophia who died at the age of 33. The classical design is based on the Temples of Vesta at Rome and Tivoli.
Grant Recipient/Owner: The Earl of Yarborough
Access contact: Mr H A Rayment
Tel: 01469 560214
Opening Arrangements: Exterior viewable from permissive paths through Mausoleum Woods 1 April - 31 August at all reasonable times, interior (excluding private crypt) by prior arrangement with the Estate Office. Parking in village or walks car park about a quarter of a mile from Mausoleum.
Heritage Open Days: No
🅿 See above
♿ No. Disabled WC: No. Guide Dogs: Yes
💷 Yes
Adult: £2.00 (to view interior)

Burghley House

Stamford, Lincolnshire PE9 3JY
Large country house built by William Cecil, Lord High Treasurer of England, between 1565 and 1587, and still lived in by descendants of his family. Eighteen State Rooms, many decorated by Antonio Verrio in the 17th century, housing a collection of artworks including 17th Italian paintings, Japanese ceramics, European porcelain and wood carvings by Grinling Gibbons and his followers. There are also four State Beds, English and continental furniture, and tapestries and textiles. 'Capability' Brown parkland.
Grant Recipient/Owner:
Burghley House Preservation Trust
Access contact: Mr David Parratt
Tel: 01780 752451   **Fax:** 01780 480125
Email Address: burghley@burghley.co.uk
Opening Arrangements: 1 April - 7 October: daily (except 8 September) 11am - 4.30pm. By guided tour only apart from Saturday and Sunday afternoons when there are guides in each room. Partially accessible for wheelchair users, please telephone for information. Disabled parking available close to visitors' entrance.
Heritage Open Days: No
🅿 Yes. Spaces: 500
♿ Partial. Disabled WC: Yes. Guide Dogs: Yes
💷 Yes
Adult: £6.80
Child: £3.30
Other: £6.30 (senior)

Doddington Hall

Lincoln LN6 4RU
Late Elizabethan mansion with original garden walls, gatehouse and outbuildings. Contents, including furniture, textiles, porcelain and pictures, reflect 400 years of domestic use.
Website Address:
www.doddingtonhall.free-online.co.uk
Grant Recipient/Owner: Mr Antony Jarvis
Access contact: Mr Antony Jarvis
Tel: 01522 694308   **Fax:** 01522 685259
Email Address: estateoffice@doddingtonhall.free-online.co.uk
Opening Arrangements: House & Gardens: May - September, Wednesdays, Sundays and Bank Holiday Mondays 2 - 6pm; Gardens only: February - April, Sundays 2 - 6pm. Opening arrangements provisional at time of going to print, please check with Mr Antony Jarvis or Miss Fiona Cairns-Watson at the Hall for current details. Wheelchair access to Gardens and ground floor of Hall only.
Heritage Open Days: No
🅿 Yes. Spaces: 250
♿ Partial. Disabled WC: Yes. Guide Dogs: Yes
💷 Yes
Adult: £4.50 (£2.25 garden only)
Child: £2.25 (£1.50 garden only)
Other: £12.50 (family ticket)

Harding House

48-54 Steep Hill, Lincoln, Lincolnshire
Grade II listed house of the 16th century, remodelled in the 18th and restored in the 20th. Built of coursed rubble and brick with a pantile roof, now houses a craft studio.
Grant Recipient/Owner:
The Chief Executive, Lincoln City Council
Access contact: Mr Mark Wheater
Tel: 01522 873464
Opening Arrangements: Open during normal shop opening hours.
Heritage Open Days: No
🅿 No
♿ No. Disabled WC: No. Guide Dogs: Yes
💷 No

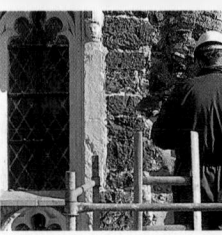
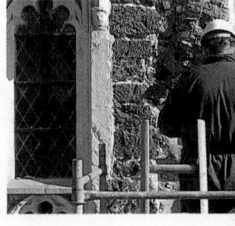
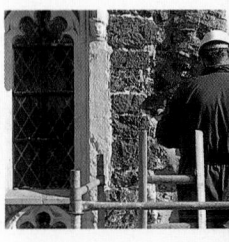
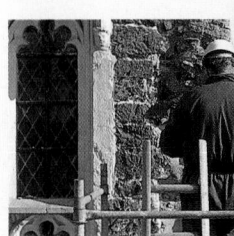
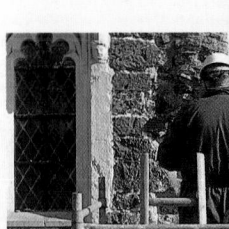
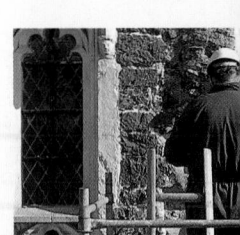
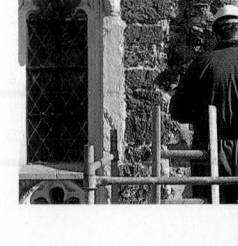
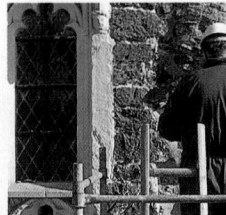
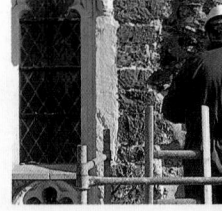
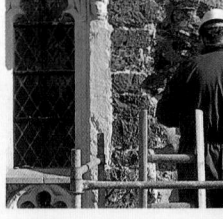

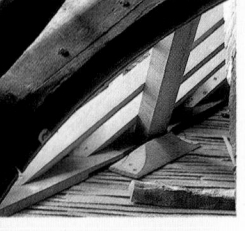
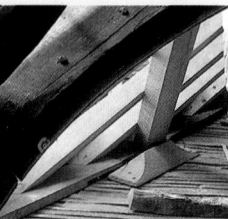
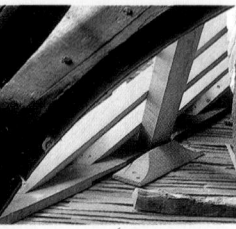
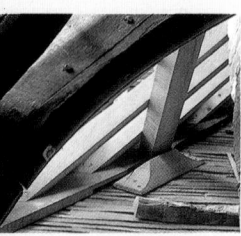
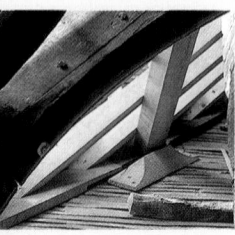
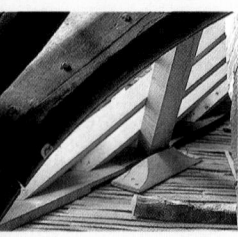
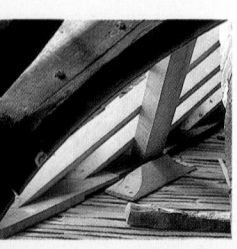

Heggy's Cottage

Hall Road, Haconby, nr. Bourne, Lincolnshire PE10 0UY

Built c1500 of mud and stud construction, a good example of early conversion to two storeys. Restored to its original state in 1995.

Grant Recipient/Owner: Mrs J F Atkinson
Access contact: Mrs J F Atkinson
Tel: 01778 570790
Opening Arrangements: By prior written arrangement with Mrs J F Atkinson, Haconby Hall, nr. Bourne, Lincolnshire PE10 0UY.
Heritage Open Days: No
P Yes. Spaces: 1
No. Disabled WC: No. Guide Dogs: No
£ No

Kyme Tower

Manor Farm, South Kyme, Lincoln, Lincolnshire LN4 4JN

23.5m high tower with four storeys and a stair turret. Remainder of a fortified medieval manor house, built on the site of an Augustinian priory, itself built on an Anglo-Saxon religious establishment. There are also visible earthworks of the former moat and fishponds on the site.

Grant Recipient/Owner: Kathy Hayward
Access contact: Mr W B Lamyman
Tel: 01526 860603
Opening Arrangements:
By prior telephone arrangement.
Heritage Open Days: No
P Yes. Spaces: 3
No. Disabled WC: No. Guide Dogs: No
£ No

Maud Foster Windmill

Boston, Lincolnshire PE21 9EG

Built 1819 and still working daily as a commercial flour mill. Access to all 7 floors, a tea-room and shop.

Grant Recipient/Owner: Mr T E Waterfield
Access contact: Mr James Waterfield
Tel: 01205 352188
Opening Arrangements: All year: Wednesdays and Saturdays 11am - 5pm, Sundays 1 - 5pm; July and August: Thursdays and Fridays 11am - 5pm; Bank Holidays 10am - 5pm. Closed Christmas and New Year.
Heritage Open Days: No
P Yes. Spaces: 16
No. Disabled WC: No. Guide Dogs: No
£ Yes
Adult: £2.50
Child: £1.50
Other: £2.00 (senior citizens)

Tattershall Castle

Tattershall, Lincoln, Lincolnshire LN4 4LR

A vast fortified and moated red-brick tower, built c1440 for Ralph Cromwell, treasurer of England. The building was rescued from becoming derelict by Lord Curzon 1911-14 and contains four great chambers with enormous Gothic fireplaces, tapestries and brick vaulting. Gatehouse with museum room.

Website Address: www.nationaltrust.org.uk
Grant Recipient/Owner: The National Trust
Access contact: The Custodian
Tel: 01526 342543   **Fax:** 01526 342543
Email Address: etcxxx@smtp.ntrust.org.uk
Opening Arrangements: 1 April to 4 November: daily except Thursdays and Fridays 10.30am - 5.30pm. 10 November to 16 December: Saturdays and Sundays 12 - 4pm. Ground floor of castle may occasionally be closed for functions or events. Wheelchair access to ground floor only via ramp.
Heritage Open Days: No
P No
Partial. Disabled WC: Yes. Guide Dogs: Yes
£ Yes
Adult: £3.00
Child: £1.50
Other: £7.50 (family). Accompanied children free July & August.

Uffington Manor Gatepiers

Main Street, Uffington, nr. Stamford, Lincolnshire

Pair of Grade II* listed gate piers, possibly by John Lumley c1700, surmounted by urns with wrought iron entrance gates with a coat of arms over of later 19th century date.

Grant Recipient/Owner: Mr David Pike
Access contact: Mr David Pike
Tel: 01780 751944   **Fax:** 01780 764256
Opening Arrangements: Can be viewed from public roadway, otherwise by prior written arrangement.
Heritage Open Days: No
P Yes. Spaces: 2
Yes. Disabled WC: No. Guide Dogs: Yes
£ No

Waltham Windmill

Brigsley Road, Waltham, Grimsby, Lincolnshire DN37 0JZ

Grade II listed six-sailed tower mill, one of only three in the country. Built in 1880 by John Sanderson of Louth, 90ft high with 6 publicly accessible floors. Museum of rural life at site.

Grant Recipient/Owner: Waltham Windmill Trust
Access contact: Mrs M A Stennett
Tel: 01472 822236
Opening Arrangements: Easter - September: Saturdays and Sundays 10am - 4pm and Bank Holiday Mondays. Group visits can be arranged by contacting Mrs Diana Le-Core (01472 752122 or fax 01472 316788). Wheelchair and guide dog access to ground floor only.
Heritage Open Days: Yes
P Yes. Spaces: 30
Partial. Disabled WC: No. Guide Dogs: Yes
£ Yes
Adult: £1.00
Child: 50p

LONDON

Bruce Castle

Lordship Lane, London N17 8NU

Originally built in the 16th century but altered extensively in the 17th, 18th and 19th centuries. Now a museum containing displays about the building and local district, and an archive.

Website Address: www.brucecastlemuseum.org.uk
Grant Recipient/Owner: London Borough of Haringey
Access contact: Ms Sian Harrington
Tel: 020 8808 8772   **Fax:** 020 8808 4118
Email Address: museum.services@haringey.gov.uk
Opening Arrangements: Wednesday - Sunday 1 - 5pm plus Easter Monday, May Day, late May Bank Hoilday and August Bank Holiday. Closed Good Friday, Christmas Day, Boxing Day and New Year's Day. Groups at other times by prior arrangement. Archive open by prior arrangement.
Heritage Open Days: Yes
P Yes. Spaces: 15
Yes. Disabled WC: Yes. Guide Dogs: Yes
£ No

College of Arms

Queen Victoria Street, London EC4V 4BT

Built in 1670s/1680s to the design of Francis Sandford and Morris Emmett to house the Heralds' offices, on the site of their earlier building, Derby Place, which was destroyed in the Great Fire of 1666. The principal room is Earl Marshal's Court which is two floors high with gallery, panelling and throne. New record room added 1842 and portico and terrace in 1867.

Website Address: www.college-of-arms.gov.uk
Grant Recipient/Owner: College of Arms
Access contact: Officer in Waiting
Tel: 020 7248 2762   **Fax:** 020 7248 6448
Email Address: enquiries@college-of-arms.gov.uk
Opening Arrangements: Earl Marshal's Court only: all year (except Public Holidays and State and Special Occasions), Monday - Friday 10am - 4pm. Group visits (up to 10) by prior arrangement with the Officer in Waiting. Group tours of Record Room (up to 20) also by prior arrangement.
Heritage Open Days: Yes
P No
No. Disabled WC: No. Guide Dogs: No
£ No

Dissenters' Chapel

Kensal Green Cemetery, London

Grade II* building within Grade II* cemetery. Cemetery dates from 1832 and is London's oldest. The Chapel was designed in Greek Revival style by John Griffith in 1834. It is now used by the Friends of Kensal Green Cemetery as a headquarters, exhibition space and art gallery.

Website Address: www.hct.org.uk
Grant Recipient/Owner: Historic Chapels Trust
Access contact: Mr Henry Vivian-Neal
Tel: 020 8960 1030
Opening Arrangements: Cemetery: daily; Dissenters' Chapel: weekends and at other times by prior arrangement. Guided tours of chapels and cemetery at weekends for modest charge. Parking in adjacent streets, disabled parking in cemetery.
Heritage Open Days: Yes
P See above
Yes. Disabled WC: Yes. Guide Dogs: Yes
£ See above

Garrick's Temple

Hampton Court Road, Richmond-upon-Thames, London TW12 2EJ

The actor-manager David Garrick built the Temple in 1756 to celebrate the genius of William Shakespeare. The Temple was restored between 1997-1999 and now houses an exhibition of Garrick's acting career and life at Hampton, while the grounds have been landscaped to echo their original 18th century layout.

Website Address: www.hampton.online.co.uk
Grant Recipient/Owner:
London Borough of Richmond-upon-Thames
Access contact: The Curator
Tel: 020 8892 0221   **Fax:** 020 8744 0501
Email Address: leisure@richmond.gov.uk
Opening Arrangements: Temple: Sundays: first Sunday in April to last Sunday in September 2 - 5pm. Bank Holiday Mondays 2 - 5pm. London Open House weekend Saturday and Sunday 10am - 5pm. Also pre-arranged visits for small groups throughout the year (tel: 020 8892 0221). Lawn: open all year 7.30am - dusk. Wheelchair access only to lawn gardens.
Heritage Open Days: No
P No
See above. Disabled WC: No. Guide Dogs: Yes
£ No

Great Stanmore Old Church

Church Road, Stanmore, London HA7 4AQ

Early all red brick church attributed to Nicholas Stone and consecrated in 1632 by William Laud, later Archbishop of Canterbury. Used until partial demolition in 1851. Contains the tombs of the 4th Earl of Aberdeen, Victorian Prime Minister, and the Marquess of Abercorn.

Grant Recipient/Owner: Dr Frederick Hicks
Access contact: Dr Frederick Hicks
Tel: 020 8954 1677
Opening Arrangements: April - September: Saturdays 2.30 - 4.30pm. At other times by prior arrangement with Dr Frederick Hicks, 30 Elm Park, Stanmore, London HA7 4BJ (tel.020 8954 1677). Wheelchair access may be difficult as there is some 50 metres of grass from car park to church.
Heritage Open Days: Yes
P Yes. Spaces: 10
See above. Disabled WC: No. Guide Dogs: Yes
£ No

Highgate Cemetery

Swain's Lane, London N6 6PJ

Western, older cemetery, opened in 1839, has good examples of Victorian funerary architecture. Eastern cemetery opened in 1854. Some 168,000 persons are buried in the cemetery including many notables.

Grant Recipient/Owner:
Friends of Highgate Cemetery Ltd
Access contact: Mrs J A Pateman
Tel: 020 8340 1834
Opening Arrangements: Western cemetery: March - November daily tours at 12, 2 & 4pm, weekends tours hourly 11am - 3pm (winter) and 11am - 4pm (summer); Eastern cemetery: daily (unescorted) weekdays 10am - 3.45pm (winter) and 10am - 4.45pm (summer), weekends always. Both cemeteries closed 25 & 26 December, plus during funerals. Wheelchair access to Eastern cemetery only. Some street parking.
Heritage Open Days: No
P See above
Partial. Disabled WC: No. Guide Dogs: Yes
£ Yes
Adult: £3.00 Tour of West (£1.00 small cameras only);
Child: £2.00 East (£1.00 small cameras only).
Other: £1.00 (9-15) West; East free, but donations welcome.

Highpoint

North Hill, Highgate, London N6

Two blocks of flats built in 1935 and 1938 by Lubetkin and Tecton. Constructed of reinforced concrete with decorative features.

Grant Recipient/Owner: Mr Gamble
Access contact: Mr Stephen Ellman
Tel: 020 7554 5800
Opening Arrangements: By prior arrangement with Mr Stephen Ellman of Gross Fine, 14/16 Stephenson Way, London NW1 2HD (tel.020 7554 5800).
Heritage Open Days: No
P No
No. Disabled WC: No. Guide Dogs: Yes
£ No

The House Mill

Three Mill Lane, Bromley-by-Bow, London E3 3DU

Industrial water mill, originally built 1776 as part of a distillery. Contains 4 floors with remains of unrestored machinery, 4 water wheels and gearing. Originally had 2 pairs of millstones and has unique survival of Fairbairn-style "silent millstone machinery".

Grant Recipient/Owner: River Lea Tidal Mill Trust
Access contact: Mr Brian Strong
Tel: 020 8440 3654
Email Address: brian.strong@tesco.net

Opening Arrangements: Sunday of National Mills Weekend, Heritage Open Days and the first Sunday of each month April - December 11am - 4pm. Groups by prior arrangement with Mr Brian Strong, 14 Eversleigh Road, New Barnet, Hertfordshire EN5 1NE (tel.020 8440 3654). For further information ring 020 8980 4626. Car park nearby.
Heritage Open Days: Yes
P See above
♿ Yes. Disabled WC: Yes. Guide Dogs: Yes
£ Yes
Adult: £3.00
Child: Free
Other: £1.00

Prendergast School Murals
Hilly Fields, Adelaide Avenue, London SE4 1LE
Painted in the school hall in the 1930s by students of the Royal College of Art, they depict classical tales and incorporate local features.
Grant Recipient/Owner:
Governors of Prendergast School
Access contact: Miss E Pienaar
Tel: 020 8690 3710 **Fax:** 020 8690 3155
Opening Arrangements: By prior written arrangement during school hours in term-time.
Heritage Open Days: Yes
P No
♿ Yes. Disabled WC: No. Guide Dogs: Yes
£ No

The Queen's Chapel of the Savoy
Savoy Hill, Strand, London WC2R 0DA
Originally part of a hospital founded in 1512 by Henry VII. Rebuilt by Robert Smirke after a fire in 1864, from which time dates the ceiling covered with heraldic emblems. Recently restored.
Grant Recipient/Owner: Duchy of Lancaster
Access contact: John Robson
Tel: 020 7836 7221 **Fax:** 020 7379 8088
Opening Arrangements:
All year except August and September: Tuesday - Friday 10.30am - 3.30pm; Sundays for Morning Service only. Closed the week after Christmas Day and the week after Easter Day. Parking on meters in adjoining streets.
Heritage Open Days: No
P See above
♿ No. Disabled WC: No. Guide Dogs: Yes
£ No

Royal Geographical Society
(with the Institute of British Geographers), Lowther Lodge, 1 Kensington Gore, London SW7 2AR
Norman Shaw building in the Queen Anne style, built in the 1870s as a private house with a two acre garden for the Lowthers. Owned by the Royal Geographic Society since 1912 and houses their large collection of geographical material, which comprises archives, books, maps and pictures, dating from the 15th century to the present day. The Lecture Theatre extension was built in 1930 in order to mark the Society's centenary.
Grant Recipient/Owner: Royal Geographical Society
Access contact: Ms Denise Prior
Tel: 020 7591 3090 **Fax:** 020 7591 3091
Email Address: d.prior@rgs.org
Opening Arrangements: Weekdays (except Bank Holidays) 9.30am - 5.30pm. Closed between Christmas and New Year. Use of collections, library, map room and picture library by prior arrangement only: Mondays - Fridays 11am - 5pm; archives on Thursdays and Fridays 11am - 5pm. Charges levied for use of collections. Parking by prior arrangement only. Wheelchair access to all areas except Council Room and Lecture Theatre balcony.
Heritage Open Days: No
P Yes. Spaces: 1
♿ Partial. Disabled WC: Yes Guide Dogs: Yes
£ No

The Royal Institution of Great Britain
21 Albemarle Street, London W1X 4BS
Houses the Michael Faraday Museum and a 200 year old lecture theatre. Regular public lectures on scientific themes.
Grant Recipient/Owner:
Royal Institution of Great Britain
Access contact: Mr Alan Winter
Tel: 020 7409 2992 **Fax:** 020 7670 2920
Address: alanw@ri.ac.uk
Opening Arrangements: Monday - Friday 9am - 5pm. Public lectures/events on various days of the week usually starting at 6.30pm or 7.30pm. Lecture lists published on RI website (www.ri.ac.uk). Entry charge for Faraday Museum only. Parking available on meters on street.
Heritage Open Days: Yes
P See above
♿ Yes. Disabled WC: Yes. Guide Dogs: Yes
£ Yes
Adult: £1.00 (museum), £5.00 (lecture).
Child: £1.00 (museum), £3.00 (lecture).
Other: Schools free.

St Pancras Chambers
Euston Road, London NW1 2QR
Grade I listed Gothic-style building fronting St Pancras Station. Built as the Midland Grand Hotel between 1868 and 1876 to designs by Sir George Gilbert Scott.
Grant Recipient/Owner: British Railways Board/London & Continental Stations & Property Ltd
Access contact: Ms Lynda Nolan
Tel: 020 7304 3900 **Fax:** 020 7304 3901
Email Address: lnolan@lcsp.co.uk
Opening Arrangements: The front entrance and former ground floor coffee lounge are generally open each weekday 11.30am - 3.30pm without charge. For information on guided tours of the remainder of the building contact 020 7304 3900. Please note that tours involve climbing several flights of stairs and that there are no working lifts or other facilities for disabled visitors.
Heritage Open Days: Yes
P No
♿ No. Disabled WC: No. Guide Dogs: No
£ Yes
Adult: £7.50 for tour.

Sutton House
2-4 Homerton High Street, Hackney, London E9 6JQ
A unique survival in London's East End, Sutton Hosue was built in 1535 by Ralph Sadlier, Principal Secretary of State for Henry VIII. Rare example of a Tudor red brick house with 18th century alterations and later additions. Features include original linenfold panelling and 17th century wall paintings.
Website Address: www.nationaltrust.org.uk
Grant Recipient/Owner: The National Trust
Access contact: The Property Manager
Tel: 020 8986 2264
Opening Arrangements: 7 February to 28 November: Wednesdays and Sundays only and Bank Holiday Mondays 11.30am - 5.30pm. Gallery, shop and café: 10 January to 21 December Wednesday to Sunday 11am - 5pm. Wheelchair access to ground floor. On street parking.
Heritage Open Days: No
P See above
♿ Partial. Disabled WC: Yes. Guide Dogs: Yes
£ Yes
Adult: £2.10
Child: £0.60
Other: £4.70 (family)

Walpole's House
St Mary's College, Strawberry Hill, Waldegrave Road, Twickenham, London TW1 4SX
Bought by Horace Walpole in 1749 and over the next half century converted into his own vision of a 'gothic' fantasy. Reputedly the first substantial building of the Gothic Revival.
Grant Recipient/Owner: St Mary's, Strawberry Hill
Access contact: Conference Officer
Tel: 020 8240 4114/4044 **Fax:** 020 8255 6174
Email Address: evansn@smuc.ac.uk
Opening Arrangements: Easter - mid-October: Sundays 2 - 3.30pm. Guided group tours (minimum 10 people) by prior arrangement on any day except Saturday. Wheelchair access to ground floor and grounds.
Heritage Open Days: Yes
P Yes. Spaces: 60
♿ Partial. Disabled WC: Yes. Guide Dogs: Yes
£ Yes
Adult: £5.00
Other: £4.25

MERSEYSIDE

Bluecoat Chambers
School Lane, Liverpool, Merseyside L1 3BX
Queen Anne building dated 1716 housing contemporary art gallery, café bar, crafts centre and shops. Reputedly the oldest arts centre in the country.
Grant Recipient/Owner: Bluecoat Arts Centre Ltd
Access contact: Mr A Hurley
Tel: 0151 709 5297 **Fax:** 0151 707 0048
Email Address: bluecoat@dircon.co.uk
Opening Arrangements: All year (except Sundays and Bank Holidays) Monday - Saturday 9am - 5.30pm. Wheelchair access to ground floor only.
Heritage Open Days: No
P No
♿ Partial. Disabled WC: Yes. Guide Dogs: Yes
£ No

Broughton Hall Conservatory
Convent of Mercy, Yew Tree Lane, West Derby, Liverpool, Merseyside L12 9HH
Victorian conservatory of rectangular shape with an entrance porch at one end and an access bay to main building, at the other. The cast iron structure is mounted on a stone plinth. The elevations are divided into a series of panels with decorated cast iron circular columns. From the capitols spring semi-circular arches. These form the bases of the frieze moulding which runs round the periphery of the building. The flooring is of quarry tiles.
Grant Recipient/Owner:
Institute of Our Lady of Mercy
Access contact: Sister Superior
Tel: 0151 228 9232
Opening Arrangements: By prior written arrangement only, Monday - Saturday 10am - 4pm. No access on Sundays, Religious Holidays and Bank Holidays. Wheelchair and guide dog access by prior arrangement.
Heritage Open Days: No
P Yes. Spaces: 4
♿ See above. Disabled WC: Yes. Guide Dogs: Yes
£ No

Liverpool Collegiate Apartments
Shaw Street, Liverpool, Merseyside L6
Grade II* former school built 1843 of red sandstone in Tudor Gothic style, gutted by fire and now converted into residential block.
Website Address: www.urbansplash.co.uk
Grant Recipient/Owner: Mr Bill Maynard
Access contact: Mr Bill Maynard
Tel: 0151 707 1493 **Fax:** 0151 708 0479
Email Address: design@urbansplash.co.uk
Opening Arrangements: Exterior only.
Heritage Open Days: No
P No
♿ No
£ No

Speke Hall
The Walk, Liverpool, Merseyside L24 1XD
One of the most important timber framed manor houses in the country, dating from 1490. The interior spans many periods: the Great Hall and priest holes evoke Tudor times, the Oak Parlour and smaller rooms, some with William Morris wallpapers, show the Victorian desire for privacy and comfort. There is some Jacobean plasterwork and intricately caved furniture. Restored garden and woodland walks.
Website Address: www.nationaltrust.org.uk
Grant Recipient/Owner: The National Trust
Access contact: Simon Osborne
Tel: 0151 427 7231 **Fax:** 0151 427 9860
Opening Arrangements: House: 28 March to end October, Wednesdays to Sundays (open Bank Holidays). November and December, Saturdays and Sundays only. Times: March to mid October 1 - 5.30pm, mid October to December 1 - 4.30pm. Woodland and garden: open daily throughout the year except Mondays (open Bank Holidays), closed 24-26 and 31 December, 1 January. Times: March to mid October 11am - 5.30pm., mid October - end March 2002 11am - 4pm. Wheelchair access to ground floor of house. Car park is 500 yards from the property. Courtsey shuttle service available.
Heritage Open Days: No
P Yes. Spaces: 400
♿ Partial. Disabled WC: Yes. Guide Dogs: Yes
£ Yes
Adult: £4.50
Child: £2.50

Turner Memorial Home of Rest
Dingle Lane, Liverpool, Merseyside L8 9RN
Grade II listed red sandstone ashlar building with tile roof, c1881-3, by Alfred Waterhouse. Used as a nursing home for elderly men. Contains a chapel.
Grant Recipient/Owner:
Trustees of the Turner Memorial Home of Rest
Access contact: Mrs Alison Charlesworth
Tel: 0151 727 4177 **Fax:** 0151 727 7788
Opening Arrangements: By prior arrangement.
Heritage Open Days: No
P Yes. Spaces: 10
♿ Yes. Disabled WC: Yes. Guide Dogs: Yes
£ No

NORFOLK

Billingford Cornmill
Scole, Norfolk
Built in 1860. One pair of stones have been repaired to full working order and are run occasionally.
Grant Recipient/Owner: Norfolk Windmills Trust
Access contact: Miss A L Jaques
Tel: 01603 222708 **Fax:** 01603 224413
Email Address: amanda.jaques.pt@norfolk.gov.uk

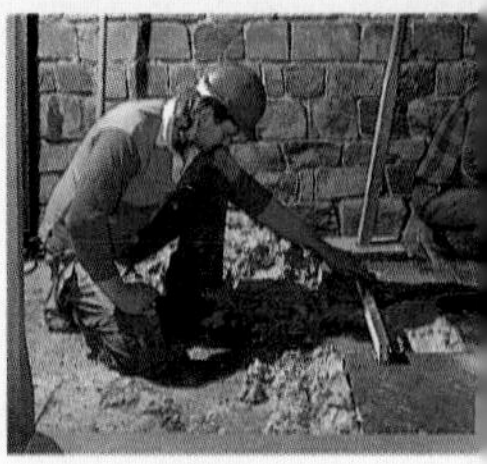
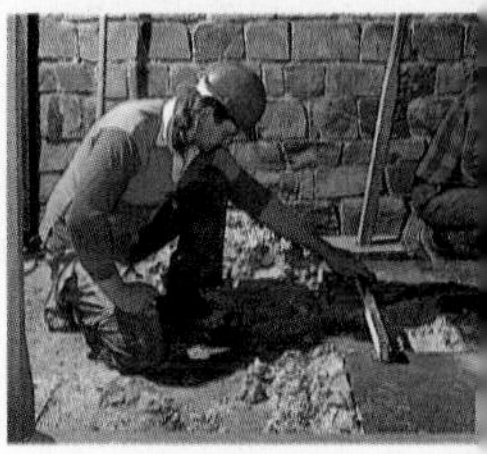
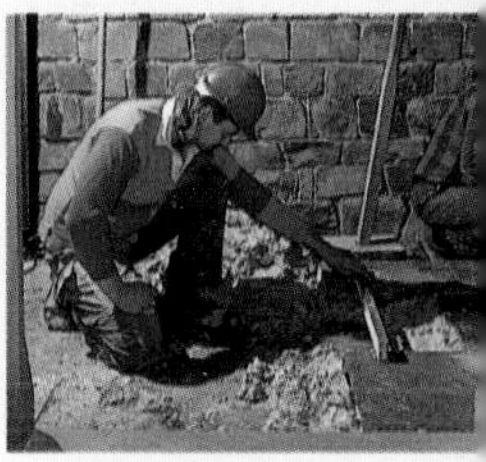
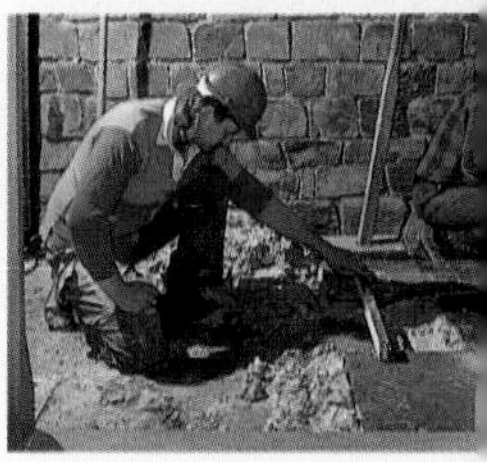
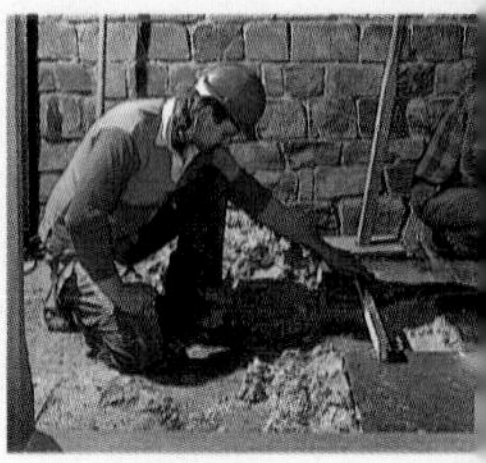
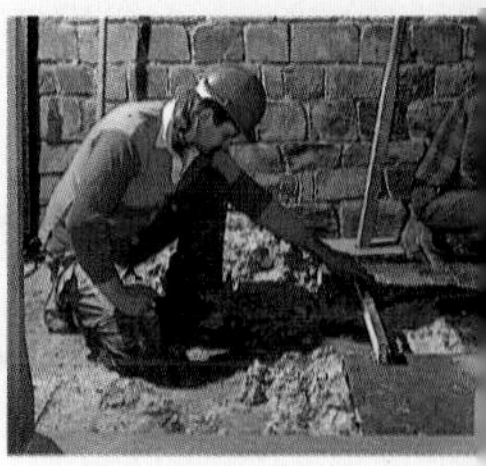
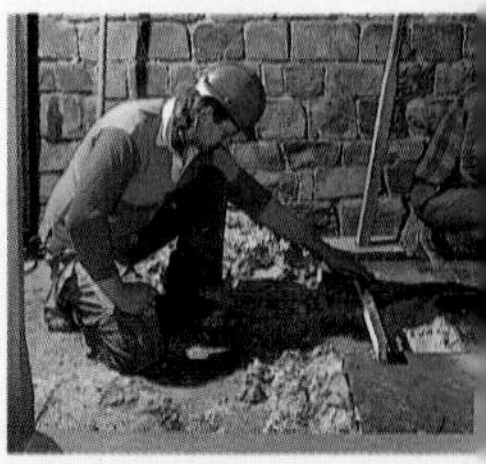

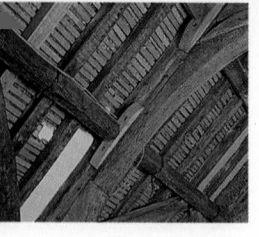
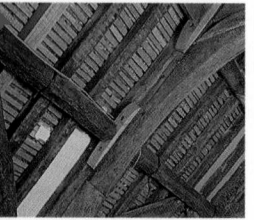
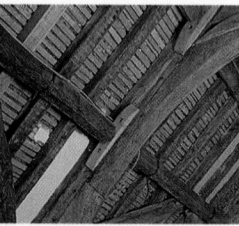
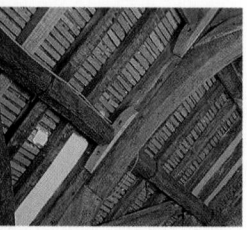
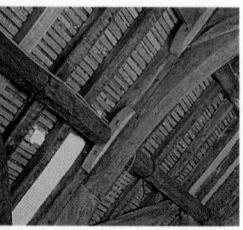
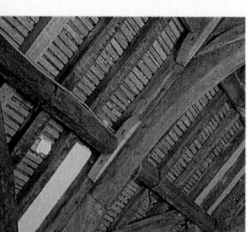
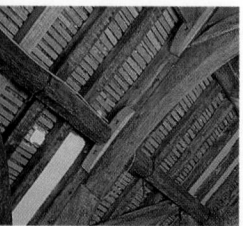

⊞ Opening arrangements at properties grant-aided by English Heritage

Opening Arrangements: For current opening arrangements please contact, Miss A L Jaques, Conservation Officer, Building Conservation Section, Department of Planning and Transportation, Norfolk County Council, County Hall, Martineau Lane, Norwich, Norfolk NR1 2SG (tel.01603 222708). Admission charges are also provisional at time of going to press, please check with Miss Jaques for up-to-date information.
Heritage Open Days: No
P Yes. Spaces: 2
No. Disabled WC: No. Guide Dogs: No
£ Yes
Adult: 70p (provisional)
Child: 30p (provisional)

Churchman House
71 Bethel Street, Norwich, Norfolk NR2 1NR
Georgian town house with Victorian additions, contains plastered and panelled rooms, and carved fireplaces.
Grant Recipient/Owner: Norwich City Council
Access contact: Superintendent Registrar
Tel: 01603 767600   **Fax:** 01603 632677
Opening Arrangements: By prior arrangement on Tuesday or Thursday afternoons. Wheelchair access to ground floor only. Parking for disabled only.
Heritage Open Days: No
P See above
Partial. Disabled WC: Yes. Guide Dogs: Yes
£ No

Denver Windmill
Sluice Road, Denver, Downham Market, Norfolk PE38 0EG
Working windmill on edge of the fens, built in 1835 and recently restored.
Website Address: www.denvermill.co.uk
Grant Recipient/Owner: The Norfolk Windmills Trust
Access contact: Mr Richard Townsley
Tel: 01366 384009
Opening Arrangements: 1 April - end of October: Monday - Saturday 10am - 5pm, Sunday 12 - 5pm; 1 November - end of March: Monday - Saturday 10am - 4pm, Sunday 12 - 4pm. Wheelchair access to ground floor of windmill only, there is a video shown of the mill in the new visitor facilities which are accessible to wheelchair users.
Heritage Open Days: No
P Yes. Spaces: 50
Partial. Disabled WC: Yes. Guide Dogs: Yes
£ Yes
Adult: £2.50
Child: £1.20
Other: £2.25

Dragon Hall
115-123 King Street, Norwich, Norfolk NR1 1QE
Medieval timber-framed merchant's hall. The 15th century great hall has a crown post roof with an intricately carved and painted dragon.
Website Address:
http://freespace.virgin.net/dragon.hall/index.htm
Grant Recipient/Owner:
Norfolk & Norwich Heritage Trust
Access contact: Mr Neil Sigsworth
Tel: 01603 663922   **Fax:** 01603 663922
Email Address: dragon.hall@virgin.net
Opening Arrangements: 1 November - 31 March: Mondays - Fridays 10am - 4pm; 1 April - 31 October: Mondays - Saturdays 10am - 4pm; closed Bank Holidays and 22 December - New Year's Day. Wheelchair access to ground floor only.
Heritage Open Days: Yes
P Yes. Spaces: 6
Partial. Disabled WC: No. Guide Dogs: Yes
£ Yes
Adult: £1.50
Child: 50p
Other: £1.00

Felbrigg Hall
Felbrigg, Norwich, Norfolk NR11 8PR
17th century house containing its original 18th century furniture and paintings. The walled garden has been restored and features a working dovecote and fine and aged trees.
Website Address: www.nationaltrust.org.uk
Grant Recipient/Owner: The National Trust
Access contact: Property Manager
Tel: 01263 837444   **Fax:** 01263 837032
Email Address: atgusr@smtp.ntrust.org.uk
Opening Arrangements: House: 31 March to 4 November: daily except Thursdays and Fridays. Times: 1 - 5pm, Bank Holiday Sundays and Bank Holiday Mondays 11am - 5pm. House will close at 4pm on and after 29 October. Garden: 31 March to 4 November: daily except Thursdays and Fridays. Times: 11am to 5.30pm. Estate walks: daily, dawn to dusk. Wheelchair access to ground floor, photograph album on first floor, garden, shop and bookshop (ramp), tea room and restaurant accessible.

Visitors with disabilities may be set down at Reception by arrangement.
Heritage Open Days: No
P Yes. Spaces: 200
Partial. Disabled WC: Yes. Guide Dogs: Yes
£ Yes
Adult: £5.80
Child: £2.90
Other: £14.50 (family). £2.20 (gardens only).

Gowthorpe Manor
Swardeston, Norwich, Norfolk NR14 8DS
Small family house, built in brick in 16th century by Augustine Steward, thrice Mayor of Norwich and MP. Some original features remain but has been altered over the years, especially in early 19th century.
Grant Recipient/Owner: Mrs D M Watkinson
Access contact: Mrs D M Watkinson
Tel: 01508 570216
Opening Arrangements: By prior arrangement on Mondays and occasionally at other times, such as groups in the evening.
Heritage Open Days: No
P Yes. Spaces: 15
No. Disabled WC: No. Guide Dogs: Yes
£ No

Hales Hall Barn
Loddon, Norfolk NR14 6QW
Late 15th century brick and thatch barn 180ft long, built by James Hobart, Henry VII's Attorney General. Queen post roof, and crown post roof to living accommodation, and richly patterned brickwork. The Barn and similar sized gatehouse, ranged around defended courtyards, are all that remain of the house that once stood on this site.
Grant Recipient/Owner: Mr Terence Read
Access contact: Mr Terence Read
Tel: 01508 548395   **Fax:** 01508 548040
Opening Arrangements: All year: Tuesday - Saturday 10am - 5pm (or dusk if earlier); plus Easter - October: Sunday afternoons and Bank Holiday Mondays 11am - 4pm. Closed 25 December - 5 January and Good Friday. Garden with yew and box topiary included in admission charge. Parties and guided tours by prior arrangement with Mr Terence Read, Hales Hall, Loddon, Norfolk NR14 6QW (tel.01508 548395).
Heritage Open Days: No
P Yes. Spaces: 40
Yes. Disabled WC: No. Guide Dogs: Yes
£ Yes
Adult: £1.50
Child: Free
Other: £1.50, £2.50 (guided tours).

King's Lynn Custom House
Purfleet Quay, King's Lynn, Norfolk PE30 1HP
Built 1683 as a merchants exchange, become official Custom House in 1703. Building purchased by the Crown in 1717 for £800 and was used by HM Customs until 1989. The Borough Council of King's Lynn and West Norfolk obtained a lease of the building in 1995 and restored it.
Grant Recipient/Owner:
King's Lynn & West Norfolk Council
Access contact: Mr Tim Hall
Tel: 01553 774297   **Fax:** 01553 772361
Email Address: gaolhouse@west-norfolk.gov.uk
Opening Arrangements: Easter - end of October: Monday - Saturday 9.15am - 5pm, Sunday 10am - 4pm; November - March: daily 10.30am - 4pm. Wheelchair access to ground floor only. Parking in public car parks.
Heritage Open Days: Yes
P See above
Partial. Disabled WC: No. Guide Dogs: Yes
£ No

Old Buckenham Cornmill
Green Lane, Old Buckenham, Norfolk
Mill with the largest diameter tower in England, which had five sets of stones when it was working. Once owned by the Colmans of Norwich and Prince Duleep Singh. Built by John Burlingham in 1818.
Grant Recipient/Owner: Norfolk Windmills Trust
Access contact: Miss A L Jaques
Tel: 01603 222708   **Fax:** 01603 224413
Email Address: amanda.jaques.pt@norfolk.gov.uk
Opening Arrangements: May - September: second Sunday of each month 2 - 5pm. Groups at other times by prior arrangement with Miss A L Jaques, Conservation Officer, Building Conservation Section, Department of Planning and Transportation, Norfolk County Council, County Hall, Martineau Lane, Norwich, Norfolk NR1 2SG (tel.01603 222708).
Heritage Open Days: No
P Yes. Spaces: 6
No. Disabled WC: No. Guide Dogs: No
£ Yes
Child: 70p
Adult: 30p

Old Hall
Norwich Rd, South Burlingham, Norfolk NR13 4EY
Small Elizabethan manor house with a painted stucco fireplace, painted stucco mermaids and scrollwork on the front porch, and a long gallery of hunting scenes in grisaille, c1600.
Grant Recipient/Owner: Mr P Scupham
Access contact: Mr P Scupham
Tel: 01493 750804   **Fax:** 01493 750804
Email Address: goodman@dircon.co.uk
Opening Arrangements: By prior telephone arrangement with Mr P Scupham or Ms M E Steward. No access for guide dogs to the Long Gallery.
Heritage Open Days: Yes
P Yes. Spaces: 8
No. Disabled WC: No. Guide Dogs: Yes, see above.
£ No

Old Meeting House/ Congregational Church
Colegate, Norwich, Norfolk NR3 1BW
Built 1693 in brick with classical dressings and black glazed pantile roof. Unusual sun dial with date of building on front elevation, which is a feature of Free Church buildings. Contains tiered pews to a gallery on three sides and an organ in working order dating from 1650. External paving mirrors the Dutch influence.
Grant Recipient/Owner: Norwich City Council
Access contact: Mr G F D Eve
Tel: 01603 212211   **Fax:** 01603 212345
Email Address: property@norwich.gov.uk
Opening Arrangements: April - September: Wednesdays 12.30 - 4pm. At other times by prior arrangement with Mr G F D Eve, Property Services, St Giles House, St Giles Street, Norwich NR2 1UZ (tel.01603 212343).
Heritage Open Days: Yes
P Yes. Spaces: 2
Partial. Disabled WC: Yes. Guide Dogs: Yes
£ No

Oxburgh Hall
Oxborough, King's Lynn, Norfolk PE33 9PS
Moated manor house with tudor gatehouse, was built in 1428 by the Bedingfeld family who still live there. The rooms show the development from medieval austerity to Victorian comfort, and include a display of embroidery done by Mary, Queen of Scots. Gardens include a French Parterre and woodland walks, as well as a Catholic chapel.
Website Address: www.nationaltrust.org.uk
Grant Recipient/Owner: The National Trust
Access contact: Property Manager
Tel: 01366 328258   **Fax:** 01366 328066
Email Address: aohusr@smtp.ntrust.org.uk
Opening Arrangements: House: 31 March to 4 November daily except Thursdays and Fridays. Times: 1- 5pm, Bank Holidays 11am - 5pm. Last admission 4.30pm. Garden: 3 to 25 March Saturdays and Sundays; 31 March to 4 November: daily except Thursdays and Fridays; August: daily. Times: March 11am - 4pm, 31 March to 4 November 11am - 5.30pm. Wheelchair access to ground floor rooms (shallow ramp), difficult stairs to upper floors, garden largely accessible, tea room and shop accessible.
Heritage Open Days: No
P Yes. Spaces: 100
Partial. Disabled WC: Yes. Guide Dogs: Yes
£ Yes
Adult: £5.30
Other: Family discounts.

Ruined Church of St Mary the Virgin
Houghton-on-the-Hill, Norfolk
Ancient church at least 900 years old. Many original features remain including double splay windows, keyhole chancel, arch built with Roman brick, 12th century North door and early wall paintings.
Grant Recipient/Owner: Norfolk County Council
Access contact: Mr & Mrs R Davey
Tel: 01760 440470
Opening Arrangements: All year at any reasonable time.
Heritage Open Days: Yes
P Yes. Spaces: 40
Yes. Disabled WC: No. Guide Dogs: Yes
£ No

St Andrew's Hall
St Andrew's Street, Norwich, Norfolk
Remains of medieval friary, including the nave (St Andrew's Hall), choir (Blackfriars Hall), crypt, cloisters, private chapel (Beckets) and chapter house. Hammerbeam roof in nave, medieval bosses in choir and a 13th century 7 light East Window. A civic hall in use since 1540.
Grant Recipient/Owner: Norwich City Council
Access contact: Mr Tim Aldous
Tel: 01603 628477   **Fax:** 01603 762182

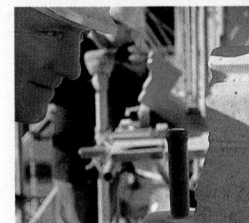

Email Address: taldous.ncc.sah@gtnet.gov.uk
Opening Arrangements: Monday - Saturday 9am - 5pm, subject to events. Wheelchair access to ground floor only. Parking in multi-storey car park in city centre. Green Badge on site, Orange Badge if space is available.
Heritage Open Days: No
Ⓟ See above
♿ Partial. Disabled WC: Yes. Guide Dogs: Yes
💷 No

St Benet's Level Mill

Ludham, Norfolk
Typical example of a Broadland drainage mill with tapering red brick tower, white boat shaped cap, sails and fantail. Built in 18th century and altered over the years, it became redundant in the 1940s. Ground and first floors accessible. Information boards on site.
Grant Recipient/Owner:
Crown Estates Commissioners
Access contact: Mr D L Ritchie
Tel: 01692 678232   **Fax:** 01692 678055
Email Address: d.l.ritchie@farmline.com
Opening Arrangements: Open days: second Sunday in May and first Sunday in August. At other times by prior arrangement with Mr D L Ritchie at Hall Farm, Ludham, Great Yarmouth, Norfolk NR29 5NU (tel.01692 678232) or Miss Jenny Henderson, Carter Jonas, 6-8 Hills Road, Cambridge CB2 1NH (tel.01223 368771). Guide dog access to ground floor only.
Heritage Open Days: No
Ⓟ No
♿ No. Disabled WC: No. Guide Dogs: Yes, see above.
💷 No

St Mary's Abbey

West Dereham, Norfolk
The present six bay house is the remains of the service block of Sir Thomas Dereham's renaissance style mansion, which he built after 1689 incorporating the surviving parts of a Premonstratensian Abbey founded in 1188 by Hubert Walter. Had become a ruin and was only recently restored, with the building re-roofed, re-fenestrated and a first floor and stair tower added. The house is now a private residence.
Grant Recipient/Owner: Mr G Shropshire
Access contact: Miss Sue Watkins
Tel: 01353 727200
Opening Arrangements: By prior arrangement with Miss Sue Watkins, G's Marketing Ltd, Barway, Ely, Cambridgeshire CB7 5TZ (tel.01353 727200). Toilet facilities for the disabled are available on request, although they are not specifically designed.
Heritage Open Days: No
Ⓟ Yes. Spaces: 20
♿ Yes. Disabled WC: Yes. Guide Dogs: Yes
💷 No

St Peter

Dunton, Norfolk
Grade II* redundant medieval church constructed of flint with stone dressings. Has Victorian stained glass, rebuilt porch of 1896, 15th century tower, 14th century nave and remains of previous building. Occasionally used for services.
Grant Recipient/Owner: Norfolk Churches Trust
Access contact: Mr Malcolm Fisher
Tel: 01603 767576
Opening Arrangements: At any reasonable time.
Heritage Open Days: Yes
Ⓟ Yes. Spaces: 3
♿ Yes. Disabled WC: No. Guide Dogs: Yes
💷 No

Shotesham Park Dairy Farm Barn

Newton Flotman, Norfolk
Built c1500 with later additions, part weather-boarded and part-rendered 5-bay timber framed barn with double queen post thatched roof.
Grant Recipient/Owner:
Norfolk Historic Buildings Trust/ Mr Christopher Bailey
Access contact: Mr John Nott
Tel: 01508 470113
Opening Arrangements: All year by prior arrangement with either Mr John Nott (tel.01508 470113) or Mr Christopher Bailey (tel.01508 499285). The Barn is in a busy farmyard but parking can usually be found (apart from at harvest time) for at least two cars by prior arrangement.
Heritage Open Days: No
Ⓟ Yes. Spaces: 2
♿ No. Disabled WC: Yes. Guide Dogs: Yes
💷 No

Thornage Hall Dovecote

Thornage, Holt, Norfolk NR25 7QH
Square dovecote, dated 1728, built of red brick in English bond with hipped roof in red black and black glazed pantiles terminating in square wooden glover. Contains 20 tiers of holes on all 4 sides and on brick spokes projecting from each corner toward the centre.
Grant Recipient/Owner: Norfolk Dovecote Trust/ Camphill Communities East Anglia
Access contact: Ms A Gimelli
Tel: 01263 860305
Opening Arrangements: Open for village fete in July, plus first Sunday in September, 2 - 5pm. At other times by prior written arrangement with Ms A Gimelli at Thornage Hall.
Heritage Open Days: No
Ⓟ Yes. Spaces: 50
♿ No. Disabled WC: No. Guide Dogs: Yes
💷 No

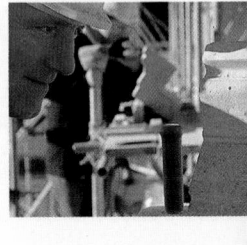

NORTH YORKSHIRE

Beningbrough Hall

**Shipton-by-Beningbrough,
North Yorkshire YO30 1DD**
Country house, 1716, contains an impressive baroque interior. A very high standard of craftmanship is displayed throughout, most of the original work surviving with extremely fine woodcarvings and unusual central corridor running the full length of the house. Over 100 pictures on loan from the National Portrait Gallery are on display. There is a fully equipped Victorian laundry and walled garden.
Website Address: www.nationaltrust.org.uk
Grant Recipient/Owner: The National Trust
Access contact: Property Manager
Tel: 01904 470666   **Fax:** 01904 470002
Email Address: ybbrgb@smtp.ntrust.org.uk
Opening Arrangements: House; 31 March to 30 June, 1 September to 31 October daily except Thursdays and Fridays (but open Good Friday); July and August daily except Thursdays. Times: House: 12 noon - 5pm last admission 4.30pm, grounds 11am - 5.30pm. Wheelchair access (ramped) to ground floor only.
Heritage Open Days: No
Ⓟ Yes. Spaces: 250
♿ Partial. Disabled WC: Yes. Guide Dogs: Yes
💷 Yes
Adult: £5.20 (house). £3.60 (garden & exhibition).
Child: £2.60 (house). £1.80 (garden & exhibition).
Other: £13.00 (family: house). £9.00 (family: garden & exhibition). Discount for cyclists.

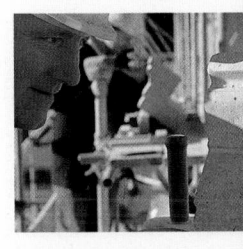

Braithwaite Hall

East Witton, Leyburn, North Yorkshire DL8 4SY
17th century stone farmhouse with fine original features including fireplaces, panelling and oak staircase.
Website Address: www.nationaltrust.org.uk
Grant Recipient/Owner: The National Trust
Access contact: Mrs David Duffus
Tel: 01969 640287
Opening Arrangements: By arrangement with the tenant Mrs David Duffus. No access for coaches. No WC.
Heritage Open Days: No
Ⓟ Yes. Spaces: 10
♿ No. Disabled WC: No. Guide Dogs: Yes
💷 Yes
Adult: £1.00 (including leaflet)
Child: £1.00 (including leaflet)

Castle Howard

York, North Yorkshire YO60 7DA
Large stately home dating from the beginning of the 18th century and designed by Sir John Vanbrugh. Situated in 1000 acres of landscaped grounds which include numerous monuments.
Website Address: www.castlehoward.co.uk
Grant Recipient/Owner: The Hon. Simon Howard
Access contact: Mr D N Peake
Tel: 01653 648444   **Fax:** 01653 648529
Email Address: estatemanager@castlehoward.co.uk
Opening Arrangements: 16 March - 4 November: daily 11am - 4.30pm (Grounds only from 10am); November - mid-March: grounds open most days but please telephone for confirmation in November, December and January. Wheelchair access to all but chapel and first floor of exhibition wing.
Heritage Open Days: No
Ⓟ Yes. Spaces: 300
♿ Partial. Disabled WC: Yes. Guide Dogs: Yes
💷 Yes
Adult: £7.50
Child: £4.50
Other: £6.75

Cawood Castle

nr. Selby, North Yorkshire
This decorated gatehouse, and wing to one side, is all that remains of the castle, once a stronghold of the Archbishops of York. Visitors have included Thomas Wolsey, Henry III, Edward I, and Henry VIII. In the 18th century it was used as a courtroom eventually ending up in domestic use. Extremely steep spiral staircase.

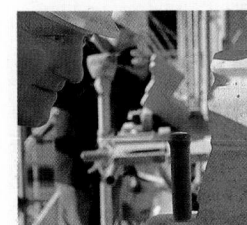

Website Address: www.landmarktrust.co.uk
Grant Recipient/Owner: The Landmark Trust
Access contact: Ms Victoria Piggott
Tel: 01628 825920   **Fax:** 01628 825417
Email Address: vpiggott@landmarktrust.co.uk
Opening Arrangements: The Landmark Trust is an independent charity, which rescues small buildings of historic or architectural importance from decay or unsympathetic improvement. Landmark's aim is to promote the enjoyment of these historic buildings by making them available to stay in for holidays. Cawood Castle can be rented by anyone, at all times of the year, for periods ranging from a weekend to three weeks. Bookings can be made by telephoning the Booking Office on 01628 825925. As the building is in full-time use for holiday accommodation, it is not normally open to the public. However the public can view the building by prior arrangement by telephoning the access contact (Victoria Piggott on 01628 825920) to make an appointment. Potential visitors will be asked to write to confirm the details of their visit.
Heritage Open Days: No
Ⓟ Yes. Spaces: 1
♿ No. Disabled WC: No. Guide Dogs: No
💷 No

Church Cottage

Studley Royal, Ripon, North Yorkshire
Situated adjacent to St Mary's Church, Church Cottage is the original Rectory, designed by Burges to complement the high Victorian Gothic church. It has a muscular, ornate style with intricate heraldic carving above the main entrance. The house sits by the main vista of the Deer Park which visually links St Mary's Church with Ripon Cathedral.
Website Address: www.fountainsabbey.org.uk
Grant Recipient/Owner: The National Trust
Access contact: Sarah Kay
Tel: 01765 608888   **Fax:** 01765 608889
Email Address: yfnsak@smtp.ntrust.org.uk
Opening Arrangements: Viewing on request Monday to Friday 10am - 4pm.
Heritage Open Days: No
Ⓟ Yes. Spaces: 100
♿ No. Disabled WC: No. Guide Dogs: Yes
💷 No

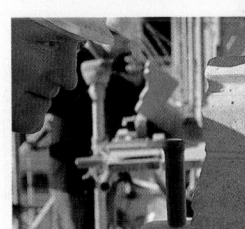

Duncombe Park

Helmsley, York, North Yorkshire YO62 5EB
Recently restored family home of Lord and Lady Feversham. Originally built in 1713 and then rebuilt after a fire in 1879 largely to the original design. Early 18th century gardens.
Website Address: www.duncombepark.com
Grant Recipient/Owner: Lord Feversham
Access contact: The Agent
Tel: 01439 770213   **Fax:** 01439 771114
Email Address: sally@duncombepark.com
Opening Arrangements: House and Gardens: Friday 13 April - 28 October, Sundays - Thursdays 10.30am - 6pm (hourly tours 11am - 4pm). Free flow visits (visitors do not need to join a guided tour) Sundays and Bank Holidays. For group and school visits contact the Estate Office. Special events. Wheelchair access to ground floor only.
Heritage Open Days: No
Ⓟ Yes. Spaces: 200
♿ Partial. Disabled WC: Yes. Guide Dogs: Yes
💷 Yes
Adult: £6.00
Child: £3.00 (10-16)
Other: £5.00

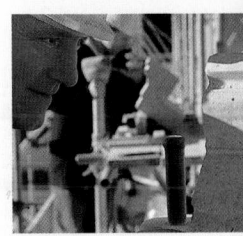

Farnley Hall

Farnley, Otley, North Yorkshire LS21 2QF
Grade I listed building, older part of the house (generally referred to as the Manor House) dates from the mid-17th century. It was Jacobeanized in the 1840s and in recent years has been renovated and modernised and is now let as a separate assured shorthold. The chief visitor interest lies in the Reception Wing added in 1785, designed and built by John Carr of York. The Carr Wing houses a collection of gouache drawings by J M W Turner depicting the Hall itself and the surrounding countryside. Also collections of 18th and early 19th century furniture.
Grant Recipient/Owner: Mr G N Le G Horton-Fawkes
Access contact: Mr G N Le G Horton-Fawkes
Tel: 01943 467905   **Fax:** 01943 463031
Email Address: farnley.hall@farming.co.uk
Opening Arrangements: May - August by prior written arrangement. Some assistance may be required for wheelchair users at certain points, please check with the Farnley Hall Estate.
Heritage Open Days: No
Ⓟ Yes. Spaces: 20
♿ Partial. Disabled WC: Yes. Guide Dogs: Yes
💷 Yes
Adult: £5.00

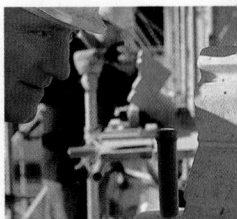

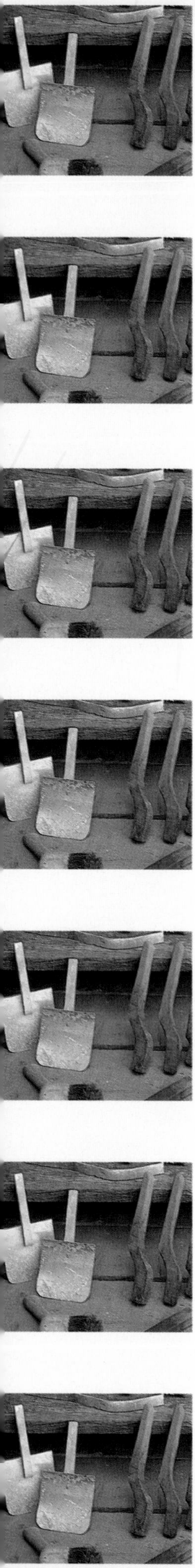

Opening arrangements at properties grant-aided by English Heritage

Fountains Hall

Studley Royal, Ripon, North Yorkshire HG4 3DY

Elizabethan mansion, built between 1589 and 1604 for Stephen Proctor. Two rooms; the Stone Hall and the Arkell Room, both unfurnished, are open to the public. During summer 2001 a third room, the Great Chamber, will be opened to guided tours. This upper room features an ornate chimney piece depicting the Biblical story of the Judgement of Solomon.

Website Address: www.fountainsabbey.org.uk
Grant Recipient/Owner: The National Trust
Access contact: Sarah Kay
Tel: 01765 608888 **Fax:** 01765 608889
Email Address: yfnsak@smtp.ntrust.org.uk
Opening Arrangements: Open as part of the Fountain's Abbey and Studley Royal estate. January to March: 10am - 4pm; April to September 10am - 6pm; October to December 10am - 4pm. Estate closed 24, 25 December and Fridays in January, November and December.
Heritage Open Days: No
P Yes. Spaces: 500
Yes. Disabled WC: Yes. Guide Dogs: Yes
£ Yes
Adult: £4.30
Child: £2.10
Child: £10.30 (family).

Giggleswick School Chapel

Giggleswick, Settle, North Yorkshire BD24 0DE

Built 1897-1901 by T G Jackson for Walter Morrison as a gift to the school to commemorate the Diamond Jubilee of Queen Victoria. Constructed of Gothic Banded rockfaced millstone grit sandstone and limestone, with copper hipped roof to nave and copper covered terracotta dome to chancel. Contains Italian sgrafitto work throughout.

Website Address: www.giggleswick.n-yorks.sch.uk/chapel
Grant Recipient/Owner: The Governors of Giggleswick School
Access contact: The Bursar and Clerk to the Governors
Tel: 01729 893000/893012 **Fax:** 01729 893150
Email Address: bursar@giggleswick.n.yorks.sch.uk
Opening Arrangements: By prior arrangement, apart from July to September when restoration works are due to be undertaken.
Heritage Open Days: No
P Yes. Spaces: 25
Partial. Disabled WC: No. Guide Dogs: Yes
£ No

Grand Assembly Rooms

Blake Street, York, North Yorkshire

Important surviving early Palladian style building (exact model of his Egyptian Hall, based on Vitruvius) designed by Lord Burlington and built by public subscription between 1732 and 1736. Originally used for balls and assemblies, after World War II and in the last 10 years the Rooms have been fully restored and now house a restaurant.

Grant Recipient/Owner: Director of Environment & Development Services, City of York
Access contact: Shona Davies
Tel: 01904 637254
Opening Arrangements: Daily 12 noon - 12 midnight. Closed Christmas Day only. Parking at Marygate car park 5 minutes away, disabled parking adjacent in Blake Street.
Heritage Open Days: No
P See above
Yes. Disabled WC: Yes. Guide Dogs: Yes
£ No

Jervaulx Abbey

East Witton Without, York, North Yorkshire

Ruins of Cistercian Abbey moved to this site in 1156, built of sandstone ashlar in Early English style. Remains of nave, transepts and choir, with a cloister on the south side of the nave, flanked by a chapter house to the east and a kitchen and dorter to the south.

Grant Recipient/Owner: Mr Burdon
Access contact: Mr Ian Burdon
Tel: 01677 460391
Opening Arrangements: At any reasonable time. Wheelchair access is limited by uneven terrain and steps to various parts of the site.
Heritage Open Days: Yes
P Yes. Spaces: 55
Partial. Disabled WC: Yes. Guide Dogs: Yes
£ Yes
Adult: £2.00 (honesty box)
Child: £1.50 (honesty box)

Merchant Taylors Hall

Aldwark, York, North Yorkshire YO1 2BX

Guildhall of the Merchant Taylors' Company, c1400 with late 15th century wing. Mainly timber-framed and refaced in brick with tile roofs and brick chimney stacks. Refenestrated early 17th century and extended, reface and porch added 1714-15, entrance front and wing refaced c1730. Restored with some rebuilding and further extensions in 20th century. Contains painted glass, c1700, by Henry Gyles.

Grant Recipient/Owner: Company of Merchant Taylors
Access contact: Mrs Audrey Lambert
Tel: 01904 632967
Opening Arrangements: May - September: Tuesdays 10am - 4pm. At other times by prior arrangement. For Hall bookings (apart from visits) contact 01904 624889.
Heritage Open Days: No
P No
Yes. Disabled WC: Yes. Guide Dogs: Yes
£ No

The Mount School - Lindley Murray Summerhouse

Dalton Terrace, York, North Yorkshire YO24 4DD

Grade II* listed summerhouse built c1774, formerly situated in the grounds of Holgate House, York. Octagonal timber structure on raised stepped circular base with lead ogee roof and decorated with Doric columns. Restored in 1997.

Website Address: www.mount.n-yorks.sch.uk
Grant Recipient/Owner: The Mount School
Access contact: Ms Anne Bolton
Tel: 01904 667506 **Fax:** 01904 667524
Email Address: abolton.mount@talk21.com
Opening Arrangements: By prior arrangement Monday - Friday all year (except Bank Holidays) 9am - 4.30pm.
Heritage Open Days: No
P Yes. Spaces: 3
Yes. Disabled WC: Yes. Guide Dogs: Yes
£ No
Donations welcome.

Newburgh Priory

Coxwold, York, North Yorkshire YO6 4AS

Priory originally built in 1145 with alterations in Tudor, Jacobean and Georgian periods. Tomb of Oliver Cromwell in the House, extensive grounds, walled garden and walks with views across the lake to the White Horse. Tea rooms.

Access contact: Sir George Wombwell Bt
Tel: 01347 868372
Opening Arrangements: April, May and June: Wednesdays and Sundays, Easter Sunday and Bank Holiday Monday and May Bank Holiday Mondays. Guided tours every 30 minutes starting at 2.30pm. Last tour 4.30pm. Grounds open 2 - 6pm. Coach parties and groups by arrangement. Wheelchair access to ground floor of house, parts of garden.
Heritage Open Days: No
P No
Partial. Disabled WC: Yes. Guide Dogs: No
£ Yes
Adult: £2.00 (house). £2.00 (grounds).
Child: £1.00 (house). Free (grounds).

Norton Conyers Hall

nr. Ripon, North Yorkshire HG4 5EQ

Medieval house with Stuart and Georgian additions. 18th century walled garden nearby. Family pictures, furniture and costumes. Visited by Charlotte Bronte in 1839, a family legend of a mad woman confined in an attic room inspired the mad Mrs Rochester in 'Jane Eyre' and the Hall was the model for 'Thornfield Hall'.

Grant Recipient/Owner: Sir James Graham Bt
Access contact: Sir James Graham Bt
Tel: 01765 640333 **Fax:** 01765 640333
Email Address: norton.conyers@ripon.org
Opening Arrangements: House and Garden: 13 May - 9 September Sundays, 9 - 14 July daily, Easter Sunday and Monday, Bank Holiday Sundays and Mondays. House 2 - 5pm, Garden (no admission charge but donations welcome) 11.30am - 5pm. Wheelchair access to ground floor only.
Heritage Open Days: No
P Yes. Spaces: 60
Partial. Disabled WC: Yes. Guide Dogs: Yes
£ Yes
Adult: £4.00
Child: £3.00 (10-16)
Other: £3.00 (senior citizens)

Ormesby Hall

Church Lane, Ormesby, Middlesbrough TS7 9AS

A mid-18th century Palladian mansion, notable for its fine plasterwork and carved wood decoration. The Victorian laundry and kitchen with scullery and game larder are interesting. 18th century stable block, attributed to Carr of York, is leased to the Cleveland Mounted Police. Large model railway and garden with holly walk.

Website Address: www.nationaltrust.org.uk
Grant Recipient/Owner: The National Trust
Access contact: Property Manager
Tel: 01642 324188 **Fax:** 01642 300937
Email Address: yorkor@smtp.ntrust.org.uk
Opening Arrangements: 1 April to 4 November daily except Mondays, Fridays and Saturdays (but open Good Friday and Bank Holiday Mondays) 2 - 5pm. Wheelchair access to: ground floor of house (shallow step at entrance), shop, tea room and garden. Car park is approximately 100 metres from house.
Heritage Open Days: No
P Yes. Spaces: 100
Partial. Disabled WC: Yes. Guide Dogs: Yes
£ Yes
Adult: £3.50. £2.20 (garden, railway and exhibition only).
Child: £1.70. £1.00 (garden, railway and exhibition only).
Other: £8.50 (family).

The Pigsty

Fyling Hall, Fylingthorpe, North Yorkshire

Two pigs were the excuse for this exercise in primitive classicism, inspired by buildings seen by Squire Barry of Fyling Hall on his travels around the Mediterranean in the 1880s. Uneven steps from parking place.

Website Address: www.landmarktrust.co.uk
Grant Recipient/Owner: The Landmark Trust
Access contact: Ms Victoria Piggott
Tel: 01628 825920 **Fax:** 01628 825417
Email Address: vpiggott@landmarktrust.co.uk
Opening Arrangements: The Landmark Trust is an independent charity, which rescues small buildings of historic or architectural importance from decay or unsympathetic improvement. Landmark's aim is to promote the enjoyment of these historic buildings by making them available to stay in for holidays. The Pigsty can be rented by anyone, at all times of the year, for periods ranging from a weekend to three weeks. Bookings can be made by telephoning the Booking Office on 01628 825925. As the building is in full-time use for holiday accommodation, it is not normally open to the public. However the public can view the building by prior arrangement by telephoning the access contact (Victoria Piggott on 01628 825920) to make an appointment. Potential visitors will be asked to write to confirm the details of their visit.
Heritage Open Days: No
P Yes. Spaces: 1
No. Disabled WC: No. Guide Dogs: No
£ No

St Paulinus

Brough Park, Richmond, North Yorkshire DL10 7PJ

Catholic neo-Gothic chapel designed by Bonomi with priest's accommodation and school room in undercroft.

Grant Recipient/Owner: Mr Greville Worthington
Access contact: Mr Greville Worthington
Tel: 01748 812127
Email Address: tote@grev.demon.co.uk
Opening Arrangements: By prior arrangement.
Heritage Open Days: No
P Yes. Spaces: 2
No. Disabled WC: No. Guide Dogs: Yes
£ No

St Saviour's Church

(Archaeological Resource Centre)
St Saviourgate, York, North Yorkshire YO1 8NN

Church on site by late 11th century, present building dates from the 15th and extensively remodelled in 1845. Now houses the Archaeological Resource Centre which contains an archaeological collection excavated by the York Archaeological Trust and promotes access to archaeological material through hands-on displays.

Grant Recipient/Owner: Dr R A Hall
Access contact: Miss Christine McDonnell
Tel: 01904 643211 **Fax:** 01904 627097
Email Address: cmcdonnell@yorkarchaeology.co.uk
Opening Arrangements: School holidays: Monday - Friday 11am - 15.30pm; groups by prior arrangement only during school term. For further details please check with Miss Christine McDonnell, York Archaeological Trust, Cromwell House, 13 Ogleforth, York, North Yorkshire YO1 7FG (tel.01904 643211). Visitors who simply want to view the building may look round free of charge, otherwise admission charged for entrance to Archaeological Resource Centre, £3.60 for adults and children (carers/enablers free when helping disabled person). Disabled parking just outside entrance, otherwise public car parks close by. Sensory garden on architectural theme.
Heritage Open Days: No
P See above
Yes. Disabled WC: Yes. Guide Dogs: Yes
£ No

Scampston Hall

Scampston, Malton, North Yorkshire, YO17 8NG

Late 17th century country house, extensively remodelled in 1801 by Thomas Leverton. Contains Regency interiors and an art collection. Set in a parkland designed by

'Capability' Brown with 10 acres of lakes and a Palladian bridge.
Website Address: www.scampston.co.uk
Grant Recipient/Owner: Sir Charles Legard Bt
Access contact: Sir Charles Legard Bt
Tel: 01944 758224 **Fax:** 01944 758700
Email Address: legard@scampton.co.uk
Opening Arrangements: 27 May - 10 June and 22 July - 5 August (closed Saturdays), 1.30 - 5pm. Groups at other times by prior arrangement. Wheelchair access to ground floor only.
Heritage Open Days: No
P Yes. Spaces: 50
♿ Partial. Disabled WC: Yes. Guide Dogs: Yes
£ Yes
Adult: £5.00 House, Garden & Park.

Temple of Victory

Allerton Park, nr. Knaresborough, North Yorkshire HG5 0SE
Attributed to Henry Holland, architect for the Duke of York, but possibly by James Payne. Late 18th century octagon tower in the Grecian style. The entrance is by a double flight of steps secured by iron palisades.
Grant Recipient/Owner: The Gerald Arthur Rolph Foundation for Historic Preservation & Education
Access contact: The Gerald Arthur Rolph Foundation for Historic Preservation & Education
Tel: 01423 330927
Opening Arrangements: Easter Sunday - end of September: Sundays and Bank Holiday Mondays 1 - 5pm. Parking half a mile away.
Heritage Open Days: No
P Yes. Spaces: 30
♿ No. Disabled WC: No. Guide Dogs: No
£ No

Thompson Mausoleum

Little Ouseburn Churchyard, Little Ouseburn, North Yorkshire YO26 9TS
18th century Mausoleum in magnesian limestone. It is a rotunda encircled by 13 Tuscan columns, above which a frieze and cornice support a plain drum and ribbed domed roof. Listed Grade II*.
Grant Recipient/Owner: Mr H Hibbs
Access contact: Mr H Hibbs
Tel: 01423 330414
Email Address: helier@clara.net
Opening Arrangements: Always available to view from the outside but no access to interior at present as it is awaiting repair.
Heritage Open Days: No
P Yes. Spaces: 4
♿ Partial. Disabled WC: No. Guide Dogs: Yes
£ No

NORTHAMPTONSHIRE

Hall Farmhouse

Hall Yard, Kings Cliffe, Peterborough, Northamptonshire PE8 6XQ
Former medieval open hall. Music room, c1795, with coved and ornamented ceiling. Home of William Law 1740-61.
Grant Recipient/Owner: Mr J A R Grove
Access contact: Mr J A R Grove
Tel: 01780 470748
Opening Arrangements: By prior arrangement.
Heritage Open Days: No
P Yes. Spaces: 3
♿ No. Disabled WC: No. Guide Dogs: Yes
£ No

Laxton Hall

Corby, Northamptonshire NN17 3AU
Built in 18th century. Formerly a boys school, now a Polish residential care home.
Grant Recipient/Owner:
Polish Benevolent Housing Association Ltd
Access contact: Mr J Palmi
Tel: 01780 444292 **Fax:** 01780 444574
Opening Arrangements: By prior written arrangement with Mr J Palmi, PBF Housing Association, 2 Devonia Road, London N1 8JJ, in the early afternoon of the first Monday of each month (except during Religious Festivals).
Heritage Open Days: No
P Yes. Spaces: 10
♿ No. Disabled WC: No. Guide Dogs: No
£ No

The Manor House

Hardwick, Wellingborough, Northamptonshire PE8 5HZ
Manor house dating back to the 12th century. The exterior of the building has been restored including a fine example of a Collyweston roof. Now part of a modern working farm.
Grant Recipient/Owner: Mr Siddons
Access contact: Mr Siddons
Tel: 01933 678785 **Fax:** 01933 678166
Email Address: siddons@siddons.fsbusiness.co.uk
Opening Arrangements: Exterior only. Opening arrangements under review at time of going to print, please check English Heritage website for current information.
Heritage Open Days: No
P Yes. Spaces: 4
♿ No. Disabled WC: No. Guide Dogs: No
£ No

Nunnery Cottages

1/2 The Maltings, Desborough Road, Rothwell, Northamptonshire NN14 6JZ
Farmhouse, now two houses, built 1660 (part may be earlier, mid-16th century) of ironstone with limestone and brick dressings, plain tile and thatched roofs.
Grant Recipient/Owner: Rothwell Preservation Trust
Access contact: Mrs C E Mackay
Tel: 01536 713252/711086 **Fax:** 01536 713252
Opening Arrangements: By prior written arrangement with Mrs C E Mackay, Secretary of the Rothwell Preservation Trust, 23 High Street, Rothwell, Northamptonshire NN14 6AD.
Heritage Open Days: No
P No
♿ No
£ No

The Prebendal Manor House

Nassington, nr. Peterborough, Northamptonshire PE8 6QG
Reputedly the oldest manor house in Northamptonshire, dating from the early 13th century and on the site of a Saxon hall. The House has been much altered over the centuries. The Prebend of Nassington was established in Lincoln Cathedral in the 12th century and the House was occupied by the Prebendary and his tenants until 1836 when the Prebend was dissolved. Also on site is a tithe barn museum, 15th century dovecote, fish ponds and a recreated medieval garden.
Website Address: www.prebendal-manor.demon.co.uk
Grant Recipient/Owner: Mrs Jane Baile
Access contact: Mrs Jane Baile
Tel: 01780 782575
Email Address: info@prebendal-manor.demon.co.uk
Opening Arrangements: May, June and September: Wednesdays and Sundays 1 - 5.30pm; July and August: Wednesdays, Thursdays and Sundays 1 - 5.30pm; Bank Holiday Mondays 1 - 5.30pm. Closed Christmas. Groups by prior arrangement. Free audio tours.
Heritage Open Days: No
P Yes. Spaces: 14
♿ Partial. Disabled WC: No. Guide Dogs: Yes
£ Yes
Adult: £4.00
Child: £1.20
Other: £3.50 (groups 20+), free (National Archaeology Days).

NORTHUMBERLAND

Bamburgh Castle

Bamburgh, Northumberland, NE69 7DF
Rocky fortress with Norman keep, Kings Hall, Cross Hall, bakehouse, Victorian scullery, armoury and dungeon containing a collection of fine china, porcelain, glassware, paintings, furniture, tapestries, arms and armour. Home of the Armstrong family.
Website Address: www.bamburghcastle.com
Grant Recipient/Owner:
Trustees of Lord Armstrong Deceased/ Lady Armstrong
Access contact: Mr R Bewley
Tel: 01668 214515 **Fax:** 01668 214060
Email Address: bamburghcastle@aol.com
Opening Arrangements: 17 March - 31 October: daily 11am - 5pm (last admission 4.30pm). Wheelchair access to first 5 rooms only.
Heritage Open Days: No
P Yes. Spaces: 100
♿ Partial. Disabled WC: Yes. Guide Dogs: Yes
£ Yes
Adult: £4.50
Child: £1.50
Other: £3.50 (senior citizens)

Belford Hall

Belford, Northumberland NE70 7EY
Country house, 1754-56 by James Paine, wings and rear entrance added 1818 by John Dobson. The property stood derelict for 40 years until it was restored by the North East Civic Trust and the Monument Trust between 1984-87.
Grant Recipient/Owner: North East Civic Trust
Access contact: Ms Sheila Fairbairn
Tel: 01668 213794
Opening Arrangements: Every day in the months of May and September to include the spring and summer bank holidays from 12 noon to 6pm. Wheelchair access to ground floor with assistance (three steps to main entrance). No public toilets.
Heritage Open Days: No
P Yes. Spaces: 8
♿ Partial. Disabled WC: No. Guide Dogs: Yes
£ No

Brinkburn Mill

Longframlington, Rothbury, Northumberland NE65 8AR
Brinkburn Priory was founded c1135 within a loop of the River Coquet. The Mill was built c1800 near the site of its medieval predecessor, but dressed up later to improve the view from the house. The wheel and grinding stones are still in place, although long unused.
Website Address: www.landmarktrust.co.uk
Grant Recipient/Owner: The Landmark Trust
Access contact: Ms Victoria Piggott
Tel: 01628 825920 **Fax:** 01628 825417
Email Address: vpiggott@landmarktrust.co.uk
Opening Arrangements: The Landmark Trust is an independent charity, which rescues small buildings of historic or architectural importance from decay or unsympathetic improvement. Landmark's aim is to promote the enjoyment of these historic buildings by making them available to stay in for holidays. Brinkburn Mill can be rented by anyone, at all times of the year, for periods ranging from a weekend to three weeks. Bookings can be made by telephoning the Booking Office on 01628 825925. As the building is in full-time use for holiday accommodation, it is not normally open to the public. However the public can view the building by prior arrangement by telephoning the access contact (Victoria Piggott on 01628 825920) to make an appointment. Potential visitors will be asked to write to confirm the details of their visit.
Heritage Open Days: No
P Yes. Spaces: 1
♿ No. Disabled WC: No. Guide Dogs: Yes
£ No

Chillingham Castle

Chillingham, Northumberland NE66 5NJ
Medieval castle owned by the same family for 800 years, housing collection of antiques and artefacts from all over the world and a museum. Set in grounds designed by Sir Jeffrey Wyatville. Due to its strategic position close to the Scottish border the Castle was often besieged and was visited many times by royalty.
Website Address: www.chillingham-castle.com
Grant Recipient/Owner: Sir Humphry Wakefield Bt
Access contact: Mr A S de Courtenay-Wellum
Tel: 01668 215359 **Fax:** 01668 215463
Email Address: enquiries@chillingham-castle.com
Opening Arrangements: May - September: daily 12 noon - 5pm. Closed Tuesdays in May, June and September. Limited wheelchair access to parts of ground floor only due to varying floor levels, steep and spiral staircases.
Heritage Open Days: No
P Yes. Spaces: 50
♿ Partial. Disabled WC: Yes. Guide Dogs: Yes
£ Yes
Adult: £4.50
Child: Free
Other: £4.00 (senior citizens), £3.80 (groups).

Cragside

Rothbury, Morpeth, Northumberland NE65 7PX
High Victorian mansion by Norman Shaw, with original furniture and fittings including William Morris's stained glass and earliest wallpapers. Built for the inventor-industrialist and armaments manufacturer, Lord Armstrong, who installed the world's first hydro-electric lighting. The mansion is set in a 1,000-acre wooded estate, with rock garden, formal garden, man-made lakes and hydro-electric machinery.
Website Address: www.nationaltrust.org.uk
Grant Recipient/Owner: The National Trust
Access contact: Mr John O'Brien
Tel: 01669 620333 ex 101 **Fax:** 01669 620066
Email Address: nrcjob@smtp.ntrust.org.uk
Opening Arrangements: 31 March to 4 November: Tuesday - Sunday (and Bank Holiday Mondays). Times: House 1- 5.30pm (last admission 4.30pm); estate and gardens 10.30am - 7pm (last admission 5pm). Winter opening (estate only) 7 November to 16 December: Wednesday - Sunday 11am - 4pm. Wheelchair access to ground floor of house and one landing area on first floor.
Heritage Open Days: No
P Yes. Spaces: 400
♿ Partial. Disabled WC: Yes. Guide Dogs: Yes
£ Yes
Adult: £6.70 (house & estate). £4.20 (estate only).
Child: £3.40 (house & estate). £2.10 (estate only).
Other: £16.80 (family: house & estate). £10.50 (family: estate only). No admission charge to estate during winter opening.

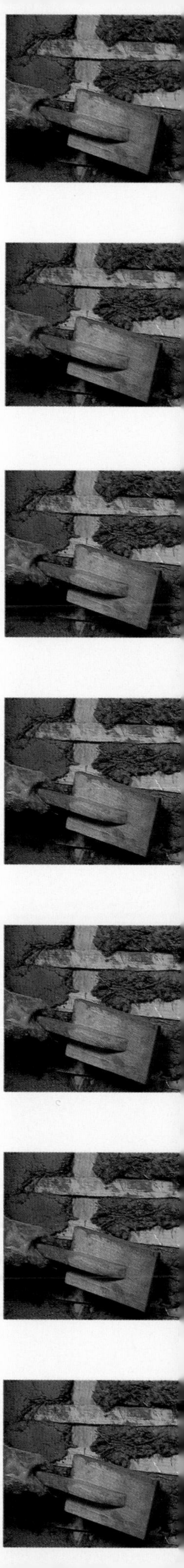

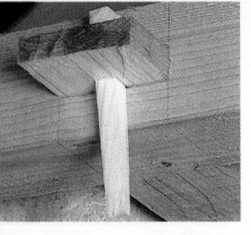
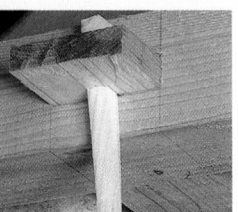
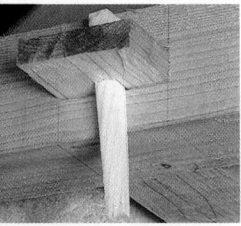
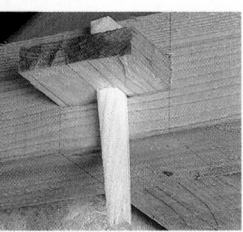
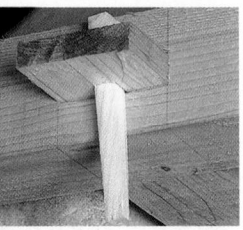
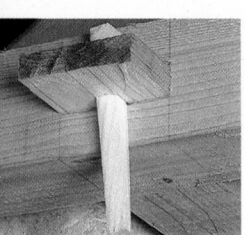
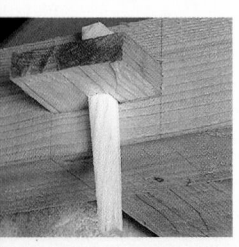

⌗ Opening arrangements at properties grant-aided by English Heritage

Cruck Barn

Towhouse, Bardon Mill, Hexham, Northumberland NE47 7EQ
Grade II* 17th century heather-thatched cruck barn.
Grant Recipient/Owner: Mrs J G Hayward
Access contact: Mrs J G Hayward
Tel: 01434 344473   **Fax:** 01434 344473
Opening Arrangements: By prior arrangement.
Heritage Open Days: No
Ⓟ Yes. Spaces: 2
♿ Yes. Disabled WC: No. Guide Dogs: Yes
£ No

Hexham Moot Hall

Market Place, Hexham, Northumberland NE46 3NH
Built c1400 and used as a home, office and court for the Archbishop of York's bailiff who administered Hexhamshire from the Hall. The former stores on the ground floor are now an art gallery, the first floor courtroom houses the Border Library and the second floor hall is used for community activities.
Grant Recipient/Owner: Tynedale District Council
Access contact: Ms Janet Goodridge
Tel: 01434 652351   **Fax:** 01434 652425
Email Address: museum@tynedale.gov.uk
Opening Arrangements: Mondays, Tuesdays, Thursdays and Fridays 10am - 12.30pm and 1.30 - 3pm. Closed Christmas to New Year.
Heritage Open Days: No
Ⓟ No
♿ No. Disabled WC: No. Guide Dogs: Yes
£ No

High Meadows Cottage Barn

Whitshields, Bardon Mill, Northumberland NE47 7BN
18th century stone walled, cruck roofed heather thatched barn with flagged floor. Perhaps a unique survival of a once-common vernacular building type, remaining virtually unaltered.
Grant Recipient/Owner: Mr D W Collinson
Access contact: Dr M Crick
Tel: 0777 1996 838
Opening Arrangements: By prior telephone arrangement. Wheelchair access not without difficulty.
Heritage Open Days: No
Ⓟ Yes. Spaces: 4
♿ Partial. Disabled WC: No. Guide Dogs: Yes
£ No

High Staward Farm

Langley-on-Tyne, Hexham, Northumberland NE47 5NS
Georgian farmhouse standing inside a walled garden surrounded by the farm steading. Has a ging gang, threshing machine, pig stys with stone troughs and a blacksmiths shop. Most of the house and buildings are of dressed stone and the house has flagged floors, ceiling hooks, cheeseboard and rail, large pantry and servants staircase. Still a working hill farm.
Grant Recipient/Owner: Mr R J Coulson
Access contact: Mr R J Coulson
Tel: 01434 683619
Opening Arrangements: By prior arrangement.
Heritage Open Days: No
Ⓟ Yes. Spaces: 2
♿ No. Disabled WC: No. Guide Dogs: Yes
£ No

Lady's Well

Holystone, Harbottle, Northumberland
The Lady's Holy Well is considered to be of Roman origin and is located on a halting place along the Roman road. The main feature of the well today is a rectangular stone tank which is fed by a natural spring.
Website Address: www.nationaltrust.org.uk
Grant Recipient/Owner: The National Trust
Access contact: Mr John O'Brien
Tel: 01669 620333 ex 101   **Fax:** 01669 620066
Email Address: ncrjob@smtp.ntrust.org.uk
Opening Arrangements: Open all day throughout the year.
Heritage Open Days: No
Ⓟ No
♿ No. Disabled WC: No. Guide Dogs: Yes
£ No

Lambley Viaduct

Lambley, Tynedale, Northumberland
17 arch stone viaduct, 100ft high and 1650ft long, spanning the South Tyne river. Originally carried single track, now used as a footpath.
Grant Recipient/Owner: British Rail Property Board/ North Pennines Heritage Trust
Access contact: Mr David Flush
Tel: 01434 382045

Email Address: np.ht@virgin.net
Opening Arrangements: At all times as part of the South Tyne Trail between Featherstone Park and Alston. Wheelchair access from Coanwood End.
Heritage Open Days: No
Ⓟ Yes. Spaces: 30
♿ Yes. Disabled WC: No. Guide Dogs: Yes
£ No

Lindisfarne Castle

Holy Island, Berwick-upon-Tweed, Northumberland TD15 2SH
Built in 1550 to protect Holy Island harbour from attack, the castle was converted into a private house for Edward Hudson by Sir Edwin Lutyens in 1903. Small walled garden was designed by Gertrude Jekyll. 19th century lime kilns in field by the castle.
Website Address: www.nationaltrust.org.uk
Grant Recipient/Owner:
Access contact: Property Manager
Tel: 01289 389244   **Fax:** 01289 389349
Opening Arrangements:
1 April to 31 October: daily except Fridays (but open Good Friday). Opening times 12 noon - 3pm, but sometimes earlier or later as the tide allows. Council car park one mile from site.
Heritage Open Days: No
Ⓟ See above
♿ No. Disabled WC: No. Guide Dogs: Yes
£ Yes
Adult: £4.20
Child: £2.10
Other: £10.50 (family). NT members free.

Little Harle Tower

Kirkwhelpington, Newcastle-upon-Tyne, Northumberland NE19 2PD
Medieval tower with 17th century range and a Victorian wing which contains a recently restored 1740s drawing room. It has been one family's home since 1830 though part is now let.
Grant Recipient/Owner: Mr J P Palmer Anderson
Access contact: Mr John Clark
Tel: 01434 320363   **Fax:** 01434 320675
Email Address: post.haltwhistle@csh.co.uk
Opening Arrangements: By prior arrangement (at least two weeks notice required) with Mr John Clark of Clark Scott Harden, Market Place, Haltwhistle, Northumberland NE49 0BP (tel.01434 320363).
Heritage Open Days: No
Ⓟ Yes. Spaces: 6
♿ Partial. Disabled WC: No. Guide Dogs: Yes
£ No
Donations to the church requested.

Mitford Hall Camellia House

Morpeth, Northumberland
East wing and conservatory of country house built c1820 by John Dobson, detached from main house by demolition of north-east wing in 20th century.
Grant Recipient/Owner: Shepherd Offshore plc
Access contact: Mr B Shepherd
Opening Arrangements: By prior written arrangement during the summer. Wheelchair access by prior arrangement. Ordinary toilet on site may be accessible for some disabled persons, please contact Hall for further information.
Heritage Open Days: No
Ⓟ Yes. Spaces: 3
♿ Yes. Disabled WC: Yes. Guide Dogs: Yes
£ No

St Cuthbert's Chapel

Farne Islands, Northumberland
St Cuthbert's Chapel was completed in 1370. By the early 19th century it was in a ruinous condition. Restored in 1840 by Archdeacon Thorp it includes some fine 17th century woodwork from Durham Cathedral and a memorial to Grace Darling. Remains of an original window.
Website Address: www.nationaltrust.org.uk
Grant Recipient/Owner: The National Trust
Access contact: Mr John Walton
Tel: 01665 720651   **Fax:** 01665 720651
Email Address: john.walton@ntrust.org.uk
Opening Arrangements: 1 to 30 April, 1 August to 30 September: daily, Inner Farne Island (St Cuthbert's Chapel) and Staple Island 10.30am - 6pm (Low Season). 1 May to 31 July: daily, Staple Island 10.30am - 1.30pm, Inner Farne Island 1.30pm - 5pm (High Season). Inner Farne Island is accessible for wheelchairs, Staple Island is not accessible. Lavatory for disabled on Inner Farne Island. Guide dogs are allowed on boat but not on islands. Parking in Seahouse (nearest mainland village).
Heritage Open Days: No
Ⓟ See above
♿ Partial. Disabled WC: Yes. Guide Dogs: See above
£ Yes

Adult: £3.00 (Low Season). £4.00 (High Season). Provisional
Child: £1.50 (Low Season). £2.00 (High Season). Provisional.

The Tower

Elsdon, Northumberland NE19 1AA
14th century Tower House, residence of the Rector until 1961 and originally used as a refuge against Border raids.
Grant Recipient/Owner: J F Wollaston
Access contact: J F Wollaston
Fax: 01830 520904
Opening Arrangements: By previously arranged guided tour, weekends only, 1 April - 30 October. Parking in village.
Heritage Open Days: No
Ⓟ Yes. Spaces: 30
♿ No. Disabled WC: No. Guide Dogs: Yes
£ Yes
Adult: £3.00

Wallington Hall & Clock Tower

Cambo, Morpeth, Northumberland NE61 4AP
House was built in 1688 on site of a former pele tower for Sir Walter Blackett, a wealthy Newcastle upon Tyne merchant. It served as a shooting box until Sir Walter's grandson, Sir Walter Calverley Blackett decorated the interiors and erected the Clock Tower and stable buildings.
Website Address: www.nationaltrust.org.uk
Grant Recipient/Owner: The National Trust
Access contact: Property Manager
Tel: 01670 774283   **Fax:** 01670 774420
Email Address: nwabmp@smtp.ntrust.org.uk
Opening Arrangements: House: 31 March to 30 September: daily except Tuesdays 1 - 5.30pm (last entry 5.00pm). 1 to 28 October: daily except Tuesdays 1 - 4.30pm (last entry 4pm). The grounds are open 365 days a year. No wheelchair access to first floor of house.
Heritage Open Days: No
Ⓟ Yes. Spaces: 500
♿ Partial. Disabled WC: Yes. Guide Dogs: Yes
£ Yes
Adult: £5.50 (house, garden & grounds). £4.00 (garden & grounds only).
Child: £2.75 (house, garden & grounds). £2.00 (garden & grounds only).
Other: £13.75 (family).

NOTTINGHAMSHIRE

Kiln Warehouse

Castle Station, Newark, Nottinghamshire
Grade II* former warehouse. Early example of the use of massed concrete construction. Interior completely destroyed by fire in the early 1990s, the exterior walls have been restored and warehouse converted into offices.
Grant Recipient/Owner: The Regional Director
Access contact: Mr Edward Vanstone
Tel: 0115 950 7577   **Fax:** 0115 950 7688
Email Address: edwardv@fhp.co.uk
Opening Arrangements: The exterior walls for which the property is notable can be viewed without arrangement. Access to internal courtyard is by prior arrangement with Mr Edward Vanstone of Fisher Hargreaves Proctor, Chartered Surveyors, 10 Oxford Street, Nottingham NG1 5BG (tel.0115 950 7577). Parking available on adjacent land.
Heritage Open Days: No
Ⓟ See above
♿ Yes. Disabled WC: No. Guide Dogs: Yes
£ No

Newdigate House

Castle Gate, Nottingham, Nottinghamshire NG1 6AF
House, c1675, built for Thomas Newdigate. Stucco with ashlar dressings, hipped slate roof, sash windows, panelled rooms and Adam-style plasterwork. Crested wrought-iron railings, central gateway and overthrow, probably by Francis Foulgham, to the exterior. Marshal Tallard was held prisoner here after the battle of Blenheim. The ground floor is now a restaurant.
Grant Recipient/Owner: Mr Alan Trease
Access contact: Mr Ashley Walters
Tel: 0115 8475587
Opening Arrangements: Daily 11am - 11pm. Some assistance may be required for wheelchair access, please check with Mr Walters on 0115 8475587.
Heritage Open Days: No
Ⓟ No
♿ Partial. Disabled WC: No. Guide Dogs: Yes
£ No

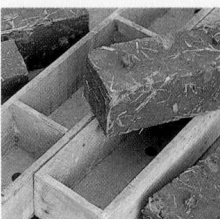

OXFORDSHIRE

Blenheim Palace & Park

Woodstock, Oxfordshire OX20 1PX

Ancestral home of the Dukes of Marlborough and birthplace of Winston Churchill. Built between 1705-22 for John Churchill, the 1st Duke, in recognition of his victory at the Battle of Blenheim in 1704. Designed by Sir John Vanbrugh, the house contains in its many state rooms a collection of paintings, furniture, bronzes and the Marlborough Victories tapestries. A five-room Churchill Exhibition includes his birth room. 'Capability' Brown park and gardens.

Website Address: www.blenheimpalace.com
Grant Recipient/Owner: Duke of Marlborough
Access contact: Mr N Day
Tel: 01993 811325   **Fax:** -1993 813527
Email Address: nickday@blenheimpalace.com
Opening Arrangements: Palace: 12 March - end of October, daily 10.30am - 5.30pm (last admission 4.45pm). Park: daily (except Christmas Day) 9am - 6pm (last admission 4.45pm). High Lodge may be visited by prior written arrangement with the Estate Office.
Heritage Open Days: No
P Yes. Spaces: 10000
♿ Yes. Disabled WC: Yes. Guide Dogs: Yes
£ Yes
Adult: £9.30
Child: £4.80
Other: £7.50 (senior citizens). £23.00 (family ticket)

Broughton Castle

Banbury, Oxfordshire OX15 5EB

Originally built c1300, the castle stands on an island site surrounded by a 3 acre moat. Greatly enlarged in 1550 and decorated with plaster ceilings, panelling and fireplaces. Ancestral home of the Lords Saye and Sele since 1450.

Website Address: www.broughtoncastle.demon.co.uk
Grant Recipient/Owner: Lord Saye & Sele
Access contact: Lord Saye & Sele
Tel: 01295 262624   **Fax:** 01295 276070
Opening Arrangements: 20 May - 12 September: Wednesdays and Sundays, plus Thursdays in July and August and Bank Holiday Mondays (including Easter) 2 - 5pm. Groups at any time throughout the year by prior arrangement. Wheelchair access to ground floor only.
Heritage Open Days: No
P Yes. Spaces: 150
♿ Partial. Disabled WC: Yes. Guide Dogs: Yes
£ Yes
Adult: £4.50
Child: £2.00 (5-15)
Other: £4.00 (seniors/students)

Clattercote Priory Farm

Claydon, Banbury, Oxfordshire OX17 1QB

Founded c1150, the Priory is now a family house - part farmhouse, part tenanted. A rare example of a Gilbertine Priory with cellars and 'chapel', probably medieval.

Grant Recipient/Owner: Mr Adrian Taylor
Access contact: Mr Adrian Taylor
Tel: 01295 690476   **Fax:** 01295 690476
Email Address: clattercote1@aol.com
Opening Arrangements: By prior written arrangement. Donations requested, with proceeds to charity.
Heritage Open Days: No
P Yes. Spaces: 4
♿ No. Disabled WC: No. Guide Dogs: Yes
£ No

The Cottage

Aston Street, Aston Tirrold, Oxfordshire OX11 9DQ

House dating back to 1286, with later 16th and 17th century alterations and additions. Timber-framed with water reed thatched roof. The 13th century west wing is one of very few known domestic timber-framed buildings of this date in which aisled construction is not used.

Grant Recipient/Owner: Mr B C Bateman
Access contact: Mr B C Bateman
Fax: 01235 850351
Email Address: bateman5@supanet.com
Opening Arrangements: By prior written arrangement.
Heritage Open Days: No
P No
♿ No. Disabled WC: No. Guide Dogs: Yes
£ No

Farnborough Hall

Farnborough, Banbury, Oxfordshire OX17 1DU

Mid-18th century honey-coloured stone built home of the Holbech family for over 300 years, contains impressive plasterwork. Set in grounds with 18th century temples, a terrace walk and an obelisk.

Website Address: www.ntrustsevern.org.uk
Grant Recipient/Owner: The National Trust
Access contact: Mr & Mrs G Holbech

Tel: 01295 690002
Opening Arrangements: April - end of September. House and grounds: Wednesdays and Saturdays 2 - 6pm, also 6 & 7 May 2 - 6pm; Terrace walk: Thursdays and Fridays 2 - 6pm (closed Good Friday). Wheelchair access to ground floor of house, Terrace walk may be difficult as it is very steep.
Heritage Open Days: No
P Yes. Spaces: 10
♿ Partial. Disabled WC: No. Guide Dogs: Yes
£ Yes
Adult: £3.40. £1.70 (Garden). £1.00 (Terrace walk only).
Child: £1.70. £1.35 (Garden).

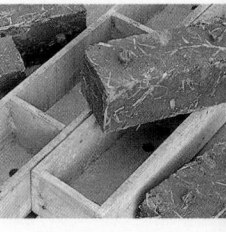

Pope's Tower & Chapel

The Manor House, Stanton Harcourt, Witney, Oxfordshire OX8 1RJ

Over the Chapel, the Tower was used by Alexander Pope during the summers of 1717 and 1718, while he translated the 5th volume of Homer's Illiad and was the inspiration for other houses planned by Pope. The Chapel has a fan-vaulted Chancel roof and wooden moulded ceiling in the Nave. Still used by both Parish and Manor House.

Grant Recipient/Owner: The Hon. Mrs Gascoigne
Access contact: The Hon. Mrs Gascoigne
Tel: 01865 881928   **Fax:** 01865 880117
Opening Arrangements: Open 15, 26 & 29 April; 3, 6, 17, 20, 24 & 27 May; 14, 17 & 28 June; 1, 5, 8, 19 & 22 July; 2, 5, 16, 19, 23 & 26 August; 6, 9, 20 & 23 September; and Bank Holiday Mondays 2 - 6pm. Groups by prior arrangement with the Hon. Mrs Gascoigne at the Manor House.
Heritage Open Days: No
P Yes. Spaces: 15
♿ Yes. Disabled WC: Yes. Guide Dogs: Yes
£ Yes
Adult: £5.00 House & Garden, £3.00 Garden only.
Child: Under 12 £3.00 House & Garden, £2.00 Garden only.
Other: £3.00 (senior) House & Garden , £2.00 Garden only.

Shotover Park

Wheatley, Oxfordshire OX33 1QS

Early 18th century garden follies. The Gothic Temple (designer unknown) lies east of the house at the end of a long canal vista. Has a battlemented gable with a central pinnacle and a rose-window, below which is an open loggia of three pointed arches. The other Temple west of the house, designed by William Kent, is of a domed octagonal construction.

Grant Recipient/Owner: Sir John Miller
Access contact: Sir John Miller
Tel: 01865 872450
Opening Arrangements: Access to Temples at all reasonable times (lie close to public rights of way). Parking for a few cars at the Gothic Temple, otherwise other arrangements can be made in advance with Sir John Miller on 01865 872450 or Mrs Price on 01865 874095. Wheelchair access to the Gothic Temple with assistance.
Heritage Open Days: Yes
P Yes. Spaces: 50
♿ Partial. Disabled WC: No. Guide Dogs: Yes
£ No

Stonor Chapel

Stonor Park, Henley-on-Thames, Oxfordshire RG9 6HF

Medieval Catholic Chapel used throughout the years of Catholic repression.

Grant Recipient/Owner: Lord Camoys
Access contact: Ms Lisa Absalom
Tel: 01491 638587   **Fax:** 0870 128 6834
Email Address: lisa@stonorpark.demon.co.uk
Opening Arrangements: April - September: Sundays and Bank Holiday Mondays, plus Sundays and Wednesdays in July and August; also Saturdays 26 May and 25 August 2 - 5.30pm (last admission 5pm). Groups by prior arrangement Tuesday - Thursday. Open for Mass 10.30am on Sundays and Days of Holy Obligation. Admission charge to House, Chapel and Gardens (£4.50 for adults, children are free) but none to visit Chapel only. Wheelchair access to Chapel very limited and none to House.
Heritage Open Days: No
P Yes. Spaces: 100
♿ Partial. Disabled WC: No. Guide Dogs: No
£ No

Swalcliffe Tithe Barn

Shipston Road, Swalcliffe, nr. Banbury, Oxfordshire

15th century barn built by New College, Oxford, for estates in north Oxfordshire. Built for the Rectorial Manor of Swalcliffe by New College, who owned the Manor. Constructed between 1400 and 1409, much of the medieval timber half-cruck roof remains intact.

Grant Recipient/Owner: Oxfordshire Building Trust Ltd

Access contact: Mr Martyn Brown
Tel: 01993 814114   **Fax:** 01993 813239
Email Address: martyn.brown@oxfordshire.gov.uk
Opening Arrangements: Easter - end of October: Sundays and Bank Holidays 2 - 5pm. At other times by prior arrangement (contact Jeff Demmar 01295 788278).
Heritage Open Days: Yes
P Yes. Spaces: 10
♿ Yes. Disabled WC: Yes. Guide Dogs: Yes
£ No

Tudor House

East Hagbourne, Oxfordshire OX11 9LR

Early 17th century barn with thatched roof and queen post construction. Three bays and an aisle on one side. Original wattle and daub infill at ends only.

Grant Recipient/Owner: Mr I C Barfoot
Access contact: Mr I C Barfoot
Tel: 01235 818968   **Fax:** 01235 818968
Opening Arrangements:
By prior arrangement. Parking on street.
Heritage Open Days: No
P See above
♿ Partial. Disabled WC: No. Guide Dogs: Yes
£ No

Tusmore Park Old Granary & Dovecote

Tusmore, nr. Bicester, Oxfordshire OX27 7SP

Timber framed structure of a type peculiar to Oxfordshire. 16th century but may be earlier, the top storey was converted into a dovecote probably in the 18th century.

Grant Recipient/Owner: Tusmore Park Holdings SA
Access contact: A D T Barkas
Tel: 01869 346075   **Fax:** 01869 346003
Opening Arrangements: By prior arrangement in August.
Heritage Open Days: No
P Yes. Spaces: 5
♿ Yes. Disabled WC: No. Guide Dogs: Yes
£ No

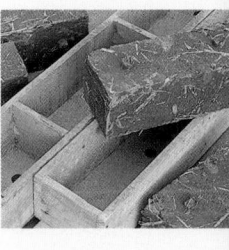

SHROPSHIRE

2/3 Milk Street

Shrewsbury, Shropshire

Timber-framed 2 and a half storey building dating from the 15th century with later alterations and additions. Medieval shop front to rear. Still a shop.

Grant Recipient/Owner: Mr M J Cockle
Access contact: Mr Peter Napier
Tel: 01743 236789
Opening Arrangements: Ground floor shop open 6 days a week all year, upper floor flats can be visited only by prior arrangement with Mr Peter Napier, Pooks, 26 Claremont Hill, Shrewsbury, Shropshire SY1 1RE (tel.01743 236789). Wheelchair access to ground floor only.
Heritage Open Days: No
P No
♿ Partial. Disabled WC: No. Guide Dogs: No
£ No

Attingham Park

Atcham, Shrewsbury, Shropshire SY4 4TP

Built 1785 by George Steuart for the 1st Lord Berwick, with a picture gallery by John Nash. Contains Regency interiors, Italian neo-classical furniture and Grand Tour paintings. Park landscaped by Repton in 1797.

Grant Recipient/Owner: The National Trust
Access contact: The Property Manager
Tel: 01743 708162   **Fax:** 01743 708175
Email Address: matsec@smtp.ntrust.org.uk
Opening Arrangements: House: 30 March - 28 October; daily except Wednesdays and Thursdays 1 - 4.30pm (last admission 4pm). Park: all year, except Christmas Day; March - October 9am - 8pm, November - February 9am - 5pm.
Heritage Open Days: No
P Yes. Spaces: 150
♿ Yes. Disabled WC: Yes. Guide Dogs: Yes
£ Yes
Adult: £4.30
Child: £2.15
Other: £10.75 (family)

Benthall Hall

Broseley, Shropshire TF12 5RX

16th century stone house situated on a plateau above the gorge of the River Severn, with mullioned and transomed windows, carved oak staircase, decorated plaster ceilings and oak panelling. Also has a restored plantsman's garden, old kitchen garden and a Restoration church.

Grant Recipient/Owner: The National Trust
Access contact: The Custodian
Tel: 01952 882159
Opening Arrangements: 1 April - 30 September: Wednesdays, Sundays and Bank Holiday Mondays 1.30 -

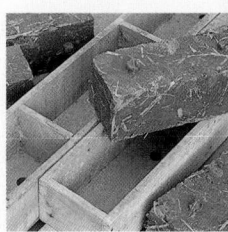

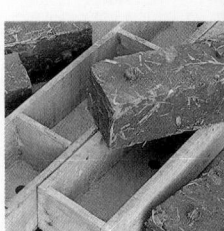

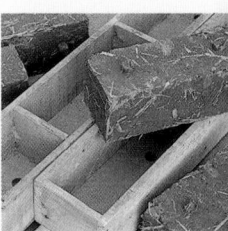

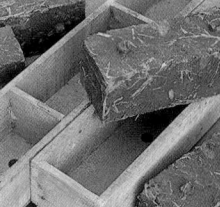

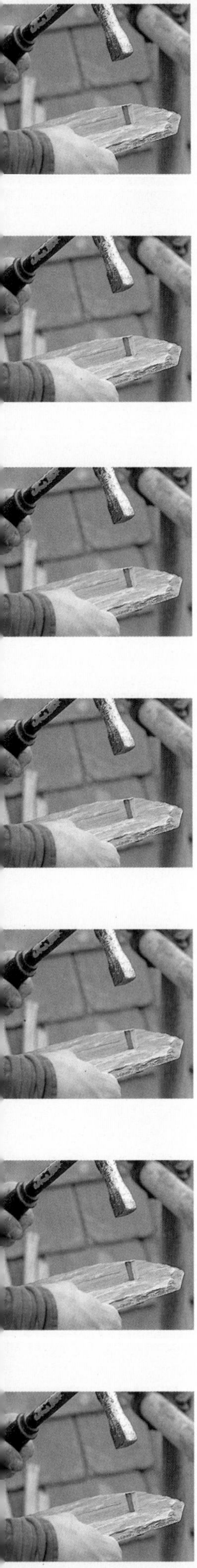

5.30pm. Groups by prior arrangement with the Custodian. Wheelchair access to ground floor of Hall and part of garden only.
Heritage Open Days: No
P Yes. Spaces: 50
♿ Partial. Disabled WC: No. Guide Dogs:Yes
£ Yes
Adult: £3.50
Child: £1.75
Other: £2.25 (garden only)

Blodwell Summerhouse
Blodwell Hall, Llanyblodwell, Oswestry, Shropshire SY10 8LT
Square red brick summerhouse with ashlar dressings and slate roof, built 1718, at end of terrace in a restored formal garden.
Grant Recipient/Owner:
Trustees of the Bradford Estate
Access contact: Mr R J Taylor
Tel: 07977 239955
Opening Arrangements: By prior arrangement.
Heritage Open Days: No
P Yes. Spaces: 2
♿ Yes. Disabled WC: No. Guide Dogs: Yes
£ No

Bromfield Priory Gatehouse
nr. Ludlow, Shropshire
The Benedictine monks of Bromfield Priory added a new stone gatehouse before 1400, and after the Dissolution a timber-framed upper storey was added to this. The main room over the arch was used for the manorial court; then as the village school, ending up as the parish recreational room.
Website Address: www.landmarktrust.co.uk
Grant Recipient/Owner: The Landmark Trust
Access contact: Ms Victoria Piggott
Tel: 01628 825920 **Fax:** 01628 825417
Email Address: vpiggott@landmarktrust.co.uk
Opening Arrangements: The Landmark Trust is an independent charity, which rescues small buildings of historic or architectural importance from decay or unsympathetic improvement. Landmark's aim is to promote the enjoyment of these historic buildings by making them available to stay in for holidays. Bromfield Priory Gatehouse can be rented by anyone, at all times of the year, for periods ranging from a weekend to three weeks. Bookings can be made by telephoning the Booking Office on 01628 825925. As the building is in full-time use for holiday accommodation, it is not normally open to the public. However the public can view the building by prior arrangement by telephoning the access contact (Victoria Piggott on 01628 825920) to make an appointment. Potential visitors will be asked to write to confirm the details of their visit.
Heritage Open Days: No
P Yes. Spaces: 1
♿ No. Disabled WC: No. Guide Dogs: Yes
£ No

Dudmaston
Quatt, Bridgnorth, Shropshire WV15 6QN
Queen Anne mansion of red brick with stone dressings, situated in parkland overlooking the Severn. Contains furniture, Dutch flower paintings, contemporary paintings and sculpture.
Grant Recipient/Owner: The National Trust
Access contact: The Administrator
Tel: 01746 780866 **Fax:** 01746 780744
Email Address: mduefe@smtp.ntrust.org.uk
Opening Arrangements: 1 April - 30 September. House & Garden: Tuesdays, Wednesdays, Sundays and Bank Holiday Mondays 2 - 5.30pm; Garden: Mondays, Tuesdays, Wednesdays and Sundays 12 - 6pm. Groups by prior arrangement on Monday afternoons only. Tea Room open same days as garden, 11.30am - 5.30pm; Shop open same days as garden, 1.30 - 5.30pm. Wheelchair access to main and inner halls, Library, oak room, No 1 and Derby galleries, old kitchen, garden and grounds (some estate walks).
Heritage Open Days: No
P Yes. Spaces: 150
♿ Partial. Disabled WC: Yes. Guide Dogs: Yes
£ Yes
Adult: £3.85
Child: £2.30
Other: £9.00 (family), £2.80 (garden only).

Hawkstone Hall
Marchamley, Shrewsbury, Shropshire SY4 5LG
Grade I Georgian mansion and restored gardens set in spacious parkland. Ancestral home of the Hill family from 1556-1906.
Grant Recipient/Owner: Rector & Trustees of Hawkstone Hall/ Redemptorists
Access contact: Guest Mistress
Tel: 01630 685242 **Fax:** 01630 685565
Opening Arrangements: 5 - 31 August 2 - 5pm, plus Spring Bank Holiday Monday.
Heritage Open Days: No
P Yes. Spaces: 40
♿ Yes. Disabled WC: No. Guide Dogs: Yes
£ Yes
Adult: £3.50
Child: £1.00

Hospital of the Undivided Trinity
Clun, Shropshire
Founded in 1607 by Henry Howard, Earl of Northampton and built in 1618 with alterations of 1857. Dwellings and other rooms arranged around a square courtyard. A well preserved example of a courtyard-plan almshouses.
Grant Recipient/Owner:
The Trustees of Trinity Hospital
Access contact: Mr B Corley
Tel: 01588 640830
Opening Arrangements: By prior arrangement with the Warden, Mr Corley. Gardens and chapel open each day apart from Christmas Day.
Heritage Open Days: No
P Yes. Spaces: 4
♿ Yes. Disabled WC: No. Guide Dogs: Yes
£ No

Langley Gatehouse
Acton Burnell, Shropshire
This gatehouse has two quite different faces: one is of plain dressed stone; the other, which once looked inwards to long demolished Langley Hall, is timber-framed. It was probably used for the Steward or important guests. It was rescued from a point of near collapse and shows repair work of an exemplary quality.
Website Address: www.landmarktrust.co.uk
Grant Recipient/Owner: The Landmark Trust
Access contact: Ms Victoria Piggott
Tel: 01628 825920 **Fax:** 01628 825417
Email Address: vpiggott@landmarktrust.co.uk
Opening Arrangements: The Landmark Trust is an independent charity, which rescues small buildings of historic or architectural importance from decay or unsympathetic improvement. Landmark's aim is to promote the enjoyment of these historic buildings by making them available to stay in for holidays. Langley Gatehouse can be rented by anyone, at all times of the year, for periods ranging from a weekend to three weeks. Bookings can be made by telephoning the Booking Office on 01628 825925. As the building is in full-time use for holiday accommodation, it is not normally open to the public. However the public can view the building by prior arrangement by telephoning the access contact (Victoria Piggott on 01628 825920) to make an appointment. Potential visitors will be asked to write to confirm the details of their visit.
Heritage Open Days: No
P Yes. Spaces: 2
♿ No. Disabled WC: No. Guide Dogs: Yes
£ No

Porch House
Bishop's Castle, Shropshire SY9 5BE
Originally built as "L" shaped timber-framed building, probably house, 1565 and subsequently infilled and partly re-built. Now used as owner's house with shop and self-contained flats. Ground floor front wall recently completely re-built.
Grant Recipient/Owner: Mrs J McColl
Access contact: Mrs J McColl
Tel: 01588 638854 **Fax:** 01938 555851
Opening Arrangements: By prior written arrangement.
Heritage Open Days: No
P No
♿ No. Disabled WC: No. Guide Dogs: Yes
£ No

St Winifred's Well
Woolston, nr. Oswestry, Shropshire
St Winifred was a 7th century Welsh princess who was brought back to life after being decapitated by an angry suitor. The well here has been venerated for centuries and the little building above was the well chapel, a miraculous survival preserved since the Reformation as a court house and then cottage. Approached by a public footpath.
Website Address: www.landmarktrust.co.uk
Grant Recipient/Owner: The Landmark Trust
Access contact: Ms Victoria Piggott
Tel: 01628 825920 **Fax:** 01628 825417
Email Address: vpiggott@landmarktrust.co.uk
Opening Arrangements: The Landmark Trust is an independent charity, which rescues small buildings of historic or architectural importance from decay or unsympathetic improvement. Landmark's aim is to promote the enjoyment of these historic buildings by making them available to stay in for holidays. St Winifred's Well can be rented by anyone, at all times of the year, for periods ranging from a weekend to three weeks. Bookings can be made by telephoning the Booking Office on 01628 825925. As the building is in full-time use for holiday accommodation, it is not normally open to the public. However the public can view the building by prior arrangement by telephoning the access contact (Victoria Piggott on 01628 825920) to make an appointment. Potential visitors will be asked to write to confirm the details of their visit. Roadside parking only.
Heritage Open Days: No
P Yes. Spaces: 1
♿ No. Disabled WC: No. Guide Dogs: Yes
£ No

Weston Park
Weston-under-Lizard, Shifnal, Shropshire TF11 8LE
Stately home, built 1671, designed by Lady Wibraham. Houses collection of paintings by Van Dyck, Gainsborough, Lely and Stubbs, and is surrounded by 1000 acres of 'Capability' Brown parkland and formal gardens. Formerly home to the Earls of Bradford, now held in trust for the nation by The Weston Park Foundation.
Website Address: www.weston-park.com
Grant Recipient/Owner: Weston Park Foundation
Access contact: Mr Colin Sweeney
Tel: 01952 852100 **Fax:** 01952 850430
Email Address: enquiries@weston-park.com
Opening Arrangements: Easter 14-16 April - 30 June: weekends only; 30 June - 31 August: daily; 31 August - 16 September: weekends only, 11am - 5pm. Wheelchair access to all areas except open parkland and some formal gardens.
Heritage Open Days: No
P Yes. Spaces: 300
♿ Partial. Disabled WC: Yes. Guide Dogs: Yes
£ Yes
Adult: £2.50
Child: £1.50
Other: £2.00

SOMERSET

Bath Assembly Rooms
Bennett Street, Bath, Somerset BA1 2QH
Built in 1771 by John Wood the Younger, now owned by the National Trust and administered by Bath and North East Somerset District Council. Each of the rooms has a complete set of original chandeliers. The Museum of Costume is located on the lower ground floor.
Grant Recipient/Owner:
Bath City Council/National Trust
Access contact: Mrs P C Ruddock
Tel: 01225 477752 **Fax:** 01225 444793
Email Address: penny_ruddock@bathnes.gov.uk
Opening Arrangements: Daily 10am - 5pm when not in use for pre-booked functions. Telephone in advance (01225 477789) to check availability. There are no pre-booked functions during the day during August. Closed Christmas Day and Boxing Day. On-street car parking available with pre-paid voucher.
Heritage Open Days: No
P See above
♿ Yes. Disabled WC: Yes. Guide Dogs: Yes
£ No

Dovecote
adjacent to Church Memorial Garden, Priory Green, Dunster, Somerset
Scheduled medieval circular tower dovecote 8.5 metres high with internal diameter of 4.5 metres. Probably 13-14th century part of the monastic estate of the Benedictine Priory of Dunster, a cell of Bath Priory, sent to build the church of St George in 1150. Contains over 500 nest sites lining the 4' thick round stone wall, which was served by a revolving ladder from a central vertical ash post with two alighting platforms for feeding the birds when enclosed.
Grant Recipient/Owner: Dunster Parish Council
Access contact: M P Grantham
Tel: 01643 821812
Opening Arrangements: Interior can be viewed all year from barred doorway, otherwise access by arrangement with the Reverend M P Grantham, The Rectory, St George's Street, Dunster, Somerset TA24 6RS (tel.01643 821812) or the Churchwarden (tel.01643 708056).
Heritage Open Days: No
P No
♿ No. Disabled WC: No. Guide Dogs: Yes
£ No

Dunster Castle
Dunster, nr. Minehead, Somerset TA24 6SL
Sited atop a wooded hill, there has been a castle on the site since Norman times. The 13th century gatehouse survives, but the present building was remodelled in 1862-72 by Antony Salvin for the Luttrell family.
Website Address: www.nationaltrust.org.uk

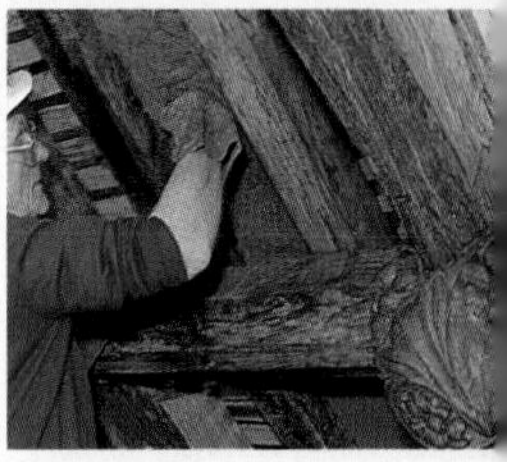

Grant Recipient/Owner: The National Trust
Access contact: The Property Manager
Tel: 01643 821314 **Fax:** 01643 823000
Opening Arrangements: Castle: 31 March to 4 November: daily (except Thursdays and Fridays) at the following times: 31 March to 26 September 11am - 5pm; 29 September to 4 November 11am - 4pm. Garden and park: daily (closed 25/26 December) at the following times: January to March, 29 September to 31 December 11am - 4pm; 31 March to 28 September 10am - 5pm. Castle is a ten-minute steep climb from car park. Multi-seater vehicle available for lifts if required. Castle is accessible to manual wheelchairs via stairclimber. Castle and garden on steep hill.
Heritage Open Days: No
P Yes. Spaces: 180
♿ Partial. Disabled WC: Yes. Guide Dogs: Yes
£ Yes
Adult: £6.00 (Castle, garden & park). £3.00 (garden & park).
Child: £3.00 (Castle, garden & park). £1.50 (garden & park).
Other: £15.00 (family: Castle, garden & park). £7.50 (family: garden & park). Separate rates for booked groups.

Empire & Commonwealth Museum

Clock Tower Yard, Temple Meads, Bristol BS1 6QH
Museum housed in world's earliest surviving railway terminus, which was completed in 1840 and was originally part of the Great Western Railway designed by I.K. Brunel. Over 220ft long with timber and iron roof spans of 72ft, this Grade I listed building has been nominated as a world heritage site. Contains the Passenger shed and the adjoining former Engine and Carriage shed, the latter currently holds the Museum's temporary exhibitions until a permanent gallery opens in 2002.
Website Address: www.empiremuseum.co.uk
Grant Recipient/Owner: Empire Museum Ltd
Access contact: Ms Holly Bown
Tel: 0117 925 4980 **Fax:** 0117 9254983
Email Address: staff@empiremuseum.co.uk
Opening Arrangements: Daily 10am - 6pm.
Heritage Open Days: Yes
P Yes. Spaces: 25
♿ Yes. Disabled WC: Yes. Guide Dogs: Yes
£ No

Englishcombe Tithe Barn

Rectory Farmhouse, Englishcombe, Bath, Somerset BA2 9DU
Early 14th century cruck framed tithe barn. Recently restored with new crucks, masonry and straw lining to the roof, and filigree windows unblocked. There are masons and other markings on the walls. Now used as a venue, principally for wedding receptions.
Website Address: www.barnhire.com
Grant Recipient/Owner: Mrs Jennie Walker
Access contact: Mrs Jennie Walker
Tel: 01225 425073
Email Address: tithebarn@ntlworld.com
Opening Arrangements: 15 - 20 April, 6 - 11 May, 27 May - 1 June, 25 - 29 June and 26 - 30 August, 3 - 6pm. At other times by prior arrangement.
Heritage Open Days: Yes
P Yes. Spaces: 34
♿ Yes. Disabled WC: Yes. Guide Dogs: Yes
£ No
£1 per person donation requested from groups.

Eyre Mortuary Chapel

Perrymead Cemetery, Bath, Somerset
Mid-19th century Gothic Revival Catholic building, built as a mortuary chapel for the Eyre family. Constructed of Bath stone from the designs of Charles Hanson. The interior has recessed arches supported on columns of Devonshire marble, a screen of hammered ironwork and an elaborate marble altar with a Minton tile floor.
Grant Recipient/Owner: Trustees of the Eyre Mortuary Chapel
Access contact: Mrs B Carruthers
Tel: 01684 292600 **Fax:** 01684 292042
Opening Arrangements: By prior arrangement with Mrs B Carruthers, Walton Cardiff Manor, nr. Tewkesbury, Gloucestershire GL20 7BL (tel.01684 292600). Donation requested.
Heritage Open Days: No
P Yes. Spaces: 4
♿ No. Disabled WC: No. Guide Dogs: Yes
£ No

Forde Abbey

Chard, Somerset TA20 4LU
Cistercian monastery founded in 1140 and dissolved in 1539 when the church was demolished. The monks quarters were converted in 1640 into an Italian style "palazzo" by Sir Edmund Prideaux. Interior has plaster ceilings and Mortlake tapestries.
Website Address: www.fordeabbey.co.uk
Grant Recipient/Owner: Trustees of the Roper Settlement
Access contact: Mrs Clay
Tel: 01460 220231
Opening Arrangements: Gardens: daily 10am - 4.30pm. House: April - October; Tuesday - Thursday, Sunday and Bank Holidays 1 - 4.30pm. Access for wheelchairs and guide dogs to garden only.
Heritage Open Days: No
P Yes. Spaces: 500
♿ See above. Disabled WC: No. Guide Dogs: See above
£ Yes
Adult: £5.20 house & garden, £4.00 gardens (provisional).
Child: Free
Other: £5.00 (seniors) house and garden, £3.80 gardens only (provisional).

Gants Mill

Gants Mill Lane, Bruton, Somerset BA10 0DB
Working watermill with deeds dating back to owner John le Gaunt in 1290. The documents were saved for posterity by the model for "Tom Jones's" Sophia Weston. Corn grinding demonstrations, historical displays and timeline of a millennium of milling - corn, wool and silk.
Website Address: www.gantsmill.co.uk
Grant Recipient/Owner: Mr Brian Shingler
Access contact: Brian & Alison Shingler
Tel: 01749 812393
Email Address: shingler@gantsmill.co.uk
Opening Arrangements: Mill: Easter - end of May, Thursdays and Bank Holiday Mondays; Mill & Garden: June - end of September, Sundays, Thursdays and Bank Holiday Mondays 2 - 5pm. Groups by prior arrangement. Refreshments available.
Heritage Open Days: No
P Yes. Spaces: 20
♿ No. Disabled WC: No. Guide Dogs: Yes
£ Yes
Adult: £3.50
Child: £1.00
Other: Group reductions by arrangement.

Great House Farm

Theale, Wedmore, Somerset BS28 4SJ
17th century farmhouse with Welsh slate roof, oak doors and some original diamond paned windows. Inside is a carved well staircase with two murals on the walls. There are four servants rooms at the top, three of which are dark and occupied by Lesser Horseshoe bats.
Grant Recipient/Owner: Mr A R Millard
Access contact: Mr A R Millard
Tel: 01934 713133
Opening Arrangements: April - August: Tuesdays and Thursdays 2 - 6pm by prior telephone arrangement.
Heritage Open Days: No
P Yes. Spaces: 6
♿ No. Disabled WC: No. Guide Dogs: Yes
£ Yes
Adult: £2.00

Gurney Manor

Cannington, Somerset TA5 2MW
Late medieval house built around a courtyard. Used as a tenant farm before converted into flats in the 1940s, now restored to its original undivided state.
Website Address: www.landmarktrust.co.uk
Grant Recipient/Owner: The Landmark Trust
Access contact: Ms Victoria Piggott
Tel: 01628 825920 **Fax:** 01628 825417
Email Address: vpiggott@landmarktrust.co.uk
Opening Arrangements: The Landmark Trust is an independent charity, which rescues small buildings of historic or architectural importance from decay or unsympathetic improvement. Landmark's aim is to promote the enjoyment of these historic buildings by making them available to stay in for holidays. Gurney Manor can be rented by anyone, at all times of the year, for periods ranging from a weekend to three weeks. Bookings can be made by telephoning the Booking Office on 01628 825925. As the building is in full-time use for holiday accommodation, it is not normally open to the public. However the public can view the building by prior arrangement by telephoning the access contact (Victoria Piggott on 01628 825920) to make an appointment. Potential visitors will be asked to write to confirm the details of their visit.
Heritage Open Days: No
P Yes. Spaces: 3
♿ No. Disabled WC: No. Guide Dogs: Yes
£ No

Hall Farm High Barn

Stogumber, Taunton, Somerset TA4 3TQ
17th century Grade II* listed building with seven bays of red local sandstone rubble with jointed cruck roof. South wall supported by four buttresses but there are none on the North wall. There are blocked windows on the South wall and two stub walls extend north. Lines of joist holes were provided for internal flooring and the two main entrances were to the north and south.
Grant Recipient/Owner: Mr G R Hayes
Access contact: Mr G R Hayes
Tel: 01984 656321
Opening Arrangements: By prior arrangement with Mr G R Hayes at Hall Farm.
Heritage Open Days: No
P Yes. Spaces: 4
♿ Yes. Disabled WC: No. Guide Dogs: Yes
£ No

Hestercombe

Cheddon Fitzpaine, Taunton, Somerset TA2 8LG
Formal gardens, featuring terraces, rills and an orangery, designed by Sir Edwin Lutyens and Gertrude Jekyll. The newly restored Landscape Garden was designed by Bampfylde in 1750 and comprises 40 acre pleasure grounds with classical temples and a Great Cascade.
Website Address: www.hestercombegardens.com
Grant Recipient/Owner: Somerset County Council
Access contact: Mrs J Manning
Tel: 01823 413923 **Fax:** 01823 413747
Email Address: info@hestercombegardens.com
Opening Arrangements: Every day of the year, including Christmas Day, 10am - 5pm (last admission). Limited wheelchair access.
Heritage Open Days: No
P Yes. Spaces: 100
♿ Partial. Disabled WC: Yes. Guide Dogs: Yes
£ Yes
Adult: £3.60
Child: £1.00 (5-15yrs)

Lancin Farmhouse

Wambrook, Chard, Somerset TA20 3EG
14th century farmhouse with old oak beams, fireplaces with the original smoking thatch, flagstone floors and breadoven.
Grant Recipient/Owner: Mr S J Smith
Access contact: Mrs R A Smith
Tel: 01460 62290
Opening Arrangements: June - October: Monday - Thursday 2 - 5pm by prior arrangement.
Heritage Open Days: No
P Yes. Spaces: 5
♿ No. Disabled WC: No. Guide Dogs: No
£ Yes
Adult: £3.00

Lytes Cary Manor

nr. Charlton Mackrell, Somerton, Somerset TA11 7HU
Manor house with a 14th century chapel and Tudor Great Hall, much added to in the 16th century and rescued from dereliction by Sir Walter Jenner in the 20th century. The interiors have been refurbished in period style.
Website Address: www.nationaltrust.org.uk
Grant Recipient/Owner: The National Trust
Access contact: Property Manger
Tel: 01985 843600 **Fax:** 01985 843624
Email Address: wlybxp@smtp.ntrust.org.uk
Opening Arrangements: 2 April to 31 October: Monday, Wednesday and Saturdays 2- 6pm or dusk if earlier; also Fridays in June, July and August 2 - 6pm. Wheelchair access to garden only.
Heritage Open Days: No
P Yes. Spaces: 50
♿ Partial. Disabled WC: Yes. Guide Dogs: Yes
£ Yes
Adult: £4.50
Child: £2.00

Merefield House Gazebo

East Street, Crewkerne, Somerset TA18 7AB
18th century garden house/gazebo, set in walled terraced town garden, approached by flight of steps. The stucco faced cube building has steep Dutch gable, supporting large lead eagle and sundial to the front. Virtually complete 18th century interior with hemispherical dome in the centre with vine leaves and grapes, set in a square moulded frame, with views over Crewkerne and the Dorset Hills.
Grant Recipient/Owner: Mr Roger Rousell
Access contact: Mr Roger Rousell
Tel: 01460 73222
Opening Arrangements: By prior arrangement with Mr Rousell at Merefield House.
Heritage Open Days: Yes
P No
♿ No. Disabled WC: No. Guide Dogs: Yes
£ No

The Old Manse

14 Bath Road, Beckington, Somerset BA3 6SW
Late 16th/early 17th century gabled stone built dwelling

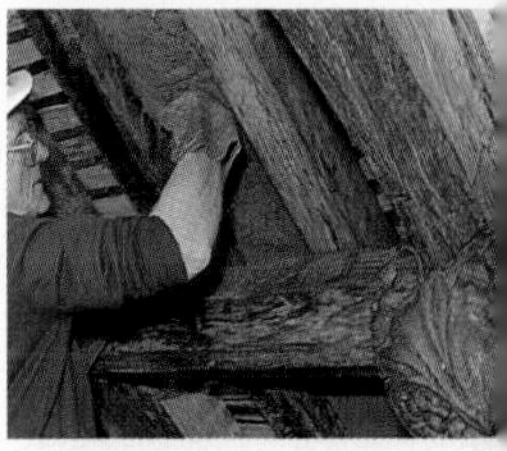
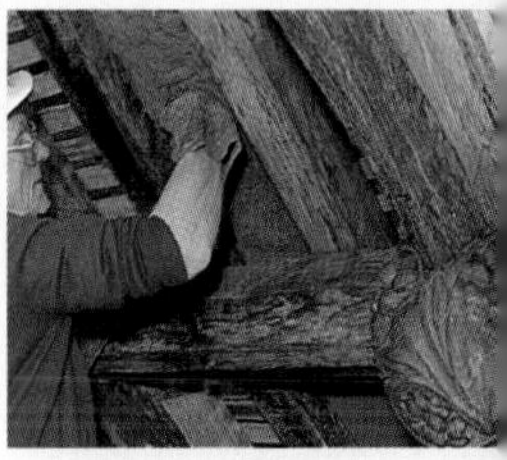
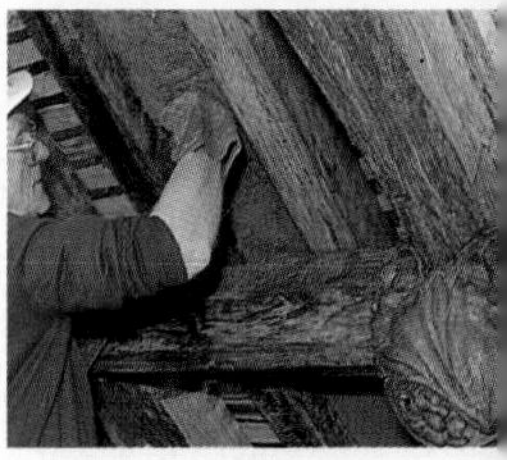
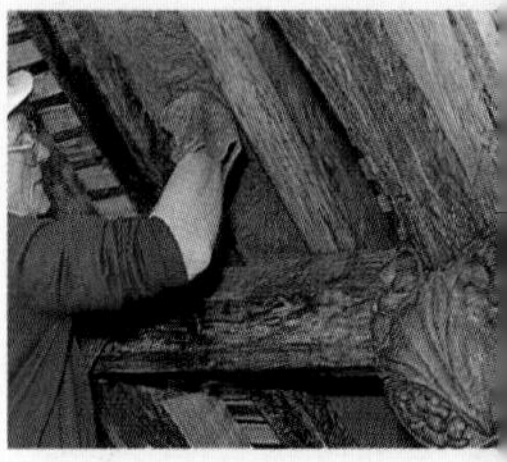
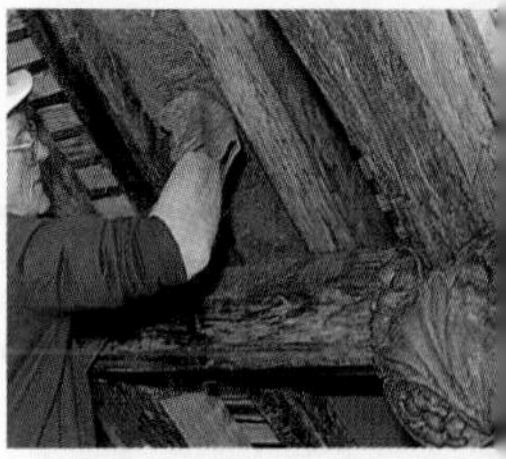
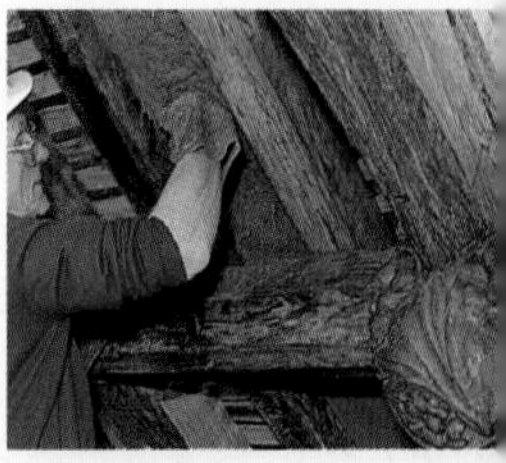

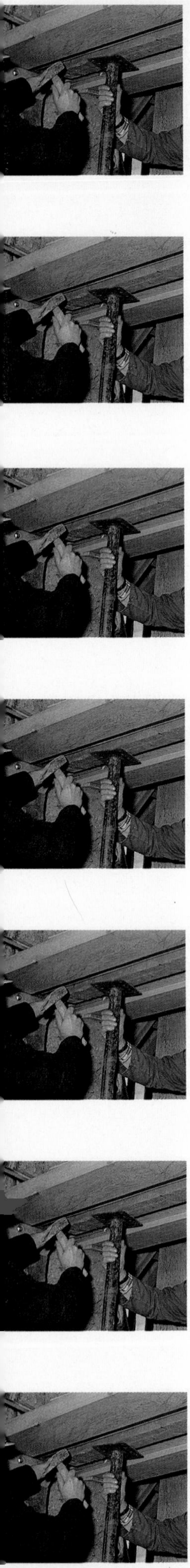

with mullioned windows with transoms to front elevation and stone tiled roof. Contains 2 large Plantagenet/Tudor fireplaces, 16th century oak staircase, strapwork ceilings and transitional rococo fireplaces. Gallery of attic rooms reveal an unusual roof structure.
Grant Recipient/Owner: Mr J Evans
Access contact: Mr J Evans
Tel: 01373 831401 **Fax:** 01373 831401
Email Address: jennie@stackridge.com
Opening Arrangements: By prior arrangement. On street parking.
Heritage Open Days: Yes
P See above
♿ No. Guide Dogs: Yes
£ No

Orchard Wyndham

Williton, Somerset TA4 4HH
Manor house, originally medieval but with many subsequent alterations and additions. Family home of the Wyndhams and their ancestors, the Orchards and Sydenhams, for 700 years.
Grant Recipient/Owner: Wyndham Estate
Access contact: Estate Office
Tel: 01984 632309 **Fax:** 01984 633526
Email Address: wyndhamest@talk21.com
Opening Arrangements: August: Thursdays and Fridays 2 - 5pm, Bank Holiday 11am - 5pm, by guided tour (groups of maximum 8 persons, last tour 4pm). At other times by prior arrangement (at least 2 weeks notice requested). Wheelchair access to ground floor and gardens only.
Heritage Open Days: No
P Yes. Spaces: 25
♿ Partial. Disabled WC: No. Guide Dogs: Yes
£ Yes
Adult: £5.00
Child: £1.00 (under 12)

Penniless Porch

Market Place, Wells, Somerset BA5 2RB
Comprising the upper two floors of the mid-15th century gateway to the Close, together with the 17th/18th century eastward extension associated with it. The gatehouse belongs to the improvements to the Close and Market Place under Bishop Thomas Bekynton, c1451, the adjoining eastern extension may incorporate fifteenth and sixteenth century fabric, but is ostensibly of the following two centuries, containing a good 18th century stair to the rear.
Grant Recipient/Owner:
Dean & Chapter of Wells Cathedral
Access contact: Mr Peter Bird
Tel: 01749 677561 **Fax:** 01749 676207
Email Address: wells@caroe.co.uk
Opening Arrangements: By prior telephone arrangement.
Heritage Open Days: No
P No
♿ No. Disabled WC: No. Guide Dogs: No
£ No

Priest's House

Muchelney, Langport, Somerset TA10 0DQ
A late medieval hall house, built by Muchelney Abbey in 1308 for the parish priest and little altered since the hall was divided in the early 17th century. Interesting features include the Gothic doorway, beautiful tracery windows and a massive 15th century stone fireplace. The house is occupied and furnished by tenants.
Website Address: www.nationaltrust.org.uk
Grant Recipient/Owner: The National Trust
Access contact: Sir Anthony Denny
Tel: 01458 252621
Opening Arrangements: 1 April to 30 September: Sunday and Mondays 2.30 - 5.30pm; last admission 5.15pm. Parking in nearby roads.
Heritage Open Days: No
P See above
♿ No. Disabled WC: No. Guide Dogs: Yes
£ Yes
Adult: £2.00
Child: £2.00

Prior Park College Chapel

Mansion & Old Gymnasium, Ralph Allen Drive, Bath, Somerset BA2 5AH
Built for Ralph Allen in the mid-18th century as an early and successful demonstration of the quality of Bath stone. The Chapel and Old Gymnasium are part of the mid-19th century additions to adapt the property as a Catholic seminary for Bishop Baines. Now a boarding and day school.
Website Address: www.priorpark.co.uk
Grant Recipient/Owner:
Governors of Prior Park College
Access contact: C J Freeman
Tel: 01225 837491 **Fax:** 01225 835753
Email Address: bursar@priorpark.co.uk
Opening Arrangements: Chapel: Sundays throughout the year for public worship, plus 17 June (to be confirmed), 2 - 5pm, otherwise by prior arrangement. Mansion: certain Sundays March - July 11.30am - 6pm, please telephone or e-mail for details, plus 17 June (to be confirmed) 2 - 5pm; also limited number of group tours in July and August by prior arrangement. Old Gymnasium: 10 July - 18 August, Monday - Fridays 10am - 4pm but please telephone in advance. Limited wheelchair access.
Heritage Open Days: No
P Yes. Spaces: 50
♿ Partial. Disabled WC: No. Guide Dogs: Yes
£ Yes
Adult: £2.50
Child: £2.50
Other: £2.50

Robin Hood's Hut

Halswell Park, Goathurst, nr. Bridgwater, Somerset TA5 2DH
Thatched banqueting house, built in the 1760s to designs probably by Henry Keene, Surveyor of the Fabric at Westminster Abbey. Designed to look like a hermit's hut from the South, its Northern Italianate loggia has views over the Bristol Channel.
Grant Recipient/Owner:
Somerset Building Preservation Trust Ltd
Access contact: Mr D R Miller
Tel: 01460 52604
Opening Arrangements: Access to the exterior of the building and umbrello at all times. Access to the interior by prior arrangement with Mr D R Miller of the Somerset Building Preservation Trust, Acacia House, 37 Station Road, Ilminster, Somerset TA19 9BG (tel.01460 52604) or The Landmark Trust, Shottesbrooke, Maidenhead, Berkshire SL6 3SW (tel.01628 825920). One mile country walk with stiles.
Heritage Open Days: Yes
P No
♿ No. Disabled WC: No. Guide Dogs: Yes
£ No

Rowes Leadworks

('Wildscreen at Bristol' and Firehouse restaurant), Deanery Road, Harbourside, Bristol BS1 5DB
A former leadworks built in 19th century. One of a few surviving structures associated with the industrial character of this area with a goods station and nearby warehouses. Now transformed into a restaurant/bar, 'The Firehouse Rotisseries'. Attached to this is a modern canopied, large open structure, the entrance to 'Wildscreen at Bristol' which features imagery and interactive exhibits of the natural world. It includes an Imax cinema and living botanical house.
Website Address: www.at-bristol.org.uk
Grant Recipient/Owner: Bristol City Council
Access contact: Mr Gerwyn House
Tel: 0117 9092000 **Fax:** 0117 9157202
Email Address: gerwyn.house@at-bristol.org.uk
Opening Arrangements: All venues: 10am - 6pm. Possible late openings for August (ring for confirmation). Parking is operated by Bristol City Council and there is a charge.
Heritage Open Days: No
P Yes. Spaces: 500
♿ Yes. Disabled WC: Yes. Guide Dogs: Yes
£ No. Charges for access to 'Wildscreen at Bristol'.

Rowlands Mill

Rowlands, Ilminster, Somerset TA19 9LE
Grade II* stone and brick 3-storey millhouse and machinery, c1620, with a mill pond, mill race, overshooting wheel and waterfall. The millhouse is now a holiday let but the machinery has separate access and is in working condition.
Grant Recipient/Owner: Mr P G H Speke
Access contact: Mr P G H Speke
Tel: 01460 52623 **Fax:** 01460 52623
Opening Arrangements: Millhouse Fridays and machinery Monday - Friday 10am - 4pm by prior written arrangement (at least 1 week's notice required). Heritage Open Days machinery only unless a Friday, then whole building.
Heritage Open Days: Yes
P Yes. Spaces: 7
♿ No. Disabled WC: No. Guide Dogs: Yes
£ Yes
Adult: £3.00
Child: Free
Other: Free

Temple of Harmony

Halswell Park, Goathurst, nr. Bridgwater, Somerset TA5 2DH
18th century folly, a copy of the Temple of Verilis, forms part of the 18th century Pleasure Gardens at Halswell House. Restored in 1994.
Website Address: www.somersite.co.uk/temple.htm
Grant Recipient/Owner: Halswell Park Trust
Access contact: Mr H M Humphreys
Tel: 01823 443955
Email Address: mick@somersite.co.uk
Opening Arrangements: 1 June - end of September: Saturdays and Sundays 2 - 5pm, plus Easter Weekend and May Day Bank Holiday. Any other day by prior arrangement with Mr H M Humphreys, Honorary Secretary, The Halswell Park Trust, Creech Barn, Creech St Michael, Taunton, Somerset TA3 5PP (tel.01823 443955).
Heritage Open Days: Yes
P Yes. Spaces: 4
♿ No. Disabled WC: No. Guide Dogs: Yes
£ Yes
Adult: £1.00
Child: 50p
Other: 50p (senior citizens)

Wells Old Almshouses

Chamberlain Street, Wells, Somerset
Comprises 4 unchanged almshouses, the oldest dating from 1435, with a Guild Room, chapel and gardens.
Grant Recipient/Owner: Wells Old Almshouses Trust
Access contact: Mr Adrian I'Anson
Tel: 01749 677499
Email Address: adrian.ianson@virginnet.co.uk
Opening Arrangements: Heritage Open Days, and at other times by prior arrangement with the Secretary, Wells Old Almshouses Trust, 66 Portway, Wells, Somerset BA5 2BP (tel.01749 677499).
Heritage Open Days: Yes
P No
♿ Yes. Disabled WC: No. Guide Dogs: Yes
£ No

Westbury College

Westbury-on-Trym, Bristol, Somerset
The 15th century gatehouse of the College of Priests (founded in the 13th century), of which John Wycliff was prebend.
Website Address: www.nationaltrust.org.uk
Grant Recipient/Owner: The National Trust
Access contact: Rev G M Collins
Tel: 0117 926 1536
Opening Arrangements: Access by key only, to be collected by written or telephone appointment with Rev GM Collins, The Vicarage, 44 Eastfield Road, Westbury on Trym, Bristol, BS9 4AG (tel: 0117 926 1536, or the National Trust Wessex Regional Office: 01985 843600). Wheelchair access to ground floor only. Street parking only.
Heritage Open Days: No
P See above
♿ Partial. Disabled WC: No. Guide Dogs: Yes
£ Yes
Adult: £1.10
Child: £0.50
Other: £0.50

SOUTH YORKSHIRE

Cusworth Hall

Museum of South Yorkshire Life, Cusworth Lane, Doncaster, South Yorkshire DN5 7TU
Grade I listed 18th century country house designed by George Platt with additions by James Paine, set in a landscaped park designed by Richard Woods. Home of the Battie-Wrightson family until 1952, now converted into a museum of South Yorkshire life.
Grant Recipient/Owner:
Doncaster Metropolitan Borough Council
Access contact: Mr F Carpenter
Tel: 01302 782342 **Fax:** 01302 782342
Email Address: museum@doncaster.gov.uk
Opening Arrangements: Monday - Friday 10am - 5pm, Saturdays 11am- 5pm, Sundays 1 - 5pm. Early closing at 4pm in December and January. Closed Christmas Day, Boxing Day and Good Friday. Wheelchair access to ground floor, tea room, shop and Great Kitchen. Refreshments available.
Heritage Open Days: No
P Yes. Spaces: 150
♿ Partial. Disabled WC: Yes. Guide Dogs: Yes
£ No

The Mansion House

High Street, Doncaster, South Yorkshire DN1 1DG
One of only 3 Mansion Houses in the country, the others being in London and York. Originally built as a residence for the Mayor in the late 1740s, now used as a meeting place for the local authority. Contains ballroom with many paintings of local dignitaries, a banqueting room which is now used as the Council Chamber, the Peace Window at the top of the main staircase depicting local history and the coat of arms, and a kitchen with many original fittings.
Grant Recipient/Owner: The Chief Executive
Access contact: Mr Horace Shillito
Tel: 01302 734032 **Fax:** 01302 734040
Opening Arrangements: Monday - Friday 8.30am - 5pm and evenings by prior arrangement only with

Doncaster Metropolitan Borough Council, 2 Priory Place, Doncaster, South Yorkshire DN1 1BN (tel.01302 734032). Wheelchair access to upper floors restricted by small lift which will not accommodate large wheelchairs, for further information please check with council. Parking in town centre car parks during the day, street parking in evening. Disabled parking adjacent to property day and night.
Heritage Open Days: No
P See above
♿ Partial. Disabled WC: No. Guide Dogs: No
£ Yes
Adult: £2.00 (evenings only)

Moated Site & Chapel

Thorpe Lane, Thorpe-in-Balne, nr. Doncaster, South Yorkshire, DN6 ODY
Medieval chapel, moated site and fishponds. Built 12th century with 13th, 14th, 15th and 19th century alterations. Restored and reroofed in 1994/5. In 1452 the chapel was the scene of the forcible abduction of Joan, wife of Charles Nowel, by Edward Lancaster of Skipton in Craven, which resulted in the passing of an Act of Parliament for the redress of grievance and the better protection of females.
Grant Recipient/Owner: Mr Attey
Access contact: Mrs Attey
Tel: 01302 883160
Opening Arrangements: By prior arrangement with Mrs Attey at the Manor House.
Heritage Open Days: Yes
P Yes. Spaces: 10
♿ No. Disabled WC: No. Guide Dogs: Yes
£ No
Donation for charity welcomed.

STAFFORDSHIRE

10 The Close

Lichfield, Staffordshire WS13 7LD
Early 15th century timber-framed house, originally one-up one-down and part of a five-dwelling range in the Vicar's Close. Notable doors and solid tread staircase remains in attic. Currently residence of assistant cathedral organist.
Grant Recipient/Owner:
Dean & Chapter of Lichfield Cathedral
Access contact: Mr Robert Sharpe
Tel: 01543 306201
Opening Arrangements: By prior written arrangement.
Heritage Open Days: No
P No
♿ No. Disabled WC: No. Guide Dogs: Yes
£ No

2-6 The Close

Lichfield, Staffordshire WS13 7LD
External steps and handrails to (mainly) early 18th century houses in the Cathedral Close.
Grant Recipient/Owner:
The Dean & Chapter of Lichfield Cathedral
Access contact:
The Dean & Chapter of Lichfield Cathedral
Tel: 01543 306100 **Fax:** 01543 306109
Email Address: enquiries@lichfield-cathedral.org
Opening Arrangements: At all reasonable times (exterior only).
Heritage Open Days: No
P No
♿ Yes. Disabled WC: No. Guide Dogs: Yes
£ No

7 Vicar's Close

Cathedral Close, Lichfield, Staffordshire
Grade II* listed building forming part of the medieval complex constructed for the Lay Vicars' Choral of the Cathedral and arranged around two courtyards. Mostly 15th century timber-frame with brick stacks and brick rebuilding. Now a private residence.
Grant Recipient/Owner:
The Dean & Chapter of Lichfield Cathedral
Access contact:
The Dean & Chapter of Lichfield Cathedral
Tel: 01543 306100 **Fax:** 01543 306109
Email Address: enquiries@lichfield-cathedral.org
Opening Arrangements: By prior arrangement (21 days notice requested) with the Dean & Chapter of Lichfield Cathedral, 19a The Close, Lichfield, Staffordshire WS13 7LD (tel.01543 306100). Wheelchair access to ground floor only.
Heritage Open Days: No
P No
♿ Partial. Disabled WC: No. Guide Dogs: Yes
£ No

8/9 Vicar's Close

Lichfield, Staffordshire
Grade II* listed building forming part of the medieval complex constructed for the Lay Vicars' Choral of the Cathedral and arranged around two courtyards. Mostly 15th century timber-frame with brick stacks and brick rebuilding. Now a private residence.
Grant Recipient/Owner:
The Dean & Chapter of Lichfield Cathedral
Access contact:
The Dean & Chapter of Lichfield Cathedral
Tel: 01543 306100 **Fax:** 01543 306109
Email Address: enquiries@lichfield-cathedral.org
Opening Arrangements: By prior arrangement (21 days notice requested) with the Dean & Chapter of Lichfield Cathedral, 19a The Close, Lichfield, Staffordshire WS13 7LD (tel. 01543 306100). Wheelchair access to ground floor only.
Heritage Open Days: No
P No
♿ Partial. Disabled WC: No. Guide Dogs: Yes
£ No

Barlaston Hall

Barlaston, nr. Stoke-on-Trent, Staffordshire ST12 9AT
Mid-18th century Palladian villa attributed to Sir Robert Taylor, with public rooms containing some fine examples of 18th century plasterwork. Extensively restored during the 1990s.
Grant Recipient/Owner: Mr James Hall
Access contact: Mr James Hall
Fax: 01782 372391
Opening Arrangements: 6 March - 11 September: Tuesdays, entrance at 2,3,4 & 5pm.
Heritage Open Days: Yes
P Yes. Spaces: 6
♿ No. Disabled WC: No. Guide Dogs: No
£ Yes
Adult: £2.50
Child: £1.50
Other: No charge for Historic House Association members.

Biddulph Grange Garden

Biddulph, Stoke-on-Trent, Staffordshire ST8 7SD
Garden with series of connected apartments designed to display specimens from James Bateman's extensive and wide ranging plant collection. Visitors are taken on a miniature tour of the world featuring the Egyptian court, China, a Scottish glen, as well as a pineture and rock areas. West Wing also built by James Bateman houses the tea room, shop and toilets.
Website Address: www.nationaltrust.org.uk
Access contact: Christine Belford/Andrew Humphris
Tel: 01782 517999 **Fax:** 01782 510624
Email Address: mbgwxm@smtp.ntrust.org.uk
Opening Arrangements: 28 March to 4 November: Wednesdays to Fridays 12 noon - 6pm, Saturdays and Sundays 11am - 6pm (High Season). 10 November to 16 December: Saturdays and Sundays 12 noon to 4pm (Low Season). Wheelchair access to Lime Avenue, Lake, Pinetum, Cheshire Cottage, Egypt and East Terrace. West Wing open as for garden.
Heritage Open Days: No
P Yes. Spaces: 100
♿ Partial. Disabled WC: Yes. Guide Dogs: Yes
£ Yes
Adult: £4.40 (High Season). £2.00 (Low Season).
Child: £2.30 (High Season). £1.00 (Low Season).
Other: £11.00 (High Season). £5.00 (Low Season).

Claymills Pumping Engines

The Victorian Pumping Station, The Sewage Works, Meadow Lane, Stretton, Burton-on-Trent, Staffordshire DE13 0BA
Large Victorian steam-operated sewage pumping station built in 1885. Four beam engines housed in two Italianate engine houses, one operational on steaming weekends. Boiler house with range of five Lancashire boilers, large Victorian steam-operated workshop with blacksmith's forge, steam hammer, and steam driven machinery. 1930s dynamo house with very early D.C. generating equipment, earliest dynamo 1889 (all operational).
Grant Recipient/Owner: Severn Trent Water Ltd
Access contact: Mr Roy Barratt
Tel: 01283 534960
Email Address: roybarratt@yahoo.co.uk
Opening Arrangements: Steaming weekends: 31 December 2000 & 1 January, 15 - 16 April, 16 - 17 June, 26 - 27 August, 22 - 23 September, 20 - 21 October; otherwise open every Saturday throughout the year. Admission charged for steaming weekends, donations requested on other open days. Refreshments available. Wheelchair access to ground floor only (workshop, boiler house and engine house), shop and refreshment area. Parking for 6 coaches.
Heritage Open Days: Yes
P Yes. Spaces: 100
♿ Partial. Disabled WC: Yes. Guide Dogs: Yes
£ Yes
Adult: £2.00
Child: £1.00

Goat Maltings

Clarence Street Mill, Clarence Street, Burton-on-Trent, Staffordshire DE14 3LG
Grade II* listed maltings, built 1883 by Sir Peter Wacker. First octagonal malting to be built. Then owned by Yeomans, Cherry and Curtis and now partly used as an animal food manufacturing facility and storage depot. Weathervane in the shape of a goat on top of the octagonal malting kiln.
Grant Recipient/Owner: Mr Geo L White Ltd
Access contact: Mr George White
Tel: 01283 564641 **Fax:** 01283 511967
Email Address: gw-glw@freezone.co.uk
Opening Arrangements: All year 9am - 4.30pm (excluding weekends and Bank Holidays except by prior written arrangement). Guide dog access to ground floor only.
Heritage Open Days: No
P Yes. Spaces: 6
♿ No. Disabled WC: No. Guide Dogs: Yes
£ No

Ingestre Pavilion

Tixall, nr. Stafford, Staffordshire
The pavilion was built in 1752 as part of a formal garden layout subsequently altered by 'Capability' Brown. The façade is a powerful and distinguished one, although the architect is not known. The building behind it had been demolished by 1802 and so there are now new ones including an octagonal saloon.
Website Address: www.landmarktrust.co.uk
Grant Recipient/Owner: The Landmark Trust
Access contact: Ms Victoria Piggott
Tel: 01628 825920 **Fax:** 01628 825417
Email Address: vpiggott@landmarktrust.co.uk
Opening Arrangements: The Landmark Trust is an independent charity, which rescues small buildings of historic or architectural importance from decay or unsympathetic improvement. Landmark's aim is to promote the enjoyment of these historic buildings by making them available to stay in for holidays. Ingestre Pavilion can be rented by anyone, at all times of the year, for periods ranging from a weekend to three weeks. Bookings can be made by telephoning the Booking Office on 01628 825925. As the building is in full-time use for holiday accommodation, it is not normally open to the public. However the public can view the building by prior arrangement by telephoning the access contact (Victoria Piggott on 01628 825920) to make an appointment. Potential visitors will be asked to write to confirm the details of their visit.
Heritage Open Days: No
P Yes. Spaces: 2
♿ No. Disabled WC: No. Guide Dogs: Yes
£ No

Kinver Edge (Hill Fort)

nr. Stourbridge, Staffordshire
A sandstone ridge covered in woodland and heath with Iron Age hill fort with views across surrounding countryside.
Grant Recipient/Owner: The National Trust
Access contact: The Warden
Tel: 01384 872418
Opening Arrangements: Kinver Edge is open at all times.
Heritage Open Days: No
P Yes. Spaces: 100
♿ No. Disabled WC: No. Guide Dogs: Yes
£ No

Newton's College

The Close, Lichfield, Staffordshire WS13
Grade II* range of 10 almshouses built 1800 for widows and unmarried daughters of clergymen who had served the Cathedral. Faced in Hallington stone to a classical style, 2 storeys with central pedimented break. Now private residences.
Grant Recipient/Owner:
The Dean & Chapter of Lichfield Cathedral
Access contact:
The Dean & Chapter of Lichfield Cathedral
Tel: 01543 306100 **Fax:** 01543 306109
Email Address: enquiries@lichfield-cathedral.org
Opening Arrangements: By prior arrangement (21 days notice requested) with the Dean & Chapter of Lichfield Cathedral, 19a The Close, Lichfield, Staffordshire WS13 7LD (tel.01543 306100).
Heritage Open Days: No
P No
♿ No. Disabled WC: No. Guide Dogs: Yes
£ No

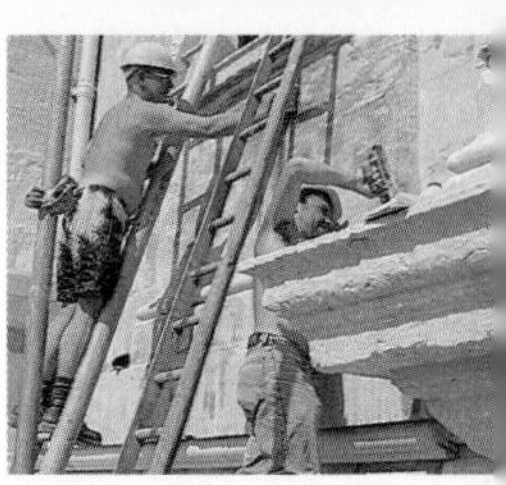
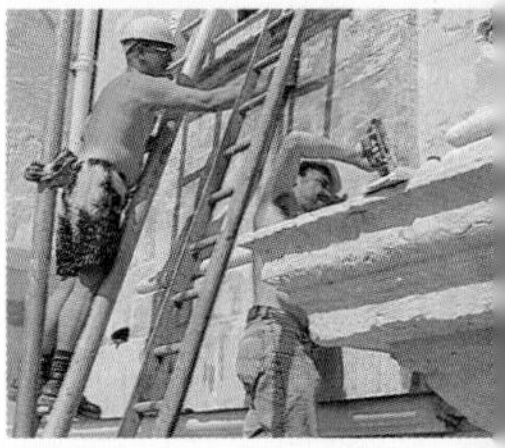
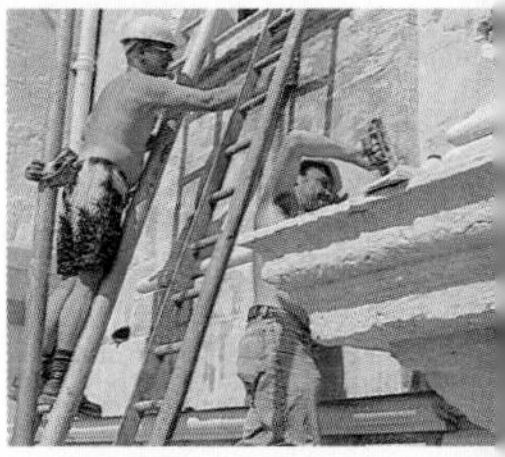
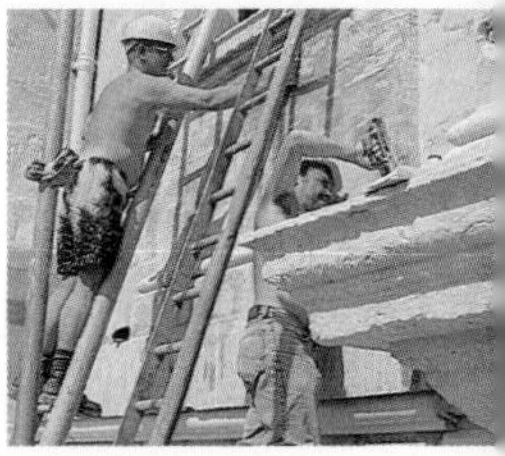
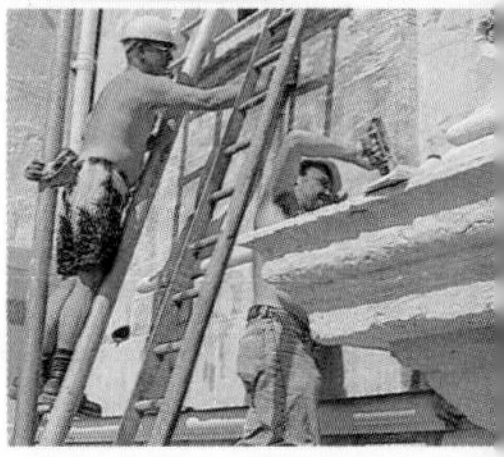
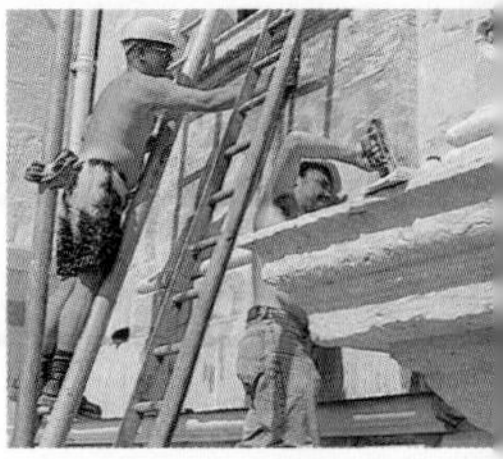
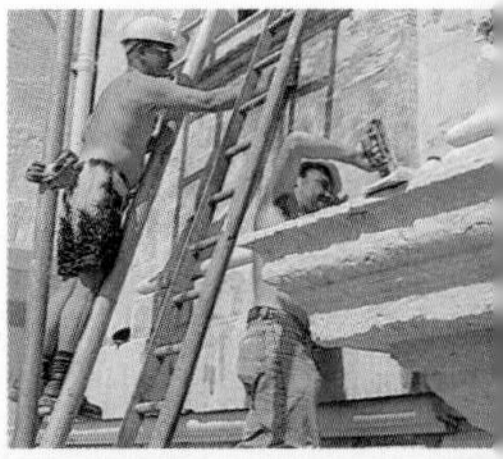

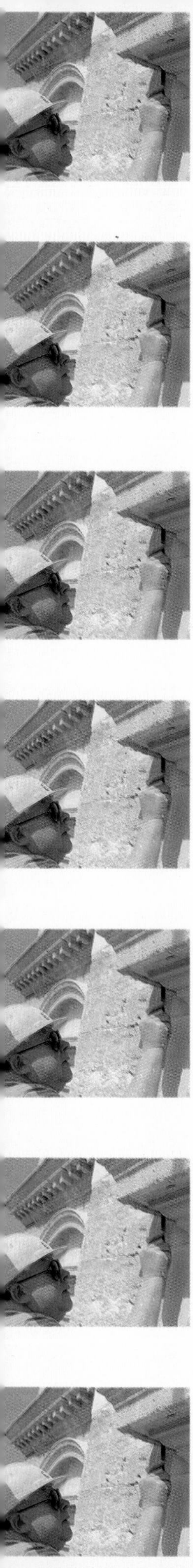

Shugborough

Milford, Stafford, Staffordshire ST17 0XB

The present house was begun circa 1695. Between 1760 and 1770 it was enlarged and again partly remodelled by Samuel Wyatt at end of 18th century. The interior is particularly notable for its plaster work and other decorations. Ancestral home of the Earls of Lichfield. Houses the Staffordshire County Museum, Georgian working farm and Rare Livestock Breed project.

Grant Recipient/Owner: The National Trust
Access contact: Staffordshire County Council
Tel: 01889 881388
Opening Arrangements: Saturday 31 March to Sunday 30 September 2001: Mansion House, County Museum, farm and gardens: open daily except Mondays (but open Bank Holiday Mondays) 11am - 5pm; October Sundays only. Open to booked parties only: Monday 1 October to Friday 29 March 2002: Mansion house, County Museum, farm and gardens Monday to Friday 10.30am - 4pm. Wheelchair access to ground floor of house, museum and farm.
Heritage Open Days: No
P Yes. Spaces: 600
♿ Partial. Disabled WC: Yes. Guide Dogs: Yes
£ Yes
Adult: £4.50 (per site). £9.00 (to all sites).
Child: £3.00 (per site). £6.00 (to all sites).
Other: £12.00 (per site). £22.00 (to all sites).

Sinai Park

Branston, Shobnall, Staffordshire

Timber-framed E-shaped house, two-thirds derelict, on moated hill-top site, dating from the 13th century. House built variously during 15th, 16th and 17th centuries with later additions, including wall paintings and carpenters marks. 18th century bridge and plunge pool in the grounds.

Grant Recipient/Owner: Ms C A Newton
Access contact: Ms C A Newton
Tel: 01283 544161
Email Address: knewton@brookes-vernons.co.uk
Opening Arrangements: By prior arrangement only.
Heritage Open Days: No
P No
♿ No. Disabled WC: No. Guide Dogs: Yes
£ No

SUFFOLK

Culford School Iron Bridge

Culford, Bury St Edmunds, Suffolk IP28 6TX

Constructed for the second Marquis Cornwallis in the late 1790s by Samuel Wyatt, brother of James, to a design patented by Wyatt. The bridge, in Culford Park, is one of the earliest surviving bridges with an unmodified cast iron structure, being the earliest known example with hollow ribs.

Grant Recipient/Owner: Mr J W Beaty
Access contact: Michael Woolley
Tel: 01284 729318 **Fax:** 01284 729077
Email Address: bursary@culfordschool.freeserve.co.uk
Opening Arrangements: Access to the iron bridge and Culford Park is available at any time throughout the year. Disabled access may be difficult as over grass and toilet facilities are limited, being only available when Culford Hall is open and the facility having low steps at the entrance to the Hall and the toilets. Temporary ramps will be provided at the entrance to the Hall on Heritage Open Days.
Heritage Open Days: Yes
P Yes. Spaces: 100
♿ Yes. Disabled WC: Yes. Guide Dogs: Yes
£ No

Elms Farm Wallpaintings

Old Station Road, Mendlesham, Suffolk IP14 5RS

Wealden hall house dating from 1480, wallpaintings consist of 16th century floral design and Biblical texts in the upper hall and solar and 17th century armorial patterning in the parlour.

Grant Recipient/Owner: Mrs Pamela Gilmour
Access contact: Mrs Pamela Gilmour
Opening Arrangements: By prior written arrangement.
Heritage Open Days: No
P Yes. Spaces: 10
♿ No. Disabled WC: No. Guide Dogs: No
£ No

Flatford Mill & Willy Lott's Cottage

Flatford, East Bergholt, Suffolk CO7 6OL

Flatford watermill, 1733 datestone, incorporating possibly earlier but altered former granary range to rear and further C19 range adjoining granary. Later alterations. The mill was in the possession of the Constable family from the mid C18. Willy Lott's farmhouse, late C16-C17. Grade I listing of both buildings reflects their significance in the life and work of John Constable. Both buildings are leased by the National Trust to the Field Studies Council. Flatford Bridge Cottage 16th century thatched cottage, upstream from Flatford Mill houses an exhibition on John Constable.

Website Address: www.nationaltrust.org.uk
Grant Recipient/Owner: The National Trust
Access contact: Property Manager
Tel: 01206 298260 **Fax:** 01206 299193
Email Address: atdcykx@smtp.ntrust.org.uk
Opening Arrangements: Public access to Flatford Mill and Willy Lott's Cottage is to the exterior and by virtue of their use as a course centre for the Field Studies Council (for information on courses tel: 01206 298283). The Field Studies Council will also arrange tours for groups. (Flatford Bridge Cottage is open March and April daily except Mondays and Tuesdays 11am - 5.30pm; May to end September daily 10am - 5.30pm; October daily 11am - 5.30pm; November and December daily except Mondays and Tuesdays 11am - 3.30pm. Closed Christmas. Car park 200 metres from cottage. Parking near cottage available for disabled visitors. Lavatory for disabled available in car park owned by Babergh DC, 25 yards from the cottage. For further information contact the Property Manager 01206 298260).
Heritage Open Days: No
P Yes. Spaces: 200
♿ Partial. Disabled WC: Yes. Guide Dogs: Yes
£ No

Hadleigh Deanery

Hadleigh, Ipswich, Suffolk IP7 5DT

Built 1495 by the then Dean, William Pykenham. Ornate red brick building, originally constructed as a gateway but became a study/library (on first floor) for subsequent Deans. The present house was built onto it in 1831. Has a spiral staircase, dovecot, turrets, vaulted oratory and secret chamber.

Grant Recipient/Owner:
Diocese of St Edmundsbury and Ipswich
Access contact: Canon David Stranack
Tel: 01473 822218
Opening Arrangements: Sunday 16 September 2 - 5pm. Other opening arrangements under review at time of going to print, please check English Heritage website for current information. Also by prior arrangement. Parking in Magdalen Street.
Heritage Open Days: No
P See above
♿ No.
£ No
Donations requested.

Hall Farm Barn

Withersfield, Suffolk

100ft long by 30ft wide thatched barn built c1400, with later alterations. Floor is split into 3 levels with the east wall having been bricked inbetween the timbers and the west wall still consisting of horsehair, lathe and plaster. Situated in working farmyard.

Grant Recipient/Owner: Mr C R W Bradford
Access contact: Mr T Mytton-Mills
Tel: 01440 702146 **Fax:** 01440 702552
Email Address: tom@hall-farm.fsnet.co.uk
Opening Arrangements: By prior telephone arrangement.
Heritage Open Days: No
P Yes. Spaces: 12
♿ Yes. Disabled WC: Yes. Guide Dogs: Yes
£ No

Horseman's House

Boundary Farm, Framsden, Suffolk IP14 6LH

Mid 17th century brick stable. Gable ended with brick pinnacles along upper edge with panels of diaper work in dark headers below round vents/owl holes. Original three bay, two storey structure housed horseman above his charges in unusually ornate accommodation for all. Now horse and rider holiday accommodation.

Grant Recipient/Owner: Mr Bacon
Access contact: Mr Bacon
Tel: 01728 860370 **Fax:** 01728 860370
Email Address: info@boundaryfarm.co.uk
Opening Arrangements: By prior arrangement only. Wheelchair access to ground floor only.
Heritage Open Days: No
P Yes. Spaces: 4
♿ Partial. Disabled WC: Yes. Guide Dogs: Yes
£ No

Ickworth House

Ickworth, Horringer, Bury St Edmunds, Suffolk IP29 5QE

The Earl of Bristol created this eccentric house, with its central rotunda and curved corridors, in 1795 to display his collections. These include paintings by Titian, Gainsborough and Velasquez and a Georgian silver collection. The house is surrounded by an Italianate garden set in a 'Capability' Brown park with woodland walks, deer enclosure, vineyard, Georgian summerhouse and lake.

Website Address: www.nationaltrust.org.uk
Grant Recipient/Owner: The National Trust
Access contact: Property Manager
Tel: 01284 735270 **Fax:** 01284 735175
Email Address: arore@smtp.ntrust.org.uk
Opening Arrangements: House: 24 to 28 October: daily except Mondays and Thursdays (but open Bank Holiday Mondays) 1 - 5 (last admission 4.30pm). Closes 4.30pm in October. Garden: 24 March to 28 October: daily; 29 October to end March 2002: daily except Saturdays and Sundays. Times: 10am - 5pm (last admission 4.30pm) 1 November to end March 2002; 10am to 4pm. Park daily. Wheelchair access to House: ramped access (restricted access in House for large powered vehicles/chairs); lift to first floor; stairlift to basement (shop and restaurant) suitable to wheelchair users able to transfer; wheelchair on each floor; garden largely accessible, some changes of level, gravel drive and paths.
Heritage Open Days: No
P Yes. Spaces: 2000
♿ Partial. Disabled WC: Yes. Guide Dogs: Yes
£ Yes
Adult: £5.70. £2.50 (park & garden only).
Child: £2.50. £0.80 (park & garden only).
Other: £4.70 (group rate). No group rates Sundays & Bank Holiday Mondays. Family discounts.

Melford Hall

Long Melford, nr. Sudbury, Suffolk CO10 9AA

Elizabethan house, little changed externally since 1578 and with panelled banqueting hall. Regency library, Victorian bedrooms and collections of furniture and porcelain. Garden and parkland.

Website Address: www.nationaltrust.org.uk
Grant Recipient/Owner: The National Trust
Access contact: Property Manager
Tel: 01787 880286
Opening Arrangements: April and October: Saturdays, Sundays and Bank Holidays; May to end September: daily except Mondays and Tuesdays (but open Bank Holiday Mondays) 2 - 5.30pm. Wheelchair access to ground floor (ramps on request). Stairlift to first floor.
Heritage Open Days: No
P Yes. Spaces: 50
♿ Partial. Disabled WC: Yes. Guide Dogs: Yes
£ Yes
Adult: £4.40
Other: £3.30 (per-booked groups daily except Sundays, Mondays & Tuesdays).

St Peter

College Street, Ipswich, Suffolk

Large medieval church near the docks, owned by Ipswich Borough Council and redundant since the 1970s. Noted for a Tournai font and adjacent to Thomas Wolsey's gateway.

Grant Recipient/Owner:
Ipswich Historic Churches Trust
Access contact: Mr J S Hall
Tel: 01473 232300 **Fax:** 01473 230524
Opening Arrangements: By prior arrangement with Mr J S Hall, Secretary, Ipswich Historic Churches Trust, 24-26 Museum Street, Ipswich, Suffolk IP1 1HZ (tel.01473 232300). Wheelchair access to all of the church apart from the vestry and parts of the chancel.
Heritage Open Days: Yes
P No
♿ Partial. Disabled WC: No. Guide Dogs: Yes
£ No

Samson's Tower (Abbey Visitor Centre) and 1-3 West Front

Great Churchyard, Bury St Edmunds, Suffolk IP33 1RS

Ruined Grade I medieval west front of the Abbey of St Edmund, now converted into a visitor centre interpreting the life of Edmund and private residences.

Grant Recipient/Owner:
St Edmundsbury District Council
Access contact: Director of Leisure Services, St Edmundsbury Borough Council
Tel: 01284 764667 **Fax:** 01284 757084
Email Address: steve.palframan@stedmundsbury.gov.uk
Opening Arrangements: Abbey Visitor Centre (Samson's Tower): January - Easter, weekends 11am - 4pm; Easter - October, daily except Tuesdays and Thursdays 11am - 4pm; closed November and December. Opening arrangements for Visitor Centre may change, please check English Heritage website for up-to-date information. Opening arrangements for no.s 1,2 & 3 West Front under review at time of going to print, again please check English Heritage website for up-to-date information. Wheelchair access only to visitor centre. Disabled parking available within 10yds by prior arrangement and disabled toilets 150 metres away. Parking at pay and display car park on Angel Hill 150 metres away. Open Heritage Open Days at time of going to print but again this may change, please check English Heritage website for up-to-date information.

Heritage Open Days: Yes
P See above
♿ Partial. Disabled WC: No. Guide Dogs: Yes
£ No

Somerleyton Hall & Gardens

Somerleyton, Lowestoft, Suffolk NR32 5QQ
Early Victorian stately home, built in Anglo-Italian style for Sir Morton Peto by John Thomas upon former Jacobean mansion. Contains carved stonework and state rooms. Has 12 acres of gardens with a yew hedge maze.
Website Address: www.somerleyton.co.uk
Grant Recipient/Owner:
The Rt Hon Lord Somerleyton GCVO
Access contact: Mr Ian Pollard
Tel: 01502 730224 **Fax:** 01502 732143
Email Address: enquiries@somerleyton.co.uk
Opening Arrangements: Easter Sunday - end of September: Thursdays, Sundays and Bank Holidays, plus Tuesdays and Wednesdays in July and August, 12.30 - 5.30pm. Admission charges are provisional at time of going to print, please check with Hall for current rates.
Heritage Open Days: No
P Yes. Spaces: 200
♿ Yes. Disabled WC: Yes. Guide Dogs: Yes
£ Yes
Adult: £5.00 (see above)
Child: £2.50
Other: £4.80 (senior citizens), £14.20 (family).

Theatre Royal

Westgate Street, Bury St Edmunds, Suffolk IP33 1QR
A rare example of a late Georgian playhouse. Built 1819, later used as a warehouse but restored and re-opened as a theatre in 1965. Constructed of white brick and stucco with a slate roof.
Website Address: www.theatreroyal.org
Grant Recipient/Owner: The National Trust
Access contact: The Administrator
Tel: 01284 755127 **Fax:** 01284 706035
Email Address: admin@theatreroyal.org
Opening Arrangements: By guided tour only by prior arrangement: Mondays and Wednesdays 11am - 1pm and 2 - 4pm, Saturdays 11am - 1pm. Limited wheelchair access, please ring 01284 769505 for details. Limited parking in Westgate Street.
Heritage Open Days: No
P See above
♿ Partial. Disabled WC: No. Guide Dogs: No
£ Yes
Adult: £2.00
Child: £1.00

Woodbridge Lodge

Rendlesham, nr Woodbridge, Suffolk IP12 2RA
Late 18th century small gothic folly. Originally a gatehouse to Rendlesham Hall, now part of a dwelling house.
Grant Recipient/Owner: Dr C P Cooper
Access contact: Dr C P Cooper
Tel: 01394 460642
Opening Arrangements: Exterior only by prior arrangement..
Heritage Open Days: No
P Yes. Spaces: 3
♿ No. Disabled WC: No. Guide Dogs: No
£ No

SURREY

Carshalton Water Tower

West Street, Carshalton, Surrey
18th century garden building with an Orangery, Saloon, plunge-bath lined with Delft tiles, part-restored water wheel and stone pump chamber. Built 1721 for Sir John Fellowes, sub-Governor of the South Sea Company.
Grant Recipient/Owner: Carshalton Water Tower Trust
Access contact: Mrs Julia Gertz
Tel: 020 8647 0984
Opening Arrangements: First Sunday in April - last Sunday in September 2.30 - 5pm, plus local and national Heritage Open Days. Private tours by prior arrangement with the Friends of Carshalton Water Tower, 136 West Street, Carshalton, Surrey SM5 2NR (tel.020 8647 0984). Parking available by arrangement.
Heritage Open Days: Yes
P See above
♿ Yes. Disabled WC: Yes. Guide Dogs: Yes
£ Yes
Adult: 75p
Child: 25p

Clandon House

West Clandon, Guildford, Surrey, GU4 7RQ
Palladian mansion, built c1730 by Venetian architect Giacomo Leoni. Two-storeyed Marble Hall, collection of 18th century furniture, porcelain, textiles, carpets, the Ivo Forde Meissen collection of Italian comedy figures and a series of Mortlake tapestries.
Grant Recipient/Owner: The National Trust
Access contact: Mr David Brock-Doyle
Tel: 01483 222482 **Fax:** 01483 223479
Email Address: sclsea@smtp.ntrust.org.uk
Opening Arrangements: House: 1 April - 4 November; daily except Monday, Friday and Saturday (but open Good Friday, Easter Saturday and Bank Holiday Mondays) 11am - 5pm (last admission 4.30pm). Museum: as for house 12 - 5pm. Garden: all year as for house 11am - 5pm. Wheelchair access to lower ground floor and five steps to ground floor.
Heritage Open Days: No
P Yes. Spaces: 200
♿ Partial. Disabled WC: Yes. Guide Dogs: Yes
£ Yes
Adult: £5.00
Child: £2.50
Other: £12.50 (family), £4.00 (group rate, per head Tuesdays, Wednesdays & Thursdays only).

Claremont House

Claremont Drive, Esher, Surrey KT10 9LY
Built 1772 in Palladian style by 'Capability' Brown for Clive of India. Henry Holland and John Soane were responsible for the interior decoration. For over a century it was a royal residence, home to Charlotte, Princess of Wales, the young Queen Victoria, and the Duke and Duchess of Albany.
Website Address: www.claremont-school.co.uk
Grant Recipient/Owner:
Claremont Fan Court Foundation Ltd
Access contact: Mrs C Bradley
Tel: 01372 467841 **Fax:** 01372 471109
Email Address: library@intonet.co.uk
Opening Arrangements: Guided tours: 1 & 2 April, 6 & 7 May, 3 & 4 June, 2 July, 5 & 6 August, 2 & 3 September and 7 & 8 October, 2 - 5pm (last tour 4.30pm). Groups and individuals at other times by prior arrangement. Wheelchair access also by prior arrangement.
Heritage Open Days: No
P Yes. Spaces: 100
♿ Partial. Disabled WC: No. Guide Dogs: Yes
£ Yes
Adult: £3.00
Child: £1.50
Other: £2.00

Great Hall

Virginia Park, Christchurch Road, Virginia Water, Surrey GU25 4BM
By W H Crossland for Charas Holloway and opened 1884. Built of red brick with Portland stone dressings and slate roofs in Franco-Flemish Gothic style. Formerly part of the Royal Holloway Sanatorium.
Grant Recipient/Owner: Octagon Virginia Ltd
Access contact: Mr John Ellams
Tel: 01344 845276 **Fax:** 01344 842428
Email Address: virginiapark@aol.com
Opening Arrangements: Entrance Hall, Staircase and Great Hall of former Sanatorium open on the following Wednesdays and Sundays 10am - 4pm: February 21 & 25, March 28, April 1, 18, 25 & 29, May 16, 23 & 27, June 20, 24 & 27, July 18, 25 & 29, August 15, 22 & 26, September 19, 26 & 30, October 17,24 & 28, November 21 & 25 and December 5 & 9. At other times by prior telephone arrangement with the Estate Office. Public car park nearby. No coach parties. Wheelchair access with assistance (steps into building to be negotiated).
Heritage Open Days: No
P See above
♿ Partial. Disabled WC: Yes. Guide Dogs: Yes
£ Yes
Adult: £3.00

Hospital of the Blessed Trinity (Abbot's Hospital)

High Street, Guildford, Surrey GU1 3AJ
17th century almshouse with enclosed courtyard and turreted tower entrance. Rear gardens with other 17th century buildings and matching new development. Tour visitors may also view the panelled common rooms with interesting furniture and paintings and the Chapel, which has well-known painted-glass windows.
Grant Recipient/Owner:
Governors of the Hospital of the Blessed Trinity
Access contact: Mr John W Moss
Tel: 01483 562670
Opening Arrangements: 1 May to end September: Mondays and Wednesdays 2.30pm only guided walks of chapel courtyard and terrace. Special organised guided walks with the Master's permission Monday to Saturdays 10.30am to 5pm (contact the Master, John Moss, 01483 562670). Wheelchair access to lower rooms and gardens, please notify if intending to use a wheelchair.
Heritage Open Days: Yes
P No
♿ Partial. Disabled WC: No. Guide Dogs: Yes
£ No

Kingston Grammar School – Lovekyn Chapel

70 London Road, Kingston-upon-Thames, Surrey KT2 6PY
Chapel of St Mary Magdalene, known as the Lovekyn Chantry Chapel, was consecrated in 1310 and is one of the oldest buildings in Kingston. Built by Edward Lovekyn in 1299 and restored and re-endowed in 1352 by his son John, twice Lord Mayor of London. In 1561 Queen Elizabeth established her grammar school in the Chapel. The school continues to use it for a wide variety of activities and public use.
Website Address: www.kingston-grammar.surrey.sch.uk
Grant Recipient/Owner:
Governors of Kingston Grammar School
Access contact: Mr A G Howard-Harwood
Tel: 020 8939 8825 **Fax:** 020 8974 5177
Email Address: bursar@kingston-grammar.surrey.sch.uk
Opening Arrangements: By prior written arrangement with Mr A G Howard-Harwood, Bursar & Clerk to the Governors at the school. Public car park nearby.
Heritage Open Days: Yes
P See above
♿ Yes. Disabled WC: Yes. Guide Dogs: Yes
£ No

The Old Mill

Outwood Common, nr. Redhill, Surrey RH1 5PW
England's oldest working windmill, built in 1665. Houses museum of bygones.
Website Address: www.outwoodwindmill.co.uk
Grant Recipient/Owner: Mrs Sheila Thomas
Access contact: Mrs Sheila Thomas
Tel: 01342 843644 **Fax:** 01342 843458
Email Address: sheila@outwoodwindmill.co.uk
Opening Arrangements: Easter - October: Sundays and Bank Holidays 2 - 6pm, plus parties by prior arrangement. Wheelchair access to museum and ground floor of mill only.
Heritage Open Days: No
P Yes. Spaces: 2
♿ Partial. Disabled WC: Yes. Guide Dogs: Yes
£ Yes
Adult: £2.00
Child: £1.00

The Old Palace School

Old Palace Road, Croydon, Surrey CRO 1AX
Residence of Archbishop's of Canterbury between 12th and 18th centuries. Contains 15th century banqueting hall, guard room and chapel, a Norman undercroft, a Tudor long gallery, Elizabeth I's bedroom and some of the earliest medieval brickwork in England. Currently home of the Old Palace School of John Whitgift.
Grant Recipient/Owner: Whitgift Foundation
Access contact: Dr Andrew Bradstock
Tel: 020 8688 2414
Opening Arrangements: By guided tour only: 17-21 April, 28 May - 1 June, 16-21 & 23-28 July. Doors open 1.45pm, last tour commences 2.15pm. Groups by prior arrangement on these dates, please contact Dr Andrew Bradstock on 020 8680 0467. Refreshments available.
Heritage Open Days: Yes
P No
♿ No. Disabled WC: No. Guide Dogs: No
£ Yes
Adult: £4.00
Child: £3.00 (senior citizens)
Other: £10.00 (family ticket)

Oxenford Farm

Milford Road, Elstead, Godalming, Surrey GU8 6LA
1840 Gothic-style stone barn by Pugin with cowsheds and gatehouse.
Grant Recipient/Owner: Mr C F Baker
Access contact: Mr A C Baker
Tel: 01252 702109 **Fax:** 01252 702109
Opening Arrangements: 1 - 24 December: daily 9am - 5pm. At other times by prior written arrangement. Wheelchair access to barn and cowsheds.
Heritage Open Days: No
P Yes, Spaces: 10
♿ Partial. Disabled WC: No. Guide Dogs: Yes
£ No

Painshill Park

Portsmouth Road, Cobham, Surrey KT11 1JE
Restored Grade I 18th century landscape garden of 150 acres, designed by Charles Hamilton between 1738 and 1773. Contains a Gothic temple, Chinese bridge, ruined abbey, Turkish tent, grotto and 14 acre serpentine lake fed by a large waterwheel.
Website Address: www.brainsys.com/cobham/painshill
Grant Recipient/Owner: Painshill Park Trust Ltd
Access contact: Mrs Harriet Richards
Tel: 01932 868113 **Fax:** 01932 868001
Opening Arrangements: April - October: Tuesday -

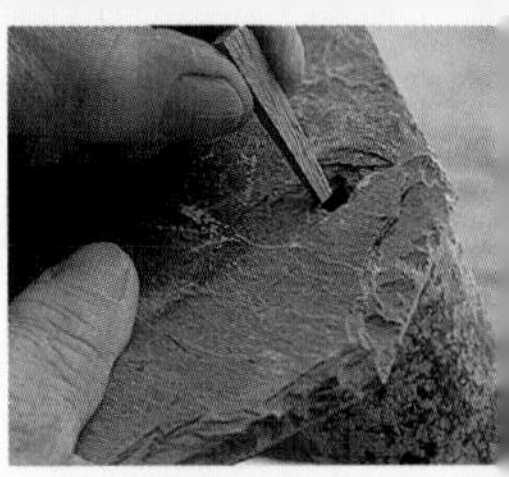
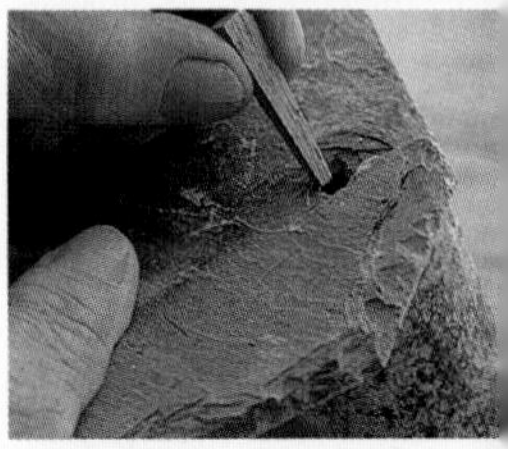
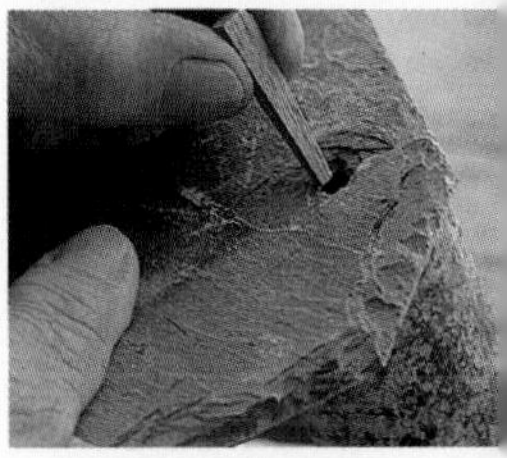
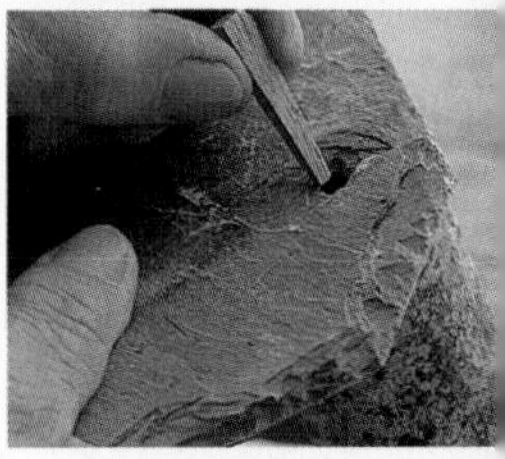
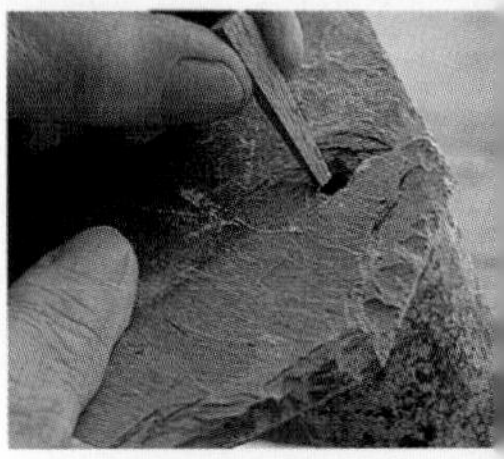
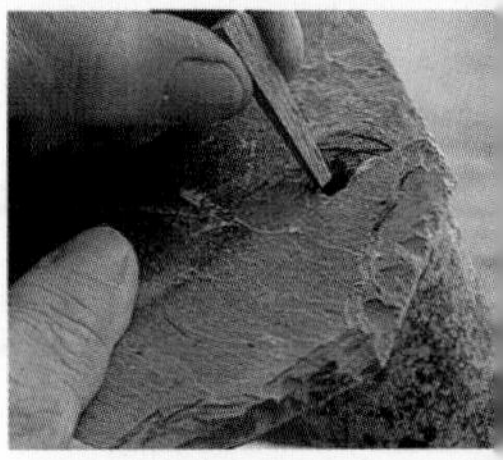
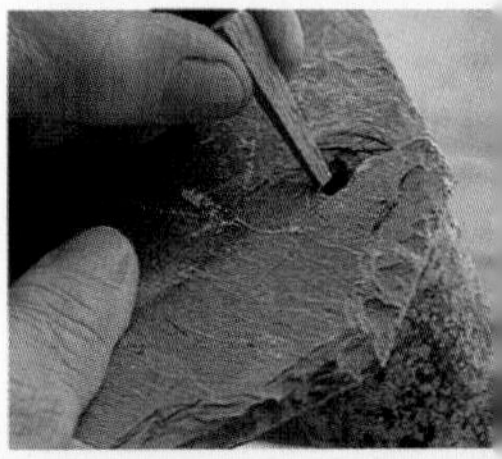

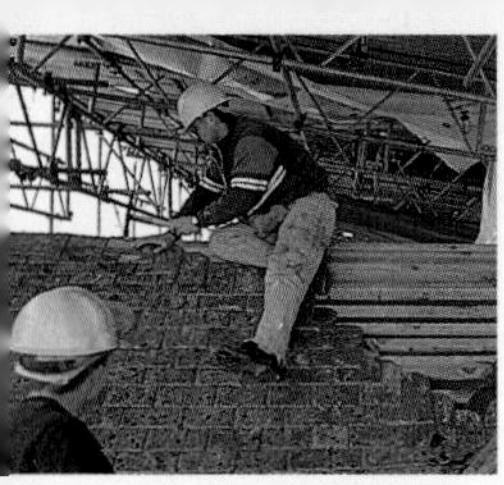
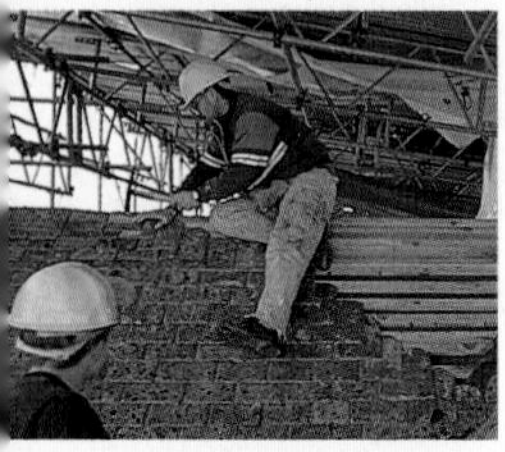
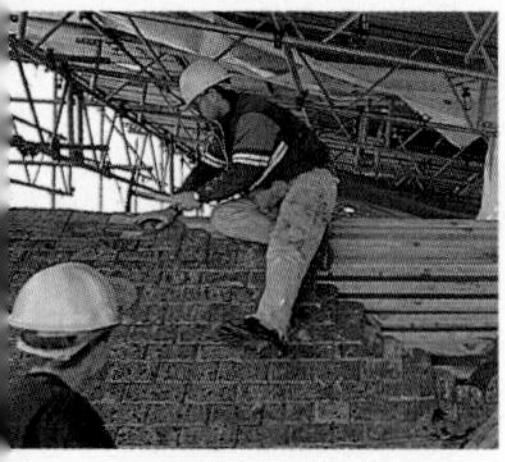
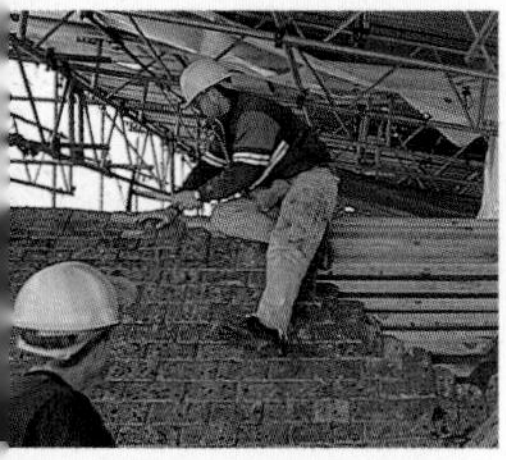
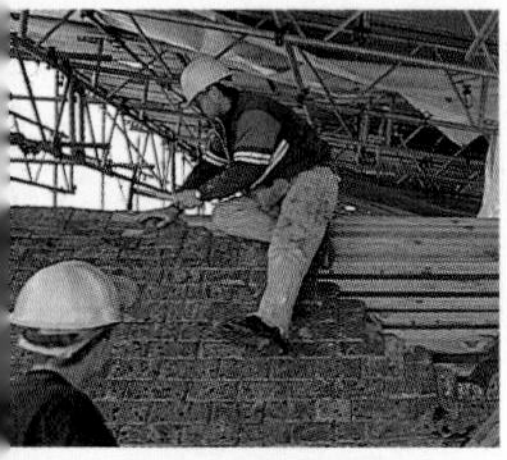
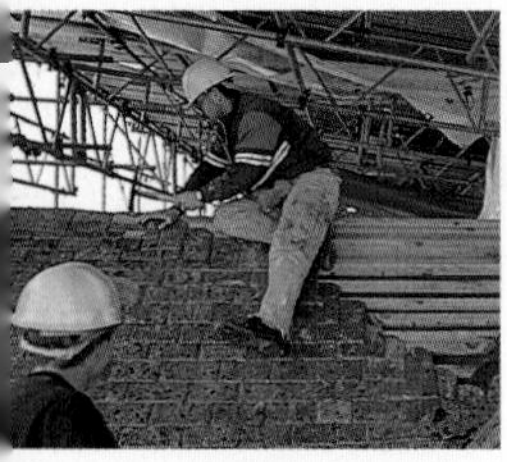
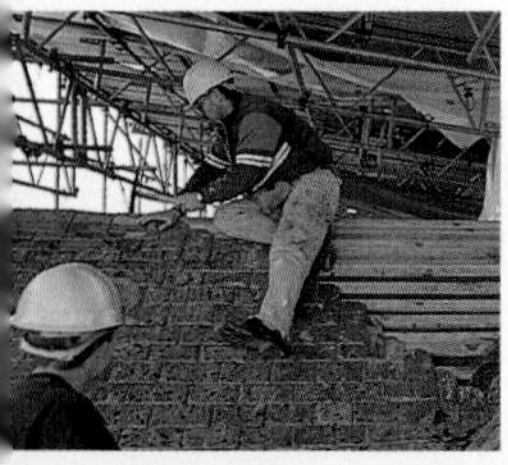

Sunday and Bank Holidays 10.30am - 6pm (last admission 4.30pm); November - March (except Christmas Day and Boxing Day): Tuesday - Thursday, Saturdays, Sundays and Bank Holidays 11am - 4pm or dusk if earlier (last admission 3pm). Guided tours by prior arrangement. Wheelchair access to most of the site, apart from the grotto and Alpine Valley. Admission charges are provisional at time of going to print, please check with Park for current rates. Parking for 8 coaches.
Heritage Open Days: No
P Yes. Spaces: 400
♿ Partial. Disabled WC: Yes. Guide Dogs: Yes
£ Yes
Adult: £4.20 (see above)
Child: £1.70 (free under five)
Other: £3.65

Red House
Frith Hill Road, Godalming, Surrey GU7 2DZ
Built by Lutyens 1897-9 for Revd Evans. An irregular mass built into steep hill with Jekyll garden. Each façade contrasting: North, street entrance low Georgian; West, English vernacular; East, romantic; South, keep-like with two bays accentuating the elevation, similar to the later Castle Drogo. Wide top-lit ramp-like staircase with rooms off to each façade on three split levels. Drawing room and dining room fireplaces are also contrasting features, with the former baroque and the latter neo-Georgian.
Grant Recipient/Owner: Mr H A Laws
Access contact: Mrs Shula Laws
Tel: 01483 429284 **Fax:** 01483 429284
Opening Arrangements: By prior written arrangement (at least 4 weeks in advance) in April, May, June, July and September (excluding Wednesdays, Thursdays and Sundays). Additional street parking.
Heritage Open Days: Yes
P Yes. Spaces: 2
♿ No. Disabled WC: No. Guide Dogs: Yes
£ No

TYNE & WEAR

21-23 Leazes Terrace
Newcastle-upon-Tyne, Tyne & Wear NE1 4LY
Elongated square of houses built 1829-34 in classical style. Now owned by the University of Newcastle and used as halls of residence.
Grant Recipient/Owner: University of Newcastle
Access contact: Miss Helen Stonebank
Tel: 0191 222 7565
Opening Arrangements: Exterior accessible at all times, only one room of the interior can be viewed (Room 21F, which is in near original condition) by prior arrangement with Miss Helen Stonebank, Accommodation Manageress, 10 Leazes Terrace, Newcastle-upon-Tyne, Tyne & Wear (tel.0191 222 7565). Parking at off street car park (metered).
Heritage Open Days: No
P See above
♿ No. Disabled WC: No. Guide Dogs: No
£ No

Fulwell Mill
Newcastle Road, Sunderland, Tyne & Wear
Grade II* listed mill built in 1821 using local limestone, remaining in use until 1949. Restoration of Mill to full working order and to provide visitor facilities expected to be completed early this year.
Grant Recipient/Owner:
Tyne & Wear Industrial Monuments Trust
Access contact: Mr Les Milne
Tel: 0191 553 1279 **Fax:** 0191 553 1460
Email Address: les.milne@sunderland.gov.uk
Opening Arrangements: Mill expected to re-open after restoration at Easter and then be open weekends and Bank Holidays until end of September, Sundays rest of the year, 10am - 4pm. Specialist groups/school parties by prior arrangement. Admission charges yet to be confirmed at time of going to print, please check with Mr Les Milne of the City of Sunderland Planning Implementation Section, PO Box 102, Civic Centre, Sunderland, Tyne & Wear SR2 7DN (tel.0191 553 1279). Wheelchair access to ground floor and visitor centre.
Heritage Open Days: No
P Yes. Spaces: 13
♿ Partial. Disabled WC: Yes. Guide Dogs: Yes
£ See above

Gibside Chapel & Column of Liberty
Gibside, nr. Rowlands Gill, Burnopfield, Tyne & Wear NE16 6BG
Palladian Chapel 1760-69; completed 1812 designed by James Paine for George Bowes, MP and coal owner, and Column of Liberty 1750-57 by Daniel Garrett until 1753; then James Paine, situated in extensive landscape. Much of the landscape is SSSI, and embracing many miles of riverside and forest walks. A forest garden is under restoration. The estate is the former home of the Queen Mother's family, the Bowes-Lyons.
Website Address: www.nationaltrust.org.uk
Grant Recipient/Owner: Regional Director
Access contact: Visitor Services Manager
Tel: 01207 542255
Email Address: joan.gardner@ntrust.org.uk
Opening Arrangements: Chapel: 1 April to 31 October 11am - 4.30pm. Winter by appointment only. Grounds: open Tuesdays to Sundays and Bank Holiday Mondays 10am. Last admission 4.30pm summer and 3.30pm winter. Wheelchair access to tea room, shop, toilets and part of the grounds. Wheelchair access is difficult to Chapel and the Avenue. Staff very happy to assist. Telephone the Visitor Services Manager (01207 542255) in advance. Parking for disabled near the site.
Heritage Open Days: Yes
P Yes. Spaces: 1000
♿ Partial. Disabled WC: Yes. Guide Dogs: Yes
£ Yes
Adult: £3.00
Child: £1.50
Other: £8.00 (family (2+4)). £5.00 (family (1+3)).

Old Town Hall
Market Place, South Shields,Tyne & Wear
Built 1768 by the Dean and Chapter of Durham in the centre of the Market Place. Square two-storey building with an open arcaded ground floor and a central pillar on steps supporting what may have been a former market cross. Upper floor reached by a symmetrical, double branch stone staircase. Restored 1977.
Grant Recipient/Owner: The Chief Executive
Access contact: Director of Community Services
Tel: 0191 4271717 **Fax:** 0191 4270469
Opening Arrangements: Access to ground floor at all reasonable times, first floor by prior arrangement with the Director of Community Services, South Tyneside Metropolitan Borough Council, Central Library Building, Prince George Square, South Shields, Tyne & Wear NE33 2PE (tel.0191 4271717). Wheelchair and guide dog access to ground floor only. Paid parking locally, with disabled parking close to site.
Heritage Open Days: No
P Yes. Spaces: 450
♿ Partial. Disabled WC: No. Guide Dogs: Yes
£ No

Washington Old Hall
The Avenue, Washington Village, District 4, Washington, Tyne & Wear NE38 7LE
17th century manor house, incorporating the 12th century remains of the home of George Washington's ancestors. Recreated 17th century interiors and displays of 'Washingtonabilia' celebrating the close connection with the USA. Permanent exhibition on the recent tenement period of the property. Jacobean knot-garden.
Website Address: www.nationaltrust.org.uk
Grant Recipient/Owner: The National Trust
Access contact: Property Manager
Tel: 0191 4166879 **Fax:** 0191 4192065
Opening Arrangements: 1 April to 31 October: Sundays to Wednesdays (but open Good Friday) 11am to 5pm (last admission 4.30pm). Wheelchair access to ground floor of house and upper garden.
Heritage Open Days: No
P Yes. Spaces: 10
♿ Partial. Disabled WC: Yes. Guide Dogs: Yes
£ Yes
Adult: £2.80
Child: £1.40
Other: £7.00 (family).

WARWICKSHIRE

The Bath House
Walton, Stratford-upon-Avon, Warwickshire
Designed in 1748 by the architect Sanderson Miller. The upper room, where the bathers recovered, is decorated with dripping icicles and festoons of sea shells - the work of Mrs Delaney, better known for her flower pictures. Narrow steep staircases.
Website Address: www.landmarktrust.co.uk
Grant Recipient/Owner: The Landmark Trust
Access contact: Ms Victoria Piggott
Tel: 01628 825920 **Fax:** 01628 825417
Email Address: www.landmarktrust.co.uk
Opening Arrangements: The Landmark Trust is an independent charity, which rescues small buildings of historic or architectural importance from decay or unsympathetic improvement. Landmark's aim is to promote the enjoyment of these historic buildings by making them available to stay in for holidays. The Bath House can be rented by anyone, at all times of the year, for periods ranging from a weekend to three weeks. Bookings can be made by telephoning the Booking Office on 01628 825925. As the building is in full-time use for holiday accommodation, it is not normally open to the public. However the public can view the building by prior arrangement by telephoning the access contact (Victoria Piggott on 01628 825920) to make an appointment. Potential visitors will be asked to write to confirm the details of their visit.
Heritage Open Days: No
P Yes. Spaces: 1
♿ No. Disabled WC: No. Guide Dogs: No
£ No

Charlecote Park
Wellesbourne, Warwick, Warwickshire CV35 9ER
Owned by the Lucy family since 1247, Sir Thomas built the house in 1558. Now, much altered, it is shown as it would have been a century ago. The balustraded formal garden gives onto a deer park landscaped by 'Capability' Brown.
Website Address: www.ntrustsevern.org.uk
Grant Recipient/Owner: The National Trust
Access contact: Property Manager
Tel: 01789 470277 **Fax:** 01789 470544
Email Address: charlecote@smtp.ntrust.org.uk
Opening Arrangements: House and Garden: 24 March to end June: daily except Wednesday and Thursday (open Good Friday). July and August: daily except Thursdays. September to 4 November: daily except Wednesdays and Thursdays. Grounds: 3 February to 18 March Saturdays and Sundays. Times: House 12 - 5pm; grounds 11am-6pm. Grounds only: November and December Saturdays and Sundays 11am to 4pm. Wheelchair access to ground floor of house, restaurant and shop. Parking for disabled near house.
Heritage Open Days: No
P Yes. Spaces: 200
♿ Partial. Disabled WC: Yes. Guide Dogs: Yes
£ Yes
Adult: £5.60 (house & grounds).
Child: £2.70 (house & grounds).
Other: £14.00 (family). £4.60 (group rate, max 40).

Lord Leycester Hospital
High Street, Warwick, Warwickshire CV34 4BH
14th century chantry chapel, Great Hall, galleried courtyard and Guildhall. Acquired by Robert Dudley, Earl of Leicester in 1571 as a home for his old soldiers. Still operating as a home for ex-servicemen.
Grant Recipient/Owner:
Patron & Governors of Lord Leycester Hospital
Access contact: D I Rhodes
Tel: 01926 491422 **Fax:** 01926 491422
Opening Arrangements: Tuesday - Sunday 10am - 4pm (winter), 10am - 5pm (summer) plus Bank Holiday Mondays. Closed Good Friday and Christmas Day. Wheelchair access to ground floor only.
Heritage Open Days: No
P Yes. Spaces: 15
♿ Partial. Disabled WC: No. Guide Dogs: Yes
£ Yes
Adult: £3.00
Child: £2.00
Other: £2.50

Nicholas Chamberlaine's Almshouses' Pump House
All Saints Square, Bedworth, Nuneaton, Warwickshire
Built 1840 of English bond brick with sandstone dressings and stone pyramid roof in Tudor Gothic style. Contains original cast iron pump. Stands in front of the almshouses and originally provided water for the residents, illuminated at night.
Grant Recipient/Owner:
Nicholas Chamberlaine's Hospital Charity
Access contact: Mr David Dumbleton
Tel: 024 76227331 **Fax:** 024 76221293
Opening Arrangements: Two sessions Saturday and Sunday of Heritage Open Days weekend and at other times by prior arrangement with Mr David Dumbleton, Clerk to the Governors, Nicholas Chamberlaine's Hospital Charity, Rotherhams and Co, 8/9 The Quadrant, Coventry, Warwickshire CV1 2EG (tel.024 76227331). Exterior visible from All Saints Square at all times. Parking at public car parks nearby.
Heritage Open Days: Yes
P See above
♿ Yes. Disabled WC: Yes. Guide Dogs: Yes
£ No

Packwood House
Lapworth, Solihull, Warwickshire B94 6AT
Originally a 16th century house, Packwood has been much altered over the years and today is a vision of Graham Baron Ash who recreated a Jacobean house in the1920s and 30s. Collection of 16th century textiles and furniture. Yew garden based on Sermon on the Mount.
Website Address: www.ntrustsevern.org.uk
Grant Recipient/Owner: The National Trust
Access contact: Mr Alan Langstaff
Tel: 01564 783294 **Fax:** 01564 782706
Email Address: baddesley@smtp.ntrust.org.uk
Opening Arrangements: House: 28 March to 28 October: daily except Mondays and Tuesdays (but open Bank Holidays and Good Friday) 12 - 4.30pm. Gardens:

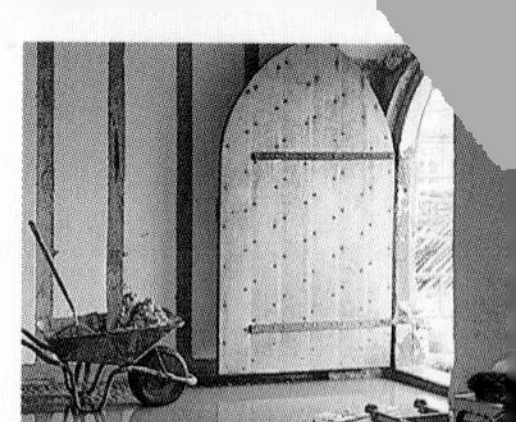

3 to 25 March Saturdays and Sundays. 28 March to 28 October: daily except Mondays and Tuesdays (but open Bank Holiday Mondays and Good Friday). Times: March, April and October 11am to 4.30pm; May to September 11am to 5.30pm.
Heritage Open Days: No
P Yes. Spaces: 140
♿ Yes. Disabled WC: Yes. Guide Dogs: Yes
£ Yes
Adult: £5.00 (house & garden). £2.50 (grounds).
Child: £2.50 (house & garden). £1.25 (grounds).
Other: £12.50 (family). £4.00 (groups 15+). Discount for combined ticket to Packwood House & Baddesley Hall.

Polesworth Nunnery Gateway

22-24 High Street, Polesworth, nr. Tamworth, Warwickshire
Abbey gatehouse, late 14th century with later alterations. Upper floors now in residential use.
Grant Recipient/Owner: Mr W E Thompson
Access contact: Mr W E Thompson
Tel: 01827 706861
Opening Arrangements: Exterior at all reasonable times, ground floor interior by prior arrangement with Mr W E Thompson, 46 Kiln Way, Polesworth, nr. Tamworth, Warwickshire B78 1JE (tel. 01827 706861). Wheelchair access to ground floor only. Parking in Abbey driveway. For further information contact Mr Thompson.
Heritage Open Days: Yes
P See above
♿ Partial. Disabled WC: No. Guide Dogs: Yes
£ No

Ragley Hall

Alcester, Warwickshire B49 5NJ
Family home of the Marquess and Marchioness of Hertford. Built in 1680 to a design by Robert Hooke in the Palladian style, with portico added by Wyatt in 1780. Contents include baroque plasterwork by James Gibb, family portraits by Sir Joshua Reynolds and a mural by Graham Rust completed in 1983. Surrounding gardens designed by 'Capability' Brown.
Grant Recipient/Owner:
Marquess of Hertford & Earl of Yarmouth
Access contact: Mr G Timms
Tel: 01789 762090 **Fax:** 01789 764791
Email Address: ragley.hall@virginnet.co.uk
Opening Arrangements: 9 April - 30 September. House: Thursday - Sunday and Bank Holiday Monday; Thursday, Friday and Sunday 12.30 - 5pm, Saturday 11am - 3.30pm and Bank Holiday Monday 11am - 5pm. Park, Gardens and Adventure Wood: Thursday - Sunday and Bank Holiday Monday 10am - 6pm; also every day 9 April - 22 April, 24 May - 3 June and 19 July - 2 September.
Heritage Open Days: No
P Yes. Spaces: 4000
♿ Yes. Disabled WC: Yes. Guide Dogs: Yes
£ Yes
Adult: £5.50 House & Garden, £4.50 Garden only.
Child: £4.00 House & Garden, £3.50 Garden only.
Other: £5.00 House & Garden, £4.00 Garden (seniors/Orange Badge); £20.00 (family) House & Garden, £15.00 (family) Garden only.

St Peter & St Paul

The Presbytery, Friars Lane, Lower Brailes, Warwickshire OX15 5HU
Roman Catholic chapel built in 1726 on first floor of old malthouse. Contains Victorian stained glass, an 18th century crucifixion painting over the altar and original altar rails and pews.
Grant Recipient/Owner: St Philip's Presbytery
Access contact: Anthony Sims
Tel: 01608 682241
Opening Arrangements: Chapel open daily 9am - 6pm.
Heritage Open Days: Yes
P Yes. Spaces: 30
♿ No. Disabled WC: No. Guide Dogs: Yes
£ No

WEST MIDLANDS

Baddesley Clinton Hall,

Rising Lane, Baddesley Clinton, Knowle, Solihull, West Midlands B93 0DQ
A moated manor house, dated from the 15th century. The interiors reflect the house's heyday in the Elizabethan era, when it was a haven for persecuted Catholics. There are three priest-holes. Garden, lake walk and nature walk.
Website Address: www.ntrustsevern.org.uk
Grant Recipient/Owner: The National Trust
Access contact: Mr Alan Langstaff
Tel: 01564 783294 **Fax:** 01564 782706
Email Address: baddesley@smtp.ntrust.org.uk
Opening Arrangements: House: 28 February to 28 October: daily except Mondays and Tuesdays (open Bank Holiday Mondays but closed Good Friday). Times: February, March, April and October 1.30 - 5pm; May to end September 1.30 - 5.30pm. Grounds: 28 February to 16 December: daily except Mondays and Tuesdays (open Bank Holidays and Good Friday). Times: February, March, April and October 12 - 5pm; May to end September 12 - 5.30pm; November to 16 December 12 - 4.30pm. Wheelchair access to ground floor of house and garden.
Heritage Open Days: No
P Yes. Spaces: 500
♿ Partial. Disabled WC: Yes. Guide Dogs: Yes
£ Yes
Adult: £5.60
Child: £2.80
Other: £14.00 (family). £4.50 (groups 15+). Discount for combined ticket to Baddesley Hall & Packwood House.

Bratch Pumping Station

Bratch Lane, Wombourne, Wolverhampton, West Midlands
Built 1895 of red brick and hipped slate roof in a castellated style with elements of Venetian Gothic. Contains re-furbished steam engines and adjoining workshop with achival photographs, news items and artefacts.
Grant Recipient/Owner: Severn Trent Water Ltd
Access contact: Mr Carlos Abraham
Tel: 0121 722 4563 **Fax:** 0121 722 4800
Opening Arrangements: Arrangements to be confirmed on the establishment of a charitable trust to manage the building. Please contact Mr Carlos Abraham, Conservation, Access & Recreation Adviser, Severn Trent Water Ltd, 2297 Coventry Road, Birmingham, West Midlands B26 3PU (tel.0121 722 4563) for the latest information. Engine room not accessible to wheelchair users.
Heritage Open Days: Yes
P Yes. Spaces: 200
♿ Partial. Disabled WC: Yes. Guide Dogs: Yes
£ Yes
Adult: £1.00
Child: 50p

St James

Great Packington, Meriden, nr. Coventry, West Midlands CV7 7HF
Red brick building with four domes topped by finules in neo-classical style. Built to celebrate the return to sanity of King George III. The organ was designed by Handel for his librettist, Charles Jennens, who was the cousin of the 4th Earl of Aylesford, who built the church.
Grant Recipient/Owner:
St James Great Packington Trust
Access contact: Packington Estate Office
Tel: 01676 522020 **Fax:** 01676 523399
Opening Arrangements: Monday - Friday 9am - 5pm, key can be obtained from the Estate Office at Packington Hall, preferably by phoning in advance on 01676 522020. At other times by prior arrangement with Lord Guernsey (tel. 01676 522274). Wheelchair access with assistance (entrance steps and heavy door to be negotiated).
Heritage Open Days: No
P Yes. Spaces: 10
♿ Yes. Disabled WC: No. Guide Dogs: Yes
£ Donations towards restoration welcomed.

St Mary's Convent

Hunters Road, Handsworth, Birmingham, West Midlands
Highly original and carefully detailed Tudor-Gothic style building. 1840-41 by A W N Pugin. The cloister to the rear has simple exposed timber truss roof and tiled floors. The original chapel was destroyed in the war. The convent is contemporary with a group of Pugin's innovatory rationally designed religious houses.
Grant Recipient/Owner: Sr Evelyn Gallagher
Access contact: Kyran Rigney/Mary Leonard
Tel: 0121 554 3271
Opening Arrangements: By appointment only, written or telephone. Parking on road only.
Heritage Open Days: No
P No
♿ No. Disabled WC: No. Guide Dogs: No
£ No

Wightwick Manor

Wightwick Bank, Tettenhall, Wolverhampton, West Midlands
Built 1887, the house is a notable surviving example of the Arts and Crafts Movement. Contains original William Morris wallpapers and fabrics, Pre-Raphaelite paintings, Kempe glass and de Morgan ware. Also has a 17 acre Victorian/Edwardian garden designed by Thomas Mawson.
Grant Recipient/Owner: The National Trust
Access contact: The Property Manager
Tel: 01902 761400 **Fax:** 01902 764663
Email Address: mwtman@smtp.ntrust.org.uk
Opening Arrangements: By guided tour only 1 March - 31 December: Thursdays and Saturdays (also Bank Holiday Sunday and Monday to ground floor only) 1.30 - 4.30pm. Also family open days Wednesdays in August 1.30 - 4.30pm. Admission by timed ticket issued from 1pm at front door. Garden: Wednesdays, Thursdays, Saturdays and Bank Holiday Sunday and Monday 11am - 6pm. Wheelchair access to ground floor only (up 2 steps).
Heritage Open Days: No
P Yes. Spaces: 50
♿ Partial. Disabled WC: No. Guide Dogs: Yes
£ Yes
Adult: £5.50
Child: £2.75 (children and students)
Other: £13.00 (family)

WEST SUSSEX

Hammerwood Park

nr. East Grinstead, West Sussex RH19 3QE
Designed by Benjamin Latrobe in 1792 as a grand hunting lodge with porticos dedicated to Apollo. Latrobe's White House portico in Washington D C is based on those at Hammerwood. The 18th century parkland incorporates subsequent gardens around the house.
Website Address: www.name.is/hammerwood
Grant Recipient/Owner: Mr David Pinnegar
Access contact: Mr David Pinnegar
Tel: 01342 850594 **Fax:** 01342 850864
Email Address: latrobe@mistral.co.uk
Opening Arrangements: By guided tour Easter Bank Holiday Monday - end of September: Wednesdays, Saturdays and Bank Holidays (tours start at 2.05pm).
Heritage Open Days: No
P Yes. Spaces: 60
♿ Yes. Disabled WC: Yes. Guide Dogs: Yes
£ Yes
Adult: £5.00
Child: £2.00
Other: £5.00

Hiorne Tower

Arundel Park, Arundel, West Sussex BN18 9AB
Constructed 1789 to design by Hiorne of Warwick, it was originally just a decorative landscape feature and lookout but was converted into a keeper's cottage in the mid 19th century when the boundary wall was built. Restored 1992.
Grant Recipient/Owner: Earl of Arundel & Surrey
Access contact: Mr M C G Baxter
Tel: 01903 883400 **Fax:** 01903 884482
Opening Arrangements:
Arundel Park is open to the public daily (except 24 March). Access to the interior of the Hiorne Tower by prior arrangement with the Duke of Norfolk's Estate Office, Arundel, West Sussex BN18 9AS (tel.01903 883400).
Heritage Open Days: No
P No
♿ No. Disabled WC: No. Guide Dogs: Yes
£ No

Parham House

Parham Park, nr. Pulborough, West Sussex RH20 4HS
Granted to the Palmer family in 1540 by Henry VIII, the foundation stone of this grey-stone Elizabethan house was laid in 1577. From the panelled Great Hall to the Long Gallery running the length of the roof-space, the house contains a collection of paintings, furniture and needlework.
Website Address: www.parhaminsussex.co.uk
Grant Recipient/Owner: Parham Park Ltd
Access contact: Ms Patricia Kennedy
Tel: 01903 742021 **Fax:** 01903 746557
Email Address: parham@dial.pipex.co.uk
Opening Arrangements: 1 April - 31 October: Wednesdays, Thursdays, Sundays and Bank Holiday Mondays (also Saturdays 19 May, 14 July and 1 September). Gardens open at 12 noon, House at 2pm with last entry at 5pm. Wheelchair access to ground floor only by prior arrangement, there is a reduced admission charge for wheelchair users and free loan of recorded tour tape. Disabled parking close to house. Admission charges are provisional at time of going to print, please check with House for current rates.
Heritage Open Days: No
P Yes. Spaces: 300
♿ Partial. Disabled WC: Yes. Guide Dogs: Yes
£ Yes
Adult: £5.25 (see above)
Child: £1.00 (5-15)
Other: £4.50 (senior citizens)

Petworth House

Petworth, West Sussex GU28 0AE
Late 17th century mansion in 'Capability' Brown parkland. The house contains the Trust's largest collection of pictures including Turners and Van Dycks. Sculptures, furniture and Grinling Gibbons carvings. Servants' quarters including interesting kitchens and other service

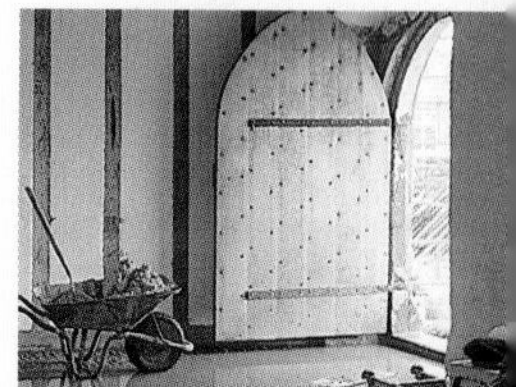

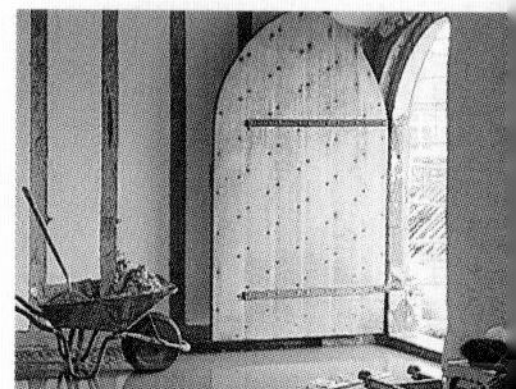

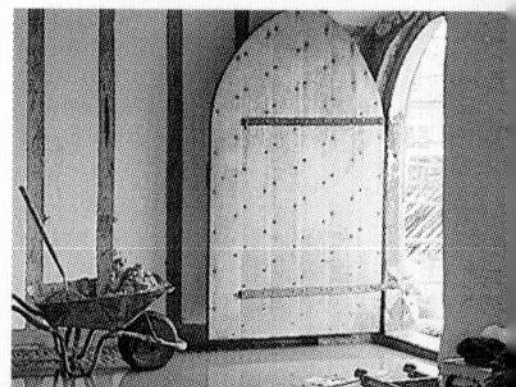

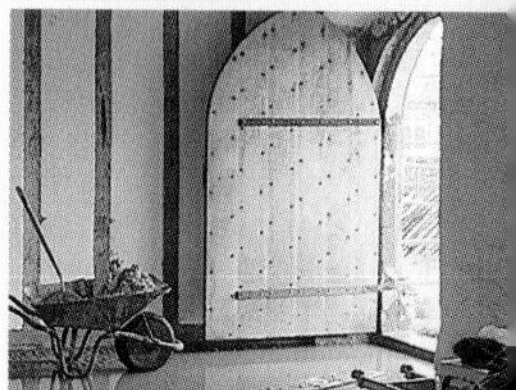

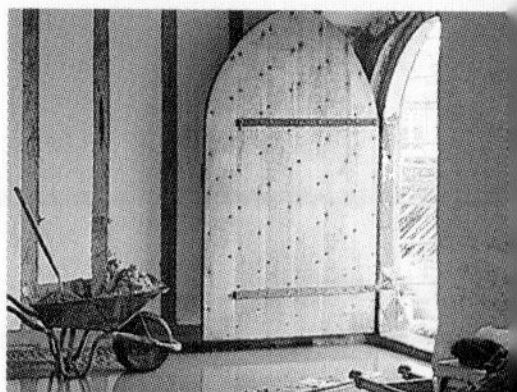

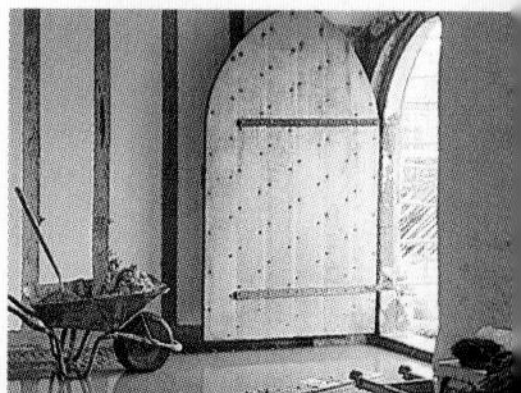

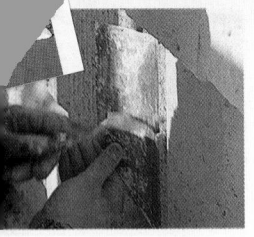

rooms. Extra rooms open at the weekend by kind permission of Lord and Lady Egremont.
Website Address: www.nationaltrust.org.uk
Grant Recipient/Owner: The National Trust
Access contact: Dr Diana Owen
Tel: 01798 342207   **Fax:** 01798 342963
Email Address: spegen@smtp.ntrust.org.uk
Opening Arrangements: House and Servants' Quarters: 31 March to 4 November: daily except Thursdays and Fridays (but open Good Friday and every Friday in July and August). Extra rooms shown weekdays (but not Bank Holiday Mondays) as follows: Mondays, White and Gold Room and Library; Tuesdays and Wednesdays, three bedrooms on first floor. Times: 1 - 5.30pm. Last admission to house 4.30pm; Servants' Quarters 5pm. Wheelchair access to ground floor of house, shop and tea room.
Heritage Open Days: No
🅿 Yes. Spaces: 150
♿ Partial. Disabled WC: Yes. Guide Dogs: Yes
💲 Yes
Adult: £6.00
Child: £3.00
Other: £15.00 (family). £5.00 (booked groups of 15+, per head).

St Hugh's Charterhouse

Henfield Road, Partridge Green, nr. Horsham, West Sussex RH13 8EB
Large monastery covering 10 acres. One large cloister of over 100 sq yds comprising 34 four-room hermitages where the monks live. The fore part is a smaller cloister about 200ft square which contains the cells of the Brothers and their work places. There is also a large church, library, refectory, Brothers Chapel and other monastic buildings. The large quad encloses a cemetery. The spire is 203ft high and has a five-bell chime.
Grant Recipient/Owner: St Hugh's Charterhouse
Access contact: Fr Cyril Pierce
Tel: 01403 864231   **Fax:** 01403 864231
Opening Arrangements: By prior arrangement, with due respect for the rules of the Charterhouse monastery. For further details please contact the monastery.
Heritage Open Days: No
🅿 Yes. Spaces: 20
♿ No. Disabled WC: No. Guide Dogs: Yes
💲 No

Sackville College

East Grinstead, West Sussex RH19 3AZ
Early Jacobean almshouse with original furniture, hall, chapel, common room, John Mason Neale study and library. Built with Sussex sandstone around a quadrangle. Founded in 1609 and still in use, providing 15 flats for elderly people together with the Warden's lodging.
Grant Recipient/Owner:
Warden & Trustees of Sackville College
Access contact: Mr David Russell
Tel: 01342 326561   **Fax:** 01342 326561
Opening Arrangements: June, July and August: Wednesday - Sunday 2 - 5pm. Groups by prior arrangement April - October.
Heritage Open Days: Yes
🅿 Yes. Spaces: 8
♿ Yes. Disabled WC: Yes. Guide Dogs: No
💲 Yes
Adult: £2.50
Child: £1.00
Other: £2.50

The Shell House

Goodwood House, Chichester, West Sussex PO18 0PX
One room Shell House dating from 1740s. Walls and ceiling decorated with hundreds of thousands of shells in classical design, with coffering, niches and cornucopia. Floor with inset horses teeth.
Grant Recipient/Owner:
Goodwood Estate Company Ltd
Access contact: Mrs Rosemary Andreae
Tel: 01243 755018   **Fax:** 01243 755005
Email Address: ra@goodwood.co.uk
Opening Arrangements: By pior written arrangement, usually on set Connoisseurs' Days (15 May, 3 July, 25 September and 23 October) or on Sunday mornings April - September. Two weeks' notice preferred. Bookings can be made with Rosemary Andreae or Kathryn Bellamy (tel. 01243 755048, email: kathryn@goodwood.co.uk). Large car park 40 metres from house. Lavatory for disabled only available when Goodwood House is open to the public.
Heritage Open Days: No
🅿 Yes. Spaces: 4
♿ No. Disabled WC: Yes. Guide Dogs: No
💲 Yes
Adult: £3 on Connoisseurs' Days as part of House visit, £5 on otheer days.
Child: Free for under 12s

Shipley Windmill

Shipley, nr. Horsham, West Sussex RH13 8PL
Grade II* listed Smock mill with five floors, built 1879 and restored in 1990 to full working order. Once owned by the Sussex writer and poet, Hilaire Belloc, who lived nearby. The milling process is demonstrated on open days for the benefit of visitors.
Grant Recipient/Owner:
Shipley Windmill Charitable Trust
Access contact: Ms Penny Murray
Tel: 01243 777642   **Fax:** 01243 777848
Email Address: penny.murray@westsussex.gov.uk
Opening Arrangements: April - October: first and third Sunday of each month, plus Bank Holiday Mondays. Also National Mills Day, Shipley Festival (May), Horsham and District Arts Fanfare (June) and the Sunday of the Heritage Open Days weekend. It is planned to open the windmill on more Sundays, please check current opening arrangements with Ms Penny Murray, Assistant Clerk to the Trustees, Shipley Windmill Charitable Trust, County Hall, Chichester, West Sussex PO19 1RQ (tel.01243 777642).
Heritage Open Days: Yes
🅿 Yes. Spaces: 10
♿ No. Disabled WC: No. Guide Dogs: No
💲 Yes
Adult: £1.50
Child: 50p
Other: £1.00 (senior citizens)

WEST YORKSHIRE

Bankhouse

Bankhouse Lane, Halifax, West Yorkshire
16th century yeomans hall with cross wing and lower end cottages.
Grant Recipient/Owner: Mr H Haigh
Access contact: Mr H Haigh
Tel: 01422 354589
Opening Arrangements: By prior arrangement.
Heritage Open Days: No
🅿 Yes. Spaces: 2
♿ No. Disabled WC: No. Guide Dogs: Yes
💲 No

Bramham Park Lead Lads Temple

Wetherby, West Yorkshire LS23 6ND
18th century open temple in the classical style in Bramham Park (about a mile from the house in woodland called Black Fen, close to a public footpath).
Grant Recipient/Owner: Mr G F Lane Fox
Access contact: Mr G F Lane Fox
Tel: 01937 846004   **Fax:** 01937 846001
Opening Arrangements: Accessible at all times, close to a public footpath.
Heritage Open Days: No
🅿 No
♿ No. Disabled WC: No. Guide Dogs: No
💲 No

Crossley Pavilion

The People's Park, King Cross Road, Halifax, West Yorkshire
Grade II* listed building, designed by Sir Joseph Paxton and constructed in 1857. Contains seating and a statue of the park's benefactor, Sir Francis Crossley (1860), by Joseph Durham. Four gargoyle fountains supply pools flanking each side of the pavilion, set on formal terrace, balustrades and steps.
Grant Recipient/Owner:
Calderdale Metropolitan Borough Council
Access contact: Miss Deborah Comyn-Platt
Tel: 01422 359454   **Fax:** 01422 348301
Email Address: d.a.comyn-platt@calderdale.gov.uk
Opening Arrangements: By prior arrangement with Calderdale Metropolitan Borough Council Leisure Services, Wellesley Park, Halifax, West Yorkshire (tel.01422 359454). Exterior viewing all year during park opening hours 8am - dusk. Street parking available on Park Road. Information Centre and toilets, including disabled toilets, due to be completed by June.
Heritage Open Days: Yes
🅿 See above
♿ Yes. Disabled WC: Yes. Guide Dogs: Yes
💲 No

Friends Meeting House

off Bolton Road, Addingham, nr. Ilkley, West Yorkshire LS29
Land for burial ground purchased in 1666, followed by construction of Meeting House in 1669. A simple single cell building with rubblestone walls, mullioned windows, stone-slated roof and stone-flagged floor. Contains loose benches and an oak minister's stand of an unusual panelled design with turned balusters.
Website Address: www.hct.org.uk
Grant Recipient/Owner: Historic Chapels Trust

Access contact: John Spencer
Tel: 01756 710225
Opening Arrangements: At all reasonable times by application to keyholders Mr & Mrs John Spencer, who live opposite the Meeting House at Cook's Cottage, 3 Farfield Cottages, Bolton Road, Addingham, nr. Ilkley, West Yorkshire LS29 0RQ (tel.01756 710225).
Heritage Open Days: Yes
🅿 Yes. Spaces: 2
♿ No. Disabled WC: No. Guide Dogs: Yes
💲 No

Harewood House

Harewood, Leeds, West Yorkshire LS17 9LQ
Designed in neo-classical style by John Carr and completed in 1772. Contains Adam interiors, Chippendale furniture and art collection. Home of the Earl and Countess of Harewood.
Website Address: www.harewood.org
Grant Recipient/Owner:
The Trustees of Harewood House Ltd
Access contact: The Trustees of Harewood House Ltd
Tel: 0113 218 1010
Opening Arrangements: Daily 14 March - 4 November: Grounds & Bird Garden open 10am - 4.30pm (last admission 4pm); House and Terrace Gallery 11am - 4.30pm (last admission 4pm). Grounds close at 6pm. Grounds and Bird Garden also open weekends between 10 November and 17 December. Disabled visitors can alight at entrance. Wheelchair access to most facilities but with some steep inclines. Wheelchair available at house and Bird Garden. Special concessions for disabled groups. Guide dogs are not allowed in the Bird Garden but a free sound guide is available for the partially sighted visitor and a babysitter for the dog.
Heritage Open Days: No
🅿 Yes. Spaces: 200
♿ Yes. Disabled WC: Yes. Guide Dogs: See above
💲 Yes
Adult: £7.50
Child: £5.00
Other: £6.75 (senior), £26.00 (family), (annual season tickets also available).

Holdsworth House Gazebo

Holdsworth, Halifax, West Yorkshire HX2 9TG
Probably built, c1633, at about the same time as the house at the corner of the sunken garden.
Grant Recipient/Owner: Cavalier Country Club
Access contact: Mr Peter Phillips
Tel: 01422 240024   **Fax:** 01422 245174
Email Address: info@holdsworthhouse.co.uk
Opening Arrangements: Hotel open throughout the year (except Christmas).
Heritage Open Days: No
🅿 Yes. Spaces: 40
♿ No. Disabled WC: No. Guide Dogs: Yes
💲 No

Ledston Hall

Hall Lane, Ledston, Castleford, West Yorkshire WF10 2BB
17th century mansion with some earlier work.
Grant Recipient/Owner: Mr G H H Wheler
Access contact: Mr J F T Hare
Tel: 01423 523423   **Fax:** 01423 521373
Email Address: james.hare@carterjonas.co.uk
Opening Arrangements: May - August: Monday - Friday 9am - 4pm. At other times by prior arrangement with Mr J F T Hare, Carter Jonas, Regent House, 13/15 Albert St, Harrogate, West Yorkshire HG1 1JF (tel.01423 523423).
Heritage Open Days: Yes
🅿 Yes. Spaces: 5
♿ Yes. Disabled WC: No. Guide Dogs: Yes
💲 No

Marlborough Hall

Crossley Street, Halifax, West Yorkshire HX1 1UG
Built in 1857 as a Mechanics Institute, which it remained until 1932. From 1917 to 1922 it doubled as the Gem Cinema, the first permanent cinema in Halifax. Contains four floors with many meeting rooms and an auditorium, the frontage hall and stairways have many original features.
Grant Recipient/Owner: Halifax & District YMCA
Access contact: Mr C F Love
Tel: 01422 353626
Email Address: admin@halifax.ymca.co.uk
Opening Arrangements: Daily 10am - 4pm (except Bank Holidays and weekends). Wheelchair access to ground floor and lower ground floor only.
Heritage Open Days: No
🅿 No
♿ Partial. Disabled WC: Yes. Guide Dogs: Yes
💲 No

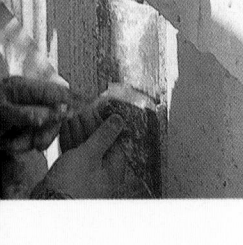
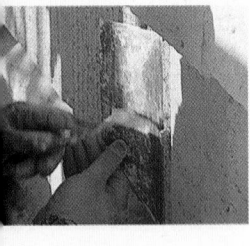
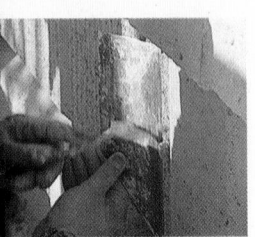
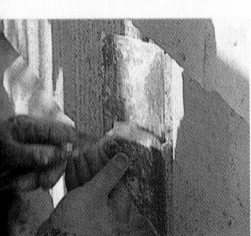
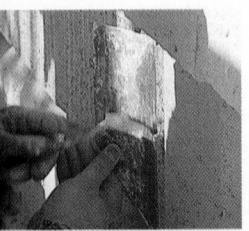

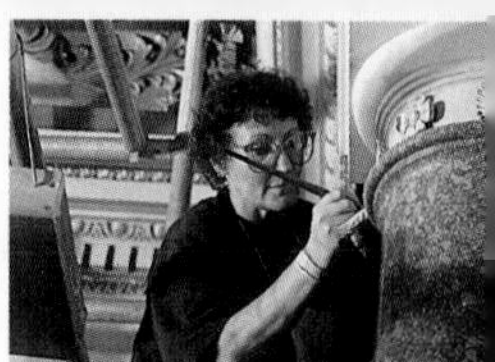

Marshall Mill

Marshall Street, Leeds, West Yorkshire LS11 9YJ
Textile mill built c1800 and now converted to offices containing lobby, external and common areas.
Grant Recipient/Owner: Marshall Mill Ltd
Access contact: Mr John Wright
Tel: 0113 245 3324 **Fax:** 0113 245 3317
Opening Arrangements: By prior arrangement.
Heritage Open Days: No
P No
♿ Yes. Disabled WC: Yes. Guide Dogs: Yes
£ No

Nostell Priory

Doncaster Road, Nostell, Wakefield, West Yorkshire WF4 1QE
Country house, 1736-1750, by James Paine for Sir Rowland Winn 4th baronet. Later Robert Adam was commissioned to complete the State Rooms. On display is a collection of Chippendale furniture, designed especially for the house, an art collection with works by Pieter Breughel the Younger and Angelica Kauffmann, and an 18th century dolls house, complete with its original fittings and Chippendale furniture. Lakeside walks.
Website Address: www.nationaltrust.org.uk
Grant Recipient/Owner: The National Trust
Access contact: Property Manager
Tel: 01924 863892 **Fax:** 01924 865282
Email Address: yorknp@smtp.ntrust.org.uk
Opening Arrangements: House: 31 March to 4 November: daily except Mondays and Tuesdays (but open Bank Holiday Mondays) 1- 5.30pm; 10 November to 9 December: Saturdays and Sundays 12 - 4.30pm. Grounds: open same days as house 11am - 6pm. Wheelchair access to ground floor of house with lift to first floor, tea room, children's playground and shop.
Heritage Open Days: No
P Yes. Spaces: 120
♿ Partial. Disabled WC: No. Guide Dogs: Yes
£ Yes
Adult: £4.50. £2.50 (grounds only).
Child: £2.20. £1.20 (grounds only).
Other: £11.00 (family). (No family ticket for grounds only).

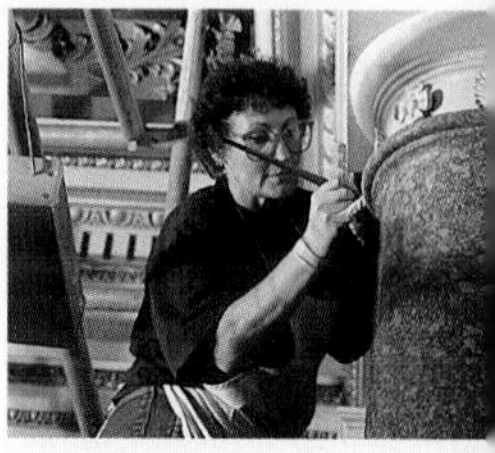

The Roundhouse

Wellington Road, Leeds, West Yorkshire LS12 1DR
Grade II* railway roundhouse built in 1847 for the Leeds and Thirsk Railway by Thomas Granger. In full use by the North-Eastern Railway until 1904, now home to Leeds Commercial Van and Truck Hire.
Grant Recipient/Owner: Wellbridge Properties Ltd
Access contact: Mr J D Miller
Tel: 0113 2435964 **Fax:** 0113 246 1142
Email Address: sales@leedscommercial.co.uk
Opening Arrangements: By prior written arrangement with the occupiers, Leeds Commercial, who manage the property as a working garage.
Heritage Open Days: No
P Yes. Spaces: 30
♿ Yes. Disabled WC: Yes. Guide Dogs: Yes
£ No

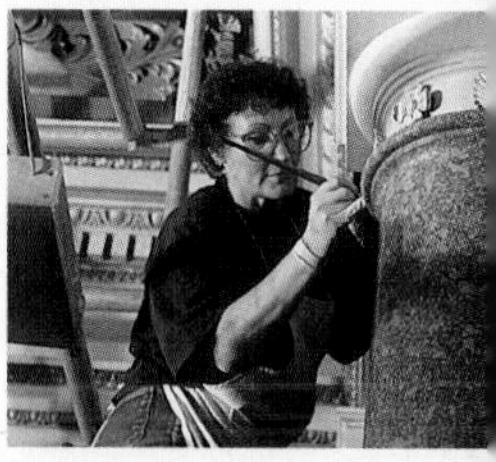

Todmorden Unitarian Church

Honey Hole Road, Todmorden, West Yorkshire OL14 6LE
Grade I church with a large wooded burial ground and ornamental gardens designed by John Gibson, 1865-69. Victorian Gothic style with tall tower and spire. Detached smaller burial ground nearby and listed lodge in churchyard.
Website Address: www.hct.org.uk
Grant Recipient/Owner: Historic Chapels Trust
Access contact: Mr Rob Goldthorpe
Tel: 01706 815648
Opening Arrangements: At all reasonable times by application to the keyholder, Mr Rob Goldthorpe, at 14 Honey Hole Close, Todmorden, West Yorkshire OL14 6LH (tel.01706 815648) or by calling at the caretaker's house, Todmorden Lodge, at the entrance to the churchyard.
Heritage Open Days: Yes
P Yes. Spaces: 50
♿ Yes. Disabled WC: Yes. Guide Dogs: Yes
£ No

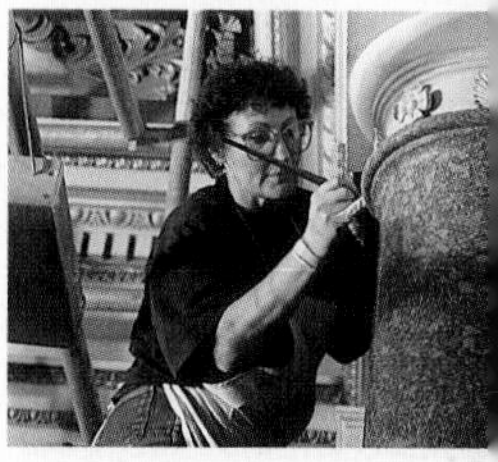

WILTSHIRE

Cherhill Monument

Cherhill Down, Wiltshire
Cherhill Monument (also known as Lansdowne Monument) is situated on the summit of the chalk ridge at Cherhill Down. Built in 1845 by the 3rd Marquis of Landsdowne in memory of the economist Sir William Petty.
Website Address: www.nationaltrust.org.uk
Grant Recipient/Owner: The National Trust
Access contact: The National Trust
Tel: 01985 843600 **Fax:** 01985 843624
Opening Arrangements: Open access via footpaths and bridleways across the Down. Parking available in laybys off the A4.
Heritage Open Days: No
P See above
♿ No. Disabled WC: No. Guide Dogs: Yes
£ No

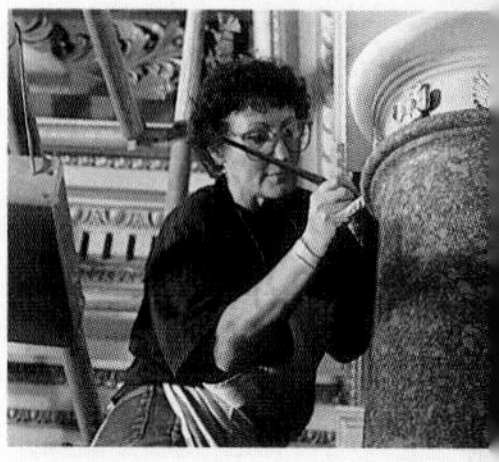

The Cloisters

Iford Manor, Bradford-on-Avon, Wiltshire BA15 2BA
Small stone-built cloister in gardens of Manor, completed 1914 by Harold Peto and based on 13th century Italian style. Interesting early contents.
Website Address: www.iford.manor@which.com
Grant Recipient/Owner: Mrs E Cartwright-Hignett
Access contact: Mrs E Cartwright-Hignett
Tel: 01225 863146 **Fax:** 01225 862364
Email Address: iford.manor@which.com
Opening Arrangements: Gardens only: April - October, Sundays and Easter Monday 2 - 5pm; May - September, daily (except Mondays and Fridays) 2 - 5pm. Children under 10 not admitted at weekends. Coaches and groups by prior arrangement only. Wheelchair access by prior arrangement to Cloisters and part of the gardens.
Heritage Open Days: No
P Yes. Spaces: 100
♿ Partial. Disabled WC: No. Guide Dogs: Yes
£ Yes
Adult: £3.00
Child: £2.50 (10-16, under 10 free).
Other: £2.50 (seniors & students)

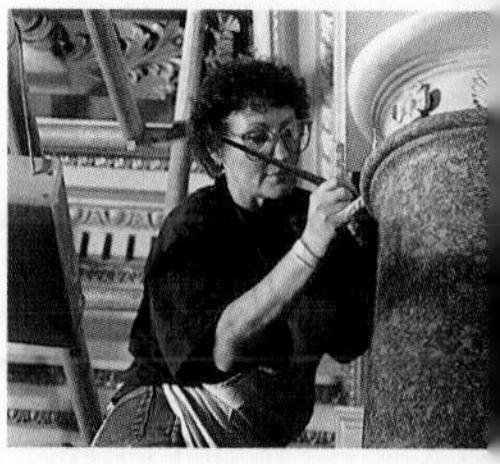

Dyrham Park

nr. Chippenham, Wiltshire SN14 8ER
17th century house set within an ancient deer park, woodlands and formal garden. The house was furnished in the Dutch style and still has many original contents including paintings, ceramics, furniture and 17th century tapestries. The Victorian domestic rooms include the kitchen, larder, bakehouse, dairy and tenants hall.
Grant Recipient/Owner: The National Trust
Access contact: The Property Manager
Tel: 01179 372501 **Fax:** 01179 372501
Email Address: wdymxa@smtp.ntrust.og.uk
Opening Arrangements: House: 31 March - 4 November: daily except Wednesday and Thursday 12-5.30 (last admission to house 4.45pm). Garden: as for house 11am - 5.30pm or dusk if earlier. Park: daily (closed 25 December) 12 - 5.30pm or dusk if earlier (when gardens are open, the park opens at 11am). Winter opening for Domestic Rooms: 10 November - 16 December: Saturday and Sunday 12 - 4.00pm. Note: property is closed 6-9 July for concerts. Wheelchair access to all but four upstairs rooms. A photograph album of these rooms is available. A free bus takes visitors from the car park to the house.
Heritage Open Days: No
P Yes. Spaces: 250
♿ Partial. Disabled WC: Yes. Guide Dogs: Yes
£ Yes
Adult: £7.80, £3.00 (grounds only), £1.90 (Park only when house & garden closed). £4.00 (Winter: Park & Domestic Rooms).
Child: £3.90, £1.50 (grounds only), 90p (Park only when house and garden closed), £2.00 (Winter: Park & Domestic Rooms).
Other: £19.00 (family).

Fonthill Underground Bath House

Fonthill Bishop, Salisbury, Wiltshire SP3 5SH
18th century boathouse or water temple of aisled 'basilica' plan with transepts and apsidal west end, the wet dock being the 'nave' and 'crossing' and the walkways the 'aisles'. Constructed of limestone ashlar with vaulted roof covered in earth.
Grant Recipient/Owner: Lord Margadale
Access contact: Resident Agent
Tel: 01747 820246
Opening Arrangements: 1 March - 31 July: by prior written arrangement with the Estate Office, Fonthill Bishop, Salisbury, Wiltshire SP3 5SH. Wellington boots will be required by visitors.
Heritage Open Days: No
P No
♿ No. Disabled WC: No. Guide Dogs: No
£ Yes
Adult: £2.50
Child: Free
Other: Free

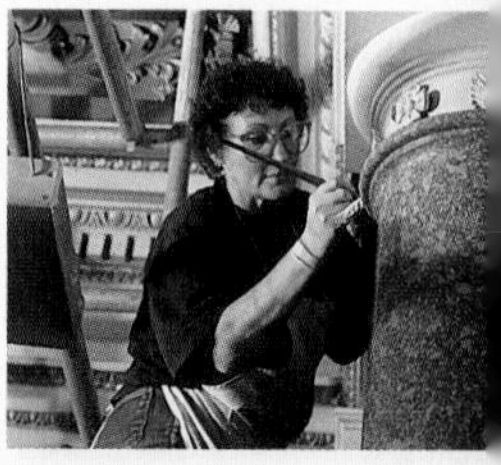

Lacock Abbey

Lacock, nr. Chippenham, Wiltshire SN15 2LG
Founded in 1232 and converted into a county house c1540, the fine medieval Cloisters, Sacristy, Chapter house and monastic rooms of the Abbey have survived largely intact. The 16th century stable courtyard has half timbered gables, a clock house, brewery and bakehouse. Victorian garden, Former residents include William Fox Talbot 'the father of modern photography'.
Website Address: www.nationaltrust.org.uk
Grant Recipient/Owner: The National Trust
Access contact: Property Manager
Tel: 01249 730141 **Fax:** 01249 730501
Opening Arrangements: Abbey: 13 March to 4 November: daily 1 - 5.30pm (closed Tuesdays and Good Friday). Museum, cloisters and garden: 3 March to 4 November: daily 11am - 5.30pm (closed Good Friday). Museum also open winter weekends, but closed 22/23 December to 30 December, telephone the Property Manager for details. Wheelchair access to Abbey is difficult as four sets of stairs. Garden, cloisters and museum are accessible. Short walk from car park to Abbey. Limited parking in Abbey courtyard by arrangement.
Heritage Open Days: No
P Yes. Spaces: 300
♿ Partial. Disabled WC: Yes. Guide Dogs: Yes
£ Yes
Adult: £6.00 (Abbey, museum, cloisters & garden). £4.80 (Abbey & garden). £3.80 (garden, cloisters & museum).
Child: £3.30 (Abbey, museum, cloisters & garden). £2.70 (Abbey & garden). £2.30 (garden, cloisters & museum).
Other: £16.30 (family: Abbey, museum, cloisters & garden). £12.30 (family: Abbey & garden). £10.90 (Abbey: garden, cloisters & museum). Group rates. Free NT members.

Lydiard Park

Lydiard Tregoze, Swindon, Wiltshire SN5 9PA
Ancestral home of the Bolingbrokes, the restored Palladian mansion contains family furnishings and portraits, plasterwork, rare 17th century painted window and room dedicated to 18th century society artist Lady Diana Spencer.
Grant Recipient/Owner: Swindon Borough Council
Access contact: Mrs Sarah Finch-Crisp
Tel: 01793 770401 **Fax:** 01793 877909
Opening Arrangements: House: Monday - Friday 10am - 1pm & 2 - 5pm, Saturdays and school summer holidays 10am - 5pm, Sundays 2 - 5pm. November - February early closing at 4pm. Grounds all day, closing at dusk. Admission prices may increase, please check with the Park.
Heritage Open Days: Yes
P Yes. Spaces: 400
♿ Yes. Disabled WC: Yes. Guide Dogs: Yes
£ Yes
Adult: £1.20 (provisional)
Child: 60p (provisional)

Manor Farm

Coate, Wiltshire SN10 3LP
16-17th century thatched farmhouse.
Grant Recipient/Owner: Roy Stokes & Company
Access contact: Roy & Ann Stokes
Tel: 01380 860234 **Fax:** 01380 860234
Opening Arrangements: By prior arrangement from May to September. As the building is part of a working farm, visitors are requested not to bring their pets.
Heritage Open Days: No
P Yes. Spaces: 2
♿ No. Disabled WC: No. Guide Dogs: No
£ Donation to a charity

Merchant's House

132 High Street, Marlborough, Wiltshire SN8 1HN
17th century town house built by the Bayly family, mercers between 1653 and c1700. Situated prominently in the High Street it contains a unique stripe-painted dining room c1665, painted balustrading to the oak staircase and a panelled chamber of the Commonwealth period.
Website Address: www.themerchantshouse.co.uk
Access contact: Mr Michael Gray
Tel: 01672 511491 **Fax:** 01672 511491
Email Address: manager@themerchantshouse.co.uk
Opening Arrangements: Saturdays all year 10am - 4pm. Public parking outside building in High Street.
Heritage Open Days: Yes
P See above
♿ No. Disabled WC: No. Guide Dogs: Yes
£ No

Old Bishop's Palace

Salisbury Cathedral School, 1 The Close, Salisbury, Wiltshire SP1 2EQ
13th century building, much altered over the centuries, with 13th century undercroft, Georgian drawing room and a chapel.
Grant Recipient/Owner: Salisbury Diocesan Board of Finance
Access contact: A J Craigie
Tel: 01722 555300 **Fax:** 01722 410910
Email Address: aspire@salisbury.enterprise-plc.com
Opening Arrangements: Opening arrangements under review at time of going to print, please check the English Heritage website or with Mr Craigie for current information.
Heritage Open Days: Yes

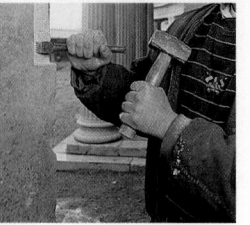

⌗ Opening arrangements at properties grant-aided by English Heritage

P No
🦽 No. Disabled WC: No. Guide Dogs: No
£ Yes
Adult: £2.00

Sarum College

19 The Close, Salisbury, Wiltshire SP1 2EE
Grade I listed house, c1677, attributed to Sir Christopher Wren. In the 1870s collegiate buildings were added, designed by William Butterfield. The college is an ecumenical education, training and conference centre.
Website Address: www.sarum.ac.uk
Grant Recipient/Owner: Trustees of Salisbury & Wells Theological College/Sarum College
Access contact: Mrs Linda Cooper
Tel: 01722 424800   **Fax:** 01722 338508
Email Address: admin@sarum.ac.uk
Opening Arrangements: Daily during term-time, please check with College for details of term-times. Wheelchair access to ground floor only.
Heritage Open Days: No
P Yes. Spaces: 37
🦽 Partial. Disabled WC: Yes. Guide Dogs: Yes
£ No

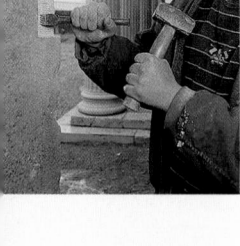

Stourhead

nr. Warminster, Wiltshire BA12 6QH
Country house, built 1721-24 for Henry Hoare by Colen Campbell. Following fire in 1902, central block was rebuilt between 1902-06. Set in landscaped parkland and with the fine Stourhead Gardens to the west. Landscape garden laid out between 1741 and 1780. Classical temples including the Pantheon and Temple of Apollo are set around the lake. King Alfred's tower is an intriguing red-brick folly. Woodlands with collection of exotic trees.
Website Address: www.nationaltrust.org.uk
Grant Recipient/Owner: The National Trust
Access contact: Property Manager
Tel: 01747 841152   **Fax:** 01747 841152
Email Address: wstest@smtp.ntrust.org.uk
Opening Arrangements: House: 31 March to 4 November: daily (except Thursdays and Fridays) 12 - 5.30pm. Garden: daily 9am - 7pm or sunset if earlier. King Alfred's Tower: 31 March to 4 November daily except Mondays (but open on Bank Holiday Mondays) at following times: Tuesdays to Fridays 2 - 5.30pm, Saturday, Sunday and Bank Holiday Mondays, 11.30am - 5.30pm or dusk if earlier. Wheelchair access to: house with use of stairclimber (must be booked in advance); 1 ½ mile path around lakes, but steep in places. Parking close to house for Orange Badge holders.
Heritage Open Days: No
P Yes. Spaces: 500
🦽 Partial. Disabled WC: Yes. Guide Dogs: Yes
£ Yes
Adult: £8.50 (house & garden). £4.80 (house). £4.80-£3.70 (garden). £1.60 (King Alfred's Tower).
Adult: £4.00 (house & garden). £2.60 (house). £2.60-£1.80 (garden). £0.80 (King Alfred's Tower).
Adult: £20.00 (family: house & garden). £12.00 (family: house). £12.00-£9.00 (family: garden). £4.00 (family: King Alfred's Tower). Group rates. Free NT members.

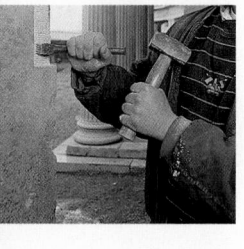

Tottenham House

Savernake Forest, Marlborough, Wiltshire SN8 3HP
Great house built of Bath stone in 1820 by Thomas Cundy for the 1st Marquess of Ailesbury. Most of the house is unfurnished, and it is currently leased to the Amber Foundation, a charity for homeless/jobless young people.
Grant Recipient/Owner: Trustees of the Savernake Estate
Access contact: Earl of Cardigan
Tel: 01672 512161   **Fax:** 01672 512105
Opening Arrangements: By prior arrangement with the Savernake Estate Office. Wheelchair access with assistance (entrance steps to be negotiated).
Heritage Open Days: No
P Yes. Spaces: 30
🦽 Partial. Disabled WC: No. Guide Dogs: Yes
£ No

Wilton House

Wilton, Salisbury, Wiltshire SP2 0BJ
Ancestral home of the Earls of Pembroke for 450 years, rebuilt by Inigo Jones and John Webb in the Palladian style with further alterations by James Wyatt c1801. Contains 17th century state rooms and an art collection including works by Van Dyck, Rubens, Joshua Reynolds and Brueghel. Surrounded by landscaped parkland.
Website Address: www.wiltonhouse.com
Grant Recipient/Owner: Wilton House Charitable Trust
Access contact: Mr Ray Stedman
Tel: 01722 746720   **Fax:** 01722 744447
Email Address: tourism@wiltonhouse.com
Opening Arrangements: 4 April - 28 October 10.30am - 5.30pm (last admission 4.30pm).
Heritage Open Days: No
P Yes. Spaces: 200
🦽 Yes. Disabled WC: Yes. Guide Dogs: Yes
£ Yes
Adult: £7.25
Child: £4.50
Other: £6.25 (senior citizens)

Wilton Windmill

East Grafton, Wiltshire, SN8 3SS
Built 1821. Only working windmill in Wiltshire, standing on a chalk ridge 550ft high.
Grant Recipient/Owner: Wiltshire County Council
Access contact: Mr John Talbot
Tel: 01672 870072
Email Address: jctalbot@waitrose.com
Opening Arrangements: Easter - end of September: guided tours on Sundays and Bank Holidays 2 - 5pm.
Heritage Open Days: No
P Yes. Spaces: 8
🦽 No. Disabled WC: No. Guide Dogs: Yes
£ Yes
Adult: £2.00
Child: 50p
Other: £1.50 (senior), £4.00 (family).

WORCESTERSHIRE

Detton Hall

Neen Savage, Cleobury Mortimer, Kidderminster, Worcestershire DY14 8LW
Large farmhouse built between the late 16th and early 18th centuries. Part half-timbered, part local stone and with roofs of clay tiles. There are 4 tall Tudor star chimney stacks and the main stairs have fretted panels. Extensively restored between 1991 and 1996.
Grant Recipient/Owner: Mr E C Ratcliff
Access contact: Mr E C Ratcliff
Tel: 01299 270387   **Fax:** 01299 270387
Opening Arrangements: By guided tour only by prior telephone or written arrangement with Mr E C or Mr E B Ratcliff. Wheelchair access to ground floor only with assistance (a few steps). Admission charges include light refreshment if required. Please note that the property is in Shropshire.
Heritage Open Days: Yes
P Yes. Spaces: 10
🦽 Partial. Disabled WC: No. Guide Dogs: Yes
£ Yes
Adult: £5.00
Child: £3.00

Edgar Tower

Worcester, Worcestershire
Gateway dates from mid-14th century and consists of a central block containing a larger arched opening for vehicular access to the precinct and a smaller pedestrian doorway. Blocks to north and south provided accommodation while the corner turrets contained stairs, garderobes, etc.
Grant Recipient/Owner: Dean & Chapter of Worcester Cathedral
Access contact: Cathedral Steward
Tel: 01905 28854   **Fax:** 01905 611139
Email Address: worcestercathedral@compuserve.com

Opening Arrangements: The Tower is one of the entrances through which visitors pass when approaching the Cathedral from the south. Visits to the interior (King's School Library) during school holidays by prior written arrangement to the Cathedral Steward, Chapter Office, 10a College Green, Worcester WR1 2LH. Please note that visits to the Tower can be physically demanding as the stairway is steep and narrow.
Heritage Open Days: Yes
P No
🦽 No. Disabled WC: No. Guide Dogs: No
£ No

Hanbury Hall

Hanbury, Droitwich, Worcestershire WR9 7EA
Built in 1701, this William and Mary-style house contains painted ceilings and staircase. It has an orangery, ice house and Moorish gazebos. The re-created 18th century garden is surrounded by parkland and has a parterre, wilderness, fruit garden, open grove and bowling green pavilions.
Website Address: www.ntrustsevern.org.uk
Grant Recipient/Owner: The National Trust
Access contact: Mr Stewart Alcock
Tel: 01527 821214   **Fax:** 01527 821251
Email Address: hanbury@smtp.ntrust.org.uk
Opening Arrangements: 1 April to 31 October: Sunday to Wednesday 1.30 - 5.30pm (but open Good Friday) last admission 5pm or dusk if earlier. Garden opens at 12.00pm. Car parking 200 metres from house. Parking for disabled near house.
Heritage Open Days: No
P Yes. Spaces: 80
🦽 Yes. Disabled WC: Yes. Guide Dogs: Yes
£ Yes
Adult: £3.00
Child: £1.60
Other: £7.50 (family).

Hopton Court Conservatory

Cleobury Mortimer, Kidderminster, Worcestershire DY14 0EF
Grade II* listed conservatory, c1830, of cast iron with a rounded archway leading to a rear room roofed with curved glass. Two rooms either side, one housing the boiler beneath to supply heat by way of cast iron grilles running around the floor of the interior.
Grant Recipient/Owner: Mr C R D Woodward
Access contact: Mr Christopher Woodward
Tel: 01299 270734   **Fax:** 01299 271132
Email Address: hoptoncourt@hotmail.com
Opening Arrangements: Weekend of 23/24 June and at other times by prior arrangement.
Heritage Open Days: No
P Yes, Spaces: 150
🦽 Yes. Disabled WC: Yes. Guide Dogs: Yes
£ Yes
Adult: £3.50

Worcester Assembly Rooms

Shaw Street, Worcester, Worcestershire WR1 3QQ
Built c1740 for the Hoppole Hotel. Such rooms were fashionable throughout the 18th century, Worcester had 3 all of which remain. Constructed over stables with 1st floor access and tea rooms. Survives virtually unaltered with much of its fine interior decoration intact. Possibly among the best early 18th century inn assembly rooms remaining in England.
Grant Recipient/Owner: Mr J Rudge
Access contact: Mr J Rudge
Tel: 01886 821190
Opening Arrangements: By prior arrangement with Mr J Rudge, Pacemark Developments Ltd, The Old School, Knightwick, Worcester WR6 5PJ (tel.01886 821190).
Heritage Open Days: No
P No
🦽 No
£ No

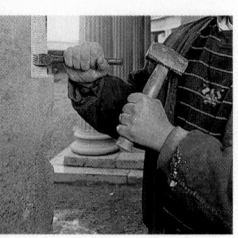

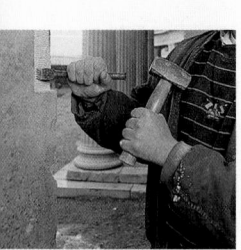

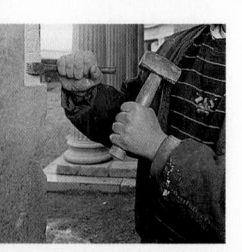

Information carried in this Section is based on that supplied by English Heritage. Every effort has been made to ensure that the information given is accurate and while believed to be at the time of going to press, opening times, entrance charges and facilities available at properties may be changed at the discretion of the owners. If long journeys are involved, visitors are advised to telephone the property to ensure the opening times are as published. The publishers do not accept responsibility for any consequences that may arise from errors or omissions.

No part of this publication may be reproduced, transmitted or used in any form or by any means graphic, electronic or mechanical, including photocopying, recording, taping or information storage and retrieval systems unless written permission of English Heritage and of the publisher has been given beforehand.

All photographic images have been supplied by English Heritage. © English Heritage Photo Library.

© English Heritage 2000/01.   www.english-heritage.org.uk

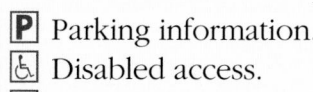

P Parking information.
🦽 Disabled access.
£ Admission prices.

London Detail

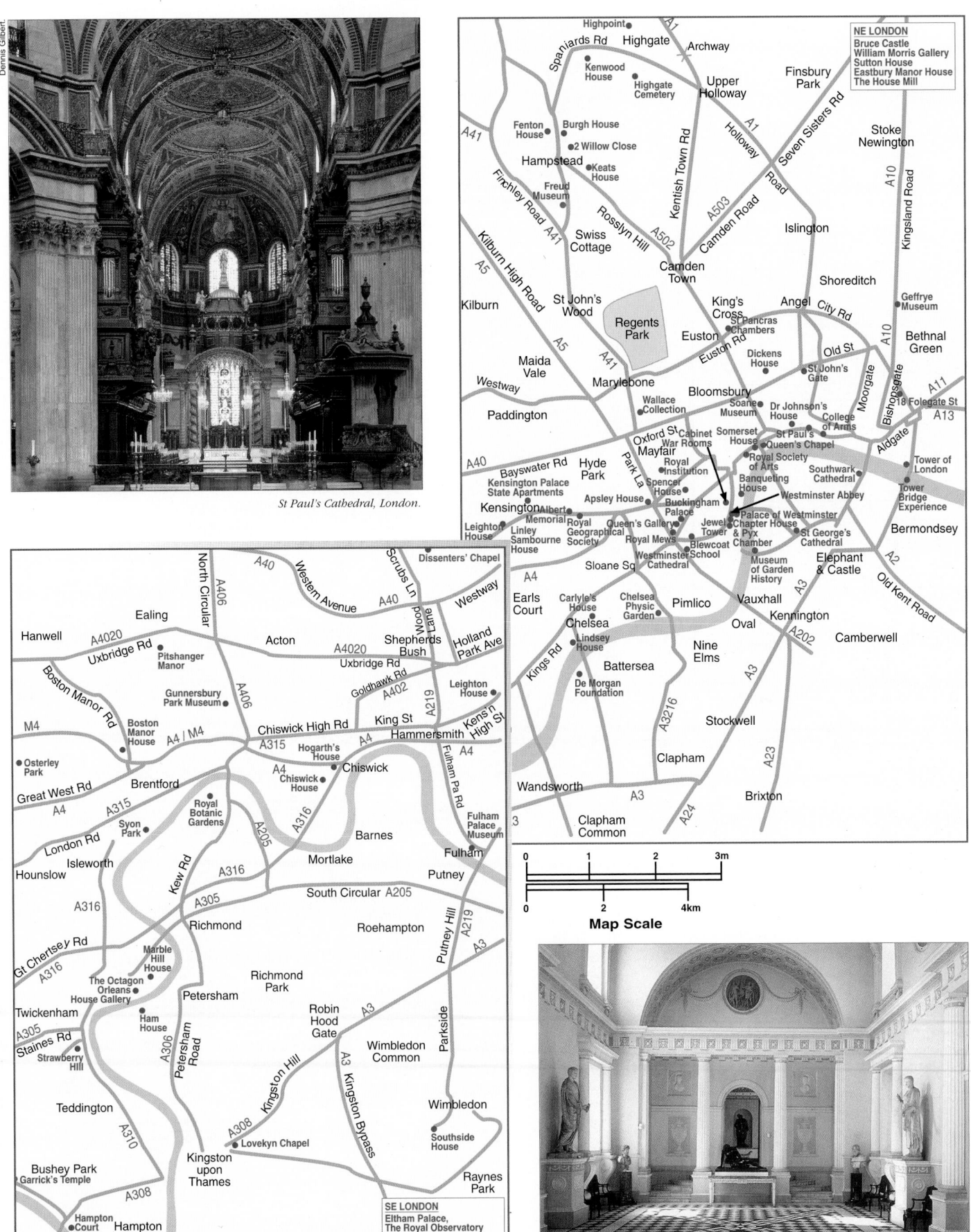

St Paul's Cathedral, London.

Dennis Gilbert.

NE LONDON
Bruce Castle
William Morris Gallery
Sutton House
Eastbury Manor House
The House Mill

Highpoint
Spaniards Rd
Highgate
Archway
A1
Kenwood House
Highgate Cemetery
Upper Holloway
Finsbury Park
A1
Fenton House
Burgh House
2 Willow Close
Keats House
Freud Museum
Hampstead
Holloway
Seven Sisters Rd
A503
Camden Road
Stoke Newington
A10
Kingsland Road
Finchley Road A41
Kilburn High Road
A5
Swiss Cottage
Rosslyn Hill
A502
Camden Town
King's Cross
St Pancras Chambers
Euston
Euston Rd
Islington
Angel
City Rd
Shoreditch
Geffrye Museum
Bethnal Green
A10
A11
Kilburn
St John's Wood
Regents Park
Maida Vale
Westway
A5
A41
Marylebone
Bloomsbury
Wallace Collection
Soane Museum
Dickens House
Old St
St John's Gate
Dr Johnson's House
College of Arms
St Paul's
Moorgate
18 Folegate St
Bishopsgate
A11
A13
Paddington
A40
Bayswater Rd
Hyde Park
Park La
Mayfair
Oxford St
Cabinet War Rooms
Somerset House
Queen's Chapel
Royal Society of Arts
Banqueting House
Aldgate
Tower of London
Kensington Palace State Apartments
Kensington
Albert Memorial
Leighton House
Royal Institution
Spencer House
Apsley House
Buckingham Palace
Queen's Gallery
Royal Mews
Southwark Cathedral
Tower Bridge Experience
Linley Sambourne House
Royal Geographical Society
Jewel Tower
Chapter House & Pyx Chamber
Westminster Abbey
Palace of Westminster
St George's Cathedral
Bermondsey
Sloane Sq
Westminster Cathedral
Blewcoat School
Museum of Garden History
Elephant & Castle
A2
Old Kent Road
Earls Court
A4
Carlyle's House
Chelsea Physic Garden
Pimlico
Vauxhall
A3
Chelsea
Lindsey House
Battersea
Nine Elms
Oval
Kennington
Camberwell
Kings Rd
De Morgan Foundation
A3
A202
Stockwell
A3216
Clapham
A23
Wandsworth
A3
A24
Brixton
Clapham Common

Map Scale

0 1 2 3m
0 2 4km

A40
North Circular
A406
Western Avenue
A40
Scrubs Ln
Dissenters' Chapel
Wood Lane
Westway
Ealing
Acton
Shepherds Bush
Uxbridge Rd
Holland Park Ave
Hanwell
A4020
Uxbridge Rd
Pitshanger Manor
Goldhawk Rd
A402
A219
Leighton House
Boston Manor Rd
Gunnersbury Park Museum
A406
Chiswick High Rd
King St
Kens'n High St
M4
Boston Manor House
A4 / M4
A315
Hogarth's House
A4
Hammersmith
A4
Osterley Park
Brentford
Chiswick House
Chiswick
Fulham Pa Rd
Great West Rd
A315
Royal Botanic Gardens
A316
Barnes
Fulham Palace Museum
A4
London Rd
Syon Park
A205
Fulham
Hounslow
Isleworth
Kew Rd
A316
Mortlake
Putney
A316
A305
South Circular A205
Putney Hill
A219
Richmond
Roehampton
A3
Gt Chertsey Rd
Marble Hill House
Richmond Park
Parkside
A316
The Octagon Orleans House Gallery
Petersham
Robin Hood Gate
A3
Wimbledon Common
Twickenham
Ham House
A305
A306
Petersham Road
Kingston Hill
Kingston Bypass
Staines Rd
Strawberry Hill
Wimbledon
Teddington
A310
A308
Lovekyn Chapel
Southside House
Bushey Park
Garrick's Temple
A308
Kingston upon Thames
Raynes Park
Hampton Court Palace
Hampton Court Park
Surbiton

SE LONDON
Eltham Palace,
The Royal Observatory
& Queens House,
Ranger's House,
Prendergast School Murals

Syon Park, London.

M I
579

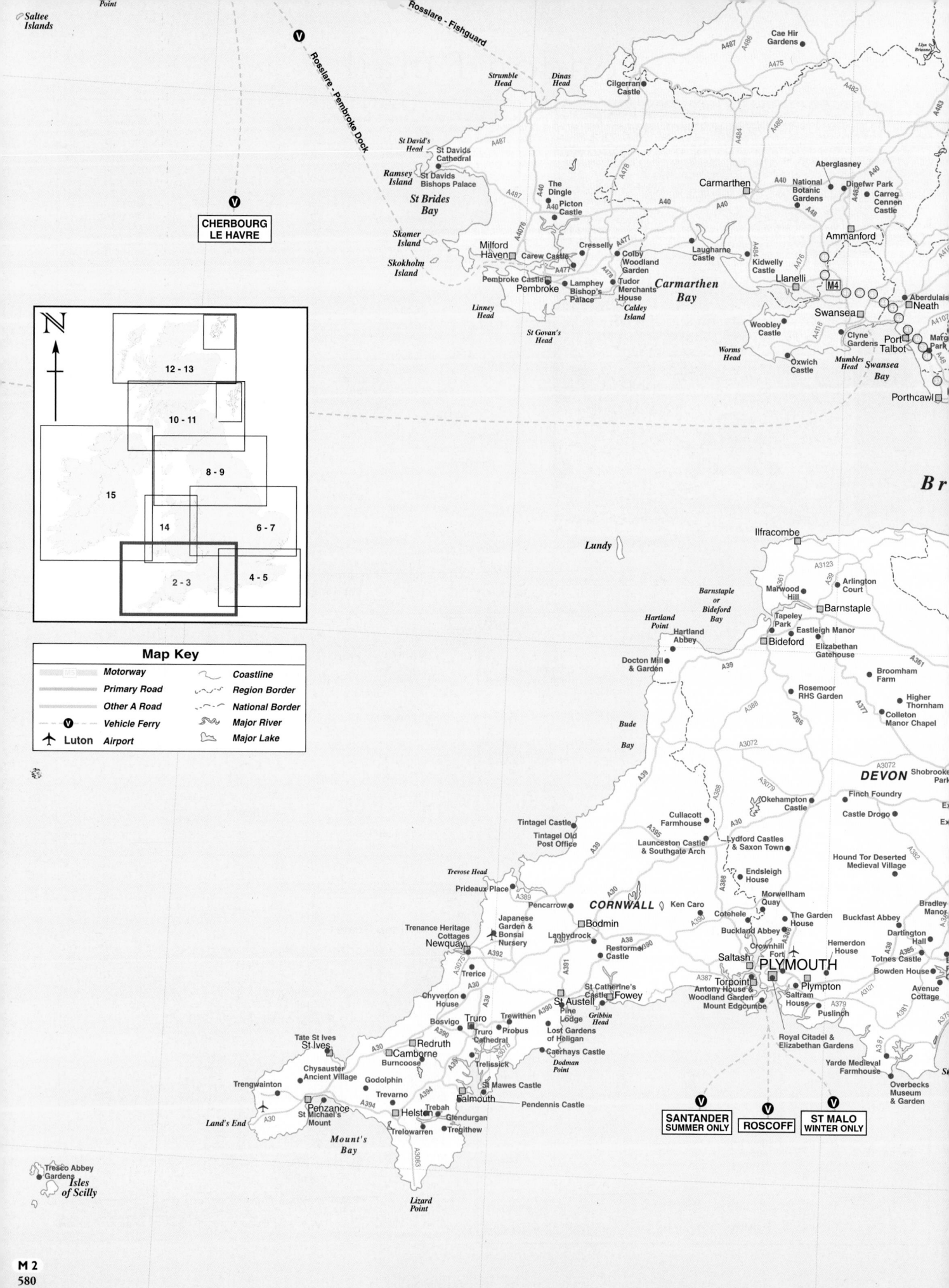

Saltee
Islands

Point

Rosslare - Fishguard

Rosslare - Pembroke Dock

Ⓥ CHERBOURG
LE HAVRE

*Strumble
Head*

*Dinas
Head*

Cilgerran
Castle

*St David's
Head*

St Davids
Cathedral

*Ramsey
Island*

St Davids
Bishops Palace

*St Brides
Bay*

The
Dingle

Picton
Castle

Aberglasney

Carmarthen

National
Botanic
Gardens

Dinefwr Park

Carreg
Cennen
Castle

*Skomer
Island*

Milford
Haven

Carew Castle

Cresselly

Colby
Woodland
Garden

Laugharne
Castle

Ammanford

*Skokholm
Island*

Pembroke Castle

Lamphey
Bishop's
Palace

Tudor
Merchants
House

*Carmarthen
Bay*

Kidwelly
Castle

Llanelli

M4

Aberdulais

Neath

*Linney
Head*

Pembroke

*Caldey
Island*

Weobley
Castle

Swansea

Clyne
Gardens

Port
Talbot

Marg
Park

*St Govan's
Head*

*Worms
Head*

Oxwich
Castle

*Mumbles
Head*

*Swansea
Bay*

Porthcawl

Cae Hir
Gardens

B r

Map inset (grid index):

N

12 - 13

10 - 11

8 - 9

15

14

6 - 7

2 - 3

4 - 5

Map Key

	Motorway		Coastline
	Primary Road		Region Border
	Other A Road		National Border
Ⓥ	Vehicle Ferry		Major River
✈ Luton	Airport		Major Lake

Lundy

Ilfracombe

A3123

*Barnstaple
or
Bideford Bay*

Marwood
Hill

Arlington
Court

Tapeley
Park

Eastleigh Manor

Barnstaple

*Hartland
Point*

Hartland
Abbey

Bideford

Elizabethan
Gatehouse

Docton Mill
& Garden

Broomham
Farm

Rosemoor
RHS Garden

Higher
Thornham

Colleton
Manor Chapel

*Bude
Bay*

A3072

A3072

DEVON

Shobrooke
Park

Finch Foundry

Okehampton
Castle

Castle Drogo

Ex

Tintagel Castle

Tintagel Old
Post Office

Cullacott
Farmhouse

Launceston Castle
& Southgate Arch

Lydford Castles
& Saxon Town

Hound Tor Deserted
Medieval Village

Trevose Head

Prideaux Place

Endsleigh
House

Morwellham
Quay

Bradley
Manor

Pencarrow

Ken Caro

CORNWALL

The Garden
House

Buckfast Abbey

Dartington
Hall

Trenance Heritage
Cottages

Japanese
Garden &
Bonsai
Nursery

Bodmin

Lanhydrock

Cotehele

Buckland Abbey

Hemerdon
House

Newquay

Restormel
Castle

A38

A390

Crownhill
Fort

Saltash

PLYMOUTH

Totnes Castle

Bowden House

Trerice

St Catherine's
Castle

Torpoint

Plympton

Avenue
Cottage

Chyverton
House

Truro

Pine
Lodge

Fowey

Antony House &
Woodland Garden
Mount Edgcumbe

Saltram
House

Puslinch

Bosvigo

Trewithen

Probus

Gribbin
Head

Lost Gardens
of Heligan

Royal Citadel &
Elizabethan Gardens

Tate St Ives

St Ives

Redruth

Camborne

Burncoose

Truro
Cathedral

St Austell

Trelissick

Caerhays Castle

*Dodman
Point*

Yarde Medieval
Farmhouse

Trengwainton

Chysauster
Ancient Village

Godolphin

Trevarno

St Mawes Castle

Overbecks
Museum
& Garden

Land's End

Penzance

St Michael's
Mount

Helston

Trebah

Glendurgan

Falmouth

Pendennis Castle

Ⓥ SANTANDER
SUMMER ONLY

Ⓥ ROSCOFF

Ⓥ ST MALO
WINTER ONLY

Trelowarren

Tregithew

*Mount's
Bay*

A3083

Tresco Abbey
Gardens

*Isles
of Scilly*

*Lizard
Point*

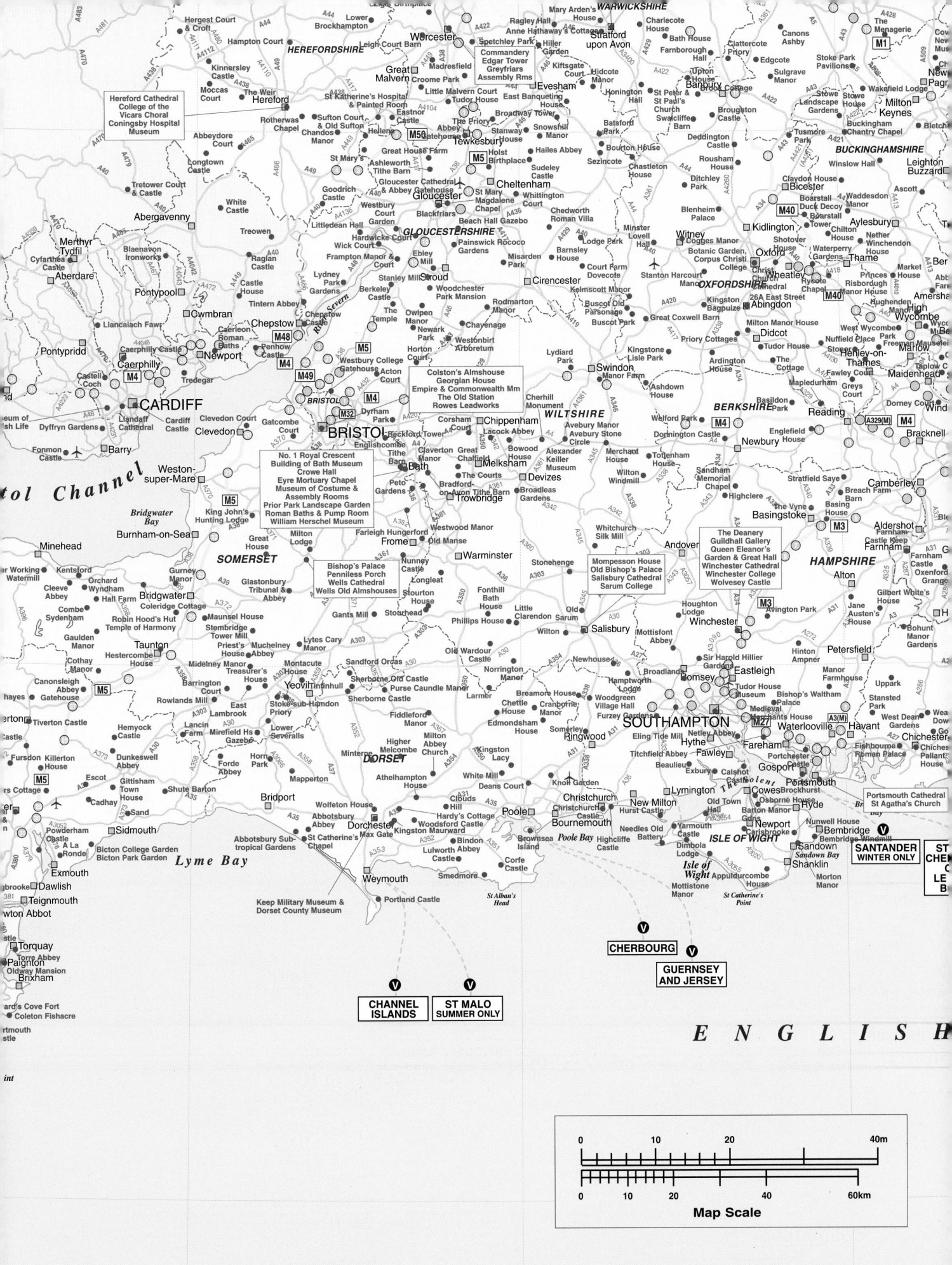

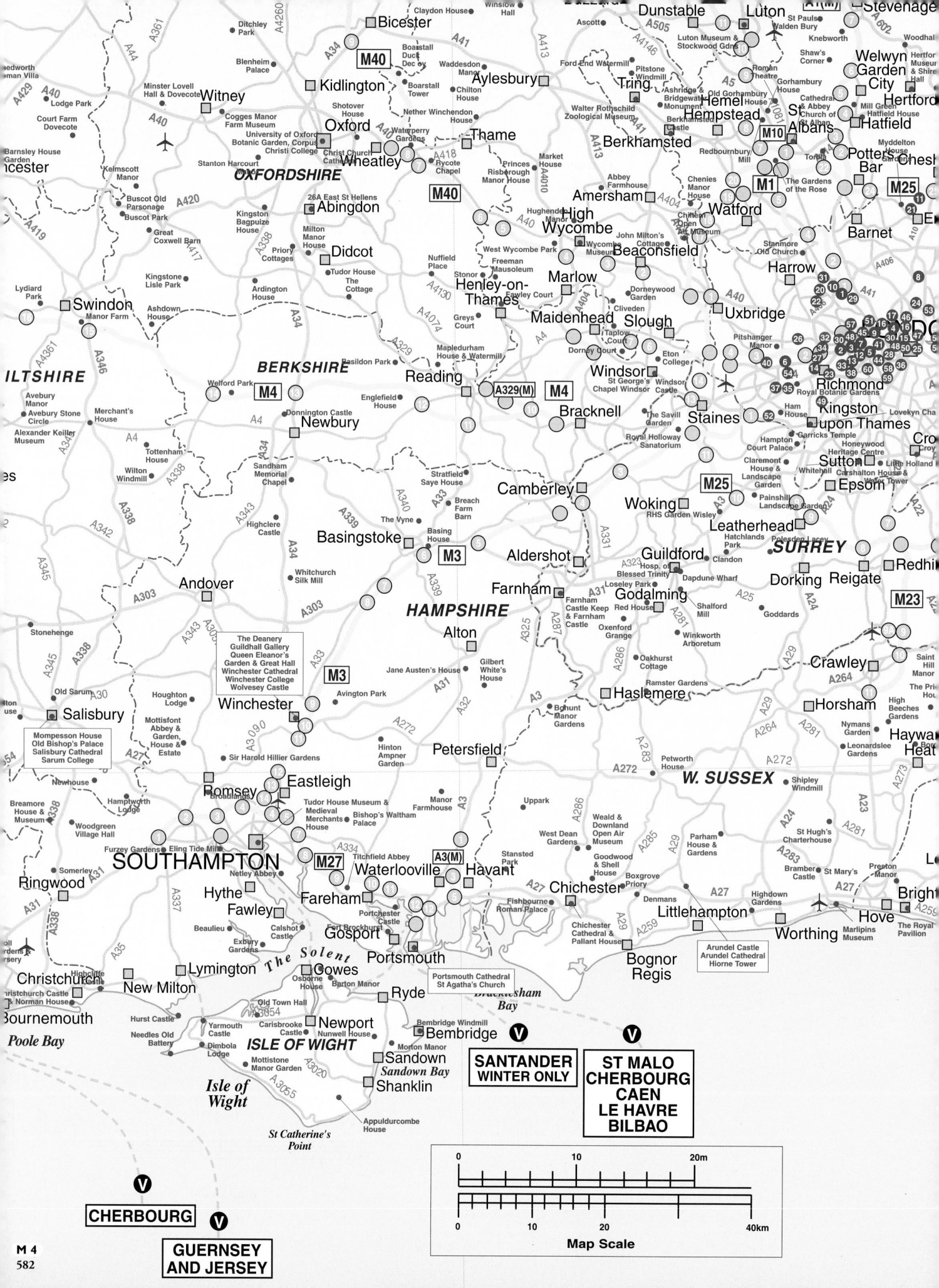

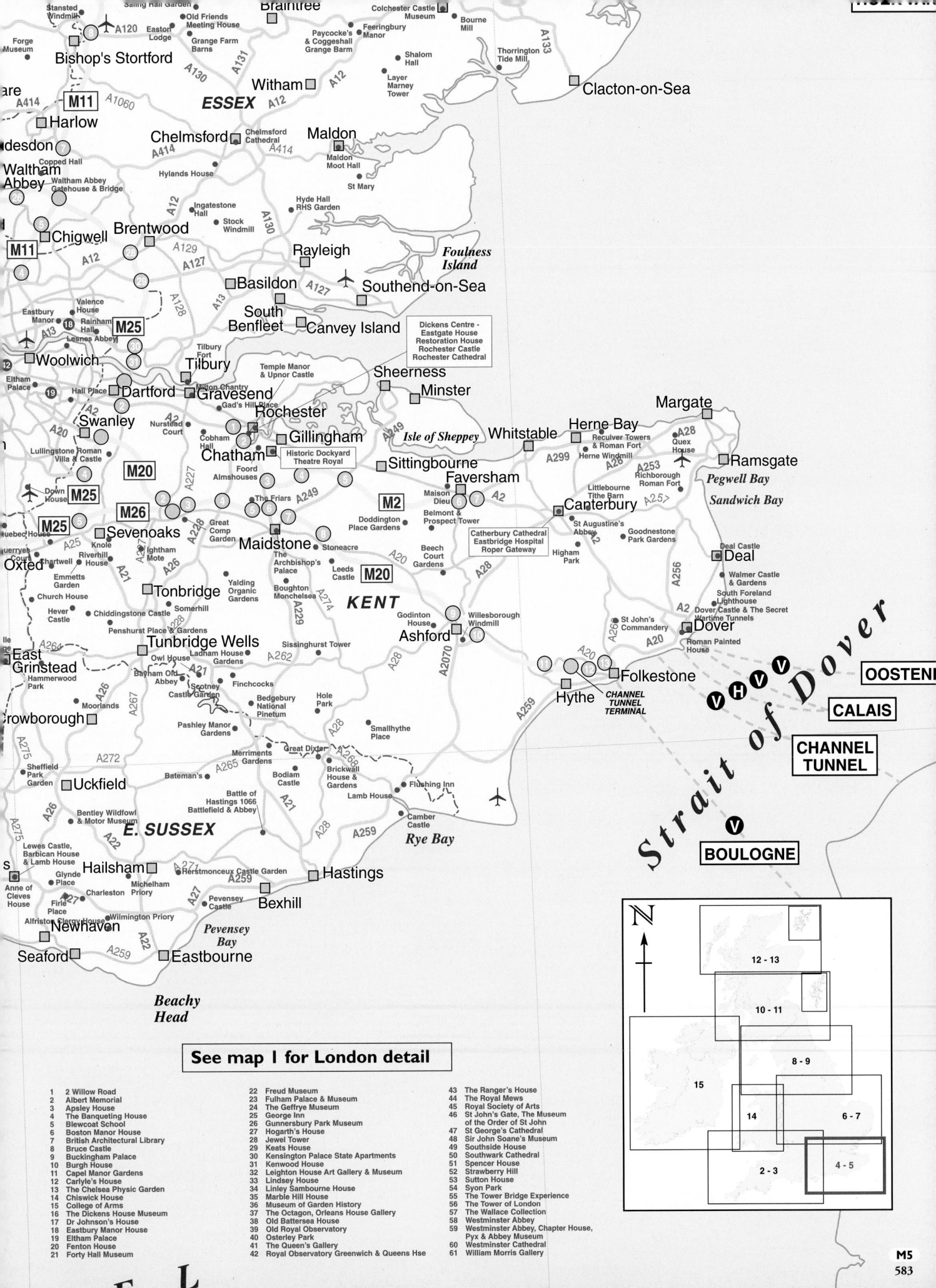

See map 1 for London detail

1 2 Willow Road
2 Albert Memorial
3 Apsley House
4 The Banqueting House
5 Blewcoat School
6 Boston Manor House
7 British Architectural Library
8 Bruce Castle
9 Buckingham Palace
10 Burgh House
11 Capel Manor Gardens
12 Carlyle's House
13 The Chelsea Physic Garden
14 Chiswick House
15 College of Arms
16 The Dickens House Museum
17 Dr Johnson's House
18 Eastbury Manor House
19 Eltham Palace
20 Fenton House
21 Forty Hall Museum
22 Freud Museum
23 Fulham Palace & Museum
24 The Geffrye Museum
25 George Inn
26 Gunnersbury Park Museum
27 Hogarth's House
28 Jewel Tower
29 Keats House
30 Kensington Palace State Apartments
31 Kenwood House
32 Leighton House Art Gallery & Museum
33 Lindsey House
34 Linley Sambourne House
35 Marble Hill House
36 Museum of Garden History
37 The Octagon, Orleans House Gallery
38 Old Battersea House
39 Old Royal Observatory
40 Osterley Park
41 The Queen's Gallery
42 Royal Observatory Greenwich & Queens Hse
43 The Ranger's House
44 The Royal Mews
45 Royal Society of Arts
46 St John's Gate, The Museum of the Order of St John
47 St George's Cathedral
48 Sir John Soane's Museum
49 Southside House
50 Southwark Cathedral
51 Spencer House
52 Strawberry Hill
53 Sutton House
54 Syon Park
55 The Tower Bridge Experience
56 The Tower of London
57 The Wallace Collection
58 Westminster Abbey
59 Westminster Abbey, Chapter House, Pyx & Abbey Museum
60 Westminster Cathedral
61 William Morris Gallery

M5
583

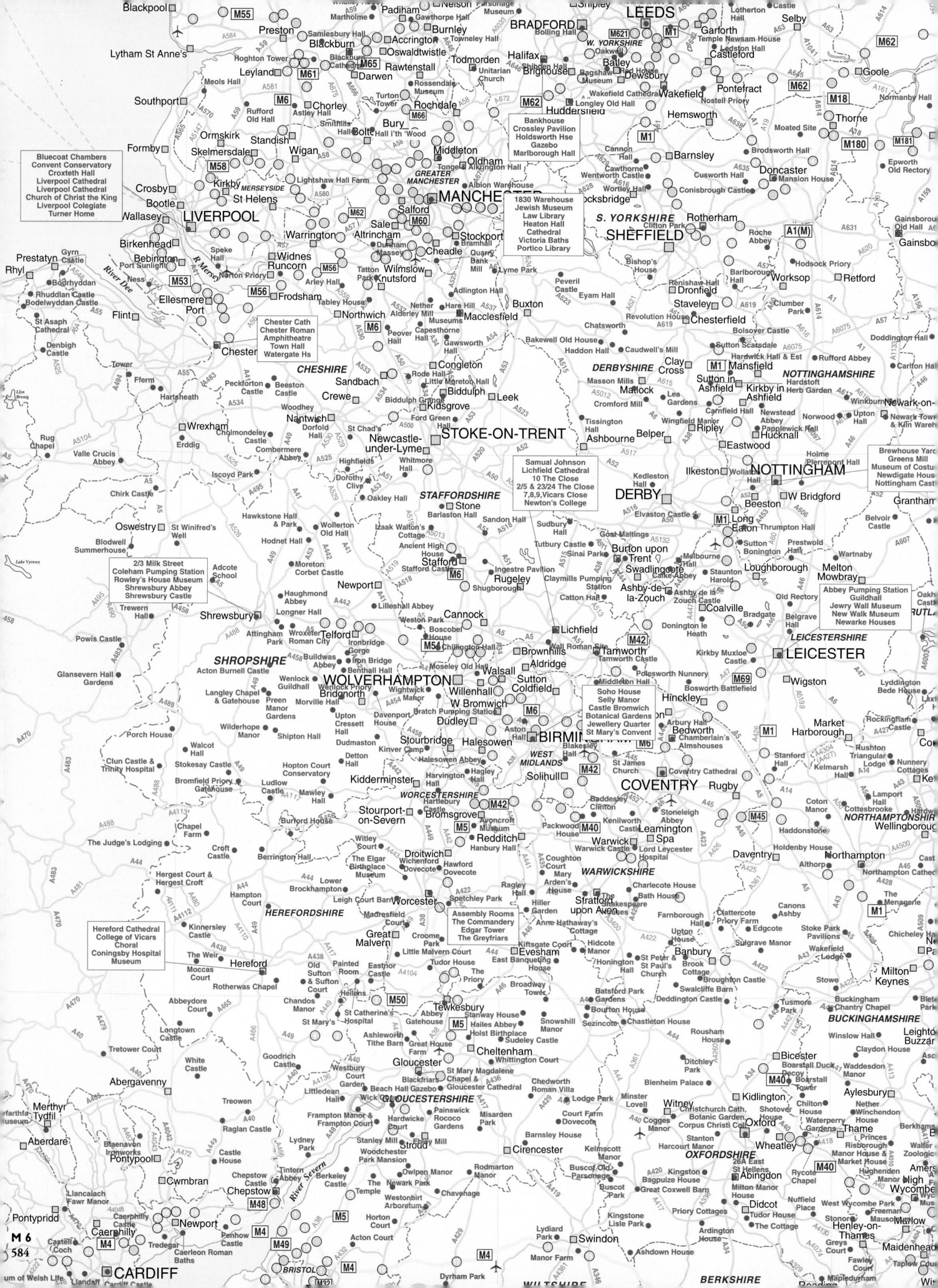

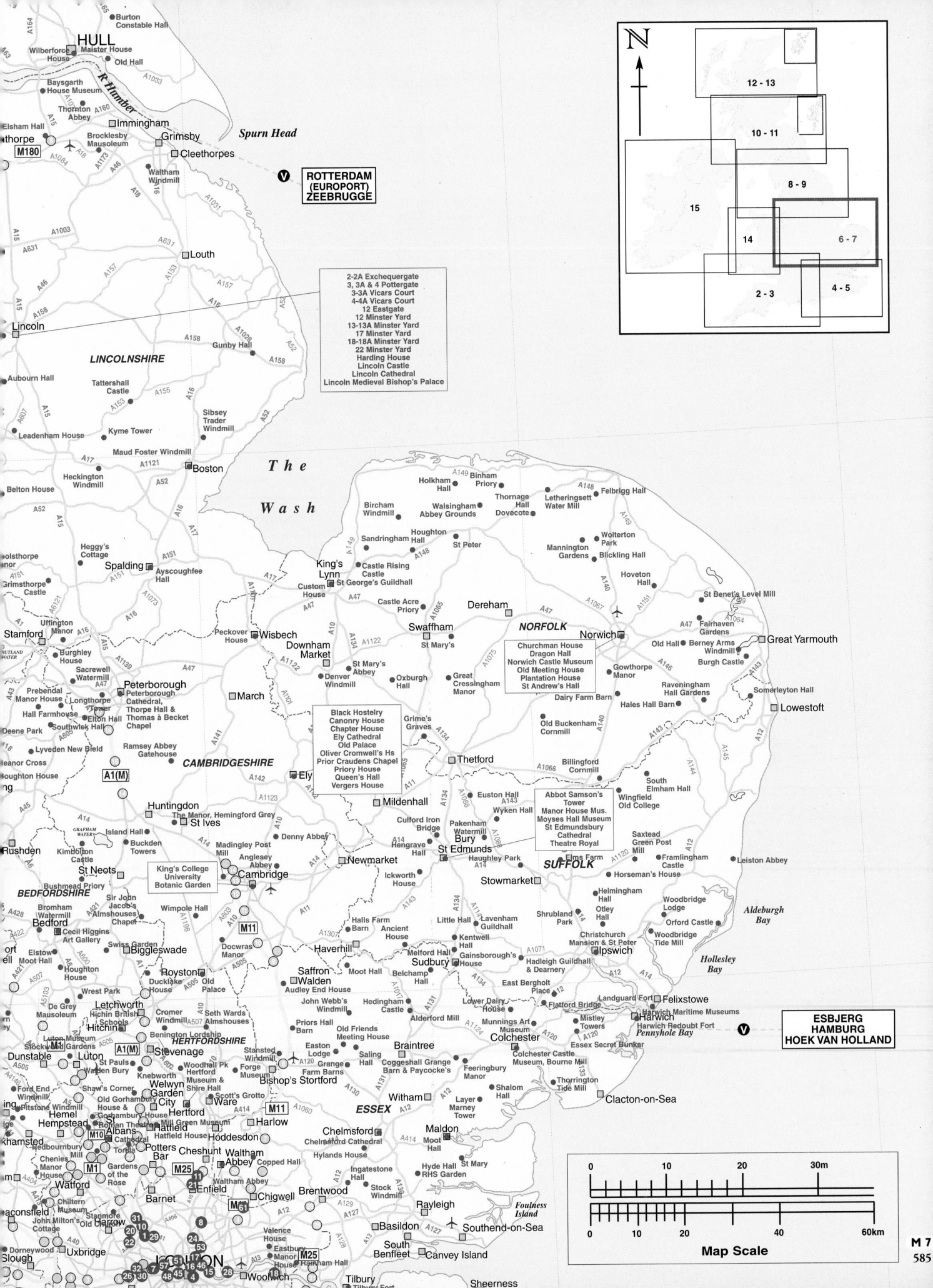

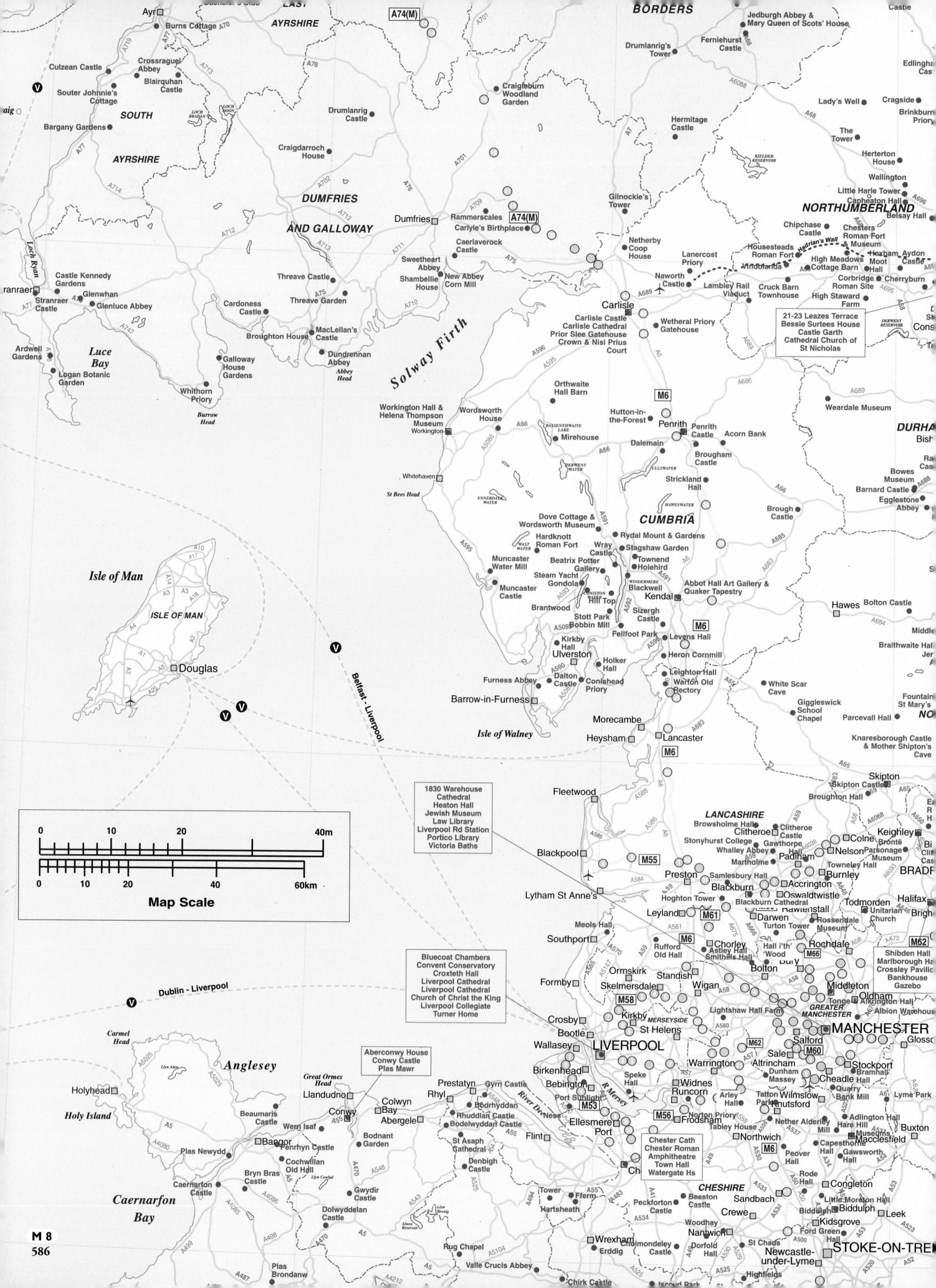

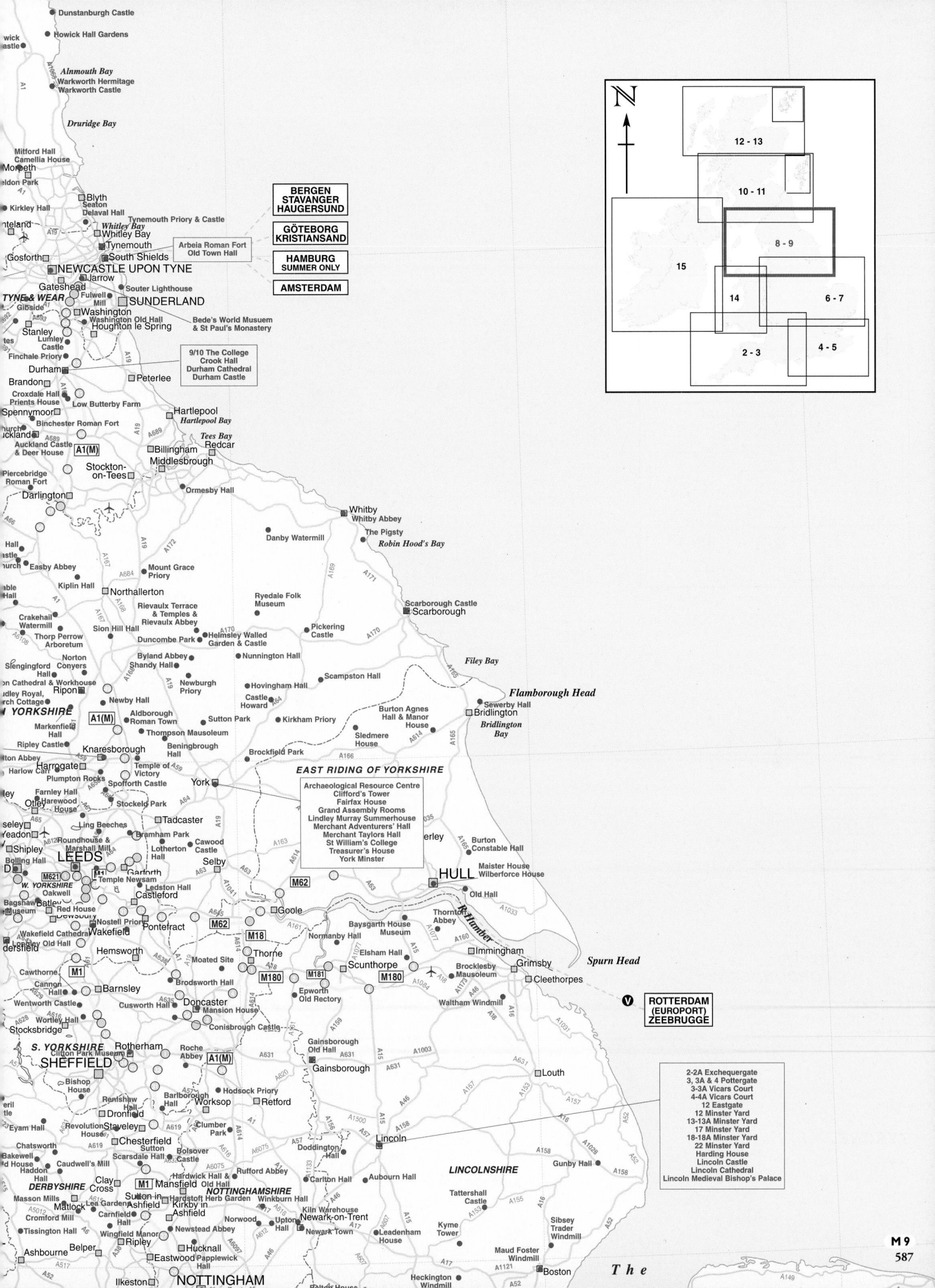

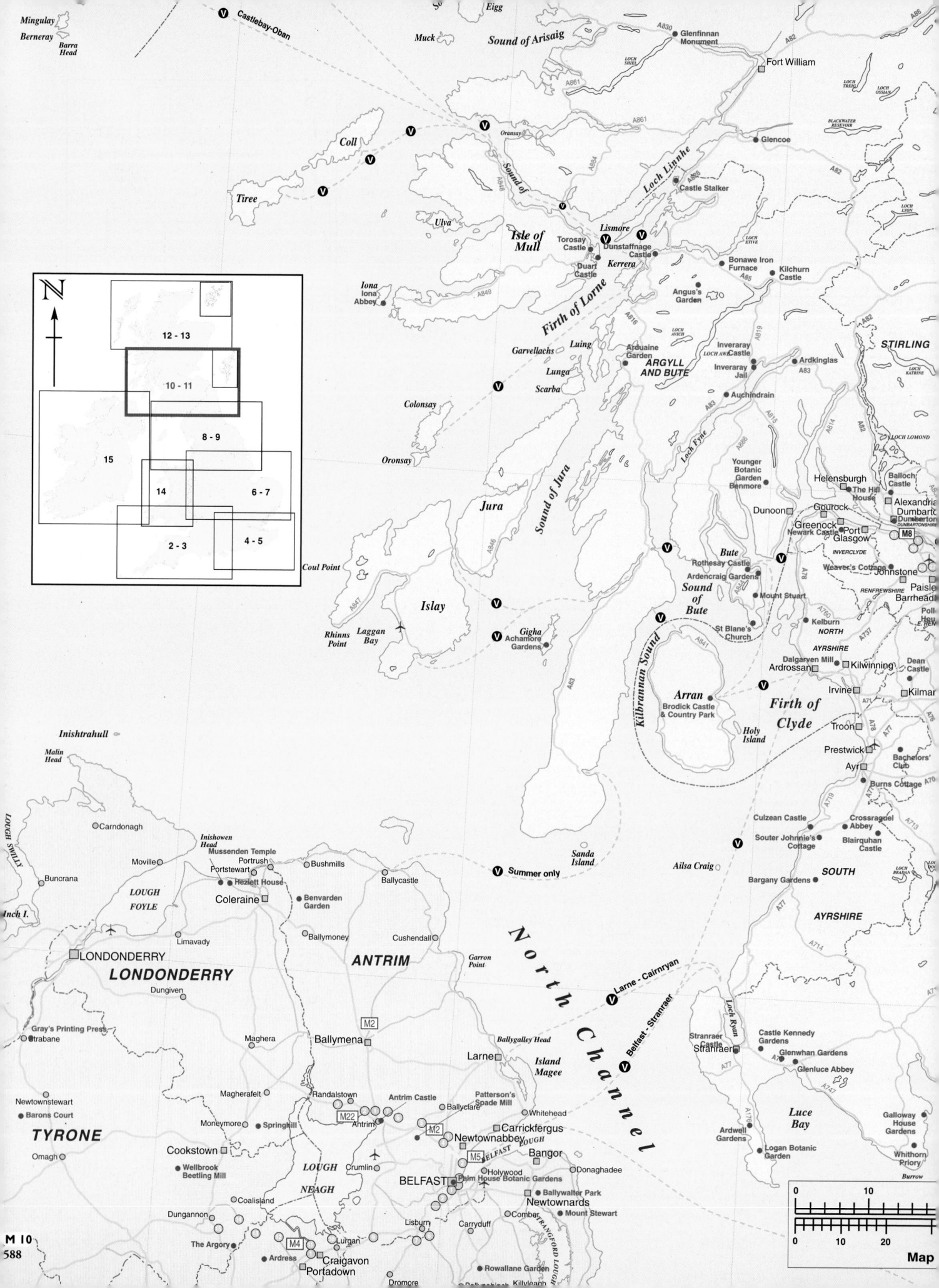

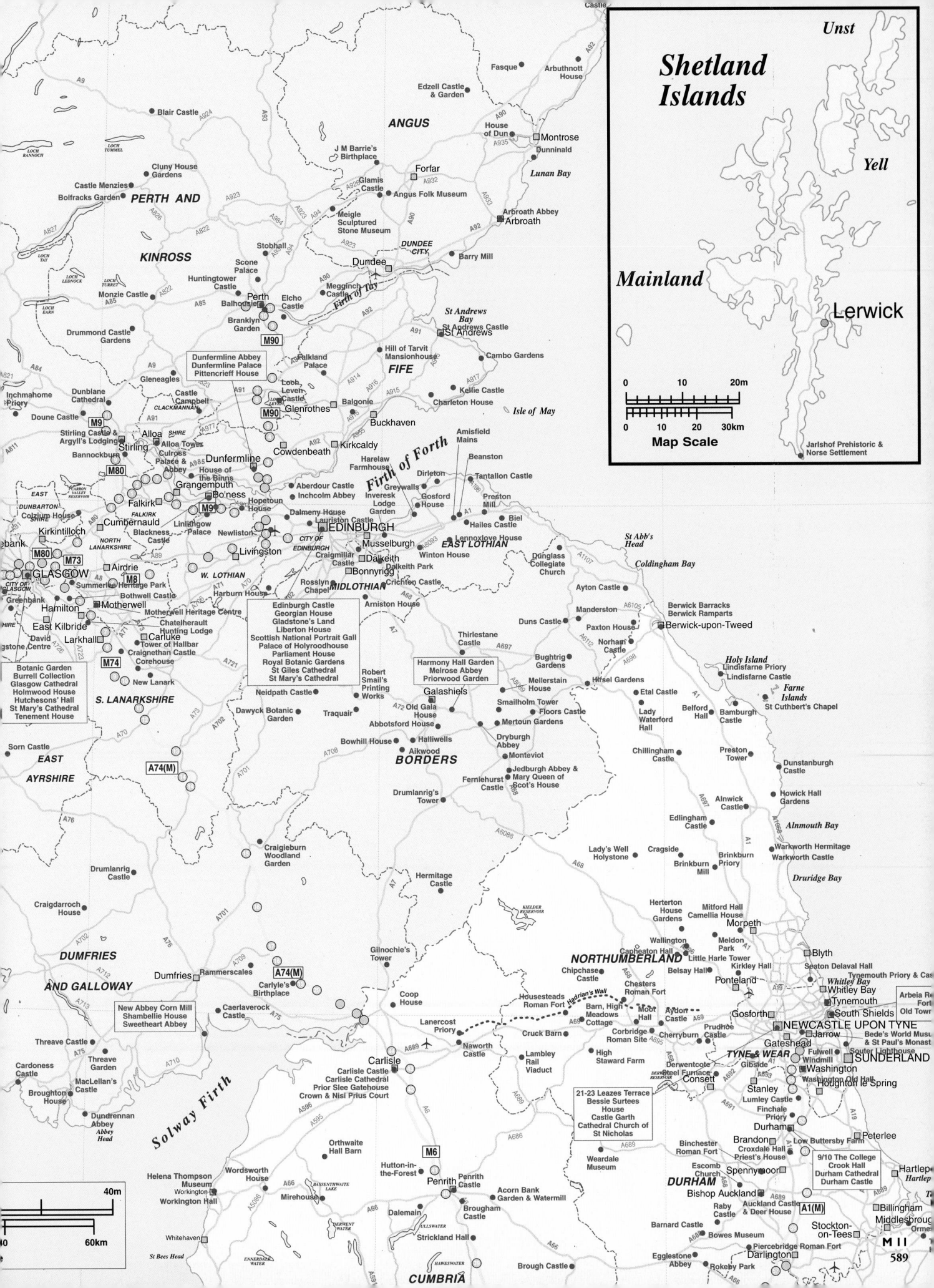

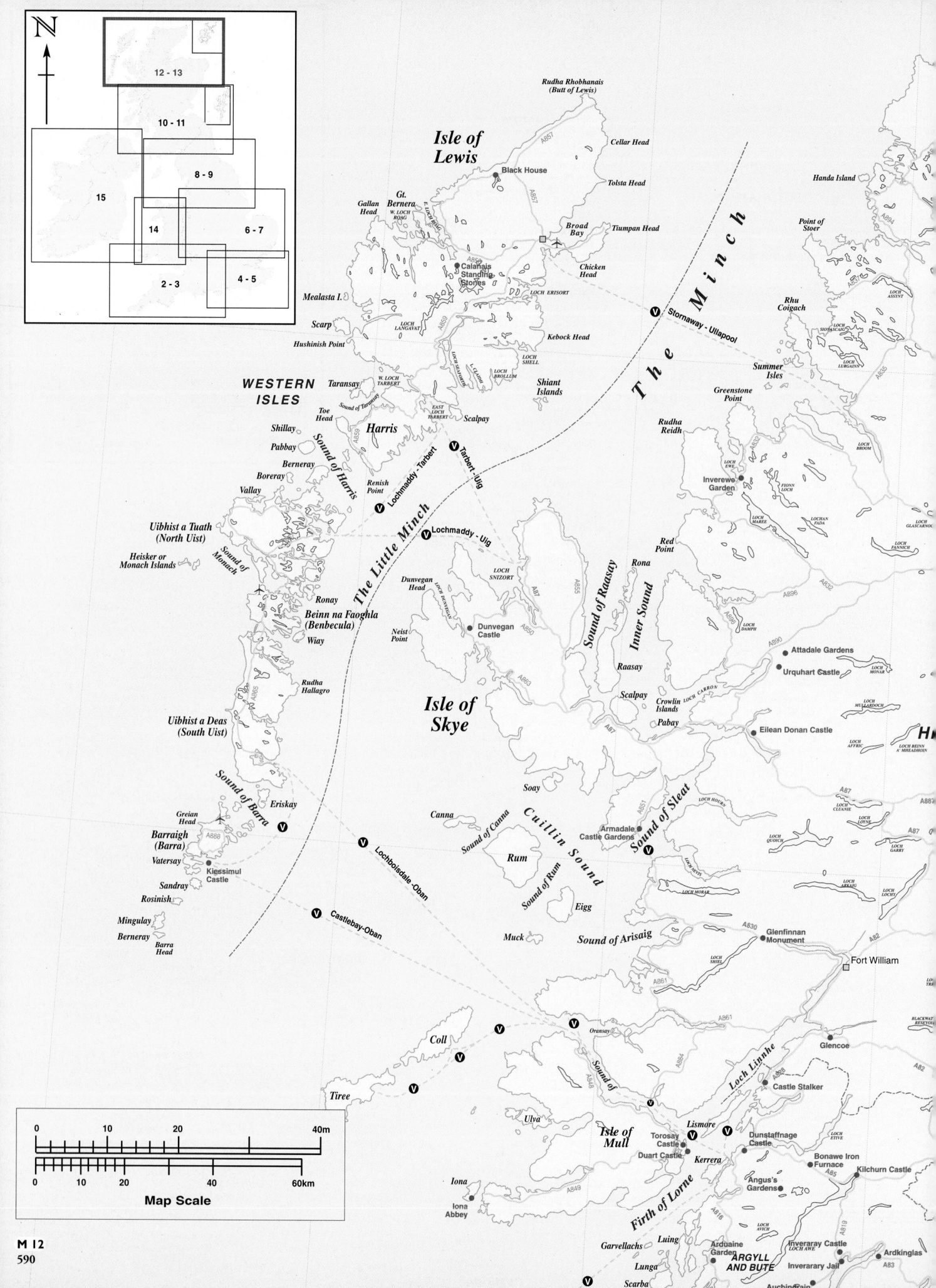

N

12 - 13

10 - 11

8 - 9

15

14

6 - 7

2 - 3

4 - 5

Rudha Rhobhanais
(Butt of Lewis)

**Isle of
Lewis**

Cellar Head

Black House

Tolsta Head

Handa Island

A857

A858

Broad
Bay

Tiumpan Head

Point of
Stoer

Gt.
Bernera

W. LOCH
ROAG

E. LOCH ROAG

Gallan
Head

Chicken
Head

Calanais
Standing
Stones

LOCH ERISORT

Rhu
Coigach

A859

LOCH
ASSYNT

Mealasta I.

Kebock Head

V Stornaway - Ullapool

The Minch

Scarp

LOCH
LANGAVAT

LOCH
SHELL

LOCH
SIOPHACHAIN

Hushinish Point

L. CLIANN

LOCH
BROLLUM

Shiant
Islands

Summer
Isles

LOCH
LURGAINN

**WESTERN
ISLES**

Taransay

W. LOCH
TARBERT

Greenstone
Point

LOCH
BROOM

Toe
Head

Sound of Taransay

Scalpay

Rudha
Reidh

Harris

EAST
LOCH
TARBERT

Shillay

LOCH
EWE

LOCH
MAREE

LOCHAN
FADA

LOCH
GLASCARNOCH

Pabbay

A859

Renish
Point

V Tarbert - Uig

Inverewe
Garden

FIONN
LOCH

Berneray

V Lochmaddy - Tarbert

Boreray

Sound of Harris

Vallay

The Little Minch

LOCH
FANNICH

Red
Point

**Uibhist a Tuath
(North Uist)**

V Lochmaddy - Uig

LOCH
DAMPH

Heisker or
Monach Islands

Sound of Monach

Dunvegan
Head

LOCH
SNIZORT

Sound of Raasay

Rona

Inner Sound

A890

Ronay

LOCH
DUNVEGAN

Dunvegan
Castle

Attadale Gardens

A863

A890

**Beinn na Faoghla
(Benecula)**

Neist
Point

LOCH
MONAR

Urquhart Castle

Wiay

Raasay

LOCH
CARRON

LOCH
MULLARDOCH

Rudha
Hallagro

A865

Scalpay

Crowlin
Islands

Eilean Donan Castle

H

Pabay

LOCH
AFFRIC

LOCH BEINN
A' MHEADHOIN

**Uibhist a Deas
(South Uist)**

**Isle of
Skye**

A87

Soay

Sound of Sleat

A87

LOCH
HOURN

LOCH
CLUANIE

LOCH
LOYNE

Sound of Barra

Greian
Head

Eriskay

Canna

Sound of Canna

Cuillin Sound

Armadale
Castle Gardens

V

LOCH
QUOICH

LOCH
GARRY

A888

V Lochboisdale - Oban

**Barraigh
(Barra)**

Rum

LOCH
ARKAIG

LOCH
LOCHY

Vatersay

Kiessimul
Castle

Sound of Rum

Sound of Arisaig

Eigg

Sandray

V Castlebay - Oban

Muck

Glenfinnan
Monument

A830

Rosinish

LOCH
SHIEL

A861

LOCH
MORAR

Mingulay

Fort William

Berneray

Barra
Head

BLACKWAT...
RESERVOIR

Glencoe

Coll

V

Oransay

A861

A82

V

Sound of

Castle Stalker

Loch Linnhe

Tiree

Ulva

A848

Lismore

Dunstaffnage
Castle

LOCH
ETIVE

Bonawe Iron
Furnace

Kilchurn Castle

**Isle of
Mull**

Torosay
Castle

V

V

A85

Duart Castle

Kerrera

Angus's
Gardens

Iona

Firth of Lorne

LOCH
AVICH

A816

A819

Ardkinglas

Iona
Abbey

Inveraray Castle

LOCH AWE

Garvellachs

Luing

Arduaine
Garden

Inverarary Jail

A83

**ARGYLL
AND BUTE**

Lunga

Scarba

V

Auchin...

0	10	20	40m
0	10	20	40	60km

Map Scale

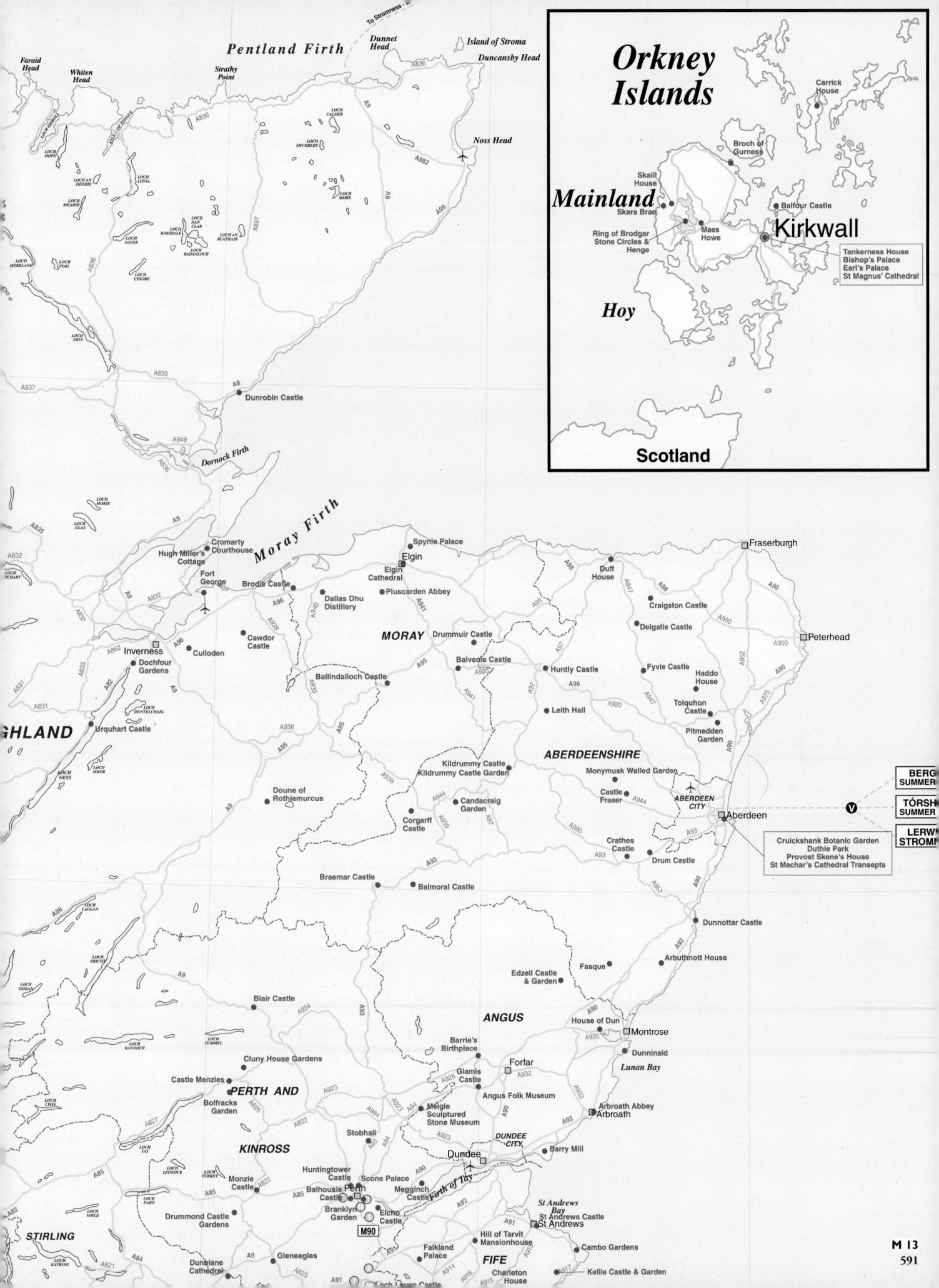

Orkney Islands

Mainland

Hoy

Carrick House

Broch of Gurness

Skaill House

Skara Brae

Balfour Castle

Ring of Brodgar Stone Circles & Henge

Maes Howe

Kirkwall

Tankerness House
Bishop's Palace
Earl's Palace
St Magnus' Cathedral

Scotland

Pentland Firth

Faraid Head

Whiten Head

Strathy Point

Dunnet Head

Island of Stroma

Duncansby Head

LOCH HOPE

LOCH LOYAL

LOCH CALDER

Noss Head

LOCH AN DEERIE

LOCH MEADIE

LOCH SHURRERY

LOCH MORE

LOCH MERKLAND

LOCH NAVER

LOCH NAN CLAR

LOCH RIMSDALE

LOCH BADANLOCH

LOCH AN RUATHAIR

LOCH FIAG

LOCH CHOIRE

Dunrobin Castle

LOCH SHIN

Dornock Firth

LOCH MORIE

Moray Firth

LOCH GLAS

Cromarty Courthouse

Hugh Miller's Cottage

Spynie Palace

Fraserburgh

Elgin

Elgin Cathedral

Duff House

Fort George

Brodie Castle

Dallas Dhu Distillery

Pluscarden Abbey

Craigston Castle

Delgatie Castle

Peterhead

MORAY

Drummuir Castle

Cawdor Castle

Inverness

Culloden

Balvenie Castle

Huntly Castle

Fyvie Castle

Haddo House

Dochfour Gardens

Ballindalloch Castle

Leith Hall

Tolquhon Castle

HIGHLAND

Urquhart Castle

LOCH DUNTELCHAIG

Pitmedden Garden

ABERDEENSHIRE

LOCH NESS

LOCH MHOR

Kildrummy Castle
Kildrummy Castle Garden

Monymusk Walled Garden

Doune of Rothiemurcus

Candacraig Garden

Castle Fraser

ABERDEEN CITY

BERG SUMMER

TÓRSH SUMMER

Corgarff Castle

Aberdeen

LERW STROMN

Crathes Castle

Cruickshank Botanic Garden
Duthie Park
Provost Skene's House
St Machar's Cathedral Transepts

Braemar Castle

Balmoral Castle

Drum Castle

Dunnottar Castle

LOCH LAGGAN

Arbuthnott House

Fasque

Edzell Castle & Garden

Blair Castle

House of Dun

ANGUS

Montrose

Dunninald

LOCH RANNOCH

Cluny House Gardens

Lunan Bay

LOCH TUMMEL

Barrie's Birthplace

Castle Menzies

Glamis Castle

Forfar

Bolfracks Garden

Meigle Sculptured Stone Museum

Angus Folk Museum

Arbroath Abbey

Arbroath

LOCH LYON

Stobhall

DUNDEE CITY

Barry Mill

KINROSS

Dundee

Firth of Tay

St Andrews Bay

LOCH TAY

Huntingtower Castle

Monzie Castle

Scone Palace

Perth

Megginch Castle

St Andrews Castle

St Andrews

LOCH LEDNOCK

Balhousie Castle

Branklyn Garden

Elcho Castle

Hill of Tarvit Mansionhouse

Drummond Castle Gardens

M90

LOCH TURRET

LOCH EARN

Falkland Palace

Cambo Gardens

STIRLING

Dunblane Cathedral

Gleneagles

FIFE

Kellie Castle & Garden

LOCH VOILE

LOCH KATRINE

Charleton House

M 13

591

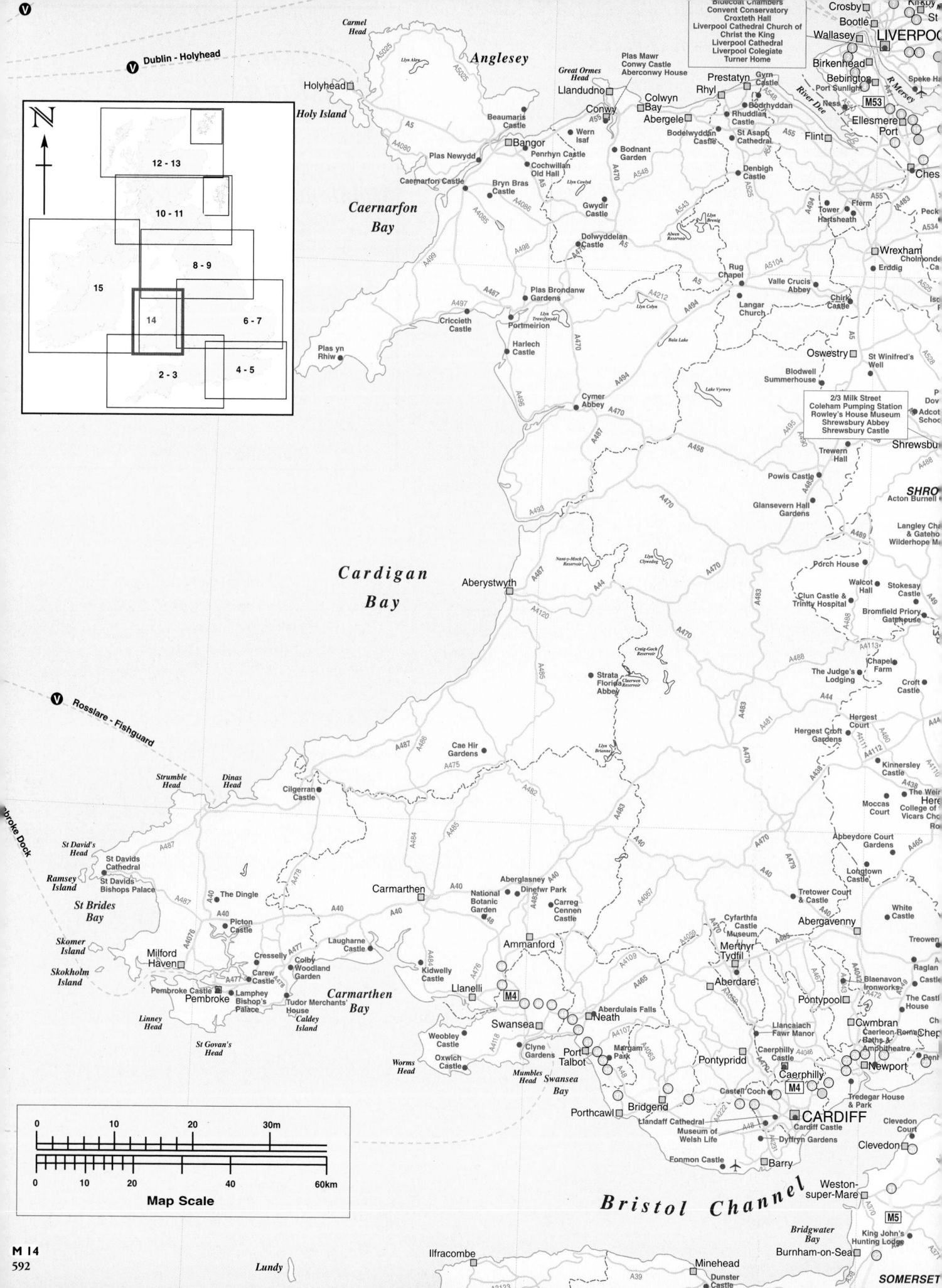

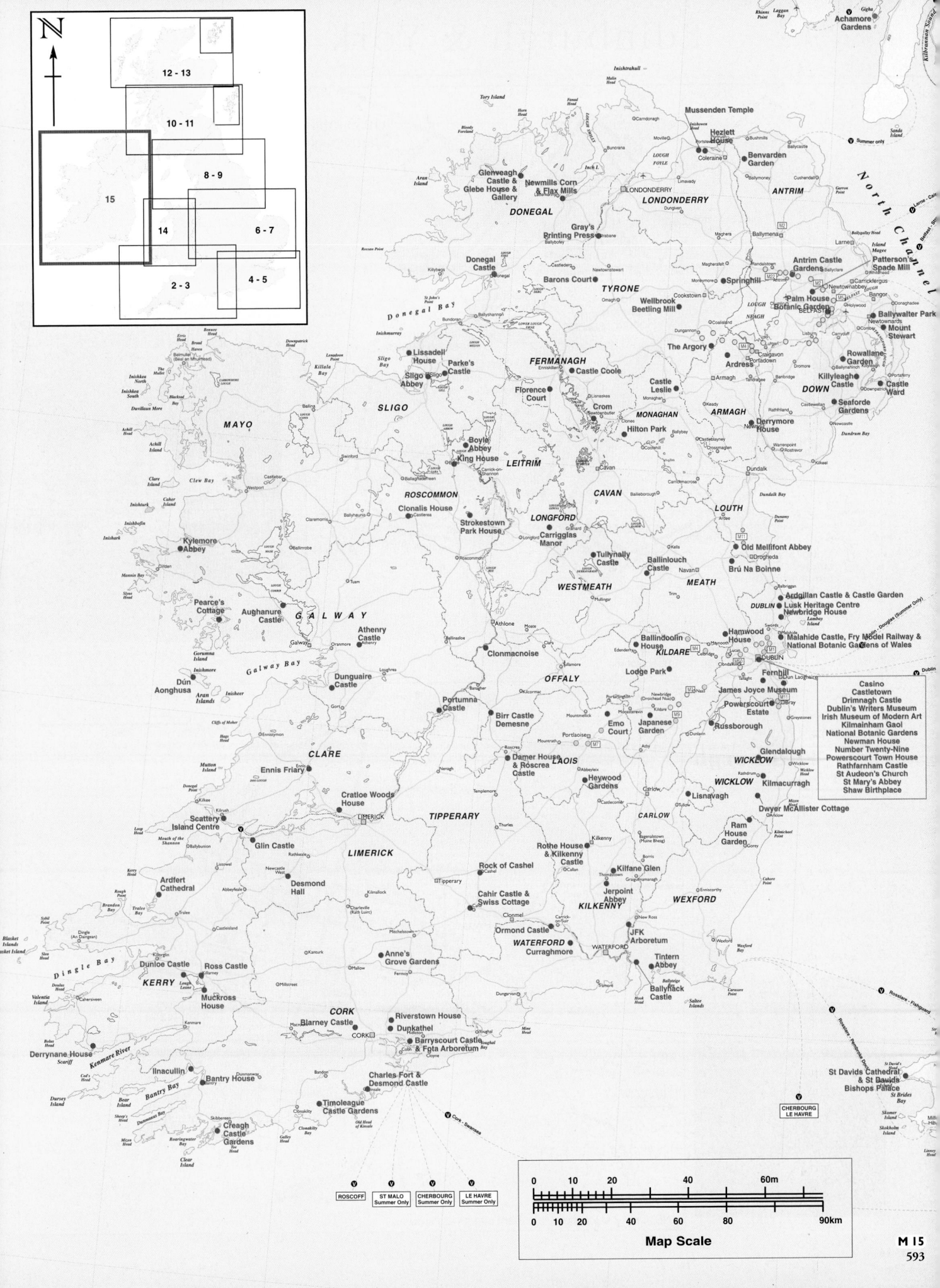

Edinburgh & York Detail

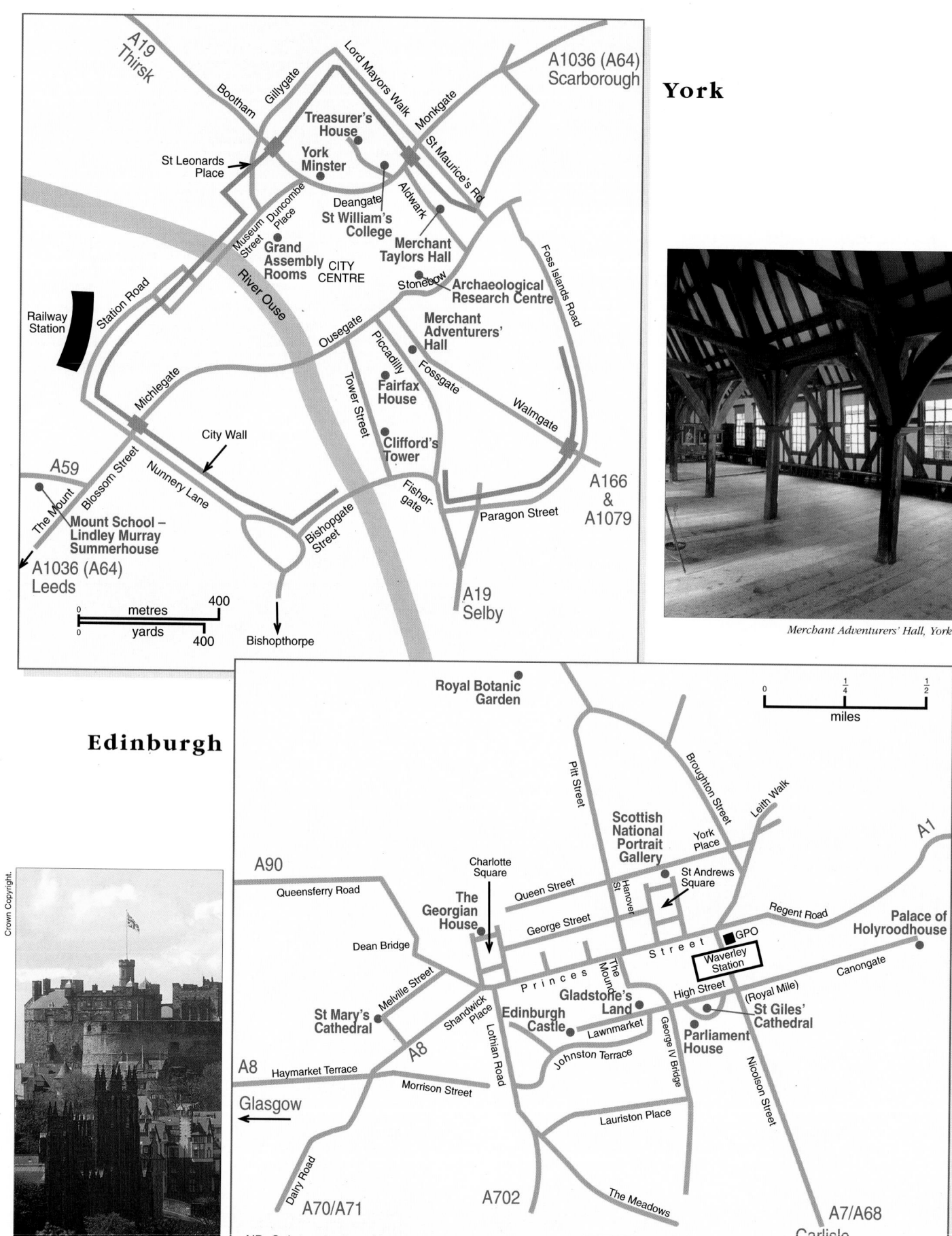

York

A19 Thirsk

A1036 (A64) Scarborough

Bootham
Gillygate
Lord Mayors Walk
Monkgate
St Maurice's Rd

Treasurer's House
York Minster
St Leonards Place
Museum Street
Duncombe Place
Deangate
Aldwark
St William's College
Grand Assembly Rooms
CITY CENTRE
Merchant Taylors Hall
Stonebow
Archaeological Research Centre
Foss Islands Road

Station Road
Railway Station
River Ouse
Ousegate
Piccadilly
Fossgate
Merchant Adventurers' Hall

Michlegate
Tower Street
Fairfax House
Walmgate

A59
Blossom Street
Nunnery Lane
City Wall
Clifford's Tower

The Mount
Mount School – Lindley Murray Summerhouse
Bishopgate Street
Fisher-gate
Paragon Street
A166 & A1079

A1036 (A64) Leeds

metres 400
yards 400

Bishopthorpe

A19 Selby

Merchant Adventurers' Hall, York.

Edinburgh

Royal Botanic Garden

Pitt Street
Broughton Street
Leith Walk

Scottish National Portrait Gallery
York Place
A1

A90
Queensferry Road
Charlotte Square
Queen Street
Hanover St
St Andrews Square
Regent Road
Palace of Holyroodhouse

The Georgian House
George Street
GPO

Dean Bridge
Street
Waverley Station
Canongate

Melville Street
Princes
The Mound
High Street
(Royal Mile)

St Mary's Cathedral
Shandwick Place
Edinburgh Castle
Gladstone's Land
St Giles' Cathedral

A8
Lothian Road
Lawnmarket
George IV Bridge
Parliament House

A8
Haymarket Terrace
Johnston Terrace
Nicolson Street

Morrison Street

Glasgow
Lauriston Place

Dairy Road
A70/A71
A702
The Meadows
A7/A68
Carlisle

Crown Copyright.

Edinburgh Castle.

NB. Only a selection of important streets are shown.

Index of all Properties

Index of all Properties

Index of all Properties

Index of all Properties

Index of all Properties

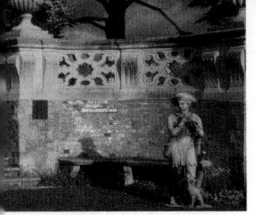
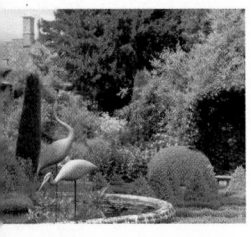
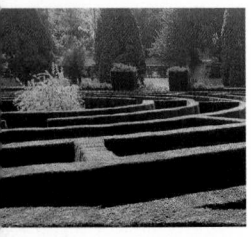
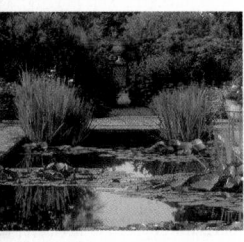
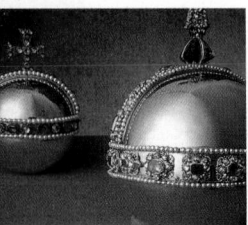
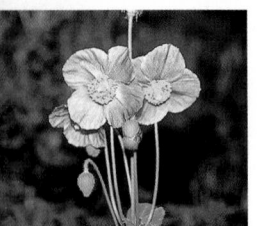
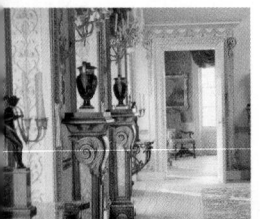

Acknowledgments

The publishers are grateful to the following for permission to reproduce the photographs on the pages listed below.

Page No.	Position on page	Description/Property	Photographer/Owner/ Organisation
Front cover		Charlecote Park, Warwickshire	NTPL/Matthew Antrobus
Frontispiece		Bourton House Garden, Gloucestershire	Mr & Mrs Richard Paice
6	Main image	Tintinhull House Garden, Somerset	NTPL/Nick Meers
7	Bottom left	Urn with cherubs, Lanhydrock, Devon	NTPL/Jerry Harpur
7	Main image	The Triton Fountain, Lytes Carey, Somerset	NTPL/Nick Meers
8	Top left	Blickling Hall, Norfolk	NTPL/Nick Meers
8	Top right	Wallington, Northumberland	NTPL/Marianne Majerus
8	Middle right	Colby Woodland Garden, Wales	NTPL/Andrew Butler
8	Lower right	Beningbrough Hall, Yorkshire	NTPL/Stephen Robson
8	Left central image	(detail) Anglesey Abbey, Cambridgeshire	NTPL/Nick Meers
8	Middle central image	(detail) Emmetts Garden, Kent	NTPL/Jerry Harpur
8	Right central image	(detail) Fenton House, London	NTPL/Jerry Harpur
8	Bottom main image	Prior Park Landscape Garden, Somerset	NTPL/David Norton
9	Top right	Ham House, London	NTPL/Stephen Robson
9	Bottom right	Dunham Massey, Cheshire	NTPL/Neil Campbell-Sharp
9	Main left	Powis Castle, Wales	NTPL/Andrew Butler
15	Main image	Maze at Chatsworth, Derbyshire	Chatsworth House Trust
16	Top centre	Maze at Leeds Castle, Kent	Leeds Castle Enterprises Limited
16	Bottom centre	Sun Maze & Lunar Labyrinth at Longleat, Wiltshire	City Photography
17	Top centre	Love Labyrinth at Longleat, Wiltshire	City Photography
17	Bottom left	Maze at Leeds Castle, Kent	City Photography
18	Main image	Tudor Rose Maze at Kentwell Hall, Suffolk	Kentwell Hall
19	Top centre	Maze at Chatsworth, Derbyshire	Chatsworth House Trust
19	Middle left	Maze at Leeds Castle, Kent	Leeds Castle Enterprises Limited
19	Bottom right	Archbishop's Maze at Greys Court, Oxfordshire	NTPL/Nick Meers
20 & 21	Top spread	Water Maze at Hever Castle, Kent	Hever Castle Limited
20	Middle right	Maze at Blenheim Palace, Oxfordshire	Chris Andrews
20	Bottom right	(detail) Hedge Maze at Longleat, Wiltshire	Longleat
21	Bottom centre	Hedge Maze at Longleat, Wiltshire	Longleat
22	Top centre	Veronica's Maze at Parham House & Gardens, Sussex	Walter Gardiner Photography
57	Main image	The Long Gallery, Parham House & Gardens, Sussex	Parham Park Trust
58 & 59	Main image	The Tower of London, London	Crown Copyright HRP
60	Main image	Raven Master & Raven, Tower of London, London	Crown Copyright HRP
61	Left	Sceptre with Cross, Tower of London, London	Crown Copyright HRP
61	Top right	Scaffold Site, Tower of London, London	Crown Copyright HRP
61	Middle	Imperial Crown of India, Tower of London, London	Crown Copyright HRP
61	Middle right	Orbs, Tower of London, London	Crown Copyright HRP
61	Bottom right	Gun Salutes, Tower of London, London	Crown Copyright HRP
62	Top left	Henry VII's Armour for Man & Horse, Tower of London, London	Crown Copyright HRP
62	Top centre	The White Tower, Tower of London, London	Crown Copyright HRP
62	Bottom left	Wakefield Tower, Tower of London, London	Crown Copyright HRP
62	Bottom right	Tower Menagerie, Tower of London, London	Crown Copyright HRP
63	Main image	Sir Thomas More's Cell, Tower of London, London	Crown Copyright HRP
88 & 89	Main image	Kingston Bagpuize, Oxfordshire	Mr & Mrs Francis Grant
90	Main image	Kingston Bagpuize, Oxfordshire	Mr & Mrs Francis Grant
91	Top left	(detail) Cantilevered Staircase, Kingston Bagpuize, Oxfordshire	Mr & Mrs Francis Grant
91	Top right	Kingston Bagpuize, Oxfordshire	Mr & Mrs Francis Grant
91	Middle right	The Dining Room, Kingston Bagpuize, Oxfordshire	Mr & Mrs Francis Grant
91	Bottom right	The Library, Kingston Bagpuize, Oxfordshire	Mr & Mrs Francis Grant
92	Top right	(detail) Magnolia *soulangeana*, Kingston Bagpuize, Oxfordshire	Mr & Mrs Francis Grant

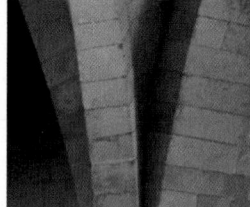

Page No.	Position on page	Description/Property	Photographer/Owner/ Organisation
92	Top centre	The drive looking west from the house, Kingston Bagpuize	Mr & Mrs Francis Grant
92	Middle centre	(detail) Colchicum, Kingston Bagpuize, Oxfordshire	Mr & Mrs Francis Grant
92	Bottom right	View of the house in winter, Kingston Bagpuize, Oxfordshire	Mr & Mrs Francis Grant
93	Main image	The Drawing Room, Kingston Bagpuize, Oxfordshire	Mr & Mrs Francis Grant
184 & 185	Main image	View of bridge, and bank of bluebells, Minterne Gdns, Dorset	The Lord Digby
186	Main image	View of the house, Minterne Gardens, Dorset	The Lord Digby
187	Top right	(detail) *Davidia Involcrata*, Minterne Gardens, Dorset	The Lord Digby
187	Middle right	(detail) *Pieris Forrestii*, Minterne Gardens, Dorset	The Lord Digby
187	Bottom right	Acer *brillantissimum*, Minterne Gardens, Dorset	The Lord Digby

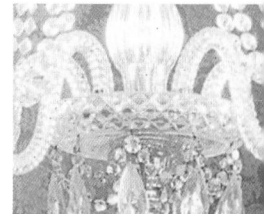

188	Top right	(detail) of page 184 & 185	
188	Top middle	Rhododendrons, Minterne Gardens, Dorset	The Lord Digby
188	Bottom right	Lake with maple trees in background, Minterne Gdns, Dorset	The Lord Digby
189	Main image	Stream with yellow bog irises, Minterne Gardens, Dorset	The Lord Digby
248 & 249	Main image	The annual border, Helmingham Hall, Suffolk	Jerry Harpur/Lord Tollemache
250	Main image	Helmingham Hall, Suffolk	Jerry Harpur/Lord Tollemache
251	Top left	(detail) Lupin 'Galaxy White' & daisies, Helmingham Hall, Suffolk	Jerry Harpur/Lord Tollemache
251	Top right	(detail) Irises & roses, Helmingham Hall, Suffolk	Jerry Harpur/Lord Tollemache
251	Middle right	The Knot Garden, Helmingham Hall, Suffolk	Jerry Harpur/Lord Tollemache

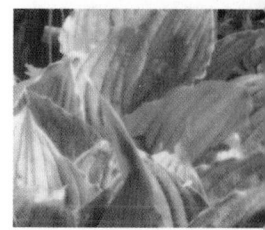

251	Bottom right	The Gourd Tunnel, Helmingham Hall, Suffolk	Jerry Harpur/Lord Tollemache
252	Top left	(detail) Poppies 'Patty's Plum', Helmingham Hall, Suffolk	Jerry Harpur/Lord Tollemache
252	Top right	(detail) Sweetpeas, Helmingham Hall, Suffolk	Jerry Harpur/Lord Tollemache
252	Bottom left	(detail) White Daisies, Helmingham Hall, Suffolk	Jerry Harpur/Lord Tollemache
253	Main image	The old bridge to the apple walk, Helmingham Hall, Suffolk	Jerry Harpur/Lord Tollemache
282	Main image	The Wild Garden, Cottesbrooke, Northamptonshire	Captain John Macdonald-Buchanan
284 & 285	Main image	Cottesbrooke Hall & Gardens, Northamptonshire	Hugh Palmer
285	Top right	Pine Court, Cottesbrooke Hall & Gardens, Northamptonshire	Captain John Macdonald-Buchanan
285	Top left	Back of house, Cottesbrooke Hall & Gardens, Northamptonshire	Captain John Macdonald-Buchanan

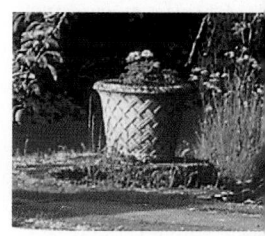

285	Middle left	Statue Walk, Cottesbrooke Hall & Garden, Northamptonshire	Captain John Macdonald-Buchanan
285	Bottom left	Rose Garden, Cottesbrooke Hall & Garden, Northamptonshire	Captain John Macdonald-Buchanan
286	Top right	(detail) Pine Court, Cottesbrooke Hall & Gardens	Captain John Macdonald-Buchanan
286	Top middle	View of Spouting Fountain, Cottesbrooke Hall & Gardens	Captain John Macdonald-Buchanan
286	Bottom centre	Bronze of Empress Elizabeth, Cottesbrooke Hall & Gardens	Captain John Macdonald-Buchanan
287	Main image	Steps with sphinx and agapanthus, Cottesbrooke Hall	Captain John Macdonald-Buchanan
318 & 319	Main image	Summer perennial border, Dorothy Clive Gardens, Staffordshire	Dorothy Clive Gardens
320	Main image	Sundial with flower border, Dorothy Clive Gardens, Staffordshire	Dorothy Clive Gardens
321	Top left	Statue with yellow laburnam, Dorothy Clive Gardens	Dorothy Clive Gardens
321	Top right	Waterfall in woodland glade, Dorothy Clive Gardens	Dorothy Clive Gardens

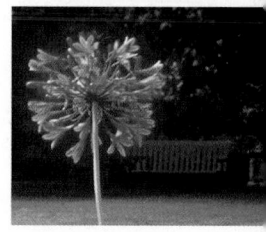

321	Bottom right	Heather Garden, Dorothy Clive Gardens, Staffordshire	Dorothy Clive Gardens
322	Top left	Child on a swing, Dorothy Clive Gardens, Staffordshire	Dorothy Clive Gardens
322	Top centre	Rhododendrons, Dorothy Clive Gardens, Staffordshire	Dorothy Clive Gardens
322	Bottom left	Lily Pond, Dorothy Clive Gardens, Staffordshire	Dorothy Clive Gardens
323	Bottom right	Photograph of Dorothy Clive, Dorothy Clive Gardens	Dorothy Clive Gardens
323	Main image	Autumn foliage, Dorothy Clive Gardens, Staffordshire	Dorothy Clive Gardens
362 & 363	Main image	Herbaceous border, Beningbrough Hall, Yorkshire	NTPL/Stephen Robson
364	Main image	Beningbrough Hall, Yorkshire	NTPL/Horst Kolo
365	Top left	(detail) Flowers in garden, Beningbrough Hall, Yorkshire	NTPL/Stephen Robson
365	Top right	Walled Kitchen Garden, Beningbrough Hall, Yorkshire	NTPL/Stephen Robson

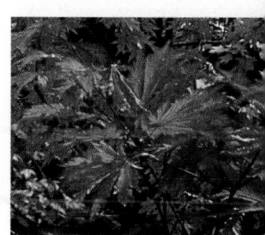

365	Middle centre	Drawing Room, Beningbrough Hall, Yorkshire	NTPL/Andreas von Einsiedel
365	Middle right	The Countess of Chesterfield, Beningbrough Hall, Yorkshire	NTPL/Andreas von Einsiedel
365	Bottom right	Drawing Room, Beningbrough Hall, Yorkshire	NTPL/Andreas von Einsiedel
366	Top right	(detail) Flower Garden, Beningbrough Hall, Yorkshire	NTPL/Stephen Robson
366	Top centre	View of house flanked by formal borders, Beningbrough Hall	NTPL/Ian Shaw
366	Bottom left	The Saloon, Beningbrough Hall, Yorkshire	NTPL/Andreas von Einsiedel
367	Main image	Walled Garden, Beningbrough Hall, Yorkshire	NTPL/Stephen Robson
392 & 393	Main image	Shrub border, Holker Hall, Cumbria	Lord & Lady Cavendish
394	Main image	Holker Hall, Cumbria	Lord & Lady Cavendish
395	Top left	(detail) Summer Garden, Holker Hall, Cumbria	Lord & Lady Cavendish
395	Top right	(detail) North West view of Holker Hall, Cumbria	Lord & Lady Cavendish

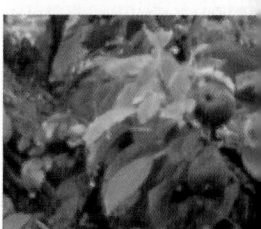

395	Middle right	The Water Fountain, Holker Hall, Cumbria	Lord & Lady Cavendish
395	Bottom right	Laurel Arch, Holker Hall, Cumbria	Lord & Lady Cavendish
396	Top left	(detail) Water Fountain, Holker Hall, Cumbria	Lord & Lady Cavendish
396	Top right	Summer Garden, Holker Hall, Cumbria	Lord & Lady Cavendish
396	Bottom right	"Texture", Holker Hall, Cumbria	Lord & Lady Cavendish

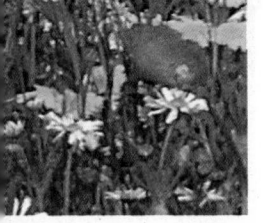
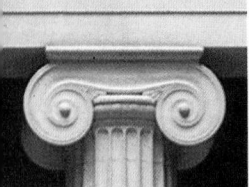
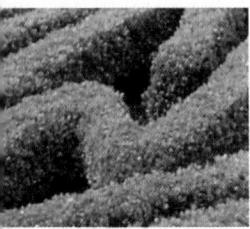
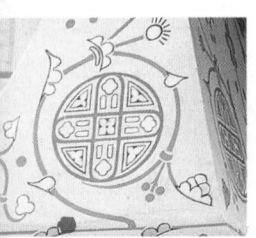
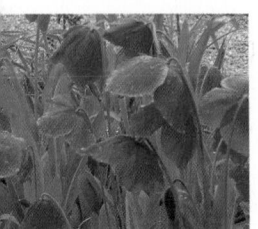
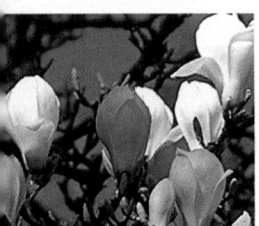
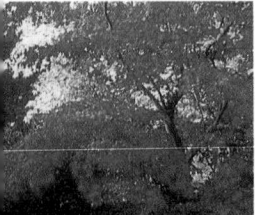

Page No.	Position on page	Description/Property	Photographer/Owner/ Organisation
397	Main image	Wild Flowers at Holker Hall, Cumbria	Lord & Lady Cavendish
422 & 423	Main image	The Quarry Garden, Belsay Hall, Northumberland	English Heritage Photo Library
424	Main image	East Front of Belsay Hall, Northumberland	English Heritage Photo Library
425	Top left	(detail) The Quarry Garden, Belsay Hall, Northumberland	English Heritage Photo Library
425	Top right	View of Belsay Castle, Belsay Hall, Northumberland	English Heritage Photo Library
425	Middle centre	The Archway in the Quarry Garden, Belsay Hall, Northumberland	English Heritage Photo Library
425	Bottom right	The Quarry Garden, Belsay Hall, Northumberland	English Heritage Photo Library
426	Top left	Pathway in Quarry Garden, Belsay Hall, Northumberland	English Heritage Photo Library
426	Top right	The Quarry Garden in summer, Belsay Hall, Northumberland	English Heritage Photo Library/Clay Perry
426	Bottom left	The Quarry Garden, Belsay Hall, Northumberland	English Heritage Photo Library
426	Bottom right	Face carving on latrine, Belsay Hall, Northumberland	English Heritage Photo Library
427	Main image	Pillar Hall, Belsay Hall, Northumberland	English Heritage Photo Library
441	Main image	The Drawing Room, Scone Palace, Perthshire	The Earl of Mansfield
442 & 443	Main image	Dirleton Castle Gardens, Edinburgh	Historic Scotland
444	Main image	Castle Campbell, West Highlands & Islands	Historic Scotland
445	Top left	(detail) Stirling Castle, West Highlands & Islands	Historic Scotland
445	Top right	The Topiary Garden, Edzell Castle, Perthshire, Dundee & Kingdom of Fife	Historic Scotland
445	Middle right	Herbaceous border, Dirleton Castle, Edinburgh	Historic Scotland
445	Bottom right	The Topiary Garden, Edzell Castle, Perthshire, Dundee & Kingdom of Fife	Historic Scotland
446	Top left	(detail) Formal planting, Dirleton Castle, Edinburgh	Crown Copyright reserved/Historic Scotland
446	Top right	The King's Knot, Stirling Castle, West Highlands & Islands	Historic Scotland
446	Bottom right	(detail) Summer border, Dirleton Castle, Edinburgh	Historic Scotland
447	Main image	Edzell Castle, Perthshire, Dundee & Kingdom of Fife	Historic Scotland
494	Main image	Aerial view of Cawdor Castle, Highlands & Skye	The Dowager Countess Cawdor
495	Top left	(detail) The Staircase, Cawdor Castle, Highlands & Skye	Christopher Sykes
495	Top right	Bedroom, Cawdor Castle, Highlands & Skye	Cawdor Castle (Tourism) Limited
495	Middle right	Snow covered scene of Cawdor Castle, Highlands & Skye	Cawdor Castle (Tourism) Limited
495	Bottom right	The Drawing Room, Cawdor Castle, Highlands & Skye	Christopher Sykes
496	Top left	(detail) Fireplace in the Drawing Room, Cawdor Castle	Christopher Sykes
496	Top right	Herbaceous border with Irish yews, Cawdor Castle	The Dowager Countess Cawdor
496	Bottom left	The Cawdor Tree, Cawdor Castle, Highlands & Skye	The Dowager Countess Cawdor
497	Main image	Cawdor Castle viewed through trees, Highlands & Skye	The Dowager Countess Cawdor
505	Main image	The Long Gallery, Powis Castle, North Wales	NTPL/Andreas von Einsiedel
506 & 507	Main image	The Drawing Room ceiling, Castell Coch, South Wales	CADW (Welsh Historic Monuments) Photo Library
508	Main image	Castell Coch, South Wales	CADW (Welsh Historic Monuments) Photo Library
509	Top left	(detail) The Banqueting House, Castell Coch, South Wales	CADW (Welsh Historic Monuments) Photo Library
509	Top right	The Entrance to Castell Coch, South Wales	CADW (Welsh Historic Monuments) Photo Library
509	Middle right	(detail) Dado panelling, Castell Coch, South Wales	CADW (Welsh Historic Monuments) Photo Library
509	Bottom right	(detail) The Three Fates, Castell Coch, South Wales	CADW (Welsh Historic Monuments) Photo Library
510	Top centre	The Drawing Room, Castell Coch, South Wales	CADW (Welsh Historic Monuments) Photo Library
510	Top left	(detail) Drawing room dado panelling, Castell Coch	CADW (Welsh Historic Monuments) Photo Library
510	Middle right	(detail) Zodiac tiles in Drawing Room fireplace, Castell Coch	CADW (Welsh Historic Monuments) Photo Library
510	Bottom left	The Lady's Bedroom, Castell Coch, South Wales	CADW (Welsh Historic Monuments) Photo Library
510	Bottom right	The Kitchen, Castell Coch, South Wales	CADW (Welsh Historic Monuments) Photo Library
511	Main image	(detail) Lord Bute's Bedroom, Castell Coch, South Wales	CADW (Welsh Historic Monuments) Photo Library
525	Main image	Staircase at The Argory, Ireland	NTPL/Andreas von Einsiedel
526 & 527	Main image	Rowallane Garden, Co Down, Ireland	NTPL/Stephen Robson
528	Main image	View of the Walled Garden, Rowallane Garden, Co Down	NTPL/Stephen Robson
529	Top left	(detail) Walled Garden, Rowallane Garden, Co Down, Ireland	NTPL/Jerry Harpur
529	Top right	Pump in Walled Garden, Rowallane Garden, Co Down	NTPL/Stephen Robson
529	Middle right	Gateway to the Old Wood, Rowallane Garden, Co Down	NTPL/Stephen Robson
529	Bottom right	Rock Garden, Rowallane Garden, Co Down	NTPL/Jerry Harpur
530	Top left	(detail) Walled Garden, Rowallane Garden, Co Down	NTPL/Jerry Harpur
530	Top right	Azaleas and rhododendrons, Rowallane Garden, Co Down	NTPL/Stephen Robson
530	Bottom left	Azaleas and rhododendrons, Rowallane Garden, Co Down	NTPL/Jerry Harpur
531	Main image	Blue *meconopsis betonicifolia* flowers at Rowallane Garden	NTPL/Jerry Harpur
IBC		View of the Saloon at Uppark, Sussex	NTPL/Nadia Mackenzie
Back cover	Left image	(detail) Agapanthus plant at Cottesbrooke Hall, Northants	Captain John Macdonald-Buchanan
Back cover	Middle image	Bride and Groom	Sarah Ward-Hendry Photography
Back cover	Right image	(detail) Helmingham Hall, Suffolk	Jerry Harpur/Lord Tollemache